MACMILLAN
COMPENDIUM

AFRICAN-AMERICAN HISTORY

MACMILLAN
COMPENDIUM

AFRICAN-AMERICAN HISTORY

SELECTIONS FROM THE
FIVE-VOLUME
Macmillan Encyclopedia of African-American Culture and History

JACK SALZMAN
Editor-in-Chief

MACMILLAN LIBRARY REFERENCE USA

Simon & Schuster Macmillan
New York

Prentice Hall International
London Mexico City New Delhi Singapore Sydney Toronto

Cover Images: Frederick Douglass, Mary McLeod Bethune, and W. E. B. Du Bois © Corbis-Bettmann; Martin Luther King, Jr. © Flip Schulke/Corbis; Booker T. Washington © Oscar White/Corbis; American flag © 1997 PhotoDisc, Inc.

Designed by Kevin Hanek
Cover photo illustration by George Berrian

Macmillan Library Reference USA
Simon & Schuster Macmillan
1633 Broadway, 5th Floor
New York, NY 10019

Manufactured in the United States of America.

printing number
1 2 3 4 5 6 7 8 9 10

Library of Congress Cataloging-in-Publication Data

Encyclopedia of African-American culture and history. Selections.
African-American history / Jack Salzman, editor-in-chief.
p. cm. — (Macmillan compendium)
"Selections from the five-volume Encyclopedia of African-American culture and history."
Includes bibliographical references and index.
ISBN 0-02-864979-6 (alk. paper)
1. Afro-Americans—History—Dictionaries. I. Salzman, Jack.
II. Title. III. Series.
E185.E545 1998
973′.0496073′003—dc21 98-36730
CIP

This paper meets the requirements of ANSI/NISO Z39.48-1992 (Permanence of Paper).

African-American History

Table of Contents

sive to popular agitation. When antislavery gained the support of William Wilberforce, Granville Sharp, and other Anglican evangelicals, it acquired respectable voices in Parliament. While advancing the view that slavery was obsolete and immoral, English leaders ensured that no fundamental threat to property rights was associated with abolition. Slave owners retained their human property during a six-year transitional "apprenticeship," and they received compensation for their losses. Having abolished its own immoral institution, England assumed responsibility for campaigns against the slave trade on the high seas, in the Islamic world, and in India. These campaigns had the effect of spreading British imperial influence and promoting British views of civilization.

As British antislavery approached its great triumphs, it began to send speakers, books and pamphlets, and some financial support to its American counterparts. Some Americans viewed British encouragement of American antislavery efforts as unwelcome meddling that endangered American independence and welfare. Both black and white abolitionists venerated names like Wilberforce and applauded the British example, but there was little resemblance between slavery in the two economies and political systems. American antislavery was compelled to address issues affecting a growing black population, a prosperous domestic economic institution, and sectional animosities in a federal political system for which England's experience offered little precedent. On the other hand, there was no existing English equivalent to the network of organizations among northern free blacks, who sought to embolden white reformers to pursue the cause of abolition more aggressively and to combat racial discrimination wherever it occurred.

As they had in England, Quakers took early leadership in American antislavery activities; and they were joined, sometimes, by insurgent evangelical movements to whom old institutions no longer seemed sacred and unchanging. Unlike England, the United States experienced a revolution that supplemented religious reform motivations with strong new reasons for opposing traditional inequalities. Slavery not only violated the law of God, but in an age of liberation and enlightenment, it contradicted the rights of man. Neither religious nor secular arguments necessarily obliged whites to combat racial prejudice or extend humanitarian aid to free blacks. Though black abolitionists would often accuse whites of coldhearted bigotry it may be the case that the Revolution "doomed" slavery.

In the 1780s, abolitionist societies were formed in most states (including the upper South). A national abolitionist "convention" met annually from 1794 to 1806 and periodically thereafter. In the decades after the Revolution, northern states abolished slavery, often after organized antislavery campaigns. In 1808, Congress, which had previously prohibited slavery in the Northwest Territory, ended the foreign slave trade. This was assumed to be a blow to North American slavery (though some slave owners supported the measure, and later experience showed that the slave population grew rapidly without imports). Appeals to the great principles of republican government seemed ready to transform American society.

Those who believed in an optimistic scenario of revolutionary liberation underestimated the ways in which persistent white hostility to blacks would impede antislavery activity. They also overlooked obstacles imposed by the Constitution. Most abolitionists accepted the prevailing consensus that the federal government lacked any constitutional power over slavery in the states. While antislavery coalitions prevailed in states like New York and Pennsylvania, residents of a northern state had no way of influencing legislatures in South Carolina or Tennessee. When controversies over slavery arose in the U.S. Congress, as in debates over fugitive slave acts from 1793 to 1817, proslavery forces won repeated victories. With the elimination of slavery in northern states, abolition societies lost membership and purpose.

The Colonizationist New Departure

Only a change of direction, one that attracted support among southern slaveholders as well as black and white Northerners, revitalized antislavery commitments in the 1820s. Some Southerners had for years entertained hopes of deporting freed slaves (a solution to racial problems somewhat analogous to Indian removal). If ex-slaves could be relocated in the West, perhaps, or Africa, or Central America, slaveholders might be less reluctant to free them, nonslaveholding whites might be less anxious about competition for work, and northern and southern townspeople might show less fear of social consequences of EMANCIPATION. Some northern reformers believed that American society would never accept blacks as equals. Appealing simultaneously to those who hated or feared free blacks and those who deplored or regretted American racism, removal schemes raised hopes of forging an irresistible coalition that might, once and for all, end slavery.

The premier organization advancing these schemes was the AMERICAN COLONIZATION SOCIETY (ACS), founded in 1816, which rapidly won the approval of prominent leaders of church and government in both the North and South. It sent only a few thousand blacks to its colony Liberia before 1830, however, and it failed to get federal funding for its efforts. Enthusiasm for the movement began to subside (though the ACS survived into the twentieth century) as doubts of its practicality grew. Modern scholars frequently dismiss its efforts as futile and its objectives as racist—both irrefutable charges. Less often pointed out are that slavery's most implacable champions hated the ACS; that with its decline, hopes for a national antislavery movement virtually disappeared; and that its predictions of enduring racism and misery for free blacks were realistic. If it included in its numbers slaveholders like Henry Clay, it also included many Northerners who would hold fast to abolitionist purposes for decades to come. It attracted the support of some northern blacks, including John B. Russwurm, a Bowdoin College graduate who spent much of his life in Liberia, and free southern blacks like those who appealed to Baltimore's white community in 1826 for help in leaving a republic where their inequality was "irremediable." Not only did they seek for themselves rights and respect that America seemed permanently to withhold, but they also upheld an antislavery vision: "Our absence will accelerate the liberation of such of our brethren as are in bondage."

Black support for colonization was undeniable. It was also extremely limited, while rejection of such schemes by prominent black abolitionists intensified during the 1820s. As early as 1817, a Philadelphia meeting had protested against the ACS's characterizations of blacks as a "dangerous and useless" class; linking manumission to colonization, the meeting continued, would only strengthen slavery. Even black leaders like James FORTEN, who privately favored emigration and believed African Americans would "never become a people until they come out from amongst the white people," joined in the protest. By 1829, militant documents like David Walker's Appeal denounced "the Colonizing Plan" as evidence of the pervasive racism that caused "Our Wretchedness."

The Immediatist New Direction

Anticolonizationist societies were launched in free black communities throughout the North, and several efforts were made to establish national newspapers to coordinate the movement. (Russwurm edited one before his conversion to colonizationism.) It was clear, however, that blacks could never sink the ACS without enlisting white allies. This meant, in practice, that blacks would have to speak in a less militant voice than Walker and other leaders might have preferred: they could not stress the virulence of racism or doubt the responsiveness of whites to conciliatory tactics. They could not advocate violent resistance to slavery or discrimination. They might also have to accept subsidiary roles in a coalition movement led by whites. These risks seemed tolerable, however, in light of the emergence in the early 1830s of a new, radical, and interracial antislavery movement that defined itself in opposition to the ACS. What for whites was a bold new departure was for blacks an episode in prudent compromise and coalition building.

Black abolitionists discovered a white champion in William Lloyd Garrison. It is likely that James Forten and other blacks influenced Garrison, at that time a colonizationist editor in Philadelphia and Baltimore, to embrace the idea of human equality. Black readers enabled Garrison in 1831 to launch his Boston-based newspaper, the *Liberator*, and they made up the great majority of subscribers to this weekly organ of immediate abolitionism throughout its early years. David WALKER was one of several blacks who named children after Garrison; others gave him financial support or protected him as he walked home at night. Many viewed the *Liberator* as their voice in American public life. Maria Stewart was one of many blacks who contributed articles condemning slavery, prejudice, and colonizationism. Garrison adopted a style of denunciation thrilling to his friends and infuriating to those whom he opposed: "I will be as harsh as truth, and as uncompromising as justice. . . . I will not equivocate—I will not excuse—I will not retreat a single inch—AND I WILL BE HEARD," proclaimed his first issue. He took up the view of the ACS that blacks had urged in the previous decade and gave it powerful and influential expression. In its first year, the *Liberator* published ten times as many articles denouncing the ACS as explaining immediate abolition. Garrison's *Thoughts on African Colonization* (1832), a withering critique of racist and proslavery quotations from colonization leaders, was widely distributed and persuaded many young reformers to change loyalties and follow a new course.

The attack on the ACS was a means of redefining antislavery strategy that appealed to a new generation of reformers in the early 1830s. Besides Garrison, the most influential of these was Theodore Dwight Weld, a restless and charismatic leader from upstate New York who had traveled extensively and worked for causes ranging from religious revivals to educational reform. As a student at Cincinnati's Lane Seminary in the early 1830s, he worked with blacks in the student body and local community, precipitating a crisis by forcing discussion of slavery and racial prejudice. He had no peer at a style of earnest, emotional antislavery lecturing, facing down mobs and winning converts to the cause, that he taught to other abolitionist speakers. Though Garrison and Weld were (in a not fully acknowledged sense) rivals, the former's uncompromising editorial stance and the latter's confrontational lecture style joined in shaping an exciting new era for abolitionism. Other important abolitionist leaders included the brothers Lewis and Arthur Tappan, merchants in New York City, well con-

nected with prominent evangelical reform movements, who furnished a sober counterpoint to Weld's and Garrison's romantic outbursts. John Greenleaf Whittier, early in a career that led to great fame as a poet, was a valued new convert.

Despite condemnation by Andrew Jackson and other public figures, anticolonizationism spread with remarkable velocity. In 1832 eleven persons formed the New England Anti-Slavery Society, "the first society of this kind created on this side of the Atlantic," as the South Carolina political leader James Henry Hammond later recalled. Though slaveholders initially mocked this news, by 1837, Massachusetts had 145 societies, and New York and Ohio, where the Tappans and Weld held influence, had 274 and 213, respectively. In December 1833, sixty-three men (three of them black) formed the American Anti-Slavery Society (AASS). Earlier that year, interracial female antislavery societies were formed in Boston and Philadelphia, and in 1837 there occurred the first "national" (northern) women's antislavery convention. By 1838, the AASS claimed 1,350 affiliated societies, with membership approaching a quarter million. Important new voices, including those of ex-Southerners James G. Birney and Angelina and Sarah Moore Grimké, added to the excitement of the mid–1830s.

The positive meaning of the immediatist, anticolonizationist doctrines that stirred up so much commotion was never a simple matter to establish. For decades scholars have argued over which of two strategies—political coercion or nonviolent persuasion—was more consistent with the immediatist commitment of the early 1830s. The truth is that immediatism had more than two potential meanings, as it blended rather unrealistic expectations of religious transformation with cautious recognition of obstacles to reform. On the one hand, some abolitionists wished to persuade slaveholders to let their slaves go free, or they hoped, at least, to encourage antislavery majorities to form in southern states. Conceding the lack of federal authority to interfere with state institutions, founders of the AASS were obliged to adopt a conciliatory stance toward the South. In particular, they denied any intention to use coercion; slavery must end by "moral suasion." On the other hand, the harsh, categorical denunciations of slavery that distinguished the new movement from the ACS were hardly conciliatory. In letters of instruction and training sessions for antislavery lecturers, Weld (who injured his own voice and retired from the field) insisted that they should not get bogged down in political or economic issues: "the business of abolitionists is with the heart of the nation, rather than with its purse strings." Slavery was, he taught, "a *moral* question," and the conviction to drive home was simply that "*slavery is a sin.*" Once convinced of that, clergymen and other opinion leaders would exert pressure on slaveholders to give up their sin. The slaveholders, similarly convinced, would be impelled to change their lives. If they did not, morally awakened democratic majorities had to compel them.

Schism and Variation

By decade's end, it was obvious that slavery was not going to succumb to northern condemnation, no matter how conciliatory or intemperate. Disagreements among abolitionists, subdued during years of enthusiasm, took on new seriousness. The AASS split in two at its 1840 convention when the Tappans and other prominent reformers walked out after a woman, Abby Kelley, was elected to a committee. They protested that under Garrison's leadership the movement was too defiant of social conventions, thus offending the clergy and other respectable leaders of society, and too enthusiastic about new radical causes, especially a new form of nonviolent anarchism called "nonresistance." The departing abolitionists believed the cause could gain popular support by shunning "extraneous," controversial positions. Many on this side were moving toward more active participation in politics. For Garrison's loyal cadres in the AASS, including radical pacifists like Henry C. Wright, abolitionist commitments led toward broad condemnation of coercive behavior and institutions. The AASS survived as a separate organization, open to all who chose to join, while in the *Liberator* and in speeches and writings, Garrisonians gave increasing attention to nonviolence, utopian communities, women's rights, and other enthusiasms of the 1840s. (They showed less sympathy with working-class reforms.) They remained adamant in opposing political ventures, some out of anarchistic convictions, others out of dismayed assessment of the receptiveness of American politicians to antislavery principles.

Many black abolitionists continued to admire Garrison, but they, too, often criticized the lengths to which he carried the logic of moral suasion. Some agreed with the charge that he depleted antislavery energy by his romantic penchant for adopting new causes. But he, at least, was unwilling to compromise the principle of equality in order to appease northern majorities. Though blacks tended to favor political action, they appreciated Garrison's scorn when political abolitionism bowed to necessity by accepting slavery where it existed in the South and segregation as it worsened in the North. They complained repeatedly that all factions of white abolitionists relegated blacks to subsidiary roles, at best, in their organizations. Such inability to

accept blacks in visible leadership positions showed that white abolitionists had not really understood the links between bigotry and slavery. It was difficult, moreover, to interest whites in combating JIM CROW in northern streetcars with the zeal aroused by movements to keep slavery (and African Americans) out of the territories. After the schism of 1840, black abolitionists met more frequently in their own organizations, held their own conventions, and supported their own newspapers, like Samuel E. Cornish's *Colored American* and Frederick DOUGLASS's paper.

In a powerful 1843 address to slaves, Henry Highland Garnet urged, *"Resistance! Resistance! Resistance!"* His controversial text was suppressed until 1848, but in the following years, similar militancy among other black leaders became increasingly noticeable. Talk of moral suasion gave way to insistence on the universal right of revolution. If whites did not concede to blacks the right to self-defense, some leaders asked, and if blacks never showed their willingness to fight, then how could southern slavery and northern injustice ever be ended? Blacks (with limited white support) engaged in civil disobedience against segregated schools and streetcars, and they used all available means to assist fugitives from slavery. But such militancy coincided with renewed interest in emigration, either to Canada, where tens of thousands of blacks, many of them fugitives, lived in constant rebuke to conditions in the northern and southern United States, or perhaps to Liberia (despite continuing black denunciation of the ACS), or Haiti, favored by Garnet as late as 1861. Douglass, James Mccune Smith, and other black leaders deplored any possible abandonment of the cause of civil rights for free blacks and emancipation of the slaves.

After the war with Mexico from 1846 to 1848, a series of political events and court decisions—particularly events and decisions returning fugitives to bondage—struck abolitionists as calamities. Not only were some black leaders resigned to emigration, but many white Garrisonians denounced the political system dominated by proslavery leaders. Theodore Parker,

Wood engraving portrait of the fugitive slave Anthony Burns, 1855, surrounded by scenes from his life. Copyrighting works such as this print under the name of the subject was a common abolitionist practice. (Prints and Photographs Division, Library of Congress)

pilots, such as Willie "Suicide" Jones and Dorothy Darby, made a living as barnstorming daredevils. Chauncey C. Spencer became well known after a parachute jump at a black air show in Chicago in 1939.

Perhaps the most influential African-American pilots and teachers were Cornelius R. Coffey and his wife, Willia B. Brown, who founded the Coffey School of Aeronautics at Harlem Airport in southwest Chicago. Coffey, an African American, was a certified aircraft and engine mechanic and instructor as well as the holder of a limited commercial pilot's license. Brown, a licensed mechanic and pilot, later became a lieutenant, the first African-American officer, in the Civil Air Patrol. She and Janet Bragg became the first African-American women to earn commercial pilot's licenses.

During the 1930s African Americans managed to make a series of long-distance flights. In 1932 pilot James Herman Banning and aircraft mechanic Thomas C. Allen were the first blacks to fly across the continent. Pilots Charles Alfred "Chief" Anderson and Dr. Albert E. Forsythe completed the first round-trip transcontinental flight by African-American pilots: in 1933 they flew between Atlantic City and Los Angeles in a Fairchild 24 named "Pride of Atlantic City." A year later Anderson and Forsythe made a well-publicized Pan American Goodwill flight in a Lambert Monocouple, the "Spirit of Booker T. Washington," stopping at numerous locations in the Caribbean and South America.

The first black woman pilot in the United States was Bessie Coleman, who had to go to France to receive training because of racial discrimination in the United States.

The military buildup of the United States prior to WORLD WAR II brought about an enormous expansion of the U.S. Army Air Corps. However, the Air Corps remained closed to blacks. In 1940, Coffey, Brown, and Enoch P. Waters started the National Airmen's Association of America to push for the inclusion of blacks in the federal government's Civilian Pilot Training Program (CPTP), which trained reserve pilots who could later be activated for military service. Association pilots Chauncey Spenser and Dale White, supported by the *Chicago Defender,* flew 3,000 miles roundtrip from Chicago to Washington on a whirlwind lobbying trip to meet with members of Congress to request the inclusion of African Americans in the CPTP. In 1941 the CPTP set up an emergency training program at black colleges and the Coffey school, which trained 2,000 black pilots. Four hundred fifty of them eventually saw combat in WORLD WAR II.

The pressure exerted by blacks and their white allies led to a small initial project. On March 22, 1941 the (newly-renamed) U.S. Army Air Force activated the highly successful and now-famous all-black 99th Pursuit (later Fighter) Squadron, organized by pilots already trained by the CPTP, at Tuskegee Army Air Field under Anderson. The creation of the "Tuskegee Airmen" unit was opposed by many in the Air Corps, the War Department, and Congress. In 1942 the 99th was put under the command of an African-American officer, Col. Benjamin O. DAVIS, Jr. Racism was so pervasive in the training of African-American fighter pilots and officers that riots occurred at several training sites in the South and Midwest. Despite inadequate training and small numbers, the "Tuskegee Airmen" were sent to North Africa. Attached to the white 33rd Fighter Group in the Mediterranean theater, the 99th performed creditably. On July 2, 1943, Charles Hall became the first African-American pilot to shoot down an enemy fighter. Hall later received the Distinguished Flying Cross, as did pilot Wendell Pruitt. Late in 1943, the 99th Squadron merged with three other Fighter squadrons trained at Tuskegee to form the 332nd Fighter Group (the 447th Bombardment Group, which never saw combat, was created the same year). The 332nd was sent to Europe, where its African-American pilots distinguished themselves as bomber escorts.

On July 26, 1948, President Harry S. Truman officially terminated segregation in the armed forces when he signed Executive Order 9981. African-American pilots were slowly integrated into formerly all-white units. Jessie L. Brown, who became the first naval air pilot, received a posthumous Distinguished Flying Cross and Air Medal for his flying during the Korean War, and his colleague Thomas J. Hudner won the Medal of Honor. By the close of the Korean War, blacks were participating in all activities of the U.S. Air Force and U.S. Army Air Cavalry units. African Americans held officer rank at all levels. Benjamin O. Davis, Jr. was promoted to lieutenant general of the Air Force in 1954. In the years following the Vietnam War, Daniel "Chappy" James was promoted to four-star general, and made head of the North American Defense Command (NORAD).

Following the Korean War, African Americans began to be active in commercial aviation as fixed wing pilots, rotorcraft pilots, flight attendants, aircraft owners, airline operators, and executives. In 1956 New York Airways hired Perry H. Young, Jr., a former civilian flight instructor at Tuskegee Air Field, as a licensed helicopter pilot. Young remained the only African-American helicopter pilot for many years. More recent helicopter pilots of distinction and achievement have been Julian Council and Jerry R. Curry. In 1958, following years of effort by the New York State Commission Against Discrimination, Mohawk Airlines hired Ruth Carol Taylor of Ithaca, N.Y., as the first African-American flight attendant. In 1965 a notable antidiscrimination lawsuit by Marlon D. Green against Continental Airlines forced airlines to hire black pilots, and Continental, Eastern Airlines, and Trans World Airlines soon hired black commercial pilots, executives, and mechanics and engineers. Shortly thereafter, Capt. David Harris of American Airlines became the first black captain of a major airline. Texas International Airlines hired Jill Brown as the first African-American woman airplane captain in 1971. James O. Plinton, Jr., another Tuskegee Air Field veteran, was vice president of Eastern from 1971 to 1979. Meanwhile, Warren Wheeler, a former pilot for Piedmont Airlines (1967–69), began Wheeler Flight Services, Inc., the first black-owned airline, in 1969.

U.S. aircraft manufacturers also recognized the value of black aerospace engineers. Beginning in the early 1950s, Douglas Aircraft Company and the Northrop Corporation led the way in hiring. Beginning in the mid-1960s, African Americans became active in all areas of the U.S. aerospace industry, EDUCATION, and government. Black men and women have been valued performers in all aspects of America's aerospace activities. They include outstanding scientists and technologists such as Drs. George Carruthers, Christine Darden, Wesley L. Harris, Robert L. Norwood, Lonnie Reid, and Woodrow Whitlow. Also active have been Dr. Julian Earls, Isaac Gilliam, IV, John Hines, Wanda A. Sigur, and Earl Washington. Within this group of outstanding African Americans, Wesley L. Harris was the first to obtain the rank of full professor in the Department of Aeronautics and Astronautics at the Massachusetts Institute of Technology (MIT) and the first to be elected Fellow of the American Institute of Aeronautics and Astronautics. Woodrow Whitlow, a student of Harris's, is the first African American to receive a Ph.D. in aeronautics and astronautics from MIT and the first to be a branch chief at the National Aeronautics and Space Administration (NASA) Langley Research Center.

An outstanding group of black astronauts and scientists have supported America's space program. In 1962 Dr. Vance H. Marchbanks, Jr. was a mission control specialist during astronaut John Glenn's orbital flight. Edward Dwight, Jr., who in 1963 became the first African American accepted into the United States space program, was eventually passed over by NASA, a move that sparked widespread protest. In 1967 Major Robert Lawrence was selected for the Department of Defense's Manned Orbital Laboratory (MOL) program. He died six months later in a plane crash. Guion S. Bluford, Jr., a Vietnam War veteran who has a Ph.D. in aerospace engineering, was the first African American in space (August 30, 1983, on board the space shuttle *Challenger*). Frederick D. Gregory became the first African American to pilot a space mission on April 29, 1985 at the controls of the space shuttle *Challenger/Spacelab 3*. Ronald E. McNair was the first African American to conduct experiments in space (aboard *Challenger*, February 3, 1984). McNair was killed in the *Challenger* explosion on January 28, 1986. Other African American astronauts with flight experience include Charles F. Bolden and Mae C. JEMISON, who in September 1992 became the first African-American woman in space.

Black men and women have been valued performers in all aspects of America's aerospace activities.

In the 1980s and '90s the rich heritage of African-American aviation has received increased attention. In 1982, "Black Wings," an exhibit on black aviation pioneers, appeared at the Smithsonian Institution in Washington, D.C. The Tuskegee Airmen have been recognized in several books and a television documentary.

BIBLIOGRAPHY

Gropman, Alan L. *The Air Force Integrates: 1945–1964.* Washington, D.C., 1978.

Hardesty, Von and Dominick Pisano. *Black Wings: The American Black in Aviation.* Washington, D.C., 1983.

Osur, Alan M. *Blacks in the Army Air Forces During World War II: The Problem of Race Relations.* Washington, D.C., 1977.

Sandler, Stanley. *Segregated Skies: All-Black Combat Squadrons of World War II.* Washington, D.C., 1992.

Stinson, Sonya. "African Americans in Aerospace and Defense." *Journal of the National Technical Association* 63, no. 2 (Fall 1989): 50–68.

— WESLEY L. HARRIS

AFFIRMATIVE ACTION

Affirmative action is an act, policy, plan or program designed to remedy the negative effects of wrongful discrimination. "Affirmative action" can remedy the perceived injustice of discrimination on the basis of a person's race, national origin, ethnicity, language, sex, religion, disability, sexual orientation, or affiliation. As a civil rights policy affecting African Americans, "affirmative action" most often denotes race-conscious and result-oriented efforts undertaken by private entities and government officials to correct the unequal distribution of economic opportunity and education that many attribute to slavery, segregation and racism.

What counts as affirmative action varies from one field to the next. Affirmative action in employment has generally meant seeking to hire a racially mixed and balanced workforce that includes a representative number of Americans of African, Latin, Asian-Pacific, or native ancestry, using the distribution of minority groups in the national or local population to gauge adequate representation. Self-described "equal opportunity/affirmative action" employers may voluntarily seek to hire African Americans, sometimes with explicit numerical goals and timetables in mind. For example, an employer whose workforce is 2 percent African American begins to hire additional blacks aiming at a workforce that will eventually include 10 percent African Americans, 3 percent of whom will occupy management positions within three years.

Employers may base affirmative-action programs on the assumption that they can achieve racially balanced workforces through race-conscious hiring and promotion preferences. Preferential employment strategies involve affirmative action on behalf of a racial minority group when a person's minority race results in employment for which race is not otherwise a significant qualification. A person's race may sometimes be a bona fide job-related qualification (Fullinwider 1980). For instance, undercover police work in black neighborhoods may require black police officers; realistic filmmaking about African-American history may require black actors. In such instances, preferring black workers is not affirmative action.

Not all racial preferences involve affirmative action and not all affirmative action involves racial preferences. For example, to attract more African-American job applicants, an employer with a mainly white workforce begins to advertise job openings in the city's neighborhood newspapers, including newspapers circulated in black neighborhoods. This change in practice is potentially effective affirmative action, but it is not preferential treatment in the sense of according blacks employment advantages over whites or other groups (Greenawalt 1983). However, if the same employer committed itself to hiring blacks over similarly qualified or better qualified whites, or by exempting blacks from the adverse impact of seniority rules, one could describe the employer as according blacks preferential treatment as an affirmative-action measure.

Affirmative action in public and private education has focused on such race-conscious programs as "desegregation," "integration," "diversity," and "multiculturalism." Whether voluntarily or pursuant to court orders, to achieve desegregation in public primary and secondary schools formerly subject to state-imposed racial segregation, school officials have expressly mandated numerical goals, ratios and quotas for faculty hiring and pupil enrollment. At some schools, voluntary affirmative action has meant allocating financial resources to recruiting and retaining minority students with special scholarships, curricula, and social programs. At others, it has also meant admissions procedures that deemphasize standardized test scores and other traditional qualifications. Some colleges and universities have adopted legally controversial minority admissions quotas or diversity criteria aimed at enrolling a representative percentage of nonwhite students each year. In many schools the ideal of a diverse, multicultural student body is thought to require affirmative action to employ teachers and to enroll and retain students of varied racial and ethnic backgrounds.

Beyond employment and education, the distribution of public or private benefits on the basis of race for the remedial purpose of redressing group discrimination fits the definition of affirmative action. Hence, minority "set-aside" requirements that reserve a percentage of public contracts for minority businesses qualify as affirmative action. The concept also reaches special effort made by public and private scientific, humanistic, and arts organizations to disburse a share of their grants, awards, and prizes to members of once-neglected minority groups. The concept even reaches redistricting to aggregate minority voters into district that remedy a history of inadequate political representation. Telling evidence of the link some see between affirmative-action quotas and voting rights was exemplified in 1993 when University of Pennsylvania law professor Lani Guinier's scholarly explorations of cumulative voting and other novel strategies to strengthen minority voting rights earned her the epithet "Quota Queen" among conservatives, who successfully thwarted her presidential appointment to head the Civil Rights Division of the Justice Department.

Viewing affirmative action goals as quotas is often designed to suggest "that they, like yesterday's quotas, serve an immoral end" (Erzorsky 1991). Indeed, the affirmative action practiced in employment, education and other fields has excited intense moral and legal debate. The debate centers on the charges that race-conscious remedies designed to redress invidious discrimination against some groups amount to wrongful "reverse discrimination" against others (Steele 1990). Opponents of affirmative action raise particular concern about any form of affirmative action that involves numerical mandates, especially goals and quotas. Although *goals* often connotes flexible guidelines for group inclusion and *quotas* often connote rigid limits with discriminatory intent, both entail optimal percentages or numbers of persons belonging to specific groups targeted to serve in specific capacities (Fullwinder 1980). The strongest proponents of affirmative action argue that numerical mandates, whether termed "goals" or "quotas," are just and effective remedies for persistent discrimination (Johnson 1992).

History

The idea that special effort is needed to remedy discrimination on the basis of race is as old as President Abraham Lincoln's Emancipation Proclamation and the Thirteenth Amendment to the Constitution ending slavery. However, affirmative action as a distinct race-relations policy did not come about until the crest of the Civil Rights Movement of the 1960s. The term "affirmative action" quietly made its debut in American law in 1935, the year Congress passed the Wagner Act, expressly requiring "affirmative action" of employers guilty of discrimination against workers on the basis of union membership.

In June 1941, President Franklin D. Roosevelt issued Executive Order 8802, a precursor of affirmative-action policies in the arena of race relations, which called for "special measures" and "certain action" to end "discrimination in the employment of workers in the defense industries or government [occurring] because of race, creed, color, or national origin." Roosevelt's historic move was intended to boost the wartime economy and reduce severe black unemployment, as urged by A. Philip Randolph and other leaders. Executive Order 8802 was not consistently enforced, but in some states sudden black competition for traditionally white jobs prompted hostility and violence against blacks.

Internal White House discussions of employment policy during the presidency of Dwight D. Eisenhower included consideration of mandatory affirmative action. On March 8, 1961, President John F. Kennedy issued Executive Order 10925 establishing a President's Committee on Equal Employment Opportunity to expand and strengthen efforts to promote full equality of employment opportunity across racial lines. Order 10925 also required that all government contractors agree not to "discriminate against any employee or applicant for employment because of race, creed, color or national origin" and to "take affirmative action to ensure that applicants are employed, and that employees are treated during employment, without regard to their race, creed, color, or national origin."

The monumental Civil Rights Act of 1964 outlawed the most blatant forms of racial discrimination in employment, education, housing, public accommodations, and voting. The 1964 Act desegregated restaurants, cinemas, retail stores, hotels, transportation, and beaches. Building on BROWN V. BOARD OF EDUCATION (1954), the historic Supreme Court decision that ended legal racial segregation of public primary and secondary schools and pronounced that school desegregation should occur "with all deliberate speed," the Act blocked federal aid to segregated schools. The Act banned unequal application of the requirements of voter registration. The Voting Rights Act of 1965 went even further in protecting the franchise, restricting literacy tests and authorizing federal election supervision in the states. Title VII of the 1964 Act banned discrimination by employers of twenty-five or more, labor unions and employment agencies, and created the Equal Employment Opportunity Commission (EEOC). Title VII empowered the federal courts to order "affirmative action as may be appropriate" to remedy past workplace discrimination.

Finally, on September 28, 1965, in the wake of the Civil Rights Act of 1964, President Lyndon B. Johnson's Executive Order 11246 launched affirmative action as the centerpiece of national employment policy and race relations. Aimed at "the full realization of equal employment opportunity," Executive Order 11246, like Kennedy's earlier order, required that firms conducting business with the federal government and these firms' suppliers "take affirmative action to ensure that applicants are employed, and that employees are treated during employment, without regard to their race, creed, color, or national origin." Order 11246 was amended by Executive Order 11375 and implemented by Labor Department Revised Order No. 4, requiring that government contractors in "good faith" set "goals" and "time-tables" for employing previously "underutilized" minority group members available and qualified for hire. The Labor Department's Office of Federal Contract Compliance, awarded responsibility for implementing Order 11246 and its amendments, developed regulations defining a program of "affirmative action" as "a set of specific and result-oriented procedures" undertaken with "every good faith effort" to bring about "equal employment opportunity." Vice President Hubert Humphrey coordinated the Johnson administration's civil rights and affirmative action policies. On Au-

The monumental Civil Rights Act of 1964 outlawed the most blatant forms of racial discrimination in employment, education, housing, public accommodations, and voting.

gust 20, 1965, at a White House conference on equal employment opportunity, Humphrey had revealed a broad understanding of the economic plight of blacks. Humphrey said America had "neglected the Negro too long" and that "government, business and labor must open more jobs to Negroes [and] must go out and affirmatively seek those persons who are qualified and begin to train those who are not."

In 1967, the Department of Health, Education and Welfare (HEW) began requiring colleges and universities receiving federal funds to establish affirmative-action goals for employing female and minority faculty members. In 1972, HEW issued guidelines for higher education requiring both nondiscrimination and efforts to recruit, employ, and promote members of formerly excluded groups "even if that exclusion cannot be traced to particular discriminatory actions on the part of the employer." The HEW guidelines also indicated that colleges and universities were not expected to lower their standards or employ less qualified job candidates. The HEW guidelines distinguished affirmative-action "goals," which its directives required as an indicator of probable compliance, from "quotas" which its directives expressly prohibited. Critics of HEW have argued that a firm distinction is untenable since "a positive 'goal' for one group must be a negative 'quota' for another" (Goldman 1977). Numerous efforts to distinguish goals from quotas have left some analysts unpersuaded: although the purpose of goals may be inclusion and quotas exclusion, "getting people in, where the shape of the 'in' is fixed, will be possible only by keeping others out" (Fullinwider 1980).

By the early 1970s affirmative action in employment became a full-fledged national policy. The EEOC had taken the stand that an obligation of result-oriented affirmative action extended to all employers within its jurisdiction, not just federal contractors or educational institutions receiving federal funds. Political support for the federal government's affirmative action initiatives was initially strong and broad based. Some maintained that affirmative action utilizing numerical goals and timetables was a necessary complement to the 1964 Civil Rights statutes. A century after the formal abolition of slavery, African Americans as a group remained substantially poorer, less well educated, and politically less powerful than whites as a group. Legally enforced segregation had intensified black inequality.

The leadership of the NAACP, the Congress on Racial Equality, the NAACP Legal and Educational Defense Fund, and the National Urban League quickly endorsed affirmative action. Diverse sectors of the economy promptly responded to Washington's affirmative action programs. For example, in 1966, the city of New York, the Roman Catholic Church in Michigan, and the Texas-based retailer Neiman Marcus were among the organizations announcing voluntary plans requiring that their suppliers and other contractors to take affirmative steps toward hiring African Americans.

The political popularity of affirmative action during the Johnson administration subsequently yielded to controversy. An erosion of political support in Congress and the White House for higher education affirmative action programs was evident as early as 1972, seemingly prompted by opposition from faculty members and administrators fearing the demise of traditional standards of scholarly merit. In 1975, the United States Attorney General Edward H. Levi publicly stated that affirmative action constitutes "quotas" and is "not good government." After 1976 both during and after the one-term presidency of the pro-affirmative action Democrat Jimmy Carter, disagreements over the legality, morality, and efficacy of affirmative action strained African-Americans' relationships with labor unions, the Republican Party, and white liberal Democrats, including Jewish liberals who supported the Civil Rights Movement but who were suspicious of government-backed racial quotas that historically had been used to exclude Jews.

Ronald Reagan and George Bush campaigned for the presidency on opposition to affirmative-action "quotas." President Reagan spoke out against affirmative action's numerical goals and quotas, and this opposition became one of the cornerstones of his public policy agenda on issues affecting African Americans. High-profile conservatives defended the ideal of a colorblind society and characterized blacks as overly dependent upon welfare, affirmative action, and other government programs promulgated chiefly by liberal democrats. *Time* and *Newsweek* magazines, as well as other mainstream media, lavished more publicity on affirmative-action controversies than any other topic related to blacks, including unemployment, health, hunger, and homelessness (Daniel and Allen 1988). The NAACP and the National Urban League maintained their support for affirmative action and the civil rights laws. Consistent with the Reagan agenda, however, the federal government lessened its enforcement of federal contracts compliance programs in the 1980s and a number of Supreme Court cases curbed affirmative action in employment and other key fields.

In the 1990s some were prepared to attribute significant gains for blacks to affirmative action, including an increase in black employment and promotion at major corporations, in heavy industry, in police and fire departments, and in higher education (Erzorsky 1991). Yet, persistent critics converted "affirmative action" into a virtual perjorative, along with "preferential treatment," "reverse discrimination," and "quotas." Symoblic of the era, Democrat Bill Clinton, a supporter of affirmative-action policies, after election to the presidency in 1992 abruptly withdrew the nomination of Lani Guinier to the Justice Department after her critics labeled her affirmative-action policies as outside the mainstream.

Moral and Policy Debates

Reflecting ties to the Civil Rights Movement, the stated goals of affirmative action range from the forward-looking goal of improving society by remedying distributive inequities, to the backward-looking goal of righting historic wrongs (Erzorsky 1991; McGary 1977–78). Affirmative action on behalf of African Americans often was, and often is, defended by scholars as compensation or reparation owed to blacks by whites or a white-dominated society (Boxhill 1984; Thomson 1977). In particular, it is argued that after two centuries of legally enforced slavery, racial segregration, and racism, African Americans now deserve the jobs, education, and other benefits made possible through affirmative action. Beyond compensatory or reparative justice, goals ascribed to affirmative action include promoting economic opportunity for minority groups and individuals; eradicating racial subordination; neutralizing the competitive advantages many whites enjoy in education, business, and employment; educating a cadre of minority professionals for service in underserved minority communities; creating minority role models, intellectuals, artists, and civic leaders; and, finally, acknowledging society's cultural diversity (Goldberg 1994; Erzorsky 1991; Boxhill 1984; Greenawalt 1983).

The stated goals of affirmative action range from improving society by remedying distributive inequities, to righting historic wrongs.

African Americans widely support affirmative action-policies. To be sure, some African-American neoconservatives, such as Glen Loury, Thomas Sowell, and Clarence THOMAS, have rejected affirmative action on the grounds that it is incompatible with a "colorblind" civil rights policy. Other African Americans sometimes have also criticized affirmative action, often on pragmatic grounds (Carter 1991; Steele 1990; Wilson 1987). They have joined those who argue that preferential treatment in education and employment mainly benefits middle-class blacks, leaving the problem of profound rural and urban black poverty untouched (Goldman 1979; Cohen 1980). Critics say affirmative action reinforces pervasive negative stereotypes of blacks as inferior to whites (Jencks, 1983). African Americans have noted this and have argued that racial preferences are demeaning or dispiriting to minorities; that they compromise African-Americans' self-esteem or self-respect (Sowell 1976). Some reject affirmative action because it has proven to be socially divisive, having bred resentment among white Americans (Nagel 1977).

As an antidote to simmering white resentments, William J. Wilson (1987) has proposed promoting race-neutral "universal policies" aimed at the health and employment problems of the poor rather than merely promoting affirmative action for racial minorities. The search for factors beyond race and racism to explain persistent black inequality in the post civil rights era has led some politically conservative opponents of affirmative action to advance the argument that minority economic inequality stems from a pervasive breakdown in work, family, and community values in minority communities.

Supporters of affirmative action offer pertinent replies to all of these arguments (Erzorsky 1991). To the contention that affirmative action does not help the poorest blacks, a reply has been that affirmative action nonetheless enhances the lives of some deserving blacks. To the argument that affirmative action lowers esteem for blacks and blacks' self-esteem, a reply is that blacks are held in very low esteem already and are vulnerable to low self-esteem due to their inferior education and employment. To the argument that affirmative action is racially divisive and breeds resentment, a reply is that blacks should not be deprived of the benefits of affirmative action simply because of white resentment, unless that resentment can be shown to stem from genuine racial injustice. Finally, to the "fingerpointing" argument that blacks' problems result from lapses of individual responsibility, one reply is that communities of poverty, drugs, and violence result from decades of private and public decision making concerning legal, economic, and social policy.

Gertrude Erzorsky (1991), who supports affirmative action, has noted a libertarian argument against affirmative action: employers should be free to choose their own workers as a basic moral freedom, comparable to the freedom to choose one's own spouse. The more common libertarian argument asserts that social and economics benefits should be distributed solely in accordance with colorblind principles of entitlement, merit, and personal. In liberal academic and intellectual circles, opponents of affirmative action have questioned the coherence of the idea that blacks as a group are entitled to, merit or deserve affirmative action as compensation or reparations for past wrongdoing (Sher

under Title VI. They ascertained that the plain language of the statute prohibiting discrimination was sufficient justification for nullifying the program.

The dissenting opinion of Justices Brennan, White, Marshall, and Blackmun cautioned that the nation's "colorblind" values were purely aspirational. They argued that a reading of the history and purpose of Title VI did not rule out race-conscious remedies. Taking up the constitutional issues, these justices rejected strict scrutiny review in favor of a lower, "intermediate" level of scrutiny. They reasoned that intermediate scrutiny permits racial classification "substantially related to an important government objective" and concluded that the university's purpose of counteracting an actual or potential disparate racial impact stemming from discrimination was sufficiently important to justify race-conscious admissions. Justice Marshall also separately wrote a dissenting opinion expressing his sense of irony at the Court's reluctance to uphold race-conscious remedies: "[i]t is unnecessary in 20th century America to have individual Negroes demonstrate that they have been victims of racial discrimination; the racism of our society has been so pervasive that none, regardless of wealth or position, has managed to escape its impact."

In 1982 the Supreme Court again took up the subject of affirmative action in professional school admissions in *Mississippi University for Women* v. *Hogan.* The nursing school of the university denied full admission to male students (admitted only as auditors) on the grounds that the education of women was "educational affirmative action" intended to mitigate the adverse effects of discrimination on women. A man denied admission brought suit under the Equal Protection Clause. A five-justice majority that included Justices Marshall and O'Connor invalidated the single-sex policy on his behalf. Justice O'Connor wrote for the Court, applying the intermediate scrutiny standard of review. This same standard is the one the Court normally applies to gender classification cases brought under the Fourteenth Amendment's Equal Protection Clause. It is also the standard that Justice Marshall defended as appropriate for affirmative action cases involving *remedial* racial classifications. The Court required that Mississippi advance an "exceedingly persuasive justification" for its gender distinction in nursing education, that included a claim that the distinction was substantially related to an important government goal. Finding no such relationship or justification, the Court disparaged the ideal of a single-sex learning environment in nursing as a "self-fulfilling prophecy" based on the stereotype that nursing is "women's work." Dissenting Justices Powell, Blackmun, Rehnquist, and Chief Justice Burger denied that the case raised a serious question of gender discrimination. Powell stressed that no woman had complained about the school and that coed nursing education was available elsewhere in the state. Although the majority limited its holding to the nursing school, the dissenters raised concerns about the implication of the case for traditional same-sex higher education in the United States. It appears that affirmative action for women may not be used as a rationale for excluding men from women's traditional provinces.

Title VII Permits Voluntary Quotas

In a significant decision, the Supreme Court reconciled Title VII of the Civil Rights Act of 1964 with voluntary affirmative action programs in *United Steel Workers* v. *Weber* (1979). With a vote of 5 to 2 (two justices did not participate in the decision), the *Weber* case upheld an employer's affirmative-action plan that temporarily required a minimum of 50 percent African-American composition in a skill-training program established to increase African-American representation in skilled positions. The lower courts had ruled that *any* racial preferences violated Title VII, even if they were established in the context of an affirmative action plan. Importantly, the Court held that Title VII's ban on all racial discrimination did not apply to affirmative-action plans. Dissenting justices Burger and Rehnquist disagreed, arguing in separate opinions that the plain language of Title VII and its legislative history banned voluntary racial preferences, even those employed as affirmative-action remedies. *Newsweek* magazine reported the *Weber* decision as a "Victory for Quotas." Eleanor Holmes Norton, the African-American head of the EEOC, declared that "employers and unions no longer need fear that conscientious efforts to open job opportunities will be subjected to legal challenge." Senator Orrin Hatch responded differently, asserting that the purpose of the Civil Rights Act had not been to "guarantee any racial group a fixed proportion of the positions and perquisites available in American society" and that the "American dream" of true liberty was "in real danger."

In *Johnson* v. *Transportation Department* (1987) the court held (6 to 3) that Title VII permits affirmative consideration of employees' gender when awarding promotions. In *Johnson* the Court upheld the promotion of Diane Joyce, made according to the Transportation Agency of Santa Clara County's voluntarily adopted affirmative-action plan. Permitting the use of sex, minority status, and disability as factors for promotional consideration, the plan survived a challenge under Title VII by a man passed over for a "road dispatcher" position. In another case, *Local No. 93, International Association of Firefighters* v. *Cleveland* (1986), the Court held that parties to a consent decree may agree to relief that might not be within a court's ordering authority under Title VII. An African-American and Latino firefighters' organization, the Vanguards, had filed a complaint against the city of Cleveland for intentional discrimination in "hiring, assignment and promotion." Since the city had previously been unsuccessful in defending other discrimination suits, it sought to settle with the Vanguards. Local 93 (Union) intervened, not bringing any claims for or against either party, but voicing strenuous opposition to a settlement including any race-conscious action. When a consent decree, which provided for the action was agreed upon and entered, the Union filed its unsuccessful formal complaint that the decree exceeded a court's authority under Title VII.

Title VII permits affirmative action that includes numerical goals, and may permit courts to order it. In *Local 28 of the Sheet Metal Workers' International Association* v. *EEOC* (1986), the Supreme Court upheld a court-ordered membership plan for a trade union found guilty of racial discrimination violating Title VII. The plan included a membership goal of 29 percent African American and Latino. The Court was again willing to permit a numerically based affirmative-action remedy in *United States* v. *Paradise* (1987). There the Court validated a temporary affirmative-action plan ordered by a lower court that required a one-for-one promotion ratio of whites to qualified blacks in the Alabama Department of Public Safety. The department had been found guilty of discrimination in 1972, but had failed to adopt promotion procedure that did not have a disparate impact on blacks. Justice William Brennan wrote an opinion arguing that the affirmative-action order was a narrowly tailored means to achieve a compelling government purpose, and it therefore met the requirements of strict scrutiny imposed by Fourteenth Amendment equal protection.

Noncongressional Business Set-Asides Set Aside

A year after the *Weber* case, in *Fullilove* v. *Klutznick* (1980), the Court upheld a provision of the congressional Public Works Employment Act, which mandated that ten percent of $4 billion in federal funds allocated for local public construction projects go to "minority business enterprises," statutorily defined as at least 50 percent owned by citizens who are "Negroes, Spanish-speaking, Oriental, Indians, Eskimos, and Aleuts." The provision had been challenged under equal protection principles. Chief Justice Burger delivered the judgment of the Court, joined by Justices White and Powell. Justice Marshall, concurring in the judgment in *Fullilove* and joined in his opinion by Justices Brennan and Blackmun, argued that "Congress reasonably determined that race-conscious means were necessary to break down the barriers confronting participation by minority enterprises in federally funded public works projects." *Fullilove* survived contest in the Court at a time when critics of federal support for minority business enterprises argued that, in addition to raising questions of fairness raised by all affirmative action, the disbursal of funds under the 1977 Public Works Employment Act by the Commerce Department's Economic Development Administration was subject to abuse (Ross 1979). The Government Accounting Office uncovered hundreds of instances of federal dollars being awarded both to minority brokers serving as go-betweens for nonminority firms and government administrators; and to nonminority firms feigning minority ownership with the help of minority "fronts" installed as phony partners or owners.

Richmond v. *J. A. Croson Co.* (1989) successfully attacked an affirmative-action plan reserving specific numerical percentages of a public benefit for minorities. The invalidated "minority set-aside" plan required prime contractors with the city of Richmond to "subcontract at least 30 percent of the dollar amount of the contract to one or more Minority Business Enterprises." The plan was challenged under 42 U.S.C. §1983, a civil rights statute, by a nonminority firm who lost a contracting opportunity due to noncompliance with the program. The justices widely disagreed about the outcome and the reasoning of the case. Thus, Justice O'Connor delivered the opinion of the Court with respect to three of its parts, joined by Chief Justice Rehnquist and Justices Stevens, White, and Kennedy; Justices Stevens and Kennedy field separate partial concurrences; Justice Scalia field a concurring opinion; Justice Marshall dissented, joined in his opinion by Justices Brennan and Blackmun; finally, Justice Blackmun filed a dissenting opinion, joined by Justice Brennan. A major task for the majority was to explain how they could invalidate the set-aside in *Croson* when the Court had previously validated a similar set-aside in *Fullilove.* Justice O'Connor distinguished the *Fullilove* case on the ground that its set-aside had been created by Congress and involved an exercise of federal congressional power, whereas the set-aside in *Croson* was a creature of municipal government. Justice Thurgood Marshall dissented from the judgment in *Croson,* warning that the Court's ruling threatened all affirmative action plans not specifically enacted by Congress—virtually all plans.

Metro Broadcasting, Inc. v. *FCC* (1990) upheld two race-conscious Federal Communications Commission programs designed to enhance program diversity. The race-conscious set-asides were challenged under equal protection principles by a nonminority broadcasting company that had lost its bid to acquire a broadcasting license to a minority-owned company. The Court argued that programming diversity, a goal both the FCC and Congress linked to ownership diversity, was derived from the public's First Amendment interest in hearing a wide spectrum of ideas and viewpoints. The interest was a sufficiently important one to justify race-conscious allocation policies. Justice O'Connor and three other justices dissented from what they considered excessive deference to Congress and a refusal to apply strict scrutiny to an instance of race-conscious thinking grounded in racial stereotypes.

Future Directions

Decided by the slimmest majority and largely on unusual First Amendment grounds, *Metro Broadcasting* leaves standing the basis for Justice Marshall's concerns about the future of all affirmative action. So, too, does *Shaw* v. *Reno* (1993). This case held that white voters stated a legitimate Fourteenth Amendment equal protection claim against North Carolina for creating a voter redistricting plan described as "so irrational on its face that it c[ould] be understood only as an effort to segregate voters" on the basis of race. Justices White, Souter, and Stevens dissented. In an attempt to comply with the Voting Rights Act, North Carolina had created a redistricting plan with two irregularly shaped "majority-minority" (majority Black and Native American) districts. In reversing the lower court, the Court invoked the ideal of a "colorblind" society and warned of the dangers of "political apartheid." Nonetheless, the constitutionality of the districts was subsequently upheld by a federal judicial panel.

The ideal of a colorblind society continues to vex proponents of race-conscious remedies to discrimination.

The ideal of a colorblind society continues to vex proponents of race-conscious remedies to discrimination. The greatest consistency in the evolving law of affirmative action is that, at any given time, its precise contour mirrors the mix of perspectives represented on the Court concerning the deepest purposes and meaning of the 1964 Civil Rights Act and the Fourteenth Amendment of the Constitution. The Supreme Court has upheld key affirmative-action measures in the past, and may again in the future, although a series of rulings in the the spring and summer of 1995 have cast considerable doubt on the allowable scope of affirmative action. Notably, in the case of *Adarand Constructors* v. *Peña* (1995) the Court ruled, 5 to 4, that the federal government's affirmative-action programs must be able to meet the same strict standards for constitutional review as had previously been applied by the Court to state and local programs. Outside the courts, controversy continues.

BIBLIOGRAPHY

Erin Fatica assisted with the legal research for this entry.

Belz, Herman. *Affirmative Action from Kennedy to Reagan: Redefining American Equality.* Washington, D.C., 1984.

Berry, Mary Francis, and John W. Blassingame. *Long Memory: The Black Experience in America.* New York, 1982.

Boxhill, Bernard. *Blacks and Social Justice.* Totowa, N.J., 1984.

Capaldi, Nicholas. *Out of Order: Affirmative Action and the Crisis of Doctrinaire Liberalism.* Buffalo, N.Y., 1985.

Cashman, Dean Dennis. *African Americans and the Quest for Civil Rights, 1900–1990.* New York, 1990.

Daniel, Jack, and Anita Allen. "Newsmagazines and the Black Agenda." In Geneva Smitherman-Donaldson and Teun A. van Dijk, eds. *Discrimination and Discourse.* Detroit, 1988, pp. 23–45.

Eastland, Terry, and William Bennett. *Counting by Race: Equality from the Founding Fathers to Bakke and Weber.* New York, 1979.

Erzorsky, Gertrude. *Racism and Justice: The Case for Affirmative Action.* Ithaca, N.Y., 1991.

Finch, Minnie. *The NAACP: Its Fight for Justice.* Metuchen, N.J., 1981.

Fullinwider, Robert K. *The Reverse Discrimination Controversy: A Moral and Legal Analysis.* Totowa, N.J., 1980.

Goldman, Alan. *Justice and Reverse Discrimination.* Princeton, N.J., 1979.

Gross, Barry. *Discrimination in Reverse: Is Turn-about Fair Play?* New York, 1978.

Green, Kathanne. *Affirmative Action and Principles of Justice.* New York, 1989.

Greenawalt, Kent. *Discrimination and Reverse Discrimination.* New York, 1983.

Horne, Gerald. *Reverse Discrimination: the Case for Affirmative Action.* New York, 1992.

Johnson, Alex M. "Defending the Use of Quotas in Affirmative Action: Attacking Racism in the Nineties." *University of Illinois Law Review* 1992 (1992): 1043–1073.

Kull, Andrew. *The Color-Blind Constitution.* Cambridge, Mass., 1992.

Livingston, John C. *Fair Game? Inequality and Affirmative Action.* San Francisco, 1979.

Loury, Glenn. "Why Should We Care About Group Inequality?" *Social Philosophy and Policy* 5 (1988): 249–271.

McGary, Howard, Jr., "Justice and Reparations." *Philosophical Forum* 9 (1977–78): 250–263.

Mosley, Albert G. "Affirmative Action and the Urban Underclass." In *The Underclass Question.* Philadelphia, 1992, pp. 140–151.

Neiman, Donald G. *Promises to Keep: African Americans and the Constitutional Order, 1776 to the Present.* New York, 1991.

Newton, Lisa. "Reverse Discrimination as Unjustified." *Ethics* 83 (1973): 1–4.

Rosenfeld, Michel. *Affirmative Action: a Philosophical and Constitutional Inquiry.* New Haven, Conn., 1991.

Rossum, Ralph A. *Reverse Discrimination: The Constitutional Debate.* New York, 1980.

Schwartz, Bernard, *Behind Bakke: Affirmative Action and the Supreme Court.* New York, 1988.
Steele, Shelby. "A Negative Vote on Affirmative Action." *New York Times Magazine,* May 13, 1990.
———. *The Content of Our Character: A New Vision of Race in America.* New York, 1990.
"A Stricter Standard for Affirmative Action." *New York Times,* July 21, 1995.
Thomson, Judith J. "Preferential Hiring." In Marshall Cohen, Thomas Nagel, and Thomas Scanlon, eds. *Equality and Preferential Treatment.* Princeton, N.J., 1977, pp. 19–39.
Wilson, William Julius. *The Truly Disadvantaged.* Chicago, 1987.

– ANITA LAFRANCE ALLEN

AFRICA

This article deals with the African background of African Americans as a means of understanding the ecological aspects of the continent from which the ancestors of this population came, and the history and nature of the major biological, linguistic, and sociocultural processes that produced those Africans. Although many of these processes were continent-wide, specific attention is paid to West and Central Africa, the regions that contributed most of the ancestors of Africans in the New World.

African Americans may have more reasons than other people to ponder the symbolism in the very shape of Africa—a question mark. After pondering the question of their connection to Africa for several centuries, as did Countee CULLEN in his classic poem "Heritage," most African Americans now fully affirm their link with what Cullen described as a land of "Copper sun or scarlet sea/Jungle star or jungle track/Strong black men or regal black/Women from whose loins I sprang/When the birds of Eden sang." Today, African Americans point with pride to their many pan-African links, especially with black South Africans, whose political emancipation they view as ending the long, bitter years of alien domination of the continent. Many proudly wear articles associated with Ghana's "kente-cloth complex" (the royal colors of kings and queens).

Almost as soon as African Americans had mastered elements of European culture, they fought against the notion that "the superior white man must bear the burden of civilizing colonial peoples of the world, if necessary against the will of those peoples" (Drake and Cayton 1970, p. 47). They especially resented and resisted the assertion that "The very existence of social order [in America] is believed to depend upon 'keep[ing] the Negro in his place' " (ibid., 756). African Americans were determined to disprove the implications of the belief that "it would be a matter of a thousand years before Africans could develop high forms of civilization or become dangerous to the white race" (Beale 1956, p. 44). The issue for African Americans was not to become "dangerous to the white race," but to liberate themselves and Africa from the control of those who questioned their very humanity. African Americans were determined to disprove the common belief that Africa had no history.

African Americans were among the first persons of African origin to insist that the brilliance of the Egyptian past is only one episode in the history of a continent that gave the world so much. Furthermore, while most of the ancestors of African Americans came from the Atlantic coasts of the continent, their cultural background undoubtedly shared many aspects of a widespread and ancient civilization. More than most continents, Africa has always been a veritable museum where kaleidoscopic cultural patterns from various epochs and their syntheses have coexisted. To avoid confusion, it is best to describe many aspects of Africa in the past tense—as part of history, since the African background often resonates as a heritage in the lives of its now far-flung peoples.

The Geography of Africa

A realm of abundant sunshine, Africa bisects the equator; 80 percent of its land mass falls between the Tropics of Cancer and Capricorn. The continent's 11.7 million square miles makes it more than three times the size of the United States, including Alaska. Its northern part borders the Mediterranean. To its east lie the Red Sea and the Indian Ocean; South Africa is surrounded by a confluence of the Indian and the Atlantic oceans. The Atlantic borders all of the western coasts of Africa. Madagascar, the largest of the continent's islands, lies to the southeast, surrounded by the Indian Ocean, and the other African islands—São Tomé, Principe, Bioko, Cape Verde, and the Canaries—are westward in the Atlantic Ocean.

Some geologists believe that Africa was the geomorphological core of an ancient supercontinent known as Gondwanaland. Around 200 million years ago this enormous land mass, averaging about 2,500 feet above sea level, fractured, leaving Africa as a high plateau of ancient Precambrian rocks sloping toward the north, while the other pieces drifted away to form South America, the Indian subcontinent, Australia, and Antarctica. Although this giant fracture created very few mountain ranges and water basins within Africa, it did create a system of spectacular trenches known as the Great Rift valley in eastern Africa. Starting in Anatolia of northern Turkey, the rift goes south for a distance of some six thousand miles, through what are now the Jordan Valley and the Dead Sea; through the Gulf of Aqaba and the length of the Red Sea; bisecting the Ethiopian Massif and continuing down into East Africa, where it divides into two branches in which are found

Lakes Kivu, Edward, Rudolf (Turkana), Albert, Victoria (the source of the Nile River and the second largest of the world's freshwater lakes), Malawi, and Tanganyika, whose bottom is several thousand feet below sea level; and finally ending at the mouth of the Zambezi River.

The majestic glacier-tipped Kilimanjaro, 19,340 feet above sea level and the highest mountain in Africa, was formed, like the other mountain ranges, by tectonic forces after the ancient faulting. The Atlas range in the northwest rises to some 13,000 feet, the Tibesti Massifs in the Sahara are over 13,000 feet, and the Cameroon Highlands in the west are comparable in height. In East Africa there are the Ethiopian Highlands with Mount Ras Dashan (15,158 feet), and further south are the great extinct volcanoes of Mounts Elgon, Kenya, and Ruwenzori (the Mountains of the Moon), which average about 17,000 feet high. The Drakensberg Mountains in southeast Africa rise to more than 11,000 feet.

Large inland basins, which are drained by the continent's spectacular rivers, often extend from the base of these mountain ranges. Characteristically, most African rivers are navigable for great distances across the continent's interior plateau until they plunge over impassable rapids or cataracts as they approach an extraordinarily narrow and relatively straight coastal plain. The advantage here is that the points at which these rivers leave the plateau can be the sites for hydroelectric dams. The disadvantage is that the rivers enter the ocean through deltas and shifting sandbars rather than through estuaries, thereby depriving the African continent of a large number of bays and gulfs that provide natural harbors in other parts of the world.

African Americans may have more reasons than other people to ponder the symbolism in the very shape of Africa—a question mark.

For example, the Zambezi drops some 343 feet over the spectacular Victoria Falls—more than twice the height of Niagara—before it heads for the sea. The Nile, along whose banks early civilizations bloomed, flows northward out of Central Africa and drops over several cataracts before joining the Mediterranean. The Niger River rises in the Liberian Highlands and goes east and then south, picking up such tributaries as the Benue and Cross rivers before emptying into the Atlantic. The great Congo River with its huge tributaries, the Kasai and the Ubangi, drains thousands of square miles before tumbling over falls to flow into the Atlantic. Many of Africa's smaller river systems, such as the Limpopo, Orange, Senegal, Vaal, and Voltas, exhibit the same pattern. Without outlets to the sea, such internal drainage systems as Lake Chad in the north and the Okavango Swamp in the south end up in shallow, brackish lakes or salt marshes.

Africa has basically seven climatic and vegetation zones. There is a central equatorial zone, and, radiating both north and south, replicating subtropical savanna zones, low-altitude desertlike zones, and Mediterranean zones. All of these are influenced by the contour of the land, and by monsoons and coastal currents. Africa's humid equatorial zone, though often referred to as "jungle," is smaller than those found either in South America or in parts of Asia. It covers central Africa, strips along the Guinea coast, and parts of Gabon, Cameroon, and northern Zaire. Here the temperatures range between 90°F during the day and 70°F during the nights. Rainfall is highest following the equinox (March and September), with an annual amount of about 50–70 inches. In some coastal areas where moisture-laden winds ascend steep slopes, the total can rise to more than 200 inches. The East African Highlands, situated on the equator, have lower temperatures and rainfall than the lowlands. In the lowlands there are tropical rain forests characterized by liana and dense vegetation, as well as species of valuable palm trees, mahogany, ebony, teak, sapele, niangnon, and kolas. The vegetation in the East African Highlands includes deciduous forests and evergreens.

The subtropical savanna ecological zones, which lie both north and south of the equatorial zone, occupy the largest area on the continent and differ only by altitude and proximity to the oceans. The fairly large northern ecological zone, which is also incidentally lower and wider, covers parts of Nigeria, the Sudan, and Chad. The temperatures can range up to 100°F, especially from March to May, just before the rains, but are usually between 70 and 50 degrees; temperatures in December and January are lower, especially during the harmattan, a dry, dusty wind that blows from the Sahara southward. Temperatures are lower in the southern subtropical zone because of the higher elevation and decreased width. The annual rainfall in both zones is 30–60 inches. Both subtropical zones are marked by the preponderant vegetation cover of the continent—grass—and within grasslands are found scattered trees of species such as the baobab and (where rainfall permits) acacia. At particularly high elevations such as the Cameroon Highlands, or the highlands and rolling plateaus of Kenya (Mounts Kilimanjaro and Ruwenzori have permanent ice fields), the upland grasslands are replaced by forests, such as the High Veldt of Transvaal, or by steep mountain slopes. Taken as a whole, this region is the one that supports many of the continent's herbivores, and pastoral activities play an important role in the economies of the indigenous peoples.

Low, dry, hot ecological zones are found both north and south as one moves further away from the equator. The Sahel in West Africa gradually shades into the Sahara, the desert of the Horn, and the Kalahari and Namid deserts are found in the south. The temperatures in the desert areas are quite variable, with great changes in daily temperature, except near the coasts. And while annual precipitation in the northern desert ranges from only 4 inches downward to zero, the popular image of the African deserts as barren rock and sand dunes bereft of vegetation is incorrect. The deserts actually support scrub and, on the margins, even grass for pasturage. The Sahara, in particular, is dotted with oases that support intensive agriculture, and in the east there is the fertile Nile Valley. The Namid Desert, which borders the Atlantic coast of southwestern Africa, is more desolate, receiving less than 10 inches; but the Kalahari, inland from the Namid, is really only a semidesert, receiving as much as 15 inches per year. It comes to quick life with the first sprinkling of rain, and often has stands of grasses and inland pans of water.

Mediterranean subtropical ecological zones are the next latitudinal regions. Characteristic of these are winter rains (from 25 to 32 inches) and summer droughts. The winters are mild, between 50°F and 60°F, and the summers around 70°F. The variable rainfalls and temperatures in these zones permit the growth of forests and brush.

The climate of Madagascar, Africa's largest island, ranges from tropical to largely subtropical. Its coastal lowlands are wet, hot, and covered with tropical forests, while the Central Highlands are drier, fairly cool, and covered with grass and interspersed woodlands. Bioko (the former Fernando Po) and São Tomé possess equatorial ecologies; the Cape Verde Islands share the ecology of the Sahel and are often plagued by droughts.

The distribution of African soils reflects the belts of temperature and especially rainfall. Approximately 36 percent of Africa, especially the equatorial zone of Zaire and the Guinea coast, may be characterized as humid, 22 percent semiarid, 26 percent arid, and 16 percent desert. This means that nearly two-thirds of Africa has a moisture deficiency during all or part of the year. The amount of water available is a function of regional and seasonal swings; it ranges from excess water, due to persistent rainfall and high humidity, to too little rainfall and high evaporation. The result is that if the soil is suddenly exposed to the elements by either humans or nature, there is severe erosion and a loss of the fertility so necessary for crop cultivation. Nevertheless, most, if not all, African soils are good for short periods, provided that they have a long fallow. The soils in humid and semiarid areas, while initially rich in humus content, lose their fertility and become lateritic if cultivated continuously. The soils of the arid lands are relatively rich in inorganic minerals but low in humus content, and need additional water in order to be usable. Typically, seasonal variation in moisture distribution sets limits on the types and amounts of crops grown. Several parts of Africa have suffered from droughts and "hungry periods" due to shortages of food.

Mineral, Plant, and Animal Resources

Africa is immensely rich in minerals, in flora, and in fauna. The continent has about two-thirds of the world's phosphorites, some 45 percent of the world's bauxite, 20 percent of its copper, 16 percent of its uranium, and substantial reserves of iron ore, manganese, chromium, cobalt, platinum, and titanium. The food crops of Africa include coffee, ensete (a banana-like fruit), varieties of yams and rice, millets, sorghums, varieties of oil palms, the kola nut, and melons, all of which are believed to be indigenous to the continent; wheat, barley, and oats, of Middle Eastern origin; varieties of bananas and plantains, thought to be of Southeast Asian origin; and maize, manioc, peanuts, tomatoes, varieties of potatoes, and some tubers and cocoa beans—all cultigens that arrived in Africa as a result of the post-Columbus great plant migration. Cotton is common in the northern savanna belt and species of trees produced bark used for making cloth. In addition, the hardwoods and lianas of the tropical forests have been utilized by human beings for shelter and for many useful products over generations.

The domestic animals of the continent include varieties of cattle, sheep, goats, horses, donkeys, camels, pigs, dogs, chickens, ducks, and the semidomesticated guinea fowl. Africa is famous for its wide variety of animals representing thousands of species of mammals, reptiles, amphibians, fish, birds, and insects. Huge herds of a variety of antelopes, giraffes, and zebras roam the savannas, providing the prey for cheetahs, leopards, and lions. Herds of elephants still roam parts of eastern and southern Africa, having been largely eliminated in the north and west. The hippopotamus still lives in tropical rivers; varieties of water birds, such as the flamingo, are among the enormous range of African birds. Many of the animals in Africa, such as the rhinoceros, are now under stress for survival as a result of excessive hunting and the growth of the human populations.

Africa and the Origin of Human Beings

A growing number of paleontologists and human geneticists now believe that the origins of the billions of human beings on Earth can be traced to a woman who lived in Africa some 200,000 years ago and left an unmistakable signature on the DNA of all *Homo sapiens.* This was the most important stage in a process that started some 4 million years ago, when the genus *Homo* emerged from the *Australopithecus,* giving rise to *Homo erectus, Homo neanderthalensis,* and other varieties of *Homo.* Then, some 250,000 to 100,000 years ago, modern humans—with lighter skeletons, "their more capacious brains, and their softer brows" and possibly "with language"—radiated out from "their African homeland and overwhelmed or supplanted the many more primitive humans who were then living in Asia and Europe" ("New Debate Over Humankind's Ancestress," *New York Times,* October 1, 1991, sec. C). That such a theory is gaining ground is all the more remarkable since in the past, the prejudice against all things African was pronounced. Charles Darwin suggested that in view of the abundance of animal life there, especially that of the primates, it would be wise to look to Africa as the possible cradle of humankind, but this was rejected by his contemporaries, who were convinced of white supremacy.

Biologists now believe that as human beings moved about within and outside the African continent, they retained the ability to interbreed, but their geno-phenotypes (often referred to as geographical "races") emerged as adaptations to different ecological zones. No one knows what the earliest *Homo sapiens* in Africa looked like, but the so-called Negro-appearing people became the dominant physical type in sub-Saharan Africa (pockets of these Negroid people also lived in the oases of the Sahara). The Negroes in the Nile Valley tend to be taller and darker; eastward, in the Horn of Africa, the people appear to be a mixture of Negroids and the so-called Caucasoids. Caucasoid populations live in northern Africa and in the northern parts of the Sahara and the Nile valley. A short variety of Negroids, popularly known as Pygmies, live scattered among their taller neighbors in the central regions, and in southern Africa live another fairly short population, yellowish in skin color and possessing wiry hair, known as the Khoisan. Also in southern Africa and parts of east-central Africa are found Caucasoid and Caucasoid-like populations of European and Indian provenance; Malayo-Polynesian populations are settled in Madagascar.

Challenges to Human Life

The human populations in Africa have had to cope with a variety of insect-borne and other diseases that flourish in the tropics, and in a few cases they have adapted geno-phenotypically to these. Yellow fever and malaria, carried by mosquitoes, have been widespread, and some populations, especially in West Africa, have acquired a certain immunity to sicklemia (sickle cell anemia), caused by malaria. Trypanosomiasis, or sleeping sickness, whose vector or carrier is the tsetse fly, is found primarily in humid forested or savanna areas and is dangerous to both human beings and animals, especially cattle and horses. Schistosomiasis, by far the most widespread of African diseases, is caused by parasites of the genus *Schistosoma* which live in running water and enter the human body through the skin after a complex life cycle that includes the snail as an intermediate host. Also associated with river valleys is onchocerciasis, or river blindness, which is carried by a species of fly, *Simulium damnosum.* In addition to these, there are varieties of diseases caused by nematodes such as guinea worms, liver flukes, and tapeworms. AIDS is the most recent virulent disease to have appeared. In contrast to many other parts of the world, where it is often associated with homosexuality and intravenous drug use, in Africa AIDS is often associated with heterosexual activities. While no cure has been found for AIDS, such diseases as schistosomiasis, malaria, yellow fever, and trypanosomiasis are less morbid than in the past, and yaws and leprosy have been largely eliminated from African populations.

African Languages

Africa's 750 to 800 different languages not only represent the largest group of languages found on any continent but are spoken by populations differing in physical types and cultures. The debate about the classification, nature, and number of African languages continues, due to the lack of agreement among scholars as to criteria used to determine genetic relationships and differences between languages and their dialects. One major consensus, however, is that all African languages fall into four major families. The languages of the largest family, the Niger-Kordofanian, are spoken in western, central, eastern, and southern Africa. The Bantu languages—one of six subgroups of the Benue-Congo languages—are believed to have recently spread over most of central and southern Africa, since they are closely related to each other. Swahili, spoken in many parts of East Africa, is an Arabized Bantu language. In southern Africa and in parts of Tanganyika are found a small but important group of languages belonging to the *Khoisan* family. This family is believed to be the source of the "clicks" found in the Bantu languages. The *Nilo-Saharan* languages are not only the second largest group of African languages, but members are found widely separated in the Nile Valley and in the Niger basin of West Africa. Also widely distributed are members of the *Afroasiatic* family, which include Semitic languages such as Arabic and Hebrew spoken outside of Africa, Berber, Hausa, and ancient Egyptian, in addition to such Cushitic languages as Amharic, found in Ethiopia. Malayo-Polynesian languages are found in Madagascar; Germanic and Latin languages were brought into Africa by the incoming Europeans.

Peoples and Cultures of Africa

Africa was the site not only of important steps in the evolution of the human species, but of a parallel development; the evolution of culture, a distinctive human characteristic. Some of the earliest traces of human cultural activities—such as stone assemblages—subsequently spread, and the evolution of these artifacts both within the African continent and outside of it, with frequent interchange, attest to the processes by which African cultures subsequently developed. Initially, all African populations lived by foraging, but by 13,000 before the present (B.P.) there is evidence that the Mesolithic (Middle Stone Age) population, which lived in the valley of the Nile around Khartoum, included harvested wild cereals in its diet. By 6000 B.P. the peoples in the Nile Valley shared the practice of crop cultivation and animal domestication with those in other parts of the Fertile Crescent, which extended eastward to the Tigris and Euphrates river valleys. Within the limits of ecological constraints, these food-production techniques involving plants and animals specific to Africa spread to various parts of the continent, replacing but not totally eliminating earlier foraging patterns. The same generalization can be made about the invention and spread of Iron Age technologies and other traits important to early African peoples (Wai Andah 1981, p. 592; Posnansky 1981, pp. 533–534).

Africa was the site not only of important steps in the evolution of the human species, but of a parallel development; the evolution of culture.

Partly as a result of the interchange of indigenous cultural elements within Africa and the addition of those from exogenous regions, it has never been strange to find Africans with differing physical types, speaking different languages, and having different sociocultural systems living contemporaneously in the same or neighboring ecological niches. For example, in central Africa, foraging populations such as the Batwa (Bantu-speaking Pygmies) have lived in contact with the pastoral Hima and agricultural Hutu (both of which are also Bantu speakers). And while these borrowed sociocultural traits from each other, they did not necessarily change their ways of life. In other cases, groups in contact changed their physical types, languages, and sociocultural traits such as economic, political, and religious systems. In this way, Africa often presented a picture of a veritable museum where the surviving evidence of important stages in the evolution of humans and culture could be witnessed. It is partly because of the interdigitation of African peoples that the classification of their societies has proved difficult—made more so by the cultural, ethnic, and biological chauvinism of Africans themselves and of foreigners who used notions about the level of cultural attainment of Africans as rationalizations for conquest, colonization, and exploitation.

Regional variations of Paleolithic, Mesolithic, and Neolithic cultural assemblages appeared in all parts of Africa, a function of both indigenous development and external influences. From the Neolithic period onward, the cultural assemblages in the Nile Valley had a brilliant florescence as a result of this mingling of indigenous development and external contacts. And while until recently—for racist, historical, and political reasons and because of various strictures peculiar to particular academic disciplines—Egyptian civilization was viewed strictly in terms of its relationship to Asia and the Mediterranean, that view is now changing. One well-known scholar recently remarked that "If the history of early Africa is unthinkable without Egypt, so too is the history of early Egypt inexplicable without Africa. Ancient Egypt was essentially an African civilization" (Davidson 1991, p. 49; Diop 1974). Nevertheless, it is also true that during certain epochs many parts of Africa were firmly linked to external civilizations, and that at other times some external areas were viewed as African. How these links were seen was very much a function of military and political power relations of the world in a given period.

Many early scholars and even contemporary ones have been so impressed by the remarkable similarities of the sociocultural institutions throughout Africa that some have speculated incessantly about whether the migrating "children of the sun" from Egypt diffused such traits as divine kingship, dual monarchies, and matriliny to all parts of the continent, and in some cases to outside areas. One may even postulate the existence of a widespread early "Ur-African" culture, or proto-African cultural elements that constituted a foundation upon which elaborate cultural complexes or centers in such areas as Egypt, the Upper Nile, the Niger, the Congo/Zaire, and the Zambezi were constructed. What follows is a description of African sociocultural institutions, especially those of the western and central regions, which most nearly resemble those of the millions of Africans who were transported to the New World during the terrible transatlantic slave trade.

Economic Organization

Most Africans, including the ancestors of those who came to the New World, were slash-and-burn horticulturists or agriculturists who often used irrigation techniques where warranted. Wheat, barley, and oats were commonly produced in the Nile Valley and North Africa by plow agriculture with irrigation. In other savanna regions, in East, Central, and South Africa and the western Sudan, cereals such as the millets, sorghums, and—to a limited extent—varieties of rice and legumes were cultivated by means of the hoe. Root crops, such as yams and other tubers, and varieties of rice and bananas were widely cultivated in the more tropical regions of West Africa and Zaire. Cotton was widely cultivated in the drier regions, and bark for bark cloth processing was produced in the forested regions such as Ashanti.

Most Africans were slash-and-burn horticulturists or agriculturists who often used irrigation techniques where warranted.

And while pastoralism based on the herding of cattle, sheep, goats, camels, donkeys, and horses was an important food-producing strategy, it was feasible primarily in the savanna areas that were free from the tsetse fly. Nevertheless, few of the so-called classic pastoralist societies such as the Masai, the Nuer, the Dinka, the Kabbabish Arabs, and the Somali, lived only by the products of their herds. Most of them, including the cattle-keeping people of East, central, and southern Africa and the Fulani of West Africa, lived in symbiotic relations with their cultivator neighbors. Especially in West Africa, many cattle herders often became sedentary cultivators when disease or droughts decimated their herds. This was not so difficult for them, since they moved in transhumance cycles among horticulturists between the forest zones and the desert, as pasturage and rainfall permitted. (Islamic practices appear to have limited the rearing of pigs, even in those areas where climatic factors made this possible.) In many parts of southern and East Africa, there were populations with mixed economies of horticulturists and pastoralists, though in many cases animals were the most valued products.

A minuscule number of African societies, such as the Batwa of Zaire, the Hadtsa and Sandawe of East Africa, and the Kung-San of southern Africa, retained an early adaptation to hunting and general foraging activities, but these economic strategies largely gave way to fishing, pastoralism, and horticulture. Hunting remained only an ancillary economic pursuit among all Africans, including the Mande, Akan, Mossi, Bakongo, and Baluba peoples of West and Central Africa. Fishing, too, declined as the major economic activity, except for a few riverine and coastal populations such as the Ebrie people of coastal West Africa and the Bozo people of the inland Niger River area.

A marked division of labor based on gender existed among all African food producers. Among the cultivators in most West and central African societies, males were primarily responsible for the heavy work of clearing and preparing the land, and growing specific crops. Women generally did most of the actual cultivation, harvesting and processing food. In addition they often cultivated certain crops, often viewed as "women" crops. Families who needed additional food for ceremonial or fiscal reasons obtained labor from voluntary organizations of youths and adults, which they paid or entertained. In the more complex Mande, Bakongo, and Fon societies, free persons and war captives who had become serfs and slaves were obliged to produce foodstuffs for their masters. In certain parts of the Sudan and the Sahel, horticulturists kept animals when conditions permitted, or traded vegetable products for animal products from neighboring pastoralist populations or foragers who hunted wild animals. The pastoralists, such as the Fulani of West Africa and the Kabbabish Arabs of the eastern Sudan, moved their herders in transhumance cycles between the tsetse-infected forest zones and the drier savannas. Males did most of the herding, leaving women to milk animals and to process and trade milk products. Hunting, whether among cultivators, pastoralists, or foragers, was the occupation of males, while women among all of these groups gathered wild products for food. Both males and females kept chickens, ducks, and small domestic animals.

Crafts, Manufactured Products, and Systems of Exchange

Almost all African cultivators used iron implements produced by male blacksmiths whose wives often made pots. These persons were often the only specialists in small-scale subsistence societies. Nevertheless, even these small-scale societies often produced surplus goods and interacted economically with the larger African societies, where specialization gave rise to other smiths who worked such metals as tin, copper, silver, and gold, procured either by mining or by placer washing. This was especially prevalent in West Africa, the Nile Valley, and the Zimbabwe region in southeastern Africa. Weavers, carpenters, glassmakers, and other specialists—especially in North Africa, the Nile Valley, Ethiopia, and

West Africa—produced surpluses for high-status persons or for trade in local periodic markets and with long-distance caravaners who supplied complex economies. Many producers of craft goods—for example, smiths, weavers, potters, and leather workers in the western Sudan—were organized into endogamous castelike guilds that posted members along trade routes. And while most of the guilds were egalitarian, others gave unequal access to their economic assets.

Barter persisted in small African communities that were largely self-sufficient, but also continued to play an economic role in some of the larger communities. Silent trade involving barter for gold and other products—as, for instance, between the ancient Malians and Phoenicians—persisted for a long time in many parts of Africa where vast differences in language and culture made face-to-face trade hazardous. Also employed were various types of currencies that ran the gamut from iron implements, lengths of cloth, beads, necklaces, bracelets, anklets, and waist bands to cowrie shells, gold dust, and slaves. In the Niger river areas, merchant guilds took goods on consignment, and used credit to procure goods for sale.

The notion of profit was well developed in various parts of North, East, and West Africa, except where inhibited by Islam. Also in parts of West Africa, destitute persons could pawn themselves or dependents for money. Those pawns who were unredeemed were often married, if female, by the creditors, or became serfs or slaves if male. The urban, or palace- and temple-based, complex economies in Egypt, the western Sudan, and East Africa were often the transit points for international products leaving from or arriving in many African ports of trade. Many West Africans were involved in the economic complex of the Niger river described below:

Lying between the desert and the forest regions of West Africa was a veritable *sahil* (an Arabic word for shore), part of a well-known ecosystem that facilitated the rise of a complex sociocultural system serving as a transit point for persons and products coming from north, south, and east. This region had among its characteristics a large floodplain suitable for cereal agriculture and livestock rearing; many waterways that provided easy transportation for natural resources and manufactured products; and an extensive savanna rich in minerals and in faunal and floral resources. Here arose the core states or empires of Ghana, Mali and Songhay, whose influence radiated throughout western and central Africa.

Leo Africanus described Jenne, one of the most important cities of the Mali empire, as a "place exceedingly aboundeth with barlie, rice, cattel, fishes, and cotton: and their cotton they sell unto the merchants of Barbarie, for cloth of Eirope, for brazen vessels, for armor and other such commodities. Their coine is of gold without any stampe or inscription at all" (Epaulard 1956, p. 468). A number of traditions hold that the gold used to mint the first English coin, the guinea, came from Jenne (Jennie or Guinea). A local scholar, al-Sadi, writing about 1655, described Jenne as "large, flourishing and prosperous; it is rich, blessed and favoured by the Almighty. . . . There one meets the salt merchants from the mines of Teghazza and merchants carrying gold from the mines of Bitou. . . . The area around Jenne is fertile and well populated; with numerous markets held there on all the days of the week. It is certain that it contains 7077 villages very near to one another" (Al-Sadi 1987, p. 97).

These reports from West Africa could easily be replicated from other parts of the continent with complex economies such as the Congo/Zaire, Zimbabwe, the Swahili coast, and Mogadishu in East Africa, North Africa—which at one time served as the granary of Rome—and, of course, Egypt and the Sudan.

Social Organization

There was a basic notion that the complementary relationship, or what is now being called "complementarity," between females and males lay at the center of the social organization of most African societies. Again, with very few exceptions, the people in African societies always emphasized the "extended family": that is, a group of married and unmarried males, females, and children, living in common or contiguous habitations, normally under the directorship of men. In most cases these men were descended from a common ancestor or ancestress, and the adults tended to interact most frequently with persons of their own gender except for purposes of reproduction. This is contrasted to the so-called nuclear family, where males and females maintained close relations for economic purposes as well as for reproduction and the rearing of children. A common domestic cycle was for a woman (rarely a man) to leave her natal family on marriage, join the extended family of a spouse, and return to her own natal family before death or, in spirit, after death.

The overwhelming majority of African societies emphasized corporate descent groups that were patrilineal: Both females and males traced their descent in the male line to a known apical ancestor, and children belonged to the husband's lineage. The size of the lineages varied in different societies, with subsidiary branches made up of descendants of subordinate known ancestors. In contrast were a small number of matrilineal societies such as the Akan in the Côte d'Ivoire and Ghana, the Lele in Zaire, and the Tonga in east Central Africa, where descent was traced to apical female ancestors and children belonged to the lineages of mothers. Where, as

pastoral societies, such as the Kipsigis and the Masai, were especially bellicose, having to protect themselves and their herds, they used kinship solidarity for such purposes. The Somali used what was called *dia-paying* groups of kinsmen to pay for damages and seek revenge. The pastoral Fulani and Tuareg of West Africa utilized powerful individuals, sometimes known as sheiks, to maintain order. Among the Nuer and Dinka of the Nilotic Sudan, recourse was also had to ritual specialists such as "leopard-skin chiefs" and "prophets," who restored peace (Evans-Pritchard 1940, pp. 209, 134; Herskovits 1948, p. 32).

Some of the small-scale African horticultural groups organized in village communities, such as the Alur, Lugbara, Tiv, Igbo, Kpelle, and Tallensi, used such institutions as shrines, rain medicines, and medicine men for maintaining peace (Southall 1956, pp. 181–196; Middleton and Tait 1958, pp. 131, 224; Fortes 1945, p. 53). Some of these societies used marriage alliances, common ritual paraphernalia, and myths that they had requested governors from larger and imperialistic African societies in order to live in peace and security. These myths also provided legitimacy for dominant or domineering groups.

The institution of the divine king, who ruled with the legitimacy of heaven and with the support of royal ancestors, appears throughout Africa. Examples are the Pharaohs in Egypt, the Ethiopia negus who had the title "King of Kings and Lion of the Tribe of Judah," the "reth" of the Shilluk in the Sudan, the "kabaka" of the Baganda, the king of the Bakongo in Zaire, the kings of the Ashante, the Alafin of Oyo among the Yoruba, the mais of the Kanuri, and the Mogho Naba of the Mossi of the western Sudan. Often complementing these rulers were royal women who, as in Egypt, the Sudan, and Angola, ruled in their own right but were also royal consorts, queen mothers, queen sisters, or princesses. The Candances and the Cleopatras of the Sudan and Egypt are well known; their counterparts such as Queen Nzinga of Angola, and Amina of the Hausa are less renowned. Both male and female rulers often had shrines, groups of priests, and religious paraphernalia that helped legitimize their rule.

These rulers had elaborate courts or temple complexes, as in the Nile Valley, from which they ruled over provinces, districts, and villages. Quite common was the tendency of rulers to shift their capitals when they assumed power, and in the case of the Egyptians and Sudanese were not above erasing the names of predecessors on the stelae about the kingdom. It was also quite common for monarchs to use royal relatives to rule outlying provinces and districts. But neither was it uncommon to see these personages replaced by administrative officials when the state became more secure. Many were the mechanisms used by African rulers to take censuses and to obtain the revenue to support their thrones and their states. Children were counted during puberty rites; priests reported the number of protective devices given to peasants to save animals from disease; spies reported the riches of subordinate rulers. In this manner, bureaucrats knew the amount of taxes to expect. These taxes included custom receipts from traders and manufacturers, products from fields cultivated for the state, and part of temple tithes and presents destined for local deities and for the rulers themselves. Rulers received wives not only for their bedchambers but to be used as pawns in dynastic marriages or to cultivate fields.

Scholars have been impressed by what is considered to be an African court tradition that was remarkably similar throughout the continent. With respect to West Africa, some of the early court traditions of Ghana, Mali, and Songhay still persist among the Mossi and Ashanti. The Malian king held court in a domed pavilion in which stood ten horses covered with gold-embroidered materials; behind him stood ten pages holding shields and swords decorated with gold, and on his right were the sons of vassal kings wearing splendid garments, with their hair plaited with gold. Before him sat the governor of the city and his ministers, and guarding the pavilion were pedigreed guard dogs that wore gold and silver collars studded with balls of the same metals. When the beating of a drum announced that the king would receive his visitors, those who professed the king's religion (that is, all except the Muslims) approached him, fell on their knees in greeting, and sprinkled dust on their heads. Visitors reported the Malians to be "the humblest of people before their king and the most submissive towards him. They swear by his name, saying: *Mansa Sulayman ki* (the king has spoken)" (Levtzion and Hopkins 1981, p. 291). The revenue of this king included all gold nuggets found in the country; he received one golden dinar on every load of salt that entered the kingdom, and two dinars when this amount was exported.

African communities and polities used a range of devices to maintain peace internally and to wage war against outsiders. Small village communities such as those in Igbo land used ridicule, various types of ordeals, expulsion, and belief in the efficacy of supernatural entities, often disguised as masked figures, to sanction evildoers. The acceptance of the decision of moot courts in larger societies was often enough to restore social harmony, in the absence of bodies that could enforce the law. State-level societies permitted the use of many informal legal devices at local levels, but all insisted upon judicial review at higher levels, with the monarch sitting as judge. Women often had parallel quasi-judicial and judicial institutions. The death penalty was often meted out for heinous crimes such as rape, murder, and treason. The legal philosophy in most African societies was based on concern for what "reasonable persons" would do if provoked, or expect as punishment for crimes.

Of course, African judges were not infallible, and the complaints of those who believed that they were treated unjustly have come down to us. The legal codes of dwellers in the Nile Valley are well known, and ethnographers have furnished details of legal decisions in other societies. In addition, one reporter from fourteenth-century Mali cited the "lack of oppression," and "the security embracing the whole country, so that neither traveller there nor dweller has anything to fear from thief or usurper." We are told that the ancient Malians "do not interfere with the wealth of any white man who dies among them, even though it be *quintar* [coins] upon *quintar.* They simply leave it in the hands of a trustworthy white man until the one to whom it is due takes it." Persons suspected of wrongdoing were subject to the poison ordeal. The innocent was applauded and the guilty punished (Levtzion and Hopkins 1981, p. 217).

The smaller African polities had no standing armies and waged war only when the men had completely taken in the harvest. In contrast, an aggressive ruler such as Shaka of the Zulus used his society's age-set/age-grade system to build a standing army as a vehicle for conquest. Ancient rulers in Egypt and the Sudan used standing armies not only to unify the valley of the Nile, but to wage war against the ancient Libyans and Assyrians. Hannibal took his elephants across France and the Alps to wage war on Rome, and in revenge the Romans destroyed Carthage in what is now Tunisia. Then when Arab armies conquered Egypt and their converts waged war in the western Sudan, they found that the king of Ghana could put an army of 200,000 soldiers in the field, including 40,000 archers and cavalry. West African soldiers served in the Muslim armies that conquered Spain and governed it until the *Reconquista* ended their rule.

Religion

Beliefs in the supernatural are often the oldest aspects of human cultures. Therefore, it is not surprising that certain African beliefs were continent-wide. And while God and other deities were ready references to most Africans, the conduct and fate of human beings appeared to remain the center of their religious concerns. In this context it is not surprising that for one critic, religion is a language that "allows humans to insert themselves into intimate relationships with the universe" (Mudimbe 1991, p. 9). Myths featuring a creator-god, who lived in the sky and was often personified as the sun, the earth, the moon, and all things that ever lived and will live, were almost universal throughout Africa. The Re/Osiris/Isis/Horus mythic complex of the Nile shares many features with Amma among the Dogon, Mangala among the Mande, Oludarame/Olorum (who came down to earth in an ark) among the Yoruba, Winnam/Naba Zid Winde among the Mossi, and Nyame among the Akan—all creator-gods associated with the sky and the sun. In the larger state societies important rulers such as the Pharaohs, and Yoruba/Nago kings such as Sango, were deified. Also participating in aspects of the divine were deities responsible for death dealing diseases such as smallpox. Other tutelary deities included the serpent and religious referents in *bori, mammy water, orisha,* vodun, and other possession cults through which spirits and humans expressed their will.

The Mande creation story tells how Mangala, the creator, made "the egg of the world" in which were pairs of seeds and pairs of twins, prototypes of future people. One male twin, Pembe, desiring to dominate creation, erupted from the egg, tearing away a piece of his placenta as he plunged through empty space. That piece of placenta became the dry, barren, and polluted earth, but Pembe could not fructify it, and so returned to the sky for seeds. Meanwhile Mangala, who had created the sun, sacrificed another male twin to account for Pembe's sin. Mangala cut Faro's body into sixty pieces and scattered them through space until they fell to earth, becoming vegetation, symbols of resurrection. Faro was restored to heaven in human form, and Mangala, using part of his placenta, created an ark in which he sent eight ancestral pairs of human beings, plants, and animals down to earth. These human ancestors, like Faro himself, had a common vital force (soul), and complementary male and female spiritual forces. Emerging from the ark, the ancestors watched for the first time the rising of the sun (Dieterlen 1957, pp. 124–138).

As the Mande myth indicates, human beings possessed elements of the divine such as souls, the "breath of life," and "shadows," whose fates and needs could be divined and propitiated when deemed necessary. Belief that one's fate or destiny could be known and influenced was found in the cult of *Fa* among the Yoruba/Nago, and the notion of *chi* (personality characteristics) in Igbo country. There was often the need for people to protect themselves against evildoers (sorcerers), who were believed capable of bringing harm and even death by magical means. There were priests who also knew how to acquire the power to heal—aided, of course, by the more powerful ancestors.

there were raids conducted from the north by the Moors, who were linked to Morocco, which had ambitions in the Senegal valley region.

A second mode of enslavement came from banditry. Senegambian bandits were often off-duty soldiers. The *ceddo,* royal slaves who governed and staffed the armies of the states, routinely conducted raids on the population of the area. While these raids were illegal, authorities often cooperated with the soldiers in the acquisition and sale of slaves. The *sofa,* professional soldiers of Segu and Kaarta, engaged in the same pattern of unofficial and illegal enslavement with official collusion. Popular resentment against this activity was strong, and on two occasions, in the 1670s and again in the 1770s, popular movements with Islamic leadership revolted against the leadership, although without long-term success.

The many "Bambara" slaves who were imported to Louisiana in the early eighteenth century probably were obtained through these means as were the many Senegambians who appear in the inventories of the last part of the eighteenth century.

In Sierra Leone, small-scale piracy was widespread on the many creeks and rivers of the coast where forests provided hideouts for raiders. This piracy coexisted with petty wars, but the most important source for eighteenth-century enslavement was the "holy war" (jihad) of the Muslim Fulbe cattle herders of Futa Jallon following 1726. While in its initial stages, the jihad was aimed at redressing grievances of the Fulbe and establishing a reformed Islamic polity; in time it became a source of wars, as the new state in Futa Jallon raided its neighbors and sent the fruits of its efforts overseas on the slave ships. The timing of the arrival of Sierra Leonean slaves in South Carolina suggests that the wars of the jihad period played a major role in the burst of exports from the region.

Before the late seventeenth century, the Gold Coast was divided into dozens of small states. Wars were frequent in the area, often occasioned by commercial disputes and unpaid debts. European trading companies, which came to the coast to buy gold, often became involved in the disputes both in an effort to settle their own commercial affairs and also to act as mercenaries hired by African states. It was only in the late seventeenth century, with the rise of larger imperial states in the interior, that the region became a major supplier of slaves to the Atlantic region. The rise of Denkyira, Asante, and Akwamu in the 1670s and later occasioned wars of expansion by these states, which were able to mobilize large armies, and forced the coastal states to operate in conjunction with each other to meet the challenge. Although the petty disputes and wars continued into the eighteenth century, major wars in which tens of thousands of people were captured and exported became more important as the interior kingdoms fought coastal states and each other. By the 1720s Asante had emerged as the most powerful state in the area, but warfare was still common. Many of the areas that Asante had conquered revolted frequently, and Asante itself was beset with civil wars especially upon the death of a ruler, as occurred in the 1750s.

Slaves from the Gold Coast, who were widely known in English-speaking America as "Coromantees" (from one of the exporting ports), were particularly valued in the West Indies for their strength and spirit, and their relatively limited numbers in America everywhere outside of the Chesapeake area reflected the greater purchasing power of the West Indian planters. On the other hand, their largely military enslavement made Coromantees capable of rebellion, and indeed, they were behind a large number of plots, conspiracies, and rebellions in both the West Indies and North America (such as the New York Slave Revolt of 1712).

Slaves from the Gold Coast were particularly valued in the West Indies for their strength and spirit.

The pattern of the Gold Coast was primarily repeated on the nearby Slave Coast. Indeed, mercenaries from the Gold Coast were often involved in the politics of the petty states of the coast in the late seventeenth century. However, the rise of the kingdom of Dahomey in the 1680s increased the frequency of large-scale wars in the area. Almost every year Dahomey launched a campaign toward the coast and against the Mahi and the Nagos, loosely structured confederations of states that lay east and west of Dahomey's core. Slaves were taken from the Mahi and the Nagos if the Dahomean armies were successful, or from Dahomey itself if the campaigns failed, as they frequently did. The Empire of Oyo, lying inland from Dahomey, occasionally intervened in the affairs of its coastal neighbors in an attempt to control Dahomey, its nominal vassal since the 1720s, or to act in conjunction with it. Oyo also conducted its own wars, about which few details are known, and many of the people captured or lost in these campaigns were also exported.

Remarkably, few Slave Coast slaves found their way to North America except for those who arrived through French shipping in Louisiana. British shippers maintained posts on the Slave Coast and slaves from these posts and formed a portion of the population in Jamaica and other West Indian islands, but they were not notable in the cargos arriving at any North American port.

Relatively few slaves were taken from the coastal areas of the Bight of Biafra, although piracy along its many rivers and creeks was quite common. Instead, people who were enslaved from the interior were exported from the coastal ports. The river network of the region provided cheap and easy transportation, while the population density of the interior regions was probably the greatest of any in Atlantic Africa.

In the early eighteenth century the kingdom of Benin, which dominated the western part of the area, underwent a lengthy civil war between government factions that lasted into the 1730s. Benin exported many of the victims of these wars through its own port of Ughoton, while many others found their way to other ports such as Warri or New Calabar on the main channel of the Niger River. New Calabar, one of the major exporting ports of the area along with its neighbor Bonny, drew most of its slaves from the Igbo areas that lay up the rivers in the interior. Olouadah Equiano, enslaved around 1760, provided a description of the area from which he originated in his autobiography. As he described it, people were enslaved as a result of many intertown wars or were captured by pirates who operated along the rivers and from bases in the thickly wooden regions. In the Cross River region which was served by the port of Old Calabar, a religious association called the Arochukwu often contributed to the supply of slaves. (The Arochukwu was an oracle which settled disputes and had branches over a wide network.) In addition to their religious services, for which they often demanded slaves in payment for adjudication, they also operated a more conventional trading network. Sometimes the oracle or its agents were reputed to kidnap people as well as engage in religious and commercial operations.

The Angola coast was largely supplied in the eighteenth century by the civil war in the kingdom of Kongo. Although there was an active slave trade from the ports of Luanda and Benguela, relatively few slaves exported from these ports or from the hinterland they served in the Kimbundu speaking interior found their way to North America. Instead, they were primarily shipped to Brazil while a few were smuggled to Kongo's ports and taken as slaves by French shippers. A few English crafts worked this coast in the late eighteenth century.

Dynastic disputes of the late seventeenth century lay at the root of Kongo's civil war. Although they were never quite resolved by force, some of these disputes were settled by monarchs in 1715, in the 1760s, the mid-1780s, after 1794, and again in 1805. The violent episodes of royal contest were interspersed with periods of smaller scale violence, because authority was not very centralized. Local wars enforcing shaky authority figures were frequent. This civil unrest and subsequent breakdown of authority led to the rise of bandits who either allied themselves with those in power or else operated on their own.

Just as Muslim reformers in Senegambia sought to mobilize popular support to oppose the oppression of the military bandits and state officials in their area, so the Christian kingdom of Kongo had its own movement of reform. Led by Beatriz Kimpa Vita, who claimed to be possessed by Saint Anthony, the movement sought an end to the civil wars and the enslavement that resulted; they also sought the restoration of Kongo under a new mystical Christian leadership. Although the movement succeeded in occupying the capital, the leader was soon captured and burned at the stake as a heretic in 1706.

After 1750 captives from the civil war in Kongo were joined by increasing numbers of people enslaved from both the north and the east of the kingdom. The slaves from the north seem to have been captured during the petty wars between commercial states, while the slaves from the east were taken as a result of the emergence and raiding of the Lunda empire which extended its authority, or at least its ability to raid, as far as the Kwango River by 1760. All these slaves from Kongo or elsewhere were sold to merchants who served North America largely through ports north of the Zaire River, often under the kingdom of Loango.

Africans who arrived in America came with specific cultural backgrounds that related to their region of origin in Africa.

Angolans made up a significant portion of the slaves imported into all American regions, but they were particularly numerous in Louisiana and South Carolina. Because so many had served in wars, they, like the Gold Coast Coromantees, were often implicated in revolts and rebellions in America. Angolans led the STONO REBELLION in 1739, and they also played an important role in the other revolts in America such as those in Brazil and in the Haitian Revolution.

Africans who arrived in America came with specific cultural backgrounds that related to their region of origin in Africa. This was particularly true of their linguistic background, for their ability to communicate with other people was limited at first to those of their own ethno-linguistic group. Unlike African social organization, which tended to be based on kinship and locality or citizenship in a state, the social organization of Africans in America was based on common languages. American "nations" or "countries," as they were called in contemporary records, formed social and mutual self-help groups from among people of their own background to bury their dead or to celebrate occasional holidays. They sometimes formed shadow governments with kings and queens, either independently or, in Spanish and Portuguese America, through membership in lay organizations created by the Catholic Church.

The presence of these ethnic social groups, helped to preserve African culture in America. They also provided a cross-state network which could allow coordinated action in larger areas and sometimes played an important role in conspiracies and revolts.

BIBLIOGRAPHY

Eltis, David. *Economic Growth and the Ending of the Transatlantic Slave Trade.* Cambridge, U.K., 1987.

Inikori, J.E., ed. *Forced Migration: The Impact of the Export Slave Trade on African Societies.* New York, 1982.

Lovejoy, Paul. *Transformations in Slavery: A History of Slavery in Africa.* Cambridge, U.K., 1983.

Rodney, Walter. *A History of the Upper Guinea Coast, 1545–1800.* London, 1970.

Thornton, John. *Africa and Africans in the Making of the Atlantic World, 1400–1680.* Cambridge, U.K., 1992.

———. *The Kingdom of the Congo: Civil War and Transition, 1641–1718.* Madison, Wis., 1983.

– JOHN THORNTON

AFRICAN METHODIST EPISCOPAL CHURCH

Richard ALLEN (1760–1831), founder of the African Methodist Episcopal (AME) Church, was born a slave in Philadelphia, Pa., on February 14, 1760. Slaveholder Benjamin Chew sold Allen, his parents, and three siblings to Stokley Sturgis of Kent County, Del. METHODIST CHURCH circuit riders frequently preached in the area, and Allen responded to their evangelism—perhaps also to their antislavery reputation—and joined the Wesleyan movement. His piety deepened because Sturgis permitted him to attend Methodist services regularly and to hold religious gatherings in the slave owner's own home. Sturgis also allowed Allen and his brother to buy their freedom, a task which was accomplished in 1783. For three years, Allen traveled through the Middle Atlantic as an itinerant Methodist preacher, then settled in Philadelphia to preach to blacks at the St. George Methodist Episcopal Church. The founding of the Free African Society of Philadelphia in 1787 and a racial altercation caused him to leave St. George, which in turn led to the building of Philadelphia's Bethel African Methodist Episcopal Church in 1794, often known as the Mother Bethel Church. In 1807, efforts by several pastors at St. George to control the congregation moved Allen to gain judicial recognition of Bethel's independence. A final attempt in 1815 by a St. George pastor to assert authority at Bethel Church induced Daniel Coker, the leader of Baltimore's black Methodists, to preach a sermon the following year commending Allen for his successful stand. Not long after, Allen drew Coker and other blacks from Baltimore; Salem, N.J.; and Attleborough, Pa., to meet with his Philadelphia followers to form the AME Church.

At the Philadelphia conference in 1816, Coker was elected bishop but declined the offer, perhaps because of his light skin color. Allen was then chosen bishop, and under his leadership the denomination rapidly expanded. African Methodism spread north to New York and New England; south through Maryland, the District of Columbia, and (for a time) South Carolina; and west to the Ohio Valley and the old Northwest Territory. During the antebellum period, the denomination included congregations in the slave states of Kentucky, Missouri, and Louisiana. Missionaries such as William Paul Quinn 1788?–1873), an AME bishop after 1844, founded scores of congregations in the Midwest in the 1830s and 1840s. Along the Pacific Coast, the AME church spread from Sacramento and San Francisco in the early 1850s and to other locations in California and adjoining territories. AME loyalists also had success in Canada and made some inroads into Haiti. In 1864, thirty-three years after Allen's death, the AME church had a membership of 50,000 in 1,600 congregations.

During the antebellum period, while the AME Church was largely restricted to the northern states, numerous clergy and congregations gave direct aid to abolitionism. Morris Brown, who became the second bishop of the church after Allen's death, had been implicated in Denmark Vesey's abortive slave insurrection in South Carolina in 1822. Vesey himself was an AME preacher who, according to white authorities, planned the slave revolt during AME church services. The abolitionist stances of Allen, Quinn, and Brown were reaffirmed at the 1840 Pittsburgh annual conference. Stating that "slavery pollutes the character of the church of God, and makes the Bible a sealed book to thousands of immortal beings," the delegates resolved that their denomination should use its "influence and energies" to destroy black bondage.

Daniel A. Payne, who became a bishop in 1852, greatly influenced the development of the AME church. Freeborn in 1811 in Charleston, S.C., Payne in his early adult years was a schoolteacher until a South Carolina state law forbade the education of blacks and forced him to close his school. In 1835 he moved north and matriculated at Gettysburg Theological Seminary in Pennsylvania. After his ordination into the AME ministry in 1843, Payne pastored in Baltimore, later serving the denomination as historiographer, and crusaded for an educated clergy. In 1863, Payne convinced reluctant AME leaders to commit to a daring venture in higher education by founding WILBERFORCE UNIVERSITY, the first black college started by African Americans. Wilberforce was only the first of several colleges founded by the AME. Others include Allen University (1880) in South Carolina, Morris Brown College (1881) in Georgia, Paul Quinn College (1881) in Texas, and Kittrell College (1886) in North Carolina.

The period of the CIVIL WAR and RECONSTRUCTION proved pivotal to AME church development. Recruitment of black soldiers occurred on the premises of AME congregations such as Israel Church in Washington, D.C. Four AME ministers—Henry M. Turner, William H. Hunter, David Stevens, and Garland H. White—served with ten other black chaplains in the Union Army. Additional AME clergy, including some who would become bishops, also fought on the Union side.

As northern victories liberated Confederate strongholds in Virginia and North Carolina, the Baltimore annual conference dispatched AME preachers in 1864 to those states to attract blacks into African Methodism. In 1865, Bishop Daniel A. Payne sailed from New York City to his hometown, Charleston, S.C., to establish the AME mission in the South. The rapid acquisition of members and congregations from Virginia to Texas swelled the denomination in 1880 to 387,566 persons in 2,051 churches.

The development of the AME church in Alabama is illustrative of the denomination's expansion in the postbellum South. Mobile had the first, though shortlived, AME congregation as early as 1820. The denomination revived when two AME ministers preached in the state

In this post–Civil War engraving, a depiction of Richard Allen, the founder of the AME Church, is surrounded by those of later church bishops. The vignettes in the corners of the engraving depict the educational and missionary endeavors of the church. (Prints and Photographs Division, Library of Congress)

and art of ballet and modern dance. Courses have been offered in dance technique and history, music for dancers, dance composition, and theatrical design. In 1974 the Alvin Ailey Repertory Ensemble, a professional performance ensemble, was formed under the direction of Sylvia Waters as a bridge between study and membership in professional dance companies. In 1984 the Alvin Ailey Student Performance Group was created under the direction of Kelvin Rotardier. The Student Performance Group has offered lecture-demonstrations to communities traditionally underserved by the arts. In 1989 Dance Foundation Inc., the umbrella organizations for the AAADT and the Ailey School, initiated the Ailey Camps program, an outreach program designed to "enhance the self-esteem, creative expression, and critical thinking skills of inner-city youth through dance." Success of the initial venture in Kansas City, Mo., led to similar programs begun in New York City (1990) and Baltimore, Md. (1992).

Ailey created the AAADT to feature the talents of his African-American colleagues, though the company was never exclusively black. Ailey integrated his company to counter the "reverse chauvinism in being an all-black anything." He told the *New York Times,* "I am trying to show the world that we are all human beings and that color is not important. What is important is the quality of our work." In the last interview conducted before his death, he commented that the essence of the Ailey enterprise was that "the dancers be fed, kept alive, interested" in the work. "We're trying to create a whole spectrum of experience for the dancer as well as the audience," he said, dramatically understating the realities of his achievements.

Ailey stopped dancing in 1965 and slowed his choreographic assignments in the 1970s to attend to the administrative and fund-raising operations associated with his ever expanding company. Upon Ailey's death, Judith Jamison was appointed artistic director of the company, to work closely with rehearsal director and longtime company member Masazumi Chaya. The AAADT finally emerged from financial difficulties in 1992, when *Dance Magazine* proclaimed it "recession-proof" due to powerful development efforts on the part of the Dance Foundation Inc.'s board of directors.

Although Ailey gave numerous interviews throughout his career, he was decidedly private about his personal life. He described himself as "a bachelor and a loner" to writer John Gruen and hardly ever allowed outsiders into his most private thoughts. In 1980 Ailey was briefly hospitalized for stress-related conditions. His death followed a long, solitary struggle that had taken him out of the limelight for some time. Ailey's legacy to the dance world was to foster a freedom of choice—from ballet, modern, and social dance performance—to best express humanity in movement terms suited to the theatrical moment.

BIBLIOGRAPHY

Emery, Lynne Fauley. *Black Dance in the United States from 1619 to 1970.* Palo Alto, Calif., 1972.

Goodman, Saul. "Brief Biographies: Alvin Ailey." *Dance Magazine* (December 1958): 70.

Gruen, John. "Interview with Alvin Ailey." Transcript of interview, collection of New York Public Library, 1972.

Latham, Jacqueline Quinn. A Biographical Study of the Lives and Contributions of Two Selected Contemporary Black Male Dance Artists—Arthur Mitchell and Alvin Ailey. Texas Women's University diss., 1973.

Long, Richard. *The Black Tradition in American Dance.* New York, 1989.

Mazo, Joseph H., and Susan Cook. *The Alvin Ailey American Dance Theater.* New York, 1978.

Moore, William. "Alvin Ailey (1931–1989)." *Ballet Review* 17, no. 4 (1990): 12–17.

– THOMAS F. DEFRANTZ

ALI, MUHAMMAD

Muhammad Ali (January 17, 1942–), boxer. Muhammad Ali was born Cassius Marcellus Clay, Jr. in Louisville, Ky. He began BOXING at the age of twelve under the tutelage of Joe Martin, a Louisville policeman. Having little interest in school and little affinity for intellectual endeavors, young Clay devoted himself wholeheartedly to boxing. He showed great promise early on and soon developed into one of the most impressive amateurs in the country. He became the National Amateur Athletic Union (AAU) champion in 1959 and in 1960, and also won a gold medal in the light-heavyweight division at the 1960 Olympics in Rome. As a result of his boyish good looks and his outgoing personality—his poetry recitations, his good-natured bragging, and his undeniable abilities—Clay because famous after the Olympics. Shortly after returning from Rome, he turned professional and was managed by a consortium of white Louisville businessmen. Carefully nurtured by veteran trainer Angelo Dundee, he accumulated a string of victories against relatively mediocre opponents and achieved a national following with his constant patter, his poetry, and his boyish antics. At 6′3″ and a fighting weight of around 200 pounds, he astonished sportswriters with his blazing hand and foot speed, his unorthodox style of keeping his hands low, and his ability to avoid punches by moving his head back. No heavyweight in history possessed Clay's grace or speed.

On February 25, 1964, Clay fought as the underdog for the heavyweight title against Sonny Liston. Liston, an ex-convict, was thought by many to be virtually invincible because of his devastating one-round victories against former champion Floyd Patterson. An air of both the theater of the absurd and of ominousness surrounded the bout in Miami. Publicly, Clay taunted and comically berated Liston. He called him "the Bear," harassed him at his home, and almost turned the weigh-in ceremony into a shambles as he seemingly tried to attack Liston and appeared on the verge of being utterly out of control. Privately, however, Clay was seen with MALCOLM X and members of the NATION OF ISLAM (NOI). Rumors started that he had joined the militant, mysterious sect. Soon after, it was discovered that he had been secretly visiting NOI mosques for nearly three years and that he had indeed become a friend of Malcolm X, who sat ringside at the Liston fight.

Clay beat Liston fairly easily in seven rounds, shocking the world by becoming heavyweight champion. Immediately after the fight, he announced that he was a member of the NOI and that his name was no longer Cassius Clay but Muhammad Ali. The response from the white press, white America, and the boxing establishment generally was swift and intensely hostile. The NOI was seen, largely through the rhetoric of Malcolm X, its most stylish spokesman, as an antiwhite hate group. (When Malcolm X broke with the NOI, shortly after the Liston fight, Ali remained loyal to Elijah MUHAMMAD and ended his friendship with Malcolm X.) Following his public conversion to Islam, Ali was publicly pilloried. Most publications and sports journalists refused to call him by his new name. Former champion Floyd Patterson nearly went on a personal and national crusade against the NOI in his fight against Ali on November 22, 1965, but Patterson later became one of the few fighters to defend Ali publicly during his years of exile. Indeed, not since the reign of Jack JOHNSON was the white public and a segment of the black population so enraged by the opinions and life of a black athlete.

After winning his rematch with Liston in Lewiston, Me., on May 25, 1965, in a bizarre fight that ended with Liston apparently being knocked out in the first round, Ali spent most of the next year fighting abroad, primarily because of his unpopularity in this country. Among his most important matches during this period were a fifteen-round decision over George Chuvalo in Toronto, a sixth-round knockout of Henry Cooper in London, and a fifteen-round decision over Ernest Terrell in Houston. While Ali was abroad American officials changed his draft status from 1–Y (unfit for Army services because of his low score on Army intelligence tests) to 1–A (qualified for induction). Many saw this change as a direct response to the negative public opinion concerning Ali's political views and the mounting war in Vietnam. Ali refused to serve in the Army on the grounds that it was a violation of his religious beliefs. (Elijah Muhammad, leader of the NOI, had served time in prison during World War II for refusing to serve in the armed services.) In 1967, Ali was convicted in federal court of violation of the Selective Service Act, sentenced to five years in prison, and immediately stripped of both his boxing title and his boxing license. For the next three and one-half years, Ali, free on bond while appealing his case (which he eventually won on appeal to the U.S. Supreme Court), was prohibited from boxing. Still, Ali had inspired black athletes to become more militant and more politically committed. Medal-winning track stars John Carlos and Tommie Smith gave a clenched-fist salute during the playing of the National Anthem at the Olympic Games in Mexico City in 1968, and Harry Edwards became one of the more outspoken leaders of a new cadre of young black athletes who saw Ali as a hero.

By 1970, with public opinion decidedly against the Vietnam War, and a growing black influence in several southern state governments, Ali was given a license to fight in Georgia. He returned to the ring on October 26 to knock out Jerry Quarry in the third round. Although he was still a brilliant fighter, the nearly four year lay-off had diminished some of Ali's abilities. He took far more punishment in the ring during the years of his return than he had taken before. This was to have dire consequences for him as he grew older.

In the early 1970s Ali fought several of his most memorable matches. On March 8, 1971, he faced the undefeated Philadelphian Joe Frazier in New York City. Frazier had become champion during Ali's exile. The fifteen-round fight, which Frazier won in a close decision, was so fierce that both boxers were hospitalized after it. Many have speculated that this fight initiated Ali's neurological deterioration. In July of that year Ali won the North American Boxing Federation (NABF) heavyweight title by knocking out Jimmy Ellis in twelve rounds. His next major boxing challenge came in March 1973, when Ken Norton captured the NABF title from Ali in a twelve-round decision. Ali regained the title six months later with a twelve-round decision over Norton. In January of the following year, Ali and Frazier staged their first rematch. This nontitle bout at Madison Square Garden ended with Ali victorious after twelve hard-fought rounds. Ali finally regained the World Heavyweight title in Kinshasa, Zaire, on October 30, 1974, when he knocked out a seemingly indestructible George Foreman in eight rounds. To counter Foreman's awesome punching power, Ali used what he called his "rope-a-dope" strategy, by which he leaned back against the ropes and covered his head, allowing

Foreman to punch himself out. The next year, Ali and Frazier faced off one last time in what Ali dubbed "The Thrilla in Manila." Both boxers received tremendous punishment during this bludgeoning ordeal. Ali prevailed, however, when Frazier's trainer refused to let the boxer come out for the fifteenth round.

During the 1970s Ali was lionized. No longer seen as a race demon, he virtually became a national icon. He appeared in movies—including the film *The Greatest* (1977), based on his autobiography of the same name (1975). Like Jackie ROBINSON and JOE LOUIS before him, Ali played himself in the film—he also appeared in television programs and in commercials. He was one of the most photographed and interviewed men in the world. Indeed, Ali even beat Superman in the ring in a special issue of the comic devoted to him. Part of Ali's newfound popularity was a result of a shift in attitude by the white public and white sportswriters, but part of it was also a reflection of Ali's tempered approach to politics. Ali became a great deal less doctrinaire in the political aspects of his Islamic beliefs and he eventually embraced Wallace D. Muhammad's more ecumenical form of Islam when the NOI factionalized after the death of Elijah Muhammad in 1975. Finally, as befitting a major celebrity, Ali had one of the largest entourages of any sports personality in history, resembling that of a head of state.

On February 15, 1978, Ali again lost the title. His opponent this time was Leon Spinks, an ex-Marine and native of a north St. Louis housing project. Spinks fought in only eight professional bouts before he met Ali. Ali, however, became the first heavyweight in history to regain the title for a third time when he defeated Spinks on September 15 of the same year.

In 1979, Ali was aged and weary; his legs were shot, his reflexes had slowed, and his appetite for competition was waning as a result of the good life that he was enjoying. Ali retired from the ring at that time, only to do what so many other great champions have so unwisely done, namely, return to battle. His return to the ring included a savage ten-round beating on October 2, 1980, at the hands of Larry Holmes, a former sparring partner who had become champion after Ali's retirement. His next fight was a ten-round decision lost to Trevor Berbick on December 11 of the following year. After the Berbick fight, Ali retired for good. His professional record stands at: 56 wins, 37 of which were by knockout, and 5 losses. He was elected to the Boxing Hall of Fame in 1987.

During Ali's later years, his speech became noticeably more slurred, and after his retirement he became more aged: moving slowly, speaking with such a thick tongue that he was almost incomprehensible, and suffering from attacks of palsy. There is some question as to whether he has Parkinson's disease or a Parkinson's-like deterioration of the neurological system. Many believe that the deterioration of his neurological system is directly connected to the punishment he took in the ring. By the early 1990s, although his mind was still sound, Ali gave the appearance of being a good deal older and more infirm than he actually was. He found it difficult to write or talk, and often walked slowly. Despite this, he is living a full life, travels constantly, and seems to be at peace with himself.

It would be difficult to overestimate Ali's impact on boxing and on the United States as both a cultural and political figure.

His personal life has been turbulent. He has been married four times and has had several children as well as numerous affairs, especially during his heyday as a fighter. His oldest daughter, Maryum, is a rap artist, following in her father's footsteps as a poet—Ali made a poetry recording for Columbia Records in 1963 called *The Greatest*—Maryum has recorded a popular RAP dedicated to her father.

It would be difficult to overestimate Ali's impact on boxing and on the United States as both a cultural and political figure. He became one of the most recognized men in the world, an enduring, if not always appropriate, stylistic influence on young boxers, and a man who showed the world that it was possible for a black to speak his mind publicly and live to tell the tale.

BIBLIOGRAPHY

Gilmore, Al-Tony. *Bad Nigger! The National Impact of Jack Johnson.* Port Washington, N.Y., 1975.

Hauser, Thomas. *Muhammad Ali: His Life and Time.* New York, 1991.

Mailer, Norman. *The Fight.* New York, 1975.

McCallum, John D. *The World Heavyweight Boxing Championship: A History.* Radnor, Pa., 1974.

Olsen, Jack. *Black Is Best: The Riddle of Cassius Clay.* New York, 1967.

Plimpton, George. *Shadow Box.* New York, 1977.

Roberts, Randy. *Papa Jack: Jack Johnson and the Era of White Hopes.* New York, 1983.

Sammons, Jeffrey T. *Beyond the Ring: The Role of Boxing in American Society.* Urbana, Ill., 1988.

Sheen, Wilfred. *Muhammad Ali.* New York, 1975.

Torres, Jose. *Sting Like a Bee: The Muhammad Ali Story.* New York, 1971.

– GERALD EARLY

ALLEN, RICHARD

Richard Allen (February 14, 1760–March 26, 1831), minister and community leader. As a reformer and institution builder in the post-Revolutionary period, Richard Allen was matched in achievements by few of his white contemporaries. At age twenty, only a few months after buying his freedom in Kent County, Del., Allen was preaching to mostly white audiences and converting many of his hearers to Methodism. At twenty-seven, he was a cofounder of the Free African Society of Philadelphia, probably the first autonomous organization of free blacks in the United States. Before he was thirty-five, he had become the minister of what would be PHILADELPHIA's largest black congregation—Bethel African Methodist Episcopal Church. Over a long lifetime, he founded, presided over, or served as officer in a large number of other organizations designed to improve the condition of life and expand the sphere of liberty for African Americans. Although he received no formal education, he became an accomplished writer, penning and publishing sermons, tracts, addresses, and remonstrances; compiling a hymnal for black Methodists; and drafting articles of organization and governance for various organizations.

The Rev. Richard Allen, founder and first bishop of the African Methodist Episcopal Church. (Photographs and Prints Division, Schomburg Center for Research in Black Culture, The New York Public Library, Astor, Lenox and Tilden Foundations)

Enslaved at birth in the family of the prominent Philadelphia lawyer and officeholder Benjamin Chew, Allen was sold with his family to Stokely Sturgis, a small farmer near Dover, Del., in about 1768. It was here, in 1777, that Allen experienced a religious conversion, shortly after most of his family had been sold away from Dover, at the hands of the itinerant Methodist Freeborn Garretson. Three years later he and his brother contracted with their master to purchase their freedom.

For a short time, Allen drove a wagon carrying salt for the Revolutionary army. He also supported himself as a woodchopper, brickyard laborer, and shoemaker as he carried out a six-year religious sojourn as an itinerant Methodist preacher. In something akin to a biblical journey into the wilderness, Allen tested his mettle and proved his faith, traveling by foot over thousands of miles, from North Carolina to New York, and preaching the word to black and white audiences in dozens of villages, crossroads, and forest clearings. During this period of his life, it seems, Allen developed the essential attributes that would serve him the rest of his career: resilience, toughness, cosmopolitanism, an ability to confront rapidly changing circumstances, and skill in dealing with a wide variety of people and temperaments.

Allen's itinerant preaching brought him to the attention of white Methodist leaders, who in 1786 called him to Philadelphia to preach to black members of the Methodist flock that worshiped at Saint George's Methodist Church, a rude, dirt-floored building in the German part of the city. Allen would spend the rest of his life there.

In Philadelphia, Allen's career was marked by his founding of Mother Bethel, the black Methodist church that opened its doors in 1794, and by the subsequent creation, in 1816, of the independent AFRICAN METHODIST EPISCOPAL CHURCH (AME Church). Soon after his arrival in 1786, he began pressing for an independent black church. His fervent Methodism brought him into contention with other emerging black leaders who wished for a nondenominational or "union" church, and thus within a few years two black churches took form. Both were guided by the idea that African Americans needed "to worship God under our own vine and fig tree," as Allen put it in his autobiographical memoir. This was, in essence, a desire to stand apart from white society, avoiding both the paternalistic benevolence of its racially liberal members and the animosity of its racially intolerant members. Allen's Bethel church, after opening its doors in a converted blacksmith's shop in

African Americans in the U.S. Cavalry, the famed "Buffalo Soldiers," helped end Indian resistance, enforce reservation policy, and control the "hostiles."

The most significant African-Native American leader was Seminole John Horse, a master marksman and diplomat in Florida and Oklahoma and, by the time of the Civil War, the Black Seminole chief in Mexico and Texas. In 1870 he signed a treaty with the United States that brought his people from Mexico to Texas so that his skilled desert soldiers could serve as army scouts. On July 4, 1870, when his Seminole nation crossed into Texas, it was a historic moment: As a result of treaty negotiations with the United States an African people had arrived intact as a nation on this soil, and under the command of their ruling monarch, Chief John Horse.

As African Americans have explored their roots, they have also found Indian ancestors. Today, as a result of further mixture and marriage, virtually every African-American family in the United States—from those of Frederick DOUGLASS, Langston HUGHES, and Alex Haley to those of the Rev. Dr. Martin Luther KING, Jr., Jesse JACKSON, and Alice WALKER—can claim an Indian branch in its family tree.

BIBLIOGRAPHY

Forbes, Jack D. *Black Africans and Native Americans.* London, 1988.

Katz, William Loren. *Black Indians: A Hidden Heritage.* New York, 1986.

Opala, Joseph A. "Seminole-African Relations on the Florida Frontier." *Papers in Anthropology* 22, no. 1 (Spring 1981): 11–51.

Porter, Kenneth Wiggins. *The Negro on the American Frontier.* New York, 1971.

Price, Richard. *First-Time: The Historical Vision of an Afro-American People.* Baltimore, 1983.

———, ed. *Maroon Societies: Rebel Slave Communities in the Americas.* Baltimore, 1979.

Woodson, Carter G. "The Relations of Negroes and Indians in Massachusetts." *Journal of Negro History* 1 (January 1920): 40–57.

– WILLIAM LOREN KATZ

AMERICAN REVOLUTION

The American Revolution, in which the colonies that became the United States cast off dependence on the mother country, was an important event not only in the history of America but of the world. The Americans' successful struggle for independence was an important development in the formation of the modern social and political conception of humanity. America's liberation was made possible by large-scale support from African-American soldiers, sailors, and laborers, who nevertheless faced racial discrimination within the military and society.

In 1770, shortly before the outbreak of the American Revolution, about one-fifth of the population of the thirteen colonies was African American, of which two-thirds was native-born, one-third African-born. About 5 percent of the African-American population—much of which was in part white or Native American—was free and had varying but limited rights as citizens. All the rest were property of their white masters. SLAVERY existed, all but unchallenged, in every colony. Approximately 90 percent of the slave population lived in the South, where their labor was essential to the economy. Slaves cultivated tobacco, indigo, rice, and sugar—major sources of profit in internal and external trade. They were also used in the South and the mid-Atlantic colonies as personal servants and artisans producing a wide range of clothes and equipment. They were less numerous in New England than elsewhere, but there too, they worked as servants and laborers, or as boatmen and longshoremen in the seaport towns of the region. Slavery not only meant that the body, labor, clothes, and housing of the slave belonged to the master, but that the slaves had no role in the political process and no independent social existence.

America's liberation was made possible by large-scale support from African-American soldiers, sailors, and laborers.

All this changed with the coming of war. The emergency situation created by the conflict meant that African Americans, both individually and as a class, gained levels of respectful attention and importance not reached again except in subsequent wars. The labors and loyalties of blacks were crucial to the comfort, security, and military success of several colonies; they had to be officially recognized.

Furthermore, the existence of slavery met widespread challenge for the first time. The rheteoric of the patriots was suffused with comparisons to slavery, and frequent allegations that the King of England was trying to reduce them, through the Stamp Act (1765), the Townshend Acts (1767), and the quartering of garrisoned British troops, to a condition of slavery and abject bondage. The Boston Massacre in March 1770, in which five Bostonians were killed in a fracas with British troops, marked the first deaths in the conflict. Among those killed was Crispus ATTUCKS, a mulatto. Committees of Correspondence in Massachusetts led to similar confrontations in other colonies. Following the famous "Boston Tea Party" of December 16, 1773, harsh British repression led to the convening in June 1774 of the Continental Congress. Sensitive to the apparent contradition of calls for liberty in the midst of slavery, Virginia delegates moved successfully to suspend the SLAVE TRADE, whose continued existence the Americans blamed on England. The trade resumed following the end of the war.

In April 1775, war broke out in Massachusetts. The colony's blacks had presented five antislavery petitions to the General Court (the colonial legislature) between 1773 and 1775, but the lawmakers had failed to act on them. Nevertheless, freemen and slaves fought with other patriots at Lexington and Concord and at Bunker Hill. Twelve, including Peter Salem, Salem Poor, and Lemuel Haynes, went on to fight in further battles and made names for themselves by their exploits. When Gen. George Washington arrived in Massachusetts to lead the first Continental Army, the slaveholding Virginian convinced the Continental Congress to bar enlistment by blacks in the Army and to dismiss slave soldiers, though he allowed free blacks already serving to finish their enlistments. Many states barred blacks from militia service. Black soldiers strongly protested.

In November 1775, Lord Dunmore, the royal governor of Virginia, issued a proclamation promising freedom for enslaved blacks in Virginia who joined the British armed forces to put down the revolt. Patriot forces throughout the colonies reacted strongly to the "infamous proclamation," and many slaveholders now saw revolution as the only way of avoiding slave insurrection. Virginia and Maryland tightened slave patrols and searched for runaways. News of the proclamation traveled swiftly. Three hundred slaves joined Dunmore's forces within a month and were designated "Lord Dunmore's Ethiopian Regiment." By mid-December, however, after an unsuccessful attack on Norfolk, Va., Dunmore fled to an offshore ship, and blacks who wished to join him were forced to steal boats and travel to asylum offshore. Still, some 2,000 were able to make their way to the British ships. Once on board, though, many of the black recruits were stricken by fever and died, and the Ethiopian Regiment disbanded.

In January 1776, in the wake of Dunmore's Proclamation, Washington changed his mind. Fearing that blacks once discharged would join the British, he permitted the "faithful" free black soldiers already in the Army to reenlist, and African-American soldiers fought that year in battles in such places as Fort Ticonderoga in New York and around New York City.

The Americans' struggle for liberty and equality, as well as the military service of African-American soldiers, brought about a significant change in the image of slavery and the condition of African Americans. Many patriots, even slaveholders, began viewing the institution as evil. When one of James Madison's slaves was caught trying to flee behind British lines, Madison refused to punish him "for coveting that liberty" that white Americans proclaimed the "right & worthy pursuit of every human being." In 1775, the same year the war broke out, the first antislavery society in America was formed in Philadelphia. Thomas Jefferson's original draft of the Declaration of Independence in 1776 charged that the King of England had "waged cruel war" on humanity by taking an unoffending people from their native land and selling them into slavery in the colonies. No section of the Declaration caused more debate than this. The passage was struck out to appease the delegates of Georgia and South Carolina. In essence, the United States was created amid a fundamental contradiction: A government based on Enlightenment principles of universal liberty and equality was established by people who denied the same freedoms to enslaved African Americans.

General Washington opposed allowing further blacks to join the Army. While Washington was impressed by the black soldiers' military prowess, he refused to allow slaves to enlist out of a combination of republican principle and concern for slaveholder sensibilities. However, this policy also changed in the face of the Continental Army's desperate need for soldiers, and on January 2, 1777, he issued an order allowing all freemen to enlist. While individual states had laws against black military service, opposition to free blacks in the army, even in Virginia, soon dissolved as the personnel shortage grew. By 1777, new enlistments were few, and conscription was largely ineffective. States were forced to hire and pay bounties to meet their enlistment quotas. Many whites refused service and hired free blacks as substitutes. In October 1777 Connecticut allowed slavemasters to manumit slaves who substituted for reluctant whites. In February 1778, Rhode Island, hard-pressed to find soldiers, passed a Slave Enlistment Act, by which the state freed slave recruits and compensated masters. The state's black regiment eventually served with distinction. By 1781 all the New England states, New York, and Maryland had authorized slave enlistments.

In spring 1779, as the war turned southward, Congress recommended enlisting southern slaves, and sent a representative, John Laurens, to convince South Carolina and Georgia to recruit slaves. Slaves were too valuable as agricultural laborers, however, and slaveholders feared arming any blacks and stirring thoughts of freedom among enslaved African Americans. Laurens's mission was unsuccessful, although both states used proceeds from sales of Loyalist-owned slaves to support military operations. The only black troops to fight in the Deep South were some five hundred black and mulatto soldiers from St. Domingue (later Haiti), includ-

Killed in the Boston Massacre of 1770, Crispus Attucks, of mixed African-American and American Indian descent, has long been honored as a patriotic hero. On this commemorative column, Attucks's name heads the list of massacre victims. (Photographs and Prints Division, Schomburg Center for Research in Black Culture, The New York Public Library, Astor, Lenox and Tilden Foundations)

ing future Haitian king Henri Christophe, who joined the French forces at the siege of Savannah, Ga., in 1779.

Many blacks, James FORTEN being probably the most famous, joined the crews of sailing ships, either in the fledgling American Navy or in merchant ships, and in privateers granted letters of marque. Many African Americans were experienced sailors who navigated ships through treacherous coastal passages. Some were veterans of the Royal Navy. Most were better prepared than whites to face the harsh and restrictive conditions of maritime life. Southerners who refused to arm black soldiers had no objection to free blacks and even slaves fighting under white control on ships in the mid-Atlantic. A few blacks escaped to freedom on the high seas.

Eventually, five thousand or more blacks enlisted in the American armed forces. They fought at Trenton, Brandywine, Saratoga, and in other important battles. Several blacks won special notice in the military: Cornelius Lenox Remond, Barzillai Lew, Cuff Whitmore, Tack Sisson, Prince Whipple (later immortalized in Emanuel Leutze's famous painting *Washington Crossing the Delaware*), Abner Dabney, and others. Other blacks served the cause as military laborers, cooks, guides, spies, drivers, and roadbuilders. The largest contingents came from the northern states that had the smallest black populations, but substantial numbers of free blacks. Together, they made a decisive contribution to the American cause.

Some African Americans served on the British side, even after the fiasco of Lord Dunmore's Ethiopian Regiment. At first, a few joined the Loyalist brigades in the North. However, white Loyalists, many of them slaveholders, decried the use of black troops. Both they and British regulars looked down on blacks and were anxious to crush rebel forces on their own. Even in the war's southern campaigns, only a few blacks enlistees were active in the British Army. The British considered blacks hard to control and undependable, and feared slave revolts. Blacks, conversely, had no confidence that joining the British Army would improve their situation. Several dozen served, however, in the Royal Navy, as pilots and seamen. After the war ended, the "Black Loyalists" who had served the British were evacuated to Nova Scotia. However, many found conditions unsuitable there and emigrated to the African colony of Sierra Leone.

While the British armed few African Americans, they made full use of the labor of slave "property," which they captured from Americans. They also put to work African Americans who ran behind their lines to freedom. When the British took New York and Philadelphia, a large percentage of those cities' enslaved blacks were liberated. After the war turned south in 1779, tens of thousands of slaves ran from plantations despite strict laws and whites' efforts to hinder runaways. Other slaves were conscripted into the king's service, constructing military fortifications in Savannah and Charleston. Slaves worked as cooks, spies (some were double agents for the Americans), and military servants. The most shocking use of blacks was for biological warfare at Yorktown. Blacks stricken with smallpox were sent to plantations in order to infect rebels. Dunmore and a few others drew up plans to arm slaves in order to augment shorthanded British forces, but nothing ever came of them.

With the end of the American Revolution in 1783, African Americans left the Army. Many veterans, particularly in the North, were emancipated by legislative enactment. Some veterans had only verbal promises of manumission from their masters. Many of these agreements were kept; some were not. Occasionally courts and state legislatures were forced to secure the emancipation of individual veterans to prevent masters from attempting to reenslave ex-soldiers because some did not wait to see whether their masters would keep their promises. Slaves bought up by states for wartime public works projects were resold. Enslaved blacks who had fled to the British were taken by them out of the country, but not necessarily to freedom. Some were claimed as compensation by Loyalist slaveholders or sold in the British West Indies. Others, abandoned, went to the West Indies, Florida, Nova Scotia, England, or Africa. A few migrated to the northern states.

As the treatment of black individuals was mixed, so was the institution of slavery, brought into question for the first time in the Revolutionary era. The territory of Vermont outlawed it in 1777, but for the balance of the war most northern states avoided antislavery action that would alienate Southerners. In 1783, a Massachusetts judge declared that slavery violated the state's constitution. The Northwest Ordinances of 1784 and 1787 banned it, and Congress came within one vote of banning it in the southern territories as well. All northern states banned slave trading, but none of the thirteen original states' legislatures banned slavery outright during the Articles of Confederation period. By the end of the war, however, slavery was discredited, and all the northern states eventually adopted gradual emancipation plans. Even Southerners, whose economy depended on it and who imported large numbers of new slaves to replenish depleted stocks, made manumission easier and allowed the formation of abolitionist societies. However, revolutionary abolitionism was a weak force, and many northern slavemasters simply sold their slaves south to the Cotton Belt.

The African-American role in the American Revolution, though ignored by most whites, then and now, became not only a major abolitionist political weapon, but a sign of historical legitimacy. Beginning with William Cooper Nell in the 1850s, African-American historians have often focused on blacks in the American Revolution. Later contributions by William Wells Brown in the 1860s, George Washington Williams in the 1880s, Benjamin Brawley in the 1920s, Luther P. Jackson in the 1940s, and Benjamin QUARLES in the 1960s added to the body of knowledge, but still, it has taken almost two centuries for full-scale consideration and discussion to take place. Today, documents, facts, analyses, and other data on the war for independence have begun to appear in large quantities.

The most important effect of the war on African Americans was the creation of a large self-conscious class of free blacks who began to organize their own communities. Under leaders such as Richard ALLEN, they formed independent religious denominations. Around their churches grew fraternities, social and literary organizations, and abolitionist societies. Martin R. Delaney, Frederick DOUGLASS, and others used the efforts of their patriot predecessors and the egalitarian language of the revolution as weapons against slavery, as well as against segregation and discrimination. Still, most blacks had to wait for the second American revolution of the Civil War to see even temporary recognition as citizens of the land in which they were born and for which they fought.

BIBLIOGRAPHY

Berlin, Ira, and Ronald Hoffman, eds. *Slavery and Freedom in the Age of the American Revolution.* Charlottesville, Va., 1983.

Foner, Philip S. *Blacks in the American Revolution.* Westport, Conn., 1976.

Frey, Silvia R. *Water From the Rock: Black Resistance in a Revolutionary Age.* Princeton, N.J., 1991.

Kaplan, Sidney, and Emma Nogrady Kaplan. *The Black Presence in the Era of the American Revolution.* Rev. ed. Amherst, Mass., 1989.

Nash, Gary B. *Race and Revolution.* Madison, Wisc., 1990.

Quarles, Benjamin. *The Negro in the American Revolution.* Chapel Hill, N.C., 1961.

Wilson, Ellen Gibson. *The Loyal Blacks.* New York, 1976.

— ALLAN D. AUSTIN

AMISTAD MUTINY

The *Amistad* mutiny was a rebellion of African captives that occurred off the northern coast of Cuba in July 1839. The mutineers had been seized in Africa, herded onto a Portuguese slave ship along with hundreds of others, and then transported illegally from the African island of Lombokor to Cuba (then a Spanish colony).

missions, and emigration. The national convention sites—including Buffalo (1843); Troy, N.Y. (1847); Cleveland (1848); and Rochester, N.Y. (1853)—marked the geographical shift away from the Atlantic coastal cities. A new generation of black leaders—many of them former slaves—came forward to claim positions of leadership in the convention movement. Frederick DOUGLASS, Henry Highland Garnet, James McCune Smith, and others sought to imbue the movement with a more practical outlook and a militant, independent spirit. Racial progress through moral reform, the staple of the conventions of the previous decade, was subsumed by the call for more forceful tactics and political action.

Not all black leaders welcomed a renewal of the convention movement. Those who held to strict integrationist principles counseled against convening separate black assemblies or establishing racially separate organizations. Others considered it wasteful of time and scarce resources to revisit the well-worn, intractable issues debated at past conventions. But most blacks favored continuing the convention process. The disagreements, often intense, centered mainly on form, agenda, and leadership.

David Ruggles's revival of the national convention movement at New Haven in 1840 and New York City in 1841 attracted only a few delegates. Poor organization, vague objectives, and editorial opposition from the *Colored American* contributed to the dismal outcome. Henry Highland Garnet had more success in promoting the 1843 national convention. The Buffalo convention set the new tenor for the movement with Garnet's controversial call for slave insurrection (disapproved by a narrow majority of the assembly) and the heated discussion of a resolution endorsing the Liberty party. The 1847 and 1848 national conventions in Troy and Cleveland highlighted the theme of black independence. James McCune Smith and Frederick Douglass addressed the delegates on the symbolic and practical need for self-reliance and independent black initiatives. These insightful speeches on independence and racial identity, affirmed their reputation as two of the leading black intellectuals of the antebellum period.

Just as in the 1830s, these later national conventions served primarily as a forum for competing ideas and leadership. The delegates approved plans for a national black press, an industrial-arts college, and other proposals of a practical nature. But without adequate resources, none of these objectives could be achieved. The conventions also sought continuity through the establishment of a permanent national organization. In the early 1840s, Ruggles anticipated the need for a national body with the short-lived American Reform Board of Disfranchised Commissioners. A more elaborate proposal—the National Council of the Colored People—emerged a decade later. By the 1850s, even racial assimilationists like Douglass and Smith had come to accept the idea of a separate black national organization. Douglass promoted this as part of an ambitious agenda for the 1853 national convention in Rochester.

The Rochester convention marked the high point of the antebellum convention movement. Over 160 representatives from ten northern states attended. The convention established the National Council of the Colored People, a major advance in black organization, even if it suffered from a contentious leadership and lack of popular support. The National Council faded quietly after the 1855 convention at Philadelphia—the last national convocation before the Civil War. The Philadelphia convention appeared lackluster and unproductive in comparison with the previous meeting in Rochester. Dominated by the seventy-member Pennsylvania delegation, the convention deferred substantial issues and engaged in a lively debate on procedural questions, particularly the propriety of seating a woman delegate, Mary Ann Shadd Cary.

Several conventions in the 1850s reflected the growing pessimism among African-Americans. As hopes faded for racial progress in the United States, a black emigration movement gained increasing support. The North American Convention (1851) reflected the growth and growing influence of black communities in Canada West. Canadian and American delegates meeting in Toronto considered the recent enactment of the FUGITIVE SLAVE ACT OF 1850 and its ramifications. They recognized that the law threatened all African Americans, not just former slaves, with arbitrary arrest and enslavement. The convention highlighted the advantages of Canadian and Jamaican emigration, and urged blacks living in the United States to come under the fair and equitable rule of British law. At the national emigration conventions of 1854 and 1856 in Cleveland, delegates weighed proposals for settlement in Haiti, Central America, and Africa. The interest in emigration continued well into the early 1860s.

In shaping a more practical agenda, blacks brought the convention movement to the state level in the 1840s and 1850s. The state meetings were better suited to address specific civil rights issues. Much of the struggle against racial discrimination involved state laws and municipal ordinances. The black vote, where permitted, weighed more heavily in state and local elections. State conventions made protection and expansion of black voting rights their primary concern. New York blacks held the first state convention at Albany in 1840 to launch a petition campaign against a property requirement that severely limited their franchise. Blacks in Pennsylvania, Michigan, New Jersey, and Connecticut followed with a similar agenda at state conventions during the 1840s.

Ultimately the convention movement enhanced the sense of racial unity, identity, and purpose among black communities.

Emerging black communities in the western states—Ohio, Indiana, Illinois, and California—also challenged voting rights restrictions and proscriptive black laws at state conventions in the 1850s. California blacks focused on restrictions against black testimony in court as well as the suffrage issue. Maryland blacks held the only convention permitted in a slave state before the Civil War. The 1852 Maryland convention, closely scrutinized by the Baltimore press, discussed colonization, the enslavement of free blacks, and petitioning the state legislature on civil rights issues. The convention's careful deliberations and guarded resolutions reflected the delegates' anxiety over white response to their gathering.

Despite the energetic and determined efforts made by the many state and national conventions, blacks achieved few of their avowed goals. But in the process, the conventions provided a sounding board for new ideas, strategies, and tactics. Many blacks established their credibility and their leadership through participation in these conventions. And ultimately the convention movement enhanced the sense of racial unity, identity, and purpose among black communities across the North American continent.

BIBLIOGRAPHY

Bell, Howard H. *Proceedings of the National Negro Conventions, 1830–1864.* New York, 1969.

Foner, Philip S., and George E. Walker, eds. *Proceedings of the Black State Conventions, 1830–1865.* 2 vols. Philadelphia, 1979–1980.

– MICHAEL F. HEMBREE

APOSTOLIC MOVEMENT

From its origins only seventy-five years ago, the Apostolic Pentecostal churches now number more than 1,500,000 members and, from a minor role on the fringe, are now emerging as a major force in world religion. With roots in the HOLINESS MOVEMENT and PENTECOSTALISM, Apostolics hold a unique "Oneness" doctrine, dating from 1914, which rejects the traditional Christian Trinitarian formula of God in three persons in favor of a belief in "Jesus Only." Apostolics hold that Jesus Christ is God: Father in creation, Son in redemption, and Holy Spirit operating the church as his mystical body.

Apostolics trace their beginnings to the Azusa Street Revival of 1906–1909 in Los Angeles under the leadership of William J. Seymour, in which participants experienced glossolalia (speaking in tongues), which they believed to be the baptism of the Holy Ghost as recorded in the Book of Acts. The necessity for this baptism is held by all Apostolics. Also descended from Wesleyan Holiness groups, Apostolics nevertheless reject the Arminian doctrine of the "three works of grace," which holds that sanctification is a gradual process not requiring the Holy Ghost. To Apostolics, in contrast, justification and sanctification occur at once when a believer receives the gift and power of the spirit.

The Apostolic Movement appealed from the beginning to working-class people, who contributed generously to building and maintaining churches. The majorities of most congregations consist of women members, although ministerial leadership positions are generally held by men. The movement is often referred to as "leader centered" because the minister's charisma and personality, displayed especially through dynamic preaching, are the most important criteria for establishing recognition and determining success in congregations with little denominational structure.

One of the early Apostolic leaders was Garfield T. Haywood (1880–1931), who reported receiving the gift of the Spirit in 1908 in the Indianapolis church of Henry Prentess, who had been at Azusa Street. Originally a Trinitarian, Haywood accepted the Oneness (or "New Issue") doctrine in 1915 under the preaching of evangelist Glen Cook, and he began to baptize in "Jesus' Name." He served as secretary of the Pentecostal Assemblies of the World, from which many white members withdrew in 1924, and in 1925 he became presiding bishop.

At Haywood's death, Robert Clarence Lawson (1883–1961) became the most notable African-American advocate for Oneness Apostolicism. Lawson stated that he was miraculously healed of tuberculosis and that he experienced the Spirit in 1914 under Haywood's ministry. Lawson became a general elder in the Pentecostal Assemblies of the World but resigned in 1919 in a dispute with Haywood over women preachers and divorce, both of which he opposed. He founded the Refuge Churches of Our Lord, later known as the Church of Our Lord Jesus Church of the Apostolic Faith, Inc., a denomination now of nearly 500 congregations in the United States, Africa, Europe, the West Indies, and Canada.

Out of Lawson's branch of the movement came the Church of the Lord Jesus Christ Apostolic, established in 1930 by Sherrod Johnson (1897–1961) of Philadelphia. Johnson became famous by publicly debating doctrinal issues on the radio; many Apostolics were pioneers in early radio ministries. Johnson's disagreement with Lawson centered on women's dress; Johnson advocated cotton stockings and ankle-length dresses and opposed hair plaiting and straightening; Lawson maintained it was not clothes that made for righteousness but whether one's life is sanctified.

Other leaders who emerged from the Lawson movement include Henry C. Brooks (c. 1895–1968), founder in 1927 of the Way of the Cross Churches of Christ, Inc.; J. P. Shields, who founded the Zion Assembly Churches in 1938; and Lymus Johnson, who established the Evangelistic Churches of Christ. From these groups have come further splits and divisions, notably the United Churches of Jesus Apostolic (1970) of James C. Richardson, Sr.; the United Way of the Cross Churches of Christ of the Apostolic Faith (1974) of Joseph H. Adams; and United Church of Jesus Christ (Apostolic) (1965) of Monroe Saunders.

From its origins only seventy-five years ago, the Apostolic Pentecostal churches now number more than 1,500,000 members.

Perhaps the most important person to split from Lawson was Smallwood E. Williams (1907–1991), who in 1957 founded the Bible Way Church of Our Lord Jesus Christ World Wide. Williams was a participant in the CIVIL RIGHTS MOVEMENT, served as head of the Washington, D.C., SOUTHERN CHRISTIAN LEADERSHIP CONFERENCE, and on the board of the NAACP, and was a sponsor of low- and middle-income housing projects, all despite criticism from many African-American Apostolics for his secular political involvement. At Williams's death in 1991, the Bible Way organization numbered over 350 churches. Williams was succeeded as presiding bishop by Laurence D. Campbell of Danville, Va.

William L. Bonner (c. 1929–) was, after Hubert J. Spencer, the actual successor to Lawson, supervising the denomination's 450 congregations. Beginning as Lawson's chauffeur, Bonner became assistant pastor of Refuge Temple in New York and later built "Solomon's Temple," a 3,000–member congregation in Detroit. A gifted radio and television producer, Bonner has established large congregations across the country and is himself pastor of four, including the 4,000–member Greater Refuge Temple in New York.

These numerous schisms are sometimes over personal power and the bishopric, but many are the result of controversies over doctrinal positions. Serious disagreements have divided Apostolics over such issues as clothes, jewelry and beauty products; the question of whether women's heads should be covered during worship; marriage and divorce; the question of women ministers, methods of water baptism; governance by one leader or several; and the role of Apostolic Pentecostals in social reform.

Although many Apostolic debates have concerned the role and position of women in the church, women have served as many of the movement's members and workers, and some have achieved leadership positions. Mattie Poole (1903–1968) conducted a healing ministry in Chicago and via radio. Carrie F. Lawson (1891–1946), R. C. Lawson's first wife, was known as the "Praying Mother of the Air." Delphia Perry (c. 1901–c. 1984) founded the International Women's Council of the Church of Our Lord Jesus Christ. Pearl Williams Jones (1931–1991) was a prominent academic and musician.

Music has played an important part in the movement, inspiring songs, anthems, and songbooks. Garfield Haywood composed many Pentecostal hymns in his book *Bridegroom Songs,* and R. C. Lawson wrote many lyrics and melodies that were compiled in *The Songs of Christ.* Full and enthusiastic congregational participation in singing is a major characteristic of Apostolic worship, and the entire church may stand, sing, and clap hands simultaneously with the choir or song leader. In the movement's early period, washboards, tambourines, and guitars were used as percussion instruments, but with greater prosperity pianos and organs and now multiranged amplification systems and computer-controlled music systems have become more prevalent.

BIBLIOGRAPHY

DuPree, Sherry S. *Biographical Dictionary of African-American Pentecostals, 1880–1990.* Washington, D.C., 1990.

Jones, Charles E. *Black Holiness: A Guide to the Study of Black Participation in Wesleyan Perfectionist and Glossolalic Pentecostal Movements.* Metuchen, N.J., 1987.

Richardson, James C. *With Water and Spirit.* Washington, D.C., 1980.

— ROBERT C. SPELLMAN

ARCHITECTURE

African Americans have been involved in building and architecture since the colonial era. The colonial plantation system relied heavily on slave craftsmen imported from Africa, who brought with them skills in ironworking, woodcarving, and the use of earth and stone to produce buildings, furniture, and tools. Written records and physical examination of building technologies indicate slave involvement in most early plantation construction throughout Louisiana, such as Magnolia in Plaquemines Parish in 1795, Oakland in Bermuda, and the mansion in Cloutierville that became the home of the nineteenth-century novelist Kate Chopin. Gippy Plantation, in South Carolina, and Winsor Hall, in Greenville, Ga., were also built by slave artisans. Some of these slave artisans were hired out to other owners as well, such as James Bell of Virginia, who was sent to Alabama to construct three spiral staircases for the Watkins-Moore-Grayson mansion.

The colonial plantation system relied heavily on slave craftsmen imported from Africa.

A number of free blacks also designed and built in the antebellum South. Charles, a free black carpenter, woodworker, and mason, contracted with Robin de Logny in 1787 to build Destrehan Plantation in St. Charles Parish, La. Free black planters in Louisiana built plantation houses that include Mignon Carlin's Arlington (1850), Pierre Cazelar's Cazelar House, and Andrew Drumford's Parrish Plantation. Louis Metoyer, one of fourteen children of a former slave, studied architecture in Paris and designed the Melrose house and several other later buildings in Isle Breville, a settlement of "free people of color." Central African influences are noticeable in most of his work, especially the African House (c. 1800), recently designated a landmark as the only structure of its type standing in the United States.

This period of African-American activity in building and construction came to an abrupt end after the CIVIL WAR. Increasing industrialization, developing trade unions in the cities of the North that excluded blacks, and the economic depression that accompanied RECONSTRUCTION largely eliminated the free black planter class and with it the independent artisan and craftsman. Many free black landowners, such as the Metoyers, either lost or had their property holdings significantly reduced.

During the second half of the nineteenth century, EDUCATION throughout the United States became increasingly formalized in all disciplines; it became progressively more difficult for a craftsman to construct a building independently. However, the majority of the states did not establish formal requirements for licensing or professional identification until well into the twentieth century.

The Massachusetts Institute of Technology (MIT), founded in 1861, inaugurated the first formal architecture program in the United States in 1867. In 1868 the Freedman's Bureau founded HAMPTON INSTITUTE in Virginia to train black men and women, many of them former slaves, to "go out and teach and lead their people." From the start, Hampton offered a full building-skills program, and a number of campus buildings were designed and built by faculty and students.

Booker T. WASHINGTON modeled Tuskegee Institute (now TUSKEGEE UNIVERSITY) in Alabama on Hampton, his alma mater, and expanded his normal school to include training in architecture and the building trades. By 1893 the school had been renamed Tuskegee Normal & Industrial Institute and, under the direction of Robert R. Taylor, offered a complete architectural drawing program in its Department of Mechanical Industries. Tuskegee's early buildings were designed by department faculty members and built under their supervision by students with student-made bricks. School records indicate that the department was established to make a profit—though this proved elusive—and that it took on design and construction jobs outside the school.

The Tuskegee program differed significantly from Hampton's in two ways; it employed a black faculty and it promoted a strong service ethic. Washington linked his architecture program to the school's primary mission to uplift a people. His program also sought to reinstate the role of the black artisan in the skilled trades. Speaking in 1901, Washington stated, "We must have not only carpenters, but also architects; we must not only have people who do the work with the hand but persons who at the same time plan the work with the brain." Aside from the work done at Hampton and Tuskegee, he continued, there were few African Americans trained in the basic principles of architecture. Indeed, in Washington's time (and to this day), the number of practicing black architects in the United States was (and is) disproportionately low. In the 1890 census, which was the first to provide a separate tabulation for architects of color, there were only forty-three black architects, a number that would rise slowly over the succeeding decades.

A number of the earliest recognized black architects began their careers at Tuskegee as students or as faculty. Washington recruited Robert R. Taylor in 1892 to develop the Department of Mechanical Industries. Taylor had been among the first blacks to graduate from the architecture program at MIT. During his forty-one-year tenure at Tuskegee he became a vice president and confidant of Washington, designed many of Tuskegee's major buildings, and supervised overall campus planning. Other Tuskegee architecture faculty included Wallace A. Rayfield, William Sidney Pittman, Walter T. Bailey, and William Augustus Hazel.

Wallace A. Rayfield taught at Tuskegee from the 1890s until 1907. Like Taylor, he designed several campus buildings but eventually left to establish the first known black architectural office in Birmingham, whose successful practice was focused on church design, one of the major areas of the field then open to blacks. He became the national architect for the African Methodist Episcopal (AME) Zion Church. Other Rayfield church designs include the Ebenezer Baptist Church in Chicago and Birmingham's Sixteenth Street Baptist Church, a landmark of the CIVIL RIGHTS MOVEMENT of the 1960s.

John A. Lankford, one of Taylor's first pupils, established one of the first black architectural offices in Washington, D.C., in 1897. In 1898 he designed and supervised the construction of the $100,000 Coleman Cotton Mill in Concord, N.C. He later worked as an instructor in architecture at several black colleges and served as superintendent of the Department of Mechanical Industries at Shaw University. He served as the national supervising architect for the AFRICAN METHODIST EPISCOPAL CHURCH, for which he designed Big Bethel, a landmark of atlanta's Auburn Avenue. He also designed churches in West and South Africa. The Grand Fountain United Order of the True Reformers, organizers of one of the first black-owned banks, commissioned his office to design their national office in Washington. Lankford also participated in the creation of the School of Architecture at HOWARD UNIVERSITY in the 1930s. Both he and Rayfield published their work in leading black journals of the time, including the CRISIS and *Opportunity*.

William Sidney Pittman, after earning degrees at Tuskegee and Drexel institutes, was a member of the Tuskegee faculty from 1899 to 1905. In 1905 Pittman moved to Washington, D.C., to establish an architectural office. In 1907 he married Booker T. Washington's daughter Portia. Pittman's output included designs for schools, libraries, lodges, and other public buildings from 1907 to 1913, which established his reputation as one of the nation's most promising black architects. The frequent "Negro Exhibits" held at national expositions following the World's Columbian Exposition at Chicago in 1893 gave Pittman and many other black architects a chance to display their skills. Pittman won the national competition for the design of the Negro Building for the Jamestown Exposition in Virginia in 1907, a building that was erected by an all-black team of contractors and workmen. In 1913 Pittman and his family moved to Dallas, Tex., where he lived until his death in 1958.

George Washington Foster, Jr. (1866–1923), studied at Cooper Union in New York (1888–1889) and worked as a draftsman in Henry J. Hardenberg's firm; it is generally believed that he later worked on the Flatiron Building (1903) in New York City as a member of Daniel Burnham's firm. In 1902 he became the first black architect licensed to practice in New Jersey. After meeting Vertner Woodson Tandy through the Elks' "colored branch," the two established a partnership in 1909 that lasted until 1915. One of the highest achievements from the latter period of Foster's life was the commission to build the Mother African Methodist Episcopal Zion Church on 137th Street in Harlem.

Vertner Woodson Tandy became the first African-American architect licensed in New York State. A Tuskegee alumnus (1905), Tandy was also the first black graduate of Cornell University's School of Architecture (1907), where he helped found Alpha Phi, the first fraternity for African Americans. The most significant commissions of Tandy and Foster's practice in New York include St. Philip's Episcopal Church and its Queen Anne-style Parish House (1910–1911) and the Harlem townhouse of Madame C. J. WALKER. After their partnership dissolved, Tandy designed Madame Walker's country house, the Villa Lewaro in Irvington-on-Hudson, New York (1917–1918); the Harlem Elks Lodge; Smalls' Paradise; and the Abraham Lincoln Houses in the Bronx, N.Y., a joint venture with Skidmore, Owings & Merrill in the 1940s.

John Lewis Wilson (1898–1989), who worked for Tandy, came from a prominent Mississippi family. He was inspired to study architecture by Wallace Rayfield, who designed a church for his father, a well-known minister. In 1923 Wilson became the first black student to attend the School of Architecture at Columbia University, N.Y., but after graduating, he was unable to find work at any of the white firms to which he applied. After the HARLEM RIOTS OF 1935, Wilson was the single African American appointed to a team of seven architects to design the Harlem River Houses, one of the first federal housing projects. His appointment came after protests from the black community.

Julian Francis Abele came from a privileged family and graduated from the University of Pennsylvania School of Fine Arts and Architecture in 1904. Following graduation, he worked for Horace Trumbauer & Associates in Philadelphia. It was Trumbauer who sent Abele to the École des Beaux Arts in Paris, where he received his diploma in 1906. Abele worked for Trumbauer for the next thirty-one years, becoming the firm's chief designer. Abele was responsible for the Gothic design of Duke University. Following the death of Trumbauer, Abele established his own office and became one of the few black members of the American Institute of Architects (AIA) in 1941.

Paul Revere Williams was discouraged by his teacher at Los Angeles Polytechnic High School from pursuing a career in architecture because of his race. Ignoring this advice, he worked his way through the University of Southern California's School of Architecture and went on to achieve considerable fame. He is best known for his designs for the houses of such Hollywood celebrities as Tyrone Power, Betty Grable, Julie London, Frank Sinatra, Cary Grant, Bill "Bojangles" robinson, Barbara Stanwyck, Bert Lahr, and William Holden. For middle-class homeowners, he published *Small Homes of Tomorrow* (1945) and *New Homes for Tomorrow* (1946). In addition, Williams designed the Los Angeles International Airport restaurant building and the Freedmen's Hospital at Howard University. In 1926 he became the first black member of the AIA and was also named by President Calvin Coolidge to the National Monument Commission. In 1956 Williams became the first black to be elected to the AIA College of Fellows. Over the years, Williams received numerous awards for his residential designs, as well as honorary degrees from Atlanta, Howard, and Tuskegee universities.

WORLD WAR II had a profound effect on the progress of African Americans in the architectural profession. In a milestone decision for black architects, the War Department awarded a $4.2 million contract in 1941 to McKissack & McKissack, a black architecture, engineering, and construction firm, founded in 1909, for the construction of Tuskegee Air Force Base. Hilyard Robinson, an architect practicing in Washington, D.C., won the architectural-design portion of the job. In 1943 Allied Engineers, Inc., a California firm organized by Paul Williams, received a $39 million contract for the design and construction of the U.S. Navy base in Long Beach, Calif. Williams also contributed to the establishment of the Standard Demountable Homes Company of California, which focused on providing housing for war workers.

With funds newly available through the GI Bill of 1944, returning African-American veterans from World War II were eligible for educational opportunities far exceeding those open to previous generations. Racial segregation still limited their choices, however, creating unprecedented enrollments at Howard, Hampton, and Tuskegee. In 1949 Howard University's School of Architecture became the first predominantly black architecture school to be accredited. However, a series of U.S. Supreme Court cases culminating in the 1954 BROWN V. BOARD OF EDUCATION OF TOPEKA, KANS., opened the doors of white architectural schools to black students.

Model church designed by John A. Lankford, a successful architect based in Washington, D.C., who participated in the founding of Howard University's School of Architecture. (R. K. Dozier Collection)

Whitney M. Young, Jr., the civil rights leader and executive director of the NATIONAL URBAN LEAGUE, forced the architectural profession to reconsider its wider social responsibilities when he delivered his famous keynote address "Man and His Social Conscience" at the annual national convention of the American Institute of Architects in 1968. Young told his audience:

> You are not a profession that has distinguished itself by your social and civic contributions to the cause of civil rights, and I am sure that does not come to you as a shock. . . . You are most distinguished by your thunderous silence and your complete irrelevance. . . . You are employers, you are key people in the planning of our cities today. You share the responsibility for the mess we are in, in terms of the white noose around the central city. We didn't just suddenly get this situation. It was carefully planned.

Soon after Young's speech, the Ford Foundation established scholarships for black architecture students as part of a far-reaching program that included grants to schools for the upgrading of facilities. The AIA itself created a Task Force on Equal Opportunity and formed a joint venture with the Ford Foundation to establish the Minority/Disadvantaged Scholarship Program (this replaced the Ford Foundation program when the latter was discontinued in 1973). In 1982 an endowment was created to support that program. In 1983 a program report stated that more than three hundred students in fifty schools had been assisted, with a considerable success rate.

In 1968 Howard University still had the only predominantly black, accredited architecture school, prompting the AIA and the Association of Collegiate Schools of Architecture (ACSA) to join forces to accredit other programs. In the mid-1990s eight institutions identified as historically black colleges and universities (HBCUs) offered accredited, professional architecture degrees, and two offered degrees in architectural engineering. Those eight schools were Howard University, Washington, D.C.; Hampton University, Hampton, Va.; Southern University, Baton Rouge, La.; Tuskegee University, Tuskegee, Ala.; Florida A&M University, Tallahassee, Fla.; Morgan State University, Baltimore, Md.; Prairie View A&M University, Prairie View, Tex.; and the University of the District of Columbia.

The Whitney M. Young, Jr., Citation Award was established in 1970 by the AIA's Social Concern Task Force. It is awarded to an architect or an architecturally focused organization in recognition of a significant contribution to social responsibility. Robert Nash was the first recipient of the citation, and he became the AIA's first African-American vice president in 1970.

In 1971 the National Organization of Minority Architects (NOMA) was founded in Chicago when a caucus of twelve black architects met at the AIA Convention in Detroit and resolved to "specifically address the concerns of black and other minority architects [in order to] add a needed dimension to the scope of the minority architects' sphere of influence." The organization strives to promote the design and development of a living, working, and recreational environment of the highest quality, as well as to increase the numbers of black architects by supporting the recruitment and education of new architects. In 1994 NOMA's membership reached approximately five hundred. Its forerunner was the National Technical Association, founded in 1926 in Chicago by Charles S. Duke.

Whitney M. Young, Jr., the civil rights leader and executive director of the National Urban League, forced the architectural profession to reconsider its wider social responsibilities.

Another resource group for black architects, founded since the 1970s, is the AIA's Minority Resources Committee (MRC), known until 1985 as the Minority Affairs Task Group (MATG). The MRC collects and disseminates information and oversees policies at the national level, as well as acting as a clearinghouse for the AIA, ACSA, and NOMA.

The tradition of African-American involvement in community-based and public building that began with the public housing and military projects of the 1930s and 1940s expanded in the 1960s and 1970s with the advent of the free clinic for architectural and urban design problems. The first prototype of the free clinic was the Architecture Renewal Committee in Harlem, or ARCH, founded by two white architects, Richard Hatch and John Bailey, in 1965 to address issues of "advocacy planning" (a phrase coined by urban planner Paul Davidoff); Max Bond was ARCH's first black director. The free-clinic concept was eventually adopted by the federal government as Community Design Centers, or CDCs. In President Lyndon Johnson's War on Poverty, CDCs provided services for the disadvantaged, primarily in urban areas. By the end of the 1960s it was clear that a substantial market for nonprofit services of this kind existed, extending beyond minority groups to many segments of society.

The recession of the mid-1970s severely affected the entire architectural profession, as did President Nixon's moratorium on construction of low- and moderate-income housing, one of the mainstays of black architectural practices. During this fallow period, architects were forced to search elsewhere for projects. However, William Coleman, a black lawyer from Philadelphia who was the Nixon administration's secretary of transportation, established a landmark affirmative action program in public works, which mandated that 15 percent of federal funds for mass transit projects must be allocated to minority firms. However, the withdrawal of much federal support for urban social programs and for low- and moderate-income housing under Presidents Reagan and Bush had a negative impact on the black architectural community.

In 1991 the Directory of African-American Registered Architects identified some 877 black architects in forty-three states. Of these, only 49 are women. In 1993 black architects made up only 7.5 percent of the AIA; in the profession as a whole, their numbers are estimated at only 1 percent. Furthermore, the majority of black architects work in the public sector on government projects, since institutional and professional biases continue to restrict their ability to obtain private commissions. Two recent reports commissioned by the AIA and the ACSA reiterate the fact of low numbers in the profession and focus on the problems faced by minorities in the architectural profession. Major obstacles that were identified for both students and practicing professionals included racism, depressed social communities, lack of role models, the high cost of education, isolation from resources, a decrease in minority set-asides, poor representation in the AIA, the absence of publicity of accomplishments in the field, tokenism in joint ventures to pursue commissions, and a high attrition rate among black students.

In addition, the century-old vocational/professional split still plagues blacks in the architecture profession. Related to the entrenched division between design and production maintained in the schools of architecture, there is even now a noticeable division in large majority firms, where larger numbers of African-American architects work on the production or technical side of building rather than in the design studios.

Black architects are also currently engaged in a fierce debate on the merits of assimilation versus a more explicitly Afrocentric architecture, with a third group focused on the professional and artistic concerns of the profession itself. A resurgence of interest in HBCUs, designs that incorporate traditional African elements, and interest in working almost exclusively within the black community characterize the Afrocentrist position, as opposed to the integrationists, who wish to be perceived as architects first and African Americans second.

The third group in the debate focuses on the role of African Americans in the architectural profession as a whole. This group deals less with political concerns and more with issues of social responsibility and community orientation. Their approach is based on the complex cultural and artistic history of black architects in the context of modern American society. In a situation in some ways analogous to the history of jazz, the proponents of this third position tend to draw upon African elements in their work, but they filter them through the lens of contemporary American culture.

One of the most visible contemporary black architects is Jack Travis, editor of the widely acclaimed book *African-American Architects in Current Practice* (1991). Travis earned his B. Arch. from Arizona State University in 1977. After working for Skidmore, Owings & Merrill, he established his own firm in New York in 1985. Travis served as a professional adviser on director Spike LEE's *Jungle Fever* (1991), a film that featured Wesley Snipes as a black architect trying to succeed in a white professional world. Travis frequently brings African-inspired elements into his sleek, modernist designs. His work includes Spike Lee's office headquarters in Brooklyn, N.Y.; many corporate projects, including retail showrooms for designer Giorgio Armani; and various private residences. He is currently an adjunct professor at the Fashion Institute of Technology, New York.

Lou Switzer is the founder and chairman of the Switzer Group, a corporate space-planning and design firm located in New York, whose clients include IBM, Con Edison, and Citibank. After working as an office messenger and then a draftsman for various design firms, Switzer attended night architecture courses at Pratt Institute, New York. Switzer worked at E. F. Hutton as assistant director of facilities planning worldwide, then began his own firm in 1975 with a minimum of capital and employees. Since the 1980s it has become a major mainstream design firm, not bound to any particular design philosophy. The firm is developing a $1.5 billion multiuse complex near the United Nations.

Harvey B. Gantt, a founding partner of Gantt Huberman Architects in Charlotte, N.C. (1971), harbored an ambition to become an architect since the ninth grade. He went on to earn his B. Arch. from Clemson University in 1965 (he was the architecture department's first black graduate) and his M. Arch. in city planning from MIT in 1970. Major works include the First Baptist Church in Charlotte, N.C. (1977) and the C. G. O'Kelly Library at Winston-Salem State University, N.C. (1990). Since the 1980s Gantt has become active in politics. He was mayor of Charlotte from 1983 to 1987 and ran for the U.S. Senate in 1990 but was narrowly defeated by incumbent Jesse Helms.

J. Max Bond, Jr., a partner in Davis Brody & Associates Architects of New York, has distinguished himself as both a teacher and practitioner in the architectural profession. Bond earned his M. Arch. from Harvard University in 1958 and spent several years during the 1960s teaching and designing buildings in Ghana, West Africa. From 1969 to 1984 Bond was professor in and then chairman of Columbia University's Division of Architecture. Since 1985 he has been dean of the School of Architecture and Environmental Studies at City College of New York. A recipient of the Whitney M. Young, Jr., Citation Award in 1987, Bond has long been active in urban renewal efforts in New York City, serving as a member of the City Planning Commission from 1980 to 1986 and as executive director of the Division of Architects Renewal Committee of Harlem. Well-known projects include the Martin Luther King, Jr., Center for Nonviolent Social Change in atlanta (1981) and the Studio Museum in Harlem (1982).

Harry L. Overstreet decided he wanted to be an architect in high school and then gained practical building experience in the U.S. Army Corps of Engineers. Overstreet worked as a self-employed designer in San Francisco and later became a licensed architect. He was appointed to the planning commission of the city of Berkeley, Calif., and served as the national president of NOMA from 1988 to 1990. Currently a principal in Gerson/Overstreet, Overstreet's work includes the Williard Junior High School in Berkeley (1980) and the Veterans Administration Medical Center in San Francisco (1991).

Roberta Washington is known for her work in Harlem salvaging neglected buildings and turning them into social-service and health-care facilities. Her twelve-person practice, Roberta Washington Architects, has taken on numerous renovation projects since its founding in 1983, including Astor Row, Hotel Cecil, Hale House Homeward Bound Residence, and Sarah P. Huntington House. Washington attended Howard University, then earned her M. Arch. from Columbia University. She worked in Mozambique from 1977 to 1981, designing a prototype for a medical center for women and children.

Shortly after the landmark U.S. Supreme Court decision *Sweatt* v. *Painter* (1950), which integrated graduate programs, John S. Chase entered the University of Texas Graduate School of Architecture in Austin in 1950 as that institution's first black student. Weathering intense racial prejudice and isolation at the university, Chase earned his M. Arch. in 1952. After graduation, no Houston architecture firms were willing to hire him, so Chase opened his own practice, becoming the first African American licensed to practice architecture in Texas, the first accepted into the Texas Society of Architects, and the first accepted into the Houston chapter of the AIA. Today Chase is the chairman and president of his own firm, with offices in Washington, D.C. and Houston, Dallas, and Austin, Tex. Appointed by President Carter as the first African American to serve on the U.S. Commission of the Fine Arts (1980), he received the Whitney M. Young, Jr., Citation Award in 1982 and has also received the NOMA Design Excellence Award four years consecutively. Chase's striking modernist designs include the School of Education Building at Texas Southern University, Houston (1977), and the Federal Reserve Bank of Dallas (associate architect; 1992).

Norma Merrick Sklarek earned her B. Arch. from Columbia University in 1950. Thirty years later she became the first black female fellow of the AIA (1980). She was also the first black female licensed to practice architecture in California. She is currently a principal in the Jerde Partnership, Inc., Los Angeles. Her work includes Downtown Plaza, Sacramento, Calif. (1993), the all-glass Pacific Design Center in Los Angeles (1978), the Queens Fashion Mall in Queens, N.Y. (1978), and the U.S. Embassy in Tokyo, Japan (1976). An architectural scholarship award has been founded in her name at Howard University.

Robert Traynham Coles has been the president and CEO of his own firm since 1963, with offices in Buffalo, N.Y., and New York City. He received his B. Arch. from the University of Minnesota (1953) and his M. Arch. from MIT (1955). Coles has taught architecture at the University of Kansas (1989) and at Carnegie Mellon University in Pittsburgh, Pa. (1990–1995). The recipient of a Whitney M. Young, Jr., Citation Award (1981), he has worked to increase the representation of blacks in the architectural profession, serving as the AIA's deputy vice president for minority affairs (1974–1976), then becoming a founding member of NOMA. His work includes the Providence Railroad Station in Providence, R.I. (1986), the Frank D. Reeves Municipal Center in Washington, D.C. (1987), and the Human Services Office Building in Canandaigua, N.Y. (1988).

Notable African-American architectural partnerships include Donald L. Stull and M. David Lee of Stull and Lee, Inc., Architects & Planners in Boston, Mass. Stull and Lee founded their firm in 1966, shortly after obtaining their M. Arch.'s from Harvard University. Their work includes the Ruggles Street Station in Boston (1986) with its giant glass arched entry; Roxbury Community College, Mass. (1987); and Harriet Tubman

House, Boston (1974). Their design for a Middle Passage Memorial (1990) consists of several giant, tangential, and abstract geometric forms, whose ominous shapes evoke a slave ship. Stull has served as president of the FAIA in addition to teaching design at Harvard University (1974–1981) and winning numerous awards from the AIA. Lee has served as vice president of the AIA and has taught urban design and architecture at Harvard and at MIT (1974–1983).

Three generations of the Fry family comprise Fry & Welch Associates, P.C., Architects & Planners. The firm was founded in 1954 and maintains offices in Washington, D.C., Atlanta, Richmond, Va., and Baltimore. The Frys—Louis E. Fry, Sr., Jr., and III—have completed such projects as the Tuskegee Chapel, Tuskegee University, Ala. (1960), and the Coppin State Athletic Center at Coppin State College, Baltimore (1986).

Wendell J. Campbell and Susan M. Campbell are the husband-and-wife team that make up Wendell Campbell Associates, Inc., of Chicago, Ill., and Gary, Ind. Wendell Campbell, the firm's president, was a founding member and the first president of NOMA (1972) and a recipient of the Whitney M. Young, Jr., Citation Award in 1976. Susan M. Campbell, the firm's vice president, received her M. Arch. from the Illinois Institute of Technology in 1992. The Campbells have designed St. Mark's Zion Church in East Chicago, Ind. (1973), the Genesis Convention Center in Gary, Ind. (1982), and the Dr. John Price House in Downers Grove, Ill. (1990), among other projects.

Black architects share not only the disadvantages but also the rich cultural heritage of African Americans.

There has been an increasing professional self-awareness among black architects. Robert Coles's speech "Black Architects: An Endangered Species," Richard Dozier's research and lectures, Jack Travis's pioneering book *African-American Architects in Current Practice,* Harry Robinson's implementation of archives at Howard University, Sharon E. Sutton's seminal work on architectural theory, and Harry Overstreet's energizing term as president of the NOMA have been critical elements in creating a climate that supports discussions of blacks in architecture.

For three hundred years, the black experience in architecture has been inseparable from the social history, political involvements, and educational opportunities of African Americans. Black architects share not only the disadvantages but also the rich cultural heritage of African Americans. As the American population grows increasingly "minority," the architecture profession has the opportunity to enrich itself by becoming more representative of the nation as a whole.

BIBLIOGRAPHY

Adams, Michael. "A Legacy of Shadows." *Progressive Architecture* (February 1991): 85–87.

Bond, J. Max, Jr. "The Black Architect's Experience." *Architectural Record* (June 1992): 60–61.

Coles, Robert Traynham. "Black Architects: An Endangered Species." *Journal of Architectural Education* (Fall 1989): 60–62.

Craig, Lois, ed. *The Federal Presence: Architecture, Politics, and Symbols in United States Government Building.* Cambridge, Mass., 1981.

Crosbie, Michael J. "Howard University School of Architecture." *Architecture* (April 1991): 52–53.

Dean, Andrea Oppenheimer. "A Values-Added Practice: Equal Measures of Conviction and City Smarts Underlie the Success of Harlem-Based Roberta Washington Architects." *Progressive Architecture* (October 1993): 54–57.

Dozier, Richard K. "The Black Architectural Experience in America." In Jack Travis, ed. *African-American Architects in Current Practice.* Princeton, N.J., 1991, pp. 8–9.

Engle, Claude. "Minorities in Practice." *Progressive Architecture* (June 1991): 59–62.

Gorman, Jean. "Southern Savvy: The Switzer Group Plays a Defining Role in the Corporate Big League." *Interiors* (July 1993): 54–56.

Grant, B. C., and D. A. Mann. *Directory of African-American Registered Architects.* Cincinnati, Ohio, 1991.

Kay, Jane Holtz. "Invisible Architects." *Architecture* (April 1991): 106–113.

Patterson, Terry. "Education: The Reconcilable Duality." *Progressive Architecture* (September 1990): 69.

Russell, Beverly. "Diversity in the Big Apple: With His Outspoken Personality, Jack Travis Is a Much Sought-After Architect." *Interiors* (July 1993): 50–53.

Ryder, Donald P. "Diverse School with a Special Mission." *Architecture* (August 1987): 48–51.

Sutton, Sharon E. "The Progress of Architecture." *Progressive Architecture* (October 1993): 76–79.

Travis, Jack, ed. *African-American Architects in Current Practice.* Princeton, N.J., 1991.

— RICHARD DOZIER AND GRETCHEN G. BANK

ARCHITECTURE, VERNACULAR

Defined as the ordinary buildings and spaces constructed, shaped, or inhabited by a particular group of people, vernacular architecture characterizes a place by giving it a specific social identity. Consequently, vernacular architecture is more than a segment of the manmade environment; it also entails an overall perception, a sense of place. Vernacular buildings and landscapes are thus especially important in the study of African-American history and culture, since as a group, African Americans left very little in the way of written documentation about the intimate day-to-day features of their domestic experiences. Encoded within any artifact is its design—its cultural base—as well as evidence of manufacture and use—its social narrative. Vernacular architecture, while a diffuse sort of data demanding cautious interpretation, affords scholars entry into the spatial realms established by certain groups of African Americans.

The Africans brought to the United States during the seventeenth century were, contrary to dismissive prejudicial stereotypes, fully equipped with the conceptual and technological skills required to build their own houses. Forced to labor on plantations along the shores of the Chesapeake and in the Carolina low country, they responded to the need for reasonable shelter by constructing small mud-walled dwellings. Archaeological remains indicate that these houses were generally rectangular in shape, and from various written accounts one can further surmise that they had roofs covered with a thatch made from tree branches or long grasses. Looking like houses straight out of Africa, these buildings did not pose, at first, the threat to a slaveholder's sense of command that one might suppose. Similar rectangular buildings with earthen walls and thatched roofs were commonplace as well in the British Isles, where they were usually identified as cottages suitable for the peasant classes who performed the bulk of the agricultural labor. The African houses with clay walls were thus allowed to stand for at least a generation.

The colonial period was characterized by a syncretic encounter between African and British cultures that fostered what the Africans would likely have interpreted as an opportunity to carry out their own ideas about house and home. What remained hidden within these buildings was an African feeling for appropriate space; the dimensions of the rooms were set according to the codes that their builders carried deep within their cultural personalities. In much of West and Central Africa, houses are built with small square rooms averaging 10' x 10'. These same dimensions discovered in the earliest slave quarters, whether they were built with earthen walls or constructed out of hewn logs, are perhaps an African signature that signals a significant degree of cultural continuity. Where Europeans saw only a small house built by people of little consequence, the enslaved Africans saw a good house constructed according to an appropriate plan. That its rooms were the right size for their style of social interaction should be seen as a subtle, but important, means of cultural preservation.

Overt African expressions of all sorts were met with increasing hostility over the course of the eighteenth century as planters initiated thoroughgoing campaigns to "improve" their properties. Even slave quarters were upgraded as slaveholders had new houses constructed with wooden frames covered with milled boards. Mud-walled houses, however, were still encouraged by some planters both for quarters and other service buildings. Robert Carter of Virginia, for example, asked his slave dealer to find him an artisan who "understood building mud walls . . . an Artist, not a Common Laborer." But the appreciation of such skills was clearly on the decline by the middle of the nineteenth century. When James Couper, owner of Hopeton Plantation in Georgia, discovered that his African slave Okra had built an African hut plastered with mud and thatched with palmetto leaves, he had the building torn down immediately.

Nevertheless, mud continued to be used in the building of chimneys on into the early twentieth century, when bricks could not be obtained and small outbuildings intended as animal shelters, particularly in the Sea Island areas of South Carolina, were still covered with a thatching of palmetto branches. While this can be seen simply as the methodology of poor people who had to make do with the materials that were easily available, African memories should not be discounted.

By 1860, 2.6 million blacks were living on plantations all across the South, and close to two-thirds of them were held on the larger estates in groups of fifty or more. Thus the plantation was not only a familiar place in the black experience; it also provided a primary context in which a distinctive African-American identity would take place. An extensive repertoire of African-American cultural traits was nurtured in the quarters communities where blacks lived largely in the exclusive company of one another. The testimony of former slaves who lived at such places describes their quarters as "little towns."

These were black places that were not merely left to the slaves, but were also, as repeated testimony confirms, places claimed by black people. Similar to the hidden African values found in the early slave houses was the sense of territorial imperative expressed by African Americans living on plantations. Out in the quarters, the fields, the work spaces, and in the woods at the margins of the plantation, too, some slaves reappropriated themselves. One Mississippi planter reported with a discernible measure of dismay that his slaves took pride in crops and livestock produced on his estate as *theirs.* With such possessive territorial gestures, slaves defined space for themselves.

In addition to distinctive expressions of music, oral literature, dance, folk art and craft, religion, and kinship that evolved within the plantation context, slave communities also developed sets of house types. While their designs were determined chiefly by the slave owners, the various clusters of slave cabins ultimately were understood by their occupants as home places. Historian

Leslie Howard Owens has recognized that the vigorous culture created by enslaved African Americans was contingent, in large measure, on a secure sense of place. "The Quarters," writes Owens, "sometimes partially, sometimes entirely, and often mysteriously, encompassed and breathed its own special vitality into these [social] experiences, frequently assuring that bondage did not snuff out the many-sided existence slaves created for themselves."

Under the watchful eyes of planters and overseers, quarters communities were fashioned that contained a variety of housing options. All these house types were derived from the basic square room also known as a "pen." A single pen could stand alone as a one-room cabin or could be combined with other pen units to form larger houses. Single- and double-pen cabins were the most frequently used, but also common was the so-called "dogtrot cabin" (two pens with a wide passage between them). Occasionally, two-story houses were provided; these buildings were basically double-pen cabins stacked one on top of another. These houses, meant to provide shelter for four slave families, resembled a building type known as the I-house, the dwelling form used as residences by the majority of planters. Larger quarters buildings were sometimes created by linking smaller cabins into a single structure; four- and six-pen barracks were built in this way. In the French areas of southern Louisiana, slaves were housed in distinctive buildings with relatively exotic features that one might expect to see in Quebec or even Normandy. During the 1820s on the larger rice plantations along the coasts of South Carolina and Georgia, a specialized quarters house was developed that had an asymmetrical three-room plan consisting of one narrow but deep general-purpose room that was flanked to one side by two smaller bedrooms. The loft, which could be entered by a ladder from the larger room, was intended as a sleeping area for children. Referred to as "tenement houses," dwellings of this sort were built in either single or double configurations.

With possessive territorial gestures, slaves defined space for themselves.

By 1860 most slave housing was constructed with wooden frames that were covered with siding. Nevertheless, many were also being built with tiers of corner-notched logs, in brick and stone masonry, and, in coastal Georgia and Florida, with tabby concrete. In addition to this variety of building techniques, slave quarters, particularly those within sight of the planter's residence, might be finished in one of several fashionable styles. Touches of Grecian, Gothic, or Italianate decoration might be added to the windows, doors, and eaves. One sees in slave housing the extensive efforts by slave owners to impose their will—indeed, their cultural values—upon their human property. These persistent attempts at discipline and control resulted in the architectural assimilation of African Americans, at least with respect to building repertoire.

By the mid-nineteenth century, blacks were thoroughly familiarized with Euro-American building forms and construction techniques. Significantly, the cabins used as quarters on plantations were not exclusively plantation structures; the same buildings were used by white yeoman farmers for the residences on their modest holdings. As slaves became accustomed to living in and building these houses, they transformed themselves essentially into black Southerners. When some of them were able to acquire their own land after 1865, they usually chose a standard plantation building like double-pen or dogtrot houses as the models for their new homes. What was different was that now they occupied both halves of the house, whereas previously a whole family had been confined to only one room. Further, they appended all manner of sheds and porches to their dwellings—personalizing touches that expressed a sense of self-empowerment and a degree of autonomy plainly suppressed in the slave cabins that were, on the outside at least, merely unadorned boxes with roofs. On the plantation, a slave quarter was an outbuilding in which property was sheltered. With the end of the plantation era, black builders transformed quarters into homes, a significant social achievement.

Throughout the nineteenth century, white and black vernacular traditions merged into a single regional entity so that differences along racial lines were manifested more as a function of relative wealth than as a matter of design choice. One instance will serve as an example of the merger of cultures in the saga of African-American vernacular architecture. Sometime about 1910 an unknown black farmer living near Darien, Ga., built what appeared to be nothing more than a slightly larger-than-usual single-pen house with a mud-and-stick chimney at one end. But in plan the house was actually a miniature version of a planter's house, consisting of four rooms divided by central passageway. Black notions of appropriate form and the highbrow southern ideal had become thoroughly integrated.

There remained, however, one African-American house form that signaled an alternate tradition: the shotgun house, a building one-room wide and three or more deep, oriented with its gable end to the front, stood apart from dwellings derived from the Anglo-

class living near the center of the city and the poor (both black and white) on the urban periphery. Emerging black settlements in Atlanta, as in many other southern cities, were further relegated to the most undesirable areas of the city: back alleys; low-lying, flood-prone ground; industrial sites; and tracts of land adjacent to railroads, cemeteries, city dumps, and slaughter houses. These locations not only tended to separate black settlements from surrounding white neighborhoods, but also contributed in some cases to very high black-mortality rates.

By 1880, several large and distinctive black communities had emerged within the city limits—most notably, Jenningstown on the west side of Atlanta, Summer Hill to the south, Shermantown on the east side, and Mechanicsville in the southwestern quadrant of the city. Other smaller black communities were scattered throughout the city, and in some areas whites and blacks continued to live in close proximity. Nonetheless, the emerging pattern in the late nineteenth century was one of separation and increasing racial division as black settlements became more concentrated and well defined. W. E. B. DU BOIS said that Atlanta's black population by the turn of the century "stretched like a great dumbbell across the city, with one great center in the east and a smaller one in the west, connected by a narrow belt."

For African Americans in Atlanta after the Civil War, employment opportunities were largely confined to unskilled labor, domestic service, or to jobs that whites did not want. Rural blacks migrating to the city tended to swell the ranks of unskilled workers, and even those freedmen who enjoyed positions as craftsmen or artisans before the war were often denied the opportunity to use those skills by prevailing white prejudice and an increasingly specialized urban job market. As a result, the vast majority of the city's unskilled labor positions (over 76 percent in 1870 and almost 90 percent in 1890) were filled by African Americans.

The economic insecurity facing back Atlantans during this period was further reflected in the relative scarcity of African Americans who owned property and the number of black women employed in personal and domestic service. In 1870 only 311 black men and 27 black women (about 3 percent of the adult population) were property owners. Ten years later, the number of black property owners had almost doubled but still lagged far behind the total for whites. Because of the low average earning power of black males, black women worked in much larger numbers than their white counterparts. The vast majority of black working women (92 percent in 1890) were confined to low-paying domestic service positions.

On the few occasions in the nineteenth century that black workers in Atlanta organized to negotiate for more pay, better working conditions, or increased job security, their efforts were usually unsuccessful. In 1881 an estimated 3,000 of Atlanta's black washerwomen joined forces to strike for higher wages and the establishment of a citywide charge of $1 per dozen pounds of wash. The city government and enraged white employers responded to these demands with arrests, fines, and threats of economic reprisals and incarceration. Under the weight of this government hostility and economic pressure, the strike eventually collapsed. Nine years later, protest by black firemen at the Georgia Pacific Railroad collapsed when the striking workers were replaced by white applicants.

Despite the considerable obstacles facing them, some black Atlantans did succeed during this period in establishing thriving businesses and accumulating wealth and property. Among these were undertaker David T. Howard, barbers Moses H. Bentley and Alonzo F. Herndon (who was also the founder of Atlanta Life Insurance Company), grocer James Tate, and hotel owner and grocer Moses Calhoun. These businessmen made their mark in a hostile economic environment in part by catering to black clients or by providing services to whites that were not in direct competition with white businesses.

White Atlantans and the city government were equally unwilling to address the social and EDUCATIONal needs of the city's growing black population. It was not until 1908 that the city established its first social service agencies and programs for African Americans. In the interim, black community needs were met instead through the actions of individuals or the programs of a growing array of black self-help, fraternal, and religious organizations. Carrie Steele Logan founded the city's first black orphanage. Self-help agencies such as the mutual aid societies organized to provide medical and death benefits for their members. The Neighborhood Union (founded by Lugenia Hope, wife of a Morehouse College president) established health centers, boys' and girls' clubs, and vocational classes for children; it also lobbied for improved public facilities for blacks. Fraternal organizations such as the Odd Fellows and the Good Samaritans raised thousands of dollars for the poor and infirm of the city.

The black churches of Atlanta likewise organized programs to meet the pressing social and economic needs of their communities. The First Congregational Church of Atlanta under the leadership of the Reverend Henry Hugh Proctor, for example, sponsored a home for black working women, business and cooking schools, a kindergarten, and an employment bureau. Similar community services and programs were provided by the city's other prominent black churches such as Big Bethel A.M.E. Church and Wheat Street Baptist.

In the area of education, black churches and religious organizations also played a prominent role. Atlanta University, the first black institution of higher learning in the city, was founded by the American Missionary Association in 1865. Atlanta Baptist College for men (MOREHOUSE COLLEGE) followed two years later, and CLARK UNIVERSITY, supported by the Freedmen's Aid Society of the Methodist Episcopal Church, was established in 1870. The final two schools of what would later become the Atlanta University Center—Morris Brown College, affiliated with the AFRICAN METHODIST EPISCOPAL CHURCH (A.M.E.), and Spelman Seminary (SPELMAN COLLEGE) for women, a Baptist school—opened in 1881. Although many of these schools were, at first, little more than advanced grammar or secondary schools, this nucleus of black higher education, unmatched in any other city in the United States, provided important educational and training opportunities for Atlanta's black students and contributed to the growth of what would become a sizable and well-educated black middle class.

Black Atlantans were less successful in the nineteenth century in establishing public elementary and secondary schools for their children, partly because of a sudden decline in the political strength of the city's African-American population following a signal achievement. In 1870, Republicans in the Georgia state legislature succeeded in changing the election system in the state's cities from an at-large selection process to a ward system. In the elections that followed in Atlanta that year, two African Americans—William Finch and George Graham—won seats on the city council. Finch used this opportunity to push for the establishment of black public schools; despite strong Democratic opposition and obstruction, he succeeded in incorporating into the city's school system two schools for black children organized and run by the American Missionary Association.

The following year, however, Democrats regained control of the state legislature, repealed the election law, and swept Finch and other Republican leaders out of office. The city continued to maintain separate public schools for its black students until the 1960s, but these schools remained few in number, and were overcrowded and understaffed. For many years, blacks were limited to grammar schools; not until the 1920s did Atlanta construct its first black public high school.

Efforts in Atlanta to segregate African Americans and restrict their political rights intensified in the period from 1890 to 1920 as the city's black population more than doubled. In 1892, local Democratic officials enacted a "white primary" law, effectively limiting voting in primary elections to white males. That same year, the city passed its first segregation ordinance, which authorized and mandated the separation of black and white passengers on streetcars. In 1913, Atlanta became the first city in Georgia to try to extend segregation to housing patterns through use of a residential segregation ordinance. Although this law was struck down by the state supreme court two years later, the city council passed a similar statute in 1917 and in 1922 tried to institute and formalize segregated housing through use of a comprehensive zoning ordinance.

Not until the 1920s did Atlanta construct its first black public high school.

Violence or threats of violence often accompanied attempts in the South during this period to disfranchise and segregate African Americans. A dramatic example of the ever-present potential for racial violence occurred in the Atlanta Riot of 1906. Racial tensions that year were intensified by a long and bitter campaign for governor in which both candidates called for the complete exclusion of blacks from the political process. Following a series of unsubstantiated reports in the local newspapers of wanton black attacks on white females, a race riot erupted in the city. Spurred on by lurid newspaper accounts of black rapists and rumors of black insurrection, roving gangs of white males attacked African Americans wherever they could find them in the downtown area and in nearby black neighborhoods.

Estimations of the number of blacks and whites killed and wounded in this riot vary widely among contemporary accounts, but the impact of this disturbance on black housing and business patterns was more clear. The riot hastened the city's move toward the economic exclusion and residential segregation of African Americans. Following the riot, African Americans were more likely to settle in established black communities, particularly those located on the eastern fringe of downtown or on the west side of the city near Atlanta University. And black businesses, which had once been interspersed among white commercial concerns on Peachtree Street, were now increasingly located to the east on Auburn Avenue, where a thriving but separate black business district soon developed.

Modest efforts to promote biracial understanding followed in the wake of the riot, culminating in the formation of the Commission on Interracial Cooperation in 1919. Overtures such as this, however, remained the exception in the 1920s and 1930s, as white supremacist organizations made their presence felt in the city. The

KU KLUX KLAN, reborn on nearby Stone Mountain in 1915, designated Atlanta as its headquarters (renaming it the "Imperial City of the Invisible Empire"). By 1923 the city's Nathan Bedford Forrest Klan No. 1 had a membership of over 15,000, including many notable local businessmen, educators, clergy, and politicians. In 1930, in the midst of growing unemployment, another white supremacist organization—the "Order of the Black Shirts"—surfaced in the city and pushed for the replacement of all black workers with unemployed whites. Although the Black Shirts' influence was short-lived, the organization nonetheless helped contribute to a restriction of the opportunities for African Americans during the years of the Great Depression.

Amazingly, in the midst of this repressive JIM CROW system, Atlanta's African Americans still managed to register some impressive gains. In 1921, for example, blacks used their ability to vote in city bond referendums and negotiations with the Commission on Interracial Cooperation to gain a commitment from the board of education to build the city's first black high school. The school was eventually constructed on the west side of town, where pioneer black businessman, banker, realtor, and builder Heman Perry was already developing new homes for Atlanta's blacks. Though Perry's overextended business empire collapsed later in the decade, his efforts on the west side helped pave the way for subsequent residential expansion in that area.

Ironically, the economic exclusion of Atlanta's African Americans from white business transactions also contributed to the growth of the city's middle class and the development of a black business and cultural mecca on Auburn Avenue that *Fortune* magazine would later describe as "the richest black street in the world." By 1920, Auburn Avenue was already home to a wide range of black-owned and -operated businesses, such as insurance companies, banks, a newspaper, barber and beauty shops, restaurants, grocery stores, photo studios, and funeral homes that provided African Americans the services denied them in the larger urban community. Freed from competition with white businessmen and assured the patronage of Atlanta's black community, many black entrepreneurs and their businesses prospered under Jim Crow.

By 1930, Jim Crow and the color line had been firmly established in the city. In the period from 1940 to 1960, however, black leaders began negotiating with city hall and white business leaders to weaken Jim Crow's hold. That city hall and the white business elite were even willing to discuss the issue with black leaders was a reflection of two important post-World War II developments: increased black voting strength and a rapidly deteriorating housing situation.

The repeal of the poll tax by the Georgia legislature in 1945 and the invalidation of the white primary by the state supreme court the following year removed two important barriers to black political participation, and Atlanta's black community responded in 1946 with a voter registration drive that added almost 18,000 new black voters to the city's rolls in only fifty-one days. Three years later, in an effort to coordinate and concentrate their newfound political strength, black Republicans and Democrats joined together to form the Atlanta Negro Voters League—a body which was soon openly courted by the mayor and by white candidates for office.

This increased black voting power and the severe housing shortage facing black Atlantans brought city hall, black leaders, and the white business elite together in behind-the-scenes meetings to negotiate such issues as the range and location of black residential expansion, redevelopment of the central business district, and city plans for annexation and growth. Each side succeeded in taking something away from the table. Mayor William Hartsfield gained important black electoral support for the city's 1951 annexation of northside suburbs (which added an estimated 100,000 residents, most of them white, to the city's population). White business leaders solicited general support for urban renewal plans that would remove low-income blacks and whites from the fringe of the central business district. They also received assurances that black residential expansion would not proceed into northside Atlanta. Black leaders got land for expansion and the construction of new housing and commitments from the city to build additional low-income housing. They also got promises from Mayor Hartsfield for a gradual phase-out of Jim Crow and increased protection against white violence.

By 1930, Jim Crow and the color line had been firmly established in the city.

The concessions gained on black housing were important for African Americans of all income levels, as dwelling units in most of the city's black neighborhoods were overcrowded and in poor condition. As late as 1959, blacks made up over one-third of the city's total population, yet occupied only about 16 percent of the developed residential land. Not surprisingly, almost three-fourths of the dilapidated housing in the city was found in black communities.

Yet as important as these negotiated agreements were, they did little to break the rigid color line in Atlanta.

Interstate highway construction and urban renewal programs in the 1950s and 1960s, for example, wiped out many inner city neighborhoods, displacing thousands of black residents who then relocated in nearby, already overcrowded, black communities. Similarly, while low-income public housing in Atlanta was increased during these decades, facilities remained strictly segregated and most new public housing was located in existing black residential areas. As a result, public housing tended not to disperse the black population throughout the metropolitan area but instead to confine it to existing areas of black residential concentration. Finally, although the 1951 annexation held certain benefits for Atlanta's black population, it also initially diluted black voting strength by adding thousands of white voters.

The peaceful biracial negotiations of this era contributed to Atlanta's emerging image as the most racially progressive city in the South. In 1961, this national reputation was further enhanced by the peaceful desegregation of four of the city's white high schools. Atlanta, ever mindful of the value of a good image, promoted itself during this decade as "the city too busy to hate."

Signs were already emerging, however, that suggested that the era of backstage biracial negotiations and gentlemen's agreements was fast coming to a close. SIT-INS in 1961 by black students to desegregate Atlanta's downtown restaurants threatened to upset relationships and alliances forged between black leaders and the white business elite and exposed generational cleavages within the black community. Martin Luther KING, Jr., who had personally led one of the sit-in demonstrations, soon found himself in the unenviable position of mediating between the more radical college students and older black leaders like his father, "Daddy" King.

One year later, changes in black leadership and tactics became even more apparent in the response of African Americans to the so-called "Peyton Road barricades." In that year, as blacks moved into the new white-only subdivision in southwest Atlanta, the city responded much as it had in the past by erecting barriers to slow and contain further black expansion (in this instance, by putting up street barricades). The resulting uproar in the black community and the accompanying national press coverage embarrassed the city and forced city hall to recognize that the days of a tightly segregated housing market in Atlanta, kept in place by overt discrimination and racial barriers, was over. While segregation practices would continue in more discreet forms—through the use of real estate tactics like blockbusting, racial steering, and discriminatory loan and mortgage policies—the right of African Americans to housing on an equal opportunity basis was now officially acknowledged.

This acknowledgment and the accelerated movement of African Americans into formerly all-white communities in south and east Atlanta contributed to a dramatic outmigration of white Atlantans in the 1960s. During this decade, the city's white population declined by 60,000 while its black population increased by 70,000. The result, as documented in the 1970 census, was that Atlanta had a black majority for the first time in its history.

This dramatic population change was reflected in black political gains in the city's 1973 elections. Not only was the city council evenly divided between whites and blacks for the first time, but the school board now had a slim African-American majority and Maynard Jackson was elected the city's first black mayor. One hundred and twenty-five years of white rule in Atlanta had come to an end.

In the years following Jackson's 1973 victory, significant gains have been made in minority participation in city government and business. Andrew YOUNG and, most recently, Bill Campbell have continued Atlanta's black mayoral presence, and efforts have been instituted to encourage the city's black and white business elite's involvement in city planning and development.

Atlanta's population base has also changed dramatically in the last few decades with the infusion of a growing cultural and ethnic diversity in what has traditionally been a biracial society. Both the city and the larger metropolitan area, however, retain a high degree of racial segregation as the city remains over two-thirds black while the surrounding suburbs are over two-thirds white. The increasing suburbanization of new jobs and business growth (particularly on the north side) has also left Atlanta, like many other cities, with a declining economic base and decreased job opportunities for those other than white-collar workers.

The growing multicultural nature of Atlanta's population, the presence of internationally recognized business concerns (e.g., CNN and Coca-Cola) and the city's selection as the site for the 1996 Olympics underlie Atlanta's current claims to being "the next great international city." How well the city succeeds at this task may be determined by Atlanta's success in overcoming the racial divisions, both social and geographical, that have historically divided the city.

BIBLIOGRAPHY

Dittmer, John. *Black Georgia in the Progressive Era.* Chicago, 1977.

Rabinowitz, Howard N. *Race Relations in the Urban South, 1865–1890.* Chicago, 1980.

Russell, James Michael. *Atlanta, 1847–1890: City Building in the Old South and the New.* Baton Rouge, La., 1988.

Stone, Clarence N. *Regime Politics: Governing Atlanta, 1946–1988.* Lawrence, Kans., 1988.

and Georges Simenon, who worked as her secretary. In 1927 "La Bakair" opened at the *Folies Bergère* in her famous costume of a few rhinestoned bananas.

That same year she met the café-society habitué "Count" Pepito de Abatino (actually a Sicilian stonemason). He became her lover and manager, taught her how to dress and act, trained her voice and body, and sculpted a highly sophisticated and marketable star. They toured Europe and South America. In Vienna, Baker was preached against for being the "impure incarnation of sex." She provoked hostility fueled by economic frustration, moral indignation, xenophobia, and racism.

When she returned to France, Abatino had done what he had promised: turned the diamond-in-the-rough of 1925 into the polished gem of 1930. There followed a ten-year reign of Baker in the music halls of Paris. Henri Varna of the Casino de Paris added to her image a baby leopard in a $20,000 diamond necklace and the song which would become her signature "J'ai deux amours, mon pays et Paris." Her name was linked with several Frenchmen, including singer Jacques Pills, and in 1934 she made her best motion picture, *Zouzou,* costarring Jean Gabin, followed by *Princess Tam Tam* in 1935.

Baker returned to New York to play in the 1936 *Ziegfield Follies,* but the show was a fiasco. She learned America would neither welcome her nor look on her with color-blind eyes as France did. Abatino died of cancer before she returned to Paris. Baker married Jean Lion, a wealthy sugar broker, in 1937, and divorced him fourteen months later. By 1939, Baker had become a French citizen. When the Nazis occupied France during World War II, Baker joined the Resistance, recruited by the head of French intelligence. For her activities in counterintelligence, Baker received the Croix de Guerre and the Légion d'Honneur. After operating between Marseilles and Lisbon under cover of a revival of her operetta *La Creole,* she was sent to Casablanca in January of 1940 to continue intelligence activities.

In 1941 Baker delivered a stillborn child, the father unknown. Complications from this birth endangered her life for more than nineteen months, and at one point her obituary was published. She recovered and spent the last years of the war driving an ambulance and entertaining Allied troops in North Africa. After the war, she married orchestra leader Jo Bouillon and adopted four children of different races that she called her "Rainbow Tribe." She turned her château, Les Milandes, into her idea of a multiracial community. In 1951, she attracted wide attention in the United States, and was honored by the NAACP, which organized a Josephine Baker Day in Harlem.

She continued to be an outspoken civil rights advocate, refusing to perform before segregated audiences in Las Vegas and Miami, and instigating a notorious *cause célèbre* by accusing the Stork Club of New York of discrimination. Her controversial image hurt her career, and the U.S. State Department hinted they might cancel her visa. Baker continued to tour outside America as her Rainbow Tribe grew to twelve. Between 1953 and 1963, she spent more than $1.5 million on Les Milandes, her financial affairs degenerated into chaos, her fees diminished, and she and Bouillon separated.

Though a popular performer in black musicals in New York City in the early 1920s, Josephine Baker had her greatest acclaim in Paris, where she achieved legendary success as a dancer after her Paris debut in 1925. (© Lidoff/Rapho/Black Star)

In 1963, Baker appeared at the March on Washington, and after performing in Denmark, had her first heart attack. In the spring of 1969, she declared bankruptcy and

Les Milandes was seized. Baker accepted a villa in Monaco from Princess Grace, began a long series of farewell performances, and begged in the streets when she couldn't work. In 1975, she summoned all her resources and professionalism for a last farewell performance at the Olympia Theatre in Paris. Baker died two days into her performance run on April 14. Her televised state funeral at the Madeleine Church drew thousands of people and included a twenty-one-gun salute.

BIBLIOGRAPHY

Chase-Riboud, Barbara. "Josephine Baker: Beyond Sequins." *Essence* (February 1975).

Hammond, Bryan. *Josephine Baker.* London, 1988.

Haney, Lynn. *Naked at the Feast.* New York, 1981.

– BARBARA CHASE-RIBOUD

BALDWIN, JAMES

James Baldwin (August 2, 1924–November 30, 1987), author and civil rights activist. Born in New York City's Harlem in 1924, James Baldwin, who started out as a writer during the late 1940s rose to international fame after the publication of his most famous essay, *The Fire Next Time,* in 1963. However, nearly two decades before its publication, he had already captured the attention of an assortment of writers, literary critics, and intellectuals in the United States and abroad. Writing to Langston HUGHES in 1948, Arna BONTEMPS commented on Baldwin's "The Harlem Ghetto," which was published in the February 1948 issue of *Commentary* magazine. Referring to "that remarkable piece by that 24–year-old colored kid," Bontemps wrote, "What a kid! He has zoomed high among our writers with his first effort." Thus, from the beginning of his professional career, Baldwin was highly regarded and began publishing in magazines and journals such as the *Nation,* the *New Leader, Commentary,* and *Partisan Review.*

Much of Baldwin's writing, both fiction and nonfiction, has been autobiographical. The story of John Grimes, the traumatized son of a tyrannical, fundamentalist father in *Go Tell It on the Mountain,* closely resembles Baldwin's own childhood. His celebrated essay "Notes of a Native Son" describes the writer's painful relationship with his stepfather. Born out of wedlock before his mother met and married David Baldwin, young Jimmy never fully gained his stern patriarch's approval. Raised in a strict Pentecostal household, Jimmy became a preacher at age fourteen, and his sermons drew larger crowds than his father's. When Jimmy left the church three years later, the tension with his father was exacerbated, and, as "Notes of a Native Son" reveals, even the impending death of David Baldwin in 1943 did not reconcile their mutual disaffection. In various forms, the problems of father-son conflict, with all of its Old Testament connotations, became a central preoccupation of Baldwin's writing.

Baldwin's career, which can be divided into two phases—up to *The Fire Next Time* (1963) and after—gained momentum after the publication of what were to become two of his more controversial essays. In 1948 and 1949, respectively, he wrote "Everybody's Protest Novel" and "Many Thousands Gone," which were published in *Partisan Review.* These two essays served as a forum from which he made pronouncements about the limitations of the protest tradition in American literature. He scathingly criticized Harriet Beecher Stowe's UNCLE TOM'S CABIN and Richard WRIGHT's *Native Son* for being firmly rooted in the protest tradition. Each writer failed, in Baldwin's judgment, because the "power of revelation . . . is the business of the novelist, that journey toward a more vast reality which must take precedence over all other claims." He abhorred the idea of the writer as a kind of "congressman," embracing Jamesian ideas about the art of fiction. The writer, as Baldwin envisioned himself during this early period, should self-consciously seek a distance between himself and his subject.

Baldwin's criticisms of *Native Son* and the protest novel tradition precipitated a rift with his mentor, Richard Wright. Ironically, Wright had supported Baldwin's candidacy for the Rosenwald Fellowship in 1948, which allowed Baldwin to move to Paris, where he completed his first novel, *Go Tell It on the Mountain* (1953). Baldwin explored his conflicted relationship with Wright in a series of moving essays, including "Alas, Poor Richard," published in *Nobody Knows My Name.*

Baldwin left Harlem for Paris when he was twenty-four. Although he spoke little French at the time, he purchased a one-way ticket and later achieved success and fame as an expatriate. Writing about race and sexuality (including homosexuality), he published twenty-two books, among them six novels, a collection of short stories, two plays, several collections of essays, a children's book, a movie scenario, and *Jimmy's Blues* (1985), a chapbook of poems. Starting with his controversial *Another Country* (1962), many of his books, including *The Fire Next Time* (1963), *If Beale Street Could Talk* (1974), and *Just Above My Head* (1979), were best-sellers. His play *Blues for Mr. Charlie* (1964) was produced on Broadway. And his scenario *One Day When I Was Lost: A Scenario Based on Alex Haley's "The Autobiography of Malcolm X"* was used by the movie director Spike LEE in the production of his feature film on MALCOLM X.

Baldwin credits Bessie SMITH as the source of inspiration for the completion of his first novel *Go Tell It on the Mountain* (1953). In "The Discovery of What It Means to Be an American," he writes about his experience of living and writing in Switzerland: "There, in that alabaster landscape, armed with two Bessie Smith records and a typewriter, I began to re-create the life that I had first known as a child and from which I had spent so many years in flight . . . Bessie Smith, through her tone and cadence . . . helped me dig back to the way I myself must have spoken when I was a pickaninny, and to remember the things I had heard and seen and felt. I had buried them very deep."

Go Tell It on the Mountain recaptures in some definitive ways the spirit and circumstances of Baldwin's own boyhood and adolescence. John Grimes, the shy and intelligent protagonist of the novel, is remarkably reminiscent of Baldwin. Moreover, Baldwin succeeds at creating a web of relationships that reveals how a particular character has arrived at his or her situation. He had, after all, harshly criticized Stowe and Wright for what he considered their rather stereotypical depiction of characters and their circumstances. His belief that "revelation" was the novelist's ultimate goal persisted throughout his career. In his second and third novels—*Giovanni's Room* (1956) and *Another Country* (1962)—he explores the theme of a varying, if consistent, American search for identity.

In *Giovanni's Room* the theme is complicated by international and sexual dimensions. The main character is forced to learn a harsh lesson about another culture and country as he wrestles with his ambivalent sexuality. Similarly, in *Another Country* Baldwin sensationally calls into question many American taboos about race, sexuality, marriage, and infidelity. By presenting a stunning series of relationships—heterosexual, homosexual, interracial, bisexual—he creates a *tableau vivant* of American mores. In his remaining novels, *Tell Me How Long the Train's Been Gone* (1968), *If Beale Street Could Talk* (1974), and *Just Above My Head* (1979), he also focuses on issues related to race and sexuality. Furthermore, he tries to reveal how racism and sexism are inextricably linked to deep-seated American assumptions. In Baldwin's view, race and sex are hopelessly entangled in America's collective psyche.

Around the time of *The Fire Next Time*'s publication and after the Broadway production of *Blues for Mr. Charlie,* Baldwin became known as a spokesperson for civil rights and a celebrity noted for championing the cause of black Americans. He was a prominent participant in the March on Washington at which the Rev. Dr. Martin Luther KING, Jr., gave his famous "I Have a Dream" speech. He frequently appeared on television and delivered speeches on college campuses. Baldwin actually published two excellent collections of essays—*Notes of a Native Son* (1955) and *Nobody Knows My Name* (1961)—before *The Fire Next Time.* In fact, various critics and reviewers already considered him in a class of his own. However, it was his exhortative rhetoric in the latter essay, published on the one hundredth anniversary of the Emancipation Proclamation, an essay that anticipated the urban riots of the 1960s, which landed him on the cover of *Time* magazine. He concluded: "If we—and now I mean the relatively conscious whites and the relatively conscious blacks who must, like lovers, insist on or create the consciousness of the others—do not falter in our duty now, we may be able . . . to end the racial nightmare, and achieve our country, and change the history of the world."

Just as he had been the leading literary voice of the civil rights movement, he became an inspirational figure for the emerging gay rights movement.

After the publication of *The Fire Next Time,* several black nationalists criticized Baldwin for his conciliatory attitude. They questioned whether his message of love and understanding would do much to change race relations in America. Eldridge CLEAVER, in his book *Soul on Ice,* was one of Baldwin's more outspoken critics. But Baldwin continued writing, becoming increasingly more dependent on his early life as a source of inspiration, accepting eagerly the role of the writer as "poet" whose "assignment" was to accept the "energy" of the folk and transform it into art. It is as though he was following the wisdom of his own words in his story "Sonny's Blues." Like Sonny and his band, Baldwin saw clearly as he matured that he was telling a tale based on the blues of his own life as a writer and a man in America and abroad: "Creole began to tell us what the blues were all about. They were not about anything very new. He and his boys up there were keeping it new at the risk of ruin, destruction, madness, and death, in order to find new ways to make us listen. For, while the tale of how we suffer, and how we are delighted, and how we may triumph is never new, it always must be heard. There isn't any other tale to tell, it's the only light we've got in all this darkness."

Several of his essays and interviews of the 1980s discuss homosexuality and homophobia with fervor and forthrightness, most notably "Here Be Dragons." Thus, just as he had been the leading literary voice of the civil rights movement, he became an inspirational figure for the emerging gay rights movement. Baldwin's nonfiction was collected in *The Price of the Ticket* (1985).

During the final decade of his life, Baldwin taught at a number of American colleges and universities—including the University of Massachusetts at Amherst and Hampshire College—frequently commuting back and forth between the United States and his home in St. Paul de Vence in the south of France. After his death in France on November 30, 1987, the *New York Times* reported on its front page for the following day: "James Baldwin, Eloquent Essayist in Behalf of Civil Rights, Is Dead."

BIBLIOGRAPHY

Campbell, James. *Talking at the Gates: A Life of James Baldwin*. New York, 1991.

Leeming, David. *James Baldwin: A Biography*. New York, 1994.

Porter, Horace. *Stealing the Fire: The Art of Protest and James Baldwin*. Middletown, Conn., 1989.

– HORACE PORTER

BALTIMORE, MARYLAND

When Baltimore was established as a town in 1729, many African Americans already lived in the area which, like most of Maryland, was rural. As the town grew during the eighteenth century, its African-American population increased gradually. Both slaves and free blacks worked as house servants, laborers, and craftsmen. Trades such as barbering, blacksmithing, and coach driving came to be almost exclusively black.

In Baltimore, as elsewhere, African Americans fought on both sides of the AMERICAN REVOLUTION. Before free blacks were allowed to enlist in the Maryland militia, 250 black men helped build the batteries and mount the guns around Whetstone Point, where Fort McHenry is now located, at the entrance to the port of Baltimore. Many enslaved blacks manumitted during the Revolutionary era settled in Baltimore. In 1789 a group of prominent Baltimoreans formed the Society for the Abolition of Slavery and the Relief of Poor Negroes and Others Unlawfully Held in Bondage. Although these abolitionists did not win a legal end to slavery, by 1810 free blacks, their numbers augmented by free black and mulatto refugees from Haiti, outnumbered slaves in the city 3,973 to 3,713. The city's most notable abolitionist in the nineteenth century was Benjamin Lundy, editor of the journal the *Genius of Universal Emancipation*. The famous abolitionist leader William Lloyd Garrison began his antislavery career in Baltimore as one of Lundy's assistants.

The African-American experience in Baltimore during the antebellum era was unique. Although Maryland was a slave state, slavery declined rapidly in urban areas. By 1820 Baltimore had the largest free black population of any city in the antebellum United States. The first independent black institutions in Baltimore were churches. In the 1780s African-American religious congregations began to separate from white-controlled churches. As early as 1787, blacks left white Methodist congregations and formed the Baltimore African Church on Sharp Street. In 1793 an African School opened on Sharp Street with financial help from local Quakers. A few years later, operation of the school was taken over by the African-American congregation of the Sharp Street African Methodist Church. An outstanding preacher from Sharp Street, Daniel Coker, formed the African Bethel Church (later Bethel African Methodist Episcopal Church), became its first ordained Methodist preacher in 1811, and helped form the AFRICAN METHODIST EPISCOPAL (AME) Conference in 1816.

When Baltimore was established as a town in 1729, many African Americans already lived in the area.

Other congregations, Sunday schools, and day schools were set up during the ensuing years. In 1824 a group of free and enslaved blacks led by William Levington, an Episcopal priest from New York City, founded St. James Episcopal Church. The church building, finished in 1827, is a landmark which still stands in Lafayette Square in West Baltimore, though it was damaged in a major fire in 1994. In 1829, a group of black Catholics led by Elizabeth Lange, an educated Haitian mulatto who had opened a school for black children, founded the Oblate Sisters of Providence, the first black women's Catholic order, with the assistance of Sulpician priest Father Jacques Hector Nicholas Joubert. That same year, the Oblate nuns established on Richmond Street the first black girls' school in the United States, Saint Frances of Rome Academy. Another school, the William Watkins Academy for Negro Youth, operated until 1850, and boasted Baltimore native Frances E. Watkins HARPER as its most distinguished graduate. In 1860 the Madison Avenue Presbyterian Church had Hiram Revels, later a senator, as its pastor, and Henry McNeal Turner, later an AME bishop, was a deacon at Bethel AME Church.

Slavery continued in Baltimore, though on a small scale, throughout the antebellum period. By 1860 there

before the Civil War, owned a farm near Mayesville, S.C., when Mary was growing up. Mary McLeod attended the Trinity Presbyterian Mission School near her home from 1885 until 1888, and with the help of her mentor, Emma Jane Wilson, moved on to Scotia Seminary (later Barber-Scotia College), a Presbyterian school in Concord, N.C.

Her stunning successes as a leader made Bethune one of the most influential women of her day and a premier African-American leader.

McLeod set her sights on serving as a missionary in Africa and so entered the Bible Institute for Home and Foreign Missions (later known as the Moody Bible Institute) in Chicago. She was devastated when she was informed that the Presbyterian Church would not support African-American missionaries to Africa. Instead, McLeod turned her attentions and talents to the field of education at home.

From 1896 through 1897, McLeod taught at the Haines Institute, a Presbyterian-sponsored school in Augusta, Ga., an experience that proved meaningful for her future. At Haines, McLeod worked with Lucy Craft Laney, the school's founder and a pioneering African-American educator. McLeod took away examples and skills she would put into action throughout her life.

From Haines, McLeod moved on to another Presbyterian school, the Kendall Institute in Sumter, S.C., where she met and married Albertus Bethune in 1898. The couple moved to Savannah, Ga., and in 1899 their only child, Albert Bethune, was born. Although Albertus and Mary McLeod Bethune remained married until Albertus's death in 1918, they were no longer together by 1907. In 1900 Bethune moved to Palatka, Fla., where she founded a Presbyterian school and later an independent school that also offered social services to the community.

In 1904 Bethune settled in Daytona, Fla., in order to establish a school for African-American girls. She opened her Daytona Educational and Industrial Institute in a rented house with little furniture and a tiny group of students. Students at the school learned basic academic subjects, worked on homemaking skills, engaged in religious activities, and worked with Bethune in the fields of a farm she bought in 1910. Through the farm, Bethune and her students were able to feed the members of the school community, as well as sell the surplus to benefit the school. The Daytona Institute also emphasized connections with the community, offering summer school, a playground for children, and other activities. All of this made Bethune an important voice in her local community.

The school's reputation began to grow at the national level through a visit by Booker T. WASHINGTON in 1912 and the addition of Frances Reynolds Keyser to the staff in the same year. Keyser had served as superintendent of the White Rose Mission in New York and was a well-known activist. After World War II, the school grew to include a high school and a nurses' training division. In 1923 the school merged with the failing Cookman Institute of Jacksonville, Fla., and embarked on a coeducational program. In 1929 it took the name BETHUNE-COOKMAN COLLEGE. By 1935 Bethune's school, founded on a tiny budget, had become an accredited junior college and, by 1943, a fully accredited college, awarding bachelor's degrees. This success gained Bethune a national reputation and won her the NAACP's prestigious Spingarn Medal in 1935.

In addition to her success as an educator, Bethune also made a major mark on the black women's club movement in America. In 1917 she was elected president of the Florida Association of Colored Women, a post she retained until 1924. Under her leadership, the organization established a home for young women in Ocala. In 1920 Bethune organized the Southeastern Federation of Colored Women and guided this group through 1925. From 1924 to 1928, she served as president of the NATIONAL ASSOCIATION OF COLORED WOMEN (NACW), the most powerful organization of African-American women's clubs in the country. During this period, she toured Europe as the NACW's president and established the organization's headquarters in Washington, D.C., in 1928. Bethune's crowning achievement in the club movement was the 1935 founding of the NATIONAL COUNCIL OF NEGRO WOMEN (NCNW). This organization served to coordinate and streamline the cooperative work of a wide variety of black women's organizations. During Bethune's fourteen years as president, the NCNW achieved this goal, began to work closely with the federal government on issues facing African Americans, and developed an international perspective on women's lives.

Bethune's influence with the Franklin D. Roosevelt administration led her to activities that made her an even greater public figure on behalf of African Americans. In 1936 she organized the Federal Council on Negro Affairs, popularly known as the Black Cabinet, a group of black advisers who helped coordinate government programs for African Americans. In this same period, she became deeply involved in the work of the National Youth Administration (NYA), serving on the advisory committee from its founding in 1935. In 1936 Bethune began functioning as director of the NYA's Division of Negro Affairs, a position which became official in 1939 and which she held until 1943. This appointment made her the highest ranking black woman in government up to that point. Bethune's goals in the NYA were to increase the representation of qualified African Americans in leadership in local and state programs and to ensure that NYA benefits distributed to whites and to blacks achieved parity.

In addition to Bethune's many other achievements, she served as the president of the Association for the Study of Negro Life and History from 1936 to 1951, established the Mary McLeod Bethune Foundation, and wrote a column for the *Pittsburgh Courier*. Bethune's career is testimony to her leadership skills, her commitment to justice and equality for African Americans, her unfailing dedication to the ideals of American democracy, and her philosophy of service.

BIBLIOGRAPHY

Bethune, Mary McLeod. "My Last Will and Testament." *Ebony*, August 1955.

Holt, Rackham. *Mary McLeod Bethune: A Biography*. New York, 1964.

Smith, Elaine. "Mary McLeod Bethune and the National Youth Administration." In Mabel E. Deutrich and Virginia C. Purdy, eds. *Clio Was a Woman: Studies in the History of American Women*. Washington, D.C., 1980.

— JUDITH WEISENFELD

BETHUNE-COOKMAN COLLEGE

On October 3, 1904, African-American educator and activist Mary McLeod BETHUNE founded a normal and industrial school for African-American girls in Daytona Beach, Fla. Though she began with only five students in a small rented house, in less than two years Bethune attracted 250 pupils and founded the Daytona School for Girls in a building she erected on top of a garbage dump. By 1916, the school had grown into the Daytona Normal and Industrial Institute, and was affiliated with the United Methodist Church. After absorbing the Cookman Institute for Boys, previously located in Jacksonville, the school, newly christened Bethune-Cookman College, was established as a high school with junior college courses in 1924. Bethune, who continued as president of the college until 1947, raised funds for the school from middle-class blacks and liberal white philanthropists. Committed to integration and interracial cooperation, Bethune sought out a mixed-race board of directors, but she opposed white directors who favored a vocational curriculum. Bethune pushed for the inclusion of a full liberal arts program, and the school continuously upgraded its standards and facilities. Despite a heavy financial squeeze during the Great Depression, Bethune-Cookman became a two-year junior college in 1939 and a four-year institution shortly after, receiving a Grade A accreditation in 1947, the last year of Bethune's presidency. In 1990 Bethune-Cookman, the only historically black college founded by a woman, had a student body of approximately 2,200 and had thirty-two buildings on fifty-two acres, and offered degrees in subject areas as diverse as biology, business, and communications.

BIBLIOGRAPHY

Bethune, Mary McLeod. "A College on a Garbage Dump." In Gerda Lerner, ed. *Black Women in White America: A Documentary History*, pp. 134–143. New York, 1972.

Holt, Rackham. *Mary McLeod Bethune: A Biography*. New York, 1964.

— MARGARET D. JACOBS

BIRMINGHAM, ALABAMA

Birmingham's African-American community came into existence with the founding of the city in 1871. Its initial growth was rapid, but in 1873, the outbreak of cholera and a national economic panic substantially reduced both black and white populations. Recovery was slow.

In the early 1880s, with the advent of a viable coal and iron industry, came a revitalized economy and a renewal of population growth. Thousands of African Americans flocked to the Birmingham area to mine coal or work in the iron mills. In both the 1890 and 1900 censuses, African Americans constituted 43 percent of the total population. After a slight decline in the years between 1910 and 1940, the percentage of African Americans in the city's total population began a steady increase, reaching 55 percent in 1980 and 63 percent in 1990.

Most African-American immigrants in Birmingham came from cotton farms in south Alabama and from the virtual enslavement represented by the sharecropper system. The city's lure was the promise of regular wages paid in cash, but what these migrants found available were generally the most menial jobs or those that were lowest paying. For African-American males, who worked in the mines and mills, the jobs they received were invariably the most dangerous. For females, job opportunities meant domestic work as maids or cooks or employment as dishwashers, laundresses, seamstresses, waitresses, or in the kitchens.

Despite the hard work, low pay, and discrimination that African Americans experienced, however, life in

Birmingham was generally an improvement over what they had known on the farm. They had more money, a more active social life, more freedom from white domination, and better education for their children. The best evidence of Birmingham's attractiveness to blacks exists in the census, which shows a reasonably sustained growth of the city's black population.

Most African-American immigrants in Birmingham came from cotton farms in south Alabama and from the virtual enslavement represented by the sharecropper system.

Most African Americans lived in the areas that were generally, but not strictly, segregated. New arrivals often moved into a "company house": a three- or four-room rental structure owned by a coal or steel company. Usually identical in design, company houses stood in rows; several rows made up a company "village." Blacks and whites were segregated by rows of houses, but a black row and a white row often stood back to back. Thus, company villages respected segregation in principal, but in reality they did not keep the races very far apart.

Until the 1960s the largest single concentration of blacks in one neighborhood was Birmingham's Southside, the area immediately south of the downtown business district. Before the mid-1960s urban renewal program, "shotgun" houses covered much of the area. Domestics, furnace and foundry workers, and a smattering of teachers occupied the houses, though few owned their homes.

Several large, predominantly white neighborhoods in Birmingham had distinct black sections that were sometimes considered—especially by their own residents—as separate neighborhoods. Tuxedo Junction in Ensley, Collegeville in North Birmingham, Zion City in Woodlawn, and Kingston in East Birmingham were all black enclaves in otherwise white neighborhoods.

Among the purely black neighborhoods were several that were middle class in character. Enon Ridge, just northwest of Interstates 59 and 65 near downtown, became the fashionable place for the few black professionals in the city in the 1890s. Shortly after the turn of the century, the neighborhood of Smithfield—southwest of Enon Ridge—was developed; large numbers of black teachers and some other professionals bought homes there. In the 1940s South Titusville, to the west of Southside, began to attract working-class African Americans who could afford to own their own homes.

Once settled in a job and a neighborhood, African Americans usually joined a church. Each black neighborhood had at least one, and usually several churches. By far the most popular denomination among African Americans was the Baptist, which had perhaps three times as many members as its nearest rival, the METHODIST. The various Pentecostal sects had the next largest number of members. The Presbyterians, Catholics, Episcopalians, and Congregationalists each had at least one, but not more than four, black congregations in the Birmingham area.

The typical black church in Birmingham at the turn of the century closely resembled the country churches of rural south Alabama. Several larger churches had a somewhat different character from the smaller neighborhood ones, primarily because of the higher economic status of their congregations. The Sixteenth Street Baptist Church, the first black church downtown (1873), always had many professionals among its members. Its services, conducted by highly educated ministers, rarely had the emotionalism seen in many other black churches.

The Sixth Avenue Baptist Church on the Southside was for decades the largest working-class church in Birmingham. In recent decades, however, it has added many professional members, and in the early 1990s, was the largest black congregation in the state.

Birmingham's African Americans encountered both prejudice and discrimination from the time the city was first established, but they especially suffered in the years just before the turn of the century. The rapid growth of the black population in Birmingham frightened local whites at a time when racist fears were on the rise nationally. In 1901, all but a few blacks lost the right to vote when a new state constitution established a poll tax, literacy tests, and "good character"—as defined by whites—as prerequisites for voting.

In 1911, the city of Birmingham began the enactment of segregation ordinances, outlawing saloons in black neighborhoods and making ones owned by whites separate black and white customers by using partitions. Other ordinances followed, including an encompassing JIM CROW statute in the 1920s.

In the early years of Birmingham's African-American community, educational concerns centered less on professional degrees than on establishing grammar schools. The first black public grammar school in Birmingham was Lane School, founded in 1886 on the Southside. Carrie A. Tuggle built Tuggle Institute, a popular private school and orphanage, on Enon Ridge in 1903.

There was no black high school in Jefferson County before 1900. Parents who wanted to educate their children beyond grammar school sent them to TUSKEGEE

INSTITUTE or Talladega College, which had high schools at the time. In 1899, however, a group led by William R. Pettiford, a local minister and businessman, requested that the city establish a public high school for blacks. The next year the board of education appointed Arthur Harold Parker as the first principal of "Industrial High School."

The local black community took great pride in the school for which Parker had responsibility, and justifiably so. In the 1930s, for example, Industrial was recognized as the largest black high school in the world. Nowhere, however, was discrimination against African Americans more evident than in education. In 1911 Birmingham spent $18.86 for each white child of school age but only $1.81 for each black child. White teachers had an average of thirty-six students per class. Black teachers, who earned much less than their white counterparts, had fifty-eight. Moreover, the school buildings provided for African Americans were grossly inferior to those for whites. Until 1925, for instance, the Industrial High School building was nothing more than two rows of shotgun houses connected by ramps.

Discrimination kept many African Americans from attempting business enterprises. Among those that did, a number located their businesses along Fourth Avenue North between Sixteenth and Eighteenth Streets, an area that became Birmingham's central black commercial district.

Most African-American businesses provided services to other black Americans not provided by white busi-

Steel mills and worker housing, Birmingham, Ala., 1936. Unlike many industrial cities in the south, heavy industry in Birmingham actively recruited black labor. This in turn helped to shape a unique tradition of African-American political and union radicalism in the city. (Prints and Photographs Division, Library of Congress)

and contemporary black heroes such as Muhammad ALI, W. E. B. DU BOIS, Malcolm X, Marcus GARVEY, Nina Simone, Amiri Baraka, and Gwendolyn BROOKS. This mural galvanized the imaginations of community people, and based on their comments, the artists made various revisions on the mural. The appeal of public art notwithstanding, this privately owned building was eventually razed, and *The Wall of Respect* passed into legend.

Despite its brief existence, the mural sparked a local and national movement. Numerous cities soon produced their own equivalents, such as *The Wall of Dignity* in Detroit, several murals by artists including Dana Chandler and Gary Rickson in Boston, and similar projects in New York, Philadelphia, and San Francisco, among others. Needless to say, the mural movement had roots going back to the 1930s in the WPA public art projects and especially in the powerful work created by the Mexican artist Diego Rivera. The Black Arts movement also echoed the 1930s in that the vogue of murals was seized upon by state and federal arts agencies. While black artists could see such murals as "committed and committing," government agencies saw them as a fine combination of public art and social control mechanisms for urban youths who could be organized into painting teams during the incendiary summers of the 1960s. Artists such as Bill Walker and Dana Chandler organized mural projects in several cities, but the political impact of these projects diminished as their frequency increased, and when government support evaporated in the arid 1970s, the mural movement withered away.

Nevertheless, the movement launched the careers of many artists. Five of the OBAC artists—Jeff Donaldson, Jae Jarrell, Wadsworth Jarrell, Barbara B. Jones, and Gerald Williams—formed their own organization, COBRA (Coalition of Black Revolutionary Artists) in 1968. The next year they became AfriCobra (African Commune of Bad Relevant Artists), adding Napoleon Henderson and Nelson Stevens to their ranks. By the time of the first AfriCobra show at Harlem's Studio Museum in July 1970, Sherman Beck, Omar Lama, and Carolyn M. Lawrence had joined the group, bringing the number to ten. For many people, AfriCobra came to epitomize the new black art. Their work used vivid, basic colors. It was representational, usually incorporating the faces of black people, and it was explicitly political. In direct rebellion against the elitist norms of establishment art, these artists endeavored to produce work that was immediately comprehensible and appealing to common people. As Jeff Donaldson put it, "This is 'poster art'—images which deal with concepts that offer positive and feasible solutions to our individual, local, national, international, and cosmic problems. The images are designed with the idea of mass production." This statement captured the spirit of the black aesthetic as many artists understood it.

The music of the Association for the Advancement of Creative Musicians, was arguably even more dazzling, iconoclastic, and influential than the poetry, fiction, and art of OBAC. AACM resembled OBAC in that it was independent and community based. Both groups consisted mostly of younger artists, in college or recently graduated, but both received leadership from older, established figures. Three band leaders, Muhal Richard Abrams, Phil Cohran, and Jodie Christian, for example, conceived AACM and called its founding meeting on May 8, 1965. Abrams, a noted pianist and composer, was elected president of AACM and served in that capacity for over a decade. The initial impetus for AACM was more economic than political. By the mid-1960s most of Chicago's important jazz clubs had closed, and jazz was everywhere in decline. These musicians saw a cooperative as the best way for musicians to take control of their own professional destinies.

AACM soon attracted many of the best young musicians in Chicago. The group established an educational program (in 1967) and an AACM orchestra that met (and continues to meet) weekly to perform new compositions by AACM members. Most importantly, AACM provided a setting in which young musicians could meet, perform together, and exchange ideas. AACM members and groups performed frequent concerts around Chicago's South Side during the late 1960s and early '70s. Ensembles formed, dissolved, and reconfigured around AACM, a few of which soon distinguished themselves: the various groups led by Abrams; the Fred Anderson Quintet; the Art Ensemble of Chicago; the Creative Construction Company; and (in the 1970s) Air.

Each of these groups had its own unique character but they had some traits in common. They were profoundly influenced by the "free jazz" innovations of Cecil Taylor and Ornett COLEMAN, by the intense instrumental styles of John COLTRANE and Eric Dolphy, by the musical eclecticism of Charles MINGUS, and by the theatrical staging and grand vision of Sun Ra. Unlike the populist OBAC, AACM produced difficult, challenging, unabashedly avant-garde work. While these musicians could play blues and conventional jazz, their interests lay in extending the frontiers of musical possibility. They experimented with extended and free-form compositions, and with exotic instruments; they even tried to redefine what constitutes music. Some compositions by the Art Ensemble, for example, incorporate bicycle horns, bird whistles, street noises, poetry, sermons, screams, and nonsense conversation.

The Art Ensemble is the group that most epitomizes AACM as an aspect of the Black Arts movement. The group consists of Roscoe Mitchell and Joseph Jarman, reeds; Lester Bowie, trumpet; Malachi Favors, bass; and Famodou Don Moye, percussion. While performing, Jarman, Favors, and Moye wear facial paint and African-style costumes; Bowie wears a white lab coat; and Mitchell dresses in ordinary street clothes (jeans, turtlenecks, etc.). Usually, the Art Ensemble packs the stage with batteries of standard instruments (sopranino to bass saxophones, soprano to bass clarinets, various flutes, and often bassoons); a standard drum kit, plus congas, gongs, and marimbas; and countless "little instruments" (whistles, bells, tambourines, conch shells, maracas, and various noisemakers). Art Ensemble concerts are visual spectacles and unpredictable musical events, reflecting the group's motto: "Great Black Music: Ancient to the Future." Their compositions, such as *People in Sorrow* (1969), exemplify the devotional parodic, evocative, experimental, lyrical eclecticism of the Art Ensemble.

In contrast to the Art Ensemble, which has flourished for three decades, the Creative Construction Company—Anthony Braxton, reeds; Leroy Jenkins, violin; Leo Smith, trumpet; Muhal Richard Abrams, piano; Richard Davis, bass; and Steve McCall, drums—persisted only for a few years. However, all of these men became major figures in the new music. Their concerts and albums were celebrated for their dazzling ensemble playing, which emphasized collective improvisation rather than solos. Both these bands developed aesthetics based upon the Black Arts precept of committed collectivity.

Chicago also developed notable and enduring black theater groups, such a KUUMBA and Ebony Talent Theater (ETT), but New York was clearly the more important city for theater and dance, and most of the famous Black Arts plays premiered there. However, the proliferation of black theater groups on campuses and in communities throughout the country guaranteed that plays by established authors, local talents, and emerging stars were quickly disseminated. Although Amiri Baraka, due to his broad range of literary and political activities, was the best known of the Black Arts playwrights, he had many talented peers. Ed Bullins, Ron Milner, Lonne Elder, Charles Fuller, Douglass Turner Ward, Adrienne Kennedy, Melvin Van Peebles, Loften Mitchell, and Ben Caldwell all wrote provocative work that challenged audiences and incited lively debate.

These authors worked in a variety of styles, and their political and cultural views differed. Nonetheless, they shared a vision of American society in crisis and a conviction that drama should challenge the complacency of audiences by exposing racism, economic exploitation, social conflict, and false consciousness. Some of these plays were satirical, while others were intensely confrontational; some relied on dialogue, while others bristled with shocking language. Furious assaults on whites were at times matched by blistering arguments between father and son, brother and sister. Black Arts theater was the theater of a people becoming aware of and rebelling against their own oppression. However, it was also a theater that sought solutions, new understandings, and transformed social relations. In keeping with the idea of an art derived from and directed to the black community, nearly all of the Black Arts theaters instituted discussion forums immediately following their productions, involving the director, cast, audience, and sometimes the author. Black art was to be educational, not just entertaining.

Black dance also proliferated during this period. The Alvin AILEY group, though founded in 1960, just before the advent of BAM, exemplified the visual and rhythmical ideals of the black aesthetic. Several other major companies were formed during the movement: among others, Dayton Contemporary Dance Company in Ohio (1968); the Dance Theater of Harlem in New York City (1969); the Philadelphia Dance Company, or Phildanco (1970); Garth Fagan's Bucket Dance in Rochester, N.Y. (1970); the Cleo Parker Robinson Dance Ensemble in Denver (1971); and the Joel Hall Dancers in Chicago (1974). While all of these troupes specialize in African-American dance, most of them have been multiethnic in composition. This conflict between the nationalist impulse to form all-black companies and the pluralist impulse to include qualified people who, regardless of their background, have the talent and disposition to make a contribution reflects a larger tension in the movement. African-American culture is inherently an amalgam, including European elements as well as African. Most black artists have been trained in institutions with European orientations. How, then, can black artists come honestly to terms with the complex nature of their own cultural heritage? Dance embraced the pluralist reality of American culture more forthrightly than the other black arts generally did.

At the same time, black dance immersed itself deeply in the cultures of Africa, the Caribbean, and black America. Unlike the literary artists and theorists of the BAM, whose acquaintance with Africa was too often only through cursory reading and vigorous fantasy, dancers had a highly developed tradition of African dance technique to draw upon. Since the early 1930s, African dancers such as Asadata Dafora and Shologa Oloba had taught African dance in New York. Nana Yao Opare Dinizulu had begun teaching African dance and culture in Harlem in 1947 and founded a company in the same year. Subsequently, the companies of Charles Moore and Chuck Davis extended this tradition. African percussion masters such as Babatunde Olatunji also traveled to the United States, imparting their vast knowledge of African music and dance. African traditions as developed in Haiti, Jamaica, and Trinidad had been studied, adapted, and taught since the 1930s by influential dancers such as Katherine DUNHAM, Pearl Primus, and Jean-Léon Destine. Even costuming and stage design had transcended mere ethnographic imitation and instead, borrowing the vivid colors and basic styles of African tradition, had evolved—preeminently in the work of Geoffrey Holder—into dazzlingly imaginative modes of expression. Thus, when large numbers of dancers began traveling to study in Africa during the late 1960s and '70s, their challenge was not to introduce new forms to American dance but rather to refine and extend a firmly established tradition.

To explain companies like Bucket Dance and the Dance Theater of Harlem as products of BAM would be simplistic and inaccurate. Clearly, however, the desire to create black cultural institutions and the desire to engage artists and audiences in a rediscovery of African and African-American expressive modes links the efforts of choreographers such as Garth Fagan and Arthur Mitchell to the broader BAM. These dancers also shared the educational commitments of the movement. In addition to training young dancers for their own companies in the traditional manner of independent dance ensembles, choreographers like Fagan, Mitchell, and Davis have always maintained vigorous public outreach programs, including workshops for children. Furthermore, since dance often captured the aesthetics of the movement without its polemics, many of the works created by Ailey, Mitchell, Fagan, Talley Beatty, Eleo Pomare, and other choreographers of that period have remained fresh and compelling, while by contrast, many popular literary works of the era now seem shrill and dated. The greatest artists of BAM may not be its acknowledged spokespersons.

Similarly, many artists who came of age during the movement have continued to develop, leaving behind many of the themes, modes, and attitudes of their own earlier work. In the visual arts, for example, many artists relied on chains and distorted images of American flags to make overtly political points. The sculptor Melvin Edwards, for example, created a series of works in the late 1960s called *Lynch Fragments.* One installation of it appeared at the Whitney in 1970, consisting of strands of barbed wire strung from the ceiling and attached to loops of heavy chain. Such work is pointed but aesthetically limited. By contrast, Edwards's work of subsequent years is large-scale, welded-steel sculptures, often in abstract forms but sometimes incorporating chain or chainlike figures as well. The growth in imaginative complexity and aesthetic appeal is immediately obvious.

Faith Ringgold, a painter with strong political commitments, was actually convicted in 1970, along with two other artists, for desecrating the American flag. Her flag paintings such as "The Flag Is Bleeding" (1967) and "Flag for the Moon: Die Nigger" (1969) are effective polemics about American violence and racism. Nonetheless, outside the angry context of the late 1960s, these works appear strident and facile. Her later works that utilize folk-art forms (as she had begun to do even in the 1960s), textiles, quilting, and various other media embody artistic maturity, not just effective visual rhetoric. David Hammons made heavy use of both flags and chains in his works of the late 1960s. Indeed, his body prints such as "Pray for America" (1969) and "Injustice Case" (1970), the latter regarding the Chicago Seven case, are among the most memorable American art images of that era. Like Edwards and Ringgold, however, Hammons discovered profounder aesthetic possibilities and resources when he moved away from the obvious symbolism and unambiguous political sentiments of BAM. Hammon's work of the 1980s and '90s, from his spade sculptures to his basketball installations, is playful, ironic, and much more deeply grounded in African-American culture. Like many other artists of their generation, Edwards, Ringgold, and Hammons were BAM artists, but their artistic growth did not terminate at the boundaries of the movement.

Some critics of the BAM have focused exclusively on a few extremist works, artists, or tendencies of the movement, thereby defining the movement only in terms of its most egregious features. While the extremes of the movement are shocking indeed, its fecundity and diversity have not been sufficiently recognized. Much has been written, for example, about the political assertiveness of BAM works. The humor of the movement, in all of its genres, has not generally been acknowledged. Much of Baraka's work is bitingly satirical. Douglass Turner Ward's *Day of Absence,* a coon show performed in whiteface, is slapstick comedy in the ministrel tradition. Cecil Brown, Sam Greenlee, and Ishmael Reed are all comic novelists. David Hammons, the Art Ensemble, and Garth Fagan have made humor a major element of their works. Haki Madhubuti and Nikki GIOVANNI, even at their most earnest, are playful and witty poets.

Despite the stern dogmatism of some Black Arts theory, the movement always encompassed diverse voices and perspectives. Some critics have dismissed the BAM as a sexist outpouring, dominated by misogynistic men. Actually, many of the iconic BAM figures were women, such as Sonia Sanchez, Nikki Giovanni, Carolyn Rodgers, Audre Lorde, Toni Cade Bambara, Faith Ringgold, June Jordan, and Adrienne Kennedy. These and other women within the movement vigorously debated gender issues among themselves and with their male counterparts, in their works, in public forums, and in organizational meetings. The common claim that women's voices were suppressed by the BAM is belied by a reading of the anthologies, periodicals, museum show catalogs, playbills, and other documents of the period.

In fact, one might argue that the most direct literary legacy of the BAM was the explosion of black women's writing in the late 1970s and '80s. For instance, while Ntozake Shange's play *for colored girls who have considered suicide/when the rainbow is enuf* (1976) anticipates in its themes and attitudes the feminism and womanism of the 1980s and '90s, its aesthetic roots—especially its use of vernacular language, color, music, and dance—are clearly in the BAM tradition. Toni Cade Bambara's intricate masterpiece *The Salt Eaters* (1980) is certainly the most sophisticated and probing book yet written on how this black nationalist political and aesthetic movement shaped the lives of its participants. Finally, womanist critics of the BAM have rejected many aspects of the movement, including some of its fundamental social values. Nevertheless, their conception of art, especially literature, as a tool of consciousness raising and community building is a direct echo of Black Arts theory.

BAM even had within it a vigorous multiculturalist tendency, which was most forcefully represented by Ishmael Reed and his San Francisco Bay Area cohorts, such as Al Young. In his poems, essays, and novels, Reed advocated a vision of multicultural pluralism, social freedom, and political tolerance. Spurning the dogmatic nationalism of many BAM adherents, Reed declared himself a multicultural artist more than a decade before the idea of multiculturalism became fashionable. Through his editing of periodicals such as *Yardbird Reader, Y'bird,* and *Quilt,* which published writers of numerous ethnic backgrounds and his leadership in multicultural collectives such as the Before Columbus Foundation, Reed acted decisively to implement his pluralist commitments. Furthermore, Reed has written devastating satires on and criticisms of Black Arts dogmas and excesses. Yet as an alumnus of the Umbra Workshop, Reed is himself a foundational figure of the movement. Clearly, the BAM was large enough, in the best Whitmanesque tradition, to contain contradictions and multitudes.

BIBLIOGRAPHY

Baraka, Amiri. *The Autobiography of LeRoi Jones.* New York, 1984.

Brooks, Gwendolyn, ed. *A Broadside Treasury: 1965–1970.* Detroit, 1971.

Donaldson, Jeff. "Ten in Search of a Nation." *Black World* 19, no. 12 (October 1970): 80–89.

Fabre, Geneviéve. *Drumbeats, Masks, and Metaphor: Contemporary Afro-American Theatre.* Cambridge, Mass., 1983.

Fine, Elsa Honig. *The Afro-American Artist: A Search for Identity.* New York, 1982.

Fowler, Carolyn. *Black Arts and Black Aesthetics: A Bibliography.* Published by author, 1981.

Gayle, Addison, ed. *The Black Aesthetic.* Garden City, N.Y., 1971.

Jones, LeRoi, and Larry Neal, eds. *Black Fire: An Anthology of Afro-American Writing.* New York, 1968.

Lewis, Samella. *African American Art and Artists.* Berkeley, Calif., 1990.

Long, Richard. *The Black Tradition in American Dance.* New York, 1989.

Parks, Carole, ed. *Nommo: A Literary Legacy of Black Chicago (1967–1987).* Chicago, 1987.

Redmond, Eugene B. *Drumvoices: The Mission of Afro-American Poetry.* Garden City, N.Y., 1976.

Smith, David Lionel. "The Black Arts Movement and Its Critics." *American Literary History* 3, no. 1 (Spring 1991): 93–110.

– DAVID LIONEL SMITH

BLACK BUSINESS COMMUNITY

Traditionally, typical firms in the black business community have included the barbershop, the beauty parlor, or the mom-and-pop food store. Such small retailing and personal-service lines of business were concentrated in African-American residential areas and served a neighborhood clientele. This type of traditional black enterprise has been in a state of continuous decline since the 1960s.

The growing lines of black business are dominated today by larger-scale firms that are likely to serve a racially diverse clientele; increasingly these enterprises sell to other businesses, including large corporations, and to units of government. They are commonly run by black entrepreneurs who have attended college. Particularly rapid growth areas include skill-intensive service industries: finance, business services, and various professional services. Such growth industries are commonly called "emerging" lines of black enterprise. They are emerging in the sense that the presence of African-American owners in these industries has historically

years of the 1920s. The black population increased particularly in the largest northern cities—during the 1920s it rose 115 percent in New York, 194 percent in Detroit, and 114 percent in Chicago (U.S. Bureau of the Census 1935).

The increased population was accompanied by a concentration of blacks in constricted sections of northern cities. Perhaps like the European migrants before them, blacks from the agrarian deep South initially preferred residential segregation in order to ease the transition from subsistence agriculture to an urban way of life. The clusters of racially mixed neighborhoods where black community life had been concentrated before World War I rapidly lost their white populations. Housing construction had nearly halted during the war years, and afterward the demand remained unfulfilled; existing black sections filled up and rents for all kinds of accommodations skyrocketed. As blacks sought housing in adjoining neighborhoods, whites increasingly spoke of the black "invasion" of their communities. Black-white competition for housing created antagonisms that paralleled those emerging in the labor market right after the war. The return of soldiers seeking jobs in 1919 coincided with the fading of war-induced prosperity; blacks and whites viewed each other as competitors for scarce jobs as well as scarce housing. In this tense milieu, 1919 produced at least twenty-six race riots in U.S. cities. Some of these took place in the South, but the largest outbreaks of violence occurred in northern cities. In Chicago, periodic bombings and attacks on blacks venturing into white communities were merely a prelude to the great 1919 race riot. Five days of violence caused mainly by white gangs took at least 38 lives, caused over 500 injuries, destroyed much property, and left over 1,000 people homeless.

Once the color line had been drawn around black neighborhoods, the ghetto had been defined and the fight for additional housing was waged block by block. As growing spatial separation reduced contacts between the races, black institutions expanded and flourished. Partly by choice and partly as a means to avoid white rejection and possible conflict, blacks increasingly patronized their own churches, stores, and places of amusement. The decline of normal and spontaneous black-white interactions tended to lessen racial tolerance and mutual understanding, reinforcing the acceptance of ghetto existence in people's minds.

Aspiring African-American leaders in the urban North sought to channel heightened black consciousness in various directions. All could agree with A. Philip Randolph when he warned African-Americans not to "depend on white men and white women to work out the problem. We have too long relied on whites. . . . You have got to get it yourself" (Stein 1986, p. 47). While black socialists such as Randolph judged unions to be the most effective vehicle for attaining racial power, Marcus GARVEY and others stressing a "race first" ideology attempted to tie black community militancy to the development of black business. Garvey's Black Star Line, a proposed transatlantic steamship enterprise, typified the goal of racial independence in business operations.

In the turmoil of 1919, many black professionals, intellectuals, and small businessmen supported the Black Star Line as a strategy to anchor the new racial consciousness in a large-scale business venture. Such enterprises would, according to Garvey, "make it possible for the youth of the race to find suitable employment . . . and remove the need for our high school and college graduates seeking jobs among the whites." In explaining his ambition to create a great enterprise that would produce both commercial opportunity and self-respect for African Americans, Garvey stated, "We had no monetary considerations or reward before us but the good we could do for our race" (Stein 1986, pp. 85, 200). But large-scale businesses, financed and operated by African Americans or any other group, require considerable financial capital and expertise. Garvey's unsuccessful line possessed neither: neither he nor any members of his board of directors had practical experience in the shipping business.

The Black Star Line notwithstanding, the growth of the black business community in the 1920s was most rapid. Black professionals, often moving north along with their clients, saw their practices and incomes rise as segregation increased. After 1920, black businessmen were commonplace in urban black communities. Previously concentrated in a few fields—as barbers, restaurant owners, undertakers—blacks were now participating in many lines of business within black residential areas. By 1930, an estimated 70,000 black-owned businesses were operating in the United States, a 700 percent increase over 1900 (Pierce 1947). Black entrepreneurs had penetrated retailing widely, but successes in manufacturing and wholesaling were still not widespread. In finance, progress was particularly apparent in the life-insurance industry: thirty-two firms employed 6,000 agents and controlled assets of over $18 million in 1928 (Harmon, Lindsay, and Woodson 1929). The 1920s were golden years for urban black business.

That community was vibrant in many southern as well as northern cities. The Hayti district of Durham, N.C., had by the 1920s become home of a substantial and widely diversified black business community. Commercial activities were concentrated on two main streets, ensuring a high level of pedestrian traffic for retailers. Black-owned banks encouraged development by providing business and real-estate loans. In addition to the many types of black-owned retail operations, the district included hotels, restaurants, personal services, repairs, finance, insurance, real estate, professional services, a library, and trade schools—all black-owned and -operated.

The Great Depression destroyed much of the ground gained during the previous decade. Black retailers benefited heavily from the "buy black" campaigns of the 1920s, and they were hit hardest by the depression. White ghetto merchants had always enjoyed greater access to financial capital and trade credit, and this advantage often proved decisive in the trough of the Great Depression. The viability of the black retailer had often been predicated on the loyalty of the black consumer; during hard times, this loyalty weakened. Black merchants, failing in droves, cried that they were being abandoned by their race. Black consumers responded that they were being exploited by the self-serving racial appeals of the black merchant. Economist Abram Harris wrote that "what the Negro businessman wants is to monopolize and exploit the market the black population provides" (1936, p. 184).

The Great Depression did create one noteworthy black entrepreneurial success story. In urban black communities, policy syndicates organized and controlled daily lotteries in which participants bet on certain numbers. These syndicates had great influence over economic life in the ghettos of the 1930s, and some of the largest black enterprises in the United States today were financed initially by the profits of policy. In the late 1930s, it was estimated, nearly one-quarter of the biggest black businesses in Chicago were either owned or controlled by the policy syndicate (Drake and Cayton 1962).

Harlem, in the depth of the Great Depression, saw small-business success materialize from a tightly knit religious cult, FATHER DIVINE's Peace Mission Movement. The Peace Mission Movement Cooperatives were started to provide employment for Father Divine's growing membership. Groups of the faithful pooled their capital and their labor to set up businesses and purchase real estate. Recruits to the movement had to abandon their worldly names, promise celibacy and chastity, turn over all of their earnings, and subscribe to the proposition that "Father Divine is God." Father Divine's followers in Harlem operated 25 restaurants, 10 barbershops, 10 dry-cleaning establishments, a coal company, and numerous other firms. His restaurants sold thousands of wholesome ten-cent meals to the unemployed (Light 1972). In addition, the restaurants provided 2,500 free meals a day in Harlem alone. Followers established similar operations in Newark, Bridgeport, Baltimore, and other cities. Father Divine's small-business empire, which he called "God, Incorporated," continued to expand after the end of the Great Depression. It dissolved only after his death in 1965.

In 1944, under the sponsorship of Atlanta University, the first large-scale quantitative study of the black business community was undertaken. Joseph Pierce's survey of 3,866 black firms in twelve cities revealed a clear picture of the state of urban black enterprise. Six lines of personal services and retailing dominated the sample: beauty parlors and barbershops, 1,005; eating places, 741; food stores, 293; cleaning and pressing establishments, 288; shoeshine and repair operations, 183; funeral parlors, 126 (1947, pp. 33–35). Except for funeral parlors and grocery stores, this list could be a survey of the enterprises that dominated the black business community in the antebellum South.

For a subsample of firms operating in nine cities, Pierce collected additional information describing financial capitalization, the age of firms, and the operational problems of business ownership as expressed by the owners themselves. The median value for initial capitalization was an incredibly low $549. This paucity of financial capital was heavily responsible for the very small size that typified the businesses described by Pierce. The median initial capitalization for all sampled retail firms was $544, and the median age was 5.3 years. For firms operating in service industries the median age was 7.1 years, and for the six most common lines of black enterprise, funeral parlors were oldest (22.6 years), while shoeshine and repair shops were youngest (3.2 years). When asked to rank the most significant obstacles to progressive business operation among blacks, the entrepreneurs identified lack of financial capital as their single greatest barrier. Other commonly mentioned obstacles were the lack of African-American patronage and a shortage of trained personnel.

Outstanding among the few large-scale types of black business, black-owned life-insurance companies weathered the Great Depression, and by 1942 they carried nearly $500 million in insurance, an increase of nearly 40 percent since 1928. Black-owned commercial banks had never been particularly successful, and they were devastated during the 1930s. Between 1888 and 1934, 134 black banks had opened; in 1934, only 12 were still operating (Ofari 1970).

The history books have nothing to say about the black business community of the 1950s; this is indicative of the lack of developments. A 1964 survey of black business in Philadelphia revealed a pattern of very small firms concentrated in personal services and retailing: the most common were beauty parlors and barbershops (35 percent) and restaurants (11 percent). Black firms were concentrated in the same lines of business that had been reported by Pierce in 1944, and mean growth in sales had barely outpaced inflation (Foley 1966).

The Late 1960s: Renewed Interest in Black Enterprise

Twentieth-century black urban ghettos have always had an active black entrepreneurial class in their midst, but they have been more often noted for such phenomena as high rates of unemployment and poverty, inadequate school systems, and substandard housing units. Destructive civil disorders in the mid-1960s in South Los Angeles, Detroit, Cleveland, and other cities drew national attention to the socioeconomic status of the black ghetto. It was precisely at this point that leaders from government and business began discussing black entrepreneurship. Heightened awareness of both the plight of blacks and their potential for urban disruption led various interest groups to endorse a proliferation of black economic-development programs. Presidential candidate Richard Nixon, in 1968, made government promotion of "black capitalism" the centerpiece of his civil rights platform. First under President Lyndon Johnson and then under the Nixon administration, the Small Business Administration (SBA) was mandated to promote black business development.

Since the mid-1960s, the SBA has initiated two major types of programs to assist minority entrepreneurs: (1) provision of loan assistance and (2) preferential procurement of federal contracts. Despite recurring problems in the SBA's programs, promoting minority-owned business development has wide appeal across the political spectrum, and Republicans and Democrats alike throughout the 1970s expanded procurement, financial, and managerial assistance programs for minorities (Bates 1981).

First under President Lyndon Johnson and then under the Nixon administration, the Small Business Administration (SBA) was mandated to promote black business development.

The vast publicity given to black capitalism in the 1960s was quite out of proportion to realistic prospects for alleviating ghetto problems via black business development. Black-owned firms as a group had been stagnant since the 1920s. Yet after 1965, federal dollars were increasingly available to assist black enterprise, and efforts to promote minority-owned businesses were taken up in the 1980s by many state and local governments.

A highly influential (and very pessimistic) assessment of the development prospects of the black business community was authored by Andrew Brimmer in the late 1960s. A member of the board of governors of the Federal Reserve System, Brimmer had a broad impact because he was the highest-ranking black economist serving in government at that time. According to Brimmer, the typical African-American firm lacked the technical, managerial, and marketing competence needed to compete successfully in the business world (1966). Black businesses existed in niches where whites were reluctant, or unwilling, to compete for black customers. The resultant segregation provided protected markets, which directly benefited black enterprise. "Behind the wall of segregation which cut Negroes off from many public services, there grew up a whole new area of opportunity. Behind this wall of protection emerged the Negro physician, the Negro lawyer, and above all, the Negro businessman" (Brimmer 1968, p. 34).

This segregated market, serving as a protective tariff, was the foundation for a business community of personal services, professional services, and public accommodations. In fields where black customers had relatively free access to retail establishments (such as department stores), black-owned businesses were typically nonviable. Progress toward desegregation, according to Brimmer, would merely undermine black businesses. Specifically, the erosion of segregation and discrimination was giving blacks greater access to public accommodations, and white firms were catering to buyers increasingly without regard to race. As the tariff wall fell, Brimmer suggested that most black firms would face very hard times. Government assistance to the black business community, by implication, was a strategy doomed to failure.

Could blacks expand beyond their few lines of traditional personal-service and retailing enterprise? Caplovitz, in his 1968 study of retail businesses operating in central Harlem, found that white business owners had higher educational levels than black owners. Furthermore, whites were much more likely to have had managerial or sales experience prior to their entry into self-employment. Black business owners operated small establishments, and they were generally less successful than their white Harlem cohorts. A later study by Brimmer suggested that the job-creation potential of black enterprise, even under "optimistic" assumptions, was minimal. These estimates assumed that no jobs would be created by black firms in the construction, manufacturing, and transportation industries. "This omission was not accidental; rather it resulted from the fact that there are few Negro-owned firms competing in these types of businesses" (Brimmer and Terrell 1971, pp. 304–306).

The pessimists, including Andrew Brimmer, were not at all surprised when the SBA's efforts to provide long-term credit access to minority-owned businesses produced very high rates of loan delinquency and default. The major government lending effort targeted to assist self-employed blacks was the Economic Opportunity Loan (EOL) program. Prior to 1968, virtually all SBA loans to minority borrowers were EOL loans, and in the five fiscal years 1969–1973, 24,422 of the 36,782 SBA loans to minorities were EOLs. In 1973, the average SBA loan for minority borrowers came to $19,795 under the EOL program and $61,157 under all other programs; the mean SBA loan for all nonminority borrowers exceeded $100,000 (Bates 1975). The EOL program was designed to help low-income persons who either owned or wanted to establish very small businesses. A high personal income and/or any evidence of past or present aptitude for success in business was grounds for loan denial, since the EOL program was designed to serve minorities who were unlikely candidates for success in business. Hence, the high default rate followed logically from the underlying philosophy of the program. The availability of EOL loans at low interest rates encouraged many blacks to enter businesses that were not viable. The resulting events—failing in business and defaulting on loan obligations—placed severe hardships on many unsuccessful entrepreneurs.

The EOL program, of course, could not be used to judge the potential of black enterprise because it was merely a massive case study of institutionalized failure. Studies contrasting successful with unsuccessful black-owned businesses have provided something of a model portrait, a description that typifies the successful black business owner of the 1970s and 1980s. A college graduate with an above-average income enters business—usually outside such traditional areas as personal services, often in an emerging field such as finance. In terms of firm size (sales volume, total assets), the business is above average. Cash flow is strong relative to debt-repayment obligations. The size of the owner's financial investment at the point of business entry is the strongest single predictor of firm viability (Bates 1989). The model owner is likely to be over thirty-five but under sixty.

The model portrait that typifies black business failure follows logically from the above analysis: A low-income individual who has not graduated from high school enters business—most likely in a small-scale retail operation or a service line of business that is not skill-intensive. Financial investment is low and the firm size is small. The firm is often unable to achieve a scale of operation that is sufficient to provide the entrepreneur with a decent income. With or without a loan, discontinuance of the business is likely.

The world of small business, finally, is rife with highly educated entrepreneurs whose ventures have gone belly-up. There are no guaranteed formulas for success.

Brimmer's pessimistic view of the black business community has not withstood the test of time. One fundamental flaw in his analysis was the assumption that the emerging black firms of the 1970s would be replicas of the existing species; the possibility of evolution and progress was not considered. Brimmer's observation that segregation and discrimination had protected black business, although not devoid of insight, is a one-sided interpretation of the historical development of black entrepreneurship in America. His "protected markets" thesis failed to explore causal relationships between racism and the stunted state of the black business community. Among the more important causal relationships was the fact that financial capital sources—such as commercial banks—had frequently been closed to black firms. Discrimination in the labor market made it difficult to generate the initial equity investment for business formation, which partially explained the black business community's small size and industry orientation. Constraints limiting educational and training opportunities similarly thwarted many potential lines of enterprise. Indeed, the erosion of discrimination ushered in a new era of opportunity for black entrepreneurs.

A lessening of discrimination reduced key constraints that historically have thwarted black business progress. In the survey by Pierce cited above, for example, black entrepreneurs identified their inability to obtain credit as a serious handicap in the competitive struggle for success. Scarcity of financial capital caused the overwhelming majority of black firms to concentrate in lines of business requiring little capital. When capital markets began to open up, black businesses predictably expanded into fields where they theretofore had been unable to compete on an equal basis. Project OWN, the initial 1968 government effort to encourage commercial-bank lending to black enterprise, achieved a broadening of the black industry base. The industry distribution of black firms receiving bank loans sharply differed from the distribution of all black businesses: few of the borrowers were in traditional fields; most operated in emerging lines of business (Bates 1973).

Easing the Historical Constraints

The constraints that shaped the traditional black business community—limited capital access, barriers to education and training, and so forth—have changed substantially since the 1960s. The availability of government loan guarantees (against default risk) induced thousands of banks to extend business loans, thus eroding a tradition of minimal contact between blacks and commercial-bank lending departments. College enrollments by black students increased dramatically in the 1960s and 1970s; enrollment growth in business-related fields was particularly rapid.

The constraints that shaped the traditional black business community—limited capital access, barriers to education and training, and so forth—have changed substantially since the 1960s.

While increased loan availability typified black (and other minority) business promotion efforts in the 1960s, the use of procurement dollars and "set-asides" targeted to minority firms by corporations and government units did not become a major force until the late 1970s. Large corporations in the consumer-products industries routinely targeted procurement dollars to minority firms, advertised in minority-owned publications, and deposited funds in minority-owned banks. Set-asides and preferential procurement programs targeting minority enterprise, widely utilized by local governments in the 1980s and 1990s, reflect the growing political power of blacks (and Hispanics) in many central cities. Atlanta, Chicago, Los Angeles, Philadelphia, Detroit, New Orleans, Dallas, and Minneapolis are among the large cities that have shown major support for minority business development activities.

While the traditional black business community consisted predominantly of very small firms serving a ghetto clientele, the lure of market opportunity in recent years has induced entrepreneurs to create larger firms that are oriented toward corporate and government clienteles (Bates 1985). The finance, insurance, and real-estate field typifies the above trends in black entrepreneurship. Among all self-employed blacks in this field in 1980, 66 percent had attended college (versus 28 percent of all self-employed blacks) and the majority of these had graduated from four-year colleges or universities (Bates 1987). In the universe of all self-employed individuals, the incidence of college attendance has risen steadily through time; among blacks, however, growth in the reported frequency of college attendance has been relatively more rapid than among nonminorities. A comparison of 1970 and 1980 census data indicates a 120 percent increase in the incidence of college attendance among self-employed blacks, versus a 91.7 percent increase for their nonminority cohorts.

The importance of well-educated, highly skilled blacks in explaining growth in entrepreneurship is emphasized by findings of a study by Handy and Swinton (1983). In explaining growth in the number of black-owned firms between 1972 and 1977, Handy and Swinton found that three closely related variables most accurately predicted growth in a particular metropolitan area: (a) growth in the available pool of black professional and managerial manpower; (b) the initial level of black professional and managerial manpower; and (c) the level of education among blacks within the metropolitan area.

A longer-term perspective on the changing composition of the minority business community is highlighted in Table 1's comparison of 1960 and 1980 U.S. Census data on minority self-employment. Two lines of business—personal services and retailing—accounted for well over half of all minority enterprises in 1960. Lesser concentrations of minorities were working in miscellaneous other services (such as entertainment, lodging, and repair services), and construction. Collectively, these four most common fields—personal services, retail, construction, and miscellaneous other services—accounted for 81.3 percent of self-employed minorities in 1960. Between 1960 and 1980, all of the growth in relative self-employment shares—as measured by the proportions of minority entrepreneurs in various lines of business—took place *outside* these four areas (Bates 1987). Self-employment growth was most rapid in four fields that collectively more than doubled their relative share of the entrepreneur pool: business services; finance, insurance, and real estate; transportation, communication, and utilities; and wholesale. Moreover, within certain broad industry categories, the distribution of black-owned firms has changed markedly. Special trade contractors in areas such as painting and carpentry have decreased in incidence, while general contracting and heavy construction firms have increased substantially. These shifts reflect a movement toward more skill- and capital-intensive lines of business within the broad industrial groupings.

Although marginal operations are undoubtedly numerous within the black business community, data from the U.S. Bureau of the Census reveal a clear trend toward more skill-intensive lines of business. In 1960,

Table 1

PERCENTAGE OF ALL MINORITY SELF-EMPLOYED IN VARIOUS INDUSTRIES, 1960–1980*

Industry	1960	1980	% Change since 1960	Industry Growth Rate
Construction	16.7%	16.5%	−1.2%	Stagnant
Manufacturing	4.1	6.0	46.3	Moderate
Transportation, communications, and utilities	3.9	6.0	53.8	Rapid
Wholesale	1.7	3.6	111.8	Rapid
Retail	25.4	25.4	0.0	Stagnant
Finance, insurance, and real estate	1.4	4.0	185.7	Rapid
Business services	2.4	6.6	175.0	Rapid
Repair services	5.2	6.9	32.7	Moderate
Personal services	28.9	14.7	−49.1	Declining
Other services	10.3	10.3	0.0	Stagnant
Total	100.0%	100.0%		

* Excludes agriculture, doctors, and lawyers.
Source: U.S. Bureau of the Census unpublished data.

nearly 30 percent of self-employed blacks ran personal-services firms and fewer than 10 percent operated in skill-intensive areas such as finance, insurance, and real estate; business services; and professional services. Among black-owned firms that began operations in the 1976–1982 period, 25 percent were in these skill-intensive service industries; only 10.3 percent of start-ups were in personal services. In 1960, blacks in skill-intensive areas were concentrated in several specialties: medicine, law, insurance. By the 1990s, common lines of business include not only these fields but consulting firms, ad agencies, engineering services, accounting firms, employment agencies, and computer-software operations. The data on black business reflect trends toward diversity that are vitally important for comprehending the trajectory of black entrepreneurship.

Growing numbers of experienced, financially sophisticated black entrepreneurs are manifested in business dealings that are thrusting some enterprises into the mainstream of corporate America. In 1987, Reginald Lewis completed the largest transaction ever negotiated by an African American when he purchased the International Foods Division of Beatrice, Inc., which had annual sales of $1.8 billion. J. Bruce Llewellyn (with his partner, Julius Erving) owns the Philadelphia Coca-Cola Bottling Company. The very largest of the black-owned businesses today compete in the open marketplace: they do not typically target a minority clientele. In contrast, the largest black-owned enterprises of the mid-twentieth century—firms selling life insurance and hair-care products—catered almost exclusively to minority clients. These giants of an earlier era, as noted by Brimmer, flourished in market niches that were generally overlooked by corporate America. Black-owned businesses reliant on such protected markets have experienced growing competition from mainstream corporate America since the 1960s. Their changing fortunes are a reflection of the same basic social forces that have permitted emerging black-owned firms to compete successfully in the nonminority marketplace.

The black business community is profoundly different today than it was in the 1960s. Its size and scope have expanded; industry diversity has flourished; highly educated entrepreneurs are the norm in many lines of business; bank credit is more widely available. Black emerging businesses are progressing rapidly overall, but they must still contend with a range of problems that typify small business in general, as well as several that disproportionately affect black firms. A key factor responsible for black enterprise growth is the rising incidence of highly educated entrepreneurs in nontraditional lines of business; a key factor that continues to retard growth is the paucity of equity capital available for investment in small firms. Personal-wealth holdings are traditionally a major source of capital for small-business creation and expansion. Disparities in such holdings discourage entry into self-employment and handicap black business startups.

Data describing family-wealth holdings in 1984 indicate that black households had a median net worth of $3,397, versus $39,135 for white households: for every dollar of wealth in the median white family, the median black family had nine cents (Jaynes and Williams 1989, 292). While only 8.6 percent of the white households had zero or negative net worth, 31 percent of the black households held absolutely no wealth.

Wealth in the form of business equity was most commonly observed among black households whose income exceeded $24,000. Business equity was held by 3.5 percent of the black upper-middle-income ($24,000–$48,000) households, and by 14.0 percent of the black high-income households. In contrast, the fraction of white households with business equity ownership surpassed that of black households at every income level. At the upper-middle and high income levels, respectively, 11.0 percent and 21.5 percent of the white households held wealth in the form of small business equity. The greatest disparity in business equity holdings, however, derived from the fact that higher-income white households are relatively much more numerous than higher-income blacks. Disparities in personal-wealth holdings, therefore, continue to handicap black business startups today. In the 1990s as in the 1890s, black business creation has been concentrated in industries where formation requires relatively little financial capital. Lacking assets, and therefore lacking borrowing capacities, blacks are too often ill equipped to exploit economic opportunities.

The financial capital constraint facing black-owned businesses is unlikely to ease anytime soon. The low net-worth holdings that typify most black households will be alleviated, at best, only gradually over a period of many years. Low levels of personal wealth restrict business viability in several ways. Commercial banks lend most freely to those who possess significant amounts of equity capital to invest in their businesses. Beyond banks, the second and third most important sources of debt capital for small business are family and friends, respectively (Bates 1991). The low net-worth holdings of black households in general restrict the availability of debt capital that family and friends can invest in small business operations.

Access to credit has been expanded for black firms in recent decades. Relative to the situation in 1944 described by the Pierce survey, the fact that over 25 percent of African-American businesses beginning operations between 1976 and 1982 received commercial bank loans is noteworthy (Bates 1991). But credit access is certainly not approaching parity with that of white businesses. Black college graduates are least disadvantaged relative to white business owners, but black firms as a group are less likely to get loans, and the loans that are extended are much smaller than those afforded to their white cohorts (Ando 1988; Bates 1991).

An entirely different sort of barrier to continued black business progress has emerged in the federal courts. Challenges to the constitutionality of minority business assistance programs threaten to reverse the process of broadening the range of markets served by black-owned enterprises. Minority business set-asides at the state and local levels are being cut back due to the judicial constraints imposed on these programs by the Supreme Court's 1989 *Richmond* v. *Croson* ruling.

Another constraint on black business viability is location-based. Inner-city black communities are increasingly being left out of the business development process. All the basic elements of black business viability—talented entrepreneurs, financial capital, and markets—are threatened in the inner-city milieu: banks redline, better-educated entrepreneurs are pulling out, and markets are weak (Bates 1989). In light of the reorientation of emerging black enterprises toward racially diverse or largely nonminority clienteles, choice business locations are increasingly found outside of minority neighborhoods.

The lessening of discriminatory barriers has not been a smooth and steady social process.

The nature of the black business community is largely derivative of broad social forces. Slavery and the social milieu of the antebellum South shaped black entrepreneurship in the nineteenth century. Urbanization, northern migration, and the growing intensity of segregation that followed World War I shaped a black business community in the 1920s that was profoundly different from its nineteenth-century predecessor. Finally, a lessening of segregation and discrimination in recent decades has generated an entirely new growth dynamic in the black business community of the 1990s. The lessening of discriminatory barriers has not been a smooth and steady social process. The future composition of the black business universe may derive from the expanded opportunities offered by a less segregated society, or it may reflect growing constraints imposed by evolving discriminatory barriers.

BIBLIOGRAPHY

Ando, Faith. "Capital Issues and Minority-Owned Business." *Review of Black Political Economy* 16 (1988): 77–109.

Bates, Timothy. *Black Capitalism: A Quantitative Analysis.* New York, 1973.

———. "Black Entrepreneurship and Government Programs." *Journal of Contemporary Studies* 4 (1981): 59–70.

———. "Commercial Bank Lending to Black and White-Owned Businesses." *Quarterly Review of Economics and Business* 31 (1991): 64–80.

———. "Government as Financial Intermediary for Minority Entrepreneurs." *Journal of Business* 48 (1975): 541–547.

———. "Impact of Preferential Procurement Policies on Minority-Owned Businesses." *Review of Black Political Economy* 14 (1985): 51–66.

———. "Self-Employed Minorities: Traits and Trends." *Social Sciences Quarterly* 68 (1987): 539–551.

———. "Small Business Viability in the Urban Ghetto." *Journal of Regional Science* 29 (1989): 625–643.

Bates, Timothy and Daniel Fusfeld. *The Political Economy of the Urban Ghetto.* Carbondale, Ill., 1984.

Brimmer, Andrew. "The Negro in the National Economy." In John Davis, ed. *American Negro Reference Book.* Englewood Cliffs, N.J., 1966, pp. 251–336.

———. "Desegregation and Negro Leadership." In *Business Leadership and the Negro Crisis.* New York, 1968.

Brimmer, Andrew, and Henry Terrell. "The Economic Potential of Black Capitalism." *Public Policy* 19 (1971): 289–308.

Caplovitz, David. *The Merchants of Harlem: A Study of Small Business in the Black Community.* Beverly Hills, Calif., 1973.

Drake, St. Clair, and Horace Cayton. *Black Metropolis.* New York, 1962.

Du Bois, W. E. B. *The Philadelphia Negro: A Social Study.* New York, 1967.

Fleming, G. James, and Bernice Sheldon. "Fine Food for Philadelphia." *Crisis* 45 (1938): 111–116.

Foley, Eugene. "The Negro Businessman: In Search of a Tradition." Talcott Parsons and Kenneth Clark, eds. In *The Negro American.* Boston, 1966, pp. 555–579.

Handy, John, and David Swinton. "The Determinants of the Rate of Growth of Black-Owned Businesses." *Review of Black Political Economy* 12 (1984): 85–110.

Harmon, J., Arnett Lindsay, and Carter Woodson. *The Negro as Businessman.* College Park, Md., 1929.

Harris, Abram. *The Negro as Capitalist.* Philadelphia, 1936.

Holsey, Albon. "Seventy-Five Years of Negro Business." *Crisis* 45 (1938): 231–247.

Jaynes, Gerald, and Robin Williams. *A Common Destiny: Blacks and American Society.* Washington, D.C., 1989.

Kelsey, Carl. "The Evolution of Negro Labor." *Annals of the American Academy of Political and Social Science* 21 (1903): 59–74.

Light, Ivan. *Ethnic Enterprise in America.* Berkeley, Ca., 1972.

Myrdal, Gunnar. *An American Dilemma.* New York, 1944.

Ofari, Earl. *The Myth of Black Capitalism.* New York, 1970.

Pierce, Joseph. *Negro Business and Business Education.* New York, 1947.

Ransom, Roger, and Richard Sutch. *One Kind of Freedom.* New York, 1977.

Stein, Judith. *The World of Marcus Garvey.* Baton Rouge, La., 1986.

U.S. Bureau of the Census. *Negroes in the United States, 1920–1932.* Washington, D.C., 1935.

Walker, Juliet. "Racism, Slavery and Free Enterprise: Black Entrepreneurship in the United States before the Civil War." *Business History Review* 60 (1986): 343–382.

Washington, Booker T. *The Negro in Business.* Boston, 1907.

– TIMOTHY BATES

BLACK CODES

Black codes were laws passed to regulate the rights of free African Americans in the antebellum and post–Civil War eras. Before the Civil War, a number of midwestern states adopted black codes (or black laws) to inhibit the migration of free blacks and in other ways limit black rights. After the Civil War, most southern states adopted far more severe black codes to prevent former slaves, called freedmen at the time, from having the full rights of citizens and to reimpose, as much as possible, the labor and racial controls of slavery.

In 1804, Ohio passed an act to "regulate black and mulatto persons." This law became the prototype for subsequent laws passed in Ohio, Indiana, Illinois, and the Michigan Territory. It required that blacks migrating to Ohio show proof of their freedom and exacted a fifty-dollar fine from any white hiring a black who did not have such proof. On its face, this law could be seen as a good-faith effort to prevent fugitive slaves from entering the state. In fact, it was primarily designed to discourage black migration. An 1807 law raised the fine to one hundred dollars and required migrating blacks to find two sureties to guarantee their "good behavior" and assure that they would not require public assistance. Subsequent amendments to these laws prevented blacks from serving on juries and testifying against whites and severely limited their access to public schools. Although discriminatory, these laws did not prevent blacks from owning real estate, entering professions—including law and medicine—or exercising freedom of speech, press, assembly, and worship. Moreover, once blacks were legally present in a state, the black codes of the North did not inhibit their geographic mobility.

These laws were generally ineffective in limiting the growth of the free black population. From 1803 to 1860, Ohio's black population actually grew at a slightly faster rate than did its white population. Between 1830 and 1860, Indiana, Illinois, and Ohio all saw growth in their black populations of over 300 percent. There is little evidence that migrating blacks were usually asked to prove their freedom or that anyone enforced the requirement that migrating blacks find sureties to sign bonds for them. There are, in addition, no recorded cases of any whites being fined for hiring blacks who failed to provide proof of their freedom.

In 1849, Ohio repealed most of its black codes, including those provisions discouraging black migrants from coming to the state. The repeal was part of an elaborate legislative compromise that also sent the abolitionist Salmon P. Chase to the U.S. Senate. Indiana and Illinois retained their discriminatory laws until after the Civil War. Iowa, California, and Oregon also adopted some aspects of the northern black codes, but Iowa and California dropped virtually all these rules before or during the Civil War.

By the end of the Civil War, blacks in the North had substantial equality under the law, with the exceptions that in most states they could not vote or serve on juries. These disabilities based on race disappeared after the ratification of the FIFTEENTH AMENDMENT in 1870. After 1870, some northern states still prohibited marriages between blacks and whites, but otherwise most remnants of the black codes were no longer on the books.

In the South, the situation was far different. The loss of the war and the Emancipation of four million slaves immediately and dramatically affected southern society. Emancipation upset the system of racial control that had kept blacks subordinate to whites since the seventeenth century, and also destroyed the economic relationship that had allowed planters to count on a pliable and ever-present source of labor. With slavery gone, the legal status of the freedmen and their role in the postwar South were uncertain. Immediately after the war, southern legislatures began to adopt "black codes" to define the status of former slaves and to cope with the emerging problems resulting from Emancipation.

Northerners assumed that after Emancipation ex-slaves would have the same rights as other free people. But southerners did not hold such views. Before the war, the rights of free blacks were severely restricted, and usually enumerated in slave codes, underscoring the antebellum southern view that free blacks were an anomalous and inherently dangerous class of people. Thus, when the war ended the ex-slaves of the former Confederate states lacked most legal rights. The black codes changed this but in a way that rigorously limited the rights of freedmen.

At the personal level, the black codes allowed African Americans to marry each other (but not whites) and furthermore declared that all slaves who had lived as married couples would be considered legally married. Mississippi's laws of 1865–the first adopted in the postwar South—illustrate how the black codes gave former slaves some rights, while at the same time denying them many others that whites had. The end result was to give former slaves most of the responsibilities, but few of the benefits, of freedom.

An 1865 law, with the misleading title "An Act to confer Civil Rights on Freedmen, and for other Purposes," declared that blacks could "sue and be sued, implead and be impleaded" in all state courts, but only allowed them to testify in cases involving other blacks and prohibited them from serving on juries. The law allowed freedmen to acquire and dispose of property "to the same extent that white persons may," but prohibited them from renting any land except in "towns or cities." In other words, free blacks could not rent farmland. In overwhelmingly rural Mississippi, this meant freedmen would become a peasant class, forced to work for white landowners and unable to acquire land on their own. Another provision of this law required that all labor contracts made with freedmen for more than a month had to be in writing, and that any freedman who quit before the end of the term of a contract would "forfeit his wages for the year," including those earned up to the time he quit. In a provision similar to the antebellum slave codes, this law obligated "every civil officer" to "arrest and carry back to his or her legal employer any freedman, free negro or mulatto, who shall have quit the service of his or her employer before the expiration of his or her term of service." This in effect made the free blacks of Mississippi slaves to their employers, at least for the term of their employment. Anyone attempting to hire a black under contract to someone else was subject to fine, jail terms, and civil damage suits. Another Mississippi statute allowed counties to apprentice African-American children if their parents were declared to be too poor to support them. To many, this appeared to be an attempt to re-enslave the children of the freedmen. Still another statute, also enacted in 1865, declared that any black who did not have a labor contract would be declared a vagrant and would be subject to fines or imprisonment. This law provided punishment for free blacks who were "found unlawfully assembling themselves together either in the day or night time," for whites who assembled with such blacks, and for whites and blacks who married or cohabited.

Other states adopted laws with similar intent but different provisions. Rather than prohibiting blacks from renting land, South Carolina prohibited them from working in nonagricultural jobs without paying special taxes that ranged from ten to one hundred dollars. South Carolina also enacted harsh criminal laws to suppress African Americans. Stealing a hog could lead to a thousand-dollar fine and ten years in jail. Other crimes had punishments of whipping, the stocks, or the treadmill, as well as fines and long imprisonment. Hired farm workers in South Carolina could not even sell farm produce without written authorization from their employers. Other provisions of the law created special taxes and fines for blacks with imprisonment or forced labor for those who lacked the money to pay them. Like Mississippi, South Carolina provided for the apprenticing of black children. These and similar laws created something close to a reimposition of slavery in South Carolina. In 1865, Louisiana and Alabama adopted laws similar to those of South Carolina and Mississippi.

The black codes of 1865 shocked many Northerners. In South Carolina, Gen. Daniel E. Sickles suspended the law, as did Union troops in the Mississippi military. Even some white governors, including William L. Sharkey of Mississippi and Robert Patton of Alabama, opposed some of the more blatantly discriminatory laws. In Congress, Republicans responded by introducing legislation that led to the Civil Rights Act of 1866 and eventually to the FOURTEENTH AMENDMENT.

In 1866 the rest of the former Confederacy adopted black codes. Florida's code was as harsh as those of Mississippi and South Carolina, providing whipping, the pillory, and forced labor for various offenses. Florida prohibited any blacks from moving into the state, prohibited African Americans from owning firearms, and, though allowing the creation of schools for blacks, prohibited the use of state money to pay for them.

Other states were more discreet in their legislation, trying to avoid giving ammunition to Republicans in Congress who were growing increasingly impatient with the South's attempts to reimpose bondage and oppression on the freedmen. Virginia's vagrancy law carefully avoided any reference to race, but still punished offenders with forced labor, and was clearly directed at the freedmen. Not surprisingly, Gen. Alfred H. Terry suspended its operation, although two other generals, in other parts of Virginia, allowed it to go into force. Tennessee's new criminal code provided the death penalty for breaking and entering with the intent to rob, for robbery itself, and for horse stealing. This law did not use any racial terms, but was clearly aimed at blacks. Similarly, Georgia and North Carolina tried to avoid the use of racial terms that might have jeopardized their chances of readmission to the Union. Nevertheless, none of the former Confederate states was ready to have racially blind statutes, much less racially blind justice. North Carolina's law, arguably the least offensive of the new black codes, nevertheless provided a death penalty for black rapists when the victim was white, but not for white rapists, no matter what the color of the victim.

Like the 1865 laws, those passed in 1866 regulated the movement of blacks, their ability to live where they wished, and their ability to sell their labor on an open market. All of the 1866 laws also tried to create racial controls to keep African Americans in a subordinate role, even as they tried to avoid the appearance of racial discrimination. By 1867, southern legislatures had repealed most of the provisions that designated specific punishments by race. Even without racially specific language, courts continued to apply solely to African Americans provisions of the black codes regulating vagrancy, contracts, and children.

Although these laws remained on the books in one form or another throughout RECONSTRUCTION, their enforcement was sporadic. Congress, the Freedmen's Bureau, and the military opposed them. Nevertheless, the laws remained a symbol of the oppression that the postbellum South offered African Americans. After 1877, the South gradually reimposed those provisions of the black codes that segregated blacks and regulated labor contracts. Such laws led to peonage and a second-class status for southern blacks in the late nineteenth and early twentieth centuries.

BIBLIOGRAPHY

Berwanger, Eugene D. *The Frontier Against Slavery.* Urbana, Ill., 1967.

Erickson, Leonard. "Politics and Repeal of Ohio's Black Laws, 1837–1849." *Ohio History* 82 (1973): 154–175.

Finkelman, Paul. "Prelude to the Fourteenth Amendment: Black Legal Rights in the Antebellum North." *Rutgers Law Journal* 17 (1986): 415–482.

———, ed. *Race, Law, and American History, 1700–1990.* Vol. 3, *Emancipation and Reconstruction.* New York, 1992.

Nieman, Donald. *To Set the Law in Motion: The Freedmen's Bureau and the Legal Rights of Blacks, 1865–1868.* Millwood, N.Y., 1979.

Wilson, Theodore B. *The Black Codes of the South.* University, Ala., 1965.

— PAUL FINKELMAN

BLACK PANTHER PARTY FOR SELF-DEFENSE

Huey P. Newton and Bobby Seale founded the Black Panther Party for Self-Defense in October 1966, and despite periods of imprisonment, they remained leaders as the party expanded from its Oakland, Calif., base to become a national organization. Assuming the posts of defense minister and chairman, respectively, of the new group, Newton and Seale drafted a ten-point program and platform that included a wide range of demands, summarized in the final point: "We want land, bread, housing, education, clothing, justice and peace." Rather than on its program, however, the party's appeal among young African Americans was based mainly on its brash militancy, often expressed in confrontations with police. Initially concentrated in the San Francisco Bay area and Los Angeles, by the end of 1968 the Black Panther party ("for Self-Defense" was dropped from its name) had formed chapters in dozens of cities throughout the United States, with additional support chapters abroad. Although most of its leaders were male, a substantial proportion of its rank-and-file members were female. Influenced by the ideas of Marx and MALCOLM X, the Black Panther Party's ideology was not clearly defined, and the party experienced many internal disputes over its political orientation. The FBI's covert Counterintelligence Program (COINTELPRO) and raids by local police forces exacerbated leadership conflicts, resulted in the imprisonment or death of party members, and hastened the decline of the group after 1968.

After joining the party in 1967, Eldridge CLEAVER, a former convict and author of a book of essays called *Soul on Ice,* became one of the party's main spokespersons and a link with white leftist supporters. Arrested in May 1967 during a protest at the California state capitol in Sacramento against pending legislation to restrict the carrying of weapons, Cleaver remained affiliated with the Panthers despite repeated efforts of authorities to return him to prison for parole violations. His caustic attacks on white authorities combined with media images of armed Panthers wearing black leather jackets attracted notoriety and many recruits during the summer of 1967. Cleaver's prominence in the Black Panther party increased after October 28, 1967, when Newton was arrested after an altercation that resulted in the death of an Oakland police officer. The Panthers immediately mobilized to free Newton, who faced a possible death sentence if convicted. As part of this support effort, Cleaver and Seale contacted Stokely CARMICHAEL, former chairman of the STUDENT NONVIOLENT COORDINATING COMMITTEE (SNCC) and a nationally known proponent of black power. SNCC activists and representatives from other black militant groups participated in "Free Huey" rallies during February 1968, helping to transform the Panthers from a local group into a national organization. When Cleaver was arrested during an April 6 raid that resulted in the killing of party treasurer Bobby Hutton, his parole was revoked, and his legal defense, as well as that of Newton, became a major focus of Panther activities.

Although the Black Panther party gradually shifted its emphasis from revolutionary rhetoric and armed confrontations with police to "survival programs," clashes with police and legal prosecutions decimated the party's leadership.

Serious conflicts accompanied the party's rapid growth, however, for its leaders divided over ideological and tactical issues. Cleaver and Seale were unsuccessful in their effort to forge an alliance with SNCC, whose members distrusted the Panthers' hierarchical leadership style. When relations between the two groups soured during the summer of 1968, Carmichael decided to remain allied with the Panthers, but his advocacy of black unity and Pan-Africanism put him at odds with other Panther leaders, who advocated class unity and close ties with the white New Left. Although his presence helped the Panthers to establish strong chapters in the eastern United States, Carmichael severed ties with the party after he established residency in Africa in 1969. The party's relations with southern California followers of black nationalist Maulana Karenga also deteriorated, a result both of the FBI's COINTELPRO efforts and the Panthers' harsh criticisms of Karenga's cultural nationalist orientation. In January 1969, two members of Karenga's U.S. organization killed two Panthers during a clash at UCLA.

Although the Black Panther party gradually shifted its emphasis from revolutionary rhetoric and armed confrontations with police to "survival programs," such as free breakfasts for children and educational projects, clashes with police and legal prosecutions decimated the party's leadership. Soon after finishing his 1968 presidential campaign as candidate of the Peace and Freedom party, Cleaver left for exile in Cuba and then Algeria to avoid returning to prison for parole violation. In March 1969, Seale was arrested for conspiracy to incite rioting at the 1968 Democratic convention in Chicago, and in May, Connecticut officials charged Seale and seven other Panthers with murder in the slaying of party member Alex Rackley, who was believed to be a police informant. In New York, twenty-one Panthers were charged with plotting to assassinate policemen and blow up buildings. Though nearly all charges brought against Panther members either did not result in convictions or were overturned on appeal, the prosecutions absorbed much of the party's resources. An effort during 1969 to purge members considered disloyal or unreliable only partly succeeded.

In 1970, when Newton's conviction on a lesser manslaughter charge was reversed on appeal, he returned to find the party in disarray. Seale still faced murder charges (they were dropped the following year). Chief of staff David Hilliard awaited trial on charges of threatening the life of President Richard Nixon. Some chapters, particularly those in the eastern United States, resisted direction from the Oakland headquarters. In 1971, Newton split with Cleaver, in exile in Algeria, charging that the latter's influence in the party had caused it to place too much emphasis on armed rebellion. In 1973, Seale ran an unsuccessful, though formidable, campaign for mayor of Oakland. The following year Newton, facing new criminal charges and allegations of drug use, fled to Cuba. After Newton's departure, Elaine Brown took over leadership of the ailing organization. The Black Panther party continued to decline, however, and, even after Newton returned in 1977 to resume control, the group never regained its former prominence.

BIBLIOGRAPHY

Brown, Elaine. *A Taste of Power: A Black Woman's Story.* New York, 1992.

Cleaver, Eldridge. *Eldridge Cleaver: Post-Prison Writings and Speeches.* New York, 1969.

Heath, G. Louis, ed. *Off the Pigs! The History and Literature of the Black Panther Party.* Metuchen, N.J., 1976.

Hilliard, David. *Side of Glory: Autobiography of David Hilliard and the Story of the Black Panthers.* Boston, 1993.

Newton, Huey P. *Revolutionary Suicide.* New York, 1973.

– CLAYBORNE CARSON

BLACK TOWNS

African-American town promoters established at least eighty-eight, and perhaps as many as two hundred, black towns throughout the United States during the late nineteenth and early twentieth centuries. Black towns, all-black incorporated communities with autonomous black city governments and shopkeeper economies, were created out of a combination of economic and political motives. The founders of towns such as Boley, Okla., and Mound Bayou, Miss., like the entrepreneurs who created Chicago, Denver, and thousands of other municipalities across the nation, hoped their enterprises would be profitable, and appealed to early settlers with the promise of rising real estate values. However, they added special attractions to African Americans: the ability to escape racial oppression, control their economic destinies, and prove black capacity for self-government.

The first attempts at establishing all-black communities were in Upper Canada (later Ontario), as an offshoot of the abolitionist movement. In 1829 the settlement of Wilberforce was created to resettle black refugees expelled from Cincinnati. Wilberforce, as well as most of the later Canadian settlements such as Dawn and Elgin, were operated largely by white charities, and were designed to give African Americans land and teach them usable skills. However, they were poorly funded and managed, and none survived long. The first black town in the United States was created in 1835, when Free Frank McWhorter, an ex-Kentucky slave, founded the short-lived town of New Philadelphia, Ill. More black towns were settled in the first years after the Civil War. Texas led the way in the late 1860s, with the founding of Shankleville in 1867 and Kendleton in 1870. These arose from the desire of emancipated slaves to own land without interference.

However, the vast majority of black towns emerged following the end of RECONSTRUCTION. Like whites, blacks were lured by the promise of the West, and many towns were planned in western areas. African Americans, largely unable to secure land and economic opportunity in settled areas, looked to the West, with its reserves of land obtainable cheaply, or free through the Homestead Act. Furthermore, the society of the frontier had a reputation for egalitarianism and individual autonomy. To blacks in the ex-Confederate states, who had briefly tasted political power before being overwhelmed by white regimes, the possibility of black-run areas was attractive. Among these dozens of black communities, six representative towns will be discussed in depth.

Nicodemus, Kans., was the first all-black community that gained national attention. Nicodemus was founded by W. R. Hill, a white minister and land speculator, who during the mid-1870s joined three black Kansas residents—W. H. Smith, Simon P. Rountree, and Z. T. Fletcher—in planning a black agricultural community in western Kansas, near the frontier. They founded a land company to create Nicodemus, named after a legendary African slave prince who purchased his freedom, and recruited settlers from the South.

The first group, thirty colonists, arrived from Kentucky in July 1877. Undaunted by the treeless, windswept countryside, another 150 Kentucky settlers reached the site in March 1878, and more newcomers arrived later in the year from Tennessee, Missouri, and Mississippi as part of the "EXODUSTER" migration. By 1880, 258 blacks and 58 whites resided in the town and surrounding township. Both the townspeople and the farmers, who grew corn and wheat, helped Nicodemus emerge as a small, briefly thriving community. The first retail stores opened in 1879. Town founder and postmaster Z. T. Fletcher opened the St. Francis Hotel in 1885. Two white residents established the town's newspapers, the *Nicodemus Western Cyclone* in 1886 and the *Nicodemus Enterprise* one year later. By 1886 Nicodemus had three churches and a new schoolhouse.

The town's success attracted other African Americans, including Edwin P. McCabe, who would soon become the most famous black politician outside the South. A Troy, N.Y., native born in 1850, McCabe arrived in Nicodemus in 1878 and began working as a land agent, locating settlers on their claims. In 1880, when Kansas governor John P. St. John established Graham County (which included Nicodemus), McCabe was appointed acting county clerk, beginning a long career of elective and appointive officeholding. In November 1881, McCabe was elected clerk for Graham County, and the following year, at age thirty-two, he became the highest-ranking African-American elected official outside the South when Kansas voters chose him as state auditor. Nicodemus's fortunes, however, began to decline in the late 1880s. An 1885 blizzard destroyed 40 percent of the wheat crop, prompting the first exodus from the area. By 1888 three railroads had bypassed the town, despite its commitment of $16,000 in bonds to attract a rail line. Moreover, toward the end of the decade Oklahoma began to appeal to prospective black homesteaders.

Oklahoma was the most important center of black town activity. Thirty-two all-black towns, the largest number in the nation, emerged in the Twin Territories, Oklahoma Territory and Indian Territory, that became the state of Oklahoma in 1907. The two most famous towns were Langston City in Oklahoma Territory and Boley in Indian Territory. Though the specific reasons for town founding varied, most grew out of the tradition of autonomy among the black ex-slaves of Indian peoples; antiblack violence in the South, which encouraged migration to the Twin Territories; and the political maneuvers of Edwin McCabe and other black politicians who settled in Oklahoma. The government-owned land in Oklahoma was a primary focus of black leaders, who lobbied for the creation of an all-black territory there in the years before 1889. For African Americans like McCabe, Oklahoma Territory, whose former Native American reservations were opened to non-Indian settlement in 1889, represented not only the last major chance for homesteading but also a singular opportunity to develop communities where black people could achieve their economic potential and exercise their political rights without interference. McCabe, who emerged as the leading advocate of black settlement, would also become a town promoter, combining political and racial objectives with personal profit.

McCabe and his wife, Sarah, moved to Oklahoma in April 1890 and six months later joined Charles Robbins, a white land speculator, and William L. Eagleson, a black newspaper publisher, in founding Langston City, an all-black community about ten miles northeast of Guthrie, the territorial capital. Langston City was named after the Virginia black congressman who supported migration to Oklahoma. The McCabes, who owned most of the town lots, immediately began advertising for prospective purchasers through their newspaper, the *Langston City Herald,* which was sold in neighboring states. The *Herald* portrayed the town as an ideal community for African Americans. "Langston City is a Negro City, and we are proud of that fact," proclaimed McCabe in the *Herald.* "Her city officers are all colored. Her teachers are colored. Her public schools furnish thorough educational advantages to nearly two hundred colored children." The *Herald* also touted the agricultural potential of the region, claiming the central Oklahoma prairie could produce superior cotton, wheat, and tobacco. "Here is found a genial climate, about like that of . . . Northern Mississippi . . . admirably suited to the wants of the Negro from the Southern states. A land where every staple . . . can be raised with profit." By February 1892 Langston City had six hundred residents from fifteen states including Georgia, Maryland, and California, with the largest

Headquarters of the Mound Bayou Foundation, an all-black town in Mississippi, subsidized by the Tazoo Mississippi Valley Railroad, January 1939. (Prints and Photographs Division, Library of Congress)

numbers from neighboring Texas. The businesses established included a cotton gin, a soap factory, a bank, and two hotels. An opera house, a racetrack, a billiard parlor, three saloons, masonic lodges, and social clubs provided various forms of entertainment.

Like Nicodemus, Langston City residents hoped a railroad would improve their town's fortunes. Between 1892 and 1900 McCabe waged a steady but ultimately unsuccessful campaign to persuade the St. Louis & San Francisco Railroad to extend its tracks through the town. When the rail line bypassed the town, Langston residents believed they lost their main opportunity to grow. Throughout the railroad campaign, however, town promoters urged other reasons for migration to their community. The *Herald* (no longer owned by the McCabes) continued to emphasize the superior racial climate of the area. McCabe, using his political connections as chief clerk of the territorial legislature in 1896, was able to obtain for Langston City the Colored Agricultural and Normal School (later Langston University). The location of the school, the only publicly supported black educational institution in the territory, in Langston City ensured the town's permanence.

Boley, the largest all-black town in Indian Territory, was founded in the former Creek Nation in 1904 by two white entrepreneurs, William Boley, a roadmaster for the Fort Smith & Western Railroad, and Lake Moore, an attorney and former federal commissioner to the region's Indian tribes. Boley and Moore chose Tom Haynes, an African American, to handle promotion of the town. Unlike Langston City, Boley was on a rail line and in a timbered, well-watered prairie that easily supported the type of agriculture familiar to most prospective black settlers. The frontier character of the town was evident from its founding. Newcomers, who usually arrived by train, were forced to live in tents until they could clear trees and brush to construct homes and stores. During the town's first year, Creek Indians rode several times through Boley's streets on shooting sprees that killed several people. T. T. Ringo, a peace officer appointed by townsite officials, stopped the violence. However, Boley's reputation for lawlessness continued into 1905, when a second peace officer, William Shavers, was killed while leading a posse after a gang of white horse thieves who terrorized the town.

By 1907 Boley had a thousand residents, as well as more than two thousand farmers in the surrounding countryside, and was beginning to take on a permanent air. Boley's businesses included a hotel, sawmill, and cotton gin. Churches, a school, fraternal lodges, women's clubs, and a literary society attest to the cultural development of the town. A community newspaper, the *Boley Progress*, was founded in 1905 to report on local matters and promote town growth. After a visit in 1905, Booker T. WASHINGTON described Boley as a "rude, bustling, Western town [that nonetheless] represented a dawning race consciousness . . . which shall demonstrate the right of the negro . . . to have a worthy place in the civilization that the American people are creating."

Boley's spectacular growth was over by 1910. When the Twin Territories became the state of Oklahoma in 1907, the Democrats emerged as the dominant political party. They quickly disfranchised black voters and segregated public schools and accommodations. Their actions eliminated the town's major appeal as a political center, part of a territory where African Americans escaped the JIM CROW restrictions they faced in southern states. Although blacks continued to vote in local elections, political control at the local level could not compensate for marginal influence at the courthouse or the state capital, where crucial decisions affecting the town's schools and roads were routinely made by unsympathetic officials. Moreover, after the initial years of prosperity, declining agricultural prices and crop failures gradually reduced the number of black farmers who were the foundation of the town's economy. Although Boley remained the center of a famous black rodeo, it ceased to be an important center of black life.

Mound Bayou, Miss., was the most successful all-black town. Founded by the Louisville, New Orleans & Texas Railroad in 1887, the town was situated along the rail line that extended through the Yazoo-Mississippi delta, an area of thick woods, bayous, and swamps that nonetheless contained some of the richest cotton-producing lands in the state. When the fear of swamp-land diseases deterred white settlement, the railroad hired two prominent African-American politicians, James Hill and Isaiah Montgomery, as land promoters. Hill had once been Mississippi's secretary of state, while Montgomery was the patriarch of a family of ex-slaves of Joseph Davis. After the CIVIL WAR, the Montgomery family had acquired the Davis Bend plantations of their former master and of his more famous brother, Confederate president Jefferson Davis. The Davis heirs reclaimed the lands in the 1880s, prompting the Montgomery family to seek other business opportunities.

The railroad, which wanted settlers on the least populated lands along its route, chose a site fifteen miles east of the Mississippi River and ninety miles south of Memphis to establish a town. The four-square-mile area selected included two bayous and several Indian burial mounds, inspiring Montgomery to name the town and colony Mound Bayou. Montgomery, the more active of the two promoters, sold the first town lots to relatives and friends from the Davis Bend plantations. In the fall of 1887 he led the first twelve settlers to Mound Bayou. By 1888 the town had forty residents, and about two hundred people had settled in the surrounding countryside. Twelve years later it had grown to 287 residents, with 1,500 African Americans in the vicinity.

With rail transportation assured and a sizable population of black farmers nearby, Montgomery and other promoters concentrated on efforts to increase business development. Those efforts were helped by his close association with Booker T. Washington. Montgomery and Washington met in 1895 when the Mississippi planter served as a commissioner for the Atlanta Exposition, at which Washington gave the speech that launched his national career. Washington, who saw in Montgomery and Mound Bayou the embodiment of his philosophy of black economic self-help, featured the Mississippian in exhibitions and conferences sponsored by Tuskegee Institute (now TUSKEGEE UNIVERSITY). Montgomery, in turn, used the Tuskegee educator's fame and contacts to attract investors. While Montgomery accepted a federal post in Jackson in 1902 and ceased his direct involvement in Mound Bayou promotional activities, Washington's interest in the town remained strong. He switched his support to merchant-farmer Charles Banks, who settled there in 1904 and founded the Bank of Mound Bayou. In 1908, following a visit to Mound Bayou, the Tuskegee educator prompted a number of flattering articles on the town in national magazines and profiled the community in books he published in 1909 and 1911.

Mound Bayou's population reached eleven hundred in 1911, with nearly eight thousand in the rural area. The sizable population ensured economic support for the town, which featured the largest number of African-American-owned businesses of any of the all-black towns. Mound Bayou's businesses included its bank, a savings and loan association, two sawmills, three cotton gins, and the only black-owned cottonseed mill in the United States. By 1914, however, some businesses, including the Bank of Mound Bayou, closed, and the town experienced its first population losses. Booker T. Washington's death in 1915 initiated a period of estrangement between Isaiah Montgomery and Charles Banks, the promoters most closely identified with the town's fortunes. By the early 1920s the town lost its vitality and began to resemble other small delta communities.

In 1908 white and black land speculators combined to create the westernmost all-black town, Allensworth, Calif. The town was initiated by the California Colony and Home Promoting Association (CCHPA), a black, Los Angeles-based land development company. CCHPA hoped to encourage black settlement in California's rapidly growing San Joaquin Valley, and it envisioned a town as the commercial center of a thriving agricultural colony. Since CCHPA had no resources to purchase land, it joined with three white firms, the Pacific Farming Company (owners of the site of the prospective town), the Central Land Company, and the Los Angeles Purchasing Company, to create an eighty-acre townsite in Tulare County along the Santa Fe Railroad, about halfway between Fresno and Bakersfield. Allensworth was named for Lt. Col. Allen Allensworth, chaplain of the all-black Twenty-fourth Infantry Regiment, and the highest-ranking African American in the U.S. Army. After his retirement, Allensworth settled in Los Angeles, and he became president of the association in 1907.

Initial sales were slow, and by 1910 the town had only eighty residents. Most of the adult residents worked on ten-acre farms nearby, which they purchased for $110 per acre on an installment plan. The town's slow growth prompted Allensworth to intensify his promotional efforts. In January 1912 he sent a lengthy letter to the *New York Age,* the nation's largest African-American newspaper, promoting the townsite and linking it to Booker T. Washington's call for black economic self-help. Allensworth also suggested that his town's objectives were similar to those of Mound Bayou. By May Allensworth began to concentrate recruiting efforts on his former soldiers, issuing a promotional newspaper, *The Sentiment Maker,* which specifically targeted black military personnel.

The town of Allensworth had one hundred residents in 1914. Despite their small numbers, they owned dozens of city lots and three thousand acres of nearby farmland. Oscar O. Overr, a migrant from Topeka, Kans., was the community's most prosperous resident native, with a 640-acre farm and four acres of town lots. In 1914 Overr became California's first elected black justice of the peace. Allensworth also had a twenty-acre park named after Booker T. Washington, and a library named for Colonel Allensworth's wife, Josephine, and which received as its first holdings the family's book collection. After the colonel's death on September 14, 1914, Overr and William A. Payne, the town's first schoolteacher, attempted to establish the Allensworth Agricultural and Manual Training School, modeled after Tuskegee, to train California's black youth in practical skills. They failed to obtain state funding, however, because urban black political leaders feared the school would encourage segregation. The school promotion scheme was the last concerted effort to lure settlers to Allensworth. Except for a brief period in the 1920s, the town's population never exceeded one hundred residents.

One all-black Colorado town, Dearfield, emerged in Weld County. Dearfield was conceived by O. T. Jackson, who arrived in the state in 1887 and became a messenger for Colorado governors. Inspired by Booker T. Washington's book *Up from Slavery,* Jackson went into business. He believed successful farm colonies were possible in Colorado and chose as his first site a 40-acre tract 25 miles southeast of Greeley, which he homesteaded. Jackson attracted other black Denver investors who made additional land purchases. Among them was Dr. J. H. P. Westbrook, a physician, who suggested the name Dearfield. The town's population peaked at seven hundred in 1921, with families occupying nearly fifteen thousand acres in the area. Dearfield's farmers grew wheat, corn, and sugar beets, and like their Weld County neighbors, prospered during WORLD WAR I because of the European demand for American foodstuffs. Town founder Jackson was also its most prominent businessman. He owned the grocery store, restaurant, service station, and dance hall. The war years were the apex of the town's prosperity. Declining agricultural prices and the attractiveness of urban employment caused Dearfield to steadily lose population. Only a handful of "pioneers" remained when Jackson died in Dearfield in 1949.

No town could successfully compete with the attraction of larger cities, which lured millions of Americans from farms and small towns during the twentieth century.

None of the surviving all-black towns are the thriving, prosperous communities envisioned by their promoters. Many, like Nicodemus, Allensworth, and Dearfield, have long been emptied of residents. In the 1990s Boley, Mound Bayou, and Langston City continue, but they are not dynamic centers of economic or cultural activity for their regions. Like thousands of small towns throughout the United States, black communities were subject to the vagaries of transportation access, unpredictable agricultural productivity, detrimental county or state political decisions, and shifting settlement patterns. Moreover, towns such as Nicodemus, Allensworth, and Dearfield, which had few black farmers in their hinterlands to sustain their prosperity, were especially vulnerable to decline.

No town, however, could successfully compete with the attraction of larger cities, which lured millions of Americans from farms and small towns during the twentieth century. Most of these communities began declining in about 1915, the first year of the Great Migration of hundreds of thousands of southern African Americans to northern cities. Moreover, the initial reason for the creation of the towns may have hastened their demise. Blacks could now gain some of the political rights and job opportunities they sought by moving to northern cities rather than small southern or southwestern towns, while the racial insularity of these communities, which seemed attractive to one generation, proved restricting to another. For one brief period in the late nineteenth and early twentieth centuries, a handful of all-black communities throughout the nation symbolized the aspirations of African Americans for political liberty and economic opportunity.

BIBLIOGRAPHY

Crockett, Norman L. *The Black Towns.* Lawrence, Kans., 1979.

Franklin, Jimmie Lewis. *Journey Toward Hope: A History of Blacks in Oklahoma.* Norman, Okla., 1982.

Hamilton, Kenneth Marvin. *Black Towns and Profit: Promotion and Development in the Trans-Appalachian West, 1877–1915.* Urbana, Ill., 1991.

Smallwood, James M. *Time of Hope, Time of Despair: Black Texans During Reconstruction.* Port Washington, N.Y., 1981.

Wayne, George H. "Negro Migration and Colonization in Colorado—1870–1930." *Journal of the West* 15 (1976): 102–120.

— QUINTARD TAYLOR

BLAKE, JAMES HUBERT "EUBIE"

James Hubert "Eubie" Blake (February 7, 1883–February 12, 1983), jazz pianist, composer. Born in Baltimore, Md., the son of former slaves, Eubie Blake began organ lessons at the age of six and was soon syncopating the tunes he heard in his mother's Baptist church. While in his teens he began to play in the RAGTIME style then popular in Baltimore sporting houses and saloons. One of his first professional jobs was as a dancer in a minstrel show, *In Old Kentucky.* During this time Blake also began to compose music, with his first published piece, "Charleston Rag," appearing in 1899. While in his twenties Blake began performing each summer in Atlantic City, where he composed songs ("Tricky Fingers," 1904) and came in contact with such giants of ragtime and stride piano as Willie "The Lion" Smith, Luckey Roberts, and James P. JOHNSON. His melodic style and penchant for waltzes were influenced by the comic operettas of Victor Herbert, Franz Lehar, and Leslie Stuart. During this time Blake began to perform songs in his mature style, which was marked by broken-octave parts and arpeggiated figures, as well as sophisticated chord progressions and altered BLUES chords. In 1910 Blake married Avis Lee, a classical pianist.

In 1916, with the encouragement of bandleader James Reese EUROPE, Blake began performing with Noble Sissle as "The Dixie Duo," a piano-vocal duet. Sissle and Blake performed together on the B. F. Keith vaudeville circuit, and also began writing songs together. In 1921 Sissle and Blake joined with the well-known comedy team of Flournoy Miller and Aubrey Lyles to write *Shuffle Along,* which became so popular in both its Broadway and touring versions that at one point three separate companies were crisscrossing the country performing it. In 1924 Sissle and Blake teamed up with Lew Payton to present *In Bamville,* which later was known as *The Chocolate Dandies.* After the closing of the show in 1925, Sissle and Blake returned to vaudeville, touring the United States, Great Britain, and France. In 1927 Sissle remained in Europe, and Blake teamed up with Henry Creamer to write cabaret shows. In 1928 Blake joined with Henry "Broadway" Jones and a cast of eleven performers to tour the United States on the Keith-Albee Orpheum circuit with *Shuffle Along Jr.* In that year he also wrote "Tickle the Ivories." Two years later Blake set to music lyrics by Andy Razaf for Lew Leslie's *Blackbirds of 1930,* which included "Memories of You," which became one of the best known of Blake's many songs. In 1932, after the death of Lyles, Sissle and Blake reunited with Miller to present *Shuffle Along of 1933,* but the show closed after only fifteen performances. During the Great Depression, Blake wrote several shows with Milton Reddie. *Swing It,* which included the songs "Ain't We Got Love" and "Blues Why Don't You Leave Me Alone," was produced by the WORKS PROGRESS ADMINISTRATION. During the war years Blake performed in U.S.O. shows and wrote *Tan Manhattan* (1943). When "I'm Just Wild About Harry," from *Shuffle Along,* became popular during the 1948 presidential campaign of Harry Truman, Sissle and Blake reunited to update the show. The new version failed to gain popularity, and Blake retired from public life.

James Hubert "Eubie" Blake. (Photographs and Prints Division, Schomburg Center for Research in Black Culture, The New York Public Library, Astor, Lenox and Tilden Foundations)

In the 1960s there was a renewed public interest in ragtime, and Blake recorded *The Eighty-Six Years of Eubie Blake* (1969), an album that led to a resurgence in his career. Thereafter, Blake performed regularly in concert and on television, and continued to compose ("Eubie's Classic Rag," 1972). He performed at jazz festivals in New Orleans (1969) and Newport R.I. (1971). Even in his last years, he retained his remarkable virtuosity on piano, vigorously improvising melodic embellishments to a syncopated ragtime beat. In 1978 the musical revue *Eubie!* enjoyed a long run on Broadway. Blake also established a music publishing and recording company and received numerous honorary degrees and awards, including the Presidential Medal of Freedom in 1981. Blake, whose more than three hundred compositions brought a sophisticated sense of harmony to the conventions of ragtime-derived popular song, was active until his ninety-ninth year, and his centennial in 1983 was an occasion for many tributes. However, the 1982 death of his wife, Marion, to whom he had been married since 1945—his first marriage had ended with the death of his wife, Avis—led to a decline in his own health. He died on February 12, 1983 in Brooklyn, N.Y., only five days after his hundredth birthday.

BIBLIOGRAPHY

Berlin, E. *Ragtime: A Musical and Cultural History.* Berkeley, Calif., 1984.

Bolcom, William, and R. Kimball. *Reminiscing with Sissle and Blake.* New York, 1973.

Graziano, John. "Black Musical Theater and the Harlem Renaissance Movement." In Samuel A. Floyd, Jr., ed. *Black Music in the Harlem Renaissance.* Westport, Conn., 1980.

Rose, A. *Eubie Blake.* New York, 1979.

— JOHN GRAZIANO

BLAKEY, ART

Art Blakey (Buhaina, Abdullah Ibn) (October 11, 1919–October 16, 1990), drummer and bandleader. Born in Pittsburgh, Pa., and orphaned as an infant, Blakey learned enough piano in his foster home and school to organize a group and play a steady engagement at a local nightclub while in his early teens. He later taught himself to play drums, emulating the styles of Kenny Clarke, Chick Webb, and Sid Catlett. Blakey left Pittsburgh for New York City with Mary Lou Williams's band in the fall of 1942, leaving her band in 1943 to tour with the Fletcher Henderson Orchestra. After his stint with Henderson, he briefly formed his own big band in Boston before heading west to St. Louis to join Billy Eckstine's new big bebop band. Blakey remained with the band for its three-year duration, working with other modern JAZZ musicians including Dizzy GILLESPIE, Charlie PARKER, Sarah VAUGHAN, Miles DAVIS, Dexter Gordon, and Fats Navarro.

After Eckstine disbanded the group in 1947, Blakey organized another big band, the Seventeen Messengers. At the end of the year, he took an octet including Kenny Dorham, Sahib Shihab, and Walter Bishop, Jr., into the studio to record for Blue Note Records as the Jazz Messengers. In the same year Blakey joined Thelonious MONK on his historic first recordings for Blue Note, recordings that document both performers as remarkably original artists. The next year Blakey went to Africa to learn more about Islamic culture and subsequently adopted the Arabic name Abdullah Ibn Buhaina. During the early 1950s Blakey continued to perform and record with the leading innovators of his generation, including Charlie Parker, Miles Davis, and Clifford Brown. With his kindred musical spirit, Horace Silver, Blakey in 1955 formed a cooperative group with Kenny Dorham (trumpet), Doug Watkins (bass), and Hank Mobley (tenor saxophone), naming the quintet the Jazz Messengers. When Silver left the group in 1956, Blakey assumed leadership of the seminal hard bop group, renowned for combining solid, swinging jazz with rhythm and blues, gospel, and blues idioms.

Blakey's commitment to preserving the quintessence of the hard bop tradition lasted unflaggingly for over thirty-five years. His group toured widely, serving both as a school for young musicians and the definitive standard for what has become known as "straight-ahead jazz." Blakey's Jazz Messengers graduated from its ranks many of the most influential figures in jazz, including Wayne Shorter, Freddie Hubbard, Donald Byrd, Jackie McLean, Lee Morgan, Johnny Griffin, Woody Shaw, Keith Jarrett, JoAnn Brackeen, Branford, Delfayo, and Wynton MARSALIS, Donald Harrison, and Terence Blanchard. A drummer famous for his forceful intensity, hard swinging grooves, and an inimitable press roll, Blakey also adopted several African drumming techniques—including rapping the sides of his drums and altering the pitch of the tom-toms with his elbow—which expanded the timbral and tonal vocabulary of JAZZ drumming. His drumming style as an accompanist is characterized by an unwavering cymbal beat punctuated by cross-rhythmic accents on the drums. A distinctive soloist, Blakey exploited the full dynamic potential of his instrument, often displaying a command of rhythmic modulation and a powerful expressiveness that incorporated polyrhythmic conceptual influences from West Africa and Cuba. In addition to his singular achievements as a drummer and bandleader, Blakey also served as a catalyst in bringing together percussionists from diverse traditions to perform and record in a variety of ensembles. His versatility as a drummer outside of the context of his own group received global recognition during his 1971–1972 tour with the Giants of Jazz, which included Dizzy Gillespie, Sonny Stitt, Thelonious Monk, Kai Winding, and Al McKibbon. Blakey died in New York City in 1990.

BIBLIOGRAPHY

Porter, Lewis. "Art Blakey." In Barry Kernfeld, ed. *The New Grove Dictionary of Jazz.* London, 1988, pp. 115–116.

Southern, Eileen. "Art Blakey." *Biographical Dictionary of Afro-American and African Musicians.* Westport, Conn., 1982, p. 37.

— ANTHONY BROWN

BLUES, THE

A type of African-American musical art that was first developed in the Mississippi Delta region of Louisiana at the end of the nineteenth century, the blues, like many musical expressions, is difficult to define. Some people think of the blues as an emotion; others regard it primarily as a musical genre characterized by a special blues scale, containing twelve bars and three chords in a particular order. Besides embodying a particular feeling (the "blues") and form, the blues also involves voice and movement: poetry set to dance music. It is vocal not only in the obvious sense that most blues songs have lyrics, but in that even in purely instrumental blues, the lead instrument models its expressivity on the singing voice; and it involves dance because it quite literally moves listeners—even when they are sitting down. Its influence on JAZZ, GOSPEL MUSIC, theater music, rock, and almost every subsequent form of popular music in the twentieth century has been incalculable.

Early blues singers composed their own songs, inventing verses and borrowing from other singers, and they were among the first Americans to express feelings of *anomie* characteristic of modern life and to rise above it through art. By singing about frustration, mistreatment, and misfortune and often overcoming it with irony, blues singers helped themselves and their listeners to deal with the problems of life, whether frustrated and angered by cheating lovers, ignorant bosses, hypocritical churchgoers, crooked shopkeepers, an unjust legal system, racism and prejudice, police brutality, inadequate pay, unemployment, or the meaninglessness of menial labor. Blues singers fought adversity by asserting human creativity, by turning life into art through ironic signification, by linking themselves through their traditional art to others in the community, and by holding out a future hope for freedom and better times down the road. The blues as music and poetry can convey a tremendous range of emotions succinctly and powerfully. Blues lyrics represent an oral poetry of considerable merit, one of the finest genres of vernacular poetry in the English language.

The blues is a distinct musical type. It is an instrumentally accompanied song-type with identifying features in its verse, melodic, and harmonic structures, composition, and accompaniment. Most blues lyrics are set in three-line or quatrain-refrain verses. In the three-line verse shown below, the second line repeats the first, sometimes with slight variation, while the third completes the thought with a rhyme.

> I'm gonna dig me a hole this morning, dig it deep down in the ground;
> I'm gonna dig me a hole this morning, dig it deep down in the ground;
> So if it should happen to drop a bomb around somewhere, I can't hear the echo when it sound.
> ("Lightnin' " Hopkins, "War News Blues")

In the quatrain-refrain verse shown below a rhymed quatrain is followed by a two-line refrain. Each verse form occupies twelve measures or bars of music; in the quatrain-refrain form the quatrain occupies the first four of the twelve.

> I got a job in a steel mill,
> a-trucking steel like a slave.
> For five long years every Friday
> I went straight home with all my pay.
> If you've ever been mistreated, you know just what I'm talking about:
> I worked five long years for one woman; she had the nerve to throw me out.
> (Eddie Boyd, "Five Long Years")

The tonal material in the blues scale (illustrated herewith) includes both major and minor thirds and sevenths and perfect and diminished fifths. Blues shares this tonal material with other African-American music such as work songs, lined hymnody, gospel music, and jazz. A sharp rise to the highest pitch followed by a gradual descent characterizes the melodic contour of most vocal lines in each verse. Blues shares this contour with the field holler, a type of work song.

Blues has a distinctive harmonic structure. The first line of the verse (or the quatrain in the quatrain-refrain form) is supported by the tonic chord (and sometimes the subdominant, resolving to the tonic at the end of the line), the second line by the subdominant (resolving to the tonic), and the third line by the dominant seventh and then the subdominant before resolving to the tonic. Urban blues and jazz musicians modify this harmonic structure with altered chords and chord substitutions. The blues also has characteristic contents and performance styles. Most blues lyrics are dramatic monologues sung in the first person; most protest mistreatment by lovers and express a desire for freedom. Early blues singers improvised songs by yoking together lines and verses from a storehouse in their memories; most of today's singers memorize entire songs.

Most early down-home blues singers accompanied themselves on piano or on guitar, on the latter supplying a bass part with the right-hand thumb and a treble part independently with the right-hand fingers. Early vaudeville or classic blues singers were accompanied by pianists and small jazz combos. In the 1930s or after, blues "shouters" were accompanied by jazz and RHYTHM 'N' BLUES bands, and this led in the 1940s to urban blues singers who played electric guitar and led their own bands. After WORLD WAR II, most down-home blues singers played electric guitar, sometimes with a small combination of bass, drums, second guitar, harmonica, or piano.

The beginning of blues cannot be traced to a specific composer or date. The earliest appearance of music recognizable as the blues was the publication of W. C. HANDY's "The Memphis Blues" (1912) and the "St. Louis Blues" (1914), but by his own testimony, Handy first heard the blues along the lower Mississippi River in the 1890s, and many historians agree with Handy that this was the likeliest environment for the origin of the blues. However, just when and where one locates the origin of blues depends upon what is considered sufficient to the genre. Some cultural historians locate the essence of the blues in resignation or in protest against mistreatment, and they believe that since slaves sung about their condition, these songs must have been blues, even though there is no evidence that they were called blues or that the verse or musical forms resembled later blues. Folklorists and musicologists, on the other hand, have constructed a narrower definition, essentializing structural aspects of the blues as well as their subject and relying for evidence on a combination of oral history, autobiography, and the first blues music recorded by the oldest generation of African Americans.

W. C. Handy and "Jelly Roll" MORTON, well-known and accomplished African-American musicians who were very much involved in music before the turn of the twentieth century, recalled in their autobiographies that blues began along the Mississippi in the 1890s as a secular dance music, accompanied by guitars and other portable instruments or piano, with more or less improvised verses, among the river roustabouts in the juke joints and barrelhouses and at picnic and other roadside entertainments. About 1900, folklorists first collected this music, but did not realize they were witnessing the formation of a new genre. Verse patterns varied, the only standard feature being the repetition of the first line; sometimes once, sometimes twice, sometimes three times. The verses were aphoristic, and their subjects concerned lovers, traveling, and daily aspects of life. Harmonic support often was confined to the tonic. The collectors did not call those songs blues, and we may suppose that the singers did not, either.

The first recordings of African Americans singing blues were not made until the 1920s, but it is clear that between 1890 and 1920 the blues developed into a named and recognizable musical genre. In this period the blues developed and diffused wherever there were African Americans in the United States, in the rural areas as well as the towns and cities and among the traveling stage shows. Ma Rainey, the "mother of the blues," claimed to have begun singing blues from the stage in 1902, while "Jelly Roll" Morton identified a blues ballad, "Betty and Dupree," as popular fare in New Orleans during the last years of the nineteenth century. Handy's "Memphis Blues" was used in the 1912 mayoralty campaign, while "St. Louis Blues" was a show tune designed to elevate blues to a higher class. Rural songs at country dance parties gradually consolidated toward three-line verse forms with twelve-measure stanzas and the typical harmonic pattern indicated above, while many of the stage songs featured two sections, an introduction followed by a section in recognizable blues form. The stage songs later became known as "classic" or "vaudeville" blues.

African Americans recorded vaudeville blues beginning with Mamie Smith in 1920. Women with stage-show backgrounds, accompanied by pianists and small combos, sang blues songs composed by professional tunesmiths. The best of the vaudeville blues singers, Ma Rainey and Bessie SMITH, appealed across racial and class boundaries, and their singing styles revolutionized American popular music. In some of their blues, Rainey and Smith sang about strong, independent women who put an end to mistreatment. Rainey in particular, who sang about such subjects as prostitution, lesbianism, and sadomasochistic relationships, may be viewed as a spokesperson for women's rights. Other vaudeville blues singers, such as Mamie Smith, Sippie Wallace, Ida Cox, and Alberta Hunter, were also very popular in the 1920s, but the era of vaudeville or "classic" blues came to an end during the Great Depression. The down-home or country-flavored blues was recorded beginning in 1926, when record companies took portable recording equipment to southern cities and recorded the local men who sang the blues and accompanied themselves on guitars and pianos in the juke joints and at the country dance parties. Some of the older singers like Charley Patton and Henry Thomas (1874–c. 1959) sang a variety of traditional songs, not all blues; others, like "Blind" Lemon Jefferson, specialized in blues; yet others, like Blind Blake, achieved instrumental virtuosity that has never been surpassed. The variety of traditional music recorded by the older generation reveals the proto-blues as well as the blues and helps to show how the form evolved.

Geographic regions featured their own particular instrumental guitar styles before WORLD WAR II. The down-home blues of Florida, Georgia, and the Carolinas tended toward rapidly finger-picked accompaniments: "ragtime" styles in which the right-hand thumb imitated the stride pianist's left hand, while the right-hand fingers played melody. Blind Blake, Blind Boy Fuller (c. 1909–1941), and Blind Gary Davis (1896–1972) were among the first exponents of this East Coast style. In Mississippi, on the other hand, chord changes were not as pronounced, and accompaniments featured repeated figures, or riffs, rather than the melody of the verse. Charley Patton, "Son" House (1902–1988), Robert JOHNSON, and Muddy Waters (McKinley Morganfield) were outstanding guitarists in the Mississippi Delta style. Piano styles equally reflected regional differences. All embodied genuine innovations, such as bottleneck or slide guitar or imitating the expressiveness of the voice, and an inventiveness and technical accomplishment unparalleled in vernacular American music.

Down-home blues became so popular in the late 1920s that talent scouts arranged for singers to travel north to make recordings in the companies' home studios. Blues music was available on what were called "race records," 78-rpm records for African Americans, and they were advertised heavily in black newspapers like the Chicago *Defender*.

While early recordings offer the best evidence of the sound of blues music in its formative years, they can only begin to capture the feel of an actual performance. Because down-home blues usually was performed in barrelhouses, juke joints, at parties, and picnics where the bootleg whiskey flowed, gambling took place, fighting was not uncommon, and sexual liaisons were formed, the music became associated with those who frequented these places. Churchgoers shunned blues because it was associated with sin, while middle-class blacks kept blues at a distance. Most communities, whether rural or urban, had their local blues musicians and entertainments, however. In the 1920s, blues was the most popular African-American music.

The depression cut heavily into record sales and touring stage shows, and most of the classic blues singers' careers ended. The increasing popularity of jazz music provided an opportunity for their successors to tour and record with jazz bands. The down-home blues continued unabated in the rural South and in the cities. A small number of outstanding down-home singers, including Tommy McClennan (1908–1960) Memphis Minnie (McCoy), and Robert Johnson, made commercial recordings, but the big-band blues of Count BASIE and other jazz bands, featuring blues "shouters" like Walter Brown, Jimmy Rushing, and "Hot Lips" Page, rode radio broadcasts and records to national popularity later in the 1930s. The blues form became a common ground for jazz improvisors, and jazz artists of the highest stature, from Louis ARMSTRONG through Duke ELLINGTON, Billie HOLIDAY, and Charlie PARKER, Sarah VAUGHAN, Miles DAVIS, John COLTRANE, and Wynton MARSALIS, composed and improvised a great many blues. For Charles MINGUS, one of the most important jazz innovators of the 1950s and 1960s, blues and church music were the twin African-American cornerstones of jazz, and much of his music successfully integrated these roots into contemporary "soul" music. Indeed, since the 1940s, periodic reinvigorations of jazz have taken blues for their basis, and it appears that they will continue to do so: bop, hard bop, funk, and other jazz movements all looked for inspiration in blues roots.

Besides the jazz bands, blues in the 1940s and '50s was featured in the urban and rhythm 'n' blues bands led by such guitarists-singers as (Aaron) "T-bone" Walker and (Riley) B. B. [Blues Boy] King, whose spectacular instrumental innovations virtually defined the genre and influenced countless blues and rock guitarists. Electronic amplification of the guitar allowed it to be heard above the piano and brass and reed instruments; Walker's pioneering efforts virtually invented the modern blues band, the core of which is an electric guitar accompanied by a rhythm section. King's live performances combined instrumental virtuosity in the service of great feeling with a powerful, expressive voice that transformed daily experience into meaningful art, and he spoke to and for an entire generation. His album *B. B. King Live at the Regal* (1965) is often cited as the finest blues recording ever made.

Down-home blues was well served in the years just after World War II by a host of new recording companies. Among the outstanding singer-guitarists were Sam "Lightnin' " Hopkins from Houston and John Lee Hooker from Mississippi (and later Detroit) who, along with West Helena and Arkansas harmonica-player "Sonny Boy Williamson" (Rice Miller), contributed a magnificent body of original blues lyric poetry. The Mississippi Delta connection led to such singers as Muddy Waters and Howlin' Wolf (Chester Burnett), who led small combos in Chicago after 1945 that helped create the Chicago blues style, basically a version of the Delta blues played on electrified and amplified instruments. Muddy Waters' band of the early 1950s, featuring "Little" Walter (Jacobs) on amplified harmonica, defined a classic Chicago blues sound that many think was the high point of the genre. With his horn-influenced, amplified harmonica solos, "Little" Walter invented a completely new sound, and his work stands as another influential example in a music with a history of astonishing technological innovation in the service of greater expressivity. A cluster of post-World War II artists including Waters, Wolf, Jimmy Reed (1925–1976), John Lee Hooker, Elmore James, Little Walter, Sonny Boy Williamson (Rice Miller), and others greatly influenced rock 'n' roll in the 1960s, while a number of similar artists, relying heavily on blues, such as Fats Domino and Chuck Berry, helped to define ROCK 'N' ROLL in the 1950s.

In the 1960s, the African-American audience for blues declined, while the white audience increased and the first "blues revival" occurred. Young white musicians and researchers rediscovered older down-home blues singers such as Son House and Mississippi John Hurt, and blues singers and bands became featured acts in coffeehouses, clubs, and festivals that catered to a college-age white audience. Many blues singers' musical careers were extended by this attention. Young white musicians began to play and sing the music, and, along with traditional blues musicians, found a new audience. Earlier recordings were reissued for collectors, research magazines devoted to blues appeared, and cultural historians and scholars began writing about the music. Although black musicians continue to perform blues in traditional venues—bars, juke joints, etc.—particularly in Chicago and in the Mississippi Delta, since the 1960s, newer styles such as MOTOWN, soul music, disco, funk, RAP, and hip-hop eclipsed blues as popular music among African Americans.

In the early 1990s, another blues revival began to take place. As a resurgence of interest in blues occurs, older blues recordings are being reissued on CD, and some recordings, such as those of Robert Johnson, sell extremely well, while younger singers and musicians, black and white, increasingly choose to perform and record blues. Blues radio shows, such as the one hosted on National Public Radio by Ruth Brown, have increased the music's visibility and popularity. Blues now appears as background music for ads on radio and television. Nightclubs featuring blues can now be found in many American cities, and older artists such as Robert Jr. Lockwood (1915–) and Buddy Guy (1936–) have had new careers, while younger artists such as the Holmes Brothers and Robert Cray have come to prominence. Some southern cities and states, such as Memphis and Mississippi, have set up a significant tourist industry around blues, and there are blues museums and monuments as well. Thirty years ago, it was a music in decline, known outside African-American culture only to a small number of aficionados; but today the blues is historicized, an official part of American and African-American culture. Thirty years ago, literary critics and cultural historians saw little use for the blues, viewing it as a music of slave-consciousness and resignation; but today a new generation of African-American writers, such as Henry Louis Gates, Jr., and Houston Baker, see blues as a source of black pride and a root tradition. As such, blues has had a profound effect upon African-American life and, lately, upon popular culture throughout the world where it and its musical offspring have spread.

Thirty years ago, it was a music in decline; today the blues is historicized, an official part of American and African-American culture.

BIBLIOGRAPHY

Baker, Houston. *Blues, Ideology and Afro-American Literature: A Vernacular Theory.* Chicago, 1984.

Evans, David. *Big Road Blues: Tradition and Creativity in the Folk Blues.* Berkeley, Calif., 1982.

Gates, Henry Louis, Jr. *The Signifying Monkey: A Theory of African-American Literary Criticism.* New York, 1988.

George, Nelson. *The Death of Rhythm and Blues.* New York, 1988.

Hart, Mary, et al., eds. *The Blues: A Bibliographical Guide.* New York, 1989.

Lieb, Sandra. *Mother of the Blues: A Study of Ma Rainey.* Amherst, Mass., 1981.

Oliver, Paul, ed. *The Blackwell Guide to Blues Recordings.* New York, 1989.

Palmer, Robert. *Deep Blues.* New York, 1981.

Pearson, Barry Lee. *"Sounds So Good to Me": The Bluesman's Story.* Philadelphia, 1984.

Sawyer, Charles. *The Arrival of B. B. King.* London, 1982.

Titon, Jeff Todd. *Early Downhome Blues: A Musical and Cultural Analysis.* Urbana, Ill., 1977.

Titon, Jeff Todd, ed. *Downhome Blues Lyrics: An Anthology from the Post-World War II Era.* 2nd ed. Urbana, Ill., 1990.

– JEFF TODD TITON

BOND, JULIAN

Julian Bond (January 14, 1940–), activist, elected official. Julian Bond was born in Nashville, Tenn., of a prominent family of educators and authors. He grew up in the town of Lincoln University, Pa., where his father, Horace Mann Bond, was then president of the university, and later in Atlanta, when his father became president of Atlanta University. While attending Morehouse College in the early 1960s, Julian Bond helped found the Committee on Appeal for Human Rights. He dropped out of Morehouse to join the STUDENT NONVIOLENT COORDINATING COMMITTEE (SNCC), of which he became communications director in 1962. In 1964 he traveled to Africa and upon his return became a feature writer for the *Atlanta Inquirer.* Later he was named its managing editor. He eventually received his B.A. from Morehouse in 1981.

Bond won election to the Georgia House of Representatives in 1965, triggering controversy. On January 10, 1966, fellow legislators voted to prevent him from taking his seat in the house when he refused to retract his widely publicized support of draft evasion and anti-Vietnam activism. Protest in defense of Bond's right to expression was strong and widespread. Both SNCC and the SOUTHERN CHRISTIAN LEADERSHIP CONFERENCE (SCLC) sought mass support for Bond through community meetings, where discussion and ferment strengthened African-American awareness of the relationship between peace activism and the civil rights struggle. The Rev. Dr. Martin Luther KING, Jr., rallied to Bond's defense, Vice President Hubert Humphrey publicly supported Bond, and noted cultural figures took out ads for pro-Bond campaigns.

After nearly a year of litigation, the U.S. Supreme Court ruled that Bond's disqualification was unconstitutional. The Georgia house was forced to seat Bond, and he remained in the house until 1975. In 1968 Bond was presented as a possible vice presidential candidate by opposition Democrats at the Democratic Convention in Chicago. He was too young, however, to qualify for the office, and his name was withdrawn. In 1972 he published *A Time to Speak, a Time to Act: The Movement in Politics,* in which he discussed ways of channeling civil rights activism into the electoral system. In 1975 Bond was elected to the Georgia state senate, where he served for twelve years. His activities during this period included the presidency of the Atlanta NAACP, where he served until 1989, and service as the narrator of both parts of the popular PBS documentary series about the CIVIL RIGHTS MOVEMENT, "Eyes on the Prize" (1985–1986, 1988–1989).

In 1986 Bond ran for U.S. Congress from Georgia and narrowly lost in a bitter contest with John Lewis, his former civil rights colleague. In the early 1990s Bond served as visiting professor and fellow at various colleges, including the University of Pennsylvania, Drexel University, Harvard University, and the University of Virginia, and was a frequent essayist and commentator on political issues. He also was, in the early 1990s, the host of a syndicated television program, *TV's Black Forum.* In 1996 Bond was elected Chair of the Board of the NAACP.

BIBLIOGRAPHY

Lewis, Amy. "Julian Bond." In William McGuire and Leslie Wheeler, eds. *American Social Leaders.* Santa Barbara, Calif., 1993.

Neary, John. *Julian Bond: Black Rebel.* New York, 1971.

– EVAN A. SHORE AND GREG ROBINSON

BONTEMPS, ARNA

Arna Bontemps (October 13, 1902–June 4, 1973), writer. Arna Bontemps—poet, playwright, novelist, critic, editor, and anthologist—was a leading figure in the HARLEM RENAISSANCE of the 1920s and 1930s. His work is distinguished by a passionate struggle for liberation and a mystical faith in the unseen. The latter may derive from his early religious training, for his parents were Seventh-Day Adventists. Born in Alexandria, La., in 1902, Bontemps grew up in Los Angeles. The early death of his mother left him in the care of an austere father and his grandparents. Upon his graduation from San Fernando Academy in 1920, he enrolled in Pacific Union College, another Seventh-Day Adventist institution, where he earned an A.B. degree in 1923.

In 1924 Bontemps went to New York, where he met other young writers, including Langston HUGHES, Countee CULLEN, and Claude MCKAY. He was stimulated by the cultural vitality of New York—its theater, its music, its concern with world affairs, and the struggle of its black people for social recognition and cultural realization. Bontemps taught in Adventist schools, such as the Harlem Academy, and began his serious career as a writer. His first novel, *God Sends Sunday,* published in 1931, is the story of Little Augie, a jockey who earns a great deal of money and spends it lavishly on brothels, women, and fancy cars. The character was suggested by a great-uncle of Bontemps. Bontemps and Countee Cullen transformed the story of Little Augie into a musical, *St. Louis Woman,* which played on Broadway in 1946.

Bontemps's historical novel *Black Thunder* (1936), among the first of the genre in African-American literature, was based on a Virginia slave revolt in 1800. *Drums at Dusk* (1939), more superficial and romantic than *Black Thunder,* deals with the Pierre Toussaint-Louverture uprising in Haiti. Other historical works include *We Have Tomorrow* (1945) and the biography *Frederick Douglass: Slave, Fighter, Freeman* (1958). In collaboration with Jack Conroy, Bontemps wrote a history of black migration, *They Seek a City* (1945; updated in 1966 as *Any Place but Here.*)

In 1932 Bontemps coauthored, with Langston Hughes, *Popo and Fifine: Children of Haiti.* He and Conroy also produced a series of original tales for children: *The Fast Sooner Hound* (1942); *Slappy Hooper, the Wonderful Sign Painter* (1946); and *Sam Patch, the High, Wide and Handsome Jumper* (1951). In writing books for children, Bontemps made a major contribution, since juvenile literature written by and for African Americans was virtually nonexistent at the time. In 1956 he received the Jane Addams Children's Book Award for *Story of the Negro* (1948).

Bontemp's work is distinguished by a passionate struggle for liberation and a mystical faith in the unseen.

Throughout his career, Bontemps produced original poetry, notable for its brooding quality and its suggestive treatment of protest and black pride. "A Black Man Talks of Reaping," which won a *Crisis* magazine first prize in 1926, is one of the strongest of his protest poems. "Golgotha Is a Mountain" and "The Return" won the Alexander Pushkin Award for Poetry offered by *Opportunity* magazine in 1926 and 1927, respectively. *Personals,* a collection of his poems, was published in 1963 by Paul Bremen in London.

In 1943 Bontemps became head librarian at Fisk University in Nashville, Tenn.; in 1965, he became director of university relations. From 1966 to 1969 he was a professor at the Chicago Circle campus of the University of Illinois and in 1969 served as visiting professor and curator of the James Weldon Johnson Collection at Yale University. In 1970 he returned to Fisk as writer-in-residence; he died there in 1973.

BIBLIOGRAPHY

Bontemps, Arna. *The Harlem Renaissance Remembered.* New York, 1972.

———. *The Old South.* New York, 1973.

Hughes, Langston, and Arna Bontemps. *Book of Negro Folktales.* New York, 1958.

– CHARLES H. NICHOLS

BOXING

Despite the fact that professional prizefighters and sites for professional BOXING matches are found all over the world, the origins of modern BOXING can be traced to one country and era: late eighteenth- and early nineteenth-century England.

Although proto-forms of combat or blood sports existed in ancient Greece and Rome, they have little connection with the sport of boxing as practiced and understood today. The antecedent of modern boxing was bare-knuckle prizefighting, which sprang up in England almost simultaneously with that country's emergence as a major capitalist world power.

To be sure, the less restrictive moral atmosphere accompanying the decline of Puritanism in the mid-1600s permitted a revival of the rough sports of antiquity. Early on, boxing had close ties to the city, as it was supported by urban wealth when local squires migrated to the metropolis along with increasing numbers of working-class men. Boxing's rise came in large part from the growth of commercialized leisure and popular recreation.

Before the rules formulated by Jack Broughton, one of the earliest of the new breed of "scientific boxers" who appeared on the English sporting scene in the early 1730s, bare-knuckle fighting largely consisted of butting, scratching, wrestling, and kicking. Under the Broughton Rules, elements of wrestling remained, but there was more emphasis on the fists, on skilled defensive maneuvers, and on different styles of throwing a punch effectively. Broughton, for instance, developed the technique called "milling on the retreat," or moving backward while drawing one's opponent into punches, a technique Muhammad ALI used to great effect during his reign as heavyweight champion over two hundred years later. Broughton also used gloves or "mitts" for training his pupils, many of whom were among England's leading citizens.

Under the Broughton Rules, which were superseded by the London Prize Ring Rules in 1838, boxers fought for indeterminate lengths of time, a fight not being declared ended until one could not come up to the scratch mark in the center of the ring. A round lasted until one fighter was felled; both men then returned to their corners and were given thirty seconds to "make scratch" again. London Prize Ring Rules governed the sport of prizefighting as a bare-knuckle contest until the coming of gloves and the Marquis of Queensberry Rules. The first heavyweight championship fight under Queensberry Rules was held between the aging John L. Sullivan and James J. "Jim" Corbett on September 7, 1892. Not only did the fight usher in the age of Queensberry, it also ushered in the age of American domination of the sport, as both Sullivan and Corbett were Americans.

The golden age of bare-knuckle fighting in England, overlapping with the Regency period, occurred between 1800 and 1824, an era captured by Pierce Egan, one of the earliest boxing journalists, in his classic work *Boxiana.* It is during this era that there is record of the first black boxers of note. Bill Richmond was a slave who learned to box by sparring with British seamen. He was taken to England in 1777 by Gen. Earl Percy, a commander of British forces in New York during the American Revolution. Richmond, known as "the Black Terror," became the first American to achieve fame as a prizefighter. He stood about five feet tall and weighed between 155 and 170 pounds. Richmond beat such established British fighters as Paddy Green and Frank Mayers. Among his losses was one in 1805 to the British champion Tom Cribb, who was a title aspirant at the time. Richmond, who died in London, is probably best known not for his fighting but for being a second to the first black fighter to challenge for the championship.

That man, also an American ex-slave, made an even bigger name for himself as a prizefighter. Tom Molineaux apparently came from a boxing family, as it has been claimed that his father was an accomplished plantation scrapper. While there is no record of Molineaux's career before his arrival in England, it is well established that many planters engaged their more athletic slaves in sports. Since most young planters had taken the obligatory European tour and discovered boxing to be the rage among British gentlemen, it is little wonder they imported it to America.

Molineaux, who became known in England as "the Moor," arrived in England in 1809 and quickly defeated Bill Burrows and Tom Blake. Molineaux was matched with Tom Cribb, the champion, for the first time on

December 18, 1810, a bitterly cold day (during the bare-knuckle era, most fights took place outdoors). It was one of the most talked-about and eagerly anticipated sports events in British history. Molineaux apparently won the fight, knocking Cribb out in the twenty-eighth round. However, Cribb's seconds accused Molineaux of illegal tactics. During the pandemonium that ensued, Cribb was able to recover, finish the fight, and beat Molineaux, largely because the black boxer had become chilled by the damp cold. The two men fought a rematch in 1811, with Cribb the easy winner, as Molineaux had failed to train and had generally succumbed to dissipation. He went downhill rapidly after his second loss to Cribb and died in Ireland in 1818, a shell of the figure he had been in his prime.

Despite the impact of Richmond and Molineaux, blacks did not constitute a significant presence in boxing until the late nineteenth and early twentieth centuries, when the United States became the principal venue for professional matches. This era can be referred to as the pre-Jack JOHNSON age, as the coming of Johnson signified a new epoch not only in boxing but in American sports history. The years 1890 and 1905 are considered among the worst in American race relations, when blacks experienced JIM CROW and American racist practices in their most virulent, oppressive, and blatant forms. Life for black fighters was far from easy: They often were denied fights against whites or, if permitted, found they were expected to throw the fight. They were paid less and fought far more often than did their white counterparts.

Among the important black fighters of this era were Peter Jackson, George Dixon, Joe Gans, and Jersey Joe Walcott. The latter three were all champions in the lighter weight divisions. Boxing under the Queensberry Rules had evolved to the point where there were now firmly established weight divisions, unlike during the bare-knuckle days of Richmond and Molineaux, when boxers fought at "open weight," and there were sometimes great weight disparities between the contestants.

Peter Jackson was arguably the best heavyweight of his generation. Many experts felt he could have taken the measure of the then-champion, John L. Sullivan, had not Sullivan—in keeping with the intense racism of the times—drawn the color line and refused to meet Jackson. The "Black Prince," as Jackson was called, was born in St. Croix, Virgin Islands. His family emigrated to Australia when he was twelve years old and returned to the Virgin Islands three years later. Jackson did not come back with them, opting to seek his fortune as a sailor. During his years as a sailor, Jackson developed his boxing skills. He became the Australian heavyweight champion, but on discovering that America was a place to make one's name, he emigrated in 1888.

At the age of thirty, in 1891, Jackson fought contender Jim Corbett to a sixty-one-round draw, but it was Corbett who fought Sullivan for the title the following year. Although Jackson enjoyed success as a fighter, he left the ring for the stage, as he was unable to obtain a title match against either Sullivan or Corbett once Corbett defeated Sullivan for the championship. Jackson toured with a stage production of *Uncle Tom's Cabin* for several years. At thirty-seven, out of condition and well past his prime, he tried a comeback against Jim Jeffries, only to be knocked out in three rounds. Despite the frustration Jackson endured, he was widely admired by many white sports enthusiasts for his gentlemanly demeanor, and he was idolized by blacks. The abolitionist Frederick DOUGLASS in his old age hung a portrait of Jackson in his home. Jackson died of consumption in Australia in 1901.

George Dixon, known to the world as "Little Chocolate," was a smooth and cagey boxer who began his professional career on November 1, 1886. He first became bantamweight champion, although there was dispute about the exact weight qualification for this division. He eventually became the world featherweight champion, a title he held from 1892 to 1900. Dixon was a popular fighter, often featured in white sporting publications such as the *National Police Gazette,* as well as being seen in the haunts of the black entertainment world. Life in the sporting world eventually dissipated Dixon, who was knocked out by Terry McGovern in New York in 1900. He lost his last fight to Monk Newsboy in 1906 and died penniless and broken in health in 1909.

Joe Gans, "the Old Master," is considered by many historians of boxing to be one of the greatest lightweights of all time. He was born in Baltimore on November 25, 1874, and launched his professional career in 1891. He reigned as lightweight champion from 1902 to 1908. Gans was plagued by ill health, eventually losing his title to Battling Nelson in a rematch. In 1909, he tried to win his title back in another battle against Nelson, but he was sick and aging and easily beaten. Gans died a year later of tuberculosis. It has been suggested that he became a follower of FATHER DIVINE before his death. Gans died in Baltimore, and Divine was living there at the time, although at this stage in his career, Divine was virtually unknown as a black religious leader. As Divine was known as a healer (it is not clear whether, at this stage, his followers believed he was God, as they later did) and Gans was afflicted with a disease with no known cure that ravaged the black community, he may have been drawn to Divine as a last-ditch effort to seek a cure.

Joe Walcott was born in Barbados on March 13, 1873. Called "the Barbados Demon" because of his whirlwind punching power and ability to endure punishment (a style that can be likened to that of the popular 1970s junior welterweight champion Aaron Pryor), Walcott held the welterweight title from 1898 to 1906. He retired from the ring in 1911 and worked for a time as a janitor, winding up, as many black fighters did, with no money from his ring efforts. He was killed in an automobile accident in 1935.

From 1908 to the present, the history of blacks in boxing can be divided into three periods: the Jack Johnson era (1908–1915), the Joe Louis era (1937–1949), and the Muhammad Ali era (1964–1978). There have been many impressive and important black fighters aside from these heavyweight champions: Henry Armstrong, a dominant force in the 1930s, who became champion of the featherweight, lightweight, and welterweight divisions simultaneously, the first fighter to achieve such a feat; Sugar Ray Robinson, welterweight champion and winner of the middleweight title on five different occasions, who dominated his weight division in the 1950s and was probably one of the most stylish and influential boxers in history; Archie Moore, "the Old Mongoose," who was champion of the light heavyweight division from 1952 and 1962; Floyd Patterson, Olympic champion in 1952, heavyweight champion from 1956 to 1962, one of the youngest men ever to hold that title; Sugar Ray Leonard, Olympic champion in 1976, champion in the welterweight, junior middleweight, middleweight, and super middleweight divisions, one of the most popular fighters in the 1980s; and the controversial Mike Tyson, who was imprisoned for rape, the youngest man ever to win the heavyweight championship when he won the belt in 1986, and one of the most ferocious and unrelenting fighters ever to enter the ring.

Billy Jordan, introducing Jack Johnson in Reno, Nev., July 4, 1910, prior to his heavyweight title defense against former champion James J. Jeffries. Jeffries, the most accomplished of the "white hopes" put forward to defeat Johnson, was knocked out in the fifteenth round. (Prints and Photographs Division, Library of Congress)

These are a few of the notable black fighters of the twentieth century. But none of these men exercised the social and political impact on American society that Johnson, Louis, and Ali did. These three not only changed boxing, but their presences reverberated throughout the world of sport and beyond. People who normally had no interest in either boxing or sport took an interest in the careers of these three.

Jack Johnson learned the craft of boxing as a child in the same manner many black youngsters were forced to: through participating in battles royal, where five, six, or seven black youngsters were blindfolded and fought against one another in a general melee. The toughest survived the ordeal and made the most money. It may be argued that battles royal were not necessarily more brutal than ordinary prizefights, but they were surely far more degrading.

Johnson fought his first professional fight at the age of nineteen, and the defensive skills he learned to survive the battle royal stood him in good stead when he challenged white fighters in the early twentieth century. Black fighters at this time were expected not to win many fights against white opponents; if they did win, they did so on points. Johnson was among three other black heavyweights who fought during this period: Joe Jeanette, Sam McVey, and Sam Langford, also known as "the Boston Tarbaby." Johnson became a leading contender for the title. After much wrangling and many concessions, he fought Tommy Burns for the heavyweight championship in December 1908 in Sydney, Australia.

Although the color line had been drawn against black challengers to the heavyweight title, Johnson succeeded in part because he was in the right place at the right time. Many in the white sporting public felt it was time to give a black a shot at the title, and Johnson was, at that point, well liked by the white sporting fraternity. Publications such as the *National Police Gazette,* not noted for any enlightened racial attitudes, campaigned vigorously for him to get a title fight. When Johnson defeated Burns, he became the first black heavyweight champion, the most prized title in professional sports.

Soon, however, the white sporting public soured on Johnson. His arrogance and his public preference for white women provoked a cry for "a great white hope" to win the title back for whites. In 1910, Jim Jeffries, a former champion, was lured out of a six-year retirement to take on Johnson in the Nevada desert, a fight that was the most publicized, most heatedly discussed, and most fervently anticipated sporting event in American history at that time. It was the first prizefight to take on significant political overtones, as many whites and blacks saw it as a battle of racial superiority. Johnson was easily the most famous, or the most notorious, black man in America, and the fight occurred at the height of American and Western imperialism, when racial segregation and oppression in this country were fiercely enforced and severely maintained. Johnson easily won the fight, although the victory caused race riots around the country as angry whites brutalized rejoicing blacks. This was Johnson's last great moment as a professional athlete.

In 1912, Johnson's first white wife, Etta Duryea, committed suicide at the champion's Chicago nightclub. In 1913, on the testimony of a white prostitute with whom Johnson had once been intimate, he was convicted under the Mann Act and sentenced to a year and a day in federal prison. Johnson's personal life was now in shambles, and he had no future as a fighter because he was thoroughly hated by the white public. He left the country for Paris.

Johnson lost the title to Kansan Jess Willard in Cuba in 1915, a fight Johnson claimed he threw in order to regain entry to the United States. In fact, he did not return until 1920, when he served his time in prison with little fanfare or notice. Johnson went on to become a museum raconteur, an autobiographer, a fight trainer, and an occasional participant in exhibitions. He died in an automobile accident in 1946.

When Joe Louis defeated Jim Braddock in June 1937 to win the heavyweight title, he was the second black to become heavyweight champion, the first permitted even to fight for the championship since the end of Johnson's tenure in 1915. During the ensuing twenty-two years, there were only three black champions of any division, and two had brief reigns: West African Battling Siki was light heavyweight champion from September 1922 to March 1923, Tiger Flowers was middleweight champion for six months in 1926, and Kid Chocolate was featherweight and junior lightweight champion from 1931 to 1933.

Joe Louis's father was institutionalized for mental illness and his mother remarried. The family relocated from Alabama to Detroit because of job opportunities in the automobile industry. Louis had little interest in school and was attracted to boxing. He had a distinguished amateur career before turning professional in 1934 under the management of John Roxborough and Julian Black, both African Americans. Louis's trainer Jack Blackburn, a former fighter of considerable accomplishment, was also black. With Mike Jacobs, an influential New York promoter, serving as the entrée into big-time fights, Louis's career was carefully guided to the championship in three years.

Louis's most important fight was his rematch against German heavyweight Max Schmeling in 1938.

Image was everything for Louis, or at least for his handlers. In order to be accepted by the white public, he had to be the antithesis of Johnson in every respect. Johnson had bragged and consorted with white women publicly; Louis was taciturn and seen only with black women. Louis went about his business with dispatch, never relishing his victories or belittling his opponents. This latter was an especially sensitive point, as all of Louis's opponents, before he won the championship, were white.

Louis came along at a time when blacks were more assertively pushing for their rights, unlike the era of Johnson. A. Philip Randolph scored a significant victory when he achieved recognition for his union from the Pullman Car Company and achieved further gains when his threatened March on Washington forced President Franklin D. Roosevelt to issue Federal Order 8802 in 1942, integrating defense industry jobs. Louis came of age after the HARLEM RENAISSANCE and after Marcus GARVEY'S UNIVERSAL NEGRO IMPROVEMENT ASSOCIATION movement, both of which signaled greater militancy and race awareness on the part of blacks.

Louis's most important fight was his rematch against German heavyweight Max Schmeling in 1938. Louis had lost to Schmeling in 1936 and for both personal and professional reasons wanted to fight him again. Because Schmeling was German and probably a Nazi, the fight took on both racial and political overtones. Louis became the representative of American democracy against German arrogance and totalitarianism, as well as of American racial fair play against Schmeling's image of racial superiority and intolerance.

Louis won the fight easily, smashing Schmeling in less than a single round. As a result, he became the first black hero in American popular culture. During World War II, he served in the U.S. Army and donated purses from his fights to the war effort. He retired in 1949, after holding the title longer than any other champion and defending it successfully more times than any other champion. Money problems, particularly back income taxes, forced him to make a comeback in 1950. He retired permanently after his loss to Rocky Marciano in 1951. In later years, Louis became a greeter in a Las Vegas hotel. He suffered from mental problems as well as a period of cocaine addiction. He died in Las Vegas in 1981, probably the most revered black boxer, arguably the most revered black athlete, in American history.

Muhammad Ali, born Cassius Clay, Jr., had a distinguished career as an amateur, culminating in a gold medal at the 1960 Olympic Games. Always outgoing with a warm but theatrical personality, the photogenic young boxer spouted poetry, threw punches with greater grace and speed than any heavyweight before him, and was generally well received by the public. Although many people disliked his showy, sometimes outrageous ways, others thought him a breath of fresh air in boxing. The young Clay fought an aging but still intimidating Sonny Liston for the championship in 1964, defeating the older man in a fight in which Clay was the decided underdog.

It was after this fight that Clay announced his conversion to the NATION OF ISLAM. Shortly afterward, he changed his name to Muhammad Ali, probably one of the most widely and thoroughly discussed and damned name changes in American history. Ali's popularity among whites plummeted as a result of his conversion.

But he was not through provoking the white American public. In 1967 he refused induction into the armed services on religious grounds. His spiritual leader, Elijah MUHAMMAD, had served time in prison during World War II for taking the same stand. Ali was stripped of his title, and his license to fight was revoked. Despite outcries from more liberal sections of the white public, Ali was, in effect, under a kind of house arrest for three and a half years, not permitted to fight in this country and not permitted to leave the country to fight abroad while his case was being appealed.

Ali was finally permitted to fight again in late 1970 in Georgia against journeyman heavyweight Jerry Quarry, whom he dispatched in a few rounds. During the interval of Ali's exile, the sentiments of the white public had changed significantly. Many turned against the VIETNAM WAR. The deaths of Rev. Dr. Martin Luther KING, Jr., and Robert Kennedy only two months apart in 1968, made many think the country was on the verge of collapse, and as a result there was a greater sense of tolerance and understanding. Ali's religious beliefs did not strike so many as being as bizarre and threatening as they had a few years earlier. Finally, blacks had achieved some political leverage in the South, and this was instrumental in getting Ali a license to box again. Ali eventually won his case in the U.S. Supreme Court when his conviction was overturned as one of a series of decisions that broadened the allowable scope for conscientious objection to war.

Ali lost his claim to the title when he suffered his first professional defeat at the hands of Joe Frazier in March 1971, the first of three epic battles between the two great fighters. But Ali eventually regained his title in 1974 when he defeated George Foreman in a shocking upset in Zaire. He lost the title again in 1978 to Olympic champion Leon Spinks, but regained it a few months later in a rematch, becoming the first heavyweight to win the championship three times.

Ali was by far the most popular champion in the history of boxing. His face was, and still is, recognized more readily in various parts of the world than that of virtually any other American. Ali has been particularly important in creating a stronger sense of kinship between American blacks and people of the Third World. He is the most renowned Muslim athlete in history.

Like many before him, Ali fought too long, disastrously trying a comeback in 1981 against champion Larry Holmes, who badly thrashed him over ten rounds. Ali's health deteriorated throughout the 1980s. It was finally revealed that he suffers from Parkinson's disease, induced by the heavy punishment he took in the ring. Although physically not what he once was, Ali remains a formidable physical presence, a man of great warmth and humor, and an athlete who is still honored around the world for his courage both in and out of the ring.

With Ali's departure from boxing, the heavyweight division was dominated for a considerable period by Holmes, a formidable fighter but a man of little personality, wit, or engagement. Although Holmes enjoyed considerable popularity during his reign, it was fighters from the lighter weight divisions who attracted media attention and huge purses during the late 1970s through the 1980s. Sugar Ray Leonard, Marvelous Marvin Hagler, Matthew Saad Muhammad, Aaron Pryor, Dwight Muhammad Qawi, Thomas "Hitman" Hearns, Marvin Johnson, Mike "the Body Snatcher" McCallum, Livingstone Bramble, and Michael Spinks were among the best and most highly publicized fighters of the day.

Relying on the popularity of several highly skilled Latin American fighters, including the redoubtable

Roberto Duran, Alexis Arguella, Pipino Cuevas, and Victor Galindez, which enabled fight promoters to once again use ethnic and cultural symbolism as a lure for a diverse and fragmented public, these black fighters were able to bring greater attention and larger sums of money to boxing arenas in the 1980s than ever before.

After Holmes, the heavyweight class fell into complete disarray, similar to the 1930s before the coming of Joe Louis. A succession of undistinguished champions paraded before the public. Not until the emergence of Mike Tyson did the category reclaim its position as the glamour division of the sport. Tyson enjoyed greater financial success than any other heavyweight in history. However, he was poorly advised, surrounded by cronies who did not protect his interests or their own. Tyson pursued a self-destructive path of erratic, violent behavior and suspected substance abuse, and was finally imprisoned for an assault on a black beauty contestant.

BIBLIOGRAPHY

Fleischer, Nat. *Black Dynamite: The Story of the Negro in the Prize Ring from 1782 to 1838.* 5 vols. New York, 1938.

Gorn, Elliott. *The Manly Art: Bare-knuckle Prize Fighting in America.* Ithaca, N.Y., 1986.

McCallum, John D. *The World Heavyweight Boxing Championship: A History.* Radnor, Pa., 1974.

Mead, Chris. *Champion—Joe Louis, Black Hero in White America.* New York, 1985.

Reid, J. C. *Bucks and Bruisers: Pierce Egan and Regency England.* London, 1971.

Roberts, Randy. *Papa Jack: Jack Johnson and the Era of White Hopes.* New York, 1983.

Sammons, Jeffrey. *Beyond the Ring: The Role of Boxing in American Society.* Urbana, Ill., 1988.

Young, A. S. "Doc." *Negro Firsts in Sports.* Chicago, 1963.

– GERALD EARLY

BROOKS, GWENDOLYN ELIZABETH

Gwendolyn Elizabeth Brooks (June 7, 1917–), poet, novelist, teacher, and reader/lecturer. Taken to Topeka, Kans., to be born among family, Brooks was reared in Chicago, where she continues to reside. In her autobiography, *Report from Part One* (1972), she describes a happy childhood spent in black neighborhoods with her parents and younger brother, Raymond. "I had always felt that to be black was good," Brooks observes. School awakened her to preferences among blacks, the "black-and-tan motif" noted in her earlier works by critic Arthur P. Davis. Her father, David Anderson Brooks, was the son of a runaway slave, a janitor with "rich Artistic Abilities" who had spent a year at Fisk University, Nashville, hoping to become a doctor, and who sang, told stories, and responded compassionately to the poverty and misfortune around him; her mother, Keziah Wims Brooks, had been a fifth-grade teacher in Topeka and harbored a wish to write. They nurtured their daughter's precocious gifts. When the seven-year-old Gwendolyn began to write poetry, her mother predicted, "You are going to be the *lady* Paul Laurence DUNBAR." Years later, Mrs. Brooks took her daughter to meet James Weldon JOHNSON and then Langston HUGHES at church. Hughes became an inspiration, friend, and mentor to the young poet.

Brooks was graduated from Wilson Junior College (now Kennedy-King) in 1936. She was employed for a month as a maid in a North Shore home and spent four months as secretary to a spiritual adviser (see the "Prophet Williams" section of the story "In the Mecca"). In 1939, she married Henry Lowington Blakely II, a fellow member of Inez Cunningham Stark's poetry workshop in the South Side Community Art Center and himself a poet and writer. Motherhood (Henry, Jr., 1940; Nora, 1951), early publishing (*A Street in Bronzeville,* 1945), warm critical reception, careful supervision of her career by her editor at *Harper's,* and a succession of honors and prizes helped her overcome her reticence about public speaking. The first African American (or "Black," her articulated preference) to win a Pulitzer Prize, for poetry (*Annie Allen,* 1950), Brooks also received two Guggenheim Fellowships. Upon the death of Carl Sandburg (in 1968), she was named the poet laureate of Illinois. She was the first black woman to be elected to the National Institute of Arts and Letters (1976); to become consultant in poetry to the Library of Congress (1985–1986, just before the title was changed to poet laureate); to become an honorary fellow of the Modern Language Association; and to receive the Poetry Society of America's Shelley Memorial Award and its Frost Medal. She was elected to the National Women's Hall of Fame and given the National Endowment for the Arts Lifetime Achievement Award in 1989. In Illinois, the Junior High School at Harvey, the cultural center at Western Illinois University, and the center and a chair as Distinguished Professor of English at Chicago State University all bear her name. The number of her honorary doctorates already exceeds seventy.

Brooks's work is notable for its impeccable craft and its social dimension. It marks a confluence of a dual stream: the black sermonic tradition and black music, and white antecedents such as the ballad, the sonnet, and conventional and free-verse forms. Influenced early by Hughes, T. S. Eliot, Emily Dickinson, and Robert Frost, she was propelled by the Black Arts movement of the 1960s into black nationalist consciousness. Yet her poetry has always been infused with both humanism and heroism, the latter defined as extending the concept of leadership, by both personality and art. In 1969 she moved to Dudley Randall's nascent, historic Broadside Press for the publication of *Riot* and subsequent works.

Brooks's books span six decades of social and political changes. *A Street in Bronzeville* addresses the quotidian realities of segregation for black Americans at home and in WORLD WAR II military service; *Annie Allen* ironically explores postwar antiromanticism; *Maud Martha,* her novel (1953), sketches a bildungsroman of black womanhood; *Bronzeville Boys and Girls* (1956) presents sturdy, home-oriented black children of the 1950s; *The Bean Eaters* (1960) and new poems in *Selected Poems* (1963) sound the urgencies of the Civil Rights Movement. In 1967, at the second Fisk University Writers' Conference at Nashville, Brooks was deeply impressed by the activist climate, personified by Amiri BARAKA. Though she had always experimented with conventional forms, her work subsequently opened more distinctly to free verse, a feature of the multiform *In the Mecca* (1968), which Haki R. Madhubuti calls "her epic of Black humanity" (*Report from Part One,* p. 22).

Upon returning to Chicago from the conference at Fisk, Brooks conducted a workshop with the Blackstone Rangers, a teenage gang, who were succeeded by young writers such as Carolyn M. Rodgers and Madhubuti (then don l. lee). Broadside published *Riot* (1969), *Family Pictures* (1970), *Aloneness* (1971), and *Beckonings* (1975). Madhubuti's Third World Press published *The Tiger Who Wore White Gloves* (1974) and *To Disembark* (1981). In 1971 Brooks began a literary annual, *The Black Position,* under her own aegis, and made the first of her two trips to Africa. Beginning with *Primer for Blacks* (1980), she published with her own company *The Near-Johannesburg Boy* (1986), the omnibus volume *Blacks* (1987), *Gottschalk and the Grande Tarantelle* (1988), and *Winnie* (1988, a poem honoring Winnie Mandela). Her books are also being reissued by Third World Press. The adult poems of *Children Coming Home* (1991) express the perspective of contemporary children, and may be contrasted with the benign ambience of *Bronzeville Boys and Girls* among her works for children.

Brooks's work is notable for its impeccable craft and its social dimension.

Brooks supports and promotes the creativity of other writers. Her annual Poet Laureate Awards distribute considerable sums of her own money, chiefly to the schoolchildren of Illinois. She visits prisons, where her readings have inspired poets such as the late Ethridge Knight. Lauded with affectionate respect in two tribute anthologies, recognized nationally and internationally as a major literary figure, Brooks continues to claim and to vivify our democratic heritage.

BIBLIOGRAPHY

Kent, George E. *A Life of Gwendolyn Brooks.* Lexington, Ky., 1990.

Melhem, D. H. *Gwendolyn Brooks: Poetry and the Heroic Voice.* Lexington, Ky., 1987.

———. *Heroism in the New Black Poetry: Introductions and Interviews.* Lexington, Ky., 1990.

Shaw, Harry. *Gwendolyn Brooks.* New York, 1980.

– D. H. MELHEM

BROTHERHOOD OF SLEEPING CAR PORTERS

The Brotherhood of Sleeping Car Porters (BSCP), organized in secret on August 25, 1925, became the first successful African-American labor union. From its inception in 1867, the Pullman Company had employed black porters because company officials believed their subservience could be depended upon and because they would work for low wages. Pullman thereby created an occupation over which African Americans had a monopoly. While steady employment and travel experience made porters the elite of black labor, they were not unionized and were often exploited and underpaid. Capitalizing on the fact that he was not a porter and hence could not be fired, socialist journalist A. Philip Randolph seized on the porters' complaints, educated them about collective bargaining and the value of trade unionism, and began organizing them in 1925. The question of unionization to the average porter, however, meant a choice between steady, albeit low, pay and reprisals by the company, so organizing had to be carried on covertly and employees' wives were often utilized for the job. Loyal assistants, like Milton P. Webster in Chicago, Ashley Totten and Benjamin McLauren in New York, C. L. Dellums in Oakland, and E. J. Bradley in St. Louis, took care of the daily details and organizing while Randolph obtained outside publicity and funding.

Porters had legitimate complaints, working long hours for little pay. They made the railroad car ready, assisted with luggage, waited on passengers, converted seats into beds that they then made up, polished shoes, and remained on call twenty-four hours a day. Nevertheless, because they had been inculcated with the idea of company benevolence, and because of their fear of reprisal, most porters were reluctant to jeopardize their jobs by joining the union. Many did not understand

Alfred Macmillan, a Pullman porter, at work in 1942. The Brotherhood of Sleeping Car Porters, which reached a labor agreement with the Pullman Company in 1937, was the most influential of black unions. The success of the union led to increased wages and improved working conditions for porters such as Macmillan. (Prints and Photographs Division, Library of Congress)

the difference between the company union, the Employee Representation Plan (ERP), and a trade union like the BSCP.

Still, despite obstacles, BSCP membership increased, and Pullman attempted to undermine its success with a series of retaliatory measures, including frame-ups, beatings, and firings. The company had previously dealt with labor unions, but now resisted bargaining with African Americans as equals. Company propaganda identified Pullman as a benefactor of African Americans, which led many prominent blacks to oppose the BSCP. Organized labor was anathema to others because they believed, with justification, that black workers were discriminated against by white unions.

Although initially opposed to its craft-union stance, Randolph began taking a more conciliatory tone toward the American Federation of Labor (AFL) in his writings as early as 1923. After he began organizing the porters, Randolph continually sought the advice of William Green, head of the AFL. The BSCP first applied for an international charter from the AFL in 1928. Because of jurisdictional disputes with white unions, most likely prompted by racism, the AFL refused the international charter, granting instead federal charters to individual locals. Brotherhood officials were unhappy with federal status, but the weak BSCP needed the support of the AFL. For his part, Green, concerned about Communist infiltration of black labor, considered the BSCP an acceptable alternative, not only to communism but also to masses of African-American laborers remaining outside the federation, where they acted as potential strikebreakers.

Realizing that the success of the union ultimately depended on its ability to correct grievances and provide job security, Randolph employed various strategies to force the company to the bargaining table. First, in 1926, he attempted to bring the dispute before the federal Board of Mediation under the Watson-Parker Railway Labor Act. Although the board recommended arbitration, under the act arbitration was voluntary and the company demurred. Second, believing that depending on tips was a degrading practice and because the uncertainty of the amount to be expected was one of the porters' primary grievances, Randolph brought the tipping system before the Interstate Commerce Commission in 1927. A ruling prohibiting tipping in interstate travel would have compelled a wage increase, but the ICC ultimately decided it did not have jurisdiction. Thus the BSP was forced to call a strike in 1928, but, accustomed to finding jobs as strikebreakers, African Americans knew other blacks would be eager to take what many considered a plush position and consequently were reluctant to actually walk off the job. In response to a rumor that Pullman had nearly five thousand Filipinos ready to take the places of brotherhood members, Willie Green advised Randolph to postpone the strike.

After the aborted strike, membership dropped and the BSCP almost ceased to exist. The more favorable labor legislation under President Franklin D. Roosevelt, however—especially passage of the amended Railway Act of 1934, which outlawed company unions—revived the BSCP. Although Pullman responded by replacing its ERP with the Pullman Porters and Maids Protective Association, the situation for labor had changed. The AFL granted the brotherhood an international charter in 1935. After twelve years, the Pullman Company finally signed a contract with the BSCP on August 25, 1937, bringing improved working conditions and some two million dollars in income to the porters and their families.

Beginning with the 1932 AFL convention, Randolph started denouncing racism within the federation and attacking federal unions designed for African Americans. Although well disposed to John L. Lewis and the industrial unionism of the unions that left the AFL in 1937 to form the Congress of Industrial Organizations (CIO) Randolph—who had long advocated industrial unions—held the BSCP in the AFL, saying he thought it wiser to remain and fight for equality than to leave and let the federation continue its racist policies undisturbed. BSCP officers contented themselves trying to prevent the split in the union movement and later working for reunification, but competition from the CIO forced the AFL to a more egalitarian position on racial equality. When the two federations merged in 1955, Randolph became a vice president of the newly created AFL-CIO, and the BSCP became instrumental in pushing the combined federation to financially back civil rights activity.

Not only did the BSCP successfully negotiate a series of favorable wage agreements between Pullman and its porters through the years, but the union provided support for civil rights activity by contributing its labor and some fifty thousand dollars to Randolph's various equality movements as well. By the fall of 1940, fueled by defense contracts, the American economy was beginning to emerge from the Great Depression. But because of racial discrimination, African Americans found themselves locked out of the new job opportunities opening in defense industries. Randolph, backed by the brotherhood, threatened a march on Washington of one hundred thousand blacks the following July 1, to demand jobs in defense plants and integration of the armed forces. While integration of the military was not achieved, the Roosevelt administration was sufficiently concerned to issue Executive Order 8802 in June 1941, creating the wartime Fair Employment Practices Committee (FEPC) in exchange for cancellation of the march. Although weak, the FEPC did provide job training and economic improvement for many African Americans. In 1948, the porters' union assisted, albeit more reluctantly, Randolph's threat of a black boycott of universal military training; the Truman administration capitulated with integration of the military by Executive Order 9981. The BSCP supported Randolph's prayer pilgrimage in 1957, marches in Washington for integrated schools in 1958 and 1959, and the march on Washington for Jobs and Freedom in 1963. (Many organizers for the BSCP went on to assume important roles in the CIVIL RIGHTS MOVEMENT, such as E. D. Nixon, who played an instrumental part in the Montgomery bus boycott of 1955–1956.)

The BSCP stimulated black participation in unions and fought to end discrimination in organized labor.

BSCP officers realized early on the threat to Pullman travel presented by the rise of commercial aviation; the drop was precipitous after World War II, with the porters becoming a diminished and aging group. Bowing to the decline of the railroad industry, in 1978 the BSCP merged with the Brotherhood of Railway and Airline Clerks. The brotherhood, however, had served its members well. Although porters were often absent from home because of long runs and usually missed holidays as well, the brotherhood helped the porters' domestic situation by providing job security, higher wages, and improved working conditions. Furthermore, during its heyday, under Randolph's leadership the BSCP became more than an instrumentality of service to the porters. From its inception in 1929 Randolph utilized the union's organ, the *Black Worker,* in the fight against communism to educate porters to fight for civil rights and to cajole them to abide by such middle-class virtues as thrift, cleanliness, and abstinence from alcohol. He organized the porters' wives into a Ladies' Auxiliary and their children into Junior Auxiliaries. The union thus encircled its members' lives and built their self-esteem. Trained in trade-union methods of collective bargaining, porters refused to beg for favors from the white power structure. Hence, the BSCP stimulated black participation in unions and fought to end discrimination in organized labor. The BSCP left an important legacy to both organized labor and the struggle for civil rights.

BIBLIOGRAPHY

Brazeal, Brailsford Reese. *The Brotherhood of Sleeping Car Porters: Its Origin and Development.* New York, 1946.

Harris, William H. *Keeping the Faith: A. Philip Randolph, Milton P. Webster, and the Brotherhood of Sleeping Car Porters, 1925–37.* Urbana, Ill., 1977.

Pfeffer, Paula F. *A. Philip Randolph, Pioneer of the Civil Rights Movement.* Baton Rouge, La., 1990.

Santino, Jack. *Miles of Smiles, Years of Struggle: Stories of Black Pullman Porters.* Urbana, Ill., 1989.

Wilson, Joseph F. *Tearing Down the Color Bar: A Documentary History and Analysis of the Brotherhood of Sleeping Car Porters.* New York, 1989.

– PAULA F. PFEFFER

BROWN, JAMES JOE, JR.

James Joe Brown, Jr. (May 3, 1933–), singer and songwriter. Born near Barnwell, S.C., to Joe Brown, a turpentine worker, and Susan Behlings. After his mother left the family when the boy was four years of age, Brown spent his formative years in a brothel run by his aunt Handsome Washington in Augusta, Ga. After the authorities closed the brothel in 1943, he lived with his aunt Minnie Walker, receiving occasional tutoring on drums and piano from neighbors and showing early promise on harmonica and organ. He absorbed the music of the black church and of the minstrel shows that passed through Augusta; he heard the blues his father learned in the turpentine camps, and he listened to pop music on the radio. Fascinated by "soundies" (filmed musical numbers that preceded the feature at movie theaters), he paid close attention to those of Louis Jordan and His Tympany Five, who performed jump blues and novelty songs with great showmanship. Singing Jordan's "Caldonia," Brown entered and won local talent contests while not yet in his teens. At thirteen, he formed the Cremona Trio, his first musical group, performing the songs of such RHYTHM AND BLUES artists as Jordan, Amos Milburn, Wynonie Harris, Charles Brown, and the Red Mildred Trio.

These early musical endeavors were cut short when Brown's habit of stealing clothes and other items from unlocked automobiles earned him a harsh eight-to-sixteen-year prison sentence, which he began serving at Georgia Juvenile Technical Institute (GJTI) in Rome, Ga., in 1949. In GJTI, he formed a GOSPEL quartet with three other inmates, including Johnny Terry, who would later become one of the original Famous Flames. After serving three years, he was paroled in Toccoa, the small town in northeast Georgia to which GJTI had been moved. He soon formed a gospel group with several youthful Toccoa musicians including Bobby Byrd, a talented keyboard player, who would remain a central figure in James Brown's musical endeavors into the early 1970s.

The fledgling gospel group soon began playing rhythm and blues and performed for dances and in small clubs throughout eastern Georgia and neighboring areas of South Carolina until Little Richard's manager induced them to come to the vital music scene centered in Macon, Ga. At a Macon radio station, the group, soon to be known as the Famous Flames, recorded a demo of "Please, Please, Please," which attracted the attention of Cincinnati-based King records. Rerecorded in Cincinnati and released in 1956, the song eventually climbed to number six on the rhythm and blues record chart. During the next two years, Brown sought to duplicate the success of "Please," essaying a number of rhythm and blues styles and occasionally imitating the differing approaches of Little Richard and King labelmates Hank Ballard and the Midnighters and the Five Royales. In 1958, with the recording of "Try Me," a pleading ballad steeped in gospel, he achieved the number one position on the rhythm-and-blues chart, and began to realize his own distinctive style.

Brown soon became a headliner at Harlem's Apollo Theater and toured tirelessly, playing as many as 300 dates annually and presenting a stage revue complete with comedians, warmup acts, dancers, and a full orchestra. As a singer, he developed a powerful shouting style that owed much to gospel, but his rhythmic grunts and expressive shrieks harked back farther still to ring shouts, work songs, and field cries. As a band leader, he developed one of the most disciplined bands in entertainment and maintained it for more than three decades. He reimported the rhythmic complexity from which rhythm and blues, under the dual pressure of rock 'n' roll and pop, had progressively fallen away since its birth from jazz and blues. As one of the greatest vernacular dancers in rhythm and blues, he integrated the latest dance crazes with older black popular dance styles and integrated them into a seamless whole that came to be known as "the James Brown." He became one of the most exciting live performers in popular music, capping his performances with a collapse-and-resurrection routine that became his trademark.

With the album *Live at the Apollo* (1963), Brown brought the excitement of his stage show to record buyers throughout the world. Through the mid-1960s, he enjoyed enormous success with such compositions as "Out of Sight" (1964), "I Feel Good (I Got You)" (1965), "Papa's Got a Brand New Bag" (1965), and "Cold Sweat" (1967). These infectious, rhythmically complex dance hits propelled him to international stardom and heralded funk, his most original and enduring contribution to popular music around the world. Dispensing almost entirely with chord changes, Brown, by the late 1960s, stripped the music to its rhythmic essence. Horns, guitars, and voices—including Brown's rich assortment of grunts, groans, shrieks, and shouts—were employed percussively. Rhythmic emphasis fell heavily on the downbeat at the beginning of each measure, imparting a sense of overwhelming propulsiveness to the music while leaving ample room for complex rhythmic interplay.

From the late 1960s through the mid 1970s, Brown and his band, assisted by gifted arrangers Pee Wee Ellis and Fred Wesley, produced powerful, polyrhythmic funk music that included inspired dance tracks as heard on albums such as *Sex Machine* (1970) and *Super Bad* (1971). He also wrote inspirational, political and social commentary such as the anthem of black pride "Say It Loud—I'm Black and I'm Proud" (1968). Brown also became something of a political figure; several presidential candidates sought his endorsement. Following the murder of the Rev. Dr. Martin Luther KING, Jr. in April 1968, Brown helped quell riots in Boston and Washington, D.C. In 1971 he produced a single about the dangers of drug use, "King Heroin."

Although Brown's records sold well through the early 1970s, the magnitude of his accomplishment was obscured by the rise of disco. Plagued by personal problems, including the break-up of his second marriage, the death of his oldest son, a federal tax case, and troubles with his numerous business enterprises, he briefly went into semiretirement, though he never entirely stopped performing, and he recorded numerous albums during this period, including *Hot* (1976) and *Bodyheat* (1976).

In the early 1980s he staged a successful comeback. He made cameo appearances in numerous motion pictures such as *The Blues Brothers* (1980). A series of retrospective albums, including *The Federal Years* (*Part 1 and 2,* 1984) and *Dead on the Heavy Funk* (1985) traced the development of his music from 1956 to 1976, and he returned to extensive recording and performing. His music was also widely sampled by rap artists. In 1986 he performed "Living in America" in the film *Rocky IV* and that year became one of the first performers inducted into the Rock and Roll Hall of Fame.

In 1988, after leading police in Georgia and South Carolina on a high-speed chase that ended when the police fired some two dozen bullets into his truck, Brown was sentenced to six years in prison for failing to stop for a police officer and aggravated assault. Although the lengthy sentence sparked a national outcry for Brown's pardon, he remained incarcerated for more than two years, earning early release in 1991. Nevertheless, he re-emerged to be seen as one of the towering figures of popular music throughout the world. His musical innovations inform rock and jazz-funk hybrids, dance pop, reggae, hip-hop, and much African and Latin popular music. Critics, formerly ignoring him, now generally recognize him as one of the most influential American musicians of the past half century. His output has been prodigious, including more than seventy albums. In 1991 he released *Star Time,* a 71–song, 4–CD compilation of his greatest hits. He has also produced hundreds of recordings by other artists and continues to record (*Love Over-Due,* 1991).

BIBLIOGRAPHY

Brown, James, with Bruce Tucker. *James Brown: The Godfather of Soul.* New York, 1986.

Hirshey, Gerri. " 'We Sang Like Angels' " and "Superbull, Superbad." In *Nowhere to Run: The Story of Soul Music.* New York, 1984, pp. 54–63, 265–293.

– BRUCE TUCKER

BROWN, STERLING ALLEN

Sterling Allen Brown (May 1, 1901–January 13, 1989), poet, scholar. Sterling A. Brown, who expressed the humor and resilience of the black folk tradition in his poetry, teaching, and public persona, was born on the HOWARD UNIVERSITY campus. Except for a few years spent elsewhere as student and teacher, he remained at Howard most of his life. His father, Sterling Nelson Brown, born a slave, became a distinguished clergyman in Washington, D.C., as pastor of the Lincoln Temple Congregational Church and professor of religion at Howard, beginning in the 1890s. Rev. Brown died shortly before his son followed his example by joining the Howard faculty in 1929, a post that he held until his retirement forty years later, in 1969.

Sterling A. Brown, who expressed the humor and resilience of the black folk tradition in his poetry, teaching, and public persona, was born on the Howard University campus.

As a youngster Brown attended the Lucretia Mott School and Dunbar High School, which was generally acknowledged as the finest black high school in the country. Upon graduation Brown accepted the scholarship that Williams College in Massachusetts offered to the Dunbar valedictorian each year. At Williams he joined the debating team, earned Phi Beta Kappa membership, and became the doubles tennis partner of Allison Davis, subsequently a distinguished social scientist and University of Chicago professor. After graduating from Williams in 1922, Brown earned his master's degree in English from Harvard University the following year. Before returning to Howard in 1929, he taught for three years at Virginia Seminary in Lynchburg, Va., for two years at Lincoln University in Missouri; and for a year at Fisk University in Nashville.

Brown achieved an enduring reputation as a poet, scholar, and teacher. His most celebrated volume of poems was *Southern Road* (1932). Unlike such HARLEM RENAISSANCE contemporaries as Claude MCKAY and Countee CULLEN, who wrote sonnets imitating Keats and Shakespeare, Brown eschewed traditional high literary forms and subjects, preferring instead the folk-ballad form and taking common black people as his subjects. In this he was like Langston HUGHES. Brown was influenced by realist and narrative poets such as A. E. Housman, Edwin Arlington Robinson, and Edgar Lee Masters, as well as by African-American folklore, blues, and work songs. The characters of Brown's poems, such as Slim Greer, Scrappy, and Old Lem, are tough, worldly, and courageous. Some are fighters and troublemakers; some are pleasure-seekers or hardworking farmers; and some are victims of racist mobs. At once unsentimental and unapologetic, these characters embody the strength and forthrightness that was typical of Brown's work in every genre.

As a scholar, Brown is best remembered for two books: *The Negro in American Fiction* (1937) and *Negro Poetry and Drama* (1937). These are both exhaustive works that document the African-American presence in American literature from the beginnings to the 1930s. The former book has been especially influential as the first and most thorough work of its kind, and has been a foundation for all subsequent studies of blacks in American fiction. From 1936 through 1940 Brown served as national editor of Negro affairs for the Federal Writers' Project (FWP). In this position he was involved with reviewing how African Americans were portrayed in the publications of the FWP, especially the series of state guidebooks. Although the task was frustrating—especially where the Deep South states were concerned—the appointment reflected how highly Brown, not yet forty, was regarded. During this same period, Brown also edited, along with Arthur P. Davis and Ulysses Lee, *The Negro Caravan* (1941), which remains one of the most useful and comprehensive anthologies of African-American writing ever published. All in all, the 1930s was the most intensely productive decade of Brown's life.

As a teacher, Brown has been broadly influential. He was a pioneer in the teaching of African-American literature, and a startling number of black writers, scholars, and political figures have studied with him. Outside the classroom, Brown for many years held informal listening sessions, using his own massive record collection to introduce students to jazz, the blues, and other black musical forms. Alumni of those sessions include LeRoi Jones (Amiri BARAKA) and A. B. Spellman, both of whom subsequently wrote important books about JAZZ. Similarly, Stokely CARMICHAEL and Kwame Nkrumah were students of Brown who have often acknowledged their debt to him. His power as a teacher derived in part from his erudition but especially from his rare ability to combine the vernacular, scholarly, and literary traditions of the United States with progressive political values and a blunt, unpretentious personal style.

Brown's literary productivity decreased after the 1940s, partly due to recurrent illnesses. He nonetheless remained active as a guest lecturer and poetry recitalist, and taught at several universities during his forty-year tenure at Howard, including Vassar College, Atlanta University, and New York University. In 1980 Michael S. Harper edited Brown's *Collected Poems,* which was awarded the Lenore Marshall Prize for the oustanding volume of poetry published in the United States that year. Brown's memoir, "A Son's Return: 'Oh, Didn't He Ramble,'" published in *Chant of Saints* (1979), recounts his early years, especially his life at Williams College, and is, despite its short length, one of the most compelling of African-American literary memoirs. Brown died in Takoma Park, Md.

BIBLIOGRAPHY

Brown Sterling A. "A Son's Return: 'Oh, Didn't He Ramble.' " In Michael S. Harper and Robert B. Stepto, eds. *Chant of Saints.* Urbana, Ill., 1979.

Gabbin, Joanne V. *Sterling A. Brown: Building the Black Aesthetic Tradition.* Westport, Conn., 1985.

Redmond, Eugene B. *Drumvoices: The Mission of Afro-American Poetry.* Garden City, N.Y., 1976.

Stuckey, Sterling. "Introduction." In Michael S. Harper, ed. *The Collected Poems of Sterling A. Brown.* New York, 1980.

– DAVID LIONEL SMITH

BROWNSVILLE, TEXAS, INCIDENT

On the night of August 13, 1906, some 250 rounds of ammunition were fired into several buildings in Brownsville, Tex. One man was killed and two others were wounded. The townspeople's suspicions immediately fell upon the members of Companies B, C, and D of the First Battalion of the United States 25th Infantry, Colored. The African-American soldiers had arrived sixteen days before the shooting and were stationed at Fort Brown, just outside of town and near the site of the incident. Tensions between the black troops and some openly racist Brownsville residents flared. Although the soldiers and their white commander consistently denied any knowledge of the "raid," as it came to be called, subsequent investigations sustained the townspeople's opinion of their guilt.

President Theodore Roosevelt appointed an assistant inspector general to investigate. Two weeks later the inspector reported that it "can not be doubted" that the soldiers were guilty but that their white officers were not responsible. He recommended that "all enlisted men" be discharged from service because some of the soldiers "must have some knowledge of the guilty parties." Roosevelt then appointed Gen. E. A. Garlington inspector general to discover the guilty soldiers; all continued to proclaim their innocence. In his report, Garlington referred to "the secretive nature of the race, where crimes charged to members of their color are made." By the end of November all soldiers in the battalion were discharged without honor from the U.S. Army, because no one would point a finger at the supposed guilty parties. Those who were able to prove their innocence of participation in the raid were allowed to reenlist, and fourteen did so.

However, when an interracial civil rights organization, the Constitution League, reported to Congress that the evidence demonstrated the innocence of the soldiers, Senate hearings were held and Brownsville became a national issue. In March 1910 a Senate committee issued a majority report concluding that the shooting was done by some of the soldiers, who could not be identified, and upheld the blanket discharge of the battalion. Two minority reports were also issued. The first asserted that there was no evidence to indict any particular soldier, and that therefore there was no justification for discharging the entire battalion. The second minority report argued that the weight of the testimony showed that *none* of the soldiers participated in the shooting. Military courts-martial of two white officers found them not guilty of responsibility for the affray.

The incident had assumed national importance largely because Sen. Joseph Benson Foraker of Ohio charged that Theodore Roosevelt had allowed a decision based on flimsy evidence to stand. Thus, the Brownsville affray became an issue in Foraker's lengthy but ultimately unsuccessful campaign against Roosevelt for the 1908 presidential nomination.

The Brownsville incident also divided the African-American community. A split in 1905 that had resulted in the establishment of the anti-Booker T. WASHINGTON group, the NIAGARA MOVEMENT, forerunner to the NATIONAL ASSOCIATION FOR THE ADVANCEMENT OF COLORED PEOPLE (NAACP), sharpened appreciably. Washington's unwillingness to criticize Roosevelt publicly—although privately he tried to dissuade the president from discharging the soldiers—induced many of his previous supporters to desert him. On the Brownsville issue, the division soon became those committed to the Republican party versus everyone else.

It is possible that some of the soldiers of the Twenty-fifth Infantry were guilty of the attack; it is also possible they were not. What is clear is that the soldiers were not proved guilty. When the incident was over, Roosevelt and Washington, if not unscathed, at least survived. Foraker risked his career on a bid for the presidency and lost. The black community lapsed into political silence. The soldiers of the Twenty-fifth remained penalized until 1973, when they were granted honorary discharges. Only one soldier was still alive.

BIBLIOGRAPHY

Lane, Ann J. *The Brownsville Affair: National Crisis and Black Reaction.* Port Washington, N.Y., 1971.

Tinsley, James A. "Roosevelt, Foraker and the Brownsville Affray." *Journal of Negro History* 41 (January 1956): 43–65.

– ANN J. LANE

BROWN V. BOARD OF EDUCATION OF TOPEKA, KANSAS

Brown, 347 U.S. 483 (1954), was the most important legal case affecting African Americans in the twentieth century and unquestionably one of the most important Supreme Court decisions in U.S. constitutional history. Although directly involving segregated public schools, the case became the legal underpinning for the CIVIL RIGHTS MOVEMENT of the 1950s and 1960s and the dismantling of all forms of statutory segregation.

Brown combined separate cases from Kansas, South Carolina, Virginia, and Delaware that turned on the meaning of the FOURTEENTH AMENDMENT's requirement that states not deny their citizens "equal protection of the law." The Court also heard a similar case from Washington, D.C., *Bolling* v. *Sharpe,* which involved the meaning of the Fifth Amendment's due process clause.

Brown, *347 U.S. 483 (1954), was the most important legal case affecting African Americans in the twentieth century.*

In 1954, laws in eighteen states plus the District of Columbia mandated segregated schools, while other states allowed school districts to maintain separate schools if they wanted to do so. Although theoretically guaranteeing blacks "separate-but-equal" education, segregated schools were never equal for blacks. Linda

Brown, whose father, Rev. Oliver Brown, sued the Topeka, Kans., school system on her behalf, had to travel an hour and twenty minutes to school each way. If her bus was on time, she was dropped off at school a half hour before it opened. Her bus stop was six blocks from her home, across a hazardous railroad yard; her school was twenty-one blocks from her home. The neighborhood school her white playmates attended was only seven blocks from her home, and required neither bus nor hazardous crossings to reach. The *Brown* companion cases presented segregation at its worst. Statistics from Clarendon, S.C., where one of the cases began, illustrate the inequality of separate but equal. In 1949 and 1950, the average expenditure for white students was $179, but for blacks it was only $43. The county's 6,531 black students attended school in 61 buildings valued at $194,575; many of these schools lacked indoor plumbing or heating. The 2,375 white students in the county attended school in twelve buildings worth $673,850, with far superior facilities. Teachers in the black schools received, on average, salaries that were one-third less than those of teachers in the white schools. Finally, Clarendon provided school buses for white students in this rural county but refused to provide them for blacks.

The plaintiffs could easily have won orders requiring state officials to equalize the black schools, on the grounds that education was separate but *not* equal. Since the 1930s the Court had been chipping away at segregation in higher education, interstate transportation, housing, and voting. In *Brown* the NAACP Legal Defense Fund, led by Thurgood MARSHALL, decided to directly challenge the whole idea of segregation in schools.

Marshall's bold challenge of segregation per se led the Court to reconsider older cases, especially PLESSY V. FERGUSON, that had upheld segregation. The Court was also compelled to consider the meaning of the Fourteenth Amendment, which had been written at a time when most states allowed some forms of segregation and when public education was undeveloped in the South. The Court ordered attorneys for both sides to present briefs and reargument on these historical matters. In the end, the Court found the historical argument to be

> at best . . . inconclusive. The most avid proponents of the post-War Amendments undoubtedly intended them to remove all legal distinctions among "all persons born or naturalized in the United States." Their opponents, just as certainly, were antagonistic to both the letter and the spirit of the Amendments. . . . What others in Congress and the state legislatures had in mind cannot be determined with any degree of certainty.

After reviewing the histories of the Fourteenth Amendment, public education, and segregation, Chief Justice Earl Warren, speaking for a unanimous Court, concluded, "In approaching this problem, we cannot turn the clock back to 1868 when the Amendment was adopted, or even to 1896 when *Plessy* v. *Ferguson* was written. We must consider public education in the light of its full development and its present place in American life throughout the Nation." Warren found that "in the field of public education the doctrine of 'separate but equal' has no place. Separate education facilities are inherently unequal." *Brown* did not technically overturn *Plessy* (which involved seating on railroads) or the separate-but-equal doctrine. But that technicality was unimportant. *Brown* signaled the end to the legality of segregation. Within a dozen years the Supreme Court would strike down all vestiges of legalized segregation.

Brown did not, however, lead to an immediate end to segregated education. The Court instead ordered new arguments for the next year to determine how to begin the difficult social process of desegregating schools. The NAACP urged immediate desegregation. However, in a second case, known as *Brown II* (1955), the Court ordered its mandate implemented with "all deliberate speed," a process that turned out to be extraordinarily slow. Linda Brown, for example, did not attend integrated schools until junior high; none of the plaintiff children in the Clarendon County case ever attended integrated schools.

BIBLIOGRAPHY

Finkelman, Paul, ed. *Race Law and American History.* Vol. 7, *The Struggle for Equal Education.* New York, 1992.

Kluger, Richard. *Simple Justice.* New York, 1975.

Tushnet, Mark. *The NAACP's Campaign Against Segregated Education.* Chapel Hill, N.C., 1987.

— PAUL FINKELMAN

BUNCHE, RALPH JOHNSON

Ralph Johnson Bunche (1904–1971), scholar, diplomat, and international civil servant. Ralph Bunche was born in Detroit, Mich., to Fred and Olive Johnson Bunch. His father, a barber, abandoned the family when his son was young. Bunche moved with his mother to Albuquerque, N. Mex., where she died in 1917. He then went to Los Angeles to be raised by his maternal grandmother, Lucy Taylor Jackson. During his teen years, he added a final "e" to his name to make it more distinguished. Bunche lived in a neighborhood with relatively few blacks, and he was one of only two blacks in his class at Jefferson High School, where he graduated first in his class, although Los Angeles school authorities barred him from the all-city honor roll because of his race. Bunche's valedictory address was his first public speech. Bunche entered the University of California at Los Angeles (UCLA) on scholarship, majoring in political science and philosophy. He was active on the debating team, wrestled, played football and baseball, and was a standout basketball player. In 1927, he graduated *summa cum laude* and again, first in his class.

Assisted by a tuition fellowship and a $1,000 scholarship provided by a group of African-American women in Los Angeles, Bunche enrolled at Harvard University in 1927 to pursue graduate study in political science. He received a master's degree in 1928, and then accepted an invitation to join the faculty of Howard University. Bunche was only twenty-five when he created and chaired Howard's political science department. His association with Howard continued until 1941, although he pursued graduate work at Harvard during leaves.

Bunche's graduate work combined his interest in government with a developing interest in Africa. He conducted field research in western Africa in 1932 and 1933, and wrote a dissertation on the contrast between European colonial and mandatory governments in Africa. The dissertation, completed in 1934, won a Harvard award as the best political science dissertation of the year, and Bunche was awarded the first Ph.D. in political science ever granted an African American by an American university. Bunche undertook postdoctoral studies in 1936 and 1937, first at Northwestern University, then at the London School of Economics and at South Africa's University of Cape Town. In 1936 he published a pamphlet, *A World View of Race.* His notes, taken during fieldwork in South Africa and detailing the political and racial situation were published in 1992 under the title *An African American in South Africa.*

During Bunche's time at Howard in the 1930s, he was deeply involved in civil rights questions. He believed that black people's principal concerns were economic, and that race, though significant, was secondary. While he participated in civil rights actions—notably a protest he organized against segregation in Washington's National Theater in 1931—Bunche, a principled integrationist, warned that civil rights efforts founded on race would collapse over economic issues. He felt that the best hope for black progress lay in interracial working-class economic improvement, and he criticized Franklin Roosevelt both for his inattention to the needs of black people and for the New Deal's failure to attack existing political and economic structures. In 1936, Bunche and others founded the NATIONAL NEGRO CONGRESS, a broad-based coalition he later termed "the first sincere effort to bring together on an equal plane Negro leaders [and] professional and white-collar workers with the Negro manual workers and their leaders and organizers." The Congress was eventually taken over by Communist Party workers. Bunche, disillusioned, resigned in 1938.

In 1939, Bunche was hired by the Swedish sociologist Gunnar Myrdal to work on what would become the classic study of race relations in the United States, *An American Dilemma: The Negro Problem and Modern Democracy* (1944). Over the next two years Bunche wrote four long research memos for the project (one was published in 1973, after Bunche's death, as *The Negro in the Age of FDR*). The final report incorporated much of Bunche's research and thought. The unpublished memos, written for the Carnegie Corporation, have remained an important scholarly resource for researchers on black America, both for their exhaustive data and for Bunche's incisive conclusions.

In 1941, after the United States entered World War II, Bunche left Howard to work for the Office of the Coordinator of Information for the Armed Service, and later joined the newly formed Office of Strategic Services, the chief American intelligence organization during WORLD WAR II, precursor of the Central Intelligence Agency. Bunche headed the Africa section of the Research and Analysis Branch. In 1944, Bunche joined the U.S. Department of State's Postwar Planning Unit to deal with the future of colonial territories.

From this point forward, Bunche operated in the arena of international political affairs with an ever-increasing degree of policy-making power. In 1945, he was appointed to the Division of Dependent Area Affairs in the Office of Special Political Affairs, becoming in the process the first African American to head a State Department "desk."

In 1944, Bunche was a member of the U.S. delegation at the Dumbarton Oaks Conference in Washington, D.C., which laid the foundation for the United Nations. Appointed to the U.S. delegation in San Francisco in 1945 and in London in 1946, Bunche helped set up the U.N. Trusteeship system to prepare colonies for independence. His draft declaration of principles governing all dependent territories was the basis of Chapter XI, "Declaration Regarding Non-Self-Governing Territories," of the United Nations Charter.

Bunche went to work in the United Nations Secretariat in 1946 as head of the Trusteeship Department. In 1947, he was assigned to the U.N. Special Commission on Palestine which was a United Nations Trusteeship. The outbreak of the First Arab-Israeli War in 1948, and the assassination of U.N. mediator Folke Bernadotte by Jewish militants, propelled Bunche, Bernadotte's assistant, into the position of acting mediator. Bunche brought the two sides together, negotiating with each in turn, and succeeded in arranging an armistice. Bunche's actions earned him the 1950 Nobel Prize for Peace. He was the first United Nations figure, as well as the first African American, to win a Nobel Prize. Bunche also won the NAACP's Spingarn Medal (1950), and other honors. In 1953 the American Political Science Association elected him its president, the first time an African American was so honored. In 1950, President Truman offered him the post of Assistant Secretary of State. Bunche declined it, and in a rare personal statement on racism, explained that he did not wish to raise his family in Washington, a segregated city.

Bunche remained at the United Nations until shortly before his death in 1971. In 1954, he was appointed United Nations Undersecretary General for Special Political Affairs, and served as a roving specialist in U.N. work. Bunche's most significant contribution at the United Nations was his role in designing and setting up U.N. peacekeeping forces, which supervise and enforce truces and armistices and have arguably been the U.N.'s most important contribution to global peace. Building on the truce supervising operation he put into place after the 1949 Middle East armistice, Bunche created a United Nations Emergency Force in 1956, after the Suez crisis. U.N. peacekeepers played a major role in Lebanon and Yemen, later in the Congo (now Zaire), in India and Pakistan, and in Cyprus. Sir Brian Urquhart, Bunche's assistant and successor as U.N. Undersecretary General for Special Political Affairs, said: "Bunche was unquestionably the original principal architect of [what] is now called peacekeeping . . . and he remained the principal architect, coordinator, and director of United Nations peacekeeping operations until the end of his career at the U.N."

While Bunche remained primarily involved as an international civil servant with the United Nations, promoting international peace and aiding developing countries, he also remained interested in the civil rights struggle in America.

While Bunche remained primarily involved as an international civil servant with the United Nations, promoting international peace and aiding developing countries, he also remained interested in the civil rights struggle in America. Indeed, Bunche demanded and received special dispensation from the United Nations to speak out on racial issues in the United States. Bunche served on the board of the NAACP for many years, and served as an informal adviser to civil rights leaders. In 1963, he attended the March on Washington, and two years later, despite poor health, he traveled to Alabama and walked with the Rev. Dr. Martin Luther KING, Jr., in the front row of the Selma-to-Montgomery Voting Rights March.

BIBLIOGRAPHY

Bunche, Ralph. *An African-American in South Africa.* Athens, Ohio, 1992.

———. "A Critical Analysis of the Tactics and Programs of Minority Groups." *Journal of Negro Education* (July 1935). In August Meier, Elliot Rudwick and Francis L. Broderick, eds. *Black Protest Thought in the Twentieth Century.* Indianapolis, Ind., 1971.

Mann, Peggy. *Ralph Bunche, U.N. Peacemaker.* New York, 1975.

Rivlin, Benjamin, ed. *Ralph Bunche: The Man and His Times.* New York, 1988.

— C. GERALD FRASER

BUREAU OF REFUGEES, FREEDMEN, AND ABANDONED LANDS

Bureau of Refugees, Freedmen, and Abandoned Lands, the federal agency that oversaw Emancipation in the former slave states after the CIVIL WAR, commonly known as the "Freedmen's Bureau." Officially designed to protect the rights of the ex-slaves against intrusion by their former masters, now seen by many historians as paternalistic. In this view, the Freedmen's Bureau pursued "social control" of the freedpeople, encouraging them to return to work as plantation wage laborers.

The Freedmen's Bureau developed out of wartime private relief efforts directed at the "contrabands" who had fled to Union lines. At the suggestion of the American Freedmen's Inquiry Commission, a body set up by the War Department to investigate issues relating to the freedpeople, Congress established the bureau on March 3, 1865, as a military agency. Intended as a temporary organization to exist for one year after the official end of the rebellion, the bureau had "control of all subjects relating to . . . freedmen from rebel States." In addition, it would undertake white refugee relief and manage confiscated Confederate property. The commissioner of the bureau, Oliver Otis Howard, was known as the "Christian general" for his philanthropic interests and Congregationalist religious enthusiasm. Howard eventually presided over a network of almost 1,000 local military and civilian agents scattered across the South, nearly all of them white.

Initially, Howard and his subordinates hoped to provide the rumored FORTY ACRES AND A MULE to at least some freedpeople from plantations seized by the government during the war. The legislation creating the bureau had authorized some land redistribution, and Howard's office drafted Circular 13, which would have implemented the distribution of land in bureau possession. However, Pres. Andrew Johnson countermanded the proposal, and his policy of widespread pardons for ex-Confederates restored most property to its former owners. Stymied, Howard then felt obliged to evict the freedpeople from the lands given them during the war under the "Sherman grant." These were located on the Sea Islands and coastal areas of South Carolina and Georgia. Thus, by the late summer of 1865, Howard abandoned land redistribution and turned his attention to more attainable goals.

The bureau's remaining areas of activity were broad. It assumed the responsibility for aiding the destitute—white and black—and for the care of ill, aged, and insane freedpeople. It also subsidized and sponsored educational efforts directed at the African-American community, developed both by the freedpeople themselves and by the various northern missionary societies. The postwar years witnessed an explosive growth in black education, and the bureau encouraged this development in the face of white southern opposition. The bureau's agents also assumed the duty of securing minimal legal rights for the freedmen, especially the right to testify in court.

Perhaps the bureau's most enduring, and controversial, aspect was its role in overseeing the emergence of free labor. While it attempted to protect the freedpeople from impositions by their former masters, the freedpeople were also enjoined to labor diligently. The favored bureau devise for adjusting plantation agriculture was the annual labor contract, as approved by the local bureau agent. Tens of thousands of standardized contracts were written and enforced by the bureau in 1865 and 1866. The contracts it approved generally provided for wage labor under circumstances reminiscent of slavery: gang labor, tight supervision, women and children in the work force, and provisions restricting the physical mobility and deportment of the freedmen.

In practice, bureau agents spent much of their time encouraging diligent labor by the freedmen, quashing rumors of impending land redistribution, and even punishing the freedmen for refractory behavior. In some cases, agents issued and enforced vagrancy codes directed at the freedpeople. Despite encouraging the freedmen to act as disciplined wage laborers, the bureau soon incurred the enmity of the planters. It insisted that corporal punishment be abandoned, and backed this policy up with frequent arrests. It also established a dual legal structure, with local agents acting as judges in those instances where the civilian courts refused to hear blacks' testimony or committed flagrant injustice. Finally, the bureau and the military opposed the efforts of the conservative presidential RECONSTRUCTION governments to reimpose harsh vagrancy laws, through the BLACK CODES and similar legislation. President Andrew Johnson heeded the complaints of the planters, and in February 1866 vetoed legislation providing for the extension of bureau activities.

The bureau's most enduring, and controversial, aspect was its role in overseeing the emergence of free labor.

The Freedmen's Bureau became a focus of the emerging political struggle between Johnson and Congress for the control of Reconstruction. With the increasing power of the Republican party and especially the Radical faction, the bureau secured powerful political sponsorship. Its functions were extended over Johnson's veto in July 1866. With the enactment of congressional Reconstruction in March 1867, Freedmen's Bureau personnel tended to become involved with the political mobilization then sweeping the black community. For example, in South Carolina, Assistant Commissioner Robert K. Scott was elected the state's first Republican governor, and in Alabama four of the six Republican congressmen elected in February 1868 were bureau officials. Though they were widely denounced as "carpetbaggers," bureau officials exercised an important role in the politicization of the freedpeople through Republican groups such as the Union League.

The restoration of most of the southern states under the military Reconstruction acts furnished the immediate cause of the bureau's demise. With southern governments now granting the freedpeople equal legal rights, there no longer appeared any need for interference in local legal functions. The expansive powers of the Freedmen's Bureau had long violated states' rights taboos, and, moreover, the expense of the bureau's programs proved unpopular with the northern public. The renewal bill of July 1866 provided for the organization's essential termination in two years' time. Later legislation changed that date to the end of 1868, and after that time only the bureau's Education Division and efforts to secure bounties owed to black veterans continued. On June 30, 1872, these operations ended, and the Freedmen's Bureau ceased to exist.

Many of the bureau's aims were certainly laudable, and its accomplishments in promoting black legal rights and education substantial, but the overall record is mixed. In abandoning land redistribution, and in promoting the return of ex-slaves to plantation agriculture as hired labor under the contract system, the bureau also assisted in the survival of the plantation economy.

BIBLIOGRAPHY

Bently, George R. *A History of the Freedmen's Bureau.* Philadelphia, 1955.

Foner, Eric. *Reconstruction: America's Unfinished Revolution, 1863–77.* New York, 1988.

McFeely, William S. *Yankee Stepfather: General O. O. Howard and the Freedmen.* New York, 1968.

– MICHAEL W. FITZGERALD

C

CALLOWAY, CABELL "CAB"

Cabell "Cab" Calloway (December 25, 1907– November 18, 1994), jazz singer and bandleader. Born in Rochester, N.Y., Calloway was raised in Baltimore, Md. In high school he sang with a local vocal group called the Baltimore Melody Boys. The Calloway family, including Cab's sister, singer Blanche Calloway, then moved to Chicago, where he attended Crane College. Calloway began his career as a singer, drummer, and master of ceremonies at nightclubs in Chicago and other midwestern cities. In the late 1920s in Chicago, Calloway worked with the Missourians, a big band; in the male vocal quartet in *Plantation Days*; and as leader of the Alabamians. In 1929, he took the Alabamians to Harlem's Savoy Ballroom, and that same year was featured in Fats Waller and Andy Razaf's *Hot Chocolates* revue.

In 1929 Calloway began to lead the Missourians under his own name ("St. James Infirmary," 1930). In 1931, they replaced Duke ELLINGTON as the COTTON CLUB's house band. During the 1930s Calloway became a household name, the country's prototypical "hipster," renowned for his infectious vocal histrionics, his frenzied dashing up and down the stage in a white satin zoot suit, and leading audience sing-a-longs, particularly on his biggest hit, "Minnie the Moocher" (1931). That song, with its "Hi-de-ho" chorus, was a million-copy seller and earned him the nickname "Hi-de-ho Man."

Calloway's talents were not limited to comic entertainment. During the swing era Calloway's band was one of the most popular in the country ("At the Clambake Carnival," 1938; "Jumpin' Jive," 1939; "Pickin' the Cabbage," 1940), and he nurtured some of the best instrumentalists of the day, including saxophonists Ben Webster and Chu Berry, trumpeters Jonah Jones and Dizzy GILLESPIE, bassist Milt Hinton, and drummer Cozy Cole. The orchestra held its own in competitions throughout the 1930s with the bands of Count BASIE, Duke Ellington, Chick Webb, and Jimmy Lunceford. Calloway's orchestra left the Cotton Club in 1934 for a European tour. In addition to its success in nightclubs and on the concert stage, the Calloway orchestra also appeared in movies, including *The Big Broadcast* (1932), *The Singing Kid* (1936), *St. Louis Blues* (1939), and *Stormy Weather* (1943). Calloway disbanded the orchestra in 1948, and worked with a sextet before touring England as a solo.

Calloway returned to his roots in musical theater in 1952 for a two-year run in the role of Sportin' Life in a touring version of George Gershwin's *Porgy and Bess.* Throughout the 1950s and 1960s, Calloway continued to perform both as a solo act and as the leader of big bands. In the mid-1960s he toured with the Harlem Globetrotters comic basketball team. In 1974 Calloway appeared in an all-black version of *Hello, Dolly!,* and two years later he published his autobiography, *Of Minnie the Moocher and Me.* Calloway appeared on Broadway in *Bubbling Brown Sugar* in 1975, and his cameo in *The Blues Brothers* (1980) brought a revival of interest in him. In 1984 he sang with his vocalist daughter, Chris, in an engagement at New York's Blue Note nightclub. In 1987 he again appeared with Chris Calloway, this time in *His Royal Highness of Hi-de-ho* in New York.

During the 1930s Calloway became a household name, the country's prototypical "hipster," renowned for his infectious vocal histrionics and his frenzied dashing up and down the stage in a white satin zoot suit.

BIBLIOGRAPHY

Papa, J. *Cab Calloway and His Orchestra.* Zephyrhills, Fla., 1976.
Simon, G. T. *The Big Bands.* New York, 1981.

– MICHAEL D. SCOTT

CAMBRIDGE, GODFREY MACARTHUR

Godfrey MacArthur Cambridge (February 26, 1933– November 29, 1976), actor. Godfrey Cambridge was born in New York City in 1933 and grew up in Harlem with his parents, Sarah and Alexander. He attended Flushing High School, where he excelled as both a student and a leader of extracurricular activities. Cambridge won a scholarship to Hofstra College (now Hofstra University) on Long Island, where he majored in English and had his first acting experience, appearing in a school production of *Macbeth.* After racial threats forced him to leave Hofstra during his junior year, Cambridge attended City College in New York City.

Upon graduating, he worked at a number of jobs including stints as an airplane wing cleaner, a judo instructor, a cab driver, and clerk for the New York City Housing Authority.

In 1956 Cambridge landed his first professional role, as a bartender in an Off-Broadway revival of Louis Peterson's *Take a Giant Step*. The play ran for nine months and led to television appearances in shows such as *The United States Steel Hour, Naked City*, and *You'll Never Get Rich* (with Phil Silvers as Sergeant Bilko). In 1961 Cambridge appeared in Jean Genet's *The Blacks*, a savage drama about racial hatred, and for his efforts received the *Village Voice*'s Obie Award for best performer of 1961. The following year he appeared in Ossie DAVIS's *Purlie Victorious*, for which he earned a Tony nomination. Cambridge went on to perform in other plays, including *A Funny Thing Happened on the Way to the Forum* (1962), *The Living Promise* (1963), and *How to Be a Jewish Mother* (1967), in which he played every part but the title role.

After a successful appearance on *The Jack Paar Program* in 1964, Cambridge was able to choose his roles and began turning down film parts which stereotyped him. Instead he played a wide variety of movie characters, including a reprise of his role in the film version of *Purlie Victorious*, entitled *Gone Are the Days* (1963), an Irishman in *The Troublemaker* (1964), a Jewish cab driver in *Bye, Bye, Braverman* (1968), and a concert violinist in *The Biggest Bundle of Them All* (1968). Cambridge is probably best known for his leading roles in the popular films *Watermelon Man* (1970) and *Cotton Comes to Harlem* (1970).

In addition to his film appearances, Cambridge was a successful stand-up comedian. His sense of humor, while not alienating to white audiences, did not lack bite. Essentially a social satirist, his comedy often dealt with ordinary people, black and white, struggling with the problems of everyday life.

During the CIVIL RIGHTS MOVEMENT, Cambridge performed at rallies and organized support for the employment of more African Americans in the entertainment industry. A compulsive eater who at times weighed as much as 300 pounds, in 1976 Cambridge collapsed and died on the set of the TV movie *Victory at Entebbe*, in which he played the Ugandan dictator Idi Amin.

BIBLIOGRAPHY

Bogle, Donald. *Blacks in American Films and Television*. New York, 1988.

New York Times Biographical Services. November 30, 1976, p. 1521. New York, 1976.

— THADDEUS RUSSELL

CARMICHAEL, STOKELY

Stokely Carmichael (July 29, 1941–), activist. Born in Port of Spain, Trinidad, Stokely Carmichael graduated from the Bronx High School of Science in 1960 and Howard University in 1964. During his college years, he participated in a variety of civil rights demonstrations sponsored by the CONGRESS OF RACIAL EQUALITY (CORE), the Nonviolent Action Group (NAG), and the STUDENT NONVIOLENT COORDINATING COMMITTEE (SNCC). As a freedom rider, he was arrested in 1961 for violating Mississippi segregation laws and spent seven weeks in Parchman Penitentiary. After college, he worked with the Mississippi Summer Project, directed SNCC voter-registration efforts in Lowndes County, Ala., and helped organize black voters through the Lowndes County Freedom Organization.

Carmichael proffered an outspoken, militant stance that helped distance SNCC from the moderate leadership of competing civil rights organizations.

Elected SNCC chairman in 1966, he proffered an outspoken, militant stance that helped distance SNCC from the moderate leadership of competing civil rights organizations. A chief architect and spokesperson for the new Black Power ideology, Carmichael coauthored (with Charles V. Hamilton) *Black Power* (1967) and published a collection of his essays and addresses, *Stokely Speaks* (1971). He left his SNCC post in 1967. The next year he was made prime minister of the BLACK PANTHER PARTY; in 1969, he quit the Black Panthers and became an organizer for Kwame Nkrumah's All-African People's Revolutionary Party. Studies with Nkrumah of Ghana and Sékou Touré of Guinea confirmed his Pan-Africanism and, in 1978, moved him to change his name to Kwame Toure. Since 1969, he has made Conakry, Guinea, his home. He has continued his work in political education, condemning Western imperialism, and promoting the goal of a unified socialist Africa.

BIBLIOGRAPHY

Carmichael, Stokely. *Stokely Speaks: Black Power Back to Pan-Africanism*. New York, 1971.

Carmichael, Stokely, and Charles V. Hamilton. *Black Power: The Politics of Liberation in America*. New York, 1967.

— WILLIAM L. VAN DEBURG

CARPETBAGGERS

Devised by opponents of RECONSTRUCTION as a term of abuse for Northerners who came to the South after the Civil War and joined the REPUBLICAN PARTY, the word *carpetbagger* has remained part of the lexicon of American politics. Today it refers to those, regardless of region, who run for office in a district to which they have only recently moved.

During Reconstruction, the term implied that Republican newcomers were men from the lower echelons of northern society who had packed all their belongings in a suitcase and left their homes in order to reap the spoils of office in the South. This image was reinforced by anti-Reconstruction scholars early in the twentieth century, who charged that carpetbaggers poisoned the South's allegedly harmonious race relations by turning gullible African Americans against their former masters and using them as stepping-stones to office.

Some carpetbaggers undoubtedly were corrupt adventurers. The large majority, however, hardly fit the traditional image. Most tended to be well educated and middle-class in origin. Some had been lawyers, businessmen, newspaper editors, and other pillars of northern communities. The majority (including fifty-two of the sixty who served in Congress during Reconstruction) were veterans of the Union army who simply decided to remain in the South when the war ended in 1865. At this time, blacks did not enjoy the right to vote, and the possibility of office for northern newcomers was remote.

For most carpetbaggers, the lure of the South was the same that drew thousands of Americans to settle in the West during the nineteenth century—economic opportunity. With cotton prices high and the South starved of capital, numerous army veterans purchased land or went into business with impoverished southern planters. They hoped to combine personal economic gain with a role in helping to mold the "backward" South in the image of the modern, industrializing North, substituting, as one wrote, "the civilization of freedom for that of SLAVERY." Other groups of carpetbaggers were teachers, Freedmen's Bureau officers, and those who came to the region genuinely hoping to assist the former slaves.

A variety of motives led these Northerners to enter politics in 1867. Crop failures had wiped out many who had invested in cotton land, and politics offered a livelihood. Some had earned the former slaves' goodwill, or proved more willing to work politically with African Americans than were native-born white Southerners. Indeed, in some localities, carpetbaggers were the only Republicans with political experience, and a number ran for office because they had been asked to do so by the former slaves. Generally, carpetbaggers were more likely than white southern Republicans to support black aspirations for equality before the law, and laws prohibiting racial segregation in public accommodations. As proponents of the North's "free labor" ideology, they strongly favored Reconstruction programs promoting railroad development and economic modernization, and tended to oppose measures to use the power of the state to distribute land to the former slaves.

No accurate figures are available as to how many Northerners came to the South during Reconstruction, but in no state did those born in the North represent even 2 percent of the total population. Nonetheless, carpetbaggers played a major role in Republican politics. Generally representing Black Belt constituencies, they held a major share of Reconstruction offices in Florida, Louisiana, and South Carolina, whose Republican parties attracted little support from white Southerners. Their ranks included such Republican governors as Robert K. Scott (who came south from Ohio with the Army and directed the Freedmen's Bureau in South Carolina) and Henry C. Warmoth and William P. Kellogg of Louisiana (army veterans from Illinois). In Mississippi, when black leaders became dissatisfied with the moderate policies of "scalawag" Gov. James L. Alcorn, they turned to Maine native Adelbert Ames, who had demonstrated a commitment to equal rights when he commanded the fourth military district under the Reconstruction Act of 1867. Ames was elected governor in 1873. Another prominent carpetbagger was Albion W. Tourgée, who, as a judge in North Carolina, waged a courageous campaign against the Ku Klux Klan.

Although the term *carpetbagger* generally applies to whites, a considerable number of black Northerners also came south during this period. Reconstruction was one of the few occasions in American history when opportunities for black men of talent and ambition were greater in the South than in the North. The ranks of "black carpetbaggers" included veterans of the Union army, ministers and teachers who had come south to work for the Freedmen's Bureau or for northern aid societies, and the children of southern free blacks who had been sent north years before for an education. Quite a few were veterans of the antislavery struggle in the northern states or Canada.

Over 100 public officeholders after the Civil War were African Americans who had been born in the North or lived there for a substantial period before the war. Born in Philadelphia, Mifflin Gibbs and Jonathan Gibbs held major positions in Arkansas and Florida, respectively. Tunis G. Campbell, who had lived in New York before the Civil War, was the political "boss" of

McIntosh County, Ga., during Reconstruction, and Stephen A. Swails, a veteran of the Fifty-fourth Regiment of Massachusetts Voluntary Infantry, became the most prominent political leader in Williamsburg County, S.C. A number of "black carpetbaggers" had been born abroad, including South Carolina congressman Robert B. Elliott, apparently a native of Great Britain, and Martin F. Becker, a South Carolina constitutional convention delegate, who hailed from Dutch Guiana (now known as Suriname).

After the end of Reconstruction, most white carpetbaggers appear to have returned to the North, as did many of their black counterparts.

BIBLIOGRAPHY

Current, Richard N. *Those Terrible Carpetbaggers: A Reinterpretation.* New York, 1988.

Foner, Eric. *Freedom's Lawmakers: A Directory of Black Officeholders During Reconstruction.* New York, 1993.

Harris, William H. "The Creed of the Carpetbaggers: The Case of Mississippi." *Journal of Southern History* 40 (1974): 199–224.

Overy, David H. *Wisconsin Carpetbaggers in Dixie.* Madison, Wis., 1961.

Powell, Lawrence N. *New Masters: Northern Planters during the Civil War and Reconstruction.* New Haven, Conn., 1980.

– ERIC FONER

CARVER, GEORGE WASHINGTON

George Washington Carver (c. 1864–January 5, 1943), scientist and educator. Born in Diamond, Mo., George Washington Carver did not remember his parents. His father was believed to be a slave killed accidentally before Carver's birth. His mother was Mary Carver, a slave apparently kidnapped by slave raiders soon after he was born. He and his older brother were raised by their mother's former owners, Moses and Susan Carver, on their small, largely self-sufficient farm.

Denied admission to the neighborhood school because of his color, Carver was privately tutored and then moved to nearby Neosho to enter school in the mid-1870s. He soon realized he knew more than the teacher and left with a family moving to Fort Scott, Kans. After witnessing a lynching there, he left that town and for over a decade roamed around the Midwest seeking an education while supporting himself by cooking, laundering, and homesteading.

In 1890 Carver enrolled in Simpson College in Indianola, Iowa, where he was an art major and the only African-American student. After his teacher convinced him that a black man could not make a living in art, Carver transferred to Iowa State College at Ames in 1891 to major in agriculture. Again the only black student on campus, Carver participated fully (except for dating) in extracurricular activities and compiled such an impressive academic record that he was hired as a botany assistant to pursue postgraduate work. Before he received his master of agriculture degree in 1896, he was placed in charge of the greenhouse and taught freshmen students.

An expert in mycology (the study of fungi) and plant cross-fertilization, Carver could have remained at Iowa and probably would have made significant contributions in one or both fields. However, he felt an obligation to share his knowledge with other African Americans and accepted Booker T. WASHINGTON's offer to become head of the agricultural department at Tuskegee Normal and Industrial Institute in 1896.

When he arrived at Tuskegee, Carver intended only to stay a few years and then pursue doctoral work. Instead, he spent his remaining forty-six years there. Although he once considered matrimony, he never married and instead "adopted" many Tuskegee students as his "children," to whom he provided loans and guidance. For the first half of his tenure, he worked long hours in administration, teaching, and research. The focus of his work reflected the needs of his constituents rather than his personal talents or interests. As director of the only all-black-staffed agricultural experiment station, he sought answers to the debt problems of small-scale farmers and landless sharecroppers. Thus, in his teaching, extension work (carried on with a wagon equipped as a movable school), and agricultural bulle-

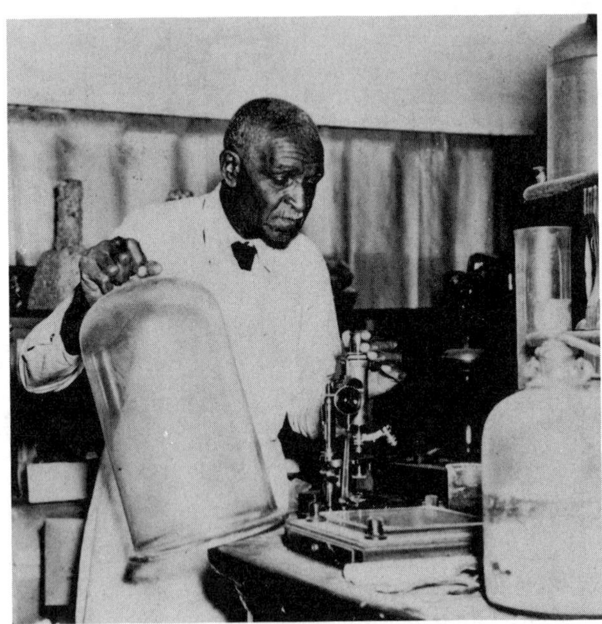

George Washington Carver. (Photographs and Prints Division, Schomburg Center for Research in Black Culture, The New York Public Library, Astor, Lenox and Tilden Foundations)

tins, Carver preached the use of available and renewable resources to replace expensive, purchased commodities. He especially advocated the growing of peanuts as a cheap source of protein and published several bulletins with peanut recipes.

After twenty years at Tuskegee, Carver was respected by agricultural researchers but largely unknown to the general public. His rise to fame began with his induction in 1916 into Great Britain's Royal Society for the Arts and the growing realization of his usefulness by the peanut industry. In 1921, a growers' association paid his way to testify at tariff hearings in Congress. There his showmanship in demonstrating peanut products drew national press coverage. Two years later, some Atlanta businessmen founded the Carver Products Company, and Carver won the Spingarn Medal of the NAACP. Although the company failed, it generated publicity. Then in 1933 an Associated Press release exaggerated Carver's success in rehabilitating polio patients with peanut-oil massages. Soon he was perhaps the best known African American of his generation.

The increasing publicity caught the attention of numerous people who found Carver's rise from slavery and his personality appealing. Articles began to appear describing the flowers in the lapels of his well-worn jackets and his rambles in the woods to commune with his "Creator," through which he expressed his devout but nonsectarian belief. Because he took no public stand on political or racial matters, many diverse groups could adopt him as a symbol of their causes. Thus he was appropriated by advocates of racial equality, the "New South," religion, the "American Dream," and even segregation. His significant work as an agricultural researcher and educator was obscured by the myth of the "peanut wizard."

Relishing the publicity, Carver did little to correct the public record, aside from general statements of his "unworthiness" of the honors that came with increasing frequency. Some symbolic uses of his life helped to perpetuate white stereotypes of African Americans, but most of the publicity had a positive impact on both white and black Americans. Indeed, Carver became a potent tool for racial tolerance after the Commission on Interracial Cooperation and the YMCA began to sponsor his lecture tours of white college campuses in the 1920s and 1930s. On these tours, Carver added dozens of whites to his adopted "family." To them he was no "token black" but a trusted father figure to whom they wrote their innermost thoughts. Many, such as white clergyman Howard Kester, became outspoken advocates of racial justice.

Because of his compelling personality, Carver had a profound impact on almost everyone—black or white—who came in contact with him. His "special friends" ranged from white sharecroppers to Henry Ford. Most of his major publicists were true disciples of Carver's vision of the interrelatedness of all human beings and their environment. Because of his extreme frugality, he was also able to leave a substantial legacy by giving about sixty thousand dollars to establish the George Washington Carver Foundation, which continues to support scientific research at Tuskegee University. Although his scientific contributions were meager relative to his fame, and he could not single-handedly save the black family farm, Carver's work and warmth greatly enriched the lives of thousands.

BIBLIOGRAPHY

Kremer, Gary R. *George Washington Carver in His Own Words.* Columbus, Mo., 1987.

Mackintosh, Barry. "George Washington Carver: The Making of a Myth." *Journal of Southern History* 42 (1976): 507–528.

McMurry, Linda O. *George Washington Carver: Scientist and Symbol.* New York, 1981.

– LINDA O. MCMURRY

CHARLES, RAY

Ray Charles (Ray Charles Robinson) (September 23, 1930–), musician. Ray Charles's achievement over the past forty-five years marks him as one of the most important and influential figures of American music in the postwar period. He is often called the "Father of Soul," both for his innovative blending of gospel, blues, and jazz, and his enormous versatility as a singer, pianist, songwriter, composer-arranger, saxophonist, and band leader.

Born into a poor family in Albany, Ga., Ray Charles was raised in Greenville, Fla. At the age of five he contracted glaucoma; left untreated, it soon blinded him. His mother, Aretha, sent him to the School for the Deaf and Blind in St. Augustine, where he spent the next eight years studying composition, learning to write musical scores in braille, and mastering various instruments (the trumpet, alto saxophone, clarinet, organ, and piano). After his mother died in 1945, he left school to form a combo; after he had saved enough money, he moved to Seattle, where he played in a number of jazz trios, gradually developing a piano and vocal style heavily influenced by Nat "King" COLE. At around this time, Ray Charles decided to drop his surname in order to avoid being confused with prizefighter Sugar Ray Robinson.

Charles developed a significant following in Seattle, and soon began to record for various labels. His first hits, "Baby Let Me Hold Your Hand" (1951) and "Kiss

Me Baby" (1952) were recorded for the Swing Time label. In 1952 Charles began to record for Atlantic Records, where he made his first musical breakthrough with "I've Got a Woman" (1955), a blend, startlingly unconventional for the time, of a coarse bluesy sexuality with the intense emotionality of gospel. Many of his musical ideas in this period were taken from GOSPEL music, but his adaptations provoked much criticism for their combination of the vocal techniques of "testifying" with sexually explicit lyrics. This style nevertheless provided Charles with some of his most successful songs, among them, "Hallelujah, I Love Her So" (1956), "The Right Time" (1959), and "What'd I Say" (1959).

Ray Charles is often called the "Father of Soul," both for his innovative blending of gospel, blues, and jazz, and his enormous versatility as a singer, pianist, songwriter, composer-arranger, saxophonist, and band leader.

As his fame increased, Charles increasingly found favor with white audiences. In 1959 he left Atlantic for ABC/Paramount; the move signaled a turn toward country-and-western music and popular standards. While his early recordings with ABC (such as "Georgia on My Mind," "Hit the Road Jack," and "I Can't Stop Loving You") are generally considered the equals of those of his Atlantic period, some critics charged that his music was gradually becoming conventional and uninspired. Nevertheless, throughout the 1960s Charles turned out scores of Top-Ten hits (including "You Are My Sunshine," "Let's Go Get Stoned," and "Here We Go Again"), and a number of successful LPs.

Charles's rise to fame was not without its struggles. Along the way he developed an addiction to heroin, and in 1955, 1961, and 1965, he was arrested for the possession of narcotics. He never served a long prison term, but he stopped performing for a year after his last arrest, during which time he worked successfully to overcome the seventeen-year-long addiction. Since then the record shows a steady series of successes and honors. In 1966, the U.S. House of Representatives passed a special resolution honoring Charles for his musical achievement. In the late 1960s he founded his own record label and music publishing firm. In 1979, Hoagy Carmichael's "Georgia on My Mind," perhaps Charles's best-known recording, was adopted as the official song of Georgia. In 1986, Charles was among the first ten artists inducted into the Rock and Roll Hall of Fame.

During his career, Charles has appeared in several films, including *Blues for Lovers* (a.k.a. *Ballad in Blue,* 1965) and *The Blues Brothers* (1980), and has performed on the soundtracks of many more, including *The Cincinnati Kids* (1965) and *In the Heat of the Night* (1967); his song "What'd I Say" was the subject of *Cosmic Ray,* an experimental film by Bruce Conner, in 1961.

In recent years, Charles has been active in various social causes, including civil rights issues, African famine relief, and aid to the disabled. In 1985, he attributed the presence of several bombs found under a bandstand where he was to perform to his public statements opposing racism. In 1987 he made an appeal to Congress for federal aid for the deaf and established the Robinson Foundation for Hearing Disorders with an endowment of $1 million.

In addition to making frequent concert appearances and appearing in several popular commercials (most notably the phenomenally successful Diet Pepsi ads in the early 1990s), Charles has remained active in producing and recording his own albums. His LP *Friendship* rose to number one on the country-and-western charts in 1985. In 1990, he performed with B.B. King in the Philip Morris Superband, and released an album, *Would You Believe?* Charles's autobiography *Brother Ray* (1978, with David Ritz), was published in a revised and updated edition in 1992. Charles has won eleven Grammy Awards, the title of Commandeur de l'Ordre des Arts et des Lettres from the French Republic, an NAACP Hall of Fame Award (1983), and a Lifetime Achievement Award from the National Academy of Recording Arts and Sciences (1989).

BIBLIOGRAPHY

Balliett, Whitney. *American Singers.* New York, 1979.

Brelin, Christa, and William C. Matney, Jr., eds. *Who's Who Among Black Americans.* 7th ed. Detroit, 1992.

Marsh, Dave. "Ray Charles." In *The New Grove Dictionary of American Music.* H. Wiley Hitchcock and Stanley Sadie, eds. London and New York, 1986.

Shaw, Arnold. *Black Popular Music in America.* New York, 1986.

— ROBERT W. STEPHENS

CHARLESTON, SOUTH CAROLINA

The presence of blacks in Charleston dates from 1526, when a Spanish expedition from the West Indies arrived in the low country. For the next hundred years blacks fought alongside both the French and the Spanish as these two competed for the region, but an English colony of settlers from Barbados arrived to found the first permanent settlement (Charles Towne) in 1670. The Barbadians had long relied on slave labor from Africa to grow food, and the early presence of Africans and West Indians brought as slaves, mixed with European elements, helped in creating the unique cultural mix that distinguishes the city and the surrounding Sea Islands area.

The successful introduction of rice in the late 1690s paralleled the emergence of a fixed reliance upon African slave labor that resulted in the colony's having a black majority population by 1700. Legend has it that an African enslaved woman brought rice to the colony aboard ship. Certainly, there were Africans skilled in the cultivation of rice, a staple crop in parts of West Africa, and both the baskets for collecting the crop and the methods of cleaning it were of African origin. Africans from different tribes had skills in ironwork, carpentry, and other trades. This expertise was desperately needed in a colony with a small white labor force, and one less able than Africans to withstand the humid, malarial climate. Along with the slaves came African styles of art, cloth, and cuisine. Perhaps the most enduring carryover from Africa is the GULLAH language still spoken by some low-country African-Americans, related to the Krio tongue of Sierra Leone.

Charleston, meanwhile, was growing in size and in importance, both as a center of trade and as a port. White Charlestonians traded heavily with their West Indian partners, and much of the traffic was in slaves. An estimated 40 percent of all enslaved persons brought to the English colonies between 1700 and 1775 came through Charleston's Sullivan Island harbor. The customs and quarantine facilities on the island have caused it to be dubbed "the Ellis Island of Black America."

Enslaved blacks lived in the city and surrounding areas in large numbers. Neither the STONO REBELLION of 1739, in which an armed group of slaves killed 31 whites in an engagement, nor the American Revolution, with its egalitarian message, provoked widespread abolitionist sentiment in Charleston. During the antebellum period, some three-quarters of the city's white families owned slaves, as did a small number of mulatto families. Enslaved blacks generally lived in their masters' houses, or in nearby cabins. Within the large city, enslaved blacks often hired themselves out as laborers or craftsworkers, sometimes saving enough money to buy their freedom. The City Council made repeated efforts to control the enslaved population through labor registries and ordinances against blacks dressing "up" above their station.

Charleston also boasted a large free black population. Miscegenation was relatively open and widespread, and many white men kept black mistresses. After 1800, a free, mixed-race "brown elite" grew up around mutual aid and benevolent organizations such as the Brown Fellowship Society and Friendly Moralist Society. Most free women of color worked as domestics, and men worked as carpenters, bakers, sawyers, among other jobs. Prior to the Civil War, between eighty and ninety percent of Charleston's skilled trades were entrusted to black labor. Charlestonian Edward Jones, a second-generation free black whose parents operated the renowned Jones Boarding House, was one of America's first black college graduates (Amherst, 1839). The free blacks were second-class citizens, and after 1815 they faced increasing pressure and legal disabilities, including "black taxes" on nonresidents, and denial of all-black church services, as whites grew frightened of slave revolts. In 1822, a conspiracy was uncovered. A free black carpenter named Denmark Vesey was charged with having plotted with slave assistants to start an uprising to kill all the whites in Charleston. Though the extent of the plot has long been disputed by historians, Vesey and twenty-two slaves were hanged. More often slaves resorted to arson, poisoning, work stoppage, and running away to resist enslavement.

As a result of the DENMARK VESEY CONSPIRACY, further harsh laws were imposed on free blacks, including the notorious order providing for the detention of black sailors while their ships were in port. Nevertheless, the free black population had developed sufficient personal ties with influential whites to feel reasonably secure. After 1822, white immigration was encouraged. By 1860, Charleston had a white majority population and was fervently secessionist. Even before the Civil War began in the city, the secessionist backlash led to harassment of the free black population. White workers resenting black competition instigated a "crackdown" on free blacks. White groups instituted house-to-house searches, and those blacks unable to show identification proving their status were enslaved. Many free people of color fled the city.

Even before the Civil War began in the city, the secessionist backlash led to harassment of the free black population.

Charleston was hit hard economically by the Civil War and the Union naval blockade, and the port never regained its former importance after 1865. After the Civil War ended, newly freed blacks poured into

Charleston from the ravaged countryside, seeking work. The city became a center of African-American life. Blacks, finally able to found their own churches, split from whites to found St. Mark's Church (Episcopal), Centenary Methodist Church, Morris Street Baptist Church, and other congregations. These became the centers of black life. The black community also set up many businesses and community institutions. The Avery Normal Institute, founded in 1865, was the symbol of white elite efforts to aid black uplift, producing academically superior students and teachers until it closed in 1954. The Longshoremen's Protective Association, which lasted until 1905, was a majority black group whose efforts assured dockworkers the highest wages of all South Atlantic ports. Blacks from Charleston and the low country, such as Robert B. Elliott and Robert Smalls, were influential in the state's black majority state assembly, which first met in the city in 1866. Richard Harvey Cain, a state senator later elected to Congress, in 1871 founded Lincolnville, a colony for free blacks, just outside the city. While the corruption in South Carolina's government was later held up by whites as an example of black incompetence, and the state was "redeemed" by white Democrats in 1870, the progressive state constitution that blacks had helped to draft remained in force until 1895.

After its "redemption," Charleston continued as a black center. Blacks continued to occupy postmaster and customs jobs through the 1880s, and there were no fewer than seven black newspapers in the nineteenth century's last two decades. The Wainwright Printing Company (1897) exists as the oldest surviving black business. Institutions such as the Jenkins Orphanage (1892; it was later famous for its band) and the Charleston Training School for Colored Nurses (1897) were founded. Only after 1895, under the racist regime of Ben Tillman, was large-scale segregation instituted. Discrimination was rampant. When Theodore Roosevelt appointed Dr. William D. Crum, an African American, as Collector of the Port in 1903, white opposition in the city drew national attention. Crum's appointment was eventually rescinded, and he was made ambassador to Liberia, the African nation first settled by black Charleston expatriates in 1820.

During most of the twentieth century, Charleston was a small southern town with a unique integrated housing pattern. Unlike the image of blacks living in rundown tenements such as Cabbage Row (immortalized as Catfish Row in DuBose Heyward's *Porgy*), black Charlestonians lived throughout the city, and many owned their homes. Total social segregation existed nevertheless. Public schools were poor, and job discrimination kept most blacks in menial labor. Low cotton and agricultural prices forced many blacks to migrate. According to some sources, the "geechee dance," which black Charlestonians brought to northern cities, gave rise to the popular 1920s dance the Charleston. Some prominent twentieth-century Charlestonians include HARLEM RENAISSANCE portrait painter Edwin Harleston (founder of the local branch of the NAACP), famed marine biologist Dr. Ernest E. JUST, and the human rights activist Septima Poinsette CLARK.

Change started in the 1940s, when Federal Judge J. Waties Waring abolished the state's Democratic "white primary" and ordered the equalization of teachers' pay. The NATIONAL ASSOCIATION FOR THE ADVANCEMENT OF COLORED PEOPLE (NAACP), with support from other organizations like the SOUTHERN CHRISTIAN LEADERSHIP CONFERENCE led the CIVIL RIGHTS MOVEMENT in the city. Community members worked with Mayor Palmer Gaillard to peacefully integrate the city. Gaillard picked black aldermen to run with him, and ensured that desegregation laws were obeyed. In 1970, Herbert Fielding became the first black Charlestonian since Reconstruction elected to the state assembly, and Lonnie Hamilton was elected to the city council. The economic problems of the city's blacks remained, and were highlighted by the 1969 strike of the largely black workforce at the Medical University of South Carolina and Charleston County hospitals, which fought for better wages and union recognition.

In the 1990s, Charleston is paying greater attention to its rich black past, with the Avery Research Center for African American History and Culture, housed in the original Avery Institute building on the College of Charleston campus, being the chief institutional agent. However, the preservationist movement has aroused opposition as well as appreciation from blacks, who fear that their neighborhoods and homes may be invaded and taken over by those seeking to preserve the past at the expense of genuine black economic development.

BIBLIOGRAPHY

Drago, Edmund Lee. *Initiative, Paternalism, and Race Relations: Charleston's Avery Normal Institute.* Athens, Ga., 1990.

Newby, I. A. *Black Carolinians: A History of Blacks in South Carolina from 1895–1968.* Columbia, S.C., 1973.

Rosen, Robert N. *A Short History of Charleston.* San Francisco, 1982.

Wood, Peter H. *Black Majority: Negroes in Colonial South Carolina from 1670 Through the Stono Rebellion.* New York, 1974.

– MILLICENT E. BROWN

CHESNUTT, CHARLES WADDELL

Charles Waddell Chesnutt (June 20, 1858–November 15, 1932), writer. Born in Cleveland, Ohio, to freeborn mulattoes, Chesnutt was raised mostly in Fayetteville,

N.C., by his father, Andrew; his mother, Ann Maria, died when he was only thirteen. Though Chesnutt attended the Howard School and received a fairly sound general education, he proved to be a model autodidact, teaching himself advanced mathematics, ancient languages, history, and shorthand. His first teaching assignments in Charlotte, N.C., and Spartanburg, S.C., from 1875 to 1877, served as a proving ground for what he had learned. He rose in 1879 from being first assistant to the principal of the State Colored Normal School of North Carolina to become its principal, serving also as Sunday-school superintendent of the renowned Evans Chapel African Methodist Episcopal Zion Church. Despite his success, Chesnutt was determined to escape the harsh racism of the South. In 1883, peddling his shorthand skills, he sought work with northern newspapers, such as the *New York Mail and Express;* he stayed there only five months before moving on to Cleveland to try his luck in this city of his birth, soon to become his permanent place of residence. While working in the law offices of a railroad company, Chesnutt studied law, and in 1887 passed the Ohio bar examination. Pleased with his accomplishments, he began operating a stenographic service for the courts and was well rewarded for his efforts. Having secured a foothold on this trade, he sent for his wife, Susan, whom he married in 1878, and his children, who were left behind in Fayetteville while he traveled from the South to the North and back again—a pattern of departures and returns that would later play a subtle role in most of his fiction.

Novelist and short-story writer Charles W. Chesnutt was one of the few African-American authors in the early twentieth century whose works were widely published. Chesnutt's evocative depictions of black southern life received widespread critical acclaim. (Mary O. H. Williamson Collection, Moorland-Spingarn Research Center, Howard University)

Rankled by racist or insensitive southern white writers and their depictions of miscegenation and the black experience, Chesnutt vowed to render a more accurate and faithful account of the issues. In 1887, his tale of magic, witchcraft, and slavery "The Goophered Grapevine," brought him to the nation's attention, though by now he had already published approximately sixteen short stories in a variety of magazines and newspapers. With the heavy-handed assistance of his publisher's editors, Chesnutt produced *The Conjure Woman* (1899), a collection of tales connected by their plots' depiction of magical events and unified by their portrayal of the horrors of slavery while raising troubling questions regarding the complex attachments that linked the ex-slaves to their slave forebears and to their masters. It was a stunning success, preceded a few months earlier by *The Wife of His Youth and Other Stories of the Color Line* (1899)—a collection of tales wherein irony and inexplicable coincidences, rather than magic, represent the controlling literary technique, and where blacks confront the lessons of the "color line": color prejudice among blacks, which is as much about race as it is about kinship and familial affiliation. This too was very well received.

Though Chesnutt appears to have been steadfast against any temptation to pass as white himself, he flirted very much with this topic in his fiction. Thus, the pathos aroused in his first novel, *The House Behind the Cedars* (1900), is created by the choice a young woman must make between passing as white, thereby enjoying the apparent benefits of white society, and remaining with her mother to live among those of the black race with whom she was raised, but among whom she would be forever blocked from enjoying the fruits due her as an American citizen.

In the wake of his early successes, Chesnutt closed his stenographic offices and devoted himself full-time to writing fiction. By now it appeared that he had joined that diverse group of regional writers called "local colorists"; but with a compulsory life of Frederick DOUGLASS (1899) behind him, his next literary efforts proved too realistic and bitter for his newfound audience. Though readers may be moved by the sibling rivalry of two women, one black and one white, depicted in *The Marrow of Tradition* (1901), in his second novel, their kinship is eclipsed by the highly charged politics of the post-Civil War period, a polarized time that left little room for moderating sentiments in the North or the South. The plot depicts strange bedfellows brought together by political goals based more on postbellum fears than on any alliance they might have forged during the antebellum era or any indignity they might have suffered in common. Forced by poor sales, Chesnutt returned in 1901 to stenography, consequently remaining sorely underrated during his lifetime.

As a witness to events that took place in the South during the 1890s, Chesnutt could no longer believe that paternalistic, well-meaning whites were able or willing to do anything more for blacks. In his last published novel, *The Colonel's Dream* (1905), the white colonel returns to his southern home with the belief that he can forestall the return to slave conditions into which many blacks and poor whites are falling. Having failed, the colonel returns north with the belief that blacks cannot win the war of "Redemption," as this era was dubbed, with or without the assistance of white patrons. With Reconstruction over, blacks were, during this nadir of their odyssey in America, on their own.

Chesnutt's light complexion, erudition, sophistication, and accomplishments, however, gave him an entrée into the upper ranks of Cleveland society, where he observed activities satirized in that highly ironic short story "Baxter's Procrustes." As one of the wealthiest black men in the city, Chesnutt was among the most successful political forces in Cleveland, though he never held political office. He often took the middle ground in racial affairs, whether the issue was between blacks and whites or among blacks: He was a member of both the NATIONAL ASSOCIATION FOR THE ADVANCEMENT OF COLORED PEOPLE (NAACP), founded in part by the militant W. E. B. DU BOIS, and the Committee of Twelve, steered by the cautious and conciliatory Booker T. WASHINGTON.

Nevertheless, until his death, Chesnutt was so outspoken in defense of blacks against discrimination and illegal practices that in 1928 he was awarded the NAACP Spingarn Medal for the most "distinguished service" of any black person that year who had acted to advance the cause of blacks in America.

Besides his two published collections of short stories, Chesnutt wrote and/or published an additional twenty-nine short stories, sixteen "tales," ten "anecdotes," seven occasional poems, and numerous essays, articles, and book reviews. He continued to write and publish until 1930 ("Concerning Father" was his last short story), despite poor critical reception and sales, not to mention poor health. As Chesnutt's reputation grows, he will be seen as the first African-American master of the short story.

BIBLIOGRAPHY

Andrews, William L. *The Literary Career of Charles W. Chesnutt.* Baton Rouge, La., and London, 1980.

———. "A Reconsideration of Charles Waddell Chesnutt: Pioneer of the Color Line." *CLA Journal* 19, no. 2 (December 1975): 137–151.

Chesnutt, Helen. *A Biography of Charles Waddell Chesnutt.* Chapel Hill, N.C., and New York, 1952.

Render, Sylvia. *Charles W. Chesnutt.* Boston, 1980.

———. Introduction to *The Short Fiction of Charles W. Chesnutt.* Washington, D.C., 1974.

Thompson, Gordon. Charles W. Chesnutt, Zora Neale Hurston, Melvin B. Tolson: Folk and Non-Folk Representation of the Fantastic. Ph.D. diss., Yale University, 1987.

– GORDON THOMPSON

CHICAGO, ILLINOIS

Chicago's African-American community emerged in the 1840s, sixty-one years after the arrival of Jean Baptiste Pointe du Sable, an Afro-French immigrant and Chicago's first non-Native American settler. Excluded from most manufacturing and mercantile employment and lacking capital to establish businesses, black Chicagoans filled less promising and rewarding roles in the city's growing economy. Resisting marginalization, these African Americans agitated against slavery, formed vigilance committees to defend fugitives, lobbied for the repeal of the Illinois Black Laws, and developed a skeletal institutional life.

The implications of RECONSTRUCTION legislation forced state legislators to reconsider legal constraints on black citizens: Black men won the franchise (1870), while legislation overturned de jure school segregation (1874) and prohibited discrimination in public accommodations (1885). Integrationist in orientation, business and professional leaders had strong ties to white Chicagoans and established the legitimacy of black participation in civic life. They published Chicago's first black newspaper, built churches, and engineered the election of the city's first black public official in 1871.

Between 1890 and 1915, migration—largely from the upper South—tripled Chicago's black population to fifty thousand. Employers' assumptions regarding particular aptitudes of the various races relegated eastern and southern European immigrants to the least skilled jobs in the dynamic industrial sector; African Americans—supposedly incapable of regular, disciplined industrial work—were virtually excluded except as temporary strikebreakers. Black men overwhelmingly labored in service positions. Black women, more likely than other women to enter the paid labor force, were even more concentrated in these dead-end occupations.

African Americans earned less than their white counterparts, but paid higher housing prices in Chicago's increasingly rigid dual housing market. Racially distinct blocks gradually consolidated into enclaves during the late nineteenth century. Limited to residences in these areas, black Chicagoans concentrated in two emerging ghettos—a long thin sliver on the South Side and a smaller area on the West Side.

In response to exclusion coupled with population growth, Chicago's black male leadership turned inward. Between 1890 and 1915 a new generation of leaders focused its energies on developing black institutional life. Women were more likely than men to be active in interracial reform movements, but men occupied positions of power within the community. Oscar Depriest, the first black alderman in a city where power resided in the city council, won election in 1915. By then black Chicago had its own YMCA, settlement houses, hospital, military regiment, and bank, and a vital business and entertainment district along the State Street "Stroll."

Looking inward did not imply a retreat from nineteenth-century traditions of asserting citizenship rights. Chicago's black leadership honored both Booker T. WASHINGTON and W. E. B. DU BOIS. George Cleveland Hall presided over the National Negro Business League one year and sat on the NAACP committee on grievances the next. Chicago Defender editor Robert Abbott venerated Tuskegee Institute and its founder, while advising black Southerners to answer white violence with armed opposition.

The economic and demographic dislocations of World War I transformed Chicago and other manufacturing centers. Industrial demand jumped while immigration dwindled, forcing industrialists to lay aside assumptions about black workers. To black Southerners, the North offered opportunities to fulfill aspirations for complete citizenship; the new jobs made the move possible. Approximately sixty thousand black Southerners—largely from the deep South—relocated in Chicago.

With men earning factory wages and women maintaining high rates of labor-force participation, the material base for a "black metropolis" complemented the existing South Side institutional infrastructure. Men worked in steel mills, packinghouses, other heavy industries, and traditional service niches. Women worked in light industry and domestic service. Postal workers and Pullman porters anchored a middle class defined more by lifestyle and institutional affiliation than by income. Chicago had more black-owned stores by the end of the 1920s than any other city in the United States. A thin professional and business elite occupied the top of an attenuated class structure. Black politicians sat in the city council, the state legislature, and, by 1929, the U.S. House of Representatives.

This community's rapid growth exacerbated tensions rooted in competition over neighborhood turf, political influence, and unionization. Middle- and upper-class white Chicagoans mobilized financial and legal resources to "protect" their neighborhoods from black "invasion"; the white working class looked to political clout and physical intimidation. Violence escalated during the Great Migration, erupting into a massive riot in 1919. Retaliating after whites attacked black citizens, first at a beach and subsequently on streetcars and in the streets, black Chicagoans suffered the brunt of both the attacks and the arrests.

The weight of the Great Depression fell with similarly unequal force. Last admitted through the factory gates, black workers were the first sacrificed to the business cycle. Eviction often followed unemployment. Little new housing opened for black Chicagoans until the first public-housing project was completed in 1940.

Black Chicagoans responded to the depression with renewed activism. Resurrecting "Don't Buy Where You Can't Work" campaigns initiated during the 1920s, ghetto residents successfully picketed stores and office buildings. Black politicians, however, found their clout diminished, as a dominant Democratic organization replaced competitive politics. No longer brokers between black voters and white factional leaders, a new generation of black politicians accepted places in William Dawson's "submachine." Eschewing confrontation, black politicians concentrated on expanding the community's niche in government employment.

The New Deal, industrial recovery during World War II, and the emergence of the Congress of Industrial Organization (CIO) opened new economic and political opportunities. By the end of the war, thousands of black Chicagoans held union jobs, and a new generation of black activists emerged from the CIO and, later, the Negro American Labor Council.

This energy had its counterpart in the arts, producing a cultural efflorescence often referred to as the "Chicago Renaissance." Extending beyond the jazz and blues innovations customarily associated with Chicago musicians like Muddy Waters and Dizzy GILLESPIE, this creative terrain included literature (Richard WRIGHT, Arna BONTEMPS, Willard Motley, Margaret Walker, and

Gwendolyn BROOKS), dance (Katherine DUNHAM), and art (Archibald Motley, George Neal, Richmond Barthé and Margaret Taylor Goss [Burroughs]).

Migration from the South surged during the 1940s and 1950s, with the ghetto expanding along its margins. Attempts to leapfrog across boundaries, whether by individuals or within the context of Chicago Housing Authority initiatives, attracted violent resistance. By the early 1950s a reconstructed housing authority had shifted from being a force for integration to becoming a developer of high-rise ghettos constructed in black neighborhoods. In 1959 the U.S. Commission on Civil Rights labeled Chicago "the most residentially segregated city in the nation."

Riots in 1966 and 1968 articulated rage and provoked temporary civic concern about racial injustice and poverty, but left mainly devastation in their wake.

Residential segregation combined with gerrymandered public-school districts to dominate the agenda of Chicago's postwar civil rights movement. The formation of the Coordinating Council of Community Organizations in 1962 established an institutional foundation for accelerated mobilization, focusing mainly on school desegregation and led by Albert Raby and Dick GREGORY. The entrance of the SOUTHERN CHRISTIAN LEADERSHIP CONFERENCE and the Rev. Dr. Martin Luther KING, Jr., in 1965 and 1966 shifted the focus toward open housing. Marches through white neighborhoods encountered violent opposition, bringing Mayor Richard Daley to the bargaining table, but black leaders lacked the resources to secure more than rhetoric and promises. By 1967 only Jesse JACKSON's employment-oriented Operation Breadbasket was winning tangible concessions. Riots in 1966 and 1968 articulated rage and provoked temporary civic concern about racial injustice and poverty, but left mainly devastation in their wake.

Continued organizing efforts paid dividends in 1983, with the election of Chicago's first African-American mayor, Harold Washington. Frequently stymied by an obstructionist city council, Washington had begun to wield effective power only two years before his death in 1988. Washington's coalition divided after his death, but its elements remained a force in city politics and within the black community into the 1990s.

In the 1990s, Chicago's African-American population remained largely on the South and West Sides. Block after block of working-class bungalows and apartment buildings housed families struggling to maintain their standard of living amid deteriorating public schools, a declining industrial base, and a vulnerable public sector. The implications of unemployment or low-wage service jobs were visible nearby, in neighborhoods characterized by deteriorated housing and dwindling business activity. Public-housing projects held a population skewed toward children and unemployed or underemployed women. But prosperous middle-class neighborhoods, while losing some residents to increasing opportunities in the suburbs, continued to include a black elite that has maintained its commitment to black institutions while taking its place among the city's power brokers.

BIBLIOGRAPHY

Drake, St. Clair, and Horace Clayton. *Black Metropolis: A Study of Negro Life in a Northern City.* New York, 1945.

Grossman, James R. *Land of Hope: Chicago, Black Southerners, and the Great Migration.* Chicago, 1989.

– JAMES R. GROSSMAN

CHRISTIAN METHODIST EPISCOPAL CHURCH

The Colored Methodist Episcopal Church in America (CME) was organized December 16, 1870, in Jackson, Tenn., by former slaves who had been members of the Methodist Episcopal (ME) Church, South. After their emancipation, however, they realized that continued membership in the church of their former masters was neither desirable nor practical and requested their own separate and independent church "regularly established," as Isaac Lane said, "after our own ideas and notions." With careful attention to what was pointed to as the "desires of our colored members," the ME Church, South, provided the basic ecclesiastical, legal, and practical means that enabled them, in the words of Lucius H. Holsey, to establish their "own separate and distinct ecclesiasticism."

Between 1866 and 1870 several hundred black preachers were ordained, an official periodical, *The Christian Index,* began publication, five black annual conferences were established, delegates empowered to set up their "separate ecclesiastical jurisdiction" were called to meet, the ordination of bishops was authorized, and transfer to the new church of all properties that had been used by slave congregations was sanctioned. On December 21, 1870, William H. Miles and Richard H. Vanderhorst—two black preachers elected bishops and ordained by Robert Paine, Senior Bishop of the ME Church, South—assumed the Episcopal oversight of the new jurisdiction, and an independent church of African Americans became a reality.

The CME Church soon emerged as one of the more influential churches in African-American communities throughout the South. Beginning with approximately 78,000 members, competent leaders, several hundred congregations, and title to hundreds of pieces of church property, it had, by the turn of the century, expanded beyond the Mason-Dixon Line following the migrations of African Americans to the North, Midwest, and the Pacific Coast. At the close of World War I, the CME Church was established wherever significant numbers of African Americans were located. After World War II, as CMEs found themselves in more racially inclusive communities and the civil rights struggle intensified, the term "colored" took on the stigma of discrimination and JIM CROW-ism. Consequently, in 1954 the name was changed to the Christian Methodist Episcopal Church. By 1990 it had more than 812,000 communicant members, congregations throughout the United States, and conferences in Nigeria, Ghana, Liberia, Haiti, and Jamaica.

The CME Church soon emerged as one of the more influential churches in African-American communities throughout the South.

The CME Church is the ecclesiastical outgrowth of the grafting of nineteenth-century Protestantism, as practiced by American METHODISTS, and African slave religion, as found in the peculiar institution of SLAVERY. In confronting slavery, Protestant denominations endeavored to "save" the souls of slaves rather than free them from their bondage. Preaching the Gospel to the slaves was the means to this end. The Methodists were highly effective in slave evangelism. Methodism, begun by John Wesley in England and established on the American continent in 1784 as the Methodist Episcopal Church, was appealing to slaves. Methodists preached a plain and simple Gospel that gave meaning and hope to the desperate conditions of the slave experience, practiced styles of preaching and worship that encouraged the expression of deep feelings and strong emotions, and provided a system of licenses and ordination that enhanced the status of slave preachers.

Early American Methodists had opposed slavery, but as more Southerners and slaves joined the church, irreconcilable conflicts developed, and in 1844 Methodism split over the slavery issue. The southern branch of Methodism promoted such an extensive program of slave evangelism that by the beginning of the Civil War more than 207,000 slaves—almost 50 percent of all slaves who embraced Christianity—were members of the ME Church, South. Among them were those who would organize the CME Church in 1870.

The Christianity that the slaves embraced, however, was reshaped in accordance with the realities of their slave experiences and the remnants of their African heritage. Residual elements of African religion such as belief in one supreme being, the union of the spiritual and the material, a strong affirmation of the present life, and certitude of life after death, molded the Gospel preached to the slaves into African-American religion, the most powerful force of African-American life. Though the scion of African-American religion would flourish from the sap of orthodox Christian faith, it would nonetheless have a shape all its own. And it would sprout the varied branches of African-American religion, such as the CME Church, as former slaves, finally set free, established their separate churches, giving institutional meaning to the religion that had sustained them in the darkest days of slavery.

The CME Church perceived the social concerns of African Americans to be a significant part of its mission. CMEs have been in the vanguard of black America's "stride toward freedom" in demanding their own church, sharing in RECONSTRUCTION governments, protesting the enactment of Jim Crow laws, helping establish and support civil rights organizations, and participating fully in the civil rights struggle. It has been a leader in the education of black youth as many of its early church buildings were used as schools. Twenty-one educational institutions have been under its auspices; and four colleges and a school of theology are presently under its sponsorship. CME churches helped to meet the needs of African Americans through ministries such as low-income housing projects, credit unions, senior citizens' homes, child care centers, Project Head-Start, and antipoverty and drug prevention programs. The CME Church has been a pioneer participant in the ecumenical movement through the National Council of Churches, the World Council of Churches, and the National Congress of Black Churches.

Influential African Americans of the CME Church include William H. Miles, its first bishop; Lucius H. Holsey, the leader in establishing CME schools; Charles H. Phillips, the major influence in expanding the church; Helena B. Cobb, founder of an institute for black girls and an early proponent of women's rights; Channing H. Tobias, chairman of the board of the

NAACP; John Hope FRANKLIN, historian of African Americans; William Y. Bell, who served as Dean of the School of Religion of Howard University; B. Julian Smith, a leader in the ecumenical movement; Joseph A. Johnson, Jr., a black theologian; and Alex Haley, author.

BIBLIOGRAPHY

Lakey, Othal Hawthorne, *The History of the CME Church.* Memphis, Tenn., 1985.

Phillips, C. H. *The History of the Colored Methodist Episcopal Church in America.* Jackson, Miss., 1900.

– OTHAL HAWTHORNE LAKEY

CHURCH OF GOD IN CHRIST

In 1895, the Rev. Charles Harrison Mason and the Rev. Charles Price Jones, both former Baptists, organized a Holiness church in Lexington, Miss. Mason named the new body the Church of God in Christ, based on 1 Thess. 2:14. A national organization was chartered in Memphis two years later with Jones as general overseer. Mason and Jones heard of the great religious revival that broke out on Azusa Street in Los Angeles in 1906, and Mason, along with ministers D. J. Young and J. A. Jeter, traveled to California in March 1907 to investigate.

They met the Rev. William Joseph Seymour, the African-American leader of the revival, whose Pentecostal sermons proclaimed a new doctrine: "Baptism in the Holy Spirit" was essential to salvation and sanctification, and evidence of this baptism was glossolalia, or speaking in tongues. Mason and Young accepted the Pentecostal doctrine, but Jones and Jeter did not and Mason and Jones separated over the issue. Lawsuits ensued over ownership of church properties, and when they were concluded in 1909, Mason controlled a national church in which local congregations had lost much of their independence. Jones and his followers established the Church of Christ (Holiness) U.S.A. in 1910 in Selma, Ala.

The church included both black and white members, reflective of the interracial character of Azusa Street. Many early preachers received their credentials from Mason, and some white members split off to form independent or Assembly of God churches. Mason and the church supported conscientious objectors during World War I, which resulted in spying by the FBI and harrassment by the federal government.

Bishop Ozro Thurston Jones, Sr. (1891–1972), succeeded as leader of the church at Mason's death in 1961. He had been national leader of the youth department. He was followed by Bishop J. O. Patterson, Sr. (1912–1989), Mason's son-in-law, who established the C. H. Mason Theological Seminary, a unit of the Interdenominational Theological Center in Atlanta, in 1970. During Patterson's administration, ministers' standard dress of dark suits and ties began to be replaced as bishops and elders in the pulpit started wearing robes and vestments. Patterson was instrumental in founding the World Fellowship of Black Pentecostal Churches in 1984. Bishop Louis Henry Ford (1914–) of Chicago became leader in December 1989. Ford's administration reopened The Saints Academy School in Lexington, Miss. in September 1993.

The Church of God in Christ, as the major African-American Pentecostal denomination, has participated in the phenomenal growth of worldwide Pentecostalism since Azusa Street.

Mason had appointed Mother Lizzie Roberson as national supervisor of women, and she was followed by Mother Lillian Coffey, Mother Annie L. Bailey, and Mother Mattie Carter McGlothen. The church's headquarters building, Mason Temple in Memphis, was the site of Rev. Martin Luther KING, Jr.'s last speech, in support of striking garbage workers, and is now a historic landmark.

The Church of God in Christ, as the major African-American Pentecostal denomination, has participated in the phenomenal growth of worldwide Pentecostalism since Azusa Street. In 1925 the church's membership was 250,000. In 1945 there were 1,850 churches in the United States. By 1961, membership was 382,679 in 4,500 congregations, and in 1982 the church reported 9,982 congregations and 3,709,661 members. By 1991 there were 5.5 million members in 30,000 churches in the United States, plus an additional two million members in other countries.

BIBLIOGRAPHY

DuPree, Sherry Sherrod. *Biographical Dictionary of African-American, Holiness-Pentecostals, 1880–1990.* Washington, D.C., 1989.

DuPree, Sherry Sherrod, and Herbert C. DuPree. *Exposed!: Federal Bureau of Investigation (FBI) Unclassified Reports on Churches and Church Leaders.* Washington, D.C., 1993.

Kelley, Frances, and German R. Ross. *Here Am I, Send Me: The Dramatic Story of Presiding Bishop J. O. Patterson.* Memphis, Tenn., 1970.

Official Manual with the Doctrine and Discipline of the Church of God in Christ. Memphis, Tenn., 1973.

– SHERRY SHERROD DUPREE

CINCINNATI, OHIO

Cincinnati is located in the southwest corner of Ohio, adjacent to Indiana and across the Ohio River from Kentucky. One of the white settlers of 1788 named the proposed town Losantiville, from the Latin *os* (mouth), Greek *anti* (opposite), and French *ville* (city), because of its position opposite the mouth of the Licking River. On January 2, 1790, Governor St. Clair, a loyal member of the old Revolutionary Army Society of Cincinnatus, changed the name to Cincinnati. In the early nineteenth century, the city was nicknamed "Porkopolis" because of its large pork industry. By 1900, Cincinnati was better known as a flourishing arts and business center and called "the Paris of the Midwest," "the Queen City," and "Blue Chip City."

In 1800, 337 African Americans, many of whom had been slaves fleeing to free states, were living in Ohio. In 1802 the state constitution of Ohio upheld the Northwest Ordinance of 1787, which prohibited slavery in the state but divested African Americans of political and civil rights. Two years later, Ohio's first Black Law prohibited African Americans from settling there without written proof of freedom. In 1807, the next Black Law required African Americans to post bond of five hundred dollars as guarantee of good behavior and forbade testimonials against white men in court.

Despite discriminatory legislation, African Americans began to develop religious and educational communities in Cincinnati. In 1810, numbering 80 out of the total city population of 2,540, they built the first African-American church, with William Allen as its preacher. Reportedly a station of the UNDERGROUND RAILROAD from 1812 to 1815, the church was burned and rebuilt three times. In 1824, pastors from the Bethel Church formed the AFRICAN METHODIST EPISCOPAL CHURCH. It was renamed the Allen Temple A.M.E. Church, and followers later built a permanent place of worship at Sixth and Broadway. In 1825, Henry Collins established the first African-American school in an old pork house one block away. In the 1820s, most African Americans lived in wooden shanties in "Bucktown," "Little Bucktown," or "Little Africa," the small area between Fifth and Seventh streets and Broadway and Eggleston avenues. Within twenty years the crowded, disease-infested district was known as "the Swamp."

Fearing the rapidly growing African-American population (9.4 percent in 1829), 120 white men of the Cincinnati Colonization Society, begun in 1826, advocated its deportation to Africa. They insisted on more rigid enforcement of the Black Laws and demanded bond payment in 1829. During a three-day riot, whites insulted, attacked, and killed African Americans who could not pay within the allotted sixty days. Between 1,000 and 1,200 African Americans then fled to Canada and established the settlement of WILBERFORCE. Two years later, Black Laws were passed forbidding African Americans to serve in the state militia or on juries in Ohio.

Sympathetic white abolitionists at Lane Seminary hosted eighteen nights of antislavery debates. When ordered to suspend their activities in 1834, students staged a walkout. The Lane rebels then enrolled at Oberlin College in Oberlin, Ohio, which subsequently became an abolitionist center and accepted students of all races. The same year, Virginia-born Owen T. B. Nickens founded the first successful African-American elementary school in Cincinnati.

By the 1840s, most African Americans worked as day laborers, barbers, menial servants, roustabouts, and steamboat laborers along the riverfront. Many lived in "Bucktown" between the Ohio River and Third Street east of Sycamore, bordered by Broadway and Main. The neighborhood gained a reputation for drinking, gambling, thieving, and prostitution. At the same time, wealthy African Americans lived on the "fashionable thoroughfare" of McAllister Street (north of Fourth Street).

Fearing the advancement of African Americans, Charles McMicken bought 10,000 acres in Africa between Liberia and Sierra Leone (which he called "Little Ohio") for their emigration in 1836. After his colonization plan failed, he inserted a clause in his will excluding African Americans from sharing his endowment to the University of Cincinnati (he also granted his slaves freedom after his death if they chose to go to Liberia). In spite of McMicken, African Americans became some of the University of Cincinnati's most successful graduates. They include William H. Parham (first African-American graduate of the law school, in 1874), biologist Charles Turner (1891), and educator Jennie D. Porter (U.C.'s first African-American Ph.D., 1928, and founder of the Harriet Beecher Stowe School). In 1969 Lawrence Hawkins, assistant supervisor of Cincinnati public schools since 1967, became U.C.'s first African-American dean.

In 1844 the Rev. Hiram S. Gilmore, an English clergyman, established Cincinnati High School, Ohio's first private African-American high school. He was succeeded by McMicken's mulatto son, John. The institution's role was later eclipsed by the partial repeal of a Black Law in 1849, providing African Americans with free public EDUCATION. Elected African-American trustees were unable to organize their educational system, however, when local authorities refused to provide funds. African American John I. Gaines, a wealthy provision-store owner, led the case to victory at the Supreme Court in 1852, and a colored school board and superintendency were created. In 1857 the first African-American public high school, Gaines High School, was founded in his honor. Attendance there dwindled after 1887, when a new law permitted the integration of white common schools.

Throughout the nineteenth and early twentieth centuries, African Americans struggled for education and freedom of speech. Bloody riots erupted in Cincinnati in 1836 and 1841, when whites destroyed the press of the antislavery *Philanthropist* newspaper published by James G. Birney, a former southern slave owner. African-American Cincinnatians published their own newspapers thereafter, including the *Disfranchised American* (begun 1843), *Colored Citizen* (1866–1873), *Declaration* (founded in 1866), *American Catholic Tribune* (1844–1894), and the *Cincinnati Herald* (founded in 1953).

White philanthropists aided African Americans in their struggle for equality. Levi Coffin, arriving in Cincinnati in 1847, became the "national president" of the Underground Railroad. He led slaves across the Ohio River to free states. One woman whom Coffin aided was immortalized as Eliza Harris in UNCLE TOM'S CABIN. This novel by white Cincinnatian Harriet Beecher Stowe played a crucial role in igniting antislavery activity. White abolitionists also commissioned portraits from African-American artists such as painter Robert S. DUNCANSON and daguerreotypist James P. Ball. Their patronage allowed Duncanson, one of the most acclaimed landscape painters of the nineteenth century, to study abroad. Duncanson painted murals of the Ohio Valley in the home of his benefactor Nicholas Longworth; these are now in the Taft Museum.

Although Cincinnati's African-American population had decreased substantially with the emigration to Canada in 1829, it slowly rose to 2.7 percent (5,900 of 216,239) in 1870. While African-American men began to enter professional occupations, women worked primarily as domestics, washers, seamstresses, and prostitutes from the 1850s to the 1880s. A middle-class white clientele paid for their services in "Rat Row" (between Walnut and Main) and "Sausage Row" (between Broadway and Ludlow), where African Americans and poor whites lived. One-third of African Americans resided in single-family homes, 12 to 15 percent were live-in domestics, and the remainder lived in multiple-family tenements. Although African Americans began to move to the West End and Walnut Hills in the 1860s, one-third of all transport workers still lived in "Bucktown" by 1880. By 1900, however, industrial and commercial buildings displaced most African Americans to the West End.

African-American Cincinnatians began to gain political power after the EMANCIPATION proclamation of 1863, with the men among them acquiring the right to vote in Ohio in 1870. Historian George Washington Williams became the first African American elected to the Ohio Legislature, in 1879, and the Black Laws were completely repealed in 1887. Yet African Americans still experienced gross political inequality.

In 1893, Wendell Phillips Dabney (Cincinnati's first African-American paymaster) helped found the Douglass League, a Republican organization, to pressure for reforms. His newspaper, the *Union* (1907–1952), kept African Americans informed. In 1915 Dabney became the first president of the Cincinnati chapter of the National Association for the Advancement of Colored People. While he and his associates fought for civil rights, others, who believed racial equality was impossible in the United States, worked for a faction of Marcus GARVEY's "Back to Africa" movement. (The Ohio Colonization Society had sent the last African-American emigrant to Liberia in 1902.)

Under the African-American leader William Ware, membership in the Cincinnati chapter of the UNIVERSAL NEGRO IMPROVEMENT ASSOCIATION reached almost 8,000. Ware then founded the Welfare Association for Colored People, in 1917. On one day in that year, at the height of the Great Migration, 1,022 migrants arrived in the city. Cincinnati's African-American population nearly doubled within a decade; by 1920, it had reached 7.5 percent (30,079 of 401,207). Almost 60 percent of these people, many of whom worked in paper mills and factories during the 1920s, lived in the West End. They later resided in federally funded houses in the Laurel Homes and Lincoln Court projects, built in the 1930s and 1940s.

As the African-American population grew (to 12.2 percent in 1940), so did its political representation, with the City Council elections of Frank A. B. Hall in 1931, Jesse D. Locker in 1941 (President Eisenhower appointed Locker ambassador to Liberia in 1953), and Theodore M. Berry in 1942. In 1944 the Lincoln Heights community became incorporated as the nation's only city with a 100 percent African-American population. In 1963, William A. McClain was appointed to the city's top legal post as city solicitor. African-American mayors of Cincinnati include Berry (1972–1975), J. Kenneth Blackwell (1979–1980), and Dwight Tillery (elected 1991). In 1975 Berry was one of the founding members of the Committee of Fifty, a group of anonymous African Americans who demanded justice for the city council's vice-mayor, William Chenault, accused of embezzlement. The committee was also concerned about the general well-being of African Americans in the city. Many had been forced to move to the suburbs in the 1950s because Queensgate Project I demolished more than half the housing in downtown's West End for industry development and the Mill Creek Expressway. Between 1935 and 1970, 62,500 persons were removed from the area. Most resettled in the Over-the-Rhine and Mt. Auburn neighborhoods, where race riots erupted during the summer of 1967, as in 116 other cities across the nation. The Queensgate Project II of 1973 displaced still more families. By then, African Americans made up 27.7 percent of Cincinnati's population. That figure rose to over a third (138,132 of 364,040) in 1990.

Other notable African-American Cincinnatians include Granville T. Woods (inventor of a steam-boiler furnace and fifteen appliances used by electric railways); artist Antonio Blackburn, Jr. (awarded the medal of the Swedish State School of Arts, Crafts, and Design, 1960); jazz musician Artie Matthews (founder of the Cosmopolitan Conservatory of Music, 1921–1958); poet Nikki GIOVANNI; and athletes William DeHart Hubbard (Olympic broad-jump champion, 1924), Ezzard Charles (world heavyweight boxing champion, 1949–1951), Wallace (Bud) Smith (world lightweight boxing champion, 1955–1956), and Oscar Robertson (All-American athlete, 1958).

BIBLIOGRAPHY

Dabney, William Phillips. *Cincinnati's Colored Citizens: Historical, Sociological, Biographical.* 1926. Reprint. Cincinnati, 1988.

Edwards, Ethel. *Ringside Seat on Revolution.* Cincinnati, 1972.

Hurley, Daniel. *Cincinnati, the Queen City.* Cincinnati, 1982.

Koehler, Lyle. *Cincinnati's Black Peoples: A Chronology and Bibliography.* Cincinnati, 1986.

McKee, Dan M. *A Comparison of Appalachian, Black, and White Neighborhoods of Cincinnati, 1960–1970.* Cincinnati, 1977.

Taylor, Henry Louis, Jr. The Building of a Black Industrial Suburb: The Lincoln Heights, Ohio Story. Thesis, State University of New York, Buffalo, 1979.

Washington, Michael, Sr. *Segregation in Cincinnati During the Early Twentieth Century.* Cincinnati, 1985.

— THERESA LEININGER-MILLER

CITIZENSHIP SCHOOLS

During the mid-1950s through the 1960s, citizenship schools—established under the auspices of the Highlander Citizenship School—played a vital role in promoting literacy, increasing voter registration, and cultivating community leadership skills among African Americans in the South. Under the direction of Myles Horton (1905–1990), a white Appalachian, the Highlander Citizenship School—which focused on labor education since its founding in 1932 in Monteagle, Tenn.—had emerged as a champion of racial equality and integration by the early 1950s. Horton believed that the progress of unionization in the South was stymied by a lack of racial cooperation and that illiteracy was one of the greatest barriers between black people and first-class citizenship. In 1953, a grant from the Schwartzhaupt Foundation gave Horton the resources to create adult education programs that would focus on providing African Americans with the tools they needed to become informed voters. These programs became known as citizenship schools.

Horton participated in discussions with black community activists in Highlander workshops to devise education strategies that would encourage and sustain their voter registration efforts. In attendance at one of the early workshops were two activists from South Carolina who played central roles in defining the ideology behind the citizenship school program: Septima CLARK and Esau Jenkins. Clark, an NAACP activist and Johns Island schoolteacher who would be appointed Highlander's director of education in 1957, believed that the goal of citizenship schools should not be limited to increasing literacy among African Americans.

Clark was a staunch advocate of black political empowerment, and she argued that citizenship schools should teach students that they had a right to be part of the body politic and had the power to change the government. She believed that a central goal of the program was to create and nurture black activism and that the schools themselves should be built upon the groundwork laid by local activists.

During the mid-1950s through the 1960s, citizenship schools played a vital role in promoting literacy, increasing voter registration, and cultivating community leadership skills among African Americans in the South.

Clark brought Horton's attention to the poverty and isolation of black residents on the Sea Islands and the efforts of Esau Jenkins, a former student who had developed into a local leader and activist, to increase black voter registration on Johns Island. Through discussions with Jenkins and Clark, Horton became convinced that Johns Island should be the site of the first citizenship school. After many months of community-based meetings and events to mobilize support for the project, the Johns Island Citizenship school was founded in 1957.

The school had an initial enrollment of fourteen students registered for classes held two times a week during the three-month layover between crops. Unable to afford formal structures or a paid staff, classes were held in the back room of a small cooperative store and Bernice Robinson, Septima Clark's niece, volunteered to be the first teacher of the school. Robinson, an NAACP member who had attended Highlander workshops, was committed to breaking down traditional classroom hierarchies. She allowed her students to play an integral role in determining what was taught to them. She created a culturally familiar environment in her classroom by incorporating music based on the traditional folk culture of the Sea Islands into her lessons.

Students were taught practical skills that they needed in their daily lives—such as reading the Bible, signing their names, and filling out money orders and voter registration forms. However, the classroom curriculum centered on teaching students to address the social conditions in their community and challenge their oppression. The school served as a site of political discussion, where students were encouraged to speak up and take a more critical view of the world. The knowledge students gained at the school allowed them to tackle problems differently and make better uses of local resources. As the school began to "graduate" successful new voters and community political awareness grew, enrollment rapidly increased. Due to the efforts of Robinson, the philosophy of Clark, and the support of Jenkins and other Sea Island blacks, the school was a success. From 1956 to 1960, voter registration on Johns Island increased 300 percent.

Citizenship schools were created on the other South Carolina Sea Islands as the success of the Johns Island's school became evident and the CIVIL RIGHTS MOVEMENT spread throughout the South. Teacher-training workshops at Highlander brought together experienced teachers with new and prospective teachers. Teachers varied widely in experience, training, and age, and included farmers, domestic workers, and college students. The workshops were forums for discussions of current events and local politics and created a sense of community and shared problems among participants. By early 1961, eighty-two teachers had been trained by Highlander and were teaching in citizenship schools in Alabama, Georgia, South Carolina, and Tennessee.

Believing that voting was only the first step toward the empowerment of African Americans, Esau Jenkins traveled throughout the South encouraging citizenship school students to initiate "Second Step" political action groups for developing strategies to address community problems. Associations following this philosophy sprang up alongside citizenship schools on six islands and on two mainland communities. By 1961, citizenship schools had registered hundreds to vote and could be credited with helping to develop and sustain the tide of black protest of the early civil rights movement.

Just as the citizenship school program seemed poised for major expansion, the Tennessee legislature's persistent efforts to disrupt Highlander's activities and undermine their programs increased in pace. In February 1961, Horton, anticipating that the citizenship school program would soon outgrow Highlander's funding capabilities, negotiated the transfer of the program to the SOUTHERN CHRISTIAN LEADERSHIP CONFERENCE(SCLC) to ensure the program's survival and continuance. An obscure turn-of-the-century law prohibiting integration in private schools was used to revoke the school's charter and confiscate its property a few months later.

Septima Clark joined the staff of SCLC in July 1961 as director of workshops and, with Andrew YOUNG and Dorothy Cotton, two committed SCLC activists, administered the newly renamed Citizenship Education Project (CEP). Later that year, SCLC opened the Dorchester Cooperative Community Center in Dorchester, Ga., to serve as a CEP teacher-training center. During this same time period, the Kennedy administration pledged to support voter-registration projects in an attempt to steer the focus of the Civil Rights Movement away from volatile direct action protests. CEP became a central part of the Voter Education Project organized in 1962 by the CONGRESS OF RACIAL EQUALITY, SCLC, and the NAACP, to promote black voter registration in the South. Despite receiving little promised federal support or protection, by 1966, the project had trained more than 10,000 citizenship school teachers.

Citizenship schools grew to become a key grass-roots base of support for the Civil Rights Movement throughout the deep South. They provided African Americans with the knowledge they needed to challenge southern voter registration laws and the racial status quo. By 1970, thirteen years after the first citizenship school was formed with only fourteen students, 800 citizenship schools graduating more than 100,000 African Americans in the South—including some of the veterans of the Civil Rights Movement like Fannie Lou HAMER—had been formed.

As time progressed, however, many Civil Rights Movement participants on the front line of southern racial violence became disillusioned with the pace of social change, and involvement in local politics was no longer a central goal of the splintering movement. Despite the continued overall success of CEP in training teachers, many of the schools closed, due to a lack of funding and because there was often little long-term commitment to doing follow-up work with the students. Septima Clark often complained that too much of SCLC's energies were focused on the excitement of protests rather than on the daily rigors of citizenship education. These factors, combined with the passage of the Voting Rights Act of 1965, led to the decline of CEP. By 1970, the schools faded out of existence, and Clark retired from her position in SCLC.

BIBLIOGRAPHY

Glen, John M. *Highlander: No Ordinary School, 1932–1962.* Lexington, Ky., 1988.

Horton, Aimee. *The Highlander Folk School: A History of Its Major Programs, 1932–1961.* Brooklyn, N.Y., 1989.

– MICHAEL A. COOKE

CIVIL RIGHTS MOVEMENT

The African-American Civil Rights Movement has roots in the earliest resistance by blacks to their involuntary arrival in America and their unequal treatment. As slaves in America, blacks protested through work slowdowns and sabotage, escapes, and rebellions; while free blacks in the North opposed racial discrimination through petitions, litigation, and more aggressive nonviolent tactics such as boycotts from 1844 to 1855 that pressured Boston authorities to desegregate public schools.

The South, where slavery endured until 1865 and where at least 90 percent of black Americans lived until 1910, posed the crucial testing ground for civil rights activism. The newly freed slaves asserted their rights in ways ranging from participation in southern electoral politics, as voters and public officials, to nonviolent protests against segregated horsecars. These protests triumphed in New Orleans, Richmond, Va., and Charleston, S.C., in 1867, in Louisville in 1871 (all involving confrontations with passengers and police), and in Savannah, Ga., in 1872 (through a boycott that placed economic pressure on the traction company).

The rise of JIM CROW laws throughout the South beginning in the late nineteenth century triggered black resistance in every state of the former Confederacy; most of this resistance centered on boycotts of segregated streetcars. These protests postponed the spread of segregation in some cities, but ultimately they failed everywhere amid a surge of white racial violence and legal repression, including disfranchisement of most southern blacks by 1900. Black civil rights activity also succumbed to a national resurgence of racism, evident in the Supreme Court verdict in PLESSY V. FERGUSON (1896) that sustained a Louisiana segregation statute for affording blacks separate-but-equal facilities. The preeminent southern black spokesman, Booker T. WASHINGTON, accommodated these bleak trends by appealing to whites for economic toleration and racial peace while publicly renouncing agitation for social and political rights.

Because of the long odds and mortal risks facing black dissidents in the South, civil rights militance in the early twentieth century remained chiefly the province of northern blacks such as the Massachusetts natives William Monroe TROTTER and W. E. B. DU BOIS. In 1905 Du Bois began a movement in Niagara Falls, N.Y., to urge redress of racial injustices. Poorly attended and funded, the NIAGARA MOVEMENT lived four years in obscurity before dissolving into a new, interracial organization that formed in the wake of white racial rioting in Springfield, Ill., the city of Abraham Lincoln's youth. In 1910 the NAACP began its long crusade for racial equality, operating through the courts and the trenchant pen of Du Bois, the group's first black officer and the editor of a new journal for black rights, the *Crisis.*

The African-American Civil Rights Movement has roots in the earliest resistance by blacks to their involuntary arrival in America and their unequal treatment.

In the 1915 case *Guinn* v. *United States,* attorneys for the NAACP persuaded a unanimous Supreme Court to declare unconstitutional the "grandfather clause," by which some states had disfranchised blacks through harsh registration tests while exempting citizens—almost invariably whites—whose grandfathers had voted. This ruling did not clearly exhaust the South's legal strategems for denying blacks the ballot, but it encouraged the NAACP's reliance on the courts—the branch of government best insulated from political pressures—and on constitutional appeals for colorblind justice.

During the 1930s the NAACP sued for equal school facilities for blacks, in accord with the Supreme Court sanction of separate-but-equal treatment. In this way the NAACP secured the desegregation of all-white law or graduate schools in Maryland, Missouri, and other states unable to convince federal courts of an equal commitment to black and white students. The NAACP also beat down the formal exclusion of blacks from party primary elections in the South, through litigation culminating with the Supreme Court case *Smith* v. *Allright* in 1944.

Beginning in the 1930s elected officials received increasingly vigorous tutoring from the NAACP and other black groups on the need for protection of civil rights. Strong federal anti-lynching bills passed the House of Representatives in 1937 and again in 1940, though each time succumbing to southern filibusters in the Senate. In 1941 the black union leader A. Philip Randolph planned a march on Washington to protest racial discrimination in the armed forces and defense industries. To persuade Randolph to call off the march, President Franklin Roosevelt in July 1941 created an advisory committee, the Fair Employment Practices Committee, to promote racial integration in munitions factories. A limited step, it was also the first presidential order for civil rights since RECONSTRUCTION—and the first intended chiefly to quiet an emerging black mass movement.

Civil rights activity quickened after the end of WORLD WAR II, in 1945, in an increasingly open society that could not easily justify segregation after years of propaganda denouncing Nazi Germany for its vicious racial policies. The registration of over two million blacks by the late 1940s, many of them migrants from the rural South to northern cities, further undermined the racial status quo. So did the growing numbers of religious, civil, labor, intellectual, and white minority leaders who termed racism a challenge to national democratic values. Their words gained added force from the competition between the United States and the Soviet Union for support from emerging nonwhite nations, which made evidence of American racism a damaging embarrassment.

In December 1946 President Harry Truman appointed a committee to investigate violations of black rights. Three months later he endorsed the resulting report, entitled "To Secure These Rights," which prescribed a comprehensive federal assault on JIM CROW. In 1948 Truman acceded to a strong civil rights plank that liberal delegates had inserted in the Democratic national platform. He then weathered defections by a minority of southern whites to win a second term, aided by 70 percent of the northern black vote. Two years later he began desegregation of the armed forces to heighten military efficiency for the KOREAN WAR and to quiet restive black leaders.

By the late 1940s the NAACP's chief legal counsel, Thurgood MARSHALL, felt emboldened to attack directly the principle of segregation in public education. In several cases before the Supreme Court, Marshall argued that segregation denied blacks "equal protection of the laws" as guaranteed by the Fourteenth Amendment to the Constitution. In 1954 Chief Justice Earl Warren wrote for a unanimous Court, in BROWN V. TOPEKA, KANSAS BOARD OF EDUCATION, that in the area of public education "the doctrine of 'separate but equal' has no place."

By threatening white supremacy the Brown case intensified southern resistance to civil rights progress. The KU KLUX KLAN and other fringe hate groups experienced overnight revivals, congressmen and governors vowed "massive resistance," and state district attorneys sought injunctions to ban NAACP branches (they were entirely successful in Alabama by 1957). In May 1955 the Supreme Court tempered its original ruling in *Brown* by requiring no timetable for school desegregation, only that school districts move "with all deliberate speed." Compliance proved minimal, and when President Dwight D. Eisenhower sent federal troops in 1957 to guard nine blacks attending a formerly all-white high school in Little Rock, Ark., the prolonged furor discouraged further national intervention for desegregation.

In 1954 Chief Justice Earl Warren wrote for a unanimous Court, in Brown *v.* Topeka, Kansas Board of Education, *that in the area of public education "the doctrine of 'separate but equal' has no place."*

Despite its limited tangible impact, *Brown* did confer a symbol of legitimacy on black activists, who prepared bolder assaults on segregation in the South. In December 1955 blacks in Montgomery, Ala., organized a bus boycott after a former NAACP secretary, Rosa PARKS, was arrested for refusing to yield her seat on a segregated bus to a white man. The boycott leader was a twenty-six-year-old, northern-educated minister originally from Atlanta, the Rev. Dr. Martin Luther KING, Jr. King gained national attention for the protest against segregation by invoking Christian morality, American ideals of liberty, and the ethic of nonviolent resistance to evil exemplified by Mohandas Gandhi of India in his campaign against British colonial rule. Like Gandhi, King advocated confronting authorities with a readiness to suffer rather than inflict harm, in order to expose injustice and impel those in power to end it. In November 1956, despite growing white violence, the boycott triumphed with aid from the NAACP, which secured a Supreme Court decision (in *Gayle* v. *Browder*) that overturned Montgomery's laws enforcing bus segregation.

The signs of growing black restiveness in the South encouraged new civil rights initiatives. In January 1957 King organized the SOUTHERN CHRISTIAN LEADERSHIP CONFERENCE (SCLC), a network of nonviolent civil rights activists drawn mainly from the black church. In September of that year Congress passed the first Civil Rights Act since Reconstruction; the act created a commission to monitor civil rights violations and authorized the Justice Department to guard black voting rights through litigation against discriminatory registrars. This act (and a follow-up measure in April 1960) nonetheless failed to curb the widespread disfranchisement of southern blacks.

The failure to implement federal civil rights edicts increasingly spurred blacks to shift their struggle for equality from the courts and cloakrooms to the streets. During the late 1950s blacks, often affiliated with local NAACP youth chapters, conducted scattered, short-lived SIT-INS at lunch counters that served whites only. On February 1, 1960, a sit-in by four students at the Woolworth's lunch counter in Greensboro, N.C., triggered a host of similar protests throughout the South, targeting Jim Crow public accommodations from theaters to swimming pools. Strict conformity to nonviolent Christian and Gandhian tenets characterized the demonstrators, many of whom courted arrest and even imprisonment in order to dramatize the evils of segregation.

In April 1960 several hundred student activists gathered in Raleigh, N.C., at the invitation of Ella Baker, the executive director of the Southern Christian Leadership Conference. Baker urged the students to preserve their grass-roots militancy by remaining independent of established civil rights groups, and they responded by forming the STUDENT NONVIOLENT COORDINATING COMMITTEE (SNCC, pronounced "snick") to promote Gandhian resistance to Jim Crow. By the summer of 1960 the sit-ins, which were often reinforced by boy-

Harlem demonstration for the passage of the Anti-Lynching Bill, 1936. (Photographs and Prints Division, Schomburg Center for Research in Black Culture, The New York Public Library, Astor, Lenox and Tilden Foundations)

cotts of offending stores, had desegregated dozens of lunch counters and other public accommodations, mainly in southern border states.

Black protests intensified during the presidency of John F. Kennedy, a Democrat elected in 1960 with heavy black support. Kennedy early directed the Justice Department to step up litigation for black rights, but he avoided bolder commitments that he feared would trigger southern white racial violence and political retaliation. Civil rights leaders therefore increasingly designed campaigns to pressure their reluctant ally in the White House. In May 1961 James Farmer, who had cofounded the CONGRESS OF RACIAL EQUALITY (CORE) nearly two decades earlier, led fourteen white and black CORE volunteers on a freedom ride through the South, testing compliance with a Supreme Court order to desegregate interstate bus terminal facilities. White mobs abetted by police beat the riders in Birmingham, Ala., on May 14; six days later federal marshals saved the riders from a mob in Montgomery. As the freedom rides proliferated, Kennedy quietly persuaded southern communities to desegregate their bus terminals.

Although the Kennedy administration strove to balance the competing pressures of black activists and their southern white opponents, growing racial tensions impelled the president to take stronger civil rights initiatives. In October 1962 Kennedy sent federal marshals to protect a black student, James Meredith, who had registered at the all-white University of Mississippi at Oxford. After mobs killed two people at the campus and besieged the marshals, the president reluctantly troops to restore order.

Racial polarization worsened in 1963, as demonstrations throughout the South precipitated 15,000 arrests and widespread white violence. On May 3 and for several days afterward, police in Birmingham beat and unleashed attack dogs on nonviolent black followers of Dr. King, in full view of television news cameras. The resulting public revulsion spurred President Kennedy to address the nation on June 11, to confront a "moral issue" that was "as old as the Scriptures" and "as clear as the American Constitution." He urged Congress to enact a strong civil rights law that would allow race "no place in American life."

A coalition of African-American groups and their white allies sponsored a march on Washington on August 28, 1963, to advance the civil rights bill then before Congress. Reflecting the growing national stature of the Civil Rights Movement, the rally secured the participation of diverse political, cultural, and religious figures. Standing before the Lincoln Memorial, Dr. King told several hundred thousand blacks and whites at this event of his "dream" for interracial brotherhood. Afterward President Kennedy praised the goals and peaceful character of the march.

When Lyndon B. Johnson succeeded to the presidency on November 22, 1963, he made passage of the civil rights bill his top priority and effectively linked this goal to the memory of the martyred President Kennedy. A broad-based federation called the Leadership Conference on Civil Rights coordinated the lobbying efforts of over a hundred groups on behalf of the legislation, centered on extraordinary activity by Protestant, Catholic, and Jewish ministers. On July 2, 1964, Johnson signed the omnibus Civil Rights Act, which barred segregation in public accommodations, ended federal aid to segregated institutions, outlawed racial discrimination in employment, sought to strengthen black voting rights, and extended the life of the UNITED STATES COMMISSION ON CIVIL RIGHTS.

SNCC remained in the vanguard of civil rights activism in 1964 by organizing rural blacks in Mississippi, a state whose history was pockmarked with the casual shootings of black people. About a thousand college students, most of them white, volunteered for the FREEDOM SUMMER project to further the nonviolent, integrationist ideals of the Civil Rights Movement. The project workers set up "Freedom Schools" to give black children a positive sense of their history and identity, and an interracial party, the "Freedom Democrats," to give otherwise disfranchised blacks a political voice. The project also exposed the extreme dangers daily facing civil rights workers, after a federal manhunt recovered the bodies of three volunteers—Michael Schwerner, Andrew Goodman, and James Chaney—who had been murdered by a mob led by the deputy sheriff of Philadelphia, Miss. In late August the project workers helped the Freedom Democrats try to unseat Mississippi's lily-white delegation at the Democratic national convention. Despite considerable northern support, their challenge failed because of strong resistance by President Johnson, who feared the loss of southern white voters in an election year. This harsh coda to the Freedom Summer spurred younger black activists to question the wisdom of alliances with white liberals and to stress instead the importance of black solidarity.

The fraying civil rights coalition rallied in 1965 behind Dr. King's campaign in Selma, Ala., for equal voting rights. On March 7 black marchers setting out from Selma toward Montgomery suffered assaults by state and local police. The televised scenes of violence galvanized national support for protection of blacks seeking the ballot, a view that President Johnson reinforced in a special appearance before Congress on March 15. Ten days later twenty-five thousand black and white marchers reached Montgomery escorted by federal troops. On August 6, 1965, Johnson signed a strong Voting Rights Act, which authorized the attorney general to send federal examiners to supersede local registrars and regulations wherever discrimination occurred. The act also directed the attorney general to challenge poll taxes for state and local elections in the courts (the Twenty-fourth Amendment to the Constitution, adopted in 1964, had already banned such taxes in national elections).

After 1965 the Civil Rights Movement fragmented in the absence of an overriding goal to unify and inspire it. During a march with King through Mississippi in June 1966, SNCC's Stokely CARMICHAEL ridiculed faith in nonviolence and white good will and demanded "black power," a militant slogan that alienated white liberals and divided blacks. As the focus of the Civil Rights Movement increasingly turned from de jure segregation, to economic inequality and patterns of de facto segregation in the North, agreement on a strategy for addressing and solving these problems became more elusive. Ghetto riots, including a six-day rampage in South Central Los Angeles in August 1965, further split the movement by harming its nonviolent image and by shifting its focus from constitutional rights to problems of slum housing and poverty, for which no reform consensus existed. On April 4, 1968, the assassination of King in Memphis, Tenn., touched off riots that left Washington, D.C., in flames for three days. The following week, partly in tribute to the slain King, Congress passed the Civil Rights Act of 1968, which banned discrimination in the sale and rental of most housing.

The 1970s witnessed the emergence of expressly race-conscious government programs to redress the legacy of racial discrimination. In the 1971 case *Swann* v. *Charlotte-Mecklenburg* the Supreme Court acknowledged the failures of earlier approaches to school desegregation by sanctioning the busing of children to other neighborhoods as a tool to achieve racial balance. The federal government also promoted AFFIRMATIVE ACTION to afford blacks (and, increasingly, other minorities and women) preference in school admissions and employment. These developments reflected the limitations of civil rights legislation in affording access to the economic mainstream; but they provoked fierce opposition. Violence in Boston and other cities over racial busing confirmed that the race problem was truly national rather than southern. And in *Regents of University of California* v. *Bakke* in 1978 the Supreme Court reflected the national acrimony over affirmative action by ruling five to four to strike down racial quotas in medical school admissions while allowing (by an equally slim margin) some race-conscious selection to achieve educational "diversity."

During the 1980s a conservative shift in national politics frustrated civil rights leaders, especially in the NAACP and the Urban League, who relied on federal activism to overcome state, municipal, and private acts of discrimination. Ronald Reagan, a Republican who won the presidency for the first of two terms in 1980, sought to trim federal authority in racial matters. From 1981 to 1985 his administration reduced the number of lawyers in the Justice Department's Civil Rights Division from 210 to 57, and also vainly attempted to disband altogether the United States Commission on Civil Rights. On January 8, 1982, Reagan restored the federal tax exemptions for segregated private schools that had been ended in 1970. The following year the Supreme Court, by an eight-to-one vote, overturned this ruling as a violation of the Civil Rights Act of 1964; in 1986 Reagan appointed the lone dissenter, William Rehnquist, to be Chief Justice of the Supreme Court.

During the 1980s a conservative shift in national politics frustrated civil rights leaders, especially in the NAACP and the Urban League.

The Rehnquist Court increasingly chipped away at government safeguards of black rights, a pattern evident from several employment discrimination cases in 1989: in *Patterson* v. *McLean Credit Union* the Court ruled that the Civil Rights Act of 1866 protected blacks merely in contracting for jobs but did not protect them from racial harassment by employers; in *Wards Cove Packing Co.* v. *Atonio* the Court shifted the burden of proof from employers to employees regarding job discrimination; in *City of Richmond* v. *J. A. Croson Co.* the Court rejected a program setting aside 30 percent of city contracts for minority businesses in the absence of flagrant evidence of discrimination, although Richmond had a history of official segregation and although minority contractors held fewer than 1 percent of the city contracts in Richmond, where minorities constituted half the population; in *Price Waterhouse* v. *Hopkins* the Court exonerated an employer who had committed acts of racial discrimination but who also cited other, legitimate reasons for such actions. In October 1990 the Republican president, George Bush, vetoed a civil rights bill that expressly restored the earlier, tougher curbs on job discrimination, and the Senate sustained his veto by a single vote. In November 1991, President Bush signed a milder version of this same bill while restating his opposition to quotas to promote minority hiring.

The central goal of the Civil Rights Movement—full equality between blacks and whites—remains a distant vision. Residential segregation, seen in the persistence of inner-city black ghettos and lily-white suburbs, has easily survived federal open-housing statutes. De facto segregation of churches, social centers, and private schools also remains routine; and wealth, too, is largely segregated along racial lines, with the median family income of blacks in 1990 barely three-fifths that of whites, and with blacks three times as likely to be poor. Many civil rights leaders have urged comprehensive government remedies; but black political power remains limited with regard to national office holding and access to the circles that make foreign and domestic policy.

Despite its limitations, the Civil Rights Movement has in key respects transformed American race relations. In communities throughout the South during the 1960s, "whites only" signs that had stood for generations suddenly came down from hotels, rest rooms, theaters, and other facilities. School desegregation by the mid-1970s had become fact as well as law in over 80 percent of all southern public schools (a better record than in the North, where residential segregation remains pronounced). The federal government has also vigorously checked groups promoting racial hatred: Beginning in 1964 the FBI infiltrated the Ku Klux Klan so thoroughly that by 1965 perhaps one in five members was an informant; federal indictments and encouragement of private lawsuits helped reduce Klan membership from 10,000 in 1981 to less than 5,500 in 1987.

Protection of the suffrage represents the Civil Rights Movement's greatest success: When Congress passed the Voting Rights Act in 1965 barely 100 blacks held elective office in the country; by 1989 there were more than 7,200, including 24 congressional representatives and some 300 mayors. Over 4,800 of these officials served in the South, and nearly every Black Belt county in Alabama had a black sheriff. Mississippi, long the most racially repressive state, experienced the most dramatic change, registering 74 percent of its voting-age blacks and leading the nation in the number of elected officials (646). The unexpectedly strong showing by the Reverend Jesse JACKSON in seeking the Democratic presidential nomination in 1984 and 1988 reflected the growing participation by blacks in mainstream politics.

Having leveled the formal barriers of a legal caste system during the early 1960s, the Civil Rights Movement has since expanded its aims to include substantive equality of opportunity in all areas of American life. The NAACP and the Urban League have for decades urged federal measures to reconstruct the inner cities, create jobs, extend job training to all poor Americans, and strengthen affirmative action to help minorities overcome a legacy of exclusion. Beginning in the 1980s, however, a growing minority of blacks have gained national influence (highlighted by the appointment of Clarence Thomas to the Supreme Court in 1991) by emphasizing private rather than government initiatives and by deploring quotas and other race-conscious programs as politically divisive. The movement for racial equality is now struggling to forge a program that can both unify black activists and also capture the nation's moral high ground and its reform impulses as convincingly as earlier civil rights campaigns.

BIBLIOGRAPHY

Howell, Raines, ed. *My Soul Is Rested: Movement Days in the Deep South Remembered.* New York, 1983.

Kluger, Richard. *Simple Justice.* New York, 1977.

Sellers, Cleveland, with Robert Terrell. *The River of No Return: The Autobiography of a Black Militant and the Life and Death of SNCC.* New York, 1973.

Sitkoff, Harvard. *The Struggle for Black Equality, 1954–1980.* New York, 1981.

Weisbrot, Robert. *Freedom Bound: A History of America's Civil Rights Movement.* New York, 1991.

Williams, Juan, with the "Eyes on the Prize" Production Team. *Eyes on the Prize: America's Civil Rights Years, 1954–1965.* New York, 1987.

– ROBERT WEISBROT

CIVIL WAR

On April 12, 1864, three years to the day after the Civil War began with the firing on Fort Sumter in Charleston harbor, George W. Hatton, a former slave who had risen to the rank of sergeant in Company C, First Regiment, United States Colored Troops, encamped near New Bern, N.C., sat down to write a letter and reflect upon the circumstance in which he found himself. Hatton, his fellow soldiers, and their families had lived generations as slaves in the American South. Now they were part of a liberating army and serving a government that, through a combination of intent and necessity, waged total war on the South in order to destroy SLAVERY. Hatton struggled to find the right words for his sentiments. "Though the Government openly declared that it did not want the Negroes in this conflict," he wrote, "I look around me and see hundreds of colored men armed and ready to defend the Government at any moment; and such are my feelings, that I can only say, the fetters have fallen—our bondage is over."

A month later, Hatton's regiment was encamped close to Jamestown, Va., when several African-American freedwomen entered their lines showing evidence that they had been severely whipped. Members of Hatton's company managed to capture "a Mr. Clayton," the man who had allegedly administered the beatings. The white Virginian was stripped to the waist, tied to a tree, and given twenty lashes by one of his own former slaves, a William Harris, now a member of the Union army. In turn, each of the women Clayton had beaten was given her chance to lay the lash on the slaveholder's back. The women were given leave to, in Sgt. Hatton's words, "remind him that they were no longer his, but safely housed in Abraham's bosom, and under the protection of the Star Spangled Banner, and guarded by their own patriotic, though once down-trodden race." Again Hatton felt almost lost for words to describe the transformations he witnessed. "Oh that I had the tongue to express my feelings," he declared, "while standing on the banks of the James River, on the soil of Virginia, the mother state of slavery, as a witness of such a sudden reverse! The day is clear, the fields of grain are beautiful, and the birds are singing sweet melodious songs, while poor Mr. C. is crying to his servants for mercy."

Such acts of violent retribution by ex-slaves against their former masters were rare in the wake of Emancipation. Most freedpeople simply sought a portion of land, freedom of movement, and security for their families in circumstances of hardship and uncertainty. But Hatton's eloquence allows us to see many elements in the meaning of the Civil War in African-American history. It was the extraordinary time when blacks, free and ex-slave alike, came to identify their own fate closely with the fate of the Union—the United States "Government" (blacks frequently capitalized the word as Hatton did) and its military and political fortunes. Because the war to save the Union became the war to free the slaves, and because so many southern blacks liberated themselves when the opportunity came, many thousands serving as soldiers and sailors in Union uniforms, the Civil War and black Emancipation became inextricable parts of the same epic event. Because the sectional balance of political and economic power was fundamentally altered for a century in great part out of the destruction of slavery, and because, simply put, the terrible conflict would not have happened were it not for the presence of over four million slaves and the array of contradictions they caused for the meaning of America, the Civil War may rightly be considered, as many historians now consider it, the "Second American Revolution."

The drama of Emancipation—four million people liberated from chattel slavery in the midst of the world's first total war—is all the more striking because for black leaders the 1850s had been a decade of discouragement and division combined with unpredictable political crisis. Some black abolitionists like Martin Delany, Henry Highland Garnet, and Mary Ann Shadd struggled to organize emigration plans by which free blacks could start life over again in Africa, the Caribbean, or Canada. Most antebellum free blacks living in the North (a quarter million in the 1850s) followed the lead of Frederick DOUGLASS, James McCune Smith, or Sojourner TRUTH, who insisted that the future for African Americans lay in America. This was not an easy position to sustain by the late 1850s, especially in the wake of the DRED SCOTT DECISION in 1857, wherein Chief Justice of the U.S. Supreme Court Roger B. Taney proclaimed that blacks were "beings of an inferior order . . . so far inferior, that they had no rights which the white man was bound to respect." But black and white abolitionists condemned such ideas, and hope could also be found in the mounting sectional conflict over the expansion of slavery into the West, and in the new antislavery REPUBLICAN PARTY to which it gave birth. Blacks welcomed the news of JOHN BROWN'S RAID on Harpers Ferry in 1859; some had actively participated in the ill-planned and ill-fated raid on a federal arsenal in northern Virginia. Plotting slave insurrections, however, had always been easier in theory than in practice, as many fugitive slaves in the North knew from experience. Larger hopes rested in the idea that somehow the conflict between North and South would boil into disunion and political confrontation sufficient enough to cause the federal government to move, militarily and legally, against slavery.

The drama of Emancipation is all the more striking because for black leaders the 1850s had been a decade of discouragement and division.

So, after the election of Abraham Lincoln in 1860, the secession crisis the following winter, and the outbreak of war in the spring of 1861, African Americans could take heart that the longed-for "jubilee" of black freedom that they had sung and written about for years might now happen. Although prophecy and reality would not meet easily, nor without ghastly bloodshed, most would have agreed with Douglass's editorial of March 1861. "The contest must now be decided, and decided forever," he wrote, "which of the two, Freedom or Slavery, shall give law to this Republic. Let the conflict come." In a few short years and through untold suffering, the rest of the American people, with differing degrees of satisfaction or resistance, would be forced to see in the war the same meaning that Douglass proclaimed. In the wake of the outbreak of war, Douglass captured the anxiety and the hopes of his people as well as their antislavery friends: "For this consummation we have watched and wished with fear and trembling. God be praised! that it has come at last."

Black responses to the outbreak of war ranged from an ecstatic willingness to serve to caution and resistance. Across the North, free black communities sent petitions to state legislatures, organized militia companies, and wrote to the secretary of war offering their services on the battlefield. Only two days after President Lincoln's call for volunteers, the Twelfth Baptist Church in Boston hosted a meeting that the abolitionist William Wells Brown called "crowded as I had never seen a meeting before." In one resolution after another, these black Bostonians declared their support. "Our feelings urge us to say to our countrymen," they announced, "that we are ready to stand by and defend the Government with our lives, our fortunes, and our sacred honor." From Pittsburgh came the offer of a black militia company called the "Hannibal Guards," who insisted on being considered "American citizens." Although "deprived of all our political rights," this group of eager soldiers understood the moment as a historic main chance: They wished "the government of the United States sustained against the tyranny of slavery." From Philadelphia came the news that the sizable black population of that city would raise two full regiments of infantry. In New York City, blacks rented a hall to hold meetings and drill their own militia in preparation for service. In Albany, Ohio, a militia company organized, calling itself the "Attucks Guards" and flying a handmade flag presented by the black women of the town. In Detroit a full black military band under the command of a Capt. O. C. Wood sought to enlist. And from Battle Creek, Mich., a black physician, G. P. Miller, wrote to the War Department asking for the privilege of "raising from 5,000 to 10,000 freemen to report in sixty days to take any position that may be assigned to us (sharpshooters preferred)."

But as promptly as blacks volunteered, their services were denied during the first year of the war. Most states explicitly prohibited black participation in their militias. The policy of the federal government reflected widespread white public opinion: that the war was for the restoration of the Union and not the destruction of slavery. On a deeper level, most white Northerners held the view that "this is a white man's war," as the police in Cincinnati told a large gathering of blacks attempting to find a hall in which to hold their patriotic meetings. Amid this fear, confusion, and bravado, the deep-seated racism of the mid-nineteenth century prevailed as the United States Congress and the War Department made it federal policy to deny enlistment to black soldiers. All of this occurred amid widespead assumptions in the North that secession and rebellion would be easily put down in one summer. But underneath all such social currents rested the fear that white men simply would not shoulder muskets next to black men. Soon, a tragically divided people would be forced to see how historical forces had been unleashed that would compel them to act both because of and above their prejudices.

A vigorous debate about support for the war ensued among blacks during the first year of the conflict. Stung by the rejection of their early enthusiasm for enlistment, some blacks turned away in anger, declaring—as did a man in Troy, N.Y.—that "we of the North must have all the rights which white men enjoy; until then we are in no condition to fight under the flag which gives us no protection." An "R.H.V." from New York City was even more explicit in opposing black participation. "No regiments of black troops," he said, "should leave their bodies to rot upon the battle-field beneath a Southern sun, to conquer a peace based upon the perpetuity of human bondage." Black newspaper editors divided over the issue. The *Anglo-African* (New York) vehemently urged support for the war as a crusade against the slaveholding South, and therefore in blacks' long-term interests. Frederick Douglass, in his *Douglass Monthly* (Rochester, N.Y.), demanded black enlistment from the first sounds of war. The exclusion policy angered him deeply, and by September 1861, he attacked the Lincoln administration's "spectacle of blind, unreasoning prejudice," accusing it of fighting with its "white hand" while allowing its "black hand to remain tied." The *Christian Recorder,* the African Methodist Episcopal Church newspaper in Philadelphia, dissented from Douglass's call for troops. "To offer ourselves now," wrote its editor Elisha Weaver, "is to abandon self-respect and invite insult." Blacks should not fight, said Weaver, in a war where "not only our citizenship, but our common humanity is denied." The war was not yet the social revolution it would become; and no black leader could see the end from the beginning.

In the South, the bulk of African Americans found themselves living in the Confederate States of America, a hastily created nation mobilizing for war on a scale no one had imagined, determined to preserve slavery as the basis of its socioeconomic system, and soon under siege and invasion. All of these circumstances made for what would eventually become—especially when the Yankee armies came in large numbers to Virginia, the coast of the Carolinas, the Mississippi River Valley, and the Tennessee-Georgia region—a mass exodus of both military and self-emancipation from 1862 to 1865. But at the outset of the war, motivated by local pride, protection of the home place, or fear of reprisal, some southern blacks actually offered their services to the Confederate armies. Two Louisiana regiments of blacks were enlisted in 1861, but were never allowed to serve in active duty.

In March 1861, in a speech in Savannah, Ga., Vice President of the Confederacy Alexander H. Stevens stated, at least implicitly, what all Southerners would come to know—that it was black Southerners who might have the most at stake in this war. Comparing the Confederacy to the federal government created in 1787, Stevens declared that the South's move for independence "is founded upon exactly the opposite ideas; its foundations are laid, its cornerstone rests, upon the great truth that the Negro is not equal to the white man; subordination to the superior race is his natural and moral condition." Stevens knew, as did the masses of slaves anticipating "de Kingdom comin' an' de year ob Jubilo," that the status of slavery was central to the war. Before it was over in 1865, that founding Constitution of 1787 would undergo the beginnings of a process of fundamental change.

One of the few economic strengths in the Confederacy's war-making capacity was its huge supply of black labor. Tens of thousands of slaves were pressed into service to build fortifications and to work as teamsters, cooks, boatmen, blacksmiths, laundresses, and nurses. Slaves had long performed these tasks in the South; so, as the massive mobilization took place all across the Confederacy, black forced labor became one of the primary means by which the South waged war. Blacks were "hired out" by their owners to work in ordnance factories, armories, hospitals, and many other sites of military production and transport. In Georgia alone, an estimated ten thousand blacks worked on Confederate defenses. In some twenty-nine hospitals across northern Georgia in 1863, blacks comprised 80 percent (nearly one thousand people) of the workers, especially the nurses, cooks, and laundresses. Early in the war many slaveholders were quite willing to offer the labor of their slaves to the South's cause. But as the conflict endured, and the displacement of people became ever more chaotic, many owners began to transfer (or, as this process became known, "refugee") their slaves to the interior.

Huge numbers of slaves were set in motion by these removals. Many blacks experienced separation of families as men were forced into Confederate labor gangs and women and children were often left to their own devices back on the home place, or themselves were eventually caught up in refugee movement in the face of advancing Union armies. But especially for males, this social flux, however great the hardship, provided enormous opportunity for escape to Union lines. Especially in the upper South and along the coasts, but eventually in the South's heartland as well, many slaves would find freedom by slipping away from Confederate railroad crews or joining Union forces after decisive battles.

Indeed, thousands of blacks were "employed" (not always with compensation) as military laborers on the Union side as well. Wherever Union forces advanced into the South, so important were blacks as foragers, wagon masters, construction workers for fortifications and bridges, and cooks and camp hands that a visitor to any Yankee army camp would see hundreds and sometimes thousands of black faces. Ex-slaves who were familiar with the southern countryside also served numerous Union officers as spies and sources of military intelligence. Harriet TUBMAN, famous for her earlier career as a "conductor" on the UNDERGROUND RAILROAD, was one of the countless blacks who served the Union cause as guides and spies. She was formally commended by the secretary of war and at least five high-ranking Union officers for her two years' work in the Sea Islands as a nurse and a daring scout.

Nothing so typified the eventual antislavery character of the Civil War as the black soldier in Union blue.

Driven by human will and military necessity, an enormous exodus of liberation ensued throughout the first three years of the war. The black Union soldier and later historian George Washington Williams observed both motivations. "Whenever a Negro appeared with a shovel in his hands," wrote Williams, "a white soldier took his gun and returned to the ranks." "It was an exodus whose Moses was multiple," wrote historian Benjamin QUARLES, "an Odyssey whose Ulysses was legion."

Nothing so typified the eventual antislavery character of the Civil War as the black soldier in Union blue. As the war dragged on, events moved so quickly that Emancipation and black enlistment became inseparable realities. From the first designation of fugitive slaves as "contrabands" (confiscated property of war) in 1861, abolitionists demanded that blacks be recruited as soldiers. The initial exclusion policy proved untenable in the face of total war, and by 1862, due to mounting white casualties, northern public opinion was increasingly favorable to the employment of black troops. That sentiment grew even stronger in the spring of 1863, when the federal government instituted a much-despised conscription law.

In the wake of the bloody and unsuccessful Peninsular campaign in July 1862, Congress enacted the Second Confiscation Act, empowering Lincoln to "employ . . . persons of African descent . . . for the suppression of the rebellion." Under vague authority, initial black regiments had already been organized by zealous Union commanders in Louisiana and Kansas. But by August 1862, the War Department authorized the recruitment of five regiments of black infantry in the Sea Islands of South Carolina and Georgia. By Thanksgiving Day, Thomas Wentworth Higginson, the commander of the FIRST SOUTH CAROLINA VOLUNTEERS (the first regiment of ex-slaves), looked out of the broken windows of an abandoned plantation house in the Sea Islands, "through avenues of great live oaks," and observed that "all this is the universal Southern panorama; but five minutes walk beyond the hovels and the live oaks will bring one to something so un-Southern that the whole Southern coast at this moment trembles at the suggestion of such a thing—the camp of a regiment of freed slaves."

Following Lincoln's Emancipation Proclamation in January 1863, the governors of Massachusetts, Connecticut, and Rhode Island were authorized to raise black regiments. Gov. John Andrew of Massachusetts had been especially instrumental in convincing the Lincoln administration to make such moves. Abolitionist George L. Stearns was commissioned to organize black recruiters, and by April black abolitionists such as Douglass, Martin Delany, Henry Highland Garnet, John Mercer Langston, William Wells Brown, Charles Lenox Remond, and O. S. B. Wall were enlisting young free blacks from across the North and sending them to Readville, Mass., where they became part of the FIFTY-FOURTH MASSACHUSETTS COLORED REGIMENT. That spring, as a recruiting document, Douglass published his "Men of Color to Arms!," a pamphlet that captured the revolutionary character of the war now imagined in black communities. "I urge you to fly to arms and smite with death the power that would bury the government and your liberty in the same hopeless grave," Douglass demanded of young recruits, of whom his own first two were his sons Lewis and Charles.

The Fifty-fourth Massachusetts became the famous test case of what the northern press still viewed as the experiment with black troops. Its valorous assault on Fort Wagner on the sands around Charleston harbor in South Carolina, July 18, 1863, where the regiment suffered 100 dead or missing and 146 wounded, served as a tragic but immensely symbolic demonstration of black courage. Indeed, many white Northerners, as well as Confederate soldiers, discovered that black men would and could fight. Blacks who served in the Union army and navy during the Civil War fought for many reasons. They fought for the simplest and deepest of causes: their own freedom and that of their families. They fought because events had seemed to provide an opening to a new future, to the achievement of the birthright of *citizenship* through military service. They also fought for the right to fight, for a sense of human dignity. They fought because they lived in a world that so often defined "manhood" as that recognition gained by the act of soldiering.

In May 1863 the War Department established the Bureau of Colored Troops, and from then until the end of the war, quartermasters and recruiting agents labored competitively to maximize the number of black soldiers throughout the South. The manpower needs of the Union armies were endless, and black enlistment became the most direct way to undermine and destroy SLAVERY. By the end of the war in April 1865, the nearly 180,000 blacks in the Union forces included 33,000 from the northern free states. The border slaveholding states of Delaware, Maryland, Missouri, and Kentucky provided a total of 42,000, half that number from Kentucky alone. Tennessee sent 20,000; Louisiana, 24,000; Mississippi, nearly 18,000; and the remaining states of the Confederacy, almost 40,000. These statistics demonstrate that Emancipation and black enlistment became twin functions of the Union war effort. Wherever northern armies arrived first and stayed the longest, there the greatest numbers of black men became Yankee soldiers.

In desperation, some slaveholders offered wages and other privileges in order to induce their slaves to stay. As the war dragged on, some black men eagerly enlisted with the Union, but others were forced into service by impressment gangs—sometimes composed of black soldiers—as a means of filling the ranks. Like their white comrades, black soldiers suffered untold hardships. But they sometimes received inadequate medical care compared with white troops, faced possible re-enslavement or execution if captured, and encountered several overt forms of discrimination within the Union ranks. Virtually all commissioned officers in black units were white, and though promises had been made to the contrary during the early recruiting period, the federal government capitulated to racism with an explicitly unequal pay system for black soldiers. White privates in the Union army received $13 per month plus $3 for clothing, while black men received only $7 plus clothing. As a matter of both principle and dire hardship for their families, the unequal pay issue angered black soldiers and recruiters more than any other form of discrimination. During 1863 many black regiments resisted the policy, refusing to accept any pay until it was equalized. Open revolt resulted in at least one regiment, the Third South Carolina Volunteers, being led by black sergeant William Walker. Walker led his company in stacking their arms at their commanding officer's tent in protest of unequal pay. After a lengthy court-martial, Walker was convicted of mutiny, and in February 1864 he was executed by a firing squad before the audience of his own brigade. The strictures of military law, mixed with racism, made war in this instance an extremely unforgiving business.

Black families, especially women, suffered not only the dislocations of war, but tremendous physical and financial hardship as well. Many, like Rachel Ann Wicker of Piqua, Ohio, wrote in protest to governors and President Lincoln. In September 1864, Wicker informed Governor Andrew of Massachusetts (her husband was in the Fifty-fifth Massachusetts) that "i speak for myself and Mother and i know of a great many others as well as ourselve are suffering for the want of money to live on." She demanded that Andrew explain "why it is that you Still insist upon them takeing 7 dollars a month when you give the Poorest White Regiment that has went out 16 dollars." Under pressure from such women, from black communities, abolitionists, and governors, Congress enacted equal pay for blacks and whites in June 1864.

In spite of ill treatment, black soldiers—motivated by their own sense of freedom, feeling a sense of dignity that perhaps only military life could offer, and politicized as never before—participated in some 39 major battles and 410 minor engagements during the last two years of the war. Many vocal white critics were silenced when black units fought heroically and suffered terrible casualties in such battles as Port Hudson, La., in May 1863; Milliken's Bend in June 1863; Fort Wagner the next month; and various stages during the siege of Petersburg, Va., in 1864. Sometimes Confederate troops gave no quarter to their captured black opponents. At Fort Pillow, Tennessee, in April 1864, Confederate general Nathan Bedford Forrest gave orders that led to the massacre of at least 200 black soldiers. In all, nearly 3,000 blacks died in battle during the Civil War, and another staggering 33,000 died of disease. Again and again, many of the white officers who led black units testified to the courage and devotion of their men. Higginson declared that he never had to "teach the principles of courage" to his regiment of freed slaves. And he especially marveled at one of his black sergeants, Prince Rivers, who had been a "crack coachman" in Beaufort, S.C., before Emancipation. "There is not a white officer in this regiment," wrote Higginson, "who has more administrative ability, or more absolute authority over the men; they do not love him, but his mere presence has controlling power over them. He writes well enough . . . if his education reached a higher point, I see no reason why he should not command the Army of the Potomac." By the time Abraham Lincoln spoke of a "new birth" of freedom at Gettysburg in November 1863, and called Emancipation the "result so fundamental and astounding" in his second inaugural address in March 1865, there was no better symbol emerging of that regeneration than the anguished sacrifices of black soldiers and their families in the crusade for their own freedom.

With the passage of the Thirteenth Amendment in February 1865, slavery was legally abolished in America.

With the passage of the THIRTEENTH AMENDMENT in February 1865, slavery was legally abolished in America; the institution from which all blacks had been forced to derive social identity had been destroyed. For blacks the ending of the Civil War was a season of great hope and anxiety. Freedom, and at least the promise of the right to vote and equality before the law, was now possible. Millions of ex-slaves dreamed of land ownership amid their ambiguous new status in the conquered and devastated South. The years ahead during RECONSTRUCTION and beyond would bring great advancement in black politics, civil rights, and institution-building, as well as great disappointment and betrayal. But Emancipation had come at last.

In its own context, the meaning of the Civil War for African Americans had no more poignant illustration than the fall of Richmond, the capital of the Confederacy, in the first week of April 1865. Black troops were among the first Union forces to triumphantly occupy the city, and the freed population welcomed them in what the black newspaper correspondent T. Morris Chester called "a spectacle of jubilee." Jubilant black folk also welcomed Lincoln when he visited Richmond on April 4, only two days after Confederate evacuation. There was "no describing the scene along the route," reported Chester. "The colored population was wild with enthusiasm." There were whites in the crowd, but "they were lost in the great concourse of American citizens of African descent." To the black soldiers, many of whom were recently slaves, as well as to the masses of freedpeople, such a revolutionary transformation, such an apocalyptic moment, could only be the work of God in union with his people. Garland H. White, a former Virginia slave who had escaped to Ohio before the war, now marched into Richmond as the chaplain of the Twenty-eighth United States Colored Troops. After making a triumphant speech "amid the shouts of ten thousand voices" on Broad Street, White, overcome by joyful tears, wandered the streets of Richmond, where later that day he found his mother, whom he had not seen in twenty years. Even more telling, though, was the liberation of Richmond's remaining slave pens and auction rooms. As the black troops approached the abandoned "Lumpkin's Jail" (owned by the notorious slave trader Robert Lumpkin), the prisoners behind the barred windows began to chant:

> Slavery chain done broke at last!
> Broke at last! Broke at last!
> Slavery chain done broke at last!
> Gonna praise God till I die!
>
> Now no more weary trav'lin',
> 'Cause my Jesus set me free,
> An' there's no more auction block for me
> Since he give me liberty.

BIBLIOGRAPHY

Berlin, Ira, et al., eds. *Freedom: A Documentary History of Emancipation, 1861–1867.* Series 2, *The Black Military Experience.* New York, 1983.

Blight, David W. *Frederick Douglass' Civil War: Keeping Faith in Jubilee.* Baton Rouge, La., 1989.

Litwack, Leon F. *Been in the Storm So Long: The Aftermath of Slavery.* New York, 1979.

McPherson, James M. *The Negro's Civil War: How American Negroes Felt and Acted during the War for the Union.* New York, 1965.

Quarles, Benjamin. *The Negro in the Civil War.* New York, 1953.

— DAVID W. BLIGHT

CLARK, SEPTIMA POINSETTE

Septima Poinsette Clark (May 3, 1898–December 15, 1987), educator and civil rights activist. Septima Poinsette was born and reared in Charleston, S.C. Her mother, Victoria Warren Anderson, was of Haitian descent and worked as a laundress, and her father, Peter Porcher Poinsette, was a former slave who worked as a cook and a caterer. Her parents deeply influenced Poinsette and instilled in her a willingness to share one's gifts and a belief that there was something redeeming about everyone. In addition, Poinsette's early education, which brought her into contact with demanding black teachers who insisted that students have pride and work hard, left a positive and lasting impression on her. Partly as a result of these influences, Poinsette pursued a career in education. In 1916, she received her teaching certificate from Avery Normal Institute, a private school for black teachers founded after the end of the Civil War by the American Missionary Association in Charleston.

Poinsette's first teaching position was on Johns Island, S.C., from 1916 to 1919, because African Americans were barred from teaching in the Charleston public schools. She tried to address the vast educational, political, and economical inequities that faced Johns Island blacks by instituting adult literacy classes and health education and by working with the NAACP. In 1919, she returned to Charleston to work at Avery and spearheaded a campaign against Charleston's exclusionary education system that resulted, one year later, in the overturning of the law barring black teachers from teaching in public schools. In May 1920, Poinsette married Nerie Clark, a black Navy cook. She had two children, one of whom died at birth. After her husband died in 1924, Clark sent her other child, Nerie, Jr., to live with his paternal grandmother because she could not support him financially.

Shortly thereafter, Clark returned to Columbia, S.C., became active in various civic organizations, and continued her education, receiving a B.A. from Benedict College (1942) and an M.A. from Hampton Institute (1945). She led the fight for equal pay for black teachers in South Carolina. Her efforts attracted the attention of the NAACP, which initiated litigation and won a 1945 ruling mandating equal pay for black teachers in South Carolina. In 1947, Clark returned to Charleston to teach in public schools and continued her civic activities until she was fired in 1956 because of her membership in the NAACP. Unable to find another position in South Carolina, Clark moved to the Highlander Folk School, in Monteagle, Tenn., an interracial adult education center founded by Myles Horton in 1932 to foster social activism and promote racial equality. There Clark became director of education. Together with Horton and South Carolina black activists such as Esau Jenkins from Johns Island, she devised educational strategies to challenge black illiteracy and encourage black voter registration. Clark, guided by the belief that literacy was integral to black equality, instituted the citizenship school program, an adult literacy program that focused on promoting voter registration and empowering people to solve their own problems through social activism.

The first citizenship school, founded on John's Island in 1957, was a success, and Clark traveled throughout the deep South, trying to make links with other local activists to foster the expansion of the schools. In 1961, the citizenship school program was transferred to the SOUTHERN CHRISTIAN LEADERSHIP CONFERENCE (SCLC) after the Tennessee legislature's persistent efforts to disrupt Highlander activities resulted in the school's charter being revoked and its property being confiscated. Clark joined SCLC to oversee the newly renamed Citizen Education Project, and by 1970 over 800 Citizenship schools had been formed that graduated over 100,000 African Americans who served as a key grass-roots base for the CIVIL RIGHTS MOVEMENT throughout the deep South. In 1971, however, she retired from SCLC because long-term commitment to the schools had faded.

Clark, guided by the belief that literacy was integral to black equality, instituted the citizenship school program.

Clark remained an outspoken spokesperson for racial, as well as gender, equality. She chronicled her life of activism in her autobiography, *Echo in My Soul,* in 1962. In 1966, she spoke at the first national meeting of the National Organization of Women (NOW) about the necessity of women challenging male dominance. In 1976, she was elected to the Charleston, S.C., school board. Three years later, she was awarded the Living Legacy award from President Jimmy Carter in honor of her continuing dedication to black empowerment through education. In 1987, she received an American Book Award for her second autobiography, *Ready from Within: Septima Clark and the Civil Rights Movement.* Later that year, Septima Clark died in Charleston, S.C.

BIBLIOGRAPHY

Clark, Septima. *Echo in My Soul,* 1962.

Clark, Septima, with Cynthia Stokes Brown. *Ready from Within: Septima Clark and the* CIVIL RIGHTS MOVEMENT. Navarro, Calif., 1986.

Crawford, Vicki, Jacqueline Rouse, and Barbara Woods, eds. *Trailblazers and Torchbearers: Women in the* CIVIL RIGHTS MOVEMENT. Brooklyn, N.Y., 1990.

– CHANA KAI LEE

CLARK-ATLANTA UNIVERSITY

In 1988, two historic black colleges, Clark College and Atlanta University, merged to form Clark-Atlanta University. Atlanta University was founded on October 16, 1867, when the trustees of Atlanta University received a charter from the state of Georgia. Edmund Ware, appointed by the American Missionary Association (AMA) to head up freedmen's education in Atlanta in 1866, was encouraged to find a black school already in operation when he arrived. The school had been founded in 1865 by two former slaves who turned it over to the leadership of newly arrived northern missionaries. Under Ware's guidance, enrollment grew and a new school house was built.

After the charter was granted and funds were raised (including $10,000 from the Freedman's Bureau), fifty acres were purchased and the cornerstone of the first building was set in June 1869. The first completed building housed the Normal School, which opened in October 1869. Both a grammar and secondary school were maintained on the premises until after the turn of the century.

Academic standards were high and the curriculum was patterned after the model of New England colleges. The educators were committed to the belief that African Americans deserved and were capable of an education equal to that offered to white students. Atlanta University was open to students of all races and colors. Initially, both black and white children attended (the white students were the children of faculty members). White and black faculty and students dined together in the tradition of the New England colleges. This scandalized Atlanta whites, who boycotted the university and everyone connected with it. In 1887 the state of Georgia cut off the land grant appropriations because of the interracial mixing.

After the turn of the twentieth century, the missionary societies did not get the contributions they once had received and so they were no longer able to provide much financial support to black colleges. The philanthropic organizations that gradually took the missions societies' place as the primary benefactor of black colleges and universities were skeptical of higher education for African Americans. As a result, Atlanta University experienced a constant battle for financial stability. This situation led to the affiliation with MOREHOUSE COLLEGE and SPELMAN COLLEGE in 1929. Part of the agreement stipulated that Spelman and Morehouse would remain undergraduate institutions while Atlanta University would function solely as a graduate school. (The first graduate degree, an M.A., was awarded in 1931.) This affiliation eventually grew into the Atlanta University Center in 1957. In 1988 Clark College and Atlanta University merged to form Clark-Atlanta University.

Atlanta University's most famous professor was W. E. B. DU BOIS, who taught there twice, from 1897 to 1910 and from 1932 to 1944. In addition to his many other responsibilities and accomplishments, Du Bois headed up the Atlanta University Studies program. This program began in 1896 as a sociological study of the urban condition of black Americans by a white businessman, George Bradford. Bradford began his study in response to the annual conference on the needs of rural black Americans, which was hosted by HAMPTON and TUSKEGEE institutes. Du Bois took the project over in 1897 and completely changed its focus. Instead of continuing the theme of the first two conferences—that African-American urban life would improve if blacks worked harder and improved their moral character—Du Bois sought to systematically study all possible sociological topics of African-American urban life. Topics and studies of the two-day conferences included "The Negro in Business" (1899), "The Negro Artisan" (1902), "The Negro Church" (1903), and "The Negro American Family" (1908). The proceedings from most of these conferences were published.

The conferences grew in prestige and fame and many experts from around the world participated in them. Max Weber, the great German sociologist, joined in the conference on crime in 1904. In spite of the tremendous financial difficulties of the program, Du Bois, almost singlehandedly, placed the Atlanta University Studies program in the forefront of American social science research on African Americans.

In addition to the contract of affiliation, 1929 also saw another milestone for Atlanta University. John Hope was selected as the first African-American president of the university. Hope was already the president of Morehouse College. He served as president of both schools until 1931 when he retired from Morehouse (after a twenty-five-year tenure as its president) and devoted the rest of his life (he died in 1936) to the presidency of Atlanta University.

The many distinguished graduates from Atlanta University include James Weldon JOHNSON, appointed U.S. Consul in Venezuela in 1906 by President Theodore Roosevelt and executive secretary of the NATIONAL ASSOCIATION FOR THE ADVANCEMENT OF COLORED PEOPLE (NAACP) from 1920 to 1930, and Walter WHITE, who was the Executive Secretary of the NAACP from 1931 to 1955.

Clark College was founded in 1869 as the Summerhill School by the Freedmen's Aid Society of the Methodist Episcopal Church. It became Clark University in 1870, named after Bishop Davis W. Clark the first president of the Freedmen's Aid Society. The school was chartered by the state of Georgia in 1877. Clark was a coeducational institution which taught elementary and secondary levels exclusively in its early years. The first baccalaureate degree was issued in 1883. It remained a private, undergraduate liberal arts institution committed to providing its students with the intellectual knowledge and skills necessary to excel in the field they chose to pursue.

In 1883 a department of theology was opened which separated from Clark University in 1886 and became Gammon Theological Seminary. Though not a party to the original contract of affiliation between Atlanta University, Morehouse College, and Spelman College in 1929, Clark began to participate in closer relations with the new university system, thereafter. In 1940 Clark University changed its name to Clark College and in 1957, it became one of the six founding members of the Atlanta University Center. In 1992 Clark-Atlanta University had an enrollment of 4,480 students, 86 percent of whom were African American.

BIBLIOGRAPHY

Bacote, Clarence A. *The Story of Atlanta University.* Atlanta, 1969.

Lewis, David Levering. *W. E. B. Du Bois: Biography of a Race, 1868–1919.* New York, 1993.

McPherson, James M. *The Abolitionist Legacy.* Princeton, N.J., 1975.

Roebuck, Julian B., and Komanduri S. Murty. *Historically Black Colleges and Universities.* Westport, Conn., 1993.

– DEBI BROOME

CLEAVER, ELDRIDGE LEROY

Eldridge Leroy Cleaver (August 31, 1935–), writer, political activist. Eldridge Cleaver was born in Wabbaseka, Ark., where he attended a junior college. From 1954 to 1957 and again from 1958 to 1966 he was incarcerated on drug and rape charges, and furthered his education while in prison. In 1965, Cleaver became the most prominent "Black Muslim" prisoner to break with Elijah MUHAMMAD's NATION OF ISLAM after MALCOLM X's assassination. Just as FBI director J. Edgar Hoover had begun to target the BLACK PANTHERS as the nation's "greatest threat," Cleaver became the party's minister of information in 1966, calling for an armed insurrection to overthrow the United States government and replace it with a black socialist government. During the late 1960s and early '70s, he also was an assistant editor and contributing writer to *Ramparts* magazine.

In 1968, Cleaver published *Soul on Ice,* which remains his primary claim to literary fame. A collection of autobiographical and political essays in the form of letters and meditations, *Soul on Ice* articulated the sense of alienation felt by many black nationalists who refused to work within an inherently corrupt system. Cleaver viewed his own crimes as political acts and spelled out how racism and oppression had forged his revolutionary consciousness.

Later that year, while on parole, Cleaver was involved in a shootout with Oakland police during which a seventeen-year-old Black Panther, Bobby Hutton, was killed; Cleaver and a police officer were wounded. Cleaver's parole was revoked and he was charged with assault and attempted murder. Although he received worldwide support and was chosen to run as the presidential candidate for the Peace and Freedom Party, Cleaver feared for his safety if he surrendered to the authorities. He fled the country, jumping a $50,000 bail, and lived for the next seven years in Cuba, France and Algiers. He also visited the Soviet Union, China, North Vietnam, and North Korea during these years of exile. But in 1975 he returned to the United States and struck a deal with the FBI. Although he faced up to seventy-two years in prison, he was sentenced instead to 1,200 hours of community service.

In 1978, Cleaver published *Soul on Fire,* a collection of essays on his newly acquired conservative politics, and in 1979 he founded the Eldridge Cleaver Crusades, an evangelical organization. In 1984 he ran as an independent candidate for Congress in the eighth Congressional District in California. In the 1980s, he lectured on religion and politics, and published his own poetry and polemical writings. In March 1994, his struggle with drugs came to national attention when he underwent brain surgery after he had been arrested in Berkeley, Calif., late at night with a serious head injury, in a state of drunkenness and disorientation.

In 1965, Cleaver became the most prominent "Black Muslim" prisoner to break with Elijah Muhammad's Nation of Islam.

Cleaver has been a prolific writer and speaker and was seen by some in the late 1960s as a black leader capable of organizing and leading a mass movement. *Soul on Ice* won the Martin Luther King Memorial Prize in 1970. Most of his work consists of nonfiction writing: *Eldridge Cleaver: Post-Prison Writings and Speeches* (1969), *Eldridge Cleaver's Black Papers* (1969), the introduction to Jerry Rubin's *Do It!* (1970), and contributions to *The Black Panther Leaders Speak: Huey P. Newton, Bobby Seale, Eldridge Cleaver, and Company Speak Out Through the Black Panther Party's Official Newspaper* (1976) and to *War Within: Violence or Nonviolence in Black Revolution* (1971). He has also authored and coauthored numerous pamphlets for the Black Panther party and the People's Communication Network. Some of his work has also appeared in anthologies such as the *Prize Stories of 1971: The O. Henry Awards.*

Cleaver has had both his critics and his followers. There are those who felt that his commitment to violence and his use of rape as a political weapon in the 1960s had no place within society. Others have questioned the sincerity and credibility of his later *volte face* to right-wing politics and fundamentalist Christianity, and Cleaver has often felt compelled to explain and defend himself. According to him, combined with his growing disenchantment with communism and radical politics was a mystical vision resulting in his conversion to Christianity. When accused of having mellowed with age, Cleaver replied, "That implies that your ideas have changed because of age. I've changed because of new conclusions."

BIBLIOGRAPHY

Baranski, Lynne, and Richard Lemon. *People* (March 22, 1982).

Hunter, Charlayne. "To Mr. and Mrs. Yesterday," *New York Times Book Review* (March 24, 1968): 3.

— AMRITJIT SINGH

CLEVELAND, OHIO

Cleveland has had African-American connections from its earliest days. The city and the surrounding Western Reserve area were founded in 1798 by explorers from the Connecticut Land Company, who brought along an African American, "Black Joe," as guide and interpreter. While a fugitive slave named Ben spent several months in Cleveland in 1806, the first African-American Clevelander, George Peake, arrived with his family in 1809. Peake, a farmer and ex-soldier from Maryland, later invented an improved hand mill for grinding corn. Few blacks settled in the growing community, however. In 1820 there were only fifty-four blacks in the vicinity, and just three were within city limits. White residents were not particularly friendly to them, though in 1819 a Cleveland jury convicted two white men on kidnapping charges for the attempted recapture of a FUGITIVE SLAVE from Virginia. In 1827, despite strong black opposition, the Cuyahoga County Colonization Society was formed to support efforts at sending blacks to Africa.

There were still only seventy-six blacks in Cleveland in 1830, most of them living in the town's eastern section, when Cleveland's first black church, St. John's African Methodist Episcopal (AME) Church, was organized. During the next two decades, the area's black population grew to over three hundred. Under the leadership of John Malvin, a sailor and merchant from Cincinnati, the city's black community organized the School Fund Society, which ran schools intermittently until city funding was granted in 1843. In 1839 the Young Men's Union Society (later the Colored Young Men's Lyceum), a literary and political club, was founded.

During this period, Cleveland, along with the rest of the surrounding Western Reserve, was settled by masses of white New Englanders, many of whom were reformers and evangelicals with powerful antislavery convictions. In 1833 the Cleveland (later the Cuyahoga County) Anti-Slavery Society was formed. Cleveland soon became a center of abolitionist activity and a primary station on the UNDERGROUND RAILROAD. Black activists included John Malvin, William Howard Day, editor of Cleveland's first black newspaper, the *Alienated American* (1853–1855), and barber John Brown, the city's wealthiest African American. They joined whites such as Joshua Giddings (elected to Congress on the Free Soil ticket in 1850) to aid fugitive slaves and lobby for civil rights and suffrage. In 1849 they helped bring about the repeal of most of the state's Black Laws.

Under abolitionist influence, Cleveland's white population developed a distinctive racial liberalism, and a large part of its white population supported black equality. By the end of the 1840s, the city's public schools and most of its churches were integrated. Segregation in public places was rare, and blacks were able to find housing throughout the city. Numerous African Americans found jobs as skilled laborers. Others entered the professions; notable among them was Robert Boyd Leach, one of the few antebellum black doctors. A few African Americans, such as Brown, cattle dealer Alfred Greenbrier, and contractor Madison Tilley, occupied prominent places in the city economy.

An important result of Cleveland's racial tolerance was that the city's black population shared the facilities of the larger community, and separate black institutions were thus few and poorly supported. While a National Emigration Convention of Colored Men was organized in the city in 1854, most community leaders were integrationist.

The outbreak of the CIVIL WAR in 1861 prompted widespread excitement in Cleveland, and black leaders called for the Union Army to accept black soldiers. However, it was not until 1863 that blacks were accepted into the Army. As many as fifteen hundred blacks fought in the 127th Ohio Volunteer Infantry (later absorbed into the Fifth Ohio United States Colored Troop). In honor of African-American contributions to the victory, a black soldier is depicted in the city's Soldiers & Sailors Monument, dedicated in 1894.

In the years after the Civil War, a modest number of blacks, largely from the Upper South, migrated to Cleveland, but African Americans remained less than 2 percent of the total population. In 1870 all black males in Ohio were enfranchised, and three years later Republican John P. Green was elected justice of the peace, becoming Cleveland's first black officeholder. In 1882, with the aid of white votes, he won election to the state legislature. In 1891 Green was elected to the state senate. However, at the same time, Cleveland's tradition of racial tolerace began to decline. Discrimination restricted black job prospects. Between 1865 and 1890, the proportion of black homeowners fell from over 33 percent to 15 percent. Segregation of public facilities grew increasingly common despite the 1887 Ohio civil rights law.

As housing segregation increased, the East Side's Central Avenue district became largely a black area. In the face of exclusion, black Clevelanders organized within their own community. St. John's AME church grew in size, and three more churches, including Mount Zion Congregational Church and Cory Methodist Church, were established by 1890. Institutions such as the Cleveland Home for Aged Colored People (1896) were created.

Cleveland also featured a lively black cultural scene at the end of the nineteenth century. Lyceums and debating clubs, such as the Coral Builders Society and the Wide Awake Literary Society, sprang up. In 1883 Harry Clay Smith, a twenty-year-old from West Virginia, founded the *Cleveland Gazette,* a weekly black newspaper that became the voice of black Cleveland. Despite competition from various short-lived journals, it remained in circulation for over seventy years. Black theater, beginning in the 1850s with the Dramatic Temple, remained popular. Many important musicians came from Cleveland, including Charles McAfee, bassoonist with the Cleveland Orchestra and also the leader of the Excelsior Band and the McAfee and Bowman Orchestra; concert singer Rachel Turner Walker, "the Creole Nightingale"; opera composer Harry Lawrence Freeman; and Justin Miner Holland, famed for his guitar instruction manual.

The most eminent black Clevelander of the late nineteenth century was lawyer/novelist Charles W. CHESNUTT, who came to the city in 1883. Admitted to the Ohio bar in 1887, he made his living as a lawyer and court reporter. Meanwhile, he became nationally known for his speeches, novels, and short stories. Chesnutt was the first African-American member of the Cleveland Chamber of Commerce, and in 1912 he helped found the Cleveland branch of the NATIONAL ASSOCIATION FOR THE ADVANCEMENT OF COLORED PEO-

PLE (NAACP). Another notable resident was Garrett Morgan, who came to Cleveland in 1895; a businessman and newspaper editor, he was best known for his inventions.

Cleveland's black population doubled during the 1890s as large-scale migration from the South began, and the city continued to receive migrants during the first part of the century. However, white immigrants from Europe also settled in Cleveland, and the proportion of blacks in the population remained under 2 percent. Although Cleveland managed to avoid the extremes of racial violence that occurred elsewhere, the city became heavily segregated. While the public schools remained integrated, industrial jobs were closed to blacks due to employer and union exclusion, and most poor blacks were forced into low-paying menial labor. Middle-class African Americans were denied equal access to civil service and white-collar jobs, and black businessmen were forced to redirect their services towards an all-black market. A few wealthy blacks, such as barber George Myers, continued to be accepted among the city's elite.

Cleveland's black population doubled during the 1890s as large-scale migration from the South began, and the city continued to receive migrants during the first part of the century.

The concentration of blacks in the Central Avenue area heightened black influence in politics. The leading black politicians were George Myers and Harry Clay Smith, two disciples of Republican political boss Mark Hanna. Smith, who founded the Afro-American Republican Club in 1892, served three terms in the state assembly, while Myers (son of Baltimore labor leader Isaac Myers) served as a delegate to three Republican national conventions. In 1910 Thomas Fleming, an African American, was appointed to Cleveland's city council, and with the aid of saloonkeeper and political boss "Starlight" Boyd, he was elected to a regular term five years later. Meanwhile, in 1901 the First Johnson Negro Democratic Club, headed by Walter L. Brown, was formed. Although blacks were unable to win Democratic support for citywide office until the 1920s, in 1909 Brown won the party's nomination for justice of the peace.

During the Great Migration, beginning around 1915, Cleveland was a principal destination of southern black migrants. By 1930 the black population was almost nine times larger than it had been in 1910. The migration had wide-reaching economic, political, and social consequences for black Cleveland. The civilian labor shortage that occurred during World War I forced industrial employers to hire black male workers; by 1920 a higher percentage of African Americans worked in industry in Cleveland than in any other city except DETROIT. While blacks remained largely excluded from unions and were unable to move beyond low-level positions, median family income increased. The wages of these workers made possible a growing black middle class. In 1921 Herbert Chauncey founded the Empire Savings & Loan Company, the city's first black-owned bank.

At the same time, the migration strained scarce city housing resources. Blacks were forced into already crowded and unhealthy housing in the Central-Woodland district. The migrants paid high rents for space in the district's tenements and apartment houses (many of which were owned by middle-class blacks). Attempts by blacks to move outside the district were met by violence. In 1925, when Charles Garvin, a black doctor and community leader, bought a house in an all-white neighborhood, it was destroyed by a bomb.

The growing population increased black political power and assertiveness. Under the leadership of Claybourne George, the Cleveland NAACP, which boasted sixteen hundred members by 1922, instituted dozens of civil rights suits to challenge black exclusion and campaigned for the hiring of black workers by city business. Marcus Garvey's Universal Negro Improvement Association also had a powerful Cleveland chapter, organized by Leroy Bundy. Black institutions were formed to aid the migrants. The most notable were the Negro Welfare Association (later the Cleveland Urban League), founded in 1917, and the Phillis Wheatley Association, a settlement house for black women, founded in 1913. Another institution was the *Cleveland Call & Post* newspaper, formed by the merger of two small journals in 1927 and still in publication in the 1990s.

At the same time, black representation and influence on the city council increased. By 1929 a "black triumvirate" of George, Bundy, and Lawrence Payne had been elected. Since the three controlled the balance of power in an often deadlocked council, they were able to trade votes during the following three years for the integration of City Hospital and for committee chairmanships. Over the subsequent decade, they used these chairmanships to obtain welfare aid and city services for the black community as well as the appointment of blacks to city commissions.

Despite the unpleasant conditions in the Central-Woodland district, a strong entertainment culture developed in the "Roaring 3rd" section in the 1920s and '30s. Dance halls, such as the Golden Slipper (later the Trianon), and jazz dance clubs, such as Val's in the Valley (renowned during the early 1930s for the presence of pianist Art Tatum), grew up in the area. Cleveland also launched the careers of jazz artists such as violinist Hezekiah "Stuff" Smith. Another important cultural resource was the nationally known Karamu House, a white-run interracial theater and settlement house founded as the Playhouse Settlement in 1915. The Karamu Theater, opened in 1927, sponsored dance and acting classes as well as amateur theatrical productions written by such African Americans as Shirley Graham and Langston HUGHES (who spent some of his youth in Cleveland).

Sports were also a popular pastime. Cleveland fielded several professional black baseball teams, notably the Cleveland Buckeyes, Negro American League champions of the 1940s. The city's most celebrated athlete was Jesse OWENS, who became a national hero after winning four gold medals in track and field in the 1936 Olympics.

The Great Depression led to widespread unemployment among Cleveland's blacks, and the African-American population declined slightly as residents left the city in search of work. Many black businesses, including the Empire Savings & Loan, were forced to close. Several insurance companies developed financial problems, and in 1936 four companies merged into the Dunbar Mutual Insurance Company, which became the city's largest black-owned business. Despite the efforts of such groups as the Future Outlook League, which successfully used boycotts to fight job discrimination, inequality remained a chronic problem. During the decade, many blacks were able to find emergency employment through New Deal social programs, and the community's political allegiance swung to the Democratic party.

The industrial surge that accompanied WORLD WAR II and the postwar prosperity drew new waves of black migrants to Cleveland in search of industrial employment. The city's black population grew from 84,504 to 250,818 in twenty years. With help from the federal Fair Employment Practices Committee, blacks were able to find jobs and to advance into previously all-white positions. The migration also made possible advances in black political power; by 1960 there were ten blacks on Cleveland's city council, and blacks were active in city commissions. No large city had a higher level of black political representation. Civil rights activity also increased. By 1945 the NAACP's membership jumped to ten thousand. The same year, the Cleveland Community Relations Board was founded. It drafted a city ordinance, enacted in 1946, revoking the licenses of public facilities which were found to have excluded blacks.

The new migration prompted recurring housing shortages in the deteriorating Central-Woodland area where most blacks were forced to live. In the years after the war, blacks began to expand into the Glenville and Mount Pleasant neighborhoods, which had long had black residents. During the 1950s blacks began to move into the once fashionable, previously all-white Hough neighborhood. The area became largely black within ten years. Black residents in these areas of Cleveland were faced with poor city services, deteriorating schools, and police repression. (A warrantless police search of the home of Dollree Mapp, a black woman, led to the landmark 1961 U.S. Supreme Court case *Mapp* v. *Ohio.*)

The CIVIL RIGHTS MOVEMENT dramatically expanded in Cleveland during the 1960s. In 1963 the NAACP organized the United Freedom Movement (UFM), an alliance of some fifty groups. In 1963 and 1964 the UFM launched a campaign against de facto school segregation. Leaders sued to halt construction of new schools, and interracial contingents demonstrated at schools in white areas that segregated black students bused from inner-city areas. On several occasions violence erupted when white mobs confronted the protesters, and in April 1964 a small riot broke out after a white demonstrator was accidentally killed during a construction site protest. Leaders organized a school boycott, but Mayor Ralph Lochner and city leaders refused to meet with UFM representatives. Split by factionalism, by 1966 the UFM had virtually disintegrated.

On July 18, 1966, the frustration over inequality that had been building up in black Cleveland overflowed, and full-scale rioting broke out in the Hough neighborhood. A crowd of blacks destroyed a tavern after an altercation inside. Police were called in, but the rioting intensified. Mayor Lochner called in units of the Ohio National Guard and closed all the city's bars, but the rioting continued for six nights. Four people were killed, thirty were injured, and three hundred were arrested.

In 1967 Carl Stokes, a state legislator who had run for mayor as an independent two years previously and narrowly lost, ran again, this time on the Democratic ticket. Stokes's narrow victory, based on a near-unanimous black vote (African Americans made up about a third of the city's population) and one-fourth of the white vote, made him the first black mayor of a large city. The following year his brother, Louis Stokes, ran for Congress from a newly created black-majority district and was elected Cleveland's first black congressman. The victories of the Stokes brothers were important symbols of black political power in the city. Carl Stokes put through important reforms; he implemented affirmative action through an equal employment opportunity ordinance, increased spending for housing and welfare (with the help of federal funding frozen under previous administrations), and created Cleveland:Now! a joint public-private program for community rehabilitation, which raised more than $100 million in funds.

Since the end of the 1960s, Cleveland has had many of the same problems as other deindustrializing cities.

However, Stokes's administration was crippled by the Glenville Shootout of July 23, 1968, a gun battle in Glenville between police and black militants led by Fred "Ahmad" Evans. It left seven dead (including three policemen) and set off rioting by local blacks. Stokes called in National Guard troops, then cordoned off the area, ordering only black police and community leaders inside to calm rioters. However, the rioting continued for three days, demonstrating that the election of a black mayor was not sufficient to eliminate racial tension and violence. Cleveland:Now! was discredited when it was revealed at Evans's trial that he had purchased guns with money obtained indirectly through the program. Stokes was reelected in 1969, but he was unable to persuade voters to approve higher income taxes for better city services or to reform the city police department. He declined to run again in 1971. Though blacks continued to occupy positions of power on the city council, it was not until 1990 that the city elected another black mayor, Michael White.

Since the end of the 1960s, Cleveland has had many of the same problems as other deindustrializing cities. The poor economy and racial tension have led whites and middle-class blacks to migrate to nearby suburbs. (As a result, Shaker Heights has developed a large black population.) By 1990 the city of Cleveland had a near majority of blacks in its population. Most of Cleveland's blacks, concentrated in East Cleveland, faced decrepit housing and schools. A 1983 report identified Cleveland as one of the nation's three most segregated cities. (In 1976 a U.S. District Court ordered busing to assure desegregated schools.) The city economy remained sluggish. In 1978 Cleveland briefly went into default on its obligations. Despite economic development through such programs as the Gateway Project, a nonprofit public construction firm with significant minority participation, black unemployment remained high. The closing of the First National Bank Association in 1990 was a blow to black business in Cleveland.

Barriers to advancement notwithstanding, there have been many black success stories. In 1974 Frank Robinson of the Cleveland Indians was hired as major league baseball's first black manager. In 1990 Thomas Greer became editor of the *Cleveland Plain Dealer,* the city's main newspaper. Clevelanders, in fact, have achieved some success in many fields in recent decades. Notable figures include musicians Tadd Dameron and jazz avant-gardist Albert Ayler, stage figures Dorothy Dandridge and Ruby Dee, promoter Don King, and writers Chester HIMES and Russell Atkins.

The city's complex black history has been preserved at the city's Afro-American Cultural and Historical Society Museum, founded in 1953 and established in a permanent building in 1983.

BIBLIOGRAPHY

Black, Lowell Dwight. *The Negro Volunteer Militia Units in the Ohio National Guard, 1870–1954.* Cleveland, 1976.

Davis, Russell H. *Black Americans in Cleveland.* Washington, D.C., 1972.

Kusmer, Kenneth. *A Ghetto Takes Shape: Black Cleveland, 1870–1930.* Urbana, Ill., 1976.

Porter, Philip W. *Cleveland: Confused City on a Screw.* Columbus, Ohio, 1976.

Van Tassel, David D., and John J. Grabowski, eds. *The Encyclopedia of Cleveland History.* Bloomington, Ind., 1987.

— GREG ROBINSON

COLE, NAT "KING"

Nat "King" Cole (Nathaniel Adams Cole) (March 17, 1919–February 15, 1965), singer and pianist. Born in Montgomery, Ala., Nat Cole moved with his family to Chicago when he was two years old. His father, the Rev. Edward James Cole, Sr., was a pastor at the True Light Baptist Church. His parents encouraged the musical talents of young Cole and his four brothers. All but one eventually became professional musicians. Cole had his earliest musical experiences in his father's church, where he sang and played the organ. While in high school, he played in the Rogues of Rhythm, a band led by his brother Eddie, at a Chicago night spot called the Club Panama. In 1936 he played piano in a touring production of Noble Sissle and Eubie BLAKE's *Shuffle Along.* The tour ended in Long Beach, Calif., in 1937. Cole stayed in southern California, and played piano in Los Angeles-area clubs.

In 1938 he organized a trio with Oscar Moore on guitar and Wesley Prince on bass. About this time he adopted the name Nat "King" Cole. The trio began to gain popularity largely due to Cole's sophisticated, swinging piano style. In 1943 Cole signed a contract with the newly organized record company Capitol.

On his first hit recording "Straighten Up and Fly Right" (1943), Cole sang for the first time. The song, based on a sermon of his father's, was taken from a traditional black folktale. In 1944, Cole achieved a national reputation as a pianist, taking part in "Jazz at the Philharmonic," a series of touring jazz concerts.

Eventually, Cole's singing came to dominate his piano playing. His 1946 recording of "The Christmas Song," which added a string section to Cole's singing, was a turning point in the evolution of his career. By 1949 he was recording primarily with orchestral accompaniment, and his piano playing was relegated to a secondary role. Cole achieved great success with such vocal recordings as "Mona Lisa" (1950) and "Unforgettable" (1951). Cole's singing style was, like his piano playing, relaxed, disarming, and authoritative. His performances remained impressive even with the most banal material, and they always retained their integrity, shunning both pseudodramatic straining for effects and coy mannerisms. His singing had an immense popularity with both white and black audiences. Cole's was the first black jazz combo to have its own sponsored radio program (1948–1949), and in 1956 and 1957 he became the first black performer to have his own series on network television. (The program was canceled, however, because of the difficulty in finding sponsors for it.) Cole also made several films, including *St. Louis Blues* (1958, a life of W. C. HANDY), and *Cat Ballou* (1965).

In the early 1960s Cole was sometimes criticized by black activists for his failure to actively participate in the struggle for civil rights. Cole resented the accusations, noting that he had made substantial financial contributions to civil rights organizations. By this time, Cole was a headliner at Las Vegas casinos and was one of the most financially successful performers in popular music. He died of lung cancer in 1965 at the height of his popularity. He was the most successful black performer of the postwar era. The appreciation of his contribution to popular music has increased since his death. His television show has been syndicated and many of his recordings have been reissued.

Cole's first marriage, to Nadine Robinson in 1937, ended in divorce. He married Maria Ellington (no relation to Duke Ellington) in 1948. They had four children, and also adopted Maria's niece. One of their children, Natalie Cole, has had a successful career as a pop singer. In 1991, Natalie Cole achieved considerable recognition for her album *Unforgettable,* an ingeniously recorded album of duets with her late father, which won Grammies for best album and best song.

– ROBERT W. STEPHENS

COLEMAN, ORNETTE

Ornette Coleman (c. March 9, 1930–), jazz saxophonist and composer. Born in Fort Worth, Tex., on a date that remains in dispute, Ornette Coleman's early musical influences included gospel, rhythm and blues, and bebop. Coleman, whose father was a singer, began playing saxophone at age sixteen, and had little formal music instruction. His earliest performances were in local churches, and he was expelled from his high school

The avant-garde jazz of tenor saxophonist Ornette Coleman, a pioneer of "free jazz" in the late 1950s and early '60s, challenged almost all conventional assumptions about the sound of jazz. A restless innovator, Coleman expanded the vocabulary of jazz for more than thirty years. (Photographs and Prints Division, Schomburg Center for Research in Black Culture, The New York Public Library, Astor, Lenox and Tilden Foundations)

band for improvising during a performance of John Philip Sousa's "Washington Post March." Coleman at first played tenor saxophone in a honking rhythm-and-blues style influenced by Illinois Jacquet and Big Jay McNeely. His first professional work came in 1949 with the Silas Green Minstrels, a tent show that toured the South and Midwest. Coleman also traveled with blues singer Clarence Samuels, and blues singer and guitarist "Pee Wee" Crayton. By this time, Coleman had been inspired by bebop to start playing with a coarse, crying tone, and a frantic, unrestrained sense of rhythm and harmony. The reception in the jazz community to his controversial style kept him from working for a decade.

In 1950 Coleman moved to Los Angeles and began to recruit a circle of associates, including drummers Edward Blackwell and Billy Higgins, trumpeters Don Cherry and Bobby Bradford, bassist Charlie Haden, and pianist Paul Bley. Coleman married poet Jayne Cortez in 1954; unable to support himself as a musician, he took a job as a stock boy and elevator operator at a Los Angeles department store. Despite his reputation as an eccentric who had unusually long hair, wore overcoats in the summer, and played a white saxophone, in 1958 Coleman was invited to make his first recording, *Something Else!* which included his compositions "Chippie" and "When Will the Blues Leave." Pianist John Lewis brought Coleman and Cherry to the Lenox (Mass.) School of Jazz in 1959, which led to a famous series of quartet performances at New York's Five Spot nightclub.

The albums Coleman made over the next two years, including *Tomorrow Is the Question, The Shape of Jazz to Come, This Is Our Music,* and *Free Jazz,* were vilified by traditionalists, who heard the long, loosely structured, collective improvisations and adventurous harmonies as worthless cacophony. However, among his admirers, those performances, which included his compositions "Focus on Sanity," "Peace," "Lonely Woman," and "Beauty Is a Rare Thing," were also recognized as the first significant development in jazz since bebop. Although modeled on the wit and irreverence of bebop, Coleman's pianoless quartets broke out of traditional harmonies, as well as rigid theme-and-improvisation structures. Coleman began to call this style "harmolodics," referring to a musical system, since developed in a vast, unpublished manuscript, in which improvised melodies need not obey fixed harmonies.

In the 1950s Coleman had been shunned by the jazz world, but in the 1960s he found himself hailed as one of the greatest and most influential figures in jazz. Yet Coleman, who was divorced from Cortez in 1964, scaled back his activities in order to study trumpet and violin. In the mid-1960s Coleman most frequently appeared in trio settings (*At the Golden Circle,* 1965–1966), often including bassist David Izenzon and drummer Charles Moffett. In 1967 Coleman became the first jazz musician to win a Guggenheim fellowship. During the late 1960s and early 1970s, Coleman often played with the members of his old quartet, plus tenor saxophonist Dewey Redman, with whom he had first become acquainted in Fort Worth (*Science Fiction,* 1971).

Coleman, who had been composing classical music since the early 1950s, also saw performances in the 1960s of his string quartet *Dedication to Poets and Writers* (1961), his woodwind quintet *Forms and Sounds* (1967), and *Saints and Soldiers* (1967), a chamber piece. Coleman's *Skies of America* symphony was recorded in 1972 with the London Symphony Orchestra. In 1973 he traveled to Morocco to record with folk musicians from the town of Joujouka.

Coleman's next breakthrough came in 1975, when he began to play a style of electric dance music that recalled his early career in rhythm-and-blues dance bands. Using Prime Time, a new core group of musicians that often included his son, Denardo, a drummer, born in 1956, Coleman recorded *Dancing in Your Head,* an album-length elaboration of a theme from *Skies of America* in 1975, and recorded *Of Human Feelings* in 1979. During this time Coleman also founded Artists House, a collective that helped introduce guitarists James "Blood" Ulmer and bassist Jamaaladeen Tacuma.

The mid-1980s brought a revival of interest in Coleman. His hometown, Fort Worth, honored him with a series of tributes and performances, including the chamber piece *Prime Design/Time Design* (1983). A documentary by Shirley Clarke, *Ornette: Made in America,* was released in 1984, and Coleman collaborated with jazz-rock guitarist Pat Metheny (*Song X,* 1985), and rock guitarist Jerry Garcia (*Virgin Beauty,* 1987). On *In All Languages* (1987) he reunited with his 1959 quartet, and in 1991 Coleman, who had composed and performed on the film soundtracks for *Chappaqua* (1965) and *Box Office* (1981), recorded the score for *Naked Lunch.* Coleman, who has lived in Manhattan since the early 1960s, continues to compose regularly, though performing and recording only sporadically with Prime Time.

BIBLIOGRAPHY

Davis, Francis. *In the Moment: Jazz in the 1980s.* New York, 1986.

Litweiler, John. *Ornette Coleman: The Harmolodic Life.* London, 1992.

Spellman, A. B. *Four Lives in the Bebop Business.* New York, 1970.

– BILL DIXON

COLTRANE, JOHN WILLIAM

John William Coltrane (September 23, 1926–July 17, 1967), jazz tenor and soprano saxophonist. Born in Hamlet, N.C., Coltrane moved with his family to High Point, N.C., when he was only a few months old. His father was a tailor, and his mother was an amateur singer. Coltrane received his first instrument, a clarinet, when he was twelve, though he soon began to play the alto saxophone, which was his primary instrument for a number of years.

After high school, Coltrane moved to Philadelphia, where he studied at the Ornstein School of Music and the Granoff Studios, where he won scholarships for both performance and composition. He played in the Philadelphia area until 1945, when he entered the Navy for two years, playing in Navy bands. His exposure at this time to bebop and the playing of Charlie PARKER proved a major and lasting influence on Coltrane's music. Coltrane was so awed by Parker's abilities on the alto saxophone that he switched to playing the tenor saxophone, on which he felt he wouldn't be intimidated by the comparison. When Coltrane returned to Philadelphia, he started playing in blues bands, and in 1948 he was hired by Dizzy GILLESPIE. But Coltrane began drinking heavily and using drugs, and in 1951 he lost his job with the Gillespie band.

The recognition of Coltrane as a major jazz figure dates from his joining the Miles DAVIS Quintet in 1955, an association that would last, on and off, until 1959. In 1957, Coltrane overcame his drinking and narcotics problem, and in the process underwent a spiritual rebirth. Also in 1957 he began to play with Thelonious MONK, and recorded his first album as a leader, *Blue Train.* Other important albums from this period include *Giant Steps* and *Coltrane Jazz,* both from 1959.

Coltrane left Davis in 1959 and thereafter led his own ensemble. The key personnel in Coltrane's definitive quartet of the period, which stayed together from 1961 to 1965, included McCoy Tyner on piano, Elvin Jones on the drums, and Reggie Worhman on bass. Alto saxophonist Eric Dolphy played regularly with the ensemble until his death in 1964. In 1959 Coltrane started playing the soprano saxophone (an instrument that, except for Sidney Bechet, had been rarely used by jazz musicians). He soon recorded his most famous soprano sax solo, "My Favorite Things." Coltrane developed a distinctive soprano style, different from the one he favored on the tenor saxophone. His best-known works of this period include *A Love Supreme* (1964) and the collective free jazz improvisation *Ascension* (1965). In 1965 Coltrane's band underwent another change. His regular band members included Rashied Ali on drums, Pharoah Sanders as a second tenor saxophone, and on the piano, his second wife, Alice Coltrane. With this ensemble, Coltrane explored free jazz improvisation until his death from cancer on July 17, 1967.

Coltrane, often simply called "Trane," was by far the most popular jazz musician to emerge from the New York City jazz avant-garde of the late 1950s and 1960s.

In the little more than ten years of his active career, Coltrane's music underwent a number of metamorphoses. He first achieved renown as bluesy hard-bop tenor saxophonist. After 1957 he began to develop a new approach in which his solos were filigreed with myriad broken scales and arpeggios played extremely rapidly—this became known as his "sheets of sound" approach. In 1961 Coltrane began to play solos of unprecedented length, often lasting twenty or thirty minutes. If some found these solos to be soporific and self-indulgent, others were mesmerized by their sweep and intensity, and Coltrane acquired a number of avid fans. His best solos in the early 1960s were often gentle and powerfully introspective. By the mid-1960s Coltrane was playing free jazz, where his former lyrical style was often replaced by a harsh and turbulent soloing.

Coltrane, often simply called "Trane," was by far the most popular jazz musician to emerge from the New York City jazz avant-garde of the late 1950s and 1960s. His personal and communicative style, his spiritual quest, and his early death, in addition to the virtuosity and grace of his solos, contributed to a Coltrane "cult" that has not abated in the decades since his passing. His influence on subsequent musicians, which has been immense, includes not only his musical ideas but his taking of extended solos and his view of jazz as an ongoing quest for spiritual knowledge and self-wisdom.

BIBLIOGRAPHY

Simpkins, C. O. *Coltrane: A Musical Biography.* New York, 1975.

Taylor, Cecil. "John Coltrane." *Jazz Review* (January 1959): 34.

Thomas, John. *Chasin the Trane: The Music and Mystique of John Coltrane.* Garden City, N.Y., 1975.

— WILLIAM S. COLE

COMMUNIST PARTY OF THE UNITED STATES

When the Communist Party of the United States (CPUSA) was founded in 1921, few people realized the critical role it would play in African-American politics and culture. The product of several splinter groups emerging out of the Socialist party's left wing in 1919, it was founded by people who (like the Socialists before them) viewed the plight of African Americans as inseparable from the class struggle. However, pressure from the newly formed "Third" International, or Comintern, and popular support for black nationalist movements within African-American communities compelled the CPUSA to reconsider its approach to the "Negro question." In 1921, V. I. Lenin assailed the American Communist leadership for neglecting the plight of black workers; one year later, Comintern officials insisted that African Americans were a "nationality" oppressed by worldwide imperialist exploitation and called on American Communists to work within the Garvey movement. In 1928 the Comintern, with input from Harry Haywood and South African Communist James La Guma, passed a resolution asserting that African Americans in the southern Black Belt counties constituted an oppressed nation and therefore possessed an inherent right of self-determination.

An emerging black Left, deeply touched by the Bolshevik revolution as well as by postwar workers' uprisings and racial violence, also shaped the Communist position toward African Americans in the 1920s. The African Blood Brotherhood (ABB), founded in 1918 by Cyril Briggs, eventually joined the CPUSA en masse during the early 1920s. Formed as a secret, underground organization of radical black nationalists, the ABB supported collective working-class action, and advocated armed defense against lynching as well as racial equality and self-determination for Africans and peoples of African descent. After being absorbed by the CPUSA, the ABB ceased to exist as an independent entity. In its place the party in 1925 created the American Negro Labor Congress (ANLC), an organization led chiefly by ex-ABB leaders intent on building interracial unity in, and black support for, the labor movement. When the ANLC disintegrated after failing to gain popular support, it was replaced by the League of Struggle for Negro Rights in 1930. This proved to be somewhat more successful due to the popularity of its newspaper, the *Liberator.* Under the editorship of Cyril Briggs, it became a journal of black news tailor-made for the African-American community and a forum for radical black creative writers.

The self-determination slogan may have inspired a few black intellectuals already in the CPUSA, but it was not the key to building black working-class support during the 1930s. However, the party's fight for the concrete economic needs of the unemployed and working poor, its role in organizing sharecroppers in Alabama, its militant opposition to racism, and its vigorous courtroom battles in behalf of African Americans through the International Labor Defense (ILD) attracted a considerable section of America's black working class and intelligentsia. In particular, the ILD's defense of nine young black men falsely accused of raping two white women in Alabama, known as the SCOTTSBORO CASE, crystallized black support for the CPUSA in the 1930s.

Black support during this period typified black working-class life and culture, and many rank-and-file Communists were churchgoing Christians who combined the party's politics and ideology with black folk culture. Moreover, in spite of the CP's highly masculine language of class struggle and self-determination, black women played central roles in both the leadership and the rank and file. African-American working women participated in relief demonstrations, resisted evictions, confronted condescending social workers, and fought utilities shutoffs. The Communist party produced a significant group of black women leaders, including Louise Thompson Patterson, Claudia Jones, Audley Moore, and Bonita Williams.

In 1935, in accordance with the Comintern's Seventh World Congress, the CPUSA called for a Popular Front against fascism, deemphasized its Marxist ideology, and eventually supported Roosevelt's New Deal coalition. While southern Communists chose to play down race in order to build alliances with southern white liberals, the Popular Front led to more support from African Americans in the urban North. The party gained a larger black following in such places as Harlem and Chicago because of its opposition to Italy's invasion of Ethiopia in 1935, and when African-American radicals were unable to join Haile Selassie's army, because of U.S. government restrictions against the enlistment of U.S. citizens in a foreign army, many closed ranks with the Left and fought in the Spanish Civil War. Communists were also the primary force behind the NATIONAL NEGRO CONGRESS (1935–1946) and the Southern Negro Youth Congress (1937–1948), both of which represented hundreds of black organizations. Finally, during the Popular Front black Communist labor organizers—among them, Hosea HUDSON, Ebb Cox, James Hart, and Ferdinand C. Smith—played a critical role in the formation of the Congress of Industrial Organizations (CIO), particularly in the steel, mining, marine transport, and meat-packing industries.

During this period the party attracted a considerable number of black artists, including Paul ROBESON and Langston HUGHES. Communist cultural critics collected African-American music, began to write jazz criticism, and insisted that black culture was the clearest expression of "American culture." This newfound appreciation of black culture opened up potential space for creative expression within CPUSA circles. Communist papers published poems and short stories by black writers and carried articles and cartoons on black history; CPUSA auxiliaries sponsored plays by black playwrights, art exhibits, benefit jazz concerts, and dances. Nevertheless, many projects were constrained by ideological imperatives or failed due to lack of support. In 1932, for example, the Soviet Union invited a group of black artists (including Langston HUGHES) to make a film about African-American life, but the Soviets soon abandoned the project.

The Nazi-Soviet Pact of 1939, the CPUSA's sudden shift to an extreme antiwar position, the Dies Committee's investigation into "un-American" activities, and the rising anticommunism among CIO leaders weakened the party's base of support on the eve of World War II, but its relationship to black workers and artists remained fairly strong, especially in Harlem. Between 1939 and 1940, for instance, black Communists led a boycott of the film *Gone with the Wind,* initiated a campaign to "End Jim Crow in Sports" and collected 10,000 signatures to demand the integration of blacks in major league BASEBALL, organized numerous plays and jazz concerts, and persuaded blues composer W. C. HANDY to lecture at the Workers School.

When Communists shifted to a prowar position after Germany invaded Russia in 1941, the African-American leadership, for the most part, adopted an uncompromising stance vis-à-vis the war effort, insisting on a "double victory" against racism at home and fascism abroad. While the CPUSA essentially opposed the "Double V" campaign, arguing that too much black militancy could undermine the war effort, rank-and-file Communists continued to fight on the civil rights front throughout the war, demanding, among other things, the full integration of the armed forces and implementation of the Fair Employment Practices Committee. In spite of these measures, the party's opposition to the Double V slogan left many African Americans feeling that it had abandoned them for the sake of the war.

After the war, the Communists worked to rebuild ties to black working-class communities, a strategy that included resurrecting the self-determination thesis. The Civil Rights Congress, led by Communist William L. Patterson, gained notoriety for its militant defense of African Americans falsely accused of crimes and Communists accused of "un-American" activities, and for its historic petition to the United Nations charging the U.S. government with genocide against African Americans. However, McCarthyite repression and the party's leftward turn in the wake of Secretary Earl Browder's expulsion and William Z. Foster's rise to power weakened the CPUSA considerably. As the state arrested Communists for violating the Smith Act (including black leaders such as Henry Winston, Ben J. Davis, Jr., Claudia Jones, and Pettis Perry), the party experienced its own factional disputes and expulsions. As the country moved right, the party under Foster moved farther left and further into isolation. By 1956, the CPUSA had become a shadow of its former self, never to achieve the status it had enjoyed in the 1930s and 1940s.

During the next three decades, black Communists and ex-Communists such as Jack O'Dell, Mae Mallory, Abner Berry, and Hosea Hudson (to name but a few) participated in various civil rights organizations, antiwar movements, labor unions, and black nationalist struggles. As an organization, however, the CPUSA maintained a significant black constituency only in New York City, Detroit, and California—with the latter regarded as a renegade state by the CPUSA Central Committee. While the national leadership attacked black nationalism during the height of the Black Power movement, the California cadre, under the guidance of leaders such as Charlene Mitchell and Dorothy Healey, not only gave support to various nationalist movements but established an all-black youth unit called the Che-Lumumba Club, in defiance of Central Committee directives. The movement to free Angela DAVIS, the last nationally renowned black Communist of the twentieth century, further strengthened the CPUSA's black support in California.

With the collapse of the Soviet Union in 1991, the CPUSA practically fell apart. Virtually every leading African-American cadre member, including Angela Davis, James Jackson, and Charlene Mitchell, quit the party altogether with the hope of reconstituting a new democratic left-wing movement.

BIBLIOGRAPHY

Allen, James S., and Philip Foner, eds. *American Communism and Black Americans: A Documentary History, 1919–1929.* Philadelphia, 1987.

Haywood, Harry. *Black Bolshevik: Autobiography of an Afro-American Communist.* Chicago, 1978.

Horne, Gerald. *Communist Front? The Civil Rights Congress, 1946–1956.* London and Toronto, 1988.

Kelley, Robin D. G. *Alabama Communists During the Great Depression.* Chapel Hill, N.C., 1990.

Naison, Mark D. *Communists in Harlem during the Depression.* Urbana, Ill., 1983.

— ROBIN D. G. KELLEY

COMPROMISE OF 1850

The COMPROMISE OF 1850 actually consists of five separate legislative acts that affected African Americans.

These included a new FUGITIVE SLAVE LAW, the admission of slaves into some of the new western territories, the admission of California to the Union as a free state, and the prohibition of the public sale of slaves in Washington, D.C.

The compromise helped preserve the Union for another decade, while at the same time underscoring the impossibility of solving the problem of slavery through the political process.

In 1850 the United States faced its greatest sectional crisis since the MISSOURI COMPROMISE. The Mexican-American War had led to the acquisition of vast new western territories and to virtual political paralysis over the status of SLAVERY in those territories. Meanwhile, southern dissatisfaction over the Fugitive Slave Act of 1793 and the Supreme Court decision in *Prigg* v. *Pennsylvania* led to demands for stronger federal support for the return of runaway slaves, while northern hostility to slavery led to calls for secession in the South. Meanwhile, the population boom in California that came as a result of the discovery of gold there led to a demand for immediate statehood.

In early 1850, Sen. Henry Clay of Kentucky tried to resolve these problems with his "omnibus bill." This bill had provisions designed to appease the South, including a new fugitive slave law, and provisions to please the North, such as the immediate admission of California as a free state. Clay hoped legislators from both sections would support the bill. However, in July Congress defeated it, with members from each section opposing the law because of what it gave to the other.

In September, Sen. Stephen A. Douglas of Illinois guided the compromise through Congress, not as a single bill but as a series of five separate laws—two antislavery, three proslavery.

The most significant antislavery provision was the admission of California as a free state. For the first time since the Missouri Compromise, the Union would have a majority of free states. While not immediately changing the balance of power in the nation, this was an enormous potential threat to the South and to slavery. Thereafter the North would have a permanent and growing majority in the Senate. The compromise also abolished the SLAVE TRADE in the District of Columbia. This was an important moral victory for antislavery northerners but one with little practical impact; private sale of slaves in the district remained legal, while slave trading still existed in neighboring Maryland and Virginia.

Two statutes allowed slavery in the newly created Utah and New Mexico territories, although few slaves were actually brought to either place. More important was the new fugitive slave law, which simplified the process of returning fugitive slaves to their masters and provided federal protection and support for masters seeking their escaped slaves.

The compromise was an abject failure. Some northern compromisers, like Daniel Webster of Massachusetts, were vilified for their votes in favor of the new fugitive slave law. Like the compromise it symbolized, the fugitive slave law failed in its purpose while exacerbating sectional tensions. It failed to secure the return of significant numbers of slaves, while leading to violent confrontations in the North and to northern states openly refusing to cooperate with the federal government. The compromise helped preserve the Union for another decade, while at the same time underscoring the impossibility of solving the problem of slavery through the political process.

BIBLIOGRAPHY

Freehling, William. *Secessionists at Bay: 1776–1854.* New York, 1991.

Potter, David. *The Impending Crisis.* New York, 1976.

— PAUL FINKELMAN

COMPROMISE OF 1877

The Compromise of 1877 refers to the settlement which resolved the disputed presidential election of 1876. The REPUBLICAN candidate for president, Rutherford B. Hayes, was declared elected in exchange for the national Republican administration's promise to remove federal troops from southern states. The bargain represented the end of RECONSTRUCTION and the end of substantial black participation in southern politics.

In the presidential election of 1876, the DEMOCRATIC candidate, Samuel J. Tilden, in fact won a majority of the popular vote. However, 184 undisputed votes in the electoral college left him one vote short of a necessary majority. The outcome would be determined by the results in three southern states—Louisiana, South Carolina, and Florida, still under Republican state governments. Republican-dominated election officials in all three states declared majorities for Hayes, after invalidating returns reflecting intimidation and fraud against black voters. At the same time, new Democratic state regimes, claiming election in the 1876 canvass, announced that their states had voted for Tilden. As the electoral college prepared to meet in Washington to name the president, the possibility of a violent confrontation over the disputed succession loomed—and the memory of the recent CIVIL WAR made that possibility palpable.

The procedures for counting electoral votes under the Twelfth Amendment to the federal Constitution were ambiguous. To resolve the crisis, Congress established a bipartisan Electoral Commission in January 1877 to determine the actual returns. It soon became apparent that the Republicans enjoyed a narrow majority on the commission, and that Hayes would be declared the winner. Fearing a continuing constitutional crisis, Hayes moved to reassure southern Democrats that if inaugurated, he would prove amenable to their interests.

The precise content of the numerous private meetings between Hayes's intermediaries and southern Democrats is not known. On February 26, the most important of these meetings occurred at the Wormley House, a black-owned Washington, D.C., hotel. Hayes's personal representative announced that if inaugurated, Hayes would recognize the Democratic gubernatorial candidates as elected, and pursue a policy of noninterference in affairs in the southern states. Other Republican promises were made regarding federal sponsorship of a proposed southern railroad line to the Pacific; southern Democrats abandoned congressional obstruction of the final electoral count to secure Hayes's election, and he was peacefully inaugurated on March 4, 1877.

The following month Hayes withdrew the last federal troops sustaining the Reconstruction governments, which immediately dissolved in the face of a possible bloodbath. In essence, Hayes left southern Republicans—who had helped make him President—to fend for themselves in the future. This marked the end of Reconstruction and the eclipse of federal efforts to secure voting and other civil rights for the southern freedpeople.

BIBLIOGRAPHY

Foner, Eric. *Reconstruction, America's Unfinished Revolution, 1863–1877.* New York, 1988.

Woodward, C. Vann. *Reunion and Reaction: The Compromise of 1877 and the End of Reconstruction.* Rev. ed. Garden City, N.Y., 1956.

– MICHAEL W. FITZGERALD

CONGRESSIONAL BLACK CAUCUS

The Congressional Black Caucus was a product of the growth in black political power in the 1960s and '70s. The creation of an institutional base for black Americans within the U.S. Congress had been encouraged by the passage of the Civil Rights Act of 1964 and the Voting Rights Act of 1965. In 1969 Rep. Charles Diggs (D-Mich.) formed the Democratic Select Committee (DSC), the precursor of the Congressional Black Caucus, as a means by which the nine black members of the House of Representatives could address their common political concerns. Later that year Diggs and his colleagues played a role in defeating the nomination of Clement Haynesworth to the U.S. Supreme Court, and they investigated the killings of BLACK PANTHER party members in Chicago. They boycotted President Richard Nixon's 1970 State of the Union Address and pressured Nixon into meeting with the DSC concerning civil rights, antidrug legislation, welfare reform, and Vietnam.

The creation of an institutional base for black Americans within the U.S. Congress had been encouraged by the passage of the Civil Rights Act of 1964 and the Voting Rights Act of 1965.

On June 18, 1971, at its first annual dinner in Washington, D.C., the group was formally organized as the Congressional Black Caucus (CBC), and Diggs became its first chairman. In March 1972 the CBC helped sponsor the National Black Political Convention in Gary, Ind., but distanced itself from the convention because of its dominance by militant activist groups. In June of that year, in order to make the 1972 Democratic national convention more attentive to black concerns, the CBC drafted the Black Declaration of Independence and the Black Bill of Rights. The Black Declaration of Independence demanded that the DEMOCRATIC PARTY and its nominee commit themselves to full racial equality. The Black Bill of Rights called for, among other items, a full employment program; a guaranteed-annual-income system; an end to American military involvement in Vietnam and all African countries; and a setting aside of 15 percent of all government contracts for the use of black businesses. However, the CBC failed to win the official support of the Democratic party or its nominee, George McGovern, for these demands.

In 1973 Rep. Louis Stokes (D-Ohio) succeeded Diggs as caucus chairman. Stokes worked to get individual CBC members greater seniority and more powerful committee chairs in Congress. Rep. Charles Rangel-

(D-N.Y.) became the CBC chair in 1974, serving until 1976. Over the next twenty years, Rangel became one of the leading congressional authorities on urban housing and narcotics control. During that same period, the CBC extended its influence both within and outside of Congress. CBC members became chairs of seven out of twenty-seven congressional committees. It developed nationwide networks of black voters and business leaders and "brain trust" networks addressing EDUCATION, health, the justice system, and foreign affairs. In 1976 it established the Congressional Black Caucus Foundation, which conducts and funds studies relating congressional politics to the concerns of the black community. In 1977 the CBC established TransAfrica; headed by Randall Robinson, TransAfrica became the major lobbying body in Washington on behalf of the Anti-Apartheid Movement in South Africa and of other African policy issues. The CBC was also involved in the successful efforts to pass the 1977 Full Employment Act, the 1982 Martin Luther King Holiday legislation, and the 1986 sanctions against South Africa.

The growth of black political power has expanded the size of the CBC. In 1992 an unprecedented forty African Americans were elected to Congress. This increase in size has tested and transformed the CBC in other ways as well. In 1993 Carol Moseley-Braun (D-Ill.) became the first black senator in fourteen years and one of ten black women in Congress. In 1990 Gary Franks (R-Conn.) became the first black Republican elected to the House of Representatives since 1932. A conservative Republican, Franks has been at odds with the policies of the CBC and has attacked it for its liberal slant and allegiance to the DEMOCRATIC PARTY.

There has been a growing ideological diversity within the CBC, its chairs ranging from such centrists as Charles Rangel (D-N.Y.) and Edolphus "Ed" Towns (D-N.Y.) to such left-liberals as Ron Dellums (D-Calif.). In 1993, Kweisi Mfume (D-Md.) became chair and has been active in publicizing the activities of the CBC. He has also been its most controversial chair. In 1993 he advocated the formation of a "sacred covenant" between the CBC and the NATION OF ISLAM with its leader, Louis FARRAKHAN. The other members of the CBC subsequently renounced this covenant, and Mfume eventually followed the rest of the Black Caucus in doing so.

Although controversial, Mfume helped to make the CBC more aggressive in influencing domestic and foreign policy. When the House of Representatives, without consulting the CBC, moved to give President Clinton the line-item veto (a tool that governors had used in the past to keep civil rights measures out of legislative bills), Mfume led the CBC in blocking the effort. Mfume also helped change President Clinton's policy toward Haiti. Mfume's pressure persuaded Clinton to extend more aid to Haitian refugees, place stronger sanctions on Haiti's military government, and consider returning Haiti's democratic government to power by force.

The Congressional Black Caucus has become one of the most influential voting blocks within Congress. While it has been divided on certain issues, such as the 1993 North American Free Trade Agreement (NAFTA), on many other issues, such as health care, African and Caribbean issues, and crime, the CBC has emerged as a shrewd and pragmatic advocate for African-American interests.

BIBLIOGRAPHY

Barnet, Marguerite Ross. "The Congressional Black Caucus." In Harvey C. Mansfield, ed., *Congress Against the President: Proceedings of the Academy of Political Science.* New York, 1975.

Clay, William L. *Just Permanent Interests: Black Americans in Congress, 1870–1991.* New York, 1992.

Ruffin, David C., and Frank Dexter Brown. "Clout on Capitol Hill." *Black Enterprise* 14 (October 1984): 97–104.

– DURAHN TAYLOR

CONGRESS OF RACIAL EQUALITY

Congress of Racial Equality (CORE), civil rights organization. With a political and ideological legacy that spans six decades from interracial nonviolent direct action in the 1940s and '50s, militant black nationalist separatism in the late '60s, and black capitalism in the '70s, '80s, and '90s, the Congress of Racial Equality (CORE) is one of the most important civil rights organizations in the history of the United States. It was founded in Chicago in 1942 as the Committee of Racial Equality (the name was changed to the present one in 1943) by a group of ten white and five black student activists who were influenced by the Christian Youth Movement, rising industrial unionism, and the antiracist political activism of black and white communists in the 1930s. The founders of CORE were staunch believers in pacifism. Many of them were members of the Chicago chapter of the Fellowship of Reconciliation (FOR), an interracial and pacifist civil rights organization committed to social change through the transformation of racist attitudes, led by A. J. Muste (1885–1967). Deeply influenced by the strategies of social change championed by Indian activist Mahatma Gandhi as described in Krishnalal Shridharani's *War Without Violence* (1939), CORE founders believed that through interracial organizing and nonviolent direct action they could attack racism at its "core."

CORE was an informal, decentralized organization. Members drafted a "Statement of Purpose" and "CORE Action Discipline," both of which served as a constitution for the organization and proclaimed the members' commitment to working for social change through nonviolent direct action in a democratic, nonhierarchical organization. Guidelines for new members demanded familiarity with Gandhian ideas and active participation in the organization. Voluntary contributions from the members served as the organization's only source of funding. The leadership of CORE was shared by George Houser, a white student at the University of Chicago, and James Farmer, a black Methodist student activist. James Robinson, a white Catholic pacifist, and Bernice Fisher, a white divinity student at the University of Chicago, also provided inspirational and organizational leadership.

In their first year, CORE activists organized sit-ins and other protests against segregation in public accommodations, but white recalcitrance and a weak membership base left them with few victories. In 1942, at a planning conference to discuss organizational growth, CORE activists declared their commitment to expanding nationally by forming alliances with local interracial groups working to defeat racism through nonviolent direct action. Farmer argued that CORE would not grow as a mass-based activist organization unless it severed its ties to FOR and disassociated itself from the organization's pacifism. Under the rubric of FOR's Department of Race Relations, he and Bayard RUSTIN, a black FOR field secretary, traveled around the country and met with activists sympathetic to Gandhian ideology, to foster interest in forming CORE chapters among those present at FOR events.

As a result of their efforts, CORE had seven affiliates by the end of 1942. Most chapters were located in the Midwest; they contained fifteen to thirty members who were usually middle-class college students and were predominantly white. Local groups retained primary membership affiliation and control over local funds. As a result, chapter activities varied widely and were not centrally coordinated. Chapters where pacifists dominated focused almost entirely on educating and converting racists, rather than on direct action. The repressive atmosphere of the South in the 1940s severely curtailed the activity of CORE's few southern affiliates. New York, Chicago, and Detroit were the most active and militant chapters, conducting training workshops in nonviolent direct action for volunteers in selected northern cities as well. They also organized SIT-INS—a tactic pioneered by CORE activists—and picket lines at segregated restaurants, swimming pools, movie theaters, and department stores.

CORE had some success in integrating public accommodations and recreational areas, but it was clear to CORE's founders that to mount a sustained assault on racism they would have to create a stronger national structure. In 1943, Farmer was elected the first chairman of CORE and Bernice Fisher was elected secretary-treasurer. By 1946, due to both the reluctance of local chapters to relinquish their independence or share their funds and to the infrequency of national planning meetings, CORE faced an organizational crisis. After much debate, CORE revamped its national structure: Farmer resigned and George Houser occupied the newly created leadership position of executive secretary. Houser played a central role in defining the ideology of CORE as editor of the *CORE-lator,* the organizational newsletter, and author of almost all CORE literature. He focused CORE's organizational energy and limited resources on a closer coordination of local activities among its thirteen affiliates, with the ultimate goal of building a mass movement.

The culmination of Houser's efforts was CORE's first nationally coordinated action, the Journey of Reconciliation—a two-week trip into the upper South to test the 1946 *Morgan* decision by the U.S. Supreme Court outlawing segregation in interstate travel. In April of 1947, sixteen men—eight white and eight black—traveled by bus through the region challenging segregated seating arrangements that relegated blacks to the back of the bus. The protesters were confronted by some violence and overt hostility, but in general they were faced with apathy from most whites, who were unaware of the Morgan decision. In many instances, black passengers on the bus followed suit when they saw racial mores being successfully challenged. The arrest of four of the protesters in Chapel Hill, N.C.—with three of them, Bayard Rustin, Igal Roodenko, and Joe Felmet forced to serve thirty days on a chain gang—catapulted CORE and the Journey of Reconciliation to national attention.

In 1947, CORE took further steps to strengthen their organizational structure by creating an office of field secretaries to travel around the country to organize new CORE chapters. Two years later they created the National Council—a policy-making body with one representative from each local chapter—to improve communication between the local and the national chapters. In 1951, CORE hired James Robinson to coordinate fund-raising efforts. Despite these efforts, the early fifties marked another period of organizational decline for CORE, as the number of affiliated chapters dropped from a high of twenty at the end of the 1940s and fluctuated around eleven during the early 1950s.

Weakened by continuing debates over the role of pacifism and the national organizational structure, CORE's growth was further stunted by anticommunism. Although CORE's executive committee had drafted a "Statement on Communism" in 1948 saying that it would not work with communists, CORE's civil rights activities were attacked as "subversive" and "un-American" in the hostile racial climate of the 1950s. At this organizational nadir, Houser resigned and the national structure was once again reorganized to divide his duties among three people: Billie Ames, a white activist from CORE's St. Louis chapter, became group coordinator and took charge of organizational correspondence; James Peck, a white Journey of Reconciliation veteran, was in charge of editing the *CORE-lator;* and James Robinson continued to serve as treasurer. Wallace Nelson, who had held the salaried position of field secretary, was replaced by four volunteers.

CORE found a renewed sense of purpose in the mid-1950s. In 1954, the BROWN V. BOARD OF EDUCATION OF TOPEKA, KANSAS decision declared separate but equal educational facilities unconstitutional. One year later, the Montgomery bus boycott mobilized thousands of African Americans to challenge segregated buses. CORE activists—as pioneers of the strategy of nonviolent direct action—provided philosophical resources to the boycott and dispatched LeRoy Carter, a black field-secretary, to Montgomery to provide support. Electrified by rising black protest, CORE decided to channel the majority of the organization's energy into expanding into the South.

To facilitate this expansion, there was a revival of the national staff. In 1957, James Robinson, whose tireless fund-raising efforts had boosted organizational finances, was appointed executive secretary. He worked closely with the National Action Committee, comprising influential members based in New York who made policy decisions. CORE created a staff position for a public relations coordinator, who was in charge of promoting CORE as a major civil rights organization alongside the NAACP and the SOUTHERN CHRISTIAN LEADERSHIP CONFERENCE (SCLC), which was founded after the Montgomery bus boycott. In addition, the *CORE-lator* was transformed from an organizational organ into an informative newsmagazine that reported on the social movements emerging in the South.

Most importantly, CORE directly confronted its relationship to the black community for the first time. Although its predominantly white leadership structure remained firmly in place, African Americans such as James McCain, who was appointed field secretary in 1957, were sought out for prominent and visible positions. Publicity for CORE also was sought in the black press. Nonetheless, CORE'S ideological commitment to interracialism continued to be unwavering. McCain, for example, worked closely with James Carey, a white field secretary, to demonstrate the viability of interracial organizing to potential new affiliates. However, the fundamental nature of the organization had begun to change. Interracialism—which had been defined since CORE's inception as racial diversity within chapters—was redefined on a regional level. To reflect the probability of minimal white support for CORE in the South, as well as the continued inability of majority white chapters on the West Coast to secure a black membership base, the interracial requirement for chapters was removed from the constitution. In addition, although CORE retained its base among white and black middle-class college students, its class and age composition was radically altered as many younger and poorer African Americans, with few ideological links to pacifism, joined its ranks.

By 1960, the number of CORE chapters had risen to twenty-four, with new chapters springing up in Virginia, Tennessee, South Carolina, Florida, Kentucky. With a stable national structure, growing income, new constituencies, and increased visibility, CORE finally seemed poised to join the ranks of the major civil rights organizations. In February 1960, when four college students sat in at a lunch counter in Greensboro, N.C., to protest segregation and ignited a wave of student protest that spread throughout the South, CORE activists scrambled to provide guidance. In Florida, CORE members pioneered the "jail-in" technique when five members chose to serve out their sentences rather than pay bail after being arrested for sitting in at a department store counter. One year later, CORE activists organized another "jail-in" in Rock Hill, S.C., which received national attention, helped galvanize the black community, and set a precedent of "jail-no bail" that became an important direct action strategy in the Civil Rights Movement. In the North, affiliates started sympathy demonstrations for the student demonstrators and called for nationwide boycotts to attempt to place economic pressure on national chains to desegregate their facilities.

In May 1961, CORE mounted its most militant challenge to segregation: the Freedom Rides. Modeled on the earlier Journey of Reconciliation, the Freedom Rides were protests against segregated interstate buses and terminals in the South. Seven white and six black activists, including James Farmer (who had been appointed CORE executive director earlier that year), participated in the Freedom Rides. After successfully challenging segregation in Virginia and North Carolina, the Freedom Riders faced harassment, intimidation, and violence from racist southern whites in the deep South. Two riders were attacked in Rock Hill, S.C.; two were arrested in Winnesboro, S.C.; and in a violent climax, riders were beaten and their bus bombed by a white mob near Birmingham, Ala. After this event, which was recorded by the press for a shocked nation to see, CORE terminated the rides. SNCC activists resumed the Freedom Rides in Mississippi, unleashing a white backlash so virulent that the Kennedy administration was forced to intervene with federal protection. Though SNCC activists—with some resentment on the part of CORE officials—took the leadership of the protest and received most of the credit for the remaining Freedom Rides, CORE continued to provide guidance to the freedom riders and stationed field secretaries in key southern cities to assist riders. Many CORE activists, including Farmer, rejoined the rides when SNCC continued them. The freedom riders finally triumphed in September 1961 when the Interstate Commerce Commission issued an order prohibiting segregated facilities in interstate travel.

In May 1961, CORE mounted its most militant challenge to segregation: the Freedom Rides.

The Freedom Rides placed CORE in the vanguard of the Civil Rights Movement. As a result of the national attention that the rides had generated, James Farmer joined SNCC's John Lewis and SCLC's Rev. Dr. Martin Luther KING, Jr., as a national spokesperson for the CIVIL RIGHTS MOVEMENT. By the end of 1961, CORE—with fifty-three affiliated chapters, rising income, and increased visibility—was able to mount new activities. CORE was an active participant in the wave of direct action protest that swept through the South in 1962 and 1963. In 1962, CORE worked closely with the local NAACP to launch the Freedom Highways project to desegregate Howard Johnson hotels along North Carolina highways. Faced with retaliatory white violence, and locked into increasingly contentious competition with the other civil rights organizations, CORE broadened the scope of its activities. In 1962, CORE joined the Voter Education Project (VEP) initiated by President John F. Kennedy and mounted vigorous voter registration campaigns in Louisiana, Florida, Mississippi, and South Carolina.

CORE activists played a pivotal role in many of the leading events of the Civil Rights Movement. In 1963, CORE joined the NAACP, SCLC, and SNCC in sponsoring the March on Washington. As a part of the Council of Federated Organizations (COFO), a statewide coalition of civil rights organizations engaged in voter registration, CORE played a crucial role in the Freedom Summer in 1964 in Mississippi. James Chaney and Michael Schwerner, two of three civil rights workers killed in June 1964 by racist whites in the infamous case that focused national attention on the South, were members of CORE.

By 1963, CORE activities—severely curtailed by arrests and racial violence—shifted from the South to the North. Two thirds of CORE's sixty-eight chapters were in the North and West, concentrated mainly in California and New York. In the North, CORE chapters directly confronted discrimination and segregation in housing and employment, using tactics such as picketing and the boycott. As they began to address some of the problems of economically disadvantaged African Americans in the North—among them, unemployment, housing discrimination, and police brutality—they began to attract more working class African-American members. To strengthen their image as a black-protest organization, leadership of northern chapters was almost always black, and CORE chapters moved their headquarters into the black community. As member composition changed and CORE acquired a more militant image, CORE's deeply held ideological beliefs and tactics of social change were increasingly challenged by black working-class members. These members were willing to engage in more confrontational tactics, such as resisting arrest, obstructing traffic, all night sit-ins, and other forms of militant civil disobedience. Drawing on different ideological traditions, they viewed nonviolence as a tactic to be abandoned when no longer expedient—not as a deeply held philosophical belief. They often identified with MALCOLM X, who preached racial pride and black separatism, rather than with Gandhian notions of a beloved community.

By 1964, the integrationist, southern-based civil rights coalition was splintering, and consensus over tactics and strategy within CORE was destroyed. Vigorous debates emerged within CORE about the roles of whites (by 1964 less than 50 percent of the membership) in the organization. Infused with heightened black pride and nationalism, angered by the paternalism of some white members, and believing that black people should lead in the liberation of the black community, many black CORE members pushed for the diminution of the role of whites within the organization; an increasingly vocal minority called for the expulsion of whites.

As CORE struggled for organizational and programmatic direction, old tensions between rank and file members of the national leadership resurfaced as local chapters, operating almost autonomously, turned to grass-roots activism in poor black communities. In the South, CORE activities centered on building self-supporting community organizations to meet the needs of local communities. Activists organized projects that ranged from job discrimination protests, to voter registration, to securing mail delivery for black neighborhoods. In the North, CORE activists continued in the tradition of direct action. They fostered neighborhood organizations with local leadership, started community centers and job placement centers, and organized rent strikes and welfare rights protests.

In 1966, the National CORE convention endorsed the slogan of Black Power. Under the leadership of Farmer and Floyd McKissick—elected in 1963 as CORE national chairman—CORE adopted a national position supporting black self-determination, local control of community institutions, and coalition politics. In 1967 the word "multiracial" was deleted from the constitution, and whites began an exodus from the organization. One year later, Roy Innis, a dynamic and outspoken leader of CORE's Harlem chapter, replaced Farmer and under the new title of national director took control of the organization. Innis staunchly believed in separatism and black self-determination and argued that blacks were a "nation within a nation." He barred whites from active membership in CORE and centralized decision-making authority to assert control over local chapter activities. By this point, however, CORE was a weakened organization with a handful of affiliated chapters and dwindling resources.

Innis's economic nationalism and support for black capitalism led to an extremely conservative political stance for CORE on issues ranging from civil rights legislation and foreign policy to gun control and welfare. In 1970 he met with southern whites to promote separate schools as a viable alternative to court imposed desegregation and busing. In the late 1970s and early '80s, almost all CORE activities ground to a halt as Innis and CORE came under increasing criticism. In 1976, Farmer severed all ties with CORE in protest of Innis's separatism and his attempt to recruit black Vietnam veterans to fight in Angola's civil war on the side of the South-African-backed National Union for the Total Independence of Angola (UNITA). In 1981, after being accused by the New York State attorney general's office of misusing charitable contributions, Innis agreed to contribute $35,000 to the organization over a three-year period in exchange for not admitting to any irregularities in handling funds. In the early 1980s, former CORE members, led by Farmer, attempted to transform CORE into a multiracial organization, but Innis remained firmly in command. In 1987, Innis supported Bernhard Goetz, a white man who shot black alleged muggers on the subways in New York; and Robert Bork, a conservative Supreme Court nominee.

CORE chapters have mounted only sporadic activities in the 1990s, but Innis—at this point, one of the leading black conservatives—has maintained visibility as national director of the organization.

BIBLIOGRAPHY

Bell, Inge Powell. *CORE and the Strategy of Nonviolence.* New York, 1968.

Farmer, James. *Lay Bare the Heart: An Autobiography of the Civil Rights Movement.* New York, 1985.

Meier, August, and Elliot Rudwick. *Black Protest in the Sixties.* Chicago, 1970.

———. *CORE: A Study in the* CIVIL RIGHTS MOVEMENT. New York, 1975.

Peck, James. *Cracking the Color Line: Nonviolent Direct Action Methods of Eliminating Racial Discrimination.* New York, 1962.

Van Deburg, William. *New Day in Babylon: The Black Power Movement and American Culture, 1965–1975.* Chicago, 1992.

– CAROL V. R. GEORGE

COSBY, WILLIAM HENRY, JR. "BILL"

William Henry "Bill" Cosby, Jr. (July 12, 1937–), comedian and philanthropist. Bill Cosby was born in Germantown, Pa., to William and Annie Pearle Cosby. After a stint in the Navy (1956–1960), Cosby studied at Temple University in Philadelphia, but dropped out to pursue a career as a stand-up comic.

During the 1960s, Cosby worked in network television as a comedian featured on late-night talk shows. In 1965 he became the first African-American network television star in a dramatic series when producers named him to costar with Robert Culp in *I Spy* (1965–1968). Cosby's character, Alexander Scott, did not usually address his blackness or another character's whiteness. As with other forms of popular entertainment with black characters at the time, Cosby's character was portrayed in a manner in which being black merely meant having slightly darker skin. He won Emmy awards for the role in 1966 and 1967.

From 1969 through 1971, Cosby appeared as Chet Kincaid, a bachelor high school coach, on the situation comedy series *The Bill Cosby Show.* Cosby portrayed Kincaid as a proud but not militant black man. The series was moderately successful. A few years later, Cosby and CBS joined forces in a television experiment, *Fat Albert and the Cosby Kids* (1972–1977), a cartoon series for children. The series set the course for television in the vital new area of ethics, values, judgment, and personal responsibility. By the end of its three-year run, *Fat Albert* had inspired a number of new directions in children's television.

In 1972 and 1973, Cosby starred in *The New Bill Cosby Show,* a comedy-variety series. Cosby's Jemmin Company, which he had recently established, produced the shows, allowing him to have more control over the productions. As he did in all his television series, Cosby made great use of other black artists who had had few opportunities to practice their craft elsewhere.

For a few months in late 1976, largely because of his success as a regular guest on the PBS educational series *The Electric Company,* where he demonstrated great skill at working with and entertaining youngsters, ABC hired Cosby to host a prime time hour-long variety series oriented toward children, *Cos.* It did not catch on with viewers, however, and was canceled after a few months.

In the fall of 1984, *The Cosby Show* began on NBC, featuring Cosby as Cliff Huxtable, an obstetrician living with his wife and four children in a New York City brownstone. Their fifth child, away at college most of the time, appeared sporadically in featured parts. The show put black images on the screen that many people admired. The characters on *The Cosby Show* represented a real African-American upper-middle-class family, rarely seen on American television. Cosby sought black artists who had not been seen on network television in years for cameo roles (Dizzy GILLESPIE and Judith JAMISON, for example). He also included black writers among his creative staff, and by the third year, he insisted on using a black director for some of the episodes. In its first year, *The Cosby Show* finished third in the ratings; from the second season through the fourth season, it was the number-one-rated show in the United States.

Bill Cosby during his opening night performance at New York's Radio City Music Hall, March 1987. (AP/Wide World Photos)

Conscious of the need to lead the networks toward more equitable treatment of African Americans, Cosby used his position to require that more doors be opened. He had a presence in almost every area of television programming: He was a mass volume spokesman and star presenter for advertisements and public relations image campaigns that included Jello, Coca-Cola, Delmonte, Kodak, and E. F. Hutton. He appeared in drama, action-adventure stories, comedies, and children's programs. In 1992 he also entered into prime time syndication with Carsey-Werner Productions with a remake of the old Groucho Marx game series, *You Bet Your Life.* The show lasted only one season. That same year, however, Cosby made public his bid to purchase the National Broadcasting Corporation (NBC-TV), a television network worth $9 billion. Cosby was determined to call attention to the proliferation of negative images of black people and the titillation of viewers with sex and violence. All television viewers, he argued, were diminished by the spate of "drive-by-images" that reinforced shallow stereotypes.

Throughout his career, Cosby appeared at highly popular concert performances across the United States. His comedy focused on his own life as a reflection of universal human needs. He also produced more than twenty comedy/musical record albums, many of which have won Grammy awards, including *Bill Cosby Is a Very Funny Fellow* (1963), *I Started Out as a Child* (1964), *Why Is There Air?* (1965), *Wonderfulness* (1966), *Revenge* (1967), *To Russell, My Brother, Whom I Slept With* (1968), *Bill Cosby* 1969, *Bill Cosby Talks to Children About Drugs* (1971), and *Children, You'll Understand* (1986). Cosby has written many best-selling books, including *The Wit and Wisdom of Fat Albert* (1973), *You Are Somebody Special* (1978), *Fatherhood* (1986), *Time Flies* (1987), and *Love and Marriage* (1989). He has served on numerous boards, including the NAACP, Operation Push, the UNITED NEGRO COLLEGE FUND, and the National Sickle Cell Foundation.

Cosby, who in 1993 was listed in *Forbes* magazine as one of the 400 richest people in the world with a net worth of more than $315 million, has been one of the most important benefactors to African-American institutions. In 1986 he and his wife gave $1.3 million to FISK UNIVERSITY; the following year they gave another $1.3 million to be divided equally among four black universities—Central State, HOWARD, Florida A & M, and Shaw; in 1988 they divided $1.5 million between Meharry Medical College and Bethune Cookman College. In 1989 Bill and Camille Cosby announced that they were giving $20 million to SPELMAN COLLEGE, the largest personal gift ever made to any of the historically black colleges and universities. In 1994 the couple donated a historic landmark building in downtown Washington, D.C. to the NATIONAL COUNCIL OF NEGRO WOMEN to help them establish a National Center for African-American Women. Cosby himself has been the recipient of numerous awards, including the NAACP's Spingarn Medal (1985). He holds an M.A. (1972) and a doctorate (1976) in education from the University of Massachusetts at Amherst. In 1976 he also finally received a B.A. from Temple University. Cosby, who married Camille Hanks in 1964, has lived in rural Massachusetts since the early 1970s. Beginning in 1996, Cosby produced and starred in a successful comedy series called *Cosby.* His life was disrupted the following year by the murder of his son, Ennis, and the charge by Autumn Jackson that she was Cosby's illegitimate daughter. Cosby's popularity continued unabated through this period.

BIBLIOGRAPHY

Lane, Randall. "Bill Cosby, Capitalist." *Forbes* (September 28, 1992): 85–86.

Smith, Ronald L. *Cosby.* New York, 1986.

Zoglin, Richard. "Cosby Inc." *Time* (September 28, 1987): 56–60.

– JANNETTE L. DATES

COTTON CLUB

First opened in 1920 as the Club Deluxe, the venue at Lenox Avenue and West 142nd Street in HARLEM took on new ownership and its permanent name in 1922. Owney Madden, who bought the club from heavyweight boxing champion Jack JOHNSON, intended the name Cotton Club to appeal to whites, the only clientele permitted until 1928. The club made its name by featuring top-level black performers and an upscale, downtown audience. It soon became a leading attraction for white "tourists" from high society wanting to see the much publicized, risqué Harlem cultural life.

Following the death in 1927 of Andy Preer, leader of the house band, the Cotton Club Syncopators, Duke ELLINGTON and his orchestra were brought in as replacements and began a four-year rise to prominence on the Cotton Club's stage. Soon after Ellington took over as bandleader, the Cotton Club Orchestra was broadcast nightly over a national radio network.

Responding to local protests, the club's management opened its doors to black patrons for the first time in the winter of 1928. Nonetheless, prices were kept prohibitively high and the club's audience remained virtually all white. The nightly revues, which were generally more popular than the orchestra, featured scantily clad, light-skinned women dancing to Ellington's "jungle music."

The Cotton Club made its name by featuring top-level black performers and an upscale, downtown audience.

In 1931 Ellington and his orchestra left the club and were replaced by Cab CALLOWAY's Missourians. Calloway, like Ellington, established himself as a major figure in mainstream JAZZ during his Cotton Club years. Calloway's Missourians remained the house band until 1934, when they were replaced by Jimmie Lunceford's acclaimed swing band. Most of the renowned jazz performers of the period appeared at the Cotton Club, including Louis ARMSTRONG, Ethel WATERS, and dancers Bill "Bojangles" Robinson and the NICHOLAS BROTHERS.

Following riots in Harlem in 1935, the club was forced to close due to a widespread perception among whites that the area was unsafe. It reopened in 1936 downtown at 200 West 48th Street, where it remained until its final closing in 1940.

BIBLIOGRAPHY

Charters, Samuel Barclay, and Leonard Kunstadt. *Jazz: A History of the New York Scene.* 1962. Reprint. New York, 1981.

Schuller, Gunther. *The Swing Era: The Development of Jazz, 1930–1945.* New York, 1989.

– THADDEUS RUSSELL

CRISIS, THE

The Crisis magazine is the official organ of the NATIONAL ASSOCIATION FOR THE ADVANCEMENT OF COLORED PEOPLE (NAACP) founded in 1910 by its first editor, W. E. B. DU BOIS. The publication's original title for many years was *The Crisis: A Record of the Darker Races,* and its contents throughout time have reflected its historical importance as the chronicler of African-American history, thought, and culture. The title, Du Bois later wrote, was the suggestion of William English Walling, a founder of the NAACP.

Du Bois said his object in publishing *The Crisis* was "to set forth those facts and arguments which show the danger of race prejudice, particularly as manifested today toward colored people. It takes its name from the fact [that] the editors believe that this is a critical time in the history of the advancement of men." The monthly issues contained subject matter ranging from literary works, editorial commentary, feature stories, and reports on NAACP activities to articles on current events. In the first decades two regular features were "American Negroes in College" and "Along the NAACP Battlefront."

Du Bois served as editor for twenty-four years before retiring in 1934. By that time, *The Crisis* could boast among its contributors such luminaries as George Bernard Shaw, Mahatma Gandhi, Sinclair Lewis, Langston HUGHES, and James Weldon JOHNSON. Although founded with the objective of being the official organ of the NAACP, it was also intended to be as self-supporting as possible. But when Du Bois retired as editor in 1934, its circulation had dropped from 100,000 (1918) to only 10,000. His successor as editor was Roy WILKINS, who served in that role until 1949 before being succeeded by James W. Ivy (1949–1967), who was at the helm during the peak civil rights era years.

The Crisis *magazine is the official organ of the National Association for the Advancement of Colored People.*

During the transition years, *The Crisis* shifted its focus from the issues of wartime discrimination against African Americans in the U.S. armed forces, lynchings, and other manifestations of JIM CROW policies, to the courts, where rights were being upheld in voter registration, school desegregation, and housing discrimination. By 1988 circulation had risen to 350,000 subscribers. The magazine's basic editorial philosophy changed little over time from that established by Du Bois, but it had attracted enough major national corporate advertisers to place it on solid financial footing. Moreover, the NAACP had changed its policy to require both members and nonmembers to pay the subscription fee.

The Crisis continues with contributors from all walks of African-American life, including leadership in the clergy, academe, business, law, medicine, and other professions. It continues the tradition of serving as the cultural and social "record of the darker races."

BIBLIOGRAPHY

Du Bois, W. E. B. *The Autobiography of W. E. Burghardt Du Bois.* New York, 1968.

Emery, Edwin, and Michael Emery. *The Press and America.* Englewood Cliffs, N.J., 1978.

– CLINT C. WILSON II

CRUMMELL, ALEXANDER

Alexander Crummell (March 3, 1819–September 19, 1898) nationalist, abolitionist, and missionary. Alexander Crummell was the son of Boston Crummell, who had been kidnapped from his homeland in Temne country, West Africa, and enslaved in New York. Boston Crummell was never emancipated, his son later wrote, but obtained his freedom simply by announcing to his master that "he would serve him no longer." Boston Crummell married Charity Hicks, a freeborn woman from Long Island, and established an oyster house in lower Manhattan. It was in the Crummell home that the African-American newspaper *Freedom's Journal* was founded.

The Crummells were members of the Protestant Episcopal church, and Alexander came early under the influence of Rev. Peter Williams, Jr. Williams was a supporter of back-to-Africa movements, and had been friendly with the repatriationists Paul Cuffe and John Russwurm. Crummell attended school in Williams's church and in the African Free School until his early teens, when he enrolled in the Noyes Academy in Canaan, N.H. Shortly after it opened, the academy was closed by mob violence and Crummell resumed his studies at the Oneida Institute in Whitesboro, N.Y.

Encouraged by Williams to become a candidate for ordination, Crummell applied to the General Theological Seminary in New York City but was rejected. He informally attended lectures at Yale University, and studied privately with clergymen in New England. While in New England he married Sarah Mabritt Elston of New York, ministered to congregationists in New Haven and Providence, and worked as a correspondent for the *Colored American.* Crummell was ordained to the Episcopal priesthood in 1842, and labored with small congregations in Philadelphia and New York. He went to England in 1848, ostensibly to raise funds for his parish; almost immediately, however, he began preparing with a tutor to enter Cambridge University. His familial obligations and lecturing activities detracted from his academic performance, and he failed his first attempt at the university examinations, but he was among the eleven out of thirty-three candidates who passed the "additional examination," and he was awarded the bachelor's degree in 1853.

Desiring to bring up his children "under black men's institutions," he embarked on his missionary career in West Africa under the auspices of the Protestant Episcopal church. Over the ensuing decades he was often in conflict with his immediate superior, Rev. John Payne, the bishop of Cape Palmas, especially when

In the year before his death, Crummell organized the American Negro Academy, which was dedicated to the pursuit of the higher culture and civilization for black Americans.

Crummell attempted to organize another diocese in the Liberian capital city of Monrovia. Crummell at first showed little interest in working with the native population. Many of his writings during these years addressed such statesmanlike topics as "God and the Nation" and "The Relations and Duties of Free Colored Men in America to Africa." These, along with a number of his other essays on black-nationalist themes, were collected for his first book, *The Future of Africa* (1862).

Crummell spent sixteen years between 1853 and 1872 in Liberia, although he returned to the United States twice during those years for fund-raising purposes. The assassination of Liberian president Edward James Royce and threats against Crummell's own life led to his hasty and final departure in 1872. Sarah Crummell died in 1878 and he was remarried, to Jennie M. Simpson, on September 23, 1880. Crummell established St. Luke's Episcopal Church in Washington in 1879, and retained the pastorate until 1894, when he retired. He continued to write and lecture actively until his death in 1898. Among his important writings during the Washington years were "The Destined Superiority of the Negro" and "The Black Woman of the South, Her Neglects and Her Needs" (1883). These and other sermons were collected in his books *The Greatness of Christ and Other Sermons* (1882) and *Africa and America* (1891).

Crummell's theological writings are dominated by the idea that salvation cannot be achieved solely by the acceptance of grace. He believed that God works actively in history and that the good are punished and the evil rewarded in this life. Crummell was contemptuous of enthusiastic revivalism and believed that the struggle for salvation must remain an arduous task, even after the Christian has experienced conversion. Although a notorious Anglophile, and hostile to the cultural expressions of the black masses, he never wavered in his black-nationalist chauvinism, apparently seeing no contradictions in his position. His essay "The Destined Superiority of the Negro" revealed his confidence that the African race was a "chosen people."

In the year before his death, Crummell organized the American Negro Academy, which was dedicated to the pursuit of the higher culture and civilization for black Americans. He influenced W. E. B. DU BOIS, whose sentimental and somewhat inaccurate eulogy, "Of Alexander Crummell," was reprinted in *The Souls of Black Folk* (1903). Other Crummell protégés were William H. Ferris and John E. Bruce, both of whom became prominent Garveyites during the 1920s.

Crummell's papers are widely scattered, and a complete bibliographic survey is beyond the scope of this article. The main repository is in the Schomburg Collection of the New York Public Library. A number of important letters are in the American Colonization Society Papers in the Library of Congress and in the Domestic and Foreign Missionary Society Papers in the Archives of the Episcopal Church at Austin, Tex. Additional important materials are in the Massachusetts and Maryland State Historical Societies.

BIBLIOGRAPHY

Moses, Wilson J. *Alexander Crummell: A Study of Civilization and Discontent.* 1989.

Oldfield, John. *Alexander Crummell and the Creation of an African-American Church in Liberia.* 1990.

Rigsby, Gregory U. *Alexander Crummell: Pioneer in Nineteenth Century Pan-African Thought.* 1987.

Scruggs, Otey M. *We the Children of Africa in This Land.* 1972.

— WILSON J. MOSES

CULLEN, COUNTEE

Countee Cullen (March 30, 1903–January 9, 1946), poet, novelist, and playwright. It has been difficult to place exactly where Countee Cullen was born, with whom he spent the very earliest years of his childhood, and where he spent them. New York City and Baltimore have been given as birthplaces by several scholars. Cullen himself, on his college transcript at New York University, listed Louisville, Ky., as his place of birth. A few years later, when he had achieved considerable literary fame during the era known as the NEW NEGRO OF HARLEM RENAISSANCE, he was to assert that his birthplace was New York City, a claim he continued to make for the rest of his life. Both Cullen's second wife, Ida, and some of his closest friends, including Langston HUGHES and Harold Jackman, all said he was born in Louisville, although one Cullen scholar, Beulah Reimherr, in her M.A. thesis, claims that Ida Cullen gave her husband's place of birth as Baltimore. As James Weldon JOHNSON wrote in *The Book of American Negro Poetry* (revised edition, 1931), "There is not much to say about these earlier years of Cullen—unless he himself should say it." And Cullen—revealing a temperament that was not exactly secretive but private, less a matter of modesty than a tendency toward being encoded and tactful—never in his life said anything more clarifying.

What we know for certain is that he was born on March 30, 1903, and that sometime between his birth and 1918 he was adopted by the Rev. Frederick A. and Carolyn Belle (Mitchell) Cullen of the Salem Methodist Episcopal Church in Harlem. It is impossible to state with any degree of certainty how old Cullen was at the time, or how long he knew the Cullens before he was adopted. Apparently, he went by the name of Countee Porter until 1918. He became Countee P. Cullen by 1921, and eventually just Countee Cullen. According to Harold Jackman, the adoption was never really "official"; that is to say, it was never formally consummated through the proper state-agency channels. It is difficult, indeed, to know whether Cullen was ever legally an orphan at any stage in his childhood.

Frederick Cullen was one of the pioneer black activist-ministers; he moved his Salem Methodist Episcopal Church from a storefront mission—where it was in 1902, when he first arrived in New York City—to the site of a former white church in Harlem in 1924, where he could boast of a membership of over 2,500. Since Countee Cullen himself stated in his 1927 anthology of black American poetry. *Caroling Dusk*, that he was "reared in the conservative atmosphere of a Methodist parsonage," it is clear that his foster father, particularly, was a strong influence. The two men were very close, often traveling abroad together. But as Cullen evidences a decided unease in his poetry over his strong and conservative Christian training and the attraction of his pagan inclinations, his feelings about his father may have been somewhat ambivalent. Frederick Cullen was, on the one hand, a puritanical Christian patriarch, and Countee was never remotely that. On the other hand, it has been suggested that Frederick was also something of an effeminate man. (He was dressed in girl's clothing by his poverty-stricken mother well beyond the acceptable boyhood age for such a practice and was apparently effeminate in his manner as an adult.) Some scholars, especially Jean Wagner, have argued that Countee Cullen's homosexuality, or decidedly ambiguous sexual nature, may have been attributable to his foster father's contrary influence as both fire-breathing Christian and latent or covert transsexual. To be sure, in his poetry Cullen equated paganism with various sensual postures, including homosexuality. Cullen was a devoted and obedient son, and the fact that the Cullens had no other children made this attachment much easier to achieve.

Cullen was an outstanding student both at DeWitt Clinton High School (1918–1921)—where he not only edited the school's newspaper but also assisted in editing the literary magazine, *Magpie*, and wrote his first poetry that achieved notice—and at New York University (1921–1925), where he wrote most of the major work that was to make up his first two volumes, *Color* (1925) and *Copper Sun* (1927). It was also while at NYU that he wrote *The Ballad of the Brown Girl* (1927). In high school Cullen won his first contest, a citywide competition, with the poem "I Have a Rendezvous with Life," a nonracial poem inspired by Alan Seeger's "I Have a Rendezvous with Death." If any event signaled the coming of the Harlem Renaissance, it was the precocious success of this rather shy black boy who, more than any other black literary figure of his generation, was being touted and bred to become a major crossover literary figure. Here was a black man with considerable academic training who could, in effect, write "white" verse—ballads, sonnets, quatrains, and the like—much in the manner of Keats and the British Romantics (albeit, on more than one occasion, tinged with racial concerns), with genuine skill and compelling power. He was certainly not the first African American to attempt to write such verse, but he was first to do so with such extensive education, with such a complete understanding of himself as a poet, and producing poetry that was not trite or inferior. Only two other black American poets before Cullen could be taken so seriously as self-consciously considered and proficient poets: Phillis WHEATLEY and Paul Laurence DUNBAR.

If the aim of the Harlem Renaissance was, in part, the reinvention of the native-born African American as a being who could be assimilated while decidedly retaining something called a "racial self-consciousness," then Cullen fit the bill better than virtually any other Renaissance writer. And if "I Have a Rendezvous with Life" was the opening salvo in the making of Cullen's literary reputation, then the 1924 publication of "Shroud of Color" in H. L. Mencken's *American Mercury* confirmed the advent of the black boy wonder as one of the most exciting American poets on the scene. After graduating Phi Beta Kappa from NYU, Cullen earned a master's degree in English and French from Harvard (1927). Between high school and graduation from Harvard he had become the most popular black poet—virtually the most popular black literary figure—in America. It was after one of his poems and his popular column appeared in *Opportunity* magazine that A'lelia Walker (heiress of Madame C. J. WALKER's hair-care-products fortune) named her salon, where the black and white literati gathered in the late 1920s, the Dark Tower.

Cullen won more major literary prizes than any other black writer of the 1920s: the first prize in the Witter Bynner Poetry Contest in 1925; *Poetry* magazine's John Reed Memorial Prize; the Amy Spingarn Award of *The Crisis* magazine; second prize in *Opportunity* magazine's first poetry contest; second prize in the poetry contest of *Palms.* He was the second African American to win a Guggenheim Fellowship. His first three books—*Color, Copper Sun,* and *The Ballad of the Brown Girl*—sold well and made him a hero for many blacks. Lines from Cullen's popular poems, such as "Heritage," "Incident," "From the Dark Tower," and "Yet Do I Marvel," were commonly quoted.

Cullen won more major literary prizes than any other black writer of the 1920s.

Cullen was also at the center of one of the major social events of the Harlem Renaissance; on April 9, 1928, he married Yolande Du Bois, only child of W. E. B. DU BOIS, in one of the most lavish weddings in black New York history. This wedding was to symbolize the union of the grand black intellectual patriarch and the new breed of younger African Americans who were responsible for much of the excitement of the Renaissance. It was an apt meshing of personalities, as both Cullen and Du Bois *père* were conservative by nature and ardent traditionalists. That the marriage turned out so disastrously and ended so quickly—Yolande and Cullen divorced in 1930--probably adversely affected Cullen. (He remarried in 1940.) Cullen published *The Black Christ and Other Poems* in 1929, receiving lukewarm reviews from both black and white presses. He was bitterly disappointed that *The Black Christ,* his longest and in many respects his most complicated poem, the product of over two years' work, was considered by most critics to be his weakest and least distinguished.

From the 1930s until his death, Cullen wrote a great deal less, partly hampered by his job as a French teacher at Frederick Douglass Junior High (his most famous student was James BALDWIN). But he wrote noteworthy, even significant work in a number of genres. His novel *One Way to Heaven,* published in 1934, rates among the better black satires, and is one of the three important fictional retrospectives of the Harlem Renaissance, the others being Wallace Thurman's *The Infants of the Spring* and George Schuyler's *Black No More;* his translation of *The Medea* is the first major translation of a classical work by a twentieth-century black American writer; the children's books *The Lost Zoo* and *My Lives and How I Lost Them* are among the more clever and engaging books of children's verse, written at a time when there was not much work published for children by black writers; and his poetry of the period includes perhaps some of his best, certainly some of his more darkly complex, sonnets. He was also working on a musical with Arna BONTEMPS called *St. Louis Woman* (based on Bontemps's novel, *God Sends Sunday*) at the time of his death from high blood pressure and uremic poisoning.

For many years after his death, Cullen's reputation was eclipsed by those of other Harlem Renaissance writers, particularly Langston HUGHES and Zora Neale HURSTON, and his work had gone out of print. More recently, however, there has been a resurgence of interest in his life and work, and his books are being reissued.

BIBLIOGRAPHY

Bontemps, Arna, ed. *The Harlem Renaissance Remembered.* New York, 1972.

Davis, Arthur P. *From the Dark Tower: Afro-American Writers, 1900 to 1960.* Washington, D.C., 1974.

Early, Gerald, ed. *My Soul's High Song, The Collected Writings of Countee Cullen, Voice of the Harlem Renaissance.* New York, 1991.

Ferguson, Blanche F. *Countee Cullen and the Negro Renaissance.* New York, 1966.

Huggins, Nathan. *Harlem Renaissance.* New York, 1971.

Wagner, Jean. *Black Poets of the United States: From Paul Laurence Dunbar to Langston Hughes.* Translated by Kenneth Douglas. Champaign, Ill., 1973.

– GERALD EARLY

D

DANCE THEATER OF HARLEM

Dance Theater of Harlem, classical dance company. The Dance Theater of Harlem (DTH) was founded on August 15, 1969, by Arthur Mitchell and Karel Shook as the world's first permanent, professional, academy-rooted, predominantly black ballet troupe. Mitchell created DTH to address a threefold mission of social, educational, and artistic opportunity for the people of Harlem, and to prove that "there are black dancers with the physique, temperament and stamina, and everything else it takes to produce what we call the 'born' ballet dancer." During its official 1971 debut, DTH triumphantly debunked opinions that black people could not dance ballet. By 1993 DTH had become a world-renowned company with forty-nine dancers, seventy-five ballets in its repertory, an associated school, and an international touring schedule.

DTH's extensive repertory has included technically demanding neoclassic ballets (George Balanchine's 1946 *The Four Temperaments*); programmatic works (Mitchell's 1968 *Rhythmetron* and Alvin AILEY's 1970 *The River* to music by Duke ELLINGTON); and pieces that explore the African-American experience (Louis Johnson's 1972 *Forces of Rhythm* and Geoffrey Holder's 1974 *Dougla* created in collaboration with DTH conductor-composer Tania Leon). DTH also excels in its own versions of classic ballets, including a sumptuous, Geoffrey Holder-designed production of Stravinsky's *Firebird* (1982) choreographed by John Taras, and a stunning Creole-inspired staging of *Giselle* (1984) created by Mitchell, designer Carl Mitchell, and artistic associate Frederic Franklin. This highly acclaimed *Giselle* set the Romantic-era story in the society of free black plantation owners in pre–Civil War Louisiana. DTH is perhaps best known for its revivals of dramatic ballets, including Agnes de Mille's 1948 *Fall River Legend* and Valerie Bettis's 1952 *A Streetcar Named Desire,* both of which have starred principal ballerina Virginia Johnson. Other important classical dance artists associated with DTH include Lydia Arbaca, Karen Brown, Stephanie Dabney, Robert Garland, Lorraine Graves, Christina Johnson, Ronald Perry, Walter Raines, Judith Rotardier, Paul Russell, Eddie J. Shellman, Lowell Smith, Mel Tomlinson, and Donald Williams.

In 1972 the DTH school moved to its permanent home at 466 West 152nd Street, where training in dance, choreography, and music supplemented outreach programs bringing dance to senior citizens and children of the Harlem community with special needs. The international celebrity achieved by DTH began with a Caribbean performance tour in 1970, an engagement at the Spoleto Festival in 1971, and an auspicious 1974 London debut at Sadler's Wells. In 1988 DTH embarked on a five-week tour of the U.S.S.R., playing sold-out performances in Moscow, Tbilisi, and Leningrad, where the company received a standing ovation at the famed Kirov Theatre. In 1992, DTH successfully performed in Johannesburg, South Africa.

Mitchell created DTH to address a threefold mission of social, educational, and artistic opportunity for the people of Harlem.

In 1990, faced with a $1.7 million dollar deficit, DTH was forced to cancel its New York season and lay off dancers, technicians, and administrative staff for a six-month period. Mitchell and the board of directors responded with increased efforts to enlarge corporate support and strengthen their African-American audience base. In 1994 DTH completed a $6 million expansion and renovation project, which doubled classroom and administrative space and confirmed the DTH commitment to provide access to the disciplined training necessary for a career in classical ballet.

BIBLIOGRAPHY

Kendall, Elizabeth. " 'Home' to Russia: Dance Theatre of Harlem on Tour in the Soviet Union." *Ballet Review* V. 16 No. 4, Winter 1989: 3–49.

Maynard, Olga. "Dance Theatre of Harlem: Arthur Mitchell's 'Dark and Brilliant Splendor.' " *Dance Magazine* (May 1975): 52–64.

– THOMAS F. DEFRANTZ

DAVIS, ANGELA YVONNE

Angela Yvonne Davis (January 26, 1944–), political activist. Angela Davis lived in a section of Birmingham, Ala., known as "Dynamite Hill" because of the violent attacks by white nightriders intent on maintaining the residential demarcation line between blacks and whites.

Both of her parents were educators, worked actively for the NAACP, and taught their children not to accept the socially segregated society that existed at the time. She attended Brandeis University, where she was influenced by the teachings of Marxist philosopher Herbert Marcuse. After graduating in 1961, she spent two years in Europe, where she was exposed to student political radicals. Her own radicalism, however, came into focus with the murder in 1963 of four young black Sunday school children in a Birmingham, Ala., church bombing. In California, where she went to pursue graduate study with Marcuse (who was now at the University of California, San Diego), Davis began working with the STUDENT NONVIOLENT COORDINATING COMMITTEE (SNCC), the Black Panthers, and the Communist party, of which she became a member in 1968.

Hired in 1969 by UCLA to teach philosophy, Davis not long after was fired by the Board of Regents and then-Governor Ronald Reagan because of her Communist party affiliation. Ultimately, her case went to the Supreme Court, which overturned the dismissal. By that time, however, Davis herself was in hiding as a result of an incident at the Soledad state prison. In August 1970, George Jackson, a prisoner and member of the Black Panthers, assisted by his brother Jonathan, attempted to escape using smuggled guns. Both brothers were killed, and some of the guns were traced to Davis. Fearful for her safety and distrustful of the judicial system, Davis went underground. For two months she was on the FBI's Ten Most Wanted list before being apprehended and incarcerated. She remained in jail for sixteen months before being tried for murder and conspiracy. In June 1972 she was acquitted of all charges against her. Davis resumed her academic career at San Francisco State University and again became politically active, running as the Communist party candidate for vice president in 1980 and 1984. In 1991 she joined the faculty of the University of California, Santa Cruz, as professor of the history of consciousness. She is the author of several books, including *If They Come in the Morning* (1971), *Women, Race, and Class* (1983), and *Women, Culture, and Politics* (1989). Her autobiography, *Angela Davis: An Autobiography,* originally published in 1974, was reissued in 1988.

BIBLIOGRAPHY

Lanker, Brian. *I Dream a World: Portraits of Black Women Who Changed America.* New York, 1989.

– CHRISTINE A. LUNARDINI

DAVIS, BENJAMIN OLIVER, JR.

Benjamin Oliver Davis, Jr. (December 18, 1912–), general. Benjamin O. Davis, Jr., son of the first African-American general in the U.S. Army, had a long and distinguished career of his own in the U.S. Air Force. Following his long MILITARY service, he spent a number of years working as an important administrator in the Department of Transportation.

The younger Davis was born in Washington, D.C. He spent many of his early years watching or participating in his father's military activities. In the 1920s, he lived with his parents and attended school in Tuskegee, Ala., and Cleveland, Ohio. One of his most vivid memories from those days involved his father facing down a KU KLUX KLAN march while the family lived at Tuskegee. As an adolescent, Davis, Jr., was an excellent scholar and displayed leadership qualities. He was one of the few African-American students at Central High School in Cleveland and was elected president of his graduating class. He attended college at Western Reserve University (Cleveland, Ohio) and the University of Chicago, but then decided on a military career. Despite the handicaps that had faced his father, he felt that it was a profession where he could advance on his merits. In 1932 his father asked the assistance of Oscar DePriest, congressman from Illinois, who nominated Davis, Jr., to the United States Military Academy. Subsequently he passed the entrance examination and entered West Point in 1932.

Life at the military academy had change little since the last African-American had graduated in the 1880s. The presence of blacks was resented, and almost all the cadets ignored Davis. The only time he had any companionship was when he was allowed to leave West Point. During his years at the academy he began to develop an interest in flying, an area the Army had closed to African Americans. When he graduated in 1936, ranking thirty-fifth in a class of 276, he requested assignment to the Army Air Corps. The Army refused because there were no African-American flying units and they would not assign a black officer to a white unit.

During the next few years he performed a variety of duties, similar to those of his father. In 1938 he received an appointment as Professor of Military Science at Tuskegee Institute. Two years later he was detached to work as an aide to his father, who was then commanding the 2nd Cavalry Brigade at Fort Riley, Kans.

His interest in flying never waned, and in 1941, he received his opportunity. Bowing to pressure, the Army decided to allow African Americans into the Army Air Corps, established a flight training program at Tuskegee Institute, and ordered Davis to command the first class. After he graduated in 1942, he was rapidly promoted to the rank of major and given command of the 99th Pursuit Squadron, the first African-American air unit.

In April 1943, the unit was transferred to North Africa and in June flew its first combat mission. Most of the ensuing missions were rather routine, but not everyone was persuaded of their effectiveness. A number of white officers were convinced that no African-American air unit could ever measure up to the quality of the white units.

Later in the year Davis was ordered back to the United States and assigned command of the 332nd Fighter Group, a larger all-black flying unit. More important, he was able to answer the many questions that army staff officers posed about the effectiveness of the 99th Squadron. Enough of these officers were convinced to the extent that they decided to continue the African-American flying program and transferred the 332nd to the Italian theater. During the last year of the war, Davis was promoted to the rank of colonel, flew sixty combat missions, mainly escorting bombers, and received several awards, including the Distinguished Flying Cross. At the end of the war he returned to the United States and was placed in command of the 477th Composite Group. Among the problems he had to face in his new assignment were segregated base facilities, poor morale, and continued evidence of the detrimental impact of segregation.

During the next few years Davis continued to deal with those problems while advocating an end to segregation. When President Harry S. Truman issued Executive Order 9981 in 1948, ending racial discrimination in the armed forces, Davis became a key officer in the Air Force. He helped draft desegregation plans and put them into practice at Lockbourne Air Base. Subsequently he was assigned to the new Air War College. During the Korean War he served at the Pentagon as deputy for operations in the Fighter Branch. Later he was given a variety of command assignments throughout the world, including Formosa, Germany, and the Philippines. In 1965 he was promoted to lieutenant general, the first African American to reach that rank. He retired from the Air Force in 1970.

During the following years he served in a variety of positions within civilian government. For several months in 1970 he was director of public safety in Cleveland, Ohio, but found he could not work well with Mayor Carl Stokes. Adapting to the world of urban politics proved to be quite difficult for a man who had spent the previous thirty years in the military. In June 1970 Davis became a member of the President's Commission on Campus Unrest. From 1970 to 1975, he served as an administrator in the Department of Transportation. As assistant secretary of transportation, he headed the federal programs developed to deal with air hijacking and highway safety. In 1978 he became a member of the Battle Monuments Commission, a position his father had held twenty-five years earlier. During the next few years, he remained busy with a variety of activities, including programs designed to tell people about the role of African Americans in aviation, and the writing of his autobiography, which was eventually published in 1991.

BIBLIOGRAPHY

Davis, Benjamin O., Jr. *American: An Autobiography.* Washington, D.C., 1991.

Nalty, Bernard C. *Strength for the Fight: A History of Black Americans in the Military.* New York, 1986.

— MARVIN E. FLETCHER

DAVIS, BENJAMIN O., SR.

Benjamin O. Davis, Sr. (May 28, 1880–November 26, 1970), general. Benjamin O. Davis, Sr., was born in Washington, D.C. During his fifty years of duty as an enlisted man and officer in the United States Army, he strove to help others surmount the barrier of racism.

Davis, the youngest of three children, grew up in Washington, D.C. After graduating from high school, he volunteered for service in the SPANISH-AMERICAN WAR. The Army appointed him a second lieutenant in the Eighth United States Volunteer Infantry. After the unit was deactivated at the end of the war in 1899, Davis decided to continue his military career and joined the regular army. Two years later, he successfully passed a competitive examination and became an officer. On October 22, 1902, he married his childhood sweetheart, Elnora Dickerson. During the next few decades he served in a variety of positions, usually removed from active duty with his regiment. This included duty as military attaché to Liberia (1909–1911), teacher of military science at Wilberforce University (1906–1911, 1915–1917, 1929–1930, 1937–1938), instructor with the Ohio National Guard (1924–1928), and professor of military science at Tuskegee Institute (1921–1924, 1931–1937). In 1912 a son, Benjamin O. DAVIS, Jr., was born. The elder Davis's wife died in 1917 after the birth of their third child, and three years later he married Sadie Overton. In late October 1940, President Franklin D. Roosevelt appointed Davis as brigadier gen-

During his fifty years of duty as an enlisted man and officer in the United States Army, Davis strove to help others surmount the barrier of racism.

eral, making him the first African American to reach that rank.

During World War II, Davis carried out a variety of assignments in Washington and Europe, all generally connected with racial issues. For much of the period he was assistant inspector general. He conducted investigations of racial incidents, tried to encourage the advancement of African-American soldiers and officers, and made efforts to convince the Army to face the consequences of its policies of segregation and discrimination. As a member of the Committee on Negro Troop Policies, Davis quietly worked toward these ends. In 1942 and again in 1944–1945, he served in England and dealt with racial problems in the European theater of operations. One of his most notable contributions occurred as a result of the manpower shortage created by the German attack in the Ardennes in December 1944. He advanced a proposal for retraining black service troops as combat soldiers and inserting these men into white units on an individual basis. Though Gen. Dwight Eisenhower, the theater commander, found this unacceptable, he was forced to accept integration of African-American platoons into white units. It was a significant breakthrough in the wall of segregation.

Following the conclusion of the war, Davis served in a variety of positions before his retirement in 1948. He continued to stress the inequities of segregation and was pleased when President Harry Truman ordered its removal. In the next decade he worked for the government of the District of Columbia and the American Battle Monuments Commission. He resided in Washington with Sadie until her death in 1966, and spent the last years of his life with his younger daughter, Elnora McLendon, in her home in Chicago.

BIBLIOGRAPHY

Fletcher, Marvin E. *America's First Black General: Benjamin O. Davis, Sr., 1880–1970.* Lawrence, Kans., 1989.

Nalty, Bernard C. *Strength for the Fight: A History of Black Americans in the Military.* New York, 1986.

— MARVIN E. FLETCHER

DAVIS, MILES DEWEY, III

Miles Dewey Davis, III (May 26, 1926–September 28, 1991), jazz trumpeter and composer. One of the most influential musicians in America in the 1950s and 1960s, Davis was a restlessly innovative performer, a central figure in several post-bebop jazz styles, including cool, hard-bop, modal, fusion, and electric jazz. Born in Alton, Ill., Davis grew up in East St. Louis. His mother was a classically trained pianist and violinist. Davis received his first trumpet at the age of thirteen from his father, a successful dentist. In high school he studied with Elwood Buchanan. Trumpeter Clark Terry also served as a mentor. Davis began playing dates in the St. Louis area in his mid-teens, and in 1943 and 1944 he played with Eddie Randle's Rhumboogie Orchestra. He also performed with Adam Lambert's Six Brown Cats in Chicago, and with Billy Eckstine in St. Louis, before moving to New York in 1944. Davis's ostensible reason for coming to New York was to study at the Juilliard School, but he gained his real education in the jazz clubs of Harlem and 52nd Street.

One of the most influential musicians in America in the 1950s and 1960s, Davis was a restlessly innovative performer.

Once in New York, Davis began associating with the young musicians beginning to popularize bebop. He made his first recordings in 1945 with vocalist Rubberlegs Williams. Later that year he recorded with alto saxophonist Charlie PARKER ("Billie's Bounce," "Now's the Time"). Parker became Davis's mentor and roommate, and over the next few years the two made many important and influential bebop recordings, including "Yardbird Suite," "Ornithology," "A Night in Tunisia," "Donna Lee," "Chasin' the Bird," and "Parker's Mood." On these recordings Davis distinguished himself by his intimate tone and sparse, hesitant style of improvisation. During this time Davis was a fixture on 52nd Street, performing and recording with pianist Tadd Dameron, pianists Bud Powell and Thelonious MONK, vocalist Billy Eckstine, and saxophonist Coleman HAWKINS. He first recorded as a band leader in 1947 ("Milestones" and "Half Nelson," with Parker on tenor saxophone), and the next year left Parker to form an experimental nine-piece group in collaboration with arranger Gil Evans. The ensemble, which included a French horn and tuba and featured advanced harmonies and unusual compositional forms, was short-lived, performing at the Royal Roost nightclub for only two weeks. Nonetheless, its recordings from 1949–1950 ("Move," "Venus de Milo," "Boplicity," and "Israel") spawned the cool jazz movement of the 1950s, and became particularly popular upon their 1954 rerelease in LP form as *The Birth of the Cool.*

Despite a period of heroin addiction from 1949 to 1953, Davis continued to perform and record in a cool style, often with saxophonist Sonny Rollins ("Morpheus," "Dig," "The Serpent's Tooth," "Tune Up," and

"Miles Ahead"). His career took another leap forward with the 1954 recording of "Walkin'." That recording, with its more extroverted approach, inaugurated hard bop, a rugged and bluesier version of bebop. In 1955 Davis formed his first significant quintet, including tenor saxophonist John COLTRANE, bassist Paul Chambers, pianist Red Garland, and drummer Philly Joe Jones. They recorded the landmark *Round About Midnight* (1955) and performed and recorded until 1957, when Davis added alto saxophonist Cannonball Adderley to the group. In 1957 Davis went to France to record the soundtrack for Louis Malle's film *Elevator to the Gallows.* Back in the United States the next year, Davis recorded *Milestones,* which introduced the concept of modal jazz, in which modes or scales, as opposed to chord changes, determine a song's harmonies. In 1959 Davis recorded perhaps his greatest record, *Kind of Blue,* which included the modal compositions "So What," "All Blues," and "Freddie Freeloader," with an ensemble that included drummer Jimmy Cobb and pianists Wynton Kelly and Bill Evans. In the late 1950s Davis also renewed his association with arranger Gil Evans. They produced three acclaimed orchestral works, *Miles Ahead* (1957), *Porgy and Bess* (1958), and *Sketches of Spain* (1959–1960). During this time Davis achieved his mature instrumental style, delicate and tentative on ballads, boldly lyrical on up-tempo numbers.

Davis's trumpet style resembled, in a famous description, "a man walking on eggshells," but he was often belligerent and profane, on stage and off. He refused to announce titles, walked off the stage when sidemen soloed, and rarely acknowledged applause. Nonetheless, he openly demanded the respect he felt was appropriate to jazz musicians. During the 1950s Davis also became an internationally known public figure noted for his immaculate attire, his interest in sports cars, and for taking up boxing as a hobby.

In 1960, Adderley and Coltrane left the ensemble, which underwent a number of personnel shifts until 1963, when Davis hired pianist Herbie Hancock, bassist Ron Carter, and drummer Tony Williams. With saxophonist Wayne Shorter's arrival the next year, Davis began featuring churning, lengthy improvisations built around Shorter's quirky compositions (*E.S.P.,* 1965; *Miles Smiles,* 1966).

During the late 1960s Davis became disenchanted with the poor reception his music found among black audiences, and he began to search for a new, more commercially appealing style. He found inspiration in the funk rhythms of James BROWN and Sly Stone, as well as in Karlheinz Stockhausen's vast electric-mystic soundscapes. Davis added Keith Jarrett and Chick Corea on electric pianos and John McLaughlin on electric guitar to his regular ensemble, and recorded *In a Silent Way* (1969) and the bestselling *Bitches Brew* (1969), albums that introduced the style that has become known as jazz-rock or "fusion," using loud rock instruments and funk rhythms to accompany extended solo and group improvisations. Davis continued in this vein on *Big Fun* (1969), *Live-Evil* (1970), *On the Corner* (1972), *Agharta* (1975) and *Pangea* (1975). Although Davis gained many fans of rock music, jazz fans were perplexed and unsympathetic. Health problems due to drug abuse and a 1972 car accident convinced Davis to retire in 1975.

In 1980 Davis returned to music, but to the disappointment of many of his fans he continued using popular forms of electric instruments. In his best performances, Davis still communicated with the intensity and fire he had in the 1950s, but his recordings, including *The Man with the Horn* (1981), *Star People* (1982), *Tutu* (1986), and *Amandla* (1989), were largely panned by critics, who were particularly harsh on his undistinguished accompanists. Davis, who lived in New York and Malibu, continued to perform and record in the late 1980s and early 1990s. In 1982 Davis married his third wife, the actress Cicely Tyson; they were divorced in 1989.

He published an outspoken memoir, *Miles, the Autobiography,* in 1989. After many years of battling alcoholism, drug addiction, and circulatory and respiratory ailments, Davis died in 1991 in New York.

BIBLIOGRAPHY

Carr, Ian. *Miles Davis: A Critical Biography.* London, 1982.

Chambers, Jack. *Milestones,* 2 vols. Toronto, 1983, 1985.

Cole, Bill. *Miles Davis: A Musical Biography.* New York, 1974.

Davis, Miles, with Quincy Troupe. *Miles, the Autobiography.* New York, 1989.

— WILLIAM S. COLE

DAVIS, OSSIE

Ossie Davis (December 18, 1917–), actor and playwright. Ossie Davis was born in Cogdell, Ga., to Kince Charles Davis, a railroad construction worker, and Laura Cooper Davis. After finishing high school in Waycross, Ga., he hitchhiked north and attended Howard University. In 1937, Davis left Howard and went to New York City, where he worked at odd jobs before joining Harlem's Rose McClendon Players in 1939.

Davis was drafted into the Army in 1942, and after his discharge in 1945, he again pursued his acting career. In 1946, he successfully auditioned for Robert Ardrey's *Jeb,* in which he starred opposite actress Ruby Dee. Davis and Dee were married in 1948.

In 1953, Davis wrote *Alice in Wonder,* a one-act play, produced in Harlem, that dealt with the politics of the McCarthy era. Blacklisted for left-wing associations, Davis and Dee supported themselves by staging readings at colleges. In 1955, Davis starred in a television production of Eugene O'Neill's *The Emperor Jones,* and two years later appeared on Broadway opposite Lena HORNE in *Jamaica!*

In the 1960s, Davis achieved broad success in the performing arts. In 1960, he replaced Sidney POITIER and appeared with Ruby Dee in Lorraine HANSBERRY'S play *A Raisin in the Sun.* The following year, his play *Purlie Victorious,* a satire on southern racism, opened on Broadway to an enthusiastic response. Davis also wrote and starred in the film version of *Purlie Victorious,* entitled *Gone Are the Days* (1963). He appeared in several other films during this period, including *The Cardinal* (1963), *The Hill* (1964), *The Scalphunters* (1968), and *Slaves* (1969). He also appeared on several television shows, wrote an episode for the popular series *East Side/West Side,* and narrated National Education Television's *History of the Negro People* (1965). In 1969, Davis was nominated for an Emmy award for his performance in the Hallmark Hall of Fame special *Teacher, Teacher.* That same year Davis directed, cowrote, and acted in the film *Cotton Comes to Harlem,* based on a novel by Chester HIMES.

During these years, Davis continued his political activities. In 1962, he testified before Congress on racial discrimination in the theater, and joined the advisory board of the CONGRESS OF RACIAL EQUALITY (CORE). The following year, he wrote a skit for the 1963 March on Washington, and in 1965 Davis delivered a eulogy at the funeral of his friend, MALCOLM X. In 1972, he served as chairman of the Angela Davis Defense Fund. While Davis has strong affinities with black nationalism, he has nonetheless rejected black racism and separatism.

Through the 1970s, '80s, and early '90s, Davis continued his performing career, notably in a radio series, the *Ossie Davis and Ruby Dee Hour* (1974–1976); in the public television series *With Ossie and Ruby* (1981); in the role of Martin Luther King, Sr., in Abby Mann's television miniseries *King* (1977); and in the Spike LEE films *Do the Right Thing* (1989) and *Jungle Fever* (1991). Throughout the early 1990s, he was a semiregular on the television series *Evening Shade.* Davis also has written several children's books, which include plays based on the lives of Frederick DOUGLASS and Langston HUGHES, and a novel, *Just Like Martin* (1992), about a southern boy, inspired by the life of the Rev. Dr. Martin Luther KING, Jr.

BIBLIOGRAPHY

Landay, Eileen. *Black Film Stars.* New York, 1973.

McMurray, Emily J., and Owen O'Donnell, eds. *Contemporary Theater, Film and Television.* Detroit, 1992.

– SUSAN MCINTOSH AND GREG ROBINSON

DAVIS, SAMMY, JR.

Sammy Davis, Jr. (December 8, 1925–May 19, 1990), singer, dancer, and actor. Sammy Davis, Jr., was born in Harlem in New York and began performing with his father, a vaudeville entertainer, before his fourth birthday. Davis made his first film, *Rufus Jones for President* (1933) when he was eight years old. By the time he was fifteen, he had traveled widely throughout the United States as a full partner in the Will Mastin Trio, comprised of Davis, his father, and Davis's adopted "uncle" Will Mastin. Although they often played at white venues, the trio was compelled to eat and room at Negro establishments; yet Davis, who had received an informal education at the hands of family and friends, was unprepared for the virulent racism he encountered upon joining the Army in 1943. During his tenure in the military, he produced and performed in shows with other service personnel, including the singer and songwriter George M. Cohan, Jr.

Following WORLD WAR II, Davis returned to the Will Mastin Trio. The group played to segregated audiences and, despite their rising popularity, were forbidden to sleep or socialize in the hotels and casinos where they worked. Davis began recording songs for Capitol Records in 1946; one of his first cuts, "The Way You Look Tonight," was named *Metronome*'s Record of the Year. An extremely versatile performer, adept at tap dancing, singing, impersonations, and comic and serious acting, he received his first big break when Frank Sinatra asked the trio to open for his show at Manhattan's Capitol Theater. Davis went on to perform at Slapsie Maxie's and Ciro's in Los Angeles and at the Copacabana in New York, in addition to appearing on *The Ed Sullivan Show* and Eddie Cantor's *The Colgate Comedy Hour.*

In November 1954, Davis, who had become a celebrity with white and black audiences alike, was involved in a near-fatal car accident while driving from Las Vegas to Los Angeles. He lost his left eye and was hospitalized for several months; during this time, he was visited by a rabbi, who urged him to reflect on the consequences of the accident and the meaning of his previous actions. After a period of intense study, Davis, who claimed to have found an "affinity" between blacks and Jews as oppressed peoples, converted to Judaism.

Davis's popularity was much enhanced by his brush with death. He performed in Philadelphia, Chicago, and Los Angeles, before taking the lead role in *Mr. Wonderful,* a musical comedy that opened on Broadway in 1956. Two years later, Davis, who had been nicknamed "Mr. Wonderful" after the Broadway show, was featured in a serious dramatic role in the movie *Anna Lucasta.* In the 1959 film of *Porgy and Bess,* Davis gave a memorable performance as the character Sportin' Life. That year, he married Loray White, an African-American dancer whom he later left for the Swedish actress Mai Britt. Davis's interracial romance with Britt was highly publicized, and the couple married in 1960.

Davis is perhaps best known for the films he made during the 1960s, when he worked and socialized with the "Rat Pack," a group of Hollywood actors that included Sinatra, Dean Martin, Peter Lawford, and Joey Bishop, who were featured, along with Davis, in such films as *Oceans Eleven* (1960), *Sergeants Three* (1962), *Robin and the Seven Hoods* (1964), *Salt and Pepper* (1968), and *One More Time* (1970). Davis also appeared in such films as *Johnny Cool* (1963), *A Man Called Adam* (1966), *Sweet Charity* (1969), and the German remake of *The Threepenny Opera* (1964), in which he sang "Mack the Knife." In addition, he continued to perform in clubs and on Broadway, where he was praised for his rendering of the title character in *Golden Boy,* Clifford Odets's play about an African-American boxer struggling to free himself from the constrictions of ghetto life. Davis appeared on television in numerous comic and guest-artist roles, as well as in serious dramatic series like the *Dick Powell Theatre* and *General Electric Theater.* In 1966, he hosted a television variety and talk show called *The Sammy Davis Jr. Show,* which ran for less than a year. He also continued to record albums and produced such hit songs as "Candy Man," "Hey There," "Mr. Bojangles," and "The Lady Is a Tramp."

Throughout the 1960s, Davis worked to promote civil rights and African-American/Jewish relations by giving benefit performances and substantial donations. His first autobiography, *Yes I Can,* was published in 1965; three years later, he was awarded the Spingarn Medal by the NAACP for his work in civil rights. Davis's marriage to Mai Britt ended in 1968, and two years later, he married the African-American actress Altovise Gore. In 1971, he was awarded an honorary doctorate of fine arts by Wilberforce University in Ohio. A controversy erupted the following year when Davis, a registered Democrat and supporter of left-wing causes, allowed himself to be photographed with President Richard Nixon at the 1972 Republican Convention; he publicly endorsed Nixon for a time but then renounced their affiliation in 1974.

Sammy Davis, Jr. (center), with James Baldwin (left), and Martin Luther King, Jr. (right), at the Majestic Theater, New York, 1964. (© George West)

During the early 1970s, Davis, by then almost as well known for his extravagant spending habits and hard-drinking lifestyle as for his stage presence and vitality, began to experience liver and kidney problems, for which he was eventually hospitalized in 1974. However, he rebounded fairly quickly and was back onstage a few months later in a revue called *Sammy on Broadway.* From 1975 to 1977, he starred in the television show *Sammy and Company.* He performed regularly on the Las Vegas club circuit, and in 1979, became the first recipient of *Ebony* magazine's Lifetime Achievement Award.

Throughout the 1960s, Davis worked to promote civil rights and African-American/Jewish relations by giving benefit performances and substantial donations.

Davis's second autobiography, *Hollywood in a Suitcase,* was published in 1980; throughout the decade he continued to appear, albeit less frequently, in films, on television, and onstage. In 1986, he received an honorary degree from Howard University. Two years later, he embarked on a national tour with Frank Sinatra, Dean Martin, and Liza Minnelli. Davis was featured in the movie *Taps* (1989), a tribute to showbiz entertainers, and published a third autobiographical work, *Why Me?* (1989), before dying of throat cancer in spring 1990.

BIBLIOGRAPHY

Davis, Sammy, Jr. *Yes I Can.* New York, 1980.

Mortiz, Charles, ed. *Current Biography Yearbook,* New York, 1978.

– JESSE RHINES

DECARAVA, ROY

Roy DeCarava (December 9, 1919–), photographer. Born and raised by his mother in Harlem, Roy DeCarava graduated with a major in art from the Straubenmuller Textile High School in 1938. While still in high school he worked as a sign painter and display artist and in the poster division of the WORKS PROGRESS ADMINISTRATION (WPA) project in New York City. In his senior year he won a competition to design a medal for the National Tuberculosis Association's high school essay contest and upon graduation received a scholarship for excellence in art.

Supporting himself as a commercial artist, DeCarava studied painting at Cooper Union with Byron Thomas and Morris Kantor from 1938 to 1940, and lithography and drawing at the Harlem Art Center from 1940 to 1942. He attended the George Washington Carver Art School in 1944 and 1945, studying painting with Charles White. In 1946 his serigraph won the print award at the Atlanta University Fifth Annual Exhibition of Painting and Sculpture (a national juried exhibition for black artists), and the following year he had a one-man show at the Serigraph Gallery in New York.

In 1946, DeCarava began to use photography as a means to sketch ideas for paintings, and by 1947 he had decided to concentrate exclusively on it. Although he lacked formal training, DeCarava approached photography as "just another medium that an artist would use"; he quickly established a distinctive style and chose a subject—the people of Harlem—that engaged him deeply and productively. Some of his strongest work dates from the late 1940s and early 1950s, such as *Graduation* (1949) and *Gittel* (1950). His first photographic exhibition was in 1950 at New York's Forty-fourth Street Gallery, and that year he sold three prints to the Museum of Modern Art. In 1952, DeCarava became the tenth photographer and among the earliest black artists to be awarded a Guggenheim Fellowship. Continuing his work in Harlem during the fellowship year, DeCarava produced over 2,000 images; he wanted to show, he has said, "[African Americans'] beauty and the image that we presented in our being." In 1955 four of his photographs appeared in the Museum of Modern Art's famous *Family of Man* exhibition and best-selling book. In the same year, 141 photographs were published with a text by Langston HUGHES in their much-acclaimed classic *The Sweet Flypaper of Life* (1955), a tale of everyday events in the lives of a fictional yet representative Harlem family.

DeCarava formed his style at a time in photographic history when the social documentary ethos of the 1930s was giving way to a more formalist aesthetic which especially appreciated a photographer's manipulation of the unique qualities of the medium. He was influenced by the French photographer Henri Cartier-Bresson, whose theory of the "decisive moment" credits formal organization equally with factual content in conveying essential meaning in a photograph. Like Cartier-Bresson, DeCarava uses a small camera, avoids contrived settings, often shooting in the street, and achieves important, often metaphorical, effects through composition, as in *Sun and Shade* (1952) and *Boy Playing, Man Walking* (1966). Indeed, DeCarava has taken pains throughout his career to foster interpretations that see more in his style than literal and programmatic documentary. His titles are always brief and uninflected, and he insists that his work is not political and that "the definition of truth is a personal one." Dismayed that so few galleries showed photography as a fine art, DeCarava operated the Photographer's Gallery from 1954 to 1956, exhibiting work by such artists as Berenice Abbott, Harry Callahan, and Minor White.

DeCarava felt keenly that black people were not seen as "worthy subject matter" for art; he was determined that African Americans be portrayed in ways that were "serious," "artistic," and "human." His dual commitment—to content representing the beauty and diversity of the African-American experience and to full formal mastery of his medium—has deeply influenced younger photographers, who have seen him as the first to develop "the black aesthetic" in photography. From 1963 to 1966, he directed the Kamoinge Workshop for black photographers and chaired the Committee to End Discrimination Against Black Photographers of the American Society of Magazine Photographers. In 1968 DeCarava picketed the Metropolitan Museum of Art's controversial *Harlem on My Mind* exhibition, protesting its emphasis on documentary, rather than artistic, representation of the Harlem Community. In 1972 DeCarava received the Benin Award for contributions to the black community.

DeCarava's work was included in six group shows at the Museum of Modern Art during the 1950s and '60s, and he had a one-man show at the Studio Museum in Harlem in 1969. In 1958 he gave up commercial art to support himself as a free lance photographer for magazines, advertising agencies, museums, and nonprofit organizations. From 1968 to 1975, DeCarava was a contract photographer for *Sports Illustrated* magazine, and in 1975 he was appointed associate professor of art at Hunter College, attaining the rank of City University distinguished professor in 1989.

DeCarava's impressive exhibition record continued in the 1970s and '80s with solo shows at the Museum of Fine Arts in Houston, the Corcoran Gallery of Art in Washington, D.C., and the Museum of Modern Art in Sweden. *The Sound I Saw,* an exhibition of 100 jazz photographs at the Studio Museum in Harlem, was accompanied by a publication of the same title (1983). In 1982, the Friends of Photography published *Roy DeCarava: Photographs,* a major monograph with eighty-two pictures.

In the course of his career DeCarava has traveled and photographed in Paris, London, Stockholm, and Bangkok. His developing interest in abstraction has suggested to some critics that DeCarava feels an increasing emotional detachment from his subjects. Most viewers, however, have appreciated the artist's occasional experiment with blur or soft focus in later work as evidence of his ongoing creative exploration of his medium.

An exhibition of DeCarava's works is to be held at the Museum of Modern Art in January 1996.

BIBLIOGRAPHY

Blue, Carroll. "Conversations with Roy DeCarava." A 58-minute film distributed by First Run/Icarus Films. New York, 1983.

Coleman, A. D. "Roy DeCarava: 'Thru Black Eyes.' " In *Light Readings: A Photography Critic's Writings 1968–78.* New York, 1979, pp. 18–28.

DeCarava, Sherry Turner. "Celebration." In *Roy DeCarava: Photographs.* Carmel, Calif., 1981, pp. 7–20.

Fraser, C. Gerald. "For Roy DeCarava, 62, It's Time for Optimism." *New York Times,* June 6, 1982, p. 60.

Wallen, Ruth. "Reading the Shadows—The Photography of Roy DeCarava." *Exposure* 27, no. 4 (Fall 1990): 13–26.

— MAREN STANGE

DEMOCRATIC PARTY

Among the many ironies of African-American history, few are as startling as the transition in the position of blacks in the Democratic party. Throughout the nineteenth century and into the twentieth century, the Democratic party consistently supported white supremacy. While it sometimes courted black support, party leaders never offered more than minor patronage. However, beginning in the 1930s, increasing numbers of African Americans were drawn into the New Deal Democratic coalition. The alliance between blacks and Democrats was cemented in the late 1940s, when the Democrats emerged as the primary civil rights party. By the mid 1960s, blacks voted overwhelmingly for Democratic candidates, and black officeholders and concerns had made important inroads into party policy. Since the 1960s, blacks have consistently been the most loyal supporters of the Democrats, often providing over ninety percent of their votes for the party's candidates. In more recent times, the relationship between blacks and Democrats has been remade by black elected officials and party activists in such efforts as the campaigns of the Rev. Jesse JACKSON.

Prior to the Civil War, the few African Americans who could vote involved themselves with the precursors of the REPUBLICAN party. There were alignments with the Federalists and later the Whigs. On the minor party level, there was identification with the various antislavery parties—i.e., the Liberty party, the Free Soilers, and the Political Abolitionists, some of which had antislavery Democrats—such as former President Martin Van Buren—in active roles. For the most part, these minor parties not only permitted African Americans to attend and participate in their national conventions, but also addressed the issue of slavery. Still, they often ignored other issues, such as suffrage, which had an impact on the roles of black people as citizens of the evolving Republic. The Republican party itself, virtually from its birth, took up the cudgels for the African-American community. In its maiden national effort in 1856, and subsequently in the 1860 presidential election, the Republican party attracted the attention and the support of a considerable segment of the African-American community.

Among the many ironies of African-American history, few are as startling as the transition in the position of blacks in the Democratic party.

However, the Republican party's chief competitor, the Democratic party, took a negative and inimical position toward the African-American community. It had done so in prior years and continued to do so in later years. In the South, the Democratic majority firmly supported SLAVERY. In the North and later in the midwestern states, Democratic leaders denigrated the entire African-American community and its political aspirations. All during the antebellum period, the Democratic party opposed the extensions of suffrage rights to that portion of the African-American community that could vote. Historian Phyllis Field, observing the Democrats in New York, wrote: "Whenever the Democratic party was strong . . . there one would find little sentiment to extend the rights of blacks." Similarly, midwestern Democrats' sentiments about suffrage and slavery, epitomized in the rhetoric of Stephen Douglas during the famous Lincoln-Douglas debates in Illinois in 1858, were virtually uniformly negative. Throughout the period, the racist posture of the Democrats pushed the African-American community away from the party.

During the presidential election of 1860, Democratic orators reached new heights of racist demagoguery to stigmatize blacks and their Republican allies, reaching a nationwide audience via newspaper articles, books, and pamphlets. In the 1864 election, Democrats sympathetic to the South, known as "Copperheads," declared that the Republicans favored racial intermarriage, and published political cartoons depicting President Lincoln involved with African-American women at the inaugural ball.

These attitudes continued during RECONSTRUCTION, when the reconstituted southern Democratic party sought to wrest control from the coalition of white and African-American Republicans who headed the local governments. In state after state Democratic "redeemers" used violence and fraud to restore white supremacy. Black Republicans and their white allies were unable to resist without outside intervention, since conservative Democrats controlled the money, the land, and the credit-system. Eventually, white rule was restored in the former Confederate states in the early 1870s, with South Carolina, Louisiana, and Florida in 1876 as the last to be "redeemed." The disputed presidential election of 1876 and the COMPROMISE OF 1877 that followed permitted the southern Democrats to regain these three remaining states and put the fragile Republican coalition to rest as a political force in state governments in the region.

Yet in the post-Reconstruction era in the South, an alliance did begin to take root. It was during this "redemption" drive that African-American Democrats first emerged. During the political struggle for control, white Democrats reached out to the African-American community for voters, political representatives, and finally, political appointees for a few offices. This was a clever maneuver, and here and there it worked. It split the African-American community and drained off crucial support for the Republican coalition. The promise of offices provided another avenue for politically ambitious blacks who had not found rewards or political mobility under the Republican banner. African-American Democrats, such as Thomas Hamilton of South Carolina, were elected to the state legislature, and held minor political offices on the county and city level. The black voters of their communities provided significant support, although not at the level of that for Republicans.

By 1900, the tenuous African-American Democratic pact with southern white Democrats had dissolved, although a few southern black conservatives, notably William H. Councill and Henry McNeal Turner, collaborated with the Democrats during the 1890s. For a variety of reasons—ranging from the rising tide of racial bigotry throughout the country to the fears of elite whites of class-based alliances between blacks and poor whites (conservatives beat off Populist challenges, ironically, with the aid of black votes obtained through bribery or fraud)—white candidates campaigned for votes by championing white supremacy, and government officials succeeded in disfranchising almost all black voters.

The second part of this tentative alliance of blacks with the Democratic party—which continued despite the rising tide of racism in the South—was African-American support of national tickets. By the early 1800s, black dissatisfaction with the failure of Republicans outside the South to provide sufficient patronage or support black rights led leaders to seek deals with the Democrats. A few black leaders such as Peter H. Clark of Cincinnati and Edwin Garrison Walker and James

Monroe Trotter of Boston, left the Republicans and led their followers into the Democratic party. (Such defectors were termed "mugwumps" beginning in 1884.) At the same time, independents such as George T. Downing of Rhode Island, T. Thomas Fortune of New York and James Milton Turner of Missouri became involved in Democratic party affairs. The 1884 and 1892 elections of Democrat Grover Cleveland to the presidency provided African Americans with the opportunity to emerge at the national level. Cleveland appointed them to minor, but highly visible, jobs in the national government. What evolved after Cleveland's second election was the creation of two national African-American Democratic organizations, the National Colored Democratic Association and the Negro National Democratic League. These groups functioned in various capacities to sustain the party's evolving position in the African-American community, as well as to sponsor the party's standard bearer, William Jennings Bryan, in two national elections.

In 1912, African Americans became fully involved in the national Democratic party, when presidential candidate Woodrow Wilson reached out in a minor way to secure the African-American vote. Many blacks were disillusioned with the Republicans over patronage discrimination and inaction on civil rights issues and they felt especially betrayed by Presidents Theodore Roosevelt and William Howard Taft, Roosevelt's secretary of war during the BROWNSVILLE, TEXAS INCIDENT of 1906. The Wilson strategy was threefold. First, he appealed to key African-American leaders such as William Monroe Trotter and W. E. B. DU BOIS with promises of fair treatment. Second, he recognized several African-American political organizations and groups and their publications as official campaign organs. Finally, he spent money ($52,255.95) to mobilize the northern African-American vote. With these actions, a rudimentary alliance between the African-American community and the national Democratic party took root. Wilson's antiblack actions once in office, such as the segregation of the federal workforce, stalled the emerging alliance, but did not shatter it.

Meanwhile, in the first years of the century, urban African-American communities saw a gradual rebirth of the Democratic party. The migration of African Americans to northern cities to find better opportunities put them into a situation where they could be recruited en masse into the urban Democratic political machines. Local clubs such as St. Louis's Negro Jefferson League (c. 1900) and New York's United Colored Democracy (1898) were formed. These organizations tended to be adjuncts of white political clubs which worked to elect Democratic candidates. A new African-American Democratic machine came into being, notably in Chicago and New York. In exchange for electoral support, patronage was dispensed to the African-American community through black leaders, and an occasional black was selected for office at the state and local levels.

This local rebirth led inevitably to a reappearance of African-American Democrats at the national level in the late 1920s and 1930s as full participants in party organizations. The black-Democratic alignment took place slowly in some northern urban areas, in part as a byproduct of involvement in urban and labor union politics, and in a cyclical fashion alternated between fast and slow in other areas. The switch from the Republicans to the Democrats during the Depression years was aided by several other factors: First, the Republicans continued during the 1920s to subordinate black concerns to white unity. They provided limited patronage and refused to act against LYNCHING. Second, the federal government social welfare programs of the 1930s provided massive aid to African Americans hard hit by the economic crisis and improved their living and working conditions. While sometimes conducted on a discriminatory basis, federal relief and work programs were run more fairly than previous state and local initiatives, and they offered blacks a source of income independent of regional elites. Third, Eleanor Roosevelt and other Democratic reformers spoke out against discrimination and made visible gestures of support for blacks.

However, there was no general shift of Democratic party policy during the 1930s. White Southerners remained a fundamental element in the Democratic coalition, and civil rights was not a part of the central New Deal agenda. Despite this, President Franklin D. Roosevelt did reach out to blacks by appointing a "Black Cabinet" following the 1932 election. For the first time, African Americans received visible appointments at the presidential level. Although they were confined to the narrow role of "Negro advisers," this was an important step beyond the minor appointments of Presidents Wilson and Cleveland.

The culmination of the shift in party allegiance was the election of African-American Democrats to Congress, beginning with Chicago's Arthur Mitchell in 1934. This was a harbinger of things to come. African-American Democratic congresspersons steadily increased in number, although there were only a handful of blacks in Congress until the 1970s. The rise to power of Adam Clayton POWELL, Jr., first elected in 1944, signaled a corresponding gain in black presence in party circles. The achievements of African Americans in national Democratic party politics not only solidified and reconstructed the evolving African-American alliance with the Democrats, but eventually played a large part in pulling remaining African-American Republican voters away from that party and into the Democratic coalition.

Beginning with the election of 1936, a majority of African Americans voted for Democratic candidates for president of the United States and other offices, although a majority still identified themselves as Republicans. The solidification of the black-Democratic alliance followed the Democratic party's emergence as a civil rights party. The Roosevelt administration took a few cautious steps, such as the creation of the Fair Employment Practices Commission (FEPC) in 1941, but refused to actively challenge its important white southern constituency. It was in the late 1940s, during the presidency of Harry S. Truman, that party leaders first developed a strong civil rights agenda, such as the creation of the Civil Rights Commission in 1946 and the integration of the armed forces in 1948.

By 1948, the majority of blacks identified themselves as Democrats, and black voters, particularly in the urban North and Midwest, were an important source of electoral support. Partly in recognition of northern black support, the national Democratic party adopted a civil rights plank at its convention that year. It prompted a southern walkout, but a strong black vote helped reelect Truman nonetheless.

The election played an important role in shifting the balance of power in the party toward blacks and their white liberal allies. Still, during the 1950s, the Democratic party rested uneasily between its competing constituencies. It was only gradually, in the shadow of the CIVIL RIGHTS MOVEMENT, that the party began to come to terms with its role as defender of black freedom and advancement. Meanwhile, the liberal racial platform of the national party caused some influential white Southerners, beginning with Strom Thurmond in 1964, to leave the Democrats and join the Republican party. The Republican "southern strategy," pioneered by presidential candidate Richard Nixon in 1968, involved the slowing of desegregation and the downplaying of civil rights activity in return for white support. By the end of the 1960s, the majority of white Southerners were no longer reliably Democratic voters.

The most obvious area of civil rights activity was legislation, notably the 1957, 1960, 1964, and 1972 civil rights acts, which the Democratic party sponsored. The 1972 act was championed by an African-American Democrat, Rep. Augustus F. Hawkins. When a conservative Supreme Court circumscribed the 1964 and 1972 acts in 1987, the Democratic party sponsored the 1988 and 1991 Civil Rights Restoration Acts. These latter acts maintained the intent and integrity of the original ones and emerged at least to some extent as a result of the influence of African-American Democrats.

Besides these landmark pieces of legislature, the Democrats made major appointments that altered the future for African Americans. Starting with President John Kennedy and continuing through President Bill Clinton, Democratic presidents have made major appointments to the bureaucracy and executive staff and put members of the black community into critical and powerful positions. President Lyndon Johnson, a white Southerner with strong black support, appointed the first African American (Robert WEAVER) to a Cabinet position, and the first African American (Thurgood MARSHALL), to the Supreme Court. The number of African-American appointees increased under another Southerner, President Jimmy Carter, whose election had been assured by a strong black vote, before declining under Presidents Reagan and Bush.

While urban northern blacks remained tied to the Democrats via unions and machine politics, an important element of the absorption of African Americans throughout the South into the Democratic party, once the effort to attach themselves to the national party and its political elites began, was their attempts to reshape and refocus southern "whites only" Democratic state parties. Gradually, African-American satellite Democratic parties began to emerge at the grassroots level. The first major example of this was the South Carolina Progressive Democratic Party (SCPDP), formed in 1944. The SCPDP went to the national Democratic convention that year to urge the party leadership to have the state party in South Carolina change its membership policies, stance, and position on segregation. Although the party did not get far with its challenge, it set the stage for the Mississippi Freedom Democratic Party (MFDP), organized by African Americans and whites in 1964. That year, the MFDP offered a seating challenge to the "whites only" Democratic party at the National Convention in Atlantic City. While its members had little more success than their predecessors, they received the promise of a study commission, and of an integrated state delegation at the next convention, in Chicago.

The MFDP, in turn, inspired the creation of the National Democratic Party of Alabama in 1968. This party was organized by African Americans in the state who had watched the MFDP on national television in 1964 and then carried their own challenge to the National Convention in 1968. They were seated, and their efforts set off a rash of political organizations in other southern states by African Americans to change the composition, outlook, and procedures of the South's white state Democratic parties.

The efforts of black activists, plus the shift of white conservatives to the Republican party, transformed the Democratic parties of the South. White Democrats with liberal racial views predominated. Strong black support helped elect many U.S. senators and state governors who received a minority of white votes; so, too, in 1976 Jimmy Carter carried the South despite winning only a minority of the white southern vote. Additionally, parties became more inclusive and sponsored black candidates. Mississippi even named an African American, Ed Cole, as state party chair in 1992.

During the seventies and eighties, African-American Democrats made unprecedented gains. As political machines and urban white populations declined, African Americans began to be elected to political office. By 1990, the nation's three largest cities had Democratic African-American mayors. Similarly, African-American community organization, augmented by population shifts and legislative redistricting, made possible the election of thirty-nine African Americans to Congress by 1992.

The alliance between the African-American community and the Democratic party has been strained in recent years.

During this time, there were also new and innovative efforts by African-American Democrats to transform the party and put the alliance on a stronger basis. Black Democratic organizations and caucuses mushroomed in number and size. As early as 1968, there were convention maneuvers to nominate certain delegates as presidential candidates. Efforts were made to nominate Georgia representative Julian BOND as vice president, while Rev. Channing Philips of Washington, D.C., gathered the largest number of presidential delegates among blacks. The effort soon fizzled. In January 1972, Shirley Chisholm announced that she would run in the Democratic primaries for president. This novel venture signaled a shift for African-American national politics; previously, blacks had run for the presidency only on minor party tickets, but now an African American launched a major effort on the Democratic ticket. Chisholm ran in nearly half the state primaries and captured more than 350,000 votes and 35 delegates, although she released them during the convention.

Chisholm's efforts foreshadowed the most significant black Democratic effort at remaking the party, the presidential campaigns of Jesse JACKSON in 1984 and 1988. In 1984, Jackson was never in contention for the nomination (the majority of blacks supported front runner Walter Mondale), but ran a strong campaign, capped by a well-received speech at the Democratic Convention. His presence sparked increases in black interest and voter registration. In 1988, Jackson, acting as the leader of a "Rainbow Coalition" of liberals and dispossessed groups, was a serious candidate, and received over seven million votes, winning several primaries. The success of Jackson's 1988 effort was partly responsible for the naming of an African American, Ron Brown, as national party chairman. Jackson's campaigns established him (and, symbolically, blacks in general) as a powerful though ambiguous figure in the party. While his assistance in rallying voter support was sought, his conservative opponents criticized him for splitting the party and making radical demands. Jackson helped make other African-American candidates credible. In the 1992 primaries, another African American, Gov. L. Douglas Wilder of Virginia, made an abortive effort, withdrawing shortly before the start of the primary season.

The alliance between the African-American community and the Democratic party has been strained in recent years, as blacks resist having their votes taken for granted and white Democrats seeking conservative and moderate white votes distance themselves from black issues at times. Bill Clinton, for example, was accused by black leaders of downplaying black interests in his successful bid for the presidency in 1992. Still, a larger proportion of the black vote than that of any other large ethnic group continued to go to the Democrats. Clinton's own victory in the Democratic primaries was made possible partly by large-scale black electoral support, and in the general election, an estimated 82 percent of blacks who voted did so for the Democratic candidate. Clinton responded by appointing more blacks to his cabinet than any previous president. Whether the black-Democratic alliance will continue or dissolve depends on the new urban crisis and the response of new generation Democrats to the challenges that these issues present. To date, however, African-American Democrats have achieved much in and through their political party.

BIBLIOGRAPHY

Bunche, Ralph J. *The Political Status of the Negro in the Age of FDR.* Chicago, 1983.

Field, Phyllis. *The Politics of Race in New York: The Struggle for Black Suffrage in the Civil War Era.* Ithaca, N.Y., 1982.

Frye, Hardy. *Black Parties and Political Power: A Case Study.* Boston, 1980.

Grossman, Lawrence. *The Democratic Party and the Negro: Northern and National Politics, 1868–1892.* Urbana, Ill., 1976.

Holt, Thomas. *Black over White: Negro Political Leadership in South Carolina During Reconstruction.* Urbana, Ill., 1977.

Link, Arthur S. "The Negro as a Factor in the Campaign of 1912." *Journal of Negro History* 32 (January 1947): 81–89.

Miller, J. Erroll. "The Negro in National Politics in 1968." In P. W. Romero, ed. *In Black America.* Washington, D.C., 1969.

Walton, Hanes, Jr. *Black Politics : A Theoretical and Structural Analysis.* Philadelphia, 1972.

———. "The Democrats and African Americans: The American Idea." In Peter B. Kovler, ed. *Democrats and the American Idea: A Bicentennial Appraisal.* Washington, D.C., 1992, pp. 333–348.

———. "The National Democratic Party of Alabama and Party Failure in America." In Kay Lawson and Peter Merkl, eds. *When Parties Fail.* Princeton, N.J., 1988.

Weiss, Nancy J. *Farewell to the Party of Lincoln: Black Politics in the Age of FDR.* Princeton, N.J., 1983.

Wood, Forrest G. *Black Scare: The Racist Response to Emancipation and Reconstruction.* Berkeley, Calif., 1983.

— HANES WALTON, JR. AND MERVYN DYMALLY

DENMARK VESEY CONSPIRACY, THE

Denmark Vesey (c. 1767–1822), born in Africa or the Caribbean, was an enslaved carpenter in Charleston when he won $1,500 in a lottery in 1799 and bought his freedom for $600 from slave trader Joseph Vesey. Passing up a chance to return to Africa, he opened a woodworking shop in Charleston and committed himself to the African-American freedom struggle. Vesey was an avid Bible reader, fluent in several languages, and he continually preached to his friends that blacks should be equal to whites. In the winter of 1821–1822 he began organizing for an armed revolt. He recruited enslaved artisans from diverse occupations—carters, sawyers, mechanics, lumberyard workers—and blacks from different religious, ethnic, and language groups within the area's varied community.

Vesey met with his recruits in the carpentry shop and in the local African church, formed several years earlier after whites had expelled blacks from the Methodist Church. He exhorted them to action, using the Bible, the French and Haitian revolutions, and the U.S. congressional debates about slavery in Missouri to support his argument. The planners apparently wrote several letters to Saint-Dominique requesting assistance in the uprising scheduled for mid-July. They planned to take the arsenal and guardhouse in Charleston and then start several fires. As whites left their homes, Vesey and his lieutenants would kill them before they could assemble.

But one recruit approached by Vesey's allies informed his master on May 30, and white authorities, disbelieving at first, questioned suspects until the full outline emerged. When word leaked out, Vesey moved the date forward to the night of Sunday, June 16. The organizers destroyed all papers regarding their design, but it was too late. Further slave confessions and testimony of a black spy in the African Church soon revealed details of the revolt, and arrests began.

During the summer of 1822, the authorities executed thirty-seven black Carolinians and deported forty-three more. Vesey was captured on July 2, after refusing to confess. Gullah Jack Pritchard, the respected conjure man responsible for mobilizing less acculturated African newcomers in the countryside, tried to continue the revolt and free the jailed rebels, but he, too, was captured and hanged. Officials also imposed fines and short prison terms on four white participants found guilty of "inciting slaves to insurrection."

In the year following the revolt, frightened South Carolina legislators passed a series of laws restricting the movement of African Americans, including a Negro Seamen Act ordering all free black sailors to be jailed while their ships were in port. Other southern states followed suit, and when federal courts eventually ruled such laws unconstitutional, it only fueled the debate over states' rights. The fearful white reaction to Vesey's plot has led a few historians to suggest that the conspiracy was imaginary—entirely the product of paranoia among slaveholders. While white hysteria cannot be discounted, neither can the evidence and logic for a well-planned revolt. Some Americans have recalled Vesey as a patriot and martyr; others portray him as a dangerous agitator. Not surprisingly, a proposal in modern Charleston to commemorate Denmark Vesey with a public portrait aroused heated debate.

BIBLIOGRAPHY

Aptheker, Herbert. *American Negro Slave Revolts.* New York, 1943.

Killens, John Oliver. *The Trial Record of Denmark Vesey.* Boston, 1970.

Lofton, John. *Denmark Vesey's Revolt: The Slave Plot That Lit a Fuse to Fort Sumter.* Revised ed. Kent, Ohio, 1983.

Wade, Richard C. "The Vesey Plot: A Reconsideration." *Negro Digest* 15 (1966): 28–41.

— PETER H. WOOD

DETROIT, MICHIGAN

Detroit was founded in 1701 by Antoine de la Mothe Cadillac, as part of the French Empire in North America. Acquired by the British at the end of the French and Indian War in 1763, the city remained under English control until 1796, when after Jay's Treaty it was turned over to the United States. It is not clear when the first blacks arrived in Detroit, but they began migrating to Michigan in the early 1800s. White Detroiters owned slaves, although the Northwest Ordinance of 1787 officially banned slavery in the territories. The

1810 census reported seventeen slaves in the city. In the 1820s there were sixty-seven blacks in town, 4.7 percent of the population.

In 1827 Michigan passed a BLACK CODE that required all African Americans to have a valid, court-attested certificate of freedom and to register with the county clerk. Blacks were required to pay a $300 bond of good behavior, although most actually evaded paying. The law's ostensible purpose was to protect blacks from slavehunters, but its real purpose was to discourage black migration. In 1833 the city had its first major racial disturbance, called the Blackburn riot. After law enforcement officials arrested a fugitive slave couple, Thornton and Ruth Blackburn, in order to return them to Kentucky, blacks attacked the sheriff, who later died from his injuries, and a riot ensued. The Blackburns escaped to Canada. Although more than thirty blacks were arrested, some uninvolved in the conspiracy, none was convicted.

In 1837, the same year that Michigan became a state, its state legislature abolished slavery. The Detroit Anti-Slavery Society was founded that year. Detroit established itself as a major terminal of the UNDERGROUND RAILROAD. Black abolitionists—such as Episcopal Rev. William Monroe, who eventually emigrated to Liberia; George DeBaptiste, a prominent businessman; William Lambert, later a supporter of John Brown; and Henry Bibby, a fugitive slave who eventually sought refuge in Canada—were active in the Colored Vigilance Committee, formed in 1840.

Black migration to Detroit was small until the mid-1840s, but by 1850 there were 587 blacks in the city. The first black community was located on the banks of the Detroit River, at the foot of Woodward Ave. The black area would expand north and a little east over time, but never west across Woodward. The first black church, Second Baptist, was established in 1836, in reaction to segregation in white churches. Bethel African Methodist Episcopal was organized in 1841, and St. Matthew's Episcopal, with Monroe in the pulpit, in 1846. In 1843 the community offered a Young Men's Debating Club, a reading room, a library, and a temperance society. An Afric-American Philharmonic Association opened in 1850. The churches also housed black schools and served as political halls. While blacks were denied suffrage, in 1855 they were given the right to vote in school board elections.

The CIVIL WAR was a turning point in Detroit's history. Many Michiganites opposed slavery, but many were also frankly racist. Detroit had pockets of immigrants from the South, and Confederate sympathizers, but the most hostile forces toward blacks in the city were the group of white immigrants from Ireland and Germany, who resented black labor competition. In 1863, Detroit had a race riot, the West's only major racial disturbance of the war. A black man, William Faulkner, was accused of molesting two nine-year-old girls, one white and one black. Convicted of rape, he was sentenced to life in prison, whereupon a white mob, mostly Irish and German, attempted to lynch him. Militia officers who came to protect Faulkner fired at the mob in self-defense, and one man was killed. The mob, frustrated in its lynch attempt, moved to the black area of Beaubien St., where they beat the residents, killing two and injuring over twenty, and burned down more than thirty of their houses. White Detroiters condemned the mob and reimbursed blacks for their losses, but Frederick DOUGLASS used the defenselessness of Detroit blacks as an example of the need for black soldiers. After 1863, 895 black Michiganites, many from Detroit, joined the Union Army.

The Civil War was a turning point in Detroit's history. Many Michiganites opposed slavery, but many were also frankly racist.

Between 1860 and 1870, Detroit's black population increased sevenfold, and continued to climb thereafter, due largely to migrants from Canada, rural Michigan, and elsewhere. Twenty-eight percent of the overall black population, representing the majority of the non-native-born Michiganites, came from Virginia and Kentucky. The migrants from Kentucky had generally been enslaved and had worked in agriculture. Mostly illiterate single people, they found jobs as unskilled laborers. The Virginians were free black family groups, among them a few professionals and many mechanics and tradespeople, who left the industrialized areas of Virginia to escape the state's harsh black codes. Between the two groups there were class tensions, and they frequented different churches.

By 1870, 85 percent of Detroit's blacks lived in the old quarter and an enclave called Kentucky, around Kentucky St., north of Jefferson Ave. Although the neighborhood was not majority black, blacks were confined to shabby tenements and dilapidated houses. Although blacks of mixed ancestry could vote as early as 1866, and some blacks did so illegally, black efforts to secure the vote were repeatedly voted down in Michigan until 1870, when the FIFTEENTH AMENDMENT was passed. The public schools, despite orders of the state legislature, remained segregated until the following year.

Once blacks were enfranchised, however, they immediately organized a Colored Republican Club at the ward level. In 1875 and 1876, Samuel Watson became Detroit's first African-American elected official when he was elected to the Board of Estimate, the city legislature's upper house. In 1884, Watson became the first northern black delegate to the Republican National Convention. In 1883, a group of blacks started the weekly *Plaindealer* as the voice of black protest, black business, and black Republicanism. It was one of the first organs to substitute the term "Afro-American" for "Negro." One of its founders, and the organizer of the protest group Afro-American League, was Robert Pelham, Jr., Detroit's leading black politician in the 1880s. After he left to take a position in the Federal Land Office in 1889, David Augustus Straker became Detroit's chief black leader. Straker, a former dean of Allen University Law School in South Carolina, argued civil rights cases and helped found the Detroit Industrial and Financial Cooperative Association and the National Federation of Colored Men. In 1892 he was elected Wayne County circuit court commissioner (judge). The same year, William W. Ferguson was elected to the Michigan legislature. The seat would be held by blacks until 1900.

After the turn of the century, the demography of black Detroit again shifted, as blacks from the deep South began to migrate. The southern-born population, which had been stable for thirty years, increased by 10 percent, relative to the Michigan-born population, between 1900 and 1910. The automobile and other industries, which hired few blacks, spurred the growth of secondary industries which used black labor. By 1915, increased industrial demand due to World War I, as well as a cutoff of immigration from Europe, induced Henry Ford and other industrialists to employ blacks in large numbers. The availability of jobs at $5 per day, advertised by handbills and by labor agents sent south by Ford, provoked a mass migration to Detroit. Black organizations like the Detroit Urban League were set up to find jobs and housing for the new arrivals. The city's black population, 5,000 in 1910, reached 120,000 in 1930.

While blacks toiled in the most difficult and unpleasant positions in industry, with abysmal housing conditions, the relatively high industrial wages they received, and their separation from white society made possible the growth of an independent black economy. Detroit's black middle class, built on the patronage of black workers, was one of the largest in the nation. Black Republicans, thanks partly to contributions by Henry Ford, were increasingly influential in the party. In 1930, Charles Roxborough was elected to the Michigan state senate, the first African American to serve there.

Competition for jobs and housing sparked widespread racial tension. Detroit was a center of the KU KLUX KLAN in the 1920s. In 1925, when Dr. Ossian Sweet, an African American, bought a house in a white neighborhood, a white mob surrounded his house. Sweet fired out in self-defense and killed a white man. Defended by Clarence Darrow, Sweet and his relatives charged in the shooting were acquitted. During the 1930s, right-wing antiblack leaders Father Coughlin and Gerald L. K. Smith were based in the Detroit area.

The collapse of the economy during the 1930s left many blacks unemployed and ill-housed. Since the flow of friends and relatives from the South looking for work continued, conditions for Detroit blacks worsened. As competition for housing increased, many blacks were forced into the Black Bottom neighborhood, also known as Paradise Alley. The automobile industry cut down its hiring of blacks. Nevertheless, the black community continued to develop. In 1936, publisher/entrepreneur John Sengstacke, who later put together a chain of black newspapers, created the *Michigan Chronicle,* which became the major source of news for black Detroit. Both mainstream and heterodox black religious denominations flourished in Detroit. The Rev. James Francis Marion Jones (Prophet Jones), who arrived in the city in 1938, became a popular cult leader/radio evangelist, although his claim of six million followers seems exaggerated. Of more lasting significance was the NATION OF ISLAM, founded by W. D. FARD about 1930 and led after his death by Elijah MUHAMMAD.

However, by far the best-known black Detroit resident in the first half of the twentieth century was Joe Louis, who moved to Detroit at the age of twelve. The heavyweight BOXING champion from 1935 through 1949, Louis began his career in local Detroit clubs, and his swift rise to boxing eminence was aided by John Roxborough, a black Detroit businessman.

In 1938, the United Auto Workers (UAW) was able to get a contract with General Motors. Despite the hostility of white workers, the union promoted black unionists such as Horace Sheffield, Robert Battle, Coleman Young, and Sheldon Tappes to leadership positions. In part through union registration drives, blacks in Detroit, as elsewhere, became an important part of Franklin D. Roosevelt's New Deal coalition. In 1936, blacks elected their first Democratic state Representative, Charles Diggs, Sr.

The coming of WORLD WAR II and the awarding of lucrative defense contracts to Detroit industries sparked massive renewed migration to Detroit. Walter WHITE of the NAACP estimated that 350,000 people, including

50,000 blacks, entered the city between March 1942 and June 1943. Hate strikes by white workers against blacks, and the past refusal of many blacks to join unions in strikes, had left great bitterness. In February 1942, blacks turned to protests and violence when the Sojourner Truth Homes, a federal housing project built for blacks, was suddenly reassigned to whites. The change was eventually canceled, but racial tensions grew as job competition and the housing crisis intensified. The tensions finally exploded into the DETROIT RIOT OF 1943.

After the war, the African-American population of Detroit climbed, doubling again between 1940 and 1950, and reaching 482,000 in 1960, 29 percent of the city's population. The black middle class expanded. In 1959 Berry Gordy founded the MOTOWN Record Corporation, which would become a cultural force, and the city's first black-owned multimillion dollar corporation. It created the "Motown sound," tuneful pop-oriented RHYTHM AND BLUES, and features such groups as the Supremes, the Temptations, the Four Tops, and the Jackson Five. Black performers such as Diana Ross, Smokey Robinson, and Aretha FRANKLIN became superstars in the music industry. Churches also expanded, and the Rev. C. L. Franklin and the Rev. Charles Hill became legends in their own time. The Rev. Albert Cleague also began the Black Messiah Movement in Detroit in 1952, turning his United Church of Christ into the Shrine of the Black Madonna. Detroit had the largest NATIONAL ASSOCIATION FOR THE ADVANCEMENT OF COLORED PEOPLE chapter in America, and blacks were key members of the DEMOCRATIC PARTY coalition led by the UAW. In 1954, blacks elected Charles Diggs, Jr., to the U. S. House of Representatives, and in 1957 they elected the first black city councilman, William Patrick.

However, large-scale discrimination persisted. The Interracial Commission, renamed the Detroit Commission on Community Relations (CCR) in 1953, had no enforcement powers, and the UAW failed to win Fair Employment Practices clauses in its contracts. Decentralization in the auto industry led to rising unemployment. Detroit's police, segregated and almost all white, were notorious for bigotry. Only 3 percent of the 300,000 units of new housing built in the 1950s in Detroit were given to blacks. While large numbers of blacks moved into the formerly Jewish neighborhood on 12th Street, those who tried to move into other all-white neighborhoods were met by mobs and brick-throwers.

Local white residents picket in February 1942 to prevent blacks from moving into the Sojourner Truth Homes, a newly opened federal housing project in Detroit. The disturbances at the site were a grim foreshadowing of the massive Detroit riot of June 20, 1943, during which more than thirty people died. (Prints and Photographs Division, Library of Congress)

During the 1960s, Detroit achieved a somewhat undeserved reputation as a "model city" in terms of race relations. Reform Mayor Jerome Cavanaugh, whose 1961 campaign had been supported in large numbers by blacks angered at his incumbent opponent's policy of random police searches, installed a liberal police commissioner. In five years, Cavanaugh brought in an estimated $230 million in federal money for programs, some designed by city officials, for black Detroiters. Groups such as the Citizen's Committee for Equal Opportunity, founded by UAW head Walter Reuther, worked against discrimination. In June 1963, after black militants planned a civil rights protest march, Mayor Cavanaugh persuaded more moderate groups to participate, and invited the Rev. Dr. Martin Luther KING, Jr., to speak. About 125,000 people participated in the Walk to Freedom, making it the largest civil rights protest up to that time. In 1964, a militant black lawyer, John Conyers, was elected to Congress.

Nevertheless, discrimination persisted. Whites resisted housing integration, and schools were chronically underfunded. Police bigotry proved resistant to change. Poor, unemployed inner-city blacks resented the high prices they faced in stores owned both by whites and by the black middle class, whom they felt were "collaborators" with an oppressive white power structure.

The DETROIT RIOT OF 1967, a gigantic urban rebellion, scarred Detroit physically and destroyed its "model city" image. The alliance of African Americans and white liberals cut, the black community concentrated on electing African-American officials. In 1969, Richard Austin, an African American, ran unsuccessfully for mayor, but in 1973 Coleman Young was elected to the first of five terms as mayor. Mayor Young has reshaped the police force and brought blacks into city government.

Around 1975, Detroit became a black majority city. By 1990, the city had the largest percentage of African Americans of any big city in the United States, but it had lost one-third of its population in the previous twenty years as the auto industry and manufacturing sector declined and more affluent whites and blacks moved to nearby suburbs. Despite the mayor's efforts to stimulate development, symbolized by the Renaissance Center, and revive the local economy through job-creating projects, 34 percent of Detroit's residents were receiving public assistance in 1987. Detroit's large black middle class gave it the highest black median household income in America in the 1980s. Nevertheless, the city experienced chronic double-digit unemployment through the early 1990s as crime rose and neighborhoods decayed.

BIBLIOGRAPHY

Aberbach, Joel. *Race in the City: Political Trust and Public Policy in the New Urban System.* Boston, 1973.

Fine, Sidney. *Violence in the Model City: The Cavanaugh Administration, Race Relations, and the Detroit Riot of 1967.* Ann Arbor, Mich., 1989.

Katzman, David. *Before the Ghetto: Black Detroit in the Nineteenth Century.* Urbana, Ill., 1973.

Levine, David Alla. *Internal Combustion: The Races in Detroit, 1915–1926.* Westport, Conn., 1976.

Rich, Wilbur C. *Coleman Young and Detroit Politics.* Detroit, 1989.

Shogan, Robert, and Tom Craig. *The Detroit Race Riot; A Study in Violence.* Philadelphia, 1964.

Thomas, Richard Walter. *Life for Us Is What We Make It: Building Black Community in Detroit, 1915–1945.* Bloomington, Ind., 1992.

— WILBUR C. RICH

DETROIT RIOT OF 1943

The beginning of WORLD WAR II brought about large movements of African Americans and whites to Detroit to seek employment in defense industries. The city was unprepared to handle the influx, and racial tensions in Detroit were exacerbated by competition for inadequate city housing and recreational facilities. On June 20, 1943, blacks and whites seeking to escape the heat at Belle Isle, Detroit's municipal resort, came to blows. Rumors of violence spread to Paradise Alley, the city's black section, and to working-class white neighborhoods, and that night the city erupted into a full-fledged racial conflict. It would later be considered the first large-scale "modern" urban riot, since African Americans were not simply victims of mob assaults. Instead of concentrating on self-defense against attack, as previously, they themselves actively attacked property and white bystanders.

Meanwhile, blacks outside their own neighborhoods were also victimized by violence, which the city's police were unable, or unwilling, to stop. City authorities were taken by surprise and were slow to call in outside aid. Federal authorities, conversely, were unsure of their authority to intervene without declaring a state of emergency. Admitting that the city was out of control, they believed, would give America's wartime enemies a powerful propaganda weapon. Finally, late on June 21, military police squads were called in to restore order. The riot claimed 34 victims, of whom 25 were black. There were also some 675 injuries and 1,893 arrests. White investigators such as the governor's Fact-Finding Committee blamed the riots on blacks' "militant appeals for equality." However, in response to the riots Mayor Edward Jeffries set up the Mayor's Interracial Committee—the first government group of its kind in the nation—with authority to investigate complaints and to use the courts to enforce antidiscrimination laws.

BIBLIOGRAPHY

Shogan, Robert, and Tom Craig. *The Detroit Race Riot: A Study in Violence.* Philadelphia, 1964.

Thomas, Richard Walter. *Life for Us Is What We Make It: Building Black Community in Detroit, 1915–45.* Bloomington, Ind., 1992.

— GAYLE T. TATE

DETROIT RIOT OF 1967

During the 1960s, Detroit enjoyed a somewhat exaggerated reputation as a model city for race relations. Its liberal mayor, Jerome Cavanaugh, attracted federal aid for antipoverty programs, and city authorities, supplemented by private and church groups, made conscious attempts to reach out to black leaders. However, serious problems of economic inequality, poor housing, and police brutality remained unaddressed.

In the early morning of July 23, 1967, police raided a "blind pig," an illegal drinking establishment, on 12th Street. Patrons were led outside, handcuffed, and forced to wait, as police wagons were delayed reaching the site. A crowd, partly aroused by the shouts of black militants, gathered and confronted the police, who withdrew from the area. Aroused blacks rioted, looting and burning large white-owned sections of the 12th Street area, then moving to other parts of the city. Before long, downtown Detroit was in flames. Police and firefighters were soon overwhelmed. At first, police were ordered not to fire on rioters in hopes that tensions would die down, but as the rebellion spread, the order was reversed. The riot continued through July 23 and 24. Mayor Cavanaugh and Michigan Gov. George Romney were reluctant to authorize federal intervention, but on the morning of July 25, National Guard units, later supported by infantry troops, were brought in. Eventually, rioters targeted both black-owned and white-owned stores. The riot wound down over the following two days. In all, there were 43 deaths, 1,189 injuries, and 7,231 arrests. The riot, the largest during the 1960s, ended Detroit's liberal-black coalition. The riots and the slump in the economy prompted large numbers of Detroiters, mostly white, to move from the city to nearby suburbs. By the mid-1970s, Detroit had an African-American majority and a black mayor, Coleman Young, whose main electoral constituency was poor blacks.

In the early morning of July 23, 1967, police raided a "blind pig," an illegal drinking establishment, on 12th Street. Before long, downtown Detroit was in flames.

BIBLIOGRAPHY

Fine, Sidney. *Violence in the Model City: The Cavanaugh Administration, Race Relations, and the Detroit Riot of 1967.* Detroit, 1989.

– GAYLE T. TATE

DISCIPLES OF CHRIST

The Christian Church (Disciples of Christ) has its roots in the religious movements of the early nineteenth century known as the Great Revival and the Restoration. These movements, involving various new Protestant denominations, shared a concern for the restoration of primitive Christianity and a revival of simple piety. These groups wanted to abolish the rigid demarcations between denominations, an attitude that at times drew hostility from rival PRESBYTERIANS, METHODISTS, and BAPTISTS. The Disciples of Christ was formed in 1832, when the Christians in Kentucky, led by Barton W. Stone (1772–1844), joined with the Disciples, led by Thomas Campbell (1763–1854) and his son, Alexander (1781–1866). Groups with similar beliefs, such as the O'Kelly Christians and the Freewill Baptists, spread such doctrines to the South and West in areas that would later attract many of the Disciples of Christ.

The Disciples initially encouraged African Americans' religious participation, both by slaves who joined their masters' congregations and by free blacks. Alexander Campbell was a slave owner and did not allow the church to oppose slavery, but free blacks were encouraged to join the church; they worshipped in his first congregation at Brush Run, Pa., after 1820. Free blacks in the North and South joined the movement and helped establish interracial congregations in such places as Wheatland, Mich.

The position of African Americans in the Disciples of Christ reflected the complex nature of Campbell's attitudes toward slavery. Blacks who were ordained or appointed as deacons could only serve other blacks. While churches with interracial memberships like the one in Uniontown, N.C., flourished, segregation was maintained internally. If permitted inside the churches, free blacks and slaves most often had to sit in the back in a segregated balcony or gallery. The first wholly African-American congregation was organized in 1834 at Midway, Ky. Black membership there had swelled to the point where the white women's missionary group bought a slave (also named Alexander Campbell) and gave him enough education to lead the church. He later earned enough money to buy the freedom of his wife, Rosa Campbell, who became a leader among women Disciples. By 1860, there were probably about 7,000 black Disciples, most of them in North Carolina, Kentucky, and Tennessee. Since the heritage of the Disciples included searching for freedom from restrictive creeds and exclusion from mainstream churches, African Americans may have used the experience of the Disciples to speak to their condition in American society, despite their treatment in the church.

After EMANCIPATION, many African Americans sought to restructure their lives free of white domination. Many black Disciples left the church for denominations with strong African-American constituencies, such as the Baptist or African Methodists. White Disciples were increasingly uneasy in integrated congregations. As a result, the number of African-American independent Disciples congregations increased. Blacks acquired roles of local consequence and developed regional structures to support their churches. In 1878, Preston Taylor (1849–1931) and H. Malcolm Ayers organized a national convention of black Disciples, called the National Convention of Churches of Christ, which met intermittently through the end of the nineteenth century. Born in slavery, Taylor became a preacher and businessman after the Civil War. He mastered stonecutting and managed a mortuary, cemetery, and recreational park besides going about his work building churches and congregations in Kentucky and Tennessee. In the Carolinas, loose associations of black Disciples were organized, and from this base many churches were established in other states in the East. In other places, local prayer meetings grew in size and importance and were formalized as regional state conventions in the 1890s. However, African Americans neither shared leadership on a national level nor became autonomous within the church as an organized group.

Within the official church hierarchy, the group most active in the black community was the Board of Negro Education and Evangelization, founded in 1890 as a subsidiary of the American Christian Missionary Society. Because the developing black congregations were hampered by their lack of trained ministers, the board tried throughout the second half of the nineteenth century to start a college that would draw a national student body to train for the ministry. Southern Christian Institute (SCI) opened in 1881 in Edwards, Miss. Though it trained ministers, it followed the HAMPTON INSTITUTE model of a self-sustaining industrial school and maintained segregation on campus to please its white benefactors. It merged with the Congregationalist Tougaloo College in 1954. The only remaining black Disciples college is Jarvis Christian College at Hawkins, Tex., established in 1912. SCI was able to train evangelical ministers to serve the African-American communities rapidly dispersing throughout the South and Midwest.

The EXODUSTERS of the late 1870s brought new black populations to Texas, Arkansas, Missouri, and Kansas in the West and to Piedmont Virginia, and West Virginia, and the Carolinas in the East. By the end of the nineteenth century, African Americans comprised about 4 to 5 percent of the Disciples of Christ. The great migration of southern blacks to northern cities, which began in 1914, further depopulated southern black congregations. Because the Disciples of Christ had been an almost entirely rural church, black congregants who left the countryside found few churches in the cities.

The twentieth century brought a gradual restructuring of the church that gave black members more power. African-American congregations were permanently organized as the National Convention of the Disciples of Christ in Nashville in 1917 in response to the formation of the International Convention of the Disciples of Christ, which was established to govern the whole church. The National Convention elected President Taylor its president and agreed to convene once a year as an auxiliary to the International Convention. The convention initiated a period of growth in programs for African Americans in the church, most notably in education, women's groups, and missionary projects. Another prominent leader of the National Convention was Rosa Brown Bracy, who had gained prominence in the church through the Christian Women's Board of Missions. She helped organize the convention and was elected its executive secretary in 1942, the year it changed its name to the National Christian Missionary Convention. In 1945 the body convinced white missionary agencies to work with it collaboratively. This resulted in a large funding increase for work in the black community.

In the 1990s, between 5 and 10 percent of all Disciples of Christ are African Americans. They are active and serve at all levels of church leadership.

In 1968–1969, the church was restructured and renamed the Christian Church (Disciples of Christ). The formal convention structure merged with the General Assembly (formerly the International Convention) and an all-inclusive National Convocation was created, ensuring African Americans fellowship, leadership training, and discussion of issues related to their church life in the context of the total mission of the church. In addition, the Fund for Reconciliation was established to promote black entrepreneurship and the reintegration of African Americans into the church. In response to James Forman's Black Manifesto in 1969, the church doubled its endowment fund to $4 million. In the 1990s, between 5 and 10 percent of all Disciples are African Americans. They remain active and have served at all levels of church leadership.

BIBLIOGRAPHY

Barber, William Joseph. *Disciples Assemblies of Eastern North Carolina.* St. Louis, 1966.

Bracy, Rosa Brown. *A History of the Negro Disciples.* St. Louis, 1938.

Cardwell, Brenda, and William K. Fox. *Journey Toward Wholeness: A History of Black Disciples of Christ in Mission of the Christian Churches.* Vol. I, *From Convention to Convocation: No Longer 'Objects of Mission' but 'Partners in the Work' (1700–1988).* N.p., 1990.

Fox, William J., ed. *The Untold Story: A Short History of Black Disciples.* St. Louis, 1976.

Henry, Kenneth E. "The Black Disciples Heritage: Authentic, Vital and Enduring." *Discipliana* 36, no. 2 (1976).

Lyda, Hap. A History of Black Christian Churches (Disciples of Christ) in the United States Through 1899. Ph.D. Vanderbilt University, 1972.

McAllister, Lester G., and William E. Tucker. *Journey in Faith.* St. Louis, 1989.

— KENNETH E. HENRY

DOBY, LAWRENCE EUGENE "LARRY"

Lawrence Eugene "Larry" Doby (December 13, 1923–), baseball player. Larry Doby was the second African American to play major league baseball and the second to manage a major league team. Born and raised in Camden, S.C. Doby moved to Paterson, N.J., in 1938, where he starred in three sports at Eastside High. During his high school years, he also played semipro baseball. In 1942, after graduation, Doby joined the Newark Eagles of the Negro National League, playing under the name "Larry Walker" to protect his amateur status. During the off-season, Doby attended Long Island University and Virginia Union University. Doby's career was interrupted by naval service from 1944 to 1945. In 1946, he returned to the Eagles, made the league all-star team, and helped lead them to the NNL pennant. According to surviving statistics, Doby hit .378 in the NNL, with 25 home runs in 139 games.

Doby played during the winter of 1946 and '47 with the San Juan Senators in Puerto Rico. In spring 1947, while Doby was playing with the Eagles, the Cleveland Indians of the American League recruited him for their outfield and purchased his contract. Doby joined the team on July 4, 1947, several months after Jackie Robinson had broken the color line of major league baseball with the Brooklyn Dodgers of the National League. Although he faced much of the same brutal racist treatment from fans and other players that Robinson did, Doby received little media attention playing in Cleveland. He batted .301 in 1948, and .318 in that season's World Series. In eleven seasons, playing for Cleveland, Chicago, and Detroit, he batted .283, twice led the league in home runs (1952 and 1954, with 32), and made the all-star team six times. In 1962, at age 38, after retiring briefly, Doby went to Japan to play two seasons for the Chunichi Dragons. He was the second American to play in Japan.

After returning from Japan, Doby worked in Cleveland's Center Field Lounge, and operated a liquor store. In 1967, he was appointed Director of Bicycle Safety for Essex County, N.J. When the Montreal Expos were organized in 1969, Doby joined them as a scout and batting coach. In the winter of 1971 and in 1972, Doby managed a team in Venezuela, but lost his job when he refused to throw a game. In 1978 Doby was named manager of the Chicago White Sox, but he held that position for only 87 games, winning 37 and losing 50. In 1980, Doby became director of community relations with the National Basketball League's New Jersey Nets.

BIBLIOGRAPHY

Moore, Joseph Thomas. *Pride Against Prejudice: The Biography of Larry Doby.* Westport, Conn., 1988.

— GREG ROBINSON

DORSEY, THOMAS ANDREW "GEORGIA TOM"

Thomas Andrew "Georgia Tom" Dorsey (July 1, 1899–January 23, 1993), GOSPEL composer. Born in Villa Rica, Ga., the oldest of three children of Rev. Thomas Madison and Etta Plant Dorsey, Thomas Dorsey obtained his education in the public schools of Villa Rica and Atlanta. His first piano teacher was his mother, from whom he learned enough by age eight to play the pump organ for church services at which his father preached. In his early teens he began piano lessons, four times weekly, with a Mrs. Graves, from whom he learned not only piano technique and musical reading but enough music theory to be able to jot down musical ideas he was already creating. He was encouraged in this aspect of musicianship by the band members who accompanied acts at the 81 Theater, a vaudeville house on Atlanta's Decatur Street, where, since age eleven, he had worked selling soda pop. It was in this capacity that, at age thirteen, he met the legendary Ma Rainey. Other performers he met who were to influence him were pianists Eddie Heywood and Ed Butler, and the comedy team Butterbeans and Susie. Shortly thereafter, Dorsey began playing the house-party circuit in Atlanta.

Desiring a better musical education, Dorsey migrated to Gary, Ind., in 1916, where he worked in a steel mill and played piano in various jazz bands. After returning to Atlanta for the winters of 1917 and 1918, he settled permanently in Chicago in 1919, where he studied for a short while at the Chicago Musical College. From 1923 until 1924, he served as pianist and arranger for

Les Hite's Whispering Serenaders. During this time he composed "Riverside Blues" (1923), recorded by King Oliver's Creole Jazz Band. Around 1924, Dorsey organized his own group, the Wildcats Jazz Band, at the request of J. Mayo ("Ink") Williams of Paramount Records. This group accompanied Ma Rainey on recordings and on tour. While he accompanied Rainey irregularly for a number of years, Dorsey also began a successful association with Tampa Red (born Hudson Whittaker) in 1925. This duo produced the 1928 hit "Tight Like That." It was during this time that Dorsey became known as "Georgia Tom" and "Barrelhouse Tom," because of the raunchy nature of the songs he played.

Although he continued to play in and conduct jazz and blues bands throughout the 1920s, Dorsey's interest was steadily growing toward the new GOSPEL MUSIC created by the southern pentecostal churches, and a prominent form of music in Chicago at this time.

Dorsey then wrote his first gospel song, "If I Don't Get There," which was published in the National Baptist Convention's *Gospel Pearls.* Despite this new conviction, Dorsey returned to the blues world until 1928, when he suffered a nervous breakdown. His second conversion to Christianity—he had been converted as a child in Georgia but in the terminology of the African-American church of the era "backslid" when he began to play secular music—occurred in Chicago, at the 1932 annual meeting of the National Baptist Convention, the largest organization of African-American Christians. During the convention, Rev. A. W. Nix of Birmingham, Ala., delivered a stirring GOSPEL rendition of Edwin O. Excell's "I Do, Don't You?" Not only did Dorsey join the church again, but he decided that he wanted to dedicate his life to writing GOSPEL music.

Though only a few of Dorsey's songs helped to initiate new trends in gospel music, he is nevertheless remembered as the most important person in gospel music to date.

In 1930 Dorsey renounced secular music and became a full-time gospel musician, composing GOSPEL pieces and peddling "song sheets" throughout Chicago. The response was discouraging and he was often the butt of jokes. Notwithstanding these initial rejections, Dorsey organized one of the first GOSPEL choirs at Chicago's Pilgrim Baptist Church in 1931, where his accompanist was the young Roberta Martin, and whose future members included Eugene Smith, leader of the Roberta Martin Singers, and James Cleveland, later known as the "Crown Prince of Gospel." In the next year, Dorsey opened the first publishing house for the exclusive sale of GOSPEL music by African-American composers in the country. The same year, along with Sallie Martin and others, he organized the National Convention of Gospel Choirs and Choruses, which, along with Cleveland's Gospel Music Workshop of America (organized in 1968), annually draws the largest number of GOSPEL musicians and music lovers in the United States. In addition to Martin, Dorsey was aided in the early GOSPEL movement by composers Theodore R. Frye and Kenneth Morris and singer Willie Mae Ford Smith.

In 1932, Dorsey and Frye traveled from Chicago to Indianapolis to organize a gospel choir. When Dorsey arrived in Indianapolis, a telegram informed him that his wife had given birth to a child, but had not survived. Dorsey returned to Chicago, only to find that his newly born daughter had died as well. In his grief, he sat alone in a dark room for three days, emerging to write the song that—after "Amazing Grace"—is the second most popular song in African-American Christendom:

> Precious Lord, take my hand, lead me on, let me stand.
> I am tired, I am weak, I am worn;
> Through the storm, through the night, lead me on to
> the light.
> Take my hand, precious Lord, lead me on.

Dorsey taught this song to his choir at Pilgrim Baptist, and in less than a year it had moved into the folk category, with congregations singing all three stanzas without the benefit of sheet music. Since then, it has been translated into more than fifty languages, and Dorsey conducted it throughout the world.

"Precious Lord" is not unlike most of Dorsey's compositions, in that the text is that of the poor, disfranchised African-American Christian but also speaks to all people. He has a special penchant for imbuing his songs with catchy phrases, such as "I'm Going to Live the Life I Sing About in My Song," "If We Ever Needed the Lord Before, We Sure Do Need Him Now," and the song written for Mahalia JACKSON, who served as his song demonstrator from 1935 to 1946, "There Will Be Peace in the Valley for Me." His melodies were simple, supported by harmonies that did not detract from the text. Dorsey was so instrumental in the development of gospel music that there was a period during the 1930s and '40s when GOSPEL songs were referred to as "Dorseys." For his contributions he was, early on, dubbed the "Father of Gospel."

Though only a few of Dorsey's songs helped to initiate new trends in gospel music, he is nevertheless remembered as the most important person in GOSPEL music to date. He organized gospel music's first chorus and its first annual national convention, founded its first publishing house, established the gospel-music concert tradition, and in recognition of this, he was celebrated in the 1982 documentary *Say Amen, Somebody.*

BIBLIOGRAPHY

Boyer, Horace Clarence. "Analysis of His Contributions: Thomas A. Dorsey, 'Father of Gospel Music.' " *Black World* 23 (1974): 20.

Heilbut, Anthony. *The Gospel Sound: Good News and Bad Times.* 1971. Reprint. New York, 1985.

– HORACE CLARENCE BOYER

DOUGLAS, AARON

Aaron Douglas (May 26, 1899–February 24, 1979), painter and educator. Born in Topeka, Kans., Aaron Douglas graduated from Topeka High School in 1917, then earned his B.F.A. from the University of Nebraska in 1922. While he taught art at Lincoln High School in Kansas City, Mo. (1923–1925), his social circle included future civil rights leader Roy WILKINS, future classical music composer William Levi Dawson, and Ethel Ray (Nance), who became Charles S. Johnson's assistant at *Opportunity* magazine. Ray and Johnson persuaded Douglas to postpone study in France to work in New York. Douglas soon became one of the leading artists of the NEW NEGRO movement, developing a geometric, monochromatic style of depicting African Americans in dynamic silhouettes by synthesizing formal and symbolic elements of West African sculpture with European-American traditions and modern design into a hard-edged, Art Deco-like style.

In 1925, Douglas earned three important distinctions that launched his career—first prize for a front cover illustration of *Opportunity,* first prize in drawing (for *The African Chieftain*) from *Crisis* magazine, and a commission to illustrate Alain LOCKE's anthology *The New Negro.* The following year, Douglas married his high school classmate, educator Alta Sawyer, and illustrated *The Emperor Jones* and the short-lived magazine of African-American art and literature *Fire!!* In 1927, he illustrated *Plays of Negro Life,* edited by Locke and Montgomery Gregory, and *God's Trombones: Seven Sermons in Negro Verse* by James Weldon JOHNSON. Six works in the latter book, along with a portrait, were exhibited at the Harmon Foundation in 1928. Over the next decade, Douglas would illustrate books by Charles S. Johnson, Claude MCKAY, Paul Morand, and Andre Salmon, as well as numerous magazine covers.

In the late 1920s, Douglas studied privately with Fritz Winold Reiss, a German-American artist whose modernist work Douglas had admired in the New Negro issue of *Survey Graphic* (edited by Locke in March 1925). Reiss and Locke encouraged Douglas to look to African art for inspiration and develop his own racially representative work. Through their influence, Douglas received a one-year scholarship (1928–1929) to the Barnes Foundation in Merion, Pa., where he studied both African and modern European art.

In 1930, Douglas painted heroic murals of African-American culture and history in the library at Fisk University in Nashville, the Sherman Hotel in Chicago, and Bennett College in Greensboro, N.C. In 1931 he went to Paris for one year to study independently and with Charles Despiau and Othon Friesz at the Académie Scandinave. While Douglas worked diligently, only one piece from his time abroad is known: *Forge Foundry,* a black-and-white illustration published in the French journal *Revue du monde noir* (1931).

In the 1930s, Douglas based himself in New York as an arts leader and muralist. The year after he was elected president of the Harlem Artists' Guild (1935), he addressed the First American Artists Congress. With sponsorship from New Deal art programs and various grants, Douglas completed several murals, most notably *Aspects of Negro Life,* at the 135th Street Harlem Branch of the New York Public Library (1934); those for the Hall of Negro Life exhibited at the Texas Centennial Exposition (1936); and *Education of the Colored Man,* at the Atlanta City Housing Project (1938). In 1938, Douglas received a travel fellowship to the American South and Haiti from the Julius Rosenwald Fund. He exhibited his paintings of Haitian life at the American Contemporary Art Gallery in New York the following year.

In 1939, Douglas began teaching art at FISK UNIVERSITY, where he served as professor and chair of the Department of Art Education for nearly three decades. During this period, he often divided his time between Nashville and New York, where he completed his M.A. in Art Education at Columbia University Teachers College in 1944 (his fraternal affiliations included Sigma Pi Phi and Kappa Alpha Psi) and received a Carnegie teaching grant in 1951. From the 1930s until the '50s, the Douglases frequently entertained artists and writers at their home at 409 Edgecombe Avenue, known as "the White House of Harlem," because the building's residents included prominent intellectuals and civil rights leaders. Douglas painted many of their portraits, in addition to landscapes.

As founder of the Carl Van Vechten Gallery (1949) at Fisk, Douglas acquired a major gift from Georgia O'Keefe, the Alfred Steiglitz Collection (1949), as well as an important series of portraits of African-Americans, the Winold Reiss Collection (1952), and he brought numerous artists to the university for lectures and exhibitions. Noted for these achievements and his art, Douglas was honored by President John F. Kennedy at a White House reception commemorating the centennial of the Emancipation Proclamation in 1963. In 1972 he became a fellow of the Black Academy of Arts and received its outstanding achievement award. The following year, Fisk University awarded Douglas an honorary degree of Doctor of Fine Arts. After retiring as professor emeritus in 1966, Douglas lectured widely and continued to paint until his death in 1979.

Douglas's work has appeared in many major American museums and galleries and in university and community center exhibitions. Additional solo exhibitions were held at D'Caz-Delbo Gallery (1933); University of Nebraska, Lincoln (1941); People's Art Center, St. Louis (1947); Chabot Gallery, Los Angeles (1948); Riley Art Galleries, New York (1955); University of California, Berkeley (1964); and Mulvane Art Center, Topeka (1970).

BIBLIOGRAPHY

Driskell, David, David Levering Lewis, and Deborah Willis Ryan. *Harlem Renaissance: Art of Black America.* New York, 1987.

Huggins, Nathan Irvin. *Harlem Renaissance.* New York, 1971.

Igoe, Lynn Moody, with James Igoe. *250 Years of Afro-American Art: An Annotated Bibliography.* New York, 1981.

Lewis, David Levering. *When Harlem Was in Vogue.* New York, 1979.

– THERESA LEININGER-MILLER AND LINDA NIEMAN

DOUGLASS, FREDERICK

Frederick Douglass (February 1818–February 20, 1895), abolitionist, journalist, orator, and social reformer. Born Frederick Augustus Washington Bailey to Harriet Bailey, a slave, and an unacknowledged father (perhaps his master Aaron Anthony) in Tuckahoe, Md., Frederick Douglass—he assumed this name in 1838 when he escaped north to freedom—soon became the most famous African American of the nineteenth century. Separated from his family while young, he was a personal slave to several whites during his formative years. Consequently, he early learned self-reliance and began honing the arts of survival. At the same time, he found a sense of belonging through his relationships with various families and individuals, white and black, who liked and encouraged the bright and precocious youth. Ultimately, the lure of freedom and equality proved irresistible and propelled him on an extraordinary journey of both individual achievement and service to his people and his nation.

Taken in 1826 to Baltimore—where, as an urban slave, he could expand his horizons greatly—he taught himself how to read and write with the witting and unwitting assistance of many around him. Similarly, this more open urban environment, with its large and expanding free African-American population, further whetted his desire to learn as much as possible about freedom, including runaway slaves and the abolitionist movement.

Frederick Douglass soon became the most famous African American of the nineteenth century.

Around the age of thirteen, he converted to Christianity, but over time he became increasingly disillusioned with a religious establishment that compromised with and supported evil and injustice, especially slavery and racial prejudice and discrimination. Also around that age, he purchased his first book, *The Columbian Orator,* which deepened not only his understanding of liberty and equality but also the enormous power of rhetoric, as well as literacy. Indeed, throughout his life he firmly believed in the power of the written and spoken word to capture and to change reality.

As a rapidly maturing eighteen-year-old, developing spiritually and intellectually as well as physically, he revealed an intensifying longing to be free that led him to plan an unsuccessful runaway scheme with several fellow slaves. Several months previously he fought Covey, the "Negro breaker"—one versed in subduing unruly slaves—another sign of the depth of that longing. He later portrayed his triumph over Covey as a turning point in his struggle to become a free man. With the aid of Anna Murray, a free African-American woman in Baltimore with whom he had fallen in love, he escaped to freedom. They moved to New Bedford, Mass. (1838); Lynn, Mass. (1841); Rochester, N.Y. (1847); and Washington, D.C. (1872).

In the North, Douglass found it very hard to make a living as a caulker because of racial discrimination and often had to resort to menial jobs. Anna worked hard as well, creating a comfortable domestic niche for a family that eventually included five children: Rosetta, Lewis Henry, Frederick, Jr., Charles Remond, and Annie. Frederick's speeches within the local black communities brought him to the attention of the mostly white abolitionists allied with William Lloyd Garrison, and in 1841 they asked him to join them as a lecturer. An increasingly powerful lecturer and draw for the Garrisonian Massachusetts Anti-Slavery Society, Douglass learned a great deal from his work with such people as Garrison and Wendell Phillips. Most important, he adopted their pacificism and moral suasionist approach to ending slavery and was deeply influenced by their interrelated perfectionism and social reformism. As a good Garrisonian, he argued for disunion and rejected the political approach to ending slavery as a compromise with a proslavery Constitution.

Douglass also began to come into his own as an activist and a thinker. Drawing upon his experiences as a slave, he lambasted slavery and its notorious effects, most notably antiblack prejudice and discrimination in both North and South. As the living embodiment of a small measure of success in the enormous struggle against slavery, he spoke eloquently with uncommon authority. In 1845, his *Narrative of the Life of Frederick Douglass, an American Slave* was published and its huge success, followed by a successful speaking tour of Great Britain, heightened his celebrity immeasurably. Ever conscious of his public persona and his historical image, he carefully crafted both. *My Bondage and My Freedom* (1855) and *Life and Times of Frederick Douglass* (1881; revised 1892), fuller autobiographies, were likewise crucial in this regard.

His stirring narrative and equally stirring oratory derived much of their power and authenticity from Douglass's deep-seated engagement with the plethora of issues confronting blacks north and south, free and slave. His strong involvement in the national Negro convention movement, as well as with various state and local black conferences, furthered his impact and by 1850 made him the principal spokesman for his race. His fierce commitment to egalitarianism, freedom, and justice similarly led him to embrace the women's-rights movement, notably women's suffrage, and to become one of the most important male feminists of the nineteenth century. He attended the first Women's Rights Convention, in Seneca Falls, N.Y., in 1848; on the day of his death, February 20, 1895, he had earlier attended a meeting of the National Council of Women.

Shortly after his return from Great Britain in 1847, Douglass embarked upon a distinguished career in journalism. He edited the *North Star* (1847–1851), *Frederick Douglass' Paper* (1851–1860), *Douglass' Monthly* (1859–1863), and, for a time, the *New National Era* (1870–1874). Complementing the other aspects of his varied public voice and extending its reach and influence, Douglass's work as a journalist furthered his use of the printed word as a tool for agitation and change. Stressing self-reliance, hard work, perseverance, education, and morality, Douglass exemplified the embrace by many African Americans of middle-class values and the American success ethic. Likewise, invoking America's revolutionary tradition, he emphasized the imperative of full black liberation within the confines of the American nation. After 1851, when he formally broke with the Garrisonians and accepted political action against slavery as viable and necessary, he became more politically engaged. By the outbreak of the CIVIL WAR, he supported the REPUBLICAN PARTY.

The tumultuous events of the 1850s convinced Douglass, like untold numbers of his compatriots, that war was unavoidable, the Union cause just, and slave emancipation inevitable. He urged his audience, most notably President Abraham Lincoln, to further ennoble the Union cause by accepting black troops into the Union army and treating them fairly. He exhorted his people to support fully the Union cause and to struggle ceaselessly to ensure that Union victory would mean emancipation and the necessary conditions for black progress. His often arduous efforts to recruit black Union troops, who braved strong white hostility and mistreatment, showed him grappling intensely with the central and complex issue of African-American identity. African Americans, he cogently argued, honored their group as well as national heritage and mission through vigorous support of an abolitionist Union cause.

Douglass emerged from the war even more widely known and respected. He continued to urge his nation to deal justly and fairly with his people, even after the nation reneged on its insufficient and short-lived efforts to do so during RECONSTRUCTION. While many blacks questioned his continuing allegiance to the Republican party, Douglass valiantly—albeit unsuccessfully—endeavored to help the party rediscover its humanistic and moral moorings. Appointed to serve as the United States marshal for the District of Columbia (1877–1881), recorder of deeds for the District of Columbia (1881–1886), and chargé d'affaires for Santo Domingo and minister to Haiti (1889–1891), he remained a stalwart Republican.

Over the years, Douglass's status as a comfortable middle-class elder statesman tended on occasion to blind him to the harsh conditions confronting rural, impoverished, and migrant blacks. Still, as in his fiery condemnation of the alarming growth in the number of lynchings of black men in the 1880s and 1890s (often upon the false accusation of an attack on a white woman), it was clear that his commitment to justice never wavered. Likewise, while many women's-rights advocates criticized him for supporting the FIFTEENTH AMENDMENT, which failed to enfranchise women as it enfranchised black men, Douglass contended that the greater urgency of the black male need for the vote and its greater likelihood of passage made support imperative. After its passage, he continued his efforts on behalf of women's rights and sought to heal the rift within the movement.

When Douglass married Helen Pitts, his white secretary, in January 1884, a year and a half after the death of his first wife, they endured much criticism from many blacks and whites, including close family members. Nonetheless, Douglass, the quintessential humanist, steadfastly articulated his commitment to a composite American nationality, transcending race, as an integral component of his vision of a democratic and egalitarian country. When others criticized him for a lack of race spirit, Douglass, refusing to be imprisoned within a racialist universe, claimed ultimate allegiance to the human race.

Yet he also fully understood and vividly personified his people's struggle from slavery to freedom, from obscurity and poverty to recognition and respectability. His enduring legacy to his people and all Americans is best captured in his lifelong and profound dedication to the imperative of agitation and concerted action: "If there is no struggle," he declared, "there is no progress."

BIBLIOGRAPHY

Andrews, William L., ed. *Critical Essays on Frederick Douglass.* Boston, 1991.

Blassingame, John W., et. al., eds. *The Frederick Douglass Papers.* New Haven, Conn., 1979–.

Blight, David W. *Frederick Douglass' Civil War: Keeping Faith in Jubilee.* Baton Rouge, La., 1989.

Douglass, Frederick. *Life and Times of Frederick Douglass: Written by Himself.* 1892. Reprint. New York, 1962.

———. *The Life and Writings of Frederick Douglass.* 5 vols. New York, 1975.

———. *My Bondage and My Freedom.* 1855. Reprint. New York, 1969.

———. *Narrative of the Life of Frederick Douglass, an American Slave, Written by Himself.* 1845. Reprint. New York, 1968.

Martin, Waldo E., Jr. "Frederick Douglass: Humanist as Race Leader." In Leon Litwack and August Meier, eds., *Black Leaders of the Nineteenth Century.* Urbana, Ill., 1988, pp. 59–84.

———. *The Mind of Frederick Douglass.* Chapel Hill, N.C., 1984.

McFeely, William S. *Frederick Douglass.* New York, 1990.

Preston, Dickson J. *Young Frederick Douglass: The Maryland Years.* Baltimore, 1980.

Quarles, Benjamin. *Frederick Douglass.* 1948. Reprint. New York, 1968.

Sundquist, Eric J., ed. *Frederick Douglass: New Literary and Historical Essays.* New York, 1990.

— WALDO E. MARTIN, JR.

DOVE, RITA

Rita Dove (August 28, 1952–), poet. Rita Dove was born in Akron, Ohio. She graduated *summa cum laude* from Miami University in Oxford, Ohio in 1973, then spent the following year in Tubingen, Germany, as a Fulbright scholar. In 1975 she enrolled in the Writers' Workshop at the University of Iowa, where she received her Master's in Fine Arts degree two years later. In 1981 Dove joined the English Department at Arizona State University, where she continued to teach creative writing until 1989. In that year she accepted a position at the University of Virginia, which named her Commonwealth Professor of English in 1992.

Dove's first volume of poems, *Yellow House on the Corner,* was published in 1980. It was followed in 1983 by *Museum,* which displays a more conscious awareness of the conventions of artistic and historical practice. Three years later, Dove published *Thomas and Beulah* (1986), two versions of the story of two ordinary African Americans. The volume, which loosely narrates the lives of Dove's grandparents, was awarded the Pulitzer Prize in Poetry in 1957. *Thomas and Beulah* is a turning point in Dove's career for more reasons than its award-winning status. Not coincidentally, its narrative style emerges just after Dove's first published foray into fiction, *First Sunday* (1985), a collection of stories. Dove had also published one novel, *Through the Ivory Gate* (1992), the story of a black woman whose work as a puppeteer evokes painful childhood memories of disturbing cultural significance. What *First Sunday* and *Through the Ivory Gate* may lack in believable dialogue and depth of characterization is made up for in the echoes of *Grace Notes* (1989). In these poems, each moment is filled by the persistent ringing of carefully culled metaphor.

Dove's gifts as a poet were most fully acknowledged in 1993 when she was appointed Poet Laureate of the United States, the first black writer ever to have been so honored.

More public attention has fallen on Dove's career than on that of any other contemporary African American poet. Recognized for her virtuoso technical ability, Dove represents a generation of poets trained in university writers' workshops who are sometimes chastised for their formal competence at the expense of emotional depth. Dove has distinguished herself in her capacity to filter complex historical and personal information through precise selections of poetic form. In this, she is most closely allied to black poets such as Gwendolyn BROOKS, Michael S. Harper, and Robert Hayden. Her unusual range of subject matter, thematically and geographically, has earned her a reputation as as black writer unafraid to set African-American culture within a global context. Dove's gifts as a poet were most fully acknowledged in 1993 when she was appointed Poet Laureate of the United States, the first black writer and the youngest poet ever to have been so honored.

BIBLIOGRAPHY

Rampersad, Arnold. "The Poems of Rita Dove." *Callaloo* 9, no. 1 (Winter 1986): 52–60.

Taleb-Khyar, Mohamed B. "An Interview with Maryse Condé and Rita Dove." *Callaloo* 14.2 (Spring 1991): 347–366.

— GINA DENT

DRAKE, ST. CLAIR

St. Clair Drake (January 2, 1911–June 14, 1990), sociologist. St. Clair Drake was born in Suffolk, Va., where his father was a Baptist pastor in small rural parishes. Although Drake knew his father only during his first thirteen years, the elder Drake had a decisive influence on his son's later development. John Gibbs St. Clair Drake had been born in Barbados, but studied for the Baptist ministry in Lynchberg, Va. During World War I, Reverend Drake followed his congregation to Pittsburgh, where many had migrated to work in the steel mills.

In Pittsburgh, the family lived in a "middle class" house, with access to a well-stocked library. There Drake formed his habit of wide reading on many subjects. He attended a school where he was the only African-American child, and listened, fascinated, to discussions of religion and race between his father and other preachers.

His parents were divorced in 1924, and Drake accompanied his mother back to Virginia. He attended Booker T. Washington High School in Staunton, Va., where he had his first encounters with southern segregation.

From 1927 through 1931, Drake attended Hampton Institute, in Virginia, where he was an outstanding student. Central to his subsequent career was the influence of a young professor, W. Allison Davis, who introduced him to anthropology. After graduating, Drake taught high school in rural Virginia, traveling to Philadelphia every summer and investing his small earnings in a few books on anthropology. During those summers, he worked and studied with the American Friends Service Committee, a Quaker organization.

In summer 1931, he demonstrated the quiet courage that remained characteristic of him. Some of the Friends initiated a "peace caravan," and Drake and his friend, Enoch Waters, traveled with it through the South, attempting to win support for disarmament and international cooperation. Remarkably, the trek did not terminate in disaster.

In 1935, while still teaching in Virginia, Drake became a member of a research team that was making a social survey of a Mississippi town. Davis had questioned whether the ideas of the white anthropologist, W. Lloyd Warner, concerning class and caste, were applicable to blacks and whites in the South. The outcome was Drake's earliest published research, which was incorporated into Davis's *Deep South.* Working with senior anthropologists, Drake conducted much of the research and prepared the manuscript for publication. After *Deep South,* Drake's closeness to those whom he studied caused him always to describe himself as a "participant-observer."

In 1937 Drake entered the University of Chicago on a Rosenwald Fellowship for further studies in anthropology. Intermittently, he continued to study there over the next fifteen years. In 1942 he married Elizabeth Johns, a white sociologist. *Black Metropolis,* his best-known work, appeared in 1945. Coauthored with Horace Cayton, it is a pathbreaking work of description and analysis of African-American life in Chicago.

In 1946, Drake joined the faculty of the newly established Roosevelt College (later University) in Chicago, where he remained until 1968. This college had been created as a protest against the racially restrictive Central YMCA College, its predecessor.

Drake was increasingly interested in Africa and the African diaspora. His doctoral dissertation for the University of Chicago, "Value Systems, Social Structure, and Race Relations in the British Isles," involved one year of research of the "colored" community of Cardiff, Wales, placing that community into the larger context of Africa and the South Atlantic. During that year in Britain, Drake became a close associate of George Padmore, the West Indian pan-Africanist and advisor to Kwame Nkrumah. After Ghana's independence, from 1958 to 1961, Drake became Professor of Sociology at the University of Ghana, while still holding his professorship at Roosevelt University.

In 1969 he accepted a long-standing invitation to become Professor of Sociology and Anthropology and Director of African and Afro-American Studies at Stanford University in California. The Stanford period was most notable for the publication of the vast and erudite *Black Folk Here and There* (two vols., 1987–1990). Using an enormous array of sources, it presents the thesis that prejudice against blacks is a relatively recent phenomenon, arising first during the Hellenistic period.

BIBLIOGRAPHY

Drake, St. Clair. "In the Mirror of Black Scholarship. W. Allison Davis and *Deep South.*" *Harvard Educational Review,* Monograph #2 (1974): 42–54.

———. Autobiographical manuscripts held in the Schomburg Collection, New York Public Library.

— FRANK UNTERMYER

DRAMA

African-American drama draws from at least two sources: the heritage of Africa and that of Europe. On the North American continent, those cultures met, interacted with Native American traditions and a new physical environment, and produced a culture that, while related to both AFRICA and Europe, is nonetheless distinct from both. For the historian of African-American drama, this heritage poses a series of complex questions: What kinds of events count as drama, in that Europeans have come to define drama primarily as a written text, while Africans have placed more value on the communicative capacity of such ephemeral elements as dance, music, and spectacle? If one focuses on written forms, then for whom have black playwrights written? What are the indicators—in terms of content and/or style—that signify the choice of a primarily black, white, or mixed audience? How have dramatists coded or masked their intentions so as to speak to these different audiences simultaneously?

If emphasis is placed on performance rather than upon a written script, then African-American drama begins on the slave ships, when Africans were forced to sing and dance in order to ensure their health and salability and to provide entertainment for white crewmen. SLAVE NARRATIVES and travelers' accounts attest to the fact that plantation owners encouraged their property to perform because they thought that occasional merry-making increased productivity and lessened the possibility of revolt, and because they seemed genuinely fascinated by the musical idioms, gestures, and the black body itself, all of which were radically different from what they knew of European tradition.

African-American drama draws from at least two sources: the heritage of Africa and that of Europe.

Long before black men were allowed on American stages, a caricature stage Negro made an appearance. The English dramatist Isaac Bickerstaff introduced a lazy, rambunctious West Indian slave in *The Padlock* in 1769; in 1795 the white American James Murdoch followed suit with *The Triumph of Love,* in which a stupid buffoon known as Sambo delighted audiences and initiated a derogatory stereotype that the American public seemingly will not let die. To counter this representation with spectacles more pleasing to "ladies & gentlemen of color," a free black man named Mr. Brown (first name unknown) opened the African Grove Theatre in lower Manhattan in New York City in 1821. This first, professional black theater company mounted productions of Shakespeare, dance and pantomime interludes, and *King Shotaway* (1823), thought to be the first play written and performed by African Americans. Though no script remains today, records indicate that it concerned a slave insurrection in the Caribbean. Produced within a year of the Denmark Vesey slave insurrection in Virginia, the play roused the ire of white spectators to the extent that a group of rowdies intent on "wanton mischief" destroyed the theatre building and forced the company's closure in 1823. With its demise, Ira Aldridge, who had been inspired to join the group after seeing the West Indian actor James Hewlett in *Richard III,* left for Europe where he eventually won gold medals from the Prussian and Austrian heads of state for his superior artistry in Shakespearean tragedies as well as in popular comedies. Sadly, Aldridge became the first of a long line of African-American expatriate artists who found greater acceptance abroad than at home.

The Sambo stereotype would solidify in the 1840s into the minstrel show. According to conventional theater history, minstrelsy began in 1828 when a young white performer named Thomas D. Rice observed an old, deformed Negro singing and dancing. He is said to have borrowed the man's entire performance (including his clothing), thereby initiating what would become an extremely popular form of entertainment—and a pattern of exploitation repeated by many other white performers who reaped great profit from their imitations of black art. More recent scholarship, however, argues that minstrelsy originated not with Rice and his colleagues who claimed that they were accurately depicting real African-American customs, but with black people themselves. In gathering to sing and dance, enact stories, and mock the cultured pretensions of their masters, slaves were creating a form in which improvisation and ecstatic response based upon the interactions of those assembled were more important than a fixed or written text wherein all elements are related to each other by an inviolable logic that does not give any space to the unplanned or unexplained. They were pioneering a form in which language was treasured for its power to stimulate the imagination and emotions. Given slave conditions, they were projecting a metaphysical stance and style that enabled them to survive with their intelligence, humor, and dignity relatively intact. But in performing for white observers, these slaves masked their behavior so that the owners could interpret their efforts as black incompetence rather than as a critique of what appeared to the slaves as white ridiculousness. Thus, white minstrel performers were offering white audiences a parody of black behavior that was, unbeknownst to them, already a parody of white customs. By the 1860s when black men were allowed to perform onstage, audiences had grown so accustomed to the black-face image that African Americans had to black up—adding yet another layer of parody.

Because of its topicality, improvised quality, and general construction as entertainment aimed at the masses, the minstrel show is usually not considered drama. Yet, it was particularly significant for what would follow, because any playwright wishing to represent African Americans onstage would have to confront the enduring legacy of minstrelsy's grinning darky. Furthermore, it signaled that performance modes rooted in African-American culture were likely to be characterized by masking, evocative language, improvisation grounded in a mastery of technique, episodic structure shaped as much by performer-audience interactions as by logic, as well as by ecstasy, and an ethical/aesthetic stance that seeks to affirm the humane even while it holds opposites in balanced tension.

Masking is at the core of *The Escape; or a Leap for Freedom* by William Wells Brown, who is generally considered the first African American to have a play published. First read from Northern, abolitionist platforms in 1857 by Brown, who was a successful fugitive, this text appears double-voiced, offering contradictory representations to audience members. Undoubtedly, abolitionist attendees at a reading agreed with the representation of slave owners as exploitative and religiously hypocritical, and they sympathized with the mulatto couple who, in fine diction, vow to seek freedom. They probably also found comic relief in Cato, the stereotypical buffoon who uses nonsensical words, pursues gluttonous pleasures, and apes white mannerisms. But Cato is also a trickster who, when beyond his owners' presence, sings freedom songs (in standard English) and cunningly schemes to turn every situation to his own advantage. Thus, when freedom is almost at hand, he jettisons the grinning mask, helps the runaway couple, and makes his own leap to freedom. In his trickstering, Cato seems to represent an independent spirit that will not be contained by social conventions not of his own making. That position could hardly have been a comforting prospect to those Northerners who, despite their antiSLAVERY convictions, believed in black inferiority, and yet, presumably it accurately reflected one attitude found among pre-Civil War blacks. Though the figure of the manipulative buffoon found no place in the theaters patronized by whites, its appearance in one of the earliest black plays identifies masking as an important African-American survival strategy. It is a representation to which African Americans have periodically returned in the musical comedies of Bert Williams and George Walker (*Abyssinia,* 1906; *Bandanna Land,* 1908), and in dramas as different as Garland Anderson's *Appearances* (1925), LeRoi Jones's (Amiri BARAKA's) *The Slave* (1964), Douglas Turner Ward's *Day of Absence* (1965), and Ed Bullins's *The Gentleman Caller* (1969).

The use of theater as an arena for advancing social change continued in the first decades of the twentieth century, when W. E. B. DU BOIS and others organized the pageant *The Star of Ethiopia.* Seeking to teach history to both blacks and whites, Du Bois and his pageant master Charles Burroughs crafted a series of tableaux linking Egyptian and Yoruba cultures with African-American heroes like Nat Turner and with the quest for freedom. Between 1913 and 1925, this pageant involved approximately three thousand people as performers and was performed in four cities before more than thirty thousand people. Not only did the pageant mobilize often competitive community energies, foster racial pride, and indulge a love of spectacle, but it also provided a model of nonprofessional, socially charged art that others would utilize. Thus, for example, inhabitants of Los Angeles mounted "50 Years of Freedom" in 1915 to combat the negative imagery of D. W. Griffith's film *The Clansman,* and in 1974, people dressed in Ku Klux Klan outfits appeared in San Francisco City Hall chambers as part of an effort to ban the display of regalia of groups advocating hate and genocide.

Angelina Weld Grimké's *Rachel* is the first twentieth-century full-length play written, performed, and produced by blacks. In this sometimes melodramatic coming-of-age play, a high-spirited young woman rejects marriage and the possibility of motherhood because she fears that future generations will be unable to escape the racism she has personally experienced. The production provoked a storm of controversy when sponsored by the District of Columbia branch of the NATIONAL ASSOCIATION FOR THE ADVANCEMENT OF COLORED PEOPLE (NAACP) in 1916, because it implicitly defied the NAACP philosophy of racial progress led by an educated, black elite, whom Du Bois had termed "the talented tenth." For some, the play reduced art to the level of propaganda. Thus, when Alain LOCKE, one of the leading theoreticians and promoters of the HARLEM RENAISSANCE, and educator Montgomery Gregory founded HOWARD UNIVERSITY's dramatic art department in 1921, they explicitly espoused an aesthetic that privileged technical beauty or art over social concerns. W. E. B. Du Bois took a different position, arguing both in his writings and his organization of the amateur Krigwa Players that the two were not so easily separated.

Though short-lived (1925–1927), this drama group was significant because it extended Du Bois's efforts and those of Charles JOHNSON to foster formal cultural production and increase readership through contests and publication in the NAACP and Urban League magazines, *Crisis* and *Opportunity.* Additionally, the theater's manifesto propounded a standard of evaluation that would be echoed in the militant sixties. Namely, an authentic black theater had to be "about us . . . by us . . . for us . . . and near us."

Also differing with Locke's and Montgomery's emphasis on art divorced from a strong social referent were a number of women who won most of the drama prizes in the *Crisis* and *Opportunity* contests sponsored between 1925 and 1927. Protest against lynching, the lack of birth-control information, and racial discrimination against returning black World War I veterans were some of the issues that women like Alice Dunbar Nelson, Georgia Douglas Johnson, Mary Burrill, and May Miller dramatized in plays like *Mine Eyes Have Seen* (1918), *Sunday Morning in the South* (1925), *Safe* (c. 1929), *Blue-Eyed Black Boy* (c. 1930), *Nails and Thorns* (1933), *They That Sit in Darkness* (1919), and *Aftermath* (1919). The antilynching dramas are of particular importance because these women, largely deprived of leadership roles in organizations like the NAACP or the Urban League, seemingly viewed the stage as an arena for advancing an important social agenda. Their work formed a continuum with the direct, antilynching campaigns launched by Ida B. WELLS and other black women active in the Women's Club movement from the turn of the century to the early decades of the twentieth century. Additionally, the antilynch play was a genre in which black women predominated, producing more plays than either black men, white women, or white men.

The Great Depression of the 1930s largely stymied African-American efforts to establish their own theaters. One outlet for theatrical interests was the black church, where folk dramas such as "The Old Ship of Zion," "Heaven Bound," or "In the Rapture" began. Popular throughout the Midwest, East, and South, these dramas took their plots from the Bible. Often a given church would mount the same play over a number of years, so that novelty of story line was not an objective. Rather, dramatic appeal rested in the improvisational space allotted to comic byplay, the artistry with which spirituals were rendered, and the affirmation of a sense of communal solidarity in terms of both religious emotions aroused by the actual event and the creative energies marshalled in preparing costumes, sets, and participants for performance. The aesthetic evident in these folks dramas has parallels with such African traditions as festivals, for in both instances a community, sharing a set of beliefs and symbols, gathers to enact itself in a performance balancing fixed and fluid elements. That is, the broad parameters of a known plot, familiar spirituals, and performers whose personalities both onstage and offstage are known to the community are balanced against fluid performance specifics like the particular placement and rendition of individual songs and narrative episodes, the spontaneous extension of humorous moments, and the emotional dynamic between audience and performers. Through this symbolic practice, a value system is reaffirmed, and the individual is offered an opportunity to experience his or her relationship to a community. Started during the Great Depression, folk dramas like *Heaven Bound, Noah's Ark,* or *The Devil's Funeral* can still be witnessed in some black Baptist and fundamentalist churches.

The government inadvertently became another sponsor for dramatic activity during the Depression. Faced with the collapse of financial markets and the unemployment of millions of Americans, in 1935 the federal government established a relief program known as the Works Progress Administration. It included the Federal Theatre Project (FTP) that during its four years of operation annually employed some thirteen thousand theater workers who performed before approximately 65 million people in theaters, parks, schools, hospitals, and churches. With black units in twenty-two cities, FTP not only offered work to black performers, but also provided many of them with their first formal training in acting, directing, writing, and technical design. Offerings ran the gamut from adaptations of mainstream plays to musicals and dramas addressing contemporary social issues. One of its most popular shows with white and black audiences was a "voodoo" *Macbeth* directed by Orson Welles for the New York Negro unit of FTP. In setting this classic in the tropics, Welles was not only continuing the practice of making Shakespeare accessible to people with varying degrees of formal education, but he was also furthering a theatrical convention in which aspects of African-related culture are used to make mainstream fare more exotic or appealing. "Voodoo" *Macbeth* was soon followed by *Swing Mikado,* a jazz version of the Gilbert and Sullivan light opera; in more recent years, black "remakes" of white standards have resulted in such musicals as *The Wiz* (1975; adapted from *The Wizard of Oz*) and Lee Breuer's *The Gospel at Colonus* (1983; adapted from the fifth-century Greek drama *Oedipus at Colonus*).

In addition to delightful spectacles, the FTP also produced serious drama that questioned the fabric of American life. One such drama, *Big White Fog* by Theodore Ward, is a good example of a play that speaks simultaneously to both white and black audiences. Its realistic style with an immediately recognizable physical setting, operation of cause-and-effect within family relationships, and the hero's movement toward greater self-knowledge locates the text within the mainstream of American dramaturgy. The play's cultural specificity resides in its focus on the competing promises of Marcus GARVEY's Back-to-Africa movement, a black capitalism derived from Booker T. WASHINGTON, and socialism within the context of the Depression. Furthermore, its dramatization of intraracial (as well as interracial) color prejudice adds powerful depth, because it captures a reality known painfully well by African Americans, but for the most part hidden from the view of the larger society. Produced first in 1938 by the FTP black unit in Chicago, it aroused a certain degree of controversy because of its seeming support of communism. It was subsequently remounted in New York in 1940 by the short-lived Negro Playwrights Company, which Ward had helped to organize along with other playwrights like Langston HUGHES and Abram Hill (*On Striver's Row,* 1940; *Walk Hard,* 1944). Theodore Ward subsequently found critical praise and limited audience success with his historical drama about Reconstruction, *Our Lan'.* Begun in 1941, it was first produced off-Broadway at the Henry Street Settlement Playhouse in 1946.

Started during the Great Depression, folk dramas like Heaven Bound, Noah's Ark, *or* The Devil's Funeral *can still be witnessed in some black Baptist and fundamentalist churches.*

Further fueling conservative concern about art and politics was a form of experimental theater known as the Living Newspaper. The format was initially conceived by FTP director Hallie Flanagan, who, like many other white American artists had been impressed by the theatrical experimentation she witnessed in Germany and Russia in the 1920s. The Living Newspaper hired unemployed workers to research current events that were then enacted by large casts in an episodic, panoramic fashion with minimal sets or costumes, in effect producing a kind of theatricalized newsreel. One of the first Living Newspapers to run afoul of its government sponsors was *Ethiopia,* which was closed after an initial preview because of fears that its powerful dramatization of Benito Mussolini's invasion of the African nation of Ethiopia would provoke protests and jeopardize relations with the Italian government, with which the nation was then at peace. Politics also seems to have been the explanation for not producing Abram Hill and John Silvera's script *Liberty Deferred* (1938), which utilized many of the Living Newspaper techniques to dramatize the African-American history. Though FTP fare was very popular with the American public, it nonetheless drew the suspicions of congressmen who regarded this first attempt at subsidized public art as a haven for allegedly anti-American, communist sympathizers. With the economy improving as the nation moved toward active participation in WORLD WAR II, the Dies Committee killed the Federal Theatre Program in 1939.

Langston Hughes's *Don't You Want to Be Free?* (1937) stands in marked contrast to Ward's *Big White Fog.* While Ward's play had been sponsored by the Federal Theatre, Hughes's was produced by his own leftist-affiliated Harlem Suitcase Theatre. Like much of the agitprop, or agitation-propaganda play writing of the Great Depression, his play utilizes minimal scenery, a small pool of actors to play a large number of roles, and direct address to the audience, designed to encourage them to undertake a specific action. In this case, the text argues for an acceptance of working-class solidarity across racial barriers. The play's distinctiveness is marked by its use of poetry, gospel and blues songs, dance, and vignettes to suggestively chronicle black history from Africa to the United States. The validation of culture that Hughes had begun in experimenting with poetic form in *The Weary Blues* (1926) was here extended to the theater; his use of an episodic structure, knitted together and propelled by the emotional energy of black music as well as by the evocative intensity of language, provided a model that more contemporary playwrights like Amiri Baraka and Ntozake Shange would emulate in the 1970s. Hughes's later deployment of religious experience, which found commercial success in *Black Nativity* (1961), helped inaugurate the contemporary gospel drama genre, practiced by such artists as Vinnette Carroll with *Your Arms Too Short to Box with God* (1975) and Ken Wydro and Vi Higgensen with *Mama I Want to Sing* (1980).

World War II (1939–1945) brought in its wake increased militancy at home and abroad, as African Americans agitated for fair-employment practices, the elimination of restricted housing, and an end to segregated schools, and as Africans mobilized to gain their independence from colonial masters. This new aggressiveness was mirrored in Lorraine HANSBERRY's *A Raisin in the Sun* (1959). Using Langston Hughes's poetic query, "What happens to a dream deferred?", the young playwright explored the conflicting aspirations of the Youngers, a Chicago tenement family eagerly awaiting the arrival of a $10,000 insurance check paid upon the death of the father. Thirty-year-old Walter Lee's dream of owning a liquor store and hence of functioning as a man in terms espoused by the American middle class clashes with Mama's desire to purchase a comfortable house with a small garden, while Beneatha's medical studies and humanist philosophy come into conflict with her brother's chauvinism and her mother's religiosity. Sister-in-law Ruth's decision to seek an illegal abortion marks the battering that the older generation's Southern, sharecropping values have taken in the industrial North. Paradoxically, Mama's spiritual faith, rooted in the American slave experience, is congruent with Asagai's progressive social commitment based in contemporary, African anticolonial movements, for in wooing Beneatha, this Nigerian student speaks of the necessity of belief in human potential and the consequence struggle for human betterment.

Produced five years after the historic BROWN V. BOARD OF EDUCATION OF TOPEKA, KANSAS decision outlawing segregated schools, *A Raisin in the Sun* seemed to signal the nation's willingness to live up to its credo of equality. It constituted a number of landmarks: the first time that an African-American woman's work had been produced at the Ethel Barrymore Theatre on Broadway; the directorial debut of African-American Lloyd Richards in such a prestigious venue; widespread recognition for actors Claudia McNeil, Ruby Dee, Sidney POITIER, and Diana Sands; and encouragement for other artists to articulate their visions of black America. In addition, it won the New York Drama Critics Circle Award, beating out such mainstream competitors as Tennessee Williams's *Sweet Bird of Youth,* Eugene O'Neill's *A Touch of the Poet,* and Archibald MacLeish's *J.B.* Thus, the play's ending was interpreted, for the most part, as a ringing endorsement of integration. But at the time of its twenty-fifth-anniversary production in 1984, optimism had waned; the reinsertion of the character of the chatty neighbor, who brings news of a racial bombing, along with the final action of the play, namely Mama's retrieving her sickly plant for the family's move into a white neighborhood, clarified Hansberry's call for continued struggle for dignity.

In both its content and structure, *Raisin* speaks to the white mainstream and to black audiences. In fact, critics have compared this drama to the Depression-era *Awake and Sing* (1935), written by the white author Clifford Odets, because not only do both feature families dominated by women, but they also deploy ethnic slang and the metaphors of a cramped physical environment as a sign of moral constriction and of money from an insurance check as the vehicle for exercising personal integrity. Ephemeral, performance-based yet nonetheless significant elements, along with the written text, serve, however, to simultaneously locate this drama within an African matrix. Rather than arguing, as did critics influenced by the federally sponsored MOYNIHAN REPORT on black families, that Mama is an emasculating matriarch because the Youngsters do not conform to the 1950s norm of the nuclear family, one can more profitably understand them as fitting the pattern of an extended African family in which great respect is due elders. At moments of extreme crisis, Mama and Walter Lee each evoke the dead patriarch's memory in halting, yet repetitive linguistic rhythms (that are merely suggested in the written script) seemingly to gain access to his moral support in their decision making. Their actions in these instances are akin to African customs of conjuring the spiritual energies of departed relatives in order to solve current, material problems. Similarly, Beneatha and Walter Lee's fanciful creation of a dance welcoming African warriors home from battle constitutes a writing of culture on the body that provides them a dignity denied them by the American environment; as such, it conforms to African assertions that knowledge is kinesthetic and subjective as well as cerebral.

In both its content and structure, A Raisin in the Sun *speaks to both the white mainstream and to black audiences.*

If Hansberry's hero could be aligned with the southern CIVIL RIGHTS MOVEMENT in his attempt to find a place within the American mainstream, then LeRoi Jones's (a.k.a. Amiri Baraka) protagonists in *Dutchman* and *The Slave* were related to the NATION OF ISLAM and its fiery spokesman MALCOLM X, for at the time of the plays' premieres in 1964, spectators saw these characters as determined to destroy the social system. In the former drama, a twentyish African-American man and older, white woman engage in a bizarre dating game on a subway car that never reaches its final destination. Claiming to know both everything and nothing concerning Clay's life history, this stranger named Lula alternately describes a tantalizing sexual liaison that they will enjoy and hurls racial taunts at the would-be poet until he sheds his polite, middle-class demeanor and acknowledges a deep hatred of white America. But Clay fails to act upon his murderous knowledge, preferring instead to use art as a safety valve that tempers rebellious impulses. Once Lula has exposed this rage, she kills Clay and enlists the aid of the hitherto passive onlookers in throwing his body off the train. Like the mythic captain of the *Flying Dutchman,* who was fated to sail the world looking for absolution for his crimes, Lula begins to seek out another young black male as the play closes. Seemingly, the play functioned as a cautionary tale demonstrating to blacks that death was the price for inaction upon their justifiable anger and warning whites of the rage they could expect if they continued to deny full citizenship to African Americans. Largely unnoted at the time was the text's gender politics, which accuses the white woman rather than fingering the actual holders of oppressive power in the United States.

In contrast, the black man is no longer the victim and the white man is visible in *The Slave.* Walker has invaded the home of his white former wife in order to take his daughters to safety behind the lines of his revolutionary army advancing on the city—or, so he alleges, because it seems as though Walker's real purpose is to exorcise those feelings that bind him to Grace and Easley, Grace's present (white) husband and Walker's former professor. In the ensuing literal and figurative battle, Walker kills Easley, a beam fatally hits Grace, and Walker departs, apparently leaving the children upstairs crying.

But social psychiatrist Frantz Fanon, whose writings on anticolonial struggles in Algeria provided intellectuals in the 1960s with an important framework for conceptualizing Black Power movements, has argued that it is easier to proclaim rejection than to reject. Fanon's analysis is pertinent to the Baraka text, for despite his aggressive stance, Walker agonizes that he has no language with which to construct a new world, his sole epistemology or frame of reference is a Western system that enforces hatred of black people.

The ambiguity of his position has, in fact, been signaled at the outset by a prologue in which an actor, dressed as a stereotypical old field slave, addresses viewers directly, arguing that whatever he and they understand as reality may be a lie told for survival purposes. What is needed, he suggests, is a superstructure that will enable communication among blacks and whites by ensuring that their common language has the same undeniable referents; otherwise, a black man's legitimate quest for control over his destiny may be understood by a white man as senseless terrorism. The rest of the play then argues that this enabling structure is violence, undertaken by the exploited black masses in defense, as Fanon argued, against the violence waged upon them by the state. But as a playwright, Baraka is caught in a problematic position, for his primary tool of communication with audiences is language itself, suspect because of its inherent capacity to simultaneously convey multiple references and values. Yet, given the *extra*-theatrical, social backdrop of armed confrontations waged by groups like the BLACK PANTHER PARTY, most spectators and readers at the time of the drama's initial productions focused their attention on the text's revolutionary rhetoric rather than its ambivalence.

At the heart of both these plays is an examination of hegemony or the power of a ruling class to enforce throughout the entire society perspectives that maintain its privileged status through noncoercive means like education, the arts, or certain everyday practices. In *Dutchman* the dominance of the elite, as embodied in Lula, is maintained in part because art functions as a passive mode of resistance that deflects direct confrontation. In *The Slave* and subsequent dramatic works like *Four Black Revolutionary Plays, Arm Yrself or Harm Yrself* (1967), or *The Motion of History* (1977), art is defined as counterhegemonic; it is seen as a weapon that can be utilized to attack sociopolitical hierarchies. In rejecting, as Du Bois had done previously, the opposition of art to propaganda, Amiri Baraka became a major proponent of the BLACK ARTS MOVEMENT (1964–1974), functioning as a role model for a younger generation eager to assert a positive sense of their black identity.

In an atmosphere of civil rights demonstrations and urban rebellions, entitlement programs designed to bring about what President Lyndon Johnson termed "the Great Society," Vietnam war protest, and the beginnings of a renewed feminism, African-American drama, with its implicit critique of the dominant social structure, briefly flourished. Playwrights like Ed Bullins, Richard Wesley, Clay Goss, Ron Milner, Ben Caldwell, Sonia Sanchez, and Marvin X followed Baraka's example. Artists like Robert Macbeth, Barbara Ann Teer, and Woodie King, Jr. established companies that advocated a black nationalist position (New York's the New Lafayette, National Black Theatre, and Concept East in Detroit respectively), while more moderate practitioners like Douglas Turner Ward, Hazel Bryant, C. Bernard Jackson, John Doyle, and Nora Vaughn, and such companies as the Negro Ensemble, the Richard Allen Cultural Center in New York, the Inner City Cultural Center in Los Angeles, and the Grassroots Experience and Black Repertory Group Theatre in the San Francisco Bay Area also found governmental funding and receptive audiences for their efforts.

Another of the most prolific playwrights of this period was Ed Bullins, who has written in a variety of styles, including comedy (*The Electronic Nigger,* 1968), theater of the Absurd (*How Do You Do?* 1965), fictionalized autobiography (*A Son Come Home,* 1968), and a realism whose seemingly photographic accuracy does

Ntozake Shange's highly successful for colored girls who have considered suicide/when the rainbow is enuf *(1976) marked new visibility for black feminist themes in the theater. (Prints and Photographs Division, Library of Congress)*

not reveal the playwright's evaluation of his source material (*Clara's Ole Man,* 1965). Unlike virtually any other black dramatist before him, Ed Bullins placed onstage—and thereby validated—in plays like *Goin' a Buffalo* (1966), *In the Wine Time* (1968), and *The Taking of Miss Janie* (1975) lower-class hustlers, prostitutes, pimps, and unemployed teens as well as lower-middle-class community college students, veterans, musicians, and would-be artists and intellectuals, virtually all of whom aggressively pursue an individually-oriented materialism shorn of any rhetoric of concern for a shared, common good.

In disavowing the espoused social values of the American mainstream, Bullins's playwriting style in his full-length dramas also demanded a mode of criticism that was outside the Aristotelian-derived, mainstream preference for tightly organized, linear dramatic structures. Thus, these dramas may be more productively analyzed in terms of jazz, a musical idiom that originated among African Americans and was until relatively recently held in low regard by the American public. Like a jazz composition in which individual musicians improvise a solo or "riff" off a shared melodic line, a play such as *The Fabulous Miss Marie* (1971) has a basic narrative concerning a group of black Los Angelenos who party unconcernedly while a civil rights demonstration is being broadcast on television. The seemingly endless rounds of drinking, meandering conversations, verbal sparring, and sexual repartee function as a base line from which action is periodically stopped in order for individual characters to step from the shadows into a spotlight and address the audience directly with their own solos on the theme of trying to "make it" in the United States.

Adrienne Kennedy is another playwright whose work demanded different critical tools. Like Baraka, Kennedy confronts, in plays like *The Owl Answers* (1965) and *Rat's Mass* (1963), questions of representation and identity formation, offering a black woman's account of the cultural schizophrenia induced by American racial constructions. Thus, protagonists like Sarah in *Funnyhouse of a Negro* (1963) are paralyzed by devotion to European culture, symbolized in this text by Queen Elizabeth and the Duchess of Hapsburg, and by psychosexual confusion centered on a father figure, associated here with blackness, encroaching jungles, civilizing missions in Africa, and contradictorily, the anticolonialist Congolese hero Patrice Lumumba. Adding to the ambiguity is Kennedy's consistent decision to distribute the female protagonist's story amongst a number of different characters, thereby producing an identity or voice that does not come together in a single, coherent whole. Though her earliest plays were produced during the same time period as Baraka's, the ideological demand for positive valorization of "the black experience" in the sixties' Black Arts and Black Power movements meant that her frighteningly powerful dramatizations of the anguished sensibility Du Bois had termed "double consciousness" won a few supporters among African-American theatergoers. Notwithstanding, her highly abstract style found positive response within the limited circles of the white avant-garde in New York. Given subsequent critiques of identity and relationships of domination and marginality launched from theorists of feminism, literary deconstruction, postcoloniality, and postmodernism, a space has been cleared, and Kennedy's work is presently garnering from white and black critics alike the attention it deserves.

Exploding on the theatrical scene in 1976 with *for colored girls who have considered suicide/when the rainbow is enuf,* Ntozake Shange builds upon examples set by Hughes, Baraka, and Kennedy in black theater as well as those offered by Europe's Antonin Artaud and Bertolt Brecht. Coining the term "choreopoem," Shange creates a total theater in which unscripted elements like music and dance become equal partners with the written word—i.e., poetry. Thus, in *for colored girls . . .* not only do the women talk about their encounters with men, but they also utilize 1960s Motown tunes, Afro-Cuban rhythms, nonsensical chants, and GOSPEL cadences in order to break out of a social world in which they have been devalued as "a colored girl an evil woman a bitch or a nag." With this first text, Shange placed African-American women's experiences of rape, abortion, domestic abuse, sexual desire, and self-affirmation center stage, and she helped fuel an intense debate within black communities concerning the relevance of feminism—understood at that time as the preoccupation of white, middle-class women—to the lives of African Americans. Seeking in *Spell #7* (1979) to confront the power of the minstrel mask that has determined representations of blacks in American popular imagination she crafts a provocative theater whose implications refuse to remain within the illusionary space created by drama. Shange has continued in texts like *Boogie Woogie Landscapes* (1979), *From Okra to Greens/ A Different Kinda Love Story* (1978), and *The Love Space Demands: A Continuing Saga* (1992) to utilize poetry, music, and dance in a nonlinear fashion to explore ways in which a sense of personal integrity and nobility can be harmonized with the realities of racist and sexist social constructions of black (female) identity. Playwrights like Alexis Deveaux, Aishah Rahman, and George C. Wolfe have followed Shange's lead in experimenting with dramatic form, while the last has parodied the feminist content of Shange's dramas in *The Colored Museum* (1986).

Closer to the American mainstream's penchant for realism is August WILSON, who has benefited from a virtually unique, creative collaboration with Lloyd Richards, the same director who brought Hansberry's *A Raisin in the Sun* to Broadway some thirty-five years earlier. Each of his plays has been "workshopped" (read aloud by professional actors and a director, critiqued, and re-written) at the National Playwrights Conference of the Eugene O'Neill Theater, run by Richards, before receiving productions (and further revisions) and national media attention at various, mainstream regional theaters and on Broadway.

A skilled storyteller, Wilson has taken on the challenge of writing a play for each decade of the twentieth century. Thus, *Ma Rainey's Black Bottom* (1984) focuses on the renowned 1920s blues singer and her band, who, through their casual reminiscences, reveal a collective history of discrimination. *Fences* (1985) centers on an overbearing man's relationship to his son and other family members at the point in the 1950s when African Americans were being allowed entry into white, professional sports organizations; and *Joe Turner's Come and Gone* (1986) dramatizes the search by various boardinghouse occupants for a sense of wholeness and sustaining purpose in the first decade of the twentieth century, when thousands of rural black people moved north seeking employment in an industrializing economy. In *The Piano Lesson* (1987), set in the 1930s, a brother and sister fight for possession of the family's piano, which seems to symbolize conflicting ideas concerning uses of the past in charting present courses of action; while set against the backdrop of Malcolm X's militancy of the 1960s, *Two Trains Running* (1990) features the regular patrons of a modest diner who pursue their own dreams of advancement by playing the numbers (i.e., illegally betting on the outcome of horse races) or consulting Aunt Esther, a local fortune teller whose alleged, advanced age happens to correspond to the numbers of years African-Americans have lived in the United States.

Like the novelist Toni MORRISON, August Wilson crafts a world in which the pedestrian often assumes grand, mythic proportions, nearly bursting in the process the neat, explanatory rationales implicit in the genre of dramatic realism. Characters regularly fight with ghosts, make pacts with the Devil, or talk to Death; seemingly, they quest for a spiritual center or standpoint from which to confront a material world hostile to their presence. Arguing the importance of blues music in shaping the identity of African Americans, Wilson seems to create characters whose very lives are a blues song: improvisatory, ironic, yet simultaneously affirmative, grounded in a bedrock of belief in the possibility of human integrity.

Seemingly with the post-sixties integration of some public school systems, (sub)urban neighborhoods, job sites, and mass media, the hybrid character of African-American—and indeed, American—culture has accelerated. Those comfortable with a postmodernism that often finds its inspirations in a global eclecticism of "high" and "low" cultures, can enjoy such African-American performance artists as Robbie McCauley (*My Father and the Wars,* 1985; *Sally's Rape,* 1991), and Laurie Carlos who, in the tradition of Ntozake Shange, work individually and collaboratively to fuse personal narratives with larger feminist issues. Also termed a performance artist, Anna Deavere Smith offers in her *On the Road: A Search for American Change* series solo performances of edited interviews with people, both famous and obscure, on topics like gender and racial tensions in professional organizations, urban neighborhoods, and on university campuses. She has also focused on the increasingly multicultural, fractious character of American cities, for her *Fires in the Mirror: Crown Heights, Brooklyn and Other Identities* (1992) and *Twilight: Los Angeles, 1992* (1994), in which she performs the words of more than thirty women and men within an hour and a half, challenges audiences to grapple with notions of community in the context of competing demands for racial and economic justice. They can also sample dramas by Suzan-Lori Parks (*The Death of the Last Black Man in the Whole Entire World,* 1990; *Imperceptible Mutabilities in the Third Kingdom,* 1989), who cites the white, American expatriate writer Gertrude Stein and "The Wild Kingdom" television program among her influences; or work by Eric Gupton, Brian Freeman, and Bernard Branner (*Fierce Love: Stories from Black Gay Life,* 1991), collectively known as AfroPomoHomo, a shortening of the identificatory tags, African-American, postmodernist, and homosexual. Or, spectators can attend a concert by Urban Bush Women, Bill T. Jones/Arnie Zane Dance Company, or David Rousseve, whose mixture of modern dance choreography, pedestrian gestures, athleticism, and narrative communicated through both movement and spoken text blur conventional Western distinctions between drama and dance. What all these artists share is a sensibility that does not reach for some grand, master truth. Rather, juxtaposing elements as diverse as European high art, Georgia Sea Island chants, television programs, West African religions, and popular music, they recognize that African-American identity is varied, and no one can claim to represent black authenticity without doing violence to other perspectives found in these communities.

In the early 1990s, approximately 200 companies were dedicated to the production of African-American theater and drama.

Indeed, for those theatergoers in the 1990s who find the choreopoem form of an Ntozake Shange, the mythic reach of an August Wilson, or the puzzling symbolism of a Suzan-Lori Parks not to their liking, other options are available. They can attend a performance of *Beauty Shop, Living Room,* or *Beauty Shop, Part 2,* all of which have been written, produced, and directed by Shelly Garrett. Starting in 1987 with the intention of simply creating dramatic pieces that would leave audiences exhausted with laughter, Garrett is said to have targeted his attentions primarily toward an underserved population of black women, ages 25 to 54 who watch soap operas and rarely frequent theater. Thus, his scripts are closer to TV sitcoms in their representations of everyday life; stereotypes abound, with the women portrayed as materialist, classist, sexually repressed or rapacious. Men are represented as self-centered sex objects, financially secure but dull, or flamboyant homosexuals outgossiping the most catty (yet hilarious) women. Seemingly, considerable advertising on black-oriented radio stations, the dramas' verbal play, the performers' zestful aura, a mixture of some recognizable truths, and cheerful confirmation of spectators' misogynist and homophobic attitudes have attracted thousands of spectators, enabling Garrett to tour at least fifty cities nationwide for more than two years with one show. But those disturbed by what they may perceive as rampant sexuality in these shows also have an option in the commercial arena, for producers have created a religious version, like Michael Mathews's *I Need a Man* (1993), wherein some of these lively stereotypes undergo spiritual conversion aided by the performance of GOSPEL music. As with much black art, the form is elastic, so that local, gospel radio personalities occasionally make guest appearances onstage during the performance; the predictability of plot and character types is offset by the dynamics of the performer-viewer interactions. Whether participants undergo a religious experience in this highly commercialized venue depends, as it does in church, upon their own belief systems and sensibilities.

In the early 1990s, approximately 200 companies were dedicated to the production of African-American theater and drama. As the foregoing account suggests, audiences can experience a wealth of themes, perspectives, and styles, all of which seek to articulate aspects of African-American culture. This diversity is indeed a cause for celebration. Yet, given the nation's difficult economic conditions that promise no easy solution, the arts in general and black and other so-called minority expressive cultures in particular will be under intense pressure to obtain the financial resources that enable artistic production. Perhaps artists from earlier generations would have spoken of the economic constraints upon their work, too, and advised their descendants that the challenge remains constant: To create a tasty "soul" food of dramatic fare, one must utilize the diverse materials at hand, seasoning them with attention to technique, intelligence, passion, an occasional bit of humor, openness to inspiration, and most important, grace under pressure.

BIBLIOGRAPHY

Abramson, Doris E. *Negro Playwrights in the American Theatre, 1925–1959.* New York, 1969.

Boskin, Joseph. *Sambo: the Rise and Demise of an African Jester.* New York, 1986.

Brown-Guillory, Elizabeth, ed. *Their Place on the Stage: Black Women Playwrights in America.* Westport, Conn., 1988.

———. *Wines in the Wilderness: Plays by African American Women from the Harlem Renaissance to the Present.* New York, 1990.

Carter, Steven R. *Hansberry's Drama.* Urbana, Ill., 1991.

Craig, E. Quita. *Black Drama of the Federal Theatre Era: Beyond the Formal Horizons.* Amherst, Mass., 1980.

Fabre, Genevieve. *Drumbeats, Masks, and Metaphor.* Translated by Melvin Dixon. Cambridge, Mass., 1983.

Fanon, Frantz. *Black Skins, White Masks.* Translated by Charles Lam Markmann. New York, 1967.

———. *The Wretched of the Earth.* Translated by Constance Farrington. New York, 1963.

Fletcher, Winona L. "Witnessing a 'Miracle': Sixty Years of 'Heaven Bound' at Big Bethel in Atlanta." *Black American Literature Forum* 25, no. 1 (Spring 1991): 83–92.

Harrison, Paul Carter. "Introduction: Black Theater in Search of a Source." In *Kuntu Drama: Plays of the African Continuum.* New York, 1974, pp. 5–29.

———. *Totem Voices: Plays from the Black World Repertory.* New York, 1989.

Hatch, James V., ed. *Black Theater, U.S.A.: Forty-Five Plays by Black Americans, 1847–1974.* New York, 1974.

———. *The Roots of African American Drama.* Detroit, 1991.

Hill, Errol, ed. *The Theatre of Black Americans.* New York, 1990.

Mitchell, Angela. "Cheap Laughs: Bad Taste, Big Bucks." *Emerge* 4, no. 5 (March 1993): 49–51.

Mollette, Carlton, and Barbara Mollette. *Black Theatre: Premise and Presentation.* 1986. Reprint. Briston, Ind., 1992.

Neal, Larry. *Visions of a Liberated Future: Black Arts Movement Writings.* New York, 1989.

Perkins, Kathy A. *Black Female Playwrights: An Anthology of Plays Before 1950.* Bloomington, Ind., 1989.

Rampersad, Arnold. *The Life of Langston Hughes, Volume 1, 1902–1941: I, Too, Sing America.* New York, 1986.

Sanders, Leslie Catherine. *The Development of Black Theater in America.* Baton Rouge, La., 1988.

Scott, Freda L. "The Star of Ethiopia: A Contribution Toward the Development of Black Drama and Theater in the Harlem Renaissance." In Amritijit Singh, William S. Shiver, and Stanley Brodwin, eds. *The Harlem Renaissance: Revaluations.* New York, 1989.

Turner, Darwin T., ed. *Black Drama in America: An Anthology.* Washington, D.C., 1993.

Wiggins, William H., Jr. "Pilgrims, Crosses, and Faith: The Folk Dimensions of 'Heaven Bound'." *Black American Literature Forum* 25, no. 1 (Spring 1991): 93–100.

Wilkerson, Margaret B. *Nine Plays.* New York, 1986.

———. "Redefining Black Theatre." *The Black Scholar* 10, no. 10 (July/August 1979): 322–342.

Williams, Mance. *Black Theatre in the 1960s and 1970s.* Westport, Conn., 1985.

Woll, Allen. *Black Musical Theatre: From "Coontown" to "Dreamgirls."* Baton Rouge, La., 1989.

– SANDRA L. RICHARDS

DRED SCOTT V. SANDFORD

In the Dred Scott decision of 1857 the Supreme Court ruled, in a 7–2 vote, that free blacks were not citizens of the United States and that Congress lacked the power to prohibit SLAVERY in the western territories.

Scott was a Virginia slave, born around 1802, who moved with his master, Peter Blow, to St. Louis in 1830. Blow subsequently sold Scott to Dr. John Emerson, an army surgeon, who took Scott to Fort Armstrong in Illinois, a free state, and Fort Snelling in the Wisconsin Territory, where slavery was prohibited by the MISSOURI COMPROMISE. In 1846, after Emerson's death, Scott sued for his freedom (and that of his family). In 1850 a St. Louis court ruled that Scott became free by residing in Illinois and the Wisconsin Territory. In 1852 the Missouri Supreme Court, articulating the South's proslavery ideology, rejected precedents of its own that went back more than twenty-five years and reversed the lower court decision:

> Times are not as they were when the former decisions on this subject were made. Since then not only individuals but States have been possessed of a dark and fell spirit in relation to slavery, whose gratification is sought in the pursuit of measures, whose inevitable consequence must be the overthrow and destruction of our government.

Thus, Missouri would not recognize the freedom a slave might obtain by living in a free state.

In 1854 Scott began a new suit in United States District Court against John F. A. Sanford, a New Yorker who became the executor of Emerson's estate after Emerson's widow, the initial executor, remarried. Scott claimed he was a citizen of Missouri, suing Sanford in federal court because there was a diversity of state citizenship between the two parties. Sanford answered with a plea in abatement, arguing that no black, free or slave, could ever sue as a citizen in federal court. Federal District Judge Robert W. Wells ruled that *if* Scott was free, he was a citizen of Missouri for purposes of a diversity suit. However, Wells's ruling after the trial was that Scott was still a slave. Scott then appealed to the U.S. Supreme Court. At issue was more than his status: the Missouri Supreme Court's decision challenged the constitutionality of the Missouri Compromise. The central political issue of the 1850s—the power of the federal government to prohibit slavery in the territories—was now before the Supreme Court.

In the Dred Scott decision of 1857 the Supreme Court ruled that free blacks were not citizens of the United States and that Congress lacked the power to prohibit slavery in the western territories.

The ardently proslavery Chief Justice Roger B. Taney used *Dred Scott* v. *Sandford* to decide this pressing political issue in favor of the South. Taney asserted that (1) the Missouri Compromise was unconstitutional because Congress could not legislate for the territories; (2) freeing slaves in the territories violated the Fifth Amendment prohibition on taking of property without due process; and (3) blacks, even those in the North with full state citizenship, could never be U.S. citizens. Taney asked: "Can a negro, whose ancestors were imported into this country, and sold as slaves, become a member of the political community formed and brought into existence by the Constitution of the United States, and as such become entitled to all the rights, privileges, and immunities guaranteed by that instrument to the citizens?" Taney answered his own question in the negative. He asserted that at the nation's founding blacks were considered "beings of an inferior order, and altogether unfit to associate with the white race, either in social or political relations; and so far inferior, that they had no rights which the white man was bound to respect; and that the negro might justly and lawfully be reduced to slavery for his benefit." Taney thought his lengthy decision would open all the territories to slavery and destroy the Republican party. In essence, he had constitutionalized racism and slavery. America, in Taney's view, was thoroughly a "white" nation.

Justice Benjamin Robbins Curtis of Massachusetts protested Taney's conclusions. Curtis noted: "At the time of the ratification of the Articles of Confederation [1781], all free native-born inhabitants of the States of New Hampshire, Massachusetts, New York, New Jersey, and North Carolina, though descended from African slaves, were not only citizens of those States, but such of them as had the other necessary qualifications possessed the franchises of electors, on equal terms with other citizens." Curtis concluded that when the Constitution was ratified, "these colored persons were not only included in the body of 'the people of the United States,' by whom the Constitution was ordained and established, but in at least five of the States they had the power to act, and doubtless did act, by their suffrages, upon the question of adoption." Curtis also argued that under a "reasonable interpretation of the language of the Constitution," Congress had the power to regulate slavery in the federal territories.

Northern Republicans and abolitionists were stunned and horrified. Horace Greeley, writing in the *New York Tribune*, called Taney's opinion "atrocious," "abominable," and a "detestable hypocrisy." The *Chicago Tribune* was repelled by its "inhuman dicta" and "the wicked consequences which may flow from it." Northern Democrats, on the other hand, hoped the decision would destroy the Republican party by undermining its "free soil" platform and by finally ending the national debate over slavery in the territories. The New York *Journal of Commerce* hopefully declared that the decision was an "authoritative and final settlement of grievous sectional issues."

Ultimately, it was neither authoritative nor final. By 1858, northern Democrats faced a politically impossible dilemma. Their answer to the problem of slavery in the territories had been popular sovereignty —allowing the settlers to vote slavery up or down. But Taney's opinion denied both Congress and the settlers of a new territory the power to prohibit slavery. This made popular sovereignty meaningless. Stephen A. Douglas, the most prominent proponent of popular sovereignty, told his Illinois constituents that settlers could still keep slavery out of most of the territories by not passing laws that would protect slave property. This simply led to southern demands for a federal slave code for the territories and a split within the Democratic party in 1860.

Republicans made Taney and the decision the focus of their 1858 and 1860 campaigns. Abraham Lincoln argued in his "house divided" speech (1858) that Taney's opinion was part of a proslavery conspiracy to nationalize slavery. He predicted "another Supreme Court decision, declaring that the Constitution of the United States does not permit a *state* to exclude slavery from its limits." He told Illinois voters that "we shall *lie down* pleasantly dreaming that the people of Missouri are on the verge of making their state *free;* and we shall *awake* to the *reality*, instead, that the Supreme Court has made *Illinois* a *slave* state."

Such arguments helped lead to a Republican victory in 1860. During the Civil War the Lincoln administration gradually reversed many of Taney's assertions about the status of blacks. This Republican policy culminated with the adoption of the FOURTEENTH AMENDMENT, which explicitly overruled *Dred Scott,* declaring, "All persons born or naturalized in the United States . . . are citizens of the United States and of the State wherein they reside."

BIBLIOGRAPHY

Erlich, Walter. *They Have No Rights: Dred Scott's Struggle for Freedom.* Westport, Conn., 1979.

Fehrenbacher, Don E. *The Dred Scott Case: Its Significance in American Law and Politics.* New York, 1978.

Finkelman, Paul. *An Imperfect Union: Slavery, Federalism, and Comity.* Chapel Hill, N.C., 1981.

———. *Slavery in the Courtroom.* Washington, D.C., 1985.

Potter, David M. *The Impending Crisis: 1848–61.* New York, 1976.

— PAUL FINKELMAN

DU BOIS, WILLIAM EDWARD BURGHARDT

William Edward Burghardt Du Bois (February 23, 1869–August 27, 1963), historian, sociologist, novelist, and editor. W. E. B. Du Bois was born in Great Barrington, Mass. His mother, Mary Burghardt Du Bois, belonged to a tiny community of African Americans who had been settled in the area since before the Revolution; his father, Alfred Du Bois, was a visitor to the region who deserted the family in his son's infancy. In the predominantly white local schools and Congregational church, Du Bois absorbed ideas and values that left him "quite thoroughly New England."

From 1885 to 1888 he attended Fisk University in Nashville, where he first encountered the harsher forms of racism. After earning a B.A. (1888) at Fisk, he attended Harvard University, where he took another B.A. (1890) and a doctorate in history (1895). Among his teachers were the psychologist William James, the philosophers Josiah Royce and George Santayana, and the historian A. B. Hart. Between 1892 and 1894 he studied history and sociology at the University of Berlin. His dissertation, *The Suppression of the African Slave-Trade to the United States,* was published in 1896 as the first volume of the Harvard Historical Studies.

Between 1894 and 1896, Du Bois taught at Wilberforce University, Ohio, where he met and married Nina Gomer, a student, in 1896. The couple had two children, Burghardt and Yolande. In 1896, he accepted a position at the University of Pennsylvania to gather data for a commissioned study of blacks in Philadelphia. This work resulted in *The Philadelphia Negro* (1899), an acclaimed early example of empirical sociology. In 1897, he joined the faculty at Atlanta University and took over the annual Atlanta University Conference for the Study of the Negro Problems. From 1897 to 1914 he edited an annual study of one aspect or another of black life, such as education or the church.

Appalled by the conditions facing blacks nationally, Du Bois sought ways other than scholarship to effect change. The death of his young son from dysentery in 1899 also deeply affected him, as did the widely publicized lynching of a black man, Sam Hose, in Georgia the same year. In 1900, in London, he boldly asserted that "the problem of the Twentieth Century is the problem of the color line." He repeated this statement in *The Souls of Black Folk* (1903), mainly a collection of essays on African-American history, sociology, religion, and music, in which Du Bois wrote of an essential black double consciousness: the existence of twin souls ("an American, a Negro") warring in each black body. The book also attacked Booker T. WASHINGTON, the most powerful black American of the age, for advising blacks to surrender the right to vote and to a liberal education in return for white friendship and support. Du Bois was established as probably the premier intellectual in black America, and Washington's main rival.

His growing radicalism also led him to organize the NIAGARA MOVEMENT, a group of blacks who met in 1905 and 1906 to agitate for "manhood rights" for African Americans. He founded two journals, *Moon* (1905–1906) and *Horizon* (1907–1910). In 1909 he published *John Brown,* a sympathetic biography of the white abolitionist martyr. Then, in 1910, he resigned his professorship to join the new NATIONAL ASSOCIATION FOR THE ADVANCEMENT OF COLORED PEOPLE (NAACP) in New York, which had been formed in response to growing concern about the treatment of blacks. As its director of research, Du Bois founded a monthly magazine, the *Crisis.* In 1911 he published his first novel, *The Quest of the Silver Fleece,* a study of the cotton industry seen through the fate of a young black couple struggling for a life of dignity and meaning.

In 1900 Du Bois boldly asserted that "the problem of the Twentieth Century is the problem of the color line."

The *Crisis* became a powerful forum for Du Bois's views on race and politics. Meanwhile, his developing interest in Africa led him to write *The Negro* (1915), a study offering historical and demographic information on peoples of African descent around the world. Hoping to affect colonialism in Africa after World War I, he also organized Pan-African Congresses in Europe in 1919, 1921, and 1923, and in New York in 1927. However, he clashed with the most popular black leader

of the era, Marcus GARVEY of the UNIVERSAL NEGRO IMPROVEMENT ASSOCIATION. Du Bois regarded Garvey's "back to Africa" scheme as ill-considered, and Garvey as impractical and disorganized.

Du Bois's second prose collection, *Darkwater: Voices from Within the Veil* (1920), did not repeat the success of *The Souls of Black Folk* but captured his increased militancy. In the 1920s, the *Crisis* played a major role in the HARLEM RENAISSANCE by publishing early work by Langston HUGHES, Countee CULLEN, and other writers. Eventually, Du Bois found some writers politically irresponsible; his essay "Criteria of Negro Art" (1926) insisted that all art is essentially propaganda. He pressed this point with a novel, *Dark Princess* (1928), about a plot by the darker races to overthrow European colonialism. In 1926 he visited the Soviet Union, then nine years old. Favorably impressed by what he saw, he boldly declared himself "a Bolshevik."

The Great Depression increased his interest in SOCIALISM but also cut the circulation of the *Crisis* and weakened Du Bois's position with the leadership of the NAACP, with which he had fought from the beginning. In 1934, he resigned as editor and returned to teach at Atlanta University. His interest in Marxism, which had started with his student days in Berlin, dominated his next book, *Black Reconstruction in America* (1934), a massive and controversial revaluation of the role of the freedmen in the South after the Civil War. In 1936, Du Bois commenced a weekly column of opinion in various black newspapers, starting with the *Pittsburgh Courier.* He emphasized his continuing concern for Africa with *Black Folk: Then and Now* (1939), an expanded and updated revision of *The Negro.*

In 1940, Du Bois published his first full-length autobiography, *Dusk of Dawn: An Autobiography of a Concept of Race,* in which he examined modern racial theory against the major events and intellectual currents in his lifetime. In 1944, his life took another dramatic turn when he was suddenly retired by Atlanta University after growing tension between himself and certain administrators. When the NAACP rehired him that year, he returned to New York as director of special research. In 1945 he was honored at the Fifth Pan-African Congress in Manchester, England, and published a bristling polemic, *Color and Democracy: Colonies and Peace.* A year later, he produced a controversial pamphlet, "An Appeal to the World," submitted by the NAACP on behalf of black Americans to the United Nations Commission on Civil Rights. In 1947 came his *The World and Africa,* an examination of Africa's future following World War II.

By this time Du Bois had moved to the left, well beyond the interests of the NAACP, which generally supported the Democratic party. In 1948, when he endorsed the Progressive party and its presidential candidate, Henry Wallace, he was fired. He then joined Paul ROBESON, who was by this time firmly identified with radical socialism, at the Council on African Affairs, which had been officially declared a "subversive" organization. In 1950, Du Bois ran unsuccessfully for the U.S. Senate from New York on the American Labor party ticket. Also that year, in another move applauded by communists, he accepted the chairmanship of the Peace Information Center, which circulated the Stockholm Peace Appeal against nuclear weapons.

Early in 1951, Du Bois and four colleagues from the Peace Information Center were indicted on the charge of violating the law that required agents of a foreign power to register. On bail and awaiting trial, he married Shirley Lola Graham, a fellow socialist and writer (his first wife had died in 1950). At the trial in November 1951, the judge heard testimony, then unexpectedly granted a motion by the defense for a directed acquittal. Du Bois was undeterred by his ordeal. In 1953, he recited the Twenty-third Psalm at the grave of Julius and Ethel Rosenberg, executed as spies for the Soviet Union. For such involvements, he found himself ostracized by some black leaders and organizations. "The colored children," he wrote, "ceased to hear my name."

Returning to fiction, he composed a trilogy, *The Black Flame,* about the life and times of a black educator seen against the backdrop of generations of black and white lives and national and international events (the trilogy comprised *The Ordeal of Mansart,* 1957; *Mansart Builds a School,* 1959; and *World of Color,* 1961). After the government lifted its ban on his foreign travel in 1958, Du Bois visited various countries, including the Soviet Union and China. In Moscow on May 1, 1959, he received the Lenin Peace Prize.

In 1960 Du Bois visited Ghana for the inauguration of Kwame Nkrumah as its first president. He then accepted an invitation from Nkrumah to return to Ghana and start work on an *Encyclopedia Africana,* a project in which he had long been interested. In October 1961, after applying (successfully) for membership in the COMMUNIST PARTY, he left the United States. He began work on the project in Ghana, but illness the following year caused him to go for treatment to Romania. Afterward, he visited Peking and Moscow. In February 1963, he renounced his American citizenship and officially became a citizen of Ghana. He died in Accra, Ghana, and was buried there.

BIBLIOGRAPHY

Aptheker, Herbert. *Annotated Bibliography of the Published Writings of W. E. B. Du Bois.* Millwood, N.Y., 1973.

Lewis, David Levering. *W. E. B. Du Bois: Biography of a Race 1868–1919.* New York, 1993.
Rampersad, Arnold. *The Art and Imagination of W. E. B. Du Bois.* New York, 1973.

– ARNOLD RAMPERSAD

DUNBAR, PAUL LAURENCE

Paul Laurence Dunbar (June 27, 1872–February 9, 1906), writer. Dunbar, the child of ex-slaves, was the first African-American writer to attain widespread fame for his literary activities. Known chiefly for his dialect poetry, Dunbar also broke new ground in several ways for the further development of an African-American literary tradition.

Born and raised in Dayton, Ohio, Dunbar showed early signs of literary ambition. He served as editor of his high school newspaper, and at the same time began a short-lived newspaper of his own, the Dayton *Tattler,* focusing on matters of interest to the black community. Like most young black men, and despite a good school record, he confronted upon graduation a world with few opportunities, and had to take work as an elevator operator; but he also became increasingly dedicated to his literary activity, especially to poetry. Encouraged by several white friends in Dayton as well as by the noted popular poet James Whitcomb Riley, Dunbar published locally his first book of poetry, *Oak and Ivy,* in 1892. However, he achieved real fame in 1896, when an expanded and revised collection, *Majors and Minors*—also published mainly for a local audience—came to the attention of the prominent American writer William Dean Howells. Howells admired it and saw to the publication that year of a larger volume, *Lyrics of Lowly Life,* by the established American firm Dodd, Mead. It was the first of five major collections to be published by the company during Dunbar's lifetime.

Known chiefly for his dialect poetry, Dunbar also broke new ground in several ways for the further development of an African-American literary tradition.

Singled out for praise by Howells, and serving as the basis for Dunbar's fame, was his dialect verse. Fitting broadly into the popular, mainly white-authored, plantation-tradition literature of the time, Dunbar's dialect poetry created a sentimental portrait of African-American folklife in the antebellum South, treating a variety of themes, from love and courtship to social life and folk ideas. Although the dialect Dunbar used owed more to its literary antecedents than to actual folk speech, he also drew heavily on folk traditions for his own subjects and themes, and thus often succeeded in giving real life to the form, freeing it from the stereotypes that dominated the works of white practitioners. The publication of this work, together with successful public readings of it throughout the United States and abroad, made Dunbar among the most popular poets, regardless of race, in America at the turn of the twentieth century.

Dunbar's success with dialect poetry had a powerful impact on black American literature during its time. He had few black predecessors in the form—although such early black dialect writers as James Edwin Campbell and Daniel Webster Davis were his exact contemporaries—but as his fame grew, so did the volume of dialect poetry in African-American literature. It began to appear frequently in black newspapers and magazines, and few collections of African-American poetry over the next two decades lacked at least some examples of dialect verse. Many were dominated by it.

Dunbar himself was ambivalent about his success with the dialect form. He wrote a great deal of poetry in standard English, and felt that this was his most important work. Much of this verse is significant, especially for its time, as Dunbar not only addressed such contemporary issues as southern racial injustice and violence, but broke notably from conventions of piety and gentility that had earlier dominated poetry by black Americans. Still, it was the dialect poetry that critics, black and white, praised during Dunbar's lifetime, a fact that the poet found greatly frustrating. His frustration spilled over into a personal life marked by real difficulties, including problems in his marriage to the talented writer Alice Moore Dunbar, and the alcoholism and chronic ill health, culminating in tuberculosis, that led to his early death.

Although Dunbar made his reputation as a poet, his literary production during his brief life showed real diversity. It included a large number of short stories that appeared in popular magazines and in four major collections published by Dodd, Mead. Much of this short fiction complemented the popular dialect poetry, some of it written entirely in dialect and most of it featuring dialect-speaking folk characters. A few stories, however, moved in directions of protest, or of exploring issues of urbanization and cultural conflict. Dunbar also did some writing for the theater, including the highly popular musical comedy *Clorindy,* on which he collaborated with the composer William Marion cook.

But some of his most important work, outside his poetry, lay in his novels. Dunbar published four novels; one, *The Love of Landry* (1900), was a sentimental work set in the American West, but the other three focused on questions of culture and identity in ways that allowed him to explore the issues affecting him as an individual and as an artist. These included *The Uncalled* (1899), tracing a young man's efforts to deal with pressures exerted on him to enter the ministry; *The Fanatics* (1901), a tale of Civil War-era Ohio; and *The Sport of the Gods* (1902), describing the travails of a black family forced to flee the South and to make its way in the more complex setting of urban New York. Only the last novel featured black protagonists, and it has often been considered the pioneering work in literary realism by a black writer. But all, excepting *The Love of Landry,* looked significantly and innovatively at the kinds of forces, cultural and psychological, that confront and constrain the individual in an effort to create a satisfying personal identity, and, at least implicitly, at the meaning of race in American life.

Dunbar's work has not always fared well in the hands of critics in the years after his death. Not without justification, many have found too much of the dialect work, despite the writer's efforts to the contrary, to be uncomfortably close to that of white plantation-tradition writers, contributing to the same stereotypes the plantation tradition helped to spread. But Dunbar's influence and originality remain important milestones in the subsequent evolution of an African-American literary tradition.

BIBLIOGRAPHY

Baker, Houston A., Jr. "The 'Limitless' Freedom of Myth: Paul Laurence Dunbar's *The Sport of the Gods* and the Criticism of Afro-American Literature." In *Blues, Ideology, and Afro-American Literature: A Vernacular Theory.* Chicago, 1984, pp. 114–138.

Martin, Jay, ed. *A Singer in the Dawn: Reinterpretations of Paul Laurence Dunbar.* New York, 1975.

Revell, Peter. *Paul Laurence Dunbar.* Boston, 1979.

Wagner, Jean. *Black Poets of the United States from Paul Laurence Dunbar to Langston Hughes.* Translated by Kenneth Douglas. Urbana, Ill., 1973, pp. 73–125.

— DICKSON D. BRUCE, JR.

DUNBAR-NELSON, ALICE

Alice Dunbar-Nelson (July 19, 1875–September 18, 1935), writer. Alice Dunbar-Nelson was born Alice Ruth Moore in New Orleans, La. From her father, Joseph Moore, a sailor who never lived with the family, she inherited the light-colored skin and hair which enabled her to pass as white when she wished. Her mother, Patricia Wright Moore, an ex-slave who was part black and part Native American, supported the family as a seamstress. After attending public schools, Dunbar-Nelson graduated from the teachers' training program at Straight College (now Dillard University) in her hometown in 1892. In addition to her teaching, she worked as a stenographer and bookkeeper for a black printing firm. She was interested in theater, played the piano and cello, and presided over a literary society. In 1895, *Violets and Other Tales,* her first collection of stories, essays, and poetry, was published.

In 1896 she moved with her family to West Medford, Mass. The following year she moved to New York, where she taught public school in Brooklyn while she helped her friend Victoria Earle Matthews found the White Rose Mission (later the White Rose Home for Girls in Harlem), where she also taught. On March 8, 1898, she married the poet Paul Laurence DUNBAR, and moved to Washington, D.C., where he lived. Their romance had been conducted through letters. He first wrote to her after seeing her picture alongside one of

Alice Dunbar-Nelson. (Photographs and Prints Division, Schomburg Center for Research in Black Culture, The New York Public Library, Astor, Lenox and Tilden Foundations)

her poems in a poetry review. At their first meeting they agreed to marry.

Although it was a stormy marriage, it significantly aided Dunbar-Nelson's literary career. In 1899 her husband's agent had her second collection, *The Goodness of St. Roque,* published as a companion book to Dunbar's *Poems of Cabin and Field.* The couple separated in 1902 and Dunbar-Nelson moved to Wilmington, Del., where she taught English at the Howard High School. Paul Dunbar died in 1906. In 1910 Dunbar-Nelson married a fellow teacher, Henry Arthur Callis, but that union soon dissolved. In 1916, she married Robert J. Nelson, a journalist with whom she remained until her death in 1935.

Dunbar-Nelson's writings, published continually throughout her life, displayed a wide variety of interests. After studying English literature as a special student at Cornell University, she published "Wordsworth's Use of Milton's Description of Pandemonium" in the April 1909 issue of *Modern Language Notes.* She also published several pedagogical articles, including "Is It Time for the Negro Colleges in the South To Be Put into the Hands of Negro Teachers?" (*Twentieth Century Negro Literature* 1902) and "Negro Literature for Negro Pupils" (*The Southern Workman* February 1922). The *Journal of Negro History* published her historical essay "People of Color in Louisiana" in two parts; the first appeared in October 1916 and the second in January 1917. From 1920 to 1922 she and Nelson published and edited the *Wilmington Advocate.* In addition, she wrote columns for the Pittsburgh *Courier* (1926, 1930) and the Washington *Eagle* (1926–1930) in which she reviewed contemporary literature and delivered political analyses.

In 1920, Dunbar-Nelson lost her job at Howard High School due to her political activity on behalf of women's and civil rights. That year she founded the Industrial School for Colored Girls in Marshalltown, Del., which she directed from 1924 to 1928. From 1929 to 1931 she served as Executive Secretary of the American Inter-Racial Peace Committee, a subsidiary of the American Friends (Quakers) Service Committee. She used this position to organize the National Negro Music Festival in 1929, and to engage in a ten-week cross-country speaking tour in 1930. In 1932 she moved to Philadelphia, where her husband was a governor appointee to the Pennsylvania Athletic Commission. Her lifelong interest in the African-American oral tradition prompted her to publish *Masterpieces of Negro Eloquence* in 1914 and *The Dunbar Speaker and Entertainer* in 1920. She was a member of the Delta Sigma Theta sorority and the Daughter Elks. Dunbar-Nelson is often considered a poet of the Harlem Renaissance. Her two most anthologized poems are "Sonnet" (often called "Violets"), and "I Sit and Sew." Her diary, published in 1984, is an invaluable source of information about her life.

BIBLIOGRAPHY

Hull, Gloria T. *Color, Sex, and Poetry: Three Women Writers of the Harlem Renaissance.* Bloomington, Ind., 1987.

Hull, Gloria, T., ed. *Give Us Each Day: The Diary of Alice Dunbar-Nelson.* New York, 1984.

– MICHEL FABRE

DUNCANSON, ROBERT S.

Robert S. Duncanson (1821–December 21, 1872), painter. In this thirty-year career from the antebellum era through Reconstruction, Robert S. Duncanson progressed from being a humble housepainter to an artist of international stature who marked the emergence of the African-American practitioner into the Anglo-European art world. Duncanson was the first American artist of African descent to appropriate the landscape as an expression of his cultural identity. He was born into a family of mulatto freepeople who worked as painters, carpenters, and handymen in Fayette, N.Y. The family moved to Monroe, Mich., around 1830; there Duncanson apprenticed in the trade and then worked as a housepainter. By 1841 he had moved to Cincinnati, "the Athens of the West," to learn the art of painting. Throughout the 1840s he worked as an itinerant artist traveling between Cincinnati, Monroe, and Detroit painting portraits, historical subjects, and still lifes.

While working in Detroit, Duncanson received a commission to paint *The Cliff Mine, Lake Superior* (1848)—an event that altered the course of his career. The commission, from the Pittsburgh abolitionist Rev. Charles Avery, launched Duncanson's career as a landscape painter and established a lifelong relationship with abolitionist patrons. In this formative stage of his art, Duncanson was influenced by a group of Cincinnati landscape painters, including T. Worthington Whittredge (1820–1910) and William Louis Sonntag (1822–1900), to pursue the so-called Hudson River School style and create important early landscapes such as *Blue Hole, Flood Waters, Little Miami River* (1851; Cincinnati Art Museum). In 1853, he became the first African-American artist to take the traditional grand tour of Europe when abolitionist patron Nicholas Longworth sponsored his journey. Upon his return, Duncanson emerged as the principal landscape painter in the Ohio River Valley with such important pictures as *Landscape with Rainbow* (1859; National Museum of American Art). At this time he and James Pressley

Ball, a daguerreotypist, formed the nucleus of a group of African-American artists in Cincinnati who actively participated in the antislavery movement and created a monumental antislavery panorama that toured the United States.

In the months preceding the Civil War, Duncanson created the largest easel painting of his career, *The Land of the Lotus Eaters* (1861), which prophesied the imminent civil conflict. When he unveiled this vast tropical landscape, critics were moved to proclaim him "the best landscape painter in the West" (*Cincinnati Gazette,* May 30, 1862). Deeply troubled by the war, Duncanson exiled himself from the United States and traveled to Canada in 1863 on a journey to exhibit his "great picture" in England. Canadians warmly received the distinguished African-American painter without any reservations due to his race; he was therefore encouraged to remain there for two years, and contributed to founding a national landscape-painting school. He then toured the British Isles, where he was actively patronized by the aristocracy and where he extensively exhibited *The Lotus Eaters,* which English critics also praised as a "masterwork."

The success of Duncanson's second European tour crowned his career with international acclaim. Upon his return to Cincinnati in 1866, he began a series of Scottish landscapes inspired by English romantic literature, the finest being *Ellen's Isle, Loch Katrine* (1870). In his final years the artist suffered a tragic dementia, perhaps caused by lead poisoning, that led him to believe that he was possessed by the spirit of a master painter. His illness, combined with the pressures of racial oppression and his lofty artistic ambitions, proved too great for the artist to manage; he collapsed while hanging an exhibition in October 1872, dying in a Detroit sanatorium shortly thereafter.

BIBLIOGRAPHY

Hartigan, Linda. "Robert Scott Duncanson." In *Sharing Traditions: Five Black Artists in Nineteenth Century America.* Washington, D.C., 1985, pp. 51–68.

Ketner, Joseph D. *The Emergence of the African-American Artist: Robert S. Duncanson 1821–1872.* Columbia, Mo., and London, 1993.

———. "Robert S. Duncanson (1821–1872): The Late Literary Landscape Paintings." *American Art Journal* 15 (Winter 1983): 35–47.

McElroy, Guy. *Robert S. Duncanson: A Centennial Exhibition.* Cincinnati, 1972.

Porter, James A. "Robert S. Duncanson: Midwestern Romantic-Realist." *Art in America* 39 (October 1951): 99–154.

Pringle, Allan. "Robert S. Duncanson in Montreal, 1863–1865." *American Art Journal* 17 (Autumn 1985): 28–50.

– JOSEPH D. KETNER

DUNHAM, KATHERINE

Katherine Dunham (June 22, 1909–), choreographer and dancer. Born in Chicago, and raised in Joliet, Ill., Katherine Dunham did not begin formal dance training until her late teens. In Chicago she studied with Ludmilla Speranzeva and Mark Turbyfill, and danced her first leading role in Ruth Page's ballet *La Guiablesse* in 1933. She attended the University of Chicago on scholarship (B.A., Social Anthropology, 1936), where she was inspired by the work of anthropologists Robert Redfield and Melville Herskovits, who stressed the importance of the survival of African culture and ritual in understanding African-American culture. While in college she taught youngsters' dance classes and gave recitals in a Chicago storefront, calling her student company, founded in 1931, "Ballet Nègre." Awarded a Rosenwald Travel Fellowship in 1936 for her combined expertise in dance and anthropology, she departed after graduation for the West Indies (Jamaica, Trinidad, Cuba, Haiti, Martinique) to do field research in anthropology and dance. Combining her two interests, she linked the function and form of Caribbean dance and ritual to their African progenitors.

The West Indian experience changed forever the focus of Dunham's life (eventually she would live in Haiti half of the time and become a priestess in the *vodoun* religion), and caused a profound shift in her career. This initial fieldwork provided the nucleus for future researches and began a lifelong involvement with the people and dance of Haiti. From this Dunham generated her master's thesis (Northwestern University, 1947) and more fieldwork. She lectured widely, published numerous articles, and wrote three books about her observations: *Journey to Accompong* (1946), *The Dances of Haiti* (her master's thesis, published in 1947), and *Island Possessed* (1969), underscoring how African religions and rituals adapted to the New World.

And, importantly for the development of modern dance, her fieldwork began her investigations into a vocabulary of movement that would form the core of the Katherine Dunham Technique. What Dunham gave modern dance was a coherent lexicon of African and Caribbean styles of movement—a flexible torso and spine, articulated pelvis and isolation of the limbs, a polyrhythmic strategy of moving—which she integrated with techniques of ballet and modern dance.

When she returned to Chicago in late 1937, Dunham founded the Negro Dance Group, a company of black artists dedicated to presenting aspects of African-American and African-Caribbean dance. Immediately she began incorporating the dances she had learned into her choreography. Invited in 1937 to be part of a notable New York City concert, *Negro Dance Evening,* she premiered "Haitian Suite," excerpted from choreography she was developing for the longer *L'Ag'Ya.* In 1937–1938 as dance director of the Negro Unit of the Federal Theater Project in Chicago, she made dances for *Emperor Jones* and *Run Lil' Chillun,* and presented her first version of *L'Ag'Ya* on January 27, 1938. Based on a Martinique folktale (ag'ya is a Martinique fighting dance), *L'Ag'Ya* is a seminal work, displaying Dunham's blend of exciting dance-drama and authentic African-Caribbean material.

What Dunham gave modern dance was a coherent lexicon of African and Caribbean styles of movement.

Dunham moved her company to New York City in 1939, where she became dance director of the New York Labor Stage, choreographing the labor-union musical *Pins and Needles.* Simultaneously she was preparing a new production, *Tropics and Le Jazz Hot: From Haiti to Harlem.* It opened February 18, 1939, in what was intended to be a single weekend's concert at the Windsor Theatre in New York City. Its instantaneous success, however, extended the run for ten consecutive weekends and catapulted Dunham into the limelight. In 1940 Dunham and her company appeared in the black Broadway musical, *Cabin in the Sky,* staged by George Balanchine, in which Dunham played the sultry siren Georgia Brown—a character related to Dunham's other seductress, "Woman with a Cigar," from her solo "Shore Excursion" in *Tropics.* That same year Dunham married John Pratt, a theatrical designer who worked with her in 1938 at the Chicago Federal Theater Project, and for the next forty-seven years, until his death in 1986, Pratt was Dunham's husband and her artistic collaborator.

With *L'Ag'Ya* and *Tropics and le Jazz Hot: From Haiti to Harlem,* Dunham revealed her magical mix of dance and theater—the essence of "the Dunham touch"—a savvy combination of authentic Caribbean dance and rhythms with the heady spice of American showbiz. Genuine folk material was presented with lavish costumes, plush settings, and the orchestral arrangements based on Caribbean rhythms and folk music. Dancers moved through fantastical tropical paradises or artistically designed juke-joints, while a loose storyline held together a succession of diverse dances. Dunham aptly called her spectacles "revues." She choreographed more than ninety individual dances, and produced five revues, four of which played on Broadway and toured worldwide. Her most critically acclaimed revue was her 1946 *Bal Nègre,* containing another Dunham dance favorite, *Shango,* based directly on *vodoun* ritual.

If her repertory was diverse, it was also coherent. *Tropics and le Jazz Hot: From Haiti to Harlem* incorporated dances from the West Indies as well as from Cuba and Mexico, while the "Le Jazz Hot" section featured early black American social dances, such as the Juba, Cake Walk, Ballin' the Jack, and Strut. The sequencing of dances, the theatrical journey from the tropics to urban black America implied—in the most entertaining terms—the ethnographic realities of cultural connections. In her 1943 *Tropical Revue,* she recycled material from the 1939 revue and added new dances, such as the balletic "Choros" (based on formal Brazilian quadrilles), and "Rites de Passage," which depicted puberty rituals so explicitly sexual that the dance was banned in Boston.

Beginning in the 1940s, the Katherine Dunham Dance Company appeared on Broadway and toured throughout the United States, Mexico, Latin America, and especially Europe, to enthusiastic reviews. In Europe Dunham was praised as a dancer and choreographer, recognized as a serious anthropologist and scholar, and admired as a glamorous beauty. Among her achievements was her resourcefulness in keeping her company going without any government funding. When short of money between engagements, Dunham and her troupe played in elegant nightclubs, such as Ciro's in Los Angeles. She also supplemented her income through film. Alone, or with her company, she appeared in nine Hollywood movies and in several foreign films between 1941 and 1959, among them *Carnival of Rhythm* (1939), *Star-Spangled Rhythm* (1942), *Stormy Weather* (1943), *Casbah* (1948), *Boote e Risposta* (1950), and *Mambo* (1954).

In 1945 Dunham opened the Dunham School of Dance and Theater (sometimes called the Dunham School of Arts and Research) in Manhattan. Although technique classes were the heart of the school, they were supplemented by courses in humanities, philosophy, languages, aesthetics, drama, and speech. For the next ten years many African-American dances of the next generation studied at her school, then passed on Dunham's technique to their students, situating it in dance mainstream (teachers such as Syvilla Fort, Talley Beatty, Lavinia Williams, Walter Nicks, Hope Clark, Vanoye Aikens, and Carmencita Romero; the Dunham technique has always been taught at the Alvin AILEY studios).

During the 1940s and '50s, Dunham kept up her brand of political activism. Fighting segregation in hotels, restaurants and theaters, she filed lawsuits and made public condemnations. In Hollywood, she refused to sign a lucrative studio contract when the producer said she would have to replace some of her darker-skinned company members. To an enthusiastic but all-white audience in the South, she made an after-performance speech, saying she could never play there again until it was integrated. In São Paulo, Brazil, she brought a discrimination suit against a hotel, eventually prompting the president of Brazil to apologize to her and to pass a law that forbade discrimination in public places. In 1951 Dunham premiered *Southland,* an hour-long ballet about lynching, though it was only performed in Chile and Paris.

Toward the end of the 1950s Dunham was forced to regroup, disband, and reform her company, according to the exigencies of her financial and physical health (she suffered from crippling knee problems). Yet she remained undeterred. In 1962 she opened a Broadway production, *Bambouche,* featuring fourteen dancers, singers, and musicians of the Royal Troupe of Morocco, along with the Dunham company. The next year she choreographed the Metropolitan Opera's new production of *Aida*—thereby becoming the Met's first black choreographer. In 1965–1966, she was cultural adviser to the President of Senegal. She attended Senegal's First World Festival of Negro Arts as a representative from the United States.

Moved by the civil rights struggle and outraged by deprivations in the ghettos of East St. Louis, an area she knew from her visiting professorships at Southern Illinois University in the 1960s, Dunham decided to take action. In 1967 she opened the Performing Arts Training Center, a cultural program and school for the neighborhood children and youth, with programs in dance, drama, martial arts, and humanities. Soon thereafter she expanded the programs to include senior citizens. Then in 1977 she opened the Katherine Dunham Museum and Children's Workshop to house her collections of artifacts from her travels and research, as well as archival material from her personal life and professional career.

During the 1980s, Dunham received numerous awards acknowledging her contributions. These include the Albert Schweitzer Music Award for a life devoted to performing arts and service to humanity (1979); a Kennedy Center Honor's Award (1983); the Samuel H. Scripps American Dance Festival Award (1987); induction into the Hall of Fame of the National Museum of Dance in Saratoga Springs, N.Y. (1987). That same year Dunham directed the reconstruction of several of her works by the Alvin Ailey American Dance Theater and *The Magic of Katherine Dunham* opened Ailey's 1987–1988 season.

In February 1992, at the age of eighty-two, Dunham again became the subject of international attention when she began a forty-seven-day fast at her East St. Louis home. Because of her age, her involvement with Haiti, and the respect accorded her as an activist and artist, Dunham became the center of a movement that coalesced to protest the United States's deportations of Haitian boat-refugees fleeing to the U.S. after the military overthrow of Haiti's democratically elected President Jean-Bertrand Aristide. She agreed to end her fast only after Aristide visited her and personally requested her to stop.

Boldness has characterized Dunham's life and career. And, although she was not alone, Dunham is perhaps the best known and most influential pioneer of black dance. Her synthesis of scholarship and theatricality demonstrated, incontrovertibly and joyously, that African-American and African-Caribbean styles are related and powerful components of dance in America.

BIBLIOGRAPHY

Beckford, Ruth. *Katherine Dunham: A Biography.* New York, 1979.

Dunham, Katherine. *A Touch of Innocence.* New York, 1969.

— SALLY SOMMER

DURHAM, NORTH CAROLINA

Located in a north-central piedmont area of North Carolina, which includes much of the Research Triangle Park, Durham is the state's fifth largest city. In 1990 it had a population of 136,611, about 46 percent African American. A center of black enterprise, it is touted as a beacon of progressive race relations. Its significance is comparable to larger southern cities such as RICHMOND, ATLANTA, and Nashville.

Durham was organized in the 1850s, in the middle of a slave-holding region, the antebellum hamlet boasting scarcely more than a post office and railroad station. Slaves and free people of color helped to cultivate its tobacco and other cash crops. Incorporated in 1866, it drew numerous black residents. Black life centered on the St. Joseph's African Methodist Episcopal and White Rock Baptist Churches.

By the 1880s, tobacco and textile factories and railroads began turning Durham into a model New South town. In 1890 the American Tobacco Company was formed. It soon controlled 75 percent of the national market. In 1898 blacks were hired in large numbers by tobacco factories. Soon after, black entrepreneurs established cotton mills, and in 1902 white tycoon Julian S. Carr opened a cotton mill with all black employees. Compared to many southern factory towns, which

shunned black laborers, an unusual number of black Durhamites worked in factories.

A center of black enterprise, Durham is touted as a beacon of progressive race relations.

A black middle class emerged. John Merrick, an ex-slave barber, bought the rights to the Royal Knights of King David, a fraternal order and used this framework to start an insurance business. After major white insurers like Prudential Life Insurance Company decided during the 1890s to stop accepting black policyholders, Merrick and several business partners formed a syndicate to develop the North Carolina Mutual and Provident Association, chartered in 1898. Mutual was unsuccessful at first, but under the leadership of Charles C. Spaulding it grew swiftly until it was the largest black-owned business in America. Its directors parlayed its capital and experience into other ventures, including drug stores, a real estate firm, textile mill, and the Mechanics and Farmers Bank, which opened in 1908. The black Durham elite was instrumental in founding North Carolina College (NCC) in 1910 (now North Carolina Central University). Commentators as diverse as Booker T. WASHINGTON and W. E. B. DU BOIS wrote magazine articles hailing the development of black enterprise in Durham. By 1919, when Mutual declared itself the North Carolina Mutual Life Insurance Company, Durham had become virtually the "capital" of the black middle class, a term popularized by sociologist E. Franklin FRAZIER in *The New Negro* (1925). During the 1920s, the Bankers Fire Insurance Company, the Mutual Savings and Loan Association, and the National Negro Finance Corporation were founded there as well.

Despite Durham's reputation for interracial cooperation and economic backing from white businessmen, which buttressed black progress, JIM CROW remained strong in the city through the first half of the twentieth century. Health and labor conditions for black workers were poor. The Durham Committee on Negro Affairs (DCNA), a civil rights organization controlled by the black business elite, was launched in 1935. In 1942, the Durham NAACP, one of the state's oldest branches, joined the DCNA to support a meeting of southern black leaders at North Carolina College, out of which came the "Durham Manifesto" demanding the abolition of segregation in the South. Five years later, during the Journey of Reconciliation, an early effort by the CONGRESS OF RACIAL EQUALITY (CORE) to test compliance with a Supreme Court decision against segregated interstate buses, Durham police beat and arrested freedom riders. In 1949, black parents won a school equalization suit against the city's board of education, although token school integration did not begin until 1959. The DCNA's voter registration efforts made it a political power.

In 1960, African-American students from NCC sat-in at lunch counters and forced city officials to take steps "quietly" to desegregate downtown stores. Student-led boycotts and mass demonstrations, assisted by Durham attorney Floyd B. McKissick, later head of CORE, led by 1963 to a fair hiring ordinance and nonracial admissions to policy at nearby Duke University. In 1968, Durham was swept by violent African-American protest after the assassination of the Rev. Dr. Martin Luther KING, Jr. Black power advocates recruited hospital workers into unions and struggled to empower poor people. In 1981, black activists formed the National Black Independent Political Party. The DCNA, renamed the Durham Committee on Black Affairs, sponsored the election of blacks to various offices.

In the 1990s, one-fourth of Durham's black residents live in poverty. However, the city remains a hub of black capitalism. North Carolina Mutual is the largest black insurance company in America, while Mechanics and Farmers Bank and Mutual Savings and Loan are nationally prominent. Durham is also a cultural locus, home of the African American Dance Ensemble and the Thelonious Monk Institute of Jazz. In 1992, the predominantly black area of Durham was included in a newly drawn congressional district, and the city's first African-American Representative, Melvin L. Watt, was elected.

BIBLIOGRAPHY

Anderson, Jean Bradley. *Durham County: A History of Durham County, North Carolina.* Durham, N.C., 1990.

Gavins, Raymond. "The Meaning of Freedom: Black North Carolina in the Nadir, 1880–1900." In *Race, Class, and Politics in Southern History: Essays in Honor of Robert F. Durden.* Baton Rouge, La. 1989, pp. 175–215.

Jones, Beverly W. "Durham, North Carolina" In *The Statistical and Geographical Abstract of the Black Population in the United States.* College Park, Md., 1992.

Weare, Walter B. *Black Business in the New South: A Social History of the North Carolina Mutual Life Insurance Company.* Urbana, Ill., 1973.

— RAYMOND GAVINS

DYER BILL

In response to mob violence and the frequent brutal lynching of African Americans, the Dyer antilynching bill was first introduced in the United States Congress in April 1918. Leonidas Dyer, a Missouri Republican serving the Twelfth Congressional district, which included the large black electorate in St. Louis's South Side, was the bill's architect and sponsor.

After securing earlier support from the NAACP, which was intensifying its own crusade against lynching at the time, Dyer submitted legislation to make lynching a federal crime. In its original form, the bill invoked the equal-protection-of-the-laws clause of the Fourteenth Amendment to safeguard American citizens against lynching by federal statute. The bill defined a lynch mob as a group of three or more individuals, made them liable to prosecution for a capital crime, and also subjected state officials to fine and imprisonment for failing to prosecute individuals whom they knew were involved in lynching. During the same session, Merrill Moores of Indiana submitted another bill that was also intent on making lynching a federal crime. Neither bill, however, initially satisfied the NAACP. Moorfield Storey, the Association's first president and noted constitutional lawyer, believed both bills were unconstitutional because they employed the Fourteenth Amendment to seek federal redress for the crime of murder, the jurisdiction of which resided with the states. Accordingly, the association failed to lobby vigorously for the bill in 1918, and the matter did not reach a congressional vote.

The following year, however, the NAACP and Storey dropped their opposition and supported Dyer's bill with an intensive lobbying campaign. This resulted partly from Storey's growing recognition that state governments were not punishing lynchers and from his new argument that the federal government could prosecute lynchers under its wartime and national emergency powers. The NAACP's motives stemmed from the worsening conditions facing African Americans in the United States following World War I. Rather than ushering in a new climate of racial tolerance, the war's aftermath had produced more virulent racism and excessive violence. Blacks returning from the war were lynched while still in uniform in some southern communities, and America experienced major race riots during the Red Summer of 1919. NAACP support for the Dyer Bill became one facet of a crucial new drive for civil rights in a time of intensified oppression. Despite the turnaround and strenuous campaigning by the NAACP, the bill languished. Dyer faithfully submitted it annually, through 1929, only to have a mixture of constitutional questions, southern filibusters, and general political indifference block a fail vote on its passage.

Although the Dyer Bill never became law, its legacy was revived by the introduction of new antilynching measures, the Costigan-Wagner bill of 1935 and the Wagner-Gavagan bill of 1940, both of which were substantially the same as the Dyer Bill, except that the former sought state rather than federal relief. As President, Franklin D. Roosevelt failed to support these antilynching laws out of fear that his support would cause southern resentment and irrevocably shatter his New Deal coalition. Neither of these measures was successful, but collectively all three proposed bills kept the NAACP active in its antilynching crusade and kept the issue before the nation.

BIBLIOGRAPHY

Zangrando, Robert L. *The NAACP Crusade Against Lynching, 1909–1950.* Philadelphia, 1980.

– MARSHALL HYATT

E

EAST ST. LOUIS, ILLINOIS, RIOT OF 1917

The East St. Louis, Ill., riot of 1917 was the first in a number of riots that occurred between 1917 and 1919, a period of economic disruption amid massive black migration northward. East St. Louis, dubbed by some "the Pittsburgh of the West," was a town of sixty-eight thousand people across the Mississippi River from St. Louis, with stockyards and aluminum iron factories. Living conditions were dreadful, and law enforcement was lax in the "open" town. Still, African Americans fleeing the South settled there. The town's black population went from six thousand in 1910 to ten thousand in 1920.

In April 1917, the white labor force went on strike at the Aluminum Ore Company. Employees attempting to form a union were frozen out and replaced by strikebreakers, a small percentage of whom were black. At the same time, during an electoral campaign, local Democratic leaders charged that Republicans were encouraging blacks to settle in East St. Louis to swell the Republican vote. Stories of black vice and crime were prominently reported in newspapers.

On May 28, a labor union delegation called upon the mayor to request that blacks no longer be allowed to migrate to the city. As the delegation was leaving city hall, news reached its members that a black man had accidentally killed a white man during a holdup. Soon rumors spread of white women being insulted and white girls shot. Over three thousand whites gathered to retaliate. Angry mobs invaded the downtown area, attacking African-American residents. Mobs used oil-soaked rags to burn down African-American shanties, and six people were shot, none fatally. Police remained neutral or assisted rioters, and National Guard troops mobilized during the strike refused to intervene. The next day, there were further beatings and a shooting death. Instead of protecting black citizens, police entered blacks' houses to search for concealed weapons.

During the following month, racially motivated crime continued in East St. Louis. Black laborers going to work were attacked and had to get police escorts; blacks crossing the bridge to St. Louis were tormented; and, especially following the calling off of the strike late in June, blacks were randomly beaten. The mayor failed to listen to NATIONAL ASSOCIATION FOR THE ADVANCEMENT OF COLORED PEOPLE (NAACP) warnings of rising racial tension, or even to produce a riot plan. Police and the press cheered on violent whites, and no incidents were investigated or rioters charged. A labor committee sent to investigate the May 28 riot blamed employers for importing "an excessive and abnormal number" of blacks, and on blacks themselves.

On the evening of July 1, as rumors swirled among all races of plans for July 4 uprisings, a carload of whites drove through a black area, spraying bullets into homes. Police remained inactive until the car drove through again, and blacks returned the fire. Blacks, believing a police car was the marauders returning, opened fire, killing two detectives in the process.

The East St. Louis riot was the first in a number of riots that occurred between 1917 and 1919, a period of economic disruption amid massive black migration northward.

On July 2, after viewing the bullet-ridden police car, white crowds marched through the city, beating and shooting blacks. Men were lynched, women and children clubbed. The police refused to act, and some of the National Guard troops and police stationed in the area joined in the rioting. Black houses were set afire, their occupants were shot as they tried to escape, and their corpses were dumped in Chokia Creek. A large crowd of African Americans fled across the bridge to St. Louis. Once the National Guard units left, the violence escalated. At least thirty-nine blacks, and possibly up to a hundred were killed, along with nine whites, making it one of the deadliest riots in African American history. Hundreds were injured, and the black neighborhood was heavily damaged.

The negative publicity the riot generated led Illinois Attorney General C. W. Middlekauf to indict eight-two whites and twenty-three blacks for rioting and murder. Only nine whites were ever sent to prison. Seven police officers charged with murder or assault pleaded guilty to lesser charges and were collectively fined $150. Meanwhile, ten blacks who were arrested in the detectives' deaths received fourteen-year sentences from all-white juries. On July 28, 1917, a silent parade of 10,000, organized by the NAACP, passed through New York City's Harlem neighborhood to protest the riot and killings. The NAACP's relief and protest activities brought it high visibility among African Americans.

The riot demonstrated the defenselessness of black Americans against white violence in the growing urban areas outside the South. It would be only the first in a series of racial incidents in the following two years.

BIBLIOGRAPHY

Rudwick, Elliott M. *Race Riot at East St. Louis, July 2, 1917.* 2nd ed. Urbana, Ill., 1982.

— GAYLE T. TATE

EBONY

Published by the Johnson Publishing Company, *Ebony* is the largest circulation African-American periodical. Founded in 1945, it grew out of an attempt by publisher John H. JOHNSON to please two staff members who wanted to start an entertainment magazine, *Jive.* Johnson agreed to a three-way partnership on the project, but the two staffers were unable to put up money, so Johnson assumed full ownership. Johnson changed the style of the proposed magazine into one whose philosophy would be to highlight the positive side of African-American life, emphasizing black pride and achievements, rather than oppression and poverty. Recognizing the widespread appeal of photos, Johnson planned a monthly glamor magazine on glossy paper, in the style of the popular weekly *Life,* filled with pictures of prominent and successful blacks. The new magazine, which Johnson named *Ebony* (after the beautiful and strong black wood) was planned during World War II, but due to paper restrictions, the first issue did not appear until November 1, 1945. Johnson had pledged to accept no advertisements until circulation reached 100,000; the magazine was an immediate success and the first ads appeared in the May 1946 issue. By May 1947, when *Ebony* became the first African-American periodical large enough to be audited by the Audit Bureau of Circulation, its circulation had reached 309,715. Despite its prestige and large circulation, however, poor advertising revenues made it unprofitable until Johnson secured advertising contracts from white firms previously reluctant to purchase space in African-American publications.

Ebony has drawn some criticism over the years for the showy, escapist nature of its features, and its emphasis on the activities of wealthy blacks, although the magazine took a more activist direction starting in the era of the CIVIL RIGHTS MOVEMENT. Over time, the magazine has added sections on cooking, health, and gossip. The enormous success of *Ebony* has inspired numerous competitors over the years, and the magazine has had numerous spinoffs, including the periodicals *Ebony Man,* the now defunct *Ebony Jr.,* the Ebony Fashion Fair traveling fashion show, and the syndicated television program *Ebony/Jet Showcase.*

In the early 1990s, the magazine's circulation was about 1.9 million, of which 12 percent were white. It was distributed in some forty countries, including many in Africa.

BIBLIOGRAPHY

Graves, Earl. "Johnson Celebrates 50th," *Black Enterprise* 23 (November 1992): 26.

Johnson, John H., and Lerone Bennett, Jr. *Succeeding Against the Odds.* New York, 1989.

— GREG ROBINSON

ECONOMICS

After the Civil War, four million freed slaves joined one-half million free blacks in a twilight status somewhere between full citizenship and slavery. African Americans and their white allies understood that without economic property and voting rights for the ex-slaves, the Emancipation would have little practical meaning for African Americans or American democracy. Political citizenship for African-American men was theoretically achieved in the Thirteenth, Fourteenth, and Fifteenth Amendments to the Constitution and the civil rights acts of 1866 and 1875. Later, however, that status was voided as, state by state, the South disfranchised African-American voters toward the end of the nineteenth century. Moreover, the ex-slaves received no financial reparations for the two and a third centuries of bondage they and their predecessors had endured. In particular, Congress refused to confiscate valuable farmlands from supporters of the Confederacy, who were perceived as a competent managerial elite, for redistribution to the freedmen, who were perceived as unskilled and inexperienced independent farmers. Nor would the federal government risk lending money to plantation owners so that the war-ravaged South could reconstitute its economy on a sound basis.

Reconstruction to 1900

FROM SLAVERY TO SHARECROPPING. Overwhelmingly, the ex-slaves entered freedom with nothing but their labor to sell to former slave owners who were bereft of capital and low on credit and whose prior experience had given them absolute power over that same labor. Between the two groups stood the freed blacks' newfound mobility and the BUREAU OF FREEDMEN, REFUGEES AND ABANDONED LANDS, commonly called the Freedmen's Bureau, which Congress had created as a compromise between forces for and against land confiscation to ensure a smooth and just transition from slave to free labor and a speedy return to large crops of cotton, sugar, tobacco, and rice.

AFRICAN-AMERICAN AGRARIANISM. A complex interaction between politics and African-American self-help was at work throughout the Reconstruction period. Black reconstruction began during the Civil War when thousands of runaway slaves wreaked havoc on the Confederacy's war effort and economy. Many of them were convinced that they had a right to the new homesteads they had established on land abandoned by slave owners in the wake of the advancing Union armies, land from which they were subsequently removed by military force. Blacks now enjoyed the freedom of migration; many former slaves from the upper South and Southeast moved to the Southwest where the fertile cotton lands of Arkansas, Mississippi, and Louisiana allowed planters to offer higher wages than elsewhere. Between 1860 and 1910 the southern Atlantic states' share of the African-American population declined from 46 percent to 42 percent while the share of the western south central states rose from 15 percent to 20 percent.

African Americans and their white allies understood that without economic property and voting rights for the ex-slaves, the Emancipation would have little practical meaning.

Blacks and their Republican allies continued the quest for economic security for the ex-slaves at the state and local levels. African-American politicians in southern state legislatures were strong backers of the rights of labor and the small farmer. They and other Republicans campaigned for homestead laws to enable landless families to acquire unsettled federal land. African-American leaders and their white allies, many of them Union army veterans, started societies that raised money to buy and work land. The legislatures of a number of states passed laws that were decidedly prolabor and as such raised the ire of large owners of property. For example, states such as South Carolina, Alabama, and Georgia passed laws that gave the laborer first right to cotton and other cash crops as a lien on his or her claims for wages or a share of the crop.

FROM GANG LABOR TO FAMILY SHARECROPPING. Sharecropping evolved as a system that neither freedpeople nor planters considered optimal. During the initial years of Reconstruction, former slaves and slave owners faced off in a struggle to determine the new labor-management relations. The ex-slaves rebelled against the attempt by the owners of large plantations to approximate the labor relations of the slave regime. In the immediate postbellum period large cotton plantations would employ several work gangs under the supervision of a headman or overseer; decision making was a hierarchical function. (Such a structure had been typical of the slave economy.) Freedmen (including women and adolescents) were organized into these work gangs, but many refused to work under gang foremen who in many cases had been "drivers" who enforced discipline with whips. African Americans demanded and won more freedom in the performance of their daily tasks and especially in the conduct of their private affairs.

The Freedmen's Bureau adjudicated thousands of labor disputes between planters and laborers. The vast majority involved labor turnover as African Americans attempted to exercise their new rights of mobility. Labor turnover was most frequently due to harsh supervision—whipping and the like—and to the inability of a great many formerly well-to-do planters to pay laborers their wages at the end of the year. Additionally, the bureau was also involved in many arguments over work rules and payment arrangements.

Of the heavily capitalized sugar plantations of Louisiana and, to a lesser extent, the larger rice plantations of South Carolina and Georgia, those that survived Reconstruction intact were generally able to maintain closely supervised work crews that were paid money wages. However, the majority of laborers on tobacco and cotton plantations (usually one-third to one-half their numbers) worked in gangs for a share wage of the net proceeds of a crop that was to be divided between anywhere from ten to fifty workers after it was harvested and sold by the planter. Moreover, in those cases where African Americans did contract to work for money wages, these sums were due in a lump at the end of the crop year. In either case, during the year, laborers obtained subsistence food and clothing (usually on credit) from either plantation stores or independent merchants.

In 1866 and 1868 large-scale crop failures due to disastrous weather conditions left many planters unable to pay their debts to creditors and laborers. As a result, most laborers received only partial wages or no wages at all for a full year's work. This experience led to wholesale abandonment of plantations as laborers searched for employers who could pay them during the harvest season. Furthermore, it led to extreme distrust between African Americans and their employers. These problems of no pay and low pay led to a large reduction in the labor supply of African-American women and children; seeing their work efforts bear little fruit for two years, they reallocated their time to activities such as household chores and school.

At this point the Freedmen's Bureau ruled that, while workers promised money wages were employees and could be paid after the employer had sold the crop, share laborers were part owners of the crop and had the right to demand crop division in the field, after which they could dispose of their share as they wished. Given the huge number of landlords defaulting on payments to laborers, this ruling, which the bureau enforced with the military, led laborers to demand shares because that form of payment provided greater security to the laborer than did postharvest wages. By 1867 only those planters with the greatest reputations for solvency and access to cash or credit could hire labor for wages, since African Americans were as a rule demanding to work where, in their words, they were "part owners of the crop."

But the system of paying laborers one-half the crop while still working them in large gangs led to severe incentive problems and inefficient work. Because all workers received a portion of the entire gang's share, better workers felt that they were being cheated and refused to work with those they considered inefficient. Moreover, some workers recognized that, since they each were just one member of a large work gang, their share of the crop would not be substantially reduced if they shirked their responsibilities. These developments increased absenteeism and other poor work habits, thus causing many arguments. To avoid this problem of the free rider, the size of work gangs was reduced and workers were allowed to choose their coworkers.

During approximately the ten-year period from 1865 to 1875, planters and laborers experimented with many types of labor systems. By the late 1860s many aspects of managerial authority had flowed from planters to laborers as small groups of men and women formed work groups that collectively contracted with planters for a group share of the crop. These work collectives, called variously "squads," "associations," and "clubs," were in a real sense democratic, majority-rule worker collectives that seriously threatened the managerial authority of the planters.

By the mid-to-late 1870s, throughout the cotton and tobacco areas of the South, the scaling down of work-group size to better meet demands for efficiency and equity among workers, the practice of allowing self-selection of coworkers, and African Americans' demand for family autonomy led to the proliferation of share-tenancy for one half the crop by groups of families working a small farm for themselves. Whether the planters anticipated it or not, the individualism inherent in family share-tenancy destroyed the collective esprit of the cotton and tobacco laborers, and unlike the wage hands on sugar plantations who continued to agitate and sometimes lead insurrections against employers and the state for better working conditions, share tenants became a conservative workforce whose deep but unvoiced animosity for its plight only occasionally led to activism.

Extreme violence and terrorism was used by the Ku Klux Klan to drive African Americans from the political process.

The agrarianism and political participation among African Americans that preceded full institution of family sharecropping should be understood as twin activities whose common objective was to transfer economic and political power from the landowning and former slaveholder class to the working classes of the South. This attempt to institute economic and political democracy in the South posed a serious threat to the established property interests. The story of their violent reply has often been told. The planters and their allies managed to focus all questions on the issue of race by defining the political and economic contest as one that would determine which *race* as opposed to which *classes* would control the South's political and economic institutions. Extreme violence and terrorism was used by the KU KLUX KLAN and other terrorist organizations to drive African Americans from the political process and from any collective efforts to improve their economic status.

A major cost of the race relations of discrimination and segregation was the failure of blacks and the descendants of the nonslaveholding whites to forge a political bond. Devastated by the Civil War and the credit famine and crop failure of the war's immediate aftermath, small white farmers in the upland regions of the cotton South also became impoverished. The racial segregation of southern life was well illustrated in the geographical division of black and white agricultural labor. From the latter third of the nineteenth century onwards, relatively small farms owned and worked by white families produced increasing quantities of cotton in the piedmont regions of the upper South; labor on large cotton plantations in the lower South, however, was almost exclusively black. White and black cotton producers became victims of a brutal economic system wherein low cotton prices (which persisted into the mid-twentieth century) tied them to a cycle of credit advances, poverty, and debt to landowners and merchants, a cycle that became for many a cruel form of debt peonage.

INDUSTRIAL LABOR. According to the census of 1890, a huge majority of African-American men and women were employed as agricultural laborers or in personal service. In the northern states the discriminatory conditions that had existed before the Civil War persisted. In cities like Chicago, New York, Philadelphia, and Baltimore and in hundreds of smaller towns, blacks, with few exceptions, were proscribed from employment in all but menial laboring and personal-service positions. Blacks with education and skills had to accept employment well below their abilities or had to find some way to operate a business within the segregated African-American community. For example, W. E. B. DU BOIS wrote of a young African American who had graduated from the University of Pennsylvania with a degree in engineering but could only find employment as a restaurant waiter in the Philadelphia of the late 1890s.

By 1900 employment in the South was dominated by a pattern of segregation wherein one race, through economic competition, politics, or violence, essentially drove the other race from the industry or from many occupations within it. The textile industry, which hardly existed in the South before the Civil War, was almost completely staffed by white men, women, and children. Economic segregation exhibited a perverse symmetry—black and white families in cotton production were separated by geography, whereas black and white families in cotton manufacturing were separated by the refusal of textile employers to hire African Americans.

Many African Americans worked outside the plantations. They found employment with the railroads, in coal mining, in the growing lumber mill and turpentine industries that became important to the southern economy, and in the nonfarm tobacco industry centered in the upper South. Moreover, black labor, because it could be obtained cheaply from plantations, was a major factor in the rise of the southern iron and steel industries. Many of these industries managed to keep wages low and working conditions barbarous by hiring convict labor from the state.

TRADE UNIONS. Before the Civil War skilled slaves, hired out by their masters, often competed with white craftsmen for work. Competition from slaves lowered wages and impeded unionization. Southern white workers generally became antagonistic toward the slaves instead of toward the slavery that was responsible for the adverse conditions; even in the North blacks were despised by the white working classes. Expectations that this antagonism between black and white working-class people would continue after emancipation were strengthened during the draft riots of 1863 when thousands of rioting working-class New Yorkers, protesting class-biased draft laws and the Republican party, attacked African Americans, injuring many; subsequently, in 1865, white workers in the Baltimore shipyards and docks staged a long and victorious strike to drive blacks from the better jobs. In Washington, D.C., the white bricklayers' union in 1869 expelled four members found working with blacks on a government job.

Only in industries where large numbers of African Americans had acquired experience as slaves, where there were no significant technological changes in work conditions to disadvantage blacks (i.e., since they were discriminated against when seeking training), and where unionization among whites was not strong were blacks able to maintain an employment presence. Indeed, blacks were often hired specifically to break unions that were forming or were existent but weak. For example, during the decades after 1870, blacks pushed many whites from the iron and coal industries as producers in Georgia, Alabama, and Tennessee recruited black labor for semiskilled jobs in order to break the strength of incipient labor organizations among whites. On the other side of the ledger was the contract construction industry where, throughout the South, thousands of freed slave craftsmen were a strong economic force well into the twentieth century. From their ranks arose many black contractors who, along with the skilled workers, were later gradually squeezed out of the industry mainstream by white contractors and craftsmen, who generally refused to work with or for blacks. Moreover, the discriminatory training and educational opportunities in the private and public sectors prevented African Americans from adapting the skills they had to technologically changing crafts. This was especially true in the newer electrical, plumbing, and mechanical trades, which developed in the late nineteenth and early twentieth centuries.

Such disabilities meant that African Americans were generally forced to compete against white unions or had to accommodate themselves to white dominance of union privileges. Thus, in Baltimore black craftsmen driven from the shipyards organized a cooperative shipbuilding company and operated it successfully for two decades until a combination of changing conditions in the industry and racism caused it to fail. The leader of the Baltimore shipyard workers, Isaac Meyers, became president of the Colored National Labor Union, which sought to organize African-American laborers and was a major national force in black union activity during the late nineteenth century. But the Colored National Labor Union, tied to the Republican party's philosophy that employers and workmen should cooperate and that laborers' greatest achievement was to become business proprietors themselves, largely became a middle-class organization that provided no sound basis for a trade union movement among African Americans.

During the late nineteenth century two disparate philosophies of trade unionism were in conflict to determine the character of the labor movement in the United States. The more conservative craft union philosophy was represented by the American Federation of Labor (AFL), which sought to organize workers into independent (and largely self-interested) craft unions that sought to improve their members' working conditions by erecting barriers to competition. The alternative was to organize workers by industry so that the interests of an industrial union would be tied to every craft practiced therein. This philosophy was represented by the Knights of Labor, who, as they put it, sought to "promote [the] welfare of the masses." In 1893, the AFL national convention unanimously resolved that working people must unite regardless of "creed, color, sex, nationality, or politics." But its organizational structure and philosophy, which gave so much power to local crafts, allowed rabid racism and exclusion of blacks to persist in most locals. Few African Americans gained entry to the AFL. By contrast, the Knights of Labor organized independent of race, but they too could not overcome the specter of racial animosity. Many chapters of the Knights of Labor had separate black and white locals.

Here and there, however, biracial unions arose, suggesting that an accommodation between the races could be reached. Numerous dockworkers along the southeastern seaboard in places such as Charleston, New Orleans, and Mobile had biracial unions that shared employment and union offices through a kind of racial quota system. Frequently whites received more than the share warranted by their numbers. In the coal fields of southern Ohio, western Pennsylvania, and West Virginia, the United Mine Workers arrived at a similar accommodation. Even so, at the end of the nineteenth century, the relationship between the labor movement and African Americans was primarily a contentious and competitive affair that weakened the economic goals of both.

WOMEN'S EMPLOYMENT. African Americans' strongest asset in a discriminatory environment was their willingness to work harder, longer, and for less pay than whites—simply because they had to. The labor market condition of African-American women typified this status. According to the censuses of 1890 and 1900, black women were overwhelmingly employed in domestic service and on farms. The 1900 census showed that 96 percent of African-American women working for wages were employed as field workers, house servants, waitresses, or laundresses. The nationwide discrimination against blacks in general kept African Americans in such poverty that even lower-middle-class whites could afford to hire black women as cooks and housecleaners. These positions involved long hours under close supervision and offered the lowest of wages. In a city such as Cincinnati, Ohio, a typical occupation for African-American women was to set up a business by contracting to wash the clothes of a number of white families each week. This backbreaking labor was often the main support of African-American households.

African Americans' strongest asset in a discriminatory environment was their willingness to work harder, longer, and for less pay than whites.

Black women were also employed in factories to some extent. It appears that in the few instances when African-American women could obtain alternative employment, they chose to abandon domestic service. Along the southeastern seaboard they found seasonal employment, usually involving dirty and difficult working conditions, in various factories in the seafood processing industry. In many seaport towns African-American women and men engaged in the excruciatingly dirty, smelly, and physically demanding task of shucking oysters. During the busy season of September through April, domestic servants in such towns were difficult to hire. However, the seasonality of the work meant that some of the women would have to return to domestic work.

Slaves had been the primary labor source in antebellum Virginia tobacco plants, and after the Civil War African Americans remained a significant factor in the tobacco factories of the upper South. By 1910 the eleven former Confederate states employed over eight thousand African-American women in the least desirable and lowest-paying occupations in tobacco factories. They were primarily restricted to the cigar and chewing-tobacco sectors of the industry. The newer, more mechanized, and higher-paying cigarette industry came to be dominated by white labor. This practice was replicated when black men and women were virtually shut out of the cotton textile industry, which became the major employer of white women.

Labor and Blacks: 1900–1940

THE FIRST URBANIZATION. Between 1880 and 1910 nearly seventeen million Europeans emigrated to the United States. These immigrants overwhelmingly entered the country through the ports of New York and New Jersey and thence spread throughout the northeastern United States, where they swelled the labor force and precipitated a great competition for jobs, housing, and other resources. There was little demand for African-American labor outside the South, and migration of blacks out of the South during this period was relatively low. But the beginning of World War I in 1914 halted the European migration and also created a boom for industry in the United States. Northern employers, starved for labor, turned to the laborers of the South. Black and white southerners responded positively, and a great competition for agricultural labor developed. Hundreds of labor agents from northern and southern factories scoured the rural South for laborers while evading the landlords and local authorities who fought, sometimes with violent extralegal methods, to retain them. Approximately 525,000 African Americans migrated to the urban North between 1910 and 1920 in search of the promised land of the urban labor agents' exaggerated depiction.

Prior to the war African-American migrants to the urban North had mostly found employment as janitors, porters, and servants, but during the war, blacks, both newcomers and older residents alike, were hired for jobs that had previously been restricted to whites. For the most part, however, African-American men were still at best employers' second choice to white labor, and the jobs they could obtain often were in areas "designated" for blacks because they required work in conditions of extreme heat, moisture, dust, or some other undesirable feature. For example, African-American men were typically preferred as asphalt workers, who were required to speedily and efficiently perform heavy and exacting labor with hot asphalt and heated tools during the summer, and in such similar work as the acid bath in the iron and steel industry.

In Chicago in 1910, over 51 percent of African-American men were in domestic and personal service. In 1920 this figure had fallen to 28 percent, even though the black population had increased significantly, because factory work had become the most important source of employment for black men, who had even managed to increase their representation in semiskilled jobs.

Opportunities for African-American women were not so good. While more jobs opened in manufacturing and trade, they were still overwhelmingly restricted to domestic service, where 64 percent of employed African-American women labored. These restrictions applied regardless of skill and qualifications. City-born women with high school and college educations were often no more able to obtain work other than domestic service than were illiterate peasants from a tobacco plantation.

Throughout urban America unionization only benefited white workers, who did their best to exclude blacks from occupations over which unions had control. By the late 1920s in the South—where at the end of the nineteenth century, African Americans could be found in various occupations—growing union control and a resumption of immigration from Europe resulted in losses of jobs for blacks. Railroad work is illustrative: In the late nineteenth and early twentieth centuries blacks had been employed by railroads as firemen, brakemen, and even engineers, but unionization led to their ouster in a campaign to make these occupations all white. In some cases, the desire to rid an occupation of black competition led to extreme violence, as when the Brotherhood of Railroad Workers in Memphis, Tenn., placed a bounty of three hundred dollars on the heads of black firemen. Three African-American firemen were kidnapped and murdered for the reward.

Employment conditions for African Americans in New England were no better. In New Haven, Conn., blacks were excluded from all of the city's primary industries. In 1930 not even a dozen African Americans had jobs in the city's clock, rubber, paper and printing, and ammunition factories, although they employed thirteen hundred workers. A study of the area's labor market reported:

> There were none in the cigar and tobacco factories, employing another two hundred and fifty. In the iron and steel industry, a large one in New Haven, the Negroes have had throughout the generation only a few of the two thousand to three thousand semiskilled jobs; at the peak in 1920 their share was less than three-tenths of their due. A smelting plant reported none: "They had always been able to get all the white men they needed, even for the heat jobs." A steel wire manufactory with a force of nearly five hundred employed only one Negro who had insulated himself by serving for a time as a janitor. An informant at a rubber firm said there were no Negroes at all in the new, modern factory, although in the badly ventilated old one both colored men and women had worked in some of the dusty places to which white people objected.

Thus, in 1930, as the Great Depression began, African Americans' economic position had improved to the extent that they were less concentrated in the rural South and were better represented in manufacturing and trade industries. Still, they remained severely underrepresented as artisans and operatives and in clerical, business, and professional positions. Overwhelmingly, African-American women had few opportunities outside domestic and personal service occupations, and black men were relegated to positions as common laborers.

DEPRESSION. Between 1929 and 1932 the real value of the total volume of goods and services produced by the U.S. economy fell by one-third, from $96 billion to $64 billion. This catastrophic event led to hundreds of bank and business failures, mass unemployment on a scale of one in four Americans looking for work, and conditions of poverty that affected the U.S. population in every class. African Americans, who were for the most part at the bottom of the economic order, were destined to face especially bleak prospects. Moreover, the nature of the electoral process further weakened their economic position. The great majority of African Americans were industrially and politically disfranchised. This disability made them an easy target for exclusion from the councils of industrial and political decisions that would affect their economic future. Despite a number of important overtures to black voters by the Democratic party—overtures that ultimately led to increased political representation of African Americans in local and national politics—the economic philosophy of the New Deal may have worsened the suffering that African Americans experienced during the 1930s.

As the Great Depression began, African Americans' economic position had improved to the extent that they were less concentrated in the rural South and were better represented in manufacturing and trade industries.

Through most of the decade, the Roosevelt administration believed that the depression was primarily a problem of "ruinous competition" between businesses and workers, which caused prices and wages to be too low to maintain adequate aggregate purchasing power and "American standards of living." Thus, the administration sought to solve this problem. The foundation of the economic policy was the National Industrial Recovery Act (NIRA) of 1933, whose purpose, according to President Roosevelt, "was to put people back to work, . . . to raise the purchasing power of labor by limiting hours (of work) and increasing wages. It was to elevate labor standards by making sure that no employer would suffer competitive disadvantages as a result of paying decent wages or establishing decent working conditions." But the act went far beyond protection of labor and industry from mere business fluctuations to an attack against "unfair competition" by businessmen who took advantage of pools of unemployed, desperate laborers willing to accept jobs at almost any price. This unfair competition consisted in cutting wages and prices to restore profit margins and forcing other firms to follow, willingly or otherwise. Disfranchised African-American men and women had little or no voice in determining the specific policies used to attack these problems. The chosen policies left them highly vulnerable.

Both the rhetoric and the legislation of what historian Arthur Schlesinger, Jr., dubbed the "first" and "second" New Deals aimed at and succeeded for a time in repealing the law of supply and demand. As a consequence, the policy deprived the economically dispossessed of the only weapon they had in the fight to make a living: their ability to offer their labor for lower wages and longer working hours than their more privileged white countrymen could or would. Without this ability African Americans were left with no active agency to force unions and white workers generally to accept black coworkers on terms at least partially determined by blacks. African Americans were forced to apply for employment on the terms set both by employers acting in concert with or in reaction to unions and by the level of discrimination that the public conscience and social institutions would tolerate.

The National Recovery Administration (NRA)—with its voluminous codes of fair competition that legislated minimum prices (for everything from safety pins to automobiles), output quotas, and labor standards—became a bureaucratic, economic, and political failure and was declared unconstitutional by the U.S. Supreme Court in 1935. Nevertheless, its lines of emphasis signaled the major directions that the New Deal would continue to explore. While much attention was given to the argument that price codes hurt small businesses and stifled economic recovery by, in Justice Hugo Black's terms, "making it a crime to produce too much, and to sell too cheaply," no one was listening to the symmetric argument that the legislation robbed the unemployed laborer of his most effective measure for gaining employment precisely because it became a crime to work too much and to sell one's labor cheaper than the competition.

The impact of the new labor market structure upon the black worker was felt immediately, grimly forecasting the shape of things to come. In 1933, after passage of the NIRA, the NAACP reported that "the first effect of the . . . President's agreement was the displacement of many Negro workers throughout the South where employers decided that if they had to pay the minimum wage of twelve dollars a week they would not pay it to Negroes." By way of illustration, the NAACP's journal, the *Crisis,* reported the "dismissal of fourteen colored women from a [Memphis] factory where they had been getting seven dollars a week and the employment of fourteen white women to take their places at twelve dollars a week."

If the minority worker faced the problem of being displaced in industries where white workers were willing to enter under the new improved conditions, the new social welfare legislation to protect the American worker was not applicable in just those industries where blacks were so numerically dominant that they could not be feasibly displaced and therefore might benefit from improved conditions. Agriculture, casual, and domestic labor were not covered by social security or fair labor legislation.

Indeed, the Agricultural Adjustment Act of 1933, whose objective was to improve the economic condition of the U.S. farm population, dealt a tremendous blow to the economic condition of African Americans. Landowners were paid by the acre to reduce the amount of land they tilled. A proportion of the funds received was supposed to go to sharecroppers and renters, but the political organizations that oversaw the distributions were in the hands of whites and controlled by the landlords, so few croppers or renters received funds. Moreover, the reduction in crop acreage drastically reduced the landowners' need for labor, and many thousands of rural laboring families were thrown out of work. Loans from the government set in motion a demand for farm capital that led to mechanization of plantations, which in turn, by the late 1940s and 1950s, would lead to continuing mass unemployment of southern farm laborers.

Empirical evidence suggests that the very structure of how labor markets allocated jobs and earnings was drastically altered during the 1930s. For example, the infamous two-to-one relationship between nonwhite and white unemployment rates, a relationship that has remained relatively stable for forty years, may well have been a result of labor market intervention in the 1930s. The unemployment rates (in nonfarm industries) for whites and nonwhites respectively were 7.9 percent and 8.6 percent in the spring of 1930, giving a ratio of 1.09. By 1940 the rates were 9.3 percent and 13.4 percent, forming a ratio of 1.44, and the ratio climbed during the next three decades. The inclusion of agricultural unemployment makes the overall nonwhite rate in 1930 lower than that for whites—the last time that result occurred.

Poverty was common in the United States at the beginning of the 1940s, but it was far more prevalent among blacks.

The emphasis of the fair labor legislation of the second phase of the New Deal (after 1935)—protection of the market position of the employed—was consistent with the position of the old craft unions, which preached a philosophy of membership exclusion and closed bargaining to maintain and enhance the living standard of a protected few employees. As a consequence, while the labor legislation looked progressive at the time, it allowed the protectionist elements in the union movement, largely represented by the American Federation of Labor (AFL), to gain dominance over the more democratic philosophy of inclusion that was advocated by the Congress of Industrial Organizations (CIO), which had inherited part of the philosophy of unions such as the Knights of Labor. The CIO's attempts to organize black and white labor in the South were brutally crushed during the thirties. It eventually adopted much of the AFL's outlook, though it remained less hostile to black workers than the AFL. In the mid 1950s the AFL and CIO merged.

Thus, in 1934 the marginal position of the black laborer in the New Deal's social compact was determined. The labor market became the province of white laborers who relinquished places to others only on their own terms. These terms increasingly forced African Americans into situations where lack of demand for their services from the private sector made them ever more dependent on the public sector. By 1940 so many African Americans either were working on government works projects or were on welfare relief that in African-American communities the NRA was remembered as the Negro Relief Act.

Poverty was common in the United States at the beginning of the 1940s, but it was far more prevalent among blacks. As a consequence of discrimination in education and in the labor market, black men and women worked long and arduous hours for very little income. Still, four of five black families were headed by two parents; even so, by present-day standards adjusted for inflation, 81 percent of black families, compared with 48 percent of white families, lived in poverty.

1940–1990: An Age of Prosperity and Despair

After substantial economic gains during the era of World War I, African Americans experienced little progress during the interwar period. But since World War II there have been great changes. First, while African Americans' economic status, both in absolute terms and relative to whites, improved during the period from 1940 to 1973, it has since, again relative to whites, leveled off or even deteriorated. Indeed, for many blacks at the lowest economic strata, their absolute economic well-being has deteriorated since the mid-1970s. For example, African Americans' real per capita income and average family income were 58 percent of whites' in the late 1960s and in the late 1980s; the proportion of African-American families with incomes below $10,000 (in constant dollars) rose from 23.9 to 25.6 percent between 1967 and 1990. Second, concurrent with this deterioration has been a drop in the employment of black males; and third, the level of inequality within the black population has heightened.

Changes in the mean annual earnings of men and women and in the relative earnings of blacks to whites at ten-year intervals (plus 1984) are displayed in table 1. Each race-sex group enjoyed substantial increases in real earnings from 1939 into the early 1970s. After 1973, however, growth in real mean earnings stagnated for all groups, and by the middle 1980s real annual earnings had declined below the 1970s peak for each group. Changes in mean weekly wages behaved similarly. Between 1939 and 1984 mean weekly wages for blacks relative to whites increased twenty-six percentage points for males and fifty-six points for females. Overall, black men earned mean weekly wages that had risen to 67 percent of white men's, while mean weekly wages for black women had reached 97 percent of white women's. The rising black-white ratios from 1939 through 1979 indicate that mean earnings for blacks were rising faster than for whites over this time, while the decline in the 1984 ratios indicate that those forces leading to reductions in the real annual earnings of American women and men must have affected labor market opportunities for blacks more severely than for whites. To gain some understanding of these trends in average incomes requires study of the historical conditions that produced them.

During the 1940s African Americans competed in the labor market under very adverse conditions. A majority of white Americans approved of job discrimination against blacks. In a 1944 national survey 55 percent of all white Americans and 80 percent of those living in the South responded that "white people should have the first chance at any kind of job" over blacks. Furthermore, largely because of discrimination in the provision of public education, the median schooling completed by black females and males in 1940 was just 6.2 and 5.4 years, respectively, compared to white female and male medians of 8.8 and 8.7 years, respectively. The primary source of black employment remained agriculture: Two-fifths of black working men labored in agriculture, mostly as sharecroppers, renters, and day laborers, and 50 percent of the black population lived on farms or in farm areas of the South. Nearly three-quarters of employed African-American women were still in domestic or personal service.

Despite these obstacles, black men and women, with higher employment-to-population ratios than whites, were more likely to be working, and they did so for far lower wages. Even so, in 1939 African-American men's mean weekly wage was less than one-half (47%) of the mean wage paid white men and three-quarters (72%) of that paid white women, while black women earned

Table 1

MEAN ANNUAL EARNINGS OF BLACK AND WHITE WOMEN AND MEN, 1939–1990

	1939	1949	1959	1969	1979	1984	1990*
Women							
Black	$2,070	$3,632	$4,764	$8,347	$10,496	$10,252	$14,404
White	5,192	6,647	7,870	9,966	10,420	10,354	15,424
Ratio	.40	.54	.60	.84	1.0	.99	.93
Men							
Black	$3,833	$6,655	$9,540	$14,177	$15,160	$13,218	$18,783
White	8,745	12,596	18,079	22,860	23,032	20,457	27,630
Ratio	.44	.53	.53	.62	.66	.65	.68

* Earnings for 1939–1979 are standardized to 1984 prices. Earnings in 1990 are for 1990 prices. Source: U.S. Bureau of the Census.

a mean wage a fourth (27%) of white men's and less than one-half (41%) of white women's. Differentials in educational attainment can explain part of the earnings gaps, but striking evidence of the pervasive public sanction of labor market discrimination against African Americans is the fact that in 1939 the mean weekly earnings of black men and women college graduates ($201 and $159 in 1985 prices) were far less than the earnings of white men and women high school graduates ($393 and $270).

A wartime economy again proved to be a source of economic mobility for many African Americans. Pulled by the strong demand for workers in wartime factory production and many other industries, African Americans again left the rural South in search of opportunity. Many found improved job conditions as semiskilled and even some skilled jobs opened to blacks in expanding industries such as munitions and steel. As during World War I, though, equal opportunity did not prevail.

MINORITY EXCLUSION FROM MID-CENTURY TO 1973. Although labor scarcity and government pressure against discrimination in defense-related industries alleviated the problems somewhat, employers and labor unions remained virtually free to practice systematic and overt discrimination against African Americans during the period from 1940 through the mid-1960s. With few exceptions white-collar clerical jobs and higher-paying blue-collar positions were still unavailable to blacks. Discrimination was invoked against minorities regardless of their qualifications. In the early 1940s, for example, African Americans were so proscribed in labor markets that personal-service and janitorial jobs with elite employers were often positions of high prestige among urban African Americans. Such jobs were held by black graduates of northern high schools and predominantly white colleges. African Americans who had attended "integrated" public schools all their lives and whose families had lived in a city for generations often found access to economic opportunity as blocked as did newly arrived migrants. Thus, while blacks again found themselves much in demand to fill the lower job rungs in many industries—itself a step up from farm work or other work outside the factory—they were still closed off from the better jobs, and some of the industries providing the best jobs continued to bar African Americans altogether.

For example, from its beginnings the aircraft industry refused to employ African Americans. Even those with the necessary skills and educational requirements for the work found that discrimination barred their way. In the spring of 1940, *Fortune* magazine reported that the aircraft industry had "an almost universal prejudice against Negroes . . . you almost never see Negroes in aircraft factories . . . [and] there is little concealment about the anti-Negro policy." By way of illustration, the article in *Fortune* quoted the president of an aircraft firm called Vultec (shortly afterward a division of General Dynamics, which had a large plant in the Fort Worth, Tex., area) as telling a Negro organization that "it is not the policy of this company to employ people other than of the caucasian race. . . ." Similarly, the president of North American Aviation stated that

> we will receive applications from both white and Negro workers. However, the Negroes will be considered only as janitors and in other similar capacities . . . it is against the company policy to employ them as mechanics or aircraft workers. . . . We use none except white workers in the plant . . . at Inglewood [Calif.] and the plant in Dallas and we intend to maintain the same policy in Kansas City. . . .

Throughout the 1940s and into the 1950s, conditions improved somewhat in the North, but in the Southwest plants hired few African Americans, and when they did, they frequently operated segregated facilities. In such plants African Americans were usually refused admittance to training or else given segregated and inferior training. In some cases they were provided training that omitted preparation for key jobs.

During the 1950s, despite three major recessions, the U.S. economy managed to create job growth that raised millions of Americans out of poverty. But during the 1950s and 1960s the rapid mechanization of farming methods throughout the South, encouraged by the improved availability of farm credit due to the Agricultural Adjustment Act created during the New Deal era, greatly decreased the need for farm workers. Thousands of the poorest laborers, black and white, were pushed out of the rural South where they had quickly become an economically redundant population. Spilling into urban areas across the nation, many African Americans found themselves undereducated and discriminated against in an economy plagued with high unemployment.

Government was still a major part of the problem. State employment offices, such as those in the greater Washington, D.C., and Baltimore area, maintained segregated services until the early 1960s. Switchboard operators often asked prospective employers who had failed to request a particular office whether they wanted "white or Negro workers." After the Baltimore office stopped accepting discriminatory requests from employers, the volume of job orders dropped off. Directors of the program attributed this to a "switch by employers from the public to the private employment agencies" where presumably they could still discriminate. However, at the public employment bureaus some personnel acknowledged that they continued to send "discriminating" businesses only the workers they wanted to hire. In the District of Columbia, private agencies proudly touted their ability to avoid black labor. An official audit in the district found that a "substantial proportion (if not a majority) of the job orders placed by private business [were] discriminatory." Similar blatant practices were in place throughout the nation. The U.S. Civil Rights Commission, investigating racial conditions in Cleveland, Ohio, during the late 1960s, found newspaper ads for vacant job positions that required applicants to live on the "West Side only" or specified "West Side residents preferred." Because of segregation, nearly all blacks lived on the east side of the city.

Discrimination against minorities in public education by state and local governments was equally significant. Inferior, segregated schooling put minorities at a great disadvantage in competing in the labor market. The State Advisory Committees of the U.S. Civil Rights Commission, referring to vocational training, found in 1961 that most communities offered African Americans only inferior, segregated vocational training, if any at all, throughout the United States; even if African Americans did become skilled, discrimination in the skilled trades made black employment difficult or impossible.

A major obstacle to black economic progress during the postwar period was the continued hostility of unions. A study of unions undertaken in the early 1940s discovered that the constitutions or rituals of fourteen national unions explicitly prohibited African-American members. Among these were the machinists' and railroad brotherhoods. Eight others refused admittance to blacks by "tacit consent," and nine more admitted African Americans only in segregated "auxiliary" unions that were affiliated with white parent unions. These segregated relationships put blacks in subordinate positions that gave the white branches most of the best jobs, seniority, and a more than proportionate share of employment. During the 1940s there were many instances when white unions went on strike to protest the hiring or skill upgrading of blacks. In some cases the military had to be called in to desegregate a plant and force white workers back to work so that war production could be continued.

Despite these difficulties, African Americans made inroads into CIO unions. Postwar industrial growth led to an increase in employment in the automobile industry and others that depended on it, such as steel and rubber. By the late 1950s a kind of blue-collar elite of high-wage, unionized workers (belonging to such CIO unions as the United Auto Workers and United Steel Workers) had emerged in many African-American communities. Often these workers, frequently semiliterate migrants from rural communities and farms, were better paid than African-American college graduates; at that time, such educated blacks were restricted to positions serving segregated black communities or in jobs well below their qualifications in the "mainstream" labor market. This desegregation imbalance set up very strong disincentives for young blacks to place a premium on education.

But even among CIO unions black employment was slowed because of racial animosity. During the fifties the CIO's renewed attempts to organize white workers in the South led it to de-emphasize its policies of racial equality, and its 1955 merger with the AFL to create the AFL-CIO implied the tacit acceptance of the discriminatory policies of the AFL's craft unions. In the late 1950s George Meany, then president of the AFL-CIO, acknowledged, "Right here in the District of Columbia . . . there are local unions whose membership . . . [is] closed to Negro applicants." Two-thirds of the way through the twentieth century, minority participation in the craft trades was negligible nationwide. In 1965 the President's Commission on Equal Employment Opportunity surveyed 989 construction industry contractors, 281 employer associations, and 731 unions. In the thirty southern cities surveyed, only 26 of 3,696 persons—less than 1 percent—selected for apprenticeship programs of plumbers', electricians', sheet-metal workers', ironworkers', and carpenters' unions were members of a minority group; 20 of those 26 were in the carpenters' union. In the nonsouthern states and cities, 133 of 5,906 persons (2%) in apprenticeship programs for the same five trades were black; 70 were carpenters. Nevertheless, among industrial unions African Americans' power was growing with their numbers.

ANTIDISCRIMINATION AND AFFIRMATIVE ACTION. The urban migration of African Americans greatly increased their political power, and with their civil rights organizations they lobbied local, state, and federal officials to end job discrimination. In the 1940s the Fair Employment Practices Committee (FEPC) held hearings throughout the nation to investigate allegations of discrimination. Large war contractors, such as steel, aircraft, and shipbuilding firms, were targeted by the FEPC as they were thought to be especially susceptible to federal government coercion. The FEPC was, however, largely an investigative body with limited enforcement powers, and historians have been divided on whether it actually increased opportunities for blacks beyond those jobs that would have arisen anyway due to the wartime shortage of labor. During the 1950s many states and localities passed antidiscrimination legislation, but most economists and historians have assessed these laws as ineffective in reducing job discrimination against minorities.

In the late 1950s President Eisenhower, responding to the findings of discrimination of the Civil Rights Commission (whose members he had appointed) and using the apparatus of the FEPC, created the President's Commission on Equal Employment Opportunity, which was chaired by Vice President Richard Nixon. This commission investigated hiring practices in defense-related industries and used the contracting powers of the federal government to "encourage" contractors to institute affirmative-action hiring programs for blacks. While the commission enjoyed some success, it was largely ineffective against the areas of deepest resistance to equal-employment opportunities for African Americans.

For example, during the 1950s pressure from the federal government persuaded General Electric to desegregate its jet engine facility near Dallas, Tex. Even so, by 1960 the facilities of some large plants were still segregated, and major aircraft companies in the Dallas-Fort Worth area employed few African Americans other than in laboring and service jobs. The African-American proportion of all skilled operatives in the industry in 1968 was 7.5 percent in the Southwest (it was 13.5% nationally). Fort Worth, with a population that was about 16 percent black in 1960, employed a lower percentage of blacks than did Seattle with a 5 percent black population.

Then, in the early 1960s, the government of the United States, swept up in the tide of a national CIVIL RIGHTS MOVEMENT and growing black political power, initiated a series of legislative, executive, and judicial actions designed to redress and correct the effects of over three hundred years of exclusion and discrimination. Strengthening the programs initiated by President Eisenhower, President Kennedy in 1961 banned discrimination by government contractors with executive order 10925, and his administration established guidelines to promote the hiring of minorities by these contractors. Against this background the U.S. Congress, under strong pressure from President Lyndon Johnson and the civil rights coalition of blacks, liberals, and national unions, enacted the Civil Rights Act of 1964, which attempted to remedy discrimination against people of color in employment, housing, access to credit, public accommodation, and association, as well as to promote a more general enjoyment of constitutional rights. Title VII of the act created the Equal Employment Opportunity Commission (EEOC), which became the major antidiscrimination enforcement agency of the federal government in matters of employment. As was the FEPC of the late 1940s, the EEOC was initially limited to fact-finding and conciliation, although it did encourage private parties to sue employers and labor unions and it could recommend that the U.S. Attorney General initiate law suits when a pattern or practice of discrimination was found. In the 1970s Congress gave the EEOC the power to sue alleged discriminators.

In 1965 President Johnson extended legal procedures through executive order 11246, which established rules for nondiscrimination by federal contractors. Contractors with fifty or more employees and contracts of $50,000 or more were required to develop and submit affirmative-action compliance programs with goals and timetables for the hiring and promotion of minorities. In the late 1960s and early 1970s President Richard Nixon—who, it will be recalled, had chaired Eisenhower's commission—institutionalized affirmative-action policies even further through more explicit reliance on the concept of goals and timetables in hiring by federal contractors.

THE KENNEDY-JOHNSON SIXTIES. During the Kennedy and Johnson administrations, expansionary economic policies generally and spending for the war in Vietnam particularly had the economy growing at an unprecedented rate. During the ten-year period between 1963 and 1973, incomes and earnings of the American population reached all-time historical highs. Thus, adjusted for inflation, in 1959 the mean weekly earnings of American white men were $398; that figure had risen to $504 by 1969. The mean weekly earnings of white women rose from $217 to $271 during the same ten years. Nearly all segments of society shared in the economic prosperity. The poverty rate fell from 22.2 percent in 1960 to 12.6 percent in 1970 before reaching its all-time low of 11.1 percent in 1973.

As members of the American population, African Americans shared in this period of economic prosperity. Largely through their own initiative, blacks responded to the growing economy by completing the migration, from south to north and from rural areas to cities, that they began decades earlier, causing a concurrent movement from agricultural employment to other industries. Against a backdrop of high rates of employment, job creation, and growth of real output, there were increases in the schooling of blacks. In addition, through their increasing electoral influence, the moral authority of the Civil Rights Movement, and the urban riots of the 1960s, African Americans forced the political system to afford them greater participation in areas of the economy previously closed to them. Affirmative action and antidiscrimination enforcement were important components, making it possible for more blacks to gain access to "good" jobs, whose numbers had been increased by the steady economic growth.

Perhaps encouraged by the fact that six consecutive presidential administrations, both Democrat and Republican—albeit with varying degrees of vigor—had endorsed a civil rights agenda of fighting employment discrimination and advancing the economic position of minorities towards equality with whites, the U.S. Supreme Court, in a series of cases, strengthened both antidiscrimination forces and affirmative-action policies. In the important 1971 cases, *Griggs* v. *Duke Power Co.,* the Court, arguing that "Congress directed the thrust of the act [title VII] to the consequences of employment practices, not simply the motivation," ruled that employment and hiring practices (such as tests) that led to disparate impact on minorities must be shown to have a strictly business necessity.

Largely through their own initiative, blacks responded to the growing economy by completing the migration, from south to north and from rural areas to cities.

Successful litigation against businesses and unions attacked discrimination at its heart while affirmative-action policies in government and the private sector gave African Americans new opportunities. By the mid-1960s strong government pressure against discrimination had opened employment to blacks in the previously all-white southern textile industry. White-collar occupations were opened to black women in many areas of the economy.

The strongest proof of the success of this push for egalitarian race relations was the emergence of a new black middle class. This group was three to four times the size it had been in 1960, but more important, post-1960 entrants were no longer confined to occupations in segregated black society. After the 1960s black ministers, teachers, and the small group of professionals and proprietors serving almost all-black clienteles came to be outnumbered by black professionals and white-collar employees working for organizations and institutions primarily run by whites. This widened job access was matched by increased rates of matriculation at predominantly white colleges. For the first time in American history, the black poor, although numerically significant and highly visible, became a distinct minority of the African-American population.

FROM THE VIETNAM WAR ERA TO 1990. The economics of the 1960s proved to be as much an aberration as its politics. The combination of low-unemployment domestic policies, the War on Poverty, and the expanding Vietnam War defense budgets produced an inflation that by the end of the decade was squeezing the purchasing power of middle-class Americans. Richard Nixon gained the presidency partially on the basis of a promise to bring budgets under control and put a stop to inflation. But the commitment of his administration (and Ford's and Carter's) to fight inflation with high-unemployment policies proved weak. In 1970, one year after the end of the Kennedy-Johnson economic program, inflation and unemployment stood at 5.7 and 4.8 percent, respectively. Ten years later, in 1980, inflation and unemployment were 13.5 and 7 percent, respectively. In between had come a decade of slow economic growth accompanied by the great energy crisis of 1973–1975, when oil and gas shortages increased industrial costs and sent the economy into what was then the worst recession of the postwar period, with unemployment reaching 8.5 percent.

In addition, the European and Japanese economies had fully recovered from the war and were competing effectively with domestic manufactures in the United States. Hard hit by the competition were autos, steel, rubber, and similar industries. The spectacular economic growth of the sixties—coming on the heels of the modest growth, tempered by three recessions, of the Eisenhower years—camouflaged the shrinking manufacturing base that had alarmed many economists during the 1950s. Thus, manufacturing, which employed a major portion of American middle-income families and practically all middle-income African Americans, was evaporating in many eastern and midwestern cities.

The twenty-seven years of relative economic growth from 1946 to 1973 produced many victories and achievements for African Americans as millions of them reached the middle class. However, the conditions of prosperity did not lift all white Americans out of poverty, nor were they sufficient to do so for all African Americans, who continued to bear the legacy of economic discrimination and inferior schooling. Economic growth, affirmative action, antidiscrimination enforcement, and a determination to make it in the economy had not been enough to overcome inadequate educational and employment incentives, let alone the import-market competition from abroad that reduced the availability of high-paying blue-collar jobs.

THE REAGAN-BUSH YEARS. In the early 1980s Ronald Reagan, elected president on the promise to reinvigorate American society, initiated a policy-induced recession that drove unemployment above 8 percent and slowed the inflation rate. Afterwards, Reagan's much-heralded income tax cut, combined with significant increases in defense spending, created an aggregate demand in service, real estate, and financial markets that led to renewed prosperity for many sectors of the economy. But the economic program also created enormous federal budget deficits, which led to a frenzy of public and private borrowing and spending. In addition, the growth favored those with higher incomes, while the deterioration in the average wages of American men and women continued during the 1980s. As the loss of manufacturing jobs proceeded at a rapid pace, the economy replaced them with service-sector jobs that either required high education and skills or offered very low wages. Changes in U.S. immigration policy in 1965 and again in 1986, as well as substantial increases in illegal immigration, resulted in an unprecedentedly large influx of immigrants, many of whom filled the lower paying jobs. Reductions in real earnings were generally greatest for those men and women with the least education. Black and white men with less than a high school education actually earned real mean weekly wages in 1984 that were less than their respective wages in 1960, and the earnings of black male high school graduates fell from two-thirds those of black male college graduates in the period from 1939 to 1969 to one-half in 1984.

RACE RELATIONS, FALLING REAL WAGES, AND EMPLOYMENT. Changing employment patterns were similar for black and white men, although declining employment among black men was especially severe. The really significant reductions in labor-force participation and employment occurred between 1970 and 1980. The heralded recovery of the mid-1980s apparently improved the position of white low-skilled men but not black. Thus, although in 1970 there was no difference between the employment rates of black high school and college graduates, by 1985 high school graduates had an employment rate twelve percentage points lower. The employment rate of high school dropouts was nearly thirty points lower.

As a result, the later 1970s and especially the 1980s were times when poor Americans were finding it ever more difficult to escape from poverty. Poverty rates rose dramatically as the American economy faltered. In 1973 the poverty rate among whites was 8.4 percent; in 1992 it was 11.6 percent. For blacks the increase during this period was from 31.5 percent to 33.3 percent. No group was safe: The rate among Latinos went from 21.9 percent in 1973 to 29.3 percent by 1992, and though 1973 figures for Asian Americans are not available, their 12.5 percent poverty rate in 1992 is higher than that of the preceding years. Declining real wages and rising unemployment discouraged many young Americans as successive cohorts of high school graduates entered an economy that appeared to promise them a standard of living worse than that of their parents.

FEMINIZATION OF POVERTY. By the 1990s Americans with poor educations and few skills found it particularly difficult to succeed under these harsh economic conditions. Many gave up the attempt to do so and turned to crime and public assistance as a way of life. Although socially disadvantaged individuals of all racial groups were susceptible to these troubles and temptations, hundreds of thousands of black youths lived in social conditions that made them especially vulnerable. Lack of mainstream economic opportunity and the choice of crime or public assistance spawned a subculture that has now produced two or three generations of low-income, low-skilled African Americans. One-parent black families became nearly as prevalent as two-parent black families. Poverty became highly feminized; overall, a third of black families lived in poverty, but the rate was much higher for mother-only families.

Lack of mainstream economic opportunity spawned a subculture that has now produced two or three generations of low-income, low-skilled African Americans.

A major factor in this predicament was the continuing discrepancy in economic opportunities available to men and women. Thus, in 1990 black and white women working year-round and full-time earned 58 and 65 percent, respectively, of what white men similarly employed earned. The low mean earnings of women high school graduates working year-round and full-time—$16,026 for black women and $19,356 for white women, compared with $29,257 and $22,644 for white and black men, respectively—made it exceedingly difficult for women heading families with children to escape poverty. For African-American women in this educational group, the poor economic position of similarly educated black men insured continuing high rates of dependence on public assistance.

GOVERNMENT POLICY TOWARD THE POOR DURING THE EIGHTIES. In this economic environment many voters became disgruntled with government policies on affirmative action and aid to the poor. The Reagan administration launched a counterattack on affirmative-action programs. The federal judiciary, whose new appointees were more conservative, rejected the approach to antidiscrimination law that had been followed in the previous decades. Pushed by vigorous lobbying from the Reagan Justice Department, the courts began to shift the burden of proof in discrimination cases back onto employees, weakening the *Griggs* ruling that had set up the standard of disparate impact as prima facie evidence of discrimination. While virtually all white Americans publicly espoused the principle of equal opportunity for all citizens, employment discrimination against African Americans nonetheless remained a significant problem. Using techniques that involved black and white job seekers with identical résumés, researchers in Chicago, Los Angeles, and the District of Columbia found considerable evidence of unequal treatment.

The slowing of economic growth, the continuing shift from heavy manufacturing to service jobs, and a concurrent decline in real wages have produced great economic and social distress. Increased competition for jobs has increased the number of discouraged workers who discontinue an active job search for extended periods. Government transfer programs probably abetted their decisions, but there is little theoretical or empirical evidence for believing that transfers were the major factor. Similarly, activity in the underground economy and crime probably serve as a safety valve for those whose market opportunities have declined most.

The economic history of the United States since Reconstruction shows that the status of blacks and the opportunities available to them and to other minorities have generally moved in a direction consistent with that of the larger American society. This common destiny and the difficult economic conditions since the early 1970s best explain the present conditions among the African-American population.

BIBLIOGRAPHY

Du Bois, W. E. B. *Black Reconstruction in America, 1860–1880.* New York, 1935.

Harris, William H. *The Harder We Run: Black Workers Since the Civil War.* New York, 1982.

Jaynes, Gerald. *Branches Without Roots: Genesis of the Black Working Class, 1862–1882.* New York, 1986.

Jaynes, Gerald, and Robin M. Williams, eds. *A Common Destiny: Blacks and American Society.* Washington, D.C., 1989.

Jones, Jacqueline. *The Dispossessed: America's Underclasses from the Civil War to the Present.* New York, 1992.

———. *Labor of Love, Labor of Sorrow: Black Women, Work, and the Family from Slavery to the Present.* New York, 1988.

Mandle, Jay R. *Not Slave, Not Free: The African Economic Experience Since the Civil War.* Durham, N.C., 1992.

Wolters, Raymond. *Negroes and the Great Depression: The Problem of Economic Recovery.* Westport, Conn., 1970.

– GERALD D. JAYNES

EDELMAN, MARIAN WRIGHT

Marian Wright Edelman (June 6, 1939–), attorney and founder of the Children's Defense Fund. The daughter of Arthur Jerome Wright, minister of Shiloh Baptist Church, and Maggie Leola Wright, a community activist, Marian Edelman was born and raised in Bennetsville, S.C. She attended Spelman College, from which she graduated as valedictorian in 1960. During her senior year, Edelman participated in a sit-in at City Hall in Atlanta. Responding to the need for civil rights lawyers, Edelman entered Yale Law School as a John Hay Whitney Fellow in 1960. After graduating from law school in 1963, she became the first black woman to pass the bar in Mississippi. From 1964 to 1968 she headed the NAACP Legal Defense and Education Fund in Mississippi, where she met her husband, Peter Edelman, a Harvard Law School graduate and political activist. In 1971, she became director of the Harvard University Center for Law and Education. She was also the first black woman elected to the Yale University Corporation, where she served from 1971 to 1977.

Edelman is best known for her work with the Children's Defense Fund (CDF), a nonprofit child advocacy organization that she founded in 1973. The CDF offers programs to prevent adolescent pregnancy, to provide health care, education, and employment for youth, and to promote family planning. In 1980, Edelman became the first black and the second woman to chair the Board of Trustees of Spelman College. She has been the recipient of numerous honors and awards for her contributions to child advocacy, women's rights, and civil rights, including the MacArthur Foundation Prize Fellowship (1985) and the Albert Schweitzer Humanitarian Prize from Johns Hopkins University (1988). Edelman has published numerous books and articles on the condition of black and white children in America, including *Children Out of School in America* (1974), *School Suspensions: Are They Helping Children?* (1975), *Portrait of Inequality: Black and White Children in America* (1980), *Families in Peril: An Agenda for Social Change* (1987), and *The Measure of Our Success: A Letter to My Children and Yours* (1992).

BIBLIOGRAPHY

Ploski, Harry A., and James William, eds. *The Negro Almanac: A Reference Work on the African American.* 5th ed. Detroit, 1989.

Smith, Jessie Carney, ed. *Notable Black American Women.* Detroit, 1992.

– SABRINA FUCHS

EDUCATION

The Africans enslaved in the New World were heirs to the rich and varied educational traditions of their homelands. Like young people everywhere, young Africans were given instruction in their artistic, religious, and cultural heritages by their parents, extended kinship networks, and local communities. Africans from different language groups shared much in common with each other, including related forms of social and political organization, marriage and family customs, and sculptural and musical traditions, as well as related folklore and other leisure activities.

At the same time, there were many divisions within the cultures of western and central Africa, the two areas from which slaves were captured and transported to the New World. While most Africans were followers of traditional African religions, some slaves had been Islamicized, and a handful of slaves (primarily from Portuguese areas) had some experience of Christianity in Africa. Most slaves had had no exposure to written language in Africa, but a small number were literate in Arabic. Some copied Islamic legal texts and made phonetic transcriptions of the Gospels.

A continuing debate surrounds the question of the extent to which African cultural and educational traditions have survived in America. "Probably never before in history has a people been so nearly completely stripped of its social heritage as the Negroes who were brought to America," the African-American sociologist E. Franklin FRAZIER wrote in 1939. His contention was vigorously disputed by Melville Herskovits and others and has since largely fallen from favor. Numerous scholars have provided substantial evidence of the continued retention of African folkways and educational traditions among early generations of Africans in the New World. African retentions are most apparent in the arts, in crafts, and in certain aspects of language and family customs. With regard to religious and political organization, however, the evidence is less clear-cut. For slaves in the New World, the role of African traditions had to be balanced against another, less tangible, yet crucial educational concern: the need to learn about the strange and frightening world of the slave owners.

Despite wariness on both sides, slaves and their masters learned about each other informally, and their education was a two-way process. The procedures for South Carolinian rice cultivation were probably taught to planters by slaves familiar with rice agriculture in Africa. Of primary importance to slaves was the acquisition of the English language. Not surprisingly, the slaves who had direct and extended contact with whites gained a more rapid and superior knowledge of standard English, while those with less contact—for instance, the slaves living in the Sea Islands of South Carolina—developed English dialects in which Africanisms were more prominent. Some were forced to learn languages and other aspects of European culture at the bidding of their masters. Numerous slaves were taught the violin, in order to play at dances and cotillions; in many instances, these musicians not only acquired a standard repertory and technique but also were able to incorporate, and introduce to their hearers, elements from their African musical traditions.

Slave owners were generally made extremely uneasy by the prospect of literate slaves.

Slaves also received other kinds of training. Some were informally apprenticed in various technical disciplines. James Derham, a slave who had been trained as an assistant to a doctor and was later freed, became a practicing physician, and was judged competent in his learning by the late-eighteenth-century Philadelphia abolitionist Benjamin Rush. Rush also praised the abilities of Thomas Fuller, an illiterate Virginia slave who had mastered the principles of "lightning calculation," and astounded his listeners by performing such feats as calculating, without paper and in the space of two minutes, the number of seconds in a year and a half.

Such accomplishments were exceptional. The vast majority of slaves had no opportunity to gain advanced knowledge of European culture because they had no formal education and therefore were unable to acquire the basic tools needed for learning, such as the ability to read. Slave owners were generally made extremely uneasy by the prospect of literate slaves, both for practical reasons—literacy made escapes and insurrections easier to arrange—and for the less tangible ways in which literacy would force slave owners to confront the immorality of human enslavement. Many laws were passed in southern states, banning slave literacy in the aftermath of an insurrectionary scare. In 1740 the STONO REBELLION prompted the institution of antiliteracy laws in South Carolina. In 1770 Georgia made it a crime to teach slaves to read and write, and in the early 1830s, following NAT TURNER'S REBELLION and other alleged provocations, Louisiana, North Carolina, Virginia, and Alabama banned teaching slaves to read, while Georgia and South Carolina reinforced the laws they had previously passed.

The existence of these laws did not prevent slaves from acquiring literacy, and the extent and impact of antiliteracy laws have probably been exaggerated. Very few people were prosecuted for this "crime." The laws appear to have done little more than affirm the common prejudice against slave literacy. Like most aspects of the slave code, enforcement was primarily left in the hands of individual slave owners. Masters could be barbarous in reacting against slaves who gained the ability to read or write; some went so far as to amputate their fingers. These savage gestures did little to curb the hunger for learning of many slaves, and many masters accommodated or even welcomed slave literacy. At least three of the earliest African-American poets—Jupiter HAMMON, Phillis WHEATLEY, and George Moses Horton—published collections of verse while enslaved, with the tacit approval of their masters. Though accurate figures will probably never be available, it is estimated that 10 percent of slaves could read by 1860.

Before 1800, almost all slaves were largely self-taught. Free blacks—for example, the Maryland astronomer, surveyor, and almanac maker Benjamin BANNEKER—also acquired their knowledge from informal instruction and such printed matter as they were able to acquire. For many slaves, literacy began by finding a friendly white person, often a slave mistress or a generational cohort to the slave (and increasingly, after 1830, a fellow black) who was willing to give instructions in the rudiments of reading. This was usually followed by the careful and intense private reading and rereading of a selected text. At age twelve, Frederick DOUGLASS purchased a copy of *The Columbian Orator* and proceeded to memorize its forms of speech in what was the first step toward his becoming perhaps the most gifted public speaker of his time. For slaves as for their white contemporaries, literacy began with the acquisition of a Bible or a copy of Noah Webster's "blue-black" speller, although the similarities between the ways in which slaves and other students acquired knowledge of reading (and of the even more dangerous art of writing) ended with these texts. For slaves the act was invariably covert. As a former slave related in an interview, many slaves could read but "de kep' dat up deir sleeve, dey played dumb lack dey couldn't read a bit till after surrender." Slaves developed elaborate strategies for hiding reading material from their masters; as Frederick DOUGLASS noted, the fact that such knowledge was forbidden made its acquisition that much sweeter.

Religion

The dissemination of the Christian religion played a major role in providing both the motivation and the practical means for blacks, slave and free, to acquire an education. "The frequent hearing of my mistress reading the Bible aloud," Frederick DOUGLASS wrote in his autobiography, ". . . awakened my curiosity with respect to this *mystery* of reading." In the Protestantism that most African Americans adopted during the antebellum period, great emphasis was placed on the word of God and the biblical text as the center of the religious experience. Many slave owners questioned whether, given the admonitions against slavery in the Bible, a convert to Christianity could legally be owned. This problem was addressed in a number of colonial legislatures—in Maryland as early as 1644—and by various ministers throughout the succeeding two centuries; however, in every instance, a person's religious orientation was found to have no bearing on his or her status as a slave.

No serious institutional effort at proselytizing Africans was made before the establishment of the Society for the Propagation of the Gospel in Foreign Parts (SPG) by the Church of England in 1701. The SPG embraced as its mission the expansion of Christianity to unconverted blacks, Native Americans, and whites, and the expansion of Anglicanism to strongholds of other Christian denominations, such as Congregationalism in New England. Believing that literacy was a requirement for baptism, in 1704 the SPG established the first North American school for educating blacks, in New York. By 1708 its founder, Elias Neau, reported that it had two hundred students, male and female, free and slave. Despite a threat of closure in the aftermath of the New York Slave Revolt of 1712, the school survived until the AMERICAN REVOLUTION. Another SPG school, in which two black slaves provided instruction in Christian principles and basic education, was founded in Charleston in 1743, and remained open until 1763.

The conversion of Africans to Christianity did not take place on a large scale until the middle of the eighteenth century, when a movement known as the Great Awakening occurred. Many leaders of the Great Awakening, such as the white Virginian Presbyterian Samuel Davies, emphasized the need for black converts to read the word of God. Throughout the antebellum period a number of white religious leaders, including many staunch defenders of slavery, favored black literacy and the distribution of religious texts as a way of spreading the faith, and doubtless as a means of making slaves more tractable. White ministers, missionaries, and teachers initially believed that they could control the forms and purposes of black literacy; but the emergence of independent black congregations and denominations (which after the end of the eighteenth century usually had literate ministers) soon proved their hopes vain. Throughout and indeed beyond the antebellum period, the church remained a main arena for the advancement of African-American literacy. The ministry was a magnet for literate and ambitious young men, and most congregations tried to foster basic "Bible literacy" among its members.

Schools and Teachers

Not surprisingly, almost all formal education for African Americans in the North and South during the antebellum period was reserved for a small group of free blacks, comprising about 5 percent of the total black population. In New England and the mid-Atlantic colonies or states, schools for blacks became fairly common toward the end of the eighteenth century. Many were founded by abolitionist societies and Quakers. In New York City, the New York Manumission Society opened the New York African Free School in 1787. New Jersey Quakers had established schools for blacks in Burlington, Salem, and Trenton by 1800. Philadelphia had seven black schools by 1797. Schools stressing basic literacy were established over a wide range of places, including Newport, R.I.; Charleston, S.C.; Savannah, Ga.; Georgetown, Md.; Wilmington, Del.; Richmond, Alexandria, and Norfolk, Va.

Almost all formal education for African Americans during the antebellum period was reserved for a small group of free blacks, comprising about 5 percent of the total black population.

Free blacks also opened a number of schools independently of abolitionist groups. In 1798, Primus Hall, son of the pioneer black Freemason Prince Hall, established a school in his Boston home. Catherine Ferguson, an ex-slave who had purchased her own freedom, opened a school in New York City in 1793. Maria Becraft opened the first boarding school for black girls, in Washington, D.C. Becraft later joined the Sisters of Providence, and by the 1830s, Roman Catholic teaching orders had established schools for black girls in Baltimore, Nashville, and New Orleans. Other late eighteenth-century and early nineteenth-century black mutual aid organizations, such as the African Union Society in Newport and the Free African Society of Philadelphia, also established schools. The elite mulatto Brown Fellowship Society in Charleston, S.C., supported two schools, one for the children of its members, another for darker free blacks and orphans. In Philadelphia in 1860, there were fixty-six private schools for blacks, only twelve of which were led by whites.

Schools for blacks were often underfunded, and faced other obstacles as well. In 1829 Daniel Payne, who later became the senior bishop of the AFRICAN METHODIST EPISCOPAL CHURCH, opened an innovative school in Charleston and charged his students fifty cents a month. But Payne was obliged to close the school in 1835, after South Carolina had tightened its restrictions against teaching blacks, and whites rioted against the free black community. In 1834 the building housing Noyes Academy in Canaan, N.H., was torn from its foundations and hauled into a swamp by local whites who objected to its integrated student body. Probably the most famous instance of racism of this sort was that encountered by the white Quaker operator of a boarding school in Canterbury, Conn., in 1833. Prudence Crandell lost all of her white students after she admitted a black girl. She then advertised for black girls to attend the school, and thereafter Crandell and the school faced violence by local residents and legal harassment by the state of Connecticut. Crandell refused to post bond and served time in jail. Though she was subsequently vindicated legally, Crandell abandoned the school after 1834.

The establishment of public funding for primary education raised a new series of questions concerning the funding and exclusion of blacks from public schools. Public funding for education began in the 1820s. In some states—as, for instance, Ohio in the 1830s—blacks were excluded altogether from common schools, and they had to fight for a share of tax revenue to establish their own schools in many cities and towns. From 1830 onward, black leaders were divided in their opinions as to whether African Americans should press for admission to the more prestigious and better-funded white schools, or establish public schools of their own. In 1847 Frederick Douglass led an unsuccessful fight for equal funding for a local black public school in Rochester, N.Y. Nine years later, the same black school was closed after the city fathers agreed to integrate the local school system. Lockport, a small New York State city on the Erie Canal, and the northern terminus of the UNDERGROUND RAILROAD, chose to segregate its African-American population and the public schools in 1835. It was not until 1870 that the Rev. C. W. Mossell succeeded in renewing the black assault on Lockport's segregated schools. In a series of petitions to the Lockport school board, then to the New York State Superintendent, Mossell, joined by others in the black community, reminded the school board that it was "extravagant to continue the school."

In 1876 the black school "quietly closed its doors and blacks entered the public schools without a murmur of protest from the white community." The most publicized and protracted fight for educational integration of the antebellum period was carried out by prominent black and white abolitionists in Boston, who succeeded in integrating Massachusetts public schools in 1855, after a decade-long struggle.

The Civil War, Emancipation, and the First Schools

In the first half of the nineteenth century, the proliferation of numerous mutual aid societies, fraternal organizations, and black-owned libraries and reading rooms all promoted African-American literacy and education, as did the emergence of the black press and black publishing houses. The hundreds of slave narratives published in antebellum America, many proudly claiming "written by himself or herself," were, among other things, defiant assertions of the importance of literacy. These cultural developments, as well as the formal establishment of schools, contributed to the gathering sectional conflict over the status of slavery, which culminated in the CIVIL WAR.

So great was the need for literacy that efforts on behalf of African-American education persisted even after the country had erupted into war. Indeed, many of the roughly 180,000 black soldiers who served in the Union Army, a large number of them ex-slaves, saw army service as a way of acquiring reading skills. Classes were supervised by the army chaplain, and those who had some reading ability also served as instructors. A number of commanders reported a total reversal of illiteracy rates in their companies and regiments in a period of little more than a year.

The education of freed and runaway slaves who had not enlisted as soldiers also began almost immediately upon contact with the Union Army. Teachers worked in the many "contraband" camps that sprang up behind the Union lines. The earliest of these camps, established by Mary Chase in Alexandria, Va., on September 1, 1861, later became HAMPTON INSTITUTE. When a school for contrabands and freed slaves was established by the American Missionary Association (AMA) near Fortress Monroe at Hampton, Va. the AMA's Lewis Lockwood found that Mary S. Peake, a black Virginian educated in the private schools of Washington, D.C., already had begun a school for 45 children one month

Well into the twentieth century, because of inadequate funds for education and school construction, churches were often used as classrooms, such as this church in Gee's Bend, Ala., in 1937. (Prints and Photographs Division, Library of Congress)

after Confederate forces had evacuated Hampton, Va., in September 1861. Schools were created by the Union Army directly after taking control of rebel territory. One of the best-known examples is the school established on the Sea Islands of South Carolina, at Port Royal, which was captured by Union forces early in 1862. There, both white and black northern teachers—including Charlotte Forten, a black teacher from Philadelphia who wrote a widely circulated account of the aptitude of the freedmen as students—participated in what was termed a successful "rehearsal for Reconstruction."

In the aftermath of the Civil War, education emerged as one of the most prominent and basic concerns of the freed slaves. As Booker T. WASHINGTON wrote, "few people who were not right in the midst of the scenes can form any exact idea of the intense desire which the people of my race showed for education . . . it was a whole race trying to go to school. . . . Few were too young, and none too old, to make the attempt." Although many expressed a great interest in reading the Bible, students also saw literacy as the key to full citizenship. Their passion for education remained unchanged throughout the century after EMANCIPATION. It is striking how many African-American leaders in the succeeding century—Washington, W. E. B. DU BOIS, Mary McLeod Bethune, Benjamin MAYS, Alain LOCKE, and Anna Julia Cooper, to name a few—were educators. Perhaps the greatest tribute to the tenacity of African-American education is that by 1950, despite inadequate funding, the indifference or outright hostility of most government bodies, and the myriad indignities and injustices of southern segregation, 90 percent of African Americans in the South were literate.

The original Freedmen's Bureau Act of 1865 made no provision for education; however, the Civil Rights Act of 1866 enlarged the bureau's power in this area, and appropriated more than $500,000 for the building and repair of schoolhouses. The extensive educational system that the bureau then established became the framework for African-American common schools. By 1866 the percentage of ex-slaves attending schools in the South was equal to that of blacks in the North, and far above that of southern white students. There were 975 schools with more than 1,400 teachers for freedmen; the number of teachers jumped to 2,000 the following year. Most of the teachers were originally northern, female, and white; however, the Freedmen's Bureau devoted considerable energy to engaging African Americans, and by 1869 a majority of the instructors were black. Many of the whites involved in teaching had backgrounds in ABOLITION and church missionary work, and the underfunded educational efforts of the Freedmen's Bureau were supported by such secular abolitionist organizations as the National Freedmen's Relief Association of New York and the Indiana Emancipation League, as well as religious bodies such as the Scotch Convenanters Church and at least eight regional meetings of the Quakers. After 1868, reconstructed southern state governments also began to contribute to black education. Perhaps the most important alternative source of funding was the AMA, which supported the efforts of the Freedmen's Bureau in addition to establishing its own network of schools. Northern black denominations and organizations such as the African Civilization Society were also extremely active in sponsoring schools for the freedmen after emancipation.

However, many freed slaves, conscious of their lack of education and its relevance to their new status, founded schools without any prompting from outside authority. When John Alvord, the superintendent of schools for the Freedmen's Bureau, conducted a survey trip to the South in 1865, he discovered that at least 500 schools had been independently established by the freed slaves. Not all of these schools were new; some served as continuations of schools that had operated secretly under slavery. In most areas, blacks were expected to supplement other sources with their own funds. By 1867, the direct and voluntary contributions of blacks greatly augmented, and in some cases far exceeded, the contributions of the Freedmen's Bureau in all southern states. Freed slaves also invested in their schools by purchasing schoolbooks, boarding and protecting teachers, and constructing school buildings.

Whereas the support of public or common schools through taxation had become a fixture of northern society, southern support of education was tenuous at best. Ex-slaves struggled to ensure the political survival of universal public education. As W. E. B. Du Bois wrote, "Public education for all at public expense was, in the South, a Negro idea." Numerous black RECONSTRUCTION era politicians made public education a key element in their political program, and joined with white members of the REPUBLICAN PARTY to include a public school provision in the new state constitutions. Other literacy-related institutions, such as newspapers and printing operations, were established by southern African Americans at this time. "Freedom and school books and newspapers go hand in hand. Let us secure the freedom we have received by the intelligence that can maintain it," admonished an editorial in an 1865 edition of the *New Orleans Black Republican.*

Educating the newly freed slaves was a burden keenly felt by many northern missionaries who regarded education as a key means of regenerating the South. As one Illinois educator remarked in 1865, it was "now up to the teacher to finish the work the soldier had begun." Northern educators sought to inculcate in both white and black Southerners the Protestant values of hard work, sobriety, self-control, and piety. The schools they founded were based on the traditional New England model of liberal education. Arithmetic, reading, writing, Greek, Latin, history, geography, science, music, and philosophy were all included in the curriculum. In addition, missionary instruction was supplemented by moral teachings, biblical readings, prayer meetings, and other methods designed to shape the ethical as well as the intellectual development of black students.

Many of the missionary educators who went to the South to teach during this period did so at tremendous sacrifice. They frequently taught in inadequate and dangerous conditions and faced indifference or hostility from most southern whites. Although they frequently showed a lack of understanding of the cultural background of their black students, most missionary teachers believed that African Americans were their spiritual equals, and considered education the first step toward achieving political and legal reform.

Colleges

Since the problem of secondary education for African Americans was largely ignored by the southern states, missionary societies concentrated increasingly on creating secondary schools. In the 1870s these societies began to address the need for institutions in which blacks could be trained as teachers; by 1895, more than forty colleges and sixty secondary schools for blacks, most of them supported by northern missionaries, had been established in the South.

Most of the so-called historically black colleges and universities (HBCUs) were founded in the years immediately following the Civil War, and almost all of these were founded by missionary organizations in the North. The American Missionary Association, affiliated with the Congregational Church, established FISK UNIVERSITY (1866), Straight University (1869), Talladega College (1867), Tougaloo College (1869), and Tillotson College (1875). The Freedmen's Aid Society of the Methodist Episcopal Church, North, sponsored Bennett College (1873), CLARK UNIVERSITY (1869), Claflin College (1869), Morgan College (1867), New Orleans University (1869), Philander Smith College (1877), and Meharry Medical College (1876). The mostly white American Baptist Home Mission Society was responsible for the founding of Benedict College (1870), Bishop College, Hartshorn Memorial College (1884), MOREHOUSE COLLEGE (1867), Shaw University (1865), and Spelman Seminary (1881) (now SPELMAN COLLEGE). The Presbyterian-sponsored colleges were Biddle University (1867), now Johnson C. Smith University, Knoxville College (1875), and Stillman Seminary (1876). Among the colleges founded by black denominations were Allen University (1880), Morris Brown College (1881), Wilberforce College (1856) (now WILBERFORCE UNIVERSITY), Paul Quinn College (1881), Edward Waters College (1888), and Shorter College (1886), all organized by the African Methodist Episcopal Church. The African Methodist Episcopal Zion Church founded Livingstone College (1882), and the Colored Methodist Episcopal Church founded Lane College (1879), Paine College (1884), Texas College (1895), and Miles Memorial College (1907). Black Baptists were responsible for the creation of Arkansas Baptist College (1885), Selma University (1878), and Virginia College and Seminary (1888). Three independent, nondenominational colleges were founded during this time: Atlanta University (1872), HOWARD UNIVERSITY (1868), and Leland University (1870). Most African Americans received their higher education at the missionary colleges, despite the fact that these institutions acquiesced to segregation on campus and were controlled financially and administratively by whites.

Private, church-affiliated colleges were supplemented by state colleges and land-grant institutions. The first land-grant school, Alcorn Agricultural and Mining (A&M) College, was authorized in 1871. In 1890 the federal government passed the Second Morrill Act, which extended land-grant provisions to sixteen southern states. In many instances, black colleges were established solely to obtain funding for white colleges under the act. The financial resources of the state land-grant schools were even more limited than those of the private schools. However, unlike the missionary schools, the faculty and administration of the state land-grant institutions were predominantly black. By 1915, sixteen land-grant colleges for African Americans had been established, and almost every southern state supported some type of school for black higher education. Many of these institutions were normal schools, and had as their primary purpose the training of black teachers for a segregated primary education system.

Although this spate of college funding appears impressive, it gives a misleading impression of the state of black collegiate education in the postemancipation period. Most of these colleges and universities were institutes of higher education in name only; very few actually taught courses at the college level. For the most part, these colleges were used for secondary and/or remedial instruction. Many white Southerners feared that higher education would increase the political and economic expectations of African Americans and did all they could to ensure that black colleges obtained as little support as possible from state governments.

As of 1915, only 33 of the nearly 100 black colleges were able to provide college-level courses for their students. A number of early twentieth-century surveys, undertaken by persons of varying ideological perspectives, concluded that the network of black colleges was overextended. In 1900, W. E. B. Du Bois found a total college-level enrollment of only 726 students. Ten years later, in his book *The College Bred Negro,* Du Bois recommended reducing the total number of black colleges from 100 to 32 to strengthen and improve black higher education. In his view, the only "first-grade colored colleges" were Fisk, Howard, Atlanta, Morehouse, and Virginia Union—while Lincoln, Talladega, and Wilberforce served as examples of "second-grade colored colleges." Those who were more skeptical of black higher education, and wished to replace it with industrial training, reached even more sweeping conclusions. Thomas Jesse Jones, the director of the Phelps-Stokes Fund, visited and studied black institutions over a period of two years, and in 1917 published a two-volume survey that claimed that the only colleges worth saving were Fisk and Howard.

Northern philanthropies performed a vitally needed function at a time when neither the state nor the federal government showed a serious interest in the education of African Americans.

While these debates over state-funded institutions were taking place, private black colleges were forced to seek new sources of funding. The missionary societies had fallen on hard times, and by the end of the century their finances had been greatly curtailed. Their resources were replaced with those of new philanthropies, such as the John T. Slater Fund (1881); the Anna T. Jeannes Foundation (1907); the Phelps-Stokes Fund (1910); and the Carnegie Foundation, Julius Rosenwald Fund, and Laura Spelman Rockefeller Fund (all founded between 1902 and 1917). Unlike the older missionary societies, the newer philanthropies were predominantly secular in their goals and skeptical of the need for, and possibilities within, black education. Like many northern whites of their era, these philanthropical societies wished to bring about a reconciliation with southern whites; and in their eagerness to be sensitive to southern white concerns, they gave scant consideration to the feelings, needs, and aspirations of southern blacks. To be sure, some northern philanthropies—in particular, the Rosenwald Fund—continued to support serious intellectual work by blacks. Whatever their biases, they performed a vitally needed function at a time when neither the state nor the federal government showed a serious interest in the education of African Americans.

Industrial vs. Academic Education

Chronic lack of funding provided the backdrop for the late nineteenth-century controversy between industrial and academic training, as exemplified by Booker T. Washington and W. E. B. Du Bois, respectively. The concept of industrial education for African Americans was not a new one. Vocational education for artisans had long been favored by both black and white educators. For blacks, the need to acquire an education outside the discriminatory influence of craft unions was a necessity. In 1853, Frederick Douglass had favored industrial schooling as a means of overcoming this problem, and during the post-Civil War period his solution was taken up by such prominent African-American leaders as T. Thomas Fortune.

The kind of industrial education favored by Douglass was related to, but differed significantly from, the model of industrial training that became associated with Booker T. Washington. Douglass favored an industrial education that would enable black laborers to become competent in any skill they chose, even if their skills placed them in direct competition with whites. Washington's method, by contrast, consisted primarily in training blacks for teaching in segregated schools and for working in traditionally black occupations (such as agriculture and domestic service).

One of the earliest industrial schools was Hampton Normal Agricultural Institute (now HAMPTON INSTITUTE), founded in 1868 by Gen. Samuel Chapman Armstrong, a Civil War officer who had spent his formative years in Hawaii as the son of missionary parents. There, future teachers worked six days a week to learn "the dignity of labor" before going out to preach the values of hard toil to the South's future labor force. Many white people viewed this form of education as a means of ensuring racial harmony, since it provided blacks with useful skills without challenging the existing racial order.

In 1881 Booker T. Washington, Armstrong's most illustrious pupil, founded Tuskegee Institute (now TUSKEGEE UNIVERSITY) in Alabama. Washington's role in African-American education, like his role in black history in general, remains extremely controversial. His stated goal for his students was to enable them to become economically independent and self-sufficient. Washington advised the Tuskegee students against openly challenging the status quo, and suggested instead that they become responsible citizens by seeking to establish themselves in a job or a trade. Thereafter, he asserted, white society would concede equality. While Washington was not opposed to academic higher education as such, he looked on it as a secondary task. "It is well to remember," he claimed in a speech in 1904, ". . . that our teachers, ministers, lawyers, and doctors will prosper just in proportion as they have about them an intelligent and skillful producing class."

Washington's great opponent in educational philosophy was W. E. B. Du Bois, the author of *The Souls of Black Folk* (1903) and a Harvard Ph.D. Du Bois, who had begun his undergraduate career at Fisk, was a strong supporter of academic education and the missionary colleges. He placed great emphasis on the importance, within the African-American tradition, of creating what he called "the Talented Tenth," college-educated blacks who would assume leadership roles in the community. For Du Bois, the missionary colleges, and the northern missionaries themselves, had played a critical role in creating educated black college undergraduates. In 1918 Du Bois described the northern missionaries as "men radical in their belief in Negro possibility" who by 1900 had "trained in Greek, Latin, and math 2,000 men, and these men trained fully 50,000 in morals and manners, and they in turn taught the alphabet to 9 million men." Du Bois believed that college-bred African Americans would lead all blacks to an awareness of their full capabilities, and ultimately to equal status with the white population. While he readily acknowledged the faults of the black colleges, he nevertheless insisted on weighing these faults against their potential for creating a black leadership class.

The difference between the philosophies of education for the Negro that were held by Du Bois and Washington became the major source of the debate and enmity between the two Negro educators. Du Bois's major objection to Washington's philosophy was Washington's, and the northern abolitionists', efforts to educate Negro young people for menial jobs and "to farm land that they would seldom own" (Levering Lewis, 1993).

Historian John Hendrik Clarke counsels against taking sides in the Washington-Du Bois debate, since black people were in need of workmen and technicians as well as educators and politicians accountable to the needs of black people.

After 1900, as the influence of missionary societies waned, Booker T. Washington's theories were championed by most of the northern philanthropists. Washington was also supported by an emerging group of white middle-class Southerners who became known as advocates of the "New South." Both groups sought to maintain white supremacy through the creation of a literate and skilled black workforce that would increase economic prosperity without threatening the existing social structure. Hampton and Tuskegee became the well-funded showcases for industrial education. It should be noted, however, that however popular industrial education might have been with white philanthropists, neither the concept nor the institutions were popular among black educators or among southern blacks as a whole. As James Anderson points out in *The Education of Blacks in the South, 1860–1935,* academic education was in greater demand, and it, rather than the few highly publicized examples of industrial education, became the model for almost all of the hundred colleges established in the South.

The controversy between Washington and Du Bois was fueled by the positive reactions of white philanthrophists to Washington's educational views. In a climate in which scientific racism, doubts about the intellectual ability of blacks, and the acceptance of blacks as an inferior, politically negligible caste were nearly universal among the whites in power, the prospect of academic education for blacks was discounted as threatening or irrelevant. Consequently, funding for black academic institutions (e.g., Atlanta University) was curtailed, while Hampton Institute and Tuskegee garnered the larger share of the philanthropists' money.

However, philanthropical discrimination against black colleges, and such criticisms as those expressed by Jones in his 1917 survey, did not force black colleges to close, but led instead to an upgrading of their academic programs. Starting in 1913, accreditation agencies pressured many schools either to eliminate or to separate higher education from their secondary programs of instruction in order to be considered full-fledged colleges or universities. State teaching examinations also caused a number of black colleges—including Hampton and Tuskegee—to introduce a broader liberal arts curriculum so their graduates could pass the teacher certification tests.

The faculties of many black colleges remained predominantly, at times exclusively, white through the end of the nineteenth century. In 1894 only one black faculty member was employed at Fisk, and none at Atlanta University. By 1915, black professors made up 69 percent of the faculty at Howard University, 58 percent at Clark University, 93 percent at Meharry Medical College, and 31 percent at Fisk. Still, most of the presidents of the black colleges were white, and some—who owed their positions to northern philanthropists—were vehemently opposed to political activism and social change. Fayette McKenzie, the president of Fisk after 1915, eliminated the black educators and northern missionaries serving on the Board of Trustees, closed the student government and newspaper, and refused to allow a chapter of the NATIONAL ASSOCIATION FOR THE ADVANCEMENT OF COLORED PEOPLE (NAACP) on campus. In March 1925 a student strike supported by the alumni, the national black press, and local black leaders forced McKenzie to resign. At Hampton in 1929, students forced the president to resign and demanded an academic curriculum. The unrest at these and other black colleges in the 1920s marked a crucial transition in the history of the HBCUs. By the 1930s the colleges were predominantly staffed and administered by black educators and had become increasingly self-conscious with regard to their African-American orientation.

Primary and Secondary Education

Due to the controversy surrounding the Washington-Du Bois debate on black colleges, little attention was paid to primary and secondary education in the late nineteenth and early twentieth centuries. The commitment to African-American education by parents, teachers, and students was not matched by southern state governments, which discriminated against black schools by underfunding them on a regular basis. In 1900 only 36 percent of black children in the South attended school, and of these, 86 percent went for less than six months per year. The gains in school attendance and literacy were fewer for blacks than for whites. From 1876 to 1895 black enrollment increased 59 percent, while white enrollment was up 106 percent. About one-third of all southern blacks were literate by 1900—a sign of both how much had been achieved through black education (from a 90 percent illiteracy rate immediately after the Civil War) and how much was yet to be done.

In *The Common School and the Negro American* (1910), Du Bois accused the U.S. government of not giving sufficient funds and authority to the U.S. Bureau of Education and thereby refusing "to tell the whole truth concerning our efforts to educate the children of freedmen as well as our general educational system." Those black children who did attend school, Du Bois contended, were poorly taught, by teachers who were half prepared, ill-trained, and employed only three to six months a year. Schoolhouses and school equipment were inadequate if not downright wretched. According to Du Bois, the reduction of funds for black schools lowered the efficacy of course studies and served to eliminate competent teachers in favor of instructors who would act as "willing tools who do not and will not complain." Moreover, the introduction of manual and industrial training—however valuable or necessary—had created an excess of ill-considered and unrelated work, which detracted from the time and attention needed for the critical disciplines of reading, writing, and arithmetic. All of these things, Du Bois wrote, were deliberately aimed at "training Negroes as menials and laborers and cutting them off from the higher avenues of life."

Not until the first third of the twentieth century did the majority of black children have access to elementary school. The economic depression of the late nineteenth century and the increasingly virulent racism of most southern whites had prevented further developments in the educational programs initiated by the freedmen and northern missionaries right after the Civil War. What little money was available for public education was spent on the children of poor whites. After 1900, philanthropies such as the General Education Board frequently merged their programs for white and black education into a combined southern education directive—a process that resulted, as Booker T. Washington charged, in money "actually being taken from the colored people and given to the white schools."

Not until the first third of the twentieth century did the majority of black children have access to elementary school.

Following 1915, a "public" primary education system emerged through the support of local governments, white philanthropies, and black communities. The philanthropies often demanded that black communities pay a large portion of the school costs, through the levying of special taxes and the donation of labor, materials, and land. This practice, documented by Richard R. WRIGHT, Jr., in *Self-Help in Negro Education* (1909), demonstrated yet again the sacrifices African Americans were willing to make for education. Of all the philanthropies, the Rosenwald Fund was the most active in establishing common schools. Between 1913 and 1935, 15 percent of the total costs for school construction in the South were provided by the Rosenwald Fund, and 17 percent were covered by blacks themselves.

While state governments contributed, albeit meagerly and with reluctance, to primary schools, they made a concerted effort to prevent the building of high schools for African Americans. In 1934, 54 percent of southern white children attended high school, as compared to 18 percent of black youth in the South. There were almost no high schools in rural areas until 1915.

That blacks were being denied educational opportunities was made clear in the case of *Cumming* v. *School Board of Richmond County, Georgia,* heard by the U.S. Supreme Court in 1899. Upon the closing of the only black high school in the county, local black residents sued for equal segregated facilities. The courts ruled against the plaintiffs, despite the precedent set by the 1896 PLESSY V. FERGUSON decision, which upheld the segregation of railway carriages on interstate lines but asserted that blacks and whites should be accommodated on "separate but equal" terms. A black high school did not reopen in Richmond County until 1945.

In the South as a whole, the building of black high schools did not begin in earnest until 1920. Southern governments and northern philanthropists were determined to develop curricula that would train black youth to become laborers, although in many cases blacks managed to have an academic regimen included in the school programs. County normal schools, modeled on the Hampton and Tuskegee institutions, were cited as an alternative to academic normal schools by most philanthropies until 1930, after which these county normal schools either died out or were converted into public high schools.

Preparatory Elementary and Secondary Schools Founded by African-American Women

In the late nineteenth century and early twentieth century as blacks were migrating from the South to the North, four prominent African-American women founded elementary and secondary preparatory schools for black youths. The schools existed over long periods of time and successfully educated generations of black students.

The Haines Normal and Industrial Institute was chartered in 1886 and closed in 1949. It was founded by Lucy Craft Laney, the seventh of ten children in a slave family. Lucy Craft Laney was educated by a daughter of the Campbells, a slave-holding family. Later she graduated from Ballard Normal School and, aided by the American Missionary Association, entered Atlanta University, graduating in 1873. For the next ten years she taught in the public schools of several Georgia towns and cities, including Augusta and Savannah.

With the support and help of the Presbyterian Board of Missions, Lucy Craft Laney opened a school in a lecture room of the Christ Presbyterian Church in Augusta. In 1886, the school was chartered by the state of Georgia. By 1931, Haines Institute had grown to 27 teachers, 300 high school students, and 413 elementary school students. Mary McLeod BETHUNE began her teaching career at Haines Institute.

The Palmer Memorial Institute (1902–1971) was founded by Charlotte Hawkins Brown, an educator and civil rights activist. Charlotte Hawkins was born in rural Henderson, N.C., to parents who had lived with a part of a white family called Hawkins. When she was about seven years old, the family moved to Boston. Charlotte was educated in the public schools of Cambridge (the Allison Grammar School); she was an excellent student, and was chosen graduation speaker. She graduated from the Cambridge English High and Latin School, where the principal became one of her lifelong supporters. She wanted to attend Radcliffe College but her mother was not sympathetic toward Radcliffe, so she decided to prepare for a career in teaching and enrolled in the Massachusetts State Normal School at Salem.

Charlotte Hawkins began her career in teaching at Bethany Institute in McLeansville, N.C. She then returned north for further education at Harvard, Simmons College in Boston, and Temple University in Philadelphia. In 1902, seeking to help break down the walls of segregation in American life, she founded the Palmer Memorial Institute in Sedalia, N.C. The school became known for its emphasis on cultural education.

Charlotte Hawkins Brown also started the movement to establish the State Training School for Negro Girls in Rocky Mount, N.C. This school was organized into elementary, high school, and junior college instruction, with both cultural and academic courses. The campus was one of the first public interracial meeting places in North Carolina, in accordance with Brown's adamant opposition to racial segregation, which also resulted in her frequent ejection from Pullman berths and seats on southern trains.

The National Training School for Girls (1909–1961) was founded by Nannie Helen Burroughs, who had a long history of involvement in industrial education and throughout her life was associated with causes related to the African-American working woman.

In 1909 she founded the National Training School for Women and Girls in Washington, D.C. The school became well known for the emphasis Burroughs placed on spiritual training. She stressed the three "B's": the Bible, the bath, and the broom, which she regarded as tools for the advancement of the race.

The school continued to operate in its original format until after Burroughs's death in 1961, although in 1934 its name was changed to the National Trades and Professional School for Women. In 1964 the trade school curriculum was abandoned and the school was reestablished as the Nannie Helen Burroughs School, for students of elementary school age.

A tireless advocate of the education of African Americans, especially women, Burroughs also worked toward securing equality in the workplace for black women. She was a member of the National Association of Colored Women, which later became the NATIONAL COUNCIL OF NEGRO WOMEN, under the leadership of Mary McLeod Bethune.

Mary McLeod Bethune founded the Daytona Normal and Industrial School in Daytona Beach, Fla., in 1904. The school is now called BETHUNE-COOKMAN COLLEGE.

After serving in national positions under Presidents Calvin Coolidge and Herbert Hoover, Bethune became best known as an adviser to President Franklin D. Roosevelt, Eleanor Roosevelt, and President Harry Truman. Bethune was appointed by President Roosevelt to the directorship of the National Youth Administration. Well-known for her forceful speaking style, she became one of the most sought-after speakers of her day.

The Great Depression of the 1930s marked a turning point in the history of black education. The wholesale firing of blacks in menial positions in order to create work for unemployed whites demonstrated the futility of educating blacks for specifically "black" jobs. A growing militancy, which first found expression in the college disturbances of the previous decade, led blacks to demand control over the staffing and administrative policies of their institutions. In *The Mis-Education of the American Negro,* Carter WOODSON criticized industrial education for shortchanging blacks and academic education for its failure to address the specific needs of black students, who were not offered courses in African-American history and culture.

The Educational Impact of the Great Migration

Beginning in the 1920s, blacks began migrating in large numbers to northern states and cities. In 1910, 90 percent of African Americans lived in the South; by 1970, only a bare majority resided in the southeastern and southern states. The movement north was part of a broader transformation from a largely rural into a largely urban population. Cities became the dominant dwelling places for southern as well as northern blacks. These two related migrations, from the South to the North and from the farm to the urban center, changed almost every aspect of African-American life. Migration from rural areas to southern and southwestern cities allowed many blacks to attend school for the first time. In 1910, 46.6 percent of all black children between ages ten and fifteen were working in agriculture, domestic employment, or industry, as compared to 14.3 percent of whites. By 1930, the figures for blacks had dropped to 16.1 percent. Not until 1930 did the percentage of fourteen- and fifteen-year-old blacks attending school reach 78.1 percent, a level approximating that which white children had reached (77.4 percent) two decades earlier. Southern educational authorities, fearful of rural depopulation, started more and somewhat better-funded schools in rural areas after 1915, in hopes of enticing African Americans to stay. (Nonetheless, these new schools remained segregated, underfunded, and were inferior to the schools established for whites.)

Migration from rural areas to southern and southwestern cities allowed many blacks to attend school for the first time.

Integrated education was possible for those blacks who left the South for the North. By 1910, seven northern states prohibited segregated schools: Illinois, Massachusetts, Nevada, New Jersey, New York, Ohio, and Pennsylvania. Within these systems, differential treatment of black students was hardly a rarity. Nevertheless, there was far less likelihood that black children seeking a fair opportunity for education would be met with instant opposition. The centralization of public schools in northern urban, industrialized areas not only promised lower costs per pupil (as compared to costs in the South overall, and in rural areas in particular) but also precluded the maintenance of racially separate school systems (though not of racially isolated schools).

For African Americans, education in northern cities was in many ways a vast improvement over what was available in the South. Because most northern cities were formally integrated, black students could obtain funding and term lengths that were equal to those of whites, and many were able to excel in this new setting. However, in spite of the fact that segregation was not *de jure* (as it was in the South), segregated housing patterns often led to *de facto* segregation and consequently, to the inequitable distribution of funds for predominantly black schools. Blacks were frequently encouraged to take vocational rather than academic courses. In integrated schools they sometimes faced hostility from teachers and fellow students, and were discouraged from participating in extracurricular activities. High-school dropout rates remained higher for blacks than for whites, and quotas—if not outright bars—limited black entrance and matriculation in northern colleges.

By 1940 the percentage of black students between five and twenty years of age who were attending school had risen from 44.7 percent (in 1910) to 64.4 percent, while white attendance had climbed from 61.3 percent to 71.6 percent during those same years. The median schooling completed by persons aged 25 was 5.7 years for blacks and 8.7 years for whites. This discrepancy was accounted for by the fact that 41.8 percent of blacks had spent fewer than five years in elementary school, as compared to 10.9 percent of whites. By 1950 the percentage of blacks with fewer than five years of primary schooling had dropped to 36.2 percent; not until 1980 would there be a rough parity in the median number of school years completed by blacks (12.2 years) and whites (12.5 years).

During the middle decades of the twentieth century, the federal government became increasingly involved in African-American education. As part of his 1930s New Deal, President Franklin D. Roosevelt created the WORKS PROJECT ADMINISTRATION (WPA), which developed literacy programs and hired black writers to participate in such special projects as documenting the lives of former slaves. WPA classes were attended by more than 100,000 African Americans. From 1936 to 1943, the Division of Negro Affairs of the National Youth Administration (NYA), headed by noted black educator Mary McLeod Bethune, aided hundreds of thousands of black students both in the North and in the still-segregated South. Bethune's was the first federal program to address the needs of black students by providing direct aid, and as such served as an important precedent for later federal educational assistance programs. The federal government continued to voice its support for African-American education throughout the 1940s, and in 1947 the President's Commission on Higher Education issued a report calling for the full integration of all colleges and universities.

Perhaps the most significant indication of the government's commitment to creating educational opportunities for blacks was the appearance of the 1947 report by the Presidential Committee on Civil Rights. The report, titled *To Secure These Rights,* charged the government with failing to eliminate "prejudice and discrimination from the operation of either our public or our private schools and colleges." After examining the seventeen southern states and the District of Columbia, the committee concluded that "whatever test is used—expenditure per pupil, teachers' salaries, the number of pupils per teacher, transportation of students, adequacy of school buildings and educational equipment, length of school term, extent of curriculum—Negro students are invariably at a disadvantage." A single example of these inequities is the disparity in salaries between white and black teachers in Alabama and Mississippi for the school year 1943–44: In Alabama, white teachers earned $1,158 to black teachers' $661; in Mississippi, white teachers earned $1,107 to black teachers' $342. As the report noted, relatively little had changed since Du Bois cited very similar statistics in his 1911 work *The Common School and the Negro American.*

The Assault of Social Science and Law on "Separate but Equal" Education

The U.S. Supreme Court case of *Plessy* v. *Ferguson,* which upheld segregation by establishing the constitutionality of "separate but equal" facilities for whites and blacks, was decided in 1896, but it was not until the late 1930s that segregation became a legal issue in the South. In the subsequent assault on segregation, the great majority of cases involved education, primarily because this was the area in which state-provided facilities were most patently and grossly unequal. Starting with *Missouri ex. rel. Gaines* v. *Canada* (1938), the NAACP Legal Defense and Educational Fund (LDEF) began to chip away at the foundations of segregation on a case-by-case, aspect-by-aspect basis. The rulings in *Gaines* and such cases as *McLaurin* v. *Oklahoma State Regents for Higher Education* (1950) and *Sweatt* v. *Painter* (1950) forced white institutions to admit black students into their graduate and professional programs because no comparable institutions for blacks existed; however, it was the landmark case of BROWN V. BOARD OF EDUCATION OF TOPEKA (1954) that challenged segregation both in principle and as social policy.

Brown v. *Board of Education of Topeka*

The case brought to the U.S. Supreme Court by the NAACP Legal Defense and Educational Fund in 1952 was a consolidation of five school cases from the states of South Carolina, Virginia, Kansas, Delaware, and the District of Columbia. Named for the litigants in the Kansas case, the case challenged the legality of segregated public schools, and in so doing, the validity of the ruling in *Plessy* v. *Ferguson* in 1896 (Kluger, *Simple Justice,* 1976; Franklin and Moss, *From Slavery to Freedom,* 1988).

On May 17, 1954, the Court ruled for the plaintiffs, writing, ". . . in the field of public education the doctrine of separate but equal has no place. Separate educational facilities are inherently unequal" (Kluger, *Simple Justice,* p. 707).

The following year, on May 7, 1955, the Court issued its implementation order, directing the desegregation of all public facilities and accommodations ". . . with all deliberate speed."

Sharing Responsibilty: A New Federal Role

Despite the *Brown* decision, and the telling need for massive improvement in elementary and secondary education, the federal government showed a great reluctance to intervene in school desegregation matters. Indeed, President Dwight D. Eisenhower failed to support the opinions expressed in *Brown,* and in so doing subtly encouraged the segregationists in their efforts to limit its impact on state and local policies. However, in 1957 a crisis was precipitated in Little Rock, Ark., when Gov. Orval Faubus openly defied a federal court order by using the Arkansas National Guard to prevent the desegregation of schools. Faubus finally backed down and withdrew the National Guard, but it was promptly replaced by white supremacist mobs, who gathered to stop nine black students from entering the all-white Central High School. Eisenhower responded by federalizing the National Guard and ordering them to protect those students. In the ensuing case, *Cooper* v. *Aaron* (1958), the Supreme Court ruled that state authorities must uphold the *Brown* decision.

Despite the Brown *decision, the federal government showed a great reluctance to intervene in school desegregation matters.*

The Little Rock incident spurred the passage of the Civil Rights Act of 1957, the first new civil rights legislation since Reconstruction. The 1957 act established the UNITED STATES COMMISSION ON CIVIL RIGHTS, whose duties included the investigation and appraisal of situations that denied blacks equal protection under the law. Although southern senators managed to strip the bill of almost all of its federal enforcement provisions, its enactment marked the first attempt by the federal government to take responsibility for the protection of civil rights.

The real turning point in the establishment of a federal civil rights policy occurred with the passage of the Civil Rights Act of 1964, which allowed the U.S. attorney general to take legal action in achieving school desegregation and authorized federal assistance for districts desegregating their schools.

President Lyndon B. Johnson's energetic support of the act preceded his administration's landmark Elementary and Secondary Education Act of 1965, authorizing federal assistance in providing teaching materials and special services for school districts with large numbers of poor.

The Elementary and Secondary Education Act of 1965

The Elementary and Secondary Education Act (ESEA) of 1965 was a landmark piece of legislation because its enactment marked a major incursion into state prerogatives and responsibilities for providing elementary and secondary education.

Although the federal government had enacted several statutes affecting the preparation of teachers in elementary and secondary schools and the development of new curricula under the National Defense Education Act of 1958, it had left control of elementary and secondary education to the states.

The passage of the Elementary and Secondary Education Act of 1965 formally established the doctrine of equal educational opportunity as a national priority and gave millions of dollars to state education and local education authorities (SEAs and LEAs) to use in specified ways under the guidelines of the five titles of the act.

Title I made available an initial allocation of $775 million for the education of children of low-income families (Keppel, *The Necessary Revolution in Education,* 1966). Though allocation of the money was under federal control, it was administered through the states. Title I was changed to Chapter I by the 1981 reauthorization of ESEA. Of the poor children served by Chapter I, an estimated 47 percent have represented the black urban and rural poor. Though an insufficient amount of money was provided to alleviate the "savage inequalities" in local funding between wealthy white suburban school districts and largely black and poor urban school districts (Kozol, *Savage Inequalities,* 1991), Chapter I of ESEA has provided increased educational resources for poor children.

Funds also were provided to strengthen state departments of education (under Title V) in monitoring the spending of federal ESEA allocations by local school districts and to encourage states to provide additional monies for the education of poor pupils. State money was to be used to supplement, not supplant, federal funds.

With the passage of these acts, the federal government obtained the fiscal and legal leverage necessary to overcome the massive resistance to desegregation in the South and in other parts of the country. In 1964, 2.3 percent of southern black students attended integrated schools; percentages increased to 7.5 in 1965 and to 12.5 in 1966. The U.S. Supreme Court's ruling in *Green* v. *County School Board* (1968), ordering the immediate desegregation of schools, succeeded in greatly accelerating this process. Whereas in 1968–69 only 32 percent of southern black students were attending integrated schools, 79 percent were attending integrated schools in 1970–71.

As *de jure* segregation was being brought to an end in the South, civil rights activists turned their attention to the *de facto* segregation persisting elsewhere. While some legislators insisted that *de facto* segregation represented only residential ethnic clustering, and argued against applying civil rights legislation to the affected schools, civil rights advocates noted a more than passing resemblance between the quality of education in largely black inner city schools and the inferior schooling to which blacks were subjected in the segregated South.

Beginning in the mid-1960s, a number of studies were undertaken to assess the overall quality of African-American education. As a consequence of Section 402 of the Civil Rights Act of 1964, the U.S. commissioner of education was required to provide the president and Congress with a report on "the lack of availability of equal educational opportunities for individuals by reason of race, color, religion, or national origin in public educational institutions at all levels in the United States, its territories and possessions, and the District of Columbia." The report, titled *Equality of Educational Opportunity* and delivered on July 2, 1966, concluded that "American public education remains largely unequal in most regions of the country, including all those where Negroes form any significant part of the population." It had been shown that, among minority groups, blacks were subjected most frequently and in the greatest numbers to segregation; when all groups were taken into account, the same held true for white children. Eighty percent of white first-to-twelfth-grade pupils attended schools that were 90 percent to 100 percent white. Segregation also held for teaching staffs nationwide: Where the races of teachers and pupils were not matched, white teachers often taught black children, but black teachers seldom taught white children. Finally, where integration existed, it involved the enrollment of a few black pupils in predominantly white schools, almost never the enrollment of a few whites in predominantly black schools.

The study, which came to be known as the Coleman Report—after James S. Coleman, the Johns Hopkins University professor who headed the research team—found that minority students scored "distinctly lower" than the average white student on tests that measured such basic skills as reading, writing, calculating, and problem-solving. Moreover, findings indicated that "the deficiency in achievement is progressively greater for minority pupils at higher grade levels." Little wonder, then, that in metropolitan areas of the North and West, 20 percent of black students sixteen and seventeen years of age dropped out of school.

In 1967, a year after the Coleman Report appeared, the Commission on Civil Rights issued a report titled *Racial Isolation in the Public Schools,* which stressed that redistricting would have little impact on the *de facto* segregation of housing and schools in large parts of the country. Studies showed that 83 percent of white elementary school students were enrolled in all-white schools, and 75 percent of black children were enrolled in all-black schools. The commission highlighted the liabilities of educating children in racial isolation. Not only did black students achieve less than white students, but also the longer they remained in school, the farther behind they fell. Black students were less likely to attend schools with adequate libraries, strong academic curricula, and competent teachers. Furthermore, black children who attended desegregated schools performed better than those attending racially segregated schools. The commission also recommended that the federal government take action by establishing a uniform standard of racial isolation in schools, and that schools with a black enrollment in excess of 60 percent be judged unsatisfactory.

As a solution to the problem of *de facto* segregation, the Commission on Civil Rights proposed the creation of "magnet schools," which would attract students from a wider area to inner-city schools, and "metropolitan school districts," which would draw on both urban and suburban student populations. Although, in the case of small cities, magnet schools proved successful as part of a citywide desegregation plan, their effectiveness was extremely limited in large cities such as New York, Chicago, Los Angeles, and Philadelphia. In these instances, federal funding was provided at the outset for desegregation planning, but that funding did not cover the costs of constructing new schools or converting large older schools, or of the special programs, equipment, and transportation needed to accommodate all the students who wished to attend. In addition, many poor and minority children lacked the preparation required to pass the entrance standards established for the magnet school programs. As a result, only middle-class children, or the most strongly motivated of the poor, were able to avail themselves of the magnet schools in their system.

The formation of metropolitan school systems has proven even more controversial, and has faced stiff resistance from those who insist on the primacy of neighborhood schools. The intensification of urban-suburban segregation following WORLD WAR II, when federal programs such as those offered by the Federal Housing Program (FHA) deliberately encouraged the development of all-white suburbs, presented an insuperable barrier to the establishment of integrated metropolitan districts. In *Milliken* v. *Bradley* (1974), the U.S. Supreme Court declared in a 5 to 4 vote that a metropolitan plan for Detroit could not be enforced, since to do so would be punitive to suburban whites, who could not be held responsible for the *de facto* segregation of inner-city schools. However, in *Milliken II* (1977), the Supreme Court overturned *Milliken I* and granted federal courts authority over metropolitan desegregation "when the plans were remedial in nature" and where suburban residents had directly influenced the distribution of races in a particular area. In the appeal of a Delaware case brought by the Delaware NAACP's Louis Redding (*Evans* v. *Buchanan,* 1969, 1978), the Court ruled that Delaware's Educational Advancement Act (1968) had limited school district consolidation to districts with fewer than 15,000 pupils, thereby excluding the possibility of merging Wilmington with any other suburban district. The U.S. District Court found that the state of Delaware and suburban real estate interests had colluded in preventing blacks from moving into the suburban districts bordering on Wilmington. It was impossible, therefore, for the Wilmington school district (which was 84 percent black, 4 percent Hispanic, and 12 percent white) to be desegregated within its own boundaries. The solution proposed by Wilmington for desegregating New Castle County schools resulted in the merging of ten of the eleven suburban school systems in that county with the Wilmington school system into a single consolidated school district.

In a county as small as New Castle County, busing was not too lengthy, since no school destination was more than forty minutes away. The same did not hold true for other states and communities, where busing was opposed on the basis of distance and length of the bus ride.

Gary Orfield and colleagues, in a 1993 study on school desegregation, *The Growth of Segregation in American Schools: Changing Patterns of Separation and Poverty Since 1968,* names Delaware (Wilmington), North Carolina (large county-city desegregation), Virginia (large county desegregation), Kentucky (Louisville), Nevada (Clark County), Indiana (Indianapolis), and Colorado (Denver) as states that have large proportions of African-American students attending integrated schools. He cites metropolitan desegregation orders—usually city with suburbs, or city with adjoining county—as being responsible factors. "When examining the most integrated states for African-American students, it is obvious that there have been long-term impacts of court orders, particularly those that provide for city-suburban desegregation."

In 1995, the U.S. Supreme Court ruled that the U.S. District Court was in error when it held that ". . . Missouri and the Kansas City school system were jointly liable for having run a segregated school system that they had failed to dismantle" (*New York Times,* June 13, 1995, p. 29). The case was remanded to the lower court for solution.

The effect of the ruling was to absolve the state of Missouri of the responsibility for paying for magnet schools and higher teachers' salaries in Kansas City, the remedy that the lower court had prescribed in order to attract white students to the Kansas City schools.

In 1982 the state of Delaware, with permission of the U.S. District Court, was allowed to divide the consolidated school district into four districts radiating from the center of the city of Wilmington, but did not relieve the state of Delaware of the obligation to maintain racial integration across the districts. Now, with the Kansas City ruling, the future of metropolitan solutions (city-suburbs or city-county plans) to help desegregate city school systems looks increasingly dim.

School Busing

Busing, the means by which white and black students were transported from their home neighborhoods to outside schools, became the most popular, and at the same time the most controversial, means of creating integrated school settings in northern cities. In the 1971 case of *Swann* v. *Charlotte-Mecklenburg Board of Education,* the U.S. Supreme Court voted unanimously to direct school authorities in North Carolina to achieve "the greatest possible degree of actual desegregation" by redistributing 14,000 of the 24,000 black students remaining in all-black or nearly all-black schools. The *Swann* case affirmed the Court's pledge, previously articulated in *Green,* to enforce desegregation posthaste, even if—as in this instance—it meant forcing students to travel to schools outside their own district. In the aftermath of *Swann,* many who had been stalwart in their opposition to *de jure* segregation in the South reversed their position and argued against busing in the North by charging that busing was an infringement on the authority of local school districts and on the prerogatives of parents. Arguments against busing ranged from pragmatic worries about the length and cost of bus trips, to principled concerns as to its effect on the children themselves, since those who were bused had to struggle to adjust in an alien and often hostile environment. The public controversy over busing, which Rich-

Busing became the most popular, and at the same time the most controversial, means of creating integrated school settings in northern cities.

ard M. Nixon invoked as a central issue in his successful 1968 and 1972 presidential campaigns, peaked in the early 1970s. In 1974–75, a series of violent riots by white residents of South Boston who objected to the busing of blacks to their neighborhood high school attracted national attention and demonstrated the extent of racial animosity in the North.

For many blacks, the busing controversy highlighted the limitations of northern liberals with regard to their commitment to integration. As Carl Holman, president of the National Urban Coalition, observed, "racism comes much more naturally, and to a much broader spectrum of whites, than we could have imagined." Sen. Abraham Ribicoff of Connecticut charged the North with "monumental hypocrisy" in a speech on segregation that he delivered to the Senate in 1970. Senator Ribicoff's home state, Connecticut, did not adopt a comprehensive statewide school desegregation plan until 1993, when metropolitan school districts came into being under the forceful leadership of Gov. Lowell Weicker. Attempts to end *de facto* segregation in the North, once *de jure* segregation had been terminated in the South, had a curious result. Statistics from 1971 show a clear predominance of segregated education in northern schools: There, 57 percent of all black students attended largely black schools, while the same might be said of only 32 percent of black students in the South.

Dilemmas of Isolation and Integration

Two major migratory waves following WORLD WAR I and WORLD WAR II brought more than one million African Americans to the major cities of the northern, north-central, and northeastern United States.

After World War II, the movement of blacks into such cities as New York, Boston, Detroit, and Seattle was accompanied by an exodus of whites to newly created suburbs. Because of racially discriminatory lending policies and restricted neighborhoods (Bradford, 1993), it was difficult for blacks to gain access to suburban housing. Neighborhood organizational patterns and the absence of whites in the cities caused urban school systems to become *de facto* racially segregated.

The opposition to school busing by the white majority and the difficulty of proving that *de facto* racial isolation in the North was caused by state or local governmental policies or action brought a growing disenchantment with busing as a means of improving the educational opportunities of black youth.

In the late 1960s and early '70s, a number of black and white liberal educators began to examine the research reporting on the dramatic gains that early childhood education could have on subsequent schooling, as a means of ensuring successful learning for poor urban and rural children, white and black.

Head Start

Head Start, begun in May 1965 and placed in the federal Office of Economic Opportunity, became one of the most durable and successful educational initiatives of President Johnson's administration. It was the most prominent component of Johnson's War on Poverty. Enrolling preschool children aged three to five years, Head Start is a program for poor children—a racially and ethnically diverse group—designed not only to motivate them and improve their conceptual and verbal skills but to motivate parents as well, by involving them in the educational process and educating them as to their children's health and nutritional needs.

Opponents of Head Start claimed it did not bring about the results its creators had supposed—namely, that it would raise IQ levels significantly in as brief a period as eight weeks. In addition, it was feared that the educational advantages of Head Start would tend to "fade out" if they were not reinforced in elementary and secondary education. However, numerous long-term studies have demonstrated Head Start's effectiveness as a preschool program, and despite past and present political opposition, it has been retained as a model for educational spending for successive administrations.

Another preschool program, the Perry Preschool Educational Project, beginning in 1962 with an original group of 123 African-American preschoolers from poor families in Benton Harbor, Mich., has developed a research paradigm that has allowed the project to track the progress of the original group through the twenty-seventh year of the program. The results show greatly reduced rates of delinquency and adolescent pregnancy and higher rates of school completion than those achieved in the nontreatment group.

Community Control of Local Schools

The call for community control of local schools is a more controversial, but not radical, approach to improving education in low-income urban neighborhoods.

When the parents and community called for control of a new intermediate school, I.S. 201, in the East Harlem community of New York City, in whose planning they had participated since 1958, the parents and community reflected the participatory political atmosphere of the 1960s.

As a precedent, parent advisory councils were mandated and had a defined participatory role with professional educators and planners in many federal education programs. Secondly, parents and community representatives were often members of community action agencies and corporations; therefore, while recognizing the professional roles of teachers and school administrators, the parents in the I.S. 201 community sought a similar participatory role in the operation of their new school.

A two-year study by Dr. Kenneth B. Clark, a professor of psychology at City College of New York—who, with his wife, Mamie Phipps Clark, completed social science research that contributed to the landmark decision in *Brown* v. *Board of Education of Topeka* (1954)—had produced evidence of the significant decrease in academic achievement in the schools in the Harlem Community (*Youth in the Ghetto,* 1964; *Dark Ghetto,* 1965).

Black parents and community members maintained that black schools and black students had suffered gravely under a centralized school system that was unsympathetic to their particular needs.

The call for community control of local schools is a more controversial, but not radical, approach to improving education in low-income urban neighborhoods.

As a means of improving the performance of black students, they suggested placing schools under the community's jurisdiction and allowing parents, in concert with administrators and teachers, to exert a direct influence on school organization, curriculum, staffing, and policymaking.

In 1958, in one of a series of planning meetings with school officials about the building of a new intermediate school in the East Harlem community, the superintendent of schools, Bernard Donovan, promised parents a role in naming the school and selecting the principal; he said the school would be integrated and would function as a magnet school.

In the fall of 1966, I.S. 201 opened; however, it failed to draw white students from the Bronx or the West Side of Manhattan. When this failure became apparent, and other promises had been broken, the parents and community demanded "control of the school" (D. Jones, 1966). Black groups in New York City and in other parts of the country mobilized to support the East Harlem residents in their call for community action. Preston Wilcox, an assistant professor at the Columbia University School of Social Work, had worked with the parents for many years and suggested that the opening of I.S. 201 should be regarded as an opportunity to experiment with a new approach to relations between the community and the public educational system.

In the spring of 1967, in response to the crisis at I.S. 201, city officials, with planning grants and the help of consultants from the Ford Foundation, created seven demonstration projects designed to "improve the instruction programs for children in the schools concerned by bringing the parents and community into a more meaningful participation with the schools." Three of the projects (I.S. 201; Two Bridges, on Manhattan's Lower East Side; and Ocean Hill-Brownsville, in the East New York section of Brooklyn) included intermediate or junior high schools.

In the spring of 1968, Rhody McCoy, the supervisor of the Ocean Hill-Brownsville project, ordered nineteen teachers and supervisors to report to the city's central Board of Education offices for reassignment. McCoy claimed that these teachers were unsympathetic to the educational reforms advocated by the local school board. His action prompted a power struggle between the Ocean Hill-Brownsville school board and the city teachers' union—the United Federation of Teachers (UFT)—which escalated when the UFT's president, Albert Shanker, called a citywide strike. During the strike, teachers opposed to the UFT tried to keep schools open in Brooklyn and in other parts of the city, with varying degrees of success. Race relations in the city suffered considerably over the next two months as the supporters of Ocean-Hill Brownsville accused their opponents of racism, while the UFT, which was predominantly Jewish, maintained that community control advocates were anti-Semitic. The strike ended after the central school board dismissed McCoy and the Ocean Hill-Brownsville board. It was decided that local schools should not be given the right to transfer teachers; at the same time, however, it was acknowledged that a centralized system could not meet the students' needs, and plans to decentralize New York City's schools were passed by the New York State legislature in the fall of 1969. The decentralization law allowed for the creation of thirty to thirty-three districts of approximately twenty thousand pupils each. The central board retained control over the high schools and citywide educational programs; the community boards were given control over the elementary, middle, and junior high schools within their boundaries. The chancellor was given limited authority over the community boards (N.Y. Education Law, chap. 2590, 1969).

New York City's school system became a model for other metropolitan school systems throughout the nation because decentralization conformed to the requirements of the Elementary and Secondary Education Act of 1965. Title I of the act required organized parental participation—distinct from that of the schools—in the allocation of more than $2.6 billion in funds designed to assist economically disadvantaged children of rural and urban, white and minority groups alike. Despite occasional instances of corruption on local boards and the periodic failure of some schools to lift performance levels (measured by the Board of Education, New York State Regents, and SAT tests), this form of governance, overseen by an active citywide chancellor, continues to be favored in New York City by many parents, community members, teachers, and politicians.

The action of the I.S. 201 parents and community must be evaluated in the political context of the times. This was a period of government-sanctioned, and -aided, community participation in quality of life areas by poor people, mainly black and Latino. The areas of health and education were targeted as those that would reduce crime and welfare dependency. The process was disruptive to the established structure of the school system but resulted in a school system design that brought the system closer to the people it served.

A declining commitment to integration, evidenced by the controversy over decentralization, was also manifested in federal policy during the Nixon presidency.

Milwaukee and Chicago are examples of other cities for which New York was a model. The Milwaukee school system was partially decentralized in 1993.

In 1988, the Illinois state legislature enacted into law the School Reform Act, the first in a series of bills designed to decentralize the Chicago public schools. In 1991, the Illinois legislature passed a bill which originated in the State Senate as SB10 and was enacted into law as Public Act 87-454. The legislation determined the governance of the Chicago school system, decentralized the Chicago public schools into local attendance units, or multiattendance units, and designated each Local School Council, previously established, as the policymaking body for each school. The authority of the Local School Councils included responsibility for budget making, for allocation of federal funds to federal and state programs, and for special education and bilingual programs. The design of each school council, the council's authority, and a prescribed mode of operation is described in the publication *LSC Council Sourcebook: Basics for the Local School Council (1993).*

A declining commitment to integration, evidenced by the controversy over decentralization, was also manifested in federal policy during the Nixon presidency. Presidential adviser Daniel Patrick Moynihan suggested that the administration pursue a policy of noninterference in local affairs and racial matters, which he termed "benign neglect." Nowhere was Nixon's lack of commitment to desegregation more apparent than in the wording of his statement of March 24, 1970, that announced the allocation of $1.5 billion "to mitigate the effects of segregated schools." Although the allocation provided financial assistance to segregated minority school districts or "racially impacted" areas, no effort was made to address the problem of their segregation per se. In 1972 Congress passed the Emergency School Aid Act, aimed at funding minority students according to their special needs. The act supported desegregation in principle; but the passage of the Equal Opportunity Act in 1974 sharply limited the initiatives the federal government could take in ending *de facto* segregation.

Higher Education Since 1954

The *Brown* ruling, which paved the way for drastic changes in public primary and secondary school systems, did little to change the funding and structure of historically black colleges, which continued to subsist on meager funds from state, federal, and private sources. Four years prior to *Brown,* in *Sweatt* v. *Painter* and *McLaurin* v. *Oklahoma State Regents for Higher Education* (1950), two cases involving the admission of African Americans to all-white universities for graduate study, the U.S. Supreme Court ruled that blacks were not receiving the higher educational opportunities to which they were entitled under the "separate but equal" ruling of *Plessy* v. *Ferguson.* The Court's decisions, which ordered that Herman Sweatt be admitted to the all-white University of Texas Law School, and ruled unconstitutional the treatment of George W. McLaurin, who had been admitted to the University of Oklahoma's doctoral program in education on the condition that segregation be maintained (he was obliged to sit in a separate row "for Negroes" in class, eat at a separate table in the cafeteria, and study at a separate desk in the library), anticipated *Brown* insofar as they implied that equality for blacks could not be attained under the segregated state-supported system of higher education. However, the rulings were narrowly applied, and neither law schools nor graduate schools made haste to welcome black students.

During the 1950s and 1960s, HBCUs persisted in their dual function of providing students with a college-level education and offering secondary-level curricula to compensate for the incomplete preparation most graduates of southern public schools received. An emerging generation of well-trained academics, including some whites, brought a newly sustained level of college instruction to many of these institutions. However, only three HBCU's—Atlanta University, the Interdenominational Theological Center, and Meharry Medical College—were devoted solely to graduate study. Meharry and Howard University remained the primary academic institutions for training blacks as doctors, while Howard and Atlanta were the only institutions offering a Ph.D. degree.

Throughout the 1970s and '80s, HBCUs continued to confront the unique problems of providing substantial compensatory education, building and retaining highly trained faculty at salaries lower than the national norm, and attracting student bodies large enough to keep them in operation. Nevertheless, the importance of these institutions increased significantly with the dramatic rise in black college attendance during these two decades. In 1972 an estimated 727,000 black students were enrolled in college and graduate and professional schools. By 1984 this number had risen to 1,274,000, an increase of 75 percent. Black enrollment in higher education programs continued to rise, reaching 1,477,000 in 1991—more than doubling since 1972. At this time, African Americans constituted approximately 11 percent of the nation's total enrollment. Of the 1,480,000 pursuing higher education, roughly 89,000 were in graduate programs and 17,000 in professional schools. Of the 1,330,000 undergraduates, roughly 16 percent (213,904) were attending HBCUs. Also attending HBCUs were 31,085 white, 2,131 Hispanic, 2,009 Asian-American, and 388 Native-American students. While African Americans constitute 8 percent of the total enrollment of non-black institutions of higher education, white students now make up 13 percent of the total enrollment at HBCUs.

In 1992 the U.S. Supreme Court found in *United States* v. *Fordice* that HBCUs had received unequal treatment in Mississippi because the state had not eliminated its dual system of public higher education, first established under segregation. The ruling, which affected eighteen other southern states, had the same impact on public higher education that *Brown* had had on secondary schools; but where *Brown* had been enthusiastically received, *Fordice* elicited widespread skepticism and dismay. According to the Supreme Court, the state of Mississippi had failed to abolish segregation by retaining a system of higher education that favored predominantly white colleges and universities over HBCUs. The state's admissions and funding policies were called into question, as was the number of its institutions, since it was found that programs were being duplicated at white colleges and HBCUs, and that such duplications perpetuated segregation.

The *Fordice* ruling required that action be taken to end *de facto* segregation by integrating Mississippi's eight state-sponsored colleges and universities. At the same time, the Court held that HBCUs should not be accorded preferential treatment in the desegregation process if they intended to remain exclusively black institutions. Many legislators and educators feared that instead of protecting the constitutional rights of African Americans, the Court's call for integration would result in the dismantling of HBCUs in favor of the larger, better-funded, and more "comprehensive" state-sponsored predominantly white schools. The lesson to be learned from *Brown,* opponents to the ruling claimed, was that integration had not been carried out as a two-way process; on the contrary, African Americans had had to bear the burden of adjusting to, and being educated in, white-majority schools. The loss of HBCUs, which African Americans had struggled for more than a century to maintain, would mean the loss of a crucial aspect of their education and history.

In response to the *Fordice* ruling, Mississippi's Board of Trustees of Institutions of Higher Learning proposed closing Mississippi Valley State, a predominantly black university, and merging the other existing black schools. Previously, the Mississippi Black Legislative Caucus had sought a special appropriation of $55 million for academic programs and school renovation at Mississippi Valley State, Alcorn, and Jackson universities; but they were forced to settle for $11 million after failing to obtain legislative support. A similar battle ensued in the Alabama legislature, where internecine competition between Auburn University and the state's two public historically black colleges led to the killing of appropriations of $38 million in educational aid. Decisions regarding the funding and closure of HBCUs continue to be contested as plans for desegregation are decided in these and other states.

The 1990s controversy over desegregation and the budgetary disputes in state legislatures have brought to light the financial inequities against which HBCUs have been struggling since their inception. Reductions in the 1990s in federal as well as state educational budgets have also contributed to the financial difficulties with which HBCUs must contend. It has been shown that HBCUs lag behind other institutions in their reception of specialized funds. For example, in 1990 a study published by the President's Board of Advisers on Historically Black Colleges showed that more than $1.5 billion in research grants had been given to five predominantly white colleges, while $330 million had been divided among 117 predominantly black colleges during that one year. As a means of challenging these inequities, the fledgling Institute for College Research and Development was established by a consortium of six HBCUs. The purpose of the institute, which is supported by the Office of Minority Impact of the Department of Energy, is to increase the number of research grants and thereby diminish the operating costs for these six universities.

Public Education's Perilous New Status

The liberal approach to education, which emerged during the 1960s and received strong federal support, was eroded under the presidential administrations of Richard Nixon (1969–1974) and Gerald Ford (1974–1977), before undergoing a brief revival during the presidency of Jimmy Carter (1977–1981). Under Carter, Head Start received its first budget increase since 1967. However, the administrations of Ronald Reagan (1981–1989) and George Bush (1989–1993) marked a conservative reaction against liberal educational reforms. During his campaign for the presidency, Reagan pledged to abolish the Department of Education, which had been established as a separate arm of the government by Jimmy Carter. Reagan did not succeed in fulfilling his pledge, but he managed to limit the federal government's role in education severely by making the states responsible for many federal assistance programs. In addition to reducing social services and low-income assistance drastically, Reagan's Omnibus Budget Reconciliation Act of 1981 placed state governments in charge of elementary and secondary educational funding, administration, and policies. For the working poor with children in urban school systems, this shift from federal to state control meant larger classrooms and fewer teachers, and reductions in such related services as Aid to Families with Dependent Children (ADFC), Medicaid, food stamps, job training, and compensatory education.

As cuts in federal spending were being implemented, educators and politicians expressed a growing concern over the obvious steady decline in the quality of education that American schools were able to provide. In a 1983 report titled *A Nation at Risk,* the National Commission on Excellence in Education noted that "the educational foundations of our society are presently being eroded by a rising tide of mediocrity that threatens our very future as a nation and a people." The report, which spawned a plethora of national and regional studies, recognized that the poor and minority groups comprised the nation's youth who were most at risk (*A Nation at Risk,* p. 32), but left to the states the responsibility for addressing the specific needs of the most affected groups. The studies noted especially the academic problems of minority students in urban schools. While reporting that American public education must reach higher academic standards and reach higher levels of achievement if America's schoolchildren were to compete successfully with students in other industrial nations of the world, the studies offer no additional funding or funding strategies, such as urging states to develop school funding policies that would provide greater equity in funding between suburban communities and cities, or recommending that corporations and businesses hire and train minority youth.

As cuts in federal spending were being implemented, educators and politicians expressed a growing concern over the obvious steady decline in the quality of education.

A comprehensive study of African-American education was carried out by the National Research Council and published under the title *A Common Destiny: Blacks in American Society* (1989). Three of its most important findings were, first, although substantial progress had been made since World War II with regard to some aspects of equality of achievement, participation, and rewards for African Americans, many remained "separated from the mainstream of national life under conditions of great inequality." Second, among the many factors that contribute to measurable gaps between the levels of education, employment, and housing enjoyed by blacks and whites, a remarkable measure of these differences is attributable to the continuation of private and public discrimination. Third, the progress that has been made over the past fifty years in closing these gaps between blacks and whites is the result, in large part, of "purposeful actions and policies by government and private institutions." In the absence of such actions, including national policy initiatives, "further progress is unlikely," the report concludes.

The Resegregation of Public Education

The impact of these years on African-American children in elementary and secondary schools was increasing isolation, whether in predominantly black schools or in desegregated schools, and a decline in the quality of educational opportunity available to them. A statistical analysis based on a 1985–1986 study of the nation's large urban school districts of 15,000 or more students confirms a resegregation in education through ability grouping, curriculum tracking, special education, and discipline. In every case these result in the placement of most black students in lower academic level groups and few black students in the higher level, "gifted" academic groups. Black students are nearly twice as likely to receive corporal punishment or suspension; they are three times more likely to be expelled. A black student is 18 percent more likely to drop out of school and 27 percent less likely to graduate. "This pattern," say the authors, "is consistent with a denial of equal educational opportunities for black students" (Meir, Steward, and England, 1989). As desegregation was being achieved in the South, segregation increased in the Northeast, now the most segregated region in the country. Studies have shown that because of their racial isolation, black and Hispanic students in urban areas are much less likely to become computer literate—a fact that has serious economic consequences. According to the National Bureau of Economic Research, the inability to use computers accounted for nearly one-third of the increase in the earnings gap between blacks and whites during the period from 1976 to 1990.

Such problems are rooted in early education. Statistics from 1990 show that black fourth graders scored 28.6 percent lower than white fourth graders in all areas of mathematics. In that same subject, blacks scored 31.3 percent lower in the eighth grade and 30.9 percent lower in the twelfth grade.

A similar disparity exists in tests reflecting their command of historical information: In 1988, black students scored 15.6 percent lower than whites in the fourth grade, and 31 and 15.4 percent lower in the eighth and twelfth grades, respectively.

Disproportionate Assignments to Special Education for Black and Latino Males: Classification/Placement of African-American and Latino Students

One very significant failing of America's big-city school systems to serve African-American children adequately is the disproportionate assignment of African-American male children to special education classes, especially those for the mentally retarded and for the emotionally disturbed. This pattern of assignment applies also to Latino males and is found in almost every big-city school system.

Many children are placed in special education classes because they perform below their grade in reading and/or for behavioral problems, rather than for organicity. For most children, placement in special education leads to permanent classification, despite state and federal regulations that mandate decertification examinations every three years.

According to a 1991 report (Walter Stafford et al., *Cause for Alarm: The Condition of Black and Latino Males in New York City*, pp. 13–14), "Black males accounted for 28 percent of special education students (33,787 black males, 27,668 Latino males, and 14,309 white males)." Within special education programs, black males (and Hispanic males) were enrolled in two programs: for those with learning disabilities and for those with emotional disturbance. These special education placements are especially damaging to the educational progress of black males, because return to the educational mainstream is virtually impossible; therefore, such placements often lead black male students to drop out of school without sufficient education or educational credentials.

Jay Gottlieb and colleagues, in a 1994 study of special education placements in urban school systems, "Special Education in Urban America: It's Not Justifiable for Many," find that "for children who reside in inner cities, the vast majority of whom are poor and members of minority groups, special education referral, evaluation, and placement practices are not more effective now than they were 25 years ago" (p. 453).

These findings, despite the passage of P.L. 94-142 (1975), legislation generated by the CIVIL RIGHTS MOVEMENT giving people with handicaps the right to be educated in public education and in "the least restricted environment," indicate that urban public school systems continue to misdiagnose and mislabel minority children, black and Latino, and place them in special education classes, when analysis of the placements "reveals the powerful effects of poverty among the minority groups that predominate in urban schools."

Many of these children are classified as learning disabled, a medically oriented categorical designation, to ensure reimbursement for excess costs and special education services and programs. Such assignments are not in conformity with state and federal regulations and demonstrate the necessity for additional reforms in special education placement policies by urban school systems nationwide.

The Gottlieb study concludes:

> . . . the vast majority of children who are classified as learning disabled and placed in special education in many urban school districts are not disabled in the sense demanded by legislation and regulation. Instead, they are children who suffer the many ravages of poverty, not the least of which is its effect on academic performance. (p. 456)

African-American Teachers

The publication of *A Nation at Risk* brought a new focus on the nation's teachers as a critical resource in the performance of the nation's schools and students. Two special studies, *A Nation Prepared: Teachers for the 21st Century*, by the Carnegie Forum on Education and the Economy (1986), and *Tomorrow's Teachers,* a 1986 report of the Holmes Group (a consortium of deans of schools of education in large universities), critically examined the preparation and practice of elementary and secondary teachers. Both reports spoke to the past roles of minority teachers educating children in the nation's public schools, and to the need for minority teachers in the future.

As noted in *A Nation Prepared* and *Teaching's Next Generation* (1993), there is a need to prepare a larger number of minority group members to become teachers. Minority students, mainly black and Latino, represent a majority in twenty-three of twenty-five of the nation's largest cities, but the number of black teachers in the United States is only 8.6 percent. The percentage is expected to decrease to 5 percent if drastic steps are not taken in training and recruitment of black teachers.

By the year 2000, black and Latino students will represent the majority of students in the 25 central cities and metropolitan areas of the United States. The present teaching force is predominantly Caucasian. Many teachers will retire within the next several years, and will have to be replaced with significant numbers of minority teachers.

As the number of minority public school students is rising, the minority teaching force is shrinking in number. The Carnegie Report recognized the role that the historically black colleges and state black colleges had performed over the years in the preparation of teachers and teacher educators and proposed collaborative relationships. Both the Carnegie and the Holmes Group reports noted the need to recruit and prepare bright minority students for teaching, now that desegregation had opened many other career choices for them.

A new emphasis now has been placed on teacher preparation. It requires a "knowledge base" in the liberal arts, with concomitant emphasis on the quantitative subjects, and the development of "pedagogical skills": studies in human development and theories of teaching and learning, the knowledge of discrete teaching technologies appropriate to a given subject, as well as knowledge and recognition of a range of student needs.

Throughout the nation, teacher education is being strengthened to meet new state certification requirements by collaborations among education and liberal arts departments in their own colleges and universities and by participation in regional and national teacher education networks.

Preteaching programs and collaborations between and among colleges and high schools are being developed to encourage and recruit students to the teaching profession.

The DeWitt Wallace-Reader's Digest Fund is a major private sponsor of programs to prepare and recruit new minority teachers.

The federal government is providing funds to the states under Chapter V of ESEA, and in separate block grant programs, under Chapter II of the same legislation, for minority teacher education and recruitment.

To be successful, the programs will have to prepare recruits at every level to pass the state examination for certification or the National Teachers Examination from the Educational Testing Service. Failure to pass the required examinations has presented a major barrier to minority candidates in the past.

Bernard Watson and Fasha Traylor express concern about the reform movement in teaching, specifically about the outcome of greater professionalization of teachers. While having no doubt that individual teachers will benefit from the "professionalization" process that the Holmes Group recommends, they warn that greater professionalization of teachers may not necessarily "result in an educational system that is accessible, responsive, and responsible to all American children."

Watson and Traylor offer two bases for this conclusion. First, conceptualization of the National Board for Professional Teaching Standards does not indicate that the board will attend to the specific needs of individual local school districts. Second, given the certainty that the system of rewards for acquiring greater professionalization will find its way into collective bargaining agreements (as they already have in some school systems), it is questionable whether these superbly prepared teachers will seek positions in the schools of minority communities in urban centers or in rural America (Watson and Traylor, "Tomorrow's Teachers: Who Will They Be, What Will They Know?" 1988).

If either the board or the teachers fail to respond appropriately, minority students in the nation's big-city school systems will not benefit from the professionalization of the teaching profession.

Following World War II, large sections of New York City, Philadelphia, Chicago, Detroit, and Atlanta had school subdistricts that enrolled a majority of African-American students. In the late 1960s, the growing percentages of African-American pupils in urban school systems, plus the call for community control of schools, intensified the demand for black administrators in systemwide positions, including the general superintendency.

By March 1974 there were forty-four city or county African-American superintendents, a superintendent of the Virgin Islands (by presidential appointment), and two African-American state superintendents of public instruction, one in Michigan and the other in California (Scott, 1980).

By 1975 Detroit, Washington, D.C., Chicago, Atlanta, and Wilmington, Del., had black superintendents of public schools. New York City appointed its first black chancellor (the title of the system-wide superintendency), Richard Green, in 1985.

The graduate schools of education of Harvard, Columbia, Atlanta, and Fordham Universities, several aided by the Rockefeller and Ford Foundations, among others, recruited to their existing doctoral programs, or developed special programs for the academic and professional preparation of minority candidates for system-wide administrative positions.

Though well prepared, minority superintendents faced the same order of financial and educational problems as did their Caucasian colleagues and predecessors: shrinking budgets, municipal overburden, decaying and asbestos-filled school buildings; and the perpetual problems of racial balance and the underachievement of large numbers of minority pupils.

Afrocentrism and Multiculturalism

A resurgent interest in and support of Afrocentric studies, in part as one form of antidote to alienation from education, has been challenged by some educators as divisive, while the perpetuation of an emphasis on Eurocentric studies is not considered divisive in a culturally pluralistic nation such as ours. But neither an Afrocentric nor a Eurocentric education provides us with the "core around which a truly multicultural education can be developed," Gordon argues.

With increasing frequency we are required, as citizens of our national society, "to function in more than a single language, adapt to the demands of more than a single culture, meet the behavioral demands of more than a single situation, and understand the symbols and rituals of people other than those with whom most of us have been socialized." It is from these multidisciplinary, multiculturalist, multiperspectivist learning experiences that competencies in critical analysis, critical interpretation, and critical understanding will allow for responsibly discharging future decisions and judgments. Gordon concludes that "no matter what core knowledge is chosen as the vehicle . . . educators are beginning to realize that the teaching of dogma (either hegemonic or resistant) is no longer appropriate for the optimal development of learners." ("Conceptions of Africentrism and Multiculturalism in Education: A General Overview").

Where multiculturalism emphasizes the diversity of groups within a particular culture, Afrocentrism insists on the primacy of an African-based cultural tradition. Proponents of this method argue that black youngsters must develop a strong sense of their African heritage if they are to survive in a hostile, white-dominated environment.

One Afrocentric approach is the creation of all-male, Afrocentric schools. Advocates of such schools point to the high levels of violence, and low levels of education, among many black males, and stress the benefits of instilling in young black men a sense of pride in their cultural roots.

Where multiculturalism emphasizes the diversity of groups within a particular culture, Afrocentrism insists on the primacy of an African-based cultural tradition.

The prospect of creating these schools has been hotly debated, with critics charging that a segregated environment would damage students by further alienating them from the cultural mainstream. Not only would the gender exclusive schools be ineligible for federal funding, but evidence suggests that many black male and female students have succeeded academically and developed positive self-images in racially integrated public schools (Clark, *A Possible Reality,* 1972; Edmonds, *Educational Leadership,* 1982).

American blacks have long been divided between Afrocentrist and American nationalist philosophies. Perhaps the time has come for a rapprochement between these two philosophical positions.

W. E. B. Du Bois, in *Souls of Black Folk* (1903), stated the dilemma of the African American: "An American, a Negro; two souls, two thoughts, two unreconciled strivings. . . ."

The dilemma Du Bois described will be resolved when the African heritage of the African American takes its rightful and respected place alongside the other cultures of this intercontinental, international, multicultural nation.

School Choice

There has always been choice in American education, usually divided into three major sectors: public, parochial, and independent. Until choice became an issue in national efforts to improve the academic performance of poor children in public urban and rural schools, the sectors operated as separate islands, with the "separation clause" of the First Amendment to the U.S. Constitution as the arbiter.

The First Amendment to the U.S. Constitution prohibits funding religious schools with public monies. However, according to some legal experts, the "wall" between church and state, private and public schools, has been breached by the "child benefit theory," which was devised by the conceptualizers of the 1965 Elementary and Secondary Education Act to allow funding of poor children in parochial and nonpublic schools, under Title I, now Chapter I, of the act (Hughes and Hughes, 1972).

Under this theory, providing federal money to private schools is legal as long as the money follows the child who otherwise would be eligible in public school. The federal money, or program, therefore benefits the child, not the nonpublic school. A sizable proportion of the American public favors providing public money to private and parochial schools. Rather than equity and access, the battle is being based on quality of education.

There is a general consensus that public schools in city school systems are failing to give poor, racially isolated, language-different students the quality education that will prepare them for a future in the technologically oriented world-society of the twenty-first century. By contrast, suburban schools and private and parochial schools with smaller student bodies (and in the case of wealthy suburbs, different funding formulas) are providing such education.

The implications of choice plans, public and private, are grave for black parents and their children in urban school systems. There is usually an additional monetary cost for the family, if only for transportation to a school in another district or community. At the extreme, the costs are great if the parent has to make up the difference between the public voucher amount and the tuition of the private school.

This is particularly troubling to African Americans who remember that tuition grants for funding private education was the device resorted to in 1955 by Prince Edward County, Va., in defiance of the U.S. Supreme Court's 1954 *Brown* decision. Under this arrangement a system of private schools for white students was established, but none for blacks. Does "school choice" amount to nothing more than a present-day analogue for Prince Edward County's gambit of 1955?

Some educators regard tuition grants or vouchers as flawed policy for dealing with the problems of public education. They argue that school choice allows for winners and losers, and that a national policy that assures there will be losers is unacceptable, unconstitutional, and unsound.

School choice can be exercised within the public schools or outside of public education. The latter is the smaller sector, with a relatively stable 10 to 11 percent of the nation's school-age children in private schools. This sector is augmented slightly by such experiments as Whittle Schools, driven by an interest in both quality in education and the profit to be derived from such educational ventures. A similar experiment is being carried out by Educational Alternatives, Inc., for a group of privatized Baltimore schools and for the public schools of Hartford, Conn. Privatization of public schools raises questions about the equitable distribution of resources and funding among corporation-managed and non-corporation-managed schools. Another important concern is making students and teachers a captive audience for a commercial enterprise paid for with public monies.

Choice within the public sector includes special programs within schools, school pairing (a limited choice), magnet schools, examination schools, choice among schools within a district (a wider choice), choice among districts within a system, and schools funded by business.

Whatever the form of choice, considerations including accountability and governance, effectiveness, equity, and the allocation of resources are inescapable. In matters of accountability and governance, will private schools receiving public money be held to the same accreditation, affirmative action, open records requirements, health and safety statutes (including insurance), and accountability reporting required of the public sector? What is the meaning of claims that "choice works," as President Bush said, when experimental studies over the past twenty years have shown little evidence that choice brings educational improvement, greater parental involvement, or increased pupil learning? With a number of researchers finding that in New York, Chicago, Boston, and Philadelphia choice in education worked to the detriment of low-achieving students, what are the claims to be made for it on the basis of equity? Is it fair that students with learning problems or limited proficiency in English be excluded from magnet schools or that students who simply are average achievers are informally or formally returned to their neighborhood school without recourse? What is to be done about the failure of these schools to educate a student body representative of those cities? Since, according to a wide range of cost estimates and investigations, choice will not be low-cost school improvement, what are the benefits the new investments will bring as a result of choice, that is, benefits that could not be more readily achieved through the expenditure of these new investments on public education alone?

There are those who argue that any such new investments in choice, particularly if it involves public/private school vouchers, violate the long-held belief in the "American social contract," which, it is claimed, makes the entire society responsible for the elementary and secondary education of its children and youth.

There can be serious debits to school choice for black children—and others among the rising number of racial and ethnic minority children—and their parents in urban school systems if, in the name of excellence, better students are siphoned off to magnet and private schools and all other students are dumped into public education. This, as is evident from the history of other forms of tracking, will spawn a self-perpetuating vicious cycle erosive of effective public education.

For African Americans, the prospects of quality education remain a problem of equal educational rights.

A number of new academic models have proven to work effectively for black students. The College Board's Equity 2000 project, which has carried out pilot programs in California, Tennessee, Maryland, Rhode Island, Texas, and Wisconsin, trains teachers and guidance counselors to address the special needs of poor and minority students, and maintains a curriculum that emphasizes algebra and geometry as the "gatekeeper" subjects for all middle- and high-school students. A similar and more specialized mathematics program, called the Algebra Project, initiated by Robert P. Moses in the Roxbury neighborhood of Boston, Mass., has been carried out successfully in California and Mississippi.

One of the most celebrated and successful models for developing effective schools was instituted in the New Haven school system by Dr. James Comer, a member of the faculty of psychiatry at Yale University. The School Development Program is a comprehensive school program that involves parents, mental health professionals, teachers, and administrators in a mutually supportive relationship that in turn drives the academic program and assessment in an improved school climate (Comer, 1980).

Each of the programs is skills-based and provides students with the confidence to draw on their personal experiences to understand and resolve academic problems.

It should be noted, however, that successful models for public education are few, and many public school systems continue to struggle with increasing limitations in financial resources, lower academic standards, lack of discipline, and escalations of violence.

Perhaps the clearest indication of the nation's disillusionment with public education is the currency of school choice—a "public" system that would offer a better education to a select few. This will not respond to a pervasive concern among the nation's parents that their children gain the skills and assurance they will need to sustain themselves in the competitive multinational economy of their adulthood in the twenty-first century. For African Americans especially, the prospects of quality education remain a problem of equal educational rights.

In big cities across the nation attention is being focused on the improvement of public education at all levels. In New York, Chicago, and Philadelphia the Annenberg Foundation is helping principals, teachers, parents, communities, and boards of education to create smaller, theme-based, alternative primary and secondary schools.

Whatever the structure of the local school system, or the agreed-upon organizing theme of each school, however, preparation for a productive future in the modern world requires that students master the basic skills of English comprehension, writing and mathematics and an understanding of science and computer technology. Public education remains the most certain system for ensuring equity, quality, and personal empowerment. Federal, state, and local education officials, with the help of the private sector, must continue to be held responsible for the effective education of all of the nation's children, whatever their color or socioeconomic status.

BIBLIOGRAPHY

American Council on Education. *Minorities on Campus.* Washington, D.C., 1989.

American Council on Education and Education Commission of the States. *One Third of a Nation.* Washington, D.C., 1988.

Anderson, James D. *The Education of Blacks in the South, 1860–1935.* Chapel Hill, N.C., 1988.

Asante, Molefi K., and Mark T. Mattson. *Historical and Cultural Atlas of African Americans.* New York, 1992.

Ascher, Carol. *Changing Schools for Urban Students.* New York, 1993.

The Atlanta University Publications. 1911. Reprint. Atlanta, 1968.

Berry, Mary Frances. *The Politics of Parenthood.* New York, 1993.

———. "Unfinished Business of Carter G. Woodson." *City Sun,* March 20–26, 1991, p. 31.

Berry, Mary Frances, and John W. Blassingame. *Long Memory.* New York, 1982.

Bracey, John H., Jr., August Meir, and Elliott Rudwick. *Black Nationalism in America.* Indianapolis, Ind., 1970.

Bradford, William D. "Money Matters: Lending Discrimination in African-American Communities." In *The State of Black America 1993.* New York, 1993, pp. 109–123.

Bullock, Henry Allen. *A History of Negro Education in the South.* Cambridge, Mass., 1967.

Carleton, George W. *The Suppressed Book About Slavery.* 1863. Reprint. New York, 1968.

Carmichael, Stokely, and Charles V. Hamilton. *Black Power.* New York, 1967.

Carnegie Forum on Education and the Economy. *A Nation Prepared: Teachers for the 21st Century.* Washington, D.C., 1986.

Carson, Clayborne. *In Struggle.* Cambridge, Mass., 1981.

Clark, Kenneth B. *A Possible Reality.* New York, 1972.

———. *Dark Ghetto.* New York, 1965.

———. *Youth in the Ghetto.* New York, 1964.

Clarke, John Henrick. *Education for a New Reality in the African World.* New York, 1994.

Comer, James P. *School Power.* New York, 1980.

Comer, James P., et al. "School Power: A Model for Improving Black Student Achievement." In Willy DeMarcell Smith and Eva Wells Chunn, eds. *Black Education.* New Brunswick, N.J., 1991.

Cornelius, Janet Duitsman. *When I Can Read My Title Clear.* Columbia, S.C., 1991.

Cremin, Lawrence A. *American Education: The National Experience, 1783–1876.* New York, 1980.

———. *The Metropolitan Experience, 1976–1980.* New York, 1988.

Davidson, Basil. *The African Slave Trade: Precolonial History, 1450–1850.* Boston, 1961.

Davis, Arthur P., J. Saunders Redding, and Joyce Ann Joyce. *The New Calvacade: African-American Writing from 1760 to the Present.* Washington, D.C., 1991.

Douglas, Carlyle C. "Outlook for Young Black Males Called Bleak." *New York Times,* May 19, 1985, p. 34.

Du Bois, W. E. B., ed. *The Common School and the Negro American.* Atlanta, Ga., 1911.

Edelman, Marian Wright. *Families in Peril.* Cambridge, Mass., 1987.

Edmonds, Ron. "Programs of School Improvement: An Overview." *Educational Leadership* (December 1982): 4–11.

Foner, Eric. *Reconstruction: America's Unfinished Revolution, 1863–1877.* New York, 1988.

Franklin, John Hope, and Alfred A. Moss, Jr. *From Slavery to Freedom.* New York, 1994.

Garibaldi, Antoine M. "The Role of Historically Black Colleges in Facilitating Resilience Among African-American Students." *Education and Urban Society* 24 (1991): 103–111.

Gordon, Edmund W. "Conceptions of Africentrism and Multiculturalism in Education: A General Overview." *Journal of Negro Education* 61, no. 3 (1992): 235–236.

Gottlieb, Jay, Mark Alter, Barbara W. Gottlieb, and Jerry Wishner. "Special Education in Urban America: It's Not Justifiable for Many." *The Journal of Special Education* 27, no. 4 (1994): 453–465.

Gutman, Herbert G. *The Black Family in Slavery and Freedom, 1750–1925.* New York, 1976.

Hacker, Andrew. *Two Nations.* New York, 1992.

Hare, Bruce R. "Black Youth at Risk." In *The State of Black America, 1988.* New York, 1988.

Holmes Group. *Tomorrow's Teachers.* East Lansing, Mich., 1986.

Hughes, John F., and Anne O. Hughes. *Equal Education.* Bloomington, Ind., 1972.

Jackson, Edward M. *Black Education in Contemporary America.* Briston, Ind., 1986.

Jaynes, Gerald David, and Robin M. Williams, Jr., eds. *A Common Destiny: Blacks and American Society.* Washington, D.C., 1989.

Jones, Dorothy S. "Intermediate School 201 Controversy." Report No. 1 to the Church and Race Secretariat of the Protestant Council of the City of New York, September 12, 1966.

Jones, Faustine Childress. *The Changing Mood in America.* Washington, D.C., 1977.

Jones-Wilson, Faustine C. "Equity in Education: A Low Priority in the School Reform Movement." In Willy DeMarcell Smith and Eva Wells Chunn, eds. *Black Education.* New Brunswick, N.J., 1991.

Kearney, C. Phillip, and Elizabeth VanderPutten, eds. *Grants Consolidation: A New Balance in Federal Aid to Schools?* Washington, D.C., 1979.

Keppel, Francis. *The Necessary Revolution in American Education.* New York, 1966.

Kluger, Richard. *Simple Justice.* New York, 1976.

Kozol, Jonathan. *Savage Inequalities.* New York, 1992.

Larner, Jeremey. "I.S. 201: Disaster in the Schools." *Dissent* 45, no. 1 (1967): 21.

Lazar, Irving, and Richard B. Darlington. *Lasting Effects After Preschool.* Washington, D.C., 1978.

Lightfoot, Sara Lawrence. *The Good High School.* New York, 1993.

Logan, Rayford W., and Michael R. Winston. *Dictionary of America Negro Biography.* New York, 1982.

Mandle, Jay R. *Not Slave, Not Free: The African-American Experience Since the Civil War.* Durham, N.C., 1992.

Marable, Manning. *How Capitalism Underdeveloped Black America.* Boston, 1983.

———. *Race, Reform, and Rebellion.* Jackson, Miss., 1991.

Meir, K.J., Joseph Steward, Jr., and Robert E. England. *Race, Class and Education: The Politics of Second Generation Discrimination.* New York, 1989.

Mills, Johnnie R., Jo Ann Dauzat, and Burnett Joiner. *Improving Teacher Education: A Conscious Choice.* Dubuque, Iowa, 1989.

Minter, Thomas K. *Intermediate School 201, Manhattan: Center of Controversy.* Cambridge, Mass., 1967.

Munger, Frank J., and Richard Fenno, Jr. *National Politics and Federal Aid to Education.* Syracuse, N.Y., 1962.

Nathan, Richard P., and Fred Doolittle. *The Consequences of Cuts.* Princeton, N.J., 1983.

National Commission on Excellence in Education. *A Nation at Risk: The Imperative for Educational Reform.* Washington, D.C., 1983.

Niane, D. T., ed. *UNESCO General History of Africa: Africa from the Twelfth to the Sixteenth Century.* London, 1984.

Orfield, Gary. *Public School Desegregation in the United States, 1968–1980.* Washington, D.C., 1983.

Porter, Dorothy. *Early Negro Writing, 1760–1837.* Boston, 1971.

Prettyman, Alfred E. "The Ring of *The Bell Curve:* Resonances and Reverberations." New York, 1995.

Ravitch, Diane. *The Great School Wars.* 1974. Reprint. New York, 1968.

———. *The Troubled Crusade.* New York, 1983.

Rogers, David. *110 Livingston Street.* New York, 1968.

Scott, Hugh J. *The Black School Superintendent: Messiah or Scapegoat?* Washington, D.C., 1980.

Snowden, Frank M., Jr. *Blacks in Antiquity.* Cambridge, Mass., 1970.

Stafford, Walter, et al. *Cause for Alarm: The Condition of Black and Latino Males in New York City.* New York, 1991.

Sterling, Dorothy, ed. *We Are Your Sisters: Black Women in the Nineteenth Century.* New York, 1984.

Suffrin, Sidney C. *Administering the National Defense Education Act.* Syracuse, N.Y., 1963.

Swanson, Dena Phillips, and Margaret Beale Spencer. "Youth Policy, Poverty, and African Americans: Implications for Resilience." *Education and Urban Society* 24 (1991): 148–161.

U.S. Department of Education, National Center for Education Statistics. *America's Teachers: Profile of a Profession.* Washington, D.C., 1993.

———. *The Condition of Education, 1991.* Washington, D.C., 1991.

———. *The Condition of Education, 1992.* Washington, D.C., 1992.

Vergon, Charles B. "The Context of School Desegregation Policy." *Education and Urban Society* 23, no. 1 (1990): 3–21.

Watson, Bernard C. and Traylor, Fasaha M. "Tomorrow's Teachers: Who Will They Be, What Will They Know?" In *The State of Black America 1988.* New York, 1988.

Weikert, David P. *Quality Preschool Programs: A Long-Term Social Investment.* New York, 1989.

West, Cornel. *Race Matters.* Boston, 1993.

Winfield, Linda F., ed. "Resilience, Schooling, and Development in African-American Youth." *Education and Urban Society* 24 (1991): 5.

Wood, Forrest G. *The Arrogance of Faith.* New York, 1990.

Woodson, Carter G., and Charles H. Wesley. *The Education of the Negro Prior to 1861.* Washington, D.C., 1915.

———. *The Miseducation of the Negro.* Washington, D.C., 1933.

———. *The Negro in Our History.* Washington, D.C., 1972.

Wright, Donald R. *African Americans in the Colonial Era.* Carbondale, Ill., 1990.

———. *African Americans in the Early Republic, 1789–1831.* Carbondale, Ill., 1993.

– THOMAS K. MINTER AND ALFRED E. PRETTYMAN

ELLINGTON, EDWARD KENNEDY "DUKE"

Edward Kennedy "Duke" Ellington (April 29, 1899–May 24, 1974), composer, band leader, JAZZ pianist. One of the supreme composers of the twentieth century, Edward Kennedy Ellington was born into a comfortable middle class family in Washington, D.C. The son of a butler, Ellington received the nickname "Duke" as a child because of the care and pride he took in his attire. As he grew older, his aristocratic bearing and sartorial elegance made the nickname stick. Although he took piano lessons starting in 1906, he was also a talented painter, and before he finished high school he was offered an NAACP-sponsored painting scholarship for college. By this time, however, his interests were again turning toward music, especially RAGTIME and stride piano. By 1918, when Ellington married Edna Thompson, he was leading a band that played popular tunes in a ragtime style at white "society" events. To support his wife and son, Mercer, who was born in 1919, Ellington also worked as a sign painter.

In 1923, Ellington, encouraged by pianist Fats Waller, moved to New York as pianist and arranger of the Washingtonians. When the leader of the ensemble, Elmer Snowden, left in 1924, Ellington took over and led the band in what were his first appearances on record. The Washingtonians had extensive stays at the Club Hollywood, later called the Kentucky Club, from 1924 to 1927. In this formative period, Ellington's key influence was trumpeter Bubber Miley, whose guttural, plunger-muted style added a robust, blues-tinged element to Ellington's previously genteel compositions and arrangements. Miley's growling, mournful solos inspired Ellington's most important compositions in the 1920s, including "East St. Louis Toodle-O" (1926), "Black and Tan Fantasy" (1927), and "The Mooche" (1928). Another important composition from this period, "Creole Love Call" (1927), features a wordless obligato by vocalist Adelaide Hall.

Ellington was one of the supreme composers of the twentieth century.

On December 4, 1927, Ellington's band debuted at Harlem's COTTON CLUB, an all-white nightclub. The engagement lasted on and off for four years, and gave Ellington a national radio audience, as well as the chance to accompany a variety of chorus and specialty dance numbers and vocalists, often portraying "primitive" and "exotic" aspects of African-American culture. It was in that environment that he perfected the style, marked by energetic climaxes and haunting sonorities, that became known as his "jungle music."

The Cotton Club engagement made Ellington one of the best-known musicians in jazz, famed not only for his eminently danceable tunes, but also for compositions that attracted the attention of the classical music world. During the 1930s the orchestra toured the U.S. extensively, and made trips to Europe in 1933 and 1939. Ellington's 1930s recordings, which achieved huge success among both white and black audiences, include "Ring Dem Bells" (1930), "Mood Indigo" (1930), "Rockin' in Rhythm" (1931), "It Don't Mean a Thing If It Ain't Got That Swing" (1932), "Sophisticated Lady" (1932), "Daybreak Express" (1933), "Solitude" (1934), "In a Sentimental Mood" (1935), trombonist Juan Tizol's "Caravan" (1937), "I Let a Song Go out of My Heart" (1938), and "Prelude to a Kiss" (1938). Ellington's early 1940s band is often considered the best he ever led. Bolstered by tenor saxophonist Ben Webster, bassist Jimmy Blanton, and Ellington's assistant, composer and arranger Billy Strayhorn, the orchestra recorded a number of masterpieces, including "Ko-Ko" (1940), "Concerto for Cootie" (1940), "In a Mellotone" (1940), "Cotton Tail" (1940), "Perdido"

(1942), and "C-Jam Blues" (1942), as well as Strayhorn's "Chelsea Bridge" (1941) and "Take the A Train" (1941). Ellington also recorded in groups led by clarinetist Barney Bigard, trumpeters Cootie Williams and Rex Stewart, and saxophonist Johnny Hodges.

In the 1940s Ellington became increasingly interested in extended composition. Though he was the greatest master of the four-minute jazz composition, he chafed against the limitations of the length of a 78-rpm record side. As early as 1934 he wrote the score for the short film *Symphony in Black,* and the next year recorded *Reminiscing in Tempo,* a contemplative work taking up four sides. His greatest extended composition was the fifty-minute *Black, Brown and Beige,* which premiered at Carnegie Hall on January 23, 1943. This work, which included the hymnlike "Come Sunday" passage, depicted African Americans at work and at prayer, with vignettes on aspects of history from emancipation to the development of Harlem as a black community. Other extended works from this period include *New World-a-Comin'* (1943), *The Liberian Suite* (1947), and *The Tattooed Bride* (1948). Ellington continued to issue shorter recordings, but there were fewer memorable short compositions after the mid-1940s, though "The Clothed Woman" (1947) and "Satin Doll" (1953) were notable exceptions. In addition to composing and conducting, Ellington was an excellent pianist in the Harlem stride tradition, and he made memorable duets with bassist Jimmy Blanton in 1940.

During the bebop era of the late 1940s and early '50s, Ellington's band declined in influence. However, their performance at the 1956 Newport Jazz Festival, featuring saxophonist Paul Gonsalves's electrifying solo on "Diminuendo and Crescendo in Blue," reaffirmed their reputation, and earned Ellington a cover article in *Time* magazine. Ellington thereafter took the orchestra to Europe, Japan, the Middle East, India, South America, and Africa. The orchestra also made albums with Louis Armstrong, Coleman Hawkins, Count Basie, Ella Fitzgerald, and John Coltrane, and as a member of a trio Ellington recorded with Max Roach and Charles Mingus. Among his many later extended compositions are *Harlem* (1951), *A Drum Is a Woman* (1956), *Such Sweet Thunder* (1957), *The Queen's Suite* (1959), *The Far East Suite* (1967), and *Afro-Eurasian Eclipse* (1971). Ellington also composed film scores for *Anatomy of a Murder* (1959) and the Oscar-nominated *Paris Blues* (1961). He composed music for ballets by choreographer Alvin AILEY, *The River* (1970) and *Les Trois rois noirs,* including a section dedicated to the Rev. Dr. Martin Luther King, Jr., composed in Ellington's final years and premiered in 1976. In his last decade, Ellington also wrote religious music for three events he called "Sacred Concerts" (1965, 1968, 1973), vast productions that evoked his strong sense of spirituality through GOSPEL and choral music, dancing, and thankful hymns.

Starting with the 1943 *Black, Brown and Beige,* many of Ellington's extended works were tributes to his African-American heritage, and demonstrations of his pride in the accomplishments of African Americans. His many shorter depictions of Harlem range from the elegiac "Drop Me Off in Harlem" (1933) to the boisterous "Harlem Airshaft" (1940). Perhaps his most personal tributes are his two musicals, *Jump for Joy* (including "I Got It Bad and That Ain't Good," 1942), and *My People* (1963), both dealing with the theme of integration. The latter includes the song "King Fit the Battle of Alabam."

Ellington's music was collaborative. Many of his works were written by band members, and many more were written collectively, by synthesizing and expanding riffs and motifs into unified compositions. Ellington's compositions were al-

Duke Ellington Band, on RKO lot, Culver City, Calif., 1930. (Frank Driggs Collection)

most always written with a particular band member's style and ability in mind, and his collaborator Strayhorn remarked that while Ellington played piano, his real instrument was his orchestra. Ellington was an exceptionally original musical thinker, whose orchestral sound was marked by instrumental doublings on reeds, ingenious combinations of instruments, and the carefully crafted use of a variety of muted brasses. The diversity of the band was remarkable, containing an extraordinary variety of masterful and distinctive soloists, ranging from the smooth, sensuous improvisations of saxophonist Johnny Hodges to the gutbucket sounds of trumpeter Cootie Williams and trombonist "Tricky Sam" Nanton.

In the ever-changing world of the big bands, the Ellington orchestra's core roster seldom changed. The most important of his band members, with their tenures parenthetically noted, include trumpeters William "Cat" Anderson (1944–1947, 1950–1959, 1961–1971), Bubber Miley (1924–1929), Rex Stewart (1934–1945), Arthur Whetsol (1923–1924, 1928–1936), and Cootie Williams (1929–1940, 1962–1973); violinist and trumpeter Ray Nance (1940–1963); trombonists Lawrence Brown (1932–1951, 1960–1970), Joe "Tricky Sam" Nanton (1926–1946), and Juan Tizol (1929–1944, 1951–1953); alto saxophonists Otto Hardwick (1923–1928, 1932–1946), Johnny Hodges (1928–1951, 1955–1970), and Russell Procope (1946–1974); tenor saxophonists Paul Gonsalves (1950–1970, 1972–1974) and Ben Webster (1940–1943, 1948–1949); baritone saxophonist Harry Carney (1927–1974); clarinetists Barney Bigard (1927–1942) and Jimmy Hamilton (1943–1968); vocalists Ivy Anderson (1931–1942) and Al Hibbler (1943–1951); drummer Sonny Greer (1923–1951); bassist Jimmy Blanton (1939–1941); and composer and arranger Billy Strayhorn (1939–1967).

During his lifetime Ellington was celebrated as a commanding figure in American culture. He cherished the many awards and honorary degrees he earned, including the Spingarn Medal (1959) and eleven Grammy Awards. Ellington remained gracious, though many were outraged by the refusal of a 1965 Pulitzer Prize committee, firmly opposed to recognizing "popular" music, to give him a special award for composition. In 1970 Ellington was awarded the Presidential Medal of Freedom by President Nixon and was feted with a seventieth-birthday celebration at the White House. He died of cancer on May 24, 1974.

Since Ellington's death, his orchestra has been led by his son, Mercer, himself a trumpeter and composer of note. In 1986, Duke Ellington became the first African-American jazz musician to appear on a U. S. postage stamp. The 1980s and '90s have witnessed a growing interest in Ellington among scholars who are increasingly interested in the extended compositions, and among jazz fans gaining access to a wealth of previously unreleased recordings. Such attention inevitably confirms Ellington's status not only as the greatest composer and bandleader in jazz, but as a figure unique in the history of twentieth-century music.

BIBLIOGRAPHY

Collier, James Lincoln. *Duke Ellington.* New York, 1987.
Dance, Stanley. *The World of Duke Ellington.* New York, 1970.
Ellington, Duke. *Music Is My Mistress.* New York, 1973.
Schuller, Gunther. *Early Jazz.* New York, 1968.
———. *The Swing Era.* New York, 1988.
Tucker, Mark. *Ellington: The Early Years.* Chicago, 1991.
———, ed. *The Duke Ellington Reader.* New York, 1993.
Williams, Martin. *The Jazz Tradition.* New York, 1983.

— MARTIN WILLIAMS

ELLISON, RALPH

Ralph Ellison (March 1, 1914–April 16, 1994), writer. Ralph Ellison was born to Lewis and Ida Millsap Ellison in Oklahoma City, Okla., a frontier town with a rich vernacular culture. As a child, he worked at Randolph's Pharmacy, where he heard animal tales and ghost stories. The local all-black high school provided rigorous training in music, and the Aldridge Theatre featured many of the leading blues, ragtime, and jazz musicians of the day. Ellison played in high school jazz bands and in 1933 enrolled as a music major at Tuskegee Institute, Ala. He involved himself in the other arts as well and on his own discovered T. S. Eliot's *Waste Land,* where he found a range of allusions "as mixed and varied as that of Louis Armstrong."

At the end of his third college year, Ellison went to New York to earn money. He never returned to Tuskegee. He met Langston HUGHES, whose poetry he had read in high school, and Richard WRIGHT, who urged him to write for *New Challenge,* which Wright was editing. Ellison wrote a review for the magazine in 1937, his first published work. In 1938 he took a Works Progress Administration job with the New York Writer's Project and worked at night on his own fiction. He read Hemingway to learn style.

Ellison wrote book reviews for the radical periodicals *Direction, Negro Quarterly,* and *New Masses,* which in 1940 printed at least one review by him every month. His first short stories were realistic in the manner of Richard Wright and presented fairly explicit political solutions to the dilemmas of Jim Crow. By 1940 he had begun to find his own direction with a series of stories in the Huck Finn/Tom Sawyer mold—tales of black youngsters who were not so much victims as playmakers in a land of possibility. "Flying Home" (1944) offers wise old Jefferson as a storyteller whose verbal art helps lessen the greenhorn Todd's isolation and teaches him a healthier attitude toward the divided world he must confront. That story set the stage for Ellison's monumental 1952 novel *Invisible Man,* which received the National Book Award the following year.

Set between 1930 and 1950, *Invisible Man* tells of the development of an ambitious young black man from the South, a naïf who goes to college and then to New York in search of advancement. At first Invisible Man, unnamed throughout the novel, wants to walk the narrow way of Booker T. Washington, whose words he speaks at his high school graduation as well as at a smoker for the town's leading white male citizens. At the smoker he is required to fight blindfolded in a free-for-all against the other black youths. In this key chapter, all the boys are turned blindly against one another in a danger-filled ritual staged for the amusement of their white patrons. That night the young man dreams of his grandfather, the novel's cryptic ancestor-wise man, who presents him with "an engraved document" that seems an ironic comment on his high school diploma and its costs. "Read it," the old man tells him. " 'To Whom It May Concern,' I intoned. 'Keep This Nigger Boy Running.' "

> *Rich in historical and literary allusions, the* Invisible Man *stands both as a novel about the history of the novel and as a meditation on the history of the United States.*

Whether a student in the southern college or a spokesman in New York for the radical political movement called the Brotherhood (modeled on the Communist party of the 1930s or some other American political organization that exploited blacks and then sold them out), Invisible Man is kept running. Quintessentially American in his confusion about who he is, he mad-dashes from scene to scene, letting others tell him what his experience means, who he is, what his name is. And he is not only blind, he is invisible—he is racially stereotyped and otherwise denied his individuality. "I am invisible," he discovers, "simply because people refuse to see me. Like the bodiless heads you see sometimes in circus sideshows, it is as though I have been surrounded by mirrors of hard, distorting glass. When they approach me they see only my surroundings, themselves, or figments of their imagination—indeed, everything and anything except me."

After encounters with remarkable adults—some wisely parental, some insane but brilliant, some sly con men—he learns to accept with equipoise the full ambiguity of his history and to see the world by his own lights. "It took me a long time," he says, "and much painful boomeranging of my expectations to achieve a realization everyone else appears to have been born with: That I am nobody but myself. But first I had to discover that I am an invisible man!" He had to find out that very few people would bother to understand his real motives and values; perhaps not all of these mysteries were knowable, even by himself. And yet in this novel of education and epiphany, Invisible Man decides he can nonetheless remain hopeful: "I was my experiences and my experiences were me," he says. "And no blind men, no matter how powerful they became, even if they conquered the world, could take that, or change one single itch, taunt, laugh, cry, scar, ache, rage or pain of it."

Rich in historical and literary allusions—from Columbus to World War II, from Oedipus and Br'er Rabbit to T. S. Eliot and Richard Wright—*Invisible Man* stands both as a novel about the history of the novel and as a meditation on the history of the United States. In doing so, it presents a metaphor for black American life in the twentieth century that transcends its particular focus. It names not only the modern American but the citizen of the contemporary world as tragicomically centerless (but somehow surviving and getting smarter): *Homo invisibilis.* It is Ellison's masterwork.

Shadow and Act (1964) and *Going to the Territory* (1987) are collections of Ellison's nonfiction prose. With these books he established himself as a preeminent man of letters—one whose driving purpose was to define African-American life and culture with precision and affirmation. The essays on African-American music are insider's reports that reflect Ellison's deep experience and long memory. Whether discussing literature, music, painting, psychology, or history, Ellison places strong emphases on vernacular culture—its art, rituals, and meanings—and on the power of the visionary individual, particularly the artist, to prevail. These books offer a strong challenge to social scientists and historians to consider African-American life in terms not just of its ills and pathologies but of its tested capacity to reinvent itself and to influence the nation and the world.

BIBLIOGRAPHY

Benston, Kimberly, ed. *Speaking for You: The Vision of Ralph Ellison.* Washington, D.C., 1985.

O'Meally, Robert G. *The Craft of Ralph Ellison.* Cambridge, Mass., 1980.

– ROBERT G. O'MEALLY

EMANCIPATION

Few events in American history can match the drama and the social significance of black emancipation in the midst of the CIVIL WAR. Since the early seventeenth century, when African-born slaves were first brought ashore in Virginia, through the long development of the South's plantation economy and its dependence upon slave labor, emancipation had been the dream of African-American people. Beyond the age of the American Revolution, when the northern states freed their relatively small numbers of slaves, and into the antebellum era of abolitionism, the writing of fugitive slave narratives, and increasing free black community development in the North, emancipation became a matter of political and religious expectation. To be a black abolitionist, a fugitive slave desperately seeking his or her way through the mysterious realities of the Underground Railroad, or one of the millions of slaves cunningly surviving on southern cotton plantations was to be an actor in this long and agonizing drama. The agony and the hope embedded in the story of emancipation is what black poet Francis Ellen Watkins tried to capture in a simple verse written in the wake of John Brown's execution in 1859 and only a little over a year before the outbreak of the Civil War:

Make me a grave where'er you will,
In a lowly plain, or a lofty hill,
Make it among earth's humblest graves,
But not in a land where men are slaves.

Soon, by the forces of total war, which in turn opened opportunities for slaves to seize their own freedom, emancipation became reality in America. Black freedom became the central event of nineteenth-century African-American history and, along with the preservation of the Union, the central result of the Civil War.

On Emancipation day, January 1, 1863 (when Abraham Lincoln's Emancipation Proclamation was to go into effect), "jubilee meetings" occurred all over black America. At Tremont Temple in Boston, a huge gathering of blacks and whites met from morning until night, awaiting the final news that Lincoln had signed the fateful document. Genuine concern still existed that something might go awry; the preliminary proclamation had been issued in September 1862, a mixture of what appeared to be military necessity and a desire to give the war a new moral purpose. Numerous luminaries from throughout antebellum free black leadership spoke during the day; the attorney John Rock, the minister and former slave John Sella Martin, the orator and women's suffragist Anna Dickinson, author William Wells Brown, and Boston's William Cooper Nell as presiding officer were among them. The most prominent of all black voices, Frederick DOUGLASS, gave a concluding speech during the afternoon session punctuated by many cries of "Amen." In the evening, tension mounted and anxiety gripped the hall, as no news had arrived from Washington. Douglass and Brown provided more oratory to try to quell the changing mood of doubt. Then a runner arrived from the telegraph office with the news: "It is coming!" he shouted, "it is on the wires!" An attempt was made to read the text of the Emancipation Proclamation, but great jubilation engulfed the crowd. Unrestrained shouting and singing ensued. Douglass gained the throng's attention and led them in a chorus of his favorite hymn, "Blow Ye the Trumpet, Blow." Next an old black preacher named Rue led the group in "Sound the loud timbel o'er Egypt's dark sea, Jehovah has triumphed, his people are free!" The celebration lasted until midnight, when the crowd reassembled at pastor Leonard A. Grimes's Twelfth Baptist Church—an institution renowned among black Bostonians for its role in helping many fugitive slaves move along the road to liberty—to continue celebrating.

Few events in American history can match the drama and the social significance of black emancipation in the midst of the Civil War.

From Massachusetts to Ohio and Michigan, and in many Union-occupied places in the South where ex-slaves were now entering the Yankee army or beginning their first year as free people, such celebrations occurred. Full of praise songs, these celebrations demonstrated that whatever the fine print of the proclamation might say, black folks across the land knew that they had lived to see a new day, a transforming moment in their history. At a large "contraband camp" (center for refugee ex-slaves) in Washington, D.C., some six hundred black men, women, and children gathered at the superintendent's headquarters on New Year's Eve and sang through most of the night. In chorus after chorus of "Go Down, Moses" they announced the magnitude of their painful but beautiful exodus. One newly supplied verse concluded with "Go down, Abraham, away down in Dixie's land, tell Jeff Davis to let my people go!" Many years after the Tremont Temple celebration in Boston, Douglass may have best captured the meaning of Emancipation day for his people: "It was not logic, but the trump of jubilee, which everybody wanted to hear. We were waiting and listening as for a bolt from the sky, which should rend the fetters of four millions of slaves; we were watching as it were, by the dim light of stars, for the dawn of a new day; we were longing for the answer to the agonizing prayers of centuries. Remembering those in bonds as bound with them, we wanted to join in the shout for freedom, and in the anthem of the redeemed." For blacks the cruel and apocalyptic war finally had a holy cause.

The emancipation policy of the Union government evolved with much less certitude than the music and poetry of jubilee day might imply. During the first year of the war, the Union military forces operated on an official policy of exclusion ("denial of asylum") to escaped slaves. The war was to restore the Union, but not to uproot SLAVERY. But events overtook such a policy. Floods of fugitive slaves began to enter Union lines in Virginia, in Tennessee, and along the southern coasts. Thousands were eventually employed as military laborers, servants, camp hands, and even spies. Early in the war, at Fortress Monroe, Va., in May 1861, the ambitious politician-general Benjamin F. Butler declared the slaves who entered his lines "contraband of war." The idea of slaves as confiscated enemy property eventually caught on. In early August 1861, striking a balance between legality and military necessity, the federal Congress passed the First Confiscation Act, allowing for the seizure of all Confederate property used to aid the war effort. Although not yet technically freed by this law, the slaves of rebel masters came under its purview and an inexorable process toward black freedom took root. Into 1862 the official stance of the Union armies toward slaves was a conflicted one: exclusion where the slaveholders were deemed "loyal," and employment as contrabands where the masters were judged "disloyal." Such an unworkable policy caused considerable dissension in the Union ranks, especially between abolitionist and proslavery officers. But wherever Union forces gained ground in the South, the institution of slavery began to crumble.

By the spring and summer of 1862, Congress took the lead on the issue of emancipation policy. In April it abolished slavery in the District of Columbia, and a large sum of money was allocated for the possible colonization of freed blacks abroad. The Lincoln administration, indeed, pursued a variety of schemes for Central American and Caribbean colonization during the first three years of the war. The sheer impracticality of such plans and stiff black resistance notwithstanding, this old idea of black removal from America as the solution to the revolutionary implications of Emancipation died hard within the Lincoln administration and in the mind of the president himself. But Lincoln, as well as many other Americans, would be greatly educated by both the necessity and the larger meanings of Emancipation. A black newspaper in Union-occupied New Orleans declared that "history furnishes no such intensity of determination, on the part of any race, as that exhibited by these people to be free." And Frederick Douglass felt greatly encouraged by an evolving emancipation movement in early 1862, whatever its contradictory motives. "It is really wonderful," he wrote, "how all efforts to evade, postpone, and prevent its coming, have been mocked and defied by the stupendous sweep of events."

In June 1862, Congress abolished slavery in the western territories, a marvelous irony when one remembers the tremendous political crisis over that issue in the decade before the war, as well as the alleged finality of the DRED SCOTT DECISION of 1857. In July, Congress passed the Second Confiscation Act, which explicitly freed slaves of all persons "in rebellion," and excluded no parts of the slaveholding South. These measures provided a public and legal backdrop for President Lincoln's subsequent Emancipation Proclamation, issued in two parts, maneuvered through a recalcitrant Cabinet, and politically calculated to shape northern morale, prevent foreign intervention (especially that of the British), and keep the remaining four slaveholding border states in the Union. During 1862, Lincoln had secretly maneuvered to persuade Delaware and Kentucky to accept a plan of compensated, gradual Emancipation. But the deeply divided border states bluntly refused such notions. In the preliminary proclamation of September 21, 1862, issued in the aftermath of the bloody battle of Antietam (a Union military success for which Lincoln had desperately waited), the president offered a carrot to the rebellious South: in effect, stop the war, reenter the Union, and slavery would go largely untouched. In his State of the Union address in December, Lincoln dwelled on the idea of gradual, compensated Emancipation as the way to end the war and return a willful South to the Union. None of these offers had any chance of acceptance at this point in what had already become a revolutionary war for ends much larger and higher than most had imagined in 1861.

Lincoln had always considered slavery to be an evil that had to be eliminated in America. It was he who had committed the Republican party in the late 1850s to putting SLAVERY "on a course of ultimate extinction."

At the outset of the war, however, he valued saving the Union above all else, including whatever would happen to slavery. But after he signed the document that declared all slaves in the "states of rebellion . . . forever free," Lincoln's historical reputation, as often legendary and mythical as it is factual, became forever tied to his role in the emancipation process. Emancipation did indeed require presidential leadership to commit America to a war to free slaves in the eyes of the world; in Lincoln's remarkable command of moral meaning and politics, he understood that this war had become a crucible in which the entire nation could receive a "new birth of freedom." The president ultimately commanded the armies, every forward step of which from 1863 to 1865 was a liberating step, soon by black soldiers as well. On one level, Emancipation had to be legal and moral, and, like all great matters in American history, it had to be finalized in the Constitution, in the THIRTEENTH AMENDMENT (passed in early 1865). But black freedom was something both given and seized. Many factors made it possible for Lincoln to say by February 1865 that "the central act of my administration, and the greatest event of the nineteenth century," was Emancipation. But none more than the black exodus of self-emancipation when the moment of truth came, the waves of freedpeople who "voted with their feet."

The actual process and timing of Emancipation across the South depended on at least three interrelated circumstances: one, the character of slave society in a given region; two, the course of the war itself; and three, the policies of the Union and Confederate governments. Southern geography, the chronology of the military campaigns, the character of total war with its massive forced movement of people, the personal disposition of slaveholders and Union commanders alike, and the advent of widespread recruitment of black soldiers were all combined factors in determining when, where, and how slaves became free. Thousands of slaves were "hired out" as fortification laborers, teamsters, nurses, and cooks in the Confederate armies, eventually providing many opportunities for escape to Union lines and an uncertain but freer future. Thousands were also "refugeed" to the interior by their owners in order to "protect" them from invading Yankee armies. Many more took to the forests and swamps to hide during the chaos of war, as Union forces swept over the sea islands of the Georgia or South Carolina coast, or the densely populated lower Mississippi Valley region. Many of those slaves eventually returned to their plantations, abandoned by their former masters, and took over agricultural production, sometimes under the supervision of an old driver, and sometimes by independently planting subsistence crops while the sugar cane rotted.

Many slaves waited and watched for their opportunity of escape, however uncertain their new fate might be. Octave Johnson was a slave on a plantation in St. James Parish, La., who ran away to the woods when the war came. He and a group of thirty, ten of whom were women, remained at large for a year and a half. Johnson's story, as he reported it to the American Freedmen's Inquiry Commission in 1864, provides a remarkable example of the social-military revolution under way across the South. "We were four miles in the rear of the plantation house," said Johnson. His band stole food and borrowed matches and other goods from slaves still on the plantation. "We slept on logs and burned cypress leaves to make a smoke and keep away mosquitoes." When hunted by bloodhounds, Johnson's group took to the deeper swamp. They "killed eight of the bloodhounds; then we jumped into Bayou Faupron; the dogs followed us and the alligators caught six of them; the alligators preferred dog flesh to personal flesh; we escaped and came to Camp Parapet, where I was first employed in the Commissary's office, then as a servant to Col. Hanks; then I joined his regiment." From "working on task" through survival in the bayous, Octave Johnson found his freedom as a corporal in Company C, Fifteenth Regiment, Corps d'Afrique.

For many slaves, the transition from bondage to freedom was not so clear and complete as it was for Octave Johnson. Emancipation was a matter of overt celebration in some places, especially in southern towns and cities, as well as in some slave quarters. But what freedom meant in 1863, how livelihood would change, how the war would progress, how the masters would react (perhaps with wages but perhaps with violent retribution), how freedpeople would find protection in the conquered and chaotic South, how they would meet the rent payments that might now be charged, how a peasant population of agricultural laborers deeply attached to the land might now become owners of the land as so many dreamed, and whether they would achieve citizenship rights were all urgent and unanswered questions during the season of Emancipation. Joy mixed with uncertainty, songs of deliverance with expressions of fear. The actual day on which masters gathered their slaves to announce that they were free was remembered by freedpeople with a wide range of feelings and experience. Some remembered hilarity and dancing, but many remembered it as a sobering, even solemn time. A former South Carolina slave recalled that on his plantation "some were sorry, some hurt, but a few were silent and glad." James Lucas, a former slave of Jefferson Davis in Mississippi, probed the depths of human nature and ambivalence in his description of the day of liberation: "Dey all had diffe'nt ways o' thinkin' 'bout it. Mos'ly though dey was jus' lak me, dey didn' know jus' zackly what it meant. It was jus' somp'n dat de white folks an' slaves all de time talk 'bout. Dat's all. Folks dat ain' never been free don' rightly know de *feel* of bein' free. Dey don' know de meanin' of it." And a former Virginia slave simply recalled "how wild and upset and *dreadful* everything was in them times."

The actual day on which masters gathered their slaves to announce that they were free was remembered by freedpeople with a wide range of feelings and experience.

But in time, confusion gave way to meaning, and the feel of freedom took many forms. For many ex-slaves who followed Union armies freedom meant, initially, life in contraband camps, where black families struggled to survive in the face of great hardship and occasional starvation. But by the end of 1862 and throughout the rest of the war, a string of contraband camps became the first homes in freedom for thousands of ex-slaves. At LaGrange, Bolivar, and Memphis in western Tennessee; at Corinth in northern Mississippi; in "contraband colonies" near New Orleans; at Cairo, Ill.; at Camp Barker in the District of Columbia; on Craney Island near Norfolk, Va.; and eventually in northern Georgia and various other places, the freedpeople forged a new life on government rations and through work on labor crews, and received a modicum of medical care, often provided by "grannies"—black women who employed home remedies from plantation life. For thousands the contraband camps became the initial entry into free labor practices, and a slow but certain embrace of the new sense of dignity, mobility, identity, and education that freedom now meant. Nearly all white Northerners who witnessed or supervised these camps, or who eventually administered private or government work programs on confiscated southern land, organized freedmen's aid societies and schools by the hundreds, or observed weddings and burials, were stunned by the determination of this exodus despite its hardships. In 1863, each superintendent of a contraband camp in the western theater of war was asked to respond to a series of interrogatives about the freedmen streaming into his facilities. To the question of the "motives" of the freedmen, the Corinth superintendent tried to find the range of what he saw: "Can't answer short of 100 pages. Bad treatment—hard times—lack of the comforts of life—prospect of being driven South; the more intelligent because they wished to be free. Generally speak kindly of their masters; none wish to return; many would die first. All delighted with the prospect of freedom, yet all have been kept constantly at some kind of work." All of the superintendents commented on what seemed to them the remarkable "intelligence" and "honesty" of the freedmen. As for their "notions of liberty," the Memphis superintendent answered: "Generally correct. They say they have no rights, nor own anything except as their master permits; but being freed, can make their own money and protect their families." Indeed, these responses demonstrate just what a fundamental revolution Emancipation had become.

Inexorably, Emancipation meant that black families would be both reunited and torn apart. In contraband camps, where women and children greatly outnumbered men, extended families sometimes found and cared for each other. But often, when the thousands of black men across the South entered the Union army they left women and children behind in great hardship, sometimes in sheer destitution, and eventually under new labor arrangements that required rent payments. Louisiana freedwoman Emily Waters wrote to her husband, who was still on duty with the Union army, in July 1865, begging him to get a furlough and "come home and find a place for us to live in." The joy of change mixed with terrible strain. "My children are going to school," she reported, "but I find it very hard to feed them all, and if you cannot come I hope you will send me something to help me get along. . . . Come home as soon as you can, and cherish me as ever." The same Louisiana soldier received a subsequent letter from Alsie Thomas, his sister, reporting that "we are in deep trouble—your wife has left Trepagnia and gone to the city and we don't know where or how she is, we have not heard a word from her in four weeks." The choices and the strains that Emancipation wrought are tenderly exhibited in a letter by John Boston, a Maryland fugitive slave, to his wife, Elizabeth, in January 1862, from Upton Hill, Va. "[I]t is with grate joy I take this time to let you know Whare I am i am now in Safety in the 14th regiment of Brooklyn this Day i can Adres you thank god as a free man I had a little truble in giting away But as the lord led the Children of Isrel to the land of Canon So he led me to a land Whare Fredom Will rain in spite Of earth and hell . . . i am free from al the Slavers Lash." Such were the joys of freedom and the agonies of separation. Boston concluded his letter: "Dear Wife i must Close rest yourself Contented i am free . . . Write my Dear Soon . . . Kiss Daniel For me." The rich sources on the freedmen's experience do not tell us whether Emily Waters ever saw her husband again, or whether the Bostons were reunited. But these letters demonstrate the depth with which freedom was embraced and the human pain through which it was achieved.

The freedpeople especially gave meaning to their freedom by their eagerness for education and land ownership. In the Sea Islands of South Carolina, the Port Royal Experiment was a large-scale attempt, led by northern philanthropists interested as much in profits as in freedmen's rights, to reorganize cotton production by paying wages to blacks. But amid this combination of abolitionists' good works and capitalist opportunity, thousands of blacks of all ages learned to read. So eager were the freedmen to learn that the teachers from the various freedmen's-aid societies were sometimes overwhelmed. "The Negroes will do anything for us," said one teacher, "if we will only teach them." Land ownership was an equally precious aim of the freedmen, and they claimed it as a right. No one ever stated the labor theory of value more clearly than Virginia freedman Bayley Wyat, in a speech protesting the eviction of blacks from a contraband camp in 1866: "We has a right to the land we are located. For Why? I tell you. Our wives, our children, our husbands, has been sold over and over again to purchase the lands we now locates upon; for that reason we have a divine right to the land. . . . And den didn't we clear the land, and raise de crops ob corn, ob cotton, ob tobacco, ob rice, ob sugar, ob everything?" The redistribution of land and wealth in the South would remain a largely unrealized dream during RECONSTRUCTION, and perhaps its greatest unfinished legacy. But armed with literacy, and an unprecedented politicization, southern blacks accomplished much against great odds in the wake of Emancipation.

Many of the twentieth-century triumphs in America's never-ending search for racial democracy have their deep roots in the story of Emancipation and its aftermath.

By the end of the war in 1865, the massive moving about of the freedpeople became a major factor in Confederate defeat. Thousands of white Union soldiers who witnessed this process of Emancipation became, despite earlier prejudices, avid supporters of the recruitment of black soldiers. And no one understood just what a transformation was under way better than the former slaveholders in the South, who now watched their world collapse around them. In August 1865, white Georgian John Jones described black freedom as the "dark, dissolving, disquieting wave of EMANCIPATION." That wave would abate in the turbulent first years of Reconstruction, when the majority of freedmen would resettle on their old places, generally paid wages at first, but eventually working "on shares" (as sharecropping tenant farmers). Reconstruction would bring a political revolution to the South, a great experiment in racial democracy, led by radical Republicans in the federal government and by a new American phenomenon: scores of black politicians. This "disquieting wave" would launch black suffrage, citizenship rights, civil rights, and widespread black officeholding beyond what anyone could have imagined at the outset of the Civil War. That the great achievements in racial democracy of the period 1865–1870 were betrayed or lost by the late nineteenth century does not detract from the significance of such a passage in African-American history. Many of the twentieth-century triumphs in America's never-ending search for racial democracy have their deep roots in the story of Emancipation and its aftermath.

BIBLIOGRAPHY

Berlin, Ira, et al., eds. *Freedom: A Documentary History of Emancipation, 1861–67.* Series 1, vol. 1, *The Destruction of Slavery.* Series 1, vol. 3, *The Wartime Genesis of Free Labor.* Series 2, *The Black Military Experience.* New York, 1982–1990.

Foner, Eric. *Nothing but Freedom: Emancipation and Its Legacy.* Baton Rouge, La., 1983.

Litwack, Leon F. *Been in the Storm So Long: The Aftermath of Slavery.* New York, 1979.

— DAVID W. BLIGHT

ENTREPRENEURS

African economic practices in food production and distribution provided the basis for the initial entrepreneurial expression of black people in this nation. A vibrant commercial culture existed in western and central Africa during the transatlantic slave trade era. The economic structures of African societies were exceedingly sophisticated. Internal market systems proliferated, regulated by central authorities at the national, regional, and local levels. International trade—including trade in slaves—was controlled by kings and wealthy merchants, while local economies required the participation of men and women as producers, wholesalers, and retailers in markets overseen by guilds.

1619–1789

Africans who were brought to the United States as slaves first made use of the surplus commodities from their own provision grounds—land either allotted to them or surreptitiously appropriated by them for food growing and, occasionally, tobacco cultivation—to create local produce markets where goods were sold or bartered. These were the first business ventures that provided slaves with money. Successful slave entrepreneurs could earn enough money to purchase freedom for themselves and their families and subsequently acquire land. In mid-seventeenth-century Virginia the Anthony Johnson family secured its freedom and opened a commercial farm producing tobacco for both local and international markets. The Johnsons also had a number of indentured servants and slaves.

Although there were relatively few free blacks with holdings in land or slaves, their numbers did increase during the eighteenth century. In colonial cities African Americans were particularly active as entrepreneurs in the food-service industry, first as market people and then as street food vendors and cook- and food-shop owners. In 1736, in Providence, R.I., Emanuel Manna Bernoon opened the first African-American catering establishment with the capital from his wife's illegal whiskey distillery business. One of the leading caterers of nearby Newport was "Dutchess" Quamino, a pastry maker who conducted her business in a small house. The catering activities of blacks in these towns placed Rhode Island at the center of African-American enterprise and contributed significantly to the state's early development as a resort area.

One of the most renowned innkeepers in eighteenth-century America was Samuel Fraunces (1722–1795). While there is some dispute whether Fraunces was of African descent, there is no doubt that he was a West Indian who migrated to New York City in the 1750s. His tavern and inn, which opened in 1761, earned him a reputation as a leading restaurateur with "the finest hostelry in Colonial America." Four years later Fraunces established Vaux-Hall (named after the famous English pleasure gardens), a resort with hanging gardens, waxworks, concerts, fireworks, and afternoon dances, which set the standard for pleasure gardens in colonial America; during the 1780s, when New York City was the nation's capital, Fraunces' Tavern in lower Manhattan served as a meeting place for the new government and was the site of George Washington's farewell to his troops.

A number of northern blacks were successful tradesmen or artisans. Peter Williams, Sr., who was born a slave in New York and helped found the African Methodist Episcopal Zion Church in 1800, was a successful tobacconist. With the profits from his earnings, Williams purchased his freedom in 1786. African-born Amos Fortune (1710–1801) purchased his freedom at age sixty and established a successful tannery business with a clientele that extended to New Hampshire and Massachusetts.

Black entrepreneurs were also to be found at the American frontier. In 1779 Jean Baptiste Pointe Du Sable established a trading post on the site of what later became the city of Chicago. In addition to importing merchandise from the East, Du Sable owned a bake house, mill, dairy, smokehouse, and lumberyard. His mercantile activities serviced a wilderness hinterland with a two-hundred-mile radius.

Beginning in the late eighteenth century, blacks developed enterprises in sports and music. In Newport, R.I., African-born Occramer Marycoo, later known as Newport Gardiner (1746–?), established a successful music school based on his reputation as a musician and composer. In 1780 Gardiner cofounded the African Union Society, which kept community records, found training and jobs for black youth, and supported members in time of financial need. Gardiner led thirty-two other African Americans to Liberia, with support from the AMERICAN COLONIZATION SOCIETY, in 1826. The most famous late-eighteenth-century black sports figure was boxer Bill Richmond (1763–1829), who achieved recognition in both America and England. Born a slave in New York, Richmond left for London during the Revolution, where his fame in BOXING grew. Upon retiring from the ring, he established a popular inn in London known as the Horse and Dolphin and opened a BOXING academy.

1790–1865

The entrepreneurial efforts of African Americans became increasingly pronounced in the early national and antebellum years. Throughout this period African-American entrepreneurs were prominent in crafts and personal services, which required limited capital for the development of enterprise. Blacks also established profitable businesses in transportation, manufacturing, personal services, catering, restaurants and taverns, real estate, finance, commercial farming, merchandising, mining, and construction. Unlike later black entrepreneurs, most antebellum businessmen had a consumer base that was primarily white. By the advent of the Civil War, at least twenty-one black entrepreneurs had accumulated holdings of over $100,000.

A prominent figure in transportation and commodity distribution was Paul Cuffe (1759–1817), a native of New Bedford, Mass., who founded a shipping line, owned several vessels, and held an interest in several others. Cuffe purchased his first ship in 1785 and had constructed a wharf and warehouse by 1800. His shipping enterprises extended from whaling to coastal and transatlantic trade vessels, which carried cargo and passengers to the West Indies, Africa, England, Norway, and Russia. Cuffe's most notable voyage was undertaken in 1815, when he transported thirty-eight African Americans to Sierra Leone at his own expense. He died two years later and left an estate valued at $20,000. Like Cuffe, the Philadelphia entrepreneur James FORTEN (1766–1842) actively supported the abolitionist movement and agitated for the rights of free blacks. Forten, whose estate was valued at $100,000, invented a new sail-making device and ran a factory that employed over forty workers, both white and black. Other antebellum inventors and manufacturers included Henry Boyd (c. 1840–1922) and William Ellison (1790–1861). Boyd, a native of Cincinnati, patented a bedstead and employed some thirty people in his bed-making factory. Slave-born William Ellison of South Carolina established a successful cotton gin factory after he was freed. He invented a device which substantially increased the gin's efficiency, and his market extended to most of the South's cotton-producing regions. He invested his profits in slaves and real estate holdings.

Antebellum blacks became leading innovators in the personal-service and hair-care industry, establishing luxurious barbershops, bathhouses, and hotels. In Mississippi, where there were fewer than a thousand free blacks and over four hundred thousand slaves, slave-born William Johnson (1809–1851) purchased his freedom and founded a successful barbershop and bathhouse in Natchez. Johnson used his profits to develop other enterprises, such as money brokerage, real estate leasing, a toy shop, a drayage business, and agriculture. He owned slaves, some of whom worked in his barbershop and on his plantation, while others were hired out. The most successful hairdresser in the North was Joseph Cassey of Philadelphia, whose estate was valued at $75,000 in 1849. Cassey's wealth also included profits from moneylending enterprises.

Another prominent African American in the hair-care business and an early African-American philanthropist was Pierre Toussaint (1766–1853), a Haitian immigrant who became one of New York's leading hairdressers. Toussaint was generous in his support of the Roman Catholic church and the education of young men studying for the priesthood. During the 1840s the three Remond sisters, Cecilia, Maritcha, and Caroline Remond Putnam—members of a prominent African-American abolitionist and business family (their mother was a successful caterer)—established the exclusive Ladies Hair Works Salon in Salem, Mass. In addition to promoting the sale of Mrs. Putnam's Medicated Hair Tonic and other products both locally and nationally (through mail-order distribution), they opened the largest wig factory in the state.

Black entrepreneurs also flourished in the clothing industry, as African-American tailors and dressmakers became leading designers in American fashion. Perhaps best known was Mary Todd Lincoln's dressmaker, Elizabeth Keckley (1818–1907), who employed twenty seamstresses at the height of her enterprise.

During the antebellum period Philadelphia and New York became the leading centers for black catering businesses. The most prominent caterers of Philadelphia were Robert Bogle, Peter Augustine, the Prossers, Thomas DORSEY, Henry Minton, and Eugene Baptiste. Much of the $400,000 in property owned by free Phila-

Elizabeth Keckley, a dressmaker, purchased her freedom in 1855 through a loan from her customers. She eventually moved from St. Louis to Washington, D.C., where she became one of the capital's elite dressmakers and in 1868 worked in the White House as Mary Todd Lincoln's dressmaker. (Moorland-Spingarn Research Center, Howard University)

delphia blacks in 1840 belonged to caterers. New York's Edward V. Clark was listed as a jeweler in the R. G. Dun mercantile credit records; yet he operated a successful catering business, which included lending out silver, crystal, and china for his catered dinners. In 1851 Clark's merchandise was valued at $5,000.

During the War of 1812, Thomas Downing established a famous oyster house and restaurant on Wall Street, which became a noted attraction for foreign tourists and the haunt of the elite in business and politics. In 1844 Thomas's son, George T. Downing (1819–1903), founded the Sea Girt Hotel, housing businesses on the first floor and luxury rooms above. Twelve years after the Civil War, Downing expanded his food-service business to Washington, D.C., where he was known as "the celebrated colored caterer."

Samuel T. Wilcox of Cincinnati, who established his business in 1850 and relied primarily on the Ohio and Mississippi riverboat trade, was the most successful black entrepreneur in wholesale food distribution. Before the Civil War Wilcox's annual sales exceeded $100,000; his estate was valued at $60,000. Solomon Humphries, a free black in Macon, Ga., owned a grocery valued at $20,000. In upstate New York William Goodridge developed a number of diverse enterprises, including a jewelry store, an oyster company, a printing company, a construction company, and a large retail merchandise store, while running a train on the Columbia Railroad. In 1848 Goodridge earned a reported business capital of $20,000 in addition to real estate holdings in both New York and Canada. In Virginia the slave Robert Gordan managed his owner's coal yard and established a side business whose profits amounted to somewhere around $15,000. After purchasing his freedom, Gordan used the capital to start a profitable coal business in Cincinnati and by 1860 reported annual earnings of $60,000 from coal and real estate profits.

The extractive industries proved to be a source of wealth for slave-born Stephen Smith (1797–1873), a Pennsylvania lumber and coal merchant, bank founder, and investor in real estate and stock who was known as "Black Sam." The R. G. Dun mercantile credit records list his wealth at $100,000 in 1850 and $500,000 in 1865. Smith, whose wife ran an oyster house, obtained his start in business as the manager of his owner's lumberyard. William Whipper (1804–1876), Smith's partner in the lumber business from 1835 to 1836, started out in the steam-scouring business. Whipper, who, like Smith, had extensive real estate holdings, was a cashier in the Philadelphia branch of the Freedman's Savings Bank from 1870 to 1874, with reported assets (registered in the 1870 census) amounting to $107,000. Both men were leaders in abolitionist activities and provided financial support to black institutions.

Eight of the wealthiest antebellum African-American entrepreneurs were slaveholders from Louisiana who owned large cotton and sugar plantations. Marie Metoyer (1742–1816), also known as Coin-Coin, the daughter of African-born slaves, was freed in 1796 at the age of forty-six and acquired several hundred slaves as well as ten thousand acres of land. The Metoyer family's wealth amounted to several hundred thousand dollars. Urban black businessmen and women in Louisiana also owned productive slaves: CeCee McCarty of New Orleans, a merchant and money broker who owned a train depot and used her slaves as a traveling sales force, accumulated $155,000 from her business activities. Most of the wealthy black entrepreneurs lived in New Orleans: the Soulie Brothers, Albin and Bernard, accumulated over $500,000 as merchants and brokers; Francis La Croix, a tailor and real estate speculator, declared assets of $300,000; and Julien La Croix, a grocer and real estate speculator, reported assets totaling $250,000.

The developing frontier continued to provide entrepreneurial opportunities to African Americans. William Leidesdorff, a rancher and businessman in San Francisco during the last years of Mexican rule, died in debt in 1848; shortly afterward, gold was discovered on his property, and the value of his estate leaped to well over a million dollars. While still a slave, "Free" Frank McWorter (1777–1854) established a saltpeter factory in Kentucky during the War of 1812. Profits from the mining of crude niter, the principal ingredient used in the manufacture of gunpowder, enabled McWorter to purchase freedom for his wife in 1817 and for himself two years later. After he was freed, McWorter expanded his saltpeter enterprise and engaged in commercial farming and land speculation activities. In 1830 he moved to Illinois, where in 1836 he founded the town of New Philadelphia, the first town promoted by an African American, though both blacks and whites purchased New Philadelphia town lots. By the time he died, McWorter had been able to free a total of sixteen family members from slavery.

Antebellum blacks, both slave and free, profited significantly from the construction industry. The most resourceful slave entrepreneur in this field was Anthony Weston, who built rice mills and improved the performance of rice-thrashing machines. By 1860 Weston's property in real estate and slaves—purchased in his wife's name, since she was a free black—was valued at $40,075. Slave-born Horace King (1807–1885) worked as a covered-bridge builder in Alabama and Georgia. After being freed in 1846, King established a construction company that was eventually expanded to include construction projects for housing and commercial institutions. After King's death the company was renamed the King Brothers Construction Company and overseen by his sons and daughter.

1865–1929

By the time the Civil War ended in 1865, over twenty-five hundred African-American businesses had been established by slaves and free blacks. Despite the difficulties that blacks experienced with regard to continuing social, political, and economic inequalities, the end of slavery did bring about a much wider range of prospects for budding African-American entrepreneurs. It was during this time that the first black millionaires emerged.

Health and beauty-aid enterprises, real estate speculation, and the development of financial institutions such as banks and insurance companies provided the basis for the wealth accumulated by many of the most successful black entrepreneurs. The food- and personal-service industries continued to be sources of income. Durham, N.C., and Atlanta, Ga., became the commercial centers for black America. The numbers of blacks involved in business steadily increased: In 1890, 31,000 blacks were engaged in business; their numbers rose to 40,455 in 1900 and to 74,424 in 1920.

Many leading black entrepreneurs of this era were either slave-born or had slave-born parents. Others had only limited formal educations and often started as unskilled workers or laborers. A number of African-American businesses were farm related. In 1900 Junius C. Graves, who owned five hundred acres of Kansas land valued at $100,000, became known as the Negro Potato King. Perhaps the most successful black entrepreneur of the Reconstruction era was Benjamin Montgomery (1819–1877), a slave of Joseph Davis (brother of the Confederate president, Jefferson Davis). In 1866 Joseph Davis sold his cotton plantations to Montgomery for $300,000. In addition to establishing a retail store on the Davis plantation in 1842, Montgomery had managed the Davis plantation from the 1850s on. In 1871 Dun gave Montgomery—who continued to run both enterprises with his sons as commission merchants—an A credit rating, ranking his family among the richest planter merchants and noting: "They are negroes, but negroes of unusual intelligence & extraordinary bus[iness] qualifications." The Montgomerys registered a net worth of $230,000 in 1874 but suffered severe setbacks several years later when crops failed and cotton prices declined. In 1881 the family was unable to make payments on interest and capital and the property reverted to the Davis family by auction. In 1887 Benjamin Montgomery's son Isaiah Montgomery migrated to Mississippi and founded the all-black town of Mound Bayou, where black enterprise was encouraged and where, in 1904, Charles Banks (1873–1923) founded the Bank of Mound Bayou and the Mound Bayou Loan and Investment Company.

By the turn of the century, some of the most successful black entrepreneurs had already begun to discover a national black consumer market. In 1896 Richard H. Boyd, a Baptist minister (1843–1922), established the National Baptist Publishing House in Nashville, Tenn., with a printing plant that covered half a city block. In 1910 the annual company payroll amounted to $200,000. Under Boyd's management the publishing house earned $2.4 million in just under ten years and by 1920 was one of the largest black businesses in the nation. But Boyd did not limit his business enterprises to religious publishing. His holdings included the One Cent Savings and Bank Trust, which he founded in 1904 (and which became the Citizens Savings Bank and Trust in 1920), the *Nashville Globe* (established in 1905), the National Negro Doll Company (1909–1929), the National Baptist Church Supply Company, and the Union Transportation Company. Union Transportation owned five steam-driven buses and fourteen electric buses, carrying twenty passengers each. This company was founded in 1905 to support a black bus boycott in response to the segregated streetcar ordinance that Nashville had passed that year. By 1993 four generations of Boyds had continued their ownership of the publishing house and Citizens Bank; as of that year the assets of the bank alone totaled $118.3 million.

Urban real estate investment and speculation ventures continued to be the major source of wealth for some of the leading black entrepreneurs during this era. In New Orleans Thomy La Fon (1810–1893), whose real estate activities began before the Civil War, left an estate valued at over $700,000. In St. Louis slave-born James Thomas (1827–1913) used the profits from his exclusive barbershop to invest in real estate; his property holdings exceeded $400,000 by 1879. In Memphis slave-born Robert Church (1839–1912) accumulated over $700,000 from real estate investments and speculation. His first enterprises were a bar, gambling hall, and pawnshop. Church Park, which he developed on Beale Street as a recreation center, included an auditorium used for annual conventions of black organizations and a concert hall that featured black entertainers. Church also founded the Solvent Bank and Trust Company.

The late nineteenth century marked the founding of large-scale black banks and insurance companies. In

1899 slave-born John Merrick (1859–1919) of Durham founded the North Carolina Mutual and Provident Company, which as of 1993 still ranked first on *Black Enterprise*'s list of black-owned insurance companies with assets of nearly $218 million. Merrick had little formal education and was a barber by trade; his initial business activities included a chain of barbershops as well as real estate investments. He also founded a land company, the Mechanics and Farmers Bank (1907), and the Durham Textile Mill. Indeed, while Chicago and New York were only emerging as important centers of African-American enterprise in the early decades of the twentieth century, Durham's black business district had come to be known as the Capital of the Black Middle-Class. "At the turn of the century," John Sibley Butler noted, "commentators were as excited about North Carolina as they are today about the Cuban-American experience in Miami." Atlanta was also rapidly rising to prominence as a center for black business. Slave-born Alonzo Franklin Herndon (1858–1927), who founded the Atlanta Life Insurance Company in 1905, left an estate valued at more than $500,000. Herndon's real estate investments and lavishly appointed barbershops—which catered to an elite white clientele—provided profits for the start-up and expansion of Atlanta Life.

In some cases, the overly rapid expansion of business enterprises led to bankruptcy. Atlanta businessman Edward Perry (1873–1929) established the Standard Life Insurance Company in 1913 and the Citizens Trust Bank in 1921. With the income from his Service Realty Company and Service Engineering and Construction Company, both founded in the 1920s, Perry purchased land on Atlanta's west side and constructed some five hundred homes. By 1925 he had established eleven different businesses together valued at $11 million and providing employment for twenty-five hundred people. Perry lost all of his holdings within four years. His contemporaries blamed his bankruptcy on imprudent expansion, limited capital reserves, and injudicious business decisions. An insurance company founder and winner of the NAACP's Spingarn Medal in 1927, Anthony Overton (1865–1945) was another black businessman whose success in the early decades of the century was followed by bankruptcy in the depression years.

Real estate, an enterprise crucial to the growth of northern black communities, offered similar opportunities for rapid expansion, sometimes with disastrous results. Jesse Binga (1865–1950) began his real estate operations on the south side of Chicago in 1905. Three years later he founded the first black-owned bank in the North, which in 1921 became the Binga State Bank. In 1929 he constructed the five-story Binga Arcade to revitalize the deteriorating black business district. Later that year, when his bank failed, Binga's wealth was assesssed at more than $400,000; he was convicted of fraudulent bank practices in 1933 and spent three years in jail. Like Herman Perry and James Thomas, Binga spent the rest of his life in poverty and obscurity. The same fate befell Harlem's Phillip A. Payton, Jr. (1876–1917), who organized a consortium of black investors to found the Afro-American Realty Company in 1904. Within two years the company controlled $690,000 in rental properties. Payton was largely responsible for opening Harlem as a community to African Americans; subsequently, however, his stockholders charged him with fraudulent practices, and he went bankrupt.

Hair and beauty care, a less risky industry, proved especially profitable for black entrepreneurs. Annie M. Turnbo-Malone (1869–1957), founder of the Poro Company (1900) and a pioneer in the manufacture of hair- and skin-care products, is considered the first self-made American female millionaire. She began her business in Lovejoy, Ill., and eventually expanded to St. Louis, where she built a five-story manufacturing plant in 1917. The plant housed Poro College, a beauty school with branches in most major cities. In 1930 Turnbo-Malone moved her operations to Chicago and purchased a square city block on the South Side. She franchised her operations and, with national and international markets, reportedly provided employment opportunities for some seventy-five thousand people.

C. J. Sarah Breedlove Walker (1867–1919) was a Poro agent before she initiated her own hair-care-products and cosmetics business in St. Louis in 1905. The "Walker system" for hair included an improved steel hot comb that revolutionized hair straightening for black women. The business strategies of the company—which employed over five thousand black women as agents who disseminated information on the Walker hair-care system in a marketing and employee-incentive program that utilized a national and international network of marketing consultants—presaged the practices of modern cosmetics firms.

The World War I era also witnessed the growth of black-owned publishing businesses. In 1905 Robert Abbott (1870–1940) founded the *Chicago Defender*, the first black newspaper with a mass circulation. The *Defender* used sensationalized news coverage to attract a large audience and was outspoken in its condemnation of racial injustice. By 1920 it had a circulation of over 200,000, with national circulation exceeding local sales. At Abbott's death the *Defender* was valued at $300,000. Abbott's successor, his nephew John H. Sengstacke, went on to establish Sengstacke Enterprises, which, with the *Defender* and ten other papers, became the largest black newspaper chain in America.

As media opportunities grew, African Americans became increasingly visible in the entertainment industry. One of the most successful black entrepreneurs in this field was Harry Herbert Pace (1884–1943). After founding Pace and Handy Music (1917), a sheet music company whose publications included W. C. HANDY's "St. Louis Blues," he founded the New York-based Black Swan Record Company (1921), the first record company owned by an African American. Black Swan's first success was Ethel WATERS's "Oh Daddy" in 1921, which sold 600,000 copies in six months. Pace, who wanted to tap a national market for his records, refused to record Bessie SMITH because he thought her music "too colored." By 1923 Black Swan was cutting six thousand records a day. Pace sold the company, at a hefty profit, to Paramount later that year. In addition, Pace's creative management and financial strategies promoted the growth of several black financial institutions, including Robert Church's Memphis Solvent Savings Bank (whose assets he increased from $50,000 to $600,000 in the years from 1907 to 1911) and Herman Edward Perry's Standard Life Insurance Company. In 1929 Pace engineered the merger of three northern black insurance companies to form Supreme Liberty Life Insurance.

In most cases African Americans could not gain access to the capital markets and financial resources needed for developing industrial enterprises.

Even as African-American entrepreneurs were branching out into new lines of business, many remained active in the catering and hotel fields. James Wormley (1819–1884), a caterer and restaurateur who built the five-storied Wormley's Hotel (1871) in Washington, D.C., ranked among the most fashionable black hoteliers. Wormley's hotel was patronized by leading politicians and foreign dignitaries, and he left an estate exceeding $100,000 in assets. In Philadelphia the tradition of catering, long an African-American resource, reached a pinnacle with the Dutrieulle family. Their catering business, established by Peter Dutrieulle (1838–1916) in 1873, lasted for almost a century, flourishing under the management of his son Albert (1877–1974) until 1967.

African Americans also profited in new areas of the food industry. C. H. James & Company of Charleston, W.V., a wholesale food processing and distribution enterprise founded in 1883, lasted for four generations of family ownership. From the time of its inception, the company's suppliers and buyers were primarily white; it was initially headed by Charles Howell James (1862–1929) and included a traveling dry goods retail operation. However, once the family decided to abandon the retail operation (in 1916) and limit the enterprise solely to the distribution of wholesale produce, the profits escalated to over $350,000. After a brief period of bankruptcy—caused by the stock market crash of 1929—the company was resuscitated by Edward Lawrence James, Sr. (1893–1967), and began to show a profit by the end of the 1930s. The company's survival was due largely to innovations in wholesale food distribution methods. Now headed by Charles H. James III (1959–), it remains one of the most successful black businesses in the country.

Up to the onset of the Great Depression, black entrepreneurial efforts were concentrated primarily on the service industry, since in most cases African Americans could not gain access to the capital markets and financial resources needed for developing industrial enterprises. The few blacks who attempted to capitalize on the demand for such modern industries as auto manufactures, movie production, and airline companies did not succeed. Nevertheless, the Great Migration of the early twentieth century caused a dramatic rise in northern urban black populations, and entrepreneurs were quick to seize the opportunities afforded by a new and rapidly expanding African-American consumer base. This growth was not matched in the South, where Jim Crow laws and societal racist practices restricted black enterprise to the same, increasingly depleted markets.

1930–1963

During the Great Depression the number of black businesses declined from 103,881 in 1930 to 87,475 in 1940. Among the few who prospered in those years was Texan Hobart T. Taylor, Sr., who used family money from farm property to start a cab company in 1931. The company continued to flourish during World War II, and Taylor added considerably to his wealth by investing the proceeds in rural and urban real estate. By the 1970s Taylor's assets were valued at approximately $5 million.

The food-processing industries remained a fairly stable resource for black entrepreneurs before, during, and after World War II. In the late 1930s California businessman Milton Earl Grant (1891–) started companies in rubbish hauling and hog raising. In 1947 he founded the Broadway Federal Savings and Loan Association in Los Angeles. By 1948 Grant had grossed some $200,000 from the sale of hogs; he invested the profits in real estate, and by 1970 his holdings exceeded more than $1.5 million. In Buffalo, N.Y., Cornelius Ford founded the C. E. Ford Company, a cattle brokerage firm, during the 1920s. Ford's business survived the depression and in the 1950s was yielding over $1 million annually from livestock trade and sales. His company was one of the chief buyers for Armour and Company for some twenty-five years. In addition, Ford became president of the Buffalo Livestock Exchange (the fifth largest in the nation), speculated in the Canadian cattle market, and leased railroad yards from New York Central.

George McDermmod, a potato chip maker and chief executive officer of Community Essentials, established a manufacturing plant in Crescent City, Ill., and a distribution plant in Detroit during the 1940s. As of 1950 McDermmod was selling his products to fourteen hundred dealers in nine states with gross business receipts amounting to over $100,000 annually. In Chicago Kit Baldwin established an ice-cream company that catered primarily to the black community and was reporting annual business receipts of $75,000 by the late 1940s. During this same period Detroit entrepreneur Sydney Barthwell established a drugstore chain of nine stores and manufactured ice cream. In 1948 Barthwell reported a staff of eighty full-time employees and gross business receipts in excess of $1.5 million.

The hair-care and cosmetic-manufacturing business also continued to attract black entrepreneurs. In Harlem Rose Morgan and Olivia Clark established the Rose Meta House of Beauty in 1947. Three years later they were earning $3 million from the sale of cosmetics and hair-care products in national stores and via international mail. Morgan and Clark's chain of beauty shops proliferated in major American cities as well as in Monrovia, Liberia; Cayenne, British Guiana; Puerto Rico; Cuba; and Jamaica. In New York City alone, their three shops employed three hundred people.

One of the most successful and wealthiest black entrepreneurs of the WORLD WAR II era was S. B. Fuller (1905–1988), whose Chicago business empire, Fuller Products, comprised health and beauty aids as well as cleaning products and real estate. Fuller's many investments included the famous Regal Theater, the Pittsburgh *Courier,* Fuller Guarantee Corporation, the Fuller Department Store, and various livestock operations. In 1947 he secretly purchased a cosmetic factory owned and operated by whites. By 1960 Fuller, who had begun his career in 1935 as a door-to-door salesman, reported a payroll of five thousand employees, white and black, and a three-hundred-product line that brought in over $10 million in sales. However, when Fuller's ownership of the cosmetic factory—the products of which were tailored to the needs of southern white consumers—was discovered in the early 1960s, his cosmetics were boycotted by whites, and he was unable to raise sufficient capital to offset his losses. In 1964 the SEC charged Fuller with the sale of unregistered securities and forced him to pay $1.5 million to his creditors. Although Fuller Products was resurrected from bankruptcy in 1972, it never recovered as a major black business.

Another financier who rose to prominence after the depression was Arthur George Gaston (1892–) of Birmingham, Ala. Gaston's business activities began with the founding of a burial society, which he incorporated in 1932 as the Booker T. Washington Insurance Company. Seven years later, with the proceeds from life and health insurance sales, Gaston established the Booker T. Washington Business College, the Gaston Motel, and the Gaston Construction Company. In 1952 he expanded his holdings with the Vulcan Realty and Investment Corporation, a real estate firm that financed the construction of office and apartment buildings, as well as the development of housing subdivisions. Gaston's Citizens Federal Savings and Loan Association—ranked seventeenth on the 1993 *Black Enterprise* list of financial companies—was founded in 1957. Additional enterprises included Booker T. Washington Broadcasting and a soft-drink bottling company. In 1987 Gaston sold ownership of his insurance, radio, and construction companies to the employees. In 1993 the Booker T. Washington Insurance Company ranked sixth on the *Black Enterprise* list of insurance companies, with assets over $43 million.

The 1940s and 1950s witnessed an increase in manufacturing opportunities for African-American entrepreneurs. The Grimes Oil Company of Boston, a petroleum products distributor, was founded in 1940 by Calvin M. Grimes; as of 1993, its sales had reached $37 million. In 1949 Dempsey Travis (1920–) founded the H. G. Parks Sausage Company in Baltimore. Subsequently, in 1990, Travis initiated the development of a middle-class townhouse project on Chicago's South Side.

1964–1994

The 1960s marked the emergence of a national network of large black businesses, many of which were founded on minute initial capital outlays. Johnson Publications began in 1942 with an investment of $250; the H. J. Russell Construction Company began in 1952 with a $150 truck; Berry Gordy started Motown for $700 in 1958. As the Civil Rights Movement gathered momentum in the late 1950s and early '60s, it became easier for blacks to obtain more substantial business financing; however, undercapitalized joint ventures persisted as a major method in the founding and development of new enterprises by African-American entrepreneurs. With few exceptions enterprises founded by black entrepreneurs remain relatively small private or family-owned companies. As of 1993 only eleven of the *Black Enterprise* top 100 businesses employed more than a thousand people.

In 1964, for the first time in the history of this country, the federal government took steps to provide assistance to black entrepreneurs by creating the Office of Minority Business Enterprises (OMBE), a division of the Small Business Administration (SBA), which was overseen in turn by the Department of Commerce. In 1969 President Richard M. Nixon issued executive order no. 11458, calling for the "strengthening of minority business enterprise"; by 1976 surveys showed that over two-thirds of the top black businesses had been started with support from the SBA. However, under Presidents Reagan and Bush progress toward business parity for blacks was visibly slowed.

The 1960s marked the emergence of a national network of large black businesses, many of which were founded on minute initial capital outlays.

While African-American businesses have continued to tap an African-American consumer market, black entrepreneurs have slowly expanded sales to include mainstream national and international markets. One ironic consequence of black economic success has been that some of the most profitable black-owned companies—such as Johnson Products and Motown Records—have since been acquired by larger, white-owned organizations. The first black company to have its stock publicly traded was the Johnson Products Company, which was founded by George S. Johnson (1927–) in 1954; it was listed for the first time on the American Stock Exchange in 1969. Johnson Products greatly increased its sales when it introduced a non-lye-based hair relaxer, Ultra-Sheen (developed by George Johnson), into the market in 1966. During the late 1960s Johnson developed another best-selling hair product, Afro-Sheen, in response to the newly popular Afro hair style; so successful were these and other items that his company controlled the market in black hair products throughout the mid-1960s and into the early 1970s. By the mid-1970s, however, a series of setbacks—mostly in the form of competition from new black- and white-owned companies—cost Johnson the leading market share; in 1989 he lost control of the company to his ex-wife, Joan B. Johnson, who then sold Johnson Products to IVAX for $67 million dollars in 1993. In its final year as a black company, Johnson Products ranked twentieth in the *Black Enterprise* top 100 of 1992, registering $46.2 million in sales.

The most prominent rival for Johnson Products was Edward G. Gardner's (1925–) Soft Sheen Products, established in 1964. Soft Sheen's most successful product, Care Free Curl, was introduced in 1979. Like Johnson, Gardner also had to compete with white companies—most notably Revlon and Alberto Culver—which controlled 50 percent of a $1 billion black hair-care market in 1988. By this time black enterprises were seriously theatened with losing the market to white corporations that had only recently entered the field. Black manufacturers launched an aggressive campaign to prevent white companies from gaining control and received support from Jesse JACKSON's Operation Push, as well as from John H. JOHNSON, publisher of EBONY and *Jet* magazines, and *Essence* founder Edward T. Lewis, both of whom refused to accept advertisements from white-owned companies in their publications. The white cosmetic giants escalated their strategies; by 1993 only five of the nineteen cosmetic companies in the black hair-care market were African-American owned. Black hair-care products remain an extremely profitable field. In 1993 Soft Sheen reported $96.6 million in sales and ranked ninth in the *Black Enterprise* top 100; Luster Products, reporting $46 million, ranked twenty-ninth; and Pro-Line, with $40.5 million, ranked thirty-fourth.

Berry Gordy's company, Motown Records, a subsidiary of Motown Industries, was the largest and most successful African-American enterprise in the entertainment field and the first to profit from the introduction of black music into the mainstream consumer market. Gordy's eight record labels, which recorded such groups as the Supremes and the Temptations, produced numerous hits on the pop and R&B charts. Almost from its inception Motown included Motown Productions, Hitsville, and the music publishing company Jobete. Most of Motown's holdings were sold to MCA Records for $61 million in 1988, and the company's listing was removed from *Black Enterprise.* As of 1993 Motown's gross business receipts totaled $100 million.

Motown's success served as a catalyst for African-American participation in the entertainment industry. Dick Griffey Productions, a concert-promotion and record company founded in 1975, has continued to flourish in recent years. Its founder, Dick Griffey (1943–) expanded into international markets by investing the company's proceeds in the African Development Public Investment Corporation, as well as in an African commodities and air-charter service, which he founded in 1985. In 1993 Dick Griffey Productions ranked fifty-seventh on *Black Enterprise*'s listing with sales of $26.5 million, while the African Development Corporation, registering sales of $57.8 million, ranked twenty-second.

Perhaps the most successful African-American entrepreneur of the postwar era was John H. Johnson (1918–), the owner of Johnson Publications. Johnson's business empire extends to various media corporations, Fashion Fair (a cosmetic company), radio stations, and television production companies. Founded in the 1970s, Fashion Fair has become the largest black-owned cosmetic company of the 1990s.

Black enterprise was greatly stimulated by an increasingly diversified African-American reading audience. Essence Communications, the parent company of *Essence,* a black woman's magazine, was founded in 1970 by four African-American men. Edward T. Lewis (1940–), the company's publisher and CEO, also established a direct-mail catalogue business before joining with J. Bruce Llewellyn and Percy Sutton in the purchase of an American Broadcasting Company (ABC) affiliate TV station in Brooklyn. In 1993 Essence Communications reported $71.1 million in sales.

In 1970 Earl G. Graves (1933–) launched *Black Enterprise,* a publication designed to address African-American interests in business and to report on black economic development. Soon afterward, Graves expanded his business interests by acquiring both a marketing and research company and EGG Dallas Broadcasting. In 1990 he joined Earvin "Magic" Johnson in purchasing the Washington, D.C., Pepsi-Cola franchise, of which Graves is CEO. In 1993 the franchise reported $49.3 million in sales, placing it twenty-sixth on the *Black Enterprise* listing; Earl G. Graves, Limited, ranked seventy-second, with sales of $22.4 million.

By the 1970s black entrepreneurs had managed to gain access to capital markets and were able to invest their wealth in a variety of business ventures. Some of the earliest black advertising agencies included the Chicago-based Proctor & Gardner Advertising, founded in 1970 by Barbara Gardner Proctor (1932–), and Burrell Communications Group, founded by Thomas J. Burrell (1939–) in 1971. In 1992 Burrell's client list included such megafirms as Coca-Cola, McDonalds, and Crest and registered assets in excess of $77 million.

One of the most promising businessmen to emerge during this period was New Yorker J. Bruce Llewellyn (1927–), who purchased FEDCO Foods Corporation, a Bronx chain of ten supermarkets, for $3 million. Llewellyn sold FEDCO for $20 million in 1984; the next year he joined basketball star Julius Erving and actor Bill COSBY in purchasing the Philadelphia Coca-Cola Bottling Company. Four years later Llewellyn bought Garden State Cable Television. By 1993 Garden State's assets registered $96 million, while Philadelphia Coca-Cola reported sales of $290 million, making it the third most profitable company on the *Black Enterprise* top 100 list.

By the 1970s black entrepreneurs had managed to gain access to capital markets and were able to invest their wealth in a variety of business ventures.

Entertainment entrepreneur Percy E. Sutton (1920–) pursued a political career (he was Manhattan borough president for several years) in addition to founding the Inner City Broadcasting Company in 1970. Sutton, who controlled the Inner City Cable and the Apollo Theater Group, expanded his interests with Percy Sutton International, which has built manufacturing plants in such countries as Nigeria. In 1989 Sutton estimated his net worth at $170 million.

Black participation increased significantly in the area of finance. Perhaps the most profitable business enterprise was the TLC Group, established by securities lawyer Reginald Lewis (1942–1993). Lewis purchased the McCall Pattern Company for $1 million in cash and $24 million in borrowed money; four years later he sold the company for $63 million. Aided by financing from Manufacturers Hanover Trust and Drexel Burnham Lambert, he then engineered a $985 million leveraged buyout of Beatrice International Companies, a large multinational corporation. Beatrice became the first billion-dollar black company, and in 1993 ranked first on the *Black Enterprise* top 100 list with $1.7 billion in sales (five times as much as the second company on the list).

Construction and land development executive Herman J. Russell (1930–), founder and CEO of H. J. Russell & Company of Atlanta, Ga., started out in 1952 as the owner of the H. J. Russell Plastering Company, a small private business. In 1959 Russell established the H. J. Russell Construction Company, which specialized in building single-family homes and duplexes. His involvement in large-scale private-sector commercial projects began in 1969, when he was commissioned to construct the thirty-four story Equitable Life Assurance Building in Atlanta. In the 1970s Russell obtained financing from the Department of Housing and Urban

Development (HUD) in order to construct twenty-nine housing projects with four thousand units for low- and middle-income families, while he maintained ownership of the properties. Other large-scale construction projects followed: the Atlanta Stadium, the Atlanta City Hall Complex, the Martin Luther King Community Center, and the Carter Presidential Center. In joint-venture projects with white construction companies, Russell built the parking deck for Atlanta's Hartsfield Airport, the Georgia Pacific fifty-two-story office building, and the addition to the Atlanta Merchandise Mart. He also joined with another African-American-owned construction company, C. D. Moody Construction, to place the winning bid for the $209 million Olympic Stadium contract in Atlanta for the 1996 games.

Russell has expanded his conglomerate to include many diverse businesses. H. J. Russell & Company is the parent company of several subsidiary firms, including Williams-Russell and Johnson, an engineering, architecture, and construction management firm. Russell also owns Russell-Rowe Communications, an ABC affiliate in Macon, Ga. In addition, the City Beverage Company and the Concessions International Corporation, which oversees food concessions in several major airports, are owned by Russell. In 1972 he secured the management rights to Atlanta's Omni sports-convention complex and a 10 percent ownership share of the National Basketball Association's Atlanta Hawks, anticipating by almost two decades the 37.5 percent interest, $8 million purchase of the Denver Nuggets by black entrepreneurs Bertram Lee and Peter Bynoe (1989).

During the past three decades many black athletes and entertainers have assumed entrepreneurial management positions by using their million-dollar salaries to develop new enterprises both inside and outside the sports and entertainment industries. For example, former Green Bay Packer football player Willie D. Davis (1934–) went on to earn an M.B.A. from the University of Chicago and found his own business, Willie Davis Distributing Company, in 1970. He sold the highly successful company (averaging annual sales of $25 million) in the late 1980s. Among Davis's multimillion-dollar enterprises are part ownership of five radio stations, significant shares in several companies, and the Alliance Bank of Culver City, Calif. Another successful athlete was football star Gale Sayers, who founded Crest Computer Supply in 1984, and by 1993 became the owner of a company whose annual sales amounted to $43 million.

One of the few very successful female entertainment entrepreneurs is television talk-show host Oprah WINFREY. In 1992 Winfrey became the highest paid U.S. entertainer, with earnings of $98 million. She has amassed a fortune of more than $250 million by controlling syndication of her talk show and founding the Harpo Production Company, a movie investment firm.

Naomi Sims (1949–), one of America's first successful black models, capitalized on the black hair-care-product market by designing and manufacturing wigs that approximated the hair texture of black women. In 1973 she established the Naomi Sims Collection. With sales of $5 million the first year, Sims expanded distribution to include an international market. A cosmetic line, Naomi Sims Beauty Products, Limited, was introduced in 1986, and by 1988 sales from those products exceeded $5 million.

Historically, black entrepreneurs have participated in the clothing industry as tailors and dressmakers but seldom as manufacturers of mass apparel. In 1989 Carl Jones (1955–) formed the first African-American-owned clothing manufacturing firm, the Los Angeles-based Threads 4 Life Corporation, doing business as Cross Colours. Cross Colours, which reported sales of $93 million in 1993, capitalized on the urban hip-hop, Afrocentric focus in dress, which came to prominence in the early 1990s. The company now has five clothing lines, including Cross Colour Classics, a line tailored to older and more conservative buyers. Jones's innovative Cross Colours Home, a home-furnishing line in which African fabrics and African-designed bed and table linens are featured prominently, is sold in Marshall Fields, I. Magnin, and Macy's.

New Jersey-based H. F. Henderson Industries, founded in 1954 by Henry F. Henderson (1928–), is an example of black participation in America's high-tech industries. Henderson specializes in automatic weighing systems, although most of the revenue for the company—which earned a reported $25.7 million in 1993—comes from defense contracts for the design and manufacture of control panels for the U.S. military. He began expanding his business in the 1970s with the Small Business Association's 8(a) program and a $125 million government contract; by the mid-1980s government contracts amounted to 50 percent of his business, with the private domestic sector accounting for 25 percent and the remaining 25 percent coming from an international market that included the People's Republic of China, Japan, Canada, Spain, and England.

Increasingly, black entrepreneurs are tapping markets on a global scale. Henderson, Sutton, Griffey, and George H. Johnson have all found international markets for their products. Soft Sheen's global expansion has taken place under the leadership of Edward G. Gardner's son, Gary, who purchased Britain's black-owned Dyke and Dryden, an import and manufacturing company that specializes in the distribution—primarily in Africa—of black personal-care products. Soft

Sheen West Indies was also established in Jamaica. In the 1960s and '70s entrepreneur Jake Simmons, Jr. (1901–1981), had used his earnings from the southwestern petroleum industry to invest in oil leases in West Africa.

Despite the development of multimillion-dollar businesses by African-American entrepreneurs, black business-participation rates remain low; only 3 percent of all companies in the United States are black owned, and in 1987 earnings from African-American businesses comprised only 1 percent of American gross receipts. And while black entrepreneurial participation in manufacturing has increased, only 1 percent of all black businesses are involved in this area of the economy. Publicly traded black companies remain few; indeed, only three black companies have taken this route. In 1971 Parks Sausage of Baltimore went public; it was taken over by a white private investment group in 1977 but was reacquired by the former black owners in 1980. In 1993 its sales reached almost $23 million. Robert Johnson, the founder of the Black Entertainment Channel, placed his company in public trading in order to expand his holdings. "It's time for African-Americans to think of company control in terms other than just percentage of black ownership," Johnson explained. "We should start thinking in terms of black control through the creation of value."

Despite the development of multimillion-dollar businesses by African-American entrepreneurs, black business-participation rates remain low.

The future of privately held black businesses in the late twentieth century remains unclear. It has been argued that in the 1990s access to capital and strategic alliances has led some black-owned companies to either go public or become amalgamated within larger, interracial concerns. Whether exclusive black ownership of black enterprises will remain central to the black economy is one of many questions black entrepreneurship will face as it enters the twenty-first century.

BIBLIOGRAPHY

Amos, Wally, and Leroy Robinson. *The Famous Amos Story: The Face That Launched a Thousand Chips.* New York, 1983.

Bailey, Ronald. *Black Business Enterprise.* New York, 1973.

Bates, Timothy, and William Bradford. *Financing Black Economic Development.* New York, 1979.

Butler, John Silbey. *Entrepreneurship and Self-Help Among Black Americans: A Reconsideration of Race and Economics.* Albany, N.Y., 1991.

Cross, Theodore. *Black Capitalism.* New York, 1969.

Du Bois, W. E. B. *Economic Co-operation Among Negro Americans.* Atlanta, 1907.

———. *The Negro in Business.* Atlanta, 1899.

Gatewood, Willard. *Aristocrats of Color: The Black Elite, 1880–1920.* Bloomington, Ind., 1990.

George, Nelson. *Where Did Our Love Go? The Rise and Fall of the Motown Sound.* New York, 1986.

Green, Shelley, and Paul Pryde. *Black Entrepreneurship in America.* New Brunswick, N.J., 1990.

Hamilton, Kenneth Marvin. *Black Towns and Profit: Promotion and Development in the Trans-Appalachian West.* Urbana, Ill., 1991.

Harmon, J. H., Jr., Arnett G. Lindsay, and Carter G. Woodson. *The Negro as Businessman.* 1929. Reprint. New York, 1969.

Harris, Abram L. *The Negro Capitalist: A Study of Banking and Business Among Negroes.* 1936. Reprint. New York, 1968.

Henderson, Alexa Benson. *Atlanta Life Insurance: Guardians of Black Economic Dignity.* Tuscaloosa, Ala., 1990.

———. "Henry E. Perry and Black Enterprise in Atlanta, 1908–1925." *Business History Review* 61 (Summer 1987): 216–242.

Hund, James. *Black Entrepreneurship.* Belmont, Calif., 1970.

Johnson, Frank J. *Who's Who of Black Millionaires.* Fresno, Calif., 1984.

Johnson, John H., and Lerone Bennett, Jr. *Succeeding Against the Odds.* New York, 1989.

Kinzer, Robert, and Edward Sagarin. *The Negro in American Business: Conflict Between Separatism and Integration.* New York, 1950.

Oak, Vishnu V. *The Negro's Adventure in General Business.* Yellow Springs, Ohio, 1949.

Ofari, Earl. *The Myth of Black Capitalism.* New York, 1970.

Osborne, Alfred. "Emerging Entrepreneurs and the Distribution of Black Enterprise." In *Managing Take-off in Fast Growth Companies: Innovations in Entrepreneurial Firms.* New York, 1986.

Pierce, Joseph A. *Negro Business and Negro Business Education: Their Present and Prospective Development.* New York, 1947.

Schweninger, Loren. *Black Property Owners: The South, 1790–1915.* Urbana, Ill., 1991.

———, ed. *From Tennessee Slave to St. Louis Entrepreneur: The Autobiography of James Thomas.* Columbia, Mo., 1984.

Walker, Juliet E. K. "Entrepreneurs, Slave." In the *Dictionary of Afro-American Slavery.* Westport, Conn., 1988.

———. "Entrepreneurs [Women] in Antebellum America." In *Black Women in America: An Historical Encyclopedia.* New York, 1993.

———. *Free Frank: A Black Pioneer on the Antebellum Frontier.* Lexington, Ky., 1983.

———. "Prejudices, Profits, Privileges: Commentaries of 'Captive Capitalists': Antebellum Black Entrepreneurs." *Economic and Business History* 8 (1990): 399–422.

———. "Racism, Slavery, and Free Enterprise: Black Entrepreneurship in the United States Before the Civil War." *Business History Review* 60 (1986): 343–382.

Washington, Booker T. *The Negro in Business.* 1907. Reprint. Chicago, 1969.

Weare, Walter B. *Black Business in the New South: A Social History of the North Carolina Mutual Life Insurance Company.* Urbana, Ill., 1973.

Whitten, David O. "A Black Entrepreneur in Antebellum Louisiana." *Business History Review* 45 (1971): 210–219.

— JULIET E. K. WALKER

EPISCOPALIANS

Although the first African-American Episcopal Church, St. Thomas African Episcopal Church in Philadelphia, was consecrated on July 29, 1794, with Absalom JONES as the first priest, the history of the African-American affiliation with the Episcopal Church began with the baptism of African slave children in seventeenth century Virginia, Maryland, and the Carolinas, where most eastern seaboard planters belonged to the Church of England. While some devout masters baptized slave children, others, suspecting that Christianity might legally or morally undermine their slaves' subordinate status, expressed indifference to religious training for slaves and resisted slave conversions. In spite of resistance in the colonies, several Anglican missionaries began training and baptizing slaves as early as 1695. The Church of England Christianized slaves and Native Americans through the English Society for the Propagation of the Gospel in Foreign Parts (SPG), which was founded in 1701. The first schools for blacks in the colonies were organized by the SPG in the early eighteenth century. Through the SPG, the Church of England became the first church to take Christianity to slaves in the British North American colonies and became the earliest denomination to train blacks to be missionaries.

During the colonial period the Church of England and the SPG established Sunday schools and catechetical schools for missionary training and adult education of slaves. Since baptism and religious instruction depended upon the masters' and mistresses' attitude, SPG efforts to induce masters to send slaves to regular catechetical instructions met with inconsistent results. While some masters encouraged slave baptism and conversion, many other colonists and Anglican ministers continued to ignore the religious lives of slaves throughout the colonial period. Other colonists apprehensively questioned SPG activities, rejected slave presence at the communion table, and doubted the qualifications of African Americans for Christian salvation and church participation.

An Easter procession exiting an Episcopal church in Chicago in 1941. Black Episcopal congregations were favored places of worship of the black middle class. (Prints and Photographs Division, Library of Congress)

Though at midcentury the Church of England had the most extensive work of any denomination among slaves in the southern colonies, the AMERICAN REVOLUTION disrupted the church's work and led to the complete reorganization of the Church of England in America into a separate denomination, the Protestant Episcopal Church of America, in 1787. In addition to losing the momentum and experience of seven decades of work among slaves, the church lost the most influential catalyst for bringing slaves into the Episcopal Church: the large number of Anglican southern aristocrats who were British sympathizers and loyalists. This contributed to the decay and disestablishment of the church in the southern states and the subsequent decline of their membership and the rise of the Baptists and Methodists.

Whereas in the colonial period black participation in the Anglican Church had been centered among slaves in eastern seaboard cities and on plantations, antebellum black Episcopalians were predominantly free blacks living in northern cities who saw themselves as role models of black achievement, activism, and independence for other blacks, and as members of a higher social class, differentiated from the masses of illiterate, rural slaves.

Given the identification of the Episcopal Church with the middle and upper classes, the bulk of the antebellum free black community rejected the Episcopal Church in favor of affiliation with the Methodists and Baptists, whose egalitarian message and ease of conversion offered greater access to membership and the ministry. Catechetical teaching and literacy requirements inhibited black membership in the Episcopal Church and especially denied African Americans access to the Episcopal ministry. With no literacy requirements for membership in Methodist and Baptist churches, blacks could not only join these denominations, they could become ministers to their own people. While Episcopalians recoiled at the emotional expressiveness of black worship in song, dance, and shout, the Methodist and

Baptist evangelical traditions included these same worship styles. Free to lead their own congregations, black ministers could preach a message of liberation, and their congregations could claim this niche of cultural and political autonomy.

For the vast majority of antebellum blacks who were slaves, Methodist and Baptist membership and ministry were infinitely more accessible than Episcopalian affiliation on the expanding frontiers of plantation slavery. The farmers, planters, and slaves of Alabama, Mississippi, Tennessee, and other new states did not inherit the Anglican traditions of the eastern seaboard colonial aristocracy, but were instead claimed by the Second Great Awakening of Methodist and Baptist revivalism which not only brought slaves into Christianity in large numbers, but also provided fertile ground for the invisible slave church, led by black ministers and embraced by slaves who created African-American religious traditions.

By the end of the CIVIL WAR, these developments—limited access to membership and the ministry; rejection of African and evangelical traditions; and early geographic containment of the church on the eastern seaboard—placed black Episcopalians wishing to proselytize the freed slaves in the disadvantageous position of being in a church which required a highly literate ministry; rejected African folk traditions; afforded African Americans little independence or automony compared to the black Baptist church or the independent black Methodist denominations; and appealed to northern urban black communities rather than the majority of blacks in the rural South. Nonetheless, some of the most important leaders of African-American cultural and religious life were Episcopal priests, including James Holly (1829–1911), and Alexander CRUMMELL (1819–1898), both of whom, somewhat surprisingly given their denominational background, became ardent black nationalists.

In the two decades following the Civil War, the Episcopal Church's Freedman's Commission operated schools, hospitals, and churches, but failed to compete effectively against the missionary campaign launched by the predominantly black denominations whose membership swelled. To make matters worse, the black membership of the Episcopal Church drastically declined during RECONSTRUCTION when the Episcopal Church failed to accept black Episcopalians' demands for black ministers. For example, in South Carolina between 1860 and 1868 black membership in the Episcopal Church declined from 3,000 to less than 300.

By the 1880s, a slight increase in black membership from the small but growing black middle class in southern cities alarmed southern Episcopalians who had embraced the widespread reestablishment of white supremacy and segregation of the post-Reconstruction South. In 1883 the Sewanee Conference of Southern Bishops met in Sewanee, Tenn., and unanimously authorized diocesan segregation and placed the care of black congregations and ministers under missionary organizations. In response to this and other forms of church discrimination, Alexander Crummell, rector and founder of St. Luke's in Washington, D.C., founded the Conference of Church Workers Among Colored People in 1883 and the Women's Auxiliary to the Conference in 1894. Although the Negro Conference failed in its appeal to the General Convention to change the Sewanee Canon's endorsement of church segregation, they succeeded in getting the General Convention to appoint a Church Commission for Work Among the Colored People. The meetings of the Conference of Church Workers Among Colored People also provided black Episcopalians a forum in which they could meet each other, share their grievances, and formulate solutions to their ambiguous and limited role in the church.

As black Episcopalians entered the twentieth century, they confronted an ironic, complex dilemma which discouraged growth of black membership: While their own predominantly white denomination continued to discriminate against them by denying black clergy and lay persons full voting rights on diocesan councils and in the General Convention, the black denominations saw the majority of black Episcopalians as elite, privileged, and snobbish. From the 1880s to the 1930s, the Episcopal Church did not decide if black communicants should be separated into racial dioceses and missionary districts with their own bishops or if they should remain in a diocese and be given equal representation and perhaps a black suffragan bishop (a bishop without the right to become archbishop). In 1903 the Conference of Colored Workers asked that black churches be placed under the general church rather than the diocesan conventions composed of the same local white leaders who supported and upheld secular racial segregation and discrimination. Requests for redress of the inequality within the church at the 1905 General Convention went unanswered and revealed that sentiments among northern white Episcopalians were little better than those of the Sewanee Conference. Northern dioceses questioned African-American ordinations and promoted the idea of placing black congregations under the supervision of white parishes or under the direction of the bishop.

The question of independence was even more complicated, because black churches were not self-supporting. Black clergy salaries and black school supplies were paid by the Domestic and Foreign Missionary

Society or the American Church Missionary Society and their auxiliaries until 1912. In 1918 Edward T. Demby and Henry B. Delany became the first black suffragan bishops.

By 1921 the Episcopal Church had two black bishops, 176 black ministers, 288 African-American congregations and 31,851 communicants concentrated along the eastern seaboard from New York to Georgia. The church had failed to respond adequately to requests for a black ministry, though it had established schools during the late nineteenth century—not only primary and secondary schools, but also schools to train teachers, ministers, and missionaries to go to Africa. Like the churches, the schools also had a welfare status and received at least half of their funding from the American Church Institute for Negroes, Inc., the agency that disbursed general church funds for black education. In spite of extensive efforts for black education, these schools created few black members, churches, or ministers. Black students felt no necessary allegiance to or affiliation with the Episcopal Church. Rather, their training led to secular jobs and their membership remained with the predominantly black denominations. After decades of training blacks, the church continued to impede African-American ordinations and to maintain the dependent status of black congregations as subordinate churches.

The large urban African-American migrations following World Wars I and II failed to increase the numbers of black Episcopalians. Rather, the rural folkways of black Southerners made black Episcopalians even more estranged from the black southern working class that filled northern cities. As ever larger numbers of black Southerners entered the urban North, black Episcopal scholars and clergy attacked the spontaneous, emotional music and folk traditions of rural black southern church culture in the Methodist and especially the Baptist churches.

The CIVIL RIGHTS MOVEMENT of the 1950s and '60s and the Black Power movements of the 1960s and '70s evoked increasing racial consciousness among blacks within predominantly white denominations, including Episcopalians. Black Episcopalians confronted their historical dual identity crisis—one within the Episcopal church where black members and clergy had felt alienated, excluded, and invisible for almost two centuries, and the other in trying to identify with other black Christians, especially those in independent black churches.

Black Episcopalians responded to this new climate of racial awareness by forming the Episcopal Society of Cultural and Racial Unity and the General Convention Special Program in 1967. Formed out of the merger of the Conference of Colored Church Workers and Summer Schools of Religious Education, the Union of Black Episcopalians was founded in 1968 to confront the historically diminished role of African Americans in the Episcopal Church. More than twenty chapters in the United States serve 150,000 black members out of 3,500,000 Episcopalians. In 1972 the Union of Black Episcopalians had the church establish the Absalom Jones Theological Institute at the Interdenominational Theological Center in Atlanta. In 1973 the General Convention formed the Commission for Black Ministries, now the Office of Black Ministries, which compiles a directory of black clergy, convenes the Black Diocesan Executives, and acts as a clearinghouse for African-American clergy. In 1981 the church published an official supplementary hymnal *Lift Every Voice and Sing: A Collection of Afro-American Spirituals and Other Songs.* Since the 1960s a large influx of black Anglicans from the Caribbean and the development of new liturgies directed toward black parishioners have revitalized the African-American presence in the Episcopal Church.

Whereas the National Baptist Convention could claim a tradition of independence and the largest black Methodist denominations could embrace a strong tradition of protest, it seemed that the black Episcopal tradition could claim neither independence nor protest. Beginning in the 1960s black Episcopalians affirmed the strains of independence and protest within the African-American religious traditions by celebrating being Episcopalian and black. In recent years women have taken a more active role in the church. In 1976 the social activist, lawyer, and poet Pauli Murray became the first black female priest in the Episcopal Church; in 1980 Barbara Harris—a black woman—became the first female Episcopal bishop. Black Episcopal clergy joined the National Council of Black Churches in its attack on white domination of the National Council of Churches and in its efforts to improve the lives of urban blacks. Since 1973 the Episcopal liturgical calendar has included the celebration of Absalom Jones, the first black Episcopal priest.

BIBLIOGRAPHY

Bennett, Robert A. "Black Episcopalians: A History from the Colonial Period to the Present." *Historical Magazine of the Protestant Episcopal Church* 22 (1979): 312–321.

Bragg, George F. *Afro-American Church Work and Workers.* Baltimore, Md., 1904.

———. *History of the Afro-American Group of the Episcopal Church.* Baltimore, Md., 1922.

Brydon, George MacLaren. *The Episcopal Church Among the Negroes of Virginia.* Richmond, Va., 1937.

Hood, R. E. "From a Headstart to a Deadstart: The Historical Basis for Black Indifference Toward the Episcopal Church, 1800–1860." *Historical Magazine of the Protestant Episcopal Church* 51 (1982): 269–296.

Spencer, Jon Michael. "The Episcopal Church." In *Black Hymnody: A Hymnological History of the African-American Church.* Knoxville, Tenn., 1993, pp. 165–181.

– LILLIE JOHNSON EDWARDS

EUROPE, JAMES REESE

James Reese Europe (February 22, 1881–May 9, 1919), composer and conductor. Born in Mobile, Ala., Europe spent his formative years in Washington, D.C., where his father held a position with the U.S. Postal Service. The family was unusually musical; his brother, John, became a noted ragtime pianist, and his sister, Mary, was an accomplished concert pianist, choral director, and music teacher in the Washington public schools. James Europe attended M Street High School and studied violin, piano, and composition with Enrico Hurlie of the Marine Corps Band and Joseph Douglass, grandson of Frederick DOUGLASS. Other musical influences included Harry T. Burleigh (especially his arrangements of African-American spirituals), organist Melville Charlton, and composer Will Marion Cook.

Like Cook and Burleigh—who had both studied with the celebrated Bohemian composer Antonín Dvořák while he was directing the Prague National Conservatory of Music—Europe accepted Dvořák's assessment of the importance of African-American folk music as a basis for an American national music. He did not believe, however, as did many at the time, that popular forms of musical expression were necessarily vulgar or "lowbrow" and therefore lacked potential musical value. He was a consistent champion of African-American music and musical artistry at every level and in any form, including those (like jazz) that had yet to emerge fully.

After moving to New York City in 1903, Europe established himself as a leading composer and music director in black musical theater, contributing to such productions as John Larkins's *A Trip to Africa* (1904), Ernest Hogan's *Memphis Students* (1905), Cole and Johnson's *Shoo-fly Regiment* (1906–1907) and *Red Moon* (1908–1909), S. H. Dudley's *Black Politician* (1907–1908), and Bert Williams's *Mr. Lode of Koal* (1910). In April 1910, Europe and several fellow professionals (including Ford Dabney, William Tyers, and Joe Jordan) formed the Clef Club, a union and booking agency that substantially improved the working conditions for black musicians in New York City. Europe was elected president and conductor of the club's concert orchestra, a 125–member ensemble whose unusual instrumentation (consisting primarily of plucked or strummed instruments) he felt to be better suited to the performance of authentic African-American music than that of the standard symphony orchestra. The orchestra's 1912 Concert of Negro Music at Carnegie Hall was a historic event, and Europe and the orchestra repeated their appearance on New York's most famous stage in 1913 and 1914.

Europe was a consistent champion of African-American music and musical artistry in any form, including those (like jazz) that had yet to emerge fully.

In addition to developing "an orchestra of Negroes which will be able to take its place among the serious musical organizations of the country," Europe realized the practical importance to black musicians of taking advantage of the increasing demand for popular music to support the expansion of nightlife. Between 1910 and 1914, he built the Clef Club (and later, the Tempo Club) into the greatest force for organizing and channeling the efforts of black musicians in New York, providing musicians for vaudeville orchestras, hotels, cabarets, and dance halls, as well as for private society parties and dances. In 1913, as a result of his success in providing dance orchestras for the eastern social elite, Europe was recruited as musical director for the legendary dance team of Vernon and Irene Castle. Between them, they revolutionized American social dancing by making the formerly objectionable "ragtime" dances (turkey trots, one-steps, etc., which had been derived from traditional African-American dance practice) widely acceptable to mainstream America. The most lasting of the Castle dances, the fox-trot, was conceived by Europe and Vernon Castle after a suggestion by W. C. HANDY. Europe's association with the Castles led to a recording contract with Victor Records, the first ever for a black orchestra leader.

Late in 1916, Europe enlisted in the Fifteenth Infantry Regiment (Colored) of New York's National Guard and was commissioned as a lieutenant. Largely as an aid to recruitment, he organized a regimental brass band that became, when the Fifteenth was mobilized and sent overseas, one of the most celebrated musical organizations of World War I. As a machine-gun company commander, Europe also served in the front lines and was the first black American officer in the Great War to lead troops into combat. Upon his return to the United States in early 1919, he was hailed as America's "jazz king" for incorporating blues, ragtime, and jazz elements into his arrangements for the band. He received another recording contract and embarked upon a nationwide tour. During a performance in Boston, however, Europe was cut in a backstage altercation with a mentally disturbed member of the band. The injury did not appear serious at first, but his jugular vein had in fact been punctured, and he died before the bleeding could be stopped. Europe's funeral was the first public funeral ever held for an African American in New York City; he was buried with full military honors in Arlington National Cemetery.

Though Europe was not a composer of major concert works, his more than one hundred songs, rags, waltzes, and marches include several ("On the Gay Luneta," "Castle House Rag," "Castle Walk," "Hi There," "Mirandy") that exhibit unusual lyricism and rhythmic sophistication for their day. But it was as an organizer of musicians, as a conductor who championed the works of other African-American composers, and as an arranger and orchestrator that his genius was most pronounced and his influence the greatest. In this regard, Europe may properly be seen as an original catalyst in the development of orchestral jazz, initiating a line of development that would eventually lead to Fletcher Henderson and Duke ELLINGTON. Among the many individuals who acknowledged his pioneering influence were Eubie BLAKE and Noble Sissle (whose epoch-making 1921 musical *Shuffle Along* helped restore black artistry to the mainstream of American musical theater) and composer George Gershwin.

BIBLIOGRAPHY

Badger, R. Reid. "James Reese Europe and the Prehistory of Jazz." *American Music* 7 (1989): 48–68.

Welborn, Ron. "James Reese Europe and the Infancy of Jazz Criticism." *Black Music Research Journal* 7 (1987): 35–44.

— R. REID BADGER

EXODUSTERS

The exodusters were about 20,000 southern African Americans who migrated spontaneously to Kansas from Mississippi, Louisiana, Texas, Kentucky, and Tennessee in the spring of 1879 in fear that they would be reenslaved when Democrats consolidated control as RECONSTRUCTION ended. The Exodus to Kansas was the most spectacular manifestation of a widespread anxiety among southern freedpeople who sought bodily safety, personal autonomy, and their rights as citizens. They had seen enough of their former masters' conception of freedom to realize they were in danger.

Even before the violent campaigns that ended Reconstruction made hundreds of former slaves into refugees, white supremacists had inflicted frightful injustices upon freedpeople; farming arrangements and credit practices kept black families poor and landless. Political violence subverted attempts to engender meaningful democracy in state that had been run as oligarchies by the rich. The rights to vote, hold office, and send children to school all came under intense pressure—much of it blatantly illegal. The withdrawal of federal support, after the Panic of 1873, signaled to white supremacists that the freedpeople were fair game. Thus began a process, called "Redemption," that wrested control of southern states from blacks and Republicans by any means necessary.

The Exodusters were about 20,000 southern African Americans who migrated spontaneously to Kansas in the spring of 1879 in fear that they would be reenslaved.

To overthrow Reconstruction, white supremacists used murder, rape, arson, fraud, and intimidation. These terrorist campaigns indicated that after Reconstruction, not only would black men not be able to vote, but black people generally would lose the relative autonomy they had come to identify with freedom. Many blacks saw only one alternative to literal or virtual reenslavement: migration. In the late 1870s, black Southerners began a process of interstate migration that would eventually take one-half of the African-American population out of the South.

Exodusters headed to Kansas, which they knew as the quintessential free state, in hopes of homesteading on free government land and becoming independent farmers. To people who vividly recalled the oppression of slavery, farming their own land meant being their own masters. Although few of the migrants of the Kansas Fever Exodus (as it was called at the time) were able to claim and keep land as homesteaders in the long term, as Kansans they were able to achieve much more economic and political autonomy than they would have in the South. Given that Kansas eventually became a segregated state (one of the five U.S. Supreme Court cases that together are known as BROWN V. BOARD OF EDUCATION, which paved the way for the desegregation of American life after 1954, originated in Topeka, Kans.), the Exodus to Kansas was qualified, though a real success.

Some confusion exists over the issue of leadership of the Exodus to Kansas. The migration of 1879 was a leaderless, unplanned, millenarian movement, in which migrants trusted in God and the federal government to restore their rights as citizens. But Benjamin "Pap" Singleton (1809–c. 1889) of Kentucky and Henry Adams (1843–?) of Louisiana are often identified as its leaders. Both were champions of migration and poor men who had been slaves.

Singleton was a cabinetmaker from Nashville, Tenn., who had come to advocate migration to Kansas in the early 1870s—a sentiment he shared with Sojourner TRUTH, who visited Lawrence, Kans., in 1871. Although Truth did not actually guide migrants to Kansas, Singleton and his co-workers had some success in the business of migration. He made three trips to Kansas from Tennessee and in 1879 established the Singleton Colony in Dunlap, Morris County. His faith in migration out of the South continued in the 1880s, as he vainly sought refuge for his people overseas.

Henry Adams was a traditional healer, businessman, and political organizer from Caddo Parish, La., who turned to migration only after realizing that hundreds of blacks in northern Louisiana had lost their lives trying to vote or organize politically. In and around Shreveport, Adams and his fellow Union army veterans set up two grassroots networks during Reconstruction: The first, called simply the Committee, rallied voters and kept account of the casualties of white supremacist terrorism; its successor, the Colonization Council, corresponded with the American Colonization Society toward the goal of moving black Southerners to Liberia. Kansas was never Adams's destination of choice, for he remained convinced that only West Africa offered a safe haven for American blacks. Unlike Singleton, who felt his wisdom was divinely inspired, Adams was a tireless political activist whose work came to an end when political violence drove him into exile in New Orleans.

Both Singleton and Adams testified before a joint committee of the United States Senate designated to investigate the Exodus. While these two figures did not lead the Exodus to Kansas, they symbolized black Southerners' well-founded conviction that Democratic rule was against their best interests. After Reconstruction, blacks throughout the South sought sanctuary in Kansas, Indiana, and West Africa. The spectacular, millenarian Exodus of 1879 was merely the most visible indication that black Southerners had no faith in the self-designated "wealth and intelligence," the would-be natural leaders of the southern states.

In 1879, black and white observers divided over whether to support the Exodus to Kansas. In general, old abolitionists and radical Republicans of both races supported the exodusters' bid for freedom, but often with reservations. Blacks, especially, approved of migration out of the South, given the facts of political violence and economic exploitation, yet many would have preferred a carefully planned movement with educated leadership. While Henry Highland Garnet, Wendell Phillips, Sojourner Truth, William Lloyd Garrison, George T. Downing, John Mercer Langston, and Richard T. Greener supported the Exodus, the grand old man among black statesmen, Frederick DOUGLASS, was its unbending critic. Douglass had fled Maryland as a fugitive slave in 1838, but by 1879 he had become a high-ranking federal official; he excoriated the Exodusters for acting out of cowardice. Former confederates first denigrated the exodusters as dupes, then attempted to persuade them to come back home and work. In general, the exodusters' supporters were most concerned with what happened to black people. Critics thought in terms of the interests of the South as an economic whole that depended on the very low wage labor of black families who had no political rights.

BIBLIOGRAPHY

Athearn, Robert G. *In Search of Canaan: Black Migration to Kansas, 1879–80.* Lawrence, Kans., 1978.

Painter, Nell Irvin. *exodusters: Black Migration to Kansas After Reconstruction.* New York, 1976.

— NELL IRVIN PAINTER

F

FARD, WALLACE D.

Wallace D. Fard (?-c. 1934), religious and political leader. Little is known about the mysterious Wallace D. Fard, credited with founding the NATION OF ISLAM. Only the years of 1930 to 1934 are clearly documented. He claimed to have been born in Mecca, a member of the tribe of Kureish, to which the Prophet Muhammad belonged, and to have been educated in England and at the University of California. His detractors claimed he had been jailed in California for dealing in narcotics. Neither of these accounts of his life was ever confirmed.

Fard appeared in Detroit some time before 1930, peddling silks and raincoats and declaring that he was on a mission to secure justice, freedom, and equality for American blacks. He professed that he was an Islamic prophet and that redemption would come through Islam. Fard quickly gained a following, especially among recent immigrants from the South who were undergoing severe economic hardship. In 1930, he set up permanent headquarters for what he called the "Lost-Found Nation of Islam" in the Temple of Islam. He also organized the Fruit of Islam, a defense corps; the Muslim Girls Training Corps Class; and the University of Islam, a radically unconventional elementary and high school that Muslim children attended instead of public schools. Fard began the practice of substituting *X* for black Muslims' last names—disavowing their identities as slaves. The names were intended to be replaced later by their "original" Arabic names.

Little is known about the mysterious Wallace D. Fard, credited with founding the Nation of Islam.

Fard asserted that blacks were the first people on Earth, indicating their superiority to whites, whom he castigated as devils. Fard was a reputed nationalist, calling for racial separatism and self-determination in the form of an independent black republic within current U.S. borders.

The Nation of Islam gained mainstream public attention in Detroit in November 1932 when one of its members, Robert Karriem, "sacrificed" his boarder by plunging a knife into his heart. Press reports tried to link this crime to his involvement in the Nation of Islam. The movement, however, continued. After converting an estimated 8,000 Detroit blacks to the Nation of Islam, Fard disappeared in late 1933 or 1934. His followers used the mysterious circumstances of Fard's disappearance to deify him further, maintaining that he was God, although his successor as the Nation's head, Elijah MUHAMMAD, claimed to have accompanied him to the airport when he was deported.

While Wallace Fard clearly was important in the 1930s, his legacy in the large and influential Nation of Islam is most significant. Although his tenure with the organization was short, he continued to be revered as its spiritual leader. The Nation of Islam stated in an official publication in 1942, "We believe that Allah appeared in the person of Master W. Fard Muhammad, July 1930; the long-awaited 'Messiah' of the Christians and the 'Mahdi' of the Muslims."

BIBLIOGRAPHY

Evanzz, Karl. *The Judas Factor: The Plot to Kill Malcolm X.* New York, 1992.

White, John. *Black Leadership in America: From Booker T. Washington to Jesse Jackson.* New York, 1990.

— SIRAJ AHMED

FARRAKHAN, LOUIS ABDUL

Louis Abdul Farrakhan (May 17, 1933–). Louis Eugene Walcott was born in the Bronx, N.Y., but was raised in Boston by his West Indian mother. Deeply religious, Walcott faithfully attended the Episcopalian church in his neighborhood and became an altar boy. With the rigorous discipline provided by his mother and his church, he did fairly well academically and graduated with honors from the prestigious Boston English High School, where he also participated on the track team and played the violin in the school orchestra. In 1953, after two years at the Winston-Salem Teachers College in North Carolina, he dropped out to pursue his favorite avocation of music and made it his first career. An accomplished violinist, pianist, and vocalist, Walcott performed professionally on the Boston nightclub circuit as a singer of calypso and country songs. In 1955, at the age of twenty-two, Louis Walcott was recruited by MALCOLM X for the NATION OF ISLAM. Following its custom, he dropped his surname and took an *X*, which meant "undetermined." However, it was not until he had met Elijah MUHAMMAD, the supreme leader of the Nation of Islam, on a visit to the Chicago headquarters that Louis X converted and dedicated his life to building the Nation. After proving himself for ten years, Elijah Muhammad gave Louis his Muslim name, "Abdul Farrakhan," in May 1965. As a rising star within the Nation, Farrakhan also wrote the only song, the popular "A White Man's Heaven is a Black Man's Hell," and the only dramatic play, *Orgena* ("A Negro" spelled backward), endorsed by Mr. Muhammad.

After a nine-month apprenticeship with Malcolm X at Temple No. 7 in Harlem, Minister Louis X was appointed as the head minister of the Boston Temple No. 11, which Malcolm founded. Later, after Malcolm X had split with the Nation, Farrakhan was awarded Malcolm's Temple No. 7, the most important pastorate in the Nation after the Chicago headquarters. He was also appointed National Spokesman or National Representative after Malcolm left the Nation in 1964 and began to introduce Elijah Muhammad at Savior Day rallies, a task that had once belonged to Malcolm. Like his predecessor, Farrakhan is a dynamic and charismatic leader and a powerful speaker with an ability to appeal to masses of black people.

In February 1975, when Elijah Muhammad died, the Nation of Islam experienced its largest schism. Wallace Dean Muhammad, the fifth of Elijah's six sons, was surprisingly chosen as supreme minister by the leadership hierarchy. In April 1975 Wallace, who later took the Muslim title and name of Imam Warith Deen Muhammad, made radical changes in the Nation of Islam, gradually moving the group toward orthodox Sunni Islam. In 1975 Farrakhan left the New York Mosque. Until 1978 Farrakhan, who had expected to be chosen as Elijah's successor, kept silent in public and traveled extensively in Muslim countries, where he found a need to recover the focus upon race and black nationalism that the Nation had emphasized. Other disaffected leaders and followers had already formed splinter Nation of Islam groups—Silas Muhammad in Atlanta, John Muhammad in Detroit, and Caliph in Baltimore. In 1978, Farrakhan formed a new organization, also called the Nation of Islam, resurrecting the teachings, ideology, and organizational structure of Elijah Muhammad, and he began to rebuild his base of followers by making extensive speaking tours in black communities. Farrakhan claimed it was his organization, not that of Wallace Muhammad, that was the legitimate successor to the old Nation of Islam.

In 1979, Farrakhan began printing editions of *The Final Call,* a name he resurrected from early copies of a newspaper that Elijah Muhammad had put out in Chicago in 1934. The "final call" was a call to black people to return to Allah as incarnated in Master Fard Muhammad or Master Fard and witnessed by his apostle Elijah Muhammad. For Farrakhan, the final call has an eschatological dimension; it is the last call, the last chance for black people to achieve their liberation.

Farrakhan became known to the American public via a series of controversies which were stirred when he first supported the Rev. Jesse JACKSON's 1984 presidential campaign. His Fruit of Islam guards provided security for Jackson. After Jackson's offhand, seemingly anti-Semitic remarks about New York City as "Hymietown" became a campaign issue, Farrakhan threatened to ostracize *Washington Post* reporter Milton Coleman, who had released the story in the black community. Farrakhan has also become embroiled in a continuing controversy with the American Jewish community by making anti-Semitic statements. Farrakhan has argued that his statements were misconstrued. Furthermore, he contends that a distorted media focus on this issue has not adequately covered the achievements of his movement.

Farrakhan's Nation of Islam has been successful in getting rid of drug dealers in a number of public housing projects and private apartment buildings; a national private security agency for hire, manned by the Fruit of Islam, has been established. The Nation has been at the forefront of organizing a peace pact between gang members in Los Angeles and several other cities. They have established a clinic for the treatment of AIDS patients in Washington, D.C. A cosmetics company, Clean and Fresh, has marketed its products in the black community. Moreover, they have continued to reach out to reform black people with the Nation's traditional dual emphases: self-identity, to know yourself; and economic independence, to do for yourself. Under Farrakhan's leadership, the Nation has allowed its members to participate in electoral politics and to run for office, actions that were forbidden under Elijah Muhammad. He has also allowed women to become ministers and public leaders in the Nation, which places his group ahead of all the orthodox Muslim groups in giving women equality. Although the core of Farrakhan's Nation of Islam continues to be about 20,000 members, his influence is much greater, attracting crowds of 40,000 or more in speeches across the country. His group is the fastest growing of the various Muslim movements, largely through the influence of RAP groups like Public Enemy and Prince Akeem. International branches have been formed in Ghana, London, and the Caribbean. In the United States, however, Farrakhan has remained an immensely controversial figure, as was best exemplified by the response to the Million Man March held in Washington, D.C. on October 16, 1995.

BIBLIOGRAPHY

Essien-Udom, E. *Black Nationalism: A Search for an Identity in America.* Chicago, 1962.

Farrakhan, Louis. *Seven Speeches by Minister Louis Farrakhan.* New York, 1974.

———. *A Torchlight for America.* Chicago, 1993.

Lincoln, C. Eric. *The Black Muslims in America.* Boston, 1963.

Lomax, Louis F. *When the Word is Given.* New York, 1963.

Mamiya, Lawrence H. "From Black Muslim to Bilalian: The Evolution of a Movement." *Journal for the Scientific Study of Religion* 21, no. 2 (1982): 138–151.

Marsh, Clifton E. *From Black Muslims to Muslims: The Transition from Separatism to Islam, 1930–1980.* Metuchen, N.J., 1984.

Muhammad, Warith Deen. *As the Light Shineth From the East.* Chicago, 1980.

– LAWRENCE H. MAMIYA

FATHER DIVINE

Father Divine (c. 1880–September 10, 1965), minister. Born George Baker to ex-slaves in Rockville, Md., he endured poverty and segregation as a child. At age twenty he moved to Baltimore, where he taught Sunday school and preached in storefront churches. In 1912, he began an itinerant ministry, focusing on the South. He attracted a small following and, pooling his disciples' earnings, moved north and purchased a home in 1919 in the exclusively white Long Island community of Sayville, N.Y. He opened his doors to the unemployed and homeless.

By 1931, thousands were flocking to worship services in his home, and his white neighbors grew hostile. In November they summoned police, who arrested him for disturbing the peace and maintaining a public nuisance. Found guilty, he received the maximum fine and a sentence of one year in jail. Four days later, the sentencing judge died.

The judge's sudden death catapulted Father Divine into the limelight. Some saw it as evidence of his great powers; others viewed it as sinister retribution. Although Father Divine denied responsibility for the death, the incident aroused curiosity, and throughout the 1930s the news media continued to report on his activities.

Father Divine's Peace Mission Movement grew, establishing extensions throughout the United States and in major cities abroad. He relocated his headquarters to Harlem, where he guided the movement, conducted worship services, and ran an employment agency. During the Great Depression, the movement opened businesses and sponsored a national network of relief shelters, furnishing thousands of poor people with food, clothes, and jobs.

Father Divine's appeal derived from his unique theology, a mixture of African-American folk religion, Methodism, Catholicism, Pentecostalism, and the ideology based on the power of positive thinking, New Thought. He encouraged followers to believe that he was God, to channel his spirit to generate health, prosperity, and salvation. He demanded they adhere to a strict moral code, abstaining from sexual intercourse and alcohol. Disciples cut family ties and assumed new names. His worship services included a banquet of endless courses, symbolizing his access to abundance. His mind-power theology attracted many, especially those suffering from racism and economic dislocation, giving disciples a sense of control over their destinies in a time filled with chaos and confusion.

Father Divine's appeal derived from his unique theology, a mixture of African-American folk religion, Methodism, Catholicism, Pentecostalism, and New Thought.

His social programs also drew followers. Although rigid rules governed the movement's shelters, they were heavily patronized. An integrationist, Father Divine campaigned for civil rights, attracting both African-American and Euramerican disciples. Challenging American racism, he required followers to live and work in integrated pairs.

With economic recovery in the 1940s, Father Divine's message lost much of its appeal; membership in the movement declined and Peace Missions closed. In 1946 he made headlines with his marriage to a white disciple named Sweet Angel. He spent his declining years grooming her for leadership. Upon his death in 1965, she assumed control of the movement, contending that Father Divine had not died but had surrendered his body, preferring to exist as a spirit. The movement perseveres with a small number of followers and businesses in the Philadelphia area.

BIBLIOGRAPHY

Watts, Jill. *God, Harlem U.S.A.: The Father Divine Story.* Berkeley, Calif., 1992.

Weisbrot, Robert. *Father Divine and the Struggle for Racial Equality.* Urbana, Ill., 1983.

– JILL M. WATTS

FAUSET, JESSIE REDMON

Jessie Redmon Fauset (April 27, 1884–April 30, 1961), writer and teacher. As literary editor of the CRISIS, the official journal of the NATIONAL ASSOCIATION FOR THE ADVANCEMENT OF COLORED PEOPLE (NAACP), Fauset published the early writings of Arna BONTEMPS, Langston HUGHES, and Jean TOOMER. She promoted the work of poets Georgia Douglas Johnson and Anne Spencer. But, although she is more often remembered for her encouragement of other writers, she was herself among the most prolific authors of the HARLEM RENAISSANCE. In addition to her poems, reportage, reviews, short stories, and translations that appeared regularly in the *Crisis,* she published four novels in less than ten years.

Born in what is now Lawnside, N.J., Fauset grew up in Philadelphia. Her widowed father, a minister, was the primary influence on her childhood. Her outstanding academic record won her admission to Cornell University, where she was elected to Phi Beta Kappa; she graduated in 1905. She taught high school French and earned an M.A. from the University of Pennsylvania, before W. E. B. DU BOIS hired her for the *Crisis* in 1919.

Her contributions to the *Crisis* were numerous and diverse: biographical sketches of blacks across the diaspora, essays on drama and other cultural subjects, and reports on black women activists and political causes. One of the few women to participate in the 1921 Pan-African Congress, Fauset recorded her vivid impressions of that meeting. Several of her best essays describe her travel to Europe and North Africa during 1925 and 1926. She reviewed and translated works by Francophone writers from Africa and the Caribbean.

Although she subtitled one of them "A Novel without a Moral," all of Fauset's books convey strong messages. *There Is Confusion* (1924) depicts the struggle of an educated, idealistic young woman to achieve her professional goal of becoming a concert singer without compromising her personal and racial pride. Fauset's best novel, *Plum Bun* (1929), uses the subject of "passing" to explore issues of race and gender identity. Its protagonist, another aspiring artist, learns that no success is worth betraying one's selfhood. In the foreword to *The Chinaberry Tree* (1931), Fauset explains that her purpose is to write about the "breathing-spells, in-between spaces where colored men and women work and love and go their ways with no thought of the 'problem.' " Blacks and whites were not so different after all. But as her final novel, ironically titled *Comedy: American Style* (1934), demonstrates, she did not ignore the problems of racism and sexism endemic to early twentieth-century American life. In general, however, Fauset's novels present sentimental resolutions to the complex problems they raise.

After resigning from the *Crisis* in 1926, Fauset returned to teaching. In 1929 she married businessman Herbert Harris and later moved to Montclair, N.J. She ceased thereafter to play a public role. Yet even after her death in 1961, her example continued to inspire. Not only had she probably published more than any black American woman before her, her fiction confirmed that not all the drama in African-American life revolved around interracial conflict.

BIBLIOGRAPHY

McDowell, Deborah E. Introduction to *Plum Bun* by Jessie Redmon Fauset. Boston, 1990.

Sylvander, Carolyn W. *Jessie Redmon Fauset, Black American Writer.* Troy, N.Y., 1981.

– CHERYL A. WALL

FEDERAL WRITERS' PROJECT

The Federal Writers' Project (FWP) was an arm of the New Deal's WORKS PROGRESS ADMINISTRATION (WPA) that gave employment between 1935 and 1939 to some 4,500 American writers, 106 of them (as of 1937) African-American. The great majority of FWP writers were hired to work on the American Guide Series, a collection of state guidebooks describing the distinctive folkways and histories of the country's different regions, both rural and urban.

A number of prominent African-American writers participated in the FWP. The Illinois project hired Margaret Walker, Richard WRIGHT, Willard Motley, Frank Yerby, William Attaway, Fenton Johnson, Arna BONTEMPS, and Katherine DUNHAM. The New York project hired Wright, Claude MCKAY, Ralph ELLISON, Tom Poston, Charles Cumberbatch, Henry Lee Moon, Roi Ottley, Helen Boardman, Ellen Tarry, and Waring Cuney. Zora Neale HURSTON briefly directed the Florida project, and Charles S. Johnson contributed to the *Tennessee State Guide.*

Because of the cutoff in federal funding in 1939, after which various FWP projects reverted to individual states, much FWP material never saw publication. But in addition to the sections on Negro history in several state guides, a number of important studies of black culture were generated by FWP writers on FWP-based research. Urban studies include: McKay, *Harlem: Negro Metropolis* (1940); Wright, *Twelve Million Black Voices* (1941); Ottley and William Weatherby, *New World A-Comin': Inside Black America* (1943); Ottley, *The Negro in New York: An Informal History* (1967); Bontemps and Jack Conroy, *Anyplace but Here* (1966); St. Clair DRAKE and Horace Cayton, *Negro Metropolis: A Study of Negro Life in a Northern City* (1945); Moon, *Balance of Power: The Negro Vote* (1948); and Gilbert Osofsky, *Harlem: The Making of a Ghetto* (1965).

Rural studies, drawn from the FWP's massive interviewing project of over two thousand ex-slaves from eighteen states, include the North Carolina project's *These Are Our Lives* (1939); the Savannah project's *Drums and Shadows: Survival Studies among the Georgia Coastal Negroes* (1940); Roscoe Lewis, *The Negro in Virginia* (1940); Benjamin Botkin, *Lay My Burden Down: A Folk History of Slavery* (1945); Charles L. Perdue, *Weevils in the Wheat: Interviews with Virginia Ex-Slaves* (1976); and George P. Rawick's nineteen-volume *The American Slave: A Composite Autobiography* (1972), subsequently supplemented (1977, 1979) by twenty-two additional volumes.

The materials gathered in the slave narrative collection, while flawed, continue to be widely used in studies of U.S. slavery. Sterling BROWN, the FWP's national editor of Negro affairs, encountered resistance from various state project heads who were reluctant to hire black interviewers or to adhere to Brown's goal of eliminating "racial bias . . . [that] does not produce the accurate picture of the Negro in American social history" (Gabbin 1985, p. 69). But Brown received support from other project directors and managed to insert substantial material about African-American history and culture into many state guides, as well as to foster the ex-slave interviewing project.

Some historians of slavery insist that because most of the FWP interviewers were white, the former slaves engaged in a self-censorship that "lead[s] almost inevitably to a simplistic and distorted view of the plantation as a paternalistic institution where the chief feature of life was mutual love and respect between masters and slaves" (Blassingame 1975, p. 490). Other historians, however, argue that "a blanket indictment of the interviews is as unjustified as their indiscriminate or uncritical use" and that the interviews constitute "the single most important source of data used to examine the 'peculiar institution' and its collapse" (Yetman 1984, pp. 189, 209).

In addition to contributing to the state guides and the slave narrative collection, a number of African-American writers wrote and published works of their own during their FWP tenure. Hurston published *Their Eyes Were Watching God* (1937), *Tell My Horse* (1938), and *Moses, Man of the Mountain* (1939); Attaway worked on *Blood on the Forge* (1941); Wright published *Uncle Tom's Children* and wrote *Native Son* (both in 1940); Bontemps published *Drums at Dusk* (1939); Walker wrote an unpublished novel about Chicago ghetto life, *Goose Island*, as well as an early draft of *Jubilee* (eventually published in 1966).

Zora Neale Hurston holding a copy of American Stuff *at the Federal Writers' Project booth at the* New York Times *Bookfair, November 1937. (Photographs and Prints Division, Schomburg Center for Research in Black Culture, The New York Public Library, Astor, Lenox and Tilden Foundations)*

The FWP experience did not simply provide these writers with financial support but significantly shaped the content and perspective of their writing. The project provided Hurston with recording equipment and transportation, enabling her to deepen her already established interests as a folklorist. Attaway's *Blood on the Forge* and Wright's *Twelve Million Black Voices,* which depict the cultural dislocation of southern sharecroppers in the industrial North, reflect central concerns of the Illinois project. Wright's *Native Son* was profoundly shaped by the FWP-based urban sociology of Cayton's and Drake's emerging Chicago School. Ellison's *Invisible Man* (1953), which treats black experience as both distinctly African American and broadly human, reflected the FWP's characteristic insistence that the United States is a harmonious blend of distinct cultural particularities.

The work performed by black writers in the FWP showed the project's preoccupation with the nation's diverse folkways. The FWP's distinct approach to diversity cannot be fully understood, however, apart from the influence of the cultural politics espoused by the Left—specifically, the COMMUNIST PARTY of the United States—in the era of the Popular Front (1935–1939). The FWP was not, as was claimed in 1939 by House Un-American Activities Committee head Martin Dies, "doing more to spread Communist propaganda than the Communist Party itself" (Penkower 1977, p. 195). But a number of FWP writers, black and white, worked in the orbit of the Left. The admixture of localism and universalism pervading many works of the FWP was strongly influenced by the cultural Left's pluralistic project of seeking the "real America" in "the people."

BIBLIOGRAPHY

Blassingame, James W. "Using the Testimony of Ex-Slaves: Approaches and Problems." *Journal of Southern History* 41 (1975): 473–492.

Gabbin, Joanne V. *Sterling A. Brown: Building the Black Aesthetic Tradition.* Westport, Conn., 1985.

Mangione, Jerre. *The Dream and the Deal: The Federal Writers' Project, 1935–1943.* Boston and Toronto, 1972.

Penkower, Monty Noam. *The Federal Writers' Project: A Study in Government Patronage of the Arts.* Urbana, Ill., 1977.

Yetman, Norman R. "Ex-Slave Interviews and the Historiography of Slavery." *American Quarterly* 36 (Summer 1984): 181–210.

– BARBARA CLARE FOLEY

FESTIVALS

From early colonial times to the present day, African Americans have created and observed an impressive calendar of celebratory and commemorative events: jubilees, festivals and anniversaries, "frolics" and seasonal feasts, fairs and markets, parades, and pilgrimages, not to speak of more private or secret ceremonies such as church meetings and revivals, family reunions, baptisms and funerals, and spiritual cults. These customs have received the casual or sustained attention of travelers, visitors, or local observers. They have been praised or disparaged, extolled as the epitome of a festive spirit that should prevail in any society and as the expression of an enduring, authentic culture, or dismissed as primitive, low-brow manifestations of a subculture, an unsophisticated, burlesque imitation of mainstream life, or, at best, an adaptation or appropriation of Euro-American customs.

This festive mood with which African Americans have been credited has encouraged the persistence of many prejudices and stereotypes fostered by the minstrel tradition, which represented blacks as a happy-go-lucky, careless, lighthearted people, prone to dancing and singing. This inclination for mirth has been interpreted as a sign that the predicament of slaves and their descendants should not be such a burden to the white mind and that their sufferings and the wrongs committed against them have been exaggerated.

Yet African-American celebrations, with all their unacknowledged complexities of forms and functions, are powerful symbolic acts that express, vehemently and with exuberance, not acquiescence to fate but needs, desires, and utopian will, disenchantment, anger, and rebelliousness. Communal, playful, or carnivalesque in character, they are events through which the community endeavors to build its identity, in self-reflective scrutiny and in constant confrontation with "the black image in the white mind," to question or challenge its basic assumptions. These feasts not only give the lie to and articulate the pain of certain truths, the ambivalence of a dream always deferred; they also define unexamined propositions in performances infused with subtle ironies and double entendre.

Among the "hallowdays" observed by northern slaves and free blacks, the coronation festivals or "negro elections" set the pattern for many civic feasts and festivals. Once a year in colonial New England, slaves were allowed to accompany their masters to election festivities where whites organized the election of their governors. In the 1750s, blacks started to organize their own similar celebrations, in which a leader, preferably African-born and of known royal ancestry, quick-witted and ready of speech, was elected king or governor, a title that endowed him with authority among both blacks and whites. (The title "king" or "governor" was used by blacks according to each New England colony's specific status: Governors were elected in colonies that were relatively autonomous, whereas kings were elected in colonies more closely tied to England. According to this custom, which endured through the 1850s, bondsmen confronted their African origin—the king was intermediary to the ancestors. Bondsmen also expressed their desire to have their separate institutions and to prove their ability for self-government.

Elections were prepared for by weeks of debates and meetings. A strong political message was conveyed to the community and to white rulers in a spirit that blended parodic intent and high seriousness. By ritually transferring power from the hands of the masters to those of one of their fellows, slaves were paving the way for their emancipation. Election days were perhaps the first freedom celebrations that combined the memory of the freedom and power Africans enjoyed before their capture with an anticipation of the freedom to come. The official recognition of African royalty and gentility reversed old stereotypes, which associated Africanness with savagery and lack of culture. The king was regarded as a civilized "negro" (the term "black" was not in usage as a noun then), composed and refined. These elections, prompted by the desire to counter forces of fragmentation and to ease conflicts, sought a consensus and struck a note of unity.

Coronation festivals were also indicative of white-black relations. The elected was often the slave of a prominent master, and slaves devised strategies to gain the support of masters to organize their ceremonies. The wealthier the slave owner, the greater the chance of having a grand festival, and, conversely, the greater the display, the stronger the evidence of the master's influence. While these feasts increased antagonism between blacks and poor whites, they offered an occasion to redefine slave-master relations, based on mutual claims and obligations. Negro kings held many roles as opinion leaders, counselors, justice makers, and mediators who could placate black insurgency or white fearfulness when faced with such a display of autonomy and self-rule.

There were other occasions when blacks gathered around a self-appointed leader. Pinkster is another well-known festival. Derived originally from the Dutch Whitsuntide celebration "pfingster," which the "Africs" took over in the late eighteenth century, the pinkster reached its peak in the early 1800s in Albany, N.Y. There the choice of a hill as the site for the celebration had many symbolic meanings. From the top of this hill, the low could look down on the world—an interesting reversal of the usual situation and a mock imitation also of the hills on which rulers like to set their capitols. Pinkster Hill was close to the place where many executions of blacks (accused in 1793 of having set fire to the city) had been staged. It was also close to the burial grounds, a military cemetery, and an all-black cemetery.

Thus death presided over the festivities, reminding blacks of the limits set on their freedom, of punishments inflicted on black rebels, of the failure to acknowledge or reward the achievements of black soldiers who had participated in the nation's wars, and of the intricate game of integration and segregation. The epitaphs and names inscribed on the graves emphasized the enduring character of African customs and rites. Cemeteries may have been the ultimate freedom sites, since only in death could blacks reach the absolute freedom they were celebrating.

Coronations and the pinkster exemplify a significant trend in the role granted to feasts: the official recognition of blacks' special gift for creating festive performances and their capacity for infusing it into other groups. (Native Americans, Germans, Dutch, and French attended the pinkster.) Feasts thus offered an arena for interaction and for the dream of a utopian and pluralistic order in a society divided by many social and political conflicts. Feasts were also an ironic comment on a republic that claimed to be dedicated to freedom but could still enslave part of its population, on the indignity of those who dared establish their power through the subjugation of others, and on the resilience of victims whose spirits could not be crushed.

Through the postrevolutionary era and in the antebellum years. African Americans evolved a tradition of emancipation celebrations that charted the different stages toward gradual, then complete liberation. This tradition, however, initiated at a time when blacks were experiencing a sense of betrayal and of the enduring precariousness of their situation, was conditional—the ought and the should prevailed. The future that was at stake was not only that of slaves and freed blacks, it was also the destiny of the nation and its aspiring democracy. These yearly occurrences were not marginal to black life; they were a political manifestation of jeremiad and claim making that was pursued deliberately, was announced and debated in the press, and involved major institutions, societies, and associations (churches, societies for mutual relief, temperance and benevolent societies, freemasons, etc.).

Emancipation celebrations were occasions for public appearances in marches and parades or at universal exhibitions. Many leaders, religious or political, seized these opportunities to address the world in sermons, speeches, orations, or harangues, developing race pride and race memory. There they assessed the contribution of black people in the building of the nation, their progress, their capacity for self-government, their commitment to liberty as a universal right. These feasts were not merely opportunities to celebrate on a large scale; they held out a promise to fashion new roles in a better world and wield new power, and they heralded a season of change, from enslavement and invisibility to liberation and recognition.

Both freedom and power were present in the ceremonies, not as mere allegorical figures but as fully developed ideas whose force needed to be conveyed to large audiences. Images and symbols were evolved and played out—in words, gestures, movements, and visual forms, with much ado and the will to adorn. The talents and gifts of black folks were put to use in a collective effort to stir and arouse consciousness and encourage action.

In the black calendar of feasts, Independence Day was the most controversial as well as the bleakest celebration. The solemnities of the Fourth of July encouraged African Americans to organize their own separate ceremonies and formulate their own interpretation of the meaning of these national commemorations. One is reminded here of Frederick DOUGLASS's famous 1852 address, "What Is to the American Slave Your Fourth of July?" Many black leaders urged their members not to observe that unholy day and proclaimed that persecution was not over and final emancipation still out of reach. July 4 thus became a menacing and perilous day, one on which blacks were more tempted to plan insurrection than to celebrate the republic, a day also when they were most exposed to violence, riots, arrests, and murder, as in New York in 1834 or New Hampshire in 1835. No wonder they looked for other sites and landmarks to construct an alternative memory.

After 1808, January 1 was adopted as a day of civic celebration. The time, New Year, coming right after the Christmas festivities, and the date, in commemoration of the official end of the SLAVE TRADE, seemed most appropriate. Yet, as in similar feasts, thanksgiving was tempered by ardent protest, and rejoicing by mourning and memories of the hardships of the Middle Passage. January 1 induced a heightened consciousness of Africa, where the black odyssey had begun. Africa became the central symbol and the subject of heated debate, especially when the colonization movement encouraging free blacks to return to Africa divided the community.

Curiously, January 1 never became a black national holiday. It was celebrated as such for only eight years in New York, was abandoned in the 1830s in Philadelphia, and only after general EMANCIPATION was proclaimed on January 1, 1863, did it assume new significance. The strengthening of the "peculiar institution," the development of the much dreaded domestic slave trade and its illegal perpetuation and that of the foreign trade, may explain the decline in popularity of this memorial celebration. Many states chose instead the days when emancipation law was passed into their constitutions: July 14 was adopted in Massachusetts, while after 1827 New York institutionalized July 5 as its freedom day, setting it apart from the American Fourth of July.

The abolition of slavery in the British West Indies by an act of Parliament on August 1, 1834, brought new hopes, and henceforth this memorable date became a rallying point for all freedom celebrations and for the black abolitionist crusade. State emancipations were indicted for having brought little improvement in the conditions of slaves and free blacks: The rights of blacks were trampled in the North, and racial violence and tensions continued to rise, while in the South slavery was entrenched more solidly than ever.

England and Canada became the symbols of the new celebration; the former (the perfidious and despotic tyrant at the time of the Revolutionary War) was praised for setting an example for the American republic, the latter was hailed as the land of the free and a refuge for the fugitives. Black orations became more fiery, urging the righting of wrongs and of all past errors. Orations also called for self-reliance, respectability, and exemplary conduct among blacks, for a distrust of whites, and for a stronger solidarity with the newly freed population of the West Indies and between the slaves and free blacks in the United States.

Increasingly, blacks sought sites that would commemorate events or figures more related to the African-American diaspora or to their community and its own distinctive history. Sometimes towns set the calendars—Baltimore for the Haitian Revolution, or Cleveland for NAT TURNER'S REBELLION, or Boston in the late 1850s for Crispus ATTUCKS. In 1814, Wilmington, Del., created its own celebration, Big Quarterly, which has been observed until very recently. Held at the close of the harvest season, it honored the founder of the Union Church of Africa, Peter Spencer.

Similar to religious revivals and patterned after the early meetings of the Quakers, Big Quarterly celebrated the struggles endured by leaders to achieve full ecclesiastical autonomy. This feast can be seen as the prototype of many religious services: praying, singing, the clapping of hands and stomping of feet, the beating of drums and tambourines, the playing of guitars, violins, and banjos. There was a characteristic use of space at such gatherings: The feast began in the church, then moved outside on the church grounds, and finally moved out to the open—Baltimore's famous French Street, for instance—where late in the century, as the feast grew more popular (in Baltimore attendance reached 10,000 in 1892, 20,000 in 1912), revival preachers took their stands to urge repentance from sin, and wandering minstrel evangelists played spirituals on odd instruments.

It was then also that educated "colored people" criticized the celebrations for giving way to weird cult practices and worldly pleasures, and for being outdated relics of old slavery times. In antebellum days, this religious feast was closer to a freedom celebration. Occurring in a region where slave-catching activities were intense, where slaves—who had to have a pass from the master to attend—were tempted to escape to Philadelphia or to the free states, Big Quarterly became a "big excursion on the Underground Railroad," with the presence among the pilgrims, who became potential fugitives, of both vigilant spies and marshals in addition to helpful railroad conductors.

Blacks sought sites that would commemorate events or figures related to the African-American diaspora or to their community and its own distinctive history.

In Syracuse in 1851 another major festival emerged in protest against the 1850 Fugitive Slave Law and after the rescue of a slave named Jerry. Jerry Rescue Day, which established Syracuse as the slaves' City of Refuge, embodied the spirit of defiance, of bold resistance to "iniquitous power" and to an infamous act that prevailed in the prewar years. Significantly, black leaders, rebels, warriors, and fugitives became heroic figures in celebrations and were chosen as signs that could demonstrate the unending fight against tyranny and for freedom. The oratory became more exhortative, the mood more impatient and indignant.

Freedom celebrations culminated in the early 1860s in Emancipation Jubilees and in the famous "Juneteenth" still observed today in Texas and surrounding states. In Texas, emancipation was announced to slaves eighteen months after its proclamation. This oddity of American history explains why Juneteenth and not January 1 became a popular celebration in those parts, in defiance of the official calendar and in reaction to the contempt in which part of the slave population had been held at a time when the proclamation event was a major breakthrough in the nation's history.

Thus, from Election Day to freedom celebrations, African Americans created a ritual tradition of religious and community life. Momentous appearances in public places became challenges to the established order, calling attention to the danger of overlooking or forgetting iniquities, setbacks, and sufferings as well as heroic acts. By reiterating a commonality of origin, goals, and strivings, feasts served to correct the inconsistencies of history and to cement a unity that was always in jeopardy.

Feasts also emphasized the necessary solidarity between the enslaved and the free, between African-born and American-born black people. Although most celebrations occurred in the North, they were symbolically and spiritually connected with slaves in the South, and a dense network of interaction was woven between various sites, places, and times. Former celebrations were often referred to and used as examples to follow or improve upon. The feasts themselves became memorable events to be passed on for generations to come and to be recorded in tales, song, and dance and in physical, verbal, kinetic, or musical images. The festive spirit became ingrained in African-American culture as something to celebrate in black speech, where it is inscribed in so many words, in the literature and the arts that bear incessant testimony to the tradition.

The tradition created by colonial and antebellum celebrations has continued well into the twentieth century, still in anticipation of a freedom and justice that general emancipation failed to accomplish. Numerous associations founded after the CIVIL WAR resorted to ceremonial and commemorative rites to continue to enforce the idea of freedom, and they patterned their meetings and conventions on earlier gatherings. Freedom celebrations remained a model for the great marches and demonstrations—the protest against the 1917 riots, or the parades of the Garvey movement, or the marches of the CIVIL RIGHTS MOVEMENT. The persistence of the tradition attests to the participation of African Americans in the struggle for democracy and to the crucial significance of these ritual stagings in cultural, intellectual, and political life.

Yet civil celebrations underwent some dramatic changes. More and more they became occasions of popular rejoicings. Boisterous festivity, screened out at first, crept in. Abundance and plentifulness replaced the earlier sobriety. As they grew in scope (the most popular were in urban centers where the population was largest), they sometimes lost their original meaning and became essentially social occasions for convivial gatherings. It was the orator's and leader's duty and the role of the black press to remind participants of the seriousness of the purpose, and they did so with authority and eloquence. Nevertheless, the celebrations sometimes got out of control. With the changes brought by migration and demographic shifts, by the development of the media and of mass culture, and by the impunity of profit-seeking sponsors, some feasts turned into large commercial and popular events and lost their civil and political character, while others continued to meet white opposition and censure.

Rituals played an important role in celebrations and, whatever the occasion, shared certain features. They included the same speeches and addresses or sermons; parades and marches or processions; anthems, lyrics, and songs; banquets or picnics; dances and balls. They used all black people's skills—from the oratorical to the culinary, from the gift to adorn to polyrhythmic energy—to create their own modes, styles, and rhythms, always with an unfailing sense of improvisation and performance. And as they drew more people, many folkways, many rites of ordinary life (the habit of swapping songs, of cracking jokes, or "patting juba") found their way into the ceremonies, blending memories of Africa with New World customs and forms, in a mood that was both solemn and playful, sacred and secular, celebratory and satiric. In many respects also, feasts were a privileged space for the encounters between cultures, favoring reciprocal influences, mergings and combinations, syncretism and creolization.

Nowhere is the creolization of cultures more evident than in the carnivalesque tradition, which emerged in the New World in Brazil, Trinidad, Jamaica, and the other islands, is found in its earlier forms mostly in the South, and continues its modern forms in the great Caribbean festivals of Brooklyn and Toronto. These carnivals, perceived as bacchanalian revelry or weird saturnalia, were often associated with a special season and with rites of renewal, purification, or rebirth. Usually seen as more African, and therefore as more "primitive" and exotic, more tantalizing than the more familiar Anglo-European feasts, they have elicited ambiguous responses, ranging from outright disparagement on moral and aesthetic grounds (indecency and lewdness are judged horrid and hideous) to admiration for the exuberant display of so many skills and talents.

These "festivals of misrule" were often banned or strictly regulated by city ordinances and charged with bringing disturbances and misconduct—boisterous rioting and drunkenness, gambling and undue license of all sorts. The same criticism, phrased in similar words, was leveled by some members of the black community itself, especially those concerned with respectability and with the dignity of the "race," every time they suspected any feast of yielding too much to the carnivalesque propensity of their people.

Nowhere is the creolization of cultures more evident than in the carnivalesque tradition, which emerged in the New World in Brazil, Trinidad, and Jamaica.

Yet the carnivalesque is always present in festive rituals to correct excesses—of piety, fervor, power—and as an instrument of emancipation from any form of authority. In the African-American quest for liberation, it became an essential means of expression, allying humor, wit, parody, and satire. It had ancient roots in African cultures; and in North American society, where the weight of puritanism was strong, where work, industriousness, sobriety, and gravity were highly valued and had become ideological tools to enforce servitude, the carnivalesque tradition became part of the political culture of the oppressed. Artistically it developed also as a subversive response to the Sambo image that later prevailed in the minstrel tradition: It created, as coronation festivals did, possibilities for the inversion of stereotypes and challenged a system of representation that was fraught with ideological misinterpretations. Paradoxically, black carnivalesque performances may have nourished white blackface minstrelsy, providing it with the artistic devices on which it thrived.

The most notorious manifestations of the tradition are perhaps to be found in the North Carolina Jon-Konnu (John Canoe) Festival or in the Zulu and Mardi Gras parades of New Orleans. JonKonnu probably originated in Africa on the Guinea coast, was re-created in Jamaica in the late seventeenth century, spread through the Caribbean, where it was widely observed, and was introduced by slaves in the States in isolated places, on plantations like Somerset Place, or in city ports like Wilmington, N.C., or Key West, Fla. Meant to honor a Guinean folk hero, the festival became an elaborate satirical feast, ridiculing the white world with unparalleled inventiveness and magnificence.

The festival could last weeks, but it climaxed on Christmas Day and was attended by huge crowds. The procession, which took a ragman and his followers from house to house and through the streets, came to be known as a unique slave performance. "Coonering," as it was called, was characterized most of all by spectacular costumes and by extravagant dance steps to the music of "sinful" tunes. The rags and feathers, the fanciful headdress and masks, the use of ox or goat horns and cow and sheep bells, and the handmade instruments wove a complex web of symbolic structure, ritualization, and code building. The dressing in white skin encouraged slaves to claim certain prerogatives, even to organize revolts. In many feasts an implicit analogy was established between the "beaten" skin of the (often forbidden) drums and that of whipped slaves.

Christmas, the season of merrymaking and mobility that favored big gatherings and intense communication, became a dreaded time for planters who tried to stifle the subversive and rebellious spirit of Coonering and to change a disquieting performance into a harmless pageant. Still held today but now mostly controlled and observed by whites, it has lost part of its magnificence.

In its heyday, in antebellum America, the carnival was an artistic and political response of the slave population to its situation; it echoed in its own mode the freedom celebrations of the North. The lampooning liberty and grotesque parody of southern festivals turned them into arenas in which to voice anger and protest.

In New Orleans, when the carnival came into existence in the late 1850s, blacks were not supposed to participate. The Zulu parade, which grew out of black social life, was created by a section of the population concerned about publicly asserting its status. It developed into a wholly separate street event, a parody of the white Krewes. The African Zulu, a new king of misrule, precedes Rex and mocks his regal splendor. The carnival figures—shrunken heads of jungle beasts, royal prognosticator or voodoo doctor—the masked or painted faces, and the coconuts emphasize both the African and minstrel motifs. Neither elite nor low-brow, neither genuinely African nor creole, the Zulu parade came under attack as too burlesque; later, in the 1960s, it was criticized as exemplifying an "Uncle Tom on Wheels" and not fitting the mood of the times.

Yet the Zulu is a complex ritual that brings together several traditions: satire and masking, minstrelsy and vaudeville, brass bands, song, and dance. Another version of the coronation festival, the Zulu fuses elements of the European carnival with African, Caribbean, and Latin American practices. It establishes African Americans' rights to participate in the city's pageant, not as mere onlookers or indispensable entertainers, whose various skills as musicians and jugglers had often been used to increase the glamor of white parades, but as creators and full-fledged citizens who could thus demonstrate both their role in the city's history and their potential role in its future.

The Mardi Gras Indians, consisting of ritual chiefs, each with a spy, flagboys, and followers, march in mock imitation of the king's court and follow secret routes through the city. They enact their own rituals of violent physical and verbal confrontations between tribes. These wild warriors chant disquieting songs and speak in tongues, accompanied by haunting drumbeats and an array of other percussive sounds, as old as ancestral memories (in preference and contrast to the orderly military music of the official bands). They dance weird dance steps (e.g., the famous spy dance) and wear elaborate costumes made of beads, sequins, rhinestones, ribbons, and lace.

The tradition of Indian masking is old; originally found in Brazil, it appeared in the Caribbean in 1847. Meant to celebrate the Indian's fighting spirit and resistance, it also relates to communal rites of ancestral worship and to Dahomean ceremonial dances found also in jazz funerals. It is no accident that Mardi Gras Indians perform in the same area of New Orleans where jazz emerged out of the brass bands of Congo Square dances. Their festival may be a resurgence of the early drum gatherings that started in 1730 near the marshes of Congo Square, a market site where slaves bought merchandise from Native Americans and danced to African beats.

Now, the black Indians also appear on another festive day, March 19, at the intermission of the Lenten season. St. Joseph Day, originally an Italian Catholic feast that stylized altar building, blends the cult of saints (St. Joseph, "Queen Esther") with that of Indian heroes (Black Hawk) as well as that of voodoo spirits. Thus religious and pagan rites, cult and carnival practices, indoor ceremonies and outdoor parades complement each other, converge, and merge.

Later in the year, Easter Rock, another feast that is still observed in rural Louisiana, celebrates the Resurrection and similarly blends pagan and Christian elements. Its hero and emblem is both son and sun. The Son of God's rise from the dead is likened to that of the sun "rocking from the earth." All night long, prayer, "the shout," and dance herald and accompany the rocking of the sun/son.

Although the South has been the cradle of a diverse black carnivalesque tradition, in the prejazz and jazz ages another form of carnival celebration found its way to the North. The modern West Indian festivals of Brooklyn, N.Y., and of Toronto, Canada, give further evidence of a process of Caribbeanization that has always been at work and that repeatedly intensified during periods of great migration. The importation of slaves from the Carib Basin, the arrival of many slaves from Santo Domingo after the Haitian Revolution in the early nineteenth century, and the late twentieth-century West Indian migration to the United States have all in various degrees brought many changes to "black" celebrations. They have intensified the creolization that brought together people of African, Hispanic, Indian, and French descent. The recent festivals are also generating a pan-West Indian consciousness that expresses itself artistically through costumes, masks, music, and dance. On a much-contested terrain they enact their own rituals of rebellion, resistance and protest, inclusion and exclusion. Chaotic, playful, or violent, carnivals offer a delicate balance between many complementary or contradictory elements.

African-American celebratory performances are special occasions to celebrate freedom; they consist of various cycles of ritualized events that have rich semantic and symbolic meaning, fully a part of African-American and American history and culture. They invite us to reconsider stereotyped representations of "the race" and to revise the assumptions upon which conceptions of important figures, events, and places have themselves become objects of celebration and commemorative fervor. They are potent weapons and arenas through which to voice anger, strivings, and desire. They are efficacious and eloquent tools to educate, exhort, or indict. They are witty parodies and satires that help distance reality and change "mentalities." Crucial agents of change, celebratory performances demonstrate a people's faith in words and ideas, in the force of collective memory and imagination, in the necessity of finding powerful display. These entertaining and instructive ceremonies exhibit a gift for adornment and an inventiveness that emphatically proclaim the triumph of life over all the forces that tend to suppress or subdue "the souls of black folk."

BIBLIOGRAPHY

Abrahams, Roger, and John Szwed, eds. *Discovering Afro-America.* Leiden, Netherlands, 1975.

Blassingame, John W. *The Slave Community: Plantation Life in the Antebellum South.* New York, 1972.

Genovese, Eugene D. *Roll, Jordan, Roll: The World the Slaves Made.* New York, 1974.

Levine, Lawrence W. *Black Culture and Black Consciousness.* New York, 1977.

Southern, Eileen. *The Music of Black Americans.* New York, 1971.

Stuckey, Sterling. *Slave Culture.* New York, 1987.

— GENEVIÈVE FABRE

FIFTEENTH AMENDMENT

The Fifteenth Amendment to the U.S. Constitution provides that voting rights shall not be abridged by the federal government or any state "on account of race, color, or previous condition of servitude." The amendment reflected the federal government's emergence during Reconstruction as the guarantor of civil rights against state intrusion.

Having granted most southern black men the right to vote, at least temporarily, by the Military Reconstruction acts of 1867, the Republican majority in Congress wanted to render black suffrage nationwide and permanent. Congressman George S. Boutwell of Massachusetts proposed a constitutional amendment in January 1869. Controversy arose over the wording, with many supporters of civil rights fearing that a vague amendment would permit later disenfranchisement through indirect means.

Other Republicans, however, insisted that northern states must remain able to restrict the suffrage on the basis of literacy of education, often for nativist reasons. In addition, some Congressmen feared granting unrestricted authority in the area to the federal government. In response to such concerns, a relatively limited form of the amendment passed Congress in February 1869, over vehement Democratic opposition. It was ratified by the states in March 1870, aided by the presence of Reconstruction governments in most southern states.

A more radical amendment, calling for an end to disenfranchisement based on "race, color, nationality, property, education, or religious beliefs," was rejected, as were feminist calls for women's suffrage. Furthermore, the amendment did not guarantee the right of blacks to hold office.

As feared, southern Democratic state governments did almost eliminate black voting through poll taxes, literacy tests, residency requirements, and similar means. The Fifteenth Amendment permanently secured voting rights in the northern states, several of which still did not permit black voting at the time. The amendment was also of long-term significance in that it declared equal suffrage an ideal, if not a reality, in the nation's fundamental law. The effort actually to secure black suffrage took more than this amendment. The NAACP fought successfully against the many abridgments to black suffrage in the early twentieth century, but it was not until the Voting Rights Act of 1965 that the vast majority of eligible southern blacks were registered to vote.

BIBLIOGRAPHY

Foner, Eric. *Reconstruction: America's Unfinished Revolution, 1863–1877.* New York, 1988.

Hyman, Harold M. *A More Perfect Union: The Impact of the Civil War and Reconstruction on the Constitution.* Boston, 1973.

Maltz, Earl M. *Civil Rights, the Constitution, and Congress, 1863–1869.* Lawrence, Kans., 1990.

— MICHAEL W. FITZGERALD

FIFTY-FOURTH REGIMENT OF MASSACHUSETTS VOLUNTEER INFANTRY

The "Fifty-fourth Massachusetts Regiment" was the first regular army unit of African Americans raised in the North during the CIVIL WAR. For northern blacks, the Fifty-fourth assumed enormous significance: "The eyes of the whole world are upon you," one black newspaper announced, "civilized man everywhere waits to see if you will prove yourselves." Blacks hoped that the unit's valor would discredit charges of racial inferiority and advance the antislavery cause; failure might jeopardize the struggle for black freedom.

Massachusetts's abolitionist governor John A. Andrew organized the regiment between January and May 1863, choosing as officers white men with military experience who opposed slavery and embraced the idea of black military service. Andrew worked closely with black leaders such as Lewis Hayden to win the confidence of the African-American community and declared his own commitment to the regiment, announcing that his honor "as a man and a magistrate" would "rise or fall" with the Fifty-fourth. Enlistees came from across the North, including the well-educated sons of such black leaders as Frederick DOUGLASS, who overcame their initial resentment over the Lincoln administration's refusal to commission black officers. Black communities braved the threats and assaults of racist mobs to assist in recruitment efforts and to collect money and supplies for the troops.

The Fifty-fourth quickly proved its fighting ability in the South Carolina Sea Islands, in one case saving a white Union regiment from annihilation. The unit led the attack on Fort Wagner, a key Confederate fortification in Charleston's defensive network. Although the July 18, 1863, assault failed—the Fifty-fourth's colonel, Robert Gould Shaw, was killed, and nearly half of the attacking forces became casualties—the unit's valor won the right for blacks to serve in the army. Approximately 178,000 African Americans subsequently enlisted and played a crucial role in the victory over slavery and the South.

The Fifty-fourth Massachusetts Regiment was the first regular army unit of African Americans raised in the North during the Civil War.

The Wagner attack decimated the regiment; months passed before recruits filled the unit and its new colonel, Edward N. Hallowell—who was seriously wounded at Wagner—assumed command. The regiment's palmy first days never returned and many new officers lacked the commitment of the original ones, although Hallowell was a genuine abolitionist and closely identified with his men. Irksome fatigue duty preoccupied the regiment until February 1864, when it fought in the disastrous Olustee, Fla., campaign. More important, the unit led other black regiments in an eighteen-month pay strike against the federal government's offer of unequal pay. Although promised the same pay and benefits as whites, all blacks, regardless of rank, received less pay than white privates. Near-mutinous conditions prevailed in the Fifty-fourth until Congress bowed to pressure and adopted legislation equalizing the pay of black and white troops. In the closing months of the war, members of the Fifty-fourth were the first Union soldiers to occupy Charleston, the seat of secessionist fervor. The unit also destroyed valuable rail stock and liberated hundreds of slaves in the back country of northern Georgia and South Carolina before being mustered out in August 1865.

BIBLIOGRAPHY

Adams, Virginia M., ed. *On the Altar of Freedom: A Black Soldier's Civil War Letters from the Front.* Amherst, Mass., 1991.

Burchard, Peter. *One Gallant Rush: Robert Gould Shaw and His Brave Black Regiment.* New York, 1965.

Emilio, Luis F. *A Brave Black Regiment: History of the Fifty-fourth Regiment of Massachusetts Volunteer Infantry, 1863–1865.* 1894. Reprint. New York, 1968.

– DONALD YACOVONE

FILM

Motion pictures and large numbers of African Americans arrived in American cities simultaneously in the late nineteenth century. Black Americans came to cities in flight from the southern peonage that had replaced the institution of slavery after the Civil War. Their Great Migration in turn coincided with a similar migration from Europe. Movies, in their "primitive" days, when techniques of cutting and editing as a means of conveying a narrative had not yet been perfected, became the first medium of mass communications for the poor, teeming populations that filled northeastern cities toward the end of the nineteenth century.

Movies had played the Cotton States Exposition in Atlanta in 1895, and in the following year opened at Koster and Bial's music hall in New York. Strikingly, in these early years African Americans often appeared on the screen in unmediated, unedited form, and therefore devoid of some of the worst stereotypes with which they had been maligned by decades of southern novels, advertising logos, and popular songs. A shot of, for example, black soldiers watering their horses or dockers coaling a ship appeared on the screen untrammeled by the pejorative images of the past.

These topical vignettes were the result of a rage for news of events in the corners of the world. Thomas Edison filmed life in the Caribbean; others caught black "buffalo soldiers" on their way to the Spanish-American War, tribal ceremonies in Africa, and Theodore Roosevelt on safari.

Gradually after the turn of the century, the medium changed, both technically and economically. As the prospects for a profitable future opened up, producers began to cultivate more sophisticated techniques that allowed them to edit scenes into narratives along the lines set down by novelists and dramatists. The trend pointed toward a future cinema that would play to middle-class rather than poor audiences, in picture palaces rather than storefront nickelodeons, and at length rather than in the brief snippets with which the medium had begun its life.

For African Americans, this meant a resumption of many conventions inherited from the nineteenth-century melodramatic, comic, and musical stage. Indeed, in 1903 William S. Porter brought UNCLE TOM'S CABIN to the screen, complete with overambitious attempts at spectacle—cakewalks, pursuits across ice floes, and even a race between miniature steamboats. Tom himself was more a figure drawn from the sentimental stage than from Harriet Beecher Stowe's staunch hero.

Other restorations of familiar racial material gradually dominated the screen just as the medium began to emerge from a primitive, limited visual rhetoric. In *A Bucket of Cream Ale* (1904), a stock, obstreperous black-faced servant appeared; *The Fights of Nations* (1907) featured a razor fight; and comedies about chicken thieving and life in "coontown" became routine. From 1911 through 1915, movies sentimentalized the Civil War during the five years of its semicentennial. Rarely was there an opportunity for a genuine black portrayal to show through in *A Slave's Devotion* (1913), *Old Mammy's Secret Code* (1913), or *For the Cause of the South* (1914). Typical of the era was D. W. Griffith's *His Trust* (1911) and its sequel, a tale of the Civil War in which a slave is first entrusted with managing his master's estate while the latter is away fighting and then, after the master dies a hero's death, gives his own "savings" toward sending the master's daughter to finishing school so that she may meet and marry someone in her class.

It was at this moment that African Americans took their first steps toward an indigenous cinema. Local black entrepreneurs in Lexington, Ky., as early as the first decade of the century booked all-black films in their theaters. By 1912, William Foster in Kansas made *The Railroad Porter* with a black audience as his target. About the same time in Florida, James Weldon JOHNSON wrote two scripts for a company bent upon making films with an African-American angle.

Unfortunately for small-time entrepreneurs, the economic setting of moviemaking had begun to rationalize into competing oligopolies, even "trusts," in which ever-fewer sellers drove out competition for customers who gradually included more demanding middle-class, urbane tastemakers. Edison's Motion Picture Patents Trust, for example, formed a pool of patents through which it hoped to control the entire nation's film output by licensing the use of cameras and projectors. In such a richly capitalized economic field, African Americans only a half century removed from slavery had little chance.

The Birth of a Nation

Then in 1915, D. W. Griffith—after years spent learning filmmaking and extending its range into techniques unforeseen in the primitive years—released his Civil War epic The Birth Of A Nation. An evocative combination of conventional racial attitudes, a celebration of the Civil War and of the forbearance of the white South during Reconstruction, and a genuinely avant-garde piece of filmmaking, *The Birth of a Nation* galvanized African Americans and their white allies into a nationwide protest campaign. At issue were two major factors: first, its depiction of Reconstruction as a tale of black cupidity, corruption, and vindictiveness toward the prostrate white South, and second, the unprecedented nationwide advertising campaign, which further heightened the film's impact. It was this *combination* that nettled blacks. Most literate Americans believed the account of Reconstruction as portrayed therein, complete with its venal freedmen who did the bidding of scalawags and carpetbaggers (Woodrow Wilson had retold it in his multivolume history of the nation), but the couching of it in a blaring ad campaign and in an emotionally charged movie made the difference.

The Birth of a Nation *galvanized African Americans and their white allies into a nationwide protest campaign.*

The NAACP fruitlessly conducted a national campaign against the movie, demanding cuts of scenes that "slandered" blacks, advocating strict legal codes against maligning races and groups, and instigating a plan to make its own movie, to be titled *Lincoln's Dream*. But despite the protesters' best efforts, by the end of 1915 *The Birth of a Nation* could be seen almost anywhere its makers wished, and *Lincoln's Dream* foundered for want of an "angel."

Nonetheless, the struggle against Griffith's film confirmed a number of African Americans in their embracing of a strategy of making movies alternative to those of the mainstream. Even Booker T. WASHINGTON, the famous founder of TUSKEGEE Institute and a reputed accommodationist in racial matters, took up the idea of making black movies. At first he feared that the makers of *The Birth of a Nation* might profit from the notoriety that would follow from a vigorous black protest, but soon, through his secretary Emmett J. Scott, he committed resources to a film eventually titled *The Birth of a Race.*

The Birth of a Race

Washington and Scott's movie seemed to possess everything: the endorsement of national worthies of the Republican party; a script that traced the progress of humankind, while allocating a prominent place in it for African Americans; and a panel of rich angels led by Julius Rosenwald, a Sears and Roebuck vice president. But things fell apart. First, Washington died on November 15, 1915. Then, acting on rumors of unscrupulous practices among the project's Chicago fund-raisers, Rosenwald and other prestigious figures withdrew. And finally, with the onset of World War I, the thrust of the already episodic movie veered wildly from a pacifist theme to its ideological opposite—a justification of the American entry into the war. Thus, after almost three years of scrabbling for money, shooting in Tampa, and cutting through the thicket of cross-purposed story lines, the project changed. And yet the completed movie reached a level of accomplishment never previously attained by black moviemakers. They had actually completed a feature-length film, albeit one burdened by seemingly endless title frames that slowed its pace and shouldered aside its African-American premise in favor of militaristic themes.

The Lincoln Company

Moreover, readers of the black press noticed. Indeed, one man in particular, a postman in Omaha named George P. Johnson, saw the film as more than a grand flop. Together with his brother Noble Johnson, a contract player at Universal, he assembled a circle of black investors in Los Angeles into the Lincoln Company. Between 1916 and 1922 they turned out an impressive string of films (of which only a fragment survives), all of them celebrations of the black aspiration embedded in one of the company's titles: *The Realization of a Negro's Ambition.*

Indeed, aspiration was emblazoned on the Johnsons' battleflags. It marked or guided everything they made, whether tales of black "buffalo soldiers" fighting Mexican *insurrectes* along the border or go-getters scoring successes in capitalist circles that few blacks would have had access to in the reality of American life. The Johnsons' rivals during the booming 1920s not only followed their example but extended its reach. Among these were the Frederick Douglass Company (with its Republican namesake on its letterhead), Sidney P. Dones's Democracy Company, and regional operations such as Gate City in Kansas, Ker-Mar in Baltimore, and Norman in Jacksonville and later Boley, Okla. In the pages of the African-American press there appeared dozens of announcements of additional companies, most of which did not survive long enough to see their first film to the screen.

Some studios, such as Norman, were conduits for the investments of white "angels" or were in fact white firms. Robert Levy's Reol Studio, for example, was a white-owned company that made films from well-known black classics such as Paul Laurence DUNBAR's *The Sport of the Gods.* To some extent this rush of activity merely testified to the wealth that had reached even black strata of urban life during the 1920s. But it also suggested the presence of a maturing film culture, drawing in a sector of the black population that was not only well off enough to buy tickets but also literate enough to read the growing amount of advertising copy, reviews, and show-business gossip that had begun to fill the pages of the African-American press.

The Black Audience

In other words, an audience had been formed by the black migrations to the urban centers of America, both North and South. The names of the theaters signaled the identity of the audience. No Bijous, Criterions, or Paramounts there. But rather a Douglass or an Attucks to honor famous heroes, a Lenox, Harlem, or Pekin to provide linkages to increasingly well-known centers of black urban culture. This sort of social, institutional, and cultural density suggested the nature of this newly arrived audience: urban, literate, employed, affiliated in a circle of lodges and clubs, and church members. In short, the audience constituted a thin layer of bourgeoisie to whom movies spoke of aspiration, racial pride, and heroism, and cautioned against the evils of drink and sloth—much like a Booker T. Washington commencement address with pictures.

We can sense these social traits not only from the themes of the movies themselves but also from the critics who wrote about them: D. Ireland Thomas in the Mississippi Valley, Lester Walton of the New York *Age,* Theophilus Lewis on several papers in the New York area, Billy Rowe on the *Pittsburgh Courier,* Romeo Daugherty in the *Amsterdam News,* Fay Jackson for Claude A. Barnett's Associated Negro Press service, and other regulars on the *Afro-American* chain and even smaller papers. Augmenting their own acute criticism that seemed to be maturing toward a genuine African-American posture toward cinema were the syndicated columnists, who wrote gossipy copy for the *Los Angeles Sentinel* and the *California Eagle*—Ruby Berkeley Goodwin, Harry Levette, and Lawrence LaMar.

Micheaux and the Colored Players

Playing to this emerging audience in the 1920s were the elite of "race" film companies, either staunchly black firms such as that of Oscar MICHEAUX or white firms with a feel for the audience, such as David Starkman's Colored Players in Philadelphia. Micheaux, a peripatetic author who sold his own novels from door to door, entered the movie business in 1919 after a failed negotiation with Lincoln to produce his autobiographical novel *The Homesteader*. For much of the ensuing quarter century and more, he audaciously if not always artfully reached for effects and messages left untouched by his forebears. In his *Body and Soul* (1924) he featured the singer Paul ROBESON in his only appearance in a race movie. In *Within Our Gates* (1921) he put his own spin on the infamous Leo Frank murder case in Atlanta. And throughout his career Micheaux played on themes of racial identity, often hinging his plots upon revelations of mixed parentage.

The Colored Players differed from Micheaux's group in that they not only calculatedly played to urban, eastern audiences but seemed to have a capacity for putting every dollar on the screen, with handsomely—even densely—dressed sets and more polished levels of acting. They did Dunbar's *A Prince of His Race* (1926), a black version of the temperance tract *Ten Nights in a Bar Room* (1926), and an original screenplay entitled *The Scar of Shame* (1927).

More than any other race movie, *The Scar of Shame* addressed the concerns of the urban black middle class. Although it teased around the theme of color caste snobbery among African Americans, its most compelling argument was a call to rise above the lot that blacks had been given and to strive for "the finer things" despite adversity. But at the same time, as critic Jane Gaines has argued, their poor circumstances were given them not by a natural order but by a white-dominated system that blacks knew as the real puppeteer working the strings off camera.

Hollywood's Blacks

For its part, Hollywood in the 1920s rarely departed from conventions it had inherited from southern American racial lore. Its high moments included *In Old Kentucky* (1926), in which the black romance was in the hands of the enduring clown Stepin Fetchit. In most

Scene from Oscar Micheaux's Within Our Gates. *(Photographs and Prints Division, Schomburg Center for Research in Black Culture, The New York Public Library, Astor, Lenox and Tilden Foundations)*

movies blacks merely lent an atmosphere to the sets: Sam Baker as a burly seaman in *Old Ironsides,* Carolynne Snowden as an exotic dancer in Erich von Stroheim's Ruritanian romances, and so on. The decade also produced its own obligatory version of *Uncle Tom's Cabin.*

But with the coming of the cultural crisis wrought by the Great Depression of 1929 and after, blacks and whites shared at least fragments of the same depths of despair and were thrust together in the same breadlines and federal programs such as the WORKS PROGRESS ADMINISTRATION (WPA). In Hollywood the result was a run of socially and artistically interesting black roles, and even a couple of tolerable all-black homages to the hard life the race lived in the South: *Hallelujah!* and *Hearts in Dixie* (both in 1929).

At the same time, Hollywood had also matured into a corporate system that had rationalized moviemaking into a vertically integrated mode of production, distribution, and exhibition. The result was a manufactured product marked by so many family traits that it could be labeled by some historians "the classic Hollywood movie." Typically, such movies told an uncomplicated tale in which engaging characters embarked on a plot that obliged them to fill some lack, solve a mystery, or complete a quest resulting in a closure that wrapped all the strands into a fulfilling denouement.

Unavoidably, the African-American roles that filled out these plots owed more to the conventions of the moviemaking system than to the authentic wellsprings of everyday black life. Moreover, supporting this industrial/aesthetic system were the proscriptions set forth by Hollywood's self-censorship system, the Production Code Administration or "the Hays Office." These dos and don'ts discouraged full black participation in any plot forbidding racial slander or miscegenation, so that almost no African-American "heavy" or villain could appear. Nor could any black person engage in any sort of close relationship other than that of master and servant.

Stepin Fetchit, for example, enjoyed a flourishing career during the Great Depression, but one severely limited in its range. In *The World Moves On* (1934) he had a rare opportunity to play a soldier in the French army, but only as a consequence of following his master into combat; in *Stand Up and Cheer* (1934) he joined the rest of the cast in fighting off the effects of the depression, but was absent from pivotal scenes that centered on the white principals; and in the middle of the decade he appeared in a brief string of rural fables as a sidekick to Will Rogers's folksy *Judge Priest* or *David Harum.* Women had their moments as wise or flippant servants, notably Louise Beavers in *Imitation of Life* (1934) and Hattie McDaniel in *Alice Adams* (1935). Such a role eventually won McDaniel the first Oscar ever won by an African American: her "Mammy" in *Gone with the Wind* (1939). Whenever the script called for a character of mixed heritage, such as Tondelayo in *White Cargo* or Zia in *Sundown,* the Hollywood self-censorship system, the Hays office, pressed the studios toward the cautious choice of casting white actors in the roles.

For African Americans, the combination of an increasingly factory-like Hollywood system and a lingering economic depression provided only scant hope of improved roles. And yet the coming of sound film technology opened a window of opportunity for black performers.

Already, theatrical audiences had been introduced to African-American musical performance in the form of rollicking revues such as the *Blackbirds* series and Marc Connelly's Pulitzer Prize fable *The Green Pastures,* which he had drawn from Roark Bradford's book of tales, *Ole Man Adam and His Chillun.* Fleetingly, two major Hollywood studios—Fox and Metro—had responded with *Hearts in Dixie* and *Hallelujah!* And both the majors and the independents offered hope for an African-American presence in sound films in the form of a rash of short musical films that lasted well past the decade.

The most famous of these one- or two-reel gems were Bessie SMITH and Jimmy Mordecai's *St. Louis Blues* (1929)—which used not only W. C. HANDY's title song but incidental choral arrangements by J. Rosamond Johnson, who, with his brother James Weldon, had written the "Negro national anthem," *Lift Ev'ry Voice and Sing*—and Duke ELLINGTON's films *Black and Tan* and *The Symphony in Black* (1929 and 1935, respectively). Throughout the decade and beyond, stars of the jazz scene—Cab CALLOWAY, Louis ARMSTRONG, and the NICHOLAS BROTHERS, among others—appeared in these shorts, which culminated with Lena HORNE, the duo pianists Albert Ammons and Pete Johnson, and the pianist Teddy Wilson in *Boogie Woogie Dream* (1944). By then such films had attracted the attention of white aesthetes such as the photographer Gjon Mili, who cast Illinois Jacquet, Sid Catlett, Marie Bryant, and others in his *Jammin' the Blues* (1946), which became a *Life* magazine Movie of the Week.

Late Race Movies

As for race-movie makers, the times were harder. Of the African Americans only their doyen, Oscar Micheaux, worked through the entire decade of the 1940s, albeit as a client of white capital sources such as Frank Schiffman, manager of the Apollo Theater. Now and again a newcomer such as William D. Alexander's All America firm or George Randol with his *Dark Manhattan*

(1947) entered the field, but race movies too had matured into a system led mainly by white entrepreneurs such as Ted Toddy of Atlanta, Alfred Sack of Dallas, Bert and Jack Goldberg of New York, and Harry and Leo Popkin of Hollywood, whose loose federation was modeled on the classic Hollywood system.

As a result, race movies soon imitated Hollywood genres such as the gangster film and the Western. *Paradise in Harlem* (1940), for example, featured a tale of a black gang bent upon taking over Harlem. The community, led by an actor (Frank Wilson), mounts a jazz version of *Othello* as a fund-raiser, and the play is so compelling that even gangsters are won over by its seductive beat and a black-themed Shakespeare. Westerns—*Two Gun Man from Harlem, Bronze Buckaroo,* and *Harlem Rides the Range*—also borrowed their formulas from Hollywood, particularly their satisfying closures that promised happy lives to the good people of the cast.

The Impact of World War II

No political event affected moviemaking more profoundly than did World War II. Even before the war reached America, Hollywood responded to it by forming an Anti-Nazi League and by cleansing its movies of the worst of racist traits, much as David O. Selznick tried to do when he told his writer to place African Americans "on the right side of the ledger during these Fascist-ridden times" as they began work on *Gone with the Wind.* Indeed, so successful was he that blacks were divided in their response to the Southern epic for which Hattie McDaniel became the first black ever to win an Oscar. In less splashy movies a similar impact of the war was felt. John Huston and Howard Koch included a strong black law student who stands up to a ne'er-do-well daughter of the southern gentry in their movie of Ellen Glasgow's Pulitzer Prize novel in *In This Our Life.* And Walter WHITE of the NATIONAL ASSOCIATION FOR THE ADVANCEMENT OF COLORED PEOPLE (NAACP) helped to adapt Walter Wanger's *Sundown* (1941) to fit the changing politics brought on by the war.

No political event affected moviemaking more profoundly than did World War II.

The war provided a cultural crisis that weighed upon African Americans in several ways: The Allies' war aims included anticolonialism, the nation needed black soldiers and war workers, and black journalists campaigned to insist on such linkages, as the *Pittsburgh Courier* did in calling for a "Double V," a simultaneous victory over foreign fascism and domestic racism. Together with the NAACP, liberals within the Office of War Information and the Pentagon joined in a campaign to make appropriate movies. Two new trends resulted: government propaganda such as *The Negro Soldier, Wings for This Man,* and *Teamwork,* which asserted a black place in the war effort, and Hollywood films such as *Crash Dive, Sahara, Bataan,* and *Lifeboat,* which often integrated the armed forces before the services themselves acted to do so. Along with federal measures such as a Fair Employment Practices Commission, the movies contributed to a new political culture that reintroduced the issue of racism to the arena of national politics.

After the war, filmmakers emerged from their military experience to form a new documentary film culture bent upon making films of liberal advocacy, much as they had done during the war. The NAACP continued to lead this movement by urging wartime agencies to send their surplus films to schools, trade unions, and civil rights groups, constituting audiovisual aids for, as Roy wilkins of the NAACP said, "educating white people now and in the future." Thus, informational films such as *The Negro Soldier* entered the civilian marketplace of ideas. In the same period, a wartime antiracist tract by Ruth Benedict and Gene Weltfish became *The Brotherhood of Man,* an animated cartoon endorsed and distributed by the United Auto Workers. Another film of the era was *The Quiet One,* an account of a black boy of the streets who enters Wiltwyck School, an agency charged with treating such children. The fact that it enjoyed an unprecedented run in urban theaters perhaps contributed to Hollywood's decision to resume attention to the racial issues it had taken up during the war.

By 1949, Hollywood majors and some independent companies that had sprung up following the war produced peacetime versions of the war movies. The results were mixed. Louis DeRochemont's "message movie" *Lost Boundaries* focused on a New England village "black" family that had been passing as white, thereby blunting the main point, racial integration; Stanley Kramer's *Home of the Brave* did somewhat better by introducing a black soldier into an otherwise white platoon; Dore Schary's *Intruder in the Dust* faithfully rendered William Faulkner's book into film, including its portrayal of African Americans as icons of a sad past who could teach white people the lessons of history; Darryl F. Zanuck's *Pinky* provided a closure in which a black nurse learns the value of building specifically black social institutions; and Zanuck's *No Way Out* carried the genre into the 1950s, focusing tightly on a black family and neighborhood and their willingness to defend themselves against the threat of racism.

Postwar Hollywood

Taken as a lot, these message movies perpetuated the integrationist ideology that had emerged from the war and gave Sidney POITIER, James Edwards, Juano Hernandez, and others a foothold in Hollywood. Indeed, if anything, Hollywood only repeated itself in the ensuing decade, hobbling efforts to press on. Poitier, for example, after a few good films in the integrationist vein—*The Blackboard Jungle* (1954), *The Defiant Ones* (1959), and *Lilies of the Field* (1963)—was given few challenging scripts. Typical of the era was Alec Waugh's novel *Island in the Sun,* a book specifically about racial politics in the Caribbean, bought by 20th Century-Fox only to have its most compelling black spokesman written entirely out of the script. Black women fared little better, mainly because they were assigned only a narrow range of exotic figures, such as Dorothy Dandridge's title role in the all-black *Carmen Jones* (1954).

Not until the era of the CIVIL RIGHTS MOVEMENT—when such events as the Greensboro, N.C., student SIT-INS of 1960 became daily fare on national television—would Hollywood try to catch up with the pace of events and TV's treatment of them. Even then, the most socially challenging themes were in movies made outside the Hollywood system, on East Coast locations or even in foreign countries. These included Shirley Clarke's harsh film of Harlem's streets *The Cool World* (1964); Gene Persson and Anthony Harvey's London-made film of Amiri BARAKA's *Dutchman* (1967); Larry Peerce's cautionary tale about the stresses of interracial marriage, *One Potato Two Potato* (1965); Marcel Camus's Afro-Brazilian movie of the myth of Orpheus and Eurydice, *Orfeo Negro* (1960); and Michael Roemer's *Nothing but a Man* (1964), a pastoral film that was named by *Black Creation* magazine as the "greatest" of black movies.

Parallel to the civil rights movement, Hollywood itself experienced key changes in its institutional structure. Its production system became less vertically integrated and more dependent on sound marketing; federal laws began to require the active recruiting of blacks into studio guilds and unions from which they had been excluded by "grandfather clauses"; the old Hays Office censorship gave way to legal challenges and eventually to a liberalized system of ratings; and television assumed the role of seeking the steady audiences that B movies once had done. All these factors would alter the ways Hollywood treated race, but television had a particular impact.

In the 1960s television shows *East Side/West Side, The Store Front Lawyers, Mod Squad,* and *Julia,* social workers, idealistic attorneys, dedicated cops, and self-sacrificing hospital workers struggled on behalf of their clients, often against the social order itself. Television news and documentaries provided a tougher image for Hollywood to strive to emulate. Daily camerawork from southern streets and courtrooms recorded the agony of the region as it resisted African-American challenges to the status quo. The documentaries, whether on commercial or public television, occasionally emerged from black origins, such as William Greave's black journal. "TV Is Black Man's Ally," said the *Los Angeles Sentinel,* while *Variety* reported a new black stereotype: an "intensely brooding, beautiful black rebel."

"Blaxploitation" Films

Hollywood had little choice but to take the point, particularly since several studios were close to collapse. They stood on the verge of what came to be called the era of blaxploitation films. Black youth flocked to this cycle of jangling, violent, and shrilly political movies. Timidly at first, the majors fell to the task. But first, there were easily digestible crossover movies, such as the pastoral tales *Sounder* and *The Learning Tree* (both 1968), the latter an autobiography by the photographer Gordon Parks, Jr. Then came the urban, picaresque heroes most often thought of as "blaxploitation" icons, who combined the cynicism of 1940s film noir style with the kinetic yet cool mode of the black streets. The most famous and probably the highest earner of rentals was Parks's MGM film *Shaft* (1970). The movies that followed, such as Melvin van peebles's *Sweet Sweetback's Baadasssss Song* (1971), constituted calls for direct and sometimes violent retribution against brutal police and exploitative mobsters.

Other movies in the cycle tried to remake white classics by reinventing them in African-American settings—*Cool Breeze* (from *The Asphalt Jungle*), *Blacula* (*Dracula*), *The Lost Man* (*The Informer*). Some were derived from original material angled toward blacks, such as the cavalry Western *Soul Soldier.*

Still another genre—"crossover" movies—sought a wider sector of the market spectrum in the form of material, such as biographies of performers—Billie HOLIDAY, Leadbelly (Huddie LEDBETTER—who had enjoyed followings among whites.

Yet whatever their uneven merits, the blaxploitation movies lost touch with the market. Their place was taken by Chinese martial-art fables, the work of purveyors such as Raymond Chow and Run Run Shaw, featuring impossibly adept warriors whose revenge motifs touched a nerve in the psyches of black urban youth.

Soon the domestic makers of blaxploitation movies lost their market entirely, so that African Americans reached the screen only as functionaries in conventional Hollywood features—police, physicians, and the like—or in prestigious, even reverent treatments of classics or successes from other media, such as Eli Landau's movie of Kurt Weill and Maxwell Anderson's South African musical *Lost in the Stars,* Charles Fuller's *A Soldier's Story,* and E. L. Doctorow's *Ragtime.*

Black Independent Film

Nonetheless, the era had revealed a previously unmeasured black marketplace that seemed ready for either the raffish or the political. Moreover, the combined impact of a thin wedge of black in the Hollywood guilds, an increase in African Americans' numbers in the university film schools, and the opening of television as a training ground resulted in a greater number of filmmakers and, eventually, a steady flow of independently made black films. Madeleine Anderson's combination of journalism and advocacy; St. Clair Bourne's access to black institutions, as in *Let the Church Say Amen;* Haile Gerima's syncretism of the pace and rhythms of East African life and the stuff of African-American life, mediated by film school experience, resulting in his *Bush Mama;* and William Miles's classically styled histories such as *Men of Bronze* and *I Remember Harlem* reflected the catholicity of the movement.

In addition to this focused sort of journalism of advocacy, the 1980s also resulted in a black cinema of personal dimensions, represented by Ayoka Chenzira's *A Film for Nappy Headed People,* Charles Burnett's *Killer of Sheep,* Kathleen Collins's *The Cruz Brothers and Miss Malloy,* and Warrington Hudlin's *Streetcorner Stories* and *Black at Yale.*

By 1990 one of this generation of filmmakers, Spike LEE, had—most notably because of his flair for self-advertisement and for shrewd dealing with established Hollywood—crossed over into the mainstream system. A product of film school as well as the most famous African-American association of the craft, the Black Filmmakers Foundation, Lee managed to glaze his movies of black life with a certain universalist charm that earned the sort of rentals that kept Hollywood financing coming. Somehow he conveyed the urgency, extremity, and drama of the arcana of black life—courtship, Greek letter societies, neighborhood territoriality, the tensions of interracial marriage—into a crescendo of ringing cashboxes. From *She's Gotta Have It, School Daze, Do the Right Thing,* and *Jungle Fever,* he moved toward being entrusted with a Holy Grail of black filmmakers, a biography of MALCOLM X that had been stalled for almost a quarter of a century by fears that its protagonist's memory and mission would be violated if placed in the wrong hands.

More than at any other moment in African-American film history, Lee's access to black life, classical training, black associations, and commercial theaters promised the continued presence and vision of African Americans in cinema, rather than a reprise of the peaks and troughs of faddishness that had marked all previous eras of the medium.

The most insidious threat to their work continued to be that which touched everyone in Hollywood, not only the latest generation of African-American moviemakers: the unyielding fact that Hollywood was a system, a way of doing business that obliged newcomers to learn its conventions and the rules of its game. This was how fads and cycles were made: an innovative spin placed upon a familiar genre revivified it, drew new patrons into the theaters, and inspired a round of sequels and imitators that survived until the next cycle drew attention to itself. After all, even the most dedicated outlaws, Oscar Micheaux and Melvin Van Peebles, either borrowed money from the system or used it to distribute their work. Unavoidably their benefactors expected to shape their products to conform to the codes of conduct by which all movies were made.

Lee's access to black life, classical training, black associations, and commercial theaters promised the continued presence and vision of African Americans in cinema.

Spike Lee and his age-cohorts were particularly successful, since many of them had gone to film school where learning the trade meant in many ways learning the Hollywood system. Lee's *Malcolm X* was a case in point. In order to celebrate, render plausible, and retail his hero and his image, Lee was drawn into the dilemma of not only making a Hollywood "bioepic" but also marketing it as if it were a McDonald's hamburger. The result was remarkably faithful to its Hollywood model: its protagonist is carried along by his own ambition, revealing slightly clayed feet, as though more a charming flaw than a sin, faces implacable adversaries, is misunderstood by his friends and family, undergoes a revelatory conversion experience, is cast out by his coreligionists for having done it, and finally meets a martyr's death and a last-reel apotheosis. This formula, as stylized as a stanza of haiku poetry, in the hands of

Lee was transformed into a vehicle for carrying a particularly reverentential, yet engaging black political idiom to a crossover audience.

Could Lee's successors and age-mates not only endure but also prevail over their medium? Lee himself fretted over their future: "We seem to be in a rut," he told a black film conference at Yale in the Spring of 1992. His concern was not so much directed at the Hollywood establishment but rather to the young African-American filmmakers who had followed him to Hollywood: John Singleton, who at age twenty-three had made *Boyz N the Hood;* Matty Rich, who while still a teenager had made *Straight Out of Brooklyn;* and Lee's own cameraman, Ernest Dickerson, who had made *Juice;* each one of them set in a black ghetto, each centered on a protagonist at risk not so much from forces outside his circle but from within, and each marked by a fatalism that precluded tacking on a classic Hollywood happy ending.

Indeed, forces of daunting economic power seemed to hover over the new black filmmakers even as old-line Hollywood producing companies turned out attractive packages in which black themes and characters held a secure place. First, despite various gestures, the studios had hired woefully few black executives so that every project was pitched to persons uncommitted to its integrity. Second, the top-most owners of the system were more remote than ever, as in the case of the Japanese firm Sony which owned both Columbia Pictures and Tri-Star. Third, each new film, upon its release, faced a round of rumors of impending violence that would mar its opening. Fourth, some movies drawn from black material seemed lost in the welter of ghetto movies, much as Robert Townsend's chronicle of the careers of a black quintet of pop singers, *The Five Heartbeats,* sank from view without having reached the audience it deserved. Fifth, some black films, such as Julie Dash's *Daughter of the Dust,* a rose-tinted history of an African-American family in the Sea Islands of the Carolina low country, were so unique in texture, pace, and coloring that they were played off as esoteric art rather than popular culture. Sixth, Hollywood itself seemed ever more capable of portraying at least some aspects of black life or at least drawing black experiences into closer encounters with white. John Badham's *The Hard Way* (1992) featured the rapper LL Cool J as an undercover policeman of such depth that the actor felt "honored" to play him. Black critics almost universally admired the quiet depth of Danny Glover's role as a steady, rock-solid tow-truck driver in *Grand Canyon* (1992). And in the work of Eddie Murphy at Paramount (where he sponsored "fellowships" designed to add to the talent pool of minority writers) and in other movies such as *White Men Can't Jump,* the absurdities of race and racism in America were portrayed with arch humor.

At its height during the gestation period of Lee's *Malcolm X,* the trend toward a Hollywood-based African-American cinema seemed problematic and open either to a future of running itself into the ground as the moviemakers of the *Super Fly* era had done, falling prey to cooptation by the Hollywood system, or constantly searching out new recruits who might be the answer to Susan Lehman's rhetorical query in her piece in *GQ* (February 1991): "Who Will Be the Next Spike Lee?"

BIBLIOGRAPHY

Bogle, Donald. *Toms, Coons, Mulattoes, Mammies & Bucks.* New York, 1973.

Bourne, St. Clair. *The Making of Spike Lee's Do the Right Thing* (film). New York, 1989.

Carbine, Mary. " 'The Finest Outside the Loop': Motion Picture Exhibition in Chicago's Black Metropolis, 1905–1928." *Camera Obscura* 23 (May 1990): 9–42.

Cripps, Thomas. *Black Film as Genre.* Bloomington, Ind., 1978.

———. *Black Shadows on a Silver Screen* (film). Washington, D.C., 1976.

———. "*Casablanca, Tennessee Johnson,* and *The Negro Soldier*—Hollywood Liberals and World War II." In K. R. M. Short, ed. *Feature Films as History.* London, 1981, pp. 138–156.

———. "Making Movies Black." In Jannette L. Dates and William Barlow, eds. *Split Image: African Americans in the Mass Media.* Washington, D.C., 1990, pp. 125–154.

———. "Movies, Race, and World War II . . ." *Prologue: The Journal of the National Archives* 14 (Summer 1982): 49–67.

———. "*Native Son* in the Movies." *New Letters* 28 (Winter 1972): 49–63.

———. *Slow Fade to Black: The Negro in American Film, 1900–1942.* New York, 1977.

———. "*Sweet Sweetback's Baadasssss Song* and the Changing Politics of Genre Film." In Peter Lehman, ed. *Close Viewings: Recent Film.* Tallahassee, Fla., 1990, pp. 238–261.

———. "Winds of Change: *Gone with the Wind* and Racism as a National Issue." In Darden Asbury Pyron, ed. *Recasting: Gone with the Wind in American Culture.* Miami, 1983, pp. 137–153.

Gaines, Jane. "*The Scar of Shame:* Skin Color and Caste in Black Silent Melodrama." *Cinema Journal* 26 (Summer 1987): 3–21.

Hall, Stuart. "Gramsci's Relevance for the Study of Race and Ethnicity." *Journal of Communications Inquiry* 10 (Summer 1986): 5–27.

Hooks, Bell. "Black Women Filmmakers Break the Silence." *Black Film Review* 2 (Summer 1986): 14–15.

Klotman, Phyllis Rauch. *Frame by Frame-A Black Filmography.* Bloomington, Ind., 1979.

———. *Screenplays of the African American Experience.* Bloomington, Ind., 1991.

Leab, Daniel J. *From Sambo to Superspade: The Black Experience in Motion Pictures.* Boston, 1975.

Maynard, Richard A., ed. *The Black Man on Film: Racial Stereotyping.* Rochelle Park, N.J., 1974.

Merod, Jim. "A World Without Whole Notes: The Intellectual Subtext of Spike Lee's *Blues.*" *Boundary* 2 (1991): 239–251.

Patterson, Lindsay, ed. *Black Films and Filmmakers: A Comprehensive Anthology.* New York, 1975.

Peavy, Charles D. "Black Consciousness and the Contemporary Cinema." In Ray B. Browne, ed. *Popular Culture and the Expanding Consciousness.* New York, 1973, pp. 178–200.

Sampson, Henry T., comp. *Blacks in Black and White: A Source Book on Black Films.* Metuchen, N.J., 1977.

Taylor, Clyde. "Visionary Black Cinema." *Black Collegian* (October/November 1989): 226–233.

Waller, Gregory A. "Another Audience: Black Moviegoing in Lexington, Ky., 1907–1916." *Cinema Journal* 31 (Winter 1992): 3–44.

Woll, Allen L., and Randall M. Miller, comps. *Ethnic and Racial Images in American Film and Television: Historical Essays and Bibliography.* New York, 1987.

– THOMAS CRIPPS

FIRST SOUTH CAROLINA VOLUNTEER REGIMENT

As the first Union regiment of ex-slaves organized in the South during the CIVIL WAR, the First South Carolina Volunteers assumed the burden of proving to a skeptical North that blacks could be effective soldiers. Although officially mustered on November 7, 1862, the regiment emerged from earlier independent efforts of Gen. David Hunter (1802–1886) to organize black troops in the Department of the South. Hunter's unit never received authorization from the War Department, and within a few months he disbanded all but one company of his men. Gen. Rufus Saxton (1824–1908), supervisor of freed slaves in Hunter's department, took control of the unit, and on August 25, 1862, he gained Secretary of War Edwin M. Stanton's approval to enlist "volunteers of African descent as you may deem expedient, not exceeding five thousand." According to Stanton, the soldiers—and their families—would be granted their freedom and were entitled to receive "the same pay and rations as are allowed, by law, to volunteers in the service."

The First South Carolina Volunteers assumed the burden of proving to a skeptical North that blacks could be effective soldiers.

Thomas Wentworth Higginson (1823–1911), the fiery Massachusetts abolitionist, commanded the regiment and led it on daring raids from Port Royal, S.C., to Palatka, Fla. Higginson and his men understood that they "fought with ropes around their necks." They faced execution or enslavement if captured by Southerners, who considered black soldiers to be rebellious slaves and their white officers as treacherous criminals. Perhaps more galling, they were subjected to scurrilous charges of racial inferiority from the northern press. Nevertheless, Higginson sought to test his men in combat to dispel racist accusations that blacks could not or would not fight. The men, former slaves from South Carolina and Florida, quickly proved their ability and Higginson published stirring accounts of their exploits, laying the groundwork for full-scale black recruitment. Both Higginson and Saxton proclaimed that the men fought as bravely as any other regiment in the army. Moreover, Higginson maintained that the unit, the first to fight alongside whites under the same command in regular duty, helped to reduce racism in the army.

The regiment was authorized to draft former slaves into service, which led to some illegal impressments. But the overwhelming number of blacks volunteered for service to win freedom for themselves and their families. The government's refusal to grant the promised equal pay caused dissension in the "First," as it did among nearly all black regiments, but Higginson claimed that he never resorted to harsh measures to maintain discipline. The men, he believed, had joined out of the deepest sense of patriotism, a hatred of slavery, and "a love of liberty."

On February 8, 1864, the "First" was redesignated the Thirty-third United States Colored Troops (USCT) and subsequently took part in battles at Pocotaligo and James Island, in South Carolina. The Thirty-third USCT performed provost guard duty at Charleston, S.C., and Savannah, Ga., in February and March 1865, and was mustered out on February 9, 1866.

BIBLIOGRAPHY

Cornish, Dudley Taylor. *The Sable Arm: Negro Troops in the Union Army, 1861–1865.* New York, 1966.

Higginson, Thomas Wentworth. *Army Life in a Black Regiment.* 1869. Reprint. Boston, 1962.

– DONALD YACOVONE

FISHER, RUDOLPH JOHN CHAUNCEY

Rudolph John Chauncey Fisher (1897–1934), fiction writer, dramatist, and essayist. The youngest child of a Baptist minister, Fisher was born in Washington, D.C. He lived briefly in New York City as a small boy but was raised and educated largely in Providence, R.I., where he graduated from Classical High School and Brown University. An undergraduate of many talents, he was chosen by fellow students to be Class Day orator and by the faculty to be commencement speaker. He wrote his first published short story, "The City of Refuge" (1925), in his final year at Howard Medical School, initiating simultaneous vocations in literature and science. When Fisher's internship ended at Freedman's Hospital in Washington, D.C., a National Research Council Fellowship brought him to New York City in 1925 to work in bacteriology with Dr. Frederick P. Gay at the College of Physicians and Surgeons of Columbia University. At the pivotal moment of HARLEM RENAISSANCE in the mid–1920s, he consolidated his medical and literary careers with scientific articles in the *Journal of Infectious Diseases* and *Proceedings of the Society of Experimental Biology and Medicine* and short stories in the *Atlantic Monthly, Survey Graphic,* and *McClure's* magazine. He married Jane Ryder in 1925, and their son Hugh was born in 1926.

One of the more prolific writers of the Harlem Renaissance, Fisher produced in less than a decade fifteen published and seven unpublished short stories, two novels, half a dozen book reviews, a magazine feature article, and a play—while maintaining a medical practice, administering a private X-ray laboratory, and chairing the department of roentgenology at the International Hospital in Manhattan. Harlem is at the center of his literary project. "I intended to write whatever interests me. But if I should be fortunate enough to be known as Harlem's interpreter," he said in response to a radio interviewer's question on WINS in 1933, "I should be very happy." *The Walls of Jericho* (1928), his first novel, interweaves genre elements of color-conscious 1920s Harlem fiction—country-rooted southern migrants, slick Harlemites, and West Indians with their distinctive dialects and repartee; block-busting scenarios; racist uplifters of the race; rival lovers and their Arcadian conflicts; passing—and brings it all together amid the converging vectors of social and racial distinction at a Harlem ball. His other novel, *The Conjure Man Dies* (1932), is regarded as the earliest example of a detective novel published in book form by an African-American author.

Fisher's place among the writers of the Harlem Renaissance rests, however, on the excellence of his short fiction. In short stories, focused on tensions between West Indians and native-born Americans ("Ringtail"); alienation and reconciliation ("Fire by Night" and "The Backslider"); divisions between youth and age, the modern and the traditional, spirituals and blues ("The Promised Land"); and black consciousness and jazz in a battle of the bands ("Common Meter"), he conveys what Arthur P. Davis called a "fuller" picture of Harlem life viewed with "an understanding and amused eye," and what Sterling BROWN termed "a jaunty realism . . . less interested in that 'problem' than in the life and language of Harlem's poolrooms, cafes, and barbershops."

Two short stories in particular, "The City of Refuge" and "Miss Cynthie" (1933)—both anthologized in *The Best American Short Stories*—are Fisher's most highly regarded achievements. "The City of Refuge" concerns the arrival in Harlem of King Solomon Gillis, "a baby jess in from the land o' cotton . . . an' ripe f' the pluckin." Gillis is betrayed by everyone who seems to befriend him, yet when he is arrested by a black policeman, the symbol of Harlem's possibility he saw when he first arrived, Gillis, who "plodded flat-footedly" on "legs never quite straightened," can stand "erect" and "exhultant" as he submits to an icon of black authority. In "Miss Cynthie," Fisher's last published work, he matches his undisputed ability to evoke locale and character with what Robert Bone calls a newly discovered sense of "how to *interiorize* his dramatic conflicts, so that his protagonists have the ability to grow." Miss Cynthie struggles to embrace the success of the grandson she hopes is a doctor or at least an undertaker, but who turns out to be a song-and-dance virtuoso.

In 1934, Rudolph Fisher underwent a series of operations for an intestinal disorder—associated by some sources with his early work with X-rays—and died on December 26 of that year.

BIBLIOGRAPHY

Bone, Robert. "Three Versions of Pastoral." In *Down Home: A History of Afro-American Short Fiction from Its Beginnings to the End of the Harlem Renaissance.* 1975. Reprint. New York, 1988, pp. 139–170.

Brown, Sterling. "The Urban Scene." In *Negro Poetry and Drama and The Negro in American Fiction.* New York, 1969, pp. 131–150.

Davis, Arthur P. "Rudolph Fisher." In *From the Dark Tower: Afro-American Writers, 1900–1960.* Washington, D.C., 1974, pp. 98–103.

McCluskey, John, Jr. "Introduction." In *The City of Refuge: Collected Stories of Rudolph Fisher.* Columbia, Mo., 1987, pp. xi-xxxix.

Perry, Margaret. "The Brief Life and Art of Rudolph Fisher." In *The Short Fiction of Rudolph Fisher.* New York and Westport, Conn., 1987, pp. 1–20.

– JAMES DE JONGH

FISK UNIVERSITY

Fisk University is a private, coeducational, and independent liberal arts institution in Nashville, Tenn. It was founded in October 1865 by Erastus Milo Cravath, field secretary for the American Missionary Association (AMA); John Ogden, superintendent of education, Freedmen's Bureau, Tenn.; and the Rev. Edward P. Smith, district secretary, Middle West Department, AMA, at Cincinnati. Cravath and Smith had been sent to Nashville by the AMA to establish an elementary school for freedmen in the area. The two men joined forces with Ogden, who was named principal of the Fisk School, or the Fisk Free Colored School, when it opened on January 1, 1866, in former Union hospital barracks. The buildings and land had been purchased with much financial and moral support from the assistant commissioner of the Freedmen's Bureau for Tennessee and Kentucky, Gen. Clinton Bowen Fisk, for whom the school was named. The American Missionary Association and the Freedmen's Bureau also helped to fund the school.

Although at first it functioned mainly as an elementary and normal school, Fisk was incorporated as Fisk University on August 22, 1867, following the founders' desires for a "first-class college" to educate black teachers. The college curriculum was organized by Adam K. Spence, a Scottish-born professor of foreign languages who left the University of Michigan in 1870 to replace Ogden as principal. Fisk graduated its first four college students in 1875, awarding them the B.A. degree for successfully completing courses in such liberal arts subjects as classical and foreign languages, mathematics, natural sciences, philosophy, history, and political science. In keeping with Fisk's religious orientation, weekly Bible classes were also required.

Fisk's income derived primarily from sporadic donations, as well as what could be raised from the modest tuition rates. Under Spence's leadership it experienced dire financial problems, and had often to delay salary payments to its hardworking and dedicated teaching staff, which was originally composed primarily of white missionaries sent by the AMA. The buildings were deteriorating and in need of repair. George L. White, Fisk's treasurer and self-taught music instructor, set out on October 6, 1871, with a group of nine of his best students for a fund-raising singing tour of the North and East. White named the group the Jubilee Singers.

The Jubilee Singers introduced "slave songs" or SPIRITUALS to audiences and returned the following year with $20,000 to purchase a forty-acre campus site. Groundbreaking ceremonies were held July 1, 1873, for the erection of Jubilee Hall, now a historic landmark. The Singers remained a Fisk tradition for many years.

In 1875, Erastus Milo Cravath became the first president of Fisk University when the position of principal was eliminated, and the AMA gave up direction of the institution, transferring titles and buildings to the Fisk trustees. Spence continued at Fisk as professor of Greek until 1900. He joined other members of Fisk's white faculty in enrolling his own child at the increasingly reputable university.

Under Cravath's presidency Fisk's reputation grew, and as early as 1875 black professors joined the staff. Among the students who came from the North to study at Fisk was W. E. B. DU BOIS, one of the university's most famous alumni, who received his B.A. in 1888. When Cravath died in 1900, Fisk had graduated more than 400 students who spread Fisk's fame across the U.S. in their careers as lawyers, professors, businessmen, ministers, and editors.

During the presidency of James G. Merrill (1900–1908), Fisk added a summer school for black teachers who wanted to improve their training, as well as many new science courses. When Merrill resigned, Fisk was again experiencing money troubles, since philanthropies at that time were more interested in investing in vocational and industrial schools such as the Tuskegee Institute. Many educators followed the line of reasoning that favored a "practical" education for blacks—training to enter the work force. But Fisk remained staunchly in favor of offering the best liberal arts education it could to blacks in order to produce leaders for the black community.

Under the administration of George A. Gates, president from 1909 to 1912, Fisk established the social science department for which it would become well known. It also began to receive considerable donations from such philanthropists as Andrew Carnegie, Julius Rosenwald, and John D. Rockefeller. These donations were largely results of tireless campaigning on behalf of the university by Booker T. WASHINGTON, whose wife and son were alumni of Fisk.

The presidency of Fayette Avery McKenzie, who took office after Gates's untimely death, brought with it an "expansion of the curriculum and raising of standards," as well as a $2 million endowment campaign. By July 19, 1924, McKenzie was successful in securing half of the endowment. Although the school showed growth, McKenzie's dictatorial administration and strict student discipline led in 1924 and 1925 to one of the first student rebellions on a black college campus. Du Bois fueled the fire of the revolt by speaking out to other alumni against McKenzie. McKenzie was especially resented for his ingratiating behavior toward prominent white citizens of Nashville, and his insistence on unobtrusive, passive behavior from the black students even in the face of antiblack violence. McKenzie resigned on April 16, 1925.

Thomas Elsa Jones, a Quaker missionary, became the last white president in 1926. His years are viewed as one of the most productive periods in Fisk history. He eradicated the stricter regulations imposed on students until then. The $2 million endowment was attained. Black faculty increased to more than one-half, and the first black dean, Ambrose Caliver, was named when Jones took office. Jones placed emphasis on increasing graduate studies at the university and attracting research-oriented professors. One of these professors was Charles Spurgeon Johnson, who became the head of the department of social science in 1928 and established the Institute of Race Relations at Fisk in 1944, drawing white and black leaders to campus annually for intensive three-week conferences. In 1947 Johnson became Fisk's first black president, replacing Jones, who'd resigned to become president of his alma mater, Earlham College. Johnson's administration ended abruptly in 1956 when he died of a heart attack.

During these formative years, Fisk garnered a number of historical firsts among black colleges and universities. It was the first black college to gain full accreditation by the Southern Association of Colleges and Schools (1930); to be on the approved list of the Association of American Universities (1933); to establish a university archive (1948); to be approved by the American Association of University Women (1951); to be granted a chapter of the honorary society Phi Beta Kappa (1952); and to be accredited for membership in the National Association of Schools of Music (1954).

The 1960s brought an expansion in educational programs and buildings. A centennial celebration was held in 1966, and James Raymond Lawson, an alumnus and scientist, was inaugurated as president, replacing Stephen Junius Wright, Jr., who had been named president after Johnson's death. Enrollment reached 1,559 in 1972, the largest in the University's history. In 1977, the campus was designated by the Department of the Interior as an historical site in the National Register of Historical Places by the National Parks Service.

Ironically, in the early 1970s, school desegregation had an adverse effect on Fisk's finances, as government funding was cut back and competition for students increased as formerly segregated schools lured potential black applicants. In July 1975, Fisk's financial situation reached a crisis point as eleven percent of full-time faculty and forty staff members were laid off. Those remaining took a twenty-percent salary abatement.

With the resignation of Lawson that same year, the school was without a president until 1977, when Walter Jewell Leonard, an attorney, was selected. Inheriting serious financial woes, Leonard's administration was also a target of faculty and student disgruntlement. Student enrollment dropped and a number of faculty resigned.

When a cold homecoming day on November 12, 1983, found dormitories without heat, it became public that the Nashville Gas Company had discontinued service in April because of an overdue bill of $157,000. The financial crisis worsened as the Nashville Electric Service threatened to cut off the university's electricity if $140,000 of their bill was not met immediately. At the same time the Internal Revenue Service was threatening to put a lien on Fisk's property, since the university owed $500,000 in back payroll taxes. When Leonard suddenly resigned on November 23, 1983, the school, which had been $2.2 million in debt at his inauguration, owed some $2.8 million.

The crisis alarmed the nation, and leaders rallied to "save Fisk." President Ronald Reagan donated $1,000, and the United States Secretary of Education, Terrel H. Bell, created a task force from the public and private sectors "to review financial difficulties facing Fisk University."

As in 1871, Fisk once again withstood the tide of financial disaster, receiving scores of donations from alumni and friends. Henry Ponder, an economist, took the reins of the beleaguered institution in July 1984 as the tenth president, and set out to pare back to a "bare-bones" operation.

Despite financial hardships, the university has continued to maintain its position as a flagship among historical black colleges and universities with a tradition of academic excellence. Fisk's $10 million Alfred Stieglitz Collection of Modern Art, presented to the university in 1949 by Georgia O'Keeffe, widow of Stieglitz, as well as its library of valuable research collections and rare books, attracts visitors from all over the world. Fisk alumni, among some of the most distinguished in the nation, include the aforementioned W. E. B. Du Bois, the historian Charles H. Wesley, Congressman William Levi Dawson, and the novelist Frank Yerby. Enrollment for 1993 numbered 861.

BIBLIOGRAPHY

Collins, L. M. *One Hundred Years of Fisk University Presidents.* Nashville, Tenn., 1989.

Richardson, Joe M. *A History of Fisk University, 1865–1946.* 1980.

– ANN ALLEN SHOCKLEY

FITZGERALD, ELLA

Ella Fitzgerald (April 25, 1918–June 15, 1996), jazz vocalist. In a career lasting half a century, Ella Fitzgerald's superb pitch and diction, infallible sense of rhythm, and masterful scat singing have all become part of the fabric of American music, and she has been recognized as one "First Lady of Song." While her background and technique were rooted in jazz, she has always been a popular singer, with a soothing yet crystalline sound that brought wide acclaim. Born in Newport News, Va., she came north as a child to Yonkers, N.Y., with her mother. In 1934, on a dare, she entered a Harlem amateur-night contest as a dancer, but became immobile with stage fright when called on to perform. Instead, she sang two songs popularized by the Boswell Sisters, "Judy" and "The Object of My Affection," and won first prize.

After she had won several more amateur competitions, an opportunity came in February 1935, when she appeared at the Apollo and was spotted by Bardu Ali, the master of ceremonies for Chick Webb's band, who persuaded Webb to hire her. Fitzgerald began performing with Webb's band at the Savoy Club, and cut her first record, "Love and Kisses," with them in June 1935. Inspired by a nursery rhyme, Fitzgerald cowrote and recorded "A-Tisket, A-Tasket" with Webb's group in 1938; it became one of the most successful records of the swing era and transformed the young singer into a national celebrity.

Ella Fitzgerald's superb pitch and diction, infallible sense of rhythm, and masterful scat singing have all become part of the fabric of American music.

When Webb died suddenly in 1939, Fitzgerald assumed nominal leadership of his band, which broke up two years later. During the 1940s she gained prominence as a solo performer through hit records that showcased her versatility. Influenced by Dizzy GILLESPIE and bebop, in 1947 Fitzgerald recorded, "Oh, Lady Be Good" and "How High the Moon," two songs that utilized her scat singing, the wordless vocal improvising that became her signature style. By the early 1950s, she had appeared around the world with the star-studded Jazz and the Philharmonic tours organized by Norman Granz, a record producer and impresario who became her manager in 1954. Under his supervision and on his Verve label, she recorded *The Cole Porter Songbook* in 1956, followed by anthologies devoted to George and Ira Gershwin, Duke Ellington, Irving Berlin, and other popular composers. Heavily arranged and cannily designed to promote both songwriter and performer, Fitzgerald's "songbooks" extended her appeal.

By the 1960s, she was one of the world's most respected and successful singers. In the following years, she became something of an institution, regularly honored. She was named "Best Female Vocalist" by *Down Beat* magazine several times, and she has more Grammy Awards than any other female jazz singer. Following heart bypass surgery in 1986, she suffered from erratic health, but she intermittently recorded and gave concerts.

BIBLIOGRAPHY

Colin, Sid. *Ella: The Life and Times of Ella Fitzgerald.* London, 1986.

Kliment, Bud. *Ella Fitzgerald.* New York, 1988.

Pleasants, Henry. "Ella Fitzgerald." In *The Great American Popular Singers.* New York, 1974, pp. 168–180.

— BUD KLIMENT

FOLK ARTS AND CRAFTS

The folk arts and crafts created by African Americans are, perhaps, the least acknowledged of their cultural traditions. Worldwide recognition of black achievement in music and dance has overshadowed significant accomplishments in the area of material culture so that while black Americans are seen as gifted performers, they are rarely described as even adequate producers of objects.

Vernacular Traditions

In times past, black artisans were numerous, and they are to be credited with making a wide array of artifacts, particularly in the southern states. It is important to recall that during the preindustrial era most rural people made things: tools, utensils, containers, clothes, food, houses, toys. Whether as slaves or as free people, blacks created a multitude of necessary, useful, and sometimes beautiful, objects.

The reasons why African Americans would be skilled at making domestic arts and crafts are not hard to fathom. On plantations they often had little choice when they were ordered to learn particular trades by their owners. But more often, because they were provided with so few domestic items, they either had to make most of their furnishings and utensils, or do without. After Emancipation the folk arts and crafts that blacks had developed in the plantation setting continued to prove useful. Reduced to a condition of near servitude by continued racial exploitation and poverty, African-American artisans used their traditional skills to get themselves and their families through tough times, and some still do today. Folk arts and crafts have always played dual roles in the black community, serving both as a means of making a living and as a means for creative self-expression. While many items of folk art and craft produced by African Americans are indistinguishable in form, technique, and style from works produced by white Americans, there is a stream of African inspiration that runs through traditional black material culture in the South. The most distinctive works of African-American black folk art, in cultural terms, are those that manifest a linkage to African origins. This article provides a survey of these expressions.

BASKETRY. Coiled-grass baskets have been produced in the United States by black artisans for more than three centuries. Once integral items on plantations, particularly along the so-called "rice coast" that once extended from North Carolina to Florida's northern border, the craft is today most publicly on display in and around Charleston, S.C. Here hundreds of "sewers" are at work fashioning baskets. Using "sweetgrass," rush, pine needles, and strips of leaves from the palmetto tree as their primary materials, they produce a seemingly limitless variety of forms which they sell on street corners, in the central open-air market, and at more than fifty stands along the main highway entering the city.

What one sees here are "show baskets," a subgenre within this tradition that was initiated probably in the mid-nineteenth century. Included under this category are all sorts of decorative containers: flower baskets, serving trays, purses, sewing baskets, casserole holders, umbrella stands, and cake baskets. As is evident from this partial inventory, the show basket is intended to be used in the home where it will be prominently displayed. As these items are made, then, to be fancy, the basketmakers explore, at every opportunity, new creative possibilities in form and decoration. A show basket is a highly personalized artwork shaped extensively by individual imagination.

The most distinctive works of African-American black folk art, in cultural terms, are those that manifest a linkage to African origins.

Yet matriarch basketmaker Mary Jane Manigault explains, "All baskets begin as a hot plate," meaning that all works, no matter how imaginative and seemingly without precedent, trace back to a common ancestry rooted in basic forms and techniques: all coiled baskets start out as a disk form. The oldest African-American coiled baskets were "work baskets." They were made with bundles of stiff rushes and often sewn with strips of oak. With coils generally an inch in diameter, these were tough, durable baskets intended to be used outside, either in the fields or in the farmyard. They are easily distinguishable from the lighter, more delicately formed show baskets. Most work baskets were large, heavy, round containers made to carry produce; they all had flat bottoms and straight walls that flared out slightly from the base. One specialized work basket, the fanner, was a large tray about two feet in diameter, with a low outer rim. Primarily an implement for processing the rice harvest, it was also used as a basic kitchen tool. Rice could not be properly cooked unless it had first been fanned to separate the kernels from the husks.

These baskets were but one element in a set of African practices upon which the production of rice was based. Planters specifically sought out slaves from the rice-growing regions of West and Central Africa and with these people came not only a knowledge of rice cultivation, but also the basic technology for its harvest and preparation as food. While planters were generally wary about allowing overt African expressions among their slaves, they tolerated this mode of basketry when they realized that it basically enhanced the productivity of their estates.

Unwittingly, then, these planters actually facilitated the maintenance of decidedly African tradition. While the end of the plantation era understandably brought an end to the work basket tradition, it did not cause coiled basketry to disappear altogether. These baskets remained a feature of home craft on small black farms in the area and there was from 1910 to 1950 an attempt at the Penn School on St. Helena Island to revive the practice. While this particular effort ended with disappointing results, the tradition was able to flourish in the Charleston area, where show baskets became exceedingly popular among tourists who assiduously sought them as souvenirs of their visits.

The basketmaking tradition was necessarily transformed as artisans shifted from a rural to an urban venue as artisans made baskets more often for sale than for domestic use. Yet venerable traditions were still honored. The sewing baskets and serving trays were old-time baskets, too, even if their origins did not trace all the way back to Africa, as did those of the work baskets. But the entrepreneurial energies that were released in this commercial effort led mainly to freewheeling displays of personal imagination. Soon basketmakers were as proud of new unprecedented forms that they called "own style baskets" as they were of more conventional flower baskets or clothes hampers.

But even within this spirited and open-ended creativity there are still signs of historical memory. Fanner baskets, for example, can occasionally be found for sale in the Charleston market, albeit as lightweight show basket facsimiles. But more important, the techniques for coiling and stitching remain unchanged regardless of the type of basket. This continuity of process allows contemporary basketmakers to place themselves in the flow of a tradition that traces back through time and space to African roots. The personal satisfaction that these artisans derive from making coiled baskets is amplified by a keen awareness of that history, and as a result they are all the more motivated to preserve this custom.

BOATBUILDING. That African-American competence in agriculture was matched by maritime abilities should not be surprising. Most African slaves were captured, after all, from either coastal or riverine environments, and thus they had extensive experience with a variety of small craft. When set to work on plantations, often located near coasts or along prominent rivers, these Africans had ample opportunity to display their navigation skills. Eighteenth-century commentators were quick to acknowledge how adept slaves were in paddling log canoes, which often proved difficult to maneuver in swift currents and to keep upright. In the Charleston area, black watermen working out of hewn dugouts called "pettiaugers" (an Anglicized version of the French *piroques*) had by 1750 achieved almost complete domination of the local fishing trade. White people depended on black boating skills from Georgia to Maryland as slaves literally provided the backbone for the local transportation system during the period when there were few roads.

In this context, slaves also built boats, and while their surviving descriptions tend to be somewhat vague with respect to details, it seems that West Indian watercraft, and thus in some measure African-derived maritime traditions, provided the basic models. The pettiauger was a well-known Caribbean vessel with a hull consisting of a log dugout extended by the addition of extra planks. Fitted with sails for open-water voyaging, it could also be propelled by teams of oarsmen. Boats of this sort are described repeatedly as the usual type of plantation "barge" used to ferry people, supplies, and produce. A second type of plantation vessel was a canoe hewn from a single log. Derived from either African or Native American precedents, it was less than twenty feet in length and relatively light due to the thinness of the hull. This was an excellent vessel for navigating the shallow marshes and streams surrounding the barrier islands of the South Carolina and Georgia coasts. Plantation mistress Fannie Kemble recorded in 1838 that two slave carpenters on her Butler Island estate had made such a canoe which they sold for the sum of $60. A type of multilog dugout, common to the waters of the Chesapeake Bay, is credited to a slave from York County, Va., remembered only as Aaron. In form this craft, a log canoe with a hull shaped from as many as nine logs, seems related to the West Indian pettiaugers.

In Virginia and Maryland, African Americans were extensively involved in a full range of shipbuilding trades as ship's carpenters, caulkers, sailmakers, and blacksmiths. A remarkable account from the *Raleigh Star* in 1811 describes how a brig launched in Alexandria, Va., was "drafted by a coloured man belonging to Col. Tayloe and under his superintendence built from her keel to her topmast." Here the design sources were unquestionably Anglo-American, but the fact that a slave was given such broad authority suggests that he was working in a context in which most of the men under his command must have been slaves as well. This event suggests that blacks might have been able to do quite well as shipbuilders had they simply been afforded the chance. But there were few opportunities as African-American waterman were diverted mainly to fishing and oyster dredging, where they would be employed for their brawn rather than their designing and woodworking skills.

MUSICAL INSTRUMENT MAKING. In the testimony of former slaves there is frequent mention of homemade musical instruments. Litt Young from Mississippi recalled exciting events around 1860, when "Us have small dances Saturday nights and ring plays and fiddle playin' and knockin' bones. There was fiddles made from gourds and banjos from sheep hides." The inventory here of stringed and percussive instruments identifies two of the main classes of musical instruments frequently made by African-American artisans. To Young's short list one can add rattles, gongs, scrapers, fifes, whistles, pan pipes, and drums. All of these had verifiable African antecedents, as did many of the songs they were used to play and the dances the instruments were intended to accompany.

The drums that were so essential not only to African musical performance but to religious and healing rituals were frightening to slave holders, for they realized that these instruments could be used to send private messages that they would not be able to decipher. Laws were passed in South Carolina after the STONO REBELLION of 1739 and later in other colonies banning the playing of drums expressly to eliminate this means of communication. But such prohibitions were less than effective as deterrents, and well into the nineteenth century, slaves, particularly those who were more recently arrived from Africa, were still making drums. They commonly affixed some type of animal skin with thongs or pegs across the open end of a hollowed log or large gourd. Apparently such drums were made often enough that even as late as the 1930s elderly blacks living in the coastal regions of Georgia could still describe the practice in detail. Even though the custom was fast fading into obscurity by that time, a few of these informants claimed even to have made drums themselves.

The banjo is a very old black folk instrument that continues to enjoy considerable popularity among white aficionados of so-called "country music." This is an instrument which, according to no less an authority than Thomas Jefferson, black people "brought hither from Africa." In the earliest examples, the body of the instrument was shaped from gourd sliced in half lengthwise that was then covered with a stretched animal skin. A fretless neck was inserted at one end and four gut strings were run from its top to the base of the gourd. Today's banjos made in factories are different in every respect, except that they continue to have membrane-covered drums underneath the strings. Thus when the instrument is strummed one can still hear the distinctive combination of melodic tone and percussive thrump that was present in the original plantation instruments. The mainstay of African-American folk music through the early twentieth century, when it was largely supplanted by the blues guitar, the banjo is rarely played today by black musicians, and the only reported contemporary makers of banjos with gourd bodies are white.

The mainstay of African-American folk music through the early twentieth century, the banjo is rarely played today by black musicians.

The experience among fife makers, however, is more positive. In the delta area of northwestern Mississippi a small number of families continue to play fifes or, as they might say, "blow canes," as the entertainment at local picnics and barbecues. These people make their fifes as well. The process seems relatively simple: A foot-long section of bamboo cane is hollowed out and a mouth hole and four finger holes are pierced into it with a red-hot poker. There is considerable difficulty in calculating the correct placement for the holes so that notes of the correct pitch can be played. Considerable experimentation is required, since each piece of cane has a slightly different tonal range. In Mississippi, the fife is played as the lead instrument together with an ensemble of drums; it is a performance that resonates with similar performances among the Akan peoples of Ghana.

POTTERY. Slave potters made two very different types of wares. The earliest were earthenware vessels shaped by hand and fired to very low temperatures in open bonfires. These pots, recovered from the sites of many eighteenth-century plantations in South Carolina and Virginia, consisted mainly of small, round-bottomed bowls suitable for eating and drinking and larger round-bottomed cooking vessels. For decades these sorts of vessels were believed to be Native American in origin and thus were labeled as "Colono-Indian wares." Subsequent investigation has shown that given the sheer quantity of Colono shards at the sites of slave occupation and their relative absence in Indian villages during the same period, there can be no other conclusion than that this type of pottery was being made by slave artisans. Comparisons with African wares lend further support to the claim of slave manufacture so that some of this eighteenth-century earthenware is now referred to as Afro-Colono pottery. Many plantation-made bowls have a cross or an "X" scratched into their bases. While the function of these intriguing marks remains open to speculation, these are signs that have mystical association in Central Africa, where they are used in acts of prayer, particularly in summoning the protective power of ancestral spirits. As scholars have puzzled through the significance of these marks, they have surmised that the first slaves must have looked to their own inventory of cultural forms when they had to find an adequate way to feed themselves and they simply turned to a familiar African craft tradition. When slaves next discovered that their owners would not interfere in their efforts, some of these Africans may have gone even further and used their African pots to regenerate their interrupted religious traditions.

By the middle of the nineteenth century, the production of earthenware on plantations had ended. There were by then relatively few Africans in the slave population left to carry on the practice. More important, slave owners were now providing more food preparation items like cast-iron cooking pots. The first quarter of the nineteenth century witnessed as well an upsurge in the production of stoneware pottery, a durable type of ware shaped on a potter's wheel and fired to very high temperatures in a kiln. This type of pottery was produced mainly at small family-run shops. Occasionally slaves were employed in these shops, but chiefly as the laborers who cut the firewood or dug and mixed the clay; the more prestigious role of potter or turner was reserved for a white artisan. There was, however, one site where blacks were allowed more extensive participation, and it is there that one can identify a nineteenth-century tradition for African-American pottery.

About 1810, Abner Landrum, a prosperous white man living in the Edgefield District of west-central South Carolina, opened a pottery shop and was soon producing high-quality wares recognized as superior to any in the region. His shop would quickly grow into a booming industrial village and before long Landrum was selling stock in his operation. His financial success, however, did not go unchallenged. Other entrepreneurs also set up potteries in the area, luring away many of Landrum's skilled artisans. When he solved this crisis by training slaves to make pottery, other pottery owners soon followed his example.

Most of these African-American artisans remain unnamed, but various records suggest that about fifty slaves were employed at various shops throughout the Edgefield District. The best known of this group was a man named Dave who had once belonged to Abner Landrum. Trained first as a typesetter at Landrum's newspaper, Dave continued to display the fact that he was literate on his pots by signing and dating them and occasionally inscribing them with rhymed couplets. These vessels, unlike most, carry terse captions describing the time of manufacture and their maker's identity. More important, that they publicly carry words at a time when it was illegal for slaves to be literate makes these pots statements of overt resistance. Other slaves, upon seeing Dave's works, were likely to know that one of their own was mocking the white man's law, and they may have derived some measure of inspiration from his audacious example.

Certainly many would have noticed Dave's pots, for he made some of the largest vessels known in Edgefield. The largest one, inscribed "Great and Noble Jar," has a capacity of almost forty-five gallons and stands thirty inches in height. Many of his other pots are in this same size range and are distinctively shaped, with walls that flare boldly from a relatively narrow base to a wide shoulder close to the top of the vessel. While white potters also made large storage jars, none of their works seem as daring. With their widest sections nearer their middles, they appear to squat safely on the floor, while Dave's pots seemingly leap up and threaten to teeter back and forth. The form of Dave's pot thus emphasizes the rebelliousness signaled by his inscriptions.

Even though Dave's work is a reflection of commonplace African-American experiences of chattel slavery in the South, his pieces, as objects, are basically expressions of European ceramic traditions. The pot forms for which he is now so famous appear to take their lines ultimately from the bread pots of northeastern England, and his use of pottery wheels, kilns, and glazes are all manifestations of standardized Anglo-American ceramic technology. Yet within the community of black potters in Edgefield there were opportunities for artisans to revisit ancestral aesthetic forms. In series of small vessels, averaging about five inches in height, slave potters were apparently able to rekindle memories of African sculpture.

Pots decorated with faces are known in every ceramic tradition on the globe, but those attributed to black people in Edgefield have several attributes not seen elsewhere. Their most distinctive feature is the use of a different clay body to mark the eyes and teeth: White porcelain clay contrasts sharply with the dark glaze covering the rest of the stoneware vessel. The riveting gaze and seeming snarl that results from this mode of decoration recalls the mixed-media approach to sculpture found in West and Central Africa, where all sorts of contrasting materials are applied to a wooden form for dramatic effect, particularly in the rendering of eyes and teeth on statues and masks. That a white substance is used in Edgefield is very significant, for the same visual effect might have been achieved by simply coloring the eyes and teeth with a light colored slip. That the look of an Edgefield face jug was created by the rather difficult technique of embedding an entirely different clay body into the walls of the pot suggests that both the material and the behavior are charged with important symbolic meanings. In Central Africa, homeland to 75 percent of all slaves imported into South Carolina, white clay has sacred associations with ancestral authority.

Among the Central African Kongo people, for example, white is the color of the dead, so that white objects are offered to them and effigies of the dead are marked with white eyes. The strong stylistic affinities between Kongo sculpture and Edgefield vessels suggest that the enslaved artisans took advantage of their access to ceramic technology and used it to enhance African-inspired religious ceremonies held on the plantations in the region. These rituals could be carried on without detection because during the antebellum period blacks outnumbered whites in the Edgefield District by more than four to one. The Africanity of slave life in this area was ironically sustained as well by constant illegal smuggling operations of new African captives into the area; in fact, one of the last known cargoes of slaves to the United States was a group of Kongo captives landed on the Georgia coast, carried up the Savannah River, and sold into Edgefield County in 1858. The face vessels of Edgefield are evidence, then, of how African-American artisans could, when circumstances allowed, counter the assimilationist trajectory of their experiences and use new foreign means to reestablish ties to their African roots.

WOODCARVING. The prodigious woodcarving skills of African artisans are widely recognized, and their masks and statues are granted honored places in first-rank museums along with noteworthy masterpieces of western art. Since these works, so abundant in Africa, seem to be noticeably absent in the United States, assessments of African-American culture often begin by lamenting the loss of these skills. However, this carving tradition, while diminished in scale, is not altogether absent.

African slaves seem to have remembered their traditions for woodcarving. According to an old African-American man from Georgia who was interviewed in the late 1930s: "I remember the African men used to all the time make little clay images. Sometimes they like men, sometimes they like animals. Once they put a spear in his hand and walk around him and he was the chief. . . . Sometimes they try to make the image out of wood." In 1819 a banjo was seen in Congo Square in New Orleans by architect Benjamin Latrobe, which had an unmistakable African figure carved at the top of the instrument's neck just above the tuning pegs. A remarkable table was built sometime in the 1850s on a plantation in north-central North Carolina with each of its legs carved into figures highly reminiscent of African figures. A drum, now in the collections of the British Museum, was collected in 1753 in Virginia that is in every respect an excellent example of an Akan-Ashanti *apentemma* drum. However, since it was carved from a piece of American cedar, it is American rather than African in origin. From this smattering of examples, one can conclude that African proclivities for working creatively in wood did not simply end upon Africans' arrival in the Americas. These skills were carried on when and wherever possible.

Most often, African woodcarving skills were turned in other directions—generally to the production of useful household objects like bowls, trays, mortars and pestles, and handles for various metal tools. The severely functional nature of these items did not provide much of an opportunity for creative expression even if the artisan did his work with diligence and commitment. Yet in the carving of wooden canes some degree of African inspiration was seemingly able to reemerge. Numerous walking sticks carved by African Americans, from the nineteenth century to the present, sometimes bear distinctive marks that may relate to African traditions kept alive mainly among country people. These canes are often decorated with a wide range of media, including brass tacks, colored beads and marbles, aluminum foil, and other shiny materials. In one case from Mississippi, the carver attached a silver thermometer to the handle of a cane that was already elaborately carved with figures of humans and serpents. Yet it was not judged as complete without the bit of flash that a seemingly incongruous temperature gauge could provide. While this decorative gesture could be nothing more than a whimsical act of personal innovation, the fact that such acts are so commonplace among African-American canemakers in the South implies the presence of a shared style. Certainly one senses in the construct of these decorated canes a parallel to the African use of mixed-media assembly in sculpture.

Closer African affinities are seen in the selection of certain motifs. Reptiles dominate the shafts of most of the walking sticks that have clear attributions to African-American carvers; in addition to snakes (which are common to decorators of canes everywhere), black carvers also render alligators, turtles, and lizards, and as they are often combined with figures of human beings, the contrast may be read as symbolic of supernatural communication. According to widely held African beliefs, reptiles are appropriate symbols of messages between the spirit and human domains because they are creatures able to travel in two realms (in the water and on the land, or underground and above ground). They, like spiritual messages, move between the human environment and another, unseen place. The chief linkage between this symbolism and African-American traditions in woodcarving may lie in the fact that throughout the nineteenth century, traditional healers or "root doctors" are said to have carried carved walking sticks decorated with reptiles as a sign of their authority. Since their cures are likely to have been based on African practices, it follows that the rest of their paraphernalia (which was often as instrumental in affecting a cure as the medicines administered) was also African-derived. Consequently, when an African-American carved a snake or an alligator on a walking stick, it may have carried a different meaning and function than a similar animal carved by a white artisan.

QUILTING. Quilted bedcovers are objects that are unknown and unnecessary in tropical Africa. However, some West African ceremonial textiles are decorated with colorful appliqué figures, and large pieces of cloth for everyday use are assembled by sewing narrow strips together. Thus enslaved African women may have been somewhat prepared to make quilts since they already had the requisite skills needed to piece quilt tops from scraps and remnants. While the actual quilting process was, for the most part, new and different—that is, the binding of two large pieces of cloth together with a layer of batting in between by means of thousands of geometrically patterned stitches—extant quilts alleged to be slave-made show that these women were certainly capable of mastering the task.

Very little about the oldest surviving African-American quilts seems to demonstrate any affinity for African textile traditions. Mainly what one sees is the strict guidance of the plantation mistress. However, during the last decades of the nineteenth century, Harriet Powers of Athens, Ga., produced two quilts filled with images that seem to come straight out of Dahomey, a prominent kingdom on the West African coast. While her links to Africa are less than certain and would have been, at best, indirect, the figures on her two "bible" quilts compare closely with appliqué figures found on sewn narrative textiles of the Fon people. More commonplace and perhaps even more profoundly associated with African textiles are the so-called "strip quilts," which appear with great regularity wherever African Americans make quilts. In this type of bedcover, long, thin strip units are sewn edge-to-edge to form the large square or rectangular quilt top. The "strips" may be single pieces, or may be assembled from blocks, from thin remnants called "strings," or from assorted remnants. Regardless of the technique, the overall linear composition of the top cannot be missed. Since most contemporary African-American quilters claim that quilts of this type are the oldest pattern they know, there is a good possibility that such quilts were made during slavery. Certainly they resemble in form and technique the strip cloths of West and Central Africa. These textiles are assembled from narrow pieces about five inches wide and eight feet long that are sewn edge-to-edge to create a large rectangular panel. This tradition is seemingly perpetuated in a modified form in the African-American strip quilt.

In all of its variety, African-American folk art is a vital and enduring contribution to the artistic achievement of the United States.

Even if this mode of quilt assembly proves not to be African in origin, it is certainly a marker of African-American style. While such quilts are made by white quilters, too, they will usually protest that they were a simple type made when they were "just learning" or they were quilts merely "thrown together" and thus were nothing to be proud of. Black quilters, on the other hand, celebrate strip patterns as among the most significant in their repertories and produce them from childhood to old age. They constantly work at refining the form as they explore the nuances of the genre. These quilters are fully aware of the geometric patterns common in Euro-American quilting, patterns usually generated from block units, but they prefer to use strips. The strip format is by nature innovative and open-ended, and thus, unlike Euro-American quilt genres, is considerably less bound by formal conventions. There is, then, a sense of design permission about strip quilts, even a sense of liberation. In all of its variety, African-American folk art is a vital and enduring contribution to the artistic achievement of the United States.

Twentieth-Century Folk Art

The names of only a handful of early African-American folk artists have survived. By the middle of the nineteenth century, however, there are increasing numbers of artists whose names have been recorded. Two of the most impressive examples of nineteenth-century African-American carved walking sticks were made by a slave blacksmith named Henry Gudgell (c. 1826–1895) in Livingston County, Mo., during the 1860s. They are in the collections of the Yale University Art Gallery and of Allan and Anne Weiss, Louisville, Ky. Each version has a slender, tapering shaft with a handle carved in powerful spiral grooves and depicts a slender serpent carved in relief and entwined around the bottom of the stick. A lizard and a tortoise appear near the top of the shaft in each example, and a series of carved bands may be seen directly below the handle. The combination of motifs on the Gudgell walking sticks is undoubtedly African, and their existence was sometimes related to African beliefs in witchcraft, healing, and conjuring.

EARLY TWENTIETH-CENTURY AFRICAN-AMERICAN FOLK ART. The earliest national recognition of an individual African-American folk artist occurred when the limestone sculptures of William Edmondson (1882–1951), a tombstone carver from Nashville, Tenn., were exhibited in 1937, at the Museum of Modern Art in New York. Although the show consisted of only ten objects and no catalogue was published, it was the first one-man exhibition of works by an African-American artist to be held at the Museum of Modern Art.

The most celebrated early twentieth-century African-American folk artist is Horace PIPPIN, (1881–1946), who lived in West Chester, Pa. Pippin began painting ca. 1930, following a World War I-related disability, and was represented by the Carlen Gallery in Philadelphia. Widely collected during his lifetime, the majority of Pippin's paintings are in the permanent collections of major museums. He was the subject of the first monograph on an African-American artist. *Horace Pippin: A Negro Artist in America* by Seldom Rodman was published in 1947, the year following Pippin's death. In 1972, a revised, updated edition, *Horace Pippin: The Artist as a Black American,* was published by Seldon Rodman and Carole Cleaver.

CONTEMPORARY AFRICAN-AMERICAN FOLK ART. A revival of interest in African-American folk art occurred in 1982, when the Corcoran Gallery of Art in Washington, D.C., mounted the exhibition "Black Folk Art in America, 1930–1980," which included the works of twenty African-American artists. This exhibition was the first comprehensive show of African-American folk art to be mounted by a major museum.

Within the broad spectrum of contemporary American folk art, works produced by African Americans exist as a unique category with distinct characteristics. The majority of African-American folk artists were born and lived in the deep South. States that have produced unusually large numbers of African-American folk artists are South Carolina, Georgia, Alabama, Mississippi, Louisiana, and Texas. Many prominent African-American folk artists who live in northern and midwestern cities moved there from the South. They usually began producing art late in life, following retirement, widowhood, or a work-related disability. Some produced art sporadically: however, it is usually not until their retirement that their styles reach maturity.

A deep religiosity is one of the most common characteristics of African-American folk art. Many of the artists are ministers, missionaries, and self-styled prophets, and others insist that God instructed them to produce art. They credit their intuitive artistic abilities to God, and state that He is actually producing art through their hands. One of the most private and enigmatic examples of African-American religious folk art is *The Throne of the Third Heaven of the Nation's Millennium General Assembly,* created in a downtown Washington, D.C., garage by James Hampton (1911–1964) over a period of fourteen years. The throne is an assembly of furniture, light bulbs, and other discarded objects that were carefully covered with silver and gold metallic paper. There are few known facts concerning Hampton or his motivation for creating the throne. The glittering monument was virtually unknown before Hampton's death, and has now been permanently installed at the Smithsonian Institution, National Museum of American Art. Religious subjects occur frequently in works by African-American folk artists who are not vocally expressive of their religious convictions. The church has always been a powerful institution in African-American communities, and the belief in an afterlife is frequently more fervent among African Americans than among those of other ethnic groups, owing to its perception by them as a sphere of material comforts not attainable on earth.

A predilection for bird, animal, and serpent imagery is also a common denominator of African-American folk art. Many of the artists state that they are recalling the barnyard menageries of their childhood in the rural South. Entwined serpent and reptile motifs on carved canes and staffs are similar to examples carved in Africa many centuries ago. Animals, birds, and reptiles fashioned from tree trunks and limbs are conceived as protector figures related to a spirit world often understood only by the artist. The paramount role of animals in West African religions, folklore, and mythology suggests that the predominance of animal themes in African-American folk art is another example of African "survivals" in America.

An unusual ingenuity for transforming cast-off and scrap objects into artifacts is another general characteristic of African-American folk art. Originating from the necessity of surviving from cast-offs and leftovers, such improvisational practices can be traced back to slavery. African-American slave cooks converted cast-off pork parts into "soul food" delicacies, and leftover rice and stale bread scraps into moist, succulent puddings. Scraps of calico were converted into quilts and bedcovers. In a similar display of creativity, African-American folk artists frequently employed unusual materials in the creation of their art. These materials include chewing gum, styrofoam trays and packing panels, sawdust, mud, roots and tree trunks, animal and fish bones, broken glass, umbrella frames, costume jewelry, bottles, wooden spools, house paint, scrap pieces of masonite and paneling, bottle caps, aluminum beverage cans, and other commonplace objects which are converted into art.

Figures associated with emancipation and civil rights appear frequently in African-American folk art. George Washington, Abraham Lincoln, the Rev. Dr. Martin Luther King, Jr., John F. Kennedy, and Robert Kennedy are the most frequently represented subjects. President John F. Kennedy is the most frequently depicted non-black subject in African-American folk art. Most African-American folk artists are keenly aware of both their African heritage and their American heritage. Elderly African-American folk artists often produced scenes of slavery, slave auctions, cotton picking, and other scenes of plantation life which are commentaries on their own feelings. Louisiana artist Clementine Hunter (1885–1988) rarely depicted whites in her paintings, even in her religious figures, evidencing a rare and astonishing expression of black pride for a rural woman from the deep South who lived beyond the century mark.

African-American folk art is deeply reflective of childhood experiences. An endless repertory of baptisms, funerals, weddings, parties, barnyard scenes, cotton pickings, slavery scenes, Saturday shindigs, honky-tonk scenes, and other events which are remembered or relayed by parents and grandparents are visually recorded by African-American folk artists. This art is vibrant, pulsing with rhythm, and little attempt is made to model form three-dimensionally. Scale relationships are frequently inaccurate, and vertical perspective is usually employed.

Indulgence in flights of fantasy and desire to satisfy unfulfilled lifelong career ambitions often motivate African-American folk artists. Leslie Payne (1907–c. 1985) of Reedsville, Va., was fascinated by airplanes and ships. He dreamed of a career as a pilot and built an airplane, powered by an automobile engine, that he hoped to fly. When the plane would not lift off, Payne drove it—automobile-style—and indulged in imaginary flights which he carefully recorded in a log book. John Landry (1912–1986) grew up in New Orleans, was fascinated by Mardi Gras floats since his childhood, and often competed with other youths for the coveted positions of carrying flambeaux in Mardi Gras parades. Following his retirement as a longshoreman, Landry began fashioning miniature replicas of Mardi Gras floats using wire and discarded Mardi Gras beads. These carefully constructed shoebox-sized floats have wheels which roll, and their durability attests to Landry's desire to become an architect.

Simplicity and unpretentiousness are two of the inherent characteristics which contribute to the widespread appeal of African-American folk art. No tedious academic or intellectual mental exercises are necessary to comprehend or enjoy it. Childlike but not childish, simplistic but not always simple, twentieth-century African-American folk art is a spontaneous and untutored mode of expression. Because it is free from influences of academic art and "mainstream" movements, it is not surprising to note that a number of academically trained African-American artists have been influenced by folk art forms of African Americans.

BIBLIOGRAPHY

Benberry, Cuesta. *Always There: The African-American Presence in American Quilts.* Louisville, Ky., 1992.

Chase, Judith Wragg. *Afro-American Art and Craft.* New York, 1971.

Dallas Museum of Art. *Black Art—Ancestral Legacy: The African Impulse in African American Art.* Dallas, 1989.

Ferguson, Leland. *Uncommon Ground: Archaeology and Early African America, 1650–1800.* Washington, D.C., 1992.

Ferris, William H., ed. *Afro-American Folk Art and Crafts.* New York, 1993.

Georgia Council for the Arts and Humanities. *Missing Pieces: Georgia Folk Art 1770–1976.* Atlanta, 1977.

Greenville County Museum of Art. *Early Decorated Stoneware of the Edgefield District, South Carolina.* Greenville, S.C., 1976.

Horne, Catherine Wilson, ed. *Crossroads of Clay: The Southern Alkaline-Glazed Stoneware Tradition.* Columbia, S.C., 1990.

Leon, Eli. *Who'd A Thought It: Improvisation in African-American Quiltmaking.* San Francisco, 1987.

Livingston, Jane, and John Beardsley (with a contribution by Regenia Perry). *Black Folk Art in America, 1930–1980.* New York, 1982.

Myers, Lynn Robertson, and George D. Terry. *Carolina Folk: The Cradle of a Southern Tradition.* Columbia, S.C., 1985.

———. *Southern Make: The Southern Folk Heritage.* Columbia, S.C., 1977.

Perry, Regenia. *Selections of Nineteenth-Century Afro-American Art.* New York, 1976.

———. *Spirits or Satire: African American Face Vessels of the 19th Century.* 1985.

———. *What It Is: Black American Folk Art from the Collection of Regenia Perry.* Richmond, Va., 1982.

Rosengarten, Dale. *Row Upon Row: Sea Grass Baskets of the South Carolina Low Country.* Columbia, S.C., 1986.

Seibels, Eugenia, and JoAnne McCormick. *Southern Folk Arts.* Columbia, S.C., 1988.

Thompson, Robert F. "African Influences on the Art of the United States." In Armistead L. Robinson, et al., eds. *Black Studies in the University.* New York, 1969, pp. 128–177.

———. *Flash of the Spirit: African and Afro-American Art.* New York, 1983.

Vlach, John Michael. *The Afro-American Tradition in the Decorative Arts.* 1978. Reprint. Athens, Ga., 1990.

———. *By the Work of Their Hands: Studies in Afro-American Folk Life.* Charlottesville, Va., 1991.

Webb, Robert Lloyd. *Ring the Banjar!: The Banjo from Folklore to Factory.* Cambridge, Mass., 1984.

Wood, Peter H. *Black Majority: Negroes in Colonial South Carolina from 1670 through the Stono Rebellion.* New York, 1974.

– REGENIA A. PERRY AND JOHN MICHAEL VLACH

FOLKLORE

African-American folklore is a mode of creative cultural production that manifests itself in expressive forms such as tales, songs, proverbs, greetings, gestures, rhymes, material artifacts, and other created products and performances. Although African-American folklore is most often thought of in terms of these expressive forms, it is in reality a dynamic process of creativity that arises in performative contexts characterized by face-to-face interaction. The performative aspects of this folklore is what distinguishes it from other modes of creative cultural production within an African-American context. In other words, unlike other modes of African-American creative cultural production, such as literary and popular culture, folklore gains its meaning and value as a form of expression within unmediated performances on an ongoing basis in African-American communities.

Although African-American folklore should be conceptualized as a performed medium, it has an important historical dimension as well. That is, its performance even in contemporary settings entails the creative manipulation of historical forms of indefinite temporal origin. As such, it is intricately linked to processes of black culture-building in that it has historically served as an important means of communicating shared cultural attitudes, beliefs, and values of and within an ever-changing African community in the United States. As interrelated phenomena, African folklore creation and culture-building are both dynamic creative processes with roots in the diverse African cultures from which contemporary African Americans originated.

Among scholars of African-American folklore, however, the existence of a dynamic relationship between African and African-American processes of folklore creation has historically been controversial. The controversy arose in large part from the intricate link that folklorists envisioned between folklore creation and culture-building. Early in the study of African-American culture and folklore, scholars postulated that African people were so traumatized by the process of enslavement that they arrived in the New World culturally bankrupt and, therefore, dependent on Europeans for new cultural capital. In early studies, this view of a lack of African cultural retention contributed to a conception of the products of African-American folklore as mere imitations of European expressive forms. Although this view has been challenged over the years by the discovery of African cultural forms in the United States, these cultural expressions have been disparaged further by being identified as "Africanisms," isolated cases that somehow survived in the New World despite the trauma of enslavement. In fact, however, "Africanisms" represent the most obvious evidence that African culture and cultural forms have had a profound influence on black culture-building and folklore creation in the United States (Roberts 1989, p. 9).

African people who were forcibly unrooted from their homelands and transplanted in America as slaves brought with them cherished memories of their traditional lifestyles.

Historically, the difficulty of appreciating and recognizing the influence of African culture and cultural forms on African-American folklore has been exacerbated by the fact that Africans brought to the United States as slaves did not themselves share a coherent culture. Only recently have scholars begun to realize the irrelevance of this perspective to an understanding of black culture-building in African communities throughout the New World. For example, Sidney Mintz and Richard Price (1972, p. 5) have suggested that although Africans enslaved in the New World did not share a common culture or folk tradition upon arrival, they did share "certain common orientations to reality which tended to focus the attention of individuals from West African cultures upon similar kinds of events, even though the ways of handling these events may seem quite diverse in formal terms." While these "common orientations to reality" may not have been sufficient to support the re-creation of African cultural institutions in their pristine form, they could and did serve as a foundation for culture-building in a new environment.

African people who were forcibly unrooted from their homelands and transplanted in America as slaves brought with them cherished memories of their traditional lifestyles and cultural forms that served as the foundations of African-American folk tradition. To understand the dynamic processes that characterized the development over time of an African-American folk tradition, we must recognize that both black culture-building and folklore creation have proceeded as recursive rather than linear processes of endlessly devising solutions to both old and new problems of living under ever-changing social, political, and economic conditions. While both culture-building and folklore creation are dynamic and creative in that they adapt to social needs and goals, they are also enduring in that they change by building upon previous manifestations of themselves. Cultural transformation is a normative process experienced and carried out by all groups. In the process, the institutional and expressive forms by which a group communicates and upholds the ideals by which it lives are equally subject to transformation.

As James Snead (1984, p. 61) has argued, however, the failure to recognize the dynamic and transformational properties of African cultures in the New World has been influenced historically by the view that African cultures are static. Only by recognizing that such cultures are and always have been dynamic (i.e., capable of transforming themselves in response to the social needs and goals of African people) is it possible to envison African-American folklore as a continuous process of creativity intricately linked to a historical tradition of black culture-building with roots in Africa. During the period of black SLAVERY in the United States, enslaved Africans began the process of building a culture based on their "common orientations to reality." Despite their lack of a sense of shared identity and values upon arrival, the similarity of the conditions and treatment that they faced in the slave system facilitated their ability to envision themselves as a community. To communicate their shared identity and value system, they transformed many of their African cultural forms by focusing on the common elements within them. In the process, their creative efforts as well as the final expressive products that they created were greatly influenced by the differences in their situations in the United States from those they had known in Africa. In other words, the transformation of African cultural forms involved a process of creating new forms based on common elements from diverse African cultures and their infusion with insights and meanings relevant to contemporary situations in the United States. That these new forms did not always resemble some African original did not negate the debt they owed to African cultural roots.

The beginnings of an African-American folk tradition can be traced to the slavery period and to the efforts of African people from diverse cultural backgrounds to maintain a sense of continuity with their past. Throughout the period of slavery, scattered references to African-American folklore appeared in written records. Systematic efforts to collect and study such folklore, however, did not begin until the late nineteenth century. The earliest efforts to collect it were carried out primarily by white missionaries who flocked into the South following Emancipation to assist black freedpeople. Although these early efforts were motivated in large part by a desire to use African Americans' creative cultural production to demonstrate their humanity and fitness for freedom, such activities nevertheless preserved for posterity a vast body of African-American oral tradition.

An equally important motive for early collectors of black folklore was the prevalent belief in the late nineteenth century that folklore as a mode of creative cultural production was rapidly disappearing. In the case of African Americans, many envisioned the growing rate of literacy among freedpeople as a sure sign that the African-American folk tradition would soon disappear. Although contemporary folklorists realize the falsity of this perspective, it nevertheless provided a primary impetus for the collection of African-American folklore in the late nineteenth century and influenced a concentration on those forms that had obvious roots in slavery. During this productive period of African-American folklore gathering, collectors focused most of their attention on three forms: SPIRITUALS, animal-trickster tales, and folk beliefs.

Spirituals received a great deal of attention, especially from northern missionaries, in the late nineteenth century. The first book-length collection of African-American folklore published was *Slave Songs of the United States* which primarily contained spirituals. The spiritual song tradition of African Americans developed during the late eighteenth and early nineteenth centuries with the conversion of large numbers of enslaved African-Americans to Christianity. Spirituals as a body of songs were developed primarily around the actions of Old Testament figures whose faith in God allowed them to be delivered from bondage and persecution in dramatic ways. The songs followed a pronounced leader/chorus pattern known as call and response, which in performance created a kind of communal dialogue about the power of faith and belief in an omnipotent God. While the songs often portrayed Heaven as the ultimate reward of faith in God, their primary focus was on earthly deliverance from bondage and persecution. Through analogy to Old Testament stories of persecution and divine deliverance, the songs constantly reiterated the power of God to deliver the faithful.

Spirituals provided enslaved Africans with an alternative expressive form for communicating their vision of the power of God and the rewards of faith in Christianity to that offered by the slavemasters. As enslaved Africans freely and often testified, the masters frequently attempted to use slave's Christian conversion and participation in white religious services to reinforce the masters' view of enslavement. The dominant message that enslaved Africans received from white preachers was "Servants, obey your masters." In the spirituals, enslaved Africans were able to convey to members of their community a more empowering and liberating vision of God and the Christian religion. Of equal importance, the creation and performance of spirituals allowed them to incorporate more of their African cultural heritage into Christian worship. Despite general prohibitions against unsupervised worship, enslaved Africans created opportunities for separate worship in slave cabins, "hush harbors," and even their own churches, where they created and performed spirituals in a style and manner that incorporated African performance practices. These practices included the development of the "shout," a religious ritual characterized by a counterclockwise shuffling movement reminiscent of African ritual dancing. The primary purpose of the "shout" was to induce spirit possession, a form of communion with the supernatural valued by many people of African descent.

Spirituals provided enslaved Africans with an alternative expressive form for communicating their vision of the power of God and the rewards of faith.

In the late nineteenth century, the collection of spirituals was rivaled only by the collection of animal-trickster tales. With the publication of Joel Chandler Harris's *Uncle Remus: His Songs and Sayings* in 1881, the collection of animal-trickster tales by various individuals escalated. By the end of the nineteenth century, literally hundreds of these tales had been collected and published. Early collectors of black folktales often expressed amazement over the variety of animal-trickster tales created by enslaved Africans. That tales of the animal trickster would become central in the narrative performances of enslaved Africans is not surprising, however. In the cultures from which enslaved Africans originated, folktales in which clever animals acted as humans to impart important lessons about survival were ubiquitous. Although various animals acted as tricksters in different

African traditions, the tales of their exploits showed important similarities throughout sub-Saharan Africa. In fact, even the same plots could be found in the trickster-tale traditions of diverse African groups (Feldmann 1973, p. 15).

In the United States, the animal trickster was most often represented by Brer Rabbit, although other animals acted as tricksters in some tales. Although a number of trickster tales found in the repertory of enslaved Africans retained plots from African tradition, many transformed the African trickster in ways that reflected the situation of enslavement. The impetus for transforming the African trickster was not only the need to create a single tradition out of many but also the differences in the situations faced by Africans in the New World from those in Africa that had given the exploits of tricksters there meaning and value. In the trickster tales of enslaved Africans, the trickster was an actor particularly adept at obtaining the material means of survival within an atmosphere similar to that in which enslaved Africans lived. Unlike African tricksters, whose behavior was often conceptualized as a response to famine or other conditions in which material shortage existed, the trickster of enslaved African Americans acted in a situation of material plenty.

The primary obstacle to the acquisition of the material means of survival for the trickster of enslaved Africans was the physical power and control wielded by the dupe. This situation reflected the conditions under which enslaved Africans lived, in which the material means of survival were readily available but were denied by the control of the slavemasters. In these tales, the trickster was portrayed as developing clever strategies for obtaining material goods, especially food, despite the efforts of his dupes to deny access. As historians of the slave experience have noted, the concern with the acquisition of food was a common one during slavery (Blassingame 1972, p. 158; Genovese 1976, pp. 638–639). In tale after tale, Brer Rabbit proved to be a masterful manipulator of his dupes, who appeared most often in the guise of the wolf or the fox. The tales often portrayed situations in which cleverness, verbal dexterity, and native intelligence or wit allowed the trickster to triumph over the dupes. For enslaved Africans, this provided a model of behavior for dealing with the power and control of the slavemasters over the material means of survival.

Often reported as case studies, the folk beliefs of enslaved Africans also seemed widespread to collectors in the late nineteenth century. In many ways, the concerns of collectors reflected a stereotypical view of many white Americans that African Americans were inordinately superstitious. The collection of folk beliefs centered primarily around the practice of conjuration. At the core of this practice was the conjurer, a figure transformed by enslaved Africans but based on African religious leaders such as medicine men. While the conjurer in different parts of the South was known by different names, including root doctor, hoodooer, and two-heads, the practice of conjuration was remarkably similar wherever it was found (Bacon and Herron 1973, pp. 360–361). In most instances, conjurers were believed to be individuals possessed of a special gift to both cause and cure illness. Although the source of the conjurer's powers was usually believed to be mysterious, some believed it came from an evil source, others believed it came from God, and still others believed it could be taught by those possessed of it.

During the period of slavery, conjurers played a prominent role among enslaved Africans, especially as healers. Although most slavemasters attempted to provide for the health needs of enslaved Africans, their efforts often fell short. In general, the state of scientific medicine during the period of slavery was so poorly developed that, even under ideal conditions, doctors were ineffective in treating many diseases. The importance of conjurers for enslaved Africans also had to do with beliefs about the causes of illness, beliefs deeply influenced by their African cultural heritage. Like their ancestors, many enslaved Africans continued to believe that illness was caused by the ill-will of one individual against another through an act of conjuration. Individuals could induce illness either through their own action or by consulting a conjurer, who could be persuaded to "lay a spell." In these cases, only the power of a conjurer could alleviate the illness.

In their practices, conjurers used both material objects, such as charms and amulets, and verbal incantations in the form of curses and spells. However, theirs was primarily an herbal practice; hence, the common name of root doctor for these practitioners. The frequent use of verbal incantations derived from African beliefs about the power of the spoken word to influence forces in nature for good or ill. Although conjurers have often been associated with unrelieved evil, their role was a culturally sanctioned one. Within the belief and social system that supported the practice of conjuration, social strife, believed to be the dominant cause of illness, was seen as disruptive to the equilibrium and harmony of the community. The conjurer's role was to discover the identity of the individual responsible for the disruption and to restore harmony. For both the social and physical well-being of enslaved Africans, the conjurer's abilities in this regard proved beneficial. Not only did the presence of conjurers provide them with a means of tending to their own health needs, it also provided a mechanism for addressing issues of social strife within the group without the intervention of slavemasters.

Although spirituals, trickster tales, and folk beliefs were the focus of most early collecting, the folklore of enslaved Africans included more than these genres. Collectors seldom noted other vibrant genres that developed during slavery, including proverbs, courtship rituals, prayers, sermons, and forms of folktale other than trickster narratives. But while there was no concerted effort to collect these genres, examples sometimes found their way into collections. In addition, folklorists and other scholars have begun to utilize various kinds of records, including plantation journals, slave narratives, and diaries of various sorts in an effort to better understand the nature of black vernacular creativity during the slave period (Joyner 1984; Ferris 1983). These types of resources have proven particularly useful in the study of black material culture. Because slavemasters were generally responsible for the material needs of enslaved Africans, the importance of knowledge possessed by Africans and applied to the production of various material objects has generally been overlooked. However, African skill and knowledge were responsible for the production of many material objects used in everyday life on farms and plantations. It has become evident, for example, that African knowledge and skill in rice cultivation were responsible for the profitable rice industry that thrived along the coast of Georgia and South Carolina. In addition, African knowledge of basketry and textiles was responsible for the development of a unique tradition of basketry and quilting that continues to be practiced today (Ferris, 1983, pp. 63–110 and 235–274). Of equal importance, many enslaved Africans who served as blacksmiths, carpenters, cooks, and seamstresses on farms and plantations used African techniques in the production of the material products for which they were responsible.

Despite early predictions of the demise of an African-American folk tradition with the advent of freedom and literacy, African Americans have continued to create and perform various genres of folklore. In many ways, the success of early collectors was a testament to the vibrancy and importance of vernacular creativity among African Americans. Although Emancipation brought about important changes in lifestyle, it did not alter many of the conditions that had made the forms of folklore created by enslaved Africans meaningful. In the post-Emancipation era, the development of the sharecropping system and the imposition of JIM CROW laws created patterns of economic and social oppression similar to those that had existed during slavery. In fact, the similarities in the conditions of freedpeople in the late nineteenth and early twentieth centuries to those endured by enslaved Africans allowed them to simply alter many of the forms they had created during slavery to reflect new realities.

As the conditions that would influence black culture-building in the post-Emancipation era became clear, African Americans began the process of both transforming existing forms and creating new ones to communicate their perceptions of the economic, social, and political realties that informed their lives as freedpeople. With the failure of Reconstruction and growing patterns of segregation following Emancipation, African Americans came to realize that conditions imposed on them that inhibited their progress in society had to be addressed differently. In a general sense, the powerful role that the law played in the lives of freedpeople made many of the strategies developed during slavery for dealing with white power and control no longer effective or in the best interest of African Americans. For example, the tales of the animal trickster, which had provided an important model of behavior for dealing with white economic exploitation and social oppression during slavery, gradually lost their effectiveness as the expressive embodiment of a strategy for freedpeople. In some animal-trickster tales collected in the late nineteenth century, contests between the animal trickster and dupe were settled in the courts.

Despite the decline of animal-trickster-tale narration, African Americans retained the trickster as a focus for folklore creation. In the late nineteenth and early twentieth centuries, the trickster was transformed into the badman, a character whose primary adversary was the law, personified by the white policeman or sheriff (Roberts 1989, pp. 171–220). The emergence of white lawmen as powerful and often brutal defenders of white privilege made it extremely problematic for African Americans to retaliate directly against whites for their exploitation. At the same time, the proliferation of patterns of segregation and economic exploitation and the rise of Jim Crow laws made the black community an arena for the actions of badmen. Therefore, although badmen spent much of their energy attempting to elude the law, they found their dupes in members of the black community. As tricksters, they attempted to dupe members of the black community into participating in illegal activities such as gambling, bootlegging, prostitution, numbers-running, and drug-dealing. That is, badmen as tricksters sought material gain by outwitting both African Americans and the law. In this sense, the black badmen of the post-Emancipation era faced a double bind not unknown to many African Americans.

Folklore creation surrounding black badmen in the late nineteenth and early twentieth centuries reflected changed conditions faced by African Americans in society. As the law in both its abstract and personified forms became a powerful force in maintaining white privilege, African Americans were forced to turn increasingly to their own communities for solutions to their economic and social oppression. Because the law was often brutal in its treatment of African Americans, they made avoidance of the law a virtue and attempted to keep the law out of their communities. In so doing, they assumed a great deal of responsibility for maintaining harmony and peace among themselves. In economically deprived black communities, however, the means of enhancing one's economic status were extremely limited. The rise of secular entertainment establishments such as jukes and bars served as a focus for many of the activities associated with black badmen. In these establishments, many African Americans found activities by which they had the potential to enhance their economic well-being, such as gambling and numbers-playing, as well as offering psychological escape in whiskey and drugs from the oppressive conditions of their lives. Despite their illegal nature, these activities posed little danger to the black community as long as individuals who participated in them played by the unwritten rules. However, the consumption of alcohol and the existence of games of chance created an environment in which violence often erupted and the law intervened.

The exploits of black badmen typically unfolded in jukes and bars. The badman emerged in folklore as an individual who, in defense of his trade, committed an act of murder. The badman's exploits were celebrated in legends and ballads, narrative songs that told of their deeds. For example, the notorious gambling badman Stackolee purportedly shot Billy Lyons, who was cheating him in a card game. Duncan shot the white policeman, Brady, to end his bullying of patrons at Duncan's bar. Invariably caught and punished, the badman was treated sympathetically in folklore. The sympathy engendered by the badman derives from the importance to some members of the black community of the activities with which he became associated, as well as the individuals he killed. The badman's victims were usually cheaters or bullies whose actions threatened to bring the power and force of the law down on the community. In the late nineteenth and early twentieth centuries, many African Americans endured economic conditions that made the activities identified with black badmen important to their material well-being. At the same time, they recognized the potential and real consequences of participating in these activities.

In many ways, the focus of folklore creation surrounding black badmen reflects the nature of black folklore since Emancipation. In a profound sense, expressive celebration of the black badman reflected a general pattern of forms that focused on conditions faced by African Americans on a recurrent basis yet suggested that the solutions lie within the black community. The most common types of folktale performed by African Americans since Emancipation attempt to identify the origins of conditions that inhibit black progress in society. These often humorous narratives attempt through suggestion and persuasion to address intragroup attitudes and behaviors perceived as responsible for the conditions faced by African Americans. At the same time, they suggest that when African Americans recognize their own role in maintaining behaviors not in their best interest, they gain the ability and power to change them.

In many narratives the focus of the tales is on the origins of certain animal characteristics. These tales were developed during slavery and usually involved animals from the trickster cycle. In some instances, the animal trickster is made the dupe. The best known of these tales purport to explain why the rabbit has a short tail or the buzzard a bald head. While these tales often seem to be naive explanations for the physical characteristics of different animals in reality they impart useful lessons about African-American moral and social values. In most instances, the tales reveal that the acquisition of the physical characteristics came about as a result of obsessive pride and vanity, or a failure to evaluate the motives of one known to be an adversary.

In many ways, the focus of folklore creation surrounding black badmen reflects the nature of black folklore since Emancipation.

The didactic intent of African-American origin tales is even more evident in those that involve human actors. Many of these tales, which also originated in slavery, continue to be performed in African-American communities today (Dance 1978, pp. 7–11). The focus is on the development of certain physical features associated with African Americans as a race. For example, the performer purports to explain why African Americans have big feet or hands, nappy hair, black skin, etc. The stories are invariably set at the beginning of time when God, a principal actor in the tales, gave out human traits. African Americans are envisioned as always getting the "worse" characteristics because they arrived late, were playing cards and did not hear God calling them, or were too impatient to wait for God. Despite the humor often evoked in these tales, they speak to

African Americans about certain negative patterns of behavior stereotypically associated with the race—laziness, tardiness, impatience, etc. Rather than being self-deprecating, as some scholars have suggested, these tales attempt in a humorous way to call attention to certain behavioral patterns perceived by some members of the black community as inhibitive to the advancement of African Americans. In addition, they reveal one of the ways in which African Americans have historically attempted to communicate in intragroup contexts the nature and consequences of negative stereotypes of them.

Closely associated with tales of origin is a large group of tales that revolves around the character of "Colored Man" (Dorson 1956, pp. 171–186). These tales often purport to explain the origins of conditions experienced by African Americans in society. From all internal evidence, Colored Man tales are a post-Emancipation invention that thrived in the early and mid-twentieth century. In this group of tales, Colored Man is pitted in a contest with White Man and a member of another racial or cultural group, either Jew or Mexican. In some instances, the three actors are given a task by God, usually involving the selection of packages of different sizes; in others, they are involved in a scheme of their own making. In the former case, Colored Man makes the wrong decision, whether he selects the largest or the smallest package. His choices are most often conceptualized as a result of his greed, his ability to be deceived by appearances of easy gain, his laziness, or even his efforts not to be outsmarted. The tales almost invariably revolve around some stereotype associated with African Americans. By portraying situations in which a generic African American acts out a stereotype, the performers of these tales implicitly call for critical self-examination. On the other hand, by setting these tales at the beginning of time, performers suggest that conditions experienced by African Americans in the present result from systemic sources.

Throughout the twentieth century, African Americans have created and performed folktales that deal realistically with their situation in society. Many function as jokes that revolve around stereotypes. However, these tales function to constantly remind African Americans that one of the most problematic aspects of their existence in American society derives from negative images of them held by other groups. In many of these tales, the African American appears as the dupe of the non-blacks, who use stereotypes to manipulate him into making bad choices. In other tales, African-American performers celebrate certain stereotypical images that seem to allow them to gain an advantage over other groups. This type of narrative usually revolves around sexual stereotypes; blacks triumph over members of other groups because they demonstrate superior sexual prowess or larger sexual organs. In their celebration of an image of self generally evaluated negatively in society, African Americans reveal an interesting ambivalence about such images and possibly a different value orientation.

Besides narrative, other forms of African-American folklore created since Emancipation reveal an intimate concern with intragroup problems and solutions. Of the genres created and performed by African Americans, the BLUES is concerned directly with conditions and situations within the black community. As a body of song, the blues touches on various problematic areas of black life like unemployment, homelessness, sharecropping, police brutality, and economic exploitation (Titon 1977; Keil 1966; Oliver 1963). However, it concentrates primarily on the problems of black male/female relationships. Although the blues celebrates the joys of being in a successful relationship, it most often focuses on the problems involved in sustaining one. These problems often revolve around economic issues, especially the inability of black males to provide for the material well-being of lover, wife, or family.

In the late nineteenth century and the early decades of the twentieth, the blues served as an ongoing commentary on conditions faced by many African Americans. As an expressive form, the blues did not often propose solutions to the problems it identified but rather focused on defining the contours of situations shared by large numbers of African Americans. When the blues did offer a solution, it most often proposed mobility: either moving out of a troubled relationship or moving out of town. It might be suggested that the idea of mobility as a solution to problematic situations often found in the blues simply reflected a solution embraced by thousands of African Americans in the early twentieth century. During the heyday of the blues, African Americans witnessed the migration of thousands from the rural South into urban centers in search of better economic and social conditions.

For many African Americans, the blues reflected much about the nature of black culture-building in the early twentieth century. It emerged as the first solo form of musical expression created by African Americans and signaled the growing diversity of the black population. In the midst of the Great Migration and other changes in black life, the blues revealed the difficulty of speaking about a common African-American experience in post-Emancipation America. It envisioned a community beset by various problems of identity, values, and even beliefs arising from mobility as well as economic and social upheaval. Although blues performers spoke from a first-person point of view, their popularity derived from their ability to use personal experience as a metaphor for shared realities. Despite its popularity with a large segment of the black population, however, the blues was not valued by all members of the community. Due to its association with secular entertainment establishments in which drinking alcohol, dancing, gambling, and often violent crimes occurred, as well as to its often sexually explicit lyrics, it was sometimes strongly disparaged by religious and socially conscious members of the black community.

However, in the early twentieth century, the blues had its expressive and religious counterpart in the emergence of GOSPEL MUSIC (Heilbut 1975; Allen 1991). The development of modern gospel can be attributed to two interrelated influences, which can be conceptualized as, on the one hand, musical and, on the other, social and religious. Although spirituals continued to be performed well after Emancipation, the message of deliverance from bondage and persecution through analogy to Old Testament figures and events lost much of its meaning for freedpeople. In addition, performance of spirituals in the post-Emancipation era was greatly influenced by efforts of some African-American religious leaders to make black religious practices more closely resemble those of white Americans. As a result, many black churches banned the "shout," an important context for spiritual song performance, and began to encourage the singing of European hymns to the neglect of spirituals. At the same time, the emergence of Europeanized arrangements and performances of spirituals proliferated, especially with touring college choirs such as those organized at Fisk University and Hampton Institute. The success of these choirs, as well as the barbershop-quartet craze of the nineteenth century, influenced the organization of hundreds of black harmonizing quartets that sang primarily arranged spirituals.

While these changes in the religious and musical life of African Americans in the South greatly influenced the attitude toward and performance of spirituals, the Great Migration confronted many African Americans with a new lifestyle and environment that threatened their ability to maintain the spiritual values that many had traditionally associated with black religion. In urban areas, many African Americans embraced not only new social and economic patterns but also modes of worship in churches that did not fulfill social and spiritual needs as southern churches had. In both South and North, many African Americans in the late nineteenth and early twentieth centuries turned to the newly developing SPIRITUAL CHURCH MOVEMENT and HOLINESS MOVEMENT and the STOREFRONT CHURCHES that arose to house them. In these churches, many African Americans found patterns of worship more conducive to their religious sensibilities, and an emerging musical style that came to be known as gospel. Unlike the spirituals of enslaved Africans, gospel songs tended to emphasize the New Testament message of love and faith in God as the solutions to human problems. As such, gospel relies less on analogy to Old Testament personalities and events and more on the abstract New Testament promise of rest and reward for the faithful.

In an important sense, gospel, like the blues, envisions a diverse black community, whereas spirituals relied on the existence of a coherent community sharing a single condition: slavery. As such, gospel songs tend to abstract the nature of the problems for which Christian faith provides a solution. In essence, the lyrics of gospel songs seldom identify specific conditions but, instead, speak of burdens, trials, and tribulations and offer faith in God as a solution. In this regard, gospel is genre that gains its meaning in performance. Through performance, its apparent abstract message is concretized in messages delivered as sermons, prayers, and testimonies, which provide numerous illustrations of the situations of which gospel music speaks. Although gospel songs are usually written by individuals and recorded by commercial companies, a development that goes back to the 1920s and 1930s, gospel remains a vernacular form performed in African-American communities in churches and concert halls throughout the United States on a regular basis.

Gospel, like the blues, envisions a diverse black community, whereas spirituals relied on the existence of a coherent community sharing a single condition: slavery.

The study of African-American folklore in the twentieth century remains vital. The focus of collection in recent years has turned from the rural South to urban communities in both North and South where viable traditions of African-American oral expressive culture continue to thrive. In the process, folklorists continue to produce important collections of African-American folklore reflective of both historical and contemporary concerns. For example, the toast tradition, which involves the recitation of long narrative poems revolving around the actions of black badmen, has been collected extensively (Jackson 1974; Wepman, Newman, and Binderman 1976). These poems, which have been collected in prisons and on the streets, chronicle the lives of individuals involved in criminal activities and warn of the consequences of their behavior. Although a large number of toast texts have been published, the toast as a genre is not widely known among African Americans. In fact, it seems to be known and performed primarily by individuals who participate in a criminal lifestyle or individuals who have connections with it. While toasts seem to celebrate criminality and the peculiar brand of "badness" associated with it, these poems tend to be highly moralistic and realistic in terms of the consequences of criminal activity. In addition—despite their often offensive language, violent imagery, and seeming disregard for legal and moral authority in the black community and society—toasts give expressive embodiment to behavioral and economic strategies and reflect attitudes embraced by some individuals in African-American communities with regard to drug-dealing, prostitution, gambling, and other so-called victimless crimes.

Although not primarily or exclusively an urban genre, the dozens has been the focus of much study in recent years (Abrahams 1970). The dozens is a generic name for a form of verbal artistry known variously in African-American communities as joning, wolfing, busting, breaking, and cracking, and by a host of other names. Although the art of playing the dozens is generally associated with adolescent males, the practice in different ways is one that knows no age limit or gender. Generally speaking, younger males tend to play more often and to rely more on formulaic rhymes and phrases in their performances. Often discussed as verbal exchanges that disparage the mother through implications of sexual impropriety, playing the dozens just as often involves apparent insults to one's opponent. While playing the dozens has been associated with the acquisition of verbal skill, especially among young African-American males, it also serves as an intragroup mechanism for communicating information with negative import for individuals. Regardless of who plays the dozens or how it is played, the content of the exchanges focuses on behaviors that violate certain norms generally accepted by African Americans, whether they relate to sexual activity, personal habits, physical characteristics, modes of dress, etc.

A concern with playing the dozens in recent years has been accompanied by a general focus on other forms of African-American folklore that reveal a rich tradition of verbal play. Forms such as signifying, marking, and loud-talking have been discussed as a reflection of the art of everyday life in African-American communities (Mitchell-Kernan 1972). The artistry of these forms derives from the ability of individuals to encode messages with serious import in humorous and witty forms. In addition, the rise of rap music, which transforms many African-American expressive forms into a flourishing narrative tradition, reflects the continuing verbal artistry in black communities. Rap, which exists as both a narrative and a musical tradition, reflects a continuing concern in African-American expressive culture with identifying conditions and situations that impact negatively on the black community. Though a diverse group, rap songs frequently point to the need for self-evaluation, criticism, and change in the black community itself without denying the impact of systemic causes for many of the conditions it identifies.

African-American folklore reflects many of the ways in which African Americans have historically communicated their attitudes, beliefs, and values in artistic forms in everyday life. Although the roots of the study of this folklore lie in beliefs about its ultimate demise, the African-American tradition of vernacular creativity and performance remains vital. While the genres that constitute the African-American folk tradition are too numerous to be examined in a short discussion, the basic categories of narrative, song, verbal artistry, and material culture suggest the tradition's contours. With African culture and cultural forms providing the tradition-rich source of African-American folklore, it has been endlessly transformed to both aid and reflect black culture-building in the United States. On an everyday basis, African-American folklore continues to provide individuals with a rich creative outlet for expression and performance.

BIBLIOGRAPHY

Abrahams, Roger. *Deep Down in the Jungle: Negro Narrative Folklore from the Streets of Philadelphia.* Chicago, 1970.

Allen, Ray. *Singing in the Spirit: African-American Sacred Quartets in New York City.* Philadelphia, 1991.

Allen, William F., Charles P. Ware, and Lucy McKim Garrison. *Slave Songs of the United States.* 1867. Reprint. New York, 1951.

Bacon, Alice M., and Leonora Herron. "Conjuring and Conjure-Doctors." In Alan Dundes, ed. *Mother Wit from the Laughing Barrel: Readings in the Interpretation of Afro-American Folklore.* Englewood Cliffs, N.J., 1973.

Blassingame, John W. *The Slave Community.* New York, 1972.

Dance, Daryl C. *Shuckin' and Jivin': Folklore from Contemporary Black America.* Bloomington, Ind., 1978.

Dorson, Richard M. *American Negro Folktales.* Greenwich, Conn., 1956.

Feldmann, Susan. *African Myths and Tales.* New York, 1973.

Ferris, William. *Afro-American Art and Crafts.* Boston, 1983.

Genovese, Eugene. *Roll, Jordan, Roll: The World the Slaves Made.* New York, 1976.

Harris, Joel Chandler. *Uncle Remus: His Songs and Sayings.* 1881. Reprint. Detroit, 1971.

Heilbut, Tony. *The Gospel Sound: Good News and Bad Times.* Garden City, N.Y., 1975.

Jackson, Bruce. *Get Your Ass in the Water and Swim like Me: Narrative Poetry from Black Oral Tradition.* Cambridge, Mass., 1974.

Joyner, Charles. *Down by the Riverside: A South Carolina Slave Community.* Urbana, Ill., 1984.

Keil, Charles. *Urban Blues.* Chicago, 1966.

Lovell, John, Jr. *Black Song: The Forge and the Flame.* New York, 1972.

Mintz, Sidney W., and Richard Price. *An Anthropological Approach to the Afro-American Past: A Caribbean Perspective.* Philadelphia, 1972.

Mitchell-Kernan, Claudia. "Signifying, Loud-Talking, and Marking." In Thomas Kochman, ed., *Rappin' and Stylin' Out.* Urbana, Ill., 1972.

Oliver, Paul. *The Meaning of the Blues.* New York, 1963.

Roberts, John W. *From Trickster to Badman: The Black Folk Hero in Slavery and Freedom.* Philadelphia, 1989.

Snead, James. "Repetition as a Figure in Black Culture," In Henry Louis Gates, Jr., ed. *Black Literature and Literary Theory.* New York, 1984, pp. 59–80.

Titon, Jeff Todd. *Early Downhome Blues: A Musical and Cultural Analysis.* Urbana, Ill., 1977.

Wepman, Dennis, Ronald B. Newman, and Murray B. Binderman. *The Life: The Lore and Folk Poetry of the Black Hustler.* Philadelphia, 1976.

– JOHN W. ROBERTS

FOLK MEDICINE

Folk medicine has been a significant feature of the cultural and social heritage of African Americans since colonial times. Its origins trace back to traditions brought to the New World by slaves. African-based religious and medical customs were often closely intertwined, reflecting an effort to understand relationships between metaphysical and physical phenomena and to apply this knowledge in promoting the health and well-being of an individual or community. "Root doctor" is perhaps the best-known type of folk practitioner. Other types include "witch doctor," "hoodoo doctor," and "voodoo doctor." While the practice of folk medicine involves a complex, eclectic array of belief systems and therapies, the most common ingredient is a combination of incantations (the spiritual element) and herbal concoctions (the physical element).

Prior to Emancipation, planters tolerated and sometimes encouraged folk practice in order to save the expense of hiring white practitioners to treat slaves. Thus, a special class of folk practitioner evolved within the slave community. A number of these practitioners were women, the so-called "Negro doctoresses," entrusted with health-care responsibilities ranging from midwifery to minor surgery and the preparation and dispensing of medicines.

After Emancipation, folk practitioners were confronted by two major obstacles. The first concerned developments in modern medicine, particularly the evolving notion of disease as a largely physical process involving specific tissues and organs, and distinct from religious or spiritual traditions. Second, mainstream practitioners erected legal, educational, and other hurdles as part of the effort to increase professionalization of the field and to reduce competition from those using alternative approaches. The mainstream medical press highlighted instances of alleged malpractice by "unqualified" folk practitioners. In 1899, for example, the *Journal of the American Medical Association* noted: "A colored 'voodoo doctor' . . . was put on trial for manslaughter during the past week. In a raid of the man's house by the police, there was found a weird collection of things, including animal remains, herbs, charms, and medicines."

Folk medicine has been a significant feature of the cultural and social heritage of African Americans since colonial times.

Despite such pressures, folk practices continued to play a significant role in health care in the twentieth century. Deeply rooted in cultural experience, they provided options for those whose access to health care was otherwise limited. Tensions between folk practitioners and advocates of "community standards" in religious and health practice persist, as in legal actions in Florida, for example, against the Santeria cult for violation of animal-sacrifice statutes during the late 1980s and early 1990s. A common thread that links these worlds—the promotion and preservation of health—is often buried under disputes over philosophy and methodology. Nevertheless, connections occur in unexpected ways, especially within the African-American community, where folk traditions run deep. Numa Pompilius Garfield Adams, a graduate of Rush Medical College (1924) and the first African-American dean of the Howard Medical School, always acknowledged the influence of his grandmother, Mrs. Amanda Adams, in his choice of a career. Mrs. Adams, a folk practitioner and midwife in rural Virginia, had introduced him as a child to the therapeutic properties of herbs.

BIBLIOGRAPHY

Hurston, Zora Neale. *Mules and Men.* 1935. Reprint. Bloomington, Ind., 1978.

Journal of the American Medical Association 33 (December 16, 1899): 1559.

Puckett, Newbell Niles. *Folk Beliefs of the Southern Negro.* 1926. Reprint. Montclair, N.J., 1968.

Watson, Wilbur H. *Black Folk Medicine: The Therapeutic Significance of Faith and Trust.* New Brunswick, N.J., 1984.

– KENNETH R. MANNING

FOLK RELIGION

The folk religious traditions of blacks in the United States have roots in a number of sources, but it is their African origins that have left the most indelible and distinctive cultural imprint. Of the 400,000 Africans who were held in bondage on the North American mainland during the SLAVE TRADE, most if not all were influenced by some indigenous philosophical or sacred system for understanding and interpreting the world. Religion for Africans, however, was more a way of life than a system of creeds and doctrines. The African religious experience allowed for meaningful relations between members of the human community and personal interaction with the world of ancestors, spirits, and divinities, who closely guided mortal existence and provided their adherents with explanations and protections within the realm of earthly affairs. African religions, although differing according to their national origins, provided an overall theological perspective in which spirituality was infused into every aspect of life.

In the colonies, Africans came into contact for the first time with the customs and cultures of white Europeans and Native Americans. Although strange and unfamiliar, the perspectives of these groups did share certain aspects, particularly in the realm of beliefs surrounding the supernatural. Both whites and Indians had worldviews that encompassed mythical perceptions of the universe and powers that pervaded human life and nature. Spiritual beings, holy objects, and the workings of the enchanted world were thought to be powerful and efficacious. Evil and misfortune were perceived as personalized agents of affliction.

Such beliefs were expressed, for the most part, in folklore and legend. Africans themselves had corresponding ideas concerning the supernatural that included sacred entities, charms, and places—although it is difficult to disengage these beliefs from their primary religious framework. We can speculate that from their initial periods of contact, blacks, whites, and Indians exchanged and adopted compatible ideas and visions of the world, each group drawing from the cultures of the others.

It was during the colonial era that enslaved Africans were first exposed to Christian missionary activity, although up to the mid-eighteenth century few blacks were actually converted. Evangelical revivalism, exploding among white Americans in the early national period, had a significant impact on blacks. Adopting their own interpretations and understandings of the message of the Christian faith, black preachers and laypersons developed unique and creative styles of religious devotion. It is here that one of the prominent strands of African-American folk religion developed.

African-American religion, however, was characterized by diversity from the start. Scattered references to the activity of "sorcerers," "doctors," and "conjurers" from the 1700s and early 1800s indicate that black religious beliefs were miltifaceted. Traditional African spirituality recognized the roles of individuals who were sacred practitioners, diviners, and healers, dynamic intermediaries between the unseen realm of spirits and the world of the living. Although they had been separated from the structures and institutions of their national homelands, African specialists recreated aspects of their religious identities within New World environments. Adapting their native beliefs and practices to the American context, these early black practitioners formed yet another thread in the evolving tapestry of African-American religion.

By the antebellum era, the second generation of blacks born in the United States had developed an indigenous culture. Although the overseas slave trade was declared illegal by 1808, most black Americans in the mid-nineteenth century had some knowledge or acquaintance with recently arrived or native-born Africans who recalled the traditions and ways of their homeland. To the American-born slaves, these Africans represented the presence and mystery of a powerful sacred past. While some blacks converted to Christianity and a few adhered to Islam, others maintained the beliefs of their forebears through their observance of modified African ceremonies. Accordingly, the religion of slaves consisted of widely differing innovations of traditions and beliefs.

African-American folk religion thus emerged as a composite creation, drawn from scattered elements of older cultural memories and grafted New World traditions which were later passed on from generation to generation. An "invisible institution," the folk Christianity of the slave quarters developed as a religion of the vernacular. As a community, slaves prayed, sang, "shouted," and preached to one another in the manner and styles reminiscent of their African heritage. The emphasis on the verbal medium in performance generated the distinctive vocal traditions that became characteristic of African-American liturgy, including the inventive oral repertory of chanted sermon and song.

Other traditions made real the power and presence of the supernatural in human life. Belief in a variety of mysterious beings, including hags, witches, and ghosts, suggests that for many African Americans the spiritual world was alive and immediate, active with forces ominous and threatening. Sacred folk beliefs were derived from Old and New World sources: local variations of Haitian-derived vodun, the interpretation of signs, the usage of charms, and the mystical knowledge of conjurers, root workers, and hoodoo practitioners, who tapped supernatural forces for prediction and protection. Although many of these traditions were deeply embedded in black folklore, they reflected viable perspectives on spirituality, the need for control and explanation that leads to religious thought.

African-American folk religion emerged as a composite creation, drawn from scattered elements of older cultural memories and grafted New World traditions.

Healing, another prominent dimension of African-American folk religion, was practiced by specialists who combined knowledge of traditional remedies with holistic therapy. As in Africa, the onset of sickness was understood by many blacks to have both physical and spiritual implications. Folk religion undergirded African-American faith in skilled practitioners who were able to counteract ailments with herbal and natural medicines, as well as techniques such as prayer. Folk beliefs also offered a theory of explanation for why such afflictions might occur. For example, illness was often thought to be caused by negative spiritual forces. In the early twentieth century, some of these latter impulses would find their way into sectarian Christianity, within groups like the HOLINESS MOVEMENT, and PENTECOSTALISM, churches that emphasized faith healing and physical wholeness through spiritual power.

With the drastic demographic shifts and movements in black life during the late nineteenth and early twentieth centuries, from South to North and from countryside to city, African-American folk religion took on a broader significance. The "old-time" revivalist traditions of worship in the rural churches would no longer be restricted to the South, as thousands of migrants made their way to northern urban areas. Relocating in search of new prospects and new lives, they brought their local traditions and beliefs with them, establishing new religious institutions within storefronts and homes. Many of these transplanted folk churches recalled features of African religion, especially the emphasis on emotional styles of worship, call and response, spirituals, and Holy Ghost spirit possession.

The folk religion of blacks also lived on in noninstitutionalized forms within urban centers. African-American conjurers, healers, and other specialists underwent a metamorphosis, some reemerging as leaders within the so-called cults and sects of the cities, and others setting up within occult shops and botanicas as spiritual advisers. This vast network of urban practitioners attracted devotees from diverse religious backgrounds, including members of the mainstream Christian denominations, who found in these traditions resolution and assistance for day-to-day concerns.

Although black folk religion continues to be varied and eclectic in its manifestations, it demonstrates a common orientation toward spirituality that is dynamic, experimental, and intensely pragmatic. Characterized by pluralism, folk beliefs fulfill diverse needs and functions that cut across doctrinal barriers and creedal differences. They constitute a way of life that is at the heart of the African-American religious experience.

BIBLIOGRAPHY

Fauset, Arthur Huff. *Black Gods of the Metropolis: Negro Cults in the Urban North.* Philadelphia, 1944.

Hurston, Zora Neale. *The Sanctified Church.* Berkeley, Calif., 1981.

Levine, Lawrence. *Black Culture and Black Consciousness: Afro-American Folk Thought from Slavery to Freedom.* New York, 1977.

Puckett, Newbell Niles. *Folk Beliefs of the Southern Negro.* Chapel Hill, N.C., 1926.

Raboteau, Albert J. *Slave Religion: The Invisible Institution in the Antebellum South.* New York, 1978.

– YVONNE P. CHIREAU

FOOTBALL

American-style, intercollegiate football emerged from the English sport of rugby during the 1870s and 1880s. Almost immediately, African Americans distinguished themselves on college gridirons.

Black Pioneers at Predominantly White Colleges, 1889–1919

William Henry Lewis and William Tecumseh Sherman Jackson were two of the first blacks to play football at a predominantly white college. Both of these Virginians played for Amherst College from 1889 through 1891. Jackson was a running back, while Lewis was a blocker. In 1891 Lewis served as captain of the Amherst squad. After graduation, he attended Harvard Law School, and because of the lax eligibility rules of the time, played two years for Harvard. In 1892 and 1893, Yale coach Walter Camp named Lewis to the Collier's All-American team at the position of center. After his playing days, Lewis became an offensive line coach at Harvard, the first black coach at a predominantly white college. He left football when President William Howard Taft appointed him as United States Assistant Attorney General in 1903.

William Arthur Johnson, George Jewett, and George Flippin were other early black players. Johnson appeared as a running back for MIT in 1890. That same year, Jewett played running back, punter, and field-goal kicker for the University of Michigan. Flippin, who played running back for the University of Nebraska from 1892 to 1893, was an intense athlete who would not tolerate foul play. The press reported that in one game he "was kicked, slugged, and jumped on, but never knocked out, and gave as good as he received." Flippin went on to become a physician. Other African Americans who played in the 1890s included Charles Cook (Cornell), Howard J. Lee (Harvard), George Chadwell (Williams), William Washington (Oberlin), and Alton Washington (Northwestern).

After the turn of the century, numerous blacks played football for northern and midwestern schools. Two of the most talented stars were Edward B. Gray of Amherst and Robert Marshall of the University of Minnesota. A halfback and defensive end, Gray earned selection to Camp's All-American third team in 1906. Marshall was another skillful end and field-goal kicker who played from 1903 to 1906. In 1904, Minnesota defeated Grinnell College 146–0. Marshall scored 72 points in that contest, a record that still stands. He was named to the second All-American team in 1905 and 1906.

As intercollegiate football gained in popularity during World War I, two black players won national acclaim. Frederick Douglass "Fritz" Pollard entered Brown University in 1915. By mid-season, the 5′6″ freshman had excelled as a kicker, runner, and defensive back. He helped take his team to the second Rose Bowl game in 1916, a 14–0 loss to Washington State. The following year also proved successful. Pollard starred in games against Rutgers, Harvard, and Yale, scoring two touchdowns in each contest. In naming Pollard to the All-American team in 1916, Walter Camp described him as "the most elusive back of the year, or any year. He is a good sprinter and once loose is a veritable will-o'-the-wisp that no one can lay hands on."

The son of a Presbyterian minister, Paul ROBESON of Princeton, N.J., enrolled at Rutgers University in 1915 on an academic scholarship. Tall and rugged (6′3″, 225 pounds), he played tackle and guard as a freshman and sophomore. In his final two seasons he was switched to end, where he gained All-American honors. Walter Camp described him in 1918 as "the greatest defensive end who ever trod a gridiron." Besides football, Robeson lettered in track, baseball, and basketball. He also excelled academically, earning election to Phi Beta Kappa. Although he was excluded from the college glee club for racial reasons, he was named to Cap and Skull, a senior society composed of four men "who most truly and fully represent the finest ideals and traditions of Rutgers." After graduation, he played professional football to finance his way through Columbia Law School. He also began an acting and singing career which brought him international recognition.

Almost all of the pioneer African-American players experienced both subtle and overt forms of discrimination. Pollard was forced to enroll at several universities before he found one willing to let him play football. Often black players were left off their squads at the request of segregated opponents. And football, a violent game at best, provided ample opportunities for players to vent racial animosities at black players. Paul Robeson, for example, suffered a broken nose and a dislocated shoulder as a result of deliberately brutal tactics by opposing players. Despite the drawbacks, there probably was no venue of major sporting competition of the era that had as few impediments to black participation as major collegiate football.

Pioneers at Black Colleges, 1889–1919

The first football game between black colleges occurred in North Carolina in 1892 when Biddle defeated Livingstone, 4–0. Owing to inadequate funding, it took nearly two decades for most black colleges to establish football programs. On New Year's Day in 1897, as a forerunner of the bowl games, Atlanta University and Tuskegee Institute met in what was billed as a "championship game." But major rivalries eventually developed between Fisk and Meharry in Tennessee, Livingstone and Biddle in North Carolina, Tuskegee and Talladega in Alabama, Atlanta University and Atlanta Baptist (Morehouse), and Virginia Union and Virginia State. By 1912, Howard and Lincoln in Pennsylvania, Hampton in Virginia, and Shaw in North Carolina had organized the Colored (later Central) Intercollegiate Athletic Association (CIAA).

Almost all of the pioneer African-American players experienced both subtle and overt forms of discrimination.

The black press began to select All-American teams in 1911. Two of the players on that first team were Edward B. Gray, a running back from Howard who had played the same position from 1906 to 1908 at Amherst, and Leslie Pollard, older brother of Fritz, who had played halfback for one year at Dartmouth before resuming his career at Lincoln University. Two other standout athletes who played for black colleges were Floyd Wellman "Terrible" Terry of Talladega and Henry E. Barco of Virginia Union.

Pioneers: Black Professionals, 1889–1919

Charles Follis of Wooster, Ohio, is credited with being the first African-American professional football player. He was recruited by the Shelby, Ohio, Athletic Club, where he played professionally from 1902 to 1906. One of his teammates during the first two years was Branch Rickey, who would, as general manager and president of the Brooklyn Dodgers in 1947, desegregate major league baseball by signing Jackie ROBINSON. A darting halfback, Follis often experienced insults and dirty play. In one game in 1905 the Toledo captain urged fans to refrain from calling Follis a "nigger." By 1906 the abuse had become unendurable and Follis quit the game. He died of pneumonia in 1910, at the age of 31. Three other blacks appeared on professional club rosters prior to 1919. Charles "Doc" Baker ran halfback for the Akron Indians from 1906 to 1908, and again in 1911. Gideon "Charlie" Smith of Hampton Institute appeared as a tackle in one game in 1915 for the Canton Bulldogs. And Henry McDonald, probably the most talented black professional during the early years, played halfback for the Rochester Jeffersons from 1911 to 1917. In one game against Canton in 1917, Earle "Greasy" Neale hurled McDonald out of bounds and snarled, "Black is black and white is white . . . and the two don't mix." Racial incidents and segregation would become even more severe in the interwar years.

Black Stars at Predominantly White Colleges, 1919–1945

Following World War I, a number of blacks gained national celebrity for their football skills. John Shelburne played fullback at Dartmouth from 1919 through 1921. During those same years, Fred "Duke" Slater was a dominant tackle at the University of Iowa. In the early 1920s, Charles West and Charles Drew played halfback for Washington and Jefferson (in Washington, Pa.) and Amherst, respectively. West became the second African American to appear in a Rose Bowl game. After their football careers, both men became medical doctors. Drew achieved international acclaim for perfecting the method of preserving blood plasma. Toward the end of the decade, David Myers appeared as a tackle and end for New York University and Ray Kemp played tackle for Duquesne.

Although scores of blacks played football for major colleges, they constantly faced racial prejudice. Some colleges denied blacks dormitory space, thus forcing them to live off campus. Others practiced a quota system by limiting the number of black players on a squad to one or two. Others benched minority athletes when they played segregated southern schools. In 1937, Boston College surrendered to southern custom when it asked Louis Montgomery to sit out the Cotton Bowl game against Clemson. One sportswriter complained that "even Hitler, to give the bum his due, didn't treat Jesse Owens the way the Cotton Bowl folk are treating Lou Montgomery—with the consent of the young Negro's alma mater. . . ." African Americans also encountered excessive roughness from white players. Jack Trice of Iowa State was deliberately maimed by Minnesota players in 1923 and died of internal bleeding. Finally, minority players were snubbed by white sportswriters. No blacks were named first-team All-Americans from 1918 to 1937, including Duke Slater, probably the best tackle of that era.

In the 1930s, dozens of black players had outstanding careers. The Big Ten Conference featured a number of gifted running backs, especially Oze Simmons of Iowa and Bernard Jefferson of Northwestern. Talented linemen included William Bell, a guard at Ohio State, and Homer Harris, a tackle at the University of Iowa. Two of the best black athletes at eastern colleges were Wilmeth Sidat-Singh, a rifle-armed quarterback at Syracuse, and Jerome "Brud" Holland, an exceptional end at Cornell. Named first-team All-American in 1937 and 1938, Holland was the first black to be so honored since Robeson two decades earlier. In the West, Joe Lillard was a punishing running back at Oregon State in 1930 and 1931. And Woodrow "Woody" Strode and Kenny Washington starred for UCLA from 1937 to 1940. Strode was a 220–pound end with sure hands and quickness. Washington, a 195–pound halfback, was one of the nation's premier players. In 1939, he led all college players in total yardage with 1,370, but failed to win first-team All-American honors.

During the war years, there were five exceptional African-American college players. Marion Motley was a bruising 220–pound fullback at the University of Nevada. Two guards, Julius Franks of the University of Michigan and Bill Willis of Ohio State, were named to several All-American teams. And Claude "Buddy" Young was a brilliant running back at the University of Illinois. As a freshman in 1944, the diminutive, speedy halfback tied Harold "Red" Grange's single-season scoring record with 13 touchdowns. He spent the next year in the armed service, but continued his career after the

Kenny Washington, a teammate of Jackie Robinson on UCLA's football teams of the late 1930s, preceded Robinson in breaking the color barrier in major professional sports when he played with the NFL's Los Angeles Rams in 1946. (Photographs and Prints Division, Schomburg Center for Research in Black Culture, The New York Public Library, Astor, Lenox and Tilden Foundations)

war. Finally, Joe Perry was a standout running back at Compton Junior College in southern California.

Black College Play, 1919–1945

Although black colleges lacked sufficient funds for equipment and stadiums, football grew in popularity after World War I. Black conferences sprang up throughout the South, but the CIAA, created in 1912, fielded the most talented teams. In the immediate postwar period, Franz Alfred "Jazz" Bird of Lincoln was the dominant player. A small but powerful running back, Bird was nicknamed "the black Red Grange."

Morgan State University was the dominant black college team of the 1930s and early 1940s. Coached by Edward Hurt, Morgan State won seven CIAA titles between 1930 and 1941. Running backs Otis Troupe and Thomas "Tank" Conrad were the star athletes for the Morgan State teams. In the deep South, Tuskegee Institute overwhelmed its opponents, winning nine Southern Intercollegiate Athletic Conference (SIAC) titles in ten years from 1924 through 1933. Tuskegee's team was led by Benjamin Franklin Stevenson, a skilled running back who played eight seasons from 1924 through 1931. (Eligibility rules were not enforced at the time.) In the more competitive Southwest Athletic Conference (SWAC), Wiley University boasted fullback Elza Odell and halfback Andrew Patterson. Langston College in Oklahoma, which won four championships in the 1930s, featured running back Tim Crisp. The Midwestern Athletic Conference (MWAC), started in 1932, was dominated by Kentucky State, which topped the conference four times in the 1930s. Its key players were ends William Reed and Robert Hardin, running back George "Big Bertha" Edwards, and quarterback Joseph "Tarzan" Kendall. During the war years, fullback John "Big Train" Moody of Morris Brown College and guard Herbert "Lord" Trawik of Kentucky State were consensus picks for the Black All-American team.

Black Professionals, 1919–1945

In 1919 several midwestern clubs organized the American Professional Football Association, the forerunner of the National Football League (NFL) created two years later. The first African Americans to play in the NFL were Robert "Rube" Marshall and Fritz Pollard. Over forty years old, Marshall performed as an end with the Rock Island Independents from 1919 through 1921. Pollard appeared as a running back with the Akron Pros during those same years. Racial incidents were commonplace. Pollard recalled fans at away games taunting him with the song "Bye, Bye, Blackbird." Occasionally, they hurled stones at him. Even at home games, fans sometimes booed him. Besides playing, Pollard served as the first black NFL coach, directing Akron in 1920, Milwaukee in 1922, Hammond in 1923 and 1924, and Akron again in 1925 and 1926. Other blacks who performed in the NFL during the 1920s were Paul Robeson, Jay "Inky" Williams, John Shelbourne, James Turner, Edward "Sol" Butler, Dick Hudson, Harold Bradley, and David Myers. Those athletes did not compete without incident. In 1926, the New York Giants refused to take the field until the Canton Bulldogs removed their quarterback, Sol Butler, from the game. Canton obliged. The last three minority athletes to play in the desegregated NFL were Duke Slater, Joe Lillard, and Ray Kemp. An exceptional tackle who often played without a helmet, Slater performed for Milwaukee (1922), Rock Island (1922–1925), and the Chicago Cardinals (1926–1931). Joe Lillard also starred for the Cardinals from 1932 to 1933. He was a skillful punt returner, kicker, and runner, but his contract was not renewed after the 1933 season. Ray Kemp, a tackle with the Pittsburgh Pirates (later renamed the Steelers), met a similar fate.

In 1933, NFL owners established an informal racial ban that lasted until 1946. The reasons for the exclusionary policy are not entirely clear. Probably NFL moguls were attempting to please bigoted fans, players, and owners. In addition, professional football hoped to compete with baseball for fans and adopted that sport's winning formula on racial segregation. Southern-born George Preston Marshall, who owned the Boston franchise, was especially influential in the shaping of NFL policy. A powerful personality with a knack for innovation and organization, Marshall in 1933 spearheaded the reorganization of the NFL into two five-team divisions with a season-ending championship game. Four years later, he moved his Boston team to Washington, D.C., a segregated city. Marshall once vowed that he would never employ minority athletes. Indeed, the Redskins was in fact the last NFL team to desegregate, resisting until 1962.

Other owners implausibly attributed the absence of African-American athletes to the shortage of quality college players. The NFL draft was established in 1935, but owners overlooked such talented stars as Oze Simmons, Brud Holland, Wilmeth Sidat-Singh, Woody Strode, and Kenny Washington. Owners also lamely argued that they purposely did not hire blacks in order to protect them from physical abuse by bigoted white players.

Denied an opportunity in the NFL, blacks formed their own professional teams. The New York Brown Bombers, organized in 1935 by Harlem sports promoter Hershel "Rip" Day, was one of the most talented squads. Taking their nickname from the popular heavyweight fighter Joe LOUIS, the Brown Bombers recruited Fritz Pollard as coach. Pollard agreed to coach, in part, to showcase minority athletes. He signed Tank Conrad, Joe Lillard, Dave Myers, Otis Troupe, Hallie Harding, and Howard "Dixie" Matthews. The Bombers competed mainly against semipro white teams such as the New Rochelle Bulldogs. Pollard coached the Bombers to three winning seasons, but he resigned in 1937 when the team was denied use of Dyckman Oval Field in the Bronx. The Brown Bombers continued for several more years as a road team and then disappeared.

During the war years, blacks played professionally on the West coast. In 1944 both the American Professional League and the Pacific Coast Professional Football League fielded integrated teams. Kenny Washington starred for the San Francisco Clippers and Ezzrett Anderson for the Los Angeles Mustangs. In the Pacific Coast League, Jackie Robinson, who would integrate major league baseball, represented the Los Angeles Bulldogs, and Mel Reid performed for the Oakland Giants. The following year the two leagues merged into the Pacific Coast League. The Hollywood Bears, with Washington, Anderson, and Woody Strode, won the title.

The Postwar Years: Blacks at Predominantly White Colleges

World War II and the Cold War proved instrumental in breaking down racial barriers. After all, how could Americans criticize Nazi Germany and then the Soviet Union for racism and totalitarianism when blacks were denied first-class citizenship in the United States? During the 1940s and 1950s, blacks worked diligently to topple segregation in all areas, including athletics. In football, their efforts met with considerable success.

During the postwar years, several minority athletes performed admirably at big-time schools. Buddy Young returned to the University of Illinois and helped lead his team to a Rose Bowl victory over UCLA. Levi Jackson, a fleet running back, became the first African American to play for Yale and was elected team captain for 1949. Wally Triplett and Denny Hoggard became the first blacks to play in the Cotton Bowl when Penn State met Southern Methodist in 1948. And Bob Mann, Len Ford, and Gene Derricotte helped the University of Michigan trounce the University of Southern California in the 1949 Rose Bowl, 49–0.

Blacks continued to make their mark in intercollegiate football in the 1950s. Ollie Matson excelled as a running back at the University of San Francisco from 1949 through 1951. The following year he won two medals in track at the Olympics in Helsinki. Jim Parker was a dominant guard at Ohio State. In 1956 he became the first African American to win the Outland Trophy, awarded to the nation's foremost collegiate lineman. Bobby Mitchell and Lenny Moore starred at halfback for the University of Illinois and Penn State, respectively. Prentiss Gautt took to the gridiron for the University of Oklahoma in 1958, the first black to perform for a major, predominantly white southern school. And Jim Brown, perhaps the greatest running back in the history of the game, debuted at Syracuse University in 1954. There, Brown lettered in basketball, track, lacrosse, and football and was named All-American in the latter two sports. As a senior, he rushed for 986 yards, third highest in the nation. In the final regular season game he scored 43 points on 6 touchdowns and 7 conversions. In the 1957 Cotton Bowl game against Texas Christian University, he scored 21 points in a losing cause and was named MVP. Brown would go on to have a spectacular career in the NFL.

Literally and figuratively, African Americans made great strides on the gridiron in the 1950s. Yet barriers continued to exist. Dormitories at many colleges remained off limits. Blacks were denied access to most major colleges in the South. They were virtually excluded from some football positions, especially quarterback. And they were not seriously considered for the Heisman Trophy, an award presented to the best collegiate player.

In the 1960s, a landmark decade in the advancement of civil rights, black gridiron stars abounded. Ernie Davis, Brown's successor at fullback for Syracuse, was an exciting and powerful runner who shattered most of Brown's records. As a sophomore in 1959, Davis averaged 7 yards per carry and helped lead Syracuse to its first undefeated season. Ranked first in the nation, Syracuse defeated Texas in the Cotton Bowl and Davis was named MVP. The following year, Davis gained 877 yards on 112 carries and scored 10 touchdowns. As a senior, he had another outstanding season and became the first African American to win the Heisman Trophy. Tragically, he was diagnosed with leukemia in 1962 and never played professional football. He died at the age of twenty-three.

The 1960s produced a number of sensational black running backs. Leroy Keyes of Purdue and Gale Sayers of Kansas twice earned All-American recognition. Floyd Little and Jim Nance proved worthy successors to Brown and Davis at Syracuse. And Mike Garrett and O. J. SIMPSON, both of USC, won Heisman awards. The decade's greatest breakaway runner, Simpson rushed for 3,295 yards and 22 touchdowns in only 22 games. Blacks also excelled as linemen, receivers, and defensive backs. Bobby Bell and Carl Eller both won All-American acclaim as tackles with the University of Minnesota. Bell also captured the Outland Trophy in 1962. Bob Brown of Nebraska and Joe Greene of North Texas State also were All-American tackles. Paul Warfield was a crafty wide receiver for Ohio State. And George Webster of Michigan State twice earned All-American distinction as a defensive back. Also from Michigan State was the feared defensive end Charles "Bubba" Smith, who joined the Baltimore Colts in 1967.

In the 1960s bastions of bigotry collapsed. The last three lily-white college conferences—the Southwest, Southeast, and Atlantic Coast—all desegregated. Blacks, too, put the lie to the stereotype that they lacked the intellectual necessities to perform as quarterbacks. Sandy Stephens was voted an All-American at Minnesota and Marlin Briscoe and Gene Washington called signals at the University of Omaha and Stanford, respectively. Yet the NFL showed little or no interest in Stephens, and the other two were converted to wide receivers.

During the 1970s, 1980s, and 1990s, major colleges actively recruited African-American athletes. Considered essential to the success of the football program, blacks at some schools were illegally offered monetary and material inducements. Meager grade-point averages and low graduation rates also brought accusations that universities were exploiting minority athletes. After all, the vast majority of varsity players do not go on to enjoy lucrative professional athletic careers. To blunt the criticism, the NCAA instituted Proposition 48 in 1983. That directive required entering freshman varsity athletes to achieve a combined score of 700 on the Scholastic Aptitude Test (SAT) and to maintain at least a C average.

From 1970 through the 1993 season, blacks have won the Heisman Trophy 17 times. The vast majority of selectees have been running backs. Beginning with Ohio State's Archie Griffin in 1974 and 1975, minority athletes won the Heisman ten consecutive years: Tony Dorsett (1976), Earl Campbell (1977), Billy Sims (1978), Charles White (1979), George Rogers (1980), Marcus Allen (1981), Herschel Walker (1982), and Michael Rozier (1983). Running backs Bo Jackson (1985) and Barry Sanders (1988) also were recipients. The only non-running backs to capture the prize were receivers Johnny Rodgers (1972), Tim Brown (1987), and Desmond Howard (1991), and quarterbacks Andre Ware (1989) and Charlie Ward (1993). Outland trophy winners for the best interior lineman have included Rich Glover (1972), John Hicks (1973), Lee Roy Selmon (1975), Ross Browner (1976), Greg Roberts (1978), Mark May (1980), and Bruce Smith (1984).

From 1970 through the 1993 season, blacks have won the Heisman Trophy 17 times.

Blacks have only slowly been hired as collegiate coaches. The first African-American head coach at a major college football program was Dennis Green, who was head coach at Northwestern (1981–1985) and at Stanford (1989–1991) before being named head coach of the Minnesota Vikings in the NFL. In the early 1990s the only African-American coaches at Division 1–A colleges were Ron Cooper at Eastern Michigan University, Ron Dickerson at Temple University, and Jim Caldwell at Wake Forest University.

Black College Play in the Postwar Era

Although football programs at black colleges continued to be strapped financially, they still produced some superb players and coaches. Eddie Robinson of Grambling, Ed Hurt and Earl Banks of Morgan State, and Jake Gaither of Florida A & M were four of the most successful black college coaches. Each won several conference titles and sent numerous players to the NFL. Morgan State produced three premier NFL players—Roosevelt Brown, a guard with the New York Giants in the mid-1950s, Leroy Kelly, a running back with the Cleveland Browns in the mid-1960s, and Willie Lanier, a linebacker with the Kansas City Chiefs from 1967 to 1977—among numerous other stars. Florida A & M yielded Willie Gallimore, a running back with the Chicago Bears (1957–1963), and Bob Hayes, a sprinter who played wide receiver for the Dallas Cowboys (1965–1974). Grambling has sent more than seventy players to the NFL, including quarterback James Harris, running backs Paul Younger and Sammy White, wide receiver Charlie Joiner, defensive tackles Ernest Ladd and Junious "Buck" Buchanan, defensive backs Everson Walls, Roosevelt Taylor, and Willie Brown, and the outstanding defensive end for the Green Bay Packers, Willie Davis.

Two of the greatest offensive players in NFL history graduated from black colleges in Mississippi. NFL career rushing leader Walter Payton attended Jackson State before joining the Chicago Bears in 1975, and the San Francisco '49ers' Jerry Rice, the holder of the career record for touchdown receptions, graduated from Mississippi Valley State in 1985. Other notable products of black colleges include defensive specialists David "Deacon" Jones and Donnie Schell from South Carolina State, defensive end Elvin Bethea from North Carolina A & T, wide receivers John Stallworth and Harold Jackson of Alabama A & M and Jackson State, respectively, and guard Larry Little of Bethune Cookman. Prairie View A & M produced safety Ken Houston and wide receiver Otis Taylor. Maryland State delivered defensive back Johnny Sample and two dominant linemen, Roger Brown and Art Shell. Savannah State yielded tight end Shannon Sharpe.

The NFL in the Postwar Years

The democratic idealism of World War II and the emergence of a rival professional league, the All-America Football Conference (AAFC), proved instrumental in the toppling of the racial barrier in 1946. That year the Los Angeles Rams of the NFL hired Kenny Washington and Woody Strode, and the Cleveland Browns of the AAFC signed Marion Motley and Bill Willis. Washington and Strode were beyond their prime, but Motley and Willis were at their peak. They helped lead the Browns to the first of four consecutive league championships. Both athletes were named first-team All-Pros, an honor which became perennial. Both would also be inducted into the Pro Football Hall of Fame.

The success of the Browns prompted desegregation among other teams, especially in the AAFC, which lasted until 1949. The football New York Yankees signed Buddy Young and the gridiron Brooklyn Dodgers took Elmore Harris of Morgan State. The Los Angeles Dons recruited Len Ford, Ezzrett Anderson, and Bert Piggott. Ford would go on to star as a defensive end for the Cleveland Browns. The San Francisco '49ers, originally an AAFC team, in 1948 signed Joe Perry, who would, in his second season, lead the league in rushing. After the '49ers joined the NFL, he became the first back to amass back-to-back thousand-yard rushing seasons in 1953 and 1954.

Among NFL teams, only the Rams, the New York Giants, and the Detroit Lions took a chance on African-American athletes in the 1940s. The Lions signed Melvin Grooms and Bob Mann, and the Giants acquired Emlen Tunnell, one of the sport's greatest safeties. In the early 1950s, the Giants also obtained Roosevelt Brown, a superior tackle. The Baltimore Colts acquired Buddy Young from the Yankees, and the Chicago Cardinals signed Wally Triplett, Ollie Matson, and Dick "Night Train" Lane. Matson was a crafty runner and dangerous receiver who rushed for 5,173 yards and caught 222 passes in 14 NFL seasons. He was inducted into the Pro Football Hall of Fame in 1972. Dick Lane, another Hall of Fame inductee, excelled as a cornerback for the Cardinals and Lions. The Washington Redskins, the last NFL team to desegregate in 1962, acquired Bobby Mitchell from the Cleveland Browns for the draft rights to Ernie Davis. Mitchell was a gifted wide receiver and an explosive kick returner. He, too, was elected to the Pro Football Hall of Fame in 1983.

Jim Brown, Lenny Moore, and John Henry Johnson were all premier running backs in the 1950s and early 1960s. In nine seasons with Cleveland, Brown led the NFL in rushing eight times, amassing 12,312 yards and 126 touchdowns, a career record. He was selected Rookie of the Year in 1957, and MVP in 1958 and 1965. He was also voted to nine All-Pro teams. At 6′2″ and 230 pounds, Brown ideally combined power, speed, and endurance. Lenny Moore was the epitome of a runner-receiver. He gained 5,174 yards as a halfback and another 6,039 yards as a receiver. He was named Rookie of the Year in 1956 and helped propel the Baltimore Colts to NFL championships in 1958 and 1959. He was elected to the Pro Football Hall of Fame in 1975. John Henry Johnson, a powerful running back and ferocious blocker, played for San Francisco, Detroit, and Pittsburgh (1954–1966). In 13 seasons, he totaled 6,803 yards on 1,571 carries.

The formation of the American Football League (AFL) in 1959 presented opportunities on the new teams for scores of African Americans. Prior to its merger with the NFL in 1966, the AFL produced many exciting black players. Carlton "Cookie" Gilchrist of the Buffalo Bills became the league's first thousand-yard rusher in 1962. Other excellent running backs included Abner Haynes of the Dallas Texans, Paul Lowe of Oakland, Jim Nance of Boston, and Mike Garrett of Kansas City. Lionel Taylor of Denver, Art Powell of Oakland, and Otis Taylor of Kansas City were all gifted receivers. Willie Brown and Dave Grayson were prominent defensive backs for Oakland. And three future Hall of Famers all played for Kansas City: Buck Buchanan, Bobby Bell, and Willie Lanier.

Minority athletes also excelled in the NFL during the 1960s. Roosevelt Brown of New York and Jim Parker of Baltimore were frequent All-Pros on the offensive line. The successful Green Bay teams were anchored on defense by Willie Davis at end, Herb Adderly at cornerback, and Willie Wood at safety. Other defensive standouts were Roger Brown and Dick Lane of Detroit, Abe Woodson of San Francisco, Roosevelt "Rosey" Grier of New York and Los Angeles, and Carl Eller and Alan Page of Minnesota.

Gale Sayers of the Chicago Bears was probably the most electrifying offensive star of the 1960s. A graceful back with breakaway speed, he won Rookie of the Year honors in 1965, scoring 22 touchdowns. The following year, he led the NFL in rushing with 1,231 yards. After leading the league in rushing for a second time in 1969, injuries ended his career. The decade also yielded two superior pass receivers: Paul Warfield and Charlie Taylor. Playing 13 seasons for Cleveland and Miami, Warfield caught 427 passes for 8,565 yards. Another Hall of Famer, Taylor played his entire thirteen-year career for Washington, totaling 649 passes for 9,140 yards.

The 1970 merger of the AFL and NFL set the stage for the emergence of professional football as America's most popular spectator sport. Since the merger, the NFL has been split into two divisions, the National Football Conference (NFC) and the American Football Conference (AFC). During the era of the unified league, African Americans have managed to topple virtually every existing sports barrier. In football, they have continued to dominate the skill positions of running back, receiver, and defensive back. In the 1970s, Orenthal James "O. J." Simpson became the dominant back. A slashing and darting runner for the Buffalo Bills, Simpson led the AFC in rushing in 1972, 1973, 1975, and 1976. In 1973 he shattered Jim Brown's single-season record by rushing for 2,003 yards. In eleven seasons he rushed for 11,236 yards and caught 232 passes for 2,142 yards. Walter "Sweetness" Payton became the game's most statistically accomplished running back, establishing an NFL record of 16,726 yards in 13 seasons with the Chicago Bears. A durable player who missed only four of 194 games, he also holds the record for most thousand-yard seasons (10), most hundred-yard games (77), most yards rushing in a single game (275), and is second to Jim Brown for most touchdowns (125).

Erick Dickerson led the NFC in rushing with the Los Angeles Rams in 1983, 1984, 1986, and with the Indianapolis Colts in 1988. In 1984 he broke Simpson's record by gaining 2,007 yards in a single season. Earl Campbell, a barrel-thighed fullback with the Houston Oilers, led the AFC in rushing from 1978 to 1981. In 1978 he captured both the Rookie of the Year and the MVP awards. In eight seasons he gained 9,407 yards. Tony Dorsett of the Dallas Cowboys was another leading ground-gainer who accumulated more than 10,000 yards rushing. In a game against Minnesota in 1983 he sprinted for a 99-yard touchdown run, establishing an NFL record. In the 1970s, Franco Harris helped spark the Pittsburgh Steelers to four Super Bowl victories, and in the 1980s, Marcus Allen helped the Oakland Raiders win the Super Bowl in 1984. The following year Allen led the NFL in rushing and was named MVP. Ottis Anderson, Roger Craig, and Herschel Walker have been successful ground-gainers and pass receivers. Thurmond Thomas of the Buffalo Bills is another quality dual-purpose back. In the early 1990s, three of the NFL's most gifted runners were Thomas, Barry Sanders of Detroit, and Emmitt Smith of Dallas, who won rushing titles in 1991, 1992, and 1993.

A number of blacks have gained recognition as receivers. Possessing both blocking and pass-catching ability, Kellen Winslow, Ozzie Newsome, Shannon Sharpe, and John Mackey have served as model tight ends. Mackey was elected to the Pro Football Hall of Fame in 1991—an honor long overdue and probably denied him earlier because of his union fights against management and the NFL office. Notable wide receivers have included Otis Taylor, Paul Warfield, Harold Jackson, Cliff Branch, Drew Pearson, Mel Gray, Lynn Swann, John Stallworth, Isaac Curtis, James Lofton, Charlie Joiner, Mike Quick, Art Monk, Al Toon, Andre Rison, Andre Reed, John Taylor, Ahmad Rashad, Mark Duper, Mark Clayton, Michael Irvin, and Sterling Sharpe. In 1993, Sharpe of the Green Bay Packers caught 112 passes, surpassing his own single-season record established the year before. Sure hands, breathtaking quickness, and an incomparable ability to run with the ball make Jerry Rice of the '49ers a peerless receiver. In Super Bowl XXIII against Cincinnati, Rice won the MVP by catching 11 passes for a record 215 yards. The following year, in Super Bowl XXIV against Denver, he caught 7 passes for 148 yards and 3 touchdowns. Barring injury, Rice seems certain to break Jim Brown's record for career touchdowns and Art Monk's record for career pass interceptions.

Blacks have also distinguished themselves as defensive backs, interior linemen, and linebackers. Art Shell, Gene Upshaw, Bob Brown, Leon Gray, Reggie McKenzie, Anthony Munoz, and Larry Little all have excelled on the offensive line. Little was selected to the Pro Football Hall of Fame in 1993. A frequent All-Pro selection, Dwight Stephenson of the Miami Dolphins became the first outstanding black center in the mid-1980s. Claude Humphrey, Leroy Selmon, Joe Greene, Bruce Smith, Reggie White, and Charlie Johnson have all been standout defensive linemen. Defensive backs include Ronnie Lott, Mel Blount, Lem Barney, Jimmy Johnson, Emmitt Thomas, Donnie Schell, Louis Wright, Mike Haynes, Albert Lewis, and Ron Woodson. And some of the best linebackers in the game have been minority athletes such as George Webster, David Robinson, Willie Lanier, Robert Brazille, Lawrence Taylor, Mike Singletary, Cornelius Bennett, Seth Joyner, Hugh Green, Andre Tippett, Derrik Thomas, Vincent Brown, Junior Seau, and Rickey Jackson.

Blacks, too, have dispelled the myth that they lack the intellectual gifts to play certain positions, especially quarterback. In 1953 the Chicago Bears signed a black Michigan State signal caller appropriately named Willie Thrower. He appeared in several games but did not distinguish himself and was released at the end of the year. George Taliaferro of Indiana University appeared as a quarterback for Baltimore in 1953, but he also failed to make an impression. Two years later, the Green Bay Packers signed Charlie Brackins from Prairie View A & M, but he was used sparingly. Marlin Briscoe of the University of Omaha quarterbacked several games for the Denver Broncos in 1968, but was released the following year and became a wide receiver for Buffalo. James Harris of Grambling took snaps for Buffalo in 1969, and led the Los Angeles Rams to a division title in 1974. Joe Gilliam played adequately for Pittsburgh in 1974, but lost the job to Terry Bradshaw, who became the offensive leader of the Super Bowl champions.

The performance of Doug Williams for the Washington Redskins in the 1988 Super Bowl against Denver demonstrated that a black possessed the athletic and intellectual necessities to direct an NFL football team. In Super Bowl XXII Williams captured the MVP award by completing 18 of 29 passes for a record 340 yards and 4 touchdowns. Nonetheless, within a year Williams was out of professional football, receiving little reward or lasting recognition for his accomplishment.

In 1988, Randall Cunningham demonstrated dazzling running and passing ability and directed the Philadelphia Eagles to their first division title since 1980. And in the early 1990s, Warren Moon, leader of the high-powered "run and shoot" Houston Oiler offense, was one of the most accomplished passers in football. In 1990, his receiving corps of Haywood Jeffries, Drew Hill, Ernest Givens, and Curtis Duncan each caught more than 65 passes, an unparalleled gridiron feat.

While distinguishing themselves at every playing position and earning salaries commensurate with their performances, blacks in football management positions are still a novelty. There are no black owners and few African Americans in NFL front office jobs. Minority head coaches are rare, even though by the 1990s sixty percent of the players were black. Art Shell was named head coach of the Los Angeles Raiders in 1989, becoming the first black NFL coach since Fritz Pollard. The Raiders also hired a minority candidate, Terry Robiskie, to become their offensive coordinator. In 1992, Minnesota appointed Dennis Green, formerly the coach of Northwestern and Stanford, to direct the team. Green named Tony Dungy as defensive coordinator. And that same year, the Green Bay Packers employed two black coordinators, Sherman Lewis and Ray Rhodes. Gene Upshaw was elected president of the NFL Players Union, but he came under fire when he led the membership in an unsuccessful one-game strike against the owners in 1987.

While distinguishing themselves at every playing position, blacks in football management positions are still a novelty.

The status of African Americans in football in recent decades has been impressive, though many problems remain. Their entrance into leadership roles has been slow. The adjustment to the high-pressure world of top-level collegiate and professional football has proved difficult for many. Too many African Americans have developed drug problems, or have become burnt-out cases after their football careers have ended. For many, the adjustment to the largely white world of professional football has been jarring. In recent years football players have been more willing to speak out about racial problems. When the state of Arizona decided not to recognize the Martin Luther King, Jr., holiday, blacks helped persuade the NFL to transfer the site of the 1993 Super Bowl from Phoenix to Los Angeles.

In the past, high-salaried minority players have been criticized for being aloof. In part, blacks have been reluctant to speak out for fear of alienating the white majority. "A lot of people, myself included," Lawrence Taylor once observed, "don't want to give up their status in white America. You learn how to deal with certain situations, how to play the game." But Taylor and other highly visible minority athletes are increasingly speaking out on social issues in order to improve the human condition for athletes and nonathletes alike.

BIBLIOGRAPHY

Ahse, Arthur R., Jr. *A Hard Road to Glory: A History of the African-American Athlete, 1619–1987.* 3 vols. New York, 1988.

Carroll, John M. "Fritz Pollard and the Brown Bombers." *The Coffin Corner* 12 (1990): 14–17.

Chalk, Ocania. *Black College Sport.* New York, 1976.

———. *Pioneers of Black Sport.* New York, 1975.

Edwards, Harry. "Black Athletes and Sports in America." *The Western Journal of Black Studies* 6 (1982): 138–144.

Henderson, Edwin B. *The Black Athlete: Emergence and Arrival.* New York, 1968.

———. *The Negro In Sports.* Washington, D.C., 1949.

Johnson, William Oscar. "How Far Have We Come?" *Sports Illustrated* 75 (August 5, 1991): 39–46.

Pennington, Richard. *Breaking the Ice: The Racial Integration of Southwest Conference Football.* Jefferson, N.C., 1987.

Roberts, Milton. "Black College All-Time, All-Star Football Team." *Black Sports* (June 1976): 47–50.

Smith, Thomas G. "Civil Rights on the Gridiron: The Kennedy Administration and the Desegregation of the Washington Redskins." *Journal of Sport History* 14 (1987): 189–208.

———. "Outside the Pale: The Exclusion of Blacks from the National Football League." *Journal of Sport History* 15 (1988): 255–281.

Spivey, Donald. "The Black Athlete in Big-Time Intercollegiate Sports, 1941–1968." *Phylon* 44 (1983): 116–125.

– THOMAS G. SMITH

FORTEN, JAMES

James Forten (September 2, 1766–March 15, 1842), businessman and abolitionist. Born free in Philadelphia in 1766, James Forten attended a Quaker school in Philadelphia headed by abolitionist Anthony Benezet. At the age of fourteen he went to sea and became a powder boy on the *Royal Louis,* a colonial privateer under the command of Captain Stephen Decatur, father of the nineteenth-century naval hero of the same name. After one successful sortie against the British, the *Royal Louis* was captured by a group of British ships; Forten and the rest of the crew were taken prisoner. Had he not befriended the son of the British captain, Forten, like many African Americans in his situation, might have been sent into slavery in the West Indies. Instead the British captain ensured that Forten would be transferred to the *Jersey,* a prison hulk in New York harbor; after seven months, Forten was released. On the prison hulk, many succumbed to rampant disease; Forten luckily avoided serious illness.

Shortly after his release, Forten began to work under the tutelage of Robert Bridges, a Philadelphia sail maker. Forten's skill and aptitude guaranteed his success in the industry: by the age of twenty he was the foreman of Bridges's shop. Upon Bridges's retirement in 1798, Forten became the undisputed master of the shop and developed a reputation for excellent service and innovative sail handling techniques. His business grew; some estimates suggest that he had a fortune of over $100,000 by the early 1830s.

Forten used both his fortune and his fame to forward his agenda for the destruction of slavery.

Forten used both his fortune and his fame to forward his agenda for the destruction of slavery. One of the most prominent and vocal Philadelphians on the issue, Forten was a lifelong advocate of immediate abolition. In 1800 he was a petitioner to the U.S. Congress to change the terms of the 1793 Fugitive Slave Law which permitted suspected runaways to be seized and arrested without a warrant and access to due process. Forten refused to rig sails for ships that had participated in or were suspected of participating in the slave trade. In 1812, along with well-known Philadelphians Richard ALLEN and Absalom JONES, he helped raise a volunteer regiment of African Americans to help defend Philadelphia were the city to be threatened by the British.

In September 1830, Forten was a participant in the first National Negro Convention in Philadelphia. Its goal was to "consider the plight of the free Negro" and to "plan his social redemption." At the next annual convention, Forten used his influence to oppose funding for the American Colonization Society which supported black emigration to Liberia; at other times, however, Philadelphia's black elite, including Forten, had advocated emigration to Haiti and Canada.

In 1832 Forten and several other African Americans forwarded another petition to the Pennsylvania legislature asking it not to restrict the immigration of free blacks into the state nor to begin more rigorous enforcement of the 1793 federal Fugitive Slave Law. Much of their argument was based on two main principles: a moral argument based on the evils of slavery and an economic argument—that free blacks were extremely productive members of the Philadelphia and Pennsylvania communities. As one of the organizers of the American Anti-Slavery Society in 1833, Forten provided support, especially economic, to abolitionist activities. Forten's generous support greatly aided the continuing publication of William Lloyd Garrison's abolitionist *Liberator.* Around 1838 he also went to court in a vain attempt to secure the right to vote.

Forten was a founder and presiding officer of the American Moral Reform Society. The society stressed temperance, peace, and other Garrisonian ideals, which included the full and equal participation of women in antislavery activism and society in general. Forten's reputation for good works was well known: he received an award from the city of Philadelphia for saving at least four, and perhaps as many as twelve, people from drowning in the river near his shop. When he died in 1842, thousands of people, many of whom were white, reportedly attended his funeral.

Even before his death in 1842, the legacy of Forten's deep belief in abolition was carried on by his family. Forten's children, and later his grandchildren, would figure as prominent abolitionists and civil rights activists throughout the nineteenth century. Forten's son James, Jr., and his son-in-law Robert Purvis were very active in the abolitionist movement from the 1830s onwards, and often collaborated with the elder Forten in his various activities. All of Forten's daughters were involved in antislavery affairs, and Charlotte Forten GRIMKÉ, Forten's granddaughter, became a well-known author, educator, and activist for civil rights.

BIBLIOGRAPHY

Aptheker, Herbert, ed. *A Documentary History of the Negro People in the United States.* New York, 1951, pp. 126–133.

"The Forten Family." *Negro History Bulletin* 10, no. 4 (January 1947): 75–79.

Purvis, Robert. *Remarks on the Life and Character of James Forten Delivered at Bethel Church, March 30, 1842.* Philadelphia, 1842.

Winch, Julie. *Philadelphia's Black Elite: Activism, Accommodation, and the Struggle for Autonomy, 1787–1848.* Philadelphia, 1988.

– EVAN A. SHORE

FORTY ACRES AND A MULE

After the CIVIL WAR, many freedmen expected the federal government to provide them with enough land (forty acres) to establish themselves as independent farmers. This, they felt, was owed to them as restitution for their past labor. The hope for land redistribution sprung from a number of sources, including the wartime experiments at the Sea Islands of South Carolina and at Davis Bend. Expectations were also sparked by Union Gen. William T. Sherman's victorious march through Georgia. On January 12, 1865, Sherman and Secretary of War Edwin Stanton met with twenty leaders of the black community in Savannah, Ga. Four days after the meeting, Sherman issued Special Field Order No. 15, which set aside a thirty-mile portion of the lowcountry rice coast from South Carolina to Georgia for settlement by blacks. Families of freedmen would receive forty acres and, possibly, the loan of a mule—many historians claim this to be the origin of the phrase. Further indication that the government would assist blacks in their effort to become independent farmers came with the formation of the Freedmen's Bureau in March 1865. Along with distributing food and clothing, the bureau was authorized to divide abandoned and confiscated land into forty-acre plots for rental to freedmen and loyal refugees. Complicating these efforts was the fact that the federal government's legal title to southern land was still not clear.

The phrase "forty acres and a mule" suggests empty promises made by the U.S. government and the debt owed to its black citizens.

In the summer of 1865, President Andrew Johnson ordered land in federal hands to be returned to former owners. Thaddeus Stevens, Charles Sumner, and other Radical Republican congressmen tried to pass a bill upholding the Sherman land titles; however, it was vetoed by Johnson. In July 1866 Congress ratified another attempt at land redistribution, with the Southern Homestead Act. Unfortunately, this, too, proved to be of little help to the freedmen. Many blacks had signed long-term restrictive labor contracts, and others were unable to afford the implements, seed, and rations needed to work the land. By mid-1867, Radical Republican congressmen had limited their focus to securing political rights for blacks (in particular the right to vote), rather than sweeping land reform.

The phrase "forty acres and a mule" has been used since the nineteenth century for a number of black causes. It suggests that African Americans deserve restitution for the work of black slaves. More generally, the term suggests empty promises made by the U.S. government and the debt owed to its black citizens.

BIBLIOGRAPHY

Oubre, Caude F. *Forty Acres and a Mule: The Freedmen's Bureau and Black Land Ownership.* Baton Rouge, La., 1978.

– WALTER FRIEDMAN

FOURTEENTH AMENDMENT

Coming approximately ten years after the DRED SCOTT DECISION had ruled that all slaves and their descendants were not citizens of the United States, the Fourteenth Amendment, ratified on July 28, 1868, granted both state and federal citizenship to "all persons born or naturalized in the United States" (with the notable exception of Native Americans living on reservations). It also pledged that no state shall "abridge the privileges or immunities" of citizens, nor "deny to any person within its jurisdiction the equal protection of the laws." Along with the FIFTEENTH AMENDMENT, which sought to extend the franchise to all blacks, the Fourteenth Amendment was drafted by Radical Republican members of Congress, who were uneasy with President Andrew Johnson's lenient policies toward the South in the wake of the CIVIL WAR. These Republicans aimed at giving meaning to the freedom which had been legally granted to slaves by the THIRTEENTH AMENDMENT. In particular, they hoped to invalidate the discriminatory black codes that had been passed by various state legislatures.

Radical Republicans were also concerned that, with the emancipation of slaves, southern representation in Congress would dramatically increase when the former Confederate states reentered the Union—according to Article I, Section 2 of the Constitution, only three-fifths of the slave population had previously been counted for purposes of representation. To ensure that newly freed blacks would have a voice in choosing their political leaders, Section 2 of the amendment promised to reduce congressional representation proportionately for each male citizen denied suffrage. (Despite severe restrictions placed on black suffrage, however, this section was never applied.)

Section 3 of the Fourteenth Amendment excluded former Confederates from holding political office even if they had previously taken an oath to support the U.S. Constitution. This section aimed at keeping former Confederate officers from regaining political office. It had only a temporary effect. Section 4 declared the government of the United States not liable for the Confederate debt.

The intentions of the Radical Republicans were undermined by a series of conservative Supreme Court decisions. In the *Slaughterhouse Cases* (1873), the Court held that state law, rather than federal law, controlled the basic civil liberties of citizens. Further, it interpreted the "privileges and immunities" of citizens in a narrow way, covering such matters as protection on the high seas. The Court also declared that states were not required to enforce the liberties guaranteed in the Bill of Rights. In the 1883 Civil Rights cases, the Court ruled that the Fourteenth Amendment did not ensure citizens equal access to public accommodations, and in PLESSY V. FERGUSON (1896), that racial segregation of railways was not a violation of the amendment's "equal protection" clause.

After World War II, a different interpretation of the Fourteenth Amendment evolved from a less conservative Supreme Court. The "equal protection" clause began to be used to fight racial discrimination in such cases as BROWN V. THE BOARD OF EDUCATION OF TOPEKA, KANSAS (1954), against school segregation, and the *Reapportionment Cases* (1964), against unfairly drawn state legislative districts. As well, the Court came to hold a broader interpretation of the civil rights protected under the Fourteenth Amendment. *Shelley* v. *Kraemer* (1948) outlawed racially restrictive covenants in housing. *U.S.* v. *Guest* (1966) applied the Fourteenth Amendment to cover private violence that was racially motivated. Under Chief Justice Earl Warren, the Court ruled, in a series of cases, that most of the Bill of Rights had to be respected by the states. The liberal Court of the late 1960s and early '70s found other rights guaranteed by the amendment, such as the right to use birth control devices (*Griswold* v. *Connecticut,* 1965) and the right to an abortion (*Roe* v. *Wade,* 1973). The appointees of several conservative Republican presidents from the 1970s and 1980s, however, have interpreted the rights protected under the amendment more narrowly.

It took approximately a century before the federal government was willing to enforce the provisions of the Fourteenth Amendment as its authors had envisioned. The amendment will no doubt continue to be interpreted in ways that will either broaden or narrow federal protection of civil rights, according to the political climate of the nation and the makeup of the Court.

BIBLIOGRAPHY

Berger, Raoul. *The Fourteenth Amendment and the Bill of Rights.* Norman, Okla., 1989.

Nelson, William E. *The Fourteenth Amendment: From Political Principle to Judicial Doctrine.* Cambridge, Mass., 1988.

— WALTER FRIEDMAN

FRANKLIN, ARETHA LOUISE

Aretha Louise Franklin (March 25, 1942–), singer. Known as "Lady Soul" and "The Queen of Soul," Aretha Franklin brought the undiluted power of black gospel singing to American popular music beginning in the late 1960s. Born March 25, 1942, in Memphis, Tenn., and raised in Detroit, Mich., she was the fourth of five children of Barbara Siggers Franklin and the well-known gospel preacher and singer, the Rev. C. L. Franklin of Detroit's New Bethel Baptist Church. Her mother, also a gospel singer, left her husband and children in 1948 when Aretha was six, and died shortly thereafter.

Aretha's formative years were spent singing in her father's church choir and traveling with him on the gospel circuit. Numerous jazz and gospel figures visited the Franklin's home, and James Cleveland boarded with the family and worked with Aretha as she practiced playing the piano and singing. Clara Ward sang at an aunt's funeral, and Franklin was so moved she decided to become a professional singer herself. At fourteen she recorded a selection of gospel songs including Thomas A. Dorsey's "Precious Lord, Take My Hand." She became pregnant at fifteen and dropped out of school.

At eighteen Franklin was brought to the attention of John Hammond, the producer at Columbia Records who had "discovered" Bessie SMITH, Billie HOLIDAY, and other African-American musicians. Hammond praised Franklin's voice as the best he had heard in twenty years. Franklin signed with Columbia and moved to New York but achieved only marginal success as a pop singer because of Columbia's material and arrangements, a confused hodgepodge of jazz, pop, and standards.

Her breakthrough came in 1966 when her Columbia contract expired and she signed with Atlantic Records, where she was teamed with veteran producer Jerry Wexler. He constructed simple, gospel-influenced arrangements for her, often based on her own piano playing. In these comfortable musical settings her true voice emerged with intensity and emotion. Wexler said, "I took her to church, sat her down at the piano, and let her be herself." Franklin's first record with Wexler was "I Never Loved a Man (The Way I Love You)" in February 1967. It was an immediate success and topped *Billboard's* charts. Her second hit, "Respect," was sung with such conviction it became a call for black and feminist pride and empowerment.

Often compared to Ray CHARLES for her fusion of sacred and secular styles, Franklin came to personify African-American "soul" music. She produced a series of top records including "Chain of Fools," "Think," and "Don't Play That Song." She has won fifteen Grammy Awards, three American Music Awards, and a Grammy Living Legend Award. With thirty-five albums, she has had seventeen number one rhythm-and-blues singles, and more million-selling singles than any other woman singer. In 1980 she switched to the Arista label.

Throughout her career, her dominant public voice has been contrasted with her private, even reclusive, personality, although she carefully monitors her career and the music industry. Her personal life has at times been difficult, with her mother's abandonment, her own pregnancy at age fifteen, several unsuccessful marriages, and, particularly, the fact that her father, to whom she was very close, spent five years in a coma from a gunshot wound in 1979 until his death in 1984.

BIBLIOGRAPHY

Bego, Mark. *Aretha Franklin: The Queen of Soul.* New York, 1989.

— BUD KLIMENT

FRANKLIN, JOHN HOPE

John Hope Franklin (January 2, 1915–), historian and educator. John Hope Franklin was born in Rentiesville, Okla., an exclusively African-American town. At an early age he came to be introduced to white custom, law, and justice in the South. His father, a lawyer, was expelled from court by a white judge who told him that no black person could ever practice law in his court. Young Franklin was himself ejected, along with his mother (an elementary school teacher) and sister, from a train because his mother refused to move from the coach designated for whites. After moving to Tulsa in 1926, Franklin attended Booker T. Washington High School and learned the meaning of a "separate but equal" education—inferior facilities and a sharply limited curriculum. His avid interest in music introduced him to the JIM CROW seats in the local concert hall. He went on to receive his B.A. at FISK UNIVERSITY in 1935 and his Ph.D. in history at Harvard University in 1941.

Throughout his career, Franklin combined scholarship with social activism. As student body president at Fisk University, he protested the lynching of a local black man to the mayor, the governor, and President Franklin D. Roosevelt. Having once been barred from entering the University of Oklahoma to pursue graduate studies, he readily agreed to the NAACP's request that he be an expert witness for a black student seeking admission to the graduate program in history at the University of Kentucky. At the request of Thurgood Marshall, he served on the research team whose work led to the Supreme Court's BROWN V. BOARD OF EDUCATION decision outlawing school segregation. In 1965, he joined more than thirty other historians on the civil rights march into Montgomery, Ala.

Like Carter WOODSON and W. E. B. DU BOIS, Franklin demonstrated to a skeptical or indifferent profession that the history of black Americans was a legitimate field for scholarly research. His first book, *The Free Negro in North Carolina, 1790–1860* (1943), explored the anomalous position of free blacks in the slave South. *Reconstruction After the Civil War* (1961) was a revisionist treatment of the unique experiment in biracial democratic government in the postwar South, particularly in its depiction of blacks as active participants and leaders, not simply as victims or passive tools of white politicians. In *The Militant South* (1956) and *A Southern Odyssey* (1976), Franklin explored different facets of the southern experience and varieties of southern white expression. His Jefferson Lecture in the Humanities for 1976, *Racial Equality in America,* probed that troubled and elusive search. In a turn to biography, his *George Washington Williams* (1985) traced the life of a historian who wrote in the 1880s the first substantial and scholarly history of black Americans. For hundreds of thousands of students, Franklin's *From Slavery to Freedom* (first published in 1947) introduced them to African-American history. In *Race and History* (1989), he brought together his most important essays and lectures, including his autobiographical sketch and reflections, "A Life of Learning."

In his books, as in his teaching, Franklin transcends the distinction between African-American and American history. He has underscored the unique quality of the history of African Americans even as he has viewed that history as an intimate part of American history, inseparable from and a central theme in the national experience. Rejecting the need to replace old distortions with new myths and eulogistic sketches of heroes and heroines, he has demonstrated his full appreciation of the complexity and integrity of the American and African-American past.

Throughout his career, Franklin combined scholarship with social activism.

His early teaching career included Fisk University, St. Augustine's College, North Carolina Central College, and HOWARD UNIVERSITY. In 1956 he went to Brooklyn College as chairman of the department of history—a department of fifty-two white historians. (The appointment made the front page of the *New York Times;* Franklin's troubled search for housing did not.) In 1964, he joined the history faculty of the University of Chicago, serving as chair from 1967 to 1970 and as the John Matthews Manly Distinguished Service Professor from 1969 to 1982. Moving to Durham, N.C., he chose to diversify rather than retire, becoming the James B. Duke Professor of History and professor of legal history in the law school at Duke University.

Franklin has been elected to the presidencies of the American Studies Association, the Southern Historical Association, the United Chapters of Phi Beta Kappa, the Organization of American Historians, and the American Historical Association. More than seventy colleges and universities have awarded him an honorary degree. He has served on numerous national commissions, was chairman of the Advisory Board of President Bill Clinton's Initiative on Race, and in 1980 was a United States delegate to the 21st General Conference of UNESCO. In 1978 the state that initially forced John Hope Franklin to undergo the humiliating rites of racial passage elected him to the Oklahoma Hall of Fame.

BIBLIOGRAPHY

Franklin, John Hope. *Race and History: Selected Essays, 1938–1988,* especially "John Hope Franklin: A Life of Learning," Baton Rouge, La., 1989, pp. 277–291.

– LEON F. LITWACK

FRATERNITIES AND SORORITIES

"Greek-letter" organizations, so called because each takes a series of three letters from the Greek alphabet for its name, have played an important role in African-American college life.

Devoted primarily to socializing among members (women in sororities and men in fraternities), campus chapters provide young people with a structured environment in which to adjust to college life and, often, to form lasting friendships. African-American fraternities and sororities share with similar white organizations a culture that features exclusiveness (members must be invited to join and meet both objective and subjective requirements regarding scholastic achievement and desirable personal and social qualities); secret rituals, grips, and passwords; humiliating and sometimes even physically dangerous initiation rites (though these have been discouraged by the national organizations at least since the 1930s); and an emphasis on parties and socializing for their own sake. However, they also encourage good scholarship, teach their members social skills, and instill a sense of character and service to society. In doing so these organizations have constituted one of the chief training grounds of what has been called the "community of striving blacks."

Moreover, many college graduates remain active in alumni chapters, swelling the ranks of the national organizations and giving them a central place in the institutional infrastructure of the black middle class. Graduate members usually provide the leadership of the national organizations, which over the years have distinguished themselves in both the provision of social services and the struggle for civil rights. Sorority and fraternity presidents have included such significant figures as Sadie T. M. Alexander and Dorothy I. Height (both of Delta Sigma Theta) and Charles Wesley, Rayford W. Logan, and Ernest Morial (all of Alpha Phi

Alpha). Patricia Roberts Harris was Delta Sigma Theta's first executive director before she went on to become the first black woman cabinet secretary. Marian ANDERSON, Violette Anderson, Countee CULLEN, W. E. B. DU BOIS, John Hope FRANKLIN, John Hope, Lena HORNE, Barbara JORDAN, Thurgood MARSHALL, Ralph Metcalfe, Jesse OWENS, Adam Clayton Powell, Sr., Leontyne PRICE, Paul ROBESON, Georgiana Simpson, and Walter WHITE were just a few of the prominent blacks to join African-American fraternities and sororities.

Nevertheless, critics such as the eminent sociologist E. Franklin FRAZIER have taken the Greek-letter organizations to task for their elitism, social snobbishness, and frivolity, which, as Frazier charged in *Black Bourgeoisie,* "divert the students from a serious interest in education." Moreover, their detractors argue, black fraternities and sororities have at times reinforced pernicious class and color divisions within the black community. In particular, some have accused the Greek-letter organizations of favoring light-skinned candidates for membership. Those with darker complexions, they charge, are forced to demonstrate superior academic, athletic, or social prowess to gain admittance. The organizations themselves, however, have denied harboring this sort of prejudice.

The social and cultural opportunities offered by fraternities and sororities were especially important for African Americans at predominantly white schools.

Administrators at black colleges originally opposed the establishment of fraternities and sororities on their campuses, fearing that secret societies would divide student bodies and distract students from the Christian and literary activities preferred by the administrators. In 1910, for example, the trustees of Atlanta University voted to "disapprove entirely" of secret organizations and gave the administration and faculty the right to do whatever they deemed necessary to suppress such groups. Before 1925 FISK UNIVERSITY also prohibited fraternities. Both of these schools eventually lifted their bans on Greek-letter societies, but a similar prohibition remained in effect at SPELMAN COLLEGE until at least 1964.

Despite their critics, however, Greek-letter organizations have provided many important benefits to their members. Although popular also at historically black colleges and universities, the social and cultural opportunities offered by fraternities and sororities were especially important for African Americans at predominantly white schools at a time when black students were few in number and excluded from general campus activities. Chapter houses provided housing for many students; at times this was the only adequate housing available to blacks barred from regular dormitories. On the campuses of black colleges, Greek-letter organizations often formed formidable political machines, dominating student government and controlling access to coveted positions in student clubs and publications. While this provoked the opposition of some, it also influenced others to seek membership.

The first African-American Greek-letter organization was not, strictly speaking, a college fraternity, though it was patterned after existing white societies. Sigma Pi Phi was founded in Philadelphia in 1904 by two physicians, a dentist, and a pharmacist. Open only to those with college degrees, it aimed to provide a space for social interaction for the most successful men in the African-American community. Self-consciously elitist, Sigma Pi Phi quickly spread to other cities, but its membership remained small—177 in 1920, 500 in 1954. Each chapter was called a *boulé,* a Greek term referring to a deliberative body, and the national organization soon also became known informally as Boulé. (Other sororities and fraternities use this word to describe their national conventions.) In 1992 Sigma Pi Phi claimed three thousand members in ninety-one chapters.

The years between 1906 and 1922 saw the founding of all of the eight major African-American Greek-letter student societies. Five of the eight were established at HOWARD UNIVERSITY, though in most cases they quickly spread to white campuses as well. These were Alpha Kappa Alpha Sorority (1908), Omega Psi Phi Fraternity (1911), Delta Sigma Theta Sorority (1913), Phi Beta Sigma Fraternity (1914), and Zeta Phi Beta Sorority (1920). The other three, Alpha Phi Alpha Fraternity (1906), Kappa Alpha Psi Fraternity (1911), and Sigma Gamma Rho Sorority (1922), were established at Cornell (Ithaca, N.Y.), Indiana (Bloomington, Ind.), and Butler universities (Indianapolis), respectively.

Alpha Phi Alpha, the first black Greek-letter fraternity, was established by a group of seven students at Cornell University in 1906, emerging out of a literary society founded earlier. In 1907 students at Howard formed the fraternity's second chapter, and in 1908 a chapter at the University of Toronto made Alpha Phi Alpha an international organization (the Toronto chapter lasted until 1912). Also in 1908, the fraternity held its first convention, adopting as its stated ideals, "manly deeds, scholarship, and love for all mankind."

Founded at Howard on January 15, 1908, Alpha Kappa Alpha became the first black sorority and the first Greek-letter organization established at a black school. The nine founders were all students in the university's School of Liberal Arts. Their leader, Ethel Hedgeman, was encouraged in this undertaking by Ethel Robinson, a graduate of Brown University who had been a sorority sister there. In its first year Alpha Kappa Alpha set standards for membership, requiring that candidates complete the first half of their sophomore year and maintain an average of 75 percent or better. The organization's early activities centered on concerts and cultural events, often relying on the talents of the members themselves.

Two fraternities were formed in 1911, Kappa Alpha Psi at Indiana University and Omega Psi Phi at Howard. The former typified the strength of fraternities and sororities among African-American students on predominantly white Midwestern campuses, where they were greater in numbers than at Eastern white schools but faced social isolation. The founders of Omega Psi Phi, on the other hand, received encouragement from Ernest E. JUST, a biologist and prominent member of the Howard faculty.

By 1913 dissatisfaction had spread among some members of the Howard chapter of Alpha Kappa Alpha who wanted to put more emphasis on involvement in community affairs and building a national organization. They also opposed the pompous Greek titles given officers (basileus, anti-basileus, grammateus, epistoleus, tamiouchos). Based largely in Howard's Teachers College, many of the dissident members were also members of a circle of friends that included men in Omega Psi Phi. After an unsuccessful attempt to reform the older organization, twenty-two women left Kappa Alpha and founded a new sorority called Delta Sigma Theta.

The following year, Howard saw the founding of a new fraternity, Phi Beta Sigma, which adopted the motto "Culture for service and service for humanity." In 1920 members of Phi Beta Sigma played an important role in the establishment of a new sorority, Zeta Phi Beta, which became a sister organization to the fraternity from which it took part of its name and on whose constitution it based its own. Finally, in 1922 Sigma Gamma Rho Sorority became the last of the major black Greek-letter organizations to be founded. Originally established at Butler University as a professional sorority for teachers and students of education, Sigma Gamma Rho expanded beyond this constituency by the end of the decade. By the early 1920s the African-American fraternities and sororities claimed a total membership of several thousand in dozens of chapters.

Competition for members and honors characterized the interaction among the various Greek-letter societies on campus. The close relationship between Alpha Kappa Alpha and Delta Sigma Theta led to an especially heated rivalry that became part of the sororities' traditions. Attracting the boyfriend of a member of the other organization was considered a particular coup. Each group strove to best the other in academic pursuits as well; when Alpha Kappa Alpha established an award for the woman graduating from Howard with the highest grade point average, Deltas made a special effort to win the prize—and often did. Partly in an effort to control this sort of rivalry, black sororities and fraternities founded the National Interfraternal Council in 1922. The council also sought to develop common membership standards for the Greek-letter organizations. It was replaced in 1930 by the National Pan-Hellenic Council, which, in addition to setting academic standards for membership, worked to secure black representation in predominantly white interfraternal organizations and fought discrimination in dormitory housing.

Social service and the promotion of education have provided the national organizations with their main focus of activities. Together with both campus and graduate chapters, they have sponsored a variety of projects in the United States and abroad (especially in Africa).

Alpha Phi Alpha pioneered with its annual campaign to promote higher education among black youth. Inaugurated on a national level in 1916, this effort was broadened in 1919 under the title "Go to High School, Go to College." Carried out each year during the first week in June, this campaign featured the dissemination of literature, speeches by fraternity members, and counseling sessions with individual students and parents. Under the influence of its education director, the noted historian Rayford W. Logan, Alpha Phi Alpha replaced "Go to High School, Go to College" in 1933 with "Education for Citizenship." Designed to inform blacks of both the "rights" and the "responsibilities" of citizenship, Logan hoped that the campaign would help African Americans challenge their disfranchisement by preparing them to vote. Similarly, Kappa Alpha Psi established its "Guide Right Program" to help youth with "discovering and developing their potentials."

The sororities, in particular, initiated a number of notable social welfare programs. Alpha Kappa Alpha, for example, began its Mississippi Health Project in 1935. Continued for eight years, the project sent teams of doctors and nurses to rural areas of the state to provide treatment and education. In the 1940s and 1950s Sigma Gamma Rho sponsored "Teen Towns," where black youths ages thirteen to seventeen could spend their leisure time at "worthwhile activities." In 1937 Delta Sigma Theta initiated its National Library Program to send bookmobiles throughout the South. Ten years later the Detroit chapter of Delta Sigma Theta opened the Delta Home for Girls to provide a residential alternative to the local juvenile detention home.

Since 1965 Alpha Kappa Alpha has operated the Jobs Corps Center in Cleveland under contract with the government. In the 1970s Phi Beta Sigma initiated Project SAD (Sigma Attacks Defects) to promote infant health by educating men concerning the importance of proper prenatal and neonatal health care, as well as the dangers of tobacco, alcohol, drugs, and venereal disease. Both sororities and fraternities continued to sponsor a wide range of social welfare programs into the 1990s.

The sororities also took a particular interest in international affairs. In the late 1940s Alpha Kappa Alpha became an accredited observer at the United Nations. In Africa Sigma Gamma Rho started Project Africa to provide agricultural assistance to African women and ran several campaigns to send books to educational institutions on the continent. Alpha Kappa Alpha chapters "adopted" more than three hundred African villages in conjunction with the international-aid organization Africare. And in 1965 Zeta Phi Beta opened a Domestic Science Center in Monrovia, Liberia. Delta Sigma Theta has aided hospitals and other projects in Kenya and Uganda, as well as in India and Haiti.

All the Greek-letter organizations encouraged education among young African Americans by providing scholarships and fellowships to both members and nonmembers. They also sponsored essay contests and other competitions for high school and college students, ran tutoring, counseling, and placement programs and undertook leadership training seminars for college members and graduates. Phi Beta Sigma had an affiliated Sigma Beta Club for young men in high school. Alpha Phi Alpha's Education Foundation encourages scholarship, promotes research, and aids the publication of works by African Americans. Over the years the fraternities and sororities have also contributed millions of dollars to educational, scientific, charitable, and civil rights causes, including the United Negro College Fund, and many individual black schools.

African-American fraternities and sororities have differed from their white counterparts in their stress on political involvement, particularly in support of civil rights. One of Delta Sigma Theta's first public activities after its founding in 1913 was to participate in the mass march on Washington for women's suffrage. (Later that year the sorority sent a delegate to the national conference of the Intercollegiate Socialist Society, where, as the only African-American present, she was called upon to comment on the question of civil rights for blacks.)

By the 1930s many of the organizations put considerable emphasis on civil rights work, lobbying for progressive legislation, participating in litigation, and working closely with such organizations as the NATIONAL ASSOCIATION FOR THE ADVANCEMENT OF COLORED PEOPLE (NAACP), the NATIONAL URBAN LEAGUE, the Joint Council on National Recovery, and the NATIONAL COUNCIL OF NEGRO WOMEN. Alpha Phi Alpha helped initiate Donald Murray's legal battle for admission to the law school of the University of Maryland. Following his court-ordered admission in 1936, the fraternity paid Murray's tuition and book costs. After campaigning actively for the Costigan-Wagner Anti-Lynching Bill, Alpha Kappa Alpha Sorority established a full-time civil rights lobby in 1938. In 1948 Alpha Kappa Alpha (which, ironically, had been viewed as too insular and conservative by the members who had split off to form Delta Sigma Theta in 1913) invited the seven other major African-American Greek-letter societies to join it in forming the American Council for Human Rights (ACHR), whose aim it was to eliminate racial discrimination and inequality. The ACHR pressed for fair employment legislation, desegregation in the armed forces, bans on poll taxes and lynching, and the integration of transportation and public accommodations in Washington, D.C. The council was dissolved in 1963.

African-American fraternities and sororities have differed from their white counterparts in their stress on political involvement.

In the late 1940s several of the organizations removed any reference to color or race from their membership requirements, enrolling a small number of students of non-African descent. Nevertheless, they remained overwhelmingly African-American and committed to work in the black community. The societies also continued to educate the public on the achievements of black men and women. In the 1940s Delta Sigma Theta produced a series of publications on black heroes, and in the 1960s Alpha Kappa Alpha published a series on black women in the judiciary, politics, business, medicine, and dentistry.

In the late-1960s, a period in which black and student militancy converged, sororities and fraternities suffered a decline in popularity among students who dis-

Table 1

MAJOR AFRICAN-AMERICAN COLLEGE SORORITIES AND FRATERNITIES

Organization	Place and Date of Founding	Headquarters	Membership*	Number of Chapters†
Alpha Kappa Alpha *Sorority*	Howard 1908	Chicago	110,000	Campus: 410 Alumnae: 420
Alpha Phi Alpha *Fraternity*	Cornell 1906	Chicago	100,000 (since founding)	Campus: 290 Alumni: 274
Delta Sigma Theta *Sorority*	Howard 1913	Washington, D.C.	175,000	Active: 760
Kappa Alpha Psi *Fraternity*	Indiana 1911	Philadelphia	80,000	Active: 323 Alumni: 308
Omega Psi Phi *Fraternity*	Howard 1911	Washington, D.C.	50,000	Active: 511 Alumni: 259
Phi Beta Sigma *Fraternity*	Howard 1914	Washington, D.C.	65,000	N.A.
Sigma Gamma Rho *Sorority*	Butler 1922	Chicago	50,000†	Active: 350†
Zeta Phi Beta *Sorority*	Howard 1920	Washington, D.C.	75,000	550 (College and alumnae)

* As reported in Julia C. Furtaw, ed., *Black Americans Information Directory 1992–93,* 2nd ed. (Detroit, 1992).
† As reported in Darren L. Smith, ed., *Black Americans Information Directory 1990–91,* (Detroit, 1990).

dained their elitism and stress on purely social activities. Even within the organizations themselves, members advocated reforms that would deemphasize their exclusive nature. Several societies, for example, did away with the minimum-grade-point-average requirements that had helped define their elite character. However, society members were often in the forefront of the black campus activism of the era. Cultural historian Paula Giddings, who joined Delta Sigma Theta at Howard University in 1967, recalls that most of the leaders of the student revolt there the following year were members of Greek-letter organizations.

By the early 1980s observers noted the resurgence of student interest in fraternities and sororities. To some extent, this was a consequence of collegians' increased concern for personal advancement and the realization that society membership could help them fulfill their aspirations in this regard. At the same time, however, organizational leaders, both on campus and among graduates, sought to reemphasize the societies' commitments to political action and social service within the black community and overcome their negative image as "noncaring, social-activity prone" groups. During this period Alpha Kappa Alpha carried out its "Black Faces in Public Places" campaign to build monuments to important African Americans in parks and government buildings. It also supported "Black Family Month" and "Black Dollar Day," the latter as part of an effort to encourage African Americans to patronize black-owned businesses.

Despite their temporary dip in popularity in the late 1960s and early 1970s, black sororities and fraternities have grown steadily since their inception, as more and more African Americans have attended college and as graduate members have accumulated. By 1990 the eight major black fraternities and sororities claimed a membership of more than 700,000 in thousands of campus and alumni chapters. In 1981 the Council of Presidents was established to promote better relations among organizations on campus and augment its constituents' political influence.

In addition to the major college-based fraternities and sororities, there have been a number of much smaller Greek-letter societies recruiting from among practitioners and students of particular professions. These organizations provide their members with social activities, professional enrichment, and in some cases, scholarships and loan funds. They also sponsor charitable programs and recruit young people to their respective professions. These include Alpha Pi Chi Sorority (business and professional women, established in 1963), Chi Delta Mu Fraternity (physicians, dentists and pharmacists, est. 1913), Chi Eta Phi Sorority (registered and student nurses, est. 1932), Eta Phi Beta Sorority (businesswomen, est. 1942), Iota Phi Lambda Sorority (est. 1929), and the National Sorority of Phi

Delta Kappa (women in education, est. 1923). In 1990 they ranged in membership from six hundred fifty to eight thousand.

BIBLIOGRAPHY

Baird's Manual of American College Fraternities. Various editions, authors, and publishers, 1898–1968.

"A Dramatic Comeback on Campus." *Ebony* (December 1983): 93–98.

Dreer, Herman. *The History of the Omega Psi Phi Fraternity.* Washington, D.C., 1940.

Giddings, Paula. *In Search of Sisterhood: Delta Sigma Theta and the Challenge of the Black Sorority Movement.* New York, 1988.

Little, Monroe. "The Extra-Curricular Activities of Black College Students, 1868–1940." *Journal of Negro History* (September 1980): 135–148.

Parker, Marjorie. *Alpha Kappa Alpha Through the Years, 1908–1988.* Chicago, 1990.

Wesley, Charles. *The History of Alpha Phi Alpha: A Development in Negro College Life.* Washington, D.C., 1948.

———. *History of Sigma Psi Phi.* Washington, D.C., 1954.

White, Pearl Schwartz. *Behind These Closed Doors—a Legacy: The History of Sigma Gamma Rho Sorority.* Chicago, 1974.

Wright, Charles. "Phi Beta Sigma Fraternity: Yesterday's Tradition—Tomorrow's Innovation." In Lennox S. Yearwood, ed. *Black Organizations: Issues on Survival Techniques.* Washington, D.C., 1980.

Wright, Willie J. "The Role of the Omega Psi Phi Fraternity in the Survival of Black Organizations." In Lennox S. Yearwood, ed. *Black Organizations: Issues on Survival Techniques.* Washington, D.C., 1980.

Ya Salaam, Kalamu, and Brenda Reese. "Is Pledging Passé?" *Black Collegian* (November-December 1974): 50–53.

– DANIEL SOYER

E. Franklin Frazier. (Photographs and Prints Division, Schomburg Center for Research in Black Culture, The New York Public Library, Astor, Lenox and Tilden Foundations)

FRAZIER, EDWARD FRANKLIN

Edward Franklin Frazier (September 24, 1894–May 17, 1962), essayist and activist. Born in Baltimore in 1894, the year in which W. E. B. DU BOIS was completing his doctoral degree at Harvard and 135 blacks were lynched in the South, E. Franklin Frazier was encouraged in his formative years by his parents, especially his working-class father, to seek upward mobility and social justice through education. With a scholarship from Colored High School he went on to Howard University, where he graduated *cum laude* in 1916 after four years of rigorous education and political activism at the "capstone of Negro education." For the rest of his academic career, he taught primarily in segregated, African-American schools and colleges, first in the South in the 1920s and early '30s, then for most of his career in Howard's sociology department. In between teaching jobs, he received scholarships that enabled him to get a master's degree at Clark University (1920) and a Ph.D. in sociology from the University of Chicago (1931). Despite his election as the first African-American president of the American Sociological Association (1948) and his recognition by UNESCO in the 1950s as a leading international authority on race relations, Frazier was never offered a regular faculty appointment by a predominantly white university.

With minimal institutional and foundation support, Frazier managed to produce eight books and over one hundred articles. He is best known for his pioneering studies of African-American families, especially *The Negro Family in the United States* (1939), which demonstrated that the internal problems of black families were socially created within and by Western civilization, not by the failure of Africans to live up to American standards. Building upon Du Bois's 1908 essay, *The Negro American Family,* Frazier refuted the prevailing social scientific wisdom which, in his words, "most often dealt with the pathological side of [black] family life. . . ." In contrast, Frazier's family is a broad spectrum of households, constantly in a process of change and reorganization, sometimes disorganized and demoralized, sometimes tenacious and resourceful. To Frazier the serious problems within African-American families—"the waste of human life . . . delinquency, desertions, and broken homes"—was not due to cultural backwardness, but rather to economic exploitation and the social damage inflicted by racism.

Frazier also made a variety of other important intellectual contributions: as an ethnographer and historian of everyday life in black communities; as a trenchant and subtle critic of the dynamics and etiquette of racism; as an influential consultant to Gunnar Myrdal's *An American Dilemma* (1944); as the author of the first systematic textbook on *The Negro in the United States* (1949); and as a critic of overly specialized, narrowly conceived studies in the social sciences. Frazier's popular reputation was made by *Black Bourgeoisie* (first published in the United States in 1957), but he explored the controversial relationship between class, politics, and culture all his life, beginning with a polemical essay on "La Bourgeoisie Noire" in 1928 and ending with his scholarly assessment of *Race and Culture Contacts in the Modern World* (1957). In this body of work he challenged monolithic portraits of African-American communities and documented their socioeconomic diversity; in particular, he exposed the collaborative and opportunistic role played by the black middle class in holding back the struggle for social equality and ensuring that "bourgeois ideals are implanted in the Negro's mind." Instead of being "seduced by dreams of final assimilation," Frazier called upon black leaders to envision "a common humanity and a feeling of human solidarity" in which "racial and cultural differentiation without implications of superiority and inferiority will become the basic pattern of a world order."

Frazier was part of a cadre of activists, intellectuals, and artists who after World War I formed the cutting edge of the NEW NEGRO movement that irrevocably changed conceptions of race and the politics of race relations. Though a loner who distrusted organizations, Frazier had close and respectful relationships with civil rights leaders such as W. E. B. Du Bois, Paul ROBESON, and A. Philip Randolph, as well as with scholars, such as Ralph BUNCHE and Abram Harris, who tried to bridge the gap between university and community, theory and practice. From his undergraduate days at Howard, when he was a vigorous opponent of U.S. entry into World War I, until his last years, when he welcomed a revitalized civil rights movement, Frazier was a politicized intellectual who believed that "a moral life is a life of activity in society."

BIBLIOGRAPHY

Edwards, G. Franklin, ed. *E. Franklin Frazier on Race Relations.* Chicago, 1968.

Frazier, E. Franklin. *The Negro in the United States.* New York, 1949.

———. *The Negro Family in the United States.* Chicago, 1939.

Platt, Anthony M. *E. Franklin Frazier Reconsidered.* New Brunswick, N.J., 1991.

– ANTHONY M. PLATT

FREE BLACKS IN THE NORTH

As in the South, free blacks in the northern states prior to the Civil War straddled the boundaries of SLAVERY and freedom. While searching for the social, legal, and political liberties whites enjoyed, free blacks in the North reached back to help liberate African-American slaves. Whites in the North used every measure of control to squeeze black liberty, making free black existence akin to slavery. Still, such people were free, earned their own livelihood, created their own cultural and religious institutions, and formed a shadow political order dedicated to the overthrow of the slavocracy.

Slavery constantly affected free black life in the North. It existed in all northern colonies until the American Revolution. In the states with the largest black populations—Pennsylvania, New Jersey, and New York—the gradual introduction of emancipation meant that servitude affected the lives of African Americans into the antebellum era. Although the numbers of free blacks grew steadily, from a few in the colonial era to virtually the entire black population in the antebellum period, they were denied political equality; hampered by poverty and by segregation in work, housing, and property ownership; and buffeted by worsening racism. Free blacks, organizing of churches and benevolent societies and their indefatigable struggle against slavery and racism combated white presumptions of racial inferiority. By the Civil War, free blacks in the North established strong church-based communities in the urban areas, owned hard-won farm property, and created a distinguished, politically minded intelligentsia.

Enumeration of free blacks in the colonial era is difficult because censuses did not differentiate between slave and emancipated. In New England, where the vast majority of blacks were slaves working in the seaports, the African-American population reached its zenith of 15,400, or 2.6 percent of the area's population of 581,100, in 1770. Blacks in New England gained freedom by working as indentured servants. A Rhode Island statute of 1652 limited servitude to ten years. Masters grateful for good service manumitted some, while keen-minded slaves used legal loopholes to win freedom from their masters in court, or negotiated an end to slavery through private contract. A few purchased their liberty. Estimates of the free black population included about 2,000 in Massachusetts in 1764 and 500 (a rough estimate) in Rhode Island in 1774.

The enactment of gradual emancipation laws in New England after the American Revolution immediately multiplied the free black population. Among the most notable was sea captain Paul Cuffe. In 1790 in Massachusetts, New Hampshire, Maine, and Vermont, free blacks outnumbered slaves by 6,804 to 157. Slavery retained a stronger grip in Rhode Island, with 3,484 free blacks to 958 slaves. Only in Connecticut did slavery retain real consequence, with 2,771 slaves to 2,648 free blacks. Although the last slaves were not completely freed in New England until 1840, the words *free* and *black* became firmly linked. On the eve of the Civil War, more than 23,000 free blacks lived in New England.

New Jersey, New York, and Pennsylvania—the middle colonies—had a larger enslaved population of 35,000 in 1770; nearly 21,000 of these lived in and around New York City. The oldest free black population in colonial America emerged in the 1640s in New Amsterdam, later New York. This original group expanded to about 100 people living in the city and its hinterlands. Traces of the first group of free black settlers existed in rural New York and New Jersey throughout the slavery era. Present in New Amsterdam, slavery became codified in the half century after the English conquest in 1664. Struggling against the tightening noose of bondage, blacks used loopholes in the law and sued successfully for their freedom.

New York and New Jersey both curtailed black suffrage, harbored hostile social attitudes, and openly practiced discrimination in work and housing.

In 1713, the colonial government stymied emancipations by requiring a £200 insurance bond and sharply restricting blacks' property rights. Despite these legal curbs, about 140 blacks were freed by wills from 1667 to 1770. The English government freed an additional 100 Spanish slaves in court decisions affected by international diplomacy between 1747 and 1760. Other, very rare means of obtaining freedom included financial redemption, military service, and special grants. The Quakers' antislavery position began to erode slavery during the AMERICAN REVOLUTION, as over 100 blacks became free through testaments. British proclamations exchanging freedom for military service freed about 600 New York and New Jersey blacks during the American Revolution. At the end of the war in 1783, these black loyalists left for Nova Scotia and Great Britain.

After 1783, blacks gained freedom through favorable court decisions, confiscation of Loyalist estates, self-purchase, and a rising political antislavery sentiment. The abolition of slavery was contentious in New York and New Jersey; Dutch slave owners were the most recalcitrant. In 1790, slaves in the two states outnumbered free blacks by 32,616 to 7,444. Gradual emancipation in 1799 in New York and 1804 in New Jersey made long-term chances for freedom better, but as late as 1830, New Jersey had 2,254 slaves out of a black population of 20,557. On the eve of the Civil War, 75,000 free blacks and 18 slaves lived in the two states.

Conditions for free blacks in New York and New Jersey were characteristic of those in northern states. Both states curtailed black suffrage, harbored hostile social attitudes, openly practiced discrimination in work and housing, tolerated murderous disease climates, and encouraged free blacks to emigrate to Liberia. Rioters periodically attempted to destroy black institutions.

Despite depressing social conditions, a staunch black middle class constructed a community in New York City. By 1830, three years after final abolition, New York's blacks could proudly point to significant churches in all denominations except the Dutch Reformed and to schools, newspapers, and a politically progressive intelligentsia from the clergy and antislavery activists. The 1830s was the decade of an African-American renaissance in New York as blacks battled slave-catchers, conducted an UNDERGROUND RAILROAD, published magazines and newspapers, wrote poetry, and opened schools. The successes of the middle class did not always ameliorate poverty for the mass of free blacks. Although black activists constantly railed against inequality, basic jobs such as carting were segregated and factories rarely hired blacks. Mortality rates were far higher than those of whites, and few blacks lived past fifty years of age. New York's free black population rose to 49,005 by 1860, but the percentage of blacks in the total population dipped to less than 5 percent. In New Jersey, free blacks lived more constricted lives as lack of opportunity, tenant farming, and residual bigotry blighted their freedom. The persistence of slavery, which did not end in New Jersey until passage of the THIRTEENTH AMENDMENT in 1865, meant that most free blacks lived and worked as employees on white farms. With few prospects, the young left for the cities. As late as 1860, only 25,318 free blacks lived in New Jersey.

Pennsylvania was more liberal to free blacks. While Quaker antislavery agitation became more effective by 1760, free blacks were few in the eighteenth century. Political and economic restrictions were powerful impediments. By 1770 there were about 300 free blacks in Philadelphia; in the next six years, masters freed another 175. British enticements and black opportunism helped at least 80 Philadelphians to gain freedom and leave for Nova Scotia. In 1780, Pennsylvania enacted gradual emancipation. Despite limits to immediate freedom, by 1790 freepeople outnumbered slaves in Pennsylvania by 6,531 to 3,707. Freedom by degrees meant that even in 1840 there were 64 slaves in the state, but Philadelphia in particular became a beacon for free blacks. As in New York, community was based on church. Richard ALLEN and Absalom JONES established important congregations. Philadelphia became a city of refuge for already free, newly freed, and fugitive slaves. By 1810, 9,653, or 40 percent, of the state's blacks lived in Philadelphia. Proprietors, artisans, mariners, and domestics composed a fragile middle class. As in New York City, there was a free black serving the community in every trade. Less segregated than New York, Philadelphia offered better support to the unskilled black.

Pennsylvania became cooler to free blacks by the 1820s. Racism, competition for jobs, and the steady stream of unskilled fugitives from the South tested the limits of the state's egalitarianism. Riots, nasty public attitudes, and stark discrimination made the state gradually less attractive. But despite rising bigotry, the middle class flourished intellectually and spiritually. Richard Allen headed the first conventions of black Methodists and, later, the first Colored National Conventions between 1830 and 1833. Aiming at the extinction of slavery, black activists welcomed fugitive slaves and fought for black civil rights.

By the 1850s, the issues of slavery and its aftermath consolidated free black aims in the North. Working with sympathetic whites, black political and abolitionist societies lobbied for the emancipation of slaves in the South and advancement of black civil liberties in the North. For ordinary people, the Fugitive Slave Act of 1850, the DRED SCOTT DECISION of 1857, and bigotry's unceasing irritant made life in the North less palatable. The allure of the city faded in the antebellum period as other free blacks sought refuge and land in the West, Canada, or Liberia. As the Civil War unfolded, northern free blacks beseeched Abraham Lincoln to enroll them in the Union army. After 1863, tens of thousands of northern blacks served with distinction and courage in the war to end slavery. Passage of the thirteenth, fourteenth and fifteenth amendments validated their efforts and those of their ancestors to earn full citizenship.

BIBLIOGRAPHY

Cottrol, Robert J. *Providence's Black Community in the Antebellum Era.* Westport, Conn., 1982.

Curry, Leonard P. *The Free Black in Urban America, 1800–1850.* Chicago, 1981.

Horton, James O., and Lois E. Horton. *Black Bostonians: Family Life and Community Struggle in the Antebellum North.* New York, 1979.

Litwack, Leon. *North of Slavery.* Chicago, 1961.

Nash, Gary B. *Forging Freedom: The Formation of Philadelphia's Black Community.* Cambridge, Mass., 1987.

Nash, Gary B., and Jean Soderlund. *Freedom by Degrees: Emancipation in Pennsylvania and Its Aftermath.* New York, 1991.

White, Shane. *Somewhat More Independent: The End of Slavery in New York City, 1770–1810.* Athens, Ga., 1991.

Zilversmit, Arthur. *The First Emancipation: The Abolition of Slavery in the North.* Chicago, 1967.

– GRAHAM RUSSELL HODGES

FREEDOM SUMMER

In the summer of 1964, the Council Of Federated Organizations (COFO)— a Mississippi coalition of the CONGRESS OF RACIAL EQUALITY (CORE), the STUDENT NONVIOLENT COORDINATING COMMITTEE (SNCC), and the NATIONAL ASSOCIATION FOR THE ADVANCEMENT OF COLORED PEOPLE (NAACP) invited Northern white college students to spearhead a massive black voter registration and education campaign aimed at challenging white supremacy in the deep South. This campaign, which became known as Freedom Summer, was the culmination of COFO's efforts to attack black disfranchisement in Mississippi. COFO had been formed in 1962 in response to the Kennedy administration's offer of tax-exempt status and funding from liberal philanthropies to civil rights organizations that focused their activities on increasing black voter registration. The considerable success of COFO activists in sparking the interest of black Mississippians in voter registration during the summer of 1963 prompted them to propose an entire summer of civil rights activities in 1964 to focus national attention on the disfranchisement of blacks in Mississippi, and to force the federal government to protect the civil rights of African Americans in the South.

SNCC played the largest role in the project and provided most of its funding. Robert MOSES of SNCC was the guiding force behind the summer project, and the overwhelming majority of COFO staff workers were SNCC members who were veterans of the long fight for racial equality in Mississippi.

Approximately 1,000 northern white college students, committed to social change and imbued with liberal ideals, volunteered to participate in the Freedom Summer campaign. Under the direction of SNCC veterans, these volunteers created community centers that provided basic services such as health care to the black community, and initiated voter education activities and literacy classes aimed at encouraging black Mississippians to register to vote. SNCC activists also directly challenged the segregated policies of the all-white Mississippi Democratic party by supporting the efforts of local black leaders to run their own candidates under the party name Mississippi Freedom Democratic Party (MFDP). The MFDP efforts encouraged over 17,000 African Americans to vote for the sixty-eight delegates who attended the national Democratic Convention in Atlantic City in the summer of 1964 and demanded to be seated in replacement of the regular Democratic organization. The MFDP challenge, though unsuccessful, focused national attention on Mississippi and propelled Fannie Lou HAMER, a local activist, into the national spotlight.

Another focus of the Freedom Summer was institutionalized educational inequities in Mississippi. Thirty COFO project sites created "Freedom Schools," administered under the direction of Staughton Lynd, a white Spelman College history professor, to provide an alternative education to empower black children to challenge their oppression. These schools provided students with academic training in remedial topics, as well as in more specialized subjects like art and French. A key goal of the schools was to develop student leadership and foster activism through discussions about current events, black history, the philosophy behind the civil rights movement, and other cultural activities. Despite the overcrowding and the perennial lack of facilities, over 3,000 African-American students attended the Freedom schools.

Violence framed the context of all COFO activities and created a climate of tension and fear within the organization. White supremacists bombed or burned sixty-seven homes, churches, and black businesses over the course of the summer, and by the end of the project, at least three civil rights workers—James Chaney, Michael Schwerner, and Andrew Goodman—had been killed by southern whites, four had been critically wounded, eight hundred had been beaten, and over a thousand had been arrested. The reluctance of the state government to prosecute the perpetrators of these acts of violence and the failure of the federal government to intervene to provide protection for civil rights workers left many activists disillusioned about the federal government's ability or desire to ensure racial justice.

The impact and legacy of the Freedom Summer stretched far beyond the borders of Mississippi. Many Freedom Summer programs lived on when the project ended and COFO disbanded. Freedom Summer community centers provided a model for federally funded clinics, Head Start programs, and other War on Poverty programs. Freedom schools served as models for nationwide projects in alternative schooling. The barriers to black voting uncovered and publicized during the summer project provided stark evidence of the need for the Voting Rights Act of 1965, which made literacy tests and poll taxes illegal.

The Freedom Summer facilitated the development of a radical new political consciousness among many white volunteers, who found the summer to be a powerful experience of political education and personal discovery. At least one-third of the volunteers stayed on in Mississippi to continue the struggle for black equality. Many volunteers who returned to the North were disillusioned with the promises of the federal government and became activists in the New Left and the antiwar movement. Mario Savio, a Freedom Summer veteran, emerged in the fall of 1964 as the principal spokesperson of the free speech movement at the University of California at Berkeley, a key event in the emergence of the New Left.

The Freedom Summer experience was also an important catalyst for the women's liberation movement. Group consciousness of gender oppression among white women grew markedly during the summer as male volunteers were assigned more visible organizing tasks. In November 1964, at a SNCC staff meeting in Waveland, Miss., Mary King and Casey Hayden, two white staff members, presented an anonymous position paper criticizing the enforced inferiority of women in the Freedom Summer project and their exclusion from the decision-making process. This memo was one of the first discussions of the issues that would form the basis of the emerging women's movement within the New Left.

The Freedom Summer's most enduring legacy was the change of consciousness it engendered among black Mississippians.

The experience of the Freedom Summer also radicalized black civil rights workers—though in quite different ways from white radicals. The summer helped steer black radicals in SNCC away from interracial movements and toward a suspicion of white participation that came to characterize the black power movement. Subsequent debates in the CIVIL RIGHTS MOVEMENT about the doctrine of interracialism were fueled by what the Freedom Summer revealed about the successes, and inherent limitations, of interracial civil rights activity. From the inception of the project, some black SNCC activists contested the Freedom Summer's premise that national attention could only be garnered by exposing white people to the violence and brutality that black people faced daily. These blacks were veterans of the long battle with white racists that SNCC had waged in Mississippi since 1961, were increasingly skeptical of liberal politics, and believed that the presence of white volunteers—who often tended to appropriate leadership roles and interact with black people in a paternalistic manner—would undermine their goal of empowering Mississippi blacks and hamper their efforts to foster and support black-controlled institutions in Mississippi. Tensions and hostility between black and white COFO activists were further inflamed by interracial liaisons which were often premised on the very racial stereotypes and misconceptions that they sought to surmount.

However, the Freedom Summer's most enduring legacy was the change of consciousness it engendered among black Mississippians. The Freedom Summer succeeded in initiating thousands of African Americans into political action, providing thousands of black children with an antiracist education and creating black-led institutions like the Mississippi Freedom Democratic Party. Fannie Lou Hamer provided a fitting testament to the impact of the Freedom Summer when she stated in 1966, "Before the 1964 summer project there were people that wanted change, but they hadn't dared to come out. After 1964 people began moving. To me it's one of the greatest things that ever happened in Mississippi."

BIBLIOGRAPHY

Cagin, Seth, and Philip Dray. *We Are Not Afraid: The Story of Goodman, Schwerner, and Chaney and the Civil Rights Campaign for Mississippi.* New York, 1988.

McAdam, Doug. *Freedom Summer.* New York, 1988.

Weisbrot, Robert. *Freedom Bound: A History of America's Civil Rights Movement.* New York, 1990.

— ROBYN SPENCER

FUGITIVE SLAVE LAWS

From the colonial period to the adoption of the THIRTEENTH AMENDMENT, African Americans sought to escape their bondage. Masters found the recovering of runaways to be time-consuming, expensive, and often impossible. Colonial governments occasionally agreed to help recover slaves from other jurisdictions, but generally such cooperation was ineffective.

During the American Revolution, those states dismantling slavery usually exempted fugitive slaves from their emancipatory schemes. The Articles of Confederation (1781) did not obligate the states to return fugitive slaves, but in 1787 the Confederation Congress adopted the first national fugitive slave law as part of the Northwest Ordinance. The ordinance prohibited slavery in the Northwest Territory but also provided that a fugitive slave "may be lawfully reclaimed and conveyed to the person claiming his or her labor or service."

Late in the Constitutional Convention of 1787, without serious debate or a recorded vote, the delegates adopted what became the fugitive slave clause, providing that "No Person held to Service or Labour in one State, under the Laws thereof, shall, in Consequence of any Law or Regulation therein, be discharged from such Service or Labour, but shall be delivered up on Claim of the Party to whom such Service or Labour may be due" (U.S. Constitution, Art. IV, Sec. 2, Par. 3). The framers apparently contemplated enforcement by state and local governments, or through individual action. The location of the clause in Article IV, with other clauses dealing with interstate relations, supports this analysis.

However, in the Fugitive Slave Act of 1793 Congress spelled out procedures for returning runaway slaves. This law emerged from a controversy between Pennsylvania and Virginia over the status of a black named John Davis. In 1788 three Virginians seized Davis in Pennsylvania, claiming him as a fugitive slave, and took him to Virginia. When Virginia's governor refused to extradite the three men charged with kidnapping in Pennsylvania, the governor of Pennsylvania complained to President Washington, who brought the problem to Congress. This eventually led to the 1793 law, which regulated both the extradition of fugitives from justice and the return of fugitive slaves.

Under this law, the slave owners or their agents (claimants) seized runaways and brought them to any federal, state, or local judge or magistrate and presented "proof to the satisfaction" of the judge that the person seized was the claimant's fugitive slave. A claimant could establish this proof orally or through a certified "affidavit taken before . . . a magistrate" of the claimant's home state. If the judge upheld the claim, he issued a certificate of removal to the claimant. Anyone interfering with the seizure or rendition of a fugitive slave was subject to a five-hundred-dollar penalty, plus the value of any slaves lost and any costs a master incurred trying to reclaim the slave.

This law never worked well. All responsibility for capturing slaves rested with owners, who were not guaranteed any aid from police officials. Northern judges sometimes declined to participate in fugitive slave cases. In *Jack* v. *Martin* (1835), New York's highest court declared the federal law unconstitutional but returned Jack to slavery under the constitutional clause itself. In 1836, in an unpublished opinion, New Jersey's Chief Justice Joseph Hornblower declared the 1793 law unconstitutional and also freed the black before him.

Starting in the 1780s, northern legislatures passed "personal-liberty laws" to protect free blacks from kidnapping or mistaken seizure. These laws also provided state procedures to facilitate the return of bona fide fugitives. Laws passed after 1793 often added procedural and evidentiary requirements to the federal law. The northern states balanced protecting free blacks from kidnapping with fulfilling their constitutional obligation to return fugitive slaves.

In 1837 a local judge in Pennsylvania refused to take cognizance of a case involving an alleged fugitive slave named Margaret Morgan and her children. Edward Prigg, a professional slavecatcher, then acted on his own, taking Morgan and her children to Maryland in violation of Pennsylvania's 1826 personal-liberty law. In *Prigg* v. *Pennsylvania* (1842), United States Supreme Court justice Joseph Story held the 1793 law constitutional and determined that state personal-liberty laws interfering with rendition were unconstitutional. Story characterized the fugitive slave clause as "a fundamental article" of the Constitution necessary for its adoption, even though the history of the clause, by that time available to Story, shows this was not true. Story urged state officials to continue to enforce the 1793 law, but stated they could not be required to do so. A number of states soon passed new personal-liberty laws, prohibiting their officials from acting under the federal law.

Congress amended the 1793 law as part of the COMPROMISE OF 1850. Under this act, alleged fugitives could not testify on their own behalf or have a jury trial. In reaction to state refusals to participate in the rendition process, the Fugitive Slave Act of 1850 provided for enforcement by federal commissioners to be appointed in every county in the country. They received five dollars if they decided that the black before them was not a slave, but were paid ten dollars if they found in favor of the claimant. Popular opposition to the law increased after the publication of Harriet Beecher Stowe's fictional attack on slavery, UNCLE TOM'S CABIN (1852), which partially centered on the fugitive slave Eliza.

The 1850 law led to riots in Boston; Syracuse, N.Y.; Oberlin, Ohio; and elsewhere. Federal prosecutions of rescuers often failed. In Christiana, Pa., federal officials obtained treason indictments of over forty men after a group of fugitives fought their would-be captors and killed a slave owner. The prosecutions failed when United States Supreme Court justice Robert Grier ruled in *United States* v. *Hanway* (1851) that opposition to the fugitive slave law did not constitute treason. After these incidents, the Fugitive Slave Act was a dead letter in much of the North. In *Ableman* v. *Booth* (1859) the Supreme Court affirmed the constitutionality of the 1850 law and the supremacy of the federal courts.

CAUTION!!
COLORED PEOPLE
OF BOSTON, ONE & ALL,
You are hereby respectfully CAUTIONED and advised, to avoid conversing with the
Watchmen and Police Officers of Boston,
For since the recent ORDER OF THE MAYOR & ALDERMEN, they are empowered to act as
KIDNAPPERS
AND
Slave Catchers,
And they have already been actually employed in KIDNAPPING, CATCHING, AND KEEPING SLAVES. Therefore, if you value your LIBERTY, and the *Welfare of the Fugitives* among you, *Shun* them in every possible manner, as so many *HOUNDS* on the track of the most unfortunate of your race.
Keep a Sharp Look Out for KIDNAPPERS, and have TOP EYE open.
APRIL 24, 1851.

The passage of a new, more effective Fugitive Slave Law in 1850 ushered in a decade of anxiety for many northern blacks. This poster appeared in April 1851, two months after Shadrach, an escaped ex-slave from Virginia, was liberated from his imprisonment by Boston blacks. (Prints and Photographs Division, Library of Congress)

Peaceful enforcement of the 1850 law was more common than violent opposition. Some removals required a show of federal force and the use of troops. Over nine hundred fugitives were returned under the act before 1862. However, Southerners estimated that as many as ten thousand slaves escaped during that period.

Ultimately, the fugitive slave laws did little to protect southern property, but did much to antagonize sectional feelings. Southerners saw the North as unwilling to fulfill its constitutional obligation. Northerners believed the South was trying to force them to become slavecatchers, and in the process undermining civil liberties in the nation. In 1864, after the issuance of the Emancipation Proclamation, Congress repealed both the 1793 and 1850 laws.

BIBLIOGRAPHY

Finkelman, Paul. *An Imperfect Union: Slavery, Federalism, and Comity.* Chapel Hill, N.C., 1981.

———. "The Kidnapping of John Davis and the Adoption of the Fugitive Slave Law of 1793." *Journal of Southern History* 56 (1990): 397–422.

———, ed. *Articles on American Slavery.* Vol. 6, *Fugitive Slaves.* New York, 1989.

Morris, Thomas D. *Free Men All: The Personal Liberty Laws of the North, 1780–1861.* Baltimore, 1974.

Wiecek, William M. *The Sources of Antislavery Constitutionalism in America, 1760–1848.* Ithaca, N.Y., 1977.

– PAUL FINKELMAN

FUGITIVE SLAVES

Many of the stories of fugitive slaves who managed to reach the free states in the antebellum period have entered the realm of legend. The dangers and sacrifice inherent in their efforts to reach free soil have been acknowledged and have become part of the historical record. Most scholars would agree, however, that only a small minority of the runaway slave population in any given year even attempted to reach the free states. Their stories are much more difficult to tell. This article will discuss the individual histories of fugitive slaves; a separate article discusses FUGITIVE SLAVE LAWS.

The principal source for the study of fugitive slaves is the advertisements published in local newspapers. (There is little reason to assume, however, that all slave runaways were advertised.) Information can also be gleaned from the diaries, logbooks, correspondence, and other personal papers of slave owners. Newspapers in both free states and slave states gave a great deal of attention to the more spectacular cases where violence or the threat of violence occurred in the recovery process. Newspapers also gave considerable coverage of efforts to subvert legal process in the return of fugitive slaves, particularly in the decade before the CIVIL WAR. Part of the record has also been preserved in legal documents and court records. The owners dispassionately, and in considerable detail, described the personal characteristics of the fugitives and noted whether or not they were habitual runaways, the names of their previous owners or employers, their motives for running away, and whether they were expected to be fleeing beyond state lines.

The advertisements provided elaborate descriptions noting age, height, date of running away, date of the advertisement, home county or city, any scarring, four or five gradations of skin color, marital status, literacy, speech impediments, whether the runaway had been charged with a crime, motivations, and work skills, along with the names of employers and previous owners by county. The advertisements of sheriffs and town jailers revealed the date and county of incarceration of those who had been "taken up."

The owners of fugitive slaves usually described their runaways with great care. Distinguishing marks were carefully noted. In the *Richmond Enquirer,* Robert Lewis, of Albemarle County, Va., described his runaway in the following manner:

> Eighty dollars reward—Ran away from the Subscriber on the 4th of April, in the city of Richmond, a mulatto fellow, about 30 years of age, 5 feet 6 or 8 inches high; is remarkable on account of having red curly hair & grey eyes which generally appear to be sore; one of his legs somewhat shorter than the other, though scarcely to be perceived without nice observation; when standing, is very apt to stand fast on his right leg, and rather extend the left. In pronouncing the word whiskey, which he is very fond of, and apt to call for at a public house, he pronounces it whisty. He is a very humble, obedient fellow, and when spoken to, has a downlook. It is not improbable that he may obtain free papers, to endeavor to pass as a free man, having absconded from his boat in the basin at Richmond, with about $120 in cash (June 24, 1817).

Scholars have often noted the frequency of stuttering or other speech impediments in the runaway slave population. In the Virginia sample, the frequency was 7 percent, seven times greater than the norm for the population as a whole.

The interpretations of this phenomena are controversial. Kenneth Stampp (1956) suggested that the "down look" and the speech impediments were caused by stress resulting from fear (pp. 381–382). While Eugene Genovese (1974) did not disagree that slaves had been conditioned to fear white men, he argued that the stuttering was also an expression of "smoldering anger and resentment" (p. 647). John W. Blassingame (1979) disagreed. He argued that the incidence of stuttering and other speech impediments may have resulted from the slaves' "unfamiliarity with European languages, missing teeth, and other physical infirmities" (p. 203). Another plausible explanation for the speech impediments is that stuttering was an acceptable form of aggression, a result of which was to make the listener suffer.

An analysis of the 1,433 fugitive advertisements in the Richmond *Enquirer* published between 1804 and 1830 revealed an interesting profile. In this record, 84.9 percent were males; 13.02 percent were females. Only 2 percent were children. James Benson Sellers, in *Slavery in Alabama* (1964), reported that of 562 fugitives advertised between 1820 and 1860, 84.1 percent were males; and 15.4 percent were females (p. 293). Eugene D. Genovese noted in *Roll, Jordan, Roll* that, between 1850 and 1860, the percentage of North Carolina runaways was 82 percent male (p. 798, note 2). The percentage of female runaways from New Orleans in 1850 was higher. Judith Kelleher Schafer reported in *The Journal of Southern History* that 31.7 percent were women (1981, pp. 33–56). All the sources seem to agree that the great majority of fugitives was made up of relatively young men. The average age in the Virginia sample was 27.

A possible explanation for the preponderance of males is suggested by the dangers inherent in running away. Successful flight demanded planning, ingenuity, bravery, and opportunity. In most southern states, the law provided that any black person could be stopped and checked for documentation of free status or possession of a "free pass." Any slave beyond a given distance from home without a "free pass" could be taken into custody and returned. The law also provided that the owner was obligated to pay a prescribed reward, based upon mileage, for the return of his slave. Even if those dangers were avoided, slave patrols had to be eluded and slave catchers frustrated. The rigor of successfully avoiding arrest and the fear of returning to face certain punishment were such that women, especially those with children, were discouraged from running away.

Although they were predominantly male, the runaways represented fieldhands, skilled artisans, the more privileged, and the less privileged. Roughly one-third of the fugitives were skilled or had some training and education. Fieldhands represented 70 percent of the Virginia slaves. Owners advertised for the return of runaways in Virginia every month, but the most popular months were between May and August. The least popular month was November. Owners demonstrated no hurry to advertise their runaways. A time lapse of six weeks to six months occurred between the date of running away and the date of advertisement. In January 1811, for example, Archer Hankins reported that his slave George had run away the previous July. In April 1811, John S. Payne of Campbell County reported that three of his slaves had absconded in January. The most plausible reason for the delay in advertising runaways was the assumption that the slaves would return of their own accord. Several instances on the record indicate that an owner knew where his slave was lurking; but rather than go after the fugitive himself, he offered a reward for someone else to return his slave to him, or "secure him in jail so that I get him again." Whatever the motivation for running away, large numbers returned of their own accord or were apprehended within days, or sometimes in weeks. Of 1,151 runaways advertised in Virginia, 831 were single men and 111 were single women. Married men numbered 154 and married women 55. The advertisements in the Richmond *Enquirer* also made a point of identifying fugitives by color: black, mulatto, tawny, yellow, and "pass for white." Only about 2.5 percent of the Virginia sample could read or write.

The rigor of successfully avoiding arrest and the fear of returning to face certain punishment were such that women were discouraged from running away.

The motivations for running away discussed in the literature are complex. Gerald W. Mullin (1972) classified motives by objective. The first group were little more than truants who ran off to visit wives, friends, or family on other plantations. The second group included those slaves who absconded to the towns and cities to find employment and pass as free men. A third smaller group was made up of those slaves who preferred freedom to bondage and attempted, by whatever means, to reach the free states (p. 106). Stampp argued that slaves had a heightened sense of dignity that was easily insulted. Running away was a means of expressing a personal grievance (Stampp 1956, p. 112). There is general agreement on an extended list of reasons for running away that include fear of sale, loneliness resulting from sale out of state, the desire to reestablish family ties, to escape overwork, and simply to be free. In the Virginia advertisements, the single most important reason for running away was the desire not to be free, but to "pass as free."

Motivation for slaves who ran away was in many cases a great mystery to their owners. Kenneth Stampp (1956) reported several owners who stated that their slaves had run away for no apparent reason and without provocation (pp. 111–112). But William K. Scarborough has argued that a more common explanation was fear of the whip (Scarborough 1984, pp. 89–90). The cruelty of some masters and overseers in the treatment of slaves is well documented. While only a small minority of slaves in the Virginia sample was described as scarred, the scars were often noteworthy. Robert Dickenson of Nottoway County described the scars of Isaac, an "habitual" runaway. He had a scar "over his right eye and . . . a lump as large as the finger on the fore part of the right shoulder." The scars, he said, were "caused by whipping" (*Richmond Enquirer*, December 23, 1809). Many of the slaves had been scarred by smallpox. A few of the scars were inflicted with branding irons. A recently purchased slave of John Sanders had been "lately branded on the left hand" (*Richmond Enquirer*, March 12, 1814). Thomas Coleman of Lunenburg County branded his slave, Charles, on the forehead, on each cheek, and his chest with the letter C (*Richmond Enquirer*, July 1, 1823).

The treatment of runaway slaves was often callous; but occasionally the advertisements expressed concern for the welfare of the fugitive, especially the younger ones. Edmund Lewis had taken a thirteen-year-old boy into custody in Buckingham County. The boy told his captor that he had been stolen from his father, George Belew, when "very young" and thought he had been sold "about ten times." The object of the notice, said Lewis, was to notify "his parents or friends to attend to his case," which was pending before the court of Buckingham County (*Richmond Enquirer*, October 27, 1818). Samuel Carter of Halifax County expressed concern for a ten-year-old whom he had "taken up" after being lost from a slave-trading expedition. Carter did not place the boy in jail because he was too ill and too young (*Richmond Enquirer*, April 18, 1817).

A large category of fugitives comprised those who had been hired out. Because of the surplus of slave labor in Virginia, many slaveholders were forced either to sell their surplus slaves or to hire them out. The services of the slaves were usually rented for six months or a year, and many of them ran away during that time. Slaves were hired as boatmen on the river and laborers in the coal pits, brick yards, and rope walks. Some were hired because they had special skills. They worked as ostlers, carriage drivers, and house servants.

Those who hired slaves did not always find it a happy experience. P. V. Daniel of Richmond hired the services of John Brown, who was a "good house servant, ostler and driver, and a pretty good barber." One evening, Brown requested a pass to go into town and had not been heard from since (*Richmond Enquirer*, July 8, 1823). Nelson Patterson of Kanawha County hired John and Reuben from Thomas Logwood of Gloucester County. Patterson "carried them" to Buckingham County to make salt. At the first opportunity, they ran away (*Richmond Enquirer*, December 19, 1816).

The advertisements contain frequent expressions of fear that slaves had been "enticed off" by a white man or some other person. William B. Johnson could explain Isabella's elopement in no other way for "such was her attachment for her mistress and fellow-servants, that she would not have eloped had she not been taken off by some white man." Nathaniel Price believed that Kitty had been "inveigled off by her husband" (*Richmond Enquirer*, June 17, 1808).

A few African Americans engaged in an interesting racket. Lewis informed his owner William Fisher of Chesterfield County that a white man with whom Lewis had worked the previous year tried to decoy him off by promising to sell him and then later meet at some designated place, divide the money, and thus continue on (*Richmond Enquirer*, September 19, 1826). Jerman Baker in Cumberland County had a similar experience when a young fellow who called himself John Irvin came up to Baker's plantation on foot with two African-American men. He claimed that his horse had foundered on the road and that he was on his way to Richmond to deliver one of the slaves. The other slave, he said, belonged to his father, a merchant in Campbell County. Baker bought this slave for $430. He gave Irvin a horse valued at $130, paid $100 in cash, and gave him a note for $200. The slave absconded shortly thereafter, and adding insult to injury, took a horse with him. Baker warned: "I forewarn all persons from trading for the note I executed to said John Irvin" (*Richmond Enquirer*, March 3, 1812).

White people aided and abetted relatively few slaves in their escapes. Some slaves received permission to visit their wives or families in other locations and never returned. Without help from other slaves, runaways could not remain away from their owners for long periods of time. Literate slaves provided forged passes that made it possible for fugitive slaves to lurk around the smaller towns or simply disappear in the larger cities. Owners could do little to prevent such aid. Free papers could be checked against the court records in the fugitive's home county; but if he was caught and returned to his master, another opportunity to escape usually presented itself.

The objective of the fugitives who remained within the state was usually the larger towns. Spencer Roane of Hanover complained that Betsy, one of his servants, "was so much pleased with Richmond, as to abscond, when his family returned from thence" (*Richmond Enquirer*, July 26, 1811). Joseph Ingraham sent Billy into Richmond with a load of wheat. Billy sold the wheat for $40 and disappeared (*Richmond Enquirer*, October 1, 1824). The chances of being detected in the cities were considerably reduced. In Virginia, Richmond, Manchester, Petersburg, Williamsburg, and Norfolk were the principal towns for which many fugitives aimed. Work could more readily be secured in the towns, and the townspeople were less suspicious of a strange black face. Hiding in the cities was easier and less dangerous than in the countryside.

Methods used to deter running away varied. William Scarborough has argued that overseers were more inclined to use harsh discipline in order to create fear. At least two overseers resorted to shooting their "recalcitrant" runaways (Scarborough 1984, pp. 90–91). A more common deterrent was the use of dogs. The practice of running away was so widespread that some men became professional slavecatchers who used hounds to hunt down fugitives. This practice was more likely to be used in the deep South than in the border states. Other methods were less violent. For example, in South Carolina, one planter restricted the privileges of the slaves who did not run away in order to induce the runaways to return (Scarborough 1984, p. 92).

All slave states enacted laws both to deter and to aid in the recovery of fugitive slaves. The laws in Virginia were fairly typical. The laws to suppress runaway slaves before the Revolution were extremely harsh. In 1680 a law was passed making it lawful to kill any fugitive who resisted arrest. A 1723 law provided for punishment by "dismembering, or any other way not touching life." Laws designed to restrict the movement of slaves were amended very little over the years; only refinements were added. These laws required slaves who were away from the plantation to have written permission. The unfortunate slave without such permission was subject to punishment of ten lashes for every offense. In 1748, slave stealing was defined as a capital offense punishable by "death without benefit of clergy." Laws that made it a crime to transport a slave out of the colony or state without the consent of the owner were enacted and amended many times. A Virginia law enacted in 1805 prohibited a master of a vessel from taking any African American on board without checking his status. The penalties for violation of this law were severe. If the master of a vessel was convicted, his fine was to be $500 for every African American found on his vessel without a pass. The master was also liable for an additional $200 fine: "one third thereof shall go to the master or owner of such slave, one third to the informer, and one third to the overseers of the poor, for the use of the poor." Upon conviction of removing a slave out of the county, the master could be imprisoned for a period of up to four years.

Laws for the apprehension and return of fugitive slaves depended upon the goodwill and support of the white population. The function of these laws was to ensure, so far as possible, the return of the runaway to his master. A schedule of rewards was established by state legislatures to encourage compliance. Usually a basic fee was required, plus mileage. If a fugitive was caught in Maryland or Kentucky, the reward was to be $25 plus $0.25 per mile for traveling to the residence of the owner, or the jail to which the fugitive was committed. The reward for apprehending runaways in Delaware, New Jersey, New York, Pennsylvania, or Ohio was to be $50. Between 1800 and 1830 in Virginia, rewards offered for the return of fugitive slaves ranged from $3 to $150.

A system of confining and selling unclaimed runaways developed during the years preceding the AMERICAN REVOLUTION. After 1726, it was permissible to hire out such slaves with an iron collar around their necks stamped with the letter "P.G." (for "Public Gaol"). This procedure of confining slaves and hiring them out changed little except that after the Revolution, treatment of runaways became somewhat less stringent. After 1782, slaves were forbidden to hire themselves out in order to pay their masters money in lieu of services. After 1807, the owner became liable to a fine of $10 to $20 for permitting his slaves to hire themselves out.

Every free African American was forced to register with the county clerk and obtain a copy of the register certifying that he or she was free. This law facilitated the recognition of runaways and placed the burden of enforcement on the free population and not on the slaves. The fine for employing or harboring an African American without a pass was $5 for each offense, and the offender was liable to a suit for damages by the aggrieved party. The most severe penalties were reserved for those convicted of "enticing off" or stealing slaves. As late as 1799, the penalty was still death "without benefit of clergy." After 1805, however, the punishment for slave stealing was reduced to a fine of between $100 and $500 and imprisonment for not less than two years and not more than four. The convicted felon was also required to pay the owner an amount double the value of the slave, plus double the amount of costs.

The literature on fugitive slaves provides extended discussion of slave crime. Stampp (1956) argued that petty theft was almost universal. Other crimes discussed were arson, deliberate injury and self-mutilation, and acts of violence. The most frequent targets for arson were the slave quarters, cotton gins, and other farm buildings. Some slaves were willing to suffer personal injury and great pain rather than return to slavery. Attempts to arrest and return fugitive slaves frequently resulted in violence. A few slaves even resorted to murder (pp. 124–132). Genovese (1974) argued that some caution must be exercised concerning charges of arson. He asserted that in many cases, planters simply assumed that the arsonists were slaves. He further contended that arson committed by slaves was more likely to occur in the cities than on the plantations (pp. 613–615). Slaves were capable of the most violent crimes if provoked. A servant shot and killed Virginia Frost of Richmond, Va., when reproached for "insolent language" (Genovese 1974, pp. 361–362). In the period between 1710 and 1754, Mullin found evidence that only 2 slaves had been tried for murder before county courts (Mullin 1972, p. 61). Only 26 fugitives were charged with crimes in the Virginia advertisements between 1800 and 1830: 17 for theft, 1 for arson, 6 for robbery, 1 for assault, and 1 for murder. In Richmond, a double murder was committed when a runaway name Jack broke into the home of Daniel Ford. Both Ford and his wife were shot and killed (*Richmond Enquirer*, October 17, 1820). However outrageous these crimes were perceived to be, the percentage of runaways charged with crime in Virginia was low. The number of crimes runaways committed after absconding is not known.

There is good reason to believe that many thousands of slaves slipped their shackles and successfully made their way to the free states.

The fugitives who were believed by their owners in Virginia to be headed out of state were much more diligently pursued. The record indicates that, in many cases, the owners had a fairly clear idea of their runaway slaves' destinations. Mullin found a high correlation between the estimates of fugitives' destinations and the counties where they were intercepted and incarcerated (Mullin 1972, pp. 188–189). If the owners' estimates can be believed, only a small percentage of the runaways advertised in Virginia between 1800 and 1830 were headed north. In a sample of 1,253 fugitives, only 113, or 9 percent, were thought to be headed for the Mason-Dixon Line. During that period, 294, or 23.4 percent, were captured. Twelve northward-bound fugitives were advertised in 1823. Typical was an advertisement in January. John Taylor of Brunswick County, Va., advertised in the *Richmond Enquirer* for his runaway named Granderson. Granderson, "a first rate house and body servant," had been hired the previous year to Gen. Robert R. Johnson of Warrentown, N.C., from whom he had run away. Taylor believed that the slave was headed for Petersburg, "where it is feared he will attempt to procure a conveyance to the north" (January 14, 1823). Thirteen were thought to be headed north in 1826. Abner Mitchell of Richmond had hired a slave named Robin, alias Robert Chamberlayne, from his owner in New Kent County. Mitchell asserted that the fugitive "will endeavour to get to New-York, or some other Northern cities" (January 3, 1826). In 1826, 56 fugitives were advertised, and 20, or 35.7 percent, were captured and placed in jail. It must be understood that the 20 fugitives who were captured in 1826 had not necessarily run away that year.

Between the founding of the Republic and the Civil War, there is good reason to believe that many thousands of slaves slipped their shackles and successfully made their way to the free states; many went on to Canada. Despite the most stringent efforts of both the state and national governments to deter the efforts of slaves to become free, the flow of fugitives to the North continued. The numbers of fugitives going north was only a small portion of the runaways. However, the impact of fugitive slaves on the African-American and white communities in the North and their role in shaping the antebellum anti-slavery discourse were out of proportion to their numbers.

BIBLIOGRAPHY

Blassingame, John W. *The Slave Community: Plantation Life in the Antebellum South.* Revised and enlarged edition. New York, 1979.

Campbell, Stanley W. *The Slave Catchers: Enforcement of the Fugitive Slave Law, 1850–1860.* Chapel Hill, N.C., 1970.

Finkelman, Paul. *An Imperfect Union: Slavery, Federalism, and Comity.* Chapel Hill, N.C., 1981.

Genovese, Eugene D. *Roll, Jordan, Roll: The World the Slaves Made.* New York, 1974.

Mullin, Gerald W. *Flight and Rebellion: Slave Resistance in Eighteenth-Century Virginia.* New York, 1972.

Richmond Enquirer. September 1804–December 1830.

Scarborough, William Kauffman. *The Overseer: Plantation Management in the Old South.* Athens, Ga., 1984.

Schafer, Judith Kelleher. "New Orleans Slavery in 1850 as Seen in Advertisements." *Journal of Southern History* 47 (1981): 33–56.

Sellers, James Benson. *Slavery in Alabama.* New York, 1964.

Stampp, Kenneth M. *The Peculiar Institution: Slavery in the Antebellum South.* New York, 1956.

Sydnor, Charles. *Slavery in Mississippi.* New York, 1933.

— STANLEY W. CAMPBELL

FULLER, META VAUX WARRICK

Meta Vaux Warrick Fuller (June 9, 1877–March 18, 1968), sculptor. Named for one of her mother's clients (Meta, daughter of Pennsylvania senator Richard Vaux), Meta Vaux Warrick Fuller was born in Philadelphia, the youngest of three children of William and Emma (Jones) Warrick, prosperous hairstylists. She enjoyed a privileged childhood, with dancing and horseback-riding lessons. While attending Philadelphia public schools, Fuller took weekly courses at J. Liberty Tadd, an industrial arts school. At eighteen, she won a three-year scholarship to the Pennsylvania Museum and School for Industrial Art. In 1898 she graduated with honors, a prize in metalwork for her *Crucifix of Christ in Anguish,* and a one-year graduate scholarship. The following year, she was awarded the Crozer (first) Prize in sculpture for *Procession of the Arts and Crafts,* a terracotta bas-relief of thirty-seven medieval costumed figures.

From 1899 to 1903, Fuller studied in Paris, at first privately with Raphael Collin, and then at the Colarossi Academy. Among her supporters in France were expatriate painter Henry O. TANNER and philosopher W. E. B. DU BOIS, who encouraged her to depict her racial heritage. Fuller produced clay, painted-plaster, and bronze figurative works based on Egyptian history, Greek myths, French literature, and the Bible.

In 1901, sculptor Auguste Rodin praised Fuller's clay piece *Secret Sorrow* (or *Man Eating His Heart*). With his sponsorship, Fuller began to receive wider notice. Art dealer Samuel Bing exhibited twenty-two of her sculptures at his L'Art Nouveau Gallery in June 1902. *The Wretched,* a bronze group of seven figures suffering physical and mental disabilities (as well as other macabre pieces, such as *Carrying the Dead Body* and *Oedipus,* in the latter of which the figure is blinding himself), earned Fuller the title "delicate sculptor of horrors" from the French press. She later enlarged a plaster model of *The Impenitent Thief,* which she had shown at Bing's gallery. Although she never finished the piece, Rodin saw that it was exhibited at the prestigious Société National des Beaux Arts Salon in April 1903.

Among Meta Vaux Warrick Fuller's supporters were painter Henry O. Tanner and philosopher W. E. B. Du Bois, who encouraged her to depict her racial heritage.

Upon Fuller's return to Philadelphia, she established a studio on South Camac Street in a flourishing artistic neighborhood. Her sculptures were exhibited at the Pennsylvania Academy of Fine Arts in 1906, 1908, 1920, and 1928. In 1907 the Jamestown Tercentennial Exposition commissioned Fuller to create fifteen tableaux of 24-inch-high plaster figures depicting African-American progress since the Jamestown settlement in 1607. She received a gold medal for *The Warrick Tableaux,* a 10-foot-by-10-foot diorama.

The artist's career slowed considerably after her marriage in 1909 to the Liberian neurologist Solomon C. Fuller and a fire in 1910 that destroyed the bulk of her work in storage. By 1911, Fuller was the devoted mother of two sons (the last was born in 1916), an active member of Saint Andrew's Episcopal Church, and host to prominent guests who frequently visited the family in the quiet town of Framingham, Mass.

Fuller began to sculpt again in 1913, when Du Bois commissioned a piece for New York state's celebration of the fiftieth anniversary of the Emancipation Proclamation. *The Spirit of Emancipation* represented Humanity weeping for her freed children (a man and woman) as Fate tried to hold them back. Positive public response promoted Fuller to continue working. In 1914, the Boston Public Library exhibited twenty-two of her recent works. Among the numerous requests and awards that followed from African-American and women's groups were a plaster medallion commissioned by the Framingham Equal Suffrage League (1915); a plaster group, *Peace Halting the Ruthlessness of War* (for which she received second prize from the Massachusetts branch of the Women's Peace Party in 1917); and a portrait relief of the NAACP's first president, Moorfield Storey, commissioned by Du Bois in 1922. The same year, the New York Making of America Exposition displayed Fuller's *Ethiopia Awakening,* a one-foot-high bronze sculpture of a woman shedding mummy cloths. This Pan-Africanist work symbolized the strength of womanhood, the emergence of nationhood, and the birth of what Alain LOCKE would call three years later the "NEW NEGRO." One of Fuller's most poignant works, *Mary Turner: A Silent Protest Against Mob Violence* (1919), commemorates both the silent parade of ten thousand black New Yorkers against lynching in 1917 and the lynching of a Georgian woman and her unborn child in 1918. Fuller never finished the piece because she believed Northerners would find it too inflammatory and Southerners would not accept it. She created numerous other works that depicted symbolic and actual African and African-American culture, including her celebrated *Talking Skull* (1937), based on an African fable. She also produced portrait busts of friends, family members, and African-American abolitionists and other black leaders, such as educator Charlotte Hawkins Brown, composer Samuel Coleridge Taylor, and Menelik II of Abyssinia. The Harmon Foundation exhibited Fuller's work in 1931 and 1933. She later served as a Harmon juror.

Fuller participated in numerous local organizations; she was a member of the Boston Art Club, an honorary member of the Business and Professional Women's Club, chair of the Framingham Women's Club art committee, and the only African-American president of Zonta, a women's service club. Additionally, she designed costumes for theatrical groups and produced "living pictures": re-creations of artistic masterpieces with actors, costumes, sets, and lighting.

In the 1940s, Fuller's husband went blind and became increasingly ill. She nursed him until his death in 1953, then contracted tuberculosis herself and stayed at the Middlesex County Sanatorium for two years. She wrote poetry there, too frail to create more than a few small sculptures.

By 1957, Fuller was strong enough to continue her work. She produced models of ten notable African-American women for the Afro-American Women's Council in Washington, D.C. She also created a number of sculptures for her community, including several religious pieces for Saint Andrew's Church, a plaque for the Framingham Union Hospital, and the bronze *Storytime* for the Framingham Public Library. For her achievements, Livingstone College (her husband's alma mater) awarded her an honorary doctorate of letters in 1962, and Framingham posthumously dedicated a public park in the honor of Meta and Solomon Fuller in 1973. Since then, Fuller's sculptures have been included in numerous exhibitions.

BIBLIOGRAPHY

Gordon, Joy L., and Harriet Forte Kennedy. *An Independent Woman: The Life and Art of Meta Warrick Fuller.* Framingham, Mass., 1985.

Kerr, Judith Nina. God-Given Work: The Life and Times of Sculptor Meta Vaux Warrick Fuller, 1877–1968. Ph.D. diss., University of Massachusetts, 1986.

— THERESA LEININGER-MILLER

G

GABRIEL PROSSER CONSPIRACY

During 1800 Gabriel Prosser worked in secret to recruit and organize thousands of enslaved Virginians. He sketched out an elaborate plan to overthrow the slavery regime, and it came within hours of execution. But on the chosen day—Saturday, August 30—a hurricane destroyed bridges and flooded roads. The violent downpour washed out the proposed attack on the state capitol at Richmond, allowed time for word of the plan to leak to white authorities, and foiled what could have become a brilliant move in the dangerous chess game to force an end to SLAVERY.

Gabriel was born into bondage about 1775 around the time that white Virginians declared their political independence. The authorities who executed him said he showed "courage and intellect above his rank in life." As the property of tavernkeeper Thomas Prosser, he worked regularly as a blacksmith in the Richmond area, where, inspired by stories of the recent HAITIAN REVOLUTION, he framed his desperate plan. Aided by his wife and his brothers Martin and Solomon, he worked to procure weapons and rally recruits (Martin, a preacher, found recruits at funerals and secret religious gatherings, where he employed biblical accounts of the Israelites' escape from Egypt to inspire potential conspirators). According to testimony in subsequent trials, from two to ten thousand African Americans knew of the design and looked to Gabriel as their leader to, in Solomon's words, "conquer the white people and possess ourselves of their property." The insurrectionists intended to spare METHODISTS, Quakers, and local Frenchmen because of their emancipationist leanings, and they expected poor whites and nearby Catawba Indians to join their cause when it gathered strength.

The plan called for several hundred participants (advised by a veteran from the successful siege at Yorktown) to gather at a spot outside Richmond. Behind a banner invoking the American, French, and Haitian Revolutions with the words Death or Liberty, they would march on the city in three contingents. One group would light fires in the dockside warehouses to divert whites from the heart of the city, while the other two groups would seize the capitol armory and take Gov. James Monroe hostage. When the "white people agreed to their freedom," Gabriel "would dine and drink with the merchants of the city," and a white flag would be hoisted above the capitol, calling other blacks in the countryside to join them.

Betrayal by informers presented a huge danger, with so many persons approached about such an overwhelming plan. When torrential rains forced last-minute postponement of the march on Richmond, several slaves had already alerted whites to the impending action, and Gov. Monroe moved swiftly. The state militia arrested scores of suspects, and several dozen persons were executed. Prosser took refuge on the schooner *Mary,* captained by a sympathetic white Methodist. But in late September he was betrayed by two slave crewmen and captured in Norfolk. After a brief show trial in which the leader remained silent, he was hanged on October 7.

In the aftermath of the foiled insurrection, the Virginia Assembly acted to restrict the movement of all blacks—enslaved and free—and to set up a white public guard in Richmond. Such precautions proved ineffective, however. In 1802 authorities discovered further black plans to fight for freedom in Virginia and North Carolina. In 1936 the publication of Arna Bontemps's novel *Black Thunder* offered an interesting literary treatment of Prosser's revolt.

BIBLIOGRAPHY

Egerton, D. R. "Gabriel's Conspiracy and the Election of 1800." *Journal of Southern History* 56 (1990): 191–214.

Marszalek, John F. "Battle for Freedom: Gabriel's Insurrection." *Negro History Bulletin* 39 (1976): 540–543.

Mullin, Gerald W. *Flight and Rebellion: Slave Resistance in Eighteenth-Century Virginia.* New York, 1972.

— PETER H. WOOD

GAINES, ERNEST J.

Ernest J. Gaines (1933–), writer. The oldest son of a large family, Ernest Gaines was born on January 15, 1933, on the River Lake Plantation in Point Coupée Parish, La. His parents separated when he was young, and his father's absence led to a permanent estrangement. More important than his parents in his childhood was a maternal great-aunt who provided love and served as an example of strength and survival under extreme adversity. The older people in the close-knit community of the plantation "quarters" exemplified similar qualities, passing on to the child the rich oral tradition that figures prominently in his fiction.

At the age of fifteen Gaines moved from this familiar environment to Vallejo, Calif., where he could receive a better education. Lonely in these new surroundings, he spent much of his time in the town's public library and began to write. After high school he spent time in a junior college and the military before matriculating at San Francisco State College. An English major, he continued to write stories and graduated in 1957. Encouraged by his agent, Dorothea Oppenheimer, and (while in the creative writing program at Stanford) by Malcolm Cowley, Gaines committed himself to a literary career. In 1964 he published his first novel, *Catherine Carmier.* His subsequent books are *Of Love and Dust* (1967), *Bloodline* (1968), *The Autobiography of Miss Jane Pittman* (1971), *In My Father's House* (1978), and *A Gathering of Old Men* (1983). In a collection of interviews published as *Porch Talk with Ernest Gaines* (1990), he discussed his work in progress, a novel about an uneducated black man on death row and a black teacher in a Louisiana plantation school titled *A Lesson Before Dying.*

In the 1960s and '70s, except for a year at Denison University, Gaines lived and wrote in San Francisco. Since the early 1980s he has been associated with the University of Southwestern Louisiana, although he has continued to summer in San Francisco.

South Louisiana, the region of Gaines's youth and literary imagination, is beautiful and distinctive with unique cultural, linguistic, and social patterns. Like George Washington Cable and Kate Chopin before him, Gaines has been fascinated by the interplay of caste and class among the ethnic groups of the area: blacks, mixed-race Creoles, Cajuns, white Creoles, and Anglo whites. Once fairly stable as subsistence farmers, blacks and mixed-race Creoles have been dispossessed of the best land or displaced altogether by Cajuns, who are favored by the plantation lords because they are white and use mechanized agricultural methods. Under such socioeconomic conditions, young blacks leave, as Gaines himself did, though they often find themselves drawn back to Louisiana.

Such is the case in *Catherine Carmier.* In this novel the protagonist is the educated and alienated Jackson Bradley, who returns to his native parish to claim the love of the title character, daughter of a mixed-race Creole whose racial exclusivism, attachment to the land, and semi-incestuous feelings toward her cannot condone such an alliance. Nor do Jackson's fellow blacks approve. Jackson cannot recapture his love or his homeland because, for all its pastoral charm, the world of his childhood is anachronistic. In *Of Love and Dust* Gaines moves from Arcadian nostalgia to a tragic mode. Marcus Payne, the rebellious protagonist, defies social and racial taboos by making love to the wife of a Cajun plantation overseer, Sidney Bonbon, after being rejected by Bonbon's black mistress. As Marcus and Louise Bonbon prepare to run away together, the Cajun, a grim embodiment of fate, kills him with a scythe.

If *Catherine Carmier* is a failed pastoral and *Of Love and Dust* a tragedy, *The Autobiography of Miss Jane Pittman* is a near-epic account of a centenarian whose life has spanned slavery, RECONSTRUCTION, JIM CROW, and the CIVIL RIGHTS MOVEMENT. Her individual story reflects the experience of oppression, resistance, survival, and dignity of an entire people. Although the protagonist of *In My Father's House* is a minister and civil rights leader in Louisiana and his unacknowledged son is an urban militant, this work's central theme is more private than public—the search for a father who has abdicated parental responsibility. In this grim tale, the son commits suicide and the father survives but without dignity. The mood of *A Gathering of Old Men,* on the other hand, is more comic than grim, but the old men who gather with shotguns to protect one of their own from unjust arrest achieve in this act of resistance the dignity that has been missing from their lives. White characters, too, achieve moral growth as social and racial change finally catches up with the bayou country. It is Gaines's most hopeful novel and in some ways his best.

In 1972 Gaines received the Black Academy of Arts and Letters Award. He was given the annual literary award of the American Academy and Institute of Arts and Letters in 1987.

BIBLIOGRAPHY

Babb, Valerie Melissa. *Ernest Gaines.* Boston, 1991.

— KENNETH KINNAMON

GARVEY, MARCUS MOSIAH

Marcus Mosiah Garvey (August 7, 1887–June 10, 1940), founder and leader of the Universal Negro Improvement Association (UNIA), the largest organized mass movement in black history. Hailed in his own time as a redeemer, a "black Moses," Garvey is now best remembered as champion of the Back-to-Africa movement that swept the United States in the aftermath of World War I.

Garvey was born on August 17, 1887, in the town of St. Ann's Bay on the north coast of the island of Jamaica. He left school at fourteen, worked as a printer's apprentice, and subsequently joined the protonationalist National Club, which advocated Jamaican self-rule. He participated in the printers' union strike of 1912, and following its collapse, he went to Central America, working in various capacities in Costa Rica, Honduras, and Panama. He spent over a year in England during 1913–14, where he teamed up for a time with the pan-Negro journalist and businessman Duse Mohamed Ali, publisher of the influential *African Times and Orient Review.* After a short tour of the European continent, he returned to England and lobbied the Colonial Office for assistance to return to Jamaica.

Garvey arrived back in Jamaica on the eve of the outbreak of World War I. He lost little time in organizing the UNIA, which he launched at a public meeting in Kingston on July 20, 1914. Content at first to offer a program of racial accommodation while professing strong patriotic support for British war aims, Garvey was a model colonial. He soon aspired to establish a Tuskegee-type industrial training school in Jamaica. In spring 1916, however, after meeting with little success and feeling shut out from political influence, he came to America—ostensibly at Booker T. Washington's invitation, though Garvey arrived after Washington died.

Garvey's arrival in America was propitious. It coincided with the dawn of the militant NEW NEGRO era, the ideological precursor of the Harlem Renaissance of the 1920s. Propelled by America's entry into World War I in April 1917, the New Negro movement quickly gathered momentum from the outrage that African Americans felt in the aftermath of the infamous East St. Louis race riot of July 2, 1917. African-American disillusionment with the country's failure to make good on the professed democratic character of American war aims became widespread.

Shortly after his arrival in America, Garvey embarked upon a period of extensive travel and lecturing that provided him with a firsthand sense of conditions in African-American communities. After traveling for a year, he settled in Harlem, where he organized the first American branch of the UNIA in May 1917.

With the end of the war, Garvey's politics underwent a radical change. His principal political goal now became the redemption of Africa and its unification into a United States of Africa. To enrich and strengthen his movement, Garvey envisioned a black-owned and -run shipping line to foster economic independence, transport passengers between America, the Caribbean, and Africa, and serve as a symbol of black grandeur and enterprise.

Accordingly, the Black Star Line was launched and incorporated in 1919. The line's flagship, the SS *Yarmouth,* rechristened the SS *Frederick Douglass,* made its maiden voyage to the West Indies in November 1919; two other ships were acquired in 1920. The Black Star Line would prove to be the UNIA's most powerful recruiting and propaganda tool, but it ultimately sank under the accumulated weight of financial inexperience, mismanagement, expensive repairs, Garvey's own ill-advised business decisions, and ultimately, insufficient capital.

Within a decade of founding the Universal Negro Improvement Association (UNIA) in Jamaica in 1914, Marcus Garvey built the UNIA into the largest independent African-American political association. (Prints and Photographs Division, Library of Congress)

Meanwhile, by 1920 the UNIA had hundreds of divisions and chapters operating worldwide. It hosted elaborate annual conventions at its Liberty Hall headquarters in Harlem and published the *Negro World,* its internationally disseminated weekly organ that was soon banned in many parts of Africa and the Caribbean.

At the first UNIA convention in August 1920, Garvey was elected to the position of provisional president of Africa. In order to prepare the groundwork for launching his program of African redemption, Garvey sought to establish links with Liberia. In 1920 he sent a UNIA official to scout out prospects for a colony in that country. Following the official's report, in the winter of 1921 a group of UNIA technicians was sent to Liberia.

Starting in 1921, however, the movement began to unravel under the economic strain of the collapse of the

Black Star Line, the failure of Garvey's Liberian program, opposition from black critics, defections caused by internal dissension, and official harassment. The most visible expression of the latter was the federal government's indictment of Garvey, in early 1922, on charges of mail fraud stemming from Garvey's stock promotion of the Black Star Line, though by the time the indictment was presented, the Black Star Line had already suspended all operations.

The pressure of his legal difficulties soon forced Garvey into an ill-advised effort to neutralize white opposition. In June 1922 he met secretly with the acting imperial wizard of the Ku Klux Klan in Atlanta, Ga., Edward Young Clarke. The revelation of Garvey's meeting with the KKK produced a major split within the UNIA, resulting in the ouster of the "American leader," Rev. J. W. H. Eason, at the August 1922 convention. In January 1923 Eason was assassinated in New Orleans, La., but his accused assailants, who were members of the local UNIA African Legion, were subsequently acquitted. Following this event and as part of the defense campaign in preparation for the mail fraud trial, Garvey's second wife, Amy Jacques Garvey (1896–1973), edited and published a small volume of Garvey's sayings and speeches under the title *Philosophy and Opinions of Marcus Garvey* (1923).

Shortly after his trial commenced, Garvey unwisely assumed his own legal defense. He was found guilty on a single count of fraud and sentenced to a five-year prison term, though his three Black Star Line codefendants were acquitted. (The year following his conviction, Garvey launched a second shipping line, the Black Cross Navigation and Trading Co., but it too failed.)

Thanks to an extensive petition campaign, Garvey's sentence was commuted after he had served thirty-three months in the Atlanta federal penitentiary. He was immediately deported to Jamaica upon release in November 1927 and never allowed to return to America. A second and expanded volume of *Philosophy and Opinions of Marcus Garvey* was edited and published by Amy Jacques Garvey in 1925 as part of Garvey's attempt to obtain a pardon.

Back in Jamaica, Garvey soon moved to reconstitute the UNIA under his direct control. This move precipitated a major split between the official New York parent body and the newly created Jamaican body. Although two conventions of the UNIA were held in Jamaica, Garvey was never able to reassert control over the various segments of his movement from his base in Jamaica.

Although he had high hopes of reforming Jamaican politics, Garvey went down to defeat in the general election of 1930 in his bid to win a seat on the colonial legislative council. He had to content himself with a seat on the municipal council of Kingston. Disheartened and bankrupt, Garvey abandoned Jamaica and relocated to London in 1935. A short time after arriving in England, however, fascist Italy invaded Ethiopia, producing a crisis that occasioned a massive upsurge of pro-Ethiopian solidarity throughout the black world, in which movement UNIA divisions and members were at the forefront. Garvey's loud defense of the Ethiopian emperor Haile Selassie soon changed to scathing public criticism, thus alienating many of Garvey's followers.

Garvey melded black aspirations for economic and cultural independence with the traditional American creed of success.

Throughout the thirties Garvey tried to rally his greatly diminished band of supporters with his monthly magazine, *Black Man.* Between 1936 and 1938 he convened a succession of annual meetings and conventions in Toronto, Canada, where he also launched a school of African philosophy as a UNIA training school. He undertook annual speaking tours of the Canadian maritime provinces and the eastern Caribbean.

In 1939 Garvey suffered a stroke that left him partly paralyzed. The indignity of reading his own obituary notice precipitated a further stroke that led to his death on June 10, 1940. Although his last years were spent in obscurity, in the decades between the two world wars, Garvey's ideology inspired millions of blacks worldwide with the vision of a redeemed and emancipated Africa. The importance of Garvey's political legacy was acknowledged by such African nationalists as Nnamdi Azikiwe of Nigeria and Kwame Nkrumah of Ghana. In 1964 Garvey was declared Jamaica's first national hero.

While he failed to realize his immediate objectives, Garvey's message represented a call for liberation from the psychological bondage of racial subordination. Drawing on a gift for spellbinding oratory and spectacle, Garvey melded black aspirations for economic and cultural independence with the traditional American creed of success to create a new and distinctive black gospel of racial pride.

BIBLIOGRAPHY

Cronon, Edmund David. *Black Moses: The Story of Marcus Garvey and the Universal Negro Improvement Association.* Madison, Wis., 1955.

Hill, Robert A., ed. *The Marcus Garvey and Universal Negro Improvement Association Papers.* Los Angeles and Berkeley, 1983–1991.

Jacques-Garvey, Amy, ed. *Philosophy and Opinions of Marcus Garvey.* New York, 1923–1925. Reissued with an introduction by Robert A. Hill. New York, 1992.

Lewis, Rupert. *Marcus Garvey: Anti-Colonial Champion.* Trenton, N.J., 1988.

Martin, Tony. *Race First: The Ideological and Organizational Struggles of Marcus Garvey and the Universal Negro Improvement Association.* Westport, Conn., 1976.

Stein, Judith. *The World of Marcus Garvey: Race and Class in Modern Society.* Baton Rouge, La., 1986.

Vincent, Theodore G. *Black Power and the Garvey Movement.* 2nd ed. Trenton, N.J., 1992.

– ROBERT A. HILL

GIBSON, ALTHEA

Althea Gibson (August 25, 1927–), tennis player. Althea Gibson was the first black tennis player to win the sport's major titles. Born in Silver, S.C., to a garage hand and a housewife, she came to New York City at age three to live with an aunt. The oldest of five children, she was a standout athlete at Public School 136 and began playing paddleball under Police Athletic League auspices on West 143rd Street in Harlem. In 1940, she was introduced to tennis by Fred Johnson, a one-armed instructor, at the courts (now named after him) on 152nd Street. She was an immediate sensation.

Gibson became an honorary member of Harlem's socially prominent Cosmopolitan Tennis Club (now defunct) and won her first tournament—the American Tennis Association (ATA) junior girls title—in 1945. (The ATA is the oldest continuously operated black noncollegiate sports organization in America). Though Gibson lost in the finals of the ATA women's singles in 1946, she attracted the attention of two black physicians: Dr. Hubert Eaton of Wilmington, N.C., and Dr. R. Walter Johnson of Lynchburg, Va., who tried to advance her career.

In September 1946 Gibson entered high school in Wilmington while living with the Eatons, and she graduated in 1949. She won the ATA women's single title ten years in a row, from 1947 to 1956. As the best black female tennis player ever, she was encouraged to enter the U.S. Lawn Tennis Association (the white governing body of tennis) events. Jackie Robinson had just completed his third year in major league baseball, and pressure was being applied on other sports to integrate. Though she was a reluctant crusader, Gibson was finally admitted to play in the USLTA Nationals at Forest Hills, N.Y., on August 28, 1950.

Alice Marble, the former USLTA singles champion, wrote a letter, published in the July 1950 issue of *American Lawn Tennis* magazine, admonishing the USLTA for its reluctance to admit Gibson when she was clearly more than qualified. Gibson's entry was then accepted at two major events in the summer of 1950 before her Forest Hills debut. She was warmly received at the Nationals, where she lost a two-day, rain-delayed match to the number-two-seeded Louise Brough in the second round.

Gibson's breakthrough heralded more to come. The ATA began a serious junior development program to provide opportunities for promising black children. (Out of that program came Arthur ASHE, who became the first black male winner of the sport's major titles.) Sydney Llewelyn became Gibson's coach, and her rise was meteoric. Her first grand slam title was the French singles in Paris in 1956. Before she turned professional, she added the Wimbledon and the U.S. singles in both 1957 and 1958, and the French women's doubles and the U.S. mixed doubles. She was a Wightman Cup team member in 1957 and 1958. After her Wimbledon victory, she was presented her trophy by Queen Elizabeth II, she danced with the queen's husband, Prince Philip, at the Wimbledon Ball, and New York City accorded her a ticker-tape parade.

The poise she showed at Wimbledon and at other private clubs where USLTA-sanctioned events were played was instilled by Dr. Eaton's wife and by her time spent as an undergraduate at Florida A&M University in Tallahassee, Fla. Jake Gaither, FAMU's famed athletic director, helped secure a teaching position for her in physical education at Lincoln University in Jefferson City, Mo. In the winter of 1955–56, the State Department asked her to tour Southeast Asia with Ham Richardson, Bob Perry, and Karol Fageros.

In 1957 Gibson won the Babe Didrickson Zaharias Trophy as Female Athlete of the Year, the first black female athlete to win the award. She also began an attempt at a career as a singer, taking voice lessons three times a week. While singing at New York City's Waldorf-Astoria Hotel for a tribute to famed songwriter W. C. HANDY, she landed an appearance on the *Ed Sullivan Show* in May 1958. Moderately successful as a singer, she considered a professional tour with tennis player Jack Kramer, the American champion of the 1940s. She also became an avid golfer, encouraged by Joe LOUIS, the former world heavyweight champion, who was a golf enthusiast. Louis had also paid her way to her first Wimbledon championships.

The Ladies Professional Golfers Association (LPGA) was in its infancy and purses were small. But Gibson was a quick learner and was soon nearly a "scratch" player. She received tips from Ann Gregory, who had been the best black female golfer ever. Gibson, a naturally gifted athlete, could handle the pressure of professional sports. But the purses offered on the LPGA tour were too small to maintain her interest.

In 1986, New Jersey Governor Tom Kean appointed Gibson to the state's Athletic Commission. She became a sought-after teaching professional at several private clubs in central and northern New Jersey and devoted much of her time to counseling young black players. The first black female athlete to enjoy true international fame, Gibson was elected to the International Tennis Hall of Fame in 1971.

BIBLIOGRAPHY

Gibson, Althea. *I Always Wanted to Be Somebody.* New York, 1958.

Gibson, Althea, with Richard Curtis. *So Much to Live For.* New York, 1968.

– ARTHUR R. ASHE, JR.

GIBSON, JOSHUA "JOSH"

Joshua "Josh" Gibson (December 21, 1911–January 20, 1947), baseball player. If any one man personified both the joy of Negro League BASEBALL and the pathos of major league baseball's color line, it was catcher Josh Gibson, black baseball's greatest hitter. Born to sharecroppers Mark and Nancy (Woodlock) Gibson in Buena Vista, Ga., Josh moved to Pittsburgh in 1924 when his father found employment at the Homestead Works of the Carnegie-Illinois Steel Company. On the diamond, the solidly built Gibson astounded fans and players with his feats for two decades, but he never got the chance to play in the major leagues.

As a youth on the Northside of Pittsburgh, Gibson attended a vocational school where he prepared for the electrician's trade. But it was on the city's sandlots, playing for the Gimbel Brothers and Westinghouse Airbrake company teams, that he prepped for his life's work. Joining the Pittsburgh Crawfords in 1927 when this team of local youths was still a sandlot club, Gibson soon attracted the attention of Homestead Grays owner Cumberland Posey.

Gibson starred for the Grays in the early 1930s, returning to the Pittsburgh Crawfords for the 1934–1936 campaigns. By then, the Crawfords were owned by numbers baron Gus Greenlee, who remade them into the 1935 Negro National League champions. With future Hall of Famers Gibson, Satchel PAIGE, Judy Johnson, Oscar Charleston, and "Cool Papa" Bell on the team, the Crawfords were quite possibly the best team ever assembled.

In 1937, after breaking his contract and joining many of his Crawford teammates in the Dominican Republic, Gibson was traded back to the Grays. There, he and Buck Leonard were considered black baseball's equivalent to Babe Ruth and Lou Gehrig. The Grays won nine NL pennants in a row after Gibson returned, a mark equaled only by the Tokyo Giants.

Although a fine defensive catcher, the muscular 6′1″, 215-pound Gibson is remembered best for his legendary swings at the plate. Perhaps the greatest slugger ever, he hit balls out of parks across the United States and the Caribbean basin, where he played each winter between 1933 and 1945. His home runs at Forbes Field and Yankee Stadium are thought to have been the longest hit at each. During his career, Gibson never played for a losing team.

His lifetime .379 batting average in the Negro and Caribbean leagues is the highest of any Negro Leaguer. He won batting championships, most-valuable-player awards, and/or home run titles in the Negro Leagues, Cuba, Mexico, the Dominican Republic, and Puerto Rico. His home run blasts are still recalled throughout these lands.

The second-highest-paid Negro Leaguer, Gibson also was its second-best attraction, behind Satchel Paige in both categories. Promoters often advertised for Negro League games by guaranteeing that Gibson would hit a home run. He rarely let them down.

Although fellow Negro Leaguers remember Gibson with fondness and a respect that borders on awe, his personal life was touched by tragedy. His young bride, Helen, died delivering their twin children, Josh, Jr., and Helen, in 1930. Gibson himself died in 1947, soon after the Brooklyn Dodgers signed Jackie ROBINSON. He was only thirty-five at the time. In 1972, he joined batterymate Satchel Paige in the Baseball Hall of Fame.

BIBLIOGRAPHY

Holway, John B. *Josh and Satch: A Dual Biography of Josh Gibson and Satchel Paige.* Westport, Conn., 1991.

Ruck, Rob. *Sandlot Seasons: Sport in Black Pittsburgh.* Champaign-Urbana, Ill., 1987.

– ROB RUCK

GILLESPIE, JOHN BIRKS "DIZZY"

John Birks "Dizzy" Gillespie (October 21, 1917–January 6, 1993), jazz trumpeter and composer. Born in Cheraw, S.C., John Birks Gillespie, or Dizzy, as he was later known, took up trombone in his early teens and began playing trumpet shortly thereafter. When he began to play trumpet, he puffed out his cheeks, a technical mistake that later became his visual trademark. Starting in 1932, Gillespie studied harmony and theory at Laurinburg Institute, in Laurinburg, N.C., but in 1935 he broke off studies to move with his family to

Philadelphia. Frank Fairfax gave Gillespie his first important work, and it was in Fairfax's band that Gillespie earned his nickname, Dizzy, for his clowning onstage and off.

In 1937 Gillespie moved to New York and played for two years with Teddy Hill's band. Through the early 1940s his experience was mostly with big bands, including those of Cab CALLOWAY, Ella FITZGERALD, Benny Carter, Charlie Barnet, Les Hite, Lucky Millinder, Earl Hines, Duke ELLINGTON, and Billy Eckstine. Among his important early recordings were "Pickin' the Cabbage" (1940) with Calloway and "Little John Special" (1942) with Millinder. Gillespie, who married Lorraine Willis in 1940, began leading small ensembles in Philadelphia and New York shortly thereafter. In 1945 he joined with saxophonist Charlie PARKER to lead a bebop ensemble that helped inaugurate the modern JAZZ era.

Although in the early 1940s younger jazz musicians had played in a bebop style in big bands and in after-hours jam sessions at clubs in HARLEM, it was not until Parker and Gillespie's 1945 recordings, including "Dizzy Atmosphere," "Shaw 'Nuff," and "Groovin' High," that the new style's break from swing became clear. Bebop reacted to the at times stodgy tempos of the big bands and was instead characterized by adventurous harmonies and knotty, fast lines played in stunning unison by Gillespie and Parker, with solos that emphasized speed, subtlety, and wit.

Gillespie's trumpet style during this time was enormously influential. By the mid-1940s he had broken away from his earlier emulation of Roy Eldridge and arrived at a style of his own, one which he maintained for the next five decades. He had a crackling tone, and his endless flow of nimble ideas included astonishing runs and leaps into the instrument's highest registers. Although many of Gillespie's tunes were little more than phrases arrived at spontaneously with Parker, Gillespie composed many songs during this time that later became jazz standards, including "A Night in Tunisia" (1942), "Salt Peanuts" (1942), and "Woody 'n' You" (1943). In addition to his virtuosity on trumpet, Gillespie continued to display his masterful sense of humor and instinct for gleeful mischief both onstage and off. Starting in the mid-1940s he affected the role of the jazz intellectual, wearing a beret, horn-rimmed glasses, and a goatee. He popularized bebop slang and served as the hipster patriarch to the white beatniks.

After his initial successes with Parker in the mid-1940s, Gillespie went on to enormous success as the leader of a big band. He hired Tadd Dameron, George Russell, Gil Fuller, and John Lewis as composers and arrangers; some of the band's recordings include "Things to Come" (1946), "One Bass Hit" (1946), and "Our Delight" (1946). The band's celebrated appearance at the Salle Pleyel in Paris, France, in 1948 yielded recordings of " 'Round About Midnight," "I Can't Get Started," and "Good Bait." The latter date included the Cuban percussionist Chano Pozo, and during this time Gillespie began to explore Afro-Cuban rhythms and melodies. Gillespie's composition "Manteca" (1947) and his performance of George Russell's "Cubana Be, Cubana Bop" (1947) were among the first successful integrations of jazz and Latin music, followed later by his composition "Con Alma" (1957). In the late 1940s and early '50s Gillespie also continued to work on small group dates, including reunions with Charlie Parker in 1950, 1951, and 1953 and a return to the Salle Pleyel as a leader in 1953.

Dizzy Gillespie had a crackling tone and his endless flow of nimble ideas included astonishing runs and leaps into the instrument's highest registers.

Although Gillespie never lost his idiosyncratic charm and sense of humor—after 1953 he played a trumpet with an upturned bell, supposedly the result of someone having bent the instrument by sitting on it—he outgrew the role of practical joker and instead became a figure of respect and genial authority. He released "Love Me" and "Tin Tin Deo" in 1951 on his own short-lived Dee Gee record label and became a featured soloist on many performances by the popular traveling sessions known as Jazz at the Philharmonic (JATP). In 1956 Gillespie's integrated band became the first to tour overseas under the sponsorship of the U.S. State Department, and in the following years he took them on tours to the Middle East, South America, and Europe. In 1959 Gillespie, always an outspoken opponent of segregation, performed at the first integrated concert in a public school in his hometown of Cheraw, S.C. The next year he refused to back down when Tulane University in New Orleans threatened to cancel a concert unless he replaced his white pianist with an African American. Gillespie's political activities took another twist in 1964 when he went along with a tongue-in-cheek presidential campaign. During this time Gillespie continued to record, both with small groups (*Swing Low, Sweet Cadillac,* 1967) and with big bands (*Reunion Big Band,* 1968). He also worked extensively in film and television.

In the 1970s and '80s, Gillespie maintained his busy schedule of touring and recording both in the United States and abroad as a leader of small and large bands and as a guest soloist. He appeared with the Giants of Jazz tour (1971–2) and recorded with Mary Lou Williams (1971), Machito (1975), Count BASIE (1977), Mongo Santamaria (1980), Max ROACH (1989), and often with his trumpet protégé, John Faddis. During this time he also appeared on television shows such as *Sesame Street* and *The Cosby Show.* In 1979 he published his autobiography, *To BE or Not to BOP,* in which he explained his longstanding interest in Africa, which influenced his politics, music, and style of dress, and also recounted his involvement in the Baha'i faith, to which he had converted in the late 1960s.

By the late 1980s Gillespie had long been recognized as one of the founding figures of modern jazz. In 1989 he won the U.S. National Medal of the Arts and was made a French Commandeur d'Ordre des Arts et Lettres. Although his instrumental style was largely fixed by the mid-1940s, he won four Grammy Awards in the 1970s and '80s, and his career as a trumpeter ranked in influence and popularity with Louis ARMSTRONG and Miles DAVIS; along with Armstrong he became jazz's unofficial ambassador and personification around the world. Gillespie, who lived in Queens, N.Y., and then in Camden, N.J., continued giving hundreds of concerts each year in dozens of countries until his death at the age of seventy-four.

BIBLIOGRAPHY

Gillespie, Dizzy, and Al Fraser. *To BE or Not to BOP.* New York, 1979.

Gitler, Ira. *Jazz Masters of the Forties.* New York, 1966.

Horricks, Raymond. *Dizzy Gillespie.* Tunbridge Wells, U.K., 1984.

— JONATHAN GILL

GILPIN, CHARLES SIDNEY

Charles Sidney Gilpin (November 20, 1878–May 6, 1930), actor and singer. Born and raised in Richmond, Va., Charles Gilpin worked as an apprentice in the *Richmond Planet* print shop before finding his vocation in the theater and becoming one of the most highly regarded actors of the 1920s.

Gilpin first appeared onstage as a singer when he was only twelve. In 1896, he joined a MINSTREL show and left Richmond, thus beginning the life of an itinerant performer that he would lead for many years. Between engagements in restaurants, variety theaters, and fairs, he worked at various odd jobs and was, among other things, a printer, barber, boxing trainer, and railroad porter.

In 1903, Gilpin joined the Canadian Jubilee Singers of Hamilton, Ontario. In 1905 and 1906, he performed with the Abyssinia Company and the Original Smart Set, two traveling musical troupes. From 1907 to 1911, he appeared with Robert Motts's Pekin Theatre in Chicago, where he played his first dramatic roles and became a well-known character actor. He toured Canada and the United States with the Pan-American Octette from 1911 to 1913. Afterward he performed for one season with Rogers and Creamer's Old Man's Boy Company in New York.

In 1915, Gilpin joined the Anita Bush players, one of the first black stock companies in New York City, as its star performer. He accompanied the troupe when it moved within the year from the Lincoln Theater in Harlem to the neighboring Lafayette Theatre, where it became known as the Lafayette Stock Company and eventually launched the careers of many famous black performers.

In January 1916, Gilpin made a memorable appearance in whiteface as Jacob McCloskey, a slave overseer and villain of Dion Boucicault's *The Octoroon.* He starred in several more successful productions before leaving the company over a salary dispute in April 1916. As a result of the reputation Gilpin earned with the Lafayette players, he was given the role of the Rev. William Custis, modeled after Frederick DOUGLASS, in the 1919 Broadway premiere of John Drinkwater's *Abraham Lincoln.*

Gilpin's first Broadway role led to a far greater one: Eugene O'Neill saw him in *Lincoln* and recommended Gilpin for the lead in his new play, *The Emperor Jones.* The play opened in November 1920 in Greenwich Village and, following favorable reviews, moved to the Princess Theatre on Broadway. Gilpin, having beaten out numerous white actors for the part, became famous overnight. He played the title role for four years to great critical and popular acclaim. *The Emperor Jones* marked O'Neill's first great success and, more important, it greatly advanced the case for the public acceptance of black performers in serious drama.

For his work in *The Emperor Jones,* the Drama League of New York named Gilpin in 1920 as one of the ten people who had done the most for the American theater. Gilpin was the first African American so honored. His invitation to the league's presentation dinner, however, created a public controversy that ended with his attendance, following the Drama League's refusal to rescind the invitation and Gilpin's refusal to decline it. Gilpin received a standing ovation of unusual length on accepting the award.

In 1921, the NAACP awarded Gilpin its Spingarn Medal for his achievement, and he was received at the

White House in a private audience by President Warren G. Harding. In 1922, the Dumas Dramatic Club (now the Karamu Players) in Cleveland renamed itself the Gilpin Players in his honor.

In 1924, Gilpin starred as the Rev. Cicero Brown in Nan Steven's *Roseanne,* a drama about black life in the South, produced in Greenwich Village in New York City. In 1925, he appeared in a brief run of J. B. Totten's *So That's That.*

Although he never again achieved the success he had with his portrayal of Brutus Jones, Gilpin continued to perform after 1926, mainly in revivals of *The Emperor Jones.* Gilpin was on the road with the play when his health failed in 1929. He died of pneumonia a year later in Eldridge Park, N.J.

BIBLIOGRAPHY

Hughes, Langston, and Milton Meltzer. *Black Magic: A Pictorial History of the African-American in the Performing Arts.* New York, 1967.

Isaacs, Edith. *The Negro in the American Theatre.* New York, 1947.

Monroe, John G. "Charles Gilpin and the Drama League Controversy." *Black American Literature Forum* (Winter 1982): 139–141.

Thompson, Francesca. "The Lafayette Players." In Errol Hill, ed. *The Theatre of Black Americans.* New York, 1987.

– ALEXIS WALKER

GIOVANNI, YOLANDA CORNELIA "NIKKI"

Yolanda Cornelia "Nikki" Giovanni (June 7, 1943–), poet. Nikki Giovanni was born in Knoxville, Tenn. Her father, Jones Giovanni, was a probation officer; her mother, Yolanda Cornelia Watson Giovanni, was a social worker. The Giovannis were a close-knit family, and Nikki felt a special bond with her younger sister, Gary, and her maternal grandmother, Louvenia Terrell Watson. Watson instilled in Giovanni a fierce pride in her African-American heritage.

After graduating from Fisk University in 1967, Giovanni was swept up by the Black Power and BLACK ARTS movements. Between 1968 and 1970 she published three books of poetry reflecting her preoccupation with revolutionary politics: *Black Judgment* (1968), *Black Feeling, Black Talk* (1970), and *Re: Creation* (1970).

But *Re: Creation* also introduced more personal concerns. In the spring of 1969, Giovanni gave birth to a son, Tom. The experience, she said, caused her to reconsider her priorities. Her work through the middle 1970s concentrated less overtly on politics and confrontation and more on personal issues such as love and loneliness. Yet Giovanni would always deny any real separation between her "personal" and her "political" concerns. During this time she began writing poetry for children. *Spin a Soft Black Song: Poems for Children* appeared in 1971, *Ego-Tripping and Other Poems for Young People* in 1973, and *Vacation Time: Poems for Children* in 1980.

In the 1970s, Giovanni expanded her horizons in other ways. Between 1971 and 1978 she made a series of six records, speaking her poetry to an accompaniment of gospel music (the first in the series, *Truth Is on Its Way,* was the best-selling spoken-word album of 1971). She published essays and two books of conversations with major literary forebears: *A Dialogue: James Baldwin and Nikki Giovanni* (1973) and *A Poetic Equation: Conversations Between Nikki Giovanni and Margaret Walker* (1974). She was also a sought-after reader and lecturer.

Critical reaction to Giovanni's work has often been mixed. While some have praised her work for its vitality and immediacy, some have felt that her early popularity and high degree of visibility worked against her development as a poet. Others have criticized her work as politically naive, uneven, and erratic. Some of these reactions were due in part to Giovanni's very public growing up as a poet and the diversity of her interests. These criticisms have never bothered Giovanni, who believes that life is "inherently incoherent."

Other works of Giovanni's include *My House* (1972), *The Women and the Men* (1972), *Cotton Candy on a Rainy Day* (1978), *Those Who Ride the Night Winds* (1983), and a collection of essays, *Sacred Cows and Other Edibles* (1988).

BIBLIOGRAPHY

Bailey, Peter. "I Am Black, Female, Polite, . . ." *Ebony* (February 1972): 48–56.

Tate, Claudia. *Black Women Writers at Work.* New York, 1983.

– MICHAEL PALLER

GOLF

Despite limited access to public courses, exclusion from private clubs, and the absence of professional role models, substantial numbers of African Americans have played the game of golf since its introduction to America. They have also established and maintained many of the social institutions associated with the sport. According to a 1990 study by Mediamark Research, of the nearly eighteen million adults in the United States who play golf, about 2.5 percent, or 450,000, are black Americans.

Ironically, considering the elitist origins of golf in this country, one of the first American-born golf professionals was an African American—John Shippen, who competed in the 1896 U.S. Open, held at Shinnecock Hills on Long Island. Shippen, then eighteen years old, worked as an assistant to Willie Dunn, the professional at Shinnecock Hills. His participation was protested by a group of foreign-born professionals who threatened to withdraw if Shippen and Oscar Bunn, a Shinnecock Indian golfer from the reservation, were allowed to play. Theodore Havemeyer, the president of the United States Golf Association (USGA), informed the disgruntled golfers that the tournament would be run even if Shippen and Bunn were the only competitors.

Shippen shot a 78 in the morning round of the thirty-six-hole, one-day event and was tied for the lead. In the end, he tied for fifth. He played in four other U.S. Opens, continued to compete in local and national tournaments, and became the golf professional at several black-run clubs in Philadelphia and in Laurel, Md. For thirty-five years he served as the professional at the Shady Rest Country Club in Scotch Plains, New Jersey. He died at the age of ninety in a nursing home in Newark, N.J., in 1968.

Most African-American golfers developed an interest in the game through caddying. In the early 1920s, a golf boom fueled a demand for caddies at both private and public courses. Traditionally, clubs allowed caddies to play golf one day a week when the course was closed to members for maintenance. This allowed some black teenagers the chance to play on courses at clubs that would not have allowed them as members.

Despite limited access to public courses and exclusion from private clubs, substantial numbers of African Americans have played the game of golf since its introduction to America.

While blacks were able to gain limited access to America's golf courses, they faced many obstacles when they attempted to make a living at golf. The original Professional Golfers' Association (PGA) constitution in 1934 stipulated that only "golfers of the Caucasian race" were eligible for membership. Dewey Brown, who was playing golf in the 1920s, became the first black member of the PGA. However, there is no indication of the exact date or explanation of how he was exempted from the "Caucasian clause." He served as golf professional at several black clubs but was most closely associated with the Buckwood Inn at Shawnee-on-the-Delaware.

Despite this limited opportunity to play golf, enough African Americans developed an interest in the game to support a number of black-operated clubs by the second decade of the twentieth century. One was the Shady Rest Golf Club in Westfield (now Scotch Plains), N.J., established in 1921, which is generally considered to be the first black country club—that is, a club incorporating golf and tennis with a full schedule of social events. A colony of black resident cottages had sprung up on either side of what was the Westfield Country Club, and eventually the course itself was sold to a group of African Americans and renamed Shady Rest. The membership, according to the *New York Sun* in July 1922, consisted of "prosperous Negro merchants, lawyers, doctors, Pullman porters, waiters and janitors."

At about the same time, black golfers in Washington, D.C., found it difficult to gain access to courses in the area. So strong was their interest in the game that, during the 1920s, several of them secured summer cottages in Stow, Mass., where they established the Mapledale Country Club, one of the significant early black golf courses. Other black-owned clubs included Sunset Hills Country Club in Kankakee, Ill,; Lincoln Country Club in Atlanta; and the Asbury Park Course in New Jersey.

In 1926, Robert Hawkins (a resident of Stow) invited players from black clubs throughout the United States to a tournament at Mapledale. On Labor Day weekend of that year, thirty-five black golfers came to play the seventy-two-hole tournament. The winners of the professional division, Harry Jackson of Washington, D.C., and Marie Thompson of Chicago, were paid one hundred dollars each; the amateurs received medals. The tournament was repeated in 1927 and 1928, when the players came together to establish the United Golfers Association (UGA). Through UGA tournaments, a number of black golfers gained prominence; they included Robert "Pat" Ball (who won the UGA title in 1927, 1929, 1934, and 1941) and Walter Speedy of Chicago; Howard Wheeler (who won the UGA title five times between 1933 and 1958) of Atlanta; John Dendy of Asheville, N.C.; and A. D. V. Crosby and R. G. Robinson of Ann Arbor, Mich.

Black women also demonstrated a strong desire to gain access to golf facilities. In 1937, an all-black women's club, Wake Robin Golf Club, was formed in Washington, D.C., followed soon afterward by the Chicago Women's Club. Lucy Williams of Indianapolis and Laura Osgood of Chicago emerged as leading women golfers, as did Thelma Cowan (who won the UGA national tournament in 1947, 1949, 1954, and 1955), Anne Gregory (who won in 1950, 1953, 1957, 1965, and 1966), and Ethel Funches, who won seven times, beginning in 1959.

While the UGA provided an opportunity for black club pros and amateurs to test their skills against other club players, it had little success in introducing black golfers into the white mainstream. The USGA did not reserve any place in its annual championship for members of the UGA (as the United States Lawn Tennis Association did for the all-black American Tennis Association). There was little interaction between the USGA and the UGA. It wasn't until 1959 that any USGA championship was won by an African American. In that year, Bill Wright won the Public Links Championship. In 1982, Charles Duhon won the USGA Senior Amateur Championship.

Military service and black colleges were two other avenues for the development of black golfers. For some, the Army offered the only opportunity to play on an eighteen-hole course that approached championship caliber. Pvt. Calvin Searles (who subsequently died in World War II) played in the 1944 Tam O'Shanter All American event. This was the only mainstream tournament that allowed blacks to compete during the war years. Other prominent players during the 1940s included Ed Jackson and Bennie Davis of Detroit; Calvin Ingram and Frank Radcliffe of Chicago; Peter Fortunes of Suffolk, Va.; and Hoxey Hazzard of Montgomery, Ala.

The only black college with its own course was TUSKEGEE INSTITUTE, which had a three-hole course built in 1920 that was expanded to nine holes approximately a decade later. Tuskegee sponsored the first black intercollegiate tournament in 1938 and, on a larger scale, established a national intercollegiate event in 1940.

African Americans were also making efforts to increase access to public courses. In a number of court cases around the country, blacks sued to gain equal access to public facilities, paralleling other civil rights efforts of the period. A black dentist, P. O. Sweeny, sued the Louisville, Ky., Parks Department in 1947 for the right to play unrestricted on local municipal courses. The decision ruled, in essence, that the courts could not enforce social equality, and the suit was dismissed. Other lower court cases yielded similar results or, in some, modified rules for access. There were some exceptions, however. A federal judge in Baltimore opened city courses to African Americans in 1948, and in 1950 the U.S. Supreme Court overturned a Florida State Supreme Court ruling that had restricted black access to local courses to one day per week. Finally, in 1955, the U.S. Supreme Court reaffirmed its rejection of "separate but equal" accommodations for public golf and recreational facilities. In this decision, the Court vacated a ruling by a lower court that allowed Atlanta to legally segregate blacks and whites if the facilities were of equal quality. However, the ruling did not immediately open up public courses to black golfers.

A similar struggle occurred over the integration of professional organizations. In 1948, Ted Rhodes, Bill Spiller, and Gunter Madison, accomplished black golfers, forced the PGA to rethink its exclusionary rule. These golfers brought suit against the PGA for discrimination when they were not allowed to compete in the Richmond Open in Richmond, Calif. The case was settled out of court in September 1948 when the PGA, through attorney Dana Murdock, declared that it would not discriminate or refuse tournament-playing privileges to anyone because of color. But discrimination on the professional tour continued.

At the 1952 San Diego Open, former boxing champion Joe LOUIS, himself an accomplished amateur golfer, was invited by a local Chevrolet sponsor to participate in the tournament. A PGA committee notified Louis that he was banned from participation. While the PGA constitution prohibited non-Caucasians from membership, Louis had been invited, according to the rules, by the local sponsor as one of five amateur golfers allowed, without the need for qualification. Non-Caucasians were prohibited from membershp in the PGA, but an individual sponsor could invite up to five members or nonmembers (amateurs or pros) to compete.

Horton Smith, PGA president, polled the members of the executive committee to gain an exemption for Louis to compete. The PGA added a clause to its bylaws that allowed one PGA-approved "Negro" amateur (under five handicap) and one PGA-approved "Negro" professional of "recognized standing and ability" to be designated by local sponsors to compete in its events. Louis accepted these conditions because at the time he had no other choice. Despite the national attention afforded the San Diego Open racial controversy, it would be nine years before the PGA would officially rescind its "Caucasian only" clause.

The black golfer who played the most prominent public role in bringing African-American golf to the attention of the sporting world was Lee Elder.

In 1960, after receiving a letter protesting PGA policies from black tour professional Charles Sifford, the attorney general of California, Stanley Mosk, announced, "We intend to take every step available to us, both in and out of the courts, to force the PGA either to eliminate this obnoxious restriction or to cease all activity of any kind within our state" (*New York Times,* November 23, 1960). Eventually, the executive committee of the PGA voted to eliminate racial restrictions for membership. The full membership ratified the committee's decision in November 1961.

Charles Sifford was the most prominent black professional golfer of the postwar decades. Other than John Shippen, he accomplished the most "black firsts" in golf. After dominating the annual UGA professional championship, winning a record five championships in a row between 1952 and 1956, he became the first black player to win a significant title in a predominantly white event, the Long Beach (California) Open, in 1957. While Pete Brown, another early black professional, also helped pave the way for black professional golfers by being the first black pro to win a PGA tournament, the 1964 Waco Turner Open, Sifford was the first black player to win a major PGA event, the 1969 Los Angeles Open.

The Ladies Professional Golfers Association (LPGA) was established in 1948, and although there was no written clause in its constitution barring blacks from membership and tournament play, it was not until 1963 that an African-American tennis champion, Althea GIBSON, competed on the LPGA tour, and not until 1967 that an African American, Renee Powell, became a regular member of the tour.

The black golfer who played the most prominent public role in bringing African-American golf to the attention of the sporting world was Lee Elder. After competing mainly in UGA tournaments, Elder earned his PGA card in 1967. He is best known as the first black golfer to compete in the Masters, the tournament most symbolic of the inability of African-American golfers to break into major tournament golf. Throughout the early 1970s, Elder was the focal point of the effort to obtain equality in entrance to the Masters. In 1971 the Masters changed earlier policies, which had invited players on the basis of a complicated point system and by ballot of former Masters champions. The new policy granted an invitation to anyone who won a PGA tournament in the year prior to the Masters. In 1974, Elder won the Monsanto Open, which qualified him to compete in the 1975 Masters.

In 1982 Calvin Peete became the first black multiple winner, capturing the Greater Milwaukee Open for the second time, the Anheuser-Busch Classic, the BC Open, and the Pensacola Open and had his best finish in a grand slam event, placing third in the PGA championship.

Eldrick "Tiger" Woods has become an enormous success in the late 1990s. Woods, whose father is black and mother is Asian, won the U.S. Amateur Championship in 1994, 1995, and 1996. He was PGA Player of the Year in 1997, his first full year as a professional golfer, winning the prestigious Masters tournament and four other tournaments during the year. He was voted Associated Press 1997 Male Athlete of the Year and he is expected to be a champion for years to come.

Despite considerable progress by black golfers on the professional tour, African Americans are still denied equal access to private country-club memberships. During an interview before the 1990 PGA championship at the Shoal Creek Country Club in Alabama, Hall Thompson, president of Shoal Creek, openly stated that his club did not allow black members. The ensuing controversy prompted both the PGA and the USGA to review site-selection policies for all future championships and coaxed several discriminatory clubs to open their doors. This open public discussion has exposed the racial intolerance that has long been associated with the game of golf but has at least begun the exploration of ways to eliminate the barriers that have restricted African-American golfers.

BIBLIOGRAPHY

Ashe, Arthur R., Jr. *A Hard Road to Glory: The History of the Black Athlete.* Vol. 2. New York, 1988.

Barkow, Al. *The History of the PGA Tour.* New York, 1989.

Graffis, Herbert. *The PGA: The Official History of the Professional Golfers Association.* New York, 1975.

Hannigan, Frank. "A Champion Against the Odds." *U.S.G.A. Journal* (August 1982): 38–41.

Jones, Guilford. "Past Greats." *Black Sports* (July 1973): 65–68.

McRae, Finley F. "Hidden Traps Beneath the Placid Greens." *American Visions* (April 1991): 26–29.

Martin, H. B. *Fifty Years of American Golf.* London, 1966.

Williams, Lena. "Renee Powell on Tour." *Black Sports* (July 1973): 43–45.

Young, A. S. *Negro Firsts in Sports.* Chicago, 1963.

— LAWRENCE J. LONDINO

GOSPEL MUSIC

The African-American religious music known as gospel, originating in the field hollers, slave songs, spirituals, and Protestant hymns sung on southern plantations, and later at camp meetings and churches, has come to dominate not only music in black churches, but singing and instrumental styles across the spectrum of American popular music, including jazz, blues, rhythm and blues, soul, and country. Exemplified in songs such as "Take My Hand, Precious Lord" and "Move On Up a Little Higher," gospel music encourages emotional and jubilant improvisation on songs of thanksgiving and praise as well as sorrow and suffering.

Musically, gospel is distinguished by its vocal style, which in both male and female singers is characterized by a strained, full-throated sound, often pushed to guttural shrieks and rasps suited to the extremes of the emotion-laden lyrics. Melodies and harmonies are generally simple, allowing for spontaneity in devising repetitive, expressive fills and riffs. The syncopated rhythms of gospel are typically spare, with heavy, often hand-clapped accents.

The Founding Years

Although the roots of gospel can be traced to Africa, and the earliest arrival of Africans in the New World, the main antecedent was the "Dr. Watts" style of singing hymns, named for British poet and hymnist Isaac Watts (1674–1748), who emphasized a call-and-response approach to religious songs, with mournful but powerful rhythms. Thus, in the nineteenth century, African-American hymnody in mainstream denominations did not differ considerably from music performed in white churches. The earliest African-American religious denominations date back to the late eighteenth century, when black congregations split off from white church organizations in Philadelphia. In 1801 the minister Richard ALLEN, who later founded the AFRICAN METHODIST EPISCOPAL (AME) denomination, published two collections of hymns designed for use in black churches. These collections were the forerunners of similar collections that formed the basis for the music performed in most nineteenth-century black churches, yet they were quite similar to the slow-tempo, restrained white Protestant hymnody. Around the middle of the nineteenth century a new type of music known as "gospel hymns" or "gospel songs" was being composed in a new style, lighter and more songlike than traditional hymnody, written by white composers such as Dwight Moody (1837–1899), Ira Sankey (1840–1908), Philip Paul Bliss (1838–1876), Robert Lowry (1826–1899), and William Batchelder Bradbury (1816–1868).

Gospel music encourages emotional and jubilant improvisation on songs of thanksgiving and praise as well as sorrow and suffering.

Another important nineteenth-century influence on gospel music was the idea, increasingly popular at a minority of nineteenth-century black churches, that spiritual progress required a deeper and more directly emotional relationship with God, often through the singing of white "gospel hymns," although gospel as an African-American form would not take that name for decades. These congregations, often led by charismatic ministers, began searching for a religion based on "Holiness or Hell" and were early participants in the Latter Rain movement, which sought to "irrigate the dry bones" of the church. The first congregation known to accept this doctrine, based on the activities of the Day of Pentecost (though, confusingly, this is *not* what is now called Pentecostalism) was the United Holy Church of Concord, S.C., which held its first meeting in 1886 and had its first convention in 1894 under the leadership of Brother L. M. Mason (1861–1930). Another early congregation to accept that doctrine and encourage early forms of gospel music was the Church of the Living God, in Wrightsville, Ark., under the leadership of William Christian (1856–1928) in 1889.

The Holiness doctrine proved controversial within black churches, as did the music associated with Holiness. In 1895 Charles Harrison Mason and Charles Price Jones were forced from the Baptist church, and together they proceeded to organize the CHURCH OF GOD IN CHRIST in Lexington, Miss., where the music was heavily influenced by the performance style at Los Angeles's Azusa Street Revival, a black congregation that marked the beginning of PENTECOSTALISM, under the leadership of William Joseph Seymour. The Azusa Street Revival featured highly charged services involving "speaking in tongues" as a manifestation of the Holy Ghost. Such activities were eventually integrated into the mainstream of black church activity, but around the turn of the century, Holiness-style services, and even the singing of spirituals, were strenuously opposed by conservative black church elders who had fought to "elevate" the musical standards of their congregations. Jones, for example, was opposed to the Azusa Street style, and eventually split from Mason to organize the Church of Christ, Holiness.

Early forms of gospel music such as sung or chanted testimonials and sermons were used to complement prayers in Holiness churches. Drawing on the call-and-response tradition that dated back to slavery times, members of a congregation would take inspiration from a phrase from the sermon or testimony and out of it spontaneously compose a simple melody and text. A chorus of congregants would repeat the original phrase, while the leader interpolated brief extemporized choruses. For example, in Charles Harrison Mason's 1908 "I'm a Soldier," the leader and congregation begin by alternating the following lines: "I'm a soldier/In the army of the Lord/I'm a soldier/In the army." Succeeding choruses differ only in the lead line, with the leader interpolating such phrases as "I'm fighting for my life," "I'm a sanctified soldier," or "I'll live and I'll die," and the congregation repeating "In the army" as a refrain. The length of such songs often stretched to fifteen minutes or more. Along with simple "homemade" harmonies came hand-clapping, foot-stomping, and holy dancing, also known as "shouting."

Holiness, Sanctified, and Pentecostal congregations sprang up rapidly all over the South, particularly in rural, poor communities, starting around the turn of the century, and in less than a decade gospel music, then known as church music, was being sung in Baptist and Methodist congregations as well. During this time the most popular gospel hymns were by a new generation of black composers, including William Henry Sherwood; Jones, who composed "Where Shall I Be?" and "I'm Happy with Jesus Alone"; Mason, who in addition to "I'm a Soldier" wrote "My Soul Loves Jesus" and the chant "Yes, Lord"; and Charles Albert Tindley, who composed "What Are They Doing in Heaven," "Stand by Me," and "I'll Overcome Someday," which was the forerunner of the civil rights anthem "We Shall Overcome." Since at this time there were no publishing houses for black gospel, these composers began to establish their own. They also depended on recordings and traveling preachers to spread their music. Preachers who popularized their own songs included J. C. Burnett ("Drive and Go Forward," 1926), Ford Washington McGhee ("Lion of the Tribe of Judah," 1927), J. M. Gates ("Death's Black Train Is Coming," 1926), and A. W. Nix ("The Black Diamond Express to Hell," 1927).

The Birth of Gospel Music

The 1920s were a crucial time in the development of gospel music. In 1921 the National Baptist Convention, USA, the largest organization of black Christians in the world, not only formally recognized gospel as a legitimate sacred musical form but published a collection of hymns, spirituals, and gospel songs under the title *Gospel Pearls,* edited by Willa A. Townsend (1885–1963). That hymnal contained six songs by Tindley, the first gospel composer successfully to combine the conventions of white evangelical music with the simple, often sentimental melodies of black spirituals. The 1921 convention also marked the emergence of the composer Thomas A. DORSEY (1899–1993), who would go on to become the Father of Gospel because of his indefatigable songwriting, publishing, organizing, and teaching. Three years later the National Baptist Convention published the *Baptist Standard Hymnal,* another important step toward bringing gospel into the mainstream of African-American church worship. Other important gospel composers who came to prominence during this time were Lucie Campbell (1885–1963) and William Herbert Brewster (1897–1987).

Despite the publication of these hymnals and the dissemination of individual songs in both print and by record, it was by word of mouth that gospel spread, particularly in working-class communities in the rural South. In Jefferson County, Ala., workers in coal mines and factories used their lunch hours to organize quartets to sing this new type of religious song. In some respects these groups were inspired by the tradition of the secular Fisk Jubilee and Tuskegee vocal quartets, but the new groups emphasized the powerful emotional experiences of conversion and salvation. One of the first such groups, the Foster Singers, organized in 1916, stressed equality between the vocal parts. However, it was a Foster Singers spinoff group, the Birmingham Jubilee Singers, led by one of the members of the Foster Singers, that inspired gospel quartets that soon started all over the South. The Birmingham Jubilee Singers allowed the bass and tenor more prominence and freedom, raised tempos, and used more adventurous harmonies, including "blue" notes. The vocal quartets organized in this style in the 1920s include the Fairfield Four (1921), which as of 1992 still included one of its original members, the Rev. Samuel McCrary; the Blue Jay Singers (1926); the Harmonizing Four (1927); and the Dixie Hummingbirds (1928). In the 1930s, new quartets included the Golden Gate Quartet (1934), which went on to become the most popular group of the 1930s and '40s, and the Soul Stirrers (1936). The following year, Rebert H. Harris (b. 1916) joined the groups, and over the next fourteen years he became their most famous singer. In 1938 Claude Jeter Harris (b. 1914) organized the Four Harmony Kings, who later changed their name to the Swan Silvertones to acknowledge their sponsorship by a bakery.

By the 1930s, gospel music had been firmly planted in northern cities. This was due not only to the Great Migration of rural blacks following World War I but also to the fact that, increasingly, record companies and publishing houses were located in northern cities, and particularly in Chicago, then the focal point for gospel music. Thomas Andrew Dorsey opened his publishing house in 1932, the same year he composed "Take My Hand, Precious Lord" (popularly known as "Precious Lord, Take My Hand"). Through composing, publishing, organizing, and teaching gospel choirs, Dorsey was given the sobriquet Father of Gospel.

Starting in the 1920s, gospel music was taken up by many different types of ensembles, in addition to vocal quartets. In urban areas, blind singers often came to prominence by performing on street corners and in churches. One of the most important of these was Connie Rosemond, for whom Lucie Campbell composed "Something Within Me." Others were Mamie Forehand and the guitarists and singers Blind Joe Taggard and Blind Willie Johnson. The blind Texan singer Arizona Dranes accompanied herself on piano and is credited with introducing that instrument to recorded gospel music. Among the gospel singers who sang with piano accompaniment as early as the 1920s were Willie Mae Ford Smith, Sallie Martin, Clara Hudmon (1900–1960), Madame Ernestine B. Washington (1914–1983), and guitarist and singer Sister Rosetta Tharpe, the first important performer to find a large audience outside the gospel circuit. Male-accompanied singers included Brother Joe May (1912–1973) and J. Robert Bradley (b. 1921). The greatest of the accompanied singers was Mahalia JACKSON, who was born in New Orleans and found her calling in Chicago at age sixteen. Her 1947 recording of "Move On Up a Little Higher," by Herbert Brewster, featuring her soaring contralto, came to define the female gospel style.

In the late 1930s, accompanied gospel ensembles consisting of four to six women, four or five men, or a mixed group of four to six singers, became popular. Clara Ward (1924–1973) organized the earliest notable accompanied ensemble, the Ward Singers, in 1934. The year before, Roberta Martin had joined with composer Theodore Frye (1899–1963) to form the Martin-Frye Quartet, later known as the Roberta Martin Singers. Sallie Martin organized the Sallie Martin Singers in 1940. Three years later the Original Gospel Harmonettes were formed, with pianist Evelyn Stark. They later came to prominence when singer Dorothy Love Coates joined the group and introduced "hard" gospel techniques, such as singing beyond her range and straining the voice for dramatic effects. Other accompanied ensembles included the Angelic Gospel Singers and the Davis Sisters, with pianist Curtis Dublin.

During this time vocal quartets and quintets continued to be popular. Archie Brownlee (1925–1960) organized the Five Blind Boys of Mississippi in 1939, the same year that Johnny L. Fields (b. 1927) formed the Five Blind Boys of Alabama, featuring Clarence Fountain (b. 1929). James Woodie Alexander (b. 1916) began leading the Pilgrim Travelers in 1946.

In the years between the wars, women, who from the start had been pillars of African-American religious institutions, became increasingly involved as publishers and organizers. In 1932, Dorsey, Sallie Martin, and Willie Mae Ford Smith formed the National Convention of Gospel Choirs and Choruses. Roberta Martin, the composer of "God Is Still on the Throne," opened her own publishing house in 1939. Sallie Martin opened hers along with Kenneth Martin (1917–1989), the composer of "Yes, God Is Real," in 1940.

The Golden Age

By 1945, gospel was becoming recognized not only as a spiritual experience but also as a form of entertainment, and this became known as gospel's golden era. Singers, appearing on stage in attractive uniforms, had established and refined a popular and recognizable vocal sound. Gospel pianists such as Mildred Falls (1915–1975), Herbert Pickard, Mildred Gay, Edgar O'Neal, James Herndon, and James Washington and organists such as Little Lucy Smith, Gerald Spraggins, Louise Overall Weaver, and Herbert "Blind" Francis were working in exciting styles derived from ragtime, barrelhouse, and the blues, with chordal voicing, riffs, and complicated rhythms. Finally a group of composers including Doris Akers (b. 1923), Sammy Lewis, and Lucy Smith could be depended on to come up with fresh material. Just as early gospel composers relied on traveling from church to church to popularize their songs, so too did the first early popular gospel singers find it necessary to go on the road. Sister Rosetta Tharpe performed at nightclubs and dance halls, but far more typical was the experience of Mahalia Jackson, who by 1945 had quit her regular job and joined a growing number of traveling professional gospel singers performing in churches and schools, moving on to auditoriums and stadiums. These singers were able to support themselves, and some, like Jackson, were quite successful, especially in the context of touring companies.

By 1945, gospel was becoming recognized not only as a spiritual experience but also as a form of entertainment.

After the war the recording industry and radio played a large part in popularizing gospel. At first, small companies such as King, Atlantic, Vee-Jay, Dot, Nashboro, and Peacock were the most active in seeking out gospel singers. Apollo Records recorded Jackson and Roberta Martin before they moved to larger labels. The Ward Sisters, the Angelic Gospel Singers, and the Davis Sisters first recorded for Gotham Records. The Original Gospel Harmonettes recorded first for RCA Victor. With the proliferation of recordings, gospel radio programs became popular. In New York, the gospel disk jockey Joe Bostic was extraordinarily successful, as were Mary Manson in Philadelphia, Irene Joseph Ware in Chicago, Mary Dee in Baltimore, Goldie Thompson in Tampa, and John "Honeyboy" Hardy in New Orleans. Other cities with gospel shows in the postwar years included Atlanta, Los Angeles, Louisville, and Miami.

Among the more prominent performers and leaders who emerged during gospel's postwar golden era were Madame Edna Gallmon Cooke (1918–1967), Julius "June" Cheeks (1928–1981), who joined the Sensationales in 1946, "Professor" Alex Bradford (1927–1978), Robert Anderson (b. 1919), and Albertina Walker (b. 1930), who in 1952 formed the Caravans. Among the members of the Caravans were Shirley Caesar and Inez Andrews (b. 1928), who had a hit record with "Mary, Don't You Weep." Marion Williams left the Ward Singers in 1958 to form the Stars of Faith. Willie Joe Ligon (b. 1942) organized the Mighty Clouds of Joy in 1959. Perhaps the best-known singer to emerge from the golden era was Sam Cooke, who joined the Soul Stirrers in 1950 and revitalized the male gospel quartet movement with his hits "Nearer to Thee" and "Touch the Hem of His Garment" before going on to fame as a popular singer starting in 1956.

The most significant figure from this time was the Rev. James Cleveland, who began singing in Dorsey's children's choir at the age of eight. By the age of sixteen, Cleveland had composed his first hit for the Roberta Martin Singers. He accompanied the Caravans, formed his own group, and in 1963 began recording with the Angelic Choir of Nutley, N.J. Cleveland's recordings were so successful that they sparked a new phase in gospel music dominated by gospel choirs. Prominent choirs following Cleveland's lead included those led by Thurston Frazier, Mattie Moss Clark (b. 1928), and Jessy Dixon (b. 1938).

By the end of the 1950s, gospel was becoming ubiquitous, not only in black communities but as a part of mainstream American culture. Mahalia Jackson recorded "Come Sunday" as part of Duke Ellington's *Black, Brown and Beige* in 1958 and the next year appeared in the film *Imitation of Life*. Langston Hughes, who in 1956 wrote *Tambourines to Glory: A Play with Spirituals, Jubilees, and Gospel Songs,* wrote the gospel-song play *Black Nativity* in 1961, for a cast that included Marion Williams and Alex Bradford. In 1961, a gospel category was added to the Grammy awards, with Mahalia Jackson the first winner. During the 1960s, costumed groups and choirs began to appear on Broadway, at Carnegie Hall, and in Las Vegas, as well as on television shows. In addition to Sam Cooke, many singers trained in the gospel tradition helped popularize gospel-style delivery in popular music. Rhythm-and-blues doo-wop groups from the late 1940s and 1950s, such as the Ravens, the Orioles, and the Drifters, used close harmonies and a high-crooning-male-lead style borrowed from gospel. Singers such as Dinah Washington, Ray CHARLES, Al Green, Aretha FRANKLIN, James BROWN, Little Richard, and Stevie WONDER used gospel techniques to cross over to enormous international popularity on the rock, soul, and rhythm-and-blues charts.

Gospel music was a crucial part of the civil rights movement. There had been a political thrust in sacred black music since the abolitionist hymnody of the nineteenth-century, and in the 1960s musicians such as Mahalia Jackson, Fannie Lou HAMER, Guy Carawan, the Montgomery Trio, the Nashville Quartet, the CORE Freedom Singers, the SNCC Freedom Singers, and Carlton Reese's Gospel Freedom Choir appeared at marches, rallies, and meetings. Gospel musicians had always reworked traditional material at will, and in the 1960s gospel songs and spirituals originally intended for religious purposes were changed to apply to secular struggles. For example, "If You Miss Me from Praying Down Here" became "If You Miss Me from the Back of the Bus." Other popular songs were "We Shall Overcome," "This Little Light of Mine," "We'll Never Turn Back," "Eyes on the Prize," "Ninety-Nine and a Half Won't Do," "O Freedom," and "Ain't Nobody Gonna Turn Me Around." For many leaders of the civil rights movement, such as Hamer, the Rev. Dr. Martin Luther King, Jr., and the Rev. Wyatt Tee Walker, gospel music was an essential part of their organizing work. "Precious Lord" was a favorite of Martin Luther King, Jr., and Mahalia Jackson sang the song at his funeral.

The Contemporary Sound and Beyond

The next phase in the history of gospel music came in 1969, when Edwin Hawkins released his rendition of "Oh Happy Day," a white nineteenth-century hymn, in which he eschewed the gritty timbres of Cleveland in favor of smooth pop vocals, soul harmonies, and jazz rhythms, including a conga drum. The song, which became the number one song on Billboard's pop chart, represented a fusion of the traditional gospel style of Mahalia Jackson, Thomas Andrew Dorsey, and the Dixie Hummingbirds, with elements of jazz, rhythm and blues, and soul. Record producers, inspired by the crossover potential of what became known as contemporary gospel, began encouraging gospel groups toward a more contemporary sound, igniting a long-running controversy within the gospel community.

After Hawkins, one of the principal figures of contemporary gospel throughout the 1970s was the composer and pianist Andrae Crouch, the cousin of critic Stanley Crouch. Also important were Myrna Summers, Danniebell Hall, Douglas Miller, Bebe and Cece Winans, the Clark Sisters, and the ensemble Commissioned. At the same time, gospel came to Broadway again in the widely acclaimed musical *Your Arms Too Short to Box with God* (1976).

In 1983 *The Gospel at Colonus* was a popular stage production in New York, and in the 1980s and '90s gospel, particularly contemporary, has continued to attract large audiences. The unaccompanied vocal sextet Take 6 combined gospel-style harmonies with mainstream jazz rhythms to achieve huge popular success in the late 1980s. Other popular contemporary singers from this time included Richard Smallwood, who uses classical elements in his songs, Bobby Jones, Keith Pringle, and Daryl Coley. Walter Hawkins (b. 1949), the brother of Edwin Hawkins, combines elements of traditional and contemporary styles, especially on recordings with his wife, Tremaine (b. 1957). The Hawkins style was taken up by the Thompson Community Choir, the Charles Fold Singers, the Barrett Sisters, and the Rev. James Moore, as well as mass choirs in Florida, New Jersey, and Mississippi. The choral ensemble Sounds of Blackness has been popular in recent years, as have contemporary vocal quartets such as the Williams Brothers, the Jackson Southernaires, and the Pilgrim Jubilees. These groups often use synthesizers and drum machines in addition to traditional gospel instruments. Prominent contemporary gospel composers include Elbernita Clark, Jeffrey LeValle, Andrae Woods, and Rance Allen.

Gospel-style singing, at least until the advent of rap music, dominated African-American popular music. One indication of the importance of gospel to the music industry is the fact that as of 1993 there were six Grammy categories devoted to gospel music. Gospel, which started out as a marginal, almost blasphemous form of musical worship, now has a central place in African-American church activity. Not only Holiness and Pentecostal churches but Baptist and Methodist denominations have fully accepted gospel music. Its striking emotional power has enabled gospel music to remain a vital part of African-American culture.

BIBLIOGRAPHY

Boyer, Horace Clarence. "A Comparative Analysis of Traditional and Contemporary Gospel Music." In Irene W. Jackson, ed. *More Than Dancing: Essays on Afro-American Music and Musicians.* Westport, Conn. 1985.

Burnim, Mellonee V. "Gospel Music Tradition: A Complex of Ideology, Aesthetic and Behavior." In Irene W. Jackson, ed. *More Than Dancing: Essays on Afro-American Music and Musicians.* Westport, Conn., 1985.

Harris, Michael W. *The Rise of Gospel Blues: The Music of Thomas Andrew Dorsey in the Urban Church.* New York, 1992.

Heilbut, Anthony. *The Gospel Sound: Good News and Bad Times.* New York, 1971. Revised, 1985.

Lovell, John, Jr. *Black Song: The Forge and the Flame: The Story of How the Afro-American Spiritual Was Hammered Out.* New York, 1972.

Maultsby, Portia K. *Afro-American Religious Music: A Study in Musical Diversity.* Springfield, Ohio, 1986.

Reagon, Bernice Johnson, ed. *We'll Understand It Better By and By.* Washington, D.C., 1992.

Ricks, George R. *Some Aspects of the Religious Music of the U.S. Negro: An Ethnomusicological Study with Special Emphasis on the Gospel Tradition.* New York, 1977.

Walker, Wyatt Tee. *"Somebody's Calling My Name": Black Sacred Music and Social Change.* Valley Forge, Pa., 1979.

– HORACE CLARENCE BOYER

GREGORY, RICHARD CLAXTON "DICK"

Richard Claxton "Dick" Gregory (October 12, 1932–), comedian, activist, and rights advocate. Dick Gregory was born and raised in a St. Louis slum. Abandoned by his father when he was a child, Gregory worked at odd jobs to help support his family. In high school, he distinguished himself as a talented runner and demonstrated the quick wit and gift for satire that would ultimately catapult him toward stardom. With the aid of an athletic scholarship, he attended Southern Illinois University at Carbondale (1951–1954 and 1956), where he became a leading track star and began to dream of becoming a comedian.

Drafted into the army in 1954, Gregory returned briefly to Carbondale after completing his term of service in 1956 and then traveled to Chicago to pursue his goal of becoming a comedian. He admired and was influenced by Timmie Rogers, Slappy White, and Nipsey Russell. In the late 1950s, Gregory worked in small black clubs like the Esquire Show Lounge, where he met his future wife, Lillian Smith, and struggled to gain popular recognition. His efforts won him a cameo appearance in "Cast the First Stone," a 1959 ABC television documentary.

Gregory's breakthrough occurred in January 1961, when the Playboy Club in Chicago hired him to replace the unexpectedly ill white comedian "Professor" Irwin Corey. Gregory's bold, ironic, cool, and detached humor completely disarmed and converted his audience, which included many white southern conventioneers. After this success, his contract with the Playboy Club was quickly extended from several weeks to three years. Against the backdrop of the intensifying pace of the CIVIL RIGHTS MOVEMENT, Gregory's candid, topical humor signaled a new relationship between African-American comedians and white mainstream audiences. By 1962 he had become a national celebrity and the first black comic superstar in the modern era—opening the doors for countless black comedians. He also became an author, publishing *From the Back of the Bus* (1962) and, with Robert Lipsyte, *Nigger: An Autobiography* (1964).

His celebrity status secured, Gregory emerged as an outspoken political activist during the 1960s. As an avid supporter of the civil rights movement, he participated in voter registration drives throughout the South, marched in countless parades and demonstrations, and was arrested numerous times. He also began to entertain at prisons and for civil rights organizations, using his biting humor as a powerful tool to highlight racism and inequality in the United States. The assassinations of John F. Kennedy, the Rev. Dr. Martin Luther KING, Jr., and others led Gregory to believe in the existence of a large framework of conspiracies to thwart civil rights and liberties in the United States. He took to the lecture circuit, espousing the ideas of Mark Lane, a leading conspiracy theorist.

Gregory found numerous ways to dramatize his chosen causes. He fasted for lengthy periods to demonstrate his commitment to civil rights and to protest the VIETNAM WAR, the abuse of narcotics, and world hunger. In 1967 he campaigned unsuccessfully in a write-in effort to be mayor of Chicago, and in 1968 he was the presidential candidate for the U.S. Freedom and Peace party, a split-off faction within the Peace and Freedom party, whose candidate for president in 1968 was Eldridge CLEAVER. By the late 1960s, Gregory was increasingly devoting his attention to the youth of America, lecturing at hundreds of college campuses each year and making fewer and fewer night club appearances; he released his last comedy album, *Caught in the Act,* in 1973.

During the 1970s, Gregory wrote several books, including *No More Lies: The Myth and Reality of American History* (published as by Richard Claxton Gregory with James R. McGraw, 1971); *Code Name Zorro: The Murder of Martin Luther King, Jr.* (with Mark Lane, 1971); and *Dick Gregory's Political Primer* (1972). After moving with his wife and ten children to a farm in Massachusetts in 1973, he became a well-known advocate of vegetarianism. Often limiting himself to a regimen of fruit and juices, he became a nutritional consultant, often appearing on talk shows in his new role, and wrote (with Alvenia Fulton) *Dick Gregory's Natural Diet for Folks Who Eat, Cookin' with Mother Nature* (1974). He also wrote *Up from Nigger,* with James R. McGraw, the second installment of his autobiography (1976).

Gregory made a decision to place his celebrity status in the service of his fierce and uncompromising commitment to human rights.

In 1984 Gregory founded Health Enterprises, Inc., successfully marketing various weight-loss products. Three years later he introduced the Slim-Safe Bahamian Diet, a powdered diet mix that proved extremely popular, and expanded his financial holdings to hotels and other properties. These economic successes were abruptly reversed after the failure of a financing deal and conflicts with his business partners. Gregory was evicted from his Massachusetts home in 1992. In the same year, he returned to his home town of St. Louis to organize the Campaign for Human Dignity, whose stated purpose was to reclaim predominantly African-American neighborhoods from drug dealers and prostitutes. In October 1993, Gregory was arrested for illegally camping—along with members of his "Dignity Patrol"—in a crime-ridden park in Washington, D.C. In 1993 he also coauthored, with Mark Lane, *Murder in Memphis,* another book about the assassination of Rev. Dr. Martin Luther King, Jr.

After Gregory achieved the pinnacle of success in the world of stand-up comedy, he made a decision to place his celebrity status in the service of his fierce and uncompromising commitment to human rights. Throughout the various shifts and turns of his career for more than three decades, he has kept faith with those commitments.

BIBLIOGRAPHY

Gregory, Dick, with Martin Lipsyte. *Nigger: An Autobiography.* New York, 1964.

Gregory, Dick, with James R. McGraw. *Up from Nigger.* New York, 1976.

Hendra, Tony. *Going Too Far.* New York, 1987.

Watkins, Mel. *On the Real Side: Laughing, Lying and Signifying—The Underground Tradition of African-American Humor That Transformed American Culture from Slavery to Richard Pryor.* New York, 1994.

– JAMES A. MILLER

GRIGGS, SUTTON ELBERT

Sutton Elbert Griggs (1872–1933), novelist and preacher. Born in Chatfield, Tex., Sutton E. Griggs was raised in Dallas, and attended Bishop College in Marshall, Tex. Following the path of his father, the Rev. Allen R. Griggs, he studied for the Baptist ministry at the Richmond Theological Seminary (later part of Virginia Union University) and was ordained in 1893. Griggs's first pastorate was in Berkley, Va., and he went on to serve more than thirty years as a Baptist minister in Nashville and Memphis, Tenn. In addition to his career as a pastor, he soon established himself as an author of novels, political tracts, and religious pamphlets. In the period following Reconstruction, marked by a fierce resurgence of segregation, disfranchisement, and antiblack violence in the South, Griggs—along with such African-American writers as Charles W. CHESNUTT, Paul Laurence DUNBAR, W. E. B. DU BOIS, and Frances Ellen Watkins HARPER—responded with positive portrayals of black Americans and demands for civil rights.

Griggs wrote more than thirty books, most of which he published himself and vigorously promoted during preaching tours of the South, as he describes in *The Story of My Struggles* (1914). His five novels are technically unimpressive, weakened by stilted dialogue, flat characterizations, and sentimental and melodramatic plot lines. Even as flawed polemics, however, they are distinguished by their unprecedented investigation of politically charged themes of African-American life in the South, such as black nationalism, miscegenation, racial violence, and suffrage. Above all else a religious moralist, Griggs was critical of assimilationist projects, calling instead for social equality and black self-sufficiency, but he was equally impatient with radical militancy in the quest for civil rights.

In the period following Reconstruction, marked by a fierce resurgence of segregation, disfranchisement, and antiblack violence, Griggs responded with positive portrayals of black Americans.

His fiction often centers on such ethical concerns. In *Imperium in Imperio* (1899), Griggs's best-known work and one of the first African-American political novels, the integrationist Belton Piedmont chooses to die rather than support a militaristic plot to seize Texas and Louisiana from the United States as a haven for African-Americans. In *Overshadowed* (1901), Astral Herndon, discouraged by the "shadow" of racial prejudice both in the United States and in Africa, chooses exile as a "citizen of the ocean." Dorlan Worthell in *Unfettered* (1902) wins the hand of the beautiful Morlene only by offering a plan for African-American political organization. *The Hindered Hand* (1905) is pessimistic about the possibilities of reforming southern race relations: The Seabright family encounters violent tragedy in striving to "pass" in white society in order to transform white racist opinions, and their one dark-skinned daughter, Tiara, flees to Liberia with her husband, Ensal, who has refused to participate in a "Slavic" conspiracy to destroy the Anglo-Saxons of the United States through germ warfare. While Baug Peppers attempts inconclusively to fight for voting rights for southern blacks before the Supreme Court in *Pointing the Way* (1908), Letitia Gilbreth, who believes that "whitening" the race through assimilation is the only way to effect racial equality, is driven mad when her niece refuses the mulatto Peppers and marries a dark-skinned man.

Similar themes also appear in Griggs's political treatises, most notably *Wisdom's Call* (1909), an eloquent argument for civil rights in the South that comments on lynching, suffrage, and the rights of black women, and *Guide to Racial Greatness; or, The Science of Collective Efficiency* (1923), with a companion volume of biblical verses entitled *Kingdom Builders' Manual* (1924); these together offer a project for the political organization of the African-American southern population, stressing education, religious discipline, employment, and land ownership. At the end of his life, Griggs returned to Texas to assume the position his father had held, the pastorate of the Hopewell Baptist Church in Denison. He soon departed for Houston and, at the time of his death, was attempting to found a national religious and civic institute there.

BIBLIOGRAPHY

Fleming, Robert E. "Sutton E. Griggs: Militant Black Novelist." *Phylon* 34 (March 1973): 73–77.

Gloster, Hugh M. "Sutton E. Griggs: Novelist of the New Negro." *Phylon* 4 (Fourth Quarter 1943): 333–345.

— BRENT EDWARDS

GRIMKÉ, CHARLOTTE L. FORTEN

Charlotte L. Forten Grimké (August 17, 1837–July 22, 1914), abolitionist, teacher, and writer. Charlotte Forten was born into one of Philadelphia's leading African-American families. Her grandfather, James FORTEN, was a well-to-do sail-maker and abolitionist. Her father, Robert Bridges Forten, maintained both the business and the abolitionism.

Charlotte Forten continued her family's traditions. As a teenager, having been sent to Salem, Mass., for her education, she actively joined that community of radical abolitionists identified with William Lloyd Garrison. She also entered enthusiastically into the literary and intellectual life of nearby Boston, and even embarked on a literary career of her own. Some of her earliest poetry was published in antislavery journals during her student years. And she began to keep a diary, published almost a century later, which remains one of the most valuable accounts of that era.

Completing her education, Forten became a teacher, initially in Salem, and later in Philadelphia. Unfortunately, she soon began to suffer from ill health, which would plague her for the rest of her life. Nevertheless, while unable to sustain her efforts in the classroom for any length of time, she did continue to write and to engage in antislavery activity. With the outbreak of the

CIVIL WAR, she put both her convictions and her training to use, joining other abolitionists on the liberated islands off the South Carolina coast to teach and work with the newly emancipated slaves.

On the Sea Islands, she also kept a diary, later published. This second diary, and two essays she wrote at the time for the *Atlantic Monthly,* are among the most vivid accounts of the abolitionist experiment. Like many teachers, Forten felt a cultural distance from the freedpeople but worked with dedication to teach and to prove the value of emancipation. After the war, she continued her work for the freedpeople, accepting a position in Massachusetts with the Freedmen's Union Commission.

She also continued her literary efforts, which included a translation of the French novel *Madame Thérèse,* published by Scribner in 1869. In 1872, after a year spent teaching in South Carolina, Forten moved to Washington, D.C., where she worked first as a teacher and then in the Treasury Department. There she met the Rev. Francis Grimké, thirteen years her junior, and pastor of the elite Fifteenth Street Presbyterian Church. At the end of 1878, they married.

The marriage was long and happy, despite the death in infancy of their only child. Apart from a brief residence in Jacksonville, Fla., from 1885 to 1889, the Grimkés lived in Washington, D.C. and made their Washington home a center for the capital's social and intellectual life. Although Charlotte Grimké continued to suffer from poor health, she maintained something of her former activism, serving briefly as a member of the Washington school board and participating in such organizations as the NATIONAL ASSOCIATION OF COLORED WOMEN. She did a small amount of writing, although little published. Finally, after about 1909, her failing health led to her virtual retirement from active life.

BIBLIOGRAPHY

Charlotte Forten Grimké Papers. In Francis James Grimké Papers, Manuscript Division, Moorland-Spingarn Research Center, Howard University, Washington, D.C.

Cooper, Anna J. *Life and Writings of the Grimké Family.* 2 vols. 1951.

Stevenson, Brenda, ed. *The Journals of Charlotte Forten Grimké.* New York, 1988.

— DICKSON D. BRUCE, JR.

GULLAH

The Gullah are a community of African Americans who have lived along the Atlantic coastal plain and on the Sea Islands off the coast of South Carolina and Georgia since the late seventeenth century. Comprised of the descendants of slaves who lived and worked on the Sea Islands, Gullah communities continue to exist in the late twentieth century, occupying small farming and fishing communities in South Carolina and Georgia. The Gullah are noted for their preservation of African cultural traditions, made possible by the community's geographic isolation and its inhabitants' strong community life. They speak an English-based Creole language also referred to as Gullah, or among Georgia Sea Islanders as Geechee.

The etymology of the term *Gullah* is uncertain. Among the most widely accepted theories is that it is a shortened form of Angola, a region of coastal central Africa (with different boundaries from the contemporary nation-state and former Portuguese colony of the same name). Many of South Carolina's slaves were imported from the older Angola. Equally plausible is the suggestion that the term is a derivation of the West African name *Golas* or *Goulah,* who were a large group of Africans occupying the hinterland of what is present-day Liberia. Large numbers of slaves were brought to South Carolina from both western and central Africa, lending both explanations credibility. The word *Geechee* is believed to have originated from *Gidzi,* the name of the language spoken in the Kissy country of present-day Liberia. Whatever the origins of these terms, it is clear that the Gullah community that developed in the Sea Islands embodied a mixture of influences from the coastal regions of West Africa.

The slave communities of the Sea Islands developed under unique geographic and demographic conditions that permitted them to maintain a degree of cohesion and autonomy denied slave communities in other regions of the South. A geographical shift in the production of rice within the South Carolina low country during the mid-1700s brought a major shift in population. South Carolina's slave population had been concentrated in the parishes surrounding Charleston, but in the 1750s, South Carolina rice planters abandoned the inland swamps for the tidal and river swamps of the coastal mainland. At the same time, new methods in the production of indigo stimulated settlement of the Sea Islands, where long-staple cotton also began to be produced in the late eighteenth century.

As a result, the coastal regions of South Carolina and the adjacent Sea Islands became the center of the plantation economy, and the demand for slave labor soared. Concurrent with this shift in agricultural production was a change in the African origins of the slaves imported into South Carolina. During the last half of the eighteenth century, imports from the Kongo-Angola region declined, and the majority of slaves introduced into the Sea Islands came from the Windward Coast (present-day Sierra Leone, and Senegal, and Gambia) and the Rice Coast (part of present-day Liberia). South Carolina planters apparently preferred slaves from these regions because of the Africans' familiarity with rice and indigo production. These African bondsmen and women brought with them the labor patterns and technical skills they had used in Africa. Their knowledge of rice planting had a major impact in transforming South Carolina's methods of rice production.

The geographic isolation of the Sea Islands and the frequency of disease in the swampy, semitropical climate of the region kept white settlement in the area to a minimum. Meanwhile, a constant, growing demand for slaves and their concentration on tremendous plantations created a black majority in the South Carolina coastal region. In 1770 the population in the South Carolina low country was 78 percent black, and the proportion of blacks along the coast and the Sea Islands probably was even higher.

The relative isolation and numerical strength of the slaves and their freedom from contact with white settlers permitted them to preserve many native African linguistic patterns and cultural traditions. The constant influx of African slaves into the region throughout the remainder of the eighteenth century, likewise permitted the Gullah to maintain a vital link to the customs and traditions of West Africa.

The end of slavery brought significant changes to the Gullahs' traditional way of life, but the unique geographic and demographic conditions on the Sea Islands ensured that the Gullah community would retain its distinctiveness well beyond the CIVIL WAR. Blacks remained a majority in the South Carolina low country. In 1870, the population was 67 percent black; by 1900 it had decreased only marginally.

The Gullahs' experiences during and after the Civil War differed from those of blacks across the South. While the Port Royal Experiment, established on the Sea Islands during the Union's wartime occupation to provide the Gullah with experience in independent farming, was ultimately a failure, many Gullah in the decades following the Civil War nevertheless were able to become independent farmers.

Due to the declining market for the Sea Islands' long-staple cotton, many white landowners began to desert the area shortly after the war's end. Agricultural production in the low country first suffered from war-related devastation of the land; then, in the early 1900s, competition from rice plantations in the western United States further crippled South Carolina's market position. As whites abandoned their former plantations and blacks took over the land, some cotton production for the market continued, but subsistence farming and fishing dominated the Sea Island economy.

Whites' abandonment of the coastal region and the Sea Islands left the Gullah even more isolated than before. While black residents of the Sea Islands during the first half of the twentieth century, like other African Americans across the South, were denied basic civil rights, they benefitted from their geographic isolation and numerical dominance. Unlike blacks in most other regions of the South, the Gullah were able to maintain cohesive, largely independent communities well into the twentieth century.

The distinctiveness of the Gullah community is perhaps best reflected in its language.

Most of what we know of the Gullah comes from studies conducted by anthropologists and linguists in the 1930s and '40s. The Gullah culture described by these observers reflects a blending of various African and American traditions. Gullah handicrafts such as basket weaving and wood carving demonstrate African roots, both in their design and their functionality. Wooden mortars and pestles, rice "fanners," and palm leaf brooms were introduced into the Sea Islands by the Gullah and were used in ways that reflected African customs. The Gullah, for example, used their palm-leaf brooms to maintain grass-free dirt yards—a tradition they still maintain in the late twentieth century. The Gullah diet similarly reflects the African origins of the original Gullah slave community. Based heavily on rice, the Gullah make gumbos and stews similar to West African dishes such as *jollof* and *plasas.*

The distinctiveness of the Gullah community is perhaps best reflected in its language. Gullah, or Geechee, a predominantly oral language, is the offspring of the West African Pidgin English that developed along the African Coast during the peak of the slave trade. Pidgin languages developed in Africa as a merger of the English language and the native languages spoken on the African coast and served as a means of communication among Africans and British slave traders. Many of the slaves from the coastal regions of West Africa that were brought to South Carolina in the eighteenth century were familiar with pidgin language and used it to communicate with one another in the New World. Over time, the pidgin mixed with the language spoken by the South Carolina planter class and took on new form. Gullah, the creole language that developed, became the dominant and native language of the slave community of the Sea Islands. Like most unwritten creole languages, Gullah rapidly evolved, and by the time it was first seriously studied in the 1930s, it undoubtedly had more in common with standard English than antebellum or eighteenth-century Gullah.

The Gullah language derives most of its vocabulary from the English language, but it also incorporates a substantial number of African words, especially from the Krio language of present-day Sierra Leone. The Gullah used names, for example, that reflected personal and historical experiences and that carried specific African meanings. Naming practices of the Gullah served, as they do for West Africans, as symbols of power and control over the outside world. The pronunciation of Gullah and its sentence and grammatical structures, moreover, deviate from the rules of standard English, reflecting instead West African patterns. Gullah is spoken with a Caribbean cadence, reflecting the common African background of the Gullah and West Indian slaves.

Gullah, though less widely spoken in the late twentieth century, remains prevalent throughout the Sea Islands. Lorenzo Dow Turner, the first linguist to study Gullah speech in the 1940s, found a number of African words and phrases being used among the inhabitants of the Sea Islands in the 1940s. In 1993, William A. Stewart, a linguist at the City University of New York, estimated that 250,000 Sea Islanders still spoke Gullah and at least a tenth of this number spoke no other language. Gullah also has had a significant impact upon the language spoken among inhabitants across the southeastern region of the United States. Such Gullah words as *buckra* (a white person), *goober* (peanut), and *juke* (disorderly) can be found in the vocabulary of black and white southerners.

Other aspects of Gullah language observed by Turner and such scholars as Ambrose E. Gonzales and Guy B. Johnson also exhibit African roots. Gullah proverbs demonstrate an adaptation of the African tradition of speaking in parables, and the oral tradition of storytelling among the Gullah also has been identified with African patterns. Trickster tales such as those about Brer Rabbit, which were popularized in the late nineteenth and early twentieth centuries by the white folklorist Joel Chandler Harris, are still part of Gullah and Geechee folklore. These tales, often moral in tone and content, are an important form of entertainment.

Religion played a dominant role within the Gullah slave community and continued to regulate community life into the twentieth century. Church membership predicated membership in the community at large, and one was not considered a member of the plantation community until one had joined the "Praise House." Praise Houses, originally erected by planters in the 1840s as meetinghouses and places of worship for slaves, functioned as town halls among the Gullah well into the late twentieth century, possibly as late as the 1970s. The Praise House essentially took the place of the white-controlled Baptist churches as the slave community's cultural center. Even after blacks assumed control of their churches during and after the war, the Praise House remained the locus of community power.

Everyone in the community was expected to abide by the Praise House customs and regulations, enforced by a Praise House Committee, which held them to certain standards of behavior and trust. This method of defining the borders of the community reinforced the Gullahs' close-knit community structure; some argue that it mirrored West African traditions of establishing secret societies.

This utilization of the Praise House to fit the needs of the Gullah community illustrates the adaptive nature of the Gullah's religious practices. Gullah slaves applied a mixture of African customs and beliefs to Christian principles introduced by their masters to create a religion that served a vital function within their community. The Gullah incorporated certain African religious traditions into their Christian beliefs. While accepting Christianity, for example, they maintained their belief in witchcraft, called *wudu, wanga, joso,* or *juju,* and continued to consult "root doctors" for protection and for their healing powers.

The Gullahs' physical forms of worship also continued to follow West African patterns. Gullah spirituals, both religious and secular in nature, for example, incorporated a West African pattern of call-and-response. In addition to being sung in church and at work, these highly emotional spirituals often were used as accompaniments to the Gullah "ring shout," a syncretic religious custom that combined Africanisms with Christian principles. During the ring shout, onlookers sung, clapped, and gesticulated, while others shuffled their heels in a circle. The performance started slowly but gained speed and intensity as it progressed. The ring shout, which has largely disappeared in the late twentieth century, served as a religious expression linked to natural and supernatural forces. While the trance-like atmosphere of the ring shout is believed to be of West African origin, the practice itself and the way it functioned within the community are Gullah creations.

The strength and endurance of the Gullah community and culture is evident in the cultural traditions of the Seminole Blacks, a group strongly tied to the original Sea Island Gullah community. From the late 1700s to the early nineteenth century, Gullah slaves escaped from the rice plantations and built settlements along the remote, wooded Florida frontier. Over time, these maroon communities joined with other escaped slaves and surrounding Native Americans to form a loosely organized tribe with shared customs, food, and clothing. Along with the Native Americans, the escaped slaves were removed from Florida in the nineteenth century and were resettled on reservations in the West. During the late twentieth century, groups of these Seminole Blacks were found throughout the West, especially in Oklahoma, Texas, and Mexico. Some of these groups, who have retained numerous African customs, continue to speak Afro-Seminole, a creole language descended from Gullah.

While Gullah communities still exist in the Sea Islands of Georgia and South Carolina, they have begun to disintegrate in recent decades. The social cohesion of the community was first threatened in the 1920s when bridges were built between the mainland and the islands. Outmigration from the Sea Islands accelerated during WORLD WAR II as defense spending created new economic opportunities. During the 1950s and '60s, outside influence increased as wealthy developers began buying up land at cheap rates and building resorts on Hilton Head and other islands. While this development opened some job opportunities for black Sea Islanders, the openings tended to be in low-paying, service jobs with little opportunity for advancement.

Many Gullah traditions have largely disappeared, and many community members criticize the now predominantly white public schools for deemphasizing the history and culture of the Gullah people.

One benefit of this development has been to break down the Gullah's isolation and to increase their awareness of trends within the larger African-American community. In the 1940s, Esau Jenkins, a native of Johns Island, led a movement to register voters, set up community centers, and provide legal aid to members of the island's African-American community. In an effort to register black voters, Jenkins, with the help of Septima Clark of Charleston, established the South's first Citizenship School on Johns Island in 1957. Jenkins' efforts helped break down the isolation of black Sea Islanders and involved them more directly in the struggle for civil rights among African Americans across the country.

The modernization of the Sea Islands and the Gullahs' subsequent loss of isolation, however, has caused the community to lose some of its cultural distinctiveness and cohesion. From a predominantly black population on Hilton Head in 1950, whites outnumbered blacks five to one by 1980. Many Gullah traditions, such as the ring shout, have largely disappeared, and many community members criticize the now predominantly white public schools for deemphasizing the history and culture of the Gullah people. In response to the negative impact of these modernizing changes, there have been efforts in recent years to increase public awareness of Gullah traditions and to preserve them.

In 1948, the Penn Center on St. Helena Island, S.C., formerly a school for freed slaves, was converted into a community resource center. It offers programs in academic and cultural enrichment and teaches Gullah to schoolchildren. In 1979, the Summer Institute of Linguistics, a professional society of linguists, and the nondenominational Wycliffe Bible Translators undertook projects on St. Helena Island to translate the Bible into Gullah, to develop a written system for recording Gullah, and to produce teaching aids for use in schools. The project director, Ervin Greene, a Baptist minister on nearby Daufuskie Island, estimated in 1993 that 75 percent of the New Testament already had been translated and that the New Testament would be completed by 1996, the Old Testament within five years of that date. In 1985, Beaufort, S.C., began an annual Gullah Festival to celebrate and bring recognition to the rich Gullah culture.

Increasingly, national attention has been focused on the Sea Islands. In 1989, "In Living Color," a dance-theater piece about Gullah culture on Johns Island, S.C., premiered in New York City at the Triplex Theater. Set in a rural prayer meeting, the piece offers a memoir of life among the Gullah during the late 1980s. *Daughters in the Dust,* a 1992 film about a Gullah family at the turn of the century, perhaps provided greatest national recognition for the Gullah. Written and directed by Julie Dash, whose father was raised in the Sea Islands, the film's dialogue is primarily in Gullah, with occasional English subtitles.

Such projects have helped increase public awareness of the importance of understanding and preserving Gullah traditions, and in 1994 the children's network, Nickelodeon, began work on a new animated series called *Gullah Gullah Island,* which focuses on a black couple who explore the culture of the Sea Islands. Black

Sea Islanders hope that these efforts will bring the necessary national recognition to help protect the Gullah community from further cultural erosion.

BIBLIOGRAPHY

Burden, Bernadette. "A Bible to Call Their Own: Gullah Speakers Put Verses in Native Tongue." *Atlanta Journal and Constitution,* June 11, 1993, p. 6.

Creel, Margaret Washington. *"A Peculiar People": Slave Religion and Community-Culture Among the Gullahs.* New York, 1988.

Crum, Mason. *Gullah: Negro Life in the Carolina Sea Islands,* 1940. Reprint. New York, 1968.

Jacobs, Sally. "The Sea Islands' Vanishing Past." *Boston Globe,* March 24, 1992, p. 61.

Joyner, Charles. *Down by the Riverside: A South Carolina Slave Community.* Urbana, Ill., 1984.

Rose, Willie Lee. *Rehearsal for Reconstruction: The Port Royal Experiment.* New York, 1964.

Turner, Lorenzo D. *Africanisms in the Gullah Dialect.* Ann Arbor, Mich., 1949.

Wood, Peter H. *Black Majority: Negroes in Colonial South Carolina from 1670 Through the Stono Rebellion.* New York, 1974.

— LOUISE P. MAXWELL

H

HAITIAN REVOLUTION

The Haitian Revolution of 1789–1804 began as a political struggle among the free inhabitants of Saint Domingue, a French colony on the island of Hispaniola. The French Revolution of 1789 provided the occasion for class and racial antagonisms to surface in Saint Domingue. Each of the colony's social castes seized the moment to address its grievances. The *grand blancs*—planters and wealthy merchants—sought greater autonomy in managing the colony's economic and political affairs. The French Revolution's declared egalitarianism appealed to the *petit blancs*—lower class whites—as it did to the *gens de couleur*—the mulattoes and free blacks who resented the barriers of legal and social discrimination. While colonial representatives solicited support from various political factions in Paris, the struggle turned violent on the island. The *gens de couleur*, led by Vincent Ogé, attempted an unsuccessful revolt in the spring of 1791. In August, the colony's slave population joined in the struggle and turned the Haitian Revolution into a war for emancipation and national independence.

Saint Domingue's slave population—over 400,000—produced the sugar, coffee, cotton, and indigo that made it the richest colony in the French Empire. Estimates suggest that a third of France's foreign trade in the 1780s came from this one colony. The constant toil in a tropical climate and the brutality of the slaveowners made conditions for the slaves among the worst in the Western Hemisphere. The slave insurrection of August 1791 began with attacks against several plantations. Among the leaders in the initial uprising, the most prominent was a Jamaican fugitive and voodoo priest, John Boukman. Voodoo practices, widespread among the slaves, provided a means for defining leadership, organizing, and communicating among the insurgents. Within a few months the insurrection had engulfed the entire colony. The Haitian Revolution primarily divided the inhabitants along racial lines, but political and military exigencies led to shifting alliances that at times pitted free blacks against insurgent slaves and poor whites against wealthy planters.

The success of the slave insurrection was due in large part to the leadership of Toussaint Louverture (c. 1744–1803). Although born a slave, he benefited from paternalistic owners. He acquired a rudimentary education and assumed steward's responsibilities on the plantation. Toussaint joined the slave insurrection of August 1791 as an aide to one of the insurgent commanders. At first Toussaint was recognized for his skills as an herbalist and healer, but he quickly established his reputation as a military organizer and battlefield tactician. He molded the black insurgents into a military force capable of challenging the best troops of Europe. Through the 1790s, he successfully opposed the armies of England, Spain, and France as they intervened in the colony's revolution.

Toussaint's efforts to rid the island of slavery were inexorably bound to European imperial rivalries and the politics of the French Revolution. Toussaint initially sided with the Spanish in Santo Domingo, but he went over to the French side when the National Convention in Paris, controlled by the Jacobin faction, abolished slavery in February 1794. French colonial authorities rewarded their new ally by making him lieutenant governor and allowing him to expand his army to 20,000. In May 1797, Toussaint became governor general of Saint Domingue. That same year, he thwarted a British invasion and two years later, in a rare outburst of vindictiveness, he brutally suppressed the mulatto opposition led by André Rigaud. In 1801, Toussaint invaded Santo Domingo, and with this quick, relatively bloodless campaign, he brought the entire island of Hispaniola under his control.

Toussaint's regime was tainted by authoritarian tendencies and corruption in the military. Nor did former slaves find relief from oppression; despite the benefits of emancipation and progressive labor reforms, they remained tied to the plantation through long-term contracts, vagrancy laws, and government oversight. Under the Constitution of 1801, Toussaint ruled as governor-general for life, but Saint Domingue remained a French colony. Toussaint apparently believed that total independence from France was untenable without the support of Britain or the United States, and he also hoped that French planters and professionals would remain on the island. He was one of the few leaders who seemed insulated from the intense hatreds generated by decades of slavery and oppression, and a brutal ten-year race war. His rule held out genuine prospects for racial reconciliation among former slaves, mulattoes, and whites.

In his tireless work habits, administrative skills, and military genius, Toussaint mirrored his contemporary and adversary, Napoleon Bonaparte. The army of 40,000 sent by Napoleon to reestablish slavery and direct French control over the island forced Toussaint's capitulation in May 1802. He retired to his plantation, but French authorities, perceiving him as a lingering threat, had him arrested and deported. He spent his last months confined in a prison near the French-Swiss border.

Following Toussaint's deportation, Jean-Jacques Dessalines (1758–1806) gained overall command of the insurgent army. Charismatic and militarily astute, Dessalines had been one of Toussaint's most loyal and capable military commanders. He harassed the French forces while tropical diseases decimated their ranks. The heavy losses forced the French to withdraw, and Dessalines inaugurated the independent republic in January 1804. The new nation adopted the indigenous Arawak name for the island, Haiti. By the new constitution Dessalines held the position of governor-general, but in September he assumed the title Emperor Jacques I. His intense hatred of the French and fear of a pro-French sentiment in Haiti led him to carry out a systematic extermination of the remaining white inhabitants. The massacre was the final chapter in a vicious race war that at times seemed genocidal. Dessalines had little education or understanding of government administration. His regime, authoritarian and built on personal loyalties and family ties, provided a troubling precedent for Haitian political life. Dessalines's rule ended abruptly in 1806, when he was assassinated near Port-au-Prince by several military leaders opposed to his dictatorship.

Southern slaveholders, ever haunted by the specter of slave revolt, saw this apparition materialize in Haiti.

Haitian-American relations in the early 1800s were tied closely to U.S. relations with the European powers and territorial expansion on the North American continent. American designs on the Louisiana Territory and the Floridas meant conceding at times to French, English, and Spanish concerns in the Caribbean. Ironically Napoleon's failure to reestablish slavery in Haiti opened the way for the total withdrawal of French interests in North America and the sale of the Louisiana Territory in 1803. Pressure to improve relations with Haiti came from New England merchants who had developed a lucrative trade with the former French colony. But southern slaveholders generally carried the debate on Haitian-American relations in the antebellum period. Southern congressmen were particularly appalled by the prospect of a Haitian diplomatic presence in Washington, D.C., and blocked initiatives to normalize relations with the new nation. In the end, the United States refused to recognize the Haitian government, despite compelling economic and diplomatic considerations, until 1862.

Americans discovered in the Haitian Revolution their deepest fears and aspirations. Southern slaveholders, ever haunted by the specter of slave revolt, saw this apparition materialize in Haiti. The "horror stories" from white colonial refugees, graphically detailed in the southern press, fueled obsessive fears of a bloody race war. During the 1790s, southern states increased slave patrols, restricted importation of slaves from Hispaniola, and readily attributed any sign of slave discontent to the insidious influence of Haitian agents. Even those Southerners troubled by the existence of slavery harbored greater anxieties about a large, free black population in the South. The Haitian Revolution penetrated deep into southern consciousness, hardening proslavery convictions and stifling sentiment for gradual emancipation. The memory of the Haitian revolution was heightened by the emigration of thousands of refugees—slaves, free blacks, and whites—to the United States, especially to Louisiana.

Proslavery apologists saw in the Haitian Revolution the triumph of barbarism over civilization. Through the antebellum period, they pointed to Haiti's economic and political failures to foster the theory that slavery was a positive good. The results of the Haitian Revolution, they insisted, demonstrated that African slaves were a dependent people, unfit for freedom. Abolitionists countered these proslavery myths by arguing that the Haitian Revolution was the inevitable result of slavery. Most white abolitionists carefully avoided any endorsement of slave violence, but they suggested that the revolution's brutality and terror were a natural consequence of a brutal and oppressive institution. Moreover, they considered any progress in Haiti remarkable given the island's uneducated and politically inexperienced population.

African Americans were even more forthright in celebrating the Haitian Revolution. The "second republic" in the Western Hemisphere provided an unprecedented example of black political achievement. African-American writers and speakers frequently invoked the Haitian Revolution and its leaders to generate a sense of racial pride and accomplishment. The Haitian Revolution was a landmark in the history of black nationality. Many African Americans, despairing of any hope for racial progress in the United States, looked to Haiti as a place to create a viable black nation. The Haitian government supported several initiatives beginning in the 1820s to encourage African-American settlement. Several thousand immigrants accepted the invitation. J. Theodore Holly, an Episcopal priest, was foremost among the advocates of Haitian immigration. On the eve of the Civil War, he helped revive interest in Haiti and founded an African-American colony on the island. Most of the surviving immigrants eventually returned from the island disillusioned by their experience. The Civil War diverted the attention of African Americans from Haiti, but despite its diminished appeal as an African homeland, Haiti has remained an influential source of black political life and culture.

BIBLIOGRAPHY

Fick, Carolyn E. *The Making of Haiti: The Revolution from Below.* Knoxville, Tenn., 1990.

Hunt, Alfred N. *Haiti's Influence on Antebellum America.* Baton Rouge, La., 1988.

James, C. L. R. *The Black Jacobins: Toussaint L'Ouverture and the San Domingo Revolution.* 1938. Reprint. New York, 1963.

Jordan, Winthrop. *White Over Black.* Chapel Hill, N.C., 1968.

Miller, Floyd J. *The Search for a Black Nationality.* Urbana, Ill., 1975.

Ott, Thomas O. *The Haitian Revolution, 1789–1804.* Knoxville, Tenn., 1973.

Robinson, Donald R. *Slavery and the Structure of American Politics, 1765–1820.* New York, 1971.

– MICHAEL F. HEMBREE

HAMER, FANNIE LOU

Fannie Lou Hamer (Townsend, Fannie Lou) (October 6, 1917–March 14, 1977), civil rights activist. Fannie Lou Townsend was born to Ella Bramlett and James Lee Townsend in Montgomery County, Miss., in 1917. Her parents were sharecroppers, and the family moved to Sunflower County, Miss., when she was two. Forced to spend most of her childhood and teenage years toiling in cotton fields for white landowners, Townsend was able to complete only six years of schooling. Despite wrenching rural poverty and the harsh economic conditions of the Mississippi Delta, she maintained an enduring optimism. She learned the value of self-respect and outspokenness through her close relationship with her mother. In 1944, she married Perry Hamer, moved with him to Ruleville, and worked as a sharecropper on a plantation owned by W. D. Marlowe.

During her years on the Marlowe plantation, Hamer rose to the position of time- and record-keeper. In this position she acquired a reputation for a sense of fairness and a willingness to speak to the landowner on behalf of aggrieved sharecroppers. She began to take steps to directly challenge the racial and economic inequality

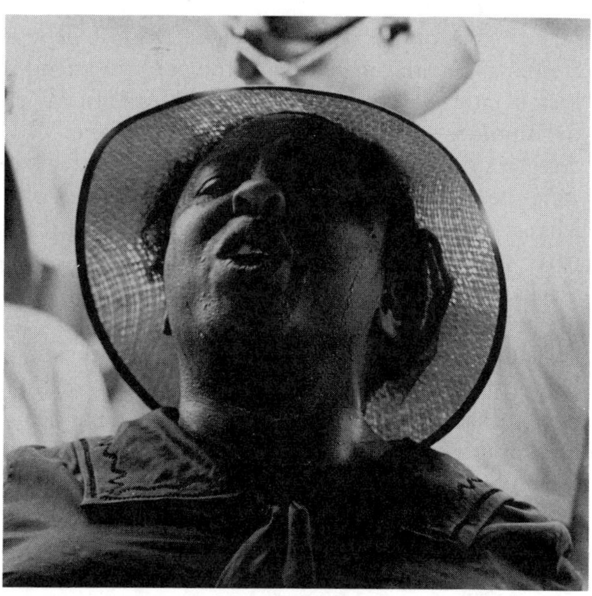

Fannie Lou Hamer singing at a gathering at Enid Dam Campsite, Miss., on June 12, 1966, during the march to Jackson, Miss., in the wake of the attack on James Meredith. (© Charmian Reading)

that had so circumscribed her life after meeting civil rights workers from the Student Nonviolent Coordinating Committee (SNCC) in 1962. In Mississippi, SNCC was mounting a massive voter registration and desegregation campaign aimed at empowering African Americans to change their own lives.

Inspired by the organization's commitment to challenging the racial status quo, Hamer and seventeen other black volunteers attempted to register to vote in Indianola, Miss., on August 31, 1962, but were unable to pass the necessary literacy test, which was designed to prevent blacks from voting. As a result of this action, she and her family were dismissed from the plantation, she was threatened with physical harm by Ruleville whites, and she was constantly harassed by local police. Eventually, she was forced to flee Ruleville and spent three months in Tallahatchie County, Miss., before returning in December.

In January 1963 Hamer passed the literacy test and became a registered voter. Despite the persistent hostility of local whites, she continued her commitment to civil rights activities and became a SNCC field secretary. By 1964, Hamer had fully immersed herself in a wide range of local civil rights activities, including SNCC-sponsored voter registration campaigns, and clothing- and food-distribution drives. At that time she was a central organizer and vice-chairperson of the Mississippi Freedom Democratic Party (MFDP), a parallel political party formed under the auspices of SNCC in response to black exclusion from the state Democratic Party.

Hamer was one of the sixty-eight MFDP delegates elected at a state convention of the party to attend the Democratic National Convention in Atlantic City in the summer of 1964. At the convention the MFDP delegates demanded to be seated and argued that they were the only legitimate political representatives of the Mississippi Democratic Party because unlike the regular party which formed and operated at the exclusion of blacks, their party was open to all Mississippians of voting age.

Hamer's televised testimony to the convention on behalf of the MFDP propelled her into the national spotlight. A national audience watched as she described the economic reprisals that faced African Americans who attempted to register to vote and recounted the beating that she and five other activists had received in June 1963 in a Winona County, Miss., jail. Hamer's proud and unwavering commitment to American democracy and equality inspired hundreds of Americans to send telegrams supporting the MFDP's challenge to the southern political status quo. Although the MFDP delegates were not seated by the convention, Hamer and the party succeeded in mobilizing a massive black voter turnout and publicizing the racist exclusionary tactics of the state Democratic Party.

By the mid-sixties, SNCC had become ideologically divided and Hamer's ties to the organization became more tenuous. However, she continued to focus her political work on black political empowerment and community development. Under her leadership, the MFDP continued to challenge the all-white state Democratic party. In 1964 Hamer unsuccessfully ran for Congress on the MFDP ticket, and one year later spearheaded an intense lobbying effort to challenge the seating of Mississippi's five congressmen in the House of Representatives. She played an integral role in bringing the Head Start Program for children to Ruleville, and organized the Freedom Farm Cooperative for displaced agricultural workers. In 1969 she founded the Freedom Farm Corporation in Sunflower, a cooperative farming and landowning venture to help poor blacks become more self-sufficient. It fed well over 5,000 families before collapsing in 1974. Three years later, after over a decade of activism, she died from breast cancer and heart disease.

Fannie Lou Hamer was a symbol of defiance and indomitable black womanhood that inspired many in the civil rights movement. Morehouse College and Howard University, among others, have honored her devotion to African-American civil rights with honorary doctoral degrees. Her words "I'm sick and tired of being sick and tired" bear testament to her lifelong struggle to challenge racial injustice and economic exploitation.

BIBLIOGRAPHY

Crawford, Vicki L., Jacqueline Anne Rouse, and Barbara Woods. *Women in the* CIVIL RIGHTS MOVEMENT. New York, 1990.

Hamer, Fannie Lou. *To Praise My Bridges: An Autobiography.* Jackson, Miss., 1967.

Jordan, June. *Fannie Lou Hamer.* New York, 1972.

Kling, Susan. *Fannie Lou Hamer.* Chicago, 1979.

– CHANA KAI LEE

HAMMON, JUPITER

Jupiter Hammon (1711–c. 1806), poet, preacher. Jupiter Hammon was born on Long Island, N.Y., and raised in slavery to the Lloyd family. Little is known about his personal circumstances; scholars speculate that he attended school and was permitted access to his master's library. He is known to have purchased a Bible from his master in 1773. A favored slave in the Lloyd household, he worked as a servant, farmhand, and artisan. In early 1761, Hammon published the first poem by a black person to appear in British North America, titled "An Evening Thought. Salvation by Christ with Penitential Cries: Composed by Jupiter Hammon, a Negro belonging to Mr. Lloyd of Queen's Village, on Long Island, the 25th of December, 1760." When British troops invaded Long Island, Hammon fled with the Lloyd family to Hartford, where he remained for the

Even as Hammon urged African Americans to "obey our masters," he questioned whether slavery was "right, and lawful, in the sight of God."

duration of the Revolutionary War. His second extant poem, "An Address to Miss Phillis Wheatly [sic], Ethiopian Poetess, in Boston, who came from Africa at eight years of age, and soon became acquainted with the gospel of Jesus Christ," was published there in 1778. In 1779, a work called *An Essay on Ten Virgins* was advertised, but no copy of it remains. Hammon's sermon, *A Winter Piece: Being a Serious Exhortation, with a Call to the Unconverted; and a Short Contemplation on the Death of Jesus Christ,* to which is appended the seventeen-quatrain verse, "A Poem for Children, with Thoughts on Death," appeared in Hartford in 1782. Hammon returned to Oyster Bay, Long Island, later that year, and a second prose work, *An Evening's Improvement, Shewing the Necessity of Beholding the Lamb of God,* which concludes with "A Dialogue, Entitled, the Kind Master and the Dutiful Servant," was published in 1786. Hammon spoke to members of the African Society in New

York on September 24, 1786. The text of that speech, *An Address to the Negroes of the State of New York,* was printed in New York early in 1787.

Hammon's poems follow a strict, mechanical rhyme scheme and meter, and, like his sermons, exhort the reader to seek salvation by obeying the will of God. He appears to have extended this notion of Christian piety to his domestic situation, and refused to speak out in public against slavery. However, even as he urged African Americans to "obey our masters," he questioned whether slavery was "right, and lawful, in the sight of God." "I do not wish to be free," he said at age seventy-five, "yet I should be glad, if others, especially the young negroes were to be free." The exact date of his death, and the place of his burial, are not known.

BIBLIOGRAPHY

Kaplan, Sidney. *The Black Presence in the Era of the American Revolution 1770–1800.* Greenwich, Conn., 1973.

– QUANDRA PRETTYMAN

HAMPTON, LIONEL LEO

Lionel Leo Hampton (April 12, 1908–) jazz vibraphonist, bandleader. Lionel Hampton was born in Louisville, Ky., and raised in Birmingham, Ala., and then in Chicago. Most sources list his birth year as 1909; his autobiography, however, states that he was born in 1908. Hampton introduced the vibraphone to jazz and is widely regarded as a virtuoso performer. Like many jazz musicians, he received his first musical experiences in the black church, learning to play drums in his grandmother's Birmingham Holiness congregation. He received his first formal lessons on percussion while in elementary school. Hampton later joined the Chicago Defender Youth Band, directed by Major N. Clark Smith, an influential educator who nurtured many famous jazz musicians, among them Milt Hinton and Nat "King" COLE. By his second year of high school, Hampton was playing drums regularly with local musicians, including Les Hite and Detroit Shannon.

In the mid-1920s, Hampton moved to Culver City, Calif., where he joined Reb's Legion Club Forty-Fives and made some of his first recordings. On the West Coast he met Gladys Riddle, who later became his wife and business partner until her death in 1971. In 1930 he began a series of recordings with Louis ARMSTRONG and His Sebastian's Cotton Club Orchestra, his first recordings on vibraphone. During this time, he also made appearances in movies with Les Hite (the Columbia film *Depths Below*) and Louis Armstrong (*Pennies from Heaven*).

In the mid-1930s, Hampton formed his own group and worked regularly along the West Coast. In 1936, he joined Benny Goodman's Quartet, which included Teddy Wilson, Gene Krupa, and later guitarist Charlie Christian. The series of Goodman engagements (such as the famous 1938 Carnegie Hall concert) and recordings catapulted him to stardom as jazz's most influential vibraphonist. Through Hampton's performances, the vibraphone became a jazz instrument of recognition. During this same period, he also continued to record as the leader of his own sessions until leaving Goodman in 1940. Hampton performed and recorded continuously with great commercial success for the next forty-five years in the United States and abroad with various groups, one of the jazz world's most popular and highly regarded musicians.

Throughout his long career, Hampton recognized and nurtured young talent. A partial list of musicians who have played in his groups over the years reads like a Who's Who of jazz history: Howard McGhee, Dexter Gordon, Fletcher Henderson, Oscar Peterson, Ben Webster, Coleman HAWKINS, Johnny Griffin, Quincy JONES, Benny Carter, Dinah Washington, Betty Carter, Nat "King" Cole, and Joe Williams, among others. Hampton is perhaps best known for his showy, energetic stage presence and his hard-driving swing style, which can be heard in such compositions as "Flying Home," "Stompology," and "Down Home Stomp." Over the years, he joined Goodman and Wilson for reunion concerts and remained actively engaged in philanthropic and civic activities.

BIBLIOGRAPHY

Hampton, Lionel, with James Haskins. *Hamp: An Autobiography.* New York, 1989.

– GUTHRIE P. RAMSEY, JR.

HAMPTON INSTITUTE

In 1868 in Hampton, Va., Samuel Chapman Armstrong founded Hampton Normal and Agricultural Institute as a nondenominational and coeducational school where young African Americans were to be trained as teachers. Armstrong, a white man, was convinced that most freedmen's schools were failures because they did not address blacks' most pressing needs. He believed that the experience of slavery had caused African Americans to degenerate into a morally deficient caste, and he accepted the stereotypical image of the freedman as poor, lazy, insolent, and lawless. To succeed, he argued, educators had to respond to these harsh realities by developing an entirely new approach to education for blacks. In addition to offering academic instruction, schools had to contribute to their pupils' moral development and had to help them attain material prosperity. Armstrong intended Hampton to be a model school, where generations of black teachers would be indoctrinated with his ideas.

Because Armstrong believed that blacks would continue to serve as the South's laboring class in the foreseeable future, Hampton Institute became the first school for African Americans to adopt a comprehensive system of industrial education. All students were required to labor in the school's farms and trade shops for two full days each week. The stated goal of this manual-education program was not to train skilled craftsmen but to develop "character" and to foster a spirit of self-reliance among the students. Hampton's white teachers reported that the work system helped their pupils to appreciate the dignity of labor and to understand that prosperity could be gained only through hard work.

Students' academic pursuits were closely coordinated with their work in the shops and fields. Hampton's supporters argued that "book learning" was useful to most African Americans only to the extent to which it could make them more productive and prosperous workers. Therefore, the institute's teachers emphasized only the development of "practical" skills like writing, botany, and simple arithmetic. As a result, by the time students completed the three-year normal program, they had received educations equivalent only to grammar-school programs in the North.

To supplement the institute's academic and industrial work, Armstrong developed a system of social instruction designed to "civilize" the students. Since Hampton was primarily a boarding school, its teachers could control their students' behavior every hour of the day. In their dormitories, students received instruction in Christian morality, personal hygiene, housekeeping, and etiquette. Above all, they learned to emulate the behavior and seek the respect of their white neighbors.

The influence of Armstrong's educational philosophy, known as the Hampton Idea, soon spread throughout the South as Booker T. WASHINGTON and hundreds of other graduates applied the lessons they had learned at the institute to their own schools. Substantial financial support from whites in the North enabled Hampton and its imitators to grow rapidly. Many whites found Hampton's pragmatic approach, with its emphasis on manual labor and self-help rather than social and political activism, enormously appealing. The institute offered the hope that the nation's "race problem" could be solved without disrupting the socioeconomic status quo. The General Education Board and other philanthropic foundations used their financial influence to guide Hampton's growth along even more conservative directions, and to encourage other schools to adopt similar curriculums. Their support helped the institute to develop into one of America's largest and wealthiest black schools, and guaranteed that the Hampton Idea would become ascendant in the field of African-American education by the start of the twentieth century.

Hampton Institute has always been criticized by African Americans who believed that it served only to perpetuate their socioeconomic subordination. The school appeared to be training its students to fill precisely the same roles that blacks held under slavery. As the Hampton Idea gained widespread support among whites, it seemed increasingly likely that industrial education would soon be the only form of schooling available to blacks. As a result, criticism of the institute grew sharper, especially among black intellectuals.

In 1903 W. E. B. DU BOIS published his first major attack on industrial education, and was soon recognized as the leading critic of the Hampton Idea. While Du Bois and other critics conceded that many African Americans could benefit from "practical" education, they felt that blacks also needed access to higher education in order to progress. They urged the institute to place greater emphasis on academics and to encourage its students to aspire to something more than life as manual laborers. They complained that in its pursuit of material prosperity and white approval, Hampton too often sacrificed black dignity.

These criticisms had little direct impact on the institute's curriculum until the 1920s. After World War I, many states embarked on crusades of educational reform, and began to demand that teachers be better educated. Increasing numbers of Hampton's graduates failed to meet these higher standards. Institute officials first attempted to solve the problem by making only slight modifications to the academic program; eventually, however, they were forced to raise their admissions standards and to offer college-level courses. By 1927, over 40 percent of Hampton students were enrolled in the collegiate program. These students, who were more sympathetic to Du Bois's arguments than their predecessors had been, became increasingly critical of their school.

In 1927, a protest over a relatively minor social issue quickly grew into a general strike. Student leaders demanded that the institute raise the quality of its teaching, abolish key elements of the industrial system, hire more African Americans, and grant students an expanded role in administration. The strike was quickly crushed, but Hampton officials had no alternative but to respond to the students' demands. In 1929, the institute declared that it would no longer accept students who had not already completed high school. The following year, to emphasize its shift from Armstrong's industrial model to a more traditional program of higher education, the school formally changed its name from Hampton Normal and Agricultural Institute to Hampton Institute. In 1984, the school—having developed into a prominent liberal-arts and teachers' college with over four thousand students—changed its name to Hampton University.

BIBLIOGRAPHY

Anderson, James D. *The Education of Blacks in the South, 1860–1935.* Chapel Hill, N.C., 1988.

Peabody, Francis G. *Education for Life: The Story of Hampton Institute.* Garden City, N.Y., 1919.

– GREGORY J. MURPHY

HANDY, WILLIAM CHRISTOPHER "W. C."

William Christopher "W. C." Handy (November 16, 1873–March 28, 1958), anthologist and composer. While a child in his native Alabama, W. C. Handy studied music in school; in his teens, he joined a traveling minstrel show as a cornetist. After returning to finish his basic schooling, Handy embarked on a varied career as a teacher, factory worker, college bandmaster, dance-orchestra leader, and minstrel musician. He eventually settled in Memphis in 1908, where he cofounded a music-publishing company with Harry Pace.

After moving to New York in 1918, the Pace and Handy Music Company became the leading publisher of music by African Americans. In 1920, the two owners discontinued their partnership and started separate enterprises, Pace his Black Swan Records, and Handy his Handy Brothers, Inc., and short-lived Handy Record Company. In addition, Handy served variously as a musical consultant, concert program producer, and booking agent. Meanwhile, he continued playing trumpet, composing, arranging, touring, and recording. During his life as a performer, Handy played with such popular groups as W. A. Mahara's minstrels, with Jelly Roll MORTON and with other jazz and popular-music luminaries. He appeared at theaters, dance halls, and concert venues as an instrumentalist and as a bandleader.

Handy's first published blues, "Memphis Blues," in 1912, started a fad; by 1914 he had published the song for which he is best known, "St. Louis Blues." Later he published "Beale Street Blues," making a third Handy "standard" in America's published blues canon. A consensus among jazz historians is that some compositions popularly attributed to Handy are derivative. Some esteem him more highly as a collector, publisher, and popularizer than as a creator of blues. His transcribing and arranging of blues and spirituals led to his books *Blues: An Anthology* (1926; reprinted as *Treasury of the Blues,* 1930), and *Book of Negro Spirituals* (1938).

Handy was a pioneer in bringing folk blues to the public. This led to his being called "the Father of the Blues," which was later used as the title of his autobiography. In 1928, Handy organized a concert at Carnegie Hall to present black music from plantation songs to concert compositions. During the 1930s he organized other concerts of black music for the Chicago World's Fair, the New York World's Fair, and the Golden Gate Exposition in San Francisco.

Handy's productivity declined after he was accidentally blinded in 1943. He died in New York in 1958 of bronchial pneumonia, having suffered an impairing stroke several years earlier. He was honored and memorialized by, among other things, all-Handy musical programs; a movie, *St. Louis Blues;* a 1957 birthday party attended by over eight hundred persons; W. C. Handy Park in Memphis; a postage stamp; and names of institutions and places, including a housing development in his hometown of Florence, Ala.

BIBLIOGRAPHY

Handy, W. C. *Father of the Blues: An Autobiography.* New York, 1941.

Kay. G. W. "William Christopher Handy: Father of the Blues." *Jazz Journal* 24, no. 3 (1971): 10.

Southern, Eileen. *The Music of Black Americans: A History.* 2nd ed. New York, 1983.

– THEODORE R. HUDSON

HANSBERRY, LORRAINE

Lorraine Hansberry (May 19, 1930–January 12, 1965), playwright. Lorraine Hansberry was the youngest child of a nationally prominent African-American family. Houseguests during her childhood included Paul Robeson and Duke Ellington. Hansberry became interested in theater while in high school, and in 1948 she went on to study drama and stage design at the University of Wisconsin. Instead of completing her degree, however, she moved to New York, worked at odd jobs, and wrote. In 1959 her first play, *A Raisin in the Sun,* was produced and was both a critical and commercial success. It broke the record for longest-running play by a black author and won the New York Drama Critics Circle Award. Hansberry was the first African American and the youngest person ever to win that award. The play, based on an incident in the author's own life, tells the story of a black family that attempts to move into a white neighborhood in Chicago. Critics praised Hansberry's ability to deal with a racial issue and at the same time explore the American dream of freedom and the search for a better life. The play was turned into a film in 1961, and then was adapted as a musical, *Raisin,* which won a Tony Award in 1974.

Hansberry's second play, *The Sign in Sidney Brustein's Window,* focuses on white intellectual political involvement. Less successful than *A Raisin in the Sun,* it closed after a brief run at the time of Hansberry's death from cancer in 1965. After her death, Hansberry's former husband, Robert B. Nemiroff, whom she had married in 1953, edited her writings and plays, and produced two volumes: *To Be Young, Gifted and Black* (1969) and *Les Blancs: The Collected Last Plays of Lorraine Hansberry* (1972). *To Be Young, Gifted and Black* was presented as a play and became the longest-running Off-Broadway play of the 1968–1969 season.

BIBLIOGRAPHY

Metzger, Linda, ed. *Black Writers: A Selection of Sketches from Contemporary Authors.* Detroit, 1989.

– LILY PHILLIPS

HARLEM, NEW YORK

Roughly bounded by 110th Street and running north to 155th Street, bordered on the west by Morningside Drive and St. Nicholas Avenue and on the east by the East River, Harlem during the twentieth century became the most famous African-American community in the United States. Prior to 1900, Harlem had been primarily a white neighborhood. In the 1870s it evolved from an isolated, impoverished village in the northern reaches of Manhattan into a wealthy residential suburb with the growth of commuter rail service.

With the opening of the Lenox Avenue subway line in the early years of the twentieth century, a flurry of real estate speculation contributed to a substantial increase in building. At the time the population of Harlem was largely English and German, with increasing numbers of Jewish immigrants. By 1904, however, the economic prosperity and expansion ceased as a result of high rental costs and excessive construction. In that same year, Phillip A. Payton, Jr., a black realtor, founded the Afro-American Realty Company with the intention of leasing vacant white-owned buildings and then renting them to African Americans. Although the Realty Company survived for only four years, due to Payton's unwise financial investments, it played a pivotal role in opening up the Harlem community to African Americans.

Coupled with this development, black migration from the South during the early years of the new century dramatically altered Harlem's composition, until by 1930 it had become a largely all-black enclave. In 1890 there were approximately 25,000 African Americans in Manhattan. By 1910 that number had more than tripled to 90,000. In the following decade the black population increased to approximately 150,000 and more than doubled by 1930 to over 325,000. In Harlem itself the black population rose from approximately 50,000 in 1914 to about 80,000 in 1920 to about 200,000 by 1930.

From a social perspective, Harlem was labeled a "city within a city," because it contained the normal gamut of classes, businesses, and cultural and recreational institutions traditionally identified with urban living. By the 1920s, moreover, Harlem's place in American intellectual and political history had progressed significantly. This transition was fueled on the cultural scene by the literary and artistic activity which is collectively called the HARLEM RENAISSANCE. Emerging after the promise of racial equality and egalitarianism in return for black military service in WORLD WAR I had been squelched by renewed racism and a series of race riots during the Red Summer of 1919, the Renaissance reflected the evolution of a "New Negro" spirit and determination. As one of its acknowledged leaders, Alain LOCKE, explained, self-respect and self-dependence became characteristics of the NEW NEGRO movement, which were exemplified in every facet of cultural, intellectual, and political life.

Harlem during the twentieth century became the most famous African-American community in the United States.

Represented by poets such as Claude MCKAY, Langston HUGHES, and Countee CULLEN; novelists like Zora Neale HURSTON, Jean TOOMER, and Jessie FAUSET; artists like Aaron DOUGLAS; photographers like James VANDERZEE; and social scientists and philosophers like E. Franklin FRAZIER, Alain Locke, and W. E. B. DU BOIS, the Renaissance was national in scope, but it came to be identified with the emerging African-American cultural capital, Harlem. The outpouring of literary and artistic production that comprised the Renaissance led as well to a number of social gatherings at which the black intelligentsia mingled and exchanged ideas. Many of the most celebrated of these events were held at the home of A'Lelia Walker Robinson, daughter of Madame C. J. WALKER, who had moved the base of her multimillion-dollar beauty care industry to Harlem in 1913.

Also fostering Harlem's growth in the 1920s were a series of political developments. Both the NATIONAL ASSOCIATION FOR THE ADVANCEMENT OF COLORED PEOPLE (NAACP) and the NATIONAL URBAN LEAGUE established offices in the area. Moreover, by 1920 two major New York black newspapers, *The New York Age* and *The New York Amsterdam News,* moved their printing operations and editorial offices to Harlem. Socialists A. Philip Randolph and Chandler Owen established their offices in Harlem as well and from there they edited and published their newspaper, the *Messenger,* after 1917. Nothing, however, caught the attention of Harlemites as quickly as the arrival in 1916 of Marcus GARVEY, who established the headquarters of the UNIVERSAL NEGRO IMPROVEMENT ASSOCIATION (UNIA) in the district. Garvey's emphasis on race pride, the creation of black businesses and factories, and his appeal to the masses awakened and galvanized the Harlem community.

By 1915, in fact, Harlem had become the entertainment capital of black America. Performers gravitated to Harlem and New York City's entertainment industry. Musicians such as Willie "The Lion" Smith, Fats Waller, and James P. JOHNSON created a version of early JAZZ piano known as the Harlem Stride around the time of World War I. After 1920, bandleaders such as Fletcher Henderson, Duke ELLINGTON, and Chick Webb laid the foundation for big-band jazz. (Early in the 1940s, at clubs such as Minton's Playhouse and Monroe's, a revolution would occur in jazz. Individuals such as Thelonious MONK, Charlie PARKER, and Dizzy GILLESPIE moved away from swing, using advanced harmonies and substitute chords, creating be-bop jazz.)

Harlem also became a major center of popular dance. On the stage, Florence Mills was perhaps Harlem's most popular theatrical dancer in the 1920s; 150,000 people turned out for her funeral in 1927. TAP DANCE flourished in Harlem as well. The roster of well-known performers included the Whitman Sisters, Buck and Bubbles, the NICHOLAS BROTHERS, Earl "Snake Hips" Tucker, and Bill "Bojangles" ROBINSON, who carried the honorary title of "The Mayor of Harlem."

Theatrical life was also vibrant in Harlem. From the early years of the century through the Great Depression, the center of popular entertainment in Harlem was the Lincoln Theatre on 135th Street off Lenox Avenue. After 1934, the Lincoln was superseded by the Apollo Theater. Harlem attracted vaudevillians such as Bert Williams, George W. Walker, Flournoy Miller, and Aubrey Lyles, and a later generation of comedians including Dewey "Pigmeat" Markham and Dusty Fletcher, who popularized the "Open the Door, Richard" routine.

After 1917, the Lafayette Theater grew in prominence as a home of serious drama, due to the success of such actors as Paul ROBESON, Richard B. Harrison (famous for his role as "De Lawd" in *Green Pastures*), and Abbie Mitchell. Harlem was also a center of nightclubs. The best known included the black-owned Smalls Paradise, the COTTON CLUB, and the mobster-connected and racially exclusive Connie's Inn. The best-known dance hall was the Savoy Ballroom, the "Home of Happy Feet," which presented the best in big-band jazz after 1926. Harlem's cultural vitality was celebrated in plays including Wallace Thurman's *Harlem* (1929), Langston Hughes's *Mulatto* (1935), *Little Ham* (1935), and *Don't You Want to be Free?* (1936–1937), and Abram Hill's *On Strivers' Row* (1939). Musical performers celebrated Harlem's social scene through such compositions as "The Joint is Jumping," "Stompin' at the Savoy," "Harlem Airshaft," "Drop Me Off in Harlem," and "Take the A Train."

As Harlem became a political and cultural center of black America, the community's black churches became more influential as well. Most were Protestant, particularly BAPTIST and METHODIST, and the Abyssinian Baptist Church became the most famous during the interwar period. The Rev. Adam Clayton Powell, Sr. moved the church from West 40th Street in midtown Manhattan to West 138th Street in Harlem in 1923. He combatted prostitution, organized classes in home economics, built a home for the elderly, and organized soup kitchens and employment networks during the Great Depression. He was succeeded as senior pastor in 1937 by his son, Adam Clayton POWELL, Jr., who expanded the scope of the Abyssinian church's community activism. Harlem's scores of storefront churches, many of which proliferated during the interwar period, imitated Abyssinian's community aid efforts on a smaller scale. Harlem's most famous heterodox religious leader of the 1930s, FATHER DIVINE, established a series of soup kitchens and stores in the community through his Peace Mission and his Righteous Government political organization.

The 1930s were a period of stagnation and decline in Harlem, as they were throughout the nation. Civil rights protest increased during the decade, and much of it originated in Harlem. In response to white businessmen's unwillingness to hire black workers for white-collar jobs in their Harlem stores, a series of "Don't Buy Where You Can't Work" boycott campaigns commenced in 1933 and became an effective method of protesting against racial bigotry throughout the decade. Harlem community leaders such as Adam Clayton Powell, Jr. often joined with the NAACP, the National Urban League, the COMMUNIST PARTY OF THE U.S.A., and the Citizens' League for Fair Play (CLFP) in leading these protests. Under the aegis of the Communist party, major demonstrations were also held on Harlem streets in the early 1930s in support of the Scottsboro Boys and Angelo Herndon.

Major party politics thrived in Harlem as much as radical politics did during the first half of the century. In the 1920s the REPUBLICAN PARTY (led in black communities by Charles Anderson) and the DEMOCRATIC PARTY (led by Ferdinand Q. Morton under Tammany Hall's United Colored Democracy), competed fiercely for black votes. Within the black community itself, African Americans and Caribbean Americans competed for dominance over the few available instruments of political control. Caribbeans were particularly prominent in the struggle to integrate Harlem blacks into the main organization of the Democratic party; J. Raymond Jones (an immigrant from the Virgin Islands who would ultimately become head of Tammany Hall) led an insurgent group called the New Democrats in this effort during the early 1930s.

Civil disturbances played an important role in Harlem's growing political consciousness. In 1935 a riot, fueled by animosity toward white businesses and the police, left three dead, and caused over 200 million dollars in damage. New York City Mayor Fiorello LaGuardia later assigned his Mayor's Commission on Conditions in Harlem (led by E. Franklin Frazier) to study this uprising; the commission revealed a great number of underlying socioeconomic problems that were giving rise to racial animosities in Harlem. In 1943 Harlem experienced another major race riot, which left five dead. This second riot was fueled by race discrimination in war-related industries and continuing animosities between white police officers and Harlem's black citizens.

These events helped shape the emerging political career of Adam Clayton Powell, Jr., who was elected to the New York City Council in 1941 and to the United States Congress in 1944, representing Harlem's newly created Eighteenth District. Powell's intolerance of race discrimination, and his vocal and flamboyant style brought national attention to the community, and he remained a symbol of Harlem's strength and reputation until his expulsion from Congress in 1967. He was reelected by his loyal Harlem constituency in 1968.

By the end of World War II, Harlem experienced another transition. The migration of middle-class blacks to more affluent neighborhoods destabilized the class balance of earlier decades. Many of the remaining businesses were owned not by black residents but by whites who lived far removed from the ghetto. At the same time, most of the literati associated with the Renaissance had left the district. However, Harlem's literary life was preserved by a number of dedicated authors, such as Ralph ELLISON (whose 1952 novel *Invisible Man* was centered in Harlem) and Harlem native James BALDWIN. The HARLEM WRITERS GUILD was founded in 1950 by John Killens, Maya ANGELOU, John Henrik Clarke, and others, and has for over four decades offered writers in the community a forum for the reading and discussion of their works. Photographers such as Austin Hansen and Gordon PARKS, Sr. continued to capture and celebrate Harlem's community on film.

Civil disturbances played an important role in Harlem's growing political consciousness.

For most of those who remained in Harlem after the war, however, a sense of powerlessness set in, exacerbated by poverty and a lack of control over their community. The quality of Harlem housing continued to be an acute problem. Paradoxically, as the quality of Harlem's inadequately heated, rat-infested buildings continued to deteriorate, and as housing health ordinances were increasingly ignored, the rents on those units continued to rise. People were evicted for being unable to keep up with the costs, but having no other place to go, many either entered community shelters or joined the swelling ranks of the homeless.

Heroin addiction and street crime were increasingly serious problems. The 1950s saw Harlem deteriorate, both spiritually and physically. Dependent on welfare and other social services, many Harlemites longed for a chance to reassert some degree of hegemony over their community.

The 1964 Harlem Youth Opportunities Unlimited Act (HARYOU) represented an attempt to provide solutions. After an intensive study of the community from political, economic, and social perspectives, HARYOU proposed a combination of social action for the reacquisition of political power and the influx of federal funds to redress the increasing economic privation of the area. From the beginning, however, the project suffered from personnel conflicts at the leadership level. Social psychologist Dr. Kenneth B. Clark, who originally conceived and directed the project, resigned after a struggle with Congressman Adam Clayton Powell, Jr. Following Clark's tenure, a Powell ally, Livingston Wingate, led the project through a period of intensifying government scrutiny regarding its financial administration.

As a political attempt to increase local control through community action while remaining dependent upon government largess for funding, HARYOU failed. It was also unable to ameliorate the alienation and decline into delinquency that plagued Harlem's youth. Illustrative of its failure was the 1964 riot, ignited like its predecessors by an incident of alleged police brutality; this latest riot underscored the troubles that continued to plague the community.

By the late 1960s, Harlem precisely fit the conclusion reached by the 1968 National Commission of Civil Disorders report. It was a ghetto, created, maintained, and condoned by white society. Literary works of the postwar era, from Ann L. Petry's *The Street* (1946) to Claude Brown's *Manchild in the Promised Land* (1965), reflected this progressively deteriorating state of affairs as well.

It was in this period of decay that another charismatic organization emerged in the community, the NATION OF ISLAM (NOI). MALCOLM X, the head of Harlem's mosque, blended the intellectual acumen of the literati of the 1920s with the political sophistication and charisma of Garvey. Malcolm X galvanized the masses and rekindled in them a sense of black pride and self-determination, appealing to their sense of disgruntlement with a message that was far more angry and less conciliatory than that offered by other major civil rights leaders. He was assassinated on February 21, 1965, in the Audubon Ballroom in Upper Manhattan.

Throughout Harlem's history there has been a wide gap between the social, intellectual, and artistic accomplishments of the community's elite and the poverty and neglect of its masses.

Harlem since the 1960s has been severely affected by the same external forces that plagued many other American urban centers. As the mainstay of the United States economy underwent a critical transition from heavy manufacturing to service and information technologies, large-scale industry left urban areas. Large numbers of the Harlem population followed this exodus from the community, settling in suburban areas in Queens, the Bronx, and other boroughs. The resultant unemployment among those who remained further eviscerated Harlem. The community had long lost its position as the population center of black New York to the Bedford-Stuyvesant area of Brooklyn. Community vital statistics have been no more encouraging; it was estimated in 1992 that the average African-American male born in Harlem would have a life expectancy of sixty-four years, dying before becoming eligible for most Social Security or retirement benefits.

The Harlem Commonwealth Council (HCC), a nonprofit corporation begun in 1967 and founded through the Office of Economic Opportunity and the private sector, sought to develop Harlem economically and empower its community leaders politically. Yet, in its first twenty-five years, bad investments and an uncertain economy have reduced its real estate holdings, and virtually all its large-scale enterprises have gone bankrupt.

In 1989 David N. Dinkins, a product of Harlem's Democratic clubs, became the first African-American mayor of New York City. One of his biggest supporters was Charles Rangel, who in 1970 had succeeded Adam Clayton Powell, Jr., as Harlem's congressman. In his four years as mayor, Dinkins sought to reestablish an atmosphere of racial harmony and cooperation, to realize his vision of New York City as a "gorgeous mosaic" of diverse ethnicities.

Residents continued to reassert control over their community in the 1990s, as the Harlem Chamber of Commerce led efforts to revitalize Harlem's businesses and reclaim the community's physical infrastructure (a process sometimes referred to as "ghettocentrism"). A plan to spend over 170 million dollars to build permanent housing for the poor and homeless began early in the decade, and such landmark structures as the Astor Row houses on West 130th Street were rehabilitated as well. The Schomburg Center for Research in Black Culture, established in 1926 on 135th Street as a branch of the New York Public Library, remained the nation's leading resource of African-American scholarship, as well as the location of academic conferences and meetings of the HARLEM WRITERS GUILD. The Studio Museum of Harlem on 125th Street was a focus for African-American and Caribbean-American folk art. The Apollo Theater on 125th Street was reopened in 1989, and it continued to showcase the current and future leaders of black entertainment. The nearby Hotel Theresa no longer served as a hotel but continued as the Theresa Towers, a modern office center and community landmark.

Throughout Harlem's history there has been a wide gap between the social, intellectual, and artistic accomplishments of the community's elite and the poverty and neglect of its masses. At the same time, however, there remains in Harlem, as there has been in every decade of its existence, an inner energy and spirit.

BIBLIOGRAPHY

Anderson, Jervis. *This Was Harlem: A Cultural Portrait, 1900–1950.* New York, 1981.

Capeci, Dominic. *The Harlem Riot of 1943.* Philadelphia, 1977.

Clarke, John Henrik, ed. *Harlem: A Community in Transition.* New York, 1969.

Cruse, Harold. *The Crisis of the Negro Intellectual: From Its Origins to the Present.* New York, 1967.

Greenberg, Cheryl. *"Or Does It Explode?" Black Harlem in the Great Depression.* New York, 1991.

Hamilton, Charles V. *Adam Clayton Powell, Jr.: The Political Biography of an American Dilemma.* New York, 1991.

Huggins, Nathan. *The Harlem Renaissance.* New York, 1971.

Johnson, James Weldon. *Black Manhattan.* 1930. Reprint. New York, 1991.

Lewis, David Levering. *When Harlem Was in Vogue.* New York, 1981.

Locke, Alain, ed. *The New Negro.* Reprint. New York, 1925.

McKay, Claude. *Harlem: Negro Metropolis.* 1940. Reprint. New York, 1968.

Naison, Mark. *Communists in Harlem During the Depression.* Urbana, Ill., 1986.

Osofsky, Gilbert. *Harlem: The Making of a Ghetto.* New York, 1963.

– MARSHALL HYATT

HARLEM BOYCOTTS

During the 1930s, African Americans in several cities organized boycotts of stores in black neighborhoods which refused to hire blacks. In New York City's Harlem neighborhood, the center of America's black life, pressure for a boycott movement had begun after 1929, when a successful boycotting campaign was organized in Chicago under the slogan "Don't Buy Where You Can't Work." In 1931, black nationalists called for a cross-class campaign, but Harlem businessmen and influential ministers refused. During the summer of 1933, members of the Negro Industrial and Clerical Alliance, led by Sufi Abdul Hamid, a black nationalist disciple of Marcus GARVEY and veteran of the Chicago campaign, picketed small stores on Harlem's 135th Street in order to obtain jobs for blacks. His boycotts were accompanied by anti-Semitic speeches against Jewish merchants.

In 1934, at the height of the Great Depression, members of St. Martin's Protestant Episcopal Church complained to their minister, the Columbia University-trained Rev. John H. JOHNSON, about the conspicuous absence of black salespeople at Blumstein's department store, the largest store on Harlem's 125th Street. Johnson approached the owner of the store, William Blumstein, and requested that he hire black salespeople, since the majority of his customers were black. When the owner refused, Johnson appealed to the Harlem community to create a united front to protest Blumstein's hiring practices. The newspaper *New York Age* actively took up the cause, and as a result, the Citizen's League for Fair Play (CLFP) was established. The League, whose members included sixty-two of Harlem's social, religious, and business groups, was committed to ending job discrimination and obtaining white-collar jobs for blacks. The CLFP also included some radical black nationalists such as Sufi Hamid, Arthur Reid, and Ira Kemp.

The boycott began in June 1934. It became known as the Jobs-for-Negroes-Campaign, and borrowed the slogan that had been used in Chicago. After six weeks of active picketing, mostly by the more radical members of the CLFP, Blumstein capitulated. On July 26, 1934, an agreement was reached in which Blumstein agreed to hire blacks as sales clerks. After the success of the boycott, a number of other stores along 125th Street, such as Koch's, began to employ blacks in clerical positions.

After this initial success, the CLFP fell into disunity. The radical nationalists, such as Sufi Hamid and Kemp, charged that middle-class, light-skinned blacks, who had been trained by the Urban League, were being hired over the dark-skinned, lower-class blacks who had actually done the picketing. A "Rebel Picketing Committee" separated itself from the CLFP, and began picketing small stores along 125th Street, even those that had just hired light-skinned blacks. They recommended that merchants hire only dark-skinned blacks. This new movement, led by the CLFP's radicals, agitated for all jobs in Harlem, rather than just a few token positions. When the other members of the CLFP discovered that Sufi Hamid had collected dues from picketers in return for promising them jobs, they accused him of "racketeering" and expelled him from the group. Kemp and Reid then made the "Rebel Picketers" an entirely dues-paying organization. When they approached A. S. Beck shoe store demanding it hire black workers, the store sued the picketers, stating that they were not a labor union and had no right to make such demands. In November 1934, the New York courts decided the dispute in favor of A. S. Beck. Until the decision was overturned the next year, the movement ebbed. The NAACP and moderate leaders, disgusted by the radicals' mercenary actions, supported the court action. At the same time, Sufi Hamid began to call himself the "Black Hitler," and became more openly hostile to Jews. He was arrested for "spreading anti-Semitism in Harlem," but was later acquitted.

Meanwhile, in 1935, the COMMUNIST PARTY started its own boycott of the Empire Cafeteria. Party activists, who favored interracial labor organization, had participated in small numbers in the Blumstein's boycott, carrying signs demanding no white workers be fired. Their success in securing jobs for four black countermen at Empire, without any other workers losing jobs, made the party a power in boycott organizing.

In 1936, Kemp and Reid obtained a charter for the Harlem Labor Union (HLU), and resumed picketing on a small scale as part of their goal of becoming sole bargaining agent for black workers. The HLU was not really a labor union. Middle-class in its objectives, it aimed to build up black business power through worker dues. Labor leaders and the NAACP decried the HLU's strikebreaking and sweetheart contracts to business, which assured that HLU members would be hired over other workers. However, Kemp and Reid remained popular with the workers for whom they found jobs.

The next large boycott was not organized until 1938, when two of Harlem's influential ministers, the Rev. Adam Clayton POWELL, Jr., of the Abyssinian Baptist Church, and the Rev. Lloyd Imes of St. James Presbyterian Church, provided the impetus for the formation of the Greater New York Coordinating Committee for Employment (GNYCC). Within his CLFP-like coalition of some 200 groups, Powell secured the backing of both the HLU and the communists, who despised each other. Neither of them could afford to oppose the popular Powell. The GNYCC was committed to fighting discriminatory practices throughout the city, including in the utility companies. After some unsuccessful attempts by the GNYCC to force the New York Telephone Company to hire blacks, a rival group was formed, which was called the Harlem Job Committee (HJC). Led by A. Phillip Randolph of the BROTHERHOOD OF SLEEPING CAR PORTERS, the HJC began to boycott stores around Harlem, and suggested the GNYCC confine itself to the utility companies. Eventually, under pressure from GNYCC, Consolidated Edison Electric Company agreed to hire a few trainees. In 1939, a GNYCC boycott of the New York World's Fair resulted in the hiring of 700 blacks. While most of the jobs were menial, this represented a much higher number than the organizers' target of forty.

The last major boycott of the era was of the Fifth Avenue Coach Company and the Omnibus Corporation, which began in 1941. Powell led the United Negro Bus Strike Committee, which brought together the HLC and the Communists, whose NATIONAL NEGRO CONGRESS participated. After months of active boycotting and intermittent violent confrontations with white unionists, Powell announced victory. The bus companies agreed to hire thirty-two black trainees immediately and set a black employment quota.

The boycotts' results were mixed. The coalitions that fostered them were unstable, and their leaders were not always motivated by principle in conducting them. They did help break the job ceiling and discriminatory hiring practices which either kept blacks in menial jobs or excluded them completely. However, in 1941, African-American social scientist Ralph BUNCHE concluded that the "Don't buy where you can't work" boycotts and other racial campaigns had mostly aided middle-class blacks. During the Depression their long-term effect on poor blacks was simply to increase competition with displaced white workers, which meant that wages dropped and blacks working in white areas would be fired. Perhaps its most important legacy was that, by the 1940s, blacks could be seen working in white-collar positions all over the city.

BIBLIOGRAPHY

Hamilton, Charles V. *Adam Clayton Powell, Jr.: The Political Biography of an American Dilemma.* New York, 1991.

Muraskin, William. "The Harlem Boycott of 1934: Black Nationalism and the Rise of Labor Union Consciousness." *Labor History* 13, no. 3 (1972): 361–373.

Naison, Mark. *The Communists in Harlem During the Great Depression.* New York, 1984.

— MANSUR M. NURUDDIN AND GREG ROBINSON

HARLEM GLOBETROTTERS

The Harlem Globetrotters were founded in 1926. At that time, Abe Saperstein (1902–1966), an English-born Jewish Chicagoan who had coached semipro basketball in the Chicago area, took over coaching duties of an African-American team, the Savoy Big Five (formerly Giles Post American Legion). Saperstein decided the team would be more popular with better marketing. To emphasize its racial composition and its barnstorming, he renamed the team the Harlem Globetrotters, though they had no connection to the New York City neighborhood. The newly-renamed team debuted on January 7, 1927, in Hinckley, Ill., wearing red, white, and blue uniforms that Saperstein had sewn in his father's tailor shop. The first starting team consisted of Walter "Toots" Wright, Byron "Fat" Long, Willis "Kid" Oliver, Andy Washington, and Al "Runt" Pullins.

The Globetrotters played the itinerant schedule of barnstorming basketball teams, taking on black and white squads of greatly varying levels of ability, with many memorable games against their archrivals, the New York Rens. Players boosted the team's popularity by clowning—drop-kicking balls, spinning them on fingertips, and bouncing them off teammates' heads. In 1939, the Globetrotters finished third in the *Chicago Herald American*'s World Professional Tournament; in 1940, they became World Champions. In 1943, the team traveled to Mexico City (the first indication that the team would soon justify their "Globetrotter" name) and won the International Cup Tournament. During the mid-1940s, a white player, Bob Karstens, joined the Globetrotters (the team has briefly had two other white players).

After World War II, as professional all-white basketball leagues began slowly integrating, the Globetrotters, led by Marques Haynes, were so popular that rumors spread that Saperstein opposed integration in order to keep control of the market for black players. Meanwhile, they continued to hold their own against white teams in exhibition games. In February 1948, the Globetrotters, following a 52-game winning streak, played George Mikan and the Minneapolis Lakers evenly in two exhibition games in Chicago. The team's skill and popularity belied black exclusion policies.

By 1950, NBA teams had three black players, including ex-Globetrotter Nat "Sweetwater" Clifton. After the integration of professional basketball, the Globetrotters' playing style changed dramatically. Clowning now became predominant. Players such as Reece "Goose" Tatum, Meadowlark Lemon, and Fred "Curly" Neal were hired not only for playing ability but for trick shooting, dribbling, and comedic talent. The Globetrotters, now billed as "The Clown Princes of Basketball," became best known for already familiar routines, such as the pregame "Magic Circle." In this act, players stand in a loose circle and display their skill and deftness with the ball, accompanied by the team's theme song, "Sweet Georgia Brown."

In 1950, the Globetrotters began annual coast-to-coast trips with squads of college All-Americans, which lasted until 1962. The same year, the team began annual European summer tours, playing to enormous crowds. In 1951, they played before 75,000 spectators in Berlin's Olympic Stadium, still one of the largest crowds ever to see a basketball game. During this period, they appeared in two movies, *Go Man Go* (1948) and *The Harlem Globetrotters* (1951). In the early 1950s, after the Globetrotters lost consecutive games to Red Klotz's Philadelphia Spas, Abe Saperstein decided to dispense with playing local teams and to barnstorm with the Spas (later renamed the Washington Generals), who play some 250 games with the Globetrotters each year, and serve as straight men for their stunts. The Generals, following an agreement with the Globetrotters, allow several trick-shot baskets per game. The last time the Generals beat their rivals was in 1971. In the 1950s, the Globetrotters split into two squads, one of which played on the East coast, while the other focused on the West. In 1958–1959, the same year that Wilt Chamberlain, after the end of his college career, spent playing with the team (often as a 7′1″ guard!), the Globetrotters toured the Soviet Union as goodwill ambassadors. Other famous athletes who played with the team included Bob Gibson and Connie Hawkins. The team has retained its interracial popularity, though during the 1960s some blacks criticized team members for their clownish image, which reinforced racial stereotypes, and the team's silence on civil rights issues.

The Harlem Globetrotters Basketball Team, 1930–1931 season. Standing (left to right) Abe Saperstein, Toots Wright, Byron Long, Inman Jackson, William Oliver; seated is Al Pullins. (Photographs and Prints Division, Schomburg Center for Research in Black Culture, The New York Public Library, Astor, Lenox and Tilden Foundations)

After Abe Saperstein's death in 1966, the team was sold to three Chicago businessmen for $3.7 million. In 1975, Metromedia purchased the team for $11 million. The Globetrotters remained popular into the 1970s, when they starred in cartoon and live-action TV series, but their popularity declined some years later, especially after stars such as Meadowlark Lemon left the team after contract disputes. In 1985, the first female Globetrotter, Lynette Woodward, was hired. In December 1986, Metromedia sold the team (as part of a package that included the Ice Capades) to International Broadcasting Corp. (IBC) for $30 million. In 1993, IBC entered bankruptcy and Mannie Johnson, a former Globetrotter, bought the team. It was another Globetrotter, Curly Neal, who best captured the team's appeal: "How do I know when we played a good 'game'?" he said. "When I look up at the crowd and I see all those people laughing their heads off. It's a hard world and if we can lighten it up a little, we've done our job."

BIBLIOGRAPHY

Gutman, Bill. *The Harlem Globetrotters.* Champaign, Ill., 1977.

Lemon, Meadowlark. *Meadowlark.* Nashville, Tenn., 1987.

Weiner, Jay. "Meadowlark Lemon Comes Home to Roost with Globetrotters." Chicago *Star Tribune,* March 1, 1993.

— GREG ROBINSON

HARLEM RENAISSANCE

If the Harlem Renaissance was neither exclusive to Harlem nor a rebirth of anything that had gone before, its efflorescence above New York's Central Park was characterized by such sustained vitality and variety as to influence by paramountcy and diminish by comparison the similar cultural energies in Boston, Philadelphia, and Washington, D.C. During its earliest years, beginning about 1917, contemporaries tended to describe the Harlem phenomenon as a manifestation of the New Negro Arts Movement. However, by the time it ended in the winter of 1934–1935—with both a whimper and a bang—the movement was almost universally regarded as indistinguishable from its Harlem incarnation.

As the population of African Americans rapidly urbanized and its literacy rate climbed, HARLEM, NEW YORK, the "Negro capital of America," rose out of the vast relocation under way from South to North. A combination of causes propelled the Great Black Migration: southern white mob violence, the economics of discrimination, crop failure, the interruption of European immigration after 1914 and a consequent labor vacuum in the North, and the aggressive recruitment of black labor for work at wartime wages by northern industrialists. With the vast welling of black people from Georgia, the Carolinas, Virginia, and elsewhere, their numbers rose from 60,534 in all of NEW YORK CITY in 1910 to a conservative 1923 estimate of the NATIONAL URBAN LEAGUE (NUL) that placed the number at 183,428, with probably two-thirds in Harlem. Although this section of the city was by no means wholly occupied by people of color—never more than 60 percent during the 1930s—it soon became distinctively black in culture and in the mainstream perception. If the coming of black Harlem was swift, its triumph had been long anticipated by the increasing numbers of African Americans living in midtown Manhattan's teeming Tenderloin and San Juan Hill districts. The Tenderloin (so called from a police captain's gustatory graft), stretching roughly from West Fourteenth to Forty-second streets, had become home to the city's nonwhites during the early nineteenth century, after they forced their way out of the old Five Points area east of today's Foley Square, where City Hall stands.

By the 1890s, blacks were battling the Irish for scarce turf north of Fiftieth Street in what came to be called San Juan Hill, in honor of African-American troops in the Spanish-American War. Influx and congestion had, as the African-American newspaper the *New York Age* predicted, great advantages: "Influx of Afro-Americans into New York City from all parts of the South made . . . possible a great number and variety of business enterprises." The example of Lower East Side Jews accumulating money and moving on, in the 1890s, to solid brownstones on wide, shaded streets in Harlem was enviously watched by African Americans. The area had undergone a building boom in anticipation of the extension of the subway, but by the turn of the century many apartment buildings were sparsely occupied. A few white landlords broke ranks around 1905 to rent or sell to African Americans through Philip A. Payton's pioneering Afro-American Realty Company.

Two institutional activities were outstandingly successful in promoting the occupation of Harlem—churches and cabarets. Saint Philip's Episcopal Church sold its West Twenty-fifth Street holdings for $140,000 in 1909 and disposed of its Tenderloin cemetery for $450,000 two years later. The Abyssinian Baptist Church, presided over by the charismatic Adam Clayton Powell, Sr., negotiated a comparable disposal of its property in order to build one of Protestant America's grandest temples on 138th Street. Nightclubs such as Banks's, Barron's, and Edmond's transported music and a nightlife style from the Tenderloin that gave Harlem its signature. Barron's Little Savoy featured "Jelly Roll" MORTON, Willie "the Lion" Smith, James P. JOHNSON, Scott JOPLIN, and other legends of the era. Barron Wilkins took his club uptown before the country entered the European war.

Precisely why and how the Harlem Renaissance materialized, who molded it and who found it most meaningful, as well as what it symbolized and what it achieved, raise perennial American questions about race relations, class hegemony, cultural assimilation, generational-gender-lifestyle conflicts, and art versus propaganda. Notwithstanding its synoptic significance, the Harlem Renaissance was not, as some students have maintained, all-inclusive of the early twentieth-century African-American urban experience. There were important movements, influences, and people who were marginal or irrelevant to it, as well as those alien or opposed. Not everything that happened in Harlem from 1917 to 1934 was a Renaissance happening. The potent mass movement founded and led by the charismatic Marcus GARVEY was to the Renaissance what nineteenth-century populism was to progressive reform: a parallel but socially different force, related primarily through dialectical confrontation. Equally different from the institutional ethos and purpose of the Renaissance was the black church. An occasional minister (such as the father of poet Countee CULLEN) or exceptional Garveyites (such as Yale-Harvard man William H. Ferris) might move in both worlds, but black evangelism and its cultist manifestations, such as Black Zionism, represented emotional and cultural retrogression in the eyes of the principal actors in the Renaissance. If the leading intellectual of the race, W. E. B. DU BOIS, publicly denigrated the personnel and preachings of the black church, his animadversions were merely more forthright than those of other New Negro notables like James Weldon JOHNSON, Charles S. Johnson, Jessie Redmon FAUSET, Alain LOCKE, and Walter Francis WHITE.

The relationship of music to the Harlem Renaissance was problematic, for reasons exactly analogous to its elitist aversions to Garveyism and evangelism. When Du Bois wrote, a few years after the beginning of the New Negro movement in arts and letters, that "until the art of the black folk compels recognition they will not be rated as human," he, like most of his Renaissance peers, fully intended to exclude the blues of Bessie SMITH and the jazz of "King" Oliver. Spirituals sung like lieder by the disciplined Hall Johnson Choir—and, better yet, lieder sung by conservatory-trained Roland Hayes, recipient of the NAACP's prestigious Spingarn Medal—were deemed appropriate musical forms to present to mainstream America. The deans of the Renaissance were entirely content to leave discovery and celebration of Bessie, Clara, Trixie, and various other blues-singing Smiths to white music critic Carl Van Vechten's effusions in *Vanity Fair.* When the visiting film director Sergei Eisenstein enthused about new black musicals, Charles S. Johnson and Alain Locke expressed mild consternation in the Urban League's *Opportunity* magazine. They would have been no less displeased by Maurice Ravel's fascination with musicians in Chicago dives. As board members of the Pace Phonograph Company, Du Bois, James Weldon Johnson, and others banned "funky" artists from the Black Swan list of recordings, thereby contributing to the demise of the African-American-owned firm. But the wild Broadway success of Miller and Lyles's musical *Shuffle Along* (it helped to popularize the Charleston) or Florence Mills's *Blackbirds* revue flaunted such artistic fastidiousness.

The very centrality of music in black life, as well as of black musical stereotypes in white minds, caused popular musical forms to impinge inescapably on Renaissance high culture. Eventually, the Renaissance deans made a virtue out of necessity; they applauded the concert-hall ragtime of "Big Jim" EUROPE and the "educated" jazz of Atlanta University graduate and big-band leader Fletcher Henderson, and they hired a Duke ELLINGTON or a Cab CALLOWAY as drawing cards for fund-raising socials. Still, their relationship to music remained beset by paradox. New York ragtime, with its "Jelly Roll" Morton strides and Joplinesque elegance, had as much in common with Chicago jazz as Mozart with "Fats" Waller. The source of musical authenticity and the reservoir of musical abundance lay in those recently urbanized and economically beleaguered men and women whose chosen recreational environments were raucous, boozy, and lubricious. Yet these were the men and women whose culture and condition made Renaissance drillmasters (themselves only a generation and a modest wage removed) uncomfortable and ashamed, men and women whose musical pedigrees went back from Louis ARMSTRONG and Sidney Bechet through Chicago to New Orleans's Storyville and its colonial-era Place Congo.

The Renaissance relished virtuoso performances by baritone Jules Bledsoe or contralto Marian ANDERSON, and pined to see the classical works of William Grant STILL performed in Aeolian Hall. It took exceeding pride in the classical repertory of the renowned Clef Club Orchestra. On the other hand, even if and when it saw some value in the music nurtured in prohibition joints and bleary rent parties, the movement found itself pushed aside by white ethnic commercial co-optation and exploitation—by Al Capone and the mob. Thus, what was musically vital was shunned or deplored in the Harlem Renaissance from racial sensitivity; what succeeded with mainstream audiences derived from those same shunned and deplored sources and was invariably hijacked; and what was esteemed as emblematic of racial sophistication was (even when well done) of no interest to whites and of not much more to the majority of blacks. Last, with the notable exception of Paul ROBESON, most of the impresarios as well as the featured personalities of the Renaissance were more expert in literary and visual-arts matters than musical.

The very centrality of music in black life, as well as of black musical stereotypes in white minds, caused popular musical forms to impinge inescapably on Renaissance high culture.

The purpose of emphasizing such negatives—of stressing whom and what the Harlem Renaissance excluded or undervalued—serves the better to characterize the essence of a movement that was an elitist response to a rapidly evolving set of social and economic conditions demographically driven by the Great Black Migration, beginning in the second decade of the twentieth century. The Harlem Renaissance began "as a somewhat forced phenomenon, a cultural nationalism of the parlor, institutionally encouraged and constrained by the leaders of the civil rights establishment for the paramount purpose of improving 'race relations' in a time of extreme national reaction to an annulment of economic gains won by Afro-Americans during the Great War" (Lewis 1981). This mobilizing elite emerged from the increasing national cohesion of the African-American bourgeoisie at the turn of the century, and of the migration of many of its most educated and enterprising to the North about a decade in advance of the epic working-class migration out of the South. Du Bois indelibly labeled this racially advantaged minority the "Talented Tenth" in a seminal 1903 essay. He fleshed out the concept biographically that same year in "The Advance Guard of the Race," a piece in *Booklover's Magazine:* "Widely different are these men in origin and method. [Paul Laurence] DUNBAR sprang from slave parents and poverty; [Charles Waddell] CHESNUTT from free parents and thrift; while [Henry O.] TANNER was a bishop's son."

Students of the African-American bourgeoisie—from Joseph Willson in the mid-nineteenth century through Du Bois, Caroline Bond Day, and E. Franklin FRAZIER during the first half of the twentieth to Constance Green, August Meier, Carl Degler, Stephen Birmingham, and, most recently, Adele Alexander, Lois Benjamin, and Willard Gatewood—have differed about its defining elements, especially that of pigment. The generalization seems to hold that color was a greater determinant of upper-class status in the post–Civil War South than in the North. The phenotype preferences exercised by slaveholders for house slaves, in combination with the relative advantages enjoyed by illegitimate offspring of slavemasters, gave a decided spin to mulatto professional careers during Reconstruction and well beyond. Success in the North followed more various criteria, of which color was sometimes a factor. By the time of Booker T. WASHINGTON's death in 1915, however, a considerable amount of ideological cohesion existed among the African-American leadership classes in such key cities as Atlanta, Washington, Baltimore, Philadelphia, Boston, Chicago, and New York. A commitment to college preparation in liberal arts and the classics, in contrast to Washington's emphasis on vocational training, prevailed. Demands for civil and social equality were espoused again after a quietus of some fifteen years.

The once considerable power of the so-called Tuskegee Machine now receded before the force of Du Bois's propaganda, a coordinated civil rights militancy, and rapidly altering industrial and demographic conditions in the nation. The vocational training in crafts such as brickmaking, blacksmithing, carpentry, and sewing prescribed by Tuskegee and Hampton institutes was irrelevant in those parts of the South undergoing industrialization, yet industry in the South was largely proscribed to African Americans who for several decades had been deserting the dead end of sharecropping for the South's towns and cities. The Bookerites' sacrifice of civil rights for economic gain, therefore, lost its appeal not only to educated and enterprising African Americans but to many of those white philanthropists and public figures who had once solemnly commended it. The Talented Tenth formulated and propagated the new ideology being rapidly embraced by the physicians, dentists, educators, preachers, businesspeople, lawyers, and morticians comprising the bulk of the African-American affluent and influential—some 10,000 men and women, out of a total population in 1920 of more than 10 million. (In 1917, traditionally cited as the natal year of the Harlem Renaissance, there were 2,132 African Americans in colleges and universities, probably no more than 30 of them attending "white" institutions.)

It was, then, the minuscule vanguard of a minority—0.02 percent of the racial total—that constituted the Talented Tenth that jump-started the New Negro Arts Movement. But what was extraordinary about the Harlem Renaissance was that its promotion and orchestration by the Talented Tenth were the consequence of masterful improvisation rather than of deliberate plan, of artifice imitating likelihood, of aesthetic deadpan disguising a racial blind alley. Between the 1905 "Declaration of Principles" of the NIAGARA MOVEMENT and the appearance in 1919 of Claude MCKAY's electrifying poem "If We Must Die," the principal agenda of the Talented Tenth called for investigation of and protest against discrimination in virtually every aspect of national life. It lobbied for racially enlightened employment policies in business and industry; the abolition through the courts of peonage, residential segregation ordinances, JIM CROW public transportation, and franchise restrictions; and enactment of federal sanctions against lynching. The vehicles for this agenda, the NAACP and the NUL, exposed, cajoled, and propagandized through their excellent journals, the CRISIS and *Opportunity,* respectively. The rhetoric of protest was addressed to ballots, courts, legislatures, and the workplace: "We urge upon Congress the enactment of appropriate legislation for securing the proper enforcement of . . . the thirteenth, fourteenth and fifteenth amendments," the Niagara Movement had demanded and the NAACP continued to reiterate. Talented Tenth rhetoric was also strongly social-scientific: "We shall try to set down interestingly but without sugar-coating or generalizations the findings of careful scientific surveys and facts gathered from research," the first *Opportunity* editorial would proclaim in January 1923, echoing the objectives of Du Bois's famous Atlanta University Studies.

It is hardly surprising that many African Americans, the great majority of whom lived under the deadening cultural and economic weight of southern apartheid, had modest interest in literature and the arts during the first two decades of the twentieth century. Even outside the underdeveloped South, and irrespective of race, demotic America had scant aptitude for and much suspicion of arts and letters. Culture in early twentieth-century America was paid for by a white minority probably not a great deal larger, by percentage, than the Talented Tenth. For those privileged few African Americans whose education or leisure inspired such tastes, therefore, appealing fiction, poetry, drama, paintings, and sculpture by or about African Americans had become so exiguous as to be practically nonexistent. With the rising hostility and indifference of the mainstream market, African-American discretionary resources were wholly inadequate by themselves to sustain even a handful of novelists, poets, and painters. A tubercular death had silenced poet-novelist Dunbar in 1906, and poor royalties had done the same for novelist Chesnutt after publication the previous year of *The Colonel's Dream.* Between that point and 1922, no more than five African Americans published significant works of fiction and verse. There was *Pointing the Way* in 1908, a flawed, fascinating civil rights novel by the Baptist preacher Sutton GRIGGS. Three years later, Du Bois's *The Quest of the Silver Fleece,* a sweeping sociological allegory, appeared. The following year came James Weldon Johnson's well-crafted *The Autobiography of an Ex-Colored Man,* but the author felt compelled to disguise his racial identity. A ten-year silence fell afterward, finally to be broken in 1922 by McKay's *Harlem Shadows,* the first book of poetry since Dunbar. In "Art for Nothing," a short, trenchant think piece in the May 1922 *Crisis,* Du Bois lamented the fall into oblivion of sculptors Meta Warrick FULLER and May Howard Jackson, and that of painters William E. Scott and Richard Brown.

Although the emergence of the Harlem Renaissance seems much more sudden and dramatic in retrospect than the historic reality, its institutional elaboration was, in fact, relatively quick. Altogether, it evolved through three stages. The first phase, ending in 1923 with the publication of Jean TOOMER's unique prose poem *Cane,* was dominated by white artists and writers—bohemians and revolutionaries—fascinated for a variety of reasons with the life of black people. The second phase, from early 1924 to mid-1926, was presided over by the civil rights establishment of the NUL and the NAACP, a period of interracial collaboration between "Negrotarian" whites and the African-American Talented Tenth. The last phase, from mid-1926 to 1934, was increasingly dominated by African American artists themselves—the "Niggerati."

When Charles S. Johnson, new editor of *Opportunity,* sent invitations to some dozen African-American poets and writers to attend an event at Manhattan's Civic Club on March 21, 1924, the movement had already shifted into high gear. At Johnson's request, William H. Baldwin III, white Tuskegee trustee, NUL board member, and heir to a railroad fortune, had persuaded *Harper's* editor Frederick Lewis Allen to corral a "small but representative group from his field," most of them unknown, to attend the Civic Club affair in celebration of the sudden outpouring of "Negro" writing. "A group of the younger writers, which includes Eric Walrond, Jessie Fauset, Gwendolyn Bennett, Countee Cullen, Langston HUGHES, Alain Locke, and some others," would be present, Johnson promised each invitee. All told, in addition to the "younger writers," some fifty persons were expected: "Eugene O'Neill, H. L. Mencken, Oswald Garrison Villard, Mary Johnston, Zona Gale, Robert Morss Lovett, Carl Van Doren, Ridgely Torrence, and about twenty more of this type. I think you might find this group interesting enough to draw you away for a few hours from your work on your next book," Johnson wrote the recently published Jean Toomer almost coyly.

Although both Toomer and Langston Hughes were absent in Europe, approximately 110 celebrants and honorees assembled that evening, included among them Du Bois, James Weldon Johnson, and the young NAACP officer Walter Francis White, whose energies as a literary entrepreneur would soon excel even Charles Johnson's. Locke, professor of philosophy at Howard University and the first African-American Rhodes scholar, served as master of ceremonies. Fauset, literary editor of the *Crisis* and Phi Beta Kappa graduate of Cornell University, enjoyed the distinction of having written the second fiction (and first novel) of the Renaissance, *There Is Confusion,* just released by Horace Liveright. Liveright, who was present, rose to praise Fauset as well as Toomer, whom he had also published. Speeches followed in rapid succession—Du Bois, James Weldon Johnson, Fauset. White called attention to the next Renaissance novel: his own, *The Fire in the Flint,* shortly forthcoming from Knopf. Albert Barnes, the crusty Philadelphia pharmaceutical millionaire and art collector, described the decisive impact of African art on modern art. Poets and poems were commended—Hughes, Cullen, Georgia Douglas johnson of Washington, D.C., and, finally, Gwendolyn Bennett's stilted yet appropriate "To Usward," punctuating the evening: "We claim no part with racial dearth, / We want to sing the songs of birth!" Charles Johnson wrote the vastly competent Ethel Ray Nance, his future secretary, of his enormous gratification that Paul Kellogg, editor of the influential *Survey Graphic,* had proposed that evening to place a special number of his magazine at the service of "representatives of the group."

Two compelling messages emerged from the Civic Club gathering. Du Bois asserted that the literature of apology and the denial to his generation of its authentic voice were now ending; Van Doren said that African-American artists were developing at a uniquely propitious moment. They were "in a remarkable strategic position with reference to the new literary age which seems to be impending," Van Doren predicted. "What American literature decidedly needs at this moment is color, music, gusto, the free expression of gay or desperate moods. If the Negroes are not in a position to contribute these items," Van Doren could not imagine who else could. It was precisely this "new literary age" that a few Talented Tenth leaders had kept under sharp surveillance and about which they had soon reached a conclusion affecting civil rights strategy. Despite the baleful influence of D. W. Griffith's *The Birth of a Nation* and the robust persistence of Uncle Tom, "coon," and Noble Savage stereotypes, literary and dramatic presentations of African Americans by whites had begun, arguably, to change somewhat for the better.

The African American had indisputably moved to the center of mainstream imagination with the end of the Great War, a development crucially assisted by chrysalis of the Lost Generation—Greenwich Village bohemia. The first issue of Randolph Bourne's *Seven Arts* (November 1916), featuring, among others of the Lyrical Left, Waldo Frank, James Oppenheim, Paul Rosenfeld, Van Wyck Brooks, and the French intellectual Romain Rolland, incarnated the spirit that informed a generation without ever quite cohering into a doctrine. The inorganic state, the husk of a decaying capitalist order, was breaking down, these young white intellectuals believed. They professed contempt for "the people who actually run things" in America. Waldo Frank, Toomer's bosom friend and literary mentor, foresaw not a bloody social revolution in America but that "out of our terrifying welter or steel and scarlet, a design must come." There was another Village group decidedly more oriented toward politics: the Marxist radicals (John Reed, Floyd Dell, Helen Keller, Max Eastman) associated with *Masses* and its successor magazine, *Liberator,* edited by Max and Crystal Eastman. The inaugural March 1918 issue of *Liberator* announced that it would "fight for the ownership and control of industry by the workers."

The African American had indisputably moved to the center of mainstream imagination with the end of the Great War, a development crucially assisted by chrysalis of the Lost Generation.

Among the Lyrical Left writers gathered around *Broom, S4N,* and *Seven Arts,* and the political radicals associated with *Liberator,* there was a shared reaction against the ruling Anglo-Saxon cultural paradigm. Bourne's concept of a "trans-national" America, democratically respectful of its ethnic, racial, and religious constituents, complemented Du Bois's earlier concept of divided racial identity in *The Souls of Black Folk.* Ready conversance with the essentials of Freud and Marx became the measure of serious conversation in MacDougal Street coffeehouses, Albert Boni's Washington Square Book Shop, or the Hotel Brevoort's restaurant. There Floyd Dell, Robert Minor, Matthew Josephson, Max Eastman, and other *enragés* denounced the social system, the Great War to which it had ineluctably led, and the soul-dead world created in its aftermath, with McKay and Toomer, two of the Renaissance's first stars, participating.

From such conceptions, the Village's discovery of Harlem followed logically and, even more, psychologically. For if the factory, campus, office, and corporation were dehumanizing, stultifying, or predatory, the African American—largely excluded from all of the above—was a perfect symbol of cultural innocence and regeneration. He was perceived as an integral, indispensable part of the hoped-for design, somehow destined to aid in the reclamation of a diseased, desiccated civilization. The writer Malcolm Cowley would recall in *Exile's Return* that "one heard it said that the Negroes had retained a direct virility that the whites had lost through being overeducated." Public annunciation of the rediscovered Negro came in the fall of 1917, with Emily Hapgood's production at the old Garden Street Theatre of three one-act plays by her husband, Ridgely Torrence. *The Rider of Dreams, Simon the Cyrenian,* and *Granny Maumee* were considered daring because the casts were black and the parts were dignified. The drama critic from *Theatre Magazine* enthused of one lead player that "nobody who saw Opal Cooper—and heard him as the dreamer, Madison Sparrow—will ever forget the lift his performance gave." Du Bois commended the playwright by letter, and James Weldon Johnson excitedly wrote his friend, the African-American literary critic Benjamin Brawley, that *The Smart Set*'s George Jean Nathan "spoke most highly about the work of these colored performers."

From this watershed flowed a number of dramatic productions, musicals, and several successful novels by whites, and also, with great significance, *Shuffle Along,* a cathartic musical by the African Americans Aubrey Lyles and Flournoy Miller. Theodore Dreiser grappled with the explosive subject of lynching in his 1918 short story "Nigger Jeff." Two years later, the magnetic African-American actor Charles GILPIN energized O'Neill's *The Emperor Jones* in the 150-seat theater in a MacDougal Street brownstone taken over by the Provincetown Players. *The Emperor Jones* (revived four years later with Paul Robeson in the lead part) showed civilization's pretensions being moved by forces from the dark subconscious. In 1921, *Shuffle Along* opened at the 63rd Street Theatre, with music, lyrics, choreography, cast, and production uniquely in African-American hands, and composer Eubie Blake's "I'm Just Wild About Harry" and "Love Will Find a Way" entering the list of all-time favorites. Mary Hoyt Wiborg's *Taboo* was also produced in 1921, with Robeson in his theatrical debut. Clement Wood's 1922 sociological novel *Nigger* sympathetically tracked a beleaguered African-American family from slavery through the Great War into urban adversity. T. S. Stribling's *Birthright,* that same year, was remarkable for its effort to portray an African-American male protagonist of superior education (a Harvard-educated physician) martyred for his ideals after returning to the South. "Jean Le Negre," the black character in e. e. cummings' *The Enormous Room,* was another Noble Savage paradigm observed through a Freudian prism.

But Village artists and intellectuals were aware and unhappy that they were theorizing about Afro-America and spinning out African-American fictional characters in a vacuum—that they knew almost nothing firsthand about these subjects. Sherwood Anderson's June 1922 letter to H. L. Mencken spoke for much of the Lost Generation: "Damn it, man, if I could really get inside the niggers and write about them with some intelligence, I'd be willing to be hanged later and perhaps would be." At least the first of Anderson's prayers was answered almost immediately, when he chanced to read a Jean Toomer short story in *Double-Dealer* magazine. With the novelist's assistance, Toomer's stories began to appear in the magazines of the Lyrical Left and the Marxists, *Diak, S4N, Broom,* and *Liberator.* Anderson's 1925 novel *Dark Laughter* bore unmistakable signs of indebtedness to Toomer, whose work, Anderson stated, had given him a true insight into the cultural energies that could be harnessed to pull America back from the abyss of fatal materialism. Celebrity in the Village brought Toomer into Waldo Frank's circle, and with it criticism from Toomer about the omission of African Americans from Frank's sprawling work *Our America.* After a trip with Toomer to South Carolina in the fall of 1922, Frank published *Holiday* the following year, a somewhat overwrought treatment of the struggle between the races in the South, "each of which . . . needs what the other possesses."

Claude MCKAY, whose volume of poetry *Harlem Shadows* made him a Village celebrity also (he lived on Gay Street, then entirely inhabited by nonwhites), found his niche among the *Liberator* group, where he soon became coeditor of the magazine with Michael Gold. The Eastmans saw the Jamaican poet as the kind of writer who would deepen the magazine's proletarian voice. McKay increased the circulation of *Liberator* to 60,000, published the first poetry of e. e. cummings (over Gold's violent objections), introduced Garvey's UNIVERSAL NEGRO IMPROVEMENT ASSOCIATION (UNIA), and generally treated the readership to experimentation that had little to do with proletarian literature. "It was much easier to talk about real proletarians writing masterpieces than to find such masterpieces," McKay told the Eastmans and the exasperated hard-line Marxist

Gold. McKay attempted to bring Harlem to the Village, as the actor Charlie Chaplin discovered when he dropped into the *Liberator* offices one day and found the editor deep in conversation with Hubert Harrison, Harlem's peerless soapbox orator and author of *When Africa Awakes.* Soon all manner of Harlem radicals began meeting at the West Thirteenth Street offices, while the Eastmans fretted about Justice Department surveillance. Richard B. Moore, Cyril Briggs, Otto Huiswood, Grace Campbell, W. A. Domingo, *inter alios,* represented Harlem movements ranging from Garvey's UNIA and Brigg's African Blood Brotherhood to the Communist party, with Huiswood and Campbell. McKay also attempted to bring the Village to Harlem, in one memorable sortie taking Eastman and another Villager to Ned's, his favorite Harlem cabaret. Ned's, notoriously antiwhite, expelled them.

This was part of the background to the Talented Tenth's abrupt, enthusiastic, and programmatic embrace of the arts after World War I. In 1924, as Charles Johnson was planning his Civic Club evening, extraordinary security precautions were in place around the Broadway theater where *All God's Chillun Got Wings,* O'Neill's drama about miscegenation, starring Paul Robeson, was playing. With white Broadway audiences flocking to O'Neill plays and shrieking with delight at *Liza, Runnin' Wild,* and other imitations of *Shuffle Along,* the two Johnsons, Du Bois, Fauset, White, Locke, and others saw a unique opportunity to tap into the attention span of white America. If they were adroit, African-American civil rights officials and intellectuals believed, they stood a fair chance of reshaping the images and repackaging the messages out of which mainstream racial behavior emerged.

Bohemia and the Lost Generation suggested to the Talented Tenth the new approach to the old problem of race relations, but their shared premise about art and society obscured the diametrically opposite conclusions white and black intellectuals and artists drew from it. Stearns's Lost Generation *révoltés* were lost in the sense that they professed to have no wish to find themselves in a materialistic, Mammon-mad, homogenizing America. Locke's New Negroes very much wanted full acceptance by mainstream America, even if some—Du Bois, McKay, and the future enfant terrible of the Renaissance, Wallace Thurman—might have immediately exercised the privilege of rejecting it. For the whites, art was the means to change society before they would accept it. For the blacks, art was the means to change society in order to be accepted into it.

For this reason, many of the Harlem intellectuals found the white vogue in Afro-Americana troubling, although they usually feigned enthusiasm about the new dramatic and literary themes. Most of them clearly understood that this popularity was due to persistent stereotypes, new Freudian notions about sexual dominion over reason, and the postwar release of collective emotional and moral tensions sweeping Europe and America. Cummings, Dreiser, O'Neill, and Frank may have been well intentioned, but the African-American elite was quietly rather infuriated that Talented Tenth lives were frequently reduced to music, libido, rustic manners, and an incapacity for logic. The consummate satirist of the Renaissance, George Schuyler, denounced the insistent white portrayal of the African American in which "it is only necessary to beat a tom tom or wave a rabbit's foot and he is ready to strip off his Hart, Schaffner & Marx suit, grab a spear and ride off wild-eyed on the back of a crocodile." Despite the insensitivity, burlesquing, and calumny, however, the Talented Tenth convinced itself that the civil rights dividends of such recognition were potentially greater than the liabilities were.

For whites, art was the means to change society before they would accept it. For blacks, art was the means to change society in order to be accepted into it.

Benjamin Brawley put this potential straightforwardly to James Weldon Johnson: "We have a tremendous opportunity to boost the NAACP, letters, and art, and anything else that calls attention to our development along the higher lines." Brawley knew that he was preaching to the converted. Johnson's preface to his best-selling anthology *The Book of American Negro Poetry* (1922) proclaimed that nothing could "do more to change the mental attitude and raise his status than a demonstration of intellectual parity by the Negro through his production of literature and art." Reading Stribling's *Birthright,* an impressed Fauset nevertheless felt that she and her peers could do better. "We reasoned," she recalled later, " 'Here is an audience waiting to hear the truth about us. Let us who are better qualified to present that truth than any white writer, try to do so.' " The result was *There Is Confusion,* her novel about genteel life among Philadelphia's aristocrats of color. Walter Francis White, similarly troubled by *Birthright* and other two-dimensional or symbolically gross representations of African-American life, complained loudly to H. L. Mencken, who finally silenced him with the challenge, "Why don't you do the right kind of novel. You could do it, and it would create a sensation." White did. The sensation turned out to be *The Fire in the Flint* (1924), the second novel of the Renaissance, which he wrote in less than a month in a borrowed country house in the Berkshires.

Meanwhile, Langston Hughes, whose genius (like Toomer's) had been immediately recognized by Fauset, published several poems in the *Crisis* that would later appear in his collection *The Weary Blues.* The euphonious "The Negro Speaks of Rivers" (dedicated to Du Bois) ran in the *Crisis* in 1921. With the appearance of McKay's *Harlem Shadows* in 1922 and Toomer's *Cane* in 1923, the officers of the NAACP and the NUL saw how real the possibility of a theory being put into action could be. The young New York University prodigy Countee Cullen, already published in the *Crisis* and *Opportunity,* had his mainstream breakthrough in 1923 in *Harper's* and *Century* magazines. Two years later, Cullen won the prestigious Witter Bynner poetry prize, with Carl Sandburg as one of the three judges. Meanwhile, the *Survey Graphic* project moved apace under the editorship of Locke.

Two conditions made this unprecedented mobilization of talent and group support in the service of a racial arts and letters movement more than a conceit in the minds of its leaders: demography and repression. The Great Black Migration produced the metropolitan dynamism undergirding the Renaissance. The Red Summer of 1919 produced the trauma that led to the cultural sublimation of civil rights. In pressure-cooker fashion, the increase in Harlem's African-American population caused it to pulsate as it pushed its racial boundaries south below 135th Street to Central Park and north beyond 139th ("Strivers' Row"). Despite the real estate success of the firms of Nail and Parker and the competition given by Smalls' Paradise to the Cotton Club and Connie's (both off-limits to African-American patrons), however, this dynamic community was never able to own much of its own real estate, sustain more than a handful of small, marginal merchants, or even control the profits from the illegal policy business perfected by one of its own, the literary Caspar Holstein. Still, both the appearance of and prospects for solid, broad-based prosperity belied the inevitable consequences of Harlem's comprador economy. The Negro Capital of the World filled up with successful bootleggers and racketeers, political and religious charlatans, cults of exotic character ("Black Jews"), street-corner pundits and health practitioners (Hubert Harrison, "Black Herman"), beauty culturists and distinguished professionals (Madame C. J. WALKER, Louis T. Wright), religious and civil rights notables (Reverends Cullen and Powell, Du Bois, Johnson, White), and hard-pressed, hardworking families determined to make decent lives for their children. Memories of the nightspots in "The Jungle" (133rd Street), of Bill "Bojangles" ROBINSON demonstrating his footwork on Lenox Avenue, of raucous shows at the Lafayette that gave Florenz Ziegfeld some of his ideas, of the Tree of Hope outside Connie's Inn where musicians gathered as at a labor exchange, have been vividly set down by Arthur P. Davis, Regina Andrews, Arna BONTEMPS, and Hughes.

In the first flush of Harlem's realization and of general African-American exuberance, the Red Summer of 1919 had a cruelly decompressing impact on Harlem and Afro-America in general. The adage of peasants in Europe—"City air makes free"—was also true for sharecropping blacks, but not even the cities of the North made them equal or rich, or even physically secure. Charleston, S.C., erupted in riot in May, followed by Longview, Tex., and Washington, D.C., in July. Chicago exploded on July 27. Lynchings of returning African-American soldiers and expulsion of African-American workers from unions abounded. In the North, the white working classes struck out against perceived and manipulated threats to job security and unionism from blacks streaming north. In Helena, Ark., a pogrom was unleashed against black farmers organizing a cotton cooperative; outside Atlanta the Ku Klux Klan was reconstituted. The message of the white South to African Americans was that the racial *status quo ante bellum* was on again with a vengeance. Twenty-six race riots in towns, cities, and counties swept across the nation all the way to Nebraska. The "race problem" definitively became an American dilemma, and no longer a remote complexity in the exotic South.

The term "New Negro" entered the vocabulary in reaction to the Red Summer, along with McKay's poetic catechism: "Like men we'll face the murderous, cowardly pack / Pressed to the wall, dying, but fighting back!" There was a groundswell of support for Marcus Garvey's UNIA. Until his 1924 imprisonment for mail fraud, the Jamaican immigrant's message of African Zionism, anti-integrationism, working-class assertiveness, and Bookerite business enterprise increasingly threatened the hegemony of the Talented Tenth and its major organizations, the NAACP and NUL, among people of color in America (much of Garvey's support came from West Indians). The UNIA's phenomenal fund-raising success, as well as its portrayal of the civil rights leadership as alienated by class and color from the mass of black people, delivered a jolt to the integrationist elite. "Garvey," wrote Mary White Ovington, one of the NAACP's white founders, "was the first Negro in the United States to capture the imagination of the masses."

The *Negro World,* Garvey's multilingual newspaper, circulated throughout Latin America and the African empires of Britain and France. To the established leadership, then, the UNIA was a double threat because of its mass appeal among African Americans and because "respectable" civil rights organizations feared the spillover from the alarm Garveyism caused the white power structure. While Locke wrote in his introductory remarks to the special issue of *Survey Graphic* that "the thinking Negro has shifted a little to the left with the world trend," he clearly had Garveyism in mind when he said of black separatism, "this cannot be—even if it were desirable." Although the movement was its own worst enemy, the Talented Tenth was pleased to help the Justice Department speed its demise.

The term "New Negro" entered the vocabulary in reaction to the Red Summer.

No less an apostle of high culture than Du Bois, initially a Renaissance enthusiast, vividly expressed the farfetched nature of the arts movement as early as 1923: "How is it that an organization of this kind [the NAACP] can turn aside to talk about art? After all, what have we who are slaves and black to do with art?" Slavery's legacy of cultural parochialism, the agrarian orientation of most African Americans, systematic underfunding of primary education, the emphasis on vocationalism at the expense of liberal arts in colleges, economic marginality, the extreme insecurity of middle-class status: all strongly militated against the flourishing of African-American artists, poets, and writers. It was the brilliant insight of the men and women of the NAACP and NUL that although the road to the ballot box, the union hall, the decent neighborhood, and the office was blocked, there were two paths that had not been barred, in part because of their very implausibility, as well as their irrelevancy to most Americans: arts and letters. These people saw the small cracks in the wall of racism that could, they anticipated, be widened through the production of exemplary racial images in collaboration with liberal white philanthropy, the robust culture industry located primarily in New York, and artists from white bohemia (like themselves, marginal and in tension with the status quo).

If in retrospect, then, the New Negro Arts Movement has been interpreted as a natural phase in the cultural evolution of another American group—a band in the literary continuum running from New England, Knickerbocker New York, and Hoosier Indiana to the Village's bohemia, East Side Yiddish drama and fiction, and the southern Agrarians—such an interpretation sacrifices causation to appearance. The other group traditions emerged out of the hieratic concerns, genteel leisure, privileged alienation, or transplanted learning of critical masses of independent men and women. The Renaissance represented much less an evolutionary part of a common experience than it did a generation-skipping phenomenon in which a vanguard of the Talented Tenth elite recruited, organized, subsidized, and guided an unevenly endowed cohort of artists and writers to make statements that advanced a certain conception of the race—a cohort of whom most would never have imagined the possibility of artistic and literary careers.

Toomer, McKay, Hughes, and Cullen possessed the rare ability combined with personal eccentricity that defined them as artists; the Renaissance needed not only more like them but a large cast of supporters and extras. American dropouts heading for seminars in garrets and cafés in Paris were invariably white, and descended from an older gentry displaced by new moneyed elites. Charles Johnson and his allies were able to make the critical Renaissance mass possible. Johnson assembled files on prospective recruits throughout the country, going so far as to cajole Aaron DOUGLAS and others into coming to Harlem, where a network staffed by his secretary, Ethel Ray Nance, and her friends Regina Anderson and Louella Tucker (assisted by the gifted Trinidadian short story writer Eric Walrond) looked after them until a salary or fellowship was secured. White, the self-important assistant secretary of the NAACP, urged Robeson to abandon law for an acting career, encouraged Nella LARSEN to follow his own example as a novelist, and passed the hat for artist Hale WOODRUFF. Fauset continued to discover and publish short stories and verse, such as those of Wallace Thurman and Arna Bontemps.

Shortly after the Civic Club evening, both the NAACP and the NUL announced the creation of annual awards ceremonies bearing the titles of their respective publications, *Crisis* and *Opportunity.* The award of the first *Opportunity* prizes came in May 1925 in an elaborate ceremony at the Fifth Avenue Restaurant with some 300 participants. Twenty-four judges in five categories had ruled on the worthiness of entries. Carl Van Doren, Zona Gale, Fannie Hurst, Dorothy Canfield Fisher, and Alain Locke, among others, judged short stories. Witter Bynner, John Farrar, Clement Wood, and James Weldon Johnson read the poetry entries. Eugene O'Neill, Alexander Woollcott, Thomas M. Gregory, and Robert Benchley appraised drama. The judges for essays were Van Wyck Brooks, John Macy, Henry Goodard Leach, and L. Hollingsworth Wood. The awards ceremony was interracial, but white capital and influence were crucial to success, and the white presence in the beginning was pervasive, setting the outer boundaries for what was creatively normative. Money to start the *Crisis* prizes had come from Amy Spingarn, an accomplished artist and poet and the wife of Joel Spingarn, chairman of the NAACP's board of directors. The wife of the influential attorney, Fisk University trustee, and Urban League board chairman L. Hollingsworth Wood had made a similar contribution to initiate the *Opportunity* prizes.

These were the whites Zora Neale HURSTON, one of the first *Opportunity* prize winners, memorably dubbed "Negrotarians." These comprised several categories: political Negrotarians such as progressive journalist Ray Stannard Baker and maverick socialist types associated with *Modern Quarterly* (V. F. Calverton, Max Eastman, Lewis Mumford, Scott Nearing); salon Negrotarians such as Robert Chanler, Charles Studin, Carl and Fania (Marinoff) Van Vechten, and Elinor Wylie, for whom the Harlem artists were more exotics than talents; Lost Generation Negrotarians drawn to Harlem on their way to Paris by a need for personal nourishment and confirmation of cultural health, in which their romantic or revolutionary perceptions of African Americans played a key role—Anderson, O'Neill, Georgia O'Keeffe, Zona Gale, Frank, Louise Bryant, Sinclair Lewis, Hart Crane; commercial Negrotarians such as the Knopfs, the Gershwins, Rowena Jelliffe, Liveright, V. F. Calverton, and music impresario Sol Hurok, who scouted and mined Afro-America like prospectors.

The philanthropic Negrotarians, Protestant and Jewish, encouraged the Renaissance from similar motives of principled religious and social obligation and of class hegemony. Oswald Garrison Villard (grandson of William Lloyd Garrison, heir to a vast railroad fortune, owner of the New York *Evening Post* and the *Nation,* and cofounder of the NAACP), along with foundation controllers William E. Harmon and J. G. Phelps-Stokes, and Mary White Ovington of affluent abolitionist pedigree, looked on the Harlem Renaissance as a movement it was their Christian duty to sanction, as well as an efficacious mode of encouraging social change without risking dangerous tensions. Jewish philanthropy, notably represented by the Altmans, Rosenwalds, Spingarns, Lehmans, and Otto Kahn, had an additional motivation, as did the interest of such scholars as Franz Boas and Melville Herskovits, jurists Louis Brandeis, Louis Marshall, and Arthur Spingarn, and progressive reformers Martha Gruening and Jacob Billikopf. The tremendous increase after 1900 of Jewish immigrants from Slavic Europe had provoked nativist reactions and, with the 1915 lynching of Atlanta businessman Leo Frank, both an increasingly volatile anti-Semitism and an upsurge of Zionism. Redoubled victimization of African Americans, exacerbated by the tremendous out-migration from the South, portended a climate of national intolerance that wealthy, assimilated German-American Jews foresaw as inevitably menacing to all American Jews.

The May 1925 *Opportunity* gala showcased the steadily augmenting talent in the Renaissance—what Hurston pungently characterized as the "Niggerati." Two laureates, Cullen and Hughes, had already won notice beyond Harlem. The latter had engineered his "discovery" as a Washington, D.C., bellhop by placing dinner and three poems on Vachel Lindsay's hotel table. Some prize winners were barely to be heard from again: Joseph Cotter, G. D. Lipscomb, Warren MacDonald, Fidelia Ripley. Others, such as John Matheus (first prize in the short story category) and Frank Horne (honorable mention), failed to achieve first-rank standing in the Renaissance. But most of those whose talent had staying power were also introduced that night: E. Franklin Frazier, winning the first prize for an essay on social equality; Sterling BROWN, taking second prize for an essay on the singer Roland Hayes; Hurston, awarded second prize for a short story, "Spunk"; and Eric Walrond, third short-story prize for "Voodoo's Revenge." James Weldon Johnson read the poem taking first prize, "The Weary Blues," Hughes's turning-point poem combining the gift of a superior artist and the enduring, music-encased spirit of the black migrant. Comments from Negrotarian judges ranged from O'Neill's advice to "be yourselves" to novelist Edna Worthley Underwood's exultant anticipation of a "new epoch in American letters," and Clement Wood's judgment that the general standard "was higher than such contests usually bring out."

Whatever their criticisms and however dubious their enthusiasms, what mattered as far as Charles Johnson and his collaborators were concerned was success in mobilizing and institutionalizing a racially empowering crusade, and cementing an alliance between the wielders of influence and resources in the white and black communities, to which the caliber of literary output was a subordinate, though by no means irrelevant, concern. In the September 1924 issue of *Opportunity* inaugurating the magazine's departure from exclusive social-scientific concerns, Johnson had spelled out clearly the object of the prizes: they were to bring African-American writers "into contact with the general world of letters to which they have been for the most part timid and inarticulate strangers; to stimulate and foster a type of writing by Negroes which shakes itself free of deliberate propaganda and protest." The measures of Johnson's success were the announcement of a second *Opportunity* contest, to be underwritten by Harlem "businessman" (and numbers king) Caspar Holstein; former *Times* music critic Carl Van Vechten's enthusiasm over Hughes, and the subsequent arranging of a contract with Knopf for Hughes's first volume of poetry; and, one week after the awards ceremony, a prediction by the New York *Herald Tribune* that the country was "on the edge, if not already in the midst of, what might not improperly be called a Negro renaissance"—thereby giving the movement its name.

These were the gifted men and women who were to show by example what the potential of some African Americans could be.

Priming the public for the Fifth Avenue Restaurant occasion, the special edition of *Survey Graphic* edited by Locke, "Harlem: Mecca of the New Negro," had reached an unprecedented 42,000 readers in March 1925. The ideology of cultural nationalism at the heart of the Renaissance was crisply delineated in Locke's opening essay, "Harlem": "Without pretense to their political significance, Harlem has the same role to play for the New Negro as Dublin has had for the New Ireland or Prague for the New Czechoslovakia." A vast racial formation was under way in the relocation of the peasant masses ("they stir, they move, they are more than physically restless"), the editor announced. "The challenge of the new intellectuals among them is clear enough." The migrating peasants from the South were the soil out of which all success would come, but soil must be tilled, and the Howard University philosopher reserved that task exclusively for the Talented Tenth in liaison with its mainstream analogues—in the "carefully maintained contacts of the enlightened minorities of both race groups." There was little amiss about America that interracial elitism could not set right, Locke and the others believed. Despite historical discrimination and the Red Summer, the Rhodes scholar assured readers that the increasing radicalism among African Americans was superficial. The African American was only a "forced radical," a radical "on race matters, conservative on others." In a surfeit of mainstream reassurance, Locke concluded, "The Negro mind reaches out as yet to nothing but American events, American ideas." At year's end, Albert and Charles Boni published Locke's *The New Negro,* an expanded and polished edition of the poetry and prose from the *Opportunity* contest and the special *Survey Graphic.*

The course of American letters was unchanged by the offerings in *The New Negro.* Still, the book carried several memorable works, such as the short story "The South Lingers On," by Brown University and Howard Medical School graduate Rudolph FISHER; the acid "White House(s)" and the euphonic "The Tropics in New York," poems by McKay, now in European self-exile, and several poetic vignettes from Toomer's *Cane.* Hughes's "Jazzonia," previously published in the *Crisis,* was so poignant as to be almost tactile as it described "six long-headed jazzers" playing while a dancing woman "lifts high a dress of silken gold." In "Heritage," a poem previously unpublished, Cullen outdid himself in his grandest (if not his best) effort with its famous refrain, "What is Africa to me." The book carried distinctive silhouette drawings and Egyptian-influenced motifs by Aaron Douglas, whose work was to become the artistic signature of the Renaissance. With thirty-four African-American contributors—four were white—Locke's work included most of the Renaissance regulars. (The notable omissions were Asa Randolph, George Schuyler, and Wallace Thurman.) These were the gifted men and women who were to show by example what the potential of some African Americans could be and who proposed to lead their people into an era of opportunity and justice.

Deeply influenced, as were Du Bois and Fauset, by readings in German political philosophy and European nationalism (especially Herder and Fichte, Palacky and Synge, Herzl and Mazzini), Locke's notion of civil rights advancement was a "cell group" of intellectuals, artists, and writers "acting as the advance guard of the African peoples in their contact with Twentieth century civilization." By virtue of their symbolic achievements and their adroit collaboration with the philanthropic and reform-minded mainstream, their augmenting influence would ameliorate the socioeconomic conditions of their race over time and from the top downward. It was a Talented Tenth conceit, Schuyler snorted in Asa Randolph's *Messenger* magazine, worthy of a "high priest of the intellectual snobbocracy," and he awarded Locke the magazine's "elegantly embossed and beautifully lacquered dill pickle." Yet Locke's approach seemed to work, for although the objective conditions confronting most African Americans in Harlem and elsewhere were deteriorating, optimism remained high. Harlem recoiled from Garveyism and socialism to applaud Phi Beta Kappa poets, university-trained painters, concertizing musicians, and novel-writing officers of civil rights organizations. "Everywhere we heard the sighs of wonder, amazement and sometimes admiration when it was whispered or announced that here was one of the 'New Negroes,' " Bontemps recalled.

By the summer of 1926, Renaissance titles included the novels *Cane, There is Confusion, The Fire in the Flint,* and Walter White's *Flight* (1926), and the volumes of poetry *Harlem Shadows,* Cullen's *Color* (1924), and Hughes's *The Weary Blues* (1926). The second *Opportunity* awards banquet, in April 1926, was another artistic and interracial success. Playwright Joseph Cotter was honored again, as was Hurston for a short story. Bontemps, a California-educated poet struggling in Harlem, won first prize for "Golgotha Is a Mountain," and Dorothy West, a Bostonian aspiring to make a name in fiction, made her debut, as did essayist Arthur Fauset, Jessie's able half-brother. The William E. Harmon Foundation transferred its attention at the beginning of 1926 from student loans and blind children to the Renaissance, announcing seven annual prizes for literature, music, fine arts, industry, science, education, and race relations, with George Edmund Haynes, African-American official in the Federal Council of Churches, and Locke as chief advisors. That same year, the publishers Boni & Liveright offered a $1,000 prize for the "best novel on Negro life" by an African American. Caspar Holstein contributed $1,000 that year to endow *Opportunity* prizes; Van Vechten made a smaller contribution to the same cause. Amy Spingarn provided $600 toward the *Crisis* awards. Otto Kahn underwrote two years in France for the young artist Hale Woodruff. There were the Louis Rodman Wanamaker prizes in music composition.

Both the Garland Fund (American Fund for Public Service) and the NAACP's coveted Spingarn Medal were intended to promote political and social change rather than creativity, but three of eight Spingarn medals were awarded to artists and writers between 1924 and 1931, and the Garland Fund was similarly responsive. The first of the Guggenheim Fellowships awarded to Renaissance applicants went to Walter White in 1927, to be followed by Eric Walrond, Nella Larsen (Imes), and Zora Neale Hurston. The Talented Tenth's more academically oriented members benefited from the generosity of the new Rosenwald Fund fellowships.

The third *Opportunity* awards dinner was a vintage one for poetry, with entries by Bontemps, Sterling Brown, Hughes, Helene Johnson, and Jonathan H. Brooks. In praising their general high quality, the white literary critic Robert T. Kerlin added the revealing comment that their effect would be "hostile to lynching and to jim-crowing." Walrond's lush, impressionistic collection of short stories, *Tropic Death,* appeared from Boni & Liveright at the end of 1926, the most probing exploration of the psychology of cultural underdevelopment since Toomer's *Cane.* If *Cane* recaptured in a string of glowing vignettes (most of them about women) the sunset beauty and agony of a preindustrial culture, *Tropic Death* did much the same for the Antilles. Hughes's second volume of poetry, *Fine Clothes to the Jew* (1927), spiritedly portrayed the city life of ordinary men and women who had traded the hardscrabble of farming for the hardscrabble of domestic work and odd jobs. Hughes scanned the low-down pursuits of "Bad Man," "Ruby Brown," and "Beale Street," and shocked Brawley and other Talented Tenth elders with the bawdy "Red Silk Stockings." "Put on yo' red silk stockings, / Black gal," it began, urging her to show herself to white boys. It ended wickedly with "An' tomorrow's chile'll / Be a high yaller."

A melodrama of Harlem life that had opened in February 1926, *Lulu Belle,* produced by David Belasco, won the distinction for popularizing Harlem with masses of Jazz Age whites. But the part of Lulu Belle was played by Lenore Ulric in blackface. Drama quickened again in the fall of 1927 with Harlemite Frank Wilson (and, for one month, Robeson) in the lead role in Du Bose and Dorothy Heyward's hugely successful play *Porgy. Porgy* brought recognition and employment to Rose McClendon, Georgette Harvey, Evelyn Ellis, Jack Carter, Percy Verwayne, and Leigh Whipper. Richard Bruce Nugent, Harlem's most outrageous decadent, and Wallace Thurman, a Utah-born close second, newly arrived from Los Angeles, played members of the population of "Catfish Row." Frank Wilson of *Porgy* fame wrote a play himself, *Meek Mose,* which opened on Broadway in February 1928. Its distinction lay mainly in the employment it gave to Harlem actors, and secondarily in an opening-night audience containing Mayor James Walker, Tuskegee principal Robert Russa Moton, Alexander Woollcott, Harry T. Burleigh, Otto Kahn, and the Joel Spingarns. There was a spectacular Carnegie Hall concert in March 1928 by the ninety-voice Hampton Institute Choir, followed shortly by W. C. HANDY's Carnegie Hall lecture on the origins and development of African-American music, accompanied by choir and orchestra.

Confidence among African-American leaders in the power of the muses to heal social wrongs was the rule, rather than the exception, by 1927. Every issue of *Opportunity,* the gossipy *Inter-State Tattler* newspaper, and, frequently, even the mass-circulation Chicago *Defender* or the *soi-disant* socialist *Messenger* trumpeted racial salvation through artistic excellence until the early 1930s. *Harper's* for November 1928 carried James Weldon Johnson's article reviewing the strategies employed in the past for African-American advancement: "religion, education, politics, industrial, ethical, economic, sociological." The executive secretary of the NAACP serenely concluded that "through his artistic efforts the Negro is smashing" racial barriers to his progress "faster than he has ever done through any other method." Charles Johnson, Jessie Fauset, Alain Locke, and Walter White fully agreed. Such was their influence with foundations, publishing houses, the Algonquin Round Table, and various godfathers and godmothers of the Renaissance (such as the mysterious, tyrannical, fabulously wealthy Mrs. Osgood Mason) that McKay, viewing the scene from abroad, spoke derisively of the artistic and literary autocracy of "that NAACP crowd."

A veritable ministry of culture now presided over African America. The ministry mounted a movable feast to which the anointed were invited, sometimes to Walter and Gladys White's apartment at 409 Edgecombe Avenue, where they might share cocktails with Sinclair Lewis or Mencken; often (after 1928) to the famous 136th Street "Dark Tower" salon maintained by beauty-culture heiress A'Lelia Walker, where guests might be Sir Osbert Sitwell, the crown prince of Sweden, or Lady Mountbatten; and very frequently to the West Side apartment of Carl and Fania Van Vechten, to imbibe the host's sidecars and listen to Robeson sing or Jim Johnson recite from "God's Trombones" or George Gershwin play the piano. Meanwhile, Harlem's appeal to white revelers inspired the young physician Rudolph Fisher to write a satiric piece in the August 1927 *American Mercury* called "The Caucasian Storms Harlem."

The third phase of the Harlem Renaissance began even as the second had just gotten under way. The second phase (1924 to mid-1926) was dominated by the officialdom of the two major civil rights organizations, with their ideology of the advancement of African Americans through the creation and mobilization of an artistic-literary movement. Its essence was summed up in blunt declarations by Du Bois that he didn't care "a damn for any art that is not used for propaganda," or in exalted formulations by Locke that the New Negro was "an augury of a new democracy in American culture." The third phase of the Renaissance, from mid-1926 to 1934, was marked by rebellion against the civil rights establishment on the part of many of the artists and writers whom that establishment had promoted.

Group portrait, including (back row, left to right) Ethel Ray (Nance), Langston Hughes, Helen Lanning, Pearl Fisher, Dr. Rudolf Fisher, Clarissa Scott, Hubert Delany. (Front row, left to right) Regina M. Anderson (Andrews), Luella Tucker, Esther Popel, Jessie Fauset, Mrs. Charles S. Johnson, E. Franklin Frazier. (Photographs and Prints Division, Schomburg Center for Research in Black Culture, The New York Public Library, Astor, Lenox and Tilden Foundations)

Three publications during 1926 formed a watershed between the genteel and the demotic Renaissance. Hughes's "The Negro Artist and the Racial Mountain," appearing in the June 1926 issue of the *Nation,* served as a manifesto of the breakaway from the arts and letters party line. Van Vechten's *Nigger Heaven,* released by Knopf that August, drove much of literate Afro-America into a dichotomy of approval and apoplexy over "authentic" versus "proper" cultural expression. Wallace Thurman's *Fire!!,* available in November, assembled the rebels for a major assault against the civil rights ministry of culture.

Hughes's turning-point essay had been provoked by Schuyler's *Nation* article "The Negro Art-Hokum," which ridiculed "eager apostles from Greenwich Village, Harlem, and environs" who made claims for a special African-American artistic vision distinctly different from that of white Americans. "The Aframerican is merely a lampblacked Anglo-Saxon," Schuyler had sneered. In a famous peroration, Hughes answered that he and his fellow artists intended to express their "individual dark-skinned selves without fear or shame. If white people are pleased we are glad. . . . If colored people are pleased we are glad. If they are not, their displeasure doesn't matter either." And there was considerable African-American displeasure. Much of the condemnation of the license for expression Hughes, Thurman, Hurston, and other artists arrogated to themselves was generational or puritanical, and usually both. "Vulgarity has been mistaken for art," Brawley spluttered after leafing the pages of *Fire!!* "I have just tossed the first issue of *Fire!!* into the fire," the book review critic for the Baltimore *Afro-American* snapped after reading Richard Bruce Nugent's extravagantly homoerotic short story "Smoke, Lillies and Jade." Du Bois was said to be deeply aggrieved.

But much of the condemnation stemmed from racial sensitivity, from sheer mortification at seeing uneducated, crude, and scrappy black men and women depicted without tinsel or soap. Thurman and associated editors John Davis, Aaron Douglas, Gwendolyn Bennett, Arthur Huff Fauset, Hughes, Hurston, and Nugent took the Renaissance out of the parlor, the editorial office, and the banquet room. *Fire!!* featured African motifs drawn by Douglas and Nordic-featured African Americans with exaggeratedly kinky hair by Nugent, poems to an elevator boy by Hughes, jungle themes by Edward Silvera; short stories about prostitution ("Cordelia the Crude") by Thurman, gender conflict between black men and women at the bottom of the economy ("Sweat") by Hurston, and a burly boxer's hatred of white people ("Wedding Day") by Bennett; and a short play about pigment complexes within the race (*Color Struck*) by Hurston, shifting the focus to Locke's "peasant matrix," to the sorrows and joys of those outside the Talented Tenth. "Let the blare of Negro jazz bands and the bellowing voice of Bessie Smith . . . penetrate the closed ears of the colored near-intellectuals," Hughes exhorted in "The Negro Artist and the Racial Mountain."

Van Vechten's influence decidedly complicated the reactions of otherwise worldly critics such as Du Bois, Jessie Fauset, Locke, and Cullen. While his novel's title alone enraged many Harlemites who felt their trust and hospitality betrayed, the deeper objections of the sophisticated to *Nigger Heaven* lay in its message that the Talented Tenth's preoccupation with cultural improvement was a misguided affectation that would cost the race its vitality. It was the "archaic Negroes" who were at ease in their skins and capable of action, Van Vechten's characters demonstrated. Significantly, although Du Bois and Fauset found themselves in the majority among the Renaissance leadership (ordinary Harlemites burned Van Vechten in effigy at 135th Street and Lenox Avenue), Charles Johnson, James Weldon Johnson, Schuyler, White, and Hughes praised the novel's sociological verve and veracity and the service they believed it rendered to race relations.

The younger artists embraced Van Vechten's fiction as a worthy model because of its ribald iconoclasm and its iteration that the future of African-American arts lay in the culture of the working poor, and even of the underclass—in bottom-up drama, fiction, music, poetry, and painting. Regularly convening at the notorious "267 House," Thurman's rent-free apartment on 136th Street (alternately known as "Niggerati Manor"), the group that came to produce *Fire!!* saw art not as politics by other means—civil rights between book covers or from a stage or an easel—but as an expression of the intrinsic conditions most people of African descent were experiencing. They spoke of the need "for a truly Negroid note," for empathy with "those elements within the race which are still too potent for easy assimilation," and they openly mocked the premise of the civil rights establishment that (as a Hughes character says in *The Ways of White Folks*) "art would break down color lines, art would save the race and prevent lynchings! Bunk!" Finally, like creative agents in society from time immemorial, they were impelled to insult their patrons and to defy conventions.

To put the Renaissance back on track, Du Bois sponsored a symposium in late 1926, inviting a wide spectrum of views about the appropriate course the arts should take. His unhappiness was readily apparent, both with the overly literary tendencies of Locke and with the bottom-up school of Hughes and Thurman.

The great danger was that politics was dropping out of the Renaissance, that the movement was turning into an evasion, sedulously encouraged by certain whites. "They are whispering, 'Here is a way out. Here is the real solution to the color problem. The recognition accorded Cullen, Hughes, Fauset, White, and others shows there is no real color line,' " Du Bois charged. He then announced that all *Crisis* literary prizes would henceforth be reserved for works encouraging "general knowledge of banking and insurance in modern life and specific knowledge of what American Negroes are doing in these fields." Neither James Weldon Johnson nor White (soon to be a Guggenheim fellow on leave from the NAACP to write another novel in France) approved of the withdrawal of the *Crisis* from the Renaissance, but they failed to change Du Bois's mind.

Like creative agents in society from time immemorial, they were impelled to insult their patrons and to defy conventions.

White's own effort to sustain the civil-rights-by-copyright strategy was the ambitious novel *Flight,* edited by his friend Sinclair Lewis and released by Knopf in 1926. A tale of near-white African Americans of unusual culture and professional accomplishment who prove their moral superiority to their oppressors, White's novel was considered somewhat flat even by kind critics. Unkind critics, such as Thurman and the young Frank Horne at *Opportunity,* savaged it. The reissue the following year of *The Autobiography of an Ex-Colored Man* (with Johnson's authorship finally acknowledged) and publication of a volume of Cullen's poetry, *Copper Sun,* continued the tradition of genteel, exemplary letters. In a further effort to restore direction, Du Bois's *Dark Princess* appeared in 1928 from Harcourt, Brace; it was a large, serious novel in which the "problem of the twentieth century" is taken in charge by a Talented Tenth International whose prime mover is a princess from India. But the momentum stayed firmly with the rebels.

Although Thurman's magazine died after one issue, respectable Afro-America was unable to ignore the novel that embodied the values of the Niggerati—the first Renaissance best-seller by a black author: McKay's *Home to Harlem,* released by Harper & Brothers in the spring of 1928. No graduates of Howard or Harvard discourse on literature at the Dark Tower or at Jessie Fauset's in this novel. It has no imitations of Du Bois, James Weldon Johnson, or Locke—and no whites at all. Its milieu is wholly plebeian. The protagonist, Jake, is a Lenox Avenue Noble Savage who demonstrates (in marked contrast to the book-reading Ray) the superiority of the Negro mind uncorrupted by European learning. *Home to Harlem* finally shattered the enforced literary code of the civil rights establishment. The *Defender* disliked McKay's novel, and Du Bois, who confessed feeling "distinctly like needing a bath" after reading it, declared that *Home to Harlem* was about the "debauched tenth." Rudolph Fisher's *The Walls of Jericho,* appearing that year from Knopf, was a brilliant, deftly executed satire that upset Du Bois as much as it heartened Thurman. Fisher, a successful Harlem physician with solid Talented Tenth family credentials, satirized the NAACP, the Negrotarians, Harlem high society, and easily recognized Renaissance notables, while entering convincingly into the world of the working classes, organized crime, and romance across social strata.

Charles Johnson, preparing to leave the editorship of *Opportunity* for a professorship in sociology at Fisk University, now encouraged the young rebels. Before departing, he edited an anthology of Renaissance prose and poetry, *Ebony and Topaz,* in late 1927. The movement was over its birth pangs, his preface declared. Sounding the note of Hughes's manifesto, he declared that the period of extreme touchiness was behind. Renaissance artists were "now less self-conscious, less interested in proving that they are just like white people. . . . Relief from the stifling consciousness of being a problem has brought a certain superiority" to the Harlem Renaissance, Johnson asserted. Johnson left for Nashville in March 1928, four years to the month after his first Civic Club invitations.

Meanwhile, McKay's and Fisher's fiction inspired the Niggerati to publish an improved version of *Fire!!* The magazine, *Harlem,* appeared in November 1928. Editor Thurman announced portentously, "The time has now come when the Negro artist can be his true self and pander to the stupidities of no one, either white or black." While Brawley, Du Bois, and Fauset continued to grimace, *Harlem* benefited from significant defections. It won the collaboration of Locke and White; Roy de Coverly, George W. Little, and Schuyler signed on; and Hughes contributed one of his finest short stories, based on his travels down the west coast of Africa—"Luani of the Jungles," a polished genre piece on the seductions of the civilized and the primitive. Once again, Nugent was wicked, but this time more conventionally. The magazine lasted two issues.

The other Renaissance novel that year from Knopf, Nella Larsen's *Quicksand,* achieved the distinction of being praised by Du Bois, Locke, and Hughes. Larsen was born in the Danish Virgin Islands of mixed parentage. Trained in the sciences at Fisk and the University of Copenhagen, she would remain something of a mystery woman, helped in her career by Van Vechten and White but somehow always receding, and finally disappearing altogether from the Harlem scene. *Quicksand* was a triumph of vivid yet economical writing and rich allegory. Its very modern heroine experiences misfortunes and ultimate destruction from causes that are both racial and individual; she is not a tragic mulatto, but a mulatto who is tragic for both sociological and existential reasons. Roark Bradford, in the *Herald Tribune,* thought *Quicksand's* first half very good, and Du Bois said it was the best fiction since Chesnutt.

There were reviews (*Crisis, New Republic, New York Times*) that were as laudatory about Jessie Fauset's *Plum Bun,* also a 1928 release, but they were primarily due to the novel's engrossing reconstruction of rarefied, upper-class African-American life in Philadelphia, rather than to special literary merit. If Helga Crane, the protagonist of *Quicksand,* was the Virginia Slim of Renaissance fiction, then Angela Murray (Angele, in her white persona), Fauset's heroine in her second novel, was its Gibson Girl. *Plum Bun* continued the second phase of the Renaissance, as did Cullen's second volume of poetry, *The Black Christ,* published in 1929. Ostensibly about a lynching, the lengthy title poem lost its way in mysticism, paganism, and religious remorse. The volume also lost the sympathies of most reviewers.

Thurman's *The Blacker the Berry,* published by Macaulay in early 1929, although talky and awkward in spots (Thurman had hoped to write the Great African-American Novel), was a breakthrough. The reviewer for the Chicago *Defender* enthused, "Here at last is the book for which I have been waiting, and for which you have been waiting." Hughes praised it as a "gorgeous book," mischievously writing Thurman that it would embarrass those who bestowed the "seal-of-high-and-holy approval of Harmon awards." The ministry of culture found the novel distinctly distasteful: *Opportunity* judged *The Blacker the Berry* to be fatally flawed by "immaturity and gaucherie." For the first time, color prejudice within the race was the central theme of an African-American novel. Emma Lou, its heroine (like the author, very dark and conventionally unattractive), is obsessed with respectability as well as tortured by her pigment. Thurman makes the point on every page that Afro-America's aesthetic and spiritual center resides in the unaffected, unblended, noisome common folk and the liberated, unconventional artists.

With the unprecedented Broadway success of *Harlem,* Thurman's sensationalized romp through the underside of that area, the triumph of Niggerati aesthetics over civil rights arts and letters was impressively confirmed. The able theater critic for the *Messenger,* Theophilus Lewis, rejoiced at the "wholesome swing toward dramatic normalcy." George Jean Nathan lauded *Harlem* for its "sharp smell of reality." Another equally sharp smell of reality irritated establishment nostrils that same year with the publication of McKay's second novel, *Banjo,* appearing only weeks after *The Blacker the Berry.* "The Negroes are writing against themselves," lamented the reviewer for the *Amsterdam News.* Set among the human flotsam and jetsam of Marseilles and West Africa, McKay's novel again propounded the message that European civilization was inimical to Africans everywhere.

The stock market collapsed, but reverberations from the Harlem Renaissance seemed stronger than ever. Larsen's second novel, *Passing,* appeared. Its theme, like Fauset's, was the burden of mixed racial ancestry. But, although *Passing* was less successful than *Quicksand,* Larsen again evaded the trap of writing another tragic-mulatto novel by opposing the richness of African-American life to the material advantages afforded by the option of "passing." In February 1930, white playwright Marc Connelly's dramatization of Roark Bradford's book of short stories opened on Broadway as *The Green Pastures.* The Hall Johnson Choir sang in it, Richard Harrison played "De Lawd," and scores of Harlemites found parts during 557 performances at the Mansfield Theatre, and then on tour across the country. The demanding young critic and Howard University professor of English Sterling Brown pronounced the play a "miracle." The ministry of culture (increasingly run by White, after James Weldon Johnson followed Charles Johnson to a Fisk professorship) deemed *The Green Pastures* far more significant for civil rights than Thurman's *Harlem* and even than King Vidor's talking film *Hallelujah!* The NAACP's Spingarn Medal for 1930 was presented to Harrison by New York's lieutenant governor, Herbert Lehman.

After *The Green Pastures* came *Not Without Laughter,* Hughes's glowing novel from Knopf. Financed by Charlotte Osgood Mason ("Godmother") and Amy Spingarn, Hughes had resumed his college education at Lincoln University and completed *Not Without Laughter* his senior year. The beleaguered family at the center of the novel represents Afro-Americans in transition within white America. Hughes's young male protagonist learns that proving his equality means affirming his distinctive racial characteristics. Not only did Locke admire *Not Without Laughter,* the *New Masses* reviewer embraced it as "our novel." The ministry of culture decreed Hughes worthy of the Harmon gold medal for

1930. The year ended with Schuyler's ribald, sprawling satire *Black No More,* an unsparing demolition of every personality and institution in Afro-America. Little wonder that Locke titled his retrospective piece in the February 1931 *Opportunity* "The Year of Grace." Depression notwithstanding, the Renaissance appeared to be more robust than ever.

The first Rosenwald fellowships for African Americans had been secured, largely due to James Weldon Johnson's influence, the previous year. Beginning with Johnson himself in 1930, most of the African Americans who pursued cutting-edge postgraduate studies in the United States over the next fifteen years would be recipients of annual Rosenwald fellowships. Since 1928 the Harmon Foundation, advised by Locke, had mounted an annual traveling exhibition of drawings, paintings, and sculpture by African Americans. The 1930 installment introduced the generally unsuspected talent and genius of Palmer Hayden, William H. Johnson, Archibald Motley, Jr., James A. Porter, and Laura Wheeler Waring in painting. Sargent Johnson, Elizabeth Prophet, and Augusta SAVAGE were the outstanding sculptors of the show. Both Aaron Douglas and Romare BEARDEN came to feel that the standards of the foundation were somewhat indulgent and therefore injurious to many young artists, which was undoubtedly true. Nevertheless, the Harmon made it possible for African-American artists to find markets previously wholly closed to them. In 1931, more than 200 works of art formed the Harmon Travelling Exhibition of the Work of Negro Artists, to be seen by more than 150,000 people.

Superficially, Harlem itself appeared to be in fair health well into 1931. James Weldon Johnson's celebration of the community's strengths, *Black Manhattan,* was published near the end of 1930. "Harlem is still in the process of making," the book proclaimed, and the author's confidence in the power of the "recent literary and artistic emergence" to ameliorate race relations was unshaken. In Johnson's Harlem, redcaps and cooks cheered when Renaissance talents won Guggenheim and Rosenwald fellowships; they rushed to newsstands whenever the *American Mercury* or *New Republic* mentioned activities above Central Park. In this Harlem, dramatic productions unfolded weekly at the YMCA; poetry readings were held regularly at Ernestine Rose's 135th Street Public Library (today's Schomburg Center); and people came after work to try out for Du Bois's Krigwa Players in the library's basement. It was the Harlem of amateur historians such as J. A. Rogers, who made extraordinary claims about the achievements of persons of color, and of dogged bibliophiles such as Arthur Schomburg, who documented extraordinary claims. It was much too easy for Talented Tenth notables Johnson, White, and Locke not to notice in the second year of the Great Depression that for the vast majority of the population, Harlem was in the process of unmaking. Still, there was a definite prefiguration of its mortality when A'Lelia Walker suddenly died in August 1931, a doleful occurrence shortly followed by the sale of Villa Lewaro, her Hudson mansion, at public auction.

Meanwhile, the much-decorated Fifteenth Infantry Regiment (the 369th during World War I) took possession of a new headquarters, the largest National Guard armory in the state. The monopoly of white doctors and nurses at Harlem General Hospital had been effectively challenged by the NAACP and the brilliant young surgeon Louis T. Wright. There were two well-equipped private sanitariums in Harlem by the end of the 1920s: the Vincent, financed by numbers king Caspar Holstein, and the Wiley Wilson, equipped with divorce settlement funds by one of A'Lelia Walker's husbands. Rudolph Fisher's X-ray laboratory was one of the most photographed facilities in Harlem.

It was much too easy for Talented Tenth notables Johnson, White, and Locke not to notice that for the vast majority of the population, Harlem was in the process of unmaking.

Decent housing was becoming increasingly scarce for most families; the affluent, however, had access to excellent accommodations. Talented Tenth visitors availed themselves of the Dumas or the Olga, two well-appointed hotels. By the end of 1929, African Americans lived in the 500 block of Edgecombe Avenue, known as "Sugar Hill." The famous "409" overlooking the Polo Grounds was home at one time or another to the Du Boises, the Fishers, and the Whites. Below Sugar Hill was the five-acre, Rockefeller-financed Dunbar Apartments complex, its 511 units fully occupied in mid-1928. The Dunbar eventually became home for the Du Boises, E. Simms Campbell (illustrator and cartoonist), Fletcher Henderson, the A. Philip Randolphs, Leigh Whipper (actor), and, briefly, Paul and Essie Robeson. The complex published its own weekly bulletin, the *Dunbar News,* an even more valuable record of Talented Tenth activities during the Renaissance than the *Inter-State Tattler.*

The 1931 *Report on Negro Housing,* presented to President Hoover, was a document starkly in contrast to the optimism found in *Black Manhattan.* Nearly 50 percent of Harlem's families would be unemployed by the end of 1932. The syphilis rate was nine times higher than white Manhattan's; the tuberculosis rate was five times greater; those for pneumonia and typhoid were twice those of whites. Two African-American mothers and two babies died for every white mother and child. Harlem General Hospital, the area's single public facility, served 200,000 people with 273 beds. Twice as much of the income of a Harlem family went for rent as a white family's. Meanwhile, median family income in Harlem dropped 43.6 percent in two years by 1932. The ending of Prohibition would devastate scores of marginal speakeasies, as well as prove fatal to theaters such as the Lafayette. Connie's Inn would eventually migrate downtown. Until then, however, the clubs in "The Jungle," as 133rd Street was called (Bamville, Connor's, the Clam House, the Nest Club), and elsewhere (Pod's and Jerry's, Smalls' Paradise) continued to do a land-office business.

Because economic power was the Achilles' heel of the community, real political power also eluded Harlem. Harlem's Republican congressional candidates made unsuccessful runs in 1924 and 1928. Until the Twenty-first Congressional District was redrawn after the Second World War, African Americans were unable to overcome Irish, Italian, and Jewish voting patterns in order to elect one of their own. In state and city elections, black Harlem fared better. African-American aldermen had served on the City Council since 1919; black state assemblymen were first elected in 1917. Republican party patronage was funneled through the capable but aged Charles W. ("Charlie") Anderson, collector of Internal Revenue for the Third District. Although African Americans voted overwhelmingly for the Republican ticket at the national level, Harlemites readily voted for Democrats in city matters. Democratic patronage for Harlem was handled by Harvard-educated Ferdinand Q. Morton, chairman of the Municipal Civil Service Commission and head of the United Colored Democracy—"Black Tammany." In 1933, Morton would bolt the Democrats to help elect Fusion candidate Fiorello La Guardia mayor. Despite a growing sense of political consciousness, greatly intensified by the exigencies of the Depression, Harlem continued to be treated by City Hall and the municipal bureaucracies as though it were a colony.

The thin base of its economy and politics eventually began to undermine the Renaissance. Mainstream sponsorship, direct and indirect, was indispensable to the movement's momentum, and as white foundations, publishers, producers, readers, and audiences found their economic resources drastically curtailed (the reduced value of Sears, Roebuck stock chilled Rosenwald Fund philanthropy), interest in African Americans evaporated. With the repeal of the Eighteenth Amendment, ending Prohibition, honorary Harlemites such as Van Vechten sobered up and turned to other pursuits. Locke's letters to Charlotte Osgood Mason turned increasingly pessimistic in the winter of 1931. In June 1932, he perked up a bit to praise the choral ballet presented at the Eastman School of Music, *Sahdji,* with music by William Grant Still and scenario by Richard Bruce Nugent, but most of Locke's news was distinctly downbeat. The writing partnership of two of his protégés, Hughes and Hurston, their material needs underwritten in a New Jersey township by "Godmother," collapsed in acrimonious dispute. Each claimed principal authorship of the only dramatic comedy written during the Renaissance, *Mule Bone,* a three-act folk play that went unperformed (as a result of the dispute) until 1991. Locke took the side of Hurston, undermining the affective tie between Godmother and Hughes, and essentially ending his relationship with the latter. The part played in this controversy by their brilliant secretary, Louise Thompson, the strong-willed, estranged wife of Wallace Thurman, remains murky, but it seems clear that Thompson's Marxism had a deep influence on Hughes in the aftermath of his painful breakup with Godmother, Locke, and Hurston.

In any case, beginning with "Advertisement for the Waldorf-Astoria," published in the December 1931 *New Masses,* Hughes's poetry became markedly political. "Elderly Race Leaders" and "Goodbye Christ," as well as the play *Scottsboro, Limited,* were irreverent, staccato offerings to the coming triumph of the proletariat. The poet's departure in June 1932 for Moscow, along with Louise Thompson, Mollie Lewis, Henry Moon, Loren Miller, Theodore Poston, and thirteen others, ostensibly to act in a Soviet film about American race relations, *Black and White,* symbolized the shift in patronage and the accompanying politicization of Renaissance artists. If F. Scott Fitzgerald, golden boy of the Lost Generation, could predict that "it may be necessary to work inside the Communist party" to put things right again in America, no one should have been surprised that Cullen and Hughes united in 1932 to endorse the Communist party candidacy of William Z. Foster and the African American James W. Ford for president and vice-president of the United States, respectively. *One Way to Heaven,* Cullen's first novel—badly flawed and clearly influenced by *Nigger Heaven*—appeared in 1932, but it seemed already a baroque anachronism with its knife-wielding Lotharios and elaborately educated types. An impatient Du Bois, deeply alienated from the Renaissance, called for a second

Amenia Conference to radicalize the ideology and renew the personnel of the organization.

Jessie Fauset remained oblivious to the profound artistic and political changes under way. Her final novel, *Comedy: American Style* (1933), was technically much the same as *Plum Bun.* Once again, her subject was skin pigment and the neuroses of those who had just enough of it to spend their lives obsessed by it. James Weldon Johnson's autobiography, *Along This Way,* was the publishing event of the year, an elegantly written review of his sui generis public career as archetypal Renaissance man in both meanings of the word. McKay's final novel also appeared that year. He worried familiar themes, but *Banana Bottom* represented a philosophical advance over *Home to Harlem* and *Banjo* in its reconciliation through the protagonist, Bita Plant, of the previously destructive tension in McKay's work between the natural and the artificial, soul and civilization.

The publication at the beginning of 1932 of Thurman's last novel, *Infants of the Spring,* had already announced the end of the Harlem Renaissance. The action of the book is in the characters' ideas, in their incessant talk about themselves, Booker T. Washington, W. E. B. Du Bois, racism, and the destiny of the race. Its prose is generally disappointing, but the ending is conceptually poignant. Paul Arbian (a stand-in for Richard Bruce Nugent) commits suicide in a full tub of water, which splashes over and obliterates the pages of Arbian's unfinished novel on the bathroom floor. A still legible page, however, contains this paragraph that was in effect an epitaph:

> He had drawn a distorted, inky black skyscraper, modeled after Niggerati Manor, and on which were focused an array of blindingly white beams of light. The foundation of this building was composed of crumbling stone. At first glance it could be ascertained that the skyscraper would soon crumple and fall, leaving the dominating white lights in full possession of the sky.

The literary energies of the Renaissance finally slumped. McKay returned to Harlem in February 1934 after a twelve-year sojourn abroad, but his creative powers were spent. The last novel of the movement, Hurston's beautifully written *Jonah's Gourd Vine,* went on sale in May 1934. Charles Johnson, James Weldon Johnson, and Locke applauded Hurston's allegorical story of her immediate family (especially her father) and the mores of an African-American town in Florida called Eatonville. Fisher and Thurman could have been expected to continue to write, but their fates were sealed by the former's professional carelessness and the latter's neurotic alcoholism. A few days before Christmas 1934, Thurman died, soon after his return from an abortive Hollywood film project. Ignoring his physician's strictures, he hemorrhaged after drinking to excess while hosting a party in the infamous house at 267 West 136th Street. Four days later, Fisher expired from intestinal cancer caused by repeated exposure to his own X-ray equipment. A grieving Locke wrote Charlotte Mason from Howard University, "It is hard to see the collapse of things you have labored to raise on a sound base."

The publication at the beginning of 1932 of Thurman's last novel, Infants of the Spring, *had already announced the end of the Harlem Renaissance.*

Locke's anthology had been crucial to the formation of the Renaissance. As the movement ran down, another anthology, English heiress Nancy Cunard's *Negro,* far more massive in scope, recharged the Renaissance for a brief period. Enlisting the contributions of most of the principals (though McKay and Walrond refused, and Toomer no longer acknowledged his African-American roots), Cunard captured its essence, in the manner of expert taxidermy.

Arthur Fauset attempted to explain the collapse to Locke and the readers of *Opportunity* at the beginning of 1934. He foresaw "a socio-political-economic setback from which it may take decades to recover." The Renaissance had left the race unprepared, Fauset charged, because of its unrealistic belief "that social and economic recognition will be inevitable when once the race has produced a sufficiently large number of persons who have properly qualified themselves in the arts." James Weldon Johnson's philosophical *tour d'horizon* appearing that year, *Negro Americans, What Now?,* asked precisely the question of the decade. Most Harlemites were certain that the riot exploding on the evening of March 19, 1935, taking three lives and causing $2 million in property damage, was not an answer. By then, the Works Progress Administration had become the major patron of African-American artists and writers. Writers like William Attaway, Ralph ELLISON, Margaret Walker, Richard WRIGHT, and Frank Yerby would emerge under its aegis, as would painters Romare Bearden, Jacob Lawrence, Charles Sebree, Lois Maillou Jones, and Charles White. The COMMUNIST PARTY was another patron, notably for Richard Wright, whose

1937 essay "Blueprint for Negro Writing" would materially contribute to the premise of Hughes's "The Negro Artist and the Racial Mountain." And for thousands of ordinary Harlemites who had looked to Garvey's UNIA for inspiration, then to the Renaissance, there was now FATHER DIVINE and his "heavens."

In the ensuing years much was renounced, more was lost or forgotten; yet the Renaissance, however artificial and overreaching, left a positive mark. Locke's *New Negro* anthology featured thirty of the movement's thirty-five stars. They and a small number of less gifted collaborators generated 26 novels, 10 volumes of poetry, 5 Broadway plays, countless essays and short stories, 3 performed ballets and concerti, and a considerable output of canvas and sculpture. If the achievement was less than the titanic expectations of the ministry of culture, it was an artistic legacy, nevertheless, of and by which a beleaguered Afro-America could be both proud and sustained. Though more by osmosis than by conscious attention, mainstream America was also richer for the color, emotion, humanity, and cautionary vision produced by Harlem during its golden Age. "If I had supposed that all Negroes were illiterate brutes, I might be astonished to discover that they can write good third-rate poetry, readable and unreadable magazine fiction," was the flinty judgment of a contemporary white Marxist. That judgment was soon beyond controversy largely because the Harlem Renaissance finally, irrefutably, proved the once-controversial point during slightly more than a single decade.

BIBLIOGRAPHY

Bontemps, Arna, ed. *The Harlem Renaissance Remembered: Essays Edited with a Memoir.* New York, 1972.

Huggins, Nathan I. *Harlem Renaissance.* New York, 1971.

———, ed. *Voices from the Harlem Renaissance.* New York, 1976.

Lewis, David L. *When Harlem Was in Vogue.* New York, 1981.

Wagner, Jean. *Black Poets of the United States: From Paul Laurence Dunbar to Langston Hughes.* Urbana, Ill., 1973.

– DAVID LEVERING LEWIS

HARLEM RIOTS OF 1935 AND 1943

In 1935, a riot broke out in HARLEM, N.Y., the "capital" of African-American life. Harlem had been hard hit by the Great Depression. White storeowners, despite a black majority clientele, often refused to hire African-American clerks. Boycotts and picketing, beginning in 1933, had forced some stores to hire black workers, but in 1935 several shopkeepers obtained an injunction against picketers, stalling the boycott movement. The injunction was enforced, often with some brutality, by New York police.

On March 19, 1935, a ten-year-old dark-skinned Puerto Rican boy, Lino Rivera, was caught shoplifting a small knife by a white storeowner at the S. H. Kress store on 125th Street. A scuffle ensued, and the boy hit a clerk. Police were called, and the boy was taken into custody and later released. Wild rumors spread that the boy had been beaten, especially after an ambulance arrived for the clerk. Soon after, a hearse parked by chance in front of the store, led to rumors of the boy's death. Harlemites, egged on by streetcorner speakers, surrounded the store and took to the streets, smashing windows and looting. Passing city buses were attacked. Police arrived to relieve the besieged storeowners. The following day, rioting resumed. By the end of the disturbance, three blacks had been killed, two hundred wounded, and $2 million of damage had been done, mostly to white-owned property.

Immediately following the disturbance, New York Mayor Fiorello La Guardia appointed a biracial Mayor's Commission on Conditions in Harlem, which commissioned a panel of experts, led by sociologist E. Franklin FRAZIER, to investigate the events. In the report, entitled "The Negro in Harlem: A Report on Social and Economic Conditions Responsible for the Outbreak of March 19, 1935," Frazier recommended vigorous antidiscrimination efforts by city housing, relief, and police authorities, and fair hiring in municipal jobs. La Guardia enlisted scholar Alain LOCKE to advise on implementing the report. Over the following years, La Guardia led efforts to enlarge Harlem Hospital, build public housing for blacks, convince city agencies to curb official racism, and train city police.

Nevertheless, conditions in Harlem remained tense through the early 1940s. Harlemites, led by City Councilman Adam Clayton POWELL, Jr., complained constantly of police brutality and housing and economic discrimination. Blacks resented the hypocrisy of fighting a war for democracy in the segregated Army. In 1943, La Guardia infuriated blacks by approving a whites-only downtown housing project, Stuyvesant Town, and allowed segregated naval personnel to use facilities at city-owned Hunter College. City authorities temporarily closed down the Savoy Ballroom, a leading Harlem nightspot, on the grounds that it was a center of drug use and prostitution.

In July 1943, New Yorkers learned of the massive race riot and police repression in Detroit, and many people feared a similar disturbance in New York. Powell warned repeatedly of tensions in Harlem. He called for black self-defense efforts. La Guardia, who denounced Powell as a demagogue, attempted to reduce tension and train security forces in proper riot control.

On August 1, 1943, Harlem "boiled over," in NAACP leader Walter WHITE's words. An African-American woman, Majorie Polite, became involved in an argument at the Braddock Hotel, and grew disorderly and profane. The management called the police when she refused to leave, and a police officer arrested her. Florine Roberts and her son Robert Bandy, a uniformed soldier, observing the action, demanded her release. Bandy then either grabbed the policeman's stick or hit him and ran. The officer called for him to stop, then opened fire, wounding him slightly. Bandy then went to be treated at Sydenham Hospital.

Rumors soon spread that police officers had killed a black soldier who was trying to protect his mother. Crowds of blacks surrounded the hotel, Sydenham Hospital, and the 28th Police Precinct. Three thousand blacks called out threats to the arresting officers. Around 10:30 P.M., crowds began breaking windows, vandalizing streets, and setting fires. La Guardia called out 5,000 police, who exercised great restraint in dealing with rioters, and firemen. He also toured the riot-torn streets pleading for calm in the company of such prominent African Americans as Max Yergan, a well-known Harlem political figure. During the next twenty-four hours, the mayor made five separate radio broadcasts, calling on Harlemites to return to their homes. After midnight, the mayor ordered the area closed to nonresidents, banned street assembly, and closed all establishments serving liquor. Walter White and others rode in city sound trucks through the area to help restore order. The riot ended before dawn. Six African Americans had been killed, 185 injured, and 500 arrested.

The next day, fearing a recurrence, La Guardia imposed a partial curfew, lifted the wartime dimout, and brought emergency food supplies to relieve burned out shops and houses. The mayor called in 8,000 state guard troops (including an all-black regiment), 6,000 police, and 1,500 volunteers, almost all black, to stand by in case of trouble, though none were actually called on to patrol in Harlem.

White city authorities and black Harlemites who feared negative repercussions from the riot sought to blame the disturbance on "hoodlums," and denied that ordinary citizens took part in the riot. Even Powell sought to minimize the disturbance, denying it was a "race riot" or that racial tension was responsible. Despite his own admission that he did no more—though no less—for Harlem than for other sections of the city, the mayor was popular among New York's black population, and his swift, impartial reaction to the riots served further to increase his standing. La Guardia convened an Emergency Conference for Interracial Unity, chaired by singer Marian ANDERSON and William Jay Schieffelin, which brought together 200 distinguished New Yorkers, including Powell, Stanley M. Isaacs, Duke ELLINGTON, Ruth Benedict, and others, to suggest ways to reduce racial tension. La Guardia soon reopened the Savoy Ballroom, and opened a branch of the Office of Price Administration in Harlem to check on price-gouging merchants.

Like the Detroit riot of 1943, the Harlem riots of 1935 and 1943 began with blacks unleashing anger at police brutality and economic discrimination by destroying property. However, they were smaller affairs than the fearsome explosion in Detroit. Despite tensions between La Guardia and Powell, this was due in part to the relative restraint and responsiveness of New York officials and their cooperation with the local black leadership. The unusual level of cooperation between black Harlemites and city authorities was significant, as was the willingness of black leaders to pretend that the riots were the work of a few troublemakers rather than the community at large. The explanation probably lies in a combination of factors: fear of Detroit-style bloodshed; a desire to avoid giving America's wartime enemies propaganda points; respect for La Guardia and for moderate civil rights leadership; and confidence in the possibilities for peaceful change far greater than that present in the 1960s riots.

BIBLIOGRAPHY

Capeci, Dominic J. *The Harlem Riot of 1943.* Philadelphia, 1977.

Hamilton, Charles V. *Adam Clayton Powell, Jr.: The Political Biography of an American Dilemma.* New York, 1991.

Naison, Mark. *The Communists in Harlem During the Great Depression.* Urbana, Ill., 1983.

— GAYLE T. TATE

HARLEM RIOT OF 1964

In July 1964, Harlem and several other African-American neighborhoods of New York City erupted in violence over police brutality, in demonstrations that prefigured the major urban rebellions later in the decade. In 1964, Harlemites had been involved in many large-scale protest activities, which had heightened their racial consciousness and militancy. On July 16, 1964, a fifteen-year-old African American, James Powell, was shot and killed by Thomas Gilligan, an off-duty police officer in Manhattan's Yorkville neighborhood. That night, there was a peaceful student protest march in Harlem. Two days later, the combined New York chapters of the CONGRESS OF RACIAL EQUALITY (CORE) sponsored a protest march and rally. Black leaders had repeatedly urged the creation of a civilian review board to investigate mounting complaints of police brutality in Harlem. Posters referred to Gilligan as a "murderer," and speakers called for a review board and the firing of the city police commissioner.

In July 1964, Harlem and several other African-American neighborhoods of New York City erupted in violence over police brutality.

After the rally, militant CORE speakers regrouped, and a crowd marched to the Harlem police precinct on 123rd Street to press their demands. When minor skirmishes began between demonstrators and police, police set up barricades and sixteen leaders were arrested and brought into the police station. Demonstrators charged that the protesters were being beaten and that their cries could be heard. Another skirmish broke out between police and demonstrators, with both groups gaining reinforcements. At approximately 10:30 P.M., a riot began with youths pelting police with missiles and Molotov cocktails, and police shooting over protesters' heads in an unsuccessful attempt to disperse them.

The rebellion continued for four nights, and spread to Brooklyn's Bedford-Stuyvesant neighborhood, where there was further rioting during the next two nights. Blacks roamed the street, carrying bottles and bricks. White-owned businesses were vandalized and burned by arsonists. Whites entering Harlem unguarded were beaten. CORE chairman James Farmer organized squads from CORE chapters and walked through Harlem's streets urging an end to the violence. He was ignored by the crowd and jeered by black militants, who called the riot a justified protest.

The uprising finally petered out on July 23, but even as New York City calmed down, related rioting struck Rochester, N.Y., and three cities in New Jersey: Jersey City, Elizabeth, and Paterson. Altogether, the violence left one man killed, 144 people injured, and resulted in 519 arrests. While the explosion seems small when compared to the urban riots that were to come in the next few years, it was the first major outbreak of urban violence in a generation.

BIBLIOGRAPHY

Meier, August, and Elliott Rudwick. *CORE: A Study in the Civil Rights Movement, 1942–1968.* Urbana, Ill., 1973.

Ritchie, Barbara. *The Riot Report: A Shortened Version of the Report of the National Advisory Commission on Civil Disorders.* New York, 1969.

– GAYLE T. TATE

HARLEM WRITERS GUILD

In the late 1940s, a number of talented and ambitious young African Americans were seeking a way to simultaneously express their creativity and promote social change. Two such figures were Rosa Guy and John Oliver Killens, who had studied literature and writing at prominent institutions like New York University, but realized that the mainstream literary world was largely inaccessible to blacks. Consequently, they began meeting with Walter Christmas and John Henrik Clarke in a HARLEM storefront to critique each other's ideas and stories. By the early 1950s, this workshop became known as the Harlem Writers Guild. During the Guild's early years, meetings were frequently held in Killens's home as well as the home of artist Aaron DOUGLAS. As membership grew, the Guild influenced several generations of African-American writers, whose work spanned many genres.

Killens's *Youngblood* (1954) was the first novel published by a Guild member. Appearing to critical acclaim at the beginning of the CIVIL RIGHTS MOVEMENT, it told the story of a Southern black family struggling for dignity in the early twentieth century. Although Killens was a native of Georgia and a tireless voice protesting racial injustice in the United States, he was also involved in left-wing politics as a young man, and Guild participants, many of whom were union organizers or Progressive party members, were encouraged to think globally. Christmas and Clarke were both contributors to communist periodicals, while other writers, such as novelists Julian Mayfield and Paule Marshall, called attention to the lives and struggles of slave descendants in Cuba and the West Indies.

Although its main goals were literary, the Guild believed in political action. In 1961, for example, Guy, Marshall and Maya ANGELOU staged a sit-in at the United Nations to protest the assassination of the first Congolese premier, Patrice Lumumba. That same year, when Fidel Castro and Nikita Khrushchev met in Harlem, Guild members joined another organization, Fair Play for Cuba, in welcoming them to the African-American capital of the world.

During the 1960s, a number of Guild members found work as professional writers, journalists, and editors in the publishing industry. As a consequence, the Guild, in addition to workshops, began sponsoring writers' conferences and book parties (the celebration at the United Nations for Chester HIMES's *The Quality of Hurt* drew 700 people). More than a thousand people attended a 1965 conference, "The Negro Writer's Vision of America," which was cosponsored by the New School for Social Research. This event featured a widely reported debate between Killens and Clarke and two white intellectuals, Herbert Aptheker and Walter Lowenfels, on the proper role of the artist in the fight against racism. Playwright Ossie DAVIS, a participant at the conference, summed up his viewpoint when he wrote in *Negro Digest* that the black writer "must make of himself a hammer, and against the racially restricted walls of society he must strike, and strike, and strike again, until something is destroyed—either himself—or the prison walls that stifle him!"

In 1970 Louise Meriwether published *Daddy Was a Numbers Runner,* and the next two decades saw the publication of acclaimed books by Grace Edwards-Yearwood, Doris Jean Austin, Arthur Flowers, and Terry McMillan, famed for her popular third novel, *Waiting to Exhale* (1992). Other Guild members, such as Guy, Joyce Hansen, Brenda Wilkinson, and Walter Dean Myers, focused on writing literature for children and young adults.

In the early 1990s the Guild sponsored several literary celebrations: a centennial salute to Zora Neale HURSTON, "The Literary Legacy of Malcolm X," and two tributes to Rosa Guy for her leadership in the organization. Some former Guild members also received national attention after the election of Bill Clinton as U.S. president. Essayist and poet Maya Angelou was chosen to read her poem "On the Pulse of the Morning" at the 1993 presidential inauguration. In addition, Clinton made it known that his favorite mystery character was Walter Mosley's Easy Rawlings.

In 1991 Guild Director William H. Banks Jr. began hosting "In Our Own Words" for the *MetroMagazine* section on WNYE. This weekly television program brought many Guild members exposure in six viewing areas in the United States and Canada.

Since 1988, writing workshops have met most frequently at the SCHOMBURG Center for Research in Black Culture of the New York Public Library.

BIBLIOGRAPHY

Cruse, Harold. *The Crisis of the Negro Intellectual.* New York, 1967.

Johnson, Abby Arthur and Ronald Maberry. *Propaganda & Aesthetics.* Amherst, Mass., 1979.

– SHARON M. HOWARD

HARPER, FRANCES ELLEN WATKINS

Frances Ellen Watkins Harper (September 24, 1825–February 20, 1911), writer and activist. One of the most prominent activist women of her time in the areas of abolition, temperance, and women's rights, Frances Ellen Watkins Harper also left an indelible mark on African-American literature. Frances Watkins was born in Baltimore and raised among the city's free black community. She was orphaned at an early age and her uncle, the Rev. William Watkins, took responsibility for her care and education, enrolling her in his prestigious school for free blacks, the Academy for Negro Youth. Here Watkins received a strict, classical education, studying the Bible, Greek, and Latin. Although she left school while in her early teens in order to take employment as a domestic, she never ceased her quest for additional education. She remained a voracious reader; her love of books contributed to her beginnings as a writer.

Frances Watkins published her first of several volumes of poetry in 1845. This early work, *Forest Leaves,* has been lost, however. From 1850 until 1852, Watkins taught embroidery and sewing at Union Seminary, an African Methodist Episcopal Church school near Columbus, Ohio. She then moved on to teach in Pennsylvania. Both teaching situations were difficult, since the schools were poor and the facilities overtaxed. During this period, she was moved by the increasing number of strictures placed on free people of color, especially in her home state of Maryland, a slave state. From this point, she became active in the antislavery movement.

In 1854, Watkins moved to Philadelphia and became associated with an influential circle of black and white abolitionists. Among her friends there were William Still and his daughter Mary, who operated the key UNDERGROUND RAILROAD station in the city. The same year another collection of Watkins's verse, *Poems on Miscellaneous Subjects,* was published. Many of the pieces in this volume dealt with the horrors of slavery. The work received popular acclaim and was republished in numerous revised, enlarged editions. Watkins also published poems in prominent abolitionist papers such as *Frederick Douglass' Paper* and the *Liberator.* Later would come other collections—*Sketches of Southern Life* (1872), the narrative poem *Moses: A Story of the Nile* (1889), *Atlanta Offering: Poems* (1895), and *Martyr of Alabama and Other Poems* (1895).

With her literary career already on course, Watkins moved to Boston and joined the antislavery lecture circuit, securing a position with the Maine Anti-Slavery Society. She later toured with the Pennsylvania Anti-Slavery Society. Watkins immediately distinguished herself, making a reputation as a forceful and effective speaker, a difficult task for any woman at this time, especially an African American. Public speaking remained an important part of her career for the rest of her life, as she moved from antislavery work to other aspects of reform in the late nineteenth century.

In 1860, Frances Watkins married Fenton Harper and the two settled on a farm near Columbus, Ohio. Their daughter, Mary, was born there. Fenton Harper died four years later, and Frances Harper resumed her public career. With the close of the Civil War, she became increasingly involved in the struggle for suffrage, working with the American Equal Rights Association, the American Woman Suffrage Association, and the National Council of Women. Harper also became an active member of the Women's Christian Temperance Union. Despite her disagreements with many of the white women in these organizations and the racism she encountered, Harper remained steadfast in her commitment to the battle for women's rights. She refused to sacrifice any aspect of her commitment to African-American rights in seeking the rights of women, however. She was also a key member of the National Federation of Afro-American Women and the NATIONAL ASSOCIATION OF COLORED WOMEN.

In addition to the many poems, speeches, and essays she wrote, Frances Ellen Watkins Harper is probably best known for her novel, *Iola Leroy; or, Shadows Uplifted,* published in 1892. The work tells the story of a young octoroon woman who is sold into slavery when her African-American heritage is revealed. It is a story about the quest for family and for one's people. Through Iola Leroy and the characters around her, Harper addresses the issues of slavery, relations between African Americans and whites, feminist concerns, labor in freedom, and the development of black intellectual communities. In this book, she combined many of her lifelong interests and passions.

Harper's public career ended around the turn of the century. She died in Philadelphia in 1911, leaving an enduring legacy of literary and activist achievement.

BIBLIOGRAPHY

Carby, Hazel V. *Reconstructing Womanhood: The Emergence of the Afro-American Woman Novelist.* New York, 1987.

Smith, Frances Foster, ed. *A Brighter Coming Day: A Frances Ellen Watkins Harper Reader.* New York, 1990.

– JUDITH WEISENFELD

HASTIE, WILLIAM HENRY

William Henry Hastie (November 17, 1904–April 14, 1976), lawyer and educator. William Hastie was considered one of the best legal minds of the twentieth century. He was once suggested for the presidency of Harvard University and twice considered as a nominee for the U.S. Supreme Court, reflections of the high regard in which he was held.

Hastie was born in Knoxville, Tenn., where he spent his early years. His father, a clerk in the United States Pension Office, and his mother, a teacher until his birth, offered him early examples of resistance to discrimination. Rather than ride on segregated streetcars, they provided alternative means for young Hastie to go to school, which sometimes meant walking.

The first African-American federal appeals judge, William Hastie (left) is congratulated on his appointment by Chief Judge John Biggs, Jr., of the Third Circuit in Philadelphia in 1949. (AP/Wide World Photos)

In 1916 the family moved to Washington, D.C., which gave Hastie the opportunity to attend Dunbar High School, the best secondary school in the nation for African Americans. There he excelled athletically and academically, graduating as valedictorian of his class in 1921. He went on to Amherst College, where he again established an excellent athletic and academic record. In addition to winning prizes in mathematics and physics, he was elected to Phi Beta Kappa as a junior, and served as its president during his senior year. In 1925, he graduated magna cum laude as class valedictorian.

After teaching mathematics and general science for two years at the Bordentown Manual Training School in New Jersey, Hastie pursued legal studies at Harvard Law School, where he distinguished himself as a student. He was named to the editorial board of the *Harvard Law Review,* the second African American to earn that distinction, and was one of its most active editors. Hastie received his LL.B. degree from Harvard in 1930 and returned there to earn an S.J.D. in 1933.

His academic career close followed that of his second cousin Charles Hamilton HOUSTON, who had also excelled at Dunbar High, Amherst College, and Harvard Law School. Upon completion of his legal studies, Hastie became a lawyer and went into practice with his father William in the Washington, D.C., firm of Houston and Houston. He also became an instructor at Howard University Law School, where Houston was vice dean. Working together, the two men transformed the law school from a night school to a first-class institution. As Robert C. Weaver recalled, "It was during this time that the Houston-Hastie team became the principal mentors of Thurgood MARSHALL, as well as symbols for, and teachers of, scores of black lawyers, many of whom played a significant role in Civil Rights litigation" (Weaver 1976, p. 267).

In 1930, the year that Hastie completed his first law degree, the NAACP decided on its legal strategy for fighting against racism: to attack the "soft underbelly" of segregation—the graduate schools. Hastie, Houston, and Thurgood Marshall became the principal architects of that strategy. In 1933, Hastie was one of the lawyers who argued the first of these cases: *Hocutt* v. *University of North Carolina*. Although the case was lost, his performance won him immediate recognition; more important, it laid the groundwork for future cases that would lead to the end of legal segregation in the United States.

As assistant solicitor for the Department of the Interior (1933–1937), Hastie challenged the practice of segregated dining facilities in the department. He also played a role in drafting the Organic Act of 1936, which restructured the governance of the Virgin Islands. In 1937, as a result of his work on the Organic Act, he was appointed federal judge of the U.S. District Court for the Virgin Islands, the first African American to be appointed a federal judge. He left this post in 1939 and returned to Howard Law as a professor and dean. In 1946, he went back to the Virgin Islands as its first black governor.

In 1940, Hastie was appointed civilian aide to the secretary of war and given the charge of fighting discrimination in the armed services. While he was able to make some progress after a little more than two years, conditions remained intolerable. Hastie decided that he could fight segregation more effectively if he were outside the constraints of an official position, and he resigned in January 1943.

In 1949, Hastie left the position of governor of the Virgin Islands to take a seat as judge on the Third Circuit Court of Appeals, where he established a positive reputation. His cases were never overturned, and they often established precedents that were upheld by the Supreme Court. He served the Third Circuit as chief justice for three years before retiring in 1971 and taking a position as senior judge.

Hastie received over twenty honorary degrees, including two from Amherst College (1940, 1960) and one from Harvard (1975). He was the recipient of the NAACP's Spingarn Medal (1943), the Philadelphia Award (1975), and the Washington Bureau Association's Charles Hamilton Houston Medallion of Merit (1976). He was elected a fellow of the American Academy of Arts and Sciences (1952) and was made a lifetime trustee of Amherst College (1962). His alma maters have also honored him with portraits: One, dedicated in 1973, hangs in the Elihu Root Room of the Harvard Law Library; the other, a gift of the Amherst College class of 1992, hangs in the Johnson's Chapel.

BIBLIOGRAPHY

Wade, Harold, Jr. *Black Men of Amherst.* Amherst, Mass., 1976.

Ware, Gilbert. *William Hastie: Grace under Pressure.* New York, 1984.

Weaver, Robert C. "William Henry Hastie, 1904–1976." *The Crisis* (October 1976): 267–270.

— ROBERT A. BELLINGER

HAWKINS, COLEMAN RANDOLPH

Coleman Randolph Hawkins (November 21, 1904–May 19, 1969), jazz saxophonist. Hawkins was born and raised in St. Joseph, Mo. His mother, a schoolteacher and organist, introduced him to music. By the age of nine, he had studied piano, cello, and tenor saxophone, and by the age of fourteen he was playing frequently at dances in Kansas City. By 1921 he was performing with the orchestra of the 12th Street Theatre in Kansas City, and at the same time studying music theory both at the Industrial and Educational Institute, and at Washburn College, in Topeka, Kans.

In 1921, Hawkins quit school to tour with Mamie Smith's Jazz Hounds ("I'm Gonna Get You," 1922) and two years later he moved to New York City, where he played with clarinetist Wilbur Sweatman at Connie's Inn. That year he was hired by bandleader Fletcher Henderson. His eleven-year engagement with Henderson's orchestra made him a star. Through touring and frequent recording, both with Henderson, a Benny Carter-led group known as the Chocolate Dandies, and other ensembles ("Dicty Blues," 1923; "The Stampede," 1926; "Sugar Foot Stomp," 1931; and "New King Porter Stomp," 1932), Hawkins became one of the dominant tenor saxophonists in jazz, proving that the instrument could produce more than novelty effects. Hawkins was also a progressive composer, whose "Queer Notions" (1933), with Fletcher Henderson's orchestra, featured unusual harmonies.

In 1934, Hawkins took a six-month leave from the Henderson band, never to return. He went to England to work for British bandleader Jack Hylton, and toured Europe to tremendous acclaim. Hawkins spent five years touring Europe. "Honeysuckle Rose" and "Crazy Rhythm" document his 1937 collaborations with fellow expatriate saxophonist Benny Carter and French guitarist Django Reinhardt. With war threatening Europe, Hawkins returned to the United States in 1939 to lead a nine-piece band at Kelly's Stable. That engagement immediately reestablished his reputation as the preeminent saxophonist in jazz.

In October 1939 Hawkins recorded "Body and Soul," which became one of the great musical landmarks of the twentieth century, demonstrating the extent to which Hawkins had elevated the tenor saxophone to a central place in jazz. With its ripe tone, jagged rhythm, and arresting harmonies, "Body and Soul" remains his best known and most identifiable recording. The recording also caps a major shift that had taken place in Hawkins's solo style. Whereas his early recordings with Henderson feature his big, powerful sound, and the so-called "slap-tongue" technique, characterized by rapid syncopations and arpeggiations that produced a "herky-jerky" sound, by the late 1920s Hawkins was developing the more swaggering, legato execution of tones first heard on "One Hour" (1929), with the Mound City Blue Blowers. That mature style, with its rough tone and vertical or chordal approach to harmony, established one of the two major schools of saxophone playing; the other school was that of Lester Young, with his light, vibratoless tone, and melodic, or horizontal, style of improvisation.

In October 1939 Hawkins recorded "Body and Soul," which became one of the great musical landmarks of the twentieth century.

Always a restless experimenter, Hawkins was one of the few swing era musicians to gain new distinction during the bebop era. In 1940 he organized his own big band, one of the first to record bebop, and during the next decade he performed with bebop musicians such as Thelonious MONK, Miles DAVIS, Max ROACH, Kenny Clarke, and Dizzy GILLESPIE and with Fats Navarro. Hawkins's "Picasso" (1948) is thought to be the first unaccompanied saxophone recording in jazz.

In the late 1940s and '50s Hawkins used New York City as a base from which to tour the United States and Europe, often with trumpeter Roy Eldridge. He also toured with the "Jazz at the Philharmonic" all-star jam sessions organized by Norman Granz (1945), and appeared on the 1957 television program "The Sound of Jazz."

Although his own playing was always firmly rooted in the traditions of the swing era, Hawkins kept up with new developments. He recorded with Thelonious Monk and John COLTRANE (1957), Bud Powell (1960), Duke ELLINGTON (1962), and Sonny Rollins (1963). He also recorded prolifically as a leader, including on *Hawk Eyes* (1957), *Night Hawk* (1960), and *Wrapped Too Tight* (1965). In the late 1960s Hawkins continued to appear at major jazz festivals and to perform in jazz clubs in New York. However, liver problems due to alcoholism made his behavior increasingly erratic. He died in New York in 1969.

BIBLIOGRAPHY

Chilton, John. *The Song of the Hawk: The Life and Recordings of Coleman Hawkins.* Ann Arbor, Mich., 1990.

James, B. *Coleman Hawkins.* Tunbridge Wells, 1984.

Williams, Martin. "Coleman Hawkins: Some Comments on a Phoenix." In *The Jazz Tradition.* New York, 1970, pp. 64–70.

— EDDIE S. MEADOWS

HEALTH AND HEALTH CARE PROVIDERS

The ability of a population to maintain itself relatively healthy and free of disease is an important index of social progress. For African Americans, the struggle has been a difficult one. There have been notable successes and significant failures—a mixed record complicated by factors rarely within the control of African Americans individually or as a group.

Health in the Antebellum Period

Under slavery, living and working conditions had a deep impact on black health. These conditions included housing, sanitation, food intake, labor, physical treatment, and clothing. While they varied from state to state and from plantation to plantation, conditions on the whole were poor, and certainly unstable and unpredictable. Slaveholders paid scant attention to how such conditions might influence the health of slaves, even though economic interests alone suggested the importance of maintaining a decent standard. Consequently, morbidity and mortality rates among blacks far exceeded those of whites. Medical treatment for slaves was provided by contract physicians who worked one or more plantations (often to supplement income from private or hospital practice among whites), and usually only in severe cases. Preventive medicine was rarely practiced. On any particular plantation, inoculation or vaccination programs against epidemic diseases such as smallpox usually began only after a sizable portion of slaves were affected. A few Southern health-care establishments, such as the Georgia Infirmary (founded in Savannah in 1832), offered treatment exclusively for blacks—both free and bonded.

Under slavery, living and working conditions had a deep impact on black health.

Some slaves practiced therapies based on herbal, magico-religious, and other customs brought from Africa. Planters often relied on these slaves as cheap, effective surrogates for white practitioners. In Virginia, for example, a slave known as "old Man Docr. Lewis" had a reputation for successfully treating ailments using a "decoction of herbs." A so-called "hoodoo doctor" in Georgia was believed to have applied in certain instances an effective combination of fetishes, incantations, and sprinkling powder (ingredients unknown). A special class of female practitioners—known as "Negro doctoresses"—evolved within the ranks of slaves. These women, who combined obstetric duties with the preparation and dispensing of medicinal herbs, were the starting point for traditions of black midwifery and root doctoring that thrived well into the twentieth century. African-American midwives and root doctors provided important health-care alternatives, particularly for poor and rural blacks whose access to regular practitioners was limited at best.

Slaves are known to have contributed to the larger body of medical theory and practice. Onesimus, a slave belonging to the eminent Bostonian cleric Cotton Mather, taught his master the live-virus principle of inoculation against smallpox. "I do assure you," Mather wrote in 1716 to an officer of the Royal Society, "that many months before I met with any Intimations of treating ye Small-Pox with ye Method of Inoculation, I had from a Servant of my own, an account of its being practised in Africa." Nevertheless, Mather received the credit and Onesimus's role was ignored. Another case involved a slave named Cesar, from South Carolina. This practitioner developed an apparently effective antidote for rattlesnake poison—a concoction of roots compounded with rum and lye—that was widely publicized in the mid- and late-eighteenth-century popular press. Unlike Onesimus, Cesar received not only due credit, but also, by vote of the state legislature, his freedom and an annual stipend of one hundred pounds sterling. James Durham, born into slavery in 1762, learned medicine by observing a succession of physician-masters. After purchasing his freedom in 1783, he established his own practice in New Orleans and maintained a correspondence (1789–1802) with Benjamin Rush, one of the foremost physician-scientists of the day.

As a group, free blacks did not fare much better than slaves. In northern urban centers, where many lived and worked, the medical establishment paid little attention to their plight; for the most part, they had to fend for themselves. Black patients were denied access to Bellevue Hospital in New York City until 1841, when a group of public-spirited citizens succeeded in persuading the administration to set aside a few (albeit carefully segregated) beds. Even in relatively enlightened cities like Philadelphia, populated by prominent white liberals, Quakers, and abolitionists, the vast majority of blacks remained isolated on the bottom rung of the social and economic ladder, employed primarily as day laborers or domestic servants, or in small business. This form of segregation took a curious twist during the Philadelphia yellow fever epidemic of 1793, when blacks, originally thought to have been immune from the disease, were coopted into nursing and corpse-disposal service in infected city houses. Even as their own people started succumbing to the disease, blacks continued a vigorous campaign to provide relief not only to black victims but to white as well. Under the auspices of the African Society, and the inspired leadership of two of its officers, Absalom JONES and Richard ALLEN, the campaign was marked by acts of individual heroism and group commitment that were not always appreciated by whites who benefited. Blacks stood accused, for example, of using the epidemic as an opportunity for extortion and other forms of exploitation. Such charges were especially hurtful considering that the African Society, an organization established for the relief of destitute Negroes, had gone beyond its normal call of duty to serve whites during the crisis. Jones and Allen responded to the charges in a 1794 pamphlet entitled *A Narrative of the Proceedings of the Black People, During the Late Awful Calamity in Philadelphia, in the Year 1793: and a Refutation of Some Censures, Thrown Upon Them in Some Late Publications.*

Early African-American Practitioners

Before the Civil War, only a handful of blacks practiced medicine in the sense of participating as part of a discrete professional class within mainstream established traditions. Those who did were often denied access to normal lines of professional discourse, including membership in medical societies, or were shunted to the periphery of accepted medical practice. Nevertheless, their routes of entry to the profession tended to follow the pattern of their white counterparts. The three major routes at the time were self-education, apprenticeship, and attendance at medical school.

Among the prominent self-taught African-American practitioners in the antebellum period was James Still. Still's herbal remedies became popular, among both whites and blacks in rural New Jersey, as an alternative to the surgical and other radical techniques commonly used by school-trained physicians. Other self-taught black practitioners included David Ruggles, a hydrotherapist whose "water-cure establishment" near Northampton, Mass., attracted an interracial clientele from throughout the country; and William Wells Brown, who practiced in Boston under the self-coined designation "dermapathic and practical physician." All had close ties to the abolitionist movement. Still's brothers, William and Peter, were known for their antislavery writings, while Ruggles wrote articles for *The Emancipator* and William Brown served as an agent of the Underground Railroad.

Blacks who trained for medical careers via the apprenticeship route included John Sweat Rock. Rock acquired the rudiments of the trade while serving under white practitioners in Salem, N.J. Although he was denied admission to at least one medical school because of his race, Rock finally earned the M.D. at American Medical College, Philadelphia, in 1852 or 1853. He settled in Boston, Mass., where he practiced medicine and dentistry before taking up law in 1861. An active abolitionist, in 1865 he became the first African American admitted to argue cases before the U.S. Supreme Court. The experience of Martin Robison Delany was similar. After serving apprenticeships and under several white physicians in Pittsburgh, Delany was denied admission to medical schools in Pennsylvania and New York. The Harvard Medical School admitted him and two other blacks in 1850, but refused to let them reregister after the first term, when white students petitioned for their dismissal on racial grounds. Although he never earned a medical degree, Delany alternated the practice of medicine in Pittsburgh, Chatham (Ontario), and Charleston (S.C.) with other interests as a writer, lecturer, and antislavery activist.

A small number of blacks managed to overcome the medical school color bar and acquire formal academic training. Among these were David John Peck, who in 1847 earned the M.D. at Rush Medical College, Chicago. James Skirving Smith attended courses at Berkshire Medical College (Pittsfield, Mass.) in 1848, shortly after earning the M.D. at Vermont Medical College. In 1849, Bowdoin Medical College awarded M.D.s to John Van Surley De Grasse (1825–1868) and Thomas Joiner White, while a third student, Peter William Ray, completed medical studies without taking a degree. Rebecca Lee, believed to have been the first African-American woman to earn the M.D., graduated from New England Female Medical College in 1864.

These, however, were unusual cases. African-Americans sometimes sought professional or educational opportunity abroad. James McCune Smith attended the University of Glasgow, where he earned the B.A. (1835), M.A. (1836), and M.D. (1837) before returning to New York City to set up practice. As with Delaney and other black physicians of the time, Smith's commitment to the antislavery movement occupied at least as much time and energy as his professional duties. He achieved a degree of notoriety in the early 1840s for his public rebuttals of Senator John C. Calhoun's attempts to rationalize the institution of slavery by portraying blacks as mental defectives. Calhoun had based his ideas on the work of a white New Orleans physician, Dr. Samuel Adolphus Cartwright (1793–1863), who, among other things, believed that slaves suffered from drapetomania, "a disease causing [them] to run away . . . as much a disease of the mind as any other species of mental alienation." Besides James McCune Smith, foreign-trained African-American physicians included Alexander Thomas Augusta, who earned his medical degree in 1856 at Trinity Medical College, Toronto, after being denied admission to schools in Philadelphia and Chicago. John H. Rapier, Jr. (1835–1865), migrated to Jamaica, where he served dental and medical apprenticeships and made plans to attend the medical school of Queen's University (Kingston, Ont.) and one of the Royal Colleges in England before finally earning his degree in 1864 at the College of Physicians and Surgeons, Keokuk, Iowa.

The Civil War and Its Aftermath

At least nine African-American physicians served with the Union Army during the Civil War. These included Rapier, Augusta, and De Grasse, along with Charles Burleigh Purvis, M.D., Charity Hospital Medical College, Cleveland, 1865; Courtland Van Rensselaer Creed, M.D., Yale University, 1857; Alpheus W. Tucker; William Ellis; William Powell; and Anderson Ruffin Abbott, M.D., University of Toronto, 1863. The relatively high casualty rate among black troops was a reflection not on the competence of these practitioners, but rather on the War Department's unwillingness to aggressively seek out, train, and commission more African-American physicians. This unwillingness illustrated, in microcosm, the diffident—if not uniformly hostile—attitude of the larger society (both northern and southern) toward the health needs of African Americans.

In fact, morbidity and mortality rates among blacks soared for a decade or so after the Civil War. Health-care services on the plantation may have been meager, but at least they had been available and provided in essential cases. As emancipated slaves (the so-called "freedmen") adjusted to their new station in life, they found themselves without access to such services. Smallpox, yellow fever, and cholera epidemics took a heavy toll among them. In Charleston, S.C., the death rate for blacks between 1866 and 1871 was twice that for whites, and the disparity was even greater for children under the age of five. According to some estimates, one-quarter to one-third of the former slaves in particular locales died during the early years of Reconstruction. The BUREAU OF FREEDMEN, REFUGEES, AND ABANDONED LANDS, established in March 1865 to help emancipated slaves adjust to new conditions, quickly turned its attention to the issue of health. The Bureau established fifty-six hospitals and forty-eight dispensaries, the largest the Freedmen's Hospital in Washington, D.C., and over a four-year period was said to have provided medical assistance to at least a million African Americans.

African-American Medical Schools, Hospitals, and Professional Societies

Health issues remained a major concern for blacks as they sought access to the social and professional mainstream of American life. With education widely perceived as a critical component in this struggle, medical schools were among the earliest programs to be established—either independently or with existing African-American institutions of higher learning. HOWARD UNIVERSITY (Washington, D.C.), founded in 1867, opened its medical department on November 9, 1868 with five professors and eight students. One antebellum black college, LINCOLN UNIVERSITY (Oxford, Penn., 1854), operated a medical department briefly from 1870 to 1872. Meharry Medical College (Nashville, Tenn.) opened its doors in 1876. The next quarter century saw the establishment of other black medical schools in Southern or border states. These included Leonard Medical School of Shaw University (Raleigh, N.C., 1882); Louisville National Medical College (Louisville, Ky., 1888); Flint Medical College of New Orleans University (1889); Hannibal Medical College (Memphis, Tenn., 1889); Knoxville College Medical Department (Knoxville, Tenn., 1895); Chattanooga National Medical College (Chattanooga, Tenn., 1899); State University Medical Department (Louisville, Ky., 1899); Knoxville Medical College (1900); Medico-Chirurgical and Theological College of Christ's Institution (Baltimore, 1900); and the University of West Tennessee (Jackson, 1900; Memphis, 1907).

Small health-care facilities were commonly established in connection with these schools. The Auxiliary Hospital, for example, was attached to Louisville National Medical College and administered for many years by a black woman doctor, Sarah Helen Fitzbutler (M.D. Louisville, 1892). Such institutions served two purposes—to provide clinical material for students and to

Toward the end of the nineteenth century, African-American health practitioners established their own professional societies in addition to medical schools and hospitals.

fill the void created by white hospitals, which either refused to admit blacks or offered them inferior treatment relative to that for whites. Black hospitals also provided suitable sites for the establishment of nursing schools. The schools offered opportunities for African-American women, whose important role in health care—stretching at least as far back as the traditions of the slave midwife and root doctor—would not have been realized otherwise because of the racially exclusionary policies exercised by white nursing schools. Such policies had hardened in the years following Black Reconstruction (the period of the so-called White Redemption), and were reinforced as a result of the Supreme Court's 1896 "separate but equal" decision in the case of *Plessy* v. *Ferguson.*

As the color line separating white from black grew sharper toward the end of the nineteenth century, and through the first half of the twentieth century, African-American health practitioners established their own professional societies in addition to medical schools and hospitals. Three highly regarded black physicians—Purvis, Augusta, and Tucker—were denied admission to membership in the all-white Medical Society of the District of Columbia in 1870. A biracial medical society, the National Medical Society (NMS), was established in response. NMS members could not attend conventions of the American Medical Association, however, because the AMA recognized only a single majority society from each state or locale—a technicality that hindered blacks in certain states from gaining access to the AMA as late as the 1950s. The Medico-Chirurgical Society of the District of Columbia, a successor to the NMS, was founded on April 24, 1884. Other early black medical societies included the Lone Star State Medical Association (Texas, 1886) and the Old North State Medical Society (North Carolina, 1887). The national African-American counterpart to the AMA, the National Medical Association, was established in 1895. Its charter states that it was born out of "the exigencies of the American environment [to] band . . . together for mutual cooperation and helpfulness the men and women of African descent who are legally and honorably engaged in the practice of the cognate professions of Medicine, Surgery, Dentistry and Pharmacy." Such organizations represented means by which critical health-care and professional issues facing blacks could be tackled.

Health Status and Progress in the Twentieth Century

The decades leading up to World War I presented a series of disturbing developments. First, the health status of African Americans appeared to be making little progress despite the fact that the number of black physicians more than tripled in twenty years (from 909 in 1890 to 3,409 in 1910). A 1906 monograph by W. E. B. DU BOIS, *The Health and Physique of the Negro American,* used statistical analysis to demonstrate that disparities between the health of whites and blacks had remained stable (or had even increased slightly) and that African Americans were dying in large numbers from a variety of conditions, primarily tuberculosis. Secondly, an influential policy document, the Flexner Report (1910), called for sweeping changes in medical education throughout the United States and Canada. The report declared that the black medical schools were so weak that only two—Howard and Meharry—were worth salvaging. As a result, all but Howard and Meharry were closed by 1923, leaving these two institutions with the awesome task of training the bulk of African-American physicians. Third, hospital experience became an integral component of medical training, reflecting new and demanding requirements developed by state boards with regard to individual licensure and institutional accreditation. This development severely limited postgraduate opportunities for African Americans, whose small hospitals could not generally meet the required standards and who continued to be denied internships and residencies at white hospitals. Freedman's Hospital, one of the few black institutions offering postgraduate training in the school year 1909–1910, had only eight openings that year.

These problems persisted between the world wars, and the African-American community did not present a united front on how to tackle them. The question was how to transform a two-tiered health system—one for whites, one for blacks—into something more equitable and just. Some African Americans urged the establishment of more and better black hospitals and medical colleges, while others suggested that such measures were short-sighted and would only detract from efforts to deal with larger, more endemic issues of discrimination and segregation. A heated medico-political dialogue ensued between black health professionals in the 1930s and 1940s. The African-American surgeon Louis Tompkins Wright, for example, was critical of foundations—like the Julius Rosenwald Fund—which provided monies to revamp existing black health-care institutions and to establish new ones. The only solution, Wright felt, was radical action: desegregation of white hospitals and medical schools. On the other hand, African-American surgeon Peter Marshall Murray argued that the key to improving black health and to increasing access of African Americans to careers in the health professions was not racial integration—or the merging of African Americans into the majority community—but rather what he termed "the proper development" of uniquely black institutions.

This dialogue paralleled the debate begun years earlier by W. E. B. Du Bois and Booker T. WASHINGTON over what the goals and ambitions of African Americans should be. Du Bois insisted that blacks demand equal social status and services—without compromise, without being discouraged by the depth of racial separatism in the society—while Washington advocated a separatist model of gradual improvement through self-help programs and, most important, the avoidance of racial conflict. As a matter of fact, Washington and Du Bois had much to say themselves on the subject of African-American health. In 1915, Washington initiated a Negro Health Program at Tuskegee Institute (Ala.) to raise consciousness among African Americans about the need for sound health practices. This program blossomed into the National Negro Health Movement, which was placed on a permanent year-round basis with support from the U. S. Public Health Service and other organizations. The program was phased out in 1950, at a time when it was believed that a racially separatist approach had run its course and that American society was gearing up "to work together for mutual welfare."

W. E. B. Du Bois, on the other hand, questioned the premises on which black and white health interests were separated to begin with, and doubted the view of optimists who felt that mid-century marked a new era of racial cooperation. He argued in *The Crisis,* the official organ of the NAACP, and in other forums, for a uniform, equitable system of health care regardless of race. Du Bois shared the principles of progressives who promoted comprehensive, antidiscriminatory health legislation during the 1940s. Their proposals, including the Truman-era Wagner-Murray-Dingell Bill (which was decried by the AMA and other establishment groups as a "socialist" evil), died with the advent of the Cold War and McCarthyism. They were revived, albeit in modified form, in the establishment of the Medicare and Medicaid systems during the 1960s and '70s.

Civil Rights, Health Care, and Medicine

A system that routinely excluded African Americans from most medical schools, that denied them admission to medical societies and recognition by some specialty boards, and that channeled them into segregated health-care facilities proved resilient to change. When Louis T. Wright was elected a fellow of the American College of Surgeons in 1934 (the first African-American fellow since the noted surgeon Daniel Hale Williams became a charter member in 1913), several voting members staged a walkout in protest and some threatened to rescind their own fellowships. The National Medical Association and the National Association of Colored Graduate Nurses struggled, with mixed success, to persuade the government to admit African-American physicians and nurses to service in the armed forces during World War II. Black health professionals could serve, the government finally allowed, but only within segregated units such as the 93rd Division at Fort Huachuca, Ariz. In 1947 Charles Richard Drew, head of surgery at Howard University, wrote to the editor of the *Journal of the American Medical Association,* Morris Fishbein, urging an end to what Drew termed the "repeated humiliation" of African-American physicians resulting from the AMA's bylaw that required a member first to join a constituent state society. A decade later Dr. Leonidas Berry, the lone black fellow of the American College of Gastroenterology, boycotted the College's 1958 convention in New Orleans to protest the hotel's refusal to provide him with accommodations.

Social activism in the 1960s may have stimulated legislation and reduced obvious inequities, but it did not eliminate barriers to health services for African Americans.

Such incidents were common well into the 1960s, and underscored the tortuous path that the nascent civil rights movement had yet to negotiate. Some African-American health professionals developed their own brand of social activism. As part of the Medical Committee for Civil Rights, a biracial group founded in 1963, they organized a petition drive urging the AMA "to speak out immediately and unequivocally against racial segregation and discrimination . . . wherever [they] exist in medicine and health services" and to terminate "the racial exclusion policies of State and County medical societies." African-American physicians picketed the AMA convention in Atlantic City in 1963 to protest that organization's lack of progress on such issues. They also demonstrated outside the conventions in New York City (1965) and Chicago (1966). The Medical Committee for Human Rights (founded 1964), successor to the Medical Committee for Civil Rights, became an important source of health-care support for workers during the civil rights movement.

Social activism in the 1960s may have stimulated legislation, modified certain attitudes, and reduced obvious inequities, but it did not eliminate barriers to health services for African Americans. The period from the 1970s to the 1990s contained disturbing trends. In 1993, a quarter of a century after the KERNER REPORT (issued by a commission appointed by President Lyndon B. Johnson) warned of the consequences of a racially separate and unequal society, there is evidence to suggest that little has changed—and, in some instances, it has changed for the worse. The evidence is found in health-care data as much as in statistics relating to unemployment, poverty, income, crime, and violence. African Americans who suffer heart attacks, for example, are less likely than whites to be aggressively treated with bypass surgery. Unequal access to prenatal care is demonstrated in the finding that African-American women with small babies are nearly three times as likely to undergo premature birth as white women in the same condition. In 1989, the overall infant mortality rate for blacks was more than twice that for whites. Life expectancy for African Americans peaked at 69.5 years in 1985 and declined to 69.2 years in 1991, while that for whites was both higher and on the increase during the same period. A 1991 study found that whites suffering from AIDS were 73 percent more likely than nonwhites to procure access to the drug AZT, then thought to be an effective treatment for the disease. Thousands of African Americans, a 1990 epidemiological survey found, die in the prime of life—and at rates more than twenty times that for whites—of health conditions that could be cured or treated by routine medical care. These conditions include appendicitis, pneumonia, gall bladder infection, hypertensive heart disease, asthma, influenza, and hernia.

African-American Contributors to Modern Medicine

No overview of health and medicine in the African-American community would be complete without a glance at some of the major accomplishments of black physicians. That many struggled against the currents of racial discrimination to acquire medical training and to establish themselves as clinical practitioners is significant enough, but it is truly remarkable that some also contributed to advancing the frontiers of medical knowledge.

Among the early pathbreakers was Daniel Hale Williams, a surgeon and founder of Provident Hospital, which served primarily the African-American community in Chicago. On July 9, 1893, Williams performed one of the earliest recorded cases of successful open-heart surgery. He entered the thoracic cavity of a stabbing victim and sutured the pericardium (the sac enclosing the heart), after which the patient recovered fully. Other notable African Americans included William Augustus Hinton, a bacteriologist specializing in research on venereal disease. A member of the Harvard Medical School Faculty and (from 1915) director of the Wassermann Laboratory of the Massachusetts Department of Public Health, Hinton developed a flocculation method for detecting syphilis. This became known as the "Hinton test," which, along with the Wassermann and Kahn tests, served as a standard diagnostic technique in laboratories throughout the United States and abroad. Largely for racial reasons, Hinton felt obliged to eschew public recognition of his achievement. His fear was that the Hinton test would not gain general acceptance, should it become too widely known that its originator was an African American.

As in the white medical community, major advances tended to come out of the work of African Americans located in urban centers, where research and clinical facilities were relatively abundant. Solomon Carter Fuller, a staff member at the Westborough State Hospital near Boston, Mass., wrote widely on neurologic, pathologic, and psychiatric subjects and became known for his work on dementias and Alzheimer's disease. He was one of the earliest researchers to suggest that Alzheimer's did not result from arteriosclerosis. William Harry Barnes, an otolaryngologist attached to hospitals in Philadelphia, devised several instruments that came into widespread surgical use. The most notable, perhaps, was his hypophyscope (1926) providing easier access to the pituitary gland. Louis T. Wright, whose career at Harlem Hospital covered more than three decades (1919–1952), displayed an unusual versatility of interests. Highly regarded as a surgeon, he proposed new perspectives on skull-fracture treatment, devised implements for dealing with knee-joint and cervical vertebrae fractures, developed a method for intradermal vaccination against smallpox, oversaw the first tests on humans of the antibiotic aureomycin, and conducted important cancer research at a center founded expressly for that purpose at Harlem Hospital. The dermatologist Theodore Kenneth Lawless (1892–1971), a staff member of Cook County Hospital (Chicago) and faculty member at Northwestern University Medical School until 1941, proposed helpful correctives for tissue damage resulting from the use of new arsenical preparations in syphilis treatment during the 1920s.

Noteworthy results came out of research conducted by African-American medical scientists at predominantly black educational institutions. Charles Richard Drew and Edward William Hawthorne (1921–1986), for example, served as faculty members at Howard University. Drew is best remembered for his work in "blood banking," or methods to preserve blood for subsequent use in transfusions. His 1940 treatise, *Banked Blood: A Study in Blood Preservation* (for which he was awarded the Sc.D. degree at Columbia University), was recognized as a pioneering and definitive study. Drew headed the "Blood for Britain" project at the height of the German blitzkrieg during World War II, and in 1941 was appointed director of the American Red Cross Blood Bank. He returned to Howard following a dispute with Red Cross officials over his refusal to condone the policy of segregating blood by race of donor and recipient. Hawthorne, an acknowledged leader in the area of cardiovascular-renal physiology, pioneered the use of electronically instrumented techniques to record heart function in conscious mammals during the 1950s and 1960s. When heart surgery in humans developed to the point where diseased valves could be replaced, Hawthorne helped to advance knowledge about the relationship of valve closure to the tension of connecting cords, shortening of the papillary muscles, and pressure of blood inside the heart chambers. His interest in the relationship between stress, the cardiac cycle, and the development of high blood pressure arose out of clinical observations of a health problem affecting African Americans in disproportionately large numbers.

Women Physicians

African-American women have also played an important role in medicine. Among the nineteenth-century pioneers, in addition to Rebecca Lee (mentioned above), were Rebecca J. Cole and Susan Smith McKinney Steward (1848–1919), who earned M.D.s at the Woman's Medical College of Pennsylvania (1867) and New York Medical College for Women (1870), respectively. Over a hundred black women earned medical degrees by the turn of the twentieth century. This was possible in part because the two major medical schools open to blacks—Howard University Medical School and Meharry Medical College—had admissions policies that were relatively liberal on the issue of gender. In 1878, Eunice P. Shadd (1848–1887) became the first African-American woman to earn the M.D. at Howard (two white women had taken M.D.s there in 1872 and 1874). The first woman physician to graduate at all-black Meharry was Georgia Esther Lee Patton (1864–1900), in 1893.

The activities of these early professional women were broad—ranging from missionary work and general practice to obstetrics, nurse training, and social service—but inevitably circumscribed by limits that the society had placed on women, black and white alike. This pattern changed gradually in the twentieth century, as African-American women physicians joined their white counterparts in entering leadership positions in medical administration, research, clinical work, teaching, and specialist fields. Two early examples were May Edward Chinn and Ernest Mae McCarroll. In 1926, Chinn became the first black woman graduate of University and Bellevue Hospital Medical College (New York University). In addition to her private practice, she carried out research and clinical work on early cancer detection and care of the terminal patient. McCarroll, who earned the M.D. at Woman's Medical College of Pennsylvania in 1925, was the first African American appointed (in 1946) to the staff of Newark (N.J.) City Hospital. Margaret Morgan Lawrence, psychiatrist, was in the vanguard of developments in the field of child psychiatry. Angela Dorothea Ferguson, a faculty member in the department of pediatrics at Howard University, worked with Roland Boyd Scott (b. 1909) to unravel problems in the etiology and treatment of sickle cell disease. Helen Octavia Dickens, Dorothy Lavinia Brown, and Myra Adele Logan were the first African-American women elected to the coveted fellowship of the American College of Surgeons. When pediatrician Agnes Lattimer (b. 1928), a specialist in the effects of lead poisoning on child development, served as head of Cook County Hospital, Chicago, in the mid-1980s, she was believed to be the only black woman to hold chief executive status in a major hospital in the United States. The National Aeronautics and Space Administration (NASA) appointed surgeon Irene Long (b. 1951) to head its medical operations branch in 1982. These and other African-American women have been part of a professional community dedicated to improving the health of Americans, black and white alike.

BIBLIOGRAPHY

Beardsley, Edward H. *A History of Neglect: Health Care for Blacks and Mill Workers in the Twentieth-Century South.* Knoxville, Tenn., 1987.

Cobb, W. Montague. "The Black American in Medicine." *Journal of the National Medical Association* 73 (1981), suppl.

———. *Medical Care and the Plight of the Negro.* New York, 1947.

———. *Progress and Portents for the Negro in Medicine.* New York, 1948.

Corwin, Edward Henry Lewinski, and Gertrude E. Sturgis. *Opportunities for the Medical Education of Negroes.* New York, 1936.

Curtis, James L. *Blacks, Medical Schools and Society.* Ann Arbor, Mich., 1971.

Gamble, Vanessa Northington. *The Black Community Hospital: Contemporary Dilemmas in Historical Perspective.* New York, 1989.

Hanft, Ruth S., Linda E. Fishman, and Wendy J. Evans. *Blacks and the Health Professions in the 80s: A National Crisis and a Time for Action.* Washington, D.C., 1983.

Hayden, Robert C., and Jacqueline Harris. *Nine Black American Doctors.* Reading, Mass., 1976.

Hine, Darlene Clark. *Black Women in White: Racial Conflict and Cooperation in the Nursing Profession, 1890–1950.* Bloomington, Ind., 1989.

Jones, James H. *Bad Blood: The Tuskegee Syphilis Experiment.* New York, 1981.

Kenney, John Andrew. *The Negro in Medicine.* Tuskegee, Ala., 1912.

Lamb, Daniel Smith, comp. and ed. *Howard University Medical Department, Washington, D.C.: A Historical, Biographical, and Statistical Souvenir.* Washington, D.C., 1900.

Lightfoot, Sara Lawrence. *Balm in Gilead: Journey of a Healer.* Reading, Mass., 1988.

McBride, David. *Integrating the City of Medicine: Blacks in Philadelphia Health Care, 1910–1965.* Philadelphia, 1989.

"Minorities and Medicine." *New York State Journal of Medicine* 85 (April 1985): 125–166.

Morais, Herbert Montfort. *The History of the Afro-American in Medicine.* New York, 1968.

Organ, Claude H., and Margaret M. Kosiba, eds. *A Century of Black Surgeons: The U.S.A. Experience.* 2 vols. Norman, Okla., 1987.

Postell, William Dosite. *The Health of Slaves on Southern Plantations.* Baton Rouge, La., 1951.

Savitt, Todd L. *Medicine and Slavery: The Diseases and Health Care of Blacks in Antebellum Virginia.* Urbana, Ill., 1978.

Summerville, James. *Educating Black Doctors: A History of Meharry Medical College.* University, Ala., 1983.

Wynes, Charles E. *Charles Richard Drew: The Man and the Myth.* Chicago, 1988.

– KENNETH R. MANNING

HENDRIX, JAMES MARSHALL "JIMI"

James Marshall "Jimi" Hendrix (November 27, 1942–September 18, 1970), rock guitarist, singer, and songwriter. In a professional career that lasted less than a decade, Jimi Hendrix created music that would establish him as the most innovative and influential guitarist rock music produced.

Born in Seattle, Wash., Hendrix started to play the guitar at age eleven and was playing with local rock groups as a teenager. He left school at sixteen, and with his father's permission, joined the Army as a paratrooper a year later. While in the service he met bass player Billy Cox, with whom he would later join forces as a civilian. Hendrix's Army career ended when he was injured on a practice jump.

Once out of the Army, he hit the "chitlin" circuit as a backup guitarist for a host of popular rock and rhythm-and-blues artists including Little Richard, the Isley Brothers, Curtis Knight, Wilson Pickett, Ike and Tina Turner, King Curtis, and James BROWN. During this period, from 1962 to 1964, he began incorporating his trademark crowd-pleasers—playing his guitar with his teeth, behind his back, and between his legs. Early in his career, Hendrix played ambidextrously before he eventually settled on using a right-handed Fender Stratocaster, restrung upside down and played left-handed. He manipulated the tone and volume controls (which were now on top) to make unique effects and sounds. Hendrix's huge hands allowed him a phenomenal reach and range; his ability to play clean leads and distorted rhythm simultaneously remains a musical mystery.

Jimi Hendrix created music that would establish him as the most innovative and influential guitarist rock music produced.

In 1964 Hendrix came to New York, and using the name "Jimmy James," fronted his own band, called the Blue Flames. He became known in New York at the height of the folk music era in the mid-1960s. Holding forth as a solo act at the Cafe Wha?, a basement café on MacDougal Street in Greenwich Village, he also found time to play local venues as a sideman with a group called Curtis Knight and the Squires, and in Wilson Pickett's band, where he met young drummer Buddy Miles. In 1967, Chas Chandler (the bassist of the former Animals) convinced Hendrix to return with him to London. On the promise that he would meet Eric Clapton, Hendrix agreed. In just three weeks in England the Jimi Hendrix Experience was formed with Mitch Mitchell on drums and Noel Redding on bass. "Hey Joe," their first single, went all the way to number 6 on the British charts in 1967, and an appearance on the British television show "Ready, Steady, Go" attracted wide attention when Hendrix played their new single, "Purple Haze."

The same year, Paul McCartney persuaded the Monterey Pop Festival officials to book Hendrix, despite the fact that his first album had yet to be released. His riveting musical performance ended with his setting his guitar on fire. His action and his performance transformed the twenty-four-year-old into a rock superstar. Later that year (1967) his debut album *Are You Experienced?* was called by *Guitar Players'* Jas Obrecht "the most revolutionary debut album in rock guitar history."

In 1968 he released his second album, *Axis: Bold As Love,* which contained more of his distinctive sounds in such songs as "Little Wing," "If 6 was 9," and "Castles Made of Sand." His third album, a double set titled *Electric Ladyland,* was released just nine months later. Hendrix created a recording studio of the same name in Greenwich Village, a reflection of his belief that he was connected to a female spirit/muse of fire and electricity.

In 1969 Hendrix performed at the Woodstock Festival, the only black performer of his time to penetrate the largely white world of hard and psychedelic rock. He was pressured by black groups to take a more political stance, but Hendrix took no part in formal politics; his political statement was in his music. His electric version of the "Star-Spangled Banner," played at Woodstock, was in itself a political statement.

Later that year Hendrix formed the all-black Band of Gypsys with former Army friend Bill Cox on bass and Buddy Miles on drums. Although the group lasted only a few months, a live performance was captured on the album *Band of Gypsys.* Hendrix's management believed it was a mistake for him to forsake his white rock side, and he was pressured to make an adjustment. Hendrix finally settled on Mitch Mitchell on drums with Billy Cox on bass. They performed at the club Isle of Fehmarn in West Germany on September 6, 1970. Twelve days later Hendrix died in London after complications resulting from barbiturate use.

Though Hendrix's period as a headline performer lasted only three years, his influence on popular music has been considerable. In helping to establish the prime role of the electric guitar soloist, he was an inspiration for several generations of heavy metal musicians. His improvisatory style has inspired both jazz musicians and practitioners of avant-garde "new music."

BIBLIOGRAPHY

Henderson, David. *Jimi Hendrix: Voodoo Chile'.* New York, 1978.

———. *'Scuse Me While I Kiss the Sky: The Life of Jimi Hendrix.* New York, 1981.

– DAVID HENDERSON

HILL-THOMAS HEARINGS

In September 1991, U.S. District Judge Clarence THOMAS, nominated to the U.S. Supreme Court by President George Bush, began his confirmation hearing by the Senate Judiciary Committee. On September 27, the committee, tied in its vote on the nomination, sent the nomination to the floor without a recommendation. Despite the committee's failure to issue a recommendation, most commentators believed the Senate would confirm Thomas. On October 6, 1991, National Public Radio and *New York Newsday* ran a story about Anita Faye Hill (b. 1956), a law professor at the University of Oklahoma. Hill, who had been a staff attorney under Thomas at the Department of Education and the Equal

Employment Opportunity Commission in the early 1980s, had told FBI investigators that Thomas had sexually harassed her during her tenure. The story was based on the leak of a confidential affidavit Hill had provided the committee on September 23. Her story made public, Hill openly repeated her accusations. In a comment later echoed by many women, Hill claimed the all-male Judiciary Committee had been insensitive to the importance of sexual harassment and had not questioned Thomas about it. Meanwhile, Thomas categorically denied any such conduct. On October 8, following a long debate in the Senate, the vote on Thomas's confirmation was delayed. Committee Chair Joseph R. Biden scheduled further hearings in order to provide Hill and Thomas an opportunity to testify publicly on the issue.

On October 11, 1991, before a nationwide television audience, the hearings on Thomas's conduct began. Hill described Thomas's repeated sexual overtures to her, charging that he had boasted of his sexual prowess, frequently used prurient sexual innuendos, and had insisted on describing to her the plots of pornographic movies he had seen. When asked why, if Thomas had harassed her in such a fashion, Hill had accepted a position under him at the EEOC, she explained that the harassment had stopped for a period, and she feared she would be unable to find another job without his recommendation.

Toni Morrison asserted that black men such as Thomas wished to rise on the backs of black women, whose needs and feelings were ignored.

Thomas's testimony flatly contradicted that of Hill. While Thomas asserted he had not listened to Hill's testimony, which he angrily referred to as "lies," he denied any wrongdoing and repeatedly refused to discuss his private life. He denounced the committee's confirmation process as "un-American" and assailed it for staging what he called a "high-tech lynching" of him as an independent conservative black intellectual.

During the following days, as the Senate debated the hearings, Senate Republicans launched a furious assault on Hill's character and truthfulness in order to discredit her. Senators charged her with "fantasizing" about Thomas's interest in her. At the same time, many observers felt the Judiciary Committee had not investigated Thomas's veracity with equal zeal. Nationwide argument, which crossed ideological and gender lines, raged over whether Thomas or Hill was telling the truth, and whether Thomas's alleged sexual harassment was relevant to his confirmation.

Within the black community, debate was particularly pointed, although few, if any, blacks altered their position on Thomas's confirmation as a result of the revelations. Many, perhaps most, blacks saw the affair as an embarrassment, reviving stereotypes of blacks as sexually rapacious, vulgar, and mendacious, and the stigma of black males as rapists. Harvard sociologist Orlando Patterson assumed the essential truth of Hill's version, but thought Thomas's conduct was an example of "Rabelaisian humor," a harmless example of "down-home courting." Some suspected conspiracies, such as black conservative Arthur Fletcher, chair of the U.S. Civil Rights Commission, who claimed the hearings were a racist plot to pit blacks against each other. Yale law professor Stephen Carter called both parties victims of the confirmation process. Many black men and women considered Hill a traitor to the race for accusing Thomas publicly, and for trying to block a black man's ascension to the Supreme Court. Others defended Hill's courage. Jesse JACKSON called her the "Rosa Parks" of sexual harassment. Toni MORRISON asserted that black men such as Thomas wished to rise on the backs of black women, whose needs and feelings were ignored. Countless women, black and white, were inspired by the public discussion of sexual harassment to share their own feelings and stories of harassment.

On October 15, the Senate confirmed Thomas, 52–48, the second narrowest winning margin in history. Public opinion polls published at the time showed the majority of Americans believed Thomas and suspected Hill's allegations. Still, many women were politically energized by the hearings, and many women were elected to public office in 1992 with the support of their campaign contributions and activism. Within a year after the hearings, however, new opinion polls suggested that a majority of Americans now believed Anita Hill had told the truth. By that time, continuing public interest in the affair had been reflected in the publication of several books on the trials, including two notable anthologies of essays written by African Americans.

BIBLIOGRAPHY

Brock, David. *The Real Anita Hill.* New York, 1993.

Chrisman, Robert and Robert L. Allen, eds. *Court of Appeal: The Black Community Speaks Out on the Racial and Sexual Politics of Thomas v. Hill.* New York, 1992.

Morrison, Toni, ed. *Race-ing Justice, Engendering Power.* New York, 1992.

– GREG ROBINSON

HIMES, CHESTER

Chester Himes (July 29, 1909–November 12, 1984), novelist and short story writer. Born in Jefferson City, Mo., the youngest of three sons, he spent his first fourteen years in the South. His mother, née Estelle Bomar, the daughter of former slaves who had achieved considerable success in the construction business, was educated at a black Presbyterian finishing school in North Carolina and taught music from time to time at African-American colleges and academies. Her husband, Joseph Himes, also born of former slaves, grew up in North Carolina poverty but acquired a diploma at Claflin College in Orangeburg, S.C. A skilled blacksmith and wheelwright, he taught mechanical arts at black institutions in Georgia, Missouri, Mississippi, and Arkansas. Both parents appear as thinly disguised characters whose conflicting social and racial views bewilder the protagonist in Himes's autobiographical novel *The Third Generation* (1954).

In 1923 a freak accident blinded Himes's older brother, causing the family to move from Pine Bluff, Ark., to St. Louis to seek specialized medical treatment. Two years later they moved to Cleveland, where Chester graduated from East High School in January 1926. Following graduation he worked as a busboy at a Cleveland hotel, where he suffered a traumatic fall that left him with permanent back and shoulder injuries. In September 1926 he enrolled as a liberal arts student at Ohio State University, but he was expelled the following February for failing grades and unseemly behavior. Thereafter he drifted into a life of crime in the black ghettos of Cleveland and Columbus. In December 1927, he was sentenced to serve twenty years in the Ohio State Penitentiary for armed robbery.

While in prison, Himes began a lifelong career writing fiction; his first stories were printed in African-American publications in early 1932. In 1934 he reached a national audience in *Esquire* for "To What Red Hell," describing the 1930 fire that swept through the Ohio penitentiary, killing more than 330 convicts. He was paroled in 1936, and in August 1937 he married Jean Lucinda Johnson, a longtime friend. From 1936 to 1940 he worked mainly at manual jobs and for the FEDERAL WRITERS' PROJECT, departing for California in the fall of 1940 in hopes of writing for Hollywood. Repeated rejections at the studios, however, required him to seek work at racially tense California shipyards. These experiences are reflected in several articles he wrote in the 1940s, as well as in two bitter novels, *If He Hollers Let Him Go* (1946) and *Lonely Crusade* (1947). The interethnic, economic, social, and sexual consequences of racism are treated at some length in these books.

From 1945 to 1953 Himes lived mainly in New York and New England; he sailed for France several months after the publication of his prison novel *Cast the First Stone* (1952). For the rest of his life he lived mainly in France and Spain, making only occasional visits to the United States. Much of his subsequent fiction was published first in France before appearing elsewhere. Among his books written abroad were seven Harlem police thrillers involving Cotton Ed Johnson and Grave Digger Jones; one of these won a French literary award in 1958. Two incomplete novels, *Plan B,* dealing with a future race war, and *The Lunatic Fringe* have not yet been printed in the United States. Himes's own favorite among his works was *The Primitive* (1955), depicting an intense, troubled relationship between a black man and a white woman in post-World War II New York. Himes's only published novel with a non-American setting, *A Case of Rape* (1985), focuses on four black men being tried in Paris for the violation and death of a white woman. Because the fictional characters were modeled on well-known African Americans living in Europe, the book caused something of a stir in the expatriate community. Himes's other works written in Europe were *Pinktoes* (1961), an interracial sex comedy about the activities of a celebrated Harlem hostess, and *Run Man Run* (1966), a thriller telling of a black man's flight from a murderous New York policeman. In 1978, Himes obtained a divorce in absentia and married Lesley Packard, an English journalist.

While living in Spain, Himes wrote two volumes of an autobiography, *The Quality of Hurt* (1973) and *My Life of Absurdity* (1976). Toward the end of his life he came to view his writings as being in the absurdist tradition. Racism, he said, made blacks and whites behave absurdly. He envisioned organized violence as the only means of ending racial oppression in America. Because his literary reputation was never as high in the United States as it was in Europe, Himes lived precariously for most of his authorial years, but a resurgence of interest in his writings in the 1970s brought him a measure of financial security. Upon his death in Alicante, Spain, he left a number of unfinished projects.

BIBLIOGRAPHY

Lundquist, James. *Chester Himes.* New York, 1976.

Milliken, Stephen F. *Chester Himes: A Critical Appraisal.* Columbia, Mo., 1976.

Muller, Gilbert H. *Chester Himes.* Boston, 1989.

Skinner, Robert. *Two Guns from Harlem: The Detective Fiction of Chester Himes.* Bowling Green, Ohio, 1989.

– EDWARD MARGOLIES

HOLIDAY, BILLIE

Billie Holiday (April 7, 1915–July 17, 1959), singer. Born Eleanora Fagan in Philadelphia, the daughter of Sadie Fagan and jazz guitarist Clarence Holiday, Billie Holiday grew up in Baltimore and endured a traumatic childhood of poverty and abuse. As a teenager, she changed her name (after screen star Billie Dove) and came to New York, where she began singing in speakeasies, influenced, she said, by Louis ARMSTRONG and Bessie SMITH. In 1933 she was spotted performing in Harlem by critic-producer John Hammond, who brought her to Columbia Records, where she recorded classic sessions with such jazz greats as pianist Teddy Wilson and tenor saxophonist Lester Young.

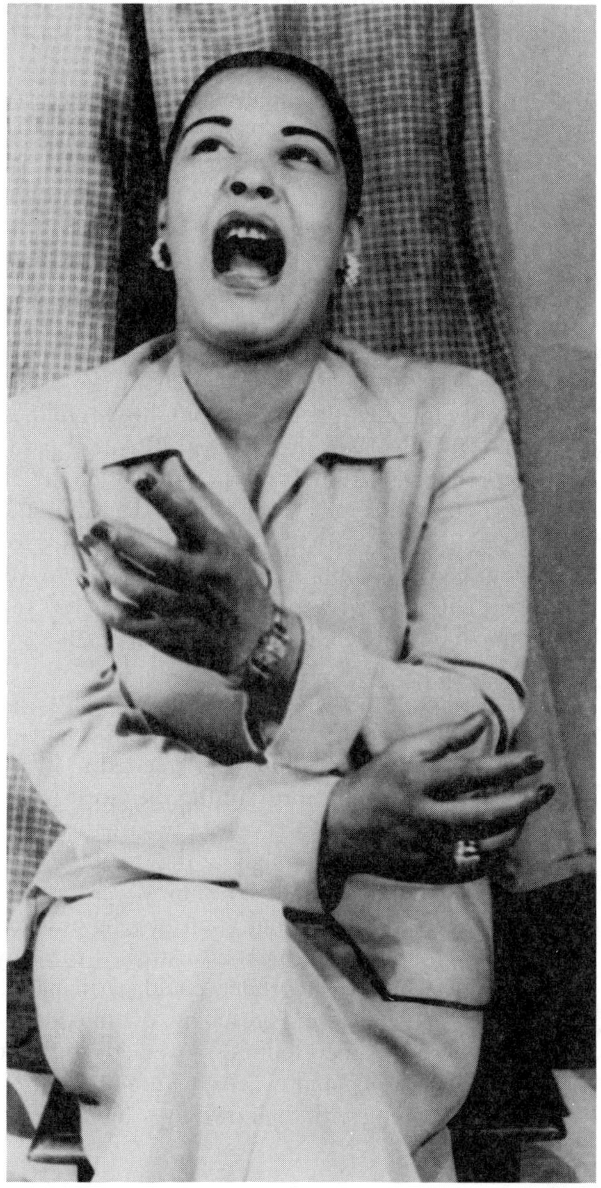

Shown here in 1949, Billie Holiday was known for the fluttering timbre and rhythmic grace of her singing voice. (Prints and Photographs Division, Library of Congress)

Following grueling tours with the big bands of Count BASIE and Artie Shaw, Holiday became a solo act in 1938, achieving success with appearances at Cafe Society in Greenwich Village, and with her 1939 recording of the dramatic antilynching song "Strange Fruit." Performing regularly at intimate clubs along New York's Fifty-second Street, she gained a sizable income and a reputation as a peerless singer of torch songs. A heroin addict, she was arrested for narcotics possession in 1947 and spent ten months in prison, which subsequently made it illegal for her to work in New York clubs. Yet despite such hardships and her deteriorating health and voice, she continued to perform and make memorable, sometimes challenging recordings on Decca, Verve, and Columbia until her death in 1959.

Although riddled with inaccuracies, Holiday's 1956 autobiography, *Lady Sings the Blues,* remains a fascinating account of her mercurial personality. A 1972 film of the same title, starring pop singer Diana Ross, further distorted her life but introduced her to a new generation of listeners. Holiday was one of America's finest and most influential jazz singers. Her voice was light, with a limited range, but her phrasing, in the manner of a jazz instrumentalist, places her among the most consummate of jazz musicians. She was distinguished by her impeccable timing, her ability to transform song melodies through improvisation, and her ability to render lyrics with absolute conviction. While she was not a blues singer, her performances were infused with the same stark depth of feeling that characterizes the blues.

BIBLIOGRAPHY

Chilton, John. *Billie's Blues.* New York, 1989.

Kliment, Bud. *Billie Holiday.* New York, 1990.

O'Meally, Robert. *Lady Day: The Many Faces of Billie Holiday.* New York, 1991.

– BUD KLIMENT

HOLINESS MOVEMENT

The Holiness movement is a significant religious movement in African-American religious history. The term *Holiness* can be confusing due to the multiplicity of its uses. Many publications use the term somewhat broadly to include PENTECOSTALISM and the APOSTOLIC MOVEMENT; however, properly used, it specifically describes that distinct Holiness movement that resulted in the founding of the Holiness church denomination.

The Holiness movement in the post–Civil War era was the result of an internal conflict within the METHODIST CHURCH. Eschewing the new, less austere standards of the postwar church, followers of the Holiness movement advocated a simple, antiworldly approach to life as well as adherence to a strict, moralistic code of behavior. The followers of the Holiness movement believed in the theological framework of John Wesley, but then went a step further in their interpretation of his writings. In addition to the first blessing of conversion which is justification by faith accepted by most Protestants, adherents of the movement declared that a second experience or blessing of complete sanctification was necessary in order to achieve complete emotional peace. The second blessing purified the believer of his inward sin (the result of Adam's original sin), and would give the believer a perfect love toward God and man. A state of earthly holiness (or perfection) was seen as possible to achieve. This experience was attained through devout prayer, meditation, the taking of Holy Communion, and fellowship with other believers. Those who had received the second blessing were characterized by a deep inner feeling of joy and ecstasy, as well as by lives that reflected a moral and spiritual purity.

At first, the Methodist Church leaders welcomed the new movement as one which would instill more pious behavior in its members. By 1894, however, those who had experienced the "second blessing" began to press for changes to church doctrine, literature, even songs used in worship services. As a result, the followers of the new movement split from Methodism and founded their own churches throughout the South, North, and Midwest. In the early Holiness churches, racial lines were obscured. Many blacks and whites served together as officials, preachers, and church members. However, under pressure to conform to social norms of segregation, divisions along racial lines were well in place by the 1890s.

Black Holiness congregations, often calling themselves the Church of God, sprang up throughout the South after 1890. One of the largest and most influential was the CHURCH OF GOD IN CHRIST, founded by C. H. Mason and C. P. Jones, which was incorporated in Memphis in 1897. It was the first Holiness church of either race to be legally chartered. Mason and Jones had come out of a Baptist Church background, as had many other black converts to the Holiness movement. Like their counterparts from the Methodist Church, they longed for a purer expression of their faith and a religion that was unfettered by the push toward worldly materialism. Because it was legally chartered, the Church of God in Christ could perform marriage ceremonies and ordinations. Many independent white Holiness ministers were ordained by Jones and Mason. It was also the denomination most receptive to musical experimentation, encouraging the use of instruments, RAGTIME, JAZZ, and the BLUES as a part of worship.

Both the black and white Holiness congregations were split after a black Holiness convert named William J. Seymour organized a church in Los Angeles in 1906, where he espoused a third blessing—the Baptism of the Holy Ghost—which would be evidenced by the Pentecostal gift of speaking in tongues. Seymour taught that it was only after having received this third blessing that a believer was truly sanctified and perfected. Thousands of Holiness believers were converted to the new Pentecostal church. Pentecostalism has gone on to attract millions of converts and eventually overshadowed its founding Holiness faith.

In 1907, Mason was converted, which resulted in a schism between him and Jones over doctrinal differences. While Mason adhered to the tenet of a required third blessing in order to receive the Holy Spirit, Jones maintained that the gift of the Holy Spirit was given by God at the time of conversion. They split into two churches and Mason's new Church of God in Christ became the largest Pentecostal church in the United States. Jones founded the Church of Christ (Holiness) USA in 1907. By 1984 there were 170 congregations with approximately 10,000 members. One of the offshoot congregations that sprang from the Church of Christ (Holiness) USA is the Churches of God, Holiness. Founded in Atlanta in 1920, by 1967 there were forty-two churches with a reported membership total of about 25,000. There are several other, smaller Holiness churches, as well.

Besides serving as the birthplace of the Pentecostal church, the Holiness movement was very important and influential in the lives of those who believed in it. The movement was brought north during the Great Migration of the first two decades of the twentieth century and continued to thrive throughout the era of the Great Depression. Simplicity and continuity were stressed over consumption and liberalization of religious standards. The Holiness movement also stressed that anyone, regardless of race or gender, could participate in church hierarchy, including preaching, on an equal basis. The believers of the Holiness movement sought to undo the materialistic and divisive nature of American society by beginning with their own lives and their own hearts.

BIBLIOGRAPHY

Ayers, Edward L. *The Promise of the New South.* New York, 1992.

DuPree, Sherry Sherrod, ed. *Biographical Dictionary of African-American Holiness-Pentecostals: 1880–1990.* Washington, D.C., 1989.

Murphy, Larry G., J. Gordon Melton, and Gary L. Ward, eds. *Encyclopedia of African American Religions.* New York, 1993.
Paris, Arthur. *Black Pentecostalism.* Amherst, Mass., 1982.
Payne, Wardell J., ed. *Directory of African-American Religious Bodies.* Washington, D.C., 1991.
Synan, Vinson. *The Holiness-Pentecostal Movement in the United States.* Grand Rapids, Mich., 1971.

– DEBI BROOME

HORNE, LENA

Lena Horne (June 30, 1917–), singer and actress. Born in New York, Lena Horne accompanied her mother on a tour of the Lafayette Stock Players as a child and appeared in a production of *Madame X* when she was six years old. She received her musical education in the preparatory school of Fort Valley College, Ga. and in the public schools of Brooklyn. Horne began her career at the age of sixteen as a dancer in the chorus line at the COTTON CLUB in Harlem. She also became a favorite at Harlem's Apollo Theatre, and was among the first African-American entertainers to perform in "high-class" nightclubs. Appearing on stages and ballrooms from the Fairmont in San Francisco to the Empire Room at the Waldorf-Astoria in New York, Horne was among the group of black stars—including Sammy DAVIS, Jr., Eartha Kitt, and Diahann Carroll—who had musicals especially fashioned for them on Broadway.

Horne's spectacular beauty and sultry voice helped to make her the first nationally celebrated black female vocalist.

Horne made her first recording in 1936 with Noble Sissle and recorded extensively as a soloist and with others. She toured widely in the United States and Europe. In 1941 she became the first black performer to sign a contract with a major studio (MGM). Her first film role was in *Panama Hattie* (1942), which led to roles in *Cabin in the Sky* (1942), *Stormy Weather* (1943), *I Dood It* (1943), *Thousands Cheer* (1943), *Broadway Rhythm* (1944), *Two Girls and a Sailor* (1944), *Ziegfeld Follies of 1945* and *1946, The Duchess of Idaho* (1950), and *The Wiz* (1978). Horne was blacklisted during the McCarthy era of the early 1950s, when her friendship with Paul ROBESON, her interracial marriage, and her interest in African freedom movements made her politically suspect. Her Broadway musicals include *Blackbirds of 1939, Jamaica* (1957), and the successful one-woman Broadway show *Lena Horne: The Lady and Her Music* (1981). The record album of the latter musical won her a Grammy Award as best female pop vocalist in 1981.

Horne's spectacular beauty and sultry voice helped to make her the first nationally celebrated black female vocalist. Her powerful and expressive voice is perhaps captured best in the title song of *Stormy Weather.* In 1984 she was a recipient of the Kennedy Center honors for lifetime achievement in the arts. She published two autobiographies: *In Person: Lena Horne* (1950) and *Lena* (1965).

BIBLIOGRAPHY

Buckley, Gail Lumet. *The Hornes: An American Family.* New York, 1986.

– JAMES E. MUMFORD

HORSE RACING

African Americans were significantly involved in professional horse racing from the sport's introduction into the United States in the mid-seventeenth century until the early twentieth century, when black jockeys and trainers were systematically driven out of the profession.

As the sport spread through the colonial South, where members of the gentry sought to emulate the pursuits of their English counterparts, slaves were most often used to train and race horses. In the colonial North racehorse owners usually imported English jockeys or hired local whites to tend the stables and ride in races. Horse racing was also popular in the United States among nonelites in the eighteenth and nineteenth centuries, with poor whites, free blacks, and even slaves participating in low-stakes races at rural social gatherings. Horse racing's increasingly black milieu contributed to its reputation as a sport of "the rabble." The Maryland General Assembly passed a law in 1747 "to prevent certain Evils and Inconveniences attending the sale of strong Liquors, and running of Horse-Races, near the yearly Meetings of the People called Quakers, and to prevent the tumultuous Concourse of Negroes and other Slaves during the said Meetings."

During the first half of the nineteenth century, however, black jockeys and trainers were increasingly hired by northern owners, and by the end of the CIVIL WAR, African Americans dominated the sport throughout the United States. In 1866, at the first Jerome Handicap at Jerome Park in what is now New York City, a black rider named Abe Hawkins won on a horse named Watson. Hawkins went on to win the third Travers Stakes at Saratoga Springs, N.Y., in 1866 aboard a horse called Merritt. Oliver Lewis, a black jockey, rode Aristides to victory in the first Kentucky Derby, held in 1875 at

Churchill Downs in Louisville. The predominance of African Americans in the sport was particularly evident that day; fourteen of the fifteen horses in the field were ridden by black jockeys. African Americans won fifteen of the first twenty-eight runnings of the Kentucky Derby.

Several black jockeys were among the sport's most prominent figures in the late nineteenth century. The leading jockey in the late 1870s was William "Billy" Walker, an African-American rider who, in 1877, won the Kentucky Derby and Dixie Handicap. Walker rode Ten Broeck—a Dutch name—to victory over Molly McCarthy in the famous 1878 Match Race in Louisville, which became the subject of the black folk song and later bluegrass standard "Molly and Ten Brooks." Isaac Murphy, who was born a slave in Kentucky, won a remarkable 44 percent of his races, including three Kentucky Derby victories (1884, 1890, 1891), in a career that spanned the years 1878 to 1891. Murphy was widely considered the greatest jockey of his generation and was perhaps the most successful and best-known black athlete of the nineteenth century. Two other exceptional black jockeys in this period were Willie Simms and James "Soup" Perkins. Simms won the Kentucky Derby twice (1896, 1898), the Latonia Derby (1896), the Belmont Stakes twice (1893, 1894), and the Second Special four times (1892, 1894, 1895, 1897). Simms was the all-time money winner for black jockeys, with lifetime earnings of more than $300,000. Perkins, who rode five winners in one day at the age of thirteen, in one two-year period won the Kentucky Derby (1895), the Clark Handicap (1895), the Tennessee Oaks (1896), and the St. Louis Derby (1896).

Black trainers were also quite successful in the late nineteenth century. Black Kentucky Derby–winning trainers included Edward "Brown Dick" Brown with Baden-Baden in 1877, William Bird with Buchanan in 1884, and Alex Perry with Joe Cotton in 1885.

At elite horse racing venues, African Americans were generally excluded from owning racehorses, but a prominent exception to this rule was Robert James Harlan (1816–1897), the businessman, civil rights leader, and the mulatto half brother of U.S. Supreme Court Justice John Marshall Harlan. Robert Harlan owned a stable of racehorses in pre–Civil War Cincinnati and was said to be the only black owner allowed to enter horses in races in southern cities.

Jimmy Winkfield, who was among the last great African-American jockeys, left the United States for Europe when a racist backlash forced blacks from the sport in the first two decades of the twentieth century. Before he was driven from racing in the United States, however, Winkfield established himself as a top jockey, winning both the 1901 and 1902 Kentucky Derbies, the last to be won by a black jockey.

The wave of antiblack discrimination that profoundly altered the face of horse racing began in the 1890s, when white jockeys began to systematically harass and bully their successful black counterparts, often purposely fouling them during races and forcing their horses to stumble and even fall. The discrimination took an official form in 1894 with the establishment of the Jockey Club, which licensed riders but systematically denied the sanctioning of African Americans. By the 1920s only a few black jockeys were still eking out careers. Jess Conley was the last black jockey in the Kentucky Derby, finishing third aboard Colston in 1911. Among the remaining black jockeys in this period was Canada Lee, the actor and boxer, who raced on major tracks in New York State from 1921 to 1923 at the beginning of his career. Black trainers also found the environment too hostile to continue and virtually vanished from the sport.

Many black jockeys and trainers turned to steeplechase racing, an obstacle-course event where the demand for competent professionals was such that discrimination was not as great as in traditional "flat track" racing. Through the 1920s and '30s several black jockeys rose to prominence as steeplechasers, including Charlie Smoot, who won several prestigious steeplechase races.

Since the early part of the twentieth century, only a handful of African Americans have maintained careers as jockeys and trainers and none have risen to prominence. In the 1940s, '50s, and '60s such riders as Hosea Lee Richardson, Robert McCurdy, and Al Brown managed to gain mounts at large tracks but never appeared in a major stakes race. Louis Durousseau, a Louisiana Cajun, was the most successful black jockey after World War II, winning more than $100,000 per year in the 1960s. Since the 1960s black jockeys have had a minimal presence in a profession dominated by whites and Latinos. In the 1980s and '90s, however, a number of wealthy African Americans, including singer Barry White, record executive Berry Gordy, Jr., and the rapper Hammer have invested in racehorses.

BIBLIOGRAPHY

Ashe, Arthur R., Jr. *A Hard Road to Glory: A History of the African-American Athlete, 1619–1918.* New York, 1988.

Betts, John Rickards. *America's Sporting Heritage: 1850–1950.* Reading, Mass., 1974.

Parmer, Charles. *For Gold and Glory.* New York, 1939.

– THADDEUS RUSSELL

HOSPITALS, BLACK

Black hospitals have been of three broad types: segregated, black-controlled, and demographically determined. Segregated black hospitals included facilities established by whites to serve blacks exclusively, and they operated predominantly in the South. Black-controlled facilities were founded by black physicians, fraternal organizations, and churches. Changes in population led to the development of demographically determined hospitals. As was the case with Harlem Hospital, they gradually evolved into black institutions because of a rise in black populations surrounding the hospitals. Historically black hospitals—the previously segregated and the black-controlled hospitals—are the focus of this article.

Until the advent of the Civil Rights Movement, racial customs and mores severely restricted black access to most hospitals. Hospitals—both in the South and in the North—either denied African Americans admission, or accommodated them, almost universally, in segregated wards, often placed in undesirable locations such as unheated attics and damp basements. The desire to provide at least some hospital care for black people prompted the establishment of the earliest segregated black hospitals. Georgia Infirmary, established in Savannah in 1832, was the first such facility. By the end of the nineteenth century, several others had been founded, including Raleigh's St. Agnes Hospital in 1896 and Atlanta's MacVicar Infirmary in 1900. The motives behind their creation varied. Some white founders expressed a genuine, if paternalistic, interest in supplying health care to black people and offering training opportunities to black health professionals. However, white self-interest was also at work. The germ theory of disease, widely accepted by the end of the nineteenth century, acknowledged that "germs have no color line." Thus the theory mandated attention to the medical problems of African Americans, especially those whose proximity to whites threatened to spread disease.

Until the advent of the Civil Rights Movement, racial customs and mores severely restricted black access to most hospitals.

Following the precedent set by other ethnic groups, African Americans themselves founded hospitals to meet the particular needs of their communities. Provident Hospital, the first black-controlled hospital, opened its doors in 1891. The racially discriminatory policies of Chicago nursing schools provided the primary impetus for the establishment of the institution. In addition, the hospital proved beneficial to black physicians, who were likewise barred from Chicago hospitals. Several other black-controlled hospitals opened during the last decade of the nineteenth century. These included Tuskegee Institute and Nurse Training School at Tuskegee Institute, Ala., in 1892; Provident Hospital at Baltimore, in 1894; and Frederick Douglass Memorial Hospital and Training School at Philadelphia, in 1895. The establishment of these institutions also represented, in part, the institutionalization of Booker T. WASHINGTON's political ideology. These hospitals would advance racial uplift by improving the health status of African Americans and by contributing to the development of a black professional class.

By 1919 approximately 118 segregated and black-controlled hospitals existed, 75 percent of them in the South. Most were small, ill-equipped facilities that lacked clinical training programs. Consequently, they were inadequately prepared to survive sweeping changes in scientific medicine, hospital technology, and hospital standardization that had begun to take place at the turn of the century.

The most crucial issue faced by the historically black hospitals between 1920 and 1945 was whether they could withstand the new developments in medicine. In the early 1920s, a group of physicians associated primarily with the National Medical Association (NMA), a black medical society, and the NATIONAL HOSPITAL ASSOCIATION (NHA), a black hospital organization, launched a reform movement to ensure the survival of at least a few quality black hospitals. The leaders of these organizations feared that the growing importance of accreditation and standardization would lead to the elimination of black hospitals and with it the demise of the black medical profession. For most African-American physicians, black hospitals offered the only places in which they could train and practice.

The NMA and NHA engaged in various activities to improve the quality of black hospitals, including the provision of technical assistance and the publication of educational materials. They also worked to raise funds for black hospitals. But funds were not readily forthcoming. Indeed, the Depression forced all hospitals to grapple with the problem of financing. However, three philanthropies, the Julius Rosenwald Fund, the General Education Board, and the Duke Endowment, responded to the plight of black hospitals and provided crucial financial support.

The activities of the black hospital reformers and the dollars of white philanthropists produced some improvements in black hospitals by World War II. One prominent black physician hailed these changes as the "Negro Hospital Renaissance." This, however, was an overly optimistic assessment. The renaissance was limited to but a few hospitals. In 1923, approximately 200 historically black hospitals operated. Only six provided internships, and not one had a residency program. By 1944, the number of hospitals had decreased to 124. The AMA now approved nine of the facilities for internships and seven for residencies; the American College of Surgeons fully approved twenty-three, an undistinguished record at best. Moreover, the quality of some approved hospitals was suspect. Representatives of the American Medical Association freely admitted that a number of these hospitals would not have been approved except for the need to supply at least some internship opportunities for black physicians. This attitude reflected the then accepted practice of educating and treating black people in separate, and not necessarily equal, facilities.

The growth of the civil rights movement also played a key role in limiting the scope of black hospital reform. In the years after World War II, the energies of black medical organizations, even those that had previously supported separate black hospitals, shifted toward the dismantlement of the "Negro medical ghetto" of which black hospitals were a major component. Their protests between 1945 and 1965 posed new challenges for the historically black hospitals and called into question their very existence.

The NMA and the NAACP led the campaign for medical civil rights. They maintained that a segregated health care system resulted in the delivery of inferior medical care to black Americans. The organizations charged that the poorly financed facilities of the black medical ghetto could not adequately meet the health and professional needs of black people and rejected the establishment of additional ones to remedy the problem. Instead, the NMA and the NAACP called for the integration of existing hospitals and the building of interracial hospitals.

Legal action was a key weapon in the battle to desegregate hospitals. Armed with the precedent set by the Supreme Court ruling in BROWN V. BOARD OF EDUCATION OF TOPEKA, KANSAS, the medical civil rights activists began a judicial assault on hospital segregation. *Simkins* v. *Moses H. Cone Memorial Hospital* proved to be the pivotal case. The 1963 decision found the separate-but-equal clause of the Hill-Burton Act unconstitutional. The 1946 legislation provided federal monies for hospital construction. The Simkins decision represented a significant victory in the battle for hospital integration. It extended the principles of the Brown decision to hospitals, including those not publicly owned and operated. Its authority, however, was limited to those hospitals that received Hill-Burton funds. A 1964 federal court decision, *Eaton* v. *Grubbs,* broadened the prohibitions against racial discrimination to include voluntary hospitals that did not receive such funds.

The 1964 Civil Rights Act supplemented these judicial mandates and prohibited racial discrimination in any programs that received federal assistance. The 1965 passage of the Medicare and Medicaid legislation made most hospitals potential recipients of federal funds. Thus, they would be obligated to comply with federal civil rights legislation.

The predominant social role of the historically black hospitals before 1965 had been to provide medical care and professional training for black people within a segregated society. The adoption of integration as a societal goal has had an adverse effect on the institutions. Civil rights legislation increased the access of African Americans to previously white institutions. Consequently, black hospitals faced an ironic dilemma. They now competed with hospitals that had once discriminated against black patients and staff. In the years since the end of legally sanctioned racial segregation, the number of historically black hospitals has sharply declined. In 1944, 124 black hospitals operated. By 1990 the number had decreased to eight and for several of them the future looks grim.

Desegregation resulted in an exodus of physicians and patients from black hospitals. Where white physicians had once used these facilities to admit and treat their black patients, they abruptly cut their ties. Furthermore, since 1965, black physicians have gained access to the mainstream medical profession and black hospitals have become less crucial to their careers. This loss of physician support contributed to declines in both patient admissions and revenues at many black hospitals. As a result of changing physician referral practices and housing patterns, black hospitals have also lost many of their middle class patients. They have become facilities that treat, for the most part, poor people who are uninsured or on Medicaid. This pattern of decreased physician support, reduced patient occupancy, and diminished patient revenues forced many black hospitals to close after 1965. It also makes the few surviving institutions highly vulnerable.

The historically black hospitals have had a significant impact on the lives of African Americans. Originally created to provide health care and education within a segregated society, they evolved to become symbols of black pride and achievement. They supplied medical care, provided training opportunities, and contributed to the development of a black professional class. The hospitals were once crucial for the survival of African Americans. They have now become peripheral to the lives of most Americans and are on the brink of extinction.

BIBLIOGRAPHY

Cobb, W. Montague. "Medical Care and the Plight of the Negro." *Crisis* 54 (1947): 201–211.

Downing, L. C. "Early Negro Hospitals." *Journal of the National Medical Association* 33 (1941): 13–18.

Gamble, Vanessa Northington. *The Black Community Hospital: Contemporary Dilemmas in Historical Perspective.* New York, 1989.

———. "The Negro Hospital Renaissance: The Black Hospital Movement." In Diana E. Long and Janet Golden, eds., *The American General Hospital.* Ithaca, N.Y., 1989, pp. 182–205.

Julius Rosenwald Fund. *Negro Hospitals: A Compilation of Available Statistics.* Chicago, 1931.

Kenney, John A. "The Negro Hospital Renaissance." *Journal of the National Medical Association* 22 (1930): 109–112.

Payne, Larah D. "Survival of Black Hospitals in the U.S. Health Care System: A Case Study." In Lennox S. Yearwood, ed. *Black Organizations: Issues on Survival Techniques.* Lanham, Md., 1980, pp. 205–211.

Taravella, Steve. "Black Hospitals Struggle to Survive." *Modern Healthcare* 20 (July 2, 1990): 20–26.

— VANESSA NORTHINGTON GAMBLE

HOUSTON, CHARLES HAMILTON

Charles Hamilton Houston (September 3, 1895–April 22, 1950), lawyer. Born in the District of Columbia the son of William L. Houston, a government worker who attended Howard University Law School and became a lawyer, and Mary Hamilton Houston, a teacher who later worked as a hairdresser, Charles Hamilton Houston attended Washington's M Street High School, and then went to Amherst College in Amherst, Mass. He graduated Phi Beta Kappa in 1915, then taught English for two years at Howard University. In 1917, Houston joined the Army and served as a second lieutenant in a segregated unit of the American Expeditionary Forces during World War I. Following his discharge, he decided on a career in law and entered Harvard Law School. Houston was the first African-American editor of the *Harvard Law Review.* He received an LL.B. degree cum laude (1922) and an S.J.D. degree (1923). He received the Sheldon Fellowship for further study in civil law at the University of Madrid (1923–1924).

In 1924, Houston was admitted to the Washington, D.C. bar, and he entered law practice with his father at Houston & Houston in Washington, D.C. (later Houston & Hastie, then Houston, Bryant, and Gardner), where he handled domestic relations, negligence, and personal injury cases, as well as criminal law cases involving civil rights matters. He remained with the firm until his death. Throughout his career, Houston served on numerous committees and organizations, including the Washington Board of Education, the National Bar Association, the National Lawyers Guild, and the American Council on Race Relations. He also wrote columns on racial and international issues for the CRISIS and the *Baltimore Afro-American.* In 1932, he was a delegate to the NAACP's second Amenia Conference.

In 1927 and 1928, after receiving a grant from the Rockefeller Foundation, Houston wrote an important report, "The Negro and His Contact with the Administration of Law." The next year, he was appointed vice dean at Howard University, where he served as professor of law and as head of the law school. He transformed the law program into a full-day curriculum that was approved by both the American Bar Association and the Association of American Law Schools. Houston mentored such students as Thurgood MARSHALL, William Bryant, and Oliver Hill. Under his direction, Howard Law School became a unique training ground for African-American lawyers to challenge segregation through the legal system.

In 1935, Houston took a leave of absence from Howard to become the first full-time, salaried special counsel of the NAACP. As special counsel, Houston argued civil rights cases and traveled to many different areas of the United States, sometimes under trying conditions, in order to defend blacks who stood accused of crimes. He won two important Supreme Court cases, *Hollins* v. *Oklahoma* (1935) and *Hale* v. *Kentucky* (1938), which overturned death sentences given by juries from which blacks had been excluded because of their race.

Houston persuaded the joint committee of the NAACP and the philanthropic American Fund for Public Service to support an unrelenting but incremental legal struggle against segregation, with public education as the main area of challenge. In 1896, the U.S. Supreme Court had ruled in PLESSY V. FERGUSON that "separate but equal" segregated facilities were constitutional. Houston realized that a direct assault on the decision would fail, and he designed a strategy of litigation of test cases, and slow buildup of successful precedents based on inequality within segregation. He focused on combatting discrimination in graduate education, a less controversial area than discrimination in primary schools, as the first step in his battle in the courts. *University of Maryland* v. *Murray* was his first victory, and an important psychological triumph. The Maryland Supreme Court ordered Donald Murray, an African American, admitted to the University of Maryland Law School, since there were no law schools for blacks in the state. Two years later, Houston successfully argued *Missouri ex rel. Gaines* v. *Canada* in the Supreme Court. The Court ordered Lloyd Gaines admitted to the University of Missouri, which had no black graduate school, ruling that scholarships to out-of-state schools did not constitute equal admission. In 1938, suffering from tuberculosis and heart problems, Houston resigned as chief counsel, and two years later he left the NAACP. However, he remained a prime adviser over the next decade through his membership on the NAACP Legal Committee. His position as special counsel was taken over by his former student and deputy Thurgood Marshall, who formed the NAACP Legal Defense and Education Fund, Inc. (LDF) to continue the struggle Houston had begun. Their endeavor culminated with the famous 1954 Supreme Court decision BROWN V. BOARD OF EDUCATION OF TOPEKA, KANSAS, which overturned school segregation. Houston remained active in the effort. Shortly before his death, he initiated *Bolling* v. *Sharpe* (1954), a school desegregation suit in Washington, D.C., which later became one of the school cases the Supreme Court decided in *Brown.*

In 1940, Houston became general counsel of the International Association of Railway Employees and of the Association of Colored Railway Trainmen and Locomotive Firemen. Houston and his co-counsel investigated complaints of unfair labor practices and litigated grievances. Houston successfully argued two cases, *Steele* v. *Louisville & Nashville Railroad* and *Tunstall* v. *Brotherhood of Locomotive Firemen and Enginemen,* involving racial discrimination in the selection of bargaining agents under the Railway Labor Act of 1934. Houston also worked as an attorney for hearings of the President's Fair Employment Practices Committee (FEPC). Appointed to the FEPC in 1944, he dramatically resigned in December 1945 in protest over President Truman's refusal to issue an order banning discrimination by Washington's Capital Transit Authority, and of the committee's imminent demise.

In the late 1940s, Houston led a group of civil rights lawyers in bringing suit against housing discrimination. He helped draft the brief for the LDF's Supreme Court case *Shelley* v. *Kramer,* and argued a companion case, *Hurd* v. *Hodge,* in which the Supreme Court barred enforcement of racially restrictive covenants in leases.

In 1948, Houston suffered a heart attack, and he died of a coronary occlusion two years later. He received the NAACP's Spingarn Medal posthumously in 1950. In 1958, Howard University named its new main law school building in his honor.

BIBLIOGRAPHY

Kluger, Richard. *Simple Justice.* New York, 1975.

McNeil, Genna Rae. " 'To Meet the Group Needs': The Transformation of Howard University School of Law, 1920–1935." In V. P. Franklin and James D. Anderson, eds. *New Perspectives on Black Educational History.* Boston, 1978, pp. 149–172.

———. *Groundwork: Charles Hamilton Houston and the Struggle for Civil Rights.* Philadelphia, Pa., 1983.

Rowan, Carl. *Dream Makers, Dream Breakers: The World of Justice Thurgood Marshall.* Boston, 1993.

Segal, Geraldine. *In Any Fight Some Fall.* Rockville, Md., 1975.

Tushnet, Mark V. *The NAACP's Legal Strategy Against Segregated Education, 1925–1950.* Chapel Hill, N.C., 1987.

— GENNA RAE MCNEIL

HOUSTON, TEXAS

Houston, long a center of African-American life in Texas, boasts one of the nation's largest black populations. African Americans have been resident there from the city's very beginnings—slaves, with Mexican prisoners, cleared land for the settlement in 1836. Their numbers grew with the city, such that by 1860 the over 1,000 slaves and handful of free blacks composed 22 percent of Houston's population. Houston's early fortunes were based not on manufacture but on commerce—particularly the marketing of crops grown by African-American labor elsewhere in Texas—and slaves not employed in domestic service often worked as teamsters, dock workers, for merchants, or in road or railway building. Authorities imposed curfews and outlawed slaves hiring their own time or living apart from their masters, but contemporaries reported a relative laxity in the enforcement of such controls. SLAVERY survived in Houston until 1865, the city remaining in Confederate hands throughout the CIVIL WAR.

Following emancipation, rural freedpeople flocked to Houston, looking for nonagricultural employment, schools, and safety in numbers. The African-American population more than tripled between 1860 and 1870, peaking at nearly 40 percent of total population (3,691 out of 9,382). Black people resided in significant numbers in all the city's wards, though they often gathered in certain districts like the fourth ward's "Freedmantown," southwest of the business district. Black churches, such as Trinity Methodist Episcopal and Antioch Baptist, played a particularly important role in the early building of this free community.

Houston, long a center of African-American life in Texas, boasts one of the nation's largest black populations.

An important coastal railroad hub, Houston thrived in the post–Civil War decades as a center of Texas's expanding cotton, timber, and grain trade. For the most part, however, African Americans were relegated to the least remunerative work—domestic and service positions or unskilled or semiskilled labor in commerce and transport. Nevertheless, freedpeople exercised considerable political leverage during RECONSTRUCTION. Aided by a mobilized black constituency, Republicans controlled the city through 1873. Black Houstonians served on the city council, as city officials, and in the state legislature, the most prominent among them being businessman and former slave Richard ALLEN.

After Reconstruction ended, African Americans continued to vote and participate in politics, but the growing numbers and power of Democrats at the state and local levels, and the dispersal of the minority black population throughout the city, prevented them from winning office. The imposition of a state poll tax after the turn of the century, the barring of black voting in crucial Democratic primaries, at-large systems of representation, and the exclusion of blacks from Republican party leadership reduced their influence still further. At the same time, state, then local, segregation ordinances expanded and institutionalized the separation of the races. The 1903 segregation of Houston streetcars prompted a black boycott, but in 1907 the city authorized more extensive discrimination in public accommodations. JIM CROW in Houston bore bitter fruit in 1917, when black soldiers of the 24th Infantry, maddened by mistreatment at the hands of local police and citizens, rioted, murdering over a dozen whites.

As segregation hardened, the city itself was being transformed by the nearby discovery of oil in 1901 and by the completion, thirteen years later, of a ship channel making Houston a deep water port. Already a bustling entrepôt, Houston became a center for the refining and marketing of petroleum and related products. Its size and wealth would multiply steadily in the following decades. As total population boomed, African Americans became a smaller portion of the whole (e.g., slightly over 20 percent of city residents in 1930—63,377 out of 292,352). Yet blacks moved to Houston in great numbers, particularly from rural Texas and Louisiana, to work for the railroads, on the docks, in the oil and cotton trade, and in service occupations. Increasingly segregated black neighborhoods expanded in the fourth ward, near downtown, and in the third and fifth wards, to the southeast and northeast respectively. Many of them lacked paved streets, indoor plumbing, and other basic amenities, indicating not only neglect on the part of the city but also that the jobs a booming economy provided black workers were, typically, not well paid. In the newer industries, as in the old, African Americans in 1940 remained clustered in less skilled positions. In spite of such circumstances, though, Houston's African Americans built a distinctly vibrant urban community. They supported a large number of service and retail businesses, black newspapers such as Clifton Richardson and Carter Wesley's *Houston Informer,* a college, founded in 1927 which grew into Texas Southern University, and such legendary cultural figures as bluesman Lightnin' Hopkins.

Houston's progress in civil rights paralleled that of the South as a whole. A local chapter of the NATIONAL ASSOCIATION FOR THE ADVANCEMENT OF COLORED PEOPLE had been formed as early as 1912, and black Houstonians had been active in the organization's litigation against the white primary and segregation in graduate education. By the 1950s, however, attention focused on public schools. Desegregation efforts mandated by federal courts began in the early 1960s, slowly and by no means thoroughly integrating schools over the course of the following twenty years (the growth of the white population in suburban districts and the continued concentration of black citizens within the city limits inevitably restricted this process). Though certain city facilities had been desegregated in the 1950s, lunch counter SIT-INS by local black college students in 1960 signaled a broader assault on discrimination in public accommodations. Black political participation had expanded after the Supreme Court's striking down of the white primary in 1944. Activists formed the Harris County Council of Organizations in 1949 to organize the black community politically as well as to challenge discrimination in its many forms. By 1958, a black woman, Hattie Mae White, had been elected to the city's school board. But only the 1965 Voting Rights Act, the federally mandated end to the poll tax, redistricting, the creation of single-member legislative districts, and voter registration drives would allow black Houstonians, after a hiatus of nearly 100 years, to be elected to the state legislature in 1966 and to the city council in 1971. In 1972, Houston's Barbara JORDAN became the first Texan of African descent elected to the U.S. Congress. She would be succeeded there by Mickey Leland, then Craig Washington. In 1991, an African American, state representative Sylvester Turner, garnered 46 percent of the vote in a mayoral runoff, his loss attributed to his failure to win a majority of the steadily growing Hispanic vote.

Houston's progress in civil rights paralleled that of the South as a whole.

In the same decades, the black population—beginning to grow more quickly than the city as a whole—multiplied several times over, reaching 458,000 (28.1

percent) in 1990. In the 1970s, no other city in the former Confederate states had a larger or faster growing African-American community. During these boom years, increasing numbers of black Houstonians found employ in white-collar and skilled professions. Yet substantive gains coexisted with lingering disparities. While faring better in terms of income and employment than black workers in many other southern cities, African Americans in 1980 were significantly less well paid and more likely to be jobless than "Anglo" Houstonians. They remained disproportionately concentrated in lower-paying service and blue-collar jobs and in impoverished, predominantly black, central city neighborhoods. The black community particularly suffered when the collapse of oil prices ravaged Houston's economy in the 1980s, unemployment far exceeding even the unusually high rates among whites. Preliminary 1990 figures suggested that black population growth had slowed as a result, though greater Houston remained among the nation's top ten metropolitan areas in numbers of African Americans.

BIBLIOGRAPHY

Beeth, Howard, and Cary Wintz. *Black Dixie: Afro-Texan History and Culture in Houston.* College Station, Tex., 1992.

Bullard, Robert. *Invisible Houston: The Black Experience in Boom and Bust.* College Station, Tex., 1987.

McComb, David. *Houston: A History.* Austin, Tex., 1981.

Wintz, Cary. "Blacks." In Fred R. von der Mehden, ed. *The Ethnic Groups of Houston.* Houston, 1984.

———. "The Emergence of a Black Neighborhood: Houston's Fourth Ward, 1865–1915." In Char Miller and Heywood Sanders, eds. *Urban Texas: Politics and Development.* College Station, Tex., 1990.

– PATRICK G. WILLIAMS

HOWARD UNIVERSITY

In December 1866, a group of Congregationalists in Washington, D.C., proposed establishing the Howard Normal and Theological Institute for the Education of Teachers and Preachers to train ministers and educators for work among newly freed slaves. After receiving some support and funding, Howard University was chartered on March 2, 1867, and given the mission of establishing a university "for the education of youth in the liberal arts and sciences."

Howard received its name from Gen. Oliver Otis Howard, head of the Freedmen's Bureau. Gen. Howard, along with several other Civil War generals and U.S. congressmen, was largely responsible for the organization of the university and its campaign to secure an annual appropriation for its maintenance from Congress. Despite substantial federal funding, Howard was governed by a privately selected board of trustees and has always maintained its independent status. In keeping with its religious mission, the board of the university decreed that anyone chosen for any position in the university "be a member of some Evangelical church."

In the first years of Howard University's operation, very few African Americans were involved in its administration or on the board of trustees. The first students enrolled at Howard, four or five young women, were also white; they graduated from the three-year Normal Department in 1870. George B. Vashon, the first black faculty member at Howard, taught in a short-lived evening school in 1867–1868. One of the first black female leaders at Howard was Martha B. Briggs (1873–1879, 1883–1889). At first an instructor in the Normal Department, Briggs would become principal of the department in 1883.

In 1868, the trustees created a Preparatory Department which served as preparation for entrance into undergraduate course work by ensuring a minimum level of achievement in basic subjects like reading and writing. They also added a collegiate department, which included a four-year curriculum; it would eventually become the mainstay of the university. In its inaugural year, the collegiate department only had one student and two professors. The first three graduates of the department received their degrees in 1872. One of the two blacks in this class, James Monroe Gregory, became a tutor in Latin and math; in 1876, he became a professor of Latin.

Several other departments rounded out the university in its early years. A medical department was established in 1868. Its first graduating class of five, in 1871, included two blacks. The nearby Freedmen's Hospital was invaluable for medical students and doctors who were often unable to secure medical privileges at other institutions. Charles Burleigh Purvis, who worked virtually without compensation for many years as a professor in the medical department, was largely responsible for guiding both the medical school and its students during his long career.

Under the tutelage of Dean John Mercer Langston, a future congressman, the Law Department first enrolled students in the spring of 1869. It graduated its first class of ten in February 1871, including African-American John Cook, a future dean of the law school. An integral part of Howard from its founding, the theology department, opened officially in 1870, never used federal funds; instead, it relied upon contributions from the American Missionary Association, which was associated with the Congregational Church.

The university struggled financially for the first several years. Much of its original funding came from the

Howard University. (Photographs and Prints Division, Schomburg Center for Research in Black Culture, The New York Public Library, Astor, Lenox and Tilden Foundations)

Freedmen's Bureau, which provided capital for operation as well as money for the purchase of land and the construction of a campus. Before the bureau closed it channeled more than $500,000 to Howard, from 1867 until 1872. After the bureau's demise, the university received no additional federal funds until 1879, when Congress began granting Howard a small appropriation.

After several years, Howard's operations increased in scope. Between 1875 and 1889, more than 500 students received professional degrees in medicine, law, and theology, and almost 300 students received certificates from the normal, preparatory, and collegiate departments. The board of trustees also made efforts to expand and increase the African-American representation among its membership. In 1871, they appointed Frederick DOUGLASS to become a trustee; he served until his death in 1895. Several other blacks were named trustees in this period. Booker T. WASHINGTON became a trustee in 1907.

By 1900, Howard University had more than 700 students. Along with FISK and ATLANTA universities, Howard was one of the most prominent black academic colleges in the country. Under the administration of President Wilbur P. Thirkield (1906–1912), the university began to stress more industrial courses of study and the sciences. Howard established one of the first engineering programs at a predominantly black college; Howard's other science programs were also generally superior. The eminent biologist Ernest E. Just (1907–1941), who taught at Howard for several decades, helped further develop Howard's reputation in the sciences.

Another leader at Howard—and one of the most important black educators in the early twentieth century—was Kelly Miller. Miller, who served Howard in various capacities from 1890 to 1934, was dean of the College of Arts and Sciences from 1908 to 1919, fought for the introduction of courses on African-American life as early as the turn of the century.

The 1920s was a decade of great growth and change. The high school that prepared students for entrance into Howard closed in 1920. Under the administration of President J. Stanley Durkee, the university budget grew from $121,937 in 1920 to $365,000, only five years later. Lucy Slowe Diggs (1922–1937) was the first dean of women at Howard; she helped to transform the role of female university officials to that of active administrators participating in shaping university policy. In 1925 students took part in a week-long strike for greater student participation in university policy-making and an end to mandatory chapel services. Another focus of student and intellectual agitation was the growing demand for the appointment of a black president to lead Howard. Mordecai W. Johnson, a Baptist minister, became Howard's first African-American president on September 1, 1926; he served until 1960.

In the 1920s and 1930s, Howard became a center of African-American intellectual life and attracted a brilliant faculty committed to finding new directions for black America. Many black scholars trained at Ivy League schools and other predominantly white institutions were unable to find employment other than in historically black colleges and universities (HBCUs). Howard attracted the cream of the crop.

One of the leading figures at Howard in the 1920s was philosopher Alain LOCKE (1912–1925, 1927–1954), popularizer of the NEW NEGRO movement. Several administration officials and faculty members urged the implementation of a curriculum that explicitly acknowledged the cultural accomplishments of African Americans. Kelly Miller had been doing so for years; William Leo Hansberry (1922–1959) became the first African-American scholar to offer comprehensive courses in the civilization and history of Africa in the 1920s.

The 1930s were a period of intellectual accomplishment at Howard, with a faculty that included the leading black scholars in the country. Led by political scientist Ralph J. BUNCHE (1928–1933), English professors Sterling BROWN (1929–1969) and Alphaeus Hunton (1926–1943), sociologist E. Franklin FRAZIER (1934–1959), and economist Abram Harris, Jr. (1927–

1945), the Howard faculty looked for ways to transcend the division between accommodationism and black nationalism. While proud exponents of the distinctiveness of black culture, they often espoused industrial unionism and multiracial working class harmony, and were sensitive to the internal divisions and class differences within the black community. Historian Rayford Logan (1938–1982), largely responsible for strengthening the history department, wrote the most comprehensive history of Howard from its founding until its centennial. Logan also served the larger cause of African-American studies by producing the ground-breaking *Dictionary of American Negro Biography* (1982). The distinguished African-American pianist Hazel Harrison (1936–1955) was one of the leading women faculty members of the period.

Charles H. Houston (1929–1935), who helped to strengthen the curriculum at the law school and became one of the most important civil rights lawyers of the 1930s and 1940s, added to Howard's position as the best black law school in the country at the time. Under Houston's capable guidance, the law school strengthened its curriculum and received accreditation from the American Association of American Law Schools in late 1931. Graduates included Thurgood MARSHALL (1933), future justice of the U.S. Supreme Court.

The 1930s were also marked by administrative controversy. President Johnson came under harsh criticism from many who felt that his managerial style was heavy-handed and autocratic. Johnson had removed several administration officials and had fired several university employees. The alumni association criticized Johnson and the board of trustees as well, arguing that the alumni should have more of a voice in choosing trustees and constructing university policy.

Given their reliance on federal funds for operation, Howard officials were often held accountable by members of Congress for perceived ideological aberrations like socialism or communism. In the early 1940s, investigations into the activities of some faculty members, among them Alphaeus Hunton, by the House Committee on Un-American Activities (HUAC) brought unwanted attention to Howard. When another HUAC inquiry occurred in the early 1950s, President Mordecai Johnson did not attempt to derail the various investigations but declared his confidence that the faculty members being investigated would be vindicated; all were. The administration at Howard often urged moderation and discouraged university employees from making overtly political statements.

Several prominent black scholars taught at Howard during the 1940s and 1950s. Margaret Just Butcher, daughter of biologist Ernest Just, taught English at Howard from 1945 until 1955; she collaborated with Alaine Locke on *The Negro in American Culture* (1956). Prominent civil rights leader Anna Arnold Hedgemann was dean of women from 1946 until 1948; she would later be instrumental in helping to plan the 1963 March on Washington. Mercer Cook (1927–1936, 1944–1960, 1966–1970), an influential translator of the Négritude poets, and the Afrocentrist Cheikh A. Diop, taught in the Department of Romance Languages for several generations.

While the 1950s was a time of relative quiet at Howard, the university experienced intellectual and political turmoil during the 1960s. In 1962, Vice President Lyndon B. Johnson spoke at the commencement; returning to Howard three years later, this time as president, Johnson renewed his pledge to struggle for equal rights for all and outlined the tenets of what would become his plans for the Great Society. Students vocally disrupted a 1967 speech by Gen. Lewis Hershey, director of the Selective Service System. They further disrupted campus operations in 1968 when students all over the country took part in demanding an end to the war in Vietnam. Howard students were also urging the implementation of a more radical curriculum. In 1969 Howard inaugurated its African-American Studies program.

President James M. Nabrit, Jr., one of the attorneys who crafted one of the briefs used to justify the decision by the U.S. Supreme Court to end segregation in the landmark 1954 BROWN V. BOARD OF EDUCATION OF TOPEKA, KANSAS, led Howard from 1960 until 1969, some of its most turbulent years. Notable faculty members included Patricia Roberts Harris (1961–1963, 1967–1969), who was an attorney, the first African-American woman to become an ambassador, and a professor in the Howard Law School for several years. Her tenure as the first black female dean of the law school, however, lasted only thirty days; outcry over student protests and conflicts with other university administrators compelled her to resign (1969).

In the mid-1980s, Howard was one of the first universities in the United States to initiate divestment from South Africa. Republican party chairman Lee Atwater resigned from the board of trustees in 1989 after protests by hundreds of students. Howard received more unfavorable publicity in early 1994 after the appearance on campus by former NATION OF ISLAM official Khalid Muhammad.

Howard has many notable facilities. The Moorland-Spingarn Center, one of the premier archival resources for studying African-American history and culture, had accumulated over 150,000 books and more than 400 manuscript collections. The center was a result of the donation of collections from trustee Jesse Moorland in 1914 and NAACP official Arthur Spingarn in 1946; they included "books, pictures, and statuary on the Negro and on slavery." An art gallery includes an extensive African-American collection of painting, sculpture, and art. A university radio and television station sought to bring in revenue and offer a valuable educational service to the larger community of the District of Columbia. The Howard University Press has published more than 100 works since its inception in 1972. Howard University Hospital, a 500-bed teaching hospital, is responsible for, among other things, pioneering research by the Howard University Cancer Center and the Center for Sickle Cell Disease.

By the early 1990s the budget of the university was approximately $500 million, and the university employed more than 6,000 people. (In 1975 the budget was about $100 million.) Howard still receives more than 40 percent of its budget from the federal government. Its enrollment in 1993 stood at almost 12,000 students distributed among various colleges, programs, and institutes.

The future, however, holds uncertainty for Howard and other HBCUs. Howard has consistently dedicated itself to providing an intellectual haven for African Americans denied opportunities elsewhere. In 1963, the board of trustees promised that

> As a matter of history and tradition, Howard University accepts a special responsibility for the education of capable Negro students disadvantaged by the system of racial segregation and discrimination, and it will continue to do so as long as Negroes suffer these disabilities.

As bars against entry of blacks into primarily white universities have disappeared, a crisis has arisen for those schools which historically relied upon having the brightest African-American students and faculty. Partly to address this problem, Howard launched its Howard 2000 reorganization program in the early 1990s. Its goal was to help Howard remain fiscally and academically competitive into the next century.

BIBLIOGRAPHY

Dyson, Walter. *Howard University, the Capstone of Negro Education: A History, 1867–1940.* Washington, D.C., 1941.

Janken, Kenneth Robert. *Rayford W. Logan and the Dilemma of the African-American Intellectual.* Amherst, Mass. 1993.

Leavy, Walter. "Howard University: A Unique Center of Excellence." *Ebony* 40 (September 1985): 140–142.

Logan, Rayford. *Howard University: The First Hundred Years, 1867–1967.* New York, 1969.

Wolters, Raymond. *The New Negro on Campus: Black College Rebellions in the 1920s.* Princeton, N.J., 1975.

— ESME BHAN

HUDSON, HOSEA

Hosea Hudson (1898–1988), union leader and communist activist. Born into an impoverished sharecropping family in Wilkes County in the eastern Georgia black belt, Hudson became a plowhand at ten, which sharply curtailed his schooling. The combination of a boll-weevil infestation and a violent altercation with his brother-in-law prompted Hudson in 1923 to move to Atlanta, where he worked as a common laborer in a railroad roundhouse. A year later he moved to Birmingham, Ala., and commenced his career as an iron molder.

Although he remained a faithful churchgoer, Hudson harbored persistent doubts about God's goodness and power, given the oppression of African Americans as workers and as Negroes. As a working-class black, however, he lacked a focus for his discontent until the COMMUNIST PARTY OF THE U.S.A. (CPUSA) began organizing in Birmingham in 1930. In the wake of the conviction of the Scottsboro boys and the Camp Hill massacre, both in Alabama in 1931, Hudson joined the CPUSA. Within a year he had lost his job at the Stockham foundry. Although he was able to earn irregular wages through odd jobs and iron molding under assumed names, much of the burden of family support in the 1930s fell on his wife, who never forgave him for putting the welfare of the Communist party before that of his wife and child.

In the wake of the conviction of the Scottsboro boys and the Camp Hill massacre, both in Alabama in 1931, Hudson joined the CPUSA.

During the Great Depression, Hudson was active with a series of organizations in and around the CPUSA. He helped the Unemployed Councils secure relief payments and fight evictions on behalf of the poor. In his first trip outside the South, he spent ten weeks in New York State at the CPUSA Party National Training School in 1934, during which he learned to read and write. As a party cadre in Atlanta from 1934 to 1936, he worked with neighborhood organizations and helped investigate the lynching of Lint Shaw. Returning to Birmingham in 1937, he worked on the WORKS PRO-

JECT ADMINISTRATION (WPA), served as vice president of the Birmingham and Jefferson County locals of the Workers Alliance, and founded the Right to Vote Club (which earned him a key to the city of Birmingham in 1980 as a pioneer in the struggle for black civil rights).

After the creation of the Congress of Industrial Organizations, Hudson joined the campaign to organize unorganized workers. As the demand for labor during World War II eased his way back into the foundries, he became recording secretary of Steel Local 1489, then organized United Steel Workers Local 2815. He remained president of that local from 1942 to 1947, when he was stripped of leadership and blacklisted for being a communist. He was underground in Atlanta and New York City from 1950 to 1956, during the height of the Cold War and McCarthyism. Imbued with a justified sense of the historical importance of his life, Hudson initiated two books on his experiences: *Black Worker in the Deep South* (New York, 1972) and *The Narrative of Hosea Hudson* (Cambridge, Mass., 1979). Active in the Coalition of Black Trades Unionists until his health failed in the mid-1980s, Hudson died in Gainesville, Fla., in 1988.

BIBLIOGRAPHY

Painter, Nell Irvin. *The Narrative of Hosea Hudson: His Life as a Negro Communist in the South.* Cambridge, Mass., 1979.

— NELL IRVIN PAINTER

HUGHES, LANGSTON

Langston Hughes (February 1, 1902–May 22, 1967), writer. James Langston Hughes was born in Joplin, Mo., and grew up in Lawrence, Kans., mainly with his grandmother, Mary Langston, whose first husband had died in John Brown's band at Harpers Ferry and whose second, Hughes's grandfather, had also been a radical abolitionist. Hughes's mother, Carrie Langston Hughes, occasionally wrote poetry and acted; his father, James Nathaniel Hughes, studied law, then emigrated to Mexico around 1903. After a year (1915–1916) in Lincoln, Ill., Hughes moved to Cleveland, where he attended high school (1916–1920). He then spent a year with his father in Mexico. In June 1921, he published a poem that was to become celebrated, "The Negro Speaks of Rivers," in the CRISIS magazine. Enrolling at Columbia University in New York in 1921, he withdrew after a year. He traveled down the west coast of Africa as a mess man on a ship (1923), washed dishes in a Paris nightclub (1924), and traveled in Italy and the Mediterranean before returning to spend a year (1925) in Washington, D.C.

Poems in journals such as the CRISIS and *Opportunity* led to Hughes's recognition as perhaps the most striking new voice in African-American verse. Steeped in black American culture, his poems revealed his unswerving admiration for blacks, especially the poor. He was particularly inventive in fusing the rhythms of jazz and blues, as well as black speech, with traditional forms of poetry. In 1926 he published his first book of verse, *The Weary Blues,* followed by *Fine Clothes to the Jew* (1927), which was attacked in the black press for its emphasis on the blues culture. A major essay, "The Negro Artist and the Racial Mountain," expressed his determination to make black culture the foundation of his art. In 1926, he enrolled at historically black LINCOLN UNIVERSITY, and graduated in 1929. With the support of a wealthy but volatile patron, Mrs. Charlotte Osgood Mason (also known as "Godmother"), he wrote his first novel, *Not Without Laughter* (1930). The collapse of this relationship deeply disturbed Hughes, who evidently loved Mrs. Mason but resented her imperious demands on him. After several weeks in Haiti in 1931, he undertook a reading tour to mainly black audiences, starting in the South and ending in the West. He then spent a year (1932–1933) in the Soviet Union, where he wrote several poems influenced by radical socialism, including "Goodbye Christ," about religious hypocrisy. In Carmel, Calif. (1933–1934), he wrote most of the short stories in *The Ways of White Folks* (1934). After a few months in Mexico following the death of his father there, Hughes moved to Oberlin, Ohio.

In New York, his play *Mulatto,* about miscegenation in the South, opened on Broadway in 1935 to hostile reviews, but enjoyed a long run. Several other plays by Hughes were produced in the 1930s at the Karamu Playhouse in Cleveland. He spent several months as a war correspondent in Spain during 1937. Returning to New York in 1938, he founded the Harlem Suitcase Theater, which staged his radical drama *Don't You Want to Be Free?* In 1939, desperately needing money, he worked on a Hollywood film, *Way Down South,* which was criticized for its benign depiction of slavery. However, he was able to settle various debts and write an autobiography, *The Big Sea* (1940).

In 1940, when a religious group picketed one of his appearances, Hughes repudiated "Goodbye Christ" and his main ties to the left. In *Shakespeare in Harlem* (1942) he returned to writing poems about blacks and the blues. After two years in California, he returned to New York. Late in 1942, in the *Chicago Defender,* he began a weekly newspaper column that ran for more than twenty years. In 1943 he introduced its most popular feature, a character called Jesse B. Semple, or Simple, an urban black Everyman of intense racial consciousness but also with a delightfully offbeat sense of humor. In 1947, his work as lyricist with Kurt Weill and Elmer Rice on the Broadway musical play *Street Scene* enabled him finally to buy a home and settle down in Harlem. Hughes, who never married, lived there with an old family friend, Toy Harper, and her husband, Emerson Harper, a musician.

As a writer, Hughes worked in virtually all genres, though he saw himself mainly as a poet. In *Fields of Wonder* (1947), *One-Way Ticket* (1949), and *Montage of a Dream Deferred* (1951), he used the new bebop jazz rhythms in his poetry to capture the mood of an increasingly troubled Harlem. With Mercer Cook, he translated the novel *Gouverneurs de la rosée* (*Masters of the Dew,* 1947) by Jacques Roumain of Haiti; he also translated poems by Nicolás Guillén of Cuba (*Cuba Libre,* 1948), Federico García Lorca of Spain (1951), and Gabriela Mistral of Chile (*Selected Poems,* 1957). The first of five collections of Simple sketches, *Simple Speaks His Mind,* appeared in 1950, and another collection of short stories, *Laughing to Keep from Crying,* came in 1952. Working first with composer William Grant STILL and then with Jan Meyerowitz, Hughes composed opera libretti and other texts to be set to music.

Hughes was widely recognized as the most representative African-American writer and perhaps the most original of black poets.

Right-wing groups, which were anti-Communist and probably also motivated by racism, steadily attacked Hughes—despite his denials—for his alleged membership in the Communist party. In 1953, forced to appear before Sen. Joseph McCarthy's investigating committee, he conceded that some of his radical writing had been misguided. Criticized by some socialists, he pressed on with his career, and later toured Africa and elsewhere for the State Department. He published about a dozen books for children on a variety of topics, including jazz, Africa, and the Caribbean. With the photographer Roy DECARAVA he published an acclaimed book of pictures accompanied by a narrative, *The Sweet Flypaper of Life* (1955). His second volume of autobiography, *I Wonder as I Wander,* came in 1956.

Perhaps the most innovative of Hughes's later work came in drama, especially his gospel plays such as *Black Nativity* (1961) and *Jericho-Jim Crow* (1964). He was also an important editor. He published (with Arna BONTEMPS) *Poetry of the Negro, 1746–1949* (1949), as well as *An African Treasury* (1960), *New Negro Poets: U.S.A.* (1964), and *The Book of Negro Humor* (1966). Hughes was widely recognized as the most representative African-American writer and perhaps the most original of black poets. In 1961, he was admitted to the National Institute of Arts and Letters. He died in New York City.

BIBLIOGRAPHY

Bloom, Harold. *Langston Hughes.* New York, 1989.

Mikolyak, Thomas A. *Langston Hughes: A Bio-Bibliography.* Westport, Conn., 1990.

Rampersad, Arnold. *The Life of Langston Hughes.* New York, 1986–1988.

– ARNOLD RAMPERSAD

HUNT, RICHARD

Richard Hunt (September 12, 1935–), sculptor, graphic artist, educator. Born and raised in Chicago, Richard Hunt saw his talent nurtured early in children's classes at the Art Institute of Chicago (AIC), which he attended from age thirteen. That institution was central to his development as a sculptor. There in 1953 he saw the work of Julio Gonzalez, a Spanish sculptor of welded metal whose technique differed radically from the traditional western methods of cast sculpture. Gonzalez' impact was so great that Hunt, still a high school student, built a studio in the basement of his father's barbershop to begin sculpting. He later taught himself to weld in two years. Also at the AIC, Hunt encountered the work of Richmond Barthé, an African-American sculptor who had graduated from the School of the AIC in 1929. Although their styles differed—Barthé modeled naturalistic representations of the human figure, while Hunt was more abstract—Hunt found the older artist to be an inspiration. In 1953, Hunt enrolled in the School of the AIC on a scholarship from the Chicago Public School Art Society. Since the school had limited welding equipment, he taught himself by talking to professional metalworkers and by taking metalcraft classes where he made jewelry. He graduated four years later with a degree in art education and was awarded a travel grant to visit England, Spain, France, and Italy.

If the school taught him techniques, another institution prompted him with ideas that have informed his entire career. From 1951 to 1957, Hunt worked part-time in the zoological experimental laboratory at the University of Chicago. From his earliest work there is a propensity for images that are biomorphic, suggesting tentacles, bones, wings, thoraxes, antennae, and tendons. One of these early works, *Arachne,* was acquired for the permanent collection of the Museum of Modern Art (MoMA) in New York in 1957, while he was still a student. His first one-person show followed in the same city the next year. Exhibitions and purchases from major museums and universities in the years immediately following his graduation indicate his early aesthetic maturity.

This early work used discarded metal parts, which Hunt welded into small-scale zoomorphic and anthropomorphic shapes whose gestures paralleled the "drawing in space" that could be found among other sculptors of the period, including David Smith, another of his influences. The angular armatures and calligraphic forms echoed the gestures of Abstract Expressionist painting. Other sources for this style were the metal African sculpture he had seen with his mother on childhood visits to the Field Museum of Natural History, as well as Greek, Roman, and Renaissance sculpture. By the late 1960s, Hunt's reputation led to numerous commissions for public sculpture. He resolved the resultant change to a larger scale by increasing the mass of his forms to give them a stronger visual presence in the out-of-doors (and to accommodate their being cast from bronze and brass as well as being welded from aluminum and cor-ten steel). Works appeared not as branch or limblike extensions, but as congealed extrusions from some geological source. The works are often designed to protrude from their own rectilinear bases as if they are being manipulated by some overwhelming force. Although different in style, this work maintains Hunt's interest in natural processes of growth and change presented, paradoxically, in the inert medium of metal. This second phase of Hunt's career has led to more than seventy commissions of public sculpture across the country in airports, schools and universities, plazas, hospitals, churches, and synagogues.

Hunt has been included in many national and international exhibitions since he began showing in 1955. Retrospectives of his career were held in 1967 at the Milwaukee Art Center and in 1971 at MoMA and at the AIC. His awards include a Guggenheim Fellowship in the year 1962–1963 and a fellowship at the Tamarind Lithography Workshop in Los Angeles in 1965. In 1964 he was a visiting professor at Yale University. In 1966 he was included in the First World Festival of Negro Arts in Dakar, Senegal. His appointments include the Illinois Arts Council (1970–1975); the National Council on the Arts (1968–1974); board of trustees, Museum of Contemporary Art (Chicago, 1975–1979); board of governors, Skowhegan School of Painting and Sculpture (1979–1984); commissioner, National Museum of American Art, Smithsonian Institution (1980–1988); advisory committee, Getty Center for Education in the Arts (1984–1988); director, International Sculpture Center, (1984–); president, founder, Chicago Sculpture Society (1985–1989); and board of governors, School of the Art Institute of Chicago (1985–1989).

BIBLIOGRAPHY

Columbia College Art Gallery. *Outside In: Public Sculpture by Richard Hunt.* Chicago, 1986.

Landau/Traveling Exhibitions, and Samella Lewis. *Richmond Barthé/Richard Hunt: Two Sculptors, Two Eras.* Los Angeles, 1992.

Museum of Modern Art. *The Sculpture of Richard Hunt.* New York, 1971.

– HELEN M. SHANNON

HURSTON, ZORA NEALE

Zora Neale Hurston (c. 1891–January 28, 1960), folklorist. Zora Neale Hurston was born and grew up in Eatonville, Fla., the first black incorporated town in America. (Her exact date of birth is uncertain. She claimed to be born in either 1901 or 1910, but a brother thinks it was as early as 1891.) Her father, a carpenter and Baptist preacher and a signer of the town's charter, was elected mayor three terms in succession. Her mother, formerly a country schoolteacher, taught Sunday school but spent most of her time raising her eight children. In Eatonville, unlike most of the South at the turn of the century, African Americans were not demoralized by the constant bombardment of poverty and racial hatred, and Hurston grew up surrounded by a vibrant and creative secular and religious black culture. It was here she learned the dialect, songs, folktales, and superstitions that are at the center of her works. Her stories focus on the lives and relationships between black people within their communities.

The untimely death of Hurston's mother in 1904 disrupted her economically and emotionally stable home life, and a year later, at age fourteen, she left home for a job as a maid and wardrobe assistant in a traveling Gilbert and Sullivan company. She left the company in Baltimore, found other work, and attended high school there. In 1918 she graduated from Morgan Academy, the high school division of Morgan State University, and entered Howard University in Washington, D.C., where she took courses intermittently until 1924. She studied there with poet Georgia Douglas Johnson and philosopher Alain LOCKE. Her first story, "John Redding Goes to Sea" (1921), appeared in *Stylus,* Howard's literary magazine.

Hurston arrived in New York in 1925, at the height of the HARLEM RENAISSANCE. She soon became active among the group of painters, musicians, sculptors, entertainers, and writers who came from across the country to be there. She also studied at Barnard College under the anthropologist Franz Boas and graduated with a B.A. in 1928. Between 1929 and 1931, with support from a wealthy white patron, Mrs. Osgood Mason, Hurston returned south and began collecting folklore in Florida and Alabama. In 1934 she received a Rosenwald fellowship and in 1936 and 1937 Guggenheim fellowships that enabled her to study folk religions in Haiti and Jamaica. She was a member of the American Folklore Society, the Anthropological Society, the Ethnological Society, the New York Academy of Sciences, and the American Association for the Advancement of Science. From her extensive research Hurston published *Mules and Men* (1935), the first collection (seventy folktales) of black folklore to appear by a black American. *Tell My Horse* (1938), a second folklore volume, came after her travels to the Caribbean. Her most academic study, *The Florida Negro* (1938), written for the Florida Federal Workers Project, was never published.

While Franz Boas and Mrs. Mason stimulated Hurston's anthropological interests that gave her an analytical perspective on black culture that was unique among black writers of her time, she was fully vested in the creative life of the cultural movement as well. Her close friends included Carl Van Vechten, Alaine Locke, Langston HUGHES, and Wallace Thurman, with whom she coedited and published the only issue of the journal *Fire!!* Appearing in November 1926, its supporters saw it as a forum for younger writers who wanted to break with traditional black ideas. Ironically, *Fire!!* was destroyed by a fire in Thurman's apartment.

Hurston's first novel, *Jonah's Gourd Vine* (1934), reveals the lyric quality of her writing, her skillfulness with and mastery of dialect. The story is about a Baptist preacher with a personal weakness that leads him to an unfortunate end. But Hurston's protagonist, modeled on her father, is a gifted poet/philosopher with an enviable imagination and speech filled with the imagery of black folk culture. He is also a vulnerable person who lacks the self-awareness to comprehend his dilemma; thus, his tragedy.

For its beauty and richness of language, *Their Eyes Were Watching God* (1937), the first novel by a black woman to explore the inner life of a black woman, is Hurston's art at its best. Her most popular work, it traces the development of the heroine from innocence to her realization that she has the power to control her own life. An acknowledged classic since its recovery in the 1970s, it has been applauded by both black and white women scholars as the first black feminist novel. *Moses, Man of the Mountain* (1939), Hurston's third and most ambitious novel, makes of the biblical Israelite deliverance from Egypt an exploration of the black transition from slavery to freedom. Taking advantage of the pervasiveness of the Moses mythology in African and diaspora folklore and culture, Hurston removes Moses from Scripture, demystifies him, and relocates him in African-American culture, where he is a conjure man possessed with magical powers and folk wisdom. The novel tells the story of a people struggling to liberate themselves from the heritage of bondage. In *Seraph on the Suwanee* (1948), Hurston's last and least successful work, she turns away from black folk culture to explore the lives of poor white Southerners. This story focuses on a husband and wife trapped in conventional sexual roles in a marriage that dooms to failure the wife's search for herself.

Following her rediscovery, a once-neglected Hurston rose into literary prominence and enjoys acclaim as the essential forerunner of black women writers who came after her.

Dust Tracks on a Road (1942), Hurston's autobiography, is the most controversial of her books; some of her staunchest admirers consider it a failure. Critics who complain about this work focus on its lack of self-revelation, the inaccurate personal information Hurston gives about herself, and the significant roles that whites play in the text. Other critics praise it as Hurston's attempt to invent an alternative narrative self to the black identity inherited from the slave narrative tradition. Poised between the black and white worlds, not as victim of either but participant-observer in both, her narrative self in *Dust Tracks* presents positive and negative qualities of each. From this perspective, *Dust Tracks* is a revisionary text, a revolutionary alternative women's narrative inscribed into the discourse of black autobiography.

Reviews of Hurston's books in her time were mixed. White reviewers, often ignorant of black culture, praised the richness of her language but misunderstood the works and characterized them as simple and unpretentious. Black critics in the 1930s and 1940s, in journals like the CRISIS, objected most to her focus on black folk life. Their most frequent criticism was the absence from her works of racial terror, exploitation, and misery. Richard WRIGHT expressed anger at the "minstrel image" he claimed Hurston promoted in *Their Eyes Were*

Watching God. None of her books sold well enough while she was alive to relieve her lifetime of financial stress.

Hurston and her writings disappeared from public view from the late 1940s until the early 1970s. Interest in her revived after writer Alice WALKER went to Florida "in search of Zora" in 1973, and reassembled the puzzle of Hurston's later life. Walker discovered that Hurston returned to the South in the 1950s and, still trying to write, supported herself with menial jobs. Without resources and suffering a stroke, in 1959 she entered a welfare home in Fort Pierce, Fla., where she died in 1960 and was buried in an unmarked grave. On her pilgrimage, Walker marked a site where Hurston might be buried with a headstone that pays tribute to "a genius of the South." Following her rediscovery, a once-neglected Hurston rose into literary prominence and enjoys acclaim as the essential forerunner of black women writers who came after her.

BIBLIOGRAPHY

Hemenway, Robert E. *Zora Neale Hurston: A Literary Biography.* Urbana, Ill., 1977.

Wall, Cheryl. "Zora Neale Hurston: Changing Her Own Words." In Fritz Fleischmann, ed. *American Novelists Revisited: Essays in Feminist Criticism.* Boston, 1982, pp. 371–393.

– NELLIE Y. MCKAY

I

IMMIGRATION

For the most part, the study of African-American history and that of American immigration history have been viewed by scholars as completely separate entities. This division is misleading and arbitrary. With the exception of AMERICAN INDIANS, the population of the United States is composed of migrants and their descendants. The study of African-American history has focused on the population created by the forced migrations of hundreds of thousands of Africans in the SLAVE TRADE lasting into the first decade of the nineteenth century. However, what is usually overlooked in the literature is the stream of voluntary migrants of persons of African descent to the United States from the late eighteenth century down to the present, a stream that has swollen significantly in the last third of the twentieth century.

The voluntary immigration from Africa and the Caribbean has produced considerable ethnic diversity within the African-American population. Among persons of African descent there are Haitians, Cape Verdeans, Jamaicans and numerous African ethnicities, among many others. (This article excludes black Latinos from detailed consideration. Given the extent of the integration of persons of African ancestry into the cultures of Cuba, Puerto Rico, and the Dominican Republic, it would be difficult to separate blacks or the African dimensions of Latino culture from broader treatments of Latino culture and history which are outside the scope of this encyclopedia.)

Because blacks in this society are often seen solely in racial terms, their distinctive cultural identities go unrecognized. In the post-1960s era, the range of cultural and linguistic backgrounds that the migrants brought with them became increasingly more diverse. How they identified themselves was often constrained by how they were viewed by both whites and native-born blacks. Would they be recognized as members of an immigrant group or just simply as black? One may call oneself a Trinidadian, speak the *patois,* eat roti and curry goat, throw a weekly hand into the *susu* (rotating credit association), and play on a cricket team, but in the eyes of the members of the host society all such expressions of cultural difference are blotted out by the blinding force of racial stereotypes.

The history of the relationship between native and foreign-born blacks in the United States has often been an uneasy one filled with ambivalence on both sides. Roy Simon Bryce-LaPorte (1993) has posed the provocative questions: "Who is or will be considered an African American?" and "When does a black person of foreign birth or ancestry become African American?" At times the realities of race have drawn the two populations together, particularly when outside discrimination has triggered a reactive solidarity. More often, however, cultural differences have superseded alliances based on color. Immigrants typically attempt to assert their cultural distinctiveness, foster ethnic solidarity, and resist identification with what has been the most subordinated sector of American society, while African Americans may exhibit resentment at the perceived preferential treatment accorded the foreigners, regarding them as a competitive threat in an economy where resources available to racial minorities are scarce.

Because blacks in this society are often seen solely in racial terms, their distinctive cultural identities go unrecognized.

As a by-product of a society that is organized on the basis of a rigid binary racial structure, official government records such as those compiled by the U.S. Census or the Bureau of Immigration are hopelessly deficient regarding black immigrant populations, further contributing to their sense of invisibility. For example, entrenched standards of "black" and "white" formed the basis of classification when the multiracial Cape Verdeans arrived during the latter part of the nineteenth and early twentieth centuries. Routinely grouped under other broader categories, those looking phenotypically most European or "white" were listed as "Portuguese" while the remainder were haphazardly labeled "African Portuguese," "Black Portuguese," and "Atlantic Islanders"—making any reasonable demographic estimates from these sources impossible. Similarly, while British West Indians were distinguished from Puerto Ricans and Cubans, they were not distinguished from French or Dutch West Indians. Moreover, the U.S. Immigration and Naturalization Service collected demographic information only on those who were perceived to be mulatto under the designation "West Indian Race";

those appearing to be darker-skinned were simply lumped under the generalized label of "African Race," and no effort was made to gather data concerning the social characteristics of this group. Finally, information on Jamaicans was not compiled separately until 1953. Rather they were consolidated under "British West Indians" and then further subsumed under the classification of "Other Caribbean." As for arrivals from the continent of Africa, it was not until the 1960s that U.S. immigration records listed them separately by country of origin. From 1890 to 1980, totals of the foreign-born black population was tabulated in the decennial Census, but the figures were not broken down by place of birth (see Table 1). These limitations in conjunction with the sizable number of undocumented black aliens, especially among those who have entered since the 1970s, mean that official calculations of population data related to black immigrants contain serious shortcomings.

Scholarship that treats the black immigrant experience in America has been exceedingly sparse. The first and only book-length overview to date on the subject is Ira Reid's now classic monograph *The Negro Immigrant,* published in 1939. The vast majority of black immigrants to the United States at that time who established the most longstanding communities were Haitians, Cape Verdeans, or British West Indians. These continuing streams of immigration were joined in the post-1960s by increasing numbers of migrants from other countries in Africa and the Caribbean, as well as by people of African descent emigrating from nations where the dominant population is not black, e.g., Afro-Cuban newcomers. Furthermore, varying proportions of other Spanish-speaking multiracial societies in Latin America who migrate may be classified as black in the United States, further swelling the percentages of those of African descent.

Table 1

THE FOREIGN-BORN BLACK POPULATION OF THE UNITED STATES

Year	Number
1890	19,979
1900	20,336
1910	40,339
1920	73,803
1930	98,620
1940	83,941
1950	113,842
1960	125,322
1970	253,458
1980	815,720

Source: U.S. Census of Population, 1890–1980.

Since the 1960s, several factors have converged to stimulate an upsurge in black immigration to the United States. The most significant development was the passage of the landmark Hart-Celler Immigration Reform Act of 1965, which established parity among independent nations in each of the hemispheres; this opened the doors to much more variegated groups in terms of race, ethnicity, religion, language, and national origin than any previous policy. Subsequent measures, most notably the liberal reforms of the Refugee Act of 1980, the Immigration and Reform Act of 1986, and the Immigration Act of 1990, reinforced this diversifying trend.

Political and policy changes during the 1960s in both the Caribbean region and in Britain roughly coincided with the implementation of Hart-Celler in this country, further contributing to the rise in black migrants. Many of the British West Indian islands with predominantly black populations moved toward independence from the British Commonwealth of Nations in this period and were thus able to circumvent the stringent visa quotas that had been allotted them as colonial possessions by the McCarran-Walter Act of 1952. In neighboring Haiti, François "Papa Doc" Duvalier's dictatorial rule caused many Haitians to relocate to the north. At about the same time, in 1962, the British Parliament enacted legislation that sharply curtailed the flow of West Indians to the United Kingdom. A final push factor was the rapid growth in population of many of the islands of the West Indies straining resources and triggering a serious unemployment crisis.

The post-1960s period also witnessed a dramatic increase in continental African blacks entering the United States from such sub-Saharan nations as Nigeria, Ghana, and Ethiopia. In the 1960s alone, the number of African-born blacks in this country increased sixfold. Most planned only a temporary stay, arriving to benefit from the higher education and technical skills training that are still unavailable to them in their native countries. Some, however, particularly those whose homelands are rife with political unrest or who hold asylum status, settled permanently. This "brain drain" of valued human resources has been cause for much concern to those acutely aware of the need for well-trained people to assist in pressing economic and social development in their countries of origin.

Between 1972 and 1992, Jamaica, among non-Hispanic countries with overwhelmingly black populations accounted for 373,972 legal entrants into this country. This was followed by 249,953 from Haiti; 161,530 from Guyana; and 109,594 from Trinidad and Tobago—all Caribbean nations. The leading source of immigrants from Africa was Nigeria with 56,144; followed by 40,694 from Ethiopia; 25,046 from Ghana; and 14,954 from Cape Verde (see Table 2). While such figures usually represent severe undercounts, another indicator of the substantive presence of foreign-born blacks is contained in the *Report on the Foreign-Born Population in the United States* derived from the 1990 census: 435,000 listed themselves as having Jamaican ancestry; 290,000, Haitian; 82,000, Guyanese; 76,000, Trinidad-and-Tobagonian. Another 92,000 declared themselves of Nigerian ancestry.

Haitians

Within the history of black migration to the United States, Haitians are particularly noteworthy. They were the earliest voluntary settlers, starting in the second half of the eighteenth century and likewise they comprised, more than two centuries later, the first major group of black refugees to arrive here. Although their official status as political refugees has been contested, the desperation of their flight out of Haiti in the last decades of the twentieth century was often significantly motivated by direct experience with political persecution at home or fear of such reprisals, as well as by the desire to escape the dire economic conditions of the most impoverished country in the Western hemisphere.

The Republic of Haiti occupies one-third of the island of Hispaniola (the Dominican Republic occupies the remainder) situated in the Caribbean sea. The Haitian people are descended from African slaves who were brought to the island in the seventeenth and eighteenth centuries by French colonists to work on sugar plantations. The slaves initiated a successful revolution, overthrowing French rule in 1804 to become an independent nation—the second oldest republic in the New World after the United States.

Haitian migration to this country has occurred in three main waves: the years of the HAITIAN REVOLUTION, 1791–1803; the era of United States occupation, 1915–

Table 2

TOP EIGHT PREDOMINANTLY BLACK IMMIGRANT GROUPS BY SELECTED COUNTRY OF BIRTH, 1972–1992

	1972	1973	1974	1975	1976	1977	1978
Jamaica	13,427	9,963	12,408	11,076	11,100	11,501	19,265
Haiti	5,809	4,786	3,946	5,145	6,691	5,441	6,470
Guyana	2,826	2,969	3,241	3,169	4,497	5,718	7,614
Trinidad and Tobago	6,615	7,035	6,516	5,982	6,040	6,106	5,973
Nigeria	738	738	670	653	907	653	1,007
Ethiopia	192	149	276	206	332	354	539
Ghana	326	487	369	275	404	454	711
Cape Verde	248	214	122	196	1,110	964	941
	1979	**1980**	**1981**	**1982**	**1983**	**1984**	**1985**
Jamaica	19,714	18,970	23,569	18,711	19,535	19,822	18,923
Haiti	6,433	6,540	6,683	8,779	8,424	9,839	10,165
Guyana	7,001	8,381	6,743	10,059	8,990	8,412	8,531
Trinidad and Tobago	5,225	5,154	4,599	3,532	3,156	2,900	2,831
Nigeria	1,054	1,896	1,918	2,257	2,354	2,337	2,846
Ethiopia	726	977	1,749	1,810	2,643	2,461	3,362
Ghana	828	1,159	951	824	976	1,050	1,041
Cape Verde	765	788	849	852	594	591	627
	1986	**1987**	**1988**	**1989**	**1990**	**1991**	**1992**
Jamaica	19,595	23,148	20,966	24,523	25,013	23,828	18,915
Haiti	12,666	14,819	34,806	13,658	20,324	47,527	11,002
Guyana	10,367	11,384	8,747	10,789	11,362	11,666	9,064
Trinidad and Tobago	2,891	3,543	3,947	5,394	6,740	8,407	7,008
Nigeria	2,976	3,278	3,343	5,213	8,843	7,912	4,551
Ethiopia	2,737	2,156	2,571	3,389	4,336	5,127	4,602
Ghana	1,164	1,120	1,239	2,045	4,466	3,330	1,867
Cape Verde	760	657	921	1,118	907	973	757

Source: Compiled from the U.S. Department of Justice, Statistical Yearbooks of the Immigration and Naturalization Service.

1934; and the period beginning with the long and repressive rule of the Duvaliers—François "Papa Doc," followed by his son, Jean-Claude "Baby Doc," 1957–1986—and continuing to the present, in late 1994, with no sign of abating. Even prior to the influx prompted by the Haitian Revolution, however, there had already been a Haitian presence in colonial America. One of the most notable émigrés was Jean Baptiste Point du Sable, who traded furs along the Mississippi River and founded with his Potawatami Indian wife Kittahaw the permanent settlement of Chicago in 1772. Later, in 1779, a battalion of 800 volunteers from Haiti fought valiantly to victory against the British in support of American independence at the Battle of Savannah.

Beginning in 1791, the number of arrivals began to increase, as the migrants sought to escape the turmoil of insurrection brewing in their homeland. The newcomers scattered along the coastal cities of New Orleans, Charleston, Philadelphia, and New York, and even as far as Boston. One such émigré, Joseph Savary, led the Second Battalion of Free Men of Color under Gen. Andrew Jackson in 1814–1815, distinguishing himself by becoming the first black to be ranked a major in the U.S. Army. Philadelphia was the cultural center of the émigré population in these years where settlers published a Haitian newspaper and ran a bookstore that served as a meeting place for compatriots.

Interestingly, the movement of blacks between Haiti and the United States has not always been one-way. At various times in the nineteenth century, African Americans left the United States for Haiti seeking a new homeland free of white domination. In the year 1824, some 13,000 black Americans emigrated to Haiti, and in 1861 another 12,000 made the journey, most departing from New Orleans. One of the first of these émigrés was a young man named Alexander Du Bois, the grandfather of W. E. B. DU BOIS, who sailed for Haiti in the early 1820s. He stayed only a few years, however, returning to the United States in 1831. Abraham Lincoln was the first American president to recognize Haiti's independence; under his administration a plan was also devised to resettle newly freed slaves to the island republic. Lincoln's policy toward Haiti, and perhaps even toward American blacks, was likely influenced by his personal barber and reputed confidant, the Haitian immigrant, William De Florville, known as "Billy the Barber."

More than a century after the Haitian revolution and in response to a succession of ineffectual presidents and continued political instability, the United States occupied the Republic of Haiti, triggering the outflow of hundreds, primarily from Port-au-Prince, to New York City. These newcomers were well educated and able to establish businesses, obtain professional employment, and assimilate fairly readily into existing urban communities. A significant proportion settled in Harlem, some joining other African Americans and West Indians in shaping the cultural movement of the HARLEM RENAISSANCE. After World War II, growing numbers of Haitian women made the journey, recruited initially as domestic workers in major cities throughout the United States. Like many immigrants these women viewed their relocation as a temporary measure, but also like so many, they ended up settling permanently in this country.

By far the largest outpouring of Haitians began as early as the late 1950s, when François Duvalier took office as president, inaugurating an era of dictatorship that lasted thirty years. Initially, the migrants from this last wave were primarily intellectuals, professionals, and political refugees of the middle and elite classes attempting to escape the brutal regime, but by the mid-1960s the high unemployment, shrinking opportunities, and oppressive rule in Haiti set in motion mass migration. This flow coincided with the liberalization of U.S. immigration policy, especially as regards provisions for family reunification.

By far the largest outpouring of Haitians began as early as the late 1950s, when François Duvalier took office as president.

The grim political and economic circumstances in Haiti made emigration a matter of life or death for many who found myriad ways, both legal and clandestine, of reaching U.S. shores, including much publicized, desperate attempts to make the crossing in leaky and overcrowded boats. Many sold everything they owned to book passage. Those who arrived by conventional means often came on tourist visas and simply overstayed their visit. By 1977 the volume of the exodus at sea escalated due to the confluence of several factors: deportation of Haitian workers from the Bahamas and a concurrent threat that they would also be expelled from the neighboring Dominican Republic; a shift in U.S. policy that made labor certification requirements more stringent for prospective entrants; and finally, severe drought in Haiti in both 1975 and 1977, as well as stepped-up internal violence. This influx was predominantly male and largely illiterate—a flight from severe rural poverty.

For the most part the migrants were unwanted in this country, however, and their journey was filled with obstacles throughout. Some of the boats were simply intercepted en route by United States Coast Guard cutters and returned to Haiti. Those that did succeed in making the crossing faced a hostile reception by the authorities. Without proper documentation and often without knowledge of their legal rights, they were incarcerated in detention centers outside Miami such as the notorious Camp Krome, a miserable, overcrowded facility where large numbers of refugees languished for indefinite periods.

There was more trouble. Public health officials had already associated Haitians with the spread of tuberculosis, and in the early 1980s, the Center for Disease Control in Atlanta singled out the migrants as one of the high-risk groups for contracting the HIV virus. Although they were later officially removed from that list, the damage had already been done, further exacerbating negative sentiments toward the Haitian newcomers.

At this juncture, the charge of racial discrimination began to be made as explanation for the differential treatment accorded Haitians—the only black population seeking political asylum—as compared to the Cubans, the other major group of Caribbean refugees reaching South Florida. Cubans were classified as political refugees, and this enabled many to make an easier transition to the United States. By contrast, although most Haitians left their homeland in this period to escape political persecution, the vast majority did not hold refugee status but rather were categorized as economic migrants. Thus, even when they did actually succeed in relocation, and despite having experienced the violent disruptions and consequent liabilities of political repression, they could not take advantage of the resettlement services that come with refugee status in the United States.

When racial bias was raised as a major factor in the mistreatment of Haitian refugees, some in the African-American community made a concerted effort to persuade lawmakers to reassess their policies. The CONGRESSIONAL BLACK CAUCUS got involved as did such established black political figures as Jesse JACKSON and Shirley Chisholm lobbying on behalf of the Haitian cause during the early 1980s. Here then, was a situation where allegiances based on race overshadowed cultural differences.

After the 1991 ouster of the democratically elected President Jean-Bertrand Aristide, political reprisals against Aristide supporters in Haiti once again led more than 50,000 to flee their homeland seeking refuge in the United States. While initially a few were screened and allowed entry, most were turned away or were intercepted at sea where they were then sent to detention centers in other parts of the Caribbean.

In the 1990s the largest concentration of Haitian immigrants was in New York City, where over half of those claiming Haitian ancestry in the United States lived. Within the metropolis, Haitians clustered in Brooklyn's low- and moderate-income neighborhoods while those who could afford it relocated to parts of Queens. Although the tendency was to reside among coethnics, these were also areas where black Americans and other Afro-Caribbeans lived. The Haitian influx into the city included migrants from a wide range of socioeconomic and educational backgrounds, but, for the most part, they worked in unskilled and semiskilled factory jobs and in service industries.

The sustained economic growth in Massachusetts during the 1980s attracted some of the Haitian population of the Northeast away from the established community in New York City, where many middle- and working-class families felt constrained by rising crime rates and congestion. The Boston area had a reputation for good schools, and its strong economy held out the promise of economic advancement and educational opportunity.

In the late 1970s and early '80s, while more than 60,000 Haitian "boat people" were arriving in South Florida, there was a secondary migration into Miami of primarily middle-class Haitians who had originally settled in New York. Together they have created a flourishing "Little Haiti" modeled after the successful ethnic economy of Miami's "Little Havana." While operating on a much smaller scale and with more obstacles than its Cuban counterpart, "Little Haiti" has grown to include enterprises from ethnic micro-businesses to more established ventures selling Caribbean and French-styled products, a well-developed community service sector, outlets for Haitian music and art, and a strong presence within the local educational system. When a new public school opened in the neighborhood, it was renamed Toussaint Louverture Elementary after the Haitian revolutionary leader. Low-cost housing is available to residents of the enclave, an area that is situated close to the garment factories and warehouses in Miami where many of the immigrants are employed. Others who fled to Florida in these years became migrant farmworkers, heading north to pick fruits and vegetables all along the southern Atlantic coast.

No matter where they ultimately settle, religious participation is high among the newcomers. While most Haitians are Catholic, increasing numbers are joining evangelical Protestant congregations, a legacy of the

Protestantism brought to Haiti by hundreds of American missions. Most of the immigrant Protestant worshipers are Baptists. Some churches serving the Haitian community offer services in Creole and some in French, while Haitian pastors are taking greater leadership roles. Many Haitian settlers have creatively combined their more institutionalized Christian practices with less formal, traditional vodoun religious beliefs. A growing number of families send their children to parochial schools.

One of the defining features of the Haitian émigré community is the extended network of radio and television outlets that broadcast Haitian programming, usually in Creole. One can listen to Haitian music and news from the homeland at any hour of the day while educational, cultural and religious programs are offered on both radio and local cable stations. Typically, the Haitian migrants remain close to their relatives in Haiti. Family members already in the United States help the others to come in classic chain migration fashion. Although there are no statistics available on the subject, it is widely understood that the money sent by Haitians from this country to their families and relatives in Haiti is one of their most important sources of revenue. When travel is not risky, Haitian immigrants, when they can afford it, often make return visits. Similarly, the children of wealthy Haitians are more likely to fly to the United States, particularly Miami, than to travel out of the city of Port-au-Prince to another part of the country. It has also become more common for wealthy Haitian parents to send their children to American schools while English/French bilingual schools in Haiti have benefited from increasing popularity. Hence, at many differing levels, the back-and-forth movement and interpenetra-

Cape Verdean immigrants in New England had a strong maritime background and many worked as sailors, often on Cape Verdean-owned packet boats and barks. In this picture from 1922, Wanderer *prepares to sail, with its captain, Antone T. Edwards, in the foreground. (Old Dartmouth Historical Society—New Bedford Whaling Museum)*

tion of Haitian and American cultures permeate the Haitian-American immigrant experience.

Coming from a highly class-stratified society, Haitians must adjust to a situation in the United States where race predominates over both social class and ethnicity. Members of the first generation are much more likely to exhibit a strong national identity, continuing to speak Haitian Creole, which is not simply a dialect of French but a language of its own, and to associate primarily with coethnics. In general, they do not actively identify with African Americans. However, studies completed in New York, Miami, and Evanston, Ill., demonstrate that the immigrant children are much more likely to shed their traditional culture, speak English exclusively, and attempt to fit into black America. Haitians also view themselves as distinctive from other Afro-Caribbean migrants. They shun identifying themselves as West Indians especially because of the difference in language from their English-speaking Caribbean counterparts and also because of their differing cultural background and their unique history of early self-rule. Faced with discrimination based on race as well as significant levels of anti-immigrant bias, Haitian Americans have had to juggle a complex mix of social, cultural, regional, and racial identifications in the process of adapting to their new communities.

Cape Verdeans

The first voluntary mass migration of a population of African descent to the United States began in the latter half of the nineteenth century when significant numbers of Cape Verdeans left their drought-stricken archipelago off the west coast of Africa, which had long been colonized by Portugal, to make southeastern New England their new home. Although little known outside of the New England region, these Afro-Portuguese settlers are of particular significance as the only major group of Americans to have made the transatlantic voyage from Africa to the United States on their own initiative.

Most historians agree that the Cape Verde Islands were uninhabited until the mid-fifteenth century, when Portuguese explorers landed there. Almost from the very beginning of settlement, West African slaves were being brought to the Cape Verdes, initially to labor on sugar and cotton plantations, but the arid climate of these Sahelian islands prevented truly successful commercial cultivation of the land. What soon became more important to the Portuguese than agricultural production was the strategic location of the archipelago as a crossroads in the expanding slave trade. Situated near the Guinea coast and on the trade winds route to Brazil, the islands served as an entry point for the distribution of goods, for supplying foreign vessels with needed supplies and salt, and for transporting slaves to the New World.

As these exchanges were taking place, the sparse Portuguese population intermingled with the greater numbers of West Africans to produce a rich and distinctive society and culture. In this mesh of African ancestry, Catholicism, and Western presence, it has not always been possible to discern whether the European or the African influence predominates. Rather the interweaving has been so complete that it is most appropriate to speak of the evolution of a separate culture with its own distinctive customs, folklore, cuisine, music, literature and finally, language. Though based in Portuguese and several West African languages, the mother tongue of the Cape Verdean people is a full-fledged, creolized language of its own, called Crioulo. Although varying in dialect from one island to another, Crioulo has become a defining feature of the Cape Verdean cultural identity that has been transmitted to the United States and other parts of the world.

The effects of the dry climate in the Cape Verde Islands was exacerbated by colonial mismanagement of the land, so that by the end of the eighteenth century, the people of the islands were experiencing severe and recurrent drought with its resulting famine and high mortality. Unable to escape overland to more favorable conditions, young Cape Verdean men seized the chance to leave home in search of a better life as crew aboard the United States whaling ships that were beginning to arrive at the archipelago's protected harbors, particularly on the island of Brava.

The Cape Verdean seamen earned a reputation as disciplined and able crews. Despite their skill as whalers, however, they were routinely allotted the lowest rates in the division of profits and were frequently subject to harsh treatment in the mariners' hierarchy because of discrimination based on race and ethnicity. Their exploitation at sea foreshadowed a similar prejudice that they would face once the immigrants began to settle more permanently in this country.

By the late nineteenth century, with the advent of steamship travel and the decline of the whaling and sealing industries, the old sailing vessels had become obsolete and were available at a very low cost. Some of the early Cape Verdean migrants took advantage of this opportunity to buy up these old Essex-built "Gloucester Fishermen." They pooled their resources and converted them into cargo and passenger ships, used as packet boats that regularly plied between the Cape Verdes and the ports of New Bedford, Mass., and Providence, R.I. With the purchase of a sixty-four-ton fishing schooner, the *Nellie May,* Antonio Coelho became the first Cape

Verdean–American packet owner. He hired a former whaleman as captain and set sail for Brava in 1892. Before long, Cape Verdean–American settlers came to own a fleet of these vessels. Thus, in a situation unlike that of most immigrant groups, black or white, the Cape Verdeans had control over their own means of passage to this country.

During this same period, cheap sources of labor were being sought for the expanding textile mills, on the cranberry bogs and in the maritime-related occupations of southern coastal New England. Increasing numbers, including women and children, were arriving to fulfill the demand, fleeing their land of continuous hunger. The movement continued steadily until the enforcement of the restrictive immigration laws of the early 1920s, which curtailed the influx.

The Cape Verdean settlers brought with them a distinctive cultural identity, thereby initially defining themselves in terms of ethnicity.

Like the records of other immigrants who do not fall readily within the dualistic confines of the United States system of racial classification, official population records have been completely inadequate in providing accurate demographic data on the Cape Verdeans. However, analysis of information recorded on the packet ship passenger lists has made it possible to calculate solid estimates of the numbers of Cape Verdean entrants as well as to construct a population profile on this group. In the years between 1820 and 1975 some 35,000 to 45,000 Cape Verdeans emigrated to the United States, with the islands of Brava and Fogo providing over 60 percent of the newcomers. In the years of the heaviest inflow, between 1880 and 1920, the overwhelming majority were male. After the islands became an independent nation in 1975, thanks to the continued liberal immigration policy of the United States, an average of 900 arrivals entered annually. Currently the estimated number of Cape Verdeans and their descendants living in the United States stands at 350,000, slightly more than the total population of the home country itself.

The Cape Verdean settlers brought with them a distinctive cultural identity, migrating freely to New England as Portuguese colonials, thereby initially defining themselves in terms of ethnicity. However, because of their mixed African and European ancestry, they were looked upon and treated as an inferior racial group. Although the Cape Verdeans sought recognition as Portuguese Americans, white society, including the other Portuguese immigrants, excluded them from their social and religious associations. They suffered similar discrimination in housing and employment. At the same time, the Cape Verdeans chose not to identify with American blacks. Their Catholicism tended to keep them apart from the primarily Protestant African-American population, but, more powerfully, they quickly perceived the adverse effects of racism on the upward mobility of anyone considered nonwhite in this country.

One noteworthy exception to this pattern is illustrated by the life of the flamboyant and charismatic evangelist leader "Sweet Daddy" Grace, perhaps the most notorious Cape Verdean American immigrant. Founder of the United House of Prayer for All People, by the late 1930s he had established hundreds of these Protestant congregations throughout the United States with an estimated half a million followers, primarily African Americans. In the process, he amassed hundreds of thousands of dollars, and by 1952, EBONY magazine called him "America's richest Negro minister." On the subject of race, Sweet Daddy declared, "I am a colorless man. I am a colorless bishop. Sometimes I am black, sometimes white. I preach to all races." Born Marceline Manoël de Graça in 1881, he sailed from his native island of Brava to New Bedford at the age of nine. Among the bishop's many teachings was the singular claim that along with his own migration, God, too, first arrived in America in the year 1900.

As in characteristic of other nonwhite immigrants to the United States, issues of identity among the Cape Verdeans are an ever-evolving and complex matter. The 1960s were watershed years for Cape Verdean Americans as the rise of black nationalism and its attendant emphasis on pride in one's African heritage had a transformative effect on many. The domestic social changes coincided with the struggles for liberation from Portuguese colonialism on the continent of Africa as well. At the time, the Cape Verde Islands, under the great revolutionary leader Amilcar Cabral, in collaboration with the Portuguese colony of Guinea-Bissau, were engaged in a protracted armed conflict to procure their independence. The process of rethinking racial identifications touched most Cape Verdean–American families in this period, often creating intergenerational rifts between the parents and grandparents, who were staunchly Portuguese, and their children, who were beginning to ally themselves with the African-American struggle not only in political thought but also in cultural expression.

Shortly after gaining its independence in 1975, the Republic of Cape Verde presented the United States with the gift of the schooner *Ernestina,* the last Cape Verdean packet boat in existence. In 1986, at the Tall

Ships celebration of the Statue of Liberty centennial, the vessel took its place at the front of the flotilla, in recognition of its unique history as the only surviving ship in the parade that had actually carried immigrants to this country.

West Indians

The term *West Indian* refers here to the Anglophone Caribbean, a group of countries that were once British territories or are still formally associated with the British Commonwealth, including Jamaica, Trinidad and Tobago (which became one nation at the time of their independence in 1962), Barbados, the Bahamas, and Guyana (formerly British Guiana), as well as the scattered smaller islands of St. Kitts and Nevis, Antigua, Montserrat, St. Vincent, St. Lucia, Dominica, and Grenada. Although Guyana, Panama, and Belize are located on the South American mainland, they are included under the British West Indian rubric because of their related history, Caribbean orientation, and substantial black population. Jamaica has always been the most populous, with roughly half of the region's inhabitants residing there. West Indians are English-speaking or speak an English-based Creole. Although their migration in large numbers did not begin until the early twentieth century, they make up the largest group of voluntary black settlers in the United States. West Indians constitute vibrant and growing ethnic communities, some of long-standing, especially in New York City and other cities of the northeast such as Boston and Hartford. They are also found along Florida's Gold Coast region, in the midwestern cities of Detroit and Chicago, and in southern California.

The English first settled the West Indies in the seventeenth century and shortly thereafter began to bring in large numbers of Africans as slaves for the enormously productive, labor-intensive sugar plantations. Before long, the black population had greatly outnumbered the white and continued to grow after slavery was abolished so that the West Indians by and large are descended from African ancestry. The only exceptions are in Trinidad and Guyana, where significant proportions of the inhabitants are Asian Indians, the legacy of labor recruitment in the nineteenth century.

Although a sprinkling of West Indians relocated to North America in the nineteenth century, the first sizable wave arrived in the early decades of the twentieth, with approximately 85,000 entering between 1900 and 1930. American investors in this period—in particular, the United Fruit Company—developed large tracts of agricultural land in the Caribbean, strengthening the connection between the two regions, while the steamship lines hauling the fruit established transportation routes, especially to the ports of the northeast. Other West Indians, chiefly from Barbados and the Bahamas, came to work as migrant laborers on farms and construction projects in the southern United States during World War I, with many choosing to stay on a permanent basis. Between 1910 and 1921, a series of damaging hurricanes hit the islands hard, heightening the level of out-migration. When passage of the restrictive U.S. immigration laws of 1921 and 1924 effectively cut off the influx from southern and eastern Europe, people from the West Indies, which were still British colonies, came in under the generous British quota.

The newcomers had considerable job skills and training upon their arrival as well as higher levels of literacy than most immigrant groups of this period. Early in the migration, the sex ratio was significantly skewed toward men, but by the 1920s more women than men were making the journey. By far, the largest concentration of West Indian settlers was in New York City. The consensus among scholars and contemporary observers has been that this wave of migrants made an extremely successful adjustment to their new society. West Indians opened small businesses as a route to upward mobility and, among the black population as a whole, were overrepresented in the professions. They thus played prominent roles in the intellectual, political, and economic leadership of the community.

The success of West Indians, especially of those who settled in New York during the earlier part of the century, has been used invidiously to demonstrate the superiority of the foreigners over resident African Americans. West Indian business acumen has been related to cultural factors such as hard work, thrift, participation in coethnic revolving credit associations, and maintenance of a strong family economy—resources that the newcomers supposedly transplanted from their countries of origin and thus are unavailable to native-born blacks. More recent research, however, has led to a reexamination of the notion that West Indians outperform native-born blacks; it has been found that, at least among the post-1965 settlers, levels of self-employment and occupational mobility as compared to African Americans have been exaggerated.

West Indians arriving to New York at the beginning of the twentieth century brought with them a legacy of political sophistication derived from the experience of living in Commonwealth territories, where class distinctions formed the primary organizing structure of society. The most influential political leader in the early period was the Jamaican-born Marcus GARVEY, who had organized plantation laborers in the Caribbean and Central America before coming to the United States in 1916. Within a few short years, Garvey mobilized hundreds of thousands of both West Indians and African Americans throughout the country to active political participation through his UNIVERSAL NEGRO IMPROVEMENT ASSOCIATION (UNIA), an organization promoting black nationalism, entrepreneurship, and solidarity. While Garvey utilized his steamship company, the Black Star Line, to transport blacks between the United States, the West Indies, and even Africa, his central aim was not solely a back-to-Africa solution to racial strife, but rather a passionate commitment to the development of strong, self-reliant, capitalist, black communities in this country and around the world. By the mid-1920s, Garvey came under federal surveillance as a possible threat to national security and was convicted of mail fraud. Because of his immigrant status—he never became a naturalized citizen of the United States—the government was able to deport him, and Garvey was expelled from the country in 1927.

During the 1920s and '30s, Caribbean intellectuals settled in Harlem, shaping leftist politics and making major contributions to the literary and artistic production of the Harlem Renaissance. Militant socialist thinkers, such as Richard B. Moore, a native of Barbados; Cyril Briggs, born on the tiny island of Nevis; and Hubert H. Harrison from the Virgin Islands, organized laborers and tenants, delivered public lectures, and published radical journals and Marxist treatises. With other West Indians, including Frank Crosswaith and the Rev. Ethelred Brown, they ran for political office on the Socialist or Communist tickets at the local, state, and even national level, though none ever succeeded in being elected. Another central figure to the Harlem Renaissance was the Jamaican-born writer and poet Claude MCKAY, whose lyrical but biting literary contributions served to define the movement. Some of the leadership actively promoted alliances between the foreign-born and native black populations based on class solidarity to jointly combat the forces of racism and capitalism.

Never large enough to constitute a separate ethnic enclave in New York, Boston and other cities, the British West Indian immigrants to the metropolis were scattered throughout African-American neighborhoods; typically, they held the same menial, unskilled, and low-paying jobs as the rest of the black population. The women almost all worked as domestics replacing the earlier Irish help and competing with native-born black women, as white employers increasingly showed a preference for hiring foreign-born blacks. In Boston, by the early 1980s, West Indians began to establish an ethnic niche for themselves within the expanding service economy, especially as health care paraprofessionals and hospital workers in the city's extensive network of medical facilities.

The primary adaptation strategy for the West Indian newcomers was to uphold their foreign-born identity as nationals of a particular colony and as British. There were community efforts to promote the celebration of the Commonwealth holidays of Empire and Coronation Day and to encourage participation in organized cricket matches; individuals expressed their differences by emphasizing their British accents. No matter how hard they tried to assert their foreignness, however, how they defined themselves was less significant ultimately than how they were defined by others. For the most part, the white majority did not differentiate West Indians from the larger black population. Yet, unlike their Haitian counterparts, those from the Anglophone West Indies have been much more likely to develop a Caribbean panethnicity in the United States, shedding strong identifications based on nationality—as Jamaican or Barbadian, for example—and manifesting instead a West Indian identity. Because the political climate in their home countries has been more stable than the situation in Haiti in the last decades, West Indians have been more free to move back and forth, maintaining strong ties and forging a transnational identity as well.

West Indian migration north to the United States skyrocketed in the post-1965 era. In New York City, the newcomers—unlike the early twentieth-century first generation of settlers who tended to disperse among the local African-American population—are establishing discrete West Indian neighborhoods with an unmistakable Caribbean flavor. The lively and elaborate carnivals celebrated at summer's end with the sounds of calypso music, the parades of flamboyant masqueraders, and the aromas of West Indian dishes are a declaration to the public that a distinctive *black* and *foreign* population makes its home in the United States.

Recent Trends

Since 1965 black immigration to the United States has expanded beyond its traditional sources in the Caribbean and Cape Verde Islands. Some European migrants are of African descent. Recent immigration from Great Britain has contained a high percentage of persons of African-Caribbean ancestry. In New York City, for example, many British newcomers have settled in neighborhoods such as Crown Heights and East Flatbush, areas with heavy recent Caribbean arrivals.

The most interesting recent trend has been the development of African immigration. There is a tradition of voluntary African immigration dating back to the mid-nineteenth century. Orishatukeh Faduma from west Africa, a nineteenth-century educator in North Carolina, was a member of the American Negro Academy in the early twentieth century and the author of a scalding critique on the lack of education evidenced among the black clergy. Chief Alfred Sam, from the Gold Coast (now Ghana), was a leader of a back-to-Africa movement in Oklahoma around 1913, where he tried to sell local black residents shares in his Akim Trading Company. Many Africans came to the United States seeking education, including John Chilembwe, leader of the revolt in Nyasaland in 1915 and Kwame Nkrumah, later the leader of Ghana. The historically black colleges and universities (HBCUs) have educated many African political and religious leaders.

Increasing immigration to the United States by persons of African descent has challenged conventional assumptions about the nature of African-American identity.

In the 1940s, there were approximately 2,000 African immigrants living in Harlem, primarily working as seamen, laborers, and cocoa importers. Their places of origin ranged from Nigeria, Dahomey (now Benin), the Gold Coast (now Ghana), the Congo (now Zaire), Liberia, to Sierra Leone. As a result of the Italian-Ethiopian war, there was some emigration of Ethiopian refugees to the United States, including Malaku E. Bayen, the editor of the *Voice of Ethiopia* in the late 1930s.

However, it was in the 1970s that African emigration commenced in substantial numbers. Although only about 2 percent of immigrants to the United States during the 1980s were from Africa (less if one excludes North Africa), African newcomers have established flourishing subcommunities, and have become an important part of the cultural and political life in many black neighborhoods. The most populous country in Africa, Nigeria, has been the source of the largest numbers of arrivals. The political troubles in Ethiopia in the 1970s and '80s contributed to an exodus of refugees and immigrants; over 5,000 Ethiopians moved to the United States in 1991 alone. The struggle against apartheid was an important factor in the sizable outmigration from South Africa. Dennis Brutus, Abdullah Ibrahim (Dollar Brand), Miriam Makeba, and Lindewe Mabuza were some of the prominent refugees from South Africa during this time. Other countries with substantial outflows, many of them former British colonies with Anglophone traditions, include the Cameroons, Ethiopia, Ghana, Ivory Coast, Kenya, Liberia, Senegal, Sierra Leone, Somalia, Sudan, Tanzania, and Uganda. The influx of African immigrants has coincided with and helped catalyze a renewed interest among many African Americans in their African roots. These settlers have played a significant part in the burgeoning African handicraft and artwork markets within black urban communities.

Increasing immigration to the United States by persons of African descent has expanded and challenged conventional notions and assumptions about the nature of African-American identity. The mingling of cultures, languages, historical backgrounds, and lifestyles has fostered a sense of multicultural diversity within black America. The common benchmarks of African-American experience have been expanded to include the full range of cultures within the wide ambit of the African diaspora. For all of the tensions and problems cultural mixing and assimilation bring, the result has already replenished African-American cultural and political life.

BIBLIOGRAPHY

Apraku, Kofi. *African Émigrés in the United States: A Missing Link in Africa's Social and Economic Development.* New York, 1991.

Bryce-Laporte, Roy S. "Black Immigrants: The Experience of Invisibility and Inequality." *Journal of Black Studies* (September 1972): 29–56.

———. "Voluntary Immigration and the Continuing Encounters Between Blacks: The Post-Quincentenary Challenge." *Annals of the American Academy of Political and Social Science* 530 (November 1993): 28–41.

Bryce-Laporte, Roy S., and Delores M. Mortimer, eds. *Caribbean Immigration to the United States.* Research Institute on Immigration and Ethnic Studies Occasional Papers No. 1. Washington, D.C., 1976. Foner, Nancy.

"The Jamaicans: Race and Ethnicity Among Migrants in New York City." In *New Immigrants in New York.* New York, 1987, pp. 195–219.

Halter, Marilyn. *Between Race and Ethnicity: Cape Verdean American Immigrants.* Urbana, Ill., 1993.

———. " 'Staying Close to Haitian Culture': Ethnic Enterprise in the Immigrant Community." In Marilyn Halter, ed. *New Migrants in the Marketplace: Boston's Ethnic Entrepreneurs.* Amherst, Mass., 1995.

Ho, Christine. *Salt-Water Trinnies: Afro-Trinidadian Immigrant Networks and Non-Assimilation in Los Angeles.* New York, 1991.

Johnson, Violet. "Culture, Economic Stability and Entrepreneurship: The Case of British West Indians in Boston." In Marilyn Halter, ed. *New Migrants in the Marketplace: Boston's Ethnic Entrepreneurs.* Amherst, Mass., 1995.

Kasinitz, Philip. *Caribbean New York: Black Immigrants and the Politics of Race.* Ithaca, N.Y., 1992.

Laguerre, Michel S. *American Odyssey: Haitians in New York City.* Ithaca, N. Y., 1984.

Lawless, Robert. "Haitian Migrants and Haitian-Americans: From Invisibility into the Spotlight." *Journal of Ethnic Studies* 14 (1986): 29–70.

Model, Suzanne. "Caribbean Immigrants: A Black Success Story?" *International Migration Review* 25 (1991): 248–276.

Portes, Alejandro, and Alex Stepick. *City on the Edge: The Transformation of Miami.* Berkeley and Los Angeles, 1993.

Reid, Ira de Augustine. *The Negro Immigrant: His Background, Characteristics and Social Adjustment, 1899–1937.* New York, 1939.

Reimers, David M. *Still the Golden Door: The Third World Comes to America.* New York, 1992.

Stafford, Susan Buchanan. "The Haitians: The Cultural Meaning of Race and Ethnicity." In *New Immigrants in New York*. New York, 1987, pp. 131–159.

Sutton, Constance R., and Elsa M. Chaney. *Caribbean Life in New York City: Sociocultural Dimensions*. New York, 1992.

Ueda, Reed. *Postwar Immigrant America: A Social History*. Boston, 1994.

Woldenmikael, Tekle Mariam. *Becoming Black American: Haitians and American Institutions in Evanston, Illinois*. New York, 1989.

– MARILYN HALTER

INVENTORS AND INVENTIONS

Historians are just beginning to uncover some of the ways in which African Americans have contributed to the development of American technology. Seventeenth-century African-American inventors left no written records of their own. But many of them were skilled in crafts and created new devices and techniques in the course of their work. Africans brought a store of technological knowledge with them to the Americas. In the West, elements of African technology merged with European and Native American technology to create new American traditions in technology. This is particularly evident in the areas of boat building, rice culture, pharmacology, and musical instrument-making.

We know more about black inventors in the eighteenth and nineteenth centuries, particularly those who enjoyed some celebrity in their time, such as Norbert Rillieux, a Louisianan who invented the multiple-effect vacuum evaporation system for producing sugar from sugar cane. The Rillieux method revolutionized the sugar industry and came to be the accepted method of sugar cane juice evaporation. Though blacks contributed to the technological development that resulted, there was little public recognition of their achievements.

In the North, many African-American men turned to the maritime trades for employment, and from these ranks came several outstanding inventors such as James FORTEN, the wealthy Philadelphia black abolitionist whose fortune was built upon his invention around the turn of the nineteenth century of a sail handling device, and Lewis Temple, who introduced the toggle harpoon to commercial whaling in Massachusetts in the 1840s.

Craftsmen who invented new devices discovered innovative techniques that improved the quality of their products or reduced the cost of producing them often went into business for themselves instead of hiring themselves out for wages. But these craftsmen-inventors still faced the problems of patenting the invention or protecting it somehow from competitors, financing its production, and marketing it.

The enactment of the U.S. Patent Act in 1970 provided for some documentation of black inventors and their inventions, but this documentation is incomplete. Because the race of the inventor was not generally recorded by the U.S. Patent Office, it is not known for certain how many blacks received patents. Thoms L. Jennings, a New York abolitionist, is the earliest African-American patent holder to have been identified so far. He received a patent for a dry-cleaning process on March 3, 1821. Further research may uncover earlier black patent holders. Slaves were legally prohibited from receiving patents for their inventions, and there are few surviving accounts in which slave inventors are fully identified.

The slave inventor found himself in an unlikely position that must have strained the assumptions of slavery to the utmost. Nothing illustrates the slave inventor's dilemma more clearly than the situation of two such inventors: "Ned" and Benjamin Montgomery. They were responsible for the federal government and the Confederate government formally taking up the "problem" of slave inventors.

Ned's owner, O. J. E. Stuart, wrote to the secretary of the interior requesting that he receive a patent for the invention of a cotton scraper that his slave mechanic, Ned, had invented. Although Stuart admitted that the concept for the invention came entirely from Ned, he reminded the secretary that "the master is the owner of the fruits of the labor of the slave both intillectual [sic], and manual." The U.S. attorney general rendered a final opinion on June 10, 1858, "that a machine invented by a slave, though it be new and useful, cannot, in the present state of the law, be patented." The attorney general also prohibited the masters of slaves from receiving patents for their slaves' inventions. The decision not to allow either slaves or their owners to receive patents for slave inventions meant that such inventions could not enjoy any legal protection or any formal recognition. The attorney general's opinion stood until the end of the Civil War and the passage of the THIRTEENTH AMENDMENT and FOURTEENTH AMENDMENT. Further mention of Ned is absent from the historical record, and nothing is known of what became of him.

Benjamin Montgomery was also a slave inventor. He was the slave of Joseph Davis (brother of Jefferson Davis, later president of the Confederacy). Montgomery served as general manager and mechanic on Davis's plantation in Mississippi. In the late 1850s Montgomery invented a propeller for a river steamboat, specifically designed for the shallow waters around the plantation. Montgomery's biographers write that both Joseph and Jefferson Davis tried to have the propeller patented, but they were prevented from doing so by the attorney general's 1858 decision barring slave inventions from being patented. After he became president of the Confederate States, Jefferson Davis oversaw Confederate legislation that allowed a master to receive patents for his slaves' inventions. Many other slaves, lost to history, invented labor saving devices and innovative techniques.

Many African Americans made contributions to the new technologies and industries developed in the nineteenth century.

After the Civil War, significant numbers of black inventors began to patent their inventions. The list of inventions patented by blacks reveals what kinds of occupations African Americans held and in which sectors of the labor force they were concentrated. Agricultural implements, devices for easing domestic chores, musical instruments, and devices related to the railroad industry were common subjects. These inventions served as a source of financial security, personal pride, achievement, and spiritual "uplift" for African Americans. Much of the struggle for black inventors of that era revolved around the battle to assert themselves upon the national consciousness. On August 10, 1894, on the floor of the House of Representatives, Representative George Washington Murray from South Carolina rose to read the names and inventions of ninety-two black inventors into the Congressional Record. Rep. Murray hoped that it would serve as a testament to the technological achievement of a people so recently emancipated.

Many African Americans made contributions to the new technologies and industries developed in the nineteenth century. Jan Matzeliger invented a shoe-lasting machine that made the skill of shoe lasting (i.e., shaping) by hand obsolete. Elijah McCoy designed hydrostatic oil lubricators that were adopted by railroad and shipping companies. His standard of quality was so rigorous that the term "the real McCoy" came to be applied to his lubricators and to stand for the highest quality product available. Garrett A. Morgan patented a safety hood (a precursor to the modern gas mask) and an automatic traffic signal. He once donned his safety hood himself to save the lives of men trapped in an underground explosion. Granville T. Woods and Lewis H. Latimer were pioneers in the newly emerging fields of electrical engineering. Woods patented many electrical and railway telegraphy systems; Latimer, with several patents to his credit, was one of the "Edison pioneers," the group of researchers who worked most closely with Thomas A. Edison.

The twentieth century brought many changes to industrial engineering and design. The rise of corporate enterprise led to more centralized research. Many of the most important inventions began to come from teams of researchers employed by large companies. As technology became more complicated, inventors in emerging fields began to have more formal education.

Today, advanced degrees in engineering and the sciences have become prerequisites for doing innovative work in some fields. Despite these changes, important inventions are still being patented by inventors who work alone—individuals who are suddenly struck by a solution to a daily encountered problem, or who laboriously work out a cheaper, quicker, or better means of producing something.

BIBLIOGRAPHY

Baker, Henry E. *The Colored Inventor: A Record of Fifty Years.* 1915. Reprint. New York, 1968.

Carter-Ives, Patricia. *Creativity and Invention: The Genius of Afro-Americans and Women in the United States and Their Patents.* Arlington, Va., 1988.

Gibbs, Carroll. *The Afro-American Inventor.* Washington, D.C., 1975.

Haber, Louis. *Black Pioneers of Science and Invention.* New York, 1970.

Hayden, Robert. *Eight Black American Inventors.* Boston, 1972.

Hermann, Janet Sharp. *Pursuit of a Dream.* New York, 1981.

James, Portia P. *The Real McCoy: African American Invention and Innovation, 1619–1930.* Washington, D.C., 1989.

Klein, Aaron. *Hidden Contributors: Black Scientists and Inventors in America.* New York, 1971.

— PORTIA P. JAMES

ISLAM

Originating as a religion in the seventh century A.D. through the revelations, visions, and messages received by the prophet Muhammad in Arabia, Islam spread rapidly throughout North Africa. Black African converts to Islam were called "Moors," and not only helped conquer southern Spain but also gained a reputation as skilled navigators and sailors. The Moors who accompanied the Spanish explorers in the fifteenth and sixteenth centuries were among the first to introduce the Islamic religion to the Americas. However, the greater impact of Islam in British North America occurred with the arrival of African Muslims (adherents of Islam) from the Islamized parts of West Africa who had been captured in warfare and sold to the European traders of the Atlantic slave trade.

The presence of Muslim slaves has been ignored by most historians, who have tended to focus on the conversion of Africans to Christianity or on the attempts to preserve aspects of traditional African religions. Yet their presence has been attested to by narrative and documentary accounts, some of which were written in Arabic. Yarrow Mamout, Job Ben Solomon, and Lamine Jay arrived in colonial Maryland in the 1730s. Abdul Rahaman, Mohammed Kaba, Bilali, Salih Bilali, and "Benjamin Cochrane" were enslaved in the late eighteenth century. Omar Ibn Said, Kebe, and Abu Bakr were brought to southern plantations in the early 1800s; two others, Mahommah Baquaqua and Mohammed Ali ben Said, came to the United States as freemen about 1850 (Austin 1984, p. 9). Abdul Rahaman, a Muslim prince of the Fula people in Timbo, Fouta Djallon, became a slave for close to twenty years in Natchez, Miss., before he was freed; he eventually returned to Africa through the aid of abolitionist groups.

Court records in South Carolina described African slaves who prayed to Allah and refused to eat pork. Missionaries in Georgia and South Carolina observed that some Muslim slaves attempted to blend Islam and Christianity by identifying God with Allah and Muhammad with Jesus. A conservative estimate is that there were close to 30,000 Muslim slaves who came from Islamic-dominated ethnic groups such as the Mandingo, Fula, Gambians, Senegambians, Senegalese, Cape Verdians, and Sierra Leoneans in West Africa (Austin 1984, p. 38). However, in spite of the much larger presence of African Muslims in North America than previously thought, the Islamic influence did not survive the impact of the slave period. Except for the documents left by the Muslims named above, only scattered traces and family memories of Islam remained among African Americans, such as Alex Haley's ancestral Muslim character, Kunta Kinte of the Senegambia, in his novel *Roots.*

By the late nineteenth century, black Christian churches had become so dominant in the religious and social life of black communities that only a few African-American leaders who had traveled to Africa knew anything about Islam. Contacts between immigrant Arab groups and African Americans were almost nonexistent at this time. After touring Liberia and South Africa, Bishop Henry McNeal Turner of the African Methodist Episcopal church recognized the "dignity, majesty, and consciousness of [the] worth of Muslims" (Austin 1984, p. 24; Hill and Kilson 1971, p. 63). But it was Edward Wilmot Blyden, the West Indian educator, Christian missionary, and minister for the government of Liberia, who became the most enthusiastic supporter of Islam for African Americans. Blyden, who began teaching Arabic in Liberia in 1867, wrote a book, *Christianity, Islam and the Negro Race* (1888), in which he concluded that Islam had a much better record of racial equality than Christianity did—a conclusion that struck him especially after he compared the racial attitudes of Christian and Muslim missionaries whom he had encountered in Africa. Islam, he felt, could also be a positive force in improving life conditions for African Americans in the United States. Though he lectured extensively, Blyden did not become a leader of a social movement that could establish Islam effectively in America. That task awaited the prophets and forceful personalities of the next century.

The massive rural-to-urban migrations by more than four million African Americans during the first decades of the twentieth century provided the conditions for the rise of a number of black militant and separatist movements, including a few that had a tangential relationship to Islam. These "proto-Islamic" movements combined the religious trappings of Islam—a few rituals, symbols, or items of dress—with a core message of black nationalism.

In 1913 Timothy Drew, a black deliveryman and street-corner preacher from North Carolina, founded the first Moorish Holy Temple of Science in Newark, N.J. Rejecting Christianity as the white man's religion, Drew took advantage of the widespread discontent among the newly arrived black migrants and rapidly established temples in Detroit, Harlem, Chicago, Pittsburgh, and cities across the South. Calling himself Prophet Noble Drew Ali, he constructed a message aimed at the confusion about names, national origins, and self-identity among black people. He declared that they were not "Negroes" but "Asiatics," or "Moors," or "Moorish Americans" whose true home was Morocco, and their true religion was Moorish Science, whose doctrines were elaborated in a sixty-page book, written by Ali, called the *Holy Koran* (which should not be confused with the Qur'an of orthodox Islam).

Prophet Ali issued "Nationality and Identification Cards" stamped with the Islamic symbol of the star and crescent. There was a belief that these identity cards would prevent harm from the white man, or European, who was in any case soon to be destroyed, with "Asiatics" then in control. As the movement spread from the East Coast to the Midwest, Ali's followers in Chicago practiced "bumping days," on which aggressive male members would accost whites on the sidewalks and surreptitiously bump them out of the way—a practice that reversed the Jim Crow custom of southern whites forcing blacks off the sidewalks. After numerous complaints to the police, Noble Drew Ali ordered a halt to the disorders and urged his followers to exercise restraint. "Stop flashing your cards before Europeans," he said, "as this only causes confusion. We did not come to cause confusion; our work is to uplift the nation"

(Lincoln 1961, p. 54). The headquarters of the movement was moved to Chicago in 1925.

The growth of the Moorish Science movement was accelerated during the post–World War I years by the recruitment of better-educated but less dedicated members who quickly assumed leadership positions. These new leaders began to grow rich by exploiting the less educated membership of the movement and selling them herbs, magical charms, potions, and literature. When Ali intervened to prevent further exploitation, he was pushed aside, and this interference eventually led to his mysterious death in 1929. Noble Drew Ali died of a beating; whether it was done by the police when he was in their custody or by dissident members of the movement is not known. After his death, the movement split into numerous smaller factions with rival leaders who claimed to be "reincarnations" of Noble Drew Ali.

The Moorish Science Temple movement has survived, with active temples in Chicago, Detroit, New York, and a few other cities. In present-day Moorish temples, membership is restricted to "Asiatics," or non-Caucasians, who have rejected their former identities as "colored" or "Negro." The term *el* or *bey* is attached to the name of each member as a sign of his or her Asiatic status and inward transformation. Friday is the Sabbath for the Moors, and they have adopted a mixture of Islamic and Christian rituals in worship. They face Mecca when they pray, three times a day, but they have also incorporated Jesus and the singing of transposed hymns into their services. The Moorish Science Temple movement was the first proto-Islamic group of African Americans, and helped to pave the way for more orthodox Islamic practices and beliefs. Many Moors were among the earliest converts to the NATION OF ISLAM, or Black Muslim movement.

While the Moors were introducing aspects of Islam to black communities, sometime around 1920 the Ahmadiyyah movement sent missionaries to the United States, who began to proselytize among African Americans. Founded in India in 1889 by Mizra Ghulam Ahmad, a self-proclaimed Madhi, or Muslim messiah, the Ahmadiyyahs were a heterodox sect of Islam that was concerned with interpretations of the Christian gospel, including the Second Coming. The Ahmadiyyahs also emphasized some of the subtle criticisms of Christianity that were found in the Qur'an such as the view that Jesus did not really die on the cross (Surah 4:157–159).

As an energetic missionary movement, the Ahmadiyyah first sent missionaries to West Africa, then later to the diaspora in the United States. Sheik Deen of the Ahmadiyyah mission was influential in converting Walter Gregg, who became one of the first African-American converts to Islam and changed his name to Wali Akram. After a period of studying the Qur'an and Arabic with the sheik, Akram founded the First Cleveland Mosque in 1933. He taught Islam to several generations of Midwesterners, including many African Americans. He also worked as a missionary in India. Although it was relatively unknown and unnoticed, the Ahmadiyyah mission movement is significant in that it provided one of the first contacts for African Americans with a worldwide sectarian Islamic group, whose traditions were more orthodox than the proto-Islamic black-nationalist movements.

About the same time that the Ahmadiyyah movement began its missionary work in the United States, another small group of orthodox Muslims, led by a West Indian named Sheik Dawud Hamed Faisal, established the Islamic Mission to America in 1923 on State Street in Brooklyn. At the State Street Mosque, Sheik Dawud taught a more authentic version of Islam than the Ahmadiyyahs because he followed the Sunna (practices) of the Prophet Muhammad; where the Ahmadiyyahs believed in the tradition of the Mahdi, or Islamic messianism, Dawud belonged to the tradition of Sunni orthodoxy. The sheik welcomed black Americans to mingle with immigrant Muslims. He taught Arabic, the Qur'an, the Sunna-Hadith tradition, and Sharia, or Islamic law, emphasizing the five "pillars" of Islam: the credo (*shahadah*) of Islam that emphasizes belief in one God and Muhammad as the messenger of Allah; prayer (*salat*) five times a day facing Mecca; charity tax (*zakat*); fasting (*saum*) during the month of Ramadan; pilgrim-

Elijah Muhammad, 1960. (Photographs and Prints Division, Schomburg Center for Research in Black Culture, The New York Public Library, Astor, Lenox and Tilden Foundations)

age to Mecca (*hajj*) if it is possible. Sheik Dawud's work was concentrated mainly in New York and New England. He became responsible for converting a number of African-American Muslims.

A smaller group and third source of African-American Sunni Muslims was the community in Buffalo, N.Y., that was taught orthodox Islam and Arabic by an immigrant Muslim, Prof. Muhammad EzalDeen, in 1933. EzalDeen formed several organizations, including a national one called Uniting Islamic Societies of America in the early 1940s.

The work of the Ahmadiyyah movement, Sheik Dawud's Islamic Mission to America and the State Street Mosque, Imam Wali Akram's First Cleveland Mosque, and Professor EzalDeen's Islamic Societies of America was important in establishing a beachhead for a more orthodox and universal Sunni Islam in African-American communities.

During the turmoil of the 1960s, young African Americans traveled abroad and made contact with international Muslim movements such as the Tablighi Jamaat. The Darul Islam movement began in 1968 among dissatisfied African-American members of Sheik Dawud's State Street Mosque in Brooklyn, and was led by a charismatic black leader, Imam Yahya Abdul Karim. Sensing the disenchantment with the lack of leadership, organization, and community programs in Sheik Dawud's movement, Imam Karim instituted the Darul Islam, the call to establish the kingdom of Allah. The movement spread to Cleveland, Baltimore, Philadelphia, and Washington, D.C. A network of over forty mosques was developed between 1968 and 1982. After a schism in 1982, the Darul Islam movement declined in influence, but it is since being revived under the charismatic leadership of Imam Jamin Al-Amin of Atlanta (the former H. Rap Brown of the STUDENT NONVIOLENT COORDINATING COMMITTEE). Other smaller Sunni organizations also came into existence during the 1960s, such as the Islamic Party and the Mosque of the Islamic Brotherhood. It is ironic, however, that the greatest impact and influence of Islam among black people were exerted by another proto-Islamic movement called the Nation of Islam.

In 1930 a mysterious peddler of sundry goods, who called himself Wali Fard Muhammad, began to spread the word of a new religion, designed for the "Asiatic black man." He soon developed a following of several hundred people and established Temple No. 1 of the Nation of Islam. Focusing on knowledge of self as the path to individual and collective salvation, Master Fard explained that black people were members of the lost-found tribe of Shabazz and owed no allegiance to a white-dominated country, which had enslaved and continuously persecuted them. When Fard mysteriously disappeared in 1934, his chief lieutenant—the former Robert Poole, now called Elijah MUHAMMAD—led a segment of followers to Chicago, where he established Muhammad's Temple No. 2 as the headquarters for the fledgling movement.

Elijah Muhammad deified Master Fard as Allah, or God incarnated in a black man, and called himself the Prophet or Apostle of Allah, frequently using the title "the Honorable" as a designation of his special status. Although the basic credo of the Nation of Islam stood in direct contradiction to the tenets of orthodox Islam, the movement's main interests were to spread the message of black nationalism and to develop a separate black nation. The Honorable Elijah Muhammad emphasized two basic principles: to know oneself, a development of true self-knowledge based on the teachings of the Nation of Islam; to do for self, an encouragement to become economically independent. He also advocated a strict ascetic lifestyle, which included one meal per day and a ban on tobacco, alcohol, drugs, and pork. From 1934 until his death in 1975, Muhammad and his followers established more than 100 temples and Clara Muhammad schools, and innumerable grocery stores, restaurants, bakeries, and other small businesses. During this period the Nation owned farms in several states, a bank, a fleet of trailer trucks for its fish and grocery businesses, and an ultramodern printing plant. Muhammad's empire was estimated to be worth more than $80 million.

Elijah Muhammad's message of a radical black nationalism, which included the belief that whites were devils, was brought to the American public by a charismatic young minister who had converted to the Nation of Islam after his incarceration in a Boston prison in 1946 for armed robbery. Upon his release from prison in 1952 and until his assassination in 1965, Minister MALCOLM X, the former Malcolm Little, had an enormous impact on the growth of the movement.

Extremely intelligent and articulate, Malcolm was an indefatigable proselytizer for the Nation, founding temples throughout the country and establishing the newspaper *Muhammad Speaks*. For his efforts, he was rewarded with the prestigious post of minister of Temple No. 7 in Harlem and appointed as the national representative by Elijah Muhammad. Malcolm led the Nation of Islam's attack on the use of the word *Negro* as depicting a slave mentality, and successfully laid the ideological basis for the emergence of the Black Consciousness and Black Power movements of the late 1960s. However, an internal dispute with Elijah Muhammad about future directions and personal moral conduct led Malcolm to leave the Nation in 1964. On his *hajj* to Mecca, Malcolm became convinced that orthodox Sunni Islam was a solution to the racism and discrimination that plagued American society. On February 21, 1965, the renamed El Hajj Malik El Shabazz was assassinated in the Audubon Ballroom in Harlem while delivering a lecture for his newly formed Organization for Afro-American Unity. Minister Louis FARRAKHAN, another charismatic speaker, replaced Malcolm as the national representative and head minister of Temple No. 7.

Islam has had a much longer history in the United States, particularly among African Americans, than is commonly known.

When Elijah Muhammad died a decade later, in February 1975, the fifth of his six sons, Wallace Deen Muhammad, was chosen as his father's successor as supreme minister of the Nation. In April 1975, Wallace shocked the movement by announcing an end to its racial doctrines and black-nationalist teachings. He disbanded the Fruit of Islam and the Muslim Girls Training, the elite internal organizations, and gradually moved his followers toward orthodox Sunni Islam. Wallace's moves led to a number of schisms, which produced several competing black-nationalist groups: Louis Farrakhan's resurrected Nation of Islam in Chicago, the largest and most well known of the groups; Silas Muhammad's Nation of Islam in Atlanta; and a Nation of Islam led by John Muhammad, brother of Elijah Muhammed, in Detroit.

In the evolution of his movement, Wallace took the Muslim title and name Imam Warith Deen Muhammad (in 1991 the spelling of his surname was changed to the British *Mohammed*). The movement's name and the name of its newspaper also changed several times: from the World Community of Al-Islam in the West (*Bilalian News*) in 1976 to the American Muslim Mission (*American Muslim Mission Journal*) in 1980; then in 1985 Warith decentralized the movement into independent masjids (*Muslim Journal*). With several hundred thousand followers—predominantly African Americans—who identify with his teachings, Mohammed has continued to deepen their knowledge of the Arabic language, the Qur'an, and the Sunna, or practices of the Prophet. Immigrant Muslims from Africa, Pakistan, and Middle Eastern countries also participate in the Friday Jumuah prayer services.

Although it adheres to the basic tenets of orthodox Sunni Islam, the movement has not yet settled on a particular school of theological thought to follow. Since every significant culture in Islamic history has produced its own school of thought, it is Mohammed's conviction that eventually an American school of Islamic thought will emerge in the United States, comprising the views of African-American and immigrant Muslims. Imam Warith Deen Mohammed has been accepted by the World Muslim Council as a representative of Muslims in the United States, and has been given the responsibility of certifying Americans who desire to make the pilgrimage to Mecca.

In its varying forms, Islam has had a much longer history in the United States, particularly among African Americans, than is commonly known. In the last decade of the twentieth century, about one million African Americans belong to proto-Islamic and orthodox Islamic groups. It has become the fourth major religious tradition in American society, alongside Protestantism, Catholicism, and Judaism. In black communities, Islam has reemerged as the dominant religious alternative to Christianity.

BIBLIOGRAPHY

Austin, Allen. *African Muslim Slaves in Ante-Bellum America.* New York, 1984.

Blyden, Edward Wilmot. *Christianity, Islam and the Negro Race.* 1888. Reprint. Edinburgh, 1967.

Essien-Udom, E. U. *Black Nationalism: A Search for Identity in America.* Chicago, 1962.

Farrakhan, Louis. *Seven Speeches.* Chicago, 1974.

Fauset, Arthur Huff. *Black Gods of the Metropolis.* 1944. Reprint. Philadelphia, 1971.

Haddad, Yvonne, ed. *The Muslims of America.* New York, 1991.

Hill, Adelaide C. and Martin Kilson. *Apropos of Africa: Afro-American Leaders and the Romance of Africa.* Garden City, N.Y., 1971.

Hill, Robert A., ed. *The Marcus Garvey and The Universal Improvement Association Papers.* 3 vols. Los Angeles, 1983–1984.

Lincoln, C. Eric. *The Black Muslims in America.* Boston, 1960.

Malcolm X and Alex Haley. *The Autobiography of Malcolm X.* New York, 1965.

Mamiya, Lawrence H. "From Black Muslim to Bilalian: The Evolution of a Movement." *Journal for the Scientific Study of Religion* 21, no. 2 (June 1982): 138–152.

Muhammad, Elijah. *Message to the Black Man in America.* Chicago, 1965.

Muhammad, Warith Deen. *As the Light Shineth from the East.* Chicago, 1980.

Perry, Bruce. *Malcolm: The Life of a Man Who Changed Black America.* Barrytown, N.Y., 1991.

Turner, Richard B. Islam in the United States in the 1920's: The Quest for a New Vision in Afro-American Religion. Ph.D. diss., Princeton University, 1986.

Waugh, Earle H., Baha Abu-Laban, and Regula B. Qureshi, eds. *The Muslim Community in North America.* Edmonton, Alberta, 1983.

– LAWRENCE H. MAMIYA

Jazz also has an inescapable political thrust. It originated during a time of enormous oppression and violence in the South against African Americans. The early African-American practitioners of jazz found racial discrimination in virtually every aspect of their lives, from segregated dance halls, cafes, and saloons to exploitative record companies. Like blackface minstrelsy, early jazz was popular with whites, in part because it reinforced "darkie" stereotypes of African Americans as happy-go-lucky and irrepressibly rhythmic. Nonetheless, many black jazz musicians used jazz as a vehicle for cultural, artistic, and economic advancement, and were able to shape their own destinies in an often hostile environment. African-American jazz was, from its earliest days, often performed for or by whites, and it was assimilated into the overall fabric of popular music, to the uneasiness of some on both sides of the racial divide. It has continued to mirror and exemplify the complexities and ironies of the changing status of African Americans within the broader culture and polity of the United States.

Played in every country of the globe, jazz is perhaps twentieth-century America's most influential cultural creation.

Early Jazz

Although its origins are obscure, early forms of jazz began to flourish around the turn of the century in cities such as New Orleans, Chicago, and Memphis. The long prehistory of jazz begins with the rhythmic music slaves brought to America in the sixteenth and seventeenth centuries and developed on southern plantations. Since the traditional drums, flutes, and horns of West Africa were largely forbidden, call-and-response singing and chanting, field hollers, foot stomping, and handclapping were common, especially in the context of fieldwork and church worship. Under those restrictions, among the earliest African-American instruments adopted were European string instruments such as the violin and guitar. The African-derived banjo was also a popular instrument. Eventually the publicly performed music that Reconstruction-era city-dwellers made an essential part of urban life demanded brass and woodwind instruments, not only for their volume, but to accompany the Spanish American War–era military marches, popular songs, and light classics that were so popular among all classes and races in the late nineteenth century.

While it is difficult to draw a precise line between jazz and its precursors, its immediate predecessors were two forms of African-American folk and popular music known as BLUES and RAGTIME. Ragtime is primarily piano music that integrates complex African-derived rhythmic practices with the harmonies of light classics, parlor music, show tunes, and popular songs. The virtuosic practice of "ragging"—altering rhythms to, in effect, "tease" variety and humor out of formal, strict patterns—was widespread by the 1880s, especially in towns along the Mississippi River like St. Louis and (eventually) New Orleans. Ragtime was also being played before the turn of the century in eastern cities such as New York and Baltimore. The greatest ragtime players, Scott JOPLIN, Eubie BLAKE, Tony Jackson, and Jelly Roll MORTON also composed, and sheet music became a central feature of home entertainments among families, black and white, who could afford pianos. Ragtime was also played by instrumental ensembles; the syncopated orchestras led in New York City by James Reese EUROPE and Will Marion Cook during the first two decades of the century owed much to the precise, contrapuntal style of piano rags. The ragtime-derived piano style proved influential on later jazz styles, especially since many of the best bandleaders of the swing era, including Duke ELLINGTON, Earl "Fatha" Hines, and Count BASIE, were heavily influenced by Harlem stride pianists such as James P. JOHNSON, Fats Waller, Willie "The Lion" Smith, and Luckey Roberts. Also deeply indebted to stride were later pianists such as Teddy Wilson, Art Tatum, and Thelonious MONK.

The blues similarly began along the Mississippi River in the 1880s and 1890s. Among the first published blues, "Memphis Blues" (1912), by W. C. HANDY, was broadly derived from black rural folk music. The sexual frankness and suggestiveness, its recognition of suffering and hardship of all kinds, and the slow, insinuating melodies soon had an impact on popular music. The 1920s saw the rise of such blues singers as Ma Rainey, Bessie SMITH, and Mamie Smith, but long before that the blues had a palpable influence on the music of early New Orleans jazz.

It was New Orleans that gave its name to the earliest and most enduring form of jazz, and bred its first masters. That Buddy Bolden, Bunk Johnson, Kid Ory, Jelly Roll Morton, King Oliver, Sidney Bechet, and Freddy Keppard all came from New Orleans attests to the extraordinary fertility of musical life in what was then the largest southern city. In New Orleans, blacks, whites, and the culturally distinct light-skinned African Americans known as creoles supported various kinds of musical ensembles by the mid-nineteenth century. Other influences included traveling cabaret and minstrel shows, funeral, carnival, and parade bands. A more or less direct African influence on New Orleans was also pervasive, no more so than in Congo Square, a onetime site of slave auctions that later became an important meeting place and open-air music hall for New Orleans blacks.

The various layers of French, Spanish, Haitian, creole, Indian, and African-American culture in New Orleans created a mixed social environment, and not only in Storyville, the legendary red-light district whose role in the birth of jazz has probably been overemphasized. Nonetheless, it was in Storyville that legalized prostitution encouraged a proliferation of brothels, gambling houses, and saloons where many of the early New Orleans jazz musicians first performed. Though many of the early New Orleans jazz bands and performers, including Sidney Bechet and Jelly Roll Morton, were creoles, very soon non-creoles such as King Oliver and Louis ARMSTRONG were integrated into creole ensembles.

By the end of the first decade of the twentieth century, these diverse musical styles had evolved into the style of music that was almost exclusively associated with New Orleans. Although there are no recordings of jazz from this period, what the music sounded like can be inferred from photographs of the period, later reminiscences, and later recordings. A typical early New Orleans jazz ensemble might include one or more cornets, trombone, clarinet, and a rhythm section of string or brass bass, piano, and guitar or banjo. The cornets, which were eventually replaced by the trumpets, took the melodic lead, while an elaborate countermelody was contributed by the clarinet, and the trombone provided a melodic bass line. The rhythm section filled in the harmonies and provided the beat. The typical repertory of these ensembles consisted largely of blues-based songs.

The two main types of improvisation in early jazz were solo and collective improvisation. Solo improvisation takes place when one musician at a time performs solo. In collective improvisation, which was the key feature of the New Orleans early jazz sound and later Chicago-related Dixieland style, more than one musician improvises simultaneously. This style can be heard in the early recordings of Kid Ory, King Oliver, and Jelly Roll Morton, as well as music made by whites such as the Original Dixieland Jazz Band, the New Orleans Rhythm Kings, the Wolverines, and Chicago's Austin High School Gang.

Jazz no doubt existed in some recognizable form from about 1905—the heyday of the legendary and never-recorded New Orleans cornetist Buddy Bolden—but the first recording by a group calling itself a "jazz" band was made in 1917, in New York, by the white, New Orleans–based ensemble the Original Dixieland Jazz Band. Though as early as 1913 James Reese Europe had recorded with his black syncopated orchestra, and by the early 1920s Johnny Dunn and Kid Ory had recorded, it was not until 1923 that the first representative and widely influential New Orleans–style jazz recordings by African Americans were made in the Midwest, by King Oliver and Jelly Roll Morton.

The movement of the best New Orleans musicians to Chicago is often linked to the closing of Storyville in 1917. Much more important was the Great Migration of southern blacks to northern cities during the World War I years. In Chicago, jazz found a receptive audience, and jazz musicians were able to develop profitable solo careers while enjoying a more hospitable racial climate than in the South.

Big Band Jazz

Jazz underwent significant changes on being transplanted to the North. By the early 1920s, when the New York–based band of Fletcher Henderson made its first recordings, jazz was being presented in a manner akin to the refined dance band orchestras of the time, with larger ensembles of ten pieces or more, working within carefully written arrangements. Whereas the early jazz repertory consisted largely of original blues, in the 1920s, jazz musicians began performing waltzes and popular songs. The style of playing changed as well. In place of the thrilling but often unwieldy polyphony of New Orleans jazz came the antiphonal big-band style, in which whole sections traded off unison or close-harmony riffs, often in a call-and-response format with a single soloist. In contrast to the instrumentation of the typical New Orleans early jazz ensemble of three horns and a rhythm section, big bands generally had a brass section consisting of three trumpets and one trombone, and three or four reeds (a variety of saxophones and clarinets). In the 1930s the size of big bands often grew to fifteen or more musicians. Providing the pulse for the swing big bands was a rhythm section, usually containing a piano, string bass and drums, and often an acoustic guitar.

If the big bands regimented and reined in the sounds of New Orleans jazz, it also permitted the emergence of the soloist, particularly on the saxophone and trumpet, probably the most important development of the era. Though featured soloists were not unknown in the New Orleans jazz style, big band jazz arrangements often used themes as mere preludes to extended solo improvisations, with both the rhythm section and the orchestra as a whole often served as accompanists to whoever was soloing. No figure exemplified this change better than Louis Armstrong. Although bred in New Orleans, his stay in Chicago taught him much about the theatrical possibilities of a well-constructed solo. During 1924 and 1925 he performed with the Henderson band in New York, where his majestic tone and unfailingly fresh phrasing almost singlehandedly turned that ensemble from a straightlaced dance band toward a New Orleans–influenced style that would eventually become known as swing. Armstrong's recordings with his own ensembles in the 1920s feature not only his brilliant trumpet, but his voice. By singing the same way that he played the trumpet, Armstrong became the model for superb jazz phrasing and popularized scat singing—using nonsense syllables instead of words. In the 1930s, his recordings of such emerging standards as "Body and Soul" and "Stardust" proved that jazz could redefine pop tunes.

In 1929 Armstrong fronted a big band in New York, a move that signaled the decline of both Chicago and Chicago-style jazz in favor of Harlem as the new capital, and swing big bands as the dominant sound. By the mid-1930s, Harlem was the undisputed center of the jazz world, and the swing era coincided with the rise of Harlem as the focal point for African-American culture. The largest black community in the world made its home along 125th Street in Manhattan, attending elegant and inexpensive dance palaces, and buying recordings also made in New York. However, it would be a mistake to focus exclusively on New York or Chicago. Many of the greatest swing big bands, known as territory bands, came from elsewhere. The Southwest, in particular Kansas City, an important railroad switching station as well as host to an extensive collection of mob-owned after-hours nightclubs, was the most important center for territory bands. In the early 1920s Bennie Moten's group had already inaugurated a Kansas City style, in its mature phase marked by looser, four-to-the-bar rhythms and freer styles of soloing. The pianist in the band, a student of Harlem stride named Count Basie, brought the core of that band to New York in 1936, and brought to prominence a whole new generation of

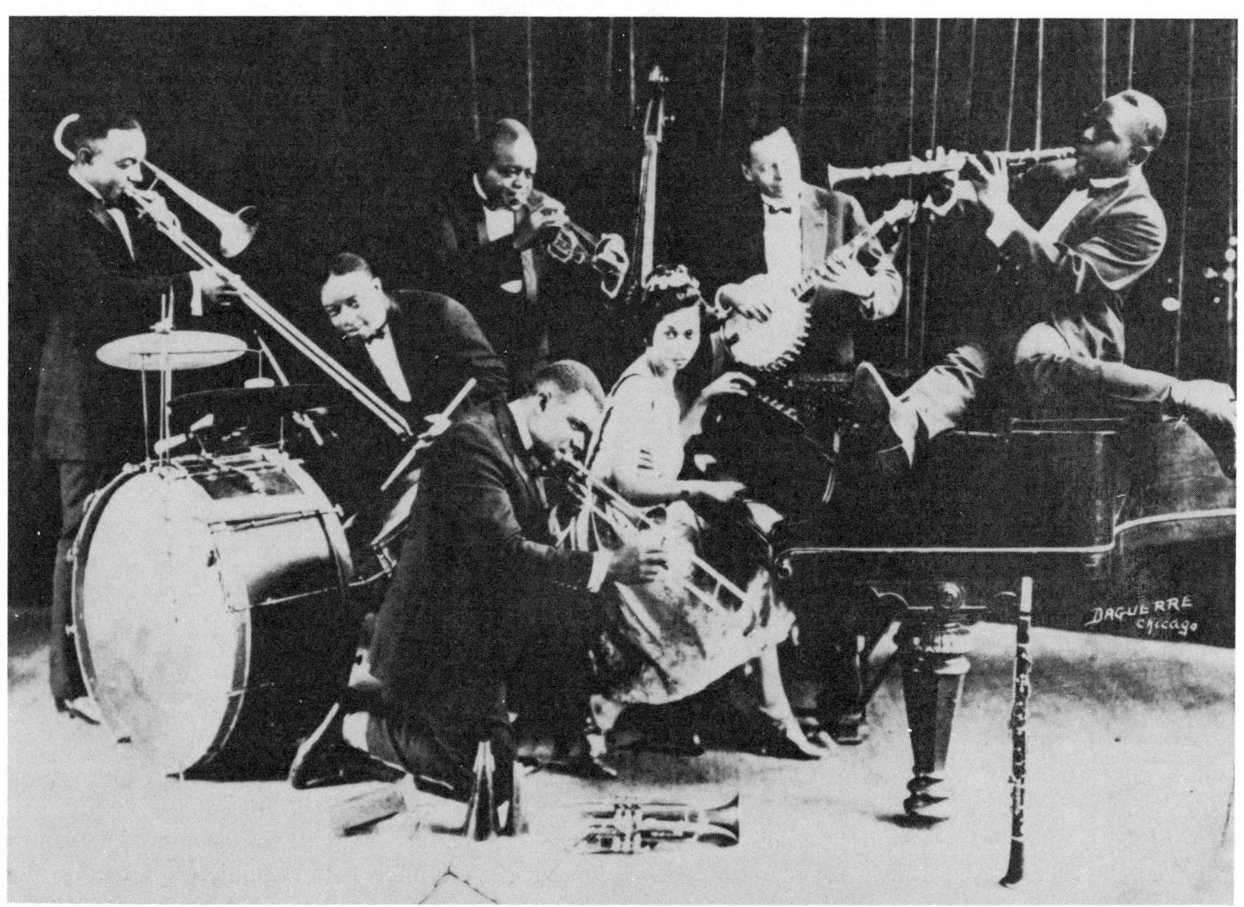

Louis Armstrong performing as a member of King Oliver's Creole Jazz Band, around 1923. (Photographs and Prints Division, Schomburg Center for Research in Black Culture, The New York Public Library, Astor, Lenox and Tilden Foundations)

hard-swinging soloists such as Lester YOUNG, Herschel Evans and Buck Clayton, as well as vocalist Jimmy Rushing.

The big band era was the only time jazz was truly America's popular music. Starting in the late 1920s, the dance bands of Ellington, Henderson, Basie, Jimmie Lunceford, Andy Kirk, Teddy Hill, Earl "Fatha" Hines, as well as those of Chick Webb, Cab CALLOWAY, and Lionel HAMPTON competed with white bands led by Benny Goodman, Paul Whiteman, Tommy Dorsey, and Artie Shaw. The prominence of the soloist during the swing era marks the emergence of celebrity jazz musicians like Louis Armstrong, who became "stars" almost on a par with the most popular white entertainers of the day, such as Bing Crosby, in both white and black communities, in Europe as well as in America. The big band era also marks the emergence of tenor saxophonist stars such as Coleman HAWKINS and Ben Webster, as well as vocalists such as Billie HOLIDAY and Ella FITZGERALD.

Jazz in the swing era gave numerous African-American performers a largely unprecedented degree of acceptance, fame, and financial success. Still, these achievements occurred within a society that was uncomfortable at best with both public and private racial interaction in any but the most controlled settings. Although some dance halls and nightclubs were integrated, many others, including the most famous ones, such as the COTTON CLUB, were not. Musicians often appeared there in less than flattering contexts, and audiences clamored for Duke Ellington's "exotic" side, known as jungle music, and for the comic, minstrel side of performers such as Louis Armstrong and Fats Waller. Through the end of the 1930s almost all jazz bands were segregated, with white bands such as those led by the Dorsey brothers, Paul Whiteman, Benny Goodman, Glenn Miller, Woody Herman, and Artie Shaw making considerably more money than their African-American counterparts.

Goodman's ensemble was the first intergrated jazz band. He hired Fletcher Henderson as an arranger and in 1936 hired Teddy Wilson as pianist and Lionel Hampton on vibes for his quartet. Goodman, the most popular bandleader of the late 1930s, played in a style quite similar to the best of the black bands, and was unfairly crowned the "King of Swing" by critics. This raised the ire of many black musicians. Although Armstrong, Ellington, Basie, and Waller became genuine celebrities, the white musicians who played in a "black" style often captured a market unavailable to blacks. This would be a persistent grievance among black jazz musicians.

Bebop

In the early 1940s, one of the last major bands from the Southwest to reach prominence in New York was led by Jay McShann, whose band contained the seeds of the next development in jazz (primarily through the innovations of its own saxophonist, Charlie PARKER). Although the emergence of the frenetic and rarified style of jazz that became known as "bebop"—so named because of the final, two-note phrase that often ended bebop solos—is frequently seen as a revolt against big band swing, all of the early bebop giants drew upon their experiences playing with swing musicians, often in big bands. Earl Hines, Billy Eckstine, Coleman Hawkins, and Cootie Williams nurtured many beboppers, and one of the first great bebop groups was a big band led by Dizzy GILLESPIE in 1945 and 1946. After Parker left Jay McShann, he worked with Gillespie in bands led by Hines and Eckstine. Thelonious Monk worked with Cootie Williams, as did Bud Powell.

The very first stirrings of bebop had come in the late 1930s, when drummer Kenny Clarke, who had worked in big bands led by Teddy Hill and Roy Eldridge, began keeping time on the high-hat cymbal, rather than on the bass drum, which was reserved for rhythmic accents, a style adopted by young drummers such as Max ROACH and Art BLAKEY. Just as timekeepers were experimenting with the rhythmical palate of the drum kit, so too were soloists extending the limits of the harmonies of standard popular songs and blues, and aspiring to a new and recondite tonal vocabulary. Inspired by the virtuosic playing and harmonic sophistication of pianist Art Tatum and tenor saxophonist Lester Young, in the early 1940s Gillespie and Parker were creating a music for musicians, noted for its complexity, with a whole new, difficult repertory. Trumpeter Fats Navarro, bassist Charles MINGUS, and pianists Thelonious Monk and Bud Powell were also prime architects of bebop, as were such white musicians as pianists Lennie Tristano and Al Haig, and alto saxophonist Lee Konitz.

Disgruntled swing musicians complained that bebop was an elitist style that robbed jazz of its place as America's popular music. Certainly, the refusal of bebop musicians to adhere to a four-to-bar bass drum rhythm meant that the music was no longer suitable for dancing. As bebop lost its function as dance music, tempos quickened even more, and solos became more rhythmically adventurous. Bebop's quirky, sophisticated compositions and fleet, witty improvisations demanded the serious and more or less undivided attention that concert music requires. Bebop came of age and reached its height of popularity not in "high-toned" Harlem dance halls, but in the nightclubs and after-hours clubs of Harlem and 52nd Street, and often the audience consisted of a small coterie of white and black jazz fans and sympathetic jazz musicians. In retrospect, however, it was not bebop that dealt the death blow to jazz as a popular music. The big bands were struggling to survive long before the bebop era began, and by the 1950s, not even Count Basie and Duke Ellington's bands could keep up with the dance rhythms of rhythm and blues and early rock and roll.

Just as New Orleans–style jazz established the basic language for what is generally considered "classic jazz," so too did the beboppers define what is still considered modern jazz. Bebop was inherently music for small ensembles, which usually included a rhythm section of piano, bass, and drums, and two or three horns, playing a new repertory of jazz standards often derived from the chord changes of Ray Noble's "Cherokee" or George Gershwin's "I Got Rhythm." In the standard bebop ensemble, after the initial statement of the theme in unison, each soloist was given several choruses to improvise on that theme. The beboppers, ever restless innovators, also experimented with Latin music, string accompaniments, and the sonorities of twentieth-century European concert music.

The latter influenced pianist John Lewis and trumpeter Miles DAVIS, bebop pioneers who forged a new style known as "cool jazz." In the late 1940s, Davis began listening to and playing with white musicians, especially arranger Gil Evans, associated with Claude Thornhill's band. Davis formed an unusual nine-piece band, including "non-jazz" instruments such as tuba and French horn for club and record sessions later known as *Cool Jazz.* The ensemble's elegant, relaxed rhythms, complex and progressive harmonies, and intimate solo styles proved enormously influential to white musicians such as Gerry Mulligan, Chet Baker, Lennie Tristano, Dave Brubeck, George Shearing, and Stan Getz, as well as to Lewis's Modern Jazz Quartet.

Davis, a prodigious creator of jazz styles, helped launch the other major trend of the 1950s, "hard bop." Inaugurated by "Walkin' " (1954), hard bop was marked by longer, more emotional solos reminiscent of 1930s cutting contests, and reaffirmation of the gospel and blues. Charles Mingus, Sonny Rollins, Clifford Brown, Horace Silver, Art Blakey, and Thelonious Monk were all major exponents of hard bop, as were Cannonball Adderley, Eric Dolphy, Mal Waldron, Jackie McLean, and Wes Montgomery later. During the late 1950s Davis led an ensemble that included some of the finest and most influential of all hard bop players, including John COLTRANE, Cannonball Adderley, and white pianist Bill Evans. Davis's landmark *Kind of Blue* (1959) introduced a popular and influential style of playing known as modal, in which modes or scales, rather than chord changes, generate improvisation. Davis also never gave up his interest in large-ensemble, arranged music, and he experimented in the late 1950s, collaborating with Gil Evans, with orchestrations derived from modern European concert music. This music, which white composer Gunther Schuller dubbed as "Third Stream," was never popular among jazz audiences, although black jazz composers such as John Lewis and George Russell embraced its concepts.

Bebop, cool jazz, hard bop, Third Stream music, and "soul" or "funk" jazz, pioneered by Horace Silver, dominated jazz in the late 1950s. However, the giants of the previous decades, playing what was to be called "mainstream" jazz, had some of their greatest popular, if not musical, successes. During that decade Louis Armstrong toured regularly in small and large ensembles, and had several enormously popular records. Basie organized a new orchestra, and also had several hit records. Ellington, who had triumphantly introduced new extended works annually in the 1940s, continued to compose for his orchestra, and also had several hits.

Avant-Garde Jazz

By the early 1960s, jazz had reached a crucial turning point. Many of the jazz masters of the swing era, such as Lester Young and Billie Holiday, were dead. Many of the most important musicians, including Charlie Parker, Bud Powell, and Clifford Brown, had died tragically young or had been devastated by heroin addiction, mental illness, or accidents. Musicians had pushed the rhythmic and harmonic conventions that had been established during the swing era to their breaking point. During the 1960s, Coltrane, Ornett COLEMAN, and Cecil Taylor led the way in beginning to abandon the swinging rhythms and melodies of traditional jazz in favor of implied tempos and harmonies, drawing on the largely unexplored reaches of their instruments, often in epic-length solos. By the mid-1960s, a whole new generation of avant-garde or free jazz musicians, including Albert Ayler, Archie Shepp, Marion Brown, Bill Dixon, Sun Ra, and Don Cherry began to abandon even the bedrock jazz convention of theme and improvisation in favor of dissonant collective improvisations related to the energetic polyphony of New Orleans–style jazz. These musicians, inspired by the civil rights movement, also began to address politics, especially race problems and black nationalism, in their music. They were often joined by musicians from the previous generation, such as Max Roach and Charles Mingus. Also in the 1960s, many jazz musicians visited Africa, and some converted to Islam, although some musicians—for example, Sadik Hakim—had converted as early as the 1940s. Many figures in the BLACK ARTS MOVEMENT, such as Amiri Baraka, hailed the extended solos of musicians such as John Coltrane as an authentic African-American art form. Ironically, at the same time, almost any connection to a large black audience in America was sundered.

The "further out" jazz became, the more harshly it was attacked by traditional musicians and listeners alike. In response, by the late 1960s many free jazz musicians were searching for ways to recapture a mass black audience. Once again, it was Miles Davis who led the way. Starting in the late 1960s, Davis began using electric instruments in his bands, and incorporating funk, rhythm and blues, and rock rhythms into his albums. Members of Davis's electric ensembles, such as Herbie Hancock, Wayne Shorter, and Chick Corea, later enjoyed tremendous popular success.

Many figures in the Black Arts Movement, such as Amiri Baraka, hailed the extended solos of musicians such as John Coltrane as an authentic African-American art form.

If the electric music Davis created, known as "fusion" or "jazz rock," inspired accusations that he was selling out, in the 1970s, the purist mantle would be carried by a group of musicians who had been playing in Chicago since the early 1960s. Striving toward the implicit racial pride and artistic and economic independence preached by Sun Ra, Mingus, and Taylor, the Association for the Advancement of Creative Musicians (AACM) was founded in 1965. The AACM, and its offshoot, the St. Louis–based Black Artists Group, have been responsible for many of the most important developments in jazz since the mid-1970s. The Art Ensemble of Chicago, pianist Muhal Richard Abrams, and saxophonist Anthony Braxton and Henry Threadgill have all been important exponents of what they term "creative music," which idiosyncratically and unpredictably draws upon everything from ragtime to free jazz.

Jazz in the 1990s

In the 1980s, the institutionalization of jazz accompanied the more general interest of universities, symphonies, and museums in many areas of African-American culture. Since the 1970s, many jazz musicians, including Mary Lou Williams, Archie Shepp, Jackie McLean, Bill Dixon, and Anthony Braxton have held university positions. Although there is a long history of formally trained jazz musicians, from Will Marion Cook to Miles Davis, a large proportion of the best young jazz musicians now come from conservatories. Such training has resulted not only in avant-gardists like Anthony Davis and David Murray, who have a healthy appreciation for the roots of jazz, but bebop-derived traditionalists like Wynton MARSALIS, who have brought mainstream jazz to the public prominence it has lacked for forty years. Further, although independent scholars compiled discographies and wrote biographies as early as the 1930s, since the 1980s there has been a burst of institutional scholarly activity, accompanied by the integration of jazz into traditional symphony repertories, as well as the creation of jazz orchestras dedicated to preserving the repertory, and developing new compositions, at the Smithsonian Institution and Lincoln Center. Jazz, as perhaps the greatest of all African-American cultural contributions, always captured the imagination of great African-American writers like Langston HUGHES and Ralph ELLISON, and it continues to suffuse the work of contemporary writers like Ishmael Reed, Toni MORRISON, Albert Murray, and Stanley Crouch.

As jazz approaches its second century, a new generation of musicians, including pianist Geri Allen and tenor saxophonist Joshua Redman, continue to improvise on the history of jazz to further address and define issues central to this particular African-American experience.

BIBLIOGRAPHY

Berendt, Joachim E. *The Jazz Book: From Ragtime to Fusion and Beyond.* Westport, Conn., 1982.

Blesh, Rudi. *Shining Trumpets: A History of Jazz.* 4th ed. London, 1958.

Charters, Samuel B., and Leonard Kunstadt. *Jazz: A History of the New York Scene.* Garden City, N.Y., 1962.

Dahl, Linda. *Stormy Weather: The Music and Lives of a Century of Jazz Women.* New York, 1984.

Driggs, Frank, and Harris Lewine. *Black Beauty, White Heat: A Pictorial History of Classic Jazz.* New York, 1982.

Feather, Leonard. *Encyclopedia of Jazz.* Revised edition. New York, 1970.

Gitler, Ira. *Jazz Masters of the Forties.* New York, 1966.

Goldberg, Joe. *Jazz Masters of the Fifties.* New York, 1966.

Hadlock, Richard. *Jazz Masters of the Twenties.* New York, 1965.

Hodeir, Andre. Translated by David Noakes. *Jazz: Its Evolution and Essence.* New York, 1956.

Jost, Ekkehard. *Free Jazz.* New York, 1981.

Leonard, Neil. *Jazz and White Americans: The Acceptance of a New Art Form.* Chicago, 1962.

Russell, Ross. *Jazz Style in Kansas City and the Southwest.* Berkeley, Calif., 1971.

Schuller, Gunther. *Early Jazz: Its Roots and Musical Development.* New York, 1968.

———. *The Swing Era: The Development of Jazz, 1930–1945.* New York, 1989.
Stearns, Marshall. *The Story of Jazz.* New York, 1970.
Stewart, Rex. *Jazz Masters of the Thirties.* New York, 1972.
Weinstein, Norman C. *A Night in Tunisia: Imaginings of Jazz in Africa.* Metuchen, N.J., 1992.
Williams, Martin. *Jazz Masters of New Orleans.* New York, 1967.
———, ed. *The Art of Jazz: Ragtime to Bebop.* New York, 1981.
———, ed. *Jazz Panorama.* New York, 1964.

– LEONARD GOINES

JEHOVAH'S WITNESSES

The New World Society of the Witnesses of Jehovah, a fundamentalist, indigenous North American religious group under the corporate behest of the Watchtower Bible and Tract Society of New York and Pennsylvania, known commonly as the Jehovah's Witnesses, has throughout much of its history consisted of some 20–30 percent African Americans. Although it has at various times and places endorsed racist and segregationist policies and practices, it has often led white society as a whole in its race-blind recruitment of members. In addition, several of the civil liberties suits argued by the Jehovah's Witnesses in the United States set important precedents for later civil rights litigation.

Founded near Pittsburgh, Pa., in 1872 by Charles Taze Russel, it relocated its headquarters to the Lighttower in Brooklyn, N.Y., in 1909. Fundamental to the Witnesses is their belief in the imminence of Har-Magedon (Armageddon)—so imminent that their second president, Judge Joseph Franklin Rutherford, declared that "many [of the Witnesses] now living will never die." For this reason, the Society requires total commitment from its members and does not permit involvement in any other organization—such as the NAACP or a political party.

The strong, supportive, and largely self-sufficient community resulting from this commitment has appealed to groups and individuals distinct or somehow excluded from dominant social groups, and to African Americans in particular. Throughout the twentieth century, the Society's aggressive recruitment activities have made Jehovah's Witnesses one of the fastest-growing religious groups in the United States, and African Americans have joined at a higher percentage rate than any other group. The Society counts some 4,289,737 members worldwide, with a year's average increase of 866,362 (peak: 904,963) in the United States.

Throughout its history, the Society has had conflicting policies towards African Americans. *The Watchtower,* one of the Society's official biweekly publications, stated in 1952 that racial divisions have no place among Witnesses. Indeed, the Witnesses have long accepted minority members more openly than most other groups. On the other hand, *Awake,* the other official biweekly publication, has counseled members against interracial marriages (April 4, 1953), and supported the policy of apartheid in South Africa (October 8, 1953). In November 1935, *The Watchtower* quoted Rutherford's decree that because blacks have less education than whites, "reading matter distributed to colored congregations would be more than half wasted. . . ." Until 1956, African Americans were not asked to attend the Jehovah's Witnesses' national conventions, though they were encouraged to conduct their own. Through the early 1960s, local assemblies, especially in the South, remained segregated.

A small group of the Church's officers and their aids appoint all supervisors, local congregational leaders, and elders. Although the Society keeps meticulous statistics, it neither responds to nor encourages inquiries about its members. Still, few African Americans have ever held important positions within the Society's hierarchy. In 1952 the NAACP's *Crisis* reported that of the 400 members on the staff of the national headquarters of the Jehovah's Witnesses, only two were African American—a mail clerk and a linotypist. In the ensuing years, more blacks worked at the Lighttower, though the upper echelons continued to exclude them.

BIBLIOGRAPHY

Cooper, Lee R. " 'Publish' or Perish: Negro Jehovah's Witness Adaptation in the Ghetto." In Irving Zaretsky, ed. *Religious Movements in Contemporary America.* Princeton, N.J., 1974.
1993 Yearbook of Jehovah's Witnesses. New York, 1993.
Stroup, Herbert Hewitt. *The Jehovah's Witnesses.* New York, 1945.
Whalen, William. *Armageddon Around the Corner: A Report on Jehovah's Witnesses.* New York, 1962.

– PETER SCHILLING

JEMISON, MAE CAROL

Mae Carol Jemison (October 17, 1956–), astronaut. Mae C. Jemison was born in Decatur, Ala., but grew up in Chicago, Ill. In 1977, she graduated from Stanford University with a B.S. in Chemical Engineering and a B.A. in African and Afro-American Studies. She received an M.D. from Cornell University Medical College in 1981. After interning at the University of Southern California Medical Center in Los Angeles, she worked in private practice until January 1983, when she joined the Peace Corps. She served in Sierra Leone and Liberia as a Peace Corps medical officer for two and a half years, returning in 1985 to Los Angeles to work as a general practitioner.

In 1987, Jemison's application to NASA's astronaut training program was accepted, and she was named the first African-American woman astronaut. After completing the one-year program, she worked as an astronaut officer representative at the Kennedy Space Center in Florida. In September 1992, Jemison became the first black woman in space when she flew as a payload specialist aboard the space shuttle *Endeavor.* During the seven-day flight, Jemison conducted experiments to determine the effects of zero gravity on humans and animals.

In September 1992, Jemison became the first black woman in space when she flew as a payload specialist aboard the space shuttle Endeavor.

In March 1993, Jemison resigned from NASA in order to form her own company, the Jemison Group, which specializes in adapting technology for use in underdeveloped nations. Her historic spaceflight brought her much adulation. In Detroit a school was named after her. And in the spring of 1993, a PBS special, *The New Explorers,* focused on her life story, while *People* named her one of the year's "50 Most Beautiful People in the World." Also in 1993, Jemison made a guest appearance as a transport operator named Lieutenant Palmer on the television series *Star Trek: The Next Generation.* This was fitting, as Jemison claimed that she was inspired to become an astronaut by the actress Nichelle Nichols, who portrayed the black Lieutenant Uhura on the original *Star Trek.*

Jemison received the CIBA Award for Student Involvement in 1979, the Essence Award in 1988, the Gamma Sigma Gamma Woman of the Year Award in 1989, and the Makeda Award for community contributions in 1993.

BIBLIOGRAPHY

"Coalition Luncheon." *Houston Chronicle,* June 30, 1993, p. 4.

Giovanni, Nikki. "Shooting for the Moon." *Essence* (April 1993): 58–60.

Hawthorne, Douglas B. *Men and Women of Space.* San Diego, Calif., 1992.

– LYDIA MCNEILL

JIM CROW

As a way of portraying African Americans, "Jim Crow" first appeared in the context of minstrelsy in the early nineteenth century. Thomas "Daddy" Rice, a white minstrel, popularized the term. Using burnt cork to blacken his face, attired in the ill-fitting, tattered garment of a beggar, and grinning broadly, Rice imitated the dancing, singing, and demeanor generally ascribed to Negro character. Calling it "Jump Jim Crow," he based the number on a routine he had seen performed in 1828 by an elderly and crippled Louisville stableman belonging to a Mr. Crow. "Weel about, and turn about / And do jis so; / Eb'ry time I weel about, / I jump Jim Crow." The public responded with enthusiasm to Rice's caricature of black life. By the 1830s, minstrelsy had become one of the most popular forms of mass entertainment, "Jim Crow" had entered the American vocabulary, and many whites, north and south, came away from minstrel shows reinforced in their distorted images of black life, character, and aspirations.

Less clear is how a dance created by a black stableman and imitated by a white man for the amusement of white audiences would become synonymous with a system designed by whites to segregate the races. The term "Jim Crow" as applied to separate accommodations for whites and blacks appears to have had its origins not in the South but in Massachusetts before the Civil War. Abolitionist newspapers employed the term in the 1840s to describe separate railroad cars for blacks and whites. Throughout the North, blacks, though legally free, found themselves largely the objects of scorn, ridicule, and discrimination. Most northern whites shared with southern whites the conviction that blacks, as an inferior race, were incapable of assimilation as equals into American society. Racial integrity demanded that blacks, regardless of class, be segregated in public transportation—that they be excluded from the regular cabins and dining rooms on steamboats, compelled to ride on the outside of stagecoaches, and forced to travel in special Jim Crow coaches on the railroads. Only in New England, prior to the Civil War, did blacks manage to integrate transportation facilities, but only after prolonged agitation, during which blacks and white abolitionists deliberately violated Jim Crow rules and often had to be dragged from the trains.

Before the Civil War, enslavement determined the status of most black men and women in the South, and there was little need for legal segregation. During RECONSTRUCTION, the Radical state governments, though several of them outlawed segregation in the new constitutions, did not try to force integration on unwilling whites. Custom, habit, and etiquette defined the social relations between the races and enforced separation. The determination of blacks to improve their position revolved largely around efforts to secure accommodations that equaled those provided the whites.

But in the 1890s, even as segregation became less rigid and pervasive in the North, the term "Jim Crow" took on additional force and meaning in the South. It

Shortly after he joined the staff of the NAACP, Johnson published his first collection of poetry, *Fifty Years and Other Poems* (1917). Like the work of Paul Laurence Dunbar, Johnson's poetry falls into two broad categories: poems in standard English and poems in a conventionalized African-American dialect. While he used dialect, he also argued that dialect verse possessed a limited range for racial expression. His poems in standard English include some of his most important early contributions to African-American letters. Poems like "Brothers" and "White Witch" are bitter protests against lynching that anticipate the poetry of Claude MCKAY in the 1920s and the fiction of Richard WRIGHT in the 1930s and 1940s.

James Weldon Johnson took an active role organizing protests against racial discrimination, including the racial violence of the "Red Summer" of 1919.

During the 1920s, Johnson's political and artistic activities came together. He was appointed secretary of the NAACP's national office in 1920. His tenure brought coherence and consistency to the day-to-day operations of the association and to his general political philosophy. He led the organization in its lobbying for the passage of the Dyer Anti-Lynching Bill and in its role in several legal cases; his report on the conditions of the American occupation of Haiti prompted a Senate investigation. Johnson's leadership helped to establish the association as a major national civil rights organization committed to accomplishing its goals through lobbying for legislation and seeking legal remedies through the courts. In 1927–1928 and again in 1929, he took a leave of absence from the NAACP. During the latter period he helped organize the consortium of Atlanta University and Spelman and Morehouse colleges.

Also in the 1920s, Johnson, with such colleagues at the NAACP as W. E. B. DU BOIS, Walter WHITE, and Jessie FAUSET, maintained that the promotion of the artistic and literary creativity of African Americans went hand in hand with political activism, that the recognition of blacks in the arts broke down racial barriers. Their advocacy of black artists in the pages of *Crisis,* and with white writers, publishers, and critics, established an audience for the flourishing of African-American literature during the HARLEM RENAISSANCE. Johnson himself published an anthology of African-American poetry, *The Book of Negro Poetry* (1922, rev. 1931), and he and his brother edited two volumes of *The Book of American Negro Spirituals* (1925 and 1926). In his introductions to these anthologies and in critical essays, he argued for a distinct African-American creative voice that was expressed by both professional artists and the anonymous composers of the spirituals. *Black Manhattan* (1930) was a pioneering "cultural history" that promoted HARLEM as the cultural capital of black America.

Johnson was not in the conventional sense either a pious or a religious man, but he consistently drew on African-American religious expressions for poetic inspiration. In early poems like "Lift Ev'ry Voice and Sing," "O Black and Unknown Bards," and "100 Years," he formulated a secular version of the vision of hope embodied in spirituals and gospel songs. His second volume of poetry, *God's Trombones* (1927), drew on the African-American vernacular sermon. Using the rhythms, syntax, and figurative language of the African-American preacher, Johnson devised a poetic expression that reproduced the richness of African-American language without succumbing to the stereotypes that limited his dialect verse.

In 1930, Johnson resigned as secretary of the NAACP to take up a teaching post at Fisk University and pursue his literary career. His autobiography, *Along This Way,* was published in 1933; his vision of racial politics, *Negro American, What Now?,* was published in 1934; and his third major collection of poetry, *St. Peter Relates an Incident,* was published in 1935. He was killed in an automobile accident on June 17, 1938.

BIBLIOGRAPHY

Fleming, Robert E., ed. *James Weldon Johnson and Arna Wendell Bontemps: A Reference Guide.* Boston, 1978.

Fleming, Robert E. *James Weldon Johnson.* Boston, 1987.

Levy, Eugene. *James Weldon Johnson: Black Leader, Black Voice.* Chicago, 1973.

— GEORGE P. CUNNINGHAM

JOHNSON, JOHN ARTHUR "JACK"

John Arthur "Jack" Johnson (March 31, 1878–June 10, 1946), boxer. The third of six surviving children, Jack Johnson was born in Galveston, Tex., to Henry Johnson, a laborer and ex-slave, and Tiny Johnson. He attended school for about five years, then worked as a stevedore, janitor, and cotton picker. He gained his initial fighting experience in battle royals, brutal competitions in which a group of African-American boys engaged in no-holds-barred brawls, with a few coins going to the last fighter standing. He turned professional in 1897. In his early years Johnson mainly fought other African-American men. His first big win was a sixth-round decision on January 17, 1902, over Frank Childs, one of the best black heavyweights of the day. The six-foot, 200-pound Johnson developed into a powerful defensive boxer who emphasized quickness, rhythm, style, and grace.

In 1903, Johnson defeated Denver Ed Martin in a twenty-round decision, thus capturing the championship of the unofficial Negro heavyweight division, which was created by West coast sportswriters to compensate for the prohibition on blacks fighting for the real crown. Johnson, who was then the de facto leading heavyweight challenger, sought a contest with champion Jim Jeffries but was rebuffed because of the color line. Racial barriers largely limited Johnson's opponents to black fighters like Joe Jeanette, whom he fought ten times. Johnson's first big fight against a white contender was in 1905, against Marvin Hart, which he lost by the referee's decision, despite having demonstrated his superior talent and ring mastery. Hart became champion three months later, knocking out Jack Root to win Jeffries's vacated title. Johnson's bid to get a title fight improved in 1906, when he hired Sam Fitzpatrick as his manager. Fitzpatrick knew the major promoters and could arrange fights that Johnson could not when he managed himself. Johnson enhanced his reputation with victories in Australia, a second-round knockout of forty-four-year-old ex-champion Bob Fitzsimmons in Philadelphia, and two wins in England.

In 1908 Canadian Tommy Burns became champion, and Johnson stalked him to Australia, looking for a title bout. Promoter Hugh McIntosh signed Burns to a match in Sydney on December 26 for a $30,000 guarantee with $5,000 for Johnson. Burns was knocked down in the first round by Johnson, who thereafter verbally and physically punished Burns until the police stopped the fight in the fourteenth round. White reaction was extremely negative, with journalists describing Johnson as a "huge primordial ape." A search began for a "white hope" who would regain the title to restore to whites their sense of superiority and to punish Johnson's arrogant public behavior. To many whites, Johnson was a "bad nigger" who refused to accept restrictions placed upon him by white society. A proud, willful man, Johnson recklessly violated the taboos against the "proper place" for blacks, most notoriously in his relationships with white women. Though much of the black middle class viewed his lifestyle with some disquiet, he became a great hero to lower-class African Americans through his flouting of conventional social standards and his seeming lack of fear of white disapproval.

Johnson defended his title five times in 1909, most memorably against middleweight champion Stanley Ketchell, a tenacious 160-pound fighter. Johnson toyed with Ketchell for several rounds, rarely attacking. Ketchell struck the champion behind the ear in the twelfth round with a roundhouse right, knocking him to the canvas. An irate Johnson arose, caught the attacking challenger with a right uppercut, and knocked him out. Johnson's only defense in 1910 was against Jim Jeffries, who was encouraged to come out of retirement by an offer of a $101,000 guarantee, split 3:1 for the winner, plus profits from film rights. When moral reformers refused to allow the match to be held in San Francisco, it was moved to Reno, Nev. The former champion, well past his prime, was overmatched. Johnson taunted and humiliated him, ending the fight with a fifteenth-round knockout. Fears that a Johnson victory would unleash racial hostilities were quickly realized as gangs of whites randomly attacked blacks in cities across the country. Some states and most cities barred the fight film for fear of further exacerbating racial tensions. Overnight the national press raised an uproar over the "viciousness" of boxing and clamored for its prohibition. Even Theodore Roosevelt, himself an avid boxer, publicly hoped "that this is the last prize-fight to take place in the United States." The reaction to Johnson's victory over a white champion proved a significant event in the history of American racism, as white fears of black male sexuality and power were manifested in a wave of repression and violence.

John Arthur "Jack" Johnson. (Prints and Photographs Division, Library of Congress)

In 1910, Johnson settled in Chicago, where he enjoyed a fast lifestyle; he toured with vaudeville shows, drove racing cars, and in 1912 opened a short-lived nightclub, the Cafe de Champion. Johnson defended his title once during the two years following the Jeffries fight, beating "Fireman" Jim Flynn in nine rounds in a filmed fight in Las Vegas, N.M. Subsequently, in response to anti-Johnson and antiboxing sentiment and concern about films showing a black man pummeling a white, the federal government banned the interstate transport of fight films.

In 1911, Johnson married white divorcee Etta Terry Duryea, but their life was turbulent and she committed suicide a year later. Johnson later married two other white women. His well-publicized love life caused much talk of expanding state antimiscegenation statutes. More important, the federal government pursued Johnson for violation of the Mann Act (1910), the so-called "white slavery act," which forbade the transportation of women across state lines for "immoral purposes." The law was seldom enforced, but the federal government chose to prosecute Johnson, even though he was not involved in procuring. Johnson was guilty only of flaunting his relationships with white women. He was convicted and sentenced to one year in the penitentiary, but fled the country to Europe through Canada. He spent several troubled years abroad, defending his title twice in Paris and once in Buenos Aires, and struggled to earn a living.

In 1915 a match was arranged with Jess Willard (6′6″ and 250 pounds) in Havana. By then Johnson was old for a boxer and had not trained adequately for the fight; he tired and was knocked out in the twenty-sixth round. The result was gleefully received in the United States, and thereafter no African American was given a chance to fight for the heavyweight title until Joe LOUIS. Johnson had hoped to make a deal with the government to reduce his penalty, and four years later claimed that he threw the fight. Most boxing experts now discount Johnson's claim and believe it was an honest fight. Johnson returned to the United States in 1920 and served a year in Leavenworth Penitentiary in Kansas. He subsequently fought a few bouts, gave exhibitions, trained and managed fighters, appeared on stage, and lectured. His autobiography, *Jack Johnson: In the Ring and Out,* appeared in 1927; a new edition was published, with additional material, in 1969. Johnson died in 1946 when he drove his car off the road in North Carolina.

Johnson's life was memorialized by Howard Sackler's play *The Great White Hope* (1969), which was made into a motion picture in 1971. Johnson finished with a record of 78 wins (including 45 by knockout), 8 defeats, 12 draws, and 14 no-decisions in 112 bouts. He was elected to the Boxing Hall of Fame in 1954. In 1987 *Ring* magazine rated him the second greatest heavyweight of all time, behind Muhammad ALI.

BIBLIOGRAPHY

Gilmore, Al-Tony. *Bad Nigger! The National Impact of Jack Johnson.* Port Washington, N.Y., 1978.

Johnson, Jack. *Jack Johnson: In the Ring and Out.* 1927. Revised. Chicago, 1969.

———. *Jack Johnson Is a Dandy: An Autobiography,* ed. Dick Schaap. New York, 1969.

Roberts, Randy. *Papa Jack: Jack Johnson and the Era of White Hopes.* New York, 1983.

Wiggins, William H. "Jack Johnson as Bad Nigger: The Folklore of His Life." *Black Scholar* 2 (January 1971): 4–19.

— STEVEN A. RIESS

JOHNSON, JOHN HAROLD

John Harold Johnson (January 19, 1918–), publisher. John H. Johnson rose from humble origins to found the country's largest African-American publishing empire and become one of the wealthiest men in the United States. Johnson was the only child of Leroy Johnson and Gertrude Jenkins Johnson and was reared in the Mississippi River town of Arkansas City. His father was killed in a sawmill accident when young Johnny (the name with which he was christened) was eight years old. The following year, 1927, his mother married James Williams, who worked as a bakery shop deliveryman.

Because the public school curriculum for blacks in Arkansas City terminated at the eighth grade and because Johnson and his mother had heard of greater opportunities in Chicago, they became part of the African-American migration to that city in 1933. Johnson enrolled in DuSable High School and proved himself an able student. Perhaps the crucial event in his life occurred when he delivered an honors convocation speech heard by Harry H. Pace, president of the Supreme Liberty Life Insurance Company.

Pace, who often helped talented black youths (among them Paul ROBESON), encouraged Johnson to attend college. Pace gave Johnson a part-time job at the insurance company that enabled his protégé to attend the University of Chicago. But Johnson's interest focused on the impressive operations of the black-owned insurance firm, and he eventually dropped his university studies, married Eunice Walker in 1941, and assumed full-time work at Supreme Liberty Life.

Among Johnson's duties at Supreme Liberty Life was to collect news and information about black Americans and prepare a weekly digest for Pace. Johnson thought that such a "Negro digest" could be marketed and sold.

In 1942 he parlayed a $500 loan using his mother's furniture as collateral to publish the first issue of *Negro Digest,* a magazine patterned after *Reader's Digest.* Although there were format similarities between the two publications, Johnson noted in his 1989 autobiography, *Succeeding Against the Odds,* that *Reader's Digest* tended to be upbeat whereas *Negro Digest* spoke to an audience that was "angry, disillusioned and disappointed" with social inequalities in the United States. Within eight months *Negro Digest* reached $50,000 a month in sales.

In 1945 Johnson launched his second publication, *Ebony,* using the format made popular by the major picture magazine *Life.* Central to his philosophy was the concept that African Americans craved a publication that would focus on black achievement and portray them in a positive manner. Six years later he created *Jet,* a pocket-sized weekly carrying news, society, entertainment, and political information pertinent to African Americans. In ensuing years Johnson added other enterprises to his lucrative empire, including new magazine ventures, book publishing, Fashion Fair cosmetics, several radio stations, and majority ownership of Supreme Liberty Life Insurance Company.

Despite the wide range and diversity of his business holdings, Johnson admitted his management style to be hands-on and direct, with every detail of operations requiring his personal approval. While tasks may be delegated, Johnson believes that his staff requires daily monitoring and oversight to ensure performance. Although he named his daughter, Linda Johnson Rice, president and chief operating officer in the late 1980s, he clearly remained in charge but asked "her opinion on decisions I plan to make."

By 1990 Johnson's personal wealth was estimated at $150 million. He has been a confidant of several U.S. presidents of both political parties and served as a goodwill ambassador to various nations throughout the world, including Eastern Europe and Africa.

BIBLIOGRAPHY

Emery, Edwin, and Michael Emery. *The Press and America.* Englewood Cliffs, N.J., 1978.

Johnson, John H. *Succeeding Against the Odds.* New York, 1989.

Wilson, Clint C. II. *Black Journalists in Paradox.* Westport, Conn., 1991.

– CLINT C. WILSON II

JOHNSON, JOSHUA

Joshua Johnson (c. 1765–c. 1830), portrait painter. Almost nothing is known about the early life of the African-American portraitist Joshua Johnson, whose name is often spelled "Johnston." Scholars have suggested that he was a Caribbean immigrant who settled in Baltimore, or that he was a freed slave, possibly once owned by the Peale family of painters. The most reliable information about Johnson's life comes from Baltimore city records, where his name first appears in the 1790s. During the late eighteenth and early nineteenth centuries, Baltimore was home to a vibrant community of free blacks and aristocratic abolitionists, a situation that surely favored Johnson's early career. Nonetheless, in a 1798 advertisement in the *Baltimore Intelligencer,* Johnson claimed that as a self-taught artist he had "experienced many insuperable obstacles in the pursuit of his studies."

Whether or not Johnson was once owned by members of the Peale family, he was stylistically allied with them throughout his career, which lasted into the 1820s, with the oil-on-canvas portrait tradition in which the Peales worked. Johnson described himself as a "limner," an early American term for a nonacademic, itinerant portrait painter in a "naive" style.

Johnson's portrait subjects included members of the working and middle classes, but he is best known for his delightful depictions of well-to-do Baltimore families and children, arranged along the length of gracefully curved and tack-studded Federal-style sofas and chairs, often complemented by domestic objects such as containers of strawberries, branches of cherries, pet dogs, red shoes, coral jewelry, and white Empire-style dresses.

Among Johnson's finest family portraits are the *Portrait of Mr. and Mrs. James McCormick and Their Children, William Lux McCormick, Sophia Pleasants McCormick, and John Pleasants McCormick* (1804–1805); *Portrait of Mrs. Thomas Everette and Her Children, Mary Augusta Everette, Rebecca Everette, John Everette, Thomas Everette, Jr., and Joseph Myring Everette* (1818); and *Mrs. Hugh McCurdy and Her Daughters Mary Jane McCurdy and Letitia Grace McCurdy* (1806–1807). Johnson's best-known portraits of children include *The Westwood Children* (1807); *Portrait of Edward Pennington Rutter and Sarah Ann Rutter* (1804); and *Charles John Stricker Wilmans* (1803–1805).

Only two Johnson paintings of African-American sitters have been identified. One of these, *Portrait of Daniel Coker* (1805–1810, in the collection of the American Museum in Bath, England), is considered Johnson's most important work, a rendering of the prominent early black Methodist and advocate of African emigration.

Johnson's painting style is characterized by a restrained palette with a silvery quality that evokes the reflected light of Baltimore's seaport. Johnson was also noted for his capturing an elegance of pose and for composition that accentuated a stiff but gentle modeling of the human form. He applied paint thinly, focusing with a fine line on details of costume, facial features, hair, and props. In his later works, Johnson was especially attentive to individual characteristics of his sitters, becoming adept at expressing their relationships through their poses and gestures. Those scholars who claim that Johnson had a West Indian or French Caribbean background—possibly coming from Saint Dominique, now known as Haiti—point to elements of French influence in those details, particularly in his representations of hair styles and costumes.

Johnson is presumed to have died sometime after 1824, since that is the last year he appears in Baltimore municipal records. No date of death or burial records have been found for Johnson, although records indicate that his second wife, Clara (or Clarissa), whom he had wed before 1803, probably survived him. Johnson's first marriage, to Sarah, sometime before 1798, resulted in two daughters, both of whom died in childhood, and two sons, who grew up in Baltimore.

Although Johnson clearly earned a living as a "limner," and even gained some local fame, his achievements came to wider public attention only during the 1940s, with the publication of a series of articles by Jacob Hall Pleasants, a genealogist and historian who had collected various accounts about the artist from the owners of a remarkable group of unsigned portraits of Baltimoreans from the late eighteenth and early nineteenth centuries. In attempting to reconcile these conflicting accounts, Pleasants drew from various Baltimore housing, tax, professional, and church directories—as well as newspaper advertisements from 1798 and 1802—to identify twenty-one portraits by Johnson.

By the 1990s, more than eighty paintings had been credited to Johnson, most of which have been acquired by major museums and private collections. Since Johnson rarely signed his paintings—his only signed work is *Portrait of Sarah Ogden Gustin* (1798–1802)—scholars and historians have continued to discover additional works. Johnson's paintings have also been featured in exhibitions at the Municipal Museum of the City of Baltimore in 1948 and at the Abby Aldrich Rockefeller Folk Art Center with the Maryland Historical Society in 1987.

BIBLIOGRAPHY

"Early Black Painter." *Colonial Homes* 8, no. 5 (September-October 1982): 124–127, 164–165.

Hartigan, Linda Roscoe. *Sharing Traditions: Five Black Artists in Nineteenth-Century America.* Washington, D.C., 1985.

Hunter, Wilbur Harvey, Jr. "Joshua Johnston: 18th Century Negro Artist." *American Collector* 17 (February 1948): 6–8.

Pleasants, J. Hall. "Joshua Johnston, the First American Negro Portrait Painter." *Maryland Historical Magazine* 37, no. 2 (June 1942): 121–149.

– LINDA CROCKER SIMMONS

JOHNSON, ROBERT LEROY

Robert Leroy Johnson (May 8, 1911?—August 16, 1938), blues guitarist and singer. The year of Robert Johnson's birth in Hazelhurst, Miss., is subject to dispute, with biographers often listing 1912 or 1914, or even 1891. Johnson grew up in the upper Mississippi Delta, mostly in Memphis, Tenn., and Robinsonville, Miss. As a child he played the Jew's harp and harmonica, and in the mid-1920s he studied guitar with Willie Brown in the Robinsonville area. He also learned about music from Charley Patton and Son House. In 1929 Johnson married Virginia Travis. She died the next year, and in 1931 Johnson married Calletta Craft.

By the early 1930s Johnson was performing professionally at parties, juke joints, and nightclubs, and occasionally on the streets of Delta towns and cities. He spent most of the rest of his life traveling, often with Johnny Shines, performing throughout the South and Midwest, and apparently visiting New York and New Jersey, and possibly Canada. During visits to Texas in 1936 and 1937 he made his only recordings—twenty-nine songs in all—only one of which, "Terraplane Blues," had any success. During his lifetime, Johnson's career was surrounded by a mystique of danger and hedonism. His virtuosity as a singer and guitarist, combined with powerful appetites for alcohol, sex, and fighting, caused a story to circulate that one night at a lonely Delta crossroads he had sold his soul to the devil. That myth was fueled by the mysterious circumstances surrounding his demise. It is not certain how Johnson died, but his biographers have generally confirmed the account that he was poisoned by the jealous husband of a woman he had met at a party near Greenwood, Miss.

After his death Johnson came to be called "King of the Delta Blues." Although the title may be somewhat misleading, Johnson's impact in the years before World War II was enormous. In his own lifetime, Johnson's influence came about largely through his encounters with the musicians who heard him during his travels. These musicians adopted Johnson's dominant seventh "turnaround" chord and his boogie woogie–style "walking" bass lines, both of which became standard aspects of every blues guitarist's style. After his death, Johnson's reputation came to rest as much on his recordings as on his myth. His piercing, high-pitched voice often came close to a moaning whine, while his songwriting encompassed simple but detailed and dramatic observations about life and travel in the Mississippi Delta ("Ramblin' on My Mind," "Love in Vain," "Terraplane Blues") and haunting visions of loneliness and almost supernatural psychological torment ("Hell Hound on My Trail," "Crossroads Blues," "Stones in My Passway"). As a guitarist, Johnson coupled a powerful rhythmic drive with stinging slide guitar solos.

Johnson was "rediscovered" in the 1960s, when folk and BLUES music became popular among white audiences, and his songs became staples of 1960s rock and roll. In the 1980s and '90s scholars uncovered many details of Johnson's life, including the only two existing photographs of him. A 1990 release of all of his recordings, *Robert Johnson: The Complete Recordings,* including forty-one sides, many never before commercially released, was a huge success. In addition, he inspired Alan Greenberg's screenplay *Love in Vain* (1983), the documentary *The Search for Robert Johnson* (1992), and Bill Harris's play *Robert Johnson: Trick the Devil* (1993).

After his death Robert Leroy Johnson came to be called "King of the Delta Blues."

BIBLIOGRAPHY

Guralnick, Peter. "Searching For Robert Johnson." *Living Blues* 53 (1982): 27–41.

Palmer, Robert. *Deep Blues.* New York, 1981.

– JONATHAN GILL

JOHNSON, WILLIAM HENRY

William Henry Johnson (March 18, 1901–April 13, 1970), painter. For most African Americans, life in a small southern town after Reconstruction hardly promised more than a succession of menial jobs, a world of hard labor, and an insular, often fearful existence. As an artistically inclined but poverty-stricken black youth growing up in Florence, S.C., during the first two decades of the twentieth century, William H. Johnson followed this all-too-familiar pattern. There were very few options in his life other than running errands for his parents at the local YMCA and train depot, or working at the local steam laundry.

With the encouragement of a few teachers and his Pullman porter uncle, however, Johnson left South Carolina around 1918 in search of a better life and migrated to New York City. From 1921 until 1926, Johnson attended the School of the National Academy of Design, where he quickly became one of the school's most outstanding students. Johnson also worked for three summers (1924–1926) with artist and teacher Charles Webster Hawthorne at his Cape Cod School of Art in Provincetown, Mass.

After failing to win the Pulitzer Traveling Scholarship in his final year at the School of the National Academy of Design, Johnson (with the financial backing of Charles Webster Hawthorne and painter George B. Luks) traveled to Paris, where he continued his art studies and experienced a sense of personal freedom for the first time. After about a year in Paris, Johnson moved to Cagnes-sur-Mer on the French Riviera, where he inaugurated an expressive and rhythmic painting style, best seen in works like *Village Houses* or *Cagnes-sur-Mer* (c. 1928–1929), *Young Pastry Cook* (c. 1928–1930), and *Jacobia Hotel* (1930).

These French-inspired paintings earned Johnson the William E. Harmon gold medal for distinguished achievements in the field of Fine Arts (1929–1930). Although his European sojourn was interrupted by a brief (and, as a result of the Harmon gold medal, widely celebrated) return to the United States in 1929, Johnson again returned to Europe—specifically, Denmark—in 1930, and maintained this Scandinavian base until 1938. During this time, Johnson married a Danish textile artist, Holcha Krake, traveled throughout Europe and North Africa, and exhibited his bold, expressionistic paintings (e.g., *Old Salt, Denmark,* c. 1931–1932; *Bazaars Behind Church, Oslo,* c. 1935; and *Midnight Sun, Lofoten,* 1937) in galleries in Denmark, Norway, and Sweden.

With the rise of the National Socialist Party in Germany and the expansion of Adolf Hitler's political dominion throughout Europe, Johnson and his wife fled Denmark in 1938 and settled in New York City. Johnson embarked on a new career in New York, based not on his European-inspired portraits and landscapes, but rather on African-American subjects and themes, all painted in a highly chromatic two-dimensional patchwork quilt-like technique.

Although he lived for much of this time (c. 1938–1946) in a humble manner (in poorly heated lofts in Greenwich Village), Johnson exhibited regularly in New York galleries as well as in all of the major "all-Negro" exhibitions that were organized around the country during this time. Johnson's paintings of rural life in the South (*Going to Church,* c. 1940–1941), Harlem's fashionable nightclubs and urban lifestyles (*Cafe,* c. 1939–1940), the black soldier during World War II (*K.P.,* c. 1942), and religious themes based on Negro spirituals (*Swing Low Sweet Chariot,* c. 1944) all reaped positive but limited critical notice in their day, and remain classic examples of an authentic African-American painting tradition during the war years.

In spite of Johnson's critical successes and personal satisfaction with his work, he sold very little during his lifetime and experienced numerous personal tragedies. In 1942, a fire broke out in his studio/loft, destroying many of his paintings and personal belongings, and forcing him and his wife to seek temporary housing in the middle of winter. In 1943, his wife was diagnosed as suffering from breast cancer, from which she died shortly thereafter, leaving Johnson profoundly bereft.

Works produced by Johnson from 1944 onward exhibit a strange, almost untutored look, stemming no doubt from these trials in his personal life and, moreover, from an encroaching paresis, brought on by a then undiagnosed case of advanced syphilis. Still, these late paintings, which examined black history (*Nat Turner,* c. 1945), the breaking down of colonial rule in the world (*Nehru and Gandhi,* c. 1945), and the major political conferences which led to the conclusion of World War II (*Three Allies in Cairo,* c. 1945), demonstrate a heightened political consciousness on Johnson's part, as well as his desire to connect the world's mid-century quest for political and economic independence with the African American's ongoing struggle for freedom.

Johnson's art career halted in 1947, when he suffered a mental breakdown and was committed to a New York State mental hospital in Central Islip, Long Island. While Johnson languished in the hospital, never to paint or lead a normal life again, his personal estate of more than a thousand paintings, drawings, and prints lay in a wooden storage bin in lower Manhattan, neglected and essentially forgotten for almost a decade. In 1956, the Harmon Foundation, a philanthropic organization that had supported Johnson earlier in his career, agreed to take possession of Johnson's estate just as it was about to be disposed of by Johnson's court-appointed lawyers.

After several years of organizing, conserving, and exhibiting Johnson's art, the Harmon Foundation ceased operation in 1966, and soon thereafter turned over the entire collection (still in need of further research and conservation) to the Smithsonian Institution's National Museum of American Art (then known as the National Collection of Fine Arts). On the eve of the opening of Johnson's first major retrospective at the Smithsonian Institution in November 1971, the exhibition organizers learned that Johnson had died at Central Islip Psychiatric Center in 1970, totally unaware that his work and extraordinary career were finally receiving the recognition and acclaim that he had sought so fervently during his active years.

The art and life of William H. Johnson, the subject of several retrospective exhibitions, numerous publications, and a film documentary, intrigue audiences who have an interest in American art produced between the Great Depression and the end of World War II, the issue of primitivism in modern art and intellectual thought, and the various modes and methods of representing African-American culture during the twentieth century.

BIBLIOGRAPHY

Powell, Richard J. *Homecoming: The Art and Life of William H. Johnson.* New York, 1991.

– RICHARD J. POWELL

JOHNSON PUBLISHING COMPANY

One of the largest black-owned businesses in the United States in the 1990s, the Johnson Publishing Company is a family-owned conglomerate of media and beauty companies based in Chicago and founded by John H. JOHNSON in 1945. In 1942, Johnson saw the possibilities for a monthly review of articles about blacks, whom the white media largely ignored. Borrowing $500 with his mother's furniture as security, he started *Negro Digest.* The success of the periodical led him to create *Ebony.* As *Negro Digest* used the format of *Reader's Digest, Ebony*'s glossy picture layout was based on that of *Life. Ebony* was an immediate success and its popularity and circulation grew steadily, making the magazine the keystone of the Johnson publishing empire and a staple in black homes. Despite its large circulation, *Ebony*'s production costs in its first years almost bankrupted the company until Johnson was able to secure advertising contracts from white-controlled corporations. *Negro Digest* remained small, with a circulation of about 60,000. In 1951, Johnson discontinued it and started the vastly successful pocket-sized news magazine, *Jet.* (*Negro Digest* was revived in 1965 and renamed *Black World* in 1970. It folded not long thereafter.)

Over the decades, Johnson has launched or acquired many enterprises, including *Copper Romance* and *Hue,* short-lived publications of the mid-1950s; *Tan Confessions,* which became the fan magazine *Black Stars; Ebony Africa* (1965), a brief attempt at developing an Africa-centered magazine, and such businesses as the Supreme Life Insurance Company. He has thus augmented the scope of his company. In the early 1990s, his holdings included *Ebony, Jet, Ebony, Jr.* (1973–), and *EM: Ebony Man* (1985–) magazines; Fashion Fair Cosmetics; Supreme Beauty Products; the syndicated television program *Ebony/Jet Showcase;* three radio stations, and the annual Ebony Fashion Fair traveling fashion show.

The Johnson Publishing Company remains entirely family owned and operated. In the early 1990s, it employed more than 2,300 people worldwide, had a total magazine circulation of more than three million, and had increased its sales from $72 million in 1980 to $274.2 million in 1992. Some black journalists and readers are critical of Johnson's refusal to print negative or analytical pieces about African-American life in his magazines, and blacks have questioned his contention that black entrepreneurs can start businesses without bank loans and credit. Still, Johnson is one of a handful of African Americans featured on *Forbes* magazine's list of 400 wealthiest Americans, and he is a man whose rise from poverty has interwoven itself into the company's mystique.

BIBLIOGRAPHY

Cohen, Roger. "Black Media Giant's Fire Still Burns." *New York Times,* November 19, 1990.

Johnson, John H., and Lerone Bennett, Jr. *Succeeding Against the Odds.* New York, 1989.

– PETRA E. LEWIS

JONES, ABSALOM

Absalom Jones (1746–1818), minister and community leader. Among the enslaved African Americans who gained their freedom in the era of the American Revolution, Absalom Jones made some of the most important contributions to black community building at a time when the first urban free black communities of the United States were taking form. Enslaved from his birth in Sussex County, Del., Jones served on the estate of the merchant-planter Benjamin Wynkoop. Taken from the fields into his master's house as a young boy, he gained an opportunity for learning. When his master moved to Philadelphia in 1762, Jones, at age sixteen, worked in his master's store but continued his education in a night school for blacks. In 1770 he married, and through unstinting labor he was able to buy his wife's freedom in about 1778 and his own in 1784.

After gaining his freedom, Jones rapidly became one of the main leaders of the growing free black community in Philadelphia—the largest urban gathering of emancipated slaves in the post-Revolutionary period. Worshiping at Saint George's Methodist Episcopal Church, Jones soon began to discuss a separate black religious society with other black Methodists such as Richard ALLEN and William White. From these tentative steps toward community-based institutions came the Free African Society of Philadelphia, probably the first independent black organization in the United States. Although mutual aid was its purported goal, the Free African Society was quasi-religious in character; beyond that, it was an organization where people emerging from the house of bondage could gather strength, develop their own leaders, and explore independent strategies for hammering out a postslavery existence that went beyond formal legal release from thralldom.

Absalom Jones made some of the most important contributions to black community building at a time when the first urban free black communities of the United States were taking form.

Once established, the Free African Society became a vehicle for Jones to establish the African Church of Philadelphia, the first independent black church in North America. Planned in conjunction with Richard Allen and launched with the assistance of Benjamin Rush and several Philadelphia Quakers, the African Church of Philadelphia was designed as a racially separate, nondenominational, and socially oriented church. But in order to gain state recognition of its corporate status, it affiliated with the Protestant Episcopal Church of North America and later took the name Saint Thomas's African Episcopal Church. Jones became its minister when it opened in 1794, and served in that capacity until his death in 1818. For decades, Saint Thomas's was emblematic of the striving for dignity, self-improvement, and autonomy of a generation of African Americans released or self-released from bondage, mostly in the North. In his first sermon at the African Church of Philadelphia, Jones put out the call to his fellow African Americans to "arise out of the dust and shake ourselves, and throw off that servile fear, that the habit of oppression and bondage trained us up in." Jones's church, like many others that emerged in the early nineteenth century, became a center of social and political as well as religious activities, and a fortress from which to struggle against white racial hostility.

From his position as the spiritual leader at Saint Thomas's, Jones became a leading educator and reformer in the black community. Although even-tempered and known for his ability to quiet controversy and reconcile differences, he did not shrink from the work of promoting the rights of African Americans. He coauthored, with Richard Allen, *A Narrative of the Proceedings of the Black People, During the Late Awful Calamity in Philadelphia, in the year 1793,* a resounding defense of black contributions in the yellow fever epidemic of 1793—Jones himself assisted Benjamin Rush in ministering to the sick and dying in the ghastly three-month epidemic—and a powerful attack on slavery and white racial hostility. In 1797, he helped organize the first petition of African Americans against slavery, the slave trade, and the federal Fugitive Slave Law of 1793. Three years later, he organized another petition to President Jefferson and the Congress deploring slavery and the slave trade. From his pulpit he orated against slavery, and he was responsible in 1808 for informally establishing January 1 (the date on which the slave trade ended) as a day of thanksgiving and celebration, in effect an alternative holiday to the Fourth of July for black Americans.

Typical of black clergymen of the nineteenth century, Jones functioned far beyond his pulpit. Teaching in schools established by the Pennsylvania Abolition Society and by his church, he helped train a generation of black youth in Philadelphia. As Grand Master of Philadelphia's Black Masons, one of the founders of the Society for the Suppression of Vice and Immorality (1809), and a founder of the literary Augustine Society (1817), he struggled to advance the self-respect and enhance the skills of the North's largest free African-American community. By the end of Jones's career, Saint Thomas's was beginning to acquire a reputation as the church of the emerging black middle class in Philadelphia. But he would long be remembered for his ministry among the generation emerging from slavery.

BIBLIOGRAPHY

Nash, Gary B. " 'To Arise Out of the Dust': Absalom Jones and the African Church of Philadelphia, 1785–95." In Nash, ed. *Race, Class, and Politics: Essays on American Colonial and Revolutionary Society.* Urbana and Chicago, 1986, pp. 323–355.

— GARY B. NASH

JONES, QUINCY DELIGHT, JR.

Quincy Delight Jones, Jr. (March 14, 1933–), music producer and composer. Born in Chicago, Quincy Jones learned to play trumpet in the public schools in the Seattle, Wash., area, where his family moved in 1945. Jones sang in church groups from an early age, and wrote his first composition at the age of sixteen. While in high school he played trumpet in RHYTHM AND BLUES groups with his friend Ray CHARLES. After graduating from high school, Jones attended Seattle University, and then Berklee School of Music in Boston. He traveled with Jay McShann's band before being hired by Lionel HAMPTON in 1951. Jones toured Europe with Hampton, and soloed on the band's recording of his own composition, "Kingfish" (1951).

After leaving Hampton in 1953, Jones, who had an undistinguished solo style on trumpet, turned to studio composing and arranging, working with Ray Anthony, Tommy DORSEY, and Hampton. During the 1950s Jones also led his own big bands on albums such as *This Is How I Feel About Jazz* (1956). In 1956 Jones helped Dizzy GILLESPIE organize his first state department big band. From 1956 to 1960 he worked as the music director for Barclay Records in Paris, and while there he studied arranging with Nadia Boulanger. He also worked with Count BASIE, Charles Aznavour, Billy Eckstine, Sarah VAUGHAN, Dinah Washington, and Horace Silver, and led a big band for recording sessions such as *The Birth of a Band* (1959). Jones served as music director for Harold Arlen's blues opera *Free and Easy* on its European tour. Back in the U.S. in the early 1960s, Jones devoted his time to studio work, attaining an almost ubiquitous presence in the Los Angeles and New York music scenes.

Jones began working as a producer at Mercury Records in 1961. After producing Leslie Gore's hit record "It's My Party" (1963), he became Mercury's first African-American vice president in 1964. He increasingly made use of popular dance rhythms and electric instruments. In 1964 he also scored and conducted an album for Frank Sinatra and Count Basie, *It Might As Well Be Swing.* He recorded with his own ensembles, often in a rhythm and blues or pop jazz idiom, on albums such as *The Quintessence* (1961), *Golden Boy* (1964), *Walking in Space* (1969), and *Smackwater Jack* (1971). Jones also branched into concert music with his *Black Requiem,* a work for orchestra (1971). Jones was the first African-American film composer to be widely accepted in Hollywood, and he scored dozens of films, including *The Pawnbroker* (1963), *Walk, Don't Run* (1966), and *In Cold Blood* (1967).

By 1994, with twenty-two Grammy awards to his credit, Quincy Jones was the most honored popular musician.

In 1974, shortly after recording *Body Heat,* Jones suffered a cerebral stroke. He underwent brain surgery, and after recovering he formed his own record company, Qwest Productions. Throughout the 1970s Jones remained in demand as an arranger and composer. He also wrote or arranged music for television shows (*Iron-*

side, The Bill Cosby Show, the miniseries *Roots,* and *Sanford and Son*), and for films (*The Wiz,* 1978). During the 1980s Jones expanded his role in the film business. In 1985 he coproduced and wrote the music for the film *The Color Purple,* and served as executive music producer for Sidney Poitier's film *Fast Forward* (1985).

Jones's eclectic approach to music, and his ability to combine gritty rhythms with elegant urban textures is perhaps best exemplified by his long association with Michael JACKSON. Their collaborations on *Off The Wall* (1979) and *Thriller* (1984) resulted in two of the most popular recordings of all time. Jones also produced Jackson's 1987 *Bad.* During this time, Jones epitomized the crossover phenomenon by maintaining connections with many types of music. His eclectic 1982 album *The Dude* won a Grammy award, and in 1983 he conducted a big band as part of a tribute to Miles DAVIS at Radio City Music Hall. The next year he produced and conducted on Frank Sinatra's *L.A. Is My Lady.* He conceived of USA for Africa, a famine relief organization that produced the album and video *We Are The World* (1985). In 1991 Jones appeared with Davis at one of the trumpeter's last major concerts, in Montreux, Switzerland, a performance that was released on album and video in 1993 as *Miles and Quincy Live at Montreux.* During this time Jones also continued to work with classical music, and in 1992 he released *Handel's Messiah: A Soulful Celebration.*

By 1994, with twenty-two Grammy awards to his credit, Jones was the most honored popular musician in the history of the awards. He also wielded enormous artistic and financial power and influence in the entertainment industry, and was a masterful discoverer of new talent. In 1990 his album *Back on the Block,* which included Miles Davis and Ella FITZGERALD in addition to younger African-American musicians such as Ice-T and Kool Moe Dee, won six Grammy awards. He continued to expand his activities into the print media, including the magazine *Vibe,* aimed primarily at a youthful African-American readership. He also produced the hit television series "Fresh Prince of Bel Air," which began in 1990. That same year Jones was the subject of a video biography, *Listen Up: The Lives of Quincy Jones* (1990).

BIBLIOGRAPHY

Horricks, Raymond. *Quincy Jones.* Tunbridge Wells, U.K., 1985.

Sanders, Charles Leonard. "Interview with Quincy Jones." *Ebony* (October 1985): 33–36.

Shah, Diane K. "On Q." *New York Times Magazine,* November 18, 1990, p. 6.

– JONATHAN GILL

JOPLIN, SCOTT

Scott Joplin (c. 1867/68–April 1, 1917), RAGTIME composer. Born in eastern Texas, some 35 miles south of present-day Texarkana, to an ex-slave father and a free-born mother, Joplin rose from humble circumstances to be widely regarded as the "King of Ragtime Composers." (Formerly thought to have been born on November 24, 1868, he is now known to have been born in late 1867 or early 1868.) In the early years of his career he worked with minstrel companies and vocal quartets, in bands as a cornetist, and as a pianist. His earliest published compositions (1895–1896) were conventional songs and marches. In 1894 he settled in Sedalia, Mo., where he attended the George R. Smith College. His "Maple Leaf Rag" (1899), which memorializes a black social club in Sedalia, became the most popular piano rag of the era. By 1901 he was famous and moved to St. Louis, where he worked primarily as a composer. Despite his success in ragtime, he wanted to compose for the theater. In 1903 he formed a company to stage his first opera, *A Guest of Honor* (now lost). He spent all his money on the unsuccessful opera tour and then returned to composing piano rags. In 1907 he moved to New York, where major music publishers were eager to issue his rags, but he still aspired to be a "serious" composer. In 1911 he completed and self-published his second opera, *Treemonisha,* in which he expressed the view that his race's problems were exacerbated by ignorance and superstition and could be overcome by education. He never succeeded in mounting a full production of this work.

Despite his efforts with larger musical forms, Scott Joplin is today revered for his piano rags, these being the most sophisticated examples of the genre. His published output includes fifty-two piano pieces, of which forty-two are rags (including seven collaborations with younger colleagues); twelve songs; one instructional piece; and one opera. Several songs, rags, a symphony, and several stage works—his first opera, a musical, and a vaudeville—were never published and are lost.

A Scott Joplin revival began in late 1970 when Nonesuch Records, a classical music label, issued a recording of Joplin rags played by Joshua Rifkin. For the record industry, this recording gave Joplin the status of a classical composer. This status was enhanced a year later when the New York Public Library issued the two-volume *Collected Works of Scott Joplin.* Thereafter, classical concert artists began including Joplin's music in their recitals. In 1972, his opera *Treemonisha* received its first full performance, staged in Atlanta in conjunction with an Afro-American Music Workshop at Morehouse College, and in 1975 the opera reached Broadway. (There have been three orchestrations of the work—by T. J. Anderson, William Bolcom, and Gunther Schuller.) In 1974, the award-winning movie *The Sting* used several Joplin rags in its musical score, bringing Joplin to the attention of an even wider public. "The Entertainer" (1902), the film's main theme, became one of the most popular pieces of the mid-1970s. Further recognition of Joplin as an artist came in 1976 with a special Pulitzer Prize, and in 1983 with a U.S. postage stamp bearing his image.

BIBLIOGRAPHY

Berlin, Edward A., *King of Ragtime: Scott Joplin and His Era*. New York, 1994.

Haskins, James, and Kathleen Benson. *Scott Joplin*. Garden City, N.Y., 1978.

— EDWARD A. BERLIN

JORDAN, BARBARA CHARLINE

Barbara Charline Jordan (February 21, 1936–January 17, 1996), congresswoman and professor. Barbara Jordan was born in Houston, Tex., the daughter of Arlyne Jordan and Benjamin M. Jordan, a Baptist minister. She spent her childhood in Houston, and graduated from Texas Southern University in Houston in 1956. Jordan received a law degree from Boston University in 1959. She was engaged briefly in private practice in Houston before becoming the administrative assistant for the county judge of Harris County, Tex., a post she held until 1966.

In 1962, and again in 1964, Jordan ran unsuccessfully for the Texas State Senate. In 1966, helped by the marked increase in African-American registered voters, she became the first black since 1883 elected to the Texas State Senate. The following year she became the first woman president of the Texas Senate. That year, redistricting opened a new district in Houston with a black majority. Jordan ran a strong campaign, and in 1972 she was elected to the House of Representatives from the district, becoming the first African-American woman elected to Congress from the South.

Jordan's short career as a high-profile congresswoman took her to a leadership role on the national level. In her first term, she received an appointment to the House Judiciary Committee, where she achieved national recognition during the Watergate scandal, when in 1974 she voted for articles of impeachment against President Richard M. Nixon. A powerful public speaker, Jordan eloquently conveyed to the country the serious constitutional nature of the charges and the gravity with which the Judiciary Committee was duty-bound to address the issues. "My faith in the Constitution is whole, it is complete, it is total," she declared. "I am not going to sit here and be an idle spectator to the diminution, the subversion, the destruction of the Constitution."

Jordan spent six years in Congress, where she spoke out against the Vietnam War and high military expenditures, particularly those earmarked for support of the war. She supported environmental reform as well as measures to aid blacks, the poor, the elderly, and other groups on the margins of society. Jordan was a passionate campaigner for the Equal Rights Amendment, and for grassroots citizen political action. Central to all of her concerns was a commitment to realizing the ideals of the Constitution.

Public recognition of her integrity, her legislative ability, and her oratorical excellence came from several quarters. Beginning in 1974, and for ten consecutive years, the *World Almanac* named her one of the twenty-five most influential women in America. *Time* magazine named Jordan one of the Women of the Year in 1976. Her electrifying keynote address at the Democratic National Convention that year helped to solidify her stature as a national figure.

In 1978, feeling she needed a wider forum for her views than her congressional district, Jordan chose not to seek reelection. Returning to her native Texas, Jordan accepted a professorship in the School of Public Affairs at the University of Texas at Austin in 1979, and since 1982 she has held the Lyndon B. Johnson Centennial Chair in Public Policy. Reflecting her interest in minority rights, in 1985 Jordan was appointed by the secretary-general of the United Nations to serve on an eleven-member commission charged with investigating the role of transnational corporations in South Africa and Namibia. In 1991, Texas Gov. Ann Richards appointed her "ethics guru," charged with monitoring ethics in the state's government. In 1992, although confined to a wheelchair by a degenerative disease, Jordan gave a keynote speech at the Democratic National Convention, again displaying the passion, eloquence, and integrity that had first brought her to public attention nearly two decades earlier.

BIBLIOGRAPHY

Haskins, James. *Barbara Jordan*. New York, 1977.

— CHRISTINE A. LUNARDINI

JORDAN, MICHAEL JEFFREY

Michael Jeffrey Jordan (February 17, 1963–), basketball player. Widely acknowledged as the most exciting player ever to pick up a basketball, Michael Jordan was born in Brooklyn, N.Y., the fourth of James and Deloris

Jordan's five children and the last of their three boys. He grew up in North Carolina, first in rural Wallace and later in Wilmington.

A late bloomer in athletic terms, Jordan was released from the Laney High School varsity basketball team in his sophomore year. Even after an impressive junior season, he received only modest attention from major college basketball programs and chose to attend the University of North Carolina.

On March 29, 1982, the nineteen-year-old freshman sank the shot that gave his school a 63–62 victory over Georgetown and its first NCAA men's basketball championship in twenty-five years. Jordan followed that by winning the college Player of the Year award from the *Sporting News* in each of the next two seasons. After announcing that he would enter the NBA draft after his junior season, he capped his amateur career by captaining the U.S. men's basketball team to a gold medal at the 1984 Olympic Games in Los Angeles.

Jordan was the third pick in the 1984 NBA draft, chosen by the woeful Chicago Bulls. The six-foot-six-inch guard immediately set about reversing their fortunes and was named the NBA Rookie of the Year after leading the team in scoring, rebounding, and assists.

After sitting out most of his second season with a broken foot, Jordan put on one of the greatest individual performances in postseason history, scoring 63 points in a playoff loss to the Boston Celtics in 1986. The following season he scored 3,041 points—the most ever by a guard—and won the first of his six successive scoring titles with a 37.1 average. In 1987–1988 he became the first player ever to win the Most Valuable Player and Defensive Player of the Year awards in the same season.

Jordan's brilliance on the basketball court, however, was almost eclipsed by his success as a commercial spokesperson. Before his rookie season he signed with the Nike sneaker company to promote a signature shoe—the Air Jordan. The shoe was an instant smash, establishing Jordan as a viable spokesperson. The commercials in which he starred with filmmaker Spike LEE helped make him a pop icon as well.

Basketball purists have criticized Jordan for indulging his individual brilliance at the expense of his teammates. But he and the Bulls shook the one-man-team tag in 1990–1991 by defeating Earvin "Magic" Johnson and the Los Angeles Lakers in five games to win the franchise's first NBA championship. The following season, they defeated the Portland Trailblazers in six games to clinch another title, and in 1993 they again won the championship when they defeated the Phoenix Suns in six games.

Chicago Bulls guard Michael Jordan slam-dunks the ball while Bulls forward Stacey King (right) and Sacramento Kings center Ralph Sampson (left) look on, February 1991. (AP/Wide World Photos)

Jordan was named the NBA's Most Valuable Player three times between 1988 and 1992. During that period he became the most successfully marketed player in the history of team sports, earning roughly sixteen million dollars in commercial endorsements in 1992 alone from such corporations as Nike, McDonald's, Quaker Oats (Gatorade), and General Mills (Wheaties). Even when controversy surrounded Jordan, as it did during the 1992 Olympic Games when he refused to wear a competing sponsor's uniform, or when he incurred sizable debts gambling on golf and poker, he regularly registered as one of the nation's most admired men and one of young peoples' most revered role models. Jordan's basketball career came to a sudden halt in October 1993 when he announced his retirement in a nationally televised news conference. He said a diminishing love for the game, the pressures of celebrity, and the murder of his father three months earlier contributed to his decision. In February 1994 he signed with the Chicago White Sox of the American League, hoping to work his way up through the White Sox farm system to major league baseball. Unhappy with the progress he was making, Jordan subsequently elected to drop out of the White Sox organization, and in the spring of 1995, he resumed his basketball career by returning to the Bulls. After his return to basketball, Jordan led the Bulls to NBA championships in 1996, 1997, and 1998. He was named the NBA's Most Valuable Player in 1996 and 1998.

BIBLIOGRAPHY

Naughton, Jim. *Talking to the Air: The Rise of Michael Jordan.* New York, 1992.

– JIM NAUGHTON

JOURNALISM

Faced with the challenge of seeking just treatment in a society that systematically restricted the lives of freed blacks as well as slaves, African Americans began publishing their own periodicals long before the Civil War, using words as weapons in their protracted struggle for equality. The crusading editors of early black newspapers constituted an intellectual vanguard with a five-pronged mission: (1) to define the identity of a people who had been stripped of their own culture in a hostile environment; (2) to create a sense of unity by establishing a network of communication among literate blacks and their white supporters throughout the country; (3) to examine issues from a black perspective; (4) to chronicle black achievements that were ignored by the American mainstream; and (5) to further the cause of black liberation.

These objectives, set forth by founders of one of the oldest black institutions in the United States, underscored the activities of African-American journalists for nearly 150 years. When blacks began to move into the mainstream during the latter part of the twentieth century, assuming positions on general-circulation newspapers and in the broadcast media, most still retained a sense of being somehow involved with a larger racial cause. Yet these modern practitioners often were torn by conflicting loyalties: Were they blacks first or journalists first? Should they strive for respect in the mainstream by avoiding stories dealing with black topics, or fill in the gaps of coverage that might be left by white reporters? Should they follow the journalistic rule that calls for objectivity and report even events that might be damaging to blacks, or be ever mindful of the effects their stories might have on attitudes toward African Americans? It was a measure of social change that no such questions would have entered the minds of their predecessors.

Origins

The first African-American newspaper, *Freedom's Journal,* was founded in New York City on March 16, 1827, in response to the persistent attacks on blacks by a proslavery white paper, the New York *Enquirer.* The purpose of this pioneering publication was to encourage enlightenment and to enable blacks in the various states to exchange ideas. Thus it provided a forum for debate on issues that swirled around the institution of slavery. Among these was the question of whether blacks should strive for full citizenship and assimilation in America—a view favored by most blacks at that time—or whether they should follow a course of separation and opt for resettlement in Africa, a position then held mostly by whites who saw this as a way to rid the country of troublesome free blacks.

The two founding editors of *Freedom's Journal* were accomplished freemen who stood on opposite sides of the colonization question. Samuel E. Cornish, an ordained minister who had organized the first African Presbyterian church in the United States, thought blacks should fight for integration in America, while the Jamaican-born John B. Russwurm, who was the nation's second black college graduate (from Bowdoin College), supported repatriation in a part of West Africa that became Liberia. However, they were united in their opposition to slavery and stood as one in their appetite for discussion. They set forth their mission clearly in the first issue of *Freedom's Journal,* stating: "We wish to plead our own cause. Too long have others spoken for us. . . . From the press and the pulpit we have suffered much by being incorrectly represented."

Six months later, when their differences over the colonization issue proved insurmountable, Cornish left. Russwurm continued publishing the paper until March 28, 1829. He then settled in Liberia, where he remained until his death in 1851. There he worked as a school administrator, government official, and editor of a newspaper called the *Liberia Herald.*

Two months after Russwurm's departure, Cornish resurrected *Freedom's Journal,* on May 29, 1829, changing its name to *The Rights of All* and infusing it with a more militant tone; publication was suspended on October 9 of the same year. Cornish remained active in both the antislavery and black convention movements, but returned to journalism in 1837, serving as editor of Philip A. Bell's newspaper, the *Weekly Advocate.* Two months after its debut, the paper was renamed the *Colored American;* it was published until 1842. Although the paper was based in New York, there is evidence that a Philadelphia edition also was produced, making it possibly the first African-American publication to serve more than one city with different editions. Scholars of the early black press have noted the quality and originality of the *Colored American,* which was uncompromising in its call for black unity and full citizenship rights for all.

After the first steps were taken, others began using journalism to establish communication links in a largely illiterate nation and to generate support in the struggle against slavery. While most of these newspapers were based in New York, the *Alienated American* was launched in Cleveland on April 9, 1853. Martin R. Delany, the first black graduate of Harvard, published his own newspaper, *Mystery,* in Pittsburgh before he became assistant editor of Frederick DOUGLASS's *North Star.* Other outstanding early publications were Stephen Myer's *Elevator* (Albany, 1842), Thomas Hamilton's *Anglo-African* (New York, 1843), and William Wells Brown's *Rising Sun* (New York, 1847).

The first black newspaper to be published in the South before the Civil War was the *Daily Creole,* which surfaced in New Orleans in 1856 but bowed to white pressure in assuming an anti-abolitionist stance. It was followed, near the end of the Civil War, by the *New Orleans Tribune,* which appeared in July 1864 and is considered the first daily black newspaper. Published three times a week in both English and French, it was an official organ of Louisiana's Republican party, then the nation's progressive political wing. The *Tribune* called for bold measures to redress the grievances of bondage, including universal suffrage and payment of weekly wages to ex-slaves.

Of the forty or so black newspapers published before the Civil War, the most influential was the North Star, *founded and edited by Frederick Douglass.*

Most of these newspapers depended on the personal resources of their publishers along with contributions from white sympathizers to supplement their meager income from subscriptions, but prosperous blacks also lent their support. A notable "angel" of the period was James FORTEN, a Philadelphia veteran of the American Revolution who had amassed a fortune as a sail manufacturer. Forten was a major backer of William Lloyd Garrison, a white journalist who became one of the leading voices in the abolitionist movement through his newspaper the *Liberator,* first published on January 1, 1831.

Of the forty or so black newspapers published before the Civil War, the most influential was the *North Star,* founded and edited by Frederick Douglass in Rochester, New York, beginning on November 1, 1847. The name was that of the most brilliant star in the night sky, Polaris, a reference point for escaping slaves as they picked their way northward to freedom. Since Douglass is a figure of major historical importance he is not regarded primarily as a journalist, but he, like the black leaders who would follow him, knew how to use the press as a weapon. In the prospectus announcing his new publication, he wrote: "The object of the *North Star* will be to attack slavery in all its forms and aspects; advocate Universal Emancipation; exact the standard of public morality; promote the moral and intellectual improvement of the colored people; and to hasten the day of freedom to our three million enslaved fellow countrymen." Thus he defined the thrust of the early black press.

A Period of Transition

The number of black newspapers increased dramatically after the end of the Civil War in 1865, as the newly emancipated struggled to survive with no resources and few guaranteed rights. Publications sprang up in states where none had previously existed. Armistead S. Pride, the leading scholar on the black press, determined in the mid-twentieth century that African Americans had published 575 newspapers or periodicals by 1890, the end of the Reconstruction period. Although most were short-lived and many were religious or political publications rather than regular newspapers, some survived—notably the *Philadelphia Tribune,* which was founded in 1884 and continues to be published. It is considered the oldest continuously produced black newspaper in the United States. This period also marks the beginning of the *Afro-American,* which originated as a four-page Baptist church publication in Baltimore on August 13, 1892. After several metamorphoses, it became the highly respected anchor of a nationally distributed newspaper chain.

This heightened journalistic activity was due to many factors, among them an increase in literacy and greater mobility on the part of blacks, though their position in society as a whole was hardly satisfactory. When federal troops were withdrawn from the South in 1877 as a matter of political expediency, African Americans were left to the mercy of bitter whites who had fought to deny them freedom. Slavery was replaced by the economic bondage of sharecropping. White dominance was sustained through a system of rigidly enforced segregation and terrorism, including lynching, or the random torture and hanging of blacks. When southern blacks fled to northern cities in the first wave of black migration, they found themselves entrapped in squalid ghettos with few opportunities for work except in the most menial of jobs. For these reasons, the black press was still fueled by the spirit of protest, but that spark often had to be carefully veiled.

The pattern for race relations in America had been set in 1895 when Booker T. WASHINGTON, a former slave who had founded Tuskegee Institute, a school providing vocational education for blacks, went before the Cotton States' Exposition in Atlanta and proclaimed that it was folly for blacks to seek equal rights: they should pull themselves up by their own bootstraps and make the best of things as they were, getting along with whites by being patient, hardworking, subservient, and unresentful. In one of the most infamous metaphors of American history, Washington raised his hand and declared, "In all things that are purely social, we can be as separate as the fingers, yet one as the hand in all things essential to mutual progress." Such rhetoric, calling for a separate but not necessarily equal society, condoned the conservative mood of the era. Ordained by whites to speak for blacks, due to his "Atlanta compromise," Washington came to wield extraordinary power. It extended to the press, as black publishers struggled to keep their papers alive. Most had a small subscription base and advertising was hard to come by; therefore, they were inordinately dependent on contributions. Washington's critics said that he exercised undue influence over the black press by controlling loans, advertisements, and political subsidies, making certain that his doctrine prevailed.

The journalist most commonly associated with Washington is T. Thomas Fortune, who was editor of the *New York Age* during a period when Washington controlled it financially and used the paper as a conduit for presentation of his views, though Fortune did not share them. But Fortune had an identity in his own right. Respected as an accomplished and aggressive writer with a sharply satiric style, he stood out as a true professional. He had learned the business by working as a typesetter and later became one of the first of his race to hold an editorial position on a white daily, writing for the New York *Sun* and the *Evening Sun,* leading turn-of-the-century newspapers. Before assuming control of the *Age,* Fortune had published two newspapers of his own, the *Globe* and the *Freeman,* which were considered the best of their type. The *Age* had grown out of a tabloid called the *Rumor,* established in 1890.

Firmly committed to the struggle for racial equality, Fortune was an activist and organizer who used the *Age* to promulgate his own ideas. He extolled black pride before the turn of the century, urging that the term *Afro-American* be used instead of *negro,* then usually spelled with a lowercase *n.* Disdaining political patronage and declaring himself an independent, he was unable to attract the political advertising that was the main source of income for black newspapers. As a result, Fortune relied increasingly on contributions from Booker T. Washington, who eventually purchased the *Age.* Obligated to write editorials espousing Washington's accommodationist views, Fortune responded by presenting his own beliefs in opposing editorials in the same edition. Researchers credit Fortune with having written or edited all of Washington's books and many of his speeches, but Washington never acknowledged him. Torn by the compromises he was forced to make, Fortune succumbed to mental illness and poverty during the latter part of his career, but he has been called the dean of black journalism.

A few intrepid journalists refused to accept a state of such uneasy compromise. One stood out from all others. While several women contributed to journalism during the formative years of the black press, Ida B. WELLS transcended gender by risking her life to expose racially motivated crimes. She taught in rural schools before migrating to Shelby County, Tennessee, where she began writing for a black newspaper called the *Living War* under the name "Iola." As a teacher in Memphis, she was fired for writing exposés about injustices in the education system. Turning to journalism on a full-time basis, she became part-owner and editor of the *Memphis Free Speech.* In May 1892, when three black Memphis businessmen were lynched after a white mob attacked their grocery store, Wells charged in her paper that the murders had been instigated by the white business community. She called for a boycott of those white businesses and urged blacks to migrate to the new Oklahoma territory, where they might find freedom from oppression. She also wrote that she had purchased a pistol and would use it to defend herself. In her last column for that paper, Wells said that the white women who accused black men of rape often were their lovers.

When Wells left town to attend a convention in Philadelphia, her newspaper office was destroyed and the building burned. Relocating to New York, she continued her crusade in Fortune's *New York Age,* of which she became a part-owner. Lecturing throughout the United States and abroad, she later published documentation of lynchings in *Redbook* magazine and helped found the Negro women's club movement. One of the most outspoken black journalists of all time, Ida B. Wells became the only woman of her profession to be commemorated by the issuance of a stamp in 1990 as part of the U.S. Postal Service's Black Heritage series.

As some blacks continued to resist Booker T. Washington's accommodationist doctrine, a militant tone was set for the twentieth century when William Monroe TROTTER founded the Boston *Guardian* in 1901 with George Forbes. Both had graduated from college in 1895, Trotter from Harvard and Forbes from Amherst. Trotter quickly became the dominant force on the paper. The product of an interracial marriage, he had grown up comfortably in a Boston suburb. At Harvard, he had become the first African American inducted into the honor society Phi Beta Kappa and went on to earn his M.A. degree there in 1896. Unwilling to accept any sort of compromise, he demanded absolute equality for blacks and used his paper to consolidate the first organized opposition to Washington and his ideas. Trotter joined with another son of Massachusetts, W. E. B. DU BOIS—who is considered by many to be the greatest intellectual produced by black America—in laying groundwork for the NIAGARA MOVEMENT, the forerunner of the NATIONAL ASSOCIATION FOR THE ADVANCEMENT OF COLORED PEOPLE (NAACP). Trotter then disdained the NAACP for being too little, too late, and too white. He carried the fight for black rights to the international arena, going before the League of Nations and the World Peace Conference in Paris, to no avail. Disillusioned and ill, Trotter either jumped or fell to his death from the roof of his Boston home in 1934, when he was sixty-two years old. But he had sounded a defiant note that set the tone for further development of the black press throughout the twentieth century.

Early black newspapers bore little resemblance to their modern counterparts. From the beginning, they had not been intended as instruments of mass communication. They were aimed at a small educated elite and emphasized commentary over news coverage. Editors exchanged copies of their publications by mail and engaged in debates over issues, with the responses appearing in their next editions. It was assumed that subscribers also read white publications and thus were informed on major national events. Yet these papers filled a void by interpreting the news from a black perspective and noting developments of particular interest to African Americans, providing information that was not available elsewhere. This included local coverage of religious and social events, a mainstay of black newspapers.

Growth and Power

The modern black press did not come into being until 1905, when Robert S. Abbott founded the *Chicago Defender,* the first African-American newspaper designed to appeal to the masses and, consequently, the first commercially successful black journalistic enterprise. Although Abbott's sole objective was to improve the plight of blacks in America, he realized that he would have to communicate with the common people if he were to help them. In this respect, Abbott followed the imperatives that have shaped the daily newspapers of the twentieth century, when it has been assumed that a publication first must capture the attention of the largest number of potential readers by playing up stories that generate immediate interest. Abbott took particular note of the practices of William Randolph Hearst, who had built the largest journalistic empire of the early twentieth century by engaging in sensationalism to boost sales. But in spite of the screaming red headlines and excited tone that came to mark the *Defender's* style, the paper, at its core, held to the same precepts that have informed black journalism since its inception.

A small, very black man who suffered the indignities imposed on those of his color during a period when dark skin was considered a major social liability even among African Americans, Abbott was a Georgian who settled in Chicago, where he decided to publish his own newspaper, although three other black papers already were being distributed there. According to Roi Ottley, Abbott's biographer, the publisher started out in a rented room with nothing but a card table, a borrowed chair, and twenty-five cents in capital, intent on producing his newspaper. Abbott, who had a law degree, called it the *Defender* because he intended to fight for the rights of black people. At that time, the black population of Chicago was concentrated in so few blocks on the South Side that Abbott could gather the news, sell advertising, and distribute his newspaper on foot by himself. That was a situation he was to change with his paper.

At first, Abbott avoided politics and other contentious topics, featuring neighborhood news and personals, but he hit his stride when he began to concentrate on muckraking, publishing exposés of prostitution and other criminal activities in the black community. Adopting the scarlet headlines favored by his white counterparts, Abbott developed a publication so popular that copies were posted in churches and barbershops where blacks congregated, so that the latest stories could be read aloud.

One of the factors that contributed to Abbott's early success was increasing literacy among blacks. By 1910, seven out of ten blacks over the age of ten could read and Chicago's black population had grown to 44,103, though still concentrated in a small area. In 1910 Abbott hired his first paid employee, J. Hockley Smiley, an editor who moved the paper more decidedly toward sensationalism and encouraged the publisher to press for national circulation. White distributors refused to carry black newspapers, but Chicago was a major railroad center, so Smiley suggested that railroad porters and waiters be used to carry bundles of papers to their destinations, smuggling them into the South, where they could be turned over to local black agents. In turn, the railroad workers brought back news, enabling the *Defender* to become the first black publication with a truly national scope. To shore up this thrust, Abbott employed Roscoe Conkling Simmons, a leading orator, to tour the country, promoting the paper. Since the stance of the *Defender* was militant, with detailed accounts of injustices committed against blacks, participants in this underground distribution system courted danger. Two agents were killed and others were driven from their homes because of their involvement with the *Defender*. Yet Abbott did not back down, engaging the redoubtable Ida B. Wells to report on riots, lynchings, and other racial wrongs.

Abbott found his place in history in 1917, during World War I, when he began to publish front-page stories with blazing headlines urging southern blacks to migrate to the North, where they could escape from the indignities of Dixie and acquire higher-paying jobs in industry. The paper offered group railroad rates to migrants and encouraged them to seek personal advice on how to adjust to the big city by following the *Defender*'s regular features. Scholars credit the *Defender* with being a major force in stimulating the tide of northern migration after the war, when blacks realized that the rights U.S. soldiers had fought for abroad were not being extended to them at home. More than 300,000 African Americans migrated to the great industrial cities of the North between 1916 and 1918, with 110,000 moving to Chicago alone, tripling the city's black population.

By 1920, the *Defender* claimed its peak circulation of 283,571, with an additional high pass-along rate. Unlike those struggling earlier black publishers, Abbott became a millionaire, moving into his own fully paid-for half-million-dollar plant on Chicago's South Side. With a broad-based national circulation, the *Defender* offered hope and inspiration to poor southern blacks like the young Johnny Johnson, who read the paper as a youth in his native Arkansas during the early 1930s and soon moved north with his family to Chicago, where he would build his own publishing empire. Though the paper eventually declined in popularity, due to its failure to keep up with the growing sophistication of blacks, it is still being published. When Abbott died in 1940, one of his nephews, John H. Sengstacke, assumed leadership. In 1956, he converted the *Defender* into a daily; it appeared four times a week with an additional weekend edition.

While Abbott carved out his empire from Chicago, publishers in other parts of the country also built journalistic enterprises that cumulatively developed into one of the most powerful institutions in black America.

At least a dozen black newspapers had come and gone in Pittsburgh by 1910, when the lawyer Robert L. Vann drew up incorporation papers for the *Pittsburgh Courier*, a publication he edited and eventually came to own. Born impoverished in 1879 in Ahoskie, N.C., Vann struggled for years to acquire an education, finally earning both baccalaureate and law degrees from the Western University of Pennsylvania, later renamed the University of Pittsburgh. A relatively small man, like Abbott, he was encouraged by friends to pass for an East Indian because he had straight hair and keen features, but Vann remained staunchly black. Though the *Courier* managed to survive, it did not gain much momentum until 1914, when Ira F. Lewis joined the staff as a sportswriter. He turned out to be a gifted salesman who built advertising and circulation, going on to become business manager of the paper and transforming it into a national institution.

In its editorial tone, the *Pittsburgh Courier* tended to be somewhat less sensational than the *Defender*, commanding attention with its distinctive peach-colored cover page. In front-page editorials, Vann led his crusades, demanding that the huge industrial firms hire African Americans as well as the European immigrants who were surging into the labor market, and criticizing unions for denying blacks membership. He called for better education and housing for blacks and urged them to boycott movie houses and stores that overcharged them or treated them disrespectfully.

A local publication during its early years, the *Courier* began to make national inroads during the 1920s, when Vann improved its quality by retaining some of the most talented black journalists of the period. George S. Schuyler, a figure of the HARLEM RENAISSANCE who was called the black H. L. Mencken due to his bitingly satiric prose, began contributing a weekly column and became chief editorial writer, a position he held for several decades. Schuyler also toured the nation to produce extensive series on the socioeconomic status of black America.

Vann sent Joel A. Rogers, a self-taught historian, to Europe and Africa, where he documented black contributions to Western civilization. Rogers later produced a column called "Your History" and collaborated with an artist on a weekly illustrated feature that stimulated pride among blacks, who had been denied evidence of prior achievements by their race. When Italy invaded Ethiopia in 1935, Rogers became one of the first black war correspondents by covering the conflict from the front. His colorful dispatches captured the attention of African Americans throughout the United States, and this boosted circulation.

Sparkling entertainment and social news were staples, but the *Courier*'s forte was its sports coverage. Excellent reportage was provided by W. Rollo Wilson, William G. Nunn, Sr., Wendell Smith, and Chester "Ches" Washington, a championship speed typist who went on in the 1970s to become the successful publisher of a chain of newspapers in California. The *Courier* secured its national stature during the 1930s by recognizing the potential of a young pugilist named Joe LOUIS and maintaining a virtual monopoly on coverage of his activities until long after Louis had become the most popular heavyweight champion in history. As a result, circulation reached 250,000 by 1937, according to figures of the Audit Bureau of Circulation, and the *Courier* supplanted the *Defender* as the nation's leading black weekly.

It was a role of the nation's top black newspapers to bridge the gap separating artists and intellectuals from the masses. The *Defender* published the early poems of the Chicagoan Gwendolyn BROOKS, who would become the first African American to win a Pulitzer Prize, and employed Willard Motley as a youth editor long before he became a bestselling novelist. The poet and humorist Langston HUGHES introduced his character Jesse B. Semple (Simple) in its pages. Similarly, the *Courier* featured commentary and reviews by James Weldon JOHNSON, while W. E. B. Du Bois wrote a column for the paper after he stepped down as editor of the *Crisis,* the official magazine of the NAACP.

It was a role of the nation's top black newspapers to bridge the gap separating artists and intellectuals from the masses.

Unlike Abbott, who relished his ties to the man in the street and especially fellow migrants from the South, Vann was an aloof, politically driven man who used his paper to promote his own career as a lawyer and to seek control of black patronage. He is perhaps best known for his defection from the Republican party, which had claimed the loyalties of black voters since the time of Abraham Lincoln. Democrats were strongly identified with their party's southern segregationist faction. By 1932, the country was in the throes of an economic depression and the yet untried Franklin D. Roosevelt was the Democratic presidential candidate. Vann, who thought that the Republicans had taken the black vote for granted for too long without responding to the needs of that constituency, delivered a speech that projected him to national prominence. Calling for the black vote to remain "liquid" rather than allied to a single party, he said, "I see millions of Negroes turning the picture of Lincoln to the wall." The line became a catchphrase in the successful Democratic campaign to get black votes and win the election.

As a result, Vann was given a position as a special assistant to the attorney general, but he found only disillusionment in Washington, where he was generally ignored. As patterns of patronage shifted toward a younger group of blacks, Vann switched back to the Republican party, failing to take the black vote with him. He died in 1940, seven months after Robert S. Abbott. Yet he had established so firm a foundation for the *Courier* that it retained its popularity for several more years under the management of Ira Lewis, with the publisher's widow, Jesse L. Vann, at the helm. Under editors P. L. Prattis and William G. Nunn, Sr., the crusades continued, with calls for integration of the armed forces during World War II and a "double V" campaign for victory abroad and against discrimination at home. In 1946 the *Courier* published fourteen editions, including local and national editions, with branch offices in twelve cities, and was the most popular black publication even in several cities with their own black newspapers. It attained a circulation of 357,212 in May 1947, a record for audited black newspapers.

Some of the paper's crusades had tangible results. *Courier* sportswriter Wendell Smith, who had been using his column to press for integration of major-league baseball since the 1920s, served as the liaison between Jackie ROBINSON and Branch Rickey, general manager of the Brooklyn Dodgers, resulting in Robinson's joining that team in 1947.

After the death of Ira Lewis in 1948, the *Courier* lapsed into a general decline, due to mismanagement and numerous other factors that affected the black press in the 1950s and '60s. On the brink of financial collapse in 1965, it was purchased by John Sengstacke, owner of the *Defender* chain. Thus the similar but separate missions of Robert S. Abbott and Robert L. Vann converged in a final irony. Continuing publication as the *New Pittsburgh Courier,* the paper was but a shadow of its old self. Sengstacke Publications, which included the *Courier* and other acquisitions, became the largest African-American newspaper chain in the country as the black press struggled for its very survival.

The third member of what could be called a triumvirate of great black national newspapers was the *Afro-American,* which evolved from its beginnings as a Baltimore church publication to become one of the most widely circulated black newspapers in the South and East, with branch offices in Washington, Philadelphia, Richmond, and Newark, N.J. Its founder was John H. Murphy, Sr., a former slave and a whitewasher by trade, who created it by merging his own Sunday-school sheet with two similar church publications, and going on to expand its coverage to include issues and events of interest to the general black population.

When Murphy died in 1922, his five sons took over the operation, with one of them, Carl Murphy, assuming control. Under his leadership, the *Afro-American* grew into a national publication with multiple editions that emphasized solid reportage and took moderate editorial positions. It became the dominant black publication in the Washington-Baltimore-Richmond triangle, focusing on political matters in a part of the country with a heavy concentration of African Americans. Though firmly patriotic in most of its views, the *Afro,* as it was known, demonstrated courage by standing up for the singer/actor Paul ROBESON and the scholar/editor W. E. B. Du Bois when both were accused of being Communists during the McCarthy era. The publisher also ignored official pressure and sent the journalist William Worthy to Communist China on assignment after the U.S. State Department had denied him a visa. From 1961 through the 1980s, the founder's grandson, John Murphy III, played a major role in the paper's fortunes, especially after the death of Carl Murphy in 1967. Over the years, successive generations of Murphys have stepped forward to assume leadership.

While these were the titans in the era of the popular black press, other newspapers distinguished themselves by serving the needs of their own urban communities. The *Amsterdam News* was established in 1909 in New York City when James H. Anderson began publishing a local sheet with $10 and a dream, giving it the name of the street on which he lived. It gained prominence and commercial success after 1936, when it was purchased by two Harlem physicians, one of whom, C. B. Powell, assumed control and developed the paper to the point where it had a circulation of more than 100,000 after World War II. The Norfolk *Journal and Guide* achieved a high level of respectability after 1910, when P. B. Young, a twenty-six-year-old North Carolinian, purchased its original entity, a fraternal organ, and transformed it into a general-circulation black newspaper. Avoiding sensationalism and maintaining a relatively conservative stance, the *Journal and Guide* was singled out for praise by mainstream scholars of the press, who considered it the most objective of black newspapers. Yet it responded readily to the needs of its readers, launching campaigns that resulted in better housing for black residents and pay scales for black teachers that equaled those of whites. W. O. Walker built the Cleveland *Call and Post* into a "bread-and-butter" paper that focused firmly on local news, while the Scott family, beginning in 1932, built the *Atlanta Daily World* into the nation's oldest black daily, one of only three that survived into the 1990s. Across the nation, from the early to mid-twentieth century, it was difficult to find a major city that was not served by a black newspaper.

The reasons for their existence were obvious. Until the late 1950s, African Americans were mostly ignored by mainstream publications, and when they did appear it was as perpetrators of crimes. If news of interest to the black population was included at all, it was in tiny, segregated columns dubbed "Afro-American," or some similar name, placed inconspicuously in back pages. Even reportage on African-American sports or entertainment figures was designed to reinforce prevailing stereotypes. Thus the black press served the palpable needs of a neglected and maligned people. Editors of black newspapers said that they hoped to change society to such an extent that they would put themselves out of business. But when this change began to take place, they were not prepared to cope with the consequences.

The Tides of Change

When the struggle for racial equality blossomed into the modern CIVIL RIGHTS MOVEMENT, beginning with the Montgomery, Ala., bus boycott in 1955, mainstream publications took steps toward covering events in which African Americans were the major players. As the movement spread from Montgomery to Birmingham to Little Rock and beyond, white newspaper editors began to realize that they were witnessing one of the biggest stories of the century. Furthermore, they were being challenged, for the first time, by television, a news medium that could provide more immediate coverage, enhanced by dramatic visual images that captured the action as it happened. This was most forcefully demonstrated on August 28, 1963, when television provided extended live coverage of the historic March on Washington and the Rev. Dr. Martin Luther KING, Jr.'s "I Have a Dream" speech. Since each day brought new developments, most black newspapers, limited to weekly publication, were unable to compete. Furthermore, few of them possessed or were willing to commit the resources that would have enabled them to deploy correspondents to the various hot spots throughout the country. Reporters who worked for the black press during that time recalled their frustration at having to cover the movement by telephone or by rewriting accounts that appeared in the leading white-owned papers.

Although the coverage provided by mainstream print and broadcast media was from a white perspective, inroads were made into a territory that had been the exclusive property of the black press. Yet black journalists were rarely employed by the white media. Even in New York City, the nation's media capital, no African Americans held full-time jobs on white newspapers until Lester A. Walton was hired by the *World* in the 1920s. No further advances were made until the late 1940s, when three veterans of the black press were hired by New York daily papers: George Streator by the *Times,* Edgar T. Rozeau by the *Herald Tribune,* and Ted Poston by the *Post.* In 1955, a year after the Supreme Court school-desegregation decision, *Ebony* magazine found only thirty-one blacks working on white newspapers throughout the country. Black journalists were so rare in the developing medium of TELEVISION that they were not even counted before 1962, when Mal Goode, a radio newscaster and former advertising salesman for the *Pittsburgh Courier,* was hired by ABC to become the first network correspondent of his race.

When the struggle for racial equality blossomed into the modern Civil Rights Movement, mainstream publications took steps toward covering events in which African Americans were the major players.

No major changes were to occur until the late 1960s, when the nation's black communities went up in flames, from Watts in Los Angeles to Harlem in New York. The 1968 *Report of the National Advisory Commission on Civil Disorders,* better known as the Kerner Commission Report, analyzed the causes of those upheavals. In a section implicating the media, the report said:

> They have not communicated to the majority of their audience—which is white—a sense of the degradation, misery, and hopelessness of living in the ghetto. They have not communicated to whites a feeling for the difficulties and frustrations of being a Negro in the United States. They have not shown understanding or appreciation of—and thus have not communicated—a sense of Negro culture, thought or history.
>
> Equally important, most newspaper articles and most television programming ignored the fact that an appreciable part of their audience was black. The world that television and newspapers offered to their black audience was almost totally white, in both appearances and attitude. As we have said, our evidence shows that the so-called "white press" is at best mistrusted and at worst held in contempt by many black Americans. Far too often, the press acts and talks about Negroes as if Negroes do not read the newspapers or watch television, give birth, marry, die and go to PTA meetings.

The riots, as they were transpiring, had driven home a message to white news managers, who realized that their reporters were ill-equipped to enter the alien world of black neighborhoods and to gain the confidence of residents to the point where they might discover what was really going on. As the flames of rage spread from the ghettos to central commercial areas, some realized that the destiny of white America was irrevocably linked to that of black America. As a result, some black reporters were hired literally in the heat of the moment. With the strong indictment of the Kerner Commission finding its mark, black reporters were recruited by the mainstream for the first time, most commonly from the black press. By the mid-1970s, nearly a hundred African-American journalists were employed by mainstream publications.

Another response to the report was the development of training programs to increase the limited supply of black journalists. The largest of these was a concentrated summer program established at Columbia University in 1968 through a $250,000 grant from the Ford Foundation. Directed by Fred Friendly, former head of CBS News and a professor at Columbia's Graduate School of Journalism, the program trained members of various minority groups, then placed from twenty to forty of them each year in both print and broadcast jobs. When one of its black graduates, Michele Clark, died in an airplane crash after working her way up to become co-anchor of the *CBS Morning News,* the minority-training program was renamed in her honor. In 1974, after substantial increases in the number of African Americans earning degrees from journalism schools, including Columbia's, this program was discontinued. The following year, it was revived through the efforts of Earl Caldwell, a leading African-American journalist and columnist for the New York *Daily News.* Relocated to the University of California at Berkeley and operated by the Institute for Journalism Education (IJE), the program continued to train and place members of minorities on mainstream newspapers into the early 1990s. Under the guidance of nationally known African-American journalists, among them Nancy Hicks, Robert Maynard, and Dorothy Gilliam, the IJE broadened its scope to include programs in editing and management training, designed to facilitate movement of black journalists into the upper echelons of the print media.

All of these changes had a devastating effect on black newspapers. Their circulations plummeted as television and mainstream newspapers encroached on their readership by providing more immediate, though often superficial and insensitive, coverage of major events affecting the African-American community. By 1977 the audited circulation of the *Chicago Defender* had shrunk to 34,000 daily and 38,000 for the weekend edition; the *New Pittsburgh Courier* dipped to 30,000 weekly; the Baltimore *Afro-American* averaged 34,000 for two weekday editions and 18,500 for a weekend national edition. A few publications fared somewhat better, but others teetered on the brink of bankruptcy or had disappeared altogether. While more than 300 black newspapers were being published in the early 1960s, only 170 remained by the late 1980s. Their overall quality also declined as most of the top talent defected to the mainstream, where the rewards included salaries that were several times larger, far better benefits, and greater prestige. Television offered not only large salaries, but high visibility and glamour, a heady kind of stardom. After 1970, few aspiring journalists entered the field with the intention of working for the black press.

Exceptions to this grim pattern were two radical newspapers that surfaced during the 1960s in the furor of the Black Revolution. *Muhammad Speaks,* the official organ of the NATION OF ISLAM, otherwise known as the Black Muslims, stemmed from a column called "Mr. Muhammad Speaks" that its leader, Elijah MUHAMMAD, had written for the *Pittsburgh Courier* during the 1950s. When Christian ministers, valuable links in the black press circulation chain, objected to Muhammad's anti-Christian rhetoric, the column was discontinued. Since Muslim followers had employed aggressive tactics to sell the paper on the streets, they took with them a huge chunk of the paper's circulation. The column resurfaced in the *Amsterdam News* during the 1960s, when MALCOLM X was galvanizing the black masses not only in Harlem but throughout the nation. By the early 1970s, the Black Muslims were publishing a popular weekly newspaper of their own called *Muhammad Speaks,* producing it in Chicago, where a staff of experienced journalists (who were not necessarily Muslims) worked out of a well-equipped plant. Featuring African-American news with a militant slant, along with dogma, and distributed through the same street-selling techniques, *Muhammad Speaks* achieved an unaudited weekly circulation of 400,000 to 600,000, an all-time record for a black newspaper. Circulation dropped sharply after the assassination of Malcolm X, the death of Elijah Muhammad, power struggles within the Muslim sect, and a general shift away from overt militance in the African-American population, but the paper continued publication under other names, including the *Bilalian News* and later the *Final Call,* in the late 1980s and early 1990s.

A shorter-lived but significant effort was the *Black Panther,* which achieved an unaudited circulation of 100,000 during the 1970s, when it was edited by Eldridge CLEAVER, author of the autobiographical militant manifesto *Soul on Ice.* Politically radical in its tone, condemning police brutality at home and America's foreign policy abroad, the paper ceased publication after the credibility of Panther leaders was undermined.

While the movement toward integration all but obliterated the power previously held by black newspapers, one genre of African-American publications flourished. These were the black magazines that had been conceived as commercial enterprises rather than instruments of protest. They were better able to adjust to the demands of an increasingly competitive marketplace.

Black Magazines and John H. Johnson

Early black newspapers so resembled magazines in tone and content that differentiation between the two often was based primarily on frequency of publication. The first black magazines seem to have been subsidized organs that originated in the black church during the early 1840s. The first general-circulation magazine owned independently by African Americans and directed to them was the *Mirror of Liberty,* published by David Ruggles, a New Yorker who was a key figure in the Underground Railroad. Forwarding the cause of abolition, it was published from 1847 to 1849. Other magazines followed. Frederick Douglass, after publishing a series of newspapers, lent his name to an abolitionist magazine, *Douglass' Monthly,* that was aimed primarily at British readers and was issued from 1860 to 1862. A forerunner of popular modern periodicals was *Alexander's Magazine,* a national publication produced in Boston from 1905 to 1909. It emphasized the positive aspects of African-American life, featuring stories about outstanding individuals with commentary on cultural, educational, and political events.

The first African-American magazine to have a lasting impact was the CRISIS, which was the brainchild of W. E. B. Du Bois. It first appeared in 1910, a year that resonates with significance due to the number of African-American organizations, institutions, and publications spawned at that time. Du Bois, who was one of the original incorporators of the NAACP, assumed the position of director of publications and research for that organization after several previous excursions into journalism. He used the *Crisis*—which remains the official organ of the NAACP—to criticize national policies that impeded the progress of blacks and to educate African Americans in the techniques of protest. After Du Bois resigned his post in 1934 following squabbles with the NAACP leadership, he launched other magazines, the most notable being *Phylon,* a scholarly journal published by Atlanta University, where he spent portions of his career as a professor and head of the sociology department.

The first African-American magazine to have a lasting impact was the Crisis, *which was the brainchild of W. E. B. Du Bois.*

Following Du Bois's inspired lead, the NATIONAL URBAN LEAGUE published *Opportunity,* a journal that documented the literary and artistic accomplishments of the Harlem Renaissance and lasted until 1949. Another notable periodical of the post–World War I period was the *Messenger,* a militantly socialist journal edited by Chandler Owen and A. Philip Randolph, the latter of whom was to become the voice of black labor as head of the Brotherhood of Sleeping Car Porters. All of these publications depended on subsidies. Commercial black magazines—meaning those that were fully self-sustaining through advertising as well as subscriptions—did not surface until the 1940s, a period when general-circulation magazines were one of the main forms of home entertainment. The engaging combination of pictures and words had made *Life* a popular chronicle of the American Dream, while *Time* provided snappily written coverage of weekly events and the *Saturday Evening Post* reinforced mainstream values in fiction and nonfiction. The *Reader's Digest* offered encapsulated extracts from the era's leading publications, including periodicals like the *Ladies' Home Journal,* which catered to the traditional interests of women. Yet African Americans remained invisible in the pages of these magazines, as they had been in mainstream newspapers.

A veritable revolution in black magazines began in 1942 when John H. Johnson began publishing *Negro Digest,* a monthly periodical roughly the size of the *Reader's Digest,* featuring stories about black accomplishments, news items of interest to African Americans, and provocative original articles by prominent whites addressing black issues. He used it as the cornerstone for the development of the most successful black publishing firm in history. Although other quality mass-circulation black magazines originated in the post–World War II period, Johnson outmaneuvered his competition and thus eliminated it by developing brilliant marketing strategies. His climb from poverty to inclusion in *Forbes* magazine's list of the four hundred richest Americans was a real-life Horatio Alger story.

Johnson was born poor in 1918 in Arkansas City, Ark., a tiny town on the banks of the Mississippi River. His father was killed in a sawmill accident when he was eight and his mother remarried a year later. Since the town offered no opportunities for a black child to be educated beyond the eighth grade, his mother, Gertrude Johnson Williams, moved the family north to Chicago in 1933 and worked as a domestic to educate her son. When he graduated from the city's DuSable High School as the most outstanding student in the class of 1936, Johnson was offered a scholarship to the University of Chicago but opted to attend part-time while working at Supreme Liberty Life Insurance Company, one of the nation's leading black businesses. Among his tasks was to produce the company's monthly newspaper. Another was to provide digests of news about blacks for the company's president, Harry Pace, who was Johnson's mentor.

When friends were fascinated by the nuggets of black-oriented news Johnson shared with them, he conceived the idea of publishing a monthly magazine based on this kind of information. Having no money, he used his mother's new furniture as collateral to borrow $500. With this sum, he paid for the mailing of an introductory subscription letter sent to Supreme's twenty thousand customers. The resultant magazine, *Negro Digest,* was so popular that Johnson was able to launch a second magazine, EBONY, in 1945. Stressing the positive aspects of African-American life and employing ample pictures in a storytelling fashion, *Ebony* eventually became the all-time leader among black magazines.

Along the way, Johnson outstripped his most promising competitor, *Our World,* which was published by John P. Davis, a Harvard Law School graduate. It was launched in 1946, just after *Ebony,* and also was a quality picture magazine printed on slick paper. *Our World* amassed a circulation of 251,599 by 1952, but went bankrupt in 1955 because it could not attract major advertising accounts, the lifeblood of commercial publications. Meanwhile, Johnson used every ounce of ingenuity he could muster to break down the barriers that led white manufacturers to dismiss black magazines as advertising venues. By Johnson's own admission, he triumphed not so much because he had a better magazine, but because he was a more inventive businessman.

Johnson also was adept at changing his tactics as the times demanded. He discontinued *Negro Digest* in 1951 when *Ebony* had usurped its audience, replacing his first publication with *Jet,* a pocket-size weekly newsmagazine. In 1965, when black militance was in vogue, he revived *Negro Digest,* changing its name to *Black World.* Under the editor Hoyt Fuller, it became a prestigious outlet for African-American literature and thought, documenting the developments of what some have called the second black Renaissance. By 1970, when the movement subsided and subscriptions dropped, Johnson again discontinued the magazine.

Responding to what he read to be public taste, Johnson published *Tan Confessions* during the 1950s and 1960s, later transforming it into *Black Stars,* a fan magazine; *Hue,* a pocket-size picture magazine of the late fifties; *Ebony, Jr.,* an educational magazine for children, produced during the late sixties; and *Ebony Africa,* which reflected the African independence movement but was discontinued after a few issues in 1965 when it foundered on differing national, linguistic, and political realities. By 1992, Johnson was publishing *Ebony,* with a monthly circulation of 1.9 million; *Jet,* with a weekly circulation of nearly 1 million; and *EM: Ebony Man,* a lifestyle magazine for the African-American man that was established in 1985 and had a monthly circulation base of 225,000.

Some criticized Johnson's publications for concentrating too heavily on entertainment and light features while paying too little attention to major issues. But *Ebony* also had its serious side, and provided a nurturing environment for the development of talented black writers. Foremost among these was Lerone Bennett, Jr., who joined the staff in 1953. A scholar as well as a journalist, Bennett produced several series of articles that interpreted and dramatized black history in a literary style accessible to the general reader. Most of these articles evolved into popular books, published by Johnson, that became a mainstay of the black studies programs instituted by American colleges and universities during the 1970s.

Johnson maintained his leadership in the field and accumulated an estimated net worth of $200 million by expanding into the areas of radio broadcasting, television production, and cosmetics manufacturing. Although he never earned a college degree, he was granted several honorary doctorates. He also became the chief stockholder of Supreme Life, where he had started his career, and served on the boards of several major corporations.

The legislative gains of the 1960s led to improvements in the overall educational and economic status of African Americans, providing fertile ground for the cultivation of magazines aimed at newly affluent black consumers. A dozen new magazines surfaced in 1970 alone, and two of them went on to become major publications: *Essence* and *Black Enterprise.*

Essence: The Magazine for Today's Black Woman was conceived when a Wall Street brokerage firm invited a group of young black businessmen to come up with ideas for business ventures. As a result, Johnathan Blount, Cecil Hollingsworth, Ed Lewis, and Clarence Smith developed a proposal for a black women's magazine. The idea was sold to financial backers and a staff was assembled. *Essence* attracted an audience from its very first issue, which appeared in April 1970, but was hampered by numerous organizational and editorial changes during its early years. By the 1980s, it had achieved stability and enormous popularity by offering fashions, fiction, self-help, and other articles addressing the interests of African-American women, especially those under forty. By 1992, *Essence* had a circulation of 900,000.

Black Enterprise reflected the improved national climate and positive mood of the post-movement period by encouraging black participation in the economic mainstream. First published by Earl Graves in August 1970, the magazine was nearly two years in the planning, with input from a board of advisers that included Whitney Young, Jr., head of the National Urban League. A major objective was to stimulate black entrepreneurship, but the concept was broader than that of a simple black business magazine. *Black Enterprise* interpreted national economic and political trends from a black perspective and provided advice on career planning and money management. Its annual listing of the one hundred biggest black businesses provided a ready reference for determining the progress of African-American entrepreneurs. Like *Essence, Black Enterprise* was able to establish a substantial advertising base and had a circulation of 250,500 in 1992.

With the expansion of the black middle class, a variety of magazines were developed to address specific tastes. By 1990, at least twenty-five black-oriented magazines were being published in the United States. Promising newcomers included *Visions,* a Washington-based quarterly focusing on the arts, history, and culture, founded in 1985; *Emerge,* a New York–based monthly newsmagazine targeting the upscale, which first appeared in 1989; and *YSB* (short for "Young Sisters and Brothers"), which was aimed at the youth market and was launched in 1991 in conjunction with the Black Entertainment Television cable network.

The boom in black magazines also provided increased opportunities for African-American photographers to have their work displayed to greater advantage. Photojournalists had contributed to black newspapers throughout the twentieth century, but under circumstances in which graphics were not stressed. Magazines, with their slick paper and more attractive layouts, offered a far better showcase, but the mainstream had been all but closed to African Americans. The only one to achieve distinction there was Gordon PARKS, Sr., who had taught himself photography while working as a railroad waiter. After honing his craft on a Rosenwald Fellowship, Parks joined the staff of *Life* magazine in 1949 and acquired a national reputation for his riveting photographs of the disadvantaged. *Ebony,* in particular, with its physical similarity to *Life,* became a showcase for the work of Moneta Sleet, Jr., who previously had been on the staff of *Our World.* He joined *Ebony* in 1955, covering major stories throughout the world, from the civil rights movement to the evolution of an independent Africa. In 1969, he became the first African-American photographer to win a Pulitzer Prize, for his picture of Mrs. Martin Luther King, Jr., with her daughter, Bernice, at the funeral of the slain leader. One of Sleet's younger colleagues at *Ebony* was Ozier Muhammad, who went on to win a Pulitzer Prize in 1969 as a staff photographer for the New York daily *Newsday.*

Mainstreaming

The last decades of the twentieth century brought a dramatic shift toward the mainstreaming of African-American journalists. Beginning in the 1970s, general-circulation daily newspapers and television stations recruited black journalists as they never had before. By 1990, nearly four thousand blacks were employed by daily newspapers; a few established national reputations. Possibly the best known of these was Carl T. Rowan, who also appeared regularly as a commentator on televised public-affairs programs. Rowan built his entire career within the mainstream. He started out in 1948 on the staff of the *Minneapolis Tribune,* where he won several awards for reporting. A distinguished author, Rowan held some high government posts in the 1960s during the Kennedy and Johnson administrations. He became a syndicated columnist for the *Chicago Daily News* in 1965, later expanding on that base. William Raspberry of the *Washington Post* also gained broad recognition through a syndicated column published in general-market newspapers throughout the country. Other African-American journalists became well known through columns in major metropolitan newspapers, among them Earl Caldwell and Bob Herbert of the New York *Daily News,* Les Payne of *Newsday,* Dorothy Gilliam of the *Washington Post,* Chuck Stone of the *Philadelphia Daily News,* and Clarence Page of the *Chicago Tribune.*

Most major newspapers had at least a few African-American reporters on their staffs by 1990, while the *Washington Post* and *New York Times* each had more than fifty. However, the *Post* responded more readily to the need for change and offered more opportunities for these journalists to move into high-level positions as editors and managers. They also were better able to establish a public identity through the prominent display of their work in the *Post.*

The last decades of the twentieth century brought a dramatic shift toward the mainstreaming of African-American journalists.

The Gannett Corporation, which was the nation's largest newspaper chain, publishing eighty-seven dailies throughout the country as well as the national *USA Today,* outstripped others in the field by implementing a strong affirmative-action policy. Under chairman Allen Neuharth, Gannett enforced strict rules ensuring that minorities were included in the coverage of news and that they were consulted as sources for stories that did not necessarily pertain to race. Through the Gannett chain, Robert Maynard, who had spent ten years at the *Washington Post* as a national correspondent, ombudsman, and editorial writer, became the first African-American publisher of a general-market daily in 1979, at the *Oakland Tribune.* Maynard went on to purchase the paper in 1983, another first. Also under the Gannett system, Pam Johnson, who held a Ph.D. in communications, was named publisher of the *Ithaca Journal* in upstate New York in 1981, becoming the first African-American woman to control the affairs of a mainstream daily newspaper. And Barbara Reynolds, who had been an *Ebony* editor and an urban-affairs writer for the *Chicago Tribune,* was featured as a columnist in *USA Today.*

Similar changes took place in television, though they did not extend to the higher levels of management. The first black journalist on television was Louis Lomax, a newspaperman and college teacher who entered the relatively new medium in 1958 at WNTA-TV in New York. The author of five books, Lomax contributed to mainstream magazines like *Harper's* and produced television documentaries before his death in an automobile accident in 1970.

Due to the visual nature of television, it often appeared that blacks were making more progress there than in print journalism. Some shifted easily from one medium to the other. In 1963, a year after Mal Goode integrated network television news, Bill Matney moved from the *Detroit News,* a general-circulation daily newspaper, to NBC, where he covered the White House for the network from 1970 to 1972. Yet no African American held a major position in television until 1978, when Max Robinson became the first of his race to become a regular co-anchor for a prime-time network newscast, heading the national desk in Chicago for the ABC nightly news. Robinson left the network five years later after being demoted, and died of AIDS in 1988, but he served as a role model for young blacks aspiring to careers in television news.

One of the most durable of network television newscasters was Ed Bradley, who joined CBS as a stringer in its Paris bureau in 1971, then became a White House correspondent in 1976. He later anchored the CBS *Sunday Night News,* was one of the chief correspondents for the top-rated *60 Minutes,* and hosted his own weekly newsmagazine program, *Street Stories.* Perhaps the most ubiquitous was Bryant Gumbel, a former sportswriter, who straddled the fence between journalism and entertainment when he became co-anchor of NBC's popular *Today* show in 1981, piloting that program into the 1990s while also hosting major network specials. Bernard Shaw carved out an important niche in the alternative outlet of cable television. After serving as a network correspondent for both ABC and CBS, he joined the Cable News Network at its inception in 1980 and became its anchor, gaining distinction as a hard-hitting interviewer on national and international issues.

Progress was uneven for women. By the late 1980s, it was common for local stations to feature African-American women as anchors, but only a few were able to break into the networks as correspondents, among them Lee Thornton, Norma Quarles, and Jacqueline Adams. Charlayne Hunter-Gault became one of the most visible woman journalists on television in 1978 when she became New York correspondent for the *McNeil-Lehrer Report,* the Public Broadcasting System's nightly news hour. Carole Simpson took the next major step in 1989, when she became the first African-American woman to anchor a network evening newscast, for ABC.

Some of these gains, in both print and broadcast journalism, were illusory, more cosmetic than substantive. While African Americans were involved in gathering and presenting the news, they seldom participated in the important decision-making process that determined what stories were to be covered and how they were to be played. A survey conducted by the American Society of Newspaper Editors in 1985 revealed that almost 95 percent of the journalists on daily newspapers were white and that 92 percent of the nation's newspapers did not have a single minority person in a news executive position. Fifty-four percent of the newspapers had no minority employees at all. While African Americans accounted for more than 11 percent of the population, only about 4 percent of newsroom employees were black.

Affairs were no better in broadcasting, where assignment editors, producers, and associate producers shape the news and the real power is held by executive producers and other top managers. In a 1982 survey of the nation's three networks, Michael Massing of the *Columbia Journalism Review* found that no blacks held high-level management positions. The highest-level job held by an African American at ABC was as an assignment editor on a nightly news show, while at CBS and NBC the top posts were held by bureau chiefs. At all the networks, about 5 percent of the producers and associate producers were black, many in lower-level jobs.

Due to the visual nature of television, it often appeared that blacks were making more progress there than in print journalism.

The efforts of black reporters often were overshadowed by general policies that resulted in a predominance of negative portrayals of African Americans in the media. While only 15 percent of the poor people in the United States in 1990 were black, newspaper and television coverage, in particular, perpetuated the impression that most criminals, prostitutes, drug addicts, welfare mothers, illiterates, and homeless persons were black. On the other hand, hardworking African Americans and those who constituted a large middle class were glossed over. For many mainstream viewers, the most astounding offshoot of the televised 1992 congressional hearings on the nomination of Clarence THOMAS to the U.S. Supreme Court was not the sensational nature of Anita Hill's accusations of sexual harassment by Thomas, but the fact that the American audience had a chance to observe several highly educated, well-spoken, and impeccably dressed witnesses who happened to be black.

There also were rumblings within the profession. Black reporters frequently complained about racist attitudes in newsrooms and sluggishness in promotions. The result was a series of lawsuits in the 1980s charging discrimination. The most notable outcome was in a case brought by four black reporters against the New York *Daily News.* In 1987, a federal court ruled on their behalf, charging that the newspaper had given them fewer promotions, worse assignments, and lower salaries than their white counterparts; they were granted sizable financial settlements.

Subtler problems also prevailed. Black journalists who had struggled to establish their credibility shuddered in 1981 when Janet Cooke, a black reporter for the *Washington Post,* admitted that she had fabricated a story about an eight-year-old drug addict that had won her a Pulitzer Prize. Cooke returned the prize, but the incident haunted black journalists, who feared that all of them subsequently would be suspect, which would not have been the case had a white journalist engaged in a similar breach of ethics.

There also were points where conflicting loyalties came into play. When the Rev. Jesse JACKSON sought the Democratic presidential nomination in 1984, his quest for broad-based support crumbled when the *Washington Post* reported that Jackson had referred to Jews as "hymies" and New York City as "Hymietown." The effect of this disclosure was all the more profound because it had been made by a black reporter, Milton Coleman. The incident, more than any other, caused many black journalists to consider whether there might be times when they should disobey the rule of objectivity in reporting the news without regard to the effect it might have on their own people. This question was addressed by Juan Williams of the *Washington Post* in the paper's July 16, 1989, edition, when he railed at criticism from black readers who accused him of being a traitor because he wrote articles that were critical of blacks, including the city's mayor, Marion Barry. Williams contended that black journalists were obligated to ask hard questions of black politicians, holding them to an absolute standard.

Beyond the problems of professional ethics, black journalists frequently found themselves isolated in the newsrooms where they worked. In the old days of the black press, most journalists had known each other, or at least had been aware of each other through a tightly woven network. They also had been devoted to a common cause: to improve the situation of their people. But modern professionals were scattered, often building careers as specialists in areas far removed from racial topics.

Fragmentation and a collective sense of isolation, along with concern for their overall effectiveness within the mainstream, led to the formation of the National Association of Black Journalists (NABJ) in Washington, D.C., on December 12, 1975. While black journalists' groups had sprung up and often withered away in various cities, this became the largest and most successful national organization, especially in terms of developing local affiliates. By 1992, the NABJ had a membership of more than two thousand, of whom 60 percent were in print and 40 percent in broadcasting. Unlike other journalism organizations, it limited membership to those involved in gathering and disseminating the news, excluding those in public relations.

Yet certain fundamental questions prevailed. Black journalists in the mainstream realized that they were merely employees, for the most part, having little power in the institutions where they worked. Meanwhile, a tide of conservatism had swept over the nation in the 1980s during the Reagan and Bush administrations, undermining affirmative-action policies and threatening to cancel out previous gains. As African Americans in general were revisited by old woes of economic instability, family deterioration, and escalating prejudice, it seemed that the clock had been turned back to an earlier time. Furthermore, black communities were beset with violent crime, drug abuse, teen pregnancy, and social disorganization. Some of these problems could not be remedied by the government and had to be addressed by blacks themselves. In earlier periods, the black press had provided a forum for honest discussion of black-on-black problems, but these publications no longer had a broad enough circulation base to be effective. The popular black magazines sometimes addressed these issues, but their major thrust was elsewhere. The challenge facing committed African-American journalists, as the twentieth century neared its end, was how they could attain greater power within the mainstream while, perhaps, beginning to build institutions of their own.

BIBLIOGRAPHY

Bennett, Lerone, Jr. *Before the Mayflower: A History of Black America.* 5th ed. Chicago, 1982.

Berger, Warren. "One Year and Counting: Wilmer Ames and 'Emerge.' " *Folio* (December 1, 1990): 35.

Black Press Handbook 1977: Sesquicentennial 1827–1977. Washington, D.C., 1977.

Britt, Donna. "The Relentlessly Upbeat Woman behind Spirit of Essence." *Los Angeles Times,* June 3, 1990, p. E14.

Buni, Andrew. *Robert L. Vann of the Pittsburgh Courier: Politics and Black Journalism.* Pittsburgh, 1974.

Carmody, Deidre. "Black Magazines See Sales in Unity." *New York Times,* May 4, 1992, p. D9.

Cohen, Roger. "Black Media Giant's Fire Still Burns." *New York Times,* November 19, 1990, p. D8.

Dann, Martin E., ed. *The Black Press 1827–1890.* New York, 1971.

Dates, Jannette, L., and William Barlow, eds. *Split Image: African Americans in the Mass Media.* Washington, D.C., 1990.

Ebony. "Negroes on White Newspapers." November 1955.

Gilliam, Dorothy. "What Do Black Journalists Want?" *Columbia Journalism Review* (May/June 1972): 47.

Hicks, Jonathan P. "More New Magazines, and These Beckon to Black Readers." *New York Times,* August 5, 1990, p. 20.

Hogan, Lawrence D. *A Black News Service: The Associated Negro Press and Claude Barnett, 1919–1945.* Cranberry, N.J., 1984.

Johnson, John H., with Lerone Bennett, Jr. *Succeeding against the Odds.* New York, 1989.
Jones, Alex S. "Oakland Publisher in Uphill Struggle." *New York Times,* June 5, 1985, p. A16.
———. "Sense of Muscle for Black Journalists." *New York Times,* August 21, 1989, p. D1.
LaBrie, Henry III. *Perspectives of the Black Press: 1974.* Kennebunkport, Maine, 1974.
Michaelson, Judith. "Black Journalists Remember Robinson as Role Model." *Los Angeles Times,* December 23, 1988, pt. 6, p. 36.
The Negro Handbook. Chicago, 1966.
Noble, Gil. *Black Is the Color of My TV Tube.* New York, 1981.
Ottley, Roi. *The Lonely Warrior: The Life and Times of Robert S. Abbott.* Chicago, 1955.
Polski, Harry A., and James Williams, eds. *The Negro Almanac: A Reference Work on the Afro-American,* 5th ed. New York, 1987.
Quintanilla, Michael. "Blacks Seek Changes in Newsrooms." *Los Angeles Times,* August 3, 1990, p. E1.
Report of the National Advisory Commission on Civil Disorders. New York, 1968.
Scardino, Albert. "Black Papers Retain a Local Role." *New York Times,* July 24, 1989, p. D1.
Shaw, David. "Critics Cite a Need to Lead in Hiring Minorities." *Los Angeles Times,* December 13, 1990, p. A1.
———. "Negative News and Little Else." *Los Angeles Times,* December 11, 1990, p. A1.
———. "Newspapers Struggling to Raise Minority Coverage." *Los Angeles Times,* December 12, 1990, p. A1.
Smith, Roger W. "Black Journalists Deplore Pace of New Media Hires." *Newsday,* March 19, 1988, p. 11.
Smythe, Mabel, ed. *The Black American Reference Book.* New York, 1976.
Strader, Jim. "Black on Black." *Washington Journalism Review* (March 1992): 33–36.
Wells, Ida B. *Crusade for Justice: The Autobiography of Ida B. Wells.* Edited by Alfreda M. Duster. Chicago, 1970.
Williams, Juan. "Being Black, Being Fair; Journalists Have to 'Do the Right Thing,' Too." *Washington Post,* July 16, 1989, p. B1.
Wolseley, Roland E. *The Black Press, U.S.A.* Ames, Iowa, 1971.

— PHYL GARLAND

JUDAISM

Estimates of the number of black people in the United States who consider themselves Jews or Hebrews range from 40,000 to 500,000. These people can be divided into three groups: individuals, such as Sammy Davis, Jr., and Julius Lester, who convert to Judaism and join predominantly white congregations—often as a result of intermarriage; African Americans who trace their Jewish heritage back to slavery and who worship in either black or white synagogues; and blacks whose attraction to Judaism is based on a racial identification with the biblical Hebrews.

The third group is by far the largest, but it is made up of many independent denominations that have a wide variety of beliefs and practices. The best known are the Black Jews of Harlem, the Temple Beth-El congregations, the Nation of Yahweh, the Original Hebrew Israelite Nation, the Israeli School of Universal Practical Knowledge, the Church of God, and the Nubian Islamic Hebrews. Reconstructionist Black Jews and Rastafarians are two groups whose relationship to Judaism or Hebrewism is so limited that they are best thought of as movements basically rooted in Christianity that have an affinity to the Old Testament and Jewish symbols.

Each of the major groups is unique and will be discussed separately. However, they generally have the following characteristics in common: They believe that the ancient Hebrews were black people, that they are their descendants, and that their immediate ancestors were forcibly converted from Judaism to Christianity during slavery. In addition, they believe that they are not converts to Judaism but have discovered or returned to their true religion. On the other hand, they believe that white Jews are either converts to their way of life, descendants of one of the biblical people whom they believe started the white race (Edomites, Canaanites, Japhites, or lepers), or that they are imposters altogether. This is the principle reason why some groups consider the term "Jew" anathema and insist on the biblical terms Hebrew or Israelite, or more commonly, Hebrew Israelite. They believe that the enslavement of and discrimination against African Americans were predicted in the Bible and are therefore a combination of divine punishment upon the children of Israel for their sins and the result of the blatant aggression of white people. Hebrew Israelites are messianic and believe that when the messiah comes, retribution will be handed down upon all sinners—but particularly upon white people for their oppression of people of color. Beyond these similarities—which a few Hebrew Israelites strongly oppose—the groups can differ widely according to the degree to which they follow rabbinic traditions, use Hebrew, conduct services, follow dress codes, and incorporate Christian or Islamic beliefs into their theology.

There have been three main phases in the use of elements of the Jewish religion in African-American worship. From exposure to evangelical Protestantism in the early nineteenth century, many African Americans identified with the enslavement, emancipation, and nation-building of the Hebrews as depicted in the Bible. Old Testament imagery was a staple of sermons and spirituals. The best-known of the latter is undoubtedly "Go Down, Moses," in which the release of the Hebrews from Egyptian captivity is seen as a sign of the redemption of blacks from slavery. This connection to the Jewish people, often strengthened by connections to Pan-African movements such as the one led by Marcus GARVEY, provided the impetus for more formal identification as Jews, often outside of a Christian context, in the late nineteenth and early twentieth centuries. Since the 1960s, another period of active black nationalism, there has been renewed identification with elements of the Jewish religion by a number of African-American religious groups. Many of these groups are quite eclectic in their theology and religious borrowings, and are often hostile to mainstream Judaism.

The Black Jews of Harlem is one of the oldest, largest, and best-known Hebrew Israelite groups in the United States. The denomination was founded in New York City by Rabbi Arnold J. Ford (1877–1935) and Rabbi Wentworth Arthur Matthew (1892–1973). Ford was the musical director of Garvey's UNIVERSAL NEGRO IMPROVEMENT ASSOCIATION (UNIA). The Black Jews based their nationalism of Ethiopianism on the belief that biblical prophecies about Ethiopia, notably Psalm 68:31 "Ethiopia shall soon stretch out her hands," referred to Ethiopia in connection with the regathering of the Children of Israel as applied specifically to black people. To achieve this Ford tried to create a Black Jewish denomination based on beliefs and customs he learned from European Jews. During the early period the group used the term Ethiopian Hebrew rather than Hebrew Israelite. Also, whereas Ford and Matthew emphatically believed that the ancient Hebrews were black, they were less certain about the origins of white Jews and would sometimes refer to them as "our fairer brothers."

The Black Jews of Harlem is one of the oldest, largest, and best-known Hebrew Israelite groups in the United States.

In 1923 Ford opened a congregation called Beth B'nai Abraham (House of the Children of Abraham) for black people in Harlem. Rabbi Matthew, who had founded The Commandment Keepers Congregation in Harlem four years earlier, became Ford's student. In 1933, Ford ordained Matthew before leaving for Ethiopia where he lived the remainder of his life. Matthew quickly instituted the Jewish knowledge he gained from Ford into his services. In the late 1940s he created the Ethiopian Hebrew Rabbinical College in New York City where he trained and ordained twenty-two other rabbis who carried their blend of black nationalist and orthodox European Judaism to black communities throughout the United States and the Caribbean. By the 1990s, this community was being led by two students of Matthew: Rabbi Levi Ben Levy, who is the chief rabbi of the Israelite Board of Rabbis, and Rabbi Yhoshua Ben Yahonatan, who is the president of the Israelite Council. The rabbis and congregation affiliated with these bodies have limited but cordial relations with mainstream white Jewish congregations in New York. The Black Jews generally conduct their services in both Hebrew and English, observe Jewish holidays such as Hanukkah and Purim, the high holy days, and ceremonies such as Bar and Bat Mitzvah. By the early 1990s, the size of the group was probably less than five thousand, though higher estimates are sometimes given.

The Temple Beth-El congregations, also known as the Church of God and Saints of Christ (CGSC), were founded by William Saunders Crowdy (1847–1908). Crowdy was born a slave and fought in the Civil War. In 1893 he had a prophetic vision on his farm in Guthrie, Okla. that told him to start a new church that had no affiliation with any religious denomination. The specific doctrines of the church evolved over time and were based on Crowdy's revelations which he called the "Seven Keys." Crowdy taught that black people were part of the "lost tribes of Israel" and that the Hebraic Laws of the Old Testament, such as Passover, were to be obeyed. Unlike the Black Jews of Harlem, Crowdy did not abandon the use of the New Testament or a belief in Jesus Christ, and he continued practices such as baptism and ritual foot washing. In 1896 he founded his first church in Lawrence, Kans. Two years later the first CGSC general assembly was held. By 1900 the church had 5,000 members. After his death in 1908 the church suffered a split. As a whole, the church was at its height in 1936 when there were over 213 tabernacles in the United States. By the 1990s the number of tabernacles had declined to fifty-three with seven branches in South Africa. Over the years the Christian component of the Beth-El tabernacle has diminished and the Jewish elements have been augmented. The Temple's national headquarters is in Philadelphia, Pa. and its international headquarters is on a 500-acre farm in Suffolk, Va. It has an estimated membership of 38,000.

The Church of God was founded by Prophet F. S. Cherry. The anthropologist Arthur Huff Fauset describes this group in *Black Gods of the Metropolis* (1944). Fauset reports that this group was located at 2132 Nicholas Street in Philadelphia, Pa. The church had less than 300 members at its founding, and there was no mention of affiliate congregations. All that is known about Prophet Cherry is that he was born in the South and worked as a seaman and on the railroads, which allowed him to travel throughout the United States and to many parts of the world. He was self-educated and taught his followers that they were the original Hebrews. They believed that Jesus was the mes-

ployment rate remained constant throughout 1941 while the white rate fell. That year, five hundred people marched against the exclusionary policy, but it was not until after March 1942, when thirteen thousand blacks met in the Municipal Auditorium to demand an end to discrimination, that the Fair Employment Practices Committee was able to force black hiring. During the war years, Fellowship House, an interracial living center sponsored by liberal whites of the Fellowship of Reconciliation (FOR) came to the city. FOR members began a small chapter of the CONGRESS OF RACIAL EQUALITY (CORE), and organized a few successful protests against segregated facilities. In 1945 the city's blacks united to elect an African-American state representative, Democrat James McKinley Neal, who served several terms.

The first small victories against discrimination came in 1951, when the city council admitted blacks to public parks and buildings, and organized a Commission on Human Relations. The same year, however, a judge refused to admit black students to a superior white school on the grounds that differences in physical plant did not negate "substantial equality." Many black parents kept their children at home (a practice tolerated by truant officers) rather than send them to overcrowded black schools. Integration finally began in 1954, after the U.S. Supreme Court's BROWN V. BOARD OF EDUCATION OF TOPEKA, KANSAS decision.

In 1960 sit-ins began in Kansas City, sponsored by an intergroup Public Accommodations Movement. While most downtown restaurants agreed to serve African Americans by the end of the year, the city council refused to pass an ordinance until 1963, and protests continued through passage of the Civil Rights Act of 1964. Throughout the decade, race relations remained tense in the face of white intransigence. Radical black groups such as the BLACK PANTHERS organized in the city, offering free school breakfast programs. In April 1968, following the assassination of the Rev. Dr. Martin Luther King, Jr., city authorities refused to close schools for a day of remembrance, although schools in nearby Kansas City, Kans., were closed. Three hundred black students marched on City Hall and were met by police with tear gas. That night, rioting broke out in black areas. Nervous white officials responded to the violence by sending in almost three thousand state troopers and members of the National Guard to augment the police force. By the end of the evening, fifty-seven people had been wounded and 275 people arrested.

Since the 1960s, African Americans in Kansas City have made significant political gains. Freedom, Inc., a political organization founded in 1962 by businessmen Leon Jordan and Bruce Watkins, organized the black vote over the following years and helped elect city council members, state legislators, judges, and others. Watkins ran unsuccessfully for mayor in 1979, but his strong finish demonstrated black community political power. In 1982 the city's district elected its first black U.S. representative, Alan Wheat. In 1991 Kansas City elected Emanuel Cleaver, a Methodist minister and onetime black radical, as the city's first African American mayor. In tribute to the city's historical role as regional political and cultural center, civil rights activist Horace Peterson III opened an archive/museum, the Black Archives of Mid-America, in 1974.

Despite these accomplishments, blacks in Kansas City continue to face many difficulties. Unemployment remains high, despite the efforts of organizations such as the Black Economic Union, founded in 1967, to stimulate investment in black business, and the city's economic base has been damaged by white flight and deindustrialization. School segregation has been a continuing problem. In 1984 a desegregation plan was implemented which created a system of magnet schools to induce whites to attend predominantly black schools, and the city council increased taxes to pay for them. Still, studies in the 1990s indicated that the magnet schools were not increasing the educational opportunities of most black students, who were doing worse, not better. In 1990 the U.S. Supreme Court, upholding a Federal Appeals court ruling, ordered Missouri to pay for the education of one-fourth of Kansas City's black students at predominantly white suburban schools. However, it will be many years before the full effects of the decision are clear.

BIBLIOGRAPHY

Brown, A. Theodore and Lyle W. Dorsett. *K.C.: A History of Kansas City, Missouri.* Boulder, Colo., 1978.

Bruce, Janet. *The Kansas City Monarchs: Champions of Black Baseball.* Lawrence, Kans., 1983.

Greene, Lorenzo, Gary F. Kremer, and Antonio F. Holland. *Missouri's Black Heritage.* Rev. ed., Columbia, Mo., 1992.

Martin, Asa Earl. *Our Negro Population: A Sociological Study of the Negroes of Kansas City, Missouri.* Kansas City, 1913. Reprint. New York, 1969.

Russell, Ross. *Jazz Style in Kansas City and the Southwest.* Berkeley, Calif., 1971.

Thomas, Tracy and Walt Bodine. *Right Here in River City: A Portrait of Kansas City.* Garden City, N.Y., 1976.

— GREG ROBINSON

KERNER REPORT

The Kerner Report was the result of a seven-month study by the National Commission on Civil Disorders to pinpoint the cause of racial violence in American cities during the late 1960s. The eleven-member panel was better known as the Kerner Commission, after its chairman, Gov. Otto Kerner of Illinois.

President Lyndon Johnson appointed the commission on July 28, 1967, in the wake of large-scale urban rioting in the United States between 1965 and 1967, which resulted in several deaths and injuries as well as widespread property damage. The commission was charged with tracing the specific events that led up to the violence, finding general reasons for the worsening racial atmosphere in the country, and suggesting solutions to prevent future disorders.

The Kerner Report was submitted to Johnson in February 1968. It concluded, in part, that the violence had its roots in the frustration and anger of poor urban blacks concerning such problems as high unemployment, discrimination, poor schools and health care, and police bias.

Stating that discrimination and segregation were deeply embedded in American society, the report warned that America was "moving toward two societies, one black, one white—separate and unequal." The report recommended a massive national commitment to sweeping reforms to improve education, housing, employment opportunities, and city services in poor black urban areas.

The Rev. Dr. Martin Luther KING, Jr., called the report "a physician's warning of approaching death, with a prescription for life." The prescription was, however, largely ignored. Many whites thought the report placed too much blame for the riots on societal problems and white racism, and not enough on the lawlessness of black rioters. Johnson accepted the report but did not support its conclusions. Few of the report's recommendations were ever implemented.

BIBLIOGRAPHY

Carson, Clayborne, ed. *Eyes on the Prize: America's Civil Rights Years.* New York, 1989.

O'Reilly, Kenneth. *Racial Matters: The FBI's Secret File on Black Americans, 1960–1972.* New York, 1989.

– RENE SKELTON

KING, CORETTA SCOTT

Coretta Scott King (April 27, 1927–), civil rights activist. Born in Marion, Ala., a rural farming community, Coretta Scott attended Lincoln High School, a local private school for black students run by the American Missionary Association. After graduating in 1945, she received a scholarship to study music and education at Antioch College in Yellow Springs, Ohio. Trained in voice and piano, she made her concert debut in 1948 in Springfield, Ohio, as a soloist at the Second Baptist Church. Scott officially withdrew from Antioch in 1952 after entering the New England Conservatory of Music in 1951 to continue her music studies.

During her first year at the conservatory, she met the Rev. Dr. Martin Luther KING, Jr., who was a doctoral candidate at Boston University's school of theology. The two were married on June 18, 1953, despite Martin Luther King, Sr.'s opposition to the match because of his disapproval of the Scott family's rural background and his hope that his son would marry into one of Atlanta's elite black families. The couple returned to Boston to continue their studies. The following year, Coretta Scott King received a bachelor's degree in music (Mus.B.) from the New England Conservatory of Music, and in September the two moved to Montgomery, Ala., despite Coretta King's misgivings about returning to the racial hostility of Alabama.

Although Coretta King aspired to become a professional singer, she devoted most of her time to raising her children and working closely with her husband after he had assumed the presidency of the Montgomery Improvement Association in 1955. She participated in many major events of the CIVIL RIGHTS MOVEMENT along with her husband, both in the United States and overseas, as well as having to endure the hardships resulting from her husband's position, including his frequent arrests and the bombing of their Montgomery home in 1956.

Early in 1960, the King family moved to Atlanta when King became copastor of Ebenezer Baptist Church with his father. Later that year, Coretta King aided in her husband's release from a Georgia prison by appealing to presidential candidate John F. Kennedy to intervene on his behalf. In 1962, Coretta King became a voice instructor at Morris Brown College in Atlanta, but she remained primarily involved in sharing the helm of the civil rights struggle with her husband. She led marches, directed fund raising for the SOUTHERN CHRISTIAN LEADERSHIP CONFERENCE and gave a series of "freedom concerts" that combined singing, lecturing, and poetry reading. A strong proponent of disarmament, King served as a delegate to the Disarmament Conference in Geneva, Switzerland, in 1962, and in 1966 and 1967 was a cosponsor of the Mobilization to End the War in Vietnam. In 1967, after an extended leave of absence, she received her bachelor of arts degree in music and elementary education from Antioch College.

On April 8, 1968, only four days after the Rev. Dr. Martin Luther King, Jr., was assassinated in Memphis, Coretta King substituted for her deceased husband in a march on behalf of sanitation workers that he had been scheduled to lead. Focusing her energies on preserving her husband's memory and continuing his struggle, Coretta King also took part in the Poor People's Washington Campaign in the nation's capital during June 1968, serving as the keynote speaker at the main rally at the Lincoln Memorial. In 1969 she helped found and served as president of the Atlanta-based Martin Luther King, Jr. Center for Nonviolent Social Change, a center devoted to teaching young people the importance of nonviolence and to preserving the memory of her husband. In 1969 she also published her autobiography, *My Life with Martin Luther King, Jr.*, and in 1971 she received an honorary doctorate in music from the New England Conservatory.

In 1983 Coretta King led the twentieth-anniversary march on Washington and the following year was elected chairperson of the commission to declare King's birthday a national holiday, which was observed for the first time in 1986. She was active in the struggle to end apartheid, touring South Africa and meeting with Winnie Mandela in 1986 and returning there in 1990 to meet the recently released African National Congress leader, Nelson Mandela.

Coretta King has received numerous awards for her participation in the struggle for civil rights, including the outstanding citizenship award from the Montgomery Improvement Association in 1959 and the Distinguished Achievement Award from the National Organization of Colored Women's Clubs in 1962. As of 1993, she retained her position as chief executive officer of the Martin Luther King, Jr. Center for Nonviolent Change, having resigned the presidency to her son, Dexter Scott King, in 1989. As she has done for many years, Coretta Scott King continues to press for the worldwide recognition of civil rights and human rights.

BIBLIOGRAPHY

Branch, Taylor. *Parting the Waters: America in the King Years, 1954–63.* New York, 1988.

King, Coretta Scott. *My Life with Martin Luther King, Jr.* New York, 1969.

– LOUISE P. MAXWELL

KING, MARTIN LUTHER, JR.

Martin Luther King, Jr. (January 15, 1929–April 4, 1968), minister and civil rights leader. Born Michael King, Jr., in Atlanta on January 15, 1929, he was the first son of a Baptist minister and the grandson of a Baptist minister, and his forebears exemplified the African-American social gospel tradition that would shape his career as a reformer. King's maternal grandfather, the Rev. A. D. Williams, had transformed Ebenezer Baptist Church, a block down the street from his grandson's childhood home, into one of Atlanta's most prominent black churches. In 1906, Williams had joined such figures as Atlanta University scholar W. E. B. DU BOIS and African Methodist Episcopal (AME) bishop Henry McNeal Turner to form the Georgia Equal Rights League, an organization that condemned lynching, segregation in public transportation, and the exclusion of black men from juries and state militia. In 1917, Williams helped found the Atlanta branch of the NAACP, later serving as the chapter's president. Williams's subsequent campaign to register and mobilize black voters prodded white leaders to agree to construct new public schools for black children.

After Williams's death in 1931, his son-in-law, Michael King, Sr., also combined religious and political leadership. He became president of Atlanta's NAACP, led voter-registration marches during the 1930s, and spearheaded a movement to equalize the salaries of black public school teachers with those of their white counterparts. In 1934, King, Sr.—perhaps inspired by a visit to the birthplace of Protestantism in Germany—changed his name and that of his son to Martin Luther King.

Despite the younger King's admiration for his father's politically active ministry, he was initially reluctant to accept his inherited calling. Experiencing religious doubts during his early teenage years, he decided to become a minister only after he came into contact with religious leaders who combined theological sophistication with social gospel advocacy. At Morehouse College, which King attended from 1944 to 1948, the college's president, Benjamin E. MAYS, encouraged him to believe that Christianity should become a force for progressive social change. A course on the Bible taught by Morehouse professor George Kelsey exposed King to theological scholarship. After deciding to become a minister, King increased his understanding of liberal Christian thought while attending Crozer Theological Seminary in Pennsylvania. Compiling an outstanding academic record at Crozer, he deepened his understanding of modern religious scholarship and eventually identified himself with theological personalism. King later wrote that this philosophical position strengthened his belief in a personal God and provided him with a "metaphysical basis for the dignity and worth of all human personality."

At Boston University, where King began doctoral studies in systematic theology in 1951, his exploration of theological scholarship was combined with extensive interactions with the Boston African-American community. He met regularly with other black students in an informal group called the Dialectical Society. Often invited to give sermons in Boston-area churches, he acquired a reputation as a powerful preacher, drawing ideas from African-American Baptist traditions as well as theological and philosophical writings. The academic papers he wrote at Boston displayed little originality, but King's scholarly training provided him with a talent that would prove useful in his future leadership activities: an exceptional ability to draw upon a wide range of theological and philosophical texts to express his views with force and precision. During his stay in Boston, King also met and began dating Coretta Scott, then a student at the New England Conservatory of Music. On June 18, 1953, the two students were married in Marion, Ala., where Scott's family lived. During the following academic year, King began work on his dissertation, which was completed during the spring of 1955.

King acquired a reputation as a powerful preacher, drawing ideas from African-American Baptist traditions as well as theological and philosophical writings.

Soon after King accepted his first pastorate at Dexter Avenue Baptist Church in Montgomery, Ala., he had an unexpected opportunity to utilize the insights he had gained from his childhood experiences and academic training. After NAACP official Rosa PARKS was jailed for refusing to give up her bus seat to a white passenger, King accepted the post of president of the Montgomery Improvement Association, which was formed to coordinate a boycott of Montgomery's buses. In his role as the primary spokesman of the boycott, King gradually forged a distinctive protest strategy that involved the mobilization of black churches, utilization of Gandhian methods of nonviolent protest, and skillful appeals for white support.

After the U. S. Supreme Court outlawed Alabama bus segregation laws in late 1956, King quickly rose to national prominence as a result of his leadership role in a successful boycott movement. In 1957, he became the founding president of the SOUTHERN CHRISTIAN LEADERSHIP CONFERENCE (SCLC), formed to coordinate civil rights activities throughout the South. Publication of King's *Stride Toward Freedom: The Montgomery Story* (1958) further contributed to his rapid emergence as a nationally known civil rights leader. Seeking to forestall the fears of NAACP leaders that his organization might draw away followers and financial support, King acted cautiously during the late 1950s. Instead of immediately seeking to stimulate mass desegregation protests in the South, he stressed the goal of achieving black voting rights when he addressed an audience at the 1957 Prayer Pilgrimage for Freedom. During 1959, he increased his understanding of Gandhian ideas during a month-long visit to India as a guest of Prime Minister Jawaharlal Nehru. Early in 1960, King moved his family—which now included two children, Yolanda Denise (born 1955) and Martin Luther III (born 1957)—to Atlanta in order to be nearer SCLC's headquarters in that city and to become copastor, with his father, of Ebenezer Baptist Church. The Kings' third child, Dexter Scott, was born in 1961; their fourth, Bernice Albertine, was born in 1963.

Soon after King's arrival in Atlanta, the lunch counter sit-in movement, led by students, spread throughout the South and brought into existence a new organization, the STUDENT NONVIOLENT COORDINATING COMMITTEE (SNCC). SNCC activists admired King but also pushed him toward greater militancy. In October 1960, his arrest during a student-initiated protest in Atlanta became an issue in the national presidential campaign when Democratic candidate John F. Kennedy intervened to secure his release from jail. Kennedy's action contributed to his narrow victory in the November election. During 1961 and 1962, King's differences with SNCC activists widened during a sustained protest movement in Albany, Georgia. King was arrested twice during demonstrations organized by the Albany Movement, but when he left jail and ultimately left Albany without achieving a victory, his standing among activists declined.

King reasserted his preeminence within the African-American freedom struggle through his leadership of the BIRMINGHAM, ALABAMA campaign of 1963. Initiated by the SCLC in January, the Birmingham demonstrations were the most massive civil rights protests that had occurred up to that time. With the assistance of Fred Shuttlesworth and other local black leaders, and without much competition from SNCC or other civil rights groups, SCLC officials were able to orchestrate the Birmingham protests to achieve maximum national impact. During May, televised pictures of police using dogs and fire hoses against demonstrators aroused a national outcry. This vivid evidence of the obstinacy of Birmingham officials, combined with Alabama Governor George C. Wallace's attempt to block the entry of black students at the University of Alabama, prompted President John F. Kennedy to introduce major new civil rights legislation. King's unique ability to appropriate ideas from the Bible, the Constitution, and other canonical texts manifested itself when he defended the black protests in a widely quoted letter, written while he was jailed in Birmingham.

King's speech at the August 28, 1963, March on Washington, attended by over 200,000 people, provides another powerful demonstration of his singular ability to draw on widely accepted American ideals in order to promote black objectives. At the end of his prepared remarks, which announced that African Americans wished to cash the "promissory note" signified in the words of the Constitution and the Declaration of Independence, King began his most quoted oration: "So I say to you, my friends, that even though we must face the difficulties of today and tomorrow, I still have a dream. It is a dream deeply rooted in the American dream that one day this nation will rise up and live out the true meaning of its creed—we hold these truths to be self-evident, that all men are created equal." He appropriated the familiar words of the song "My Country 'Tis of Thee" before concluding: "And when we allow freedom to ring, when we let it ring from every village and hamlet, from every state and city, we will be able to speed up that day when all of God's children—black men and white men, Jews and Gentiles, Catholics and Protestants—will be able to join hands and to sing in the words of the old Negro spiritual, 'Free at last, free at last, thank God Almighty, we are free at last.' "

Martin Luther King, Jr., with schoolchildren in Grenada, Miss., Fall 1966. (© Bob Fitch/Black Star)

After the march on Washington, King's fame and popularity were at their height. Named *Time* magazine's Man of the Year at the end of 1963, he was awarded the Nobel Peace Prize in December 1964. The acclaim he received prompted FBI director J. Edgar Hoover to step up his effort to damage King's reputation by leaking information gained through surreptitious means about King's ties with former communists and his extramarital affairs.

King's last successful civil rights campaign was a series of demonstrations in Alabama that were intended to dramatize the denial of black voting rights in the deep South. Demonstrations began in Selma, Ala., early in 1965 and reached a turning point on March 7, when a group of demonstrators began a march from Selma to the state capitol in Montgomery. King was in Atlanta when state policemen, carrying out Governor Wallace's order to stop the march, attacked with tear gas and clubs soon after the procession crossed the Edmund Pettus Bridge on the outskirts of Selma. The police assault on the marchers quickly increased national support for the voting rights campaign. King arrived in Selma to join several thousand movement sympathizers, black and white. President Lyndon B. Johnson reacted to the Alabama protests by introducing new voting rights legislation, which would become the Voting Rights Act of 1965. Demonstrators were finally able to obtain a court order allowing the march to take place, and on March 25 King addressed the arriving protestors from the steps of the capitol in Montgomery.

After the successful voting rights campaign, King was unable to garner similar support for his effort to confront the problems of northern urban blacks. Early in 1966 he launched a major campaign in Chicago, moving into an apartment in the black ghetto. As he shifted the focus of his activities north, however, he discovered that the tactics used in the South were not as effective elsewhere. He encountered formidable opposition from Mayor Richard Daley, and was unable to mobilize Chicago's economically and ideologically diverse black populace. He was stoned by angry whites in the suburb of Cicero when he led a march against racial discrimination in housing. Despite numerous well-publicized protests, the Chicago campaign resulted in no significant gains and undermined King's reputation as an effective leader.

His status was further damaged when his strategy of nonviolence came under renewed attack from blacks following a major outbreak of urban racial violence in Los Angeles during August 1965. When civil rights activists reacted to the shooting of James Meredith by organizing a March against Fear through Mississippi, King was forced on the defensive as Stokely CARMICHAEL and other militants put forward the Black Power slogan. Although King refused to condemn the militants who opposed him, he criticized the new slogan as vague and divisive. As his influence among blacks lessened, he also alienated many white moderate supporters by publicly opposing United States intervention in the Vietnam War. After he delivered a major antiwar speech at New York's Riverside Church on April 4, 1967, many of the northern newspapers that had once supported his civil rights efforts condemned his attempt to link civil rights to the war issue.

In November 1967, King announced the formation of a Poor People's Campaign designed to prod the nation's leaders to deal with the problem of poverty. Early in 1968, he and other SCLC workers began to recruit poor people and antipoverty activists to come to Washington, D.C., to lobby on behalf of improved antipoverty programs. This effort was in its early stages when King became involved in a sanitation workers' strike in Memphis. On March 28, as he led thousands of sanitation workers and sympathizers on a march through downtown Memphis, violence broke out and black youngsters looted stores. The violent outbreak led to more criticisms of King's entire antipoverty strategy. He returned to Memphis for the last time early in April. Addressing an audience at Bishop Charles H. Mason Temple on April 3, he sought to revive his flagging movement by acknowledging: "We've got some difficult days ahead. But it doesn't matter with me now. Because I've been to the mountaintop. . . . And I've seen the promised land. I may not get there with you. But I want you to know tonight that we, as a people, will get to the promised land."

The following evening, King was assassinated as he stood on a balcony of the Lorraine Motel in Memphis. A white segregationist, James Earl Ray, was later convicted of the crime. The Poor People's Campaign continued for a few months but did not achieve its objectives. King became an increasingly revered figure after his death, however, and many of his critics ultimately acknowledged his considerable accomplishments. In 1969 his widow, Coretta Scott King, established the Martin Luther King, Jr., Center for Nonviolent Social Change, in Atlanta, to carry on his work. In 1986, a national holiday was established to honor his birth.

BIBLIOGRAPHY

Baldwin, Lewis V. *There is a Balm in Gilead: The Cultural Roots of Martin Luther King, Jr.* Minneapolis, 1991.

Branch, Taylor. *Parting the Waters: America in the King Years, 1954–63.* New York, 1988.

Garrow, David J. *Bearing the Cross: Martin Luther King and the Southern Christian Leadership Conference.* New York, 1986.

King, Coretta Scott. *My Life with Martin Luther King, Jr.* New York, 1969.

King, Martin Luther, Sr., and Clayton Riley. *Daddy King: An Autobiography.* New York, 1980.

Lewis, David Levering. *King: A Biography.* Urbana, Ill., 1978.

Oates, Steven B. *Let the Trumpet Sound: The Life of Martin Luther King, Jr.* New York, 1982.

Reddick, L. D. *Crusader Without Violence: A Biography of Martin Luther King, Jr.* New York, 1959.

— CLAYBORNE CARSON

KOREAN WAR

When North Korea invaded South Korea on June 25, 1950, the second anniversary of President Harry S. Truman's executive order integrating the races in the armed forces was fast approaching. In the order of July 26, 1948, Truman established the President's Committee on Equal Treatment and Opportunity in the Armed Services, headed by Charles T. Fahy, an attorney and future federal judge, which reviewed and approved the integration plans of the armed forces. Once the Fahy Committee granted approval, the President let each service carry out its program with a minimum of interference.

The Korean War, which ended on July 27, 1953, did not require a mobilization of manpower, industry, and resources on the scale of World War II. Limited though it was, the Korean conflict demonstrated that racial segregation resulted in the wasteful misassignment of men and women and undermined the efficient conduct of the war. The armed services discovered that they could no longer delay compliance with the two-year-old order calling for equal treatment and opportunity regardless of race.

The impact of the war on race relations in civil society proved less decisive, because a civil rights movement, which for the present used the courtroom as a battlefield, was gathering momentum. As a consequence of the CIVIL RIGHTS MOVEMENT, the Supreme Court in 1954 decided *Brown* v. *Board of Education of Topeka* and overturned the principle of separate-but-equal, the legal foundation upon which racial segregation rested.

The Air Force

When the Air Force became independent of the Army in September 1947, Lieut. Gen. Idwal W. Edwards, a member of the Air Staff, became concerned that, in the event of wartime expansion, poorly educated blacks, products of a segregated and second-rate educational system, would not fit easily into a service heavily dependent on advanced technology. Yet Lieut. Col. Jack Marr, investigating race relations for Edwards, discovered a cadre of African-American pilots, technicians, and administrators just as competent as their white counterparts. To promote efficiency, Edwards proposed that the Air Force abolish segregation and let blacks and whites compete for all assignments, so that only the best would survive, regardless of race. Before President Truman issued his order, Edwards sold this idea to Gen. Carl Spaatz, the first Air Force Chief of Staff, and his successor, Gen. Hoyt S. Vandenberg. Secretary of the Air Force Stuart Symington agreed and placed Assistant Secretary Eugene M. Zuckert in charge of integrating the races.

Despite the authority of the Commander in Chief and endorsement by the Secretary of the Air Force and two successive Chiefs of Staff, a number of influential Air Force officers opposed racial integration. One of them, Gen. George C. Kenney, whose airmen had supported Gen. of the Army Douglas MacArthur's advance from Australia to Japan, argued that blacks would embarrass themselves in a racially mixed Air Force, while others predicted a decline in white enlistments, if not large-scale desertions. Moreover, blacks serving in segregated units worried that integration merely provided an excuse for purging them from the service. Edwards, in fact, did not expect many African Americans to compete successfully, estimating that their presence in integrated units would stabilize at about 1 percent.

The Korean conflict demonstrated that racial segregation resulted in the wasteful misassignment of men and women and undermined the efficient conduct of the war.

In May 1949, the Air Force adopted a personnel policy that ended racial segregation and prohibited the assignment of airmen outside their specialties—employing black mechanics as laborers, for example—so as to subvert integration. The fears of African-American airmen proved groundless, as the Air Force broke up the segregated units and reassigned the officers and men in accordance with their skills. The predicted exodus of whites did not occur.

The Air Force began integrating the races some thirteen months before the Korean fighting began in June 1950. By the end of 1949, roughly 60 percent of all African-American airmen either served in or were about to join racially mixed units. The Korean War confirmed the new policy, demonstrating that the needs of the service, and not race, should determine assignments. The last all-black unit disbanded in June 1952, two years after the North Korean invasion.

Edwards may well have been surprised by the ability of blacks to compete with whites, when opportunities were more or less equal. The proportion of African Americans in the Air Force, far from shrinking, increased in the course of the conflict from 6.4 percent to 7.2 percent. The representation of blacks in the officer corps (including pilots and navigators) remained minuscule, however, increasing during the war from 0.6 percent to 1.0 percent.

The Navy and Marine Corps

Although the other services had submitted integration plans that the Fahy Committee approved, none had progressed as far as the Air Force when the Korean War began. The Navy, for example, formulated a policy that theoretically opened every specialty without regard to race, but 65 percent of the African Americans in the service—more than 10,000 sailors—served in the Steward's Branch. In an attempt to make this duty more attractive, the Navy in 1949 directed that chief stewards have all the privileges of chief petty officers in the general service, and in August 1953 decreed that all senior stewards assume the status of petty officers, effective January 1.

The African-American community resented the recruitment of blacks to function essentially as cooks, servants, and waiters—in the words of Rep. Adam Clayton Powell, "fighting communism with a frying pan or shoe polish." The continued existence of a large body of black stewards raised doubts about the sincerity of the Navy's commitment to racial integration and made it difficult to recruit African Americans during the Korean War expansion. Lester Granger, formerly an adviser to the Navy Department on racial matters and a member of the Fahy Committee, warned that the Steward's Branch remained a "constant irritant" to his fellow African Americans and recommended recruiting whites for this specialty. The fighting in Korea ended, however, before the Navy in 1954 stopped recruiting expressly for the Steward's Branch and allowed any sailor to volunteer. This decision opened the branch to whites, without preventing veteran African-American stewards from reenlisting.

Despite the tardiness in accepting white stewards, the number of blacks in that specialty declined during the Korean conflict until more than half of the African-

American sailors performed other duty. A policy recommended by Anna M. Rosenberg, the Assistant Secretary of Defense for Manpower and Personnel, and adopted in April 1951 by Secretary of Defense George C. Marshall, opened a wider spectrum of assignments to African Americans in the armed forces. The new policy required that the Army, Navy, Marine Corps, and Air Force accept a share from each of four categories of recruits, groupings based on scores on the standardized qualification test then in use. Assistant Secretary Rosenberg hoped to divert into the Army a greater proportion of recruits from Categories I through III, especially those in the highest two, who formerly would have gravitated into the Air Force and Navy, and divide more equitably the members of Category IV, many of them African Americans taught in segregated schools. The Navy had no choice but to assign the resulting tide of blacks to a wide variety of occupations.

Although the Navy did provide greater opportunity for blacks during the Korean War, the specter of the Steward's Branch deterred many African Americans from enlisting. The proportion of blacks in the Navy declined by about 0.2 percent between 1950 and the end of the fighting in 1953. Not until 1960 did black Americans account for even 4.9 percent of naval personnel, a lesser proportion than the Air Force had a decade earlier. In spite of the admission of blacks to the Naval Academy—which graduated its first African American, Ensign Wesley A. Brown, in 1949—and the efforts of Lieut. Dennis D. Nelson, a graduate of the World War II officer candidate course for blacks, to stir up interest in officer training, the proportion of African-American naval officers did not exceed 1 percent when the Korean War ended.

The wartime demand for manpower forced the Marine Corps, a part of the Naval Establishment, to abandon the practice of racial segregation and conform to the Truman directive by carrying out the plan approved by the Fahy Committee. When the Korean War began in June 1950, racial integration in the Marine Corps remained confined mostly to athletic teams. With 1,605 African Americans on active duty—just 1.6 percent of the enlisted strength, and no officers—the Marine Corps easily maintained segregated units or specialties to accommodate them. A rapid wartime mobilization and a hurried deployment to the Far East resulted in the merging of blacks and whites in units being expanded to wartime strength. As the war continued—especially after the Chinese intervened, beginning in October 1950—greater reliance on the draft, together with Assistant Secretary Rosenberg's program for the qualitative distribution of manpower, increased the number of black Marines more than ninefold to 15,729, 6 percent of total strength. The number of African-American officers remained small, however, with only thirteen on active duty when the Korean conflict ended. This group included Franklin E. Petersen, Jr., the first African American to become a pilot in the Marine Corps and ultimately a four-star general. In short, the Korean struggle compelled the Marine Corps to accept large numbers of blacks, assign them where they could best help fight the war, and abandon the prewar practice of concentrating them in security and service units or employing them as stewards.

The Army

Like the Navy and Marine Corps, the Army complied slowly with President Truman's integration order. Not until April 1950, some twenty-one months after the Truman directive and within three months of the outbreak of war, did the Army abolish racial quotas for recruiting. Black males continued, nevertheless, to train in racially separate units, even though African-American women trained alongside their white counterparts. Segregated training for black males became an early casualty of the Korean War, however. The increase in white recruits forced the commanders of training divisions to assign some whites to regiments or battalions reserved for blacks. By March 1951, the sheer number of trainees defeated efforts to segregate the races in all of the Army's nine training divisions.

The largest African-American combat unit, the 24th Infantry, which traced its regimental lineage to the post-Civil War reorganization of the Army, went to war in July 1950. Like the other understrength American units trying to stop the North Korean onslaught, the 24th Infantry proved ill prepared for war, both physically and mentally. Some 62 percent of the enlisted men had general classification test scores in Categories IV and V, and this challenged the leadership and instructional skills of noncommissioned officers. Moreover, the regiment depended upon a replacement pool determined exclusively by race; it could not accept whites—except for officers, especially in command positions—even though suitably trained blacks, noncommissioned officers in particular, proved scarce. These problems ensured that the regiment would amass a mixed record of success and failure.

Racism, whether reflexive or calculated, may have magnified the flaws of the 24th Infantry and obscured its accomplishments. Prejudice against African Americans existed in American society and in the Army that fought the early battles in Korea. Alarmed by the number of courts-martial of members of the regiment, the NAACP sent Thurgood MARSHALL to investigate the administration of justice in the Army's Far East Command. He discovered that blacks, compared to whites, tended to be charged with more serious offenses, convicted more readily, and given harsher punishment.

One of the regiments sent to Korea in the summer of 1950, the 9th Infantry, had two battalions of whites and one made up of black soldiers transferred from the segregated 25th Infantry, disbanded as part of the Army's retrenchment after World War II. When casualties mounted among his white soldiers, one of the battalion commanders demanded replacements and in August accepted more than 200 African Americans, some of them also former members of the 25th Infantry, whom he assigned throughout his unit.

Prejudice against African Americans existed in American society and in the Army that fought the early battles in Korea.

As the experience of the 9th Infantry indicated, race could not determine assignments; black soldiers had to serve wherever the Army needed them, not in a particular regiment or battalion. In a limited conflict requiring only a partial mobilization, the Army could not maintain two separate channels of recruitment, training, and assignment—one for whites, the other for blacks, and each with its own overhead for administration.

Gen. Matthew B. Ridgway understood the inherent inefficiency and leveled the crumbling ramparts of racial segregation throughout the Far East. Upon taking over the Far East Command from Gen. MacArthur, Ridgway abolished segregation, which he later described as "wholly inefficient, not to say improper," and "both un-American and un-Christian." As part of his integration program, he disbanded the 24th Infantry on July 1, 1951, and reassigned the African-American soldiers to formerly all-white units.

The Army could have integrated swiftly and smoothly, if it had reassigned its African Americans, about 12 percent of aggregate strength, uniformly throughout the service. Unfortunately, not every senior commander shared Ridgway's belief in racial integration, and because he integrated first, they sent their unwanted blacks to the Far East, increasing the proportion there to 17.6 percent. The Far East Command absorbed the newcomers, however, and Ridgway's success became a source of pride to the Truman administration and the Army.

The European Command began integrating the races in 1951 but bogged down amid fears of unrest in the ranks and friction with local civilians. The Army prodded the command into acting, however, and the last all-black unit in Europe—indeed, in the entire service—integrated in November 1954. Meanwhile, the Korean fighting ended, draft calls declined, and the proportion of African Americans in the Army leveled off at about 12 percent, essentially the same as when the war began.

By the time President Dwight D. Eisenhower took office in January 1953, the armed forces had made an irrevocable commitment to integrating the races. In April, four months before the Korean armistice went into effect, the new administration undertook the racial integration of the schools operated by the Department of Defense for the children of servicemen. When the 1953 school year began, all the schools located on federal land and sustained by federal funds had integrated. Those operating off-base, or locally funded, eventually followed suit, for in May 1954 the Supreme Court, in *Brown* v. *Board of Education of Topeka,* declared segregated schools unconstitutional.

Civil Society

The mobilization for the Korean War, and the maintenance of powerful armed forces for the continuing Cold War, boosted the American economy as a whole, creating jobs, some of which went to African Americans. As President Roosevelt had done during World War II, Truman issued a series of executive orders during 1951 that barred discrimination on the part of firms under contract to the government. In December of that year, the President established the Committee of Government Contract Compliance, a faint shadow of Roosevelt's Fair Employment Practice Committee. The new organization could do no more than publicize instances of racial discrimination and advise the contracting agencies, which alone had the authority to cancel agreements with firms that violated government policy. The Korean War did not alter the fact that the racial attitudes of a community determined employment opportunities for blacks.

Nor did the pressures of war slow the shift of the black populace from southern farms to northern cities or end the exclusion of African Americans from the new suburbs springing up around America's urban centers. About 1.5 million blacks from the rural South migrated to the cities during the 1950s, as 3.5 million nonwhites moved into the inner portions of the nation's twelve largest cities and 4.5 million whites moved out, most of them to the suburbs. Although 5 percent of African Americans lived in the suburbs, they dwelt either in segregated communities or on rural tracts counted as suburban only for purposes of the census. The Supreme Court, in *Shelley* v. *Kraemer* (1948), had declared racial covenants designed to enforce segregated housing unenforceable at law, but one of the new model suburbs, Levittown in Pennsylvania, actually had no black resident until 1957.

BIBLIOGRAPHY

Dalfiume, Richard M. *Desegregation of the U.S. Armed Forces: Fighting on Two Fronts, 1939–1953.* Columbia, Mo., 1969.

Gropman, Alan L. *The Air Force Integrates, 1945–1964.* Washington, D.C., 1978.

McCoy, Donald R., and Richard T. Ruetton. *Quest and Response: Minority Rights and the Truman Administration.* Lawrence, Kans., 1973.

MacGregor, Morris J. *Defense Studies: The Integration of the Armed Forces, 1940–1965.*Washington, D.C., 1981.

Nichols, Lee. *Breakthrough on the Color Front.* New York, 1954.

Polenberg, Richard. *One Nation Divisible: Class, Race, and Ethnicity in the United States Since 1938.* New York, 1980.

— BERNARD C. NALTY

KU KLUX KLAN

To most people the words *Ku Klux Klan* mean a southern terrorist movement organized after the Civil War, with active chapters still in existence, that seeks forcibly to deny African Americans their rights. Such a perception mistakes the Klan as a monolithic movement with a continuous history. Similarities in name, costume, and ritual have hidden from view the Ku Klux Klan's separate incarnations. In four distinct movements differing in geographical base, tactics, targets, and purpose, Klansmen have organized their resources to claim power.

Confederate army veterans formed the first Klan movement in 1866 in Pulaski, Tenn. Manipulating the Greek word for circle, *kuklos,* they alliteratively created "Ku Klux Klan" as the name of what was initially designed to be only a fraternal body. Members, however, quickly became aware of the social-control power of a secret organization of armed white men. The Klan, under former Confederate General and now Imperial Wizard Nathan Bedford Forrest, soon spread throughout the South, emerging as a vehicle to combat Reconstruction and subordinate recently emancipated blacks and their white Republican allies. Masked and robed Klansmen threatened, flogged, and killed those who sought black rights and a more just distribution of wealth and power. Congress, with the support of President Ulysses S. Grant, responded to these outrages in 1870–1871 with laws protecting black voters and outlawing Klan activities. In 1871, under these laws, Grant suspended habeas corpus in parts of Klan-dominated South Carolina and ordered mass arrests and prosecutions of Klansmen. White Southerners, with the Klan's usefulness at an end, resorted to political activism and the more subtle and "acceptable" means of economic coercion inherent in their control of credit, land, and jobs to reassert influence.

Nearly half a century later, the second Ku Klux Klan appeared. On Thanksgiving Day in 1915, William Joseph Simmons, a former Methodist circuit rider and fraternal organizer and the son of a Reconstruction Klansman, convinced fifteen of his friends to follow him to the summit of Stone Mountain in Georgia. There, under an American flag and a burning cross, the men knelt and dedicated themselves to the revival of the Knights of the Ku Klux Klan. As early as 1898, Simmons had planned to re-create the Klan to honor the men of the first hooded order and to pioneer a new fraternal group. The interest generated by the fiftieth anniversary in 1915 of the end of the Civil War, and the premiere in Atlanta of the motion-picture masterpiece *Birth of a Nation,* enticed Simmons to reify his dream.

The second Klan grew slowly. By 1920, it counted only four or five thousand members in scattered chapters in Georgia and Alabama. To revitalize his dream, Simmons turned for help in promoting the Klan to E. Y. Clarke and Elizabeth Tyler of the Southern Publicity Association. They signed a contract with Simmons stipulating that the Association, henceforth the Propagation Department of the Invisible Empire, would promote and enlarge the Klan in exchange for eight dollars of every ten-dollar membership fee, or klectoken. Clarke and Tyler enlisted more than 200 organizers, known as kleagles, and directed them to exploit any issue or prejudice that could be useful in recruiting men for the movement. The kleagles fanned out across the United States. Working on a commission basis, they sought to secure as many new members for the Klan as they possibly could. The sharp rise in the secret order's membership reflected their success, for between June 1920 and October 1921, 85,000 men joined.

Directed from Atlanta by the new imperial wizard, Hiram Wesley Evans, but tuned to the local environment, the kleagles preached a multifaceted program. They portrayed the Klan as a patriotic movement determined to safeguard endangered American institutions and values. The Klan posed as the champion of the "old-time religion" and promised to unite all Protestants under a single banner. Law and order was another rallying cry. A sharp upsurge in crime in the postwar years, primarily fueled by Prohibition law violations, alarmed Americans. Many of those impatient with the police and courts turned to the Klan to enforce the laws and restore order to their communities.

The message of Americanism, Protestantism, and law enforcement was not aimed at all Americans. The Klan accused Catholics of placing their allegiance to the pope above their loyalty to the United States. Vowing to eliminate "papist power," the Klan boycotted Catholic businesses, burned crosses before churches, fired Catholic public school teachers, and defeated Catholic candidates for public office. Anti-Semitism was also a plank in the Klan program. The Jews, declared the kleagles, dominated the American economy and led those who sought to commercialize the Sabbath and exclude the Bible from the public schools. White supremacy was another tenet: Klan leaders exploited white fears of change and offered the movement as a means to maintain the racial status quo. Finally, the Klan beckoned lodge joiners by providing the fellowship, festivity, and mystery that these men craved. Simmons's creation of rituals and his titles for movement officers—kleagle, kludd, exalted cyclops—were intended to appeal to these men's imaginations.

The Klan advanced quickly in the early 1920s. In Texas, 200,000 men joined, and a Klansman was elected to the United States Senate. California's 50,000 Klansmen helped capture the statehouse for their candidate. Colorado Klan organizers counted 35,000 recruits, and elected members as governor and U.S. senator. Twenty local chapters were organized for Chicago's 50,000 Klansmen, while 35,000 wore the hood and robe in Detroit. The Klan citadel of Indiana claimed 240,000 knights, who succeeded in electing two governors and two United States senators. New York added 200,000 more Klansmen, and Pennsylvania 225,000. Only 16 percent of the membership lived in the South. The Klan population was higher in New Jersey than in Alabama; Indianapolis Klan membership was nearly double that in South Carolina and Mississippi combined. At its height in 1924, the national movement drew an estimated 3 million to 6 million men from throughout the United States.

The impact of the Ku Klux Klan on the 1924 presidential election is difficult to judge. Klan leaders' unyielding opposition at the Democratic National Convention to the presidential ambitions of New York governor Al Smith, a Catholic and antiprohibitionist, and to a platform plank specifically condemning their organization deepened divisions that the party would not bridge for years.

The Klan's response to community problems was usually political. By electing trusted officials, Klansmen would be assured that crime would be suppressed, minorities regulated, and community improvements initiated. In many cities and towns across America, Klan and government merged. Mayors, city councilmen, and police officials consulted with Klan leaders about policy, legislative agendas, and appointments. Such relationships also existed on the state level in Indiana, Oregon and Colorado. Violence, which occurred in isolated instances, was mainly perpetrated by independent bands of radicals, usually in the early days of Klan building.

The second Klan's fall was as rapid as its rise. The reasons for decline were varied: the movement's inability to fulfill its promises; members' demoralization in the face of their leaders' financial or moral corruption; and a failure to respond as the salience of past issues faded and new concerns came to the fore. By the end of the 1920s the Klan was discredited and without influence. Anti–New Deal rhetoric and a flirtation with the pro-Nazi American Bund in the 1930s did not revive the movement. In 1944, the Internal Revenue Service revoked its designation of the Klan as a charitable organization and forced William Simmons's Invisible Empire out of business with a demand for $685,000 in back taxes.

Splintering early into more than a dozen separate groups, the Ku Klux Klan resorted to bombing, arson, and murder to stop the black challenge.

Burning crosses of the third Klan movement appeared in 1946; by 1949 over 200 chapters, holding 20,000 Klansmen, had been organized. Additional growth spurts followed the Supreme Court's BROWN V. TOPEKA, KANSAS, BOARD OF EDUCATION decision in 1954 and school desegregation in Little Rock in 1957, for this was a southern campaign, focused upon African Americans' quest for racial and economic equality. Splintering early into more than a dozen separate groups, the secret order resorted to bombing, arson, and murder to stop the black challenge. The Klans competed unsuccessfully with the more respectable urban and middle-class White Citizens Councils for members and funds, and remained a secondary impulse in the 1950s and 1960s. Still, the organization became the center of national attention. In 1961, Klansmen assaulted freedom riders. In 1963, members bombed a Birmingham church, killing four black children. The following year, Klansmen murdered three civil rights workers in Mississippi.

In response, the Federal Bureau of Investigation (FBI) targeted seventeen Klan groups in 1964. Agents infiltrated chapters and paid Klansmen to disrupt activities by sowing discord among fellow members. By the early 1970s, one of every six Klansmen was on the FBI payroll. Repression was effective. Klan membership, which had grown to 50,000 in the mid-1960s, declined to 6,500 by 1975.

New Ku Klux Klans emerged in the late 1970s. College-educated leaders, proficient in their use of the media, offered a "modern" movement that rejected terrorism. Welcoming Catholics for the first time and accepting women as equal partners, the Klans opposed busing to remedy school segregation, affirmative action programs, and illegal immigration from Mexico. Klansmen spread north and west, aligning with neo-Nazi groups such as Aryan Nations and the White Aryan Resistance in a United Racist Front. Adopting the slogans of the Christian Identity movement that proclaimed white Christians as the true chosen people of God, Klansmen assailed blacks, Asians, and Hispanics as "mud people" under the rule of Satan's offspring, the Jews. Leaders, predicting a coming race war, established military training camps in the West and Midwest and organized a computer network linking members throughout the United States.

By the late 1980s, the Klan was again in retreat. Federal prosecutors brought Klansmen and their leaders to trial for violent acts, sedition, and conspiracy to overthrow the government. Groups such as the NATIONAL ASSOCIATION FOR THE ADVANCEMENT OF COLORED PEOPLE (NAACP), the Anti-Defamation League, and the Southern Poverty Law Center monitored hooded activities and filed civil lawsuits on behalf of Klan victims to collect damages and drain the movement of funds. Within the decade, the Klans had lost over half of their members, leaving approximately 5,000 men and women beneath hood and robe.

Yet the Klan's hold on America's mind has not loosened. The history of the Ku Klux Klan is a history of resurrection, and the observant search for the spark that will ignite another revival. Thus Louisiana state legislator David Duke, a former member of the American Nazi party and sometime imperial wizard of a Klan splinter group, drew the national spotlight when he ran for governor in 1991. His defeat did not ease concern, for he captured a majority of white votes. America's long history of racial and religious conflict, the eerie sight of the flaming cross, and the menacing imagery of hooded and robed men ensure that the Invisible Empire of the Ku Klux Klan will retain its powerful symbolism for friend and foe alike into the next century.

BIBLIOGRAPHY

Alexander, Charles. *The Ku Klux Klan in the Southwest.* Lexington, Ky., 1966.

Chalmers, David. *Hooded Americanism: The History of the Ku Klux Klan.* New York, 1981.

Coben, Stanley. *Rebellion against Victorianism: The Impetus for Cultural Change in 1920s America.* New York, 1991.

Goldberg, Robert A. *Hooded Empire: The Ku Klux Klan in Colorado.* Urbana, Ill. 1981.

Jackson, Kenneth. *The Ku Klux Klan in the City.* New York, 1967.

Wade, Wyn Craig. *The Fiery Cross: The Ku Klux Klan in America.* New York, 1987.

– ROBERT ALAN GOLDBERG

KWANZA

In 1966, at the height of the black self-awareness and pride that characterized the Black Power movement, cultural nationalist Maulana Karenga created the holiday of Kwanza. Kwanza, meaning "first fruits" in Swahili, is derived from the harvest time festival of East African agriculturalists. Karenga believed that black people in the diaspora should set aside time to celebrate their African cultural heritage and affirm their commitment to black liberation. His philosophy, called Kawaida, formed the ideological basis of Kwanza. The holiday was intended to provide a nonmaterialistic alternative to Christmas, and is celebrated from December 26 through January 1. Each day is devoted to one of the seven principles on which kawaida is based: *umoja* (unity), *kujichagulia* (self-determination), *ujima* (collective work and responsibility), *ujamaa* (cooperative economics), *nia* (purpose), *kuumba* (creativity), and *imani* (faith).

In 1966, at the height of the black self-awareness and pride that characterized the Black Power movement, Maulana Karenga created the holiday of Kwanza.

The attempt to honor communal heritage through ceremony is central to Kwanza. On each evening of the celebration, family and friends gather to share food and drink. The hosts adorn the table with the various symbols of Kwanza, and explain their significance to their guests. First a mkeka (straw mat) representing the African-American heritage in traditional African culture is laid down. Upon the mat, a kinara (candleholder) is lit with seven candles in memory of African ancestors.

Each of the seven candles represents one of the seven values being celebrated. A kikomba (cup) is placed on the mat to symbolize the unity of all African peoples, and finally, tropical fruits and nuts are laid out to represent the yield of the first harvest.

Although Kwanza was at first limited in practice to cultural nationalists, as more African Americans came to heightened awareness and appreciation of their African heritage, the holiday gained wider and more mainstream acceptance. In the 1990s, Kwanza is celebrated internationally, but has gained its widest acceptance and popularity among African Americans.

BIBLIOGRAPHY

Karenga, Maulana. *Kawaida Theory: An Introductory Outline.* Inglewood, Calif., 1980.

Magubane, Bernard. *The Ties That Bind: African American Consciousness of Africa.* Trenton, N.J., 1987.

Weusi-Puryear, Omoniki. "How I Came to Celebrate Kwanza." *Essence* (December 1979): 112, 115, 117.

– NANCY YOUSEF AND ROBYN SPENCER

L

LABOR AND LABOR UNIONS

African-American workers' relationship to the organized labor movement has undergone tremendous, if uneven, shifts since the CIVIL WAR. Concentrated in southern agriculture or in unskilled occupations before World War I, most black workers simply did not compete directly with whites in the economic sphere. Trade unions were dominated by white workers, whose skills and racial solidarity often enabled them to bar blacks from membership in their associations and employment in certain sectors of the economy. By World War I, however, the efforts of an ever-growing number of urban industrial black workers to advance economically undermined the success of white labor's exclusionary strategy. With the triumph of industrial unionism represented by the rise of the Congress of Industrial Organizations during the Great Depression of the 1930s, an important branch of the labor movement committed itself to interracial organizing. The modern American labor movement has both reflected and contributed to the nation's changing race relations. While never free of racial tensions or inequality, and while possessing a wide range of unions with different racial policies, practices, and degrees of commitment to racial equality, the labor movement has served as one more arena of black workers' larger struggle for racial equality in the economy.

Agriculture

In the aftermath of the Civil War, the overwhelming number of black workers made their living in southern agriculture as landless sharecroppers and tenant farmers, concentrated at the bottom of the South's economic hierarchy where they exercised little political or economic power. Black agricultural workers launched periodic collective challenges to white planters' authority in the political realm during RECONSTRUCTION and the Populist Era in the late 1880s and early 1890s, and in the economic arena in the form of strikes by rural Knights of Labor in the mid-1880s and by various sharecroppers' movements in the 1930s. But their movements and uprisings were quickly crushed. The 1887 strike by some 10,000 Knights of Labor (most of whom were black) working in the Louisiana sugar fields met with fierce state repression, as did the efforts of the black Alabama Share Croppers' Union in the 1930s. Trade unions and other movements found the rural South infertile soil in which to take root and flourish, for many reasons, including the South's racial ideology, black workers' economic weakness arising from their landlessness, the power of the planter class, the commitment of the state to repressing rural labor, and the organized labor movement's lack of interest in agricultural and black workers. The most successful black response to economic and political oppression was short-range mobility within the South and ultimately migration out of the South. Engaged overwhelmingly in rural southern agriculture at the end of the Civil War, African Americans have, by the late twentieth century, become a largely urban people, engaged in manufacturing, transportation, and service trades in the North, South, and West.

Nineteenth- and Early Twentieth-Century Trade Unions

Before and after the Civil War, trade unions of white workers in the North and South viewed skilled and unskilled urban black workers as a threat to their own economic security. Skill, independence, manliness, and a sense of racial superiority defined the contours of these skilled whites' beliefs. In white workers' thinking, black workers (slave or free) might demean a craft by working more cheaply and without regard to union work rules or customs. Accordingly, whites excluded blacks from membership in their organizations, denied blacks access to apprenticeship programs, and occasionally resorted to force to drive blacks out of employment.

Immediately after the Civil War, a new, loosely organized, and short-lived national federation of white trade unions, the National Labor Union (1866–1872), eventually admitted black delegates representing black workers to its conventions but went no further. At the same time, most of its constituent members barred blacks from their unions, urging them to organize separately into their own unions. While white workers excluded blacks from white associations, their acceptance, sometimes reluctant, sometimes not, of all-black associations was as far as most white union members were willing to go. The alternative, which was more widely practiced, was white exclusion, nonrecognition, and outright hostility toward blacks. Until the 1930s, exclusion and biracial unionism represented the white labor movement's two dominant tendencies toward African Americans.

In response to their exclusion from white organizations, black workers built upon their communities' larger institutional networks to create all-black unions that championed their members' class and racial interests. Black labor leader Isaac Myers, a Baltimore ship caulker, was a founder of another short-lived association in 1869, the black National Labor Union which brought together representatives of newly formed black unions, community leaders, and black political (Republican) officials. More enduring, if less recognized, were the dozens of smaller associations that emerged during and after Reconstruction in such southern urban centers as Richmond, Galveston, New Orleans, Mobile, and Savannah.

During the 1880s, the Knights of Labor emerged from obscurity to become the nation's most powerful labor federation. The Knights' ideology was cooperative, inclusive, and egalitarian. The organization embraced all wage earners across lines of skill, gender, religion, ethnicity, and race (with the exception of Asian immigrants). Although there are no precise figures, one contemporary estimated that blacks constituted about 10 percent (roughly 60,000) of the Knights' membership in 1886. Yet the formation of Knights' locals largely followed strict racial lines. The Order, particularly in the South, absorbed already existing black and white locals, and new locals formed along racially distinct lines. This biracial character did not prevent black and white delegates from meeting together or formulating joint strategies, but it did perpetuate existing differences and made expressions of solidarity more difficult. By 1886, the Knights' racial policies came under fierce attack from conservative southern editors, politicians, and employers as well as some white Knights. Playing upon white workers' racial fears, employers "race-baited" the Order, which, for many reasons, went into decline in the late 1880s.

The American Federation of Labor (founded in 1881) succeeded the Knights as the nation's dominant labor organization by the early 1890s. In contrast to the inclusiveness of the Knights, the social bases of the AFL rested on white craft workers who sought to protect their skills and jobs from all newcomers. Craft unions were exclusive, barring workers from membership on the basis of their lack of skills, their sex, race, and in some cases ethnicity. The AFL was formally opposed to racial discrimination in its ranks; in 1892, its New Orleans members participated in an (unsuccessful) interracial general strike on behalf of unskilled black and white workers. But by the turn of the century, AFL leaders tolerated widespread discrimination by its constituent members, explaining that the all-important principle of craft autonomy—which granted considerable power to individual unions—made it impossible for them to intervene in member unions' internal affairs. AFL officials adhered to that principle only selectively, however, for on other issues they did sometimes intervene.

The majority of union internationals in the AFL, as well as the independent, powerful railroad brotherhoods, remained all white, and a minority of union internationals admitted blacks into segregated, second-class unions. Several large internationals defied these trends. The International Longshoremen's Association and the United Mine Workers of America, while embracing biracial unions (all-black and all-white locals), espoused somewhat more egalitarian views and policies. The existence of large numbers of black workers, many of whom were organized, compelled white trade unionists in these fields to reach accommodations with African-American workers. That is, these unions' success and very existence required a coming-to-grips with racial divisions; they could little afford to exclude or ignore black workers.

During the Progressive Era, only the Industrial Workers of the World (IWW) adopted a principled stand against racial discrimination. Far to the left of the AFL, the IWW advocated the formation of industrial unions (all workers in a factory, regardless of craft, would be members of the same union) and the overthrow of capitalism, championing a working-class solidarity that transcended all lines of division. While it gained adherents among black and white southern timber workers and Philadelphia longshoremen before World War I, the IWW confronted massive government and employer repression and declined rapidly during the war.

In the late nineteenth and early twentieth century, maintaining all-white workplaces sometimes brought white workers into sharp conflict with employers and blacks. Employers used white workers' racial beliefs and practices to their own advantage by turning to black workers to break strikes or otherwise undermine union wages and work rules. Black workers, who were barred from certain sectors of employment and union membership, found strikebreaking to be one method of cracking the economic color line and securing new jobs. In this period, there were dozens of instances of small- and large-scale riots and other violence as whites in all-white unions battled black workers imported by employers to undercut union authority and power.

White workers often coexisted easily or uneasily with black workers in their trades, but upon other occasions they sought to drive blacks completely out of those jobs. For instance, the 1894–1895 strikes by white New Orleans dock workers and the 1909 strike by white Georgia railroad firemen each sought as its goal the elimination of black workers. During the World War I era, massive labor shortages in the North contributed to an unprecedented migration of African Americans out of the South. Securing a wide foothold in mass-production industries for the first time, black workers confronted often-hostile whites, especially during the postwar economic downturn. Competition for jobs was only one of the many causes of the race riots that exploded in 1919, and black workers suffered discrimination not only at the hands of unions but by employers as well.

Despite the AFL's racial practices and black leaders' condemnation of those practices, numerous black workers formed all-black unions and joined the federation. Generally representing unskilled workers (in such trades as longshoring and mining), these unions were often smaller and weaker than their white counterparts. Nonetheless, they participated in the labor upheavals of the World War I era. The years 1918 and 1919, for instance, witnessed strikes by black female domestic workers and laundry workers in Mobile and Newport News, black male longshoremen in New Orleans, Galveston, Savannah, and Key West, and black (and white) coal miners in West Virginia, Tennessee, Kentucky, Arkansas, and Alabama. These strikes failed less because of white workers' opposition (in some cases, whites and blacks struck together) than because of violent opposition by employers and government. Yet the rare union effort to bridge the racial gap in northern industry, such as the wartime drive by Chicago's multiracial and multiethnic packinghouse workers, failed not only because of the employers' hostility; in the Chicago packinghouses, racial and skill divisions proved too deep for organizers to overcome, dooming the unions' efforts.

Immediately after the war, black unionists demanded that the AFL abolish its color line and actively organize black workers. While the AFL passed lofty resolutions, the behavior of its white affiliates changed little, if at all. Although the AFL eventually did offer organizational backing to the largest all-black union in the United States, the BROTHERHOOD OF SLEEPING CAR PORTERS, founded in 1925 and led by A. Philip Randolph, it did little to challenge the racism of its other railroad unions, which remained virtually lily-white until the 1960s.

African Americans, like their white native-born and

African-American laundry workers and washerwomen organized unions as early as 1866; in Atlanta, in 1881, three thousand washerwomen went on strike. Labor organizing in large commercial laundries began before World War I. In the late 1920s the heavily female work force in commercial laundries earned, on average, less than fifteen dollars a week. (Prints and Photographs Division, Library of Congress)

immigrant counterparts, were of many minds on the subject of organized labor. Until the mid-twentieth century, most blacks worked in sectors of the economy (agriculture, domestic service, and common labor) that were not conducive to sustaining trade unions, regardless of the race of the labor force. If no one could deny the institutional racism of organized white labor, African Americans disagreed on such issues as the possibilities of positive institutional change, the relationship between black workers and white industrialists, the union movement's tactics, and the like. Conservative leader Booker T. WASHINGTON, along with many business-oriented black newspaper editors and clergymen, were extremely harsh in their evaluation of the AFL, counseling black workers to ally with the industrial leaders in the New South and in the North. Some black workers, excluded from white unions and hence certain job categories, reluctantly or enthusiastically became strikebreakers as the only way to gain access to better jobs. Other black leaders were ideologically flexible, praising organized labor when it opened its doors to blacks, condemning it when it kept those doors closed. Black proponents of black union organizing, like miner Richard L. Davis and longshoreman James Porter, worked within their respective union internationals, attempting to enlist black workers in the labor movement's ranks at the same time they sought to modify white labor's racism. Given white workers' often abusive treatment, a relative lack of skills, and economic subordination, a majority of black workers remained outside of the labor movement (as did a majority of white workers). Black workers who joined trade unions did so for many of the same reasons white workers did: to improve wages and working conditions, to eliminate or reduce abuses, to win a degree of job security and control over the conditions of their labor, and to secure a measure of dignity in their work lives. Black trade unions waged a continual struggle to carve out a place for themselves in an often reluctant labor movement dominated by whites. Until the rise of the Congress of Industrial Organizations in the 1930s, their successes were relatively few and far between.

Industrial Unionism and Unions in Modern America

The formation of the Congress of Industrial Organizations in 1935 heralded a gradual transformation in the relationship between organized labor and African-American workers. Breaking away from the AFL, CIO unions advocated industrial unionism and campaigned vigorously to organize basic industry (auto, steel, meat packing, electric, rubber). Committed to organizing all workers, regardless of skill, sex, or race, the CIO both ideologically and practically had to secure the support of black workers, whose presence in basic industry in the North had increased dramatically since the great migration of the World War I era brought hundreds of southern blacks into the northern economy. There was no single CIO perspective or practice on racial issues, for CIO unions' record on racial issues and behavior toward black workers varied by industry and region. During World War II, thousands of white workers (many of whom were themselves newcomers to industry and the labor movement) conducted unofficial, unsanctioned hate strikes against the presence or advancement of black workers in their factories, strikes that were opposed by the federal government and top union leaders. Before and after World War II, left-wing CIO unions maintained the strongest record on civil rights issues and the treatment of black members. Influenced by communist leaders and an active black rank and file, the United Packinghouse Workers, the Farm Equipment Workers, the Food, Tobacco, Agricultural, and Allied Workers, the Mine, Mill, and Smelter Workers, and, by the 1950s and 1960s, the Hospital Workers Union stood at the forefront of those in the labor movement advancing a civil rights agenda. The more centrist United Automobile Workers Union, especially in Detroit, worked in close alliance with black political leaders in the 1940s.

Since 1950, the labor movement's record on issues of black equality has remained checkered. Participating in the anti-communism of the post–World War II era, the CIO purged its left wing, firing communist organizers and expelling unions most active in the struggle for racial equality. The CIO's failed Operation Dixie in 1946–1947 left organized labor far weaker and economic segregation far stronger in the South. The merger of the AFL and the CIO in 1955 sealed the labor movement's primary organizational fault line, but on terms that left substantively untouched much of the racial conservatism of the AFL craft unions. Over the next several decades, black trade unionists founded a number of all-black organizations (the NATIONAL NEGRO LABOR COUNCIL, the Negro American Labor Council, the League of Revolutionary Black Workers, and the Coalition of Black Trade Unionists) as well as caucuses within various international unions (affecting unions in steel, the garment trade, the postal service, and education), all of which aimed at advancing African Americans' civil rights by pressuring AFL-CIO officials and employers alike. Since the 1960s, many white AFL unions have continued to discriminate against blacks and have opposed affirmative action strongly, and, in the 1980s, many white unionists participated in the "white backlash" and defected from the Democratic party, becoming "Reagan Democrats" who voted Republican in

York University's Tisch School of the Arts, where he received an M.F.A. in film production in 1983. While at New York University Lee produced several student films: *The Answer* (1980), *Sarah* (1981), and *Joe's Bed-Stuy Barbershop: We Cut Heads* (1982). *Joe's Bed-Stuy Barbershop,* his M.F.A. thesis film, was awarded a Student Academy Award by the Academy of Motion Picture Arts and Sciences in 1982, was broadcast by some public television stations, and received critical notice in *Variety* and the *New York Times.*

Lee's first feature-length film was the highly acclaimed comedy *She's Gotta Have It* (1986), which he shot in twelve days on location in Brooklyn at a cost of $175,000. The film eventually grossed $8 million. The action of the film centers on a sexually liberated young black woman who is having affairs simultaneously with three men. Interspersed with these scenes, she and the film's characters debate her conduct from ideological perspectives then current in the black community; such topics as hip-hop, color differences, sexual codes, and interracial relationships are raised. This debate spilled over into the national media. Controversy was to become a hallmark of Lee's work.

She's Gotta Have It is characterized by disjointed narrative syntax, mock–cinéma vérité technique, active camera movement, and disregard for autonomy of text. Lee has often employed the same actors and film technicians in many films, giving them a repertory effect.

Lee's second film, *School Daze* (1988), was financed by Columbia Pictures for $6.5 million and grossed more than $15 million. It also dealt with a controversial topic, the conflict at a southern black college between light-skinned students who seek assimilation into mainstream America and dark-skinned students who identify with Africa.

In 1989 Lee produced *Do the Right Thing,* which was set in Brooklyn. The film was produced for $6 million and grossed $30 million. *Do the Right Thing* focused on the relationship between an Italian-American family that operates a pizzeria in the Bedford-Stuyvesant neighborhood and the depressed black community that patronizes it. The film chronicles the racial tensions and events over a period of one day, climaxes in a riot in which one black youth is killed, and ends with the complete destruction of the pizzeria.

This highly successful film was followed by *Mo' Better Blues* (1990), the story of the love affairs, personal growth, and development of a jazz musician in New York City. *Jungle Fever* (1991), also set in New York, was Lee's treatment of interracial relationships, centering on an affair between a married black architect and his Italian-American secretary.

Lee's most ambitious film to date has been *Malcolm X,* which was released in November 1992. In this film Lee departed from his earlier technique and employed the traditional style and approach of the Hollywood epic biography. Produced by Warner Brothers, *Malcolm X* was three hours long and cost $34 million, though it had originally been budgeted for $28 million. By the end of 1994 it had grossed $48.1 million. In a highly publicized initiative Lee raised part of the additional funds needed from black celebrities Bill COSBY, Oprah WINFREY, Earvin "Magic" Johnson, Michael JORDAN, Janet Jackson, and Prince, among others. Denzel Washington, who portrayed MALCOLM X, was nominated for an Academy Award as best actor. Lee based his film on an original screenplay, written by James BALDWIN and Arnold Perl in 1968, that was based on *The Autobiography of Malcolm X* as told to Alex Haley.

In 1994 Lee collaborated with his siblings Joie and Cinque Lee in the production of *Crooklyn,* the story of a large, working-class black family growing up in Brooklyn.

Lee's other films include *Clockers* (1995), about an inner city boy who becomes involved with drug dealers, and *Girl 6* (1996), about a woman employed as a phone sex operator. Lee's 1996 film *Get on the Bus* tells the story of a group of men who travel by bus to Washington, D.C. for the Million Man March in 1995. In 1998, Lee released *He Got Game,* his third film starring Denzel Washington. Washington appears as a convict who is released from prison to convince his son, a high school basketball star, to attend college.

Spike Lee's film career has generated a film company, Forty Acres and a Mule; a chain of retail outlets that sell paraphernalia from his films; and a series of television commercials, ten of them with basketball star Michael Jordan.

BIBLIOGRAPHY

Lee, Spike. *By Any Means Necessary: The Trials and Tribulations of the Making of Malcolm X.* New York, 1992.

———. *Spike Lee's Gotta Have It: Inside Guerilla Filmmaking.* New York, 1987.

———. *Uplift the Race: The Construction of School Daze.* New York, 1988.

Lee, Spike, with Lisa Jones. *Do the Right Thing: A Spike Lee Joint.* New York, 1989.

– ROBERT CHRISMAN

LINCOLN UNIVERSITY

Lincoln University is located in Southern Chester county, four miles north of Oxford, Pa. Founded in 1854, the university is the oldest extant black institution of higher learning in the United States. The university was founded by John Miller Dickey, a white senior pastor of the Oxford Presbyterian Church. Before founding Lincoln University, Dickey had shown concern for the welfare of African Americans. In 1850, he contributed decisively to the liberation of two sisters, Rachel and Elizabeth Parker, who had been kidnapped in Oxford for sale into slavery. Dickey also supported the American Colonization Society and felt that emancipated Africans should return to the African continent as missionaries. In 1852 Dickey made unsuccessful attempts to place James Ralston Amos, an African American and the treasurer of the fund for "Negro Church" building established by Richard Allen in 1794, into Princeton University Seminary and also at a religious academy managed by the Presbyterian Synod of Philadelphia. Frustrated by a failed effort to secure admission for a "colored" student in a "white" institution, Dickey sought a solution in establishing an institution for "colored" men.

The institution Dickey established was originally chartered by the state of Pennsylvania as Ashmun Institute, named in honor of Jehudi Ashmun, the first governor of Liberia. After the Civil War and in recognition of the role that President Abraham Lincoln played in the emancipation of the enslaved, Ashmun Institute was renamed Lincoln University. The educational curriculum was originally conceived to include not only all aspects of liberal arts, but also law, medicine, and theology. Financial problems and declining enrollment, however, necessitated the closing of the seminary as well as the schools of law and medicine. The university's charters of 1854 and 1866 restricted admission to male students. However, in 1953 the university amended its charter to permit coeducation. In 1972, Lincoln University became a state-related institution within Pennsylvania's Commonwealth System of Higher Education and was placed on the same basis for state aid as Temple University and the University of Pittsburgh as well as Pennsylvania State University.

Founded in 1854, Lincoln University is the oldest extant black institution of higher learning in the United States.

Lincoln University has played a vital role in the training of leaders, not only among African Americans but also among Africans. In the first hundred years of its existence, Lincoln University graduated 20 percent of the African-American doctors, and more than 10 percent of the African-American attorneys in the United States. In the words of Dr. Niara Sudarkasa, the eleventh president of Lincoln University, "Lincoln University's alumni roster reads like a section of Who's Who of the Twentieth Century." Its distinguished alumni include Thurgood MARSHALL, who not only argued successfully the historic school desegregation case before the Supreme Court in 1954 but also became the first African-American appointed to the Supreme Court, and the poet Langston HUGHES, who was in Lincoln University's class of 1929. Two former heads of state in Africa were educated at Lincoln University: Kwame Nkrumah, Ghana's first prime minister, graduated in 1939, and Nnamdi Azikiwe, Nigeria's first president, was in Lincoln University's class of 1930. Lincoln's alumni have been presidents of thirty-six colleges and universities.

Lincoln's positive impact has particularly been felt in the Commonwealth of Pennsylvania, where many of its graduates have distinguished themselves as educators, physicians, judges, lawyers, and scientists. Harry W. Bass, Pennsylvania's first African-American legislator; Robert N. C. Nix, the state's first African-American congressman; Herbert Millen, the state's first African-American judge; and Roy C. Nichols, the first African-American Bishop of the United Methodist Church, were graduates of Lincoln University.

Lincoln University has continued the tradition of educating students from Africa who return to their continent to assume leadership positions. Namibia's first independence government cabinet had at least six Lincoln University graduates. This impressive record of Lincoln's national and international alumni in various fields of human endeavor testifies to the value of a preparation solidly rooted in an education for freedom.

Since the 1960s, Lincoln University has intensified its tradition of international involvement. In 1961, the U.S. State Department sponsored the African Languages and Area Studies Program at the university. From 1963 to 1971, the United States Peace Corps Training Program prepared volunteers on Lincoln University's campus and sent them to places in Africa and the Caribbean. Dr. Niara Sudarkasa, an internationally recognized anthropologist and the first African-American female to be appointed as Lincoln's president, has since her inauguration in 1987 highlighted the international focus of Lincoln University. Under her leadership Lincoln has established the Center for Public Policy and Diplomacy, the Center for the Study of Critical Languages, and the Center for the Comparative Study of the Humanities. These centers have become focal points for international studies at the university. Also, in addition to the European languages that are traditionally taught in colleges, Lincoln also teaches Chinese, Japanese, Russian, and Arabic languages.

Dr. Horace Mann Bond, a graduate of Lincoln University, was the institution's first African-American president. He served from 1945 to 1957. Dr. Bond was succeeded by Dr. Marvin Wachman, who was white. After Dr. Wachman, the succeeding presidents—Dr. Herman Branson (1970–1985) and Dr. Sudarkasa (1987–present)—have been black.

Lincoln University's student population has traditionally numbered about 1,400. Students are recruited from various social, economic, and national backgrounds. The university has continued to expand its physical facilities on its 400 acres of land.

BIBLIOGRAPHY

Bond, Horace Mann. *Education for Freedom: A History of Lincoln University, Pa.* Lincoln University, Pa., 1976.

Carr, George B. *John Miller Dickey.* Philadelphia, 1929.

Lewis, Thomas E. "Lincoln University—The World's First Negro School of Higher Learning." *Philadelphia Bulletin,* August 26, 1951, p. 3.

Sudarkasa, Niara. "Lincoln University's International Dimension." In Andrew Dinniman and Burkard Holzner, eds. *Education for International Competence in Pennsylvania.* Harrisburg, Pa., 1988.

– LEVI A. NWACHUKU

LITERATURE

African-American literature, like African-American culture in general, was born out of the harsh realities of black life in North America. Although the African presence in the Americas preceded both slavery and its predecessor, indentured service (which began for blacks in North America with the landing of nineteen Africans from a Dutch ship at Jamestown, Va., in 1619), blacks lived virtually from the start under severe pressures that tended to erode their African identity, although many important features of African culture and personality unquestionably persisted. These pressures also prevented the easy acquisition by blacks of the more complex aspects of European civilization. Except in rare circumstances, literacy among blacks was discouraged or forbidden on pain of punishment by the law courts, by slave owners, or by vigilante force. On the other hand, because the determination of blacks to become free and to acquire power (essentially one and the same idea) is as old as their presence in North America, the ability to read and write became quickly established as essential to the political and economic future of the group.

The earliest black writing reveals a combination of factors and influences that set African-American literature on its way. The desire for freedom and power was shaped at the start by religious rather than secular rhetoric, so that the Bible was the most important text in founding the new literature. Gradually, religious arguments and images gave way in the nineteenth century to political and social protest that eschewed appeals to scriptural authority. As blacks, increasingly estranged from their African cultural identities, sought to understand and represent themselves in the New World, they drew more and more on the wide range of European literatures to find the models and characters which they would adapt to tell their own stories. Rich forms of culture developed in folktales and other works of the imagination, as well as in music, dance, and the other arts. A major aspect of African-American literature, broadly defined, is the persisting influence of oral traditions rooted in the African cultural heritage; these traditions have probably affected virtually all significant artistic meditations by African Americans on their social and political realities and aspirations.

African-American literature, like African-American culture in general, was born out of the harsh realities of black life in North America.

The first significant black American writing emerged toward the end of the eighteenth century with the poet Phillis WHEATLEY. Born in Africa but reared as a slave in Boston, Wheatley was anomalous in that she was encouraged by her white owners not only to read and write but also to compose literature. Like the other black poet of note writing about the same time, Jupiter HAMMON, Wheatley was strongly influenced by Methodism. Unlike Hammon, however, she responded to secular themes as, for example, in celebrating George Washington and the American struggle for independence. Her volume *Poems on Various Subjects, Religious and Moral* (London, 1773) was the first book published by a black American and only the second volume of poetry published by any American woman.

One consequence of the religious emphasis in early black American writing was a tendency to deny, in the face of God's omnipotence, the authenticity of the individual self and the importance of earthly freedom and economic power. In *Autobiography,* the first literary assertion of the emerging African-American identity came in the eighteenth century from a writer ultimately committed to religion—Olaudah Equiano, born in Africa and sold into slavery in the West Indies, North America, and Great Britain. His volume *The Interesting Narrative of the Life of Olaudah Equiano, or Gustavus Vassa, the*

African (London, 1789) became the model for what would emerge as the most important single kind of African-American writing: the slave narrative.

Also in the eighteenth century appeared the first of another significant strain—the essay devoted primarily to the exposition of the wrongs visited on blacks in the New World and to the demand for an end to slavery and racial discrimination. In 1791, the gifted astronomer and almanac maker Benjamin BANNEKER addressed an elegant letter of protest to Thomas Jefferson, then secretary of state and later president of the United States. Banneker appealed to Jefferson, as a man of genius who had opposed slavery (even as he continued to own slaves) and as a signer of the Declaration of Independence, to acknowledge the claims of blacks to equal status with white Americans.

Although the United States formally abolished the importation of slaves in 1807, the first half of the nineteenth century paradoxically saw the deepening of the hold of slavery on American life, primarily because the invention of the cotton gin revived slavery as an economic force in the South. In response, African-American writers increasingly made the quest for social justice their principal theme. In 1829, George Moses Horton of North Carolina, who enjoyed unusual freedom for a slave, became the first black American to protest against slavery in verse when he published his volume *The Hope of Liberty.* Far more significant, however, was *David Walker's Appeal, in Four Articles* (1829), in which David WALKER aggressively expounded arguments against slavery and racism and attacked white claims to civilization even as that civilization upheld slavery. Walker's writing may have encouraged the most famous of all slave insurrections, led by Nat Turner in Virginia the following year, when some sixty whites were killed.

The founding by the white radical William Lloyd Garrison of the antislavery newspaper the *Liberator* in 1831 helped to galvanize abolitionism as a force among both whites and blacks. In particular, abolitionism stimulated the growth in popularity of slave narratives. A major early example was *A Narrative of the Adventures and Escape of Moses Roper* (1837), but the most powerful and effective was undoubtedly *Narrative of the Life of Frederick Douglass, an American Slave* (1845), which enjoyed international success and made Frederick DOUGLASS a leader in the antislavery crusade. One New England observer, Ephraim Peabody, hailed the narratives as representing a "new department" in literature; another, Theodore Parker, declared that they were the only native American form of writing and that "all the original romance of Americans is in them, not in the white man's novel." Slave narratives were certainly a major source of material and inspiration for the white writer Harriet Beecher Stowe when she published, in the wake of the Fugitive Slave Act of 1850, her epochal novel UNCLE TOM'S CABIN (1852). This novel, which offered the most expansive treatment of black character and culture seen to that point in American literature, would itself have a profound effect on black writing.

One autobiography largely ignored in its time, but later hailed as a major work, was Harriet JACOBS's *Incidents in the Life of a Slave Girl* (1861), published under the pseudonym Linda Brent. In its concern for the fate of black women during and after slavery, and its emphasis on personal relationships rather than on the acquisition of power, *Incidents in the Life* anticipated many of the concerns that would distinguish the subsequent writing of African-American women.

Other important writers of the antebellum period who sounded notes of protest against social injustice were escaped slaves such as William Wells Brown and Henry Highland Garnet, as well as the freeborn John Brown Russwurm (from Jamaica, West Indies) and Martin R. Delany. Of these writers, the most versatile was certainly Brown, who published as a poet, fugitive slave narrator, essayist, travel writer, dramatist, historian, and novelist. Responding to the implicit challenge of *Uncle Tom's Cabin,* Brown published the first novel by an African American, *Clotel; or, The President's Daughter* (London, 1853), in which he drew on the rumor of a long-standing affair between Thomas Jefferson and a slave. *Uncle Tom's Cabin* and *Clotel* helped to establish the main features of the black novel in the nineteenth century. These include an emphasis on the question of social justice for African Americans, on light-skinned heroes and heroines, and on plots marked by melodrama and sentimentality rather than realism.

Almost as versatile as Brown, and in some respects the representative African-American writer of the second half of the nineteenth century, was the social reformer Frances Ellen Watkins HARPER. As with the vast majority of black writers before and after the Civil War and the heyday of the abolitionist movement, Harper maintained her career by printing and distributing her own texts, almost entirely without the opportunities and rewards that came from white publishers. Her major source of her fame was her poetry, although she depended technically on the lead of traditional American poets of the age, such as Longfellow and Whittier. Antislavery sentiment formed the core of her first book, *Poems on Miscellaneous Subjects* (1854), which went through almost two dozen editions in twenty years. Harper also published the first short story by an African American, "The Two Offers," in 1859; the biblical narrative *Moses, a Story of the Nile* (1869); and a novel about an octoroon heroine, *Iola Leroy, or Shadows Up-*

who established themselves as urban realists included Nathan Heard, Robert D. Pharr, Louise Meriwether, and George Cain.

By the late 1970s, the high point of the Black Power, Black Arts, and Black Aesthetic movements had clearly passed. However, all had left an indelible mark on the consciousness of the African-American writer. Virtually no significant black writer in any major form now defined him- or herself without explicit, extensive reference in some form to race and the history of race relations in the United States. On the other hand, gender began to rival race as a rallying point for an increasing number of women writers, most of whom addressed their concern for the black woman as a figure doubly imperiled on the American scene. Zora Neale Hurston's *Their Eyes Were Watching God* and, to a lesser extent, Harriet Jacobs's *Incidents in the Life of a Slave Girl* became recognized as fountainhead texts for black women, who were finally seen as having their own distinct line within the greater tradition of American writing.

The most influential black feminist fiction writer of this period was Alice WALKER, who gained critical attention with her poetry and with her novels *The Third Life of Grange Copeland* (1970) and *Meridian* (1976). However, *The Color Purple* (1981), with its exploration of the role of incest, male brutality against women, black "womanist" feeling (Walker's chosen term, in contrast to "feminist"), and lesbianism as a liberating force, against a backdrop covering both the United States and Africa, became an international success. The novel, which won Walker the Pulitzer Prize for fiction, appealed to black and white women alike, as well as to many men, although its critical portraiture of black men led some to see it as divisive. Gloria Naylor's *The Women of Brewster Place* (1982), the interrelated stories of seven black women living in a decaying urban housing project, was also hailed as a striking work of fiction; her *Linden Hills* (1985) and *Mama Day* (1988) brought her further recognition. Audre Lorde also contributed to black feminist literature, and expanded her considerable reputation as a poet with her autobiography, or "biomythography," *Zami: A New Spelling of My Name* (1982), which dealt frankly with her commitment to lesbianism as well as to black culture. With poetry, literary criticism, and her widely admired historical novel *Dessa Rose* (1986), Sherley Anne Williams established herself as a versatile literary artist. Earlier fiction writers, such as Toni Cade Bambara and Paule Marshall, also published with distinction in a new climate of interest in women's writing. Bambara's *The Salt Eaters* (1980) and Marshall's *Daughters* (1991) found receptive audiences.

Novelist Toni Morrison (left) received the Nobel Prize for Literature from Swedish King Carl XVI Gustaf in the Concert Hall, Stockholm, Sweden, December 10, 1993. Morrison was the first black woman to receive this literature prize. (AP/Wide World Photos)

The most critically acclaimed black American writer of the 1980s, however, was Toni MORRISON. Without being drawn personally into the increasingly acrimonious debate over feminism, she nevertheless produced perhaps the most accomplished body of fiction yet produced by an African-American woman. Starting with *The Bluest Eye* (1970), then with *Sula* (1973), *Song of Solomon* (1977), *Tar Baby* (1981), and—garnering enormous praise—*Beloved* (1987), Morrison's works consistently find their emotional and artistic center in the consciousness of black women. *Beloved,* based on an incident in the nineteenth century in which a black mother killed her child rather than allow her to grow up as a slave, won Morrison the Pulitzer Prize for fiction in 1988. Her sixth novel, *Jazz,* appeared in 1992. In 1993 Morrison became the first black woman to be awarded the Nobel Prize for literature.

In some respects, the existence of a chasm between black female and male novelists was more illusion than reality. Certainly they were all participants in a maturing of the African-American tradition in fiction, marked by versatility and range, in the 1980s. In SCIENCE FICTION, for example, Samuel R. Delany, Octavia Butler, and Steven Barnes produced notable work, as did Virginia Hamilton in the area of children's literature. David Bradley in the vivid historical novel *The Chaneysville Incident* (1981), and John Edgar WIDEMAN in a succession of novels and stories set in the black Homewood section of Pittsburgh where he grew up, rivaled the women novelists in critical acclaim. Charles JOHNSON's novels *Oxherding Tale* (1982) and *Middle Passage* (1990; winner of the National Book Award) exuberantly challenged the more restrictive forms of cultural nationalism. Without didacticism, and with comic brilliance, Johnson's work reflects his abiding interests in Hindu and Buddhist religious and philosophical forms as well as in the full American literary tradition, including the slave narrative and the works of mid-nineteenth-century American writers.

The shift away from fundamental black cultural nationalism to more complex forms of expression was strongly reflected in the waning popularity of poetry. Most of the black-owned presses either went out of business or were forced by a worsening economic climate to cut back severely on their lists. The work of the most acclaimed new poet of the 1980s, Rita DOVE, showed virtually no debt to the cultural-nationalist poets of the previous generation. While Dove's verse indicated her interest in and even commitment to the exploration of aspects of black culture, it also indicated a conscious desire to explore more cosmopolitan themes; from the start, her art acknowledged formalist standards and her sense of kinship with the broad tradition of American and European poetry. In 1987, she won the Pulitzer Prize for poetry (the first African American to do so since Gwendolyn Brooks in 1950) with *Thomas and Beulah,* a volume that drew much of its inspiration from her family history in Ohio. She was named U.S. poet laureate in 1993.

Sealing the wide prestige enjoyed by African-American writers late in the twentieth century, a major playwright appeared in the 1980s to match the recognition gained by writers such as Morrison and Walker. August WILSON, with *Fences* (1986), *Ma Rainey's Black Bottom* (1988), *The Piano Lesson* (Pulitzer Prize, 1990), and *Two Trains Running* (1992), was hailed for the power and richness of his dramas of black life. George C. Wolfe, especially with *The Colored Museum* and *Jelly's Last Jam* (1992), also enjoyed significant critical success as a dramatist.

By the last decade of the twentieth century, the study of African-American literature had become established across the United States as an important part of the curriculum in English departments and programs of African-American studies. This place had been created in part by the merit of the literature, but more clearly in response to demands by black students starting in the 1960s. Still later, the prestige of black literature was reinforced in the academic community through widespread acceptance of the idea that race, class, and gender played a far greater role in the production of culture than had been acknowledged. The academic study and criticism of African-American writing also flourished. In addition to the work of anthologists, who had helped to popularize black writers since the 1920s, certain essays and books had helped to chart the way for later critics. Notable among these had been the work of the poet-scholar Sterling Brown in the 1920s and '30s, especially his ground-breaking analysis of the stereotypes of black character in American literature. More comprehensively, a white scholar, Vernon Loggins, had brought out a study of remarkable astuteness and sympathy, *The Negro Author: His Development in America to 1900* (1931).

By the last decade of the twentieth century, African-American literature had become established as an important part of the curriculum in English departments.

In 1939, J. Saunders Redding, himself a novelist and autobiographer of note, published a landmark critical study, *To Make a Poet Black;* with Arthur P. Davis, he also edited *Cavalcade,* one of the more important of African-American anthologies. Later, Robert Bone's *The Negro Novel in America* (1958; revised edition, 1965) laid the foundation for the future study of African-American fiction. In the 1960s and 1970s, academics such as Darwin Turner, Addison Gayle, Jr., Houston A. Baker, Jr., Mary Helen Washington, George Kent, Stephen Henderson, and Richard Barksdale led the reevaluation of black American literature in the context of the more radical nationalist movement. In biography, the French scholar Michel Fabre and Robert Hemenway contributed outstanding studies of Richard Wright and Zora Neale Hurston, respectively. Another French scholar, Jean Wagner, published the most ambitious study of black verse, *Black Poets of the United States* (1973). Still later, other academics such as Barbara Christian, Hortense Spillers, Frances Smith Foster, Donald Gibson, Thadious Davis, Trudier Harris, Robert B. Stepto, Robert G. O'Meally, Richard Yarborough, Deborah McDowell, Hazel V. Carby, William L. Andrews, Nellie Y. McKay, Gloria Hull, and Henry Louis Gates, Jr., provided an often rich and imaginative counterpart in criticism and scholarship to the achievement of African-American creative writers of the past and present. Gates's *The Signifying Monkey* (1988), which explores the relationship between the African and African-American vernacular traditions and literature, became perhaps the most frequently cited text in African-American literary criticism. In 1991, Houston A. Baker, Jr., became the first African American to serve as president of the Modern Language Association, the most important organization of scholars and critics of literature and language in the United States.

BIBLIOGRAPHY

Anderson, Jervis. *This Was Harlem: 1900–1950.* New York, 1981.

Bone, Robert. *The Negro Novel in America.* New Haven, 1965.

Bontemps, Arna, ed. *The Harlem Renaissance Remembered.* New York, 1972.

Cullen, Countee, ed. *Caroling Dusk: An Anthology of Verse by Negro Poets.* New York, 1929.

Davis, Arthur P. *From the Dark Tower: Afro-American Writers 1900–1960.* Washington, D.C., 1981.

Honey, Maureen, ed. *Shadowed Dreams: Women's Poetry of the Harlem Renaissance.* New Brunswick, N.J., 1989.

Huggins, Nathan I. *Harlem Renaissance.* New York, 1971.

———, ed. *Voices from the Harlem Renaissance.* New York, 1976.

Hughes, Langston, and Arna Bontemps, eds. *Poetry of the Negro, 1746–1970.* Garden City, N.Y., 1970.

Hughes, Langston. *The Big Sea.* New York, 1940.

Ikonne, Chidi. *From Du Bois to Van Vechten: The Early Negro Literature, 1903–1926.* Westport, Conn., 1981.

Johnson, James Weldon. *Along This Way.* New York, 1990.

Kellner, Bruce, ed. *The Harlem Renaissance: A Historical Dictionary for the Era.* New York, 1987.

Knopf, Marcy. *The Sleeper Wakes: Harlem Renaissance Stories by Women.* New Brunswick, N.J., 1993.

Lewis, David Levering. *When Harlem Was in Vogue.* New York, 1989.

Locke, Alain, ed. *The New Negro.* New York, 1968.

McKay, Claude. *A Long Way from Home.* New York, 1970.

Osofsky, Gilbert. *Harlem: The Making of a Ghetto.* New York, 1963.

Perry, Margaret. *Silence to the Drums: A Survey of the Literature of the Harlem Renaissance.* Bloomington, Ind., 1985.

Rampersad, Arnold. *The Life of Langston Hughes: Vol. 1, 1902–1941: I Too Sing America.* New York, 1986.

Studio Museum in Harlem. *Harlem Renaissance Art of Black America.* New York, 1987.

Wagner, Jean. *Black Poets of the United States.* Translated by Kenneth Douglas. Urbana, Ill., 1973.

Wintz, Cary D. *Black Culture and the Harlem Renaissance.* Houston, 1988.

– ARNOLD RAMPERSAD

LOCKE, ALAIN LEROY

Alain Leroy Locke (September 13, 1885–June 9, 1954), philosopher. Best known for his literary promotion of the HARLEM RENAISSANCE of the 1920s, Alain Locke was a leading spokesman for African-American humanist values during the second quarter of the twentieth century. Born into what he called the "smug gentility" and "frantic respectability" of Philadelphia's black middle class, Locke found himself propelled toward a "mandatory" professional career that led to his becoming the first African-American Rhodes scholar, a Howard University professor for over forty years, a self-confessed "philosophical mid-wife" to a generation of black artists and writers between the world wars, and the author of a multifaceted array of books, essays, and reviews.

Locke was descended from formally educated free black ancestors on both maternal and paternal sides. Mary and Pliny Locke provided their only child with an extraordinarily cultivated environment, partly to provide "compensatory satisfactions" for the permanently limiting effects that a childhood bout with rheumatic fever imposed. His mother's attraction to the ideas of Felix Adler brought about Locke's entry into one of the early Ethical Culture schools; his early study of the piano and violin complemented the brilliant scholarship that won him entry to Harvard College in 1904 and a magna cum laude citation and election to Phi Beta Kappa upon graduation three years later.

Locke's undergraduate years, during Harvard's "golden age of philosophy," culminated with his being selected a Rhodes scholar from Pennsylvania (the only African American so honored during his lifetime) and studying philosophy, Greek, and humane letters at Oxford and Berlin from 1907 to 1911. There Locke developed his lasting "modernist" interests in the creative and performing arts, and close relationships with African and West Indian students that gave him an international perspective on racial issues. Locke's singular distinction as a black Rhodes scholar kept a national focus on his progress when he returned to the United States in 1912 to begin his long professional career at Howard University. His novitiate there as a teacher of English and philosophy was coupled with an early dedication to fostering Howard's development as an "incubator of Negro intellectuals" and as a center for research on worldwide racial and cultural contacts and colonialism. He managed simultaneously to complete a philosophy dissertation in the field of axiology on "The Problem of Classification in Theory of Value," which brought him a Ph.D. from Harvard in 1918. In 1924, he spent a sabbatical year in Egypt collaborating with the French Oriental Archeological Society for the opening at Luxor of the tomb of Tutankhamen.

On his return in 1925, Locke encountered the cycle of student protests then convulsing African-American colleges and universities, including Hampton, Fisk, and Lincoln, as well as Howard. Subsequently dismissed from Howard because of his allegiances with the protestors, he took advantage of the three-year hiatus in his Howard career to assume a leadership role in the emerging Harlem Renaissance by first editing the March 1925 special "Harlem number" of *Survey Graphic* magazine. Its immediate success led him to expand it into book form later that year in the stunning anthology THE NEW NEGRO, which—with its cornucopia of literature, the arts, and social commentary—gave coherent shape to the New Negro movement and gave Locke the role of a primary interpreter.

More than just an interpreter, mediator, or "liaison officer" of the New Negro movement, however, Locke became its leading theoretician and strategist. Over the following fifteen years, and from a staggering diversity of sources in traditional and contemporary philosophy, literature, art, religion, and social thought, he synthesized an optimistic, idealistic cultural credo, a "New Negro formulation" of racial values and imperatives that he insisted was neither a formula nor a program, but that confronted the paradoxes of African-American culture, charting what he thought was a unifying strategy for achieving freedom in art and in American life.

Locke's formulation was rooted, like the complex and sometimes competing ideological stances of W. E. B. DU BOIS, in the drive to apply the methods of philosophy to the problems of race. It fused Locke's increasingly sophisticated "cultural racialism" with the new cultural pluralism advocated by Jewish-American philosopher Horace Kallen (a colleague during Locke's Harvard and Oxford years) and by Anglo-American literary radicals such as Randolph Bourne and V. F. Calverton. Locke adapted Van Wyck Brooks's and H. L. Mencken's genteel critical revolt against Puritanism and Philistinism to analogous problems facing the emergent but precarious African-American elite; and he incorporated into his outlook the Whitmanesque folk ideology of the 1930s and 1940s "new regionalism." Finally, Locke's credo attempted to turn the primitivist fascination with the art and culture of Africa to aesthetic and political advantage, by discovering in it a "useable past" or "ancestral legacy" that was both classical and modern, and by urging an African-American cultural mission "apropos of Africa" that would combine the strengths of both Garveyism and Du Bois's Pan-African congresses.

In the course of doing so, Alain Locke became a leading American collector and critic of African art, clarifying both its dramatic influence on modernist aesthetics in the West and its import as "perhaps the ultimate key for the interpretation of the African mind." In conjunction with the Harmon Foundation, he organized a series of African-American art exhibitions; in conjunction with Montgomery Gregory and Marie Moore-Forrest, he played a pioneering role in the developing national black theater movement by promoting the Howard University Players, and by coediting with Gregory the 1927 watershed volume *Plays of Negro Life: A Source-Book of Native American Drama.* From the late 1920s to mid-century, Locke published annual *Opportunity* magazine reviews of scholarship and creative expression that constitute in microcosm an intellectual history of the New Negro era.

With the onset of the worldwide Depression in 1929 and the end of the 1920s "vogue for things Negro," Locke viewed the New Negro movement to be shifting, in lockstep, from a "Renaissance" phase to a "Reformation." His commitment to adult-education programs led him to publish, for the Associates in Negro Folk Education, *The Negro and His Music* and *Negro Art: Past and Present* in 1936 and a lavish art-history volume, *The Negro in Art: A Pictorial Record of the Negro Artists and the Negro Theme in Art,* in 1940. A return to formal work in philosophy found him producing a series of essays in the 1930s and 1940s on cultural pluralism. And his early interest in the scientific study of global race relations was revived in his coediting with Bernhard Stern of *When Peoples Meet: A Study in Race and Culture Contacts* (1942). During a year as an exchange professor in Haiti, Locke had begun a potential magnum opus on the cultural contributions of African Americans, which occupied the last decade of his life, when his preeminence as a scholar and the lessening of segregation in American higher education kept him in demand as a visiting professor and lecturer within the United States and abroad. The effects of his lifelong heart ailments led to Locke's death in June 1954. His uncompleted opus, *The Negro in American Culture,* was completed and published posthumously by Margaret Just Butcher, daughter of a Howard colleague.

BIBLIOGRAPHY

Harris, Leonard. *The Philosophy of Alain Locke: Harlem Renaissance and Beyond.* Philadelphia, 1989.

Linnemann, Russell J. *Alain Locke: Reflections on a Modern Renaissance Man.* Baton Rouge, La., 1982.

Tidwell, J. Edgar, and Wright, John S. "Alain Locke: A Comprehensive Bibliography of His Published Writings." *Callaloo* 4 (February-October 1981).

– JOHN S. WRIGHT

LOS ANGELES, CALIFORNIA

The experiences of African Americans in Los Angeles have differed from those of black people in most other large American cities. Los Angeles has always been characterized by cultural diversity. This diversity has shaped the history of African Americans in Los Angeles: African Americans have frequently compared themselves to Latinos and Asian Americans, and patterns of cooperation and competition among these groups have left indelible marks on the city's politics and culture.

The first black people in Los Angeles spoke Spanish. Twenty-nine of the 46 people who established the pueblo in September 1781 could trace some ancestors to Africa. Throughout the Spanish (1781–1821) and Mexican (1821–1848) eras, black residents participated in social, cultural, and political activities. Several black men or mulattoes held positions in the pueblo's government.

The U.S. conquest of northern Mexico and the Gold Rush of 1848–1849 scarcely affected Los Angeles, which remained a small, largely Mexican town. In the 1850s and '60s, Southern California's remoteness attracted some FUGITIVE SLAVES. Biddy Mason, for example, came to Los Angeles in the 1850s. She acquired a fortune through shrewd investments in real estate, and she used some of her money to establish and support the first black community organizations. Reports of Mason's success helped Southern California to develop a reputation as a land of economic opportunity for African Americans.

The experiences of African Americans in Los Angeles have differed from those of black people in most other large American cities.

The completion of railroad lines and harbor improvements in the 1870s and '80s sparked explosive growth in Southern California. Los Angeles' population grew from 11,000 in 1880 to nearly 320,000 in 1910 and to more than 1.2 million in 1930. Among the new residents were small but significant numbers of African Americans. The black population grew from under 100 in 1870 to 7,500 in 1910 and to nearly 50,000 by 1930. In 1940, the census counted 75,000 African Americans in the area.

New black residents moved into a segregated city. The first black neighborhood, labeled "Nigger Alley" by white residents, developed in the 1870s on Alameda Street, near Chinatown. By 1910 a ghetto had formed around the Central Avenue Hotel in downtown Los Angeles. This ghetto expanded south along Central Avenue toward Watts, a community that attracted African Americans from the rural South. By 1930, some 70 percent of the city's black residents lived in the Central Avenue neighborhood. Significant numbers of African Americans also settled in the West Adams district, west of downtown.

The Central Avenue district became the center of African-American culture. Businesses, entertainment houses, restaurants, and churches served the expanding community. Notable musicians such as tenor saxophonist Dexter Gordon emerged from the jazz clubs of Central Avenue. The district's theaters regularly drew celebrated black performers such as Nat King COLE, Duke ELLINGTON, and Paul ROBESON to Los Angeles in the 1930s and '40s.

Prior to World War II, black residents were routinely denied access to public swimming pools and parks. They were also excluded from many theaters and restaurants. Employers refused to hire black people for clerical or white-collar jobs, and skilled black workers found few openings in the city's small industrial sector. Most black men worked as manual laborers, and most black women worked as domestic servants.

Despite the pervasive housing and employment discrimination, the city's African Americans were able to exercise some political power. Frederick Roberts, a black Republican, represented the "East Side" in the State Assembly from 1919 until 1933. Democrat Augustus Hawkins defeated Roberts in the 1932 election and served in the Assembly from 1933 until his election to Congress in 1962.

The growth of the Mexican-American and Asian-American communities in the 1910s and '20s led African-American leaders to conclude that black residents might achieve greater political and economic power through cooperation with other minority groups. The black "East Side" abutted "Little Tokyo" and the Mexican-American barrio of East Los Angeles, and all of these communities confronted racial prejudice and discrimination.

WORLD WAR II offered African-American leaders the opportunity to test their theories about multicultural cooperation. Federal propaganda fueled the desire of African and Mexican Americans to destroy racial discrimination in the United States. The federal government's decision to incarcerate Japanese Americans also haunted minority community leaders. Thousands of African Americans moved into the vacant houses and storefronts of Little Tokyo.

During the war years, black and Mexican-American civil rights organizations cooperated in their efforts to combat discrimination. Peaceful demonstrations and formal complaints to the President's Fair Employment Practices Committee (FEPC), which Franklin Roosevelt had created in 1941, succeeded in placing many black and Mexican-American workers in high-paying jobs in war industries. By 1945 black workers held 14 percent of the shipyard jobs in Los Angeles, even though African Americans comprised only 6.5 percent of the city's population.

The "Zoot-Suit Riots" further encouraged cooperation among African Americans and Mexican Americans. In response to rumors that gangs of young Mexican Americans had initiated a war against military men, hundreds of sailors and soldiers converged on downtown and east Los Angeles in early June 1943. Although the soldiers and sailors ostensibly sought gang members dressed in "zoot suits"—flashy outfits comprised of long, broad-shouldered jackets and pants that were baggy at the hips but tight around the ankle—their victims also included young Mexican-American and black men who were not wearing zoot suits. The sailors and soldiers dragged these young men from theaters and stores, stripped them of their clothing, beat them, and left them naked in the streets. After four nights of violence, military authorities ordered soldiers and sailors not to go downtown, and the rioting dissipated. In the wake of the riots, concerned activists and elected officials created several organizations which, along with the NATIONAL ASSOCIATION FOR THE ADVANCEMENT OF COLORED PEOPLE (NAACP) and the NATIONAL URBAN LEAGUE, were the backbone of an emerging multiracial civil rights coalition.

This coalition's strength peaked in 1945 and 1946, when Japanese Americans returned to the city. The War Relocation Authority (WRA), which operated the concentration camps during the war, later worked to reestablish the Japanese-American community in Los Angeles. In this process, WRA employees recognized the similarities between discrimination against Japanese Americans and discrimination against African Americans and Mexican Americans. WRA employees then began to combat all forms of racial discrimination. The War Relocation Authority lent strong governmental support to the civil rights coalition, which mounted successful legal challenges to housing and school segregation.

After the war ended, however, civil rights activists found it difficult to reform local institutions. Many African Americans lost their jobs, and financial support for the NAACP and other organizations diminished. Politicians and newspaper publishers attached the "communist" label on all civil rights activism. The fears of white residents dominated the 1946 election: two-thirds of Los Angeles's voters rejected an initiative that would have outlawed employment discrimination in California.

Southern California's mild climate and its image as a land of opportunity continued to attract black people from the East and the South after World War II. The area's African-American population grew from 75,000 in 1940 to 200,000 in 1950 and to approximately 650,000 by 1965. The population growth promised greater political power. Tom Bradley, a retired police officer, put together a coalition of African Americans and liberal white voters—many of them Jews—and won a seat on the City Council in 1963.

Bradley's election lifted the hopes of many of Los Angeles's black residents, but conditions in the ghetto did not improve in the 1950s and '60s. Unemployment was higher in African-American districts than in the rest of the city, and police officers routinely harassed black people, often using excessive force in arresting black suspects.

An arrest on August 11, 1965, turned into a confrontation between police and Watts residents and ignited a six-day rebellion. As many as 30,000 African Americans looted and burned hundreds of businesses. State officials mobilized more than 15,000 National Guard troops and police officers to quell the rebellion. The violence left thirty-four people—thirty-one of whom were black—dead and hundreds injured. The police arrested more than 4,000 people.

After the rebellion, government officials and community leaders called for sweeping reforms, including programs to train and employ the thousands of unemployed African Americans in south central Los Angeles. Local, state, and federal agencies, however, never fully implemented these reforms.

While unemployment and other social problems continued to fester in the ghetto, changes within U.S society helped to open new opportunities for some African Americans. Access to good schools and colleges led to the emergence of a new black middle class in Los Angeles. Pressure from the NAACP and other civil rights organizations created new opportunities for black performers in film and television. Black superstars such as Eddie Murphy and Michael JACKSON began to wield power within the entertainment industry in the 1980s. The wealth and power of these stars, however, put them out of touch with the hundreds of thousands of people

After the war, Louis's abilities as a fighter diminished as his earnings evaporated in a mist of high living and alleged tax evasion. After winning a rematch against Jersey Joe Walcott on June 25, 1948--only the second black fighter against whom Louis defended his title, indicating how much of a presence white fighters were in the sport well into the twentieth century—on the heels of winning an earlier controversial match on December 5, 1947, that most observers felt he had lost, Louis retired from the ring in 1949. At that time he made a deal with the unsavory Jim Norris and the International Boxing Club, which resulted in the removal of an old, sick Mike Jacobs from the professional boxing scene. Louis's deal with Norris created an entity called Joe Louis Enterprises that would sign up all the leading contenders for the heavyweight championship and have them exclusively promoted by Norris's International Boxing Club. Louis received $150,000 and became a stockholder in the IBC. He was paid $15,000 annually to promote boxing generally and the IBC bout specifically. In effect, Louis sold his title to a gangster-controlled outfit that wanted and eventually obtained for a period in the 1950s virtual control over both the management and promotion of all notable professional fighters in the United States. By 1950, however, an aged Louis, reflexes shot and legs gimpy, was forced back into the ring because of money problems. He lost to Ezzard Charles in a fifteen-round decision on September 27. On October 26, 1951, his career ended for good when he was knocked out in eight rounds by the up-and-coming Rocky Marciano.

In 66 professional bouts, Louis lost only 3 times (twice in the last two years of his career) and knocked out 49 of his opponents. He was elected to the Boxing Hall of Fame in 1954.

After his career, Louis, like many famous athletes who followed him, lived off of his reputation. He certainly never considered the idea of returning to the ordinary work world he left in the early 1930s when he became a fighter. He was hounded by the IRS for back taxes, began taking drugs, particularly cocaine, suffered a number of nervous breakdowns, and seemed often at loose ends, despite a third marriage to a woman of considerable maturity and substance, Martha Jefferson. Eventually, in part as a result of his second marriage (his second wife Marva Trotter was a lawyer for Teamster boss Jimmy Hoffa), Louis wound up working in Las Vegas as a casino greeter, playing golf with high-rolling customers, and serving as a companion for men who remembered him in his glory years.

On April 12, 1981, the day after he attended a heavyweight championship match between Larry Holmes and Trevor Berbick, Louis collapsed at his home in Las Vegas and died of a massive heart attack. He was, without question, one of the most popular sports figures of this century. In 1993 Louis appeared on a U.S. postage stamp.

BIBLIOGRAPHY

Anderson, Jervis. "Black Heavies." *American Scholar* 47 (1978): 387–395.

Edmonds, A. O. *Joe Louis.* Grand Rapids, Mich., 1973.

Grombach, John V. *The Saga of Sock.* New York, 1949.

Louis, Joe, with Edna and Art Rust. *Joe Louis: My Life.* New York, 1981.

Mead, Chris. *Champion: Joe Louis, Black Hero in White America.* New York, 1985.

Nagler, Barney. *Brown Bomber: The Pilgrimage of Joe Louis.* New York, 1972.

Wright, Richard. "High Tide in Harlem: Joe Louis as a Symbol of Freedom." *New Masses* (July 5, 1938): 18–20.

– GERALD EARLY

LOUISVILLE, KENTUCKY

African Americans have been an important part of Louisville since the first settlers arrived in 1778. The city's black population initially grew slowly, but by 1860 its 6,820 blacks were the largest urban concentration in Kentucky and 10 percent of the city's residents.

Despite their second-class status, antebellum Kentucky blacks—slave or free—had their best opportunities for progress in Louisville. Racism in Louisville proved slightly less harsh than throughout Kentucky, and better work opportunities existed, probably because of the size of the black population and the city's proximity to free soil.

African Americans provided much of the labor in antebellum Louisville. As slaves, men worked on the docks as stevedores, on the streets as draymen, and in woolen and cotton mills. Women toiled as cooks, housekeepers, washers, and ironers. By the 1830s, perhaps 20 percent of Louisville's black labor force consisted of hired-out slaves. Typically, owners hired out their more skilled slaves to the service industries—hotels and entertainment—the building trades, and factories. Hired women generally worked as domestics, often living in shacks in alleys behind their employers' homes. Free blacks, relegated by law to an inferior position, demonstrated a remarkable resilience within Louisville's economy. Many achieved success as teachers, ministers, barbers, tailors, carpenters, plasterers, and stewards.

The size of Louisville's African-American population enabled blacks to create a viable community with a sense of self-identity and even independence. The strong ministers of the independent black churches provided leadership and created a feeling of community. Louisville African Americans displayed an extraordinary determination to protect the few rights they possessed. Leaders advocated strong family relationships, opened schools for their children, and inaugurated social programs to assist the poor and the sick.

At the end of the CIVIL WAR, Louisville's African Americans faced four pressing problems: employment, housing, education, and civil rights. Those who possessed a skill fared best, but physical strength remained a prime necessity for employment. Within a few years African Americans became important laborers in the building trades and dominated Louisville's service industry and carrying trade. A few entrepreneurs enjoyed success in furniture and grocery stores, as barbers, and as undertakers.

African Americans have been an important part of Louisville since the first settlers arrived in 1778.

Chafing at discrimination in the marketplace, Louisville businessmen William Wright and Henry Hall founded Mammoth Life and Accident Insurance Company in 1915, and other African-American businessmen in Louisville founded the Domestic Life and Accident Insurance Company in 1921. Mammoth Life eventually opened offices in eight midwestern states and employed hundreds of agents.

Economic progress, however, moved slowly through the Great Depression. New Deal programs assisted a handful of high school and college students, but the greatest gains in employment for African Americans came during World War II when wages and opportunities increased. Samuel Plato's construction company won several sizeable federal contracts for building projects, and the city school board equalized black and white teachers' salaries; however, only a federal executive order banning discrimination brought gains in war industries jobs. Black protests in the 1950s forced the city government and several large businesses to hire African Americans for clerical and skilled positions, but as late as 1970 the median income of blacks remained 30 percent below that of whites, and in a city where blacks were 20 percent of the population they owned just 5 percent of the businesses.

African Americans flocked into Louisville from the countryside after the Civil War, crowding into shacks and shanties, many on poorly drained streets and alleys. Over the years, blacks were pushed into two large ghettos, "Smoketown" and "Brownstown." Determined to acquire better housing, Louisville blacks formed several self-help organizations designed to improve living conditions, but low-paying jobs and frequent economic panics prevented success for most. Despite arduous efforts, blacks remained poorly housed during the early twentieth century, and a 1950s housing study revealed that African Americans occupied most of Louisville's substandard housing. The greatest gains in acquiring upscale housing by blacks occurred in the 1980s and '90s, but some real estate agencies, unfortunately, continue making arbitrary decisions about where less affluent African Americans can rent or purchase homes.

Believing education to be the key to progress, Louisville African Americans quickly expanded their church schools after the Civil War and began demanding a system of public education for blacks. Pressure forced Louisville whites in 1870 to allocate funds for black public schools, four years before the creation of a state system. In 1879 Kentucky black Baptists founded the Baptist Normal and Theological Institute, which became the State University in Louisville in 1883, the first college in Kentucky for African Americans. (More recently its name was changed to Simmons University and then to Simmons Bible College, as it is known today.)

Louisville African Americans also took the lead in fighting for basic human and civil rights. In 1870–1871 a committee representative of the black community began a city-wide protest that forced an end to segregation and harassment on local streetcar lines. By 1875, however, Louisville blacks were divided over community responses to encroaching JIM CROW laws. William H. Steward, editor of the *American Baptist,* and Nathaniel P. Harper, the city's leading black lawyer, representing the conservative old guard, urged that blacks not test the federal Civil Right Act. Dr. Henry Fitzbutler, representing more militant civil rights activists, urged Louisville blacks to demand their legal rights. In 1883 the U.S. Supreme Court overturned the 1875 Civil Rights Act, leading to increasing discrimination and a growth in Jim Crow policies in Louisville, but the division between accommodationists and militants remained. In 1892, when the Louisville and Nashville Railroad Company segregated passenger cars, Louisville's African Americans led the "Anti-Separate Coach Movement," which blocked segregated railroad cars.

In the early twentieth century, the Louisville chapter of the NATIONAL ASSOCIATION FOR THE ADVANCEMENT OF COLORED PEOPLE (NAACP) made its reputation fighting for equal public accommodations, antilynching legislation, and an end to Jim Crow housing. Accommodationist leaders, such as William H. Steward, who controlled the Louisville chapter of the NAACP, working through powerful white friends, blocked three efforts to segregate public transportation between 1910 and 1918, but could not prevent Louisville's 1914 Residential Segregation Ordinance which the U.S. Supreme Court struck down in 1917.

After 1920, militant journalists I. Willis Cole and William Warley challenged the conservative African-American leadership. First under the banner of the Lincoln Independent Party, and later upon gaining control of the NAACP, they pulled back the veil of racism that dominated city services and government, forcing concessions. In the 1930s a new generation of antiaccommodationists, led by Frank Stanley, Sr., editor of the *Louisville Defender,* and Charles W. Anderson assumed leadership in Louisville. Stanley and Anderson spearheaded the fight to integrate the University of Louisville and won for blacks the right to enjoy city parks.

The hard work of Stanley and Anderson seemed to reach fruition when desegregation of public schools began during the mid-1950s; by the mid-1960s one-half of Louisville's schools had integrated. A 1963 executive order by the governor essentially ended legal discrimination, but anti-integration attitudes among whites remained largely unchanged. The home of a black couple who had purchased a house in the all-white Shively subdivision was bombed, and an angry mood gripped the black community as harassment and discrimination continued at lunch counters, at the Churchill Downs race track, and in employment. Economic boycotts and picketing of white-owned businesses turned into rock throwing and name-calling incidents. Louisville blacks watched with increasing anger as the U.S. government and the boxing establishment persecuted Louisville-born heavyweight boxing champion Muhammad ALI, and complained that no amount of effort seemed to change their status as second-class citizens. The inevitable blow-up came in May 1968 when violence erupted in Louisville's West End, leaving two black teenagers dead, ten persons injured, 472 under arrest, and $200,000 in property damage.

During the 1970s and '80s slow but permanent progress occurred in interracial relations in Louisville, even though the racial attitudes of a significant portion of whites lagged behind progressive changes. Schools were the key. In spite of desegregation efforts, early 1970s Kentucky Human Rights Commission reports indicated that 74 percent of Louisville's schools had remained largely segregated because of white flight to the suburbs, and that 15 percent of Louisville's formerly all-black schools retained a "racial identity."

The breakthrough came in 1975 when, to stop white flight to the suburbs, Louisville and Jefferson County school systems merged and inaugurated court-ordered, county-wide busing to achieve integration. Massive busing resulted in ugly protests and wanton violence, but busing permanently altered Louisville over the next decade, largely because of its effect on team sports. The addition of blacks to previously all-white basketball and football teams probably accomplished more toward bringing black and white Louisvillians together than any other development. By 1984–85, Jefferson County schools were the third-most desegregated system in the nation and race relations significantly improved.

In the early 1990s Louisville's African Americans enjoyed a richer, fuller life, if not one of total equality. Blacks were honored guests at the Kentucky Derby, enjoyed the city's rich cultural traditions, dominated team sports at all levels, and resided in some of the city's most fashionable subdivisions. Much progress remains to be made, but progressive Louisvillians, black and white, believe their city has at last taken a major step toward deserving the "liberal" designation they have so long proclaimed.

BIBLIOGRAPHY

Kentucky Commission on Human Rights. *30th Anniversary Commemoration of the Kentucky Commission on Human Rights.* Louisville, Ky., 1990.

Litwack, Leon, and August Meier, eds. *Black Leaders of the Nineteenth Century.* Urbana and Chicago, Ill., 1988.

Lucas, Marion B. *A History of Blacks in Kentucky: From Slavery to Segregation, 1760–1891.* Frankfort, Ky., 1992.

Wright, George C. *A History of Blacks in Kentucky: In Pursuit of Equality, 1890–1980.* Frankfort, Ky., 1992.

———. *Life Behind A Veil: Blacks in Louisville, Kentucky, 1865–1930.* Baton Rouge, La., and London, 1985.

— MARION B. LUCAS

LOYALISTS IN THE AMERICAN REVOLUTION

Black Loyalists were free and enslaved men, women, and children who allied with the British in the AMERICAN REVOLUTION. Blacks in each of the thirteen colonies took part in this massive movement, whose numbers range from 100,000 to 250,000. Although the proximity of the English Army afforded opportunities for slave flight, African Americans joined forces with the British throughout the war. African-American alliance with the British Army officially began on November 7, 1775, when Lord Dunmore, royal governor of Virginia, promised freedom to all "indented servants, Negroes and others . . . joining His Majesty's troops . . . for reducing the Colony to a proper sense of duty to His Majesty's crown." A weapon of war in America since the early seventeenth century, enticement of enemy servants and slaves with promises of freedom had never before been used to such devastating effect. British commanders William Howe, in 1777, and Sir Henry Clinton, in 1779, repeated Dunmore's clarion cry of freedom.

Such promises of freedom were the fundamental reason for blacks' choosing loyalism. Harshness of servitude was also a factor. For example, over 120 people, 13 percent of the black population, in Dutch-dominated Bergen County, N.J., where existence was grim, fled to Anglo-controlled New York City. In contrast, fewer departed from neighboring, Presbyterian Essex County. Slaves with Anglican, Methodist, and Quaker masters tilted toward the English. Among the evacuees were 131 free blacks, who chose more reliable futures of freedom with the English.

Black Loyalists were free and enslaved men, women, and children who allied with the British in the American Revolution.

Blacks pledged loyalty to the crown even though many Tories were slave holders; many American blacks recognized that opportunities for freedom were better among the British. One observer argued that "blacks generally want an English victory, for they believe it will secure freedom." Whereas during the colonial era the overwhelming number of fugitives were young men, black evacuees from New York City in 1783 included 1,336 men, 914 women, and 750 children. Many departed in family units formed before the war or within the British lines. In New York and Charleston, blacks created a free culture. Ministers and churches emerged; blacks held dances and frolics with British soldiers and sailors.

The British offered sanctuary to blacks to disrupt the American society and economy. Although exploitative conditions at times resembled slavery, black workers received pay and were free to create their own private lives. Some served the British as servants, laborers, mariners, wagoneers; others worked in private concerns. About twenty, for example, labored for pay in a Loyalist brewery in New York City. But the primary function of Black Loyalists was military. They served as pilots, spies, and members of black regiments. The Black Pioneers and Guides mustered in North Carolina in 1777; the Black Brigade operated around Philadelphia and New York City after 1778. Black regiments were especially effective in small raids against Patriot militia forces. Irregular forces known as "followers of the flag" mounted offenses against the patriots in Monmouth and Bergen counties in New Jersey, and outside of Charleston, S.C. In Monmouth, the legendary black raider Colonel Tye led a "motley crew" that regularly seized food, fuel, and valuable goods, robbed and kidnapped Patriots, and controlled border posts.

Despite Patriot efforts to move slaves far from the theater of war, the number of fugitives increased late in the war. After Gen. Henry Clinton's Philipsburg Proclamation in 1779, blacks from the plantations of South Carolina and Georgia and from the "neutral zone" surrounding New York City fled into the English lines.

The most certain estimates of Black Loyalists are based on the numbers leaving British-controlled ports at the end of the war. In addition to the three thousand who left New York City in 1783, another seven thousand were evacuated from southern port towns of Norfolk, Va.; Savannah, Ga.; and Charleston, S.C. Not all found freedom. Gen. Cornwallis abandoned over four thousand former slaves in Virginia. The British sold many southern blacks into bondage in the West Indies. In New York City, however, Gen. Carleton maintained a promise and, ignoring the fury of the Americans, permitted three thousand blacks to migrate to freedom in Nova Scotia. There, though liberty was often tough, they received land, jobs, and financial grants. In 1791, over one thousand, under the leadership of Samuel Peters, migrated to Sierra Leone and initiated a black variant of republicanism. The remainder stayed in Nova Scotia, joined in the 1790s by Maroons from Jamaica, and, after the War of 1812, by more refugees who fought their way out of slavery in the United States. During the nineteenth century, the Black Loyalists remained important symbols of a successful rebellion against slavery.

BIBLIOGRAPHY

Frey, Sylvia. *Water from the Rock: Black Resistance in a Revolutionary Age.* Princeton, N.J., 1991.

Quarles, Benjamin. *The Negro in the American Revolution.* Chapel Hill, N.C., 1960.

Wilson, Ellen. *The Loyal Blacks.* New York, 1976.

– GRAHAM RUSSELL HODGES

LUTHERANISM

A Christian tradition born as a consequence of the sixteenth-century Protestant Reformation in Europe, Lutheranism has always been a small religious presence in the African-American community. In 1991, approximately 132,000 African Americans belonged to several predominantly Euro-American Lutheran denominations in the United States. By comparison, the historic African-American Baptist, Methodist, and Pentecostal

M

MALCOLM X

Malcolm X (May 19, 1925–February 21, 1965), nationalist leader. Malcolm X, born Malcolm Little and also known by his religious name, El-Hajj Malik El-Shabbazz, was the national representative of Elijah MUHAMMAD'S NATION OF ISLAM, a prominent black nationalist, and the founder of the Organization of Afro-American Unity. He was born in Omaha, Nebr. His father, J. Early Little, was a Georgia-born Baptist preacher and an organizer for Marcus GARVEY'S UNIVERSAL NEGRO IMPROVEMENT ASSOCIATION. His mother, M. Louise Norton, also a Garveyite, was from Grenada. At J. Early Little's murder, Malcolm's mother broke under the emotional and economic strain, and the children became wards of the state. Malcolm's delinquent behavior landed him in a detention home in Mason, Mich.

Malcolm journeyed to Boston and then to New York, where, as "Detroit Red," he became involved in a life of crime—numbers, peddling dope, con games of many kinds, and thievery of all sorts, including armed robbery. A few months before his twenty-first birthday, Malcolm was sentenced to a Massachusetts prison for burglary. While in prison, his life was transformed when he discovered through the influence of an inmate the liberating value of education, and through his family the empowering religious/cultural message of Elijah Muhammad's nation of Islam. Both gave him what he did not have: self-respect as a black person.

After honing his reading and debating skills, Malcolm was released from prison in 1952. He soon became a minister in the Nation of Islam and its most effective recruiter and apologist, speaking against black self-hate and on behalf of black self-esteem. In June 1954, Elijah Muhammad appointed him minister of Temple Number 7 in Harlem. In the temple and from the platform on street corner rallies, Malcolm told Harlemites, "we are black first and everything else second." Initially his black nationalist message was unpopular in the African-American community. The media, both white and black, portrayed him as a teacher of hate and a promoter of violence. It was an age of integration, and love and nonviolence were advocated as the only way to achieve it.

Malcolm did not share the optimism of the CIVIL RIGHTS MOVEMENT and found himself speaking to unsympathetic audiences. "If you are afraid to tell truth," he told his audience, "why, you don't deserve freedom." Malcolm relished the odds against him; he saw his task as waking up "dead Negroes" by revealing the truth about America and about themselves.

The enormity of this challenge motivated Malcolm to attack the philosophy of the Rev. Dr. Martin Luther King, Jr. and the Civil Rights Movement head-on. He rejected integration: "An integrated cup of coffee is insufficient pay for 400 years of slave labor." He denounced nonviolence as "the philosophy of a fool": "There is no philosophy more befitting to the white man's tactics for keeping his foot on the black man's neck." He ridiculed King's 1963 "I Have a Dream" speech: "While King was having a dream, the rest of us Negroes are having a nightmare." He also rejected King's command to love the enemy: "It is not possible to love a man whose chief purpose in life is to humiliate you and still be considered a normal human being." To blacks who accused Malcolm of teaching hate, he retorted: "It is the man who has made a slave out of you who is teaching hate."

As long as Malcolm stayed in the Black Muslim movement, he was not free to speak his own mind. He had to represent the "Messenger," Elijah Muhammad, who was the sole and absolute authority in the Nation of Islam. When Malcolm disobeyed Muhammad in December 1963 and described President John F. Kennedy's assassination as an instance of "chickens coming home to roost," Muhammad rebuked him and used the incident as an opportunity to silence his star pupil. Malcolm realized that more was involved in his silence than what he had said about the assassination. Jealousy and envy in Muhammad's family circle were the primary reasons for his silence and why it would never be lifted.

Malcolm reluctantly declared his independence in March 1964. His break with the Black Muslim movement represented another important turning point in his life. No longer bound by Muhammad's religious structures, he was free to develop his own philosophy of the black freedom struggle.

Malcolm had already begun to show independent thinking in his "Message to the Grass Roots" speech, given in Detroit three weeks before his silence. In that speech he endorsed black nationalism as his political philosophy, thereby separating himself not only from the Civil Rights Movement, but more important, from

Muhammad, who had defined the Nation as strictly religious and apolitical. Malcolm contrasted "the black revolution" with "the Negro revolution." The black revolution, he said, is international in scope, and it is "bloody" and "hostile" and "knows no compromise." But the so-called "Negro revolution," the Civil Rights Movement, is not even a revolution. Malcolm mocked it: "The only revolution in which the goal is loving your enemy is the Negro revolution. It's the only revolution in which the goal is a desegregated lunch counter, a desegregated theater, a desegregated public park, a desegregated public toilet; you can sit down next to white folks on the toilet."

After his break, Malcolm developed his cultural and political philosophy of black nationalism in "The Ballot or the Bullet." Before audiences in New York, Cleveland, and Detroit, he urged blacks to acquire their constitutional right to vote, and move toward King and the Civil Rights Movement. Later he became more explicit: "Dr. King wants the same thing I want—freedom." Malcolm went to Selma, Ala., while King was in jail in support of King's efforts to secure voting rights. Malcolm wanted to join the Civil Rights Movement in order to expand it into a human rights movement, thereby internationalizing the black freedom struggle, making it more radical and more militant.

During his independence, which lasted for approximately one year before he was assassinated, nothing influenced Malcolm more than his travel abroad. His pilgrimage to Mecca transformed his theology. Malcolm became a Sunni Muslim, acquired the religious name El-Hajj Malik El-Shabbazz, and concluded that "Orthodox Islam" was incompatible with the racist teachings of Elijah Muhammad. The sight of "people of all races, colors, from all over the world coming together as one" had a profound effect upon him. "Brotherhood," and not racism, was seen as the essence of Islam.

Malcolm's experiences in Africa also transformed his political philosophy. He discovered the limitations of skin-nationalism, since he met whites who were creative participants in liberation struggles in African countries. In his travels abroad, Malcolm focused on explaining the black struggle for justice in the United States and linking it with other liberation struggles throughout the world. "Our problem is your problem," he told African heads of state: "It is not a Negro problem, nor an American problem. This is a world problem; a problem of humanity. It is not a problem of civil rights but a problem of human rights."

When Malcolm returned to the United States, he told blacks: "You can't understand what is going on in Mississippi, if you don't know what is going on in the Congo. They are both the same. The same interests are at stake." He founded the Organization of Afro-American Unity, patterned after the Organization of African Unity, in order to implement his ideas. He was hopeful of influencing African leaders "to recommend an immediate investigation into our problem by the United Nations Commission on Human Rights."

Malcolm X was not successful. On February 21, 1965, he was shot down by assassins as he spoke at the Audubon Ballroom in Harlem. He was thirty-nine years old.

No one made a greater impact upon the cultural consciousness of the African-American community during the second half of the twentieth century than Malcolm X. More than anyone else, he revolutionized the black mind, transforming docile Negroes and self-effacing colored people into proud blacks and self-confident African Americans. Preachers and religious scholars created a black theology and proclaimed God as liberator and Jesus Christ as black. College students demanded and got black studies. Artists created a new black esthetic and proclaimed, "Black is beautiful."

No one made a greater impact upon the cultural consciousness of the African-American community during the second half of the twentieth century than Malcolm X.

No area of the African-American community escaped Malcolm's influence. Even mainstream black leaders who first dismissed him as a rabble-rouser, embraced his cultural philosophy following his death. Malcolm's most far-reaching influence, however, was among the masses of African Americans in the ghettos of American cities. Malcolm loved black people deeply and taught them much about themselves. Before Malcolm, most blacks did not want to have anything to do with Africa. But he reminded them that "you can't hate the roots of the tree and not hate the tree; you can't hate your origin and not end up hating yourself; you can't hate Africa and not hate yourself."

Malcolm X was a cultural revolutionary. Poet Maya ANGELOU called him a "charismatic speaker who could play an audience as great musicians play instruments." Disciple Peter Bailey said he was a "master teacher." Writer Alfred Duckett called him "our sage and our saint." In his eulogy, actor Ossie Davis bestowed upon Malcolm the title "our shining black prince." Malcolm can be best understood as a cultural prophet of blackness. African Americans who are proud to be black should thank Malcolm X. Few have played as central a role as he in making it possible for African Americans to claim their African heritage.

BIBLIOGRAPHY

Breitman, George. *By Any Means Necessary.* New York, 1970.

———, ed. *Malcolm X Speaks.* New York, 1965.

Cone, James H. *Martin & Malcolm & America: A Dream or a Nightmare.* Maryknoll, N.Y., 1991.

Goldman, Peter. *The Death and Life of Malcolm X.* Urbana, Ill., 1979.

Malcolm X, with Alex Haley. *Autobiography of Malcolm X.* New York, 1965.

– JAMES H. CONE

MANUMISSION SOCIETIES

The manumission societies of the first half of the century after American independence were eventually eclipsed by the more radical antislavery organizations of the 1830s, '40s, and '50s. While the manumission societies looked to a day when the slave system would be uprooted and destroyed, they, unlike the "immediatists" in the camp of William Lloyd Garrison, were prepared to see EMANCIPATION proceed gradually. The rhetoric was also strikingly different. The later generation of ABOLITIONISTS would denounce slave owners as "manstealers" and "woman-whippers," while the earlier generation saw them not as moral degenerates but as misguided individuals who needed to be shown the error of their ways.

There was also the issue of who should participate in the work of emancipation. The manumission societies were exclusively male and exclusively white. There was none of the involvement of white women and African Americans that would characterize Garrisonian abolition and outrage its opponents. And yet, despite the differences, the older organizations prepared the way for their more outspoken successors, while the "gradualist" impulse was not entirely absent from the later phase of the antislavery struggle.

The Pennsylvania Abolition Society was a Quaker monopoly when it was established in 1775. It initially focused on rescuing free people unlawfully held as slaves. Moribund during the Revolutionary War, it was revived in 1784 by individuals from various religious denominations. In the interval Pennsylvania had enacted a gradual-abolition law, and monitoring its enforcement became a major part of the society's work. Other states and cities followed the lead of Pennsylvania. Between 1784 and 1791, manumission societies were established in every state except the Carolinas and Georgia, and by 1814 societies could be found as far west as Tennessee and Kentucky.

The socioeconomic status of the abolitionists varied from region to region. In the North, Benjamin Franklin, John Jay, Alexander Hamilton, and Benjamin Rush joined the antislavery ranks. In contrast, the Kentucky Abolition Society was composed of men in "low or . . . middling circumstances." The Maryland Abolition Society was made up of local merchants and skilled craftsmen—those least likely to use slaves or to lose money and prestige if slavery were abolished.

Policy on admitting slaveholders to membership varied. The Pennsylvania and Providence, R.I., societies excluded them altogether. The Maryland society made them eligible for some offices. The Alexandria, Va., society admitted them, as did the New York Manumission Society. Indeed, as Shane White points out (1991) some New Yorkers acquired slaves *after* joining. White contends that for some years the emphasis of the New Yorkers was not so much on challenging slavery as on removing the worst abuses in the slave system. They saw themselves as humane masters who were reacting against what they regarded as appalling acts of cruelty perpetrated by southern and Caribbean slave owners, and occasionally by those in their own state.

As the character of the membership varied so did the goals of the individual societies. On some things they were agreed. The foreign slave trade must be outlawed; abusive treatment of slaves should be punished; where they had been enacted, manumission laws should be enforced. In New York, New Jersey, and the upper South, where gradual-emancipation laws had not been passed, the societies attempted to exert pressure on lawmakers. There were some notable successes, although it is debatable how much was due to the humanitarian impulse. In the upper South, economic dislocation after the Revolutionary War had brought changes in labor requirements and patterns of agricultural production. In 1782 Virginia legislators repealed the ban on private manumissions, and Maryland and Delaware quickly followed suit.

The manumission societies made efforts to address the plight of the free people of color, since there was general agreement that their freedom must be safeguarded. Free blacks were offered advice about their conduct and encouraged to use their influence with slave kinfolk and friends to urge them to endure patiently. There was also practical assistance. The Pennsylvania and New York societies sponsored schools that trained a generation of African-American community leaders. The Pennsylvanians in particular developed a number of economic initiatives: would-be entrepreneurs received assistance, employment offices were established, and prosperous African Americans and sympathetic whites were encouraged to hire black indentured servants.

In 1791, there was a concerted effort by nine manumission societies to petition Congress to limit the foreign slave trade. When that effort failed, the New York society proposed the formation of a national convention to coordinate future action. In 1794 a convention was held in Philadelphia to organize the American Convention for Promoting the Abolition of Slavery and Improving the Condition of the African Race.

Conventions were annual until 1806, after which they became less frequent. At each meeting, member societies presented reports on their progress. Representatives from more distant societies were often unable to attend, but they submitted reports. There were contacts with foreign organizations such as the London-based African Institution and *les amis des noirs* in Paris. Delegates occasionally heard from influential African Americans, such as James FORTEN. As for policy decisions, in 1818 Forten denounced the work of the AMERICAN COLONIZATION SOCIETY (ACS) in an address to the convention. In 1821 the convention expressed its disapproval of the Liberian scheme, but in 1829, after many individual societies had already endorsed the ACS, the convention announced its approval of voluntary emigration.

Gradually the power and influence of the manumission societies declined. For more than two decades, the abolitionist impulse remained strong in the upper South. In 1827, for instance, the American Convention reported that while the free states had 24 societies, the slave states had 130. Many factors led to the demise of abolition societies in the region, including slave rebellions and the spread of the plantation economy south and west, which meant a lively market for "surplus" slaves.

In the North the crisis surrounding the MISSOURI COMPROMISE took a toll. The Pennsylvania Abolition Society, for instance, suffered a wave of resignations in the early 1820s. As for the American Convention, it met for the last time in 1832 and was formally dissolved in 1838, by which time it had been supplanted by a new and, in many respects, more radical antislavery movement.

BIBLIOGRAPHY

Berlin, Ira. *Slaves without Masters: The Free Negro in the Antebellum South.* New York, 1974.

Fogel, Robert. *Without Consent or Contract.* New York, 1989.

Litwack, Leon. *North of Slavery: The Negro in the Free States, 1790–1860.* Chicago, 1961.

Locke, Mary S. *Anti-Slavery in America.* Boston, 1901.

Quarles, Benjamin. *Black Abolitionists.* New York, 1969.

White, Shane. *Somewhat More Independent: The End of Slavery in New York City, 1770–1810.* Athens, Ga., 1991.

Zilversmit, Arthur. *The First Emancipation: The Abolition of Slavery in the North.* Chicago, 1967.

– JULIE WINCH

MARSALIS, WYNTON

Wynton Marsalis (October 18, 1961–), jazz trumpeter and composer. Born in New Orleans, Wynton Marsalis grew up in a musical family. His father, Ellis (pianist), and brothers, Branford (tenor and soprano saxophonist), Delfeayo (trombonist), and Jason (drummer), are themselves well-known jazz artists. From an early age, he studied privately and played in a children's marching band directed by the eminent New Orleans musician/scholar Danny Barker. As a youngster, Marsalis made notable contributions in both classical and jazz genres. He performed at the New Orleans Jazz and Heritage Festival, and at the age of fourteen he performed Haydn's *Trumpet Concerto in E-flat* with the New Orleans Philharmonic Orchestra. He attended the Berkshire Music Center at Tanglewood and enrolled at Juilliard in 1980. While a student at Juilliard, he joined Art BLAKEY's Jazz Messengers (1980) and toured in a quartet with former Miles DAVIS personnel Herbie Hancock, Ron Carter, and Tony Williams. He recorded his first album as a leader, *Wynton Marsalis,* in 1981.

After leaving Blakey in 1982, Marsalis formed his first group, a quintet that included several young and extremely talented musicians—his brother Branford (tenor saxophone), Kenny Kirkland (piano), Charles Fambrough (bass), and Jeff Watts (drums). In addition to performing with his own group, Marsalis replaced Freddie Hubbard for the V.S.O.P. II tour (1983). In 1984, he became the first musician to win Grammy Awards for both jazz (*Think of One,* 1982) and classical (Haydn, Hummel, and Leopold Mozart trumpet concertos, 1984) recordings. Since the late 1980s, Marsalis has concentrated on jazz performance with a group consisting of Wes Anderson and Todd Williams (saxophones), Reginald Veal (bass), Wycliffe Gordon (trombone), Herlin Riley (drums), and Eric Reed (piano). Marsalis has won critical acclaim for his virtuosic technique, musical sensitivity, and gift for improvisation. He has become an articulate spokesperson for the preservation of "mainstream" jazz (a style rooted in bop and hard bop) through his performances and writings, and, beginning in 1991, as artistic director of the classical jazz program at Lincoln Center in New York.

BIBLIOGRAPHY

Crouch, Stanley. "Wynton Marsalis: 1987." *Downbeat* 54, no. 11 (1987): 17–19.

Giddins, Gary. "Wynton Marsalis and Other Neoclassical Lions." In *Rhythm-a-ning.* New York, 1985, pp. 156–161.

– EDDIE S. MEADOWS

MARSHALL, THURGOOD

Thurgood Marshall (July 2, 1908–January 24, 1993), civil rights lawyer, associate justice of U. S. Supreme Court. Thurgood Marshall distinguished himself as a jurist in a wide array of settings. As the leading attorney for the NATIONAL ASSOCIATION FOR THE ADVANCEMENT OF COLORED PEOPLE (NAACP) between 1938 and 1961, he pioneered the role of professional civil rights advocate. As the principal architect of the legal attack against *de jure* racial segregation, Marshall oversaw the most successful campaign of social reform litigation in American history. As a judge on the United States Court of Appeals, solicitor general of the United States, and associate justice of the Supreme Court, he amassed a remarkable record as a public servant. Given the influence of his achievements over a long span of time, one can reasonably argue that Thurgood Marshall may have been the outstanding attorney of twentieth-century America.

Marshall was born in Baltimore, Md., where his father was a steward at an exclusive, all-white boat club, and his mother was an elementary school teacher. He attended public schools in Baltimore before proceeding to Lincoln University in Pennsylvania where he shared classes with, among others, Cabell "Cab" CALLOWAY, the entertainer, Kwame Nkrumah, who became president of Ghana, and Nnamdi Azikiwe, who became president of Nigeria. After graduating, he was excluded from the University of Maryland School of Law because of racial segregation. Marshall attended the HOWARD UNIVERSITY School of Law, where he fell under the tutelage of Charles Hamilton Houston. Houston elevated academic standards at Howard, turning it into a veritable hothouse of legal education, where he trained many of those who would later play important roles in the campaign against racial discrimination. Marshall graduated in 1933, first in his class.

After engaging in a general law practice for a brief period, Marshall was persuaded by Houston to pursue a career working as an attorney on behalf of the NAACP. Initially he worked as Houston's deputy and then, in 1939, he took over from his mentor as the NAACP's special counsel. In that position, Marshall confronted an extraordinary array of legal problems that took him from local courthouses, where he served as a trial attorney, to the Supreme Court of the United States, where he developed his skills as an appellate advocate. Over a span of two decades, he argued thirty-two cases before the Supreme Court, winning twenty-nine of them. He convinced the Court to invalidate practices that excluded blacks from primary elections (*Smith* v. *Allwright*, 1944), to prohibit segregation in interstate transportation (*Morgan* v. *Virginia*, 1946), to nullify convictions obtained from juries from which African Americans had been barred on the basis of their race (*Patton* v. *Mississippi*, 1947), and to prohibit state courts from enforcing racially restrictive real estate covenants (*Shelley* v. *Kraemer*, 1948).

Marshall's greatest triumphs arose, however, in the context of struggles against racial discrimination in public education. In 1950, in *Sweatt* v. *Painter*, he successfully argued that a state could not fulfill its federal constitutional obligation by hurriedly constructing a "Negro" law school that was inferior in tangible and intangible ways to the state's "white" law school. That same year he successfully argued in *McLaurin* v. *Oklahoma State Regents* that a state university violated the federal constitution by admitting an African-American student and then confining that student, on the basis of his race, to a specified seat in classrooms and a specified table in the school cafeteria. In 1954, in *Brown* v. *Board of Education*, Marshall culminated his campaign by convincing the Court to rule that racial segregation is invidious racial discrimination and thus invalid under the FOURTEENTH AMENDMENT to the federal constitution.

In 1961, over the objections of white supremacist southern politicians, President John F. Kennedy nominated Marshall to a seat on the United States Court of Appeals for the Second Circuit in New York. Later, President Lyndon B. Johnson appointed Marshall to two positions that had never previously been occupied by an African American. In 1965, President Johnson appointed Marshall as Solicitor General, and in 1967 he nominated him to a seat on the Supreme Court.

Throughout his twenty-four years on the Court, Marshall was the most insistently liberal of the Justices, a stance that often drove him into dissent. His judgments gave broad scope to individual liberties (except in cases involving asserted claims to rights of property). Typically he supported claims of freedom of expression over competing concerns and scrutinized skeptically the claims of law enforcement officers in cases implicating federal constitutional provisions that limit the police powers of government. In the context of civil liberties, the most controversial positions that Marshall took involved rights over reproductive capacities and the death penalty. He viewed as unconstitutional laws that prohibit women from exercising considerable discretion over the choice to continue a pregnancy or to terminate it through abortion. Marshall also viewed as unconstitutional all laws permitting the imposition of capital punishment.

The other side of Marshall's jurisprudential liberalism was manifested by an approach to statutory and constitutional interpretation that generally advanced egalitarian policies. His judgments displayed an unstinting solicitude for the rights of labor, the interests of women, the struggles of oppressed minorities, and the condition of the poor. One particularly memorable expression of Marshall's empathy for the indigent is his dissent in *United States* v. *Kras* (1973), a case in which the Court held that a federal statute did not violate the Constitution by requiring a $50 fee of persons seeking the protection of bankruptcy. Objecting to the Court's assumption that, with a little self-discipline, the petitioner could readily accumulate the required fee, Marshall wrote that

> It may be easy for some people to think that weekly savings of less than $2 are no burden. But no one who has had close contact with poor people can fail to understand how close to the margin of survival many of them are . . . It is perfectly proper for judges to disagree about what the Constitution requires. But it is disgraceful for an interpretation of the Constitution to be premised upon unfounded assumptions about how people live.

Marshall retired from the Court in 1991, precipitating the most contentious confirmation battle in the nation's history when President George Bush nominated as Marshall's successor Clarence Thomas, an ultraconservative African-American jurist.

Marshall died on January 24, 1993. His extraordinary contributions to American life were memorialized in an outpouring of popular grief and adulation greater than that expressed for any previous justice.

BIBLIOGRAPHY

Bland, Randall W. *Private Pressure on Public Law: The Legal Career of Justice Thurgood Marshall,* 1973.

Kluger, Richard. *Simple Justice: The History of Brown* v. *Board of Education and Black America's Struggle for Equality.* New York, 1977.

— RANDALL KENNEDY

MASSEY, WALTER E.

Walter E. Massey (1938–), physicist and scientific administrator. In March 1991 this theoretical physicist began a six-year term as director of the National Science Foundation (NSF). Previous to this appointment he served as vice president for research at the University of Chicago and the Argonne National Laboratory. Prior to this he was director of the laboratory and professor of Physics at the University of Chicago.

Born in Hattiesburg, Miss., Massey received a bachelor's degree in physics and mathematics from Morehouse College in 1958, and completed graduate studies there for a master's degree in 1959. He received his doctoral degree in 1966 from Washington University in St. Louis. Following seven years of research at the Argonne National Laboratory—operated by the University of Chicago for the U.S. Department of Energy—he was professor of physics and later a college dean at Brown University in Providence, R.I. His own research has focused on the many-body theories of quantum liquids and solids—more specifically, examining the behavior of various substances at very low temperatures.

Upon his return to the Argonne National Laboratory as its director in 1979, he was responsible for overseeing a wide array of basic and applied energy research projects, involving nuclear fission, solar energy, fossil fuels, and the effects of energy production on the environment. As Argonne's director he managed a staff of 5,000, including 2,000 scientists and engineers, with an annual budget of $233 million.

Walter Massey has lectured and written widely on the teaching of science and mathematics in the nation's public schools and colleges and on the role of science and technology in society. He is an ardent advocate of African-American involvement in science. "More and more, science and technology will influence our life, and people who are not able to deal with or understand such issues will not be able to play meaningful roles in society," says Dr. Massey.

In 1974 he received the Outstanding Educator in America award; the next year, the Distinguished Service Citation of the American Association of Physics Teachers was bestowed upon him.

BIBLIOGRAPHY

"Walter Massey: America's Pointperson in Science and Research." *Black Issues in Higher Education* (May 9, 1991): 8–13.

"Walter Massey: The Scientist as Manager." *Black Enterprise* (February 1981): 32.

— ROBERT C. HAYDEN

MAYORS

The area in which African Americans made the greatest political gains during the late-twentieth century was in city government. By 1990, most of the large cities in the United States, including four of the top five, had elected African-American mayors. This political shift took place with astounding swiftness. While a few black mayors were elected in small southern towns during RECONSTRUCTION, and numerous all-black towns during the JIM CROW era had black chief executives, the first African-American mayors of large cities were elected only in 1967, with the elections of Carl Stokes in Cleveland, Ohio, and Richard Hatcher in Gary, Ind. That same year, Walter Washington was appointed mayor of Washington, D.C., although he was not elected to that office until 1974.

The institution of black political control in the urban areas of the United States at the end of the twentieth century was the product of several factors, including the shifting racial demography of cities. As the industrial sector of the American economy declined, unemployment as well as taxes increased while city services declined. As a result, many affluent city residents, overwhelmingly white, moved from cities to adjacent suburbs, and black-majority or near-majority populations were created within city limits.

The other important factors were the Civil Rights and Black Power movements of the 1960s. The effects were most evident in the South, where movement efforts inspired passage of the Voting Rights Act of 1965 and other measures that ensured full political participation and provided federal protection to blacks attempting to exercise their right to vote. However, even in the areas of the country where blacks were able to vote throughout the twentieth century, the CIVIL RIGHTS MOVEMENT provided an inspiring ideology and model for black political action. Many of the black activists who went south returned as cadres and organizers responsible for voter registration and the formation of alliances. The Black Power movement, with its emphasis on black control of black areas, also proved influential. The URBAN RIOTS AND REBELLIONS of the 1960s, which publicized black powerlessness and at the same time hastened white outmigration, accelerated the election of African-American mayors.

Another factor that shaped the early black urban governments was the federal government. Federal civil rights legislation and affirmative-action programs improved the political and economic status of black communities. In addition, Great Society antipoverty programs provided black communities with sources of organization and patronage outside the control of white-dominated urban political machines and stimulated black interest in electoral politics.

African-American mayors can be divided into two main types: those from black-majority or near-majority cities (including virtually all southern cities with black mayors) and those with predominantly white electorates. The first wave of mayors, with the exception of Carl Stokes, came from black-majority industrial cities in the North and Midwest that had previously been the site of riots and other racial tensions. Elected with the help of black communities and movement organizations, they generally had little or no white voting support. Richard Hatcher (1933–), the first of these mayors, was elected mayor in the declining steel town of Gary, Ind., where blacks represented just over 50 percent of the population. Another notable figure, Coleman Young (1918–), of Detroit, a former United Auto Workers activist, was elected in 1973.

The urban riots and rebellions of the 1960s, which publicized black powerlessness and hastened white outmigration, accelerated the election of African-American mayors.

One model of this type of mayor is Kenneth Gibson (1932–) of Newark, N.J., who was elected in 1970. Newark's industrial core and population had declined through the postwar period and by the late 1960s, had a black-majority population. The city's notoriously corrupt machine-dominated government had traditionally excluded blacks. In 1967, one year after Gibson, a city councilman, ran unsuccessfully for mayor, a major racial uprising in the city occurred. In 1969, Newark's mayor, Hugh Addonizio, was convicted on federal corruption charges and removed from office. Meanwhile, black militants led by writer Amiri BARAKA organized a coalition of African-American and Puerto Rican voters and selected Gibson as a consensus candidate. In 1970, with the help of heavy black voter-registration efforts and bloc voting, Gibson was narrowly elected. Once in office, Gibson reached out to the white business community to counteract economic decline and attempted to assure a black majority on the city school board. He drew heavy criticism from black radicals over his perceived inattention to black community problems and from whites over municipal corruption, but remained a popular figure and was reelected for several terms before being defeated by another African American.

Gibson's experience in office typifies the problems of mayors of black-majority cities. Black mayors come to office amid high expectations of policy reforms in the police department, school board, and welfare agency. However, administrative change is difficult and hard to finance, particularly in declining "rust belt" cities with straitened budgets. Mayoral power over city agencies is often limited, and the health of city economies depends on relations between mayors and white-dominated business interests, state, and federal government officials. However, while disappointment is inevitable, African-American mayors of black cities tend to be reelected for several terms, and then are usually followed by other African Americans.

African-American mayors of southern cities, such as Atlanta's Maynard Jackson, elected in 1973; Ernest "Dutch" Morial of New Orleans, elected in 1978; Richard Arrington of Birmingham, elected in 1979; and Willie Herenton of Memphis, elected in 1992, have also come from black majority or near-majority cities. Little Rock, Ark., was the only predominantly white southern city of any size to elect black mayors during the 1970s and 1980s. However, they have differed in a few respects from their northern counterparts. First, not surprisingly, given the electoral history of the South, these candidates had little or no prior experience in electoral politics. Also, while some came from declining "New South" industrial cities, the southern mayors tended to inherit more viable city economies. Thus, while these mayors were elected by a united black vote, they have often run as moderates, hoping to cement links with white business interests. Also, southern black mayors, particularly in Atlanta, have developed affirmative-action programs and provided assistance that has helped expand and solidify the black middle class in their cities.

The other major type of black mayor has been the "crossover" mayor: chief executives elected with significant white support, usually in cities without dominant black populations. The best-known members of this group include Carl Stokes of Cleveland, elected in 1967; Tom Bradley of Los Angeles, elected in 1973; Wilson Goode of Philadelphia, elected in 1983; Harold Washington of Chicago, elected in 1983; and David Dinkins of New York City, elected in 1989. To this list might be added Sidney Barthelemy of New Orleans, who, in 1986, was elected mayor of a black-majority

Three African-American mayors talk with Housing and Urban Development Secretary Robert Weaver, December 1, 1967. (Left to right) Weaver; Mayor Carl B. Stokes of Cleveland; Mayor-Commissioner Walter Washington of Washington, D.C.; and Mayor Richard G. Hatcher of Gary, Ind. (UPI/Bettmann)

city over another African-American candidate. While Barthelemy's opponent gained a majority of the black vote, Barthelemy won with a small black vote and a solid white vote.

The "crossover" mayors form a diverse group. Many of these mayors, of whom David Dinkins is the most celebrated example, came to office in cities torn by racial tension, campaigned as peacemakers, and convinced white voters that a black mayor could more effectively "control" crime and urban rebellions. Through personal charisma and skill in reaching out to diverse minority and interest groups (Latinos, Jews, gays and lesbians, labor unions, women's groups, etc.), these candidates were able to forge successful coalitions.

By the early 1990s, black mayoral politics had entered a new stage of development. Black mayors were being elected to office in greater numbers of cities. Among them were several black women, representing both major cities (Sharon Sayles Belton of Minneapolis, elected in 1994; and Sharon Pratt Dixon of Washington, D.C., elected in 1990) and smaller cities (Carrie Perry of Hartford, Conn., elected in 1987; Jessie Rattley of Newport News, Va., elected in 1986; and Lottie Shackleford of Little Rock, Ark., elected in 1987).

Furthermore, by the 1990s, greater numbers of African Americans were coming to office in cities in which African Americans represented only a small percentage of the population. For example, Norman Rice of Seattle, elected in 1990; and Sharon Sayles Belton of Minneapolis presided in cities where blacks were, respectively, some 10 percent and 13 percent of the population. Previously (with the exception of Tom Bradley of Los Angeles), only a few cities without significant black populations, such as Boulder, Colo.; Spokane, Wash.; and Santa Monica, Calif.—university towns and other "liberal" areas—had had black mayors.

In some cases black mayors in nonblack majority cities were succeeded by other African Americans, but in many cities black electoral power was far from assured. By 1993, several black-majority cities, including Jackson, Miss.; Savannah and Macon, Ga.; and Harrisburg, Pa., had never elected black mayors. Moreover, most black mayors in racially mixed cities were elected by very narrow margins; their victories consisted of overwhelming percentages of the black vote along with a split white vote. For example, in his successful mayoral bid in 1983, Harold Washington won 51 percent of the vote, gaining 99 percent of the black vote, 60 percent of the Hispanic vote, and 19 percent of the white vote. Similarly, David Dinkins won the 1989 election by 47,080 votes, the closest election in city history, with 92 percent of the black vote, 65 percent of the Hispanic vote, and 27 percent of the white vote. Their electoral majorities remained vulnerable, and many of these mayors were defeated following small shifts in voter support in subsequent elections, while increasing racial polarization in large nonblack majority cities made the election of future black mayors extremely difficult. By 1993, white mayors had succeeded blacks in the nation's four largest cities—New York City, Los Angeles, Chicago, and Philadelphia. That year, following a shift of fewer than 100,000 votes, New York Mayor David Dinkins lost a close mayoral race, becoming the first big-city black mayor to fail to be reelected. Despite the setbacks, the office of mayor continues to be a main focus of black political aspiration, and African Americans have established themselves as solid, responsible chief executives in cities in every part of the country.

BIBLIOGRAPHY

Browning, Rufus, ed. *Racial Politics in American Cities.* New York, 1990.

Curvin, Robert. The Persistent Minority: The Black Political Experience in Newark. Ph.D. diss. Newark, N.J., 1975.

Greer, Edward. *Big Steel: Black Politics and Corporate Power in Gary, Indiana.* New York, 1979.

Karnig, Albert, and Susan Welch. *Black Representation and Urban Policy.* Chicago, 1980.

Moss, Larry Edward. *Black Political Ascendancy in Urban Centers, and Black Control of the Local Police.* San Francisco, 1977.

– GREG ROBINSON

MAYS, BENJAMIN ELIJAH

Benjamin Elijah Mays (August 1, 1894–March 28, 1984), educator, clergyman. Benjamin Mays was born in Ninety-Six, S.C., the eighth and youngest child of Hezekiah and Louvenia Carter Mays. His father supported the family as a sharecropper. A year at Virginia Union University in Richmond preceded Mays's matriculation at Bates College in Maine, from which he graduated with honors in 1920. At the Divinity School of the University of Chicago, he earned an M.A. degree in 1925. Ten years later, while engaged in teaching, social work, and educational administration, Mays received a Ph.D. from the Divinity School.

Mays lived in Tampa, Fla., in the early 1920s, where he was active in social work in the Tampa Urban League, exposing police brutality and attacking discrimination in public places. However, higher education soon became his principal vocation. Teaching stints at Morehouse College in ATLANTA and South Carolina State College in Orangeburg between 1921 and 1926 put Mays in the classroom as an instructor in mathematics, psychology, religious education, and English.

In 1934, with his Ph.D. nearly finished, Mays went to HOWARD UNIVERSITY in Washington, D.C., as dean of the School of Religion. He served for six years, and during that time graduate enrollment increased, the quality of the faculty improved, and its library was substantially augmented. During his tenure the seminary gained accreditation from the American Association of Theological Schools.

Mays's administrative successes at Howard University convinced the trustees of Morehouse College to elect him in 1940 as the new president of their institution.

Mays's administrative successes at Howard University convinced the trustees of MOREHOUSE COLLEGE to elect him in 1940 as the new president of their institution. He served until 1967. During his tenure the percentage of faculty with Ph.D.s increased from 8.7 percent to 54 percent and the physical plant and campus underwent numerous improvements. One of Mays's proteges at Morehouse was Martin Luther KING, Jr., who attended the college from 1944—when he entered as a fifteen-year-old—through 1948. Mays, both by example and personal influence, helped persuade young King to seek a career in the ministry. Mays remained a friend of King throughout his career, urging King to persevere in the MONTGOMERY BUS BOYCOTT. In 1965, Mays was instrumental in the election of King to the Morehouse Board of Trustees.

In addition to his activities in higher education, Mays remained involved in religious affairs. Though he was active as a pastor for only a few years in the early 1920s, he became a familiar presence in the affairs of the National Baptist Convention Inc. and in several ecumenical organizations. In 1944 he became vice president of the Federal Council of Churches of Christ, a national organization of mainline Protestant denominations. In 1948 Mays helped to organize the World Council of Churches (WCC) in Amsterdam, Holland, where he successfully pushed a resolution to acknowledge racism as a divisive force among Christians. When a delegate from the Dutch Reformed Church proposed that an all-white delegation from the WCC investigate apartheid in South Africa, Mays argued convincingly for an interracial team to report on race relations in that country.

Mays was a distinguished scholar of the black church and black religion. In 1930 the Institute of Social and Religious Research in New York City requested Mays and Joseph W. Nicholson, a minister in the Colored Methodist Episcopal Church, to survey black churches in twelve cities and four rural areas. In their study, *The Negro's Church* (1933), they argued that black churches represented "the failure of American Christianity." They found that there was an oversupply of black churches, too many with untrained clergy, and too much indebtedness. These shortcomings deprived the members and the communities that they served of adequate programs to deal with the broad range of social and economic ills they faced. Nonetheless, Mays and Nicholson praised the autonomy of black churches and their promotion of education, economic development, and leadership opportunities for African Americans.

In 1938 Mays produced a second important volume. *The Negro's God as Reflected in His Literature,* a study of how blacks conceptualized God and related the deity to their temporal circumstances. Mays argued that many blacks believed God to be intimately involved in and mindful of their condition as an oppressed group. Even those who doubted or rejected either the notion of God or the social dimension of the deity, Mays argued, were still influenced by their understanding of the social purpose of God. In later years Mays wrote an autobiography, *Born to Rebel* (1971), which was published in an abridged version in 1981 as *Lord, the People Have Driven Me On.*

After his retirement in 1967, Mays won election to the Atlanta Board of Education in 1969. He also became president of that body in 1970.

Mays married twice. His first wife, Ellen Harvin Mays, died in 1923. His second wife, whom he married in 1926, was Sadie Gray Mays. She died on October 11, 1969. In 1982 Mays was awarded the NAACP's Spingarn Medal. Benjamin E. Mays died in Atlanta, Ga., on March 28, 1984.

BIBLIOGRAPHY

Carson, Clayborne, Ralph E. Luker, and Penny A. Russell, eds. *The Papers of Martin Luther King, Jr.* Vol. 1, *January 1929–June 1951.* Berkeley, Calif., 1992.

Mays, Benjamin E. *Born to Rebel.* New York, 1971.

———. *Lord, the People Have Driven Me On.* New York, 1981.

———. *The Negro's God.* Boston, 1938.

Mays, Benjamin E. and Joseph W. Nicholson. *The Negro's Church.* New York, 1933.

— DENNIS C. DICKERSON

MAYS, WILLIE HOWARD

Willie Howard Mays (May 6, 1931–), baseball player. The son of steel-mill worker William Mays and Ann Mays, Willie Mays was born in Westfield, Ala. After his parents divorced soon after his birth, Mays was raised by an aunt in Fairfield, Ala. At Fairfield Industrial High School, Mays starred in basketball, football, and baseball.

At the age of seventeen, he began his professional career, joining the Birmingham Black Barons of the Negro National League. During three seasons with the Black Barons, he played 130 games in the outfield and compiled a batting average of .263. In 1950, he started the season with the Black Barons, but he was soon signed by the New York Giants. Mays played on the Giants' minor league teams until early in the 1951 season, when he joined the major league club. Mays was voted the NL Rookie of the Year, and acquired the nickname "the 'Say Hey' kid" when he forgot a Giants' teammate's name in 1951 and used the phrase.

In 1952 and 1953 Mays served in the U. S. Army, but he returned to baseball in 1954 to play one of his best seasons ever. He led the National League with a .345 batting average and had 41 home runs and 110 runs batted in. Mays led the Giants to the 1954 National League pennant and world championship. In the first game of the World Series with the Cleveland Indians at the Polo Grounds in New York City, Mays made one of the most famous catches in baseball history: With his back to home plate, he ran down Vic Wertz's 440-foot drive to center field, wheeled around, and fired a perfect throw to the infield, thus preventing the Indians from scoring. Mays was named the National League's Most Valuable Player for 1954. He won the award a second time in 1965.

Mays is often considered the most complete ballplayer of the postwar era, if not of all time. He excelled in every aspect of the game. He hit over .300 in ten seasons. His total of 660 career home runs is the third best to date. He was one of the game's great baserunners and a superlative fielder. (His fielding earned him twelve consecutive Gold Gloves, from 1957 to 1968). Mays played in every All-Star game from 1954 to 1973 and in four World Series (in 1951 and 1954 with the New York Giants; in 1962 with the San Francisco Giants; and in 1973 with the New York Mets).

Because of his formidable abilities, and because of racism, Mays was also the target of an inordinate number of "bean balls"—pitches thrown at the batter's head. However, Mays was one of the first black superstars to receive widespread adulation from white fans. In the 1960s, Mays was among the many black athletes who were criticized for not publicly supporting the CIVIL RIGHTS MOVEMENT. As on most controversial issues, Mays projected a naive innocence when confronted about his political silence. "I don't picket in the streets of Birmingham," he said. "I'm not mad at the people who do. Maybe they shouldn't be mad at the people who don't."

Mays played with the Giants (the team moved to San Francisco in 1958) until 1972, when he was traded to the New York Mets. The following year he retired as a player but was retained by the Mets as a part-time coach. Mays was inducted into the National Baseball Hall of Fame in 1979. Three months later, he was ordered by Major League Baseball Commissioner Bowie Kuhn to choose between his job with the Mets and fulfilling a public relations contract with the Bally's Casino Hotel. Mays, along with Mickey Mantle, chose the latter and was banned from any affiliation with professional baseball. In 1985, the new Commissioner, Peter Ueberroth, lifted the ban.

BIBLIOGRAPHY

Mays, Willie, and Charles Einstein. *Willie Mays: My Life In and Out of Baseball.* Greenwich, Conn., 1972.

— THADDEUS RUSSELL

MCKAY, CLAUDE

Claude McKay (September 15, 1889–May 22, 1948), poet and novelist. Claude MCKAY was the child of independent small farmers. In 1912 he published two volumes of Jamaican dialect poetry, *Songs of Jamaica* and *Constab Ballads.* They reflect the British imperial influences of his youth and reveal that the rebellion that characterized McKay's American poetry lay in both his Jamaican experience and his later experience of white racism in the United States. His Jamaican poetry also contains early versions of his pastoral longing for childhood innocence and his primal faith in the self-sufficiency and enduring virtues of the rural black community of his childhood and youth.

McKay left Jamaica in 1912 to study agriculture at Tuskegee Institute and Kansas State University, but in 1914 he moved to New York City, where he began again to write poetry. In 1919, he became a regular contributor to the revolutionary literary monthly the *Liberator,* and he achieved fame among black Americans for his sonnet "If We Must Die," which exhorted African Americans to fight bravely against the violence directed against them in the reactionary aftermath of World War I. Although expressed in traditional sonnet form, McKay's post–World War I poetry heralded modern black expressions of anger, alienation, and rebellion, and he quickly became a disturbing, seminal voice in the HARLEM RENAISSANCE of the 1920s. His collected American poetry includes *Spring in New Hampshire and Other Poems* (1920) and *Harlem Shadows* (1922).

The years between 1919 and 1922 marked the height of McKay's political radicalism. In 1922 he journeyed to Moscow, where he attended the Fourth Congress of the Third Communist International, but his independence and his criticisms of American and British Communists led to his abandonment of communism. In the 1930s, he became a vocal critic of international communism because of its antidemocratic dominance by the Soviet Union.

From 1923 until 1934, McKay lived in western Europe and Tangiers. While abroad, he published three novels—*Home to Harlem* (1928), *Banjo* (1929), and *Banana Bottom* (1933)—plus one collection of short stories, *Gingertown* (1932). In his novels, McKay rebelled against the genteel traditions of older black writers, and he offended leaders of black protest by writing in *Home to Harlem* and *Banjo* of essentially leaderless rural black migrants and their predicaments in the modern, mechanistic, urban West. Both were picaresque novels that celebrated the natural resilience and ingenuity of "primitive" black heroes. To McKay's critics, his characters were irresponsible degenerates, not exemplary models of racial wisdom; black critics accused him of pandering to the worst white stereotypes of African Americans.

In *Gingertown* and *Banana Bottom,* McKay retreated to the Jamaica of his childhood to recapture a lost pastoral world of blacks governed by their own rural community values. Although critics still debate the merits of McKay's fiction, it provided encouragement to younger black writers. *Banjo,* in particular, by stressing that blacks should build upon their own cultural values, influenced the founding generation of the Francophone Négritude Movement.

In 1934, the Great Depression forced McKay back to the United States, and for the rest of his life he wrote primarily as a journalist critical of international communism, middle-class black integrationism, and white American racial and political hypocrisy. He continued to champion in his essays working-class African Americans, who he believed understood better than their leaders the necessity of community development. He published a memoir, *A Long Way from Home* (1937), and a collection of essays, *Harlem, Negro Metropolis* (1940), based largely on materials about Harlem folk life he collected as a member of New York City's Federal Writers Project. In 1944—ill, broke, and intellectually isolated—he joined the Roman Catholic church, and spent the last years of his life in Chicago working for the Catholic Youth Organization.

Although he is best known as a poet and novelist of the Harlem Renaissance, McKay's social criticism in the 1930s and 1940s was not negligible, but it was controversial, and has since remained hard to grasp because he was neither a black nationalist, an internationalist, nor a traditional integrationist. He instead believed deeply that blacks in their various American ethnicities had much to contribute as ethnic groups and as a race to the collective American life, and that in the future a recognition, acceptance, and celebration of differences between peoples—and not simply individual integration—would best strengthen and bring together the American populace.

BIBLIOGRAPHY

Cooper, Wayne F., ed. *The Passion of Claude* MCKAY: Selected Poetry and Prose, 1912–1948. New York, 1973.

———. *Claude* MCKAY: Rebel Sojourner in the Harlem Renaissance: A Biography. Baton Rouge, La., 1987.

Giles, James R. *Claude* MCKAY. Boston, 1976.

– WAYNE F. COOPER

MEMPHIS, TENNESSEE

Located on a bluff overlooking the Mississippi River, Memphis, Tenn., received its first African-American settlers shortly after its founding in 1819. Its early black population was largely free, and Shelby County's state representatives opposed slavery. African Americans worked as domestics, stevedores, draymen, blacksmiths, and artisans.

As the town grew into a major port city, racial attitudes began to change. In 1834 Tennessee enacted a new state constitution, which stripped blacks of citizenship rights. The town's African-American population, which previously had enjoyed voting rights, was disenfranchised and forced to observe a curfew. Black clergymen were not allowed to preach. In the 1840s, Tennessee repealed its ban—adopted in 1812—on the domestic slave trade. Memphis, with its large port, became a center for slave trading. Nevertheless, Memphis was more cosmopolitan than most southern cities in that a large number of immigrants—mostly Irish, Italians, and Germans—had settled there. By 1860 the city's population was 17 percent black and more than 36 percent foreign-born.

In 1834 Tennessee enacted a new state constitution, which stripped blacks of citizenship rights.

As the CIVIL WAR lurked on the horizon, Memphis initially did not endorse secession, and even though local support for the Confederacy built once the war began, the city fell to advancing Union troops in 1862 and remained occupied and largely undamaged throughout the war. The Union Army established a large freedpeople's camp near Memphis, and many blacks migrated there, remaining after the end of the war. Yet, EMANCIPATION spawned economic competition between black and white immigrants; and despite efforts by the Freedmens' Bureau, interracial strife developed, particularly between the blacks and Irish who resided in many of the same neighborhoods. In 1866, for instance, struggling Irish residents turned their frustrations on many of their newly arrived black neighbors in a riot that left forty-six blacks dead, nearly twice that many injured, five women raped, approximately 100 blacks robbed, and ninety-one homes, four churches, and all twelve black schools destroyed.

Once the United States Congress enacted civil rights laws in 1866, the political situation improved. By 1875, a coalition of blacks, Irish, and Italians dominated Memphis politics. The blacks were led by the likes of militant saloon-keeper Ed Shaw and the more conciliatory Hezekiah Henley. African Americans held seats on both the elected city council and school board as well as appointed positions such as wharfmaster and coal inspector. Yet, as the JIM CROW era dawned, no African American would hold elective office from 1888 until 1960. As a matter of fact, with the exception of a few Republican primaries, no black would even seek an elected position until 1951.

Due to black in-migration as well as successive yellow fever epidemics, which took a heavy toll on the white population of Memphis and caused a white out-migration, blacks remained a significant voting bloc. Although blocked from holding public office, black suffrage was never formally restricted except by selective enforcement of a poll tax. Thus, even after southern Democrats regained political control of Tennessee, they were compelled to court black votes. Furthermore, black Republican leaders retained influence over policy and the awarding of city and federal patronage jobs.

Despite this limited political power, the social conditions of blacks in Memphis grew steadily worse as the nineteenth century drew to a close. The better-off, more cosmopolitan whites had fled the yellow fever epidemics of the 1880s and been replaced by poorer, more parochial whites from surrounding areas of rural Tennessee, Mississippi, and Arkansas. Blacks' civil and property rights were violated, and the city became increasingly segregated. In 1892, for instance, a white grocery storekeeper facing competition from the black-owned Peoples' Grocery tried to intimidate its owners, claiming a white mob would attack their neighborhood that evening. He then warned the police that blacks were intent on causing trouble. When the black store owners, their homes barricaded, were visited that evening by deputy sheriffs, they mistook the deputies for a mob and fired, fatally wounding them. Arrested the next day, they were taken from prison by a white mob and brutally lynched. When Ida B. Wells denounced the lynching in her newspaper, the *Memphis Free Speech,* a mob burned her press and forced her to flee the city, providing the impetus for her subsequent career as a crusader for African-American rights.

Memphis blacks were anything but passive in the face of the encroachment of segregation. A number of Memphis blacks resisted the day-to-day degradations of Jim Crow. In 1881, for example, prominent musician and schoolteacher Julia Hooks was arrested for her vociferous protest over not being seated in the theater's white section. And, beyond protest, when Mary Morrison was arrested for resisting streetcar segregation in 1905, a huge rally followed in Church Park and several thousand dollars was raised for her legal defense.

There were also forms of even more direct resistance. The following incidents occurred in 1915 and 1916 alone. When white men tried physically to remove Charley Park and John Knox from their trolley seats, Park stabbed one, and Knox ended up in a gun battle with another. A white trolley conductor was stabbed when he tried to collect extra fare from a black rider. Retaliatory ambush shootings and arson took place on occasion. Furthermore, lower-class blacks used a variety of physical means to resist local white police officers.

Meanwhile, despite such turmoil, Beale Street became known as the "Main Street of Negro America." The size and segregation of the black community early on had created a need for a number of black professionals and businesspersons. Black doctors, lawyers, and teachers provided essential services; while black entrepreneurs owned many of the groceries, barbershops, hair salons, funeral parlors, and even banks, open for black patronage. Beale Street, the black commercial center in its Jim Crow heyday, was lined with real estate and baking offices, dry goods and clothing stores, theaters, saloons, gambling joints, and a variety of other small shops (in the 1970s and 1980s, after decades of decline and neglect, city officials began to renovate the Beale Street area as an historic district and tourist attraction.)

In the business realm, in the early twentieth century, Bert Roddy founded the city's first black grocery chain and subsequently organized the Supreme Liberty Life Insurance Company. Included in his effort was an attempt to build on W. E. B. Du Bois's notion of developing community cooperative businesses, in this case Roddy's "Citizens' Coop" grocery stores. Roddy also was the first head of the Memphis branch of the

NAACP. Thomas H. Hayes, another example, was a successful grocer who also started the T. H. Hayes and Sons Funeral Home, the longest continuously running black business in Memphis. Other prominent black businessmen included James Clouston, Clarence Gilliss, Phillip Nicholson, David Woodruff, and N. J. Ford.

Robert Church, Sr., however, was the best known. A former slave, he arrived in Memphis in 1863. By the time of his death in 1912, he had amassed more than $1 million dollars' worth of real estate and other holdings. He was most likely the nation's first black millionaire. His Solvent Savings Bank, founded in 1906, was the first black-owned bank in the city's history; and his donations of Church Park and the adjacent Church Auditorium provided major focal points for black social and cultural life, especially during the Jim Crow period.

Beale Street became known as the "Main Street of Negro America."

Memphis gradually became an African-American cultural center. The city boasted several black theaters; concerts were held in the Church Auditorium. Memphis also contained the Julia Hooks Music School, a black-owned, interracial institution. Beale Street's saloons and gambling clubs were known for their "blues" music, and bands such as John R. Love's Letter Carrier's Band and Jim Turner's Band popularized the sound. Turner's pupil, W. C. HANDY, wrote down much of this music and brought it to the rest of the country. His "Memphis Blues," originally written as a campaign song, became the city's unofficial anthem. In more recent years, the Beale Street milieu has fostered many leading blues musicians such as B. B. King and Memphis Slim.

The Mississippi-born Irishman, Edward H. "Boss" Crump, first won city office in 1905. Although an avowed segregationist, he successfully registered large numbers of black voters, and he turned them out to vote with the help of prominent blacks such as W. C. Handy. By the late 1920s, Crump had consolidated his political power. Thereafter, although no longer actually holding the mayor's office himself, he proceeded to dominate Memphis politics until his death in 1954. Between 1928 and 1948, for instance, his mayoral candidates lost a total of two precincts, which were subsequently abolished upon redistricting. Crump's base of support was an odd mix of blacks and Irish; like most bosses of the day, he held his coalition together with selective patronage.

Blacks, then, although not allowed to rise to positions of authority within the party structure or the bureaucracy, still were marshalled to the polls and, in return, received a share of the city's largesse for delivering a critical voting bloc for the Crump machine. Black leaders such as Harry Pace, Robert Church Jr., J. B. Martin, and Matthew Thornton brokered black political support for patronage benefits. Although Republicans, as were many of the businessmen and professionals in the black leadership elite, they were able to work effectively with Boss Crump—especially while the large majority of blacks apparently remained loyal to the "Party of Lincoln."

Then, as a combination of Crump's efforts and Franklin Roosevelt's emerging coalition lured many blacks from their traditional allegiance to the Republican party, Dr. J. E. Walker organized the Shelby County Democratic Club as an independent political base for black Memphians. Although organizationally separate from the Crump machine, Walker worked with Crump until the early 1950s, when the two had a falling-out over the issue of social segregation. This drove Walker into the camp of a number of white "reformers" who emerged around the successful machine-challenging senatorial bid of Estes Kefauver.

In 1951 Walker challenged the machine himself by running for a position on the school board. In the course of the campaign, the first of many aggressive voter-registration drives was launched within the black community. Although Walker was soundly defeated, he was the first black candidate in decades, and black voter registration nearly tripled in 1951 alone. Then, as Crump died, the poll tax was eliminated and registration drives continued in earnest, and the percentage of registered blacks would triple again over the course of this decade, leaving more than 60 percent of the city's African Americans registered by 1960. By 1963, as blacks struggled for the right to vote across the South, black Memphians were already registered at the same rate as white Memphians.

Two additional pieces of the electoral puzzle were George W. Lee and O. Z. Evers. Lee, a prominent black Republican who led a local group called the "Lincoln League," was helpful in rallying black Republicans, mostly businessmen and ministers. Evers, on the other hand, headed a small group of independents, calling themselves the "Unity League." In addition, none of this should be seen as understating the central political role played by local black churches from Emancipation to the present day. In 1955, as just one example, dozens of churchmen representing every black denomination came together to form the "Ministers and Citizens League." They adopted a $2,000 registration budget, hired three full-time secretaries, and pledged themselves to utilizing other resources at their disposal to increase black voter registration. The black ministers used the pulpit to preach the need to register; they held mass meetings; and they even drove unregistered voters to the courthouse.

Throughout the 1950s, black candidates ran unsuccessfully for citywide and statewide office. Then, in 1959, Russell Sugarmon led a field of black candidates, pulling together black Republicans, Democrats and independents to support a "Volunteer Ticket." His campaign manager was law partner and emerging political leader A. W. Willis. Along with others like Benjamin Hooks, they represented a new political generation. As it turned out, this became a racially divisive election marred by much uncharacteristically overt racist rhetoric. For example, the white "Citizens for Progress" ran under the banner "Keep Memphis Down in Dixie." Meanwhile, prominent African Americans such as the Rev. Dr. Martin Luther KING, Jr. and Mahalia JACKSON appeared to help rally the black vote. Although all black candidates were defeated, Sugarmon had made a strong run for a seat on the city commission. In addition, each of the Volunteer candidates finished second, and nearly two-thirds of black voters were now registered. Sugarmon concluded, "We won everything but the election."

Finally, in 1960, Jesse Turner, also head of the Memphis NAACP, became the first African American since Reconstruction to win an elective post, winning a seat on the Democratic Executive Committee. In the same year, a number of student sit-ins took place, and a successful boycott was launched against downtown retailers. By the mid-1960s, the city of Memphis had a population that was approximately 34 percent black, and two-thirds of them were registered. Then, in 1964, A. W. Williss won a seat in the state legislature, and Charles Ware won a constable position—both plurality votes. Thus, it was not long before a runoff provision was added in order to preclude such developments. In addition, other forms of racial discrimination persisted. For example, Republican "election challenges" focused on the black community, where registrations were reviewed carefully, and this obviously intimidated some legitimately registered blacks. Or, extra field wages would be offered on election day, with the field hands being brought back from the fields too late to vote.

Nevertheless, despite the fact that Memphis elections remained exceptionally polarized by race—especially because whites so seldom voted for black candidates—victories began to occur in districts with large black constituencies. From 1963 onward, as the black voting bloc increased to nearly 100,000 voters, prospects for success increased. They increased despite fairly regular annexations of predominantly white suburbs, a practice that had begun as early as 1909. In 1974, for example, Harold Ford became the first black Tennessean ever elected to the United States Congress, while seats also were being won on the city council, school board, and the judiciary.

Since his election to Congress, Ford has developed the reputation of having the most effective political operation in Memphis. Besides personally paying overdue rents, distributing food at Christmas, contributing to church bazaars, giving graduation presents, and so on, his local congressional staff is also quite proficient at helping constituents through the maze of the federal bureaucracy. In addition, his congressional seniority and consequent committee assignments put him in a position to bring a respectable share of federal funds to Memphis. The word is that "Harold delivers," and his "deliveries" are well chronicled both in his newsletters and in the *Tri-State Defender.* Such service has helped build a core of very loyal supporters; they remained loyal to Ford during his protracted trials and eventual vindication on charges of bank fraud in the 1990s. In addition, the congressman, his staff, and a small group of loyalists regularly compose and distribute a sample ballot endorsing a variety of candidacies. Such endorsements, which often appear to require a financial contribution to the congressman's campaign fund, are believed to generate a sizable number of votes for the endorsed candidates.

Still, it has been the norm for black leaders to split—especially over which mayoral candidate to support. Over the years, these splits have been based on a variety of issues such as gender and intergenerational differences as well as personal rivalries. Such disunity has diluted the influence of the black community. This has been particularly problematic in a city where whites have managed to remain a majority, much of the black population has remained exceptionally poor and consequently difficult to mobilize, and where white allies have been few and far between.

Following the 1987 election, black union leader James Smith called for a leadership summit before the next mayoral election. In the spring of 1991, two "unity conferences" were held, one at the grass-roots level led by City Councilman Shep Wilbun and one at the leadership level led by Rep. Harold Ford. The result was a consensus black candidate, W. W. Herenton, whose Herenton campaign succeeded in uniting the various elite and mass groups under the banner of an uncompromising black political crusade. For the Memphis African-American community, Herenton's election—albeit by an extremely narrow margin of less than 200 votes—marked a high point in a political struggle that has spanned generations. That same year, blacks won a majority of seats on the city's school board and ended up only one vote shy of a majority on the city council.

Yet, despite political victories, the city's commerce and service-oriented economy has offered African Americans far more low-wage positions than higher-paying ones. This has left Memphis with arguably the poorest black underclass of any large U.S. city. By 1990, more than a third of that population was still impoverished; and as for the intensity of the poverty, six Census tracts had a median household income below $5,500. Consequently, a sizable number of black Memphians have ended up disproportionately poor, disillusioned, and militant as well as suspicious of political leaders, including many of their own black leaders.

Labor activism by black Memphians, protesting both their poverty and maltreatment, led to the best-remembered and most tragic event in the recent history of Memphis, the assassination of the Rev. Dr. Martin Luther King, Jr., on April 4, 1968. King was in Memphis to support a strike by the city's largely black staff of sanitation workers. The strikers' grievances went beyond economic issues and involved claims of maltreatment by white supervisors. The strike, which began in February 1968, became bitter and protracted. King encountered much hostility during his stay in Memphis, and the night before he died, in the city's largest black church, the Mason Temple, he seemed to publicly contemplate his own mortality. On the evening of April 4, King was fatally wounded by a rifle shot at the Lorraine Motel. In 1991 the motel reopened as a civil rights museum, dedicated to the memory of Dr. King.

BIBLIOGRAPHY

Biles, Roger. *Memphis in the Great Depression.* Knoxville, Tenn., 1986.

Capers, Gerald. *The Biography of a River Town.* New York, 1966.

Crawford, Charles. *Yesterday's Memphis.* Miami, 1976.

Jalenak, James. *Beale Street Politics.* New Haven, Conn., 1961.

Lamon, Lester. *Blacks in Tennessee, 1791–1970.* Knoxville, Tenn., 1981.

Lee, George. *Beale Street, Where the Blues Began.* College Park, Md., 1969.

McKee, Margaret. *Beale Black and Blue.* Baton Rouge, La., 1961.

Miller, William. *Mr. Crump of Memphis.* Baton Rouge, La., 1964.

Sigafoos, Robert. *Cotton Row to Beale Street.* Memphis, 1979.

Tucker, David. *Memphis Since Crump.* Knoxville, Tenn., 1980.

Wright, William. *Memphis Politics.* New York, 1962.

– MARCUS D. POHLMANN

METHODIST CHURCH

Since its appearance in the British colonies of North America, Methodism has been one of the most influential Christian denominations among African Americans—only the Baptist church has generally surpassed it in terms of black adherents. The majority of African-American Methodists have worshipped within all-black denominations: the African Methodist Episcopal Zion church (1801), the AFRICAN METHODIST EPISCOPAL CHURCH (1814), and the Colored Methodist Episcopal church (1870, known since 1954 as the CHRISTIAN METHODIST EPISCOPAL CHURCH). A number of black Methodists, however, chose to remain within the original, racially mixed Methodist Episcopal church (1794) and its subsequent incarnations, such as the METHODIST CHURCH (1940) and the United Methodist church (1968).

Methodism has been one of the most influential Christian denominations among African Americans.

Africans who were brought to colonial North America as slaves—with few exceptions—had not previously been exposed to Christianity. While some Anglicans and Quakers made attempts to convert blacks, they met with resistance, not only from southern slave owners, but also from within their own ranks. The evangelical revivals of the Great Awakening (1730 to 1760), which split older denominations and later helped the spread of Methodism and the Baptist faith, helped to change this. Often not formally educated in theology, Methodist preachers traveled on horseback and delivered highly moving sermons wherever they could assemble a crowd. Methodism, an independent denomination which arose out of the Wesleyan revival in the Church of England, proved extremely successful at gaining adherents in America. John Wesley and his followers were ardent Arminians. They opposed the predestination of Calvinism and believed in the possibility of salvation for all. Their message was one of redemption: Life was a quest for sanctification. It proved to be as powerful for free blacks in the North and slaves in the South as it was for white Americans.

Between 1766, when the first American Methodist Society was organized in New York City, and the conclusion of the American Revolution in 1783, Methodism spread to several northern cities, including New York and Philadelphia and to the southern states of Maryland and Virginia. Methodist preachers sent from England to the colonies often sought out black audiences on their travels. Robert Williams (1745–1775) and Joseph Pilmore (1739–1825) both spread their evangelical preaching to blacks, as did Richard Boardman (1738–1782) and Thomas Rankin (1738–1816).

Rankin introduced John Wesley's antislavery tract, "Thoughts on Slavery," to the Continental Congress. George Shadford (1739–1816) converted many slaves to Methodism while traveling on the Brunswick circuit through Virginia and North Carolina. It was Francis Asbury (1745–1816), however, who did the most to establish Methodism in America and to include blacks within the denomination. Ashbury's desire for a racially inclusive church helped to transform Methodism from a small group of societies into a national religious movement. Asbury preached understanding and acceptance of other races and recognized the need for indigenous evangelism. The extent of black involvement in early American Methodism is shown by the fact that thirty-six of the fifty-one societies represented at the 1784 constituting meeting (which established Methodism as a denomination independent of the Anglican church) reported black members. Asbury himself ordained the earliest African-American Methodist preacher, Harry Hosier, who was selected exclusively to promote the "black work" at St. George's Church in Philadelphia, Pa.

The evangelical efforts of Methodist preachers among African Americans did not by themselves mean that black converts would be accorded equality of treatment. In fact, the increase of African-American membership in the Methodist church went hand in hand with a rise in racial discrimination within the denomination. In attempting to solve this racial disharmony, the Methodist church explored various patterns of relationships between their white and black followers: simultaneous segregated worship, separate worship at different times, and separate worship in separate churches. None of these arrangements proved satisfactory. They failed to engage the issues of racism and the resulting lack of black ministerial and administrative participation. Schemes for voluntary separation and independent black churches emerged. African-American Methodists, already worshiping in segregated "classes," created small black church fellowships which often met in private homes and eventually began holding their own Sunday services. Two independent black churches—the Bethel Church in Philadelphia (founded in 1793) and the Zion Church in New York City (founded in 1801)—formed separate denominations which operated independently of the Methodist Episcopal church. These became, respectively, the African Methodist Episcopal church (AME) and the African Methodist Episcopal Zion church (AMEZ).

In the South, Wesley's strictures against slavery were ignored. With the rise of cotton and westward expansion of plantation agriculture, the Methodist church became conspicuously silent on the issue of slavery. Southern membership included a large number of slaveholders and slaves. Slaves modified the lessons of Methodism to suit their own circumstances, finding solace in promises of redemption in the afterlife. Their faith often found strongest expression in hymns and SPIRITUALS.

As divisions between northern and southern society deepened from the 1830s through the 1850s, sectional divisions arose within the Methodist Episcopal church. Antislavery members of the Methodist church broke from the denomination and formed the Welseyan Methodist church in Michigan (1841) and the Methodist Wesleyan Connection in New York (1842). A formal split in the denomination occurred after the 1844 General Conference in New York City, with the "Methodist Episcopal church, South" convening separately from the "Methodist Episcopal church" the following year.

During the Civil War the Methodist Episcopal church, South emerged as an arch defender of the Confederacy and all its institutions. The defeat of the South proved devastating for the church. The black membership of the Methodist Episcopal church, South, had stood at 207,766 in 1860; by 1866, it had fallen to 78,742. In 1870, the remaining black constituency of the Methodist Episcopal church, South requested and received a separate denominational status and formed the Colored Methodist Episcopal church (CME). Most freedmen who left the Methodist Episcopal church, South, joined one of the three all-black Methodist denominations: the AMEZ, AME, and the CME. Many others, however, joined the northern Methodist Episcopal church as it traveled south to seek converts. These northern Methodists formed clubs and societies in the south to aid the freedmen. In 1871, the Woman's Home Missionary Society was founded in New Orleans to work with needy black women and children. Other organizations providing financial and educational aid to African Americans included I. Garland Penn's Epworth League, the Bureau of Negro Work, and later in the 1920s, the Gulfside Assembly.

The Methodist Episcopal church also formed dozens of elementary and normal schools between 1866 and 1896 through its Freedman's Aid Society. Several of these later became accredited colleges. These included: Bennett College in Greensboro, N.C. (1873); Meharry Medical College in Nashville, Tenn. (1876); and Gammon Theological Seminary in Atlanta, Ga. (1888), now part of the Interdenominational Theological Center. African-American Methodists founded their own newspaper, the *Southwestern Christian Advocate* (originally the *New Orleans Christian Advocate*). It was edited and published privately for a decade before authorization by the 1876 General Conference. It became the *Central Christian Advocate* in 1940.

The result of the missionary thrust into the South by the northern Methodist Episcopal church was notable. At the end of the Civil War black membership had been roughly 26,000; by 1896 it had increased to 250,000. The Methodist Episcopal church expanded opportunities to some black members, though often in carefully selected roles. In 1852 the church had elected Francis Burns as its first black bishop. He was chosen to serve as a missionary bishop in Africa. In 1866, Burns was succeeded by John W. Roberts.

Toward the end of the Civil War, the Methodist Episcopal church began organizing separate black conferences. The first of these were in Delaware (1864); Washington, D.C. (1864); Mississippi (1867); Lexington, Ky. (1869); and South Carolina (1870). In 1868 the status of these organizations was changed from "mission conferences" to "annual conferences," which allowed them to elect representation to the denomination's General Conference. At the 1920 General Conference, two black bishops, Robert E. Jones (1872–1960) and Matthew W. Clair, Sr. (1865–1943), were elected to serve black Episcopal areas.

By the late 1930s, the record of growth, expansion and progress of the black constituency of the Methodist Episcopal church had been impressive in spite of its segregated structure. This scenario may have continued except for the movement to reunite the three branches of Methodism: the northern and southern divisions, as well as the Methodist Protestants, who had withdrawn in 1830 over the issue of lay rights and the power of the episcopacy. (The Methodist Protestants had relatively few black members—just over two thousand in 1936.)

Beginning in 1916, efforts had been made to reconcile the differences in the three branches by a General Conference. The future status and role of black people in the proposed church was important to the debate. In the 1939 Plan of Union the issue was settled by placing all African-American Methodists in a Central Jurisdiction. This decision, which literally wrote segregation into the constitution of the denomination, was considered disagreeable by many Methodists, both black and white. The general euphoria that pervaded the Uniting General Conference that gave birth to the new "Methodist church" obscured the fact that it was now the largest racially segregated Protestant body in the nation. African-American Methodists faced the future with faith that this anomaly would ultimately be eliminated.

Despite its obvious limitations, the Plan of Union did include provisions for the election of black bishops. From 1940 to 1968, fourteen Central Jurisdiction ministers were selected for this office. African Americans also attained the office of district superintendency. This occurred first on a temporary basis in New York, in 1962, and then in two full term appointments (one in New York and one in Chicago) in 1964. The ministerial leadership situation in the Central Jurisdiction was more problematic. The church faced a critical shortage of qualified candidates for the ministry. Fewer college-educated black youths expressed interest in becoming ministers because career promotions were limited and support benefits, such as salary, pension, and housing provisions, were unattractive and often inadequate.

Since 1972 all five of the geographic jurisdictions of the Methodist church have had one or more African-American bishops.

The membership of the Central Jurisdiction resulting from reunion in 1939 topped 315,000. The size of this Central Jurisdiction, however, did not increase after 1939, despite an annual national black population increase. Similarly, the growth in the number of black churches declined in this period. Black urban Methodist churches were unable to attract southern rural immigrants, or meet the widening spectrum of needs of urban dwellers in their midst. The Division of Home Missions tried to confront this crisis through technical and financial support to black (and other) disadvantaged communities. Also, the Woman's Division of Christian Service launched a program of spiritual and social uplift, through local church units across the nation. Finally, and most importantly, the General Board of Education through its several divisions designed and implemented a five-point program in the Central Jurisdiction. This included the improvement of church schools, the organization and development of the Methodist Youth Fellowship, the institution of a leadership education program, the development of a new approach to student work, and a new and critical look a ministerial education.

The Central Jurisdiction was never considered a satisfactory or final arrangement for race relations in the Methodist church. It functioned from 1940 to 1968 holding quadrennial sessions, electing bishops and board and agency representatives and performing the requirements of the church's Book of Discipline. From its beginning, it was an anomaly and steps were taken toward its elimination. In 1956, the General Conference decided to eradicate rather than correct the jurisdictional system. In 1962 a Central Jurisdiction "Committee of Five" developed a transfer-merger procedure which was subsequently authorized by a special meeting of the General Conference (1966). On August 20, 1967, the Central Jurisdiction ceased to be, and was merged into other Methodist jurisdictions.

Difficult challenges confronted the United Methodist church when it came into being at the Uniting Conference in Dallas, Tex., in May 1968. It had, first of all, to unite the Methodist church (1939–1968) and the Evangelical United Brethren church (1946–1968). It also had to confront the issue of inclusiveness—that is, intentionally including African Americans, Asian Americans, Latino Americans and Native Americans in the life and work of the church. Despite episodic increases, black membership in the United Methodist church declined after the merger. The new denomination began in 1968 with a black membership of about 370,000. Between 1968 and 1974 it showed small increases periodically, but began to decline after 1980 (in proportion to the decline in total membership). The African-American United Methodist churches which grew have shared several common characteristics: commitment to ministry from a black perspective; spiritually moving and highly spirited preaching, worship and music; a high degree of community accountability and involvement; a pluralistic approach to programming; and an open and fully inclusive membership.

Despite the problems, however, significant progress was made toward the goal of racial inclusiveness throughout the denomination following merger. Since 1972 all five of the geographic jurisdictions of the church have had one or more African-American bishops; and sixteen African-American bishops have been elected since 1968, including one woman. In 1984, the United Methodists elected their first black woman bishop—the Rev. Leontine Kelly, a pastor from Richmond, Va. Scores of African-American district superintendents have been appointed to serve districts on a nonracial basis in practically every annual conference of the church. Black general and annual elected positions and staff positions (including World Division missionary appointments) have tripled since merging with the former Evangelical United Brethren. The most dramatic progress has come from the Black Methodists for Church Renewal (BMCR). Founded on February 6, 1968, this group literally "renewed" the church's commitment to social justice. With its slogan, "Our Time Under God Is Now," the BMCR pursued a policy of racial inclusiveness that was legislated by the General Conference. All church bodies were made accountable to the General Conference for their race relations policies, and the use of church facilities "to preserve racially segregated education" was prohibited. General church funds were made available for black community development, and church school curriculum materials and educational programs were revised to be more inclusive. Finally, a black college fund was established to assist African-American schools in providing more adequate programs, and new loan and scholarship programs were instituted in higher and theological education institutions of the church. The actions stemming from the creation of the United Methodist church have marked a beneficient change in the long and complicated relationship between the Methodist church and its African-American members.

BIBLIOGRAPHY

Barclay, William C. *History of Methodist Missions.* 3 vols. New York, 1949.

Burke, Emory S., ed. *The History of American Methodism.* 3 vols. New York, 1958.

Clark, Elmer T., ed. *The Journals and Letters of Francis Asbury.* 3 vols. New York, 1958.

Graham, John H. *Black United Methodists: Retrospect and Prospect.* New York, 1979.

Morrow, Ralph E. *Northern Methodism and Reconstruction.* East Lansing, Mich., 1956.

Norwood, Frederick A. *The Story of American Methodism.* Nashville, 1974.

Shockley, Grant S., ed. *Heritage and Hope: The African American Presence in United Methodism.* Nashville, 1991.

Thomas, James S. *Methodism's Racial Dilemma: The Story of the Central Jurisdiction.* Nashville, 1992.

– GRANT S. SHOCKLEY

MICHEAUX, OSCAR

Oscar Micheaux (January 2, 1884–March 25, 1951), novelist and filmmaker. Oscar Micheaux was born in Metropolis, Ill., one of thirteen children of former slaves. The early events of his life are not clear and must be gleaned from several fictionalized versions he published. He evidently worked as a Pullman porter, acquiring enough capital to buy two 160-acre tracts of land in South Dakota, where he homesteaded. Micheaux's homesteading experiences were the basis of his first novel, *The Conquest: The Story of a Negro Pioneer* (1913). In order to publicize the book, Micheaux established the Western Book Supply Company and toured the Midwest. He sold most of the books and stock in his first company to white farmers, although his later ventures were financed by African-American entrepreneurs. From his bookselling experiences, he wrote a second novel, *The Forged Note: A Romance of the Darker Races* (1915). Micheaux's third novel, *The Homesteader* (1917), attracted the attention of George P. Johnson, who, with his Hollywood actor brother Noble, owned the Lincoln Film Company, with offices in Los Angeles and Omaha. The Johnson brothers were part of the first wave of African-American independent filmmakers to take up the challenge to D. W. Griffith's white supremacist version of American History, *Birth of a Nation* (1915), and to produce their own stories of African-American life. Fascinated by the new medium, Micheaux offered to sell the Johnson Brothers film rights to his novel, on the condition that he direct the motion picture version. When they refused, Micheaux decided to produce and direct the film himself, financing it through what became the Micheaux Book and Film Company, with offices located in New York, Chicago, and Sioux City, Iowa.

The film version of Micheaux's third novel, *The Homesteader* (1918), was the first of about fifty films he directed. He distributed the films himself, carrying the prints from town to town, often for one-night stands. His films played mostly in white-owned (but often black-managed) black theaters in the North and in the South. He even had some luck convincing southern white cinema owners to let him show his films at all-black matinees and interracial midnight shows in white theaters. While the black press at the time sometimes criticized Micheaux for projecting a rich black fantasy world and ignoring ghetto problems, he dealt frankly with such social themes as interracial relationships, "passing," intraracial as well as interracial prejudice, and the intimidation of African Americans by the KU KLUX KLAN. Micheaux's second film, *Within Our Gates* (1919), contains a disturbing sequence representing a white lynch mob hanging an innocent black man and his wife. When Micheaux tried to exhibit the film in Chicago, less than a year after a major race riot in the city, both black and white groups urged city authorities to ban the film. Micheaux's response to such censorship was to cut and reedit his films from town to town. Showman and entrepreneur that he was, he would promote a film that had been banned in one town by indicating in the next town that it contained "censored" footage. Produced on a shoestring, his films earned him just enough money to continue his filmmaking.

Some twelve of Micheaux's films are extant, and they give an idea, though incomplete, of his style. His interior scenes are often dimly lit, but his location scenes of urban streets are usually crisp and clear, providing a documentary-like glimpse of the period. He seldom had money for more than one take, with the result that the actors' mistakes are sometimes left on screen. However, Micheaux had a genius for negotiating around tight budgets, improvising with limited resources, and synchronizing production with distribution. In the early 1920s, in order to purchase the rights to African-American author Charles Waddell CHESNUTT's *The House Behind the Cedars* (1900), he offered the author shares in his film company.

To create appeal for his films, Micheaux features some of the most talented African-American actors of his time: Andrew Bishop, Lawrence-Chenault, A. B. Comithiere, Lawrence Criner, Shingzie Howard, and Evelyn Preer, many of whom were associated with the Lafayette Players stock company. Actor and singer Paul ROBESON made his first motion picture appearance in Micheaux's *Body and Soul* (1924), in a dual role as both a venal preacher and his virtuous brother. Micheaux returned often to the theme of the hypocritical preacher, a portrait inspired by the betrayal of his father-in-law, a Chicago minister. Of the actors Micheaux made celebrities in the black community, the most notable was Lorenzo Tucker, a handsome, light-skinned actor, dubbed "the colored Valentino." Micheaux's films also featured cabaret scenes and chorus line dancers, and, after the coming of sound, jazz musicians and comedians.

Micheaux had a genius for negotiating around tight budgets, improvising with limited resources, and synchronizing production with distribution.

Although his company went bankrupt in 1928, Micheaux managed to survive the early Depression, continuing to produce silent films. Although *Daughter of the Congo* (1930) featured some songs and a musical score, *The Exile* (1931) was thought to be the first African-American-produced all-talking picture. Micheaux went on to make a number of sound films, but many moments in these films are undercut because his technicians could not surmount the challenges produced by the new sound-recording technology. In the late 1930s, after the brief notoriety of *God's Stepchildren* (1937), Micheaux's film activities began to wind down and he returned to writing novels. He published *The Wind from Nowhere* (1941), a reworking of *The Homesteader,* and three other novels during the next five years. In 1948, he produced a large-budget version of *The Wind from Nowhere,* titled *The Betrayal* and billed as the first African-American motion picture to play in major white theaters. However, the film received unfavorable reviews in the press, including *The New York Times.* At a time of his decline in popularity as both novelist and filmmaker, Micheaux died during a promotional tour in 1951 in Charlotte, N.C.

Micheaux's work was first rediscovered by film scholars in the early 1970s. However, these critics still disdained the wooden acting and unmatched shots in his films and decried what they thought to be the escapist nature of his stories. More recent critics, however, have hailed Micheaux as a maverick stylist who understood but was not bound by classical Hollywood cutting style, who used precious footage economically, who was adept in his use of the flashback device, and whose "rough draft" films were vaguely avant-garde. Similarly, Micheaux is not recognized for his "protest" films and his use of social types to oppose caricature rather than to reinforce stereotype.

Largely ignored during his lifetime, Micheaux has received recognition in recent years. The Black Filmmakers Hall of Fame inaugurated an annual Oscar Micheaux Award in 1974. In 1985, the Directors' Guild presented Micheaux with a special Golden Jubilee Award, and in 1987, he received a star on the Hollywood Walk of Fame. The recent discovery of prints of two silent films, *Within Our Gates* (1919) and *Symbol of the Unconquered* (1920) in archives in Spain and Belgium, respectively, has increased the interest in his work.

BIBLIOGRAPHY

Cripps, Thomas. *Slow Fade to Black: The Negro in American Film, 1900–1942.* 2nd ed. New York, 1989.

Gaines, Jane M. "Fire and Desire: Race, Melodrama, and Oscar Micheaux." In Manthia Diawara, ed. *Black American Cinema: History, Theory, Criticism.* New York, 1993.

Green, Ron. "Oscar Micheaux's Production Values." In Manthia Diawara, ed. *Black American Cinema: History, Theory, Criticism.* New York, 1993.

Peterson, Bernard L., Jr. "A Filmography of Oscar Micheaux: America's Legendary Black Filmmaker." In David Platt, ed. *Celluloid Power.* Metuchen, N.J., 1992.

Regester, Charlene. "Lynched, Assaulted, and Intimidated: Oscar Micheaux's Most Controversial Films." *Popular Culture Review* 5, no. 1 (February 1994): 47–55.

— JANE GAINES AND CHARLENE REGESTER

MIDWIFERY

The evocation of the word *midwifery* calls up two images. The first is a medically trained nurse who specializes in obstetrics and gynecology and is licensed to attend childbirths in the hospital and, less frequently, in freestanding birthing centers or the homes of clients. The second and older image is the tradition of social childbirth in which women gave birth at home in the presence of other women and with the guidance of a skilled folk practitioner. Due to a number of economic, cultural, and political factors, social childbirth declined in significance for native-born northern white women relatively early. By the late 1760s, they had already begun to rely on male physicians to deliver their children. Traditional midwifery, however, continued to flourish among European immigrants who settled in the cities along the northeastern seaboard from the late nineteenth through the early twentieth century.

In the South, the midwifery tradition has been for the most part an African-American one, with the midwife mediating the reproductive experiences of both black and white women, especially in the region's rural communities from the early seventeenth to the closing decades of the twentieth century. By the 1940s, social childbirth had been largely replaced by scientific childbirth in the hospital, but a few surviving traditional African-American midwives continued to offer their services in the late 1980s as reported by Debra Susie (1988) in Florida and by Linda Holmes (1986) and Annie Logan (1989) in Alabama.

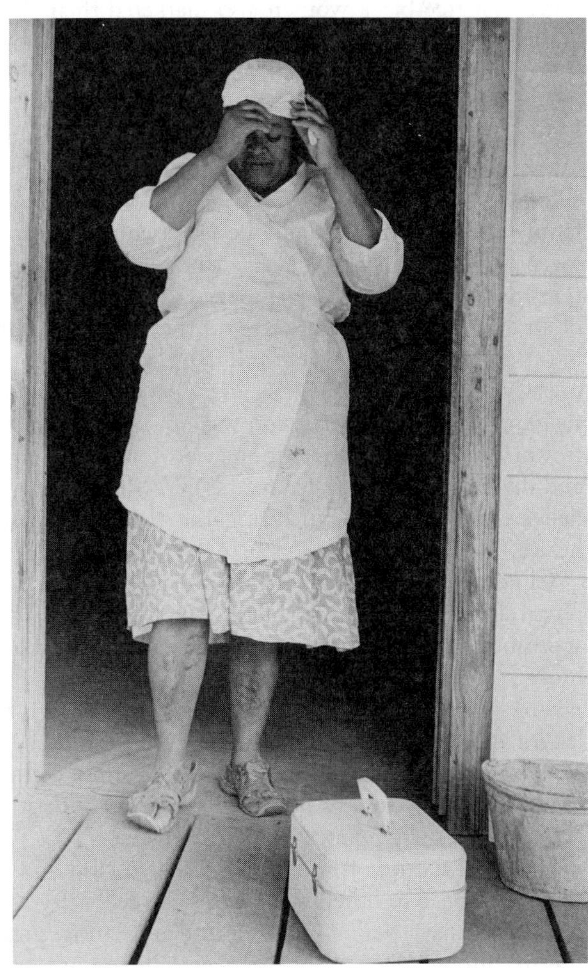

Frances Mae Carson, thirty-seven, midwife in Dallas County, Ala., getting dressed to leave on her patient rounds in the district, May 4, 1966. (© Charmian Reading)

Throughout the slaveholding South, African-American midwives had the responsibility for managing pregnancy and childbirth. Often these women were slaves practicing not only on the plantations where they resided, but also attending births on neighboring plantations, for which their owners collected a fee. In the rural areas of the South, slave midwives also delivered the children of white women. Powerful in their knowledge of the physiological, medicinal, and spiritual aspects of childbirth, slave midwives inhabited an intensely ambiguous role. They wielded an expertise that allowed them to compete successfully with "scientifically" trained white male physicians of the period while they remained classified as property, rarely receiving renumeration, and subject to sanctions should the infant or mother die. Given the close association of childbirth with other aspects of bodily functioning, slave midwives were also generally recognized as healers and attended the sick as part of their practice. Todd Savitt notes that free black women also marketed their skills as birth attendants to a white clientele, while at the same time offering their services to neighbors and kin in their own communities (Savitt 1978, 182).

In the African-American community, across historical periods, women who became midwives did so either through apprenticeship to another midwife, often a family member, or through the experience of having given birth themselves. Whatever the practical route of transmission, however, the emphasis in the articulation of an identity as a midwife was on the spiritual nature of the practice. Women were said to be called to become midwives in the same manner that a person is called to religious ministry; the decision was not under the control of the individual practitioner. So too were prayer and divine guidance crucial to the midwife's success in delivering babies and nurturing the mother back to health.

Childbirth, in this framework, did not end with the physical emergence of the infant. The midwife was responsible for postpartum care, ensuring that both mother and child—spiritually as well as physically vulnerable—were protected from harm. Though the length of time varied, new mothers were expected to refrain from normal activities, avoid eating certain foods, and keep close to home for up to a month after birth, under the guidance of their midwives.

The dual nature of midwifery as skilled craft and as spiritual service to others was intrinsic to its emergence during the slave period, and continued as an essential feature through the end of the twentieth century. It is important to recognize, then, that African-American midwives historically viewed themselves as socially embedded in the cultural and religious belief systems of their own communities, but also as having control of a set of skills that allowed them a measure of independence and authority in the broader society.

BIBLIOGRAPHY

Holmes, Linda J. "African-American Midwives in the South." In Pamela S. Eakins, ed. *The American Way of Birth.* Philadelphia, 1986, pp. 273–291.

Logan, Annie Lee, as told to Katherine Clark. *Motherwit: An Alabama Midwife's Story.* New York, 1989.

Savitt, Todd. *Medicine and Slavery: The Diseases and Health Care of Blacks in Antebellum Virginia.* Urbana, Ill., 1978.

Susie, Debra A. *In the Way of Our Grandmothers: A Cultural View of Twentieth-Century Midwifery in Florida.* Athens, Ga., 1988.

— GERTRUDE J. FRASER

MIGRATION/POPULATION

Migration has been a persistent theme throughout African-American history. Africans entered the New World as slaves, unlike European immigrants and their Asian counterparts. With the advent of the CIVIL WAR and EMANCIPATION, black population movement took on a voluntary character and slowly converged with that of other groups. Nonetheless, only with the coming of WORLD WAR I and its aftermath did blacks make a fundamental break with the land and move into cities in growing numbers. The Great Migration of the early twentieth century foreshadowed the long-run transformation of African Americans from a predominantly rural to a predominantly urban population. It reflected their quest for freedom, jobs, and social justice; the rise of new classes and social relations within the African-American community; and the emergence of new patterns of race, class, and ethnic relations in American society as a whole.

From the colonial period through the antebellum era, Africans and their American descendants experienced forced migration from one agricultural region to another. One and a half million blacks reached the United States via the international SLAVE TRADE, primarily from the west coast of Africa. Through natural increase, their numbers rose to an estimated four million by 1860. By 1750, there were more than 144,000 blacks in the tobacco-growing states of Maryland and Virginia, representing the highest concentration of slaves in the country. In the wake of the American Revolution, however, slaves experienced a dramatic relocation from the tobacco region of the upper South to the emerging cotton-growing areas of the deep South. The tobacco country slowly declined in fertility during the late eighteenth century, and planters first transported or sold their slaves to the neighboring states of Kentucky and Tennessee. After the close of the international slave trade to the United States in 1808, this movement accelerated. Between 1810 and 1820, an estimated 137,000 slaves left the Chesapeake Bay region and North Carolina for the cotton-growing states of the deep South, particularly Alabama and Mississippi.

Some slaves entered the deep South with their masters, but growing numbers came via the domestic slave trade. Whether they traveled by water or by land, they moved to their new homes in handcuffs and chains. As one ex-slave recalled, "We were handcuffed in pairs, with iron staples and bolts, with a short chain about a foot long uniting the handcuffs and their wearers." Contemporary travelers frequently commented on the sight of migrating slaves. In 1834, for example, an English traveler reported on his trip from Virginia to Alabama: "In the early grey of the morning, we came up with a singular spectacle, the most striking one of the kind I have ever witnessed. It was a camp of negro slave-drivers, just packing up to start; they had about three hundred slaves with them, who had bivouacked the preceding night in chains in the woods; these they were conducting to Natchez, upon the Mississippi River."

Although Africans, and increasingly African Americans, were the victims of coerced migrations during this period, they were by no means passive. Slaves acted in their own behalf by running away, planning rebellions, and deepening their efforts to build a viable slave community. One historian concludes, for example, that the transition from an African to a predominantly American-born slave-labor force facilitated the emergence of new forms of rebellion and demands for liberation in the new republic. As slaves learned the language, gained familiarity with the terrain, and built linkages to slaves on other plantations, they increased their efforts to resist bondage. Newspaper advertisements for runaways increased as planters and slave traders mediated the transfer of slaves from the tobacco-growing regions to the "cotton kingdom." Advertisements for runaways not only reflected the slaves' resistance, but also the harsh conditions they faced: "Bill is a large fellow, very black, shows the whites of his eyes more than usual, has a scar on his right cheek bone, several on his breast, one on his arm, occasioned by the bite of a dog, his back very badly scarred with the whip."

The Civil War and RECONSTRUCTION radically transformed the context of black migration. Black population movement accelerated, spurred by the presence of federal troops, the ending of chattel slavery, the enactment of full citizenship legislation, and rising white hostility. In the first years following Emancipation, one Florida planter informed his cousin in North Carolina, "The negroes don't seem to feel free unless they leave their old homes . . . just to make it sure they can go when and where they choose." A South Carolina family offered to pay its cook double the amount that she would receive in another village, but the woman insisted, "No, Miss, I must go. . . . If I stay here I'll never know I am free."

When the promise of freedom faded during the late 1870s, the Exodus of 1879 symbolized the new mobility of the black population. Within a few months, some six thousand blacks left their homes in Louisiana, Mississippi, and Texas for a new life in Kansas. As one black contemporary stated, "There are no words which can fully express or explain the real condition of my people throughout the south, nor how deeply and keenly they feel the necessity of fleeing from the wrath and long pent-up hatred of their old masters which they feel assured will ere long burst loose like the pent-up-fires of a volcano and crush them if they remain here many years longer." Still, the Exodus was a rural-to-rural migration, with blacks moving to Kansas when an earlier Tennessee option proved fruitless. African Americans expected to resettle on available farmland and continue their familiar, but hopefully freer, rural way of life.

Despite the predominance of rural-to-rural migration, the migration of blacks to American cities had deep antebellum roots. Boston launched its career as a slaveholding city as early as 1638, when the Salem ship *Desire* returned from the West Indies with a cargo of "salt, cotton, tobacco, and Negroes." Slavery in New York City, beginning under Dutch control in 1626, entered an era of unprecedented growth under the British in 1664. In Philadelphia in 1684, within three years after the first Quakers settled in Pennsylvania, the first fifty Africans arrived. The number of slaves in the seaports of the Northeast rose from negligible numbers during the seventeenth century to sizable proportions by the mid-eighteenth century: to over 1,500 in Boston, 1,400 in Philadelphia, and over 2,000 in New York. Southern cities such as New Orleans, Mobile, Charleston, Baltimore, Louisville, Savannah, and Richmond also had sizable antebellum black populations.

Under the impact of World War I, blacks made a fundamental break with their southern rural heritage and moved into cities in growing numbers.

Black migration to American cities escalated during the late eighteenth and early nineteenth centuries. Moreover, in the aftermath of the Civil War and Reconstruction, blacks increasingly moved into rural industrial settings such as the coalfields of Alabama, Tennessee, Kentucky, and West Virginia. Others gained increasing access to nonagricultural jobs as lumber and railroad hands in the expanding industrial order. Still, as late as 1910, nearly 90 percent of the nation's black population lived in the South, and fewer than 22 percent of southern blacks lived in cities.

Under the impact of World War I, blacks made a fundamental break with their southern rural heritage and moved into cities in growing numbers. An estimated 700,000 to one million blacks left the South between 1917 and 1920. Another 800,000 to one million left during the 1920s. Whereas the prewar migrants moved to southern cities such as Norfolk, Louisville, Birmingham, and Atlanta and to a few northern cities such as Chicago, Philadelphia, and New York, blacks now moved throughout the urban North and West. Beginning with relatively small numbers on the eve of World War I, the black urban population in the Midwest and Great Lakes region increased even more dramatically than that of the old Northeast. Detroit's black population increased by 611 percent during the war years and by nearly 200 percent during the 1920s, rising from fewer than 6,000 to over 120,000. Cleveland's black population rose from fewer than 8,500 to nearly 72,000. In St. Louis, the increase was from under 45,000 in 1910 to nearly 94,000 in 1930. In the urban West, the black population increased most dramatically in Los Angeles, growing from 7,600 in 1910 to nearly 40,000 in 1930. Nonetheless, as in the prewar era, New York City, Chicago, and Philadelphia continued to absorb disproportionately large numbers of black newcomers. Between 1910 and 1930, Chicago's black population increased more than fivefold, from 44,000 to 234,000; New York's more than tripled, from about 100,000 to 328,000; and Philadelphia's grew from 84,500 to an estimated 220,600.

Upper South and border states remained important sources of black migrants during World War I and the 1920s, but deep South states increased their importance. Blacks born in Mississippi, Alabama, Georgia, South Carolina, and Louisiana now dominated the migration stream to Illinois and Chicago, for example, making up over 60 percent of the black population increase in that area between 1910 and 1920. African Americans from the upper South predominated in New York City more so than in Chicago, but blacks from South Carolina, Georgia, and Florida came in growing numbers. In the rapidly industrializing cities of Cleveland and Detroit, the percentage of black men to women escalated from just a few more men than women in 1910 to between 120 and 140 men to every 100 women during the war years. In Milwaukee, where the ratio of men to women was 95 to 100 in 1910, the ratio reversed itself, and the number of men versus women increased between 1910 and 1920. Finally, in the northeastern cities of New York and Philadelphia, where women significantly outnumbered men before the war, the ratio evened out.

A variety of factors underlay black population movement. African Americans sought an alternative to sharecropping, disfranchisement, and racial injustice in the South. In 1917, the *AME Review* articulated the forces that propelled blacks outward from the South: "Neither character, the accumulation of property, the fostering of the Church, the schools and a better and higher standard of the home" had made a difference in the status of black Southerners. "Confidence in the sense of justice, humanity and fair play of the white South is gone," the paper concluded. One migrant articulated the same mood in verse: "An' let one race have all de South—Where color lines are drawn—For 'Hagar's child' done [stem] de tide—Farewell—we're good and gone."

African Americans were also attracted by the lure of opportunities in the North. The labor demands of northern industries, immigration-restriction legislation, and greater access to the rights of citizens (including the franchise) all encouraged the movement of blacks into northern cities. Wages in northern industries usually ranged from $3 to $5 per eight-hour day, compared with as little as 75 cents to $1 per day in southern agriculture and with no more than $2.50 for a nine-hour day in southern industries. Moreover, between 1915 and 1925, the average wages of domestics in some northern cities doubled. Northern cities also promised access to better health care. The nonwhite infant-mortality rate dropped in New York City from 176 in 1917 to 105 in 1930; in Boston, from 167 to 90; and in Philadelphia, from 193 to 100. Between 1911 and 1926, according to the Metropolitan Life Insurance Company, the incidence of tuberculosis among the nation's blacks declined by 44 percent for black males and 43 percent for black females. New York, Philadelphia, and Chicago showed similar patterns of decline.

Better social conditions, higher wages, and the franchise—it is no wonder that African Americans viewed the Great Migration to northern cities in glowing terms with references to "the Promised Land," the "flight out of Egypt," and "going into Canaan." One black man wrote back to his southern home, "The (Col.) men are making good. [The job] never pays less than $3.00 per day for (10) hours." In her letter home, a black woman related, "I am well and thankful to say I am doing well . . . I work in Swifts Packing Company." "Up here," another migrant said, "our people are in a different light." Over and over again, African Americans con-

launched the AFRICAN METHODIST EPISCOPAL CHURCH in Philadelphia, followed closely by the African Methodist Episcopal Zion church in New York, and the Baptist church in both cities. In 1886, African Americans formed the NATIONAL BAPTIST CONVENTION and spearheaded the formation of new churches.

Along with churches, blacks soon formed a variety of mutual-aid societies and fraternal orders, including the Masons, Odd Fellows, and Independent Order of St. Luke. The NATIONAL ASSOCIATION OF COLORED WOMEN, formed in 1895, emphasized service to the community. Mobilizing under its credo "Lifting as We Climb," the association organized, administered, and supported a variety of social-welfare activities: homes for the aged, young women, and children; relief funds for the unemployed; and legal aid to combat injustice before the law. Under the impact of World War I and its aftermath, new expressions of black consciousness (as reflected in the emergence of the HARLEM RENAISSANCE) and the growing participation of blacks in northern politics both demonstrated solidarity across class and status lines.

The alliance between black workers and black elites was by no means unproblematic. As the new black middle class expanded during the 1920s, for example, it slowly moved into better housing vacated by whites, leaving the black poor concentrated in certain sections. In his studies of Chicago and New York, sociologist E. Franklin FRAZIER demonstrated the increasing division of the black urban community along socioeconomic lines. While each city contained significant areas of interclass mixing, poverty increasingly characterized specific sections of the ghetto.

Moreover, the rise of working-class-oriented organizations such as the UNIVERSAL NEGRO IMPROVEMENT ASSOCIATION created substantial conflicts between black workers and established middle-class leadership. Emphasizing "race first," black pride, and solidarity with Africa, the Garvey movement struck a responsive chord among large numbers of black workers. Its Jamaican-born leader, Marcus GARVEY, frequently exclaimed, "The Universal Negro Improvement Association . . . believes that the Negro race is as good as any other race, and therefore should be as proud of itself as others are. . . . It believes in the spiritual Fatherhood of God and the Brotherhood of Man." As one migrant stated, "We will make a great mistake if we step out of the path of the Universal Negro Improvement Association." While race-conscious black business and professional people endorsed aspects of Garvey's ideas, they feared his growing appeal and often complained that his message appealed primarily to the "ignorant class" of newcomers from the South.

Despite conflicts between black workers and middle-class black leaders, African Americans continued to forge cross-class alliances. As early as 1914, Oscar DePriest defeated his white opponents and became Chicago's first black alderman. In 1928, DePriest also symbolized the growing shift of black electoral power from the South to northern urban centers when he gained the party's endorsements and won a seat in the U.S. Congress, serving the First Congressional District of Illinois. When blacks sought a similar goal in New York, they failed because skillful gerrymandering had split the black vote between the Nineteenth and Twenty-First Assembly districts. In 1944, when boundaries were redrawn, blacks elected the black minister Adam Clayton POWELL, Jr., to the House of Representatives; Harlem thus became the second northern congressional district to send a black to Congress. By then, African Americans had realigned their party affiliation from Republican to Democrat and had become an indispensable element in the New Deal coalition.

Although black electoral politics reflected the growing segregation of the urban environment, black elites retained a core of white allies. African Americans had cultivated a small number of white friends and launched the interracial NATIONAL URBAN LEAGUE in 1911 and the NATIONAL ASSOCIATION FOR THE ADVANCEMENT OF COLORED PEOPLE (NAACP) in 1909. During the 1930s and 1940s, this inter- and intraracial unity gained even greater expression with the rise of the Congress of Industrial Organizations, New Deal social-welfare programs, and the March on Washington movement. When President Franklin D. Roosevelt issued Executive Order 8802 in 1941, calling for an end to racial barriers in defense industries, African Americans achieved a major victory against racial exploitation.

As the nation entered the years after World War II, a variety of forces again transformed the context of black migration. The technological revolution in southern agriculture, the emergence of the welfare state, and the militant civil rights and Black Power movements all helped to complete the long-run transformation of blacks from a predominantly rural to a predominantly urban people. The African-American population increased from thirteen million in 1940 to over twenty-two million in 1970. The proportion of blacks living in cities rose to over 80 percent, 10 percent higher than the population at large. Beginning as the most rural of Americans, blacks had become the most urbanized.

The Great Migration helped to transform both black and white America. It elevated the issues of race and southern black culture from regional to national phenomena. It was often a volatile process, involving both intra- and interracial conflicts. Distributed almost equally among regions, by the late 1970s the black urban migration had run its familiar twentieth-century course. Increases in black urban population were now primarily the product of births over deaths rather than interregional movements. Moreover, southern-born blacks from the North and West returned home in rising numbers. During the 1980s, the proportion of African Americans living in the South increased, after declining for more than a century. At the same time, black migration to American suburbs escalated. While the outcome of this new migration is yet to be determined, the suburban migrants are faring better than their inner-city counterparts. The returning migrants are also much better off than those who left, and they envision a "New South," one that is much different from the one their forebears abandoned.

BIBLIOGRAPHY

Berlin, Ira, and Ronald Hoffman, eds. *Slavery and Freedom in the Age of the American Revolution.* Urbana, Ill., 1983.

Grossman, James R. *Land of Hope: Chicago, Black Southerners, and the Great Migration.* Chicago, 1989.

Harris, Robert L., Jr. "Coming of Age: The Transformation of Afro-American Historiography." *Journal of Negro History* 57, no. 2 (1982): 107– 121.

Harrison, Alferdteen. *Black Exodus: The Great Migration from the American South.* Jackson, Miss., 1991.

Hine, Darlene Clark, ed. *The State of Afro-American History: Past, Present and Future.* Baton Rouge, La., 1986.

Lemann, Nicholas. *The Promised Land: The Great Black Migration and How It Changed America.* New York, 1991.

Lewis, Earl. *In Their Own Interests: Race, Class, and Power in Twentieth-Century Norfolk, Virginia.* Berkeley, Calif., 1991.

Marks, Carole. *Farewell—We're Good and Gone: The Great Migration.* Bloomington, Ind., 1989.

Meier, August, and Elliot Rudwick. *Black History and the Historical Profession, 1915–1980.* Urbana, Ill., 1986.

Nash, Gary. *Forging Freedom: The Formation of Philadelphia's Black Community, 1720–1840.* Cambridge, Mass., 1988.

Painter, Nell Irvin. *Exodusters: Black Migration to Kansas after Reconstruction.* 1976. Reprint. Lawrence, Kans., 1986.

Trotter, Joe W., Jr. "Afro-American Urban History: A Critique of the Literature." In *Black Milwaukee: The Making of an Industrial Proletariat, 1915–45.* Urbana, Ill., 1985.

———, ed. *The Great Migration in Historical Perspective: New Dimensions of Race, Class, and Gender.* Bloomington, Ind., 1991.

Wilson, William J. *The Truly Disadvantaged: The Inner City, the Underclass, and Public Policy.* Chicago, 1987.

— JOE W. TROTTER, JR.

MILITARY

Military service has traditionally afforded African Americans a means of economic, social, and political advancement. In time of emergency, the British North American colonies found room in the ranks for free blacks and slaves. The United States has turned to blacks during military crises throughout its history, and today African Americans continue to help themselves by helping defend their country.

Colonial Wars and the American Revolution

In colonial times, black slaves accompanied their white masters to war, sometimes as cooks, occasionally as soldiers or sailors. South Carolina, where able-bodied male slaves outnumbered free whites of military age, enrolled trusted slaves in the militia, promising them freedom for exceptional service. Despite the shortage of white manpower, South Carolina remained wary of the slave militia, concerned that it might join in a slave rebellion. Actually, organized mutinies proved rare in colonial North America, although some individual slaves did seek vengeance by attacking the person, family, or property of the master. A planned uprising jolted the city of New York in April 1712, when some twenty slaves set fire to a building and killed nine of the whites who tried to put out the flames; the incident triggered arrests, trials, executions, and repression. South Carolina experienced a similar revolt, the Stono War of 1739, when a group of slaves from Angola rallied behind one of their number, killed several whites, and set out for the safety of Spanish Florida. White militiamen and their Native American allies tracked down and killed the fugitives. Significantly, the colony did not on this occasion call on its armed slaves, who had fought under white leaders against the Yamasee Indians in 1715.

Like the slave who might earn freedom, the free black could benefit personally from helping defend his colony. George Gire of Massachusetts earned a pension for service during the French and Indian War (1754–1763) and also enhanced his standing in the community. Moreover, the free black who shipped out in a privateer shared with other crewmen in the proceeds from the sale of captured merchantmen, money that could establish him in a craft or trade.

Military service has traditionally afforded African Americans a means of economic, social, and political advancement.

When the American colonies rebelled against Great Britain in 1775, blacks fought in the Massachusetts militia at Lexington and Concord in April and in Gen. George Washington's Continental Army at Bunker Hill in June. The rebellious southern colonies, however, refused to employ blacks except as military labor. Even

In another dramatic gesture that formed part of his reelection campaign, Roosevelt prodded the Army Air Corps into admitting blacks to pilot training. The candidates included Capt. Benjamin O. DAVIS, Jr., the son of the recently promoted general. Since the president sought to improve opportunities for black servicemen without undermining racial segregation, the younger Davis and his fellow airmen trained and served separately from whites.

After Japan attacked Pearl Harbor on December 7, 1941, the armed forces gradually discovered they would have to do more than Roosevelt anticipated. The Army found it could not afford the cost, in money and morale, of racially exclusive clubs and exchanges in the United States, and permitted a degree of integration. Overseas, black and white units, though theoretically separate, shared a common danger. Moreover, in the final months of the war in Europe, the Army ran short of white infantrymen and called for volunteers from among the black service units in that theater. Some 4,500 African Americans stepped forward, underwent a brief period of infantry training, and formed platoons assigned to formerly all-white rifle companies. The arrival of a black platoon meant that one soldier in five was an African American in a rifle company where teamwork was essential and close contact unavoidable. Racial integration inevitably resulted. The Navy and Coast Guard (a part of the wartime Navy) discovered that keeping African Americans out of combat undermined black morale as well as that of whites, who would have to endure additional sea duty because blacks could not replace them. The Coast Guard pioneered the racial integration of ships' crews, and the Navy, after experimenting with all-black crews, integrated the races on board a number of fleet auxiliaries. Only the Marine Corps, after accepting its first black recruits since the American Revolution, succeeded in maintaining racial segregation.

After the fighting ended in August 1945, the armed forces abandoned their wartime efforts at racial integration. Although a panel of senior officers predicted in 1946 that a racially integrated army would fight the next war, the military leadership feared that immediate integration would alienate white public opinion. Despite the occasional anomaly—the first black officer in the Marine Corps Reserve, or the first African-American graduate of the U.S. Naval Academy—the armed forces embraced segregation, imposing quotas on black enlistments, discharging those already in uniform who had scored poorly on the aptitude tests, and assigning the rest to menial duties. In the immediate postwar years, even the Army Air Force, in spite of its investment in black pilots, devoted more energy to isolating African Americans than to utilizing their skills.

The Decision to Integrate

Except for providing access to the benefits of the GI Bill, military service failed to help the average black advance himself, but some progress did occur. A succession of decisions by federal courts, beginning in 1938 and continuing after the war, eroded the legal foundation of racial segregation, but local authorities often ignored what the judges decreed. In the 1940 presidential election, black voters in the northern cities, rather than lawyers or the military, had triggered a change in race relations within the armed forces; a similar situation occurred in 1948. Harry S. Truman, who had become president in April 1945 after Roosevelt died early in his fourth term, faced a mutinous Democratic party. To win a close contest, Truman needed the votes of African Americans. Since a hostile Congress would not cooperate by passing civil rights legislation, Truman had no choice but to use his power as commander in chief to end segregation in the military services, providing a model for society and gaining the support of blacks. On July 26, 1948, he issued Executive Order 9981, directing the armed forces to provide equal treatment and opportunity regardless of race. His stand against racism contributed to his victory at the polls.

The Air Force, independent of the Army since September 1947, laid the foundations for integration even before the president's directive. The newest of the services, burdened with volatile concentrations of black airmen doing meaningless work, saw an opportunity to dissolve these units and force all enlisted personnel, regardless of race, to compete for technical training and useful duties. Moreover, the Air Force demanded the largest share of the defense budget to buy and operate weapons intended to deter nuclear war. So heavy an investment could scarcely be justified if the Air Force discriminated against African Americans, roughly 11 percent of the populace.

The other services lagged behind the Air Force in integrating the races. In June 1950, when North Korea invaded South Korea, the Army still maintained exclusively black combat and support units, while the Navy and Marine Corps tended to train their African-American servicemen as messmen, stewards, or members of security detachments. The demands of the KOREAN WAR changed all this. Combat ships and frontline units could not wait for the sluggish functioning of a personnel system that made race, rather than the needs of the service, the principal criterion for training and assignment. Recruits had to learn useful skills and serve wherever needed, an impossibility unless the races were truly integrated.

The need to use manpower efficiently forced the services to provide equal treatment and opportunity regardless of race, a process under way when the Korean fighting ended in July 1953. African Americans were now eligible for most specialties, though not yet all, and could expect a meaningful assignment when they completed training. Skills took time to acquire, however, and promotions did not come easily, so that blacks were underrepresented in the more demanding technical fields and among noncommissioned officers. Black commissioned officers were especially rare. As late as 1962, African Americans made up 3.2 percent of the Army's officer corps, roughly 1 percent in the Marine Corps and Navy, and 1.2 percent in the Air Force. But, despite vestiges of racial segregation that survived in the late 1950s and early 1960s, blacks as a rule enjoyed greater opportunity and better treatment in uniform than in civilian jobs.

Even as the armed forces advanced—albeit imperfectly—toward Truman's goal of racial integration, the CIVIL RIGHTS MOVEMENT, a loose coalition of black activists and their white allies, launched a struggle to regain the rights guaranteed to all citizens by the Constitution. The racial integration of the military slipped from the national consciousness as leaders such as the Rev. Dr. Martin Luther KING, Jr., challenged the federal

Gen. Benjamin O. Davis, Sr., with troops. (Prints and Photographs Division, Library of Congress)

government to protect black Americans in the exercise of their legal rights. The response of presidents John F. Kennedy and Lyndon B. Johnson culminated between 1964 and 1968 in legislation to ensure that African Americans had equal access to jobs, public accommodations, and decent housing and that they could exercise the right to vote.

A Breakdown in Racial Understanding

During 1963 and 1964, a committee headed by Gerhard A. Gesell, a Washington attorney, evaluated the progress of the armed forces toward racial integration and warned of danger. Some forms of segregation persisted, and a breakdown in communication between the races prevented the predominantly white officer corps from understanding how deeply black servicemen resented the remaining manifestations of racism. In response to the Gesell Committee's warning, Secretary of Defense Robert S. McNamara enforced equal treatment and opportunity at military and naval bases, and used moral pressure and economic leverage to integrate housing and public accommodations in nearby communities. For a brief time in the mid-1960s, the military establishment more closely approached the ideal of racial integration than any other American institution.

Scarcely had the reaction to the Gesell Committee begun when, in the spring of 1965, the United States intensified the VIETNAM WAR. As the years passed and casualties mounted, the Army and the Marine Corps relied on the Selective Service System to maintain combat strength, and the possibility of being drafted motivated young men to enlist for less dangerous duty in the Air Force or Navy. Both the volunteers and the draftees included many resentful urban blacks, bypassed by the gains of the Civil Rights Movement, and whites from a comparable social class who feared that anything they had or hoped for would be handed over to African Americans as compensation for past discrimination. Frustrated blacks rioted in Detroit, in the Watts district of Los Angeles, and, after a white gunman murdered the Rev. Dr. Martin Luther King in April 1968, in major cities throughout the nation. Since the armed forces reflected the mood of the society they defended, the mutual hatred found its way into the services and ignited worldwide race riots beginning in 1968.

Amity Restored

A riot in May 1971 at Travis Air Force Base, in California, lent urgency to a plan, drawn up under the guidance of a black Air Force officer, Col. Lucius Theus, to teach racial understanding and cooperation throughout the armed forces. The Defense Race Relations Institute (in 1979 redesignated the Defense Equal Opportunity Management Institute) began almost immediately to train instructors, who returned to their units and conducted classes to heighten racial sensitivity. In conjunction with interracial councils and fostered by the exercise of common sense on the part of commanders, the program flourished and received much of the credit for a revival of racial amity.

Success, however, stemmed in part from the suspension of the draft, reserved in 1973 for possible use in some future emergency, and the truce that ended the Vietnam fighting in January of that year. The decision to rely on volunteers instead of draftees attracted recruits who wanted to serve and would do what was expected of them—even cooperating harmoniously with members of other races. Nevertheless, the all-volunteer force included a disproportionate number of African Americans, especially when the economy faltered and jobs became scarce. In 1983, a decade after Selective Service went on the shelf, blacks in the enlisted force approached 20 percent, almost twice their proportion in society as a whole. The Army led with 33 percent; the Marine Corps followed with 22 percent; and the Air Force and Navy had 14 and 12 percent, respectively. The Army also had the greatest proportion of African Americans in the officer corps, almost 10 percent; the Air Force had 5 percent, the Marine Corps 4, and the Navy 3. The Army also had the largest proportion of African Americans among women in uniform, some 17 percent of its officers and 20 percent of enlisted women. For the Air Force, the percentages were 11 and 20; for the Marine Corps, 5 and 23; and for the Navy, 5 and 18.

As happened during the Vietnam conflict, blacks serving in the 1980s tended to gravitate toward combat units, attracted perhaps by the challenge, the status, or the premium pay. What would happen if large numbers of black Americans were killed and wounded in a future war fought mainly by the Army and Marine Corps? Just such a conflict loomed early in 1991, when a coalition led by the United States sought to expel the army of Iraq from Kuwait. Roughly 30 percent of the American force deployed to the Middle East consisted of African Americans. Fortunately, American casualties were few, since Iraqi resistance collapsed rapidly, and the war had scant effect on race relations in the United States. Military service continued to present black Americans with an opportunity to assume responsibility, learn skills, and earn respect, and compared to whites a vastly greater proportion of young blacks took advantage of the offer.

BIBLIOGRAPHY

Barbeau, Arthur E., and Florette, Henri. *The Unknown Soldiers: Black American Troops in World War I.* Philadelphia, 1974.

Berlin, Ira, ed., with Joseph P. Reidy and Leslie S. Rowlands. *Freedom: A Documentary History of Emancipation, 1861–1865.* Series II, *The Black Military Experience.* Cambridge, Mass., 1982.

Cornish, Dudley Taylor. *The Sable Arm: Negro Troops in the Union Army, 1861–1865.* 1956. Reprint. Lawrence, Kans., 1987.

Dalfiume, Richard M. *Desegregation of the U.S. Armed Forces: Fighting on Two Fronts, 1939–1953.* Columbia, Mo., 1969.

Fletcher, Marvin E. *America's First Black General: Benjamin O. Davis, Sr., 1880–1970.* Lawrence, Kans., 1989.

Fowler, Arlen. *The Black Infantry in the West, 1869–1891.* Westport, Conn., 1971.

Gropman, Alan L. *The Air Force Integrates, 1945–1964.* 1977. Reprint. Washington, D.C., 1986.

Haynes, Robert V. *A Night of Violence: The Houston Riot of 1917.* Baton Rouge, La., 1976.

Leckie, William H. *The Buffalo Soldiers: A Narrative of the Negro Cavalry in the West.* 1967. Reprint. Norman, Okla., 1975.

Lee, Ulysses. *The United States Army in World War II; Special Studies: The Employment of Negro Troops.* Washington, D.C., 1966.

MacGregor, Morris J. *Defense Studies: Integration of the Armed Forces, 1940–1965.* Washington, D.C., 1981.

MacGregor, Morris J., and Bernard C. Nalty, eds. *Blacks in the United States Armed Forces: Basic Documents.* 13 vols. Wilmington, Del., 1977.

McGuire, Phillip. *He, Too, Spoke for Democracy: Judge Hastie, World War II, and the Black Soldier.* Westport, Conn., 1988.

Nalty, Bernard C. *Strength for the Fight: A History of Black Americans in the Military.* 1986. Reprint. New York, 1989.

Osur, Alan M. *Blacks in the Army Air Forces during World War II.* Washington, D.C., 1977.

Quarles, Benjamin. *The Negro in the American Revolution.* Chapel Hill, N.C., 1961.

———. *The Negro in the Civil War.* 1953. Reprint. Boston, 1989.

Shaw, Henry I., Jr., and Ralph N. Donnelly. *Blacks in the Marine Corps.* Washington, D.C., 1975.

Singletary, Otis A. *The Negro Militia and Reconstruction.* Austin, Tex., 1971.

Weaver, John D. *The Brownsville Raid.* New York, 1970.

— BERNARD C. NALTY

MINGUS, CHARLES, JR.

Charles Mingus, Jr. (April 22, 1922–January 5, 1979), jazz musician. Born in Nogales, Ariz., Charles Mingus straddled the bebop and free jazz eras. Although he became a virtuoso bassist early in his career, his main contribution to jazz was as a composer and bandleader. For over thirty years Mingus created a body of compositions matched in quality and variety only by Duke ELLINGTON and Thelonious MONK, and ranging from somber but gritty tributes to Lester YOUNG, Charlie PARKER, and Eric Dolphy to roaring evocations of African-American gospel prayer meetings. Taking a cue from Ellington, Mingus generally wrote music for particular individuals in his superb ensembles, and such compositions were developed or "workshopped" through in-concert rehearsals rather than from fixed and polished scores prior to performance and recording. Mingus's mercurial personality thrived in these improvisational settings, but this process often made for chaos and disaster as well. He was notorious for berating audiences and musicians from the bandstand, even firing and rehiring band members during the course of performances. However, the workshops also achieved a spontaneity and musical passion unmatched in the history of jazz, as Mingus conducted and shouted instructions and comments from the piano or bass, at times in a wheelchair at the end of his life, even improvising speeches on civil rights.

Although Mingus became a virtuoso bassist early in his career, his main contribution to jazz was as a composer and bandleader.

Mingus grew up in the Watts section of Los Angeles, and in his youth studied trombone and cello before switching at age sixteen to the bass. He studied with Britt Woodman, Red Callender, Lloyd Reese, and Herman Rheinschagen, and began performing professionally while still a teenager. He played in the rhythm sections of the bands of Lee Young (1940), Louis ARMSTRONG (1941–1943), Barney Bigard (1942), and Lionel HAMPTON (1947–1948). He made his first recordings with Hampton in 1947, a session that included Mingus's first recorded composition, "Mingus Fingers." Mingus played in Red Norvo's trio from 1950 to 1951, quitting in anger after Mingus, who was not a member of the local musicians' union, was replaced by a white bassist for a television performance. Mingus settled in New York in 1951, and played stints with Duke Ellington, Billy Taylor, Stan Getz, and Art Tatum. His most important work in his early period was a single concert he organized and recorded for his own record label, Debut Records, at Toronto's Massey Hall in May 1953, featuring pianist Bud Powell, drummer Max ROACH, and the reunited team of Charlie Parker and Dizzy GILLESPIE—the definitive bebop quintet.

Mingus formed his own music workshop in 1955 in order to develop compositions for a core of performers, and it is from this point that his mature style dates. He had played in the cooperative Jazz Composers' Workshop from 1953 to 1955, but it was as the tempestuous leader of his own group that he created his most famous works, which in concerts often became long, brooding performances, building to aggressive, even savage climaxes. His compositions used folk elements such as blues shouts, field hollers, call and response, and gospel-style improvised accompanying riffs. In this middle period, which lasted from 1955 to 1966, Mingus em-

In the decades following Emancipation, the sexual coercion and assault of black women by white men continued in the South, especially as Reconstruction drew to a close. Marriages across the color line were illegal in the post-Reconstruction South, while some Northern states had repealed those laws. Other laws, in both the North and West, ranged from declaring such marriages null and void, to imposing fines, to imprisonment; they were largely enforced against white women and black men only.

People of mixed European and African ancestry have never been considered a separate "race" in this country, although both the African American and white communities of antebellum New Orleans, Charleston, S.C., Mobile, Ala., and Savannah, Ga., recognized a "mulatto" or "brown" class. By the late nineteenth century, the "one-drop rule," which proclaimed that anyone with any known African ancestry would be classified as black, prevailed nationally.

While the numbers of mixed couples have increased in the second half of the twentieth century, percentages are still small; the majority of mixed couples since the end of World War II have been white women and black men, a phenomenon that caused considerable racial tension in the CIVIL RIGHTS MOVEMENT of the 1960s. According to the U.S. Census Bureau, in 1970 there were 146 black-white married couples for every 100,000 married couples. In 1980 that number increased to 335 and in 1990, to 396. There are no reliable statistics on nonmarried couples. While recognizing legal sanctions as racist and a violation of rights, many African Americans have looked down on those who consorted with whites. As for dominant white attitudes, it was not until 1967, after nine years of trials and appeals in the case of *Loving* v. *Virginia,* that the United States Supreme Court ruled laws prohibiting marriages between blacks and whites unconstitutional; at that time, sixteen southern states had such laws.

The ongoing legacies of the legal and social history of this subject are apparent in issues ranging from the choice of racial categories on United States census forms, to the influence of racist ideology in sex crimes or alleged sex crimes, to antagonism from both white and black communities toward marriages and relationships across the color line.

BIBLIOGRAPHY

Higginbotham, A. Leon, Jr. *In the Matter of Color: Race and the American Legal Process: The Colonial Period.* New York, 1978.

Hodes, Martha. "The Sexualization of Reconstruction Politics: White Women and Black Men in the South after the Civil War." *Journal of the History of Sexuality* 3 (1993): 402–417.

Spickard, Paul R. *Mixed Blood: Intermarriage and Ethnic Identity in Twentieth-Century America.* Madison, Wis., 1989.

Williamson, Joel. *New People: Miscegenation and Mulattoes in the United States.* New York, 1980.

— MARTHA E. HODES

MISSOURI COMPROMISE

The Missouri Compromise of 1820 directly affected African Americans by prohibiting SLAVERY in the land acquired in the Louisiana Purchase north of the 36° 30′ line, but allowing slavery in Missouri itself. At the time the American Southwest belonged to Mexico. Thus the Missouri Compromise implied that the nation would eventually have more free states than slave states. Congressional debates over it signaled the beginning of public discourse over the place of slavery and the rights of free blacks in the United States.

The Missouri Compromise also allowed Maine, previously part of Massachusetts, to enter the Union as a free state. The new state of Maine had few blacks, but those who did live there had almost total equality. The state allowed blacks to vote on the same basis as whites and did not segregate its schools or any other institutions.

At the same time, Missouri would come into the Union as a slave state. When it entered the Union, Missouri adopted a constitution that prohibited the state legislature from ending slavery without the consent of slaveholders and required the legislature to prohibit the migration of free blacks into the state. Northern congressmen opposed these constitutional provisions—especially the one requiring a prohibition on the migration of free blacks. In the resolution admitting Missouri, Congress declared that the state constitution "shall never be construed to authorize the passage of any law" denying a citizen of "the privileges and immunities" of an American citizen. Despite this provision, in 1848 Missouri prohibited free blacks from entering the state.

The provisions of the Missouri Compromise were not to last. The Kansas-Nebraska Act of 1854 effectively superceded the Missouri Compromise by allowing popular sovereignty to determine the fate of slavery in the Nebraska territories. In the DRED SCOTT DECISION (1857), Chief Justice Taney declared that the entire provision violated the Constitution.

BIBLIOGRAPHY

Freehling, William W. *The Road to Disunion: Secessionists at Bay, 1776–1854.* New York, 1990.

Moore, Glover. *The Missouri Controversy, 1819–1821.* Lexington, Ky., 1953.

— PAUL FINKELMAN

MODERN JAZZ QUARTET

Comprising vibraharpist Milt Jackson, pianist-composer John Lewis, bassist Percy Heath, and drummer Connie Kay, the Modern Jazz Quartet (MJQ) epitomizes the style that came to be known as "cool jazz." Although grounded in the fiery bebop style of the late 1940s, its repertory is characterized by elegant ensemble precision, a restrained emotional atmosphere (aided by the relatively cool timbres of the vibraharp and piano), and a self-conscious attempt to bring compositional technique derived from European art music into a working relationship with jazz improvisation.

Jackson and Lewis were originally members of Dizzy GILLESPIE's big band, and occasionally performed as a quartet in the late 1940s with Kenny Clarke on drums and Ray Brown on bass. The Modern Jazz Quartet proper made its recording debut in 1952 for the Prestige label. Wearing tuxedos on stage, members of the MJQ brought jazz to audiences accustomed to European chamber music. Such early Lewis compositions as "Vendome" (1952) and "Concorde" (1955) attracted attention for their use of fugal textures, while later projects such as *The Comedy* (1962) made more ambitious use of a modern compositional idiom derived in part from contemporary European "classical" music and were associated with the Third Stream movement.

The Modern Jazz Quartet epitomizes the style that came to be known as "cool jazz."

The music of the MJQ has nevertheless remained firmly rooted in African-American culture, through the soulful improvising of Jackson and a continuous exploration of the blues (e.g., the album *Blues at Carnegie Hall,* 1966). In 1974 the group disbanded, only to reform for tours and recordings in 1981.

BIBLIOGRAPHY

Williams, Martin. "John Lewis and the Modern Jazz Quartet: Modern Conservative." In *The Jazz Tradition.* Rev. ed. New York and Oxford, 1983, pp. 172–182.

– SCOTT DEVEAUX

MONK, THELONIOUS SPHERE

Thelonious Sphere Monk (October 10, 1917–February 17, 1982), jazz pianist and composer. Thelonious Monk was born in Rocky Mount, N.C., but moved with his family to New York at age four and grew up in the San Juan Hill district of Manhattan. He began a career as a professional pianist in the mid-1930s, playing at house rent parties and touring for two years as the accompanist to a female evangelist. By 1940, he was a member of the house rhythm section at Minton's Playhouse, a nightclub in Harlem well known among musicians for its nightly jam sessions. Surviving live recordings from this period document a piano style firmly rooted in the stride-piano tradition, as well as a penchant for unusual reharmonizations of standard songs.

Monk had already written several of his best-known compositions by this period: "Epistrophy" and " 'Round Midnight" were performed and recorded by the Cootie Williams big band as early as 1944, while "Hackensack" (under the name "Rifftide") was recorded in Monk's professional recording debut with the Coleman HAWKINS Quartet in the same year. With their astringent and highly original approach to harmony, these compositions attracted the attention of the most adventurous jazz musicians, and placed Monk at the center of the emergent Bebop movement during World War II.

Although well known within the inner circle of bebop musicians, Monk did not come to more general attention until later in the 1940s. Beginning in 1947, he made a series of recordings for the Blue Note label, documenting a wide range of his compositions. These recordings, which include "Criss Cross," "Ruby, My Dear," and "Straight, No Chaser," feature him as both improviser and composer.

While Monk was admired as a composer, his unusual approach to the piano keyboard, lacking the overt virtuosity of such bebop pianists as Bud Powell and bristling with dissonant combinations that could easily be misinterpreted as "wrong notes," led many to dismiss him initially as a pianist. An incident in 1951 in which he was accused of drug possession led to the loss of his cabaret card, precluding further performances in New York City until 1957. But he continued to record for the Prestige label, including the famous "Bags Groove" session with Miles DAVIS in 1954, and he began making a series of recordings for Riverside, including *Brilliant Corners* (1956).

An extended residency at the Five Spot, a New York night club, in the summer of 1957 with John COLTRANE finally drew attention to Monk as one of the most important figures in modern jazz. From the late 1950s through the 1960s, Monk worked primarily with his quartet, featuring tenor saxophonist Charlie Rouse, touring both in this country and abroad and recording prolifically for Columbia. Increasingly, he turned to the solo piano, recording idiosyncratic performances not only of his own compositions but also of such decades-old popular songs as "Just a Gigolo." The feature-length

Thelonious Monk. (Photographs and Prints Division, Schomburg Center for Research in Black Culture, The New York Public Library, Astor, Lenox and Tilden Foundations)

film *Straight, No Chaser* (1988; directed by Charlotte Zwerin) documents Monk's music and life in the late 1960s. After 1971, he virtually retired from public life. But his reputation continued to grow, as a younger generation of musicians discovered his compositions and responded to the challenge of improvising within their distinctive melodic and harmonic framework.

BIBLIOGRAPHY

Blake, Ran. "Round About Monk: The Music." Wire 10 (1984): 23–33.

Williams, Martin. "Thelonious Monk: Modern Jazz in Search of Maturity." In *The Jazz Tradition.* New York, 1983, pp. 154–171.

– SCOTT DEVEAUX

MONTGOMERY, ALA., BUS BOYCOTT

The Montgomery, Ala., Bus Boycott began on December 5, 1955, as an effort by black residents to protest the trial that day in the Montgomery Recorder's Court of Rosa McCauley PARKS. She had been arrested on December 1 for violating the city's ordinance requiring racial segregation of seating on buses. The boycott had initially been intended to last only for the single day of the trial, but local black support of the strike proved so great that, at a meeting that afternoon, black community leaders decided to continue the boycott until city and bus company authorities met black demands: the adoption by the bus company in Montgomery of the pattern of seating segregation used by the same company in Mobile; the hiring of black bus drivers on predominantly black routes, and greater courtesy by drivers toward passengers. The leaders formed the Montgomery Improvement Association (MIA) to run the extended boycott. At a mass meeting that evening, several thousand blacks ratified these decisions.

The Mobile plan sought by the boycott differed from the Montgomery pattern in that passengers, once seated, could not be unseated by drivers. In Mobile, blacks seated from the back and whites from the front, but after the bus was full, the racial division could be adjusted only when riders disembarked. On Montgomery's buses, the front ten seats were irrevocably reserved for whites, whether or not there were any whites aboard, and the rear ten seats were in theory similarly reserved for blacks. The racial designation of the middle sixteen seats, however, was adjusted by the drivers to accord with the changing racial composition of the ridership as the bus proceeded along its route. In Rosa Parks's case, when she had taken her seat, it had been in the black section of the bus. Two blocks farther on, all white seats and standing room were taken, but some standing room remained in the rear. Bus driver J. Fred Blake then ordered the row of seats in which Parks was sitting cleared to make room for boarding whites. Three blacks complied, but Mrs. Parks refused and was arrested. She was fined fourteen dollars.

Black Montgomerians had long been dissatisfied with the form of bus segregation used in their city. It had originally been adopted, for streetcars, in August 1900, and had provoked a boycott that had lasted for almost two years. In October 1952 a delegation from the black Women's Political Council had urged the city commission to permit the use of the Mobile seating plan. In a special election in the fall of 1953, a racial liberal with strong black support, Dave Birmingham, was elected to the three-member city commission. Following his inauguration, blacks again pressed the seating proposal at meetings in December 1953 and March 1954. In May 1954, the president of the Women's Political Council, Joann G. Robinson, a professor of English at Alabama State College for Negroes, wrote to the mayor to warn that blacks might launch a boycott if white authorities continued adamant. During the municipal election in the spring of 1955, black leaders held a candidates' forum at which they posed questions about issues of interest to the black community. At the head of the list was the adoption of the Mobile seating pattern.

On March 2, only weeks before the election, a black teenager, Claudette Colvin, was arrested for violation of the bus segregation ordinance. Following this incident, representatives of the city and the bus company promised black negotiators that a seating policy more favorable to African Americans would be adopted. However, Birmingham, the racially liberal city commissioner elected in 1953, had integrated the city police force in 1954. As a result of hostility to this action and other similar ones, he was defeated for reelection in 1955 by an outspoken segregationist, Clyde Sellers. The other commissioners at once became less accommodating. By the time that Rosa Parks was arrested in December, the discussions had come to a standstill. Mrs. Parks, the secretary of the Montgomery branch of the NATIONAL ASSOCIATION FOR THE ADVANCEMENT OF COLORED PEOPLE (NAACP), shared with other black leaders the frustration that grew out of the negotiations with municipal authorities. This frustration produced her refusal to vacate her seat.

From the city jail, Parks telephoned Edgar D. Nixon, a Pullman porter who was a former president of the Montgomery NAACP branch. After Nixon had posted bail for Parks, he called other prominent blacks to propose the one-day boycott. The response was generally positive. At JoAnn Robinson's suggestion, the Women's Political Council immediately began distributing leaflets urging the action. It was then endorsed by the city's black ministers and other leaders at a meeting at the Dexter Avenue Baptist Church. The result was almost universal black participation.

At the December 5 meeting, when it was decided to continue the boycott and to form the Montgomery Improvement Association (MIA), the Rev. Dr. Martin Luther KING, Jr., was chosen as the MIA's president, principally because, as a young man who had lived in the city only fifteen months, he was not as yet involved in the bitter rivalry for leadership of the black community between Nixon and funeral director Rufus A. Lewis. Nixon was elected the MIA's treasurer, and Lewis was appointed to organize car pools to transport blacks to their jobs without having to use buses. The Rev. Ralph D. ABERNATHY was named to head the committee designated to reopen negotiations with the city and the bus company.

Initially, the renewed negotiations seemed promising. Mayor William A. Gayle asked a committee of white community leaders to meet with the MIA's delegates. But by January 1956, these discussions had reached a stalemate. The MIA's attorney, Fred D. Gray, urged that the MIA abandon its request for the Mobile plan in favor of filing a federal court lawsuit seeking to declare unconstitutional all forms of seating segregation. The MIA's executive board resisted this proposal until January 30, when Martin Luther King's home was bombed. One day thereafter, the executive board voted to authorize the suit, which was filed as *Browder* v. *Gayle* on February 1.

Meanwhile, similar strains were at work in the white community. A group of moderate businessmen, the Men of Montgomery, was attempting to mediate between the MIA and the city commission. But segregationists were pressing authorities to seek the indictment of the boycott's leaders in state court for violating the Alabama Anti-Boycott Act of 1921, which made it a misdemeanor to conspire to hinder any person from carrying on a lawful business. On February 20, an MIA mass meeting rejected the compromise proposals of the Men of Montgomery, and on February 21, the county grand jury returned indictments of eighty-nine blacks, twenty-four of whom were ministers, under the Anti-Boycott Act.

Martin Luther King, the first to be brought to trial, was convicted by Judge Eugene Carter at the end of March and was fined $500. King appealed, and the remainder of the prosecutions were suspended while the appellate courts considered his case. On May 11, a three-judge federal court heard *Browder* v. *Gayle* and on June 5, it ruled 2–1, in an opinion by Circuit Judge Richard Rives, that any law requiring racially segregated seating on buses violated the equal protection clause of the Constitution's Fourteenth Amendment. The city appealed to the U.S. Supreme Court. Both segregation and the boycott continued while the appeal was pending.

Throughout the thirteen months of negotiations and legal maneuvers, the boycott was sustained by mass meetings and its car-pool operation. The weekly mass meetings, rotated among the city's black churches, continually reinforced the high level of emotional commitment to the movement among the black population. Initially the car pool, modeled on one used during a brief bus boycott in Baton Rouge in 1953, consisted of private cars whose owners volunteered to participate. But as contributions flowed in from sympathetic Northerners, the MIA eventually purchased a fleet of station wagons, assigned ownership of them to the various black churches, hired drivers and established regular routes. Rufus Lewis administered the car pool until May 1956, when he was succeeded by the Rev. B. J. Simms.

White authorities eventually realized that the MIA's ability to perpetuate the boycott depended on its successful organization of the car pool. In November the city sued in state court for an injunction to forbid the car-pool operation on the ground that it was infringing on the bus company's exclusive franchise. On November 13, Judge Eugene Carter granted the injunction, and the car pool ceased operation the next day. But on that same day, the U.S. Supreme Court summarily affirmed the previous ruling of the lower federal court that bus segregation was unconstitutional. The city petitioned the Supreme Court for rehearing, and a final order was delayed until December 20. On December 21, 1956, the buses were integrated and the boycott ended.

The Montgomery Bus Boycott marked the beginning of the Civil Rights Movement's direct action phase, and it made the Rev. Dr. Martin Luther King, Jr., a national figure.

The city was at once plunged into violence. Snipers fired into the buses; one of the shots shattered the leg of a pregnant black passenger, Rosa Jordan. The city commission ordered the suspension of night bus service. On January 10, 1957, four black churches and the homes of the Rev. Ralph Abernathy and of the MIA's only white board member, the Rev. Robert Graetz, were bombed and heavily damaged. All bus service was then suspended. On January 27, a home near that of Martin Luther King, was bombed and destroyed, and a bomb at King's own home was defused. On January 30, Montgomery police arrested seven bombers, all of whom were members of the KU KLUX KLAN.

The arrests ended the violence, and in March full bus service resumed. However, the first two of the bombers to come to trial were acquitted in May 1957, despite their confessions and the irrefutable evidence against them. Meanwhile, in April, the Alabama Court of Appeals had affirmed on technical grounds King's conviction under the Anti-Boycott Act. Because it was now clear that the other bombing prosecutions would be unsuccessful and because the boycott had ended in any case, prosecutors in November agreed to dismiss all the remaining bombing and antiboycott-law indictments in return for King's payment of his $500 fine.

The Montgomery Bus Boycott marked the beginning of the CIVIL RIGHTS MOVEMENT's direct action phase, and it made the Rev. Dr. Martin Luther King, Jr., a national figure. Although the integration of the buses was actually produced by the federal court injunction rather than by the boycott, it was the boycott that began the process of moving the civil rights movement out of the courtroom by demonstrating that ordinary African Americans possessed the power to control their own destiny.

BIBLIOGRAPHY

Garrow, David J., ed. *The Walking City: The Montgomery Bus Boycott, 1955–1956.* In David J. Garrow, ed. *Martin Luther King, Jr., and the* CIVIL RIGHTS MOVEMENT, vol. 7. Brooklyn N.Y., 1989.

Graetz, Robert S. *Montgomery: A White Preacher's Memoir.* Minneapolis, 1991.

King, Martin Luther, Jr. *Stride Toward Freedom: The Montgomery Story.* New York, 1958.

Robinson, JoAnn Gibson. *The Montgomery Bus Boycott and the Women Who Started It: The Memoir of JoAnn Gibson Robinson.* Knoxville, Tenn., 1987.

Thornton, J. Mills, III. "Challenge and Response in the Montgomery Bus Boycott of 1955–1956." *Alabama Review* 33 (1980): 163–235.

Yeakey, Lamont H. The Montgomery, Alabama, Bus Boycott, 1955–1956. Ph.D. diss., 1979.

— J. MILLS THORNTON III

MOREHOUSE COLLEGE

In 1867 the Augusta Baptist Seminary was established in Augusta, Ga., with the aid of the Washington, D.C.–based National Theological Institute. The seminary soon became affiliated with the American Baptist Home Mission Society, which provided financial and moral support to the fledgling venture. The first class of thirty-seven men and women took courses in the Springfield Baptist Church; the class had three female missionary teachers.

In 1871, Joseph T. Robert became the first president of the institution. After seven years of pressure to move the seminary to Atlanta, the ABHMS purchased land, and the seminary moved in 1879. It was rechristened the Atlanta Baptist Seminary. Accompanying the move was an increased determination to improve the quality of education at the seminary. Within three years, the all-male institution opened a collegiate department; students could enroll in either a four-year scientific course or a six-year classical course.

By the end of the nineteenth century, school officials sought to amend the charter, changing the name of the school to Atlanta Baptist College in 1897. Nine years later, John Hope became the first African-American president; he would lead the college until 1931. Hope oversaw the rapid expansion of the institution and was largely responsible for its excellent reputation both in the region and the country. In 1913, the name of the college was again changed to honor longtime ABHMS stalwart Henry Lyman Morehouse. The newly renamed Morehouse College had about sixty students in the collegiate program in 1915.

Morehouse offered an education weighted heavily toward both spiritual and academic advancement. Teachers such as Morehouse alumnus Benjamin Brawley, who taught there in 1902–1910 and 1912–1920, provided intellectual stimulation and served as role models for the student body. During John Hope's tenure, the "Morehouse man" began to symbolize an honest, intelligent African-American male who could succeed at anything. Partially as a result of the spread of this image, the school was criticized for catering primarily to the black elite and restricting its educational efforts to the Talented Tenth.

Morehouse College, Spelman College, and Atlanta University merged some of their operations together in 1929 to streamline administrative functions and pacify philanthropists who believed the merger would simplify donations to any of the participants. Academic resources were pooled. Atlanta became solely a university for graduate study; Spelman catered to undergraduate women, and Morehouse to undergraduate men. Students could take courses at the affiliated schools. Classroom space and some faculty responsibilities were also shared.

The most notable Morehouse alumnus undoubtedly was the Rev. Dr. Martin Luther King, Jr., a 1948 graduate.

While the affiliation maintained each school's financial and administrative autonomy, the Great Depression caused Morehouse significant difficulty. John Hope's successor, Samuel Archer, turned over much of Morehouse's financial and budgetary control to Atlanta University, leaving Morehouse with almost no decision-making power.

Students and faculty at Morehouse chafed under the new arrangements. When Benjamin Elijah MAYS became president of Morehouse in 1940, he made the reempowerment of Morehouse a priority. Mays was responsible for drastically increasing the college's endowment, wresting financial control from Atlanta University, and instituting an aggressive program of construction and expansion. He was also leading Morehouse when the 1957 creation of Atlanta University Center further consolidated operations between the original three participants and the new additions of Morris Brown College, Gammon Theological Seminary, and Clark University.

Morehouse was ahead of some of its contemporaries by instituting a non-Western studies program in the early 1960s. Students at Morehouse were also active participants in the CIVIL RIGHTS MOVEMENT. The most notable Morehouse alumnus undoubtedly was the Rev. Dr. Martin Luther KING, Jr., a 1948 graduate. Julian BOND, a student at Morehouse in the early 1960s, left school to be a full-time activist with the STUDENT NONVIOLENT COORDINATING COMMITTEE (SNCC).

Mays retired in 1967, passing the torch to Hugh Gloster, who led Morehouse for the next twenty years. Gloster attempted to expand the endowment, which was always a critical issue at Morehouse. The late 1970s saw the establishment of the Morehouse School of Medicine (1978), originally a two-year institution providing a grounding in primary-care and preventive medicine to students who would then continue at four-year institutions. In 1981, the medical school, which remained autonomous from the college, switched to a four-year curriculum; its finances were bolstered by millions of dollars in donations from governmental and private donations.

Leroy Keith, Jr., became president of Morehouse in 1987. He faced many of the same problems as his predecessors had. Budget difficulties, the endowment, and other issues remained pressing crises. Other events, like fatalities caused by fraternity hazing, brought unwanted attention to the college and threatened to tarnish the image of the three thousand "Morehouse men" enrolled at the college. In September 1994, Keith resigned under pressure after a financial audit revealed that he might have received more than $200,000 in unapproved benefits. Despite these setbacks, Morehouse remained one of the most prestigious of historically black colleges, committed to academic excellence and the distinctive educational needs of African Americans.

BIBLIOGRAPHY

Brawley, Benjamin G. *History of Morehouse College.* 1917. Reprint. College Park, Md., 1970.

Butler, Addie Louis Joyner. *The Distinctive Black College: Talladega, Tuskegee, and Morehouse.* Metuchen, N.J., 1977.

Jones, Edward Allen. *A Candle in the Dark: A History of Morehouse College.* Valley Forge, Pa., 1967.

— JOHN C. STONER

MORMONS

Within the Church of Jesus Christ of Latter-day Saints, popularly known as the Mormon church, the number of African Americans has always been relatively small. This has been the case from the 1830s, the period when the denomination was first organized. African Americans, however, have exerted an influence on Mormonism far beyond their small numbers.

A handful of free northern blacks, probably no more than one or two dozen, associated themselves with Mormonism in the 1830s and 1840s, during the church's formative years in upstate New York under the leadership of Joseph Smith. The small number was largely due to limited black-white contact involving members of the still-fledgling denomination. Also limiting African-American interest were Mormon scriptural writings, as articulated by Smith, asserting that various dark-skinned peoples, including blacks, were divinely less favored or inferior to whites. These writings, which included the *Book of Mormon* and the "Book of Moses" and the "Book of Abraham," which constituted the *Pearl of Great Price*, were considered holy scripture on a level with the Old and New Testaments. In time, they helped justify denying African-American ordination to the Mormon priesthood, a lay organization open to virtually all other adult male members of the church.

In addition, Joseph Smith committed his Latter-day Saint followers to an official anti-abolitionist position during the 1830s. The reason was that the Mormons sought to adjust to local conditions following the movement of the church's headquarters, first to Kirtland, Ohio (located near the Western Reserve—a hotbed of abolitionist conflict), and then to Missouri (a slave state). Blacks thus had little incentive to join the Mormon movement.

The few blacks who did join the Mormon church, however, left their mark. Among these was Elijah Abel, who joined in Kirtland and was apparently "intimately acquainted" with and "lived in the home" of Smith. In fact, Abel, despite his African-American lineage, was ordained to the Mormon priesthood, and served as a missionary for the church on three different occasions. He was ordained during the 1830s, prior to the imposition of Mormonism's ban on black ordination. The ban itself was affirmed by Brigham Young in 1847, after he became the principal Mormon leader following Smith's death three years earlier.

Young's immediate decision to ban blacks from the priesthood was encouraged, in large part, by the disruptive behavior of William McCary, an African-Indian who was associated briefly with the church at Winter Quarters, Nebr., during the time of the Mormon migration to the western Great Basin. Young, anxious to put an end to McCary's rival prophetic claims and his practice of polygamy (a still-secret practice to those outside the church's leadership), asserted that all blacks, including McCary, were ineligible for ordination.

By the time Young and his followers settled in the Great Basin, the number of African Americans who came in contact with the Mormon church had slightly increased. In contrast to the twenty or so free blacks associated with the Mormons in Nauvoo, Ill., during the 1840s, there were over one hundred blacks living in Utah by the early 1850s—the majority being slaves belonging to Latter-day Saints who migrated west from the slaveholding South. In response to this situation, Brigham Young, in his capacity as Utah territorial governor, approved "An Act in Relation to Service," which legalized black slavery. This made Utah the only American territory west of the Mississippi River where slavery was legal prior to the Civil War. As a result, the number of blacks migrating to Utah and/or joining the Mormon church remained small in the years before and during the Civil War.

This situation continued as the number of blacks living in Utah associated with the Mormon church remained low during the next fifty to seventy-five years. Despite Emancipation, the Mormon ban on black ordination remained intact. In addition, Utah's small black population was subjected to civil restrictions upholding both de facto and de jure segregation and other forms of discrimination.

Although the number of blacks living in Utah increased from 118 to 1,235 between 1870 and 1940, their tiny percentage of the state's total population remained virtually unchanged—a mere 0.1 percent to 0.3 percent. The corresponding number of blacks within the Mormon church itself was even more negligible. Thus, both outsiders and those within the church had little need to pay attention to Utah's discriminatory civil statutes, or to Mormon ecclesiastical restrictions on black ordination during this period.

Starting in the 1950s, however, in the wake of the doubling of Utah's black population within just one decade, the state's small but active chapter of the NAACP worked for the elimination of all forms of civil discrimination. This occurred against the backdrop of a burgeoning nationwide Civil Rights Movement. Under pressure from the NAACP and other civil rights groups, the Mormon church issued a statement of support for civil rights in 1963. Two years later, as a result of further NAACP pressure, the Mormon-dominated

Utah legislature enacted both a Public Accommodations Act and a Fair Employment Act.

By the late 1960s, black activists and others exerted direct pressure on the Mormon church to lift its ban on black ordination to the priesthood. Protest was promoted mainly by black-rights activists rather than by the handful of blacks within the church. Such pressure coming from "outsiders" made Mormon officials even more resistant to change, particularly during the turbulent era of the late 1960s and early '70s.

In 1971, however, Mormon leaders did formulate a special organization for its black members known as the "Genesis group," designed to serve the needs of the estimated two hundred black Mormons living in and around Salt Lake City. In addition, room was made in the famed Mormon Tabernacle Choir for three blacks, and the church-owned Brigham Young University recruited blacks for its athletic teams. Finally, in June 1978, the church leadership lifted its black priesthood ban, allowing blacks full participation in the church. This change came less in response to Mormon-African American relations than to the emergence of the Mormon church as an international organization active in nonwhite areas outside the United States.

Indeed, during the years since the lifting of the ban, the church has enjoyed its greatest success among people of African descent Brazil, the Caribbean, and various parts of sub-Saharan Africa. By contrast, Mormonism continues to have much more limited appeal among blacks within the United States itself.

BIBLIOGRAPHY

Bringhurst, Newell G. *Saints, Slaves, and Blacks: The Changing Place of Black People Within Mormonism.* Westport, Conn., 1981.

Bush, Lester E., and Armand L. Mauss, eds. *Neither White nor Black: Mormon Scholars Confront the Race Issue in a Universal Church.* Midvale, Utah, 1984.

Launius, Roger D. *Invisible Saints: A History of Black Americans in the Reorganized Church.* Independence, Mo., 1988.

— NEWELL G. BRINGHURST

MORRISON, TONI

Toni Morrison (February 18, 1931–), writer. By the 1980s, Toni Morrison was considered by the literary world to be one of the major American novelists. In 1992—five years after she received the Pulitzer Prize for *Beloved* and the year of publication both for her sixth novel, *Jazz,* and for a series of lectures on American literature, *Playing in the Dark*—Morrison was being referred to internationally as one of the greatest American writers of all time. In 1993 she became the first black woman in history to be awarded the Nobel Prize for literature.

The road to prominence began with Morrison's birth into a family she describes as a group of storytellers. Born Chloe Anthony Wofford in Lorain, Ohio, she was the second of four children of George Wofford (a steelmill welder, car washer, and construction and shipyard worker) and Ramah Willis Wofford (who worked at home and sang in church).

Her grandparents came to the North from Alabama to escape poverty and racism. Her father's and mother's experiences with and responses to racial violence and economic inequality, as well as what Morrison learned about living in an economically cooperative neighborhood, have influenced the political edge of her art. Her early understanding of the "recognized and verifiable principles of Black art," principles she heard demonstrated in her family's stories and saw demonstrated in the art and play of black people around her, has also had its effect. Morrison's ability to manipulate the linguistic qualities of both black art and conventional literary form manifests itself in a prose that some critics have described as lyrical and vernacular at the same time.

In 1993 Toni Morrison became the first black woman in history to be awarded the Nobel Prize for literature.

After earning a B.A. from Howard University in 1953, Morrison moved to Cornell University for graduate work in English and received an M.A. in 1955. She taught at Texas Southern University from 1955 to 1957 and then at Howard University (until 1964), where she met and married Harold Morrison, a Jamaican architect, and gave birth to two sons. Those were years that Morrison has described as a period of almost complete powerlessness, when she wrote quietly and participated in a writers' workshop, creating the story that would become *The Bluest Eye.*

In 1964, Morrison divorced her husband and moved to Syracuse, N.Y., where she began work for Random House. She later moved to a senior editor's position at the Random House headquarters in New York City—continuing to teach, along the way, at various universities. Since 1988, she has been Robert F. Goheen Professor of the Humanities at Princeton University.

Morrison's first novel, *The Bluest Eye* (1970), is a text that combines formal "play" between literary aesthetics and pastoral imagery with criticism of the effects of racialized personal aesthetics. *Sula* (1973) takes the pattern of the heroic quest and the artist-outsider theme and disrupts both in a novel that juxtaposes those figurations with societal gender restrictions amid the historical constraint of racism. *Song of Solomon* (1977), *Tar Baby* (1981), and *Beloved* (1987) are engagements with the relation to history of culturally specific political dynamics, aesthetics, and ritualized cultural practices.

Song of Solomon sets group history within the parameters of a family romance; *Tar Baby* interweaves the effects of colonialism and multiple family interrelationships that are stand-ins for history with surreal descriptions of landscape; and *Beloved* negotiates narrative battles over story and history produced as a result of the imagination's inability to make sense of slavery. In *Jazz,* Morrison continues her engagement with the problems and productiveness of individual storytelling's relation to larger, public history.

Morrison's seventh novel, *Paradise* (1998), concerns an all-black township in Oklahoma and the interaction of its residents with four troubled women who live in an abandoned school nearby.

The lectures published as *Playing in the Dark* continue Morrison's interest in history and narrative. The collection abstracts her ongoing dialogue with literary criticism and history around manifestations of race and racism as narrative forms themselves produced by (and producers of) the social effects of racism in the larger public imagination.

Morrison's work sets its own unique imprimatur on that public imagination as much as it does on the literary world. A consensus has emerged that articulates the importance of Morrison to the world of letters and demonstrates the permeability of the boundary between specific cultural production—the cultural production that comes out of living as part of the African-American group—and the realm of cultural production that critics perceive as having crossed boundaries between groups and nation-states.

Morrison's ability to cross the boundaries as cultural commentator is reflected in *Race-ing Justice and Engendering Power: Essays on Anita Hill, Clarence Thomas, and the Construction of Social Reality,* a collection of essays about the nomination of Supreme Court Justice Clarence THOMAS and the accusations of sexual harassment brought against him by law professor Anita Hill. The essays in the collection were written by scholars from various fields, then edited and introduced by Morrison.

BIBLIOGRAPHY

Lubiano, Wahneema. "Toni Morrison." In Lea Baechler and A. Walton Litz, eds. *African American Writers.* New York, 1991, pp. 321–334.

Middleton, David L. *Toni Morrison: An Annotated Bibliography.* New York, 1987.

Morrison, Toni. "Memory, Creation, and Writing." *Thought* 59 (December 1984): 385–390.

— WAHNEEMA LUBIANO

MORTON, FERDINAND JOSEPH "JELLY ROLL"

Ferdinand Joseph "Jelly Roll" Morton (October 20, 1890–July 10, 1941), jazz pianist and composer. Although the facts concerning his early life remain in dispute, along with his claim to have singlehandedly invented jazz in the early years of the twentieth century, Jelly Roll Morton nonetheless remains the crucial figure in bridging nineteenth-century blues, vaudeville songs, and ragtime with the small jazz ensembles of the 1920s. He was born Ferdinand Joseph LaMothe in Gulfport, Miss. His father, a Creole carpenter and trombonist schooled in classical music, whose name has also been spelled "LeMenthe" and "Lemott," left the family when Ferdinand was a child. Ferdinand was raised in New Orleans, and took the last name of Ed Morton, his stepfather, who was a porter and trombonist. Jelly Roll played guitar and trombone before taking up piano as a teenager, performing at "sporting houses," which were bordellos in the red-light district of New Orleans known as Storyville. He also learned from pianists during his travels along the Gulf Coast as far as Florida. Morton studied with a professor of music from St. Joseph's Seminary College in Saint Benedict, La., but it was his 1902 meeting in New Orleans with the elegant ragtime pianist Tony Jackson, the composer of "Pretty Baby" and "The Naked Dance," that determined the direction of his career.

Morton left New Orleans around 1906, working in Louisiana and Mississippi as a pianist and as a small-time pool hustler, card shark, gambler, and pimp. In 1908 he moved to Memphis to work in a vaudeville show, and the next year he went on the road again, playing with vaudeville shows throughout the South, and possibly in New York, Chicago, and California. In 1911, he was performing as a pianist and comedian with McCabe's Minstrel Troubadours in St. Louis and Kansas City, and he eventually went to Chicago, where he settled for three years, leading his own band and managing a cabaret. He also published his first composition, "Jelly Roll Blues" (1915), the title referring to Morton's self-bestowed nickname, a slang term for the female genitals and sex in general. In 1915 he traveled to San Francisco, Chicago, and Detroit, and the next year he performed and ran a hotel and nightclub in Los Angeles. Between 1917 and 1923 Morton traveled and worked up and down the West Coast, from Tijuana, Mexico, to Vancouver and Alaska, as well as to Colorado and Wyoming, and finally back to Los Angeles, where he worked for a time as a boxing promoter.

Jelly Roll Morton remains the crucial figure in bridging nineteenth-century blues, vaudeville songs, and ragtime with the small jazz ensembles of the 1920s.

In 1923, Morton returned to Chicago for five years, working as a staff arranger for the Melrose Publishing House. But much more important, it was during this time that he took advantage of the growing market for "hot" records and made the recordings upon which his reputation rests. He recorded as a solo pianist in Richmond, Ind., in 1923 and 1924 ("London Blues," "Grandpa's Spell," "Milenburg Joys," "Wolverine Blues," "The Pearls"), and also with a white group called the New Orleans Rhythm Kings. Even better known are recordings he made from 1926 to 1930 in Chicago and New York ("Kansas City Stomps," "Sidewalk Blues," "Smokehouse Blues," "The Chant," "Mournful Serenade," "Shreveport Stomp," "Ponchartrain Blues") with his Red Hot Peppers, an ensemble which included trombonist Kid Ory, clarinetists Johnny Dodds and Omer Simeon, and drummer Baby Dodds. During this time Morton continued to perform, touring the Midwest with W. C. HANDY, playing second piano in Fate Marable's riverboat band, and fronting pianist Henry Crowder's band.

Morton was the first great JAZZ composer. In addition to those works already mentioned, notable compositions include "New Orleans Blues," "King Porter Stomp," "Frog-i-more Rag," "Mamanita," and "Black Bottom Stomp." Morton was also the most important pianist to emerge from early New Orleans jazz, playing in an artful blend of ornamental nineteenth-century salon music and stomping blues. His arranging provided a model for small jazz ensembles, allowing raw improvisational passages to animate sophisticated composed sections, always within the conventions of New Orleans instrumental ragtime. As an arranger and composer, Morton paid careful attention to instrumentation and ensemble effects. In this he was the prime forerunner of subsequent jazz composers.

In 1928 Morton moved to New York, where in addition to continuing recording with the Red Hot Peppers, he played for two months at Harlem's Rose Danceland, and in 1929 he led an all-girl revue in Chicago. In 1931 he again led his own ensemble in Harlem, and in 1932 he served as the accompanist for Harlem musical shows. In 1934 he worked as the house pianist at the Red Apple Club in Harlem, and recorded with the white trumpeter Wingy Manone. Despite his busy schedule, Morton found both his health and his career beginning to decline by the early 1930s. Interest in New Orleans jazz had ebbed in general, the Great Depression had caused a collapse of the record industry, and Morton was virtually financially ruined by investments in a cosmetics company.

In 1935 Morton moved to Washington, D.C., and played a two-year engagement at the Jungle Club. He worked as a nightclub manager in 1937. In 1938 he recorded eight hours of music and anecdotal reminiscences for John Lomax at the Library of Congress. While they are pioneering and indispensable as oral history, because of Morton's boastful obfuscations they raise as many historical questions as they answer. In addition to the dubious claim that he invented jazz in New Orleans in 1902 by playing four beats to the bar instead of ragtime's two, Morton, whose arrogant personality had earned him many enemies, bitterly complained that numerous famous jazz tunes had been stolen from him. Nevertheless, the interviews provide an unequaled glimpse into the creation of New Orleans jazz, along with Morton's often quite perceptive insights into the workings of his music. Alan Lomax's *Mister Jelly Roll* (1950) is a condensed version of the Library of Congress interviews.

In 1938 Morton also moved back to New York, organized a music publishing company, and began performing and recording again, just in time for a revival of interest in New Orleans jazz. In 1939 he performed solo, but a heart attack forced him into the hospital. The following year, with his health still in decline, Morton moved to Los Angeles, hoping to claim an inheritance from his godmother. There he formed a new music company and led a new group of musicians, but he was too sick to work, and died of heart disease in 1941. In 1992 Morton was the subject of a loosely biographical Broadway musical by George C. Wolfe, *Jelly's Last Jam,* which attracted national attention.

BIBLIOGRAPHY

Dapogny, James. *Ferdinand "Jelly Roll" Morton: The Collected Piano Music.* New York, 1982.

Gushee, Lawrence. "A Preliminary Chronology of the Early Career of Ferd 'Jelly Roll' Morton." *American Music* 3 (1985): 389–412.

Lomax, Alan. *Mister Jelly Roll.* New York, 1950.

Morton, Jelly Roll. "I Created Jazz." *Downbeat* 8 (1938).
Williams, Martin. *Jazz Masters of New Orleans.* New York, 1979.

– LAWRENCE GUSHEE

MOSES, ROBERT PARRIS

Robert Parris Moses (January 23, 1935–), civil rights activist, educator. Bob Moses was born in New York City and raised in Harlem. He graduated from Hamilton College in 1956 and began graduate work in philosophy at Harvard University, receiving his M.A. one year later. Forced to leave school due to his mother's death, Moses taught mathematics at a private school in New York City. He first became active in the CIVIL RIGHTS MOVEMENT in 1959, when he worked with Bayard RUSTIN, a prominent SOUTHERN CHRISTIAN LEADERSHIP CONFERENCE (SCLC) activist, on organizing a youth march for integrated schools. A meeting with civil rights activist Ella baker inspired Moses to immerse himself in the Civil Rights Movement that was sweeping the South. In 1960 Moses joined the STUDENT NONVIOLENT COORDINATING COMMITTEE (SNCC) and became the fledgling organization's first full-time voter registration worker in the deep south.

Moses, who often worked alone facing many dangerous situations, was arrested and jailed numerous times. In McComb, Miss., he spearheaded black voter registration drives and organized Freedom Schools. He grew to play a more central role in SNCC, and in 1962 he became the strategical coordinator and project director of the Congress of Federated Organizations (COFO)—a statewide coalition of the CONGRESS OF RACIAL EQUALITY (CORE), SNCC, and the NATIONAL ASSOCIATION FOR THE ADVANCEMENT OF COLORED PEOPLE (NAACP). In 1963, COFO, with Moses as the guiding force, launched a successful mock gubernatorial election campaign—"the Freedom Ballot"—in which black voters were allowed to vote for candidates of their choosing for the first time. Its success led Moses to champion an entire summer of voter registration and educational activities to challenge racism and segregation in 1964, the FREEDOM SUMMER, with the purpose of capturing national attention forcing federal intervention in Mississippi.

During the Freedom Summer, Moses played an integral role in organizing and advising the Mississippi Freedom Democratic Party (MFDP)—an alternative third party which challenged the legitimacy of the all-white Democratic party delegation at the Democratic national convention in Atlantic City. After the 1964 summer project came to an end, SNCC erupted in factionalism. Moses's staunch belief in the Christian idea of a beloved community, nonhierarchical leadership, grassroots struggle, local initiative, and pacifism made him the leading ideologue in the early years of SNCC. Finding himself unwillingly drawn into the factional struggle, Moses left the organization and ended all involvement in civil rights activities. Later that year, he adopted Parris—his middle name—as his new last name, to elude his growing celebrity.

A conscientious objector to the Vietnam War, Moses fled to Canada to avoid the draft in 1966. Two years later he traveled with his family to Tanzania, where he taught mathematics. In 1976 Moses returned to the United States and resumed his graduate studies at Harvard University. Supplementing his children's math education at home, however, led him away from the pursuit of his doctorate and back into the classroom. In 1980 he founded the Algebra Project, with grants received from a MacArthur Fellowship, to help underprivileged children get an early grounding in mathematics to better their job opportunities in the future.

Moses viewed the Algebra Project—whose classes were directly modeled on Freedom Schools and Citizenship Schools from the early 1960s—as an integral continuation of his civil rights work. He personally oversaw all teacher training to insure that the emphasis was placed on student empowerment, rather than dependence on the teachers. Creating a five-step learning method to help children translate their concrete experiences into complex mathematical concepts, Moses pioneered innovative methods designed to help children become independent thinkers. After proven success in raising students' standardized test scores in Massachusetts public schools, the project branched out to schools in Chicago, Milwaukee, Oakland, and Los Angeles, and Moses was once again propelled into the public eye. In 1992, in what he saw as a spiritual homecoming, Moses returned to the same areas of Mississippi where he had registered African-American voters three decades earlier, and launched the Delta Algebra project to help ensure a brighter future for children of that impoverished region.

BIBLIOGRAPHY

Carson, Clayborne. *In Struggle: SNCC and the Black Awakening of the 1960s.* Cambridge, Mass., 1981.
Jetter, Alexis. "Mississippi Learning." *New York Times Magazine* (February 21, 1993): 28.
McAdam, Doug. *Freedom Summer.* 1988.

– MARSHALL HYATT

MOSLEY, WALTER

Walter Mosley (January 12, 1952–), novelist. The son of an African-American janitor and a Jewish clerk, Walter Mosley was born in Los Angeles, Calif., and raised in the South Central section of that city. After graduating from high school on the west coast, he attended Goddard College and later Johnson State University, both in Vermont. Upon receiving his B.A. in 1975 from Johnson State, Mosley worked at various jobs, including that of potter and caterer. Mosley moved to New York City in 1981 and enrolled in a graduate writing program at City College, while supporting himself as a computer programmer. It was during this time that he wrote his first novel, *Gone Fishing,* for which he was unable to find a publisher. Shortly thereafter, he completed *Devil in a Blue Dress,* the first of his "Easy Rawlins" detective novels. Mosley waited for six months to show the book to his mentor, novelist Frederic Tuten. Within a week of submitting the manuscript, Mosley signed a publishing contract with the publishing company Norton, quit his job, and began writing full time.

Mosley's hero, Ezekiel "Easy" Rawlins, is an African-American detective working the South Central section of Los Angeles with his sidekick "Mouse." *Devil in a Blue Dress* (1990) finds him in his late thirties, struggling to make his way in the often violent and racist, yet colorful and endearing, working-class world of South Central just after World War II. Mosley's subsequent novels—*A Red Death* (1991), *A White Butterfly* (1992), and *Black Betty* (1994)—see Rawlins through the McCarthy era and into the early 1960s. From the outset, the series was praised by critics and sold relatively well, but it became exceptionally popular after President Bill Clinton mentioned Mosley as one of his favorite authors during his 1992 campaign. Three of the books were nominated for Gold Dagger Awards by the British Crime Writers Association; *A White Butterfly* was nominated for the Edgar Award by the Mystery Writers of America. In 1994, a film version of *Devil in a Blue Dress*—directed by Jonathan Demme and featuring Denzel Washington, Eddie Murphy, and Wesley Snipes—was in production, and two books—Mosley's fifth Rawlins novel, *The Little Yellow Dog,* and *R.L.'s Dream,* a novel about the blues—were due for publication.

BIBLIOGRAPHY

Lyall, Sarah. "Heroes in Black, Not White." *New York Times,* June 15, 1994, p. C1, 8.

McCullough, Bob. "Walter Mosley: Interview." *Publisher's Weekly* (May 23, 1994): 67–68.

— PAMELA WILKINSON

MOTOWN

Motown, which was founded in 1959 in the basement of Berry Gordy, Jr.'s Detroit home and grew to become the largest black-owned company in the United States, virtually defines the style of African-American popular music known as soul. Integrating the unrestrained vocals, hand claps, and tambourine accents of black gospel music, the strong backbeat of rhythm and blues, the heavily produced sound of white popular music, and the detailed, narrative-style love lyrics of doo-wop and vocal group songs, Motown has always signified a range of African-American pop music styles. Drawing on untrained recruits from the churches and projects of Detroit, Motown nurtured many prominent figures of postwar American popular music, including Smokey Robinson, Marvin Gaye, The Temptations, The Four Tops, Diana Ross, Stevie WONDER, the Jackson 5, and the Commodores.

Gordy, a former boxer and record store owner who had worked on the assembly line at Ford and had written several of Jackie Wilson's hits, started his musical empire with two small record labels, Tamla Records and Gordy Records. At first, Gordy worked with his brothers, sisters, and friends to produce Motown's records. By 1962 Gordy was comparing Motown with the Detroit auto industry that gave the label its name, a contraction of "Motor Town." At the height of Motown's fame starting in 1963, the production schedules at "Detroit's other assembly line," were indeed arduous, but consistently successful.

Gordy and his producers created dozens of classic soul records in Motown's cramped basement studio. Even after 1963, when the Motown sound became more elaborate, recordings were largely improvised on the spot. Motown's house band of Joe Hunter or Earl Van Dyke on piano, drummer Benny Benjamin, and electric bassist James Jamerson (1938–1983) was provided with sketchy lead sheets of chords. They responded with the inventive figures behind hits like the Temptations' "My Girl" and Martha and the Vandellas' "Nowhere to Run," on which Jamerson is virtually the lead player.

Motown virtually defines the style of African-American popular music known as soul.

Gordy also prepared his acts for performances on traveling tours known as the Motown Revue. In 1964 Gordy hired a consultant, Maxine Powell, to teach Motown's artists everything from makeup to deportment, readying them for audiences as racially diverse as those at Harlem's Apollo Theater, Las Vegas, and prime time television. In 1965 Motown hired the tap dancer Cholly

Atkins to choreograph its acts. Atkins perfected the "Temptations' Walk" and taught THE SUPREMES their demure half-turns and dance steps.

Smokey Robinson was the first of Motown's songwriter-producers, writing and producing six of Motown's first ten Top Ten hits. He specialized in wistful tunes and surprising lyrics, such as "I don't like you/ But I love you," from the Miracles' "You Really Got a Hold on Me" (1963), and "I've got sunshine on a cloudy day," from the Temptations' "My Girl" (1965). His other songs included "The One Who Really Loves You," "You Beat Me to the Punch," "Two Lovers," and "My Guy." Starting in 1964 Robinson took over the direction of the Temptations. He gave them a song he had written for himself, "The Way You Do the Things You Do," and picked Eddie Kendricks (1939–1992), whose falsetto resembled Robinson's, to sing lead. A year later he wrote "My Girl," but instead of Kendricks he chose David Ruffin (1941–1992), a gruff, raspy gospel-styled baritone, to sing lead. Robinson also had hits with Marvin Gaye and with the Marvelettes.

The most famous version of the "Motown Sound" was largely the creation of two brothers, Eddie and Brian Holland, and Lamont Dozier, usually known as Holland-Dozier-Holland, or H-D-H. Starting in 1963, while writing for and producing Martha and the Vandellas, the Four Tops, and the Supremes, they created an instantly recognizable style: drums and tambourines on all the beats, vibraphone in tandem with piano, a throaty baritone saxophone, Jamerson's pulsating bass lines, and melodic riffs that counterpointed the melody of the lyrics instead of merely marking time. H-D-H cut thirty Top Ten pop hits, among them five straight number ones for the Supremes in 1964 and 1965: "Where Did Our Love Go?" "Baby Love," "Come See About Me," "Stop! In the Name of Love," and "Back in My Arms Again."

Although black-owned, many top financial positions at the cluster of companies that made up Motown—including Tamla Records, Gordy Records, Motown Records, Jobete Music Publishing, Hitsville USA, and International Talent Management—were eventually filled by whites. Gordy was often accused of mistreating his performers financially. Motown lawyers wrote contracts that performers often never saw and paid them royalties that were well below industry standards. Motown also used the money performers made from live shows and songwriting to subsidize production costs for their next recordings, a practice known as cross-collateralization. By the end of the decade, Mary Wells, H-D-H, David Ruffin of the Temptations, and others had sued the company for keeping them in what Ruffin's lawyers called "economic peonage." Still, Motown grew steadily, and by 1965 the company was grossing $8 million a year, and had 100 employees in Detroit, New York, and Los Angeles.

By 1967, Motown was undergoing personnel and musical changes. Norman Whitfield (1943–) took charge of the Motown production line. Writing with his partner Barrett Strong (1941–) and producing by himself, he took over the Temptations in 1966 with "Ain't Too Proud to Beg." Whitfield highlighted the raspy gospel sound of David Ruffin's voice and the increasing influence of funk. New sounds like stutter-step polyrhythms, one-chord vamps, and fuzztone lead guitars all challenged the old Motown Sound, and resulted in the Temptations' "Cloud Nine" (1968), "Psychedelic Shack" (1969), and the eleven-minute "Papa Was a Rolling Stone" (1972).

The early 1970s saw important career changes for several musicians who had been with Motown almost from the start. Marvin Gaye's conceptual album, *What's Going On* (1971), originally rejected by Gordy, spawned three top-ten hits: "What's Going On," "Mercy, Mercy, Me," and "Inner City Blues." In the same year, 1971, Stevie Wonder turned twenty-one, and altered his contract with Motown in order to begin a series of albums which included *Where I'm Coming From* (1971), *Music of My Mind* (1972), *Talking Book* (1972) and *Innervisions* (1973). Wonder wrote and produced these records and played virtually every instrument himself. Motown's last discovery of the 1960s was the Jackson 5. Cut with musicians from Los Angeles, the Jackson's first four singles went to number one. Sizzling, danceable pop, the first two releases, "I Want You Back" (1969) and "ABC" (1970), featured vocals by Motown's new boy star, Michael Jackson.

As early as 1963, Gordy involved Motown in the CIVIL RIGHTS MOVEMENT, releasing *The Great March to Freedom* containing the Rev. Dr. Martin Luther KING, Jr.'s "I Have a Dream" speech. In the early 1970s Motown started a new spoken word label, Black Forum, which produced King's Grammy Award-winning *Why I Oppose the War in Vietnam* (1970), as well as *Guess Who's Coming Home: Black Fighting Men Recorded Live in Vietnam* (1970), and albums by Langston HUGHES and Margaret Danner (1970), Stokely CARMICHAEL (1970), Amiri BARAKA (1972), Ossie DAVIS and Bill COSBY (1972), and Elaine Brown (1973).

In the early 1970s Gordy moved Motown to Los Angeles, where he became increasingly involved in television specials, which were quite successful, and films, which were not. In 1973 Motown was the biggest black-owned company in the United States, and Gordy helped finance and produce *Lady Sings the Blues* (1972), *Mahogany* (1975), and *The Wiz* (1978), all of which starred Diana Ross. Despite the departure of many of Motown's key musical and financial figures, the company remained strong. Diana Ross, Stevie Wonder, the Commodores, and Rick James, continued to put Motown's records on the charts.

In 1973 Motown was the biggest black-owned company in the United States.

By the 1970s, Motown had become a financial giant as well as a dominant musical influence. In 1973 the company had grossed $40 million. Five years later, that figure was up to $60 million. In 1981 Gordy made Suzanne De Passe president of Motown Productions. She concentrated on television specials, with great success, and in 1983 the company grossed $104 million. The next year, Gordy signed a distribution agreement with MCA, an ironic return to the corporate involvement that had inspired him to start his own record company. Further ventures in television and film, including *The Last Dragon* (1985), proved largely unsuccessful. Consequently, Gordy was soon entertaining offers for Motown, and in 1988 he sold the company—then the fifth largest black-owned business in the country, with $100 million in sales and 257 employees—to MCA for $61 million. Gordy remained in control of Motown's music publishing and television and film subsidiaries. However, in 1993, MCA in turn sold the company to Polygram for $325 million. Polygram revitalized Motown, developing several major pop acts, including the singer Johnny Gill, and the vocal group Boyz II Men. Since 1985 Motown's original headquarters, the house at 2468 West Grand Boulevard in Detroit, has been a museum dedicated to the history of the company.

BIBLIOGRAPHY

Bianco, David. *Heat Wave: The Motown Fact Book.* Ann Arbor, Mich., 1988.

George, Nelson. *Where Did Our Love Go? The Rise and Fall of the Motown Sound.* New York, 1985.

Guaralnick, Peter. *Sweet Soul Music.* New York, 1986.

Hirshey, Gerri. *Nowhere to Run.* New York, 1984.

Morse, David. *Motown.* New York, 1971.

Waller, Don. *The Motown Story.* New York, 1985.

— HARRIS FRIEDBERG

MOYNIHAN REPORT

In early 1965, as the focus of government action toward African Americans turned from fighting legal segregation to the War on Poverty, Daniel Patrick Moynihan, a young sociologist from Harvard working as assistant secretary of labor, wrote a report entitled *The Negro Family: The Case for National Action.* Moynihan argued that aid for blacks must take account of the state of the black family. Relying on the African-American sociologist E. Franklin FRAZIER and other influential authorities, Moynihan argued that poor African-American families were caught in a "tangle of pathology." He noted that one-quarter of all black marriages ended in divorce, one-quarter of all black children were born out of wedlock, and one-quarter of all black households were female-headed. From the time blacks had been enslaved, Moynihan argued, their family structure had been warped, and after Emancipation it had been weakened by segregation and poverty. Black women's greater educational and employment opportunities had led to a "matriarchal" family pattern that eliminated proper role models and undermined black male self-esteem, leading to juvenile delinquency and crime. High fertility rates led to increased poverty and to welfare dependency. While blacks were not to blame for their original oppression, their pathological condition was now self-perpetuating. The report noted that instead of paralleling the unemployment rate, the number of welfare cases was now growing. Moynihan did not propose any solutions to the problems he delineated, but the report clearly looked to federal actions such as large-scale employment of black males to break the "matriarchal" mold of the black family and to curb welfare dependency. Moynihan suggested the armed forces were one arena in which black men could find masculine employment and role models.

At first, the report was circulated within the government, and portions of it were discussed by the media. President Lyndon B. Johnson covered Moynihan's main points at a commencement address at Howard University. The government officially released it in August 1965. Coming shortly after the Watts uprising in Los Angeles, the report seemed timely. Johnson called for a national conference on the black family.

The report was soon met, however, by a wave of opposition, both from social scientists debating Moynihan's conclusions and use of data and by African Americans and other civil rights activists who found it insulting. Activists felt that the emphasis on out-of-wedlock births and the "pathology" of black family relations seemed biased and demeaning. Since Moynihan had not proposed any solutions to his findings, he seemed, in the words of the white psychologist William Ryan, to be "blaming the victims" of oppression for their condition. Rather than urging federal programs for blacks, the report was interpreted as justifying inaction, since it argued that blacks were trapped in a "culture of poverty" and did not have the psychological resources to benefit from educational or employment opportunities. John Lewis of the STUDENT NONVIOLENT COORDINATING COMMITTEE criticized the report for assuming that white discrimination was no longer a factor in black life, and the nascent Black Power movement decried Moynihan's advocacy of socialization by the armed forces.

The report was also criticized by black women activists and white feminists. Dorothy Height of the National Council of Negro Women claimed the report criticized black women for holding their families together and assumed that women-headed families were inherently pathological. Social scientists have since amassed considerable statistical and demographic evidence refuting Moynihan's contention that black women enjoyed privileged employment and educational status in relation to black men, and have suggested that the problem of female-headed households arose from the fact that women were paid less than men, and could not support their families without assistance. Pauli Murray questioned why black women should be censured for working.

Rather than engendering a flood of federal action to support black families, as Moynihan had hoped, the report ended by dividing opinion. Ironically, instead of focusing attention on the black family, the report itself has continued to be the focus of huge efforts at rebuttal. Its historical premise, sociological theory, and conclusions have been repeatedly attacked. Historians such as Herbert Gutman have examined the history of the black family to demonstrate the strength of family ties despite slavery and later oppression.

The report dramatically shifted the debate among social scientists on how to fight poverty. The effect of Moynihan's conclusions has been to challenge the thesis that income redistribution alone could "solve" the problem of poverty, and to focus attention on the particular problems of inner-city blacks. Some contemporary thinkers, notably the African-American sociologist William Julius Wilson in *The Truly Disadvantaged* (1987), have devoted special attention to the problem of high unemployment among young black males and its effect on the black economy and family structure, as Moynihan discussed. The issues raised by the Moynihan report on whether black poverty is a function of inadequate "values" or socialization has echoed, in both simplistic and sophisticated fashion, in policy debates ever since.

BIBLIOGRAPHY

Gutman, Herbert. *The Black Family in Slavery and Freedom, 1750–1925.* New York, 1976.

Jones, Jacqueline. *Labor of Love, Labor of Sorrow: Black Women, Work, and the Family, from Slavery to the Present.* New York, 1985.

Lemann, Nicholas. *The Promised Land.* New York, 1991.

Rainwater, Lee, and William Yancey. *The Moynihan Report and the Politics of Controversy.* Cambridge, Mass., 1967.

– MARGARET D. JACOBS

MUHAMMAD, ELIJAH

Elijah Muhammad (October 10, 1897–February 25, 1975), religious leader. Born Robert Poole in Sandersville, Ga., Muhammad was one of thirteen children of an itinerant Baptist preacher and sharecropper. In 1919 he married Clara Evans and they joined the black migration to Detroit, where he worked in the auto plants. In 1931 he met Master Wallace FARD (or Wali Farad), founder of the NATION OF ISLAM, who eventually chose this devoted disciple as his chief aide. Fard named him "Minister of Islam," dropped his slave name, Poole, and restored his true Muslim name, Muhammad. As the movement grew, a Temple of Islam was established in a Detroit storefront. It is estimated that Fard had close to 8,000 members in the Nation of Islam, consisting of poor black migrants and some former members from Marcus GARVEY'S UNITED NEGRO IMPROVEMENT ASSOCIATION and Noble Drew Ali's Moorish Science Temple.

After Fard mysteriously disappeared in 1934, the Nation of Islam was divided by internal schisms and Elijah Muhammad led a major faction to Chicago, where he established Temple of Islam No. 2 as the main headquarters for the Nation. He also instituted the worship of Master Fard as Allah and himself as the Messenger of Allah and head of the Nation of Islam, always addressed with the title "the Honourable." Muhammad built on the teachings of Fard and combined aspects of Islam and Christianity with the black nationalism of Marcus Garvey into a "proto-Islam," an unorthodox Islam with a strong racial slant. The Honorable Elijah Muhammad's message of racial separation focused on the recognition of true black identity and stressed economic independence. "Knowledge of self" and "do for self" were the rallying cries. The economic ethic of the Black Muslims has been described as a kind of black puritanism—hard work, frugality, the avoidance of debt, self-improvement, and a conservative lifestyle. Muhammad's followers sold the Nation's newspaper, *Muhammad Speaks,* and established their own educational system of Clara Muhammad schools and small businesses such as bakeries, grocery stores, and outlets selling fish and bean pies. More than 100 temples were founded. The disciples also followed strict dietary rules outlined in Muhammad's book *How to Eat to Live,* which enjoined one meal per day and complete abstention from pork, drugs, tobacco, and alcohol. The Nation itself owned farms in several states, a bank, trailer trucks for its fish and grocery businesses, an ultramodern printing press, and other assets.

Muhammad's ministers of Islam found the prisons and streets of the ghetto a fertile recruiting ground. His message of self-reclamation and black manifest destiny struck a responsive chord in the thousands of black men and women whose hope and self-respect had been all but defeated by racial abuse and denigration. As a consequence of where they recruited and the militancy of their beliefs, the Black Muslims have attracted many more young black males than any other black movement.

Muhammad had an uncanny sense of the vulnerabilities of the black psyche during the social transitions brought on by two world wars; his *Message to the Black Man in America* diagnosed the problem as a confusion of identity and self-hatred caused by white racism. The cure he prescribed was radical surgery through the formation of a separate black nation. Muhammad's 120 "degrees," or lessons, and the major doctrines and beliefs of the Nation of Islam all elaborated on aspects of this central message. The white man is a "devil by nature," absolutely unredeemable and incapable of caring about or respecting anyone who is not white. He is the historic, persistent source of harm and injury to black people. The Nation of Islam's central theological myth tells of Yakub, a black mad scientist who rebelled against Allah by creating the white race, a weak, hybrid people who were permitted temporary dominance of the world. Whites achieved their power and position through devious means and "tricknology." But, according to the Black Muslim apocalyptic view, there will come a time in the not-too-distant future when the forces of good and the forces of evil—that is to say, blacks versus whites—will clash in a "Battle of Armageddon," and the blacks will emerge victorious to recreate their original hegemony under Allah throughout the world.

With only a third-grade education, Elijah Muhammad was the leader of the most enduring black militant movement in the United States.

After spending four years in a federal prison for encouraging draft refusal during World War II, Elijah Muhammad was assisted by his chief protégé, Minister MALCOLM X, in building the movement and encouraging its rapid spread in the 1950s and 1960s. During its peak years, the Nation of Islam had more than half a million devoted followers, influencing millions more, and accumulated an economic empire worth an estimated $80 million. Besides his residence in Chicago, Muhammad also lived in a mansion outside of Phoenix, Arizona, since the climate helped to reduce his respiratory problems. He had eight children with his wife, Sister Clara Muhammad, but also fathered a number of illegitimate children with his secretaries, a circumstance that was one of the reasons for Malcolm X's final break with the Nation of Islam in 1964.

With only a third-grade education, Elijah Muhammad was the leader of the most enduring black militant movement in the United States. He died in Chicago and was succeeded by one of his six sons, Wallace Deen Muhammad. After his death, Muhammad's estate and the property of the Nation were involved in several lawsuits over the question of support for his illegitimate children.

BIBLIOGRAPHY

Lincoln, C. Eric. *The Black Muslims in America.* Boston, 1961; rev. ed., 1973.

Muhammad, Elijah. *How to Eat to Live.* Chicago, 1972.

———. *Message to the Black Man in America.* Chicago, 1965.

– LAWRENCE H. MAMIYA

MUSIC

The African-American music tradition comprises many different genres, including SPIRITUALS, work songs, BLUES, GOSPEL MUSIC, JAZZ, and popular music. Each genre includes a complex of subdivisions and is associated with a specific cultural function, social context, and historical period. Despite these distinguishing factors, the various genres exist as part of a musical continuum of African origin. The secular and sacred forms share musical features, demonstrating that the two spheres are complementary rather than oppositional.

The web of African-American musical genres is a product of interactions between people of African descent and various environmental forces in North America. The African-American music tradition documents the ways African Americans reconciled their dual national identity and forged a meaningful life in a foreign environment, first as slaves and later as second-class citizens.

African Culture in America

When Africans arrived as slaves in America, they brought a culture endowed with many traditions for-

galvanized African Americans into political action; provided them with strength and courage; united protesters as a cohesive group; and supplied a creative medium for mass communication.

Freedom songs draw from many sources and traditions, including folk and arranged spirituals; unaccompanied congregational hymn singing; folk ballads; gospel quartets, groups, and choirs; rhythm and blues and soul music; and original creations. Protesters reinterpreted the musical repertory of African-Americans, communicating their determination to effect social and political change. The singing captured the energy and spirit of the movement. The power of the songs, according to Bernice Johnson Reagon, "came from the linking of traditional oral expression to the everyday experiences of the movement" (Reagon 1987, p. 106). Well-known freedom songs include "We Shall Overcome," "Come Bah Yah," "Ain't Gonna Let Nobody Turn Me Around," "99½ Won't Do," and "Get Your Rights, Jack."

Rhythm and Blues

During the World War II era a distinct body of African-American popular music emerged in urban areas throughout the country. Labeled rhythm and blues, this tradition consisted of many regional styles, reflecting the migration patterns of African Americans and the musical background of performers. In Los Angeles, for example, former swing band and blues musicians formed five- to eight-member combos (bass and rhythm guitar, drums, piano, saxophone, trumpet, and trombone) and created a distinctive rhythm and blues style. It was a hybrid dance form that fused the twelve-bar blues and boogie-woogie bass line with the repetitive melodic riffs and drum patterns of the southwestern and Kansas City swing bands. This tradition also featured instrumental solos by a saxophonist and vocals by a blues singer. Pioneers of this style included Louis Jordan, Joe Liggins, Roy Milton, Johnny Otis, Big Jay McNeely, Harold Singer, Paul Williams, and Wild Bill Moore.

Another artifact of the rhythm and blues style, introduced in Los Angeles in the 1940s, was the ballad. First associated with the King Cole Trio, it was performed primarily in lounges and small, intimate clubs as background or listening music. It featured a self-accompanying jazz or blues-style pianist-vocalist augmented by guitar and bass performing in a subdued or tempered style, in contrast to the high-energy sounds of the dance combos. Popularizers of this form include Cecil Gant, Charles Brown and the Three Blazers, Roy Brown, Amos Milburn, and Ray CHARLES.

In New Orleans a younger generation of performers such as Fats Domino, Little Richard, Lloyd Price, and Shirley & Lee pioneered a youthful-sounding rhythm and blues style. This tradition featured gospel-derived vocal stylings; the repeated triplet and rolling octave piano figures from the blues; and the Cuban-derived rhumba bass pattern and an underlying fast sixteenth-note cymbal pattern accented on beats two and four on the snare drum. These innovations transformed the Los Angeles rhythm and blues combo style into a contemporary sound marketed by the music industry under the label ROCK 'N' ROLL.

Freedom songs draw from folk and arranged spirituals; unaccompanied congregational hymn singing; folk ballads; gospel quartets, groups, and choirs; rhythm and blues and soul music; and original creations.

By the mid-1950s New Orleans rhythm and blues had inspired other combo styles, such as the Atlantic Sound (Atlantic Records), popularized by Ruth Brown and La Vern Baker, and those of guitarist Chuck Berry and Bo Diddley and the up-tempo vocal group styles of the Cadillacs, El Dorados, Flamingos, and Coasters. These and other artists (with their producers) borrowed elements from the New Orleans tradition and fashioned them into a personalized style.

The vocal group tradition emerged as the most popular rhythm and blues form among teenagers, especially those living on the East Coast, in Chicago, and in Detroit. In these densely populated cities teenagers formed a cappella groups that performed for school dances and other social activities. Rehearsing on street corners and in schoolyards and parks, they eventually arrived at a type of group harmony inspired by their musical training in church choirs and in gospel groups. The pioneering vocal groups of the early 1950s, the Orioles, Spaniels, and the Five Keys specialized in singing ballads that appealed to the romantic fantasies of teenagers.

By the mid-1950s vocal groups had transformed the ballad into the doo-wop style. This style highlighted the phrase "doo-doo-doo-wop" or "doo-doo-doo-doo," sung as a rhythmic accompaniment by the bass singer. The doo-wop concept, introduced by the Spaniels in the early 1950s, eventually replaced the sustained "oohs and ahs" background of the early groups, adding a rhythmic foundation to the a cappella vocal group tradition. Popularizers of the doo-wop style include the Moonglows, Monotones, Frankie Lymon and the Teenagers, Five Satins, Channels, Charts, Heartbeats, Chantels, and Crests.

Coexisting with the doo-wop style was a pop-oriented vocal group sound that featured orchestral arrangements, gospel-pop-oriented vocal stylings, sing-along (as opposed to call-response) phrases (known as "hook lines"), and Latin-derived rhythms. This style, popularized by the Platters and the post-1956 Drifters, provided some of the elements (musical arrangements and hook lines) that undergirded the 1960s vocal group sound of Smokey Robinson and the Miracles, THE SUPREMES, Four Tops, Temptations, Dells, and Impressions.

In the mid-1960s the rhythm and blues tradition began to exhibit new sounds that reflected the discontentment of many African-Americans engaged in the struggle for social and racial equality. The pop-oriented vocal stylings of the Drifters, the cha-cha beat of some rhythm and blues singers, and the youthful sound and teen lyrics of the MOTOWN groups gave way to a more spirited type of music labeled soul.

Soul Music

Soul music, distinguished by gospel music stylings and socially conscious messages, was a product of the 1960s Black Power movement, a movement led by college-age students who rejected the integrationist philosophy of the 1950s civil rights leaders. The ideology associated with this movement promoted nationalist concepts of racial pride, racial unity, self-empowerment, self-control, and self-identification. As a concept soul became associated with an attitude, a behavior, symbols, institutions, and cultural products that were distinctively black and reflected the values and worldview of people of African descent.

Many black musicians supported the Black Power movement, promoting the nationalist ideology and galvanizing African Americans into social and political action. They identified with their African heritage, wearing African-derived fashions and hairstyles; their song lyrics advocated national black unity, activism, and self-pride; and their musical styles, which captured the energy, convictions, and optimism of African-Americans, reinforced an African cultural identity.

Soul music embodies the vocal and piano stylings, call-response, polyrhythmic structures, and aesthetic conventions of gospel music. This style is represented in the recordings "Soul Finger" (1967) by the Bar-Kays; "Soul Man" (1967) by Sam and Dave; "Respect" (1967) by Aretha FRANKLIN; "We're a Winner" (1968) and "This Is My Country" (1968) by the Impressions; "Say It Loud, I'm Black and Proud" (1968) and "I Don't Want Nobody to Give Me Nothing" (1969) by James BROWN; "Freedom" (1970) by the Isley Brothers; "Respect Yourself" (1971) by the Staple Singers; "Give More Power to the People" (1971) by the Chi-Lites; and "Back Stabbers" (1972) by the O'Jays, among others.

During the early 1970s the optimism that had prevailed during the 1960s began to fade among a large segment of the African-American community. New opportunities for social and economic advancement engendered by pressures of the civil rights and Black Power movements resulted in opposition from mainstream society. Resistance to affirmative action programs, school desegregation, busing, open housing, and other federal policies designed to integrate African Americans fully into the mainstream hindered them in their progress toward social, economic, and racial equality. The musical style and lyrics of Marvin Gaye's "What's Going On" (1971) and "Inner City Blues" (1971); James Brown's "Down and Out in New York City" (1973) and "Funky President" (1974); and the O'Jays' "Survival" (1975) express mixed feelings about social change. Reflecting the disappointments and the continued struggle toward racial equality, new forms of popular expressions labeled funk, disco, and rap emerged out of the soul style during the 1970s.

Funk Music

Funk describes a form of dance music rooted in the traditions of James Brown and Sly Stone. It is characterized by group singing, complex polyrhythmic structures, percussive instrumental and vocal timbres, a horn section, and lyrics that urge "partying" or "having a good time." The primary function of funk was to provide temporary escape from the unpleasant realities of daily life. Therefore, funk performers created an ambience that encouraged black people to express themselves freely and without the restrictions or cultural compromises often experienced in integrated settings.

The therapeutic potential of funk is reflected in key recurring phrases: "have a good time," "let yourself go," "give up the funk," and "it ain't nothing but a party." Among the pioneering funk performers were Sly and the Family Stone, Kool and the Gang, Ohio Players, Graham Central Station, Bar-Kays, and Parliament.

By the mid-1970s George Clinton, the founder of Parliament and other funk groups had broadened the definition of funk to embrace a philosophy. Known as P-funk (pure funk), this philosophy emerges from the creation of an imaginary planet—the planet of funk. On this planet blacks acquire new values, a worldview, and a life style free of earthly social and cultural restrictions. Clinton's P-funk songs combined the party theme with social commentary in a comic style. This theme and the philosophy of P-funk prevail in Parliament's "Chocolate City" (1975); "P. Funk (Wants to Get Funked Up)" (1975); "Prelude" (1976); "Dr. Funkenstein" (1976); "Bop Gun (Endangered Species)" (1977); and "Funkentelechy" (1977). Musically, the P-funk style advances the concepts of Sly Stone, who achieved mood and textural variety through the use of electronic distorting devices and synthesizers.

Only a few 1970s and 1980s funk groups (including Zapp and Roger) incorporated synthesized technology into their performances. Most, such as Con Funk Shun, Rick James and the Stone City Band, Bohannon, Lakeside, Gap Band, Cameo, and Instant Funk, remained faithful to the traditional funk style of the early pioneers.

Nevertheless, George Clinton's technological concepts inspired the new breed of 1980s composers who were technician-arrangers influenced by the innovations of European avant-garde composers. Using synthesizers, drum machines, computers, and other electronic equipment, they created the techno-funk style, which employs various sound effects. Techno-funk provided the sound tracks and sound effects for many rap music records. Rap music deejays Afrika Bambaataa and the Soul Sonic Force ("Planet Rock," 1982), Planet Patrol ("Play at Your Own Risk," 1982), and the Jonzun Crew ("Space Is the Place," 1982) are pioneers of this style.

Go-Go

Another derivative funk style is go-go music, which evolved in Washington, D.C.'s inner-city neighborhoods during the mid-1970s. It is distinguished from traditional funk by its continuous audience participation and by the use of percussion instruments to extend and connect different songs into a twenty- to ninety-minute performance. Live audience participation is an essential component of the go-go tradition. The audience and performers spontaneously create and exchange phrases in an antiphonal style. Musical variety results from the percussively played horn lines and extended percussion sections. Go-go pioneer Chuck Brown popularized this style with his first hit, "Bustin' Loose" (1978), and a later hit, "We Need Some Money" (1985). Spike LEE brought national notoriety to the idiom when he featured E. U. (Experience Unlimited) performing "Da' Butt" (1988) in his film *School Daze.* Other go-go groups include Trouble Funk, Rare Essence, Little Benny and the Masters, Slim, and Redds and the Boys.

Disco

Disco is a term first used to identify dance music played in discotheques during the 1970s. The "Top 50 Disco Hits" chart that appeared in *Billboard* (a music industry publication) for the first time in 1974 indicated that the majority of these songs were soul, Latin soul, funk, and the new sounds from Philadelphia International Records (known as the Philly Sound and created by the songwriters Kenny Gamble and Leon Huff).

By the late 1970s disco referred to a new body of extended play (i.e., exceeding the standard three-minute recording) dance music distinguished by instrumental arrangements that incorporated synthesized sound effects and a distinctive drum pattern known as the disco beat. Disco, as a distinct musical style, had its origins in the orchestral arrangements and drumbeat of the Philly Sound, which combines melodic strings with percussively played horn lines over a four-to-the-bar bass drum pattern subdivided by beats of the high-hat cymbal (and variations of this pattern). The Philly groups MFSB ("TSOP," 1973, "Love Is the Message," 1974) and Harold Melvin and the Blue Notes ("Bad Luck," 1975) and Thelma Houston ("Don't Leave Me This Way," 1976) popularized this sound, which became known as disco and which became a worldwide musical phenomenon.

Both American and European disco producers and performers appropriated the Philly Sound, especially the drum pattern, to create various disco styles. They include the orchestral-style arrangements of Gloria Gaynor ("Never Can Say Good-bye," 1974, and "I Will Survive," 1978) and Salsoul Orchestra ("Tangerine," 1975); the Euro-disco styles of the Ritchie Family ("Brazil," 1975, and "The Best Disco in Town," 1976), Donna Summer ("Love to Love You, Baby," 1975), the Trammps ("That's Where the Happy People Go," 1976), and the Village People ("San Francisco," 1977, and "Macho Man," 1978); the Latin styles of Carl Douglas ("Doctor's Orders," 1974), and Van McCoy ("The Hustle," 1974, and "The Disco Kid," 1975); and the funk-based disco of Silver Convention ("Fly, Robin, Fly," 1975), B. T. Express ("B. T. Express," 1974), Taste of Honey ("Boogie Oogie Oogie," 1978), and Chic ("Good Times," 1979).

With the release of the disco film *Saturday Night Fever* (1978), disco crossed over from a primarily black and gay audience into the mainstream. The popularity of the film's sound track resulted in the disco craze. In response, record companies flooded the market with recordings that quickly reduced disco to a formula made up of the disco beat, synthesized sound effects, and repetitious vocal phrases. By the early 1980s disco had lost its originality and soon faded from the musical landscape.

The deejays in black gay basement clubs in Chicago and New York created a neodisco style known as house music in the mid-1980s. Their creations added gospel-style vocals over repetitive bass lines and drum patterns programmed on synthesizers and drum machines. Like those of disco and funk, house music lyrics encouraged dancers to have a good time. The pioneer of house music was deejay Frankie Knuckles, and its performers included Marshall Jefferson ("Move Your Body [The House Music Anthem]," 1986), Exit ("Let's Work It Out," 1987), Fast Eddie ("Yo Yo Get Funky," 1988), Inner City ("Big Fun," 1988), and Technotronic ("Pump Up the Jam," 1989, and "Move This," 1989).

Rap Music

Rap music is the product of inner-city black communities, where the proliferation of drugs and gangs, the rise in unemployment, and the lack of educational opportunities and traditional support institutions contributed to increased poverty and community decay during the years following the civil rights and Black Power movements. Between the late 1960s and the early 1970s gang violence escalated to new levels in New York City, a situation that inspired some ex-gang members to consider ways to reduce violent exchanges. They turned to rap music, which evolved in conjunction with breakdancing and graffiti art as an urban street youth culture called hip-hop. In about 1975 these artistic forms came to provide an alternative to competitive gang warfare. In turn, rap music became the vehicle through which many young people elevated their social status and developed a sense of pride, displaying their technological and verbal skills. By 1977 this music and the broader hip-hop culture dominated the expressions of inner-city youth.

Rap is defined as rhymed poetry recited in rhythm over prerecorded instrumental music. Rapping is rooted in the black oral traditions of storytelling, toasting, boasting, signifying, and "the dozens." The performance style of rappers employs the rhyming couplets, rhythmic speech patterns, and rhetorical style of black personality deejays who talked, or "rapped," over music. Rap music consists of several song types: party rap (known in the 1990s as hip-hop), novelty or humorous rap, rap ballad, Afrocentric or nationalist rap, and hardcore, or "gangsta," rap.

The first commercial rap recording—"Rapper's Delight" by the Sugarhill Gang, released in 1979—established party rap as the model for other early rap recordings. This rap style exploited the art of boasting. Rappers, while bragging about their verbal facility and the technological skills of the deejay to "rock the house," emphasized their physical attributes, material possessions, and other personal characteristics. Rappers within the same group (known as a posse or crew) verbally competed with each other as well as members of other rap groups. The groups that popularized party raps include Sequence ("Funk You Up," 1979); Curtis Blow ("The Breaks," 1980); Grandmaster Flash and the Furious Five ("Freedom," 1980, and "Birthday Party," 1981); Funky Four Plus One ("Rapping and Rocking the House," 1980); Lady B. ("To the Beat [Y'all]," 1980); Grandmaster Flash and the Furious Five and Furious Five Meets the Sugarhill Gang ("Showdown," 1981).

Rap music became the vehicle through which many young people elevated their social status and developed a sense of pride.

The early rap groups used studio bands rather than street mixes of rap deejays in their live recordings. The success of Grandmaster Flash's recording "Adventures of Grandmaster Flash on the Wheels of Steel" (1981) brought the street technology and techniques of mobile rap deejays into the studio. In this recording Flash created musical collages (combined and remixed extracts from existing records) and employed the scratching and backspinning (repetition of key musical phrases and rhythms by manipulating the record) techniques and various other sound effects. The innovations of rap deejay Afrika Bambaataa and the introduction of drum machines, synthesizers, computers, analog and digital machines, and other systems advanced the techniques and technology for rap music production. The new technology eventually replaced live musicians and arrangers on rap recordings.

During the mid-1980s a new generation of rappers from both inner cities and suburbs broadened the scope of rap. While "rockin' the house," boasting about their emcee skills, and exchanging insults, these rappers introduced new lyric themes and musical styles to the tradition. Some told humorous stories and tall tales; many recounted adolescent pranks, fantasies, and romantic encounters; and others painted graphic images of suburban and inner-city life. Rappers from inner-city communities aggressively expounded on the social ills and political issues that adversely affected the lives of African Americans, while those from the suburbs often presented parodies of the middle class.

In 1984 UTFO ("Roxanne Roxanne"), Roxanne Shante ("Roxanne's Revenge"), and the Real Roxanne ("The Real Roxanne") popularized verbal dueling, or "signifyin'," between genders. Run-D.M.C. fused rock with rap in "Rock Box" (1984) and "Walk This Way" (1986) to create the first rap crossover hit ("Walk This Way"). In "La Di Da Di" (1985), Doug E. Fresh incorporated rhythmic vocal effects in a concept known as the "human beat box," which became the trademark of the comic group the Fat Boys ("Jail House Rap," 1984, and "The Fat Boys Are Back," 1985). L. L. Cool J introduced the rap ballad in "I Need Love" (1987), which brought to rap a softer edge and a romantic dimension. Jazzy Jeff and the Fresh Prince added a humorous suburban perspective in "Girls Ain't Nothing but Trouble" (1986) and "Parents Just Don't Understand" (1988), as did De La Soul in "Potholes in My Lawn" (1989), "Plug Tunin' " (1989), and "Me Myself and I" (1989). Queen Latifah, the Real Roxanne, and Positive K introduced a feminist perspective in "Ladies First" (1989), "Respect" (1988), and "I Got a Man" (1992), respectively.

In the late 1980s rap became a public forum for social and political commentary as well as the expression of inner-city rage and X-rated behavior. Inner-city communities deteriorated throughout the 1980s due to the dismantling of government programs, the continuing rise in unemployment, the proliferation of drugs, and the relocation of the black middle class to the suburbs. As an invisible group with limited resources, inner-city residents struggled to survive. This situation, which led to chaos in inner-city communities, inspired a new aggressive tone and graphic descriptions of the harshness and diversity of inner-city life.

The first recordings that addressed the economic woes, social ills, and deteriorating conditions of inner cities were Curtis Blow's "Hard Times" (1980), Grandmaster Flash and the Furious Five's "The Message" (1982) and "New York, New York" (1983), and Grandmaster Flash and Melle Mel's "White Lines (Don't Do It)" (1983). In the late 1980s and 1990s a group of rappers expounded on these themes and promoted the 1960s black nationalism agenda associated with the NATION OF ISLAM and soul music. These rappers condemned social injustices, drugs, police brutality, violence, and black-on-black crime. Innovators of nationalist rap include Public Enemy ("It Takes a Nation of Millions to Hold Us Back," 1988, and "Fear of a Black Planet," 1989–1990); Jungle Brothers ("Straight Out of the Jungle," 1988, and "Done by the Forces of Nature," 1989); Boogie Down Productions ("By All Means Necessary," 1988, and "Ghetto Music: The Blueprint of Hip Hop," 1989); Paris ("The Devil Made Me Do It," 1989–1990); X-Clan ("To the East, Blackwards," 1990); Brand Nubian ("One for All," 1990, and "In God We Trust," 1992), and Sister Souljah ("360 Degrees of Power," 1992).

The political voices of nationalist rappers coexisted with the harsh messages of hard-core rappers who described the chaos, the rough and seedy side of inner-city life, using graphic language laced with expletives. Their raps, while portraying components of everyday life in inner-city communities, often exploited and dramatized these experiences to the point of glorifying drugs, violence, criminal acts, and misogynistic and X-rated behavior. Such rappers include Slick Rick ("Children's Story," 1988); N.W.A. ("Straight Outta Compton," 1988, and "Niggaz4life," 1991); Eazy-E ("Eazy-Duz-It," 1988); 2 Live Crew ("As Nasty As They Wanna Be," 1989); Geto Boys ("The Geto Boys," 1989, and "Uncut Dope," 1992); Ice Cube ("Amerikkka's Most Wanted," 1990); Dr. Dre ("The Chronic," 1992); and Snoop Doggy Dogg ("Doggystyle," 1993).

Hard-core and nationalist rappers occasionally have been accused of supporting racist and homophobic sentiments. Although these themes are not prominent in rap music, they are found in the lyrics of some artists, including Public Enemy ("Welcome to the Terrordome, 1989); Big Daddy Kane ("Pimpin' Ain't Easy," 1989); and Brand Nubian ("Punks Jump Up to Get Beat Down," 1992).

The musical style of nationalist and hard-core rap is aggressive, polytextured, polyrhythmic, and polysonic. Sampling, the repetitive remixing of chord sequences and rhythms from prerecorded music (especially the music of James Brown, George Clinton, and other soul and funk groups), combined with synthesized sound effects, is the primary technique used to create the distinctive sounds associated with these rap styles. The samples and the sounds of sirens, gunshots, babies crying, screams, and street noises reflect the ethos, chaos, tensions, anger, despair, and the sometimes violent nature of inner-city life. Many rappers express their commitment to improving conditions in inner-city communities. Despite the inclination of some to devalue human life, most rappers (including nationalist and some hard-core rappers) denounce behavior that negatively impacts African Americans. Dr. Jeckyll and Mr. Hyde ("Fast Life," 1984), Ice T ("I'm Your Pusher," and "High Rollers," 1988), for example, condemn drugs and criminal activity; N.W.A. "——— Tha Police," 1988) and Ice T ("Cop Killer," 1992) speak out against police brutality. Other rappers address a broader range of social issues, ranging from the plight of unwed mothers to that of the homeless and those on welfare. They include Snoop Doggy Dogg ("Keep Ya Head

Up," 1993), Arrested Development ("Mama's Always on Stage," and "Mr. Wendall," 1992), and Queen Latifah "The Evil That Men Do," 1989).

New Jack Swing

By the late 1980s new black popular styles were being created by independent producers, including Teddy Riley, Dallas Austin, and the teams of James "Jimmy Jam" Harris and Terry Lewis and Antonio "L. A." Reid and Kenneth "Babyface" Edmonds. One style that evolved from the innovations of these producers and was imitated by others was termed new jack swing. The style, pioneered by Teddy Riley, represents postmodern soul; it is defined by its sparse instrumentation and a marked underlying drum pattern blended with or sometimes above the tempered vocals. Variations of this pattern incorporate a snare drum emphasis on the second and fourth beats, giving the sound a 1970s syncopated swing associated with James Brown and Earth, Wind, and Fire. The rhythms and production techniques of new jack swing became the beat and mix of the late 1980s and 1990s. It can be heard in Guy's "Groove Me" (1988), "You Can Call Me Crazy" (1988), and "Don't Clap . . . Just Dance" (1988); Heavy D. and The Boyz' "We Got Our Own Thang" (1989); Keith Sweat's "Make You Sweat" (1990); Hi Five's "I Just Can't Handle It" (1990); the gospel group Winans' "A Friend" (1990); and Michael Jackson's "Remember the Time" (1992), among others.

Future trends in black popular music will be pioneered by individuals and groups who continue to cross traditional genres and borrow from existing styles to create music that expresses the changing ideas and ideals of the African-American community.

BIBLIOGRAPHY

Barlow, William. *Looking Up at Down: The Emergence of Blues Culture.* Philadelphia, 1989.

Bebey, Francis. *African Music: A People's Art.* Translated by Josephine Bennett. New York, 1974.

Berlin, Edward A. *Ragtime: A Musical and Cultural History.* Berkeley, Calif., 1980.

Burnim, Mellonee. "Functional Dimensions of Gospel Music Performance." *Western Journal of Black Studies* 12 (1988): 112–120.

Charters, Samuel B., and Leonard Kunstadt. *Jazz: A History of the New York Scene.* 1962. Reprint. New York, 1981.

Cone, James. *The Spirituals and the Blues.* New York, 1972.

Courlander, Harold. *Negro Folk Music, U.S.A.* New York, 1963.

De Lerma, Dominique. *Black Music in Our Culture.* Kent, Ohio, 1970.

Du Bois, W. E. B. *The Souls of Black Folk.* 1903. Reprint. Greenwich, Conn., 1961.

Epstein, Dena. *Sinful Tunes and Spirituals.* Urbana, Ill., 1977.

Fletcher, Tom. *One Hundred Years of the Negro in Show Business.* 1954. Reprint. New York, 1984.

Floyd, Samuel, Jr. *Black Music in the Harlem Renaissance.* New York, 1990.

Garland, Phyl. *The Sound of Soul.* Chicago, 1969.

George, Nelson. *The Death of Rhythm & Blues.* New York, 1988.

Gillett, Charlie. *The Sound of the City.* Rev. ed. New York, 1983.

Haas, Robert Bartlett, ed. *William Grant Still and the Fusion of Cultures in American Music.* Los Angeles, 1972.

Harris, Michael. *The Rise of Gospel Blues: The Music of Thomas Andrew Dorsey.* New York, 1992.

Harrison, Daphne Duval. *Black Pearls: Blues Queens of the 1920s.* New Brunswick, N.J., 1988.

Hurston, Zora Neale. "Spirituals and Neo-Spirituals." In Nathan Huggins, ed. *Voices from the Harlem Renaissance.* New York, 1976, pp. 344–347.

Keil, Charles. *Urban Blues.* 1961. Reprint. Chicago, 1991.

Kilham, Elizabeth. "Sketches in Color: IV." In Bruce Jackson, ed. *The Negro and His Folklore.* Austin, Tex., 1967, pp. 120–133.

Leigh, James Wentworth. *Other Days.* New York, 1921.

Levine, Lawrence. *Black Culture and Black Consciousness.* New York, 1977.

Locke, Alain. *The Negro and His Music.* 1936. Reprint. Port Washington, N.Y., 1968.

———. "The Negro Spirituals." In Alain Locke, ed. *The New Negro.* 1925. Reprint. New York, 1969, pp. 199–213.

Maultsby, Portia K. "Africanisms in African-American Music." In *Africanisms in American Culture.* Bloomington, Ind., 1990.

Myers, Robert Manson, ed. *The Children of Pride.* New Haven, Conn., 1972.

Nketia, Kwabena J. H. "African Roots of Music in the Americas: An African View." In American Musicological Society, *Report of the 12th Congress.* London, 1981, pp. 82–88.

———. *The Music of Africa.* New York, 1974.

Olmsted, Frederick Law. *A Journey in the Seaboard Slave States in the Years 1853–1854, with Remarks on Their Economy.* 1856. Reprint. New York, 1904.

Pearson, Nathan W., Jr. *Goin' to Kansas City.* Urbana, Ill., 1987.

Peretti, Burton W. *The Creation of Jazz.* Urbana, Ill., 1992.

Reagon, Bernice Johnson. "Let the Church Sing 'Freedom' " *Black Music Research Journal* 7 (1987): 105–118.

———. *We'll Understand It Better By and By.* Washington, D.C., 1992.

Rose, Trisa. *Black Noise.* Hanover, N.H., 1994.

Russell, Henry. *Cheer! Boys, Cheer! Memories of Men and Music.* London, 1895.

Schafer, William J. *Brass Bands and New Orleans Jazz.* Baton Rouge, La., 1977.

Silvester, Peter J. *A Left Hand like God: A History of Boogie-Woogie Piano.* New York, 1989.

Southern, Eileen. *The Music of Black Americans.* 2nd ed. New York, 1983a.

———, ed. *Readings in Black American Music.* 2nd ed. New York, 1983b.

Still, William Grant. "A Composer's Viewpoint." In Dominique de Lerma, ed. *Black Music in Our Culture.* Kent, Ohio, 1970, pp. 93–108.

Toll, Robert C. *Blacking Up: The Minstrel Show in Nineteenth-Century America.* New York, 1977.

Toop, David. "Changing Patterns in Negro Folk Songs." *Journal of American Folklore* 62 (1949): 136–144.

———. *The Rap Attack 2: African Rap to Global Hip, Hop.* Boston, 1992.

Work, John. *American Negro Songs and Spirituals.* New York, 1940.

— PORTIA K. MAULTSBY

MUSICAL THEATER

Musical theater—formal, staged entertainments combining songs, skits, instrumental interludes, and dances—was relatively uncommon in America before the middle of the eighteenth century. It is very likely that slave musicians occasionally took part in the earliest colonial period musical theatricals, called ballad operas, at least in the orchestra pit, since many slaves were known to be musically accomplished. Less than fully developed theatrical shows that involved satirical skits by slaves about white masters are recorded in the late eighteenth century. These skits, related to African storytelling traditions, were the seeds from which black American theatricality sprang. "Negro songs" or "Negro jigs" are also recorded in the shows of this period, suggesting the impact of an unnotated tradition of black music making on the musical theater song repertory (Southern 1983, p. 89).

Up to the Civil War

The opening of the African Grove theater in 1821 near lower Broadway in New York inaugurated the staging of plays with music "agreeable to Ladies and Gentlemen of Colour" (Southern 1983, 119). Led by playwright Henry Brown, the African Grove players produced Shakespeare's *Hamlet, Othello,* and *Richard III* (including inserted songs), popular potpourris such as *Tom and Jerry; or Life in London,* and the pantomime *Obi; or, Three Finger'd Jack.* James Hewlett was the company's principal singer and actor. Ira Aldridge, who later made his career in Europe, sang songs at the Grove. Despite the theater's popularity, it was plagued by hooligans and closed in 1829.

Various musical shows were produced with black performers periodically in Philadelphia and New Orleans, though very little information survives about these shows. New Orleans could command orchestral forces (as opposed to the modest pit band of violin, clarinet, and double bass at the African Grove) for theatricals, and it engaged black players in the 1840s. In the 1850s and '60s African-American actors became traveling entertainers or joined minstrel shows.

The Late Nineteenth Century

The Hyers Sisters touring company, founded in 1876, became the first established African-American musical comedy troupe. Managed by Sam Hyers, the company featured his two daughters, Emma Louise and Anna Madah, and a string of male comedy singer /actors: Fred Lyon, Sam Lucas, Billy Kersands, Wallace King, and John and Alexander Luca. The Hyers began as a concert-giving group but moved on to fully staged musical plays that often dealt with racial themes: *Out of Bondage* (1876); *Urlina, or The African Princess* (1879); *Peculiar Sam; or, The Underground Railroad* (1879); and *Plum Pudding* (1887). The music they presented included jubilee songs, spirituals, operatic excerpts, and new popular songs and dances.

By the 1890s a few specific plays regularly toured and featured parts for black singers, usually in the guise of "plantation slaves." Bucolic scenes or other scenarios in the cotton field, on the levee, or in a camp meeting were meant to evoke an idyllic antebellum South. Turner Dazey's *In Old Kentucky* (1892) and *The South before the War* (1893) included black singers and dancers, as did the most famous of all shows of this type, *Uncle Tom's Cabin* (based on Harriet Beecher Stowe's novel of 1852). The huge number and variety of staged versions of this powerful work made it a unique dramatic vehicle in American culture. Many African-American "jubilee" singing groups, typically male quartets, took part in the play, although early performances rarely used black actors. It served the careers of solo banjo virtuoso Horace Weston in 1877 and vaudevillian Sam Lucas, who played the role of Uncle Tom in the 1880s.

The Hyers Sisters touring company, founded in 1876, became the first established African-American musical comedy troupe.

At least a half-dozen all-black companies, as well as some integrated ones, appeared before the end of the century. Black choral singers and supernumeraries, including children, brought literally hundreds of people to the stage in productions in the 1880s and 1890s. Other festivals featuring black vaudeville acts, musical specialties, and historical tableaux, with titles like *Black America* (1895) and *Darkest America* (1897), were well-attended showcases but did not present complete plays.

The most widely acclaimed operatic singer of the period to become involved with traveling musical theatrical companies was Sissieretta Jones, known as the Black Patti (after the renowned soprano Adelina Patti). In 1896 she formed the Black Patti Troubadours and remained an important presence on the road for two decades, eventually mounting full-fledged musical comedies.

White burlesque entrepreneur Sam T. Jack formed the Creole Company in 1890 to do the skit *The Beauty of the Nile; or, Doomed by Fire,* using the novelty of black women in a minstrel line that emphasized glittery, revealing costumes and diverse musical acts. John Isham, Jack's advance man, developed his own potpourri shows presented by mixed male and female companies known as the Octoroons (1895), one of which toured in Europe. All of Isham's shows exploited the popularity of exotic costumes, operatic excerpts, musical specialties, spectacular scenery, and attractive women, while avoiding farcical minstrel show caricatures.

The First Black Musicals and the Growth of Black Vaudeville, 1897–1920

Within this world of extravagant eclecticism, full-length musical comedies—plays in which songs were frequent and newly composed if not integral—became more and more common. The first musical written by and for African Americans, "Bob" Cole and Billy Johnson's *A Trip to Coontown* (1897), was built up from Cole's songs and vaudeville turns with the Black Patti Troubadours (Cole had also managed her show in its first season) and other elements: a trio from Verdi's opera *Attila,* Sousa's new march "The Stars and Stripes Forever," a tune by Cole that was later stolen to become Yale University's fight song "Boola Boola," energetic dancing, topical humor, and social commentary. The show eschewed the Old South nostalgia typical of the earlier touring shows. Minstrel tunes were replaced by snappy up-tempo, occasionally syncopated songs written by different composers.

Florence Mills and the Florence Mills Trio. (Photographs and Prints Division, Schomburg Center for Research in Black Culture, The New York Public Library, Astor, Lenox and Tilden Foundations)

At the same time, cakewalk dancers/comedians Bert Williams and George Walker, in the course of several productions from 1898 to 1908, expanded their routines to even more ambitious dimensions, with elaborate plots and often African settings: *The Policy Players* (1899); *The Sons of Ham* (1900); *In Dahomey* (1902); *Abyssinia* (1905); and *Bandanna Land* (1907). Will Marion Cook, classical violinist and European-trained composer, wrote most of the music for these landmark shows in a unique syncopated style. Cook's sensational Broadway debut—his musical skit *Clorindy* was produced at the Casino Theatre Roof Garden in 1898—established him as a leading figure, along with its dancing star, Ernest Hogan.

In 1899 Bob Cole formed a partnership with the brothers J. Rosamond Johnson and James Weldon JOHNSON. This young trio wrote songs for many shows and performers, black and white, to great success, and later composed comic operettas for all-black casts entitled *The Shoo-Fly Regiment* (1906) and *The Red Moon* (1908); they also starred in the shows themselves. Black, white, and mixed audiences found these many early twentieth-century efforts attractive, but any hope for sustained development was dashed by the premature deaths of the leaders, Ernest Hogan, George Walker, and Bob Cole, around 1910 and the unremitting financial burden of mounting and touring with a large cast. Racism and professional jealousies among competing companies also limited the success of these shows.

Black-owned theaters rapidly increased in number in the early twentieth century, providing sites for a wide variety of musical-theater activities. Following the opening of the Pekin Theatre in Chicago in 1905, many black-owned or black-managed houses were built. By 1920 some 300 theaters around the country were serving black patrons (approximately one-third of these theaters were black-run). This in turn led to the formation of resident stock companies that provided a regular menu of musical plays and developed loyal audiences. Many short-lived shows of the 1920s and '30s filled the Lafayette, Lincoln, and Alhambra theaters in Harlem, the Howard in Washington, D.C., the Regal in Baltimore, Md., the Monogram in Chicago, the 81 in Atlanta, Ga., and the Booker T. Washington in St. Louis, Mo., among others.

A few large companies continued to tour—J. Leubrie Hill's Darktown Follies (from 1911 to 1916) and the various Smart Set shows run by S. H. Dudley, H. Tutt, and S. T. Whitney—but many acts appeared in vaudeville as well. By 1920 the Theatre Owners' Booking Association (TOBA) was formed to facilitate the book-

other matters; criminal justice, through the Capital Punishment Project; and voting rights, by its efforts to enforce the Voting Rights Act in judicial elections and to support black majority districts. The LDF also offers four scholarship programs to aid African-American law students. In the early 1990s, the LDF had twenty-eight staff lawyers in its New York, Washington, and Los Angeles offices, and a total annual budget of almost $8 million.

BIBLIOGRAPHY

Baldus, David, George Woodworth, and Charles A. Pulaski, Jr. *Equal Justice and the Death Penalty: Legal and Empirical Analysis.* New York, 1990.

Hall, Kermit, ed. *The Oxford Companion to the Supreme Court.* New York, 1992.

Kluger, Richard. *Simple Justice.* New York, 1975.

Rowan, Carl. *Dream Makers, Dream Breakers: The World of Justice Thurgood Marshall.* Boston, 1992.

Tushnet, Mark. *The NAACP's Legal Strategy Against Segregation, 1925–1950.* New York, 1987.

– GREG ROBINSON

NATIONAL ASSOCIATION FOR THE ADVANCEMENT OF COLORED PEOPLE

Since its organization in 1909, the National Association for the Advancement of Colored People (NAACP) has been the premier civil rights organization in the United States. It has been in the forefront of numerous successful campaigns on behalf of African-American rights, from the effort to suppress lynching to the long struggle to overturn legal segregation and the still-ongoing effort to secure the implementation of racial justice. The growth and evolution of the NAACP mirrors the growth of African-American political power and the vigorous debates this process engendered.

Founding and Early Days

The NAACP owes it origins to the coalescence of two political movements of the early twentieth century. The early years of the century saw the emergence of a group of black intellectuals opposed to the Accomodationism of Booker T. WASHINGTON. While William Monroe TROTTER was the first important figure to break with Washington, he was temperamentally unsuited to the uniting of political forces, and it was W. E. B. DU BOIS who soon came to be the most prominent black figure among the anti-Bookerites, as Washington's opponents were called. At the same time there was a revival of political agitation by a small group of white "neo-abolitionists," many of them descended from those who had led the antebellum fight against slavery and who were increasingly distressed by the deterioration in the legal rights and social status of African Americans.

The NIAGARA MOVEMENT, formed by Du Bois, Trotter, and twenty-eight other African-American men at a conference on the Canadian side of Niagara Falls in August 1905, was the organized expression of anti-Bookerite sentiment. The movement was forthright in its opposition to Washingtonian accommodationism and in its commitment to civil equality. At a 1906 meeting of the organization at Harpers Ferry, West Va., the site of JOHN BROWN'S RAID, the organization declared:

> We shall not be satisfied with less than full manhood rights . . . We claim for ourselves every right that belongs to a free-born American—political, civil, and social—and until we get these rights, we shall never cease to protest and assail the ears of America with the story of its shameful deeds toward us.

Despite its oratory, the Niagara Movement was loosely organized and poorly funded and was largely ineffective as a national civil rights organization during its brief history. Bruised by internal controversy and hounded by members of Washington's extensive and effective network in the black community (the "Tuskegee Machine"), the Niagara Movement's existence was tentative and brief. After its dissolution, many of its active members joined the NAACP.

The catalyst for the founding of the NAACP was a violent race riot in 1908 in Springfield, Ill., Abraham Lincoln's home town. William English Walling (1877–1936), a white socialist and labor activist, graphically described the violence he had witnessed in an article in *The Independent.* Walling invoked the spirit of Lincoln and the abolitionist Elijah Lovejoy in a call for citizens to come to the assistance of blacks and to fight for racial equality.

Walling's article was read by Mary White Ovington (1865–1951), a white journalist and social worker from a well-to-do abolitionist family who worked and lived in a black tenement in New York, doing research for her landmark sociological work *Half a Man: The Status of the Negro in New York* (1911). She responded to his plea and invited Dr. Henry Moskowitz (1879–1936), a labor reformer and social worker among New York immigrants, to join her in meeting with Walling in his New York apartment to discuss "the Negro Question." The three were the principal founders of the NAACP. Two other members of the core group were Charles Edward Russell (1860–1941), another socialist whose father had been the abolitionist editor of a small newspaper in Iowa, and Oswald Garrison Villard (1872–1949), grandson of the abolitionist William Lloyd Garrison and publisher of the liberal *New York Evening Post* journal and later the *Nation.*

Ovington also invited two prominent black New York clergymen, Bishop Alexander Walters of the African Methodist Episcopal Zion Church, a former president of the National Afro-American Council, and the Rev. William Henry Brooks, minister of Mark's Methodist Episcopal Church, to join the continuing discussions. The expanded group agreed to issue a call on February 12, 1909, Lincoln's birthday, for a conference in New York.

Since its organization in 1909, the National Association for the Advancement of Colored People (NAACP) has been the premier civil rights organization in the United States.

Written by Villard, the call reflected the Niagara Movement's platform and emphasized protection of the civil and political rights of African Americans guaranteed under the Fourteenth and Fifteenth Amendments. Of the sixty people signing the call, seven were black: Professor William L. Bulkley, a New York school principal; Du Bois; the Rev. Francis J. Grimké of Washington; Mary Church Terrell of Washington; Dr. J. Milton Waldron of Washington; Bishop Walters; and Ida B. Wells.

The founders' overriding concern was guaranteeing to all citizens the reality of equality. They demanded all rights "which underlie our American institutions and are guaranteed by our Constitution"—legal, educational, and political—as well as an end to all forms of segregation and intimidation. The organization was founded as a small elite organization which would rely primarily on agitation and legal battles rather than mass action against racial discrimination.

As a result of the call, the National Negro Conference met at the Charity Organization Hall in New York City on May 31 and June 1, 1909. The conference created the National Negro Committee (also known as the Committee of Forty on Permanent Organization and initially known as the National Committee for the Advancement of the Negro) to develop plans for an effective organization. The committee's plans were implemented a year later at a second meeting in New York, when the organization's permanent name was adopted. The organization chose to include the phrase "colored people" in its title to emphasize the broad and anti-imperialist concerns of its founders, and not to limit the scope of the organization to the United States. The NAACP's structure and mission inspired the formation of several other civil rights groups, such as South Africa's African National Congress, formed in 1912.

The NAACP's organizers created a formal institutional structure headed by an executive committee composed largely of members of the Committee of Forty. While Du Bois and a handful of other black men, largely moderates, were included, black women—notably Ida B. Wells—were excluded from the committee. Kathryn Johnson served as field secretary from 1910 through 1916 (on a volunteer basis for the first four years), becoming the first of many black women to serve as in that position; but black women were not offered leadership roles in the NAACP for several decades. Moorfield Storey (1845–1929), a former secretary to antislavery Sen. Charles Sumner, and one of the country's foremost constitutional lawyers, was named the organization's president. In addition to Storey and Du Bois, the only black and only salaried staffer, its first officers were Walling, chairman; John E. Milholland, treasurer; Villard, assistant treasurer; and Ovington, secretary. In addition to their official positions, Villard and Ovington were the principal organizers, providing direction and ideas. Francis Blascoer served as national secretary (becoming the second salaried staffer) from February 1910 to March 1911, when Ovington resumed the position pro bono for a year. May Childs Nerney took over the position in 1912.

Soon after the 1910 conference, the NAACP established an office at 20 Vesey St. in New York City (it moved to its longtime home of 70 Fifth Ave. a few years later). In its first year, it launched programs to increase job opportunities for blacks, and to obtain greater protection for them in the South by crusading against lynching and other forms of violence.

The organization's most important act by far that year was the hiring of Du Bois as director of publications and research. Du Bois's visionary ideas and militant program were his primary contributions to the NAACP. His hiring signaled the final demise of the Niagara Movement; while Du Bois brought its central vision to the new organization, the NAACP had better funding and a much more well-defined structure and program than the Niagara Movement.

In November 1910, Du Bois launched THE CRISIS as the NAACP's house journal. *The Crisis* soon became the principal philosophical instrument of the black freedom struggle. From an initial publication of 1,000 copies in November 1910 the magazine's circulation increased to 100,000 a month in 1918. In its pages, Du Bois exposed and protested the scourge of racial oppression in order to educate both his black and white audiences on the nature of the struggle and to instill pride in his people. *The Crisis* was not only known for political articles; in its pages Du Bois introduced works by African-American writers, poets, and artists.

Following the report of a Committee on Program headed by Villard, the NAACP was incorporated in New York on June 20, 1911. The organizers invested overall control in a board of directors, which replaced the executive committee. Moorfield Storey remained as president, while Villard succeeded Walling as chairman of the board of directors. The chairman of the board, rather than the president, was designated the most powerful officer in the organization, because Storey had a highly successful practice in Boston and was unable to devote much attention to the NAACP.

The executive committee centralized control of the organization in a national body, to which memberships belonged; it decentralized other significant aspects of the organization's work through local groups called vigilance committees, which became its branches. To ensure that the movement spread as quickly as possible, the committee authorized mass meetings in Chicago, Cleveland, and Buffalo.

The first local NAACP branch was organized in New York in January 1911. Joel E. Spingarn (1874–1939), former chairman of the department of comparative literature at Columbia University, became the branch's first president. His brother Arthur, a lawyer, also became active in the branch. The following year, branches were created in Boston, Baltimore, Detroit, Indianapolis, St. Louis, and Quincy, Ill. In 1913, other branch offices were created in Chicago, Kansas City, Tacoma, Wash., and Washington, D.C. Membership in the organization was contingent upon acceptance of NAACP philosophy and programs.

While the local branches were largely staffed by African Americans, the national NAACP was a largely white group during its early days. Whites had the financial resources to devote themselves to NAACP work; throughout the NAACP's early days, all of the board members contributed a considerable amount of time to the organization. Arthur Spingarn, for example, estimated that he devoted "half and probably more" of his time to the NAACP. Also, whites had the education, the administrative experience, and the access to money that were required to build the organization. For example, Villard initially provided office space for the NAACP in his *New York Post* building. He also gave his personal funds to save the infant organization from imminent collapse. Joel Spingarn paid for his own travel from city to city, soliciting memberships and funds during what were called the New Abolition tours. While he did not make sizable personal contributions to the organization until 1919, Spingarn's knowledge of the management of stocks and bonds also enabled him to direct the organization's financial policies. Furthermore, he donated funds to establish the annual Spingarn Medal, first awarded in 1915, which rapidly became the most prestigious African-American award.

While the local branches were largely staffed by African Americans, the national NAACP was a largely white group during its early days.

Despite essential contributions of white activists, blacks were increasingly uneasy about white control of an organization that was meant for African Americans. Those differences had surfaced at the founding conference, when Ida B. Wells openly expressed concern over the leading roles that whites were playing in the movement. She and William Monroe Trotter shied away from involvement in the new organization because of its domination by whites. Black resentment about white control was manifested in the frequent clashes between Du Bois and Villard, two prickly and irreconcilable personalities.

Du Bois especially resented the intrusion of whites into the editorial affairs of *The Crisis,* which he maintained as an independent, self-supporting magazine. While it remained part of the NAACP, it had its own staff of eight to ten people (led by business manager Augustus Dill, one of the NAACP's few black staff members). Many whites, including Villard, felt that *The Crisis* did not report NAACP news sufficiently. They maintained that Du Bois's often acerbic denunciations of whites were inflammatory and said his editorial style was propagandistic and unbalanced, since he refused to cover negative topics, such as black crime.

In 1914, following clashes with Du Bois, Villard resigned as chairman of the board, and Joel Spingarn succeeded him. Even after Villard's departure, the issue of white control continued, and it caused considerable conflict between Du Bois and Spingarn, his long-time friend. Though, as Du Bois admitted, his haughty personality contributed to the problem, he also interpreted his role within a racial context and felt that he could not accept even the appearance of inferiority or subservience to whites without betraying the race ideals for which he stood. Spingarn felt strongly that Du Bois devoted too much time to lecturing and writing at the expense of association work, but he and Ovington sided with Du Bois in board matters. After Ovington, a longtime ally and supporter, became NAACP chair in 1919, she too became a severe critic of Du Bois's refusal to follow board policy, though she accepted his independence in management of *The Crisis.*

The problem of white domination led to frank discussion about whether whites should continue in top-level positions in the NAACP. While Du Bois challenged any sign of black subordination, he feared that whites would refuse to aid a black-dominated organization and that it would compromise the NAACP's integrationist program. Spingarn and Ovington both acknowledged the difficulties inherent in white leadership, but felt it was a necessary evil until blacks had sufficient resources to run organizations without assistance.

In 1916 Mae Nerney resigned her post as secretary. She recommended that the board choose a black person to succeed her, but the board chose a white man, Roy Nash. It could not, however, escape the pressure to hire another black executive, so it chose James Weldon JOHNSON, a writer for the *New York Age* and a highly respected man of letters, as field secretary later that year.

Several events in the NAACP's first years combined to define and unite the fledgling organization. The first was the NAACP's ten-year protest campaign for the withdrawal of the film *Birth of a Nation,* beginning in 1915. The film, directed by D. W. Griffith, featured racist portrayals of blacks. The NAACP charged that the film "assassinated" the character of black Americans and undermined the very basis of the struggle for racial equality. The organization arranged pickets of movie theaters and lobbied local governments to ban showings of the film. The NAACP branches succeeded in leading thousands of blacks in protests and forced the withdrawal of the film from several cities and states. The struggle provided important evidence that African Americans would display opposition to racist images and actions.

The following year, upon the death of Booker T. Washington in 1915, the NAACP reached another turning point. With the end of effective opposition by those who preferred accommodation with the South's Jim Crow policies, *The Crisis,* under Du Bois's leadership, became the leading principal instrument of black opinion. As leadership passed from Washington to the militant "race men" of the North, the NAACP fully established itself as the primary black organization. Consolidating the NAACP's power, in 1916 Du Bois initiated a conference of black leaders, including Washington's men, and their friends. This was the first Amenia conference, which was held at Joel Spingarn's Troutbeck estate at Amenia, north of New York City. The fifty or so participants adopted resolutions that were aimed at breaching the division between the Washington group and the NAACP. The conference participants endorsed all forms of education for African Americans—not just the type of industrial schooling that Washington had advocated; recognized complete political freedom as essential for the development of blacks; agreed that organization and a practical working understanding among race leaders was necessary for development; urged that old controversies, suspicions and factional alignments be eliminated; and suggested that there was a special need for understanding between leaders in the South and in the North. Du Bois reiterated the African-American demand for full equality and political power.

World War I and related events combined to set the NAACP on its primary mission, a two-pronged legal and political course against racial violence. During the war, Du Bois instituted a controversial policy of black support for American military efforts, with the goal of greater recognition for civil rights afterward. However, the migration of southern blacks to northern urban areas during and after the war led to racial tension, and the clash between increasingly assertive blacks, and whites who refused to countenance changes in the racial status quo, led to violent riots, particularly during the postwar Red Summer of 1919.

Security of person was the most pressing problem that the blacks faced, since the taking of a person's life by mob action violated the most basic constitutional right. At first, the NAACP's primary strategy against lynching involved a publicity campaign backed by pamphlets, in-depth studies, and other educational activities to mobilize public support for ending the crime. From its earliest years, the NAACP devoted most of its resources to seeking an end to lynchings and other forms of mob violence; the organization's protest campaign after a lynching in Coatesville, Pa., in 1911 resulted in its first substantial publicity. In 1917 it led the celebrated silent protest parade of 15,000 people through Harlem with muffled drums to protest the violent riots that year against blacks in EAST ST. LOUIS, ILL., and discrimination in general.

The strengthening of the branch structure heightened NAACP influence. As field secretary, James Weldon Johnson was charged with organizing branches, which carried out most of the organization's protest activity. Johnson's most immediate challenge was to increase significantly the number of NAACP branches in the South, a mission that exposed him to the dangers of JIM CROW in the region. Johnson began by organizing a branch in Richmond, Va., in 1917. Initially, his progress was slow, but by the end of 1919, the NAACP

of Oklahoma could not segregate G. W. McLaurin within its graduate school once he had been admitted.

Encouraged by the decisions in *Sweatt* v. *Painter* and *McLaurin* v. *Oklahoma,* the NAACP in 1951 launched a well-planned "Equality Under Law" campaign to overturn racial separation at its roots—in elementary and secondary schools. This drive was launched with the filing of lawsuits against school districts in Atlanta; Clarendon County, S.C.; Topeka, Kans.; and Wilmington, Del.

In 1953, Dr. Channing H. Tobias, the newly elected chairman of the NAACP board of directors, launched a "Fight for Freedom Fund" campaign and a goal of "Free by '63." This slogan was designed to mobilize all of the organization's resources for what the NAACP saw as the final phase of the struggle to eliminate all state-imposed discrimination in celebration of the centennial of Lincoln's Emancipation Proclamation. Reinforcing the climate of great anticipation within the civil rights community, President Eisenhower on May 10 addressed the NAACP's "Freedom Fulfillment" conference in Washington. He pledged that wherever the federal authority extended he would do his utmost to bring about racial equality. With help from the fund-raising campaign, the NAACP's membership grew to 240,000 by 1954.

On May 17, 1954, the Supreme Court handed down its landmark ruling in the four school desegregation cases that the NAACP had initiated, plus another case challenging segregation in the District of Columbia. Reasserting the full meaning of the Fourteenth Amendment, the court declared in *Brown* v. *Board of Education* that "in the field of public education the doctrine of 'separate but equal' has no place. Separate educational facilities are inherently unequal." Shortly thereafter, the NAACP won another historic victory, when the Department of Defense reported that as of August 31, 1954, there were "no longer any all-Negro units in the services."

Implementing Brown

Less than a year after he had led the celebrations of the school desegregation case victory, Walter White died. He had developed the organization that James Weldon Johnson had passed on to him into the most powerful vehicle of its kind for achieving racial equality. *Brown* v. *Board of Education* was his crowning achievement as much as it was Thurgood Marshall's. However, in his last years, White was an increasingly embattled figure. His flamboyant style and overinvolvement in outside activities had made him many enemies on the NAACP board, and many African Americans angrily criticized his marriage to a white woman in 1949. That year White took a leave of absence and, upon his return 1950, the board sharply restricted his policy-making power.

White left a staff of experienced professionals in their prime of productivity; in addition to Wilkins, White had hired Clarence Mitchell as labor secretary, Gloster B. Current as director of branches in 1946, and Henry Lee Moon, a former newspaper reporter, as director of public relations in 1948.

Roy Wilkins, who was elected in April 1955 to succeed White as NAACP executive director, faced enormous challenges. Wilkins's first problem was pressing for the enforcement of the *Brown* decision and for passage of FEPC and other civil rights laws. NAACP lawyers participated in the formation of desegregation plans and monitored compliance with *Brown.* In 1956, under NAACP sponsorship, Autherine Lucy, an African American, won a court ruling admitting her to the University of Alabama. However, university officials expelled her on the pretext of preventing violence. The NAACP also made its struggle for passage of civil rights laws in Congress a top priority.

At the same time, the organization was forced to expend effort combatting the onslaught that the South had unleashed on the organization. The NAACP's trail-blazing victories in the courts, especially the *Brown* decision, made it a main target of the South's campaign of "massive resistance."

The resurgent KU KLUX KLAN figured strongly in the backlash of white violence, but it was not the only threat that NAACP faced from the South. Less than two months after the *Brown* decision was handed down, political leaders, businessmen and the professional elite organized the White Citizens' Council in Mississippi. Overnight, councils sprang up in other states. Regarded as "manicured kluxism," the White Citizens' Councils used economic and political pressure to prevent implementation of the *Brown* decision. In March 1956, nearly all of the southerners in Congress showed their defiance of *Brown* by signing the "Southern Manifesto," which called the Supreme Court decision "illegal."

Prior to this period, Southerners had targeted individual blacks through lynchings and other forms of violence in their campaign of terror. Now the NAACP was attacked by these groups. On Christmas night of 1951, the home of Harry T. Moore, the NAACP's field secretary in Mims, Fla., was bombed. Moore died in the blast and his wife died a few days later from injuries she received that night. In 1955, NAACP officials the Rev. George W. Lee and Lamar Smith of Belzoni, Miss. were shot to death, and Gus Courts, president of the Belzoni NAACP branch, was shot, wounded, and later forced to abandon his store and flee to Chicago.

The NAACP charged that racial violence was a manifestation of the broader pattern of opposition to civil rights and demanded that the Justice Department protect blacks in the state and elsewhere in the South. The Justice Department, however, responded that it lacked authority to prosecute suspected murderers and civil rights violaters in what it claimed were state jurisdictions.

Despite the violence, the NAACP continued to grow. The number of branches in Mississippi increased from ten to twenty-one during 1955, while membership jumped 100 percent. The NAACP took several steps to aid local blacks. In December, the NAACP board of directors voted to deposit $20,000 in the Tri-State Bank in Memphis in order to increase the bank's reserves and enable it to make more loans to embattled blacks. The board called for an investigation of the operation in Mississippi of the federal "surplus commodities" program, which provided food to the destitute, to see if it discriminated against blacks. National NAACP officials also pushed for a meeting with the Mississippi Power and Light Company to inquire about cutoffs of power to businessmen active with the NAACP and overcharges for restoration.

The South's response to desegregation made the NAACP intensify its call for President Eisenhower to enforce Brown.

In 1956, Louisiana led the South in a more deliberate assault on the NAACP when its attorney general demanded that the association's branches file their membership lists with the state. Because the NAACP refused to do so, the attorney general obtained an injunction barring the organization from operating in Louisiana. Alabama, Texas, and Georgia followed with similar punitive actions. In 1958, the Supreme Court (in *National Association for the Advancement of Colored People* v. *Alabama* ex rel. *Patterson*) overturned Alabama's fine of $100,000 against the NAACP because it refused to disclose the names and addresses of its members. But the Court then did not lift the injunction that barred the NAACP from operating in Alabama. Furthermore, the supreme courts in Arkansas and Florida held that the High Court's ruling did not affect those states. Not until June 1, 1964, after four appeals, would the U.S. Supreme Court rule unanimously that the NAACP had a right to register in Alabama as a foreign corporation. The ruling, in effect, overturned similar bans against the NAACP in other southern states and paved the way for it to resume operations in Alabama on October 29.

On January 14, 1963, for the Supreme Court in another significant case (*National Association for the Advancement of Colored People* v. *Button*) also overturned Virginia's antibarratry law, which was enacted in 1956, prohibiting the NAACP from sponsoring, financing, or providing legal counsel in suits challenging the validity of the state's segregation and other anti-civil rights laws.

One consequence of the southern crusade against the NAACP following the *Brown* decision was the splitting off of the NAACP LEGAL DEFENSE AND EDUCATIONAL FUND, a process that began in 1956 and ended in 1961. The split was caused by threats from the Southerners to rescind the LDF's tax-exempt status, and by personal differences within the NAACP. The LDF made the battle in the courts for school desegregation its main project, while the parent NAACP continued its strategy of legal and political action in numerous forms. Robert Carter, who was on the LDF's staff, was chosen as the NAACP's general counsel and he began setting up a new legal department. Carter led the NAACP's battle against the state injunctions.

The South's response to desegregation made the NAACP intensify its call for President Eisenhower to enforce *Brown,* and to provide the leadership which it regarded as essential for defeating the South's steadfast resistance to the passage of civil rights laws in Congress. NAACP leaders argued that the President's prestige could overwhelm the Southerners' use of committee chairmanships and the filibuster rule in the Senate to bottle up civil rights legislation. Eisenhower, a state's rights advocate, nevertheless supported the NAACP's demand that there should be no discrimination in federally funded programs and in the armed forces; but he was opposed to federal action to enforce *Brown.*

In 1956, responding to the NAACP's demands, election-year domestic considerations, and international pressure, Eisenhower called for civil rights legislation in his State of the Union address. The administration's package became the basis of debate in the bill H.R. 627. Senate Majority Leader Lyndon Baines Johnson of Texas, who believed that passage of some civil rights legislation was inevitable, began maneuvering to shape a compromise on the bill that would blunt its strongest provisions and break the southern filibuster. The civil rights forces were therefore left with what was essentially a weak voting rights law. Still, the 1957 Civil Rights Act created a division of civil rights in the Justice Department and a bipartisan Civil Rights Commission. Furthermore, the Civil Rights Act of 1957, the first such bill passed by Congress in eighty-two years, broke the psychological barrier to civil rights measures, making it easier for future efforts to succeed.

The encouraging breakthrough of the passage of the Civil Rights Act was somewhat overshadowed that September by the Little Rock crisis, in which Governor Orval Faubus used the Arkansas National Guard to block implementation of a federal court desegregation order at Central High School. To uphold the Constitution and end rioting, President Eisenhower federalized the Arkansas National Guard and ordered 1,000 members of the 101st Airborne Division into Little Rock. His action enabled nine black children (the "Little Rock Nine") to attend the school.

The Civil Rights Movement

The NAACP launched its "Golden Anniversary" celebrations on February 12, 1959, with services at the Community Church of New York City. One of the most promising indications of the organization's future strength was the presence of 624 youths among the 2,000 delegates who packed the New York Coliseum during the annual convention, which concluded with a rally at the Polo Grounds. In December, the NAACP held its third annual Freedom Fund dinner in New York, where it honored Marian ANDERSON, the celebrated concert singer, and Gardner Cowles, publisher of *Look* magazine. The celebrations revealed the broad acceptance of the NAACP as an institution. However, its mastery was to be challenged in the 1960s by a new generation of more militant activists.

The first sign of the tensions the NAACP would face came in 1955 and 1956, when blacks in Alabama, led by the Rev. Dr. Martin Luther King, Jr., organized the Montgomery Improvement Association to lead the boycott against segregated city buses. Although the movement was sparked by NAACP legal victories against segregation and the principal leaders of the boycott were also local NAACP leaders, the strategy of nonviolent demonstrations that they adopted was a substantial departure from the association's well-defined legal and political program. Similarly, while NAACP lawyers successfully argued the U.S. Supreme Court case *Gayle* v. *Browder* (1956), which handed victory to the boycotters, the MIA displayed impatience with the NAACP's carefully structured programs and centralized direction.

Inspired by the tactics of nonviolent protest, NAACP Youth Council chapters in Wichita, Kans., and Oklahoma City further successfully tested a new confrontation strategy in 1958 by staging "sit-downs" at lunch counters to protest segregation. The protests led to the desegregation of 60 or more lunch counters. In 1959, the NAACP chapter at Washington University in St. Louis conducted SIT-INS to end segregation at local lunch counters. The same year, the NAACP hired former CORE activist James Farmer as program director, but he was unable to move the association toward support for mass demonstrations, and he returned to CORE as executive director after less than two years.

As important as the Youth Council demonstrations were, however, they did not capture national media attention because they were not conducted in the deep South. On February 1, 1960, four students from North Carolina Agricultural and Technical College sat at a segregated store lunch counter in Greensboro and refused to leave until they were served. Two of the students, Ezell Blair and Joseph McNeil, were former officers of the NAACP's college chapter. The NAACP was heavily involved—the sit-in was conducted in consultation with Dr. George Simpkins, president of the Greensboro NAACP branch, and Ralph Jones, president of the branch's executive committee. The Greensboro actions set the stage for the sit-in movement, which spread like brush fire through the south.

The NAACP declared that it was proud that many of its youth members, from Virginia to Texas, were participating in the sit-ins. NAACP branch officials, notably Mississippi field secretary Medgar Evers, coordinated protest campaigns. Nevertheless, the students' confrontations with Jim Crow was an expression of impatience with the NAACP's carefully executed legal and political programs. There was a dramatic clash of strategies, with the NAACP adhering firmly to its philosophy of change through court action and legislation, while King and the students marched under the banner of nonviolent direct action and local change. (The problems of strategy and organizational discipline merged as early as 1959, when Roy Wilkins suspended Robert Williams, president of the NAACP's Monroe, N.C., branch, for advocating that the NAACP meet "violence with violence.") Despite the ideological clash and the intense competition for financial contributions, media attention, and historical recognition, the young activists' strategy complemented the NAACP's. The NAACP provided large sums for bail money and legal support for the demonstrators and joined more militant movement groups in local alliances, such as the Council of Federated Organizations (COFO), which sponsored voter registration and other activities in Mississippi.

Despite the media attention that the demonstrations in the South drew, by 1962 the NAACP's 388,347 members in 46 states and the District of Columbia helped it to remain the leader in civil rights. That growth was especially significant, given that repeated court injunctions, state administrative regulations, punitive legislation, and other intimidating actions prevented many people from working with the NAACP in the South. The restrictions on the NAACP opened a window of opportunity for action by groups such as the SOUTHERN CHRISTIAN LEADERSHIP CONFERENCE (SCLC) and the Student Nonviolent Coordinating Committee (SNCC; organized with the aid of NAACP veteran Ella Baker), as well as NAACP spinoffs such as the Alabama Christian Movement For Human Rights.

Meanwhile, the NAACP's board was undergoing a change. Robert C. WEAVER, an economist and national housing expert, was elected chairman in 1960. Weaver resigned in 1961 when President John F. Kennedy appointed him administrator of the Federal Housing and Home Financing Administration. He was succeeded by Bishop Stephen Gil Spottswood of the African Methodist Episcopal Zion church.

The NAACP's most outstanding contribution to the Civil Rights Movement continued to be its legal and lobbying efforts. In 1958, the NAACP forced the University of Florida to desegregate. A similar lawsuit was pending against the University of Georgia when it desegregated in 1961. In 1962, the NAACP led the battle to desegregate the University of Mississippi. The effort was directed by Constance Baker Motley, of the LDF staff. Nevertheless, the fact that the parent NAACP featured the struggle in its 1962 annual report showed the extent to which the battle to enroll James H. Meredith in the university was also its own. After Mississippi governor Ross Barnett defied a federal court order, President Kennedy was forced to send in federal troops to quell a riot and assure Meredith's admittance.

The NAACP used the President's pleas for compliance, as well as the South's brutal opposition to the nonviolent demonstrations, to reinforce its struggle in Washington for passage of a meaningful civil rights law. Following the breakthrough in 1957, the NAACP had gotten Congress to pass the 1960 Civil Rights Act. That, however, was only a weak voting rights amendment to the 1957 act. Kennedy, insisting that comprehensive civil rights legislation would not pass, refused to send any to Congress. In February 1963, Kennedy submitted a weak civil rights bill. Mobilizing a historic coalition through the LCCR, the NAACP began an all-out struggle for passage of the bill as well as the strengthening of its provisions. NAACP pickets in Lawrence, Kans., New York City, Newark, and Philadelphia helped highlight the struggle for such provisions as a national fair employment practice law.

Events in 1963 reshaped the civil rights bill and the struggle. The demonstrations in Birmingham that King led during the spring provoked national outrage. On June 11th, in response to the demonstrations, President Kennedy delivered a televised civil rights address. The following night, Medgar Evers was assassinated in Jackson, Miss. On June 19, the day Evers was buried at Arlington Cemetery, Kennedy sent Congress a revised civil rights bill that was much stronger than the one he had submitted in February.

The climactic event of 1963 was the March On Washington for Jobs and Freedom (MOW). A. Philip Randolph had initiated the call for a march in January. The NAACP, nevertheless, led in organizing it and saw to it that the march, held on August 28 at the Lincoln Memorial, broadened its focus to include the legislative struggle. From a strategic point of view, Clarence Mitchell and the NAACP Washington bureau regarded the legislative conference it held with NAACP branch leaders earlier in August as more meaningful to the struggle in Congress than the MOW had been. Both, nevertheless, served the intended purpose.

The NAACP's most outstanding contribution to the Civil Rights Movement continued to be its legal and lobbying efforts.

Following the assassination of President Kennedy in November 1963, Lyndon Johnson vowed to ensure passage of his predecessor's civil rights bill and provided the leadership that the NAACP had demanded from the executive branch. In the final, crucial phase of the struggle in the Senate, Johnson orchestrated the coordinated leadership of Majority Leader Sen. Mike Mansfield (D-Mont.) and Minority Leader Sen. Everett Dirksen (R-Ill.). Debate on the 1964 civil rights bill, H.R. 7152, began in earnest on March 10 and lasted until June 10, when the civil rights forces were finally able to break the filibuster.

The Civil Rights Act of 1964 was an immense victory for the NAACP. Following its passage, the NAACP began work on legislation to protect the right to vote. Following the Selma-to-Montgomery march, led by King, to protest the continuing disfranchisement of blacks in the South, the national climate was favorable to such a bill, and the NAACP was again left to direct the struggle in Congress for passage of the Voting Rights Act of 1965. This struggle was much less dramatic than that of 1964, perhaps because many expected its passage. Even so, as in 1957, the NAACP was hard-pressed to ward off attempts to weaken the bill. Its success in this battle was evident by the strong law that Congress passed.

Following passage of the civil rights laws, the NAACP switched its attention to enforcement, particularly in the areas of public school desegregation, employment, and housing. It also sought and won passage of strengthening provisions, such as amendments to the equal employment opportunity title of the 1964 Civil Rights Act. It won the first extension of the 1965 Voting Rights Act in 1970 with a provision extending protection for the right to vote, as well as subsequent ones. The programs remained centered in large part on the activities of the branches and its labor, education, and housing departments.

Despite the NAACP's crucial contribution to legislation which ended state-sponsored racial discrimination, the organization, with its interracial structure and integrationist philosophy, was scorned by increasing numbers of young blacks during the late 1960s as old-fashioned and overly cautious. The cycle of urban racial violence during the 1960s displayed the limits of the NAACP's program in appealing to frustrated urban blacks. President Johnson appointed Roy Wilkins a member of the National Advisory Commission on Civil Disorders, and the commission's well-known 1968 report reflected fully the NAACP's concerns.

Despite the radical criticism of the NAACP's program, the vitality of the organization's legal strategy was manifest by its success in passing legislation despite the embittered climate for black rights. While the NAACP shared credit with the other civil rights organizations for passage of the 1964 Civil Rights Act and the Voting Rights Act, there can be no doubt about its central role in 1968, when the Fair Housing Act was passed. Fearing the failure of a legislative struggle for fair housing legislation, many black leaders asked President Johnson to issue instead a comprehensive executive order barring discrimination in government-sponsored housing programs and federally insured mortgages. Johnson, however, did not want to deal with the problem piecemeal, and the NAACP supported him. The wisdom of that decision was evident on April 11, when President Johnson signed the 1968 Fair Housing Act, although its final version was somewhat weaker than the NAACP had originally intended. The final days of this struggle were overshadowed by the assassination of Dr. King in Memphis on April 4. The following day, at a meeting of civil rights leaders at the White House, the NAACP agreed to a suggestion that Congress be urged to pass the fair housing bill as a tribute to the slain leader.

During the late 1960s and early '70s, the NAACP faced new and sometimes more difficult challenges than in the past. These problems now resulted from systemic or endemic discrimination, which were more difficult to identify than state-imposed segregation and required the development of new strategies to correct. One of the organization's most important functions became the designing and implementing of affirmative action and minority hiring programs with government and private business. This struggle was led by Nathaniel R. Jones, who replaced Robert Carter as the NAACP's general counsel in 1969 (Jones served in this position for ten years, before leaving to become a judge on the United States Court of Appeals, Second Circuit, in Cincinnati. The NAACP brought suits or sent *amicus curiae* briefs in many notable affirmative action cases during the 1960s and '70s. For example, in 1969 the NAACP brought *Head* v. *Timken Roller Bearing Co., of Columbus, Ohio,* a landmark antidiscrimination lawsuit. In 1976, it won a consent decree, with a settlement by which twenty-five black workers were awarded back pay and won expanded promotional opportunities into previously all-white craft jobs. As a result of another lawsuit, filed against the Indiana State Police Department, twenty black troopers were hired, bringing the number on the thousand-man force to twenty-three.

Another aspect of the NAACP's legal struggle was the campaign against the death penalty. This struggle was led primarily by the NAACP Legal Defense and Educational Fund, which monitored death penalty cases and compiled statistics demonstrating racial disproportions in death penalty sentencing outcomes. As a result, in *Furman* v. *Georgi* (1972), the U.S. Supreme Court temporarily struck down the death penalty.

Among the NAACP's other achievements was a continuation of the thirty-eight-year-old struggle to defeat unfavorable nominees to the Supreme Court. The NAACP scored a double victory against the nomination in 1969 of Judge Clement F. Haynsworth of South Carolina and in 1970 of Judge G. Harrold Carswell of Florida as Supreme Court justices. The NAACP opposed them because of their records on racial issues. The NAACP would continue to be influential in the confirmation process—for example, in 1987 the organization led the successful opposition to the Supreme Court appointment of Robert Bork and in 1990 helped defeat the confirmation of William Lucas, an African-American conservative, as assistant attorney for civil rights.

Still another focus of NAACP efforts was its ongoing campaign against media stereotypes. NAACP pressure had succeeded in removing *Amos 'n' Andy* from network first-run television in the early 1950s; in the 1960s, NAACP pressure was partly responsible for the creation of the TV series *Julia,* the first series with a positive African-American leading character. In the 1980s, the NAACP organized protests of Steven Spielberg's film *The Color Purple* owing to its white director and negative portrayal of black men.

The Search for New Direction

By the mid-1970s, the NAACP once again was forced into a period of transition. Henry Lee Moon retired in 1974. In 1976 Roy Wilkins retired as NAACP executive director. He had devoted forty-five years to the struggle and fulfilled most of his goals. In 1978 Clarence Mitchell also retired. Meanwhile, as a sign of the growing influence of women in the organization and the Civil Rights Movement, in 1975 Margaret Bush Wilson, a St. Louis lawyer, was elected to chair the NAACP board of directors. Twenty years later, Myrlie Evers, the widow of Medgar Evers, was elected as its chair, and Hazel Dukes was named president of the powerful New York state chapter.

Along with the problems connected with the change in administration, the NAACP faced grave financial problems and some opposition to its program among blacks, who continued to criticize the NAACP as irrelevant to black needs. This opposition was an important challenge facing Benjamin L. Hooks, a minister, lawyer, and member of the Federal Communications Commission, when he became executive director of the association in January 1977. Hooks assumed command of the NAACP at a time when it was not only struggling to devise an effective strategy for new civil rights challenges but battling for its very existence.

In 1976, two adverse judgments in lawsuits against the NAACP in Mississippi had presented it with the worst crisis in its lifetime: A court awarded Robert Moody, a state highway patrolman, $250,000 as a result of a lawsuit charging libel and slander that he had filed against the NAACP. Local NAACP officials and its state field director had charged Moody with police brutality because he had allegedly beaten a black man while arresting him on a reckless driving charge. To protect its assets, the NAACP had to borrow money to post the required $262,000 bond, though it eventually won reversal of the judgment in appeals.

Then, the Hinds County chancery court in Jackson, Miss., handed down a $1.25 million judgment against the NAACP as a result of a lawsuit that local businessmen had filed against the organization following a boycott of their stores. Under Mississippi law, in order to forestall the seizure of its assets pending an appeal, the NAACP had to post a cash bond amounting to 125 percent of the judgment, which was $1,563,374. The U.S. Supreme Court reversed the judgment in 1982. However, the experience was sobering.

The NAACP was disconcerted by the Supreme Court ruling in *Regents of the University of California* v. *Bakke* in 1978. The Court ruled five to four that Title VI of the 1964 Civil Rights Act barred a university medical school's special admissions program for blacks and ordered a white applicant's admission. Although another bare majority ruled that race was a constitutionally valid criterion for admission programs, the Court had increased the difficulty of developing specific programs to meet constitutional tests.

The election of Ronald Reagan as president in 1980, at a time when the NAACP was still groping for effective programs to meet new challenges, was an even more ominous development. The Reagan administration all but destroyed the effectiveness of the U.S. Civil Rights Commission, the Civil Rights Division of the Justice Department, and the Equal Employment Commission. In 1984, Benjamin Hooks led a 125,000-person March on Washington to protest the "legal lynching" of civil rights by the Reagan administration.

Hooks assumed command of the NAACP at a time when it was not only struggling to devise an effective strategy for new civil rights challenges but battling for its very existence.

Questions concerning Hooks's leadership gained national attention in 1983 when Board Chair Margaret Wilson unilaterally suspended him. Outraged that Wilson had reprimanded Hooks without its approval, the board replaced her with Kelly Alexander, Sr., a North Carolina mortician. Following Alexander's death in 1986, the board elected Dr. William F. Gibson, a South Carolina dentist, as chairman. In order to oust Gibson, who was bitterly criticized for his leadership of the NAACP, Myrlie Evers led one of the fiercest internal battles in the organization's history.

Despite those setbacks, Hooks led the NAACP in winning several promising agreements from corporations, such as $1 billion from the American Gas Association, to provide jobs and other economic opportunities for blacks under a fair share program he inaugurated. In 1986, Hooks relocated the NAACP's national headquarters to Baltimore. Among his other accomplishments was the ACT-SO (Afro-Academic Cultural Technological Scientific Olympics) program he created to promote academic experience among minority youth through local, regional, and national competition. His goal was to seek proficiency in all academic areas, but with a special emphasis in the arts and humanities and the applied, technical, and social sciences. Hooks also continued the NAACP's political action programs with a special emphasis on voter registration.

In April 1993, Hooks retired as NAACP executive director. The board of directors had considerable difficulty deciding on a successor. Candidates included the Rev. Jesse Jackson. The board finally selected the Reverend Benjamin F. Chavis, Jr., an official of the United Church of Christ in Cleveland, who had once served more than four years in prison after being wrongly convicted on charges of conspiracy and arson for setting fire to a grocery store in Wilmington, N.C., in 1972. Chavis, much younger than his predecessor, was chosen in an attempt to revitalize the NAACP by attracting new sources of funding and reaching out to young African Americans. Chavis also called for the NAACP to expand its efforts to serve other minority interests.

Chavis's short tenure proved extremely controversial. In accord with his policy of attracting young African Americans, he shifted NAACP policy in a nationalistic direction and embraced black separatists, whom the NAACP had previously denounced. Chavis succeeded in increasing youth interest in the NAACP and was praised for his meetings with gang leaders, but he was widely criticized for inviting black radicals such as NATION OF ISLAM chair Louis FARRAKHAN to a black leadership conference, and for refusing to disassociate himself from the Nation's anti-Semitic policies. The NAACP's membership dropped significantly as a result.

Chavis also met with opposition to his administrative policies. NAACP board members were angered by his unauthorized policy statements, such as his approval of the North American Free Trade Agreement. Furthermore, Chavis was blamed for running up the organization's deficit, already swelled by declining memberships, to $1.2 million through staff salary increases. When in the summer of 1994 it was disclosed that Chavis had used organization money in an out-of-court settlement of a sexual harassment suit filed by a female staffer, there began to be calls for his resignation. On August 20, 1994, in a meeting of the board of directors, Chavis was removed as executive director.

The schism over Chavis's policies provided a forum for fundamental disagreements between blacks over the role of civil rights organizations. With full legal equality substantially achieved, the NAACP continued to face questions regarding the best use of its leadership and the appropriate strategy to employ in attacking the problems of African Americans. The departure of Chavis resulted in an invigorated NAACP. First, in 1995 Myrlie Evers-Williams replaced William F. Gibson as chair of the board, and the following year she was succeeded in the position by Julian Bond. That same year, 1996, Kweisi Mfume became President and CEO of the NAACP.

BIBLIOGRAPHY

Archer, Leonard Courtney. *Black Images in the American Theatre: NAACP Protest Campaigns—Stage, Screen, Radio & Television.* Brooklyn, N.Y., 1973.

Cortner, Richard C. *A Mob Intent on Death: The NAACP and the Arkansas Riot Cases.* Middletown, Conn., 1988.

Dalfiume, Richard M. "The Forgotten Years of the Negro Revolution," *Journal of American History* 55 (June 1968): 105–106.

Downey, Dennis, and Raymond M. Hyster. *No Crooked Death: Coatesville, Pennsylvania, and the Lynching of Zachariah Walker.* Urbana, Ill., 1991.

Finch, Minnie. *The NAACP, Its Fight for Justice.* Metuchen, N.J., 1981.

Fox, Stephen R. *The Guardian of Boston: William Monroe Trotter.* New York, 1970.

Goings, Kenneth W. *The NAACP Comes of Age: The Defeat of Judge John J. Parker.* Bloomington, Ind., 1990.

Greenberg, Jack. *Crusaders in the Courts: How a Dedicated Bunch of Lawyers Fought For the Civil Rights Revolution.* New York, 1994.

Harlan, Louis R. *Booker T. Washington: The Wizard of Tuskegee, 1901–1915.* New York, 1983.

Horne, Gerald. *Black and Red: W. E. B. Du Bois and the Afro-American Response to the Cold War.* Albany, N.Y., 1986.

Hughes, Langston. *Fight for Freedom: The Story of the NAACP.* New York, 1962.

Kellogg, Charles Flint. *NAACP: A History of the National Association for the Advancement of Colored People,* vol. 1: *1909–1920.* Baltimore, 1967.

Kellogg, Peter J. "Civil Rights Consciousness in the 1940s." *The Historian* 42, no. 1 (November 1979): 18–41.

Kluger, Richard. *Simple Justice.* New York, 1976.

Lawrence, Charles Radford. Negro Organizations in Crisis: Depression, New Deal, World War II. Ph.D. diss. Columbia University, 1953.

Lewis, David Levering. *W. E. B. Du Bois: Biography of a Race, 1868–1919.* New York, 1993.

McNeil, Genna Rae. *Groundwork, Charles Hamilton Houston and the Struggle for Civil Rights.* Philadelphia, 1983.

McPherson, James. *The Abolitionist Legacy.* Princeton, N.J., 1975.

Muse, Edward B. *Paying For Freedom: History of the NAACP and the Life Membership Program, 1909–1987.* Baltimore, 1987.

National Negro Conference. *Proceedings of the National Negro Conference.* New York, 1909.

Ovington, Mary White. "How the National Association for the Advancement of Colored People Began." *The Crisis* 8 (August 1914): 184–188.

———. *The Walls Came Tumbling Down.* 1947. Reprint. New York, 1970.

Record, Wilson. *Race and Radicalism: The NAACP and the Communist Party in Conflict.* Ithaca, N.Y., 1964.

Ross, D. Joyce. *J. E. Spingarn and the Rise of the NAACP.* New York, 1972.

Rowan, Carl. *Dream Makers, Dream Breakers: The World of Justice Thurgood Marshall.* Boston, 1992.

Rudwick, Elliott, and August Meier. "The Rise of the Black Secretariat in the NAACP, 1909–1935." In *Along the Colored Line: Explorations in the Black Experience.* Urbana, Ill., 1976.

Sitkoff, Harvard. *A New Deal for Blacks, The Emergence of Civil Rights as a National Issue: The Depression Decade.* New York, 1978.

St. James, Warren D. *NAACP: Triumphs of a Pressure Group, 1909–1980.* Smithtown, N.Y., 1980.

Tillman, Jr., Nathaniel Patrick. Walter Francis White: A Study in Interest Group Leadership. Ph.D. diss. University of Wisconsin, 1961.

Tushnet, Mark. *The NAACP's Legal Strategy Against Segregation, 1925–1950.* New York, 1987.

Vose, Clement E. *Caucasians Only: The Supreme Court, the NAACP, and the Restrictive Covenant Cases.* Berkeley, Calif., 1959.

Watson, Denton L. *Lion in the Lobby, Clarence Mitchell, Jr.'s Struggle for the Passage of Civil Rights Laws.* New York, 1990.

White, Walter. *A Man Called White.* Bloomington, Ind., 1948.

Wilkins, Roy. "The Negro Wants Full Equality." In Rayford W. Logan, ed. *What the Negro Wants.* Chapel Hill, N.C., 1944.

Wilkins, Roy, with Tom Matthews. *Standing Fast, the Autobiography of Roy Wilkins.* New York, 1982.

Wolters, Raymond. *Negroes in the Great Depression.* Westport, Conn., 1970.

Zangrando, Robert L. *The NAACP Crusade Against Lynching, 1909–1950.* Philadelphia, 1960.

– DENTON L. WATSON

NATIONAL ASSOCIATION OF COLORED WOMEN

Predating the NATIONAL ASSOCIATION FOR THE ADVANCEMENT OF COLORED PEOPLE and the NATIONAL URBAN LEAGUE, the National Association of Colored Women (NACW) was the first national black organization in the United States and has proved to be one of the longest lasting. Founded in 1896, NACW had roots that lay in decades of local political activity by African-American women. This often took the form of women's clubs, and was the result of heightened racism, a need for social services within the black community, and the exclusionary policies of many white-run organizations.

The local clubs and reform efforts of black women in churches, mutual aid societies, and literary clubs were part of a larger reform effort during the late nineteenth century. Little state assistance was available for the needy. Clubwomen provided aid to the aged, young, and other dependents, strengthened racial solidarity, and developed leadership. These local efforts, which were usually short-lived and unconnected, became the basis of a national coalition.

A series of events facilitated the emergence of the National Association of Colored Women. In 1895, a national convention of black women was called to respond to a racist letter sent by James Jacks, a southern journalist, to a British reformer. Jacks wrote that blacks lacked morality and that black women were prostitutes, natural liars, and thieves. Because of the local clubs and women's magazines that were in existence, in particular *The Woman's Era,* a national black women's journal, African-American women were able to respond quickly and effectively to the slanderous letter.

The 1895 convention led to the formation of the National Federation of Afro-American Women. Shortly thereafter, the National League of Colored Women broke from the Federation because of differences about how to deal with segregation at the Atlanta Exposition. But because of concerns about the lack of unity, the two organizations merged in 1896 to form the National Association of Colored Women. Committed to social reform and racial betterment, the NACW achieved its greatest growth from the 1890s to the 1920s. Shortly after it was founded, the NACW had 5,000 members. Twenty years later, it had 50,000 members in 28 federations and over 1,000 clubs. By 1924, it had reached 100,000 members.

The NACW was involved in a variety of projects to address problems of health, housing, education, and working conditions, and to create a social space for black women. It was the primary organization through which African-American women channeled their reform efforts. Embodied in their slogan "Lifting as we Climb" was a commitment not only to improve their own situation, but to aid the less fortunate. They built schools, ran orphanages, founded homes for the aged, set up kindergarten programs, and formed agencies in New York and Philadelphia to help female migrants from the South find jobs and affordable housing. Black women who formed the backbone of the NACW were primarily middle-class and often professional women involved in teaching or other social service occupations. Their local activities were the seeds for multiservice centers that combined the many goals of the NACW reform efforts. They provided material assistance through day care and health services and job training to help women secure jobs.

While the movement comprised many local groups with differing philosophies, the national agenda was dominated by women less interested in confrontation than in accommodation. In the early years, the NACW journal, *National Notes,* was printed at Tuskegee Institute under the direction of Margaret Murray Washington. The first president of the NACW, Mary Church Terrell, was also a supporter of Booker T. Washington and accommodationist policies. At the request of organizers in Chicago, Terrell chose not to invite outspoken anti-accommodationist Ida B. WELLS-BARNETT to the first NACW meeting.

The political orientation of women in the NACW was also evident in the programs and policies of the organization. Black clubwomen adhered to middle-class values of self-improvement and moral purity. As Terrell expressed in 1902, "Self-preservation demands that [black women] go among the lowly, illiterate, and even vicious, to whom they are bound by ties of race and sex . . . to reclaim them." They taught thrift through penny-saving societies and supported the temperance

NATIONAL COUNCIL OF NEGRO WOMEN

The National Council of Negro Women (NCNW) has been among the most influential African-American women's organizations of the twentieth century, particularly under the guidance of its founder, Mary McLeod BETHUNE, and its later president Dorothy Height. Bethune seized on the idea of an umbrella organization to bring together the skills and experience of black women in a variety of organizations. This national council would provide leadership and guidance in order to make African-American women's voices heard in every arena of social and political life. When Bethune began to pursue this goal in 1929, she met with some resistance from the leadership of other national organizations, particularly the NATIONAL ASSOCIATION OF COLORED WOMEN. But she was successful in convincing the skeptics that a National Council of Negro Women would respect the achievements and strengths of other groups and streamline the cooperative operations of black women's organizations, rather than supersede existing groups.

The NCNW was founded in New York City on December 5, 1935, after five years of planning. The true signs of Bethune's diplomatic ability were the presence at the founding meeting of representatives of twenty-nine organizations and the election of such important figures as Mary Church Terrell and Charlotte Hawkins Brown to leadership positions. Bethune was elected president by a unanimous vote. The effectiveness of the council and its leadership was immediately apparent. One of its areas of greatest success was labor issues. With Bethune's influence in the federal government, the NCNW, in conjunction with other organizations, pressed for federal jobs for African Americans, and was one of the forces behind the founding of the Fair Employment Practices Committee. Under Bethune's leadership the NCNW also established an important journal, the *Aframerican Woman's Journal,* which in 1949 became *Women United.* The council expressed an interest in international affairs, supporting the founding of the United Nations. From its founding, the United Nations has had an NCNW official observer at its proceedings.

Bethune retired from the presidency of the NCNW in 1949 and was succeeded by Dorothy Boulding Ferebee, the grandniece of Josephine St. Pierre Ruffin and former NCNW treasurer. During Ferebee's tenure, the council continued to press the issues with which it had always been concerned—civil rights, education, jobs, and health care, among others. However, the organization experienced a crisis as it moved beyond merely defining goals and issues toward providing more tangible services to its constituency. This issue carried over to the term of its third president, Vivian Carter Mason, elected in 1953. During her four years in office, Mason employed administrative skills to improve the operation of the national headquarters and to forge closer ties between the local and national councils. Under Mason, the NCNW continued to develop as a force in the struggle for civil rights. Just as Bethune led the organization to fight for the integration of the military, Mason fought for swift implementation of school desegregation.

The National Council of Negro Women has been among the most influential African-American women's organizations of the twentieth century.

In 1957, the NCNW elected Dorothy I. Height to be the organization's fourth president. Height came to her work at the council with experience on the national board of the YOUNG WOMEN'S CHRISTIAN ASSOCIATION, eight years as president of Delta Sigma Theta, and involvement in a host of organizations and institutions. Height set out to place the NCNW on firm financial ground through gaining tax-exempt status (accomplished in 1966) and through grants from foundations. She was successful in garnering support from the Ford Foundation and the U.S. Department of Health, Education, and Welfare to expand the scope of the NCNW's work.

Among Height's other major accomplishments as president was the construction of the Bethune Memorial Statue, unveiled in Lincoln Park, Washington, D.C., in 1974. The memorial pays tribute to the contributions of an extraordinary woman. The NCNW continued its commitment to preserve the history of black women through the founding of the National Archives for Black Women's History. Although the council desired such an institution from its founding, the archives did not become a reality until 1979. This collection preserves the papers of the NCNW, the National Committee on Household Employment, and the National Association of Fashion and Accessory Designers. The personal papers of a number of women are also housed there. Through this collection and through conferences sponsored by the archives, the NCNW has become an important force in preserving the records and achievements of black women in the twentieth century.

The list of organizations affiliated with the National Council of Negro Women is long and varied, reflecting the council's commitment to building bridges to create a united voice for black women. Affiliated groups include ten national sororities, the National Association of Negro Business and Professional Women's Clubs, Inc., the Auxiliary of the National Medical Association, women's missionary societies of the National Baptist Convention and the African Methodist Episcopal Church, and Trade Union Women of African Heritage. The NCNW has also developed an international component to its work. In addition to maintaining a presence at the United Nations, it has worked with women in Africa (in Togo and Senegal, for example) and other areas of the diaspora, such as Cuba.

The NCNW has been successful in creating a national organization through which African-American women can address the issues facing them and their families. It has enabled black women from a variety of backgrounds to design and implement programs and develop themselves as community leaders. The longevity and effectiveness of the council are due to the willingness of its leadership to change and to shape programs and methods to the emerging needs of African-American communities.

BIBLIOGRAPHY

Collier-Thomas, Bettye. *N.C.N.W., 1935–1980.* Washington, D.C., 1981.

Giddings, Paula. *When and Where I Enter: The Impact of Black Women on Race and Sex in America.* New York, 1984.

— JUDITH WEISENFELD

NATIONAL HOSPITAL ASSOCIATION

The National Hospital Association (NHA) was established in August 1923 by the National Medical Association at its annual meeting in St. Louis. The parent body founded this new auxiliary organization to coordinate and guide its efforts in African-American hospital reform. The NHA's specific goals included the standardization of black hospitals and of the curricula at black nurse-training schools, the establishment of additional black hospitals, and the provision of more internships for black physicians.

African-American medical leaders' concerns that the growing importance of hospital standardization and accreditation would lead to the elimination of black hospitals prompted their establishment of the NHA. They recognized that many black hospitals were inferior institutions that were ineligible for approval by certifying agencies. But these facilities were critical to the careers of African-American physicians and, in many locations, to the lives of black patients. The NHA sought to improve black hospitals by attempting to ensure proper standards of education and efficiency in them. Therefore, one of its first actions was to issue in 1925 a set of minimum standards for its member hospitals. These standards included criteria on hospital supervision, record keeping, and the operation of nurse-training schools. Compared to the guidelines of the larger and more influential American College of Surgeons, these were rudimentary. Nonetheless, the NHA hoped that its efforts would forestall the closure of African-American hospitals and demonstrate to white physicians that their black colleagues could keep abreast of changes in medical and hospital practice.

Other activities of the NHA included the provision of technical assistance to hospitals, the sponsorship of professional conferences, and the publication of literature promoting proper hospital administration. The association also lobbied major health-care organizations such as the American Medical Association, the American College of Surgeons, and the American Hospital Association, urging them to take on a role in the improvement of black hospitals.

The NHA was a short-lived organization with limited effectiveness. It never had a full-time administrator or a permanent office. During its first ten years Knoxville physician H. M. Green served as its president while maintaining a busy medical practice. The NHA ran entirely on modest membership fees and often operated at a deficit. It never received financial or programmatic support from foundations or other health-care organizations. It lacked the financial and political muscle to implement and enforce its policies and failed to convince many black physicians of the importance of its goals. By the early 1940s the NHA had disbanded.

Despite these limitations the NHA played a significant role in African-American medical history. It provided black physicians and nurses with opportunities to learn about and discuss trends in hospital care. And it helped the National Medical Association to publicize and articulate the plight of black physicians, their patients, and their hospitals at a time when few outlets for voicing such concerns existed.

BIBLIOGRAPHY

Gamble, Vanessa Northington. "The Negro Hospital Renaissance: The Black Hospital Movement." In Diana E. Long and Janet Golden, eds. *The American General Hospital.* Ithaca, N.Y., 1989, pp. 182–205.

Green, H. M. "Some Observations on and Lessons from the Experience of the Past Ten Years." *Journal of the National Medical Association* 26 (1934): 21–24.

— VANESSA NORTHINGTON GAMBLE

NATIONAL NEGRO CONGRESS

The National Negro Congress (NNC) was an organization that emerged from the May 1935 Washington,

D.C., Howard University Conference on the status of the Negro. Formally getting under way in 1936, it held meetings at irregular intervals and was composed predominantly of organizations and individuals active in the African-American community. For Ralph BUNCHE and others, the National Negro Congress held the promise of an interclass alliance which included labor, clerics, entrepreneurs, and elected officials, among others. The mission of the NNC included protesting against JIM CROW and organizing for the social, political, and economic advancement of African Americans.

Sponsors of the NNC included Charles H. Houston of the NAACP, Alain LOCKE and Ralph Bunche of Howard University, Lester Granger of the NATIONAL URBAN LEAGUE, John P. Davis of the Joint Committee on National Recovery, A. Philip Randolph of the BROTHERHOOD OF SLEEPING CAR PORTERS, who served as the organization's first president, and James Ford of the COMMUNIST PARTY OF THE U.S.A.

The participation of the Communist party within the NNC caused controversy. From the beginning, the party played a prominent role within the NNC and grew after the 1937 convention. Their point of view was that the NNC was an expression of a "united front" of African Americans (i.e., despite class and ideological differences, blacks should unite for common goals). However, by 1938, some non-communists, such as Bunche, troubled by the influence of the Communist party, left the NNC.

The mission of the NNC included protesting against Jim Crow and organizing for the social, political, and economic advancement of African Americans.

Critics of the NNC, a list that ultimately included Randolph, were of the opinion that the organization was a front for the party and that it refused to take positions at variance with those of the communists. These criticisms of the NNC became sharper after the concluding of the Nazi-Soviet pact in August 1939, which led to the German invasion of Poland and the onset of World War II.

While many communists were hesitant to criticize the pact, NNC critics (e.g., Randolph) began to drift away from the organization. Those who refused to leave the NNC felt that disputes over the pact were examples of the kind of ideological differences that should be submerged in the interest of a "united front" for the betterment of African Americans.

Despite these internecine conflicts, the NNC during its brief history rivaled the NAACP as a tribune for African Americans. It had fifty branch councils in nineteen states, published a number of communications organs, and sponsored numerous conferences.

In Harlem, where the NNC was particularly strong, it enjoyed the participation of the Rev. Adam Clayton POWELL, Jr., and the Harvard-educated communist lawyer Benjamin J. Davis, and spearheaded campaigns to secure jobs for blacks in mass transit. Across the nation, the NNC could be found boycotting department stores that engaged in racial discrimination, protesting police brutality, and demanding federal antilynching legislation and investigation of the Ku Klux Klan and Black Legion. The NNC protested vigorously the Italian invasion of Ethiopia and the perceived laggard policies of the U.S. State Department in opposing this action.

In a number of communities, the NNC worked quite closely with NAACP branches, affiliates of the Congress of Industrial Organizations (CIO), the Southern Conference for Human Welfare, and the American Committee for the Protection of the Foreign Born. After the entry of the United States into World War II in 1941, this kind of collaboration increased. Since the United States was in an alliance with the Soviet Union from 1941 to 1945, the role of communists within the NNC was not seen by many noncommunists as a bar to cooperation. As such, the NNC experienced some growth during this period after the difficulties of 1939.

The NNC played a leading role during this period in the formation of the Negro Labor Victory Committee (NLVC; 1942–1945), which in Harlem and elsewhere mobilized African Americans against fascism abroad and Jim Crow at home.

Nevertheless, neither the NNC nor the NLVC was able to survive the end of the war and the onset of the Cold War and Red Scare. By 1946, it was quite common for the NNC to be referred to as a "communist front" and "tool of Moscow." The transformation of the Soviet Union from an ally to an enemy of the United States was a leading factor in this changed perception of the NNC and its eventual demise. During the period 1946–1947 the NNC was subsumed by the Civil Rights Congress, another organization closely related to the Communist party, but one that had a broader mission, less exclusively focused on African-American affairs, of fighting political and racist repression.

BIBLIOGRAPHY

Horne, Gerald. *Communist Front? The Civil Rights Congress, 1946–56*. London, 1988.

Hughes, Cicero Alvin. "Toward a Black United Front: the National Negro Congress Movement." Ph.D. diss., Ohio University, 1982.

Streater, John Baxter. "The National Negro Congress, 1936–47." Ph.D. diss., University of Cincinnati, 1981.

– GERALD HORNE

NATIONAL NEGRO LABOR COUNCIL

The National Negro Labor Council (NNLC) was established in 1951 to promote the cause of African-American workers. Although beleaguered and ultimately extinguished by the repressive political environment of the 1950s, the organization contested economic discrimination in a variety of settings and thus helped to keep alive the battle for civil rights in the realm of labor.

During the New Deal and World War II, the Congress of Industrial Organizations (CIO), along with such allies as the NATIONAL NEGRO CONGRESS, the March On Washington Movement, and at times, the NATIONAL ASSOCIATION FOR THE ADVANCEMENT OF COLORED PEOPLE, had done much to transform organized labor from a bastion of Jim Crow into a leading agent of civil rights struggle. Mass campaigns for racial equality at work and in unions, together with the wartime mobilization, advanced the position of African Americans in the workplace and spawned a new generation of black union leadership. After the war, however, the outlook for black workers turned increasingly dismal. Peacetime reconversion, spreading mechanization, and a hardening of workplace discrimination conspired to squeeze large numbers of African Americans out of industry, even as thousands of displaced black farmers were moving from the rural South into the industrial North. Meanwhile, the conservative climate of the emerging Cold War era dampened the CIO's commitment to civil rights organizing; indeed, the expulsion from its ranks of communist-oriented unions in the late 1940s banished significant strongholds of black membership, along with many of the CIO's most energetic exponents of racial justice.

In June 1950, over 900 labor activists, predominantly black, gathered in Chicago at a National Labor Conference for Negro Rights. During the following year twenty-three Negro Labor Councils (NLCs) were established in key industrial centers around the country. In October 1951, representatives from these councils met in Cincinnati to form the National Negro Labor Council. In a founding Statement of Principles, the NNLC pledged to "work unitedly with the trade unions to bring about greater cooperation between all sections of the Negro people and the trade union movement." While it focused on equal economic opportunity, the NNLC advocated all measures essential to "full citizenship," including an end to police brutality and mob violence, the right to vote and hold public office, and the abolition of segregation in housing and in other public facilities.

The NNLC drew much of its leadership and active followers either from the unions recently expelled from the CIO—including the United Electrical, Radio, and Machine Workers; the International Mine, Mill, and Smelter Workers; the Food, Tobacco, Agricultural and Allied Workers; the National Union of Marine Cooks and Stewards; the International Fur and Leather Workers; and the International Longshoremen's and Warehousemen's Union—or from the left-wing bastions of mainstream unions, such as the United Packinghouse Workers, the Amalgamated Clothing Workers, and the United Auto Workers. (Detroit's vast UAW Local 600, a center of militant black leadership, made up a particularly vital base of the support). In cities such as San Francisco, Detroit, Washington, Chicago, Cleveland, New York, and Louisville, NLCs cultivated allies within the African-American community, as well as among sympathetic whites. William R. Hood, recording secretary of UAW Local 600, served as president of the national organization. Coleman A. Young, then organizer for the Amalgamated Clothing Workers in Detroit, served as executive secretary. World-renowned singer, actor, and civil rights leader Paul ROBESON was an active supporter.

Over the first half of the 1950s, the NNLC initiated or rallied behind a series of public campaigns around the country. Local NLCs confronted racial barriers to hiring or advancement at a number of enterprises, including the Ford Motor Company, the Statler and Sherry Netherland hotels (New York), Sears-Roebuck (Cleveland, San Francisco), General Electric (Louisville), the U.S. Bureau of Engraving (Washington), the Detroit Tigers, Drexel National Bank (Chicago), and American Airlines. Through petitions and write-in drives, picket lines and local publications, visiting committees and job-training programs, the NNLC helped to open up employment for African-American men and women as streetcar motormen and conductors, hotel workers, truck drivers, clerks and salespeople, and bank officials, and in previously unobtainable levels of skilled industrial work. The NNLC called on unions to demand the inclusion of a model "Fair Employment Practices" clause in labor contracts, and to bring African Americans into leadership positions. The NNLC also mobilized support for strikes in which black workers figured prominently, including those at International Harvester in Chicago (1952) and among sugar cane workers in Louisiana (1953).

The NNLC encountered a formidable array of obstacles. Employers remained widely resistant to the call

From 1965 until Elijah Muhammad's death in February 1975, the Nation of Islam prospered economically, but its membership never surged again. Minister Louis X of Boston, also called Louis Abdul FARRAKHAN, replaced Malcolm as the national representative and the head minister of Temple No. 7 in New York. During this period, the Nation acquired an ultramodern printing press, cattle farms in Georgia and Alabama, and a bank in Chicago.

After a bout of illness, Muhammad died in Chicago and one of his six sons, Wallace Deen Muhammad (later Imam Warith Deen Muhammad), was named supreme minister of the Nation of Islam. However, two months later Wallace shocked his followers and the world by declaring that whites were no longer viewed as devils and they could join the movement. He began to make radical changes in the doctrines and the structure of the Nation, moving it in the direction of orthodox Sunni Islam.

The changes introduced by Imam Warith Deen Muhammad led to a splintering of the movement, especially among the hard-core black-nationalist followers. In 1978, Louis Farrakhan led a schismatic group that succeeded in resurrecting the old Nation of Islam. Farrakhan's Nation, which is also based in Chicago, retains the black-nationalist and separatist beliefs and doctrines that were central to the teachings of Elijah Muhammad. Farrakhan displays much of the charisma and forensic candor of Malcolm X, and his message of black nationalism is again directed to those mired in the underclass, as well as to disillusioned intellectuals, via the Nation's *Final Call* newspaper and popular rap-music groups such as Public Enemy.

Through more than sixty years, the Nation of Islam in its various forms has become the longestlasting and most enduring of the black militant and separatist movements that have appeared in the history of black people in the United States. Besides its crucial role in the development of the black-consciousness movement, the Nation is important for having introduced Islam as a fourth major religious tradition in American society, alongside Protestantism, Catholicism, and Judaism.

BIBLIOGRAPHY

Breitman, George, ed. *Malcolm X Speaks.* New York, 1965.

Essien-Udom, E. U. *Black Nationalism: A Search for Identity in America.* Chicago, 1962.

Farrakhan, Louis. *Seven Speeches.* Chicago, 1974.

Lincoln, C. Eric. *The Black Muslims in America.* Boston, 1961.

Malcolm X and Alex Haley. *The Autobiography of Malcolm X.* New York, 1965.

Mamiya, Lawrence H. "From Black Muslim to Bilalian: The Evolution of a Movement." *Journal for the Scientific Study of Religion* 21, no. 2 (June 1982): 138–152.

Muhammad, Elijah. *Message to the Black Man in America.* Chicago, 1965.

Muhammad, Warith Deen. *As the Light Shineth from the East.* Chicago, 1980.

Perry, Bruce. *Malcolm: The Life of a Man Who Changed Black America.* Barrytown, N.Y., 1991.

Waugh, Earle H., Baha Abu-Laban, and Regula B. Qureshi, eds. *The Muslim Community in North America.* Edmonton, Alberta, 1983.

— LAWRENCE H. MAMIYA AND C. ERIC LINCOLN

NAT TURNER'S REBELLION

Nat Turner (October 2, 1800–November 11, 1831) led the most significant slave revolt in U.S. history. Undertaken in 1831 in Virginia, Turner's Rebellion claimed more lives than any similar uprising. It had repercussions throughout the South, redrawing the lines of the American debate over slavery in ways that led toward all-out civil war within a generation. Indeed, some suggest that it represented the first major battle of the long war to end slavery.

In 1831 Virginia's Southampton County, bordering on North Carolina, contained roughly 6,500 whites and 9,500 blacks. Almost all of the latter, whether young or old, lived in perpetual bondage, including Nat Turner, a slave of Joseph Travis. Turner had been born in Southampton on October 2, 1800, only five days before the execution of black revolutionary Gabriel Prosser in Richmond, and as a boy he must have heard stories of Prosser's intended insurrection. Tradition suggests his mother was born and raised in Africa. She told her son at an early age that, on the basis of his quick intelligence and the distinctive lumps on his head, he seemed "intended for some great purpose."

Turner learned to read as a small boy, and he built a strong and composite faith from listening to the African beliefs retained within his family and the Christian values of his first master, Benjamin Turner. Confident from childhood that he had a special role to play, Nat Turner found outward confirmations for his messianic thoughts and eventually determined that his personal calling coincided with the most pressing public issue of the day—the termination of racial enslavement.

Most of what we know about the man must be drawn from his *Confessions,* a remarkable autobiographical statement taken down by a young lawyer named Thomas Ruffin Gray during the rebel's final days in jail. While one can question the validity of Turner's recollections and the motivations of the disillusioned and desperate Gray (who rapidly published his lurid transcript at a profit), the confession has an underlying ring of truth and represents one of the most extraordinary firsthand texts in American history.

According to this account, Turner experienced a powerful vision in 1825 in which he "saw white spirits and black spirits engaged in battle, and the sun was darkened—the thunder rolled in the Heavens, and blood flowed in streams. . . ." Three years later, another vision told him to prepare to slay his "enemies with their own weapons." But it was not until February 1831 that a solar eclipse signaled to Turner that he must begin. He laid plans with others to act on the holiday of July 4, but when he fell ill, the date was allowed to pass. Then, on August 13, he awoke to find the sun a dim reflection of itself, changing from one hazy color to another. Taking this as another sign, he brought together a handful of collaborators on Sunday, August 21, and told them of his plan for a terrorist attack.

His intention, Turner explained, was to move through the countryside from household to household, killing whites regardless of age or sex. He hoped that this brutal show of force would be so swift as to prevent any warning and so compelling as to convince others to join in the cause. Having rallied supporters and gathered up more horses and weapons, they could march on Jerusalem, the county seat, and take the arsenal, which would give them a substantial beachhead of resistance. From there the rebellion could spread, aided by a network of enslaved black Christians, and perhaps by divine intervention as well. Turner made clear, according to the *Richmond Enquirer*, that "indiscriminate slaughter was not their intention after they obtained a foothold, and was resorted to in the first instance to strike terror and alarm. Women and children would afterwards have been spared, and men too who ceased to resist."

Among African Americans, Turner became and has remained both a martyr and a folk hero never to be forgotten.

Shortly after midnight, Turner and five others launched their violent offensive, attacking the home of Turner's master and killing the Travis household, then proceeding on to other farmsteads to wreak similar vengeance. As their ranks grew, the band became more disorderly and the element of surprise was lost, but the first militiamen who offered resistance on Monday afternoon beat a hasty retreat. By Monday night, as many as sixty or seventy African Americans had joined the cause, and on Tuesday morning Turner's army set out for Jerusalem. Behind them at least fifty-seven whites of all ages had been killed in a stretch of twenty miles.

When some rebels stopped at James Parker's farm, within three miles of Jerusalem, to win recruits and refresh themselves, the pause proved fatal, for the local militia had regrouped. They managed to attack and disperse the insurgents, who were off guard and poorly armed. Although Turner attempted to rally his followers, he never regained the initiative, and on Tuesday, white reinforcements launched a harsh and indiscriminate counteroffensive that took well over a hundred lives. One cavalry company slaughtered forty blacks in two days, mounting more than a dozen severed heads atop poles as public warnings. Turner, his force destroyed, eluded authorities for six weeks—during which time another black preacher known as David attempted to ignite an uprising in North Carolina, fueling white fears of widespread rebellion. After an enormous manhunt, authorities captured Turner in a swamp on October 30 and hanged him publicly twelve days later.

Turner's unprecedented insurgency had a complex impact. It forced Virginia's legislature to consider openly, if briefly, the prospect of gradual emancipation. It also attracted proslavery whites to the colonization movement, since many saw African resettlement as a way to remove dangerous bondsmen and reduce the free black community. For black and white abolitionists in the North, Turner's Rebellion reinforced the idea, later espoused by John Brown, that enslaved Southerners were willing and able to engage in armed revolt if only weapons and outside support could be arranged. Among churchgoing slaveholders, the uprising prompted tighter restrictions on black preaching and greater caution regarding slave access to the Gospel. Among African Americans, Turner became and has remained both a martyr and a folk hero never to be forgotten. As recently as 1969, one black Southampton resident could recall what his mother had learned in her childhood: that Nat Turner "was a man of war, and for legal rights, and for freedom."

BIBLIOGRAPHY

Aptheker, Herbert. *Nat Turner's Slave Rebellion.* New York, 1966.

Morris, Charles Edward. "Panic and Reprisal: Reaction in North Carolina to the Nat Turner Insurrection, 1831." *North Carolina Historical Review* 62 (1985): 29–52.

Oates, Stephen B. *The Fires of Jubilee: Nat Turner's Fierce Rebellion.* New York, 1975.

Tragle, Henry Irving. *The Southampton Slave Revolt of 1831: A Compilation of Source Material, Including the Full Text of 'The Confessions of Nat Turner.'* Amherst, Mass., 1971.

Wood, Peter H. "Nat Turner: The Unknown Slave as Visionary Leader." In Leon Litwack and August Meier, eds. *Black Leaders of the Nineteenth Century.* Urbana, Ill., 1988, pp. 20–40.

– PETER H. WOOD

NEWARK, NEW JERSEY

Situated on the Passaic River in northern New Jersey, Newark was founded in 1666. It remained largely agricultural for the next 150 years, and slavery was practiced on a small scale in the area through the beginning of the nineteenth century. Starting in the 1830s, industrialization caused a spurt in local economic and population growth. In 1832 the town of Newark received its charter, and four years later was incorporated as a city. As German and Irish immigrants came to Newark, the population increased almost tenfold in forty years. Slavery in Newark and New Jersey finally ended in the 1840s, though the city remained sympathetic to Southern interests and largely free of abolitionist activity.

The city's modest free black community of poor laborers and servants, which never exceeded 2,000, was molded during this period. The Baxter School, a private black school, was founded in 1828. In 1832 the city's first black church, the Thirteenth Street Presbyterian Church, was founded. St. James African Methodist Episcopal Church was founded in 1842, and St. Phillip's Episcopal Church followed not long after.

In the decades following the CIVIL WAR, small numbers of African Americans migrated to Newark, and the town's black population grew to 10,000 by WORLD WAR I, an overflow from the larger migration to nearby New York City. The thousands of immigrants from southern and eastern Europe who poured into Newark provided competition for labor and for scarce housing resources (one-fifth of the city's area was marshlands, and there was a chronic land and housing shortage). Meanwhile, the city's increasingly powerful industrial unions excluded black workers: In 1903, only six of the city's twenty-two major unions accepted black laborers.

During these decades, the city's black population remained almost exclusively trapped at the bottom of the economic ladder. In 1890 almost two-thirds of all male African Americans were engaged in unskilled labor or as servants, and 88 percent of women were maids or laundresses. Twenty years later, the picture was substantially the same. A few African Americans were able to found successful businesses. C. M. "Chicken" Brown operated a poultry stand, and Mary and Frank Anderson were the proprietors of a hotel with mostly white patrons. John S. Pinkman, who ran a furniture moving concern, became relatively wealthy.

At the same time, Newark was mostly free of overt racial tension, and the city's blacks were relatively integrated into community affairs. Housing stock, while poor, was open to blacks, and African Americans lived in integrated working-class areas throughout the city. The only all-black enclave was a district on the northern side of the downtown area. Public accommodations remained largely segregated, but schools integrated peacefully after the New Jersey Supreme Court's 1884 decision in *Pierce* v. *School Board of Burlington County,* which declared school segregation unconstitutional. In 1909, city authorities closed the all-black Baxter school, claiming separate schools were unnecessary.

The black community fostered several lasting institutions during this period. In 1871 the Bethany Baptist Church (later the city's largest black church) was founded. Bethany Church members also founded the Bethany Lodge, a masonic fraternity; the Sunday Afternoon Lyceum, a literary circle; and the Coloured Home for Aged and Orphans in nearby Montclair. In 1902, the *Appeal,* the city's first black newspaper, was founded. It was published through 1910. During the early 1900s, the Frederick Douglass Republican Club was organized to promote voting.

The Great Migration altered the face of black Newark. As the coming of World War I opened up jobs for African Americans in the city's steel mills and in war industries such as munitions plants, brickyards, and wire factories, southeastern blacks, the largest number from Georgia, poured into the city. The Negro Welfare League, an interracial group of black ministers and professionals and white businessmen founded in 1910 (transformed into the Newark branch of the NATIONAL URBAN LEAGUE in 1919) and led by African-American Thomas Puryear, attempted to find jobs and housing for the migrants, some of whom were forced into shantytowns and tent cities. The league obtained employment for black workers, who were largely excluded from white unions, often through the use of no-strike pledges. The only large protest by black workers during the period was that of the dockworkers, led by Prosper Brewer (later a political leader and the black ward's Republican ward committeeman), who struck successfully for higher wages in 1916.

The Great Migration altered the face of black Newark.

By the end of the 1920s, Newark's economy was already depressed, and its white population began to decline. Many large industrial firms left the crowded city for larger sites. Business flight cost the city well-paid jobs and tax revenue for city services, and the city's commission system of government led to unresponsive and notoriously corrupt rule. Within such an environment, racial tension grew. Downtown stores, swimming pools, and theaters continued to exclude black patrons, who were forced into segregated neighborhoods in the old downtown areas. The Third Ward, better known as the "Hill District" and considered by many commentators "the worst slum in America," was the center of Newark's black community. By 1930, 30 percent of the city's 38,880 African-American residents lived there. Antiquated zoning laws, which prevented construction of new housing, meant that few blacks owned their homes, and most were forced to settle in overcrowded dilapidated, expensive, old, white-owned housing. Sanitation was primitive, and black residents were plagued by tuberculosis and venereal disease. In 1923, the city's Board of Health tried to use the tuberculosis epidemic as a pretext for deporting black migrants. In 1927, Dr. John Kenney founded Kenney Memorial Hospital to care for poor citizens. Police harassment was a chronic problem. In 1928, police Captain George Fohs prohibited interracial contact after midnight in the district. In 1930 white city residents vetoed a proposal by the Prudential Insurance Corporation to build a black housing development in the Hill district.

Despite the depressing living conditions, a thriving black culture grew up within the "Roaring Third" Ward during the 1920s and 1930s. Religious institutions flourished, including heterodox denominations such as FATHER DIVINE's movement and Noble Drew Ali's Moorish Science Temple, founded in 1915, a black nationalist religious group that prefigured the NATION OF ISLAM. An active JAZZ scene, loosely connected with New York City's, arose in the ward. It was centered on the core intersection of Spruce Street (the "Colored Broadway") and Broome Street. There, theaters such as the Orpheum and Paramount, and such nightclubs as the Kinney Club and the Skateland Club, featured New York performers and hopefuls such as Jimmy Lunceford and Ella FITZGERALD. Newark also has been the home of many important musicians in various genres, such as Willie "The Lion" Smith, Sarah VAUGHAN, Wayne Shorter, Babs Gonzales, Larry Young, Woody Shaw, James Moody, Hank Mobley, and Dave Thomas. Another focus of black community interest during the period was Ruppert Stadium, home of the Newark Eagles of the Negro National League, who featured such players as Larry DOBY and future Hall-of-Famers Monte Irvin, Ray Dandridge, and (briefly) Satchel PAIGE.

The Great Depression devastated Newark. In the face of white competition, many blacks were unable to find work. By 1931 there were 20,000 African Americans on relief, one-third of the city's total. Although almost all welfare recipients were longtime Newark residents, in 1932 city officials organized a movement to send back all newly arrived southern blacks in order to reduce welfare rolls. Black ministers and leaders campaigned successfully against the project, and Newark Urban League president Thomas Puryear, who collaborated on it, was forced to resign.

The Depression and the struggle to remain in the city radicalized many young black Newark residents. In 1934, activist Harold Lett became director of the Newark Urban League and led protests over black job exclusion. The same year, Guy Moorehead organized the Essex County Worker's League, and in 1936 became New Jersey's first black Democratic state representative. In 1938 black community forces led by the Newark branch of the NATIONAL NEGRO CONGRESS successfully picketed chain stores to obtain jobs for African Americans. In 1939 Fred and Richard Martin bought the *Newark Herald* newspaper, renamed it the *Newark Herald-News,* and made it a powerful voice for civil rights during the 1940s.

The economic boom that followed the outbreak of World War II brought renewed black mass migration to Newark. African Americans, who had represented just 10 percent of the city's 1940 population, tripled over the next twenty years, growing to one-third of the city's total. Although black protesters won token access to public places, the rise in population was not accompanied by a rise in status. Indeed, whites actively opposed black equality. In 1949 the city Board of Education approved a policy of free transfers for white students from black majority schools, and by 1951, some 3,200 white students were attending schools outside their districts. In 1953 a reform city government was elected and replaced the corrupt city commission regime, which had systematically discriminated against blacks, with a mayor and city council.

The next year, Newark African Americans finally got their first voice in government, when former NAACP president Harry Hazelwood was named city magistrate, and newspaperman Irvine Turner was elected to the new city council, where he remained until 1970. Even so, the reform movement proved ephemeral, and Newark's Democratic machine soon regained control. Poor city services and police brutality remained chronic problems. Meanwhile, Turner became a corrupt and powerful "boss" in the black community. Famous for his fiery rhetorical denunciations of "slumlords" and racist practices, he tried to curtail efforts at reform by other blacks. The Newark NAACP, whose leaders were dependent on the machine, failed to press strongly for city action in support of black equality.

During the 1950s, even as the white population was reduced, the black population began to decline, as middle-class blacks moved to nearby suburbs. By the

nineteenth century and foreshadowed the antiabolitionist and antiblack riots of 1834 and 1835.

The position of African Americans was threatened by restrictions on their right to vote and an erosion of their economic status in the antebellum era. New York City blacks were affected after 1821 by the revised state constitution which retained a prohibitive $250 property qualification for voting for black males while eliminating property qualifications for white male voters. Occupational opportunities for free blacks also declined as they were forced out of many unskilled jobs due to competition from the increasing immigrant Irish population.

The perception of blacks as a racially inferior and degraded people coupled with the animosities fueled by economic competition resulted in numerous attacks on blacks, perhaps the most notable being the infamous CIVIL WAR draft riot of 1863 in which the Colored Orphan Asylum was burned down, almost one hundred persons were killed, and many blacks fled the city. Lincoln's Emancipation Proclamation of 1862 had turned the war from one to preserve the Union to one to end slavery. Immigrant workers unable to pay the $300 "commutation fee" to avoid the draft and fearful of the job competition from emancipated blacks much prophesied by Democratic party propaganda ventilated their racial prejudices and economic fears upon the city's small black population.

Blacks fleeing the draft riots in 1863 were driven from downtown Brooklyn and New York City. Some found refuge in the Weeksville-Carrsville area of Kings County, named after local blacks. This area is located in present-day Bedford-Stuyvesant. The Weeksville-Carrsville area dates from the 1830s and was an acknowledged neighborhood by the 1840s. A sense of racial solidarity and assertiveness existed in the neigh-

Demonstration march in New York City, early twentieth century. (Prints and Photographs Division, Library of Congress)

borhood; Weeksville blacks petitioned, albeit unsuccessfully, in 1869 to have a black appointed to the Brooklyn Board of Education so that they could have a say in the governance of the five "colored" schools. (In 1882 Phillip A. White became the first black on the Brooklyn Board of Education.) The distinctive black character of Weeksville and other parts of the Ninth Ward (which included part of present-day Bedford-Stuyvesant) was lost by 1870 as whites purchased property and moved into the area touted as excellent for "genteel suburban residences." However, more was lost than the character of the neighborhood, for as immigrants came to Brooklyn and New York City they and their offspring forced blacks out of skilled and semiskilled jobs.

Despite the contributions of black New Yorkers to the Union victory, including the formation of the Twentieth United States Colored Infantry, the referendum in New York State advocating equal suffrage was defeated. Equal suffrage for black New Yorkers would not come until the passage of the FIFTEENTH AMENDMENT to the U.S. Constitution in 1870. Between 1870 and the turn of the century African Americans continued to contribute to the establishment of new institutions and organizations in their community. The *New York Age,* founded in 1887 under the editorship of T. Thomas Fortune, became one of the leading black newspapers in the nation. In the early years of the twentieth century Charles Anderson, a close ally of Booker T. WASHINGTON, was a leading black Republican politician. During the same years Tammany Hall organized the United Colored Democracy, its black auxiliary. During these years, the city's black population rose significantly from 17,580 in 1860 to 33,888 by 1890. Nevertheless, blacks remained less than 2 percent of the total population as southern and eastern European immigrants swelled the city's population.

In 1900, after the 1898 consolidation of the five boroughs (Manhattan, Brooklyn, Queens, the Bronx, and Staten Island), New York City had 60,000 black residents. By 1920, it had the largest black population of any city in the country, though less than 3 percent of the population was black. The city's ethnic diversification was accompanied by considerable social upheaval as groups contended for jobs and living space. African Americans, who had lived in the Greenwich Village area of Manhattan, were slowly moving northward and by the 1890s were residing in substantial numbers in the infamous San Juan Hill area (centered on the West Side of Manhattan between Sixtieth and Sixty-sixth Streets on Tenth and Eleventh Avenues), so named because of the frequent interracial battles there. The worst disturbance during these years was the August 1900 antiblack riot when policemen joined the white mobs in attacking blacks all along Eighth Avenue between Twenty-seventh and Forty-second Streets.

Seeking the security of new neighborhoods, better housing stock, and the concomitant status, blacks took the opportunity to move into the middle-class community of HARLEM, created by vacant apartments in an overbuilt housing market, and the entrepreneurial skills of a black realtor, Philip A. Payton, and his Afro-American Realty Company organized in 1904. Many of the major African-American social, fraternal, and religious institutions relocated from their downtown quarters to Harlem by the early 1920s. The African Methodist Episcopal Zion ("Mother Zion"), St. Philip's Protestant Episcopal Church, and Abyssinian Baptist Church were some of the prominent churches that reestablished themselves in Harlem. The "Great Migration" of blacks from the South and the Caribbean was intensified by the demand for labor in the North during the WORLD WAR I years. The black population of New York City increased from 60,666 in 1900 to 152,407 in 1920. Of Manhattan's black population of 109,133 in 1920, two-thirds lived in Harlem.

New York City also became the center of increased Caribbean immigration. Approximately 25 percent of Harlem's black population were foreign-born by the mid-1920s, with the vast majority of the foreign-born composed of Caribbean immigrants. Although the foreign-born percentage decreased 16.7 percent by 1930 due to restrictive immigration laws, West Indian immigrants continued to play an important role in the economic, intellectual, and political life of New York City. By 1930, an estimated one-third of New York City's black professionals were from the Caribbean. Harlem was home to many prominent Caribbean intellectuals such as journalist and African Blood Brotherhood leader Cyril Briggs, socialist organizers Frank Crosswaith and H. H. Harrison, and nationalist leaders W. A. Domingo and Ethelred Brown. In 1919 Caribbean immigrants founded New York City's leading black newspaper, the *Amsterdam News.*

By this time, Harlem had become the center of New York's black life, containing not only the working class, but also the small but influential black middle class. In 1919, the Equitable Life Assurance Society placed on the market the beautiful brownstones on W. 139th Street designed by Stanford White which had been off limits to black buyers. Within eight months, members of the black bourgeoisie had purchased them and they became known as "Striver's Row." Other streets, such as Edgecomb Avenue and St. Nicholas Place, became middle- and upper-income black enclaves. The diverse black nationalities and artistic communities of Harlem contributed to its heterogeneous class composition and cosmopolitan reputation in the 1920s.

Throughout the first half of the twentieth century Harlem was the cultural and ideological capital of black America. In the 1920s, it became the center of both a literary renaissance and the black nationalistic movement of Marcus GARVEY—another Caribbean immigrant—and his UNIVERSAL NEGRO IMPROVEMENT ASSOCIATION (UNIA). From his Harlem headquarters, Garvey instilled a new racial pride while advocating the decolonization of Africa from European rule. The UNIA established several businesses, including the ill-fated Black Star Line of ships, which was intended to facilitate commerce between Africa and African-Americans. Its promoters hoped the UNIA would play a role in the repatriation of blacks from the racially repressive climate of the United States to freedom in an independent Africa. Garveyism was the nationalistic manifestation of the NEW NEGRO movement's search for racial pride and assertiveness in the struggle for freedom.

The literary ferment of the Harlem Renaissance produced numerous authors and poets who celebrated their African and African-American heritage. In such works as Langston HUGHES's *Weary Blues* (1926), Jean TOOMER's *Cane* (1923), and Countee CULLEN's poem "Heritage" (1925), black writers extolled the culture and character of Africa. The cosmopolitan nature of the Renaissance is seen in the number of West Indian artists who played an instrumental role in the literature, such as Claude MCKAY and Eric Walrond. Artists and their literary promoters, such as the black sociologist and editor of the NATIONAL URBAN LEAGUE magazine *Opportunity,* (1923–1944), Charles S. Johnson, sought to create a new and more positive image for African Americans through the arts which might be absorbed by the larger society. The NATIONAL ASSOCIATION FOR THE ADVANCEMENT OF COLORED PEOPLE, the leading civil rights organization in the United States, had its offices in Harlem, as did its journal, the CRISIS (1910–).

Throughout the first half of the twentieth century Harlem was the cultural and ideological capital of black America.

Harlem had a vibrant nightlife which was soon discovered by white theatergoers, critics, publishers, and intellectuals. The dominant form of black popular music was JAZZ. One of the roots of jazz was locally-based ragtime and Harlem stride piano, as performed by musicians such as Eubie BLAKE, Fats Waller, and James P. JOHNSON. Another root of jazz was found in New Orleans and other southern cities. Southern jazz followed black migrants north and became the popular dance music of the 1920s through the 1940s. New York City soon became a music center for jazz. White New Yorkers found black music and entertainers readily available in Harlem nightclubs. Connie's Inn and the COTTON CLUB were two of the most famous clubs in Harlem in the twenties. Owned by white underworld figures, they featured black bands, singers, and chorus-line dancers. Duke ELLINGTON and his band, and singer Lena HORNE were among the major attractions at the Harlem clubs. The appreciation of black music did not carry over into the human sphere, however, and many of the white-owned clubs excluded black patrons.

The period of the twenties and thirties was one in which the city's black population demanded greater participation or control of the institutions in their communities. In Harlem, blacks demanded positions at Harlem Hospital from which they had been excluded, as well as control of Harlem's district leaderships, clubhouses, and representation. In 1929, Charles Fillmore, a REPUBLICAN, became the city's first black district leader. In 1935, Herbert Bruce, a West Indian immigrant, became the DEMOCRATIC PARTY's first black district leader. In the first five years of the Great Depression, West Indian politicians made significant gains in the Democratic party. By 1952, four of the five Democratic district leaders in Harlem were West Indians. Four of the five founding members of the Harlem branch of the COMMUNIST PARTY were West Indians. In part these trends were the result of African-American domination of the black posts within the Republican party and the greater accessibility of the Democratic party, which had far less black involvement until the New Deal. West Indians cooperated with African-American Democrats in attempts to gain black control over the Harlem Nineteenth and Twenty-first Assembly Districts. Despite some degree of tension between African Americans and West Indians, race far more than nationality determined the condition of blacks in the city and nation. By the 1930s, the first wave of West Indian immigrants that entered the country at the beginning of the twentieth century lived in neighborhoods segregated by race but not divided by black ethnic or class differences.

By the latter half of the 1920s the Garvey movement had collapsed with his imprisonment and deportation. The stock market crash of 1929 and accompanying Depression eroded interest in the Renaissance. Still, Harlem remained dynamic, as the struggle for equality intensified as the black unemployment rate in the city grew to nearly double that of whites and threw nearly half of Harlem's families onto relief. The injustice of employment discrimination in Harlem retail and chain stores in the midst of the Depression added insult to injury. Blacks initiated successful boycotts in Harlem in the 1930s, forcing department stores, utilities, and transportation companies to reverse their policies and hire blacks. Boycotts and protest marches were important weapons in breaking down the prejudice-induced barriers that existed during the Great Depression. The 1935 riot in Harlem and the accompanying violence directed at white businesses helped sensitize political and civic leaders to the need for change. With the onset of the preparedness drive for WORLD WAR II, New York City became the headquarters for A. Philip Randolph's movement for the March on Washington in 1941 to protest discrimination in the armed forces and among federal contractors. This led to the creation of a Federal Fair Employment Practices Committee in 1941 to insure blacks their fair share of jobs in defense industries.

World War II ended the Depression and illustrated the contradiction of a country fighting against racist Nazi ideology with two armies, one white and one black. The shooting of a black soldier by a white policeman in the Hotel Braddock in Harlem touched off another riot on August 1, 1943. A critical factor contributing to the outbreak of the riot was the erroneous rumor that the soldier had been killed by the policeman. As the evening progressed crowds gathered at the local precinct, the Braddock Hotel, and at Sydenham Hospital, where he supposedly died. Rioting broke out around 10:30 P.M. with the breaking of store windows centering on 125th Street and continued for two days. The human cost of the riot was significant, with 6 people killed, all black, and 185 people injured, mostly black. Arrests of blacks numbered more than 550, with most in custody for burglary and reception of stolen goods. Estimates were that some 1,450 stores were damaged.

In comparison to the Detroit riot of June 21 of the same year, the loss of life and physical injury were considerably less, but the events of August 1st and 2nd came as a surprise in America's most cosmopolitan city in which the mayor, Fiorello La Guardia, was popular in the black community. Frustration with the continuation of racism was the underlying cause of the riot. Pictures of the earlier Detroit riot showing black victims of white mobs and police were carried by New York newspapers along with numerous articles on white violence and discrimination against black servicemen. On the local level the riot was in part sparked by black discontent with employment discrimination, with police brutality, and La Guardia's apparent retreat from liberal policies (such as his approval of the Navy's use of Hunter College as a segregated training facility for its WAVES [Women's Reserves]). La Guardia's subsequent approval of the Metropolitan Life Insurance Company's plan to build a tax-exempt quasi-public housing project (Stuyvesant Town) also incurred the wrath of blacks familiar with Metropolitan Life's policy of black exclusion and residential segregation.

Following the riot, La Guardia moved to implement policies that the black community had advocated. Within one week of the riot, the Office of Price Administration announced the opening of an office to investigate food price-gouging in Harlem. Within two weeks, La Guardia inaugurated a series of radio broadcasts to promote racial harmony. The New York City Board of Education created a course on Intercultural Relations for teachers which emphasized African-American contributions. The mayor also announced that any discrimination in tenant selection for Stuyvesant Town was illegal. The riot stimulated greater efforts at improving race relations.

WORLD WAR II had a salutary effect upon the black condition, stimulating African-American migration to the North and the acquisition of industrial jobs. In 1944, the election of Adam Clayton POWELL, Jr. to the United States Congress, and the election of Powell's successor to the New York City Council, Communist party member Benjamin J. Davis, contributed to the growth of militant black political leadership in Harlem.

In the post-World War II era, the black population grew, heavily augmented by migration from the South and the Caribbean. The passage of state and federal discrimination legislation in housing and employment aided the expansion of the black middle class and black outmigration to other boroughs and suburbs. Between 1940 and 1950, Bedford-Stuyvesant emerged as an overwhelmingly black ghetto and by 1960 black residents had expanded into the contiguous parts of Crown Heights and Brownsville. The Greater Bedford-Stuyvesant area developed into the largest black community in New York City. Nearly 40 percent of the city's blacks made their home in Brooklyn by 1970. The South Jamaica-St. Albans-Cambria Heights area of Queens also blossomed as a large area of black settlement after World War II. The black populations in other boroughs were significantly augmented by the increase in black immigration from the Caribbean following the reform of immigration laws in 1965. The 1980 census indicated that 300,000 New Yorkers were born in the non-Hispanic Caribbean, 80 percent of whom had arrived since 1965. The center of the Caribbean black community shifted in the 1970s from the Harlem and

BIBLIOGRAPHY

Aptheker, Herbert. *A Documentary History of the Negro People in the United States.* Vol. 2. Secaucus, N.J., 1951.

Fox, Stephen R. *The Guardian of Boston: William Monroe Trotter.* New York, 1970.

Harlan, Louis R. *Booker T. Washington: The Wizard of Tuskegee, 1901–1915.* New York, 1983.

– GREG ROBINSON

NICHOLAS BROTHERS

Nicholas Brothers, dancers. Fayard (1914–) and Harold (c. 1921–) Nicholas were born and reared in Philadelphia, where their parents played in a pit band called the Nicholas Collegians, which performed regularly at the Standard Theater. Fayard gravitated toward show business at a young age, claiming that the live performances and shows he saw as a child (such as Leonard Reed and his partner, Willie Bryant), were his first great influences. The children began their own professional career as the Nicholas Kids and for a short time danced with their sister Dorothy in different East Coast venues.

In 1930, the brothers danced on a popular Philadelphia radio show called the "Horn and Hardart Kiddie Hour." However, it was during an appearance at the Pearl Theater in Philadelphia that Frank Schiffman, the manager of the Lafayette Theater in Harlem, recruited the brothers to dance in New York. When they opened in New York, their name was changed to the Nicholas Brothers, and they joined the ranks of the famous "brothers" tap acts of the twentieth century.

On April 10, 1932, they moved to the COTTON CLUB, where they performed with the top bands of the period such as Jimmie Lunceford, Lucky Millinder, Duke ELLINGTON, and Cab CALLOWAY. Harold, who had a good soprano voice, did an impression of Cab Calloway that the club broadcast each night on a coast-to-coast radio show. Throughout the 1930s the Cotton Club was their "home." The Nicholas Brothers were known as "the Show Stoppers" because they literally stopped the show each night as the closing act. Perhaps because Fayard and Harold were children, they were the only African-American performers permitted to mingle with the exclusively white patrons of the club. The elegant rhythms of the young stars quickly propelled them to fame.

Fayard and Harold frequently left their regular act at the Cotton Club to tour with international shows such as Lew Leslie's *Blackbirds of 1936,* which had a successful run in London, or to perform in films. Their first film, *Pie, Pie Blackbirds* (1932), featured them in an appearance with Eubie BLAKE and his orchestra. During their career they appeared in more than fifty films including *Kid Millions* (1934), *Big Broadcast of 1936,* *Calling All Stars* (1937), *Down Argentine Way* (1940), *Tin Pan Alley* (1940), *Great American Broadcast* (1941), *Sun Valley Serenade* (1941), and *The Pirate* (1948). The brothers were among the select few who dubbed their own taps for film.

The Nicholas Brothers: Fayard (left) and Harold. (Photographs and Prints Division, Schomburg Center for Research in Black Culture, The New York Public Library, Astor, Lenox and Tilden Foundations)

From the time they were small both Fayard and Harold danced with agility, grace, and sophistication. Even when they displayed their astonishing acrobatic ability, they managed to do so with elegance. They choreographed many of their own dance routines and improvised on stage with assurance and flair. The full use of their limber bodies and the exceptional use of their hands distinguished their dancing. The Nicholas Brothers perfected the innovative technique of doing *full* splits (as opposed to jazz or half splits), and they popularized acrobatic moves such as alternately jumping over each other's heads in splits while descending a staircase, as they did in the finale of *Stormy Weather* (1943). Their "classic" tap style flawlessly blended ballet, eccentric dancing, flash, and acrobatics.

When they worked with George Balanchine on the Broadway show *Babes in Arms* (1937), the great choreographer incorporated the brothers' own moves into their routine. In the show, Harold executed a sliding split through the legs of eight lined-up chorus girls while Fayard did a flying leap over them. In 1940 they worked with choreographer Nick Castle to develop a stunt that involved climbing up a wall, doing a back flip, landing in a split and returning to their feet—all on the beat.

During their nearly five decades in show business, Fayard and Harold toured the world from Africa to Europe. In the 1960s they appeared as guests on numerous TV shows and in 1965 performed as part of Bob Hope's Christmas special for the troops in Vietnam. In the 1970s, Fayard won a Tony Award for his choreography in the Broadway hit *Black and Blue,* and in 1980 both he and Harold received an award as part of a celebration honoring fifty years of men in dance. Their Lifetime Achievement Award, presented at the Kennedy Center in 1991, crowned the brothers' career as one of the best and most popular tap acts of the twentieth century.

BIBLIOGRAPHY

Frank, Rusty. *Tap: The Greatest Tap Dance Stars and Their Stories.* New York, 1990.

Stearns, Marshall, and Jean Stearns. *Jazz Dance: The Story of American Vernacular Dance.* New York, 1964.

— JENNIFER DEVERE BRODY

NORTON, ELEANOR HOLMES

Eleanor Holmes Norton (June 13, 1937–), civil rights leader. Born in Washington, D.C., Eleanor Holmes graduated from Antioch College in 1960, received an M.A. in American history from Yale University in 1963, and a law degree from Yale in 1965. Norton was a leader of the STUDENT NON-VIOLENT COORDINATING COMMITTEE (SNCC), and was a participant in the Mississippi Freedom Democratic Party. In 1965, Holmes joined the American Civil Liberties Union (ACLU), where she served as a civil rights lawyer for five years. In 1967, she married Edward Norton, also a lawyer. The couple, who were separated in 1992, had two children. In 1968, Eleanor Holmes Norton gained attention for her active defense of freedom of speech when she represented segregationist presidential candidate George Wallace in his struggle to obtain permission from the City of New York for a rally at Shea Stadium. Keenly interested in fighting both race and gender discrimination, Norton published an article on black women in the well-known anthology *Sisterhood Is Powerful* (1970). "If women were suddenly to achieve equality with men tomorrow," she wrote, "black women would continue to carry the entire array of utterly oppressive handicaps associated with race. . . . Yet black women cannot—must not—avoid the truth about their special subservience. They are women with all that that implies."

In 1970, Norton was appointed chair of the New York City Commission on Human Rights by Mayor John Lindsay. Her achievement in detailing and correcting discriminatory practices led to a position as co-host of a weekly local television program on civil rights. In 1973, Norton helped organize a National Conference of Black Feminists, and in 1975 she cowrote *Sex Discrimination and the Law: Cases and Remedies,* a law textbook dealing with legal remedies to gender inequality.

In 1977, President Jimmy Carter appointed Norton as chair of the Equal Employment Opportunity Commission, a post she held until 1981. Charged with investigating complaints of discrimination, Norton was a visible and respected force within the Administration. In 1982, she accepted a post as professor of labor law at Georgetown University. Throughout the 1980s, she was also a regular media commentator on civil rights and affirmative action issues.

In 1990, Norton announced her candidacy for the position of District of Columbia delegate to the U.S. House of Representatives. Despite the revelation during the campaign that she owed back taxes, she was elected to Congress. She soon won praise even from her opponents for her involvement in community affairs as well as for her work in assuring Washington's fiscal viability and cutting the District's budget. She also lobbied in Congress for District statehood. In 1992, the same year Norton won reelection, she won attention for her offer to escort women seeking abortion information at clinics past antiabortion picketers, and later for her denunciation of the verdict in the Rodney King trial, which she contended was as shameful as the actual beating of King. Since the House vote in 1993 to give delegates limited voting privileges on the floor, Norton has become the first District representative to vote in Congress. In recognition of her prestige, President Bill Clinton agreed that as chair of the District of Columbia Subcommittee on Judiciary and Education, Norton would be responsible for the nomination of candidates for local U.S. Attorney and federal judgeships, the first elected District of Columbia official to be privileged.

BIBLIOGRAPHY

Hardy, Gayle S. *American Women Civil Rights Activists: Biographies of 68 Leaders, 1825–1992.* Jefferson, N.C., 1993.

Haywood, Richette, "Eleanor Holmes Norton takes D.C. Seat." *Ebony* 46 (January 1991): 105–106.

— EVAN A. SHORE AND GREG ROBINSON

NURSING

The first three American nurse-training schools were established in 1873: Massachusetts General Hospital in Boston, Bellevue Hospital in New York, and the New Haven Hospital in Connecticut. These early schools operated within hospitals, but in keeping with the "Nightingale Tradition" they enjoyed a degree of faculty autonomy and a separate funding apparatus, and they employed women as nurse supervisors. Within a very short period, however, this relatively autonomous structure was eclipsed, as hospitals came to dominate nursing education. Two factors—insufficient capital and endowment, and the demand for more science-based instruction—enabled hospital administrators quickly to gain hegemony in nursing education. Out of a desire to raise the status of the "trained nurse" and to gain control over instruction, white nurse leaders organized what would be renamed, in 1911, the American Nurses Association (ANA). Its official organ, the *American Journal of Nursing,* commenced publication in 1901.

In August 1879, Mary Eliza Mahoney became the first black graduate nurse when she received her diploma from the New England Hospital for Women and Children, in Boston. She was an exception to the rule of racial exclusion practiced by the vast majority of hospital nurse-training schools in the North and by all such institutions in the South. The pattern of widespread denial of admission to black women left African-American communities with few alternative means of training. Blacks and white philanthropists accordingly created a separate parallel network of nurse-training schools and hospitals. In 1886, John D. Rockefeller contributed the funds for the establishment of a school of nursing at the Atlanta Baptist Seminary (now Spelman College), a school for black women. This institution bears the distinction of being the country's first school of nursing established within an academic framework.

During the 1890s, the establishment of a nationwide network of black hospitals and nursing schools gained momentum as black physicians, educators, community leaders, and women's clubs grew alarmed at the high rates of black morbidity and mortality. In 1891, Daniel Hale Williams, the first surgeon to perform an open-heart suture, founded Provident Hospital and Nurse Training School in Chicago. Three years later, he was also instrumental in creating the Freedmen's Hospital and Nurse Training School in Washington, D.C. Under the aegis of Booker T. WASHINGTON, the Tuskegee Institute School of Nurse Training in Tuskegee, Ala., came into existence in 1892. In the same year, the Hampton Nurse Training School and Dixie Hospital in Hampton, Va., began accepting students. In October 1896, the black women of the Phillis Wheatley Club founded the only black hospital and nurse-training school in New Orleans. The Phillis Wheatley Sanitarium and Training School for Nurses, like its sister institutions, began rather inauspiciously, in a private residence consisting of seven beds and five patients. This institution was later renamed the Flint Goodridge Hospital and Nurse Training School and eventually incorporated into Dillard University. On October 4, 1897, Alonzo Clifton McClennan, an 1880 graduate of the Howard University Medical School, founded the Hospital and Nursing Training School in Charleston, S.C. Anna Decosta Banks, one of the first graduates of the Dixie Hospital School of Nursing, became the first head nurse of that black institution. By 1920, there were approximately two hundred black hospitals and thirty-six black nurse-training schools.

During the 1890s, black physicians, educators, community leaders, and women's clubs grew alarmed at the high rates of black morbidity and mortality.

African Americans established these institutions in order to provide black patients with access to health care and to provide black women with opportunities to enter the nursing profession. Daniel Hale Williams declared in a 1900 address before the Phillis Wheatley Club of Nashville, "In view of this cruel ostracism, affecting so vitally the race, our duty seems plain. Institute hospitals and training schools. Let us no longer sit idly and inanely deploring existing conditions."

These early black nursing schools were, for the most part, as deficient in quality and standards as were many of their white counterparts. In keeping with prevailing practices, student nurses were exploited as an unpaid labor force. In every institution they performed all the domestic and maintenance drudgery, attended the patients, and dispensed medicine. It was not inconsequential that one of the early Tuskegee catalogs noted that the major admission requirement for the nursing program consisted of a strong physique and stamina to endure hardship. In spite of the attendant difficulties and the mediocre instruction, hundreds of black women graduated from these segregated hospital nursing programs and went on to render invaluable service to black patients.

The process of becoming a nursing professional involved more than earning a diploma; as important for advancement was the acquisition of specialized training or graduate education. Black women nurses in this period encountered virtually insurmountable obstacles in their quest for more training. Indeed, for black graduate nurses, challenging career opportunities and employment in hospitals, visiting-nurses' associations, and municipal departments of health proved to be as difficult to obtain as sympathetic work environments that held out possibilities for promotion to supervisory and administrative positions. The vast majority of black graduate nurses, like their untrained predecessors, worked in private duty, usually for white families, for whom they frequently were expected to perform domestic household chores in addition to providing nursing care—all for lower wages than were paid to white nurses. Professional opportunities for black graduate nurses were often bleaker in the South than in the North. For many black women graduate nurses, however, the most galling assault to professional esteem was the denial of membership in the ANA. Only the members of the alumnae association of the Freedmen's Hospital in Washington, D.C., who had obtained ANA membership prior to 1911 escaped this most visible manifestation of professional ostracism.

Determined to repudiate the ANA's exclusionary practices, Martha Franklin, a black graduate of the Women's Hospital in Philadelphia, launched a separate black nursing organization. Franklin joined forces with Adah Belle Thoms, president of the Lincoln Hospital Nursing Alumnae Association, in August 1908, to convene a meeting of fifty-two nurses at St. Mark's Episcopal Church in New York City. Out of this meeting emerged the National Association of Colored Graduate Nurses (NACGN). In 1912, the NACGN's members numbered 125; by 1920, it boasted a membership of 500. In 1928, in order to facilitate communication and to foster a greater sense of professional involvement among black nurses, NACGN president Carrie E. Bullock founded and edited the organization's official organ, the *National News Bulletin.* She encouraged black nurses to pursue postgraduate education by persuading the Julius Rosenwald Fund to establish for them a special Rosenwald fellowship program.

From the outset, the NACGN leadership made the integration of their profession a top priority. However, it would take twenty years, the emergence of a cadre of strong and resourceful leaders, and the crisis of World War II for black nurses to gain entrée into the ANA and to win full acceptance into the profession. In the mid-1930s, the NACGN received a much-needed boost from the general education board of the Rockefeller Foundation and from the Rosenwald Fund. These timely grants enabled the NACGN to employ Mabel K. Staupers and to move into permanent headquarters at Rockefeller Center, where all the major national nursing organizations had offices. Eventually, Staupers and then-NACGN president Estelle Massey Riddle succeeded in winning recognition and acceptance for black nurses. Central to this victory was Staupers's successfully orchestrated campaign to eliminate quotas established by the Armed Forces Nurse Corps during World War II.

Initially, the War Department had established a quota for African Americans of 56 nurses, 120 doctors, and 44 dentists to tend the wards designated for black troops. In 1943, after considerable agitation, Staupers received notice that the navy, heretofore the most hostile branch of the services, had decided to place the induction of black nurses under consideration. The army took more affirmative action and raised its quota of black nurses from 56 to 160. In an effort to attract public attention to the unfairness of quotas, Staupers met with First Lady Eleanor Roosevelt in November 1944, at which time she described in detail the discrimination and humiliation black nurses suffered in the armed forces.

When in January 1945 Surgeon General Norman T. Kirk announced the possibility of a draft to remedy a nursing shortage within the armed forces, Staupers immediately challenged him, "If nurses are needed so desperately, why isn't the army using colored nurses?" Her question exposed the hypocrisy of the draft call. Afterward she encouraged nursing groups, black and white, to write letters and send telegrams protesting the discrimination against black nurses in the army and navy nurse corps. This ground swell of public support for the removal of quotas that so severely restricted the enrollment of capable and willing black women proved effective.

Buried beneath an avalanche of telegrams and seared by the heat of an inflamed public, Kirk, Navy Rear Adm. W. J. C. Agnew, and the War Department declared an end to quotas and exclusion. On January 20, 1945, Kirk stated that nurses would be accepted into the Army Nurse Corps without regard to race; five days later, Agnew announced that the Navy Nurse Corps was now open to black women. Within a few weeks, Phillis Daley became the first black woman to break the color barrier and receive induction into the navy corps. The end of discriminatory practices by a key American in-

P

PAIGE, LEROY ROBERT "SATCHEL"

Leroy Robert "Satchel" Paige (July 7, 1906–June 8, 1982). By far the best known of those who played baseball in the relative obscurity of the Negro Leagues, pitcher and coach Satchel Paige became a legendary figure from Canada to the Caribbean basin. Born in a shotgun house (a railroad flat) in Mobile, Ala., to John Paige, a gardener, and Lulu Paige, a washerwoman, he combined athletic prowess and exceptional durability with a flair for showmanship. In 1971, the Baseball Hall of Fame made Paige—Negro League ball incarnate—its first-ever selection from the (by then defunct) institution.

Paige gained his nickname as a boy by carrying satchels from the Mobile train station. Sent to the Mount Meigs, Ala., reform school at age twelve for stealing a few toy rings from a store, he developed as a pitcher during his five years there. After joining the semipro Mobile Tigers in 1924, he pitched for a number of Negro League, white independent, and Caribbean teams until he joined the Cleveland Indians as a forty-two-year-old rookie in 1948. The first African-American pitcher in the American League, Paige achieved a 6–1 record that helped the Indians to the league pennant. His first three starts drew over 200,000 fans.

But it was in the Negro Leagues and Caribbean winter ball that Paige attained his status as independent baseball's premier attraction. During the 1920s and 1930s, he starred for the Birmingham Black Barons and the Pittsburgh Crawfords, where he teamed up with catcher Josh GIBSON to form what was possibly baseball's greatest all-time battery. Between 1939 and 1947, Paige anchored the strong Kansas Monarchs staff, winning three of the Monarchs' four victories over the Homestead Grays in the 1942 Negro League World Series. Developing a reputation as a contract jumper, he led Ciudad Trujillo to the 1937 summer championship of the Dominican Republic and later pitched in Mexico, Cuba, and Venezuela.

Playing before an estimated 10 million fans in the United States, Canada, and the Caribbean, the "have arm—will pitch" Paige, according to his own estimates, threw 55 no-hitters and won over 2,000 of the 2,500 games in which he pitched.

The 6′3½″, 180-pound Paige dazzled fans with his overpowering fastball (called the "bee ball"—you could hear it buzz, but you couldn't see it), his hesitation pitch, and unerring control. Stories of him intentionally walking the bases full of barnstorming white all-stars, telling his fielders to sit down, and then striking out the side became part of a shared black mythology. "I just could pitch!" he said in 1981. "The Master just gave me an arm. . . . You couldn't hardly beat me. . . . I wouldn't get tired 'cause I practiced every day. I had the suit on every day, pretty near 365 days out of the year."

Probably the most widely seen player ever (in person), Paige was a regular at the East-West Classic (the Negro League all-star game), and also appeared on the 1952 American League all-star squad. His 28 wins and 31 losses, 476 innings pitched, 3.29 earned run average in the majors represented only the penultimate chapter of a professional pitching career that spanned five decades.

Paige ended his working life as he began it, on the bus of a barnstorming black club, appearing for the Indianapolis Clowns in 1967. In 1971, after the Hall of Fame belatedly began to induct Negro Leaguers, he led the way. As his Pittsburgh Crawfords teammate Jimmie Crutchfield put it, when Paige appeared on the field "it was like the sun coming out from behind a cloud."

BIBLIOGRAPHY

Holway, John B. *Josh and Satch: A Dual Biography of Josh Gibson and Satchel Paige.* Westport, Conn., 1991.

Ruck, Rob. *Sandlot Seasons: Sport in Black Pittsburgh.* Champaign-Urbana, Ill., 1987.

– ROB RUCK

PAINTING AND SCULPTURE

From the time of their first arrival in the New World, Africans were involved in a wide range of artistic endeavors. Much of the early art of African Americans was folk art and was a part of the routines of life and work. Africans were involved in a wide range of craft activities, including the construction of houses, the casting of iron fences, the fashioning of baskets and pottery, and the making of quilts. This art often displayed a distinctive African sensibility, and partook of traditional African practices such as the decoration of the gravesites.

African-American participation in European styles of fine artwork was slower to develop. This was both because of the unfamiliarity of Africans with the conventions of European art, and the deliberate exclusion of blacks from access to the training and clients needed for successful careers as artists. Despite these handicaps, the achievements of African Americans in painting and sculpture are rich and distinguished. Their history comprises determined individuals who, in addition to the usual struggles of artists to make a livelihood, had to overcome the additional burdens of discrimination (with black women having gender bias to contend with as well), as well as racist assumptions about the artistic abilities of persons of African descent.

It is likely that persons of African descent first created European artworks at the behest of their masters and white patrons, who wished them to make copies of works in fashionable styles. This process began surprisingly early. By 1724 the Boston print shop of Thomas Fleet had two slave artisans, Pompey and Cesar Fleet, who made woodcuts to accompany broadside ballads and small books. Most of the black artisans in eighteenth-century America were anonymous. Primarily located in cities, both free blacks and slaves worked as silversmiths, goldsmiths, watchmakers, and makers of powderhorns, among other crafts. References to them are scarce and primarily glimpsed in newspaper advertisements for their services or in notices for runaway slaves.

Those painters whose names were recorded include Neptune Thurston, an eighteenth-century Rhode Island slave whose artistic prowess, according to a nineteenth-century tradition, was an early inspiration for the renowned artist Gilbert Stuart. Scipio Moorhead, a Boston slave, almost certainly painted a portrait of Phillis WHEATLEY which served as the basis for the frontispiece to the 1773 London edition of her works. Wheatley returned the favor in her poem "To S. M. a Young African Painter, on Seeing his Works," the first recorded critical evaluation of an African-American artist:

To show the lab'ring bosom's deep intent,
And thought in living characters to paint,
When first thy pencil did those beauties give,
And breathing figures learnt from thee to live,
How did those prospects give my soul delight,
A new creation rushing on my sight?

Nineteenth-Century Art

Most of the work of nineteenth-century African-American artists is imitative of European and American conventions of technique and appropriate subject matter. The lack of a self-conscious "black aesthetic" in nineteenth-century African-American art has bothered some later critics such as Alain LOCKE, who view this period as one of relatively little importance. But this perspective slights the achievements of these artists and overlooks the efforts they made and the indignities they withstood to be accepted by their peers.

Many of these early black artists were limners—humble, often informally trained, and itinerant portrait painters. One of the first was Joshua JOHNSON or Johnston of Baltimore. His origins, parentage, and almost all other pertinent information about his life are unknown; indeed, there is considerable debate on whether Joshua Johnson was of African descent. While there were black painters in Baltimore in the early nineteenth century, the racial identity of the considerable body of work identified as that of Joshua Johnson is uncertain.

In a December 19, 1798, advertisement in the *Baltimore Intelligencer,* Joshua Johnson posted an announcement wherein he described himself as a "self-taught genius" who had overcome "many insuperable obstacles" in his efforts to become an artist. This perhaps is a reference to his African-American background; but unfortunately for historians, the advertisement is silent on the race of the artist.

Many of these early black artists were limners—humble, often informally trained, and itinerant portrait painters.

Johnson's style and some documentary evidence indicate that he came under the influence of the prominent painters Charles Wilson Peale and his nephew Charles Polk Peale. Johnson's paintings of Maryland's elite were distinguished by an individual sense of character and fine attention to detail. Critics have described Johnson as the "brass tack artist" because of his repetitive use of the same sofa, studded with brass upholstery tacks, in many of the depictions of his subjects. Johnson painted few black subjects, though he has been tentatively identified as the painter of the matched portraits of Daniel Coker and Abner Coker, two early ministers of the AFRICAN METHODIST EPISCOPAL (AME) CHURCH.

Painter, lithographer, and daguerreotypist Jules Lion was born in France and later settled in New Orleans. He was listed as a painter and lithographer in the 1838 city directory. An advertisement lists Lion as a daguerreotypist in 1840 and credits him with the introduction of this medium to New Orleans. Although there are no extant examples of his painting, he is known to have exhibited successfully at the Exposition of Paris in 1833, cofounded an art school in New Orleans in 1841, and taught drawing at the College of Louisiana. Lion typifies many early African-American artists who worked in diverse genres and media. He remained active in the New Orleans area, traveling back to France periodically until his death in 1866.

Robert Scott DUNCANSON was hailed at the height of his career as the "best landscape painter in the West" by eastern critics. Born in Seneca County in upstate New York, Duncanson was raised in Monroe, Mich., located at the western tip of Lake Erie, and by the early 1840s had moved to Cincinnati. His landscapes such as *Blue Hole, Little Moon River* (1851) and *The Land of the Lotus Eaters* (c. 1861) are excellent examples of the luminous Hudson River School landscape style.

His commissions included photographs, portraits, still lifes, and landscapes, and in the Belmont House in Cincinnati (now the Taft Museum) he executed the first murals by a black artist. In the early 1850s he probably collaborated with the African-American daguerreotypist James Presley Ball in an enormous rolling panorama (over half a mile of canvas) that depicted in its unfolding the history of African Americans in the United States.

Duncanson was fairly light-skinned and this perhaps eased his access to white artistic circles, though the snubs he did receive, such as his failure to be elected to the National Academy of Design in New York, left him greatly disturbed. His physical and mental health deteriorated toward the end of his life. He made a distinctive contribution to the tradition of American landscape painting by becoming the first African-American artist to appropriate the landscape as a vehicle to express his own cultural heritage and identity.

Boston, a major center for black cultural life in the nineteenth century, was the home of four painters of significance: William Simpson, Nelson Primus, Edward BANNISTER, and Edmonia Lewis. William Simpson was listed in the Boston directories of 1860 and 1866. Critics of the period recall his strong talents as a portrait-painter and his skill as a draftsman of exceptional ability. William Wells Brown recalled that Simpson began as a youth "drawing instead of following his class work," later studying with Matthew Wilson in 1854. Very little is known about Simpson's career, and few works are extant. Nelson Primus, born in Hartford, Conn., moved to Boston in 1864. He started out as a carriage painter in about 1858, and then professionally began a career as a portrait painter. In 1859 he won a medal for drawing at the State Agricultural Society Fair. While he received high praise in Boston, his career was only partially successful in the East, and he later moved to San Francisco, where he continued to paint.

Edward Mitchell Bannister was a first-rate landscape painter and portraitist in late nineteenth-century New England. Born in New Brunswick, Canada, to a father from Barbados and a local woman, he grew up with an early appreciation of the arts, encouraged by his mother. In 1850 he moved to Boston, where he worked as a hairdresser. As an artist he was largely self-taught, and by 1860 he had acquired a considerable local reputation. During the CIVIL WAR Bannister was a leader in the effort to obtain equal pay for black soldiers, and he painted a portrait, not extant, of Colonel Robert Gould Shaw, commander of the 54th Massachusetts Regiment.

Bannister's painting *Under the Oaks* (now lost) won a first place at the Centennial Exposition in Philadelphia in 1876. African-American newspapers and periodicals such as the *A.M.E. Church Review* proudly took note of Bannister's accomplishment. His work, influenced by the English landscape artist John Constable and the French Barbizon School, often featured seascapes and carefully textured studies of clouds and trees. In 1870 Bannister moved to Providence, R.I., where, unusually for a black professional of his era, he was fully accepted by his white peers, and was a cofounder of the socially prestigious Providence Art Club. At his death in 1901 the Providence Art Club hosted a memorial exhibition of more than one hundred of his works, a testament to his contribution to the American landscape tradition and to the high admiration of his fellow artists, patrons, and admirers.

The most prominent black sculptor of the nineteenth century was the remarkable Edmonia Lewis. Many of the specifics of her biography remain unclear. Lewis was born in upstate New York to an African-American father and a mother of mixed Chippewa and African-American descent. Orphaned at an early age, "Wildfire" (her Indian name) was raised in Canada West (now Ontario) among the Chippewa. She attended Oberlin College, but found herself embroiled in unseemly and unfounded accusations of poisoning two of her classmates, and was obliged to leave in 1863, and moved to Boston. The traumatic impact of the charges, which almost certainly had a racial basis, left Lewis distrustful of outsiders, and fostered an already strong sense of somewhat stubborn independence and self-sufficiency.

The city directory of Boston lists Lewis as a sculptor for the years of 1864 and 1865. Boston's vital black and abolitionist community provided Lewis with numerous opportunities, and she created portrait busts of many of the leading abolitionist figures. In 1866, with the money earned from sales of a plaster bust of Colonel Robert Gould Shaw, she moved to Rome. She befriended the large community of American artists in Rome and started carving in marble. *Forever Free* (1867–1868), probably her best-known work, is a commemoration of the Emancipation Proclamation. Although her work was deeply shaped by neoclassicism, she was influenced as well in both subject matter and style by her African-American and Indian backgrounds. After the 1880s she became less active and gradually cut off contacts with Americans. Lewis became a fervent Roman Catholic, and she executed some religious sculpture. Little is known about the last thirty years of her life, but it is believed that she was living in Rome as late as 1909.

Henry Ossawa TANNER was the leading African-American painter of the late nineteenth and early twentieth centuries. Born in Pittsburgh, Pa., he was encouraged in his artistic ambitions at an early age by a supportive and relatively comfortable family—his father was an AME bishop—and the intellectual community of Philadelphia. He was one of the first black artists to study at the Pennsylvania Academy of Fine Arts, studying with Thomas Eakins in 1880 and 1881, but withdrew after a racial incident. In 1891 he sailed for Europe, traveling to Italy and settling in Paris, where he experienced a freedom unknown in the United States. He would remain in Paris for the rest of his life, making brief trips home. While in France he executed two realistic genre paintings, *The Banjo Lesson* (1898) and *The Thankful Poor* (1893–1894), displaying the influence of Eakins; these painting represent Tanner's most realistic depictions of contemporary African-American life. For the remainder of his career he concentrated on visionary religious paintings in muted hues, such as *Daniel in the Lion's Den* (1895) and *The Raising of Lazarus* (1896), a prizewinner at the Paris Salon of 1897. Tanner's example and personal encouragement would be an inspiration for several generations of African-American artists. Two painters who became pupils of Tanner were William Harper and William Edouard Scott. Harper was a landscapist in the tradition of the Barbizon painters, and had admirable technical skill. Scott's landscapes displayed the influence of Turner's use of light. Scott later became known for his paintings of Haitian peasants.

Henry Ossawa Tanner was the leading African-American painter of the late nineteenth and early twentieth centuries.

The two leading black sculptors at the end of the century were Meta Vaux Warrick FULLER and May Howard Jackson. Meta Vaux Warwick, who married the pioneer African-American neurologist Solomon Carter Fuller, was born in Philadelphia and at an early age became curious about art through her older sister, an art student. Throughout her early education, her interest in art grew and her talent blossomed. She won a scholarship to the Pennsylvania School of Industrial Art and won a prize for *Process of the Arts and Crafts* (1897), a massive bas-relief composition of thirty-seven figures. After graduation she continued her studies in 1899, attending lectures at the Colarossi Academy in Paris and later working with Auguste Rodin. She was among the earliest American artists to be influenced by African sculpture and folklore in such works as *Spirit of Emancipation* (c. 1918), *Ethiopia Awakening* (1914/1921), and *The Talking Skull* (1937). Her early works had a power and fierceness that many critics found frightening. After her marriage and a devastating fire in 1910 that destroyed much of her early work, she stopped sculpting for a period of years and created stage designs for theater groups in the community. When she resumed her career her work was more technically and emotionally mature, largely consisting of themes centered on African-American culture, history, and leadership.

May Howard Jackson was educated at J. Liberty Todd's Art School in Philadelphia and won a scholarship to the Pennsylvania Academy of Fine Arts in that city. Jackson was primarily a sculptor of portrait busts and portrait groups such as *Mother and Child* (1929) and *Head of a Negro Child* (1929). In many of her works she went beyond her classical training to depict the wide range and uniqueness of African-American physiognomy. Jackson had a studio in Washington, D.C., and exhibited professionally at the National Academy of Design and the Cocoran Gallery of Art. She won a prize from the Harmon Foundation in 1928. However, the general indifference of the public, despite many critical plaudits from writers including Alain Locke and W. E. B. DU BOIS, filled her life with frustration and anger.

Charles Ethan Porter was a painter of still lifes and landscapes. Born in Connecticut, he attended the National Academy of Design and later traveled to Paris to study, evidently through the generosity of Mark Twain. Porter established a studio in Rockville, Conn., in 1884. He specialized in still lifes with elaborate floral arrangements and fruit displays, painting primarily for local white patrons. He exhibited intermittently at the National Academy of Design of New York and the American Society of Painters in Watercolor. In 1910 he became a charter member of the Connecticut Academy of Fine Arts, his only known professional association.

Laura Wheeling Waring, like Charles Ethan Porter, was a native of Connecticut. Born in Hartford, she studied at the Pennsylvania Academy of Fine Arts and at the Académie de la Grande Chaumière in Paris. In

Corter, Gordon PARKS, Archibald Motley, and Charles Sebree.

White established the medium of drawing in charcoal, ink, pencil, and collage as a means to depict semiabstract figures with intense drama. These idealized portraits and studies often had historical subject as their focus. White continued using this style throughout his life, though he became less iconographic and more individualized in his later years. He was active in the WPA as well as the SSCAC.

Burroughs was educated at the Art Institute of Chicago, was a versatile artist in painting, printmaking, and sculpture, and was a significant figure in Chicago area arts education. Cortor was primarily drawn to depictions of African-American women, reflecting their alienation from society and their introspection in positional studies using bedrooms and mirrors as stages. Sebree was a sensitive portraitist.

Another Chicago artist was Ellis Wilson. A Kentucky native, Wilson came to study at the Art Institute of Chicago. He was active in the Harmon Foundation exhibitions, the Savage Studio, and the Federal Arts Project. His mature style is based on strong color, flat figures in outline that document the black working class community.

Allan Rohan Crite was born in Plainfield, N.J., and moved to Boston to study art. He was one of the few African-American artists to be hired for the WPA Federal Arts Project in Boston. Many of Crite's early subjects were paintings of street scenes and portraits. The balance of his career was spent developing complex studies of religious and spiritual themes.

One of the most active centers for African-American art in the 1930s and 1940s was Karamu Playhouse, founded in Cleveland in 1915. Karamu Playhouse was an interracial settlement house designed to address the cultural needs of the urban poor. By the time of the Great Depression it was recognized for its theater group. It was not until funding came from the WPA that it established a strong visual arts program. Hughie Lee-Smith studied at the Cleveland Institute of Arts and became part of the Ohio Federal Arts Project. His painted imagery is figurative and realistic, with metaphysical references to surreal or romanticized landscapes. Lee-Smith was active in numerous portrait commissions and was greatly respected for his technical skill in watercolor, prints, and drawing. A significant part of his career was spent teaching at the Arts Students League in New York in addition to painting and exhibiting widely.

Elton Fax, born in Baltimore, moved to New York and worked with Augusta Savage and the Harlem Community Art Center. Later he became active in the Maryland Federal Arts Project. He was a versatile painter, printmaker, illustrator, and educator, and was the author of several books on the lives of black artists. Fax played an important role in the development of regional art programs from Baltimore to New York.

Folk Artists

One of the most important forms of African-American artistic expression in the twentieth century has been by "folk" artists. This is a difficult term to define, but generally refers to artists who have not had the benefit of formal academic training and whose work often appears "naive" in its artistic conventions, as in the handling of perspective and shadowing. Many folk artists took up art as an avocation later in their lives, after their retirement, a religious call, or a critical change in lifestyle or career.

Clementine Hunter was born on Hidden Hill Plantation in Louisiana and worked as a sharecropper. Late in life, Hunter began to paint at the encouragement of one of her guests. She had a prolific career in exhibiting and painting canvases that recalled, with humble reverence, her memories of life in Louisiana.

Horace PIPPIN, born in West Chester, Pa., began to paint later in life, despite an injury to his painting arm during World War I. He started painting by using a hot iron poker to burn the image on a piece of wood. Pippin then slowly painted in the details with numerous layers of oil paint. Many of his intensely detailed paintings relived his haunted memories of the war. His work also includes visions of childhood experiences (including his version of southern black rural life, a reality he never experienced), landscapes, interiors, and his visions of a utopian and peaceful world. During his last years, Pippin's subtle and profoundly moving art achieved great acclaim. He was an ordinary man with an extraordinary sensibility for observing the world around him.

Minnie Evans, born in Pender County, N.C., created compositions inspired by visions and dreams after a voice on Good Friday in 1935 directed her to "draw or die." Her imagery consisted of a fusion of bright colors with figurative and abstract human and plant forms. She worked in watercolor, crayon, graphite, oil, acrylic ink, collage, enamel, and tempera. Sister Gertrude Morgan, who lived most of her life in New Orleans, was adept at a wide range of other forms of expression. She was not only a gifted painted but a singer and preacher as well. After she was "called" to a missionary vocation, she used her artistic abilities to spread the word of God. Believing herself to be the bride of Jesus Christ, her paintings had large areas of white—a color of holiness—which were filled with painted images of redemption and revelation.

There have also been a number of important African-American folk sculptors. William Edmondson, born in Davidson County, Tenn., near Nashville, spent his working career as a farmhand. Upon retirement he began to carve, in part because of a command from God. He collected old limestone curbstone, and made grave-markers for people in the community who had minimal funds to lay a headstone. As his skill increased, he produced images with great spirituality, humanity, and power. Religious figures, birds, ordinary and heroic individuals, and what he called "critters and varmits (sic)" were his favorite subjects. In 1937 he became the first African-American artist to be given a one-person show by the Museum of Modern Art. Elijah Pierce was a barber, preacher, and wood carver. He was born in Baldwyn, Miss., and lived most of his life in Columbus, Ohio. Morality, ethics, and the stories of the Bible inspired many of the wooden panels he carved and painted. He painted his carvings in bright colors, energizing the message of his medium and visualizing the message of his pictorial sermons.

Perhaps the most remarkable of African-American folk sculptors was James Hampton, who migrated from Elloree, S.C., to Washington, D.C., where he worked as a janitor. A loner, he created *The Throne of the Third Heaven of the Nations' Millennium General Assembly* (c. 1950–1964), which was not known until it was found in a garage long after his death. It consists of more than 185 objects, mostly old furniture, lightbulbs, and other household objects, covered with aluminum, silver, and gold foil and ornately decorated. The heavy use of metallic paper is a symbolic reference to heavenly or celestial light. The work evokes a heavenly and spiritual place, and though Hampton drew on biblical sources, notably the book of Revelations in creating his masterpiece, the precise program is unclear.

Selma Burke working in her studio with a model. (Photographs and Prints Division, Schomburg Center for Research in Black Culture, The New York Public Library, Astor, Lenox and Tilden Foundations)

Postwar Modernism

Although one cannot define a single African-American aesthetic during the 1930s, the dominant perspective was social realism. One reason for this was the desire of most African-American artists to convey political themes in a realistic form that was programmatically consistent with the aesthetic that was typical for most WPA projects. Although figurative painting continued to predominate in the postwar period, African-American artistic expression became more diverse, and responded to the proliferation of modernist styles.

The African-American artist to be affected most directly by abstract expressionism was Norman Lewis. A native New Yorker, Lewis trained with a variety of artists, including Augusta Savage. In the 1930s he painted a number of powerful paintings in the social realist mode, demonstrating his strong sympathies for the unemployed and homeless. In the later 1930s and 1940s he experimented with the cubist simplification of form, and visually tried to convey the innovations of bebop jazz, which led to an abstract style by the late 1940s. Some critics complained that he was turning his back on depictions of African Americans, though his work often continued to comment on the CIVIL RIGHTS MOVEMENT and other important social issues. Although Lewis was among the earliest American artists to take up the cause of pure abstraction, until recently his name had been conspicuously left out of the canon of abstract expressionist innovators.

In the postwar period, African-American artistic expression became more diverse, and responded to the proliferation of modernist styles.

Jacob Lawrence was a painter and printmaker who began his career in the mid-1930s, quickly established himself as an important modernist, and developed a style based on expressive flat forms and direct color. He was greatly influenced by Augusta Savage, Charles Alston, and Henry Bouveran when he worked at the Harlem Community Art Center. His primary subject matter was African-American life and history told in a narrative format, in such works as the sixty panels of the . . . *The Migration Series* (1940–1941), a visual history of the Great Migration. Other important works include the *Toussaint Loverture* (1938) series, consisting of forty paintings; the thirty works in the *Harlem* series (1942–1943); and other connected thematic treatments of John Brown, Frederick DOUGLASS, African-American craftsmen, and a general treatment of the theme of freedom in American history. Jacob Lawrence was the first modernist painter of critical significance to emerge from the New Negro movement.

Beauford Delaney came to New York in the 1920s from Knoxville, Tenn. A sensitive portraitist, in the 1930s he experimented with brightly colored abstractions, and his subsequent portraits are highly expressionistic in their presentation. After World War II he lived in Paris. His brother Joseph Delaney was a figurative painter who was greatly influenced by the social realist painters and sought to create expressive, atmospheric compositions that reflected urban stresses in the life of large urban areas such as New York. Thomas Sills was a laborer turned painter who moved to New York City from North Carolina. He painted "brushless" canvases with abstracted forms and colors, and was active artistically from the 1950s through the early 1970s.

One of the most important African-American abstractionists was Alma Thomas, who studied at Howard University in the 1920s before beginning a long career of teaching in the Washington, D.C., public school system. In 1943 she cofounded the first integrated gallery in Washington, D.C., the Barnett-Aden gallery. Her own work was fairly conventional until the early 1950s, when she began to produce the colorful and lyrical abstract canvases she is best known for.

Elizabeth Catlett, a native of Washington, D.C., studied at Howard University and later with Grant Wood at the University of Iowa. She is a sculptor of immense power, vision, and technical skill. Her media include printmaking, wood, stone, plaster, clay, and bronze. Motherhood, women, and the struggle of oppressed people have been the central themes of her compositions throughout her life. Mexican themes were important in her art after her marriage to Mexican artist Francisco Mora and her expatriation to his country.

Like Catlett and Beauford Delaney, a number of important African-American artists expatriated themselves after World War II. Ronald Joseph moved to Europe in the 1940's, primarily living in Brussels. An abstractionist from the late 1930s, his restrained compositions received little recognition in the United States and for many decades he had little contact with American artists, though he was making a comeback at the time of his sudden death in 1992. Herbert Gentry moved to Paris after World War II and studied at the Grande Chaumière. Linear movement and biomorphic form have been among his major concerns. Though primarily abstractions, a number of his canvases have featured the representation of masks. In 1960 he settled in Stockholm, Sweden. Ed Clark moved to Paris in 1952; his paintings were often abstractions of the human figure. Other expatriates include Lawrence Potter (1924–1966), primarily a color field abstractionist, and Walter Williams (1920–), whose work often imaginatively evokes African-American childhood.

The Civil Rights Movement and the Visual Arts

The Civil Rights Movement of the 1960s was a turning point for black art and culture. A number of important artworks were directly inspired by the movement, such as Norman Lewis's *Processional* (1964), Jacob Lawrence's *The Ordeal of Mary* (1963), and Elizabeth Catlett's *Homage to My Young Black Sisters* (1968) and *Malcolm X Speaks for Us* (1969). In 1963 Romare BEARDEN contacted Norman Lewis and Hale Woodruff and formed Spiral, a group of twelve African-American artists committed to supporting the Civil Rights Movement and furthering its connection to African-American art. They held their first group show in 1964. The group had largely disbanded by 1965, though their impact as a politically conscious African-American artist collective outlived the short duration of the movement.

One of the central figures in Spiral, Romare Bearden was in his own right one of the most significant African-American artists of the postwar period. Born in Charlotte, N.C., he was raised in Harlem and was a lifelong New Yorker. He was primarily a portraitist, and Spiral had a major impact on his art, which subsequently concentrated on painted, mixed media collages that depicted the African-American experience with a strong emphasis on spirituality. Bearden was also an important writer on African-American art. His works include the posthumous *History of African-American Artists* (1993), cowritten with Harry Henderson.

Benny Andrews, like Bearden, was an activist and an expressive figurative painter who also worked in collage, with modeling paste and acrylic. Andrews was concerned that black artists express themselves on a wide range of issues. He was active in teaching in prisons in Queens, New York, and he cofounded the Black Emergency Cultural Coalition (BECC) in 1969. John Biggers, who was raised in North Carolina and who taught for many decades at Texas Southern University, was a figurative artist in the tradition of Charles White, and was profoundly influenced by numerous visits to Africa. His drawings and murals were some of his most distinguished contributions to the field.

By the late 1960s the BLACK ARTS MOVEMENT was giving rising to a new type of African-American art: community based, militant, and African-centered in its politics. In 1968 the Chicago-based Africobra (African Commune of Bad Relevant Artists) painted the *Wall of Respect* in a black Chicago neighborhood, and started a vogue of the painting of community murals in the late 1960s and 1970s. This aesthetic had other venues besides murals. Nelson Stevens, one of the founders of Africobra, painted in "Kool-Aid" colors and produced prints that contained nationalistic positive images of black males, females, and heroic icons such as MALCOLM X.

Vincent Smith was influenced by the Black Arts movement, avant-garde jazz and blues of the 1960s, and African art. Many of his oil paintings are mixed media explorations of the black experience, and his etchings and monoprints are eloquent narratives on the distinctive nuances of African-American life. Faith Ringgold, in contrast, executed huge reconfigured paintings of the American flag. She was an outspoken feminist and activist who used her art to redefine the role of women. Her paintings evolved into painted story quilts, telling complex narratives in a geometric format.

Other strategies for confronting viewers with unsettling observations on the nature of the relation between blacks and American society include those explored by Barkley Hendricks, who has painted large, portrait images of African-Americans against stark and vaguely ominous white canvases. Betye Saar uses mixed media, including found objects and advertising images, as in her *The Liberation of Aunt Jemina* (1972). Mel Edwards uses found or discarded metal objects such as parts of machines and tools to create metaphors of the exploited classes within American society, as in his *Lynch Fragment Series,* a lifelong, continuous series of explorations in form and structure.

Bob THOMPSON worked in flat, brightly colored figures and compositions that resembled the work of European masters, including Nicolas Poussin and the Fauves. His work had a strong symbolic component. His development was cut short by his untimely death. Emilio Cruz, once a studiomate of Thompson's, shared similar artistic concerns. Cruz has been occupied throughout his career with symbolism, spirituality, and the holistic sense of humanity and personal artistic development. The mood, tempo, and improvisational structure of jazz have been integral to his creative process.

Contemporary African-American Art

The diversity in medium, style, and philosophy within African-American art has burgeoned since the 1970s. In part this reflects the increasing heterogeneity of contemporary art, as well as the new prominence and confidence of black artists as they see themselves as part of the world at large.

Among the most important of recent African-American abstractionists has been William T. Williams. He works in large-scale abstractions characterized by the use of geometry, illusion, and complex surface textures, creating subtle moods and atmospheres as he attempts to realize his inner visions. Al Loving also works in an abstract idiom. Spatial relationships, color, and illusion dominate his large acrylic canvases and small watercolor collages. His forms appear suspended in space, amplifying the sense of illusion. Other abstract artists include Jack Whitten, who explores surface textures and organic structures that resemble intensely magnified sections of human skin or the tile mosaics of ancient floor patterns. Whitten is also interested in human efforts to decorate and ornament skin, as in the African practice of scarification. Oliver Jackson, a California painter, explores the power and energy of nature. In his paintings humanity is often reduced to a subordinate element within the grand scale of his oversized acrylics. Jackson is also a sculptor and woodcarver of power, skill, and vision. Raymond Saunders has developed a very personal style in which the environment around him is reflected in large studies, illuminated by iconographic messages embedded in the surface of the picture plane. Saunders uses the popular language of the community to create a visual text of ideas, images, and symbolic metaphors.

Sam Gilliam exhibited unorthodox canvases in the 1972 Venice Biennale, which broke his connection to "easel" art. The huge canvases were painted on the studio floor by pouring buckets of paint on the surface and moving the pigment across the canvas with brooms. Later he extended this process by cutting and repasting sections of these canvases, configuring them into large shaped paintings, juxtaposing bright color, texture, and form. In other commission projects he would wrap entire buildings or drape interior spaces with his creations. Gilliam has been fascinated with the processes of paint, light, color, and texture.

Another contemporary style was exemplified in the work of the highly publicized and controversial work of Jean-Michel BASQUIAT. Although often dismissed as a mere graffiti artist, he expanded and redefined the nature of abstract expressionist painting, through the use of energetic figures and text in his works. Basquiat reorganized the nature of the picture plane by using popular imagery and mixed media on grand-scale surfaces to make biting commentaries on society. He was especially concerned with the politics of African-American art within the larger society. His early stardom and the media attention he garnered, as well as his early death, have to some extent obscured his true worth, which will become clearer in passing decades.

Robert Colescott's signature style of figurative paintings is intended to place African Americans within the canons of Western art traditions. In the *Knowledge is the Key to the Past* series (1970s), Colescott re-creates famous historical compositions by European artists and replaces the subjects with black characters. The results are satirical indictments of Western society which disturb white and black viewers. Bold color and complex compositions combined with the gesturally painted figures amplify the importance of the issues involved. His sociopolitical commentaries with their deft skewering of stereotypes have often provoked controversy, negative reactions, and great debate about the relevance of his themes.

A number of recent artists have combined Afrocentric themes with a proactive stance on conceptual art. Howardena Pindell is a multitalented artist and writer who works in a wide range of media, including painting, prints, video, performance art, and installations. Her works are provocative and have often been compared to those of Colescott for their political stance. David Hammons, like Pindell, has invited controversy through his creations from hair balls, wine bottles, greasy paper bags, bottle caps, snowballs, coal, chicken wings, and barbecued ribs. Hammons treats even the most despised and hidden aspects of the black experience with a sense of reverence. Houston Conwill's inventiveness creates sculpture, installations, and performance art that recall the time, place, and memory of African and African-American cultural rituals of the past. He has been preoccupied with defining the nature of sacred space in the African-American community.

Richard HUNT and Martin PURYEAR are two of the most distinguished African-American sculptors. Both work in distinct styles. Hunt works in metal, usually steel, creating works that are derived from plant and animal forms. The metal is shaped to convey the illusion of a series of plants growing in space. Puryear creates objects and forms inspired by architectural structures and everyday objects essential to the lives of African, Asian, and American Indian peoples. His materials include wood, metal, fiber, stone, and wax. The expanded scale of the objects often sets up a psychological juxtaposition that challenges the notion of the function and role of the objects as art.

The current bounty of contemporary African-American art in some ways represents the culmination of the work of many generations of creative black painters and sculptors. African-American artists first had to struggle simply to gain access to the world of fine art. Once the barriers were beginning to be breached, they were faced with the equally important task of finding their own distinctive voice, and demanding that it be heard and given respect. Amid the turbulence of the contemporary artistic scene, few groups have been as important as African-American artists in directing the attention of artists to issues such as race, gender, identity, culture, politics, and a critical self-examination of the operations of the art world itself. At the same time, one cannot pigeonhole African-American art to one type of expression; black artists have created and are creating works in styles and forms ranging from quiet intellectual contemplation to works of militant engagement. The accomplishments of African-American art are testament to the creative expectations of black artists as they meld the complexities of their African and multiethnic American heritages with their personal artistic visions. Its achievements will endure and invent ever new forms of visual expressiveness.

BIBLIOGRAPHY

Bearden, Romare and Harry Henderson. *A History of African-American Artists: From 1792 to the Present.* New York, 1993.

Benezra, Neal. *Martin Puryear.* Chicago, 1992.

Cannon, Steve, Kellie Jones, and Tom Finkelpearl. *David Hammons: Rousing the Rubble.* Cambridge, Mass.; 1991.

Columbus Museum of Art. *Elijah Pierce: Woodcarver.* Seattle, Wash., 1992.

Connecticut Gallery, Inc. *Charles Ethan Porter.* Marlborough, Conn., 1987.

Dallas Museum of Art. *Black Art: Ancestral Legacy.* Dallas, 1989.

Driskell, David. *Two Centuries of Black American Art.* Los Angeles, 1976.

Fuller, Edmund R. *Visions in Stone: The Sculpture of William Edmundson.* Pittsburgh, 1973.

Good-Bryand, Linda, and Marcy S. Philips. *Contextures.* New York, 1978.

———. *Hidden Heritage: Afro-American Art, 1800*–1950. Bellevue, Wash., 1985.

Hartigan, Lynda Roscoe. *Sharing Traditions: Five Black Artists in Nineteenth-Century America.* Washington, D.C., 1985.

Howard University Gallery of Art. *James A. Porter: Artist and Art Historian—The Memory of the Legacy.* Washington, D.C., 1992.

King-Hammond, Leslie. *Masks and Mirrors: African-American Art, 1700–Now.* New York, 1995.

Lewis, Samella. *Art: African-American.* Los Angeles, 1993.

———. *The Art of Elizabeth Catlett.* Claremont, Calif., 1984.

Livingston, Jane, and John Beardsley. *Black Folk Art in America, 1930–1980.* Washington, D.C., 1982.

Locke, Alain. *The Negro in Art.* New York, 1940.

Newberger Museum of Art. *Melvin Edwards Sculpture: A Thirty-Year Retrospective, 1963–1993.* Seattle, Wash., 1993.

Perry, Regenia. *Free Within Our Selves: African American Artists in the Collection of the National Museum of American Art.* Washington, D.C., 1992.

Philadelphia Museum of Art. *Henry Ossawa Tanner.* Philadelphia, 1991.

Porter, James A. *Modern Negro Art.* 1943. Reprint. Washington, D.C., 1993.

Powell, Richard. *Homecoming: The Life and Art of William Henry Johnson.* Washington, D.C., 1992.

Reynolds, Gary A., and Beryl J. Wright, eds. *Against the Odds: African-American Artists and the Harmon Foundation.* Newark, N.J., 1989.

Robinson, Jontlyle Teresa and Wendy Greenhouse. *The Art of Archibald J. Motley, Jr.* Chicago, 1991.

Stein, Judith E. *I Tell My Heart: The Art of Horace Pippen.* Philadelphia, 1994.

Studio Museum in Harlem. *Beauford Delaney: A Retrospective.* New York, 1978.

———. *Harlem Renaissance: Art of Black America.* New York, 1987.

———. *Memory and Metaphor: The Art of Romare Bearden, 1940–1987.* New York, 1991.

———. *Tradition and Conflict: Images of a Turbulent Decade, 1963–1973.* New York, 1985.

Turner, Elizabeth Hutton, ed. *Jacob Lawrence: The Migration Series.* Washington, D.C., 1993.

Weekley, Carolyn J., and Stiles Tuttle Colwill with Leroy Graham and Mat Ellen Hayward. *Joshua Johnson: Freeman and Early American Portrait Painter.* Williamsburg, Va., 1988.

Wheat, Ellen Harkins. *Jacob Lawrence: American Painter.* Seattle, Wash., 1986.

Willis-Thomas, Deborah. *Black Photographers, 1840–1880: An Illustrated Bio-Bibliography.* New York, 1985.

Wilson, James L. *Clementine Hunter: American Folk Artist.* Gretna, La., 1988.

– LESLIE KING HAMMOND

PARKER, CHARLES CHRISTOPHER "CHARLIE"

Charles Christopher "Charlie" Parker (August 29, 1920–March 23, 1955), jazz alto saxophonist. Charlie Parker, often known as "Bird" or "Yardbird," was the primary architect of the style of jazz called bebop, which revolutionized jazz, taking it from dance music to a black musical aesthetic and art form. He accomplished this as performer, composer, and theorist.

Parker was born in Kansas City, Mo. When he was eleven his mother bought him an alto saxophone. By the time he was fifteen he had become a professional musician, leaving school at the same time. At first his playing was ridiculed, but after he spent some time at a retreat in the Ozark Mountains of Missouri his technique grew immensely, and during the next couple of years he played in and around the Kansas City area. During this period he learned his craft mainly by sitting in and playing in bands, where he absorbed all he could about music.

In 1939 Parker made his first visit to New York. He stayed about a year, playing mostly in jam sessions. After that he began playing in the band of Jay McShann, touring in the Southwest, Midwest, and East. It was with this band that Parker made his first recording, in Dallas in 1941. At the end of 1942 he joined the Earl Hines orchestra, which featured trumpeter "Dizzy" GILLESPIE. Bird and Dizzy began an informal partnership that launched the beginning of bebop. A strike by the American Federation of Musicians made it impossible to make records for several years, and the early period of bebop's development is largely undocumented. In 1944 Parker, along with Gillespie and other modern players, joined the Billy Eckstine band. This band was one of the first to introduce the innovations being developed in the music, and it provided a platform for Parker's new improvisations.

In 1945 Parker began to record extensively with small groups that included Gillespie. His playing became more familiar to a larger audience and to other musicians, even though the new music was criticized harshly by critics. At the end of 1945 he took a quintet to California for what turned out to be an ill-fated trip. Audiences and musicians in the West were not familiar with bebop innovations, and Parker's addiction to heroin and alcohol finally forced him into the Camarillo State Hospital. He stayed there during the second half of 1946 and was released in January 1947. He did make several important recordings for the Dial record company before and after his stay at the hospital.

Charlie Parker, often known as "Bird" or "Yardbird," was the primary architect of the style of jazz called bebop.

Parker returned to New York in April 1947 and formed a quintet featuring his protégé Miles DAVIS on trumpet, Duke Jordan on piano, Tommy Potter on bass, and Max ROACH on drums. Between 1947 and 1951 Parker left a permanent imprint on jazz. With the quintet he recorded some of his most innovative compositions: "Now's the Time," "Koko," "Anthropology," "Ornithology," "Scrapple from the Apple," "Yardbird Suite," "Moose the Mooche," "Billie's Bounce," "Confirmation," and others. In addition to playing in his own quintet, Parker worked in a variety of other musical groups, including Afro-Cuban bands and a string chorus, which he led during 1950. He was featured soloist in the Jazz at the Philharmonic series, produced by Norman Granz. Parker's main venue continued to be his quintet, which changed members several times but still was vital. Within his quintet he worked in nightclubs, recording studios, and radio broadcasts, and made his first trip to Europe in 1949, returning there the next year for an extensive stay in Sweden, where he worked with Swedish musicians.

Parker's lifestyle continued to create problems for himself and his family. In 1951 he lost his cabaret card in New York because of his constant confrontations with narcotics police. This kept him from playing in New York clubs for over two years. His alcohol and drug use precipitated a downward financial spiral from which he never recovered. In 1953 he presented a landmark concert in Toronto with Gillespie, Bud Powell on piano, Charles MINGUS on bass, and Max Roach on drums. The concert was at Massey Hall and featured many of the pieces Bird and Dizzy had created during the 1940s: "Night in Tunisia," "Hot House," "Wee," and others. This was Parker's last great musical statement. After the Toronto concert his physical and mental health deteriorated to the point where he attempted suicide several times, finally committing himself to Bellevue Hospital in New York. His last public performance was early in March 1955 at Birdland, the New York City club named after him. On March 23 he died of heart seizure in the New York apartment of his friend Baroness Pannonica de Koenigswarter.

Parker's contributions to jazz are extensive. He took saxophone playing to a level never reached before and in so doing led the way for others, not only saxophonists but all instrumentalists. He was able to weld prodigious skill with poetic content, and he left hours and hours of recordings of wondrous improvisations. Parker's playing struck fear in the hearts of many musicians and made some put down their instruments. John COLTRANE, the gifted performer of the 1950s and 1960s, moved from alto to tenor saxophone because he felt that Parker had played all that was going to be played on the alto. Parker frequently composed using the harmonic structures of established melodies as the basis of his works. He did not invent this technique but used it more than anyone else before or since. In his improvisations he used all the intervals of the scales. In his harmonic structures he consistently used chords made up of eleventh and thirteenth intervals in order to take harmony out of the diatonic system and into chromaticism. Parker was clearly one of America's most innovative and prolific artists.

BIBLIOGRAPHY

Giddins, Gary. *Celebrating Bird: The Triumph of Charlie Parker.* New York, 1987.

Morgenstern, Dan, et al. *Bird and Diz: A Bibliography.* New York, 1973.

Reiser, Robert G. *Bird.* New York, 1962.

Russell, Ross. *Bird Lives.* New York, 1973.

— WILLIAM S. COLE

PARKS, GORDON, SR.

Gordon Parks, Sr. (November 30, 1912–), photographer. A true Renaissance man, *Life* magazine photographer Gordon Parks has achieved international recognition in a wide variety of other fields including filmmaking, letters, and music. He has also pioneered as the first mainstream African-American photojournalist and as the first African American to direct a major Hollywood film.

Gordon Parks was born in Fort Scott, Kans., the youngest in a farming family of fifteen children. His mother's death when Parks was sixteen, along with his aged father's rapidly failing ability to manage a household, led to the family's break-up, and Parks moved north to live with a married sister in Minneapolis. Unwelcome in his brother-in-law's home, the teenager was soon on his own, struggling to attend high school and support himself.

The Great Depression ended his formal education, but Parks seized every opportunity to learn by reading and attending closely to the talented individuals he encountered in his various jobs. As a teenager and later as a young husband and father, he worked as a bellhop, musician, semipro basketball player, and member of the Civilian Conservation Corps, primarily in the Midwest but also for a brief time in Harlem, New York. Relative security came with a position as a railroad dining car waiter. All the while Parks wrote, composed, and read, absorbing on his own what he had been unable to study in school.

The picture magazines of the day—*Vogue, Harper's Bazaar,* and especially the brand new *Life* magazine (first issued in November 1936)—caught Parks's imagination. A newsreel cameraman's in-person presentation of his latest battle-action footage in a Chicago movie theater inspired Parks to take up photography himself, and in 1937 he acquired his first camera. Largely self-taught, he took his earliest photographs with only a few pointers from the camera salesman. Quickly mastering technique, he intuitively found the subjects most meaningful to him. The same local Minneapolis camera store soon gave him his first exhibition.

A successful fashion assignment for a stylish Minneapolis department store caught the attention of Marva (Mrs. Joe) Louis, who encouraged Parks to establish himself in Chicago. His fashion background served him well there (as it would later throughout his years at *Life*) photographing Gold Coast socialites. In his spare time, he documented the grim poverty of the city's South Side, the fast-growing Chicago enclave of African Americans displaced from the rural South who came north for jobs in the heavy industries surrounding the Great Lakes.

This socially conscious camera work won for the young photographer, now responsible for a growing family of his own, the very first Julius Rosenwald Fellowship in photography. The 1942–1943 stipend enabled Parks to work with photographic mentor Roy Stryker in Washington, D.C., at the Farm Security Administration. This was the closing years of the influential New Deal agency that had undertaken a pioneering photo documentation of depression conditions in urban and rural America.

Parks continued with Stryker until 1947, first as a correspondent for the Office of War Information, and later at the Standard Oil Company of New Jersey, photographing the face of America for the company's public relations campaign. In the brief months before he began to work for *Life* magazine in 1948, Parks photographed for *Vogue* and *Glamour* and also authored two books on photographic technique: *Flash Photography* (1947) and *Camera Portraits: The Techniques and Principles of Documentary Portraiture* (1948).

Early in his more than two decades at *Life,* Parks spent two influential years assigned to the magazine's Paris office, where he covered fashion, the arts, celebrities, and political figures. The experience was seminal, providing a rich window on the diversity of contemporary creative expression as well as an opportunity for international recognition. Moreover, like other African Americans, he found the European experience, with its relative lack of racial barriers, especially liberating.

Back in the United States during the 1950s and early '60s, Parks executed hundreds of photographic assignments for *Life* that reflect the magazine's far-ranging coverage: popular culture, high fashion, arts, entertainment, sports, national events, and the personalities of business, labor and politics. Parks's direct, realistic style of photographing life in America and abroad won him international renown as the first African-American photojournalist.

Parks's longest assignment began in 1961, when he traveled to Brazil to photograph the slums of Rio de Janeiro. His story of Flavio da Silvia, a poverty-stricken Brazilian boy whom Parks found dying of asthma, attracted international attention that resulted in Flavio and his family receiving gifts, medical treatment, and, finally, a new home. At the same time, with the emerging CIVIL RIGHTS MOVEMENT, Parks undertook a new role at *Life:* interpreting the activities and personalities of the movement, in words as well as pictures, from a personal perspective. His 1971 anthology *Born Black* is a collection of these essays and images.

A gifted storyteller, Parks began his chronological autobiographical book cycle in 1963 with *The Learning Tree,* a well-received novel that drew on the author's own childhood experiences and memories. This was followed in 1966 by *A Choice of Weapons,* a powerful first-person narrative that recounted the events and influences that enabled Parks to overcome societal prejudice and personal hardship. It is the most insightful of the series, illuminating the development of a sensitive and self-confident young man as he grows into what he will become, an artist of universal conscience and compassion.

Parks also gained distinction as a poet, composer, and filmmaker, becoming in 1969 the first African American to direct a major Hollywood film. He also produced and wrote the script for *The Learning Tree* and directed a number of other films, including the highly popular *Shaft* (1971), *Leadbelly* (1976), and *The Odyssey of Solomon Northup* (1984), about a free black sold into slavery. In addition, Parks has completed the music for a ballet about the Rev. Dr. Martin Luther KING, Jr., and has worked on a novel based on the life of J. M. W. Turner, the English nineteenth-century landscape painter.

Parks is the recipient of numerous professional awards, organization citations, and honorary degrees, among them Photographer of the Year from the American Society of Magazine Photographers (1960) and the Spingarn Medal from the NAACP (1972).

His greatest satisfaction and motivation is expressed in his prologue to *Moments Without Proper Names,* one of his three books of poems accompanied by his photographs:

> I hope always to feel the responsibility to communicate the plight of others less fortunate than myself, to show the abused and those who administer the abuses, to point up the pain of the underprivileged as well as the pleasures of the privileged—somehow to evoke the same response from a housewife in Harlem as I would from a seamstress in Paris or a butcher in Vladivostok.
>
> In helping one another we can ultimately save ourselves. We must give up silent watching and put our commitments into practice.

BIBLIOGRAPHY

Bush, Martin H. *The Photographs of Gordon Parks.* Wichita, Kans., 1983.

Hannan, Terry. *Gordon Parks, Black Photographer.* Champaign, Ill., 1972.

Turk, Midge. *Gordon Parks.* New York, 1971.

– JULIA VAN HAAFTEN

PARKS, ROSA LOUISE MCCAULEY

Rosa Louise McCauley Parks (February 4, 1913–), civil rights leader. Rosa McCauley was born in Tuskegee, Ala. She lived with relatives in Montgomery, where she finished high school in 1933 and attended Alabama State College. She met her husband, Raymond Parks, a barber, and they married in 1932. Rosa Parks worked as a clerk, an insurance salesperson, and a tailor's assistant at a department store. She was also employed at the time as a part-time seamstress by Virginia and Clifford Durr, two white residents of Montgomery who were staunch supporters of the black freedom struggle.

Parks had been active in civil rights work since the 1930s. She and her husband supported the Scottsboro defendants, a notorious case in which nine young black men were convicted in 1931 on questionable evidence for raping two white women. In 1943, Parks became one of the first women to join the Montgomery NAACP. She worked as a youth adviser, served as secretary for the local group from 1943 to 1956, and helped operate the joint office of the NAACP and the BROTHERHOOD OF SLEEPING CAR PORTERS. In addition, she worked with the Montgomery Voters League to increase black voter registration. During the summer of 1955, with the encouragement of the Durrs, Parks accepted a scholarship for a workshop for community leaders on school integration at the Highlander Folk School in Tennessee. It was an important experience for Parks, not only for the practical skills of organizing and mobilizing she learned, but because the racial harmony she experienced there nurtured and sustained her activism.

Popularly known as the Mother of the Civil Rights Movement, Parks is best known for her refusal to give up her seat for a white man on a segregated bus in Montgomery on December 1, 1955, an incident which sparked the MONTGOMERY BUS BOYCOTT. Contrary to popular belief, Parks was not simply a tired woman who wanted to rest her feet, unaware of the chain of events she was about to trigger. As she wrote in *Rosa Parks: My Story,* "the only tired I was, was tired of giving in." Parks was a veteran of civil rights activity and was aware of efforts by the Women's Political Council and the local NAACP to find an incident with which they could address segregation in Montgomery.

Parks is best known for her refusal to give up her seat for a white man on a segregated bus in Montgomery on December 1, 1955.

Parks was actively involved in sustaining the boycott and for a time served on the executive committee of the Montgomery Improvement Association, an organization created to direct the boycott. The intransigence of the city council was met by conviction and fortitude on the part of African Americans. For over a year, black people in Montgomery car-pooled, took taxis, and walked to work. The result was a ruling by the United

States Supreme Court that segregation on city buses was unconstitutional.

As a result of her involvement in the bus boycott, Parks lost her job at the department store in Montgomery. In 1957, she and her husband moved to Detroit, where she worked as a seamstress for eight years before becoming administrative assistant for Congressman John Conyers, a position she held until 1988. After she moved to Detroit, Parks continued to be active in the CIVIL RIGHTS MOVEMENT and joined the SOUTHERN CHRISTIAN LEADERSHIP CONFERENCE (SCLC). She participated in numerous marches and rallies, including the 1965 march from Selma to Montgomery.

In the mid-1980s she was a supporter of the free South Africa movement and walked the picket lines in Washington, D.C., with other antiapartheid activists. She has made countless public appearances, speaking out on political issues as well as giving oral history lessons about the Civil Rights Movement. In 1987, ten years after the death of her husband, she founded the Rosa and Raymond Parks Institute for Self-Development in Detroit, a center committed to career training for black youth. The institute, a dream of hers, was created to address the dropout rate of black youth.

Parks, an international symbol of African-American strength, has been given numerous awards and distinctions, including ten honorary degrees. In 1979, she was awarded the NAACP's prestigious Spingarn Medal. In 1980, she was chosen by *Ebony* readers as the living black woman who had done the most to advance the cause of black America. In the same year she was awarded the Martin Luther King, Jr., Nonviolent Peace Prize by the Martin Luther King, Jr., Center for Nonviolent Social Change. In addition, the SCLC has honored her by sponsoring the annual Rosa Parks Freedom award.

BIBLIOGRAPHY

Brown, Roxanne. "Mother of the Movement." *Ebony* (February 1988): 68–72.

Garrow, David, ed. *The Montgomery Bus Boycott and the Women Who Started It: The Memoir of Jo Ann Gibson Robinson.* Knoxville, Tenn., 1987.

Parks, Rosa. *Rosa Parks: My Story.* New York, 1992.

— PAM NADASEN

PENTECOSTALISM

Among scholars of Pentecostalism there are two schools of thought as to the emergence of this religious phenomenon. The first school, identified with Vinson Synan, William Menzies, and James Goff, argues that Charles Parham (1873–1929) was the founder of the Pentecostal movement and that it began in Kansas in 1901. The competing school, which includes Walter Hollenweger, James Tinney, J. Douglas Nelson, Cecil R. Robeck, and Edith Blumhofer, argues that the Azusa Street Revival in Los Angeles from 1906 to 1913 was the true beginning and William J. Seymour the pivotal person.

The second school focuses on Azusa Street and Seymour because they were the originating center of Pentecostalism throughout the United States and in Scandinavia, Great Britain, Brazil, Egypt, and India, where it spread. The revival defined Pentecostalism, shaped its interracial relations, and gave it its multicultural character. The first school designates Parham because he was the first proponent to link glossolalia with the biblical Pentecost event recounted in several chapters in the Book of Acts and to define this experience as the baptism of the Holy Spirit.

In 1901 Charles Parham operated the Bethel Bible School in Topeka, Kans. A major religious experience for him was the baptism of the Holy Spirit as described in the Bible, the Book of Acts, chapter 2. The HOLINESS MOVEMENT during the 1800s identified this experience as sanctification. The Wesleyan wing of the Holiness Movement defined the experience in terms of cleansing, while the Calvinist or Reformed wing saw it as empowerment for Christian living. Both positions understood the experience as subsequent to justification. The Reformed advocates described sanctification as a progressive process, while the Wesleyan advocates described it as an instantaneous event.

In the late 1890s Parham joined those who sought to categorize discrete experience beyond justification and sanctification. In January 1901 Parham identified glossolalia with the third experience and linked this experience instead of sanctification with Acts 2. He began preaching this new doctrine within Holiness circles in the Midwest.

In 1905 William J. Seymour, who was black, enrolled in Parham's school in Houston despite the white man Parham's enforcement of segregation laws that prevented Seymour from sitting with the white students. While Seymour adopted the new doctrine, he failed at the time to have the actual experience himself. In 1906 he carried the new doctrine to California in response to an invitation to become pastor of a small black Holiness congregation in Los Angeles headed by Julia Hutchins. Hutchins and the other members established a congregation of Evening Light Saints after withdrawing from the Second Baptist Church, which had refused to embrace their Holiness message. Hutchins, however, rejected Seymour's addition to Holiness teaching and barred him from the pulpit. Edward Lee and, later,

Richard Asberry invited Seymour to resume preaching at their homes.

After Seymour and others began speaking in tongues, they outgrew the "house church," and Seymour secured larger facilities at 312 Azusa Street, the former sanctuary of First AFRICAN METHODIST EPISCOPAL CHURCH (AME). Seymour's revival on Azusa Street attracted the attention first of local whites and blacks, especially those involved in the Holiness community. But soon participants from the Holiness Movement across the United States converged by the thousands on Azusa Street to observe events, examine the new doctrine, and experience glossolalia. Within twelve months the Azusa Street Mission spawned an international movement and began a journal, *Apostolic Faith.* From 1906 to 1908, *Apostolic Faith,* the Azusa Street Mission, and Seymour held the loosely bound movement together and provided it with a center and leadership.

Like its Holiness counterpart, Pentecostalism was basically local and regional and headed by both blacks and whites, as well as both women and men. In many places local and regional movements took over entire Holiness congregations and institutions. African-American Holiness leaders who embraced Pentecostalism along with all or some of their associated congregations included W. H. Fulford (d. 1916), William Fuller (1875–1958), Charles Harrison Mason (1866–1961), and Magdalena Tate (1871–1930).

Early Pentecostalism emerged as a strongly interracial movement and struggled with its interracial identity at a time when American society was segregated. Frank Bartleman, a white Azusa Street participant and reporter, stated that at the revival "the color line was washed away in the blood [of Jesus Christ]." While Baptist, Methodist, Presbyterian, and Holiness people lived in racially segregated congregations, associations, and denominational structures, the black and white Pentecostals pastored and preached to and fellowshipped and worshipped with each other between 1906 and 1914, and many joined the predominantly black Pentecostal-Holiness group, the CHURCH OF GOD IN CHRIST. The Pentecostal leadership was strongly anti-KU KLUX KLAN and was often the targets of Klan terrorism because of their interracial sympathies.

But racism came to counter the interracial nature of early Pentecostalism. Parham exhibited racist behavior and a patronizing attitude toward his black counterparts, especially Seymour; in 1908 blacks withdrew from the Fire-Baptized Holiness Church (later called Pentecostal Holiness Church); in 1913 another black group withdrew from the Pentecostal Holiness Church; in 1914 a white group withdrew from the Church of God in Christ; and in 1924 a white group withdrew from the half-black Pentecostal Assemblies of the World, which was led by a black minister, Garfield Thomas Haywood.

While segregation among Pentecostals came to follow the pattern of American Christianity after the Civil War, there were exceptions. Blacks and whites continued to struggle together to structure their interracial relationships during the height of segregation in the United States. In 1924 the Church of God in Christ adopted the Methodist model of establishing a minority transgeographical conference, specifically a white conference to unite the white congregations across the United States that belonged to the predominantly black denomination. In 1907 and 1931 several different groups of blacks and whites entered and withdrew from the Pentecostal Assemblies of the World.

Theologically, Pentecostalism split early into two camps over the doctrine of God: Trinitarian and Oneness. The Oneness doctrine, as opposed to the classic Christian doctrine of the Trinity, claimed that Jesus was the name of God and that God expressed Godself in the form of the Father, Son, and Holy Spirit but was not three persons in one. The Trinitarians confessed the traditional Christian doctrine of the Trinity and rejected the Oneness interpretation. While the existing black Pentecostal denominations, such as the Church of God in Christ, United Holy Church, and Church of the Living God, remained Trinitarian, many independent black Pentecostal congregations in the Midwest, especially those associated with Haywood, rejected Trinitarianism. Oneness denominations identified themselves as Apostolic churches.

Haywood and the Pentecostal Assemblies of the World are the parents of most black Apostolic denominations in the United States. Significant leaders of the movement included Robert C. Lawson (1881–1961), who organized the Church of Our Lord Jesus Christ of the Apostolic Faith in 1919, Sherrod C. Johnson (1897–1961), who organized the Church of the Lord Jesus Christ of the Apostolic Faith in 1930, and Smallwood Williams, who organized Bible Way Churches of Our Lord Jesus Christ Worldwide in 1957.

While Pentecostal denominations opened more forms of ministry to women than other Protestant denominations, only a few granted women equality with men. Among black Pentecostals, full male-female equality existed only in denominations founded by black women. Magdalena Tate's denomination, the oldest Pentecostal denomination founded by a black woman, was among the Holiness groups that joined Pentecostalism after their establishment. During 1903 she founded in Tennessee the Church of Living God, Pillar and Ground of the Truth. The other major grouping of Pentecostal denominations founded by black women withdrew from the United Holy Church of America, which ordained women to the ministry but denied them the bishopric. In 1924 Ida Robinson founded the Mt. Sinai Holy Church to rectify this inequality. In 1944 Beulah Counts (d. 1968), an associate of Robinson, organized the Greater Mt. Zion Pentecostal Church of America.

Crossing Trinitarian and Apostolic divisions is a stream within Pentecostalism called the deliverance movement. The deliverance movement grew out of the white healing movement of the 1940s associated with William Branham that produced Oral Roberts, Gordon Lindsay, and A. A. Allen. The deliverance movement among black Pentecostals is related to Arturo Skinner (1924–1975), who expanded the traditional black Pentecostal emphasis on healing to include exorcisms and heightened the accent on the miraculous. In 1956 he established the Deliverance Evangelistic Centers, with headquarters in Newark, N.J. Deliverance ministries emerged in traditional Pentecostal congregations such as Faith Temple Church of God in Christ under Harry Willis Goldsberry (1895–1986) in Chicago. In urban centers there emerged new independent congregations that competed with traditional black Pentecostals; Benjamin Smith (b. 1926), who founded the Deliverance Evangelistic Center in Philadelphia in 1960, and Richard Hinton, who founded Monument of Faith Evangelistic Center in Chicago in 1963, were two of the best-known leaders of these congregations.

Although Pentecostals are stereotyped as otherworldly, studies have shown a social activist stream within black Pentecostalism. A number of black Pentecostal denominations and leaders joined the Fraternal Council of Negro Churches and participated in the marches for black employment during the 1930s. Robert C. Lawson cooperated with Adam Clayton POWELL, Jr., and other leading Harlem ministers in campaigns for black employment. J. O. Patterson (1912–1990) of the Church of God in Christ and other ministers participated in local civil rights campaigns in Memphis, Tenn., and other southern cities and towns in the late 1950s. Smallwood Williams led the legal battle against segregated public schools during the 1950s in Washington, D.C. Arthur Brazier (b. 1921), Louis Henry Ford (b. 1914) and other Pentecostal clergy were active in the CIVIL RIGHTS MOVEMENT in Chicago and other northern cities in the 1960s.

Studies of the black Pentecostal leadership note the occurrence of a cadre of black Pentecostals who identify

Easter Sunday, April 1941, at a Pentecostal service. (Prints and Photographs Division, Library of Congress)

with twentieth-century theological liberalism. Relations between liberal Protestantism and black Pentecostalism occur on a number of levels. A significant number of Pentecostals are graduates of liberal seminaries, some as early as the 1940s. They are graduates of schools such as Temple University, Oberlin, Union Theological Seminary (New York City), Duke, Emory, and McCormick. And the first accredited Pentecostal, and only African-American, seminary, Charles Harrison Mason Theological Seminary, is a member of Interdenominational Theological Center (ITC), a consortium of African-American seminaries affiliated with mainline denominations. The Church of God in Christ, the sponsor of Mason Seminary at ITC, embraces theological liberalism from a black perspective in the preparation of an educated clergy. A number of black Pentecostal leaders are also involved in the ecumenical movement that liberal Protestantism embraces: Herbert Daughtry (b. 1931) participates in some World Council of Churches programs, and Ithiel Clemmons (b. 1921) participates in regional and local ecumenical councils.

Black Pentecostalism became the carrier of black religious folk music, noted for its call-and-response, improvisation, polyrhythms, and diatonic harmonies.

Black Pentecostalism also includes leaders who identify with evangelicalism. Black Pentecostals associated with the evangelical movement are often graduates of evangelical seminaries such as Fuller, Gordon-Conwell, and Trinity Evangelical Divinity School. Leaders such as William Bentley (b. 1926) and George McKinney (b. 1932) are active members of the National Association of Evangelicals along with the National Black Association of Evangelicals.

During the 1970s black Pentecostalism intersected with the "Word of Faith" movement spurred by Kenneth Hagin and his message of healing, prosperity, and positive confession. Fredrick Price (b. 1932) emerged as the Word of Faith leader among black Christians after establishing Crenshaw Christian Center of Los Angeles in 1973.

During the 1970s Pentecostalism influenced the historic black denominations, especially the AME Church. Neo-Pentecostal ministers occupy some major AME pulpits. The focal point for the movement during the early 1970s was St. Paul AME Church in Cambridge, Mass., under the pastorate of John Bryant (b. 1948). During the period, college campuses became centers for the growth of Pentecostalism among black students, particularly through the college gospel choir movement.

Black Pentecostals have been leaders within the black religious music movement since the early 1900s. Black Pentecostalism became the carrier of black religious folk music, noted for its call-and-response, improvisation, polyrhythms, and diatonic harmonies. By the 1920s Arizona Juanita Dranes (b. 1905) and Sallie Sanders were popular gospel singers. Dranes and Sanders began the tradition of the Baptist and Pentecostal leadership of the GOSPEL MUSIC movement. By the 1980s black Pentecostals such as Andrae Crouch, Edwin Hawkins, Walter Hawkins, Shirley Caesar, the Clark Sisters, and the Wynans dominated the gospel music movement.

From its beginning at the Azusa Street Revival in 1906, black Pentecostalism has grown to become the second-largest religious movement among African Americans and one of the fastest-growing religious movements in the United States and around the globe, especially in the Third World.

BIBLIOGRAPHY

Burgess, Stanley M., and Gary B. McGee. *Dictionary of Pentecostal and Charismatic Movements.* Grand Rapids, Mich., 1988.

Dupree, Sherry S., ed. *Biographical Dictionary of African-American Holiness-Pentecostals, 1880–1990.* Washington, D.C., 1989.

Jones, Charles Edwin. *A Guide to the Study of Black Participation in Wesleyan Perfectionist and Glossolalic Pentecostal Movements.* Metuchen, N.J., 1987.

— DAVID D. DANIELS III

PHILADELPHIA, PENNSYLVANIA

When William Penn arrived on the shores of the Delaware River in 1682 to establish the Pennsylvania Colony, the area was inhabited by Delaware Indians, Dutch, Swedes, British settlers, and free and enslaved Africans. Penn selected and named Philadelphia to be the capital of the colony. The early city was small: 1,200 acres, two miles in length from east to west between the Delaware and Schuylkill rivers, and one mile in width from north to south. The boundaries remained unchanged until the consolidation of 1854, which made the county of Philadelphia coterminous with the city, incorporating many districts and townships, including Northern Liberties, Spring Garden, Southwark, Moyamensing, Passyunk, and Blockley into the city of Philadelphia.

Scant references exist to the early presence of blacks in the colony; however, by 1720 they numbered at least 2,500 in Pennsylvania. Many were slaves. There is evidence of their collective activities by various acts of proposed and enacted legislation. The first restriction imposed in 1693 required that Africans carry passes. Later, other acts prohibited their assembly and determined where and when they could meet. The 1790 Census recorded 210 slaves in the city and 384 in the county, but Pennsylvania's Gradual Abolition of Slavery Act of 1780 applied only to children born after the act, freeing them after service to their enslaved mothers' owners for twenty-eight years. Therefore, in addition to apprenticeship, a number of black children were indentured servants, adding an additional element of separation and rendering them still not free.

Despite these limitations, Philadelphia blacks developed a community in the eighteenth century. In 1786 a petition for a burial ground was presented. A year later, the Free African Society was formed. This was the first beneficial society, established by Richard ALLEN and Absalom JONES in Philadelphia and comprised blacks and a few white Quakers. Some members of the Society were part of the group that had petitioned for a burial ground.

Richard Allen recorded that the beginning of the African Church in Philadelphia occurred in 1787. Though there is considerable scholarly disagreement on the precise sequence of events, and the date of the famous incident when Allen, Jones, and their fellow black congregants were ejected from St. George's Church, by the late 1780s a number of blacks who had previously worshipped with whites began leaving those churches to establish their own places of worship. At first they worshipped in private dwellings. Later they were able to formally dedicate their own buildings.

The African Church, later the First African Church of St. Thomas (Protestant Episcopal), was dedicated in 1794. Jones was its first pastor. Bethel Methodist Church, the oldest real estate continuously owned by blacks in the United States, was dedicated in 1796. Allen was its first pastor. In 1816 Allen and others organized the African Methodist Episcopal Church, the first black denomination. African Zoar Methodist Church was formed in 1794 by another group of blacks who left St. George's and worshipped for some time in their homes in Campingtown, an area in Northern Liberties. Later, in 1796, on ground adjacent to property owned by Lunar Brown, a member and trustee, they formally dedicated their church. METHODISTS and EPISCOPALIANS were not the only groups to lose black parishioners. In 1809 nine black men and women received a letter of dismission from the First Baptist Church of Philadelphia. They established the First African Baptist Church in that year in the Spring Garden district, near Northern Liberties. The First African Presbyterian Church was established in 1811 by men and women led by John Gloucester. These and many more black churches came into existence providing for the growing black population, schools, burial grounds, and meeting places. Not only do census figures indicate an increase in the black population, but the proliferation of institutions also attests to the population's increase and potential influence. Perhaps the most notable event in the early history of black Philadelphia was the yellow fever epidemic of the summer of 1793, which claimed about one-tenth of the city's 50,000 residents. Under the mistaken belief that African Americans had natural immunity to the disease, city leaders appealed to blacks to help treat and bury the dead. Some whites criticized blacks for trying to profit from the crisis. Jones and Allen rebutted the accusations in their jointly written *Narrative of the Proceedings of the Black People During the Late Awful Calamity in Philadelphia* (1794).

There were nineteen black churches in the city and county of Philadelphia by 1847. Eighty-four percent of black persons living in the city who were surveyed that year by the Pennsylvania Abolition Society indicated church membership. In addition to the denominations mentioned, a large percentage of blacks were members of various other denominations: Roman Catholic, African Methodist Episcopal Zion, and Society of Friends. Later, some black Philadelphians were members of the Shaker community established in Philadelphia by Rebecca Cox Jackson. Few blacks, however, attended interracial churches.

Literary and secret societies also came into existence in the 1800s. Beneficial society membership increased in every area in the city and county from 1837 to 1847. Their purpose was the relief of members who were unable to work, the interments of deceased members, and the relief of widows and orphans. Occupational organizations such as Humane Mechanics, Coachman's Benevolent Society, Union Sons of Industry, and African Porter's Benevolent Society also were formed. These institutions and real property owned by blacks were seen by whites as symbols of upward mobility and power and were targeted for violence and destruction.

Prominent black Philadelphians such as sail maker James FORTEN, the aforementioned ministers Richard Allen and Absalom Jones, educator Sarah Douglass, dentist Jacob White, and members of the Bowser and the Bustill families were well known. Indeed, they were influential in the formation, growth, and development of Philadelphia's black community. Many also raised their voices against slavery and became prominent early abolitionists. In 1830, with Allen as president, the first National Negro Convention was held in Philadelphia. Other Philadelphia abolitionists included the three granddaughters of James Forten: Margaretta, Sarah, and

Harriet Forten, and leader of the Underground Railroad, William Still.

Individual and collective economic enterprises began as early as 1810 with the founding of the African Insurance Company. Joseph Randolph was president, and Cyrus Porter and William Coleman, were treasurer and secretary, respectively. The company had capital in the amount of $5,000 in $50 shares. A financial panic in 1814 and a subsequent depression caused its failure. Two young black men, Derrick Johnson and Joseph Allen, initiated the African Fire Association (AFA) in 1818. There were more than 7,000 blacks in the city at that time, and its formation caused a "great excitement among the members of the [white] fire and hose companies." Whites successfully argued that black fire companies were unnecessary and would be unproductive. Thereafter the founders of the AFA, a potentially powerful political organization, were persuaded and encouraged to desist by some members of the black community.

Pennsylvania's Constitution in 1790 declared that a "freeman" 21 years of age who had resided in Pennsylvania for two years and paid a state or county tax "shall enjoy the rights of an elector." Though there was some African-American suffrage in the late eighteenth century and early nineteenth century in Pennsylvania, it was on a very small scale. The increasing black population in the city and county, along with their ownership of property valued at more than $300,000, caused the Pennsylvania Supreme Court in 1837 to declare that the Negro was not a "freeman" within the context of the Constitution. Revised a year later, Pennsylvania's Constitution prohibited black property owners from voting, stipulating that the vote belonged to every "white freeman," regardless of realty holdings. In 1848, blacks again petitioned for the right to vote, and in 1849, there was an election-day riot. Blacks regained the vote in 1871, and another riot ensued after that election, resulting in the murder of political leader Octavious V. Catto. The years 1829, 1835, 1838, and 1849 were tumultuous and in 1838 there were major riots against the black community which destroyed their churches, meeting halls, residences, the African Grand Lodge of Masons Hall (Pennsylvania Hall), and the Shelter for Colored Orphans.

Despite these setbacks, black Philadelphia's institutional life grew in the second half of the nineteenth century. Businessmen and philanthropists such as Stephen Smith (1797?–1873) helped found the Institute for Colored Youth, the Home for Destitute Colored Children, the House for the Aged and Infirm Colored Persons, Mercy Hospital, and the House of Refuge. Many prominent black Philadelphians such as Robert Bogle, James LeCount, James Prosser, Jeremia Bowser, and Peter Augustine made their fortunes in the catering industry. The black community supported a number of newspapers—five by the end of the nineteenth century—including the *Philadelphia Tribune,* founded in 1884, the oldest continually published black newspaper in the United States. The artistic and intellectual attainments of Philadelphia's black middle class were considerable. Benjamin T. Tanner, a bishop in the A.M.E. Church, edited the *Christian Recorder* and *AME Church Review* and made them into important forums for black intellectual and religious thought. His son, Henry Ossawa TANNER, became the leading black artist of his generation. In the middle decades of the twentieth century, the granddaughter of Bishop Tanner, Sadie Tanner Mossell Alexander and her husband, Raymond Pace Alexander, became lawyers and leaders in the civil rights struggle for Philadelphians. Arthur Huff Fauset, a distinguished folklorist and urban sociologist, also was an advocate for improving housing conditions for black Philadelphians. His sister, Jessie Redmon FAUSET, was a leading novelist of the HARLEM RENAISSANCE, and in novels such as *The Chinaberry Tree* (1931) provided a sensitive portrait of Philadelphia's black elite. Though originally from a poor background, Marian ANDERSON became active at an early age in the middle-class musical culture of her local church, and the Philadelphia community financially supported her training and early career. By the 1930s, she was one of the leading concert performers of her generation.

In 1899 W. E. B. DU BOIS's work, *The Philadelphia Negro,* was published. The monumental sociological study examined the history and present condition of blacks in Philadelphia.

After 1900 there were considerable changes in Philadelphia's black community. Between 1900 and 1960, Philadelphia's black population increased more than 800 percent. Conditions were often difficult for the new migrants. There were jobs, but new migrants met much hostility. In 1918 there was a riot that resulted in the deaths of four blacks and many injuries. Philadelphia was not prepared to house the multitude of people who came seeking refuge. Overcrowded slums quickly developed in North and South Philadelphia, and residential segregation began. Although public housing had been available to whites, it was not until 1943 that public housing became available for blacks in North Philadelphia. In response to the increase in population, neighborhoods changed, the number of public and parochial schools increased and became more segregated, and more black churches came into existence. East Calvary Methodist Church, pastored by the charismatic Charles A. Tindley, attracted a large number of migrants from the South. Purchasing property on affluent Broad Street (circa 1924), East Calvary continued to grow and later became Tindley Temple (1925).

W. E. B. Du Bois's The Philadelphia Negro *examined the history and present condition of blacks in Philadelphia.*

Although many black Philadelphians registered Republican, the New Deal attracted the loyalty of many who were less affluent, and the majority of black voters soon became Democrats. Philadelphia has long been a city of machine politics. Blacks benefited from political patronage, were elected ward leaders, and eventually won seats on city council and the courts. In 1938 Crystal Bird Fauset, running as a Democrat from a Philadelphia district, became the first black woman in the United States elected to a state legislature. The population continued to increase because of wartime employment opportunities. The many government installations, including the Philadelphia Navy Shipyard, provided jobs for migrants.

The 1960s and '70s were turbulent times for black Philadelphians. The emergence of a new militancy among them was evidenced by community protest meetings, race riots, and BLACK PANTHER PARTY rallies. Many of the rallies occurred, with the encouragement of Father Paul Washington, at the Church of the Advocate, an Episcopal church in the heart of North Philadelphia. Again, churches were influential in community improvement as evidenced by Opportunities Industrialization Center (OIC), a self-help organization founded by the Rev. Leon Sullivan.

Girard College, a segregated school in North Philadelphia, was established by the will of Stephen Girard for white male orphans and administered by the Board of City Trusts. Initial litigation to invalidate the will was begun in 1954 by attorney Raymond Pace Alexander. Later, another black attorney, Cecil B. Moore, not only renewed legal action, but rallied blacks to march around the wall of the college until it figuratively "came down." Moore was a criminal attorney known for representing indigent defendants *pro bono.* Moore increased the membership of the NAACP and eventually won election to city council. The combination of litigation and continued community pressure and moral outrage succeeded in the school's integration in 1968. (Even after the end of legal segregation, however, residential segregation patterns left the de facto segregation of Philadelphia's schools largely intact.)

With more blacks in influential positions and a large, black voting population, W. Wilson Goode was elected Philadelphia's first black mayor in 1983, with 91 percent of the black vote. Although reelected four years later, his political career was marred by the bombing of the Move compound in May 1985. After years of sparring with a black nationalist organization, MOVE, that rejected most contact with outsiders, Philadelphia police dropped bombs into its compound, killing six, and started a fire that burned down fifty adjoining homes and left 200 people homeless. All of black Philadelphia—and, indeed, most of the city's residents—were devastated at the loss of innocent lives and the destruction of a stable, black neighborhood in West Philadelphia.

Despite these difficulties, Philadelphia's black community is proud of its history as one of the centers of African-American institutional life for more than three centuries. Some of the leading monuments to black Philadelphia are the Afro-American Historical and Cultural Museum, opened in 1976, the All-Wars Memorial to Black Soldiers, unveiled in 1934, and the homes of the writer Frances Ellen Watkins HARPER and the painter Henry O. TANNER. Philadelphia has been home to a number of prominent jazz musicians, including Dizzy GILLESPIE, John COLTRANE, and the three Heath brothers: Percy, Al, and Jimmy. It also has been a center for black popular music. Other black Philadelphians who have achieved renown in recent decades include comedian Bill COSBY, and William Gray III, former congressman, ambassador to Haiti, and president of the UNITED NEGRO COLLEGE FUND.

BIBLIOGRAPHY

Allen, Richard. *The Life Experience and Gospel Labors of the Rt. Rev. Richard Allen.* Introduction by George A. Singleton. Nashville, Tenn., 1983.

Du Bois, W. E. B. *The Philadelphia Negro.* New York, 1971.

Franklin, Vincent P. "Voice of the Black Community: *The Philadelphia Tribune,* 1912–1941." *Pennsylvania History* (1984): 261–284.

Lane, Roger. *William Dorsey's Philadelphia and Ours: On the Past and Future of the Black City in America.* New York, 1991.

Lapsansky, Emma Jones. "Since They Got Those Separate Churches: Afro-Americans and Racism in Jacksonian Philadelphia." *American Quarterly 32,* (Spring 1980): 54–78.

Nash, Gary B. *Forging Freedom.* Cambridge, Mass., 1989.

Sernett, Milton C. *Black Religion and American Evangelicalism.* Metuchen, New Jersey, 1975.

Shannon, Janet Harrison. Community Formation: Blacks in Northern Liberties, 1790 to 1850. Ph.D. diss., Temple University, 1991.

Ulle, Robert F. A History of St. Thomas' African Episcopal Church, 1794–1865. Ph.D. diss., University of Pennsylvania, 1986.

Weigley, Russell W., ed. *Philadelphia: A 300–Year History.* New York, 1982.

Winch, Julie. *Philadelphia's Black Elite.* Philadelphia, 1988.

– JANET HARRISON SHANNON

PHOTOGRAPHY

African Americans shaped the practice of photography from its origin in 1840 and have participated in its history as practitioners and subjects. The larger American public was fascinated with the daguerreotype as soon as Louis Jacques Mandé Daguerre (1787–1851) publicized the process in France in 1839. The French inventor Nicéphore Niepce (1765–1833) produced the earliest extant photographic image made by a camera obscura in 1827. After the death of Niepce, Daguerre successfully fixed an image and in January 1839 announced to the Paris press his discovery, which he named the Daguerreotype. Six months after the public announcement of the process in Paris, Jules Lion, a free man of color, a lithographer, and portrait painter, exhibited the first successful daguerreotypes in New Orleans.

The African-American public was enthusiastic about Daguerre's process of making likenesses (which we now call photographs). These were numerous free black men and women who established themselves as daguerreans, photographers, inventors, artists, and artisans who had gained local and national recognition in their respective cities. Portraits of prominent and lesser-known African Americans were produced regularly in galleries and studios throughout the country. The portraits of well-known African Americans soon became popular, and the practice of private photography—the photographing of individuals for personal collections and albums—became more and more the artistic method for creating a likeness. Most of the photographs taken at this time were not intended for publication or public presentation, but noted citizens and other families from all walks of life thought it important to have their likenesses preserved for posterity.

During most of photography's early history, images produced by African-American photographers presented idealized glimpses of family members in romanticized or dramatic settings. Photographers such as C.M. Battey and James VANDERZEE sought to integrate elements of romanticism and classicism, as did the painters of the previous centuries. Most photographs taken in the early years were made to commemorate a special occasion in the sitter's life—such as marriage, birth, graduation, confirmation, and anniversaries—or the achievement of a particular social or political success.

One of the earliest known photographical studies in America of African-American physiognomy was conducted in 1850 by Harvard scientist Louis Agassiz and J. T. Zealy, a white daguerreotypist in Columbia, S.C. The latter was hired to take a series of portraits of African-born slaves on nearby plantations. The daguerreotypes were anatomical studies of the faces and the nude upper bodies of African men and women. The photographs were to give visual evidence of the "natural difference in size of limbs, heads, and configurations of muscles," thereby establishing a theory that blacks were different and inferior. Much of the work of the nineteenth-century black photographers was in sharp contrast to these scientific and stereotypical images.

The first publicized exhibition of a work by a black photographer was held on March 15, 1840, in the Hall of the St. Charles Museum in the city of New Orleans. The exhibition, reported to have drawn a large crowd, was organized and sponsored by the artist, Jules Lion. In 1854, Glenalvin Goodridge, a black photographer from York, Pa., won the prize for "best ambrotypes" (a process using a wet plate) at the York County fair. Other black photographers who won distinction in the nineteenth century at exhibitions and expositions include James Presley Ball, who exhibited his daguerreotypes in 1855 at the Ohio Mechanics Annual Exhibition, and Harry Shepherd, who won the first prize at the 1891 Minnesota State fair and later exhibited photographs of the TUSKEGEE INSTITUTE (now University) at the Paris Exposition in 1900. In 1895, Daniel Freeman, known as the first black photographer in Washington, D.C., exhibited his works in the Negro Building at the 1895 Atlanta Exposition.

The first publicized exhibition of a work by a black photographer was held on March 15, 1840, in the Hall of the St. Charles Museum in the city of New Orleans.

Between the end of the Civil War and the turn of the nineteenth century, numerous itinerant photographers flourished in the North. But even earlier, several African-American photographers were able to open their own studios. In the 1840s and '50s, James Ball and Augustus Washington (1820–?) operated galleries in Cincinnati, Ohio, and Hartford, Conn.; Jules Lion had his own studio in New Orleans. (Ball and Washington were active abolitionists who often used their photographic skills to expose the inhumane institution of slavery and promote the abolitionist movement.) Harry Shepherd opened his first portrait gallery in St. Paul, Minn., in 1887, where he employed eight attendants. He advertised that "his patrons are among all classes—from the millionaires to day wage workers." Shepherd was one of the few African-American members of the National Photographers Association of America.

Fanny J. Thompson, a musician and composer living in Memphis, Tenn., in the 1880s, studied photography and was one of the first to record African-American women working in the field. The Goodridge brothers—Glenalvin, Wallace, and William—began their careers in York, Pa., in the 1850s, before settling in East Saginaw, Mich., in 1866. They opened their first studio the following year. In 1884 they were commissioned by the U.S. Department of Forestry to photograph views of the Saginaw Valley woodlands.

At the turn of the century, photography expanded in a variety of ways. Newspapers, journals, and books published photographic images. Courses in photography were offered in schools and colleges, and correspondence courses were also available. C. M. Battey, an accomplished portraitist and fine-art photographer, was a noted educator in photography. Battey founded the Photography Division at Tuskegee Institute in Alabama in 1916. In 1917, CRISIS magazine highlighted Battey in the "Men of the Month" column as "one of the few colored photographers who has gained real artistic success." The most extensive portrait series of African-American leaders produced in the nineteenth century and early twentieth century was done by Battey. His photographic portraits of John Mercer Langston, Frederick DOUGLASS, W. E. B. DU BOIS, Booker T. WASHINGTON, and Paul Laurence DUNBAR were sold nationally and were reproduced on postcards and posters.

Between 1900 and 1919, African-American photographers flourished in larger cities, producing images of both rural and urban experiences. They included Arthur Bedou (1882–1966) of New Orleans; King Daniel Ganaway (1883–?) of Chicago, who in 1918 received first prize in the John Wanamaker Annual Exhibition of photographers; and Arthur Laidler Macbeth (1864–?) of Charlestown, S.C., Baltimore, and Norfolk. Macbeth won many awards and citations for his photographs and was among the pioneers in motion pictures. He invented "Macbeth's Daylight Projecting Screen" for showing stereopticon and moving pictures in the daytime.

In 1911, Addison Scurlock, who was HOWARD UNIVERSITY's official photographer, opened a studio in Washington, D.C., which he operated with his wife and sons, Robert and George, until 1964; after that time, his sons continued to operate the studio. In New York City, James VanDerZee, undoubtedly the best known of black studio photographers, began capturing the spirit and life of New York's Harlem in the 1920s and continued to do so for more than fifty years.

During the period of the HARLEM RENAISSANCE through the Great Depression and the New Deal, photographers began to exhibit their work widely in their communities. In the 1920s, young black photographers who viewed themselves as artists moved to the larger cities in search of education, patronage, and support for their art. Harlem was a cultural mecca for many of these photographers. In 1921 the New York Public Library's 135th Street branch in Manhattan (now known as the Schomburg Center for Research in Black Culture) organized its first exhibition of work by black artists, entitled "The Negro Artists." Two photographers, C. M. Battey and Lucy Calloway of New York, displayed six photographs in this exhibition of over sixty-five works of art. The Harmon Foundation was one of the first philanthropic organizations to give attention, cash awards, and exhibition opportunities to black photographers. These awards came to be known as the William E. Harmon Awards for Distinguished Achievement Among Negroes. In 1930, a special prize of $50 for photographic work was added in the name of the Commission on Race Relations.

A year earlier, James Latimer Allen (1907–1977) exhibited his portraits of African-American men, women, and children in a Harmon Foundation exhibition. Allen also photographed such writers of the period as Alain LOCKE, Langston HUGHES, Countee CULLEN, and Claude MCKAY. Other photographers active between 1920 and '40 included several students of C. M. Battey, among them Elise Forrest Harleston (1891–1970) of Charleston, S.C., and P. H. Polk (1898–1985) of Tuskegee, Ala. Harleston opened a photography studio with her painter husband, Edwin Harleston, after studying with Battey in 1922. Polk opened his first studio at Tuskegee in 1927. The following year he was appointed to the faculty of Tuskegee Institute's photography department, photographed prominent visitors such as Mary McLeod BETHUNE and Paul ROBESON, and made extensive portraits of scientist-inventor George Washington CARVER. Richard S. Roberts (1881–1936) of Columbia, S.C., began studying photography through correspondence courses and specialist journals, and opened his studio in the early 1920s. According to Roberts's advertisements, his studio took superior photographs by day or night. Twin brothers Morgan (1910–1993) and Marvin Smith (1910–) were prolific photographers in Harlem in the 1930s and early '40s.

They photographed members of the community, as well as political rallies, breadlines during the Great Depression, families, and "Lindy Hoppers" in the Savoy Ballroom.

During the Depression, numerous images were taken of the lives of African-Americans. The Resettlement Administration, later known as the Farm Security Administration (FSA), was created in 1935 as an independent coordinating agency; it inherited rural relief activities and land-use administration from the Department of the Interior, the Federal Emergency Relief Administration, and the Agricultural Adjustment Administration. Between 1935 and '43, the FSA photography project generated 270,000 images of rural, urban, and industrial America. Many of the heavily documented activities of the FSA were of black migrant workers in the South. In 1937, Gordon PARKS, Sr. decided that he wanted to be a photographer after viewing the work of the Farm Security Administration photographers. He was hired by the FSA in 1941, and during WORLD WAR II he worked as an Office of War Information correspondent. After the war, he was a photographer for Standard Oil Company. In 1949 he became the first African-American photographer to work on the staff of *Life* magazine.

Roy DECARAVA is the forerunner of contemporary urban photography. He studied art at Cooper Union in New York City, the Works Progress Administration's Harlem Art Center, and the George Washington Carver Art School. In 1955, DeCarava collaborated with Langston HUGHES in producing a book entitled *The Sweet Flypaper of Life,* which depicted the life of a black family in Harlem. In 1952, DeCarava received a Guggenheim Fellowship; he was one of the first black photographers to win the award. In 1954, he founded a photography gallery that became one of the first galleries in the United States devoted to the exhibition and sale of photography as a fine art. DeCarava founded the Kamoinge Workshop for black photographers in 1963.

From the 1930s through the '60s, photographers began working as photojournalists for local newspapers and national magazines marketed to African-American audiences, including *Our World,* EBONY, *Jet, Sepia,* and *Flash,* among others. Only a few African-American photojournalists, most notably Gordon Parks, Sr., Richard Saunders, Bert Miles, and Roy DeCarava, were employed for the larger picture magazines such as *Life, Look, Time, Newsweek,* and *Sports Illustrated.* Most of them learned photography while in the military and studied photography in schools of journalism.

This period also encompassed the beginning of reportage and the documentation of public pageantry and events. In the 1930s smaller hand-held cameras and faster films aided photographers in expressing their frustration and discontent with social and political conditions within their communities. The CIVIL RIGHTS MOVEMENT was well documented by photographers such as Moneta Sleet, Jr. (New York and Chicago); Jack T. Franklin (Philadelphia); Charles "Teenie" Harris (Pittsburgh); Howard Morehead (Los Angeles); Bertrand Miles (New York); Austin Hansen (New York); and U.S. Information Service Agency photographers Richard Saunders and Griffith Davis.

Between 1935 and the early 1990s, musical pioneers were the frequent subjects of Chuck Stewart (1927–), Milt Hinton, Roy DeCarava, and Bert Andrews (1931–1993), who photographed performing artists in the studio, on stage, and in nightclubs. Milt Hinton received his first camera in 1935 while he was playing in Cab CALLOWAY's band. As a jazz bassist and photographer, Hinton photographed his musician friends and colleagues. In 1950, Chuck Stewart, who studied photography at Ohio University, began photographing jazz musicians and vocalists on stage and in his studio in New York City. His photographs were used for album covers, publicity stills, and illustrations for books and articles of jazz. Stewart photographed virtually every well-known musician and vocalist between 1950 and '90; his coverage includes blues, bebop, fusion, salsa, and popular music. Bert Andrews photographed black theatrical productions on and off-Broadway from the early 1960s through the early 1990s. Among the production companies whose plays he photographed are the Negro Ensemble Company, the New Federal Theatre, and the Frank Silvera Writers' Workshop.

During the active years of the civil rights and Black Power movements—the early 1960s through the 1970s—a significant number of socially committed men and women became photographers, documenting the struggles, achievements, and tragedies of the freedom movement. STUDENT NON-VIOLENT COORDINATING COMMITTEE (SNCC) photographers Doug Harris, Elaine Tomlin, and Bob Fletcher were in the forefront in documenting the voter registration drives in the South; Robert Sengstacke, Howard Bingham, Jeffrey Scales, and Brent Jones photographed the North and West Coast activities of the BLACK PANTHER PARTY and desegregation rallies. Between 1969 and 1986, six African-American photographers received the coveted Pulitzer Prize in photography. The first to win the award was Moneta Sleet, Jr., in 1969 for his photograph of Coretta Scott KING and her daughter at the funeral of the Rev. Dr. Martin Luther KING, Jr. Following in subsequent years were Ovie Carter (1975) for international reporting for his photographs of famine in Africa and India; Matthew Lewis (1975) for his portrait studies of

Washingtonians; John White (1982) for work published in the *Chicago Sun Times;* Michel Du Cille (1985) for the photographs of the Colombian earthquake; and Ozier Muhammad (1985) for international reporting for the photographic essay "Africa: The Desperate Continent."

In the 1970s, universities and art colleges began to offer undergraduate and graduate degrees in photography, and African-American photographers began studying photography and creating works for exhibition purposes. Others studied in community centers and workshops. The symbolic and expressive images of the works produced in the 1980s and '90s offer sociological and psychological insights into the past, as well as examinations of contemporary social themes, such as racism, unemployment, child and sexual abuse, death and dying. Most of these works are informed by personal experienced. Significant contributors to the development of this genre are Albert Chong, Sulaiman Ellison, Roland Freeman, Todd Gray, Chester Higgins, Lynn Marshall-Linnemeier, Willie Middlebrook, Jeffrey Scales, Coreen Simpson, Lorna Simpson, Elisabeth Sunday, Christian Walker, Carrie Mae Weems, Carla Williams, and Pat Ward Williams.

BIBLIOGRAPHY

Coar, Valencia Hollins. *A Century of Black Photographers: 1840–1960.* Providence, R.I., 1983.

Crawford, Joe. *The Black Photographers Annual,* Vol. 1. Brooklyn, N.Y., 1972.

———. *The Black Photographers Annual.* Vol. 2. Brooklyn, N.Y., 1974.

———. *The Black Photographers Annual.* Vol. 3. Brooklyn, N.Y., 1976.

———. *The Black Photographers Annual.* Vol. 4. Brooklyn, N.Y., 1980.

DeCarava, Roy, and Langston Hughes. *The Sweet Flypaper of Life.* 1955. Reprint. Washington, D.C., 1984.

Parks, Gordon. *Born Black.* Philadelphia, 1971.

———. *A Choice of Weapons.* New York, 1966.

———. *Moments Without Proper Names.* New York, 1975.

Willis-Thomas, Deborah. *Black Photographers, 1840–1940: An Illustrated Bio-Bibliography.* New York, 1985.

———. *Black Photographers, 1940–1988: An Illustrated Bio-Bibliography.* New York, 1989.

– DEBORAH WILLIS-THOMAS

PIPPIN, HORACE

Horace Pippin (February 22, 1888–July 6, 1946), painter. One of the foremost self-taught painters of the twentieth century, Horace Pippin was born in West Chester, Pa. A disabled WORLD WAR I veteran, he initially took up art in the 1920s to strengthen his wounded right arm. By the late 1930s Pippin's distinctive and diverse images of his childhood memories and war experiences, scenes of everyday life, landscapes, portraits, biblical subjects, and American historical events had found enthusiastic local supporters such as critic Christian Brinton, artists N. C. Wyeth and John McCoy, collector Albert C. Barnes, and dealer Robert Carlen.

In the eight years between his national debut in a 1938 group exhibition at New York's Museum of Modern Art and his death at the age of fifty-eight, Pippin's productivity increased and his paintings entered major private and museum collections on the East and West Coasts. In 1947 Alain LOCKE described Pippin as "a real and rare genius, combining folk quality with artistic maturity so uniquely as almost to defy classification."

A descendant of former slaves, the artist was raised by Harriet Pippin (1834–1908). It is unknown today if Harriet was his mother or grandmother. Her eyewitness account of the 1859 hanging of the abolitionist John Brown provided the basis for Pippin's 1942 painting on that subject, which depicted her as the sole African-American woman in the crowd of onlookers.

In 1891, the family relocated to the resort town of Goshen, N.Y., where they worked as domestic servants. As a boy, Pippin showed a strong interest in drawing, winning his first set of crayons and a box of watercolors for his response to an advertising contest for an art supply company. Pippin rendered the warm family circle of his boyhood in the memory picture *Domino Players* (1943; Phillips Collection).

Horace Pippin was one of the foremost self-taught painters of the twentieth century.

He attended a segregated one-room school until 1902. After working as a porter at the St. Elmo Hotel for seven years he relocated to Paterson, N.J., finding employment crating oil paintings with a moving and storage company. Prior to his service in World War I, Pippin variously toiled in a coal yard, in an iron foundry, and as a used-clothing peddler.

In 1917, the twenty-nine-year-old Pippin enlisted in the New York National Guard, serving as a corporal in what would subsequently become the 369th Colored Infantry Regiment of the 93rd Division of the United States Army. Landing in Brest in December 1917, Pippin and his regiment first worked laying railroad track for two months prior to serving at the front lines in the Argonne Forest under French command.

While in the trenches, Pippin kept illustrated journals of his military service, but only six drawings from this period survive. He later wrote that World War I "brought out all the art in me." In October 1918 Pippin was shot through the right shoulder by a German sniper and was honorably discharged the following year. Awarded the French Croix de Guerre in 1919, he received a retroactive Purple Heart in 1945.

In 1920 Pippin married the twice-widowed Ora Fetherstone Wade, who had a six-year-old son. Supporting themselves on his disability check and her work as a laundress, they settled in West Chester, where she owned a home. A community-spirited man, Pippin helped organize a black Boy Scouts troop and served as commander of the local American Legion for black veterans. As therapy for his injured arm, he began making pictures in 1925 by burning images on wood panels using a hot iron poker. At the age of forty he expanded to oil paints, completing his first painting, *End of the War: Starting Home,* in 1930 (Philadelphia Museum of Art).

Pippin first received public attention when he exhibited two paintings in the Chester County Art Association annual of 1937. Immediately following this debut, John McCoy and Christian Brinton facilitated an exhibition for Pippin at the West Chester Community Center, a hub of local black activities. Within a year Pippin was included in Holger Cahill's "Masters of Popular Painting" at New York's Museum of Modern Art.

Art dealer Robert Carlen of Philadelphia mounted Pippin's first gallery show in 1940, comprising twenty-seven works including *Abraham Lincoln and His Father Building Their Cabin on Pigeon Creek* (Barnes Foundation), *Buffalo Hunt* (Whitney Museum of American Art), and *Cabin in the Cotton* (Art Institute of Chicago). Introduced to Pippin's work by Carlen, the renowned art collector Albert Barnes wrote two catalog essays on the artist. At his invitation, Pippin visited Barnes's Foundation to see his world-famous painting collection and to attend art appreciation lectures. This exposure did not alter his characteristic approach to his art, although from then on Pippin added still-life compositions to his repertory, of which there are many examples in Barnes's collection.

In the years between his first Philadelphia show in 1940 and his death in 1946, Pippin had solo exhibitions at New York's Bignou Gallery (1940), the Arts Club of Chicago (1941), the San Francisco Museum of Art (1942), and New York's Downtown Gallery (1944). Among the museums that purchased his work during his lifetime were the Pennsylvania Academy of Fine Arts (*John Brown Going to His Hanging*); Buffalo's Albright Knox Gallery (*Self-Portrait*); and Washington's Phillips Collection (*Domino Players*). Early collectors included Philadelphia's Main Line society and such well-known actors and writers as Edward G. Robinson, Charles Laughton, Claude Rains, John Garfield, Ruth Gordon, S. J. Perelman, and Clifford Odets.

Pippin's commissioned works were varied. For the Capehart Collection in 1943 he executed a painting inspired by Stephen Foster's "Old Black Joe" (private collection); in 1944 *Vogue* magazine requested him to paint an image on the theme of cotton (Brady Museum, Cuernavaca); his painting *The Temptation of Saint Anthony* (1945; private collection) was created for an invited competition sponsored by the film producers David L. Loew and Albert Lewin, who also asked Salvador Dali, Marc Chagall, and Giorgio de Chirico, among others, to respond to a Guy de Maupassant short story.

Mrs. Pippin was hospitalized with mental problems in March 1946. She died four months later, two weeks after the artist himself had succumbed to a stroke on July 6, 1946. Of the 137 works on paper, fabric, and wood that Pippin was known to have created, approximately ten percent are today unlocated. He once summed up his approach to paintings: "Pictures just come to my mind. I think my pictures out with my brain, and then I tell my heart to go ahead."

BIBLIOGRAPHY

Barnes, Albert. "Horace Pippin." In *Horace Pippin Exhibition,* Carlen Gallery. Philadelphia, 1940.

Bearden, Romare. "Horace Pippin." In *Horace Pippin,* The Phillips Collection. Washington, D.C., 1976.

Locke, Alain. "Horace Pippin." In *Horace Pippin Memorial Exhibition,* The Art Alliance, April 8–May 4, 1947. Philadelphia, 1947.

Rodman, Selden. *Horace Pippin: A Negro Painter in America.* New York, 1947.

Stein, Judith E., et al. *I Tell My Heart: The Art of Horace Pippin.* New York, 1993.

— JUDITH E. STEIN

PITTSBURGH, PENNSYLVANIA

Prior to the Civil War, Pittsburgh's blacks were typical of those in most northern cities—they were few in number, impoverished, and victimized by racial discrimination. Blacks arrived with the very earliest colonial settlers—as trappers, pioneers, soldiers, and slaves—once the area became a British possession in 1763, at the conclusion of the Seven Years' War. A few of these early settlers prospered. By 1800, for example, Ben Richards, a butcher, had accumulated a fortune by provisioning nearby military posts. Nonetheless, opportunities for most were quite limited, and the black population grew slowly. In 1850, blacks comprised only two thousand people—less than 5 percent of the city's population—and were centered in "Little Hayti," an area in the Lower Hill district where housing was cheap and close to downtown.

This community, although small, was active and assertive. One of its leading citizens, John Vashon, operated a fashionable bath house and barbershop. Another, John Peck, was a wigmaker and barber. Vashon, Peck, and Lewis Woodson, a barber and schoolteacher, were active in the antislavery movement. The best-known leader was Martin R. Delany, who lived in Pittsburgh from the early 1830s until 1856. He edited one of Pittsburgh's early black newspapers, *The Mystery,* from 1843 until 1847.

Despite its small size and its poverty, Pittsburgh's pre-Civil War African-American community supported a remarkable number of institutions. These included an AME (African Methodist Episcopal) church, an AME Zion church, four benevolent societies, a private school, a cemetery, a militia company, a newspaper, and a temperance society.

Prior to the Civil War, Pittsburgh's blacks were few in number, impoverished, and victimized by racial discrimination.

In the years between the Civil War and World War I, black Pittsburghers made impressive gains. From 1870 to 1900, Virginia migrants helped swell their numbers from 1,162 to 20,355, making theirs the sixth-largest black community in the nation. In 1875, following years of protests and boycotts, they forced the desegregation of the city's public schools. And, although they remained largely excluded from the city's booming iron and glass industries, by the early 1900s they boasted eighty-five businesses and supported numerous clubs dedicated to social and cultural uplift. The community erected its own Home for Aged and Infirm Colored Women, a Working Girls' Home, and a Colored Orphans' Home. Churches which catered to the district's elite—Ebenezer Baptist, Grace Memorial Presbyterian, Bethel AME, Warren ME, and St. Benedict the Moor Roman Catholic—were also active in community affairs. A number of groups—including the Aurora Reading Club, the Frances Harper League, the Wylie Avenue Literary Society, the Homewood Social and Literary Club, the Emma J. Moore Literary and Art Circle, and the Booker T. Washington Literary Society—promoted the cultural life of the community through reading and discussing literature. In addition, the prestigious Loendi Club, established in 1897, invited outstanding speakers to address its members and the black community.

African Americans in Pittsburgh also enjoyed an active musical life in the late nineteenth century. Community interest in classical music was reflected in the creation of three black concert and symphony orchestras at this time. One was founded by William A. Kelly, a coal miner and graduate of Oberlin; a second by Dr. C. A. Taylor, who had played in the Toronto Civic Orchestra; and a third by David Peeler, a local contractor and builder.

Between World War I and 1930, the city's black community grew rapidly. The cutoff of European immigration occasioned by World War I forced employers in Pittsburgh to seek out black workers to fill their depleted labor force. The iron and glass industries hired large numbers of African Americans for the first time. This touched off a migratory wave of Southerners that enlarged the region's black population. In Pittsburgh, the number of blacks rose from 25,000 to 55,000, while in the nearby mill towns of Aliquippa, Homestead, Rankin, Braddock, Duquesne, McKeesport, and Clairton, their numbers increased from 5,000 to 23,000.

Migrants brought energy and creativity to the local community. One of the most notable examples of this was Robert Vann, under whose leadership the *Pittsburgh Courier,* founded in 1910, became by the 1930s the black newspaper with the largest circulation in the country. Born in North Carolina in 1879, Vann earned his undergraduate degree at Virginia Union University in Richmond, Va. He then attended law school at the University of Pittsburgh, attracted by the availability of an Avery Scholarship for black students.

The *Courier*'s masthead—"Work, Integrity, Tact, Temperance, Prudence, Courage, Faith"—reflected Vann's faith in the American Dream. The paper endorsed the philosophy of Booker T. WASHINGTON: "Concentrate your earnings, and make capital. Hire yourselves, produce for yourselves, and sell something for yourselves." As a conservative journal, it supported World War I, opposed socialism, had no sympathy for unions, and applauded restrictive quotas on immigrants. An associate of Vann's, Daisy Lampkin (c. 1884–1965), was an active black Republican suffragist and national field secretary for the NAACP from 1935 to 1947.

The cultural life of black Pittsburgh flourished in the interwar years. By the 1930s it had two of the best teams—the Homestead Grays and the Pittsburgh Crawfords—ever to play baseball. In 1936, the Crawfords fielded five eventual Hall of Famers—Satchel

PAIGE, Josh GIBSON, James "Cool Papa" Bell, Oscar Charleston, and Judy Johnson. Pittsburgh was also an active jazz center, and prominent jazz musicians who grew up there include Lena HORNE, Billy Strayhorn, Kenny Clarke, Billy Eckstine, Roy Eldridge, Mary Lou Williams, and Art BLAKEY. The local nightlife was centered on the intersection of Wylie and Fullerton Avenues, an area of nightclubs and cabarets.

Economically and politically, however, the community suffered. Few blacks enjoyed occupational mobility in the mills, partly because of white prejudice and partly because they had entered the city just as its steel industry had stopped growing. Black migrants entered the industrial work force at the bottom and had almost no success in moving up. Abraham Epstein's 1918 study "The Negro Migrant in Pittsburgh" found that 95 percent of black industrial workers were in unskilled positions. Investigations five years later by two black graduate students, Abram Harris and Ira Reid, in "The Negro in Major Industries and Building Trades of Pittsburgh" (later incorporated into Reid's study *Social Conditions of the Negro in the Hill District of Pittsburgh of 1930*) found blacks still mired at the bottom of the job ladder, and experiencing difficulty holding on to even those lowly jobs. A situation that was bleak during the 1920s turned disastrous during the Great Depression, when 33 to 40 percent of black adults were unemployed. A study of 2,700 black families found 41 percent destitute and another 33 percent living in poverty.

Moreover, blacks were unable to exercise political influence commensurate with their numbers. Pittsburgh's hills dispersed blacks among several "minighettos," so that the Hill district—the city's major black neighborhood—housed only 41 percent of the area's black residents. This fragmentation caused political weakness and apathy that have been denounced by generations of community leaders. The distinguished career of Homer Brown as a community activist, state legislator, and local judge in the 1930s, 1940s, and early 1950s was a striking exception to this condition.

A situation that was bleak during the 1920s turned disastrous during the Great Depression, when 33 to 40 percent of black adults were unemployed.

In the 1950s, the economic and political problems of African Americans were compounded by the destruction of the Lower Hill—home to thousands of residents—for the sake of "urban renewal." Because no provision was made for their resettlement, those who were uprooted crowded into other neighborhoods, notably East Liberty and Homewood-Brushton, precipitating the abandonment of those areas by whites and more established middle-class blacks.

Nonetheless, blacks took tentative steps toward political power. In 1954 they helped elect their first city council member, Paul Jones; in 1958, they elected K. Leroy Irvis to the Pennsylvania legislature, and over the next three decades of a distinguished career Irvis served as minority whip, majority whip, and (twice by acclamation) speaker of the Pennsylvania House. Black political power was fragile, however. This was demonstrated in 1985, when blacks wound up with no representation on the city council. By 1989, following widespread protests and the abolition of an at-large electoral system, two blacks were elected to council from districts with large black majorities.

Political leadership was sorely needed, for Pittsburgh blacks suffered from many of the same social ills as their counterparts elsewhere. Indeed, in 1980, Pittsburgh blacks had a somewhat higher proportion of female-headed families and a higher infant mortality rate than blacks nationally. They also lived on an income that was only 57 percent that of local whites, and suffered an unemployment rate 2.3 times the local rate for whites.

Despite these travails, the condition of Pittsburgh's blacks was not altogether bleak. The riots following the assassination of the Rev. Dr. Martin Luther King, Jr., were less violent in Pittsburgh than in many other cities, and, at least through the 1980s, Pittsburgh was not overrun by drugs, which made its crime rate substantially lower than that of cities like Cleveland, Detroit, and Chicago, and even lower than supposedly "safe" cities like Minneapolis and Syracuse. If older black institutions, such as the great Negro League teams or the *Pittsburgh Courier,* became defunct or were greatly diminished in stature in the postwar years, black Pittsburgh has continued its cultural vitality. In jazz, Erroll Garner, Ahmad Jamal, Stanley Turrentine, Dakota Staton, and George Benson show that Pittsburgh continues to produce outstanding talent. In letters, John WIDEMAN (winner of the PEN/Faulkner Award) and August WILSON (winner of the Pulitzer Prize) have added luster through their novels and plays set in Pittsburgh. Nonetheless, black Pittsburghers still must cope with the legacy of their economic and political burdens.

BIBLIOGRAPHY

Blackett, Richard J. M. "Freedom, or the Martyr's Grave: Black Pittsburgh's Aid to the Fugitive Slave." *Western Pennsylvania Historical Magazine* 61 (January 1978): 117–134.

Bodnar, John, William Simon, and Michael P. Weber. *Lives of Their Own: Blacks, Italians, and Poles in Pittsburgh, 1900–1960.* Urbana, Ill., 1982, pp. 117, 186.

———. "Migration, Kinship, and Urban Adjustment: Blacks and Poles in Pittsburgh, 1900–1930." *Journal of American History* 66 (December 1979): 548–565.

Buni, Andrew. *Robert L. Vann of the Pittsburgh* Courier*: Politics and Black Journalism.* Pittsburgh, 1974.

Darden, Joe. *Afro-Americans in Pittsburgh: The Residential Segregation of a People.* Lexington, Mass., 1973.

Dickerson, Dennis C. "The Black Church in Industrializing Western Pennsylvania, 1870–1950." *Western Pennsylvania Historical Magazine* 64 (October 1981).

———. "Black Ecumenism: Efforts to Establish a United Methodist Episcopal Church, 1918–1932." *Church History* 52 (December 1983): 470–491.

———. *Out of the Crucible: Black Steelworkers in Western Pennsylvania, 1875–1980.* Albany, N.Y., 1986.

Edmunds, Arthur J. *Daybreakers: The Story of the Urban League of Pittsburgh: The First Sixty-Five Years.* Pittsburgh, 1983.

Epstein, Abraham. *The Negro Migrant in Pittsburgh.* Pittsburgh, 1918.

Glasco, Lawrence. "Double Burden: The Black Experience in Pittsburgh." In S. P. Hays, ed., *City at the Point.* Pittsburgh, 1989, pp. 69–109.

Gottlieb, Peter. *Making Their Own Way: Southern Blacks' Migration to Pittsburgh, 1916–1930.* Urbana, Ill., 1987.

Harris, Abram. The New Negro Worker in Pittsburgh. M.A. thesis, University of Pittsburgh, 1924.

Lubove, Roy. *Twentieth Century Pittsburgh: Government, Business, and Environmental Change.* New York, 1969.

Reid, Ira DeA. The Negro in Major Industries and Building Trades of Pittsburgh. M.A. thesis, University of Pittsburgh, 1925.

———. *Social Conditions of the Negro in the Hill District of Pittsburgh.* Pittsburgh, 1930.

Ruck, Rob. *Sandlot Seasons: Sport in Black Pittsburgh.* Urbana, Ill., 1987.

Sapolsky, Steven, and Bartholomew Roselli. *Homewood-Brushton: A Century of Community-Making.* Pittsburgh, 1987.

Sizemore, Barbara. *An Abashing Anomaly: The High-Achieving Predominantly Black Elementary School.* Pittsburgh, 1983.

Tucker, Helen A. "The Negroes of Pittsburgh." In *Charities and the Commons,* 1909. Reprinted in Paul U. Kellog, *Wage-Earning Pittsburgh* (no. 6 of *The Pittsburgh Survey*). New York, 1974, pp. 424–436.

Williams, Melvin D. *Community in a Black Pentecostal Church: An Anthropological Study.* Pittsburgh, 1974.

Wilmoth, Ann G. Pittsburgh and the Blacks: A Short History, 1780–1875. Ph.D. diss., Pennsylvania State University, 1975.

— LAWRENCE A. GLASCO

PLESSY V. FERGUSON

In *Plessy* v. *Ferguson,* 163 U.S. 537 (1896), the Supreme Court upheld an 1890 Louisiana statute that required railroads to provide separate but equal accommodations for blacks and whites, and forbade persons from riding in cars not assigned to their race. It gave constitutional sanction to virtually all forms of racial segregation in the United States until after World War II.

Plessy arose as part of a careful strategy to test the legality of the new Louisiana law. In September 1891, elite "persons of color" in New Orleans formed the "Citizens Committee to Test the Constitutionality of the Separate Car Law." They raised three thousand dollars for the costs of a test case. Albion Tourgee, the nation's leading white advocate of black rights, agreed to take the case without fee. Tourgee, a former judge, was a nationally prominent writer most noted for his novel about Reconstruction, *A Fool's Errand.*

In June 1892, Homer A. Plessy purchased a first-class ticket on the East Louisiana Railroad, sat in the "white" car, and was promptly arrested and arraigned before Judge John H. Ferguson. Plessy then sued to prevent Ferguson from conducting any further proceedings against him. Eventually his challenge reached the United States Supreme Court.

Before the Court, Tourgee argued that segregation violated the THIRTEENTH AMENDMENT's prohibition of involuntary servitude and denied blacks equal protection of the laws, which was guaranteed by the FOURTEENTH AMENDMENT. These amendments, along with the Declaration of Independence, Tourgee asserted, gave Americans affirmative rights against invidious discrimination. He asserted that the Fourteenth Amendment gave constitutional life to the Declaration of Independence, "which is not a fable as some of our modern theorists would have us believe, but [is] the all-embracing formula of personal rights on which our government is based." Joining Tourgee in these arguments was Samuel F. Phillips, a former solicitor general of the United States, who in 1883 had unsuccessfully argued the *Civil Rights Cases.*

The Court rejected Tourgee's arguments by a vote of 7 to 1. In his majority opinion, Justice Henry Billings Brown conceded that the Fourteenth Amendment was adopted "to enforce the absolute equality of the two races before the law," but asserted that the amendment "could not have been intended to abolish distinctions based upon color, or to enforce social, as distinguished from political equality, or a commingling of the two races." Ignoring the reality of the emerging JIM CROW South, the Court denied that "the enforced separation of the two races stamps the colored race with a badge of inferiority." Brown believed that segregation was not discriminatory because whites were also segregated from blacks. Thus, if segregation created a perception of inferiority "it is not by reason of anything found in the act, but solely because the colored race chooses to put that construction upon it." Reflecting the accepted social science and popular prejudices of his age, Brown argued:

> Legislation is powerless to eradicate racial instincts or to abolish distinctions based upon physical differences, and the attempt to do so can only result in accentuating the difficulties of the present situation. If the civil and political rights of both races be equal, one cannot be inferior to the other civilly or politically. If one race be inferior to the other socially, the Constitution of the United States cannot put them upon the same plane.

Thus, as long as segregated facilities were "equal" they were permissible. Segregation had now received the sanction and blessing of the Supreme Court.

In a bitter, lone dissent, Justice John Marshall Harlan, a former slave owner, acknowledged that the "white race" was "the dominant race in this country." But, as Harlan read the Constitution,

> in the eye of the law, there is in this country no superior, dominant, ruling class of citizens. There is no caste here. Our Constitution is color-blind, and neither knows nor tolerates classes among citizens. In respect of civil rights, all citizens are equal before the law. The humblest is the peer of the most powerful. The law regards man as man, and takes no account of his surroundings or his color when his civil rights as guaranteed by the supreme law of the land are involved.

Harlan protested that the Court's decision would "stimulate aggressions, more or less brutal and irritating, upon the admitted rights of colored citizens" and "encourage the belief that it is possible, by means of state enactments, to defeat the beneficent purposes which the people of the United States had in view when they adopted the recent amendments to the Constitution." In prophetic language, Harlan asserted, "The thin disguise of 'equal' accommodations for passengers in railroad coaches will not mislead any one, nor atone for the wrong this day done." Harlan argued that the Louisiana law was "inconsistent with the personal liberty of citizens, white and black" and "hostile to both the spirit and letter of the Constitution of the United States."

Harlan's voice was that of a prophet ignored by his own age. More than five decades would pass before the Supreme Court recognized the fundamental truth of his dissent. Meanwhile, the South built a social and legal system rooted in racial segregation. In January 1897, Homer Plessy pled guilty to attempting to board a "white" railroad car and paid a twenty-five-dollar fine.

BIBLIOGRAPHY

Finkelman, Paul, ed. *Race, Law, and American History.* Vol. 4, *The Age of Jim Crow: Segregation from the End of Reconstruction to the Great Depression.* New York, 1992.

Kull, Andrew. *The Color Blind Constitution.* Cambridge, Mass., 1992.

Lofgren, Charles A. *The Plessy Case: A Legal-Historical Interpretation.* New York, 1987.

Logan, Rayford W. *The Betrayal of the Negro.* Reprint of *The Negro in American Life and Thought: The Nadir, 1877–1901.* New York, 1965.

Woodward, C. Vann. *The Origins of the New South, 1877–1913.* Baton Rouge, La., 1951.

———. *The Strange Career of Jim Crow.* New York, 1955.

— PAUL FINKELMAN

POITIER, SIDNEY

Sidney Poitier (February 20, 1927–), actor, director, and filmmaker. The youngest of eight children, Sidney Poitier was born in Miami and reared on Cat Island in the Bahamas. He was forced to leave school at fifteen in order to work on his parents' tomato farm, and then moved to Miami to live with his married brother Cyril. Shortly thereafter, Poitier left for New York City, enlisted in the U.S. Army, and served as a physiotherapist until World War II ended in 1945. Upon his return to New York, he supported himself with a series of menial jobs, while studying to become an actor. After an unsuccessful audition, he spent six months trying to rid himself of his West Indian accent and eventually became a member of the American Negro Theatre, for which he often played leading roles. He also won minor parts in the Broadway productions of *Lysistrata* (1946) and *Anna Lucasta* (1948), before trying his hand at film. In 1950 he married Juanita Hardy, a dancer, with whom he had three children; Poitier and Hardy were eventually divorced.

Poitier's big break came when he was cast as a young doctor in Twentieth Century Fox's "racial problem" film *No Way Out* (1950). Leading roles followed in such films as *Cry, the Beloved Country* (1951), *Go Man Go* (1954), *Blackboard Jungle* (1955), *Band of Angels, Edge of the City,* and *Something of Value* (the last three all released in 1957). With his performance as an escaped convict in *The Defiant Ones* (1958), Poitier became the first African American to be nominated for an Oscar in the best actor category; he also won the New York Film Critics and Berlin Film Festival awards for best actor. The next year, Poitier took on the title role in Otto Preminger's motion picture version of *Porgy and Bess* (1959), for which he was also critically acclaimed.

As an actor, Poitier was known for sensitive, versatile, and eloquent interpretations and powerful on-camera presence as well as his good looks. He was one of the first African Americans to become a major Hollywood star, and during the 1960s played leads in many influential and controversial films. After originating the role of Walter Lee Younger on Broadway in Lorraine HANS-

Sidney Poitier in his Academy Award-winning performance in Lilies of the Field *(1963). (AP/Wide World Photos)*

BERRY's *A Raisin in the Sun* (1959), Poitier was featured in such diverse films as *Paris Blue* (1960), *Pressure Point* (1961), *A Patch of Blue* (1965), *The Bedford Incident* (1965), *Duel at Diablo* (1966), *Guess Who's Coming to Dinner?, In the Heat of the Night,* and *To Sir, with Love* (all 1967). In 1963, he became the first African American to win an Academy Award for best actor for his performance in *Lilies of the Field.*

The late 1960s proved a transitional period for Poitier, who was accused of portraying unrealistic "noble Negro" or "ebony saint" characters by the militant black community. He confessed to feeling himself caught between the demands of white and black audiences, and attempted to diversify his roles by taking on such films as *They Call Me Mr. Tibbs!* (1970), *A Warm December* (1973), and *The Wilby Conspiracy* (1975), and applying his talents to directing. In 1968, Poitier joined with Paul Newman, Steve McQueen, Dustin Hoffman, and Barbra Streisand to form First Artists, an independent production company. The popular western *Buck and the Preacher* (1972) marked his debut as both director and star; *A Warm December* and the hit comedy *Uptown Saturday Night* (both 1974), *Let's Do It Again* (1975), and *A Piece of the Action* (1977) all featured him in this dual role. In 1975 he was elected to the Black Filmmakers Hall of Fame; his film *Let's Do It Again* earned him the NAACP Image Award in 1976. That year, Poitier married the actress Joanna Shimkus, with whom he had two children. His autobiography, *This Life,* was published in 1980.

Over the next decade, Poitier concentrated on directing such works as *Stir Crazy* (1980), *Hanky Panky* (1982), *Fast Forward* (1985), and *Ghost Dad* (1990). In 1982 he became the recipient of the Cecil B. DeMille Golden Globe Award and the Los Angeles Urban League Whitney M. Young Award. Poitier returned to acting briefly in 1988 for starring roles in *Shoot to Kill* and *Little Nikita,* both of which were released that year.

In addition to creative filmmaking, Poitier has produced a record album called *Sidney Poitier Reads the Poetry of the Black Man* and narrated two documentaries on Paul ROBESON: *A Tribute to the Artist* (1979) and *Man of Conscience* (1986). In recognition of his artistic and humanitarian accomplishments, he was knighted by Queen Elizabeth II, and the NAACP honored him with its first Thurgood Marshall Lifetime Achievement Award in 1993.

BIBLIOGRAPHY

Ewers, Carolyn H. *The Long Journey: A Biography of Sidney Poitier.* New York, 1969.

Marill, Alvin H. *The Films of Sidney Poitier.* Secaucus, N.J., 1978.

Poitier, Sidney. *This Life.* New York, 1980.

– ED GUERRERO

POLITICS AND POLITICIANS

African-American Politics has been divided into three sections: a brief Overview, Antebellum Politics, and Reconstruction to the Present.

Overview

African-American politics has a long, complex, and frequently painful history. By definition slaves were noncitizens, outside of the political process. Yet in various ways slaves contrived to fashion a political role for themselves, such as through Negro Elections Day festivals in New England. During the Colonial period, free blacks tried to enter the political process whenever possible, but were unable to exercise significant influence on the political system. In the half century following the end of the AMERICAN REVOLUTION, free black voting was largely restricted, but through petitions, community organizations, emigrationist activities, newspapers, and eventually the ANTEBELLUM CONVENTION MOVEMENT, free blacks expressed themselves politically.

Beginning in the 1830s, at the same time that the ABOLITION movement offered blacks a voice within a national reform movement, blacks themselves set up numerous committees and organizations to struggle for suffrage, civil rights, and education. Nevertheless, the political status of African Americans remained uncertain, and it eroded during the late 1840s and 1850s as a result of growing white racism, immigrant labor competition, FUGITIVE SLAVE LAWS, and other factors. Many African Americans became convinced that freedom in the United States was unattainable, and turned their attention to colonization schemes in Africa, Canada, Haiti, and other places.

The outbreak of the CIVIL WAR galvanized blacks, who saw the war as a struggle for their liberation. Throughout the first two years of the war, African-American leaders such as Frederick DOUGLASS campaigned for blacks to be armed and devoted their attention to securing aid for freemen who escaped behind Union lines, as well as civil rights and suffrage for the free black community. By 1862 blacks were permitted to enlist in the Union Army. Thousands joined, recognizing the importance of the struggle, and black leaders served as recruiting agents.

For a brief period during RECONSTRUCTION, fortified by constitutional amendments guaranteeing equal citizenship and suffrage and white northern efforts to ensure southern compliance, black males for the first time participated fully in the electoral system. Black elected officials, sponsored by southern Republican parties in exchange for black voting support, appeared on the national scene, and black state legislators and convention delegates made decisive contributions to the political culture of their states. Meanwhile, there was widespread black involvement in municipal politics in the South's few cities of importance. Richmond, Va., had thirty-three black city council members between 1871 and 1896, while in the deep South, leaders such as William Finch of Atlanta and Holland Thompson of Montgomery, Ala., were elected to positions on city councils. In 1873 Mifflin Gibbs was elected a municipal judge in Little Rock, Ark. Many smaller towns elected black mayors. Between 1870 and 1900 twenty African Americans were elected to the House of Representatives, and two served in the Senate.

However, white Southerners never really accepted blacks as equal members of the body politic, and following the withdrawal of northern pressure—both military and political—from the South during the mid-1870s, the scope of black public participation narrowed. Black officeholding all but disappeared, and black voting power was vitiated by voting fraud, intimidation of voters, and electoral devices such as redistricting. As early as 1878 the city of Atlanta changed from ward elections to at-large voting to dilute the black vote. Other cities soon followed suit. Even where black suffrage was unfettered, the dissolution of southern Republicanism left blacks no effective weapon against one-party Democratic regimes other than through alliance with third parties such as the Populists, who were ambivalent about black support.

In the upper South, black Republicans continued to be elected in small numbers. George White, an African American, represented North Carolina in Congress into the new century, while blacks such as Richmond's John Mitchell served on city councils in Virginia into the 1890s. Violence and legislative action against black voting during the 1890s cut off even these avenues of influence.

Meanwhile, the political influence of blacks in the urban North also diminished. In the immediate postbellum period, some blacks were elected to office. In 1866, with the aid of white voters, state representatives Charles Mitchell and Edwin Walker of Boston became the first blacks elected to office from a large urban area. In 1876 George L. Ruffin was elected to Boston's Common Council. However, in most cities, the percentage of African Americans in the population remained too small for blacks to play a significant role, and as immigrant-backed machines hostile to blacks took control of city governments, black voting power diminished. Moreover, city governments were often dependent on state legislatures, which controlled budgets and selected police chiefs and other officials. These outside bodies could act to curtail or eliminate black voting strength. (Similarly, in 1871 the U.S. Congress stripped Washington, D.C., whose population was one-third black, of its elected government.) Even after many cities obtained "home rule" at the end of the century, Progressive elites instituted at-large voting and granted power to unelected city commissions and civil service workers to curb the power of blacks and white ethnics.

The Great Migration of southern blacks to northern and midwestern cities during the late 1910s and '20s brought in its wake large numbers of new voters.

Through most of the late nineteenth century, the Republican party maintained its alliance with both southern and northern black populations through government appointments and support for education. Many black voters and party leaders measured party support not through its defense of civil rights but by the amount of political patronage granted the black community. Still, as early as the 1870s many blacks grew dissatisfied with shrinking party patronage and the party's inaction over violations of black rights, and distanced themselves from the Republicans. Beginning in the 1880s some blacks flirted with joining the Democrats. However, neither party was willing to risk alienating white voters or grant more than token assistance in exchange for the black vote. Others joined third parties or attempted to build up separate black institutions but were unable to mount effective challenges to prevailing political trends.

By 1900 virtually all southern blacks were disfranchised, while their counterparts in the North were unable to exert significant influence. A few political clubs, such as New York's United Colored Democracy, were formed, but they were merely satellite party groups, given minor patronage positions in exchange for promoting white candidates. Black political power remained largely dormant for a generation, except for the influence black strongmen such as Charles Anderson in New York City, Robert Church, Jr., in Memphis, and, above all, Booker T. WASHINGTON wielded over Republican party patronage. The ratification in 1920 of the Nineteenth Amendment, which enfranchised black women as well as white women, had little discernible impact on black political strength. In the first years after the turn of the century, the border states were the only places with significant African-American influence on municipal government. For example, in 1890 Harry Smythe Cummings became the first of several blacks over the following years to sit on the Baltimore City Council.

The Great Migration of southern blacks to northern and midwestern cities during the late 1910s and '20s brought in its wake large numbers of new voters. The voting power of the increased population was strengthened by the increasing ghettoization and residential concentration of African Americans. Their votes were organized in exchange for patronage by ward leaders selected by urban machines, such as New York's J. Raymond Jones and Chicago's William Dawson. In many places, city council and other municipal elected offices remained largely powerless, and ward committeemen positions were the most powerful city jobs most blacks held. In a few areas, blacks became a large enough segment of the population to elect black officials. In 1915, after the creation of a largely black district in Chicago, Republican Oscar Depriest won election to the city's Board of Alderman. In 1919 Charles Roberts was elected to New York City's Aldermanic Board. Similarly, Frank Hall was elected to the Cincinnati City Council in 1931. The growing strength of black organizations was evidenced by DePriest's election in 1928 as the first northern black congressman. As importantly, the migration and the Great Depression helped foster increasing black community militancy, and civil rights joined patronage as a primary concern of African-American voters.

During the 1930s, as a result of aid from New Deal federal social programs, urban machine involvement, and labor union activism, the majority of black voters were drawn into the Democratic Party coalition. Meanwhile, black Democratic elected officials, beginning with Arthur Mitchell in 1934, entered Congress as well as state legislatures and municipal bodies. While the Democrats did not commit to civil rights action or provide aid proportionate to the level of black support, they made symbolic gestures toward the black community and instituted several relatively race-neutral goverment programs. While blacks backed Democratic candidates, many remained registered Republicans. A small number of blacks supported minor parties, notably the Communist Party, whose advocacy of civil rights and interracialism won it the support or approbation of many African Americans.

In the years after WORLD WAR II, black political activity increased. The war brought renewed migration to the North of southern blacks, who swelled urban voting blocs. The migration made possible the election of larger numbers of black officials such as Harlem, N.Y., minister Adam Clayton POWELL, Jr., who in 1941 became the first African-American member of the New York City Council, and who three years later was elected to Congress.

At the same time, civil rights became a national issue. In 1948, the adoption of a strong civil rights platform plank at the Democratic National Convention prompted a walkout by some white Southerners. Democratic presidential candidate Harry Truman was elected nevertheless, and his victory helped demonstrate the electoral clout of urban African Americans. Gradually, over the following years, northern Democrats championed that party's transition to a strongly problack position.

Postwar black population growth in the urban North continued to be heavy, and its effects were heightened by declining white populations, as whites migrated to nearby suburbs. In 1953 New York State assemblyman Hulan Jack was elected to the powerful position of Manhattan borough president. Soon after, Newark and Detroit, two cities with heavy concentrations of black residents, gained their first black city councilmen.

blacks, Negro Elections Day ceremonies declined, and were largely replaced with carefully staged parades that commemorated the end of local slavery. Unlike the election day ceremonies, the emancipation parades often had an explicitly oppositional political component.

REVOLUTIONARY AMERICA. When the First Continental Congress met in September 1774, African Americans' political participation, save for events such as slave revolts, had not really arrived at the stage of coherent collective action. The rare political actions of blacks were still individual, and they lacked a strong sense of community and racial consciousness. However, by the time that revolutionary America had transformed itself into an independent nation and developed a federal system, African-American politics had begun to evolve beyond the strictly individual stage, to achieve some collective bases of action.

The revolutionary struggle that led to the creation of the United States of America had a profound effect on African-American ideology and political activities. Blacks, conscious of the irony of white colonists campaigning for "liberty" while denying it to their slaves, made use of revolutionary rhetoric and the wartime needs of the country to carve out a political space for themselves. Between 1773 and 1774 African Americans in Massachusetts presented five collective antislavery petitions to the General Court, Massachusetts's governing body. One of the early petitioners, from 1773, challenged the legislators, "We expect great things from men who have made such a noble stand against the designs of their fellow-men to enslave them." Scores of other petitions protesting slavery and discrimination were presented to the legislatures of the newly independent states in the following years.

When war broke out, many free African Americans joined the fledgling American army, recognizing that military service was a traditional mark of citizenship. Partly for the same reason, white authorities soon attempted to bar blacks from military service. Once white opposition to arming slaves, at least in the northern states, melted away under pressure of military necessity, blacks enlisted in disproportionate numbers in the Continental Army. Meanwhile, slaves in Virginia, promised freedom by royal governor Lord Dunmore if they fought on the side of England, rushed in large numbers to his offshore base.

Revolution in America did little to improve the political participation of African Americans. Four of the new state constitutions denied free blacks the right to vote; five more states would eventually deny it, and only four would never deny it. Thus only four of the thirteen original colonies—plus Vermont, admitted to the Union in 1791—permitted African Americans to vote. In all of these four states—Massachusetts, New Hampshire, Rhode Island, and New York—the Negro Elections Day celebrations continued to be observed regularly, though New York imposed a discriminatory property requirement for black voters in 1821. In Connecticut, which denied African-American suffrage in 1818, the blacks' last "governor" held office shortly before the Civil War.

Nevertheless, the petitions and military service did exert an influence on the new governments in the years after the war's end. State legislatures in the North passed gradual abolition statutes, and even southern states passed laws simplifying manumission. Many veterans were freed, and some were franchised. Wentworth Cheswill of New Hampshire, probably the first person of African descent elected to office in North America, served as a justice of the peace as early as 1768, and was town selectman for New Market, N.H., several times after 1780. In 1806 he was an unsuccessful candidate for the state senate. In 1831 Alexander Twilight of Vermont became the first African American elected to a state legislature.

Only four of the thirteen original colonies permitted African Americans to vote.

Most of the states abolished the slave trade within their borders, although the U.S. Constitution delayed federal action until 1808. Meanwhile, African Americans and white antislavery allies appealed to the judiciary, bringing a handful of test cases challenging slavery in state courts. In 1783 Quock Walker brought a freedom suit in Massachusetts. Judge Richard Cushing ruled slavery incompatible with the state's constitution, resulting in the effective end of slavery in Massachusetts. By 1800 a number of northern states had passed emancipation statutes.

The development of two opposing national political parties, the Federalists and the Democratic-Republicans (later the Democratic party), increased black political involvement. To the extent that blacks participated in campaign and electoral politics, they overwhelmingly supported the Federalists, led in part by such antislavery figures as Alexander Hamilton and John Jay, over Thomas Jefferson and the Democrats, who were identified with slavery and southern interests. The Federalist Party sought the support of black leaders such as New York City's Joseph Sidney and Philadelphia's Absalom JONES, and in 1809 established a black political club, the Washington Benevolent Society, which maintained active branches in Boston and New York City. Black voting played a notable role in the Federalists' narrow victory in New York in 1813.

With the changing structure of government and electoral context came a change in political protest behavior. Not only did African Americans send their petitions and memorials to various state executives and legislatures, but by 1797 they were also sending petitions to the Congress of the United States. On January 23, 1797, four African Americans living in Philadelphia petitioned Congress though Representative John Swanwick of Pennsylvania for a redress of their grievances, which were related to a North Carolina law of 1788 that provided for the capture and reselling of illegally manumitted slaves. Seven days after the petition arrived, Congress debated whether to accept or reject "a petition from fugitive slaves." By a vote of 50–33, Congress rejected the petition. This initial petition was soon followed by another, which arrived in "the second day of the new century," in 1800. Absalom Jones had his representative, Robert Waln of Pennsylvania, present a petition to Congress to demand the banning of the SLAVE TRADE and the 1793 Fugitive Slave Act. However, Congress voted 85–1 not to consider the petition.

Thus, in this early national period, when African-American political participation was still closely circumscribed by denials of the right to vote, to serve on juries, to hold office, and to bring a legal suit against a white person, black political participation showed signs of expanding and extending itself into new directions. Not only did African Americans show increasing inclination to exert pressure and redirect their focus, they now began to take on a collective impulse. The influence of the African heritage and background was a strong spur to organization, in the form of mutual aid and fraternal organizations, educational societies, and black religious organizations, which grew up in African-American communities and served as the centers of collective effort and activism. For example, in Rhode Island, on November 10, 1780, free blacks established the African Union Society; in Massachusetts they formed The Sons of Africans Society in 1808. New York saw an African Society in 1809; Pittsburgh, an African Education Society in 1832; Boston, an African Lodge in 1787; and New York City, an African Marine Foundation in 1810. That these groups bore African names was no mere accident of simple naming. In the extant constitutions, preambles, laws, minutes, proceedings, resolutions, and reports of these African organizations, a budding "race consciousness" and sense of racial solidarity is openly expressed. Out of this sense of race-based community came the collective action that marked antebellum black pressure politics.

"Africa" did not simply provide the internal cohesion for these interest/pressure groups; it would also become a symbol of freedom and liberty. With the beginning of the emigration and colonization efforts, the influence of Africa directly reentered the contextual political realities of African Americans. The initial pioneering effort of Paul Cuffe, who personally returned thirty-eight free Negroes to Sierra Leone in 1815, was institutionalized (though substantially changed) in December 1816, when the AMERICAN COLONIZATION SOCIETY (ACS) was formed. Five years later, the society established the colony of Liberia. Although the two efforts had outwardly similar objectives, Cuffe sought Africa as a place of freedom and liberty. On the other hand, the motives of the society were at best mixed and questionable, since the society wished to send free blacks to Africa in part to eliminate what they saw as the anomalous position of the free black in the North. The implication that free blacks have no role to play in American society soon came under attack by African Americans, who saw the ACS as racist, and this served to catalyze their subsequent organizing efforts.

Finally, the late 1820s saw the beginning of African-American newspapers, which provided a forum for spokespersons who would take up the struggle on behalf of their "colored fellow citizens." (*Freedom's Journal*, founded in New York City in 1827, was the earliest.) The numerous efforts of such individuals and papers heralded not only a rising sense of solidarity and community but also vindicated the acts of pressure and protest in the revolutionary and the early national period that seemed, at first blush, so futile.

Thus elements of the African background provided the underpinning for fledgling African-American pressure group activity in the new nation by 1830. The first Negro convention was held on September 20, 1830, in Philadelphia, with delegates from seven states. Another convention met the next year, and black conventions subsequently were organized four times during the 1830s, three times in the 1840s, and twice in the 1850s. At the 1864 Syracuse, N.Y., national convention, the movement reorganized itself into the National Equal Rights League. The national convention movement directed, albeit in a rather unstable way, a mass self-help movement of the churches, mutual aid societies, and fraternal organizations, and took these efforts into the political area. With the emergence of such mass political action in both the electoral and protest areas, African-American politics had come of age.

The national organization, where possible, set up state and local affiliates. Some state and local auxiliaries pursued policies and directions independent of those of the national organization. When they were meeting and functioning properly, the national, state, and local bodies issued resolutions, petitions, prayers, and memorials addressed to state legislatures and to Congress. While their chief interest was the antislavery struggle, the conventions acted on other issues as well. Political rights such as suffrage, jury service, and repeal of discriminatory legislation were major concerns. Despite their support of abolitionist groups, the convention members also chided the American Anti-slavery Society, founded in 1833, for its unwillingness to champion "social equality."

Temperance, education, and moral reform stood high on the agenda of many Negro conventions and allied groups throughout the era. Equally important was the fight for women's equality and voting rights. As early as Maria Stewart in the 1830s, African-American women played prominent roles in black politics. Just as many white feminists became politically committed through abolitionist activities, so black leaders from Sojourner TRUTH to Frederick Douglass attended feminist conferences and pressed for the end of gender discrimination.

The convention movement was supplemented by countless local political committees and pressure groups that campaigned for civil rights and educational opportunity. Black groups formed in the early 1830s, such as the Phoenix Society in New York City and the American Moral Reform Society, based in Philadelphia, added civil rights petitioning to their temperance and educational efforts. Meanwhile, African Americans in New York City and Philadelphia organized committees to protest denials of equal suffrage and to stimulate black political involvement. African Americans in Boston successfully lobbied to overturn a state law fobidding racial intermarriage, and organized protests that desegregated most of the state's railroads. In 1855, the Legal Rights Association sued in a New York City court protesting segregated streetcars and won a judgment. In 1849 Benjamin Roberts pursued a test case challenging segregated schools in Boston to the Massachusetts Supreme Court. Although he lost, the state legislature integrated the schools in 1855.

ABOLITIONIST AMERICA. In December 1833 the American Anti-Slavery Society, the first national abolitionist organization, was founded in Philadelphia. This marked the awakening of abolition as a full-fledged sociopolitical movement, and it catapulted blacks into the center of the political system. The electoral efforts of most free blacks in this era were focused on their work for and participation in a host of antislavery third parties. They attended their conventions and served as low-level officers at the conventions, especially as secretaries. They succeeded in having resolutions and platforms adopted that called for equality. They campaigned for the standard-bearers of these parties. Where they could, they voted for these candidates. And in several states in the expanding new nation, these antislavery parties sought to have the state extend suffrage to free blacks, but to no avail.

When the first antislavery party, the Liberty party, was formed on April 1, 1840, at Albany, N.Y., it announced that its goal was "the absolute and unqualified divorce of the General Government from Slavery, and also the restoration of equality of rights, among men, in every state where the party exists or may exist." The Liberty party's leaders reached out to free blacks, and shortly after the founding of the party, influential black leaders began to associate with it, attending party conventions and providing what limited electoral support they could muster. In return, the Liberty Party welcomed black supporters into party councils and leadership positions. The brightest spot in the party's history was the election of John M. Langston on the party's ticket to a township clerk position in Ohio in 1855. Langston's nomination for office was the first ever given an African American by a political party. Despite this achievement, the Liberty Party was unable to compete with subsequent abolitionist parties. Its numbers declined through the 1850s, and it dissolved in 1860.

African Americans also became involved in the Free Soil party. At its founding convention in Buffalo, N.Y., on August 9, 1848, the party adopted a platform calling for the exclusion of slavery from the District of Columbia and the territories of the United States, though it conceded the legality of slavery in existing states. While the party called for jury trials for captured fugitive slaves, it made no commitment to expanding black equality, and many of its leaders opposed black suffrage. Free blacks participated in the convention, and later in the campaign, despite the party's limited positions on equality and the liberation of slaves. Although unsuccessful in its initial presidential bid, the party tried again in 1852. This time the national nominating convention adopted a resolution favoring black suffrage, and elected Frederick Douglass secretary of the convention. Despite the work of Douglass and other free blacks, the party polled fewer votes than it had in 1848, and dissolved after the election.

There were other antislavery parties in which African Americans participated. Frederick Douglass attended the convention of the new National Liberty party in Buffalo, N.Y., on June 14–15, 1848. The party's poor performance in the 1848 presidential election—which may have been the consequence of its stiff competition from the Liberty party and the Free Soil party—led to its collapse soon afterward. Another party, the Political Abolition party, took up the struggle in 1856. It had an even more dismal showing than expected; it collected only 484 votes for its presidential candidate. It did not again contest a presidential election.

The antislavery parties were never large organizations, although they helped swing the balance in several elections. Their failure during the 1850s was largely the result of the entry of the Republican Party into the political fray. The Republicans captured the political imagination of many free blacks, and a significant degree of their support. In 1860 the Republican party candidate, Abraham Lincoln, won the presidency, with the overwhelming support of free blacks and attentive slaves.

EMIGRATIONIST POLITICS. Beginning in the 1840s, the African heritage began to influence African-American political participation and action in a new and more direct way, through the doctrine of African-American political nationalism. The historians John Bracey, Jr., August Meier, and Elliott Rudwick describe the dynamics of this era:

> In the 1840s a number of converging developments turned Negro ideologies in more nationalist directions: the essential failure of the antislavery movement to liberate the slaves; the evidences of racism among many white abolitionists . . . increasing trends toward disfranchisement and segregation in public accommodations in many of the northeastern states, combined with the continuing pattern of discrimination in the Old Northwest that made the black man's condition there similar to that in the South; and the growing hopelessness of the economic situation. . . .

One result of the growing estrangement of African Americans from the mainstream of American politics was the national convention movement's increasing withdrawal from interracial groups and endorsement of independent black political organizations. Of course, this trend did not contradict its members' goal of equality in the United States. While blacks were nationalistic about their color, and were determined to build separate black institutions,, their nationalism did not preempt their demands for inclusion as Americans. Black institutions were created as a halfway measure, as a means to the end of integration.

The events of the 1850s aggravated the obstacles confronting African Americans. The Fugitive Slave Act of 1850 made life unsafe and dangerous for large numbers of free blacks, and the Kansas-Nebraska Act threatened to extend slavery into new territories. Finally, the U.S. Supreme Court's decision in the 1857 DRED SCOTT DECISION, that blacks had no rights as United States citizens and that a state could not forbid slavery, was responsible for convincing large numbers of black activists of the necessity for radical action. A few supported the idea of a violent overturning of the slave system, and threw their support to the white abolitionist John Brown, who planned a slave insurrection. At the same time, a number of African Americans mounted emigration and colonization efforts. Some emigrationists favored mass emigration to Africa. For them, Africa would be the place to create a great nation, a place where freedom and liberty would prevail and a place where an African nation might arise that would eventually rival that of America. Larger numbers moved to the relatively safe haven of Canada. Others favored Haiti, Central America, or other places. National emigration conventions were held in 1854, 1856, and 1858.

CONCLUSION. On the eve of the Civil War, the essential features of African-American political culture had taken form and had started to mature. The dual influences of America and Africa had converged in the era of abolitionism and black nationalism to shape a political culture that had one message: In a society where racism is a permanent feature, equality and liberty for African Americans could not be left solely to the efforts of whites; instead, in a time of political and democratic restriction, a special role had to be played by African Americans themselves.

Reconstruction to the Present

During the Reconstruction era, stretching from 1865 through 1877, the nature of African-American politics was radically transformed. The Fifteenth Amendment, ratified in 1870, gave African-American men the right to vote. Before the Civil War only a segment of the African-American community in the North was allowed to participate in politics; during the Reconstruction era, the entire community was permitted to participate. The results were striking, electing twenty African-American congressmen, two senators, a governor, six lieutenant governors, numerous local officials, state legislators, and delegates to state constitutional conventions. In addition to the figures who served in official positions, Reconstruction also energized large elements of the African-American community in political struggles. How-ever, the gains achieved during Reconstruction were largely overturned in the years after the political compromise of 1877, when federal troops were withdrawn from the southern states, where most African Americans lived.

By the turn of the century, most southern states had adopted poll taxes, literacy tests, and other measures that disfranchised the vast majority of their black populations. Segregation was rigidly imposed on African Americans, whose hard-won citizenship rights were largely ignored. Even in the northern states, where African Americans retained voting rights, de facto housing and employment discrimination eroded the dream of equality. From the 57th until the 70th congresses there were no African-Americans in the House or the Senate, and few local or state officials. In the face of such burdens, blacks organized what political protests they could.

During the Reconstruction era, stretching from 1865 through 1877, the nature of African-American politics was radically transformed.

The political struggle of African Americans from the end of Reconstruction to at least the 1960s, and in many ways to the present, has been focused on one goal: to reshape the political landscape so that the political and economic liberties of African Americans would be restored. When this goal was unworkable through major party politics, some blacks turned in independent, and sometimes separatist, directions. As early as the 1880s, many blacks, particularly in the North, grew dissatisfied with the Republican party, which refused to act effectively against deteriorating race relations or to offer the black electorate patrongae commensurate with its voting support. Black activists such as T. Thomas Fortune and Peter H. Clark urged African Americans to be politically independent and either explore the possibility of supporting the Democratic party or establish an independent political party. Neither party was generally prepared to offer significant rewards. The resulting frustration led some African Americans to eschew major party politics altogether.

THIRD PARTY POLITICS. Beginning in the 1870s, many black voters supported factions and splinter groups of the Republicans such as the National Republicans and the Greenback party, as well as statewide organizations such as Virginia's Readjusters. These groups generally opposed the tight-money, probusiness slant of the mainstream Republicans. While they supported racially liberal platforms and welcomed black electoral support, most of these groups were not interested in campaigning for black interests or soliciting black participation in party activities.

The first national third party that blacks supported was the Prohibition party, whose presidential campaigns attracted a solid core of black voters through the mid-twentieth century. The Prohibition Party did not target civil rights issues, but their radical reform message encompassed black interests. Temperance had long been a concern of black leaders in an attempt to raise the moral image and economic standing of African Americans. The elite nature of the party, particularly in the South, offered blacks with middle-class aspirations a measure of status, and the movement's strong Christian ideology contributed to general ideals of racial harmony and fairness. During the 1884 and 1888 campaigns, Prohibitionists realized that blacks represented swing votes on temperance measures, so the party reached out to them, sponsoring interracial rallies with black speakers and inviting African Americans to join organizing committees and convention delegations. For example, the African Methodist Episcopal bishop Henry McNeal Turner spoke for Prohibition Party candidates and was a delegate to the party's 1888 national convention. Philadelphia had a strong black Prohibitionist party in the late nineteenth century, at times supported by such stalwarts of black Philadelphia life as AME bishop Benjamin Tanner and physician Nathan Mossell. Also, the Prohibition Party generally opposed urban Democratic machines dominated by white ethnics, who were traditional antagonists of the black community. During the twentieth century, as the party grew more racially restrictive and black elites found other political channels, support for the Prohibitionists waned.

The Populist Party, the political arm of an agrarian movement of the 1890s, revolved around a platform of democratic reform, debt relief, and monetary expansion that appealed to southern and midwestern black farmers who supported party candidates for president and for state offices. Prominent southern blacks such as former Georgia state legislator Anthony Wilson supported the party. Many Populists, such as Tom Watson of Georgia, called for interracial economic unity and took radical positions in support of the legal rights of African Americans. Populists helped elect black officials, such as North Carolina congressman George White in 1896. Populist representatives often voted funds for black education. However many white Populists were ambivalent about black participation and voting support, fearing white racist backlash, and were cautious about challenging discrimination. With the help of voting fraud and manipulation in Black Belt areas, southern Democrats beat back Populist challenges during the 1890s. Some Populist leaders, such as the South Carolina senator "Pitchfork" Ben Tillman, had rarely disguised their racial demagoguery. Others, such as Georgia's Tom Walton, underwent a notorious transformation, from supporting interracial cooperation during the heyday of the Populist era to becoming a virulent racist and defender of lynching. Black populists also despaired of joint black-white efforts. John B. Payner, a Texas Pop-

Charles Evers leaves his car to vote in Fayette, Miss.'s municipal elections. Evers was a candidate for mayor of the city. (AP/Wide World Photos)

ulist who was one of the party's leading orators, became an embittered supporter of separate black institutions, acknowledging that the price for their survival was a subservient relation to white authorities.

As a result of their own entrenched racism, many Populists responded by supporting black disfranchisement campaigns. Despite the reversal of southern Populist leaders on black issues, small numbers of blacks continued to support the declining party during its presidential campaigns of 1900, 1904, and 1908.

During most of the twentieth century, when the vast majority of blacks in the South were unable to vote, the center of black voting strength and political influence shifted to the urban North. The record of black activity in third parties during the first half of the twentieth century reveals a strong tie between black political participation and the politics of economic protest. A few blacks offered support for candidates running on economic reform platforms, including the Progressive (Bull Moose) party in 1912 and the Progressive party in 1924, despite the refusal of party leaders to seat black delegates or to reach out to black voters. However, in 1948 Henry Wallace, running for president on the Progressive party ticket, campaigned strongly for black votes. Wallace made civil rights a centerpiece of his platform and organized integrated tours of the South. However, while he was supported by such black leaders as Paul ROBESON and W. E. B. DU BOIS, a strong Democratic party platform on civil rights sharply reduced Wallace's appeal.

Throughout this period, the Communist, Socialist, and other workers' parties repeatedly sought and gained black support for their ideologies and platforms. In the late nineteenth century a number of African-American leaders, such as Peter H. Clark of Cincinnati and T. Thomas Fortune, expressed sympathy with socialist ideas. The Socialist party, founded in 1901, gained few black converts in its first two decades, though W. E. B. Du Bois expressed strong sympathy with socialism as early as 1907 and briefly joined the party in 1912. It vigorously denounced the exploitation of workers, but subordinated race to class in its policies, refusing to recognize the special problems facing African Americans. Many of its leaders held racist views, and while the party platform opposed disfranchisement and leaders such as Eugene V. Debs publicly opposed racial discrimination, the Socialists offered no special support for black interests. After World War I, the party's platform became more inclusive. Larger numbers of blacks, inspired by African-American Socialist orators such as A. Philip Randolph, H. H. Harrison, Cyril V. Briggs, Richard Moore, Chandler Owen, and Frank Crosswaith, moved to support party candidates.

The Communist party of the U.S.A., formed in 1921, shared the class-based approach of the Socialists. By the end of the 1920s, in accordance with Moscow's ideological support of non-Western nationalism, the party developed a platform calling for worker unity in the North and African-American "self-determination" in the southern Black Belt. While black party membership was always low, the Communists attempted to exert a disproportionate influence on black life. Unlike the Socialists, the Communists'—especially in the South—actively shifting position on the Nazi-Soviet alliance destroyed its southern base. The decline of the Communist and Socialist parties after 1950 was accompanied by the formation of several minor Marxist political parties, notably the Trotskyist-influenced Socialist Workers' party, beginning in the 1950s. Probably the most influential African-American Trotskyist was the

West Indian historian and theorist C. L. R. James, who lived in the United States from 1938 until his expulsion in 1953. Tiny parties such as the Workers' World party drew black support during the 1980s. These parties have actively sought a black constituency through powerful denunciations of racism and integrated leadership but have been unable, due in part to lack of money for broad-based campaigns, to draw more than a tiny percentage of the black vote.

Beginning in the 1960s, various New Left and other radical parties without large black constituencies have sponsored black candidates for political office. For example, in 1968 during the height of the antiwar movement, Dick GREGORY, an African American, ran for president on the Freedom and Peace party's ticket. In 1992 Leonora B. Fulani, running as the presidential candidate of the New Alliance party, became the first black minor party presidential candidate to qualify for federal matching campaign funds.

SEPARATIST PARTIES. The antimainstream impulse is largely the consequence of the political discrimination that the white majority in various states has used to block the entrance of blacks into mainstream political parties. An equally significant development, however, is the appearance and growth of independent black political parties and factions throughout the twentieth century. The southern states, particularly Mississippi, have provided the most promising conditions for these independent parties. Yet the appearance of national black separatist parties in 1904, 1960, and 1992 indicates that the impulse is not limited to the South.

The first black party was the Negro Protective party, formed in Ohio in 1897, but this was not a truly independent organization. Taking advantage of black discontent over Republican inattention to black needs, the Ohio Democratic party financed a small group of black Democrats and independents, who formed a party and ran a slate of candidates for governor and lesser state offices on a platform of civil rights and control of white mobs. Many "party" candidates were paid off by Republicans to withdraw their candidacies so as not to cut into the black Republican vote. The party's gubernatorial candidate, Sam J. Lewis, received only 477 votes. The few remaining candidates for other posts did even worse.

The first nationally based black political party was the National Liberty party, which grew out of local Civil and Personal Liberty leagues. On July 5, 1904, a convention of the leagues was organized at St. Louis and was attended by delegations from thirty-six states. Iowa editor George Edwin Taylor was chosen as the party's presidential candidate. The party gained only a few votes, and it disappeared after the election.

Although two independent black presidential candidates ran in Alabama in 1960, on the ticket of the Afro-American Party, and received 1,485 votes, the next serious attempt to build a nationwide black party came with the formation of the Freedom Now Party. Organized by African-American lawyer Conrad Lynn as a national party in 1963 at a convention in Washington, D.C., during the famous March for Jobs and Freedom, it ran candidates in elections in New York, California, and Connecticut. When these candidates did poorly in November elections, it switched strategy to concentrate its efforts exclusively on Michigan. In 1964 the party ran a slate of thirty-nine candidates for statewide office in that state, hoping to demonstrate its electoral strength and to educate black voters. All the candidates were badly beaten, however, and the party dissolved soon after the election.

In the years after 1964, black activists tried on numerous occasions to establish national black parties, but without success. In 1968 the Peace and Freedom Party (not to be confused with the aforementioned Freedom and Peace party, which appeared in 7 states and got nearly 48,000 votes for Dick Gregory) was created. Run by an alliance of white leftists and members of the BLACK PANTHER PARTY, the party selected Eldridge CLEAVER as its presidential candidate. It was on the ballot in some 5 states, and Cleaver received almost 37,000 votes. However, the alliance disintegrated soon after the election, although some candidates ran on the Peace and Freedom ticket in California statewide elections in 1970. In 1976 the National Black Political Assembly, an outgrowth of the 1972 National Black Convention, formed the National Black Independent Political Party. However, handicapped by poor funding and bad management, it succeeded neither in persuading well-known black elected officials to run for president, nor in gaining sufficient signatures to place the party slate on the ballot in any state. In 1980 the National Black Independent Political party held a founding convention to form a nucleus of support for a 1984 campaign but was unable to overcome internal debate, and its platform was overshadowed by Jesse Jackson's independent black candidacy for the presidential nomination of the Democratic party. In 1992, after Jackson declined to seek the Democratic party nomination, Ron Daniels, former chair of the National Black Political Assembly, ran for president on the Campaign for a New Tomorrow ticket, but had difficulty getting his name on the ballot in many states and finished poorly.

More notably successful have been satellite black political organizations. While black-supported and -run, these have oriented themselves within existing party structures and groups. During the end of the nineteenth century and the first part of the twentieth century, this independent spirit expressed itself in the form of numerous "Black and Tan" factions in Republican parties of southern states such as Texas, Louisiana, and Tennessee. Black delegates to state conventions, opposed by "lily-white" delegations, would try to gain their groups a fair share of patronage and political influence. If defeated at the state level, they would form their own slate of delegates and candidates for local office, and appeal to the national conventions for recognition. Often, deals would be struck. Occasionally, as in Louisiana and Mississippi in the 1920s, the Black and Tan faction would win clear-cut control of patronage.

Most factions petered out by the turn of the century, however, as increasing numbers of blacks were disfranchised or left the Republicans and as the party courted white southern support. Sometimes party presidential candidates such as Theodore Roosevelt would recognize the black delegates, but once nominated refuse to award them their share of the spoils. In 1920 the Texas Black and Tans, tired of this strategy, went so far as to run their own candidates for the position of Republican presidential electors, receiving some 27,000 votes. In Virginia in the early 1920s a "lily-black" party ran newspaper editor John R. Mitchell for governor. The Tennessee and Texas Black and Tans disappeared in the early 1930s, as patronage and national party support dried up.

During the 1930s, southern blacks turned to the Democratic Party. However, excluded by white-dominated state parties, they began building shadow parties. The first example of this was the South Carolina Progressive Democratic party. Formed at a convention in Columbia in May 1944, the party was designed to build support for Franklin D. Roosevelt's Democratic candidacy while evading the state's white primary. Its representatives attended the national convention in an unsuccessful attempt to unseat the regular state delegation, and sponsored a black candidate for U.S. senator, who won some 4,500 votes in the election. While the party continued after the election, it reformed as a political caucus group, working in voter registration and unsuccessfully challenging the regular state delegation at the 1948 and 1956 conventions before being absorbed completely into the state party. (In 1970 South Carolina blacks, dissatisfied with the fused party, formed a short-lived new political party, the United Citizens' party.)

Two notable examples of satellite parties are the Mississippi Freedom Democratic party (MFDP) and the National Democratic party of Alabama (NDPA). The MFDP, created in 1964, was formed as part of an effort by the Student Nonviolent Coordinating Committee (SNCC) and other civil rights groups to dramatize the state's denial of voting rights to blacks and involve long-disfranchised Mississippi African Americans in the political process. The MFDP sponsored candidates for office in the Mississippi Democratic party primary, and sent a delegation to the 1964 Democratic national convention, urging without success that their delegation be seated in place of the white-only regular state delegation. In 1968, however, the MFDP [reorganized as the Loyal Democratic Party of Mississippi (LDPM)] succeeded in unseating the Mississippi delegation. While the party continued to operate into the 1970s, it was unable to elect large numbers of candidates to state or local office and eventually became part of the state Democratic Party, without a distinct status. The NDPA, one of a number of black political organizations in Alabama during the 1960s, was organized in 1968 to remedy the failure of the Alabama Democratic Party to open its organization to African Americans. In that year, the NDPA, inspired by the success of the MFDP, successfully fought to obtain recognition as the official state delegation at the Democratic national convention. While its platform and activity pushed the regular party into a more progressive racial posture, the NDPA was also unable to survive the 1970s as an independent black political organization.

Despite the overwhelming lack of political success of third parties and independent movements, their value has been in displaying the fitness of black candidates and sponsoring their inclusion in American political culture in periods when and in areas where, if dependent on mainstream political parties and institutions alone, African Americans would clearly have been underrepresented in this sphere of the American political process.

Separatist and independent parties reveal that African Americans have never completely forgotten or abandoned their African heritage.

The independent black political movements in particular have provided the community with its best opportunity to compete in the general election for seats in the U.S. Senate. The mainstream parties have not yet provided adequate support or opportunity. Of the twenty African-American senatorial candidates in general elections from 1920 to 1990, seventeen ran on third-party or African-American party tickets. Similarly, of all the African-American gubernatorial candidates in general elections, the vast majority were sponsored on either third-party or African-American party tickets, mostly the latter. The first such African-American gubernatorial candidate in this country was Sam J. Lewis in Ohio in the 1897 state election; he ran as the candidate of the Negro Protective Party. Through 1990, L. Douglas Wilder, Mervyn Dymally, and George Brown are the *only* African Americans to have received a major party nomination for governor or lieutenant governor and survive until the general election. At the city level, African-American mayors prior to the Voting Rights Act of 1965 had to run on small African-American or third-party tickets to play a political role. As the black percentage of the population of major cities has increased, it has become easier to elect black mayors.

Similarly, in majority black districts, for the state legislature it has been relatively easy to elect black candidates. Also, seventy-one African Americans were elected to the U.S. House of Representatives, all on major party tickets, between 1865 and 1992.

Separatist and independent parties reveal that African Americans have never completely forgotten or abandoned their African heritage. Although African Americans have more often and more strongly supported the major and minor parties, they shared the frustration and search for channels of political power that drove others to form separatist groups. Even if it remained a minor channel of blacks' political activity, the independent impulse shows a stubborn ability to survive.

THE DUAL IMPULSES IN AFRICAN-AMERICAN POLITICS IN THE FUTURE. Just why the impulses motivating African-American politics assume these patterns may be illuminated by the remarks of Samuel Du Bois Cook, who writes, "Black political parties are, after all, expressions of radically abnormal conditions and consequences—basic defects in the political system. They have had a special mission—correction of those fundamental differences. . . ." (Cook 1972). He continues, "Black political parties fostered the notion and ideal of self-help, self-propulsion, group consciousness and solidarity, and political sensitivity, awareness and appreciation."

Harold Cruse offers these thoughts on African-American political parties as a means to achieve liberation:

> The politics of ethnicity is more exactly the "politics of plurality." The demise of the civil rights era, beginning with 1980, points to political organization as the only alternative. Political organization also permits a renewed opportunity to make up for longstanding organizational deficiencies that have hampered black progress in economic, cultural, educational, and other social fields.

Cruse asserts that the "only option left" is to "organize an independent black party." Moreover, he argues, the ultimate aim of this black party would not be solely for the "expedient purposes of electoral politics." As he sees it, the African-American political party should not simply be an electoral political entity, but among other things a cultural political entity—that is, concerned with preserving those crucial values emanating from what we have here called the background impulses, such as self-help, self-propulsion, group consciousness, self-determination, and self-liberation.

Which of the two motors driving African-American politics—the mainstream or the separatist independent—will come to dominate the political lives of America's black men and black women remains to be seen. Clearly, the second impulse will continue as long as there is political discrimination and racism in the American political system. The separatist impulse, moreover, gives African-American politics much of its unique flavor and may prove to be the most enduring cultural legacy of African-American political activism.

BIBLIOGRAPHY

Amer, Mildred L. *Black Members of the United States Congress.* Washington, D.C., 1991.

Aptheker, Herbert, ed. *A Documentary History of the Negro People in the United States.* New York, 1951.

———. "Slave Guerrilla Warfare" and "Buying Freedom." In Herbert Aptheker, ed. *To Be Free: Studies in American Negro History.* New York, 1948, pp. 11–30.

Bell, Howard H. *A Survey of the Negro Convention Movement, 1830–1861.* New York, 1969.

Berlin, Ira. *Slaves Without Masters: The Free Negro in the Antebellum South.* New York, 1974.

Bracey, John, Jr., August Meier, and Elliott Rudwick, eds. *Black Nationalism in America.* New York, 1970.

Brooke, Edward. *The Challenge of Change: Crisis in Our Two-Party System.* Boston, 1966.

Cook, Samuel Du Bois, *Black Political Parties: An Historical and Political Analysis.* New York, 1972.

Cruse, Harold. *Plural but Equal: Study of Blacks and Minorities and the American Plural Society.* New York, 1987.

Draper, Theodore. *The Rediscovery of Black Nationalism.* New York, 1970.

Field, Phyllis F. *The Politics of Race in New York: The Struggle for Black Suffrage in the Civil War Era.* Ithaca, N.Y., 1982.

Fleming, G. James. *An All Negro Ticket in Baltimore.* New York, 1960.

Hamilton, Charles V., ed. *The Black Experience in American Politics.* New York, 1968.

Henry, Charles. *Culture and African American Politics.* Bloomington, Ind., 1990.

Link, Arthur S. "The Negro as a Factor in the Campaign of 1912." *Journal of Negro History* 32 (1947): 81–89.

Logan, Rayford, and Irving Cohen. *The American Negro.* Boston, 1920.

Merritt, R. L. *Symbols of American Community, 1735–1775.* New Haven, Conn., 1966.

Olbrich, Emil. *The Development of Sentiment on Negro Suffrage to 1860.* Madison, Wis., 1912.
Porter, Dorothy, ed. *Early Negro Writing, 1760–1837.* Boston, 1971.
———. *Negro Protest Pamphlets: A Compendium.* New York, 1969.
Porter, Kirk, and Donald Johnson, eds. *National Party Platforms, 1840–1964.* Urbana, Ill., 1966.
Reidy, Joseph. "Negro Election Day and Black Community Life in New England, 1750–1860." In Kenneth L. Kusmer, ed. *Black Communities and Urban Development in America 1720–1990: The Colonial and Early National Period.* New York, 1991, p. 234.
Scott, James C. *Domination and the Acts of Resistance: Hidden Transcripts.* New Haven, Conn., 1990.
Smith, Robert S. "The Black Congressional Delegation." *Western Political Quarterly* 34 (1981): 203–221.
Sweet, Leonard I. *Black Images of America, 1784–1870.* New York, 1976.
Thomas, Lamont. *Rise to Be a People: A Biography of Paul Cuffe.* Urbana, Ill., 1986.
Walton, Hanes, Jr. *Black Politics: A Theoretical and Structural Analysis.* Philadelphia, 1972.
———. "Black Presidential Participation and the Critical Election Theory." In Lorenzo Morris, ed. *The Social and Political Implications of the 1984 Jesse Jackson Presidential Campaign.* New York, 1990, pp. 49–64.
———. *The Negro in Third Party Politics.* Philadelphia, 1969.
Wesley, Charles. *Neglected History.* Washington, D.C., 1969.
White, John. *Black Leadership in America, 1895–1968.* New York, 1985.
White, Shane. " 'It Was a Proud Day': African Americans, Festivals, and Parades in the North, 1741–1831." *Journal of American History* 81 (1994): 13–50.

— HANES WALTON, JR. AND MERVYN DYMALLY

POUSSAINT, ALVIN FRANCIS

Alvin Francis Poussaint (May 15, 1934–), psychiatrist, educator, and author. Born in East Harlem in New York City, Alvin Poussaint attended Stuyvesant High School and graduated from Columbia College (B.A., 1956) and Cornell University Medical College (M.D., 1960). He took postgraduate training at the University of California's Neuropsychiatric Institute in Los Angeles, where he served as chief resident in psychiatry from 1964 to 1965. From 1965 to 1967, he was southern field director of the Medical Committee for Human Rights in Jackson, Miss., providing medical care to civil rights workers and aiding in the desegregation of health facilities throughout the South. In 1967, Poussaint became an assistant professor at Tufts University Medical School. He remained there for four years (1965–1969) before joining the faculty of the Harvard Medical School. At Boston's Judge Baker Guidance Center, he counseled families traumatized by the murder of a relative or friend.

Poussaint's research included the psychological and social adaptation of children of interracial marriages, the nature of grief, and the pharmacological treatment of smoking and bed wetting. He was a founding member and treasurer of the Black Academy of Arts and Letters in 1969. Two years later Poussaint became an initial member of the Rev. Jesse JACKSON's organization Operation PUSH (People United to Save Humanity). He also served as an advisor to Jackson during the 1984 presidential campaign.

Poussaint has written widely on such social issues of concern to African Americans as poverty, unemployment, self-esteem, parenting, and violence.

One of the nation's leading psychiatrists, Poussaint has researched and written widely on such social issues of concern to African Americans as poverty, unemployment, self-esteem, parenting, and violence. He has written several books, including *Why Blacks Kill Blacks* (1972), an examination of the effects of white racism on black psychological development. He was coauthor with James P. Comer of *Black Child Care* (1975; reissued as *Raising Black Children,* 1992), a study of the cultural biases faced by African-American youths. Poussaint also served as a consultant to *The Cosby Show* from 1984 to 1992 and *A Different World* from 1986 to 1993. He reviewed script dialogue to ensure that the two television series presented positive images of blacks and were free of stereotypes and discriminatory content. In 1993, Poussaint became professor of psychiatry and associate dean of student affairs at Harvard Medical School. A year later, he became the director of the Media Center for Children at the Judge Baker Children's Center. Poussaint has been a fellow at a number of organizations, including the American Psychiatric Association, the American Association for the Advancement of Science, and the Orthopsychiatric Association.

BIBLIOGRAPHY

Hendrix, Kathleen. "Alvin Poussaint: Upbeat About the Black Psyche." *Los Angeles Times,* June 24, 1988, Sec. 5, p. 1.
Troutt, David D. "Alvin F. Poussaint—Psychiatrist Goes Prime Time to Shape Persona of Blacks." *Los Angeles Times,* June 10, 1990, Sec. M, p. 3.

— ROBERT C. HAYDEN

POWELL, ADAM CLAYTON, JR.

Adam Clayton Powell, Jr. (November 29, 1908–April 4, 1972), congressman, civil rights activist, and clergyman. Adam Clayton Powell, Jr., was born in 1908 in New Haven, Conn. Shortly thereafter his father, Adam Clayton Powell, Sr., left New Haven for New York City to assume the pastorship of the Abyssinian Baptist Church in Harlem. The elder Powell, a prominent minister, sought the best for his only son, educating him at the elite Townsend Harris High School, then sending him to Colgate University, a largely white school in Hamilton, N.Y. In 1932 Powell received an M.A. in religious education from Columbia University Teachers College. By the time Powell had graduated from Colgate in 1930 and returned home, the United States was mired in the Great Depression. Young Powell was named an assistant pastor at the Abyssinian Church. Powell was not content, however, to concern himself exclusively with pastoral matters. With the Depression as backdrop, young Powell rallied for help for Harlemites from City Hall, and goaded the residents of Harlem to protest second-class treatment of African Americans. He declaimed from both pulpit and streetcorner, leading marchers not only to City Hall, but to the doorsteps of the ill-staffed and racially discriminatory Harlem Hospital. Older Abyssinian deacons considered him unpredictable, even impatient. But the younger members of the church adored him, and were eager to follow his lead. In the winter of 1937 Powell was named minister of the Abyssinian Baptist Church to succeed his father. He was twenty-nine years old. The congregation boasted more than 10,000 members and was probably the largest Protestant Church in the United States. During the next few years, Powell, in his forceful and flamboyant manner, became the most visible leader of the boycott campaign to break the bottleneck of discrimination that existed in stores. Melding together the often factious groups that comprised the "Don't Buy Where You Can't Work" campaign, Powell's tactics were hugely successful and emulated in other cities. He pressured New York utilities, including Consolidated Edison, to hire blacks. His boycotting tactics forced the New York City private bus companies for the first time to hire black drivers. Liberals and progressives from the world of politics were invited to appear in the Abyssinian pulpit. The mix was eclectic. They were animated by the spirit of progressive reform in the manner of Robert LaFollette and Franklin D. Roosevelt, as well as black nationalist sentiments inspired by Marcus GARVEY. Powell turned the church stage into a personal bully pulpit.

Powell was a natural for the political arena, and in 1941, running as an Independent, he became the first black to win election to the New York City Council. Although he would thereafter usually run as a Democrat, he always maintained his independence from the Democratic machine. Before his first term was over, he decided to run for Congress from a newly created district that would, for the first time, enable a black to be elected from Harlem. With help from the left-wing East Harlem Congressman Vito Marcantonio, the powerful Abyssinian church, and the vibrant artistic community of Harlem, Powell launched a two-year campaign that saw him elected the first black in 1944 to Congress from the Northeast. His Washington debut was typically controversial. In fall 1945, when the Daughters of the American Revolution (DAR) refused to allow jazz pianist Hazel Scott, the second of his three wives, to perform on the stage of Constitution Hall, Powell assailed First Lady Bess Truman in the press because of her continued connections with the DAR. President Truman was livid, and Powell was never invited to the White House while Truman was President.

Powell's talent for attracting attention and making enemies soon made him the congressional leader in the fight for civil rights legislation. Working closely with Clarence Mitchell, Jr. and the NAACP in 1950 he offered an amendment to current legislation, which came to be known as the Powell Amendment, forbidding any federal support for segregated facilities. Powell would repeatedly introduce this amendment over the next several years. Politically he was liberal, but he was also a shrewd opportunist. In 1956 Powell backed President Eisenhower's reelection bid, a move that angered Democrats. Four years later, however, Powell heartily campaigned for the Kennedy-Johnson ticket. Coinciding with Kennedy's victory, Powell had gained sufficient seniority to become chairman of the powerful House Education and Labor Committee. The influence of his powerful position, however, would not be felt until 1964, when President Johnson's heightened domestic agenda went into full action. Powell was instrumental in passage of the war on poverty legislation, on which he and Johnson collaborated. These included increased federal aid to school programs, increasing the minimum wage, and the Head Start Program for preschool children. Billions of dollars flowed through the Powell committee. In 1964 the Civil Rights Act finally saw the core of the Powell Amendment enacted into law. From 1961 to 1967 Powell was one of the most powerful politicians in the United States, and certainly the most powerful African American. He was both an American insider and outsider, working inside the halls of Congress, and identifying with the masses who remained on the outside as one of the most riveting stump speakers in the country. He often engaged in one-upmanship with Martin Luther KING, Jr. By the time his congressional career ended there would be more than sixty pieces of major legislation with his imprimatur.

Powell's political downfall began when, in 1960, he accused Esther James, a Harlem woman, of corruption. James successfully sued for libel. Powell refused to pay, and before he finally agreed to settle in 1966 Powell had accumulated enormous amounts of bad publicity because of his sometimes mercurial and sybaritic behavior. In January 1967 House members, led by southern Democrats and Republicans, refused to seat Powell until a committee could investigate his conduct, citing his indiscretions and personal lifestyle. The House committee set up to investigate Powell's conduct, the Celler Committee, chaired by New York Republican Emanuel Celler, decided to fine Powell, strip away his seniority, and have him repay money that had gone to his third wife, Yvette Diago Powell, while she had been on his payroll. The full House, however, ignored the recommendations of the Celler Committee and voted to expel Powell from Congress in March 1967. It was the first time since 1919 that the House had expelled one of its members. Powell vowed to fight the case all the way to the Supreme Court. He won a special election in March 1967 to fill his own vacant seat, and was re-elected in 1968, though he remained outside of Congress. In 1968 he barnstormed the United States, rallying black and white students on college campuses to fight for equality and end American involvement in Vietnam, peppering his defense with his catchphrase, "Keep the faith, baby." He was mentioned in 1968 as a favorite-son presidential candidate from New York. In 1969, in his last decision from the Supreme Court, Chief Justice Earl Warren ruled that Adam Clayton Powell had been unconstitutionally expelled from Congress. Back in Congress, however, Powell was without the power he had once yielded, returning as a freshman, because the Court had not ruled on the matter of his seniority and lost back pay. In 1970 he lost his last reelection bid to Charles Rangel by 150 votes. He spent the last two years of his life on the island of Bimini, in the Bahamas, where he said he was working on his memoirs, which never were published. He died of cancer in a Miami hospital on April 4, 1972, four years to the day from Martin Luther King's death.

BIBLIOGRAPHY

Haygood, Wil. *King of the Cats: The Life and Times of Adam Clayton Powell, Jr.* Boston, 1993.

Jacobs, Andy. *The Powell Affair: Freedom Minus One.* New York, 1973.

Powell, Adam Clayton, Jr. *Adam by Adam: The Autobiography of Adam Clayton Powell, Jr.* New York, 1971.

— WIL HAYGOOD

POWELL, COLIN LUTHER

Colin Luther Powell (April 5, 1937–), Army officer, chair of the Joint Chiefs of Staff. Born and raised in New York City, Colin Powell grew up in a close-knit family of Jamaican immigrants in the Hunts Point section of the Bronx. After attending public schools, Powell graduated from the City College of New York (CCNY) in 1958. Although his grades were mediocre, he discovered an affinity for the military. Participating in CCNY's Reserve Officer Training Corps (ROTC) program, he finished as a cadet colonel, the highest rank attainable. Like all ROTC graduates, Powell was commissioned as a second lieutenant after completing college.

Powell served for two years in West Germany and two years in Massachusetts, where he met his wife, Alma. In 1962, already a captain, Powell received orders to report to Vietnam. He was one of the second wave of more than 15,000 military advisers sent by the United States to Vietnam and was posted with a South Vietnamese Army unit for most of his tenure. During his first tour of duty, from 1962 to 1963, he was decorated with the Purple Heart after being wounded by a Viet Cong booby trap near the Laotian border.

After returning to the United States, Powell spent almost four years at Fort Benning in Georgia, serving as, among other things, an instructor at Fort Benning's Army Infantry School. In 1967, now a major, he attended an officers' training course at the United States Army Command and General Staff College at Fort Leavenworth, Kans., finishing second in a class of more than twelve hundred. In the summer of 1968, Powell was ordered back to Vietnam. On his second tour, Powell primarily served as a liaison to Gen. Charles Gettys of the Americal Division and received the Soldier's Medal for his role in rescuing injured soldiers, including Gen. Gettys, from a downed helicopter.

Powell returned to the United States in mid-1969 and began moving between military field postings and political appointments, a process that would become characteristic of his career. In 1971, after working in the Pentagon for the assistant vice chief of the Army, he earned an M.B.A. from George Washington University in Washington, D.C. Shortly thereafter, Powell was accepted as a White House Fellow during the Nixon administration and was attached to the Office of Management and Budget (OMB), headed by Caspar Weinberger. In 1973, after a year at OMB, Powell received command of an infantry battalion in South Korea; his mission was to raise morale and restore order in a unit plagued by drug abuse and racial problems. He then attended a nine-month course at the National War College and was promoted to full colonel in February 1976, taking command of the 2nd Brigade, 101st Airborne Division, located at Fort Campbell, Ky.

In 1979 Powell was an aide to Secretary of Energy Charles Duncan during the crisis of the nuclear accident at Three Mile Island in Pennsylvania and the oil shortage caused by the overthrow of the shah of Iran. In June of that year, while working at the Department of Energy (DOE), he became a brigadier general. Powell returned to the field from 1981 until 1983, serving as assistant division commander of the Fourth Infantry (mechanized) in Colorado and then as the deputy commanding general of an Army research facility at Fort Leavenworth. In mid-1983, he became military assistant to Secretary of Defense Caspar Weinberger. In 1986, Powell, by then a lieutenant general, returned to the field as the commander of V Corps, a unit of 75,000 troops in West Germany. The following year, in the wake of the Iran-Contra scandal, he returned to serve as President Ronald Reagan's national security adviser. During the Intermediate Nuclear Forces (INF) arms-control negotiations with the Soviet Union, Powell was heralded as being a major factor in their success.

In July 1989, Powell, a newly promoted four-star general, was nominated by President George Bush to become the first black chairman of the Joint Chiefs of Staff, the highest military position in the armed forces. As chairman, Powell was responsible for overseeing Operation Desert Storm, the 1991 international response to the 1990 Iraqi invasion of Kuwait. Through his commanding and reassuring television presence during the successful Persian Gulf War, Powell became one of the most popular figures in the Bush administration. Reappointed chairman in 1991, he was the recipient of various military decorations as well as a Presidential Medal of Freedom from Bush. In the same year, the NAACP gave Powell the Spingarn Medal, its highest award for African-American achievement.

In July 1989, Powell was nominated to become the first black chairman of the Joint Chiefs of Staff, the highest military position in the armed forces.

When Bill Clinton was elected president in 1992, he and Powell had differences over Clinton's plan to substantially reduce the defense budget. Powell also disagreed with Clinton's proposal to end the ban on homosexuals in the military and was instrumental in limiting the scope of the change. Powell retired from the Army in September 1993 at the end of his second term as chairman of the Joint Chiefs. Upon his departure, President Clinton awarded him his second Presidential Medal of Freedom.

BIBLIOGRAPHY

Means, Howard. *Colin Powell: Soldier/Statesman—Statesman/Soldier.* New York, 1992.

Powell, Colin, with Joseph E. Persico. *My American Journey.* New York, 1995.

Roberts, Steven V., with Bruce Auster and Gary Cohen. "What's Next, General Powell?" *U.S. News and World Report* (March 18, 1991): 50–53.

Rowan, Carl. "Called to Service: The Colin Powell Story." *Reader's Digest* (December 1989): 121–126.

– JOHN C. STONER

PRESBYTERIANS

The African-American constituency of the Presbyterian church dates from the 1730s, when the Rev. Samuel Davies began to evangelize slaves of Scotch-Irish Presbyterian immigrants in the Valley of Virginia. Davies reported instructing and baptizing 150 slaves in 1757. Unlike the BAPTISTS and Methodists, American Presbyterians failed to attract large numbers of blacks in either the South or the North. At the end of the nineteenth century there were fewer than 30,000 African Americans in the northern and southern Presbyterian churches combined. These two major branches of Presbyterianism had split in 1861 over the Civil War but closed ranks in 1983. The black minority has grown slowly. By 1990 it was reported that only 2.47 percent, or 64,841 of the almost three-million-member reunited Presbyterian Church in the U.S.A. (PCUSA) were African Americans.

Reputedly, Presbyterian slaves were well instructed in the rudiments of Christianity. Many were taught to read and recite the creed and passages of the Bible by their owners. The emphasis of Puritan Presbyterians on a trained clergy and a literate laity had the effect of exposing black Presbyterians to pious learning as indispensable for Christian discipleship. The Presbyterians, however, were slow to oppose slavery. The issue was first raised in 1774 at a meeting of the Synod of New York and Philadelphia, but no action was taken. In 1787 the synod approved the ultimate goal of abolition; however, successive deliverances of the General Assembly induced the practice of Presbyterians to condemn slavery in principle while warning local judicatories not to interfere with the civil order.

The first black Presbyterian preacher was John Chavis, born in Granville County, N.C., in 1763. From 1801 to 1808 he served as a missionary to slaves in Virginia and opened a school that was patronized by many leading white families. The first African-American pastor was John Gloucester, manumitted by Gideon Blackburn, a Tennessee missionary, to preach the gospel. In 1807 Gloucester was permitted by the

Presbytery of Philadelphia to organize the First African Presbyterian Church, which competed with Richard ALLEN's Bethel AFRICAN METHODIST EPISCOPAL CHURCH for members from the burgeoning black community of South Philadelphia. Gloucester's three sons entered the Presbyterian ministry. Jeremiah organized Second African of Philadelphia in 1824, James organized Siloam in Brooklyn in 1847, and Stephen served the Lombard Central church of Philadelphia. Among the earliest black congregations in the North were Shiloh in New York City (organized 1822) and Washington Street in Reading, Pa. (1823). The first black Presbyterian congregation in the South was Beaufort-Salem, organized in Sheldon, N.C. in 1828. The Ladson Presbyterian Church of Columbia, S.C. (1828), was first governed by white elders and named after the white minister who was its first pastor. The slaves of the members of the First Presbyterian Church of Macon, Georgia, organized the Washington Avenue Church of that city in 1838.

After the Civil War, blacks spurned the southern branch of the church, the Presbyterian Church in the United States (PCUS), and rallied to the northern PCUSA missionaries following the Union armies. Many became members of the northern church. Fewer than 4,000 blacks remained in the southern church, which tried to organize them into an independent Afro-American Presbyterian Church in 1874. That effort was abandoned in 1916 because of poor support from whites. During RECONSTRUCTION the northern church launched a mission to attract and minister to the recently freed people. By 1882 its Board of Missions for Freedmen sponsored two universities, Lincoln University, near Oxford, Pa., and Biddle University (later Johnson C. Smith) in Charlotte, N.C., two colleges, five boarding schools, and 138 parochial schools. Following the Presbyterian tradition of educational excellence, these institutions made a signal contribution far beyond the ranks of the black constituency. Until the church's Board of National Missions phased it out in the twentieth century, this remarkable educational system enrolled 19,166 students and 494 teachers. At its peak the board supervised 438 churches and missions, 388 schools, 272 ministers, and 27,916 communicants.

Black Presbyterians caucused for greater recognition and freedom as early as 1859, when their ministers began meeting with black Congregational clergy in Philadelphia. Prior to the Civil War Samuel Cornish, Theodore Wright, Henry Highland Garnet, and J. W. C. Pennington all Presbyterian clergy, were leading black abolitionists. Lucy Craft Laney, daughter of a Presbyterian minister and born a slave, founded the Haines Normal Institute in Augusta, Ga., in 1867. In 1891 Daniel J. Sanders became the first black president of J. C. Smith University. Blacks in the northern church became more assertive with the establishment in 1894 of the Afro-American Presbyterian Council. Its purpose was to create more fellowship among themselves in an overwhelming white church and greater influence in the boards and agencies of the denomination. At the turn of the century outspoken black pastors like Francis J. Grimké of the Fifteenth Street Presbyterian Church in Washington, D.C., and Matthew Anderson of Berean in Philadelphia consistently fought racism in the church and the proposed mergers of the northern church with the PCUS and the Cumberland Presbyterian Church, both with lingering Confederate allegiances.

Pressure from the African-American constituency moved the northern church to begin elevating blacks to key positions. In 1938 Albert B. McCoy became the first black executive of the Unit of Work for Colored People. Charles W. Talley was appointed field representative of the Atlantic Synod in 1945. During this period George Lake Imes became field representative for Negro Work in the North and West. He was followed by Robert Pierre Johnson, who served as associate stated clerk of the General Assembly in 1972. Jesse Belmont Barber, Frank T. Wilson, Emily V. Gibbes, Elo Henderson, Mildred Atris, Rachel Adams, and Bryant George were among the black men and women who served in prominent executive positions after World War II.

Lawrence W. Bottoms was an executive of the PCUS prior to his election in 1974 as its first black moderator. The PCUS began to respond to civil rights agitation after 1969. Under Bottoms's leadership in new church development in black communities and with the rising militancy of a newly formed Black Leadership Caucus, African-American membership in the southern church doubled to about 8,000 before the 1983 merger with the United Presbyterian Church (formed by the union of PCUSA and the United Presbyterian Church of North America in 1958).

Northern black Presbyterians figured prominently in the civil rights program of the National Council of Churches during the 1960s. The Afro-American Presbyterian Council of 1894 went through several reincarnations and finally developed into the Concerned Presbyterians in 1963 and Black Presbyterians United in 1968. The former caucus, with white allies, enabled the election of the controversial pastor of St. Augustine Presbyterian Church in the Bronx, Edler G. Hawkins, as the first black moderator of the United Presbyterian Church in 1964. This group was also a major factor in the creation of the Commission on Religion and Race, which steered the church through the 1960s and played a leading role in the Black Manifesto call for slavery reparations in 1969 and the Angela DAVIS crisis of 1971. Gayraud S. Wilmore, a professor at the Pittsburgh Theological Seminary, J. Metz Rollins, a pastor and civil rights activist in Tallahassee, and Robert Stone, a New York City pastor, were chosen to head this unprecedented commitment of the church to the struggle led by the SOUTHERN CHRISTIAN LEADERSHIP CONFERENCE. Since the union, Asian, Hispanic, and Native-American minorities have played a larger role in the church's program in racial and intercultural affairs. African Americans, however, came together across regional lines in 1983 to form a National Black Presbyterian Caucus, which continues to monitor church policy and practice in the field of racial and ethnic relations.

BIBLIOGRAPHY

Murray, Andrew W. *Presbyterians and the Negro: A History.* Philadelphia, 1966.

Swift, David E. *Black Prophets of Justice: Activist Clergy Before the Civil War.* Baton Rouge, La., 1989.

Wilmore, Gayraud S. *Black and Presbyterian: The Heritage and the Hope.* Philadelphia, 1983.

— GAYRAUD S. WILMORE

PRICE, MARY VIOLET LEONTYNE

Mary Violet Leontyne Price (February 10, 1927–), opera singer. Born in Laurel, Miss., the soprano Leontyne Price came to be regarded as a *prima donna assoluta* during her exceptionally long operatic career (1952–1985).

Her parents had been involved in the musical life of Laurel, and provided her with piano lessons from the age of four. Soon thereafter, she joined her mother in the church choir and, after attending a recital by Marian ANDERSON in Jackson, Miss., in 1936, she resolved on a career in music. At that time, African-American women could aspire in music only for roles in education, and it was with that major in mind that Price enrolled at Central State College in Ohio. Before she graduated in 1949, however, her vocal talent was manifest and she was encouraged to enter the Juilliard School of Music, where she studied with Florence Kimball. As Mistress Ford in a school production of Verdi's *Falstaff,* she attracted the attention of American composer Virgil Thomson, who enlisted her for the role of Cecilia in a 1952 revival of his *Four Saints in Three Acts* (1934), a work calling for an all-black cast, thus initiating her professional career and terminating her formal study.

Following this production in New York and performances at the Paris International Arts Festival, she was engaged for the role of Bess in George Gershwin's *Porgy and Bess,* with which she toured in Berlin, Paris, and Vienna into 1954. In November of that year, she made her New York debut at Town Hall. The following February she appeared in the title role of Puccini's *Tosca* on television, later adding Mozart's *Die Zauberflöte* and *Don Giovanni,* and Poulenc's *Dialogues des Carmélites* to her NBC telecasts. In 1956, she sang the role of Cleopatra in Handel's *Giulio Cesare.*

It was in the Poulenc opera as Madame Lidoine that she made her debut with the San Francisco Opera in 1957, following this with the leading soprano roles with that company in Verdi's *Il Trovatore* and Puccini's *Madama Butterfly* and debuts that year at the Arena di Verona, Covent Garden, and the Vienna Staatsoper (*Aida*). Her debut with the Lyric Opera of Chicago was as Liù in Puccini's *Turandot* (1959).

The Metropolitan Opera had only begun adding black singers to its roster in 1955 with Marian Anderson and Robert McFerrin, followed by the debuts of African-American artists Mattiwilda Dobbs (1956), Gloria Davy (1958), and Martina Arroyo (1959). Actually, Price had already appeared in the Metropolitan Opera Jamboree, a fund-raising broadcast from the Manhattan Ritz Theater, April 6, 1953, when she performed "Summertime" from *Porgy and Bess,* but her formal debut was as Leonora in Verdi's *Il Trovatore* on January 27, 1961, when she won an unprecedented forty-two-minute ovation, fully justifying her selection as the leading lady to open the next Met season (as Puccini's Minnie in *La Fanciulla del West*) and that of the next year (repeating her 1957 Vienna role of Aida, in which she was heard each season for the following five years). During the last six years of the "old Met," she particularly excelled in the Italian repertory (as Liù in Puccini's *Turandot,* Cio-Cio-San in Puccini's *Madama Butterfly,* and Elvira in Verdi's *Ernani,* which she had sung for Herbert von Karajan at the 1962 Salzburg Festival).

The new home of the Metropolitan Opera at Lincoln Center was inaugurated in 1966 with a new opera by Samuel Barber, *Antony and Cleopatra,* written specifically for her. When she concluded her career in opera performances on January 3, 1985, with *Aida* at the Metropolitan Opera, she had proved her interpretive leadership in the Italian repertories of Verdi and Puccini, but she has expanded the previously practiced limits to move far past any stereotypes, excelling in German, Spanish, French, and Slavic works, as well as in spirituals and other American literature. Her principal opera roles, in addition to those mentioned, were the Prima Donna and Ariadne (*Ariadne auf Naxos*), Amelia (*Un Ballo in Maschera*), Fiordiligi (*Così fan tutte*), Donna Anna (*Don Giovanni*), Tatiana (*Eugene Onegin*), Minnie (*La Fanciulla del West*), Leonora (*La Forza del Destino*), Manon (*Manon Lescaut*), and the title role in *Tosca.*

Her recorded legacy is extensive. In addition to many of the operatic roles in which she appeared on stage—Bizet's *Carmen,* Mozart's *Don Giovanni* and *Cosi fan tutte,* Puccini's *Madama Butterfly* and *Tosca,* Verdi's *Aida, Un Ballo in Maschera, Ernani, La Forza del Destino,* and *Il Trovatore*—she has recorded Samuel Barber's *Hermit Songs* and music of Fauré, Poulenc, Wolf, and R. Strauss, as well as Verdi's *Requiem* and Beethoven's *Ninth Symphony.* She has also recorded excerpts from *Porgy and Bess* (with her then-husband William Warfield), an album of popular songs with André Previn (*Right as Rain*), and *Swing Low, Sweet Chariot,* a collection of fourteen spirituals. In 1992 RCA reissued on compact disc forty-seven arias by Price under the title *Leontyne Price: The Prima Donna Collection,* arias which had been recorded between 1965 and 1979.

BIBLIOGRAPHY

Blyth, Alan. "Mary Violet Leontyne Price." In *The New Grove Dictionary of Music and Musicians,* vol. 15. London, 1980, pp. 225–226.

"Leontyne Price." In Nicholas Slonimsky, ed. *Baker's Biographical Dictionary of Musicians,* 7th ed. New York, 1992, p. 1363.

Lyon, Hugh Lee. *Leontyne Price: Highlights of a Prima Donna.* New York, 1973.

Sargeant, Winthrop. *Divas.* New York, 1973, pp. 134–167.

– DOMINIQUE-RENÈ DE LERMA

PROPOSITIONS 48 AND 42: NCAA BYLAW 14.3

Whether freshmen should compete in American intercollegiate athletics has been debated for a century. The issue, however, acquired distinct racial overtones only in 1983, when the National Collegiate Athletic Association (NCAA), the country's governing body for major intercollegiate athletics, adopted Proposition 48. Effective in 1986, the NCAA required that in order to be eligible to compete as a freshman, a student-athlete must have a 2.0 grade point average on a scale of 4.0 in eleven "core" courses (four English, three mathematics, and two each in social sciences and natural sciences), as well as either a 700 total score on the Scholastic Aptitude Test (SAT) or a 15 total score on the American College Test (ACT).

Historically black colleges in particular opposed Proposition 48, contending that the test scores were arbitrary and the tests themselves discriminated against lower-income minorities, often in neglected inner-city schools. Athletic grants-in-aid could still be received by "partial qualifiers"—those who had the requisite grades but not the test scores—but they could not play or practice their sport during the freshman year and lost one of their four years of eligibility.

Proposition 48, lobbied by the American Council on Education, was a reaction to the low academic standards of the previous decade, when only a 2.0 high school grade point average was required for athletic aid, without regard for the nature of the courses taken. Many athletes, often African Americans, were recruited for their athletic ability, were maintained in college while playing and then discarded upon completing their eligibility, without receiving meaningful higher education. Tony Rice, a Notre Dame quarterback among the first made ineligible under Proposition 48, expressed its rationale: "It was tough, not being able to play. . . . But . . . I was able to get a foot down on my classes."

The NCAA commenced research on the effects of Proposition 48, but before meaningful data were available, its 1989 convention passed Proposition 42, barring athletic aid to partial qualifiers. While 85 percent of the African-American athletes entering Division I schools between 1987 and 1990 qualified, African Americans constituted two-thirds of the partial qualifiers. Half of all partial qualifiers play football or men's basketball, sports in which America's colleges serve as professional development teams.

The emotional protest of Georgetown basketball coach John Thompson, who walked off the court before his team's next two games, brought massive publicity to the issue, and led to a change by the 1990 convention, prior to the effective date. While Proposition 42's bar to athletic aid was retained, need-based aid was approved. Two years later, after a prestigious commission created by the Knight Foundation refocused public attention on the commercialization of college revenue sports, additional changes were made, sponsored by a newly powerful President's Commission within the NCAA. Effective August 1995, a 2.5 average in thirteen core courses will be required, though indexing could bring it as low as 2.0 if an SAT combined score of 900 or an ACT score of 21 is achieved. More significant in terms of minimizing exploitation of major college athletes, 25 percent of whom are African-American, is requiring that athletes meet the minimum grade point average requirements throughout their college careers and complete a steadily increasing portion of their degree requirements in order to remain eligible.

BIBLIOGRAPHY

Asher, Mark. "Presidents Play the Numbers; Debate over SAT, Grades." *Washington Post,* June 30, 1991, p. B1.

Davis, Timothy. "An Absence of Good Faith: Defining a University's Educational Obligation to Student-Athletes." *Houston Law Review* 28 (1991): 743–790.

Greene, Linda S. "The New Rules of the Game: Academic Integrity or Racism?" *St. Louis University Law Journal* 28 (1984): 101–151.

Lederman, Douglas. "Arthur Ashe, Defender of Black Athletes, Urges Colleges to Help Them Meet More Stringent Standards." *Chronicle of Higher Education,* February 12, 1992, pp. A37, A40.

– GORDON A. MARTIN, JR.

PRYOR, RICHARD FRANKLIN LENOX THOMAS

Richard Franklin Lenox Thomas Pryor (December 1, 1940–), comedian. Born in Peoria, Ill., Richard Pryor overcame a troubled life in an extended family headed by his grandmother, Marie Carter, to become a preeminent comedian, film star, screenwriter, producer, and director, beginning in the early 1960s.

During Pryor's boyhood, Peoria was like the Deep South. Segregation and discrimination in housing, employment, and places of public accommodation were deeply embedded in southern Illinois. Forty percent of the black population of Peoria was unemployed, while 32 percent worked for the WORKS PROGRESS ADMINISTRATION (WPA). Odd jobs supported the rest, including the Pryor family, which ran small carting firms, pool halls, and, Pryor claimed, houses of prostitution. Peoria remained segregated for a time even after the 1954 Supreme Court decision that forbade it.

At eleven, Pryor, the son of Gertrude Thomas and Leroy "Buck" Carter Pryor, and, he once said, the seventh of twelve "Pryor kids," began acting at the Carver Community Center under the guidance of the drama teacher, Juliette Whittaker. Over the years she became the recipient of some of Pryor's performing awards; he also contributed to the private school she later founded, the Learning Tree.

After dropping out of school, Pryor joined the army in 1958, where his life was no less troublesome. After military service, he worked for his father's carting firm and the Caterpillar factory in Peoria. He also haunted the local clubs and watched television for the appearances of African-American entertainers such as Sammy DAVIS, Jr., and Bill COSBY, personalities he wanted to emulate and eventually replace.

Within a few years Pryor was playing small clubs in East St. Louis, Chicago, Windsor (Canada), Buffalo, Youngstown, and Cleveland. Much of his comic material was drawn from his army service and the early Cosby comedy routines. By 1964 he had attracted enough attention to be booked for his first national television appearance, on Rudy Vallee's *Broadway Tonight* show. Three years later, after stops on the Ed Sullivan, Merv Griffin, and Johnny Carson shows, Pryor appeared in the film *The Busy Body* with Sid Caesar and other comedians—the first of more than forty films he acted in, wrote, produced, and/or directed into the early 1990s. His first major role was in *Lady Sings the Blues* (1972), with Diana Ross, in which Pryor played a character called Piano Man.

The Richard Pryor Show ran briefly on NBC-TV for part of 1977. It was innovative and conveyed a wide range of both comedy and tenderness, but it was too daring for the executives of NBC. Amid legal wrangling, the show went off the air and, typically, Pryor laid the blame on NBC. In 1984, he played himself as a boy in *Pryor's Place,* a children's show that aired on Saturday mornings. It too was short-lived, this time without recrimination.

Richard Pryor overcame a troubled life to become a preeminent comedian, film star, screenwriter, producer, and director.

From 1970 through 1979, Pryor starred or costarred in twenty-one films. He contributed to the script of *Blazing Saddles* (1973), and in the same year wrote for and appeared on *The Flip Wilson Show* and was a cowriter for Lily Tomlin's television specials, for which he won Emmy Awards in 1973 and 1974. He continued to perform in clubs and theaters around the country; these performances provided material for his two *Richard Pryor Live in Concert* films (both in 1979). The recordings of his performances earned him three Grammy Awards: *That Nigger's Crazy,* 1974; *Is It Something I Said,* 1975; and *Bicentennial Nigger,* 1976. *That Nigger's Crazy* also became a certified gold and platinum album.

In 1980 he produced his first film, *Bustin' Loose,* starring himself and Cicely Tyson. Two years later he produced and wrote *Richard Pryor: Live on the Sunset Strip. Jo Jo Dancer, Your Life Is Calling,* which Pryor produced, directed, and helped write, was based upon his near-fatal self-immolation that occurred when he was free-basing cocaine in 1980. In 1986, Pryor, who had also survived two heart attacks, discovered that he had multiple sclerosis, but he continued to perform onstage.

Pryor was known as a "crossover" star: one who appealed to both black and white moviegoers. This label resulted from the "buddy" films he made with Gene Wilder—*Silver Streak* (1976), *Stir Crazy* (1980), and

See No Evil, Hear No Evil (1989)—although he had starred with white actors in sixteen other movies. Few of Pryor's films during the 1980s were memorable, not even the concert film *Richard Pryor: Here and Now* (1983). But *Richard Pryor: Live on the Sunset Strip,* released only the year before, most typified his pungent, raunchy comedy that echoed the African-American man in the street, which was precisely what made Pryor the great comedian he was.

When he was at his peak, few comedians could match Pryor's popularity. Most contemporary comedy is said to be "post-Pryor," because of the standards he set. His life was his act, but he shaped his personal experiences into rollicking comedy. His major themes were racism in its several forms and the battle of the sexes. Usually, the women bested the men. His topics were current and to the point, and his favorite character was an old, foul-mouthed, wise black man named Mudbone from Mississippi.

BIBLIOGRAPHY

Haskins, Jim. *Richard Pryor, a Man and His Madness: A Biography.* New York, 1984.

Williams, John A., and Dennis A. Williams. *If I Stop I'll Die: The Comedy and Tragedy of Richard Pryor.* New York, 1991.

– JOHN A. WILLIAMS

PURYEAR, MARTIN

Martin Puryear (1937–), sculptor. The oldest of seven children, sculptor Martin Puryear attended both elementary and secondary school in Washington, D.C. His father, Reginald, worked as a postal service employee, and his mother, Martina, taught elementary school. He developed strong interests in biology and art, and aspired to be a wildlife illustrator. Always interested in working with his hands, Puryear as a young man made numerous objects, including guitars, chairs, and canoes.

Puryear entered Catholic University in Washington in 1959. Although initially a biology major, he shifted in his junior year to the study of painting and sculpture. Following graduation in 1963, Puryear entered the Peace Corps and served for two years in Sierra Leone, where he taught English, French, art, and biology. In addition to his teaching, he studied the craftsmen of West Africa, particularly the carpenters, from whom he learned a wide variety of traditional techniques. In 1966 he moved to Stockholm, where he enrolled at the Swedish Royal Academy. In addition to his formal studies in printmaking, Puryear pursued an interest in Scandinavian woodworking and began to work independently, making wood sculptures in the studios of the academy. He traveled widely during his two years in Stockholm, visiting the Soviet Union and western Europe, as well as the region of Lapland in northern Scandinavia.

In 1968 Puryear returned to the United States, and the following year he entered Yale University to study sculpture at the graduate level. In addition to his exposure to the part- and full-time faculty (including James Rosati, Robert Morris, Richard Serra, and Salvatore Scarpitta) at Yale, Puryear visited New York often, familiarizing himself with recent developments in contemporary art. Following receipt of his master of fine arts degree in 1971, he taught at Fisk University in Nashville for two years. His first important sculptures were made in the early 1970s, and these were shown in a solo exhibition held in 1973 at the Henri Gallery in Washington and at Fisk.

In 1973 Puryear left Fisk and established a studio in Brooklyn. The following year he accepted a teaching position at the University of Maryland, and he commuted between New York and College Park, Md., from 1974 to 1978. It was during this period that his work became known to a larger audience. In 1977 the Corcoran Gallery of Art in Washington, D.C., organized the first museum exhibition of his work; this show included *Cedar Lodge* (1977), a large, quasi-architectural sculpture, as well as *Some Tales* (1977), a wall-mounted sculpture consisting of six linear wooden elements. In the same year, Puryear created *Box and Pole* for Art Park in Lewiston, N.Y. For this first outdoor commission, the sculptor constructed a wooden box made of milled wood with dovetailed corners, and a hundred-foot-tall pole, thereby contrasting the concentrated strength of the former with the upward, seemingly infinite reach of the latter.

If 1977 found Puryear being accorded increasing attention in the art world, it was also a time of great loss. On February 1, 1977, his apartment and studio—including virtually all of the sculptor's work to date—were lost in a fire. The following year he left the East Coast to accept a teaching position at the University of Illinois, Chicago; he lived in Chicago until 1991. During this period, Puryear achieved ever-increasing recognition and was included in numerous important group exhibitions (including the Whitney Biennial in 1979, 1981, and 1989; the Museum of Modern Art's International Survey of Recent Painting and Sculpture, in 1984; and the Walker Art Center's Sculpture Inside Outside, in 1988). In 1989 he was selected as the sole American representative to exhibit in the twentieth São Paulo Bienal in Brazil, and he received the grand prize for his installation of eight works. The same year, he received a John D. and Catherine T. MacArthur Foundation Fellowship. In the fall of 1991, a large retro-

R

RACE, CASTE, AND CLASS

In his influential 1944 study, *An American Dilemma,* Gunnar Myrdal characterized the peculiar nature of race relations in the United States as the most important problem facing the country. Social scientists have offered several theoretical frameworks to understand and conceptualize the complexities of this dilemma. Gordon Allport, for example, wrote of "prejudice" as being at the heart of American race relations (*The Nature of Prejudice,* 1958). Later theorists have written of "institutional racism" (Louis L. Knowles and Kenneth Prewitt eds., *Institutional Racism in America,* 1969), or "internal colonialism" (Robert Blauner, *Racial Oppression in America,* 1972) as frameworks for the interpretation of race relations.

Although none of these approaches has won universal acceptance, the so-called caste-class model presented by Lloyd Warner and popularized by Gunnar Myrdal has been the most influential and enduring. Beginning with a 1936 essay, "American Caste and Class," and continuing with the study of a small southern city in *Deep South* (1941), Warner and his colleagues argued that race relations in the United States could be best understood as analogous to the traditional caste system of India.

Having earlier studied a small community in New England (given the pseudonym "Yankee City"), Warner was struck by differences in intergroup relations in the two cities. Unlike Yankee City, where members of white ethnic groups experienced some mobility within the "social class" structure (even though they rarely reached the highest level), in the town they called "Deep South," all blacks seemed to be ranked below all whites, without any hope of upward mobility. This characteristic of southern race relations along with the taboo against interracial marriage suggested to Warner and his associates that a fundamentally different social structure existed in the South.

The concepts of "prejudice" and "race" were considered and rejected as explanations of this organized social system, which systematically separated the races and subordinated all blacks to whites. Warner and his associates observed that even the most liberal members of white southern society shared dominant cultural ideas about the social incompatibility of the two groups and carefully avoided social contact with blacks. They noted that race relations in the South had all the earmarks of a caste system such as existed in India. Yet southern society was not static. While blacks and whites were separated by impermeable barriers, social hierarchies existed within each community which allowed for some social mobility within each group. To express these two aspects of the town's social structure, the researchers settled on "caste and class," a nomenclature combining both aspects of community dynamics. A substantial number of community studies and essays by Warner and his colleagues provided additional plausibility to their approach to race relations in the United States and led to its widespread acceptance among social scientists. To the general public this analogy with the Indian caste system was persuasive, especially after the more popular work by Gunnar Myrdal, *An American Dilemma,* appeared a few years later.

In his influential 1944 study, An American Dilemma, *Gunnar Myrdal characterized the peculiar nature of race relations in the United States as the most important problem facing the country.*

Within this study, which became enormously popular because of its focus on the disjuncture between the American creed of equality for all and the systematic subordination of blacks, Myrdal defended the caste and class thesis. Myrdal put his greatest emphasis on the closed nature of black and white groups. He saw the ban against interracial marriage as "one expression of the still broader principle . . . that *a man born a Negro or a white is not allowed to pass from the one status to the other as he can pass from one class to another.*"

Myrdal focused on the "permanent disabilities" African Americans faced "solely because they are 'Negroes' in the rigid American definition and not because they are poor and ill-educated." His observation cut through rationalizations of white dominance based on alleged black inferiority, lack of wealth, or education. Unlike recent immigrants, he argued, African Americans were locked in their "caste" by their artificial racial definition. These arguments seemed cogent given the institutionalized system of racial separation that had developed in the South.

For all its commonsense persuasiveness, however, the caste and class model of American race relations was from the beginning seriously flawed. As a model of a system of stratification or inequality, the caste-class approach ignored fundamental distinctions already developed by both Karl Marx and Max Weber, the two authors who contributed most to this area. According to Weber, the three fundamental forms of stratifaction were "classes," "status groups," and "castes." Classes (as Marx also agreed) were groups based exclusively in the market or economy, while status groups rose out of a system which ranked individuals within a hierarchy of prestige or honor. Membership in classes was a factor of personal achievement in the marketplace through ownership of wealth or occupations held. Membership in status groups was dependent upon acceptance by their members and conformity to the groups' style of life, which frequently included in-group marriage. Castes, unlike status groups, included the added dimension of being religiously sanctioned.

Based on these distinctions, the groups about which Warner and Myrdal wrote were in reality status groups rather than classes. Warner defined a "social class" as "the largest group of people whose members have intimate access to one another," a definition that coincides exactly with Weber's definition of status groups. In practice Warner often used the terms class and status interchangeably, another indication that the difference was not one that was well grasped by him.

Neither Warner nor Myrdal appeared to comprehend the true nature of India's caste system from which they derived their analogy. Warner, a social anthropologist who spent many years studying preliterate societies in Australia, never studied up close a caste system such as that of Hindu India. He based his conclusions on secondhand observations and conversations. As the African-American sociologist Oliver Cromwell Cox pointed out in his book *Race, Caste and Class* (1948), this misunderstanding of the Indian caste system led to a fuzziness and inconsistency in the school's discussion of the hypothesized American caste system. Contradictory evidence seemed to be ignored. For example, Cox noted that though Warner adopted the definition of caste proposed by the well-known anthropologist A. L. Kroeber, he ignored Kroeber's conclusion that a caste system was not possible in Western societies. Furthermore, neither Warner nor Myrdal seemed to be aware of the essentially religious foundation of the Indian caste system. As Max Weber pointed out in *Economy and Society,* "status distinctions [in caste systems] are . . . guaranteed not merely by conventions and laws, but also by religious sanction." The complete absence of religious sanctions in maintaining racial separation in the United States was a matter not even commented on by the members of the caste-class school.

Nor was the analogy of American race relations with the Indian caste system original to either Warner or Myrdal. Cox traced the use of the analogy at least as far back as the middle of the nineteenth century. A number of prominent scholars, including William I. Thomas in 1904 and Ray Stannard Baker in 1908, made use of the analogy in their discussions of race relations in the South, sometimes applying the term "color line" and frequently the concept of "caste." So popular was the concept that it appeared in sociological textbooks early in the twentieth century. For his part, Myrdal acknowledged his own indebtedness for the concept to earlier usages in the 1930s by the Chicago University sociologist Robert E. Park.

Another area of ambiguity revolved around the perceived "form" of the caste-class social structure. While agreeing upon the existence of a "color line" or "caste line" separating all blacks from all whites, the location and even the shape of the line were disputed by members of this school. Hypotheses varied depending upon perceptions of the individual class structures of blacks and whites. Long before the writings of Warner and Myrdal, Robert E. Park argued in 1928 that the caste line had moved from an earlier horizontal to a vertical position. As the occupational structure of blacks became more differentiated, Park held, blacks and whites more and more "looked across" a vertical line rather than "up and down" along a horizontal line.

In *Deep South,* the caste line is portrayed as neither horizontal nor vertical but as *diagonal,* a position the authors argued best represented the disproportionate concentration of blacks at the bottom of their class structure. The horizontal line, Warner argued, was shifting toward a vertical position as the black class structure became similar to that of the whites and closer to "equivalency." Myrdal, on the other hand, argued that black and white class structures were shifting but would remain fundamentally asymmetrical, with blacks overrepresented in the lower classes, while whites would remain concentrated in the middle class. This situation Myrdal represented by a "diagonal curve" underscoring his conviction that a fundamental inequality would remain between blacks and whites. He further held that even in the event of a similar distribution across classes, whites of the same class would still look "down" on blacks rather than "across" as suggested by Warner's use of the term "equivalent."

Closely connected to disagreements over the position and shape of the caste line were the varying views on the essence of a "caste" system among members of the school. Cox pointed to this serious problem when he wrote that "to John Dollard, the essence of caste is 'a barrier to legitimate descent'; to W. Lloyd Warner, it is endogamy; to Guy B. Johnson, it is the achievement of 'accommodation'; to Robert E. Park, 'etiquette is the very essence of caste.' " Even the southern taboo against interracial marriage, Cox argued, was not sufficient reason for the use of the caste analogy. Classes, tribes, sects, and "any other social groups which think they have something to protect," he pointed out, have disapproved of intermarriage.

While there is still no consensus on the most accurate model of American race relations, the caste-class approach has all but disappeared from the discourse on racial inequality.

Given the many flaws in the caste-class model, why did it enjoy such longstanding popularity? While the many conceptual problems discussed above demonstrate the inadequacies of the model there is no denying its intuitive appeal at a time when 90 percent of African Americans resided in a solidly segregated JIM CROW South. It is just this intuitive appeal that may have been its undoing. As more and more African Americans moved to northern cities between the two world wars and into the 1950s, the caste-class model began losing its attractiveness. Though segregation and discrimination were widely practiced in the North, these practices lacked the legal backing of southern Jim Crow laws. Interracial marriage, for instance, though discouraged in the North by racial custom, was not proscribed by law. As St. Clair DRAKE and Horace R. Cayton observed in *Black Metropolis,* their exhaustive two-volume study of Chicago's African-American community in the mid-1940s, though a color line existed in Chicago as in the Deep South, in Chicago and other northern cities it was "not static; and sometimes the job ceiling was pierced and broken." In the North, some whites offered at least "lip service" to the democratic creed of equality. Though in a "Methodological Note" to *Black Metropolis,* Warner held that despite differences in the two cities, there was a "status system of the caste type" in *Black Metropolis,* the caste-class model nevertheless lacked persuasiveness when applied to northern cities like Chicago.

During the 1940s and '50s millions of blacks migrated to the industrial cities of the North and West in a massive population shift that eventually led almost half of the African-American population out of the South. As the CIVIL RIGHTS MOVEMENT got under way, it was the call for long denied rights, an end to segregation at lunch counters, restaurants, and other public accommodations, not an end to the legal ban on interracial marriage that dominated the movement's agenda. With rising educational levels among blacks, and increased occupational diversity and geographical dispersion, the caste-class model had lost its intuitive appeal. Lacking a firmer grounding in social facts, it could not serve as the basis of the Movement's rallying cries. Civil rights, black power, and desegregation of public accommodations proved to be more powerful images to rouse opponents of racial inequality. The term "caste" seemed absent from the vocabulary of protestors. Within the academic community, scholars tested new conceptual models of American race relations such as "institutional racism" and "internal colonialism." In the rough and tumble of the Civil Rights Movement it was increasingly the call for "black power" that brought crowds to their feet or protestors into the streets. Observations of racial inequality in housing, the job market, income and wealth continue to be made by scholars, journalists, and activists alike. And while there is still no consensus on the most accurate model of American race relations, the caste-class approach has all but disappeared from the discourse on racial inequality.

BIBLIOGRAPHY

Cox, Oliver C. *Caste, Class, and Race.* Garden City, N.Y., 1948.

Davis, Allison, Burleigh Gardner, and Mary R. Gardner. *Deep South: A Sociological Anthropological Study of Caste and Class.* Chicago, 1941.

Drake, St. Clair, and Horace R. Cayton. *Black Metropolis: A Study of Negro Life in a Northern City.* New York, 1945.

Glenn, Norvall. "White Gain from Negro Subordination." In Gary Mars, ed. *Racial Conflict.* Boston, 1971, pp. 106–16.

Landry, Bart. "The Enduring Dilemma of Race in America." In Alan Wolfe, ed. *America at Century's End.* Berkeley, Calif. 1991, pp. 185–207.

Myrdal, Gunnar. *An American Dilemma: The Negro Problem and American Democracy.* New York, 1944.

— BART LANDRY

RADIO

African-American radio can be divided into three general periods of historical development: blackface radio (1920–1941), black-appeal radio (1942–1969), and black-controlled radio (1970 to the present). Blackface radio was characterized by the appropriation of African-American music and humor by white entertainers, who performed their secondhand imitations for a predominantly white listening audience. During this period, black people were essentially outside of the commercial broadcasting loop; they were marginal as both radio entertainers and consumers. In the era of black-appeal radio, African Americans entered into the industry as entertainers and consumers, but the ownership and management of the stations targeting the black radio market remained mostly in the hands of white businessmen. This situation constrained the development of independent black radio operations, while the radio industry in general prospered from it. During the most recent period, African Americans have striven to own and operate their own radio stations, both commercial and public. In addition, they have established black-controlled radio networks and trade organizations. However, the percentage of African American-owned stations still lags far behind the percentage of black listeners.

The appropriation of black song, dance, and humor by white entertainers who blackened their faces with charcoal goes back to the early days of slavery. The resulting radical stereotypes were embedded in the blackface minstrel tradition, which dominated American popular entertainment in the antebellum period, and remained resilient enough in the postbellum years to reappear in film and radio in the early decades of the twentieth century. Popular black music styles like blues and jazz were first performed on the radio by white performers like Sophie Tucker, the first singer to popularize W. C. HANDY's "Saint Louis Blues," and Paul Whiteman, the so-called king of jazz in the 1920s. A parallel trend developed with respect to black humor with the emergence of *Amos 'n' Andy* (starring Freeman Gosden and Charles Correll) as radio's most popular comedy series.

Indeed, *Amos 'n' Andy* was radio's first mass phenomenon: a supershow that attracted 53 percent of the national audience, or 40 million listeners, during its peak years on the NBC network in the early 1930s. In addition, the series provoked the black community's first national radio controversy. Robert Abbot, editor of the Chicago Defender, defended Gosden and Correll's caricatures of black urban life as inoffensive and even humane. Robert Vann, editor of the Pittsburgh Courier, countered by criticizing the series as racist in its portrayal of African Americans. He also launched a petition campaign to have the program taken off the air that amassed 740,000 signatures—but to no avail. The petition was ignored by the Federal Radio Commission. Meanwhile, *Amos 'n' Andy* dominated black comedy on radio throughout its heyday as the "national pastime" in the 1930s. In addition to Gosden and Correll, the other major blackface radio entertainers of the era included George Mack and Charles Moran, known as the Two Black Crows on the CBS network, as well as Marlin Hunt, who created and portrayed the radio maid Beulah on the series of the same name.

During the period when blackface comedy performed by whites dominated the portrayal of African Americans over the airways, its audience was mostly white; fewer than one in ten black households owned a radio receiver. There were black entertainers and actors who managed to get hired by the radio industry in the pre-World War II era, and for the most part they were restricted to playing stereotyped roles. The renowned black comedian Bert Williams was the first important black performer to be linked to commercial broadcasting, in the 1920s; he was featured on a New York station doing the same routines he popularized while performing in blackface on the Broadway stage. During the Great Depression, as if to add insult to injury, a number of black actors and actresses who auditioned for radio parts were told that they needed to be coached in the art of black dialect by white coaches if they wanted the jobs. This perverse chain of events happened to at least three African-American performers: Lillian Randolph (*Lulu and Leander Show*), Johnny Lee (*Slick and Slim Show*), and Wonderful Smith (*Red Skelton Show*). The most famous black comic to appear regularly on network radio in the 1930s was Eddie Anderson, who played the role of the butler and chauffeur Rochester on the *Jack Benny Show.* Anderson was often criticized in the black press for playing a stereotypical "faithful servant" role, even as he was being praised for his economic success and celebrity.

Amos 'n' Andy *dominated black comedy on radio throughout its heyday as the "national pastime" in the 1930s.*

After blackface comedy, the African-American dance music called JAZZ was the next most popular expression of black culture broadcast over the airways in the 1920s and 1930s. As was the case with humor, the major radio jazz bands were made up of white musicians, and were directed by white bandleaders like Paul Whiteman, B. A. Rolfe, and Ben Bernie. The first black musicians to be broadcast with some regularity on network radio were New York bandleaders Duke ELLINGTON and Noble Sissle. A number of influential white radio producers like Frank and Ann Hummert, the king and queen of network soap operas, began to routinely include black doctors, teachers, and soldiers in their scripts. In addition, the federal government produced its own radio series, entitled *Freedom's People,* to dramatize the participation of African Americans in past wars, and it recruited Paul ROBESON as a national and then international radio spokesman for the U.S. war effort. But at the end of the war, the government withdrew from the domestic broadcasting sphere, allowing the logic of the marketplace to reassert itself. Then with the advent of the new television networks, and their subsequent domination of the national broadcasting market, radio was forced to turn to local markets in order to survive as a commercial enterprise. Inadvertently, this led to the discovery of a "new Negro market" in regions where African Americans' numbers could no longer be ignored by broadcasters. This was especially the case in large urban centers, where nine out of ten black families owned radios by the late 1940s. The result of this convergence of economic necessity and a mushrooming listening audience was the emergence of black-appeal radio stations and the rise of the African-American disc jockey—two interrelated developments that transformed the landscape of commercial radio in the postwar era.

A few black DJs were playing records over the airways in the 1930s; they worked through a brokerage system that charged them an hourly fee for airtime. The disc jockeys, in turn, solicited advertising aimed at the local black community and broadcast it in conjunction with recorded "race" music. Jack L. Cooper pioneered this approach in Chicago on his radio show *The All Negro Hour,* which first aired on WSBC in 1929. At first, he developed a live variety show with local black talent, but within two years he had switched to recorded music in order to cut costs. He played jazz discs, hosted a popular "missing persons" show, pitched ads, made community-service announcements, and also developed a series of weekend religious programs. This format was successful enough to make him into a millionaire; by the end of the 1930s, he had a stable of African-American DJs working for him on a series of black-appeal programs broadcast on two stations. In the 1940s, Cooper was challenged as Chicago's premier black disc jockey by Al Benson, who also built up a small radio empire on local outlets with his own style of black-appeal programming. Cooper targeted the middle-class African-American audience; he played the popular big-band jazz recordings of the day and prided himself in speaking proper English over the air. Benson played the down-home blues of the era and spoke in the vernacular of the new ghetto populace, most of whom were working-class southern migrants. A new era of black radio was at hand.

By the end of the 1940s, there was a growing number of aspiring DJs in urban black communities ready to take advantage of the new "Negro-appeal" formats springing up on stations throughout the country. In Memphis, Nat D. Williams was responsible for broadcasting the first African-American radio show there, on WDIA in 1948; he also created the station's new black-appeal format and launched the careers of numerous first-generation African-American DJs over WDIA's airways. Two of the most important were Maurice "Hot Rod" Hulbert, who moved on to become the dean of black disc jockeys in Baltimore, on WBEE; and Martha Jean "the Queen" Stienburg, who later became the most popular black DJ in Detroit, on WCHB. In 1950, WERD, in Atlanta, became the first African-American-owned radio station in the country when it was purchased by J. B. Blayton, Jr. He appointed his son as station manager and then hired Jack "the Rapper" Gibson as program director. Other black-appeal stations that came into prominence during the early 1950s included WEDR in Birmingham, Ala.; WOOK in Washington, D.C.; WCIN in Cincinnati; WABQ in Cleveland; KXLW in St. Louis; and KCKA in Kansas City, which became the second African American-owned radio outlet in the nation in 1952. By 1956 there were over four hundred radio stations in the United States broadcasting black-appeal programming. Each of these operations showcased its own homegrown African-American disc jockeys, who were the centerpiece of the on-air sound.

The powerful presence and influence of the African-American DJs on the airways in urban America in the 1950s stemmed from two sources. On the one hand, they were the supreme arbiters of black musical tastes; they could make or break a new record release, depending on how much they played and promoted it. On the other hand, the black disc jockeys were also the new electronic griots of the black oral tradition, posturing as social rappers and cultural rebels. As such, they collectively constituted a social grapevine that was integral not just to the promotion of rhythm and blues, but also to the empowerment of the growing CIVIL RIGHTS MOVEMENT in the South. Black-appeal radio stations like WERD in Atlanta and WDIA in Memphis, as well as Al Benson's shows in Chicago, played a vital role in informing people about the early civil rights struggles. In a speech to black broadcasters late in his life, civil rights leader the Rev. Dr. Martin Luther KING, Jr., paid special tribute to disc jockeys Tall Paul White (WEDR, Birmingham), Purvis Spann (WVON, Chicago), and Georgie Woods (WHAT, Philadelphia) for their important contributions to the civil rights efforts in their respective cities.

During the 1950s, African-American radio DJs also had a profound effect on commercial radio in general. Some stations—such as WLAC in Nashville, a high-powered AM outlet heard at night throughout the South—devoted a hefty amount of their evening schedules to rhythm and blues records. In addition, the white disc jockeys at WLAC (John R., Gene Noble, Hoss Allen, and Wolfman Jack) adopted the on-air styles, and even dialect, of the black DJs. Many of their listeners, both black and white, thought that WLAC's disc jockeys were African Americans. This was also the case on WJMR in New Orleans, where the white DJs who hosted the popular *Poppa Stoppa Show* were actually trained to speak in black dialect by the creator of the show, an African-American college professor named Vernon Winslow. Other white DJs who became popular by emulating the broadcast styles of their black counterparts included Dewey Phillips in Memphis; Zenas "Daddy" Sears in Atlanta; Phil Mckernan in Oakland, Calif.; George "Hound Dog" Lorenz in Buffalo, N.Y.; and Allen Freed in Cleveland. Freed moved on to become New York City's most famous rock and roll disc jockey, before his fall from grace as the result of payola scandals in the early 1960s.

Payola, the exchange of money for record airplay, was a common practice throughout the radio industry. It was an easy way for disc jockeys to supplement the low wages they were paid by their employers. Hence, many well-known black DJs were adversely affected by the payola exposés. Some lost their jobs when their names were linked to the ongoing investigations, and an unfortunate few were even the targets of income-tax-evasion indictments. The industry's solution to the payola problem was the creation of the "top forty" radio format, which in effect gave management complete control over the playlists of records to be aired on their stations. Formerly, the playlists had been determined by the individual DJs. This change led to the demise of both the white rock-and-roll disc jockeys and the black "personality" DJs associated with rhythm and blues, and then "soul" music. Black-appeal stations were centralized even further by the emergence of five soul radio chains in the 1960s, all of which were white-owned and -managed. By the end of the decade, these corporations controlled a total of twenty stations in key urban markets with large African-American populations like New York, Chicago, Memphis, and Washington, D.C. The chain operations not only established standardized top forty soul formats at their respective outlets, thus limiting the independence of the black DJs they employed, but they also eliminated most of the local African-American news and public-affairs offerings on the stations.

In spite of the trend toward top forty soul formats, a number of black personality DJs managed to survive and even prosper in the 1960s. The most important were Sid McCoy (WGES, WCFL), Purvis Spann (WVON), and Herb Kent (WVON) in Chicago; LeBaron Taylor and Georgie Woods (both WDAS) in Philadelphia; Eddie O'Jay in Cleveland (WABQ) and Buffalo (WUFO); Skipper Lee Frazier (KCOH) in Houston; the Magnificent Montegue (KGFJ) in Los Angeles; and Sly Stone (KSOL) in San Francisco. LeBaron Taylor and Sly Stone went on to successful careers in the music industry—Taylor as a CBS record executive and Stone as a pioneering pop musician. The Magnificent Montegue's familiar invocation, "Burn, baby, burn," used to introduce the "hot" records he featured on his show, inadvertently became the unofficial battle cry of the 1967 Watts rebellion. The new mood of black militancy sweeping the nation also found its way into the ranks of the African-American DJs, especially among the younger generation just entering the radio industry. Two of the more influential members of this "new breed," as they came to be known, were Del Shields (WLIB) in New York and Roland Young (KSAN, KMPX) in San Francisco. Both men independently pioneered innovative black music formats, mixing together jazz, soul, and salsa recordings.

The 1970s ushered in the current era of black-owned and -controlled radio operations, both stations and networks. In 1970, of the more than three hundred black-formatted stations, only sixteen were owned by African-Americans. During the next decade, the number of black-owned stations rose to 88, while the number of formatted stations surpassed 450. Some of the more prominent African Americans who became radio station owners during this era included entertainers James BROWN and Stevie WONDER, Chicago publisher John JOHNSON, and New York City politician Percy Sutton. In particular, Sutton's Harlem-based Inner City Broadcasting (WLIB-AM, WBLS-FM) has been the national trendsetter in a black-owned-and-operated radio from the early 1970s to the present. In 1977, African-American broadcasters organized their own trade organization, the National Association of Black-Owned Broadcasters. By 1990 there were 206 black-owned radio stations—138 AM and 68 FM—in the country.

It was also during the 1970s that two successful black radio networks were launched: the Mutual Black Network, founded in 1972, which became the Sheridan Broadcasting Network in 1979; and the National Black Network, started in 1973. Both of these operations provide news, talk shows, public affairs, and cultural features to their affiliate stations throughout the nation. In the 1980s, the Sheridan network had over one hundred affiliates and 6.2 million weekly listeners; in addition to news and public affairs, it offered a wide range of sports programming, including live broadcasts of black college football and basketball games. The National network averaged close to one hundred affiliates and four million weekly listeners in the 1980s; its most popular programs, in addition to its news reports, were journalist Roy Woods's *One Man's Opinion* and Bob Law's *Night Talk.*

The 1970s ushered in the current era of black-owned and -controlled radio operations, both stations and networks.

Two major formats have dominated black-owned commercial radio in the 1970s and 1980s—"talk" and "urban contemporary." Talk radio formats emerged on African-American AM stations in the early 1970s; in essence, they featured news, public affairs, and live listener call-in shows. By this time, the FM stations dominated the broadcasting of recorded music due to their superior reproduction of high fidelity and stereo signals. The AM stations were left with talk by default. Inner City Broadcasting initiated the move toward talk radio formats among African-American stations when it turned WLIG-AM, which it purchased in New York City in 1972, into "your total news and information station" that same year. The logic of the commercial radio market encouraged many of the other black AM operations, such as WOL-AM in Washington, D.C., to follow suit. Likewise, Inner City Broadcasting also pioneered the urban contemporary format on WBLS-FM during this same period. Much of the credit for the new format is given to Frankie Crocker, who was the station's program director at the time. In order to build up WBLS's ratings in the most competitive radio market in the country, Crocker scuttled the station's established jazz programming in favor of a crossover format featuring black music currently on the pop charts along with popular white artists with a black sound. The idea was to appeal to an upscale black and white audience. The formula worked to perfection; WBLS became the top station in the New York market, and scores of other stations around the country switched to the new urban contemporary format. One example was WHUR-FM, owned by Howard University in Washington, D.C. The station's original jazz and black-community-affairs format was sacked in favor of the urban contemporary approach in the mid-1970s. The new format allowed WHUR to become one of the top-rated stations in the Washington market. In the process, it gave birth to an innovative new nighttime urban contemporary style called "quiet storm," after the Smokey Robinson song of the same name. The architect of this novel format was Melvin Lindsey, a former Howard student and WHUR intern.

The 1970s and 1980s also marked the entrance of African Americans into the public broadcasting sphere. By 1990, there were thirty-two public FM stations owned and operated by black colleges around the country, and another twelve controlled by black community boards of directors. These stations are not subject to the pervasive ratings pressures of commercial radio, giving them more leeway in programming news, public affairs, talk, and unusual cultural features. Many of these stations—such as WCLK-FM, owned by Clarke College in Atlanta; WSHA-FM, owned by Shaw College in Raleigh, N.C., and WVAS-FM, from Alabama State University in Montgomery—have adopted the jazz formats abandoned by African-American-owned commercial FM stations. Others, like WPFW-FM in Washington, D.C. (the number one black public radio outlet in the country), have developed a more ambitious "world rhythms" format embracing the many musics of the African diaspora. In general, the growth of black public radio has expanded the variety and diversity of African-American programming found on the airways, while also increasing the numbers of African Americans working in radio.

BIBLIOGRAPHY

Dates, Jannette, and William Barlow, eds. *Split Image: African Americans in the Mass Media.* Washington, D.C., 1989

Downing, John. "Ethnic Minority Radio in the USA." *Howard Journal of Communication* 1, no. 4 (1989); 135–148.

Edmerson, Estelle, "A Descriptive Study of the American Negro in U.S. Professional Radio, 1922–1953." M.A. thesis, University of California at Los Angeles, 1954.

Ferretti, Frank, "The White Captivity of Black Radio." *Columbia Journalism Review* (Summer 1970); 35–39.

— WILLIAM BARLOW

RAGTIME

Ragtime was the first music of African-American origin to play a significant role in American popular culture. It had both vocal and instrumental forms, flourished from the late 1890s until the late 1910s, and had important exponents among both black and white composers.

A major element of antebellum black music in the public mind was syncopated rhythm. This and similar rhythms were used to caricature black music and were widely heard in minstrel shows that toured the nation, bringing an incipient ragtime to public consciousness. Ragtime as a distinct genre came to public notice at the 1893 World's Fair in Chicago, one piece that was played there reportedly being Jesse Pickett's "Dream Rag." The term "ragtime" first appeared in print on song publications of 1896, possibly the earliest being Ernest Hogan's "All Coons Look Alike to Me," which included a syncopated "Choice Chorus, with Negro 'Rag,' Accompaniment." As this quotation indicates, the black roots of ragtime were acknowledged from the very beginning.

Vocal Ragtime

Most early ragtime songs were known as "coon songs," "coon" being a then-widely used contemptuous term for blacks. These songs typically had lyrics in stereotypical black dialect and played upon such negative themes as black men being shiftless, lazy, thieving, gambling, and violent; of black women being mercenary and sexually promiscuous. A typical song lyric would be "I don't like no cheap man / Dat spends his money on de 'stallment plan." (Bert Williams and George Walker, 1897). Adding to the songs' negative impressions were sheet music covers that usually portrayed African Americans in grotesquely exaggerated caricatures. With the relatively insensitive ethnic climate of the time, there was little protest from the black community; black artists—including such sophisticated individuals as composer Will Marion Cook and poet-lyricist Paul Laurence DUNBAR—contributed to the genre.

Ragtime was the first music of African-American origin to play a significant role in American popular culture.

Not all early ragtime songs were abusive, even though they retained racial stereotypes. Among those whose popularity outlived the ragtime years was Howard and Emerson's "Hello! Ma Baby" (1899), which celebrates courtship over the telephone. "Bob" Cole and J. Rosamond Johnson, black artists who were sensitive to the stigma of demeaning lyrics, wrote their enormously successful "Under the Bamboo Tree" (1902) to demonstrate that a racial song could express tasteful and universally appreciated sentiments.

Around 1905, the ragtime song began to lose its overtly racial quality and came to include any popular song of a strongly hic character. Typical examples were "Some of These Days" (1910) and "Waiting for the Robert E. Lee" (1913). Irving Berlin's hit song "Alexander's Ragtime Band" (1911) which was regarded by many as the high point of ragtime, retains only slight racial suggestions in its lyrics and these are nonderogatory.

Instrumental Ragtime

Ragtime developed both as a solo-piano vehicle and as an ensemble style for virtually all instruments. Ensemble ragtime was played by marching and concert bands, by dance orchestras, and in such diverse combinations as xylophone-marimba duos and trios, piano-violin duos, and mandolin-banjo groupings. Solo-piano ragtime was heard on the vaudeville stage, in salons and brothels, in the home parlor, and on the mechanical player piano.

Ragtime was closely associated with dance. In the early days, the two-step was most common, along with such variants as the slow-drag. The cakewalk remained popular throughout the ragtime years but was a specialty dance reserved mostly for exhibitions and contests. In the 1910s many new dances joined the ragtime category, including the one-step, fox-trot, turkey trot, grizzly bear, and such waltz variants as the Boston, hesitation, and half-and-half. The tango and maxixe, though Latin-American rather than ragtime dances, were performed to syncopated music and became part of the ragtime scene in the mid-1910s.

Piano Ragtime

Ragtime was published primarily for the piano and contributed significantly to the development of American popular music and jazz piano. Piano ragtime, like the ragtime song, flourished as published sheet music, but it also existed as an improvised art, giving it a direct link to early jazz. However, since improvised ragtime was not preserved on sound recordings, we have little detailed knowledge of it.

The defining elements of ragtime were established by 1897, when the earliest piano rag sheet music appeared. Of primary importance was the syncopation, for it was from this uneven, ragged rhythmic effect that the term "ragtime" was derived. As applied to piano music, syncopation typically appeared as a right-hand pattern played against an even, metric bass. Around 1906 a new pattern, known as secondary ragtime, gained acceptance. This is not true syncopation, but the shifting accents within a three-note pattern create a polyrhythmic effect that was successfully integrated with the other ragtime gestures. After 1911, dotted rhythms made inroads into ragtime, further diluting the distinctiveness of the early ragtime syncopations.

The form into which ragtime was cast, though not a defining element, was consistent. The form followed that of the march and consisted of a succession of sixteen-measure thematic sections, each section being evenly divided into four phrases. Typically the two opening thematic sections were in the tonic key and were followed by one or two sections (known as the "trio") in the subdominant key. (As an example of the key relationships, if the tonic key were C, the subdominant key would be F.) Diagrammatically, with each section depicted with an upper-case letter, the form with repeats might appear as AA BB A CC or AA BB CC DD. To these patterns might be added four-measure introductions to A and to C and interludes between repeats of C or between C and D. Though these patterns were typical, they were not invariable; many rags used different numbers of sections and different key relationships.

Blues, another style that emerged from the African-American community, had some influence on the rags of a few composers, particularly in the use of so-called blue notes. What in later years was to become known as the classic twelve-bar blues form made its earliest appearances in piano rags. The first known example was in "One O' Them Things?" (James Chapman and Leroy Smith, 1904), in which a twelve-bar blues replaces the usual A section. Both the form and the term appear in a New Orleans ragtime publication of 1908, A. Maggio's "I Got the Blues." The first blues to achieve popularity was W. C. HANDY's "Memphis Blues" (1912), which combines twelve-bar blues and sixteen-bar ragtime sections and was subtitled "A Southern Rag." Through the rest of the ragtime era, the term "blues" was applied indiscriminately to many rags.

Though instrumental ragtime lacked the direct verbal communication possible with the lyrics of ragtime songs, early published rags conveyed a racial connotation with cover pictures that caricatured blacks, frequently in an offensive manner. As with the songs, piano ragtime's gradual acceptance as American music rather than as an exclusively racial expression was matched with the discontinuance of racial depictions.

The Composers and Performers

The first ragtime performer to acquire fame was vaudeville pianist, singer, and composer Ben Harney, who appeared in New York in 1896 with "plantation negro imitations." Though he was known as "the first white man to play ragtime," his racial origins remain uncertain.

The publication of piano ragtime began in 1897 with "Mississippi Rag," by white bandmaster William Krell. Several months later, Tom Turpin, with his "Harlem Rag," became the first black composer to have a piano rag published. Turpin, a St. Louis saloon keeper, was an important figure in the development of ragtime in that city and reportedly had composed this piece as early as 1892. The most prominent ragtime success of 1897 was Kerry Mills's "At a Georgia Campmeeting," known in both song and instrumental versions and recorded by the Sousa Band, among others.

Piano ragtime quickly caught on, and in the years 1897–1899 more than 150 piano rags were published, the most important and influential being Scott JOPLIN's "Maple Leaf Rag" (1899). Joplin was a composer with serious aspirations, and his frequent publisher John Stark adopted the term "classic ragtime" to describe the music of Joplin and others he published. These included black Missourians James Scott, Arthur Marshall, Louis Chauvin, Artie Matthews, and such white composers as J. Russel Robinson, Paul Pratt, and Joseph Lamb. Though virtually all classic rags are superior examples of the genre, the term did not embrace any single style. Nor were classic rags the best known. More popular were the easier and more accessible rags of such composers as Ted Snyder, Charles Johnson, Percy Wenrich, and George Botsford.

New York City, with its flourishing entertainment centers and music publishing industry (Tin Pan Alley), naturally attracted many ragtimers. Because of the competition and high musical standards in the city, some of the more adept ragtime pianists developed a virtuosic style known as "stride." Among the leaders of this style were Eubie BLAKE, James P. JOHNSON, and Luckey Roberts. These musicians—along with such figures as Joe Jordan, Will Marion Cook, Bob Cole, and J. Rosamond Johnson—also became involved in black musical theater, which made extensive use of ragtime.

Bandleader James Reese EUROPE, disliked the term "ragtime" but became one of the most influential musicians on the late ragtime scene in New York. In 1910 he formed the Clef Club, an organization that functioned both as a union and booking agency for New York's black musicians. As music director for the popular white dance team of Irene and Vernon Castle, beginning in 1914, Europe created a demand both for black music and for black dance-band musicians.

Many who were admired during the ragtime years left little or no record of their music. Among these were "One-Leg" Willie Joseph, Abba Labba (Richard McLean), and "Jack the Bear" (John Wilson). "Jelly Roll" MORTON was active from the early ragtime years but did most of his publishing and recording in the 1920s and 1930s. Tony Jackson was widely praised as a performer and composer but is remembered today primarily for his song "Pretty Baby." There were many black women active as performers, but they are now forgotten because they did not publish or record. Thus, the history of ragtime is slanted in favor of those who can be documented.

Reaction to Ragtime

Within the context of the genteel parlor music of the 1890s, ragtime was shockingly new. Nothing like it had ever been heard. For some, ragtime became America's statement of musical independence from Europe; it was hailed as a new expression, reflecting this nation's exuberance and restlessness. American youth, regardless of race, embraced the music as its own.

Inevitably, opposition to ragtime emerged. One sector of opposition was generational—the ever-present syndrome of the older generations rejecting the music of the younger. There was also opposition from musical elitists, those who objected to a music that lacked a proper pedigree and feared it would drive out "good music." Some denied that ragtime was at all innovative; they argued that the ragtime rhythms had been used by the European "old masters" and in various European folk musics. Then there were the blatant racists, who rejected the idea that an American music could have black origins and denied that African Americans were capable of creating anything original. Most of all, they feared that white youth was being "infected" by this developing black music.

Certain parts of African-American society also objected to ragtime. Church groups, noting that ragtime was played in saloons and brothels and used for dancing, concluded that the music contributed to sinfulness. Blacks striving for middle-class respectability were also wary of ragtime because of its lower-class associations. The *Negro Music Journal* (1902–1903), which encouraged blacks to cultivate tastes for classical music, denounced ragtime and denied that it was an African-American expression.

Despite such opposition, ragtime thrived and evolved. During the mid- to late 1910s jazz emerged as an offshoot of ragtime. At first there was little distinctiveness between the two, but by the end of WORLD WAR I jazz had replaced ragtime as the most important vernacular music in America.

BIBLIOGRAPHY

Berlin, Edward A. *Ragtime: A Musical and Cultural History.* Berkeley, Calif., 1980.

———. *Reflections and Research on Ragtime.* Brooklyn, N.Y., 1987.

Blesh, Rudi, and Harriet Janis. *They All Played Ragtime.* 4th ed. New York, 1971.

Hasse, John Edward, ed. *Ragtime: Its History, Composers, and Music.* New York, 1985.

Jasen, David A. *Recorded Ragtime, 1897–1958.* Hamden, Conn., 1973.

Jasen, David A., and Trebor Tichenor. *Rags and Ragtime.* New York, 1978.

Riis, Thomas L. *Just Before Jazz: Black Musical Theater in New York, 1890–1915.* Washington, D.C., 1989.

Schafer, William J., and Johannes Riedel. *The Art of Ragtime.* Baton Rouge, La., 1973.

Waldo, Terry. *This Is Ragtime.* New York, 1976.

— EDWARD A. BERLIN

RAP

Rap is an African-American term that describes a stylized way of speaking. Salient features of a rap include metaphor, braggadocio, repetition, formulaic expressions, double entendre, mimicry, rhyme, and "signifyin' " (i.e., indirect references and allusions). Folklorists have credited the term to the 1960s black nationalist "H. Rap" Brown, whose praise name "rap" depicted his mastery of a "hip" way of speaking, aptly called rappin'. Although Brown is lauded for the name of this genre, the roots of rap can be traced from southern oral secular traditions such as toasts, folktales, blues, game songs (e.g., "hambone") to northern urban street jive—all of which make use of many of the same features.

While rap's southern antecedents (such as the blues) developed during the antebellum period and the turn of the century, jive emerged in inner city communities as the prototype of rap. Dan Burley, a scholar of jive, discovered that jive initially emerged among black Chicagoans around 1921. The primary context of its development was in secular environs remote from the home and religious centers, such as street corners, taverns, and parks, known among urban habitats as "the streets." Jive can be defined as a metaphorical style of communicating, using words and phrases from American mainstream English but reinterpreted from an African-American perspective. For example, in rap lingo, man becomes "cat," woman becomes "chick," and house becomes "crib." The art of jive resided in its ability to remain witty and original, hence its constant fluctuation in vocabulary over the years.

Between the 1920s and 1950s, jive proliferated on all levels in the urban milieu—from the church to the street corner; but it also was incorporated in the literary works of noted black writers of the time, like Langston Hughes. Alongside its use by writers, jive became the parlance of jazz musicians. "Jam" (having a good time), "bad" (good), and "axe" (instrument) are some jive words commonplace in the jazz vernacular. By the late 1940s and 1950s, this urban style of speaking was introduced over radio airwaves by two Chicago disc jockeys, Holmes "Daddy-O" Daylie and Al Benson, who utilized jive in rhyme over music. Even the boastful poetry of former heavyweight champion boxer Muhammad ALI as well as comedian Rudy Ray Moore, known for popularizing audio recordings of toasts like "Dolemite" and "The Signifying Monkey," moved jive further into the American mainstream.

By the 1960s, jive was redefined and given a newer meaning by black nationalist "H. Rap" Brown, who laced his political speeches with signifyin', rhyme, and metaphor. Although his way of speaking inaugurated the shift from jive to rap, Brown's stylized speech soon gained popular acceptance among young urban admirers as rappin'. It was not, however, until the late 1960s that Brown's speaking style was set to a musical accompaniment by such political poets as the Watts Prophets of Los Angeles, the last poets of Harlem, and singer-pianist poet Gil Scott-Heron, who recited rhyming couplets over an African percussion accompaniment.

In the late 1960s and the 1970s, rappin' to music emerged as two distinct song styles: the soul rap and the funk-style rap. The soul rap, a rappin' monologue celebrating the feats and woes of love, was popularized by Isaac Hayes and further developed by Barry White and Millie Jackson. The funk-style rap, introduced by George Clinton and his group Parliament, consisted of rappin' monologues on topics about partying. Unlike the music of the political poets, the love and funk-style raps were not in rhyme but rather loosely chanted over a repetitive instrumental accompaniment. These artists nonetheless laid the foundation for a type of musical poetry begun primarily by African-American youth of the Bronx called rap music: a quasi-song with rhyme and rhythmic speech that draws on black street language and is recited over an instrumental soundtrack.

By the 1960s, jive was redefined by black nationalist "H. Rap" Brown, who laced his political speeches with signifyin', rhyme, and metaphor.

There are basically two factors that gave rise to rap music. With the overcommercialization of popular dance forms of the 1970s, particularly disco, and the ongoing club gang violence, African-American youth, particularly in New York City, left the indoor scene and returned to neighborhood city parks, where they created outdoor discotheques, featuring a disc jockey and an emcee. These circumstances were an impetus for the development of rap music, which is marked by four distinct phases: the mobile deejay (c. 1972–1978); the rappin' emcee and the emergence of the rap music genre (1976–1978); the early commercial years of rap music (1979–1985); and the explosive sound of rap in the musical mainstream (1986–1990s).

During the first phase, music performed in neighborhood city parks was provided by an itinerant disc jockey, the mobile deejay. Mobile jockeys were evaluated by the type of music they played as well as by the size of their sound systems. Similar to radio jockeys, mobile deejays occasionally spoke to their audiences in raps while simultaneously dovetailing one record after the other, a feat facilitated by two turntables. They were well known in their own boroughs and were supported by local followers. Popular jockeys included Pete "DJ" Jones of the Bronx and Grandmaster Flowers and Maboya of Brooklyn. The most innovative of mobile deejays, whose mixing technique immensely influenced the future sound direction and production of rap music, was Jamaican-born Clive Campbell, known as DJ Kool Herc. He tailored his disc jockeying style after the dub music jockeys of Jamaica, like Duke Reid and U Roy, by mixing collages of musical fragments, referred to as "break beats," from various recordings in order to create an entire new sound track.

Contemporaries of Kool Herc included Grandmaster Flash, Grand Wizard Theodore, and Afrika Bambaataa. Flash extended the Jamaican deejaying style with a mixing technique called backspinning (rotating one record counterclockwise to the desired beat then rotating the second record counterclockwise to the same location, thus creating an echo effect) and "phasing" (repeating a word or phrase in a rhythmic fashion on one turntable during or in between another recording). Grand Wizard Theodore popularized another mixing technique called "scratching" (the rhythmic movement of the tone arm needle of a turntable back and forth on a record). Bambaataa, on the other hand, perfected Herc's style of mixing by extending his break beats to include a variety of musical styles ranging from soul, funk, and disco to commercial jingle and television themes. But, more important, he is credited with starting a nonviolent organization called the Zulu Nation—a youth organization composed of local inner-city breakdancers, graffiti artists, and rappers—which laid the foundation for a youth mass art movement that came to be known as hip-hop.

Hip-hop not only encompassed street art forms, it also denoted an attitude rendered in the form of dress, gestures, and language associated with street culture.

The second phase of rap music began around the mid-1970s. Since mixing records had become an art in itself, some deejays felt the need for an emcee. For example, with the hiring of Clark Kent and Jay Cee, DJ Kool Herc became the Herculords, a three-man team. At many of his performances, Bambaataa was also accompanied by three emcees, Cowboy (not to be mistaken with Cowboy of the Furious Five), Mr. Biggs, and Queen Kenya. Other noted emcees during this phase were DJ Hollywood, Sweet G, Busy Bee, Kurtis Blow, Grandmaster Caz, and Lovebug Starski (the latter credited with the term "hip-hop"). Emcees talked intermittently, using phrases like "Get up," and "Jam to the beat," and recited rhyming couplets to motivate the audience to dance while the deejay mixed records. However, it was Grandmaster Flash's emcees, the Furious Five (Melle Mel, Cowboy, Raheim, Kid Creole, Mr. Ness), who set the precedent for rappin' in rhythm to music through a concept called "trading phrases"—the exchange of rhyming couplets or phrases between emcees in a percussive, witty fashion, and in synchrony with the deejay's music—as best illustrated by their hit "Freedom" (1980).

It was the music of Public Enemy that became the quintessence of sampling, from James Brown's music and vocal stylings to black nationalists' speech excerpts contributing to what rap artists refer to as a "hardcore" or street-style aesthetic.

During rap's third phase, the early commercial years from 1979 to 1985, rap music was initially recorded by independent record companies like Winley, Enjoy, and Sugar Hill Records. Of the three, Sugar Hill Records, cofounded by Sylvia and Joe Robinson, succeeded in becoming the first international rap record company, producing such artists and groups as Sequence, Spoonie G., Lady B., Grandmaster Flash and the Furious Five, and Sugarhill Gang (best known for recording the first commercial rap song "Rapper's Delight"). Other modes of commercialization included Bambaataa's introduction of "techno-pop"—music created on synthesizers and drum machines—in rap music with "Planet Rock" (1982), recorded by his group, Soul Sonic Force. By the mid-1980s, techno-pop or the electronic influence in rap gave rise to sampling, the digital reproduction of prerecorded sounds—musical or vocal—in whole or fragmentary units anywhere throughout an entire sound track. Among the most popular styles of music sampled by rap deejays is funk, primarily the music of James BROWN.

Bambaataa's musical innovation also provided the transition from the early commercial sound of rap, known as the "old school," to the "new school" rap. The former refers to earlier innovators and performers of rap music—for example, Kool Moe Dee, Melle Mel, Fat Boys, and Whodini, some of whom have continued to perform well into the 1990s. The "new school" performers are basically protégés of the pioneers; they comprise performers in the fourth phase.

In the fourth phase (1986–1990s), rap music gradually moved from the inner city into mainstream popular culture. Although independent record companies continued to dominate (e.g., Tommy Boy, Priority, Def Jam, Next Plateau), major record companies including MCA, Columbia, and Atlantic began recording rap and in some instances distributed for the independent labels. In addition, rap artists from areas outside of New York, Philadelphia, Los Angeles, Oakland, Miami, Atlanta, Houston, and Seattle, emerged as vital forces in the musical mainstream. Another factor that contributed to its growth was the fusion of rap music with hard rock, popularized by the group Run-DMC with their recording of "Rock Box" (1984) and their rendition of Aerosmith's "Walk This Way" (1986). The rap-rock fusion further evolved the new school techno-pop style through its extensive use of electronic instruments such as drum machines and samplers. However, it was the music of Public Enemy, masterminded by producer Hank Shocklee, that became the quintessence of sampling sounds, from James Brown's music and vocal stylings to black nationalists' speech excerpts. Furthermore, the use of sampling, funk-style drum rhythms with heavy bass drum, boisterous-aggressive vocal style of delivery, and/or moderate to excessive application of expletives in the text contributed to what rap artists refer to as a "hardcore" or street-style aesthetic.

Other factors that broadened the appeal of rap in popular culture were the rise of female rap artists (e.g., Roxanne Shante, the Real Roxanne, Salt-N-Pepa, MC Lyte, Queen Latifah, Yo-Yo); and the diversified sound of rap: party rap (e.g., Digital Underground, Kid 'N' Play, Hammer, De La Soul, Biz Markie, Tone Loc, and

Young MC); political rap (e.g., KRS-One/BDP, Public Enemy, Sister Souljah, Arrested Development, X-Clan); "gangsta" rap (e.g., Ice-T, Ice Cube, Geto Boys, Schoolly-D, Too Short); and eclectic rap, a cross between party and hardcore (e.g., LL Cool J, Eric B & Rakim, Naughty by Nature, EPMD, Heavy D, Kriss Kross, Das Efx); and rap/jazz fusion (e.g., Digable Planets, Us3, and Guru).

By the late 1980s, rap music had not only become musically diverse but culturally diverse as well. While a few white rap artists existed in the shadows of their African-American counterparts (e.g., Vanilla Ice), others, like the Beastie Boys,Third Bass, and House of Pain, crossed over into wider acceptance in the 1990s. Also by the late 1980s, the rap scene expanded to include Spanish-speaking performers (whose raps are aptly called Spanglish): Mellow Man Ace, Kid Frost, and Gerardo. Rap music also gained international prominence in places like England, France, Denmark, Germany, and Canada. Much of rap's popularity in these countries was due to the establishment of Zulu Nation chapters abroad and the multimedia exposure of rap artists, from recordings to the silver screen.

By the beginning of the 1990s, rap had achieved unprecedented success in the American mainstream as evidenced by its use in advertising, fashion, and other musical genres. But despite its popularity, rap had created much controversy among critics who considered its lyrics to be too hardcore and sexually explicit. Among rap's most controversial artists have been 2 Live Crew and gangsta rappers. Although much of rap's controversy remains unresolved, it continues to appeal to listeners because of its artful use of street jive and funky beats.

BIBLIOGRAPHY

Eure, Joseph D., and James G. Spady, eds. *Nation Conscious Rap.* New York, 1991.

Hager, Steven. *Hip-Hop: The Illustrated History of Breakdancing, Rap Music, and Graffiti.* New York, 1984.

Keyes, Cheryl L. *Rappin to the Beat: Rap Music as Street Culture Among African Americans.* Ann Arbor, Mich., 1992.

Nelson, Havelock, and Michael A. Gonzales. *Bring the Noise: A Guide to Rap Music and Hip-Hop Culture.* New York, 1991.

Rose, Tricia. "Orality and Technology: Rap Music and Afro-American Cultural Resistance." *Popular Music and Society.* 13, no. 4 (Winter 1989): 35–44.

Toop, David. *Rap Attack 2: African Rap to Global Hip-Hop.* Rev. ed. New York, 1991.

– CHERYL L. KEYES

RASTAFARIANS

The Rastafarian movement originated in the early twentieth century in Jamaica as a black nationalist religious phenomenon. However, its influence in the United States has been less religious and more as a cultural vehicle for a more general Afrocentrism, a political critique of colonialism, and a staple of popular music.

The first Rastafarians came together around Christian preachers in Kingston, Jamaica, who were heavily influenced by the teachings of Marcus Mosiah GARVEY. Garvey was a Jamaican labor organizer, black nationalist, and founder of the UNIVERSAL NEGRO IMPROVEMENT ASSOCIATION who came to the United States in 1916 to develop a repatriation plan for Africans in the Diaspora. That same year, Garvey predicted the rise of a powerful black king in Africa, citing from the Biblical passage that predicts that "Ethiopia shall soon stretch out her hands unto God" (Psalms 68: 31). When Prince Ras Tafari was crowned king of Ethiopia on November 2, 1930, these Garveyite Christians welcomed his coronation as a fulfillment of Garvey's prophesy. The movement became popular in some of Kingston's poorest neighborhoods among people who welcomed a promised alternative to Jamaican society.

The new king's family name, Ras Tafari (literally "Lion's Head" in the Ethiopian language of Amharic), and his royal title, Haile Selassie ("Might of the Trinity"), became significant religious symbols for these Jamaicans, who began calling themselves Rastafarians. Selassie, employing the traditional symbols and ideological supports for Ethiopian kingship, referred to himself as "the King of Kings, Lord of Lords, Conquering Lion of the Tribe of Judah"—a reference to the coming of the Messiah in the Book of Revelation—and he claimed to be a direct descendant of King Solomon and the Queen of Sheba. To the Rastafarians, this was proof of the divinity of the man they began referring to as Jah Rastari. Haile Selassie's popularity was furthered by his defiant stance in opposing the invasion of his country by Italy during the Italo-Ethiopian War of 1935–1941.

Central to Rastafarian belief are the notions that the legacy of African slavery is a reincarnation of the Biblical narrative of Exodus and that the political, social, and economic structures of Western society constitute "Babylon," the Biblical society of sin and evil that is to burn in a coming Apocalypse. Freedom and redemption for people of African descent, according to them, can only be achieved through repatriation to Africa, or more specifically Ethiopia or "Zion." For some Rastafarians, this means physical repatriation, while others interpret it as a spiritual destination. The influence of Rastafarianism was enhanced by the state visit of Haile Selassie to Jamaica in April 1966.

Rastafarians generally let their hair grow into "dreadlocks"—long, matted tresses worn both in deference to the Nazarite code in the Book of Numbers forbidding the cutting of hair and in partial imitation of the braids worn by some Ethiopian tribal warriors and priests. They openly endorse the smoking of cannabis (marijuana) as a sacrament, believing that the trancelike state induced by its ritual use creates a communion with God. The colors of the Ethiopian flag—red, gold, and green—are significant to Rastafarians, who don the color in knitted caps or "tams," belts, and badges. Rastafarians are also vegetarian and shun food that is processed or cooked with salt, a process known as "I-tal," and stress the eating of fruits and drinking of homemade juices.

In the late 1960s and early 1970s, Rastafarian culture began gaining popularity among "rude boys," rebellious youth in Kingston's ghettos. However, this was often adopted more as a style by these youths, who grew dreadlocks and danced to the increasingly Rasta-influenced Jamaican popular music, REGGAE. Referred to as "dreads," some of these young Jamaicans came to the United States in the 1970s to take part in gang warfare over the drug trade and over their allegiances to one of the two major political parties in Jamaica, the People's National Party and the Jamaican Labor Party. Throughout the decade there were a number of shootouts, murders, and bank robberies in the United States, especially in Brooklyn and the Bronx, by Jamaican dreads, giving Rastafarians a reputation among the police for extreme violence.

The Rastafarian movement began gaining adherents among African Americans and others in the United States beginning in the 1970s due to the growing popularity of reggae. Jamaican singer Desmond Dekker had a minor hit in the United States in 1972 with the American release of the 1968 song "Israelites," and the next year the film *The Harder They Come* was released, which depicted the ghettos of Kingston, Jamaica, and urban Rastafarian culture there. Reggae musicians such as Bob Marley and the Wailers and Peter Tosh toured the United States repeatedly during that decade, breathing new cultural life into black nationalism while turning dreadlocks into both a political and cultural statement.

In 1990 Rastafarians in the United States received exposure when the U.S. Supreme Court upheld the right of religious expression for Rastafarians, ruling that Rastafarians could not be required to cut their hair in prison. In 1994, Miami, Fla., was host to the International Nyahbinghi Gathering (*nyahbinghi* is Swahili for "Death to white oppressors and their black allies"), a Rastafarian meeting that brought more than 200 delegates from several countries.

Although Rastafarians can be found in almost every African-American community in the United States, actual numbers are difficult to obtain. The reason for this is that, other than a few specific sects such as the Twelve Tribes of Israel, Rastafarians have no church, no organizational structure, and no religious hierarchies. In fact, open discussion and debate about politics, African history, and biblical interpretation are much more highly valued among Rastafarians than strict dogma and structure; consequently, what it means to be a Rastafarian is continually being redefined.

BIBLIOGRAPHY

Barret, Leonard E., Sr. *The Rastafarians: Sounds of Cultural Dissonance.* Boston, 1988.

Mulvaney, Rebekah Michele. *Rastafari and Reggae: A Dictionary and Sourcebook.* New York, 1990.

Owens, Joseph. *Dread: The Rastafarians of Jamaica.* London, 1982.

– WINSTON THOMPSON

RECONSTRUCTION

Reconstruction, period that began during the CIVIL WAR and ended in 1877. One of the most controversial and misunderstood eras in American history, it witnessed far-reaching changes in the country's political and social life. For the first time, the national government assumed the basic responsibility for defining and protecting Americans' civil rights. In the South, African-American men were for the first time given the right to vote and hold office, and a politically mobilized black community joined with white allies to bring the REPUBLICAN PARTY—temporarily, as it turned out—to power. Reconstruction was America's first experiment in interracial democracy.

For much of the twentieth century, both scholarly and popular writing presented Reconstruction as an era of unrelieved sordidness in political and social life. According to this view, Abraham Lincoln, before his death, had embarked on a course of sectional reconciliation that was continued by his successor, Andrew Johnson. Their magnanimous efforts were thwarted by vindictive Radical Republicans in Congress, who fastened black supremacy upon the defeated Confederacy. An orgy of corruption and misgovernment soon followed, presided over by unscrupulous CARPETBAGGERS (Northerners who ventured south to reap the spoils of office), SCALAWAGS (southern whites who cooperated with the Republican party for personal gain), and ignorant and childlike freedpeople, who were incapable of responsibly exercising the political power that had been thrust upon them. After much needless suffering—so the interpretation goes—the South's white community banded together in patriotic organizations such as the KU KLUX KLAN to overthrow these "black" governments and restore "home rule" (their euphemism for white supremacy). Popularized through films such as *The Birth of a Nation,* this interpretation rested on the assumption that black suffrage was the gravest error of the Civil War period. It helped to justify the South's system of racial segregation and disfranchisement of black voters.

Reconstruction was America's first experiment in interracial democracy.

Although significant criticisms of the traditional interpretation were advanced earlier in the twentieth century, it was not until the 1960s that the older view was finally interred. The "second Reconstruction"—the CIVIL RIGHTS MOVEMENT—inspired a new conception of the first, and in rapid sequence virtually every assumption of the old viewpoint was swept away. In the new scholarship, Andrew Johnson, yesterday's high-minded defender of constitutional principles, was revealed as a racist politician too stubborn to compromise with his critics. Commitment to racial equality, not vindictiveness or mere partisanship, motivated his Radical Republican critics. The period of Radical Reconstruction in the South was shown to be a time of progress for African Americans and the region as a whole. The Ku Klux Klan, whose campaign of violence had been minimized by earlier historians, was revealed as a terrorist organization that beat and killed its opponents in order to deprive blacks of their newly won rights. Most strikingly, African Americans were now shown to be active agents in shaping the era's history, rather than passive recipients of the actions of others, or simply a "problem" confronting white society. Today, scholars differ among themselves on many issues, but all agree that the traditional view of the period is dead, and unlamented, and that blacks must be considered central actors in the drama of Reconstruction.

Reconstruction During the Civil War

Reconstruction began not with the Confederacy's surrender in 1865 but during the Civil War. Long before the conflict ended, Americans were debating the questions that came to form the essence of Reconstruction: On what terms should the southern states be reunited with the Union? Who should establish these terms, Congress or the president? What system of labor should replace plantation slavery? What should be the place of blacks in the political and social life of the South and the nation? One definitive conclusion emerged from the Civil War: The reconstructed South would be a society without SLAVERY.

The destruction of slavery, begun by blacks who fled the plantations in 1861 and 1862, and made into a national war aim by the Emancipation Proclamation of January 1, 1863, powerfully shaped the course of the war and the debate over Reconstruction. No longer could the Lincoln administration speak of allowing the South to return with its prewar institutions and leadership intact.

In December 1863, Lincoln announced a program for Reconstruction. He offered a pardon to all supporters of the Confederacy (except high-ranking officials) who took an oath of loyalty and pledged to accept the end of slavery. When 10 percent of a state's prewar voters took the oath, they could establish a state government and apply for readmission to the Union. New state constitutions would have to prohibit slavery, but otherwise Lincoln gave southern leaders a free hand in legislation. Voting and officeholding were limited to whites. The president, complained abolitionist Wendell Phillips, "frees the slave and ignores the Negro."

Lincoln attempted to implement his Reconstruction plan in Louisiana, portions of which had been occupied by Union troops in 1862. Two years later, elections were held for a constitutional convention, which abolished slavery and sought Louisiana's readmission to the Union. At the same time, the free African Americans of New Orleans—a self-conscious community that included many highly educated, economically successful individuals—pressed for the right to participate in Reconstruction. After meeting with two free black representatives, Lincoln in March 1864 private, and unsuccessfully, urged Louisiana's governor to allow at least some blacks to vote.

As Reconstruction proceeded in Louisiana, it became clear that many northern Republicans were unhappy with Lincoln's program. Foremost among them were the Radicals, a group that had led the opposition to slavery's expansion before the Civil War and had long favored granting equal civil and political rights to free blacks in the North. The most prominent were Rep. Thaddeus Stevens of Pennsylvania and Sen. Charles Sumner of Massachusetts, both longtime proponents of the rights of African Americans. The Radicals now insisted that the federal government had a responsibility to protect the basic rights of the former slaves. By 1864 some went further, announcing that Reconstruction could not be secure without black suffrage. Their stance combined principle and political advantage. The Radicals believed that without the right to vote, blacks would be vulnerable to domination by their former owners; they also understood that unless blacks voted, the Republican party would find it very difficult to win elections in the postwar South.

During 1864, the Radicals became convinced that Lincoln's 10-percent plan was too lenient to "rebels" and did too little to protect African Americans' rights. Enough moderate Republicans agreed that Congress passed the Wade-Davis Bill, which proposed to delay the start of Reconstruction until a majority of a state's white males—not just 10 percent—had taken an oath of loyalty. The new state governments were required to guarantee the equality before the law of black Southerners. Black suffrage, which most Republicans did not at this point support, was not mentioned. Not wishing to abandon his own approach, Lincoln pocket vetoed the bill.

Lincoln and the Radicals differed over Reconstruction, but their breach was not irreparable. Early in 1865, they worked together to secure congressional approval of the THIRTEENTH AMENDMENT, which irrevocably abolished slavery throughout the nation. Shortly thereafter Congress passed, and Lincoln signed, a bill creating the Freedmen's Bureau, an agency empowered to protect the legal rights of the former slaves, provide education and medical care, oversee labor contracts between emancipated blacks and their employers, and lease land to black families.

As the act establishing the Freedmen's Bureau suggested, there was far more to Reconstruction than the problem of forming new state governments and determining who should vote. During the Civil War, the first steps were taken toward addressing the interrelated problems of access to land and control of labor. The most famous of these "rehearsals for Reconstruction" took place on the Sea Islands of South Carolina. When the Union navy occupied the area in 1861, virtually all the white inhabitants fled to the mainland, leaving behind some 10,000 slaves, who sacked the big houses, destroyed cotton gins, and commenced planting corn and potatoes for their own consumption.

Sea Island blacks, however, were not to chart their own course to "free labor." In the navy's wake came whites from the North—military officers, Treasury agents, northern investors eager to resume plantation agriculture, and a group of young teachers and missionaries known as Gideon's Band. Many of the reformers sympathized with African Americans' desire to acquire land. Most government officials and northern investors, however, believed the Sea Island experiment provided a golden opportunity to prove that blacks would work more efficiently and profitably as free laborers than as slaves. Rather than immediately acquiring land, they believed, the former slaves should work for wages and learn the discipline of the free market. The Sea Island experiment produced many improvements in the lives of the area's black population, including access to schools and a rise in their standard of living. However, it also brought disappointment, for when plantations abandoned by their owners were auctioned off by the federal government, only a small amount of land found its way into the hands of the former slaves.

The Sea Island experiment involved a far smaller area and far fewer persons than another rehearsal for Reconstruction, which took place in the Mississippi Valley. Here many slave owners remained on their plantations, declared their loyalty to the Union, and demanded that the army compel their black laborers to remain at work. Military officials, who established "contraband camps" for black refugees, had no desire to care permanently for large numbers of former slaves. They decreed that the former slaves sign labor contracts either with planters who took an oath of loyalty or with investors from the North. They would be paid wages and guaranteed access to schools, and corporal punishment would be prohibited, but they could not leave the plantations without permission of their employers.

Inaugurated in Louisiana, this system of "compulsory free labor" was extended to the entire Mississippi Valley, the home of over half a million slaves, after the Union capture of Vicksburg in 1863. A halfway house between slavery and freedom, the system satisfied no one. Planters disliked not being able to use the whip to enforce discipline, and complained that the former slaves were unruly and refused to obey orders. The freedpeople, for their part, resented being forced to work for white employers, often their former owners, rather than being allowed access to land.

Only occasionally did glimmerings of a different policy appear. In 1863, Gen. Ulysses S. Grant directed that Davis Bend, which contained the plantations of Confederate president Jefferson Davis, be set aside for the settlement of freedpeople. By 1865, Davis Bend had become a remarkable example of self-reliance, with successful cotton farming, a series of schools, and its own system of government.

Early in 1865, a new dimension to the questions of land and labor was added by Gen. William T. Sherman. After capturing Savannah at the conclusion of his famous march to the sea, Sherman met with a group of the city's black leaders. The best guarantee of freedom, they told him, was "to have land, and turn it and till it by our own labor." Four days later, Sherman issued Field Order No. 15, setting aside the Sea Islands and a portion of the South Carolina and Georgia coasts, extending thirty miles inland, for black settlement. Each family would receive forty acres of land, and Sherman later provided that the army could loan them mules.

(Thus the phrase FORTY ACRES AND A MULE, which would echo throughout the South.) By June, some 40,000 freedpeople had been settled on 400,000 acres of "Sherman land."

In the spring of 1865, as the Civil War drew to a close, it was apparent that the federal government had not yet worked out its Reconstruction policy. In March, in his second inaugural address, Lincoln called on the nation to bind up its wounds "with malice toward none and charity toward all." But leniency to whites, for Lincoln, did not mean abandoning concern for the rights of blacks. In his last speech, just a few days before his assassination, the president endorsed the idea of limited black suffrage for the Reconstruction South. He singled out former soldiers and those with some education as particularly deserving of the right to vote. This was the first time an American president had called for granting African Americans suffrage, and it illustrated the capacity for growth that had always been the hallmark of Lincoln's leadership.

The Meaning of Freedom

Critical to the debate over Reconstruction were the complex reactions of Southerners, black and white alike, to the end of slavery. That event led inevitably to conflict between blacks seeking to bring substantive meaning to their freedom and planters seeking to retain as much as possible of the old order. Rather than being a predetermined category or static concept, "freedom" itself became a terrain of conflict during Reconstruction, its definition open to different, often contradictory interpretations, its content changing for whites as well as for blacks.

To African Americans, freedom meant independence from white control, autonomy both as individuals and as members of a community that was itself being transformed as a result of emancipation. Blacks relished the opportunity to flaunt their liberation from the innumerable regulations, significant and trivial, associated with slavery. They openly held mass meetings and religious services free of white oversight; they acquired dogs, guns, and liquor (all barred under slavery); they refused to yield the sidewalks to whites. No longer required to obtain a pass from their owners to travel, former slaves throughout the South left the plantations in search of better jobs, family members, or simply a taste of personal freedom. Many moved to southern towns and cities, where, it seemed, "freedom was free-er."

Before the war, free blacks had created a network of churches, schools, and mutual-benefit societies, and slaves had forged a semiautonomous culture centered on the family and church. With freedom, these institutions were consolidated, expanded, and liberated from white supervision.

The family stood as the main pillar of the postemancipation black community. Under slavery, most blacks had lived in nuclear family units, although they faced the constant threat of separation from loved ones by sale. Reconstruction provided the opportunity to solidify their family ties. Freedpeople made remarkable efforts to locate loved ones from whom they had been separated under slavery. One northern reporter in 1865 encountered a freedman who had actually walked more than six hundred miles from Georgia to North Carolina, searching for the wife and children from whom he had been sold away.

To African Americans, freedom meant independence from white control, autonomy both as individuals and as members of a community.

Control over their family life was essential to the former slaves' definition of freedom. Many freedwomen, preferring to devote more time to their families, and wishing to be free from the supervision of white employers (which under slavery often led to sexual exploitation), refused to work any longer in the cotton fields. Black parents strenuously resisted efforts by many planters to force their children into involuntary labor through court-ordered apprenticeships, insisting that they, rather than the employer, would decide when children went to school and when they labored in the fields.

At the same time, African Americans withdrew almost entirely from white-controlled religious institutions, where they had been excluded from a role in church governance and had often been required to sit in the back pews during services. The rise of the independent black church, with METHODISTS and BAPTISTS commanding the largest followings, redrew the religious map of the South. The church played a central role in the black community; a place of worship, it also housed schools, social events, and political gatherings, and sponsored many of the fraternal and benevolent societies that sprang up during Reconstruction. Inevitably, black ministers came to play a role in politics. Over two hundred held public office during Reconstruction.

Another striking example of the freedpeople's effort to breathe meaning into freedom was their thirst for education. Before the war, virtually every southern state had prohibited the instruction of slaves. Now, adults as well as children thronged the schools established during and after the Civil War. Northern benevolent societies, the Freedmen's Bureau, and, after 1868, state governments provided most of the funding for black education, but the initiative often lay with African Americans, who pooled their meager resources and voluntarily taxed themselves to purchase land, construct buildings, and hire teachers.

The desire for autonomy and self-improvement also shaped African Americans' economic definition of freedom. Blacks wished to take control of the conditions under which they labored and to carve out the greatest degree of economic independence. Most refused to work any longer in gangs under the direction of an overseer, and generally preferred renting land to working for wages. Above all, economic freedom meant owning land of their own. In some parts of the South, blacks in 1865 seized abandoned land, or refused to leave plantations, insisting that the property belonged to them. Many expected the federal government to guarantee them access to land.

If the goal of autonomy inspired African Americans to withdraw from social institutions controlled by whites, and attempt to work out their economic destinies by themselves, in political life "freedom" meant inclusion rather than separation. Recognition of their equal rights as citizens quickly emerged as the animating impulse of black politics. Throughout 1865, blacks organized mass meetings, parades, petitions, and conventions demanding equality before the law and the right to vote. The end of slavery, they insisted, enabled America for the first time to live up to the full implications of its democratic creed by abandoning racial proscription and absorbing blacks fully into the civil and political order.

If former slaves saw Reconstruction as heralding a new era of autonomy and equality, most southern whites reacted to military defeat and emancipation with dismay. Needing to borrow money to resume farming, many small farmers fell into debt and were forced to take up the growing of cotton. By the mid-1870s white farmers, who had cultivated only one-tenth of the South's cotton crop in 1860, were growing 40 percent, and many who had owned their land were tenants.

Planter families also faced profound changes in the aftermath of the war. In a sense, the most arduous task facing former slave owners was adjusting to the world of free labor. Planters understood that the questions of land and labor were intimately interrelated. Many were convinced, a northern visitor reported, that "so long as they retain possession of their lands they can oblige the negroes to work on such terms as they please." Between the planters' need for a disciplined labor force and the freedpeople's quest for autonomy, conflict was inevitable. Blacks, planters complained, insisted on setting their own hours of labor, worked at their own pace, and insisted on the right to conduct their personal lives as they saw fit.

With such polarized forces at work, it fell to the Freedmen's Bureau to attempt to mediate between the contending parties. The bureau's myriad responsibilities included establishing schools for freedmen, adjudicating disputes among blacks and between the races, and attempting to secure for blacks and for white Unionists equal justice from southern courts. Much to the bureau's activity, however, centered on overseeing the transition from slave to free labor.

Some bureau officials believed that the former slaves had to sign labor contracts and go back to work on the plantations. Others—such as Gen. Rufus Saxton, who directed the agency's activities in South Carolina in 1865—sympathized strongly with blacks' aspiration to own land. In the summer of 1865, however, President Andrew Johnson, who had succeeded Lincoln, ordered land in federal hands returned to its former owners. A series of confrontations followed, notably in South Carolina and Georgia, where blacks were forcibly evicted from the land they had been settled on by Sherman. In the end, the vast majority of rural freedpeople remained propertyless and poor, with no alternative but to work as laborers on white-owned plantations. The Freedmen's Bureau attempted to ensure that labor contracts were equitable, and that the former slaves were free to leave their jobs once the contracts had expired. But the ideal of forty acres and a mule was dead. The result was a deep sense of betrayal, which survived among the freedpeople and their descendants long after the end of Reconstruction.

Out of the conflict on the plantations, and with black landownership all but precluded, new systems of labor emerged in the different regions of the South. Sharecropping came to dominate the cotton South and much of the tobacco belt of Virginia and North Carolina. In the Louisiana sugar region, an influx of northern capital allowed for the repair of equipment and the resumption of production. Gang labor survived the end of slavery, with blacks working for wages and allowed access to garden plots to grow their own food. In the rice kingdom of coastal South Carolina and Georgia, planters were unable to acquire the large amounts of capital necessary to repair irrigation systems and threshing machinery destroyed by the war, and blacks continued to demand access to land they had occupied in 1865. In the end, the plantations in this region fell to pieces, and blacks were able to acquire land and take up self-sufficient farming.

The Politics of Presidential Reconstruction

To Andrew Johnson fell the task of overseeing the restoration of the Union. Johnson was ill suited for the responsibilities he now shouldered. A lonely, stubborn man, he was intolerant of criticism and unable to compromise. He lacked Lincoln's political skills and keen sense of northern public opinion. Moreover, while Johnson had supported emancipation during the war, he held deeply racist views. A self-proclaimed spokesman for the poor white farmers of the South, he condemned the old planter aristocracy, but believed African Americans had no role to play in Reconstruction.

With Congress out of session until December, Johnson in May 1865 outlined his plan for reuniting the nation. He issued a series of proclamations that inaugurated the period of Presidential Reconstruction (1865–1867). Johnson offered a pardon to all southern whites, except Confederate leaders and wealthy planters (and most of these soon received individual pardons) who took an oath of allegiance. He also appointed provisional governors and ordered conventions held, to which delegates were elected by whites alone. Apart from the requirement that they abolish slavery, repudiate secession, and abrogate the Confederate debt, the new governments were granted a free hand in managing their affairs.

To Andrew Johnson fell the task of overseeing the restoration of the Union. Johnson was ill suited for the responsibilities he now shouldered.

The conduct of the southern governments elected under Johnson's program turned most of the Republican North against the president. White voters by and large returned members of the old elite to power. Alarmed by the apparent ascendancy of "rebels," Republicans were further outraged by reports of violence against former slaves and against northern visitors in the South. But what aroused the most opposition were laws of the new southern governments that attempted to regulate the lives of the former slaves. Known as the BLACK CODES, these did grant the freedpeople certain rights, such as owning property and suing in court. African Americans could not, however, testify against whites, serve on juries or in state militias, or vote.

Responding to planters' demands that the freedpeople be forced back to work on the plantations, the Black Codes required blacks to sign yearly labor contracts. The unemployed were declared vagrants, and could be arrested, fined and hired out to white landowners. Some states limited the occupations open to blacks and tried to prevent them from acquiring land. African Americans strongly resisted the implementation of these measures, and the apparent inability of the white South's leaders to accept the reality of emancipation fatally undermined northern support for Johnson's policies.

When Congress assembled in December 1865, Johnson announced that with loyal governments functioning in all the southern states, Reconstruction was over. In response, Radical Republicans, who had grown increasingly estranged from Johnson during the summer and fall, called for the establishment of new governments with "rebels" excluded from power and black men granted the right to vote.

Most Republicans, however, were moderates, not Radicals. They believed Johnson's plan flawed but desired to work with the president in modifying it, and did not believe that either southern or northern whites would accept black suffrage. Radicals and moderates joined together in refusing to seat the Southerners recently elected to Congress. Early in 1866, Sen. Lyman Trumbull of Illinois proposed two bills, reflecting the moderates' belief that Johnson's policy required modification. The first extended the life of the Freedmen's Bureau, which had been established for only one year. The second, the Civil Rights Bill, defined all persons born in the United States as citizens and spelled out rights they were to enjoy without regard to race—making contracts, bringing lawsuits, and enjoying "full and equal benefit of all laws and proceedings for the security of person and property." The bill left the new southern governments in place, but required them to accord blacks the same civil rights as whites. It made no mention of the right to vote.

Passed by overwhelming majorities in both houses of Congress, the Civil Rights Bill represented the first attempt to define in legislative terms the essence of freedom and the rights of American citizenship. In empowering the federal government to guarantee the principle of equality before the law, regardless of race, against violations by the states, it embodied a profound change in federal-state relations.

To the surprise of Congress, Johnson vetoed both bills. Both, he said, threatened to centralize power in the national government and deprive the states of their authority to regulate their own affairs. Moreover, he believed, blacks did not deserve the rights of citizenship. The vetoes made a complete breach between Congress and the president inevitable. In April 1866, the Civil Rights Bill became the first major law in American history to be passed over a presidential veto.

Johnson had united moderate and Radical Republicans against him. Congress now proceeded to adopt its own plan of Reconstruction. In June 1866, it approved the FOURTEENTH AMENDMENT, which broadened the federal government's power to protect the rights of all Americans. It forbade states from abridging the "privileges and immunities" of American citizens or depriving any citizen of the "equal protection of the laws." In a compromise between Radical and moderate positions on black suffrage, it did not expressly give blacks the right to vote, but threatened to reduce the South's representation in Congress if black men continued to be denied the ballot. The amendment also empowered Congress to take further steps to enforce its provisions.

The most important change in the Constitution since the adoption of the Bill of Rights, the Fourteenth Amendment established equality before the law as a fundamental right of American citizens. It shifted the balance of power within the nation by making the federal government, not the states, the ultimate protector of citizens' rights. The Fourteenth Amendment, and the congressional policy of guaranteeing civil rights for blacks, became the central issue of the political campaign of 1866. Riots that broke out in Memphis and New Orleans, in which white policemen and citizens killed scores of blacks further undermined public support for Johnson's policies.

In the northern congressional elections, Republicans opposed to Johnson's policies won a sweeping victory. Nonetheless, every southern state but Tennessee, egged on by Johnson, refused to ratify the Fourteenth Amendment. The intransigence of Johnson and the bulk of the white South pushed moderate Republicans toward the proposals of the Radicals. In March 1867, over Johnson's veto, Congress adopted the Reconstruction Act, which divided the South into five military districts, temporarily barred many Confederates from voting or holding office, and called for the creation of new governments in the South with suffrage no longer restricted because of race.

The conflict between President Johnson and Congress did not end with the passage of the Reconstruction Act. In 1868 the House of Representatives impeached the president for violating the Tenure of Office Act of 1867, and the Senate came within a single vote of removing him from office. Shortly thereafter, the Republicans nominated Ulysses S. Grant as the party's presidential candidate. Reconstruction was the central issue of the 1868 campaign. Democrats denounced it as unconstitutional, and condemned black suffrage as a violation of America's political traditions. Grant's victory was a vindication of Republican Reconstruction, and it inspired Congress to adopt the era's third constitutional amendment. In February 1869, Congress approved the FIFTEENTH AMENDMENT, prohibiting the federal and state governments from depriving any citizen of the right to vote because of race.

Although it left the door open to suffrage restrictions not explicitly based on race—literacy tests, property qualifications, poll taxes—and did nothing to extend voting rights to women, the Fifteenth Amendment marked the culmination of four decades of agitation on behalf of the slave. As late as 1868, only eight northern states had allowed black men to vote. "Nothing in all history," exclaimed veteran abolitionist William Lloyd Garrison, equaled "this wonderful, quiet, sudden transformation of four millions of human beings from . . . the auction-block to the ballot-box."

Radical Reconstruction in the South

Among the former slaves, the coming of black suffrage in 1867 caused an outburst of political organization. Determined to exercise their new rights as citizens, thousands joined the Union League, an organization closely linked to the Republican party, and the vast majority of eligible African Americans registered to vote. "You never saw a people more excited on the subject of politics than are the Negroes of the South," wrote a plantation manager.

By 1870, all the former confederate states had been readmitted to the Union, nearly all under the control of the Republican party. Their new constitutions, drafted in 1868 and 1869 by the first public bodies in American history with substantial black representation (of about 1,000 delegates throughout the South, over one-quarter were black), represented a considerable improvement over those they replaced. They made the structure of southern government more democratic, modernized the tax system, and guaranteed the civil and political rights of black citizens. A few states initially barred former Confederates from voting, but this policy was quickly abandoned by the new state governments.

Throughout Reconstruction, black voters provided the bulk of the Republican party's support. Although Democrats charged that "Negro rule" had come to the South, nowhere did blacks control the workings of state government, or hold office in numbers equal to their proportion of the total population (which ranged from about 60 percent in South Carolina to around one-third in Arkansas, North Carolina, Tennessee, and Texas). In nearly every state, whites (the much-maligned "carpetbaggers" and "scalawags") controlled the machinery of the Republican party and all but monopolized the top offices—governor, U.S. senator, and major patronage positions. Nonetheless, the fact that well over fifteen hundred African Americans occupied positions of po-

terrorist societies and allowing the president to use the army against them. These laws continued the expansion of national authority during Reconstruction by defining certain crimes—those aimed at depriving citizens of their civil and political rights—as federal offenses. In 1871, President Grant authorized federal marshals, backed up by troops in some areas, to arrest hundreds of accused Klansmen. After a series of well-publicized trials, in which many of the organization's leaders were jailed, the Klan went out of existence.

Despite the Grant administration's effective response to Klan terrorism, the North's commitment to Reconstruction waned during the 1870s. Many Radical leaders, among them Thaddeus Stevens, had passed from the scene. Within the Republican party, their place was taken by politicians less committed to the ideal of equal rights for blacks. The federal government had freed the slaves, made them citizens, given them the right to vote, and crushed the Ku Klux Klan. Now, it was said, blacks should rely on their own resources, not demand further assistance from the North.

In 1872 a group of Republicans, alienated by corruption within the Grant administration, bolted the party. The Liberal Republicans, as they called themselves, believed that unrestrained democracy, in which "ignorant" voters such as the Irish immigrants of New York City could dominate politics in some locales, was responsible for such instances of corruption as the Tweed Ring. Democratic criticisms of Reconstruction found a receptive audience among the Liberals. As in the North, Liberals believed, the "best men" of the South had been excluded from power while "ignorant" voters controlled politics. The result was corruption and misgovernment. Government in the South should be returned to the region's "natural leaders."

The Liberals nominated Horace Greeley, editor of the New York *Tribune,* to run against Grant in 1872. The Democrats endorsed Greeley as well, and the continuation of Reconstruction became a major issue in the campaign. Grant overwhelmingly won reelection, but the Liberal attack on Reconstruction continued, contributing to a resurgence of racism in the North. Journalist James S. Pike, a leading Greeley supporter, in 1874 published *The Prostrate State,* an influential account of a visit to South Carolina. He depicted a state engulfed by corruption and extravagance, under the control of "a mass of black barbarism." "Negro government," he insisted, was the cause of the South's problems; the solution was to see leading whites restored to political power.

Other factors also weakened northern support for Reconstruction. In 1873, the country plunged into a severe economic depression. Distracted by national economic problems, Republicans were in no mood to devote further attention to the South. Congress did enact one final piece of civil rights legislation, the Civil Rights Act of 1875, which outlawed racial discrimination in places of public accommodation. This was a tribute to Charles Sumner, who had devoted his career to promoting the principle of equality before the law, and who died in 1874.

Nonetheless, it was clear that the northern public was retreating from Reconstruction. Meanwhile, the Supreme Court began whittling away at the guarantees of black rights Congress had adopted. In the *Slaughterhouse* cases (1873), the Court decreed that the Fourteenth Amendment had not altered traditional federalism; most of the rights of citizens remained under state control. Three years later, in *U.S.* v. *Cruikshank,* the Court gutted the Enforcement Acts by throwing out convictions of some of those responsible for the Colfax Massacre.

By the mid-1870s, Reconstruction was on the defensive. The Depression dealt the South a severe economic blow, and further weakened the possibility that Republicans could create a revitalized southern economy. Factionalism between blacks and whites and between carpetbaggers and scalawags remained a serious problem among southern Republicans. In those states where Reconstruction survived, violence again reared its head, and this time the Grant administration showed no desire to intervene. In contrast to the Klan's activities—which had been conducted at night by disguised men—the violence of 1875 and 1876 took place in broad daylight, as if to flaunt Democrats' conviction that they had nothing to fear from Washington. In Mississippi in 1875, white rifle clubs drilled in public, and Republicans were openly assaulted and murdered. When Gov. Adelbert Ames frantically appealed to the federal government for assistance, President Grant responded that the northern public was "tired out" by southern problems and would condemn any interference from Washington. On election day in 1875, armed Democrats destroyed ballot boxes and drove former slaves from the polls. The result was a Democratic landslide and the end of Reconstruction in Mississippi. "A revolution has taken place," wrote Ames, "and a race are disfranchised—they are to be returned to . . . an era of second slavery."

Similar events took place in South Carolina in 1876. Here, where blacks made up 60 percent of the population, Democrats nominated for governor Wade Hampton, one of the state's most popular Confederate veterans. Hampton promised to respect the rights of all citizens, but his supporters launched a wave of intimidation, with rifle clubs disrupting Republican meetings, and freedmen assaulted and sometimes murdered.

The collapse of Reconstruction deeply affected the future course of American development.

Events in South Carolina directly affected the outcome of the presidential campaign of 1876. To succeed Grant, the Republicans nominated Governor Rutherford B. Hayes of Ohio. His Democratic opponent was New York's governor, Samuel J. Tilden. By this time, only South Carolina, Florida, and Louisiana remained under Republican control. The election was so close that whoever captured these states (and both candidates claimed to have carried them) would become the next president. In January 1877, unable to resolve the crisis on its own, Congress appointed an electoral commission composed of senators, congressmen, and Supreme Court justices. Republicans enjoyed an 8–7 majority on the commission; the members decided that Hayes had carried the disputed southern states, and he was elected.

Democrats, who controlled the House of Representatives, could still obstruct Hayes's inauguration, but after secret discussions with representatives of the incoming president they decided not to do so. This was the famous "Bargain of 1877": Hayes would recognize Democratic control of the remaining southern states and Democrats would not block the certification of his election. Hayes became president, promised to end federal intervention in the South, and ordered United States troops, who had been guarding the statehouses in South Carolina and Louisiana, to return to their barracks (but not to leave the region entirely, as is widely believed). Reconstruction was at an end.

The collapse of Reconstruction deeply affected the future course of American development. The South long remained a bastion of one-party Democratic rule, under the control of a reactionary elite who used the same violence and fraud that had helped defeat Reconstruction to stifle internal dissent. The federal government stood by indifferently as the southern states effectively nullified the Fourteenth and Fifteenth amendments and, beginning in the 1890s, stripped African Americans of the right to vote. By the turn of the twentieth century, southern blacks found themselves enmeshed in a complex system of oppression, each of whose components—segregation, economic inequality, political disempowerment, and the pervasive threat of violence—reinforced the others. Although the black institutions created or strengthened after the Civil War—the family, church, and schools—survived the end of Reconstruction, southern governments fell far behind the rest of the nation in meeting their public responsibilities. Long into the twentieth century, the South would remain the nation's foremost economic problem, a region of low wages, stunted economic development, and widespread poverty. Not until the 1960s would the nation again attempt to come to terms with the political and social agenda of Reconstruction.

BIBLIOGRAPHY

Belz, Herman. *Reconstructing the Union: Theory and Practice during the Civil War.* Ithaca, N.Y., 1969.

Brock, William R. *An American Crisis.* London, 1963.

Drago, Edmund L. *Black Politicians and Reconstruction in Georgia.* Rev. ed. Athens, Ga., 1992.

Du Bois, W. E. B. *Black Reconstruction in America.* New York, 1935.

Fitzgerald, Michael W. *The Union League Movement in the Deep South: Politics and Agricultural Change During Reconstruction.* Baton Rouge, La., 1989.

Foner, Eric. *Reconstruction: American's Unfinished Revolution, 1863–1877.* New York, 1988.

———. *A Short History of Reconstruction.* New York, 1990.

———. *Freedom's Lawmakers: A Directory of Black Officeholders During Reconstruction.* New York, 1993.

Franklin, John Hope. *Reconstruction After the Civil War.* Chicago, 1961.

Gillette, William. *Retreat from Reconstruction 1869–1879.* Baton Rouge, La., 1979.

Holt, Thomas. *Black over White: Negro Political Leadership in South Carolina During Reconstruction.* Urbana, Ill. 1977.

Jaynes, Gerald D. *Branches Without Roots: Genesis of the Black Working Class in the American South 1862–1882.* New York, 1986.

Kaczorowski, Robert. *The Politics of Judicial Interpretation: The Federal Courts, Department of Justice, and Civil Rights, 1866–1876.* New York, 1985.

Litwack, Leon F. *Been in the Storm So Long: The Aftermath of Slavery.* New York, 1979.

Magdol, Edward. *A Right to the Land: Essays on the Freedmen's Community.* Westport, Conn., 1977.

McCrary, Peyton. *Abraham Lincoln and Reconstruction: The Louisiana Experiment.* Princeton, N.J., 1978.

Morris, Robert C. *Reading, 'Riting, and Reconstruction: The Education of Freedmen in the South 1861–1870.* Chicago, 1981.

Olsen, Otto H., ed. *Reconstruction and Redemption in the South.* Baton Rouge, La., 1980.

Perman, Michael. *The Road to Redemption: Southern Politics, 1869–1879.* Chapel Hill, N.C., 1984.

Rabinowitz, Howard N., ed. *Southern Black Leaders of the Reconstruction Era.* Urbana, Ill., 1982.

Rable, George C. *But There Was No Peace: The Role of Violence in the Politics of Reconstruction.* Athens, Ga., 1984.

Ransom, Roger L., and Richard Sutch. *One Kind of Freedom: The Economic Consequences of Emancipation.* New York, 1977.

Rose, Willie Lee. *Rehearsal for Reconstruction: The Port Royal Experiment.* Indianapolis, 1964.

Sterling, Dorothy, ed. *The Trouble They Seen.* New York, 1976.

Summers, Mark W. *Railroads, Reconstruction, and the Gospel of Prosperity: Aid Under the Radical Republicans, 1865–1877.* Princeton, N.J., 1984.

Trefousse, Hans L. *The Radical Republicans: Lincoln's Vanguard for Racial Justice.* New York, 1969.
Vincent, Charles. *Black Legislators in Louisiana During Reconstruction.* Baton Rouge, La., 1976.
Walker, Clarence E. *A Rock in a Weary Land: The African Methodist Episcopal Church During the Civil War and Reconstruction.* Baton Rouge, La., 1982.
Williamson, Joel. *After Slavery: The Negro in South Carolina During Reconstruction, 1861–1877.* Chapel Hill, N.C., 1965.

– ERIC FONER

REDDING, OTIS

Otis Redding (September 9, 1941–December 10, 1967), soul singer and composer. Otis Redding was one of the most powerful and original singer-songwriters of the 1960s and the mainstay of Stax Records, the Memphis label that became internationally successful releasing gritty southern soul. Born in Dawson, Ga., Redding grew up in Macon, 100 miles to the north. He began playing drums in school and was paid six dollars an hour on Sundays to accompany gospel groups appearing on local radio station WIBB. Redding stayed in school until the tenth grade (1957), but quit to help support his family, working variously at a gas station, as a well-digger, and occasionally as a musician. As a singer, he began to win local talent contests with his spontaneous and tough vocal style. He traveled to Los Angeles in mid-1960, where he recorded four songs, and returned to Macon in 1961, where he cut "Shout Bamalama" for the Confederate label, a minor hit that received airplay on area radio stations. His break came in 1963, when he sang his song "These Arms of Mine" at a Stax recording session of Johnny Jenkins and the Pinetoppers, a group for whom he was guest vocalist and chauffeur. When the record made it into the Rhythm-and-Blues Top Twenty in 1964, Redding's career was launched. Over the next five years, his popularity grew steadily through fiery live performances, hit singles such as "I've Been Loving You Too Long," "Try a Little Tenderness," and "I Can't Turn You Loose," and critically acclaimed LPs such as *Otis Blue, The Soul Album,* and *The Great Otis Redding Sings Soul Ballads.* Like Aretha FRANKLIN (who immortalized his song "Respect"), Redding was able to capitalize on the liberal climate of the 1960s, crossing over to white listeners on both sides of the Atlantic. His performances in England in early 1967 so enthralled audiences that he was subsequently named Best Male Vocalist in a poll sponsored by the music publication *Melody Maker,* an accolade won by Elvis Presley the previous eight years. Later in 1967, nestled between rock acts, he captivated an audience of 55,000 at the Monterey Pop Festival in California, one of the milestones of the hippie era. His death in a plane crash near Madison, Wis., on December 10, 1967, came at the peak of his career, and left fans wondering what might have been: "(Sittin' on) The Dock of the Bay," recorded three days before his death, revealed a different, introspective musical direction. It became his biggest record, heading the pop charts for four weeks and becoming a posthumous signature song.

BIBLIOGRAPHY

Guralnick, Peter. "Otis Redding" and "Stax Goes to Europe/The Big O Comes Home: Triumph and Tragedy." In *Sweet Soul Music.* New York, 1986, pp. 133–152, 308–332.

– BUD KLIMENT

REFORMED CHURCH IN AMERICA, THE

The Black people first entered New York City in 1628, the same year the first minister of the Dutch Reformed Church, the Rev. Jonas Michaelius, arrived in New York. The Reformed Church was no different from the colonial Anglican Church and the Roman Catholic Church in its acceptance of slavery as an institution. In his important book *Religion and Trade in New Netherlands,* George L. Smith expresses surprise that the Dutch accepted slavery so readily in New York and New Jersey, when slavery was not legalized in the Netherlands in the sixteenth and seventeenth centuries. He asks: "Why, then, did they so quickly resort to slavery as a scheme of social and economic organization within the Colonies?" (Smith 1973, p. 126). His reply was that the Dutch chose slavery because it was the path of least resistance. However, Smith's answer simplifies the problem.

The truth regarding the Dutch Reformed Church's response to slavery is much more complex. In his article "The Dutch Reformed Church and Negro Slavery in Colonial America" (De Jong 1971, pp. 423–436), Professor Gerald Francis De Jong points out that African slaves provided a ready-made labor force for the Dutch farmers who lived in the Hudson, Raritan, and Minisink valleys of New Jersey. According to De Jong, the Dutch Reformed were among the greatest users of African slaves in New York and New Jersey. Smith informs us that while the ministers were under the supervision of the "Classis" of Amsterdam, "they were in the financial employ of the India Company themselves; which meant that their salaries were in part made possible by the profits of the slave trade" (Smith 1973, p. 126).

In 1652, Peter Stuyvesant, the Director General of New Netherlands, was advised to import directly from Africa as many Africans as the colony needed for the cultivation of the soil. There were a few ministers, among them the Rev. Jacobus Hondius, who in 1679 criticized the slave trade; but most took the position of the Rev. Godfried Ademans, who argued in 1640 that slavery was compatible with Christianity and that the task of the Church was to minister to the soul.

There was no appreciable change in the relationship of the Reformed Church in America toward people of African descent in the eighteenth and nineteenth centuries. Although there were occasional black persons like William Johnson, who was accepted for training as a minister at the New Brunswick Theological Seminary, it was not until the twentieth century that the Church hammered out its commitment in terms of supporting missions to black people and administering a school for black youngsters at Brewton, Ala. The attitude of the Church during the seventeenth and eighteenth centuries was that the liturgy and preaching of the Reformed Church in America was too intellectually demanding for black people. Further, the Church was severely divided over the issue of slavery as an institution.

It was not until the 1950s, when black people in large numbers started to migrate North for economic opportunities and began to attend the Reformed Churches in the inner cities, that the Church was forced to respond to the black presence. The migration of black people from the South, coupled with the push for integration, which was heralded by the CIVIL RIGHTS MOVEMENT led by the Rev. Dr. Martin Luther KING, Jr., forced the Church to deal with the black presence which had infiltrated the churches in many inner cities. During the fifties and sixties, the Church responded with a mission in East Harlem and the sponsoring of storefront churches throughout New York City.

To deal with the needs of its black constituency, the Synod of 1969 asked the black membership to establish a Black Council to empower the black membership and to see that their needs were met. In 1972 the Reverend William Moses Howard was appointed executive director of the Black Council and has led it into the 1990s. He has spoken of the role of the Council as a reconciling force in the Reformed Church in America. In defining its purpose within the Reformed Church in America the Council stated: "We, the members of the Black Council, as peers of all other members of the Church, shall seek to reconcile the Church to all of God's people by leading the Church in a ministry to the holistic needs of Black people both within the Church family and beyond."

BIBLIOGRAPHY

De Jong, Gerald Francis. "The Dutch Reformed Church and Negro Slavery in Colonial America." *Church History* 40:1 (March 1971), 423–436.

Erskine, Noel Leo. *Black People and the Reformed Church in America.* Lansing, Mich., 1978.

Smith, George L. *Religion and Trade in New Netherland.* Ithaca, N.Y., 1973.

– NOEL LEO ERSKINE

REGGAE

A type of popular music that originated in Jamaica and became successful worldwide, reggae is characterized by a loping yet insistent bass rhythm. Performed largely by black musicians, reggae's appeal in America has traditionally been colorblind, finding favor originally with white listeners and then, more recently, with a core black audience.

Origins

Besides such local musical influences as calypso and mento, reggae has roots in American rhythm and blues, particularly those records made in New Orleans in the 1950s, which Jamaicans enjoyed via U. S. radio broadcasts and on "sound systems," mobile discos where records were played for dancing. To satisfy local demand, competitive sound system promoters such as Duke Reid and Clement Dodd began using primitive equipment to cut their own records, featuring island singers and musicians. Regional playing styles worked a kind of musical alchemy: the local musicians' attempts to simulate American R&B repeatedly came out skewed—they accented the second and fourth beats each measure rather than the first and third. The result, however, was no less appealing to island listeners, and the characteristic reggae rhythm was born. On the first records, released in the early 1960s, this rhythm was accelerated and the music was called "ska," after the scratchy guitar sound which propelled the songs. In subsequent years the rhythm grew slower: at medium tempo, it was called "rock steady"; then, finally, at its slowest, "reggae," after the 1968 release "Do the Reggay" by Toots and the Maytals.

Evolution

As in most popular music, the general term "reggae" actually encompasses many different styles. Two of the most distinctive, "dub reggae" and "deejaying" (also called "toasting"), began to flourish in the late 1960s and early '70s and became synonymous with the music, contributing significantly to its subsequent success, particularly in America. "Dub" refers to versions of reggae songs that have been doctored in the recording studio with echo and other sounds, records on which the vocal and instrumental tracks drop in and out suddenly and the booming bass and percussion tracks dominate. Originating on the "B" sides of reggae 45s, dub evolved considerably through the efforts of such innovative producers as Lee Perry and Augustus Pablo, who in primitive recording studios transformed existing songs into unusual aural collages.

Besides such local musical influences as calypso and mento, reggae has roots in American rhythm and blues.

"Toasting," on the other hand, originated live with sound systems, when disk jockeys began to chant boastfully and rhythmically over records to encourage dancers, imitating the staccato chatter of American radio DJs. While remarkably similar to rap music, toasting actually emerged and was recorded years earlier, the specialty of such flamboyant reggae stars as U-Roy and Big Youth. It has even been speculated that records of toasting reggae DJs, played, sold, and heard in the 1970s in American cities with large concentrations of West Indian immigrants (such as New York City) directly influenced the birth of domestic RAP.

The Rastafarian Influence

Paralleling its musical development, certain reggae lyrics began reflecting specific aspects of Jamaican life and culture. By the late 1960s, besides the songs of sex and romance common to all pop music, reggae performers sang about "rude boys" (local street toughs), the harsh lives of the local underclass, and, most notably, the RASTAFARIAN religious sect. Followers of the sect, called Rastas, wore their uncut hair in thick, matted dreadlocks, smoked marijuana as a sacrament, and revered Emperor Haile Selassie of Ethiopia as a god, because of a prediction attributed to back-to-Africa advocate Marcus GARVEY—that a black king, crowned in Africa, would be the Redeemer. Elusively complicated, with roots in mysticism as well as the Bible, Rastafarianism had been present in Jamaica since the 1930s, offering impoverished believers spiritual identity and solace by reaffirming that Africa was their true homeland, and that the captor Babylon (the ruling class or material world) must inevitably fall. Since many Jamaican musicians were Rastafarian, its terminology and beliefs were often incorporated into reggae songs. While uniquely characteristic of the music, reggae's use of Rastafarianism corresponds on a basic level to the message of heavenly deliverance found in American SPIRITUALS, and to the earthly transcendence and catharsis provided by the BLUES.

From Jamaica to the United States

Most of the Americans who discovered reggae in the 1970s were introduced to it in one of two forms. The first, *The Harder They Come,* was a 1972 Jamaican feature film directed by Perry Henzell that starred singer Jimmy Cliff as Ivan Martin, a country boy turned pop star and outlaw. Part comic book and part western, with a percolating reggae sound track, the film found a niche at midnight showings in college towns and art cinemas around the country, where it ran for several years, giving domestic viewers a vibrant first glimpse of the gritty, vibrant world of Jamaican pop. At about the same time, Americans also discovered reggae in the person of Bob Marley and the Wailers. In a career that extended from 1964 until his death from cancer in 1981, Marley was the key individual in the popularization of reggae. Through his many brilliant albums of protest and love songs (including *Catch a Fire, Natty Dread,* and *Exodus*) and his highly charged concert tours, the singer-songwriter became the face, voice, and symbol of reggae for most of the world.

The Changing American Audience

Ironically, reggae's core audience in America was at first comprised largely of white rock fans, who responded to its exoticism, its rocklike drive, and its messages of alienation. They had also heard it first: reggae's earliest inroads beyond Jamaica had been via rock-oriented radio, first in the guise of novelties like the ska song "My Boy Lollipop" or the rock-steady classic "Israelites," hits during the 1960s, and later as audible influences in the work of such premier rock artists as Paul Simon and Eric Clapton. Rock's fascination with reggae reached an apex in the late 1970s, with the international emergence of the new wave-punk rock movement. While many punks voiced solidarity with the inflammatory and apocalyptic aspects of Rastafarianism, reggae's influence was most audible in the new-style rock, which adopted many of its rhythms and recording techniques, especially dub.

In the 1980s and '90s, reggae's black audience in the United States began to increase sizably, due in part to the country's escalating West Indian immigrant population and also to a growing interest in the Afrocentric ideals the music often expresses and reflects. But the primary reason for reggae's catching on with African-American listeners is a musical one: the dominance on the charts of "dancehall style," fast-talking toasting that rose concurrently and intersects considerably with rap music, spawning such intercultural stars as Shabba Ranks.

As reggae's audience shifts and grows, developments in the music have paralleled those in other forms of pop—traditional instrumentation, for instance, has been increasingly replaced by electronic keyboards and percussion. Nevertheless, reggae's widespread popularity in America seems secure, buoyed by the growing interest in all international musics (called "World Beat") that it anticipated.

BIBLIOGRAPHY

Davis, Stephen, and Peter Simon. *Reggae Bloodlines.* New York, 1979.

———. *Reggae International.* New York, 1982.

Thomas, Michael. "Reggae: The Wild Side of Paradise." In *What's That Sound?* New York, 1976, pp. 326–350.

Ward, Ed. "Reggae." In *The Rolling Stone Illustrated History of Rock & Roll.* New York, 1980, pp. 445–450.

– BUD KLIMENT

RELIGION

Carter G. WOODSON, founder of the Association for the Study of Negro Life and History, wrote in 1939: "A definitive history of the Negro Church . . . would leave practically no phase of the history of the Negro in America untouched." Understanding African-American religion—or more accurately, the religious history of peoples of African descent in North America—is crucial for any rounded view of the African-American experience. Religion is often inseparable from culture, as was the case in traditional Africa, and encompasses more than institutional expressions. B. B. King once said that he felt closest to God when he was singing the BLUES, and African-American art, dance, and literature incorporate and reflect symbols, values, and themes. This essay will focus primarily on some of the principal issues in the study of African-American religious history and culture.

Early historical work on African-American religion, such as that of Carter G. Woodson on "the Negro Church," focused almost exclusively on the institutional history of Protestantism. Yet to view African-American religious history as merely another chapter in the expansion of European Christianity would be to ignore the special circumstances of the religious pilgrimage of African Americans and gloss over the impact of other religious traditions.

Slave Religion

Most Africans who were brought into the colonies of British North America originated from the coast and interior of West and West-Central Africa. Approximately 60 percent of the slaves imported into the territory later known as the United States arrived between 1720 and 1780. Legal United States involvement in the international SLAVE TRADE ended in 1808. Unlike what occurred in much of the New World, the growth of the slave population in the American South was largely by natural increase, and the end of the slave trade did little to retard the increase of the African-American population. In 1825 the United States had approximately 36 percent (1,750,000) of the slave population in the New World, despite the dramatic increase in the arrival of new imports. For many slaves, knowledge of AFRICA was acquired indirectly and was only one of many cultural influences. Therefore, an understanding of the formative influences on the religious experience of African Americans, while recognizing the importance of the African cultural base, must take into account the New World cultural experience. The formation of an African-American culture was a long historical process, an evolution over time.

Understanding African-American religion is crucial for any rounded view of the African-American experience.

Close examination reveals that differences within African-American religious culture are as important as similarities. The religious outlook of someone of African descent in the low country of Carolina and Georgia about 1710, before the impact of the Great Awakening, might understandably be different from that of someone subject to the religious instruction of a white Presbyterian clergyman active in organized plantation missions after 1829. The religious profiles of a member of the Mother Bethel African Methodist Church in Philadelphia in 1880, a communicant of St. Cyprian's Roman Catholic Church in Chicago in 1924, of Zion Baptist Church in rural Mississippi in 1954, and of the Pentacostal C.H. Mason Temple in Memphis today will have significant differences. Generalizations about African-American religion must account for changes over time, geographic variables, and differing population demographics.

Regional geography is an important qualifying factor in understanding the uniqueness of the African-American religious experience in the United States. *Vaudou* in Haiti, the Trinidadian cult of *Shango,* the practices of *santeria* in Cuba, and the *candomble* rituals found in Brazil exemplify a high degree of syncretism between West African traditions and Euro-Christian, principally ROMAN CATHOLIC, culture. In contrast, Africans who

HOLINESS MOVEMENT, and thereby served as a precursor for the many women who found the freedom to develop their own ministries within the orbit of the burgeoning Pentecostal and Holiness movement, which flourished in the "sanctified" storefronts of the urban North. For example, Elder Lucy Smith (1874–1952) founded All Nations Pentecostal Church in Chicago and conducted a multidimensional ministry that dealt with the material as well as the spiritual needs of her members.

Closed out of male-dominated ecclesiastical centers of power, African-American women developed auxiliary organizations. The Women's Parent Mite Missionary Society of the AME Church, founded in 1874, supported new churches in western United States and in South Africa. Baptist women led by Nannie Helen Burroughs formed the Women's Convention of the National Baptist Convention in 1900 and operated the National School for Girls in Washington. Many of these church women were also active in the club movement, which stressed self-help and charitable and civic work, and served as a focal point for women's independent identity. Beset by racism in the larger society and confronted by patriarchal attitudes within their denominations, African-American church women had to confront multiple challenges. They played an especially important role in bringing the gap between church work as traditionally defined and secular reform activity. The demands upon them intensified with the outbreak of World War I.

The centrality of women in the local congregation became all the more apparent because of external social forces in the flight from field to factory once the call for labor went out from the North. After 1910, in the early years of the Great Migration, males, particularly young males, went north lured by the promise of better jobs. Women and the young were left to carry on congregational life. Urbanization proved to be no panacea. Indeed, in poor urban areas, church adherence was increasingly the sphere of women and children. This is especially true of the independent churches, known as "storefronts." In an extensive study done in the 1980s, researchers found that in 2,150 black churches, of various denominations, women outnumbered men by a factor of 2.5 to 1. Some observers have spoken of the "feminization of the black church" because of the relative absence of males, especially young males, in urban congregations. Whether or not the disproportionate representation of females in contemporary black churches is principally a result of the urbanization of African Americans is yet to be determined. It is clear, however, that the gender question is one that black Christians, regardless of denominational affiliation, have yet to fully and adequately address.

The urbanization of African-American religion precipitated an institutional crisis in the existing black churches. In 1910 nearly 90 percent of the nation's black population lived in the South, mostly in rural regions and small towns. Since the end of the Civil War,

A river baptism in Aiken, S.C., in the early years of the twentieth century. For many African Americans, no life ceremony had so much significance as baptism. (Prints and Photographs Division, Library of Congress)

the church had assumed a dominant position in the life of southern blacks, whose institutional development in other areas was restricted by racial apartheid. By default, then, the churches served multiple purposes—worship, education, recreation, and socialization. Northern black leaders, as well as some Southern leaders (e.g., Booker T. Washington) pointed to such problems as overchurching, undereducated ministers, pastors with multiple charges, congregations too small to adequately maintain programs and property, too little emphasis on the social and political problems of the day. Carter G. Woodson referred to rural churches as "mystic shrines" while writing approvingly of northern urban churches as progressive centers of "social uplift." This debate over the mission of the black church was heightened by the Great Migration because it placed new demands upon existing denominational and local church resources and programs.

The population shift put severe strains upon existing denominational structures. Home missionary boards lacked adequate resources to cope with the need in the North, and congregations in the South were left depleted and deserted. Competition among the three major black Methodist bodies prevented a cooperative effort in addressing the needs of the migrants. The National Baptist Convention, U.S.A., Inc., underwent a contentious division in 1915, which resulted in the formation of a rival body, the National Baptist Convention of America Unincorporated, later named National Baptist Convention of America in 1916. The internecine war continued for years, draining away critically needed resources. The secretary of the Home Mission Board of the National Baptist Convention, U.S.A., Inc., reported in 1921: "We have quite a number of destitute fields both North and South and in many cases no opportunity for religious worship."

The regional shift in America's black population portended difficulties because as WORLD WAR I began the black denominations were heavily weighted to the South. In 1916 the U.S. Census of Religious Bodies credited the National Baptists with 2,939,579 members, 89 percent of whom were in the South. The AME Church had 548,355 members and was 81.2 percent southern. The AMEZ Church was 84.6 percent southern with a total membership of 257,169. The CME Church, composed principally of the descendants of ex-slaves, was 95.5 percent southern and 245,749 members strong. None of the Pentecostal or Holiness bodies, which became so important in the urban North after the Great Migration, receive recognition in the 1916 religious census.

In addition to placing strains upon ecclesiastical structures inherited from the nineteenth century and oriented primarily toward the small town and rural church, urbanization offered African Americans new religious options. Baptist and Methodist preachers now had to compete with the agents of the Pentecostal and Holiness churches. These churches played against great emphasis on an intense personal experience of the Holy Spirit. The Church of God in Christ, led by Charles Harrison Mason, held its first Pentecostal general assembly in 1907; having started as a rural church in Mississippi, the denomination grew to become a fixture in the northern city. Ill at ease in the more formal worship services of the established northern churches, many migrants organized prayer bands, started house churches, or moved into the storefronts where speaking in tongues (sometimes referred to as the practice of glossolalia) received the blessing of the Pentecostals. The Church of Christ (Holiness), U.S.A., under the leadership of Elder C. P. Jones, likewise expanded as a result of the burgeoning black populations of urban industrial America. Other Holiness and Pentecostal churches were founded by denominationally-independent religious entrepreneurs who recognized that the migrants from the South desired something that the northern black middle-class churches did not offer.

Many of the migrants wanted religious environments that reminded them of their churches back home, where they were known by name and part of an extended family. The ecstatic worship services and musical styles favored by the Pentecostal and Holiness preachers caught the attention of these ex-Southerners. When hard times befell them in the North, migrants sought out spiritual havens in the urban wilderness. Holiness and Pentecostal churches multiplied everywhere, and existing Baptist and Methodist churches split or sponsored daughter congregations as the migrant population swelled. On occasion, northern black Christians criticized their "brothers and sisters" from the South for falling short of northern cultural expectations and the existing class norms. In turn, migrants shunned some northern black churches, where the elaborate and elegant services made them feel out of place. Some fell away from organized religion all together. Others responded to their crisis of faith in the city by transplanting churches from the South led by the pastors who had followed them northward.

The tension between the two cultural streams that came together after the beginning of World War I is illustrated by the reluctance of the older African-American congregations in Chicago to readily accept GOSPEL music. Gospel music was popularized by Thomas DORSEY, the "father of gospel music," who joined Pilgrim Baptist Church in Chicago in 1921. Unlike the purveyors of commercialized gospel today, early gospel music was church centered. Yet as Mahalia JACKSON, the best-known singer of gospel, learned while growing up in New Orleans, the musical distance between the honky-tonk and a Holiness revival with its beating and tambourine shaking is not that great. Dorsey, building on the work of predecessors such as Charles Albert Tindley, was the principal force behind the introduction of blues-like gospel songs into the northern black churches. About 1930, observers of the Chicago scene reported that "Negro churches, particularly the storefront congregations, the Sanctified groups and the shouting Baptists, were swaying and jumping as never before. Mighty rhythms rocked the churches. A wave of fresh rapture came over the people." Jackson earned worldwide acclamation for her solo renditions of gospel classics, and the pioneering touring groups such as the Dixie Hummingbirds and the Five Blind Boys of Mississippi helped make gospel so popular that today it is rare to find a black church, of whatever denomination or class composition, that closes its doors to the gospel sound.

Religious diversity, even dissonance, resonated from the large, densely crowded, black urban centers after World War I. After examining data from the 1926 Federal Census of Religious Bodies, Miles Mark Fisher exclaimed: "Almost in every center, particularly urban, is some unorthodox religious group which makes a definite appeal to Negroes." The Jamaican-born black nationalist Marcus GARVEY discouraged talk of founding a new church, but he and his UNIVERSAL NEGRO IMPROVEMENT ASSOCIATION (1918–1927) had many followers who sought collective redemption in the back-to-Africa ideology. There were also some supporters, such as George Alexander Mcguire, the founder of the African Orthodox Church, who did initiate Garveyite-inspired demonstrations. The UNIA collapsed after the deportation of its "Black Moses" in 1927, but other charismatic personalities came forward offering often exotic visions of heaven on earth. FATHER DIVINE set up a series of Peace Missions during the Great Depression, offering his devotees the unusual mix of "God" in the flesh and a refuge from society's problems. Scores of religious entrepreneurs opened shop in the black ghettos, where they competed with the mainline denominations. Frequently referred to as cults and sects, the groups led by these new messiahs often died when their founders did, but some managed to survive under different leadership, as, for example, the one led by Daddy Grace (the United House of Prayer for All People). Representatives of the mainline churches frequently decried the proliferation of these alternative groups, arguing, as the Baptist Miles Mark Fisher did, that the principle message of the cults and sects was "Let us prey," not "Let us pray."

The appearance on urban street corners of black adherents of Islam and Judaism added to the perception that African-American religion was undergoing a radical reorientation in the interwar period at the expense of the historic black denominations. The first black Jewish group recognized by the federal religious census was founded in 1896 by William S. Crowdy, a Santa Fe Railroad cook, in Lawrence, Kans. African Americans wearing the yarmulke and speaking Yiddish came to the attention of a wider public in the 1920s. Located primarily in the boroughs of New York City, these teachers of black Hebraism appropriated and adapted the rituals and teachings of Orthodox Judaism. Though never large in number, the followers of Rabbi Arnold Ford and other proponents of Black Judaism generated a great deal of interest among the curious and the skeptical.

ISLAM was not entirely unheard of among African Americans before the mysterious figure of W. D. FARD appeared in the "Paradise Valley" of Detroit in 1930 to wake up the sleeping "Lost-Found Nation of Islam." There is increasing evidence that a small but not insignificant number of enslaved Africans brought knowledge of the Koran and Islamic law to North America. But modern Islam among African Americans begins with the career of Noble Drew Ali, a native of North Carolina and founder of Moorish Science in Newark, N.J., about 1913. However, the man who most popularized Islam for African Americans, was the one-time disciple of Wallace Fard, Elijah MUHAMMAD, who capitalized on the interest of urbanized blacks in the religiously exotic. Himself a migrant from Georgia, Muhammad (formerly Elijah Poole) assumed leadership of the NATION OF ISLAM after Fard's disappearance in 1934 and moved its headquarters to Chicago. The Nation's version of Islam did not fare well under the scrutiny of orthodox scholars of the Koran, and eventually the sect broke into rival factions. Nevertheless, it has had a significant impact upon many African Americans, chiefly the young and angry like MALCOLM X who believed that traditional black Christianity was a "pie-in-the-sky" religion.

Attention to the new religious options that appeared in black urban America during the period between World War I and World War II should not be at the expense of the story of the mainline black churches. Stimulated by the crisis brought about by the influx of thousands from the South, the established churches struggled with a redefinition of mission during these decades. Richard R. WRIGHT, Jr., examined the record of black church involvement within the public sphere in 1907 and concluded that only a few churches had "attacked the problems of real city Negroes." His own work in Chicago's Institutional Church and Social Settlement, founded by Reverdy Ransom, and later at Chicago's Trinity Mission and Culture Center, which Wright organized in 1905, convinced Wright that black churches needed a more compelling definition of urban mission than presently at hand. Prior to World War I, outreach primarily involved mission and charity work with the intent of recruiting new members. As Wright and Ransom discovered for themselves, pastors who addressed contemporary social problems born of urban and industrial growth were deemed too radical by denominational officials.

Attention to the new religious options that appeared in black urban America between World War I and World War II should not be at the expense of the story of the mainline black churches.

Most black preachers, urban and rural, still thought of sin and salvation in individualistic terms. The black denominations lagged behind their white counterparts in adopting the theological message of the Social Gospel movement with its focus upon the problems of urban America. Beginning with the era of the Great Migration, however, many more black churches incorporated programs into their understanding of "church work" that went beyond the traditional emphasis on praying and preaching. They assisted with needs in housing, employment, education, recreation, and health care. The instrumentalist use of the church to better the community is today so widely accepted that black clergy or congregations who show no interest in everyday problems have little appeal or credibility among African Americans.

Although black denominations were spared the bitter internecine battles that erupted in the 1920s between the white fundamentalists and modernists over such issues as the interpretation of the Creation story in Genesis, their efforts to merge have failed. Concerned about institutional inefficiency and lost oppportunities to influence the larger society and motivated by the ideal that Christ's church be one, representatives of the three principal branches of black Methodism began meetings in 1915 to discuss the possibility of merger. But leaders of the CME church (formerly the Colored Methodist Episcopal church and since 1954 the CHRISTIAN METHODIST EPISCOPAL CHURCH), balked at union because of fears of being dominated by the two larger northern black Methodist bodies: the AME and the AMEZ churches. Division among black Methodists was widened by the segregation of 315,000 in the Central Jurisdiction, a nongeographical entity, of the predominantly white United Methodist Church in 1939 after the merger of the northern and southern branches of Methodism (the segregated structure was abolished in the 1960s). Black Baptists likewise have been unable to heal the divisions within their ranks. The National Baptist Convention, U.S.A., Inc., remains the largest of all black church connections, claiming about 7.5 million members and 30,000 local churches in the late-1980s.

The contemporary black Baptist story is still best told in terms of the local congregation. Ministerial alliances at the local level have fostered interdenominational cooperation where there has been sufficient need for common action. In many congregations, the minister is still the dominant personality. Critics have argued that the domineering role played by the pastor in black congregations has retarded the development of lay leadership. The preeminence of the black minister in African-American religious culture has historical roots. Because of the class and caste attitudes of whites in the South, the ministery remained one of the few professions accessible to blacks. Even in the North, where political boundaries were defined by patterns of residential segregation and black political participation was restricted, black ministers were called upon to speak for their community before local authorities. Participation in electoral and protest politics has engaged the energies of many contemporary black clergy, but they have had to divide their time between their civic roles and their pastoral roles.

Civil Rights Era to the Present

The internal life of African-American churches probably escaped the attention of most of white America until the Rev. Dr. Martin Luther KING, Jr., began to catch the eye and ear of the news media. Rooted deep in the black Baptist tradition, King was schooled in the preaching tradition of the black church of the South. While doing advanced theological training in the North, he became proficient in the major currents of thought among liberal, socially aware Protestants. This made it possible for him to appeal to the conscience of white America during the civil rights struggle and to enlist the aid of allies from the more liberal white denominations. Yet the grassroots participation of thousands of black churchgoers who marched and sang and prayed transformed King's protest of racial segregation in Montgomery, Ala., into a mass movement. From the

of black elected officials in the United States identified themselves as Republicans, including one member of Congress, four state legislators, and five mayors.

BIBLIOGRAPHY

Bositis, David. *Blacks and the 1992 Republican National Convention.* Washington, D.C., 1992.

Burk, Robert Fredrick. *The Eisenhower Administration and Black Civil Rights.* Knoxville, Tenn., 1984.

Kousser, J. Morgan. *The Shaping of Southern Politics: Suffrage Restriction and the Establishment of the One-Party South, 1880–1910.* New Haven, Conn., 1974.

Lewinson, Paul. *Race, Class, and Party: A History of Negro Suffrage and White Politics in the South.* 1932. Rev. ed. New York, 1965.

Sherman, Richard B. *The Republican Party and Black America: From McKinley to Hoover, 1896–1933.* Charlottesville, Va., 1973.

Weiss, Nancy J. *Farewell to the Party of Lincoln: Black Politics in the Age of FDR.* Princeton, N.J., 1983.

– NANCY J. WEISS

RHYTHM AND BLUES

The term *rhythm and blues* was a product of the post-World War II music industry's effort to find a new word to replace the category that had been known for several decades as "race records." First used by *Billboard* magazine in 1949, rhythm and blues was intended to describe blues and dance music produced by black musicians for black listeners, so that rhythm and blues—often abbreviated to R&B—was more a marketing category than a well-defined musical style. In effect, R&B reflected the confluence of JAZZ, BLUES, GOSPEL, and vocal harmony group music that took place in cities such as New York, Detroit, Chicago, Memphis, Philadelphia, and New Orleans after World War II. In the 1950s successful marketing efforts that targeted white listeners made rhythm and blues, and the related category of rock and roll, the most popular music not only in the United States but in the rest of the world as well. Although much rhythm and blues music was produced by small, white-owned record labels such as Savoy, Atlantic, and Chess—in the 1960s MOTOWN would be an exception—and was aimed at a multiracial market, rhythm and blues has always drawn its core influences from African-American culture.

The Roots of Rhythm and Blues: Jazz

The most obvious ancestor of rhythm and blues was jazz, which in the 1920s and '30s was black America's popular music, produced mostly to accompany dancing. In the 1940s many big bands featured "honking" tenor saxophonists who played in a bluesy, at times histrionic style that drove dancers to ever more frenzied steps and tempos. Lionel HAMPTON's "Flyin' Home" (1943), with its famous solo by Illinois Jacquet (1922–), was the model for such performances. Many tenor saxophonists followed Jacquet's model, including Bill Doggett (1916–), Arnett Cobb (1918–1989), Ike Quebec (1918–1963), Hal "Cornbread" Singer (1919–), and Willis "Gatortail" Jackson (1928–1987). Important recordings in this style include "Juice Head Baby" (1944) and "Deacon's Hop" (1948) by Big Jay McNeely (1929–) and "The Hucklebuck" (1949) by Paul Williams.

R&B reflected the confluence of jazz, blues, gospel, and vocal harmony group music that took place in cities such as New York, Detroit, Chicago, Memphis, Philadelphia, and New Orleans.

Another jazz influence on rhythm and blues was the jump bands that were popular starting in the mid-1940s. These midsized ensembles, named for their buoyant tempos, combined the extroverted solo style of the honking tenors with the relentless momentum of shuffle and boogie-woogie rhythms of pianists Albert Ammons, Meade "Lux" Lewis, and Pete Johnson (1904–1967), whose "Roll 'Em Pete" (1938) with vocalist Big Joe Turner was one of the first great rhythm-and-blues performances. Tiny Bradshaw (1905–1958), Slim Gaillard (1916–1991), and Johnny Otis (1921–1984), the latter a white musician whose bands were largely black, all led jump ensembles. The greatest of the jump band leaders was saxophonist and vocalist Louis Jordan. His biggest hits, including "Is You Is or Is You Ain't My Baby?" (1944), "Let the Good Times Roll" (1945), "Caldonia" (1945),"Choo Choo Ch'Boogie" (1946), and "Saturday Night Fish Fry" (1940), were novelty numbers suffused with earthy humor. Jordan was a masterful saxophonist in the jazz tradition, yet most of his records were carefully composed, and his rejection of jazz improvisation became a major characteristic of rhythm and blues.

In the late 1950s and '60s, the relationship between jazz and rhythm and blues was sometimes reversed, with musicians—especially the pianist Horace Silver, who recorded "Opus de Funk" in 1953—drawing inspiration from rhythm and blues. In the 1960s, Jimmy Smith (1925–), Cannonball Adderley, David "Fathead" Newman (1933–), Eddie Harris (1934–), King Curtis (1934–1971), Stanley Turrentine (1934–), and Ramsey Lewis (1935–) all performed in the bluesy, funky style known as soul jazz. Herbie Hancock, a groundbreaking avant-garde jazz pianist in the 1960s, went on to experiment with funk music in the 1970s and rap in the '80s.

Vocal Groups

The vocal harmonizing groups of the 1940s helped develop the heavily rhythmic backing of passionate vocals that characterize rhythm and blues. Some of these groups were called "doo-wop" groups, after the wordless, nonsense-syllable accompaniments they often sang. The Ink Spots, formed in 1934, were among the earliest important rhythm-and-blues vocal groups, although the group's smooth approach on songs such as "If I Didn't Care" (1939), "To Each His Own" (1946), and "The Gypsy" (1946) was less influential in the development of rhythm and blues than the more heavily rhythmic performances of the Mills Brothers, who had hits with "Paper Doll" (1942) and "You Always Hurt the One You Love" (1944).

After World War II, dozens of important vocal groups, starting with the "bird groups," drew heavily from the gospel tradition and dominated black popular music. Groups such as the Ravens ("Ol' Man River," 1946), the Orioles ("Crying in the Chapel," 1953), The Platters ("Only You," 1955, "The Great Pretender," 1956), the Dominoes ("Sixty Minute Man," 1951), and the Clovers ("Fool, Fool, Fool," 1951; "Good Lovin'," 1953; and "Love Potion Number Nine," 1959), and the 5 Satins ("In the Still of the Night," 1956) used simple arrangements and minimal instrumental accompaniment to highlight their passionate, gospel-style vocals. The Penguins ("Earth Angel," 1954) were notable for their juxtaposition of high falsetto with deep bass voices. The Coasters had a more raucous and humorous style than other doo-wop groups, evidenced on "Riot in Cell Block No. 9" (1954) and "Charlie Brown" (1959). The Drifters were hugely popular throughout the 1950s and early '60s ("Money Honey," 1953; "Save the Last Dance for Me," 1960; "Up on the Roof," 1962; "On Broadway," 1963; and "Under the Boardwalk," 1964).

In the 1950s and '60s impromptu, street-corner doo-wop-style singing was an essential part of African-American urban life. Solo rhythm-and-blues singers who drew on gospel, vocal harmony, and doo-wop traditions were among the most popular recording artists of the era. An early member of the Drifters, Clyde Mcphatter, topped the R&B and pop charts with "Without Love" (1956), "Long Lonely Nights" (1957), and "A Lover's Question" (1958). Jackie Wilson, another falsetto tenor and Drifters' alumnus, had a huge following for his "To Be Loved" (1958), "Lonely Teardrops" (1958), and "Higher and Higher" (1959). Ben E. King (1938–) also worked with the Drifters before recording "Spanish Harlem" (1960) and "Stand by Me" (1960). Frankie Lymon (1942–1968) and the Teenagers achieved great popularity with songs such as "Why Do Fools Fall in Love?" (1956), "The ABCs of Love" (1956), and "I'm Not a Juvenile Delinquent" (1956). A doo-wop group that came to prominence relatively late was Little Anthony Gourdine (1940–) and the Imperials, whose "Tears on My Pillow" was a hit record in 1958.

Gospel music was a direct influence on many important R&B singers. Sam Cooke sang gospel with the Soul Stirrers starting in 1950 and eventually recorded such secular songs as "You Send Me" (1957), "Chain Gang" (1960), and "Another Saturday Night" (1963). Solomon Burke (1936–), who recorded "Just Out of Reach" (1960) and "Got to Get You off My Mind" (1965), also sang in a gospel-influenced R&B style. The vocals and even the themes of Curtis Mayfield and the Impressions' "I'm So Proud" (1964) and "People Get Ready" (1965) both have strong connections to black sacred music. Al Green, a child gospel sensation later known for soul recordings such as "Let's Stay Together" (1972) and "Take Me to the River" (1973), returned to the church in the late 1970s and has since concentrated solely on gospel music.

Blues

The urban blues styles of the late 1940s and early '50s, with loud, amplified guitars, anguished vocals, and churning rhythms, are also direct descendants of rhythm and blues. Perhaps the best examples of this influence are Muddy Waters, Howlin' Wolf, and B. B. King, all of whom were prominent on the rhythm and blues charts in the 1950s. Bo diddley ("Who Do You Love," 1955; "Bo Diddley," 1955, "I'm a Man," 1955) and Screamin' Jay Hawkins (1929–), who had a 1956 hit with "I Put a Spell on You," represent a less pure blues style that was nonetheless equally influential in creating rhythm and blues. Big Joe Turner, whose "Roll 'Em Pete" with pianist Pete Johnson is considered one of the founding songs of rhythm and blues, was known in the 1950s for his shouting renditions of "Chains of Love" (1951) and "Shake, Rattle and Roll" (1954), both of which are considered classic examples of a time when rock and roll was virtually synonymous with rhythm and blues. Another early rhythm and blues figure was Arthur "Big Boy" Crudup (1905–1974), a guitarist and singer who was popular throughout the 1940s but was best known for writing "That's All Right" (1946), which became a hit for Elvis Presley in 1954.

Along with the Chicago blues style, a different kind of blues, at once more derived from jazz and country music but with the same reliance on electric instruments, exerted a strong influence on early rhythm and blues. T-bone Walker, a singer and guitarist who successfully negotiated the boundary between blues and jazz on "Stormy Monday" (1945), had several hit rhythm and blues-influenced records in the early 1950s, including "Strolling with Bones" (1950) and "Street Walkin' Woman" (1951). Wynonie Harris (1915–1969), a blues shouter with a strong Louis Jordan influence, wrote "Good Rocking Tonight" and had several hits in the mid-1940s. A mellower approach was represented by Roy Brown (1925–1981), Amos Milburn (1926–1980), and Lowell Fulson (1921–), whose "Every Day I Have the Blues" (1950) later became B. B. King's signature tune.

An even more restrained, elegant blues vocal style, used by the "Sepia Sinatras," also gained a large following among rhythm and blues audiences in the 1940s and '50s. Nat "King" COLE started out as a jazz pianist but achieved his greatest acclaim as a singer, starting in 1950 with "Mona Lisa." Other singers in this genre included Cecil Gant (1915–1951) and Charles Brown (1922–).

Ray CHARLES is often grouped with blues singers, but his synthesis of many early rhythm and blues influences, in particular the melding of sacred and secular black music traditions, is unique. Starting in the mid-1950s, he combined a smooth, almost country singing style on ballads with infectious gospel inflection and solid jazz rhythms on both slow and up-tempo numbers, including "I Got a Woman" (1955), "Drown in My Tears" (1955), "What'd I Say?" (1959), "Georgia on My Mind" (1960), and "Hit the Road, Jack" (1961).

Female blues singers often landed on the rhythm and blues charts in the 1950s. Ruth Brown (1928–), who worked with Lucky Millinder (1900–1966) and Blanche Calloway (1902–1978) in the late 1940s, sang in a jump blues style on "Teardrops from My Eyes" (1950), "Mama He Treats Your Daughter Mean" (1952), and "Wild Wild Young Men" (1954). LaVern Baker (1928–), a niece of the blues singer Memphis Minnie, recorded "Jim Dandy" (1956) and "I Cried a Tear" (1958), both of which were hits on the R&B chart. Etta James, who sang blues on Chess Records, recorded "Something's Got a Hold on Me" in 1962, a song that made her reputation in a rhythm and blues vein. Dinah Washington had considerable success as a jazz singer before entering the rhythm and blues market with records such as "Baby Get Lost" (1949). Washington later crossed over into the pop field with the ballad "What a Difference a Day Makes" (1959).

New Orleans rhythm and blues almost constitutes its own genre, no doubt because of the city's unique confluence of African-American and creole cultures. Fats Domino, whose first hit was "The Fat Man" (1949), became an archetypal crossover success, whose gently rocking voice and piano playing on "Ain't That a Shame" (1955), "Blueberry Hill" (1956), "I'm Walkin' " (1957), "I Hear You Knockin' " (1958), and "I'm Ready" (1959) appealed to a large white audience. Other important New Orleans rhythm and blues musicians include Dave Bartholomew (1920–), Huey "Piano" Smith (1934–), Allen Toussaint (1938–), the Meters, Irma Thomas (1941–), and the Neville Brothers.

Rock and Roll

In the early 1950s, rock and roll—originally a euphemism for sex—was virtually synonymous with rhythm and blues. By the mid-1950s, as more and more white teenagers began to listen to rhythm and blues, the scope of the term *rock and roll* expanded and was primarily applied to white musicians such as Elvis Presley, Buddy Holly (1936–1959), Roy Orbison (1936–1988), or Bill Haley (1925–1981), whose music copied aspects of rhythm and blues styles but was aimed at white audiences. However, black musicians remained crucial to the development of rock and roll even after the term was being applied mostly to white musicians. Chuck Berry, whose country-influenced, bluesy tunes were extraordinarily successful with white audiences, exemplified the adolescent themes, rebellious sound and look, and aggressive guitar playing of early rock and roll. His "Maybellene" (1955), "Johnny B. Goode" (1958), and "Sweet Little Sixteen" (1958) became rock standards almost immediately. This was also true of Little Richard, whose "Tutti Frutti" (1955), "Long Tall Sally" (1956), and "Good Golly Miss Molly" (1958) brought to early rock and roll a frenetic, updated version of New Orleans piano styles. Chuck Berry and Little Richard were enormously influential in England. In fact, the biggest rock groups of the 1960s, including the Beatles and the Rolling Stones, rebelled against the bland, staid sounds of white pop-rockers like Pat Boone and Paul Anka and began their careers by performing mostly cover versions of black rock-and-roll songs. Other rhythm-and-blues musicians who played an important role in the development of rock and roll include Junior Parker (1927–1971), who recorded "Mystery Train" (1953), "Next Time You See Me" (1957), and "Sweet Home Chicago" (1958), as well as Ike Turner (1931–), Jackie Brenston (1930–1979), Big Mama Thornton ("Hound Dog," 1953), the Isley Brothers ("Shout," 1959; "Twist and Shout," 1962), and Chubby Checker ("The Twist," 1960). During the late 1960s, relatively few black musicians remained involved in rock and roll, notable exceptions being Richie Havens-

and Jimi HENDRIX, who had performed as an accompanist with Little Richard, the Isley Brothers, and Ike and Tina Turner before leading a popular rock ensemble.

Soul

By 1964 black popular music had acquired a new name: soul music. There is no clear chronological or stylistic division between rhythm and blues and soul music, but there are some important differences. Soul music displayed a more pronounced gospel influence, whether in up-tempo, unrestrained shouting or in slower, more plaintive styles. Furthermore, soul's general rejection of extended instrumental soloing marked the continuing retreat of jazz as the popular music of the black middle class. Finally, even though most soul music consisted of solo singing with vocal backgrounds, the influence of carefully arranged close harmonies also waned.

It is no coincidence that soul flourished alongside the black pride movement. The music was made almost exclusively by blacks, at first almost exclusively for blacks, and was part of a rising black middle-class culture that celebrated black values and black styles in hair and clothing. In addition, soul's secular stance allowed the music to directly confront political issues central to African-American culture in the 1960s. James BROWN, who had been a successful recording artist throughout the 1950s and achieved great popularity in the '60s with live performances and recordings of songs such as "I Got You" (1965) and "I Feel Good" (1965), forever linked soul music and the Black Power Movement with "Say It Loud, I'm Black and Proud" (1968).

Little Richard brought a unique sense of hectic abandon and propulsion to the rock and roll of the 1950s. Despite a highly eccentric personal style, in time he was accepted as one of the great figures of American popular entertainment. Here, in 1990, he celebrates after being awarded a star in Hollywood's Walk of Fame. (AP/Wide World Photos)

Two record companies, Atlantic and Motown, dominated the soul-style rhythm and blues markets starting in the late 1950s and defined two major approaches. Atlantic and its Stax subsidiary often concentrated on funky instrumentals. Wilson Pickett sang with a thrilling gospel feeling on songs such as "In the Midnight Hour" (1965) and "Mustang Sally" (1966). Otis REDDING's brief career included "These Arms of Mine" (1962), "I've Been Loving You Too Long" (1965), "Try a Little Tenderness" (1966), and "Sittin' on the Dock of the Bay" (1967). Ballad singer Percy Sledge (1941–) recorded "When a Man Loves a Woman" (1966) for Stax. Sam and Dave specialized in energetic, shouting vocals on hits such as "Hold On, I'm Coming" (1966), "Soul Man" (1967), and "I Thank You" (1968). Booker T. Jones (1944–) and the MG's personified the Memphis rhythm and blues sound on their instrumental hits for the Stax label, including "Green Onions" (1962) and "Hip Hug-Her" (1967). Aretha FRANKLIN reached her prime at Atlantic in the mid-1960s, when her white producer, Jerry Wexler (1917–), encouraged her to return to her gospel roots. She responded by creating perhaps the defining performances of the soul genre. Her majestic, emotional voice made songs such as "I Never Loved a Man the Way I Love You" (1967), "Respect" (1967), "Chain of Fools" (1967), and "Think" (1968) bona fide soul masterpieces.

If Stax and Atlantic musicians cultivated a funky, gritty sound, the founder of Motown, Berry Gordy, encouraged a sweeter sound, one that came to represent the classic soul sound even more than Atlantic or Stax. Those efforts produced dozens of hits during Motown's peak years in the 1960s by figures such as Marvin Gaye, Stevie WONDER, Mary Wells, and Gladys Knight. Important vocal groups included Smokey robinson and the Miracles, the Jacksons, The Four Tops, The Temptations, and THE SUPREMES.

Atlantic and Motown were by no means the only producers of soul music. Aside from James Brown, perhaps the most important, independent soul musicians of the 1960s were Tina Turner and her husband, Ike Turner, who had led his own groups and backed the blues guitarist Elmore James in the early 1950s. The duo had a string of influential hits in the 1960s, including "A Fool in Love" (1960), "It's Gonna Work Out Fine" (1961), and "River Deep, Mountain High" (1966).

In the 1970s, soul-style vocal groups remained popular, although the high lead vocals of the early vocal-harmony groups were backed with sleek, electrified rhythms. These groups included the Chi-Lites, the Stylistics, Harold Melvin (1941–) and the Bluenotes, the O'Jays, Earth, Wind and Fire, and the Spinners. Solo singers in the soul idiom in the 1970s included Roberta Flack, Barry White (1944–), Al Green, and Teddy Pendergrass (1950–), all of whom created slow, emotional ballads and love songs. In the 1980s and '90s, Whitney Houston (1963–) and Luther Vandross (1951–) have continued the tradition of the gospel-influenced singing style that characterizes soul.

Funk

In the mid-to-late 1960s a new style known as "funk," derived from the black vernacular term for anything with a coarse, earthy smell, began to dominate the rhythm and blues charts. James Brown, who had been so influential in the 1950s and early '60s in pioneering soul music, once again broke new ground, this time with stripped-down, forceful rhythms and simple, melodic riffs on "Papa's Got a Brand New Bag" (1965). This style was picked up by Sly Stone on "Dance to the Music" (1968), "Everyday People" (1968), "Hot Fun in the Summertime" (1969), and by George Clinton's work with his groups Parliament and Funkadelic in the 1970s. Other R&B musicians who adopted the funk style included Isaac Hayes (1938–), who recorded the soundtrack for *Shaft* in 1971, and Curtis Mayfield, who recorded *Super Fly* in 1972. Disco music by 1970s figures such as Donna Summer (1948–), Gloria Gaynor (1949–), Kool and the Gang, and Rick James drew directly on funk's interpretation of rhythm and blues.

Although the category of rhythm and blues, created by white music-industry executives to describe a range of musical styles, has undergone dramatic transformations, the term continues to express the essential characteristics of African-American popular music. In the 1980s and '90s, musicians such as Prince (c. 1958–), Lenny Kravitz (1964–), and Living Color have taken inspiration from Little Richard, James Brown, and Jimi Hendrix, while younger musicians such as the group Boyz II Men have updated the close-harmony vocal ensemble sound of the 1940s and '50s. Black popular music—including funk, rock, rap, and pop-gospel ballads—continues to freely borrow and mix jazz, blues, and gospel, validating rhythm and blues as the common ground of modern African-American popular music.

BIBLIOGRAPHY

George, Nelson. *The Death of Rhythm & Blues.* New York, 1988.

Gillet, Charlie. *The Sound of the City.* New York, 1984.

Gonzalez, Fernando. *Disco-File: The Discographical Catalog of American Rock and Roll and Rhythm and Blues, Vocal Harmony Groups, 1902–1976: Race, Rhythm and Blues.* New York, 1977.

Guaralnick, Peter. *Sweet Soul Music: Rhythm and Blues and the Southern Dream of Freedom.* New York, 1986.

Haralambos, Michael. *Right On: From Blues to Soul in Black America.* New York, 1975.

Shaw, Arnold. *Honkers and Shouters: The Golden Years of Rhythm and Blues.* New York, 1978.

– PETER EISENSTADT AND JONATHAN GILL

RICHMOND, VIRGINIA

Richmond's significance in American history is clear. The city has been the capital of Virginia since 1779; it was the capital of the Confederacy during the CIVIL WAR, and it has been the heart of the "myth of the Lost Cause" ever since. Its centrality to African-American history is less well known but no less important. Over the course of the nineteenth century, both before and after the Civil War, Richmond African Americans created a rich, cohesive community, grounded in industrial labor, from which they launched a series of social movements challenging the local status quo. This community and its evolving tradition of struggle enabled African Americans to survive the difficult years of the first half of the twentieth century and, in the second half of the century, to renew their quest for equal rights and justice.

In 1607, a fort was set up at the headwaters of the James River in the Virginia colony. By the 1670s, a trading post, where slaves were among the products sold, was established. Still, the outpost remained tiny for almost a century. When the town of Richmond was incorporated in 1742, it had only 250 inhabitants. Despite its small size, Richmond's central location made it a political center, and it was the site of two legislative conventions in 1775. Four years later, it became the capital of the state.

African Americans played a considerable role in Richmond's early history. Enslaved blacks, who represented nearly half the town's population and much of its skilled and unskilled labor force, built many of Richmond's houses. During the Revolutionary War, many blacks were put to labor on public projects. In 1781, fifteen slaves employed as ropewalkers fled behind British lines, following the burning of Richmond by British troops. James Lafayette, a plantation slave who had earned his freedom by spying for the Americans, became a respected resident of Richmond.

Following the end of the Revolutionary War Richmond grew steadily in size. Its black population jumped from 468 in 1782 to 2,900 in 1800. SLAVERY flourished in the city, despite the presence of a group of antislavery Quakers. As a result of liberalized manumission laws, the city's free black community grew from 40 to 607 during the same eighteen years. Free blacks (south) lived in integrated areas, and many, such as Mary Lucas and Brazil de Romo, acquired property. The most notable free black was Christopher McPherson, a real estate investor and clerk in the Court of Chancery. Blacks and whites worshipped together at the city's First Baptist Church. However, free blacks were denied voting rights and were subject to numerous petty restrictions—for example, blacks were forbidden to drink and banned from ballplaying, cockfights, and horse races. Legal curbs on both slaves and free blacks accelerated after the discovery in 1800 of Gabriel Prosser's plot for a slave revolt and takeover of Richmond. A skilled blacksmith living outside Richmond, Prosser and his accomplices were executed, but whites remained fearful of slave uprisings.

Richmond African Americans created a cohesive community from which they launched a series of social movements challenging the local status quo.

In the early nineteenth century, as Virginia's soil became depleted and tobacco farming declined, Richmond stagnated. As slavery became unprofitable, the city actually lost one-quarter of its slave population in the 1820s. In 1831, a convention met in the city to discuss abolishing slavery in Virginia, although it quickly disbanded after NAT TURNER'S REBELLION discredited EMANCIPATION efforts.

Beginning in the 1830s, as Richmond became a focal point for railroad traffic, the city was transformed into an industrial and transportation center. While some labor was performed by white immigrants, Richmond was the major urban center for industrial slavery in the antebellum South. Beginning in the 1840s, slaves were employed in large numbers, either through direct ownership or hire, in Richmond's tobacco factories, iron and flour mills (the city had the world's largest flour mill), nearby coal mines and stone quarries; in the construction of buildings, canals, and railroads; and in the hauling, unpacking, and repacking of goods along the city streets and waterways, in warehouses, and on the docks. By the 1850s, half of Richmond's slaves hired their labor, and numerous hiring agencies had emerged to handle the trade.

Tobacco manufacturing was the most labor-intensive industry in antebellum Richmond. Its fifty-two processing plants employed 3,400 slaves in the decade before the Civil War—more than half of all the slaves working in nondomestic labor. The organization of work in these factories left slaves with considerable latitude for decision making. In the chewing and plug segment of the industry, slaves often performed the most skilled work. There were no machines to set the pace. Foremen found work processes regulated by the songs of their operatives and wisely left their cat-o'-nine-tails hanging on the wall. "Overwork" bonuses were used to motivate slaves to exceed production quotas.

The iron industry was second only to tobacco in its reliance on slave labor. It more clearly restricted both the employment and the social lives of its bondsmen, who labored in the larger iron mills such as the famous Tredegar Works, founded in 1836. Only a few slaves held skilled positions; most performed the hot, heavy, and repetitive tasks around the furnaces. Still, employers resorted to "overwork" bonuses, which gave slaves some control over both their pace of work and consumption behavior.

Richmond's other "industry" was the SLAVE TRADE. As Virginia's agricultural sector contracted, "excess" slaves were sold south. Manchester, across the James River, had long been a significant slave market. With the growth of railroad traffic, slave trading became one of the city's most profitable businesses, and Richmond's market became larger than any other city except New Orleans. By 1860, there were thirty-three dealers, private slave jails, and daily slave auctions.

Factory slaves exercised considerable freedom. While many iron workers were housed in company-owned and -controlled "tenements" and enjoyed only limited freedom of movement, so many slaves worked in the tobacco factories that it was uneconomical for their employers to house them. Instead, they were provided with "board money" for lodging and food. They made their own decisions about how to spend or save their "overwork" earnings and "board money."

Slaves in other occupations also enjoyed more autonomy than they would have been allowed in plantation society. Teamsters, boatmen, stevedores, carpenters, plasterers, shoemakers, and barbers chose and controlled much of their work, earning money for themselves as well as their owners. They, too, found their own lodgings and participated in the black community. The systems of "hiring out" and "self-hire" often operated in unskilled as well as skilled work. Building trades laborers, ditch diggers, warehouse laborers, and even domestic servants (female and male) had some experience in bargaining over work conditions and selecting their own residences, spouses, food, and clothing.

The earnings of black workers were central to the development of a vital black community in Richmond. Their sense of independence, empowerment, and exploitation brought a particular cutting edge into the community. Their cash helped to support black boardinghouse keepers, grocers, barbers, tailors, seamstresses, shoemakers, churches, beneficial societies, gamblers, prostitutes, and grogshop owners. Not surprisingly, the dividing lines between slaves and free blacks in antebellum Richmond were frequently vague. Indeed, marriage and kinship, church and beneficial-society membership, and workplace and neighborhood relationships often knitted close bonds between the enslaved and the free.

Two critical social institutions were maintained by—and maintained—Richmond African Americans: the family and the church. These social institutions provided a foundation upon which they built a community that carried them from slavery through Emancipation and into RECONSTRUCTION.

All evidence points to the centrality of family in black life: the naming of children after parents, grandparents, aunts, and uncles; the efforts of free men and women to purchase the freedom of their spouses and children; the thousands of former slaves who sought to gain legal sanction for marriages in 1865 and 1866; and the recurrent laments about marriages broken by the city's numerous slave traders and by sale, particularly in the city, which served as the prime northern terminus in the internal slave trade.

No extrafamilial institution received greater attention than the church. By 1860, five thousand slaves and free blacks belonged to the city's African Baptist and African Methodist churches. In 1841, the First Baptist Church's large congregation split, and its white members left. The church became the all-black First African Baptist Church, though Dr. Robert Ryland, a white man, remained as its pastor until after the civil war. The First African Baptist Church, which had more than three thousand congregants by the eve of the Civil War, provided a public forum for voicing opinions and a vehicle for taking collective action and aiding the poor and helpless. It also gave blacks an opportunity to create their own rules for conduct and a mechanism to enforce them.

The Civil War transformed Richmond, which became the capital of the Confederacy in 1862. The war brought an influx of slaves and whites, pressures to restrict the freedoms of free blacks, material privations caused by Yankee blockades and troop movements, fears of impressment into service for the Confederate military, as well as the excitement of possible freedom. Thousands of blacks were forced into public works projects such as the reinforcement of the city's fortifications and the laying of railroad track. In 1864, amid debates by southern leaders over the question of arming slaves, a regiment of black hospital workers was formed into a makeshift regiment and paraded. Slaves, free blacks, and a handful of white Unionists maintained an underground during the war, aiding captured Union soldiers, passing information to the Union Army, and facilitating slave escapes. Black Union soldiers participated in many battles in the Richmond campaign of 1864–1865, including the successful assault on Fort Harrison. Thousands of local blacks lined the streets when black troops appropriately led the Union Army into Richmond on April 3, 1865, signaling an end to the war and the institution of slavery itself.

Race relations remained confrontational after Emancipation. In 1866, whites burned the Second African Church after blacks held a ceremony commemorating the Emancipation Proclamation. The same year, blacks engaged in several demonstrations over their exclusion from horse-drawn cars, and in 1867 federal troops were called in to quell a violent incident sparked by the exclusion.

After Emancipation, black Richmonders continued to build on the base of the extended family linked with the church. They erected a broad network of "secret societies" that fulfilled a multiplicity of purposes: funerals and death benefits, labor organization, collective self-education and self-improvement, religious advancement, political expression, socializing, and the like. The leadership of these organizations—and of the African-American community itself—emerged from the ranks of wage-earning industrial workers, especially tobacco factory workers. The most famous of the fraternal orders were the Grand Fountain United Order of True Reformers and the Independent Order of St. Luke.

The years after Emancipation witnessed the emergence of a series of popular movements grounded in the social network that honeycombed black Richmond. African Americans formed schools, notably the Richmond Theological Seminary (later Virginia Union University), which held its first classes in the former Lumpkin's slave jail in 1865. Churches expanded, and several black ministers achieved prominence in the community (including the Rev. John Jasper of the Sixth Mt. Zion Church, celebrated for his 1879 sermon "The Sun Do Move," an attack on the Copernican hypothesis of a heliocentric solar system). The movements for mutual aid and self-help were easily transformed to more overt forms of political organization and expression—parades, mass meetings, collective direct action, armed self-defense, political campaigns, labor organization, strikes, and other methods.

These new forces were concentrated in Jackson Ward, which became the geographic heart of black Richmond as housing segregation became nearly absolute. The wages of industrial workers supported black businesses such as barbershops and restaurants, and an adjacent middle-class black neighborhood developed around Marshall and Clay streets (later absorbed into Jackson ward). In 1872, the conservative "Redeemer" government gerrymandered Richmond's wards to limit black voting influence. The results were the concentration of black voting in Jackson Ward and the creation of safe "black" seats. For the rest of the century, Richmond had a full complement of African-American city councilmen and aldermen.

The years after Emancipation witnessed the emergence of a series of popular movements grounded in the social network that honeycombed black Richmond.

Black political activity heightened in the 1880s—well after the formal "redemption" of Virginia—in two movements, Readjusterism and the Knights of Labor. Both were grounded in the experiences of working-class African Americans, reflected their central leadership roles within the larger community, and were based on coalitions along class lines with disaffected whites. Black aspirations were expressed through the *Richmond Planet* newspaper, founded in 1883 and edited by journalist-politician John Mitchell, Jr., from 1884 until 1929, nine years before its demise.

Readjusterism expressed widespread frustrations with the consequences of the Depression of 1873–1878. These frustrations gave birth to a new party that gained control of state government. Blacks won several concrete gains: abolition of the whipping post, the restructuring of the tax system to lessen the burden on working people, the appointments of African Americans to the board of education and black principals to head black schools, and funding for a new black elementary school. A black regiment, headquartered in Richmond, was admitted to the state militia, although it disbanded after the SPANISH-AMERICAN WAR when its members insisted on serving under black officers.

In the mid-1880s, both white and black workers in Richmond flocked into the Knights of Labor. Organized into racially separate locals, but often supporting each other, they fought employers for higher wages, shorter hours, and better working conditions; organized producers' cooperatives; challenged convict labor through boycotts and protest movements; and promoted self-education through newspapers, reading rooms, lectures, and drama troupes. By early 1886, ten thousand Richmond workers were organized into more than thirty local assemblies, linked into two district assemblies, one white and one black.

In mid-1886, white and black leaders together led this movement into local politics, forming the Workingmen's Reform Party to contest for control over the local government. Their stunning victory at the polls, however, was soon followed by internal conflict, exacerbated by manipulative politicians from the two entrenched parties. In the midst of this turmoil, the Richmond Knights hosted the national convention of the organization, which brought more than one thousand delegates into the city. Charges of "social equality" and "race mixing" swirled, as some out-of-town delegates launched their own challenges to the emergent JIM CROW system at the Richmond Theater and in local hotels. When the dust had settled, the Knights had lost their momentum.

The Knights' demise signaled more than the end of efforts to build class-based coalitions in Richmond. In the wake of not only this defeat, but also the cooptation of the Readjusters by the mainstream Republicans and the increasing sophistication of the conservative, white elite counterattack, the local African-American community faced the loss of many of the gains they had made since Emancipation.

During the final decade of the nineteenth century and the first decade of the twentieth, the new patterns were set. African-American suffrage was restricted, by law and practice, until the last black city councilman was eliminated in 1898. When only 228 black registered voters remained on the rolls in 1903, the Jackson Ward district was broken up. Public spending confirmed that "separate" would be anything but "equal,"

gles" ROBINSON. The city's extensive black history was commemorated by the creation of the Jackson Ward National Historic District in 1981.

BIBLIOGRAPHY

Brown, W. H. *The Education and Economic Development of the Negro in Virginia.* Charlottesville, Va., 1923.

Buni, Andrew. *The Negro in Virginia Politics, 1902–1965.* Charlottesville, Va., 1967.

Chesson, Michael B. "Richmond's Black Councilmen, 1871–1896." In Howard Rabinowitz, ed. *Southern Black Leaders of the Reconstruction Era.* Urbana, Ill., 1982.

Dabney, Virginius. *Richmond: The Story of a City.* Garden City, N.Y., 1976.

Dew, Charles B. *Ironmaker to the Confederacy: Joseph R. Anderson and the Tredegar Iron Works.* New Haven, Conn., 1966.

Fink, Leon. " 'Irrespective of Party, Color, or Social Standing': The Knights of Labor and Opposition Politics in Richmond, Virginia." *Labor History* 19 (Summer 1978).

Gates, Robbins L. *The Making of Massive Resistance: Virginia's Politics of Public School Desegregation, 1954–1956.* Chapel Hill, N.C., 1962.

Jackson, Luther Porter. *Negro Officeholders in Virginia, 1865–1895.* Norfolk, Va., 1945.

Kaufman, Stuart. *Challenge & Change: The History of the Tobacco Workers International Union.* Urbana, Ill., 1986.

Knight, Charles L. *Negro Housing in Certain Virginia Cities.* Richmond, Va., 1923.

Moore, James T. "Black Militancy in Readjuster Virginia." *Journal of Southern History* 41 (May 1975).

Pinchbeck, Raymond B. *The Virginia Negro Artisan and Tradesman.* Richmond, Va., 1926.

Rachleff, Peter J. *Black Labor in Richmond, 1865–1890.* 1984. Reprint. Urbana, Ill., 1989.

Silver, Christopher. *Twentieth Century Richmond: Planning, Politics, and Race.* Knoxville, Tenn., 1984.

— PETER J. RACHLEFF

ROACH, MAXWELL LEMUEL "MAX"

Maxwell Lemuel "Max" Roach (January 10, 1924–), jazz drummer and bandleader. Born in Elizabeth City, N.C., and raised in Brooklyn, N.Y., Roach studied music as a child with his mother, a gospel singer, and received piano lessons from his aunt. He also received music lessons in public school, and by age ten was playing drums in church bands. He performed in Coney Island sideshows such as *Darktown Follies* while in high school. During this time he also began frequenting Minton's Playhouse in Harlem, where he met some of the leading jazz musicians of the day. In 1941 Roach graduated with honors from Brooklyn's Boys' High School. Soon after, he started performing regularly with Charlie PARKER at Clark Monroe's Uptown House in Harlem, and by the next year he had a strong enough reputation to fill in for Sonny Greer for several nights with Duke ELLINGTON's orchestra. In 1943–44 he recorded and performed with Coleman HAWKINS at Kelly's Stable as a replacement for Kenny Clarke ("Woody'n' You," 1944; "Bu-Dee-Daht," 1944). In 1944 he also joined Dizzy GILLESPIE's quintet at the Onyx Club, becoming a member of the first bebop band to open on 52nd Street, which had become the central location for New York jazz nightclubs. The next year Roach began working with Charlie Parker, an association that would last more than five years. On Roach's first important recording with Parker, the uptempo "Ko-Ko" (1945), Roach has already left swing drumming behind for a bebop style that keeps time on the cymbal, reserving the drums themselves for accents.

Together with Kenny Clarke, Roach redefined the rhythmical and structural architecture of jazz drumming, and created a new solo role for modern jazz drum performance. Initially influenced by the imaginative "melodic" solo style of Sid Catlett, the driving intensity of Chick Webb, and the fluid swing and finesse of Jo Jones, Roach distilled their stylistic characteristics through Clarke's polyrhythmic innovations. By the end of the 1940s, Roach was recognized as one of the leading drummers in jazz. He performed on Miles DAVIS's "Birth of the Cool" recordings (1949), and on Bud Powell's "Un Poco Loco" (1951). In the early 1950s he continued his prolific career while pursuing studies in composition and tympani at the Manhattan School of Music. From 1954 to 1956 he co-led the Clifford Brown-Max Roach Quintet, which pioneered the hard-driving style known as hard hop (*Study in Brown,* 1955; *At Basin Street,* 1956).

In the 1960s Roach began to combine his music with his politics, with a particular emphasis on racial oppression in both the United States and South Africa. His 1960 recording of *We Insist: Freedom Now Suite* used free-form musical structures, including an emotionally charged interplay between the drummer and his then-wife, vocalist Abbey Lincoln, to explore the theme of racial oppression in America. That work also used West African drumming and Afro-Cuban percussion to draw parallels between slavery in the U.S., segregation, and apartheid in South Africa.

In the 1960s Roach began to move away from appearing solely in strict jazz contexts. He began performing solo drum compositions as independent pieces, an effort dating back to his "Drum Conversation" (1953). He also recorded original works for vocal choruses and pianoless quartets. In the 1960s Roach taught at the Lenox School of Jazz, and in 1972 he assumed a faculty position at the University of Massachusetts, Amherst. Among Roach's most significant work from the 1970s are duet recordings he made with some of the leading figures from the post-bebop avant garde, including Archie Shepp, Anthony Braxton, Abdullah Ibrahim, and

Cecil Taylor. In the 1980s, Roach's astoundingly protean career included performances and recordings with a jazz quartet, the percussion ensemble M'Boom, the Uptown String Quartet (with his daughter Maxine on viola), rap and hip hop musicians and dancers. In 1980 Roach recorded an interactive drum solo with a tape recording of the Rev. Dr. Martin Luther KING, Jr.'s 1963 "I Have A Dream" speech (*Chattahoochee Red*), and in 1989 he recorded duets with Dizzy Gillespie. Roach, who wrote music as early as 1946 ("Coppin' The Bop"), has in recent years dedicated more and more of his time to composition. His *Shepardsets,* a work for the theater, received an Obie award in 1985, and he has also composed for film and television, and symphony orchestra.

Roach, who has lived in New York all of his life, has in recent years been recognized not only as one of the most important drummers in the history of jazz, but as one of the leading African-American cultural figures of the twentieth century, with a decades-long commitment to fighting racial injustice. In addition to the several honorary doctorates he has received throughout his career, in 1988 Roach became the first jazz musician to receive a MacArthur Foundation "genius award."

BIBLIOGRAPHY

Brown, Anthony. "The Development of Modern Jazz Drumset Artistry." *Black Perspective in Music* 18, nos. 1, 2 (1990): 39–58.

Roach, Max. "What Jazz Means to Me." *Black Scholar* 3, no. 2 (1972): 3.

Weinstein, Norman C. *A Night in Tunisia: Imaginings of Africa in Jazz.* Metuchen, N.J., 1992, pp. 118–126.

Whitehead, Kevin. "Max Roach: Drum Architect." *Downbeat* 52, no. 10 (1985): 16.

— ANTHONY BROWN

ROBESON, PAUL

Paul Robeson (April 9, 1898–January 23, 1976), actor, singer, and political activist. Paul Robeson was born in Princeton, N.J., where his father, William Drew Robeson, was the minister of a local Presbyterian church, and his mother, Maria Louisa Bustill, was a schoolteacher. His childhood was happy, but marred by two defining events. His mother died when he was six, after she was accidentally set on fire at home; and his father lost his church following a fierce dispute among his congregation. After working at menial jobs in Princeton, his father moved first to Westfield and then to Somerville, both in New Jersey, where he again led churches affiliated with the African Methodist Episcopal Zion Denomination.

An uncommonly brilliant student and athlete, Paul Robeson entered Rutgers College (later Rutgers University) in New Brunswick in 1916. Although he was the only black student there, he became immensely popular. He was elected to Phi Beta Kappa as a junior and selected twice (1917 and 1918) as an All-American football player by the famed journalist Walter Camp. After graduating in 1919, he moved to Harlem, and in 1920 entered the law school of Columbia University in New York. To support himself he played professional football on weekends, then turned to acting after winning a role in *Simon the Cyrenian* at the Harlem YMCA in 1921.

Graduating from law school in 1923, he was admitted to the bar and served briefly in a law firm. Then, chafing at restrictions on him as a black, and urged on by his wife, Eslanda Cardoza Goode (a fellow student, in chemistry, at Columbia), he left the law for the stage. He enjoyed immediate success, particularly with the Greenwich Village-based Provincetown Players in Eugene O'Neill's *The Emperor Jones* (1923) and *All God's Chillun Got Wings* (1925). In 1925, with his longtime accompanist Lawrence Brown, he launched his celebrated career as an interpreter of African-American spirituals and of folk songs from around the world with a concert of the former in New York. He then traveled to Europe and Great Britain (where in 1922 he had been well received as an individual and as an actor in the play *Voodoo*). Critics hailed his acting in the 1925 London production of *The Emperor Jones.*

In the 1928 London production of Jerome Kern and Oscar Hammerstein II's musical *Show Boat,* his stirring rendition of "Ol' Man River" took his popularity to new heights. Although he triumphed again when *Show Boat* opened in New York in 1930, Great Britain was the scene of many of his greatest achievements. In the following years he starred there in a number of plays, including *Othello* (1930), *The Hairy Ape* (1931), and *Stevedore* (1933). Robeson also had prominent roles in almost a dozen films, such as *Sanders of the River* (1935), *Show Boat* (1936), *King Solomon's Mines* (1935), and *Proud Valley* (1941). In most of these efforts, his depictions of a black man contrasted starkly with the images of subservience, ignorance, criminality, or low comedy usually seen on the Hollywood screen.

Handsome and blessed with a commanding physique and a voice of unusual resonance and charm, Robeson might have capitalized on his stage and screen success and ignored politics altogether. However, his resentment of racism and his attraction to radical socialism, especially after an outstanding welcome in the Soviet Union in 1934, set him on a leftward course. A frequent visitor to the U.S.S.R. thereafter, Robeson learned to speak Russian (and eventually almost two dozen other languages, in which he recorded many songs). His son, Paul, Jr., attended school there for several years. Robeson became a dependable supporter of progressive causes, including the rights of oppressed Jews and of antifascist forces in Spain. In London, he befriended several students and other intellectuals, such as Kwame Nkrumah, George Padmore, and Jomo Kenyatta, who would later be prominent in the anticolonialist movements in Africa.

In 1925, Paul Robeson launched his celebrated career as an interpreter of African-American spirituals and of folk songs from around the world.

Resettling in the United States in 1939, Robeson joined enthusiastically in the war effort and maintained his stellar position as an entertainer—although racism, including that on Broadway and in Hollywood, still disturbed him. In 1943, his critically acclaimed portrayal of Othello, in the first Broadway production of Shakespeare's play with an otherwise white cast, created a sensation. He was awarded the NAACP's Spingarn Medal in 1945. He fared less well after the war, when the Cold War intensified. In 1946, he vowed to a special committee of the California State Legislature that he had never been a member of the Communist party. However, when accusations continued, he resolutely refused to cooperate with the authorities. Despite his protests, he was identified as a communist by the House Committee on Un-American Activities. Such opposition hampered his career as a recording artist and actor.

In 1949, in a major controversy, he told a gathering in Paris that it was "unthinkable" to him that African Americans would to go war against the Soviet Union, whose fair treatment of blacks was a rebuke to racist American laws and conventions. Later that year, the announcement of his participation in a musical festival sponsored by liberals and leftists in Peekskill, N.Y., led to rioting in the town that left scores of attendees injured. The next year, the State Department impounded his passport. With Robeson refusing to sign an oath disavowing communism, his singing and acting career in effect came to an end. He was widely ostracized by whites and blacks, except those among the far left.

In 1958, the Supreme Court declared the oath and other government rules unconstitutional. That year, Robeson published *Here I Stand,* which combined autobiography with a considered statement of his political concerns and other beliefs. He sang at Carnegie Hall in what was billed as a farewell concert, and also performed in California. Leaving the United States, he was welcomed as a hero in the Soviet Union, which had awarded him the Stalin Peace Prize in 1952, but he fell ill there. Complaining of chronic exhaustion and other ailments, he entered a series of hospitals in the Soviet Union, Europe, and Britain.

In 1963, when he and his wife returned to the United States, to a home in Harlem, he announced his formal retirement. In 1965, Eslanda Robeson died. With a further deterioration in health, including a nervous breakdown, Robeson moved to Philadelphia to live with his sister. A seventy-fifth birthday celebration at Carnegie Hall in 1973 found Robeson (whose illness kept him away) saluted, in a more liberal age, by prominent blacks, liberals, and socialists as one of the towering figures of the twentieth century. In a message to the gathering, Robeson described himself as "dedicated as ever to the worldwide cause of humanity for freedom, peace, and brotherhood." He died in Philadelphia in 1976.

BIBLIOGRAPHY

Duberman, Martin B. *Paul Robeson.* New York, 1988.
Robeson, Paul. *Here I Stand.* New York, 1971.

– ARNOLD RAMPERSAD

ROBINSON, BILL "BOJANGLES"

Bill "Bojangles" Robinson (Luther Robinson) (May 25, 1878–November 25, 1949), tap dancer. The most famous of all African-American tap dancers, Bill Robinson demonstrated an exacting yet light footwork that was said to have brought tap "up on its toes" from the flat-footed shuffling style prevalent in the previous era. Born Luther Robinson in Richmond, Va., he was orphaned when both his parents, Maria and Maxwell Robinson, died in 1885; he and his brothers were subsequently reared by his grandmother, Bedilia Robinson.

Robinson gained his nickname, "Bojangles"—possibly from the slang term *jangle,* meaning "to quarrel or fight,"—while still in Richmond. It was also in Richmond that Robinson is said to have coined the phrase "Everything's copasetic," meaning "fine, better than all right." He ran away to Washington, D.C., earning nickels and dimes by dancing and singing, and then got his first professional job in 1892, performing in the "pickaninny" chorus (in vaudeville, a chorus of young African-American children performing as backup for the featured performer) in Mayme Remington's *The South Before the War.* When Robinson arrived in New York City around 1900, he challenged tap dancer Harry Swinton, the star dancer in *Old Kentucky,* to a buck-dancing contest, and won.

From 1902 to 1914, Robinson teamed up with George W. Cooper. Bound by the "two-colored" rule in vaudeville, which restricted blacks to performing in pairs, Cooper and Robinson performed as a duo on the Keith and Orpheum circuits. They did not, however, wear the blackface makeup performers customarily used. Robinson, who carried a gold-plated revolver, was a gambler with a quick temper. He was involved in a series of off-stage scrapes; it was allegedly his arrest for assault in 1914 that finally put an end to the partnership with Cooper.

After the split, Robinson convinced his manager, Marty Forkins, to promote him as a soloist. Forkins managed to book him at the Marigold Gardens Theater in Chicago by promising its star and producer, Gertrude Hoffman, Robinson's services as dance instructor; Robinson therewith launched his solo career and eventually became one of the first black performers to headline at New York's prestigious Palace Theatre.

Hailed as "the Dark Cloud of Joy" on the Orpheum circuit, Robinson performed in vaudeville from 1914 to 1927. Onstage, Robinson's open face, flashing eyes, infectious smile, easygoing patter, and air of surprise at what his feet were doing made him irresistible to audiences. His tapping was delicate, articulate, and intelligible. He usually wore a hat cocked to one side, and often exited with a Chaplinesque waddle, or with another signature step, a kind of syncopated "camel walk" (which would later be called the "moon walk" by Michael jackson). Robinson always danced in split-clog shoes, in which the wooden sole was attached from the toe to the ball of the foot and the rest was left loose, allowing for greater flexibility and tonality. Dancing upright and swinging to clean six-bar phrases, followed by a two-bar break, Robinson set new standards of performance, despite the fact that he invented few new steps.

In 1922, Robinson married Fannie Clay, who became his business manager and secretary. (The marriage was his second: in 1907, he had married Lena Chase, from whom he was divorced in 1922.) After twenty-one years he divorced Fannie and married a young dancer, Elaine Plaines.

Broadway fame came with an all-black revue, *Blackbirds of 1928,* in which he sang "Doin' the New Low Down" while dancing up and down a flight of five steps. Success was immediate: Robinson's performance was acclaimed by the major New York newspapers, and he was heralded by several as the greatest of all tap dancers. The dance Robinson performed in *Blackbirds* developed into his signature "stair dance"; notable for the clarity of Robinson's taps and for its unusual tonalities—each step yielded a different pitch—Robinson's appealing showmanship made it seem effortless. *Brown Buddies* (1930) was kept alive by Robinson's performance, as were *Blackbirds of 1933, The Hot Mikado* (1939), *All in Fun* (1940), and *Memphis Bound* (1945). Largely in recognition of his Broadway success, Robinson was named honorary "Mayor of Harlem" by Mayor Fiorello LaGuardia. In 1939, he celebrated his sixty-first birthday by tapping down Broadway, one block for each year.

Robinson turned to Hollywood, a venue largely closed to blacks, in the 1930s. His films included, *Dixiana* (1930), which had a predominantly white cast, and *Harlem Is Heaven* (1933), with an all-black cast. Robinson also appeared in the films *Hooray for Love* (1935), *In Old Kentucky* (1935), *The Big Broadcast of 1937* (1936), *One Mile from Heaven* (1937), *Road Demon* (1938), *Up the River* (1938), *By an Old Southern River* (1941), and *Let's Shuffle* (1941); in a newsreel about the 1939 World's Fair in Chicago, *It's Swing Ho! Come to the Fair;* and in a short, *Broadway Brevities* (1934). But of all his many stage and film performances, those that brought him the most fame were his appearances with child star Shirley Temple, in *The Littlest Colonel* (1935), *The Littlest Rebel* (1935), *Just Around the Corner* (1938), and *Rebecca of Sunnybrook Farm* (1938). In 1943, the all-black film *Stormy Weather,* with Robinson, Cab CALLOWAY, Lena HORNE, and Katherine DUNHAM's dance troupe, met with some success.

A founding member of the Negro Actors Guild of America, Robinson performed in thousands of benefits in the course of his career and made generous contributions to charities and individuals. Substantially, however, Robinson's career had peaked in the late 1930s, and when he died in 1949 he was in debt. According to contemporary accounts, nearly a hundred thousand people turned out to watch his funeral procession; the numbers testify to the esteem in which he was still held by his community and by the audiences who loved him. The founding of the Copasetics Club in the year that Robinson died ensured that his brilliance as a performer would not be forgotten.

BIBLIOGRAPHY

Fletcher, Tom. *100 Years of the Negro in Show Business.* New York, 1954.

Haskins, Jim, and N. R. Mitgang. *Mr. Bojangles: The Biography of Bill Robinson.* New York, 1988.

Stearns, Marshall, and Jean Stearns. *Jazz Dance: The Story of American Vernacular Dance.* New York, 1968.

– CONSTANCE VALIS HILL

ROBINSON, JACK ROOSEVELT "JACKIE"

Jack Roosevelt "Jackie" Robinson (January 31, 1919–October 24, 1972), baseball player, civil rights leader, businessman. Born in Georgia, the youngest of five children of sharecrop farmers Jerry and Mallie Robinson, Jackie Robinson was raised in Pasadena, Calif., where the Robinson family confronted the West Coast variety of American racism. White neighbors tried to drive the family out of their home; segregation reigned in public and private facilities. Robinson became an outstanding athlete at Pasadena Junior College, before transferring to U.C.L.A. in 1940, where he won renown as the "Jim Thorpe of his race," the nation's finest all-around athlete. Robinson was an All-American football player, leading scorer in basketball, and record-setting broad jumper, in addition to his baseball exploits.

Drafted into the Army in the spring of 1942 Robinson embarked on a stormy military career. Denied access to Officers' Candidate School, Robinson protested to heavyweight champion Joe LOUIS, who intervened with officials in Washington on Robinson's behalf. Once commissioned, Robinson fought for improved conditions for blacks at Camp Riley, Kans., leading to his transfer to Fort Hood, Tex. At Fort Hood, Robinson was court-martialed and acquitted for refusing to move to the back of a bus. Robinson's Army career demonstrated the proud, combative personality that would characterize his postwar life.

After his discharge from the Army in 1944, Robinson signed to play with the Kansas City Monarchs of the Negro American League. After several months of discontent in the Jim Crow league, Robinson was approached by Branch Rickey of the Brooklyn Dodgers, who offered him the opportunity to become the first black player in major league baseball since the 1890s. Robinson gladly accepted the opportunity and responsibility of this pioneering role in "baseball's great experiment."

In 1946 Robinson joined the Montreal Royals of the International League, the top farm club in the Dodger system. Following a spectacular debut in which he stroked four hits including a three-run home run, Robinson proceeded to lead the league with a .349 batting average. An immediate fan favorite, Robinson enabled the Royals to set new attendance records while winning the International League and Little World Series championships. Robinson's imminent promotion to the Dodgers in 1947 triggered an unsuccessful petition drive on the part of southern players to keep him off the team. In the early months of the season, beanballs, death threats, and rumors of a strike by opposing players swirled about Robinson. Through it all, Robinson paraded his excellence. An electrifying fielder and baserunner as well as an outstanding hitter, Robinson's assault on baseball's color line captured the imagination of both black and white Americans. He batted .297 and won the Rookie of the Year Award (since renamed the Jackie Robinson Award in his honor) en route to leading the Dodgers to the pennant.

Over the next decade Robinson emerged as one of the most dominant players and foremost gate attractions in the history of the major leagues. In 1949 he batted .342 and won the National League Most Valuable Player Award. During his ten years with the Dodgers the team won six pennants and one World Championship. Upon his retirement in 1956 Robinson had compiled a .311 lifetime batting average. He was elected to the Baseball Hall of Fame on the first ballot in 1961.

Jackie Robinson's assault on baseball's color line captured the imagination of both black and white Americans.

But Robinson's significance transcended his achievements on the baseball diamond. He became a leading symbol and spokesperson of the postwar integration crusade, both within baseball and in broader society. During his early years in Montreal and Brooklyn, Robinson had adhered to his promise to Branch Rickey to "turn the other cheek" and avoid controversies. After establishing himself in the major leagues, however, Robinson's more combative and outspoken personality reasserted itself. Robinson repeatedly pressed for baseball to desegregate more rapidly and to remove discriminatory barriers in Florida training camps and cities like St. Louis and Cincinnati. He also demanded opportunities for black players to become coaches, managers, and front office personnel. Baseball officials and many sportswriters branded Robinson an ingrate as controversies marked his career.

Upon retirement Robinson remained in the public eye. He continued to voice his opinions as speaker, newspaper columnist, and fundraiser for the NAACP. A believer in "black capitalism" through which blacks could "become producers, manufacturers, developers and creators of businesses, providers of jobs," Robinson engaged in many successful business ventures in the black community. He became an executive in the Chock Full O' Nuts restaurant chain and later helped develop Harlem's Freedom National Bank and the Jackie Robinson Construction Company. Robinson also became active in Republican Party politics, supporting Richard Nixon in 1960, and working closely with New York Gov. Nelson Rockefeller, who appointed him Special Assistant for Community Affairs in 1966. These activities brought criticism from young black militants in the late 1960s. Ironically, at this same time Robinson had also parted ways with the NAACP, criticizing its failure to include "younger, more progressive voices."

By the late 1960s Robinson had become "bitterly disillusioned" with both baseball and American society. He refused to attend baseball events in protest of the failure to hire blacks in nonplaying capacities. In his 1972 autobiography, *I Never Had It Made,* he attacked the nation's waning commitment to racial equality. Later that year the commemoration of his major league debut led him to lift his boycott of baseball games. "I'd like to live to see a black manager," he told a nationwide television audience at the World Series on October 15, 1972. Nine days later he died of a heart attack.

BIBLIOGRAPHY

Robinson, Jackie, with Alfred Duckett. *I Never Had It Made.* New York, 1972.

Rowan, Carl. *Wait Till Next Year.* New York, 1960.

Tygiel, Jules. *Baseball's Great Experiment: Jackie Robinson and His Legacy.* New York, 1983.

– JULES TYGIEL

ROMAN CATHOLICISM

Black Catholics have figured in Roman Catholic history in the continental United States since the sixteenth century. The town of St. Augustine, established in northern Florida in 1565, was composed of Spanish-speaking Catholics, both white and black. The parish registers (baptismal, marriage, and death records), which noted persons of color and their status as slave or free, reveal a multicolored society that was Catholic in religion. From 1738 to 1763, the all-black town of Gracia Real de Santa Teresa de Fort Mose served as a refuge for slaves fleeing the English colonies to the north. All who converted to Catholicism became free. In the Southwest, blacks from Mexico were also among the Spanish-speaking settlers. Africans and mulattoes made up half the original settlers of the city of Los Angeles in 1781.

Slavery was accepted by most Catholics. Catholic slaveholders included bishops, priests, religious communities of men and women, and laypersons. In the Spanish territories and in the French possessions of Louisiana, the Alabama Gulf coast, Illinois, and eastern Missouri, slave owners had to have their slaves baptized and instructed in the Catholic religion. The slave codes prohibited the separation of family members. Although these stipulations were not always carried out, they ensured a minimum of rights that did not exist in the United States. Maryland had the largest concentration of English-speaking Catholic slaves. John Carroll, first Catholic bishop in the United States, wrote in 1785 that there were about three thousand Catholic slaves in Maryland, one-fifth of the state's Catholic population. Maryland Catholics, settlers and slaves, moved to western Kentucky at the beginning of the nineteenth century. At the same period, Haitians—black as well as white Catholics—entered the United States as a result of civil unrest in the former French colony.

In the period prior to the Civil War, when many Protestant churches were divided by the issue of slavery, the Catholic bishops maintained a policy of noninvolvement. Many Catholics supported the southern cause inasmuch as they supported the Democratic party in the North or secessionists in the South. A few bishops wrote in defense of slavery. Few came out publicly for emancipation once the war began. Catholic leaders in Europe, on the other hand, were in the main opposed to slavery; in 1839 Pope Gregory XVI condemned the slave trade and slavery itself. Certain bishops, like John England of Charleston, S.C., interpreted the pope's language as referring only to international trafficking in slaves. Rome was preparing to correct this misinterpretation when the Civil War ended.

Evangelization efforts for freed slaves began immediately after the Civil War. During the Second Plenary Council of Baltimore in 1866, at the instigation of the archbishop of Baltimore, Martin J. Spalding, the Holy See presented a program whereby a bishop with nationwide jurisdiction would have responsibility for ministry to all blacks. The bishops in general opposed the plan and agreed to a less innovative (and less efficient) approach, making each bishop responsible for missions to the blacks within his diocese. Religious communities such as the Josephites, the Spiritans, the Society of the Divine Word, and the Society of African Missions took up apostolic work among American blacks.

Black lay Catholics took the initiative for evangelization even before the Civil War. The oldest known document relating to black Catholic parish life is the weekly account of a prayer meeting held each Sunday from 1843 to 1845 in the parish hall of the Baltimore cathedral. Some two hundred or more black women and men called the Society of the Holy Family prayed, sang, received spiritual instruction, began a lending library, and established a fund for charitable purposes.

As early as 1824, three free black women began to live the religious life near Bardstown, Kentucky, under the guidance of Charles Nerinckx, a frontier priest from Belgium. Unfortunately, the community was not allowed to continue. Five years later in Baltimore, five black women began to live as religious sisters. They began as schoolteachers for the children of the largely

Haitian black community that worshiped in the lower chapel of Saint Mary's Seminary, with the guidance of a French Sulpician priest.

Under the direction of Mary Elizabeth Lange, a Haitian, the first African-American community of nuns was established in 1829, today still known as the Oblate Sisters of Providence. In 1831 Rome gave final approval. Almost a dozen years later, in 1842, another community of black sisters was established, this one in New Orleans, by two women of color, Henriette Delille and Juliette Gaudin. These black sisters were known as the Sisters of the Holy Family (no connection with the parish group of Baltimore). In 1916 in Savannah, Ga., a third community of black nuns was founded, the Franciscan Handmaids of Mary, who eventually moved to Harlem. All three groups still work in the black community in education and social service.

Father Smith, a Roman Catholic priest, conducting Mass in Chicago in 1942. The number of African-American Roman Catholics doubled during the interwar years. By 1938 there were three large, well-attended Roman Catholic churches in Chicago. (Prints and Photographs Division, Library of Congress)

The first black priests in United States were three sons of an Irish-born slaveholder in Georgia, Michael Morris Healy, and a slave woman, Mary Eliza. There were ten children. Four of the sons were sent to Holy Cross College in Worcester, Mass.; three of them became priests. The eldest, James Augustine Healy, in 1875 became bishop of Portland, Me., the first black Catholic bishop in the United States. The third son, Patrick Francis Healy, became a Jesuit priest and president of Georgetown University, his African-American origins largely unknown. The first black priest who was clearly recognized as black was Augustus Tolton. Born a slave in Missouri, educated for the priesthood in Rome, and ordained for Alton, Ill., in 1886, he eventually moved to Chicago, where he became the pastor of the first black parish.

Laypersons played an important role in the development of black Catholic culture. Daniel Rudd of Bardstown, Ky., began a black Catholic weekly newspaper that for a few years had a nationwide subscription. Rudd was responsible for organizing five lay congresses of black Catholics, which met between the years 1889 and 1894 in Washington, D.C., Cincinnati, Philadelphia, Chicago, and Baltimore, respectively. These meetings were important because they revealed the social concerns and beliefs of the black Catholic community, their attachment to the Catholic church, and their determination to end racist practices within the church.

Another black Catholic lay leader and organizer of a lay Catholic organization was Thomas Wyatt Turner, who in 1924 founded the Federated Colored Catholics, a group of African-American lay leaders dedicated to the eradication of racism within the church. Turner challenged the American church and its inertia in race relations. At the same time, the Roman Curia began pressuring the American hierarchy regarding discriminatory practices. In 1920, the Society of the Divine Word began a seminary for the training of black priesthood candidates, first in Greenville and later at Bay St. Louis, both in Mississippi.

The Civil Rights Movement brought a new consciousness to black Catholics. In 1968 the National Black Catholic Clergy Caucus and the National Black Sisters' Conference were formed, and shortly thereafter the National Black Seminarians Association. In 1970, the National Office of Black Catholics was created as an umbrella organization. Gradually, the church hierarchy began to come to terms with racial matters. The United States bishops issued a pastoral letter dealing with racism and its sinfulness in 1979. Harold Perry, the second black bishop in U.S. history, was ordained in 1966 as auxiliary bishop of New Orleans. By 1991 there were thirteen black bishops, two of them heads of dioceses. In 1984 the black bishops issued a pastoral letter on evangelization within the black community. In 1987 the sixth Black Catholic Congress met in Washington, D.C. That same year a Black Secretariat was established as part of the National Conference of Catholic Bishops, with headquarters in Washington, D.C. It functions as an agency for both the bishops and the nearly two million black Catholics in the country. In most dioceses where there is a significant black population, an office of black ministry, under various titles, serves as a voice and a coordinating center for diocesan affairs and the concerns of blacks.

In 1989 a Washington, D.C., priest, George Stallings, formed a schismatic group, the Imani Temple African American Catholic Congregation. Stallings broke with the papacy and was ordained a bishop in his own church, retaining many aspects of Catholicism. Eventually, another group under Bruce Greening, likewise ordained a bishop, separated in turn from the Imani Temple.

Sanctity has been a part of the history of black Catholicism. The process of canonization was introduced for three black Catholics: Pierre Toussaint, a devout Haitian layman of New York; Mary Elizabeth Lange, the founder of the Oblate Sisters of Providence; and Henriette Delille, cofounder of the Sisters of the Holy Family.

BIBLIOGRAPHY

Davis, Cyprian. *The History of Black Catholics in the United States.* New York, 1990.

Nickels, Marilyn. *Black Catholic Protest and the Federated Colored Catholics, 1917–1933: Three Perspectives on Racial Justice.* New York, 1988.

Ochs, Stephen. *Desegregating the Altar: The Josephites and the Struggle for Black Priests, 1871–1960.* Baton Rouge, La., 1990.

What We Have Seen and Heard: A Pastoral Letter on Evangelization from the Black Bishops of the United States. Cincinnati, 1984.

— CYPRIAN DAVIS

RUDOLPH, WILMA GLODEAN

Wilma Glodean Rudolph (June 23, 1940–November 12, 1994), athlete. Wilma Rudolph, the twentieth of twenty-two children, was born in Bethlehem, Tenn., and raised in Clarksville. As a child, she suffered from scarlet fever and pneumonia and was stricken with polio, which left her without the use of her left leg. She wore a leg brace until the age of nine, when she was able to regain the strength in her legs. By age twelve, Rudolph was the fastest runner in her school. She entered Cobb Elementary School in 1947 and then attended Burt High School in Clarksville, Tenn., where she played basketball and ran track.

Rudolph met Edward Temple, track coach at Tennessee State University, while at Burt. After her sophomore year, Temple invited Rudolph to a summer training camp and began to cultivate her running abilities. In 1956, at age 16, she participated in the Olympics in Melbourne, Australia, where her team won the bronze medal in the 4 × 100-meter relay race. Two years later, Rudolph entered Tennessee State to run track and study elementary education and psychology. She was determined to return to the Rome Olympics in 1960. She trained and ran with the Tigerbelles, the Tennessee State University team, which was one of the premier teams in the country. In 1960, Rudolph became the first woman to receive three gold medals, which she won for the 100-meter race, the 200-meter race, and the 4 × 100-meter relay. She instantly became a celebrity, drawing large crowds wherever she went. The French press called her "La Gazelle." Rudolph retired from amateur running at the height of her career, in 1962.

Rudolph's achievements heightened awareness about racial and sexual barriers within sports.

Rudolph graduated from Tennessee State in 1963 and accepted a job as teacher and track coach at Cobb Elementary School. Although she has lived in many places and has held a number of different jobs, she has invariably dedicated herself to youth programs and education. She worked as the director of a community center in Evansville, Ind., with the Job Corps program in Boston and St. Louis, with the Watts Community Action Committee in California, and as a teacher at a high school in Detroit. In 1981, she started the Wilma Rudolph Foundation, a nonprofit organization which nurtures young athletes.

Wilma Rudolph has received many awards and distinctions. She was chosen in 1960 as the United Press Athlete of the Year, and the next year she was designated Woman Athlete of the Year by the Associated Press. She was inducted in 1973 into the Black Sports Hall of Fame, seven years later into the Women's Sports Hall of Fame, and in 1983 into the U.S. Olympic Hall of Fame. In 1993, she became the only woman to be awarded the National Sports Award. In addition, her autobiography, *Wilma: The Story of Wilma Rudolph,* published in 1977, was made into a television movie. Rudolph's achievements as a runner gave a boost to women's track in the United States and heightened awareness about racial and sexual barriers within sports. In addition, Rudolph has served as a role model and inspiration to thousands of African-American and female athletes, as well as people trying to overcome physical disabilities.

BIBLIOGRAPHY

Biracree, Tom. *Wilma Rudolph.* New York, 1988.

Jacobs, Linda. *Wilma Rudolph: Run for Glory.* St. Paul, Minn., 1975.

Rudolph, Wilma. *Wilma: The Story of Wilma Rudolph.* New York, 1977.

– PAM NADASEN

RUSTIN, BAYARD

Bayard Rustin (March 17, 1910–August 24, 1987), activist. Bayard Rustin was a civil rights leader, pacifist, political organizer, and controversial public figure. He was born in West Chester, Pa., in 1910, the last of nine children. He accumulated a colorful personal history, beginning with his youthful discovery that the woman he had assumed was his older sister was actually his mother. Reared by his mother and grandparents, local caterers, he grew up in the relatively privileged setting of a large mansion in town. Like the rest of his family, Rustin became a Quaker, maintaining an enduring commitment to personal pacifism as a way of life. Tall, thin, usually bushy-haired, and with an acquired West Indian accent, Rustin was noticed wherever he appeared.

He attended college at West Chester State, then moved to Harlem during the 1930s, where he cultivated a bohemian lifestyle, attending classes at City College, singing with JAZZ groups and at night clubs, and gaining a reputation as a chef. His most notable activity, however, was aligning with the COMMUNIST PARTY through the Young Communist League, a decision based on the party's position on race issues. In 1941 when asked by the party to abandon his program to gain young black recruits in favor of a singular emphasis on the European war effort, Rustin quit the party.

His public personality and organizing skills subsequently brought him to the attention of A. Phillip Randolph, who recruited him to help develop his plans for a massive March on Washington to secure equal access to defense jobs. The two men, despite brief skirmishes, remained lifelong friends. When President Franklin D. Roosevelt capitulated to Randolph's threat to hold the march—though Rustin believed that Randolph should not have canceled the march—Randolph arranged for Rustin to meet with A. J. Muste, the head of the radical pacifist Fellowship of Reconciliation (FOR). Muste came to regard the younger man almost as a son, naming him in 1941 as a field staff member for FOR while Rustin also continued as a youth organizer for the March on Washington Movement.

Now possessed of a reputation as an activist in the politics of race, Rustin was able to offer advice to the members of the FOR cell who became the nucleus for a new nonviolent action organization, the CONGRESS OF RACIAL EQUALITY (CORE). Until 1955 Rustin remained a vital figure in the FOR/CORE alliance, holding a variety of offices within both groups, conducting weekend and summer institutes on nonviolent direct action in race relations, and serving as a conduit to the March on Washington Movement for ideas and techniques on nonviolence. In 1947 he worked closely with Randolph again in a movement opposing universal military training and a segregated military, and once again believed Randolph wrong in abandoning his strategies when met with a presidential executive order intended to correct the injustice. They argued briefly and publicly, then reconciled. Rustin is sometimes credited with persuading Randolph to accept nonviolence as a strategy.

Rustin's dual commitment to nonviolence and racial equality cost him dearly. In the summer of 1942, refusing to sit in the Jim Crow section of a bus going from Louisville, Ky., to Nashville, Tenn., he was beaten and arrested. The following year, unwilling to accept either the validity of the draft or conscientious objector status—though his Quaker affiliation made that option possible—he was jailed as a draft resister and spent twenty-eight months in prison. Following his release, in 1947 he proposed that a racially integrated group of sixteen CORE/FOR activists undertake a bus trip through the Upper South to test a recent Supreme Court decision on interstate travel.

Termed the Journey of Reconciliation, the trip was essentially peaceful, although participants encountered violence outside Chapel Hill, N.C., where Rustin and three others were charged with violating the segregation laws. In a sham trial, Rustin and the others were convicted and sentenced to thirty days hard labor on a chain gang. His continuing visible role in racial policies brought him additional arrests and beatings.

After his release from the chain gang, Rustin traveled to India, where he was received by Mohandas K. Gandhi's sons. He had earlier blended strands of Gandhian nonviolence into his conception of pacifism. When the bus boycott developed in Montgomery, Ala., Rustin appeared on the scene to offer support, advice, and information on nonviolence. Martin Luther KING, Jr., accepted his help. But when word leaked of Rustin's former ties to the Communist party and his 1953 conviction on a morals charge—allegedly for homosexual activity—he was rushed out of town. The gossip led to Rustin's resignation from both CORE and FOR in

1955, although he continued the pacifist struggle in the War Resisters League.

A 1952 visit to countries in north and west Africa convinced him of the need to assist Africans in their independence struggle. And he continued to be an active though less visible force in the effort to achieve racial justice, invited by King to assist in the creation of the SOUTHERN CHRISTIAN LEADERSHIP CONFERENCE and to serve as a publicist for the group. Conservative members, however, eventually sought his ouster, and from 1960 until 1963 Rustin had little contact with King.

In 1963, as Randolph renewed his plans for a massive March on Washington, he proposed Rustin as the coordinator for the national event. Though initially opposed by some major civil rights leaders and under surveillance by the FBI, Rustin successfully managed the complex planning for the event and avoided violence. He was named executive director of the A. Philip Randolph Institute in 1964, while continuing to lead protests against militarism and segregation.

BIBLIOGRAPHY

Rustin, Bayard. *Down the Line: The Collected Writings of Bayard Rustin.* New York, 1971.

———. "On the Economic Condition of Blacks." *Crisis.* (March 1985): 24–29, 32.

– CAROL V. R. GEORGE

S

ST. LOUIS, MISSOURI

St. Louis, Mo., was founded in 1764 by French trader Pierre Laclade as a settlement and fur trading post in the Louisiana territory, then owned by Spain. African Americans, both slave and free, were present in the city virtually from the date of its creation. Few population figures are available for blacks during the colonial period. In 1772, a Spanish pastor, Father Valentine, arrived in the settlement, and in three years baptized twenty-four blacks into the Roman Catholic faith. By 1776, blacks formed about 30 percent of the rapidly growing settlement. Slaves and free blacks were employed as domestics, agricultural laborers, ship pilots, hunters, dockworkers, and craftspeople. Some free blacks, such as Jeannette Fourchet, became successful farmers.

In 1803, following the Louisana Purchase, the district of St. Louis, with its 667 slaves and 70 free black residents, became part of the United States. The number of slaves grew to 740 in St. Louis County by 1810, about 20 percent of the area's growing population. This large slave force frightened the district authorities, who passed several ordinances between 1808 and 1818 to prevent slaves from gathering in public, drinking, or associating with free blacks or whites. An 1818 ordinance prescribed jail or whipping for slaves found in public between 9:00 P.M. and daylight. The development of the steamboat and the increase in river traffic sparked sustained expansion of the settlement. In 1823, three years after Missouri became a state, and six years after the first steamboat docked at St. Louis, the city was incorporated with a population of 5,000.

Slavery continued in St. Louis throughout the antebellum period, but its rate of growth was soon checked by labor competition from white northern and European immigrants. Furthermore, some slaves—the most famous was future abolitionist William Wells Brown—escaped to free states across the Mississippi, or purchased their freedom by "hiring out" their time. In 1830, slaves still made up a fourth of the city's residents, but their numbers remained virtually static from then on, and slaves fell from 9 percent to 1 percent of the population during those years, mainly personal servants of wealthy whites in the city's third and fourth wards. The city remained solidly proslavery in its politics, and abolitionists stayed out of the area. When St. Louis slave Dred Scott tried to buy his freedom in 1846, his owner, who was part of a committee to defend slave-owner interests, refused. Forced to seek his freedom in court, with the help of white lawyers he won his freedom in 1850, before the case was overturned in the notorious 1857 U.S. Supreme Court decision, *Dred Scott* v. *Sanford.* (Soon after the case was decided, Scott was manumitted by a subsequent owner.) Even as slavery declined in St. Louis, the city remained a major slave market and was a major depot for slaves shipped to the deep South, home to such important slavetrading firms as Blakey and McAfee, and Bolton, Dickens and Company. Although the city enjoyed an unwarranted reputation, even among some abolitionists, for mild slavemasters, treatment and punishment of slaves was as cruel in St. Louis as elsewhere. Slaves were often whipped in public and sometimes beaten to death.

African Americans, both slave and free, were present in St. Louis virtually from the date of its creation.

As economic opportunity grew during the antebellum years, a local free black class sprang up in St. Louis, whose numbers surpassed those of slaves by 1860. Free blacks occupied an uncertain place in society between slaves and whites. Life for St. Louis free blacks was better than for plantation slaves, though the free black Henry Clay Bruce (older brother of Blanche K. Bruce, St. Louis school teacher and later U.S. senator) claimed that while elite free blacks looked down on slaves, they faced so many legal restrictions that their status was hardly better. Most whites despised them and made their presence difficult in numerous ways. After 1835, all free blacks had to register with county courts and have white guarantors or pay large sums as bonds of good behavior. In 1847, laws were passed prohibiting free blacks from entering Missouri and forbidding the teaching of blacks to read or write. City ordinances and state laws prohibited blacks from assembling publicly, traveling without permits, or testifying against whites in court. Their precarious position was underlined by white violence. In 1836, a white mob lynched Francis McIntosh, a free black cook accused of the fatal stabbing of a constable. McIntosh's trial judge refused to intervene, saying that the lynching was justified by "a higher law." In 1846, Charles Lyons was summarily expelled from the state for not having a license. When he protested that his constitutional rights had been violated, Circuit Judge James Krum ruled that blacks were not citizens and had no right to trial by jury. Even sympathetic white leaders such as Francis Blair favored African colonization as the best solution to racial problems.

Within the free black community, there were marked social differences. Most were poor laborers, who lived on the waterfront and attended Baptist churches with slaves, with whom they often retained family ties. At the top was "the Colored Aristocracy," as Cyprian Clamorgan termed it in an 1858 pamphlet. Largely made up of light-skinned mulattos, educated merchants, and professionals, many owning substantial property (up to $500,000 worth in one case). The "aristocrats" attended their own churches, usually either Roman Catholic or Methodist Episcopal, and sent their children to be educated in exclusive northern schools. They largely refused to socialize with the other members of the community.

Large numbers of African Americans in St. Louis, whatever their social disdain for slaves, were involved in abolitionist and racial uplift efforts. The Rev. Moses Dickson founded a secret abolitionist fraternity, the Twelve Knights of Tabor, in 1846. Several black churches and schools opened during the antebellum era. In 1845, the Roman Catholic Sisters of St. Joseph of Carandolet opened a Sunday school for one hundred black girls, but it soon closed following attacks by a white mob. In 1856, other nuns established a clandestine school. In 1858, the Jesuit priest Father Peter Loning opened a chapel and school for blacks in the upper gallery of St. Francis Xavier Church. Blacks such as Elizabeth Keckley, a mulatto seamstress and later an employee and confidante of First Lady Mary Todd Lincoln, began schools, at times using the label "sewing schools" as a front. Hiram Revels and Blanche K. Bruce, the two Reconstruction-era black U.S. senators, both taught school in St. Louis during the 1860s.

The city's most outstanding leader was John Berry Meachum, a free black from Virginia. Meachum assisted John Mason Peck, a white missionary, in establishing religious services for blacks. In 1825, following his ordination by Peck, Meachum founded and became minister of the First African Baptist (later First Baptist) Church on Third and Almond streets, probably the first independent black religious congregation west of the Mississippi River. He also established a church school in defiance of the state's ban on black literacy. In the meantime, he prospered as a carpenter and barrelmaker, and set up his shop as a training ground for enslaved blacks, whom he would buy and instruct and who would purchase their freedom from him out of their wages. After 1847, Meachum evaded the laws banning black assembly and literacy by establishing a "school for freedom" on his steamboat moored on the Mississippi River, beyond Missouri jurisdiction.

The coming of the CIVIL WAR polarized opinion on slavery. By 1860, REPUBLICAN PARTY and pro-Union sentiment, nurtured by economic as well as ideological ties, was ascendant. A small abolitionist movement set up in the city. On January 1, 1861, a slave auction was interrupted by a crowd of 2,000 men who forced the end of public sales, though newspaper advertisements for slaves continued to appear. When war broke out, St. Louis became a Union outpost. Refugees poured in, swelling the black population. They found employment in building levees and other laboring activities. In May 1863, blacks were recruited into the Army, and a Bureau of Colored Troops was set up in St. Louis. Blacks eventually volunteered in large numbers for the war effort. The American Missionary Association established a freedom school in the Missouri Hotel and in 1864 set up a Colored Board of Education to raise money for black schools.

An important partner in education was the Western Sanitary Commission (WSC), established during the war by liberal whites. Originally intended to care for wounded Union soldiers, the WSC soon devoted itself to relief efforts and the uplift of the black community. The WSC set up five tuition-supported schools, including a high school, and established a Freedmen's Orphan Home. Its members were mostly paternalistic in spirit and were unwilling to allow much black involvement in leadership. The WSC ceased operation in 1865.

The same year, following the end of the Civil War, slavery was outlawed and the ban on education was ended. St. Louis's population ballooned to 311,000 by 1870, making it the third largest city in the United States. The black population, however, grew even faster, rising from 2 percent of the 1860 population to 6 percent by 1870. Most had fled the oppressive atmosphere of the deep South and agreed with the popular adage, "Better a lamppost on Targee Street [the main street of the heavily black Near South Side] than the mayor of Dixie." They welcomed the jobs and educational opportunity available in St. Louis. In 1868, local officials successfully lobbied for the creation of a branch of the ill-fated Freedman's Bank in St. Louis to encourage black business. The black WSC schools, taken over by the St. Louis Board of Education, were funded by the city. By 1875, there were twelve black schools, although they were dilapidated, irregularly spaced in districts, and staffed by poorly paid teachers. The city did not hire its first black teacher, the Rev. Richard Cole, until 1877.

Although racial segregation was widespread, there were exceptions. Libraries and streetcars remained open to blacks throughout the century. There were even occasional incidences of interracial action. After the depression of 1873 brought widespread unemployment, an unsuccessful general strike was called to restore jobs and end wage cuts. Black levee workers marched and participated equally. The end of the RECONSTRUCTION era limited black opportunity. Outside of a few post office positions, blacks received few government jobs. When thousands of EXODUSTERS fleeing to Kansas from the South were stranded in St. Louis in spring 1879, city authorities refused to provide relief or aid for passage beyond the city. The African-American community raised three thousand dollars to support travel expenses. In response to the prejudice, blacks united politically, although they remained divided along class and occupational lines, with old-time free black St. Louisans scorning newcomers. In 1880, the *St. Louis Advance,* the city's first black newspaper, was started by publisher P. H. Murray. John W. Wheeler's successful *St. Louis Palladium* followed in 1884.

By the turn of the century, the outline of the black community in St. Louis had been clearly established. A few successful businessmen grew up, many blacks, such as future entertainer Josephine BAKER, lived in great poverty in Mill Creek Valley in the Near South Side. Others lived in "Chestnut Valley," the entertainment and vice district surrounding Chestnut, Market, and 20th streets.

There, in such establishments as Honest John Turpin's Silver Dollar Saloon, and the Hurrah Sporting Club, RAGTIME music was popularized by musicians led by Scott JOPLIN, "the King of Ragtime." In 1900, the year after he wrote the bestselling "Maple Leaf Rag," Joplin and his white publisher, John Stark, moved to St. Louis. Ragtime soon became a nationwide craze, with St. Louis its mecca. Joplin's house at 2658A Morgan Street (later Delmar Boulevard) is today a ragtime museum and center. Other ragtime artists included Tom Turpin, composer of the "St. Louis Rag" and proprietor of the Rosebud Café, and Louis Chauvin.

In the early twentieth century, blacks organized politically into the Negro Civic League, led by attorney Homer G. Phillips, which leaned toward the Republicans, and the Democratic Negro Jefferson League. The two combined to elect black candidates such as Constable Charles Turpin in 1902 and delivered black votes in exchange for patronage and protection from legal discrimination.

Even so, the political influence blacks exercised on white elites did not change their essential powerlessness in the city. In 1916 white voters easily passed a residential segregation initiative, despite a heavy campaign against it by blacks and white officials. Although the measure was annulled following legal action by the fledgling St. Louis NAACP, restrictive covenants in much of the city kept blacks from moving into white areas until the U.S. Supreme Court's 1948 *Shelley* v. *Kraemer* decision.

By the turn of the century, the outline of the black community in St. Louis had been clearly established.

The city soon improved its tattered reputation for racial harmony. After 1915, during the beginning months of the Great Migration, large numbers of southern blacks arrived in the area. Many were lured by false promises of high wages to the industrial suburb of East St. Louis, Ill., an oppressive company-dominated town whose businesses were shielded from taxes and regulation. Racial tensions grew following a failed labor strike and race baiting by Democrats fearful that the new blacks would swell the Republican vote. In July 1917, East St. Louis exploded in an enormous and bloody race riot. St. Louis, in contrast, seemed a haven for blacks; as the city's newspapers denounced the rioting, city residents organized relief efforts, and St. Louis police protected African Americans fleeing from East St. Louis.

The Great Migration transformed and revitalized St. Louis. In 1920, new voters helped elect the city's (and state's) first black legislator, Walthall Moore, and soon there were a handful of black municipal officials. Business expanded also. In 1919, the Douglass Life Insurance Company was founded. It was soon the largest insurer of Missouri blacks. Annie Malone, a beautician, established a very successful beauty business, and may have been the richest black woman in the United States during the 1920s. She founded the Poro Beauty College to teach her system and set up the Poro Music College and a black orphans' home on the proceeds of her business. The *St. Louis Argus* and the *St. Louis American* were the major African-American newspapers. While blacks continued to be excluded from white areas, two new black neighborhoods, the "Ville" and "Grove" sections, sprang up. Black commercial activity was concentrated near the shopping district of Chouteau, Franklin, and Vanderventer avenues.

Although St. Louis, musically immortalized in W. C. HANDY's 1914 "St. Louis Blues," was never to regain the central place in American music it had held in the ragtime era, the city remained enormously important to African-American music. Along with Chicago and Memphis, the greater St. Louis area, including East St. Louis, Ill., was a major midwestern center for BLUES and JAZZ before World War II. Some of its leading blues musicians were Lonnie Johnson, "St. Louis Jimmy" Oden, Roosevelt Sykes, and "Peetie Wheatstraw." Big band jazz also became quite popular after the turn of the century, especially the riverboat bands led by Fate Marable, Charlie Creath, and Dewey Jackson. Later, Nightclubs such as the Jazzland, the Plantation, and the Hummingbird were the places to find big bands, such as the Jeters-Pillars Orchestra and Cab Calloway's band. Two of the most important jazz trumpeters of all time, Clark Terry and Miles DAVIS, came from the St. Louis area.

The mass of blacks remained poor during the 1920s and were made even poorer by the Great Depression. Works Project Administration contractors in St. Louis routinely discriminated against unemployed blacks until a formal appeal was made to Washington. Still, when city leaders authorized the use of federal funds to construct Homer Phillips Hospital, a $1.3 million black hospital, black labor was excluded from the project. The hospital filled a glaring need both for health care and for graduate medical and nursing training for blacks, but it long remained underfunded, overcrowded, and unsafe.

After World War II, blacks made the first successful challenges to discrimination in St. Louis. By 1949, city swimming pools and parks were opened to blacks, and Washington University integrated, although courts refused to order city schools to desegregate. The same year, students began a nine-year campaign of sit-ins that desegregated downtown stores and lunch counters.

In the 1950s, the CIVIL RIGHTS MOVEMENT, led by students and labor activists mobilized by the CONGRESS OF RACIAL EQUALITY (CORE), hit St. Louis in force. In the late 1950s, St. Louis CORE also joined with the NAACP Youth Council, led by William Clay (who would become Missouri's first black congressman in 1969) to form the Job Opportunities Council, which inaugurated strikes and sit-ins against discriminatory hiring practices.

During the early 1960s, CORE activists expanded the use of civil disobedience to obtain jobs for blacks and made dramatic peaceful takeovers of buildings to gain attention. They also protested to improve schooling for blacks. Even after the U.S. Supreme Court's 1954 BROWN V. BOARD OF EDUCATION OF TOPEKA, KANSAS ended legal school segregation, integration lagged due to almost total residential segregation. CORE activists lay in front of school buses to end the segregation of black students bused into white schools. Despite attempted busing, in 1965 91 percent of black children were still in mostly black schools.

After civil rights protest declined, NAACP and CORE members, such as Ivory Perry, shifted toward a concentration on tenants' rights and ward electoral politics as successful strategies for change. Urban renewal projects in St. Louis not only had failed to change residential segregation patterns, but had created new problems. The Pruitt-Igoe houses, a federal housing project for blacks opened in 1954, was badly planned, with few jobs available nearby and limited transportation, play, and shopping facilities. The project (home during the 1960s to future champion boxers Leon and Michael Spinks) eventually deteriorated so badly that in 1971 officials ordered it torn down, a national symbol of the failure of urban renewal.

Since the 1960s, blacks have made many gains in St. Louis. Educational opportunities have opened up, businessmen such as David B. Price, Jr., and Wayman F. Smith III have risen to prominence, and African Americans have entered the government. In 1993, St. Louis narrowly elected its first black mayor, former circuit court clerk Freeman Bosley, Jr.

Still, black St. Louisans face enormous difficulties. As a result of continued deindustrialization, by 1990 the city had less than half its 1950 residents, and its population had become almost half African American, despite a 25 percent drop in the black population over the previous twenty years. A school desegregation plan adopted in 1976 was still not complete fifteen years later. In 1991, Project HOPE estimated black unemployment in the city at 34 percent, and black youth unemployment at 96 percent.

Despite its troubles, St. Louis has remained an important incubator of musical talent. In the 1950s many significant blues and ROCK AND ROLL musicians were based in St. Louis, including Ike Turner, Tina Turner, Chuck Berry, Albert King, and J. B. Hutto. The St. Louis-based Black Artists Group, formed in 1968 and disbanded in 1972, produced a number of extraordinary talents in avant-garde jazz, including Hamiett Bluiett, Joseph and Lester Bowie, Julius Hemphill, and Oliver Lake. The city has also been the home of such varied talents as entertainer Redd Foxx, comedian/activist Dick GREGORY, and opera singers Grace Bumbry and Felicia Weathers.

BIBLIOGRAPHY

Christensen, Lawrence O. "Race Relations in St. Louis, 1865–1916." *Missouri Historical Review* (January 1984).

Clamorgan, Cyprian. *The Colored Aristocracy of St. Louis.* St. Louis, 1858.

Day, Judy, and M. James Kedro. "Free Blacks in St. Louis: Antebellum Conditions, Emancipation and the Post War Era." *Missouri Historical Society Bulletin* (January 1974): 117–135.

Foley, William E. *The Genesis of Missouri: From Frontier Outpost to Statehood.* Columbia, Mo., 1989.

Greene, Lorenzo J., Gary R. Kremer, and Antonio F. Holland. *Missouri's Black Heritage.* Rev. ed. Columbia, Mo., 1992.

Gregory, Dick, and Robert Lipsyte. *Nigger: An Autobiography.* New York, 1964.

Lipsitz, George. *A Life in the Struggle: Ivory Perry and the Culture of Opposition.* Philadelphia, 1988.

Primm, James Neal. *St. Louis: Lion of the Valley.* Boulder, Colo., 1981.

Rainwater, Lee. *Behind Ghetto Walls: Black Families in a Federal Slum.* Chicago, 1970.

Trexler, Harrison. *Slavery in Missouri, 1804–1865.* 1914. Reprint. New York, 1986.

– GREG ROBINSON

SAN FRANCISCO AND OAKLAND, CALIFORNIA

The history of African Americans in the San Francisco Bay Area, specifically San Francisco and Oakland, is one of both success and failure. Present from its first settlement, blacks at first found San Francisco a land of opportunity and riches. The dream soon evaporated, however, and the area became hostile to black achievement. The black population, frozen out of industrial labor, remained small. During and after WORLD WAR II, the area's black population growth reached enormous levels, bringing racial tensions and conflict in its wake. At the end of the twentieth century, African Americans represented a large fraction of the Bay Area's inhabitants. Economic and social discrimination persists, despite numerous black success stories.

The Spanish settlement in San Francisco began in 1776, and it soon grew into a small town. Mexican blacks were among the settlers, and they remained after the area was turned over to Mexican control in 1821. During the Mexican period, two men of African descent served as mayors. During the 1840s, William Leidesdorff, a black man from the Danish West Indies, became a prosperous merchant and city official under the Mexicans, though he also played an important role in the American takeover. San Francisco's Leidesdorff Street was named in his honor.

In 1848, two years after the establishment of American control over California and San Francisco, gold was discovered at Sutter's Mill, in northern California. The Gold Rush of 1849 sparked massive immigration, which turned San Francisco into a city almost overnight. Black immigrants settled near the waterfront and on the "Chili Hill" slope of Telegraph Hill. The city soon acquired a somewhat exaggerated reputation as a land of hope for African Americans. Frederick DOUGLASS and others spread the newspaper reports of "black luck" on the West Coast and catalyzed further immigration. The suburb of Oakland, across the bay, also expanded during the period, first after the inauguration of ferry service in 1852, then after the city's selection as terminus of the Western Pacific and related railroads in 1869.

The history of African Americans in the San Francisco Bay Area is one of both success and failure.

Slavery became an issue in local politics as white southern Forty-Niners brought their slaves to the area as gold miners, and fugitive slaves migrated West. Even after the state of California entered the Union in 1850 and officially abolished slavery, masters used subterfuges to continue holding African Americans in bondage. For example, George Washington Dennis was brought to San Francisco by his master to work in a gambling parlor. As it happens, Dennis saved $1,000 for his freedom from the nickels and dimes he swept off the parlor's floor. He later became a wealthy livery stable owner and real estate speculator, and his son Edward Dennis became the city's first black police officer in the 1880s.

Most of San Francisco's early black settlers were free. They included Rev. John Jamison Moore, pastor of the Stockton Street African Methodist Episcopal Church, the city's first black church; William Newby, who founded the newspaper *Mirror of the Times* (1856); William Yates, a former porter for the U.S. Supreme Court who chaired the first of three California Colored State Conventions during the 1850s to organize civil rights efforts; writer/abolitionist James Madison Bell; artist/lithographer Grafton T. Brown; and merchants Peter Lester and Mifflin W. Gibbs. Isaac Flood, an ex-slave from South Carolina and one of the first black settlers in Oakland, ultimately became a wealthy landowner and community leader.

Mary Ellen "Mammy" Pleasant, an ex-slave who arrived in the city from Boston in 1847 and opened a thriving restaurant and boardinghouse (and later a bordello), rapidly became the leader of the black community. She was one of thirty-seven blacks who organized the Mutual Benefit and Relief Society in 1850 to aid new arrivals. Profiting from a chronic labor shortage, she found jobs for 300 African Americans, employing sixty herself in her restaurant and laundry. Soon thereafter, she helped the Rev. Jeremiah Sanderson set up a black school in the basement of the St. Cyprian African Methodist Episcopal Church. Pleasant also became active in civil rights efforts. A participant in the Colored Conventions, she organized the San Francisco Franchise League in 1852 to petition the legislature to grant blacks suffrage. She later became a fund-raiser for radical abolitionist John Brown.

Despite the efforts of Pleasant and her associates, legal discrimination and disfranchisement remained in San Francisco. An 1850 law, which forbade nonwhites to testify against whites in court, led to theft by unscrupulous whites and large-scale abuse of blacks and members of the growing Chinese-American community. In 1858, the state legislature passed a bill forbidding black immigration, prompting an exodus of the city's blacks to Victoria, British Columbia.

In 1866, following the end of the CIVIL WAR, blacks renewed efforts at winning equal status. At the Fourth Convention of the Colored Citizens of California that year, San Francisco's William Henry Hall moved for a concerted campaign to gain suffrage rights. The Executive Committee of San Francisco was created as a lobbying group, and it established the weekly journal *Elevator* as its organ. However, a bill to grant suffrage died in the state legislature in 1868, and blacks were not enfranchised until 1869. In 1868 Mary Ann Pleasant sued the local streetcar company after being ejected from a car and won a judgment of $500. In 1872, after black schools in San Francisco and Oakland were closed by local authorities who opposed black education, Mary Frances Ward enrolled at a white school and was rejected. She sued, and the case went to the California Supreme Court, which ruled in her favor. In 1875 the San Francisco Board of Education banned educational segregation. In 1878 David W. Ruggles became the first black to sit on a grand jury in the city.

By the last decades of the nineteenth century, San Francisco's African-American community had stabilized. The black population remained small but was extremely diverse, as black immigrants arrived from the Caribbean, Canada, Cape Verde, and other places. By 1900 San Francisco had a higher percentage of foreign-born blacks than any other American city except New York. Prejudice was widespread, although there was little overt antiblack violence. Blacks were sometimes barred or restricted in restaurants and saloons. As white labor unions such as the Building Trades Council, which mostly excluded blacks, gained unusual power in the city, African Americans found it increasingly difficult to obtain work. Most became sailors or were forced either into service trades such as barbers or into domestic service. However, several blacks were prosperous, and the literacy rate in the black community was high. While the community institutions became clustered in a black enclave in the city's Western Addition area after 1900, housing was relatively open during the period, and blacks lived in all but the most exclusive white areas. Black patients were admitted at city hospitals and health care facilities. Before police closed the Barbary Coast entertainment district in 1917, many black performers worked on its streets and in clubs such as Purcell's Elite Café and the Olympia. The most notable were vaudevillian Bert Williams and his partner George Walker. During the late 1910s, early New Orleans JAZZ musicians such as Kid Ory and Jelly Roll MORTON settled for a time in the area. Morton opened an interracial club which was quickly closed down by police.

A few African-American leaders achieved limited fame and wealth, such as Stuart T. Davison, a physician who in the early 1880s was one of the first black graduates of the University of California at Berkeley, and attorney Edward D. Mabson (later head of the activist Negro Equity League). Elite blacks formed clubs and lodges, and in 1901 they organized the Afro-American League of San Francisco under Theophilus B. Morton. Morton also founded the Afro-American Cooperative and Investment Association to spur economic unity. The Afro-American League soon became inactive, and in 1915 the Northern California branch of the NATIONAL ASSOCIATION FOR THE ADVANCEMENT OF COLORED PEOPLE (NAACP) was formed.

Throughout the period, Oakland was more welcoming to blacks than San Francisco. The railroads employed many black residents. Oakland's port, where unions were weak, accepted black workers. Oakland also provided a large number of blacks the opportunity of becoming homeowners. Community leadership was provided by various organizations, including churches such as the Beth Eden Baptist Church, founded in 1890; the California Association of Colored Women's Clubs, based in Oakland; and the *Oakland Sunshine* newspaper (1906). In 1906, after the great San Francisco earthquake and fire, over 100,000 people, some of them black, sought temporary refuge in Oakland. Many stayed, and from 1900 to 1910 the city's black population tripled, surpassing that of San Francisco.

Blacks continued to migrate to the Bay Area during the Great Migration of the mid-1910s and early '20s, although not in the massive numbers that moved to eastern cities. The great distance and the lack of established family and job contacts in the West limited the flow of new arrivals. During this period, West Oakland became established as the center of the city's evolving black community. In 1915, journalist Delilah Beasley started a twenty-year tenure as a columnist for the white-owned *Oakland Tribune.* An active crusader for civil rights, she also wrote the landmark historical study, *Negro Trail Blazers of California* (1919). E. L. Daly used real estate profits to buy and consolidate several black newspapers into the powerful and successful *California Voice.*

During the 1920s, economic opportunities for San Francisco blacks expanded somewhat. At the same time, prejudice became more marked. Increasingly, blacks were forced to settle in the Western Addition (also known as the Fillmore district), often in dilapidated homes. Even there, blacks faced exclusion. In 1924 black leaders organized the Booker T. Washington Community Center on Geary Street. When the center attempted to lease property on Divisidero Street, local whites attempted to oppose the move. Soon after the center relocated, a white group bought the building and foreclosed on the center's lease. The black community saved the center through a determined campaign of fund-raising.

Blacks organized protests against the rising tide of discrimination. The San Francisco NAACP (which was born following a split in the Bay Area branch in the early 1920s) became noted for its lawsuits and lobbying efforts. In 1921 the NAACP won an important, if temporary, victory when it persuaded Mayor Eugene Rolphe to ban a showing of the film *Birth of a Nation* (1915), which blacks considered offensive (Oakland's mayor refused to ban the film). Black political influence remained limited, though, and when the film was again shown in San Francisco in 1930, Rolphe refused to act.

The Great Depression hit blacks in the Bay Area extremely hard. By 1937 an estimated 13.7 percent of San Francisco's black laborers were unemployed, and in Oakland the figure was 15.3 percent. Large numbers of African Americans were forced to rely on public relief. Job competition with white workers led to racial tension, accompanied by police harassment.

The depression experience radicalized many Bay Area blacks, who became active in union and other left-wing activities. John Pittman's newspaper, the *San Francisco Spokesman,* criticized the NAACP for its moderation and called for such measures as cooperative health care. Pittman and lawyer William L. Patterson became active in the COMMUNIST PARTY OF THE U.S.A. The communists were the first active interracial group in San Francisco. In 1934 the radical International Longshoreman's Union, led by Harry Bridges, became the first large union in the area to admit blacks.

Through the efforts of such leaders as labor leader C. L. Dellums (uncle of future U.S. Rep. Ronald Dellums) and administrator Vivian Marsh of the BROTHERHOOD OF SLEEPING CAR PORTERS, a disproportionate number of African Americans—860 in Oakland alone by 1937—found employment in the federal jobs programs of the New Deal during the late 1930s, notably in the WORKS PROGRESS ADMINISTRATION (which also employed artist Sargent Johnson to make large sculptures for the Golden Gate exhibition) and the Negro Division of the National Youth Administration. These jobs not only allowed African Americans to earn money but offered them training for jobs from which they would ordinarily have been excluded by unions. Many of them, particularly women, were actually able to upgrade their job status in public relief employment.

The coming of WORLD WAR II largely transformed the condition of blacks in the Bay Area. Bay Area shipyards and industry rapidly expanded. Black jobseekers, as well as military personnel and their spouses, poured into the Bay Area, many from the southern states. San Francisco's black population increased more than sixfold in five years, and Oakland's rose by 341 percent. Many white employers and unions at first refused to admit blacks, and recruited migrant white workers to relieve the tremendous labor shortage. However, little by little, under the twin pressures of demand for workers and pressure from the local office of the federal Fair Employment Practices Committee (FEPC), industries began to hire black workers for well-paying jobs. In 1944 the California Supreme Court declared union segregation unconstitutional, further eroding barriers to black advancement.

The coming of World War II largely transformed the condition of blacks in the Bay Area.

Despite the black economic surge, the mass migration led to difficulties. Landlords in white neighborhoods refused to rent to large numbers of migrants, and many were unable to secure proper housing. San Francisco's Fillmore district, already a heavily black area, expanded as blacks moved into housing vacated by Japanese sent to internment camps. A new ghetto grew up in the Bayview-Hunter's Point district. Oakland's black population spilled over from West Oakland to North and East Oakland and to Richmond. Racial discrimination and exclusion from public accommodations became more frequent. Several groups, notably the Bay Area Council Against Discrimination (led by Walter Gordon, later governor of the Virgin Islands), and the white-led Council for Civic Unity, were set up by blacks and white liberals to promote equality.

A notorious episode of racial discrimination was the Port Chicago incident. In 1944 an ammunition ship explosion rocked Port Chicago, a Bay Area shipyard, killing 320 people, including 202 black sailors. When 328 black sailors were ordered to return, they refused; 258 were arrested, and 50 of them were court-martialed. Convicted of mutiny, they were sentenced to long prison terms. NAACP Legal Defense Fund director THURGOOD MARSHALL appealed the case before the Judge Advocate General of the Navy in 1945, but the convictions were upheld.

After the end of the war, migration to the Bay Area continued at a reduced pace. In 1946 the NATIONAL URBAN LEAGUE opened its first local chapter. Many blacks were released from the well-paying jobs they had occupied during the war, though black professionals, skilled laborers, and government officials found employment in increasing numbers. San Francisco hired its first black teachers, and the number of black doctors and lawyers in the city increased several times. Bay Area blacks also made their first major political gains. In 1946 physician William McKinley Thomas became Commissioner of the San Francisco Housing Authority, the city's first black high government official. In 1948 Oakland's William Byron Rumsford became the first black from Northern California to be elected to the state legislature. With the aid of white sympathizers, several interracial antidiscrimination groups were founded. The short-lived Fellowship Church, with the Rev. Howard Thurman as its pastor, was one of the first completely integrated churches in America. In 1952 the NAACP represented Mattie Banks, an African American, in her attempt to move into public housing in North Beach. Despite the Housing Authority's warning (soon borne out) that whites would leave if blacks were admitted to public housing in white areas, the state Superior Court banned segregated public housing. Nevertheless, private housing remained largely segregated during the period. When baseball star Willie MAYS moved to San Francisco with his team, the Giants, in 1958, his difficulty in finding a house was well publicized. Despite the formation of a local FEPC in 1958, job discrimination remained a chronic problem.

By the 1960s, the majority of Bay Area blacks was stuck in inner-city areas with poor housing, and faced disproportionately high unemployment rates. Ironically, the ghettoization of San Francisco blacks increased black political influence, and in 1964 Terry Francois, an African American, was named to the city's board of supervisors. The same year, Willie Brown was elected to the state legislature from San Francisco. He would remain there for thirty years and became one of the most powerful figures in California politics as Speaker of the California House. While San Francisco's black population remained static, Oakland's larger population continued to expand. As Oakland's whites began to move to nearby suburbs, African Americans became a significant proportion of the city's residents.

In the early 1960s, civil rights forces, notably the CONGRESS OF RACIAL EQUALITY (CORE), began demonstrating for employment opportunities and protesting de facto school segregation and police brutality. In 1963 a march against police brutality at San Francisco's city hall attracted two hundred people. The next year, the success of the interracial Free Speech Movement at the University of California-Berkeley, led by veterans of the Mississippi Freedom Summer, resulted in mass civil rights demonstrations. However, nonviolent protesters failed to make sufficient headway against discrimination. In 1966, following the shooting of a black teenager by police in Hunter's Point, African Americans throughout the city rioted. The rioting lasted for five days and devastated large sections of the Fillmore district.

The most notable radical black group to emerge from the Bay Area was the BLACK PANTHER PARTY, formed by Huey Newton and Bobby Seale in Oakland in 1966. The Panthers' revolutionary Marxist ideology and militant image quickly made them heroes to blacks and white leftists throughout the United States. They were particularly well regarded in Oakland for their efforts to combat police brutality and for their establishment of a free breakfast program for schoolchildren. Despite police repression and internecine conflict—which destroyed the Panther movement by the late 1970s—the Panthers helped create such institutions as the Oakland Community School and the Oakland Community Housing Center, which funded housing for homeless African Americans.

Since the 1960s, blacks in the Bay Area have benefited from increased educational and social opportunities and have become politically powerful. In 1968 the Oakland Black Caucus was formed as an umbrella community group. Three years later, Ronald Dellums became the Bay Area's first African American in Congress. In 1977, with support from the Panthers, Lionel Wilson was elected Oakland's first black mayor. (In 1991 Oakland would again elect an African American, Elihu Harris, as mayor.) In 1983 Robert Maynard bought the *Oakland Tribune,* becoming the first African-American editor of a major metropolitan daily, and in 1993 Pearl Stewart, his successor, became the first African-American woman editor. Oakland has also become a showplace of black culture, with such institutions as the Ebony Museum of Art and the Northern California Center for Afro-American History and Life. Mean-

lacked the conceptual skills necessary to plan and shape the future.

Nineteenth-century black physicians remained more or less silent about the racial dogmas advanced by their white counterparts for several reasons. First, since white organizations generally refused to admit them to membership, black physicians were kept busy developing alternative forums—their own professional societies, discussion groups, journals—to provide opportunities for shared learning and experience. The National Medical Association, the black counterpart of the American Medical Association, was founded in 1895 through the efforts of prominent physicians such as Miles Vandahurst Lynk and Robert Fulton Boyd. Second, black physicians recognized that generating racial or political controversy risked a backlash that could undermine efforts to place their own professional role and community on a solid foundation. And third, some black professionals accepted the truth of racial stereotypes and distanced themselves from the perceived taint of their race by thinking of themselves as unique, as somehow different from the "typical" African American.

Eugenics and Other Movements

In the early twentieth century, activities pursued under the guise of science continued to point to the alleged inferiority of African Americans. The eugenics movement is a good example. While it had always been present in some form (in spirit if not in name), eugenics assumed formal standing as a science with the rediscovery of Mendel's seminal paper on genetics in 1900 and the establishment in 1910 of the Eugenics Records Office at Cold Spring Harbor, Long Island. Defined as the science of improving the hereditary qualities of particular races or breeds, eugenics found devotees among geneticists and reputable practitioners in other branches of the biological sciences. It captured the public imagination, bringing issues of racial inferiority into focus not only in the realm of natural science, but in the social arena as well. Eugenics, with its growing stock of data on what were termed "weak races," fed into regressive social policies such as the anti-immigration movement and programs of coercive sterilization aimed at "purifying" the nation's population stocks. Its ideas permeated American society, promoting racial fear among whites and self-antipathy among some blacks. Although eugenics slipped out of the mainstream of American science in the 1930s following its adoption by the Germans as a social-engineering tool, its assumptions remained firmly embedded in the American social fabric.

The racial thrust underlying the work of the craniometrists, anthropometrists, physician-scientists, and eugenicists persisted past the middle of the twentieth century—in spite of the rise of the CIVIL RIGHTS MOVEMENT. In some respects, it persists down to the present day. Examples are numerous. From 1932 to 1972, the United States Public Health Service carried out the Tuskegee Study of Untreated Syphilis in the Negro Male (popularly known as the TUSKEGEE SYPHILIS EXPERIMENT). This project gathered together four hundred African-American "guinea pigs"; misled them about the nature of their illness by reinforcing the subjects' belief that they were suffering from vague ailments related to "bad blood"; and withheld treatment from them in order to observe the progress of the disease. One rationale underlying the project was the need to assess racial differences in the impact of the disease. Then there was the segregation of blood in the armed services during World War II. Still later, during the 1960s and '70s, Arthur Jensen, Richard Herrnstein, and William Shockley applied IQ and other data in studies of racial differences. These scientists drew broad conclusions, for example, about the genetic inferiority—and, in particular, the inherently lower intelligence—of blacks as compared to whites. Since the 1980s, some work in sociobiology and genetic engineering has attempted to identify genes with behavioral traits. In 1992, the National Institutes of Health awarded funds for a conference on heredity and criminal behavior but later withdrew support to placate critics who felt that linking genetics and crime in this way could add renewed authority to theories that blacks (represented disproportionately in U.S. crime statistics) were biologically inferior.

African Americans in Science

Science may have been used and abused in racially motivated ways, but this did not stop African Americans from being drawn to careers in the field. The history of blacks in American science is as old as the history of science in America. In colonial America, free blacks were known for their inventive, scientific, and technical skills. The first to achieve a national reputation in science was Benjamin BANNEKER (1731–1806), known in the latter part of the eighteenth century as a mathematician, astronomer, and compiler and publisher of almanacs. In 1791, Banneker served as part of a team of surveyors and engineers who contributed to planning the city of Washington, D.C. Other free blacks, including Thomas L. Jennings (1791–1859) and Norbert Rillieux, developed and patented technical devices in the years leading up to the Civil War. Some slaves were known for their inventive abilities, but their legal status prevented them from holding patents and from receiving widespread public recognition of their achievement.

After the Civil War, the number of blacks undertaking scientific work increased slowly. The establishment of black institutions of higher learning—necessary because white institutions did not routinely admit African-American students—provided an essential start. Nevertheless, black colleges and universities tended to focus on curricula in theology, education, medicine, and other fields that were more practical (or technical) than scientific, geared primarily toward creating a niche or foothold for African-American professionals in the social and economic mainstream. Science, in the sense of an activity devoted to pure or basic research, did not fit readily into this framework. As a result, African Americans wanting specialized science education or training were obliged to seek out programs at white institutions. It was a difficult proposition that only a few tackled successfully before the end of the nineteenth century. One of the earliest was Edward Alexander Bouchet (1852–1918), who earned a Ph.D. in physics from Yale University in 1876. Bouchet was said to have been the first African American to earn a Ph.D. from an American university. His subsequent career did not, however, include research in the sciences. He became a high-school science teacher at the Institute for Colored Youth, Philadelphia. Because of his race, professional opportunities in science were essentially closed to him. Bouchet's was nonetheless an important accomplishment, a counterexample to the widespread mythology about the mental inferiority of blacks.

Science may have been used and abused in racially motivated ways, but this did not stop African Americans from being drawn to careers in the field.

The number of blacks entering scientific fields increased markedly after the turn of the twentieth century. Among these were Charles Henry Turner, zoologist; George Washington CARVER, agricultural botanist; Ernest Everett JUST, embryologist; St. Elmo Brady, chemist; Elmer Samuel Imes, physicist; William Augustus Hinton, bacteriologist; and Julian Herman Lewis, pathologist. Percy Lavon Julian, chemist, and Charles Richard Drew, a surgeon and pioneer of the blood banking system, followed a couple of decades later. This cohort represents the first group of black scientists to receive graduate degrees from major white universities, pursue science at the research level, and publish in leading scientific journals.

World War II brought African-American scientists, as a distinct group, to public attention for the first time. Prior to this, they had worked primarily as teachers at black colleges and universities, and had not—with the notable exception, perhaps, of Ernest Just—exerted their influence widely or made their presence felt in the larger scientific community. As part of the war mobilization effort at Los Alamos and in the various branches of the Manhattan Project attached to laboratories at the University of Chicago, Columbia University, and other universities, some white scientists witnessed for the first time a sizable number of black physicists and chemists entering their world. African Americans who worked on the atom bomb project included Edwin Roberts Russell (b. 1913), Benjamin Franklin Scott (b. 1922), J. Ernest Wilkins, Jr., Jasper Brown Jeffries (b. 1912), George Warren Reed, Jr. (b. 1920), Moddie Daniel Taylor (1912–1976), and the brothers Lawrence Howland Knox (b. 1907) and William Jacob Knox, Jr. (b. 1904). At a postwar conference in 1946, one eminent white scientist, Arthur Holly Compton, remarked on how the bomb project had brought races and religions together for a common purpose.

After the war, even though a few white universities began to open up faculty appointments and graduate fellowships to blacks, racial discrimination continued to operate at many levels within the professional world of science. It was common for major associations, including the American Association for the Advancement of Science, to hold conventions in cities where segregation was both customary and legally enforced, and where hotels serving as convention sites denied accommodation to anyone of African-American origin. Blacks often relied on their own scientific associations, such as the National Institute of Science (founded in 1942) and Beta Kappa Chi Scientific Society (incorporated in 1929), to share ideas and foster collegial ties. Furthermore, most science education for African Americans—certainly at the undergraduate level—continued to take place within the confines of historically black colleges and universities.

Following passage of the 1964 U.S. Civil Rights Bill, new educational opportunities gradually opened up for blacks, and scientific careers—in both academia and industry—became more of a tangible, realistic goal. Rosters of noteworthy scientists from the 1960s to the 1990s mention a number of African Americans, including Harold Amos, bacteriologist; Shirley Ann Jackson, physicist; Edward William Hawthorne (1921–1986), physiologist; Marie Maynard Daly (b. 1921), biochemist; and Ronald Erwin Mcnair, astronautical physicist. Scientific organizations, learned societies, and educational institutions grew more inclusive during this period. David Harold Blackwell, a mathematician, was elected to the National Academy of Sciences in 1965. The physicist Walter Eugene MASSEY became the first African-American president of the American Association for the Advancement of Science in 1988 and the first African-American director of the National Science Foundation in 1990. Nevertheless, statistics indicate that African Americans continue to be underrepresented in science. Only 2 to 3 percent of American scientists are black, while African Americans constitute around 12 percent of the total U.S. population.

BIBLIOGRAPHY

Branson, Herman. "The Negro and Scientific Research." *Negro History Bulletin* 15 (April 1952): 131–136, 151.

Drew, Charles Richard. "Negro Scholars in Scientific Research." *Journal of Negro History* 35 (April 1950): 135–149.

Haber, Louis. *Black Pioneers of Science and Invention.* New York, 1970.

Klein, Aaron E. *The Hidden Contributors: Black Scientists and Inventors in America.* Garden City, N.Y., 1971.

Manning, Kenneth R. "The Complexion of Science." *Technology Review* 94 (November/December 1991): 60–69.

———. "Race, Science, and Identity." In Gerald Early, ed. *Lure and Loathing: Essays on Race, Identity, and the Ambivalence of Assimilation.* New York, 1993, pp. 317–336.

"Minorities in Science: The Pipeline Problem." *Science* 258 (November 13, 1992): 1175–1237.

Pearson, Willie, Jr. *Black Scientists, White Society, and Colorless Science: A Study of Universalism in American Science.* Millwood, N.Y., 1985.

Wright, Clarence. "The Negro in the Natural Sciences." In Jessie P. Guzman, ed. *Negro Year Book: A Review of Events Affecting Negro Life, 1941–1946.* Tuskegee, Ala., 1947, pp. 34–47.

– KENNETH R. MANNING

SCIENCE FICTION

Although the term *science fiction* originated in the 1920s, the genealogy of the form continues to be the subject of debate. British author/critic Brian W. Aldiss makes a well-argued case for Mary Shelley's *Frankenstein* (1818) as science fiction's authentic ancestor, thereby tracing the birth of the genre to the Gothic mode and the Romantic movement of which it was a part. Samuel R. Delany, the first African-American writer consciously dedicated to the science fiction enterprise, strongly demurs, arguing that science fiction has its true beginnings in pulp magazines such as *Amazing Stories,* which began publication in 1926. These two disparate views are perhaps reconciled by one quite reasonable position of current scholarship: that although what "we now call science fiction was written in earlier centuries . . . the emergence of SF as a special field, with its own subculture of writers, editors, and fans, is a phenomenon of the twentieth century" (Bainbridge 1986, p. 9). One aspect of the problem of precise definition or of pinpointing origins is that there are so many overlappings between science fiction and fantasy, a much older but still vigorous form. Indeed, the very notion of *genre* must be approached as something quite porous and impure; thus, the use of the term here will imply very soft, unstable borders.

Novelist and essayist Ishmael Reed has called George Schuyler's *Black No More* (1931) the first science fiction novel by an African American. Although the subtitle of Schuyler's book, "Being an Account of the Strange and Wonderful Workings of Science in the Land of the Free, a.d. 1933–1940," might seem to support Reed's contention, *Black No More* is in fact no more science fiction than is, for example, Jonathan Swift's *Gulliver's Travels* (1726). Both are works of satire, in which science is one of the projects being satirized. Race, as a marker of "difference," is Schuyler's actual subject; science is a target to the extent that it lends its authority to theories of race that impact invidiously on non-Europeans. If *Black No More* were to be categorized as science fiction, then works like Reed's own "Cab Calloway Stands In for the Moon" (1970), or Amiri BARAKA's stories "God and Machine" (1971) or "Answers in Progress" (1967), or "Jazz and Palmwine" (1970) by the Congolese writer Emmanuel Boundzéki Dongala might also qualify for this designation. Despite the admittedly complex and varied nature of the science fiction genre, however, the presence of elements of science fiction or fantasy in a given work is not sufficient to impress it into service as "science fiction." The aforementioned works are most appropriately situated within the context of African-American literature, the imaginative scope of which often traverses the borders of other literary territories.

A historian of science fiction's readership has claimed that there were "thousands" of black science fiction fans in the 1930s. Yet as recently as 1988–1989, an exchange of letters in the journal *Science Fiction Studies* raised these questions: Where are the black science fiction readers? Where, indeed (apart from Delany, Octavia Butler, and Steven Barnes), are the black science fiction writers? One might also ask: why have a number of African-American science fiction writers appeared since the early 1960s and not before? To the extent that the genre has been identified as "utopian," "apocalyptic," a literature of "cognitive estrangement," a mapping of alternative possibilities, it seems to have much in common, broadly speaking, with certain characteristics of African-American literature, and contemporary African-American science fiction writers have indeed exploited these points of similarity between the two literatures.

But it is also important to remember that for a long time, science fiction was considered to be a sort of paraliterature—popularly read but uncanonized by the academy, a poor but ubiquitous cousin to "serious" literature. This situation has altered dramatically with the rise of critical interest in science fiction and the inclusion of science fiction courses in university curricula. So-called minority literatures, among which African-American literature is a senior partner, have been similarly stigmatized, although the civil rights and Black Power movements, and the more recent emphasis on multiculturalism in the United States, have done much to overcome this condescension and lack of understanding. Given the struggle African-American authors waged to be taken seriously outside their own communities (and sometimes even within them), it is perhaps not surprising that they did not take on the added burden of adopting a genre that was itself marginalized in terms of respectability.

The decade of the 1960s, when Delany began publishing, was the period in which science fiction began to command attention beyond its prior constituency, gaining recognition for its frequently bold experimentalism and heightened sophistication. Some of its focus shifted from outer space to inner space, from futurological hardware to the "software" of a more human emphasis. Simultaneously, science fiction writers began to become more conscious of, and desirous of critically examining, the nature and the history of their enterprise.

Samuel Delany was a significant figure in both of these events. This "evolutionary leap" of science fiction took place, of course, during the far more general release of transformational energies that characterized the 1960s, one of the most crucial examples of which was the black cultural revolution. Though a very active participant in the "invention" of the counterculture of that era, Delany was not directly involved in the black revolution, yet he was surely among its beneficiaries to the extent that he felt free to transgress barriers to black participation in all things American, and, indeed, to refuse self-imposed limits to what one could do and be. No doubt his great success in the field was an encouragement to other black writers contemplating a career in science fiction. Still, the time was ripe for an expansion of the possible within the realm of African-American culture itself, and this, one concludes, is what made the difference. The black artist would no longer be bound by others' expectations as to what constituted his or her "proper" role. Just as the restive and yet restorative consciousness of the present has been employed by a number of African-American authors to interrogate the past, so, too, has that same consciousness been used by African-American science fiction writers to critically explore the future.

The decade of the 1960s, when Delany began publishing, was the period in which science fiction began to command attention beyond its prior constituency.

Samuel R. Delany is not only the first African-American writer committed to the field of science fiction; he is also the best known, most critically acclaimed, and most prolific, having written more than two dozen books since his first publication in 1962. Delany is, at the same time, one of the most challenging critics of the science fiction genre and its history. He is also a figure of some controversy, especially with regard to his concern with the nature and politics of sexuality, first broached explicitly in his longest and best-selling novel, *Dhalgren* (1975), and in the little-known pornographic/philosophic work *The Tides of Lust* (1973). Much of Delany's creative work could be characterized very broadly as employing archaeologies of the past and the future in order to both understand and transcend the complexities of the present.

Following Delany in importance and productivity is Octavia E. Butler, the first black woman science fiction writer. She is best known for her novel *Kindred* (1979), which, although it deals with time travel, has been celebrated as an important work of both black and feminist literature. *Kindred* is a perfect example of what could be called the de-ghettoization of science fiction, analogous to the crossover phenomenon in other cultural spheres. Butler's other works include *Patternmaster* (1976), *Mind of My Mind* (1977), *Survivor* (1978), *Wild Seed* (1980), *Clay's Ark* (1984), *Dawn* (1987), *Adulthood Rites* (1988), and *Imago* (1989), and deal imaginatively and critically with questions of race, gender, and power.

Two other writers demand mention. First is Steven Barnes, author of novels including *Streetlethal* (1983) and *Gorgon Child* (1989), as well as a number of collaborations with veteran science fiction author Larry Niven. Much of Barnes's work extrapolates dilemmas of the present into the not-so-distant future, where questions of race, gender, and sexual orientation confront increasingly blatant forms of repression. Second is Charles R. Saunders, born in the United States but living in Canada since 1969. He is a writer primarily of heroic fantasy, best exemplified by his first novel, *Imaro* (1981), which takes place in a mythical Africa. Saunders has attempted to counter Eurocentric fantasies about Africa—typified by the writings of H. Rider Haggard and Edgar Rice Burroughs—through the depiction of what could be termed Afrocentric fantasies.

It can be expected that more African-American and, indeed, other "minority" science fiction writers will emerge in the future, to join the handful of present practitioners who have already had a significant impact on a vibrant and varied genre.

BIBLIOGRAPHY

Aldiss, Brian W. *Trillion Year Spree: The History of Science Fiction.* New York, 1986.

Bainbridge, William Sims. *Dimensions of Science Fiction.* Cambridge, Mass., 1986.

Black American Literature Forum 18, no. 2 (Summer 1984). Special issue on science fiction by black writers.

Callaloo 14, no. 2 (Spring 1991). Contains section on science fiction and fantasy by black authors.

Delany, Samuel R. *Starboard Wine: More Notes on the Language of Science Fiction.* Pleasantville, N.Y., 1984.

– ROBERT ELLIOT FOX

SCOTTSBORO CASE

On April 9, 1931, an Alabama judge sentenced eight black teenagers to death: Haywood Patterson, Olen Montgomery, Clarence Norris, Willie Roberson, Andrew Wright, Ozie Powell, Eugene Williams and Charley Weems. After perfunctory trials in the mountain town of Scottsboro, all-white juries convicted the youths of raping two white women (Victoria Price and Ruby Bates) aboard a freight train as it moved across northern Alabama on March 25. The case of the ninth defendant—thirteen-year-old Leroy Wright—ended in a mistrial after a majority of the jury refused to accept the prosecution's recommendation for life imprisonment because of his extreme youth.

The repercussions of the Scottsboro case were felt throughout the 1930s; by the end of the decade, it had become one of the great civil rights cases of the twentieth century.

After the quick conviction and draconian verdict, the Communist party's legal affiliate, the International Labor Defense (ILD), took over the case from the National Association for the Advancement of Colored People. Using both propaganda and aggressive legal action, the ILD succeeded in obtaining a new trial for the eight defendants. In a landmark case, *Powell* v. *Alabama* (1932), the U.S. Supreme Court ruled that defendants in capital cases had to receive more than a pro forma defense. (One Scottsboro attorney had been drunk at the original trial; the other was elderly and incompetent.)

The April 1933 retrial of Haywood Patterson was moved to Decatur, Ala. Defense attorney Samuel Leibowitz introduced extensive evidence that the two women had concocted the charge of rape in order to avoid prosecution for prostitution and vagrancy. The highlight of the trial came when Ruby Bates—who had disappeared in 1932—dramatically renounced her earlier accusations and testified on behalf of Patterson and the other Scottsboro defendants.

But the jurors—reflecting the belief of the local white community that Bates was bribed by communist agitators ("Jew money from New York" in the words of one prosecutor)—ignored her testimony. They were particularly incensed by the willingness of Alabama's African-American population to join the defense in attacking the state's all-white jury system. (In pretrial hearings before Judge James E. Horton, Jr., ten members of Decatur's black community defied Klan cross burnings and threats to insist that they were qualified to serve as jurors but had never been called.) The jury convicted Patterson and mandated the judge to order the death penalty.

To the surprise of almost everyone, Judge Horton—convinced that Patterson and the other defendants were innocent—set aside the verdict, pointing out that the evidence "overwhelmingly preponderated" in favor of the Scottsboro defendants. He ordered a new trial and announced that the nine defendants would never be convicted in his court. In the next election, however, voters defeated Horton and elected a judge more amenable to the prosecution's case to preside over the trial of Patterson and Clarence Norris.

Many in Alabama had come to see the Scottsboro Case as a test of white Southerners' resolve against the forces of "communism" and "racial amalgamation." The guilt or innocence of the defendants thus seemed irrelevant.

The trials that followed were travesties of justice. Horton's replacement, Judge William Washington Callahan, barred critical defense evidence, bullied and belittled defense attorneys and witnesses, effectively acted as coprosecutor. In the fall of 1933, all-white juries convicted both Patterson and Clarence Norris.

ILD attorneys once again successfully appealed to the Supreme Court, this time on the grounds that African Americans had been systematically excluded from Alabama juries. In *Norris* v. *Alabama* (1935), the court accepted the defense argument, overturned the Norris and Patterson verdicts, and returned the case to Alabama for retrial. The decision, though not ending all-white juries, marked another step in the Supreme

Court's willingness to chip away at the legal system of the South.

In 1936, oversight of the case passed from the Communist party to a coalition of mainline civil rights organizations. This shift gave Alabama officials—by now embarrassed over the continuing judicial rebukes—an opportunity to compromise. The state dropped the charges against the four youngest defendants, and the other five received prison sentences from twenty years to life with the understanding that once publicity in the case had subsided, they would be quietly released. Despite the intense lobbying of national civil rights leaders (and the secret intervention of President Franklin Roosevelt), Alabama officials blocked their release. It was 1950 before the last of the Scottsboro defendants, Andrew Wright, received his parole.

For a generation of African Americans who came of age in the 1930s, the Scottsboro Case was a vivid reminder of white legal oppression, and it helped further their resolve to mobilize against JIM CROW.

BIBLIOGRAPHY

Carter, Dan T. *Scottsboro: A Tragedy of the American South.* 2nd ed. Baton Rouge, La., 1976.

Norris, Clarence, and Sybil Washington. *The Last of the Scottsboro Boys: An Autobiography.* New York, 1979.

Patterson, Haywood, with Earl Conrade. *Scottsboro Boy.* New York, 1950.

– DAN T. CARTER

SEATTLE, WASHINGTON

Soon after its founding in 1852, Seattle, Wash., attracted a small group of African-American laborers, artisans, and domestic servants. However, a black community did not emerge until the 1890s, when William Gross, the city's second African-American settler, subdivided his farm among arriving families and created the nucleus of one section of black Seattle. About the same time, another neighborhood evolved thirty blocks south, around the waterfront at Jackson Street. By 1910 the two communities had joined, forming an L-shaped pattern in the east-central section of the city known as the Central District.

Early twentieth-century black Seattle grew slowly; fewer than 4,000 of the city's 368,000 residents in 1940 were African American. Employment discrimination relegated the majority of Seattle's pre-World War II blacks to the economic periphery, where they worked as janitors, maids, railroad porters, ship stewards, and longshoremen—and persuaded other blacks to avoid the city. Nonetheless, the small community supported a number of churches, social clubs, and fraternal organizations, as well as chapters of the NATIONAL ASSOCIATION FOR THE ADVANCEMENT OF COLORED PEOPLE (NAACP), the NATIONAL URBAN LEAGUE, and, in the early 1920s, a division of the UNIVERSAL NEGRO IMPROVEMENT ASSOCIATION. This separate sphere for Seattle's blacks emerged partly from the exclusion practiced by white organizations, but also from the desire by local African Americans to control their own community-based organizations and institutions.

During World War II, black Seattle was transformed by the influx of thousands of defense workers. Between 1940 and 1950 the city's black population rose 313 percent, from 3,789 to 15,666. The beginning of this wartime influx came with the 1942 decision of the War Manpower Commission to recruit black workers for Boeing Aircraft and the numerous shipyards in and around the city. By 1945, blacks constituted 1,200 of the 42,008 aircraft construction workers in the Seattle area and 4,000 of the 60,000 shipyard workers.

The employment outlook for Seattle-area blacks after World War II was equally encouraging. Unlike most West Coast cities, Seattle retained most of its wartime jobs in the postwar era, and the black population continued to grow. Moreover, the black community registered important political gains—particularly in 1949, when a statewide Fair Practices Law was enacted, and Charles Stokes, an African American, was elected to the state legislature to represent the Thirty-seventh District, which contained a majority of Seattle's African Americans.

During World War II, black Seattle was transformed by the influx of thousands of defense workers.

Black migration to the city continued into the 1950s. However, the growth of the black community prompted greater segregation and discrimination by whites. In 1950, 69 percent of Seattle's blacks lived in 10 of the city's 118 census tracts. By 1960, 78 percent lived within the same tracts, although the total black population had increased by 11,000 residents. De facto school segregation was a direct outgrowth of the increasing residential segregation of black Seattle. In the early 1950s, no Seattle public schools were predominantly black; by 1962, six of the city's eighty-six elementary schools and one of its eight high schools had black majorities.

indentured servitude failed to meet the planters' labor needs, they imported large numbers of African slaves. As early as 1708, blacks made up a majority of the South Carolina population. By the 1730s, much of the low country had been converted to a rice culture of large plantations, with blacks outnumbering whites by almost two to one and with newly imported Africans making up a significant proportion of the black slave population.

Early on, whites and blacks in Carolina lived and worked together on small farms and stock-raising plantations, or "cow pens." To defend the colony against Indians and Spaniards, whites had even armed blacks and enlisted them in the militia. Blacks enjoyed considerable autonomy and worked in a wide variety of employments. Rice changed all that.

The heavy black presence that resulted from rice plantation culture fundamentally altered Carolina slavery. The races increasingly lived apart, and nervous whites disarmed blacks and tried to circumscribe their activities with repressive laws borrowed from Caribbean slave codes. Blacks responded with repeated individual acts of resistance and several failed uprisings. Then, in the STONO REBELLION of 1739, nearly one hundred slaves seeking to escape to Spanish Florida seized weapons and killed a score of whites before being defeated by white militia. Whites clamped down hard. The colony's government curtailed African importations for a time afterward and passed the Negro Act of 1740, which imposed the harshest slave code in the British mainland colonies.

By insisting on greater white vigilance and patrols, the slave codes in Carolina and elsewhere discouraged mass uprisings, but they did not end slave resistance or autonomy. Stono was the largest mass slave insurrection during the colonial period—and the last—although smaller rumblings occurred in South Carolina and Georgia, which instituted slavery in 1750; New York City (which had experienced a slave uprising in 1712 during which blacks had killed several whites) panicked in 1741 amid a rumor of revolt. Instead, slave resistance became more localized and individual, though no less violent at times, as slaves cultivated a new culture of their own in the quarters away from the master.

By the time of the American Revolution, slavery was firmly rooted in British North America. Every colony had slaves, and even those colonies, such as Massachusetts, with little need for mass slave labor found slaves useful in maritime trades, craft occupations, and domestic service and as common laborers. New York City and environs were especially tied to slavery, where slaves constituted over 30 percent of the city's laborers by the mid-eighteenth century and the majority of unfree workers on farms along the Hudson River, on Long Island, and in northern New Jersey. Northern colonies were further implicated in slavery by the profits their merchants earned provisioning the sugar islands and trading in slaves. Slavery's principal foothold, however, remained in the southern staple-producing colonies. There, from the Chesapeake Tidewater to the Piedmont and in the Carolinas and Georgia, American slavery acquired the character that would distinguish it thereafter.

More than anything else, dramatic slave-population growth fixed the character of British North American slavery during the eighteenth century. Several hundred thousand African slaves were brought into North America, many through the principal slave entry point of Charleston, S.C., but others to the wharves of Chesapeake planters and such ports as Philadelphia. The largest number of African-born slaves arrived at mid-century, at the same time that the native- (or "country"-) born slave population was forming families and reproducing.

The arrival of so many Africans infused African cultural identities into "country"-born slaves at a critical moment. Because the life cycles of marriage and childbirth demanded ritual, the "country"-born slaves readily adapted West African customs to New World conditions. Despite differences in language, sex ratio (the majority of African slaves imported were males), and culture, slaves in America starting families or burying their dead looked toward Africa and themselves rather than to the masters for ritual and meaning. Most slaves were native-born by mid-century, but the African influx between 1740 and 1760 made them more African and less European than they otherwise might have been.

By the early eighteenth century the construction of roads and bridges, the increased number of slaves, and larger plantation sizes all had brought slaves in closer physical contact with one another in the Chesapeake region. More significant, they had broken down language barriers that at one time had separated them. The first generation created a "pidgin" language, and the next incorporated European vocabulary into a "creole" English that retained an underlying West African grammar. Wherever large numbers of African-born slaves congregated, however, African-based language forms grew and persisted. In low-country Georgia and South Carolina, the GULLAH dialect is spoken even today. But an Afro-English had developed virtually everywhere by the mid-eighteenth century, if not earlier, providing a common tongue for slaves across British North America and smoothing the way toward building slave families and community.

The timing varied. The sexual imbalance in the Carolina and Georgia low country, where men outnumbered women two to one as late as the 1770s, retarded the process of family formation there, and the sparse slave populations in New England and the mid-Atlantic region (except for New York City) left many slave men without wives or forced them to postpone marriage. But by the time of the American Revolution, native-born slaves principally defined themselves by their family identities. Therein lay the seeds of the African-American slave community.

Slave family culture grew from West African roots, but largely in response to the demands of bondage. Demography and the strictures of Christianity worked against the transplantation of West African traditions of polygamy to British North America. More telling over the long run was the slave family's lack of security. Slave marriages had no legal standing anywhere in British North America or, later, in the United States. Prevailing norms about masters' duties to slaves and slaves' own insistence on living in and protecting their families became increasingly important factors influencing the strength and inviolability of slave families, especially during the nineteenth century. But more than anything else, the custom of the plantation and the fortunes and interests of the master determined the fate of the slave family.

Masters who fell on hard times might break up slave families by sale—a prospect so feared by slaves that they understood among themselves that they had to work hard enough to ensure the minimum solvency of the master so as to prevent the sale of family members. Slaves were sold to pay debts and to settle estates when masters died. They also were sent to develop new farms farther west or south, were sometimes rented out for years to another master, and were given away as wedding presents or to set up the master's children on a new site.

The vulnerability of slave families to disruption by sale, migration, or death led slaves to create extensive kinship networks, reviving West African cultural traditions that emphasized wide kin connections. Among the slaves on farms and plantations, aunts, uncles, cousins, and grandparents shared child-rearing duties with the slave parents or took over altogether if the parents died or were separated from their children. Women especially developed highly elaborated networks to make up, to some extent, for the absence of menfolk who lived on or had been sold to another farm or plantation.

Parents or related elders taught children crafts, proper work habits, and survival skills, later referred to by slaves as "puttin' on massa." Working in the family garden outside the slave cabin and sharing chores inside it further bound children to the family. Naming patterns identified and reinforced family ties. Boys often were named for fathers who could be sold or who lived off the plantation, while girls commonly were named for aunts or other female relatives. Kin networks stretched across neighborhoods and even states. From the mid-eighteenth century to the end of slavery, native-born slaves lived and learned within a family context, variously as members of a nuclear slave family, as individuals connected to a kinship network, and as heads of their own family households.

Two-parent households were typical for native-born slaves on plantations of twenty or more slaves. On farms with ten or fewer slaves, women usually lived with their children while their husbands lived "abroad"—that is, off the farm but nearby—visiting on Sundays and holidays or at night whenever possible. Out of self-interest alone, masters sought to keep mothers and children under the age of six or seven together. Slave fathers who lived or worked off the plantation had much less opportunity to rear their children and could not prevent their wives and children from being abused and beaten, though many of them tried to do so with individual acts of bravery. Fathers hunted, fished, tended garden, and even stole to supplement the family diet and taught their children how to do likewise, but the peculiar and persistent demands of slavery strained traditional roles and sometimes relationships within the household. Although these dynamics of family formation and interaction persisted to the last days of slavery, men quickly asserted their authority as heads of household within the black family during Reconstruction.

The rise of slave families contributed to a dramatic natural increase of population and gave it a distinctly African-American and less African cast from the mid-eighteenth century on. Slave importations virtually halted during the French and Indian War and the Revolutionary War from the 1760s through the 1780s, but South Carolina and Georgia made a burst of African slave purchases between the ratification of the U.S. Constitution and the closing of the African slave trade to the United States by law, effective January 1, 1808. Roughly forty thousand Africans were brought illegally into the United States between 1808 and 1861. Such legal and illegal importations reinvigorated African identities in the South Carolina low country and Louisiana sugar parishes where the Africans were sold, but for American slavery generally, the immediate and powerful infusion of Africans into North America had ceased by the time of the American Revolution.

As the proportion of native-born to African-born slaves went up, the male-female ratio evened out, making it easier for slaves to find partners. By the early nineteenth century the United States had the only slave population in the New World that was reproducing itself. That demographic fact made all the difference for the kind of slavery and African-American culture that developed here. Slaveholders would depend on natural increase within the context of slave families to sustain and spread their plantation interests, and slaves would look to their own families to define and defend their emerging African-American identities.

The rise of slave families contributed to a dramatic natural increase of population and gave it a distinctly African-American and less African cast.

American-born slaves responded to bondage differently than did unacculturated African-born ones. Masters sought to acculturate slaves to make them work better and be more responsive to the masters' demands. The slave who could speak English, handle farm or artisans' tools, and understand planting and craft work was more valuable than the slave who could not. Yet the more knowledge the slave acquired about the master's ways, the more independent he or she became and the more dependent the master on the slave. African-born slave resistance generally was sudden, violent, and collective; groups of African-born slaves tended to run away and try to establish maroon colonies in the interior. Colonial governments sent militia and even Indian allies to destroy such settlements and return runaways to their masters. By contrast, acculturated slaves, who were more subtle in their subversion, were less easily detected and stopped.

A slave's place in the plantation hierarchy strongly influenced his or her resistance strategies. Artisans familiar with local customs and geography from having worked off the plantation escaped to towns and seaports where they could find work. Their understanding of the whites' economy, culture, and society and their tendency to run away as individuals rather than in groups allowed them to slip into an urban anonymity that made it difficult for masters to recapture them. Field hands and domestic servants largely confined their resistance to the plantation—feigning stupidity and illness, stealing from plantation stores, and absconding to the woods for a time to escape a punishment or protest an injustice. Field hands broke tools and shirked work, and house servants pilfered from the master's larder and liquor cabinet, inflicted a host of petty nuisances when the master's eyes were turned, and on rare occasions even poisoned the master's food, but both field hands and house servants tended to stay home rather than try to flee to freedom.

Slave drivers often protected their fellow slaves in ways that kept them on the plantation. Serving as foremen on large plantations, drivers ran the day-to-day operations under the direction of an overseer or master and meted out tasks and punishment as necessary. Many drivers set work rules that allowed the weakest slaves to avoid a whipping, ignored minor lapses in the work rhythms, hid runaways, and settled quarrels among slaves so the master would not intrude.

The more the slave became like the master, the more tenuous became the "logic" of a system of bondage based on difference. For that reason, colonial masters opposed efforts by such missionary groups as the Anglican-led Society for the Propagation of the Gospel in Foreign Parts to try to convert the slaves in the early eighteenth century. Masters who did not want to be bound by Christian obligation also had reason to worry that Christian slaves would prove more restive than "heathen" ones. Only when colonial legislatures made clear that the slaves' religious status did not affect their legal one did it become possible to bring the Gospel to the slaves.

From the Great Awakening of the 1740s through the Great Revival of 1800–1805, many American-born blacks accepted the promise of salvation that evangelical preachers offered to all people regardless of color, condition, or circumstance. The impact of Baptist and Methodist preachers by the early nineteenth century was particularly decisive. The evangelical Protestant emphasis on grace and an enthusiastic "felt," as opposed to an abstract learned, religion appealed to African-American sensibilities. For the slaves, the revivalists' emphasis on being seized by the spirit recalled common West African beliefs in spirit possession, and the symbolic importance evangelicals attached to baptism as a rite of spiritual rebirth paralleled West African religious rites involving water. The laying on of hands, baptism by immersion, religious trances, and the theology of the holy Trinity also corresponded with African ancestral rituals and beliefs. Because African-American slaves could interpret evangelical religious symbols, practices, and theology within an African context, they could and did claim evangelical religion as their own.

The entry of black slaves into white churches challenged the master's absolute authority. As fellow Christians, master and slave were alike in God's eyes and, in many cases, in church discipline. The full implications of Christianizing slaves did not become evident until the nineteenth century (see below), but the antiauthoritarian, and even antislavery, thrust of early evangelicalism shook the planters' power during the eighteenth century.

By the time of the American Revolution, then, the basic contours of an African-American slave culture had been formed. Indeed, the half-century from 1740 on was probably the single most important time for the formation of African-American slave culture.

The AMERICAN REVOLUTION drastically changed the political and ideological context of slavery. In proclaiming the "rights of man," white patriots used radical language that pointed up the contradiction between slavery and their own cries for freedom. Indeed, the Enlightenment thinkers from whom the patriots drew their emphasis on natural rights already had condemned slavery as incompatible with the idea of progress. Also, slavery based on color stressed differentness, but natural rights stressed sameness, the inalienable rights of "all men." The irony was not lost on slaves, such as a group who marched through Charleston in 1766 chanting "Liberty, liberty." At the same time, the evangelical thrust that challenged the political and social assumptions underpinning the hierarchical order the planters had made brought all authority into question.

Influenced by the new political currents as well as by the Great Awakening, some white religious groups worried that slavery was corroding their own piety. Quakers sought to cleanse themselves of the sin of slaveholding, which they equated with kidnapping and avarice, and during the 1770s and 1780s they extended their antislavery witness outward by organizing antislavery societies. As historian David Brion Davis argues, slavery, which in Western thought had been linked with progress since the days of classical Greece, now was on the ideological and moral defensive.

Slaves seized the moment to assert their own independence. Thousands of slaves fled to freedom amid the confusion and upheavals of the Revolutionary War, seeking refuge in towns in the Chesapeake and among Indians in Georgia and South Carolina. Others responded to the 1775 proclamation of Lord Dunmore, royal governor of Virginia, promising freedom to any slave who bore arms against his rebel master. In the Chesapeake region virtually every slaveholding family reported at least one slave "lost to the war." Farther south, up-country Loyalists encouraged slave rebellions against low-country "patriots," and British commanders also offered slaves freedom in exchange for service. Such actions did not transform revolts into revolution. As historian Sylvia Frey has observed, the high incidence of escapes and the British commanders' own policy of restricting blacks to support rather than military roles likely "lessened the possibility of organized rebellion." Although the British often reneged on the promise of freedom, thousands of black refugees left with the British armies in 1783 to be resettled in Canada and later Sierra Leone. Desperate for men, the American armies also recruited blacks. States of the lower South resisted the call, but Maryland rewarded slaves who served with MANUMISSION and northern states eagerly met their recruitment quotas by enlisting blacks. About five thousand blacks, slave and free, served in the American armies and navy and helped lay claim to the freedom promised by the American Revolution.

Whatever blacks' claims to freedom, American political leaders remained ambivalent about slavery. Concerns about property rights, racial and social order, and political stability led the Revolutionary War generation to try to contain slavery in the hope it would die a natural death. Hating slavery but fearing any precipitous action against it, the Revolutionary War generation moved indirectly. They abolished slavery only where it was weak or thinly rooted and even then adopted policies that minimized disruption of established labor patterns and property rights. The process was slow and sometimes bitterly contested by slaveholders. Indeed, slavery was so entrenched in the Hudson River valley, where slaves made up 20 percent or more of the population, as well as in northern New Jersey and in New York City and Philadelphia, that its abolition was no foregone conclusion. But the concentration of slaves in wealthy households in cities, where it functioned as a status symbol as much as an important labor source, weakened the institution's support among artisan and laboring classes. Slavery was on the decline in Philadelphia after 1770; only in New York City, where one in five households owned at least one slave as late as 1790, and on the iron plantations in rural Pennsylvania did the institution continue to grow in the region.

Prodded by Quaker example and Revolution-era thought, Pennsylvania led the way to emancipation in 1780 with a plan for a gradual, compensated abolition that allowed slaveholders to retain control over slaves until they reached their age of majority. Likewise, other states freed only the children of slaves born after specific dates—for example, 1799 in New York and 1804 in New Jersey—so that small numbers of slaves continued to labor in several northern states into the antebellum era. In the Northwest Ordinance of 1787, however, the Revolutionary War generation moved more forthrightly to prohibit the *expansion* of slavery outright by barring it from the Northwest Territory. Slavery, which had been a "national" institution in 1776, thus became a regional one, distinguishing "North" from "South" by the early nineteenth century.

The Revolutionary War generation also closed the United States to the African slave trade, and it even raised the issue of abolition in the Chesapeake states. During the 1780s the Virginia and Maryland legisla-

a religious vision to deliver his people from bondage. Literate, highly articulate, and driven by a messianic impulse, Turner used preaching, conjuring, and cajoling to convince others to join his plan to strike one night following an eclipse of the sun. His original band of six swelled to eighty as it marched to Jerusalem, in Southampton County, killing fifty-seven men, women, and children until white authorities crushed the revolt. Turner avoided capture for over two months before he was caught and executed in November 1831.

Turner's revolt shocked the South. Hysterical white Southerners saw rebellion looming everywhere and killed as many as two hundred slaves in fits of reprisal and fear. Southern states tightened slave codes and muzzled criticism of slavery. Whites also sought to reassert their authority through closer supervision and religious instruction, even as the slaves were whispering Nat Turner's name in the same breath with those of the biblical prophets who foretold of Judgment Day and deliverance. The Turner revolt and its aftermath revealed how little the whites knew the slaves.

Deliverance came with the CIVIL WAR and the end of slavery. Once northern public opinion recognized that slavery helped sustain the Confederacy's ability to fight, the war for the Union became a war against slavery, the root cause of the conflict. From the slaves' perspective, the war meant both hardship and opportunity. By enduring the hardship and seizing the opportunity, they hastened their own liberation.

Turner's revolt shocked the South. Hysterical white Southerners saw rebellion looming everywhere.

The war made burdensome physical demands on slaves. The Confederate impressment policy of 1863, for example, forced many slaves to work away from their homes building fortifications, hauling supplies, or performing other heavy tasks under debilitating conditions that often sent them home sick or injured and sometimes killed them. However coarse and spare, the quality and quantity of food, clothes, and shoes available to slaves had improved before the war, but wartime shortages cost them the modest material "gains" they had earned in the 1850s. It also cost them their own property, as Union and Confederate "bummers" alike looted slave cabins and took the produce of slave gardens and the crops from the fields. Whatever their attitudes toward the masters and the Confederate cause, slaves had a proprietary interest in the crops they planted, the livestock and fowl they raised, and the land they tilled. The failure of Union soldiers, especially, to respect that interest sowed seeds of distrust among blacks that would make them as wary of their "liberators" as they were of their masters.

The war also created opportunities. With so many white men away from home, the masters' control over the slaves eroded steadily. Some masters entrusted slaves with running plantations; many masters relied on "faithful" slaves, such as house servants and drivers, to assist plantation mistresses in doing so. There were enough instances of slaves hiding the white family's silver from the Yankees and sharing their own produce with the master's family to fuel the postwar myth of the slaves' loyalty. In fact, trusted slaves generally joined the field hands in pursuing their own common interest. During and after the war, masters railed against the "betrayal" by their "black family," thereby acknowledging that they had never known the slaves at all. Slaves dropped their masks during the war, revealing their true feelings and selves. Everywhere they became more openly disobedient and reduced their work. Slaves spied for and gave invading Union armies information about Confederate movements and the whereabouts of the slaveholders' personal property. Even though no outright rebellions occurred, many individual acts of violence against white authority and property, especially in the sugar parishes of Louisiana, reminded whites that the slaves were a restive people. Most bided their time looking for the right moment to seize freedom.

The slaves' most dramatic response to the war was to run away. On the Sea Islands of South Carolina, as elsewhere where the masters fled from Union forces, slaves ran away by staying behind, refusing to follow their masters inland. They then took over the abandoned plantations. Wherever federal troops approached, slaves ran to them. The rush of slaves toward Union armies grew so large that it forced the Union generals to establish a policy of identifying the runaway slaves as "contraband" of war—that is, property that need not be returned to the enemy. By mid-1862 Congress had passed a confiscation act, freeing slaves who entered Union lines, but it excepted those belonging to Unionists. Slaves did not wait for Lincoln to issue his Emancipation Proclamation to seal slavery's doom. During the war, approximately one-seventh of the total slave population crossed over to Union lines. Old and young walked, swam, rode, and were carried over, pressing the issue of emancipation on the Lincoln administration more forcefully than abolitionist criticism had.

Understanding that each Union advance quickened slavery's end, many slaves joined the Union army. Almost a thousand from Florida, Georgia, and South Carolina joined a Union regiment that was formed at

Port Royal, S.C., in late 1861, well before it was official government policy to recruit or accept black troops. Over 180,000 blacks, many of them newly escaped slaves, served in the Union army and navy during the war. They fought, and 37,000 of them died, so that emancipation was not something given to slaves but something earned by their own sweat and blood. And that made all the difference in what freedom meant to blacks after the war.

Blacks emerged from the war with a vibrant African-American culture and, in their own preachers and churches, the beginnings of black leadership and institutions that provided the foundations for a successful adjustment to freedom. They readily claimed in freedom what had been denied in slavery—legal recognition of marriages, access to education, and the right to own property and keep what they produced. More important, through folklore, crafts, food, language, music, family, and religion, blacks had developed a culture in bondage that had freed them from the debasement and self-condemnation that chattel slavery encouraged. They knew where they wanted to go in freedom because they had come to know who they were as a people.

BIBLIOGRAPHY

Berlin, Ira. *Slaves without Masters: The Free Negro in the Antebellum South.* New York, 1974.

Berlin, Ira, and Ronald Hoffman, eds. *Slavery and Freedom in the Age of the American Revolution.* Charlottesville, Va., 1983.

Blassingame, John W. *The Slave Community: Plantation Life in the Antebellum South.* Rev. ed. New York, 1979.

Boles, John. *Black Southerners, 1619–1869.* Lexington, Ky., 1983.

———, ed. *Masters and Slaves in the House of the Lord: Race and Religion in the American South, 1740–1870.* Lexington, Ky., 1988.

Campbell, Edward D. C., with Kym Rice, eds. *Before Freedom Came: African-American Life in the Antebellum South.* Charlottesville, Va., 1991.

Davis, David Brion. *The Problem of Slavery in the Age of Revolution, 1770–1823.* Ithaca, N.Y., 1975.

———. *Slavery and Human Progress.* New York, 1984.

Dillon, Merton L. *Slavery Attacked: Southern Slaves and Their Allies, 1619–1865.* Baton Rouge, La., 1990.

Epstein, Dena J. *Sinful Tunes and Spirituals: Black Folk Music to the Civil War.* Urbana, Ill., 1977.

Escott, Paul D. *Slavery Remembered: A Record of Twentieth-Century Slave Narratives.* Chapel Hill, N.C., 1979.

Fox-Genovese, Elizabeth. *Within the Plantation Household: Black and White Women of the Old South.* Chapel Hill, N.C., 1988.

Frey, Sylvia R. *Water from the Rock: Black Resistance in a Revolutionary Age.* Princeton, N.J., 1991.

Genovese, Eugene. *Roll, Jordan, Roll: The World the Slaves Made.* New York, 1974.

Gutman, Herbert G. *The Black Family in Slavery & Freedom, 1750–1925.* New York, 1976.

Huggins, Nathan I. *Black Odyssey: The Afro-American Ordeal in Slavery.* New York, 1977.

Jordan, Winthrop D. *White over Black: American Attitudes toward the Negro, 1550–1812.* Chapel Hill, N.C., 1968.

Joyner, Charles. *Down by the Riverside: A South Carolina Slave Community.* Urbana, Ill., 1984.

Kolchin, Peter. *American Slavery, 1619–1877.* New York, 1993.

Kulikoff, Allan. *Tobacco and Slaves: The Development of Southern Cultures in the Chesapeake, 1680–1800.* Chapel Hill, N.C., 1986.

Levine, Lawrence W. *Black Culture and Black Consciousness: Afro-American Folk Thought from Slavery to Freedom.* New York, 1977.

Litwack, Leon F. *Been in the Storm So Long: The Aftermath of Slavery.* New York, 1979.

Miller, Randall M., and John David Smith, eds. *The Dictionary of Afro-American Slavery.* New York and Westport, Conn., 1988.

Morgan, Edmund S. *American Slavery, American Freedom: The Ordeal of Colonial Virginia.* New York, 1975.

Mullin, Gerald W. *Flight and Rebellion: Slave Resistance in Eighteenth-Century Virginia.* New York, 1972.

Mullin, Michael. *Africa in America: Slave Acculturation and Resistance in the American South and the British Caribbean, 1736–1831.* Urbana, Ill., and Chicago, 1992.

Oakes, James. *The Ruling Race: A History of American Slaveholders.* New York, 1982.

———. *Slavery and Freedom: An Interpretation of the Old South.* New York, 1990.

Owens, Leslie Howard. *This Species of Property: Slave Life and Culture in the Old South.* New York, 1976.

Parish, Peter J. *Slavery: History and Historians.* New York, 1989.

Phillips, Ulrich B. *American Negro Slavery: A Survey of the Supply, Employment and Control of Negro Labor As Determined by the Plantation Regime.* New York, 1918.

Quarles, Benjamin. *The Negro in the American Revolution.* Chapel Hill, N.C., 1961.

Raboteau, Albert J. *Slave Religion: The "Invisible Institution" in the Antebellum South.* New York, 1978.

Rose, Willie Lee, ed. *A Documentary History of Slavery in North America.* New York, 1976.

Sobel, Mechal. *The World They Made Together: Black and White Values in Eighteenth-Century Virginia.* Princeton, N.J., 1987.

Stampp, Kenneth M. *The Peculiar Institution: Slavery in the Ante-Bellum South.* New York, 1956.

Starobin, Robert S. *Industrial Slavery in the Old South.* New York, 1970.

Wade, Richard C. *Slavery in the Cities: The South, 1820–1860.* New York, 1964.

Webber, Thomas L. *Deep like the Rivers: Education in the Slave Quarter Community, 1831–1865.* New York, 1978.

White, Deborah G. *Ar'n't I a Woman? Female Slaves in the Plantation South.* New York, 1985.

Wood, Peter H. *Black Majority: Negroes in Colonial South Carolina from 1670 Through the Stono Rebellion.* New York, 1974.

Wright, Gavin. *The Political Economy of the Cotton South: Households, Markets, and Wealth in the Nineteenth Century.* New York, 1978.

– RANDALL M. MILLER

SLAVE TRADE

This entry is divided into the following sections and subsections, each of which was written by the author cited:

1. The Atlantic Slave Trade: An Overview (*Daniel C. Littlefield*)

2. The Middle Passage (*Daniel C. Littlefield*)
3. Abolition of the Slave Trade and Caribbean Slavery
   a. Abolition of British Slavery (*Petra E. Lewis*)
   b. French Abolition (*Greg Robinson*)
   c. Danish and Dutch Abolition (*Greg Robinson*)
   d. Interdiction and Iberian Abolition (*Daniel C. Littlefield*)
4. Abolition of the Slave Trade in the United States (*Greg Robinson*)

The Atlantic Slave Trade: An Overview

The Atlantic slave trade was one of the most important demographic, social, and economic events of the modern era. Extending over four centuries, it fostered the involuntary migration of millions of African peoples from their homelands in AFRICA to forced labor in the Americas and elsewhere around the globe. In the process it reshaped African societies, provided much of the raw material for constructing new social, economic, and political structures in the New World, promoted the development of a new industrial order, and furnished essential ingredients of modern world culture. It also left an unfortunate legacy of racism by establishing a connection between servility or barbarity and peoples of African descent.

The assumption from which this connection derived was advanced fairly early. The Scottish philosopher and historian David Hume wrote in 1753 that "There never was a civilized nation of any other complexion than white, nor even any individual eminent in action or speculation. No ingenious manufactures amongst them, no arts, no sciences. . . ." The passage related two crucial ideas, namely, that there was a nexus between race and culture, and that European culture was superior. Racial denigration, however, was not always the guiding principle of relationships between Africans and Europeans. There were many in eighteenth-century Europe who were familiar with achievements of African civilization. Indeed, in terms of their general world knowledge, writes historian Philip Curtin (1964, pp. 10–11) "eighteenth-century Europeans knew more and cared more about Africa than they did at any later period up to the 1950s."

The Atlantic slave trade was one of the most important demographic, social, and economic events of the modern era.

The eighteenth-century interest derived from the nature of mercantilist imperial structures based upon the production of tropical staples through plantation labor. Africa was the source of labor. Since the material or technological distance between Africa and Europe was not then as great as it was later to become, Europeans approached Africans as approximate equals.

European traders were highly dependent upon their African partners and associates to ensure an orderly trade. Since trade frequently depended upon the accident of political vagaries on the coast, European traders, to be successful, had to be aware of political and social conditions in the area where they wanted to trade. Consequently, they stationed agents (called "factors") where Africans would permit it; these factors collected slaves and forwarded reports on African conditions to mercantile companies in Europe. Although these reports are colored by ethnocentrism, factors made a serious attempt to understand the local situation because comprehension was crucial to their ability to offer trustworthy advice. In this way, Europeans disseminated important information about Africa and Africans.

Of course, the European-sponsored Atlantic trade was not the only market for bound African labor. Historians have estimated that about six million Africans were taken to Asia and the Middle East, starting as early as the seventh century a.d. but reaching a peak between 1750 and 1900. Moreover, an additional eight million slaves were involved in an internal African trade, mostly between 1850 and 1914. The Atlantic trade, starting as early as the fifteenth century but becoming important after the discovery of America and reaching its height from about 1650 to 1850, carried approximately twelve million people to captivity in the New World. It was the largest mass movement in history up to that time. It can be divided into four epochs determined by source, destination, and major carrier of slaves.

The first is the era of Iberian domination in the sixteenth century, when Portugal was practically the sole carrier. Slaves were taken from Guinea to Spanish colonies and from Congo-Angola to Brazil. In this period, slaves were only one of a number of African commodities of equal importance. The seventeenth century was a period of transition. The Dutch broke up the Spanish control of the seas, destroyed the Portuguese monopoly of the African and Indian trades, and established themselves as the leading European maritime nation. Between 1630 and 1650, Dutch control of the sea and of trade was supreme. Dutch ships carried slaves and supplies to Spanish, French, and English colonies, and New World staples from them back to Europe. After 1650, England and France moved to establish themselves in Africa and to tighten the mercantilist system in their respective imperial spheres. The eighteenth century represented a period of French and English dominance.

The French and English took most slaves from the Slave Coast, east of the Volta River, and in the Niger Delta, while maintaining important interests at the peripheries in Upper Guinea and in southern Africa, along the Loango Coast. They carried these slaves in British and French ships to their respective possessions in the West Indies and to Spanish America. This represented the height of the trade, when human cargo was the overriding European interest in Africa. Finally, there was an Iberian epoch in the nineteenth century. Northern Europeans abolished the trade north of the equator and deprecated the practice everywhere, but the demand in Brazil and Cuba continued until the middle of the century.

IBERIAN AND MEDITERRANEAN ANTECEDENTS. Although by the eighteenth century Europeans were accustomed to thinking of slaves as black, it had not always been so. Slavery did not die out in Iberia as it did in northern Europe following the collapse of the Roman Empire. It continued and was an important aspect of life on the Peninsula, especially after the Moslem invasion in the eighth century. During the reconquest, Christians as well as Moslems used slaves, generally prisoners captured from the other side, and so the institution received renewed impetus. Portugal, who freed her territory from Moslem control in the thirteenth century, continued to gain slaves through naval warfare with the Saracens in the Mediterranean and along the Spanish and Moroccan coasts. This practice of slave raiding was extended to the Canary Islands when they were conquered in the fourteenth century, and to the Atlantic coast of Africa when it was reached in the fifteenth century.

Slaves were brought to Iberia from at least as early as the eighth century, and their importation continued during the Middle Ages. They came across the Straits of Gibraltar with Moslems, and were captured through the continuing Christian-Moslem conflict on land and sea, and, occasionally, through trade with Italian city-states in the Mediterranean. The city-states of Venice and Genoa administered a commercial empire that included sugar estates in Cyprus, Crete, and Sicily, the crop eventually reaching southern Iberia. The labor force on Cyprus initially consisted of free peasants, local serfs, and a few slaves, but sugar is extremely labor-intensive. Italians utilized an already existing slave trade to fill the need. These slaves derived from several sources: Italian trading posts (*fondachi*) in the eastern Mediterranean, consisting of various eastern Europeans from the Black Sea area; through trade and conflict with Moslems in southern Iberia (consisting of both Moslem and Christian captives); and from North Africa, consisting, among others, of black Africans from the sub-Sahara. When, in the middle of the fifteenth century, Ottoman Turks cut off the Black Sea trade, Africa remained as the only external source of forced labor for Mediterranean plantations. Black slaves were a small but significant part of this early story of the European experience of slavery before the Age of Discovery.

Slaves were brought to Iberia from at least as early as the eighth century, and their importation continued during the Middle Ages.

THE PORTUGUESE HEGEMONY. Although the acquisition of slaves was not the prime motivating force of the Age of Discovery, it was an early consideration. The era is dated from the Portuguese taking of Ceuta, on the Moroccan coast across the Straits of Gibraltar, in 1415. The first black slaves reached Portugal directly from the Atlantic coast of Africa in 1442, and the first slave trading company was formed in 1444, which obtained slaves through periodic raids. But the Portuguese learned early that trade, whether in slaves or in other commodities, proceeded best in cooperation with rather than in opposition to Africans. In the fifteenth century, when the Portuguese laid claim to all of Africa, they divided the western coast into a series of regional monopolies, the right of exclusive trade in which was sold in Lisbon. They sent agents to locate on the coast. In Upper Guinea, some of these settled, intermarried with local peoples, and became middlemen in the trade between Africans and Europeans. These Afro-Portuguese had been joined by the eighteenth century by a class of Afro-French and Afro-English who operated in competing spheres of influence for the benefit of their respective metropolitan powers. Racially and culturally mixed, they achieved political influence through real or fictitious consanguineous ties to local royalty, and economic power through their control of trade.

Because of their prestige, they, in traditional African fashion, gathered to themselves full-blooded Africans, *grumetes,* who adopted their cultural affectations and became part of a hybrid trade community on the coast. Whereas in the sixteenth century these people were usually in a state of subservience to native chieftains, this condition had reversed by the eighteenth century. By this time also, they were able to repel European attempts to circumvent them and establish direct contact with local peoples in those places where they assumed hegemony.

But Portuguese activities were not uniform over all the coast. While a policy of peaceful penetration was adopted in Upper Guinea, there developed in the Gulf of Benin and in the coastal regions leading to it a relationship of power politics. The Portuguese could not move around freely, but were restricted to fortified coastal stations. The most venerable of these, São Jorge da Mina (established 1482), was important to the Portuguese as a source of gold rather than slaves; the metal was obtained through barter with local peoples. Africans brought gold from the interior, and because of long distances they had to travel, they required porters to carry inland goods secured in trade on the coast. The slave trade that developed was an internal African trade in which the Portuguese participated. To meet the demand, they brought slaves from the African kingdom of Benin, from the Portuguese settlement at São Tomé, an island farther down the coast, and from locations in Upper Guinea. The gold trade was so important that in 1610 the king forbade Portuguese subjects to take captives within several miles of the fortress so as not to disturb it.

The Portuguese utilized Africans in colonial settlements on islands off the African coast, where they produced sugar, and also supplied them to southern Europe and the Mediterranean. Between 1450 and 1500, about 30,000 Africans were shipped to Europe. Lisbon now served as entrepôt for the Mediterranean trade. In 1551, 10 percent of the city's population was servile, consisting of Moorish and Guinea slaves. At the beginning of the seventeenth century, the servile percentage was about the same, but at this period it was nearly all black.

During the sixteenth century, the center of major Portuguese slaving activity gradually shifted from Guinea to south-central Africa, in association with the development of a New World plantation system. São Tomé was entrepôt for this trade, which for most of the century centered around the Congo. Here was played out perhaps the first voluntary African attempt at westernization and Christianization when the Portuguese treated the king of the Congo (Manicongo) as an equal and sent craftsmen and missionaries to aid him. But the attempt foundered on the shoals of the slave trade as Portuguese slaving interests fomented discontent in order to encourage warfare from which they could secure captives. The kingdom broke up under the strain.

The ruler of Angola, however, was not treated as an equal. Instead, the Portuguese king granted the region to one of his nobles. In 1576 the Portuguese founded Luanda, which supplanted São Tomé as the center of slaving operations as Angola replaced the Congo as the major source of slaves. Slaving operations were different in Angola from those on the Guinea coast. Instead of setting up factories to which native chieftains brought captives, merchants sent out their own servants or employees (generally blacks or mulattoes), called *pombeiros,* who went into the interior to secure bondsmen by trading or raiding. When captives were not to be had, they incited wars or rebellions. Captives were brought to Luanda, where they were kept in barracoons, or holding stations, to recuperate until ships arrived to take them away.

As in Upper Guinea, a racially and culturally hybrid Luso-African trading community developed. Unlike their counterparts on the northern coast, however, the Afro-Portuguese in Angola kept control of their slaves through the middle passage and could benefit directly from the price of slaves in Brazil but had also to suffer the loss of slaves at sea. The latter consideration caused them to confine their interests to Africa by the end of the eighteenth century. In the three centuries between 1550 and final abolition of the Brazilian slave trade (1850), Angola furnished the majority of Brazil's captive labor.

THE DUTCH. The Dutch destroyed Portuguese pretensions to an African monopoly. By 1642, Arguim and Gorée in Upper Guinea, São Tomé in the Gulf of Benin, Luanda in Angola, and all Portuguese forts on the Gold Coast were in Dutch hands. Although Portugal recaptured São Tomé in 1648 and retained the Cape Verde Islands and Cacheu, Holland was the strongest European power in Guinea during the 1650s. Holland's advantage, however, and its virtual control of the whole European carrying trade for a time, directed at Holland the concentrated ire of the English and the French. The latter part of the seventeenth century therefore was a period of keen competition.

Dutch success derived in part from the capitalistic, joint-stock West India Company, formed in 1621. While the Portuguese, claiming all of Africa, granted individual monopolies in various parts of it, the Dutch, claiming parts of Africa, granted a monopoly of trade to one corporation in all of it. Only members of the West India Company were legally enabled to carry slaves or other goods from Africa to Dutch colonies or elsewhere. To better compete, other European nations followed the Dutch model. Most important were the French West Indies Company (1664) and the English Company of Royal Adventurers trading into Africa (1660), which was superseded by the Royal African Company (1672).

The Spanish, largely excluded from African trade but possessing large territories where slaves were useful, resorted to the *asiento.* This slave contract provided exclusive rights to importation of African bondsmen into Spanish colonies for the nation that held it. The movement of this contract from one European nation to another is to some extent a measure of its ascendancy in the slave trade. It was held successively by the Portuguese, Dutch, French, and English.

THE FRENCH AND THE ENGLISH. Although by the eighteenth century slaves were the single most important trade article, gold, ivory, beeswax, rice, camwood, and malagueta pepper saw significant exchange. The French and English followed in the Dutch wake, establishing their own companies, designated as sole carriers of their countries' trade between Europe, Africa, and the American colonies. These companies were responsible for maintaining trading posts or "factories" in areas where Africans would permit in order to secure their nation's position in trade. The British had forts along the Gambia, the French along the Senegal, and each at various other locations in the region where they engaged in competition to attract African middlemen. The two nations, along with other Europeans, had outposts along the Gold Coast and adjacent areas where competition was likewise stiff. The expense of these factories was borne by the companies as partial recompense for their monopoly.

There were generally two kinds of trading operations. One was "ships trade," wherein goods were consigned to a captain who cruised the coast, stopping at various points to dispose of his wares and take on slaves. In the seventeenth century, natives would light fires or send up smoke signals to notify ships' captains of their readiness to trade. Natives either came in canoes and boarded the ship, or waited on the shore for the arrival of the ship's party. By the eighteenth century, however, regular traders had more durable contacts, made arrangements with local merchants, and stopped at prearranged points. Another method was "factory" or "shore trade," wherein goods were consigned to a fort or outpost to which Africans came to trade and from which goods were dispensed to local traders, or, if necessary, to incoming ships that went elsewhere to find business. Slaves were collected in these factories, or in ships along the coast, until there were enough to complete a cargo.

By the end of the eighteenth century British merchants engrossed over half of the slave trade, followed by the French, Portuguese, Dutch, and Danes. The bulk of these laborers went to sugar-producing regions in tropical America, with lesser amounts reaching North America. Averaging fewer than two thousand annually before the seventeenth century, imports rose to over sixty thousand per year by the eighteenth century.

Brazil received almost 40 percent of all slave imports, the trade having begun earlier and lasted longer there than anywhere else. By contrast, the area that became the United States received only about 5 percent of the total. Individual West Indian islands, comprising smaller regions but containing more labor-intensive economies than the United States, absorbed comparatively many more slaves: Jamaica received 8 percent and Barbados 4 percent of slave imports. Nevertheless, the mechanics of crop production in the United States distinguished the region, permitting natural reproduction of the slave population, and it had the largest slave population in the Americas in the nineteenth century.

THE AFRICAN INPUT. At the height of the trade in the eighteenth century, the whole coast was regulated on the African side by middlemen who were highly conscious and jealous of their own position. They had a monopoly on trade with the interior and insisted that business be conducted through them. Moreover, they refused to be bound by any one European power and insisted on free trade with the outside world. On different parts of the coast, however, variant circumstances required distinctive considerations, all of which changed over time. In Upper Guinea, African polities competed with Afro-Europeans for trade at the posts set up by the French and English in the Senegal and Gambia rivers to attract commerce.

On the leeward coast in the Gulf of Guinea, Akan and Fon kingdoms mediated the trade. In the Niger Delta, various city-states—monarchies and republics—grew up in response to new opportunities for exchange. Ruled by special political associations, they developed a distinctive trade organization known as the "House system." K. Onwuka Dike describes this as "a kind of cooperative trading company based not so much on kinship as on commercial association between the head of a dominant family, his relatives and trading assistants, and all their followers and slaves"—a creative adaptation to business opportunities. In Congo-Angola, local governments also ruled, though the Portuguese, busily creating a colonial preserve, claimed exclusive rights in parts of the region. These disparate governments and people had their own peculiar requirements in articles, seasons, and methods of trade.

Even the trade mediums or units of accounts diverged, with Europeans adopting African practices. In Upper Guinea they used the iron bar; on the leeward coast, the ounce of gold (in the west) and the cowry shell (in the east); in the Niger Delta, the manilla, bracelet of brass or lead; in Congo-Angola, a piece of local cloth. For these reasons, European representatives had to be seriously attentive to peoples and conditions at their station or lose trade to their rivals. They had to treat Africans with considerable respect.

AFRICAN SLAVERY. Early European observers often justified slaving activities by arguing that many if not most Africans existed in some form of indigenous servitude and that the European version was preferable.

Later Europeans justified imperialism on the same basis of Africans' widespread enslavement which they now sought to abolish. Opponents sought to counter these rationales for injustice by contending that few examples of involuntary servitude existed in Africa before European contact, and that where they existed, they were of such a nature as to be scarcely comparable to the western conception, let alone the American reality. Where observers stated otherwise, they were deluded by racism, ethnocentrism, or ignorance.

Suzanne Miers and Igor Kopytoff (1977) argue that confusion results from a misapprehension of the nature of African society. Based on kinship relations that give people social existence to the extent that they belong to or are part of a local lineage, they regard as nonpersons those outside the group. Outsiders, whether slave or free, are nonpersons. Indeed, in some African societies, the words for "slave" and "outsider" are the same. There is no dichotomy between slavery and freedom (with its emphasis on autonomy and individualism) such as exists in the West, but only between nonperson and person (whose identity is found in his association and obligation to the group). Nor are the dichotomies absolute.

There are degrees of belonging connected with increasing privileges and acceptability. In Upper Guinea, for example, there were three broad categories of slaves: state, domestic, and trade. The first were at the disposition of government and performed tasks for the general good under the auspices of local authority. They lived apart, cultivated land of their own, had many rights, and suffered no marriage restrictions, though in marriages of inequality, children followed the condition of the mother. Domestics also had many rights, could not be sold, but were subject to endogamous marriage rules. Trade slaves had fewer rights and were subject to sale and endogamous marriage rules, though they were granted land to cultivate for their own use. They were the least integrated and most easily dispensable; however, if they stayed in a community long enough, and particularly if they married and had children, their situation improved. They took on the character of domestic slaves. This progression was in terms of community integration, not task specialization, as their labor activities might not change. Indeed, in most African societies there was little or no differentiation in the labor of slaves and free people.

Those slaves susceptible of sale, or trade slaves, were usually adult males captured in warfare who might never adjust to their captivity and posed a danger to their hosts. At the very least, they might run away. They could best serve the community by what they brought in trade. Women and young children, more pliable, were less likely to be sold and were apt ultimately to be absorbed by the local community. The demands of the Atlantic trade were coincident with these African outlooks in that while Atlantic slavers had more call for adult males, internal African requirements placed more value on women. Consequently, women were not equally available for trade on all parts of the coast, a consideration that slavers had to weigh.

Atlantic slave requirements influenced African societies by encouraging an increase in crimes for which people might be condemned to slavery, spurring warfare, lawlessness, and social disruption, including banditry and kidnapping, to obtain slaves, and deprived the continent of much human potential. Moreover, it accentuated the economic rather than social character of African slavery, transforming it from one among several forms of dependency in kin-based social relations to one having a more important economic role. Yet Africans who participated in the trade made their decisions within their own contexts and for their own reasons. African slaves were seldom viewed as the simple commodities which capitalism made them in the Americas.

THE AMERICAN DEMAND. New World planters, thinking of slaves as work units and interested in maximum production for the least outlay, ideally desired an adult male in his twenties or thirties. Women, who could also be worked in the fields, were in less demand. Consequently, planters normally asked for slaves in the proportion of two men for every woman. This desire for men was especially great in sugar-producing regions, which had a firm capitalist base by the seventeenth century and considered profit above everything else. Brazilian and Caribbean planters, for example, regarded harsh treatment contributing to high slave mortality in as few as five to seven years after importation to be a more economical management practice than expending either time or money to better the slave's condition and extend his life for labor. They viewed the raising of slave children as equally unprofitable and did not encourage it. Consequently, they had to depend on the slave trade to replenish their labor force for most of the period of slavery's existence in their regions. British North American planters, raising different crops, computed their finances differently, and while they also asked for slaves in the normal proportions, they had come by the first decades of the eighteenth century to recognize the value of a self-perpetuating labor force. They began to encourage reproduction, an effort which required a more equal balance between males and females.

Planters also had distinctive slave preferences, which varied with region and over time. The economy of seventeenth-century Brazil was highly dependent on bound labor from Angola, and planters described these laborers as the best that Africa had to offer. In the eighteenth century, both the source and judgment of African labor changed: Brazilian planters now rated "Sudanese" or "Mina" slaves from the leeward coast of West Africa as superior. Indeed, a special relationship developed between the northern Brazilian city of Bahia and the leeward coast, while southern Brazilian traders, centered in Rio de Janeiro, maintained an attachment to Angola. Eighteenth-century Jamaicans exhibited an affinity for Akan-speaking peoples from the Gold Coast, while South Carolina planters desired Senegambians. Virginians expressed no strong likes or dislikes.

Traders had to consider these slave fashions among other factors when they planned their voyages. They had also to figure climatological conditions and seasonal variations, the winter months in North America or the hurricane season in the West Indies creating hazards to ready sales. Slaves were in greatest demand when they could be put directly to work and sold more briskly in some seasons than in others.

The Middle Passage

The term "Middle Passage" refers to the transit or transportation of African bondspeople from the African coast to the Americas during the slave trade. It was the middle phase of the three-step passage of Africans from the interior of Africa to the coast, across the Atlantic, and then to their place of servitude in the Americas. The hellish conditions of the passage have long made it a byword for horror and a metaphor for human suffering and cruelty.

There has long been considerable debate on the numbers involved in the Middle Passage. Older estimates, influenced by moral fervor and indignant outrage, projected estimates as high as fifty million Africans transported. The actual figure is probably considerably lower. Philip Curtin's influential *The Atlantic Slave Trade: A Census* (1969) argued that about ten million people survived the passage. The subsequent twenty-five years has seen no scholarly consensus, but many scholars believe between twelve and fifteen million Africans were brought across the ocean during the four-hundred-year history of the African slave trade. There has also been debate on the effects of the slave trade on the regional population of western and central Africa. Patrick Manning (1990) has argued that without the trade, the population of Africa in 1850 would have been 100 million rather than 50 million. Joseph C. Miller (1988), by contrast, argued that high rates of reproduction offset losses taken by slave ships. The dimensions and consequences of the slave trade on African society will likely be debated for some time to come.

The slave trader was part of the commerce between Europeans and Africans. Outside of Angola, where the Portuguese began in the sixteenth century to establish a colonial preserve, Africans controlled their western coast. The cost of slaves, which rose almost steadily over the course of the trade, was determined in negotiations between Africans and Europeans. First of all, Europeans paid ground rent for the use of land in those places where they had trading posts. Monopoly companies, granted exclusive rights of trade by European imperial powers, normally absorbed these costs. In Upper Guinea, European ships paid tolls to use rivers en route to these posts. Individual traders had to hire "linguisters" to translate or act as go-betweens, and to arrange the "palavers" or conferences at which slave prices were determined. Before these conferences could be arranged, a "dash," or bribe, might have to be paid. These charges were part of the cost of doing business and had to be calculated in the accounting of profit and loss.

The term "Middle Passage" refers to the transit or transportation of African bondspeople from the African coast to the Americas during the slave trade.

Part of the greatest cost of slaves, however, involved the prices of European and Asian goods used in trade and the mix of goods comprising the standard unit of account. Europeans adopted African account formulas or standards of equivalence, derived from the barter principle. Slaves were priced in various units of account—bars (based on the iron bar), ounces (form the ounce of gold), cowries (a type of shell), or manillas (copper bracelets)—depending on the region and local practice. Traders would determine slaves' prices (for a prime male, with women and children in proportion) in bars, say, after considerable discussion. They paid for slaves in "bundles," or "assortments," of goods equal to the determined price. Not all European goods were acceptable, nor were all equally desirable. Traders spent considerable time and effort before agreeing on the composition of bundles because the mix of goods could well make the difference between a successful voyage and a failing one. Traders with better or more attractive wares had an advantage over those whose merchandise had less demand. Competition among Europeans in port increased Africans' normal advantage.

Prices differed with time and place. During the height of the trade in the eighteenth century, slave prices were higher in Upper Guinea than in Angola. Portu-

carried more slaves—a thousand or more compared to four hundred or more in sailing ships—but did not provide them extra room and often carried them too close to the boiler, adding burning or scalding to other threats of mortality. At that period, observers perceived conditions to be as bad as they had ever been.

Herbert Klein indicates that the greatest single determinant of mortality was time at sea. David Eltis, to the contrary, suggests that, within limits, even that variable was not as important as disease. Dysentery among the shackled voyagers, whether amoebic or bacillary, was the most lethal killer, and its effects seemed to be unrelated to the length of voyage. But the length of voyage, including time spent on the coast, undeniably influenced mortality, and ships traveling from East Africa consistently recorded higher death rates related to their longer passage.

Mortality varied with African region, suggesting that diet, the rigors of travel to the coast, famine, or other factors in Africa had some influence on whether a slave was likely to survive the passage. The rainy season, generally from June to August, but changing with location, was equally hard on blacks and whites, and captives contracted diseases that might flower during the Middle Passage with disastrous consequences. Indeed, the melancholy attrition that began at capture matured on the coast as slaves were kept in unhealthy holding pens—damp dungeons or "trunks" in posts on the Gold Coast; floating ship hulks or "barracoons" in the Niger Delta; open stockades, exposed to the elements, in Angola. Chained, branded, and often subjected to inadequate care, they endured the physical and psychological trauma that mistreatment and uncertainty induced, and the winnowing process that the grim rule of the survival of the fittest obliged.

Cultural transformation also began, establishing the foundations for New World social reorganization even before the Africans had landed.

Individual captains set the tone of the voyage and determined whether slaves got needless abuse or minimal consideration. Taken aboard ship, men were chained together below deck, women above. Pregnant women and children roamed free once the ship cleared the coast. Sailors took great care at leavetaking, however, as slaves were most likely to rise as they departed African shores. At sea, they fed slaves twice a day, and they allowed a period of exercise on deck unless the weather forbade. The crew occasionally washed slave platforms with vinegar and water for sanitation. African women assisted in preparing the food, making it as palatable as possible, and carrying African tastes and culinary practices to the Americas.

In the midst of these deplorable conditions began the formation of new cultures and relationships. The shipmate relationship became one that endured among those who survived transport and formed the basis for relationships ashore. Cultural transformation also began, establishing the foundations for New World social reorganization even before the Africans had landed. Along with their capacity for labor and their ability to last, survivors brought an abiding optimism and sense of self-worth that transcended physical and psychological scarring. Therein is found a moving story of human resilience and creativity.

Abolition of the Slave Trade and Caribbean Slavery

ABOLITION OF BRITISH SLAVERY. The abolition of the slave trade by Great Britain in 1807, and the subsequent passage of the British West Indian Emancipation Act in 1833, which ended British Caribbean slavery, coincided with a long-term decline in the economic importance and political influence of Caribbean sugar planters. In the first half of the eighteenth century, the sugar colonies of the British West Indies, especially Jamaica, Antigua, and Barbados, were perhaps the most prized colonial possessions of the British Empire, generating large profits from lucrative sugar exports. The wealth of the British Caribbean was derived in large part from the stability and mercantilist policies of the British imperial system, which protected Caribbean colonies as an apex of the notorious "triangular trade" with British North America and West Africa in slaves, rum, and molasses. This secure system began to unravel with the coming of the American Revolution.

The American Revolution temporarily halted the Atlantic slave trade and drove up the price of food in the West Indies, which had to be imported. Their profits destroyed, West Indian planters went deeply into debt. After American independence, the new United States traded with rival colonies such as France's St. Domingue (later Haiti). In Britain, the economic and ideological shift from mercantilism to capitalism made protectionist policies unpopular. As West Indian trade declined, British merchants and seamen turned their attention to imports of American cotton, to feed the growing textile industry. West Indian sugar, no longer protected by the British imperial system, was unable to compete with efficient, cheap sugar on the world market. New land was scarce, and absentee landlords lacked the will and capital to modernize.

In the 1780s, a massive antislavery movement, unimaginable fifty years before, began to appear in England. Abolitionist efforts were led by Quakers and by Anglican humanitarians, led by Thomas Clarkson and William Wilberforce, who formed the Society for Effecting the Abolition of the Slave Trade in 1785 and spoke against the trade as immoral and unchristian. They believed that ending the trade would lead to the amelioration or end of West Indian slavery, although abolitionists were careful to deny they wished the government to free existing slaves.

In 1789, Wilberforce introduced twelve resolutions against the slave trade in the House of Commons. The House voted to examine evidence. In 1791, the House postponed action, although it did grant Wilberforce's Society a charter to establish a colony for freed slaves in Sierra Leone. In 1792, the House of Commons officially passed a bill gradually banning the slave trade, but the Bill failed in the House of Lords. Despite Wilberforce's claim that other countries would follow England's lead in ending the slave trade, international inaction led Parliament to fear the economic consequences of unilateral action. Over the next several years, the movement slowed. The Haitian slave revolt and subsequent abolition of slavery by Revolutionary France discredited antislavery efforts as radical.

By 1804, however, the unrelenting efforts of the abolitionists and their political allies gained enough support to get a bill through the House of Commons. The House of Lords failed to pass the Bill, although the government did limit slave imports to 3 percent of the existing slave population of the islands. In 1806, the government issued Orders in Council banning the foreign slave trade, ostensibly to cut American and neutral trade with France. Planters who protested were characterized as unpatriotic. As most of the trade was with other nations, this effectively halted the trade. In 1807, after the U.S. Congress approved the closing of the slave trade the following year, easing fears of American competition, a bill for immediate abolition was introduced in the House of Lords. With government backing, it passed both houses by large margins.

The ending of the British slave trade brought lessened interest in antislavery activity, first through the focusing of national attention on the Napoleonic Wars, and then through an illiberal political climate after 1815. The British government attempted to combine humanitarianism with economic self-interest by efforts, which proved unsuccessful, to organize a worldwide end to the slave trade, first at the Congress of Vienna in 1815, and then at the Congress of Verona in 1822. By then, abolitionists realized the end of the trade had not helped the condition of West Indian slaves. In 1821, the Liverpool Antislavery Society was founded. Liberal businessmen, led by T. F. Buxton, who opposed the inefficient and feudal nature of the slave system, took control of the movement from Wilberforce and the Quakers. The "emancipists" agitated for gradual granting of civil rights to slaves. Buxton proposed that children of slaves be born free, although he avoided speaking publicly of abolition for fear of arousing slave revolts. Three sets of Orders in Council on amelioration were passed between 1823 and 1831.

By 1831, reform sentiment was high in England, and antislavery speakers and pamphleteers attracted large number of people to the cause. In December 1831, a slave revolt broke out in western Jamaica. The planter government brutally repressed it. Atrocity stories provoked widespread outrage in England. A Commission of Inquiry was appointed. In May 1832, Buxton imprudently introduced a bill in Parliament calling for an immediate end to slavery. While this measure was opposed by many antislavery moderates, it only failed by 162 to 90. This strong showing was taken by many as a sign of the antislavery movement's strength.

By 1833, when a new parliamentary session opened, liberal and antislavery forces were powerful as a result of the Reform Bill of 1832 and the commission's report. Abolitionists presented Parliament a petition signed by 1.5 million people. As antislavery delegates and West Indian lobbyists competed for attention, Buxton called for unconditional emancipation. On May 11, the new Colonial Secretary, E. G. S. Stanley, published a plan for gradual emancipation, with £15 million (later raised to £20 million) of compensation to slaveowners. Slaves would serve as "apprentices" of their former masters at three-quarters their normal work hours for twelve years (later reduced to six years for field hands and four years for domestic slaves), and slaves under six would be considered free. Slaveowners, fearing immediate abolition, decided to support the plan as the best they could obtain. The British West Indian Emancipation Act passed the House of Commons on July 1, 1833, and was adopted by the legislatures of the free colonies shortly thereafter. The apprenticeship system was waived by Antigua and Bermuda, which had too many blacks to make such a proposal feasible. In Jamaica, where the system was adopted, planters abused the system so flagrantly that, following a parliamentary inquiry in 1837, apprenticeships were abolished in favor of total emancipation on May 22, 1838.

FRENCH ABOLITION. In the late seventeenth and early eighteenth centuries, France established colonies in the Caribbean, on the Antillean islands of St. Lucie, Martinique, Guadeloupe, and St. Domingue, and on the island of Hispaniola, the largest colony. In the

tween 1837 and 1862. However, American juries often acquitted smugglers. One of the last illegal slave ship journeys, that of the *Wanderer* in 1858, became well known. Finally, in 1862, during the Civil War, the Union government, anxious to remove American warships from Africa and to placate the British, agreed to reciprocal searches. This policy effectively shut off the illegal trade.

Despite widespread evasions of the law, it was not until the 1850s that the question of reopening the trade was seriously posed. Southern radicals such as Gov. James Adams of South Carolina proposed reopening the trade as a panacea for southern ills. Importing new slaves, Adams and his allies claimed, would bring down the inflated price of labor, halt the erosion of slavery in the upper South resulting from African-Americans being sold further south, make farming labor-intensive crops such as cotton easier, increase the population of the southern states, and increase poor white farmers' prestige and stake in the slave system by making it possible for them to own slaves. The contentious question of reopening the trade would add to sectional tensions, but radicals and secessionists were delighted by such a prospect.

Notwithstanding the logical contradictions inherent in such a position, most Southerners despised the slave trade, and most influential politicians opposed reopening. While they supported slavery, and thus did not dwell so much on the immorality of the trade, they argued that legalization would split the Union and leave the South divided. Slave property values would plummet, and economic chaos would result. The upper South would still be unable to compete economically with its neighbors, and would lose the income it received from breeding and selling slaves. Increased slave competition might wipe out free white farms entirely. Adams's proposal was defeated in both houses of the South Carolina legislature. While proponents of legalization did win the backing of the powerful Southern Commercial Convention at Vicksburg in 1859, most politicians saw that the issue was not popular. Even after secession, in 1861, the Confederate congress voted to retain the ban, and the issue was eventually buried.

As the Atlantic slave trade petered to its end during the middle decades of the nineteenth century, it had already profoundly shaped three continents. It altered and likely stunted the developments of African society and political institutions in ways that are still being debated. It was the most significant population transfer of all time, creating an enormous and enduring African diaspora in the Caribbean, South America, and North America. It remains, above all, a monument to the cruelty that humans perpetrate upon their own kind. If there is any consolation to be found in its sad history, the abolition of the slave trade was the first great humanitarian reform movement. The slave trade, and later slavery itself, was ended by the combined efforts of Europeans, Africans, and Americans to redress and eliminate an enormous evil.

BIBLIOGRAPHY

Bethell, Leslie. *The Abolition of the Brazilian Slave Trade: Britain, Brazil, and the Slave Trade Question, 1807–1869.* Cambridge, U.K., 1970.

Blackburn, Robin. *The Overthrow of Colonial Slavery, 1776–1848.* London, N.Y., 1988.

Boxer, Charles. *The Portuguese Seaborne Empire, 1415–1825.* New York, 1969.

Conrad, Robert E. *World of Sorrow: The African Slave Trade to Brazil.* Baton Rouge, La., 1986.

Coughtry, Jay. *The Notorious Triangle: Rhode Island and the African Slave Trade, 1700–1807.* Philadelphia, 1981.

Craton, Michael. *Sinews of Empire: A Short History of British Slavery.* Garden City, N.Y., 1971.

Curtin, Phillip. *The African Slave Trade: A Census.* Madison, Wis., 1969.

———. *The Atlantic Slave Trade: A Census.* Madison, Wis., 1969.

———. *The Image of Africa: British Ideas and Action, 1780–1850.* Madison, Wis., 1964.

———. *The Rise and Fall of the Plantation Complex: Essays in Atlantic History.* Cambridge, U.K., 1990.

Davies, K. G. *The Royal African Company.* New York, 1970.

Davis, David Brion. *Slavery in the Age of Revolution.* New York, 1975.

Drescher, Seymour. *Capitalism and Slavery.* New York, 1987.

———. *Econocide: British Slavery in the Era of Abolition.* Pittsburgh, 1977.

Du Bois, W. E. B. *The Suppression of the African Slave Trade to the United States of America.* 1896. Reprint. New York, 1969.

Duffy, James. *Portugal in Africa.* Cambridge, Mass., 1962.

Duignan, Peter. *The United States and Africa: A History.* New York, 1984.

Duignan, Peter, and Clarence Clendenen. *The United States and the African Slave Trade, 1619–1862.* Stanford, Calif., 1963.

Eltis, David. *Economic Growth and the Ending of the Transatlantic Slave Trade.* New York, 1987.

———. "Free and Coerced Transatlantic Migrations: Some Comparisons." *American Historical Review* 88 (1983): 252–280.

Fage, John D. *A History of West Africa: An Introductory Survey.* Cambridge, U.K., 1969.

Gemery, Henry A., and Jan S. Hogendorn, eds. *The Uncommon Market: Essays in the Economic History of the Atlantic Slave Trade.* New York, 1975.

Inikori, J. E., ed. *Forced Migrations: The Impact of the Export Slave Trade on African Societies.* New York, 1982.

Klein, Herbert S. *The Middle Passage: Comparative Studies in the Atlantic Slave Trade.* Princeton, N.J., 1978.

Klein, Herbert S., and Stanley L. Engerman. "Slave Mortality on British Ships, 1791–1797." In *Liverpool, the African Slave Trade, and Abolition: Essays to Illustrate Current Knowledge and Research.* Bristol, U.K., 1976.

Klein, Herbert S., and Charles Garland. "The Allotment of Space Aboard Eighteenth-Century British Slave Ships." *William and Mary Quarterly,* 3rd Series, 42 (1985): 238–248.

Knight, Franklin K. *The Caribbean: The Genesis of a Fragmented Nationalism.* 2nd ed. New York, 1990.
Littlefield, Daniel C. "Abundance of Negroes of That Nation: The Significance of African Ethnicity in Colonial South Carolina." In *The Meaning of South Carolina History: Essays in Honor of George C. Rogers, Jr.* Columbia, S.C., 1991, pp. 19–38.
———. "The Slave Trade to Colonial South Carolina: A Profile." *South Carolina Historical Magazine* 91 (1990): 68–99.
Lovejoy, Paul E. *Africans in Bondage: Studies in Slavery and the Slave Trade.* Madison, Wis., 1986.
———. *Transformations in Slavery: A History of Slavery in Africa.* Cambridge, U.K., 1983.
Manning, Patrick. *Slavery and African Life: Occidental, Oriental, and African Slave Trades.* Cambridge, U.K., 1990.
Miers, Suzanne, and Igor Kopytoff, eds. *Slavery in Africa: Historical and Anthropological Perspectives.* Madison, Wis., 1977.
Miller, Joseph C. *Way of Death: Merchant Capitalism and the Angolan Slave Trade, 1730–1830.* Madison, Wis., 1988.
Palmer, Colin. *Human Cargoes: The British Slave Trade to Spanish America, 1700–1739.* Urbana, Ill., 1981.
Polanyi, Karl. *Dahomey and the Slave Trade: The Study of an Archaic Economic Institution.* Seattle, 1966.
Rodney, Walter. *A History of the Upper Guinea Coast, 1545–1800.* Oxford, U.K., 1970.
Takaki, Ronald. *A Proslavery Crusade: The Agitation to Reopen the African Slave Trade.* New York, 1971.
Westbury, Susan. "Slaves of Colonial Virginia: Where They Came From." *William and Mary Quarterly.* 3rd Series, 42 (1985): 228–237.

– DANIEL C. LITTLEFIELD AND GREG ROBINSON
– PETRA E. LEWIS

SMITH, BESSIE

Bessie Smith (April 15, 1894–September 26, 1937), blues singer. Bessie Smith, "Empress of the Blues," was the greatest woman singer of urban blues and, to many, the greatest of all blues singers. She was born in Chattanooga, Tenn., the youngest of seven children of Laura and William Smith. Her father, a part-time Baptist preacher, died while she was a baby, and her early childhood, during which her mother and two brothers died, was spent in extreme poverty. Bessie and her brother Andrew earned coins on street corners with Bessie singing and dancing to the guitar playing of her brother.

The involvement of her favorite brother Clarence in the Moses Stokes Show was the impetus for Smith's departure from home in 1912. Having won local amateur shows, she was prepared for the move to vaudeville and tent shows, where her initial role was as a dancer. She came in contact with Gertrude "Ma" Rainey, who was also with the Stokes troupe, but there is no evidence to support the legend that Rainey taught her how to sing the blues. They did develop a friendship, however, that lasted through Smith's lifetime.

Smith's stint with Stokes ended in 1913, when she moved to Atlanta and established herself as a regular performer at the infamous Charles Bailey's 81 Theatre.

Bessie Smith, c. 1935. (Photographs and Prints Division, Schomburg Center for Research in Black Culture, The New York Public Library, Astor, Lenox and Tilden Foundations)

By then the Theater Owners Booking Association (TOBA) consortium was developing into a major force in the lives and careers of African-American entertainers, and managers/owners often made the lives of performers miserable through low pay, poor working and living conditions, and curfews. Bailey's reputation in this regard was notorious. Smith became one of his most popular singers, although she was paid only ten dollars a week.

Smith's singing was rough and unrefined, but she possessed a magnificent vocal style and commanding stage presence, which resulted in additional money in tips. With the 81 Theatre as a home base, Smith traveled on the TOBA circuit throughout the South and up and down the eastern seaboard. By 1918 she was part of a duo-specialty act with Hazel Green but soon moved to her own show as a headliner.

Smith attracted a growing number of black followers in the rural South as well as recent immigrants to northern urban ghettos who missed the down-home style and

A typical example of the instructional song is the well-known ragtime dance ballin' the jack, which developed in about 1910. (The meaning of the title is obscure, but it probably originated from railroad slang, with the general meaning of enjoyable, rollicking good times.) As described in 1913 in its published form by two African-American songwriters, Chris Smith and Jim Burris, the dance had the following steps:

> First you put your two knees close up tight,
> then you sway 'em to the left, then you sway 'em to the right.
> Step around the floor kind of nice and light,
> then you twis' around and twis' around with all your might.
> Stretch your lovin' arms straight out in space,
> then you do the eagle rock with style and grace,
> swing your foot way 'round, then bring it back,
> now that's what I call ballin' the jack.

Between 1900 and 1920 a dance fever gripped America. Since the early 1900s couples have been moving closer together, and with the evolution of the slower, more blusey early JAZZ styles, close-clutching dances like the slow drag, which had always been done at private parties, began to surface in public places. The hip motions and languid gliding feet in such African-American dances as the grind and mooch (both a couple or solo dance) indicate that body contact and postures were already racially shifting. Certainly this prepared the way for the arrival of the tango and its immediate acceptance as a dance craze in 1913. (The tango originated in Argentina. Although its precise origins are quite complex, it was also a likely synthesis of European and African influences.) The tango is a difficult dance to do, necessitating dance lessons, a reality happily exploited by the numerous exhibition tango teams who demonstrated the dance to the eager public, then taught it to them in their studios, or at the local dance hall or tango teas. If few could afford this luxury, thousands of people nevertheless danced what they believed to be the tango. In reality, the frank sensuality of thigh and pelvic contact coincided more readily with familiar close-couple African-American dances of the juke joints, small dance halls, and white-and-tan clubs that peppered mixed neighborhoods of every American city.

By the late 1910s a flood of migrating workers moved northward, seeking jobs in urban industries built for the war effort of WORLD WAR I. As great numbers of African Americans moved into cities, they formed a critical mass of talent that erupted in a variety of artistic expressions. Their energy gave birth to the HARLEM RENAISSANCE of the 1920s and turned Harlem—and black neighborhoods in other industrial cities—into crucibles of creativity in the popular and fine arts. The golden years of black Broadway (1921–1929) began with the hugely successful *Shuffle Along* (1921), written, directed, composed, and choreographed by African Americans (its four major creators were Noble Sissle, Eubie BLAKE, Flournoy Miller, and Aubrey Lyles). This production, and subsequent road shows, brought African-American jazz music and jazz dances to a wide audience. There was little distinction between social dances and stage adaptions, and current popular dances were simply put onstage with few changes. As a result of *Shuffle Along*'s popularity, Broadway dance began to reshape itself, shifting to a jazz mode, as Florenz Ziegfeld and other producer-directors began to copy *Shuffle Along*'s choreography. A spate of new studios opened in the Broadway area to teach this African-American vernacular jazz dance to professional actors and to an eager public (one important instructor was Buddy Bradley, who taught the Astaires and a host of other Broadway and film actors, then went on to choreograph English revues).

Then with the 1923 Broadway show *Runnin' Wild*, the Charleston burst onstage and into the hearts of the American public, especially through the eponymous song James P. JOHNSON composed for the show. However, the Charleston had been a popular dance among African Americans long before the 1920s. Although its origins are unclear, it probably originated in the South, as its name suggests, then was brought north with the migrating workers. Jazz historian Marshall Stearns reports its existence in about 1904, and the late tap dancer Charles "Honi" Coles said that in about 1916 as a young child he learned a complete version of the dance, which had long been popular in his hometown of Philadelphia.

The Charleston is remarkable for the powerful resurgence of Africanisms in its movements and performance and for shattering the conventions of European partnering. The Charleston could be performed as a solo, a couple dance, partners could dance together side by side or in the closed-couple position. For women in particular, its wild movements and devil-may-care attitude broke codes of correct deportment and propriety. It was quick and decidedly angular, and the slightly crouched position of the body imparted a quality of alert wildness. The steps (and the early jazz music it was performed to) are syncopated, the knees turn in and out, the feet flick to the side, and a rapid forward-and-backward prancing step alternated with pigeon-toed shuffles and high kicks. As the arms and legs fling in oppositional balance, elbows angled and pumping, the head and hands shake in counterpoint. Knock-kneed, then with legs akimbo, body slightly squatted, this beautiful awkwardness signaled the aesthetic demise of European ideals of symmetry and grace in social dance. The fast-driving rhythms of the music smoothed the flow of broken motions into a witty dance punctuated with shimmies, rubber-legging, sudden stops, and dance elements such as the black bottom, spank the baby, or truckin'. Although these new dances often caused alarm because of their seeming anarchy of motion, and the uncontrolled freedom that that implies, the Charleston in particular roused the ire of the guardians of public morality. Warning that the Charleston would lead to sexual and political dissolution, the dance was condemned by several clerics and was banned in several cities.

Although the Charleston was immediately introduced to Europe by American jazz artists touring there, it was Josephine BAKER (she had been a chorus girl in *Shuffle Along*) who personalized the dance. She went to Paris in 1924 and became the darling of the French, and it was Josephine's charming, humorous, and slightly naughty version of the Charleston that caused such a sensation in Europe. The Charleston, and all the bold young women who performed it, came to symbolize the liberated woman of the twenties, and the rubber-legging "flapper" became an icon of the era.

Then, in 1926, the Savoy Ballroom opened in New York City's Harlem. Nicknamed "The Track" or "Home of Happy Feet," the Savoy could accommodate up to four thousand people. Because it had the reputation of being *the* place to go and hear good music and dance, all the best bands wanted to play there. It was the practice to feature two different bands on the same night, playing one after another on two different bandstands placed at opposite ends of the ballroom. This subsequent "battle of the bands" energized dancers to new heights of daring and improvisation. For thirty years the Savoy would be the center of dance in New York City, and there dances were brought to such a level of excellence that the name "the Savoy" was synonymous with the best in dancing. As its reputation grew, the Savoy also became a showplace, a kind of informal stage arena where people could go to watch the finest Savoy dancers as each tried to outdance the other.

Great dancing is inspired by great music, and the history of African-American social dance parallels the history of African-American jazz music. In truth these social dances are most accurately described as "vernacular jazz dance" (from the title and subtitle of Marshall and Jean Stearns's magnificent historical study of tap and popular dance, *Jazz Dance: The Story of American Vernacular Dance*). The juke joints of the South and the dance halls of the North served as forums where musicians and dancers worked together. The sharing of ideas, rhythms, and the heated excitement of music and movement feeding each other, produced an environment of experimentation where the spirit moved and dances got created on the spot. Certainly the arrival of big-band swing music, fathered by the great jazzmen and their groups, all of whom played the Savoy, parented the next great African-American dance as well.

Great dancing is inspired by great music, and the history of African-American social dance parallels the history of African-American jazz music.

Existing concurrently with the Charleston and evolving from it, a kind of Savoy "hop" was getting formulated on the floor of the Savoy Ballroom. Then, in 1928, the dance was christened "the lindy hop" by a well-known Savoy dancer, Shorty Snowden, in honor of Charles Lindbergh's 1927 solo flight across the Atlantic. The dance, which would become an international craze and an American classic, contained many ingredients of the Charleston—the oppositional flinging of the limbs, the wild, unfettered quality of the movement, the upbeat tempos, the side-by-side dancing of partners. But the two most outstanding characteristics were the "breakaway," when two partners split apart completely or barely held on to each other with one hand, while each cut individual variations on basic steps (a syncopated box step with an accent on the offbeat) and the spectacular aerial lifts and throws that appeared in the mid-1930s. The tradition of individual improvisation was, of course, well entrenched. However, with the lindy hop, it was *the* climactic moment of dance, and the aerial work set social dance flying. The lindy hop contained ingredients distilled during the evolution of social dance since the 1890s. It had a wide range of expressive qualities, yet it was grounded in steps and rhythms that were simple enough to be picked up readily *and* were capable of infinite variations. It would, in fact, become one of the longest lasting of all African-American social dances. Commonly known as the jitterbug in white communities, the dance adapted to any kind of music: There was the mambo lindy, the bebop lindy, and during the 1950s, the lindy/jitterbug changed tempos and syncopations and became known as rock 'n' roll; when looked at carefully, the 1970s "disco hustle" reveals itself as a highly ornamented lindy hop cut down to half time. In the 1980s and '90s, "country-western swing" looks like the lindy hop framed by fancy armwork, and in the South, "the shag" is another regional variation of the lindy hop theme.

On the floor of Harlem's Savoy Ballroom the lindy hop was brought to its highest level of performance, fueled by the big-band swing played by brilliant musicians in orchestras led by such men as Fletcher Henderson, Chick Webb, Al Cooper, Duke ELLINGTON, Earl Hines, Cab CALLOWAY, Count BASIE, Billy Eckstine, Benny Goodman, and many more. As the dynamics of swing music heated up to its full musical sound and fast, driving, propulsive "swing" beat, the dancers matched it with ever more athletic prowess. In the mid-1930s the lindy took to the air, and using steps with names such as the hip to hip, the side flip, the snatch, over the back, and over the top, the men tossed the women, throwing them around their bodies, over their heads, and pulling them through their legs until the women seemed to fly, skid-land, then rebound again.

The Savoy lindy hop was renowned for its spectacular speed and aerials. An entrepreneurial bouncer at the club, Herbert White, decided to capitalize on this dancing talent, and he formed "Whitey's Lindy Hoppers." Choosing a large group of lindy hop dancers, the best from the ballroom, White split them into smaller troupes or teams that toured the country, appearing in movies, vaudeville, on Broadway, at the 1939 World's Fair in New York City, and in many other venues. The lindy spread out to the world, first through newsreels and films, and then the dance was carried personally to Europe and Asia by American GIs during the 1940s.

As the language of jazz moved from swing to bebop, rhythmically more complex and harmonically daring, so did the nature of jazz dance. With the passing of the great dance halls, the smaller venues that featured the five- or six-piece jazz combo that was the basic form of bebop became the main site for jazz performance, and though many of these clubs had no space for dancing, bebop-influenced jazz dance nonetheless flourished.

Bebop jazz often sounded barely in control with its fast pace and solo improvisations, and bebop dancers mirrored the music. The at-times private, introverted quality of musical performance was reflected by the bebop dancer's performance, which appeared disassociated and inward. Rather than having the movement scattering outward, as in the Charleston and the lindy, the bebop dancers used footwork that slipped and slid but basically stayed in place, the dynamic of the dance was introverted and personal, and the dancer appeared to gather energy into the center of the body.

Like the music, the dance was dominated by males. And if the bebopper used many of the same steps as the lindy hopper, there were enormous stylistic differences in the focus and body language. Bebop was almost the reverse of the lindy: partners broke away for longer periods of time than they spent together. Bebop dance could be done as a solo, in a couple, or in a small group of three or four. This open relationship was perfect for a dance that placed the strongest

Interior of a juke joint on a Saturday night outside Clarksdale, Miss., November 1939. (Prints and Photographs Division, Library of Congress)

significance on individual improvisation and devalued group cooperation. The body rode cool and laid-back on top of busy feet that kept switching dynamics, tempo, flow, timing, direction, impulse, and emphasis. Off-balance and asymmetrical, the dance wobbled at the edge of stability. The dance was filled with slips and rapid splits that broke down to the floor and rebounded right back up, and the bebopper was fond of quick skating-hopping steps that appear to be running very fast while remaining in the same place. Elbows pulled into the body, shoulders hitched up, hands lightly paddled the air. Balanced on a small base—the feet remained rather close together—with swiveling body and hips, the dancer seemed made of rubber. Partners rarely touched each other or looked directly at each other. Bebop dancing influenced the dance styles of rhythm and blues and other black popular music of the 1940s. It is also known as "scat" dancing (the comparison is to the vocal freeflights of the scat singer). James BROWN is perhaps the best-known entertainer who dances in bebop mode. Watered down and simplified to rapidly rocking heel-and-toe steps that alternated with pigeon-toed motions in and out, with the occasional splits, bebop lost most of its glittering individualism when translated to the mainstream. Yet the effect of bebop dance was to give the social dancer a new "cool" persona, that of the "hipster," whose sensual slipperiness provided a rest, a contrast, to the heat and speed of the jitterbug lindy. This hip attitude had an enormous effect on Broadway jazz. Bob Fosse, Jerome Robbins, and Jack Cole, three powerful Broadway and film choreographers, would convert the physical language of bebop dance into a style of laid-back, cool jazz that would be viewed as epitomizing the best of Broadway jazz dance.

During the 1950s, with the explosion of a "teen culture" and a "teen market," an entertainment industry, led by the record companies, was established to service this market. Bepop dance influenced the dance styles of rock 'n' roll. The record industry, ever quick to seize an opportunity, made the crossover, renaming RHYTHM AND BLUES rock 'n' roll. The jitterbug got renamed as well, now called by the music's name of rock 'n' roll dance. Partners continued to split apart. With the infusion of the bebop mentality, a slippery smoothness in the footwork calmed down some of the flinging of the older forms of jitterbug, while the twisting hips were beginning to even out the sharp bouncing of the fast-paced Savoy style. Toward the end off the 1950s, gyrating hips (the trademark of Elvis Presley), previously only one movement phrase in the midst of many, would be singled out and made into an individual dance. "The twist," which became another worldwide dance fad, structured an entire dance around a single movement. Its simplicity made it easy to do, and its virtues were promoted in Chubby Checker's beguiling rock 'n' roll song "The Twist" (1960, a close copy of Hank Ballard's 1958 original.) Also in the 1950s there was a resurgence of close-clutching couple dances, similar to the older mooch and grind (now known as "dirty dancing"), danced to sweet harmonics of five-part *a cappella* singing groups who were developing a singing style that became known as doo-wop. It is notable and interesting that in the 1950s, during a period when there was a strong sense of conformity, group line dances such as the stroll and the madison became popular.

During the 1960s, the Civil Rights Movement was reflected in a re-Africanization of dance forms in such dances as the Watusi, the monkey, the bugaloo, and a series of spine-whipping, African-inspired dances such as the frug and the jerk. Animal gestures and steps reentered dances with a vengeance, formulated into dances such as the pony, the chicken, and the fish (also known as the swim). Partners did not touch. Instead, they danced face-to-face, but apart, reflecting each other's movements, using a dialogue of movement that was essentially a call-and-response mode of performance.

MOTOWN singing groups whose carefully tailored and tasty dance routines were choreographed by Cholly Atkins had an inestimable effect on dance styles. The teenagers who admired these groups and bought their records now watched them perform on television. Then they copied the Motown style, whose choreography was made to underline the message of the song. A variety of pantomimic dances was created in which the words, or story line, of the song were enacted by the dancers. For example, one of the most popular and beautiful of these tunes was Marvin Gaye's "Hitchhiker" (Atkins worked with Gaye on this tune). The major gesture-motif of this dance recurred as the dancer—feet doing little prancing steps, hips swiveling, head bobbing—circled the hand in front of the torso, then swung it off to the side, thumb stuck up, as if he or she were trying to hitch a ride on the road, watching the cars go by.

The 1970s disco explosion featured the hustle (if one strips away the ornamentation of multiple turns and sharply pointing arms and poses as the man swings out his partner, the lindy hop becomes visible). The line dance made popular by the movie *Saturday Night Fever* (1976) is actually the old madison, retooled for the 1970s (the same is true for the 1980s' bus stop and the 1990s' electric slide). However, with the explosion of breaking and electric boogie in the Bronx during the late 1970s, and popping in Sacramento and Los Angeles, dance styles underwent a radical change in the United States, then in Europe, Asia, and Africa as the

plications for the quality of life of African Americans as individuals and as a community.

Long before social work emerged as a professional field, African Americans had carried out a wide range of cooperative self-help and mutual-aid programs in order to better their lives and their communities. Throughout the eighteenth and nineteenth centuries free black women and men in the North organized benevolent societies; among the earliest was the Free African Society of Philadelphia, formed in 1787 to provide cradle-to-grave counseling and other assistance, including burial aid. Other groups raised money for educational programs or relief to widows and orphans. Northern blacks not only helped themselves, they extended aid to fugitive slaves and linked their work to a larger effort to improve the standing of African Americans in society.

Following the Civil War, the Freedmen's Bureau, a federal agency, initiated a series of social welfare policies designed to help newly freed black people in their struggle to survive; during Reconstruction many southern states promoted similar relief efforts. But in the context of emancipation, such economic, educational, and other assistance not only improved the lives of individual African Americans, it posed a challenge to the system of racial inequality itself. After Reconstruction, therefore, most states of the former Confederacy resisted adoption of programs that would alter the status quo; when local and state government did intervene on behalf of the aged, infirm, and others in need, it did so on a segregated basis.

Largely excluded from such services, African Americans in the North and the South continued to practice the kind of "social work" that had served them for centuries. Black women were often at the forefront of these efforts, pooling resources and playing a leadership role in establishing orphanages, homes for the poor and aged, educational and health-care services, and kindergartens. The abolitionist Harriet TUBMAN turned her residence in Auburn, New York, into the Home for Indigent and Aged Negroes, one of perhaps a hundred such facilities by 1915. In urban centers black women organized to aid newly arriving migrant women in finding lodging and employment; among the most prominent of these efforts was New York's White Rose Working Girls Home, founded by Victoria Earle Matthews in 1897.

Professional social work emerged around the turn of the twentieth century in response to conditions generated by the processes of industrialization, urbanization, European immigration, and southern migration. Charitable organizations, such as the National Conference of Charities and Corrections, sought to coordinate and professionalize their work, but they continued to emphasize personal misfortune or moral failing instead of larger institutional explanations for the pervasive poverty in urban industrial centers. Before the massive exodus of black people from South to North, most charity workers paid scant attention to the problems of African Americans. With the Great Migration some charitable reformers came to view black people as another immigrant group needing "Americanization," and they found ample support for their moralistic emphasis on thrift and industry from Booker T. WASHINGTON's philosophy of individual uplift. Other philanthropists insisted that black people were meant to occupy an inferior station in life and urged that they acquire industrial training suited to their "natural" limitations.

In contrast, settlement workers, mostly college-educated white women, sought to learn from immigrants and migrants themselves instead of imposing their own values and assumptions. They proposed to live in impoverished communities, providing services that would help newcomers adjust to urban industrial life without giving up their own beliefs and cultural traditions. Though settlement workers could not always mask their middle-class backgrounds, they did establish job-training and placement programs, health-care services, kindergartens, and recreation facilities. Perhaps the best-known settlement was Chicago's Hull House, founded by Jane Addams and Ellen Gates Starr in 1889.

Unlike charity workers, white activists in the settlement movement were often quicker to recognize that poor housing, educational, and job opportunities in the burgeoning black communities of the urban North were the direct result of segregation and racial discrimination. Using scientific methods to identify and analyze social problems, settlement workers pressed for government reforms in such areas as factory and tenement conditions, juvenile justice, child labor, and public sanitation. Their efforts to fuse social work with social reform also extended to race relations; one-third of the signatories of the 1909 "call" that led to the formation of the NAACP either were or had been settlement workers.

Advocating racial tolerance and an end to discrimination, however, was not the same as calling for social equality. Many social service agencies in Chicago, New York, and elsewhere either refused help to African Americans outright or offered poor quality assistance on a segregated basis; this was especially true for organizations providing lodging, board, and medical care. The settlement houses were no exception. Many were located in white immigrant communities, but a number of settlements that were easily accessible from black neighborhoods still did not serve the African-American population. Some white reformers pursued alliances with black community leaders in establishing "interracial" settlements; one notable example was the Frederick Douglass Center, founded in Chicago in 1904. But the center disdained "slum work" among the black poor. Rather, its leaders, including white minister Celia Parker Wooley and black clubwoman Fannie Barrier Williams, sought to bring together the educated elite, black and white, for lectures, concerts, and other cultural activities.

It was often African Americans themselves who, seeking to remedy the inequities in social service provision, seized the initiative in addressing individual and social problems in the black community. But such activists were faced with a stark dilemma. Without the assistance of white philanthropists, they could not hope to match "white" agencies in staffing and programming; indeed, their facilities rarely survived. Between 1900 and 1916 at least nine settlements were established in Chicago's black neighborhoods; by 1919 only one remained. In 1910 renowned antilynching agitator Ida B. WELLS-BARNETT formed the Negro Fellowship League, which offered recreational services for black men and boys, an employment agency, and later, lodging. But she was forced to disband it for lack of funds.

The alternative—support from white people—usually meant control by white people. Chicago's Wendell Phillips Center, for example, was initiated in 1907 by a group of twenty black activists, and its staff was mostly black; its board, however, was overwhelmingly dominated by whites. White reformers were thus able to limit the autonomy of black community leaders; in so doing, they often contributed to the preservation of the racial status quo. On the other hand, they helped shape the kinds of programs that were available; services for black girls, for instance, were more likely to win financial support if they emphasized morality and offered training in domestic work. On the other hand, the very involvement of whites in the creation of services "for blacks" often reflected their desire to maintain segregation in social services.

Even when forced to rely on the resources of white philanthropists whose agendas clashed with their own, African Americans often strived to translate their reform activities into a larger program of social action. In 1899 the distinguished Harvard University graduate W. E. B. DU BOIS produced *The Philadelphia Negro,* a meticulously researched study of urban African-American life. The project had been commissioned by the College Settlement Association, whose conservative wing was driven by the conviction that black people were somehow ridden with criminality and vice—an early version of the "culture of poverty" argument advanced in the 1960s to explain why economic misery persisted in much of the urban black community. But Du Bois consciously sought to set his findings within a historical and social context that acknowledged the importance of economic and political, not personal, solutions. Du Bois's sociological approach pioneered the use of scientific inquiry into the causes and effects of social problems.

The NATIONAL URBAN LEAGUE—formed in 1910–1911 as a merger of the National League for the Protection of Colored Women, the Committee for Improving Industrial Conditions of Negroes in New York, and the National League on Urban Conditions Among Negroes—represented the application of professional social work to the kinds of social services that had long been practiced in the black community. It was founded by George Edmund Haynes, the first black graduate of the New York School of Philanthropy (later the Columbia University School of Social Work), and Ruth Standish Baldwin, a wealthy white reformer. The league offered counseling and other assistance to African Americans in housing, education, employment, health, recreation, and child care. It relied on scientific research techniques to document the exclusion of African Americans and press for greater opportunities.

The league also played an important role in the training and placement of black social workers. Formal social work education made its debut in 1903 with the University of Chicago's School of Civics and Philanthropy, later known as the School of Social Service Administration. In 1917 the National Conference of Charities and Corrections became the National Conference of Social Work. (In 1956 its name was changed to the National Conference on Social Welfare.) But because of racial segregation blacks were barred from social work education and training outside the North until the 1950s, and they were denied full participation in professional bodies.

The National Urban League represented the application of professional social work to the kinds of social services that had long been practiced in the black community.

Through the able leadership of Urban League personnel, historically black educational institutions stepped in to fill the void. Under Haynes's direction Fisk University developed an undergraduate social service curriculum, including field placement with league affiliates. The Atlanta School of Social Work was founded in 1920 to provide instruction to black students, and it later affiliated with Atlanta University. By 1926 the Urban League itself employed 150 black social workers. Over the years the league continued to preserve important ties to social work education; Whitney M. Young, Jr., for example, served as dean of the Atlanta University School of Social Work before becoming the league's executive director in 1961.

The devastating economic crisis generated by the Great Depression severely strained the capacity of private social service organizations to assist individuals in need. In an extension of the reform impulse of the Progressive period, the federal government under President Franklin D. Roosevelt was forced to intervene with massive programs that placed social work firmly within the public domain. The Social Security Act of 1935 provided old age and survivors' insurance, unemployment insurance (known as entitlement benefits), and public assistance to the aged, the blind, and dependent children.

But for African Americans the impact of government involvement was contradictory, since programs aimed at affected workers automatically excluded large numbers of black people. Nearly half of all African Americans worked in agricultural labor, casual labor, and domestic service, but these occupations were not counted as part of the covered workforce. The Urban League, the NAACP, and others opposed the exclusion, arguing that it would single out black people as a stigmatized, dependent population, but their efforts were unsuccessful. They also openly criticized the unequal distribution of relief and segregated assistance programs.

The CIVIL RIGHTS MOVEMENT of the 1960s, fueled by legal and social gains achieved by African Americans during the previous decade, attacked racism and discrimination on all fronts, and social work was no exception. Concentrated in segregated enclaves, crowded into dilapidated housing, suffering from dramatically high rates of unemployment, black people in the inner cities had not reaped the benefits promised by the advent of civil rights. When Daniel Patrick Moynihan argued in 1965 that the black community was caught in a "tangle of pathology" resulting from "the deterioration of the Negro family," he was articulating a moralistic theme that had persisted in social welfare policy since at least the late nineteenth century. It was activist-oriented African Americans who led the challenge to such interpretations, defending the integrity of the black family and calling for a deeper understanding of the structural causes of poverty.

The antipoverty programs initiated under the Johnson Administration's Great Society, while in part a response to Moynihan's analysis, also created new opportunities for contesting it. African-American social workers condemned racism within the profession and demanded a greater commitment to issues of social justice. In 1967, over opposition from the leadership of the National Association of Social Workers, a nondiscrimination amendment to the association's code of ethics was presented on the floor of the delegate assembly, where it passed. The following year, in San Francisco, African Americans founded the National Association of Black Social Workers (NABSW). While some black individuals gained prominence within existing professional organizations—Whitney Young, Jr., for example, became president of the NASW in 1969—many African Americans turned to the NABSW as a vehicle for articulating the goals of effective, responsive service delivery in the black community and an end to racial exclusion and discrimination within the ranks of the profession.

Social work and social welfare programs, although widely believed to provide services on a nondiscriminatory basis, have always been influenced by larger historical trends and conditions. The historical exclusion of African Americans from social work schools and organizations virtually assured that concerned black people would continue to rely on their own methods for improving individual and community life. At the same time, the profession's dominant strategies and methodologies have reflected the racial, sexual, and class biases of the European-American middle class, often to the detriment of those most commonly under the scrutiny of social workers.

An African-American presence within the social work profession has helped to transform service delivery. Many black social workers have developed innovative models that acknowledge the importance of environmental factors—such as socioeconomic status and citizenship rights—in determining the well-being of African-American people. By asserting positive recognition of extended family formations, they have been able to respond with new flexibility to individual and family concerns. And they have sought to extend these efforts throughout the profession, working to ensure that social work education and training incorporate information about the experiences of people of color. At the same time, many African Americans in social work have rejected the notion of adjustment to the status quo, calling for change in social institutions, laws, and customs that continue to keep African-Americans from achieving their full potential.

In the 1990s the assumptions that have guided social work theory and practice demand renewed attention. The problems facing the black community continued to reflect the racism that persists in employment, health care, education, and other areas. The unemployment rate among African Americans remains twice the national average; the AIDS crisis has reached disproportionately into the black community; and drug-addicted children are now entering an educational system whose capacities are severely constrained by diminishing resources. As in the past, however, the African-American community has been left to tap its own potential in order to address these concerns. At the same time, mainstream social workers have adopted code words—diversity, multiculturalism, biculturalism—that obscure root causes and so fail to confront deep-seated racism, sexism, and class bias. Advocates of social work and social welfare can respond effectively to current problems by reclaiming a legacy of progressive social reform that acknowledges the need for structural, not personal, solutions.

BIBLIOGRAPHY

Aptheker, Herbert, ed. *A Documentary History of the Negro People in the United States.* Vol. 1. New York, 1971.

Axinn, June, and Herman Levin. *Social Welfare: A History of the American Response to Need.* 3rd ed. White Plains, N.Y., 1992.

Bell, Howard R. "National Negro Conventions of the Middle 1840s: Moral Suasion vs. Political Action." In August Meier and Elliott Rudwick, eds. *The Making of Black America: Essays in Negro Life and History.* Vol. 1. New York, 1969.

Bennett, Lerone, Jr. *Before the Mayflower: A History of Black America.* 6th ed. Chicago, 1988.

———. *The Shaping of Black America.* Chicago, 1975.

Breul, Frank R., and Steven J. Diner, eds. *Compassion and Responsibility: Readings in the History of Social Welfare Policy in the United States.* Chicago, 1980.

Clark, William E. "The Katy Ferguson Home." *Southern Workman* 52 (1923): 228–230.

Cromwell, Cheryl D. "Black Women as Pioneers in Social Welfare, 1880–1935." *Black Caucus Journal* 7, no. 1 (1976): 7–12.

Franklin, John Hope, and Alfred A. Moss, Jr. *From Slavery to Freedom: A History of Negro Americans.* 6th ed. New York, 1988.

Hornsby, Alton, Jr. *The Black Almanac: From Involuntary Servitude (1619–1860) to a Return to the Mainstream (1973–1976)?* Rev. ed. Woodbury, N.Y., 1977.

Johnson, Audreye E. "Health Issues and African Americans: Surviving and Endangered." In John S. McNeil and Stanley E. Weinstein, eds. *Innovations in Health Care Practice.* Silver Spring, Md., 1988, pp. 34–49.

———. *The National Association of Black Social Workers, Inc.: A History for the Future.* New York, 1988.

———. "The Sin of Omission: African American Women in Social Work." *Journal of Multicultural Social Work* 1, no. 2 (1991): 7–15.

———. "William Still—Black Social Worker: 1821–1902." *Black Caucus Journal* (Spring 1977): 14–19.

Lewis, David Levering. *W. E. B. Du Bois: Biography of a Race, 1868–1919.* New York, 1993.

Lide, Pauline. "The National Conference on Social Welfare and the Black Historical Perspective." *Social Service Review* 47, no. 2 (June 1973): 171–207.

Philpott, Thomas Lee. *The Slum and the Ghetto: Immigrants, Blacks, and Reformers in Chicago, 1880–1930.* Belmont, Calif., 1991.

Ross, Edyth L. *Black Heritage in Social Welfare, 1860–1930.* Metuchen, N.J., 1978.

Still, William. *The Underground Railroad.* 1872. Reprint. Chicago, 1970.

Weaver, Hilary N. "African-Americans and Social Work: An Overview of the Antebellum Through Progressive Eras." *Journal of Multicultural Social Work* 2, no. 4 (1992).

Williams, Leon F. "A Study of Discrimination in Social Work Education Programs." *Black Caucus* 14, no. 1 (Spring 1983): 9–13.

– AUDREYE E. JOHNSON

SOCIETY OF FRIENDS

Founded in England in the 1650s, the Religious Society of Friends (Quakers) first encountered Africans as slaves in Barbados and North America in the 1670s. George Fox (1624–1691), the founder of the sect, condemned the inhumane treatment of slaves and urged their religious instruction. William Edmundson (c. 1627–1712), a prominent leader, concluded by 1676 that SLAVERY itself was inherently evil. Other Friends in North America expressed similar views between 1688 and 1740: Dutch Friends in Germantown, Pa., in 1688; followers of the schismatic Pennsylvania minister George Keith in 1693; and several individuals, most notably Benjamin Lay (1677–1759) and Ralph Sandiford (c. 1693–1733).

Most Friends before 1750, however, did not challenge slavery as such or the racial assumptions behind it. Philadelphia and Newport Quakers were involved in the SLAVE TRADE. From Rhode Island to the Carolinas, Quakers owned slaves in much the same proportion as non-Quakers. Friends disowned members who treated slaves harshly, but they also disowned agitators like Lay and Sandiford.

By 1750 there was growing antislavery sentiment among American Friends, one of the fruits of a reform movement that condemned what its leaders perceived as growing religious laxness. They urged renewed emphasis on Quaker peculiarity and discipline, including freeing the society from slavery. Led by John Woolman (1720–1772) of New Jersey and Anthony Benezet (1713–1783) of Philadelphia, reformers condemned slavery both as an injustice to the slave and a temptation to sin for the owner. Gradually, their efforts succeeded. First, the various yearly meetings of Friends banned trading in slaves. By 1784, all had forbidden members to own slaves.

black education, which eventually totaled millions of dollars.

Spelman College is the oldest black women's college in the United States.

In 1883 the school moved into what were former Union Army officer barracks, which had been purchased by the American Baptist Home Mission Society (ABHMS). The school had grown to 293 students with over thirty boarders. Industrial courses, paid for by a grant from the Slater Fund, were also begun that year. A model school was opened for observation and practice teaching, and as a result, an elementary normal course was introduced.

The buildings were paid off with the help of financial gifts from Rockefeller, and the school continued to grow. In honor of Laura Spelman Rockefeller (John D. Rockefeller's wife), the name of the school was changed to Spelman Seminary in 1884. The school was officially designated for females only and had grown to over 350 day pupils and 100 boarders. The students were taught a traditional New England classical curriculum. Courses included mathematics, English grammar and literature, geography, and natural philosophy. The girls' education was comparable to the education boys were receiving at nearby Atlanta Baptist Seminary, which later became Atlanta Baptist College and (in 1913) MOREHOUSE COLLEGE. In a spelling match against the boys, the girls from Spelman took top honors. In addition, the girls were also taught cooking, sewing, general housework, and laundry skills.

A printing press was purchased as a result of another gift from the Slater Fund, and the *Spelman Messenger* began publication in March 1885. Students were trained in typesetting and composition and began to contribute articles to the publication. The first six high school graduates of Spelman Seminary completed their work in 1886.

In 1888 Spelman was incorporated and granted a charter from the state of Georgia. Two African Americans were members of the original board, and one was on the executive committee of five. In time, the school was increasingly separated from ABHMS as more and more financial resources were provided by philanthropic organizations.

In 1901 the first baccalaureate degrees were conferred upon two Spelman students who had completed the requirements by taking several college-level courses at Atlanta Baptist College. Spelman continued to grow, new buildings were built, and more lots were purchased. The new buildings led to a constant struggle to stay financially sound, and the board began to seek a source to establish a permanent endowment.

In 1924, after a science building was completed, Spelman was finally in a position to offer a full range of college-level courses. As a result, the name was changed to Spelman College. Sisters chapel was completed in 1927, and Florence Read became the new president of Spelman. Read placed tremendous emphasis on the development of a strong liberal arts college and greatly increased the college's endowment. The endowment was $57,501 in 1928 and grew to $3,612,740 by the time Read retired in 1953. The elementary school was finally abolished in 1928, as was the nurses training department. Cooperation with Morehouse College was expanded in 1928–1929. Three members of the faculty were jointly employed, other teachers were exchanged, courses on each campus were opened to juniors and seniors, and the summer school was in joint operation.

Due to constant financial pressures, in 1929 Spelman agreed to a contract of affiliation with Atlanta University and Morehouse College. This allowed them to pool their financial and administrative sources and thus eliminate redundant functions. Part of the agreement required Spelman to eliminate its high school, whose students and function were shifted to Atlanta University, though they were supported by all three affiliates.

Spelman became fully accredited in 1930 by the Association of American Colleges. The Great Depression led to a financial squeeze, but Spelman survived and maintained its standard of excellence. The 1940s saw further growth, both physically and scholastically.

In 1953 Spelman got its first African-American president with the appointment of Albert E. Manley. The contract of affiliation was expanded in 1957 to include other Atlanta area colleges, and the school became the Atlanta University Center.

Spelman students were very active in the CIVIL RIGHTS MOVEMENT of the 1960s. They participated in sit-ins at segregated public sites in Atlanta, and several were arrested. Two Spelman students were cofounders of the STUDENT NON-VIOLENT COORDINATING COMMITTEE, and in 1960 Martin Luther King, Jr., delivered the Founder's Day address. In 1961 a non-Western studies program (in cooperation with Morehouse College) was initiated with the help of a grant from the Ford Foundation. In 1969 a Black Studies program was officially added to the curriculum.

In 1976 Dr. Donald Mitchell Stewart assumed the presidency amid protests from students and faculty, who demanded the appointment of a black woman to that post. That was not to take place until 1987, when Dr. Johnnetta Betsch Cole became the first such president of Spelman College. The following year, $20 million was donated by Bill and Camille COSBY, part of which went into a new building program. In 1992 Spelman had close to two thousand students, 97 percent of whom were African Americans.

BIBLIOGRAPHY

Guy Sheftall, Beverly, and Jo Moore Stewart. *Spelman: A Centennial Celebration.* Atlanta, Ga., 1981.

Read, Florence. *The Story of Spelman College.* Princeton, N.J., 1961.

Roebuck, Julian B., and Komanduri S. Murty. *The Place of Historically Black Colleges and Universities in American Higher Education.* Westport, Conn., 1993.

– CHRISTINE A. LUNARDINI

SPIRITUAL CHURCH MOVEMENT

Although some African Americans became involved with Spiritualism in such places as Memphis, Charleston, S.C., Macon, Ga., and New Orleans during the nineteenth century, the Spiritual movement as an institutional form emerged during the first decade of the twentieth century in Chicago—a city that remains the movement's numerical center. Mother Leafy Anderson, who founded the Eternal Life Christian Spiritualist Church in Chicago in 1913, moved to New Orleans sometime between 1918 and 1921 and established an association not only with several congregations there, but also with congregations in Chicago; Little Rock, Ark.; Pensacola, Fla.; Biloxi, Miss.; Houston; and smaller cities.

Mother Anderson accepted elements from Roman Catholicism, and other Spiritual churches also incorporated elements of VOODOO. While the number of Spiritual congregations in Chicago and Detroit surpasses the fifty or so reported in New Orleans, in a very real sense the latter continues to serve as the "soul" of the Spiritual church movement.

Like many other African-American religious groups, the Spiritual movement underwent substantial growth during the Great Migration, particularly in northern cities but also in southern ones. In 1923 Father George W. Hurley, a self-proclaimed god like his contemporary, FATHER DIVINE, established the Universal Hagar's Spiritual Church in Detroit. On September 22, 1925, in Kansas City, Mo., Bishop William F. Taylor and Elder Leviticus L. Boswell established the Metropolitan Spiritual Church of Christ, which became the mother church of the largest of the Spiritual associations. Following the death of Bishop Taylor and a succession crisis that prompted a split in the Metropolitan organization, the Rev. Clarence Cobbs, pastor of the First Church of Deliverance in Chicago, emerged as the president of the principal faction, the Metropolitan Spiritual Churches of Christ. Cobbs came to symbolize the "gods of the black metropolis" (Fauset, 1971) with his dapper mannerisms and love of the "good life."

The Spiritual religion cannot be viewed simply as a black version of white Spiritualism. Initially, congregations affiliated with the movement referred to themselves as Spiritualist, but by the 1930s and '40s most of them had contracted this term to Spiritual. As part of this process, African Americans adapted Spiritualism to their own experience. Consequently, much of the social structure, beliefs, and ritual content of Spiritual churches closely resemble those of other religious groups in the black community, particularly the Baptists and Pentecostalists.

In time, the Spiritual movement became a highly syncretic ensemble that incorporated elements from American Spiritualism, Roman Catholicism, African-American Protestantism, and voodoo (or its diluted form known as "hoodoo"). Specific congregations and associations also added elements from New Thought, Ethiopianism, Judaism, and astrology to this basic core.

The Spiritual church movement has no central organization that defines dogma, ritual, and social structure. Many congregations belong to regional or national associations, but some choose to function independently of such ties. An association charters churches, qualifies ministers, and issues "papers of authority" for the occupants of various politico-religious positions. While associations sometimes attempt to impose certain rules upon their constituent congregations, for the most part they fail to exert effective control.

Instead, the Spiritual movement exhibits an ideology of personal access to power. Theoretically, anyone who is touched by the spirit can claim personal access to knowledge, truth, and authority. Although associations may attempt to place constraints on such claims by requiring individuals exhibiting a "calling" to undergo a process of legitimation, persons can easily thwart such efforts, either by establishing their own congregations or by realigning themselves with some other Spiritual group. The fissioning that results from this process means that Spiritual associations rarely exceed more than one hundred congregations.

Probably more so than even Holiness-Pentecostal (or Sanctified) churches, Spiritual congregations are small, rarely numbering over one hundred. They often meet in storefronts and house churches, and have found their greatest appeal among lower- and working-class African Americans. The larger congregations crosscut socioeconomic lines and may be led by relatively well-educated ministers. In addition to the types of offices found in black Protestant churches, Spiritual churches have mediums who are alleged to possess the gift of prophecy—that is, the ability to "read," or tell people about their past, present, and future. For the most part, mediums focus upon the wide variety of problems of living.

Like many other lower-class religious bodies, Spiritual churches are compensatory in that they substitute religious for social status. As opposed to those of many black religious groups, most Spiritual churches permit women to hold positions of religious leadership. Indeed, most of the earliest Spiritual churches in New Orleans were headed by women. Spiritual churches with their busy schedule of religious services, musical performances, suppers, and picnics also offer a strong sense of community for their adherents. Furthermore, they provide their members with a variety of opportunities, such as testimony sessions and "shouting," to ventilate their anxieties and frustrations.

Despite the functional similarities between Spiritual churches and other African-American religious groups, particularly those of the Baptist and Sanctified varieties, the former represent a thaumaturgical response to racism and social stratification in the larger society. The Spiritual church movement provides its adherents and clients with a wide variety of magico-religious rituals, such as praying before the image of a saint, burning votive candles, visualization, and public and private divination by a medium for acquiring a slice of the "American dream." While the majority of Spiritual people are lower-class, others—particularly some of those who belong to the larger congregations—are working- and middle-class. In the case of the latter, the Spiritual religion may serve to validate the newly acquired status of the upwardly mobile.

Most Spiritual people eschew social activism and often blame themselves for their miseries, faulting themselves for their failure to engage in positive thinking. Conversely, they occasionally exhibit overt elements of protest, particularly in remarks critical of business practices, politics, and racism in the larger society. Social protest in Spiritual churches, however, generally assumes more subtle forms, such as the rejection of what Spiritual people term "pie-in-the-sky" religion and a refusal to believe that work alone is a sufficient means for social mobility.

BIBLIOGRAPHY

Baer, Hans A. *The Black Spiritual Movement: A Religious Response to Racism.* Knoxville, Tenn., 1984.

Baer, Hans A., and Merrill Singer. *African-American Religion in the Twentieth Century: Varieties of Protest and Accommodation.* Knoxville, Tenn., 1992.

Fauset, Arthur. *Black Gods of the Metropolis.* Philadelphia, 1971.

Jacobs, Claude F., and Andrew F. Kaslow. *The Spiritual Churches of New Orleans: Origins, Beliefs, and Rituals of an African-American Religion.* Knoxville, Tenn., 1991.

— HANS A. BAER

SPIRITUALS

African-American sacred folk songs are known as anthems, hymns, spiritual songs, jubilees, gospel songs, or spirituals; the distinctions among these terms are not precise. "Spiritual song" was widely used in English and American tune books from the eighteenth century, but "spiritual" has not been found in print before the Civil War. Descriptions of songs that came to be known by that name appeared at least twenty-five years earlier, and African-American distinctive religious singing was described as early as 1819.

Travelers and traders in Africa in the early seventeenth century described the musical elements that later distinguished African-American songs from European folk song: strong, syncopated rhythms reinforced by bodily movement, gapped scales, improvised texts, and the universal call-and-response form in which the leader and responding chorus overlapped. To white contemporaries, the music seemed wholly exotic and barbaric, although later analysts identified elements common also to European music, such as the diatonic scale. The performance style of African music, quite distinct from familiar European styles, has persisted in many forms of African-American music to the present day.

Although the music of Africans has been documented in the West Indies and the North American mainland from the seventeenth century, conversion to Christianity was a necessary precondition for the emergence of the spiritual, a distinctive form of African-American religious music. Conversion proceeded slowly. Individual slaves were converted by the families with whom they lived in the seventeenth century, but on southern plantations, where most of the slaves lived, some planters opposed the baptism of their slaves in the belief that baptism would bring freedom. Moreover, plantations were widely separated, missionaries were few, and travel was difficult. Where religious instruction was permitted, the slaves responded with enthusiasm.

In the mid-eighteenth century a few Presbyterian ministers, led by Samuel Davies of Hanover County, Va., made special efforts to convert blacks within their neighborhoods, teaching them Isaac Watts's hymns from books sent from England. Davies wrote in 1751, "The Negroes, above all the Human Species that I ever knew, have an Ear for Musick, and a kind of extatic Delight in *Psalmody*" (Epstein 1977, p. 104). Whether the blacks injected a distinctive performance style he did not say.

Toward the end of the century, Methodist itinerants like Bishop Francis Asbury, together with his black exhorter, Harry Hosier, held protracted meetings lasting several days that drew large crowds of blacks and whites. After 1800 the camp meeting developed on the frontier, where settlements were widely scattered. From the first camp meeting, black worshipers were present, sometimes seated separately, but in close proximity to whites. In an atmosphere highly charged with emotion, both groups shared songs, parts of songs, and styles of singing in participatory services where large numbers of people needed musical responses they could learn at once. The call-and-response style of the Africans resembled the whites' time-honored practice of "lining out."

The first documented reports of distinctive black religious singing date from the beginning of the nineteenth century, about twenty years before the first organized missions to plantation slaves. Throughout the antebellum period, spirituals were mentioned in letters, diaries, and magazine articles written by Southerners, but to most Northerners they were quite unknown. As northern men and women went south during the Civil War, they heard spirituals for the first time. Newspaper reporters included song texts in their stories from the front. Individual songs were published as sheet music, although some editors were well aware that their transcriptions failed to reproduce the music fully. Lucy McKim wrote to the editor of *Dwight's Journal of Music:* "The odd turns made in the throat; and the curious rhythmic effect produced by single voices chiming in at different irregular intervals, seem almost as impossible to place on score, as the singing of birds, or the tones of an Æolian Harp" (21 [November 8, 1862]: 254–255).

When a comprehensive collection of songs, *Slave Songs of the United States,* was published in 1867, the senior editor, William Francis Allen, wrote in the introduction: "The best we can do, however, with paper and types . . . will convey but a faint shadow of the original. . . . [T]he intonations and delicate variations of even one singer cannot be reproduced on paper. And I despair of conveying any notion of the effect of a number singing together" (Allen 1867, pp. iv-v). In effect, the notational system filtered out most of the characteristic African elements, leaving versions that looked like European music. These collectors had heard the music sung by its creators, and they fully realized how defective their transcriptions were. But they feared that the music would be lost forever if the transcriptions, however unsatisfactory, were not made.

The pattern of transcribing the music in conventional notation was followed in more popular collections of songs transcribed in the 1870s from the singing of the Fisk Jubilee Singers, the Hampton Singers, and other touring groups from black schools in the South. These tours of carefully rehearsed ensembles of well-trained singers introduced audiences in the North and Europe to versions of the spirituals that eliminated many of those characteristic elements that had so attracted Lucy McKim and William Allen. The singers had been trained in European music and felt a responsibility to reflect credit on the rising black population.

The first documented reports of distinctive black religious singing date from the beginning of the nineteenth century.

By the 1890s, spirituals had become widely popular, both in the United States and in Europe, in the versions sung by the college singers. In 1892 a Viennese professor of jurisprudence, Richard Wallaschek, in a book entitled *Primitive Music,* advanced the theory that the spirituals were "mere limitations of European compositions which the negroes have picked up and served up again with slight variations" (p. 60). He never visited the United States or Africa, and his knowledge of the music was wholly derived from the defective transcriptions in *Slave Songs of the United States* and minstrel songs (p. 61). Never having heard the music, Wallaschek was unaware that there were elements that could not be transcribed, but his ideas were taken seriously by several generations of scholars.

The strongest statement of the white-origins school was made by George Pullen Jackson, a professor of German at Vanderbilt University, who explored with enthusiasm the so-called white spiritual. In his book *White Spirituals of the Southern Uplands* (1933), his discussion of black spirituals was based primarily on an analysis of transcribed versions. He cited priority in publication as certain proof of origin, overlooking the irrelevance of this fact for folk music, most especially for the music of a population kept illiterate by force of law. The white-origins theory is no longer widely accepted. Not until the advent of sound recordings was it possible to preserve the performance itself, including improvised details and performance style, for later study and analysis.

Concert arrangements of spirituals for solo singers and choirs have been made, most notably by Harry T.

Burleigh, James Weldon JOHNSON and J. Rosamund Johnson, and William Levi Dawson. Spiritual thematic materials have permeated diverse genres of American music in the twentieth century.

The musical elements that distinguished African-American spirituals from Euro-American hymnody were virtually impossible to reproduce in standard musical notation. Variable pitches; irregular strong, syncopated rhythms; and freely improvised melodic lines presented insoluble problems to the collector before the age of recording. The performance style also included humming or "moaning" in response to the solo performer (whether singer or preacher), responsive interjections, and ceaseless physical movement in response to the music—patting, hand-clapping, foot-tapping, and swaying. The overlapping of leader and responding chorus provided a complex interplay of voice qualities and rhythms. Slurs and slides modified pitch, while turns in the throat, blue notes, microtones, and sighs were equally impossible to notate. Pentatonic scales, however, and flattened fourth or seventh notes could be captured in notation.

Textual elements covered a whole spectrum of concepts, from trials and suffering, sorrow and tribulations, to hope and affirmation. Events from both the Old and the New Testaments were described, including Elijah's chariot and Ezekiel's wheel, along with more common images such as trains, shoes, wings, harps, robes, and ships. Hypocritical preachers and sinners were scorned, while death, heaven, resurrection, and triumph were often invoked.

Besides the purely religious message, there were also hidden meanings in some spirituals, exhorting the singers to resistance or freedom. Songs such as "Steal Away," "Follow the Drinking Gourd," and "Go Down, Moses"—with its refrain, "Let my people go"—could be interpreted in at least two ways. References to crossing Jordan and the trumpet blast could have both religious and secular interpretations.

BIBLIOGRAPHY

Allen, William Francis, Charles Pickard Ware, and Lucy McKim Garrison. *Slave Songs of the United States.* New York, 1867.

Epstein, Dena J. *Sinful Tunes and Spirituals: Black Folk Music to the Civil War.* Urbana, Ill., 1977.

———. "A White Origin for the Black Spiritual? An Invalid Theory and How It Grew." *American Music* 1 (1983): 53–59.

Krehbiel, Henry Edward. *Afro-American Folksongs: A Study in Racial and National Music.* New York, 1914.

Lovell, John, Jr. *Black Song: The Forge and the Flame—The Story of How the Afro-American Spiritual Was Hammered Out.* New York, 1972.

Marsh, J. B. T. *The Story of the Jubilee Singers; with Their Songs.* London, 1875.

– DENA J. EPSTEIN

SPORTS

Physical competition and display have always been an important component of African culture. In Africa, activities such as dancing and competitions such as foot racing, stone throwing, and wrestling were commonplace. Africans enslaved in the New World continued to hone their athletic abilities in both native African leisure pursuits as well in sports popular among their European masters. The conditions of slavery placed definite limits on the pursuit of sport as a leisure activity among slaves, but on Sundays and holidays many slaves enjoyed such activities as HORSE RACING, BOXING, cockfighting, and various forms of ball-playing.

African Americans attained considerable prominence in antebellum America in both boxing and horse racing. William Richmond, born on Staten Island (now part of New York City) in the late eighteenth century, achieved renown in London as a prizefighter. His protégé, Tom Molineaux, a former slave emancipated because of his fighting abilities, followed Richmond to London, where Molineaux had matches with the leading fighters of the day. Horse racing, an immensely popular sport in antebellum America, made extensive use of black jockeys, some of whom became locally celebrated and were victorious in many stake races.

Although blacks participated widely in most sports throughout the antebellum period and thereafter, the spread of JIM CROW in the late nineteenth century limited the opportunities for black participation. The familiar and discouraging pattern of radical discrimination and segregation repeated itself with distressing monotony in almost all sports between 1880 and World War II.

One of the most dramatic exclusions was in horse racing. In the 1870s, black jockeys continued to dominate the sport. Isaac Murphy, the leading jockey, won over 40 percent of his races, including three Kentucky Derby victories. In the first 1875 Kentucky Derby, fourteen of the fifteen jockeys were black men, including the winner Oliver Lewis. Such successes caused increasing concern in racing circles, and by 1894, the newly formed Jockey Club adopted a "whites only" policy. Despite the ban, black jockeys continued to dominate horse racing until about 1906, when the "whites only" policy became pervasive. Black jockeys disappeared from the Kentucky Derby in 1912 and from the sport by World War I.

The color line also fell across the path of Marshall "Major" Taylor in cycling. Cycling was a popular sport by the 1890s, and from 1896 until 1910 Taylor reigned as the best cyclist in the world. Yet his membership in the League of American Wheelmen caused the formation of the American Racing Cyclists Union in 1898, another "whites only" group that barred Taylor from its ranks because he could defeat any white cyclist. Taylor's career survived despite this.

Although blacks participated widely in most sports throughout the antebellum period, the spread of Jim Crow limited the opportunities for black participation.

A similar fate of rejection characterized the history of blacks in BASEBALL in the late nineteenth century. Before the Civil War, black people had participated in club baseball, but in 1867 the National Association of Baseball Players banned all black players, and in 1876 the newly formed National League reinforced the ban (although a few African Americans continued to play on minor league teams until the 1890s). The first all-black professional teams were also organized in the late nineteenth century.

In sports other than organized team sports, blacks did somewhat better because it was more difficult to draw a color line. By 1880, interracial boxing had gained acceptability. Boxing contests were between individuals, and the boxers were seen as surrogates of promoters and sponsors. The combatants usually met for an hour or two, and then contact was completed, nor did they travel together, share facilities, and socialize as did players in team sports.

But even in boxing, as more black men began to win in the various divisions of the sport, there were complaints about the undue prominence of black athletes. Newspaper writers such as Charles A. Dana, editor for the *New York Sun,* wrote in 1895: "We are in the midst of a growing menace. The Black man is rapidly put forward to the front ranks in athletics, especially in the field of fisticuffs. We are in the midst of a Black rise against white supremacy. . . . What America needs now is another John L. Sullivan. . . ." (Sullivan, a heavyweight champion, was noted for his negative attitudes toward blacks.)

George Dixon became the first black man to hold an American boxing title. Known as "Little Chocolate," he defeated Cal McCarthy for the bantamweight title in 1891. Joe Gans became the lightweight and welterweight champion in the first decade of the twentieth century. But the most celebrated black boxer of this era was Jack JOHNSON, who in 1908 became the first black heavyweight champion. Because Johnson flouted numerous social mores during his reign as champion, his tenure was extremely controversial. In 1915, to the relief of most white Americans, Johnson lost his heavyweight title to Jess Willard in a dubious decision. Subsequent white heavyweight champions refused to fight black contenders until 1937, when Joe LOUIS won the heavyweight championship.

Of all the team sports, FOOTBALL defied the Jim Crow influence the longest. Unlike baseball, football began in the United States as a college sport, and from its nascence in the 1800s, blacks played on the teams of northern schools such as Harvard University and Brown University. However, when professional football debuted in the 1890s, blacks were not represented. Nevertheless, as early as 1904, Charles Wallace, with the Shelby Athletic Club of Ohio, became the first black to play as a professional, and the next year the Rochester Jeffersons signed another African American, Henry McDonald. Black athletes continued in professional football—though in relatively small numbers—until 1933, when it too drew the color line. In response to the rising tide of racial exclusion, blacks had little choice but to form their own organizations.

Separate Organizations: The Black Colleges

Black colleges became a center of black athletic endeavor soon after their founding in the post-Civil War period. Although most colleges extolled physical exercise, they considered sports a frivolous distraction from serious study. Nevertheless, by the 1890s black colleges began to have intercollegiate athletic competitions, starting in football. Livingston College and Biddle College played the first game between two black colleges on December 27, 1892. By 1894, both TUSKEGEE and HOWARD, despite concerns about frivolity, began competing with other black colleges. Short of funds, the Howard team gladly accepted Harvard University's cast-off football uniforms to suit up for their game against Virginia Normal Institute on December 26, 1894.

Within a few years, other sporting events were staged at black colleges. In *A Hard Road to Glory,* Arthur ASHE suggests that the Atlanta black colleges played baseball among themselves in 1896, and that MOREHOUSE COLLEGE sponsored the first intercollegiate track meet for black colleges in the Southeast in 1907. TENNIS was one of the first sports played at black colleges; Tuskegee had its first tournament as early as 1895. BASKETBALL seems to have been the last important sport adopted by black colleges before World War I, and even after 1920 was considered a minor part of the athletic program. HAMPTON INSTITUTE, Morehouse College, and Howard University fielded the best basketball teams in the 1920s, with Morgan State College gaining ascendancy in the early 1930s. Other sports adopted by black colleges in the interwar period included GOLF and Soccer.

Because of the prohibition against interracial play, black college athletes were known mostly to the black community, with the larger white population knowing little of them until the integration era. Because of poor training facilities, performance venues, and lack of funds, few black athletes from black colleges were represented in the Olympics prior to 1928.

The Professional Black Leagues

Baseball was the first sport which developed a large number of black professional teams. The first well-known team was the Cuban Giants founded in 1885. While all-white clubs refused to play with African Americans in the United States, they often informally played against people of African ancestry from Cuba and Mexico. Knowing this, Frank Thompson formed an all-black professional team in 1885, naming it the Cuban Giants to avoid discrimination, although after 1890 even casual interracial games became a rarity. The earliest black leagues, which were organized as early as 1885, were short-lived affairs, and it was not until after World War I when Rube Foster, former pitcher of the Chicago American Giants, organized the National Negro Baseball League (NNL) with teams in Chicago, Kansas City, St. Louis, Indianapolis, and Detroit, that black professional baseball flourished. The league folded in 1931, but two years later it was revived and played in competition with the Negro American League (NAL), formed in 1936. Although both leagues continued to play against each other until the 1950s, when integration undermined their viability, they were never quite stable. Their financial success was limited because they did not own their ball parks, never made enough money to travel in comfort, and were unable to generate enough profit for reinvestment.

Nevertheless, the black community supported the black teams with great enthusiasm and consistency over the years. The always popular East-West all-star game began in 1933. Arthur Ashe described the annual all-star game as "the most well-known black sports event on earth." Many of the best-known athletes of the first half of the twentieth century played in the Negro Leagues, including Satchel PAIGE, Josh GIBSON, Cool Papa Bell, Buck Leonard, and Smokey Joe Williams. The black leagues were also responsible for a number of baseball innovators, such as Bill Monroe, inventor of shin guards, Willie Wells, who introduced the batting helmet, and J. J. Wilkinson, who promoted the first night game.

Because of the weak structure of professional basketball, there were many contests between black and white teams in the early decades of the century. Both the HARLEM GLOBETROTTERS and the Harlem Rens came into being during the 1920s. The Rens were the first black-owned and black-staffed basketball team that earned its living full-time from playing basketball. They operated successfully and profitably until 1949, when integration undermined the viability of black teams. The all-black Harlem Globetrotters, though owned by whites, continues to prosper.

Baseball was the first sport which developed a large number of black professional teams.

In tennis, too, African Americans had to create their own venues to participate in the sport. The first black tennis players learned the game at white colleges in the 1880s and '90s. By the late nineteenth century, Tuskegee Institute pioneered the game among black colleges. Just prior to World War I, black Americans organized the American Tennis Association and held ATL (American Tennis League) national championship tournaments annually, the first in Baltimore in 1917. Pressure by the NAACP in the 1920s and '30s to integrate the game had little impact, and it was not until 1950 that Althea GIBSON became the first black woman to play in the U.S. Tennis Association tournament. A few years later, in 1957, Gibson won the Ladies Singles title at Wimbledon, a feat she repeated the following year. In 1952, the U.S. Lawn Tennis Association allowed two black men to play in tournaments, and in 1963, Arthur Ashe became the first African American to win a USLTA men's event.

Patriotism

Despite their maltreatment, blacks have frequently been called upon to serve as patriotic symbols, and usually have done so willingly. During World War II, Joe Louis's picture was used on recruiting posters with a caption that read, "Private Joe Louis says, 'We're going to do our part and we'll win because we're on God's side.' " In an article written during the war, Louis was quoted as saying, "I fight for America against the challenge of a foreign invader."

Track star Jesse OWENS also was pressed into service as a patriotic role model during the war, and both Owens and Louis were used to raise money for armed-services-related charities (this despite the fact that Owens was reduced to running against race horses after winning the 1936 Olympics, and Franklin D. Roosevelt carefully refrained from acknowledging his victories). Nevertheless, despite Owens's patriotic work, the Federal Bureau of Investigation, with the personal knowledge of its director, J. Edgar Hoover, compiled an unsubstantiated negative file on Owens when the Eisenhower administration considered him in 1956 for a position in the U.S. Department of State. This file forever blocked any further serious consideration of Owens for a government job.

The patriotic activities of Owens and Louis, nonetheless, impressed the black community. Owens, Louis, and other black athletes rallied to patriotic appeals because they saw them as living refutations not merely of Nazi Aryan superiority, but of the white population's claims of superiority. They served as symbols to emulate and their successes became harbingers of better times to come. African Americans such as Michael JORDAN and Magic Johnson later would become symbols of American success at home and abroad, to some extent obscuring the sharpness of the continuing racial divisions within the United States.

Integration

Although many believe that, with the post-World War II debut of Jackie ROBINSON, professional baseball was the first major team sport to be integrated, that honor actually belongs to professional football, which erased in 1945 the color line it had drawn in 1933. In 1945, the National Football League's (NFL) Cleveland Rams moved to Los Angeles, where they signed two African Americans, Kenny Washington and Woody Strode. The next year, the Cleveland Browns, playing in the All-American Football Conference, a rival of the NFL formed in 1946, had two black players, Bill Willis and Marion Motley. Two years later, the New York Giants hired Emlen Tunnel. From the outset, several of these players, especially Washington, Motley, and Tunnel, were standouts, and the number of African Americans in the game soon increased. Blacks, however, were kept out of the positions that supposedly required the most intelligence. Not until the 1990s did African Americans play regularly at the main leadership position, quarterback.

An enlarged black college population and the growing interest of African-American athletes in basketball, produced increasing numbers of black college basketball stars after World War II. In 1950, the Boston Celtics' Chuck Cooper became the first African American in the National Basketball League (NBA). That same year, the New York Knicks raided the Harlem Globetrotters for Nathaniel "Sweetwater" Clifton. The Washington Capitols signed Earl Lloyd. By the 1980s, black men dominated the ranks of professional basketball.

In golf, the "whites only" policy of the Professional Golfers of America (PGA) continued until after World War II, when black players from the United Golfers Association (UGA) sued the PGA for its 1943 decision to have a "whites only" tour. Because of pressure from black players, the PGA finally relinquished its "whites only" policy in 1959, and Charlie Sifford became one of its first and most prominent black golfers. He won the Los Angeles Open in 1969, the first black to win on the regular tour, paving the way for such players as Lee Elder and Jim Dent to compete later.

By the mid-1950s, integration was fairly well established in professional sports and in northern colleges. Nonetheless, the increased numbers, visibility, and popularity of black athletes created problems. Blacks were still expected not to attract attention. College officials instructed them not to fight back when assaulted by prejudiced white players; to show no anger when insulted; and most of all not to date white women. Racism was not a thing of the past, either in the treatment of blacks by colleges, and fans, or in the distribution of awards. Only in 1961 did the first African American, Syracuse University's Ernie Davis, receive the Heisman Trophy for the best college football player.

There were numerous confrontations in the 1950s between integrated and nonintegrated teams. In a 1951 football game between Iowa's Drake University and Oklahoma A&M, the racist behavior of the Oklahoma A&M team against Drake's premier black quarterback caused Drake to withdraw from competition in the Missouri Valley Conference. Five years later, Georgia Tech played the University of Pittsburgh in the 1955 postseason Sugar Bowl game held in New Orleans. The governor of Georgia, Marvin Griffin, found this development intolerable since Pittsburgh had a black player on its roster. Griffin warned, "The battle is joined. . . . There is no more difference in compromising the integrity of race on the playing field than in doing so in the classroom. One break in the dike and relentless seas will rush in and destroy us." The game was played without the coming of Armageddon; but, interestingly, Tech won 7–0 on a disputed penalty called against Bobby Grier, the black player and the source of Governor Griffin's distress. Before the year was out, Louisiana legislators, sharing the governor's anguish, voted to prohibit competition between blacks and whites in athletic games within the state.

Two years after the Pittsburgh/Georgia Tech incident, the University of Oklahoma made history. The football coach, Charles "Bud" Wilkinson, had by 1958 made himself a legend in his own time. Between 1948 and 1964, he enjoyed a remarkable winning record and in 1958 became the first coach of a major southern university to recruit a black player, Prentiss Gault, who played with distinction and without incident.

Soon thereafter, the majority of southern schools recruited black football players, and within a decade after Oklahoma's precedent, the majority of southern schools integrated. The quick integration of southern college football created ambivalent responses in some segments of the black community, particularly among the coaches at the traditionally black colleges, for soon predominantly white southern schools competed for high school stars and sent their own graduates to the National Football League. Nevertheless, the black colleges, such as Grambling, Florida A&M, and Prairie View, continued to flourish and provide their own constellation of stars.

Integration came less quickly to basketball in southern schools. Despite the stellar performance of black basketball players at northern universities between 1952 and 1960, with such greats as Bill Russell and Oscar Robertson, most southern schools, including perennial standouts such as Kentucky, refused both to recruit black players and to play against them.

In 1963 at Mississippi State University in Starkville, a situation developed all too characteristic of southern white schools between 1954 and 1970. Racial conventions prohibited Mississippi State, the Southeastern Conference basketball champions in 1959, 1961, and 1962, from playing in the integrated 1963 NCAA basketball tournaments. However, the Mississippi State president, Dr. D. W. Colvard, decided the time had come to defy tradition and announced that his team would play. This caused such consternation that boosters of the university obtained an injunction prohibiting the team from leaving Mississippi. Disobeying the legal ban, the team secretly left town, arrived at East Lansing, Mich., without mishap and reached the second round against the largely black squad from Loyola of Chicago. Mississippi State lost, 61–51, and when the team returned to their campus fearing the worst, it was surprised by a warm reception from its fans. One white player, Aubrey Nichols, reflected in 1987 that "our

One of Jackie Robinson's greatest talents was his base-running ability. Here in 1946, playing for the minor league Montreal Royals, he slides into a base. When Robinson signed a contract with Brooklyn Dodger general manager Branch Rickey, he became the first African American in major league baseball in the twentieth century. (Photographs and Prints Division, Schomburg Center for Research in Black Culture, The New York Public Library, Astor, Lenox and Tilden Foundations)

game convinced a lot of people that we should have competed earlier."

Three years later, the University of Kentucky's basketball team found itself confronted with a Texas Western University (later Texas-El Paso) team with an all-black lineup. Adolf Rupp, the Kentucky coach, a committed segregationist, faced a dilemma, but since this was a championship game, he decided to let his team play. The final score was Texas Western 72 and Kentucky 65, disproving, once and for all, any doubts about the abilities of African Americans to play basketball. Ten years later, Rupp stated that the 1966 team was his all-time favorite and that it had lost the 1966 NCAA title to "a bunch of crooks." Nevertheless, the dike of segregation had been permanently burst, and five years after his defeat, Rupp signed Tom Payne, his first black player.

The 1966 loss of the University of Kentucky's basketball team to an all-black team for the NCAA championship marked a positive watershed in race relations in American sports. Two years later, new tensions emerged during the 1968 Summer Olympics in Mexico City, which took place shortly after the assassination of the Rev. Dr. Martin Luther KING, Jr. Many black athletes, such as basketball star Lew Alcindor (later known as Kareem Abdul-Jabbar), joined the Olympic boycott proposed by Harry Edwards, then a young sociology professor at the University of California at Berkeley, to protest racism in the United States. Some who chose to participate, such as Tommy Smith and John Carlos, who finished first and third in the Olympic 200-meter finals, created their own protests by raising their fists in a black-gloved black power salute on the victory stand. The black community, for the most part, welcomed the gesture as a timely condemnation of the racism at home, but the International Olympic Committee was outraged. Reprisals began immediately. Smith and Carlos were banned from the Olympic Village and for many years suffered job discrimination. So pervasive was the outrage that many black athletes, even those not supportive of this defiant protest gesture, encountered hostility at home.

Management, Ownership, Coaching

In 1966, Bill Russell became coach of the Boston Celtics, the first African-American head coach in the history of modern professional sports. (All-American football standout Fritz Pollard had briefly been player-coach for several teams in the early years of the NFL in the 1920s.) Russell had a successful tenure, coaching the Celtics for three years from the 1966–67 season through 1970, winning the NBA championship in both 1968 and 1969. He later coached the Seattle Supersonics from 1973 through the 1976–77 season. Other sports slowly followed basketball. The first black manager in baseball, Hall-of-Famer Frank Robinson, managed the Cleveland Indians, Baltimore Orioles, and San Francisco Giants in various stints between 1975 and 1984. Football was the laggard. Not until 1990, when the Los Angeles Raiders named Art Shell, did the NFL have its first black head coach.

In general, progress in the entrance of blacks into the management or the front office has been halting. On April 6, 1987, on ABC Television's *Nightline,* Al Campanis, vice president of the Los Angeles Dodgers baseball team, explaining why there were so few black managers in baseball, said, "I truly believe that they may not have some of the necessities to be, let's say, a field manager or perhaps a general manager." Campanis' statement may well have revealed the beliefs, attitudes, and prejudices of most of the owners and general managers of major league professional teams. At the time Campanis spoke, baseball had only two black managers and basketball had four head coaches out of twenty-three, also two black general managers. In football, the situation was worse: no black head coaches and few black assistant coaches. By mid-1991, the statistics had changed little, although black players made up 74 percent of professional basketball, 62 percent of football, and 18 percent of baseball.

The commissioner of the NFL, Pete Rozelle, explained the paucity of head coaches in 1986 by comparing the choice of a coach to that of a wife: "It is a very personal thing" (*Sports Illustrated,* February 23, 1987, p. 18). Black coaches were also not given a second chance at managing in any major sport after their first chance. *U.S. News and World Report* explored this topic through the case of Larry DOBY. Doby, the second black player to enter the major baseball leagues, was named manager by the Chicago White Sox during the 1978 season. But after the 1978 season, Doby was fired after compiling a 37–50 won-lost record. Doby believed his race played a great part in his dismissal, although the White Sox disputed his claim, noting that the White Sox were 90–72 in 1977, the year before Doby took over. However, as *U.S. News and World Report* pointed out, "What's important is that Doby never got a second chance."

With Frank Robinson's retirement, there was only one black manager left in baseball in 1992, perhaps proving Doby's contention that white managers with worse records routinely got second, third, and fourth chances. More important, a number of black baseball players have shown by their work as assistant coaches that they possess all the "necessities" for head coach, but have not been given a chance.

The black athlete faces formidable obstacles in obtaining managerial, coaching, and executive positions in professional sports. In the National Basketball Association (NBA), for example, where in 1991 about 75 percent of the players are black, there were five black head coaches and five general managers. Only one team, the Denver Nuggets, had black ownership. Among professional sports teams, this situation is considered exemplary, since nothing approximates it in either baseball or football. In baseball, Bill White, an African American, was chosen as president of the National League in 1991, but there were no black owners and no black general managers. In 1994, there were only two black field managers, although over 18 percent of the players were African Americans.

In football in 1994, there were only two black head football coaches, even though 62 percent of the players were black. Despite a significant number of assistant coaches, there was little indication that any of them would be invited to fill head coaching positions any time soon.

In college sports the profile was similar. In the NCAA Division I basketball in 1993, only 10 percent of the schools had African-American head coaches, although 65 percent of the players were black. The football scene was more bleak, with only two black head coaches, even though African Americans accounted for more than 55 percent of the players. Interestingly, there were no black coaches in Division I college baseball, where African Americans in general were underrepresented, accounting for only 10 percent of the players.

Athleticism

The prejudice against black athletes as potential managers, head coaches, and sports executives is directly related to the perception of African Americans as being "athletic" and not as intelligent as white people. Although whites had long thought of themselves as physically superior to blacks, this seems to have undergone a change in the 1930s, perhaps because of the achievements of Jessie Owens and Joe Louis. Blacks rapidly went from being thought of as athletic incompetents to brutishly superior. When Joe Louis defeated Primo Carnera in 1935, one white reporter described him as being "sly and sinister and, perhaps, not quite human" in his boxing prowess. Racists argued that blacks such as Louis were physically strong because of their mental inferiority. After the 1938 Joe Louis-Max Schmeling fight, newspaper columnist and high-level Roosevelt appointee Hugh S. Johnson wrote: "The average of White intelligence is above the average of Black intelligence probably because the White race is several thousand years away from jungle savagery. But for the same reason, the average White physical equipment is lower." The stereotyping has become less blatant over the decades, yet many whites still feel that black physical prowess is somehow inimical to intellectual achievements.

The predominance of the black athlete in the professional ranks of football and basketball, their disproportionate representation in those sports at the collegiate level, and their dominance of TRACK AND FIELD in the Olympics and world championships since the 1960s, have fostered the perception among many that the black athlete is naturally physically gifted. Among African Americans this view is not well received because it suggests that the black athlete need not expend the time and energy to excel or impose the discipline or sacrifice necessary to succeed. For some African Americans, the covert implication of this view is that black people, though physically gifted, are therefore less intelligent.

Still, it is difficult to account for the astonishing record of black athletic accomplishment in postwar America. There is no convincing evidence of innate African-American athletic superiority. The most plausible explanation seems to be cultural choice. Given the real or perceived lack of opportunities in other areas of the economy, sports has become an area of upward mobility. Through the influence of a few extraordinarily successful superstars, success in sports has become for many young blacks (especially males) something to emulate and a way of gaining respect among one's peers. As a result, much effort is expended to achieve success in sports.

Since the 1960s, in one of the more visible manifestations of this trend, black athletes have become increasingly dominant at white colleges. Yet the academic performance of black athletes at predominately white institutions has not been commensurate with their athletic performance. Since the 1960s, the graduation rates of black athletes have not been encouraging. Surveys taken during the 1970s and '80s, show that black athletes graduate at almost one-half the rate of white athletes.

Clearly, black athletes enter colleges and universities already disadvantaged from inferior high school training. Consequently, they are not as prepared for college life, either socially or academically. Cognizant of this, a number of universities and colleges have instituted various programs to alleviate this condition. The University of Southern California, for example, instituted the University Access Program (UAP), and reported that in 1987, 89 percent of the football team was made up of UAP students, and in 1988, 58.8 percent. U.S.C., like other schools, provides academic tutors and social counselors in the hope that graduation rates will be increased and the number of dropouts lessened. This is not a widespread approach, and apart from low graduation rates, a substantial number of black athletes who graduate do so with very marginal skills.

Black quarterbacks were a rarity in major colleges and professional teams until the 1980s. By 1990, two of the best college teams in the country, Georgia Tech and the University of Colorado, had black quarterbacks. Charlie Ward, who won the Heisman Trophy in 1993 after leading his school, Florida State University, to the national championship, was not picked in next season's college draft, perhaps indicating that the stigma of the black quarterback has not been entirely eliminated.

Media Acceptance

In the 1990s, the reception of the black athlete by the audience and media has been astonishingly positive. Black athletes now command salaries on average approximating that of whites and several superstars enjoy salaries well above the norm. Significantly, this position has been achieved without the (expected) resentment of white fans. In the 1960s, many feared that as black men began to dominate basketball and predominate football, white fans would be turned off, and both sports would suffer. This expectation has not been realized, and especially among young fans the old feelings of prejudice appear to have vanished.

A 1991 *Sports Illustrated* roundtable asked a number of outstanding former athletes if things were better for the black athlete of the 1980s. While most agreed that a number of things had improved in recent decades, a majority of the panelists (which included Hank Aaron, Anita Defrantz, and Bill Walton) believed that racism was still rampant in the treatment of black athletes in all professional and collegiate sports, and that apart from the large salaries for those superstar African Americans, the black athlete is not treated very much better than in the 1960s. More important, there remained the overriding concern that black athletes were underprepared for life after professional sports.

BIBLIOGRAPHY

Ashe, Arthur, Jr. *A Hard Road to Glory: A History of the African-American Athlete.* 3 vols. New York, 1988.

Baker, William J. *Jesse Owens: An American Life.* New York, 1986.

Berryman, Jack W. "Early Black Leadership in Collegiate Football: Massachusetts as a Pioneer." *Historical Journal of Massachusetts* 9, no. 2 (1981): 17–28.

"The Black Athlete." *Sports Illustrated* (August 5, 1991:38–41; August 12, 1991:26–28, 60–66; August 19, 1991:40–46).

Captain, Gwendolyn. "Enter Ladies and Gentlemen of Color: Gender, Sport and the Ideal of African-American Manhood and Womanhood During the Late Nineteenth and Early Twentieth Centuries." *Journal of Sport History* 19, no. 1 (1991): 81–102.

Chambers, Ted. *The History of Athletics and Physical Education at Howard University.* New York, 1986.

Davis, Lenwood G., and Belinda S. Daniels. *Black Athletes in the United States.* Greenwich, Conn., 1981.

Holway, John B. *Blackball Stars: Negro League Pioneers.* Westport, Conn., 1988.

———. *Black Diamonds: Life in the Negro Leagues from the Men Who Lived It.* Westport, Conn., 1989.

Hoose, Phillip M. *Necessities: Racial Barriers in American Sports.* New York, 1989.

Hunter, Bruce. *Quarterback: Shattering the NFL Myth.* Chicago, 1990.

Mead, Chris. *Champion: Joe Louis, Black Hero in White America.* New York, 1985.

Olsen, Jack. *The Black Athlete.* New York, 1968.

Ritchie, Andrew. *Major Taylor: The Extraordinary Career of a Champion Bicycle Racer.* San Francisco, Calif., 1988.

Sammons, Jeffrey T. *Beyond the Ring: The Role of Boxing in American Society.* Chicago, 1990.

Shapiro, Leonard. *Big Man on Campus.* New York, 1991.

Tygiel, Jules. *Baseball's Great Experiment: Jackie Robinson and His Legacy.* New York, 1983.

Wheeler, Lonnie. *I Had a Hammer: The Hank Aaron Story.* New York, 1991.

Wiggins, David K. "Sport and Popular Pastimes: Shadow of the Slavequarter." *Canadian Journal of History of Sport* 11, no. 1 (1980): 61–88.

Young, A. S. *Negro Firsts in Sports.* Chicago, 1963.

– JOHN C. WALTER

STILL, WILLIAM GRANT

William Grant Still (May 11, 1895–December 3, 1978), composer. Although he was born in Woodville, Miss., William Grant Still grew up in Little Rock, Ark. He attended Wilberforce University and Oberlin College. His private studies in composition were with George Whitefield Chadwick in Boston and Edgard Varèse in New York.

Still's musical style is perhaps best described as nationalist, successfully blending indigenous American musical elements, African-American folk materials, and the blues idiom into a range of musical genres: symphonic and operatic compositions, chamber music, and art songs. Many of his compositions were inspired by the black experience in America. Over the years, he developed an eloquent musical expressiveness in his works. An outstanding achievement was his handling of melody in his strongly lyrical pieces.

Because he was an excellent orchestrator, he was engaged by such celebrities as Paul Whiteman, Don Voorhees, Sophie Tucker, Willard Robison, and Artie Shaw to prepare orchestral arrangements. In his early years, he played in various dance orchestras and pit orchestras for musicals. Still was associated in the music industry with W. C. HANDY, Harry Pace and his Black Swan

key role in this new battle. The African-American struggle for citizenship emerged amid the political opportunity provided by a civil war within white America. Equally important, this was a civil war that broke out after it became clear to most Americans, black and white, that its party system could not resolve a public debate over slavery and its relationship to national institutions.

Until 1868, three years into Reconstruction, most African-American adult males could not and did not vote.

The path to citizenship for southern African Americans—the first of many struggles that would stretch into the late twentieth century—did not, of course, begin with voting. It began instead with daily acts of resistance, mass movement to the Union Army, and gradual self-integration by a large minority of formerly enslaved African Americans into the Union war machine. The possibility of citizenship increased during the course of the Civil War as African-American enlistment in the military conflict was widely recognized in the North as critical to the prospects of a Union military success. Military service has historically been widely recognized, in all countries that are even partly democratic, as both an obligation and a privilege of citizenship. Invariably, those who fight on behalf of democracies must also be citizens.

Still, in 1865 the right to vote was not recognized as a national right of citizenship. The 1866 Civil Rights Act and the FOURTEENTH AMENDMENT codified the understanding that such rights as the right to sue, marry, and have contracts enforced were indeed rights of being a citizen of the United States, but voting was left out. The dispute between the White House and Capitol Hill during the first stage of Reconstruction, 1865–1868, helped to establish a national right to vote. The threat posed to the Republican party by President Andrew Johnson's program for reconstructing the ex-Confederate South in turn forced Republican leaders to consider extending their increasingly national view of what citizenship meant into questions of suffrage.

The Republican party stood to lose a great deal from Johnson's plan to restore ex-Confederate states to the Union. It meant the massive reentry into American politics of former Democrats and Confederate leaders. Furthermore, in the South they would have no opposition. The playing field at the national level would thus tilt toward southern politicians. The DEMOCRATIC PARTY would be a powerful national party, and Republicans would be a regional party. In a sense, the victory won by Republicans on the battlefields might be lost in the halls of government.

One option available to Republicans to counter this threat was to promote their own plan for reconstruction of the South. This would include the development of African-American suffrage. Many Republican leaders were genuinely committed to a more egalitarian society. But they also could see that African-American suffrage helped to deal with the threat posed by Andrew Johnson's plans.

The process of building a more democratic order in a region hostile to African-American suffrage had four parts to it: (1) the military reconstruction of the South in 1867; (2) the FIFTEENTH AMENDMENT, ratified in 1870 and establishing the federal government as a guardian of state electoral rules and institutions; (3) two statutes implementing the amendment, namely, the Enforcement Act of 1870 and the Ku Klux Klan Act of 1871; (4) using the Justice Department and the U.S. Army to defend the new Republican parties from violent attack by the KU KLUX KLAN and white "rifle clubs."

Despite the violence that accompanied the rebuilding of the South, there was a high rate of adult black male electoral participation throughout the South during Reconstruction. Still, the violence that was associated with the incorporation of southern African Americans into the electoral system sharply divided many white Americans in both the North and the South. As early as 1872 the northern Republican party split over how much the national government should do to protect African Americans in the exercise of their rights. This split foretold Republican willingness to abandon the South. With the COMPROMISE OF 1877, Republicans took a big step backward from their southern commitment.

Even so, a highly participatory (if sharply contested) political order lasted in many ex-Confederate states into the late 1880s and in North Carolina into the 1890s. This was partly because Republicans stayed somewhat involved in the South and partly because there were third-party movements of economic protest that were willing to make appeals to black voters. Although African-American political participation declined in South Carolina, Georgia, Alabama, and Louisiana, in other states—including Mississippi—shifts in political opportunities were skillfully negotiated by black leaders. The state of Virginia, for instance, experienced the rise of a militant, biracial party for several years in the 1880s. George White, an African-American politician from North Carolina, to take another example, was elected to the U.S. House of Representatives as late as

1898, and he was to be the last African American to be elected from the South until 1973.

Still, conservative white Democrats had always been opposed to autonomous African-American involvement in electoral politics. Gradually, over several decades, they gained control throughout the entire South. Between about 1890 and 1910, through legislation and, in some states, constitutional conventions, they installed what has been called the "Southern system" of electoral rules. The two most important devices in this system were poll taxes, a fee to be paid prior to voting, and literacy tests. Poll taxes were a significant percentage of the annual income of small farmers, many of whom were already heavily in debt to local merchants or banks. The low rates of literacy in the region also hit many adult males hard. (See Table 1.)

State legislators and delegates to state constitutional conventions were remarkably candid, often stating their intention to disfranchise African Americans completely. But these rule changes were nevertheless designed to be, on the surface, racially neutral and thus not unconstitutional under the Fifteenth Amendment. Many southern politicians openly called for the repeal of the Fifteenth Amendment, but until repeal could occur, they were careful to make sure that the new rules did not flagrantly violate the letter of the constitutional law. In a narrow sense the rule changes *were* racially neutral, for they made it harder for poor white farmers, many of whom had supported third-party movements, to vote. However, local voter registrars often ensured that many white voters could register nonetheless, by asking far more difficult questions of blacks. Other methods used to circumvent the Fifteenth Amendment included the grandfather clause and the all-white primary.

Table 1

FEDERAL ELECTION YEARS IN WHICH POLL TAXES AND LITERACY TESTS WERE FIRST USED

States	Poll Tax	Literacy Test
Alabama	1902	1902
Arkansas	1894	
Florida	1890	
Georgia	1878*	1908
Louisiana	1898	1898
Mississippi	1890	1892
North Carolina	1900	1902
South Carolina	1896	1896
Tennessee	1890	
Texas	1904	
Virginia	1904	1902

*Note that Georgia established a poll tax in the early nineteenth century and reenacted it after Reconstruction.

Source: Adaptation of Table 6.1 in Rusk and Stucker (1978) and Kousser (1974).

Disfranchisement gathered as much momentum as it did in part because the Republican party had little need for the South after 1896. Key third-party leaders who once had supported African-American voting, such as the Georgia populist Tom Watson, became white supremacist in their outlook as a tactic for staying in the political arena. By about 1900 nearly all white resistance to disfranchisement and conservative southern Democrats had ended.

BIBLIOGRAPHY

Du Bois, W. E. B. *Black Reconstruction in America, 1860–1880.* New York, 1935.

Foner, Eric. "Blacks and the U.S. Constitution, 1789–1989." *New Left Review* 183 (September-October 1990): 63–74.

Kousser, J. Morgan. *The Shaping of Southern Politics: Suffrage Restriction and the Establishment of the One-Party South, 1880–1910.* New Haven, Conn., 1974.

Rusk, Jerrold G., and John J. Stucker. "The Effect of the Southern System of Election Laws on Voting Participation." In Joel H. Silbey, Allan G. Bogue, and William H. Flanigan, eds. *The History of American Electoral Behavior.* Princeton, N.J., 1978.

Valelly, Richard M. "Party, Coercion, and Inclusion: The Two Reconstructions of the South's Electoral Politics." *Politics and Society* 21 (March 1993): 37–67.

Walton, Hanes, Jr. *Black Political Parties: An Historical and Political Analysis.* New York, 1972.

— RICHARD M. VALELLY

SUFFRAGE, TWENTIETH-CENTURY

With the onset of the twentieth century came the eclipse of African-American suffrage in the South, where the overwhelming majority of blacks lived. The enfranchisement of black men, which began during Reconstruction, drew to a close during the 1890s and early 1900s as the former Confederate states eliminated the mass of blacks from the electorate. Poll-tax payments, literacy and understanding tests, and grandfather clauses frustrated poor and uneducated blacks, especially when administered by white registrars who arbitrarily determined whether voter applicants satisfied state requirements. Though impoverished and illiterate whites also suffered, the racial motivation behind disfranchisement was clearly evidenced in the adoption of the white primary. Winning the Democratic primary in the one-party South guaranteed election to office, a system that left blacks virtually excluded by 1910.

African Americans challenged suffrage discrimination from the beginning of the century. In 1915, the NAACP won a Supreme Court victory outlawing the grandfather clause (which had permitted illiterate whites but not blacks to qualify to vote), and it gained a victory against the white primary in 1944. In the meantime, some southern blacks continued to vote in nonpartisan municipal elections, and ratification of the

Nineteenth Amendment in 1920 opened the way for participation by black women, albeit subject to the same restrictions handicapping black men. The breakthrough for reenfranchisement came during World War II. Inspired by the war's democratic ideology and encouraged by the overturning of the white primary, black military veterans returned to civilian life intent on exercising full citizenship rights. By the end of the 1950s, nearly 30 percent of adult blacks in the South had enrolled for the ballot, up from 5 percent before World War II.

The postwar black-led CIVIL RIGHTS MOVEMENT succeeded in extending the right to vote to the majority of African Americans. In 1957 and 1960, the NAACP successfully lobbied Congress to approve civil rights laws providing the Justice Department with legal tools to enjoin voter registrars from practicing suffrage discrimination. Relying on litigation for relief, however, allowed white Southerners to devise delaying tactics to avoid compliance. The climax of the enfranchisement struggle came in 1965, when the Rev. Dr. Martin Luther KING, Jr., led nationally publicized demonstrations in Selma, Ala., resulting in passage of the powerful Voting Rights Act and registration of the majority of African Americans. Aimed at the South, the landmark law suspended literacy tests, authorized the deployment of federal registrars, and provided the federal government with a veto over proposed voting changes in covered jurisdictions, thereby effectively removing the major obstacles to black suffrage. In addition, the Twenty-fourth Amendment (1964), together with a 1966 Supreme Court ruling, eliminated the poll-tax requirement in national and state elections, respectively.

The postwar black-led Civil Rights Movement succeeded in extending the right to vote to the majority of African Americans.

Following the overthrow of these frontline barriers to voter registration, suffrage reformers attacked election rules diluting the strength of black ballots. Successful court challenges curtailed such practices as racial gerrymandering of legislatures and at-large election procedures that operated to the disadvantage of minority candidates. However, in 1993 the Supreme Court began to limit the efforts of lawmakers to shape electoral districts for the purpose of enhancing the election of blacks. Although African Americans had not reached their officeholding potential by 1990, blacks held 7,370 elected positions nationwide. More than half (4,369) governed in the South, once the bastion of white-supremacist opposition to black suffrage.

While African-American political participation expanded, black voting behavior changed significantly. The legacy of Republican-sponsored emancipation dating from the Civil War and Reconstruction eras placed those black voters who continued to exercise the franchise in the early twentieth century mainly in the GOP camp. African Americans cast their ballots solidly for the party of Abraham Lincoln until the economic crash of the Great Depression and the relief programs of Franklin D. Roosevelt's New Deal swung them into the Democratic column. President Harry Truman's civil rights policies cemented black partisan loyalties, and after 1948 African-American voters increasingly supported Democrats. In the decades following Lyndon Johnson's 1964 election, Democratic presidential candidates garnered around 90 percent of black ballots. However, this steadfast black support did not generally succeed in electing Democratic presidents, and from 1968 to 1992, Republicans captured the White House in five of seven contests.

BIBLIOGRAPHY

Hine, Darlene Clark. *Black Victory: The Rise and Fall of the White Primary in Texas.* Millwood, N.Y., 1979.

Kousser, J. Morgan. *The Shaping of Southern Politics: Suffrage Restriction and the Establishment of the One-Party South, 1880–1910.* New Haven, Conn., 1974.

Lawson, Steven F. *Black Ballots: Voting Rights in the South, 1944–1969.* New York, 1976.

———. *In Pursuit of Power: Southern Blacks and Electoral Politics, 1965–1982.* New York, 1985.

———. *Running for Freedom: Civil Rights and Black Politics in America Since 1941.* New York, 1991.

Weiss, Nancy. *Farewell to the Party of Lincoln: Black Politics in the Age of FDR.* Princeton, N.J., 1983.

– STEVEN F. LAWSON

SUPREMES, THE

The female soul vocal trio called the Supremes was one of MOTOWN's most successful rhythm and blues acts and one of the most successful recorded groups of all time. They earned twelve number-one hits and sold over twenty million records; their rise to national fame signaled the elimination of the color barrier in the pop market.

Originally a quartet known as the Primettes, the Detroit-based group had several personnel changes during its eighteen-year history. At the height of its popularity (1962–1967), the group included Diana Ross, Florence Ballard, and Mary Wilson. Their hits included "Where Did Our Love Go," "Baby Love," "Come See About Me," "Stop! In the Name of Love" (no. 1, *Billboard* charts 1965), "Back in My Arms Again" (no. 1, 1965), and "I Hear a Symphony" (no. 1, 1965), written by Motown's Holland-Dozier-Holland songwriting team. The Supremes' earliest recordings featured Ballard's strong lead vocals (produced by Smokey Robinson), but the hits from 1964 and 1965 featured Ross's bright, cooing vocals.

The Supremes were one of Motown's most successful rhythm and blues acts and one of the most successful recorded groups of all time.

In 1967 Cindy Birdsong (formerly with Patti Labelle and the Blue Belles) replaced Ballard, and the group was billed as Diana Ross and the Supremes. Their hits included "Love Child" (no. 1, 1968), "Someday We'll Be Together" (no. 1, 1969), and, with The Temptations, "I'm Gonna Make You Love Me" (no. 2, 1968). In 1970, Ross departed for a solo career and Jean Terrell led the trio, but their popularity declined by 1973. The 1981 Broadway show *Dreamgirls* supposedly depicts Ballard's perspective on the group, and in 1984 Wilson published her own memoir, *Dreamgirl: My Life as a Supreme.*

BIBLIOGRAPHY

George, Nelson. *Where Did Our Love Go? The Rise and Fall of the Motown Sound.* New York, 1985.

– KYRA D. GAUNT

won two NCAA Division II team titles. Hampton's coach, Robert Screen, and Herbert Provost, of Texas Southern University, earned national reputations. Among officials Henry Talbert became head of USTA's amateur competitions, Rodney Harmon was a player liaison with the USTA's Player Development program, and Claranella Morris became a certified match umpire.

Non-American black players have excelled. Richard Russell and Lance Lumsden played for Jamaica, and William N'Godrella of New Caledonia played for France, as did Yannick Noah, who was French-born but reared in Cameroon. Part-aboriginal Evonne Goolagong of Australia won several major titles. Yaya Doumbia of Senegal, Nduka Odizor and Tony Mmoh of Nigeria, and Peter Lamb of South Africa scored impressive wins.

In the United States, Rodney Harmon, Leslie Allen, Kim Sands, Arthur Carrington, Chip Hooper, Marcel Freeman, and Lloyd Bourne were professional tour regulars. In the early 1990s, four African-American players—Zina Garrison, Lori McNeil, Bryan Shelton, and MalVai Washington—were particularly successful tour players.

BIBLIOGRAPHY

Ashe, Arthur R., Jr. *A Hard Road to Glory.* 3 vols. New York, 1988.

———. *Off the Court.* New York, 1981.

Evans, Richard. *Open Tennis: The First 20 Years.* London, 1988.

Trengone, Alan. *The Story of the Davis Cup.* London, 1985.

– ARTHUR R. ASHE, JR.

THEATRICAL DANCE

Africans who came to the Americas brought with them a rich tradition in instrumental music, song, and dance. By the early eighteen-hundreds, not long after the official creation of the United States as a country, white men were carrying their versions of slave dances to the minstrel stage, arguably America's first indigenous theater form. According to Robert Toll, the arena in which early minstrelsy showed the strongest debt to African Americans was that of dance.

Several African-American minstrel performers were international stars and extraordinary dancers. William Henry Lane, known as Master Juba, ingeniously combined the Irish jig and reel with African derived movements and rhythms to lay the foundation for what we know as American tap dance. Billy Kersands, who introduced the Virginia Essence, was both an excellent dancer and black minstrelsy's most famous comedian. Black minstrel men and women brought fresh and original dance material to the American stage: stop time dances, various trick dances, and authentic exhibitions of the jig, the cakewalk, and the buck-and-wing.

Josephine Baker. (Photographs and Prints Division, Schomburg Center for Research in Black Culture, The New York Public Library, Astor, Lenox and Tilden Foundations)

During the last quarter of the nineteenth century, white road shows generally did not open their stages to black actors and actresses. However, during those same years, such shows as *Uncle Tom's Cabin* and *In Old Kentucky* often featured black dancers and choral groups. Some nineteenth-century traveling shows attracted new talent by holding weekly dance contests.

Many touring shows began and ended in New York around the turn-of-the-century. With more theaters than any other American city and a solid theatrical tradition for black artists, it was a logical place to plant the seeds for the development of black musical theater. Bob Coles and Billy Johnson's production of *A Trip to Coontown* (1898) was the first musical play organized, managed, produced, and written by African Americans. An excellent dancer, Coles staged several specialty acts that included dance. Will Marion Cook's *Clorindy: The Origin of the Cakewalk* (1898) closely followed *A Trip to Coontown. Clorindy* set a new standard for the Broadway stage by introducing exuberant dancing and "Negro syncopated music." Cook's model was adapted for the white stage by George Lederer, who produced *Clorindy* at the Casino Roof Garden.

At the end of the nineteenth century, the cakewalk became the rage of Manhattan, with Bert Williams and George Walker the dancing masters of white New York society. The Williams and Walker musical comedy *In Dahomey* (1902) lifted the cakewalk to the status of an international dance craze after the show's smashing London run of 1903. Walker's wife, Aida Overton Walker, was America's leading black female singer and dancer of that era. She played the female lead in and created most of the choreography for *In Dahomey* and the shows that followed and was probably the first woman to receive program credit as choreographer.

A strong influence on many twentieth-century dance steps, the cakewalk initiated the evolution of American social and theatrical dances that would upstage and then replace the nineteenth-century cotillions, schottisches, and waltzes. The long-standing impact of the cakewalk led James Weldon JOHNSON to observe in 1930: "The influence [of the cakewalk] can be seen today on any American stage where there is dancing. . . . Anyone who witnesses a musical production in which there is dancing cannot fail to notice the Negro stamp on all the movements."

Between 1910 and 1920 black theatrical development in New York took place away from Broadway, allowing African-American musical theater to develop without the constraints of white critics. *Darktown Follies* (1913), the most important musical of the decade leading into the twenties, exploded with such dances as ballin' the jack, tap air steps, the Texas Tommy, the cakewalk, and the tango. Several critics shared the *New York World*'s claim that the dancing was the best New York had ever seen. Astounded by the energy, vitality, and dynamic dancing of the cast, these critics eventually lured downtown visitors to Harlem. Florenz Ziegfeld, one such visitor, bought the rights to "At the Ball," the *Darktown Follies*' finale, and put it in his *Follies* of 1914.

In 1921 Eubie BLAKE, Noble Sissle, Flourney Miller and Aubrey Lyles joined forces and created the most important black musical comedy of the 1920s, *Shuffle Along*. The dancing in *Shuffle Along* included buck-and-wing, slow-motion acrobatics, tap air steps, eccentric steps, legomania, the soft shoe, and high kicking. Several members of the cast later became international stars, notably Josephine BAKER and Florence Mills.

Shuffle Along's greatest contribution and innovation was the dancing of its sixteen-woman chorus line. According to Marshall and Jean Stearns, "musical comedy took on a new and rhythmic life and [white] chorus girls began learning to dance to jazz." Numerous white stars of the theater learned jazz routines from downtown and uptown African-American dance instructors.

Shuffle Along was followed by a wave of African-American cast shows that continued to feature exciting dance. *Runnin' Wild* (1923) introduced the Charleston, *Dinah* (1924) introduced the Black Bottom, and *Chocolate Dandies* (1924), starring Josephine Baker, featured a female chorus line that presented swinging and complex ensemble tap sequences, a new development created by choreographer Toots Davis.

The opening of white producer Lew Leslie's *Dixie to Broadway* (1924) helped stabilize a trend that stifled the evolution of black musicals for years to come: All the performers were black, but all the producers and offstage creative talents were white. White dance directors were often credited with choreography created by black dancers. Leslie's *Blackbirds of 1928* showcased the talents of Bill "Bojangles" ROBINSON and Earl "Snake Hips" Tucker, and *Blackbirds of 1930* featured Buck and Bubbles, the Berry Brothers, and "Jazzlips" Richardson.

The musical comedy hit of 1929 was *Hot Chocolates*, which began as a revue at Connie's Inn, a Harlem cabaret. Fats Waller, Andy Razaf, and Harry Brooks provided the music and lyrics; Leroy Smith's band played in the orchestra pit; and for part of the show's run, Louis ARMSTRONG played his trumpet during intermission. Even with all the musical talent on hand, however, it was the dancing of the Six Crackerjacks, tap dancer Roland Holder, and, "Jazzlips" Richardson that prevailed in the reviews. Cecil Smith commented in 1950 that "the rhythm of Broadway musical comedies is suffused with syncopations and figures which became rooted in our national consciousness in the 1920s."

While black musicals of the twenties were revolutionizing American theatrical dance on Broadway, African-American vaudevillians were impressing theater audiences throughout the country. Since the 1900s black dance teams were rising in popularity on vaudeville stages, and many original and inventive combinations of comic, tap, and acrobatic routines thrilled audiences and inspired emerging artists. Although some black dancers performed on white theater circuits, most were restricted to black theaters. Jack Wiggins, Bill Robinson, Eddie Rector, the Berry Brothers, and a host of other star dancers served their apprenticeships on the Theater Owners Booking Association (TOBA), the black circuit. Free of the constraints imposed on aspiring artists in schools and studios, black artists in this setting could experiment and advance the development of vernacular dance at breakneck speed. The Whitman Sisters troupe (1900–1943), the greatest developer of black dancing talent, toured on the TOBA circuit for many years.

While TOBA and black musicals were enjoying their golden years, HARLEM was fast establishing itself as one of the entertainment centers of the world. In Harlem cabarets and night clubs, dancers, musicians, and singers participated jointly in revues that rivaled Broadway shows. Business was booming in Connie's Inn, Smalls Paradise, and the COTTON CLUB, where revues were usually built around popular dance fads. Many of America's most exciting dancers appear on the roll call of Cotton Club dancers: the Berry Brothers, Cora La Redd, the NICHOLAS BROTHERS, Peg Leg Bates, Bill Robinson, the Four Step Brothers, Buck and Bubbles, Whitey's Lindy Hoppers, the Three Chocolateers, Bessie Dudley, and Earl "Shakehips" Tucker.

The early thirties saw American vernacular dance slowly disappear from Broadway shows. Between the late thirties and the late fifties there were only occasional shows that featured leading dancers of authentic jazz dance: the *Hot Mikado* (1939) showcased the fancy footwork of Bill "Bojangles" Robinson and Whitey's Lindy Hoppers; the short-lived *Swingin' the Dream* (1939) presented Whitey's Lindy Hoppers, including Norma Miller and Frankie Manning; Avon Long played the role of Sportin' Life in a revival of *Porgy and Bess* (1941); and Cholly Atkins and Honi Coles stole the show every night in *Gentlemen Prefer Blondes* (1949). In addition, modern dance pioneer Katherine DUNHAM included African indigenous dances in some of her revues. For the most part, however, it was during this period that the American theater turned its back on indigenous dance.

A new performance format called "presentation" evolved in the early thirties, as vaudeville theaters slowly converted to movie theaters. By this time, radio broadcasts helped create a demand for jazz bands throughout the country at hotels, supper clubs, theaters, nightclubs, and dance halls. Big bands took center stage, and many showcased two or three dancing acts. Tap dancer Honi Coles reported that during the late twenties through the early forties, there were as many as fifty topflight dance acts. There was also a diversity of tap dancing acts, among them: eccentric dancing, a catchall term to describe dancers' use of individual styles and movements; flash dancing, which uses acrobatic combinations and fast-paced syncopations; adagio dancing, which features a slow style; comedy dancing, which includes singing, dancing, and dialogue; and acrobatic dancing, which includes somersaults, cartwheels, flips, and spins.

The fruitful years that dancers had enjoyed with jazz musicians and singers were brought to a halt in the mid-forties. Although several factors led to the separation of jazz music and classic jazz dance, the single most detrimental factor was the imposition of a 20 percent tax against dancing nightclubs by federal, state, and city governments. Many theatrical dancers turned to other jobs, such as choreographing stage routines for pop musicians. With the help of choreographer and tap dancer Cholly Atkins, these artists became the new disseminators of vernacular dance on stage. Dancing singers appeared primarily on television, in films, and in rhythm and blues concerts in the United States and abroad. In the 1990s dancing singers continue to have a major impact on American vernacular dance from the Cadillacs through James BROWN, The Temptations, the O'Jays, and Michael JACKSON to the hip-hop generation.

During the sixties vernacular dance was kept alive in part by such television variety shows as *The Ed Sullivan Show, The Lawrence Welk Show, Hollywood Palace, The Tonite Show,* and *American Bandstand.* On Broadway there remained an implied African-American presence in the work of Broadway choreographers who combined ballet and modern dance with elements of their own particular interpretations of classic jazz dance. On the concert dance stage, black choreographers Alvin AILEY, Talley Beatty, Eleo Pomare, and Donald Mckayle successfully presented works influenced by jazz dance. Ailey collaborated with Duke ELLINGTON on several projects, and in 1976 the Alvin Ailey American Dance Theater presented "Ailey Celebrates Ellington," featuring fifteen new ballets set to his music.

Fueled by the appearance of several tap masters at the 1962 Newport Jazz festival, jazz music critics began to write about rhythm tap as an art form. By the seventies, Broadway was once again embracing this genre. Tapping feet figured prominently in musicals of the 1970s and 1980s: *No! No! Nanette!* (1971), *The Wiz* (1975), *Bubbling Brown Sugar* (1976), *Eubie!* (1978), *Black Broadway* (1980), *Sophisticated Ladies* (1981), *Tap Dance Kid* (1983), and *My One and Only* (1983), which featured tap master Honi Coles. Cholly Atkins, Frankie Manning, Henry Letang, and Fayard Nicholas won Tony Awards for their tap and jazz choreography in *Black and Blue* (1989), a musical revue that also featured tap artists Bunny Briggs, Ralph Brown, Lon Chaney, Jimmy Slyde, Diane Walker, and the talented young dancer Savion Glover.

As Americans dance through the nineties, African-American vernacular dance has taken center stage on television, in films, and in American musical theater. The last jazz music critic Martin Williams made this observation in *Jazz Heritage* (1985):

> Most of the characteristics that we think of as "American" in our musicals are Afro-American. . . . The same sort of thing is true of our theatrical dance. Tap dancing is obvious enough. . . . But actually, almost any dancing in which the body moves with hips loose and flexible, with easy horizontal body movement below the waist, is Afro-influenced.

On the North American continent African-American culture has been a wellspring of new creations in music, dance, comedy, and pantomime. For well over a century, African-American theatrical dancers have graced the stages of the United States and infused American culture with elegance in movement and an unmistakable style that has been embraced worldwide.

BIBLIOGRAPHY

Boskin, Joseph. *Sambo.* New York, 1986.

Coles, Honi. "The Dance." In *The Apollo Theater Story.* New York, 1966.

Dixon-Stowell, Brenda. "Popular Dance in the Twentieth Century." In Lynne Fauley Emery, ed. *Black Dance from 1619 to Today.* 1972. Reprint. Princeton, N.J., 1988.

Epstein, Dena J. *Sinful Tunes and Spirituals: Black Folk Music to the Civil War.* Chicago, 1977.

Fletcher, Tom. *100 Years of the Negro in Show Business.* New York, 1954.

Haskins, James. *The Cotton Club.* New York, 1977.

Isaacs, Edith J. R. *The Negro in American Theater.* New York, 1947.

Johnson, James Weldon. *Black Manhattan.* 1930. Reprint. New York, 1968.

Long, Richard A. "A Dance in the Jazz Mode." In *100 Years of Jazz & Blues* [festival booklet]. New York, 1992.

Malone, Jacqui. "Let the Punishment Fit the Crime: The Vocal Choreography of Cholly Atkins." *Dance Research Journal* (Summer 1988): 11–18.

Riis, Thomas. *Just Before Jazz.* Washington, D.C., 1988.

Sommer, Sally. "Tap and How It Got That Way: Feet Talk to Me!" *Dance Magazine* (September 1988).

Stearns, Marshall, and Jean Stearns. *Jazz Dance: American Vernacular Dance.* New York, 1968.

Toll, Robert C. *Blacking Up: The Minstrel Show in Nineteenth-Century America.* New York, 1974.

———. *On with the Show.* New York, 1976.

Williams, Martin. "Cautions and Congratulations: An Outsider's Comments on the Black Contribution to American Musical Theater." In *Jazz Heritage.* New York, 1985.

Woll, Allen. *Black Musical Theater: From Coontown to Dreamgirls.* Baton Rouge, La., 1989.

– JACQUI MALONE

THEOLOGY, BLACK

The phrase "black theology" was first used by a small group of African-American ministers and religious leaders in the late 1960s. It referred to their rejection of the dominant view of Christianity as passive and otherworldly and their definition of Christianity as a religion of liberation, consistent with black people's political struggle for justice in America and their cultural identification with Africa. The origin of black theology has two contexts: the CIVIL RIGHTS MOVEMENT of the 1950s and 1960s, largely associated with the Rev. Dr. Martin Luther KING, Jr. and the rise of the Black Power Movement, strongly influenced by MALCOLM X's philosophy of black nationalism.

All persons who advocated the need for a black theology were deeply involved in the Civil Rights Movement, and they participated in the protest demonstrations led by King. Unlike most theological movements in Europe and North America, black theology's origin did not take place in the seminary or university. It was created in the context of black people's struggle for racial justice, organized in the churches, and often led by ministers.

From the beginning, black theology was understood by its interpreters as a theological reflection upon the black struggle for liberation, defined primarily by King's ministry. When King and other black church people began to connect the Christian gospel with the struggle for racial justice, the great majority of the white churches and their theologians denied that such a connection existed. Conservative white Christians said that religion and politics did not mix. Liberals, with few exceptions during the 1950s and early '60s, remained silent or advocated a form of gradualism that questioned the morality of boycotts, sit-ins, and freedom rides.

Black theology was understood by its interpreters as a theological reflection upon the black struggle for liberation.

Contrary to popular opinion, King was not well received by the white church establishment when he and other blacks inaugurated the Civil Rights Movement with the Montgomery bus boycott in 1955. Because black clergy received no theological support from white churches, they searched African-American history for the religious basis of their prior political commitment to fight for justice alongside of the black poor. Black clergy found support in Henry Highland Garnet, Nat

Turner, Sojourner TRUTH, Harriet TUBMAN, Henry McNeal Turner, and many other pre- and post-Civil War black Christians.

They discovered that the black freedom movement did not begin in the 1950s but had roots going back many years. Black Christians played major leadership roles in the ABOLITION movement, always citing their religious faith as the primary reason for their political commitment. They claimed that the God of the Bible did not create them to be slaves or second-class citizens in the United States. In order to give an intellectual account of this religious conviction, black clergy radicals created a black theology that rejected racism and affirmed black liberation as identical with the gospel of Jesus.

After the March on Washington in August 1963, the integration theme began to lose ground to the black nationalist philosophy of Malcolm X. The riots in the ghettoes of U.S. cities were evidence that many blacks agreed with Malcolm's contention that America was not a dream but a nightmare.

It was not until the summer of 1966, however, after Malcolm's assassination (1965), that the term "Black Power" began to replace the word "integration" among many civil rights activists. The occasion was the continuation of James Meredith's 1966 March against Fear (in Mississippi) by King, Stokely CARMICHAEL, and other civil rights activists. Carmichael seized the occasion to proclaim the Black Power slogan, and it was heard throughout the United States.

The rise of Black Power had a profound effect on the appearance of black theology. When Carmichael and other radicals separated themselves from King's absolute commitment to nonviolence by proclaiming Black Power, white liberal Christians, especially clergymen, urged black clergy to denounce Black Power as un-Christian. To the surprise of these white Christians, a small but significant group of black ministers refused to condemn Black Power. Instead they embraced it and wrote a "Black Power" statement that was published in the *New York Times* on July 31, 1966.

The publication of the "Black Power" statement was the beginning of the conscious development of a black theology. While blacks have always recognized the ethical heresy of white Christians ("Everybody talking about heaven ain't going there"), they still assumed that whites had the correct *understanding* of the Christian faith. However, the call of a black theology meant that black ministers, for the first time since the founding of black churches, recognized that white people's privilege in society created a defect not only in their ethical behavior but also in their theological reflections.

No longer able to accept white theology, black theologians began to make their own theology by rereading the Bible in the context of their participation in the liberation struggles of the black poor. They denounced white theology as racist and were unrelenting in their attack on the manifestations of racism in white denominations. Black clergy also created an ecumenical organization called the National Conference of Black Churchmen and black caucuses in the National Council of Churches and in nearly all the white denominations. It was in this context that the phrase "black theology" emerged.

It was one thing to proclaim the need for a black theology, however, and another to define its intellectual content. Nearly all white ministers and theologians initially dismissed it as ideological rhetoric having nothing to do with real Christian theology. Since white theologians controlled public theological discourse in seminaries and university departments of religion, they made many blacks feel that only Europeans and persons who think like them could define what theology is. In order to challenge the white monopoly on the definition of theology, many young black scholars realized that they had to carry the fight on to the seminaries and universities where theology was being taught and written.

The first book on black theology was written in 1969 by James H. Cone under the title *Black Theology and Black Power.* It identified the liberating elements of black power with the Christian gospel. Cone's second book, *A Black Theology of Liberation* (1970), made the liberation of the poor from oppression the organizing center of his theological perspective.

After Cone's works appeared, other black theologians joined him, supporting his theological project and also pointing to what they believed to be some of his limitations. In his *Liberation and Reconciliation: A Black Theology* (1971), J. Deotis Roberts, while supporting Cone's accent on liberation, claimed that Cone overlooked reconciliation as central to the gospel in black-white relations. Other black scholars argued that Cone's view of black theology was too dependent on the white European theology he claimed to have rejected and thus not sufficiently aware of the African origin of black religion. This position was taken by Gayraud S. Wilmore, author of *Black Religion and Black Radicalism* (1972).

While black scholars debated about black theology, they agreed that liberation is the central core of the gospel as found in the scriptures and the religious history of the African Americans. They claimed that the *political* meaning of the gospel is best illustrated in the Exodus, and its *spiritual* meaning is found in the ministry of Jesus. The Exodus was interpreted as analogous to Nat Turner's slave insurrection, Harriet Tubman's liberation of an estimated 300 slaves, and the black power revolution in 1960s. Slave spirituals, sermons, prayers, and the religious fervor that characterized the contemporary Civil Rights Movement expressed the spiritual character of liberation found in the ministry of Jesus.

During the early part of the 1970s, black theology in the United States influenced the development of black theology in South Africa. Black theologians in the United States also began to have contact with theologians of liberation in Latin America and Asia. Although Latin American theologians emphasized classism in contrast to black theologians' accent on racism, they became partners in their opposition to the dominant theologies of Europe and the United States and in their identification of the gospel with the liberation of the poor. A similar partnership occurred with Asians regarding the importance of culture in defining theology.

In the late 1970s, a feminist consciousness began to emerge among black women as more women entered the ministry and the seminaries. Their critique of black theology as sexist led to the development of a "womanist theology." The term "womanist" was derived from Alice Walker's *In Search of Our Mothers' Gardens: Womanist Prose* (1983) and was applied to theology by Delores Williams, Katie G. Cannon, Jacquelyn Grant, Kelly D. Brown, and other black women scholars. It has been within the context of black theologians' dialogue with women and Third World peoples that the theological meaning of liberation has been enlarged and the universal character of the Christian faith reaffirmed.

BIBLIOGRAPHY

Cone, James H. *For My People: Black Theology and the Black Church.* Maryknoll, N.Y., 1984.

———. *God of the Oppressed.* New York,1975.

Cone, James H., and Gayraud S. Wilmore, eds. *Black Theology: A Documentary History.* Vol. One: 1966–1979. Rev. ed. Maryknoll, N.Y., 1992.

———. *Black Theology: A Documentary History.* Vol. Two: 1980–1992. Maryknoll, N.Y., 1992.

– JAMES H. CONE

THIRTEENTH AMENDMENT

The Thirteenth Amendment to the U.S. Constitution, ratified in 1865, abolished SLAVERY. Its first section provided that "neither slavery nor involuntary servitude" should exist within the United States or in any place subject to its jurisdiction. The second section granted Congress the power to "enforce this article by appropriate legislation."

Early in the CIVIL WAR, President Abraham Lincoln repeatedly assured "loyal" planters that they would be able to keep their slaves, and the Emancipation Proclamation, issued in 1863, specifically exempted most slaves held in areas already under federal military occupation and the loyal border states. Yet, by encouraging abolitionist sentiment and authorizing the enlistment of African Americans in the Union Army, the Emancipation Proclamation also changed the focus of the war into a struggle against slavery itself—regardless of where it existed.

Because the Emancipation Proclamation had been issued as a war measure, some feared that it might be judged unconstitutional after the war's end. Lincoln came under increasing political pressure from within his REPUBLICAN PARTY to resolve the issue with a constitutional amendment abolishing slavery. The Republican platform of 1864 strongly supported such an amendment, and when Lincoln won in November, he began an aggressive attempt to win passage from the "lame duck" Congress in early 1865. The DEMOCRATIC opposition had the votes to prevent passage of the amendment in the House of Representatives, but Lincoln's electoral mandate served to undermine their unity. Furthermore, secret promises of administration patronage, approaching outright bribery, secured sufficient Democratic votes and absences to allow passage by a vote of 119 to 56—two votes above the required two-thirds margin.

After passage, the proposed amendment then required endorsement by three-quarters of the state legislature for ratification. It was rapidly passed by most of the northern states, and so its ratification rested with the actions of the southern states, then in constitutional limbo after the collapse of the Confederacy in April 1865. President Andrew Johnson, eager to readmit the southern states to the Union under the "lenient" terms of presidential RECONSTRUCTION, told southern legislatures that ratification of the amendment was a prerequisite for restoration to the Union. The southern constitutional conventions were very uncomfortable with this condition, especially the second section of the amendment, which apparently legitimated federal intervention to secure civil rights against state intrusion. Mississippi refused to ratify the amendment altogether, but most southern states complied with the president's emphatic instruction, and the amendment was declared ratified on December 18, 1865. Despite the end of the war, the border states of Kentucky and Delaware had refused to emancipate their slaves, so the amendment had a direct and practical effect in those states. In Oklahoma, slavery was abolished in 1866 by treaty with the Cherokee nation, thus bringing a formal end to the institution in the entire United States.

The legal interpretation of the Thirteen Amendment engenders continuing controversy, specifically the section granting Congress enforcement powers. Many proponents of the legislation offered an expansive view of the amendment, maintaining that it gave Congress the power to overturn all state legislation inconsistent with basic civil liberties. Other contemporaries took a more restrained view of the powers it granted, arguing that it only abolished slavery, narrowly defined.

BIBLIOGRAPHY

Cox, LaWanda, and John H. Cox. *Politics, Principle, and Prejudice, 1865–1866: Dilemma of Reconstruction America.* New York, 1969.

Hyman, Harold M. *A More Perfect Union: The Impact of the Civil War and Reconstruction on the Constitution.* Boston, 1975.

Maltz, Earl M. *Civil Rights, the Constitution, and Congress, 1863–1869.* Lawrence, Kans., 1990.

– MICHAEL W. FITZGERALD

THOMAS, CLARENCE

Clarence Thomas (June 23, 1948–), justice of U.S. Supreme Court. Born in Pin Point, Ga., Clarence Thomas was the second of three children of M. C. and Leola (Anderson) Thomas. M. C. Thomas left when his son was two, and Leola Thomas supported the family. They had little money, and after the family house burned down, Clarence Thomas went to live with grandparents in Savannah, Ga. Thomas attended Catholic schools, whose teachers he later credited with giving him hope and self-confidence.

In 1967, Thomas entered the Immaculate Conception Seminary in Conception, Mo., intending to become a Catholic priest. He decided to leave after hearing white classmates happily report the assassination of the Reverend Dr. Martin Luther KING, Jr. Thomas transferred to Holy Cross College in Worcester, Mass., on the school's first Martin Luther King Scholarship. At Holy Cross, Thomas majored in English literature, graduating cum laude in 1971. An admirer of MALCOLM X, Thomas helped form the Black Students League, joined the BLACK PANTHER PARTY, and ran a free-breakfast program for black children.

Rejected for military service on medical grounds, Thomas entered Yale University Law School in fall 1971 under the university's affirmative action program. He was admitted to the bar in 1974, then accepted a position as an aide to John Danforth, Missouri's attorney general. Shortly thereafter, he read the conservative African-American economist Thomas Sowell's book *Race and Economics* (1975), which he later claimed as his intellectual "salvation." Thomas adopted Sowell's pro-market, anti-affirmative action theories. In 1977, Thomas became a staff attorney for the Monsanto Company in St. Louis. In 1979, he joined Danforth, by that time a U.S. senator, as an energy and environmental specialist on his staff.

In 1980, Thomas spoke at the Fairmount Conference in San Francisco, a meeting of black conservatives. He denounced the social welfare system for fostering dependency. The publicity Thomas's conservative views received won him the interest of the Reagan administration. In 1981, despite his reluctance to be "typed" as a civil rights specialist, Thomas was named Assistant Secretary for Civil Rights in the Department of Education, where he drew criticism for refusing to push integration orders on southern colleges. In 1982, Thomas was appointed chair of the Equal Employment Opportunity Commission. Reappointed in 1986, he served until 1990. His tenure was controversial. An opponent of activist judicial action, he refused to press pending class-action suits, and opposed the use of comparable-worth guidelines in gender discrimination cases. The commission allowed thousands of age-discrimination lawsuits to lapse, through what he claimed was "bad management." Yet Thomas opposed efforts to secure tax-exempt status for racially discriminatory colleges, and in 1983 he secured an important affirmative action agreement with General Motors.

In 1989, President George Bush nominated Thomas for a seat on the U.S. Circuit Court of Appeals for the District of Columbia. The appointment was widely understood as preliminary to a possible Supreme Court appointment, as a replacement for aging African-American Justice Thurgood MARSHALL. Thomas was easily confirmed for the district court in February 1990. In July 1991, Marshall retired, and Bush nominated Thomas as his successor. Bush claimed race had nothing to do with the nomination and that Thomas was the "most qualified candidate" to succeed Marshall, an assertion widely viewed as disingenuous. Nevertheless, many blacks who opposed Thomas's conservative ideas initially felt torn by the nomination and supported him or remained neutral on racial grounds.

In his first years on the Supreme Court, Thomas voted consistently with the Court's conservative wing.

Thomas's confirmation hearings were acrimonious. He denounced the reasoning of the Court's *Brown* v. *Board of Education* (1954) desegregation case as "dubious social engineering." He refused to take a position on the *Roe* v. *Wade* (1973) abortion decision and aroused doubts by his assertion that he had never discussed it, even in private conversation. On September 27, 1991, the Senate Judiciary Committee deadlocked on Thomas's nomination, and sent it to the Senate floor without recommendation. Shortly thereafter, testimony by Anita Hill, Thomas's former assistant who claimed he had sexually harassed her, was leaked to media sources. The committee reopened hearings in order to discuss the issue. The questioning of Hill and Thomas became a national television event and a source of universal debate over issues of sexual harassment and Hill's truthfulness. Despite the damaging allegations, on October 15, Thomas was confirmed, 52–48.

In his first years on the Supreme Court, Thomas voted consistently with the Court's conservative wing. His decisions narrowed the scope of the 1965 Voting Rights Act, upheld new limits on abortion rights (he pronounced himself ready to overturn *Roe* v. *Wade*), and curbed affirmative action policies. In *Hudson* v. *McMillian* (1992), perhaps his most controversial opinion, Thomas held that the Eighth Amendment did not proscribe beating of prison inmates by guards. Thomas remained bitter about the treatment he had received during his confirmation process. In 1993 he gave a controversial speech linking society's treatment of conservative African-American intellectuals to lynching.

BIBLIOGRAPHY

"Court of Appeal: The Black Community Speaks Out on the Racial and Sexual Politics of Thomas v. Hill." *Black Scholar* (1992).

Morrison, Toni, ed. *Race-ing Justice, Engendering Power.* New York, 1992.

Phelps, Timothy, and Helen Winternitz. *Capital Games.* New York, 1992.

Toobin, Jeffrey. "The Burden of Clarence Thomas." *New Yorker* (September 27, 1993): 38–51.

— CLARENCE E. WALKER

THOMPSON, ROBERT LOUIS

Robert Louis Thompson (June 26, 1937–May 30, 1966), painter. A twenty-one-year-old student at the University of Louisville when he made his first major sale (to collector Walter Chrysler) in 1958, Bob Thompson enjoyed early recognition and acceptance at a level that was unprecedented for U. S. blacks in the visual arts. Only the African-American sculptor Richard HUNT—who sold one of his welded steel constructions to the Museum of Modern Art in 1957 at age twenty-one—anticipated Thompson's precocious success. And not until the emergence of neo-expressionist painter Jean-Michel BASQUIAT, in the 1980s, would another black artist be so thoroughly ensconced as Thompson in the cultural vanguard of his day. Photographed by Robert Frank, sketched by Larry Rivers, filmed by Alfred Leslie, and included in two of the earliest multimedia Happenings (Allan Kaprow's *18 Happenings in 6 Parts* and Red Grooms's *The Burning Building,* both 1959), Thompson was, along with such authors as Ted Joans, Bob Kaufman, LeRoi Jones, and Adrienne Kennedy, among the few blacks to gain prominence in a late 1950s/early 1960s bohemia that would profoundly alter American arts and social life. Yet because he painted in what formalist art critics and historians consider a noncanonical style, and because his death coincided with the birth of a BLACK ARTS MOVEMENT that rejected his work's integrationist content, Thompson has posthumously lapsed into relative obscurity.

Born in Louisville, Ky., Bob Thompson was the youngest of three children and the only son of Cecil DeWitt Thompson, a successful small businessman, and Bessie Shauntee Thompson, a schoolteacher. Within a year of his birth, the family moved to a small town forty miles south of Louisville. Shattered by his father's death in a 1950 automobile accident, the thirteen-year-old Thompson was sent to Louisville to live with a sister and her husband, a Fort Knox cartographer whose love of art and jazz would leave a lasting impression. Upon graduating from Louisville's Central High School in 1955, Thompson spent an unhappy year in the School of Education at Boston University, then took his brother-in-law's advice and, returning to Louisville, found work as a department store window decorator and enrolled in evening art classes. By the following spring, he had won a full scholarship to the University of Louisville's Hite Art Institute.

Thompson's training at the Hite overlapped that of painter Sam Gilliam and several other blacks, who shared a taste for modern poetry, progressive jazz, and contemporary art. Yet, awed by the Old Masters he studied in art history classes, Thompson gradually shifted from painting in a large-scale, gestural, abstract mode to figurative expressionism. His summer 1958 stay in Provincetown, Mass., proved decisive. There, he encountered a revelatory blend of brooding narrative, voluptuous color, and bluntly efficient drawing in the art of the late Jan Müller, met older, relatively established New York gestural realists Lester Johnson and Gandy Brodie, and joined a circle of younger artists, including Red Grooms, Mimi Gross, and Alex Katz, who were determined to wed their elders' stylistic candor to new, egalitarian subject matter. Precursors of pop art, these artists' adherence to a style rooted in abstract expressionism would subsequently be considered anomalous.

Encouraged by his Provincetown friends, Thompson withdrew from the University of Louisville and moved to New York in the spring of 1959. By the time his first New York solo exhibition opened less than a year later at the Delancey Street Museum, Thompson had already developed many of the elements of his signature style. Reviewing the show in *Art News,* critic Lawrence Campbell noted his use of "flat patterns, like silhouettes on rifle ranges, and synthetic colors" to create "hallucinating visions" with "the content of fairy stories" or "events ritualized by oral tradition" (Campbell 1960, p. 19).

Married to Carol Plenda in December 1960, Thompson left with her for Europe the following spring. Funded by a Walter Gutman Foundation Grant and a John Hay Whitney Fellowship, the couple spent the next two and a half years living abroad: first in Paris, then in Spain, on the island of Ibiza and at Portintiax. In Europe, Thompson refined his technique and let his debts from Old Master compositions, previously disguised or avoided, become obvious—a deliberate assertion of his desire to rival the best of Western art and to reinvent it, much in the way jazz musicians routinely appropriated and transformed standard songs.

Returning to New York in the fall of 1963, Thompson joined one of the period's top galleries, the Martha Jackson Gallery, and was given his first midtown solo show. By 1965, along with Jackson in New York, his representatives included Chicago's Richard Gray and Detroit's Donald Morris, two of the Midwest's leading dealers. Thompson's show at the Martha Jackson Gallery that year broke attendance records.

Despite this public triumph and his sustained productivity, the artist's private life was a shambles, increasingly plagued by the alcohol and drug abuse that had troubled him for years. In November 1965, he and his wife fled to Italy, hoping the changed environment might help solve his problems. Instead, on Memorial Day 1966, less than a month short of his twenty-ninth birthday, the painter was found dead in the couple's apartment in Rome, apparently the victim of a drug overdose.

Since his death, Thompson's art has been the subject of a retrospective at the New School for Social Research (1969) and a memorial exhibition at Louisville's J. B. Speed Museum (1971), as well as surveys at the University of Massachusetts at Amherst (1974), the National Collection of Fine Arts, now the National Museum of American Art, in Washington, D.C. (1975), the Studio Museum in Harlem (1978), the Wadsworth Atheneum in Hartford, Conn. (1986), and the California Afro-American Museum in Los Angeles (1990). Today his work can be found in many of the leading museums, including the Museum of the Art Institute of Chicago, the Detroit Institute of Arts, the Hirschhorn Museum and Sculpture Garden, the Metropolitan Museum of Art, the Minneapolis Institute of Art, the Museum of Modern Art, the Museum of the National Center of Afro-American Artists, the New Orleans Museum, the Solomon R. Guggenheim Museum, and the Whitney Museum of American Art.

BIBLIOGRAPHY

C[ampbell], L[awrence]. "Reviews and Previews: New Names This Month: Bob Thompson. *Art News* (February 1960): 19.

Siegel, Jeanne. "Robert Thompson and the Old Masters." *Harvard Art Review* 2 (1967): 10–14.

Wilson, Judith. "Bob Thompson." In *Novae: William H. Johnson and Bob Thompson.* Los Angeles, 1990, pp. 22–32, 54–55.

———. "Bob Thompson." In Paul Schimmel and Judith E. Stein, eds. *The Figurative Fifties: New York Figurative Expressionism.* New York, 1988, pp. 154–162.

– JUDITH WILSON

TILL, EMMETT LOUIS

Emmett Louis Till (July 25, 1941–August 28, 1955). Emmett Till was born and raised in Chicago, Ill. When he was fourteen, his parents sent him to LeFlore County, Miss., to visit his uncle for the summer. That summer Till bragged to his friends about northern social freedoms and showed them pictures of a white girl he claimed was his girlfriend. His friends, schooled in the southern rules of caste based on black deference and white supremacy, were incredulous. One evening, they dared Till to enter a store and ask the white woman inside, Carolyn Bryant, for a date. Till entered the store, squeezed Bryant's hand, grabbed her around the waist, and propositioned her. When she fled and returned with a gun, he wolf-whistled at her before being hurried away by his friends.

Emmett Till's lynching was a milestone in the emergent Civil Rights Movement.

Till's act of youthful brashness crossed southern social barriers that strictly governed contact between black men and white women. In Mississippi, where the KU KLUX KLAN was newly revived and African Americans were impoverished and disfranchised, these barriers were strictly enforced by the threat of social violence. On August 28, 1955, Carolyn Bryant's husband, Roy, and his half brother, J. W. Milam, abducted Till from his uncle's home, brutally beat him, shot him in the head, and then dumped his naked body in the Tallahatchie river. Till's mangled and decomposed body was found three days later, and his uncle named both men as the assailants. Bryant and Milam were tried for murder. Despite the fact that the two men had admitted abducting Till, they were acquitted on September 23 by an all-white jury because the body was too mangled to be definitively identified.

The verdict unleashed a storm of protest. Till's mother had insisted on an open-casket funeral, and pictures of Till's disfigured body featured in *Jet Magazine* had focused national attention on the trial. Till's age, the innocence of his act, and his killers' immunity from retribution represented a stark and definitive expression of southern racism to many African Americans. Demonstrations were organized by the NATIONAL ASSOCIATION FOR THE ADVANCEMENT OF COLORED PEOPLE (NAACP), and the BROTHERHOOD OF SLEEPING CAR PORTERS and black leaders like W. E. B. DU BOIS demanded antilynching legislation and federal action on civil rights.

Emmett Till's lynching was a milestone in the emergent CIVIL RIGHTS MOVEMENT. Outrage over his death was key to mobilizing black resistance in the deep South. In addition, black protest over the lack of federal intervention in the Till case was integral to the inclusion of legal mechanisms for federal investigation of civil rights violations in the Civil Rights Act of 1957.

In 1959, Roy and Carolyn Bryant and Milam told their stories to journalist William Bradford Huie. Only Milam spoke for the record, but what he revealed was tantamount to a confession. Huie's interviews were subsequently published in 1959 as a book entitled *Wolf Whistle.*

BIBLIOGRAPHY

Whitfield, Stephen J. *A Death in the Delta: The Story of Emmett Till.* New York, 1988.

— ROBYN SPENCER

TOOMER, JEAN

Jean Toomer (December 26, 1894–March 30, 1967), writer. Jean Toomer was born Nathan Pinchback Toomer in Washington, D.C. (He changed his name to Jean Toomer in 1920.) His maternal grandfather, Pinckney Benton Stewart Pinchback, a dominant figure in Toomer's childhood and adolescence, was acting governor of Louisiana for about five weeks in 1872 and 1873. Because Toomer's father, Nathan, deserted his wife and child in 1895, and his mother, Nina, died in 1909, Toomer spent much of his youth in the home of his Pinchback grandparents in Washington, D.C. After graduating from Dunbar High School in 1914, Toomer spent about six months studying agriculture at the University of Wisconsin. During 1916 and 1917, he attended classes at various colleges, among them the American College of Physical Training in Chicago, New York University, and the City College of New York.

By 1918, Toomer had written "Bona and Paul," a story that became part of *Cane,* his masterpiece. This early story signaled a theme that Toomer was preoccupied with in most of his subsequent writing: the search for and development of personal identity and harmony with other people. Throughout his life, Toomer, who had light skin, felt uncomfortable with the rigid racial and ethnic classifications in the United States. He felt such classifications limited the individual and inhibited personal psychic development. Having lived in both white and black neighborhoods in Washington, D.C., and having various racial and ethnic strains within him, he thought it ridiculous to define himself simplistically.

Two events early in Toomer's literary career were of great importance to his development as a writer. In 1920, he met the novelist and essayist Waldo Frank, and in 1921, he was a substitute principal at the Sparta Agricultural and Industrial Institute in Georgia. Toomer and Frank became close friends, sharing their ideas about writing, and Frank, the established writer, encouraged Toomer in his fledgling work. However, it was in Georgia that Toomer became most inspired. He was moved and excited by the rural black people and their land. He felt he had found a part of himself that he had not known well, and perhaps for the first time in his life truly identified with his black heritage. The result was an outpouring of writing, bringing forth most of the southern pieces that would be in *Cane.*

Cane, stylistically avant-garde, an impressionistic collection of stories, sketches, and poems, some of which had been previously published in *Crisis, Double Dealer, Liberator, Modern Review,* and *Broom,* was published in 1923. While only about 1,000 copies were sold, it received mostly good reviews and was proclaimed an important book by the writers who were then establishing what was to become the HARLEM RENAISSANCE. Alain LOCKE praised *Cane*'s "musical folk-lilt" and "glamorous sensuous ecstasy." William Stanley Braithwaite called Toomer "the very first artist of the race, who . . . can write about the Negro without the surrender of compromise of the artist's vision. . . . Toomer is a bright morning star of a new day of the race in literature." A review in *The New Republic* lauded *Cane* for its unstereotyped picture of the South, and Allen Tate compared Toomer's avant-garde style favorably to other modern works.

However, despite the critical praise for *Cane,* by 1924 Toomer was feeling restless and unhappy with himself.

His struggle with personal identity continued. He went to France to study at Georges I. Gurdjieff's Institute for the Harmonious Development of Man at Fontainebleau. Gurdjieff believed that human beings were made up of two parts: "personality" and "essence." Personality is superficial, created by our social environment. It usually obscures our essence, which is our true nature and the core of our being. Gurdjieff claimed that he could help people discover their essence. Toomer soon embraced Gurdjieff's ideas of personal development, and when he returned to the United States, he became an advocate of Gurdjieff's philosophy, leading Gurdjieff workshops at first briefly in Harlem and then in Chicago until 1930.

Due to Gurdjieff's influence and Toomer's continuing search for a meaningful identity, after 1923 he largely abandoned the style and subject matter he had used in *Cane.* To a great extent he abandoned black writing. From 1924 until his death, he wrote voluminously, but with little critical or publishing success. He wrote in all genres: plays, poems, essays, stories, novels, and autobiographies. While his writing became noticeably more didactic, some of it was not without interesting stylistic experimentation, especially his expressionistic drama, most notably *The Sacred Factory,* published posthumously in 1980. During this period, Toomer also wrote a number of autobiographies and provocative social, political, and personal essays, some of which were published posthumously. Works that Toomer did publish after *Cane* include: *Balo* (1927), a play of Southern rural black life, written during the *Cane* period; "Mr. Costyve Duditch" and "Winter on Earth," stories published in 1928; "Race Problems and Modern Society" (1929), an important essay on the racial situation in the United States that complements "The Negro Emergent," published posthumously in 1993; and "Blue Meridian" (1936), a long poem in which Toomer depicts the development of the American race as the coming together of the black, red, and white races.

A decade after the publication of *Cane,* Toomer had dropped into relative obscurity. It was not until the 1960s and the renewed interest in earlier African-American writing and the republication of *Cane* that Toomer began to have a large readership and an influence on the young black writers of the day. Since then, four posthumous collections of mostly previously unpublished material have appeared: *The Wayward and the Seeking* (ed. Darwin T. Turner, 1980); *The Collected Poems of Jean Toomer* (ed. Robert B. Jones and Margery Toomer Latimer, 1988); *Essentials* (ed. Rudolph P. Byrd, 1991, a republication of a collection of aphorisms originally privately printed in 1931); and *A Jean Toomer Reader: Selected Unpublished Writings* (ed. Frederik L. Rusch, 1993).

Toomer had two wives. He married Margery Latimer in 1931, and she died the following year giving birth to their daughter, also named Margery. In 1934, he married Marjorie Content. From 1936 to his death, Toomer resided in Bucks County, Pa.

BIBLIOGRAPHY

Byrd, Rudolph P. *Jean Toomer's Years with Gurdjieff: A Portrait of an Artist, 1923–1936.* Athens, Ga., 1990.

Kerman, Cynthia Earl, and Richard Eldridge. *The Lives of Jean Toomer: A Hunger for Wholeness.* Baton Rouge, La., 1987.

McKay, Nellie Y. *Jean Toomer, Artist: A Study of His Life and Work, 1894–1936.* Chapel Hill, N.C., 1984.

– FREDERIK L. RUSCH

TRACK AND FIELD

African-American men and women have played a significant role in track and field. They have won an impressive number of championships, set numerous Olympic and world records, and contributed enormously to American success in international competition. These achievements have been especially prominent in the 100-meter and 200-meter dashes and in the long jump.

Track and field competition in the United States emerged in the late nineteenth century as a popular amateur sport for men. Women did not participate extensively until the 1930s. Prior to World War I, only a few black athletes won major honors. William Tecumseh Sherman Jackson of Amherst College was the first notable black runner. Jackson regularly won the 880-yard run at collegiate meets in the Northeast from 1890 to 1892. George C. Poage was another early champion. The first African American to receive an Olympic medal, Poage captured third place in the 400-meter hurdles at the 1904 games in St. Louis. The first international star was the University of Pennsylvania's John B. Taylor, the collegiate champion and record holder in the 440-yard run. In 1908 he became the first African-American gold medalist at the Olympics, running a leg on the winning 1600-meter relay team. Howard Porter Drew was the first famous black sprinter. From 1912 to 1916 Drew dominated the sprints in the U.S. and set world records in the 100-meter and 220-yard dashes.

After World War I, African-American competitors gained increased respect. The new willingness of predominantly white northern colleges and elite track clubs to recruit and train promising black athletes greatly expanded their opportunities. Probably the most gifted black track athlete of the 1920s was William DeHart

Hubbard, a graduate of the University of Michigan. During his illustrious career as a long jumper, Hubbard earned the gold medal in the 1924 Olympics, captured two NCAA titles, won six consecutive Amateur Athletic Union (AAU) championships, and held the world record. Distance runner Earl Johnson also enjoyed considerable success. Johnson won a bronze medal in the 1924 Olympics in the 10,000-meter run and claimed three AAU titles in the event.

African-American men and women have played a significant role in track and field.

The 1930s were a golden age for African-American sprinters, especially Eddie Tolan (Michigan), Ralph Metcalfe (Marquette), and Jesse OWENS (Ohio State). Tolan won one NCAA spring championship and four AAU titles. Metcalf swept both the 100- and 220-yard NCAA championships for three straight years, and he also won seven AAU titles. But at the 1932 Olympics in Los Angeles, it was Tolan who won the head-to-head showdown, earning gold medals in both the 100- and 200-meter dashes in record time.

Owens, an Alabama native, burst onto the world scene in 1935. On May 25, at the Big Ten Championships, he delivered the greatest one-day performance in track and field history. Within the span of two hours he set three world records (long jump, 220-yard dash, and 220-yard low hurdles) and tied a fourth (100-yard dash). Owens's accomplishments at the so-called Nazi Olympics in Berlin the following year were only slightly less spectacular, as he became the first runner to earn four gold medals. He won the 100- and 200-meter dashes and the long jump, setting Olympic records in the latter two events. Owens earned his final gold medal as a late addition to the 400-meter relay squad, after U.S. coaches dropped two Jewish runners from the team. Four additional African-Americans also claimed gold medals in Berlin: Archie Williams in the 400-meter run, John Woodruff in the 800, Ralph Metcalfe in the 400-meter relay, and Cornelius Johnson in the high jump. When Johnson went to receive his award, Adolph Hitler abruptly left the stadium to avoid congratulating him, an apparent racial snub which journalists later erroneously reported to have been aimed at Owens.

Opportunities for African-American women still lagged far behind those for men. Only in the mid-1930s did black women finally gain the opportunity to demonstrate their potential. Tuskegee Institute captured its first AAU team title in 1937 and dominated national competition for a decade. Leading Tuskegee's rise to prominence was Lula Hymes, who won the AAU long jump in 1937 and 1938 and the 100-meter dash in 1938. Another Tuskegee product, Alice Coachman, became the first African-American female superstar. Coachman won three AAU 100-meter dash titles, but even more impressively she captured the AAU high jump championship every year from 1939 to 1948. She also became the first African-American woman to receive an Olympic gold medal, winning the high jump in 1948.

During the late 1940s and '50s, two black champions dominated their events—William Harrison Dillard and Mal Whitfield. The premier hurdler of his day, Dillard won two gold medals at the 1948 Olympics and two more in 1952. Whitfield was an amazingly consistent 800-meter runner and earned Olympic gold medals in both 1948 and 1952. During the 1950s African-American athletes also excelled in the decathlon. Milton Campbell took the silver medal in the event at the 1952 summer games and the gold in 1956. Rafer Johnson finished second behind Campbell in 1956 and claimed first place in 1960, setting both Olympic and world records during the year. In 1956 Charlie Dumas became the first high jumper to clear the seven-foot barrier, and later in the year he won the Olympic gold medal in the event.

During the 1950s Tennessee State University replaced Tuskegee as the women's track powerhouse. The most successful of the school's famous Tigerbelle runners was Wilma RUDOLPH. Born into a family of twenty-two children, Rudolph overcame a childhood bout with polio that forced her to wear a leg brace for several years. In 1960 she became the first American woman ever to earn three gold medals at one Olympics, winning the 100-meter and 200-meter dashes and running a leg on the champion 400-meter relay team. Her athletic success and her inspiring personal story stimulated new interest in women's track. Randolph's successor as a Tigerbelle star and queen of the sprints was Wyomia Tyus, who won the 100-meter dash in both the 1964 and 1968 Olympics, establishing a world record of 11.0 seconds in her 1968 victory.

The late 1960s were a time of widespread social protests, and sports were not exempt. The 1968 summer games in Mexico City, which sociologist Harry Edwards and other black activists had urged African Americans to boycott, combined memorable athletic achievements with political protest. Bob Beamon delivered the most spectacular individual performance, setting a world record of 29 feet, 2½ inches in the long jump. His leap, arguably the greatest single effort in track and field history, surpassed the previous mark by almost two feet and stood for twenty-four years. Three African-American sprinters also won individual gold medals while setting or tying world records at Mexico City: James Hines in the 100-meter dash, Tommie Smith in the 200-meter dash, and Lee Evans in the 400-meter run. Evans's outstanding mark of 43.8 seconds lasted for almost two decades. Also attracting considerable attention were several protests against racism by African-American athletes, especially one at the awards ceremony for the 200-meter dash winners. Standing on the victory stand during the American national anthem, Smith and John Carlos, the bronze medalist, each bowed their heads and raised one clinched fist inside a black glove in a "black power" salute, a controversial gesture for which they were suspended from the U.S. team.

The leading track superstar of the 1970s was hurdler Edwin Moses. A physics major at Morehouse College in Atlanta, Moses dominated the 400-meter hurdles, winning 122 consecutive races from 1977 to 1987. He set the world record for the event on several occasions and won gold medals in the 1976 and 1984 Olympics (the United States boycotted the 1980 Moscow games). The 1984 summer games in Los Angeles witnessed the emergence of another superstar—Carl Lewis. In a brilliant performance reminiscent of Jesse Owens at Berlin in 1936, Lewis became only the second male track competitor in history to claim four gold medals, winning individual titles in the 100-meter dash, the 200-meter dash, and the long jump, and sharing the 400-meter relay team's victory. Lewis successfully defended his 100-meter and long jump championships in 1988, and in 1992 he claimed an unprecedented third gold medal in the long jump. To do so he outdueled Mike Powell, who one month earlier had beaten Lewis and broken Bob Beamon's old long jump record with a leap of 29 feet 4½ inches.

Officials stand at attention during the playing of the U.S. National Anthem as gold medal winner Vincent Matthews (second from left) and silver medal winner Wayne Collett (left) are honored during the Munich Olympics, 1972. (Photographs and Prints Division, Schomburg Center for Research in Black Culture, The New York Public Library, Astor, Lenox and Tilden Foundations)

The top women stars of the 1980s included Florence Griffith Joyner, Jackie Joyner-Kersee, and Valerie Brisco-Hooks. At the Los Angeles games Brisco-Hooks set Olympic records in winning the 200-meter dash and the 400-meter run, adding a third gold medal with the American 1600-meter relay team. Known for her colorful running attire, Griffith-Joyner earned three gold medals (100-meter dash, 200-meter dash, and 400-meter relay) and one silver (1600-meter relay) at the 1988 Olympics and held world records in the first two events. Joyner-Kersee won the Olympic long rump competition in 1988, captured the heptathlon in 1988 and 1992, and set a new world record in the latter event.

The remarkable achievements of African-American athletes in the sprints, long jump, and hurdles, and their limited success in the distance and weight events, have perpetuated an old debate over whether sociological and cultural forces or physical tendencies help explain their success. Scholars continue to disagree vigorously over these issues. Nonetheless, they all concur that African-American men and women have made an impressive contribution to international track and field.

BIBLIOGRAPHY

Ashe, Arthur R., Jr. *A Hard Road to Glory: A History of the African American Athlete.* 3 vols. New York, 1988.

Baker, William J. *Jesse Owens: An American Life.* New York, 1986.

Edwards, Harry. *The Revolt of the Black Athlete.* New York, 1969.

Wiggins, David K. " 'Great Speed But Little Stamina': The Historical Debate over Black Athletic Superiority." *Journal of Sport History* 16 (1989): 158–185.

– CHARLES H. MARTIN

TROTTER, WILLIAM MONROE

William Monroe Trotter (April 7, 1872–April 7, 1934), newspaper editor and civil rights activist. William Monroe Trotter was born in 1872 in Chillicothe, Ohio, the son of James Monroe Trotter and Virginia Isaacs Trotter. Raised in a well-to-do white Boston neighborhood, young Trotter absorbed the militant integrationism of his politically active father, a tradition that he carried on throughout his own life.

Elected president of his senior class by his white high school classmates, Trotter worked briefly as a clerk and entered Harvard College in the fall of 1891. He graduated *magna cum laude* in June 1895, and moved easily into Boston's elite black social set. In June 1899, he married Geraldine Louise Pindell. That same year he opened his own real estate firm.

By the turn of the century, Trotter and his peers were deeply concerned about worsening race relations in the South and signs of growing racial antagonism in the North. In March 1901, Trotter helped form the Boston Literary and Historical Association, which fostered intellectual debate among prosperous African Americans; he also joined the more politically active Massachusetts Racial Protective Association (MRPA). These organizations served as early forums for his denunciation of the virtually undisputed accommodationist leadership of Booker T. WASHINGTON. In contrast to Washington, Trotter defended liberal arts education for black people, championed electoral participation as a means of securing basic rights, and counseled agitation on behalf of racial justice. With fellow MRPA member George W. Forbes, Trotter embarked on what became his life work: the uncompromising advocacy of civil and political equality for African Americans, through the pages of the Boston *Guardian.*

The *Guardian* newspaper, which began weekly publication in November 1901, offered news and analysis of the African-American condition. At the same time, it served as a base for independent political organizing led by Trotter himself. The "Trotterites" not only vilified their enemies in the pages of the *Guardian,* they also resorted to direct confrontation. On several occasions, Trotter and his supporters attempted (without success) to wrest control of the Afro-American Council from the pro-Booker T. Washington camp. More effective was their disruption of a speech Washington himself was scheduled to deliver in July 1903. Amid the fracas, Trotter delivered a litany of accusations and demanded of Washington, "Are the rope and the torch all the race is to get under your leadership?" He served a month in jail for his role in what was dubbed the "Boston Riot." After the incident, Trotter founded the Boston Suffrage League and the New England Suffrage League, through which he called for federal antilynching legislation, enforcement of the FIFTEENTH AMENDMENT, and the end of racial segregation.

Trotter embarked on the uncompromising advocacy of civil and political equality for African Americans, through the pages of the Boston Guardian.

While Trotter's editorial belligerence and unorthodox tactics were often disapproved of, many nonetheless respected his unswerving commitment to the cause of racial equality. They rose to Trotter's defense in the aftermath of the "riot" when Washington launched a malicious campaign—including surveillance, threats of libel, and the secret financing of competing publications—to intimidate and silence the *Guardian* and its editor. In this sense, Trotter's actions, and Washington's heavy-handed efforts to squelch them, helped crystallize the growing disaffection with Washington into an organizational alternative. Trotter was able to forge a successful, if temporary, alliance with W. E. B. DU BOIS and other proponents of racial integration, and he participated in founding the NIAGARA MOVEMENT in 1905.

Trotter's political independence and confrontational style went beyond the fight against Booker T. Washington, however. He clashed repeatedly with the Niagara Movement over questions of personality and leadership, and he resolved to wage the fight for racial justice under the auspices of his own virtually all-black organization, the National Equal Rights League, or NERL (originally founded as the Negro-American Political League in April 1908). While Trotter attended the founding convention of the NAACP in May 1909, he kept his distance from the white-dominated association; relations between NERL and the NAACP remained cool over the years, with occasional instances of cooperation to achieve common goals.

Trotter's zeal for direct action remained undiminished through the 1910s and 1920s. In a much-celebrated audience with Woodrow Wilson in 1914, Trotter challenged the president's segregationist policies; Wilson, viewing his adversary's candor as insolent and offensive, ordered the meeting to a close. The following year, Trotter led public protests against the showing of the film *The Birth of a Nation;* as a result of his renewed efforts in 1921, the movie was banned in Boston. In early 1919, denied a passport to travel to the Paris Peace Conference, he made his way to France disguised as a ship's cook, hoping to ensure that the Treaty of Versailles contained guarantees of racial equality; unable to influence the proceedings, he later testified against the treaty before the U.S. Congress. In 1926 Trotter again visited the White House to make the case against segregation in the federal government, this time before President Calvin Coolidge.

The *Guardian,* however, remained the primary outlet for Trotter's political convictions. Dependent largely on the contributions of black subscribers, the paper had often been on shaky financial ground. It not only absorbed Trotter's time and energy, it also drained his assets: Having abandoned the real estate business early on in order to devote himself entirely to the *Guardian,* he gradually sold off his property to keep the enterprise afloat. By 1920, with Trotter's standing as a national figure eclipsed by both the NAACP and the GARVEY movement, publication of the *Guardian* became even more difficult to sustain.

Over the years, the impassioned advocacy of militant integrationism remained the hallmark of Trotter's *Guardian.* Back in 1908, Trotter, rather than supporting the black community's creation of its own hospital, had called for integration of Boston's medical training facilities. He had insisted that short-term benefits could not outweigh the "far more ultimate harm in causing the Jim Crow lines to be drawn about us." Trotter was driven by that philosophy throughout his life, even in the face of opposition from other African Americans.

On April 7, 1934, Trotter either fell or jumped to his death from the roof of his apartment building. Although he no longer enjoyed a mass following, he was remembered as one who had made enormous personal sacrifices for the cause of racial equality.

BIBLIOGRAPHY

Bennett, Lerone, Jr. *Pioneers in Protest.* Baltimore, 1968.

Fox, Stephen R. *The Guardian of Boston: William Monroe Trotter.* New York, 1970.

Harlan, Louis R. *Booker T. Washington: The Wizard of Tuskegee, 1901–1915.* New York, 1983.

– TAMI J. FRIEDMAN

TRUTH, SOJOURNER

Sojourner Truth (c. 1797–November 26, 1883), abolitionist, suffragist, and spiritualist. Sojourner Truth was born Isabella Bomefree in Ulster County, N.Y., the second youngest of thirteen children born in slavery to Elizabeth (usually called Mau-Mau Bett) and James Bomefree. The other siblings were either sold or given away before her birth. The family was owned by Johannes Hardenbergh, a patroon and Revolutionary War patriot, the head of one of the most prominent Dutch families in late eighteenth-century New York.

Mau-Mau Bett was mystical and unlettered but imparted to her daughter strong faith, filial devotion, and a strong sense of individual integrity. Isabella Bomefree, whose first language was Dutch, was taken from her parents and sold to an English-speaking owner in 1808, who maltreated her because of her inability to understand English. Through her own defiance—what she later called her "talks with God"—and her father's intercession, a Dutch tavern keeper soon purchased her. Kindly treated but surrounded by the rough tavern culture and probably sexually abused, the girl prayed for a new master. In 1810 John I. Dumont of New Paltz, N.Y., purchased Isabella Bomefree for three hundred dollars.

Isabella remained Dumont's slave for eighteen years. Dumont boasted that Belle, as he called her, was "better to me than a man." She planted, plowed, cultivated, and harvested crops. She milked the farm animals, sewed, weaved, cooked, and cleaned house. But Mrs. Dumont despised and tormented her, possibly because Dumont fathered one of her children.

Isabella had two relationships with slave men. Bob, her first love, a man from a neighboring estate, was beaten senseless for "taking up" with her and was forced to take another woman. She later became associated with Thomas, with whom she remained until her freedom. Four of her five children survived to adulthood.

Although New York slavery ended for adults in 1827, Dumont promised Isabella her freedom a year earlier. When he refused to keep his promise, she fled with an infant child, guided by "the word of God" as she later related. She took refuge with Isaac Van Wagenen, who purchased her for the remainder of her time as a slave. She later adopted his family name.

Isabella Van Wagenen was profoundly shaped by a religious experience she underwent in 1827 at Pinkster time, the popular early summer African-Dutch slave holiday. As she recounted it, she forgot God's deliverance of his people from bondage and prepared to return to Dumont's farm for Pinkster: "I looked back in Egypt," she said, "and everything seemed so pleasant there." But she felt the mighty, luminous, and wrathful presence of an angry God blocking her path. Stalemated and momentarily blinded and suffocated under "God's breath," she claimed in her *Narrative,* Jesus mercifully intervened and proclaimed her salvation. This conversion enabled Isabella Van Wagenen to claim direct and special communication with Jesus and the Trinity for the remainder of her life, and she subsequently became involved with a number of highly spiritual religious groups.

A major test of faith followed Isabella Van Wagenen's conversion when she discovered that Dumont had illegally sold her son, Peter. Armed with spiritual assurance and a mother's rage, she scoured the countryside, gaining moral and financial support from prominent Dutch residents, antislavery Quakers, and local Methodists. She brought suit, and Peter was eventually returned from Alabama and freed.

In 1829 Isabella, now a Methodist, moved to New York City. She joined the African Methodist Episcopal Zion Church, where she discovered a brother and two sisters. She also began to attract attention for her extraordinary preaching, praying, and singing, though these talents were mainly employed among the Perfectionists (a sect of white radical mystics emerging from the Second Great Awakening who championed millennial doctrines, equated spiritual piety with morality, and social justice with true Christianity). As housekeeper for Perfectionist Elijah Pierson, Isabella was involved in "the Kingdom," a sect organized by the spiritual zealot, Robert Matthias. Among other practices he engaged in "spirit-matching," or wife swapping, with Ann Folger, wife of Pierson's business partner. Elijah Pierson's unexplained death brought public outcries of foul play. To conceal Ann Pierson's promiscuity, the Folgers suggested that there had been an erotic attachment between Matthias and Isabella Van Wagenen and that they murdered Pierson with poisoned blackberries. Challenging her accusers, Isabella Van Wagenen vowed to "crush them with the truth." Lack of evidence and prejudice about blacks testifying against whites led to dismissal of the case. Isabella Van Wagenen triumphed by successfully suing the Folgers for slander. Though chastened by this experience with religious extremism, the association with New York Perfectionists enhanced her biblical knowledge, oratorical skills, and commitment to reform.

Isabella Van Wagenen encouraged her beloved son Peter to take up seafaring to avoid the pitfalls of urban crime. In 1843 his vessel returned without him. Devastated by this loss, facing (at forty-six) a bleak future in domestic service, and influenced by the millennarian (known as the Millerite movement) ferment sweeping the Northeast at the time, she decided to radically change her life. She became an itinerant preacher and adopted the name Sojourner Truth because voices directed her to sojourn the countryside and speak God's truth. In the fall of 1843 she became ill and was taken to the Northampton utopian community in Florence, Mass., where black abolitionist David Ruggles nursed her at his water-cure establishment. Sojourner Truth impressed residents, who included a number of abolitionists, with her slavery accounts, scriptural interpretations, wit, and simple oral eloquence.

By 1846 Sojourner Truth had joined the antislavery circuit, traveling with Abby Kelly Foster, Frederick DOUGLASS, William Lloyd Garrison, and British M.P. George Thompson. An electrifying public orator, she soon became one of the most popular speakers for the abolitionist cause. Her fame was heightened by the publication of her *Narrative* in 1850, related and transcribed by Olive Gilbert. With proceeds from its sale she purchased a Northampton home. In 1851, speaking before a National Women's Convention in Akron, Ohio, Sojourner Truth defended the physical and spiritual strength of women, in her famous "Ain't I a Woman?" speech. In 1853 Sojourner's antislavery, spiritualist, and temperance advocacy took her to the Midwest, where she settled among spiritualists in Harmonia, Mich.

"I cannot read a book," said Sojourner Truth, "but I can read the people." She dissected political and social issues through parables of everyday life. The Constitution, silent on black rights, had a "little weevil in it." She was known for her captivating one-line retorts. An Indiana audience threatened to torch the building if she spoke. Sojourner Truth replied, "Then I will speak to the ashes." In the late 1840s, grounded in faith that God and moral suasion would eradicate bondage, she challenged her despairing friend Douglass with "Frederick, is God dead?" In 1858, when a group of men questioned her gender, claiming she wasn't properly feminine in her demeanor, Sojourner Truth, a bold early feminist, exposed her bosom to the entire assembly, proclaiming that shame was not hers but theirs.

Van Wagenen became an itinerant preacher and adopted the name Sojourner Truth because voices directed her to sojourn the countryside and speak God's truth.

During the Civil War Sojourner Truth recruited and supported Michigan's black regiment, counseled freedwomen, set up employment operations for freedpeople willing to relocate, and initiated desegregation of streetcars in Washington, D.C. In 1864 she had an audience with Abraham Lincoln. Following the war, Sojourner Truth moved to Michigan, settling in Battle Creek, but remained active in numerous reform causes. She supported the Fifteenth Amendment and women's suffrage.

Disillusioned by the failure of RECONSTRUCTION, Sojourner Truth devoted her last years to the support of a black western homeland. In her later years, despite decades of interracial cooperation, she became skeptical of collaboration with whites and became an advocate of racial separation. She died in 1883 in Battle Creek, attended by the famous physician and breakfast cereal founder John Harvey Kellogg.

BIBLIOGRAPHY

Fauset, Arthur H. *Sojourner Truth.* Chapel Hill, N.C., 1938.

Washington, Margaret, ed. *Narrative of Sojourner Truth.* New York, 1993.

Yellin, Jean Fagan. *Women and Sisters: The Antislavery Feminists in American Culture.* New Haven, 1989.

— MARGARET WASHINGTON

TUBMAN, HARRIET ROSS

Harriet Ross Tubman (c. 1820–March 10, 1913), abolitionist, nurse, and feminist. Harriet Ross, one of eleven children born to slaves Benjamin Ross and Harriet Green, was born about 1820 in Dorchester County in Maryland. Although she was known on the plantation as Harriet Ross, her family called her Araminta, or "Minty," a name given to her by her mother.

Like most slaves, Ross had no formal education and began work on the plantation as a child. When she was five years old, her master rented her out to a neighboring family, the Cooks, as a domestic servant. At age thirteen, Ross suffered permanent neurological damage after either her overseer or owner struck her in the head with a two-pound lead weight when she placed herself between her master and a fleeing slave. For the rest of her life, she experienced sudden blackouts.

In 1844, she married John Tubman, a free black who lived on a nearby plantation. Her husband's free status, however, did not transfer to Harriet upon their marriage. Between 1847 and 1849, after the death of her master, Tubman worked in the household of Anthony Thompson, a physician and preacher. Thompson was the legal guardian of Tubman's new master, who was still too young to operate the plantation. When the young master died, Tubman faced an uncertain future, and rumors circulated that Thompson would sell slaves out of the state.

In response, Tubman escaped from SLAVERY in 1849, leaving behind her husband, who refused to accompany her. She settled in Philadelphia, where she found work as a scrubwoman. She returned to Maryland for her husband two years later, but John Tubman had remarried.

Tubman's successful escape to the free state of Pennsylvania, however, did not guarantee her safety, particularly after the passage of the FUGITIVE SLAVE LAW of 1850, which facilitated southern slaveholding efforts to recover runaway slaves. Shortly after her escape from slavery, Tubman became involved in the ABOLITION movement, forming friendships with one of the black leaders of the UNDERGROUND RAILROAD, William STILL, and white abolitionist Thomas Garrett. While many of her abolitionist colleagues organized antislavery societies, wrote and spoke against slavery, and raised money for the cause, Tubman's abolitionist activities were more directly related to the actual freeing of slaves on the Underground Railroad. She worked as an agent on the railroad, assuming different disguises to assist runaways in obtaining food, shelter, clothing, cash, and transportation. Tubman might appear as a feeble, old woman or as a demented, impoverished man, and she was known for the rifle she carried on rescue missions, both for her own protection and to intimidate fugitives who might become fainthearted along the journey.

Tubman traveled to the South nineteen times to rescue approximately three hundred African-American men, women, and children from bondage. Her first rescue mission was to Baltimore, Md., in 1850 to help her sister and two children escape from slavery. Her noteriety as a leader of the Underground Railroad led some Maryland planters to offer a $40,000 bounty for her capture. Having relocated many runaways to Canada, Tubman herself settled in the village of St. Catharines, Canada West (now Ontario), in the early 1850s. She traveled to the South in 1851 to rescue her brother and his wife, and returned in 1857 to rescue her parents, with whom she resettled in Auburn, N.Y., shortly thereafter.

Tubman's involvement in the abolitionist movement placed her in contact with many progressive social leaders in the North, including John Brown, whom she met in 1858. She helped Brown plan his raid on Harpers Ferry, Va., in 1859, but illness prevented her from participating. Tubman's last trip to the South took place in 1860, after which she returned to Canada. In 1861, she moved back to the United States as the last of eleven southern states seceded from the Union.

When the CIVIL WAR broke out, Tubman served in the Union Army as a scout, spy, and nurse. In 1862, she went to Beaufort, S.C., where she nursed both white soldiers and black refugees from neighboring southern plantations. Tubman traveled from camp to camp in the coastal regions of South Carolina, Georgia, and Florida, administering her nursing skills wherever they were needed. Tubman also worked as a scout for the Union Army, traveling behind enemy lines to gather information and recruit slaves. She supported herself by selling chickens, eggs, root beer, and pies. After returning briefly to Beaufort, Tubman worked during the spring and summer of 1865 at a freedman's hospital in Fortress Monroe, Va.

After the war's end, Tubman eventually returned to Auburn to care for her elderly parents. Penniless, she helped support her family by farming. In 1869, Tubman married Nelson Davis, a Civil War veteran. That same year, she published *Scenes in the Life of Harriet Tubman,* written for her by Sarah H. Bradford and printed and circulated by Gerrit Smith and Wendall Phillips. Tubman received some royalties from the book, but she was less successful in her effort to obtain financial compensation for her war work. She agitated for nearly thirty years for $1,800 compensation for her service as a Civil War nurse and cook. In 1890, Congress finally awarded Tubman a monthly pension of $20 as a widow of a war veteran.

Tubman's activism continued on many fronts after the Civil War ended. She was an ardent supporter of women's suffrage and regularly attended women's rights meetings. To Tubman, racial liberation and women's rights were inextricably linked. Tubman formed close relationships with Susan B. Anthony and other feminists. She was a delegate to the first convention of the National Federation of Afro-American Women in 1896 (later called the NATIONAL ASSOCIATION OF COLORED WOMEN). The following year, the New England Women's Suffrage Association held a reception in Tubman's honor.

While living in Auburn, Tubman continued her work in the black community by taking in orphans and the elderly, often receiving assistance from wealthier neighbors. She helped establish schools for former slaves and wanted to establish a permanent home for poor and sick blacks. Tubman secured twenty-five acres in Auburn through a bank loan, but lacked the necessary funds to build on the land. In 1903, she deeded the land to the African Methodist Episcopal Zion Church, and five years later, the congregation built the Harriet Tubman Home for Indigent and Aged Negroes, which continued to operate for several years after Tubman's death and was declared a National Historic Landmark in 1974.

Tubman died on March 10, 1913, at the age of ninety-three. Local Civil War veterans led the funeral march. The National Association of Colored Women later paid for the funeral and for the marble tombstone over Tubman's grave. A year after her death, black educator Booker T. WASHINGTON delivered a memorial address in celebration of Tubman's life and labors and on behalf of freedom. In 1978, the United States Postal Service issued the first stamp in its Black Heritage USA Series to honor Tubman.

Tubman, dubbed "the Moses of her people," had obtained legendary status in the African-American community within ten years of her escape to freedom. Perhaps more than any other figure of her time, Tubman personified resistance to slavery, and she became a symbol of courage and strength to African Americans—slave and free. The secrecy surrounding Tubman's activities on the Underground Railroad and her own reticence to talk about her role contributed to her mythic status. Heroic images of the rifle-carrying Tubman have persisted well into the twentieth century as Tubman has become the leading symbol of the Underground Railroad.

BIBLIOGRAPHY

Bradford, Sara. *Harriet Tubman: The Moses of Her People.* 1886. Reprint. New York, 1961.

Conrad, Carl. *Harriet Tubman.* New York, 1943.

Litwack, Leon, and August Meier. *Black Leaders of the Nineteenth Century.* Urbana, Ill., 1988.

– LOUISE P. MAXWELL

TUSKEGEE SYPHILIS EXPERIMENT

In the early twentieth century, African Americans in the South faced numerous public health problems, including tuberculosis, hookworm, pellagra, and rickets; their death rates far exceeded those of whites. The public health problems of blacks had several causes—poverty, ignorance of proper health procedures, and inadequate medical care—all compounded by racism that systematically denied African Americans equal services. In an affort to alleviate these problems, in 1912 the federal government united all of its health-related activities under the Public Health Service (PHS). One of the primary concerns of the PHS was syphilis, a disease that was thought to have a moral as well as a physiological dimension. In 1918 a special Division of Venereal Diseases of PHS was created.

In the late 1920s, the PHS joined forces with the Rosenwald fund (a private philanthropic foundation based in Chicago) to develop a syphilis control program for blacks in the South. Most doctors assumed that blacks suffered a much higher infection rate than whites because blacks abandoned themselves to promiscuity. And once infected, the argument went, blacks remained infected because they were too poor and too ignorant to seek medical care. To test these theories, PHS officers selected communities in six different southern states, examined the local black populations to ascertain the incidence of syphilis, and offered free treatment to those who were infected. This pilot program had hardly gotten underway, however, when the stock market collapse in 1929 forced the Rosenwald Fund to terminate its support, and the PHS was left without sufficient funds to follow up its syphilis control work among blacks in the South.

Macon County, Ala., was the site of one of those original pilot programs. Its county seat, Tuskegee, was the home of the famed Tuskegee Institute. It was in and around Tuskegee that the PHS had discovered an infection rate of 35 percent among those tested, the highest incidence in the six communities studied. In fact, despite the presence of the Tuskegee Institute, which boasted a well-equipped hospital that might have provided low-cost health care to blacks in the region, Macon County was home not only to the worst poverty but the most sickly residents the PHS uncovered anywhere in the South. It was precisely this ready-made laboratory of human suffering that prompted the PHS to return to Macon County in 1932. Since they could not afford to treat syphilis, the PHS officers decided to document the damage to its victims by launching a study of the effects of untreated syphilis on black males. Many white Southerners (including physicians) believed that although practically all blacks had syphilis, it did not harm them as severely as it did whites. PHS officials knew that syphilis was a serious threat to the health of black Americans, and they intended to use the results of the study to pressure southern state legislatures into appropriating funds for syphilis control work among rural blacks.

Armed with these good motives, the PHS launched the Tuskegee Study in 1932. It involved approximately four hundred black males, who tested positive for the disease, and two hundred nonsyphilitic black males to serve as controls. In order to secure cooperation, the PHS told the local residents that they had returned to Macon County to treat people who were ill. The PHS did not inform them that they had syphilis. Instead, the men were told they had "bad blood," a catchall phrase rural blacks used to describe a host of ailments.

While the PHS had not intended to treat the men, state health officials demanded, as the price of their cooperation, that the men be given at least enough medication to render them noninfectious. Consequently, all of the men received a little treatment. No one worried much about the glaring contradiction of offering treatment in a study of untreated syphilis because the men had not received enough treatment to cure them. Thus, the experiment was scientifically flawed from the outset.

Although the original plan called for a one-year experiment, the Tuskegee Study continued until 1972 partly because many of the health officers became fascinated by the scientific potential of a long-range study of syphilis. No doubt others rationalized the study by telling themselves that the men were too poor to afford proper treatment, or that too much time had passed for treatment to be of any benefit. The health officials, in some cases, may have seen the men as clinical material rather than human beings.

The Tuskegee Study served as a cruel reminder of how class distinctions and racism could negate ethical and scientific standards.

At any rate, as a result of the Tuskegee Study approximately one hundred black men died of untreated syphilis, scores went blind or insane, and still others endured lives of chronic ill health from syphilis-related complications. Throughout this suffering, the PHS made no effort to treat the men and on several occasions took steps to prevent them from getting treatment on their own. As a result, the men did not receive penicillin when it became widely available after World War II.

During those same four decades, civil protests raised America's concern for the rights of black people, and the ethical standards of the medical profession regarding the treatment of nonwhite patients changed dramatically. These changes had no impact, however, on the

Tuskegee Study. PHS officials published no fewer than 13 scientific papers on the experiment (several of which appeared in the nation's leading medical journals), and the PHS routinely presented sessions on it at medical conventions. The Tuskegee Study ended in 1972 because a whistle-blower in the PHS, Peter Buxtun, leaked the story to the press. At first health officials tried to defend their actions, but public outrage quickly silenced them, and they agreed to end the experiment. As part of an out-of-court settlement, the survivors were finally treated for syphilis. In addition, the men, and the families of the deceased, received small cash payments.

The forty-year deathwatch had finally ended, but its legacy can still be felt. In the wake of its hearings, Congress enacted new legislation to protect the subjects of human experiments. The Tuskegee Study left behind a host of unanswered questions about the social and racial attitudes of the medical establishment in the United States. It served as a cruel reminder of how class distinctions and racism could negate ethical and scientific standards.

BIBLIOGRAPHY

Jones, James H. *Bad Blood.* New York, 1981.

"The Tuskegee Study." 3 parts. *Jet* (November 9, 16, 23, 1972).

— JAMES H. JONES

TUSKEGEE UNIVERSITY

Tuskegee University was founded in 1881 as the Normal School for colored teachers at Tuskegee in Alabama's Macon County, as the result of a political deal made between local white politicians and Lewis Adams, a leading black citizen. In exchange for black votes, Arthur Brooks and Col. Wilbur Foster, candidates for the Alabama legislature, promised to seek state appropriation for a black normal school in Tuskegee. Adams successfully rallied black support, and on February 10, 1881, House Bill No. 165 was passed, appropriating $2,000 annually for a black state and normal school in Tuskegee. The act prohibited the charge of tuition and mandated a minimum of twenty-five students to open.

Booker T. WASHINGTON was recommended to organize the school by his mentor, Gen. Samuel Chapman Armstrong, the founder of Virginia's HAMPTON INSTITUTE, although Tuskegee's trustees had specifically requested a white man. Washington had been Armstrong's best student at Hampton, where he fully accepted Armstrong's philosophy that the first step for blacks was economic and moral uplift.

When Booker T. Washington arrived at Tuskegee on June 24, 1881, there was no actual school to open, just an appropriation and authorization by the Alabama state legislature. Before selecting a location, Washington met with local white supporters, toured the area to recruit students, and investigated existing living and educational conditions for Tuskegee's black population. Washington selected a shack next to Butler Chapel, the African Methodist Episcopal church on Zion Hill, where Lewis Adams was superintendent, as the site for the school. The school officially opened on July 4, 1881, as a secondary normal school with thirty students.

By July 14, 1881, Tuskegee Normal School had more than forty students ranging in age from sixteen to forty, most of whom were already public school teachers in Macon County. As enrollment increased, Washington recruited other Hampton and Fisk graduates to teach, including Olivia A. Davidson (who served as lady principal from 1881 until her death in 1889 and who married Washington in 1886). He decided that a larger facility would soon be needed. He wrote to J. F. B. Marshall, the treasurer of Hampton Institute, and requested a loan of $200 to purchase a new farm site. While the school could not make such loans, Marshall personally loaned Washington the money, enabling him to make a down payment on the Bowen estate.

The Bowen estate, owned by William B. Bowen, was located one mile south of town. The main house had been burned down during the Civil War, leaving two cabins, a stable, and a chicken house. In keeping with his philosophy of self-knowledge, self-help, and self-control, Washington required students to clean and rebuild the Bowen estate while attending classes. By requiring such manual labor of his students, Washington was attempting to demonstrate that others were willing to help them—provided that they help themselves.

The money acquired to complete the payments on the Bowen estate came from many sources, including northern philanthropy and student fund-raisers, such as benefit suppers and student "literary entertainments," organized by Olivia Davidson. Payments on the Bowen estate were completed in April 1882.

Washington's philosophy of industrial education made Tuskegee Normal School a controversial model of black progress. Washington supported the use of manual labor as a moral training device, and he believed that manual labor would build students' character and improve their minds. In implementing a program of mandatory labor and industrial education, Washington had four basic objectives: to teach the dignity of labor, to teach the trades, to fulfill the demand for trained industrial leaders, and to offer students a way to pay expenses while attending the school (although no student, regardless of his or her economic standing was exempt from this labor requirement). Washington also considered industrial education to be valuable because it trained students in specific skills that would prepare them for jobs. However, Tuskegee's graduates primarily became members of the teaching profession. Instructors also offered academic and normal courses in botany, literature, rhetoric, astronomy, and geography in addition to the much publicized industrial courses.

Tuskegee expanded steadily over the years with money acquired from the northern speaking tours of Olivia Davidson and Booker T. Washington. Davidson began touring New England in spring 1882, soliciting support door to door on weekdays and speaking in churches and Sunday schools during the evenings and on weekends. Washington began his own fund-raising tour on May 1, 1882, in Farmington, Conn. He traveled through the North with letters of introduction from such prominent southern officials as Henry Clay Armstrong, the state superintendent, and Gov. Rufus W. Cobb. By the end of May, they had collected more than $5,000 for the expansion of Tuskegee Normal and Industrial Institute.

Porter Hall was the first new building erected, named in honor of a generous Brooklyn businessman, Alfred Haynes Porter. The three-story building housed recitation rooms on the first floor, a chapel and library on the second floor, and the girls' dormitory on the third floor. Up to this time the boys stayed with neighboring black families. Shortly after Porter Hall was completed, Washington arranged to rent several nearby cottages to house the boys, until their three-story dormitory, Armstrong Hall, was completed in 1888.

State funding for Tuskegee was increased in 1883 when the Alabama state legislature approved an additional $1,000 appropriation. The school also began receiving a $500 annual appropriation from the Peabody Fund in 1883 and $1,000 annual awards from the Slater Fund in 1884. Philanthropic funding to Tuskegee Normal and Industrial Institute signified the extent of northern support for black industrial education.

In addition to fund-raisers, grants, and philanthropic support, money was raised for Tuskegee through brick making, which Washington began at the school in 1883, though its long-term contribution to Tuskegee's financial health was more symbolic than practical.

In 1892, the Alabama legislature adopted an Act to incorporate Tuskegee Normal and Industrial Institute, legally changing the school's name. After 1895, new buildings replaced those built from northern philan-

Chemistry laboratory, Tuskegee Institute. (Prints and Photographs Division, Library of Congress)

thropy. With names like Rockefeller, Huntington, and Carnegie, these buildings indicated support from the northern, chiefly New York-based business community. Such support increased Tuskegee property value to more than $300,000 by 1901 and facilitated the growth of the faculty and student body.

On April 1, 1896, Booker T. Washington wrote to George Washington CARVER, an agricultural chemist who had just completed his M.A. from Iowa State College of Agricultural and Mechanical Arts, and offered him a position as the head of the agriculture department at a salary of $1,500. Carver arrived shortly thereafter and established the Agriculture Experiment Station, where research was conducted in crop diversification. Carver taught Tuskegee's students, emphasizing the need for improved agricultural practices and self-reliance, and also made a great effort to educate Tuskegee's black residents. He garnered national and international fame in the 1920s for his experiments with sweet potatoes, cowpeas, and peanuts.

Both Carver and Washington left a powerful legacy of manual and agricultural training at Tuskegee. Their educational philosophies had a lasting impact upon Tuskegee's curriculum and continued to influence the school's direction. After Washington's death in 1915, it had become apparent to many that Tuskegee's industrial training was increasingly obsolete in the face of rapid technological transformation in American business. The school thus entered a new era, shifting its emphasis from industrial to vocational education.

In 1915, Robert R. Moton became the second principal of Tuskegee, and although he practiced Washington's accommodationist style, he moved the school forward in directions that Washington had refused to move. Despite white opposition, Moton was instrumental in bringing a veterans' hospital to Tuskegee in 1923. He ensured that the institution, like Tuskegee Normal and Industrial Institute, was staffed entirely by blacks. Under Moton's direction, a college curriculum was developed in 1927. Two years later, Tuskegee's students demanded a shift away from "Washington's education." Moton heeded their voices and coordinated a new emphasis on science and technology.

Robert R. Moton was succeeded by Frederick D. Patterson in 1935. Patterson's administration also brought fundamental changes to the school, reflected in the name change to Tuskegee Institute in 1937. During WORLD WAR II, Patterson pursued the placement of a program for the segregated training of black pilots in Tuskegee, an action that was criticized by the NAACP. From 1939 to 1943, the Air Force trained more than 900 black pilots at Tuskegee, establishing the Tuskegee Army Airfield in 1941. Patterson also obtained significant state funding for the establishment of a graduate program (1943), a school of veterinary medicine (1945), and a school of nursing (1953).

Subsequent presidents have included Luther H. Foster (1953–1981) and Benjamin F. Payton (1981–). Foster modernized and expanded Washington's emphasis on the trade industry and established the College of Arts and Sciences and the School of Business. He led Tuskegee through the CIVIL RIGHTS MOVEMENT, when in 1968, Tuskegee students briefly held members of the board of trustees hostage in an attempt to force changes in campus policies. When Benjamin E. Payton assumed control of the school in its centennial anniversary, Tuskegee boasted 5,000 acres, 150 buildings, and an endowment of more than $22 million. Payton presided over the school's name change to Tuskegee University in 1985, and in 1989 he also undertook a major fund-raising effort for the school (seeking $150 million in donations), the largest ever attempted by a black college.

Although the school's curriculum and focus shifted over the years, the school continued to emphasize business, scientific, and technical instruction, a legacy of both Washington and Carver. In 1994, Tuskegee University had 3,598 students. It offered 45 undergraduate majors, 21 master's degrees, and a doctor of veterinary medicine degree. Distinguished alumni include novelist Ralph ELLISON, actor Keenan Ivory Wayans, and Arthur W. Mitchell, the first black Democratic congressman.

BIBLIOGRAPHY

Anderson, James. *The Education of Blacks in the South, 1865–1935.* Chapel Hill, N.C., 1988.

Bowman, J. Wilson. *America's Black Colleges: The Comprehensive Guide to Historically & Predominantly Black 4–Year Colleges and Universities.* Pasadena, Calif., 1992.

Harlan, Louis R. *Booker T. Washington: The Wizard of Tuskegee, 1901–1915.* New York, 1983.

Manber, David. *Wizard of Tuskegee: The Life of George Washington Carver.* New York, 1967.

Marable, Manning. "Tuskegee Institute in the 1920s." *Negro History Bulletin* 40 (November-December 1977): 64–68.

Norell, Robert J. *Reaping the Whirlwind: The* CIVIL RIGHTS MOVEMENT in Tuskegee. New York, 1983.

— LISA MARIE MOORE

U

UNCLE TOM'S CABIN

Harriet Beecher Stowe's fiery abolitionist novel was published in 1852. Stowe came from a prominent family of public figures that included her father, clergyman Lyman Beecher; her sister, author Catharine Beecher; and her brother, clergyman Henry Ward Beecher. The wife of clergyman Calvin Stowe, Harriet was outraged by the COMPROMISE OF 1850, the group of legislative measures that effected a compromise between North and South on the increasingly divisive issue of slavery. The most notorious article of the compromise was the provision for the legal return to their owners of escaped slaves (the FUGITIVE SLAVE LAW, enacted in 1851), which effectively legitimized the rule of slavery in the North and South. This measure, as well as the passionate advocacy of the compromise by trusted Vermont Sen. Daniel Webster, particularly infuriated Stowe and other New England intellectuals such as Ralph Waldo Emerson and John Greenleaf Whittier (whose poem "Ichabod" excoriates Webster). Stowe's first literary response to the legislation was a story called "The Freeman's Dream" (1850), about the divine retribution that visits a man who refuses to aid a group of slaves being led to market in a coffle (i.e., fastened together to form a train). Her literary career thus launched, Stowe experienced a vision, she later said, of an old black male slave being whipped to death. This image sparked the composition of *Uncle Tom's Cabin; or, Life Among the Lowly,* which was serialized in the antislavery newspaper *National Era* in 1851–1852 and published in book form on March 20, 1852.

Uncle Tom's Cabin so swarms with character, action, voice, and social detail that it defies adequate synopsis. Its multiple, intertwining plots begin with the imminent sale of the beautiful slave Eliza Harris. Her owner, Arthur Shelby, is in debt and must sell his slaves for money. Hearing of this, Eliza, with her small son and slave husband, George Harris, decides to escape, and before going informs the other slaves of Mr. Shelby's predicament. Uncle Tom, a slave on the Shelby plantation, bids Eliza to go but refuses to join her, preferring to sacrifice himself in sale for the possible preservation of the other slaves. Eliza's vividly rendered escape with her son Harry across the ice floes of the Ohio River allows Stowe to elicit sympathy for the slaves and hatred for the slave traders, even though relatively kindly masters such as Shelby are spared neither the moral taint of slavery nor Stowe's disdain. Eliza's husband George escapes separately in disguise, while Eliza is sheltered by Ohio Quakers; George and Eliza reunite at the Quaker settlement. There they fight off the slave traders who have pursued them, whereupon George makes an impassioned defense of his right to freedom. Soon, George, Eliza, and Harry escape to Canada. Meanwhile Uncle Tom is indeed sold down the river, and upon the boat of transport he meets Evangeline (Little Eva) St. Clare and her father, a New Orleans slaveowner, who buys Tom at Little Eva's behest. St. Clare is gentle, passive, but sharply reflective on the social system of slavery; he airs himself on a variety of subjects in conversation with the Vermonter Aunt Ophelia, who brings to the plantation her aid (St. Claire's wife, Marie, is perennially languid and abed) and her liberal northern perspective (some of the hypocrisies of which—for instance, advocating freedom yet feeling repulsed by slaves like Topsy—Stowe tellingly punctures). St. Clare is subject to Tom's religious influence, and under it, as well as that of the death of Little Eva, who suffers from her knowledge of slavery's oppression, decides to reform his life and to set Tom free. Before he is able to do this, however, St. Clare is killed attempting to mediate a bar fight, and once again, Tom is sold. He is purchased by Simon Legree, another Vermonter by origin, who abuses Uncle Tom the more the slave passively resists. Legree is at the same time haunted by Cassy, a slave woman on his plantation who exploits Legree's guilt over his abandonment of his mother. Cassy and another slave, Emmeline, pretend to escape but stay in an attic and drive Legree to distraction impersonating the ghosts that he believes dwell there. Legree ultimately kills Uncle Tom as young George Shelby, the son of Tom's former master, arrives; George superintends the burial of Tom and knocks Legree to the ground. He also helps Cassy and Emmeline escape, and in doing so learns that Cassy is in fact Eliza's mother. At the novel's end, everyone reunites in Canada, where they decide to voyage to Africa and establish a black Christian homeland in Liberia. George Shelby returns to Kentucky and sets all the Shelby slaves free; refusing to leave, the slaves stay to work as free people. The novel concludes with the kind of hectoring condemnations of slavery that lace the rest of the text.

So told, the novel is clearly rife with contradictions that both enrich and hobble it. For one thing the novel is misnamed, since we only see Uncle Tom's cabin briefly and most of the novel recounts Tom's painful longing to return to his family from whom he has been sold. This tale of the horrors of slavery is animated by a passion for and belief in the redemptive capacities of women. It presents a protofeminist orientation that vivifies the stories of slave and disempowered white women, and advances a feminized ethic of the antislavery struggle—most notably in the piously submissive Tom himself—even as it somewhat exploitatively uses the predicament of slaves to meditate on the oppression of women. What is more, this quite radical novel by the standards of 1852, depends on black stereotypes and seems to accept a long-discredited notion of innate racial traits (however positively rendered); thus, the blacker Uncle Tom submits while the lighter-skinned George Harris asserts the fighting spirit of his partial Anglo-Saxon blood. Finally, this story, so often accused of revolutionary intent by most of the South, is not only as hard on the North's apologists for slavery as it is on the South, it is also a fundamentally Christian novel whose social prescriptions revolve around transformations of individual feeling rather than collective struggle.

Contradictory or not, these sentimental, women-centered, radical Christian emphases achieved for *Uncle Tom's Cabin* an immediate and sustained success and influence. It sold 300,000 copies in its first year alone and inspired novelistic rebuttals and documentary defenses (one of them, *The Key to Uncle Tom's Cabin,* [1853], by Stowe herself), stage dramatizations and minstrel-show parodies, commercial take-offs, and popular-cultural iconography. The novel made national struggles over slavery—a dangerous social issue subject to persistent denial—henceforth an acknowledged fact of everyday life. Yet it was probably *Uncle Tom's Cabin*'s long stage presence in the form of the "Tom show" that was ultimately responsible for the enormity of its influence. As popularly written as the novel was, for every person who read it, very many more saw the stage play. The competing ideological inflections of *Uncle Tom*'s many dramatizations amplified the novel's political impact. With nonexistent copyright laws for stage adaptations, and Stowe declining participation in or permission for an authorized stage version, the field was open to the lowest bidder. In January 1852, attending to the novel's serialization, an anti-Tom play called *Uncle Tom's Cabin as It Is; The Southern Uncle Tom* appeared at the Baltimore Museum; in late August 1852, C. W. Taylor's crude and foreshortened version of the recently published novel ran briefly at New York's National Theatre—inspiring *New York Herald* editor James Gordon Bennett to denounce the advent of abolitionist drama. This pattern of dramatic conflict—a kind of prelude to the Civil War on stage—characterized productions of *Uncle Tom's Cabin* not only in the 1850s, but well into the 1870s.

Uncle Tom's Cabin *had a mighty and often radical cultural and social impact for over half a century.*

The chief competing productions in the 1850s were those of George Aiken and H. J. Conway. Aiken's relatively faithful version of *Uncle Tom* gestated for a year in Troy, N.Y., first recounting only Little Eva's story, then only Uncle Tom's, then combining the two into the first full-length, night-long theatrical production in history. This version, which vents many of Stowe's criticisms of slavery, opened at New York's National Theatre on July 18, 1853. Conway's much more ambiguous rendition took shape in Boston, and takes away with minstrel parody or outright racism that it occasionally renders with accuracy to Stowe's novel. P. T. Barnum heard of Conway's Compromise politics and the impressive Boston run of the show and booked this version for his American Museum beginning November 7, 1853. These adaptations, to be sure, appeared amid a dizzying array of offshoots, thefts, reworkings, rebuttals, and parodies, including (in New York alone) a "magic lantern" version (tableaux from the play) at New York's Franklin Museum; a Bowery Theatre version starring blackface originator T. D. Rice (not so outrageous as it appears, since even the "respectable" adaptations featured blackface performers in black roles); blackface lampoons such as Charles White's *Uncle Dad's Cabin* (1855), and Christy and Wood's Minstrels' *Uncle Tom's Cabin, or, Hearts and Homes* (1854); Irish parodies such as *Uncle Pat's Cabin* (by H. J. Conway) and *Uncle Mike's Cabin* (1853); and scores of others. But all this could not obscure the great theatrical rivalry that existed between the Aiken and Conway versions, encompassing everything from journalistic debate to street fights and making inescapably evident—in fact institutionalizing—the sectional conflicts that would soon eventuate in civil war. Perhaps this accounts for what Lincoln is supposed to have said upon meeting Stowe: "So this is the little lady who made this great war." Even after the war, Tom shows (which continued to be produced well into the twentieth century) and films (the first of many film versions of *Uncle Tom's Cabin* appeared in 1903) effortlessly invoked ongoing American political debate and upheavals over race and the legacy of slavery. While the novel's aesthetic and politics now seem obsolete, *Uncle Tom's Cabin* had a mighty and often radical cultural and social impact for over half a century.

BIBLIOGRAPHY

Birdoff, Harry. *The World's Greatest Hit.* New York, 1947.

Frederickson, George F. *The Black Image in the White Mind: The Debate on Afro-American Character and Destiny, 1817–1914.* New York, 1971.

Gossett, Thomas F. *Uncle Tom's Cabin and American Culture.* Dallas, 1985.

Lott, Eric. *Love and Theft: Blackface Minstrelsy and the American Working Class.* New York, 1993.

Rourke, Constance. *Trumpets of Jubilee.* New York, 1927.

Sanchez-Eppler, Karen. *Touching Liberty: Abolition, Feminism, and the Politics of the Body.* Berkeley, Calif., 1993.

Tompkins, Jane. *Sensational Designs: The Cultural Work of American Fiction, 1790–1860.* New York, 1985.

– ERIC LOTT

UNDERGROUND RAILROAD

Few aspects of the antislavery movement have been more shrouded in myth and misunderstanding than the Underground Railroad. Although white abolitionists, including Quakers, played an important role in helping to free thousands of African Americans, the degree of their involvement has been overemphasized. In the years before the Civil War, the Underground Railroad was primarily run, maintained, and funded by African Americans. Black working-class men and women collected the bulk of money, food, and clothing, and provided the shelter and transportation for the fugitives. Wealthier, better educated blacks such as Pennsylvania's Robert Purvis and William Whipper arranged for legal assistance and offered leadership, financial support, and indispensable contacts among sympathetic and influential white political leaders. Philadelphia's William STILL, who ran the city's vigilance committee and later recorded the stories of many of the people he helped, managed the pivotal point in the North's most successful underground system. He personally assisted thousands of escaping slaves and helped settle them in northern African-American communities or in Canada. As one white abolitionist leader admitted about the Underground Railroad in 1837, "Such matters are almost uniformly managed by the colored people."

Although the origins of the term are uncertain, by 1850 both those who participated in the Underground Railroad and those who sought to destroy it freely employed metaphors from the railroad business to describe its activities. More important, Northerners and Southerners understood both its symbolic and its real meanings. The numbers of African Americans who fled or were smuggled out of the South were never large enough to threaten the institutional stability of SLAVERY. Yet the number actually freed was, in a way, less important than what such activities said about the institution of slavery and the true character of southern slaves. Apologists for slavery described blacks as inferior, incapable of living in freedom, and content in their bondage. Those who escaped from the South, and the free African Americans who assisted them, undermined slavery by irrefutably disproving its racist ideology.

Most slaves who reached freedom in the North initiated their own escapes. After their initial flight, however, fugitives needed guidance and assistance to keep their hard-won liberty. Many did not have to travel far before finding help. Although the black underground's effectiveness varied over time and place, there was an astonishingly large number of semiautonomous networks that operated across the North and upper South. They were best organized in Ohio, Pennsylvania, and New York, but surprisingly efficient networks, often centered in local black churches, existed in most northern and border states, and even in Virginia. At hundreds of locations along the Ohio River, where many former slaves lived, fugitives encountered networks of black underground laborers who offered sanctuary and passed them progressively northward to other black communities. African-American settlements from New Jersey to Missouri served as asylums for fugitive slaves and provided contacts along well-established routes to Michigan, Ohio, Pennsylvania, and New York for easy transit to Canada.

Urban vigilance committees served as the hub for most of the black undergrounds. Along the East Coast, where the black underground was most effective, the Philadelphia and New York vigilance committees operated as central distribution points for many underground routes. Committee leaders such as William Still and David Ruggles directed fugitives to smaller black "stations," such as that of Stephen A. Myers in Albany, N.Y., who in turn provided transportation direct to Canada or further west to Syracuse. Vigilance committees also warned local blacks of kidnapping rings, and members hazarded their lives in searching vessels for illegal slaves. Such black leaders also maintained contacts among influential whites who covertly warned of the movement of slave owners and federal marshals. Where formal committees did not exist, ad hoc ones functioned, supplied with information from, for example, black clerks who worked in hotels frequented by slavecatchers. Black leaders such as William Still, who helped finance the famous exploits of Harriet TUBMAN, employed the latest technology to facilitate their work;

during the 1850s these committees regularly used the telegraph to communicate with far-flung "stations."

The most daring and best-organized "station" toiled in the very shadow of the U.S. Capitol. Run by free blacks from Washington, D.C., and Baltimore, this underground network rescued slaves from plantations in Maryland and Virginia, supplied them with free papers, and sent them north by a variety of land and water routes. These free blacks used their good standing among whites—as craftsmen, porters, and federal marshals' assistants—to facilitate their work. One free black used his painting business as a cover to visit plantations and arrange escapes; another employed his carriage service to transport slaves; others sustained the charges of slave owners and used their positions as plantation preachers and exhorters to pass escape plans to their "parishioners." When stealth and secrecy failed, heroic members of the Washington, D.C., "station" successfully attacked a slave pen to free some of its captives.

Members of this eastern network occasionally worked with white abolitionists such as Charles T. Torrey and the Quaker leader Thomas Garrett. But they primarily worked with other blacks, sending fugitives to Philadelphia where, either singly or in large groups, the escapees were directed to New York City and dispersed along many routes reaching into New England and Canada, or toward western New York. This network was temporarily disrupted during the 1840s, when race riots in northern cities and escalated southern surveillance forced the removal of Washington's most active agents. Nevertheless, by one estimate, between 1830 and 1860 over 9,000 fugitive slaves passed through Philadelphia alone on their way to freedom.

The Underground Railroad never freed as many slaves as its most vocal supporters claimed, and far fewer whites helped than the mythology suggests. Undeniably, however, the existence and history of the system reflect the African-American quest for freedom and equality.

BIBLIOGRAPHY

Blockson, Charles L. *The Underground Railroad: First Person Narratives of Escapes to Freedom in the North.* New York, 1987.

Gara, Larry. *The Liberty Line: The Legend of the Underground Railroad.* Lexington, Ky., 1961.

Ripley, C. Peter, et al., eds. *The Black Abolitionist Papers.* Vol. 3, *The United States.* Chapel Hill, N.C., 1991.

Siebert, Wilbur H. *The Underground Railroad: From Slavery to Freedom.* New York, 1898.

Still, William. *The Underground Railroad.* Philadelphia, 1872.

– DONALD YACOVONE

UNDERTAKERS, EMBALMERS, MORTICIANS

EBONY magazine editorialized in 1953, "Death is big business," and nowhere is it more so than in the black community, where mortality rates exceed the national average. One estimate at the time held that 3,000 black funeral parlors grossed over 120 million dollars annually from the burial of 150,000 people. Statistics, however, are emblems of a larger culture of death and dying that permeates American society and is reinforced by institutions such as the church, the insurance industry, and the funeral business. It is no accident, therefore, that undertakers became some of the most prominent, wealthy, and influential individuals in the black community.

The profession started out modestly enough and, until the end of the nineteenth century, was essentially unregulated. Just about anyone could set himself up in the mortuary business. Since disposing of corpses was a distasteful and emotionally difficult task for family members, the job often fell to operators of livery stables, who had horses and wagons to transport the dead to cemeteries. One of the earliest black funeral establishments was started by William Ragsdale, who ran a livery stable in the all-black township of Muskogee, Indian Territory (later Oklahoma). In 1889, Ragsdale purchased a horse-drawn hearse that he rented to bereaved families. The enterprise grew quickly and was incorporated as the People's Undertaking Company in 1895. Ragsdale's seven sons all followed in their father's footsteps and opened branches of the company (as Ragsdale & Sons) as far afield as San Diego and Phoenix.

The Ragsdale business first blossomed at about the time that undertaking became fully professional. The National Funeral Directors Association (NFDA) was founded in the early 1880s, and by 1910 several states had licensing requirements such as a period of internship and a course in embalming or mortuary science. William Ragsdale received training from Auguste Renouard, who toured the country giving two-week courses in embalming and who ran a school in New York. Many blacks turned to Renouard, since most other white schools excluded them. Of twenty-six undertakers identified in the first five editions of *Who's Who in Colored America* (1927–1944), eight were trained under Renouard. The others were dispersed among schools of embalming, anatomy, and sanitary science in Boston, Columbus, Cincinnati, Cleveland, Buffalo, Chicago, Philadelphia, and New York. In some cases, diplomas were granted—JIM CROW style—on the basis of a "home training course" separate from that of the other (white) graduates. A few prospective undertakers satisfied the licensing requirements by taking preclinical courses at all-black schools such as Meharry Medical College and Louisville National Medical College.

Undertaking provided blacks with a lucrative career opportunity primarily for two reasons. First, the culture demanded what Gunnar Myrdal has described as "conspicuous consumption in luxurious funerals." This stemmed in part from strong socioreligious beliefs (with traditions going back to slavery) that a decent, even opulent funeral was a fitting send-off for those who were about to enter a better world, one without struggle, poverty, and oppression. Funerals were an event in the black community. When Louis ARMSTRONG died in 1971, for example, one black periodical unfavorably compared the "white and dead" ceremony in New York to the "black, alive and swinging" one in New Orleans.

Second, black undertakers prior to 1960 exercised a virtual monopoly. Unlike other professions (e.g., medicine) where blacks often competed with their white counterparts for a share of the black clientele, undertaking remained completely segregated. Black undertakers were protected from competition because white undertakers generally refused to handle black corpses. In many small towns, the most viable black business was the funeral parlor, and the parlor's owner was often the town's wealthiest citizen. There are elements of truth in Shields McIlwaine's harsh caricature of black undertakers in *Memphis down in Dixie* (1948):

> Death and dead folks . . . have made more Negroes rich than anything else. Most Negroes crave a big funeral. They will pay their weekly burial 'inshoance' if they have to go hungry. When they quit living, as is likely some Saturday night, the Negro undertakers come running. Then the body needs a coffin and both need a hole in the ground. Result: the most prosperous Negro families . . . are undertakers or are financially interested in coffin factories or cemeteries or both.

Since black and white undertakers rarely communicated with one another on a professional basis before 1960, the black group founded its own national equivalent of the NFDA in 1938: the National Negro Funeral Directors and Morticians Association (the word *Negro* was dropped in 1957). The association remained strong despite the erosion of the competitive advantage of black undertakers following the Civil Rights Movement and the passage of antisegregation laws. In 1992, the association comprised two thousand members and twenty-six state subsidiaries.

BIBLIOGRAPHY

"The Business Side of Bereavement." *Black Enterprise* 8 (November 1977): 55–58, 61.

"Death Is Big Business." *Ebony* 8 (May 1953): 17–31.

Myrdal, Gunnar. *An American Dilemma: The Negro Problem and Modern Democracy.* New York, 1944.

– PHILIP N. ALEXANDER

UNITARIAN UNIVERSALIST ASSOCIATION

Unitarian Universalist Association, religious denomination. The Unitarian Universalist Association (UUA) was formed in 1961. It resulted from a merger of the American Unitarian Association and the Universalist Church of America. Both movements originated in opposition to Puritan theology and its Calvinist-based belief in predestination, human sinfulness, and a punitive God. Unitarianism appeared in the early nineteenth century as a quiet rebellion within the established church; its proponents insisted on the oneness and benevolence of God. Adherents to Universalism, on the other hand, posed a vocal challenge from without; emerging on the eve of the AMERICAN REVOLUTION, they proclaimed universal, rather than selective, salvation.

With their emphasis on the moral authority of the individual and the power of reason, both denominations produced prominent abolitionists. In 1784, Benjamin Rush, signer of the Declaration of Independence, and a Universalist, helped reestablish and later became president of the Pennsylvania Society for Promoting the Abolition of Slavery. William Ellery Channing (1780–1842), the preeminent Unitarian minister of his day, came to oppose slavery. Perhaps the most outspoken white Unitarian abolitionist, Theodore Parker, declared his defiance of the Fugitive Slave Law of 1850 by saying, "I have in my church black men, fugitive slaves [and] I have been obliged to take [them] into my house to keep them out of the clutches of the kidnappers." Black Unitarians included Frances Ellen Watkins HARPER, an abolitionist, writer, lecturer, and advocate of universal suffrage.

The Unitarian Universalist Association resulted from a merger of the American Unitarian Association and the Universalist Church of America.

At the same time, many Unitarians tolerated slavery or defended it outright. Thomas Jefferson, closely associated with the Unitarian theology, came to an accommodation with the institution of slavery. Unitarians John C. Calhoun and Daniel Webster argued for the COMPROMISE OF 1850, which was signed into law by another Unitarian, President Millard Fillmore.

After the Civil War, neither the Unitarians nor the Universalists were active in proselytizing African Americans. Although black converts to Unitarianism and Universalism tried to establish congregations on at least ten occasions between 1860 and 1948, they received meager support. Nonetheless, several black Unitarian ministers established churches in black communities. The Rev. Egbert Ethelred Brown (1875–1956), an activist leader in a number of Jamaican organizations in New York City and a Socialist party candidate for the New York State Assembly, founded the Harlem Unitarian Church in 1920; among those it attracted were black socialists W. A. Domingo and Frank Crosswaith. The Rev. Lewis Allen McGee (1893–1979), a former African Methodist Episcopal minister, became a leader in the American Humanist Association and established a Unitarian congregation—the Free Religious Fellowship—on Chicago's south side in 1948.

A few white ministers shared their broader vision. In 1903, Franklin C. Southworth, president of Meadville Theological School, wrote that "liberal Christianity has a mission to the blacks, whether it is labeled Unitarian or not." He wanted Meadville to "help in solving the race problem." Among its students were the Rev. Brown and Don Speed Smith Goodloe, who became the first black principal of Maryland Normal School No. 3, later Bowie State College.

The Rev. John Haynes Holmes was another visionary. The minister of the Community Church of New York, he was a founder of the NATIONAL ASSOCIATION FOR THE ADVANCEMENT OF COLORED PEOPLE (NAACP) in 1909 and soon thereafter racially integrated his own congregation. But it was not until the 1950s that other congregations—mostly major urban churches—made the effort. Their members participated in struggles for civil rights and open housing and, in 1965, hundreds of Unitarian Universalists responded to the Rev. Dr. Martin Luther King, Jr.'s call during the fight for voting rights in Selma, Ala. Among them was the Rev. James Reeb, whose brutal murder galvanized support among Unitarian Universalists. Duncan Howlett, Reeb's colleague at All Souls Unitarian Church of Washington, D.C., became the first chair of the U.S. Civil Rights Commission. Another Unitarian, educator Whitney M. Young, Jr., served as executive director of the NATIONAL URBAN LEAGUE.

Unitarian Universalist Association leaders remained at the forefront of change even as the emphasis of the CIVIL RIGHTS MOVEMENT shifted to black power. In 1967, a Black Unitarian Universalist Caucus was formed to promote social change and combat racism. A year later, in an emotional general assembly, the UUA agreed to commit $1 million to support a BUUC-sponsored Black Affairs Council. Although the measure was backed by almost 75 percent of the assembly delegates, it threatened to split the organization. In 1970, the UUA sharply reduced the resources that had been allocated for black empowerment. The organizational conflict and resulting paralysis led to the departure of a number of African Americans from the denomination.

Since it conducted an institutional racism audit in 1981, the UUA has continued to face the challenge of becoming a more inclusive movement. It remains an advocate of racial justice, continues to publish, through Beacon Press, black authors such as Marian Wright EDELMAN, James BALDWIN, Paul ROBESON, and Cornel West, and has established race awareness programs. But in 1987, of the UUA's 140,000 adult members, only 1,800 were African American.

BIBLIOGRAPHY

Morrison-Reed, Mark D. *Black Pioneers in a White Denomination.* Boston, 1984.

Robinson, David. *The Unitarians and the Universalists.* Westport, Conn., 1985

Stange, Douglas S. *Patterns of Antislavery Among American Unitarians, 1831–1860.* Rutherford, N.J., 1977.

— MARK D. MORRISON-REED

UNITED CHURCH OF CHRIST

The United Church of Christ (UCC) was formed in 1957 by the union of the Congregational Christian church (itself formed by the merger of the Congregational and Christian churches in 1931) and the Evangelical and Reformed church, a denomination formed in 1934 by the conjunction of the Lutheran and Reformed churches, two small Lutheran groups. The UCC has a continuing historical connection to African Americans, principally through the Congregational and Christian church components.

The Congregational Tradition

African Americans became involved in Congregational churches in the seventeenth century, beginning in New England, where enslaved blacks attended church with their Puritan slavemasters. The first convert, an unidentified slave woman belonging to the Rev. John Stoughton, was recorded in 1641. While religious attendance was required, only a few slaves and free blacks actually volunteered to be baptized. Congregationalism was never widely popular among blacks. Not only were

UNITED STATES COMMISSION ON CIVIL RIGHTS

The Commission on Civil Rights was established as part of the Civil Rights Act of 1957. Originally known as the President's Commission on Civil Rights, it was intended to be a temporary commission. The commission's purpose was to investigate complaints about voting rights infringement due to race, color, religion, or ethnicity; to compile information on the denial of equal protection under the law that could be used in further civil rights protection; to serve as a clearinghouse of information on equal protection in the United States; and to submit a final report and recommendations to Congress and the President within two years.

Of the first six commissioners appointed by the President and Congress, only one was black—J. Ernest Wilkins, an assistant secretary of labor in the Eisenhower administration. The first chairman was Stanley Reed, a former U.S. Supreme Court Justice who resigned almost immediately, citing "judicial improprieties" in the commission's charter. Reed was replaced by Dr. John Hannah, who served as chairman until 1969. The commission, which had its mandate extended by the Civil Rights Act of 1960, served to focus attention on the U.S. government's responsibilities regarding civil rights. The commission was also a place to which African Americans could bring complaints about legislative and extralegal, violent attempts to keep them from voting. In February 1963, the commission issued *Freedom to the Free,* a report marking the centennial of the Emancipation Proclamation. It pointed out that while the problem in the South remained de jure segregation and discrimination, in the North it was de facto: "The condition of citizenship is not yet full-blown or fully realized for the American Negro. . . . The final chapter in the struggle for equality has yet to be written." The commission's powers were enlarged and its existence extended by the 1964 Civil Rights Act to encompass investigation of allegations of denial of equal protection of any kind. Its two-volume report, *Racial Isolation in the Public Schools* (1967), pointed out increasing racial segregation in schools, especially in metropolitan areas, as whites left the cities for the suburbs, laying responsibility at the feet of housing discrimination as practiced by private citizens and local, state, and federal government. In 1969, the Rev. Theodore Hesburgh of the University of Notre Dame, a noted liberal on civil rights and segregation issues, succeeded Hannah as chairman.

During the busing crisis of the early 1970s, the commission reaffirmed the view that Congress had the responsibility for establishing a "uniform standard to provide for the elimination of racial isolation." It chided President Richard Nixon for being overly cautious about ending de facto segregation in the North in a 1970 report. Largely because of this, Nixon forced Chairman Hesburgh to resign in 1972 and replaced him with the more conservative Arthur S. Fleming the following year. The fifth report of the commission, released in November 1974, documented the failure of the government to fulfill its obligations to blacks in employment. The commission's term was extended by the Civil Rights Commission Authorization Act of 1978, as it had been previously extended every time its term was up.

The Commission on Civil Rights was established as part of the Civil Rights Act of 1957.

During Ronald Reagan's administration, the commission became the stage for a debate about affirmative action. In 1980 it endorsed racially based employment quotas in a report entitled "Civil Rights in the 1980s: Dismantling the Process of Discrimination." However, in 1981 President Reagan fired Chairman Arthur Fleming and replaced him with Clarence Pendleton, Jr., an arch-conservative and the first African American to serve as chairman; all subsequent chairpersons have also been African-American. In 1983 Reagan dismissed three other commissioners because they were critical of his administration's civil rights policies. One of the dismissed members, noted African-American historian Mary Frances Berry, successfully sued the Reagan administration to retain her position on the board, citing the commission's loss of independence. Following several months of negotiations involving the administration, Congress, and the commission itself, a compromise was reached and the body was reconstituted as the U.S. Commission on Civil Rights, with the President and Congress each appointing half the members, now numbering eight. More importantly, commissioners now had eight-year terms that could be terminated "only for neglect of duty or malfeasance in office."

In 1985 Chairman Pendleton declared that AFFIRMATIVE ACTION programs should be ended and the commission ultimately abolished. The next year he proposed that minority contract set-asides should be ended; the rest of the commission disagreed with him, as did the National Black Republican Council, so the plan did not go forward. During the George Bush administration, the debate over quotas continued. Pendleton died in 1988 and was replaced by William Barclay Allen, an African American, who was forced to resign in October

1989 following the disclosure that he had been arrested for kidnapping a fourteen-year-old girl in a child custody battle. The commission's authorization expired September 30, 1989, and the reauthorization process was an occasion for Congress to examine the body's composition and future. Its new chairman, Arthur A. Fletcher, former executive director of the NATIONAL URBAN LEAGUE, appointed in February 1990, vowed to be more active than his predecessors and to make the commission the nation's conscience once again. In August 1991 the commission issued its first significant report on discrimination on six military bases in Germany, and followed it six months later with a report on pervasive discrimination against Asians, based on barriers of language and culture.

BIBLIOGRAPHY

Blaustein, Albert P., and Robert L. Zangrando, eds. *Civil Rights and the American Negro: A Documentary History.* New York, 1968.

Lowery, Charles D., and John F. Marszalek, eds. *Encyclopedia of African-American Civil Rights: From Emancipation to the Present.* New York, 1992.

Ploski, Harry A., and James Williams, eds. *The Negro Almanac: A Reference Work on the African American.* 5th ed. Detroit, 1989.

– ALANA J. ERICKSON

UNIVERSAL NEGRO IMPROVEMENT ASSOCIATION

The Universal Negro Improvement Association (UNIA), with its motto "One God, One Aim, One Destiny" stands as one of the most important political and social organizations in African American history. It was founded by Marcus GARVEY in July 1914, in Kingston, Jamaica, West Indies.

At the time of its establishment, its full name was the Universal Negro Improvement and Conservation Association and African Communities (Imperial) League (ACL). Originally organized as a mutual benefit and reform association dedicated to racial uplift, the UNIA and ACL migrated with Garvey to the United States in 1916. Incorporated in New York in 1918, the UNIA gradually began to give voice to the rising mood of New Negro radicalism that emerged within the African-American population following the signing of the Armistice ending World War I in November 1918.

The UNIA experienced a sudden, massive expansion of membership beginning in the spring of 1919, spearheaded by the spectacular success of the stock-selling promotion of the Black Star Line, Inc. (BSL). Together with the Negro Factories Corporation and other commercial endeavors, all of which were constituted under the ACL, the BSL represented the heart of the economic program of the movement.

Outfitted with its own flag, national anthem, Universal African Legion and other uniformed ranks, official organ (*The Negro World*), African repatriation and resettlement scheme in Liberia, constitution, and laws, the UNIA attempted to function as a sort of provisional government of Africa. The result was that by 1920–1921, the UNIA became the dominant voice advocating black self-determination, under its irredentist program of African Redemption. Accompanied by spectacular parades, annual month-long conventions were held at Liberty Hall in Harlem in New York City between 1920 and 1924, at all of which Garvey presided. The document with the greatest lasting significance to emerge was the "Declaration of the Rights of the Negro Peoples of the World," passed at the first UNIA convention in August 1920.

Nearly a thousand local divisions and chapters of the UNIA were established by the mid-twenties in the United States, Canada, the West Indies, Central and South America, Africa, and the United Kingdom, causing the influence of the UNIA to be felt wherever peoples of African descent lived. With actual membership running into the hundreds of thousands, if not millions, the UNIA is reputed to have been the largest political organization in African-American history.

After Garvey's conviction on charges of mail fraud in 1923, following the ill-fated collapse of the Black Star Line, and his incarceration in the Atlanta Federal Penitentiary starting in 1925, membership in the UNIA declined rapidly. When President Calvin Coolidge commuted Garvey's sentence and he was deported from the United States in 1927, the organization found itself racked by increasing factionalization.

A new UNIA and ACL of the World was incorporated by Garvey in Jamaica at the August 1929 convention, competing with the New York-based UNIA parent body headed at the time by Fred A. Toote, who was succeeded by Lionel Francis in 1931. With the worldwide economic collapse following the 1929 stockmarket crash, however, the UNIA went into further decline, as members' resources dwindled, making it difficult to support two separate wings of the movement. Demoralization also set in as a result of the increasing fragmentation of the UNIA leadership. Garvey was able to retain the loyalty of only a part of the movement, notably the Garvey Club and the Tiger division of the New York UNIA.

When Garvey moved his headquarters in 1935 from Jamaica to London, he tried once again to revive the movement, but soon found himself confronting considerable opposition by members who were in the forefront of the pro-Ethiopian support campaign during the Italo-Ethiopian War of 1935. These members repudiated the criticisms leveled by Garvey against Ethiopia's Emperor Haile Selassie I, following invasion by Mussolini and the Fascist Italian Army.

After Garvey's death in 1940, loyalists moved the headquarters of the organization to Cleveland, Ohio, under the leadership of the new president general, James Stewart, who thereafter relocated with it to Liberia. By the 1940s and '50s, the UNIA was a mere shadow of its former strength, but it still continues to function today.

BIBLIOGRAPHY

Hill, Robert A., ed. *The Marcus Garvey and Universal Negro Improvement Association Papers.* Vols. 1–7. Berkeley and Los Angeles, Calif., 1983–1991.

Hill, Robert A., and Barbara Bair. *Marcus Garvey: Life and Lessons.* Berkeley and Los Angeles, Calif., 1987.

– ROBERT A. HILL

URBAN RIOTS AND REBELLIONS

Few social phenomena are as dramatic as urban riots and rebellions. Their ugly power displays many aspects of the negative underside of American life and their attention-grabbing force has shaped political debates. While they are as much a product of despair as of conscious political protest, they often expose long-festering social problems generally ignored or sidestepped by mainstream politics and news sources. Above all, they are often expressions of rage—by whites against blacks, blacks against whites, and blacks against their sense of hopelessness at their surroundings and situation.

Since the days of slavery, racial mob violence has been a crucial aspect of African-American history. Violence has taken two distinct forms. Up to 1940, racial rioting in the United States almost exclusively took the form of white attacks on African Americans, generally sparked by fears over black challenges to the social order. The traditional powerlessness of African Americans has made them easy scapegoats for social problems.

Since the 1940s, outbreaks of violence by African Americans have expressed frustration with the pace and efficacy of nonviolent change. Far from being simple acts of mindless violence, rebellions have been a way for a relatively powerless group to express and publicize grievances. Riots have called attention to critical problems in African-American life, such as poverty, unemployment, poor housing, price gouging, inadequate municipal services, poor medical and social services, inadequate educational and recreational facilities, and police brutality.

Since the days of slavery, racial mob violence has been a crucial aspect of African-American history.

As the aftermath of the 1992 Los Angeles riot showed, riots can shock and startle complacent people into reconsidering the underlying basis of race relations and can catalyze reform efforts. Yet in other ways they compound the problems of inner-city blacks by frightening authorities into repressive measures, obscuring nonviolent protests of grievances, destroying the local economy, and generating a white backlash for the preservation of "law and order."

Causes

Riots and rebellions, though generally sparked by specific incidents, are carried out for a variety of underlying causes. Almost all of the different studies of urban violence have discussed the fundamental causes of rioting according to one of three distinct models.

One view, developed in the 1960s and expounded by black nationalists such as the BLACK PANTHERS is the ultimate expression of collective African-American political consciousness. According to this view, uprisings are deliberate—if not actually planned—demonstrations of black community will, directed at the achievement of particular goals. Riot participants seek either to overturn established authority through revolutionary change, or to force disruptive shifts in institutional arrangements in order to demand inclusion in urban decision-making processes.

Fundamental to this view is the model of ghettos as areas of internal colonization. The theory of violent colonial revolt advocated by Frantz Fanon in *The Wretched of the Earth* (1960) was influential in 1960s black nationalist thought. African-American thinkers saw connections between the struggle of Third World peoples fighting economic and political domination by foreign whites and the state of their own communities. If black ghettos were analogous to countries whose citizens used violence to achieve independence from foreign control, then looting, sniper gunfire, and destruction of property were justifiable methods of asserting African-American control over ghetto communities and compelling outside forces to leave.

Another school of thought on urban riots claims that rebellions, whether justifiable or otherwise, are spontaneous individual expressions of African-American anger over real political or economic injustices, and protests against their involuntary segregation and marginal existence in urban ghettos. This view was popularized by the President's National Advisory Commission on Civil Disorders in its 1968 report (usually referred to as the KERNER REPORT). According to such a model, looting is a reaction to widespread price gouging by storekeepers, as well as a protest against barriers to black economic advancement and acquisition of consumer goods. Arson is an expression of anger against the merchants and landlords who live outside the community but take money from it.

History

Throughout African-American history, periods of urban racial violence have appeared. The slave conspiracies of the colonial era, the NEW YORK CITY DRAFT RIOTS OF 1863, the Atlanta Riot of 1906, the Red Summer of 1919, the DETROIT RIOT OF 1943, and the LOS ANGELES WATTS RIOT OF 1965 have all served to demarcate and separate periods of African-American history. In each new period, the position of African Americans in the United States changed, and the context and nature of the outbreaks was transformed.

The first and most fundamental expression of white violence against blacks was the institution of slavery, particularly the chattel slavery of the South. Blacks were forced against their will to toil for whites and were subject at the master's pleasure to harsh punishment for disobedience. In most cases, enslaved African Americans were unable to retaliate. On occasion they responded with direct physical violence, by beating or murdering masters. More often, their rage was expressed indirectly, either by escaping to freedom or more commonly by looting, abusing, or destroying slaveowner property.

On very rare occasions African Americans were able to organize rebellions, despite the extraordinary, near-absolute control that masters, backed by the government, exerted over slaves. Slave rebellions were violent revolts of anywhere from a dozen to 1,000 conspirators against the degradation of human enslavement. Captured insurgents were often decapitated, hanged, or put to death to serve as examples and thwart other rebellious slaves.

While some of the most famous incidents, such as NAT TURNER'S REBELLION of 1831 in Virginia, were rural affairs, most of the more celebrated slave conspiracies and revolts took place in urban environments, the most notable examples being the New York Slave Revolt of 1712, which was uncovered and foiled; the abortive GABRIEL PROSSER CONSPIRACY near Richmond, Va., in 1800; and the failed DENMARK VESEY CONSPIRACY in Charleston, S.C., 1822. City life facilitated the formulation of plans. Slaves in urban areas had greater autonomy, frequent contacts with other slaves and with free black supporters, and faster means of communication.

Urban free blacks also resorted to collective violence, particularly after the passage of the 1850 FUGITIVE SLAVE ACT, in order to protest slavecatchers and protect fugitives. African Americans formed armed bands to fight off slavenappers and rioters. They formed vigilante committees to oppose, violently if necessary, the recapture of slaves. Violent attempts to prevent the rendition of fugitive slaves to the South took place in communities as diverse as Boston, New York, Philadelphia, Detroit, and Christiana, Pa. Mobs challenged police and judicial officers to force the liberation and spiriting away of captured blacks threatened with removal south.

Large-scale urban violence in the antebellum United States was also directed against African Americans and their white allies. White resentment of African-American inhabitants in "white man's country" led to mob violence designed to force black residents to flee. Numerous antiblack outbreaks occurred during the 1830s and '40s in such cities as Philadelphia, "the northernmost southern city." The most notorious cases of racial violence were in Cincinnati in 1829 and 1841. After the disturbance of 1829, half of Cincinnati's black population departed, and in 1841, blacks were forced to seek protection from mobs in the city jail. At the same time, southerners and their northern business associates incited and often paid mobs to harass and threaten white and black abolitionists. Speakers were beaten and newspaper offices destroyed. In 1837, white abolitionist Elijah Lovejoy of Alton, Ill., was lynched by a mob. A number of blacks were also killed in antiabolitionist violence, such as in the 1842 Philadelphia riot, among other places.

By far the most bloody incident was the New York City Draft Riots of 1863, a four-day urban upheaval largely initiated by poor Irish immigrants.

As white immigrants from Ireland, Germany, and other places arrived in America, social tensions and labor unrest increased. Enraged by competition with black labor, there were racial attacks such as the 1849 Philadelphia election riot, in which Irish immigrants targeted blacks as scapegoats for the political and economic discrimination they faced. Native-born whites often condoned this violence, which eased pressure on them to improve conditions for all laborers. Antiblack violence climaxed during the CIVIL WAR in outbreaks of communal violence in such cities as Detroit, Baltimore, and Cincinnati.

By far the most bloody incident was the New York City Draft Riots of 1863, a four-day urban upheaval largely initiated by poor Irish immigrants protesting a new Union conscription law that provided for workers to be drafted into the army but allowed rich men to hire substitutes. Irish workers, indifferent or hostile to the war, were enraged by the discriminatory policy. They invaded draft offices, halted their operation, and beat ordinary bystanders. Resentful of blacks, whom they viewed as strike-breakers and the cause of the war, they targeted the black community for their rage. Blacks were beaten and hanged from lampposts, and the Colored Orphans' Home was burned to the ground. Once the rioters turned their focus from antiblack violence and threatened to overturn city authority, the rebellion was violently put down by Union troops. Over 100 deaths resulted from the rebellion, including blacks, police, militia, fire fighters, and the rioters themselves.

Post-Emancipation

RECONSTRUCTION brought renewed antiblack mob violence, particularly in the South, as white groups used extralegal means to restore conservative white-dominated governments, overturn black civil rights, and restrain blacks from exercising suffrage rights. Vigilante groups such as the KU KLUX KLAN and the Knights of the White Camellia were the most visible sources of racist violence. Riots in cities, such as in Memphis and New Orleans in 1866, followed campaigns by African Americans, many of them veterans, for suffrage and an end to racial discrimination. While blacks organized into militia for self-defense in certain areas, the urban riots clearly demonstrated the defenselessness of blacks against southern white mobs. Northern opinion was influenced by the riots into supporting the FOURTEENTH AMENDMENT and the FIFTEENTH AMENDMENT, which constitutionally guaranteed blacks the exercise of social and political rights, and into passing the Reconstruction acts which brought occupying military forces to protect blacks' constitutional rights against white terrorism.

Once the federal government withdrew its troops in 1877, and blacks lost that measure of protection, white conservatives used legal and extralegal tactics to end black political influence. By the 1890s, almost all vestiges of black political power in the South had been eliminated. A "Radical" (antiblack) movement, which called for an expanded color bar, gained influence. Radicals effectively used the specter of black-male rape of white women as a vehicle for brutal enforcement of white domination, as well as the curtailing of black economic power. In the classic "race riot" (i.e., whites attacking blacks), white mobs, usually operating with the tacit support of the police, invaded a city's black community. The attacks were directed against both persons and property, and were in many respects similar to lynch mobs with larger targets. Intimidated African Americans made sporadic efforts to defend themselves, but were quickly overwhelmed and forced to flee or retreat from their political or economic positions.

In 1892, white storeowners in Memphis, Tenn., angered by black competition, threatened mob violence. After African Americans, defending themselves against the threat, mistakenly shot a police officer, they were lynched by a white mob. In 1893, white waterfront workers in New Orleans rioted in an attempt to exclude African-American stevedores from the docks. In 1898, radical antiblack forces instigated a riot in Wilmington, N.C., a city politically controlled by blacks and white allies, as well as one of the few remaining outposts of black economic and political power in the South. Rioters overturned the city government and drove black officeholders from the area. Eight years later, in Atlanta, a center of black college and middle-class life, whites were aroused by a race-baiting gubernatorial campaign by radical demagogue Hoke Smith and by sensational newspaper stories about black rapists. Atlanta was swept by a racial uprising, as whites stormed the streets of the black community, destroyed homes and businesses, and beat and lynched residents.

A somewhat earlier outbreak in New Orleans in 1900 furnished an interesting counterpoint to the pattern. African-American Robert Charles, harassed by police, defended himself violently and shot several officers before going into hiding. While a police manhunt for Charles continued without pause, aroused whites rioted, beating blacks and destroying property. After Charles was discovered and shot, the relative painlessness of his death prompted further white retaliation against innocent blacks.

The brutality was not confined to the Deep South. Elite whites scorned blacks as inferior, and depended on their subordination for cheap labor, for which they were in turn despised by immigrant labor competition. Riots broke out in such places as New York and Brownsville, Tex. In 1908, whites of all classes in Springfield, Ill., Abraham Lincoln's hometown, exploded after a false report of a rape was spread. White rioters lynched several blacks and destroyed the entire black section of the town. The symbolism of Springfield added to the shock of the riot, and catalyzed liberal whites and blacks in New York City into the organization of the NATIONAL ASSOCIATION FOR THE ADVANCEMENT OF COLORED PEOPLE (NAACP).

Great Migration

The next cycle of riots, which lasted from 1917 into the early 1920s, was a product of the Great Migration north by southern African Americans during the era of WORLD WAR I. The wartime labor shortage and the cutoff of immigration from Europe opened up industrial and other jobs in industrial centers of the North such as Chicago, Detroit, and Pittsburgh. However, the need for African-American labor did not transform widely held white racial attitudes, and racial tensions grew apace. Furthermore, competition with white workers for better paying jobs and for housing, leisure, and health facilities remained intense. While the riots of this period, like their predecessors, tended to be instigated by whites, they differed in a number of important ways. Their size and intensity far surpassed previous outbreaks. Their savagery resulted in part from the collision of blacks catalyzed by their contribution to the war effort into demanding equal treatment with whites who remained unwilling to countenance changes in the racial status quo. After the end of World War I, widespread fears of radicalism and social change fed the hysteria of whites determined to maintain control over large black populations.

The first large riot in the cycle occurred in the drab industrial town of EAST ST. LOUIS, Ill., in the summer of 1917. Tensions following a bitter white labor strike were intensified by white fears over competition from the influx of black workers into the area. White leaders were content to allow African Americans to serve as scapegoats for worker anger. They did little to increase security measures following a small-scale riot, and a series of episodes of racial harassment ensued. In July white workers exploded into violence. Hundreds of blacks were killed, and the black section of the town was heavily damaged.

The pattern of violence escalated to a fever pitch following the end of World War I, during the Red Summer of 1919. Countless riots erupted, some in towns such as Longview, Tex., and Elaine, Ark., but most occurred in large urban areas such as CHARLESTON, S.C., WASHINGTON, and CHICAGO.

The Red Summer marked one significant change from the previous pattern of riots: African Americans frequently responded to violent attacks with organized self-defense efforts. During Red Summer, militant black leaders such as A. Philip Randolph wrote articles justifying the use of firearms against lynching and white mob violence. Blacks in several areas organized to beat off white attacks on their neighborhoods, and in Chicago gangs of black youths beat whites they caught in the black section. Black self-defense efforts intensified in the Tulsa, Okla., riot of 1921, the last in the postwar period. Black snipers shot back at white rioters, and blacks organized armed squads.

Modern Urban Rebellions

A new pattern of urban violence appeared in the HARLEM RIOTS OF 1935 AND 1943 in New York City, and in the Detroit Riot of 1943. Initiated by inner-city African Americans, and involving attacks primarily on white-owned property within the black community, this "modern" urban race riot style has come to be accepted as the standard pattern of an urban rebellion. Like subsequent outbreaks, the Harlem riots were the generalized fallout of the frustrations of ghetto life, sparked by a pattern of aggravating incidents. In both cases, acts of police brutality inspired rumors of killings, which led aroused African Americans into the streets. Rioters broke store windows and looted merchandise. Meanwhile, in Detroit, a wartime surge in population bred interracial tension over scarce housing and recreation resources. Black youths unable to escape the summer heat took out their frustration on a group of whites. As inflated rumors of conflict spread, the city erupted. Whites attacked blacks in white neighborhoods. Meanwhile, the black community actively burned and looted shops and attacked any whites whom they encountered. City police, unwilling to defend African Americans from white rioting, were massed in the black neighborhood. Nevertheless, the rebellion was so powerful that the mayor was forced to call in military assistance.

During the late 1940s and '50s, there were no major race riots in the United States, despite chronic tension in inner city African-American neighborhoods. The next wave of urban rebellions occurred in the 1960s. These established the urban race riot as a central social phenomenon. The largest rebellions were those in HARLEM (1964), Watts (1965), NEWARK (1967), and DETROIT (1967). Many "copycat" riots, inspired by these larger outbreaks, erupted in other cities. Unlike the earlier riots, black residents and community leaders justified the outbreak of riots as a natural response to ghetto living, and many militant blacks who spoke positively of violence became folk heroes in black communities.

In 1968, following the assassination of the Rev. Dr. Martin Luther KING, Jr., riots erupted in cities throughout the nation, the largest ones occurring in such cities as Baltimore and Kansas City. Inner cities throughout the United States were scarred by the results of violent action by African Americans.

A significant underlying element in the development of the urban rebellions of the mid-1960s was the CIVIL RIGHTS MOVEMENT, and the parallel development of black nationalism. The fight for equality energized masses of blacks into action in defense of equal rights, and made them acutely conscious of their right to fair treatment. The movement also inspired blacks to a new unity and pride in their identity. In the midst of important changes in the South and nationwide calls for equality, however, northern inner-city blacks saw little change or improvement, and sometimes even a decline, in their living conditions. Furthermore, the violent opposition the movement faced, and its perceived failure to achieve the goal of freedom angered and radicalized large numbers of African Americans.

Kerner Commission

Following the burst of violence that King's assassination provoked in American cities, the Kerner Commission was set up in 1968 to investigate the causes and solution to the pressing problem of collective urban violence. The resulting Kerner Report noted that while each riot was a response to a separate set of circumstances, it was possible to speak of common characteristics. Of course, it is impossible to denote the myriad individual reactions and motivations of riot participants, but the report pointed to several general factors in the riots of the 1960s.

The commission reported that riots tended to flare up in hot weather, during a "long hot summer." Racial violence has historically been slight in winter, when the cold weather presumably makes the prospect of extended activity in the street distasteful. During the summer, African Americans, unable to find adequate relief from the uncomfortable heat, were easily aroused. The contrast with affluent whites, who possessed air conditioning and could flee the city on vacations, was also the most glaring at such times.

Another common factor the commission noted was that incidents of perceived police brutality were usually the trigger for urban violence. Police brutality was a common African-American complaint. Not only was police harassment infuriating in itself, it symbolized ghetto residents' sense of being "occupied" by a foreign power. Government institutions were often biased in providing services to poor black neighborhoods and insensitive to their residents' needs and concerns. Police were the most visible (and sometimes openly racist) rep-

Armed National Guardsmen with fixed bayonets patrol Springfield Avenue in Newark, N.J., in the aftermath of three days of looting, July 15, 1967. (UPI/Bettman)

resentatives of the "outside" government, and their abuse of law enforcement authority reminded inner city residents of their powerlessness against white society and eroded African Americans' respect for "law and order."

The most common pattern of the 1960s incidents was that small numbers of ghetto blacks would become involved in altercations with police, and rumors would spread of brutal treatment. Crowds, often egged on by black militants, would confront the police with bricks, stones, and sometimes guns. Once police retreated from the area, aroused African Americans would take to the streets of ghetto neighborhoods, smashing windows, looting and setting fire to houses and stores (the popular arsonist's cry "Burn, baby, burn" is said to have originated in the Watts rebellion). Usually rioters singled out only white-owned stores; those known to be black-owned were spared. While these uprisings were generally referred to as "property riots," in which rioters attacked homes and buildings, they also featured beatings of whites in black communities (as well as reports, usually fictitious or greatly exaggerated, of sniper attacks). Police and firefighters who attempted to quench blazes were particular targets for violence.

Eventually, police coverage would be reinforced, and often martial law would be declared. National Guard or military units tended to be brought in to quell disturbances. A curfew would be put into effect, with troops ordered to shoot looters, and houses would be entered without warrant to search for snipers. After a certain amount of time, usually several days, sometimes with the help of rainstorms or cooler temperatures, the riot would wind down.

The Kerner Commission stressed the importance of daily ghetto conditions in sparking riots. Originally, many white politicians and commentators, notably the McCone Commission report after the Watts riot, shifted blame for them onto new migrants to cities or black radical groups. Yet, the epidemic of rebellions and the Kerner Commission report sparked a number of sociological studies of riots, such as Nathan Cohen's 1970 study of the Watts uprising (*The Los Angeles Riots: A Socio-Psychological View*), which indicated that many rioters were longtime ghetto residents with comparatively high levels of income and education.

After the end of the 1960s, riots more or less disappeared as part of the American urban landscape. Except for the Liberty City uprising in Miami of 1980, there were no large-scale uprisings for the following twenty years. African-American rage over inequality was not reduced, but the original hope for improvement that had fed rage subsided. The increasingly high social cost of riots, in terms of housing and business facilities lost to the black community, was another factor. Also, white flight and black electoral gains assured largely black-led or black-influenced urban governments, and in some cases police departments, which were more attentive to the troubles of black urbanites. Black militant organizations grew less popular under the pressure of official harassment and a changing black political landscape.

However, starting in the late 1970s, economic recession and reductions in federal aid devastated the black urban economy, and black-on-black crime made most ghetto neighborhoods war zones. Poor public health care, education, and safety services, coupled with an attractive underground drug economy, made inner cities ever more unlivable and oppressive. Police harassment of blacks in all areas remained a chronic concern. Discriminatory sentencing policies, and the gentle treatment given police accused of brutal acts, convinced many blacks that the legal system offered them no justice. By the 1990s, racial violence had again become a powerful threat. Rap lyrics expressed the rage of inner-city blacks, and glorified violence and guns as signs of virility. Movies such as Spike LEE's *Do the Right Thing* (1991), which dramatized a racial riot, were denounced by white critics as incitements to violence. Despite these various possible causative factors, spontaneous riots did not break out.

The Los Angeles Riots of 1992 highlighted the chronic problem of poor conditions in urban African-American communities.

In 1992, Rodney King, a black motorist, was arrested and beaten by Los Angeles police. The incident, recorded by a clandestine video camera, was played on national television along with tapes of police conversations, laced with racial epithets, transforming the incident into a *cause célèbre* of police violence against blacks. Nevertheless, when the officers were brought to trial on assault charges, an all-white suburban jury acquitted all the assailants. When news of the verdict reached the African-American area of south central Los Angeles, riots broke out. The uprising, which surpassed the 1960s riots in scope, lasted for several days. Blacks and other participants burned buildings, looted stores, and savagely beat white motorists dragged from vehicles. Local Korean-American shopowners, whom blacks perceived as unfriendly, were particularly targeted. While the 1992 riot, unlike earlier uprisings, was not confined to black areas, most outside damage was confined to commercial areas, and Los Angeles' heavily white sections were undamaged. Copycat riots erupted in several cities in the United States and Canada.

The Los Angeles Riots of 1992 demonstrated America's continuing racial difficulties, and highlighted the chronic problem of poor conditions in urban African-American communities. Urban rebellions are once again central to Americans' perception of racial issues, and the threat of rioting, a central feature of the 1993 federal trial of King's assailants, has been an element of other trial verdicts involving blacks in the early 1990s. The threat and reality of urban rebellions remains one of the touchstones of race relations in the United States. Riots serve as a chastening reminder of the lack of progress toward a final resolution of the issues of race and class in our cities despite the achievements of the Civil Rights Movement.

BIBLIOGRAPHY

Aptheker, Herbert. *American Negro Slave Revolts.* New York, 1952.

Belknap, Michael, ed. *Urban Race Riots.* New York, 1991.

Boskin, Joseph, ed. *Urban Racial Violence in the Twentieth Century.* Beverly Hills, Calif., 1969.

Brown, Richard Maxwell. *Strain of Violence.* New York, 1975.

Button, James W. *Black Violence: The Political Impact of the 1960s Riots.* Princeton, N.J., 1978.

Capeci, Dominic J. *The Harlem Riot of 1943.* Philadelphia, 1977.

Chicago Commission on Race Relations. *The Negro In Chicago: A Study of Race Relations and a Race Riot.* Chicago, 1992.

Connery, Robert H., ed. *Urban Riots: Violence and Social Change.* New York, 1968.

Feagin, Joe R., and Harlan Hahn. *Ghetto Revolts: The Politics of Violence in American Cities.* New York, 1973.

Fine, Sidney. *Violence in the Model City: The Cavanaugh Administration, Race Relations, and the Detroit Riot of 1967.* Detroit, 1989.

Graham, Hugh D., and Ted R. Gurr, eds. *Violence in America.* New York, 1969.

McCague, James. *The Second Rebellion.* New York, 1968.

Report of the National Advisory Commission on Civil Disorders. Washington, D.C., 1968.

Rudwick, Elliott M. *Race Riot at East St. Louis. July 2, 1917.* 2nd ed. Urbana, Ill., 1982.

Shogan, Robert, and Tom Craig. *The Detroit Race Riot: A Study in Violence.* Philadelphia, 1964.

Waskow, Arthur I. *From Race Riot to Sit-in, 1919 and the 1960s: A Study in the Connections Between Conflict and Violence.* Garden City, N.Y., 1966.

West, Cornel. *Race Matters.* Boston, 1993.

Williamson, Joel. *The Crucible of Race: Black-White Relations in the American South Since Emancipation.* New York, 1984.

— GAYLE T. TATE

V

VANDERZEE, JAMES AUGUSTUS

James Augustus VanDerZee (June 29, 1886–May 15, 1983), photographer. James VanDerZee was born in Lenox, Mass., the eldest son and second child of Susan Brister and John VanDerZee. He grew up in Lenox and attended the public schools there. In 1900, he won a small box camera as the premium for selling packets of sachet powder. Shortly afterward he purchased a larger camera and began photographing family members, friends, and residents in Lenox. Thus began his lifelong commitment to photography. In 1906, VanDerZee and his brother Walter moved to New York City to join their father, who was working there. By this time VanDerZee was already an accomplished photographer; however, his first New York job was waiting tables in the private dining room of a bank. In New York he met his first wife, Kate L. Brown, whom he married in 1907. The next year he and Kate moved to Phoebus, Va., then a small resort town near her home at Newport News. He worked as a waiter at the popular Hotel Chamberlin, a favored resort for the wealthy in Hampton. While in Virginia, VanDerZee continued photographing and made some of his most notable early images: photographs of the faculty and students of the Whittier School, a preparatory academy for Hampton Institute.

In 1908, after the birth of their first child, Rachel, the family returned to New York. VanDerZee continued working at a variety of jobs, including photography. For a brief period he commuted to Newark, N.J., where he operated the camera in a department-store portrait studio. In 1910, a son, Emile, was born. At the end of the first quarter-century of his life, James VanDerZee had much to celebrate—he was twice a father, happily married, and a success in the economically competitive world of pre-World War I New York. But this period of happiness did not last long. Emile died in 1911, and the following year, VanDerZee and Kate separated.

VanDerZee had recovered sufficiently by 1916 to open his first photography portrait studio. It was in Harlem, on 135th Street at Lenox Avenue. He also had a partner in the enterprise, his new wife, Gaynella Greenlee Katz. From 1916 to 1931 VanDerZee stayed at this location, and the studio became one of Harlem's most prominent photographic operations. He specialized in portraits and wedding photographs, but also took on assignments away from the studio. Among these assignments was his work for Marcus GARVEY in 1924. It was also during these years that VanDerZee began his experimental photomontage assemblages.

VanDerZee and his wife weathered the Great Depression and in 1943, in the midst of World War II, they purchased the building they had been renting at 272 Lenox Avenue. For the rest of the decade he continued his portrait work and took assignments for a variety of Harlem customers. However, a decline in business began to set in during the early 1950s. Ultimately, all he could maintain was a mail-order restoration business. Through a complicated series of loans and second mortgages, the VanDerZees were able to keep their property until 1969, when they were evicted. Ironically, VanDerZee's greatest fame and success as a photographer were yet to come.

Two years before his eviction, VanDerZee had met Reginald McGhee, who was a curator for the Metropolitan Museum exhibition *Harlem on My Mind.* Through McGhee's efforts, his work of the previous four decades became the central visual focus of the exhibition. The photographs became some of the most written-about images in the history of photography, while their maker was reduced to living on welfare. VanDerZee's fame grew when, in 1969, McGhee and other young black photographers formed the James VanDerZee Institute, which showed his work in the United States and abroad. His photographs became even more widely known when three monographs were published during the 1970s. By the second half of that decade, VanDerZee's work was being sought out by both institutional and individual collectors. By the time Gaynella died, in 1976, VanDerZee had become a symbol of artistry and courage to the Harlem community. He resumed making portraits, spoke at conferences, and gave countless interviews. In 1978, he was named the first recipient of the New York Archdiocese Pierre Toussaint Award. That year he married for the third time, to Donna Mussendon, a woman sixty years his junior.

In 1980, with his wife's help, VanDerZee began a series of portraits of African-American celebrities. Among his sitters were Eubie BLAKE, Miles DAVIS, Cicely Tyson, and Muhammad ALI. He made his last portrait, for art historian Reginia Perry, in February 1983. VanDerZee died on May 15, 1983. That day he had received an honorary doctorate of humane letters at the

Howard University commencement. He was ninety-six years old.

BIBLIOGRAPHY

De Cock, Liliane, and Reginald McGhee. *James VanDerZee.* New York, 1973.

McGhee, Reginald. *The World of James VanDerZee: A Visual Record of Black Americans.* New York, 1969.

VanDerZee, James, et al. *The Harlem Book of the Dead.* New York, 1978.

– RODGER C. BIRT

VAUGHAN, SARAH

Sarah Vaughan (March 29, 1924–April 3, 1990), jazz singer. Nicknamed "Sassy" and "the Divine One," Sarah Vaughan is considered one of America's greatest vocalists and part of the triumvirate of women jazz singers that includes Ella FITZGERALD and Billie HOLIDAY. A unique stylist, she possessed vocal capabilities—lush tones, perfect pitch, and a range exceeding three octaves—that were matched by her adventurous, sometimes radical sense of improvisation. Born in Newark, N.J., she began singing and playing organ in the Mount Zion Baptist Church when she was twelve.

In October 1942, she sang "Body and Soul" to win an amateur-night contest at Harlem's Apollo Theater. Billy Eckstine, the singer for Earl "Fatha" Hines's big band, happened to hear her and was so impressed that he persuaded Hines to hire Vaughan as a second pianist and singer in early 1943. Later that year, when Eckstine left Hines to organize his own big band, she went with him. In his group, one of the incubators of bebop jazz, Vaughan was influenced by Eckstine's vibrato-laced baritone, and by the innovations of such fellow musicians as Dizzy GILLESPIE and Charlie PARKER. Besides inspiring her to forge a personal style, they instilled in her a lifelong desire to improvise. ("It was just like going to school," she said.)

Nicknamed "Sassy" and "the Divine One," Sarah Vaughan is considered one of America's greatest vocalists.

Vaughan made her first records for the Continental label on New Year's Eve 1944, and began working as a solo act the following year at New York's Cafe Society. At the club she met trumpeter George Treadwell, who became her manager and the first of her four husbands. Treadwell promoted Vaughan and helped create her glamorous image. Following hits on Musicraft (including "It's Magic" and "If They Could See Me Now") and Columbia ("Black Coffee"), her success was assured. From 1947 through 1952, she was voted top female vocalist in polls in *Down Beat* and *Metronome* jazz magazines.

Throughout the 1950s, Vaughan recorded pop material for Mercury records, including such hits as "Make Yourself Comfortable" and "Broken-Hearted Melody" and songbooks (like those made by Ella Fitzgerald) of classic American songs by George Gershwin and Irving Berlin; she also recorded jazz sessions on the EmArcy label (Mercury's jazz label) with trumpeter Clifford Brown, the Count BASIE Orchestra, and other jazz musicians. By the mid-1960s, frustrated by the tactics of record companies trying to sustain her commercially, Vaughan took a five-year hiatus from recording. By the 1970s, her voice had become darker and richer.

Vaughan was noted for a style in which she treated her voice like a jazz instrument rather than as a conduit for the lyrics. A contralto, she sang wide leaps easily, improvised sometimes subtle, sometimes dramatic melodic and rhythmic lines, and made full use of timbral expressiveness—from clear tones to bluesy growls with vibrato. By the end of her career, she had performed in more than sixty countries, in small boîtes and in football stadiums, with jazz trios as well as symphony orchestras. Her signature songs, featured at almost all of her shows, included "Misty," "Tenderly," and "Send In the Clowns." She died of cancer in 1990, survived by one daughter.

BIBLIOGRAPHY

Giddins, Gary. "Sarah Vaughan." In *Rhythm-a-Ning,* New York, 1985, pp. 26–34.

Jones, Max. "Sarah Vaughan." In *Talking Jazz,* New York, 1988, pp. 260–265.

– BUD KLIMENT

VIETNAM WAR

The active American involvement in the Vietnam War (1961–1973) imposed demands for manpower on a populace that grew increasingly less supportive of the conflict as the fighting continued. The Selective Service System, which gathered involuntary recruits for the army and (in much smaller numbers) the Marine Corps and also persuaded potential draftees to volunteer for less dangerous duty in the navy or air force, bore down hardest on those too poor or too poorly educated to take advantage of deferments or exemptions. The draft, for example, called up a disproportionate number of black high school graduates unable to attend college.

Perceived inequities in the draft and racial animosity brought into the services from civilian life contributed to an erosion of discipline and an increase in tensions between whites and blacks. Friction in the ranks gradually abated for several reasons: the adoption in December 1969 of a lottery to reduce loopholes and exemptions in the administration of the draft; the launching in January 1972 of a formal program to assist men and women in uniform and civilian employees to put aside racial prejudice and work together in harmony; the pullout of combat troops from Vietnam in January 1973; and reliance afterward on volunteers to man the peacetime armed forces.

The Gesell Committee

The Vietnam War tested the commitment of the armed forces to racial integration. During the advisory phase (1961–1965), when the United States provided material assistance and combat support for South Vietnam against North Vietnam, a committee headed by Gerhard A. Gesell, a Washington, D.C., attorney and later a federal judge, reviewed the status of racial integration in the services, a task assigned it in the summer of 1962 by Secretary of Defense Robert S. McNamara. The committee issued two reports: the first, in June 1963, dealt with active-duty forces; the second, in November 1964, focused on the National Guard. The Gesell Committee concluded that racial discrimination undermined morale and performance. To eliminate discrimination, the panel recommended that the fight against racism become a responsibility of commanders, who would direct the campaign for equal treatment and opportunity on military and naval installations and also in nearby communities where African-American personnel and their families often had only limited access to housing and public accommodation. In addition, the committee recommended that the federal government should enforce existing civil rights laws in towns and cities near the bases and, if persuasion failed, cut off federal funds for National Guard units that persisted in racial discrimination.

Secretary McNamara tried hard to carry out the committee's recommendations. In 1967, for example, at the request of the state legislature, he had the commander at Fort Meade, Md., declare off-limits to servicemen the rental properties of landlords who discriminated against blacks. Civil rights legislation, especially the Fair Housing Act of April 1968, became part of the campaign against racism that Clark Clifford directed after succeeding McNamara as secretary of defense on March 1 of that year. The National Guard opened its ranks to African Americans, with some states launching intensive recruiting efforts, but the response proved uneven because of a lingering wariness about joining. Certain National Guard units had earned a reputation as agents of repression during the CIVIL RIGHTS MOVEMENT, and as the decade progressed, state authorities frequently called on the National Guard to deal with riots in black communities, further alienating potential African-American recruits. The urban uprisings reached their peak immediately after the murder on April 4, 1968, of the Rev. Dr. Martin Luther KING, Jr., when violence flared in 110 American cities.

The context to the racial tension within the armed forces during the Vietnam era came to be summarized in two catchphrases: black power and white backlash. Many African Americans, especially the younger generation, advocated black power and sought to take control of their own destinies, advocating the employment of violence if necessary. They had grown weary of King's nonviolent struggle, which seemed to depend on shaming an increasingly resistant white America into acknowledging the rights of black citizens and an often insensitive federal government, influenced by the hardening white attitude, into protecting them. The new defensiveness among whites reflected fear that the administration of Lyndon B. Johnson had taken power from them and redistributed it to blacks. White backlash focused on control of public schools—many of which had yet to integrate more than a decade after BROWN V. BOARD OF EDUCATION OF TOPEKA, KANSAS—and on jobs at a time when industrial employment was shrinking. As the armed forces expanded to fight the war in Vietnam, many new recruits, white and black, had attitudes shaped by these resentments. The armed forces, disproportionately composed of urban blacks and rural (often conservative) Southerners, were a cynosure for the racial tension of the 1960s.

While the racial divisions within society grew deeper, the nature of the Vietnam conflict changed. From 1965 through early 1968, the United States in effect took over the fighting from the South Vietnamese, and the resulting increase in American casualties created a demand for manpower and also strengthened opposition to the conflict. The communist Tet offensive—so called because it was timed to coincide with Tet, the celebration of the lunar new year, on January 31, 1968—disillusioned the Johnson administration, which imposed a ceiling on the American commitment and took the initial steps to return the burden of the fighting to the South Vietnamese, the policy of so-called Vietnamization. President Richard M. Nixon took office in January 1969 and soon began to implement this policy. He withdrew those Marine Corps and army forces that suffered the greatest proportion of American casualties and included a large proportion of draftees. Since the last

American ground combat troops did not leave South Vietnam until August 1972, opposition to the war and the need for manpower faded slowly.

Wartime Expansion

As the United States took over the war, commanders at every level tended to ignore the interrelationship of racism, morale, and effectiveness. Emphasis shifted from ensuring equal treatment and opportunity by carrying out the reforms recommended by the Gesell Committee to preparing for imminent combat; the former still seemed desirable, but the latter was essential. Meanwhile, the wartime expansion attracted a large number of recruits, whites as well as blacks, whose attitudes reflected the growing racial hostility. An influx of volatile individuals, most of whom entered the service reluctantly, overwhelmed the stable, professional enlisted force toward which Gesell and his colleagues had directed their reforms.

Secretary McNamara hoped to use the wartime demand for manpower to improve opportunities for poorly educated youth, especially African Americans. In August 1966 he launched Project 100,000, intended to admit that number of recruits who did not score highly enough on the classification tests to meet the usual standards for enlistment and give them training they could use to obtain jobs after leaving the service. In effect, the secretary of defense anticipated events, for by the time the Vietnam War ended, standards had so declined that the armed forces were routinely accepting persons who would have qualified for Project 100,000. He failed nonetheless to achieve his ultimate goal. Those males with the lowest scores gravitated toward assignments, such as rifleman in the army or Marine Corps, that taught few skills transferable to civilian life.

Project 100,000, along with inequities in the draft such as the liberal granting of educational deferments, enhanced the perception that the Vietnam War was a rich man's war but a poor man's fight, with African Americans doing a disproportionate share of the fighting. During the buildup of American strength, the Selective Service System inducted as many as 60 percent of the blacks eligible for the draft, compared to 30 percent of whites. The disparity may have reflected the few African Americans on draft boards throughout the nation, a mere 1.5 percent of the total membership in 1967 and only 6.6 percent after a three-year effort to increase their number. Moreover, poorer blacks lacked the opportunity to obtain deferments available to middle-class whites who could continue their education, document medical disability, or simply take advantage of counseling on ways to beat the draft. Upon entering the service, educational disadvantages resulting from second-rate schools and at times outright racism—African-American servicemen tended to emphasize the latter—steered blacks into combat units, although the prestige and extra pay associated with hazardous duty proved attractive to some. No longer did military service seem to offer better treatment and opportunity than civilian employment, as indicated by declining reenlistment rates for African Americans—from 66.5 percent in 1966 to 31.7 percent in 1967 to just 12.8 percent in 1970.

As the war intensified after 1965, opposition to American involvement became an important issue among African-American activists. In the last years of his life, Martin Luther King, Jr., was vociferous in his opposition to the war, as were many of the various groups in the Black Power movement. In 1967, when heavyweight boxing champion Muhammad ALI refused induction into the army, he was stripped of his title. However, opposition to the war was far from unanimous among African Americans. In addition to the many members of the armed forces, some leaders of the CIVIL RIGHTS MOVEMENT, including Whitney M. Young, Jr., and Bayard RUSTIN, either supported or with great reluctance criticized the Johnson administration over the war.

In the last years of his life, Martin Luther King, Jr., was vociferous in his opposition to the war, as were many of the various groups in the Black Power movement.

Racial tensions within the armed forces imposed a strain on the system of military justice as the services tried to cull out undesirables, especially those considered black militants. Many an African-American soldier accepted a general discharge under honorable conditions as an easy way out of the army only to discover that employers sometimes failed to make a distinction between a general and an undesirable, bad conduct, or dishonorable discharge. Punishment, especially that meted out by commanding officers under article 15 of the Uniform Code of Military Justice, also fell more heavily on those categorized as black militants, and a series of punishments for minor infractions made it more difficult to earn an honorable discharge. In November 1972, after investigating the administration of military justice, a majority of an interracial panel with military and civilian members warned of systemic discrimination, in which the armed forces as an institution downgraded the ability of minorities to profit from training, accept discipline, or carry out assignments.

Spreading Violence

The perception of discrimination against African Americans undermined respect for military law, and the resulting feeling of contempt reinforced the existing injustice, crowding stockades with blacks. At Long Binh in South Vietnam, overcrowding and cruel conditions—maritime shipping containers sometimes served as cells—contributed to a riot in August 1968 that pitted black prisoners against a predominantly white guard force.

Before the violence at Long Binh, the murder of Martin Luther King, Jr., in April had led to a series of racial incidents in Southeast Asia. Since the civil rights leader had denounced the war as a waste of scarce resources needed in America's cities, some white servicemen rejoiced in his death. Sailors at Cua Viet donned makeshift white robes and paraded in imitation of the KU KLUX KLAN, and Confederate flags, symbols of slavery, were unfurled over Cam Ranh Bay and Da Nang.

Racial clashes erupted wherever American forces served. In February 1969 the army had to deal with rioting at Fort Benning, Ga., where black soldiers, awaiting discharge after returning from Southeast Asia, vented their frustration at being assigned to night maneuvers or menial labor by attacking white troops. At Camp Lejeune, N.C., recurring violence in the spring of that year resulted in the death of a white marine just returned from South Vietnam. At Goose Bay, Labrador, Canada, during March 1970, a white airman, apparently angered because local white women danced with blacks serving at the air force installation, stabbed one of the African Americans, inflicting superficial wounds and triggering random beatings of whites in retaliation. In July 1970, at Great Lakes Naval Base, Ill., the shore patrol arrested four black WAVES (Women Appointed for Voluntary Emergency Service) for beating up another female sailor, also an African American. A mob of angry male sailors, whites and blacks, gathered, but the authorities defused the explosive situation by explaining that race had not been a factor and that the four women had been placed on report and released. In Europe violence occurred with such frequency that in September 1970 the Department of Defense sent an interracial team headed by Deputy Assistant Secretary of Defense Frank Render II, an African American, to investigate conditions.

To deal with the causes of these incidents and prevent further clashes, the services granted various concessions, substantial as well as symbolic. These included acceptance of a modified Afro hairstyle, toleration of the clenched-fist black power salute, a crackdown on racially offensive terms, and the stocking in exchanges of products used by African Americans and magazines of interest to them. The services also tried to ensure fairness in the administration of justice, in part by commissioning black attorneys and by monitoring article 15 proceedings and the award of other than honorable discharges. Additional measures included the removal of references to race from all records reviewed by promotion boards and further emphasis on the recommendations of the Gesell Committee to attack all forms of racial discrimination on bases and in nearby communities. Finally, the services created discussion groups and councils—ranging from advisory agencies for commanders to mere gripe sessions—to improve communication between the races.

Education in Race Relations

In November 1969 Secretary of Defense Melvin R. Laird established a task force under an African-American officer, air force Col. Lucius D. Theus, to devise a program of education in race relations. The group recommended mandatory courses taught by trained instructors. Laird approved the plan in March 1970, but momentum dissipated. Other reforms seemed to deserve a chance, among them an attempt to steer members of racial minorities into specialties where they remained underrepresented. Moreover, a growing problem of drug abuse consumed resources that might otherwise have been invested in improving race relations.

The recommendations of Theus and his colleagues remained in limbo, approved but not implemented, on May 21, 1971, when, at Travis Air Force Base, Calif., a four-day riot erupted caused by an accumulation of incidents varying from the serious to the trivial, from racial discrimination in off-base housing to a quarrel over music (country and western versus soul). On June 24 the assistant secretary of defense for manpower and reserve affairs assumed responsibility for race relations, advised by the Defense Race Relations Education Board with representatives from each of the services. In January 1972 the Defense Race Relations Institute opened its doors at Patrick Air Force Base, Fla., and began producing instructors to administer the mandatory training in racial harmony.

The program of education that radiated from the Defense Race Relations Institute (known after July 1979 as the Defense Equal Opportunity Management Institute) did not bring immediate harmony to the armed forces. Indeed, some commanders resisted the efforts of junior officers and noncommissioned officers, whose zeal was at times unalloyed with tact. Despite occasional misunderstandings, however, senior officers came to realize the value of the program in promoting racial amity.

As active American involvement in the Vietnam War drew to a close, some ten months after the Defense Race Relations Institute admitted its first class, racial violence jolted the navy. On October 12 and 13, 1972, a brawl between black and white sailors in the port of Olongapao in the Philippines reignited on board the aircraft carrier *Kitty Hawk,* but the ship's executive officer, an African American, restored order. On October 16, when the executive officer of the fleet oiler *Hassayampa* failed to move swiftly against a white sailor accused of stealing from his black shipmates, African Americans in the crew randomly attacked whites until a detachment of marines came on board and halted the violence. Yet another incident occurred on the aircraft carrier *Constellation,* where the crew included a large number of sailors whose scores on the general qualification test would have disqualified them from serving in the navy if the Vietnam conflict had not created a need for men. A decision to give general discharges under honorable conditions to a half dozen African Americans who not only scored poorly on the test but also performed indifferently inspired rumors of mass discharges, and more than a hundred sailors refused to sail with the *Constellation* when the ship left San Diego, Calif. Ten of the dissidents, including all the whites, rejoined the ship in time to sail on November 9. Of those who stayed behind, sixty-nine received new assignments and the

Between 1960 and 1975, several hundred thousand African Americans served in the United States Army in the Vietnam War. Black soldiers played a major role in all of the war's many bitter battles and skirmishes. Here a soldier participates in the battle for Hill 484. (Photographs and Prints Division, Schomburg Center for Research in Black Culture, The New York Public Library, Astor, Lenox and Tilden Foundations)

remaining fifty-one left the service, ten of them with the general discharges under honorable conditions that had triggered the incident.

Racial strife had erupted in the navy despite the vigorous efforts of the chief of naval operations, Admiral Elmo Zumwalt, to ensure equal treatment and opportunity regardless of race. Zumwalt interpreted the incidents in the fall of 1972 as evidence that his reforms were being ignored. His program had encountered strong opposition within the officer corps, and conservatives in Congress, such as Rep. F. Edward Hebert of Louisiana, blamed all the navy's troubles on Zumwalt's "permissiveness." Many of the Zumwalt reforms did not survive his tenure as chief of naval operations, but the program of education in race relations and the objective of equal treatment and opportunity prevailed.

Despite the navy's troubles, race relations in the armed forces were improving as the Vietnam War came to an end. The functioning of the Defense Race Relations Institute and the work of the instructors it trained, reinforced by statements from senior officers and civilian officials, underscored for blacks and whites the importance of racial harmony. As the program of education gathered momentum, the armed forces contracted in size and could no longer could rely on the draft, which survived after 1973 only as a possible source of manpower in some future emergency. Nevertheless, the new all-volunteer armed forces did not lack for recruits. The disappearance of high-paying industrial jobs made the services attractive to whites and blacks, and as the Vietnam War receded into the past, those who entered the service proved more willing than the wartime draftees or reluctant volunteers to conform to those rules and practices designed to promote racial amity.

The Vietnam War had an impact on African Americans and on the military. Black veterans gained access to benefits, but these, especially the payments for education, proved less generous than those allotted after WORLD WAR II, and there were fewer veterans, black or white, to take advantage of them. For many African-American officers, including the future chairman of the Joint Chiefs of Staff, Colin POWELL, the war provided the opportunity for combat commands and rapid advancement through the military hierarchy. Fears that African-American ex-servicemen might take up arms against whites proved groundless. Relative calm prevailed in civil society immediately after the war, and the armed services not only survived the turmoil of the Vietnam conflict but again attracted black recruits, in part because of poor opportunities for civilian employment. Indeed, the postwar all-volunteer armed forces had a greater proportion of African Americans than did the wartime services—15 percent in 1974 compared to 11 percent in 1970, with a higher percentage yet to come—though the numbers remained concentrated in the army and the Marine Corps and, except for the army, in the enlisted ranks, rather than being divided more evenly among the services and between commissioned and enlisted personnel.

BIBLIOGRAPHY

Boyd, George M. "A Look at Racial Polarity in the Armed Forces." *Air University Review* 21 (September-October 1970): 42–50.

Foner, Jack S. "The Vietnam War and Black Servicemen." In *Blacks and the Military in American History: A New Perspective.* New York, 1974, pp. 201–260.

Glines, C. V. "Black vs. White—Trouble in the Ranks." *Armed Forces Management* 16 (June 1970): 20–27.

MacGregor, Morris J., Jr. "Equal Treatment and Opportunity Redefined." In *Defense Studies: Integration of the Armed Forces, 1940–1965.* Washington, D.C., 1981, pp. 530–555.

Moskos, Charles C., Jr. "Surviving the War in Vietnam." In Charles R. Figley and Seymour Leventman, eds. *Strangers at Home: Vietnam Veterans Since the War.* New York, 1980, pp. 71–85.

Nalty, Bernard C. "From Nonviolence to Violence," "Turbulence in the Armed Forces," and "Emphasis on Education." In *Strength for the Fight: A History of Black Americans in the Military.* New York, 1986, pp. 287–332.

Ryan, Paul B. "USS *Constellation* Flare-Up: Was It Mutiny?" *U.S. Naval Institute Proceedings* 102 (February 1975): 68–83.

Shields, Patricia M. "The Burden of the Draft: The Vietnam Years." *Journal of Political and Military Sociology* 9 (Fall 1981): 215–228.

Spector, Ronald H. "The End of Racial Harmony." In *After Tet: The Bloodiest Year in Vietnam.* New York, 1993, pp. 242–259.

Terry, Wallace. *Bloods: An Oral History of the Vietnam War by Black Veterans.* New York, 1984.

— BERNARD C. NALTY

VOODOO

Voodoo, also spelled Vodou (following the official Haitian Creole orthography) or vodoun, refers to traditional religious practices in Haiti and in Haitian-American communities such as the sizable ones in New York City and Miami. New Orleans has the oldest Haitian immigrant community; it dates from the eighteenth century. In New Orleans priests and priestesses are sometimes called "voodoos," and throughout the southern United States the term is also used as a verb, to "voodoo" someone, meaning to bewitch or punish by magical means. More frequently "voodoo," or "hoodoo"—as well as "conjure," "rootwork," and "witchcraft"—is a term used to refer to a diverse collection of traditional spiritual practices among descendants of African slaves in the United States.

Haiti, a small, mountainous, and impoverished West Indian country, was a French slave colony and a major sugar producer during the eighteenth century. The strongest African influences on Haitian vodou came form the Fon and Mahi peoples of old Dahomey (now the Republic of Benin); the Yoruba peoples, mostly in Nigeria; and the Kongo peoples of Angola and Zaire. The term *vodun* is West African, probably Ewe, in origin and came to the Western Hemisphere with Dahomean slaves. Today, "vodun" is the most common Fon term for a traditional spirit or deity.

Haitian Vodou is said to have played a key role in the only successful slave revolution in the history of trans-Atlantic slavery, the plotters being bound to one another by a blood oath taken during a Vodou ceremony. The ceremony, conducted by the legendary priest Makandal, took place in Bois Cayman in northern Haiti. It is also claimed that word of the uprising spread via Vodou talking drums, and Vodou charms gave strength and courage to the rebels.

Voodoo refers to traditional religious practices in Haiti and in Haitian-American communities.

Haiti declared its independence in 1804, when the United States and much of Europe still held slaves. For approximately fifty years the Catholic church refused to send priests to Haiti, and for nearly a century the struggling black republic was economically isolated from the larger world. Political concerns played a major role in shaping the negative image of Haitian Vodou in the West. Vodou has been caricatured as a religion obsessed with sex, blood, death, and evil. The reality of Haitian Vodou, a religion that blends African traditions with Catholicism, is strikingly different from the stereotypes.

Following independence, large numbers of Haitians acquired small plots of land and became subsistence farmers. This agricultural base distinguishes Vodou from other New World African religions. Central to Vodou are three loyalties: to land (even urban practitioners return to conduct ceremonies on ancestral land), to family (including the dead), and to the Vodou spirits. Most Haitians do not call their religion Vodou, a word that more precisely refers to one style of drumming and dancing. Haitians prefer a verbal form. "Li sevi lwa-yo," they say, he (or she) serves the spirits. Most spirits have two names, a Catholic saint's name and an African name. Daily acts of devotion include lighting candles and pouring libations. Devotees wear a favored spirit's color and observe food and behavior prohibitions the spirits request. When there are special problems, they make pilgrimages to Catholic shrines and churches and undertake other trials. Most important, they stage elaborate ceremonies that include singing, drumming, dancing, and sumptuous meals, the most prestigious of which necessitate killing an animal. Possession, central in Vodou, provides direct communication with the *lwa,* or spirits. A devotee who becomes a "horse" of one of the spirits turns over body and voice to that lwa. The spirit can then sing and dance with the faithful, bless them, chastise them, and give advice. In Vodou persons are defined by webs of relationship with family, friends, ancestors, and spirits. The central work of Vodou ritual, whether performed in a community setting or one-on-one, is enhancing and healing relationships. Gifts of praise, food, song and dance are necessary to sustain spirits and ancestors and to enable them to reciprocate by providing wisdom and protection to the living.

The large Haitian immigrant communities that have grown up in the United States over the last forty years are thriving centers for Vodou practice. Hundreds of Vodou healers serve thousands of clients who are taxi drivers, restaurant workers, and nurse's aides. Most of the rituals performed in Haiti are now also staged, albeit in truncated form, in living rooms and basements in New York and Miami. Vodou "families" provide struggling immigrants with connections to Haitian roots and an alternative to American individualism.

Voodoo in New Orleans is more distant from its Haitian roots. Scholars believe there were three generations of women called Marie Laveau who worked as spiritual counselors in New Orleans. The first was a slave brought from Haiti to Louisiana during the time of the slave revolution. The most famous Marie Laveau, the "voodoo queen of New Orleans," born in 1827, was the granddaughter of this slave woman. Her religion was a distillation of Haitian Vodou. She kept a large snake on her altar (a representative of the spirit Danbala Wedo), went into possession while dancing in Congo Square, presided over an elaborate annual ceremony on the banks of Lake Pontchartrain on St. John's Eve (June 24), and above all, worked with individual clients as a spiritual adviser, healer, and supplier of charms, or gris-gris. Contemporary New Orleans voodoo is largely limited to these last activities.

Hoodoo, or voodoo as practiced throughout the American South, is similarly limited to discrete client/practitioner interactions. This type of voodoo is not a child of Haiti but the legacy of Dahomean and Kongo persons among North American slaves. As with Haitian Vodou, engagement with hoodoo has typically worked as a supplement to Christianity, most likely because hoodoo addresses issues Christianity ignores—issues of spiritual protection, romantic love, and luck. Harry M. Hyatt said it well: "To catch a spirit or to protect your spirit against the catching or to release your caught spirit—this is the complete theory and practice of hoodoo." The spiritual powers used in voodoo or hoodoo are morally neutral (e.g., souls of persons not properly buried) and can therefore be used constructively or destructively. Yet clear moral distinctions in how they are used are not always easy to make.

In hoodoo the illness in one person may be traced to an emotion in another, jealousy being the most destructive. In such a case, attacking the jealous person may be the only way to a cure. A related dynamic emerges in love magic, a very common type of healing that inevitably tries to control another's will. Zora Neale HURSTON collected this cure for a restless husband: "Take sugar, cinnamon and mix together: Write name of a husband and wife nine times. Roll paper . . . and put in a bottle of holy water with sugar and honey. Lay it under the back step." There have been root doctors—conjure men and women—who have used their powers unethically and maliciously, but hoodoo's fear-provoking reputation is unmerited. Most hoodoo or voodoo is of the type described in Hurston's example.

BIBLIOGRAPHY

Brown, Karen McCarthy. *Mama Lola: A Vodou Priestess in Brooklyn.* Los Angeles and Berkeley, 1991.

———. "The Power to Heal: Reflections on Women, Religion, and Medicine." In Clarissa W. Atkinson, Constance H. Buchanan, and Margaret R. Miles, eds. *Shaping New Vision: Gender and Values in American Culture.* Ann Arbor, Mich., 1987, pp. 123–141.

Deren, Maya. *Divine Horsemen: The Voodoo Gods of Haiti.* 1970. Reprint. New Paltz, N.Y., 1983.

Herskovits, Melville. *Life in a Haitian Valley.* Garden City, N.Y., 1971.

Hurston, Zora Neale. "Hoodoo in America." *Journal of American Folklore* 44 (1931): 316–417.

———. *Mules and Men.* New York, 1970.

Hyatt, Harry Middleton. *Hoodoo-Conjuration-Witchcraft-Rootwork: Beliefs Accepted by Many Negroes and White Persons, These Being Orally Recorded Among Blacks and Whites.* Hannibal, Mo., 1970.

Laguerre, Michel S. *American Odyssey: Haitians in New York City.* Ithaca, N.Y., 1984.

Metraux, Alfred. *Voodoo in Haiti.* New York, 1972.

– KAREN MCCARTHY BROWN

WALCOTT, DEREK ALTON

Derek Alton Walcott (January 23, 1930–), poet, playwright, and essayist. The son of Warwick Walcott, a civil servant and skilled painter in watercolor who wrote verse, and Alix Walcott, a school teacher who took part in amateur theater, Derek Walcott was born along with a twin brother in Castries, Saint Lucia, a small island in the Lesser Antilles of the West Indies. He grew up in a house he describes as haunted by the absence of a father who had died quite young, because all around the drawing room were his father's watercolors. His beginnings as an artist, he regards, therefore, as a natural and direct inheritance: "I feel that I have continued where my father left off." After completing St. Mary's College in his native Saint Lucia, he continued his education at the University of the West Indies in Kingston, Jamaica.

His literary career began in 1948 with his first book of verse, *25 Poems* (1948), followed not long thereafter by *Epitaph for the Young, XII Cantos* (1949), and *Poems* (1951), all privately published in the Caribbean. The decade of the 1950s, however, marked the emergence of his reputation as a playwright-director in Trinidad. His first theater piece, *Henri Cristophe* (1950), a historical play about the tyrant-liberator of Haiti, was followed by a series of well-received folk-dramas in verse. *The Sea at Dauphin* (1954), *Ione* (1957), and *Ti-Jean and His Brothers* (1958) are usually cited among the most noteworthy, along with his most celebrated dramatic work, *Dream on Monkey Mountain,* awarded an Obie, which he began in the late 1950s but did not produce until 1967 in Toronto. After a brief stay in the United States as a Rockefeller Fellow, Walcott returned to Trinidad in 1959 to become founding director of the Trinidad Theatre Workshop. He continues to work as a dramatist, and he is still more likely to be identified by a West Indian audience as a playwright.

Walcott's international debut as a poet came with *In a Green Night: Poems 1948–1960* (1962), followed shortly thereafter by *Selected Poems* (1964), established the qualities usually identified with his verse: virtuosity in traditional, particularly European literary forms; enthusiasm for allegory and classical allusion for which he is both praised and criticized; and the struggle within himself over the cruel history and layered cultural legacy of Africa and Europe reflected in the Caribbean landscape which some critics have interpreted as the divided consciousness of a Caribbean ex-colonial in the twilight of empire. A prolific quarter-century of work has been shaped by recurrent patterns of departure, wandering, and return, in his life as well as in his poetry, and a powerful preoccupation with the visual imagery of the sea, beginning with *Castaway and Other Poems* (1965), in which he establishes an imaginative topography (e.g., of "seas and coasts as white pages"), and a repertory of myths, themes, and motifs (e.g., of "words like migrating birds") for the titular exile, a repertory that recurs in later volumes.

In *The Gulf and Other Poems* (1969), reprinted with *Castaway and Other Poems* in a single volume as *The Gulf* (1970) in the United States, he sounds an ever more personal note as he considers the Caribbean from the alienating perspective of the political turbulence of the late 1960s in the southern and Gulf states of the United States. In *Another Life* (1973), his book-length self-portrait both as a young man and at forty-one, he contemplates the suicide of his mentor and alter-ego with whom he discovered the promise, and the disappointment, of their lives dedicated to art. In *Seagrapes* (1976) he identifies the Caribbean wanderer as caught up in the same ancient and unresolved dilemmas as the exiles Adam and Odysseus, whose pain the poems of a West Indian artist, like the language of the Old Testament and the Greek and Latin classics, can console but never cure.

At his most eloquent in *The Star-Apple Kingdom* (1979), Walcott fingers the rosary of the Antilles in the title poem in order to expose the inhumanity and corruption belied by the gilt-framed Caribbean pastoral of the colonialist's star-apple kingdom, and in the volume's other verse narrative, "The Schooner Flight," he finds a powerful voice in the West Indian vernacular of the common man endowed with "no weapon but poetry and the lances of palms of the sea's shiny shields." In *The Fortunate Traveler* (1981) he sounds repeated and painful notes of exhaustion, isolation, and disappointment of the peripatetic poet in exile and at home, perhaps most sharply in the satirical mode of the *kaiso* vernacular of "The Spoiler Returns."

In *Midsummer* (1984), published in his fifty-fourth year, he probes the situation of the poet as prodigal *nel mezzo del camin* of exile in fifty-four untitled stanzas of elegiac meter. In *The Arkansas Testament* (1987), divided into sections "Here" and "Elsewhere" recalling the divisions of "North" and "South" of *The Fortunate Traveler,* he succumbs once again to pangs of art's estrangement. However, in *Omeros* (1990), his overlay of his problematic but richly figured Caribbean environment with Homer's transformative Mediterranean domain in his most ambitious verse narrative yet, he weaves together the myths, themes, motifs, and imaginary geography of a prolific career to attempt a consummation and reconciliation of the psychic divisions and the spiritual and moral wounds of history and exile in the visionary and restorative middle passage of Achilles, the West Indian fisherman, to the ancestral slave coast of Africa and back to the island, once named for Helen, where he was born.

Although he has described himself as a citizen of "no nation but the imagination," and has lived as an international bard, directing plays, creating poetry, and teaching at a number of colleges and universities, he has remained faithful to the Caribbean as his normative landscape. His affirmation of identity and of the significance of myth over history for the poetic imagination is inseparable from a discussion of the historic drama played out over recent centuries across the islands of the Caribbean and from which the odyssean wayfarer ventures in a lifelong cycle of escape and return. This profound engagement with the Caribbean, explored in a series of early essays, "What the Twilight Says: An Overture," "Meanings," and "The Muse of History," and restated in his Nobel lecture "The Antilles: Fragments of Epic Memory," is summed up in a particularly poignant credo: "I accept this archipelago of the Americas. I say to the ancestor who sold me, and to the ancestor who bought me . . . and also you, father in the filth-ridden gut of the slave ship . . . to you inwardly forgiven grandfathers, I like the more honest of my race, give a strange thanks. I give the strange and bitter and yet ennobling thanks for the monumental groaning and soldering of two great worlds, like the halves of a fruit seamed by its own bitter juices, that exiled from your own Edens you have placed me in the wonder of another, that was my inheritance and your gift."

Although Walcott has described himself as a citizen of "no nation but the imagination," he has remained faithful to the Caribbean as his normative landscape.

Since 1981 Walcott has been a professor of English and creative writing at Boston University. In 1992 he was awarded the Nobel Prize for literature.

BIBLIOGRAPHY

Atlas, James. "Poet of Two Worlds." *New York Times Magazine* (May 23, 1982).

Goldstraw, Irma E. *Derek Walcott: An Annotated Bibliography.* New York: Garland, 1984.

— JAMES DE JONGH

WALKER, ALICE

Alice Walker (February 9, 1944–), novelist. Alice Walker was born in Eatonton, Ga., the eighth child of sharecroppers Willie Lee and Minnie Lou Grant Walker. The vision in Walker's right eye was destroyed when she was eight years old by a brother's BB gun shot, an event that caused her to become an introverted child. Six years later, Walker's self-confidence and commitment to school increased dramatically after a minor surgical procedure removed disfiguring scar tissue from around her injured eye. Encouraged by her family and community, Walker won a scholarship for the handicapped and matriculated at Spelman College in 1961.

After two years, Walker transferred to Sarah Lawrence College because she felt that Spelman stifled the intellectual growth and maturation of its students, an issue she explores in the novel *Meridian.* At Sarah Lawrence, Walker studied works by European and white American writers, but the school failed to provide her with an opportunity to explore the intellectual and cultural traditions of black people. Walker sought to broaden her education by traveling to Africa during the summer before her senior year. During her stay there, Walker became pregnant, and the urgency of her desire to terminate the pregnancy (she was prepared to commit suicide had she not been able to get an abortion), along with her experiences in Africa and as a participant in the CIVIL RIGHTS MOVEMENT, became the subject of her first book, a collection of poems entitled *Once* (1968).

Walker moved to Mississippi in 1965, where she taught, worked with Head Start programs, and helped to register voters. There she met and married Melvyn Leventhal, a civil rights lawyer whom she subsequently divorced (a daughter, Rebecca, was born in 1969), and wrote her first novel, *The Third Life of Grange Copeland* (1970), a chilling exploration of the causes and consequences of black intrafamilial violence. While doing research on black folk medicine for a story that became "The Revenge of Hannah Kemhuff," collected in *In*

Love and Trouble (1973), Walker first learned of Zora Neale HURSTON.

In Hurston, Walker discovered a figure who had been virtually erased from American literary history in large part because she held views—on the beauty and complexity of black southern rural culture; on the necessity of what Walker termed a "womanist" critique of sexism; and on racism and sexism as intersecting forms of oppression—for which she had herself been condemned. In Hurston, Walker found legitimacy for her own literary project. Walker obtained a tombstone for Hurston's grave, which proclaimed her "A Genius of the South," and focused public attention on her neglected work, including the novel *Their Eyes Were Watching God.*

In her influential essay "In Search of Our Mothers' Gardens" Walker asked, with Hurston and other marginalized women in mind, "How was the creativity of the black woman kept alive, year after year and century after century?" Some of the most celebrated of Walker's works—from the short stories "Everyday Use" and "1955" to the novel *The Color Purple* (1982)—explore this question. By acknowledging her artistic debt to writers like Phillis WHEATLEY, Virginia Woolf, and Hurston, as well as to her own verbally and horticulturally adept mother, Walker encouraged a generation of readers and scholars to question traditional evaluative norms.

After *In Love and Trouble,* Walker published several novels (including *Meridian, The Temple of My Familiar,* and *Possessing the Secret of Joy),* volumes of poetry (including *Horses Make a Landscape Look More Beautiful*), collections of essays, and another short story collection, *You Can't Keep a Good Woman Down* (1981). In all these works, she examined the racial and gendered inequities that affect black Americans generally and black women in particular. The most celebrated and controversial of these works is her Pulitzer Prize- and National Book Award-winning epistolary novel, *The Color Purple,* which explores, among other matters, incest, marital violence, lesbianism, alternative religious practices, and black attitudes about gender. Since the early 1980s, Walker has lived in northern California and continues to produce work that challenges and inspires its readers.

BIBLIOGRAPHY

Awkward, Michael. *Inspiriting Influences: Tradition, Revision, and Afro-American Women's Novels.* New York, 1989.

– MICHAEL AWKWARD

WALKER, DAVID

David Walker (c. 1785–June 28, 1830), civil rights activist and pamphleteer. Born free in Wilmington, N.C., the son of a free white mother and a slave father, David Walker traveled extensively in the South and observed the cruelty of slavery firsthand. Little is known about his life until he settled in Boston, where he was living as early as 1826. A tall, dark-complexioned mulatto, he operated a clothing store, selling both new and second-hand clothes, and became a leader in Boston's black community. Walker was a member of Father Snowden's Methodist Church, and was active in the Massachusetts General Colored Association formed in 1826. He was a contributor of funds to emancipate George M. Horton, a slave poet in North Carolina, and also served as an agent for *Freedom's Journal* (New York), established in 1827. Walker and his wife, Eliza, had one son, Edwin G. Walker, who later became the first black elected to the Massachusetts legislature.

Walker represented a new generation of black leaders forged by the experience of creating the first extensive free black communities in urban centers of the United States in the half-century after the American Revolution. The achievement of African Americans in establishing institutions (churches, schools, and mutual aid and fraternal societies) and in producing leaders (ministers, educators, businessmen) emboldened some in Walker's generation to challenge the reigning view among whites that African Americans, even if freed, were destined to remain a degraded people, a caste apart, better served by the removal of free blacks to Africa, which became the objective of the AMERICAN COLONIZATION SOCIETY (ACS), formed in 1817 by leading statesmen and clergy.

In an address in 1828 delivered before the Massachusetts General Colored Association, Walker laid out a strategy of opposition. Overcoming resistance to organization from within the black community, Walker and others recognized the need for a formal association to advance the race by uniting "the colored population, so far, through the United States of America, as may be practicable and expedient; forming societies, opening, extending, and keeping up correspondences" (*Freedom's Journal,* December 19, 1828). Presaging his famous *Appeal to the Colored Citizens of the World,* Walker sought to arouse blacks to mutual aid and self-help, to cast off passive acquiescence in injustice, and to persuade his people of the potential power that hundreds of thousands of free blacks possessed once mobilized.

Published in 1829, Walker's *Appeal* aimed at encouraging black organization and individual activism. It went through three editions in two years, each one longer than the previous one, the final version reaching eighty-eight pages. For many readers, the most startling aspect of the *Appeal* was its call for the violent revolt of slaves against their masters. But Walker was also vitally concerned with the institutions of free blacks in the North. Walker understood that the formation of organizations such as the Massachusetts General Colored Association and the appearance of *Freedom's Journal* in 1827 were evidence of a rising tide of black opposition to slavery and racism. Walker, along with many African-American activists of his era, was profoundly opposed to the African colonization schemes of the American Colonization Society. Colonizationists ignored and suppressed the prevailing black opposition and sought support among African Americans. For Walker, colonization represented an immediate threat to any long-term hopes of black advancement since its cardinal assumption was that such advancement was impossible.

Walker's *Appeal* was thus much more than a cry of conscience, for all its impassioned rhetoric. Despite its rambling organization, its prophetic denunciations of injustice and apocalyptic predictions, the *Appeal* forms a complex, cogent argument with political purpose: to persuade blacks to struggle with whites to abandon colonization and to strive toward racial equality. The essay culminates in an attack on colonization and concludes with an affirmation of the *Declaration of Independence.*

Few documents in American history have elicited such diverse contemporary and historical evaluations as Walker's Appeal.

Walker aimed the *Appeal* at two audiences simultaneously. His first target was blacks, whose achievements in history, Walker argued, rebutted the degraded view popularized by colonizationists and the "suspicion" of Thomas Jefferson of inherent black intellectual inferiority. Walker insisted on the importance of black self-help through rigorous education and occupational training to refute Jefferson and others. He was also unsparing in his condemnation of the ignorance and passivity of free blacks and the complicity of the enslaved, their acquiescence in helping to sustain the American racial regime. Yet in justifying physical resistance—the element which most alarmed many readers in his own day and since—Walker carefully qualified his views. He relied primarily on the power of persuasion to convince white people to recognize that slavery and racism perverted Christianity and republicanism, though his apocalyptic warnings undoubtedly were designed to stir fear in the hearts of tyrants.

Walker succeeded. He circulated copies of the *Appeal* through the mails and via black and white seamen who carried them to southern ports in Virginia, North Carolina, Georgia, and Louisiana. Southern leaders became alarmed and adopted new laws against teaching free blacks to read or write and demanded that Mayor Harrison Gray Otis of Boston take action against Walker. Otis gave assurances that Walker's was an isolated voice, without sympathy in the white community, but Walker had violated no laws. Georgians, however, placed a large sum on Walker's head. In 1830, Walker died from causes unknown amid suspicion, never confirmed, of foul play.

Few documents in American history have elicited such diverse contemporary and historical evaluations as Walker's *Appeal.* Benjamin Lundy, the pioneer abolitionist, condemned it as incendiary. William Lloyd Garrison admired the *Appeal's* "impassioned and determined spirit," and its "bravery and intelligence," but thought it "a most injudicious publication, yet warranted by the creed of an independent people." The black leader Henry Highland Garnet in 1848 proclaimed it "among the first, and . . . the boldest and most direct appeals in behalf of freedom, which was made in the early part of the Antislavery Reformation." In 1908 a modern white historian, Alice D. Adams, deemed it "a most bloodthirsty document," while in 1950 the African-American scholar Saunders Redding thought "it was scurrilous, ranting, mad—but these were the temper of the times." In their biography of their father, the Garrison children probably came closest to the truth about Walker: "his noble intensity, pride, disgust, fierceness, his eloquence, and his general intellectual ability have not been commemorated as they deserve."

BIBLIOGRAPHY

Aptheker, Herbert. *"One Continual Cry": David Walker's Appeal to the Colored Citizens of the World (1829–1830).* New York, 1965.

Garrison, W. P., and F. J. Garrison. *William Lloyd Garrison, 1805–1879. The Story of His Life, Told by His Children.* Vol. 1. New York, 1885.

Horton, James O., and Lois E. Horton. *Black Bostonians.* New York, 1979.

Litwack, Leon F. *North of Slavery: The Negro in the Free States, 1790–1860.* Chicago, 1961.

– PAUL GOODMAN

WALKER, MADAM C. J.

Madam C. J. Walker (December 23, 1867–May 25, 1919), entrepreneur, hair-care industry pioneer, philanthropist, and political activist. Born Sarah Breedlove to ex-slaves Owen and Minerva Breedlove on a Delta, La., cotton plantation, she was orphaned by age seven. She lived with her sister, Louvenia, in Vicksburg, Miss., until 1882, when she married Moses McWilliams, in part to escape Louvenia's cruel husband. In 1887, when her daughter, Lelia (later known as A'lelia Walker), was two years old, Moses McWilliams died. For the next eighteen years she worked as a laundress in St. Louis. But in 1905, with $1.50 in savings, the thirty-seven-year-old McWilliams moved to Denver to start her own business after developing a formula to treat her problem with baldness—an ailment common among African-American women at the time, brought on by poor diet, stress, illness, damaging hair-care treatments, and scalp disease. In January 1906 she married Charles Joseph Walker, a newspaper sales agent, who helped design her advertisements and mail-order operation.

While Madam Walker is often said to have invented the "hot comb," it is more likely that she adapted metal implements popularized by the French to suit black women's hair. Acutely aware of the debate about whether black women should alter the appearance of their natural hair texture, she insisted years later that her Walker System was not intended as a hair "straightener," but rather as a grooming method to heal and condition the scalp to promote hair growth and prevent baldness.

From 1906 to 1916 Madam Walker traveled throughout the United States, Central America, and the West Indies promoting her business. She settled briefly in Pittsburgh, establishing the first Lelia College of Hair Culture there in 1908, then moved the company to Indianapolis in 1910, building a factory and vastly increasing her annual sales. Her reputation as a philanthropist was solidified in 1911, when she contributed one thousand dollars to the building fund of the Indianapolis YMCA. In 1912 she and C. J. Walker divorced, but she retained his name. Madam Walker joined her daughter, A'Lelia, and A'Lelia's adopted daughter, Mae (later Mae Walker Perry), in Harlem in 1916. She left the daily management of her manufacturing operation in Indianapolis to her longtime attorney and general manager, Freeman B. Ransom, factory forewoman Alice Kelly, and assistant general manager Robert L. Brokenburr.

Madam Walker's business philosophy stressed economic independence for the 20,000 former maids, farm laborers, housewives, and schoolteachers she employed as agents and factory and office workers. To further strengthen her company, she created the Madam C. J. Walker Hair Culturists Union of America and held annual conventions.

During World War I, she was among those who supported the government's black recruitment efforts and War Bond drives. But after the bloody 1917 East St. Louis riot, she joined the planning committee of the Negro Silent Protest Parade, traveling to Washington to present a petition urging President Wilson to support legislation that would make lynching a federal crime. As her wealth and visibility grew, Walker became increasingly outspoken, joining those blacks who advocated an alternative peace conference at Versailles after the war to monitor proceedings affecting the world's people of color. She intended her estate in Irvington-on-Hudson, N.Y.—Villa Lewaro, which was designed by black architect Vertner W. Tandy—not only as a showplace but as an inspiration to other blacks.

During the spring of 1919, aware that her long battle with hypertension was taking its final toll, Madam Walker revamped her will, directing her attorney to donate five thousand dollars to the NATIONAL ASSOCIATION FOR THE ADVANCEMENT OF COLORED PEOPLE's antilynching campaign and to contribute thousands of dollars to black educational, civic, and social institutions and organizations.

When she died at age fifty-one, at Villa Lewaro, she was widely considered the wealthiest black woman in America and was reputed to be the first African-American woman millionaire. Her daughter, A'Lelia Walker—a central figure of the HARLEM RENAISSANCE—succeeded her as president of the Mme. C. J. Walker Manufacturing Company.

Walker's significance is rooted not only in her innovative (and sometimes controversial) hair-care system, but also in her advocacy of black women's economic independence and her creation of business opportunities at a time when most black women worked as servants and sharecroppers. Her entrepreneurial strategies and organizational skills revolutionized what would become a multibillion-dollar ethnic hair-care and cosmetics industry by the last decade of the twentieth century. Having led an early life of hardship, she became a trailblazer of black philanthropy, using her wealth and influence to leverage social, political, and economic rights for women and blacks. In 1992 Madam Walker was elected to the National Business Hall of Fame.

BIBLIOGRAPHY

Bundles, A'Lelia Perry. *Madam C. J. Walker—Entrepreneur.* New York, 1991.

Giddings, Paula. *When and Where I Enter.* New York, 1984.

Logan, Rayford W., and Michael R. Winston. *Dictionary of American Negro Biography.* New York, 1982.

The Textbook of the Madam C. J. Walker Schools of Beauty Culture. Indianapolis, 1928.

— A'LELIA PERRY BUNDLES

WASHINGTON, BOOKER TALIAFERRO

Booker Taliaferro Washington (c. 1856–November 14, 1915), educator. Founder of Tuskegee Institute in Alabama and prominent race leader of the late nineteenth and early twentieth centuries, Booker T. Washington was born a slave on the plantation of James Burroughs near Hale's Ford, Va. He spent his childhood as a houseboy and servant. His mother was a cook on the Burroughs plantation, and he never knew his white father. With Emancipation in 1865, he moved with his family—consisting of his mother, Jane; his stepfather, Washington Ferguson; a half-brother, John; and a half-sister, Amanda—to West Virginia, where he worked briefly in the salt furnaces and coal mines near Malden. Quickly, however, he obtained work as a houseboy in the mansion of the wealthiest white man in Malden, Gen. Lewis Ruffner. There, under the tutelage of the general's wife, Viola Ruffner, a former New England schoolteacher, he learned to read. He also attended a local school for African Americans in Malden.

From 1872 to 1875 Washington attended HAMPTON INSTITUTE, in Hampton, Va., where he came under the influence of the school's founder, Gen. Samuel Chapman Armstrong, who inculcated in Washington the work ethic that would stay with him his entire life and that became a hallmark of his educational philosophy. Washington was an outstanding pupil during his tenure at Hampton and was placed in charge of the Native American students there. After graduation he returned to Malden, where he taught school for several years and became active as a public speaker on local matters, including the issue of the removal of the capital of West Virginia to Charleston.

In 1881, Washington founded a school of his own in Tuskegee, Ala. Beginning with a few ramshackle buildings and a small sum from the state of Alabama, he built Tuskegee Institute into the best-known African-American school in the nation. While not neglecting academic training entirely, the school's curriculum stressed industrial education, training in specific skills and crafts that would prepare students for jobs. Washington built his school and his influence by tapping the generosity of northern philanthropists, receiving donations from wealthy New Englanders and some of the leading industrialists and businessmen of his time, such as Andrew Carnegie, William H. Baldwin, Jr., Julius Rosenwald, and Robert C. Ogden.

In 1882 Washington married his childhood sweetheart from Malden, Fanny Norton Smith, a graduate of Hampton Institute, who died two years later as a result of injuries suffered in a fall from a wagon. Subsequently Washington married Olivia A. Davidson, a graduate of Hampton and the Framingham State Normal School in Massachusetts, who held the title of lady principal of Tuskegee. She was a tireless worker for the school and an effective fund-raiser in her own right. Always in rather frail health, Davidson died in 1889. Washington's third wife, Margaret James Murray, a graduate of Fisk University, also held the title of lady principal and was a leader of the National Association of Colored Women's Clubs and the Southern Federation of Colored Women's Clubs.

Washington's reputation as the principal of Tuskegee Institute grew through the late 1880s and the 1890s; his school was considered the exemplar of industrial education, viewed as the best method of training the generations of African Americans who were either born in slavery or were the sons and daughters of freed slaves. His control of the purse strings of many of the northern donors to his school increased his influence with other African-American schools in the South. His fame and recognition as a national race leader, however, resulted from the impact of a single speech he delivered before the Cotton States and International Exposition in Atlanta, in 1895. This important speech, often called the Atlanta Compromise, is the best single statement of Washington's philosophy of racial advancement and his political accommodation with the predominant racial ideology of his time. For the next twenty years, until the end of his life, Washington seldom deviated publicly from the positions taken in the Atlanta address.

In his speech, Washington urged African Americans to "cast down your bucket where you are"—that is, in the South—and to accommodate to the segregation and discrimination imposed upon them by custom and by state and local laws. He said the races could exist separately from the standpoint of social relationships but should work together for mutual economic advancement. He advocated a gradualist advancement of the race, through hard work, economic improvement, and self-help. This message found instant acceptance from white Americans, north and south, and almost universal approval among African Americans. Even W. E. B. DU BOIS, later one of Washington's harshest critics, wrote to him immediately after the Atlanta address that the speech was "a word fitly spoken."

While Washington's public stance on racial matters seldom varied from the Atlanta Compromise, privately he was a more complicated individual. His voluminous private papers, housed at the Library of Congress, document an elaborate secret life that contradicted many of his public utterances. He secretly financed test cases to challenge JIM CROW laws. He held great power over the African-American press, both north and south, and secretly owned stock in several newspapers. While

Washington himself never held political office of any kind, he became the most powerful African-American politician of his time as an adviser to presidents Theodore Roosevelt and William Howard Taft and as a dispenser of REPUBLICAN PARTY patronage.

Washington's biographer, Louis R. Harlan, called the Tuskegean's extensive political network "the Tuskegee Machine" for its resemblance to the machines established by big-city political bosses of the era. With his network of informants and access to both northern philanthropy and political patronage, Washington could make or break careers, and he was the central figure in African-American public life during his heyday. Arguably no other black leader, before or since, has exerted similar dominance. He founded the National Negro Business League in 1900, to foster African-American business and create a loyal corps of supporters throughout the country. Indirectly he influenced the National Afro American Council, the leading African-American civil rights group of his day. The publication of his autobiography, *Up from Slavery,* in 1901 spread his fame even more in the United States and abroad. In this classic American tale, Washington portrayed his life in terms of a Horatio Alger success story. Its great popularity in the first decade of the twentieth century won many new financial supporters for Tuskegee Institute and for Washington personally.

Washington remained the dominant African-American leader in the country until the time of his death from exhaustion and overwork in 1915. But other voices rose to challenge his conservative, accommodationist leadership. William Monroe TROTTER, the editor of the *Boston Guardian,* was a persistent gadfly. Beginning in 1903 with the publication of Du Bois's *The Souls of Black Folk,* and continuing for the rest of his life, Washington was criticized for his failure to be more publicly aggressive in fighting the deterioration of race relations in the United States, for his avoidance of direct public support for civil rights legislation, and for his single-minded emphasis on industrial education as opposed to academic training for a "talented tenth" of the race. Washington, however, was adept at outmaneuvering his critics, even resorting to the use of spies to infiltrate organizations critical of his leadership, such as the NIAGARA MOVEMENT, led by Du Bois. His intimate friends called Washington "the Wizard" for his mastery of political intrigue and his exercise of power.

Washington's leadership ultimately gave way to new forces in the twentieth century, which placed less emphasis on individual leadership and more on organizational power. The founding of the NATIONAL ASSOCIATION FOR THE ADVANCEMENT OF COLORED PEOPLE (NAACP) in 1909 and of the NATIONAL URBAN LEAGUE in 1911 challenged Washington in the areas of civil rights and for his failure to address problems related to the growth of an urban black population. The defeat of the Republican party in the presidential election of 1912 also spelled the end of Washington's power as a dispenser of political patronage. Nevertheless, he remained active as a speaker and public figure until his death, in 1915, at Tuskegee.

Washington remained the dominant African-American leader in the country until the time of his death from exhaustion and overwork in 1915.

Washington's place in the pantheon of African-American leaders is unclear. He was the first African American to appear on a United States postage stamp (1940) and commemorative coin (1946). While he was eulogized by friend and foe alike at the time of his death, his outmoded philosophy of accommodation to segregation and racism in American society caused his historical reputation to suffer. New generations of Americans, who took their inspiration from those who were more outspoken critics of segregation and the second-class status endured by African Americans, rejected Washington's leadership role. While much recent scholarship has explored his racial philosophy and political activity in considerable depth, he remains a largely forgotten man in the consciousness of the general public, both black and white. In recent years, however, there has been some revival of interest in his economic thought by those who seek to develop African-American businesses and entrepreneurial skills. Indeed, no serious student of the African-American experience in the United States can afford to ignore the lessons that can be gleaned from Washington's life and from the manner in which he exercised power.

BIBLIOGRAPHY

Harlan, Louis R. *Booker T. Washington: The Making of a Black Leader, 1856–1901.* Urbana, Ill., 1972.

———. *Booker T. Washington: The Wizard of Tuskegee, 1901–1915.* Urbana, Ill., 1983.

Harlan, Louis R., and Raymond W. Smock, eds. *The Booker T. Washington Papers.* 14 vols. Urbana, Ill., 1972–1989.

Meier, August. *Negro Thought in America: Racial Ideologies in the Age of Accommodation, 1880–1915.* Ann Arbor, Mich., 1963.

Smock, Raymond W., ed. *Booker T. Washington in Perspective: The Essays of Louis R. Harlan.* Jackson, Miss., 1988.

Washington, Booker T. *Up from Slavery: An Autobiography.* New York, 1901.

– RAYMOND W. SMOCK

WASHINGTON, D.C., RIOT OF 1919

The 1919 riot in Washington, D.C., part of the racial violence of the Red Summer, focused national attention on the issues of violence and racial inequality in the nation's capital. The city's African-American population had increased substantially during the previous years, and racial tension was increased at the end of WORLD WAR I by the increasingly assertive demands of proud black veterans. The riot came about as a result of sensational articles which appeared in the white press, notably the *Washington Post,* during July 1919. Articles focused on an alleged black crime wave and claimed black men had attempted rapes of white women. NATIONAL ASSOCIATION FOR THE ADVANCEMENT OF COLORED PEOPLE (NAACP) officials protested the falsehoods and exaggerations to the newspaper and the federal government, and warned of possible repercussions, but to no avail.

On July 19, *Post* reporters distorted a minor interracial argument, charging that a group of blacks had sexually assaulted a white girl. White sailors and marines, seeking to lynch the black culprits, advanced into African-American areas of Washington, beating black passersby and illegally breaking into black homes. Police dispersed the mob and arrested two sailors. Eight blacks were brought in for questioning. The NAACP implored Secretary of the Navy Josephus Daniels to cancel all naval shore leave, but he refused. Despite the NAACP's demands, no action was taken against the guilty military personnel.

The next night, Sunday, brought massive violence. When police arrested a young black man on a minor charge, a large crowd of blacks and whites gathered. White rioters grabbed the man and began to beat him before he was rescued by police. Sailors and soldiers in the area roamed the streets all night, and attacked at least four other blacks. The following morning, the *Post* offered an unsubstantiated report of a major mobilization of service men in the city. During daylight hours, blacks armed themselves and began attacking whites on streetcars and shooting guns from automobiles. Monday evening the violence escalated. Over 1,000 white rioters converged on the black areas of Washington but were held back by police barricades. Blacks behind the barrier fired on the mob.

The following day, Maj. Gen. William G. Hann took control and called in provost guard troops to supplant ineffective police efforts at riot control. With help from black and white clergy, and the NAACP, the day remained peaceful. During the night, there was a heavy rain, and the riot dissipated. Black leaders were assured there would be no racial discrimination in the sentences given the hundreds of rioters arrested during the riot, but black rioters drew harsh sentences. The NAACP led an unsuccessful drive for executive clemency, and collected 30,000 signatures on a petition.

The underlying causes of the riot remain uncertain. One unique feature of Washington race relations that might have led to the riots was the rise of black economic power in the city. During the 1910s, many southern whites came to the city to take on civil service jobs in the Wilson administration. Blacks faced segregation and exclusion in government work, and left the civil service. The expanding economy during World War I made work in private industry more lucrative than public service, and soon many blacks were making more money than whites, who resented their success.

BIBLIOGRAPHY

Bergman, Peter M. *The Chronological History of the Negro in America.* New York, 1969, p. 388.

Green, Constance McGlaughlin. *The Secret City: a History of Race Relations in the Nation's Capital.* Princeton, N.J., 1967.

— GAYLE T. TATE

WATERS, ETHEL

Ethel Waters (October 31, 1896?-September 1, 1977), singer and actress. Ethel Waters was born in Chester, Pa. She came from a musical family; her father played piano, and her mother and maternal relatives sang. Her first public performance was as a five-year-old billed as Baby Star in a church program. Waters began her singing career in Baltimore with a small vaudeville company where she sang W. C. HANDY's "St. Louis Blues," becoming, apparently, the first woman to sing the song professionally. She was billed as Sweet Mama Stringbean.

About 1919 Waters moved to New York and became a leading entertainer in Harlem, where her first engagement was at a small black club, Edmond's Cellar. As an entertainer, she reached stardom during the HARLEM RENAISSANCE of the 1920s. In 1924, Earl Dancer, later the producer of the Broadway musical *Africana,* got her a booking in the Plantation Club as a replacement for Florence Mills, who was on tour. When Mills returned, Waters toured in Dancer's *Miss Calico.* By then, Waters had begun to establish herself as an interpreter of the blues with such songs as Perry Bradford's "Messin' Around." In 1921, she recorded "Down Home Blues" and "Oh Daddy" for Black Swan Records. The success of her first recording led her to embark on one of the first personal promotion tours in the United States.

In 1932 and 1933 Waters recorded with Duke ELLINGTON and Benny Goodman, respectively. Her ren-

frontier rather than the perceptible oppression of the South or East.

The history of blacks in the West begins with Afro-Spaniards in northern Mexico. These Spanish-speaking blacks accompanied Hernando Cortés and other conquistadors who superimposed Spanish rule over Mexico in 1519. Many of these Afro-Spaniards, and the slaves who were later brought to colonial Mexico, intermarried with the Indian population, generating a large Zambo (part Indian, part African) population; some of these settled on the northern frontier of Mexico, which would later become Texas, California, New Mexico, and Arizona.

The image of the West as a region of hope and opportunity evolved as a consequence of the experiences of black migrants and the attitudes of white settlers.

In 1794, for example, 23 percent of Mexican California's population was classified as mulatto or Zambo. The first census of Los Angeles, in 1781, indicated 56 percent of the original settlers as part black. During the same year, 25 percent of San Jose's population was listed as Zambo or mulatto, as was 14 percent in San Francisco. Similarly, 28 percent of Albuquerque's 1790 population was Zambo or mulatto, and in San Antonio in 1794, 35 percent fell into the two categories.

By the early years of the nineteenth century, African Americans were involved in the fur-trading industry as both traders and trappers, and consequently were responsible for exploring much of the Rocky Mountain region. Trapper Peter Ranne in 1824 was a member of the first party of Americans to reach California overland. One year later, Moses Harris was the first non-Indian to explore the Great Salt Lake region. James Beckworth and Edward Rose, among other "mountain men," traversed much of what would become Montana, Idaho, Wyoming, and Colorado.

Although some black settlers—including the farmers who migrated to Texas or the Pacific Northwest and the miners who participated in the California gold rush of the 1850s—entered the West before the Civil War, the destruction of American slavery in 1865 for the first time allowed for large-scale migration. Between 1870 and 1900, 1,000 blacks homesteaded in Colorado, 4,000 in Nebraska, 40,000 in Kansas, and over 100,000 in Oklahoma. Smaller numbers migrated to California, Montana, the Dakotas, and Arizona. Some southern African Americans organized political migrations to Kansas, Colorado, California, Montana, and Oklahoma, creating all-black settlements such as Boley and Langston in the Oklahoma Territory, Nicodemus in Kansas, and Allensworth in California, to put to practice theories of economic and political self-determination. The largest of these migrations was led by Benjamin "Pap" Singleton, a Tennessee carpenter who in 1874 distributed a circular entitled "The Advantage of Living in a Free State," which extolled the political freedom and economic opportunities in Kansas. Because of his efforts, at least 25,000 blacks settled in Kansas between 1874 and 1880.

Many African Americans manipulated their status as first settlers in a particular frontier region to achieve wealth and prominence. Barney L. Ford, a former slave who arrived in Denver in 1859, had by 1890 become one of the wealthiest men in Colorado. His property, which included a hotel, a dry-goods store, and real estate in Denver and Cheyenne, Wyo., made him a millionaire. Sarah Gammon Bickford, who from 1888 to 1931 owned and operated the water system for Virginia City, Mont., became one of the city's most prominent citizens. William Gross arrived in Seattle in 1861 and opened the city's second hotel, as well as a restaurant and barbershop, and later bought a farm that would become the site of Seattle's black community. Biddy Mason, a former slave, acquired—and donated to African-American community institutions—a fortune in Los Angeles real estate before her death in 1891.

Even those African Americans who were not wealthy often found themselves with uncharacteristic influence over white lives and fates. Wagon trains crossing the Rocky Mountains relied on experienced guides such as Moses Harris and James Beckworth to lead them. When the first settlers arrived in Oregon's Willamette Valley in the 1840s, they found themselves dependent upon two former fur traders, Winslow Anderson and James Saules, for food and provisions. When white farmers moved to the Washington Territory in the 1850s, two African-American homesteaders, George Washington Bush and George Washington Cochrane, were there to lend advice and assistance. In San Francisco in the 1850s, miners bought provisions from West Indian-born merchant William Liedesdorff.

Post-1860 African Americans worked in virtually every western industry, including mining; they participated in the gold rushes to Idaho, Montana, Colorado, and the Black Hills in South Dakota. A few blacks found gold on their claims. Californian Albert Callis amassed $90,000 in gold from his efforts in the 1850s, and John Frazier extracted $100,000 from his Colorado mine in 1866. Thaddeus Mundy, a soldier mustered out of service in Helena, Mont., in 1870, made a strike of $50,000 in nearby Dry Gulch the same year. Of course, most African Americans' experiences in mining camps were similar to that of Sarah Campbell. One of the earliest miners to reach the South Dakota Black Hills in 1874, Campbell never found gold on her claim but made a handsome living cooking, washing, and sewing for other miners.

African-American men also worked in the range cattle industry in virtually every state and territory of the West prior to 1900. They constituted nearly 25 percent, or approximately 9,000, of the 35,000 cowboys in the West between 1860 and 1895. In 1870 one black Texas trail boss, Bose Ikard, created the "Goodnight-Loving Trail" through New Mexico and Colorado, on which at least 100,000 cattle were driven north in fifteen years. Similarly, African-American soldiers after the Civil War were organized into the Ninth and Tenth cavalries and the Twenty-fourth and Twenty-fifth infantries, which were assigned to numerous locations through the West. Such assignments entailed protecting homesteaders, capturing outlaws, and quelling labor unrest. Eleven black soldiers earned the Congressional Medal of Honor while serving in the West.

The postbellum West also included political leaders and civil rights advocates such as William J. Hardin of Denver, who organized the campaign for equal suffrage in the Colorado Territory, and his Kansas counterpart, Charles Langston of Leavenworth. Western newspaper editors such as Philip Bell of the San Francisco *Elevator* and Horace Clayton of the Seattle *Republican* not only defended black rights in the West, but spoke out against the growing southern movement to segregate and disfranchise African Americans in that region.

The image of the West as a region of opportunity for African Americans continued into the twentieth century, even when that image was contradicted by racially based employment restrictions. After 1900, the urban West would be the destination for most African Amer-

Among the black troops employed by the U.S. Army in the Indian Wars in the West after the Civil War were these Seminole scouts, the descendants of escaped slaves. In 1870 they were recruited by the U.S. Army in Mexico, where they had gone before the Civil War to escape reenslavement. They served with distinction until 1881, when the unit was disabled. Most of the scouts, angered by the racism they encountered, returned to Mexico. (Photographs and Prints Division, Schomburg Center for Research in Black Culture, The New York Public Library, Astor, Lenox and Tilden Foundations)

ican western migrants. Yet blacks who moved to western cities between 1900 and 1940 usually found themselves confined to certain occupations: longshoremen, railway porters, hotel cooks and waiters, maids, ship stewards, and cannery workers. A few professionals—physicians, attorneys, ministers, and schoolteachers—provided services for black communities and many whites. Despite palpable poverty stemming from underemployment, black communities in cities such as Denver, San Francisco, Los Angeles, and Seattle nonetheless supported various community institutions—churches, social clubs, political organizations, fraternal groups, as well as civil rights defense organizations like the NATIONAL ASSOCIATION FOR THE ADVANCEMENT OF COLORED PEOPLE (NAACP), the NATIONAL URBAN LEAGUE, and the UNIVERSAL NEGRO IMPROVEMENT ASSOCIATION.

During World War II, the black West was transformed by the influx of thousands of defense workers into the region's shipyards, aircraft factories, and other war-related businesses. Between 1940 and 1950, the total number of African Americans in the region grew 49 percent, from 1,343,930 to 1,996,036. Communities in specific cities grew even more dramatically. Between 1940 and 1944, the combined African-American populations of San Francisco and Oakland jumped from 19,000 to 147,000; Portland's black population rose from 1,300 to 22,000; that in Los Angeles grew from 75,000 to 218,000. Vallejo, Calif., which became a wartime shipbuilding center in the San Francisco Bay Area, saw its black population leap from 0 to 16,000 during the war years.

It was the World War II migration, however, that brought into sharp relief underlying racial tensions and rivalries, as African Americans and Euro-Americans competed for employment and housing. Moreover, the fact that the rapidly rising black populations were now concentrated in segregated residential districts produced de facto school segregation, which exacerbated African Americans' poverty and social alienation. The black communities of the West were increasingly sharing the conditions that had long plagued eastern and southern ghettos.

By the 1960s, such conditions prompted locally based Civil Rights Movements in such cities as Seattle, Denver, and Los Angeles. Organizations such as CORE, the NAACP, and the Urban League, adopting many of the direct-action tactics successfully employed in the South, challenged the major problems of their communities—job discrimination, housing restrictions, and school segregation. As with the southern campaigns, their efforts were not always successful, but these protests registered community dissatisfaction with the evolving conditions in the region and forced political leaders to remove the most egregious examples of discrimination.

The black western migration continued into the 1980s, raising the regional population total by 1990 to 5,290,705. Such growth generated greater power and influence for specific black communities, as in the election of black mayors such as Tom Bradley in Los Angeles, Wellington Webb in Denver, and Norman Rice in Seattle. But persistent unemployment and underemployment, privation, and crime in those communities also suggest that Westerners, despite their region's reputation as the land of hope for African Americans and others, must still address the troubling nexus of race, class, and poverty in the urban milieu.

BIBLIOGRAPHY

Berwanger, Eugene. *The West and Reconstruction.* Urbana, Ill., 1981.

Franklin, Jimmie Lewis. *Journey toward Hope: A History of Blacks in Oklahoma.* Norman, Okla., 1982.

Painter, Nell Irvin. *Exodusters: Black Migration to Kansas after Reconstruction.* New York, 1977.

Porter, Kenneth W. *The Negro on the American Frontier.* New York, 1971.

Savage, W. Sherman. *Blacks in the West.* Westport, Conn., 1976.

Taylor, Quintard. "The Great Migration: The Afro-American Communities of Seattle and Portland during the 40s." *Arizona and the West* 23 (1981): 109–126.

———. "Slaves and Free Men: Blacks in the Oregon Country, 1840–1860." *Oregon Historical Quarterly* 83 (1982): 153–170.

– QUINTARD TAYLOR

WHEATLEY, PHILLIS

Phillis Wheatley (c. 1753–December 5, 1784), poet. Phillis Wheatley was born, according to her own testimony, in Gambia, West Africa, along the fertile lowlands of the Gambia River. She was abducted as a small child of seven or eight, and sold in Boston to John and Susanna Wheatley on July 11, 1761. The horrors of the middle passage very likely contributed to the persistent asthma that plagued her throughout her short life. The Wheatleys apparently named the girl, who had nothing but a piece of dirty carpet to conceal her nakedness, after the slaver, the *Phillis,* that transported her. Nonetheless, unlike most slave owners of the time, the Wheatleys permitted Phillis to learn to read, and her poetic talent soon began to emerge.

Her earliest known piece of writing was an undated letter from 1765 (no known copy now exists) to Samson Occom, the Native American Mohegan minister and one of Dartmouth College's first graduates. The budding poet first appeared in print on December 21, 1767, in the *Newport Mercury* newspaper, when the author was about fourteen. The poem, "On Messrs. Hussey and Coffin," relates how the two gentlemen of the title narrowly escaped being drowned off Cape Cod in Massachusetts. Much of her subsequent poetry deals, as well, with events occurring close to her Boston circle. Of her fifty-five extant poems, for example, nineteen are elegies; all but the last of these are devoted to commemorating someone known by the poet. Her last elegy is written about herself and her career.

In early October 1770, Wheatley published an elegy that was pivotal to her career. The subject of the elegy was George Whitefield, an evangelical Methodist minister and privy chaplain to Selina Hastings, countess of Huntingdon. Whitefield made seven journeys to the American colonies, where he was known as "the Voice of the Great Awakening" and "the Great Awakener." Only a week before his death in Newburyport, Mass., on September 30, 1770, Whitefield preached in Boston, where Wheatley very likely heard him. As Susanna Wheatley regularly corresponded with the countess, she and the Wheatley household may well have entertained the Great Awakener. Wheatley's vivid, ostensibly first-hand account in the elegy, replete with quotations, may have been based on an actual acquaintance with Whitefield. In any case, Wheatley's deft elegy became an overnight sensation and was often reprinted.

It is almost certain that the ship that carried news of Whitefield's death to the countess also carried a copy of Wheatley's elegy, which brought Wheatley to the sympathetic attention of the countess. Such an acquaintance ensured that Wheatley's elegy was also reprinted many times in London, giving the young poet the distinction of an international reputation. When Wheatley's *Poems* was denied publication in Boston for racist reasons, the countess of Huntingdon generously financed its publication in London by Archibald Bell.

Wheatley's support by Selina Hastings and her rejection by male-dominated Boston signal her nourishment as a literary artist by a community of women. All these women—the countess, who encouraged and financed the publication of her *Poems* in 1773; Mary and Susanna Wheatley, who taught her the rudiments of reading and writing; and Obour Tanner, who could empathize probably better than anyone with her condition as a slave—were much older than Wheatley and obviously nurtured her creative development.

During the summer of 1772, Wheatley actually journeyed to England, where she assisted in the preparation of her volume for the press. While in London she enjoyed considerable recognition by such dignitaries as Lord Dartmouth, Lord Lincoln, Granville Sharp (who escorted Wheatley on several tours about London), Benjamin Franklin, and Brook Watson, a wealthy merchant who presented Wheatley with a folio edition of John Milton's *Paradise Lost* and who would later become lord mayor of London. Wheatley was to have been presented at court when Susanna Wheatley became ill. Wheatley was summoned to return to Boston in early August 1773. Sometime before October 18, 1773, she was granted her freedom, according to her own testimony, "at the desire of my friends in England." It seems likely, then, that if Selina Hastings had not agreed to finance Wheatley's *Poems* and if the poet had not journeyed to London, she would never have been manumitted.

As the American Revolution erupted, Wheatley's patriotic feelings began to separate her even more from the Wheatleys, who were loyalists. Her patriotism is clearly underscored in her two most famous Revolutionary War poems. "To His Excellency General Washington" (1775) closes with this justly famous encomium: "A crown, a mansion, and a throne that shine, / With gold unfading WASHINGTON! be thine." "Liberty and Peace" (1784), written to celebrate the Treaty of Paris (September 1783), declares: "And new-born Rome [i.e., America] shall give *Britannia* Law."

Wheatley was the first African American to publish a book, the first woman writer whose publication was nurtured by a community of women, and the first American woman author who tried to earn a living by writing.

Phillis Wheatley's attitude toward slavery has also been misunderstood. Because some of her antislavery statements have been recovered only in the 1970s and '80s, she has often been criticized for ignoring the issue. But her position was clear: In February 1774, for example, Wheatley wrote to Samson Occom that "in every human breast, God has implanted a Principle, which we call Love of Freedom; it is impatient of Oppression, and pants for Deliverance." This letter was reprinted a dozen times in American newspapers over the course of the next twelve months. Certainly Americans of Wheatley's time never questioned her attitude toward slavery after the publication of this letter.

In 1778 Wheatley married John Peters, a free African American who was a jack-of-all-trades, serving in various capacities from storekeeper to advocate for African Americans before the courts. But given the turbulent conditions of a nation caught up in the Revolution, Wheatley's fortunes began to decline steadily. In 1779 she published a set of *Proposals* for a new volume of poems. While the *Proposals* failed to attract subscribers, these *Proposals* attest that the poet had been diligent with her pen since the 1773 *Poems* and that she had indeed produced some 300 pages of new poetry. This volume never appeared, however, and most of its poems are now lost.

Phillis Wheatley Peters and her newborn child died in a shack on the edge of Boston on December 5, 1784. Preceded in death by two other young children, Wheatley's tragic end resembles her beginning in America. Yet Wheatley has left to her largely unappreciative country a legacy of firsts: She was the first African American to publish a book, the first woman writer whose publication was urged and nurtured by a community of women, and the first American woman author who tried to earn a living by means of her writing.

BIBLIOGRAPHY

Davis, Arthur P. "Personal Elements in the Poetry of Phillis Wheatley." *Phylon* 13 (1953): 191–198.

O'Neale, Sondra A. "A Slave's Subtle War: Phillis Wheatley's Use of Biblical Myth and Symbol." *Early American Literature* 21 (1986): 144–165.

Robinson, William H. *Black New England Letters: The Uses of Writing in Black New England.* Boston, 1977.

———, ed. *Critical Essays on Phillis Wheatley.* Boston, 1982.

———, ed. *Phillis Wheatley in the Black American Beginnings.* Detroit, 1975.

Shields, John C. "Phillis Wheatley." In Valerie Smith, gen. ed. *African American Writers.* New York, 1991, pp. 473–491.

———. "Phillis Wheatley and Mather Byles: A Study of Literature Relationship." *College Language Association Journal* 23 (1980): 377–390.

———. "Phillis Wheatley's Struggle for Freedom in Her Poetry and Prose." In John C. Shields, ed. *The Collected Works of Phillis Wheatley.* New York, 1988, pp. 229–270, 324–336.

———. "Phillis Wheatley's Use of Classicism." *American Literature* 52 (1980): 97–111.

– JOHN C. SHIELDS

WHITE, WALTER FRANCIS

Walter Francis White (July 1, 1893–March 21, 1955), civil rights leader. Walter White, executive secretary of the NATIONAL ASSOCIATION FOR THE ADVANCEMENT OF COLORED PEOPLE (NAACP) from 1931 to 1955, was born in Atlanta, Ga. Blond and blue-eyed, he was an African American by choice and social circumstance. In 1906, at age thirteen, he stood, rifle in hand, with his father to protect their home and faced down a mob of whites who had invaded their neighborhood in search of "nigger" blood. He later explained: "I knew then who I was. I was a Negro, a human being with an invisible pigmentation which marked me a person to be hunted, hanged, abused, discriminated against, kept in poverty and ignorance, in order that those whose skin was white would have readily at hand a proof of their superiority, a proof patent and inclusive, accessible to the moron and the idiot as well as to the wise man and the genius."

In 1918, when the NAACP hired him as assistant executive secretary to investigate LYNCHINGS, there were sixty-seven such crimes committed that year in sixteen states. By 1955, when he died, there were only three lynchings, all in Mississippi, and the NAACP no longer regarded the problem as its top priority. White investigated forty-two lynchings mostly in the deep South and eight race riots in the North that developed between World War I and after World War II in such cities as Chicago, Philadelphia, Washington, D.C., Omaha, and Detroit.

In August 1946 he helped to create a National Emergency Committee Against Mob Violence. The following month, he led a delegation of labor and civil leaders in a visit with President Harry S. Truman to demand federal action to end the problem. Truman responded by creating the President's Committee on Civil Rights, headed by Charles E. Wilson, chairman and president of General Electric. The committee's report, *To Secure These Rights,* provided the blueprint for the NAACP legislative struggle.

The NAACP's successful struggle against segregation in the armed services was one of White's major achievements. In 1940, as a result of the NAACP's intense protests, President Franklin D. Roosevelt appointed Judge William H. Hastie as civilian aide to the secretary of war, promoted Colonel Benjamin O. Davis, the highest-ranking black officer in the Army, to brigadier general, and appointed Colonel Campbell Johnson special aide to the director of Selective Service. As significant as these steps were, they did not satisfy White because they were woefully inadequate. So he increasingly intensified the NAACP's efforts in this area.

White then attempted to get the U.S. Senate to investigate employment discrimination and segregation in the armed services, but the effort failed. He therefore persuaded the NAACP board to express its support for the threat by A. Philip Randolph, president of the BROTHERHOOD OF SLEEPING CAR PORTERS, to lead a march on Washington in demand for jobs for blacks in the defense industries and an end to segregation in the military. To avoid the protest, President Roosevelt on June 25, 1941, issued Executive Order 8802, barring discrimination in the defense industries and creating the Fair Employment Practice Committee. That was the first time a U.S. president acted to end racial discrimination, and the date marked the launching of the modern Civil Rights Movement. Subsequently, the NAACP made the quest for presidential leadership in protecting the rights of blacks central to its programs.

As a special war correspondent for the *New York Post* in 1943 and 1945, White visited the European, Mediterranean, Middle Eastern, and Pacific theaters of operations and provided the War Department with extensive recommendations for ending racial discrimination in the military. His book *A Rising Wind* reported on the status of black troops in the European and Mediterranean theaters.

White was as much an internationalist as a civil rights leader. In 1921 he attended the second Pan-African Congress sessions in England, Belgium, and France, which were sponsored by the NAACP and led by W. E. B. DU BOIS. While on a year's leave of absence from the NAACP in 1949 and 1950, he participated in the "Round the World Town Meeting of the Air," visiting Europe, Israel, Egypt, India, and Japan.

In 1945 White, Du Bois, and Mary McLeod BETHUNE represented the NAACP as consultants to the American delegation at the founding of the United Nations in San Francisco. They urged that the colonial system be abolished; that the United Nations recognize equality of the races; that it adopt a bill of rights for all people; and that an international agency be established to replace the colonial system. Many of their recommendations were adopted by the United Nations.

White similarly protested the menial roles that blacks were forced to play in Hollywood films and sought an end to the harmful and dangerous stereotypes of the race that the industry was spreading. He enlisted the aid of Wendell Willkie, the Republican presidential candidate who was defeated in 1940 and who had become counsel to the motion picture industry, in appealing to Twentieth Century Fox, Warner Brothers, Metro-Goldwyn-Mayer, and other major studios and producers for more representative roles for blacks in films. He then contemplated creating an NAACP bureau in Hollywood to implement the organization's programs there. Although the bureau's idea fizzled, the NAACP did create a Beverly Hills-Hollywood branch in addition to others in California.

During White's tenure as executive secretary, the NAACP won the right to vote for blacks in the South by getting the Supreme Court to declare the white Democratic primary unconstitutional; opposed the poll tax and other devices that were used to discriminate against blacks at the polls; forged an alliance between the organization and the industrial trade unions; removed constitutional roadblocks to residential integration; equalized teachers' salaries in the South; and ended segregation in higher education institutions in addition to winning the landmark *Brown* v. *Board of Education* decision in 1954, overturning the Supreme Court's "separate but equal" doctrine. Overall, White led the NAACP to become the nation's dominant force in the struggle to get the national government to uphold the Constitution and protect the rights of African Americans.

White was a gregarious, sociable man who courted on a first-name basis a vast variety of people of accomplishment and influence like Willkie, Eleanor Roosevelt, Harold Ickes, and Governor Averell Harriman of New York. In 1949 he created a furor by divorcing his first wife, Gladys, and marrying Poppy Cannon, a white woman who was a magazine food editor.

In addition to his many articles, White wrote two weekly newspaper columns. One was for the *Chicago Defender,* a respected black newspaper, and the other for white newspapers like the Sunday *Herald Tribune.* He wrote two novels, *The Fire in the Flint* (1924) and *Flight* (1926); *Rope and Faggot* (1929, reprint 1969), an exhaustive study of lynchings; *A Man Called White* (1948), an autobiography; and *A Rising Wind* (1945). An assessment of civil rights progress, *How Far the Promised Land?* was published shortly after White's death in 1955.

BIBLIOGRAPHY

Report of the Secretary to the NAACP National Board of Directors, 1940, 1941, 1942.

Sitkoff, Harvard. *A New Deal for Blacks, The Emergence of Civil Rights as a National Issue: the Depression Decade.* New York, 1978.

Watson, Denton L. *Lion in the Lobby, Clarence Mitchell, Jr.'s Struggle for the Passage of Civil Rights Laws.* New York, 1990.

Wolters, Raymond. *Negroes and the Great Depression.* Westport, Conn., 1970.

— DENTON L. WATSON

WIDEMAN, JOHN EDGAR

John Edgar Wideman (June l4, 1941–), novelist. Born in Washington, D.C., John Edgar Wideman spent much of his early life first in Homewood, Pa., and then in Shadyside, an upper-middle-class area of Pittsburgh. In 1960 he received a scholarship to the University of Pennsylvania, where he proved himself equally outstanding in his undergraduate studies and on the basketball court. He graduated Phi Beta Kappa in 1963, and his athletic achievements led to his induction into the Big Five Basketball Hall of Fame. Upon graduation, Wideman became only the second African American to be awarded a Rhodes Scholarship (Alain LOCKE had received one almost fifty-five years earlier), an honor which allowed him to study for three years at Oxford

University in England, where he earned a degree in eighteenth-century literature.

After returning to the United States in 1966 and attending the Creative Writing Workshop at the University of Iowa as a Kent Fellow, Wideman returned to the University of Pennsylvania, where he served as an instructor (and later, professor) of English. In 1967, at the age of twenty-six, he published his first novel, *A Glance Away.* The novel was well received by critics, and two years after its appearance Wideman published *Hurry Home* (1969), a novel that chronicled its protagonist's struggle to reconcile the past and the present. After publishing a third novel in 1973, a dense and technically complex work entitled *The Lynchers,* Wideman found his name was increasingly associated with a diverse set of literary forebears including James Joyce, William Faulkner, and Ralph ELLISON.

During this period, Wideman served as the assistant basketball coach (1968–1972) at the University of Pennsylvania, as well as director of the Afro-American Studies Program (1971–1973). In 1975 he left Philadelphia to teach at the University of Wyoming in Laramie. Six years later he ended a long literary silence with the publication of two books: a collection of stories, *Damballah,* and *Hiding Place,* a novel. Both books focus on Wideman's Homewood neighborhood. And with the publication in 1983 of the third book in the trilogy, Wideman's reputation as a major literary talent was assured. *Sent for You Yesterday* won the 1984 P.E.N./ Faulkner Award, winning over several more established writers.

One finds in Wideman's fiction a continuing engagement with the complexity of history as layered narrative and an ability to articulate the inner essence of events that elude us.

At this point, Wideman was drawn (by circumstance rather than choice) into the world of nonfiction after his brother, Robbie, was convicted of armed robbery and sentenced to life imprisonment. At times angry, at others deeply introspective and brooding, *Brothers and Keepers* (1984) relates the paradoxical circumstances of two brothers: one a successful college professor and author, the other a drug addict struggling to establish an identity apart from his older, famous brother. Nominated for the 1985 National Book Award, the memoir set the stage for what arguably might be called Wideman's "next phase."

In 1986, after seeing his son, Jake, tried and convicted for the murder of a camping companion, Wideman moved back east to teach at the University of Massachusetts, Amherst. The following year saw the publication of his less than successful but nonetheless intriguing novel *Reuben.* Two years later, Wideman published a collection of stories, *Fever* (1989), and followed that in 1990 with a novel, *Philadelphia Fire.* Both of these works reflect Wideman's ability to interrogate his own experiences, even as his fiction takes up pertinent social issues. In the short stories and the novel, Wideman weaves fiction into the fabric of historical events (the former involves an outbreak of yellow fever in eighteenth-century Philadelphia, and the latter the aftermath of the confrontation with and subsequent bombing by Philadelphia police of the radical group Move). In 1992 Wideman brought out *The Stories of John Edgar Wideman* (1992), which contains ten new stories written especially for the collection, themselves entitled *All Stories Are True.* What distinguishes these ten stories is their extraordinary repositioning of the reader's attention, away from the source of the stories and toward the human issues they depict. As he works to make sense of his own assets and losses, one finds in Wideman's fiction a continuing engagement with the complexity of history as layered narrative and an ability to articulate the inner essence of events that often elude us.

BIBLIOGRAPHY

Coleman, James W. "Going Back Home: The Literary Development of John Edgar Wideman." *CLA Journal* 28, no. 3 (March 1985): 326–343.

"The Novels of John Wideman." *Black World* (June 1975): 18–38.

O'Brien, John. *Interviews with Black Writers.* New York, 1973.

— HERMAN BEAVERS

WILBERFORCE UNIVERSITY

Wilberforce University, one of the oldest historically black colleges and universities, was founded by the Methodist Episcopal Church in 1856 on the site of Tarawa Springs, a former summer resort in Greene County in Ohio. The school, which had as its purpose the education of African Americans, was named for British abolitionist William Wilberforce; its first president was Richard S. Rust. From the outset, the Methodist Episcopal Church and the AFRICAN METHODIST EPISCOPAL (AME) Church had a cooperative maintenance of Wilberforce University, despite the earlier founding of an AME school, the Union Seminary, in Columbus, Ohio.

The exigencies of the CIVIL WAR led to dwindling funds, declining enrollments, and the closing of both Union and Wilberforce University. In 1863, the AME Church purchased Wilberforce University from the Methodist Episcopal Church for $10,000, sold the property of Union Seminary, and combined the faculty of the two institutions. The prime mover of the transformation, AME Bishop Daniel Payne, served as president from 1863 to 1873, the first African-American college president in the United States; Payne continued to be involved in Wilberforce's affairs until his death in 1893. Under Payne's direction, a theology department was established in 1866 (it became the autonomous Payne Theological Seminary in 1891). Payne, concerned with establishing Wilberforce as a serious academic institution, introduced classical and science departments the following year. Among the faculty members in its first decades was the classicist William Scarborough (1856–1926), born to slavery in Georgia, who was the author of a standard textbook for Greek, translator of Aristophanes, and president of Wilberforce from 1908 to 1920. Occasional lecturers included Alexander CRUMMELL and Paul Laurence DUNBAR.

In 1887, AME Bishop Benjamin W. Arnett, also a successful Ohio politician, convinced the state legislature to establish a normal and industrial department at Wilberforce with its own campus, providing Wilberforce with unusual joint denominational and public supervision and sources of financial support. Shortly thereafter, from 1894 to 1896, W. E. B. DU BOIS was an instructor at Wilberforce (he left in part because he was uncomfortable with the intense evangelical piety he found on the campus). Hallie Quinn Brown, a leader of the women's club movement, was an 1873 graduate of Wilberforce, joined the faculty in 1893 as professor of elocution (i.e., public speaking), and remained on the faculty of the English department and the board of trustees for many years. The university library was named in her honor. In 1894, a military department was created under the leadership of Charles Young, one of the most distinguished African-American military officers.

In 1922, Wilberforce instituted a four-year degree program, and in 1939 it was formally accredited. A Wilberforce graduate, Horace Henderson, gained attention for his alma mater through a student jazz band, the Wilberforce Collegians, which he founded in the early 1920s and that went on to considerable national success. From 1942 to 1947, the historian Charles Wesley was president. In 1947, the former normal and industrial department was formally separated from Wilberforce as Wilberforce State College. Later renamed Central State University, it remains a predominantly black school, with an enrollment more than triple that of Wilberforce University.

The removal of state support for Wilberforce caused a financial crisis, a decline of enrollment, and a loss of accreditation. Under the leadership of Pembert E. Stokes, Wilberforce began to return to academic and financial health, and its accreditation was restored in 1960. In 1967 construction was begun on a new campus, a quarter mile from the old campus. In 1991, Wilberforce initiated a continuing education program for nontraditional students, Credentials for Leadership in Management and Business Education (CLIMB).

BIBLIOGRAPHY

Lewis, David Levering. *W. E. B. Du Bois: Biography of the Race.* New York, 1993.

McGinnis, Frederick. *A History of an Interpretation of Wilberforce University.* Blanchester, Ohio, 1941.

Talbert, Horace. *The Sons of Allen: Together with a Sketch of the Rise and Progress of Wilberforce University.* Xenia, Ohio, 1906.

– VALENA RANDOLPH

– JACQUELINE BROWN

WILKINS, ROY OTTOWAY

Roy Ottoway Wilkins (August 30, 1901–September 8, 1981), civil rights leader, laborer, and journalist. Born in a first-floor flat in a black section of St. Louis, Mo., Roy Wilkins got his middle name from the African-American physician who delivered him, Dr. Ottoway Fields. At age four, following his mother's death, Wilkins went to St. Paul, Minn. to live with his Aunt Elizabeth (Edmundson) and Uncle Sam Williams. The Williamses wrested legal guardianship of Roy, his brother, Earl, and sister, Armeda, from their absentee, footloose father, William.

After graduating from the University of Minnesota (1923) and following a stint as night editor of the college newspaper and editor of the black weekly, the *St. Paul Appeal,* Wilkins moved to Kansas City where he was editor of the *Kansas City Call* for eight years. In 1929 in Kansas City he married Aminda Badeau. In St. Paul and Kansas City, he was active in the local NATIONAL ASSOCIATION FOR THE ADVANCEMENT OF COLORED PEOPLE chapters during a period when the NAACP was waging a full-scale attack against America's JIM CROW practices. Under Wilkins's stewardship the *Call* gave banner headline coverage to NAACP (Acting) Executive Secretary Walter WHITE's 1930 campaign to defeat President Herbert Hoover's nomination of Circuit Court Judge John J. Parker to the United States Supreme Court. Parker, in a race for North Carolina governor ten years earlier, had declared his antipathy

Woodruff moved with his mother to Nashville, Tenn., where he attended public schools. In 1920, he moved to Indianapolis to study at the John Herron Art Institute while working part-time as a political cartoonist for the black newspaper the *Indiana Ledger.* In 1927, he traveled to Europe and lived in France for the next four years. He studied with the African-American painter Henry O. TANNER and at the Académie Scandinave and Académie Moderne in 1927 and 1928. Like other American artists who sought an education in the center of the art world, Woodruff spent his time recapitulating the succession of avant-garde art movements of the previous fifty years. His landscapes and figure paintings first synthesized elements of the late-nineteenth-century styles of impressionism and postimpressionism in their interest in the nonrealistic shifts of color and the manipulation of the texture of the brushstroke. His key work of the period, *The Card Players* (1930; repainted in 1978), plays on the distortions of figure and space found in the work of Paul Cézanne and the cubists Pablo Picasso and Georges Braque. This work emphasizes Woodruff's debt to African art (which had also been a source for the cubists) in the masklike nature of the faces. Woodruff had first encountered African art in Indianapolis in the early 1920s, when he saw one of the first books on the subject. As it was written in German, he could not read it; but he was intrigued by the objects. Woodruff and the African-American philosopher and teacher Dr. Alain LOCKE visited flea markets in Paris where the artist bought his first works of African art.

In 1931, Woodruff returned to the United States to found the art department at Atlanta University. Through his pioneering efforts, the national African-American arts community developed the kind of cohesion that previously had been lacking. Woodruff himself taught painting, drawing, and printmaking. To teach sculpture, he recruited the artist Nancy Elizabeth Prophet. The works that came from the department's faculty and students came to be known as the "Atlanta School" because their subjects were the African-American population of that city. Fully representational with modernist nuances, they fall into the style of American regionalism practiced throughout the country at that time. The use of woodcuts and linoleum prints added a populist tone to these works, which dealt with everyday life. Besides teaching, he brought to Atlanta University exhibitions of a wide range of works, including those of historical and contemporary black artists and the Harmon Foundation exhibitions, providing a unique opportunity for the entire black Atlanta community, since the local art museum was then segregated. The year 1942 saw the initiation of the Atlanta University Annuals, a national juried exhibition for black artists that expanded opportunities for many who were frequently excluded from the American art scene. Woodruff's legacy can be seen in the remarkable list of his students—Frederick Flemister, Eugene Grigsby, Wilmer Jennings, and Hayward Oubré—and of the artists who showed in the Annuals, including Charles Alston, Lois Mailou Jones, Elizabeth Catlett, Claude Clark, Ernest Crichlow, Aaron DOUGLAS, William H. Johnson, Norman Lewis, Hughie Lee-Smith, Jacob LAWRENCE, and Charles White. The exhibitions continued until 1970.

During this same period, Woodruff, as part of his efforts to present a populist art, produced a series of murals. Two of his inspirations were the murals placed in public buildings across the country by WPA artists, and the Mexican mural movement. Woodruff himself received a grant to study with Diego Rivera for six weeks in the summer of 1934, when he assisted in fresco painting. After completing two WPA murals, he painted the major work of this period, the *Amistad Murals* (1938–1939) at Talladega College (Alabama). Designed in the boldly figurative style associated with social realism, the murals depict the mutiny led by Cinqué aboard the slave ship *Amistad* in 1834 and the subsequent trial and repatriation of the Africans. Other mural projects included *The Founding of Talladega College* (1938–1939), murals at the Golden State Mutual Life Insurance Company (Los Angeles) on the contribution of blacks to the development of California (1948), and *The Art of the Negro* for Atlanta University (1950–1951).

In 1946, after receiving a two-year Julius Rosenwald Foundation Fellowship to study in New York (1943–1945), Woodruff moved to that city permanently to teach in the art education department of New York University. The move was not a rejection of the South, but came as an attempt by Woodruff to be part of the new art capital which had shifted from Paris to New York. Woodruff changed his style from that of a figurative painter of the American scene to a practitioner of the ideas of abstract expressionism. While employing the gestural spontaneity of that style, he incorporated design elements from the African art he had studied since his student days in Indianapolis. Worked into his compositions are motifs from a variety of African cultural objects, including Asante goldweights, Dogon masks, and Yoruba Shango implements—a kind of aesthetic pan-Africanism. This, the third major style of his career, demonstrates the adaptability of an artist always open to new currents in both the aesthetic and political worlds. He continued to be supportive of African-American artists by being one of the founders in 1963 of Spiral, a group of black New York artists (including Charles Alston, Emma Amos, Romare BEARDEN, Norman Lewis, and Richard Mayhew) who sought to weave the visual arts into the fabric of the civil rights struggle.

Woodruff received awards from the Harmon Foundation in 1926, 1928 and 1929, 1931, 1933, and 1935, and an Atlanta University Purchase Prize in 1955. He received a Great Teacher Award at NYU in 1966 and became professor emeritus in 1968.

BIBLIOGRAPHY

Reynolds, Gary, and Beryl J. Wright. "Hale Aspacio Woodruff." In *Against the Odds: African-American Artists and the Harmon Foundation.* Newark, N.J., 1989, pp. 275–279.

Stoelting, Winifred L. Hale Woodruff, Artist and Teacher: Through the Atlanta Years. Ph.D. diss., Emory University, 1978.

Studio Museum in Harlem. *Hale Woodruff: 50 Years of His Art.* New York, 1979.

Wilson, Judith. " 'Go Back and Retrieve It': Hale Woodruff, Afro-American Modernist." In *Selected Essays: Art and Artists from the Harlem Renaissance to the 1980s.* Atlanta, 1988.

– HELEN M. SHANNON

WOODSON, CARTER GODWIN

Carter Godwin Woodson (December 19, 1875–April 3, 1950), historian, educator. He was born in New Canton, in Buckingham County, Va. Woodson probably descended from slaves held by Dr. John Woodson, who migrated from Devonshire, England, to Jamestown, Va., in 1619. He was the first and only black American of slave parents to earn a Ph.D. in history. After the Civil War, Woodson's grandfather and father, who were skilled carpenters, were forced into sharecropping. After saving for many years, the family purchased land and eked out a meager living in the late 1870s and 1880s.

Although they were poor, James Henry and Anne Eliza Woodson instilled in their son high morality and strong character through religious teachings and a thirst for education. One of nine children, the youngest boy and a frail child, Carter purportedly was his mother's favorite and was sheltered. He belonged to that first generation of blacks whose mothers did not have to curry favor with whites to provide an education for their children. As a boy Woodson worked on the family farm, and in his teens he was an agricultural day laborer. In the late 1880s the family moved to West Virginia, where Woodson's father worked in railroad construction and Woodson worked as a coal miner in Fayette County. In 1895, at the age of twenty, Woodson enrolled at Frederick Douglass High School. Perhaps because he was older than the rest of the students and felt that he needed to catch up, he completed four years of course work in two years and graduated in 1897. He then enrolled at Berea College in Berea, Ky., which had been founded by abolitionists in the 1850s for the education of ex-slaves. He briefly attended Lincoln University in Pennsylvania, but graduated from Berea College in 1903, just a year before Kentucky would pass the infamous "Day Law," which prohibited interracial education. Woodson then briefly taught at Frederick Douglass High School. Because of his belief in the uplifting power of education, and because of the opportunity to travel to another country to observe and experience its culture firsthand, he decided to accept a teaching post in the Philippines, remaining there from 1903 to 1907.

Woodson was the first and only black American of slave parents to earn a Ph.D. in history.

Experiences as a college student and high school teacher expanded and influenced Woodson's worldview and shaped his ideas about the ways in which education could transform society, improve race relations, and benefit the lower classes. Determined to obtain additional education, he enrolled in correspondence courses at the University of Chicago. By 1907 he was enrolled there as a full-time student and earned both a bachelor's degree and a master's degree in European history. His thesis examined French diplomatic policy toward Germany in the eighteenth century. He then attended Harvard University, matriculating in 1909 and earning his Ph.D. in history in 1912. He studied with Edward Channing, Albert Bushnell Hart, and Frederick Jackson Turner, the latter of whom had moved from the University of Wisconsin to Harvard in 1910. Turner influenced the interpretation Woodson advanced in his dissertation, which was a study of the events leading to secession in West Virginia after the Civil War broke out. Unfortunately, Woodson never published the dissertation.

Woodson taught in the Washington, D.C., public schools, at HOWARD UNIVERSITY, and at the West Virginia Collegiate Institute. In 1915, in Chicago, he founded the Association for the Study of Negro Life and History, and began the work that sustained him for the rest of his career. Indeed, his life was given over to the pursuit of truth about the African and African-American pasts. He later founded the *Journal of Negro History,* the *Negro History Bulletin,* and the Associated Publishers; launched the annual celebration of Negro History Week in February 1926; and had a distinguished publishing career as a scholar of African-American history.

After the publication in 1915 of *The Education of the Negro Prior to 1861,* his first book, Woodson began a scholarly career that, even if judged by output alone, very few of his contemporaries or successors could match. By 1947, when the ninth edition of his textbook *The Negro in Our History* appeared, Woodson had published four monographs, five textbooks, five edited collections of source materials, and thirteen articles, as well as five sociological studies that were collaborative efforts. With his writings covering a wide array of subjects, Woodson's scholarly productivity and range were equally broad. He was among the first scholars to study SLAVERY from the slaves' point of view, and to give attention to the comparative study of slavery as an institution in the United States and in Latin America. His work prefigured the interpretations of contemporary scholars of slavery by several decades. Woodson also noted in his work the African cultural influences on African-American culture.

One of the major objectives of his own research and the research program he sponsored through the Association for the Study of Negro Life and History was to correct the racism promoted in the work published by white scholars. Woodson and his assistants pioneered in writing the social history of black Americans, and used new sources and methods. They moved away from interpreting blacks solely as victims of white oppression and racism. Instead, blacks were viewed as major actors in American history. In recognition of his achievements, the NATIONAL ASSOCIATION FOR THE ADVANCEMENT OF COLORED PEOPLE (NAACP) in June 1926 presented Woodson with its highest honor, the prestigious Spingarn Medal. In the award ceremony, John Haynes Holmes, minister and interracial activist, cited Woodson's tireless labors to promote the truth "about Negro life and history."

Woodson suffered a heart attack and died in his sleep on April 3, 1950, in his Washington, D.C., home. He had dedicated his life to the exploration and study of the African-American past. In view of the enormous difficulties he faced battling white racism and in convincing whites and blacks alike that his cause was credible and worthy of support, the achievement of so much seminal work in black history seems almost miraculous. Through his own scholarship and the programs he launched in the Association for the Study of Negro Life and History, Woodson made an immeasurable contribution to the advancement of black history.

BIBLIOGRAPHY

Goggin, Jacqueline. *A Life in Black History.* Baton Rouge, La., 1993.

Meier, August, and Elliott Rudwick. *Black History and the Historical Profession.* Urbana, Ill. 1986.

– JACQUELINE GOGGIN

WORKS PROJECT ADMINISTRATION (WPA)

Originally the Works Progress Administration, later the Works Project Administration, began in 1935, when President Franklin D. Roosevelt established it to distribute the $4.88 billion appropriated by Congress for an emergency jobs program. Between 1935 and its ending on February 1, 1943, the WPA spent $11 billion and employed more than eight million people in a variety of construction, clerical, professional, and arts endeavors.

The WPA came at a time of critical need for African Americans. The Depression, while imposing dire hardships on people of all races and ethnic backgrounds, struck blacks with particular impact. In 1934 and 1935, one out of every three New York City workers was jobless, but in Harlem one out of every two African Americans was unemployed. Pittsburgh's black laborers had an unemployment rate of 48 percent; its white workers, 31 percent. Between 1935 and 1943, the WPA employed over a million African Americans. WPA wages became the third largest source of income for blacks, exceeded only by income from agriculture and domestic service.

The WPA not only hired African Americans; its projects contributed to the well-being of blacks in many important ways. WPA construction crews built and renovated hospitals, housing projects, schools, parks,

Jim Walker, 100 years old, learns to write at a WPA Adult Education Center in Birmingham, Ala. (Photographs and Prints Division, Schomburg Center for Research in Black Culture, The New York Public Library, Astor, Lenox and Tilden Foundations)

playgrounds, and swimming pools in African-American communities. Impoverished black children and adults received free medical and dental care at clinics staffed by black and white doctors and dentists employed by the WPA. Over 5,000 African-American instructors and supervisors worked on the WPA's education programs. They taught a quarter of a million black adults to read and write, thus helping cut the rate of black illiteracy from 16.4 percent at the start of the 1930s to 11.5 percent at its end.

An editorial in *Opportunity* in 1939 credited the WPA in northern cities with giving qualified blacks their first chances for employment in white-collar positions, and Alain LOCKE, an early chronicler of the art movement known as the HARLEM RENAISSANCE, attributed its survival in the 1930s to the WPA. The WPA FEDERAL WRITERS' PROJECT employed thousands of black poets and novelists, among them Margaret Walker, Richard WRIGHT, Sterling A. BROWN, Ralph ELLISON, Zora Neale HURSTON, and Claude MCKAY. Project employees researched and later wrote many studies of African American life, including *The Negro in Virginia* (1940); Benjamin Botkin's *Lay My Burden Down: A Folk History of Slavery* (1945); and Arna BONTEMPS's and Jack Conroy's *They Seek a City* (1945).

The WPA funded black acting troupes. For example, the Negro Theatre Project staged *Walk Together Chillun* by African-American playwright Frank Wilson at the Lafayette Theatre in Harlem and had its greatest hit with an all-black *Macbeth*. African-American musicians hired by the WPA gave concerts in schools and music halls, played for street dances, and gave free music lessons. In 1936, thirty-five hundred Harlemites were enrolled in WPA music classes. African-American artists such as Jacob LAWRENCE, Charles Alston, and Palmer Hayden painted and gave free art classes at the Harlem Community Art Center and thousands of other WPA centers across the nation. As Ralph Ellison remarked, black "writers and would-be writers, newspaper people, dancers, actors—they all got their chance" at the WPA.

Despite its substantial contributions to the welfare of African Americans, the WPA never fully met the needs of the unemployed, white or black. At no point did it hire more than one-third of the able-bodied jobless who wanted to work. Furthermore, despite orders from President Roosevelt and the national WPA directors, Harry Hopkins and Aubrey Williams, against discrimination "on any grounds, whatsoever, such as race, religion, or political affiliation," restrictive and unfair practices did occur. In the rural South, relief officials too often denied destitute African Americans certification for WPA jobs. The WPA adjusted its wage scales to prevailing rates of pay in the region. Thus, WPA laborers in the South, where about 75 percent of the black working population lived, received far lower compensation than WPA personnel in the North. Further, African Americans, even in the North, clustered in the least-skilled, poorest-paid WPA positions. In the New York City WPA in 1937, only 0.5 percent of its black employees were supervisors, while 75 percent were classified as unskilled laborers. This situation within the WPA resulted both from discriminatory practices and the generally limited educational and skill levels of African Americans on the relief rolls from which the WPA took its employees. While the WPA did try to educate and retrain its workers, especially after 1939, it never put enough resources into such efforts to upgrade substantially the skills of its common laborers.

BIBLIOGRAPHY

Blumberg, Barbara. *The New Deal and the Unemployed: The View from New York City.* Lewisburg, Pa., 1979.

Mangione, Jerre. *The Dream and the Deal: The Federal Writers' Project, 1935–1943.* Boston, 1972.

McElvaine, Robert S. *The Great Depression.* New York, 1984.

Sitkoff, Harvard. *A New Deal for Blacks.* New York, 1978.

Wolters, Raymond. *Negroes and the Great Depression: The Problem of Economic Recovery.* Westport, Conn., 1970.

— BARBARA BLUMBERG

WORLD WAR I

African Americans saw World War I as an opportunity to demonstrate their patriotism and to convince whites that they should be granted full civil rights, but these efforts faced hostility and discrimination. Eventually over 400,000 blacks would serve in segregated organizations in the U.S. armed forces, mainly as laborers, though most of the attention would be focused on the two combat divisions. African-American women faced even more barriers in their attempts to join the crusade for democracy.

When the United States entered World War I in April 1917, most African Americans were eager to take part in the war. Many accepted the concept enunciated the following year by W. E. B. DU BOIS that they should forget their grievances for the duration of the war. But from the beginning there were clear indications that the problems of discrimination would not go away. Even before American participation in the war began, Lt. Col. Charles Young, the highest ranking African-American regular army officer, was found physically unfit for duty and placed on the retired list. Many African Americans thought that he was being removed because of the possibility that he might become a general and that white officers and enlisted men might have to serve under his command. Later, the reaction of the Army to the August 1917 riot in Houston also demonstrated that African Americans would not be well treated in the armed forces. In an effort to placate the community, Secretary of War Newton Baker appointed Emmett J. Scott as his assistant for racial matters, but Scott had no real influence.

Despite the traditions established in the Spanish-American War and by the long service of the four Regular Army African-American regiments, the Army leadership believed that African Americans should not be asked to participate in combat. On the other hand, they believed that blacks made excellent laborers, especially if placed in organizations commanded by white commissioned and even noncommissioned officers. As a result, about 89 percent of all blacks who participated in World War I served in labor units both in the United States and in France. These organizations performed a variety of duties, including building training camps and loading supplies. Morale was quite low because the soldiers could see little relationship between their work and the war effort. Many of the officers did not want to be there; they saw little chance of promotion from being involved in the supply operations, and many did not like African Americans.

There was a great deal more controversy over the 11 percent of the black soldiers who were members of the combat arms. The arguments involved whether they should be allowed into combat, how the units should be organized, and who should command them. Some African Americans wanted the opportunity to fight the Germans but opposed the idea of a segregated combat division. The Army, however, was adamant that segregation must continue. Because African Americans wanted to take an active role in the war, most accepted segregation as the condition of their participation. The Army also at first refused to allow combat units to have black officers; in June 1917, it permitted the regiments to have lower-ranking African-American commissioned officers—lieutenants and captains—while keeping the control of the regiments and the divisional staff firmly in the hands of whites. The question of whether African-American officers should be trained in integrated or segregated camps also engendered controversy. Again the Army won, and established Camp Des Moines, in Iowa, as a segregated camp where all African-American officers received their training.

Initially the Army planned to create only one black division, the 92nd, and used the draft to fill its ranks. Charles Ballou, a white officer with prior service with black Regular Army units and the commander of Camp Des Moines, was appointed its leader. He made it clear that African Americans under his command were not to protest any kind of discrimination. Ballou, like many

War hero Needham Roberts of the 369th U.S. Infantry as he appeared in The Crisis *in May 1919. He is wearing the Croix de Guerre, with palm, two service stripes, and two wound stripes. (Prints and Photographs Division, Library of Congress)*

other officers, also made it clear that he did not think African-American officers were very good or that his soldiers would ever be able to perform well in combat. Division morale and effectiveness were not helped when it was forced to train at seven different sites in the United States before being shipped to France in 1918. Once in Europe the 92nd received almost no training in the front lines and had little equipment to deal with the barbed wire and machine gun emplacements that they had to face. As a result, they did not perform very well when placed into combat.

As part of the September 1918 Meuse-Argonne Offensive, the 368th Infantry, part of the 92nd Division, was given the task of acting as a connecting link with the French army on its part of the front lines. After five days of battle, the regiment was relieved of duty. According to Army reports, the regiment had not met its objectives. Then the whole division was pulled out of the front lines and spent much of the remainder of the war as reserves or on patrol duty in relatively quiet sectors of the front. Ballou believed that the solution to the problems was to remove the black officers; he proposed to court-martial many of them. Though few of these trials were actually carried out, they destroyed what little morale remained in the division. For most white officers during the war and later, the performance of the 92nd Division reinforced their stereotypes of black soldiers: they were cowards who would not perform well under the leadership of African-American officers. For African Americans the whole experience demonstrated that whites would not let them succeed.

However, the experiences of the other African-American division were different. This provisional division, the 93rd, was composed of three National Guard regiments and one regiment of draftees, largely from the South. This division never had a staff or attached artillery regiments but was essentially four regiments grouped together as a way to absorb these African-American National Guard regiments. The 15th New York Infantry became the 369th Infantry, and its regimental band, under the leadership of James Reese EUROPE, became well known in the United States and in France. A number of the African-American National Guard officers were removed, including Franklin A. Dennison, commander of the 8th Illinois, and replaced by white officers. When the provisional division arrived in France, John J. Pershing willingly turned them over to the control of the French, a policy that he rarely pursued with white divisions. As a result, the four regiments encountered a different attitude from their commanders, as the French were much more willing to treat African-American soldiers and officers as equals and wanted them to perform well in combat.

The first two African-American war heroes, Needham Roberts and Henry Johnson, came from this division. In May 1918 they were on the front lines, involved in a training exercise. They were attacked by a German raiding party. First they fired their rifles at the raiders and then used every other weapon at their disposal, including hand grenades and a bolo knife. Despite being wounded, they were successful in beating off the Germans. Both received the French *Croix de Guerre* and became heroes in the black community. Despite their heroism, Pershing still wanted to bring them to the American Army and use them as laborers. The French refused and asked for more African-American troops; Pershing declined the request.

American officers tried to impose American racial standards on the French population. They instructed them that white Americans resented good treatment for African Americans; that the black soldiers had dangerous sexual proclivities; and that they should be segregated. When news of this secret order, which had been written on August 7, 1918, reached the United States in 1919, partly through the efforts of W. E. B. Du Bois, who published the directive in May 1919, anger mounted at the American government and the military.

African-American women also tried to enter the war effort. Adah Thoms, head of the Colored Nurses Association, volunteered her organization to become part of the Nursing Corps. For a long time the Army refused to accept this offer. Not until late in the war did this barrier break when the military allowed eighteen black nurses to serve at two camps in the United States; none was permitted to go to France.

Though most African Americans served in the United States Army, a few were allowed into the Navy. The attitude of that branch of the armed forces was that African Americans made excellent stewards. Only a few older sailors were able to break out of this occupational trap. The Marines continued to refuse to allow any African Americans to serve.

BIBLIOGRAPHY

Barbeau, Arthur E., and Henri Florette. *The Unknown Soldiers: Black American Troops in World War I.* Philadelphia, 1974.

Little, Arthur W. *From Harlem to the Rhine: The Story of New York's Colored Volunteers.* New York, 1936.

Nalty, Bernard C. *Strength for the Fight: A History of Black Americans in the Military.* New York, 1986.

— MARVIN E. FLETCHER

WORLD WAR II

The Second World War and the emergency that preceded it enabled African Americans to enhance their status in both civilian life and military service. Circumstances worked to their advantage. An unprecedented threat required unprecedented mobilization, and the United States could not ignore its black citizens, who comprised roughly 10 percent of the populace. African-American men and women profited from the manpower crisis, whether in the armed forces or the civilian work force.

Better Treatment in the Segregated Armed Services

When World War II erupted in Europe in 1939, the neutral United States and its armed forces adhered to the principle of separate-but-equal, which had divided black from white since PLESSY V. FERGUSON gave it the force of law in 1896. The Navy, dependent upon black seamen until almost the end of the nineteenth century, accepted no African Americans from 1922 to 1932 and, when the ban ended, trained those it did enlist as cooks or messmen. The Army, in the 1930s, reduced its four black regiments, in existence as segregated units for some sixty years, to skeleton strength and reassigned many of the soldiers to housekeeping duties at scattered military posts. Operating within a congressionally authorized manpower ceiling, the War Department transferred some unfilled vacancies from the black regiments to the rapidly expanding Air Corps. Since Army aviation spurned African Americans, raiding the historic black regiments outraged civil rights organizations and inspired them to campaign for the admission of blacks to pilot training.

Although racial segregation permeated the military, faint signs of change appeared in 1939. Congress admitted African Americans to the Civilian Pilot Training Program administered by the Civil Aviation Administration and specified that the Air Corps cooperate in the endeavor, though not necessarily so fully as to accept the black graduates in its ranks. The Selective Service and Training Act of 1940 outlawed "discrimination against any person on account of race or color" in administering the draft, but it contained loopholes that perpetuated segregation despite the ban on discrimination. For example, black draftees could be told not to report because "suitable"—that is, segregated—quarters were not yet available. African-American leaders protested legislation that promised so much but delivered so little.

As the 1940 election approached, President Franklin D. Roosevelt, seeking an unprecedented third term, realized that he needed the support of those blacks, mainly in the large northern cities, who could exercise the right to vote. He and representatives of the War and Navy departments met with three African-American leaders: A. Philip Randolph, head of the BROTHERHOOD OF SLEEPING CAR PORTERS; Walter WHITE, of the NATIONAL ASSOCIATION FOR THE ADVANCEMENT OF COLORED PEOPLE (NAACP); and T. Arnold Hill, an adviser to the federal National Youth Administration. This meeting on September 27 produced a policy of giving black servicemen better treatment and greater opportunity within the confines of racial segregation.

Three appointments made in October 1940 symbolized the Roosevelt administration's new policy. Col. Benjamin O. DAVIS, Sr., received promotion to brigadier general, and became the first African American to attain that rank. When he reached retirement age a year later, he remained on active duty as a specialist on black troops in the office of inspector general. At the same time that Davis got his general's star, Col. Campbell C. Johnson, commander of the Reserve Officer Training Corps at Howard University, became an aide to the director of the Selective Service System, and another African American, Judge William H. HASTIE, former dean of the Howard University School of Law, was appointed a special adviser to the Secretary of War on matters pertaining to black soldiers.

Integration on the Assembly Line

"Demand the right to work and fight for our country," A. Philip Randolph urged in January 1941, three months after Roosevelt offered better treatment and broader opportunity to blacks serving in the armed forces and eleven months before Japan attacked Pearl Harbor and the United States went to war. Thus far, the President's policy had produced symbols rather than substance. Supported by other civil rights activists like Rayford Logan, of the National Urban League, and Walter White, Randolph threatened a March on Washington by 100,000 African Americans. The prospect of so massive a demonstration, scheduled for July 1, 1941, as Congress debated renewing the selective service legislation, persuaded Roosevelt to issue on June 25 Executive Order 8802, which specified that defense contracts bar discrimination and open training programs to minorities, established a Fair Employment Practice Committee to investigate violations, and resulted in cancellation of the march.

The Fair Employment Practice Committee lacked the power to subpoena witnesses or enforce compliance with the executive order and had no authority to investigate nondefense industries. Nevertheless, its deliberations publicized instances of discrimination, established the principle of federal protection of access to jobs by members of minorities, and inspired a number of northern states to establish similar agencies after the war. The committee survived bureaucratic struggles and political opposition until 1945, when segregationist opposition in Congress cut off its funding.

Despite the weakness and narrow scope of the Fair Employment Practice Committee, the African-American workforce underwent a marked change during World War II, especially in industrialized areas where labor was scarce. Overall, a million or more blacks found wartime employment, either replacing whites who entered the armed forces or occupying newly created jobs. Between January 1942 and November 1944, the percentage of African Americans in war industries increased from 3 percent to 8.3 percent.

The prospect of employment in the industrial cities of the North and West attracted both blacks and whites, as more than five million Americans exchanged a rural life for urban opportunity. In 1940, 51.4 percent of all African Americans lived in the country and 77.1 percent resided in the South, from Virginia to Texas. The next census, in 1950, revealed that only 37.6 percent still lived a rural life, with only 68.1 percent in the old Confederacy. The wartime migration intensified the competition for scarce housing and contributed to racial friction and violence in cities like Detroit, Chicago, and Los Angeles.

Whereas Randolph in 1941 demanded the right to work and fight, the black press seized upon the symbol V for Victory and in 1942 launched the Double V Campaign, seeking victory over tyranny abroad and racial segregation at home. The two objectives proved closely linked; African Americans in the armed forces, as they battled foreign tyrants, won victories over domestic racism.

The Army Air Arm

The policy adopted in 1940, improved treatment and opportunity without racial integration, resulted in the admission of African Americans to pilot training in the Army air arm. During January 1941, as Roosevelt was about to begin his third term, Assistant Secretary of War Robert P. Patterson announced the organization of a black pursuit squadron, even though the Chief of the Air Corps, Maj. Gen. Henry H. Arnold, had insisted, as recently as the previous spring, that any mixing of the races within the organization would create an impossible social problem. Very little mingling occurred. African-American pilots began training in July 1941 at segregated facilities at Tuskegee Institute, in Alabama, and completed the course by the time Japan attacked Pearl Harbor on December 7 and plunged the United States into the war.

The Tuskegee experiment produced a trained fighter unit, the 99th Pursuit Squadron, manned by African-American pilots, mechanics, and even clerks—a racial exclusiveness that reflected official policy. The Army Air Forces, which had evolved from the old Army Air Corps, flinched at the prospect of integrating the races. When the air arm reneged on a promise to integrate its officer candidate school, which produced nonflying officers, Judge Hastie, an outspoken advocate of racial integration, resigned in protest. His departure jolted the Air Forces into integrating the school, but the black graduates nevertheless served in segregated units. Hastie's replacement, Truman K. Gibson, a black attorney and civil rights advocate from Chicago, took up the fight for integration, though in a less confrontational manner.

The War Department initially planned to send the 99th Pursuit Squadron to Liberia, a thousand miles from the nearest battlefield, where it would sit out the war patrolling coastal waters for submarines. The unit, however, went to Northwest Africa, where the Allies landed in November 1942, arriving there in April of the next year. The change resulted in part from the War Department's desire to evaluate the Tuskegee experiment.

The 477th Bombardment Group, Army Air Force. (Photographs and Prints Division, Schomburg Center for Research in Black Culture, The New York Public Library, Astor, Lenox and Tilden Foundations)

The 99th Pursuit (later Fighter) Squadron encountered unique obstacles after it entered combat over the Mediterranean island of Pantelleria on June 2, 1943. The squadron lacked a cadre of veterans to pass along lessons learned in years of flying; all the pilots had learned to fly at the same time, even the commander, Maj. Benjamin O. DAVIS, Jr., the son of Brig. Gen. Davis and a 1936 graduate of West Point. The unit, moreover, had gaps in its training; because of racial segregation, few bases would provide overnight accommodations for black pilots, which eliminated the opportunity for long flights that honed navigating skills. Over Sicily and the Mediterranean, while the 99th Fighter Squadron operated as an appendage of the white 33rd Fighter Group, Maj. Davis and the others learned as they fought. They had scant hope of rest or refresher training, since Tuskegee concentrated in 1943 on producing new units—ultimately three more fighter squadrons and a medium bombardment group—rather than a steady flow of individual replacements.

Convinced that the understrength 99th could not keep pace, the commander of the 33rd Fighter Group recommended removing the squadron from combat. In October 1943, this recommendation, which could have ended the Tuskegee project, reached the War Department's Advisory Committee on Negro Troop Policy, headed by Assistant Secretary of War John J. McCloy. Maj. Davis, back from overseas, explained the circumstances that affected his unit's performance and convinced the committee, which included his father, that the 99th would improve.

Improve it did. By the time the war ended, the black 332nd Fighter Group of four squadrons—the 99th, 100th, 301st, and 302nd—was escorting bombers from airfields in Italy deep into Germany. The number of African Americans in the wartime Air Forces peaked at 145,000, but fewer than a thousand were pilots or members of air crews.

In December 1942, the Selective Service System began providing manpower for all the services, and each one, including the Army Air Forces, received its share of African-American recruits. The air arm dumped those who did not qualify for technical training, or simply seemed excess to the needs of the service, into labor or housekeeping units. This practice created an explosive concentration of underutilized and dissatisfied individuals that needed only the spark of racism to ignite it. On June 24, 1943, at Bamber Bridge in the United Kingdom, white military police, angered by the sight of black airmen dancing with white English women, struck the spark. The ensuing riot wounded five Americans, three of them blacks.

The Army Ground and Service Forces

The problems of underutilization and dissatisfaction troubled the Army Ground Forces and Army Service Forces, as well as the Air Forces, since the entire Army had to absorb large numbers of blacks who scored poorly on the aptitude tests. The War Department, because it could not waste the time and resources necessary to segregate African Americans by both test scores and race, decided to create all-black divisions, some 15,000 strong, which would absorb black junior officers and make use of enlisted men with almost every skill and level of aptitude. During 1942 and 1943, the Army activated the 92nd and 93rd Infantry Divisions and designated the 2nd Cavalry Division a black unit. Other African-American soldiers served in nondivisional outfits: regimental combat teams; separate tank, antitank, artillery, and antiaircraft battalions that could be attached to white divisions without forfeiting their racial identity; and service units of various kinds. The number of African Americans in the Army exceeded 700,000 in the summer of 1944, most of them assigned to service organizations that, among other things, helped build the Ledo Road in Burma and the Alaskan highway, loaded ships in the United States and unloaded them overseas, and drove the trucks of the Red Ball Express, which delivered cargo from the French coast to the American troops advancing toward Germany.

By the end of 1943, the Army had sent two black combat units overseas—the 24th Infantry, a regimental combat team, in the South Pacific, and the 99th Fighter Squadron, in the Mediterranean Theater. The others continued to train, often under white officers whose attitude toward African Americans combined condescension with contempt, and in parts of the country where blacks faced rigid segregation and open hostility. Indifferent leadership and the hatred expressed by local inhabitants contributed to riots by black soldiers at nine military bases during 1943. Bad morale promised to grow even worse when the War Department decided to send the 2nd Cavalry Division overseas early in 1944, disband it, and reassign the black soldiers as military laborers. The planned break-up of the cavalry division and the failure to send either of the infantry divisions into combat caused another outcry, which prominent whites echoed, among them Eleanor Roosevelt, the wife of the President.

Political pressure and the need for troops overseas failed to save the 2nd Cavalry Division but did cause the War Department to send the 93rd Infantry Division to the Pacific in January and February 1944 and the 92nd Infantry Division to Italy between July and October of that year. The 93rd Infantry Division provided one regiment that fought on Bougainville in the Solomon Islands but never campaigned as a division. Functioning mainly in general reserve, it supplied working parties and garrison forces, some of which saw action against the Japanese.

The 92nd Infantry Division pooled its best trained troops in a single combat team, built around the 370th Infantry, which sailed for Italy in July 1944 and entered combat in August. As a result, the other two regiments that followed the 370th Infantry into action were still absorbing new officers and enlisted men as they did so. Moreover, the War Department failed to provide black replacements for the casualties the racially segregated division began suffering, causing combat effectiveness to decline. As the strength of the division ebbed, the army group commander in Italy shored it up with a black regiment already in the theater, plus white and Japanese-American units.

While the 92nd Infantry Division went to war in Italy, several of the African-American combat battalions, attached to white divisions, helped liberate France and invade Germany. The War Department had precisely calculated the number of divisions it would need for a world war, but in December 1944, after savage fighting in the Huertgen Forest, an unexpected German counterattack in the Ardennes resulted in the Battle of the Bulge and inflicted additional casualties. White divisions training in the United States and United Kingdom converged on the Continent, but swifter action seemed necessary. The answer to the demand for manpower lay in the African-American service troops already in Europe.

Lt. Gen. John C. H. Lee, in charge of logistics in the European Theater of Operations, persuaded Gen. Dwight D. Eisenhower, the Allied supreme commander, to call for volunteers among the predominantly black service units to retrain as riflemen. Some 4,500 African Americans signed up, underwent training, and served in sixty-man platoons that were to join two-hundred-man white rifle companies. Except in the Seventh Army, where the platoons formed segregated companies instead of serving in white ones, this improvised racial policy integrated the fighting, though not the Army.

An attempt by the War Department to apportion officers' clubs, exchanges, and similar facilities by unit rather than race had only mixed success. As long as most units and cantonments remained racially segregated, the clubs followed suit, sometimes with the connivance of white commanders. At Freeman Field, in Indiana, the Air Forces commanding officer excluded blacks from the officers' club by reserving it for permanently assigned officers and categorizing all the African Americans as transients undergoing training. A demand by officers of the African-American 477th Bombardment Group for admission to the club triggered a confrontation that ended with the opening of the club to all officers, the transfer of the base commander, and a court-martial that imposed token punishment on one of the protesters.

The Navy

The Navy moved more slowly than the Army to provide broader opportunity and better treatment, while retaining racial segregation. The career of Doris Miller illustrated the Navy's reluctance to change. A male mess steward on the battleship USS *West Virginia,* he received the Navy Cross for shooting down two Japanese aircraft during the attack on Pearl Harbor, December 7, 1941. Instead of being reassigned to a specialty involving gunnery, he remained a mess attendant until his death in November 1943, when a Japanese submarine torpedoed the escort carrier *Liscome Bay.*

Secretary of the Navy Frank Knox believed in segregation and remained content to accept a few additional blacks as cooks and mess attendants in the rapidly expanding Navy. In January 1942, Roosevelt prodded the secretary to find better assignments for African Americans, but Knox and the General Board of the Navy, roughly the equivalent of the War Department General Staff, dragged their feet until April, when they established a quota. As a result, 277 black volunteers could enter the Navy each week and, beginning in June 1942, train at a segregated camp for recruits at the Great Lakes Naval Training Station, in Illinois. The Navy intended to assign the African American graduates of recruit training to advanced courses at the Hampton Institute, in Virginia, to learn specialties that would qualify them for general service. Even though fewer blacks volunteered than anticipated, the Navy could not easily place them in the general service and instead diverted many of them to duty as stevedores at naval ammunition depots. After December 1942, reliance on the draft dramatically increased the number of blacks in the Navy, which created new segregated units to accommodate them, including twenty-seven Naval Construction Battalions. Two navies functioned side by side, a white navy that manned the fleet, and a black one that performed heavy labor and menial work in support of the other.

The Navy moved more slowly than the Army to provide broader opportunity and better treatment, while retaining racial segregation.

Despite the growing proportion of blacks in the service, the Navy at the end of 1943 had yet to commission its first African-American officer. A dozen black college students, however, had enrolled in the V–12 officer training program and, upon graduation, would receive their commissions. To offer carefully selected black enlisted men a chance to become officers, the Navy on January 1, 1944, established a segregated officer candidate school and commissioned twelve of the sixteen graduates. The Golden Thirteen—the twelve newly minted ensigns plus another classmate who became a warrant officer—completed the course in March, and during the summer, ten other black officers, commissioned directly because of their civilian skill, reported for duty.

Since segregation confined to the galley those African Americans who served in the fleet, black morale suffered, as did the morale of white sailors who faced additional tours at sea because replacements were not available. Obviously, introducing black sailors into a greater range of seagoing specialties would improve the morale of both races. Early in 1944, the Navy tried to do this without disrupting segregation by assigning predominantly black crews to man a patrol craft, *PC 1264,* and the destroyer escort USS *Mason.* A few ships, however, could not absorb the surplus of African-American sailors.

When Knox died in April 1944, rigid segregation perished also. James V. Forrestal succeeded him as Secretary of the Navy and directed that the service integrate the crews of twenty-five fleet auxiliaries—oilers, ammunition ships, and the like—at the ratio of one black sailor in ten. Since the fleet of 75,000 ships and landing craft included 1,600 auxiliaries, the Forrestal program provided a commitment to change rather than full-fledged integration.

The Coast Guard

The Coast Guard, transferred from the Treasury Department to the Navy in November 1941, included a few African Americans who manned separate rescue stations or small craft or served in a segregated stewards' branch. Initially, the Coast Guard planned to cope with an increase in black volunteers by expanding the stewards' branch and designating additional segregated vessels and stations. The use of the Selective Service System, which raised the total number of blacks to 5,000, overwhelmed this policy.

Moreover, segregated duty, especially as a steward, imposed limits on promotion and transfer, and by 1943 sixty percent of the black Coast Guardsmen were stewards. To broaden opportunities for African Americans, Rear Admiral Russell R. Waesche, the Commandant of the Coast Guard, endorsed an experiment with racially segregated crews. The weather ship *Sea Cloud* sailed the North Atlantic in November 1943 with some twenty blacks in the crew. During successive cruises, the proportion increased until African Americans formed almost a third of the crew, including fifty petty officers and four officers. The cutter *Hoquiam,* operating in Aleutian waters, also had a thoroughly integrated crew. Other Coast Guard ships and stations had at least a few blacks assigned, some of them in charge of whites.

The Marine Corps

The Marine Corps, which recruited blacks during the American Revolution, had accepted none since its reestablishment in 1798. As late as April 1941, the commandant, Maj. Gen. Thomas Holcomb, complained that those African Americans seeking to enlist as marines were "trying to break into a club that doesn't want them." He insisted that if he had to make a choice between "a Marine Corps of 5,000 whites or 250,000 Negroes," he would choose the whites. The pressures of war did not give Holcomb a choice, and on June 1, 1942, the Marine Corps began accepting African Americans. Plans called for organizing them into a segregated and self-contained defense battalion with artillery, infantry, and light tanks.

When the draft swelled the number of black marines, the Corps increased its segregated units—another defense battalion, fifty-one depot companies, and twelve ammunition companies, plus other miscellaneous detachments and a messman's branch. In all, some 20,000 African Americans served in the wartime Marine Corps. The first black entered officer training in April 1945 but did not receive his commission in the reserve until after the fighting ended.

The Merchant Marine

When the United States entered the war, the Merchant Marine comprised 131 operating companies and 22 unions that tended to restrict blacks to the galley and the engine room. After the United States War Shipping Administration took over the Merchant Marine in 1942, racial policy changed. Thanks in part to pressure from the Fair Employment Practice Committee, Hugh Mulzac became the first of three African Americans to serve as a wartime ship's captain when he took over the SS *Booker T. Washington,* a merchantman with a racially diverse crew. To meet the demands of war, the Merchant Marine found seagoing billets for some 24,000 blacks, across a broad spectrum of nautical specialties.

Women and the War Effort

World War II did not open employment opportunities for African-American males only. Some 600,000 black women joined the wartime work force. Previously, opportunities for these women existed mainly in domestic or service jobs, but possibilities expanded during the war in sales, clerical occupations, and especially light industry, where blacks of both sexes provided a ready source of unskilled labor.

All the services recruited women during the course of the conflict. On May 14, 1942, the Army established the Women's Auxiliary Army Corps, which became the Women's Army Corps on July 1, 1943. The Navy set up the Women Accepted for Volunteer Emergency Service, the WAVES, on July 30, 1942. The Coast Guard organized the SPARS, a contraction of the motto *semper paratus,* "always prepared," on May 23, 1942, and the Marine Corps created the Women's Reserve on February 13, 1943. Only the Marine Corps refused throughout the war to accept black women, and its women's component remained exclusively white.

Since comparatively few women underwent training, the efficient use of instructional facilities required some racial integration in that phase of service, but otherwise the same policy of racial segregation applied to females as to males. As a result, few of the Army's almost 4,000 African-American women volunteers performed duties commensurate with their skills. At Fort Devens, Mass., black women trained as medical technicians refused to perform menial labor. A court-martial convicted four of their number of disobeying a lawful order, but racial prejudice was so obvious in both the order and the trial that the Judge Advocate General reversed the court's decision. The Army sent overseas just one unit made up of black women, a postal battalion that served in the United Kingdom under an African-American officer, Maj. Charity Adams.

Although the Army accepted black volunteers from the beginning of its program for women, the WAVES and SPARS did not announce their decision to admit African Americans until October 1944. The change of policy reflected the determination of Capt. Mildred H. McAfee, the director of the WAVES, and the replacement of Secretary of the Navy Frank Knox by James V. Forrestal, who favored racial integration. Pressure from black organizations also played an important role, since President Roosevelt would again need black votes when he sought a fourth term in November.

When the war began, the Army and the Navy accepted only whites as nurses. Judge William H. Hastie, before resigning as special assistant to the secretary of war, persuaded the War Department to accept black nurses, but the Army Nurse Corps commissioned only 476 African Americans during the war, roughly one percent of its strength, and tried to assign them where they would care exclusively for black troops. The wartime Navy, although acknowledging a shortage of 500 nurses in November 1943, admitted just four African-American women to that specialty.

Regression and Ultimate Integration

The wartime experience of African Americans afforded the promise of progress toward the exercise of full citizenship. The March on Washington, though it never took place, demonstrated the effectiveness of mass action, which in this instance had been planned exclusively by black leaders. The CONGRESS OF RACIAL EQUALITY (CORE), an important civil rights organization after the war, worked during the conflict for the integration of the armed forces, which, for reasons of their own, modified but did not abandon racial segregation. The war had a further impact on African-American life because military service qualified individuals for the G.I. Bill with its educational and other benefits.

As it reduced in size, the postwar Army attracted more African Americans than a segregated service could absorb. In Europe, which provided a generally benign racial climate, the number of black soldiers on duty in mid-1946 exceeded the authorization by 19,000, with another 5,000 seeking assignment there. Meanwhile, the Navy and Marine Corps attracted too few African Americans to make integration seem attractive, and, like the Army, they refused to break step with a racially segregated American society. The Air Force, established as an independent service in 1947, voluntarily undertook a measure of racial integration, but the other services avoided compliance with President Harry S. Truman's integration order of 1948 until the manpower demands of the KOREAN WAR forced them to obey.

BIBLIOGRAPHY

Dalfiume, Richard M. *Desegregation of the U.S. Armed Forces: Fighting on Two Fronts, 1939–1953.* Columbia, Mo., 1969.

Davis, Benjamin O., Jr. *Benjamin O. Davis, Jr., American: An Autobiography.* Washington, D.C., 1991.

Finkle, Lee. *Forum for Protest: The Black Press During World War II.* Cranbury, N.J., 1975.

Fletcher, Marvin E. *America's First Black General: Benjamin O. Davis, Sr., 1880–1970.* Lawrence, Kans., 1989.

Jakeman, Robert J. *The Divided Skies: Establishing Segregated Flight Training at Tuskegee, 1934–1942.* Tuscaloosa, Ala., 1992.

Lee, Ulysses. *The United States Army in World War II; Special Studies: The Employment of Negro Troops.* Washington, D.C., 1966.

MacGregor, Morris J. *Defense Studies: The Integration of the Armed Forces, 1940–1965.* Washington, D.C., 1981.

McGuire, Phillip. *He, Too, Spoke for Democracy: Judge William Hastie, World War II, and the Black Soldier.* Westport, Conn., 1988.

Nelson, Dennis D. *The Integration of the Negro into the United States Navy, 1776–1947, with a Brief Historical Introduction.* Washington, D.C., 1948.

Osur, Alan M. *Blacks in the Army Air Forces during World War II.* Washington, D.C., 1977.

Sandler, Stanley. *Segregated Skies: All-Black Combat Squadrons of World War II.* Washington, D.C., 1992.

Shaw, Henry I., Jr., and Ralph Donnelly. *Blacks in the Marine Corps.* Washington, D.C., 1975.

Stillwell, Paul, ed. *The Golden Thirteen: Recollections of the First Black Naval Officers.* Annapolis, Md., 1993.

Wynne, Neil A. *Afro-Americans and the Second World War.* London, 1970.

— BERNARD C. NALTY

WRIGHT, LOUIS TOMPKINS

Louis Tompkins Wright (July 23, 1891–October 8, 1952), physician and hospital administrator. Louis

Tompkins Wright was born in LaGrange, Ga. Both his father, Ceah K. Wright, and his stepfather, William F. Penn, were physicians. Wright received a B.A. from Clark College in Atlanta in 1911. Four years later, he graduated from Harvard Medical School, finishing fourth in his class. During his Harvard obstetrics course he was told that he could not participate in the delivery of babies at Boston-Lying-In Hospital. Wright rallied his classmates to change this policy of racial discrimination. From 1915 to 1916, he completed his internship at Freedmen's Hospital in Washington, D.C. While there, he disproved the accepted medical belief that the Schick test for diphtheria was not useful on blacks because of their dark pigmentation. Wright devised new observational techniques that allowed physicians to detect the reddening of skin necessary to judge the test's results. Wright then returned to Atlanta and entered a medical practice with his stepfather, where he also worked as treasurer of a local branch of the NAACP.

During World War I, Wright entered the U.S. Army Medical Corp at Fort McPherson near Atlanta. Commissioned a first lieutenant, he served at the Colored Officers Training Camps in Iowa and New York. During his service years, Wright introduced the intradermal method of vaccination for smallpox that was adopted by the U.S. Army Medical Corps. Assigned to the 367th Infantry Regiment in France, he suffered permanent lung damage from a phosgene gas attack on the battlefield. The recipient of a Purple Heart, Wright rose to the rank of lieutenant colonel, but was forced to resign this commission because of his injuries. He moved to New York City in 1918, married Corrine Cooke and opened an office for the general practice of surgery.

In 1919 Wright was appointed clinical assistant visiting surgeon at New York's Harlem Hospital. The hospital, in a black community, was staffed and controlled by white physicians. Four doctors resigned in protest when Wright, the first black appointed to a municipal-hospital position in New York City, joined the staff. In 1928, he became the first African-American police surgeon in the city's history. Meanwhile, at Harlem Hospital he continued to succeed, becoming director of surgery in 1943 and president of the hospital's medical board in 1948.

Wright and his researchers pioneered the use of chemotherapy to destroy cancerous cells.

Wright's interests went beyond his surgical specialty. He devised a splint for cervical fractures and a special plate for the repair of certain types of fractures of the femur bone. Using a mostly inert substance, the metal tantalum, he developed a procedure for repairing hernias. His chapter on "Head Injuries" in *The Treatment of Fractures* (1938), was one of the first contributions by an African American to a major medical text. Perhaps Wright's most significant contribution to clinical research involved the first tests on humans of the antibiotic Aureomycin. Aureomycin had been tested in laboratory mice but never on humans. After it was first isolated in the Lederle Laboratories by a former Harvard classmate in 1945, a sample was sent to Wright at Harlem Hospital to adminster to patients who had infections for which other treatments had not worked. The results of this 1947 test were positive, and he experimented with another antibiotic, Terramycin. From 1948 to 1952, Wright published some thirty papers on his trials with antibiotics. His work helped pave the way for these drugs to be approved by the Food and Drug Administration for subsequent manufacturing and widespread use.

In 1948 Wright entered the field of cancer research. Grants from the National Cancer Institute and the Damon Runyon Fund allowed him to establish the Harlem Hospital Cancer Research Foundation. Wright and his researchers, including his daughter, Jane Cooke Wright, pioneered the use of chemotherapy to destroy cancerous cells. He published fifteen papers detailing his investigations with drugs and hormones in treating cancer.

Throughout his career, Wright attacked racial prejudice and discrimination in medicine. In 1932 he opposed the establishment of a separate veteran's hospital for African Americans in the North and protested the inadequate medical care being received by black veterans. As chairman of the board of directors of the NAACP from 1935 to 1952, he established the National Medical Committee to oppose racial discrimination in medicine. The NAACP under his leadership pressed a dozen investigations into discriminatory medical training and care. As chairman, Wright often served in an advisory role to Walter White, the secretary and dominant figure of the NAACP. With speeches and writings, Wright held the powerful American Medical Association accountable for inequalities in medical care for African Americans across the country. In 1940 Wright was awarded the NAACP's Spingarn Medal for his work as a scientist, public servant, and activist.

Wright suffered a fatal heart attack in 1952. Before his death, a new medical library at Harlem Hospital was named after him. At the library dedication ceremony, Wright said, "Harlem Hospital represents the finest example of democracy at work in the field of medicine. Its policy of complete integration throughout the institution has stood the test of time."

BIBLIOGRAPHY

Cobb, W. Montague. "Louis Tompkins Wright." *Journal of the National Medical Association* (March 1953): 130–148.

Haber, Louis. "Louis Tompkins Wright." In *Black Pioneers in Science and Invention.* New York, 1970.

Hayden, Robert C. *Nine Black American Doctors.* Reading, Mass., 1976.

Logan, Rayford W., and Michael R. Winston. "Louis Tompkins Wright." *Dictionary of American Negro Biography.* New York, 1982, pp. 670–671.

– ROBERT C. HAYDEN

WRIGHT, RICHARD

Richard Wright (September 4, 1908–November 28, 1960), writer. Richard Wright was born near Roxie, Miss., the son of a sharecropper and a rural schoolteacher who supported the family when her husband deserted her. Wright's childhood, which he later described in his classic autobiography, *Black Boy* (1945), was horrific. His mother, Ella Wilson Wright, was never healthy, and she became completely paralyzed by the time her son was ten years old. Wright and his family were destitute, and their lives were sharply constricted by pervasive segregation and racism. Wright and his brother Leon moved several times to the homes of relatives in Natchez and in Memphis, Tenn., and then to their grandmother's house in Jackson. A staunch Seventh Day Adventist, Wright's grandmother discouraged his reading, destroyed a radio he had built, and unwittingly alienated him from religious practice. Wright had already had his first story published in a local newspaper, however, when he completed the ninth grade in 1925. He found employment in Memphis, where he discovered the work of H. L. Mencken. Mencken's essays spurred Wright's writing ambitions. Determined to escape the segregated South, which had plagued his childhood, Wright moved to Chicago in 1927.

Over the next several years, during the worst of the Depression, Wright supported himself and his family, which had joined him, through menial labor and at the post office, and wrote when he could find the time. He became acquainted with contemporary literature through Mencken's essays and through friends at the post office, and in 1932 he began meeting writers and artists, mostly white, at the communist-run John Reed Club. Impressed by Marxist theory, Wright became a leader of the Chicago Club and published revolutionary verse in *New Masses* and in small magazines like *Anvil, Left Front* (whose editorial board he joined), and *Partisan Review.* Recruited by communists eager to showcase African Americans in their movement, Wright became active in the party as much for literary reasons as for political ones. He wished, he later explained, to describe the real feelings of the common people and serve as the bridge between them and party theorists. Wright participated in party literary conferences, wrote poetry and stories, and gave lectures. Wright's first novel, *Lawd Today,* written during this period, was published posthumously, in 1963. In 1935, the same year he started as a journalist for *New Masses,* Wright joined the Federal Writers Project of the Works Progress Administration (WPA), helping to write a guide to Illinois, and was transferred to the local Negro Theater unit of the Federal Theater Project the next year. By this time, Wright was having doubts about the Communist party, which he believed to be promoting him only because of his skin color. He insisted on freedom from the party line for his creative work, but he remained publicly committed to the party. In 1937, eager to find a publisher for his work, Wright moved to New York, where he worked as Harlem reporter for the Communist party newspaper *The Daily Worker,* and wrote the Harlem section of the WPA's *New York City Guide* (1939).

In the Autumn 1937 issue of the leftist magazine *Challenge,* Wright wrote his influential "Blueprint for Negro Writing," in which he tried to assert and encourage black nationalism among writers, within a larger Marxist perspective. Wright called on black writers to make use of folklore and oral tradition in their work, but also to pay attention to psychological and sociological data in framing their work. Wright's own short stories, whose unsparing treatment of racism and violence in the South was couched in poetic style, were winning competitions from *Story* magazine and others, and were collected under the title *Uncle Tom's Children* (1938). Though the work was a success, Wright was dissatisfied. He thought that while he had generated sympathy for victims of racism, he had not shown its effects on all of society.

Native Son (1940), Wright's first published novel, became a Book-of-the-Month Club selection and called national attention to his compelling talent, although his unrelenting depiction of racism aroused controversy. In fact, editors had already toned down controversial material (it was not until 1992 that the unexpurgated version of the novel was published). *Native Son* is the story of a ghetto youngster, Bigger Thomas. Trapped by white racism and his own fear, Bigger accidentally murders a white woman. While he tries to cover up his deed, he is arrested, put on trial, and sentenced to death. Bigger's white communist lawyer argues that he is not responsible for his crimes, but Bigger feels that his murder and cover-up were his first creative acts, through which he has found a new freedom. The book's success won Wright the NAACP's prestigious Spingarn Medal in 1941, and a dramatization by Wright and Paul Green was produced by Orson Welles. There were two film adaptations, one a Brazilian film, *Sangre Negra* (1950), in which Wright himself played the part of Bigger Thomas, and *Native Son* (1986), starring Victor Love, but both were commercially unsuccessful.

In 1941 Wright wrote a lyrical Marxist "folk history" of African Americans, *Twelve Million Black Voices.* The following year, he finally left the Communist party. Though still a Marxist, Wright felt that the communists were unrealistic, self-serving, and not truly interested in the liberation of African Americans. During the war years, Wright worked on *Black Boy* (1945), "a record of childhood and youth," which brought him money and international fame. In *Black Boy,* Wright gives a precise, unrelenting account of how he was scarred by the poisons of poverty and racism during his early years in Mississippi. *American Hunger* (1977), a version which included Wright's Chicago years, was published posthumously.

The same year *Black Boy* appeared, Wright wrote an introduction to *Black Metropolis,* the sociological study by St. Clair DRAKE and Horace Cayton of African Americans in Chicago, in which he first expounded his major political theories. White American racism, Wright believed, was a symptom of a deeper general insecurity brought about by the dehumanizing forces of modernity and industrialization. He considered the condition of African Americans a model, and extreme example, of the alienation of the human individual by modern life.

Richard Wright at the Venice Film Festival in 1951, in front of a poster for the Argentinean film Sangre Negro, *an adaptation of his novel* Native Son. *Wright portrayed Bigger Thomas, the central character in the film. (AP/Wide World Photos)*

Wright was invited to France by the French government in 1945, and during the trip he found himself lionized by French intellectuals as a spokesperson for his race. Wright had married a white woman, Ellen Poplar, in 1941, and the couple had had a daughter, Julia. They wished to escape America's racial discrimination. He was delighted by France's apparent freedom from racial prejudice and impressed by the central role that literature and thought enjoyed in French society. Wright decided to "choose exile," and moved to Paris permanently in 1947, although he kept his American passport.

While in France, Wright became friendly with the French existentialists, although he claimed his reading of Dostoyevsky had made him an existentialist long before he met Jean-Paul Sartre and the others. Wright's thesis novel, *The Outsider* (1953), explores the contemporary condition in existentialist terms while rejecting the ideologies of communism and fascism. A posthumously published novella Wright wrote during the period, *The Man Who Lived Underground* (1971), also makes use of existential ideas. Neither *The Outsider* nor Wright's next novel, *Savage Holiday* (1954), was well received.

Wright shared the French intellectuals' suspicion of America, and participated with Sartre and the existentialists in political meetings in 1948 with the idea of producing a "third way" to preserve European culture from the Cold War struggle between American industrial society and Soviet communism. Ironically, Wright was harassed for his leftist background in America, despite his repudiation of the communists. The hostility of the Communist party to Wright grew after he published his essay "I Tried to Be a Communist" in the important anticommunist anthology *The God That Failed* (1950).

Wright had been an original sponsor of the review *Présence Africaine* in 1946, and he turned his primary attention to anticolonial questions during the 1950s. After visiting the Gold Coast in 1954, he wrote *Black Power* (1954), "a record of reactions in a land of pathos," in which he approved Kwame Nkrumah's pan-Africanist policies but stressed his own estrangement from Africa. Wright's introduction to George Padmore's *Pan-Africanism or Communism?* (1956) further disclosed his pan-African ideas. In *The Color Curtain* (1956) he reported on the First Conference of Non-Aligned Countries held in Bandung, Indonesia, in

1955, and explored the importance of race and religion in the world of politics. The same year, he helped organize, under *Présence Africaine's* auspices, the First Conference of Black Writers and Intellectuals. Papers from the conference, along with texts from the numerous lectures on decolonization Wright gave in Europe, were published as *White Man, Listen!* in 1959.

Wright's last works include *Pagan Spain* (1958), a report on Franco's Spain which included a discussion of the Catholic impact on European culture; *The Long Dream* (1959), the first novel of an unfinished trilogy dealing with the lasting effects of racism; *Eight Men* (1960), a collection of short stories; and thousands of unpublished haiku on the Japanese model. Wright died unexpectedly, on November 28, 1960, in Paris, of a heart attack. He was under emotional and mental stress at the time, partly due to spying by U.S. intelligence agents on African Americans in Paris. His sudden death fostered lasting rumors that he had been poisoned by the CIA because of his persistent fight against racial oppression and colonialism.

Wright was the first African-American novelist of international stature, and his violent denunciation of American racism and the black deprivation and hatred it causes was uncompromising. Wright inspired both African-American novelists like Ralph ELLISON and Chester HIMES and foreign writers such as the novelists Peter Abrahams and George Lanning and the political theorist Frantz Fanon. Wright's legendary generosity to other writers was both moral and sometimes financial, through the grants and jobs he found them. Wright also created for himself a role as expatriate writer and international social critic. His strong intellectual interests and earnestness, through which he melded Freudian, Marxist, and pan-African perspectives, were matched by a deep spirituality— despite his rationalist suspicion of religion—and occasional humor and comedy in his works.

BIBLIOGRAPHY

Cruse, Harold. *The Crisis of the Negro Intellectual.* New York, 1967.

Fabre, Michel. *From Harlem to Paris: Black American Writers in France, 1840–1980.* Champaign, Ill., 1991.

———. *The Unfinished Quest of Richard Wright.* Translated by Isabel Barzun. New York, 1973.

Gayle, Addison. *Richard Wright: The Ordeal of a Native Son.* Gloucester, Mass., 1980.

Walker, Margaret. *Richard Wright, Daemonic Genius.* New York, 1987.

Webb, Constance. *Richard Wright.* New York, 1968.

– MICHEL FABRE

Y

YOUNG, ANDREW

Andrew Young (October 23, 1932–), civil rights activist and politician. Andrew Young was born in New Orleans. His father was an affluent, prominent dentist, and Young was raised in a middle-class black family in a racially mixed neighborhood. He attended Howard University in Washington, D.C., and graduated in 1951. Young pursued his growing commitment to religion at Hartford Theological Seminary in Connecticut and was awarded a bachelor of divinity degree in 1955. He was ordained a Congregational minister, and from 1955 to 1959, he preached in churches in Georgia and Alabama. In the course of this work, Young experienced firsthand the wrenching poverty that shaped the lives of African Americans in the rural South. He became active in challenging racial inequality, joined the local CIVIL RIGHTS MOVEMENT and helped organize a voter-registration drive in Thomasville, Ga., one of the first of its kind in southern Georgia.

In 1959, Young went to New York to become an assistant director of the National Council of Churches and help channel New York City philanthropic money into southern civil rights activities. Two years later, he returned to Georgia and joined the SOUTHERN CHRISTIAN LEADERSHIP CONFERENCE (SCLC), a civil rights organization headed by the Rev. Dr. Martin Luther KING, Jr. Young became an active participant in the SCLC, building a reputation for coolness and rationality and often providing a moderating influence within the movement. From 1961 to 1964, he served as funding coordinator and administrator of the SCLC's Citizenship Education Program—a program aimed at increasing black voter registration among African Americans in the South.

Young grew to be one of King's most trusted aides. In 1964, he was named executive director of the SCLC and three years later took on additional responsibility as executive vice president. During his tenure, he focused on creating social and economic programs for African Americans to broaden the scope of SCLC's activism. In 1970, Young relinquished his executive positions. However, he continued his affiliation with SCLC—serving on the board of directors—until 1972.

In 1972, Young turned his energies to the political arena and launched a successful campaign to become the first African American elected to the House of Representatives from Georgia since 1870. In Congress, he served on the House Banking Committee and became familiar with the national and international business markets. In 1976, he vigorously supported the candidacy of fellow Georgian Jimmy Carter for president and vouched for Carter's commitment to black civil rights to many who were skeptical of supporting a white Democrat from the deep South. Upon Carter's election, Young resigned his congressional seat to accept an appointment as the United States Ambassador to the United Nations.

As ambassador, Young focused on strengthening the ties between the United States and the Third World. In 1979, he was forced to resign his position when it was revealed that he had engaged in secret negotiations with representatives of the Palestine Liberation Organization (PLO) in violation of U.S. policy. Young's supporters argued that Young was merely doing the job of a diplomat by speaking to all interested parties in sensitive negotiations. Many Jews and other supporters of Israel, however, believed that Young's actions gave the PLO unwarranted legitimacy. The furor that surrounded his actions forced him to submit his resignation.

In 1982, Young mounted a successful campaign for mayor of Atlanta. During his administration, he faced the same urban problems that plagued other big-city mayors, including a shrinking tax base, rising unemployment, and rising costs—all of which required difficult decisions in fund allocation. Despite these constraints, he was able to increase business investment in Georgia. He successfully ran for reelection in 1986, despite growing criticism from some African-American critics who argued that black Atlantans had been hurt by his economic development programs. In 1990, after he ran unsuccessfully for the Democratic gubernatorial nomination, Young reentered private life. He served as chairman of Law International, Inc., until 1993, when he was appointed vice chairman of their parent company, Law Companies Group, an internationally respected engineering and environmental consulting company based in Atlanta.

During the course of his career, Young has received many awards, including the Presidential Medal of Freedom—America's highest civilian award—and more than thirty honorary degrees from universities such as Yale, Morehouse, and Emory. In 1994, his spiritual memoir, *A Way Out of No Way,* was published. Young lobbied successfully to bring the 1996 Summer Olympics to Atlanta and served as cochairman of the Atlanta Committee for the Olympic Games.

BIBLIOGRAPHY

Clement, Lee, ed. *Andrew Young at the United Nations.* Salisbury, N.C., 1978.

Gardner, Carl. *Andrew Young, A Biography.* New York, 1980.

Powledge, Fred. *Free at Last? The* CIVIL RIGHTS MOVEMENT and the People Who Made It. Boston, 1991.

Young, Andrew. *A Way Out of No Way.* Nashville, Tenn., 1994.

– CHRISTINE A. LUNARDINI

YOUNG, LESTER

Lester Young (August 27, 1909–March 15, 1959), jazz tenor saxophonist. Born Willis Lester Young into a musical family headed by professor and band leader Willis Handy Young, in Woodville, Miss., he spent his childhood with his mother, sister, and brother in Algiers, La., a suburb of New Orleans, where he was introduced to jazz. At the age of ten, his father took three children, including Lester, throughout the South and Midwest with a carnival minstrel band.

Lester began playing on drums, but also played C-melody and alto saxophones before choosing the tenor saxophone as his main instrument. Although the band settled in Minneapolis in 1926, they also toured the northern plains region, playing primarily for dances. In the late 1920s, after a tour of the South, the family migrated to Los Angeles. In 1932, Young joined the original Blue Devils, based in Oklahoma City, which he left the following year to join Bennie Moten's band in Kansas City. Young also played briefly with King Oliver and Count BASIE before he gained national attention in 1934 when he replaced Coleman HAWKINS in Fletcher Henderson's band. Other members of the sax section did not welcome his unique sound, however, and Young left after a few months and returned to the Midwest. He played with Andy Kirk and with other ensembles before rejoining Count Basie in 1936, shortly before the band moved to New York City and achieved national fame.

Young remained with Basie until 1940, recording with both the full band and smaller ensembles. Many of his best known recordings were made at this time, including "Shoe Shine Boy," "Oh Lady Be Good," "Taxi War Dance," "Jive at Five," "Lester Leaps In," "Dickie's Dream," and "Way Down Yonder in New Orleans." He also recorded a number of sessions with small groups under the leadership of Teddy Wilson and Billie HOLIDAY. These records are exemplars of swing-era jazz.

After leaving Basie, Young led his own band in New York City and Los Angeles, before rejoining Count Basie from late 1943 until his induction into the Army in the fall of 1944. His military service—which led to a court-martial and a year in detention for barbituate and marijuana possession—was traumatic, and was in part responsible for his increasingly severe alcoholism. In 1946 Young joined Norman Granz's touring concert series Jazz at the Philharmonic, under whose auspices he toured extensively in the 1940s and '50s. In the 1950s he developed a new style, darker and less buoyant in tone. His playing remained at an extraordinarily high level until his death in New York on March 15, 1959, only a day after he returned from a sojourn in Paris.

Young's unique vibratoless tone, flawless execution, rhythmic excitement, and daring new lines won him legions of admirers.

Young's familiar nickname, "Pres," or "Prez," was allegedly given to him by singer Billie Holiday in the mid-1930s, but Oklahoma City Blue Devil band members remembered calling him "Pres" in 1932, before he met the famous singer. After the consummate innovator Coleman Hawkins, Young was the foremost tenor sax stylist with a unique sound and chief architect of a conception of playing alternative to that of Hawkins. Young's unique vibratoless tone, flawless execution, rhythmic excitement, and daring new lines won him legions of admirers; while he was praised for his solos, counterpoised against the riffs of the big band, he also attracted considerable attention for his peerless backing of vocalists, and the numerous riffs that were the basis of his own compositions and many of the Basie band motifs. "Lester Leaps In," "D. B. Blues," and "Up and Adam" were among his own compositions, but he also excelled at providing definitive renditions of such ballads as "These Foolish Things," "Polka Dots and Moonbeams," and "Three Little Words." The juxtaposition of relaxation ("cool") and tension ("hot") characterized much of his playing, but his performances defied simple formulaic definition. His profound influence on saxophonists Al Cohn, John COLTRANE, Stan Getz, Wardell Gray, Dexter Gordon, Charlie PARKER, and Zoot Sims was matched by his considerable impact on trumpeters Miles DAVIS and Art Farmer, as well as guitarists Charlie Christian, John Collins, Barney Kessel, and B. B. King. His contributions and influences placed him on a level with Louis ARMSTRONG and Charlie Parker.

Young's special genius extended beyond music to include his language and style of life. His life, words, and conception of music were a coherent whole. Young was complex, a man of gentle demeanor, introverted and nonviolent, but loved for his sense of humor, witty expressions, and storytelling abilities. He differed from many other band leaders in treating members of his combo as equals, staying with them in hotels on the road, and allowing ample time for them to solo on the bandstand. He also innovated in jazz slang, introducing such terms as "That's cool [all right; agreeable]," "How's the bread smell? [How much pay for the job?]," and "You dig? [Do you understand?]"; in fact, he preferred this argot, speaking standard English as little as possible. An archetypal hipster, he was famous for his adoption of the porkpie hat, a flat-crowned, wide-brimmed style popular in the 1940s. He was featured in Gjon Mili's film short "Jammin' the Blues" (1944) immortalized by Charles Mingus's tribute to him, "Goodbye Pork Pie Hat," and has been the subject of poems; a play, *The Resurrection of Lady Lester* (1980); and an opera, *Prez—A Jazz Opera* (1985). Among the numerous tributes to him are the "Pres Awards" on New York's 52nd Street; the Annual Lester Young Memorial Services in St. Peter's Lutheran Church (New York City) every March 15, which mark the day of his death; Prez Conference, a band which plays and harmonizes his solos; and numerous reissues of his recordings.

BIBLIOGRAPHY

Buchman-Moller, Frank. *You Just Fight for Your Life: The Story of Lester Young.* New York, 1990.

Daniels, Douglas Henry. "Goodbye Pork Pie Hat: Lester Young as Spiritual Figure." *Annual Review of Jazz Studies* 4 (1988): 161–177.

Porter, Lewis. *Lester Young.* Boston, 1985.

Porter, Lewis, ed. *A Lester Young Reader.* Washington, 1991.

– DOUGLAS HENRY DANIELS

YOUNG, WHITNEY MOORE, JR.

Whitney Moore Young, Jr. (July 31, 1921–March 11, 1971), civil rights leader. Whitney M. Young, Jr., was born and raised in rural Lincoln Ridge, Ky., to Whitney, Sr., and Laura Ray Young. He grew up on the campus of Lincoln Institute, a vocational high school for black students where his father taught and later served as president. In this setting, Young, who attended the institute from 1933 to 1937, was relatively isolated from external racism. At the same time, he was surrounded by black people who held positions of authority and were treated with respect. In September 1937, Young enrolled at Kentucky State Industrial College in Frankfort; he graduated in June 1941. In college he met Margaret Buckner, whom he married in January 1944; the couple later had two daughters.

After serving in World War II, Young entered a master's program in social work at the University of Minnesota in the spring of 1946, which included a field placement with the Minneapolis chapter of the NATIONAL URBAN LEAGUE (NUL). He graduated in 1947 and, in September of that year, he became industrial relations secretary of the St. Paul Urban League, where he encouraged employers to hire black workers. Two years later he was appointed to serve as executive secretary with the NUL's affiliate in Omaha, Neb.

During his tenure in Omaha, Young dramatically increased both the chapter's membership base and its operating budget. He fared less well, however, in his attempts to gain increased employment opportunities for African Americans; victories in this area continued to be largely symbolic, resulting primarily from subtle behind-the-scenes pressure exerted by Young himself. Through his Urban League experience, Young became adept at cultivating relationships with powerful white corporate and political leaders.

In early 1954 Young became dean of the Atlanta University School of Social Work. He doubled the school's budget, raised teaching salaries and called for enhanced professional development. With the 1954 BROWN V. BOARD OF EDUCATION OF TOPEKA, KANSAS, Supreme Court decision and the unfolding of civil rights activism, his activities became increasingly political. He served on the board of the Atlanta NAACP, and he played a leadership role in several other organizations committed to challenging the racial status quo, including the Greater Atlanta Council on Human Relations and the Atlanta Committee for Cooperative Action. Unlike some other black community leaders, Young supported and even advised students who engaged in sit-in demonstrations in 1960. Yet Young personally opted for a low-key approach characterized by technical support for the CIVIL RIGHTS MOVEMENT rather than activism.

Young retained close ties with NUL, and in 1960 he emerged as a top candidate for executive director of the New York-based organization. Although by far the youngest of the contenders for the position, and the least experienced in NUL work, Young was selected to fill the national post effective October 1961. Since its founding in 1910–1911, NUL had been more concerned with social services than social change; its successes had long depended on alliance with influential white corporate and political figures. However, by the early 1960s it was clear that unless it took on a more active and visible role in civil rights, the organization risked losing credibility with the black community. It was Whitney Young who, in more ways than one, would lead NUL into that turbulent decade.

For years, local Urban League activists had lobbied for a more aggressive posture on racial issues. At Young's urging, NUL's leadership reluctantly resolved to participate in the Civil Rights Movement—but as a voice of "respectability" and restraint. In January 1962, Young declared that, while NUL would not engage actively in protests, it would not condemn others' efforts if they were carried out "under responsible leadership using legally acceptable methods." By helping to plan the 1963 March on Washington, Young simultaneously hoped to confirm NUL's new commitment and ensure that the march would pose no overt challenge to those in authority. Young also furthered NUL's moderate agenda by participating in the Council for United Civil Rights Leadership (CUCRL), a consortium founded in June 1963 to facilitate fundraising and information-sharing. (CUCRL was initiated by wealthy white philanthropists concerned with minimizing competition among civil rights organizations and tempering the movement's more militant elements.)

As "black power" gained currency within the movement, new tensions surfaced inside NUL itself. Students and other Urban League workers disrupted the organization's yearly conferences on several occasions, demanding the adoption of a more action-oriented strategy. Young continued to insist on the primacy of social service provision. But in June 1968, in an address at the CONGRESS OF RACIAL EQUALITY's (CORE) annual meeting, he spoke favorably of self-sufficiency and community control. The NUL initiated a "New Thrust" program intended to strengthen its base in black neighborhoods and to support community organizing.

During his ten-year tenure, Young made his mark on NUL in other significant ways. He guided the development of innovative new programs meant to facilitate job training and placement, and he vastly increased corporate and foundation support for the organization. In the early and mid-1960s, as corporations (especially government contractors) came under fire for failing to provide equal employment opportunities, business leaders turned to the NUL and its affiliates for help in hiring black workers. At the same time, by aiding NUL financially, they hoped to demonstrate convincingly a commitment to nondiscriminatory policies.

Of the three U.S. presidents in office during Young's tenure with the League, Lyndon B. Johnson proved to be the closest ally; he drew on Young's ideas and expertise in formulating antipoverty programs, tried to bring Young into the administration, and awarded him the Medal of Freedom in 1969. Although the relationship with Johnson was important for accomplishing NUL's goals, at times it constrained Young's own political positions. In mid-1966, Young clashed with the Rev. Dr. Martin Luther KING, Jr., and other civil rights leaders who opposed the Vietnam War; Young insisted that communism must be stopped in Southeast Asia; and he disagreed that the military effort would divert resources away from urgent problems facing African Americans at home. A year later, he was no longer so sure. Nonetheless, at Johnson's request, he traveled to South Vietnam with an official U.S. delegation. Young did not speak publicly against the war until late 1969, when Richard M. Nixon was president.

In addition to overseeing NUL's "entry" into civil rights, Young heightened the organization's visibility to a popular audience. He wrote a regular column, "To Be Equal," for the *Amsterdam News,* which was syndicated through newspapers and radio stations nationwide. He published several books, including *To Be Equal* (1964), and *Beyond Racism* (1969). At the same time, Young continued to maneuver in the highest echelons of the corporate world; among other activities, he served on the boards of the Federal Reserve Bank of New York, the Massachusetts Institute of Technology, and the Rockefeller Foundation. He also remained a prominent figure in the social work profession, serving as president of the National Conference on Social Welfare in 1967 and acting as president of the National Association of Social Workers from June 1969 until his death.

In March 1971, Young traveled to Lagos, Nigeria, with a delegation of African Americans, in order to participate in a dialogue with African leaders. He died there while swimming, either from drowning or from a brain hemorrhage.

BIBLIOGRAPHY

Johnson, Thomas A. "Whitney Young Jr. Dies on Visit to Lagos." *New York Times,* March 12, 1971, p. 1.

NASW News 13, no. 4 (August 1968): 1.

Parris, Guichard, and Lester Brooks. *Blacks in the City: A History of the National Urban League.* Boston, 1971.

Weiss, Nancy J. *Whitney M. Young, Jr. and the Struggle for Civil Rights.* Princeton, N.J., 1989.

— TAMI J. FRIEDMAN

YOUNG MEN'S CHRISTIAN ASSOCIATION

Although the image of a physical fitness facility dominates the current perception of the Young Men's Christian Association (YMCA), it has long been an avenue for building community spirit and a sense of social responsibility among black Christian men. When the YMCA movement in the United States began in 1852, African-American men were excluded from membership based on local practices of segregation. Two years later, when the YMCAs in the United States joined with those in Canada to form the Confederation of North American YMCAs, U.S. racial policies became a serious issue. This confederation eventually dissolved over slavery and the Civil War. Despite the conflict, the National YMCA held fast to its assertion that local associations were autonomous bodies which could choose to exclude black men from membership.

African-American men saw possibilities in YMCA work, despite the organization's failure to take a stand against discrimination. The first black YMCA was organized in 1853 in Washington, D.C., and lasted through the Civil War. Following the War, black associations were founded in Charleston, S.C., and New York City, as well as other cities. Student YMCAs among black college students were also founded in this period. The growing interest in YMCA work among black men and the question of how best to aid the newly freed slaves moved the national YMCA to begin to encourage the formation of black YMCA branches.

African-American men saw possibilities in YMCA work, despite the organization's failure to take a stand against discrimination.

Although there was growth in this field during the late nineteenth century, it did not begin to thrive until the first black International Secretary for Colored Work was employed in 1891. William A. Hunton, who had worked in black YMCA branches in Ottawa, Canada, and Norfolk, Va., devoted his life to the expansion of YMCA work among black men. The staff later expanded to include Jesse E. Moorland, George Edmund Haynes, and Channing H. Tobias, among others. All these men opposed segregation in YMCA work but recognized the positive aspects of having the space to train young black men for leadership through volunteer and paid positions at the "Y." In addition, they felt that the problems facing young African-American men, particularly in urban areas, required knowledge of issues with which white YMCA workers had little experience dealing.

World War I proved to be a turning point for African-American men in the YMCA. During the war, the YMCA conducted successful work with black soldiers, focusing on health issues and on literacy training. Immediately following the war, the YMCA began to reevaluate its racial policies and encourage interracial dialogue. It was not until 1946, however, that the national YMCA urged local branches to desegregate, largely due to entreaties on the part of the World Alliance of YMCAs.

Although desegregation in YMCA work led to the closing of many of the all-black branches, the YMCA has remained a force in black communities. The work has expanded to include both women and men of all religious backgrounds. Local YMCAs sponsor summer camps, residence halls, adult education, job training, and a host of other activities and services. The YMCA continues to be relevant because of its longstanding commitment to creating workable communities and because of its willingness to modify its approach in changing times.

BIBLIOGRAPHY

Mjagkij, Nina. History of the Black YMCA in America, 1853–1946. Ph.D. diss., University of Cincinnati, 1990.

– JUDITH WEISENFELD

YOUNG WOMEN'S CHRISTIAN ASSOCIATION

The Young Women's Christian Association (YWCA) has been an important avenue for black Christian women's activism since the late nineteenth century. African-American women, primarily in northern urban areas, began to develop such associations with a desire to educate and train young black women and provide them with tools for survival in the city. A key component of this survival was a connection with the churches, so voting membership was restricted to young women who were members of Protestant evangelical churches. Services provided through these urban YWCA's included Bible study, lodging, trade classes, employment counseling and referrals, as well as a variety of social activities.

While the YWCA has had black members almost from the time of its founding in America in 1866, black women in the movement were segregated into a "Colored Branch" system. The YWCA operated as a biracial organization, then, rather than as an integrated one until the middle of the twentieth century. At the same time, however, a movement among students at both black colleges and at predominantly white colleges allowed for active participation in Student Christian Associations by African-American students. The student groups and the branches were brought under the jurisdiction of the National Board of the YWCA in 1906.

The segregated branch structure had both positive and negative aspects. On the one hand, these black YWCAs became important centers for educational and employment opportunities for young women and a training ground for leadership. On the other hand, colored branches were required to gain the approval of local white YWCAs in order to be recognized by the National Board. This policy clearly capitulated to the racism of many southern white women in the movement.

The Young Women's Christian Association (YWCA) has been an important avenue for black Christian women's activism since the late nineteenth century.

At the level of the National Board there were advances in representation and participation of black women in the operation of the national organization. Addie Waites Hunton and Elizabeth Ross Haynes were two of the early staff members at the national level. From World War I on, Eva Bowles, the secretary for Colored Work for the National Board, expanded the staffing of her department and encouraged growth in local branches through financial assistance. In addition, in 1924, Elizabeth Ross Haynes became the first black elected member of the board. Black women in the YWCA, with the support of black women leaders in the South, continued to call for a clear break with the biracial policies operative in the movement.

At the 1946 annual convention the YWCA adopted an "Interracial Charter," which called for pioneering in a democratic and Christian "interracial experience" in the YWCA. From this point on, despite some opposition, the YWCA moved to reorganize its previously segregated system. Positions focusing on interracial education were created at the National Board level to assist in the transition. Dorothy Height was a key figure in this area.

By 1970, the YWCA had been fairly successful in achieving the goals of the Interracial Charter but recognized the continued presence of racism, both in the organization and in society at large. At the 1970 conference, the YWCA passed a declaration that pronounced its one imperative as exerting its "collective power to eliminate racism wherever it exists and by any means necessary." Helen Jackson Wilkins Claytor, the first black president of the National Board, was instrumental in achieving this declaration.

Black women have continued to work through the YWCA out of a commitment to activism from a Christian perspective and to the possibilities of such work with women of all backgrounds.

BIBLIOGRAPHY

Lerner, Gerda. *Black Women in White America.* New York, 1972.

Salem, Dorothy. *To Better Our World: Black Women in Organized Reform, 1890–1920.* Brooklyn, 1990.

– JUDITH WEISENFELD

Z

ZYDECO

Zydeco is a style of popular dance music played by African Americans of Francophone descent in the Gulf Coast region, particularly in the bayou country of southwestern Louisiana.

Despite its frenetic tempos, often led by a buoyant singer doubling on accordion, the term *zydeco* derives from the old Louisiana song "Les Haricots Sont Pas Salés," literally translated as "the green beans aren't salted," but commonly having the meaning "times aren't good."

The origins of zydeco go back to the popular dance tunes of French settlers, or Acadians, who were expelled from Nova Scotia by the British and arrived in Louisiana in the eighteenth century. They intermarried with African Americans and Native Americans of French and Spanish descent, and their European-derived string music absorbed Afro-Caribbean rhythmic elements. The first zydeco recordings, difficult to distinguish from other forms of Cajun music, are 1934 field recordings, including "Cajun Negro Fais Dos-Dos Tune," by Ellis Evans and Jimmy Lewis, and "Les Haricots Sont Pas Salés," by Austin Coleman and Joe Washington. Accordionist Amadé Ardoin was an important early zydeco musician whose "Les Blues de la Prison" (1934) shows a strong BLUES influence.

Zydeco is a style of popular dance music played by African Americans of Francophone descent in the bayou country of southwestern Louisiana.

After World War II, RHYTHM AND BLUES began to influence zydeco, a development clearly heard on Clarence Garlow's "Bon Ton Roula" (1950), which translates as "Let the Good Times Roll." During this time accordionist Clifton Chenier, perhaps the greatest of all zydeco musicians, came to prominence. Born in Opelousas, La., in 1925, he made his first recordings in the 1950s, and pioneered the use of the piano accordion—an accordion with a keyboard—in zydeco music. Among the many popular and important records, noted for their heavy dance rhythms, that Chenier made before his death from diabetes in 1987 are "Black Gal" (1965), "Jambalaya" (1975), and *Country Boy Now* (1984).

In Louisiana, zydeco is invariably performed for dancers, often at nightclubs, dance halls, churches, picnics, and house parties known as "fais-do-do." Zydeco bands are typically led by a singer, with lead accompaniment by fiddle, button or piano accordion, or guitar, and backed by a rhythm section of bass, piano, and drums. Harmonica, washboard, "frottoir" (a metal rubbing board played with household implements), and the "bas trang" (triangle), were often used earlier in the century, but today are often replaced by electric instruments. Zydeco is sung in the patois of Creole Louisiana, with lyrics ranging from narrative tales, love songs, and laments to simple invocations to dancing and good times.

Although for a century zydeco has been, along with jazz and blues, a mainstay of the secular music scene among the Creole-descended population along the Gulf Coast from Louisiana to Texas, in recent years zydeco has achieved international popularity, and its greatest exponents have become celebrities with prolific touring and recording schedules. In addition to Chenier, other important zydeco musicians include accordionist Boozoo Chavis ("Paper In My Shoe," 1984), singer Queen Ida (*Cookin' With Queen Ida,* 1989), Rockin' Sidney ("My Toot Toot," 1984), and Lawrence "Black" Ardoin ("Bayou Two Step," 1984). Important ensembles include the Lawrence Ardoin Band, Terrence Semiens and the Mallet Playboys, and Buckwheat Zydeco's Ils Sont Partis Band.

Although zydeco and Cajun music share many musical elements and have common sociocultural origins in the late nineteenth-century contact between Creoles and Acadians, they are distinct forms, representing two aspects of the complex, multiracial culture that also produced jazz. Zydeco tends toward faster tempos, a syncopated rhythmic structure, and a deemphasis of the melodic line. Cajun's rhythms are often more rigid two-step dances or waltzes emphasizing melody. Zydeco has been documented in such films as *Zydeco: Creole Music and Culture in Rural Louisiana* (1984), and *J'ai Eté au Bal* (1991).

BIBLIOGRAPHY

Ancelet, Barry Jean, and E. Morgan. *The Makers of Cajun Music.* Austin, Tex., 1984.

Broven, John. *South to Louisiana: The Music of the Cajun Bayous.* New York, 1983.

Spitzer, Nicholas. Zydeco and Mardi Gras: Creole Identity and Performance Genres in Rural French Louisiana. Ph.D. diss., University of Texas at Austin, 1986.

— JONATHAN GILL

APPENDIX

Tables and Statistical Data

Table 1

PERSONS ARRESTED, BY CHARGE, 1972–1995*

	1972		1980		1995	
Charge	**Total**	**Black**	**Total**	**Black**	**Total**	**Black**
All Charges	6,707.0	1,847.6	9,684.0	2,375.2	10,362.8	32,124.5
Serious Crimes:	1,311.6	471.1	2,195.0	720.7	—	—
Murder	13.8	8.3	19.0	9.0	15.4	8.3
Forcible rape	17.8	8.8	29.0	14.0	24.1	10.1
Robbery	89.4	59.6	139.0	80.5	130.8	77.1
Aggravated assault	138.8	62.9	258.0	93.3	399.4	151.7
Burglary	296.2	95.9	479.0	139.4	266.3	101.2
Larceny/theft	642.3	196.9	1,123.0	342.6	1,056.1	337.9
Motor vehicle theft	110.3	37.9	130.0	38.1	137.2	52.1
Arson	n/a	n/a	18.0	3.8	13.5	3.1
All Other:						
Other assaults	290.9	111.8	456.0	145.1	883.8	300.5
Forgery & counterfeiting	40.1	12.9	72.0	23.9	84.0	27.7
Embezzlement, fraud	100.3	27.2	273.0	81.9	306.4	104.0
Stolen property	62.6	23.0	115.0	36.6	114.9	44.8
Weapons (carrying, etc.)	109.2	56.6	157.0	57.2	170.3	64.7
Prostitution & vice	40.9	25.1	83.0	45.6	74.6	26.8
Sex offenses	48.3	11.0	63.0	12.6	66.0	14.5
Drug abuse violations	402.3	84.4	532.0	125.6	1,048.3	387.8
Gambling	66.5	46.2	47.0	31.1	14.6	6.0
Offenses against family & children	51.9	15.2	50.0	18.0	84.6	27.0
Driving intoxicated	590.8	97.2	1,289.0	144.0	917.1	100.8
Liquor laws	203.5	22.6	428.0	27.5	394.6	67.0
Drunkenness	1,365.7	280.7	1,048.0	165.9	489.3	78.3
Disorderly conduct	565.1	190.1	724.0	219.4	487.0	170.4
Vagrancy	34.8	9.9	29.0	9.0	19.5	8.8
Other, except traffic	1,422.4	362.5	1,658.0	436.7	2,677.4	910.3

* In thousands.
— Data not available on a comparable basis with previous years.
Sources: *Statistical Abstract, 1980, 1972; Uniform Crime Reports: Crime in the United States, 1991.*

Table 2

AIDS DEATHS, 1982–1995

Year	Total	Black	% Black
1985 and before	12,493	3,424	27.41
1986	11,537	3,044	26.38
1987	15,451	4,525	29.29
1988	19,657	6,015	30.60
1989	26,355	7,950	33.15
1990	29,834	9,010	33.11
1991	34,551	10,722	32.22
1992	38,813	12,839	30.23
1993	41,077	14,420	28.48
1994	43,975	16,294	26.98
1995	31,256	11,879	26.31

Sources: *Black Americans: A Statistical Sourcebook* (for 1982 and 1983); *Statistical Abstract, 1992* (for 1984); *Statistical Abstract, 1993.*

Table 3

DEATH RATES BY SELECTED CAUSES, 1960–1994*

	Total				Black			
Cause of Death	**1960**	**1970**	**1980**	**1994**	**1960**	**1970**	**1980**	**1994**
Total	760.9	714.3	585.8	—	1,073.3	1,044.0	842.5	—
Diseases of the heart	286.2	253.6	202.0	281.3	334.5	307.6	255.7	235.2
Malignant neoplasms (cancer)	125.8	129.9	132.8	205.2	142.3	156.7	172.1	183.5
Cerebrovascular diseases[1]	79.7	66.3	40.8	58.9	140.2	114.5	68.5	55.2
Accidents and adverse effects	49.9	53.7	42.3	35.1	66.4	74.4	51.2	39.1
Homicide and legal intervention	—	9.1	10.8	58.9	—	46.1	40.6	37.4
Diabetes	13.6	14.1	10.1	21.8	22.0	26.5	20.3	30.1
Pneumonia, flu[2]	28.0	22.1	12.9	31.3	56.4	40.4	19.2	22.9
Chronic obstructive pulmonary diseases[3]	—	—	15.9	39.0	—	—	12.5	19.9
Cirrhosis and chronic liver disease	10.5	14.7	12.2	9.8	11.7	24.8	21.6	—
Suicide	—	11.8	11.4	12.0	—	6.1	6.4	—

* Deaths classified according to the revision of the International Classification of Diseases in use at that time; rates are per 100,000 for residential, age-adjusted population.

[1] Primarily strokes.

[2] 1960s figures for pneumonia and influenza.

[3] Such as emphysema or asthma.

— Data not available on a comparable basis with later years.

Sources: *Statistical Abstract* (1984, 1992); U.S. National Center for Health Statistics, "Vital Statistics of the United States" (annual).

Table 4

LEGAL ABORTIONS, WOMEN 15–44 YEARS OF AGE, 1975–1988

	Total*	**Black and Nonwhite***
1975		
Women, 15–44	47,606	6,749
Abortions	1,034.2	333.0
Rate	21.7	49.3
1980		
Women, 15–44	53,048	8,106
Abortions	1,553.9	460.3
Rate	29.3	56.5
1985		
Women, 15–44	56,754	9,242
Abortions	1,588.6	512.9
Rate	28.0	55.5
1988		
Women, 15–44	58,192	9,242
Abortions	1,590.8	565.1
Rate	27.3	57.3

* All data are in thousands or per 1,000.

Sources: *Statistical Abstract, 1992; Black Americans: A Statistical Sourcebook.*

Table 5

AFRICAN-AMERICAN MINISTERS RESIDENT AND CONSULS GENERAL TO HAITI, 1869–1913

Ebenezer Don Carlos Basset, 1869–1877
John Mercer Langston, 1877–1885
John Edward West Thompson, 1885–1889
Frederick Augustus Washington Bailey Douglass, 1889–1891
John Stephens Durham, 1891–1893
William Frank Powell, 1897–1905
Henry Watson Furniss, 1905–1913*

* Envoy Extraordinary and Minister Plenipotentiary
Source: David Shavit, *The United States in Latin America: A Historical Dictionary*.

Table 6

AFRICAN-AMERICAN MINISTERS RESIDENT AND CONSULS GENERAL TO LIBERIA, 1871–1948

James Milton Turner, 1871–1878
Henry Highland Garnet, 1881–1882
John Henry Smyth, 1878–1881, 1882–1885
Moses Aaron Hopkins, 1885–1886
Ezekiel Ezra Smith, 1888–1890
Alexander Clark, 1890–1891
William Henry Heard, 1895–1898
Owen Lun West Smith, 1898–1902
Ernest Lyon, 1903–1910
William Demos Crum, 1910–1912
George Washington Buckner, 1913–1915
James L. Curtis, 1915–1917
Joseph Lowry Johnson, 1918–1922
Solomon Porter Hood, 1922–1926
William Treyanne Francis, 1927–1929
Lester Aglar Walton, 1935–1945*
Raphael O'Hara Lanier, 1946–1948*

* Envoy Extraordinary and Minister Plenipotentiary
Source: David Shavit, *The United States in Africa: A Historical Dictionary;* compiled by Erica Judge.

Table 7

FIRST AFRICAN-AMERICAN PLAYERS ON MAJOR LEAGUE BASEBALL TEAMS

Player	Date	Team
Jackie Robinson	4/47	Brooklyn Dodgers
Larry Doby	4/47	Cleveland Indians
Henry Thompson	7/47	St. Louis Browns
Henry Thompson	7/49	New York Giants
Sam Jethroe	4/50	Boston Braves
Sam Hairston	7/51	Chicago White Sox
Bob Trice	9/53	Philadelphia Athletics
Gene Baker	9/53	Chicago Cubs
Curt Roberts	4/54	Pittsburgh Pirates
Tom Alston	4/54	St. Louis Cardinals
Nino Escalera	4/54	Cincinnati Reds
Carlos Paula	9/54	Washington Senators
Elston Howard	4/55	New York Yankees
John Kennedy	4/57	Philadelphia Phillies
Ossie Virgil	6/58	Detroit Tigers
Pumpsie Green	7/59	Boston Red Sox

Table 8

PROFESSIONAL ASSOCIATIONS

Name	Year Founded	Members (1997)
African-American Museums Association	1978	430
African-American Publishers, Booksellers and Writers Association	1969	—
African Heritage Studies Association	1969	—
African Literature Association	1974	800
Afro-American Police League (formerly Afro-American Patrolmen's League, 1979)	1968	2,500
Alliance of Minority Women for Business and Political Development	1982	45
American Academy of Medical Directors	1975	—
American Association for Affirmative Action	1974	1,200
American Association of Blacks in Energy	1977	900
American Black Book Writers' Association	1980	4,000
Association for the Preservation and Presentation of the Arts	1964	500
Association for the Study of Afro-American Life and History (formerly Association for the Study of Negro Life and History, 1973)	1915	2,500
Association of African American People's Legal Council	1959	—
Association of African-American Women Business Owners (formerly American Association of Black Women Entrepreneurs, 1990)	1983	725
Association of Black Admissions and Financial Aid Officers of the Ivy League and Sister Schools	1970	77
Association of Black Cardiologists	1974	500
Association of Black Foundation Executives	1971	—
Association of Black Nursing Faculty in Higher Education	1987	127
Association of Black Psychologists	1968	1,900
Association of Black Sociologists (formerly Caucus of Black Sociologists, 1976)	1968	400
Association of Black Storytellers	1984	700
Association of Black Women in Higher Education	1979	350
Association of Concerned African Scholars	1977	275
Association of Haitian Physicians Abroad	1972	900
Black Business Alliance	1979	250
Black Caucus of the American Library Association	1970	1,000
Black Entertainment and Sports Lawyers Association	1979	400
Black Psychiatrists of America	1968	1,600
Black Rock Coalition	1985	250
Black Stuntmen's Association	1966	34
Black Women in Publishing	1979	200
Black Women's Educational Alliance	1976	300
Blacks in Government	1986	6,000
Blacks in Law Enforcement	1986	900
College Language Association	1937	1,700
Conference of Minority Public Administrators (section of the American Society for Public Administration)	1971	460
Council of 1890 College Presidents	1913	18
Ethnic Employees of the Library of Congress	1973	—
Gospel Music Association	1964	6,000
Gospel Music Workshop of America	1966	18,000
International Association of African and American Black Business People	1965	*84,000
International Association of Black Professional Fire Fighters	1970	8,500
International Black Writers (formerly International Black Writers' Conference, 1982)	1970	1,800
International Black Writers and Artists	1974	500
International Rhythm and Blues Association	1966	50
Minorities in Media	1975	85
Minority Caucus of Family Service America (formerly Black Caucus of the Family Service Association of America, 1973; Minority Caucus of the Family Service Association of America, 1986)	1969	—
Music Educators' National Conference-National Black Music Caucus	1972	—
Mutual Musicians' Foundation	1917	125
National Action Council for Minorities in Engineering	1980	—
National Alliance of Black School Educators	1970	5,000
National Association for Equal Opportunities	1975	60

(continued)

Table 8 (continued)

PROFESSIONAL ASSOCIATIONS

Name	Year Founded	Members (1997)
National Association for the Advancement of Black Americans in Vocational Education	1977	900
National Association of African American Students of Law	1973	—
National Association of Black Accountants	1969	5,000
National Association of Black Catholic Administrators	1976	—
National Association of Black Consulting Engineers	1975	100
National Association of Black Geologists and Geophysicists	1981	120
National Association of Black Hospitality Professionals	1985	800
National Association of Black Journalists	1975	—
National Association of Black Owned Broadcasters	1976	150
National Association of Black Professors	1974	135
National Association of Black Real Estate Professionals	1984	—
National Association of Black Social Workers	1968	4,000
National Association of Black Women Attorneys	1972	500
National Association of Black Women Entrepreneurs	1979	3,000
National Association of Blacks in Criminal Justice	1972	3,000
National Association of Blacks Within Government	1982	—
National Association of College Deans, Registrars, and Admissions Officers (formerly National Association of Collegiate Deans and Registrars in Negro Schools, 1949; National Association of College Deans and Registrars, 1970)	1925	325
National Association of Educational Office Professionals	1934	6,500
National Extension Association of Family and Consumer Services	1931	5,100
National Association of Fashion and Accessory Designers	1949	240
National Association of Health Service Executives	1968	500
National Association of Human Rights Workers	1947	350
National Association Management Consultants	1985	30
National Association of Market Developers	1953	—
National Association of Minority Automobile Dealers	1980	500
National Association of Minority Contractors	1969	5,000
National Association of Minority Women in Business	1972	5,000
National Association of Negro Musicians	1919	2,500
National Association of Securities Professionals	1985	300
National Association of Urban Bankers	1975	3,000
National Bar Association	1925	17,000
National Beauty Culturists League	1919	10,000
National Black Bankers' Association	1927	—
National Black Catholic Clergy Caucus	1968	650
National Black Caucus of Local Elected Officials	1970	400
National Black Caucus of State Legislators	1977	575
National Black McDonalds Operators' Association	1972	169
National Black Nurses Association	1971	5,000
National Black Police Association	1972	35,000
National Black Public Relations Society	1981	—
National Black Sisters' Conference	1968	150
National Business League (formerly National Negro Business League)	1900	10,000
National Coalition of Black Meeting Planners	1983	800
National Conference of Black Lawyers	1968	1,700
National Conference of Black Mayors	1974	361
National Conference of Black Political Scientists	1969	—
National Conference of Editorial Workers	1947	600
National Council for Black Studies	1975	500
National Dental Assistants Association	1964	500
National Dental Association	1913	5,000
National Dental Hygienists' Association	1932	100
National Economic Association (formerly Caucus of Black Economists, 1975)	1969	—

(continued)

Table 8 (continued)

PROFESSIONAL ASSOCIATIONS

Name	Year Founded	Members (1997)
National Florists' Association (formerly International Flower Association, 1963; International Florists' Association, 1988)	1953	500
National Forum for Black Public Administrators	1983	3,000
National Funeral Directors' and Morticians' Association	1938	1,600
National Hypertension Association	1977	—
National Insurance Association	1921	13
National Medical Association	1895	22,000
National Naval Officers' Association	1971	2,686
National Network of Minority Women in Science	1978	250
National Newspaper Publishers' Association	1940	178
National Optometric Association	1969	350
National Organization for the Professional Advancement of Black Chemists and Chemical Engineers	1972	2,000
National Organization of Black County Officials	1982	2,000
National Organization of Black Law Enforcement Executives	1976	3,500
National Organization of Minority Architects (formerly National Organization of Black Architects, 1973)	1971	600
National Podiatric Medical Association	1971	200
National Society of Black Engineers	1975	10,000
National Society of Certified Public Accountants	—	—
National Technical Association	1926	1,500
National United Law Enforcement Association	1969	5,000
Negro Airmen International	1967	912
Organization of Black Airline Pilots	1976	900
Student National Dental Association	1972	9,000
Student National Medical Association	1964	4,000
Student National Podiatric Medical Association	1973	300
United Mortgage Bankers of America	1962	—

* 1993 Membership—1997 Membership not available

Source: Julia C. Furtaw, ed. *Black Americans Information Directory 1992–1993* (Detroit, 1992).

Table 9

AFRICAN AMERICANS ON U.S. POSTAGE STAMPS

Name	Date Appeared	Name	Date Appeared
Booker T. Washington	1940; 1956	Bill Pickett	1994
George Washington Carver	1948	Jim Beckwourth	1994
Frederick Douglass	1967	Bessie Smith	1994
Peter Salem	1968	Billie Holiday	1994
W. C. Handy	1969	Buffalo Soldier	1994
Henry O. Tanner	1973	Jimmy Rushing	1994
Paul Laurence Dunbar	1975	Muddy Waters	1994
Salem Poor	1975	Robert Johnson	1994
Harriet Tubman	1978	Ma Rainey	1994
Martin Luther King, Jr.	1979	Howlin' Wolf	1994
Benjamin Banneker	1980	Ethel Waters	1994
Whitney M. Young, Jr.	1981	Nat "King" Cole	1994
Charles Drew	1981	Charlie Parker	1995
Ralph J. Bunche	1982	Clyde McPhatter	1995
Jackie Robinson	1982	Frederick Douglass (2nd Appearance)	1995
Scott Joplin	1983	Jelly Roll Morton	1995
Carter G. Woodson	1984	Charles Mingus	1995
Roberto Clemente	1984	Louis Armstrong	1995
Mary McLeod Bethune	1985	James P. Johnson	1995
Sojourner Truth	1986	Bessie Coleman	1995
Duke Ellington	1986	Harriet Tubman (2nd Appearance)	1995
Matthew A. Henson	1986	Coleman Hawkins	1995
Jean Baptiste Pointe DuSable	1987	Eubie Blake	1995
James Weldon Johnson	1988	John Coltrane	1995
Patrick J. Healy	1989	Count Basie	1996
A. Philip Randolph	1989	Errol Garner	1996
Ida B. Wells	1990	John Henry	1996
Jesse Owens	1990	Benjamin O. Davis, Sr.	1997
Jan E. Matzeliger	1991	W.E.B. Du Bois (2nd Appearance)	1998
W. E. B. Du Bois	1992	Madam C.J. Walker	1998
Percy Lavon Julian	1993	George Washington Carver (reissue)	1998
Joe Louis	1993	Clara Ward	1998
Otis Redding	1993	Mahalia Jackson	1998
Clyde McPhatter	1993	Roberta Martin	1998
Dinah Washington	1993	Sister Rosetta Tharpe	1998
Allison Davis	1994		

Table 10

BLACK TOWNS, LISTED BY STATE

Alabama
- Cederlake
- Greenwood Village
- Hobson City
- Plateau
- Shepherdsville

Arkansas
- Edmondson
- Thomasville

California
- Abila
- Allensworth
- Bowles
- Victorville

Colorado
- Dearfield

Florida
- Eatonville
- New Monrovia
- Richmond Heights

Illinois
- Brooklyn
- Robbins

Iowa
- Buxton

Kansas
- Nicodemus

Kentucky
- New Zion

Louisiana
- Grambling
- North Shreveport

Maryland
- Fairmount Heights
- Glenarden
- Lincoln City

Michigan
- Idlewind
- Marlborough

Mississippi
- Expose
- Mound Bayou
- Renova

Missouri
- Kinloch

New Jersey
- Gouldtown
- Lawnside
- Springtown
- Whitesboro

New Mexico
- Blackdom

North Carolina
- Columbia Heights
- Method
- Oberlin

Ohio
- Lincoln Heights
- Urbancrest

Oklahoma
- Arkansas Colored
- Bailey
- Boley
- Booktee
- Canadian Colored
- Chase
- Clearview
- Ferguson
- Forman
- Gibson Station
- Grayson
- Langston City
- Lewisville
- Liberty
- Lima
- Lincoln City
- Mantu
- Marshalltown
- North Fork Colored
- Overton
- Porter
- Redbird
- Rentiesville
- Summit
- Taft
- Tatum
- Tullahassee
- Vernon
- Wellston Colony
- Wybark
- Two unnamed towns in Seminole Nation

Tennessee
- Hortense
- New Bedford

Texas
- Andy
- Board House
- Booker
- Independence Heights
- Kendleton
- Mill City
- Oldham
- Roberts
- Union City

Virginia
- Ocean Grove
- Titustown
- Truxton

West Virginia
- Institute

Sources: Adapted from Kenneth Marvin Hamilton, *Black Towns and Profit: Promotion and Development in the Trans-Appalachian West, 1877–1915* (Urbana, Ill., 1991); and Ben Wayne Wiley, Ebonyville in the South and Southwest: Political Life in the All-Black Town, Ph.D. diss., University of Texas at Arlington (1984).

Index

D

H

K

L

M

N

T

X

Y

Z